BAKER'S
BIOGRAPHICAL DICTIONARY OF
MUSICIANS

CREDITS

Laura Kuhn
Classical Editor

Dennis McIntire
Associate Classical Editor

Lewis Porter
Jazz Editor

William Ruhlmann
Pop Editor

Key to Contributors

AB	Andrew Barlett	ETA	E. Taylor Atkins	NAL	Nancy Ann Lee
AG	Andrew Gilbert	GB	Greg Baise	NC	Norene Cashen
BH	Brock Helander	GBr	Gig Brown	NS	Nicolas Slonimsky
BJH	B. J. Huchtemann	GJ	Gregg Juke	PK	Peter Keepnews
BM	Bill Moody	GK	Gregory Kiewiet	PM	Patricia Myers
BP	Bret Primack	GM	Garaud MacTaggart	PMac	Paul MacArthur
BR	Bryan Reesman	HB	Hank Bordowitz	RB	Ralph Burnett
BW	Bill Wahl	JB	Joshua Berrett	RC	Richard Carlin
CH	Chris Hovan	JC	John Chilton,	RI	Robert Iannapolto
DB	Dan Bindert		*Who's Who of Jazz*	SC	Safford Chamberlain
DCG	David C. Gross	JC-B	John Chilton,	SH	Steve Holtje
DD	David Demsey		*Who's Who of British Jazz*	SKB	Susan K. Berlowitz
DDD	Dean D. Dauphinais	JE	James Eason	SP	Sam Prestianni
DK	Dan Keener	JM	Jeff McMillan	TP	Ted Panken
DM	Dennis McIntire	JO	Jim O'Rourke	TS	Tom Smith
DO	David Okamoto	JTB	John T. Bitter	WB	Will Bickart
DPe	Damon Percy	LK	Laura Kuhn	WF	Walter Faber
DPr	David Prince	LP	Lewis Porter	WKH	W. Kim Heron
DR	Dennis Rea	MF	Michael Fitzgerald	WR	William Ruhlmann
ED	Eric Deggans	MM	*Music Master Jazz*		
EH	Ed Hazell		*and Blues Catalogue*		
EJL	Eric J. Lawrence	MS	Matthew Snyder		

BAKER'S
BIOGRAPHICAL DICTIONARY OF
MUSICIANS

VOLUME 5
PISC - STRA

Centennial Edition

NICOLAS SLONIMSKY
Editor Emeritus

LAURA KUHN
Baker's Series Advisory Editor

Schirmer Books
an imprint of the Gale Group
New York • Detroit • San Francisco • London • Boston • Woodbridge, CT

Copyright © 1900, 1905, 1919, 1940, 1958, 1971 by G. Schirmer, Inc.
Copyright © 1978, 1984, 1992 by Schirmer Books
Copyright © 2001 by Schirmer Books, An Imprint of the Gale Group

Schirmer Books
1633 Broadway
New York, New York 10019

Gale Group
27500 Drake Road
Farmington Hills, Michigan 48331-3535

Library of Congress Catalog Card Number: 00-046375

Printed in the United States of America

Printing number
1 2 3 4 5 6 7 8 9 10

Library of Congress Cataloging-in-Publication Data

Baker's biographical dictionary of musicians.—Centennial ed. / Nicolas Slonimsky, editor emeritus.

     p. cm.

  Includes bibliographical references and discographies.

  Enl. ed. of: Baker's biographical dictionary of musicians. 8th ed. / rev. by Nicolas Slonimsky.

   ISBN 0-02-865525-7 (set : alk. paper) — ISBN 0-02- 865526-5 (vol. 1) — ISBN 0-02-865527-3 (vol. 2) — ISBN 0-02-865528-1 (vol. 3) — ISBN 0-02-865529-X (vol. 4) — ISBN 0-02-865530-3 (vol. 5) — ISBN 0-02-865571-0 (vol. 6)

   1. Music—Bio-bibliography—Dictionaries. I. Slonimsky, Nicolas, 1894-
II. Slonimsky, Nicolas, 1894- Baker's biographical dictionary of musicians.

  ML105.B16 2000
  780'.92'2—dc21
  [B]

                                    00-046375

ABBREVIATIONS

A.B.	Bachelor of Arts
ABC	American Broadcasting Company
A.M.	Master of Arts
ASCAP	American Society of Composers, Authors, and Publishers
assn./Assn.	association/Association
assoc.	associate
aug.	augmented
b.	born
B.A.	Bachelor of Arts
bar.	baritone
BBC	British Broadcasting Corporation
bjo.	banjo
B.M.	Bachelor of Music
brs.	brass
bs.	bass
CBC	Canadian Broadcasting Corporation
CBS	Columbia Broadcasting System
Coll.	College
cons./Cons.	conservatory/Conservatory
d.	died
dept./Dept.	department/Department
diss.	dissertation
D.M.A.	Doctor of Musical Arts
drm.	drums
ed(s).	edit(ed), editor(s), edition(s)
enl.	enlarged
f.	formed
flt.	flute
gtr.	guitar
har.	harmonica
H.S.	High School
IRCAM	Institut de Recherche et de Coordination Acoustique/Musique
ISCM	International Society for Contemporary Music
inst./Inst.	institute/Institute

kybd.	keyboards
M.A.	Master of Arts
mdln.	mandolin
M.M.	Master of Music
MS(S)	manuscript(s)
Mus.B.	Bachelor of Music
Mus.D.	Doctor of Music
Mus.M.	Master of Music
NAACP	National Association for the Advancement of Colored People
NBC	National Broadcasting Company
n.d.	no date
NEA	National Endowment for the Arts
NHK	Japan Broadcasting Company
no(s).	number(s)
N.Y.	New York
org.	organ
op(p).	opus
orch./Orch.	orchestra/Orchestra
p(p).	page(s)
PBS	Public Broadcasting Service
perc.	percussion
perf.	performance
Ph.D.	Doctor of Philosophy
phil./Phil.	philharmonic/Philharmonic
pno.	piano
posth.	posthumously
prof.	professor
publ.	publish(ed)
RAI	Radiotelevisione Italiana
rds.	reeds
rec.	recorded
rel.	released
rev.	revised
RIAS	Radio in the American Sector
S.	San, Santo, Santa
sax.	saxophone
sop.	soprano
Ss.	Santi, Sante
St(e).	Saint(e)
sym(s).	symphony (-ies)
synth.	synthesizer
tamb.	tamborine
ten.	tenor
tr.	translate(d), translation
trmb.	trombone
trpt.	trumpet
univ./Univ.	university/University
vln.	violin
voc.	vocals
vol(s).	volume(s)
WDR	Westdeutscher Rundfunk (West German Radio)
wdwnd.	woodwinds

P

(CONTINUED)

Pischek, Johann Baptist (actually, **Jan Křtitel Pišek**), Bohemian tenor; b. Mšeno, Oct. 13, 1814; d. Sigmaringen, Feb. 16, 1873. He was trained in the law before taking up music. In 1835 he made his operatic debut in Prague. From 1840 to 1848 he toured throughout Germany, appearing in both opera and concert. He served as court singer to the King of Württemberg in Stuttgart from 1844 to 1863. In 1845 he made his London debut, and sang with the Phil. Society there in 1845, 1846–47, 1849, and 1853. In 1849 he gave a command performance before Queen Victoria and Prince Albert. —NS/LK/DM

Pischna, Josef, famous Bohemian pianist and pedagogue; b. Erdischowitz, June 15, 1826; d. Prague, Oct. 19, 1896. He was a pupil at the Prague Cons. He taught for many years in Moscow, and then at the Prague Cons. His pedagogical work for piano, *60 Exercises*, became a standard method in Europe and has been reprinted in many eds.—NS/LK/DM

Pisendel, Johann Georg, distinguished German violinist, teacher, and composer; b. Cadolzburg, Dec. 26, 1687; d. Dresden, Nov. 25, 1755. He entered the Ansbach court chapel as a chorister at 10, and became a violinist in the Court Orch. there at 16. He studied singing with Pistocchi and violin with Torelli (1709), and later was a pupil of Vivaldi in Venice (1716), becoming his close friend; completed his studies with Montanari in Rome (1717). In 1709 he appeared as a soloist in a concert by Albinoni with the Leipzig Collegium Musicum, and then deputized for Melchior Hoffmann with the ensemble and in the Opera orch. In 1712 he joined the Dresden Court Orch. He traveled with the Elector of Saxony to France (1714), Berlin (1715), Italy (1716–17), and Vienna (1718), and later assumed the duties of Konzertmeister in Dresden (1728), a title he formally received in 1730; also took that post with the orch. of the

Dresden Opera (1731). He accompanied the Elector to Berlin (1728, 1744) and Warsaw (1734). Among his outstanding pupils were J.G. Graun and Franz Benda. Albinoni, Telemann, and Vivaldi were only a few of the eminent composers who wrote works for him. Pisendel's compositions reflect German, Italian, and French characteristics. His extant works include 7 violin concertos, 4 concerti grossi, a Sinfonia, 2 sonatas for Violin and Basso Continuo, and a Sonata for Solo Violin.

BIBL.: H. Jung, *J.G. P. (1687–1755): Leben und Werk* (diss., Univ. of Jena, 1956).—NS/LK/DM

Pisk, Paul A(madeus), Austrian-born American composer, pedagogue, and musicologist; b. Vienna, May 16, 1893; d. Los Angeles, Jan. 12, 1990. He studied piano with J. Epstein, composition with Schreker and Schoenberg, and orchestration with Hellmesberger in Vienna; studied musicology with Adler at the Univ. of Vienna (Ph.D., 1916, with the diss. *Das Parodieverfahren in den Messen des Jacobus Gallus*); later studied at the Vienna Cons. (graduated, 1919). From 1922 to 1934 he taught at the Volkshochschule Volksheim in Vienna; in 1925–26, was instructor in theory at the New Vienna Cons.; from 1931 to 1933, lectured at the Austro-American Cons. in Mondsee, near Salzburg. He also wrote music criticism for the Socialist newspaper *Wiener Arbeiterzeitung*; with Paul Stefan, he founded the progressive music journal *Musikblätter des Anbruch*. He was closely associated with Schoenberg, Berg, and Webern, and espoused the tenets of the New Vienna School, adopting in many of his own works the methods of 12-tone composition. As the dark cloud of ignorance and barbarity fell on Germany and approached Austria, Pisk left Vienna and emigrated to the U.S. (1936); became a naturalized American citizen (1941). He occupied with great honor teaching posts at the Univ. of Redlands, Calif. (1937–51), the Univ. of Tex. in Austin (1951–63), and Washington Univ. in St. Louis (1963–72); he also gave courses at summer sessions at the Univ. of

Calif., Los Angeles (1966), the Univ. of Cincinnati (1969), and Dartmouth Coll. (1972). In 1973 he settled in Los Angeles. His 90th birthday was celebrated by his many disciples and admirers in 1983. He continued to compose prolifically, accumulating an impressive catalogue of works, mostly chamber music. He wrote (with H. Ulrich) *History of Music and Musical Style* (N.Y., 1963); ed. masses by Jacobus Gallus for Denkmäler der Tonkunst in Österreich. A Festschrift, *Paul A. Pisk, Essays in His Honor*, ed. by J. Glowacki, was publ. in 1966.

WORKS: DRAMATIC: *Schattenseite*, monodrama (1931); *American Suite*, ballet (Redlands, Calif., Feb. 19, 1948). **ORCH.:** *Partita* (Prague, May 17, 1925); *Suite on American Folksongs* for 24 Instruments (1944); *Bucolic Suite* for Strings (Saratoga Springs, Sept. 10, 1946); *Rococo Suite* for Viola and Orch. (1953); *Baroque Chamber Concerto* for Violin and Orch. (1953); *Canzona* for Chamber Orch. (1954); *3 Ceremonial Rites* (1957–58); *Elegy* for Strings (1958); *Sonnet* for Chamber Orch. (1960). **CHAMBER:** 4 violin sonatas (1921, 1927, 1939, 1977); String Quartet (1924); *Fantasy* for Clarinet and Piano (1925); *Rondo* for Violin and Piano (1932); *Variations on a Waltz by Beethoven* for Violin, Viola, and Guitar (1933); Piano Trio (1933–35); *Moresca Figures* for Violin, Clarinet, and Piano (1934); *Berceuse slave* for Oboe and Piano (1939); *Bohemian Dance Rondo* for Bassoon and Piano (1939); Suite for 4 Clarinets (1939); *Shanty-Boy Fantasy* for Oboe and Piano (1940); *Variations on an Old Trumpet Tune* for Brass Sextet (1942); *Little Woodwind Music* (1945); *Cortege* for Brass Choir (1945); *Variations and Fugue on an American Theme* for Violin and Cello (1946); Clarinet Sonata (1947); Suite for Oboe and Piano (1947); *Introduction and Rondo* for Flute and Piano (1948); 2 flute suites (1950, 1969); *Intermezzo* for Clarinet and Piano (1950); *Elegy and Scherzino* for Oboe, 2 Clarinets, and Bassoon (1951); Quartet for 2 Trumpets, Horn, and Trombone (1951); Horn Sonata (1953); Suite for 2 Flutes (1953); Flute Sonata (1954); Suite for Oboe, Clarinet, and Piano (1955); *Eclogue* for Violin and Piano (1955); *Idyll* for Oboe and Piano (1957); String Trio (1958); Woodwind Quintet (1958); Woodwind Trio (1960); *Music* for Violin, Clarinet, Cello, and Bassoon (1962); *Envoi* for 6 Instruments (1964); *Duo* for Clarinet and Bassoon (1966); *Perpetuum mobile* for Organ and Brass Quartet (1968); Suite for Woodwind and Piano (1970); *Variables* for Clarinet and Piano (1973); *Discussions* for Oboe, Clarinet, Bassoon, Viola, and Cello (1974); Brass Quintet (1976); Violin Sonata (1977); *Three Vignettes* for Clarinet and Bassoon (1977); *3 Movements* for Violin and Piano (1978); Trio for Oboe, Clarinet, and Bassoon (1979); *Music* for Oboe and Piano (1982); Suite for Cello (1983); piano pieces. **VOCAL:** *3 Songs* for Voice and String Quartet (Salzburg, Aug. 10, 1922); *Die neue Stadt*, "cantata for the people" (Vienna, Nov. 1926); *Der grosse Regenmacher*, scenic ballad for Narrator and Orch. (1931); *Requiem* for Baritone and Orch. (1942); *A Toccata of Galuppi* for Soprano and Orch. (1947); songs.

BIBL.: T. Collins, *The Instrumental Music of P.A. P.* (diss., Univ. of Mo., 1972).—**NS/LK/DM**

Pistocchi, Francesco Antonio Mamiliano,

noted Italian singer, teacher, and composer, known as **Il Pistocchino**; b. Palermo, 1659; d. Bologna, May 13, 1726. A precocious child, he sang in public at age 3 and publ. his first work, *Capricci puerilli*, when he was 8. He made appearances as a singer in Bologna's cappella musicale at S. Petronio (from 1670), where he was permanently engaged as a soprano (1674–75), then toured as a contralto with great success in his homeland and in

Germany. He was in the service of the Parma court (1686–95), then was Kapellmeister to the Margrave of Brandenburg in Ansbach (1696–99). After a sojourn in Vienna (1699–1700), he returned to Bologna, and once more sang in the cappella musicale at S. Petronio (1701–8); was made virtuoso di camera e di cappella to Prince Ferdinando of Tuscany (1702). He was active as a singing teacher, his notable pupils being Antonio Bernacchi, Annibale Pio Fabri, and G.B. Martini. Having been elected to membership in the Accademia Filarmonica (1687), he served as its principe (1708, 1710); took Holy Orders (1709); became honorary chaplain to the Elector Palatine Johann Wilhelm (1714); was made a member of the Congregation of the Oratory in Forli (1715).

WORKS: DRAMATIC: Opera: *Il Leandro* (Venice, May 15, 1679; 2nd version, Venice, Jan. 1682); *Il Narciso* (Ansbach, March 1697); *Le pazzie d'amore e dell'interesse* (Ansbach, June 16, 1699); *Le risa di Democrito* (Vienna, Feb. 17, 1700); *I Rivali generosi* (Reggio Emilia, April 1710; in collaboration with C. Monari and G. Cappelli). **Oratorios:** *Sant'Adriano* (Modena, 1692); *Maria vergine addolorata* (Ansbach, 1698); *Il sacrificio di Gefte* (Bologna, 1720); *I Pastori al Presepe* (Bologna, Dec. 25, 1721); *Davide* (Bologna, March 19, 1721). **Cantata:** *La pace tra l'armi, sorpresa notturna nel campo* (Ansbach, Sept. 5, 1700). **OTHER:** *Capricci puerili saviamente composti e passeggiati in 40 modi sopra un basso d'un balleto, per il clavicembalo ed altri instrumenti*, op.1 (Bologna, 1667); *Duetti e terzetti*, op.3 (Bologna, 1707); etc.—**NS/LK/DM**

Piston, Walter (Hamor, Jr.),

outstanding American composer and pedagogue; b. Rockland, Maine, Jan. 20, 1894; d. Belmont, Mass., Nov. 12, 1976. The family name was originally Pistone; his paternal grandfather was Italian. He received his primary education in Boston, then took courses in architectural drawing at the Mass. Normal Art School, graduating in 1916; then took piano lessons with Harris Shaw, and studied violin with Fiumara, Theodorowicz, and Winternitz. He played in restaurants and places of public entertainment as a youth. During World War I, he was in the U.S. Navy; after the Armistice, he entered Harvard Univ., graduating in musical subjects summa cum laude in 1924; while at Harvard, he conducted concerts of the univ. orch., the Pierian Sodality. For a time he was employed as a draftsman for Boston Elevated Railway. In 1924 he went to Paris on a John Knowles Paine Traveling Fellowship, and became a student of Boulanger; also took courses with Dukas at the École Normale de Musique (1925). Returning to the U.S. in 1926, he was appointed to the faculty of Harvard Univ.; in 1944, became a prof. of music; was named prof. emeritus in 1960. As a teacher, he was greatly esteemed, not only because of his consummate knowledge of music and pedagogical ability, but also because of his immanent humanity in instructing students whose aesthetics differed from his own; among his grateful disciples was Leonard Bernstein. As a composer, Piston followed a cosmopolitan course, adhering to classical forms while extending his harmonic structures toward a maximum of tonal saturation; he was particularly expert in contrapuntal writing. Beginning about 1965, Piston adopted a modified system of 12-tone composition, particularly in initial thematic statements; his Sym. No. 8 (1964–65) and *Variations* for Cello and Orch. (1966) are explicitly dodecaphonic. Piston rejected the narrow notion of ethnic Americanism in his music, and stated once that an artist could be as American working in the Library of the Boston Atheneum as roaming the Western prairie; yet he employed upon occasion the syncopated rhythms of jazz. He received Pulitzer Prizes in Music for his Sym. No. 3 and Sym. No. 7, and N.Y. Music Critics' Circle Awards for his Sym. No. 2, Viola Concerto, and String Quartet No. 5. He held the degree of D.Mus. *honoris causa* from Harvard Univ.; was elected a member of the National Inst. of Arts and Letters (1938), the American Academy of Arts and Sciences (1940), and the American Academy of Arts and Letters (1955). He traveled little and declined invitations to go to South America and to Russia under the auspices of the State Dept., preferring to live in his house in suburban Belmont, near Boston. His working habits were remarkably methodical; he rarely altered or revised his music once it was put on paper, and his handwriting was calligraphic. With 2 exceptions, he never wrote for voices.

WORKS: DRAMATIC: B a l l e t : *The Incredible Flutist* (Boston, May 30, 1938; suite, 1938; Pittsburgh, Nov. 22, 1940). **ORCH.:** *Symphonic Piece* (1927; Boston, March 23, 1928); 2 suites: No. 1 (1929; Boston, March 28, 1930) and No. 2 (1947–48; Dallas, Feb. 29, 1948); *Concerto for Orchestra* (1933; Boston, March 6, 1934); *Prelude and Fugue* (1934; Cleveland, March 12, 1936); 8 syms.: No. 1 (1937; Boston, April 8, 1938), No. 2 (1943; Washington, D.C., March 5, 1944), No. 3 (1947; Boston, Jan. 9, 1948), No. 4 (1950; Minneapolis, March 30, 1951), No. 5 (1954; for the 50th anniversary of the Juilliard School of Music, N.Y., Feb. 24, 1956), No. 6 (for the 75th anniversary of the Boston Sym. Orch., Nov. 25, 1955), No. 7 (1960; Philadelphia, Feb. 10, 1961), and No. 8 (1964–65; Boston, March 5, 1965); *Concertino* for Piano and Chamber Orch. (CBS Radio, N.Y., June 20, 1937); 2 violin concertos: No. 1 (1939; N.Y., March 18, 1940) and No. 2 (Pittsburgh, Oct. 28, 1960); *Sinfonietta* (Boston, March 10, 1941); *Prelude and Allegro* for Organ and Strings (CBS, Cambridge, Mass., Aug. 8, 1943); *Fugue on a Victory Tune* (N.Y., Oct. 21, 1944); *Variation on a Theme by Eugene Goossens* (1944; Cincinnati, March 23, 1945); *Toccata* (Bridgeport, Conn., Oct. 14, 1948); *Fantasy* for English Horn, Harp, and Strings (1952; Boston, Jan. 1, 1954); *Serenata* (Louisville, Oct. 24, 1956); Viola Concerto (1957; Boston, March 7, 1958); Concerto for 2 Pianos and Orch. (1959; Hanover, N.H., July 4, 1964); *3 New England Sketches* (Worcester, Mass., Oct. 23, 1959); *Symphonic Prelude* (Cleveland, April 20, 1961); *Lincoln Center Festival Overture* (N.Y., Sept. 25, 1962); *Capriccio* for Harp and String Orch. (1963; Madrid, Oct. 19, 1964); *Variations on a Theme by Edward Burlingame Hill* (Boston, April 30, 1963); *Pine Tree Fantasy* (Portland, Maine, Nov. 16, 1965); *Variations* for Cello and Orch. (1966; N.Y., March 2, 1967); Clarinet Concerto (Hanover, N.H., Aug. 6, 1967); *Ricercare* (1967; N.Y., March 7, 1968); *Fantasia* for Violin and Orch. (1970; Hanover, N.H., March 11, 1973); Flute Concerto (1971; Boston, Sept. 22, 1972); *Bicentennial Fanfare* (Cincinnati, Nov. 14, 1975); Concerto for String Quartet, Wind Ensemble, and Percussion (Portland, Maine, Oct. 26, 1976). **B a n d :** *Tunbridge Fair: Intermezzo* (1950). **CHAMBER:** *3 Pieces* for Flute, Clarinet, and Bassoon (1926); Flute Sonata (1930); Suite for Oboe and Piano (1931); 5 string quartets (1933, 1935, 1947, 1951, 1962); 2 piano trios (1935, 1966); Violin Sonata (1939); *Fanfare for the Fighting French* for Brass and Percussion (Cincin-

nati, Oct. 23, 1942); *Interlude* for Viola and Piano (1942); Quintet for Flute and Strings (1942); *Partita* for Violin, Viola, and Organ (1944); Sonatina for Violin and Harpsichord or Piano (1945); *Divertimento* for 9 Instruments (1946); *Duo* for Viola and Cello (1949); Piano Quintet (1949); Wind Quintet (1956); Sextet for Strings (1964); Piano Quartet (1964); *Souvenirs* for Flute, Viola, and Harp (1967); *Ceremonial Fanfare* for Brass and Percussion (1969; N.Y., Feb. 10, 1970); *Duo* for Cello and Piano (1972); *3 Counterpoints* for Violin, Viola, and Cello (1973). **KEYBOARD: P i a n o :** Sonata (1926); *Passacaglia* (1943); *Improvisation* (1945). **O r g a n :** *Chromatic Study on B.A.C.H.* (1940). **VOCAL:** *Carnival Song* for Men's Chorus and 11 Brasses (1938; Cambridge, Mass., March 7, 1940); *Psalm and Prayer of David* for Chorus, Flute, Clarinet, Bassoon, Violin, Viola, Cello, and Double Bass (1958).

WRITINGS: *Principles of Harmonic Analysis* (Boston, 1933); *Harmony* (N.Y., 1944; 5th ed., rev. and enl. by M. DeVoto, 1987); *Counterpoint* (N.Y., 1947); *Orchestration* (N.Y., 1955).

BIBL.: O. Daniel et al., *W. P.* (N.Y., 1964); H. Lindenfeld, *Three Symphonies of W. P.: An Analysis* (diss., Cornell Univ., 1975); H. Pollack, *W. P.* (Ann Arbor, Mich., 1981).—**NS/LK/DM**

Pistor, Gotthelf, German tenor; b. Berlin, Oct. 17, 1887; d. Cologne, April 4, 1947. He began his career as an actor in Berlin. Following vocal training from Luria, he made his operatic debut in Nuremberg in 1923. He had engagements in Würzburg (1924–25), Darmstadt (1925–27), and Magdeburg (1928–29) before serving as a principal member of the Cologne Opera (from 1929). He also made guest appearances at the Bayreuth Festivals (1925; 1927–31), at the Zoppot Festivals (1930–38), and in San Francisco (1931). In his last years, he taught voice in Cologne. Pistor was esteemed for such Wagnerian roles as Tristan, Parsifal, Siegfried, and Siegmund. —**NS/LK/DM**

Pitfield, Thomas B(aron), English composer, teacher, artist, and writer; b. Bolton, April 5, 1903; d. Nov. 11, 1999. He was educated at the Royal Manchester Coll. of Music and the Bolton School of Arts. He taught at Tettenhall Coll. (1935–45) and the Royal Manchester Coll. of Music (1947–72), and finally at the latter's successor, the Royal Northern Coll. of Music (1972–73). In addition to his musical interests, he also was active as an artist and writer. He publ. 2 autobiographical vols., *No Song, No Supper* (1986) and *A Song After Supper* (1991). His compositions were in a simple style, and included dramatic scores, orch. works, brass band pieces, chamber music, piano pieces, and choral works. —**NS/LK/DM**

Piticchio, Francesco, Italian composer who flourished in the second half of the 17th century. He was active as maestro di cappella in Palermo about 1760. From 1781 he was maestro al cembalo with an Italian opera troupe in Germany. After a sojourn in Vienna (1786–91), he returned to Italy and was in the service of the royal family in Naples. He wrote the operas *Il marchese di Verd'antico* (Rome, Jan. 1778; in collaboration with Gazzaniga), *Didone abbandonata* (Palermo, Carnival 1780), *Il militare amante* (Rome, Carnival 1781), *Gli* *amanti alla prova* or *Die Liebhaber auf der Probe* (Dresden, Jan. 4, 1785), *Bertoldo* (Vienna, June 22, 1787), and *La vendetta di Medea* (Naples, Aug. 13, 1798). Among his other works were a Sym., chamber music, oratorios, cantatas, and songs.—**LK/DM**

Pitney, Gene, successful pop-rocker of the 1960s; b. Hartford, Conn., Feb. 17, 1941. Gene Pitney grew up in Rockville, Conn., and studied piano, drums, and guitar as a child. He began writing songs and performing with his group The Genials in high school and made his first recordings for Decca in 1959 with Ginny Arnell as Jamie and Jane. He also recorded as Billy Bryan for Blaze Records and under his own name for Festival Records in 1960. His first major success came as a songwriter, composing the smash hits "Rubber Ball" for Bobby Vee, "Hello Mary Lou" for Ricky Nelson, and "He's a Rebel" for The Crystals. In 1961, Pitney dropped out of college to concentrate on music, signing with Musicor Records and scoring his first moderate hit with his own "(I Wanna) Love My Life Away," followed by Carole King and Gerry Goffin's "Every Breath I Take," coproduced by Phil Spector. His *Only Love Can Break a Heart* album yielded major hits with "Town without Pity," "Half Heaven—Half Heartache," and "True Love Never Runs Smooth," and smash hits with two Burt Bacharach–Hal David compositions, "(The Man Who Shot) Liberty Valance" and "Only Love Can Break a Heart." Pitney hit with "Mecca" and "Twenty Four Hours from Tulsa," another Bacharach-David composition, in 1963. He also toured Great Britain that year and met The Rolling Stones, subsequently scoring a moderate American and near-smash British hit with Mick Jagger and Keith Richards's "That Girl Belongs to Yesterday" and assisting The Rolling Stones in the recording of their *12 X 5* album.

In 1964, Gene Pitney had near-smash hits with "It Hurts to Be in Love" and "I'm Gonna Be Strong," the latter written by Barry Mann and Cynthia Weil, and began recording albums in foreign languages. In 1965 and 1966, he recorded country albums with George Jones and Melba Montgomery, scoring major country hits with "I've Got Five Dollars and It's Saturday Night" and "Louisiana Mama" with Jones and "Baby, Ain't That Fine" with Montgomery. Major pop hits for Pitney through 1968 included "Last Chance to Turn Around" and "She's a Heartbreaker," and the Mann-Weil compositions "Looking through the Eyes of Love" and "Backstage," both smash British hits. He also recorded the Randy Newman songs "Nobody Needs Your Love," "Something's Gotten Hold of My Heart," and "Just One Smile," all smash British hits.

Gene Pitney never achieved another major pop hit in the U.S., and his popularity faded in this country in the late 1960s. Nonetheless, he continued to tour Britain and Europe while avoiding the "oldies" revival circuit. In 1974, he cut his touring schedule to six months a year, as he became involved in real estate and stock market investments. Pitney later scored a British near- smash hit with a remake of "Something's Gotten Hold of My Heart" in duet with Marc Almond in 1988.

Disc.: GENE PITNEY: *Many Sides of Gene Pitney* (1962); *Only Love Can Break a Heart* (1962); *Sings Just for You*

(1963); *Blue Gene* (1963); *Meets the Fair Young Ladies of Folkland* (1964); *Italiano* (1964); *It Hurts to Be in Love* (1964); *I Must Be Seeing Things* (1965); *Looking through the Eyes of Love* (1965); *Español* (1965); *Backstage I'm Lonely* (1966); *Nessuno Mi Puo Giudicare* (1966); *The Gene Pitney Show* (1966); *Greatest Hits of All Time* (1966); *The Country Side of Gene* (1966); *Young and Warm and Wonderful* (1966); *Just One Smile* (1967); *Pitney Español* (1966); *Sings Burt Bacharach* (1968); *She's a Heartbreaker* (1968); *This Is Gene Pitney (Singing The Platter's Golden Platters)* (1970). GEORGE JONES AND GENE PITNEY: *George Jones and Gene Pitney* (1965); *It's Country Time Again* (1965); *Best of Country; One Has My Name* (1996). GENE PITNEY AND MELBA MONTGOMERY: *Being Together* (1966). GENE PITNEY, GEORGE JONES AND MELBA MONTGOMERY: *Famous Country Duets* (1965).—**BH**

Pitoni, Giuseppe Ottavio, Italian teacher, writer on music, and composer; b. Rieti, March 18, 1657; d. Rome, Feb. 1, 1743. He began music studies at 5, under Pompeo Natali in Rome. At 8 he was chorister at S. Giovanni de' Fiorentini, later at the Ss. Apostoli, and studied counterpoint under Foggia. In 1673–74 he was maestro di cappella at Monterotondo, from 1674 to 1676 at Assisi Cathedral, in 1676–77 at Rieti Cathedral, and, finally, in 1677, he became maestro at the collegiate church of S. Marco in Rome, retaining this post until death, though simultaneously engaged at S. Apollinare, S. Lorenzo in Damaso (1694–1721), S. Giovanni in Laterano (1708–19), and St. Peter's (1719); also in some minor Roman churches. He was an excellent teacher, and taught after the same method by which he himself rose to eminence as a composer, e.g., the writing out in score of Palestrina's works to study his style. Durante, Leo, and Feo were his greatest pupils. As a composer, he cultivated a distinct feature of the Roman school, the writing in many parts.

Works: Some 270 masses and Mass parts; more than 200 introits; over 230 graduals; about 800 Psalms; some 650 antiphons; about 250 hymns; around 235 motets; approximately 220 canticles; only a motet for 2 Voices (Rome, 1697) was publ. during his lifetime.

Bibl.: S. Gmeinwieser, *G.O. P.: Thematisches Werkverzeichnis* (Wilhelmshaven, 1976).—**NS/LK/DM**

Pitt, Percy, English conductor and composer; b. London, Jan. 4, 1870; d. there, Nov. 23, 1932. He studied with Jadassohn and Reinecke at the Leipzig Cons. and with Rheinberger at the Akademie der Tonkunst in Munich. Returning to England in 1893, he pursued his career in London. He was musical advisor (1902–07) and musical director (1907–24) of the Grand Opera Syndicate at Covent Garden, and also the first English conductor to appear at Covent Garden (1907), returning there in 1909–10 and 1919–20. He was artistic director of the British National Opera Co. (1922–24) and musical advisor to the BBC (1922–24), serving as the latter's musical director (1924–30). He wrote stage music, a *Ballade* for Violin and Orch. (1900) for Ysaÿe, a Clarinet Concerto, and a *Sérénade du passant* for Tetrazzini.

Bibl.: J. Chamier, *P. P. of Covent Garden and the BBC* (London, 1938).—**NS/LK/DM**

Pittaluga, Gustavo, Spanish composer; b. Madrid, Feb. 8, 1906. He studied law at the Univ. of Madrid and composition with Oscar Esplá. He was a member of the Grupo de los 8 in Madrid and of the Paris group of modern musicians, Triton (1935), and from 1936 to 1939 a member of the staff of the Spanish Embassy in Washington, D.C. (for the Loyalist government). He then settled in the U.S., where he was active with the film library at the Museum of Modern Art in N.Y. (1941–43).

WORKS: *Vocalise-Étude* for Voice and Piano (1932); *La Romería de los Cornudos*, ballet (1933); *El Loro*, zarzuela (1933); *Concerto militaire* for Violin and Orch. (1933); *Ricercare* for Violin, Clarinet, Bassoon, and Trumpet (1934); *Petite suite* for 10 Instruments (1935; also as *3 pièces pour une espagnolade* for Piano); *Berceuse* for Violin and Piano (1935); *6 danses espagnoles en suite* for Piano (1935); *Capriccio alla romantica* for Piano and Orch. (1936); *5 canciones populares* for Chorus and 10 Instruments (1939); *Habanera* for Violin and Piano (1942); *Lament for Federico García Lorca* for Narrator and Orch. (1942).—**NS/LK/DM**

Pittel, Harvey, American saxophonist; b. Great Falls, Mont., June 22, 1943. He studied with Kalman Bloch and Franklyn Stokes, then took courses at the Univ. of Southern Calif. in Los Angeles (1961–65), where he received his doctorate in music education. After studies with Frederick Hemke at Northwestern Univ. (1965–66), he played in the U.S. Military Academy Band (1966–69), during which time he continued his studies, with Joseph Allard. He won the silver medal at the Geneva International Competition (1970). He made his formal debut as a soloist in Ingolf Dahl's Saxophone Concerto with the Boston Sym. Orch. (1971), and his recital debut at N.Y.'s Carnegie Recital Hall (1973); subsequently toured throughout North America and Europe, appearing as a soloist with the leading orchs., as a recitalist, and as a chamber music player. —**NS/LK/DM**

Pittman-Jennings, David, American baritone; b. Duncan, Okla., Dec. 13, 1946. He studied voice with Elisabeth Parham and took his B.M. cum laude in oboe (1969) at the Univ. of Okla., and then his Masters degree in vocal performance (1974) at Calif. State Univ. in Northridge. He continued vocal training with Parham in Los Angeles, San Francisco, and Paris until 1998. In 1977 he made his operatic debut as Mozart's Count at the Graz Opera, where he sang until 1979. From 1979 to 1982 he sang at the Bremen Opera. In 1982 he appeared as Fernando at the Paris Opéra. Following his debut as a soloist in Mahler's *Lieder eines fahrenden Gesellen* in Bordeaux in 1983, he made his recital debut in Nice in 1984. From 1984 to 1986 he sang at the Netherlands Opera in Amsterdam. In 1987 he was engaged as Wozzeck at the Opéra du Rhin in Strasbourg, a role he sang in Parma in 1989. In the latter year, he also portrayed Schoenberg's Moses in Lyons. After singing Germont at the Frankfurt am Main Opera in 1991, he made his first appearance at the Vienna State Opera in 1992 as Mandryka, a role he reprised at the Semper Opera in Dresden in 1994. In the latter year, he also was engaged as Pizzaro at the Berlin State Opera, as Don Alfonso at the Hamburg State Opera, and as Renato at the Bavarian State Opera in Munich. In 1995 he again portrayed Wozzeck at the Teatro Colón in Buenos Aires

and Schoenberg's Moses at the Netherlands Opera, and then repeated the latter role at the Salzburg Festival in 1996. In 1997 he appeared as Wozzeck at the Spoleto Festival U.S.A. in Charleston, S.C., and as Mandryka at the Santa Fe Opera. He sang Jochanaan at the Berlin State Opera and Scarpia in Verona in 1998, and then Rigoletto at the Leipzig Opera and Frank in *Die tote stadt* at the Teatro Colón in 1999. On Oct. 16, 1999, he made his N.Y. debut in Dallapiccola's opera *Il Prigioniero* in a concert performance with the Montreal Sym. Orch. under Dutoit's direction. As a concert artist, he sang with many orchs. in Europe in an expansive repertoire ranging from Bach, Haydn, Beethoven, and Berlioz to Hindemith, Walton, and Zender.—**NS/LK/DM**

Pitzinger, Gertrude, Bohemian contralto; b. Mährisch-Schönberg, Aug. 15, 1904. She studied music with Joseph Marx at the Vienna Academy of Music, and voice with various teachers. After several concert tours in central Europe, she went to the U.S. and gave a N.Y. recital on Jan. 17, 1938, with excellent success. She specialized in German lieder; her repertoire included some 400 songs. She taught singing at the Hochschule für Musik in Frankfurt am Main (1960–73).—**NS/LK/DM**

Pixis, Friedrich Wilhelm, German violinist, conductor, teacher, and composer, brother of **Johann Peter Pixis;** b. Mannheim, March 12, 1785; d. Prague, Oct. 20, 1842. He studied with his father in Mannheim. After further training from Ignaz Fränzl, he made a concert tour with his brother in 1796. While in Hamburg in 1798, he received additional instruction from Viotti. Following tours in Poland, Russia, and Denmark, he returned to Mannheim and was a member of the electoral chapel orch. until 1806. After completing his studies with Albrechtberger in Vienna, he settled in Prague, where he became a prof. at the Cons. and conductor of the theater orch. in 1810. Among his students were R. Dreyschock and Kalliwoda. He composed a Violin Concerto, Variations on *War's vielleicht um eins* for Violin and Orch., and a Violin Sonata. —**LK/DM**

Pixis, Johann Peter, German pianist, teacher, and composer; b. Mannheim, Feb. 10, 1788; d. Baden-Baden, Dec. 22, 1874. Of a musical family (his father and his brother were musicians), he received his primary education at home. After touring with his brother (1796), he returned to Mannheim to study composition; continued his studies with Albrechtsberger in Vienna (1806). He went to Paris in 1823, where he established himself as a teacher. In 1840 he settled in Baden-Baden as a teacher.

WORKS: DRAMATIC: Opera: *Almazinde, oder Die Höhle Sesam* (Vienna, April 11, 1820); *Bibiana, oder Die Kapelle im Walde* (Aachen, Oct. 8, 1829); etc. **ORCH.:** Sym.; Overture; Piano Concerto. **CHAMBER:** Piano Quartet; Piano Quintet; 2 string quintets; 7 piano trios. **Piano:** Sonatas, variations, and transcriptions.

BIBL.: L. Schiwietz, *J.P. P.* (Frankfurt am Main and N.Y., 1994).—**NS/LK/DM**

Pizzarelli, John (Paul Jr.), jazz guitarist, singer; b. Paterson, N.J., April 6, 1960. A swing-styled guitarist like his father, Bucky Pizzarelli (b. Paterson, N.J., Jan. 9, 1926), his stylish Sinatra-like singing has brought him a wide audience. He was marketed similarly to Harry Connick and, like him, toured with a swing big band. His brother Martin has played bass with him for over 18 years. He has performed with Zoot Sims and Ray Brown. In 1997, he played Carnegie Hall with his father. He regularly performs at the Algonquin, N.Y.

DISC.: *My Blue Heaven* (1990); *Dear Mr. Cole* (1994); *New Standards* (1994); *Our Love Is Here to Stay* (1997); also recorded with Clark Terry, Milt Hinton, Dave McKenna, and Connie Kay.—**LP**

Pizzetti, Ildebrando, eminent Italian composer and teacher; b. Parma, Sept. 20, 1880; d. Rome, Feb. 13, 1968. He studied piano with his father, Odvardo Pizzetti, in Parma and composition with Tebaldini at the Parma Cons., graduating in 1901. He was on the faculty of the Parma Cons. (1907–08), then of the Florence Cons. (1908–24), where he became director in 1917. Fom 1924 to 1936 he was director of the Milan Cons. He then taught at the Accademia di Santa Cecilia in Rome (1936–58), from 1947 to 1952 also serving as its president. In 1914 he founded (with G. Bastianelli) in Florence a modernistic periodical, pointedly named *Dissonanza*, to promote the cause of new music. In 1930 he made a trip to the U.S. to attend the performance of his *Rondo veneziano*, conducted by Toscanini with the N.Y. Phil.; in 1931 Pizzetti conducted his opera *Fra Gherardo* at the Teatro Colón in Buenos Aires. Pizzetti's music represents the Romantic trend in 20th century Italy; in his many works for the theater, he created the modern counterpart of medieval mystery plays; the mystical element is very strong in his own texts for his operas. He employed astringent chromatic harmony, but the mainstream of his melody flows along pure diatonic lines.

WORKS: DRAMATIC: Opera: *Fedra* (1909–12; Milan, March 20, 1915); *Debora e Jaele* (1915–21; Milan, Dec. 16, 1922); *Lo straniero* (1922–25; Rome, April 29, 1930); *Fra Gherardo* (1925–27; Milan, May 16, 1928); *Orséolo* (1931–35; Florence, May 4, 1935); *L'Oro* (1938–42; Milan, Jan. 2, 1947); *Vanna Lupa* (1947–49; Florence, May 4, 1949); *Ifigenia* (RAI, Oct. 3, 1950; 1st stage perf., Florence, May 9, 1951); *Cagliostro* (RAI, Nov. 5, 1952; 1st stage perf., Milan, Jan. 24, 1953); *La figlia di Iorio* (Naples, Dec. 4, 1954); *Assassinio nella cattedrale*, after T.S. Eliot (1957; Milan, March 1, 1958); *Il calzare d'argento* (Milan, March 23, 1961); *Clitennestra* (1961–64; Milan, March 1, 1965). **Incidental Music To:** G. d'Annunzio's *La nave* (1905–07; Rome, March 1908) and *La Pisanella* (Paris, June 11, 1913); F. Belcare's *La sacra rappresentazione di Abram e d'Isaac* (1915–17; Florence, June 1917; expanded into an opera, 1925; Turin, March 11, 1926); Aeschylus' *Agamemnon* (Syracuse, April 28, 1930); Sophocles' *Le trachiniae* (1932; Syracuse, April 26, 1933); Sophocles' *Edipo a Colono* (Syracuse, April 24, 1936); *La festa delle Panatenee* (1935; Paestum, June 1936); Shakespeare's *As You Like It* (Florence, May 1938). **ORCH.:** *Ouverture per una farsa tragica* (1911); *Concerto dell'estate* (1928; N.Y., Feb. 28, 1929); *Rondo veneziano* (1929; N.Y., Feb. 27, 1930; as a ballet, Milan, Jan. 8, 1931); Cello Concerto (Venice, Sept. 11, 1934); Sym. (1940); Violin Concerto (1944; Rome, Dec. 9, 1945); *Canzone di beni perduti* (1948; Venice, Sept. 4, 1950); Harp Concerto (1958–60). **CHAMBER:** 2 string quartets (1906; 1932–33); Violin Sonata (1918–19); Cello Sonata

(1921); Piano Trio (1925). **Piano:** *Da un autunno già lontano*, 3 pieces (1911); *Sonata 1942* (1942). **VOCAL:** *Messa di requiem* (1922); *De profundis* (1937); *Epithalamium*, cantata for Soloists, Chorus, and Orch. (1939); *Oritur sol et occidit*, cantata for Brass and Orch. (1943); *Cantico di gloria "Attollite portas"* for 3 Choruses, 22 Wind Instruments, 2 Pianos, and Percussion (1948); *Vanitas vanitatum*, cantata for Soloists, Men's Chorus, and Orch. (1958); *Filiae Jerusalem, adjuro vos*, cantata for Soprano, Women's Chorus, and Orch. (1966); songs.

WRITINGS: *La musica dei Greci* (Rome, 1914); *Musicisti contemporanei* (Milan, 1914); *Intermezzi critici* (Florence, 1921); *Paganini* (Turin, 1940); *Musica e dramma* (Rome, 1945); *La musica italiana dell' 800* (Turin, 1947).

BIBL.: R. Fondi, *I. P. e il dramma musicale italiano d'oggi* (Rome, 1919); special issue of *Il pianoforte*, II (Turin, 1921); G. Tebaldini, *I. P. nelle memorie* (Parma, 1931); G. Gatti, *I. P.* (Turin, 1934; 2nd ed., 1955; Eng. tr., 1951); G. Gavazzeni, *Tre studi su P.* (Como, 1937); V. Bucchi, L. Dallapiccola et al., *Firenze a I. P.* (Florence, 1947); G. Gavazzeni, *Altri studi pizzettiani* (Bergamo, 1956); M. la Morgia, ed., *La citta d'annunziana a I. P.: Saggi e note* (Pescara, 1958); B. Pizzetti, ed., *I. P.: Cronologia e bibliografia* (Parma, 1980).—**NS/LK/DM**

Pizzi, Pier Luigi, distinguished Italian opera producer and designer; b. Milan, June 15, 1930. He was a student of architecture at the Milan Polytechnic. In 1952 he began his career as an opera designer with a production of *Don Giovanni* in Genoa. In 1959 he staged Handel's *Orlando* in Florence and acquired a notable reputation as a producer of Baroque stage works. He produced Verdi's *I due Foscari* (1979) and Gluck's *Alceste* (1989) and *Armide* (1996) at Milan's La Scala, Rameau's *Hippolyte et Aricie* in Aix-en-Provence (1983), Bellini's *Capuleti e i Montecchi* at London's Covent Garden (1984), and *Don Carlos* in Vienna (1989). In 1990 he oversaw the production of Berlioz's *Les Troyens* at the gala opening of the Opéra de la Bastille in Paris. After staging *Otello* in Chicago in 1992, he produced the first modern staging of Traetta's *Buova d'Antona* in Venice in 1993. In 1997 he produced Verdi's *Macbeth* in Verona. Pizzi's productions and designs reveal him as a master of stagecraft.

BIBL.: R. Lussan, *P.L. P.* (Paris, 1994).—**NS/LK/DM**

Pizzini, Carlo Alberto, Italian composer; b. Rome, March 22, 1905; d. there, Sept. 9, 1981. He studied with Respighi at the Accademia di Santa Cecilia in Rome, graduating in 1929. He later was an administrator there and with the RAI.

WORKS: DRAMATIC: *Dardanio*, opera (Rome, 1928); theater, film, and radio music. **ORCH.:** *Sinfonia in istile classico* (1930); *Il poema delle Dolomiti* (1931); *Strapaese* (1932); *Al Piemonte* (1941); *Grotte di Postumia* (1941); *Concierto para tres hermanas* for Guitar and Orch. (1969). **OTHER:** Chamber music; piano pieces.—**NS/LK/DM**

Plaichinger, Thila, Austrian soprano; b. Vienna, March 13, 1868; d. there, March 17, 1939. She studied with Gänsbacher at the Vienna Cons. and with Dustmann and Mampe-Babbnigg. In 1893 she made her operatic debut in Hamburg. She was a principal member of the Strasbourg Opera (1894–1901) and of the Berlin Royal Opera (1901–14). In 1904 and 1910 she was a guest artist at London's Covent Garden, and also appeared in Munich, Dresden, and Vienna. Among her finest roles were Isolde, Brünnhilde, Ortrud, Venus, and Elektra.—NS/LK/DM

Plaidy, Louis, famous German piano teacher; b. Wermsdorf, Nov. 28, 1810; d. Grimma, March 3, 1874. He began his professional career as a violinist, and performed in public in Dresden and Leipzig; at the same time he took piano lessons from Agthe, and became greatly proficient as a pianist, so that Mendelssohn engaged him in 1843 as a piano teacher at the Leipzig Cons. Plaidy concentrated on the technical problems of piano pedagogy. He taught at the Leipzig Cons. until 1865, then continued to give private lessons. He publ. a number of instructive piano studies which were widely used, his *Technische Studien für das Pianoforte-Spiel* being a standard manual. He also publ. a booklet, *Der Klavierlehrer* (1874; British ed. as *The Pianoforte Teacher's Guide*; American ed., tr. by J.S. Dwight, as *The Piano-Teacher*).—NS/LK/DM

Plakidis, Peteris, Latvian composer; b. Riga, March 4, 1947. He graduated from the Latvian Cons. in Riga (1970), where he studied composition with V. Utkins and Gederts Ramans and where he taught from 1973. He also was secretary of the Latvian Composer's Union (1978–84; from 1989). In 1990 he made a tour of the U.S. as harpsichordist of the Latvian Chamber Orch.

WORKS: ORCH.: *Music for Piano, Timpani, and Strings* (1969); Piano Concerto (1975); *Legend* (1976); *Interchanges* for a Group of Soloists (1977); Concerto for 2 Oboes and Chamber Orch. (1982); *Concerto-Ballad* for 2 Violins, Piano, and Strings (1984); *Canto* (1989). **CHAMBER:** *Improvisation and Burlesque* for Piano Trio (1966); *Prelude and Pulsation* for Wind Quintet (1975); *2 Sketches* for Oboe (1975); *Fifths,* invention for 2 Pianos (1976); *2 Retrospections* (1977); *A Short Canon and Animated Cartoon Film* for Flute, Oboe, and Piano (1979); *Romantic Music* for Piano Trio (1980); *Homage to Haydn* for Piano, Flute, and Cello (1982). **VOCAL:** *The Rifleman* for Voice and Orch. (1972); choruses; songs.—NS/LK/DM

Plamenac, Dragan, eminent Croatian-born American musicologist; b. Zagreb, Feb. 8, 1895; d. Ede, the Netherlands, March 15, 1983. He studied jurisprudence at the Univ. of Zagreb, then took courses in composition with Schreker at the Vienna Academy of Music and with Novák in Prague. In 1919 he went to Paris and attended lectures at the Sorbonne given by Pirro. He then had a seminar with Adler at the Univ. of Vienna, receiving his Ph.D. there in 1925 with the diss. *Johannes Ockeghem als Motetten- und Chansonkomponist.* From 1928 to 1939 he taught at the Univ. of Zagreb. After the outbreak of World War II, he went to the U.S., becoming a naturalized citizen in 1946. In 1947 he received a Guggenheim fellowship. He taught at the Univ. of Ill., Urbana (1954–63). Plamenac's chief accomplishment was his painstaking and fruitful research into the sources of the music of the Renaissance. He prepared a major ed. of the works of Ockeghem in the Publikationen älterer Musik, Jg. I/2 (Leipzig, 1927); a 2nd ed., rev. in 1959, was publ. in N.Y. as *Masses I-VIII in the Collected Works,* I;

Masses and Mass Sections IX-XVI appeared as vol. II (N.Y., 1947; 2nd ed., 1966).

BIBL.: G. Reese and R. Snow, eds., *Essays in Musicology in Honor of D. P. on his 70th Birthday* (Pittsburgh, 1969). —NS/LK/DM

Plancken, Corneille Vander, Belgian violinist, clarinetist, conductor, teacher, and composer; b. Brussels, Oct. 25, 1772; d. there, Feb. 9, 1849. He studied violin with Eugène Godecharles and Jean Pauwels. He pursued his career in Brussels, where he was solo violinist in the orch. of the Grand Théâtre de la Monnaie (1797–1817?). From 1820 to 1830 he was solo violinist of the Royal Chapel. He also served as conductor of the Société du Grand Concert and Société Philharmonique. Plancken was a significant figure in the development of the Belgian school of violin virtuosity. He composed violin concertos and a Clarinet Concerto, but these works are lost.—LK/DM

Plançon, Pol (-Henri), famous French bass; b. Fumay, June 12, 1851; d. Paris, Aug. 11, 1914. He was destined by his parents for a commercial career in Paris, but showed a natural vocal ability, and began to study singing with Sbriglia and Duprez. He made his operatic debut as St.- Bris in *Les Huguenots* in Lyons (1877), then appeared for the first time in Paris as Colonna in Duprat's *Petrarque* at the Théâtre de la Gaîté (Feb. 11, 1880). After a season in Monte Carlo, he made a highly successful appearance at the Paris Opéra as Méphistophélès in Gounod's *Faust* (June 23, 1883); sang that role more than 100 times during his 10 seasons at the Opéra, and was regarded as unrivaled in his dramatic delivery and vocal power. On June 3, 1891, he sang Méphistophélès for his debut at London's Covent Garden, singing there every subsequent season until 1904. His American debut took place at the Metropolitan Opera in N.Y. on Nov. 29, 1893, as Jupiter in Gounod's *Philemon et Baucis.* He then resigned from the Paris Opéra and remained a member of the Metropolitan Opera until his retirement in 1908. He had an imposing physique, mobile features, and an innate acting ability. His repertoire consisted of about 50 roles in French, Italian, German, and Eng. In some operas he sang more than one part, as in *Roméo et Juliette* (Capulet and Friar), *Aida* (Ramfis and the King), *Les Huguenots* (St.-Bris and Marcel), etc. Of Wagnerian roles, he sang the Landgrave, King Heinrich, and Pogner.—NS/LK/DM

Plánický, Josef Antonín, Bohemian composer; b. Manětín, Nov. 27, 1691; d. Freising, Bavaria, Sept. 17, 1732. He was a tutor to the children of Countess Maria Gabriela Lažanska. After travels in Bohemia, Moravia, and Austria, he entered the service of the duke-bishop's musical entourage in Freising as a singer and instrumentalist in 1722. He also was active as a teacher at the seminary. Plánický wrote the opera *Zelus divi corbinrani eccesiae frisingensis fundamentum* (Freising, Oct. 7, 1724) and a fine vol. of 12 solo motets as *Opella ecclesiantica seu Ariae duodecim nova idea exornatae.*—LK/DM

Planquette, (Jean-) Robert, French composer; b. Paris, July 31, 1848; d. there, Jan. 28, 1903. He studied at the Paris Cons. with Duprato. He wrote chanson-nettes and "saynètes" for cafés-concerts in Paris, then composed a one-act operetta, *Paille d'avoine* (Paris, March 12, 1874), and others. He achieved his first great success with the production of *Les Cloches de Corneville*, a comic opera in 3 acts, at the Folies-Dramatiques (Paris, April 19, 1877); it was performed for the 1,000[th] time there in 1886, and became one of the most popular works of its genre; in Eng., it was given as *The Chimes of Normandy* (N.Y., Oct. 22, 1877; London, Feb. 23, 1878). Other operettas were *Le Chevalier Gaston* (Monte Carlo, Feb. 8, 1879), *Rip Van Winkle* (London, Oct. 14, 1882; very successful), *Nell Gwynne* (London, Feb. 7, 1884), *Surcouf* (Paris, Oct. 6, 1887; in Eng. as *Paul Jones*, London, Jan. 12, 1889), *La Cocarde tricolore* (Paris, Feb. 12, 1892), *Le Talisman* (Paris, Jan. 20, 1893), *Panurge* (Paris, Nov. 22, 1895), and *Mam'zelle Quat'Sous* (Paris, Nov. 5, 1897). A posthumous operetta, *Le Paradis de Mahomet* (orches-trated by Louis Ganne), was produced at the Variétés in Paris on May 15, 1906.—NS/LK/DM

Planson, Jean, French organist and composer; b. probably in Paris, c. 1559; d. after 1612. He was active in Paris, where he was organist at the collegiate church of St. Germain l'Auxérrois (1575–78?) and at St. Sauveur (1586–88). He publ. a vol. of motets and sonnets for 3 to 5 and 7 Voices (Paris, 1583) and a vol. of airs for 4 Voices (Paris, 1587).—LK/DM

Plantade, Charles-Henri, French composer; b. Pontoise, Oct. 14, 1764; d. Paris, Dec. 18, 1839. As a child, he studied singing and the cello in the Royal School for the "pages de musique," and afterward took lessons with Honoré Langlé (theory), Hüllmandel (piano), and Petrini (harp). In 1797 he became a singing teacher at the Campan Inst. at St.-Denis, where Hortense de Beauhar-nais, the future Queen of the Netherlands, was his pupil. He subsequently was in the service of Queen Hortense as her representative in Paris; was a prof. at the Paris Cons. from 1799 to 1807, and again in 1815–16 and from 1818 to 1828. From 1812 to 1815 he also held the post of singing master and stage director at the Paris Opéra. He received the ribbon of the Légion d'honneur from Louis XVIII (1814); from 1816, was music master of the Royal Chapel. Losing his various positions after the revolution of 1830, he retired to Batignolles. He wrote several operas, of which *Le Mari de circonstances* (Paris, March 18, 1813) was the most successful; other operas for Paris included *Les 2 Soeurs* (May 22, 1792), *Les Souliers mordores* (May 18, 1793), *Au plus brave la plus belle* (Oct. 5, 1794), *Palma, ou Le Voyage en Grèce* (Aug. 22, 1797), *Romagnesi* (Sept. 3, 1799), *Le Roman* (Nov. 12, 1800), *Zoé, ou La Pauvre Petite* (July 3, 1800), *Lisez Plutarque* (Spring 1800), and *Bayard à la ferté, ou Le Siège de Mezières* (Oct. 13, 1811). His other works included masses, motets, etc., and he also publ. 20 sets of ro-mances, 3 books of vocal duets (nocturnes), and a Harp Sonata. His son, Charles-François Plantade (b. Paris, April 14, 1787; d. there, May 26, 1870), was also a composer; studied at the Paris Cons.; worked in the Ministry of Fine Arts; wrote romances, chansons, and chansonettes.—NS/LK/DM

Planté, Francis, French pianist; b. Orthez, Basses-Pyrénées, March 2, 1839; d. St. Avit, near Mont-de-Marsan, Dec. 19, 1934. From 1849 he was a pupil of Marmontel at the Paris Cons., winning 1st prize after 7 months' tuition. After a course in harmony in Bazin's class (1853), he retired for private study for 10 years, and then reappeared as a pianist of finished technique and style. About 1900 he suddenly vanished from concert life, vowing that he would "never be seen again in public." He created a sensation in 1915 when he was heard again in several concerts in Paris, but, in order to keep his strange vow, he was hidden from the view of the audience by a screen.

BIBL.: O. Comettant, *F. P.* (Paris, 1874); A. Dandelot, *F. P.: Une Belle Vie d'artiste* (Paris, 1920; 3rd ed., 1930); A. Lenoir and J. de Nahuque, *F. P.: Doyen des pianistes* (Paris, 1931). —NS/LK/DM

Plantinga, Leon (Brooks), American musicolo-gist; b. Ann Arbor, Mich., March 25, 1935. He was educated at Calvin Coll. (B.A., 1957), Mich. State Univ. (M.Mus., 1959), and Yale Univ. (Ph.D., 1964, with the diss. *The Musical Criticism of Robert Schumann in the "Neue Zeitschrift für Musik"*). In 1963 he joined the faculty of Yale Univ., where he served as a prof. (from 1974), acting chairman (1978–79), and chairman (1979–86) of its music dept., and director of the division of humanities (1991–97). His *Romantic Music: A History of Musical Style in Nineteenth-Century Europe* (N.Y. and London, 1984) won the ASCAP-Deems Taylor Award in 1985.

WRITINGS: *Schumann as Critic* (New Haven and London, 1967); *Muzio Clementi: His Life and Music* (London, 1977); *Romantic Music: A History of Musical Style in Nineteenth-Century Europe* (N.Y. and London, 1984); *Anthology of Romantic Music* (N.Y. and London, 1984); *Beethoven's Concertos: History, Style, Performance* (N.Y., 1999).—NS/LK/DM

Plaschke, Friedrich (real name, Bedřich Plaške), Czech bass-baritone; b. Jaroměr, Jan. 7, 1875; d. Prague, Nov. 20, 1951. He studied with Leontine von Döttcher and Ottilie Sklenář-Mala in Prague, and then with Karl Scheidemantel in Dresden. He made his operatic debut with the Dresden Court (later State) Opera as the Herald in *Lohengrin* in 1900. He was on its roster until 1939, and during his tenure there created the following roles in operas by Richard Strauss: Pöschel in *Feuersnot*, the 1st Nazarene in *Salome*, Da-Ud in *Die ägyptische Helena*, Count Waldner in *Arabella*, and Sir Morosus in *Die schweigsame Frau*. He made many guest appearances at Vienna and Munich, and also sang at Bayreuth, at Covent Garden in London, and in the U.S. with the German Opera Co. in 1923–24.—NS/LK/DM

Plasson, Michel, French conductor; b. Paris, Oct. 2, 1933. He received training in piano from Lazare-Lévy, and then studied percussion at the Paris Cons., where he took the premier prix. In 1962 he won 1st prize in the Besançon conducting competiton, and then studied conducting in the U.S. with Leinsdorf, Monteux, and Stokowski. From 1966 to 1968 he was music director of the Théâtre de Metz. In 1968 he became conductor of the

Théâtre du Capitole in Toulouse, where he served as its music and general director from 1973 to 1982. In 1974 he became music director of the Orchestre du Capitole in Toulouse, which became the Orchestre National du Capitole in 1980. He took the orch. on various tours of Europe and North America. As a guest conductor, he appeared with many of the major orchs. and opera houses of the world. In 1987 he became principal guest conductor of the Tonhalle Orch. in Zürich. In 1994 he became music director of the Dresden Phil.—NS/LK/DM

Platania, Pietro, Italian composer; b. Catania, April 5, 1828; d. Naples, April 26, 1907. He studied with P. Raimondi at the Naples Cons. He was director of the Palermo Cons. (1863–82), and later maestro di cappella at Milan (from 1882), and also director of the Naples Cons. (1885–1902). Rossini and Verdi considered him an excellent contrapuntist.

Works: DRAMATIC: Opera: *Matilde Bentivoglio* (Palermo, 1852); *Piccarda Donati* (Palermo, March 3, 1857); *La vendetta slava* (Palermo, Feb. 4, 1865); *Spartaco* (Naples, March 29, 1891); etc. **OTHER:** *L'Italia*, sym.; *Sinfonia festiva* for Voices and Orch. for the coronation tour of King Umberto I (1878); *Pensiero sinfonico*; much sacred music; secular songs; pedagogical pieces.

Bibl.: F. Guardione, *P. P.* (Milan, 1908).—NS/LK/DM

Platel, Nicolas-Joseph, French cellist, teacher, and composer; b. Versailles, 1777; d. Brussels, Aug. 25, 1835. He was one of the pages de la musique to Louis XVI. After studying singing with Louis Richer and cello with J.-L. Duport, he completed his cello studies with J.M. de La Mare. In 1796–97 he was a cellist in the orch. of the Théâtre Feydeau in Paris. Following a sojourn in Lyons (1797–1801), he returned to Paris and established himself as a virtuoso cellist. From 1805 he made tours of Europe. In 1813 he became first cellist in the theater orch. in Antwerp. In 1820 he settled in Brussels, where he became the first prof. of cello at the Royal School of Music in 1827, a position he retained when it became the Cons. in 1832. Platel publ. 5 cello concertos, Sonatas for Cello and Basso Continuo, 6 duos for Violin and Cello, 3 trios for Violin, Viola, and Cello, solo cello pieces, and vocal romances.—LK/DM

Plath, Wolfgang, German musicologist; b. Riga, Latvia, Dec. 27, 1930; d. Augsburg, March 19, 1995. He studied musicology at the Free Univ. of Berlin with Gerstenberg, and later at the Univ. of Tübingen (Ph.D., 1958, with the diss. *Das Klavierbüchlein für Wilhelm Friedemann Bach*). In 1960 he was named co-ed. (with Wolfgang Rehm) of the *Neue Mozart-Ausgabe*. His studies of Mozart autographs and texts are valuable, and he contributed important articles to the *Mozart-Jahrbuch*. —NS/LK/DM

Plato, great Greek philosopher; b. probably in Athens, c.428 B.C.; d. there, 347/348 B.C. In his *Timaeus* he formulated a system of music in which he likened the movements of music to those of the soul, whose development may therefore be influenced by the art of music.

Bibl.: T.-H. Martin, *Études sur le Timée de P.n* (Paris, 1841); J. Regner, *P.s Musik-Theorie* (Halle, 1923); E. Moutsopoulos, *La musique dans l'oeuvre de P.n* (Paris, 1959); L. Richter, *Zur Wissenschaftslehre von der Musik bei P.n und Aristoteles* (Berlin, 1961). —NS/LK/DM

Platters, The, very successful, smooth doowop group of the 1950s. **MEMBERSHIP:** Tony Williams, lead ten. (b. Elizabeth, N.J., April 5, 1928; d. N.Y., Aug. 14, 1992); David Lynch, 2nd ten. (b. St. Louis, Mo., 1929; d. Jan. 2, 1981); Paul Robi, bar. (b. New Orleans, La., 1931; d. Feb. 1, 1989); Herb Reed, bs. (b. Kansas City, Mo., 1931); Zola Taylor, contralto (b. Los Angeles, 1934). Later members included Sonny Turner (b. Cleveland, Ohio, 1939); Nate Nelson (b. N.Y., April 10, 1932; d. Boston, Mass., June 1, 1984); Monroe Powell; Gene Williams. Mentor-manager-songwriter Buck Ram was born on Nov. 21, 1907, in Chicago, Ill., and died Jan. 1, 1991, in Las Vegas, Nev., at age 83.

In 1953 in Los Angeles, Tony Williams, David Lynch, Alex Hodge and Herb Reed formed The Platters and met Buck Ram, a former writer and arranger for the big bands of the 1930s and 1940s. Becoming their manager in February 1954, Ram added female vocalist Zola Taylor, from Shirley Gunter and The Queens, in May. Paul Robi replaced Alex Hodge in July, and Ram signed the group to the Federal subsidiary of Cincinnati's King Records. The group unsuccessfully recorded Ram's "Only You" and other songs for the label, later issued on King and Deluxe. Ram next placed the group with Mercury Records and, in the fall of 1955, they scored a top R&B/smash pop hit with "Only You." The song was quickly covered by the white group The Hilltoppers for Dot, but, unlike many recordings originated by black artists, The Platters' version proved more successful.

The Platters' recording of Ram's "The Great Pretender" became the first R&B ballad to top the pop as well as R&B charts. Ram's "(You've Got) the Magic Touch" proved a smash pop and R&B hit and the standard "My Prayer" became a top pop and R&B hit in 1956. Although their sound was more akin to The Ink Spots and The Mills Brothers than the doo-wop groups of the day, The Platters appeared in several rock 'n' roll movies, including 1956's *Rock around the Clock* and *The Girl Can't Help It*. Their crossover smashes continued with "You'll Never Never Know" (co-written by Tony Williams and Paul Robi), "It Isn't Right," "On My Word of Honor," "One in a Million" (co-written by Williams), "I'm Sorry" backed with "He's Mine," and Ram's "My Dream."

Developing a widely based audience among television viewers, rock 'n' roll fans and the larger pop audience, The Platters performed at rock 'n' roll shows and supper clubs. In 1958 they scored top pop/smash R&B hits with the classic "Twilight Time" (co-authored by Ram) and the standard "Smoke Gets in Your Eyes," recorded in Paris, France. Subsequent crossover hits included "Enchanted" and the standard "Harbor Lights." The Platters' anthology album *Encore of Golden Hits*, released in early 1960, remained on the charts for more than three years.

In 1961 Tony Williams left The Platters to pursue an inauspicious solo career. He was replaced by Sonny

Turner, and the group managed major pop hits with the standards "To Each His Own" and "I'll Never Smile Again." In 1962, Zola Taylor and Paul Robi left the group, to be replaced by Sandra Dawn and Nate Nelson (lead singer of The Flamingos' 1959 crossover hit "I Only Have Eyes for You"), respectively. Switching to Musicor Records, The Platters' last major hits came in 1966–67 with "I Love You 1000 Times" and "With This Ring."

Sonny Turner left The Platters in the early 1970s, and Nate Nelson left in 1982. Buck Ram maintained the group with lead vocalist Monroe Powell and bass singer Gene Williams through the 1980s. During this time former members Paul Robi, Herb Reed, and Tony Williams each toured with their own groups as The Platters. During the 1980s, several former members died, including David Lynch (1981), Nate Nelson (1984) and Paul Robi (1989). The Platters were inducted into the Rock and Roll Hall of Fame in 1990. The two principals of The Platters, Buck Ram and Tony Williams, died in 1991 and 1992, respectively.

DISC.: *The Platters* (1955); *The Platters* (1956); *The Platters—Vol. 2* (1957); *The Flying Platters* (1957); *Around the World with The Flying Platters* (1958); *Remember When* (1959); *Reflections* (1960); *Life Is Just a Bowl of Cherries* (1961); *Encore of Broadway Golden Hits* (1962); *Sing for the Lonely* (1962); *Moonlight Memories* (1963); *Sing All-Time Movie Hits* (1963); *Sing Latino* (1963); *Christmas with The Platters* (1963); *20th Anniversary Album* (1965); *The New Soul of The Platters* (1965); *I Love You 1,000 Times* (1966); *Have the Magic Touch* (1966); *Going Back to Detroit* (1967); *Sweet, Sweet Lovin'* (1968); *I Get the Sweetest Feeling* (1968); *Singing the Great Hits Our Way* (1969); *Greatest Hits, Featuring Paul Robi* (rec. 1986; rel. 1987).—**BH**

Platti, Giovanni Benedetto, Italian composer;
b. Padua, July 9, 1697; d. Würzburg, Jan. 11, 1763. In 1722 he went to Würzburg, where he was active as an instrumentalist, tenor, singing teacher, and composer at the court of the bishops until at least 1761.

WORKS: DRAMATIC: O p e r a : *Arianna* (Würzburg, 1729). **VOCAL:** 2 oratorios; Requiem; 6 masses; cantatas; etc. **INSTRUMENTAL** (all publ. in Nuremberg): *6 sonates pour la clavessin sur le goût italien*, op.1 (1742; ed. in Istituzioni e Monumenti dell'Arte Musicale Italiana, VII, 1941, and Mitteldeutsches Musikarchiv, 1st series, III-IV, Leipzig, 1957); 6 Concerti for Harpsichord and Strings, op.1 (1742); 6 Sonate for Flute and Cello, op.3 (1743?); 6 Sonate for Harpsichord, op.4 (c. 1746; ed. in Mitteldeutsches Musikarchiv, 1st series, III-IV, Leipzig, 1957); 5 concertos for Harpsichord and Strings; 28 cello concertos; Oboe Concerto; 21 sonatas for Violin, Cello, and Bass.

BIBL.: F. Torrefranca, *G.B. P. e la sonata moderna* (Milan, 1963).—**NS/LK/DM**

Plautzius (real name, Plavic), Gabriel, Slovenian instrumentalist and composer;
b. Carniola, date unknown; d. Mainz, Jan. 11, 1641. He was Kapellmeister at the electoral court in Mainz from 1612, where he introduced the concertato style. He publ. *Flosculus vernalis sacras cantiones, missas aliasque laudes B. Mariae continens* for 3 to 6 and 8 Voices and Basso Continuo (Aschaffenburg, 1622).

BIBL.: D. Cvetko, *Les compositeurs Gallus—P.—Dolar et leur oeuvre* (Ljubljana, 1963).—**LK/DM**

Playford, Henry, English music publisher, son of
John Playford; b. London, May 5, 1657; d. there, c. 1707. He worked with his father before setting up a business of his own. His most important publications were *Wit and Mirth*, a collection of Tom D'Urfey's songs (1699, 1700), and the 2nd book of Purcell's *Orpheus Britannicus* (1702).—**NS/LK/DM**

Playford, John, English music publisher, father of
Henry Playford; b. Norfolk, 1623; d. London, Nov. 1686. He was an apprentice (1639–47) to the publisher John Benson before setting up his own business. He began publishing music in 1651, his his most important publication being *The English Dancing Master* (London, 1651; many rev. eds. to 1728). Among his other publications, all printed in London, were *A Musicall Banquet* (1651), *Musick's Recreation on the Lyra Viol* (1652; 4th ed., 1682), J. Hilton's *Catch That Catch Can* (1652; many eds. to c. 1720), *A Catalogue of All the Musik Bookes...Printed in England* (1653), his own *A Breefe Introduction to the Skill of Musick* (1654; 2nd ed., enl., 1655, with T. Campion's "Art of Composing"; many eds. to 1730), *Court Ayres* (1655; 2nd ed., rev., 1662, as *Courtly Masquing Ayres*), his own *The Whole Book of Psalmes collected into English Meeter* (1661; many later eds.), *Apollo's Banquet for the Treble Violin* (1669; many eds. to 1701), his own *Psalms and Hymns in Solemn Musick* for 4 Voices (1671), *Choice Songs and Ayres* for Voice and Theorbo or Bass Viol (5 books, 1673, 1679, 1681, 1683, 1684), and *The Whole Book of Psalmes* (1677; many eds. to 1757).—**NS/LK/DM**

Pleasants, Henry, American music critic and
writer on music; b. Wayne, Pa., May 12, 1910; d. London, Jan. 4, 2000. He was educated at the Philadelphia Musical Academy and the Curtis Inst. of Music in Philadelphia. From 1930 to 1942 he was music critic of the *Philadelphia Evening Bulletin*, and then central European music correspondent of the *N.Y. Times* from 1945 to 1955. From 1950 to 1964 he was also active with the U.S. Foreign Service. From 1967 to 1998 he was the London music critic of the *International Herald Tribune*. He also served as the London ed. of *Stereo Review*. He was active as a guest lecturer throughout the U.S. and England, and also appeared on radio and television programs of the BBC, as well as those in North America and Europe. His writings appeared in many leading American and English music magazines, and he also was a contributor to the *Encyclopaedia Britannica* and *The New Grove Dictionary of Music and Musicians*. As a tr. and ed., he publ. *Vienna's Golden Years of Music 1850–1900* (writings of Hanslick: 1950), *The Musical Journeys of Louis Spohr* (1961), *The Musical World of Robert Schumann* (1965), *The Music Criticism of Hugo Wolf* (1979), and *Piano and Song* (by Friedrich Wieck; 1988). After Pleasants's death, it was learned that during his years with the U.S. Foreign Service he had worked as the U.S. Central Intelligence Agency station chief in Bonn in the 1950s.

WRITINGS (all publ. in N.Y.): *The Agony of Modern Music* (1955); *Death of a Music? The Decline of the European Tradition and the Rise of Jazz* (1961); *The Great Singers from the Dawn of Opera to Our Own Time* (1966; 3rd ed., rev. and enl., 1985); *Serious Music, and All That Jazz* (1969); *The Great American Popular Singers* (1974); *Opera in Crisis: Tradition, Present, Future* (1989).—**NS/LK/DM**

Plé-Caussade, Simone, French pianist, pedagogue, and composer; b. Paris, Aug. 14, 1897; d. Bagnères-de-Bigorre, Aug. 6, 1985. She studied piano at the Paris Cons. with Cortot and composition with **Georges Caussade**, whom she later married. In 1928 she was appointed prof. of harmony and counterpoint at the Paris Cons.; among her students were Gilbert Amy and Betsy Jolas. She wrote a number of orch. and chamber music works in a fine impressionistic manner. —NS/LK/DM

Pleeth, William, English cellist and teacher; b. London, Jan. 12, 1916; d. April 6, 1999. He studied at the London Violoncello School and with Klengel at the Leipzig Cons. In 1932 he made his debut in Leipzig, and then returned to London, where he first appeared in 1933. In subsequent years, he appeared as a soloist with various British orchs. He also was a member of the Blech (1936–41) and Allegri (1953–67) string quartets. From 1948 to 1978 he was prof. of cello at the Guildhall School of Music in London. In 1989 he received the Order of the British Empire. Pleeth's most famous student was Jacqueline Du Pré.—NS/LK/DM

Pleshakov, Vladimir, Russian-American pianist; b. Shanghai (of Russian parents), Oct. 4, 1934. He studied piano with Russian teachers in Shanghai, and in 1949 went to Sydney, where he took piano lessons with Alexander Sverjensky. In 1955 he emigrated to the U.S. and studied medicine at the Univ. of Calif., Berkeley (A.B., 1958). Turning back to music, he entered Stanford Univ. in the graduate school of music (Ph.D., 1973). He made a special study of piano manufacture in Beethoven's era, and performed on reconstructed pianos at his concerts of classical music.—NS/LK/DM

Pleskow, Raoul, Austrian-born American composer and teacher; b. Vienna, Oct. 12, 1931. He went to the U.S. in 1939, and became a naturalized citizen in 1945. He took courses at N.Y.'s Juilliard School of Music (1950–52), with Rathaus at Queens Coll. (B.M., 1956), and with Luening at Columbia Univ. (M.M., 1958). He taught at C.W. Post Coll., Long Island Univ. (from 1959). His works combine both tonal and atonal means of expression.

WORKS: ORCH.: *2 Movements* (1968); *Music* (1980); *4 Bagatelles* (1981); *6 Epigrams* (1985); *Consort* for Strings (1988). **CHAMBER:** *Movement* for Flute, Cello, and Piano (1964); *Music* for 7 Players (1966); *Movement* for 9 Players (1967); *3 Bagatelles* for Flute, Viola, and Piano (1969); Trio for Flute, Cello, and Piano (1978); String Quartet (1979); *4 Pieces* for Flute, Cello, and Piano (1979); *Variations on a Lyric Fragment* for Cello and Piano (1980); *4 Short Pieces* for 7 Players (1981); *Divertimento: Sua sei canzoni* for 5 Players (1984); *Intrada* for Flute, Clarinet, Violin, and Cello (1984); *Composition* for 4 Instruments (1987); solo pieces for Violin, Viola, Cello, Brass, and Piano. **VOCAL:** 2 cantatas for Soloists, Chorus, and Orch. 1975, 1979); *6 Brief Verses* for 2 Sopranos and/or Women's Voices, Strings, and Piano (1983); *Paumanok* for Soprano, Chorus, and Chamber Ensemble (1985); *Serenade* for Chorus and Orch. (1988); also many settings for Solo Voice with a variety of accompaniments. —NS/LK/DM

Plessis, Hubert (Lawrence) du, distinguished South African composer, pedagogue, pianist, harpsichordist, and writer on music; b. Malmesbury District, June 7, 1922. He was a student of W. H. Bell. After training in piano at the Univ. of Stellenbosch (B.A., 1943), he studied with Friedrich Hartmann at Rhodes Univ. Coll. in Grahamstown (B.Mus., 1945) and with Alan Bush and Howard Ferguson (composition and orchestration) at the Royal Academy of Music in London (1951–54). He was on the faculty of Rhodes Univ. Coll. (1944–51), the Univ. of Cape Town (1955–57), and the Univ. of Stellenbosch (1956–82). In 1963 he was awarded the Gold Medal of the South African Academy for Arts and Sciences. He received an honorary D.Mus. degree from the Univ. of Stellenbosch in 1989. In 1994 State President F. W. de Klerk presented him with the Order for Meritorious Service, 1st class. Among his writings were *Johann Sebastian Bach* (1960), *Dagboek van "Die Dans von die Reën"* (1970), and *Letters from William Henry Bell* (1973). In his music, he followed a tonal course with some excursions into serial byways.

WORKS: DRAMATIC: Incidental music. **ORCH.:** Sym. (1953–54); *Music After 3 Paintings by Henri Rousseau* for Large Chamber Orch. (1962); *Feestelike Suite* for Chamber Orch. (1977–78). **CHAMBER:** String Quartet (1953); Trio for Piano, Violin, and Cello (1957–60); *3 Pieces* for Flute and Piano (1962–63); *Variasies Op 'n volkswysie* for Harp (1968); *4 Antique Dances* for Flute and Harpsichord or Piano (1972–74); Sonata for Solo Viola (1977); Suite for 2 Clarinets (1982); *'n Kleine hulde aan Bach* for 2 Oboes and Bassoon (1984); Sonata for Solo Cello (1991; rev. 1994). **Piano:** 4 pieces (1943–45; rev. 1962); *6 Miniatures* (1945–49); 2 sonatas (1952; 1974–75); Sonata for Piano Duet (1953); *Prelude, Fugue, and Postlude* for Piano Duet (1954–55); *Inspiré par mes chats* (1963–64); 4 pieces (1964–65); *Toe ek 'n kind was* (When I was a child), suite (1970–71). **VOCAL:** *2 Christmas Carols* for Chorus (1953); *Malay Scenes* for Chorus, Clarinet, Harp, and String Orch. (1959); *The Dance of the Rain* for Chorus and Orch. (1959–60); *Kersliedjie* for Soprano, Mezzo-soprano, Alto, and Piano (1962); *Night and Dawn* for Soprano, Chorus, and Orch. (1965–66); *Requiem aeternam* for Chorus (1974–75); *Krokos* for Chorus (1982–83); *Hugenote-Kantata* for Soloists, Chorus, and Orch. (1986–87); other choral pieces and solo songs.—NS/LK/DM

Pletnev, Mikhail, Russian pianist and conductor; b. Arkhangel'sk, April 14, 1957. He began piano lessons at age 7 with Julia Shashkina in Kazan. At 13, he entered the Moscow Central Music School as a student of Yevgeni Timakin, and later attended master classes of Yakov Flier and Lev Vlasenko at the Cons. In 1977 he won the All-Union Competition, and then captured 1st prize in the Tchaikovsky Competition in Moscow in 1978. Following appearances in England and the U.S. in 1979, he made tours of Europe and Japan. He also took up conducting. In 1990 he founded the Russian National Orch. in Moscow, which he led on its debut tour of the U.S. (1992–93). He remained its conductor until 1999, when he was made its conductor laureate. As a pianist, Pletnev's repertoire extends from Bach to contemporary scores; he has won particular distinction for his interpretations of the Classical and Romantic masterworks. Among his compositions are orch. works and chamber pieces.—NS/LK/DM

Pleyel, Ignace Joseph (actually, **Ignaz Josef**), eminent Austrian-French pianist, piano manufacturer, music publisher, and composer, father of **(Joseph Stephen) Camille Pleyel**; b. Ruppertsthal, near Vienna, June 18, 1757; d. on his estate near Paris, Nov. 14, 1831. He was the 24th of 38 children in the impoverished family of a schoolteacher; however, he received sufficient education, including music lessons, to qualify for admittance to the class of Wanhal. Thanks to the generosity of Count Ladislaus Erdödy, he became Haydn's pupil and lodger in Eisenstadt (c. 1772–77), and then was enabled to go to Rome. In 1783 he became 2nd Kapellmeister at the Strasbourg Cathedral; was advanced to the rank of 1st Kapellmeister in 1789, but lost his position during the turbulent times of the French Revolution. He conducted the "Professional Concerts" in London during the 1791–92 season, and honored his teacher Haydn by playing a work of Haydn at his opening concert (Feb. 13, 1792). After several years he returned to Strasbourg to liquidate his estate. In 1795 he went to Paris, where he opened a music store which was in business until 1834, and in 1807 founded a piano factory, which manufactured famous French pianos; the firm eventually became known as Pleyel et Cie., and continued to prosper for over a century and a half. The name Pleyel is mainly known through his piano manufacture, but he was a prolific and an extremely competent composer. His productions are so close in style to those of Haydn that specialists are still inclined to attribute certain works in Haydn's catalogues to Pleyel. He composed about 45 syms., 6 symphonies concertantes, 2 violin concertos, 5 cello concertos, other concertos, 16 string quintets, Septet, Sextet, more than 70 string quartets, many trios and duos, and some vocal music, including 2 operas, *Die Fee Urgele* for puppet theater (Eszterház, Nov. 1776) and *Ifigenia in Aulide* (Naples, May 30, 1785), and some songs.

BIBL.: L. de Fourcaud, *La Salle P.* (Paris, 1893); R. Benton, *Ignace P.: A Thematic Catalogue of His Compositions* (N.Y., 1977); R. Benton and J. Halley, *P. as Music Publisher: A Documentary Sourcebook of Early 19th-Century Music* (Stuyvesant, N.Y., 1990). —NS/LK/DM

Pleyel, (Joseph Stephen) Camille, French pianist, piano manufacturer, and composer, son of **Ignace (Ignaz Josef) Pleyel**; b. Strasbourg, Dec. 18, 1788; d. Paris, May 4, 1855. He was a pupil of his father and later of Desormery, Dussek, and Steibelt. In 1815 became a legal partner in his father's firm, which became Ignace Pleyel et Fils Aîné. In 1824 he took complete control of the business, and was joined by Kalkbrenner in 1829. Upon Camille's death, Kalkbrenner's son-in-law, A. Wolff, took over the firm. Pleyel's works include trios, sonatas, and various piano pieces. His wife, Marie-Félicité-Denise Pleyel (née Moke; b. Paris, Sept. 4, 1811; d. St.-Josse-ten-Noode, near Brussels, March 30, 1875), was a pianist, teacher, and composer. She studied with Jacques Herz, Moscheles, and Kalkbrenner, appearing as soloist in Kalkbrenner's 1st Piano Concerto in Brussels at age 14. She created a sensation with her virtuosic tour of Belgium, Austria, Germany, and Russia in her 15th year. Berlioz fell in love with her (1830), but she married the younger Pleyel that same year, only to separate from him in 1835; then she toured Europe with great success. She subsequently was prof. of piano at the Brussels Cons. (1848–72). She wrote some piano pieces. —NS/LK/DM

Plishka, Paul (Peter), American bass; b. Old Forge, Pa., Aug. 28, 1941. He studied at Montclair, N.J., State Coll. From 1961 to 1965 he was a member of the Paterson (N.J.) Lyric Opera; in 1965 he joined the Metropolitan Opera National Co., and sang with it on tour. On June 27, 1967, he made his Metropolitan Opera debut in a concert performance at the Botanical Gardens in the Bronx as the Uncle-Priest in *Madama Butterfly*; he first sang on the Metropolitan's stage as the Monk in *La Gioconda* on Sept. 21, 1967; remained on its roster for many years, most notably in such roles as King Marke, Leporello, Varlaam, Oroveso, Pimen, Gounod's Méphistophélès, and Henry VIII in *Anna Bolena*. In 1992 he celebrated his 25th anniversary at the Metropolitan Opera in an acclaimed appearance as Falstaff. In 1993 he won critical accolades as Philip II at the Seattle Opera. In 1997 he portrayed Mozart's Dr. Bartolo at the Metropolitan Opera. He also appeared as a concert singer with many of the major U.S. orchs.—NS/LK/DM

Plonsey, Dan, plays a variety of clarinets and saxophones (including soprano, alto, tenor, and baritone) in addition to more unusual horns like the Laotian mouth organ; b. Cleveland, Ohio, Sept. 1, 1958. Dan Plonsey started playing clarinet in the second grade. Three years later he picked up the alto sax. He credits his exposure to Charles Ives, Iannis Xenakis, Karlheinz Stockhausen, and Mauricio Kagel in his freshman year at Yale as "life-changing influences." A couple of years later, in 1979, he had an impressionable first encounter with Sun Ra. He took off that summer for the legendary Creative Music Studio in Woodstock, N.Y., where he studied with Roscoe Mitchell, Anthony Braxton, Leo Smith, and other luminaries of the Association for the Advancement of Creative Musicians and beyond. From 1986 to 1988, the Bay Area composer-improviser attended classes once again with Braxton, while earning an M.A. in music composition from Mills Coll. As co-founder and curator for two years (from March 1995) of the Beanbender's weekly creative-music series in Berkeley, Calif., he fueled the Bay Area improv scene. In an effort to make the venue "an otherworldly presence," he booked both up-and-coming locals and renowned innovators like Parker/Guy/Lytton, John Butcher, Rova Saxophone Quartet, and Nels Cline. As a recording artist, he is just beginning to come into his own. His ability to fuse the absurd, intellectual, and emotional sides of his personality into both compositions and improvisations gives his music a distinctive voice, which he says arises "from the drama of conflict." A wide-eyed experimentalist, his work ranges from simple melodic frameworks to extraordinary polyphony, at times incorporating elements of over-the-top Dada theater in a bid to make real the unreal.

DISC.: *Dire Images of Beauty* (1991); *Another Curiosity Piece* (1995); *Ivory Bill* (1997); *Child King Dictator Fool* (1997).—SP

Plowright, Rosalind (Anne), English mezzo-soprano, later soprano; b. Worksop, May 21, 1949. She was a student of F. R. Cox at the Royal Manchester Coll. of Music, where she made her operatic debut in the college's first British production of J. C. Bach's *Temistocle* in 1968. In 1975 she made her first appearance with the English National Opera in London as Page in *Salome*, and as Agathe with the Glyndebourne Touring Opera. In 1979 she won the Sofia International Competition and sang Miss Jessel in *The Turn of the Screw* at the English National Opera. She made her debut at London's Covent Garden as Ortlinde in 1980. In 1981 she sang at the Frankfurt am Main Opera and at the Bavarian State Opera in Munich. In 1982 she made her U.S. debut as a soloist with Muti and the Philadelphia Orch., and then her U.S. operatic debut in *Il Corsaro* in San Diego. In 1983 she appeared at Milan's La Scala, the Edinburgh Festival, and in San Francisco. She sang Aida at Covent Garden in 1984, and appeared at the Deutsche Oper in Berlin. In 1986 she sang Senta at Covent Garden. In 1987 she appeared as Gluck's Alceste at La Scala. In 1990 she made her debut at the Vienna State Opera as Amelia. She was engaged as Tosca at the English National Opera in 1994, and in 1996 she portrayed Santuzza at the Berlin State Opera. She also toured widely as a soloist with orchs. and as a recitalist. Among her other operatic roles were Médée, Rossini's Desdemona, Norma, Ariadne, and Maddalena in *Andrea Chénier*.—NS/LK/DM

Plummer, John, English composer; b. c. 1410; d. c. 1484. He was a member of the Chapel Royal by 1441. After serving as Warden or Master of the Chapel Children (1444–55), he was verger of the Royal Free Chapel of St. George at Windsor Castle from 1460. Among his extant works are a Kyrie, Gloria, antiphons, and motets.—LK/DM

Plush, Vincent, remarkable Australian composer; b. Adelaide, April 18, 1950. He studied piano, organ, and voice before embarking on regular courses at the Univ. of Adelaide (B.M., 1971), where his principal instructors in composition were Andrew McCredie and Richard Meale. From 1973 to 1980 he taught at the New South Wales State Conservatorium of Music in Sydney. In 1976 he founded the Seymour Group, an ensemble devoted to the performance of contemporary music. In 1981 he joined the staff of the Australian Broadcasting Commission (A.B.C.) in Sydney. From his earliest independent activities as a lecturer, radio commentator, and conductor, Plush dedicated his efforts to the promotion of Australian music. Thanks to a generous Harkness fellowship, he was able to spend a couple of years at Yale Univ., conducting interviews with a number of American composers for its Oral History Project; also worked at the Univ. of Minn. (1981), and participated in an Australian Arts Festival in Minneapolis (1982). He then spent a year at the Center for Music Experiment and the Computer Music Facility at the Univ. of Calif. at San Diego. Returning to Australia in 1983, he became composer-in-residence for the A.B.C., where he inaugurated a series of radio broadcasts pointedly entitled "Mainstreet U.S.A.," dedicated to new American music. A firm believer in the authentic quality of Australian folk music, he organized in Sydney the whimsically named ensemble Magpipe Musicians, which gave performances of native music in schools and art galleries, on the radio, in the concert hall, at country festivals, citizenship ceremonies, railway openings, and suchlike events, public and private. Their programs were deliberately explorative, aggressive, and exhortatory, propagandistic of new ideas, often with a decided revolutionary trend. The titles of Plush's own works often pay tribute to revolutionary or heroic events, e.g., *On Shooting Stars—Homage to Victor Jara* (a Chilean folksinger murdered by the fascistic Chilean police), *Bakery Hill Rising* (memorializing the suppression of the rebellion of Australian gold miners in 1854), *Gallipoli Sunrise* (commemorating the sacrificial attempt at capturing the Gallipoli Straits in World War I, during which thousands of Australians perished), and *The Ludlow Lullabies* (recalling the brutal attack on striking coal miners in the region of Ludlow, Colo., in 1914). The musical setting of each of these works varies from astutely homophonic to acutely polyphonic, according to the requirements of the subject.

WORKS: DRAMATIC: *Australian Folksongs*, musical theater piece for Baritone and Ensemble (Sydney, July 19, 1977); *The Maitland and Morpeth String Quartet* for Narrator and String Quartet (Sydney, April 1, 1979; rev. 1985); *Facing the Danger* for Narrator and Instruments, after the poem *Say No* by Barbara Berman (1982; Las Vegas, Jan. 18, 1983); *Grody to the Max* for "Val"-(i.e. San Fernando "Valley Girl") speaker and Trumpeter (1983); *The Wakefield Chronicles*, pageant for Narrator, Solo Trumpet and Trombone, and Ensemble, after Edward Gibbon Wakefield (Adelaide, March 5, 1986); *The Muse of Fire* for Narrator, Baritone, Trumpet, Flute, Piano, Chorus, 2 Brass Bands, Children's Chorus, and Organ, after Andrew Torning (1986–87). **ORCH.:** *Pacifica* (1986; rev. 1987; Aspen, July 10, 1988); *Concord/Eendracht* (Utrecht, May 18, 1990); *Pilbara* for Strings (1991). **Brass Band:** *The Wakefield Chorales* (1986); *March of the Dalmatians* (1987). **CHAMBER:** *Aurores* for Horn, Piano, and Ensemble (from *O Paraguay!*; Kensington, New South Wales, July 31, 1979); *Bakery Hill Rising* for Solo Horn and 8 Other Horns (1980; Ballarat, Victoria, Feb. 14, 1981); *On Shooting Stars—Homage to Victor Jara* for Ensemble (Sydney, Sept. 11, 1981); *FireRaisers*, "Concertino in the Style of a Vaudeville Entertainment" for Trumpet and Ensemble (Brisbane, Queensland, Sept. 30, 1984); *Gallipoli Sunrise* for Tenor Trombone and 7 Other Trombones (1984); *Helices* for Percussion Quartet (from *The Wakefield Chronicles*; 1985); *The Wakefield Convocation* for Brass Quintet (1985); *The Wakefield Invocation* for Trumpet and Organ (1986); *The Ludlow Lullabies* for Violin and Piano (Colorado Springs, Oct. 19, 1989); *SkyFire* for 10 Pianos and Tape (Colorado Springs, Nov. 19, 1989); *Aunt Kelly's Book of Tangos* for Violin, Cello, and Piano (1990); *Florilegium I, II, and III* (Sydney, Sept. 28, 1990); *Los Dios de Los Muertos* for Percussion Quartet (1990); *The Love-Songs of Herbert Hoover* for Horn Trio (1991); also pieces for Solo Instruments, including *Franz Liszt Sleeps Alone*, piano nocturne (1985; Budapest, March 12, 1986) and *Encompassings* for Organ (Canberra, March 16, 1975). **TAPE:** *Estuary* (1978); *Stevie Wonder's Music* for Flute and Tape (Sydney, Nov. 4, 1979); *All Ears* (1985); *Metropolis: Sydney* (WDR, Cologne, Nov. 14, 1988). **VOCAL:** *Magnificat* for Soprano, Flute, and 3 Vocal Quartets (1970; Sydney, Sept. 8, 1976); *3 Carols* for Soprano, Contralto, and Children's Chorus (1978, 1979, 1982); *The Hymn of the Winstanly Levellers* for Speaking/Singing Chorus (Sydney, May 23, 1981); *Ode to Knocks* for Mixed Voices and Instruments (Knox, Victoria, Sept. 6, 1981); *Letters from the Antipodes: 6 English Reflections on Colonial Australia* for Small

Chorus (1984; Sydney, July 9, 1989); *Letters from the Antipodes: 6 English Reflections on Colonial Australia* for Small Chorus (1984; Sydney, July 9, 1989); *All Ears*, radiophonic composition for Voices (Radio 2MBS-FM, Sydney, March 16, 1985); *The Muse of Fire*, pageant for Voices and Instruments (Penrith, New South Wales, Oct. 17, 1987); *Cornell Ceremonial Music* for Brass Instruments and Chorus (Winter Park, Fla., Nov. 10, 1988); *Andrew Torning's March to Victory* for Small Chorus and Piano (1989); *The Arraignment of Henry Lawson* for Voices and Instruments (1991); songs.—NS/LK/DM

Plutarch, famous Greek writer; b. Chaeronea, Boeotia, c.46; d. after 119. His series of essays, *Ethica* (Latin *Moralia*), includes a discussion of music. See the Loeb ed. (16 vols., 1928 et seq.).—NS/LK/DM

Pocci, Franz, Graf von, German writer on music and composer; b. Munich, March 7, 1807; d. there, May 7, 1876. Possessing versatile talents, he wrote plays with music for a puppet theater in Munich, for which he also designed the scenery. He was at his best in pieces for children (*Blumenlieder, Bildertöne für Klavier, Soldatenlieder, Jägerlieder, Alte und neue Kinderlieder,* etc.). His 2 piano sonatas were praised by Schumann for their poetic expression and fine Romantic spirit. An opera, *Der Alchymist*, was produced in Munich (1840). His grandson F. Pocci publ. a collection, *Franz Poccis Lustiges Komödienbüchlein* (Munich, 1921).

BIBL.: H. Holland, *Zur Erinnerung an F. P.* (Munich, 1877); K. Pastor, *F. P. als Musiker* (diss., Univ. of Munich, 1932). —NS/LK/DM

Poco, seminal West Coast country-rock band of the 1970s. **MEMBERSHIP:** Jim Messina, lead gtr., bs., voc. (b. Maywood, Calif., Dec. 5, 1947); Richie Furay, rhythm gtr., voc. (b. Yellow Springs, Ohio, May 9, 1944); Randy Meisner, bs., voc. (b. Scottsbluff, Neb., March 8, 1946); Rusty Young, pedal steel gtr., dobro., voc. (b. Long Beach, Calif., Feb. 23, 1946); George Grantham, drm., voc. (b. Cordell, Okla., Jan. 20, 1947). Timothy B. Schmit, bs., voc. (b. Sacramento, Calif., Oct. 30, 1947) replaced Randy Meisner; and Paul Cotton, gtr., voc. (b. Los Angeles, Feb. 26, 1943) replaced Jim Messina, in 1970. Schmit and George Grantham left in 1979, to be replaced by Steve Chapman, drm.; Charlie Harrison, bs.; Kim Bullard, kybd.

Poco did not attain the popularity of the Eagles, the first commercially successful band of the genre, until the late 1970s. By that time founders Jim Messina and Richie Furay had moved on, as had founder Randy Meisner, who subsequently joined and departed the Eagles. Despite the personnel changes, Poco maintained a remarkably consistent sound, featuring group vocal harmonies and rock instrumentation. They recorded several outstanding albums, including 1973's *Crazy Eyes*, eventually breaking through with 1979's *Legend* and its two hit singles. The group disbanded in 1984 and reunited with the original members in 1989.

Jim Messina and Richie Furay, both former members of the Buffalo Springfield, formed Poco with Rusty Young, Randy Meisner, and George Grantham in August 1968. Debuting at the Troubadour in Los Angeles in

November, Poco auditioned for Apple Records but signed with Epic. Given the chaotic career of the Buffalo Springfield, Poco's debut album was appropriately titled *Pickin' Up the Pieces*. The album sold only modestly and failed to yield a hit single. By the time of the album's release, Meisner had already departed to join Rick Nelson's Stone Canyon Band, later to help form the Eagles. Poco remained a quartet until February 1970, when Timothy B. Schmit joined the band. *Poco* and *Deliverin'* yielded minor hits with Messina's "You Better Think Twice" and Furay's "C'mon."

In November 1970 Jim Messina left Poco to form the successful Loggins and Messina duo with Kenny Loggins. He was replaced by Paul Cotton, the erstwhile leader of the Ill. Speed Press. This lineup—Furay, Young, Cotton, Schmit, and Grantham—recorded three albums and toured extensively, usually as a support act. *Crazy Eyes*, probably their finest album for Epic, sold moderately and included Furay's title song as well as excellent versions of Gram Parsons's "Brass Buttons" and J. J. Cale's "Magnolia."

Richie Furay left Poco in September 1973 to form the ill-fated Souther-Hillman-Furay Band, with singer-songwriter John David Souther and Chris Hillman, a former member of the Byrds and the Flying Burrito Brothers. An early associate of Jackson Browne and Glenn Frey, Souther had cowritten several songs for the Eagles and contributed three songs to Linda Ronstadt's album *Don't Cry Now*. Formed at the behest of Asylum Records president David Geffen as a prospective supergroup, they scored a major hit with Furay's "Fallin' in Love" from their debut album. However, the group encountered a credibility problem brought on by Asylum's massive hype campaign, and they disbanded in late 1975. Furay later recorded three solo albums for Asylum, managing a moderate hit with "I Still Have Dreams" in late 1979.

With Furay's departure, Poco continued as a four-piece, with Paul Cotton taking over as lead vocalist and Cotton and Young composing most of the material. They recorded two more albums for Epic before switching to ABC Records in 1975. They were able to achieve minor hits with "Keep On Tryin'" and the title songs to *Rose of Cimarron* and *Indian Summer*. However, by March 1978 Timothy B. Schmit had left to join the Eagles and George Grantham had left, to eventually join the Doobie Brothers. Rusty Young, the only remaining original member, and Paul Cotton reconstituted the group for their best-selling album *Legend*, which yielded the major hits "Crazy Love" and "Heart of the Night." Buoyed by the album's success (it stayed on the album charts for a year), Poco continued to tour and record until 1984, when they disbanded.

In 1989 the five original members of Poco—Jim Messina, Richie Furay, Randy Meisner, Rusty Young, and George Grantham—reunited to record *Legacy* for RCA. The album yielded a moderate hit with "Nothin' to Hide," cowritten by producer Richard Marx, and "Call It Love." They toured in 1990 with drummer Gary Mallaber, but the band soon disintegrated.

DISC.: POCO: *Pickin' Up the Pieces* (1969); *P.* (1970); *Deliverin'* (1971); *From the Inside* (1971); *A Good Feelin' to Know*

(1972); *Crazy Eyes* (1973); *Seven* (1974); *Cantamos* (1974); *Live* (1976); *Head Over Heels* (1975); *Rose of Cimarron* (1976); *Indian Summer* (1977). *Legend* (1978); *Under the Gun* (1980); *Blue and Gray* (1981); *Cowboys and Englishmen* (1982); *Ghost Town* (1982); *Inamorata* (1984); *Ghost Town/Inamorata* (1995); *Legacy* (1989). **ANTHOLOGIES:** *The Very Best of P. (1969–1974)* (1975); *The Songs of Paul Cotton* (1979); *The Songs of Richie Furay* (1979); *The Forgotten Trail (1969–1974)* (1990); *Backwards* (1983); *Crazy Loving: The Best of P., 1975–1982* (1989). **THE SOUTHER-HILLMAN-FURAY BAND:** *The Souther-Hillman-Furay Band* (1974); *Trouble in Paradise* (1975). **RICHIE FURAY** *I've Got a Reason* (1976); *Dance a Little Light* (1978); *I Still Have a Dream* (1979).—**BH**

Podéšt, Ludvík, Czech composer; b. Dubňany, Dec. 19, 1921; d. Prague, Feb. 27, 1968. He was a student of Kvapil (composition) at the Brno Cons. (1945–48) and of Racek and B. Štědroň (musicology) at the Univ. of Brno (Ph.D., 1949). After working at the Brno Radio (1947–51), he was music director of the Vit Nejedlý Army Artistic Ensemble (1953–56) and head of the music dept. of the Czech TV (1958–60).

WORKS: DRAMATIC: O p e r a : *Tři apokryfy* (3 Apocryphas; 1957–58); *Hrátky s čertem* (Frolics with the Devil; 1957–60; Liberec, Oct. 12, 1963). ORCH.: Sym. (1947–48; rev. 1964); *Raymonda Dienová*, symphonic poem (1950–51); 4 suites (1951, 1954, 1956, 1960); 2 piano concertos (1951–53; 1958–59); Violin Concerto, *Jarní Serenáda* (1953); *Advent Rhapsody* (1956–57); Cimbalom Concertino (1963); *The Seconds of a Day*, symphonic variations (1965); Concertino for 2 Cellos and Chamber Orch. (1965); *Partita* for Strings, Guitar, and Percussion (1967). CHAMBER: 2 string quartets (1942, 1942); *Litanie* for String Quartet (1944); Wind Quintet (1946); Violin Sonata (1947); Cello Sonata (1947); *Hojačky* for 2 Clarinets and Piano (1947); Suite for Viola and Piano (1955–56). P i a n o : Sonatina (1945); Sonata (1946). VOCAL: *Smrt* (Death), cantata (1942); *Písně z koncentráku* (Songs from the Concentration Camp) for Baritone and Orch. (1946); *Měsíce* (Months) for Soprano and Orch. (1948; rev. 1957–58).—**NS/LK/DM**

Podešva, Jaromír, Czech composer and teacher; b. Brno, March 8, 1927. He learned to play the piano, violin, and viola and to compose in childhood. After attending the Brno Cons. (1946–47), he pursued training in composition with Kvapil at the Janáček Academy of Music in Brno (1947–51; postgraduate studies, 1951–53). In 1960–61 he traveled abroad, studying with Copland at the Berkshire Music Center in Tanglewood and with Dutilleux in Paris. His travels are recounted in the book *Současná hudba na Západě* (Current Music in the West; Prague, 1963). From 1969 to 1987 he taught at the Ostrava Cons. He publ. the treatise *Možnosti kadence v dvanáctitónovém poli* (The Possibilities of Cadences in the Twelve-tone System; Prague, 1974). As a composer, Podešva reacted positively to his travels abroad and composed works in a style embracing both tonality and dodecaphony.

WORKS: DRAMATIC: *Bambini di Praga*, buffa-ballet-pantomime (1968). ORCH.: 10 syms.: No. 1 (1950–51), No. 2 for Flute and Strings (1961), No. 3, *Culmination—The Pearl Deep Down* (1966), No. 4, *Soláň Music*, for Flute, Harpsichord, and Small String Orch. (1967), No. 5, *3 Fragments of the Quinquennium*, for Baritone and Orch. (1967), No. 6 (1970), No. 7, *In*

memoriam J.P. jun. (1951–1972) (1982–83), No. 8, *Ostrava* (1986), No. 9 (1989), and No. 10, *Initium ultimum* (1993); *Kounic Halls* (1952); Flute Concerto (1965); Concerto for String Quartet and Orch. (1971); Piano Concerto (1973); *Beskydy Suite* (1974); Violin Concerto (1974–75); Trumpet Concerto (1975); *Homage to Léos Janáček* (1977); *Sinfonietta festiva* for Chamber String Orch. (1983); Viola Concerto (1986); *5 Pieces* for Chamber String Orch. (1994). CHAMBER: 6 string quartets (1950, 1951, 1955, 1960, 1964, 1976); 2 nonets (1954–55; 1972); Violin Sonata (1958); Cello Sonatina (1960); Wind Quintet (1961); *5 Pieces* for Violin and Piano (1967); Suite for Viola and Piano, *In Search of a Smile* (1969); Concertino for 2 Violins and Piano (1972); Quartet for Violin, Clarinet, Cello, and Piano (1977); Sonata for Solo Viola, *Circle* (1982); Clarinet Quintet (1984); Clarinet Sonatina (1984); *Fantasia quasi una sonata* for Violin and Piano (1987); Trio for Violin, Cello, and Piano (1990); *Movement* for Viola and Piano (1992); piano pieces. VOCAL: Choral works; songs. —**NS/LK/DM**

Poelchau, Georg Johann David, German tenor and music collector; b. Kremon, near Riga, June 23, 1773; d. Berlin, Aug. 12, 1836. He was educated at the Univ. of Jena. After making appearances as a soloist in Hamburg, he settled in Berlin in 1813. In 1814 he became a member of the Singakademie, where he was head of its library from 1832. He devoted much of his time to acquiring a large and valuable collection of rare books and manuscripts. The latter included items by Bach, Haydn, Mozart, and Beethoven. At his death, the collection passed into the hands of his son, who sold it to the Royal Library in Berlin in 1841.

BIBL.: K. Engler, *G. P. und seine Musikaliensammlung: Ein Beitrag zur Überlieferung Bachscher Musik in der ersten Hälfte des 19. Jahrhunderts* (Göppinge, 1974).—**LK/DM**

Poglietti, Alessandro, eminent Italian organist, teacher, and composer; b. place and date unknown; d. at the hands of the Turks during the siege of Vienna, July 1683. He served as court and chamber organist in the Vienna Kapelle of Emperor Leopold I (from 1661). He was one of the outstanding keyboard composers of his era. His works included *Endimione festeggiante*, opera (Gottweig, Jan. 12, 1677), sacred vocal works, and keyboard music, including 12 ricercares (ed. in Die Orgel, II/5–6, Lippstadt, 1957), suites, canzonas, capriccios, preludes, and fugues.—**NS/LK/DM**

Pogorelich, Ivo, provocative Yugoslav pianist; b. Belgrade, Oct. 20, 1958. He commenced piano lessons in Belgrade when he was 7, and when he was 11 he became a pupil of A. Timakin in Moscow. After studies at its Central Music School, he continued his training at the Moscow Cons., where he became a student of Aliza Kezeradze in 1976; they married in 1980. After winning 5 competitions in his homeland and the Casagrande Competition in Terni, Italy (1978), he captured 1st prize in the Montreal Competition in 1980; later that year he entered the Chopin Competition in Warsaw, where he became the center of a major controversy after he was eliminated from its final round; one of the jurors, Martha Argerich, resigned in protest and declared that Pogorelich was a "genius"; a group of Polish music

critics were moved to give him a special prize. In 1981 he made his Carnegie Hall debut in N.Y. in a recital, and that same year he made his London debut. He subsequently toured all over the world, appearing both as a soloist with orchs. and as a recitalist. His phenomenal technical mastery is well suited in showcasing his brilliant but idiosyncratic interpretations of works ranging from Bach to Bartók. He and his wife founded the Ivo Pogorelich International Solo Piano Competition, a triennial event first held in Pasadena in 1993.
—NS/LK/DM

Pohl, Carl Ferdinand, German writer on music; b. Darmstadt, Sept. 6, 1819; d. Vienna, April 28, 1887. He was a pupil of Sechter in Vienna. During his stay in London (1863–66) he gathered all available facts concerning the residence there of Mozart and Haydn, embodying this information in his publ. *Mozart und Haydn in London* (2 vols., Vienna, 1867); was archivist and librarian of Vienna's Gesellschaft der Musikfreunde (1866–87). Pohl also began an extended biography of Haydn, but publ. only one vol. (in 2 parts, 1875, 1882); the work was finished by Hugo Botstiber (Leipzig, 1927). Other publs.: *International Exhibition of 1862. Cursory Notices on the History of the Glass Harmonica* (London, 1862), an interesting historical review, *Die Gesellschaft der Musikfreunde...und ihr Conservatorium* (1871), *Denkschrift aus Anlass des hundertjährigen Bestehens der Tonkünstler-Soziat in Wien* (1871), and *Bibliographie der Musiksammelwerke des 16. und 17. Jahrhunderts* (with R. Eitner and A. Lagerberg; 1877).—**NS/LK/DM**

Pohle, David, German composer; b. Marienberg, near Chemnitz, 1624; d. Merseburg, Dec. 20, 1695. He was a student of Schütz in Dresden, and then was active at the court there and in Merseburg, Kassel, Weissenfels, and Zeitz before returning to Merseburg. In 1660 he was made Konzertmeister and in 1661 Kapellmeister in Halle. He was again active in Weissenfels and Zeitz (1674–77), serving as Kapellmeister in the latter from 1678 to 1680. From 1682 he was Kapellmeister in Merseburg. He composed several Singspiels, much sacred music, some secular vocal pieces, and 25 instrumental sonatas.

BIBL.: G. Gille, *Der Schützschüler D. P. (1624–1695): Seine Bedeutung für die deutsche Musikgeschichte des 17. Jahrhunderts* (diss., Univ. of Halle, 1973).—**LK/DM**

Pohlig, Karl, German conductor; b. Teplitz, Feb. 10, 1858; d. Braunschweig, June 17, 1928. A pupil of Liszt in Weimar, Pest, and Rome, he began his career as a pianist, touring Germany, Austria, Russia, Scandinavia, and Italy. He became 1st Kapellmeister at Graz, then asst. conductor to Mahler at the Vienna Court Opera, and conductor at London's Covent Garden (1897–98); was 1st Kapellmeister in Coburg and then in Stuttgart (1900–07). After serving as conductor of the Philadelphia Orch. (1907–12), he settled in Braunschweig as Generalmusikdirektor.—**NS/LK/DM**

Pointer Sisters, The, created a unique distillation of improvisatory jazz-style vocals, 1940s-style dress,

and campy onstage demeanor that established them as nostalgia entertainers more than recording artists in the mid-1970s. **MEMBERSHIP:** Ruth Pointer (b. East Oakland, Calif., March 19, 1946); Anita Pointer (b. East Oakland, Calif., Jan. 23, 1948); Bonnie Pointer (b. East Oakland, Calif., July 11, 1951); June Pointer (b. East Oakland, Calif., Nov. 30, 1954). Bonnie Pointer left the group in 1978.

Performing a highly eclectic repertoire, from R&B to jazz classics and original compositions, they demonstrated remarkable vocal versatility and gained a large cult following. Discarding the old image and material in 1978, the Pointer Sisters enjoyed a revitalized career under producer Richard Perry, particularly with 1983's *Breakout*. They scored a series of pop and R&B smashes with contemporary material through 1985, but subsequently languished with RCA and Motown.

The Pointer sisters grew up as daughters of ministers. They first began singing together at the West Oakland Church of God in the early 1960s. They discovered secular material during high school, and Bonnie and June began singing professionally in the late 1960s as The Pointers—A Pair. They were members of Dorothy Morrison's Northern Calif. State Youth Choir before forming the Pointer Sisters with Anita in December 1969. Stranded in Houston by their first manager, the three contacted San Francisco producer David Rubinson, who arranged their return to the Bay Area. He soon became their manager and found them session work with Cold Blood, Elvin Bishop, Taj Mahal, Boz Scaggs, and Grace Slick. In 1971 they recorded two singles for Atlantic Records, but neither proved successful.

Joined by sister Ruth in September 1972, the four Pointer sisters signed with Blue Thumb Records under David Rubinson, who produced their first three studio albums. Their debut album displayed a striking versatility of vocal talents and a diversity of musical styles and contained the originals "Sugar" and "Jada" as well as the Lambert, Hendricks and Ross classic "Cloudburst." It yielded a major pop and R&B hit with Allen Toussaint's "Yes We Can Can" and a minor crossover hit with Willie Dixon's "Wang Dang Doodle." Following a successful performance substituting for a canceled act at the Troubadour in Los Angeles in May 1973, the Pointer Sisters frequently appeared on the television shows of Helen Reddy and Flip Wilson.

The Pointer Sisters' second album, *That's a Plenty*, was even more jazz-oriented, containing vocal renditions of "Salt Peanuts" and "Black Coffee," jazz standards popularized by Dizzy Gillespie and Sarah Vaughan. The album produced a moderate country and major pop hit with Anita and Bonnie's "Fairytale," leading them to be the first black group to appear on the stage of the Grand Ole Opry, in 1976. *Steppin'* yielded a top R&B and major pop hit with their own "How Long (Betcha' Got a Chick on the Side)" and a major R&B hit with Allen Toussaint's "Going Down Slow"; it also contained Stevie Wonder's "Sleeping Alone" and "Easy Days," coauthored with Isaac Hayes. Subsequent releases fared poorly and the Blue Thumb label dissolved, leaving the sisters without a record label.

In 1978 Bonnie Pointer left the others to pursue a solo career on Motown Records. She scored a major R&B hit with "Free Me from My Freedom/Tie Me to a Tree (Handcuff Me)" and a major pop hit with Holland-Dozier-Holland's "Heaven Must Have Sent You" in 1978–1979. However, legal problems with Motown led to the end of her recording career until 1984, by which time her popularity had fizzled; she later recorded for Private Records.

In August 1978 Ruth and Anita Pointer signed with producer Richard Perry's newly formed Planet Records. They brought June back and recorded contemporary material for their debut on the label, *Energy*. The album yielded a smash pop hit with Bruce Springsteen's "Fire" and a moderate pop hit with "Happiness," and its success revived the Pointer Sisters. Subsequent hits through 1982 included "He's So Shy" and "Slow Hand" (both smash pop and near-smash R&B hits), "Should I Do It," and "American Music." Their 1983 album, *Break Out*, remained on the album charts for two years and yielded six hits, including the pop and R&B smashes "Automatic" and "Jump (For My Love)," and the pop smashes "I'm So Excited" and "Neutron Dance," the latter featured in the movie *Beverly Hills Cop*.

The Pointer Sisters' next album, *Contact*, produced hits with "Dare Me" (an R&B smash), "Freedom," and "Twist My Arm." However, subsequent releases fared less well, and by 1988 the group had switched to Motown Records. June and Anita Pointer each issued solo albums in the late 1980s. The group returned on SBK records in 1993.

DISC.: THE POINTER SISTERS: *The P. S.* (1973); *That's a Plenty* (1974); *Live at the Opera House* (1974); *Steppin'* (1975); *The Best of the P. S.* (1976); *Having a Party* (1977); *Retrospect* (1981); *Energy* (1978); *Priority* (1979); *Special Things* (1980); *Black and White* (1981); *Best, 1978–1981* (1993); *So Excited* (1982); *Greatest Hits* (1982); *Break Out* (1983); *Contact* (1985); *Hot Together* (1986); *Serious Slammin'* (1988); *P. S.'s Greatest Hits* (1989); *Sweet and Soulful* (1992); *Right Rhythm* (1990); *P. S.* (1993). **BONNIE POINTER.** *Bonnie Pointer* (1978); *Bonnie Pointer* (1979); *If the Price Is Right* (1984). **JUNE POINTER:** *Baby Sister* (1983); *June Pointer* (1989). **ANITA POINTER** *Love for What It Is* (1987).—**BH**

Poise, (Jean Alexandre) Ferdinand,

French composer; b. Nîmes, June 3, 1828; d. Paris, May 13, 1892. He studied at the Paris Cons. with A. Adam and Zimmerman, taking the 2nd Grand Prix de Rome in 1852.

WORKS: DRAMATIC: Opéras-comiques (all 1st perf. in Paris): *Bonsoir, voisin* (Sept. 18, 1853); *Le Thé de Polichinelle* (March 4, 1856); *Le roi Don Pèdre* (Sept. 30, 1857); *Le Jardinier galant* (March 4, 1861); *Le corricolo* (Nov. 28, 1868); *Les deux billets* (Feb. 19, 1870); *Les trois souhaits* (Oct. 29, 1873); *La surprise de l'amour* (Oct. 31, 1877); *L'amour médicin* (Dec. 20, 1880). **VOCAL: Oratorio:** *Cécile* (Dijon, 1888). **Other:** *Les moissoneurs*, cantata (Paris, Aug. 15, 1866); men's choruses; songs.—**NS/LK/DM**

Poissl, Johann Nepomuk, Freiherr von,

German composer; b. Haukenzell, Lower Bavaria, Feb. 15, 1783; d. Munich, Aug. 17, 1865. He was educated in Straubing, Munich, and at the Univ. of Landshut (1800); settled in Munich (1805), and studied composition with Danzi and Abbé Vogler. In 1811 he met Weber, who became a champion of his works. As a composer for the theater, he won his most notable successes with *Athalia* (June 3, 1814) and *Der Wettkampf zu Olympia oder Die Freunde* (April 21, 1815); nevertheless, he was dogged by poverty until being made asst. superintendent of court music in 1823; was also named director of the Court Theater (1825). His opera *Die Prinzessin von Provence* was first performed at the reopening celebrations of the rebuilt Nationaltheater (Jan. 23, 1825), and remains his best-known achievement. He was replaced as director of the Court Theater (1833), but was retained as director of court music until his dismissal in 1847, when he was made 1st chamberlain. His final years were marked by illness and poverty. Poissl was an important link in the development of German opera between the eras of Mozart and Weber.

WORKS: DRAMATIC: Opera (all first perf. in Munich unless otherwise given): *Die Opernprobe*, comic opera (Feb. 23, 1806); *Antigonus*, serious opera (Feb. 12, 1808); *Ottaviano in Sicilia*, dramma eroico (June 30, 1812); *Aucassin und Nicolette*, Singspiel (March 28, 1813); *Athalia*, grand opera (June 3, 1814); *Der Wettkampf zu Olympia oder Die Freunde*, grand opera (April 21, 1815); *Die wie mir oder Alle betrügen*, comic opera (1816; not perf.); *Nittetis*, grand opera (Darmstadt, June 29, 1817); *Issipile*, grand opera (1818; not perf.); *La rappresaglia*, opera semiseria (April 7, 1820); *Die Prinzessin von Provence*, magical opera (Jan. 23, 1825); *Der Untersberg*, Romantic opera (Oct. 30, 1829); *Zaide*, Romantic-tragic opera (Nov. 9, 1843). **Incidental Music:** To Heyden's *Renata* (Munich, Oct. 12, 1823), von Schenk's *Belisar* (Munich, Feb. 23, 1826) and *Kaiser Ludwigs Traum* (Munich, March 27, 1826), and Kleist's *Hermannschlacht* (1826). **ORCH.:** Clarinet Concerto (1812); Violin Concerto (1817). **VOCAL: Oratorios:** *Judith* (1824); *Der Erntetag* (Munich, April 4, 1835). **Other:** 3 masses (1812; c. 1816; 1817); *Stabat Mater* (1821); *Miserere* (1824); other sacred works; cantatas; choral music.

BIBL.: E. Reipschlager, *Schubaur, Danzi und P. als Opernkomponisten* (diss., Univ. of Rostock, 1911).—**NS/LK/DM**

Poitevin, Guillaume,

French composer; b. Boulbon, near Arles, Oct. 2, 1646; d. Aix-en-Provence, Jan. 26, 1706. He was a choirboy at St. Trophime in Arles. In 1663 he settled in Aix-en-Provence as a musician at St. Sauveur Cathedral, and then was maître de musique there from 1667 to 1693 and again from 1698. In 1665 he received the tonsure, in 1672 he was ordained, and in 1677 he was made a prebendary. Among his most notable pupils were Campra and Gilles. He was known as a composer of sacred music.

BIBL.: E. Marbot, *Gal et G. P.* (Aix-en-Provence, 1887). —**LK/DM**

Pokorny, Franz (actually, František Xaver Jan),

Bohemian clarinetist, conductor, and composer; b. Lstiboř, Dec. 22, 1797; d. Meidling, near Vienna, Aug. 7, 1850. He was a clarinetist in the Josefstadt Theater orch. from 1819 to 1822, and then in the theater orchs. in Pressburg and Baden (1822–27). In 1827 he was made conductor and in 1835 director of the Pressburg Theater.

He also was director of the Baden Theater (from 1836) and the Josefstadt Theater in Vienna (from 1837). In 1845 he purchased the Theater an der Wien in the latter city, but continued to serve as director of the Josefstadt Theater as well. He composed the successful Singspiel *Der Zauberschleier* (1842).—LK/DM

Pokrass, Dimitri, Russian composer; b. Kiev, Nov. 7, 1899; d. Moscow, Dec. 20, 1978. He studied piano at the St. Petersburg Cons. (1913–17). In 1919 he joined the Soviet cavalry during the Civil War, and wrote the song *The Red Cavalry*. This was the first of a series of many songs that acquired great popularity, among them *If War Comes Tomorrow* (1938), *March of the Tank Brigade, Farewell*, etc. He also wrote music for films.—NS/LK/DM

Polacco, Giorgio, Italian conductor; b. Venice, April 12, 1873; d. N.Y., April 30, 1960. He studied in St. Petersburg, at Venice's Liceo Benedetto Marcello, and at the Milan Cons. He became asst. conductor at London's Covent Garden (1890), then conducted in Europe and South America. He appeared in the U.S. for the first time for Tetrazzini's debut in San Francisco (1905), and also toured the U.S. with the Savage Opera Co. (1911). He made his Metropolitan Opera debut in N.Y. with *Manon Lescaut* (Nov. 11, 1912), remaining on its roster until 1917. He conducted the Chicago Grand Opera (1918–19; 1921) and in Boston (1927), and was principal conductor of the Chicago Civic Opera (1922–30). He was married twice to the soprano **Edith (Barnes) Mason.**—NS/LK/DM

Polansky, Larry, American composer, music theorist, writer, and teacher; b. N.Y., Oct. 16, 1954. He studied anthropology and music at New Coll. in Sarasota, Fla. (1974), and subsequently studied mathematics and music at the Univ. of Calif., Santa Cruz (B.A., 1976), and undertook graduate work at York Univ. in Toronto (1977). He finally majored in composition at the Univ. of Ill. at Urbana-Champaign (M.A., 1978), and also studied composition privately with James Tenney, Ben Johnston, and Ron Riddle, jazz guitar with Chuck Wayne, George Barnes, and Michael Goodwick, bluegrass mandolin with Frank Wakefield and Paul Kramer, and jazz theory and improvisation with Lee Konitz. He performed and arranged pieces in various styles, particularly jazz and folk, on guitar and other plectra, piano, and electronics (from 1966). He was a dance accompanist (1977–81), and composed works for the choreographers Ann Rodiger and Anita Feldman. He worked as a computer programmer, systems analyst, and studio engineer (from 1975). He taught at Mills Coll. in Oakland, Calif. (1981–90), where he also was involved with its Center for Contemporary Music (1981–87; interim director, 1988) and directed its Contemporary Performance Ensemble (1981–86). In 1990 he became an assoc. prof. at Dartmouth Coll., where he also co-directed its Bregman Electro-Acoustic Music Studio. He is married to **Jody Diamond**, with whom he founded and directed the American Gamelan Inst. and also ed. its journal, *Balungan*. Together they also founded the publishing firm Frog Peak Music, A Composers' Collective. His own compositions reflect sophisticated technical concerns in acoustics, intonation, and morphological processes; they are generally in variation or canonic forms, based on single ideas worked out in textures that sometimes resemble those of minimalism. His *51 Harmonies* for Percussion Trio, Live Computer Electronics, and Electric Guitar (1994) was commissioned by Cologne's Westdeutscher Rundfunk. In 1995–96 he held a Fulbright Senior Scholar/Teacher Fellowship in Melbourne, Australia, and in 2000 he received a Parsons Fund Grant from the Library of Congress for research preparatory to a monograph on Ruth Crawford Seeger. Polansky's extensive articles and reviews have appeared in the *Journal of New Music Research, Perspectives of New Music, Computer Music Journal* et al. He served as music advisor ed. to the journal *Leonardo* (from 1985) and assoc. ed. of *Perspectives of New Music* (from 1988); he also authored HMSL (Hierarchical Music Specification Language), a widely used computer music language, as well as the books *Early Works of James Tenney* (1983) and *New Instrumentation and Orchestration* (1986).

WORKS (selected listing): *Silence Study #4 for Joe Pinzarrone* for 4 Actors and Violist (1976); *Four Voice Canon #4* for 1 to 4 Marimbas (1978); *Quartet in F for Paula Ravitz* for Piano, Viola, Clarinet, and Trombone (1978); *Will You Miss Me* for Untrained Man's Voice and Harrison-Colvig "transfer" Harp (1978; also for Flute, Double Bass, Harrison-Colvig "transfer" Harp, and Untrained Man's Voice, 1980); *Unhappy Set of Coincidences for Richard Myron* for Guitar and Bass, Flute and Bass, or any 2 Melody Instruments (1979); *Another You*, 17 variations for Harp in just intonation (1980); *Four Bass Studies* for Double Bass (1983); *Sascha's Song (for the peoples of Chile)* for Tape (1983; also for Tape and 7 Instruments); *Three Monk Tunes* for Tap Dancer and Percussionist (1983); *Four Voice Canon #5* for 4 Percussionists (1984) *V'leem'shol (...and to rule...) (Cantillation Study #2)* for 5 Flutes (1984); *Milwaukee Blues* for 2 Tap Dancers and 5 Saxophones (1984); *Conversation*, electronic installation (1985; in collaboration with J. Levin and R. Povall); *Hensley Variations (Guitar Trio #1)* for Flute, Viola, and Harp (1985); *(al het) (for the people of Nicaragua)* for Soprano and Percussionist (1986); *(B'rey'sheet) (in the beginning) (Cantillation Study #1)* for Voice and Computer (1986); *Buy Some For Spare Parts*, live (HMSL) computer music installation (1986; in collaboration with P. Burk); *Simple Actions*, computer installation and performance (1986); *Study for Milwaukee Blues* for 3 Tap Dancers or 3 Percussionists (1986); *The Time is Now* for Voice, Flute, Clarinet, Viola, Guitar, and Bass, to a text by Melody Sumner (1987); *17 Simple Melodies of the Same Length* for Clarinet and Melody Instrument and Computer (1988); *Bedhaya Sadra/Bedhaya Guthrie* for Voices, Melody Instruments, Kemanak, and Gamelan (1989; rev. 1990); *Lonesome Road (The Crawford Variations)*, 51 variations for Piano (1989); *Horn* for Horn and Live Computer (1990); *Three Studies* for Performers and Live Computer (1990); *51 Melodies* for 2 Electric Guitars and Optional Rhythm Section (1991); *...slippers of steel* for 2 Electric Guitars and Computers (1991); *Roads to Cimacum* for String or Mandolin Quartet (1992); *Two Children's Songs* for Tuba and Trombone, 2 Tubas, and 2 Bassoons (1992); *Study: Anna, the long and the short of it* for Tape (1993); *51 Harmonies* for Percussion Trio and Electric Guitar (1994); *Four Voice Canon #9a (anna canon)* for Tape (1994); *The Casten Variation* for Piano or Piano and Ensemble (1994); *Always cut off the baseline* for Trumpet and Live Electronics (1995); *for jim, ben and lou*, 3 pieces for Guitar, Harp, and Percussion (1995); *Anna's Music Box*, children's MIDI software piece (1996); *Parting Hands* for 2 Percussionists (1996); *II-V-I* for 2 Electric Guitars or

Guitar Solo (1997); *Neighborhoods of Note* for 2 or 3 Suzuki Pianists (1997); *all things, beings, equal* for Saxophone (1998); *Approaching the azimuth...* for Clarinet (1998); *Cinderella* for Flute (1998); *Piker*, 5 movements for Piccolo (1998); *Essays for String Quartet, 1–3* (1999); *3 Shaker Songs* for Electric Guitar and Voice (1999); *Killing Time*, real-time Java-based computer work (2000); *3 New Hampshire Songs* for Chorus (2000); *2 Shaker Songs* for Large Ensemble including Voce and Electric Guitar (2000). —NS/LK/DM

Polaski, Deborah, American soprano; b. Richmond Center, Wisc., Sept. 26, 1949. She studied in Cincinnati and Graz. After making her operatic debut in Gelsenkirchen in 1976, she sang in Munich, Hamburg, Karlsruhe, Mannheim, and other German cities in such roles as Leonore, Sieglinde, Isolde, and Berg's Marie. In 1986 she appeared as Elektra in Oslo and as Chrysothemis in Geneva, and in 1988 as Senta at Milan's La Scala. While her portrayal of Brünnhilde at the Bayreuth Festival was cooly received in 1988, she triumphed there in that role in 1991 and 1995. In 1990 she sang Brünnhilde in Cologne and Elektra in Spoleto. Following an engagement as the *Walküre* Brünnhilde at London's Covent Garden in 1994, she sang Elektra upon her return there in 1997. Her appearance as Brünnhilde in the Berlin mounting of the *Ring* cycle in 1996 brought her further accolades. On Dec. 1, 1999, she sang excerpts from *Die Walküre* and *Fidelio* with Plácido Domingo at the gala performance of the reopening of the refurbished Royal Opera House at Covent Garden. —NS/LK/DM

Poldini, Ede (Eduard), Hungarian composer; b. Budapest, June 13, 1869; d. Corseaux, Switzerland, June 28, 1957. He studied at the Budapest Cons., and later with Mandyczewski (theory) and Julius Epstein (piano) in Vienna. In 1908 he went to live at Vevey. In 1935 he received the order of the Hungarian Cross of Merit; in 1948, was awarded the Hungarian Pro Arte Prize. He wrote the successful operas *Vagabund und Prinzessin* (Budapest, Oct. 17, 1903) and *Hochzeit im Fasching* (Budapest, Feb. 16, 1924), as well as orch. pieces, choral works, songs, and much piano music, some of which became very popular.—NS/LK/DM

Poldowski (pen name of **Irene Regine Wieniawska**; by marriage, **Lady Dean Paul**), Polish-English composer, daughter of **Henryk Wieniawski**; b. Brussels, March 18, 1879; d. London, Jan. 28, 1932. She studied at the Brussels Cons. with Gevaert, and later in London with Percy Pitt. She married Sir Aubrey Dean Paul, and then took additional courses in composition with Gédalge and d'Indy in Paris. She began writing songs to French words, in the impressionist style, setting to music 21 poems by Paul Verlaine, and 8 poems by others. She also composed *Caledonian Market*, a suite of 8 pieces for Piano, *Berceuse de l'enfant mourant* for Violin and Piano, *Tango* for Violin and Piano, *Suite miniature de chansons à danser* for Woodwind Instruments, 2 symphonic sketches (*Nocturnes* and *Tenements*), and an operetta, *Laughter*. —NS/LK/DM

Poleri, David (Samuel), American tenor; b. Philadelphia, Jan. 10, 1921; d. in a helicopter accident in Hanalei, Hawaii, Dec. 13, 1967. He studied at the Philadelphia Academy of Vocal Arts, the Berkshire Music Center in Tanglewood, and with Alberto Sciarretti. In 1945 he sang with the Philadelphia Orch. In 1949 he made his operatic debut as Gounod's Faust with Gallo's San Carlo Opera on a tour in Chicago. He subsequently was a guest artist with various opera companies and a soloist with various orchs. in the U.S. He also sang at the Edinburgh Festivals (1951, 1955) and at London's Covent Garden (1956). In 1954 he created the role of Michele in Menotti's *The Saint of Bleecker Street*. In 1955 he appeared as Cavaradossi on NBC-TV. —NS/LK/DM

Polgar, Tibor, Hungarian-born Canadian composer, conductor, pianist, and teacher; b. Budapest, March 11, 1907. He was a pupil of Kodály at the Budapest Academy of Music (composition diploma, 1925), and earned a degree in philosophy (1931). He was active as a performer and composer with the Hungarian Radio, later serving as its artistic director (1948–50). From 1962 to 1964 he was assoc. conductor of the Philharmonia Hungarica in Marl kreis Recklinghausen; then emigrated to Canada and became a naturalized citizen (1969). He conducted the Univ. of Toronto Sym. Orch. (1965–66), and later was on the staff of the Univ.'s opera dept. (1970–75). He also taught at the Royal Cons. of Music of Toronto (1966–68), and then orchestration at York Univ. in Toronto (1976–77).

WORKS: DRAMATIC: O p e r a : *Kérök* (The Suitors; 1954); *The Troublemaker* (1968); *The Glove* (1973); *A Strange Night* (1978–88). **M u s i c a l S a t i r e :** *A European Lover* (1965). **ORCH.:** *Variations on a Hungarian Folk Song* for Harp and Orch. (1969; also for Solo Harp); *Ilona's 4 Faces* for Clarinet or Saxophone and Orch. (1970; also for Clarinet or Saxophone and Piano); *Notes on Hungary* for Concert Band (1971); *Pentatonia* for Concert Band (1976; Toronto, Feb. 15, 1977); *3 Poems in Music* (1977; also for Piano); *2 Symphonic Dances in Latin Rhythm* for Trumpet and Symphonic Band (1979); *Fanfare of Pride and Joy* for Symphonic Band (1982); *Concerto romantico* for Harp and Orch. (1986); *The Voice of the Soul* for Concert Band (1989). **CHAMBER:** *Improvisazione* for 4 Horns (1962); *In Private* for Violin and Viola (1964); *Rhapsody of Kallo* for Violin and Harp (1970); Sonatine for 2 Flutes (1971); *Romantic Minutes* for Harp (1980); *Frere Jacques* for 4 Harps (1984); *Hide and Seek* for Horn and Piano (1988). **VOCAL:** *The Last Words of Louis Riel*, cantata for Contralto, Baritone, Chorus, and Orch. (1966–67); *Lest We Forget the Last Chapter of Genesis*, cantata for Low Voice and Piano or Orch. (1970); *How Long Shall the Ungodly Triumph?* for 6 Voices and Organ (1974); *Annabel Lee* for Voice, Flute, and Harp (1974); songs; arrangements.—NS/LK/DM

Poliakin, Miron, Russian violinist and pedagogue; b. Cherkassy, Feb. 12, 1895; d. Moscow, May 21, 1941. He received his early training from his father, a noted violinist, then studied with Elena Vonsovskaya in Kiev and with Auer at the St. Petersburg Cons. (1908–18). He developed a notable international career, making his N.Y. debut on Feb. 27, 1922. Returning to Russia in 1928, he became prof. of violin at the Leningrad Cons., and in 1936 joined the faculty of the

Moscow Cons. With Yampolsky and Yankelevich, he produced a pleiad of fine violinists who dominated the concert annals and competition circuits in Russia and elsewhere.

BIBL.: L. Raaben, *M. P.* (Moscow, 1963).—**NS/LK/DM**

Poliakov, Valeri(an), Russian composer and conductor; b. Orel, Oct. 24, 1913; d. Kishinev, Jan. 17, 1970. He studied clarinet and composition in Kharkov (1928–34). In 1935 he joined the staff of the Kiev Opera, and in 1937 he was appointed head of the music dept. of the Moldavian Music Theater in Kishinev, and taught at a music school there until 1940; then taught in Armenia (1941–45) and Riga (1945–51). He was music ed. and conductor of the Moldavian Radio (1951–54). He conducted the dance ensemble Zhok (1955–57) and the jazz band Bukuria (1965–66), and also taught at the Kishinev Cons. (1961–70). In 1960 he was made an Honored Artist of the Moldavian S.S.R.

WORKS: DRAMATIC: O p e r a : *Where?* (1969). **B a l l e t :** *Iliana, An Ancient Tale* (1936); *Legend of the Architect* (1959); *Eternity* (1961). **ORCH.:** *Suite on Moldavian Themes* (1938); *Moldavia,* poem (1938); *Pictures of Drinking* (1939); *Fantasia Capriccio on European Themes* (1939); 7 syms. (1944; 1946; 1947; *Chkalov,* 1950; 1958; *Heroic Fantasy,* 1961; 1966); *Triumphant Overture* (1947); 2 piano concertos (1948, 1955); *Rhapsody-Poem* (1951); *Through the Flames,* poem (1952); Violin Concerto (1953); Cello Concerto (1960); *Burleska* for Trombone and Orch. (1960); *Concerto rustico* (1963); *Vernal Garden,* sinfonietta (1969). **CHAMBER:** *3 Pieces in Memory of Prokofiev* for Violin and Piano (1962); *Ballade* for Cello and Piano (1963); String Quartet (1965); *Concert études* for Clarinet and Piano (1966) *Concert études* for Bassoon and Piano (1966). **VOCAL:** *Ballad to the Soldier* for Voices and Orch. (1948); songs.—**NS/LK/DM**

Police, The, incorporated elements of reggae, pop, punk, and jazz, and featured the intelligently crafted songs and charismatic stage presence of lead singer Sting. **MEMBERSHIP:** Sting (Gordon Sumner), lead voc., bs. (b. Wallsend, Northumberland, England, Oct. 2, 1951); Andy Summers (Andrew Somers), lead gtr. (b. Poulton-le-Fylde, Lancashire, England, Dec. 31, 1942); Stewart Copeland, drm., perc., voc. (b. Alexandria, Va., July 16, 1952).

The first British New Wave act to score a hit in America, with 1979's "Roxanne," the Police were initially rivaled by only Blondie in terms of commercial success for a New Wave act. After becoming one of the leading rock bands in the world, the Police dissolved in 1983. Sting became a highly successful solo artist and a somewhat less successful film actor. Guitarist Andy Summers became one of the pioneers in the development of guitar synthesizers, while drummer Stewart Copeland pursued soundtrack and television work in the 1980s and 1990s.

Stewart Copeland grew up in the Middle East as the son of the head of the Central Intelligence Agency's operations in the region. In 1966 the Copeland family moved to England, where Stewart attended the prestigious Millfield school in Somerset. In 1971 he returned to the United States to attend the Univ. of Calif. at Berkeley. He moved back to England at the behest of his promoter, brother Miles, in 1974 and joined the progressive-rock group Curved Air in the band's final years, as a percussionist. In late 1975 Copeland attended a performance in Newcastle by the local band Lost Exit, which included singer-bassist Sting. Born Gordon Sumner, Sting had been a semiprofessional musician around Newcastle since age 17 and had attempted music full-time in London in the early 1970s. He returned to Newcastle in 1975 and taught school for two years. By late 1976 both Curved Air and Lost Exit had broken up, and Copeland and Sting formed the Police with guitarist Henry Padovani. The group recorded the song "Fall Out" for Miles Copeland's Illegal Records label, but the single failed to sell.

Andy Summers soon replaced Henry Padovani in the Police. Summers had taken up guitar at age 14 and started playing professionally at 16, in bands such as Soft Machine and the Animals in the late 1960s. He studied classical composition and guitar at the Univ. of Calif. between 1969 and 1973 and returned to England to play with bands led by Kevin Coyne and Kevin Ayers. He met Stewart Copeland and Sting in 1977 while playing with the group Strontium 90. Signed to A&M Records, the Police recorded their debut album, *Outlandos d'Amour,* in 1978. The group financed their own tour of America in late 1978 before the record was released in this country. They achieved belated British hits with "Roxanne" and "Can't Stand Losing You," and "Roxanne" became a moderate American hit in early 1979. The album, which favored reggae rhythms and the catchy songwriting of Sting, stayed on the charts for more than a year.

The Police conducted their first British tour in summer 1979, and recorded *Regatta de Blanc* that year. It included "The Bed's Too Big without You," "Bring on the Night," and the British top hits "Walking on the Moon" and "Message in a Bottle," the latter a minor American hit. The record stayed on the American album charts for nearly two years, securing their position in this country as one of the most exciting and creative bands in contemporary music.

Notorious for their unconventional business practices under Miles Copeland, the Police established themselves with an international audience by performing in Third World cities such as Cairo, Bangkok, Athens, and Bombay in 1980. Their diverse, engaging *Zenyatta Mondatta* album yielded two near-smash American hits, "Do Do Do Do, De Da Da Da" and "Don't Stand So Close to Me"; it also contained Summers's instrumental "Behind My Camel" and Sting's "Driven to Tears" and "Shadows in the Rain." Touring diligently to sustain their enormous popularity, the Police next recorded the concept album *Ghost in the Machine,* featuring Sting's most intelligent, incisive lyrics to date. It produced the smash hit "Every Little Thing She Does Is Magic," the near-smash "Spirits in the Material World," and the moderate hit "Secret Journey," as well as "Hungry for You" and "One World (Not Three)."

By the time the Police took a break from touring and recording in 1982, they had conducted 20 tours overall, including three major world tours. During the hiatus,

Andy Summers explored the guitar synthesizer with former King Crimson guitarist and electronics wizard Robert Fripp on the *I Advance Masked* album for A&M. Sting starred in the disturbing movie *Brimstone and Treacle*, and Stewart Copeland composed the score for the Francis Ford Coppola movie *Rumblefish*.

Reconvening in 1983, the Police recorded the carefully crafted, compelling, and profound album *Synchronicity*, their masterpiece. The album includes "Walking in Your Footsteps" and yielded the top hit "Every Breath You Take," the smash hits "King of Pain" and "Wrapped Around Your Finger," and the major hit "Synchronicity II," all written by Sting. Following their stadium tour in support of *Synchronicity*, the Police announced they were taking a respite from touring and recording as the members pursued various outside projects.

Andy Summers rejoined Robert Fripp for another album of instrumentals, *Bewitched*, that contained a Dream Side and a Dance Side. He later recorded one side of the soundtrack to the 1986 movie *Down and Out in Beverly Hills* and the soundtrack to *My Weekend at Bernie's*. In the late 1980s and 1990s he recorded several solo albums.

Stewart Copeland was the most prolific former member of the Police. In 1984 he traveled to Africa to record traditional native music, assembling a film documentary and album, *The Rhythmatist*, that featured both authentic music and his own synthesizer compositions. Throughout the rest of the 1980s and 1990s he composed and performed for the movies and television; much of this work is unavailable in a recorded format. The film scores include *Out of Bounds* (1986), *Wall Street* (1987), *Talk Radio* (1988), *Men at Work* (1990), *Highlander II* (1991), and *Rappa Nui* (1994). For television, Copeland worked on the shows *The Ewoks* and *Droids* (1985), *The Equalizer* (1986), and *Babylon 5* (1993), among others. In 1988 he formed Animal Logic with jazz bassist Stanley Clarke and singer- songwriter Deborah Holland, recording two albums for I. R. S. His score for the half-hour ballet *King Lear*, featuring both orchestra and prerecorded music, was premiered by the San Francisco Ballet in 1985. In 1989 the Cleveland Opera performed Stewart Copeland's first operatic effort, the three-hour *Holy Blood and Crescent Moon*, as its season opener, but the performance was not well received by classical-music critics.

Sting continued to pursue his acting career during the 1980s, securing roles in the film adaptation of Frank Herbert's *Dune* (1984), the remake of the 1935 horror classic *The Bride of Frankenstein* as *The Bride* (1985), and *Stormy Monday* (1988). Although Sting performed credibly, none of the films were well received by critics or audiences. By 1985 Sting had assembled several of N.Y.'s finest jazz musicians for recordings that confounded rock critics and disaffected jazz fans. With Sting playing guitar, not bass, *The Dream of the Blue Turtles* was recorded with saxophonist Branford Marsalis, keyboardist Kenny Kirkland, bassist Darryl Jones, and drummer Omar Hakim. Surprisingly, the album yielded four hits: the smash "If You Love Somebody Set Them Free," the near-smash "Fortress Around Your Heart," and the major hits "Love Is the Seventh Wave" and "Russians." In the latter half of 1985 Sting toured with his new band, and the film *Bring on the Night*, an account of his early rehearsals and first concert with the band, was released. He also appeared at the Live Aid concert in 1985, and toured for Amnesty International in 1986.

In 1987 Sting returned to bass to record the double-CD set ... *Nothing Like the Sun* with Branford Marsalis and Kenny Kirkland. The album produced a near-smash hit with "We'll Be Together," a major hit with "Be Still My Beating Heart," and a minor hit with "Englishman in N.Y." It also included the gripping "They Dance Alone (Cueca Solo)," recorded with Andy Summers, Eric Clapton, and Mark Knopfler; the ballad "Sister Moon," and "History Will Teach Us Nothing." In 1988 Sting toured early in the year, formed his own record company, Panagea, performed on the Amnesty International tour, and founded the environmental group Ark with David Bowie. He made his Broadway debut in the short-lived 1989 musical production *The Threepenny Opera* and created the Save the Rain Forest Foundation while enduring an extended period of writer's block.

Sting returned to recording in 1991 with the brooding *The Soul Cages*, scoring a smash hit with "All This Time"; he toured once again. Two years later he issued his most engaging work in years, *Ten Summoner's Tales*, which included "If I Ever Lose Faith in You" and "Fields of Gold," both major hits, as well as "She's Too Good for Me" and "Love Is Stranger than Justice." At the end of 1993 Sting scored a top hit in conjunction with Bryan Adams and Rod Stewart on "All for Love," from the movie *The Three Musketeers*. A 1994 best-of set, *Fields of Gold*, includes the odd "This Cowboy Song" and one other new track.

DISC.: CURVED AIR: *Live* (1975); *Airborne* (1976); *Midnight Wire* (1975). THE POLICE: *Outlandos d'Amour* (1979); *Regatta de Blanc* (1979); *Zenyatta Mondatta* (1980); *Ghost in the Machine* (1981); *Synchronicity* (1983); *Live* (rec. 1979–1983; rel. 1995); *Every Breath You Take: The Singles* (1986); *Message in a Box: The Complete Recordings* (1993); *Every Breath You Take: The Classics* (1995). ANDY SUMMERS AND ROBERT FRIPP: *I Advance Masked* (1982); *Bewitched* (1984). ANDY SUMMERS: *Down and Out in Beverly Hills* (one side of soundtrack; 1986); *XYZ* (1987); *Mysterious Barricades* (1988); *The Golden Wire* (1989); *Charming Snakes* (1990); *World Gone Strange* (1991). STEWART COPELAND: *The Rhythmatist* (1985); *Music from The Equalizer and Other Cliff Hangers* (1988). STEWART COPELAND SOUNDTRACKS: *Rumblefish* (1983); *Out of Bounds* (1986); *Wall Street/Talk Radio* (1989); *Men at Work* (1990). ANIMAL LOGIC: *Animal Logic* (1989); *Animal Logic II* (1991). STING: *The Dream of the Blue Turtles* (1985); *Bring on the Night* (1985); ... *Nothing Like the Sun* (1987); *Box Set (above three albums)* (1992); *The Soul Cages* (1991); *Ten Summoner's Tales* (1993); *Fields of Gold* (1994); *Mercury Falling* (1996).

BIBL.: Rosetta Woolf, *Message in a Bottle* (London, 1981); Lynn Goldsmith, *The P.* (N.Y., 1983).—BH

Polignac, Armande de, French composer; b. Paris, Jan. 8, 1876; d. Neauphle-le-Vieux, Seine-et-Oise, April 29, 1962. She studied with Fauré and d'Indy. She composed the operas *Morgane* and *L'Hypocrite sanctifie, Judith de Béthulie*, dramatic scene (Paris, March 23, 1916), *La Source lointaine*, Persian ballet (Paris, 1913), *Les 1,001 Nuits*, Arabian ballet (Paris, 1914), *Chimères*, Greek ballet (Paris, June 10, 1923), *Urashima*, Japanese ballet, *La Recherche de la verité*, Chinese ballet for Small Orch., and *Petite suite pour le clavecin* (1939).—NS/LK/DM

Polin, Claire, American flutist, teacher, and composer; b. Philadelphia, Jan. 1, 1926. She studied flute with Kincaid and composition with Persichetti in Philadelphia, Mennin at the Juilliard School of Music in N.Y., and Sessions and Foss at the Berkshire Music Center in Tanglewood; held the degrees of B.Mus. (1948), M.Mus. (1950), and D.Mus. (1955). She taught at the Philadelphia Musical Academy (1949–64) and at Rutgers Univ. (1958–91). A versatile scholar, she wrote and lectured on music, and traveled and played flute in distant lands, including Israel, Russia, and Japan; advanced bold theories, suggesting, for example, a link between Hebrew and Welsh legends, and composed industriously in a cogently modernistic manner, often with recursive ancient modalities.

WORKS: ORCH.: 2 syms. (1961; *Korean*, 1976); *Scenes from Gilgamesh* for Flute and Strings (1972); *Amphion* (1978); *Mythos* for Harp and String Orch. (1982). **CHAMBER:** 3 string quartets (1953, 1959, 1969); Flute Sonata (1954); *Structures* for Flute (1964); *Consecutivo* for Flute, Clarinet, Violin, Cello, and Piano (1964); *Cader Idris* for Brass Quintet (1970); *The Journey of Owain Madoc* for Brass Quintet and Percussion (1971); *Makimono I* for Flute, Clarinet, Violin, Cello, and Piano (1972) and *II* for Brass Quintet (1972); Sonata for Flute and Harp (1972); *Aderyn Pur* for Flute, Alto Saxophone, and Bird Tape (1973); *Tower Sonata* for Flute, Clarinet, and Bassoon (1974); *Death of Procris* for Flute and Tuba (1974); *Serpentine* for Viola (1974); *Telemannicon* for Oboe and Self-Tape (1975); *Klockwork* for Alto Saxophone, Horn, and Bassoon (1977); *Synaulia* for Flute, Clarinet, and Piano (1977); *Vigniatures* for Harp and Violin (1980); *Felina* for Harp and Violin (1981); *Res naturae* for Woodwind Quintet (1982); *Kuequenaku-Cambriola* for Piano and Percussion (1982); *Freltic Sonata* for Violin and Piano (1986); *Garden of Earthly Delights* for Woodwind Quintet (1987); *Regensburg* for Flute, Guitar, and Dancer (1989); *Taliesin* for Flute, Oboe, and Cello (1993); piano pieces. **VOCAL:** *Welsh Bardic Odes* for Soprano, Flute, and Piano (1956); *Canticles* for Men's Voices (1959); *Lorca Songs* for Voices and Piano (1965); *Infinito* for Alto Saxophone, Soprano, Chorus, and Narrator (1973); *Biblical Madrigals* for Chorus (1974); *Windsongs* for Soprano and Guitar (1977); *Isaiah Syndrome* for Chorus (1980); *Mystic Rondo* for Man's or Woman's Voice, Violin, and Piano (1987–88).—NS/LK/DM

Polisi, Joseph W(illiam), American bassoonist and music educator; b. N.Y., Dec. 30, 1947. He had primary lessons in bassoon with his father, William Polisi, principal bassoonist of the N.Y. Phil. He then turned to legal studies, and took a course in political science at the Univ. of Conn. (B.A., 1969) and international relations at the Fletcher School of Law and Diplomacy at Tufts Univ. (M.A., 1970). He then resumed his musical training at Yale Univ. (M.M., 1973; M.M.A., 1975; D.M.A., 1980), and also studied bassoon with Maurice Allard at the Paris Cons. (1973–74). He per-

formed widely as a soloist and chamber music player, and also taught at the Univ. of Nev. (1975–76). He then was executive officer of the Yale Univ. School of Music (1976–80), and subsequently dean of faculty at the Manhattan School of Music (1980–83). After serving as dean of the Univ. of Cincinnati (Ohio) Coll.-Cons. of Music (1983–84), he became president of the Juilliard School in N.Y. (1984).—NS/LK/DM

Polívka, Vladimír, Czech pianist and composer; b. Prague, July 6, 1896; d. there, May 11, 1948. He studied piano at the Prague Cons., and took lessons in composition from Vítězslav Novák at the Master School there (1912–18). He traveled in Europe, America, and Japan with the violinist Jaroslav Kocián; from 1923 to 1930, taught piano in Chicago. In 1938 he returned to Prague and taught at the Cons.; was chairman of Pritomnost, an association for contemporary music. He publ. several collections of children's pieces, collaborated on a book about Smetana (Prague, 1941), and wrote a book of travels, describing his world tour (Prague, 1945).

WORKS: DRAMATIC: *Polobůh* (The Demigod), opera (1930); *A Ballad of a Deaf-Mute*, melodrama (1936); incidental music. **ORCH.:** *Jaro* (Spring), symphonic poem (1918); *Little Symphony* (1921); Suite for Viola and Small Orch. (1934); Concerto for Piano and Small Orch. (1934); Overture (1942). **CHAMBER:** 2 violin sonatas (1918, 1919); Suite for Viola and Wind Quintet (1934); String Quartet (1937); *Divertimento* for Wind Quintet (1939); *Giacona* for Viola and Piano (1944); Viola Sonata (1945). **Piano:** *Dni v Chicagu* (Days in Chicago; 1926); *3 Impromptus* (1930); *Merry Music* (1932–33); *Krajiny z let okupace* (Landscapes in the Years of Occupation), suite (1941). **VOCAL:** Choruses; songs.—NS/LK/DM

Pollack, Ben, jazz drummer, band leader; b. Chicago, Ill., June 22, 1903; d. Palm Springs, Calif., June 7, 1971. He considered joining the family fur business but instead gigged around Chicago, then in 1922 he joined the Friars' Inn Orch. (New Orleans Rhythm Kings). He also worked quite a bit in Los Angeles before 1926, then from May 1926 led his own band in Chicago, was on the West Coast in late 1927, and in N.Y. in March 1928. Benny Goodman and Glenn Miller were in his band, and later Harry James. The band did several long residencies in N.Y., Chicago, and broke up in Calif. in December 1934. Most of his sidemen formed the nucleus of the first Bob Crosby Band. He was dubbed "The Father of Swing." He led in New Orleans (1935), Chicago, and Los Angeles from 1936 until 1942, then directed a touring band for comedian Chico Marx. From August 1943, he ran his own booking agency and record company (Jewel), resuming more active performing in 1949. Later he opened his own club in Los Angeles. Pollack appeared as himself in film *The Benny Goodman Story* (1956). During the 1960s he mainly ran a restaurant in Hollywood, and later a nightclub in Palm Springs. He committed suicide by hanging. Pollack left a suicide note, explaining his act as prompted by despondency over personal and financial problems.

DISC.: *Ben Pollack and His Pick-A-Rib* (1950); *Dixieland Strut* (1960).—JC/LP

Pollak, Anna, English mezzo-soprano of Austrian descent; b. Manchester, May 1, 1912. She studied in the Netherlands and in Manchester. Following appearances as an actress and singer in musical comedy and operetta, she studied voice with Joan Cross. In 1945 she made her operatic debut as Dorabella at the Sadler's Wells Opera in London, where she was one of its leading artists until 1962. In 1952 she made her first appearance at the Glyndebourne Festival as Dorabella and at London's Covent Garden as Cherubino. Between 1962 and her retirement in 1968 she was a guest artist at the Sadler's Wells Opera. In 1962 she was made an Officer of the Order of the British Empire. She created the role of Bianca in Britten's *The Rape of Lucretia* (1946) and the title role in Berkeley's *Ruth* (1956).—NS/LK/DM

Pollak, Egon, esteemed Czech-born Austrian conductor; b. Prague, May 3, 1879; d. there (of a heart attack while conducting a performance of *Fidelio*), June 14, 1933. He studied with Knittl at the Prague Cons. He was chorus master at the Prague Deutsches Theater (1901–05); conducted opera in Bremen (1905–10), Leipzig (1910–12), and Frankfurt am Main (1912–17); also conducted in Paris and at London's Covent Garden (1914). He led Wagner's *Ring* cycle at the Chicago Grand Opera (1915–17); was able to leave the U.S. with the Austrian diplomatic legation as the U.S. entered World War I (1917). He was Generalmusikdirektor of the Hamburg Opera (1917–31); also conducted in Rio de Janeiro and at Buenos Aires's Teatro Colón (1928); appeared at the Chicago Civic Opera (1929–32) and in Russia (1932); led performances of the ensemble of the Vienna State Opera in Cairo and Alexandria (1933). He was a distinguished interpreter of the operas of Wagner and Richard Strauss.—NS/LK/DM

Pollarolo, Carlo Francesco, prominent Italian organist and composer, father of **(Giovanni) Antonio Pollarolo;** b. c.1653; d. Venice, Feb. 7, 1723. His father, Orazio Pollarolo, was organist in Brescia at the parish church of Ss. Nazaro e Celso and at the Cathedral, and it is likely that Carlo Francesco studied with him. After serving as organist at the Congregazione dei Padri della Pace and substituting for his father at the Cathedral, he was named his father's successor at the latter (1676). He was elected capo musico there (1680), and also held a similar post with the Accademia degli Erranti (1681–89). He then went to Venice, where he was elected second organist at San Marco (1690). He became its vice-maestro di cappella (1692), a position he held until his son Antonio succeeded him (1702); was also music director of the Ospedale degl'Incurabili. He composed about 85 operas, many of which are not extant; among those surviving are *Il Roderico* (1686), *Onorio in Roma* (Venice, 1692), *La forza della virtù* (Venice, 1693), *Il Faramondo* (Venice, 1699), *Semiramide* (Venice, 1713), *Ariodante* (Venice, 1716), and *Astinome* (Rome, 1719). He also wrote oratorios and many other sacred works, 19 solo cantatas with Basso Continuo or Orch., 67 arias and 5 duets with Basso Continuo or Orch., etc.

BIBL.: O. Termini, *C.F. P.: His Life, Time, and Music with Emphasis on the Operas* (diss., Univ. of Southern Calif., 1970). —NS/LK/DM

Pollarolo, (Giovanni) Antonio, Italian composer, son of **Carlo Francesco Pollarolo;** b. Brescia (baptized), Nov. 12, 1676; d. Venice, May 30, 1746. He studied with his father, for whom he began substituting as vice-maestro di cappella at Venice's San Marco (1702). He was named to that position (1723), and was acting primo maestro (1733–36) and then primo maestro (1740–46); was also maestro di coro at the Ospedale degl'Incurabili (from 1716). He wrote about 12 operas, but only *I tre voti* (Vienna, 1724) is extant. Other works include some sacred pieces, including oratorios, cantatas, and motets.—NS/LK/DM

Polledro, Giovanni Battista, Italian violinist and composer; b. Piovà, Casale Monferrato, near Turin, June 10, 1781; d. there, Aug. 15, 1853. He studied in Asti and with Pugnani in Turin, where he became a violinist in the royal orch. After touring northern Italy from 1798, he became concertmaster of the Bergamo theater orch. in 1804. Soon thereafter, he went to Moscow to play in Prince Tatishcev's serf orch. From 1811 he made successful tours of Germany. He was concertmaster of the Dresden court orch. from 1814 to 1824. From 1824 to 1844 he was maestro di cappella at the Turin court. He wrote several violin concertos, sacred music, chamber pieces, and violin studies.—LK/DM

Pollet, family of French musicians:

(1) Charles-François-Alexandre Pollet (l'aîne), citternist, guitarist, and composer; b. Béthune, 1748; d. Evreux, 1815. He was sent to Paris about 1771, where he became well known as a citternist. He wrote a method (1775), compositions, and arrangements for his instrument.

(2) (Jean-Joseph) Benoît Pollet (le jeune), harpist, music publisher, and composer, brother of the preceding; b. Béthune, 1753; d. Paris, April 16, 1823. He studied harp with J.-B. Krumpholtz. In 1791 he founded his own music shop in Paris, where he organized his own music publishing business about 1802. He wrote a method, a concerto, duos, sonatas, and arrangements for harp.

(3) Joseph Pollet, organist and choirmaster, son of the preceding; b. Paris, April 30, 1803; d. there, 1883. He served as organist and choirmaster at Notre-Dame de Paris from 1830 to 1871.—LK/DM

Pollini, Bernhard (real name, **Baruch Pohl**), German tenor, later baritone, and opera impresario; b. Cologne, Dec. 16, 1838; d. Hamburg, Nov. 27, 1897. He made his debut as Arturo in *I Puritani* in Cologne in 1857, and later sang baritone roles in an Italian opera troupe, of which he subsequently became manager and artistic director. He then undertook the management of the Italian opera at St. Petersburg and Moscow. In 1874 he became director of the Hamburg City Theater; in 1876 he also became manager of the Altona Theater and in 1894 of the Thalia Theater in Hamburg.—NS/LK/DM

Pollini, Francesco (Giuseppe), Italian pianist, singer, and composer of Slovenian birth; b. Laibach,

March 25, 1762; d. Milan, Sept. 17, 1846. He was a pupil of Mozart (who dedicated a violin rondo to him) at Vienna, and later of Zingarelli at Milan, where he was appointed a prof. of piano shortly after the opening of the Cons. (1809). He was the first to write piano music on 3 staves, a method imitated by Liszt, Thalberg, and others; a specimen of this style is one of his *32 Esercizi in forma di toccata*, op.42 (1820), a central melody surrounded by passagework for both hands. He publ. *Metodo per clavicembalo* (Milan, 1811). Among his compositions is an opera buffa, *La cassetta nei boschi* (Milan, Feb. 25, 1798), chamber music, songs, many piano pieces, and harpsichord works.—**NS/LK/DM**

Pollini, Maurizio, famous Italian pianist and conductor; b. Milan, Jan. 5, 1942. A precocious child, he began piano studies at an early age with Lonati. He made his debut at age 9, then studied with Vidusso at the Milan Cons. After sharing 2nd prize in the Geneva Competition in 1958, he took his diploma in piano at the Milan Cons. (1959); also studied with Michelangeli. After capturing 1st prize in the Chopin Competition in Warsaw (1960), he launched an acclaimed career as a virtuoso; appeared throughout Europe as a soloist with the leading orchs. and as a recitalist; made his U.S. debut at N.Y.'s Carnegie Hall (Nov. 1, 1968). In later years, he made appearances as a conductor, leading concerts from the keyboard and also mounting the podium and taking charge in the opera pit. Pollini is a foremost master of the keyboard; he has won deserved renown for making his phenomenal technical resources a means of exploring a vast repertoire, ranging from Bach to the cosmopolitan avant-garde. In 1987 he was awarded the Ehrenring of the Vienna Phil.—**NS/LK/DM**

Pololáník, Zdeněk, Czech composer; b. Brno, Oct. 25, 1935. Following training with Vladimír Malacka and František Suchý, he was a student of Josef Černocký (organ) at the Cons. (graduated,1957) and of Vilém Petrželka and Theodor Schafer (composition) at the Janáček Academy of Music (graduated, 1961) in Brno. Thereafter, he devoted himself fully to composing. In his music, Pololáník reveals an assured handling of form, structure, color, and unusual instrumental combinations.

WORKS: DRAMATIC: Melodrama: *Malá mytologická cvičení* (Small Mythological Exercises; 1991). **Ballet:** *Mechanismus* (Mechanism; 1964); *Popelka* (Cinderella; 1966); *Pierot* (About; 1976; orch. suite, 1977); *Sněhová královna* (Snow Queen; 1978); *Paní mezi stíny* (Lady Among Shadows; 1984). Also much incidental music and numerous radio, television, and film scores. **ORCH.:** Sinfonietta (1958); *Toccata* for Double Bass and Ensemble (1959); *Divertimento* for 4 Horns and Strings (1960); 5 syms.: No. 1 (1961), No. 2 for 11 Winds (1962), No. 3 for Percussion and Organ (1962), No. 4 for Strings (1963), and No. 5 (1969); *Concentus resonabilis* for 19 Soloists and Tape (1963); Piano Concerto (1966); Concerto grosso I for Clarinet or Flute, Guitar, Harpsichord, and Strings (1966) and II for Clarinet, Bassoon, and Strings (1988); Suite from the oratorio *Sheer hash sheereem* (1975); *Musica giocosa* for Violin and Chamber Ensemble (1980); Concertino for Piano and Strings (1985). **CHAMBER:** *Variations* for Organ and Piano (1956); Suite for Violin and Piano (1957); String Quartet (1958); *Scherzo contrario*

for Xylophone or Guitar, Bass Clarinet or Clarinet, and Violin (1961); *Musica spingenta I* for Double Bass and Wind Quintet (1961), *II* for String Quartet and Harpsichord (1962), and *III* for Bass Clarinet and 13 Percussion (1962); *Dodici preludii* for 2 Pianos and Organ (1963); *Tre scherzi* for Wind Quintet (1969); *Musica concisa* for Flute, Bass Clarinet, Harpsichord, Piano, and Percussion (1963); Horn Sonata (1965); *Oratio*, nonet for Key, Plucked, and Percussion Instruments (1968); *Musica trascurata* for Bass Clarinet and Piano (1970); *Ballad* for Cello and Piano (1992); *Christmas Triptych* for Bugle and 4 Trombones (1993). **KEYBOARD: Piano:** *Piano Preludes* (1957); *7 Preludes* (1960); *Seguidilla* (1983). **Organ:** *Sonata bravura* (1959); *Sonata laetitiae* (1962); *Allegro affanato* (1963); *Esultatio e pianto* (1972); *Burlesca* (1982); *Pastorale* (1986); *Preludio festivo* (1992). **VOCAL:** *Nabuchodonosor* for Chorus, 3 Trumpets, and 4 Kettledrums (1960); *Zpěv mrtvých dětí* (Cantus mortuorum liberorum) for Chorus, 3 Trumpets, and Percussion (1963); *Liturgical Mass* for Chorus, Brass, Harp, and Organ (1965); *Tiché světlo* (Silent Light) for Baritone and Organ (1965); *Cantus psalmorum* for Bass-baritone, Organ, Harp, and Percussion (1966); *Missa brevis* for Children's Chorus and Organ (1969); *Sheer hash sheereem* (Song of Songs), oratorio for Soloists, Chorus, and Orch. (1970; orch. suite, 1975); *Proglas* for Soprano, Horn, Harpsichord, Percussion, and Orch. (1980); *Slavnosti léta* (Summer Festivities) for Chorus and 2 Pianos (1985); *Vánoční poselství* (Christmas Message) for Men's Chorus, Electric Guitar, Synthesizer, and Percussion (1987); *Gloria! Co to nového...* (Gloria! What's New...), carols for Soprano, Tenor, Flute, Oboe, Cello, and Piano (1988–89; also for Men's Chorus, Piano, and Synthesizer); *Velikonoční cesta* (Easter Way), 14 songs for Soprano, Flute, Oboe, Cello, and Piano (1990; also for High Voice and Organ, 1991); *Cinderella of Nazareth*, chamber oratorio for Medium Voice and Synthesizer (1991); *Andělské poselství světu* (The Angel's Message to the World), Christmas pastoral for Soprano, Alto, Chorus, and Strings (1991); *Te Deum* for Chorus and Organ (1991); *First One Must Carry the Cross*, chamber oratorio for Medium Voice and Synthesizer (1992); *Time of Joy and Merrymaking*, cycle of 19 carols for Children's or Women's Chorus and Piano (1992); *God is Love*, chamber oratorio for Medium Voice and Synthesizer (1993); *Eulogies*, Psalms for Chorus (1993); *Cantus laetitiae*, Psalms for Children's or Women's Chorus (1993); *Encounters* for Soloists, Chorus, and Organ (1995).—**NS/LK/DM**

Pommier, Jean-Bernard, French pianist and conductor; b. Béziers, Aug. 17, 1944. He began piano lessons at 4 with Mina Kosloff. In 1958 he entered the Paris Cons., where he continued his studies with Yves Nat and Pierre Sancan. After taking the premier prix there in 1961, he completed his training with Eugene Istomin. In 1960 he won 1st prize in the Jeunesses Musicales competition in Berlin, and then began to make regular appearances in Europe. In 1971 he made his first appearance at the Salzburg Festival. During the 1973–74 season, he made his first appearances in the U.S. In subsequent years, his career took him to most of the principal music centers of the world. From 1980 he also pursued a career as a conductor.—**NS/LK/DM**

Pomus, Doc (originally, **Felder, Jerome E.**), American songwriter; b. N.Y., June 27, 1925; d. there, March 14, 1991. Pomus emerged from R&B music to become one of the most successful songwriters of the late 1950s and early 1960s, specializing in blues-based pop songs crafted for such artists as Elvis Presley and the Drifters, among them "Save the Last Dance for Me," "Surrender," and "Can't Get Used to Losing You."

Pomus was struck by polio at the age of nine and was forced to walk on crutches thereafter. Nevertheless, by his teens he was singing and playing saxophone in blues and jazz clubs. After recording unsuccessfully, he turned to writing, getting his first notable credit when "Boogie Woogie Country Girl" (music and lyrics by Doc Pomus and Reginald Asby) appeared on the flip-side of Joe Turner's R&B Top Ten single "Corrine Corrina" in 1956. Later that year Ray Charles gave him an R&B Top Ten with "Lonely Avenue." He collaborated with Jerry Leiber and Mike Stoller on "Young Blood," an R&B chart-topper in 1957 and his first Top Ten pop hit.

Pomus teamed with Mort Shuman in 1958, and mostly in collaboration with him placed many songs in the pop Top Ten over the next six years: "A Teenager in Love" (rec. by Dion and the Belmonts); "Hound Dog Man" and "Turn Me Loose" (both by Fabian) in 1959; "Go, Jimmy, Go" (Jimmy Clanton); and the #1 "Save the Last Dance for Me" (The Drifters) in 1960; the #1 "Surrender," "Little Sister," and "(Marie's the Name) His Latest Flame" (all by Elvis Presley) in 1961; "She's Not You" (music and lyrics by Doc Pomus, Jerry Leiber, and Mike Stoller) (Elvis Presley) in 1962; "Can't Get Used to Losing You" (Andy Williams) in 1963; and "Suspicion" (Terry Stafford) in 1964. (Pomus and Shuman's "This Magic Moment," a Top 40 hit by the Drifters in 1960, was revived for a Top Ten hit by Jay and the Americans in 1969.)

Shuman settled in Europe in the mid-1960s, ending the songwriting team. Pomus suffered a fall that confined him to a wheelchair for the rest of his life. Meanwhile, the ascent of The Beatles brought with it an emphasis on performers writing their own songs, thus limiting his opportunities. Pomus was inactive in the late 1960s and early 1970s, but he returned to work with a number of projects in the late 1970s and early 1980s, collaborating with Dr. John on songs for the Dr. John albums *City Lights* (1978) and *Tango Palace* (1979), and for the B. B. King album *There Must Be a Better World Somewhere* (1981), and writing with Willie De Ville for the Mink De Ville album *Le Chat Bleu* (1980). He died of lung cancer at 65 in 1991.—**WR**

Ponc, Miroslav, Czech violinist, conductor, and composer; b. Vysoké Mýto, Dec. 2, 1902; d. Prague, April 1, 1976. He studied organ with Wiedermann at the Prague Cons. (1920–22) and composition with Alois Hába there (1922–23; 1925–27).; went to Berlin and took lessons with Schoenberg. Upon returning to Prague, he studied violin with Suk at the Cons., graduating in 1930, and attended the quarter tone composition class of Hába, graduating in 1935; also took lessons in conducting with Scherchen in Strasbourg (1933). After World War II, he was active mainly as a theater conductor in Prague. He wrote a number of scores of incidental music for plays.

WORKS: *5 Polydynamic Compositions* for Piano, Xylophone, and String Quartet (1923); 2 song cycles: *A Bad Dream* (1925) and

A Black Swan (1926); *3 Merry Pieces* for Wind Quintet (1929); *Little Pieces* for Flute or Cello and Piano (1930); Piano Concertino (1930); *Overture to an Ancient Tragedy*, with the application of quarter tones in the Greek enharmonic mode (Prague, Feb. 18, 1931); Nonet (1932); *Osudy* (The Fates), 2 antique ballet pictures (1935); Suite for Piano with 2 manuals tuned in quarter tones (1935); String Trio (1937); over 100 scores of incidental music and much music for films and radio.—**NS/LK/DM**

Ponce, Manuel (Maria), distinguished Mexican composer; b. Fresnillo, Dec. 8, 1882; d. Mexico City, April 24, 1948. He studied piano with his older sister, and in 1904 went to Europe, where he took lessons in composition with Enrico Bossi at Bologna and in piano with Martin Krause in Berlin. Upon his return to Mexico, he taught piano at the Mexico City Cons. (1909–15). He gave a concert of his compositions in Mexico City on July 7, 1912, which included a Piano Concerto. In 1917 he again became a teacher at the Mexico City Cons., and also was conductor of the National Sym. Orch. (1917–19); then went to Paris for additional study, and took lessons with Dukas (1925). In 1933 he rejoined the faculty of the Mexico City Cons., serving as its director in 1934–35. His contact with French music wrought a radical change in his style of composition; his later works are more polyphonic in structure and more economical in form. He possessed a great gift of melody; one of his songs, *Estrellita* (1914), became a universal favorite, and was often mistaken for a folk song. In 1941 he made a tour in South America, conducting his own works. He was the first Mexican composer of the 20th century to employ an identifiably modern musical language, and his place in the history of Mexican music is thus very important. His works are often performed in Mexico; a concert hall was named after him in the Instituto de Bellas Artes.

WORKS: ORCH.: Piano Concerto (1912); *Balada mexicana* for Piano and Orch. (1914); *Estampas nocturnas* (1923); *Chapultepec, 3 bocetos sinfonicos* (Mexico City, Aug. 25, 1929; rev. version, Mexico City, Aug. 24, 1934); *Canto y danza de los antiguos Mexicanos* (1933); *Suite en estilo antiguo* (1935); *Poema elegiaco* for Chamber Orch. (Mexico City, June 28, 1935); *Instantáneas mexicanas* (1938); *Ferial, divertimento sinfónico* (Mexico City, Aug. 9, 1940); *Concierto del Sur* for Guitar and Orch. (Montevideo, Oct. 4, 1941); Violin Concerto (Mexico City, Aug. 20, 1943). **CHAMBER:** Piano Trio (1911); Cello Sonata (1922); *4 miniaturas* for String Quartet (1929); *Pequena suite en estilo antiguo* for Violin, Viola, and Cello (1933); Sonata for Violin and Viola (1935); numerous piano pieces, some based on Mexican rhythms; 6 guitar sonatas. **VOCAL:** About 30 songs; 34 arrangements of Mexican folk songs.

BIBL.: D. López Alonso, *M.M. P.: Ensayo biográfico* (Mexico City, 1950).—**NS/LK/DM**

Ponchielli, Amilcare, celebrated Italian composer; b. Paderno Fasolaro, near Cremona, Aug. 31, 1834; d. Milan, Jan. 15, 1886. He studied with his father, a shopkeeper and organist at the village church, and entered the Milan Cons. as a non-paying student when he was 9; his mentors included Pietro Ray (theory), Arturo Angeleri (piano), Felice Frasi (composition), and Alberto Mazzucato (music history, aesthetics, and composition). While a student there he collaborated on the operetta *Il sindaco babbeo* (Milan Cons., March 1851) and also wrote the sym. *Scena campestre* (1852). After his graduation (1854), he went to Cremona as a church organist. He was named assistant to Ruggero Manna, director of Cremona's Teatro Concordia (1855), where he brought out his opera *I promessi sposi* (Aug. 30, 1856). He was conductor of the municipal bands in Piacenza (1861–64) and Cremona (from 1864), where he also conducted opera; continued to pursue his interest in composing for the theater. He finally achieved notable success with the revised version of his *I promessi sposi* (Milan, Dec. 4, 1872), which was subsequently performed throughout Italy; his *La Gioconda* (Milan, April 8, 1876) secured his reputation. He was prof. of composition at the Milan Cons. in 1880 and again from 1881; also served as maestro di cappella at Bergamo's S. Maria Maggiore (1881–86). He married **Teresina Brambilla** in 1874. His birthplace was renamed Paderno Ponchielli in his honor. *La Gioconda* remains his only work to have acquired repertoire status; it includes the famous ballet number *Dance of the Hours*. In addition to his numerous stage works, he composed many band pieces, vocal chamber music, chamber works, and piano pieces.

BIBL.: A. Mandelli, *Le distrazioni di A. P.* (Cremona, 1897); G. Cesari, *A. P. nell'arte del suo tempo: Ricordi e carteggi* (Cremona, 1934); U. Rolandi, *Nel centenario ponchelliano: A. P. librettista* (Como, 1935); G. De Napoli, *A. P. (1834–1886): La vita, le opere, l'epistolario, le onoranze* (Cremona, 1936); A. Damerini, *A. P.* (Turin, 1940); N. Albarosà et al., eds., *A. P. 1834–1886: Saggio e ricerche nel 1507 anniversario della nascità* (Casalmorano, 1984); L. Sirch, *Catalogo tematico delle musiche di A. P.* (Cremona, 1989).—NS/LK/DM

Pond, Sylvanus Billings, American music publisher and composer; b. Milford, Vt., April 5, 1792; d. Brooklyn, March 12, 1871. He was a prominent musician of his time. He conducted the N.Y. Sacred Musical Society and the N.Y. Academy of Sacred Music, wrote songs for Sunday school, and ed. and publ. *Union Melodies* (1838), *The U.S. Psalmody* (N.Y., 1841), and *The Book of Praise, for the Reformed Dutch Church in America* (N.Y., 1866). He also composed the hymn tunes *Armenia* (1835) and *Franklin Square* (1850). Early in life, he went to Albany, where he established a piano workshop. From 1820 he was partner of the publ. house of Meacham and Pond there, and in 1832 he joined Firth & Hall of N.Y. The firm's name became Firth, Hall & Pond, and in 1848 was reorganized as Firth, Pond & Co.; it was one of the principal publishers of Stephen Foster's songs. In 1850 Pond retired, and his son, William A. Pond, became the owner. Upon the withdrawal of Firth in 1863, the firm became known as William A. Pond & Co. W.A. Pond's eldest son, William A. Pond Jr., was taken into partnership, but died in 1884; William A. Pond Sr. died the following year, and his 2 other sons, Albert Edward and George Warren Pond, succeeded him. In 1934 Joseph Fletcher acquired the catalogue; in 1946 it was purchased by Carl Fischer, Inc. For the dealings of Firth, Pond & Co. with Stephen Foster, see J.T. Howard, *Stephen Foster, America's Troubadour* (N.Y., 1931; 4th ed., 1965); consult also H. Dichter and E. Shapiro, *Early American Sheet Music, Its Lure and Its Lore, 1768–1889* (N.Y., 1941).—NS/LK/DM

Poné, Gundaris, Latvian-born American conductor and composer; b. Riga, Oct. 17, 1932; d. Kingston, N.Y., March 15, 1994. In 1944 his family went to Germany, where he studied violin. In 1950 he emigrated to the U.S., becoming a naturalized American citizen in 1956. He studied violin and composition at the Univ. of Minn. (B.A., 1954; M.A., 1956; Ph.D., 1962). In 1966 he made his conducting debut in N.Y., and subsequently appeared as a guest conductor in the U.S. and in Europe; served as music director of the Music in the Mountains Festivals (from 1981). His compositions captured 1st prizes in the Concorso Internazionale "Citta di Trieste" (1981), the Kennedy Center Friedheim Awards Competition (1982), the International Louisville Orch. Competition (1984), the International Hambach Prize Competition (1985), and the International Georges Enesco Competition (1988). His concern as a composer was to develop a musical language capable of communicating with the general audience while maintaining the high intellectual standards of contemporary composition.

WORKS: DRAMATIC: Opera: *Rosa Luxemburg* (1968). **ORCH.:** Violin Concerto (1959); *Composizione per quattro orchestre* (1967–69); *Vivos voco, Mortuos plango* (1972); *Avanti!* (1975); Horn Concerto (1976); *La Serenissima*, 7 Venetian portraits (1979–81; Trieste, Sept. 25, 1982); *American Portraits* (1982–84); *Titzarin* (1984–86); *La bella veneziana*, overture (1987). **CHAMBER:** *Hetaera Esmeraldo*, string quartet (1963); *Serie-Alea* for Flute, Oboe, Clarinet, Bassoon, and Piano (1965); Sonata for Solo Cello (1966); *San Michele della Laguna* for Clarinet, Violin, and Piano (1969); *De Mundo Magistri Ioanni* for Chamber Ensemble (1972); *Diletti dialettici*, concerto for 9 Virtuosos (1973); *Eisleriana*, concerto for 11 Players (1978); *Woodland Elegies*, 5 pieces for 5 Instruments (1980); *Propositions for Opus 32*, 6 pieces for Woodwind Quartet and Piano (1982); *Cyprian Sketches*, 4 pieces for Clarinet, Cello, and Piano (1983); *Gran duo funebre* for Viola and Cello (1987); *Pezzi del tramonto* for Violin and Piano (1989); piano pieces, including Oltre questa porta geme la terra for 3 Pianos (1969) and 3 Farewell Pieces (1984); works for solo instruments. **VOCAL:** *Quattro temperamenti d'amore* for Baritone and Orch. or Piano (1960); *Daniel Propheta* for 3 Soloists, Chorus, and Orch. (1962); *Junius Broschure* for 4 Speakers, 18 Women's Voices, and Instrumental Ensemble (1970); *5 American Songs* for Medium Voice and Small Orch. (1975).—NS/LK/DM

Pongrácz, Zoltán, Hungarian composer and teacher; b. Diószeg, Feb. 5, 1912. He studied with Kodály at the Budapest Academy of Music (1930–35); then took lessons in conducting from Nilius in Vienna (1935–38) and Krauss in Salzburg (1941). He served as director of the music dept. of Hungarian Radio in Budapest (1943–44) and then conducted the Debrecen Phil. (1946–49). He taught composition at the Debrecen Cons. (1947–58) and electronic composition at the Budapest Academy of Music (from 1975).

WORKS: DRAMATIC: Opera: *Odysseus and Nausikaa* (1949–50; Debrecen, 1960); *The Last Station* (1983). **Ballet:** *The Devil's Present* (1936). **ORCH.:** Sym. (1943); *Ballo ongaro* for Youth Orch. (1955); *3 Orchestral Etudes* (1963); *Hangok és zörejek* (Tones and Noises; 1966); *Színek és vonalak* (Colors and Lines) for Youth Orch. (1971). **CHAMBER:** *Pastorale* for Clarinet, Organ, 6 Winds, and Percussion (1941); *Javanese Music*, on a South Asiatic motif, for Chamber Ensemble (1942); *Music* for 5 Cellos (1954); Wind Quintet (1956); *Toccata* for Piano (1957); *3 Small Pieces* for Orff Ensemble (1966); *Phonothèse* for Tape (1966); *Sets and Pairs*, electronic variations for Piano and Celesta (1968); *3 Improvisations* for Piano, Percussion, and 3 Tape Recorders (1971); *3 Bagatelles* for Percussion (1972); *Zoophonia*, concrete music synthesized from animal sounds (1973); Concertino for Soprano Saxophone and Tape (1982); Concertino for Cimbalon and Electronics (1988). **VOCAL:** *Christmas Cantata* (1935); *St. Stephen Oratorio* (1938); *Apollo musagètes*, cantata (1958); *Negritude* for Speaking Chorus, Chorus, and Percussion (1962); *Ispirazioni* for Chorus, Orch., and Tape (1965); *Music from Nyírség* for Soloists, Chorus, and Folk Orch. (1965). **ELECTRONIC:** *Polar and Successive Contrasts* (1986).—**NS/LK/DM**

Poniatowski, Józef (Michal Xsawery Franciszek Jan), Prince of Monte Rotondo, Polish tenor and composer; b. Rome, Feb. 20, 1816; d. Chislehurst, England, July 3, 1873. He was a member of the Polish nobility; his uncle was a marshal in Napoleon's army. He studied in Florence, and appeared on the stage as a tenor. He then wrote operas (to Italian and French librettos). In 1848 he went to Paris and was elevated to the rank of Senator by Napoleon III; after the fall of the 2nd Empire, he went to England. In addition to operas, he also composed the popular ballad, *The Yeoman's Wedding Song.*

WORKS: DRAMATIC: Opera: *Giovanni da Procida* (Florence, Nov. 25, 1838); *Don Desiderio, ossia Il disperato per eccesso di buon cuore* (Pisa, Dec. 26, 1840); *Ruy Blas* (Lucca, Sept. 2, 1843); *Bonifazio de' Geremei* (Rome, Nov. 28, 1843); *La sposa d'Abido* (Venice, Feb. 1845); *Malek-Adel* (Genoa, June 26, 1846); *Esmeralde* (Florence, June 26, 1847); *Pierre de Médicis* (Paris, March 9, 1860); *Au travers du mur* (Paris, May 9, 1861); *L'Aventurier* (Paris, Jan. 26, 1865); *La Contessina* (Paris, April 28, 1868); *Gelmina* (London, June 4, 1872).—**NS/LK/DM**

Poniridis, Georges, distinguished Greek composer; b. Constantinople (of Greek parents), Oct. 8, 1892; d. Athens, March 29, 1982. He studied violin with Ysaÿe at the Brussels Cons. and composition with d'Indy and Roussel at the Schola Cantorum in Paris, where he remained until the outbreak of World War II; then returned to Athens and served in the Music Division of the Greek Ministry of Education (1954–58). In his music, he made use of authentic Greek motifs, at times endeavoring to emulate the simple monody of ancient Greek chants and the rhythms of classical prosody.

WORKS: DRAMATIC: Incidental music to ancient Greek plays. **ORCH.:** 2 syms. (1935, 1942); *Triptyque symphonique* (Athens, Nov. 22, 1937); *3 Symphonic Preludes* (1938); Chamber Sym. for Strings and Percussion (n.d.); *Petite symphonie* (1956); Piano Concerto (1968); Violin Concerto (1969). **CHAMBER:** Flute Sonata (1956); String Quartet (1959); Clarinet Sonata (1962); Quartet for Oboe, Clarinet, Bassoon, and Xylophone (1962); Trio for Xylophone, Clarinet, and Bassoon (1962); Trio for Flute, Oboe, and Clarinet (1962); 2 violin sonatas; Viola Sonata (1967); Cello Sonata (1967); 3 piano sonatas. **VOCAL:** Arrangements of Greek folk songs. —**NS/LK/DM**

Ponnelle, Jean-Pierre, notable French opera designer and producer; b. Paris, Feb. 19, 1932; d. Munich, Aug. 11, 1988. He received his education at the Sorbonne in Paris. In 1952 he gained early recognition as a designer with the premiere of Henze's *Boulevard Solitude* in Hannover. His first opera production followed in 1962 in Düsseldorf with his staging of *Tristan und Isolde,* and he subsequently worked in Berlin, Hamburg, Munich, Stuttgart, and other German music centers. In 1968 he brought out *Il Barbiere di Siviglia* at the Salzburg Festival, where he later worked regularly. In 1973 he produced *L'Italiana in Algeri* at the Metropolitan Opera in N.Y., returning there to oversee such productions as *Der fliegende Holländer* (1979), *Idomeneo* (1982), *La clemenza di Tito* (1984), *Le nozze di Figaro* (1985), and *Manon* (1986). He also worked at London's Covent Garden, where he produced *Don Pasquale* (1973), *Aida* (1984), and *L'Italiana in Algeri* (1988). In 1981 he produced *Tristan und Isolde* at the Bayreuth Festival. He also made many film productions of his stagings. Ponnelle was one of the most creative and influential opera designers and producers of his time. While he could be controversial, there was no denying his genius in the art of stage craft.

BIBL.: I. Fabian, *J.-P. P.* (Zürich, 1983).—**NS/LK/DM**

Ponomarev, Valery, jazz trumpeter; b. Moscow, Russia, Jan. 20, 1943. His mother was a pianist; Ponomarev began on drums and then, at age 16, switched to trumpet. He was inspired to play jazz after picking up a shortwave broadcast featuring Clifford Brown. He performed around Moscow from 1965–69 and recorded for the state label; he defected to Rome, Italy in 1971, where he worked for two years. In 1973, Ponomarev decided to move to the U.S. to meet Art Blakey. He finagled an illegal exit visa and found himself in N.Y. at an impromptu audition for Blakey, who offered him a job, which he was only able to take two years later when Blakey's then-trumpeter left the band. He spent five years with Blakey (1977–82). Since then, he has remained active in N.Y. Since 1980, he has led his own band called Universal Language. In 1992, he returned to his homeland to appear at the first Moscow International Jazz Festival.

DISC.: *Means of Identification* (1985); *Trip to Moscow* (1988); *Profile* (1991); *Live at Sweet Basil* (1993); *Live at Vartan's* (1996). —**LP**

Pons, José, Spanish composer; b. Gerona, c. 1768; d. Valencia, Aug. 2, 1818. He was a choirboy at Gerona Cathedral, where he studied with Jaime Balius. In 1791 he was made choirmaster at Córdoba Cathedral, and soon thereafter he was named its vice-choirmaster. From 1793 he served as choirmaster at Valencia Cathedral. Pons was esteemed by his contemporaries for his compositions for the church.—**LK/DM**

Pons, Juan, Spanish baritone; b. Ciutadela, Aug. 8, 1946. He received his training in Barcelona, where he commenced his career as a tenor at the Teatro Liceo. In 1979 he made his first appearance at London's Covent Garden as Alfio in *Cavalleria rusticana.* On Jan. 4, 1983, he made his Metropolitan Opera debut in N.Y. as Conte di Luna in *Il trovatore,* and also appeared that same year as Massenet's Hérode in Barcelona and as Donizetti's

Tonio at the Paris Opéra. After singing Amonasro in Vienna in 1984, he appeared as Rigoletto and Sharpless at Milan's La Scala in 1985. In 1987 he portrayed Verdi's Falstaff at the Bavarian State Opera in Munich, and in 1988 sang Germont at the Lyric Opera in Chicago. He again appeared as Falstaff in 1989 at the San Francisco Opera and at the Rome Opera. In 1992 he sang Tonio in Philadelphia and Conte di Luna in Madrid. He was engaged as Tonio in Los Angeles in 1996.—NS/LK/DM

Pons, Lily (actually, **Alice Josephine**), glamorous French soprano; b. Draguignan, April 12, 1898; d. Dallas, Feb. 13, 1976. She studied piano as a child, then took voice lessons with Alberti di Gorostiaga. She made her debut as an opera singer in Mulhouse in 1927 in the title role in *Lakmé*. After singing in provincial theaters in France, was engaged at the Metropolitan Opera in N.Y., and sang Lucia at her debut there on Jan. 3, 1931, with excellent success; she remained on its roster until 1944 (again from 1945 to 1958; on Dec. 14, 1960, made a concert appearance there). While in N.Y., she continued vocal studies with Maria Gay and Giovanni Zenatello. Her fame as an extraordinary dramatic singer spread rapidly; she was engaged to sing at the Grand Opéra and the Opéra-Comique in Paris, at Covent Garden in London, the Teatro Colón in Buenos Aires, in Mexico, and in Cuba. She went to Hollywood and appeared in films, among them *That Girl from Paris* (1936) and *Hitting a New High* (1938). During World War II, she toured the battlefronts of North Africa, India, China, and Burma; received numerous honors. So celebrated did she become that a town in Md. was named Lillypons in her honor. She was married twice (divorced both times) to the publisher August Mesritz, and once to **André Kostelanetz**. She possessed an expressive coloratura voice, which she used with extraordinary skill. In addition to Lakmé, she won great renown for her portrayals of Philine in *Mignon*, Gilda, Marie in *La Fille du régiment*, Rosina, Olympia in *Les Contes d'Hoffmann*, and Amina in *La Sonnambula*.—NS/LK/DM

Pons de Capdoil, French troubadour; b. c. 1165; d. c. 1215. He was the son of the lord of St. Julien Capdoil in Puy-Ste. Marie-en-Velay, and won distinction as a knight. He was active mainly in Marseilles, where the captivating wife of the Count of Auvergne inspired him to write several outstanding love poems. Some 27 of his poems are extant, including 4 with music. His melodies were frequently used as contrafacta.

BIBL.: M. von Napolski, *Leben und Werk des Trobadors P.d. C.* (Halle, 1879).—LK/DM

Ponse, Luctor, Swiss-born Dutch pianist, teacher, and composer; b. Geneva, Oct. 11, 1914; d. Amsterdam, Feb. 17, 1998. He studied at the Valenciennes Cons. (Prix d'Excellence for theory and solfège, 1930, and piano, 1932) and the Geneva Cons. (Prix de Virtuosité for piano, 1933). In 1936 he settled in the Netherlands. He made tours of his adopted country and abroad, and also taught piano at several conservatories. In 1964 he became a member of the Inst. for Sonology at the Univ. of Utrecht. He also founded the electronic music studio at the Groningen Cons. In 1953 and 1956 he was awarded composition prizes at the Concours Reine Elisabeth in Belgium. In some of his works from 1966 he employed electronics.

WORKS: DRAMATIC: Ballet: *Feestgericht* (1957). **ORCH.:** *Divertissement* for Strings (1946); Piano Concerto (1951–55); 3 sinfoniettas (1952, 1959, 1961); 3 syms. (1953; 1957; 1981–85); Concerto for 2 Pianos and Orch. (1961–62); *Concerto da camera* for Oboe and Strings (1962); 2 violin concertos (1963, 1965); Concerto for Piano, Orch., and Tape (1967; rev. 1980); Harp Concerto (1986); Suite for Piano and Orch. (1987); *5 études* for Piano and Orch. (1991); *Caractères* for Piano and Orch. (1993); *Triptyque III* for Wind Orch. (1994). **CHAMBER:** Trio for Flute, Clarinet, and Piano (1940–41); 2 string quartets (1941, 1947); 2 cello sonatas (1943, 1950); *2 Pieces* for Wind Quintet (1943); *Duo* for Violin and Cello (1946); Violin Sonata (1948); Quintet for Flute, Oboe, Violin, Viola, and Cello (1956); *2 Caprices* for Flute and Piano (1956); Sextet for Flute, Oboe, Violin, Viola, Cello, and Harpsichord (1958); *Variations* for Flute and Harpsichord (1962); *Euterpe Suite* for 11 Instruments (1964); *Musique concertante* for Viola, Double Bass, Piano, Percussion, and Electronics (1977); Sonata for Clarinet and Tape (1981); Suite for Piano and Percussion (1982); *Toccata* for Harpsichord (1985); *Chromatismen* for Chamber Ensemble (1997); piano pieces.—NS/LK/DM

Ponselle (real name, **Ponzillo**), **Rosa (Melba),** brilliant American soprano, sister of **Carmela Ponselle**; b. Meriden, Conn., Jan. 22, 1897; d. Green Spring Valley, Md., May 25, 1981. Her parents, who emigrated to the U.S. from southern Italy, gave her, with a prescient hope, the middle name Melba. Her father owned a grocery store in Meriden; she studied music with her mother, an amateur singer, and sang in a local church choir. Her older sister, Carmela, also learned to sing, and the 2 sisters, billed under their real name, Ponzillo, as "Italian Girls," sang in vaudeville shows in Pittsburgh and in N.Y. Later she took voice lessons in N.Y. with William Thorner, who became her manager; he introduced her to Caruso, who in turn arranged for her audition at the Metropolitan Opera. She made a fine impression, and was engaged for a debut on Nov. 15, 1918, in the role of Leonora in *La forza del destino*, opposite Caruso, who sang the male lead of Don Alvaro. Among her subsequent notable roles there were Santuzza (1918), Racehl in *La Juive* (1919), Aida (1920), Maddalena in *Andrea Chénier* (1921), Sélika (1923), Leonora in *Il Trovatore* and Gioconda (1924), Norma (1927), Violetta (1931), and Carmen (1935). She was equally successful in London when she appeared at Covent Garden as Norma (May 28, 1929). She made her last appearance at the Metropolitan Opera in N.Y. as Carmen on Feb. 15, 1937. After her retirement, she became active in social affairs. Her 80th birthday was celebrated in 1977 at her estate, with a multitude of friends and itinerant celebrities in attendance.

BIBL.: E. Aloi, *My Remembrances of R. P.* (N.Y., 1994); E. Aloi, *R. P.: A Pictorial History* (N.Y., 1996); J. Drake, *R. P.: A Centenary Biography* (Portland, Ore., 1997); M. Phillips-Matz, *R. P.: American Diva* (Boston, 1997).—NS/LK/DM

Ponta, Adamus de, South Netherlands composer who flourished in the second half of the 16th century. He was a singer in the Vienna Hofkapelle in 1563–64. He then settled in Liège, where he was succentor at St. Jean l'Evangéliste and rector of the altar of St. Ambroise (1567–69). From 1570 he was succentor and beneficiary of the altar of St. Denis. In 1576 he was elected canon of St. Materne in the Cathedral, but in 1577 he was replaced as canon and succentor. He subsequently was active at St. Jean l'Evangéliste, becoming succentor there in 1582. Ponta was an admirable composer of motets. —**LK/DM**

Pontac, Diego de, Spanish composer; b. probably in Saragossa, 1603; d. Madrid (buried), Oct. 1, 1654. He began his musical training in Saragossa when he was 9, and later studied singing and counterpoint with Juan Pujol and Francisco Berge, and counterpoint with Pedro Rimonte. In 1620 he was made maestro de capilla at Saragossa's Hospital Real. After training in composition from Nicolás Dupont in Madrid, he received a prebend as maestro de capilla in Salamanca, where he also became an examiner in singing at the Univ. Following service as chaplain in Madrid, he was made maestro de capilla at Granada's Iglesia Mayor. He was maestro de capilla at Santiago de Compostela (1644–49) and at Saragossa's Cathedral of La Seo (1649–50). Following a stay at Valencia Cathedral (1650–53), he became deputy maestro de capilla of Madrid's royal chapel in 1654. Pontac compiled 2 extensive MSS of his music for publication in 1631, but none of his works appeared in print in his lifetime. Among his works were masses, mass antiphons, motets, and responsories.—**LK/DM**

Ponte, Lorenzo da
See **Da Ponte, Lorenzo**

Pontelibero, Ferdinando, Italian violinist and composer, known as "Ajutantini"; b. Como, 1770; d. Milan, 1835. He was an orch. player in Como before joining the orch. of Milan's La Scala about 1795. In 1814 he became first violinist for the ballet there, continuing with the orch. as well until 1833.

WORKS: DRAMATIC: B a l l e t (all 1st perf. at the Teatro alla Scala, Milan): *Il Generale Colla in Roma* or *Il ballo del Papa* (Feb. 25, 1797); *Gonzalvo in America* (Jan. 1799); *I francesi in Egitto* or *Buonaparte in Egitto* (Feb. 11, 1799); *Zulima* (Jan. 1800); *Sadak e Kalasrad* (Jan. 1801); *Il sagrifizio di Curzio* (Dec. 26, 1804); *Alcina e Ruggiero* (1805); *Magri e grassi* (June 16, 1806); *Cambise in Egitto* (Sept. 30, 1807); *La morte di Whaytsong, ultimo imperatore della dinastia chinese* (Jan. 24, 1809; Acts 2–5 by G. Ferliga). **OTHER:** 3 sinfonias, various dances, 6 string quartets, and vocal pieces. —**LK/DM**

Ponti, Michael, American pianist; b. Freiburg im Breisgau (of American parents), Oct. 29, 1937. He was taken to the U.S. as a child. He studied piano with Gilmour MacDonald; in 1955 he returned to Germany to continue his studies at the Frankfurt am Main Hochschule für Musik. In 1964 he won 1st prize in the Busoni Competition in Bolzano, which launched him on a successful career. In his programs, he specialized in bringing out neglected or forgotten piano masterpieces of the sonorous Romantic past.—**NS/LK/DM**

Pontio or **Ponzio, Pietro,** Italian music theorist and composer; b. Parma, March 25, 1532; d. there, Dec. 27, 1595. He was ordained and then served as maestro di cappella at S. Maria Maggiore in Bergamo (1565–67) and at Madonna della Steccata in Parma (1567–69). From 1577 to 1582 he was maestro di cappella at Milan Cathedral. In 1582 he returned to his previous position in Parma. Pontio publ. the treatises *Ragionamento di musica...ove si tratta de passaggi...et del modo di far motetti, messe, salmi et altre compositioni* (Parma, 1588; facsimile ed. in Documenta Musicologica, XVI, 1958) and *Dialogo...ove si tratta della theorica et prattica di musica* (Parma, 1595). He also publ. 11 vols. of sacred vocal works (Venice, 1580–95), 4 of which are not extant.—**LK/DM**

Ponty, Jean-Luc, jazz-rock violinist; b. Avranches, Normandy, Sept. 29, 1942. His mother taught him piano and his father taught violin and clarinet. He began his violin studies at age five, quitting school at age 13 to focus on a concert career; he entered the Paris Conservatory, and won first prize on the instrument in 1960. While there, he began playing clarinet with some amateur jazz musicians who played once a month. He taught himself saxophone, and then one day played jazz on his violin, with great success, and began to study the recordings of Stephane Grappelli and Stuff Smith; he made his first recording with Grappelli in 1966. He was invited to play in the U.S. in 1967, and released his first U.S. recordings in 1968. Frank Zappa composed the music for and arranged his 1969 album *King Kong*, and Ponty played on Zappa's jazz-rock album, *Hot Rats*. He settled permanently in the U.S. in 1973. A year later, John McLaughlin asked him to join his second Mahavishnu Orch.; Zappa's group and Mahavishnu toured together for a month. Later, in 1976, Zappa asked ask him to join the latest version of the Mothers of Invention for a tour of the U.S. that lasted seven months. From the mid-1970s, Ponty has mostly led his own groups, playing a mix of jazz, rock, and new age music. In 1988, he met some African musicians in Paris; he recorded *Tchokola* with them in 1991, and six years later they also toured Europe. In 1995 he began working with Violectra, an English maker of four-, five- and six-string violins, to develop the perfect instrument. In addition to amplified violin, he composes and performs on the Synclavier.

DISC.: *Oeil Vision* (1962); *Jazz Long Playing* (1964); *Violin Summit* (1966); *Sunday Walk* (1967); *More Than Meets the Ear* (1969); *Live at Donte's* (1969); *King Kong: Ponty Plays Zappa* (1969); *Experience* (1969); *Canteloupe Island* (1969); *New Violin Summit* (1972); *Open Strings* (1973); *Upon the Wings of Music* (1975); *Aurora* (1975); *Imaginary Voyage* (1976); *Cosmic Messenger* (1978); *Live* (1979); *Open Mind* (1984); *Fables* (1985); *Gift of Time* (1987); *Storytelling* (1989); *Tchokola* (1991); *Jean-Luc Ponty Experience* (1991); *No Absolute Time* (1992).—**LP/MM/NS**

Ponzo, Giuseppe, Italian composer who flourished in the second half of the 18th century. He wrote the operas *Demetrio* (Genoa, Carnival 1759), *Arianna e Teseo* (Milan, Jan. 1762), *Artaserse* (Venice, Jan. 1766), and *Il rè alla caccia* (c. 1775). He also composed 6 sinfonie and other instrumental pieces, a Credo for 4 Voices and Instruments, arias, and duets.—**LK/DM**

Poole, Elizabeth, English mezzo-soprano; b. London, April 5, 1820; d. Langley, Buckinghamshire, Jan. 14, 1906. She made her debut at Drury Lane in London in 1834, and then sang in Italian opera in the U.S. (appearing with Malibran). Until her retirement in 1870, she was immensely popular as a ballad singer. Balfe wrote for her *'Tis gone, the past is all a dream*, which she introduced into *The Bohemian Girl*.—NS/LK/DM

Poot, Marcel, remarkable Belgian composer; b. Vilvoorde, near Brussels, May 7, 1901; d. Brussels, June 12, 1988. He received his first musical training from his father, then continued his studies with Gilson (1916), at the Brussels Cons. with Sevenants, Lunssens, and de Greef (1916–20), and at the Royal Flemish Cons. of Antwerp with Lodewijk Mortelmans (1921–23). In 1925, with 7 other Gilson pupils, he founded the Groupe des Synthétistes, dedicated to propaganda of new musical ideas (the group disbanded in 1930). Also in 1925, Poot was co-founder, with Gilson, of *La Revue Musicale Belge*, to which he contributed until its dissolution in 1938. He was on the staff of the Brussels Cons. from 1938 to 1966, and was its director from 1949 until his retirement. The most striking element of his music is its rhythmic vivacity; his harmony is well within the tonal sphere. His Piano Concerto (1959) was a compulsory work for finalists of 1960 Queen Elisabeth piano competition, won by Malcolm Frager.

WORKS: DRAMATIC: Chamber Opera: *Moretus* (1943; Brussels, 1944). Ballet: *Paris et les 3 divines* (1933); *Camera* (1937); *Pygmalion* (1952). Also incidental music. ORCH.: *Variations en forme de danses* (1923); *Charlot*, 3 sketches inspired by Charlie Chaplin films (1926); *Rondo* for Piano and Small Orch. (1928); *Capriccio* for Oboe and Orch. (1928); 7 syms. (1929; *Triptyque symphonique*, 1938; 1952; 1970; 1974; 1978; 1982); *Poème de l'espace*, symphonic poem inspired by Lindbergh's flight (1929; Liège, Sept. 4, 1930); *Jazz Music* (1930; Brussels, Feb. 21, 1932); *Allegro symphonique* (1935); *Fantaisie rythmique* (1936); *Ballade* for String Quartet and Orch. (1937); *Légende épique* for Piano and Orch. (1938); *Suite* for Small Orch. (1940); *Ballade* for Clarinet and Orch. (1941); *Concertstück* for Cello and Orch. (1942); *Fantasia* (1944); Sinfonietta (Chicago, Oct. 22, 1946); *Mouvement symphonique* for Wind Orch. (1946); *Divertimento* for Small Orch. (1952); *Mouvement perpétuel* (1953); *Ballade* for Violin and Orch. (1955); Piano Concerto (1959; Brussels, May 25, 1960); *2 mouvements symphoniques* (1960); *Concertstück* for Violin and Orch. (1962); *Concerto Grosso* for 11 Strings (1962); *Music for Strings* (1963); *Concerto Grosso* for Piano Quartet and Orch. (1969); Trumpet Concerto (1973); Alto Saxophone Concerto (1980). CHAMBER: Piano Quartet (1932); *3 Pièces en trio* for Piano Trio (1935); *Scherzo* for 4 Saxophones (1941); *Divertimento* for Oboe, Clarinet, and Bassoon (1942); Octet for Winds and Strings (1948); String Quartet (1952); *Ballade* for Oboe, Clarinet, and Bassoon (1954); *Fantaisie* for 6 Clarinets (1955); *Concertino* for Wind Quintet (1958); *Musique* for Wind Quintet (1964); *Legende* for 4 Clarinets or Saxophones (1967); Quartet for 4 Horns (1969); *Mosaïque* for 8 Winds (1969); *Musique de chambre* for Piano Trio (1971); several Ballades and other pieces for Solo Instruments with Piano; solo piano pieces. VOCAL: 2 oratorios: *Le Dit du routier* (1943) and *Icare* (1945); choral works; songs.—NS/LK/DM

Pop, Iggy (originally, **Osterberg, James Jewel**), vocalist for the late 1970's punk band, The Stooges; b. Ann Arbor, Mich., April 21, 1947. The Stooges, often considered the forerunner of the punk groups of the late 1970s, featured minimalist music, chaotic guitar playing, and the vituperative and insolent lyrics of Iggy Pop. MEMBERSHIP: Iggy Pop, voc.; Ron Asheton (Ronald Franklin Asheton Jr.), gtr. (b. Washington, D.C., July 17, 1948); Dave (David Michael) Alexander, bs. (b. Ann Arbor, Mich., June 3, 1947; d. Detroit, Feb. 10, 1975); Scott (Randolph) Asheton, drm. (b. Washington, D.C., Aug. 16, 1949). James Williamson, gtr. (b. Birmingham, Mich.) joined in 1972; Ron Asheton switched to bass. Scott Thurston, bs., kybd., joined in 1973.

Leader Iggy Pop's spontaneously outrageous and sadomasochistic onstage behavior made him one of the first performance artists in rock, and as such he served as a precursor to the calculated theatrical excesses of Alice Cooper and Kiss. Enduring a chaotic period of drug and psychological problems, Iggy Pop reemerged as a solo act in the late 1970s, eventually giving up his self-destructive onstage act while retaining his energetic, compelling image.

Iggy Pop played drums and sang lead with the Detroit-area high school band the Iguanas, and he later manned the Prime Movers. After a semester at the Univ. of Mich. and as a drummer for a blues band in Chicago, he returned to Detroit, where he formed the Stooges in 1967 with Asheton brothers Ron and Scott and Dave Alexander. The Stooges performed loud, three-chord rock music fronted by the vocals and disturbing onstage antics of Iggy. Over the years his notoriety grew, with deeds such as threatening and vilifying audiences, cutting himself with broken bottles, pouring hot wax over his body, intentionally smashing his teeth, and vomiting, even urinating on audiences and allowing ardent fans to perform fellatio on him.

Signed to Elektra Records, the Stooges recorded their debut album under producer John Cale of the Velvet Underground. It featured Stooges favorites such as "No Fun" and "I Wanna Be Your Dog." However, their classic second album, *Funhouse*, failed to even make the album charts and the group experienced a period of disintegration. Taken to England by mentor David Bowie in 1972, Iggy Pop and new guitarist James Williamson were joined by the Asheton brothers for the Bowie-produced *Raw Power* on Columbia. An acknowledged early heavy-metal classic, the album included the title cut as well as "Search and Destroy," "Gimme Danger," "Death Trip," and "Your Pretty Face Is Going to Hell." The Stooges broke up in early 1974 and Pop ended up in Los Angeles, where he became addicted to heroin; he kicked the habit, then entered a mental hospital in 1975.

After moving to West Berlin in spring 1976, Iggy Pop again encountered David Bowie, who managed to secure him a recording contract with RCA Records. *The Idiot* contained "Sister Midnight" and the Bowie-Pop collaboration "China Girl" (a major hit for Bowie in 1983), and *Lust for Life* included "Fall in Love with Me," "Neighborhood Threat," and the title song. Pop returned to live performance, often accompanied by Bowie on keyboards, but the albums sold modestly at best, despite critical acclaim. Iggy Pop switched to Arista Records for 1979's *New Values* and another round of disturbing, if not outrageous, live performances later that year with former Sex Pistols bassist Glen Matlock and guitarist-keyboardist Ivan Kral from the Patti Smith Group.

During the 1980s Iggy Pop abandoned his self-destructive onstage antics and recorded *Zombie Birdhouse* for Animal Records. He moved to N.Y.C. and recorded the theme song to the 1984 cult movie *Repo Man*, taking up acting and eventually securing minor roles in *Sid and Nancy* and *The Color of Money*. Pop cowrote five songs for David Bowie's *Tonight*, Bowie's last album to sell a million copies, and Bowie coproduced and coauthored five of the songs on Pop's *Blah Blah Blah* on A&M Records, hailed as his best recording in years. Former Sex Pistols guitarist Steve Jones cowrote three of the album's songs, including "Cry for Love," and the album otherwise featured "Isolation" and a remake of Johnny Kidd's "Real Wild Child." Pop conducted his first world tour in four years in 1986–1987, serving as the opening act for the Pretenders' 1987 tour. He later recorded *Instinct* with Steve Jones.

By 1990 Pop had moved to Virgin Records, where he recorded the best-selling album of his career, *Brick by Brick*. Produced by Don (Was) Fagenson, the album featured Slash and Duff McKagan from Guns N' Roses, included John Hiatt's "Something Wild," and yielded Pop's only (major) hit, "Candy," sung with Kate Pierson of the B–52's. He performed as one of the headline acts for 1990's Gathering of the Tribes festival (a precursor of the Lollapalooza tours) and toured again in 1993 in support of *American Caesar*. Skydog issued the live set *We Are Not Talking About Commercial Shit* in 1995, the year Iggy Pop recorded *Wild Animal* for New Rose Records.

DISC.: THE STOOGES: *The Stooges* (1969); *Funhouse* (1970). **IGGY POP AND THE STOOGES:** *Raw Power* (1973); *Metallic K.O.* (rec. 1973; rel. 1994). **IGGY POP:** *The Idiot* (1977); *Lust for Life* (1977); *TV Eye—1977 Live* (1978); *Choice Cuts* (1984); *New Values* (1979); *Soldier* (1980); *Party* (1981); *Zombie Birdhouse* (1983); *Blah Blah Blah* (1986); *Instinct* (1988); *Brick by Brick* (1990); *American Caesar* (1993); *We Are Not Talking About Commercial Shit* (1995); *Wake Up Suckers* (1995); *Wild Animal* (1995).

BIBL.: Per Nilsen and Dorothy Sherman, *I. P.: The Wild One* (London, 1988).—**BH**

Popov, Alexander, Bulgarian composer; b. Kolarovgrad, July 14, 1927. He studied composition with Veselin Stoyanov at the Bulgarian State Cons., graduating in 1954. He played viola in the orch. of the National Opera in Sofia, and was a member of the Sofia Soloists chamber ensemble.

WORKS: ORCH.: *Suite* (1956); *Native Land*, variations (1958); *The Artist*, suite for String Quartet and String Orch. (1961); Sinfonietta (1964); *Concerto Grosso* for Strings (1966); *Prelude and Dance* (1972); *Adagio* (1973); *Variants* for 13 Strings (1973). **CHAMBER:** 2 string quartets. **VOCAL:** 2 cantatas: *Cantata about the April Uprising* (1952) and *Land of Songs* (1969); choruses; songs.—**NS/LK/DM**

Popov, Gavriil, outstanding and original Russian composer; b. Novocherkassk, Sept. 12, 1904; d. Repino, near Leningrad, Feb. 17, 1972. He studied at the St. Petersburg Cons. with Nikolayev (piano) and Shcherbachev (composition). From his student days, he adopted the procedures of modern music; his Septet, also known as Chamber Sym. for 7 Instruments (1926; Moscow, Dec. 13, 1927), was written in a system of dissonant counterpoint then fashionable in Western Europe; his 1st Sym. (1927–32; rev. 1934; Leningrad, March 22, 1935) was in a similar vein. When modern music became the target of attack in Russia, Popov modified his style toward a more popular conception, following the tenets of socialist realism. Among his other works were 6 syms., including No. 2, *Fatherland* (Moscow, Feb. 15, 1944), No. 3 for Strings, on Spanish themes (Moscow, Jan. 31, 1947), No. 4, *Glory Be to the Fatherland* (1949), No. 5, *Pastorale* (1965), and No. 6 (Moscow, Jan. 23, 1970); Octet (1927); Violin Concerto (1937); *Divertimento* for Orch. (1938); *Hispania*, 7 fragments for Orch. (1940); Organ Concerto (1970). A 7th sym. remained unfinished at his death.—**NS/LK/DM**

Popovici, Doru, Romanian composer; b. Reşiţa, Feb. 17, 1932. He studied at the Bucharest Cons. with Constantinescu, Negrea, Andricu, Rogalski, Jora, and Vancea (1950–55) and attended the summer courses in new music in Darmstadt.

WORKS: DRAMATIC: Opera: *Prometeu* (1958; Bucharest, Dec. 16, 1964); *Mariana Pineda*, after García Lorca (Bucharest, Dec. 22, 1966); *Interogateriul din zori* (Bucharest, Feb. 6, 1975); *Noaptea cea mai lungă* (Bucharest, March 30, 1978). **ORCH.:** *Triptyque* (1955); 2 *Symphonic Sketches* (1955); *Concertino* for Strings (1956); Concerto (1960); 4 syms.: No. 1 (1962), No. 2, *Spielberg* (1966), No. 3, *Bizantina*, for Chorus and Orch. (1968), and No. 4 for Chorus and Orch. (1973); *Poem bizantin* (1968); *Codex Cajoni* for Strings (1968); *Pastorale transilvane* for Strings (1979); *Pastorale din Oltenia*, suite (1982). **CHAMBER:** Cello Sonata (1952); Violin Sonata (1953); String Quartet No. 1 (1954; rev. 1964); *Fantasy "Orphée"* for String Trio (1955); Sonata for 2 Cellos (1960); Sonata for 2 Violas (1965); *Omagiu lui Tuculescu*, quintet for Piano, Violin, Viola, Cello, and Clarinet (1967); *Musique solennelle* for Violin and Piano (1969); Trio for Violin, Cello, and Piano (1969–70); *Madrigal* for Flute, Clarinet, Violin, Viola, Cello, and Trombone (1979); piano pieces. **VOCAL:** 5 cantatas: *Porumbeii morţii* (1957), *Noapte de August* for Baritone and Orch. (1959), *In memoriam poetae Mariana Dumitrescu* (1967), *1877* (1976–77), and *Cîntec de speranţă* (1977); choruses; many songs.—**NS/LK/DM**

Popp, Lucia, esteemed Czech-born Austrian soprano; b. Uhorská Veš, Nov. 12, 1939; d. Munich, Nov. 16, 1993. She studied at the Bratislava Academy of Music (1959–63) and in Prague, her principal mentor being Anna Prosenč-Hřusková. After singing at the Bratislava Opera, she went to Vienna and appeared as Barbarina at the Theater an der Wien (1963); that same year, she joined the Vienna State Opera, where she established herself as a principal member; also became a favorite at the Salzburg Festivals. In 1966 she made her first appearance at London's Covent Garden as Oscar; then made her Metropolitan Opera debut in N.Y. in one of her finest roles, the Queen of the Night, on Feb. 19, 1967. She sang with many of the world's leading opera houses, and also won distinction as a gifted concert and lieder artist. In 1979 she was made an Austrian Kammersängerin, and was awarded the Silver Rose of the Vienna Phil. She won accolades for her roles in operas by Mozart and Strauss, especially Pamina, Despina, Zerlina, Susanna, Zdenka, Sophie, and the Countess, as well as the Queen of the Night. For some years she was married to **György Fischer**. In 1986 she married **Peter Seiffert.—NS/LK/DM**

Popper, David, famous Czech cellist and composer; b. Prague, Dec. 9, 1843; d. Baden, near Vienna, Aug. 7, 1913. He studied cello with Goltermann at the Prague Cons. He began his career with a tour in 1863, then had a highly successful appearance as a soloist at the Karlsruhe Music Festival on March 29, 1865. From 1868 to 1873 he was 1st cellist of the Vienna Court Orch. In 1872 he married **Sophie Menter**, but they were divorced 14 years later. From 1896 until his death he taught cello at the Budapest Cons. He wrote a number of extremely attractive and marvelously idiomatic pieces for the cello, which long remained in the international repertoire, among them 4 concertos (1871, 1880, 1880, 1900) and a *Requiem* for 3 Cellos and Orch. (perf. by him, with Delsart and Howell, in London, Nov. 25, 1891). He also publ. the tutors *Hohe Schule des Violoncello-Spiels* (Leipzig, 1901–5) and *10 mittelschwere grosse Etüdien* (Leipzig, c. 1905).—NS/LK/DM

Poradowski, Stefan (Boleslaw), Polish composer and pedagogue; b. Wloclawek, Aug. 16, 1902; d. Poznań, July 9, 1967. He studied composition with Opieński at the Poznań Cons. (1922–26), then took private lessons with Rezniček in Berlin (1929). Returning to Poland, he taught composition and theory at the Poznań Cons. (1930–39; 1945–67) and also gave courses (from 1956) at the Wroclaw Cons. He publ. *Nauka harmonii* (Science of Harmony; Poznań, 1931; 5th ed., rev., 1964), *Ogólne wiadomości z akustyki* (General Knowledge on Acoustics; Poznań, 1947), and *Sztuka pisania kanonów* (Art of Writing Canons; Poznań, 1965).

WORKS: DRAMATIC: *Odkupienie* (Redemption), passion play for Mezzo-soprano, Chorus, and Orch. (1939–41); *Plomienie* (Flames), opera (1961–66). ORCH.: *Sinfonietta* (1925); *Concerto antico* for Viola d'Amore and Orch. (1925); *Triptych* for Strings (1926); 8 syms. (1928; 1930; 1932; 1934; 1937–38; 1951–52; 1961; 1967); Double Bass Concerto (1929); *Capriccio on a Theme by Kreutzer* for Strings (1930); *Serenada klasyczna* for Strings (1940); *Rapsodia polska* for Violin and Orch. (1944); Concert Overture (1947); *Ratusz poznański* (The Town Hall of Poznań), symphonic poem (1950); Concerto for Flute, Harp, and String Orch. (1954); Violin Concerto (1965). CHAMBER: 4 string quartets (1923, 1923, 1936, 1947); Violin Sonata (1925); 5 trios: I and II for Violin, Viola, and Double Bass (1929, 1930), III for String Trio (1935), IV for 3 Double Basses (1952), and V for String Trio (1955); piano pieces; organ music. VOCAL: *Pieśń wiosenna* (Spring Song) for Soprano, Chorus, and

Orch. (1926); *Koń Światowida* (The Horse of Sviatovid), fantastic poem for Tenor, Baritone, Chorus, and Orch. (1931); 3 cantatas (1950, 1954, 1954); 3 masses; 4 hymns; songs; folk song arrangements.—NS/LK/DM

Porcelijn, David, Dutch conductor, teacher, and composer; b. Achtkarspelen, Jan. 7, 1947. He was a student of Vester (flute) and of Baaren and Vlijmen (composition) at the Royal Cons. of Music in The Hague, where he took the prize for composition in 1972. He then studied conducting, composition, and theory with Tabachnik in Geneva (1972–74). In 1972 he became a conductor of the Ensemble M. He also was conductor of the Radio Blazers Ensemble (1973–77), the Gewestelijk Orkest voor Zuid-Holland (1977–82), and the Nederlands Danstheater (1977–86). From 1974 to 1978 he taught at the Rotterdam Cons., and then at the Utrecht Cons. from 1984. In 1993 he became conductor of the Adelaide Sym. Orch. in Australia. From 1996 to 1998 he was conductor of the Noordhollands Phil. Porcelijn composed a number of orch. and chamber works along avant-garde lines.—NS/LK/DM

Porfetye, Andreas, Romanian composer; b. Zădăreni, July 6, 1927. He studied with Drăgoi, Constantinescu, Rogalski, and Vancea at the Bucharest Cons. (1948–54). He was ed. of the journal *Muzica* (1954–69). From 1969 he taught at the Bucharest Cons.

WORKS: ORCH.: 3 syms. (1955; 1965; *La Dramatique*, 1970); *Partita* for Strings (1958); Organ Concerto (1962; rev. 1967); *Sinfonia-Serenata* (1964); Violin Concerto (1966); *Sonata* (1971). CHAMBER: Horn Sonata (1956); Wind Quintet (1957); *Piccola sonata* for Violin and Organ (1962); Sonata for Cello and Organ (1963); *6 Pieces* for Clarinet and Harp (1965); Violin Sonata (1967); String Quartet No. 2 (1969). KEYBOARD: Piano: Sonata (1963); Sonatina (1965). Organ: *Passacaglia and Fugue* (1955); *Toccata, Chorale, and Fugue* (1957); 3 sonatas (1960–68); *Toccata* (1966); *Fantasy* (1968). VOCAL: *Cantata de camera* for Mezzo-soprano, Cello, and Chamber Orch. (1959); Cantata No. 2, *Comunistul*, for Mezzo-soprano, Chorus, and Orch. (1962); *In memorian Mihail Sadoveanu*, Requiem for Soprano, Tenor, and Orch. (1962).—NS/LK/DM

Porpora, Nicola (Antonio), famous Italian composer and singing teacher; b. Naples, Aug. 17, 1686; d. there, March 3, 1768. The son of a bookseller, he entered the Cons. dei Poveri at Naples at the age of 10 and studied with Gaetano Greco, Matteo Giordano, and Ottavio Campanile. Porpora's first opera, *Agrippina*, was presented at the Royal Palace of Naples (Nov. 4, 1708); Cardinal Grimani attended the performance and wrote a libretto on the same subject for Handel. This episode gave rise to the incorrect statement (by Fétis and others) that Handel heard Porpora's opera in Rome in 1710. Porpora produced in Naples 2 more operas: *Flavio Anicio Olibrio* (1711) and *Basilio, re d'oriente* (June 24, 1713). From 1711 until 1725, he held the title of maestro di cappella to Philip, Landgrave of Hesse-Darmstadt. He gained a great reputation as a singing teacher, and numbered among his pupils the famous castrati Farinelli, Caffarelli, Antonio Uberti (who called himself "Porporino" out of respect for his teacher), and

Salimbeni. Metastasio, who wrote librettos for several of Porpora's operas, was also his pupil. Porpora's career as a singing teacher was divided between Naples and Venice. In Naples he taught at the conservatories of Sant' Onofrio (1715–22, 1760–61) and Santa Maria di Loreto (1739–41, 1760–61); in Venice he gave lessons at the Ospedali degli Incurabili (1726–33, 1737–38), the Ospedali della Pietà (1742–46), and the Ospedaletto (1746–47). In 1718 Porpora collaborated with D. Scarlatti in the writing of the opera Berenice, regina d'Egitto, produced in Rome (1718). At about this time he succeeded in obtaining support from the Austrian court. His opera Temistocle was produced in Vienna on the Emperor's birthday (Oct. 1, 1718); his next opera, Faramondo, was staged in Naples (Nov. 19, 1719). He continued to write operas for theaters in Naples and Rome: Eumene (Rome, 1721), Adelaide (Rome, 1723), Semiramide, regina dell'Assiria (Naples, 1724), and Didone abbandonata (his 1st opera to a libretto by Metastasio; Reggio Emilia, 1725). In 1726 he settled in Venice. Among the operas he wrote during the next 8 years were Meride e Selinunte (Venice, 1726), Siroe, re di Persia (Milan, 1726), Semiramide riconosciuta (Venice, 1729), Mitridate (Rome, 1730), Tamerlano (Turin, 1730), Poro (Turin, 1731), Germanico in Germania (Rome, 1732), and Issipile (Rome, 1733). In 1733 he applied for the post of maestro di cappella at San Marco in Venice, but failed to obtain it. In the same year he was engaged by the directors of the Opera of the Nobility in London (organized as a rival company to that of Handel). For this venture Porpora wrote 5 operas: Arianna in Nasso (Dec. 29, 1733), Enea nel Lazio (May 11, 1734), Polifemo (Feb. 1, 1735), Ifigenia in Aulide (May 3, 1735), and Mitridate (Jan. 24, 1736; a different score from the earlier opera of the same title). For a while he competed successfully with Handel, but soon the Opera of the Nobility began to falter, and Porpora left London on the eve of the company's collapse. From 1747 to 1751, he was in Dresden as singing teacher to the Electoral Princess. There he became Hasse's competitor for the position of music director. Although Hasse conducted Porpora's "pastoral drama" Filandro (Dresden, July 18, 1747), their relationship was made difficult by the intrigues of Hasse's wife, the singer Faustina Bordoni. In 1751 Porpora left Dresden for Vienna, where he became the teacher of Haydn, who paid for his lessons by serving Porpora as accompanist and personal helper. Porpora returned to Naples in 1758. His last stage work, Il trionfo di Camilla, was given in Naples on May 30, 1760, with little success. In addition to his varied and numerous stage works, Porpora wrote sacred oratorios, secular cantatas, and serenatas. Among his instrumental works are 6 Sinfonie da camera for 2 Violins and Basso Continuo (London, 1736), 6 Sonatas for 2 Violins, Cello, and Basso Continuo (London, 1745, in collaboration with G.B. Costanza), a Cello Concerto, a Flute Concerto, and Ouverture roiale (1763).

BIBL.: F. Walker, A Chronology of the Life and Works of N. P. (Cambridge, 1951); A. Mayeda, N.A. P. als Instrumentalkomponist (diss., Univ. of Vienna, 1967; with thematic catalogue); E. Sutton, The Solo Vocal Works of N. P.: An Annotated Thematic Index (diss., Univ. of Minn., 1974).—NS/LK/DM

Porrino, Ennio, Italian composer and teacher; b. Cagliari, Sardinia, Jan. 20, 1910; d. Rome, Sept. 25, 1959. He studied at the Accademia di Santa Cecilia in Rome with Mule, and later took a course with Respighi (1932–35). He subsequently taught in Rome, Venice, and Naples, and from 1956 he was director of the Cagliari Cons.

WORKS: DRAMATIC: Opera: Gli orazi (Milan, 1941); L'organo di bambu (Venice, 1955); I shardana (Naples, 1959). **Ballet:** Proserpina (Florence, 1938); Altair (Naples, 1942); Mondo tondo (Rome, 1949); La bambola malata (Venice, 1959). **ORCH.:** Tartatin de Tarascon, overture (Rome, 1933); Sardegna, symphonic poem, based on Sardinian folk themes (Rome, 1933); Trumpet Concertino (1934); La visione di Ezechiele (1935); Sinfonia per una fiaba (1936); Notturna e Danza (1936); 3 canzoni italiane for Chamber Orch. (1937); Preludio in modo religioso e ostinato (1942; also for Piano); Sinfonietta dei fanciulli (1947); Sonata drammatica for Piano and Orch. (1947); Ostinato for Piano and Strings (1951; Milan, Feb. 3, 1952); Nuraghi, 3 primitive dances (1952); Concerto dell'Argentarola for Guitar and Orch. (1953); Sonar per musici for Harpsichord and Strings (1959). **OTHER:** I canti dell'esilio, 15 songs for Voice and Chamber Orch. (1947); Il processo di Cristo, oratorio (1949); other songs; chamber pieces, including Preludio, Aria e Scherzo for Trumpet and Piano (1942).—NS/LK/DM

Porro, Giovanni Giacomo, Italian organist and composer; b. Lugano, c. 1590; d. Munich, Sept. 1656. He was organist to the Duke of Savoy at the Turin court (1618–23), and then went to Rome, where he was first named maestro di cappella of S. Lorenzo in Damaso. From 1626 to 1630 he deputized as organist at St. Peter's, and then was Frescobaldi's substitute there from 1630 to 1633. In 1635 he was made vice-Kapellmeister at the Bavarian court in Munich, and shortly thereafter he was named its Kapellmeister. He composed a vast amount of sacred music amounting to some 900 works, including 187 Psalms and 208 antiphons. He also wrote operas and some 200 madrigals. Almost of all of his music is lost.—LK/DM

Porro, Pierre-Jean, famous French guitarist; b. Beziers, 1750; d. Montmorency, May 31, 1831. Through his influence the guitar became a fashionable instrument in Paris, where he had a class of pupils. He also was ed. and publ. of Journal de Guitarre (1787–1803). He publ. a guitar method, Tableau méthodique, and composed numerous divertissements, sonatas, and canzonets, for guitar solo and with other instruments. He also composed Collection de musique sacrée for 4 Voices and Organ.

BIBL.: F. Donnadieu, P., Compositeur et éditeur de musique (Béziers, 1897).—NS/LK/DM

Porsile, Giuseppe, Italian composer; b. Naples, May 5, 1680; d. Vienna, May 29, 1750. He studied in Naples at the Cons. dei Poveri di Gesù Cristo with Ursino, Giordano, and Greco. He then served as vice-maestro di cappella at the Spanish chapel in Naples. In 1695 he went to Spain to organize the music chapel of King Charles II in Barcelona; he subsequently served Charles III. When Charles III was elected Holy Roman

Emperor as Charles VI, with the seat in Vienna, Porsile followed him there. On Dec. 17, 1720, he became court composer. He continued to serve the court after Charles VI died in 1740, being granted an honorary stipend; he was pensioned on April 1, 1749. Most of his stage works were written for the court of Vienna.

WORKS (all 1st perf. in Vienna unless otherwise given): **DRAMATIC: Opera:** *Il ritorno di Ulisse alla patria* (Naples, 1707); *Il giorno natalizio dell'imperatrice Amalia Wilhelmina* (April 21, 1717); *La Virtù festeggiata* (July 10, 1717); *Alceste*, festa teatrale (Nov. 19, 1718); *Meride e Selinunte*, dramma per musica (Aug. 28, 1721); *Il tempo fermato*, componimento da camera (Oct. 15, 1721); *La Virtù e la Bellezza in lega*, serenata (Oct. 15, 1722); *Il giorno felice*, componimento da camera (Aug. 28, 1723); *Componimento a due voci* (Aug. 28, 1725); *Spartaco*, dramma per musica (Feb. 21, 1726); *Il tempio di Giano, chiuso da Cesare Augusto*, componimento per musica (Oct. 1, 1726); *La clemenza di Cesare*, servizio di camera (Oct. 1, 1727); *Telesilla*, festa teatrale (Nov. 19, 1729); *Scipione Africano, Il maggiore*, festa di camera (Oct. 1, 1730); *Dialogo tra il Decoro e la Placidezza*, festa di camera (July 26, 1732); *Dialogo* pastorale a cinque voci (Aug. 28, 1732); *Dialogo tra la Prudenza e la Vivacita*, festa di camera (Oct. 15, 1732); *La Fama accresciuta dalla Virtù*, festa di camera (Oct. 15, 1735); *Sesostri, re d'Egitto, ovvero Le feste d'Iside*, dramma per musica (Carnival 1737); *Il giudizio rivocato*, festa di camera (Oct. 15, 1737). **Oratorios:** *Sisara* (March 23, 1719); *Tobia* (March 14, 1720); *Il zelo di Nathan* (1721); *L'anima immortale creata e redenta per il cielo* (Feb. 26, 1722); *Il trionfo di Giuditta* (Feb. 18, 1723); *Il sacrifizio di Gefte* (March 9, 1724); *Mosè liberato dal Nilo* (March 1, 1725); *Assalone nemico del padre amante* (March 14, 1726); *L'estaltazione de Salomone* (March 6, 1727); *L'ubbidienza a Dio* (March 9, 1730); *Due re, Roboamo e Geroboamo* (Feb. 23, 1731); *Giuseppe riconosciuto* (March 12, 1733); *La madre de' Maccabei* (March 14, 1737). **OTHER:** Chamber cantatas; duets; instrumental pieces.—NS/LK/DM

Porta, Bernardo, Italian composer and teacher; b. Rome, 1758; d. Paris, June 11, 1829. He was a pupil of Magrini. He was the 1st maestro di cappella and director of the Tivoli orch., and then was in the service of the Prince of Salm, the prelate of Rome. About 1758 he went to Paris, where he composed several dramatic works. He also was active as a teacher until 1822.

WORKS: DRAMATIC (all 1st perf. in Paris unless otherwise given): *La principessa d'Amalfi* (Rome, 1780); *Le diable à quatre, ou La double metamorphose* (Feb. 14, 1790); *Pagamin, ou Le calendrier des vieillards* (March 29, 1792); *La blanche Haguenée* (May 24, 1793); *Alexis et Rosette, ou Les Huhlans* (Aug. 3, 1793); *La réunion du 10 août, ou L'inauguration de la République française* (April 5, 1794); *Agricole Viala, ou Le héros de 13 ans* (July 1, 1794); *Le pauvre aveugle, ou La chanson savoyarde* (July 24, 1797); *L'oracle* (1797); *Le prisonnier français, ou Le bienfait récompensé* (Oct. 2, 1789); *Deux morts qui se volent* (April 26, 1800); *Les deux statues* (April 29, 1800); *Les Horaces* (Oct. 18, 1800); *Le vieux de la montagne* (1802; unfinished; not perf.); *Le connétable de Clisson* (Feb. 9 or 10, 1804). **OTHER:** 2 oratorios, masses, motets, a cantata, and didactic instrumental pieces.—LK/DM

Porta, Costanzo, important Italian composer; b. Cremona, 1528 or 1529; d. Padua, May 19, 1601. He most likely began his religious training at the convent of Porta S. Luca in Cremona. He then went to Casalmaggiore, possibly to enter his novitiate. He was transferred to S. Maria Gloriosa dei Frari in Venice about 1549. He studied music with Willaert, the choirmaster of San Marco. In 1552 he became maestro di cappella of the cathedral in Osimo, near Ancona. On April 14, 1565, he became maestro di cappella in the Cappella Antoniana in Padua. In 1567 he became maestro di cappella of the cathedral in Ravenna. In 1574 he was called to the Santa Casa in Loreto. He publ. his first book of masses in 1578, and his *Liber motectorum* followed in 1580. He returned to Ravenna in 1580, making visits to the Este court in Ferrara and the Gonzaga court in Mantua. In 1589 he took charge of the chapel of the cathedral in Padua, but in 1592 was ordered to take up residence at the Convento del Santo. In 1595 he again became maestro di cappella at the Cappella Antoniana, a position he held until his death. Porta was one of the leading Italian composers and teachers of his time, being greatly esteemed as a contrapuntist. A modern ed. of his works, *Costanzo Porta: Opera Omnia*, was publ. in Padua (1964–70).

WORKS: VOCAL: Sacred: *37 Motectorum...liber primus* for 5 Voices (Venice, 1555); *Liber primus* [28] *motectorum* for 4 Voices (Venice, 1559; 2nd ed., rev., 1591); *Musica* [44] *introitus missarum...in diebus dominicis* for 5 Voices (Venice, 1566; 2nd ed., rev., 1588); *Musica* [40] *introitis missarum...in solemnitatibus omnium sanctorum* for 5 Voices (Venice, 1566; 2nd ed., rev., 1588); *Musica* [29] *canenda...liber primus* for 6 Voices (Venice, 1571); *Litaniae deiparae virginis Mariae* for 8 Voices (Venice, 1575); (12) *Missarum liber primus* for 4 to 6 Voices (Venice, 1578); *Liber* [52] *motectorum* for 4 to 8 Voices (Venice, 1580); *Musica* [29] *canenda...liber tertius* for 6 Voices (Venice, 1585); (44) *Hymnodia sacra totius per anni circulum* for 4 Voices (Venice, 1602); *Psalmodia vespertina omnium solemnitatem decantanda cum 4 canticis beatae virginis* for 8 and 16 Voices (Ravenna and Venice, 1605); (23) *Motectorum* for 5 Voices (Venice, 1605); also various motets, Psalms, and litanies in other collections of the period. **Secular:** *Il primo libro de* [29] *madrigali* for 4 Voices (Venice, 1555); *Il primo libro de* [28] *madrigali* for 5 Voices (Venice, 1559); *Il secondo libro de* [29] *madrigali* for 5 Voices (Venice, 1569); *Il terzo libro de* [29] *madrigali* for 5 Voices (Venice, 1573); *Il quarto libro de* [21] *madrigali* for 5 Voices (Venice, 1586); various other madrigals in other collections of the period.

BIBL.: F. Hafkemayer, *C. P. aus Cremona: Untersuchungen über seine kirchenmusikalischen Arbeiten* (diss., Univ. of Freiburg, 1953); A. Garbelotto, *Il Padre C. P. da Cremona, OFM. Conv.* (Padua, 1955); L. Pruett, *The Masses and Hymns of C. P.* (diss., Univ. of N.C., 1960).—NS/LK/DM

Porta, Giovanni, Italian composer; b. c. 1675; d. Munich, June 21, 1755. He was maestro di cappella at Vicenza Cathedral in 1710–11, and at Verona Cathedral from 1714 to 1716. His first opera, *La costanza combattuta in amore*, was premiered in Venice on Oct. 17, 1716. He then studied with Francesco Gasparini, with whom he and another composer collaborated on the opera *Il Trace in catena* (Rome, Canrival 1717). Porta's opera *L'Argippo* was given in Venice in 1717. He was commissioned to write the opera *Numitore* for the opening season of the Royal Academy of Music in London at the King's Theatre (April 2, 1720). From 1726 to 1737 he served as maestro di coro at the Ospedale della Pietà in Venice, and he also was a member of the Accademia Filarmonica in Verona from 1726. In 1737 Porta was called to

Munich by the Elector Karl Albert to serve as Hofkapell-meister at the Bavarian court, a position he retained for the rest of his life. Among his many other operas were *L'Arianna dell'isola di Nasso* (Milan, Aug. 28, 1723), *Antigone, tutore di Filippo, re di Macedonia* (Venice, Carnival 1724; in collaboration with Albinoni), *Ulisse* (Venice, Carnival 1725), *Farnace* (Bologne, 1731), *Gianguir* (Milan, Carnival 1732), *La Semiramide* (Milan, Carnival 1733), and *Ifigenia in Aulide* (Munich, Jan. 1738). He also wrote much sacred vocal music.

BIBL.: G. von Westerman, *G. P. als Opernkomponist* (diss., Univ. of Munich, 1921).—**LK/DM**

Porter, Andrew (Brian), brilliant English writer on music; b. Cape Town, South Africa, Aug. 26, 1928. He studied music at Diocesan Coll. in Cape Town, then went to England and continued his education at Univ. Coll., Oxford; became a proficient organist. In 1949 he joined the staff of the *Manchester Guardian,* and then wrote music criticism for the *Financial Times* of London (1953–74); also served as ed. of the *Musical Times* of London (1960–67). In 1972 he became the music critic of the *New Yorker.* In 1992 he became the chief music critic of *The Observer* in London. He was made a corresponding member of the American Musicological Soc. in 1993. A polyglot, a polymath, and an uncommonly diversified intellectual, Porter expanded his interests far beyond the limited surface of purely musical studies; he mastered German, Italian, and French; made an exemplary tr. into Eng. of the entire text of *Der Ring des Nibelungen,* taking perspicuous care for the congenial rendition of Wagner's words and melodic inflections; his tr. was used to excellent advantage in the performance and recording of the cycle by the conductor Reginald Goodall with the English National Opera. Porter also tr. texts of Verdi's operas, Mozart's *Die Zauberflöte,* and some French operas. His mastery of English prose and his unostentatious display of arcane erudition make him one of the most remarkable music critics writing in the English language. Selections from his reviews have been publ. in *A Musical Season* (N.Y., 1974), *Music of Three Seasons, 1974–1977* (N.Y., 1978), *Music of Three More Seasons, 1977–1980* (N.Y., 1981), *Musical Events: A Chronicle, 1980–1983* (N.Y., 1987), and *Musical Events: A Chronicle, 1983–1986* (N.Y., 1989); also was co-ed. of Verdi's *Macbeth: A Sourcebook* (N.Y., 1983).—**NS/LK/DM**

Porter, Art, jazz alto saxophonist; b. Little Rock, Ark., Aug. 3, 1962; d. Bangkok, Thailand, Nov. 23, 1996. Inspired by his musician father and by John Coltrane's music, he started playing alto saxophone at 15. He joined his father's band at local venues where he befriended Bill Clinton. While Governor of Ark., Clinton was responsible for passing legislation on behalf of artists who were too young to play in jazz venues. The legislation, known as the "Art Porter Bill," allowed underage artists to perform in bars and clubs as long as a legal guardian was present. Porter was admitted to Berklee at age 16; in January 1978, he won an IAJE young talent award. He went on to work with Jack McDuff and Pharoah Sanders and relocated to Chicago. In 1996, he was in Bangkok for the Thailand Interna-

tional Jazz Festival; his boat capsized during an outing in the Kratha Taek Reservoir in western Thailand, drowning him and at least two other passengers.

DISC.: *Pocket City* (1992); *Straight to the Point* (1993); *Undercover* (1994); *Lay Your Hands on Me* (1996).—**LP**

Porter, Cole (Albert), remarkable American composer; b. Peru, Ind., June 9, 1891; d. Santa Monica, Calif., Oct. 15, 1964. He was educated at Yale Univ. (B.A., 1913), then took academic courses at Harvard Law School, and later at the Harvard School of Music (1915–16); also received instruction in counterpoint, composition, orchestration, and harmony from d'Indy at the Paris Schola Cantorum (1919). While at Yale, he wrote football songs (*Yale Bull Dog Song, Bingo Eli Yale,* etc.) and also composed music for college functions. He first gained success as a composer for the stage with his *Wake Up and Dream* (London, March 27, 1929); his first production in N.Y. was *See America First* (March 28, 1916). There followed a cascade of musical comedies for which he wrote both the lyrics and the music, which placed him in the front rank of the American musical theater. His greatest success came with his musical comedy *Kiss Me, Kate,* after Shakespeare's *The Taming of the Shrew* (N.Y., Dec. 30, 1948). A motion picture musical biography of Porter, starring Cary Grant, was produced by Warner Bros. in 1946 as *Night and Day.* Porter was a master of subtle expression without sentimentality, a kinetic dash without vulgarity, and a natural blend of word poetry with the finest of harmonious melodies. See *The Cole Porter Song Book* (N.Y., 1959) and R. Kimball, ed., *The Complete Lyrics of Cole Porter* (N.Y., 1984).

WORKS: DRAMATIC: Musicals (all 1st perf. in N.Y. unless otherwise given): *Hands Up* (July 22, 1915); *Kitchy-koo of 1919* (revue; Oct. 6, 1919); *Fifty Million Frenchmen* (Nov. 27, 1929); *Gay Divorce* (Nov. 29, 1932); *Anything Goes* (Nov. 21, 1934); *Jubilee* (Oct. 12, 1935); *Red Hot and Blue* (Oct. 29, 1936); *Leave It to Me* (Nov. 9, 1938); *Du Barry Was a Lady* (Dec. 6, 1939); *Panama Hattie* (Oct. 30, 1940); *Let's Face It* (Oct. 29, 1941); *Something for the Boys* (Jan. 7, 1943); *Mexican Hayride* (Jan. 28, 1944); *Kiss Me, Kate* (Dec. 30, 1948); *Out of This World* (Dec. 21, 1950); *Can-can* (May 7, 1953); *Silk Stockings* (Feb. 24, 1955); etc. **Film:** Numerous, including *Rosalie* (1937), *You'll Never Get Rich* (1941), *Les Girls* (1957), and *Aladdin* (1958). **Songs:** Of his many songs, at least half a dozen became great favorites: *Begin the Beguine; It's De-Lovely; Night and Day; My Heart Belongs to Daddy; Don't Fence Me In; Wunderbar.*

BIBL.: D. Ewen, *The C. P. Story* (N.Y., 1965); C. Porter and R. Hubler, *The C. P. Story* (Cleveland, 1965); G. Eells, *The Life That Late He Led* (N.Y., 1967); R. Kimball and B. Gill, *C.* (N.Y., 1971); L. Siebert, *C. P.: An Analysis of 5 Musical Comedies and a Thematic Index of the Complete Works* (diss., City Univ. of N.Y., 1975); C. Schwartz, *C. P.* (N.Y., 1977); J. Morella and G. Mazzei, *Genius and Lust: The Creativity and Sexuality of C. P. and Noel Coward* (N.Y., 1995); W. McBrien, *C. P.: A Biography* (N.Y., 1998).—**NS/LK/DM**

Porter, Hugh, American organist and pedagogue; b. Heron Lake, Minn., Sept. 18, 1897; d. N.Y., Sept. 22, 1960. He studied at the American Cons. in Chicago (B.M., 1920), Northwestern Univ. (B.A., 1924), with Middelschulte, Farnam, Noble, and Boulanger, and at the Union Theological Seminary in N.Y. (M.S.M., 1930;

D.S.M., 1944). He taught at Northwestern Univ., the Juilliard School of Music in N.Y., N.Y.U., and the Mannes Coll. of Music in N.Y. In 1931 he joined the faculty of the Union Theological Seminary, where he was director (from 1945) and a prof. (from 1947). Porter also held many positions as a church organist, toured as a recitalist, and was organist at the Chatauqua Institution. With his wife Ethel Porter, he ed. the United Church of Christ *Pilgrim Hymnal* (1958).—NS/LK/DM

Porter, Samuel, English organist and composer; b. Norwich, 1733; d. Canterbury, Dec. 11, 1810. He was a pupil of Maurice Greene. From 1757 to 1803 he was organist at Canterbury Cathedral. After his death, his son W.J. Porter publ. his *Cathedral Music.*—LK/DM

Porter, Walter, English tenor, lutenist, and composer; b. c. 1587; d. London (buried), Nov. 30, 1659. He was a chorister at Westminster Abbey, and then may have been a pupil of Monteverdi in Italy. In 1617 he was made a tenor in the Gentlemen of the Chapel Royal. In 1639 he became Master of the Choristers at Westminster Abbey. With the outbreak of Civil War, he was compelled to seek other employment, and from 1644 to 1656 he was in the service of Sir Edward Spencer. He publ. *Madrigales and Ayres* (London, 1632) and *Mottets of Two Voyces* (London, 1657). His madrigals are some of the earliest examples of English madrigals in concertato style à la Monteverdi.—LK/DM

Porter, (William) Quincy, significant American composer and teacher; b. New Haven, Conn., Feb. 7, 1897; d. Bethany, Conn., Nov. 12, 1966. He was brought up in an intellectual atmosphere; his father and his grandfather were profs. at Yale Univ. He studied with David Stanley Smith and Horatio Parker at the Yale Univ. School of Music (B.A., 1919; B.Mus., 1921); submitted a violin concerto for the American Prix de Rome and received an honorable mention; also won the Steinert and Osborne prizes. After graduation he went to Paris, where he took courses with Capet (violin) and d'Indy (composition). Returning to America in 1922, he earned a living as a violinist in theater orchs. in N.Y. while taking a course in composition with Bloch. He taught at the Cleveland Inst. of Music (1922–28; 1931–32); played the viola in the Ribaupierre String Quartet there; also spent 3 years in Paris on a Guggenheim fellowship (1928–31). He was a prof. at Vassar Coll. and conductor of the Vassar Orch. (1932–38); in 1938 he succeeded Converse as dean of the New England Cons. of Music in Boston; from 1942 to 1946, was its director; from 1946 to 1965, was a prof. at Yale Univ. In 1954 he won the Pulitzer Prize in Music for his Concerto for 2 Pianos and Orch., later renamed the *Concerto Concertante.* His music is built on strong contrapuntal lines, with incisive rhythms; his harmonic procedures often reach stridently polytonal sonorities, while the general idiom of his works combines elements of both the modern German and the modern French styles of composition.

WORKS: ORCH.: *Ukrainian Suite* for Strings (Rochester, N.Y., May 1, 1925); Suite in C minor (1926); *Poem and Dance* (Cleveland, June 24, 1932, composer conducting); 2 syms.: No. 1 (1934; N.Y., April 2, 1938, composer conducting) and No. 2 (1961–62; Louisville, Jan. 14, 1964); *Dance in Three-Time* for Chamber Orch. (St. Louis, July 2, 1937); *Music for Strings* (1941); *Fantasy on a Pastoral Theme* for Organ and Strings (1942); *The Moving Tide* (1944); Viola Concerto (N.Y., May 16, 1948); *Fantasy* for Cello and Small Orch. (1950); Concerto for 2 Pianos and Orch., renamed *Concerto Concertante* (1952–53; Louisville, March 17, 1954); *New England Episodes*, symphonic suite (Washington, D.C., April 18, 1958); Concerto for Wind Orch. (1959); Harpsichord Concerto (1959; New Haven, Jan. 19, 1960); Concerto for Wind Orch. (1960); *Ohio*, overture (1963). CHAMBER: 10 string quartets (1923, 1925, 1930, 1931, 1935, 1937, 1943, 1950, 1958, 1965); 2 violin sonatas (1926, 1929); *In Monasterio* for String Quartet (1927); Piano Quintet (1927); *Little Trio* for Flute, Violin, and Viola (1928); Clarinet Quintet (1929); Suite for Viola (1930); *Quintet on a Childhood Theme* for Flute and Strings (1937); Horn Sonata (1946); *String Sextet on Slavic Folk Tunes* (1947); 4 pieces for Violin and Piano (1947); Duo for Violin and Viola (1954); Duo for Flute and Harp (1957); *Divertimento* for Wind Quintet (1960); Oboe Quintet (1966). P i a n o : Sonata (1930); *8 Pieces for Bill* (1941–42; nos. 2 and 8 not extant); *6 Miniatures* (1943); *Day Dreams* (1957; based on *8 Pieces for Bill*). VOCAL: *The Desolate City* for Baritone and Orch. (1950); choruses.—NS/LK/DM

Portugal (Portogallo; real name, Ascenção or Assumpção), Marcos Antônio (da Fonseca), prominent Portuguese composer; b. Lisbon, March 24, 1762; d. Rio de Janeiro, Feb. 7, 1830. A pupil at the ecclesiastical seminary at Lisbon, he continued his musical education with composition lessons from João de Souza Carvalho. Between 1784 and 1791 he wrote for Lisbon 17 stage works, mostly ephemeral. His reputation was made in Italy, where, with the exception of a short visit to Lisbon, he lived from 1792 to 1800, bringing out some 21 operas for various Italian theaters. Upon his return to Lisbon (1800), he was made mestre de capela of the royal chapel and director of the Teatro San Carlos. His *Il Filosofo seducente, ossia Non irritar le donne* (Venice, Dec. 27, 1798) was selected by Napoleon for opening the Théâtre-Italien at Paris in 1801. In 1807 the royal family fled to Brazil before the French invasion; Portugal remained until the Teatro San Carlos was closed in 1810, and then followed the court to Rio de Janeiro, where he served as mestre de capela of the royal chapel and master of music to the future John VI. The royal theater of São João, after its inauguration in 1813, produced several new operas by him. In that year he became director of the new Cons. at Vera Cruz, jointly with his brother Simão; he visited Italy in 1815, returned to Rio de Janeiro, and passed his last years there as an invalid. His masterpiece is *Fernando nel Messico* (Venice, Jan. 16, 1798; written for the famous English singer Elizabeth Billington; produced in London, in Italian, March 31, 1803); other Italian operas that had a favorable reception were *Demofoonte* (Milan, Feb. 8, 1794) and *Le Donne cambiate* (Venice, Oct. 22, 1797); of Portuguese operas, *A Castanheira* (The Chestnut Seller), produced in Lisbon in 1787, enjoyed considerable popular success. He further wrote about 100 sacred works.

BIBL.: M. Carvalhães, *M. P. na sua musica dramatica* (Lisbon, 1910).—NS/LK/DM

Porumbescu, Ciprian, Rumanian choirmaster, teacher, and composer; b. Şipote, Oct. 14, 1853; d. Stupca, Bukovina, June 6, 1883. After preliminary studies in Rumania, he went to Vienna, where he became a student of F. Krenn and Bruckner at the Cons. He publ. a collection of "social songs of Rumanian students" (Vienna, 1880) and composed an operetta, *Crai nou* (The New Moon; 1882), to a Rumanian libretto, and many songs. His death at the age of 29 deprived Rumania of the country's first national composer, but he is greatly revered as such. The town of Stupca, where he died, has been renamed Ciprian Porumbescu, and his name is attached to the official designation of several Rumanian conservatories. V. Cosma ed. the complete works (2 vols., Bucharest, 1954, 1958).

BIBL.: V. Cosma, *C. P.* (Bucharest, 1957).—NS/LK/DM

Posch, Isaac, Austrian organist, organ builder, and composer; b. place and date unknown; d. probably in Klagenfurt, c. 1622. He was active as an organist in Carinthia (from 1614) and in Carniola (from 1617). He built the organ in Oberburg for the bishops of Laibach and the organ for the Franciscan Church in Laibach in 1621. Posch publ. 2 vols. of variation suites (Regensburg, 1618, and Nuremberg, 1621), significant works in the early Baroque development of the genre. His 42 sacred concertos for 1 to 4 Voices and Basso Continuo (Nuremberg, 1623) are particularly noteworthy.
—LK/DM

Poser, Hans, German composer and teacher; b. Tannenbergsthal, Oct. 8, 1917; d. Hamburg, Oct. 1, 1970. He was a pupil of Hindemith and Grabner, and later in Hamburg of Klussmann. From 1947 he taught in Hamburg, and was made a prof. at the Hochschule für Musik there in 1962. He wrote the television chamber opera *Die Auszeichnung* (1959), instrumental works, the cantata *Till Eulenspiegel* for Soloists, Chorus, and Orch. (1956) and much other choral music, songs, and pedagogical pieces.

BIBL.: H. Wagner, ed., *H. P.: 1917–1970* (1972).—LK/DM

Pospíšil, Juraj, Slovak composer and teacher; b. Olomouc, Jan. 14, 1931. He received training in piano, organ, and theory at the Olomouc School of Music (1949–50). After studying composition with Petrželka at the Janáček Academy of Music and Drama in Brno (1950–52), he completed his studies in composition with Moyzes and Cikker at the Bratislava Academy of Music and Drama (1952–55). From 1955 to 1991 he lectured on theory and composition at the Bratislava Cons. In 1988 he received an award from the Union of Slovak Composers. Pospíšil developed a compositional style which owed much to the Second Viennese School while paying homage to Slovak tradition.

WORKS: DRAMATIC: *Inter arma,* cycle of 3 operas (1969–70); *Manon Lescaut,* scenic drama (1993). **ORCH.:** *The Mountains and the People,* symphonic poem (1954; Bratislava, Dec. 20, 1955); 6 syms.: No. 1 (1958; Bratislava, June 4, 1961), No. 2, *Nebula in Andromeda* (1963; Bratislava, June 3, 1964), No. 3 for Chamber Ensemble and Kettledrums (1967; Bratislava, Feb. 27, 1968), No. 4, *Warsaw,* for Narrator, Soprano, Chorus,

and Orch. (1978), No. 5 (1986; Bratislava, Feb. 27, 1988), and No. 6 (1996); *Reflections* (1958); *Song About a Man,* symphonic variations (1961); Trombone Concerto (1962; Bratislava, Jan. 20, 1964); Violin Concerto (1968); Clarinet Concerto (1972; also for Clarinet and Organ, 1977); 3 symphonic frescoes: No. 1 (1972; Kosice, Oct. 6, 1976), No. 2 (1976; Bratislava, Feb. 24, 1985), and No. 3 (1981; Bratislava, Feb. 10, 1985); *Concerto eroico* for Horn and Orch. (1973); *Through the Land of Childhood* (1983); Concerto for Soprano and Orch. (1984; Bratislava, Feb. 14, 1986); *Dramatic Overture* (1984); Dulcimer Concerto (1989); Sonata for Alto Trombone and Strings (1991); Tuba Concerto (1994; also for Tuba and Brass Band, 1996). **CHAMBER:** *In Reveries* for Strings (1953); Sonata for Strings (1961; Berlin, Dec. 14, 1963); *3 Inventions* for Wind Trio (1961); *Music* for Brass (1962); *Glosses* for Wind Quintet (1964); Double Bass Sonata (1964); *Contradictions* for Clarinet and String Quartet (1964); *Music* for 12 Strings (1965; Bratislava, Feb. 27, 1968); 2 sonatas for Solo Violin (1965, 1976); 4 string quartets (1970, 1979, 1985, 1990); Flute Quartet (1971); Chamber Sinfonietta for Strings and Brass (1974); 2 trios for Violin, Cello, and Piano (1977, 1987); Sonata for English Horn and String Quartet (1983); Trio for Violin, Cello, and Accordion (1985); *Melancholic Suite* for Oboe, English Horn, and Bassoon (1986); Trio for Flute, Guitar, and Cello (1986); Wind Sextet (1988); *Grand duo (quasi una sonata)* for Bass Clarinet and Piano (1989); Trio for Trombones (1990); 2 brass quintets (1991, 1996); piano pieces; organ music. **VOCAL:** *Margita and Besná* for Soloists, Chorus, and Orch. (1955); *To Bratislava* for Baritone and Orch. or Piano (1973); *Dazzlement* for Narrator and Chamber Ensemble (1973); *November Triptych* for Chamber Chorus, Wind Quintet, and Piano (1977); *The Lord's Prayer of the Hussites,* sacred cantata for Mezzo-soprano, Bass, Chorus, and Orch. (1990); *Autumn Bottling* for Bass and String Quartet (1994).
—NS/LK/DM

Poss, Georg, German trumpeter, cornet player, and composer; b. Franconia, c. 1570; d. Rothwaltersdorf, after 1633. He served as a trumpeter to Archduke Maximilian in Franconia from 1594. After his patron sent him to Venice for further training, he was in the service of Archduke Ferdinand in Graz (1597–1618). From 1618 to 1622 he was Kapellmeister to Archduke Karl, Bishop of Bixen and Breslau, at his court in Neisse, Silesia. Through his music, Poss helped to introduce the Venetian style of composition to Austria.

WORKS: *Liber primus missarum* for 6 to 8 Voices (Graz, 1607); *Orpheus mixtus, liber primus* for 8 to 16 Voices (Graz, 1607); 2 motets for 2 and 4 Voices and Basso Continuo (1615); other sacred vocal pieces.

BIBL.: H. Busch, *G. P., Leben und Werk: Ein Beitrag zur Geschichte der deutsch-venezianischen Schule in Österreich am Beginn des 17. Jahrhunderts* (Munich, 1972).—LK/DM

Posse, Wilhelm, German harpist, pedagogue, and composer; b. Bromberg, Oct. 15, 1852; d. Berlin, June 20, 1925. His father, a musician, gave him his first music lessons. He taught himself to play the harp, however, and was only 8 when he was engaged as accompanist to Adelina Patti at the Italian Opera in Berlin. Following a concert tour of Russia with his father (1863–64), he returned to Berlin and completed his training with L. Grimm at the Kullak Academy (1864–72). From 1872 to 1903 he was 1st harpist of the Berlin Phil. and the Royal Opera Orch. He also was a teacher (1890–1910) and a prof. (1910–23) at the Berlin Hochschule für Musik. In addition to his important pedagogical works, he also composed solo harp pieces and prepared various transcriptions for his instrument, including piano pieces of Liszt.—**LK/DM**

Possenti, Pellegrino, Italian composer who flourished in the first half of the 17th century. He was active in Venice during a part of his life, where he brought out 2 vols. of secular vocal music (1623, 1625) and a vol. of 18 one-movement sonatas (1628).—**LK/DM**

Postnikova, Viktoria (Valentinovna), Russian pianist; b. Moscow, Jan. 12, 1944. She studied at the Moscow Central Music School and later at the Moscow Cons., graduating in 1967. In 1966 she received 2nd prize at the Leeds Competition. She then embarked upon a major career, appearing widely as a soloist with leading orchs. and as a recitalist. She married **Gennadi Rozhdestvensky** in 1969.—**NS/LK/DM**

Poštolka, Milan, Czech musicologist; b. Prague, Sept. 29, 1932; d. there, Dec. 14, 1993. He studied with Očadlik and Sychra at the Univ. of Prague (1951–56), passing the state examination in musicology (1956), taking the C.Sc. (1966), and obtaining his Ph.D (1967; with the diss. *Leopold Koželuh: Život a dílo* [Leopold Kozeluh: Life and Works]; publ. in Prague, 1964). He worked in the music division of Prague's National Museum (from 1958), and also taught at the Univ. of Prague (1966–79); was director of a research team studying 17th- and 18th-century Czech music at the Czech Academy of Sciences (1972–86). He publ. books on Czech music of the 18th century (Prague, 1961) and on the young Haydn (Prague, 1988).—**NS/LK/DM**

Poston, Elizabeth, English pianist and composer; b. Highfield, Hertfordshire, Oct. 24, 1905; d. there, March 18, 1987. She studied piano with Harold Samuel; also took courses at the Royal Academy of Music in London. During World War II, she was in charge of music in the European Service of the BBC in London. Her works follow along neo-Classical lines.

WORKS: *The Holy Child* for Soloists, Chorus, and Strings (1950); *Concertino da Camera on a Theme of Martin Peerson* for Ancient Instruments (1950); *The Nativity* for Soloists, Chorus, and Strings or Organ (1951); Trio for Flute, Clarinet or Viola, and Piano (1958); *Peter Halfpenny's Tunes* for Recorder and Piano (1959); *Lullaby and Fiesta*, 2 pieces for Piano (1960); *Magnificat* for 4 Voices and Organ (1961); *3 Scottish Carols* for Chorus and Strings or Organ (1969); *Harlow Concertante* for String Quartet and String Orch. (1969); *An English Day Book* for Mixed Voices and Harp (1971); Sonatina for Cello and Piano (1972); hymn tunes; Christmas carols; music for films and radio.
—**NS/LK/DM**

Pothier, Dom Joseph, learned French music scholar; b. Bouzemont, near Saint-Dié, Dec. 7, 1835; d. Conques, Belgium, Dec. 8, 1923. He was ordained a priest (1858). He became a Benedictine monk in 1860 at Solesmes, in 1862, sub-prior, in 1866, prof. of theology at the Solesmes Monastery, in 1893, prior at the Benedictine monastery of Liguge, and in 1898, abbot at St.-Wandrille. When the religious orders were banned from France, he moved to Belgium. In 1904 he was appointed by Pope Pius X president of the publ. committee of the *Editio Vaticana.*

WRITINGS: EDITIONS: *Les mélodies grégoriennes d'après la tradition* (Tournai, 1880; 2nd ed., 1890); *Liber gradualis* (Tournai, 1883; 2nd ed., 1895); *Processionale monasticum* (Solesmes, 1888); *Varie preces* (Solesmes, 1888); *Liber antiphonarius* (Solesmes, 1891); *Liber responsorialis* (Solesmes, 1895); *Cantus mariales* (Paris, 1903; 3rd ed., 1924).

BIBL.: F. Velluz, *Étude bibiographique sur les mélodies grégoriennes de Dom J. P.* (Grenoble, 1881); L. David, *Dom J. P., abbé de Saint-Wandrille, et la restauration grégorienne* (St.-Wandrille, 1943).—**NS/LK/DM**

Potiron, Henri, French musicologist and composer; b. Rezé-lès-Nantes, Sept. 13, 1882; d. Roye, April 12, 1972. He settled in Paris and became a teacher at the Institut Grégorien in 1923, and also served as music director at Sacré-Coeur de Montmarte. In 1954 he took his Ph.D. at the Sorbonne with the diss. *Boèce, théoricien de la musique grecque* (publ. in Paris, 1954). Among his compositions were masses, motets, and organ pieces.

WRITINGS (all publ. in Tournai unless otherwise given): *Cours d'accompagnement du chant grégorien* (Paris, 1925; 2nd ed., rev., 1927; Eng. tr., 1933); *Leçons pratiques d'accompagnement du chant grégorien* (1938; Eng. tr., 1949); *L'origines des modes grégoriens* (1948); *L'analyse modale du chant grégorien* (1948); *Les modes grecs antiques* (1950); *La notation grecque et Boèce: Petite histoire de la notation antique* (1951); *Petit traité de contrepoint* (1951); *La composition des modes grégoriens* (1953); *L'accompagnement du chant grégorien suivant les types modaux* (Paris, 1960). —**LK/DM**

Pott, August Friedrich, German violinist and composer; b. Nordheim, Nov. 7, 1806; d. Graz, Aug. 27, 1883. He received training in violin from K. Keisewetter in Hannover, where he became a member of the court orch. Following further studies with Spohr (violin) and Hauptmann (composition) in Kassel, he was made Kammermusicus in Hannover in 1827. From 1829 he made tours as a virtuoso. During a visit to Denmark, he dedicated his concerto *Les adieux de Copenhague* to King Frederick VI, who, in turn, appointed Pott prof. of music at the Univ. of Copenhagen in 1831. From 1832 to 1848 and again from 1850 to 1861 he served as Hofkapellmeister in Oldenburg. He also continued to make tours, and played in Dresden, Berlin, and Vienna in 1834 and in London in 1838. He gave a series of benefit concerts to raise funds for a Mozart memorial in Salzburg, which was dedicated in 1842.—**LK/DM**

Potter, A(rchibald) J(ames), Irish composer and teacher; b. Belfast, Sept. 22, 1918; d. Greystones, July 5, 1980. He received training under W. Vale at the choir school of All Saints, Margaret Street, in London (1929–33), D.G.A. Fox at Clifton Coll. in Bristol (1933–36), and Vaughan Williams at the Royal Coll. of Music in London (1936–38); later he took his D.Mus. at the Univ. of Dublin (1953). From 1955 to 1973 he was a prof. of composition at the Royal Irish Academy of Music in Dublin. His output followed in the path of tradition and opted for Romantic qualities.

WORKS: DRAMATIC: O p e r a : *Patrick*, television opera (1962; RTE, March 17, 1965); *The Wedding* (1979; Dublin, June 8, 1981). **B a l l e t :** *Careless Love* (1959; Dublin, April 12, 1960); *Caitlín Bhocht* (1963; Radio Ireland, June 27, 1964). **ORCH.:** *Overture to a Kitchen Comedy* (1950); *Rhapsody Under a High Sky* (1950); *Concerto da chiesa* for Piano and Orch. (1952); *Variations on a Popular Tune* (1955); *Phantasmoraggio* (1956); *Elegy* for Clarinet, Harp, and Strings (1956); *Caonie* (Dirge; 1956); *Finnegans Wake* (1957; also for Concert Band); *Fantasia Gaelach* (1957); *Fantasie Concertante* for Violin, Cello, and Orch. (1959); *Irish Rhapsody* (1963); *Caprice* for Cello and Orch. (1964); *Hunter's Holiday* for Horn and Orch. (1964); *Sound the Sackbuts* for 3 Trombones and Orch. (1965); *Fantasie* for Clarinet and Orch. (1965); *Spanish Point* for Guitar and Orch. (1965); *Rapsóid Deireadh lae* (Rhapsody for the End of the Day) for Violin and Orch. (1966); *Concerto for Orchestra* (Dublin, March 13, 1967); *Concertino Bennio* for Trumpet and Orch. (1967); *Dance Fantasy* (1967); *Binneadán Bél* for Horn and Orch. (1967); 2 syms.: No. 1, *Sinfonia de Profundis* (1968; Dublin, March 23, 1969) and No. 2 (1976; Springfield, Mass., Dec. 11, 1981); *Madra Líath na Mara* (Grey Dog of the Sea) for English Horn and Chamber Orch. (1977); *Salala's Castle* for Winds and Percussion (1980). **CHAMBER:** String Quartet (1938); *A House Full of Harpers* for Irish Harp Ensemble and Concert Harp (1963); *Arklow Quartet* for Brass or Winds (1976–77). **VOCAL:** *Hail Mary* for Mezzosoprano, Tenor, Chorus, and Orch. (1966); *The Cornet of Horse* for Baritone, Men's Chorus, and Orch. (1975); choruses; songs.
—**NS/LK/DM**

Potter, Chris, jazz tenor and soprano saxophonist; b. Chicago, Ill., Jan. 1, 1971. He was raised in Columbia, S.C. He began playing alto saxophone and won a young talent award from the IAJE when he was 11; he performed at their Kansas City conference with other winners that year including Charnett Moffett and Harry Connick Jr. By 19, he was based in N.Y. and attracting attention for his fine work touring and recording with Red Rodney. His steadily growing reputation as a virtuosic and impassioned contemporary player has led to an increasing demand for his appearances as a sideman as well as some work as a leader.

DISC.: *Presenting Chris Potter* (1992); *Concentric Circles* (1993); *Pure* (1994); *Moving In* (1996); *Unspoken* (1997).—**LP**

Potter, (Philip) Cipriani (Hambley), distinguished English pianist, teacher, and composer; b. London, Oct. 2, 1792; d. there, Sept. 26, 1871. He began his musical training with his father, Richard Huddleston Potter (b. London, Dec. 10, 1755; d. there [buried], June 3, 1821), a founder of the Phil. Soc. of London (1813) and a violist in its orch., then studied with Thomas Attwood, Joseph Woelffl (1805–10), and Crotch (1808–9). He was made a member of the Phil. Soc. (1815), with which he made his debut as a pianist in his own Sextet for Piano, Flute, and Strings (April 29, 1816). In 1817 he went to Vienna, where he met Beethoven; at the latter's suggestion he studied counterpoint with Aloys Forster; he returned to England in 1819. He made many appearances as a pianist in London, introducing a number of Mozart's concerti and Beethoven's 1st, 3rd, and 4th

concerti. He also conducted the Phil. Soc. orch., and later was music director of the Madrigal Soc. (from 1854). In 1822 he became the first piano teacher of the men's division of the newly opened Academy of Music; was later its principal (1832–59). Potter produced several fine syms. and concertos; Wagner conducted one of his syms. at a Phil. Soc. concert in London (1855). He also wrote a set of satirical *Enigma Variations* for Piano (c. 1825), comprising "variations in the style of five eminent artists."

WORKS: ORCH.: 9 syms.: No. 1, in G minor (1819; rev. 1826), B-flat major (1821; rev. 1839), No. 6, in C minor (1826), No. 7, in F major (1826), No. 8, in E-flat major (1828; rev. 1846), No. 10, in G minor (1832), "No. 2," in D major (1833), C minor (1834), and "No. 4," in D major (1834); at least 1 other not extant; at least 3 piano concertos: "No. 2," in D minor (1832). E-flat major (1833), and E major (1835); 4 overtures: E minor (1815; rev. 1848), *Antony and Cleopatra* (1835), *Cymbeline* (1836), and *The Tempest* (1837); *Introduction and Rondo* for Piano and Orch., "alla militaire" (1827); *Duo concertant* for Piano, Violin, and Orch. (1827?); *Bravura Variations* for Piano and Orch., on a theme by Rossini (1829); *Concertante* on "Les Folies d'Espagne" for Violin, Cello, Double Bass, Piano, and Orch. (1829); *Ricercata* "on a favorite French theme" for Piano and Orch. (1830); March (1854). **CHAMBER:** 3 Grand Trios for Piano Trio (c. 1824); *Sonata di bravura* for Horn, or Bassoon, or Cello and Piano (c. 1824); Sextet for Flute and String Quartet (c. 1827); Sextet for Flute, Clarinet, Viola, Cello, Double Bass, and Piano (1836); String Quartet (n.d.); many piano works, including 3 sonatas (all 1818). **VOCAL:** *Medora e Corrado*, cantata for Solo Voices, Chorus, and Orch. (1830).

BIBL.: P. Peter, *The Life and Work of C. P. (1792–1871)* (diss., Northwestern Univ., 1972).—**NS/LK/DM**

Pougin (Paroisse-Pougin), (François-Auguste-) Arthur, French writer on music; b. Châteauroux, Indre, Aug. 6, 1834; d. Paris, Aug. 8, 1921. He studied with Alard (violin) and Reber (harmony) at the Paris Cons. and began playing violin in theater orchs. when he was 13. He became conductor of the Théâtre Beaumarchais (1855), then was asst. conductor and répétiteur of the Folies-Nouvelles (1856–59) and a member of the Opéra-Comique orch. (1860–63). He then devoted himself to writing on music, contributing articles and reviews to leading music periodicals. He was musical feuilletonist for the *Journal Officiel* (from 1878) and chief ed. of *Le Ménestrel* (from 1885), and also wrote the articles on music for Larousse's *Grand dictionnaire universel du XIXᵉ siècle* (1866–76). He edited the supplement to Fétis's *Biographie universelle* (1878–80) and revised Clément and Larousse's *Dictionnaire lyrique, ou Histoire des opéras* (1898; suppl. to 1904).

WRITINGS (all publ. in Paris unless otherwise given): *Andre Campra* (1861; 2ⁿᵈ ed., 1881); *Gresnick* (1862); *Dezèdes* (1862); *Floquet* (1863); *Martini* (1864); *Devienne* (1864); the preceding 6 were orig. publ. in *Revue et Gazette Musicale*, XXVIII (1861), XXIX (1862), XXIX (1862), XXX (1863), XXXI (1864), and XXXI (1864), respectively, and then publ. as *Musiciens français du XVIIIᵉ siècle* (1864); *Meyerbeer: Notes biographiques* (1864); *F. Halévy, écrivain* (1865); *Almanach de la musique* (1866–68); *William-Vincent Wallace: Étude biographique et critique* (1866); *De la littérature musicale en France* (1867); *De la situation des compositeurs de musique et de l'avenir de l'art musicale en France* (1867);

Bellini: Sa vie, ses oeuvres (1868); *Léon Kreutzer* (1868); *Albert Grisar: Étude artistique* (1870); *Rossini: Notes, impressions, souvenirs, commentaires* (1871); *À propos de l'exécution du "Messie" de Haendel* (1873); *Auber: Ses commencements, les origines de sa carrière* (1873); *Boieldieu: Sa vie, ses oeuvres, son caractère, sa correspondance* (1875); *Figures d'opéra-comique: Madame Dugazon, Elleviou, les Gavaudan* (1875); *Adolphe Adam: Sa vie, sa carrière, ses mémoires artistiques* (1876); *Rameau: Essai sur sa vie et ses oeuvres* (1876); *Les Vrais Créateurs de l'opéra français: Perrin et Cambert* (1881); *Verdi: Vita aneddotica* (Milan, 1881; annotated by Folchetto [pen name of J. Caponi]; rev. version in French, 1886); *Molière et l'opéra-comique* (1882); *Viotti et l'école moderne de violon* (1888); *Méhul: Sa vie, son genie, son caractère* (1889; 2nd ed., 1893); *L'Opéra-Comique pendant la Révolution* (1891); *Acteurs et actrices d'autrefois: Histoire anecdotique des théâtres de Paris depuis trois cents ans* (1896); *Essai historique sur la musique en Russie* (1897; 2nd ed., 1904; Eng. tr., 1915); *La Jeunesse de Mme. Desbordes-Valmore* (1898); *Jean-Jacques Rousseau musicien* (1901); *La Comédie-Française et la Révolution* (1902); *Un Ténor de l'Opéra au XVIIIe siècle: Pierre Jélyotte* (1905); *Hérold: Biographie critique* (1906); *Monsigny et son temps: l'Opéra-Comique et la Comédie- Italienne* (1908); *Marie Malibran: Histoire d'une cantatrice* (1911; Eng. tr., 1911); *Madame Favart: Étude théâtrale, 1727–1772* (1912); *Marietta Alboni* (1912); *Massenet* (1914); *Un Directeur de l'Opéra au XVIIIe siècle (A.P.J. de Visme): L'Opéra sous l'ancien régime: L'Opéra sous la Révolution* (1914); *Une Cantatrice "amie" de Napoléon: Giuseppina Grassini 1773–1850* (1920); *Le Violon: Les Violonistes et la musique de violon du XVIe au XVIIIe siècle* (1924).—**NS/LK/DM**

Pouishnov, Lev,

Russian-born English pianist; b. Odessa, Oct. 11, 1891; d. London, May 28, 1959. He made his public debut at age 5. After studies in Kiev, he received instruction in piano from Essipova and in composition from Liadov, Rimsky-Korsakov, and Glazunov at the St. Petersburg Cons. (graduated with the Gold Medal and the Rubinstein Prize, 1910); then toured while also being active as a teacher in Tiflis (1913–17). He left Russia as a result of the Bolshevik Revolution, and pursued a career in the West; toured widely in Europe and also made appearances in the U.S. (from 1923); made his home in England, becoming a naturalized subject in 1935. He became best known for his performances of works from the Romantic repertoire. —**NS/LK/DM**

Poulenc, Francis (Jean Marcel),

brilliant French composer; b. Paris, Jan. 7, 1899; d. there, Jan. 30, 1963. He was born into a wealthy family of pharmaceutical manufacturers; his mother taught him music in his childhood; at 16, he began taking formal piano lessons with Ricardo Viñes. A decisive turn in his development as a composer occurred when he attracted the attention of Erik Satie, the arbiter elegantiarum of the arts and social amenities in Paris. Deeply impressed by Satie's fruitful eccentricities in the then-shocking manner of Dadaism, Poulenc joined an ostentatiously self-descriptive musical group called the Nouveaux Jeunes. In a gratuitous parallel with the Russian Five, the French critic Henri Collet dubbed the "New Youths" Le Groupe de Six, and the label stuck under the designation Les Six. The 6 musicians included, besides Poulenc: Auric, Durey, Honegger, Milhaud, and Tailleferre. Although quite different in their styles of composition and artistic inclinations, they continued collective participation in various musical events. Poulenc served in the French army (1918–21), and then began taking lessons in composition with Koechlin (1921–24). An excellent pianist, Poulenc became in 1935 an accompanist to the French baritone Pierre Bernac, for whom he wrote numerous songs. Compared with his fortuitous comrades-in-six, Poulenc appears a classicist. He never experimented with the popular devices of "machine music," asymmetrical rhythms, and polyharmonies as cultivated by Honegger and Milhaud. Futuristic projections had little interest for him; he was content to follow the gentle neo-Classical formation of Ravel's piano music and songs. Among his other important artistic contacts was the ballet impresario Diaghilev, who commissioned him to write music for his Ballets Russes. Apart from his fine songs and piano pieces, Poulenc revealed himself as an inspired composer of religious music, of which his choral works *Stabat Mater* and *Gloria* are notable. He also wrote remarkable music for the organ, including a concerto that became a minor masterpiece. A master of artificial simplicity, he pleases even sophisticated listeners by his bland triadic tonalities, spiced with quickly passing diaphonous discords.

WORKS: DRAMATIC: Opera: *Les Mamelles de Tirésias,* opéra-bouffe (1944; Paris, June 3, 1947); *Dialogues des Carmélites,* religious opera (1953–56; Milan, Jan. 26, 1957); *La Voix humaine,* monodrama for Soprano (1958; Paris, Feb. 6, 1959). **Ballet:** *La Baigneuse de Trouville and Discours de Général,* 2 movements for *Les Mariés de la Tour Eiffel,* ballet-farce (Paris, June 18, 1921; other movements by members of Les Six, except for Durey); *Les Biches,* with Chorus (1923; Monte Carlo, Jan. 6, 1924); *Pastourelle,* 9th movement of an 11-movement collective ballet, *L'Eventail de Jeanne* (1927; 1st perf. of orch. version, Paris, March 4, 1929; movements by Roussel, Ravel, Ibert, Milhaud et al.); *Aubade,* choreographic concerto for Piano and 18 Instruments (private perf., Paris, June 18, 1929; public perf., London, Dec. 19, 1929); *Les Animaux modèles* (1940–41; Paris, Aug. 8, 1942) **ORCH.:** *Concert champêtre* for Harpsichord or Piano and Orch. (1927–28; Paris, May 3, 1929); Concerto for 2 Pianos and Orch. (Venice, Sept. 5, 1932); *2 marches et un intermède* for Chamber Orch. (Paris, 1937); Concerto for Organ, Strings, and Timpani (1938; private perf., Paris, June 21, 1939; public perf., Paris, June 10, 1941); Sinfonietta (1947; London, Oct. 24, 1948); Piano Concerto (1949; Boston, Jan. 6, 1950); *Matelote provençale,* movement from a collective work of 7 composers, *La Guirlande de Campra* (1952); *Bucolique: Variations sur la nom de Marguerite Long* (1954; movement from a collective work of 8 composers). **CHAMBER:** Sonata for 2 Clarinets (1918; rev. 1945); Sonata for Clarinet and Bassoon (1922); Sonata for Horn, Trumpet, and Trombone (1922; rev. 1945); Trio for Oboe, Bassoon, and Piano (1926); Sextet for Piano and Wind Quintet (1930–32; rev. 1939); *Suite française* for 9 Winds, Percussion, and Harpsichord (1935); Violin Sonata (1942–43; rev. 1949); Cello Sonata (1948); Flute Sonata (1956); *Elegie,* to the memory of Dennis Brain, for Horn and Piano (1957); *Sarabande* for Guitar (1960); Clarinet Sonata (1962); Oboe Sonata (1962). **Piano:** Sonata for Piano, 4-Hands (1918); *3 mouvements perpétuels* (1918); *Valse* (1919); *Suite in C* (1920); *6 impromptus* (1920); *Promenades* (1921); *Napoli,* suite of 3 pieces (1921–25); *2 novelettes* (1928); *3 pièces* (1928); *Pièce brève sur la nom d'Albert Roussel* (1929); *8 nocturnes* (1929–38); *15 improvisations* (1932–59); *Villageoises* (1933); *Feuillets d'album* (1933); *Les*

Soirées de Nazelles (1930–36); Mélancolie (1940); Intermezzo (1943); L'Embarquement pour Cythère for 2 Pianos (1951); Thème varié (1951); Sonata for 2 Pianos (1952–53); Elégie for 2 Pianos (1959); Novelette sur un thème de Manuel de Falla (1959). VOCAL: Choral: Chanson à boire for Men's Chorus (1922); 7 chansons for Chorus (1936); Litanies à la vièrge noire for Women's Chorus and Organ (1936); Mass in G for Chorus (1937; Paris, May 1938); Secheresses (Dryness), cantata for Chorus and Orch., after Edward James (1937; Paris, 1938); 4 motets pour un temps de penitence for Chorus (1938–39); Exultate Deo for Chorus (1941); Salve regina for Chorus (1941); Figure humaine, cantata for Double Chorus (1943); Un Soir de neige, chamber cantata for 6 Voices (1944); 2 books of traditional French songs, arr. for Chorus (1945); 4 petites prières de Saint François d'Assise for Men's Chorus (1948); Stabat Mater for Soprano, Chorus, and Orch. (1950; Strasbourg, June 13, 1951); 4 motets pour le temps de Noël for Chorus (1951–52); Ave verum corpus for Women's Chorus (1952); Laudes de Saint Antoine de Padoue for Men's Chorus (1957–59); Gloria for Soprano, Chorus, and Orch. (1959; Boston, Jan. 20, 1961); 7 répons des ténèbres for Boy Soprano, Boy's and Men's Chorus, and Orch. (1961; N.Y., April 11, 1963). Voice and Instruments: Rapsodie nègre for Baritone, String Quartet, Flute, Clarinet, and Piano (Paris, Dec. 11, 1917; rev. 1933); Le Bestiaire for Mezzo-soprano, String Quartet, Flute, Clarinet, and Bassoon, after Apollinaire (1918–19); Cocardes for Voice, Violin, Cornet, Trombone, Bass Drum, and Triangle, after Cocteau (1919); Le Bal masque for Voice, Oboe, Clarinet, Bassoon, Violin, Cello, Percussion, and Piano, after Max Jacob (1932); La Dame de Monte Carlo, monologue for Soprano and Orch. (Paris, Dec. 5, 1961). Voice and Piano: Histoire de Babar le petit éléphant for Narrator and Piano (1940–45; orchestrated by Jean Francaix, 1962). Song Cycles: Le Bestiaire (1919; arrangement); Cocardes (1919; arrangement); Poèmes de Ronsard (1924–25; later orchestrated); Chansons gaillardes (1925–26); Airs chantés (1927–28); 8 chansons polonaises (1934); 4 chansons pour enfants (1934); 5 poèmes, after Eluard (1935); Tel jour, telle nuit (1936–37); 3 poèmes, after de Vilmorin (1937); 2 poèmes, after Apollinaire (1938); Miroirs brulants (1938–39); Fiancailles pour rire (1939); Banalités (1940); Chansons villageoises (1942; orchestrated 1943); Métamorphoses (1943); 3 chansons, after García Lorca (1947); Calligrammes (1948); La Fraicheur et le feu (1950); Parisiana (1954); Le Travail du peintre (1956); 2 mélodies (1956); La Courte Paille (1960). Songs: Toréador (1918; rev. 1932); Vocalise (1927); Epitaphe (1930); A sa guitare, after Ronsard (1935); Montparnasse (1941–45); Hyde Park (1945); Paul et Virginie (1946); Le Disparu (1947); Mazurka (1949); Rosemonde (1954); Dernier poème (1956); Une Chanson de porcelaine (1958); others.

WRITINGS: Emmanuel Chabrier (Paris, 1961); Moi et mes amis (Paris, 1963; Eng. tr., London, 1978 as My Friends and Myself); Journal de mes mélodies (Paris, 1964); S. Buckland, tr. and ed., Francis Poulenc: Selected Correspondence, 1915–1963: Echo and Source (1991).

BIBL.: C. Rostand, F. P.: Entretiens avec Claude Rostand (Paris, 1954); H. Hell, P., musicien français (Paris, 1958); J. Roy, F. P. (Paris, 1964); P. Bernac, F. P.: The Man and His Songs (London, 1977); K. Daniel, F. P.: His Artistic Development and Musical Style (N.Y., 1982); F. Bloch, F. P. (Paris, 1984); M. Rosenthal, Satie, Ravel, P.: An Intimate Memoir (Madras and N.Y., 1987); G. Keck, F. P.: A Bio-Bibliography (Westport, Conn., 1990); H. Ehrler, Untersuchungen zur Klaviermusik von F. P., Arthur Honegger und Darius Milhaud (Tutzing, 1990); W. Mellers, F. P. (Oxford, 1994); J. Roy, Le groupe des six: P., Milhaud, Honegger, Auric, Tailleferre, Durey (Paris, 1994); C. Schmidt, The Music of F. P. (1899–1963): A Catalogue (Oxford, 1995); S. Buckland and M. Chimènes, eds., F. P.: Music, Art and Literature (Brookfield, Vt., 1999).—NS/LK/DM

Poulet, Gaston, French violinist and conductor, father of **Gérard Poulet;** b. Paris, April 10, 1892; d. Draveil, Essonne, April 14, 1974. He studied violin at the Paris Cons., winning the premier prix (1910). He made his debut as soloist in the Beethoven Concerto in Brussels (1911). He organized a string quartet in 1912 and gave concerts in Europe. From 1927 to 1936 he conducted the Concerts Poulet at the Théâtre Sarah-Bernhardt in Paris. From 1932 to 1944 he served as director of the Cons. of Bordeaux and conducted the Phil. Orch. there, and from 1940 to 1945 he conducted the Concerts Colonne in Paris. He was a guest conductor with the London Sym. Orch. (1947) and in Germany (1948), as well as in South America. He played the violin in the first performance of Debussy's Violin Sonata, with Debussy himself at the piano (1917). He was a prof. of chamber music at the Paris Cons. from 1944 to 1962. In 1948 he founded the famous Besançon Festival. —NS/LK/DM

Poulet, Gérard, French violinist, son of **Gaston Poulet;** b. Bayonne, Aug. 12, 1938. He entered the Paris Cons. at the age of 11 in the class of André Asselin, and won 1st prize at 12. In the same year (1950), he played 3 violin concertos with the Colonne Orch. in Paris, under his father's direction. He then appeared with other Paris orchs., and subsequently gave concerts and played with orchs. in England, Germany, Italy, Austria, and the Netherlands. In 1956 he won 1st Grand Prix at the Paganini competition of Genoa, and was given the honor of performing on Paganini's own violin, the famous Guarneri del Jesù.—NS/LK/DM

Pound, Ezra (Loomis), greatly significant American man of letters and amateur composer; b. Hailey, Idaho, Oct. 30, 1885; d. Venice, Nov. 1, 1972. He was educated at Hamilton Coll. (Ph.B., 1905) and the Univ. of Pa. (M.A., 1906). He went to England, where he established himself as a leading experimental poet and influential critic. He also pursued a great interest in early music, especially that of the troubadours, which led him to try his hand at composing. With the assistance of George Antheil, he composed the opera Le Testament, after poems by François Villon (1923; Paris, June 19, 1926); it was followed by a second opera, Calvacanti (1932), and a third, left unfinished, based on the poetry of Catullus. In 1924 he settled in Rapallo. Although married to Dorothy Shakespear, daughter of one of Yeats's friends, he became intimate with the American violinist Olga Rudge; Rudge bore him a daughter in 1925 and his wife bore him a son in 1926. Through the influence of Rudge, his interest in music continued, and he became a fervent champion of Vivaldi; he also worked as a music reviewer and ran a concert series with Rudge, Inverno Musicale. A growing interest in economic history and an inordinate admiration for the Fascist dictator Benito Mussolini led Pound down the road of political obscurantism. During World War II, he made many broadcasts over Rome Radio on topics ranging from literature to politics. His condemnation of Jewish banking circles in America and the American effort to defeat Fascism led to his arrest by the Allies after the collapse of Il Duce's regime. In 1945 he was sent to a prison camp in Pisa. In 1946 he was sent to the U.S. to stand trial for treason, but was declared insane and confined to St. Elizabeth's Hospital in Washington, D.C. Finally, in 1958, he was released and allowed to return to Italy, where he died. Among his writings on music is *Antheil and the Treatise on Harmony* (1924). He also composed several works for solo violin for Rudge, including *Fiddle Music* (1924) and *Al poco giorno* (Berkeley, March 23, 1983); he also arranged Gaucelm Faidit's *Plainte pour la mort du roi Richart Coeur de Lion*. The uncatalogued collection of Pound's musical MSS at Yale Univ. includes various musical experiments, including rhythmic and melodic realizations of his poem *Sestina: Altaforte*. Among the composers who have set his poems to music are Copland, Luytens, and Berio.

BIBL.: S. Adams, *E. P. and Music* (diss., Univ. of Toronto, 1974); R. Schafer, ed., *E. P. and Music* (N.Y., 1977; a complete collection of his writings on music).—**NS/LK/DM**

Pountney, David (Willoughby),
English opera director; b. Oxford, Sept. 10, 1947. He received his education at Radley Coll. and at the Univ. of Cambridge. In 1967 he staged his first opera, A. Scarlatti's *Il trionfo dell'onore*, with the Cambridge Opera Soc. In 1971 he produced *The Rake's Progress* at Glasgow's Scottish Opera, and in 1972 at the Netherlands Opera in Amsterdam. He first directed opera in the U.S. in 1973 when he mounted *Macbeth* at the Houston Grand Opera. From 1975 to 1980 he served as director of productions at the Scottish Opera; in collaboration with the Welsh National Opera in Cardiff, he produced a celebrated cycle of Janáček's operas. In 1977 he oversaw the production of the premiere of Blake's *Toussaint* at the English National Opera in London, and in 1980 he was responsible for the staging of the premiere of Glass's *Satyagraha* at the Netherlands Opera. Pountney garnered critical accolades during his tenure as director of productions at the English National Opera from 1982 to 1993. In 1998 he produced a new staging of *Guillaume Tell* at the Vienna State Opera. His productions have also been staged in Berlin, Rome, Paris, Chicago, and N.Y. Pountney's imaginative approach to opera production aims to create a total theater experience, running the gamut from the purely visual to the psychological.—**NS/LK/DM**

Pouplinière, Alexandre-Jean-Joseph Le Riche de La
See **La Pouplinière, Alexandre-Jean-Joseph Le Riche de**

Pousseur, Henri (Léon Marie Thérèse),
radical Belgian composer and pedagogue; b. Malmédy, June 23, 1929. He studied at the Liège Cons. (1947–52) and the Brussels Cons. (1952–53), and also had private lessons in composition from Souris and Boulez. Until 1959, he worked in the Cologne and Milan electronic music studios, where he came in contact with Stockhausen and Berio; was a member of the avant-garde group of composers "Variation" in Liège. He taught music in various Belgian schools (1950–59), and was founder (1958) and director of the Studio de Musique Electronique APELAC in Brussels, from 1970 a part of the Centre de Recherches Musicales in Liège. He gave lectures at the summer courses of new music in Darmstadt (1957–67), Cologne (1966–68), Basel (1963–64), the State Univ. of N.Y. in Buffalo (1966–69), and the Liège Cons. (from 1970), where he became director in 1975. In his music he tries to synthesize all the expressive powers of which man, as a biological species, Homo sapiens (or even Homo insipiens), is capable in the domain of art (or non-art); the technological resources of the subspecies Homo habilis (magnetic tape, electronics/synthesizers, aleatory extensions, the principle of indeterminacy, glossolalia, self-induced schizophasia) all form part of his rich musical (or non-musical) vocabulary for multimedia (or nullimedia) representations. The influence of his methods (or non-methods) of composition (or non-composition) is pervasive. He publ. *Fragments théoriques I. Sur la musique experimentale* (Brussels, 1970).

WORKS: *3 chants sacrés* for Soprano and String Trio (1951); *Seismogrammes* for Tape (1953); *Symphonies* for 15 Solo Instruments (1954–55); *Quintet to the Memory of Webern* for Violin, Cello, Clarinet, Bass Clarinet, and Piano (1955); *Mobile* for 2 Pianos (1956–58); *Scambi* for Tape (1957); *Madrigal I* for Clarinet (1958) *II* for Flute, Violin, Viola da Gamba, and Harpsichord (1961), and *III* for Clarinet, Violin, Cello, 2 Percussionists, and Piano (1962); *Rimes pour différentes sources sonores* for 3 Orch. Groups and Tape (1958–59; Donaueschingen, Oct. 17, 1959); *Electre*, "musical action" (1960); *Répons* for 7 Musicians (1960; rev. with Actor added, 1965); *Ode* for String Quartet (1960–61); *3 visages de Liège and Prospective* for Tape (1961); *Votre Faust*, an aleatory "fantasy in the manner of an opera" for 5 Actors, Vocal Quartet, 12 Musicians, and Tapes, for which the audience decides the ending (1961–67; Milan, 1969; concert version as *Portail de Votre Faust* for 4 Voices, Tape, and 12 Instruments; in collaboration with Michel Butor); *Trait* for 15 Strings (1962); *Miroir de Votre Faust* for Piano and Soprano ad libitum (Caracteres II, 1964–65); *Caractères madrigalesques* for Oboe (*Madrigal IV and Caractère III*, 1965); *Phonèmes pour Cathy* for Voice (*Madrigal V*, 1966); *Echoes I* for Cello (1967) and *II, de Votre Faust* for Mezzo- soprano, Flute, Cello, and Piano (1969); *Couleurs croisées* for Orch., a series of cryptic musical variations on the civil rights song *We Shall Overcome* (1967; Brussels Radio, Dec. 20, 1968); *Mnemosyne I*, monody, after Hölderlin, for Solo Voice, or Unison Chorus, or one Instrument (1968), and *II*, an instrumental re-creation of *Mnemosyne I*, with ad libitum scoring (1969); *Croisées des couleurs croisées* (an intensified sequel to *Couleurs croisées*) for Woman's Voice, 2–5 Pianos, Tape Recorders, and 2 Radio Receivers dialed aleatorily, to texts from Indian and Negro materials and political speeches (N.Y., Nov. 29, 1970); *Icare apprenti* for an undetermined number of instruments (1970); *Les Ephémerides d'Icare 2* for Piano and Instruments (Madrid, April 20, 1970); *Invitation à l'Utopie* for Narrator, 2 Women's Voices, Chorus, and Instruments (Brussels Radio, Jan. 25, 1971); *L'Effacement du Prince Igor*, scene for Orch. (Brussels, Jan. 18, 1972); *Le Temps des paraboles* (1972); *Die Erprobung des Petrus Herbraicus*, chamber opera (Berlin, Sept. 12,

1974); *Vue sur les jardins interdits* for Organ or Saxophone Quartet (1974); *198/4* for Cello (1975); *Les ruines de Jeruzona* for Chorus, Piano, Double Bass, and Percussion (1978); *Humeurs du futur quotidien* for Reciter and Orch. (Paris, March 12, 1978); *Tales and Songs from the Bible of Hell* for 4 Voices, Narrator, and Electronics (1979); *Les Îles déchaînées* for Jazz Group, Electroacoustic Ensemble, and Orch. (Brussels, Nov. 27, 1980); *Le Seconde Apothéose de Rameau* for Chamber Orch. (Paris, Nov. 9, 1981); *La Rose des voix* for Voice, Chorus, Reciter, and Instruments (Namur, Aug. 6, 1982); *La Passion selon quignol* for Vocal Quartet and Orch. (1982; Liège, Feb. 24, 1983; in collaboration with C. Paulo); *Cinquième vue sur les jardins interdits* for Vocal Quartet (1982); *Trajets dans les arpents du ciel* for Soloists and Orch. (Metz, Nov. 18, 1983); *Cortèjes des belles ténébreuses au jardin boréal* for English Horn, Viola, Horn, Tuba, and Percussion (1984); *L'Etoile des langues* for Chamber Chorus and Speaker (1984); *Patchwork des tribus américaines* for Wind Orch. (1984); *Nuits des Nuits* for Orch. (1985); *Sur le Qui-Vive* for Woman's Voice, Clarinet, Cello, Tuba, Keyboards, and Percussion (1985); *Arc-en-ciel de remparts* for Student Orch. and Chorus ad libitum (1986); *Un Jardin de panacailles* for Original Orchestration Globally Organized from the works of Lully, Bach, Beethoven, Brahms, and Webern with an *Original Prologue, Interlude, and Grand Finale* for 12 Musicians (1987); *Traverser la forêt*, cantata for Speaker, 2 Vocal Soloists, Chorus, and 12 Instruments (1987); *Ode No. 2, Mnemosyne (doublement) obstinée* for String Quartet and Soprano ad libitum (London, June 1989); *Leçons d'enfer*, musical theater (Metz, Nov. 14, 1991); *Dichterliebesreigentraum*, grand paraphrase after Schumann's cycle for 2 Pianos, Soprano, Baritone, Chamber Chorus, and Chamber Orch. (1992–93; Amsterdam, June 1993).—**NS/LK/DM**

Pouteau, Joseph, French organist, teacher, and composer; b. Chaumes-en-Brie, Feb. 7, 1739; d. Paris, Dec. 3, 1823. He studied organ with his great-uncle Michel Forqueray and composition with L.-C. Bordier in Paris, where he settled. He was organist at St. Martin des Champs (1753–56) and St. Jacques de la Boucherie (1756–57). Upon Forqueray's death, he was made organist at the Filles-Dieu convent in 1757. From about 1811 he taught piano at the Ursalines convent school and was organist at St. Merry. He wrote an intermède *Alain et Rosette* (Paris, Jan. 10, 1777), motets, ariettes, and harpsichord sonatas.—**LK/DM**

Powell, John, American pianist, composer, and ethnomusicologist; b. Richmond, Va., Sept. 6, 1882; d. Charlottesville, Va., Aug. 15, 1963. His father was a schoolteacher, and his mother an amateur musician. He received his primary musical education at home, then studied piano with F.C. Hahr, a pupil of Liszt. He subsequently entered the Univ. of Va. (B.A., 1901) and then went to Vienna, where he studied piano with Leschetizky (1902–07) and composition with Navrátil (1904–07). He gave successful piano recitals in Paris and London; returning to the U.S., he toured the country as a pianist, playing some of his own works. His most successful piece was *Rapsodie nègre* for Piano and Orch., inspired by Joseph Conrad's *Heart of Darkness*; Powell was the soloist in its first performance with the Russian Sym. Orch. (N.Y., March 23, 1918). The titles of some of his works disclose a whimsical propensity. Perhaps his most important achievement lies in ethnomusicology;

he methodically collected rural songs of the South; was the organizer of the Va. State Choral Festivals and of the White Top Mountain Folk Music Festivals. A man of versatile interests, he was also an amateur astronomer, and discovered a comet.

WORKS: ORCH.: Piano Concerto (n.d.); Violin Concerto (1910); *Rapsodie nègre* for Piano and Orch. (1917; N.Y., March 23, 1918); *In Old Virginia*, overture (1921); *Natchez on the Hill*, 3 Virginian country dances (1932); *A Set of 3* (1935); Sym. in A (1945; Detroit, April 23, 1947; substantially rev. version as *Virginia Symphony*, Richmond, Va., Nov. 5, 1951). **CHAMBER:** *Sonate Virginianesque* for Violin and Piano (1906); 2 string quartets (1907, 1922); Violin Sonata (1918); *From a Loved Past* for Violin and Piano (1930). **Piano:** 3 sonatas: *Sonate psychologique*, "on the text of St. Paul's 'The wages of sin is death'" (1905), *Sonate noble* (1908), and *Sonata Teutonica* (1905–13); *In the South*, suite (1906); *At the Fair*, suite (1907); *In the Hammock* for 2 Pianos, 8-Hands (1915); *Dirge*, sextet for 2 Pianos, 12-Hands (1928). **VOCAL:** Choral pieces, including the folk carol *The Babe of Bethlehem* (1934); songs, including *5 Virginian Folk Songs* for Voice and Piano (1938).—**NS/LK/DM**

Powell, Laurence, English-born American organist, conductor, teacher, and composer; b. Birmingham, Jan. 13, 1899; d. Victoria, Tex., Jan 29, 1990. He studied at Ratcliffe Coll., Leicester (1909–15), Ushaw Coll., Durham (1915–17), with Bantock at the Birmingham Midland Inst. School of Music (1919–22), and at the Univ. of Birmingham (Mus.Bac.). In 1923 he emigrated to the U.S. and in 1936 became a naturalized American citizen. He completed his education at the Univ. of Wisc. (M.A., 1926), where he also taught (1924–26). Subsequently he taught at the Univ. of Ark. (1926–34) and Little Rock Junior Coll. (1934–39). He was founder-conductor of the Little Rock Sym. Orch. (1934–39), and then conducted the Grand Rapids (Mich.) Federal Sym. Orch. (1939–41). After serving as organist at St. Mary's Church in Victoria, Tex. (1947–52), he was organist and choirmaster at St. Francis Cathedral in Sante Fe (1952–68), where he also was founder-conductor of the Sante Fe Orch., later known as the Rio Grande Sym. Orch. (1953–55). He was organist and choirmaster at Assumption Church in Albuquerque (1968–70) and at Our Lady of Victory Church in Victoria, Tex. (1970–75).

WORKS: ORCH.: *The Ogre of the Northern Fastness* (1921); *Keltic Legend* (Bournemouth, Aug. 27, 1924; rev. version, Madison, Wisc., May 20, 1931); *Charivari*, suite (1925); 2 syms. (1929, 1943); Suite for Strings (1931; Grand Rapids, May 9, 1940); *Deirdre of the Sorrows* (1933; Little Rock, March 18, 1937); *The Country Fair*, suite (1936); *Picnic* for Strings (Oklahoma City, March 21, 1936); *Variations* (Rochester, N.Y., Oct. 28, 1941); *Duo concertante* for Recorders and Orch. (1941); *Penny Overture* (1960); *Overture on French Folk Tunes* (1970); *Oracle* (1975). **CHAMBER:** Piano Quartet (1933); Quartet for Clarinets (1936); 3 recorder sonatinas (1977). **VOCAL:** *Halcyone* for Chorus and Orch. (1923); *Alleluya*, cantata for Chorus and Orch. (1926); *The Seasons* for Chorus (1928); *The Santa Fe Trail* for Baritone, Narrator, and Orch. (Santa Fe, April 22, 1958); masses; songs.—**NS/LK/DM**

Powell, Maud, esteemed American violinist; b. Peru, Ill., Aug. 22, 1868; d. Uniontown, Pa., Jan. 8, 1920. After studying violin and piano in Aurora, Ill., she received violin lessons from William Lewis in Chicago. She then studied violin with Schraideck at the Leipzig Cons. (1881–82) and theory with Charles Dancla at the Paris Cons. (1882–83); after touring England (1883), she completed her training with Joachim at the Berlin Hochschule für Musik (1884). In 1885 she appeared as a soloist with Joachim and the Berlin Phil., and with Thomas and the N.Y. Phil.; toured Europe with the N.Y. Arion Soc. (1892); subsequently performed regularly in the U.S. and Europe. She was the first American woman to found a string quartet (1894), and she also organized her own trio (1908). Powell made it a point to program works by American composers, and also introduced works by Dvorak, Lalo, Saint-Saens, Sibelius, and Tchaikovsky to the U.S. Her virtuosity won her wide recognition and praise.

BIBL.: K. Schaffer and N. Greenwood, *M. P., Pioneer American Violinist* (Arlington, Va., 1988); K. Shaffer, *M. P.: Legendary American Violinist* (Arlington, Va., 1994).—**NS/LK/DM**

Powell, Mel (real name, Melvin Epstein),

remarkable American composer and teacher; b. N.Y., Feb. 12, 1923; d. Valencia, Calif., April 24, 1998. He acquired an early fascination for American jazz, and was barely 14 when he was chosen as pianist for Benny Goodman's band. It was then that he changed his name to the more mellifluous Mel Powell, restructured from that of his paternal uncle, Poljanowsky. He was drafted into the army, where he was selected for the Air Force Band led by Glenn Miller. While playing jazz, Powell also began to compose. Tragedy struck at the height of his powers as a jazz musician and composer when he suddenly contracted muscular dystrophy; the disease affected his quadriceps, and he was ultimately confined to a wheelchair. He could still play the piano, but he could no longer travel with a band. He turned to serious composition and became an excellent teacher. While he was working with the Goodman band, he took lessons with Wagenaar and Schillinger in N.Y. (1937–39); he later studied composition privately with Toch in Los Angeles (1946–48). A turning point in his career occurred in 1948 when he entered the Yale Univ. School of Music in the class of Hindemith, from whom he acquired the matchless skill of Teutonic contrapuntal writing; he received his B.Mus. degree in 1952. From then on, Powell dedicated himself mainly to teaching. He served on the faculty of Yale Univ. (1957–69), and was dean of music at the Calif. Inst. of the Arts in Valencia (from 1969), serving as provost (1972–76) and as a prof. and fellow (from 1976). As a composer of growing strength, he revealed versatile talents, being technically at home in an incisive jazz idiom, in a neo-Classical manner, tangentially shadowing Stravinsky, and in an expressionist mode of Schoenberg, occasionally paralleling the canonic processes of Webern. He also evolved a sui generis sonorism of electronic music. In all these asymptotic formations, he nevertheless succeeded in projecting his own personality in a curious and, indeed, quaquaversal way; while absorbed in atonal composition, he was also able to turn out an occasional march tune or waltz figure. In all these mutually enhanced formulas, he succeeded in cultivating the unmistakable modality of his personal style

without venturing into the outer space of musical entropy. In 1990 he received the meritorious Pulitzer Prize in Music for his *Duplicates*, a concerto for 2 Pianos and Orch. Powell described this work as a "perpetual cadenza," an expression he attributed to Debussy.

WORKS: ORCH.: *Cantilena concertante* for English Horn and Orch. (1948); *Symphonic Suite* (1949); *Capriccio* for Concert Band (1950); *Intrada and Variants* (1956); *Stanzas* (1957); *Setting* for Cello and Orch. (1961); *Immobiles I-IV* (1967); *Settings* for Jazz Band (1982); *Modules*, intermezzo for Chamber Orch. (1985); *Duplicates*, concerto for 2 Pianos and Orch. (Los Angeles, Jan. 26, 1990); *Settings* for Small Orch. (Los Angeles, Sept. 23, 1992). **CHAMBER:** 2 string quartets: No. 1, *Beethoven Analogs* (1949) and No. 2, *String Quartet 1982* (1982); Harpsichord Sonata (1952); Trio for Piano, Violin, and Cello (1954); *Divertimento* for Violin and Harp (1954); *Divertimento* for 5 Winds (1955); Quintet for Piano and String Quartet (1956); *Miniatures for Baroque Ensemble* for Flute, Oboe, Violin, Viola, Cello, and Harpsichord (1958); *Filigree Setting* for String Quartet (1959); *Improvisation* for Clarinet, Viola, and Piano (1962); *Nocturne* for Violin (1965; rev. 1985); *Cantilena* for Trombone and Tape (1981); Woodwind Quintet (1984–85); *Setting* for Guitar (1986); *Invocation* for Cello (1987); *Amy-abilities* for Percussion (1987); *3 Madrigals* for Flute (1988). **Piano:** 2 sonatinas (1951); *Etude* (1957); *Intermezzo* (1984); *Piano Preludes* (1987). **VOCAL:** *6 Choral Songs* (1950); *Sweet Lovers Love the Spring* for Women's Voices and Piano (1953); *Haiku Settings* for Soprano and Piano (1961); *2 Prayer Settings* for Tenor, Oboe, and String Trio (1963); *Cantilena* for Voice, Violin, and Tape (1969); *Settings* for Soprano and Chamber Group (1979); *Little Companion Pieces* for Soprano and String Quartet (1979); *Strand Settings: Darker* for Soprano and Electronics (1983); *Letter to a Young Composer* for Soprano (1987); *Die Violine* for Soprano, Violin, and Piano (1987). **ELECTRONIC:** *Electronic Setting* (1958); *2nd Electronic Setting* (1961); *Events* (1963); *Analogs I-IV* (1963); *3 Synthesizer Settings* (1970–80); *Inscape*, ballet (1976); *Variations* (1976); *Computer Prelude* (1988).

DISC: *The Return of M. P.* (1987); *The Best Things in Life* (1999); *It's Been So Long* (1999).—**NS/LK/DM**

Powell, Seldon,

tenor saxophonist, flutist; b. Lawrenceville, Va., Nov. 15, 1928; d. Hempstead, N.Y., Jan. 25, 1997. He was classically trained in N.Y., and worked briefly with Tab Smith in 1949 before joining Lucky Millinder and recording with him in 1950. Powell was in the military (1950–51), then became a studio musician in N.Y. He worked and recorded with Louis Bellson, Neal Hefti, Friedrich Gulda, Johnny Richards and Billy Ver Planck in the 1950s. He also played with Sy Oliver and Erskine Hawkins, and studied at Juilliard. He traveled to Europe with Benny Goodman's band (1958), and worked briefly with Woody Herman. Powell was a staff player for ABC TV in the 1960s, and also performed and recorded with Buddy Rich, Bellson, Clark Terry and Ahmed Abdul-Malik. He did a number of soul jazz and pop dates in the late 1960s and early 1970s, among them a session with Groove Holmes and big band dates backing Gato Barbieri and Dizzy Gillespie. Powell was principal soloist in Gerry Mulligan's 16-piece band at the JVC Jazz Festival in N.Y. in 1987.

DISC.: *Seldon Powell Plays* (1955); *Seldon Powell Sextet* (1956).—**LP**

Power (Powero, Polbero, etc.**), Leonel (Lionel, Leonell, Leonelle, Leonellus, Lyonel,** etc.**),** important English composer; b. place and date unknown; d. Canterbury, June 5, 1445. He is first recorded as an instructor of the choristers and then as a clerk in the household chapel of Thomas, Duke of Clarence, brother of Henry V. On May 14, 1423, he was admitted to the fraternity of Christ Church, Canterbury, as a layman; also served as master of the choir for the non-monastic liturgical services there. He was a contemporary of Dunstable and one of the leading and most original representatives of the English style of the day; his style so approximated Dunstable's that it is not always possible to determine the authorship of a number of works by the two. He also was author of the treatise *Upon the Gamme* (c. 1450; reprinted by S. Meech in *Speculum*, July 1935). Among his works are Mass cycles, Mass movements, and various other settings of sacred Latin texts. See the complete works as ed. by C. Hamm in Corpus Mensurabilis Musicae, I (1969–76), and *The Old Hall Manuscript* as ed. by A. Hughes and M. Bent in the same series, XLVI (1969–72). See also the complete works of Dunstable as ed. by M. Bukofzer in Musica Britannica, VIII (1953; 2nd ed., rev., 1970).
—NS/LK/DM

Powers, Harold (Stone), learned American musicologist; b. N.Y., Aug. 5, 1928. He was educated at Syracuse Univ. (B.Mus. in piano, 1950) and Princeton Univ. (M.F.A. in composition and musicology, 1952; Ph.D. in musicology, 1959, with the diss. *The Background of the South Indian Rāga-System*). He taught at Princeton Univ. (1955–58) and at Harvard Univ. (1958–60). From 1961 to 1973 he was a member of the music dept. and jointly of the South Asia Regional Studies dept. at the Univ. of Pa., and then was a prof. at Princeton Univ. from 1973 to 2001. He also served as a visiting prof. at several U.S. and European univs. He was made a member of the American Academy of Arts and Sciences in 1995, an honorary member of the American Musicological Soc. in 1996, and a corresponding Fellow of the British Academy in 1999. Powers has worked in diverse fields, including Indic musicology, Italian opera, Medieval and Renaissance music theory, language and music et al. Among his important writings since 1980 are: "Language models and musical analysis," *Ethnomusicology*, 24 (1980); *India I* ("The region, its music and music history"), *India II* ("Theory and practice of classical music"), and *Mode, The New Grove Dictionary of Music and Musicians* (1980); "Tonal types and modal categories in Renaissance polyphony," *Journal of the American Musicological Society*, 34 (1981); "'La solita forma' and 'the uses of convention'," *Acta musicologica*, 59 (1987); "Reinterpretations of traditions: Omkarnath Thakur *contra* V.N. Bhatkhande on sangīta-stra and śāstrīya-sangta," in J. Katz, ed., *The Traditional Indian Theory and Practice of Music and Dance* (Leiden, 1992); "Is mode real? Pietro Aron, the octenary system, and polypohony," *Basler Jahrbuch für historische Musikpraxis*, 16 (1992); "Boito rimatore per musica," in G. Morelli, ed., *Arrigo Boito: Atti del convegno internazionale* (Florence, 1994); "La

dama velata: Act II of Verdi's 'Un ballo in maschera'," in M. Chusid, ed., *Verdi's Middle Period* (Chicago, 1997); "From psalmody to tonality," in C.C. Judd, ed., *Tonal Structures in Early Music* (N.Y., 1998).**—LK/DM**

Pownall, Mary Ann, English actress, singer, and composer; b. London, Feb. 1751; d. Charleston, S.C., Aug. 11, 1796. She was known first as Mrs. James Wrightson (her first husband was a prompter in a London theater), and she made her debut in 1770 in *The Recruiting Officer* in London. From 1776 to 1788 she was a Vauxhall favorite. In 1792 she first appeared in Boston with the Old American Co., of which she was a leading artist; later sang in subscription concerts in N.Y., and joined John Henry's N.Y. Co. She composed the text and music of numerous songs, including *Advice to the Ladies of Boston, Washington* (in honor of George Washington), and *Primroses*. Some of her songs were publ. in *Six Songs for the Harpsichord* (in collaboration with J. Hewitt; 1794) and *Kisses Sued For* (1795).**—NS/LK/DM**

Pozdro, John (Walter), American composer and pedagogue; b. Chicago, Aug. 14, 1923. He began training in piano and theory at an early age with Nina Shafran, and later studied piano with Edward Collins at the American Cons. of Music in Chicago (1941–42). After serving as a field agent in military intelligence in the U.S. Army, he pursued his training in composition with Robert Delaney at Northwestern Univ., taking B.M. and M.M. (1949) degrees. He completed his studies with Hanson, Rogers, and Barlow at the Eastman School of Music in Rochester, N.Y. (Ph.D. in composition, 1958). In 1950 he joined the faculty of the Univ. of Kans. in Lawrence, becoming chairman of theory and composition in 1961. From 1958 to 1968 he also chaired its Annual Symposium of Contemporary Music. He retired from teaching in 1992. In 1993 he served as guest composer for the International Carillon Congress in Berkeley, where he was awarded the Univ. of Calif. at Berkeley Medal for distinguished service in music. His music is inherently pragmatic, with tertian torsion resulting in the formation of tastefully enriched triadic harmony, and with asymmetric rhythms enhancing the throbbing pulse of musical continuity.

WORKS: DRAMATIC: *Hello, Kansas!,* musical play (Lawrence, Kans., June 12, 1961); *Malooley and the Fear Monster,* "family opera" (1976; Lawrence, Kans., Feb. 6, 1977). **ORCH.:** Overture (1948; Evanston, Ill., Nov. 30, 1949); 3 syms.: No. 1 (1949), No. 2 (1957; Rochester, N.Y., May 4, 1958), and No. 3 (Oklahoma City, Dec. 12, 1960); *A Cynical Overture* (1952; Austin, Tex., March 24, 1953); *Lament of Judas* (1954; Austin, Tex., March 30, 1955); *Lament in Memory of a Friend* (1956; Rochester, N.Y., April 1957); *Rondo giocoso* for Strings (1964; Pittsburg, Kans., March 9, 1965); *Music for a Youth Symphony* (Lawrence, Kans., March 4, 1969); *Waterlow Park: 1970* (Lawrence, Kans., May 8, 1972). **CHAMBER:** Wind Quintet (Evanston, Ill., Dec. 11, 1947); 2 string quartets (1947, 1952); Sextet for Flute and Strings (Evanston, Ill., Nov. 23, 1948); *Elegy* for Trumpet and Piano (1953; Lawrence, Kans., Jan. 6, 1954); *Interlude* for Winds (Lawrence, Kans., April 26, 1954); *Trilogy* for Clarinet, Bassoon, Trumpet, and Piano (Manhattan, Kans., Nov. 22, 1960); Sonata for Brass and Percussion (1966; Lawrence, Kans., Jan. 18, 1967); Violin Sonatine (1971); *Impressions* for Flute, Oboe, Clarinet,

Bassoon, and Piano (1984); *2 Movements* for Cello and Piano (1987). **KEYBOARD: P i a n o :** 6 sonatas (1947, 1963, 1964, 1976, 1979, 1982); March (1950); 8 preludes (1950–74); *3 Short Pieces* (1951); Rondo (1953); *Ballade-Fantasy* (1981); *For Nancy* (1987). **C a r i l l o n :** *Landscape I* (1954) and *II: Ostinato* (1969); *Rustic Landscape* (1981); *Variations on a Slavonic Theme* (1982); *Tryptich* (1980); *Richard's Träume* (1993); *Winds of Autumn* (1996). **VOCAL:** *John Anderson* for Women's Voices (1950; Lawrence, Kans., April 18, 1951); *All Pleasant Things* for Chorus (Lawrence, Kans., May 3, 1960); *The Creation* for Children's Voices (1967); *They That Go Down to the Sea* for Chorus (Oklahoma City, Sept. 1967); *After the Dazzle* for Chorus (1970); *This is the Hour, O Soul* for Chorus (1970); *Alleluia* for Chorus (1979); *King of Glory* for Chorus, Organ, and Piano (1983); *Spirit of Oread* for Soloists, Chorus, and Organ (1989–90); *The Lord's Prayer* for Chorus and Organ (1994).—**NS/LK/DM**

Pozo, Chino (Francisco), Latin-jazz percussionist; cousin of Chano Pozo; b. Oct. 4, 1915, Havana, Cuba; d. N.Y., April 28, 1980. He taught himself to play piano and double bass. After moving to the U.S. in 1937, he worked with Machito (1941–43) and accompanied a dance troupe (1943–49). In 1948, he performed and recorded with Tadd Dameron and Fats Navarro. While working in various Latin groups, he recorded with Dizzy Gillespie, Machito, and Charlie Parker (1950). Thereafter, he toured with Peggy Lee (1954–55), performed with Stan Kenton (1955) and Herbie Mann (1956), and recorded with Illinois Jacquet (1954), Phineas Newborn (1957), Billy Taylor (1959), and Gibor Szabo (1965). Starting in the mid-1960s, he worked as percussionist for singer Paul Anka.

DISC.: T. Dameron: *Jahbero* (1948).

Pozzoli, Ettore, Italian pianist, teacher, and composer; b. Seregno, near Milan, July 22, 1873; d. there, Sept. 9, 1957. He studied with Ferroni, Appiani, and P. Fumagalli at the Milan Cons. Following a brief career as a concert pianist, he became a teacher of solfeggio and theory at the Milan Cons. in 1899. He composed a Piano Concerto and other orch. works, the oratorio *La figlia di Jefte*, motets, chamber music, and piano pieces.—**LK/DM**

Pradas Gallen, José, Spanish composer; b. Villahermosa del Rio, Aug. 21, 1689; d. there, Aug. 11, 1757. He became a chorister at Valencia Cathedral in 1700, where he received instruction in theory from Teodoro Ortells. After serving as organist and choirmaster at the Algemesi parish church (1712–17) and the Castellón de la Plana Cathedral (1717–28), he was choirmaster at Valencia Cathedral from 1728. His large output of works included 7 masses, a Requiem, 60 Psalms, 22 motets, and over 275 villancicos.—**LK/DM**

Praeger, Ferdinand (Christian Wilhelm), German pianist, writer on music, and composer; b. Leipzig, Jan. 22, 1815; d. London, Sept. 2, 1891. His father, Heinrich Aloys Praeger (b. Amsterdam, Dec. 23, 1783; d. Magdeburg, Aug. 7, 1854), was a violinist, guitarist, and composer who served as director of the theaters in Leipzig (1818–28), Magdeburg, and Hannover. Ferdinand studied cello before taking up the piano. After moving to The Hague as a teacher in 1831, he pursued training in piano, violin, and composition. In 1834 he settled in London, where he was active as a teacher. From 1842 he was the London correspondent of the *Neue Zeitschrift für Musik*. Praeger was one of the earliest champions of Wagner. He publ. the mendacious account *Wagner as I Knew Him* (London, 1855; Ger. tr., 1892, as *Wagner, wie ich ihn kannte*). After its exposure, the German publisher withdrew it. His compositions included the overture *Abellino*, a symphonic prelude to Byron's *Manfred*, chamber music, piano pieces, and songs.

BIBL.: H. Chamberlain, *Richard Wagners echte Briefe an F. P.: Kritik der P.'schen Veröffentlichungen* (Bayreuth, 1894; 2nd ed., rev., 1908).—**LK/DM**

Praelisauer, family of German musicians, all brothers:

(1) Anton Simon Ignaz Praelisauer, organist and composer; b. Kötzting, Bavaria (baptized), Aug. 13, 1692; d. Augsburg, Jan. 5, 1746. He was organist of St. Michael's Church and vice-prefect of St. Gregory's seminary in Munich before being made organist (1725) and Kapellmeister (1736) of Augsburg Cathedral. His compositions are not extant.

(2) Coelestin (actually, **Franz Idelfons**) **Praelisauer,** organist, pedagogue, and composer; b. Kötzting (baptized), April 7, 1694; d. Tegernsee, Feb. 5, 1745. He studied at the Tegernsee seminary, and then became a member of the Benedictine order and director of music there. He composed much sacred music, including responsories for the Vigil for the Dead and the sacred folk play *Ecce Agnus Dei*.

(3) Andreas Benedikt Praelisauer, choirmaster and composer; b. Kötzting (baptized), April 7, 1699; d. Polling, Nov. 5, 1743. He studied at the Augustinian prebendary college in Polling, where he was active as a canon and coirmaster.

(4) Columban (actually, **Josef Bernhard**) **Praelisauer,** composer; b. Kötzting (baptized), Jan. 11, 1703; d. Rott am Inn, Oct. 23, 1753. He studied at the Jesuit school in Munich. In 1720 he entered the Benedictine monastery in Rott am Inn, where he served as rector chori and librarian.

(5) Robert (Martin) Praelisauer, composer; b. Kötzting (baptized), Nov. 4, 1708; d. Reinstetten, Württemberg, Oct. 18, 1771. He studied at the Jesuit school in Munich. In 1729 he took his vows at the Benedictine abbey of Ochsenhausen, Württemberg. He was ordained a priest in 1734, and then was rector chori there and later priest of various parishes. Among his extant works are *Compositiones piarum cantionum* and 3 arias for Soprano and Instruments.—**LK/DM**

Praetorius (Latinized from **Schulz, Schulze, Schultz,** or **Schultze**), family of distinguished German musicians:

(1) Jacob Praetorius, organist and composer; b. Magdeburg, c. 1530; d. Hamburg, 1586. He converted to Protestantism and settled in Hamburg, where he became clerk at St. Jacobi in 1550. He became asst. organist in 1554, then was 1st organist from 1558 until his death. He compiled a set of monophonic liturgical chants and German chorales in 1554. He also compiled a collection known as *Opus musicum excellens et novum* (1566), which contained 204 sacred compositions for 4, 5, 6, and 8 Voices by German and Netherlands composers (a majority of compositions are copies of pieces publ. by Georg Rhau). Praetorius's only extant work, a *Te Deum* for 4 Voices, is included.

(2) Hieronymus Praetorius, organist and composer, son of the preceding; b. Hamburg, Aug. 10, 1560; d. there, Jan. 27, 1629. He studied organ with his father, then with Hinrich thor Molen (1573); also had instruction with Albinus Walran in Cologne (1574–76). He was organist in Erfurt (1580–82). He became asst. organist to his father at St. Jacobi in Hamburg in 1582; upon his father's death in 1586, he became 1st organist, a position he held until his own death 43 years later. He composed masses, motets, and Magnificat settings, of which the 8 Magnificat settings for Organ (1611) are particularly noteworthy. He also prepared a collection of monophonic German and Latin service music for the churches of Hamburg under the title *Cantiones sacrae chorales* (1587), and the *Melodeyen Gesangbuch* (Hamburg, 1604), which includes 88 4-part German chorale settings; 21 of these are by him, the remaining by his son **(3) Jacob Praetorius,** Joachim Decker, and David Scheidemann.

BIBL.: B. Friederich, *Der Vokalstil des H. P.* (Hamburg, 1932); F. Gable, *The Polychoral Motets of H. P.* (diss., Univ. of Iowa, 1966).

(3) Jacob Praetorius, organist, pedagogue, and composer, son of the preceding; b. Hamburg, Feb. 8, 1586; d. there, Oct. 22, 1651. He studied organ with Sweelinck in Amsterdam. From 1603 until his death he was organist of St. Petri in Hamburg. He was a noted organ teacher and composer of organ music. He contributed 19 4-part chorale settings to his father's *Melodeyen Gesangbuch* (Hamburg, 1604). See W. Brieg, ed., *J. P.: Choralbearbeitungen für Orgel* (Kassel, 1974).

(4) Johannes Praetorius, organist and composer, brother of the preceding; b. Hamburg, c. 1595; d. there, July 25, 1660. He studied organ with Sweelinck in Amsterdam (1608–11). From 1612 until his death he was organist of the Nikolaikirche in Hamburg.—**NS/LK/DM**

Praetorius, Bartholomaeus, German cornett player and composer; b. Marienburg, c. 1590; d. Stockholm (buried), Aug. 3, 1623. He matriculated at the Univ. of Königsberg in 1608. After playing cornett at the court of the Elector Johann Sigismund of Brandenburg (1613–20), he was director of the royal chapel of King Gustavus II in Stockholm. He publ. *Newe liebliche Paduanen und Galliarden* (Berlin, 1616).—**LK/DM**

Praetorius, Christoph, German composer, uncle of **Michael Praetorius;** b. Bunzlau, Silesia, date unknown; d. Lüneburg, 1609. He matriculated at the Univ. of Wittenberg in 1551. From 1563 to 1581 he was Kantor of the Johanneum in Lüneberg. He publ. 4 vols. of sacred vocal music (1560–81) and the theoretical books *Erotemata musices* (Wittenberg, 1574) and *Erotemata renovatae musicae* (Ülzen, 1581).—**LK/DM**

Praetorius, Michael, great German composer, organist, and music theorist, nephew of **Christoph Praetorius;** b. Creuzburg an der Werra, Thuringia, Feb. 15, 1571; d. Wolfenbüttel, Feb. 15, 1621. The surname of the family was Schultheiss (sometimes rendered as Schultze), which he Latinized as Praetorius. He was the son of a Lutheran pastor. He studied with Michael Voigt, the cantor of the Torgau Lateinschule. In 1582 he entered the Univ. of Frankfurt an der Oder, and in 1584 continued his studies at the Lateinschule in Zerbst, Anhalt. From 1587 to 1590 he was organist of St. Marien in Frankfurt. In 1595 he entered the service of Duke Heinrich Julius of Braunschweig-Wolfenbüttel as an organist. In 1604 he also assumed the duties of court Kapellmeister. Upon the death of his patron in 1613, the Elector Johann Georg of Saxony obtained his services as deputy Kapellmeister at the Dresden court. He retained his Dresden post until 1616, and then resumed his duties in Wolfenbüttel. Praetorius devoted only a part of his time to Wolfenbuttel, for he had been named Kapellmeister to the administrator of the Magdeburg bishopric and prior of the monastery at Ringelheim in 1614. He also traveled a great deal, visiting various German cities. These factors, coupled with a general decline in his health, led to the decision not to reappoint him to his Wolfenbuttel post in 1620. He died the following year a wealthy man. Deeply religious, he directed that the greater portion of his fortune go to organizing a foundation for the poor. Praetorius was one of the most important and prolific German composers of his era. His *Musae Sioniae,* a significant collection of over 1,200 settings of Lutheran chorales, is a particularly valuable source for hymnology. A complete ed. of his works was prepared by F. Blume (21 vols., Wolfenbüttel, 1928–40).

WORKS (all publ. in Wolfenbüttel unless otherwise given): *Musae Sionae...geistliche Concert Gesänge über die fürnembste deutsche Psalmen und Lieder...erster Theil* for 8 Voices (Regensburg, 1605); *Sacrarum motectarum primitiae* for 4 to 16 Voices (Magdeburg, 1606; not extant); *Musarum Sioniarum motestae et psalmi latini* for 4 to 16 Voices (Nuremberg, 1607; this may be the 2nd ed. of the preceding); *Musaie Sioniae...geistliche Concert Gesänge über die fürnembste deutsche Psalmen und Lieder...ander Theil* for 8 and 12 Voices (Jena, 1607); *Musaie Sioniae...geistliche Concert Gesänge...dritter Theil* for 8, 9, and 12 Voices (Helmstedt, 1607); *Musaie Sionae...geistliche Concert Gesänge...vierdter Theil* for 8 Voices (Helmstedt, 1607); *Musae Sioniae...geistlicher deutscher...üblicher Lieder und Psalmen...fünffter Theil* for 2 to 8 Voices (1607); *Musae Sioniae...deutscher geistlicher...üblicher Psalmen und Lieder...sechster Theil* for 4 Voices (1609); *Musae Sioniae...deutscher geistlicher...üblicher Psalmen und Lieder...siebender Theil* for 4 Voices (1609); *Musae Sioniae...deutscher geistlicher...Lieder und Psalmen...in Contrapuncto simplici...gesetzet...achter Theil* for 4 Voices (1610; 2nd ed., 1612, as *Ferner Continuierung der geistlichen Lieder und Psalmen*); *Musaie Sioniae...deutscher geistlicher...Psalmen und Lieder...auf Muteten, Madrigalische und sonsten eine andere...Art...gesetzet...neundter Theil* for 2 and 3 Voices (1610; 2nd ed., 1611, as *Bicinia und Tricinia*); *Eulogodia Sionia* for 2 to 8 Voices (1611); *Hymnodia Sionia* for 3 to 8 Voices (1611; with 4 works for Organ); *Megalynodia Sionia* for 5 to 8 Voices (1611); *Missodia Sionia* for 2 to 8 Voices (1611); *Kleine und Grosse Litaney* for 5 to 8 Voices (1613); *Urania, oder Urano-Chorodia* for 2 to 4 Choirs (1613); *Epithalamium: dem...Fursten...Friedrich Ulrichen, Herzogen zu Braunschweig* for 17 Voices and Basso Continuo (1st perf., Sept. 4, 1614); *Concertgesang...dem...Fursten...Mauritio, Landgrafen zu Hessen* for 2 to 16 Voices and Basso Continuo (1st perf., June 26, 1617); *Polyhymnia caduceatrix et panegyrica* for 1 to 21 Voices and Basso Continuo (1619); *Polyhymnia exercitatrix seu tyrocinium* for 2 to 8 Voices and Basso Continuo (Frankfurt am Main, 1619); *Puernicinium...darinne 14 teutsche Kirchenlieder und anderere Concert-Gesänge* for 3 to 14 Voices (Frankfurt am Main, 1621). He also publ. a collection of French instrumental dances under the title *Terpsichore, musarum aoniarum quinta a 4 to 6* (1612).

WRITINGS: *Syntagma musicum*, his major achievement, was publ. in 3 vols. as follows: *Syntagmatis musici tomus primus* (Wittenberg and Wolfenbüttel, 1614–15; reprint, 1959), a historical and descriptive treatise in Latin on ancient and ecclesiastical music, and ancient secular instruments; *Syntagmatis musici tomus secundus* (Wolfenbüttel, 1618; 2nd ed., 1619; reprint, 1958, with an appendix, *Theatrum instrumentorum*, Wolfenbüttel, 1620; reprint, 1958), in German, a most important source of information on musical instruments of the period, describing their form, compass, tone quality, etc.; the organ is treated at great length, and the appendix contains 42 woodcuts of the principal instruments enumerated; *Syntagmatis musici tomus tertius* (Wolfenbüttel, 1618; 2nd ed., 1619; reprint, 1958), a valuable and interesting account of secular composition of the period, with a treatise on solmisation, notation, etc.

BIBL.: W. Gurlitt, *M. P. (Creuzburgensis): Sein Leben und seine Werke* (Leipzig, 1915); F. Blume, *Das monodische Prinzip in der protestantischen Kirchenmusik* (Leipzig, 1925); idem, *M. P. Creuzburgensis* (Wolfenbüttel, 1929); R. Unger, *Die mehrchörige Aufführungspraxis bei M. P. und die Feiergestaltung der Gegenwart* (Wolfenbüttel, 1941); G. Ilgner, *Die lateinischen liturgischen Kompositionen von M. P. Creuzburgensis* (Kiel, 1944); R. Fay, *The Vocal Style of M. P.* (diss., Univ. of Rochester, N.Y., 1946); A. Forcherts, *Das Spätwerk des M. P.* (Berlin, 1959); L. Abraham, *Der Generalbass im Schaffen des M. P.* (Berlin, 1961); K. Gudewill and H. Haase, *M. P. Creutzbergensis 1571 (?–1612): Zwei Beiträge su seinem und seiner Kapelle Jubilaumsjahr* (Wolfenbüttel, 1971); S. Vogelsänger, *M. P. beim Wort genommen: Zur Entstehungsgeschichte seiner Werke* (Aachen, 1987); idem, *M. P., "Diener vieler Herren: " Daten und Deutungen* (Aachen, 1991); D. Möller-Weiser, *Untersuchungen zum I. Band des Syntagma Musicum von M. P.* (Kassel, 1993).—**NS/LK/DM**

Pratella, Francesco Balilla,

Italian music critic, musicologist, and composer; b. Lugo di Romagna, Feb. 1, 1880; d. Ravenna, May 17, 1955. He studied with Ricci-Signorini, then at the Liceo Rossini in Pesaro with Cicognani and Mascagni. He taught in Cesana (1908–09). He was director of the Istituto Musicale in Lugo (1910–29), and of the Liceo Musicale Giuseppe Verdi in Ravenna (1927–45). He joined the Italian futurist movement in 1910 (Russolo's manifesto of 1913 was addressed to "Balilla Pratella, grande musicista futurista"), and in 1913 wrote his first composition in a "futurist" idiom, the choral work *Inno alla vita*. After World War I, he broke with futurism.

WORKS: DRAMATIC: O p e r a : *Lilia* (1903; Lugo, Nov. 13, 1905); *La Sina d'Vargöun* (1906–08; Bologna, Dec. 4, 1909); *L'Aviatore Dro* (1911–14; Lugo, Nov. 4, 1920); *La ninnananna della bambola*, children's opera (1920–22; Milan, May 21, 1923); *La leggenda di San Fabiano* (1928–32; Bologna, Dec. 9, 1939); *L'uomo* (1934–49; not perf.); *Dono primaverile*, comedy with music (Bologna, Oct. 17, 1923). **O t h e r :** Incidental music. **ORCH.:** *Romagna*, 5 symphonic poems (1903–04); *Musica futurista*, renamed *Inno alla vita* (1912; rev. 1933). **OTHER:** Chamber music; piano pieces; choral works; songs.

WRITINGS: *Cronache e critiche dal 1905 al 1917* (Bologna, 1918); *L'evoluzione della musica: Dal 1910 al 1917* (Milan, 1918–19); *Saggio di gridi, canzoni, cori e danze del popolo italiano* (Bologna, 1919); *Luci ed ombre: per un musicista italiano ignorato in Italia* (Rome, 1933); *Scritti vari di pensiero, di arte, di storia musicale* (Bologna, 1933); *Autobiografia* (Milan, 1971).

BIBL.: A. Ghigi, *F.B. P.* (Ravenna, 1930); *F.B. P., Appunti biografici e bibliografici* (Ravenna, 1931); R. Payton, *The Futurist Musicians: F.B. P. and Luigi Russola* (diss., Univ. of Chicago, 1974); D. Tampieri, ed., *F.B. P.: Edizioni, scritti, manoscritti musicali e futuristi* (Ravenna, 1995).—**NS/LK/DM**

Prati, Alessio,

Italian composer; b. Ferrara, July 19, 1750; d. there, Jan. 17, 1788. He studied with Pietro Marzola in Ferrara, and after further training in Naples, he completed his studies with Abate Speranza in Rome in 1774–75. He then went to France, and eventually entered the service of the Duke of Penthièvre in Paris. Following a sojourn in Russia in 1782–83, he returned to Italy and later settled once again in Ferrara as co-adjutor to Petrucci. Prati wrote the operas *L'école de la jeunesse, ou Le Barnevelt français* (Paris, Oct. 11, 1779), *L'Ifigenia in Aulide* (Florence, 1784), *Armida Abbandonata* (Munich, 1785), *La vendetta di Nono* (Florence, Carnival, 1786), *Olimpia* (Naples, June 6, 1786), *Demofoonte* (Venice, Dec. 26, 1786), and *L'Aminta* (Ferrara, 1787?). Among his other works were a Flute Concerto, an Oboe Concerto, 2 harpsichord concertos, the oratorio *Giuseppe riconosciuto*, and chamber music.—**LK/DM**

Pratt, Awadagin,

black American pianist; b. Philadelphia, March 6, 1966. He began to study the piano at the age of 6 and the violin at age 9. At 16, he became a student at the Univ. of Ill., where he received training in piano, violin, and conducting. In 1986 he entered the Peabody Cons. of Music in Baltimore, where he was its first student ever to obtain diplomas in piano, violin, and conducting. In 1992 he won the Naumburg Competition in N.Y., and in 1994 he was awarded an Avery Fisher Career Grant. As a soloist, Pratt appeared with major American orchs., including the N.Y. Phil., the National Sym. Orch. in Washington, D.C., the St. Louis Sym. Orch., the Cincinnati Sym. Orch., the Minn. Orch. in Minneapolis, and the Los Angeles Phil. He also toured widely as a recitalist at home and abroad. —**NS/LK/DM**

Pratt, Silas Gamaliel,

American composer; b. Addison, Vt., Aug. 4, 1846; d. Pittsburgh, Oct. 30, 1916. Both his parents were church singers. The family moved to Chicago when he was a child, where he received his primary music education. At 22 he went to Berlin, where he studied piano with Kullak and theory with Kiel (1868–71). He then returned to Chicago, where he served as organist of the Church of the Messiah; in 1872, established the Apollo Club. In 1875 he went to Germany once more and studied orchestration with Heinrich Dorn and also took some piano lessons with Liszt. On July 4, 1876, he conducted in Berlin his Centennial Overture, dedicated to President Grant. He also conducted at the Crystal Palace in London, when President Grant was visiting there; another work that he presented in London was *Homage to Chicago March*. Returning to Chicago, he conducted his opera *Zenobia, Queen of Palmyra* (to his own libretto) in concert form, on June 15, 1882 (stage perf., Chicago, March 26, 1883; N.Y., Aug. 21, 1883). The opera was received in a hostile manner by the press, partly owing to the poor quality of the music, but mainly as a reaction to Pratt's exuberant and immodest proclamations of its merit in advance of the production. Undaunted, Pratt unleashed a vigorous campaign for native American opera; he organized the Grand Opera Festival of 1884, which had some support. The following year he visited London again, and conducted there his symphonic work *The Prodigal Son* (Oct. 5, 1885). Returning to Chicago, he revised his early lyric opera *Antonio*, renamed it *Lucille*, and produced it on March 14, 1887. In 1888 he moved to N.Y.; there he presented, during the quadricentennial of the discovery of America, his opera *The Triumph of Columbus* (in concert form, Oct. 12, 1892); also produced a scenic cantata, *America*, subtitled *4 Centuries of Music, Picture, and Song* (Nov. 24, 1894; with stereopticon projections). Other works include *Lincoln Symphony*, a symphonic poem, *The Tragedy of the Deep* (1912; inspired by the Titanic disaster), and a cantata, *The Last Inca*. He also publ. a manual, *Pianist's Mental Velocity* (N.Y., 1903). In 1906 he settled in Pittsburgh, where he established there the Pratt Inst. of Music and Art and remained its director until his death. Pratt was a colorful personality; despite continuous and severe setbacks, he was convinced of his own significance. The story of his salutation to Wagner at their meeting—"Herr Wagner, you are the Silas G. Pratt of Germany"—may be apocryphal, but is very much in character.—NS/LK/DM

Pratt, Waldo Selden, distinguished American music historian and pedagogue; b. Philadelphia, Nov. 10, 1857; d. Hartford, Conn., July 29, 1939. He studied at Williams Coll. and at Johns Hopkins Univ., specializing in classical languages; was practically self-taught in music. He was asst. director of the Metropolitan Museum of Art in N.Y. (1880–82); in 1882 he was appointed to the faculty of the Hartford Theological Seminary, where he taught hymnology; remained there until his retirement in 1925; he also taught music history at Smith Coll. (1895–1908), and later at the Inst. of Musical Art in N.Y. He ed. the American supplement to *Grove's Dictionary of Music and Musicians* (N.Y., 1920; rev. 1928) and *The New Encyclopedia of Music and Musicians* (N.Y., 1924; 2nd ed., rev., 1929). He also publ. *The History of English Hymnody* (Hartford, Conn., 1895), *Musical Ministries in the Church* (N.Y., 1901; 4th ed., rev., 1915), *The History of Music* (N.Y., 1907; 3rd ed., aug., 1935), *The Music of the Pilgrims* (Boston, 1921), and *The Music of the French Psalter of 1562* (N.Y., 1939).—NS/LK/DM

Praupner, Jan (Josef), Bohemian violinist, choirmaster, and composer, brother of **Václav (Josef Bartoloměj) Praupner;** b. Litoměřice, Jan. 9, 1751; d. Prague, after 1824. He studied music in Litoměřice and philosophy in Prague, where he settled. From about 1778 he was a violinist in the orch. of the Prague Theater. He

also was a violinist in the Týn and Crusaders's churches, and at the Metropolitan Cathedral from about 1780. In 1807 he succeeded his brother as choirmaster at the Crusaders's Church. Among his works were 2 masses, a Requiem, and a Te Deum.—LK/DM

Praupner, Václav (Josef Bartoloměj), Bohemian violinist, organist, choirmaster, teacher, and composer, brother of **Jan (Josef) Praupner;** b. Litoměřice, Aug. 18, 1745; d. Prague, April 1, 1807. He studied music at the Jesuit Gymnasium in Litoměřice and philosophy and theology in Prague, where he settled. He was active as a director of theater orchs. and as a choirmaster at various churches, among them the Týn and Crusader's churches (from 1794). In 1803 he was elected the first director of the Tonkunstler-Sozietät. He composed the melodrama *Circe* (1789; Prague, 1794), syms., concertos, and sacred music.—NS/LK/DM

Prausnitz, Frederik (actually, **Frederick William**), German-born American conductor and teacher; b. Cologne, Aug. 26, 1920. He went to the U.S. in his youth and studied at the Juilliard School of Music in N.Y. He later served on its faculty (1947–61), and then was conductor of the New England Cons. of Music sym. orch. in Boston (1961–69). He was music director of the Syracuse (N.Y.) Sym. Orch. from 1971 to 1974. In 1976 he joined the Peabody Cons. of Music in Baltimore as conductor of its sym. orch. and opera. From 1980 he acted as director of its conducting program and conductor of its Contemporary Music Ensemble, retiring in 1997. Prausnitz appeared widely as a guest conductor in the U.S. and Europe, garnering a reputation as a leading advocate of contemporary music. He was awarded the Gustav Mahler Medal of Honor of the Bruckner Society of America (1974). He publ. *Score and Podium: A Complete Guide to Conducting* (1983) and *Roger Sessions: A Critical Biography* (1983).—NS/LK/DM

Pražák, Přemysl, Czech musicologist; b. Prague, March 19, 1908; d. there, Oct. 27, 1966. He studied musicology (with Nejedlý), literature, and law at the Univ. of Prague (L.L.D., 1931), and then pursued research on Czech composers.

WRITINGS (all publ. in Prague unless otherwise given): *Bedřich Smetana v české literatuře* (Bedrich Smetana in Czech Literature; Brno, 1939); *Neruda o hudbě* (Neruda on Music; 1941); *Neruda a Smetana* (1942); *Smetanovy zpěvohry* (Smetana's Operas; 1948); ed. with J. Bartoš and J. Plavec, *J.B. Foerster: Jeho životni pout' a tvorba 1859–1949* (J.B. Foerster: His Life and Works 1859–1949; 1949); *Bedřich Smetana* (Martin, 1956); *Světovi mistři hudby v naši vlasti* (World Famous Composers in Our Country; 1958).—LK/DM

Predieri, family of Italian musicians:

(1) **Giacomo (Maria) Predieri,** organist, cornet player, and composer; b. Bologna, April 9, 1611; d. there, 1695. He was active as a cornett player in Bologna's municipal instrumental ensemble, and also a singer at S. Petronio (1636–57), where he was vice-maestro di cappella (1650–57). He was organist at the cathedral of S. Pietro (1679–93). He was a founding member of the

Accademia Filarmonica (1666), and in 1693 was made its principe. He had 2 nephews who studied with him and pursued careers in music:

(2) **Antonio Predieri,** singer; b. Bologna, c. 1650; d. there, 1710. He began his career as a tenor in F. Bassani's *L'inganno trionfato* (1673), and then sang opera in various Italian cities. He was in the service of the dukes of Mantua (1684–87) and Parma (1687–99?), and also sang at the church of the Steccata in Parma (1689–96). He was made a member of Bologna's Accademia Filarmonica in 1685.

(3) **Giacomo Cesare Predieri,** singer and composer; b. Bologna, March 26, 1671; d. there, 1753. He studied with G.P. Colonna, becoming a member of Bologna's Accademia Filarmonica as a singer in 1688, being promoted to composer in 1690; also served as its principe (1698, 1707, 1711). He was maestro di cappella at the cathedral of S. Pietro (1696–1742). He wrote many sacred works, including 11 oratorios (only 1 extant). He had a nephew who was also a musician:

(4) **Luca Antonio Predieri,** violinist and composer; b. Bologna, Sept. 13, 1688; d. there, 1767. He studied violin with Abondio Bini and Tommaso Vitali, and counterpoint with his uncle, as well as with Angelo Predieri (b. Bologna, Jan. 14, 1655; d. there, Feb. 27, 1731), the singer and composer, and Giacomo Antonio Perti. He was an instrumentalist at the church of S. Petronio. He became a member of the Accademia Filarmonica with the rank of composer (1716), serving as its principe (1723); was maestro di cappella at S. Paolo (1725–29), Madonna della Galliera (1726), Arciconfraternitaàdella Vita (1727), and the cathedral of S. Pietro (1728–31). He went to Vienna (1737), where he served as vice-maestro (1739–41) and maestro (1741–51) at the court chapel; returned to Bologna (1765). He wrote 31 operas, of which the following are extant: *Gli auguri spiegati* (Laxenburg, May 3, 1738), *La pace tra la virtù e la bellezza* (Vienna, Oct. 15, 1738), *Perseo* (Vienna, Nov. 4, 1738), *Astrea placata, ossia La felicità della terra* (Vienna, Aug. 28, 1739), and *Zenobia* (Vienna, Aug. 28, 1740). He distinguished himself as a composer of sacred music; of his 7 oratorios, only *Il sacrificio d'Abramo* (Vienna, 1738) and *Isacco figura del Redentore* (Vienna, Feb. 12, 1740) are extant. Other extant works include masses and Mass movements, antiphons, litanies, Psalms, motets, a *Stabat Mater*, cantatas, and a Sinfonia.

BIBL.: R. Ortner, *L.A. P. und sein Wiener Opernschaffen* (Vienna, 1971).—NS/LK/DM

Prégardien, Christoph, German tenor; b. Limburg an der Lahn, Jan. 18, 1956. He gained experience as a member of the Cathedral boy's choir and later the Cathedral choir in his native city. He studied voice with Martin Gründler at the Frankfurt am Main Hochschule für Musik (graduated, 1983) and with Carla Castellani in Milan. In 1978 he won the Federal Republic of Germany vocal competition in Berlin. He sang opera in Frankfurt am Main, Stuttgart, Hamburg, Antwerp, Karlsruhe, Ghent, and other European cities, becoming well known for his roles in Baroque and Classical operas. As a concert and lieder artist, he appeared in major European music centers with notable success. In 1989 he gave a series of early music concerts in London, returning there in 1993 to make his Wigmore Hall recital debut. In 1997 he gave a London recital to mark the bicentenary of Schubert's birth. Prégardien has won particular praise for his interpretations of works by Schütz, Bach, Handel, Buxtehude, Haydn, and Mozart. —NS/LK/DM

Preindl, Josef, Austrian organist, music theorist, and composer; b. Marbach, Jan. 30, 1756; d. Vienna, Oct. 26, 1823. He settled in Vienna, where he studied with Albrechtsberger. He served as organist at the church of Maria am Gestade (1775–78), at the Carmelite church of Vienna-Leopoldstadt (1783–87), and at St. Michael's (1787), and in 1793 became Kapellmeister at St. Peter's. He later served as Vice-Kapellmeister (1795–1809) and Kapellmeister (from 1809) at St. Stephen's. He brought out a *Gesang-Lehre*, op.33 (Vienna, 2nd ed., 1833) and *Wiener Tonschule, oder Elementarbuch zum Studium des Generalbasses, des Contrapunktes, der Harmonie- und Fugen-Lehre* (ed. by I. von Seyfried, Vienna, 1827; 2nd ed., 1832, as *Anweisung zum Generalbasse*). He composed 2 piano concertos, about 14 masses and other sacred works, chamber music, and songs, but much of his output was destroyed during World War II.—NS/LK/DM

Prelleur, Peter, English organist, harpsichordist, and composer who flourished from 1728 to about 1755. He was active in London, where he became organist at St. Alban's, Wood Street, in 1728. In 1735 he was elected first organist at Christ Church, Spitalfields. He also was harpsichordist and composer at the Goodman's Fields Theatre (1728–37) and the New Wells Theatre (from 1737). His stage works included *Harlequin Hermit, or The Arabian Courtezan*, pantomime (London, 1739), *Baucis and Philemon*, interlude (London, 1740), and *Harlequin Student, or The Fall of Pantomime*, pantomime (London, 1741). Among his other works were orch. pieces, songs, and hymns. His *Introduction to Singing* (London, 1735) first appeared as Part 1 of *The Modern Musick-master, or The Universal Musician* (1731). With B. Smith, he ed. *The Harmonious Companion, or The Psalm Singer's Magazine* (London, 1732).—LK/DM

Premru, Raymond (Eugene), American trombonist, conductor, teacher, and composer; b. Elmira, N.Y., June 6, 1934; d. Cleveland, May 8, 1998. He studied at the Oberlin (Ohio) Coll. Cons. of Music, at the Eastman School of Music in Rochester, N.Y. (B.M., 1956), and with Peter Racine Fricker in London. From 1958 to 1988 he played in the Philharmonia Orch. in London, and also was a member of the Philip Jones Brass Ensemble (1960–86) and co-director of the Bobby Lamb-Ray Premru Big Band. He gave master classes in trombone virtuosity throughout the world, and taught at various institutions, including the Oberlin Coll. Cons. of Music (from 1988). In 1997 he won the Cleveland Arts Prize in Music. Among his works are a *Concerto for Orchestra* (1976), 2 syms. (1981; Cleveland, Nov. 23, 1988), Concerto for Trumpet and Strings (1983), *Celebrations* for Timpani and Orch. (1984), *Music* for 3 Trombones, Tuba, and Orch. (1985), other instrumental pieces, and choral works.—NS/LK/DM

Prendcourt, "Captain" de, organist, harpsichordist, teacher, and composer who flourished from 1686 to 1705. He was a page of honor at the court of the Elector of Saxony before being called to England by King James II to serve as Master of the Children in the Chapel Royal (1686–88). Thereafter he was active as a harpsichord teacher. He wrote a treatise on harpsichord playing and thoroughbass and composed 4 harpsichord sonatas.—LK/DM

Prenner, Georg, Austrian composer of Slovenian descent; b. Laibach, date unknown; d. St. Pölten, Feb. 4, 1590. He was active as a copyist at the Prague Kapelle of Archduke Maximilian. After his patron became Emperor Maximilian II, he served as court chaplain and almoner. From 1572 to 1578 he was abbot of the St. Dorothea Monastery in Vienna, and then of the Herzogenburg monastery. In 1587 Emperor Rudolf II made him an imperial councillor. Much of Prenner's extensive output of sacred works appeared in various contemporary anthologies.—LK/DM

Presley, Elvis, the "King of Rock and Roll," perhaps the most popular vocalist of the 20th century and the man who brought rock and roll to the masses; b. East Tupelo, Miss., Jan. 8, 1935; d. Memphis, Tenn., Aug. 16, 1977. Elvis Presley began singing with his parents at the First Assembly of God Church in Tupelo, Miss., as a child and later accompanied them to camp meetings and revivals. He obtained his first guitar for his 11th birthday and moved with his family to Memphis, Tenn., in September 1948. He sang at a high school variety show in late 1952 and became a truck driver after graduating in June 1953. The next month, in the often told story, he went to the small local Sun Records studio to make a private recording of "My Happiness" for his mother. Noticed by secretary Marion Keisker, Presley was later teamed with guitarist Scotty Moore and standup bassist Bill Black by Sun Records president Sam Phillips. The three rehearsed for several months, returning to the Sun studios on July 6, 1954 to record Bill Monroe's "Blue Moon of Kentucky" and Arthur "Big Boy" Crudup's "That's All Right (Mama)." Local disc jockey Dewey Phillips (no relation to Sam) played the latter song on his radio show and the single became a regional hit. Presley made his professional performing debut at Memphis's Overton Park on Aug. 10, 1954, and was greeted ecstatically by an audience enthralled with his rough, passionate vocals and sexually charged persona.

Elvis Presley soon began touring the South with Scotty Moore and Bill Black, billed as "The Hillbilly Cat," as his second and third Sun singles became regional hits. In October 1954 they performed on Shreveport's *Louisiana Hayride* radio show (and would continue to do so until December 1956), appearing on the show's television edition the following March. Released in April 1955, "Baby Let's Play House" became a smash country-and-western hit that summer, followed in September by the top country hit "I Forgot to Remember to Forget," backed with Junior Parker's "Mystery Train." Spotted by "Colonel" Tom Parker, a former carnival barker and erstwhile manager of Eddy Arnold and Hank Snow, Presley signed a new management deal with Parker in November 1955.

Elvis Presley's potent style and raw potential created a bidding war amongst major record labels and RCA won out with an offer of $35,000, an astoundingly high figure for 1955. In January 1956, backed by guitarists Scotty Moore and Chet Atkins, bassist Bill Black and drummer D.J. Fontana (who had joined the trio in July 1955), he completed his first recording sessions in Nashville. Presley made his national television debut on the CBS network *Dorsey Brothers Show* on Jan. 28, 1956, and, within weeks, his first RCA release, "Heartbreak Hotel," became a top pop and country-and- western and smash R&B hit. On June 5, as "I Want You, I Need You, I Love You" was becoming another three-way crossover smash, Presley appeared on *The Milton Berle Show* to an estimated audience of 40 million. Soon, his first recording with The Jordanaires, "Don't Be Cruel"/"Hound Dog," both became top hits in all three fields. Appearing on television's *Ed Sullivan Show* to an estimated audience of 54 million on Sept. 9, Elvis was shown from the waist up only.

Elvis Presley's success was phenomenal, and the three-way crossover smashes continued with "Love Me Tender," "Love Me," "Too Much" and "All Shook Up." During 1956 his first movie, *Love Me Tender,* was released, followed in 1957 by *Loving You* and *Jailhouse Rock.* On Dec. 4, 1956, Presley returned to the Memphis Sun studio to join Sun stalwarts Carl Perkins, Jerry Lee Lewis and Johnny Cash in informally singing and playing a number of gospel songs. Unknown to them, the performance was recorded. Those recordings by the so-called "Million Dollar Quartet" were bootlegged and available in Europe for years before their eventual release in the U.S. in 1990. In January 1957 Elvis recorded the four-song gospel E.P. *Peace in the Valley.* The songs were later included on *Elvis' Christmas Album,* which also contained the secular songs "Blue Christmas," "Santa Bring My Baby Back to Me" and "Santa Claus Is Back in Town."

Elvis Presley's three-way crossover smashes continued with "Teddy Bear," "Jailhouse Rock"/"Treat Me Nice" and "Don't"/"I Beg of You." He was allowed a two-month deferment to complete the movie *King Creole,* but, on March 24, 1958, he was drafted into the Army. Although he was to record only once during the next two years, the hits did not stop. However, after the three-way crossover smashes "Wear My Ring around Your Neck" and "Hard Headed Woman," his subsequent crossover smashes were restricted to two fields, pop and R&B. These included "One Night"/"I Got Stung," "(Now and Then There's) A Fool Such As I"/"I Need Your Love Tonight" and "A Big Hunk of Love," the last four being his only new recordings during his Army stint.

Discharged on March 5, 1960, Elvis Presley subsequently assembled the so-called "Memphis Mafia" entourage that served to protect and insulate him from the public until July 1976. He began recording far less exuberant and vital material with extra musicians to produce a fuller sound. Nonetheless, "Stuck on You,"

"It's Now or Never" and "Are You Lonesome Tonight" became smash pop and R&B hits. His ABC-TV television show *Welcome Home Elvis*, aired May 12, 1960, featured six minutes of Elvis, for which he was paid $125,000. The show was hosted by Frank Sinatra, a man who had earlier denounced rock 'n' roll as "the most brutal, ugly, desperate, vicious form of expression."

After making his first full album of gospel material, *His Hand in Mine*, in 1960, Elvis Presley appeared at his last public performance for eight years in Honolulu on March 25,1961. He spent the 1960s making a series of lucrative but mindless movies usually staged in exotic locations featuring numerous fleshy but virginal women and only the bare semblance of a plot. He also recorded a few non-soundtrack albums as the pop-only smash hits continued with "Surrender," "I Feel So Bad," "(Marie's The Name) His Latest Flame"/"Little Sister," "Can't Help Falling in Love," "Good Luck Charm" and "She's Not You." "Return to Sender" and "(You're the) Devil in Disguise" became his final pop and R&B smashes, with the pop-only major hits "Bossa Nova Baby," "Kissin' Cousins," "Viva Las Vegas," and "Crying in the Chapel" (rec. in 1960) ensuing. To his credit, Elvis Presley recorded perhaps the finest gospel album of his career, *How Great Thou Art*, for 1967 release. He married Priscilla Beaulieu on May 1, 1967, and his only child, daughter Lisa Marie, was born on Feb. 1, 1968.

In 1968, with the first inkling of a revival of interest in 1950s rock 'n' roll, Elvis Presley returned to television for an attempted come-back. Less than a week before the airing of his special, one of his finer later-day singles, "If I Can Dream," became a near-smash pop hit. The special, televised on NBC on Dec. 3, 1968, featured large-scale production numbers and Presley performing in front of a small audience with old associates Scotty Moore and D.J. Fontana (Bill Black had died on Oct. 21, 1965). The special was one of the five highest-rated shows of the television year and included both "If I Can Dream" and the haunting hit "Memories." It represented, in many ways, the peak of Elvis Presley's career.

Elvis Presley returned to Memphis for the first time in 14 years to record his next album, *From Elvis in Memphis*, for which he personally chose the songs. Generally regarded as one of his finest later-day albums, it yielded a smash hit with Mac Davis's socially conscious "In the Ghetto" and included "Power of Love," "Any Day Now" and "Long Black Limousine." Elvis returned to live performance on July 31, 1969 with a month-long engagement at the International Hotel (later the Hilton) in Las Vegas, backed by a 30-piece orchestra, chorus, and a five man combo featuring guitarist James Burton and keyboardist Glen D. Hardin, two of the better instrumentalists in the country. Recordings from the stand comprised the first record of *From Memphis to Vegas/From Vegas to Memphis*, while the second record (later issued as *Elvis Back in Memphis*) was taken from the Memphis sessions. The latter record included "Without Love (There Is Nothing)," "Do You Know Who I Am" and "Stranger in My Own Home." In the meantime, Presley scored a top hit with "Suspicious Minds," a smash hit with Mac Davis's "Don't Cry Daddy," and a major hit with Eddie Rabbit's "Kentucky Rain."

After a month-long appearance at the International Hotel in February 1970, Elvis Presley again toured selected venues across the U.S. until his death in 1977, although he infrequently performed in Las Vegas after 1975. He scored a near-smash country hit with "There Goes My Everything" in 1971 and a smash pop hit with "Burning Love" in 1972. On Jan. 14, 1973, Presley performed at a Honolulu benefit that produced his last major hit album, *Aloha from Hawaii*. Broadcast on NBC-TV and relayed via satellite to 40 countries, the special was viewed by an estimated audience of one billion.

Elvis Presley's fortunes again began to fade. He and Priscilla divorced on Oct. 11, 1973, and his subsequent live performances became careless and mechanical, as rumors of drug abuse and erratic personal behavior began to circulate. Most of his subsequent successes came in the country field, where he had smash hits with "I've Got a Thing about You," "Help Me," It's Midnight," "Hurt," "Moody Blue" and "Way Down." His last live performance took place in Indianapolis on June 26, 1977. On Aug. 16, 1977, Elvis Presley died in his Graceland mansion in Memphis of heart failure due to prescription drug abuse at the age of 42.

Within three months of Elvis Presley's death, his rendition of "My Way," Frank Sinatra's theme song, became a major pop and smash country hit. The spate of Elvis-related books began the month of his death with *Elvis: What Happened?*, by three former members of the "Memphis Mafia." In 1981 Albert Goldman's contemptuous biography *Elvis* was published by McGraw-Hill. The Elvis Presley estate opened Graceland to public viewing in 1982, and the mansion became the second most-visited home in America. In 1983, by means of an out-of-court settlement, "Colonel" Tom Parker severed his connection with the estate, which was overseen by ex-wife Priscilla. Through shrewd merchandising and licensing, Priscilla Presley increased the value of the Presley estate from $5 million to $100 million. In 1992, heir Lisa Marie Presley signed an agreement giving her mother the authority to run the estate for an additional five years (until 1998). "Colonel" Tom Parker died in Las Vegas on Jan. 21, 1997, at the age of 87 of complications from a stroke.

On Elvis's 50th birthday, RCA issued the six-record compilation set of live performances, *A Golden Celebration*. In 1985 Macmillan published *Elvis and Gladys* by Elaine Dundy and Putnam published Priscilla Presley's *Elvis and Me*. Elvis Presley was inducted into the Rock and Roll Hall of Fame in its inaugural year, 1986. In 1987 the Cinemax cable network broadcast *Elvis '56* perhaps the most telling of all filmic biographies. In 1988 *Elvis and Me*, based on Priscilla's book, became the top-rated miniseries of the television season and the lavish multimedia production *Elvis: An American Musical* ran in Las Vegas for two months. An Elvis television series ran on ABC television in 1990 and, in 1992, RCA released the five-CD set *The Complete 50s Masters*, arguably the single most important body of work in the history of rock 'n' roll. On Elvis's 58th birthday the U.S. Postal Service issued 500 million Elvis stamps, of which an estimated 60% were never used. During 1994 longtime

Elvis friend Joe Esposito's *Good Rockin' Tonight: Twenty Years on the Road and on the Town with Elvis* was published by Simon and Schuster, and Peter Guralnick's *Last Train to Memphis: The Rise of Elvis Presley* was published by Little, Brown. In 1996 the first ballet based on the music of Elvis Presley, *Blue Suede Shoes*, premiered in Cleveland, and the production made its West Coast debut in San Jose, Calif., in 1997.

DISC.: EARLY RECORDINGS: *Elvis Presley* (1956); *Elvis* (1956); *Elvis' Christmas Album* (1957); *For LP Fans Only* (1959); *A Date with Elvis* (1959/1989); *Elvis Is Back* (1960/1989); *I Was the One* (rec. 1956–60; rel. 1983); *The First Live Recordings* (rec. 1955–56; rel. 1984); *Rocker* (rec. 1956–57; rel. 1984); *The Complete Sun Sessions* (rec. 1954–55; rel. 1987); *Stereo '57* (1989); *The Million Dollar Quartet* (rec. Dec. 4, 1956; rel. 1990); *The Complete '50s Masters* (1992); *Elvis '56* (1996); *The Elvis Tapes* (interviews recorded in 1957; 1977). **SOUNDTRACKS:** *Loving You* (1957/1988); *King Creole* (1958); *G. I. Blues* (1960); *Blue Hawaii* (1961); *Girls! Girls! Girls!* (1962); *It Happened at the World's Fair* (1963); *Fun in Acapulco* (1963); *Kissin' Cousins* (1964); *Roustabout* (1964); *Girl Happy* (1965); *Harum Scarum* (1965); *Frankie and Johnny* (1966); *Paradise Hawaiian Style* (1966); *Spinout* (1966); *Double Trouble* (1967); *Clambake* (1967); *Speedway* (1968); *That's the Way It Is* (1970); *This Is Elvis* (selections; 1981); *Jailhouse Rock* (1997). **GOSPEL ALBUMS:** *His Hand in Mind* (1960); *How Great Thou Art* (1967); *You'll Never Walk Alone* (1971); *He Touched Me* (1972); *He Walks Beside Me* (1978); *Elvis Gospel, 1957–1971* (1989). **CHRISTMAS ALBUM:** *Elvis's Christmas Album* (1957); *Elvis Sings "The Wonderful World of Christmas"* (1971). **OTHER RCA ALBUMS 1960–77:** *Something for Everybody* (1961); *Pot Luck* (1962); *Elvis for Everyone* (1965/1990); *Elvis (TV Special)* (1968); *From Elvis in Memphis* (1969); *From Memphis to Vegas/From Vegas to Memphis* (1969); *On Stage (February 1970)* (1970); *Back in Memphis* (1970); *Elvis Country* (1971); *Love Letters from Elvis* (1971); *Elvis Now* (1972); *Live at Madison Square Garden* (1972); *Aloha from Hawaii* (1973); *Elvis* (1973); *Raised on Rock* (1973); *Good Times* (1974); *Live on Stage in Memphis* (1974); *Having Fun with Elvis on Stage* (1974); *Promised Land* (1975); *Today* (1975); *From Elvis Presley Boulevard* (1976); *Welcome to My World* (1977); *Moody Blue* (1977); *In Concert* (1977); *The Alternate Aloha* (1988); *The Lost Album* (rec. in Nashville in 1963–64; rel. 1991); *I'm 10,000 Years Old/Elvis Country* (1993).

BIBL.: J. Hopkins, *E.: A Biography* (N.Y., 1971); P. Lichter, *E. In Hollywood* (N.Y., 1975); M. Mann, *E. and The Colonel: From the Intimate Diaries of May Mann* (N.Y., 1975); R. Barry, *The E. P. American Discography* (Phillipsburg, N.J., 1976); W. A. Harbinson, *The Illustrated E.* (N.Y., 1976); P. Jones. *E.* (London, 1976); S. Zmijewsky, *The Films and Career of E. P.* (Secaucus, N.J., 1976); M. Farren, compiler, *E. In His Own Words* (N.Y., 1977); R. West, S. West, and D. Hebler, as told to S. Dunleavy, *E.: What Happened?* (N.Y., 1977); P. Lichter, *The Boy Who Dared to Rock: The Definitive E.* (Garden City, N.Y., 1978; N.Y., 1982); J. Roggero, *E. In Concert* (N.Y., 1979); J. Hopkins, *E.: The Final Years* (N.Y., 1980; 1983); M. Crumbaker with G. Tucker, *Up and Down with E. P.* (N.Y., 1981); A. Goldman, *E.* (N.Y., 1981); M. Hawkins and C. Escott, *The Illustrated Discography* (London, 1981); J. A. Whisler, *E. P. Reference Guide and Discography* (Metuchen, N.J., 1981); F. L. Worth and S. D. Tamerius, *All about E.* (N.Y., 1981); R. Carr, *E. P.: An Illustrated Record* (N.Y., 1982); D. Marsh, *E.* (N.Y., 1982, 1992); M. Torgoff, ed., *The Complete E.* (N.Y., 1982); L. Cotten and H. A. DeWitt, *Jailhouse Rock: The Bootleg Records of E. P., 1970–1983* (Ann Arbor, Mich., 1983); J. Tobler and R. Wootton, *E.: The Legend and the Music* (N.Y., 1983); W. Sauers. *E. P., A Complete Reference* (Jefferson, N.C., 1984); P. G. Hammontree, *E. P., A Bio-Bibliography* (Westport, Conn., 1985); P. Presley with S. Harmon, *E. and Me* (N.Y., 1985); L. Cotton, *All Shook Up: E. Day-By-Day, 1954–1977* (Ann Arbor, Mich., 1985); L. Cotton, *The E. Catalog* (Garden City, N.Y., 1987); A. Goldman, *E. P.* (London, 1987); D. Vellenga, *E. and The Colonel* (N.Y., 1988); F. L. Worth and S. D. Tamerius, *E.: His Life from A to Z* (Chicago, Ill., 1988; N.Y., 1992); L. Geller and J. Spector with P. Romanowski, *If I Can Dream: E.'s Own Story* (N.Y., 1989); G. McLafferty, *E. P. in Hollywood: Celluloid Sell-Out* (London, 1989); E. Greenwood and K. Tracy, *The Boy Who Would Be King: An Intimate Portrait of E. P.* (N.Y., 1990); C. Latham and J. Sakol, *"E" Is for E.: An A-to-Z Illustrated Guide to the King of Rock and Roll* (N.Y., 1990); G. Marcus, *Dead E.: A Chronicle of a Cultural Obsession* (N.Y., 1991); C. C. Thompson II and J. P. Cale, *The Death of E.: What Really Happened* (N.Y., 1991); K. Quain, ed., *The E. Reader: Texts and Sources on the King of Rock 'n' Roll* (N.Y., 1992); H. A. DeWitt, *E., The Sun Years: The Story of E. P. in the 1950s* (Ann Arbor, Mich., 1993); A. Schroer, *Private E.: The Missing Years, E. in Germany* (N.Y., 1993); W. Allen, *E.* (N.Y., 1994); J. Esposito and E. Oumano, *Good Rockin' Tonight: Twenty Years on the Road and on the Town with E.* (N.Y., 1994); P. Guralnick, *Last Train to Memphis: The Rise of E. P.* (Boston, Mass., 1994); P. J. Pierce, *The Ultimate E.: E. P. Day by Day* (N.Y., 1994); D. Stanley, *The E. Encyclopedia* (Los Angeles, Calif., 1994); A. Nash, *E. Aaron P.: Revelations from the Memphis Mafia* (N.Y., 1995); R. Gordon, *The King on the Road: E. on Tour, 1954–1977* (N.Y., 1996); G. B. Rodman, *E. after E.: The Posthumous Career of a Living Legend* (London, N.Y., 1996); P. O. Whitman, *The Inner E.: A Psychological Biography of E. Aaron P.* (N.Y., 1996); S. Moore and J. Dickerson, *That's Alright, E.: The Untold Story of E.'s First Guitarist and Manager* (N.Y., 1997); P. Guralnick, *Careless Love* (Boston, Mass., 1998).—**BH**

Presser, Theodore, American music publisher; b. Pittsburgh, July 3, 1848; d. Philadelphia, Oct. 27, 1925. He studied at the New England Cons. of Music in Boston with S. Emery, G.E. Whiting, J.C.D. Parker, and B. Lang, then at the Leipzig Cons. with Zwintscher and Jadassohn. In 1883 he founded in Philadelphia the *Etude*, a well-known music monthly of which he was ed. until 1907; James F. Cooke was its ed. from 1908 to 1949; it discontinued publication in 1957. Shortly after the foundation of the *Etude*, Presser established a publishing house, the Theodore Presser Co., for music and books about music, which has come to be one of the important firms in the U.S. It acquired the catalogues of the John Church Co. (1930), the Oliver Ditson Co. (1931), the Mercury Music Corp. (1969), Elkan-Vogel (1970), and the American Music Edition (1981). Its headquarters removed to Bryn Mawr, Pa., in 1949. In 1906 he founded the Presser Home for Retired Music Teachers, which in 1908 moved to Germantown. In 1916 he established the Presser Foundation to administer this Home, to provide relief for deserving musicians, and to offer scholarships in colleges and univs. in the U.S. Presser wrote instructive pieces and studies for piano. He was a co-founder of the Music Teachers National Assn. (1876).

BIBL.: C. Yoder, *T. P., Educator, Publisher, Philanthropist: Selected Contributions to the Music Teaching Profession in America* (diss., Univ. of Ill., 1978).—**NS/LK/DM**

Pressler, Menahem, esteemed German-born American pianist and pedagogue; b. Magdeburg, Dec.

16, 1923. He was taken to Palestine by his family after the Hiterlization of Germany, and studied piano with Eliah Rudiakow and Leo Kestenberg. He also studied with Egon Petri and Edward Steuermann. In 1946 he won the Debussy Prize at the San Francisco Piano Competition. He joined the faculty of the Ind. Univ. School of Music in Bloomington in 1955, the same year that he helped to found the Beaux Arts Trio, which subsequently acquired a distinguished place among the leading trios of the day via its many appearances in the world's major music centers and festivals. The trio also made numerous recordings, and garnered several awards for excellence. Pressler also made appearances as a soloist with orchs. and as a recitalist. On Feb. 21, 1996, he made his Carnegie Hall recital debut in N.Y. In 2000 he celebrated his 45th anniversary as the pianist of the Beaux Arts Trio, as well as a faculty member at the Ind. Univ. School of Music, where he held the title of Distinguished Prof.

BIBL.: N. Delbanco, *The Beaux Arts Trio: A Portrait* (London, 1985).—**NS/LK/DM**

Presti, Ida, French guitarist; b. Suresnes, May 31, 1924; d. Rochester, N.Y., April 24, 1967. She learned to play the guitar and the piano by the time she was 6. Soon thereafter she made her public debut as a guitarist in Paris. At age 10, she made her first recording. Following her appearance with the Société des Concerts du Conservatoire in Paris in 1936, she toured widely. Upon her marriage to **Alexandre Lagoya**, the couple formed a notable guitar duo in 1950 and toured the world. Presti died while on a tour with her husband in the U.S. Presti and Lagoya made transcriptions of keyboard works by several great masters of the past, and also commissioned works by such contemporary composers as Castelnuovo-Tedesco, Rodrígo, and Jolivet.—**LK/DM**

Preston, Simon (John), distinguished English organist, harpsichordist, conductor, and pedagogue; b. Bournemouth, Aug. 4, 1938. He was a chorister at King's Coll., Cambridge (1949–51), where he received instruction in organ from Hugh McLean. After further keyboard training from Anthony Brown at Canford School, he continued his studies with C.H. Trevor at the Royal Academy of Music in London (1956–58), and subsequently was an organ scholar at King's Coll., Cambridge (1958–62). He made his formal debut as an organist at the Royal Festival Hall in London in 1962, and from 1962 to 1967 was sub-organist at Westminster Abbey. After conducting the Oxford Bach Choir (1967–68), he was organist and lecturer at Christ Church, Oxford (1970–81); then was organist and master of the choristers at Westminster Abbey (1981–87). He toured widely as an organ virtuoso and gave master classes on both sides of the Atlantic, and also conducted much choral music. His repertoire ranges from Handel to Messiaen.—**NS/LK/DM**

Preston, Thomas, English organist and composer; b. place and date unknown; d. probably in Windsor, after 1559. He composed a Mass for Easter Day and several organ pieces for the Latin service.—**LK/DM**

Pretenders, The, one of the most successful groups to emerge from the British New Wave scene of the late 1970s. **MEMBERSHIP:** Chrissie Hynde, lead voc., rhythm gtr. (b. Akron, Ohio, Sept. 7, 1951); James Honeyman-Scott, lead gtr., kybd., voc. (b. Hereford, England, Nov. 4, 1956; d. London, England, June 16, 1982); Pete Farndon, bs. (b. Hereford, England, June 2, 1952; d. London, England, April 14, 1983); Martin Chambers, drm. (b. Hereford, England, Sept. 4, 1951). James Honeyman-Scott was replaced by Robbie McIntosh and Pete Farndon was replaced by Malcolm Foster in 1982. Foster and Martin Chambers left in 1984, to be replaced by bassist T. M. Stevens and drummer Blair Cunningham. Various musicians played with Hynde in different combinations between 1985 and 1993. In 1994 the entire group was reconstituted with Hynde, Chambers, Adam Seymour on guitar, and Andy Hobson on bass.

The Pretenders were fronted by American-born singer-songwriter Chrissie Hynde. Building on the tradition started by Patti Smith, Hynde redefined the role of women vocalists in contemporary rock by offering provocative, aggressive songs of desire, defiance, and autonomy from a distinctly female perspective as well as traditional seductive songs of romance. One of the most compelling female singers in rock, Hynde served as an inspiration to the so-called riot grrrls of the 1990s such as Courtney Love of Hole and Liz Phair.

Chrissie Hynde taught herself to sing and play guitar and wrote songs as a teenager. She studied art at Kent State Univ. for a time, and performed on the Cleveland rock circuit before moving to London in 1973. There she worked as a rock critic for the *New Musical Express* while attempting to join various bands, including two with musicians who later formed the Clash and the Damned. Finally, in 1978 she formed the Pretenders with three Hereford-based musicians, James Honeyman-Scott, Pete Farndon, and Martin Chambers. The group recorded a demonstration tape, and Nick Lowe offered to produce their first single, "Stop Your Sobbing," written by the Kinks' Ray Davies. The song became a British hit, as did the follow-ups "Kid," written by Hynde, and "Brass in Pocket (I'm Special)," cowritten by Hynde and Honeyman-Scott.

The group toured extensively around Great Britain in 1979 and recorded their debut album under producer Chris Thomas. *The Pretenders* became an instant bestseller, staying on the charts for a year and a half while yielding a major American hit with "Brass in Pocket." The stunning debut, often regarded as one of the finest rock debut albums ever, included "Kid," "Stop Your Sobbing" (a minor hit), the aggressively autonomous "Precious," and the embittered "Up the Neck," as well as "The Wait" and the ballad "Lovers of Today."

Touring incessantly and becoming a major American concert attraction by 1980, the Pretenders issued a five-song mini-album before completing *Pretenders II*. The album included the British hits "Talk of the Town" and "Message of Love" as well as "The Adultress," "Bad Boys Get Spanked," and Ray Davies's "Go to Sleep." The group again toured America in 1981 and 1982, but Pete Farndon was dismissed from the band only days before James Honeyman-Scott was found dead in a friend's apartment on June 16, 1982. Hynde and Chambers recruited Bill Bremner and Tory Butler to record "Back on the Chain Gang," and the song became a smash hit in late 1982.

Shaken by the drug-related deaths of Honeyman-Scott and then Pete Farndon, Chrissie Hynde withdrew from music for a time after the birth of her daughter by Ray Davies. Hynde and Chambers reconstituted the Pretenders with guitarist Robbie McIntosh and bassist Malcolm Foster, yet their next album, *Learning to Crawl*, was largely recorded with session musicians. The album included four hits: "Back on the Chain Gang," "Middle of the Road," "Show Me," and a powerful remake of the Persuaders' 1972 hit "Thin Line Between Love and Hate."

The Pretenders resumed touring in 1984, but personnel changes continued with the departures of Martin Chambers and Malcolm Foster, and Hynde dismantled the band in 1985. She performed solo at Live Aid in 1985 and scored a major hit that summer with a remake of Sonny and Cher's "I Got You Babe," backed by UB40. In 1986 she reconstituted the Pretenders with Robbie McIntosh and Americans T. M. Stevens and Blair Cunningham for the rather mellow *Get Close*. Dominated by love songs, the album produced a major hit with "Don't Get Me Wrong" and a minor hit with "My Baby." Other tracks included "When I Change My Life," "Tradition of Love," and "How Much Did You Get for Your Soul," the album's only angry song. In 1987 Hynde again toured, this time with McIntosh, Foster, and keyboardist Rupert Black, with Iggy Pop as her opening act.

In 1990 Chrissie Hynde recorded the inconsequential *packed!* album. She eventually reconstituted the Pretenders in 1994 with guitarist Adam Seymour, bassist Andy Hobson, and former drummer Martin Chambers for *Last of the Independents* and her first tour in seven years. With the songs largely cowritten by Hynde and Seymour, the album, hailed as the Pretenders' most cohesive in years, featured the major hit "I'll Stand by You," "Night in My Veins," and the vehement "Money Talk" and "I'm a Mother."

DISC.: *The P.* (1980); *The P. (mini)* (1981); *P. II* (1981); *Learning to Crawl* (1984); *Get Close* (1986); *The Singles* (1987); *packed!* (1990); *Last of the Independents* (1994); *Isle of View* (1995).

BIBL.: C. Salewicz, *The P.* (London, 1982); I. Tharper, *The P.* (N.Y., 1985).—**BH**

Prêtre, Georges, prominent French conductor; b. Waziers, Aug. 14, 1924. He studied at the Douai Cons., then at the Paris Cons., and also received instruction in conducting from Cluytens. He made his debut as a conductor at the Marseilles Opera in 1946, and subsequently had guest engagements in Lille, Casablanca, and Toulouse. He then was music director of the Paris Opéra-Comique (1955–59), and subsequently conducted at the Paris Opéra (from 1959), where he served as music director (1970–71). In 1959 he made his U.S. debut at the Chicago Lyric Opera; in 1961 he appeared for the first time in London. On Oct. 17, 1964, he made his first appearance at the Metropolitan Opera in N.Y., conducting *Samson et Dalila*. He appeared as a guest conductor

with many of the major opera houses and orchs. of the world in succeeding years; also served as principal guest conductor of the Vienna Sym. Orch. (1986–91). —**NS/LK/DM**

Preumayr, German-born Swedish family of musicians, all brothers:

(1) Johan Conrad Preumayr, bassoonist; b. Koblenz, Dec. 1775; d. Stockholm, March 20, 1819. He was a bassoonist in the royal orch. in Stockholm from 1811.

(2) Carl Josef Preumayr, bass, actor, cellist, and bassoonist; b. Koblenz, July 2, 1780; d. Stockholm, July 20, 1849. He appeared as a bass and an actor at the Royal Theater in Stockholm, where he became known for his portrayals of Osmin, the Commendatore, and Sarastro. He also was a cellist and bassoonist in the royal orch. in Stockholm.

(3) Frans Carl Preumayr, bassoonist; b. Ehrenbretstein, April 24, 1782; d. Stockholm, Feb. 15, 1853. He was principal bassoonist in the royal orch. in Stockholm. In 1830 he made a highly successful tour of Europe as a virtuoso.—**LK/DM**

Previn, André (George) (real name, **Andreas Ludwig Priwin**), brilliant German-born American pianist, conductor, and composer; b. Berlin, April 6, 1929. He was of Russian-Jewish descent. He showed an unmistakable musical gift as a child; his father, a lawyer, was an amateur musician who gave him his early training; they played piano, 4-hands, together at home. At the age of 6, he was accepted as a pupil at the Berlin Hochschule für Musik, where he studied piano with Breithaupt; as a Jew, however, he was compelled to leave school in 1938. The family then went to Paris, where he continued his studies at the Cons., Dupré being one of his teachers. In 1939 the family emigrated to the U.S., settling in Los Angeles, where his father's cousin, Charles Previn, was music director at Universal Studios in Hollywood. He took lessons in composition with Joseph Achron, Toch, and Castelnuovo-Tedesco. He became a naturalized American citizen in 1943. Even before graduating from high school, he obtained employment at MGM, becoming an orchestrator there and later one of its music directors; he also became a fine jazz pianist. He served in the U.S. Army (1950–52). While stationed in San Francisco, he took lessons in conducting with Monteux, then music director of the San Francisco Sym. During these years, he wrote much music for films and received Academy Awards for his arrangements of *Gigi* (1958), *Porgy and Bess* (1959), *Irma la Douce* (1963), and *My Fair Lady* (1964). Throughout this period he continued to appear as a concert pianist. In 1962 he made his formal conducting debut with the St. Louis Sym. Orch., and conducting soon became his principal vocation. From 1967 to 1969 he was conductor-in-chief of the Houston Sym. Orch. In 1968 he assumed the post of principal conductor of the London Sym. Orch., retaining it with distinction until 1979. In 1993 he was named its Conductor Laureate. In 1976 he became music director of the Pittsburgh Sym. Orch., a position he held with similar distinction until a dispute with the management led to his resignation in 1984. He had already been engaged as music director of the Royal Phil. of London in 1982, a position he held from 1985 to 1987. He then served as its principal conductor from 1987 to 1992, and thereafter was its Conductor Laureate. Previn also accepted appointment as music director of the Los Angeles Phil., after resigning his Pittsburgh position; he formally assumed his duties in Los Angeles in 1985, but gave up this position in 1990 after disagreements with the management over administrative procedures. During his years as a conductor of the London Sym. Orch., he took it on a number of tours to the U.S., as well as to Russia, Japan, South Korea, and Hong Kong. He also took the Pittsburgh Sym. Orch. on acclaimed tours of Europe in 1978 and 1982. While continuing to make regular appearances as a guest conductor with the world's leading orchs., he also continued to compose. His song cycle, *Honey and Rue* (N.Y., Jan. 5, 1992, Kathleen Battle soloist, composer conducting), became his most widely performed score. On Sept. 19, 1998, he conducted the premiere of his opera *A Streetcar Named Desire*, after Tennessee Williams, at the San Francisco Opera. Previn received an honorary knighthood from Queen Elizabeth II of England in 1996, and in 1999 he was awarded the Commander's Cross of the Order of Merit of the Federal Republic of Germany. He ed. the book *Orchestra* (Garden City, N.Y., 1979), and also publ. *André Previn's Guide to Music* (London, 1983) and the autobiographical *No Minor Chords: My Days in Hollywood* (N.Y., 1991). He was married four times (and divorced thrice): to the jazz singer Betty Bennett, to the jazz poet Dory Langdon (who made a career of her own as composer and singer of pop songs), to the actress Mia Farrow, and in 1982 to Heather Hales.

WORKS: DRAMATIC: *Every Good Boy Deserves Favor*, play for Actors and Orch. (1976); *A Streetcar Named Desire*, opera after Tennessee Williams (San Francisco, Sept. 19, 1998, composer conducting); various film scores. **ORCH.:** Cello Concerto (1960); Guitar Concerto (1971); *Principals* (Pittsburgh, Sept. 12, 1980, composer conducting); *Reflections* (Saratoga Springs, N.Y., Aug. 13, 1981); Piano Concerto (Nottingham, June 16, 1985, Vladimir Ashkenazy soloist, composer conducting). **CHAMBER:** *2 Little Serenades* for Violin and Piano (1970); *4 Outings* for Horn, 2 Trumpets, Trombone, and Tuba (London, Aug. 1974); *Peaches* for Flute and Piano (1978); *Triolet* for Horn, 4 Trumpets, 4 Trombones, and Tuba (1985); *A Wedding Waltz* for 2 Oboes and Piano (1986); Cello Sonata (Amsterdam, March 28, 1993); Trio for Piano, Oboe, and Bassoon (1994; N.Y., Jan. 31, 1996); Violin Sonata, *Vineyard* (1994; Katonah, N.Y., July 14, 1996); *Hoch soll er Leben* for Horn, 2 Trumpets, Trombone, and Tuba (N.Y., July 18, 1997); Bassoon Sonata (1997; N.Y., April 25, 1999); *Tango, Song, and Dance* for Violin and Piano (1998). **Piano:** *Paraphrase on a Theme of William Walton* (1973); *The Invisible Drummer* (1974); *Pages from My Calendar* (1974); *Matthew's Piano Book* (1979); *Variations on a Theme by Haydn* (1990). **VOCAL:** *5 Songs* for Mezzo-soprano and Piano, after Philip Larkin (1977); *Honey and Rue*, song cycle for Soprano and Orch., after Toni Morrison (1991; N.Y., Jan. 5, 1992, Kathleen Battle, soloist, composer conducting); *Sallie Chisum Remembers Billy the Kid* for Soprano and Piano (Lenox, Mass., Aug. 24, 1994; also for Soprano and Orch., 1995; Boston, March 21, 1996); *4 Songs* for Soprano, Cello, and Piano, after Toni Morisson (N.Y., Nov. 27, 1994); *Vocalise* for Soprano, Cello, and Orch. (1995; Boston,

March 21, 1996); *2 Remembrances* for Soprano, Alto Flute, and Piano (1995; Lenox, Mass., July 16, 1996); *The Magic Number* for Soprano and Orch. (1995; N.Y., April 17, 1997).

BIBL.: E. Greenfield, *A. P.* (N.Y., 1973); M. Bookspan and R. Yockey, *A. P.: A Biography* (Garden City, N.Y., 1981); H. Ruttencutter, *P.* (London, 1985).—NS/LP

Previtali, Fernando, prominent Italian conductor; b. Adria, Feb. 16, 1907; d. Rome, Aug. 1, 1985. He studied cello, piano, and composition at the Turin Cons., then was Gui's assistant at the Maggio Musicale Fiorentino (1928–36). He was chief conductor of the Rome Radio orch. (1936–43; 1945–53) and also conducted at Milan's La Scala and at other major Italian opera houses. From 1953 to 1973 he was chief conductor of the Orchestra Sinfonica dell'Accademia Nazionale di Santa Cecilia in Rome, which he led on tours abroad. On Dec. 15, 1955, he made his U.S. debut as a guest conductor with the Cleveland Orch. Previtali became well known for his advocacy of contemporary Italian composers, and conducted the premieres of numerous operas and orch. works. He was also a composer; wrote the ballet, *Allucinazioni* (Rome, 1945), choral works, chamber music, etc. He publ. *Guida allo studio della direzione d'orchestra* (Rome, 1951).—NS/LK/DM

Previte, Bobby, adventurous drummer and imaginative composer; b. Niagara Falls, N.Y., July 16, 1957. He studied at Buffalo Univ. and in 1980 moved to N.Y.C. where he quickly established himself in the "Downtown" scene, collaborating with cutting-edge innovators such as John Zorn, Wayne Horvitz, Bill Frisell, and Elliott Sharp. Previte first recorded his own music in the mid-1980s for the European label Sound Aspects. His own creations are marked by a high-spirited mixture of influences, but they generally maintain a bustling, jazz-based core. Previte has been recognized as an exceptional talent, winning the titles "Composer Deserving of Wider Recognition" (in the 1990 *Down Beat* Critics Poll) and "Hot Jazz Artist of 1991" (from *Rolling Stone*). He has performed his music at major international festivals and toured throughout the United States, Europe, Canada, Australia, and the Far East. In demand as a composer, Previte has written commissioned works for the String Trio of N.Y., the Philadelphia-based chamber ensemble Relache, and for the Moscow Circus (see his Gramavision album *Music of the Moscow Circus*). The latter piece premiered at the Gershwin Theater in N.Y.C. on Nov. 5, 1991. He arranged the Charles Mingus tune "Open Letter to Duke" for Hal Willner's *Weird Nightmare—Meditations on Mingus* recording, and created a new electronic score for the International Puppet Festival, which debuted at the Public Theater in N.Y.C. in the fall of 1992. The drummer also continues to regularly tour overseas with his various groups, has recorded during these tours, and conducted numerous workshops, lectures, and master classes in Switzerland, Germany, and Australia, as well as in the United States at the Eastman School of Music in Rochester, N.Y., and the New School in N.Y.C. He continues to work on new projects, including his band the Horse, an 11-piece ensemble that plays jazz of the early 1970s at weekly performances at the Knitting Factory in N.Y.C. The drummer established a new recording label, Depth of Field, which, in September 1997, released *Euclid's Nightmare*, a duo with John Zorn. A new quartet recording from this label was due out in spring 1998. He has released over 12 recordings as a leader and appeared on numerous others as a sideman. If you're looking for more info on Previte, see his website (http://www.bobbyprevite.com).

DISC.: *Bump the Renaissance* (1985); *Pushing the Envelope* (1987); *Dull Bang, Gushing Sound, Human Shriek* (1987); *Claude's Late Morning* (1988); *Empty Suits* (1990); *Music of the Moscow Circus* (1991); *Weather Clear, Track Fast* (1991); *Slay the Suitors* (1994); *Hue and Cry* (1994); *Too Close to the Pole* (1996); *My Man in Sydney* (1997); *Euclid's Nightmare* (1997); *Latin for Travelers* (1997).—**NAL**

Prévost, (Joseph Gaston Charles) André, Canadian composer; b. Hawkesbury, Ontario, July 30, 1934. He studied harmony and counterpoint with Isabelle Delorme and Papineau-Couture and composition with Pépin (premier prix, 1960) at the Montreal Cons. After studying analysis with Messiaen at the Paris Cons., and receiving further instruction from Dutilleux at the Paris École Normale de Musique (1961), he returned to Canada (1962) and was active as a teacher. Following studies in electronic music with Michel Phillipot at the Paris ORTF (1964), he worked with Schuller, Martino, Copland, and Kodály at the Berkshire Music Center in Tanglewood (summer, 1964); then taught at the Univ. of Montreal (from 1964). In 1986 he was made an Officer of the Order of Canada.

WORKS: ORCH.: *Poème de l'infini*, symphonic poem (1960); *Scherzo* for Strings (1960); *Fantasmes* (Montreal, Nov. 22, 1963; posthumously dedicated to President John F. Kennedy); *Pyknon*, pièce concertante for Violin and Orch. (1966); *Célébration* (1966); *Diallèle* (Toronto, May 30, 1968); *Evanescence* (Ottawa, April 7, 1970); *Hommage (à Beethoven)* for 14 Strings (1970–71); *Chorégraphie I (...Munich, September 1972...)* (1972–73; Toronto, April 22, 1975; inspired by the Munich Olympics tragedy), *II (E = MC²)* (1976), *III* (1976), and *IV* (1978; London, Ontario, Jan. 10, 1979); *Ouverture* (1975); Cello Concerto (1976; Winnipeg, Dec. 6, 1979); *Paraphrase* for String Quartet and Orch. (Toronto, April 29, 1980); *Cosmophonie* (1985); *Cantate pour cordes* for Chamber Orch. (1987). **CHAMBER:** *Pastorale* for 2 Harps (1955); *Fantasie* for Cello and Piano (1956); 2 string quartets (1958; *Ad pacem*, 1971–72); *Mobiles* for Flute, Violin, Viola, and Cello (1959–60); Violin Sonata (1960–61; arr. as a ballet as *Primordial*, 1968); 2 cello sonatas (1962, arr. for Violin and Piano or Ondes Martenot, 1967; 1985); *Triptyque* for Flute, Oboe, and Piano (1962); *Mouvement* for Brass Quintet (1963); *Ode au St. Laurent* for Optional Narrator and String Quartet (1965); Suite for String Quintet (1968); *Improvisation II* for Cello (1976) and *III* for Viola (1976); Violin Sonata (1979); Clarinet Quintet (London, England, Oct. 26, 1988). **KEYBOARD: Piano:** *4 Préludes* for 2 Pianos (1961). **Organ:** *5 Variations sur un thème grégorien* (1956); *Variations en Passacaille* (1984). **VOCAL:** *Terre des hommes* for 2 Narrators, 3 Choruses, and Orch. (Montreal, April 29, 1967); *Psaume 148* for Chorus, Brass, and Organ (Guelph, May 1, 1971); *Hiver dans l'âme* for Baritone and Orch. (1978); *Missa de profundis* for Chorus and Organ (1973); other choruses; songs.—**NS/LK/DM**

Prévost, Eugène-Prosper, French conductor and composer; b. Paris, April 23, 1809; d. New Orleans,

Aug. 19, 1872. He studied at the Paris Cons. with Le Sueur, winning the Grand Prix de Rome in 1831 with the cantata *Bianca Capello*. He conducted theatrical music in Le Havre (1835–38), then went to New Orleans, where he conducted until 1862. He was active in Paris (1862–67) before returning to New Orleans as a singing master. He produced several operas in Paris, of which *Cosimo* (Opéra-Comique, Oct. 13, 1835) was the most successful; another, *Blanche et Rene*, was given in New Orleans in 1861. He also wrote oratorios and masses.—**NS/LK/DM**

Prey, Claude, French composer; b. Fleury-sur-Andelle, May 30, 1925; d. Paris, Feb. 14, 1998. He received training in piano and organ before settling in Paris in 1945, where he studied letters and aesthetics at the Sorbonne. In 1947 he entered the Cons. and took courses with Messiaen (harmony) and Milhaud (composition). He completed his training with Mignone in Rio de Janeiro, with Frazzi in Siena, and at Laval Univ. in Quebec. In 1963 he won the Prix Italia for his chamber opera *Le Coeur révélateur*.

WORKS: *Le Phénix*, opera buffa (1957); *Lettres perdues*, radiophonic opera (1960; Paris, April 24, 1961); *La Dictée*, lyric monodrama (1961); *Le Coeur révélateur*, chamber opera (1961; Paris, Oct. 7, 1964); *L'Homme occis*, opera (1963; concert perf., Radio France, Nov. 10, 1975); *Jonas*, opera-oratorio (1963; concert perf., Paris, Nov. 3, 1966); *Mots croisés*, opera (1964; Paris, Nov. 17, 1978); *Donna mobile I*, opera (1964; Tours, Aug. 11, 1985); *Métamorphose d'Echo*, mono-mimo-mélodrame (1965); *La Noirceur du lait*, "opéra-test" (1966; Strasbourg, June 9, 1967); *On veut la lumière! Allons-y!*, opera-parody (Angers, Dec. 12, 1968); *Fêtes de la faim*, opera for comedians (Avignon, July 26, 1969); *Jeu de l'oie*, opera (1970); *Théâtrophone*, "opera a cappella" (1971); *Donna mobile II*, "opéra-kit" (Avignon, Aug. 5, 1972); *Les liaisons dangereuses*, "opéra épistolaire" (1973; Strasbourg, Feb. 5, 1974); *Young Libertad*, "opera-study" (1975; Lyons, March 5, 1976); *La Grand-mère française*, "opéra illustré" (Avignon, July 20, 1978); *Utopopolis*, "opéra-chanson" (Paris, April 11, 1980); *L'Escalier de Chambord*, opera (Tours, March 20, 1981); *Scénarios VII*, "motet-opéra" (1981); *Lunedi blu*, short opera (Paris, June 3, 1982); *Pauline*, chamber opera (Fresnoy, May 9, 1983); *O comme eau*, "ode homophone" for Voices and Early Instruments (Paris, Nov. 30, 1984); *Paysages pacifiques*, "mélo-cycle" for Soprano, Flute, Cello, and Piano (Paris, Dec. 17, 1986); *Le Rouge et le Noir*, opera (Aix-en-Provence, July 20, 1989); *Sommaire Soleil*, "melodrama" (1991; Paris, March 21, 1995); *Parlons Fric*, comic opera (1992); *Sitôt le septuor*, opera (1993).—**NS/LK/DM**

Prey, Hermann, outstanding German baritone; b. Berlin, July 11, 1929; d. Munich, July 22, 1998. He studied with Günther Baum and Harry Gottschalk at the Berlin Hochschule für Musik. He won 1st prize in a vocal competition organized by the U.S. Army (1952), and that same year made his operatic debut as the second prisoner in *Fidelio* in Wiesbaden. After appearing in the U.S., he joined the Hamburg State Opera (1953); also sang in Vienna (from 1956), Berlin (from 1956), and in Salzburg (from 1959). In 1959 he became a principal member of the Bavarian State Opera in Munich; made his Metropolitan Opera debut in N.Y. as Wolfram (Dec. 16, 1960); appeared for the first time in England at the Edinburgh Festival (1965), and later sang regularly at

London's Covent Garden (from 1973). He also appeared as a soloist with the major orchs. and as a recitalist; likewise starred in his own Munich television show. In 1982 he became a prof. at the Hamburg Hochschule für Musik. His autobiography was publ. as *Premierenfieber* (1981; Eng. tr., 1986, as *First Night Fever: The Memoirs of Hermann Prey*). Among his finest operatic roles were Count Almaviva, Papageno, Guglielmo, and Rossini's Figaro; he also sang a number of contemporary roles. As a lieder artist, he distinguished himself in Schubert, Schumann, and Brahms.—**NS/LK/DM**

Prianishnikov, Ippolit (Petrovich), Russian baritone; b. Kerch, Aug. 26, 1847; d. Petrograd, Nov. 11, 1921. He joined the Russian Imperial Navy, and later began to study voice, first at the St. Petersburg Cons. (1873–75), then in Italy, where he became a student of Ronconi in Milan. He made his debut in Milan in 1876. Returning to Russia, he joined the Maryinsky Theater in St. Petersburg in 1878, remaining there until 1886. He then went to Tiflis (1886–89) and Moscow (1892–93), where he sang and produced opera. In later years he also taught voice. Among his students were Bolshakov, Nikolai Figner, and Mravina.—**NS/LK/DM**

Přibyl, Vilém, Czech tenor; b. Náchod, April 10, 1925; d. Brno, July 13, 1990. After making his debut with an amateur opera company in Hradec Králové (1952), he pursued vocal instruction there with Jakoubková (1952–62); sang at the opera in Ústí nad Labem (1960) and at the Janáček Opera in Brno (1960); also received further training from Vavrdová at the Brno Academy of Music. He gained notable success with his portrayal of Dalibor with the Prague National Theater Opera during its visit to the Edinburgh Festival (1964); then appeared in various European music centers; also taught at the Janáček Academy of Arts in Brno (from 1969). In 1969 he was made an Artist of Merit and in 1977 a National Artist by the Czech government. His repertoire included Lohengrin, Radamès, and Otello, as well as roles in operas by Prokofiev, Martinů, and Shostakovich; he was especially esteemed for his roles in operas by Janáček.—**NS/LK/DM**

Price, Dame Margaret (Berenice), outstanding Welsh soprano; b. Blackwood, near Tredegar, South Wales, April 13, 1941. She commenced singing lessons when she was 9; then won the Charles Kennedy Scott scholarship of London's Trinity Coll. of Music at 15, and studied voice with Scott for 4 years. After singing in the Ambrosian Singers for 2 seasons, she made her operatic debut as Cherubino with the Welsh National Opera (1962); then sang that same role at her Covent Garden debut in London (1963). She made her first appearance at the Glyndebourne Festival as Constanze in *Die Entführung aus dem Serail* (1968); then made her U.S. debut as Pamina at the San Francisco Opera (1969); subsequently sang Fiordiligi at the Chicago Lyric Opera (1972). In 1973 she sang at the Paris Opéra, later joining its cast during its U.S. tour in 1976, eliciting extraordinary praise from the public and critics for her portrayal of Desdemona; made an auspicious Metropolitan Opera

debut in N.Y. in that same role on Jan. 21, 1985. In 1987 she was engaged as Norma at Covent Garden. After appearing as Adriana Lecouvreur in Bonn in 1989, she sang Amelia Grimaldi in a concert performance of *Simon Boccanegra* at the Royal Festival Hall in London in 1990. During the 1993–94 season, she sang in *Ariadne auf Naxos* at the Berlin State Opera. She also toured widely as a concert singer. Her other notable roles include Donna Anna, Aida, Adriana Lecouvreur, and Strauss's Ariadne. Price's voice is essentially a lyric soprano, but is capable of technically brilliant coloratura. She was made a Commander of the Order of the British Empire in 1982. In 1992 she was made a Dame Commander of the Order of the British Empire.—**NS/LK/DM**

Price, Florence B(eatrice née Smith), black American teacher and composer; b. Little Rock, Ark., April 9, 1888; d. Chicago, June 3, 1953. She studied with Chadwick and Converse at the New England Cons. of Music in Boston, graduating in 1906. She had been publishing her compositions since she was 11 (1899); in 1928 she won a prize from G. Schirmer for her *At the Cotton Gin* for Piano; around this time she was also writing musical jingles for radio commercials. Her first notable success came in 1932 with her 1st Sym. (winner of the Wanamaker Award; perf. by the Chicago Sym. Orch. at the Century of Progress Exhibition in 1933); she became known as the first black woman to write syms.

WORKS: ORCH.: 6 syms.: No. 1 (1931–32), *Mississippi River Symphony* (1934), D minor (n.d.), No. 3 (1940), G minor (n.d.), and *Colonial Dance Symphony* (n.d.); *Ethiopia's Shadow in America* (1932); Piano Concerto (1934); 2 violin concertos: No. 1 (n.d.) and No. 2 (1952); 2 concert overtures on Negro spirituals; Piano Concerto in 1 Movement; *Rhapsody* for Piano and Orch.; *Songs of the Oak*, tone poem. **CHAMBER:** *Negro Folksongs in Counterpoint* for String Quartet; 2 piano quintets; pieces for Violin and Piano; piano works; organ music. **VOCAL:** Choral music; songs; arrangements of spirituals.—**NS/LK/DM**

Price, Lloyd, American singer and songwriter; b. Kenner, La., March 9, 1933. Price achieved success in the early 1950s with a New Orleans–styled R&B sound on hits such as "Lawdy Miss Clawdy," then returned in the late 1950s with more mainstream hits such as "Stagger Lee," "Personality," and "I'm Gonna Get Married."

Price first sang in church and learned to play guitar, piano, and trumpet in his youth. As a teenager he led a band and appeared on local radio, writing commercial jingles for the station. He expanded one of his jingles into "Lawdy Miss Clawdy," which was recorded in New Orleans by the Hollywood, Calif.–based Specialty Records label in 1952. It topped the R&B charts in July and sold a million copies. Price hit the R&B Top Ten with four more songs in 1952–53—"Oooh-Oooh-Oooh" (music and lyrics by Lloyd Price), "Restless Heart," "Ain't It a Shame?" and "Tell Me Pretty Baby"—before being drafted and spending two years in the army performing on military bases in Asia.

Back from military service in 1956, Price initially returned to Specialty Records in Hollywood, then moved to Washington, D.C., where he founded his own KRC (Kent Record Company) label with William Boskent and his manager, Harold Logan. KRC issued his recording of "Just Because" (music and lyrics by Lloyd Price, music based on "Caro Nome" from the opera *Rigoletto* by Giuseppe Verdi) in 1956, then leased it to ABC–Paramount Records, after which it made the charts in March 1957, hitting the R&B Top Ten and the pop Top 40. After trying to continue with KRC, Price formally signed to ABC–Paramount as a recording artist in 1958 and released "Stagger Lee" (music and lyrics by Lloyd Price and Harold Logan, based on the folk song "Stack-O-Lee"), which hit #1 on the pop and R&B charts in February 1959 and sold a million copies.

Price followed "Stagger Lee" with a series of hits in 1959 and 1960: "Where Were You (On Our Wedding Day)?" (music and lyrics by Harold Logan, Lloyd Price, and John Patton; pop Top 40, R&B Top Ten); the million-selling "Personality" (music and lyrics by Lloyd Price and Harold Logan; pop Top Ten, R&B #1); "I'm Gonna Get Married" (music and lyrics by Harold Logan and Lloyd Price; pop Top Ten, R&B #1); "Come into My Heart" (music and lyrics by Lloyd Price and Harold Logan; pop Top 40, R&B Top Ten); "Wont'cha Come Home" (R&B Top Ten); "Lady Luck" (music and lyrics by Lloyd Price and Harold Logan; pop Top 40, R&B Top Ten); and "Question" (music and lyrics by Lloyd Price and Harold Logan; pop Top 40, R&B Top Ten).

Leaving ABC–Paramount, Price launched his own Double-L label, with which he returned to the pop and R&B Top 40 in 1963 with a revival of "Misty" (music by Erroll Garner, lyrics by Johnny Burke). He spent more time on business interests than his own musical career in subsequent years, purchasing the N.Y. nightclub Birdland and renaming it the Turntable, founding his own Turntable Records label, copromoting a music festival in Zaire in 1974 in connection with the Muhammad Ali–George Foreman heavyweight championship fight there, then cofounding LPG Records in 1976, both with boxing promoter Don King. Meanwhile, his songs were revived for chart entries, "Lawdy Miss Clawdy" by Gary Stites in 1960 and the Buckinghams in 1967, "Stagger Lee" by his protégé Wilson Pickett in 1967 and Tommy Roe in 1971.

Price continued to perform and record occasionally into the 1990s.—**WR**

Price, (Mary Violet) Leontyne, remarkably endowed black American soprano; b. Laurel, Miss., Feb. 10, 1927. She was taught piano by a local woman, and also learned to sing. On Dec. 17, 1943, she played piano and sang at a concert in Laurel. She went to Oak Park H.S., graduating in music in 1944; then enrolled in the Coll. of Education and Industrial Arts in Wilberforce, Ohio, where she studied voice with Catherine Van Buren; received her B.A. degree in 1948, and then was awarded a scholarship at the Juilliard School of Music in N.Y.; there she received vocal training from Florence Page Kimball, and also joined the Opera Workshop under the direction of Frederic Cohen. Virgil Thomson heard her perform the role of Mistress Ford in Verdi's opera *Falstaff* and invited her to sing in the revival of his opera *4 Saints in 3 Acts* in 1952. She subsequently performed the role of Bess in Gershwin's *Porgy and Bess*

on a tour of the U.S. (1952–54) and in Europe (1955). On Nov. 14, 1954, she made a highly acclaimed debut as a concert singer in N.Y. On Dec. 3, 1954, she sang at the first performance of Samuel Barber's *Prayers of Kierkegaard* with the Boston Sym. Orch., conducted by Charles Munch. On Jan. 23, 1955, she performed Tosca on television, creating a sensation both as an artist and as a member of her race taking up the role of an Italian diva. Her career was soon assured without any reservations. In 1957 she appeared with the San Francisco Opera; on Oct. 18, 1957, she sang Aida, a role congenial to her passionate artistry. In 1958 she sang Aida with the Vienna State Opera under the direction of Herbert von Karajan; on July 2, 1958, she sang this role at Covent Garden in London and again at La Scala in Milan in 1959, becoming the first black woman to sing with that most prestigious and most fastidious opera company. On Jan. 27, 1961, she made her first appearance with the Metropolitan Opera in N.Y. in the role of Leonora in *Il Trovatore*. A series of highly successful performances at the Metropolitan followed: Aida on Feb. 20, 1961; Madama Butterfly on March 3, 1961; Donna Anna on March 25, 1961; Tosca on April 1, 1962; Pamina on Jan. 3, 1964; Cleopatra in the premiere of Samuel Barber's opera *Antony and Cleopatra* at the opening of the new Metropolitan Opera House at Lincoln Center in N.Y. on Sept. 16, 1966. On Sept. 24, 1973, she sang Madama Butterfly at the Metropolitan once more. On Feb. 7, 1975, she appeared there in the title role of *Manon Lescaut*; and on Feb. 3, 1976, she sang Aida, a role she repeated for her farewell performance in opera in a televised production broadcast live from the Metropolitan Opera in N.Y. by PBS on Jan. 3, 1985. She then continued her concert career, appearing with notable success in the major music centers. She was married in 1952 to **William Warfield** (who sang Porgy at her performances of *Porgy and Bess*), but separated from him in 1959; they were divorced in 1973. She received many honors during her remarkable career; in 1964 President Johnson bestowed upon her the Medal of Freedom, and in 1985 President Reagan presented her with the National Medal of Arts.

BIBL.: H. Lyon, *L. P.: Highlights of a Prima Donna* (N.Y., 1973); R. Steins, *L. P., Opera Superstar* (Woodbridge, Conn., 1993).—**NS/LK/DM**

Price, Ray (Noble), American country singer, guitarist, and songwriter; b. near Perryville, Tex., Jan. 12, 1926. Price was among the most popular country singers of the 1950s and 1960s, with a style that evolved from the honky-tonk approach of his mentor, Hank Williams, to a more pop-oriented Countrypolitan sound in the 1960s, but was not inconsistent with that of protégés like Kris Kristofferson and Willie Nelson in the 1970s and 1980s. He reached the country charts 109 times between 1952 and 1989, including 46 Top Ten hits and eight #1s, the most successful of which were "Crazy Arms," "My Shoes Keep Walking Back to You," and "City Lights."

Price's parents divorced when he was four, and he spent part of his childhood on his father's farm in Cherokee County, Tex., and part with his mother in Dallas. He began attending North Tex. Agricultural Coll. in Arlington, Tex., intending to become a veterinarian, but when he turned 18 he enlisted in the Marine Corps and served in the Pacific during World War II; he returned to college in 1946. In 1948 he began singing on local radio, and in 1949, when he was hired by the *Big D Jamboree* radio show in Dallas, he left school to work in music full-time. He signed to the small Bullet Records label, which released his first single, "Jealous Lies" (music and lyrics by Ray Price) in 1950. The single was not a success, but his appearances on the *Big D Jamboree*, some of which were broadcast nationally, brought him to the attention of Columbia Records, which signed him in March 1951.

Price was befriended by Hank Williams, who facilitated his move to Nashville and his joining the *Grand Ole Opry* in January 1952, before he had scored a national hit. That hit came soon after, however, when "Talk to Your Heart" (music and lyrics by C. M. Bradley and Louise Ulrich) reached the country Top Ten in May. He had another hit that year, then struggled until scoring in March 1954 with both sides of the single "I'll Be There (If You Ever Want Me)" (music and lyrics by Rusty Gabbard and Ray Price)/"Release Me" (music and lyrics by Eddie Miller and W. S. Stevenson). There was one more country Top Ten that year, then another year off the charts.

Price returned with five Top Ten hits in 1956, including the biggest country single of the year, "Crazy Arms" (music and lyrics by Ralph Mooney and Chuck Seals), and he was in the country singles charts every year from then until 1989. He had three more #1 hits in the 1950s: "My Shoes Keep Walking Back to You" (music and lyrics by Lee Ross and Bob Wills) in September 1957; "City Lights" (music and lyrics by Bill Anderson), the biggest hit of 1958; and "The Same Old Me" (music and lyrics by Fuzzy Owen) in December 1959.

In the 1960s Price topped the country charts with the albums *Night Life* (January 1964), *Another Bridge to Burn* (November 1966), and *Touch My Heart* (April 1967). He began to add strings to his recordings, culminating in the large orchestra that accompanied him on a recording of the 1913 song "Danny Boy" (music and lyrics by Frederick Edward Weatherly, based on the 19th-century Irish traditional song "Londonderry Air") in 1967, a Top Ten country hit and his biggest crossover pop hit yet. But he achieved real crossover success and returned to the top of the country charts in September 1970 by recording Kris Kristofferson's "For the Good Times," which made the pop Top 40 and earned him a Grammy for Best Country Vocal Performance, Male. The *For the Good Times* LP topped the country charts and went gold.

His career reinvigorated, Price topped the country charts in May 1971 with "I Won't Mention It Again" (music and lyrics by Cam Mullins and Carolyn Yates), earning another Grammy nomination for Best Country Vocal Performance, Male, and hitting #1 on the country LP charts with an album of the same title. The two-record set *Ray Price's All-Time Greatest Hits*, released in August 1972, was a gold-selling album, and Price was back at #1 in the country charts with "She's Got to Be a Saint" (music and lyrics by Mario DiNapoli and Joseph Paulini) in December 1972 and "You're the Best Thing That Ever Happened to Me" (music and lyrics by Jim Weatherly) in October 1973.

Price gave up touring and turned his attention to horse-breeding on his Tex. ranch in the early 1970s, though he continued to make records. He switched to the religious Myrrh record label in 1974, to ABC/Dot in 1975, and to Monument in 1978, continuing to reach the country charts regularly. In 1980 he teamed up with Willie Nelson, who had once been a member of his backing band, for the album *San Antonio Rose*, which went gold and featured the country Top Ten single "Faded Love" (music and lyrics by Bob Wills and Johnnie Lee Wills). He moved to Dimension Records in 1981, scoring a final couple of Top Ten hits, then to Warner Bros., Clint Eastwood's Viva label, and the independent Step One label, continuing to reach the country charts through the end of the 1980s. By then he had built his own theater in the entertainment center of Branson, Mo.

Price was married twice, and had a son.

DISC.: *A Tribute to the Great Bob Wills* (1962); *Night Life* (1963); *Portrait of a Singer* (1985); *A Revival of Old-Time Singing* (1986); *Heart of Country Music* (1987); *Just Enough Love* (1988); *The Essential* (rec. 1951–62; rel. 1989); *Somes a Rose* (1992); *Los Dos* (1994).—**WR**

Pride, Charley,

one of the best-selling country performers of the 1960s and 1970s, and one of the few African-Americans to score success in this style, b. Sledge, Miss., March 18, 1938. Pride is noteworthy for being one of the few African-Americans to break through to true country stardom. Pride's interest in country music reflects the fact that in the rural South traditional country (and blues) audiences crossed racial lines; and his success reflects both the slickness of Pride's recordings and the smooth-as-silk quality of his vocals.

Pride was born one of 11 children to poor, tenant farmers. Like many other black families in rural Miss., they made their living picking cotton, for which they were paid $3.00 for each hundred pounds picked. Early on, Pride became a fan of country radio, particularly emulating the bluesy sounds of Hank Williams, and taught himself the guitar. At the same time, an early talent for athletics manifested itself, and he began playing baseball in the old Negro league in the late 1950s.

After serving in the military, Pride was hired to play for a minor-league team in Helena, Mont. He continued to perform in local bars in his free time, while he also worked off-season for Anaconda Mining as a smelter. In 1963, Red Sorvine was passing through the region and heard Pride perform; he encouraged Pride to come to Nashville to audition for RCA. Pride stalled for a year, while pursuing his dreams of big league baseball as a member of the N.Y. Mets' farm team. In 1964, he traveled to Nashville to audition for famed country producer Chet Atkins who signed him to RCA.

Pride's recording career was blessed with early success. His first single, "Snakes Crawl at Night," was an immediate Top Ten country hit, and was followed by another hit, "Just between You and Me." Within a year of the release of his first single, he was invited to join the Grand Ole Opry, where he became immediately one of the most popular performers. Atkins smothered Pride's vocals in the blend of echoey guitars and girly choruses that Nashville was becoming (in)famous for, and the country audience ate it up. Little emphasis was placed on Pride's racial identity by RCA, and no one in the audience seemed to mind that he was a lone black star among a white (and relatively conservative) group of musicians.

Pride enjoyed his greatest success in the late 1960s and early 1970s, winning numerous Grammy, CMA, and gold record awards. In addition to the standard songs of lovin' and losin', Pride also was a popular gospel recording artist, bringing the same smooth, pop delivery to his gospel recordings that he did to his songs of heartache.

A long-time resident of Dallas, Pride pretty much retired from performing in the 1980s, although he continues to record sporadically, issuing a couple of albums late in the decade for the small 16th Avenue label. He made an attempt at a comeback in 1993 with the single, "Just for the Love of It." It was typical 1960s Nashville in its conservative message and Pride's voice still sounds smooth-as-silk, even though the backing was simpler than on his earlier recordings, reflecting the influence of new country. Since then, he has been only performed irregularly.

DISC.: *Country Charley Pride* (1966); *The Pride of Country Music* (1967); *The Country Way* (1967); *Make Mine Country* (1968); *Songs of Pride...Charley, That Is* (1968); *Charley Pride-In Person* (1968); *The Sensational Charley Pride* (1969); *The Best of Charley Pride* (1969); *Just Plain Charley* (1970); *Charley Pride's Tenth Album* (1970); *Christmas In My Home Town* (1970); *From Me to You (To All My Wonderful Fans)* (1971); *Did YOu Think to Pray?* (1971); *I'm Just Me* (1971); *Charley Pride Sings Heart Songs* (1971); *The Best of Charley Pride, Vol. 2* (1972); *A Sunshiny Day with Charley Pride* (1972); *Songs of Love By Charley Pride* (1973); *Sweet Country* (1973); *The Incomparable Charley Pride* (1973); *Amazing Love* (1973); *Country Feelin'* (1974); *Pride of America* (1974); *Charley* (1975); *The Happiness of Having You* (1975); *Sunday Morning with Charley Pride* (1976); *She's Just an Old Love Turned Memory* (1977); *The Best of Charley Pride, Vol. 3* (1977); *Someone Loves You Honey* (1978); *Burgers and Fries* (1978); *You're My Jamaica* (1979); *There's a Little Bit of Hank In Me* (1980); *Roll On Mississippi* (1981); *Greatest Hits* (1981); *Charley Sings Everybody's Choice* (1982); *Live* (1982); *Night Games* (1983); *The Power of Love* (1984); *After All This Time* (1987); *I'm Gonna Love Her on the Radio* (1988); *Moody Woman* (1989); *Amy's Eyes* (1990); *Classics with Pride* (1991); *My 6 Latest & 6 Greatest* (1993); *The Very Best Of...* (1995); *Just for the Love of It* (1996); *Super Hits* (1996); *The Essential Charley Pride* (1997); *The Masters* (1998).—RC

Priestman, Brian, English conductor and music educator; b. Birmingham, Feb. 10, 1927. He received his training at the Univ. of Birmingham (B.Mus., 1950; M.A., 1952) and the Brussels Cons. (diploma, 1952). After serving as founder-conductor of the Opera da Camera and the Orch. da Camera in Birmingham, he was music director of the Royal Shakespeare Theatre at Stratford-upon-Avon (1960–63). He conducted the Edmonton (Alberta) Sym. Orch. (1964–68) and the Baltimore Sym. Orch. (1968–69), and then was music director of the Denver Sym. Orch. (1970–78). He also was principal conductor of the New Zealand National Orch. in Well-

ington (1973–76) and music director of the Fla. Phil. (1977–80). From 1980 to 1986 he was principal conductor of the Cape Town Sym. Orch., prof. and chairman of the music dept. at the Univ. of Cape Town, and director of the South African Coll. of Music. He was principal guest conductor of the Malmö Sym. Orch. (1988–90). In 1992 he became artist-in-residence, prof., and director of orch. studies at the Univ. of Kans. at Lawrence.
—NS/LK/DM

Prigozhin, Lucian (Abramovich), Russian composer; b. Tashkent, Aug. 15, 1926. He received training in piano and theory in Tashkent, and then completed his studies with Shcherbachev, Evlakhov, and Kochurov at the Leningrad Cons. He became a convinced modernist in his music, introducing the concept of "supplementary tones" in the 12-tone method of composition by allowing members of the tone-row to permutate freely. However, he preserved the basic tonality even when he no longer used the key signatures.

WORKS: DRAMATIC: *Doctor Aybolit* (Ay! It Hurts!), children's radio opera (1956); *Circle of Hades*, ballet (1964; orch. suite, 1965); *Malchish-Kibalchish*, children's radio opera (1969); *Robin Hood*, opera (1972); film music. **ORCH.:** *Sinfonietta* (1953); 3 syms. (1955, rev. 1975; 1960, rev. 1963; 1970); *Music for Flute and Strings* (1961). **CHAMBER:** 2 violin sonatas (*Sonata-burlesque*, 1967; 1969); 2 string quartets (1970, 1979); *Musica rustica* for Wind Quintet (1973); Horn Sonata (1974). **P i a n o :** Sonatina (1973); Sonata (1973); *Calendar of Nature*, 12 pieces (1974). **VOCAL:** *Stenka Razin* for 2 Soloists and Orch. (1949); *Prometheus Unbound* for Chorus and Orch. (1959–60); *The Chronicle of Igor's Campaign* for Mezzo-soprano, Bass, Chorus, and Chamber Ensemble (1966); *Snowstorm*, chamber oratorio (1968); *In Memory of the Great Battle* for Bass, Chorus, and Orch. (1975); cantatas.

BIBL.: E. Ruchyevskaya, *L. P.* (Moscow, 1977).
—NS/LK/DM

Přihoda, Váša, noted Czech violinist and teacher; b. Vodnany, Aug. 22, 1900; d. Vienna, July 26, 1960. He received his first instruction from his father, a professional violinist. He made his public debut at the age of 12 in Prague, and in 1920 he went on an Italian tour. In 1921 he appeared in the U.S., and in 1927 played in England; then gave recitals throughout Europe. He continued to concertize after the absorption of Austria and Czechoslovakia into the Nazi Reich, and was briefly charged with collaboration with the occupying powers. He eventually resumed his career, and later became a prof. at the Vienna Academy of Music.

BIBL.: J. Vratislavský, *V. P.* (Prague, 1970).—NS/LK/DM

Prima, Louis, one of rock's early forebears and pop music's great entertainers; b. New Orleans, Dec. 7, 1911; d. there, Aug. 24, 1978. Louis Prima was the son of Italian immigrants, and by the age of 11 he was leading a band in New Orleans. He had a gruff, eccentric voice that was part Louis Armstrong and part Chico Marx. He also played trumpet. While he often acted the clown, he was also a remarkable songwriter. In 1934, he and his septet started recording, cutting more than 70 sides during the 1930s alone. Among them were such hits as "I'm Living in a Great Big Way" (#13, 1935), "Chasing Shadows" (#14, 1935), "The Lady in Red" (#8, 1935), "In a Little Gypsy Tea Room" (#4, 1935), and "The Goose Hangs High" (#20, 1937). His signature song was "Way Down Yonder in New Orleans." During this prolific period, Prima wrote one of his most enduring compositions, "Sing, Sing, Sing," which became the theme song of the Benny Goodman Orch. after Goodman took it to the Top Ten in 1938.

Prima's reputation grew thanks to his appearance in a series of films through the late 1930s and early 1940s. During the 1940s, he charted with "Angelina" (#14, 1944), a version of the sea chantey "Bell Bottom Trousers" (#6, 1945) and "Civilization (Bongo, Bongo, Bongo)" (#8, 1947). In the late 1940s he started working with singer Keely Smith, who soon became his wife. Cool, classy, and sophisticated, she was the perfect foil to Prima's inspired buffoonery. They first hit with "Oh, Babe!" which went to #12 in 1950, and became a big draw in Las Vegas and showrooms around the world. In 1958, they performed the Arlen/Mercer standard "That Old Black Magic" in the movie *Senior Prom*. The subsequent single rose to #18 in 1958, taking home the first Grammy Award for Best Performance by a Vocal Group. The soundtrack to their 1959 film *Hey Boy! Hey Girl!* hit #37.

Solo again in 1960, Prima had his last chart hit with *Wonderland by Night*, the album hitting #9 while the title track rose to #15. He continued to be a force in Hollywood and Las Vegas. Supplying the voice of King Louis in Disney's animated version of *The Jungle Book*, he sang one of the film's most memorable tunes, "I Wanna Be Like You." In 1975, he underwent surgery for a brain tumor and never came out of his coma. He died in a New Orleans nursing home in 1978.

Like Louis Jordan—whose music was revived in the early 1980s by rocker Joe Jackson—Prima's music enjoyed a small renaissance during the late 1980s and 1990s. Los Lobos recorded a version of "I Wanna Be Like You" that paid as much tribute to Prima's vocal as it did the song. David Lee Roth took an almost note-for-note cover of Prima's interpolation of Irving Ceasar's "Just a Gigolo" and Roger Graham's "I Ain't Got Nobody" to #12 in 1985. The Brian Setzer Orch. turned Prima's "Jump, Jive, and Wail" into a sizable hit in the late 1990s. A documentary film on Prima's life was released in winter 2000.

DISC.: *Angelina* (1950); *Return of the Wildest* (1955); *The Wildest!* (1957); *The Call of the Wildest* (1957); *The Wildest Show at Tahoe* (1958); *Las Vegas Prima Style* (1958); *Strictly Prima* (1959); *Hey Boy! Hey Girl!* (1959); *Louis Prima* (1959); *Wonderland by Night* (1960); *Louis and Keely!* (1960); *Doin' the Twist* (1961); *The Wildest Comes Home* (1962); *Plays Pretty for the People* (1963); *Just a Gigolo* (1988); *The Capitol Recordings* (1994); *Swing with Louis Prima* (1996); *Let's Swing It* (1996); *Let's Fly with Mary Poppins* (1998); *Jump 'N' Boogie* (1998).—**HB**

Primosch, James, American composer, teacher, and pianist; b. Cleveland, Oct. 29, 1956. He studied composition with Bain Murray and Rudolph Bubalo at Cleveland State Univ. (B.A., 1978), and then with

George Crumb, Richard Wernick, George Rochberg, and Ralph Shapey at the Univ. of Pa. (M.A., 1980), during which time he also received private instruction in piano from Lambert Orkis. He completed his composition training with Mario Davidovsky and Chou Wen-Chung at Columbia Univ. (D.M.A., 1988). In 1984 he won the Tanglewood Prize in composition at the Berkshire Music Center, in 1985 he held a Guggenheim fellowship and was awarded the Charles Ives Scholarship of the American Academy of Arts and Letters, and in 1988 he was in residence at the MacDowell Colony in Peterborough, N.H. In 1988 he became an asst. prof. of music at the Univ. of Pa., where he was made an assoc. prof. of music in 1994 and where he was chairman of the music dept. from 1996 to 1998, and again in 1999–2000. In 1991–92 he held an NEA fellowship. Primosch was awarded the Cleveland Arts Prize in 1992 and held the Goddard Lieberson fellowship of the American Academy of Arts and Letters in 1993. In 1994 he served as composer-in-residence at the Marlboro (Vt.) Festival. He held a Pew Fellowship in the Arts in 1996. In 1999 he won the Elise Stoeger Prize of the Chamber Music Soc. of Lincoln Center in N.Y. In addition to teaching and composing, Primosch has been active as a pianist, particularly in contemporary music settings.

WORKS: ORCH.: *Dappled Things* (1986); Chamber Sym. (1990); *Some Glad Mystery* (1992); *Five Meditations* (1993). **CHAMBER:** *Variations* for Violin (1981); *Aria* for Oboe and Tape (1982); *Five Miniatures* for 9 Instruments (1982); 3 string quartets (1983, 1991, 1999); *Icons* for Clarinet, Piano, and Tape (1984); *Septet* (1985); *Fantasy-Variations* for Violin, Cello, and Piano (1991); *Secret Geometry* for Piano and Tape (1993); *Sacra Conversazione* for 6 Players and Tape (1994); *Dream Journal* for 2 Pianos, Percussion, and Tape (1996); Piano Quintet (1996). **KEYBOARD:** *Eighty-Eight: Homage to Gottschalk* for 44 Pianos, 176-Hands (1996); solo piano pieces; organ works. **VOCAL:** *the mystery of stillness* for Chorus and Percussion, after e.e. cummings (1979); *The Cloud of Unknowing*, cantata for Woman's Voice and Chamber Orch. (1987); *Three Sacred Songs* for Voice and Piano (1989); *Four Sacred Songs* for Soprano or Mezzo-soprano and 6 Players (1990); *Weil Alles Unsagbar Ist* for Soprano, Flute, Violin, Cello, and Piano, after Rilke (1990); *Fire-Memory/River-Memory* for Chorus and Orch., after Denise Levertov (1997); *Songs and Dances from "The Tempest"* for Soprano, Baritone, and Medieval and Renaissance Instruments, after Shakespeare (1998); *Holy the Firm* for Soprano and Piano (1999).—**LK/DM**

Primrose, William, eminent Scottish-born American violist and pedagogue; b. Glasgow, Aug. 23, 1903; d. Provo, Utah, May 1, 1982. He studied violin in Glasgow with Camillo Ritter, at London's Guildhall School of Music, and in Belgium (1925–27) with Ysaÿe, who advised him to take up viola so as to avoid the congested violin field. He was the violist in the London String Quartet (1930–35), with which he made several tours. In 1937 he settled in the U.S., and was engaged as the principal violist in the NBC Sym. Orch. in N.Y. under Toscanini, holding this post until 1942. In 1939 he established his own string quartet. In 1953 he was named a Commander of the Order of the British Empire. He became a naturalized American citizen in 1955. From 1954 to 1962 he was the violist in the Festival

Quartet. He also became active as a teacher; was on the faculty of the Univ. of Southern Calif. in Los Angeles (1962) and at the School of Music of Ind. Univ. in Bloomington (1965–72). In 1972 he inaugurated a master class at the Tokyo Univ. of Fine Arts and Music. Returning to the U.S., he taught at Brigham Young Univ. in Provo, Utah (1979–82). Primrose was greatly esteemed as a viola virtuoso; he gave first performances of viola concertos by several modern composers. He commissioned a viola concerto from Bartók, but the work was left unfinished at the time of Bartók's death, and the task of reconstructing the score from Bartók's sketches remained to be accomplished by Bartók's friend and associate Tibor Serly; Primrose gave its first performance with the Minneapolis Sym. Orch. on Dec. 2, 1949. He publ. *A Method for Violin and Viola Players* (London, 1960), *Technique in Memory* (1963), and an autobiography, *Walk on the North Side* (1978); also ed. various works for viola, and made transcriptions for the instrument.

BIBL.: D. Dalton, *Playing the Viola: Conversations with W. P.* (Oxford, 1988).—NS/LK/DM

Prin, Jean-Baptiste, French trumpet marine player, teacher, dancing master, and composer; b. England, c. 1669; d. Strasbourg, after 1742. He studied the trumpet marine with his father, and by 1689 he was active in Lyons. About 1698 he went to Paris, where he was a performer and a dancer. In 1704 he returned to Lyons and performed and taught until retiring to Strasbourg in 1737. He was the author of the method *Traité sur la trompette marine* (1742). His MS collection of works for the trumpet marine, along with those of other composers, is housed in the Lyons Library.—LK/DM

Prince (Roger Nelson), popular solo artist; b. Minneapolis, Minn., June 7, 1958. Along with Michael Jackson and Madonna, Prince was one of the most popular solo artists to emerge in the 1980s. A hugely talented yet erratic and self-indulgent musician, Prince's work shows the strong influence of rock artist Jimi Hendrix and soul/funk artists such as James Brown, Sly Stone, and George Clinton. Prince fused elements of pop, rock, soul, and funk to produce some of the most influential and best-selling albums of the 1980s. Drawing comparisons to Michael Jackson for his fusion of black and white musical styles, his shattering of racial barriers within the music industry, his ambiguous racial and sexual identity, and his reclusiveness, Prince gained his greatest success with 1984's film/album *Purple Rain*.

At age seven Prince took up piano as he was shuttled among relatives following his parents' separation. By 12 he had begun teaching himself guitar, subsequently mastering drums, bass, piano, and saxophone. While still in junior high school Prince formed with Andre Anderson the band Grand Central, which later evolved into Champagne with Anderson and Morris Day. Years later Anderson recorded as Andre Cymone, scoring a near-smash R&B hit with "The Dance Electric" in 1985. In 1976 Prince recorded demonstration tapes that led to a contract with Warner Bros. that allowed him total control over his recordings. He played all instruments

and sang all vocals on his debut album, *For You*, which yielded a major R&B hit with the sexually suggestive "Soft and Wet." His penchant for puerile lyrics was confirmed with 1979's *Prince*, again self-recorded, which featured "I Wanna Be Your Lover," a top R&B and major pop hit. Despite receiving virtually no radio airplay of his songs, Prince quickly garnered a rabid following with black audiences and established his sexually explicit image with the appropriately titled *Dirty Mind*. Staying on the charts for a year, the album contained songs about oral sex ("Head") and incest ("Sister Sister") and sparked considerable controversy for its explicitness.

In 1981, under the influence of Sly Stone and Jimi Hendrix, Prince and Morris Day formed the black rock band the Time, with bassist Terry Lewis, keyboard players Jimmy "Jam" Harris and Monte Moir, guitarist Jesse Johnson, and drummer Jellybean Johnson. In the mid-1970s Lewis had formed and played bass for the funk band Flyte Tyme in Minneapolis, recruiting Harris for the band in the late 1970s. Backed by the Time, Prince toured in 1981, but performances on the West Coast opening for the Rolling Stones were greeted with catcalls and hurled projectiles. During the year the Time released their debut album on Warner Bros., with Day singing lead vocals, writing all the lyrics, and coproducing the album. It yielded near-smash R&B hits with "Get It Up" and "Cool (Part 1)." In 1982 the Time's second album, *What Time Is It?*, yielded two R&B hits, the smash "777–9311" and "The Walk."

Meanwhile, in late 1981 Warner Bros. issued Prince's self-created *Controversy*, which effectively fused elements of funk and rock and produced R&B smashes with the title song and "Let's Work." His first crossover hits came from his next album, *1999*, which included the R&B smash title cut (a major pop hit) and the pop smashes "Little Red Corvette" and "Delirious" (both major R&B hits). The video to "Little Red Corvette" became the first by a black artist to be aired extensively on MTV and helped open the white-dominated cable TV network to blacks. The album remained on the album charts for nearly three years and eventually sold more than three million copies, establishing Prince as one of the most exciting and popular new black performers of the decade. Prince toured again in 1982 with a show replete with stunning effects and grandiose staging, centered around Prince's provocative sexual persona. However, by 1983 Prince had dismissed the Time and formed the Revolution with guitarist Wendy Melvoin, keyboardists Lisa Coleman and Matt "Dr." Fink, saxophonist Eric Leeds, and bassist Brownmark.

The Time recorded one more album, *Ice Cream Castle*, before disbanding in 1984. The album yielded three R&B hits, including "Jungle Love," also a major pop hit. Jesse Johnson and Morris Day each pursued solo careers. Johnson scored three R&B smashes in 1985 with "Be Your Man," "Can You Help Me" and "I Want My Girl," followed by the R&B smashes "Crazay" (with Sly Stone) in 1986 and "Love Struck" in 1988. Day achieved an R&B smash with "The Oak Tree" in 1985 and a top R&B (and major pop) hit with "Fishnet" in 1988. The Time eventually regrouped in 1990, with Day, Johnson,

Terry Lewis, Jimmy "Jam" Harris, Monte Moir, Jelly-bean Johnson, and 1984 member Jerome Benton, Lewis's half-brother. They scored a top R&B and near-smash pop hit with "Jerk-Out" that year. However, Day subsequently returned to solo recording with 1992's *Guaranteed*.

Terry Lewis and Jimmy "Jam" Harris formed their own production company, Flyte Tyme, in 1982, and wrote for and produced various acts beginning in 1983, including Klymaxx (1985's crossover smash "I Miss You"), the Human League (1986's crossover smash "Human"), and Robert Palmer (1986's pop smash "I Didn't Mean to Turn You On"). Their most conspicuous success came writing songs for and producing Janet Jackson. They wrote and produced her breakthrough 1986 *Control* album, 1989's *Rhythm Nation*, and 1993's *janet*. All three albums sold more than five million copies, and each produced at least five smash crossover hits. Jam and Lewis also produced Herb Alpert's 1987 comeback album *Keep Your Eyes On Me*, the New Edition's 1988 *Heart Break*, and the 1992 soundtrack to *Mo' Money*.

Prince scored his most spectacular success with the film and soundtrack *Purple Rain* in 1984. The film featured Patty "Apollonia" Kotero, the lead singer of Apollonia 6, and Morris Day as Prince's musical and romantic rival; it grossed more than $80 million at the box office. Primarily recorded with the Revolution, the soundtrack sold 11 million copies and produced five hits, including the top pop and R&B hits "When Doves Cry" and "Let's Go Crazy" and the crossover smashes "Purple Rain" and "I Would Die 4 U," both recorded "live" at the First Avenue Nightclub in Minneapolis. The film, soundtrack, and subsequent arena tour established Prince with white audiences, adolescents in particular, and made him a superstar.

Prince next announced his retirement from live performing and began building the Paisley Park recording studio near Minneapolis, which was completed in 1987. He also formed Paisley Park Records under the auspices of Warner Bros. His first album for the new label, the pretentious and insubstantial *Around the World in a Day*, yielded smash pop and R&B hits with "Raspberry Beret" and "Pop Life." His third album in less than two years, *Parade*, was issued on Paisley Park in 1986. The album was taken from the film *Under the Cherry Moon*, directed by Prince. A conspicuous failure after his popular ascension with *Purple Rain, Under the Cherry Moon* was lambasted as silly, vain, lifeless, and sexist. Nonetheless, *Parade* produced a top pop and R&B hit with "Kiss" (covered by Tom Jones in 1988), the major pop and R&B hit "Mountains," and the major R&B hit "Anotherloverholenyohead."

Prince had begun writing and producing for others beginning in 1982 with Vanity 6. The group scored a near-smash R&B-only hit with "Nasty Girl" and launched Vanity (Denise Matthews) on a marginally successful recording and film career. Apollonia 6's eponymous 1984 debut album contained the major R&B hit "Sex Shooter" from the film *Purple Rain*, and Chaka Khan scored a top R&B and smash pop hit with his "I Feel for You" that year. *The Family*, recorrded by former Time members Jerome Benton and Jellybean Johnson, yielded a near-smash R&B hit with "The Screams of Passion" in 1985, the year Prince wrote and coproduced Sheena Easton's controversial smash pop hit "Sugar Walls" under the name of Alex Nevermind. Prince also wrote the Bangles' smash 1986 pop hit "Manic Monday" as Christopher. *Wendy and Lisa*, recorded by Wendy Melvoin and Lisa Coleman of the Revolution, produced a minor pop-only hit with "Waterfall" in 1987. Percussionist-vocalist Sheila Escovedo (as Sheila E.), who began touring and recording with Prince in 1986, recorded two modest-selling albums for Paisley Park Records in 1985 and 1987, scoring a major hit in 1986 with Prince's "A Love Bizarre" from the movie *Krush Groove*, in which she starred. Mavis Staples toured with Prince in 1988 and recorded *Time Waits for No One* for Paisley Park in 1989.

By 1987 Prince had dismissed the Revolution and recorded *Sign o' the Times* by himself. The album yielded a top R&B and smash pop hit with the title song as well as a pop smash and major R&B hit with "U Got the Look" and two major R&B hits, "If I Was Your Girlfriend" and "Hot Thing," the flip of the near-smash pop hit "I Could Never Take the Place of Your Man." Several months later the concert film *Sign o' the Times* debuted to scathing reviews. Prince's next intended release, the so-called *Black Album*, was delayed and eventually withdrawn from release. Dark, sinister, and offensive, the album became quite popular as an illegal bootleg album, perhaps by design, and was eventually made available in limited release in late 1994.

Prince mounted his first full-scale American tour in four years in 1988, to support *Lovesexy*. The tour featured an eight-piece band that included Sheila E. and guitarist Levi Seacer Jr., but the album, his poorest-selling since his debut, produced only one pop hit, the smash "Alphabet Street." Prince's slide into commercial oblivion was arrested by 1989's *Batman*. Composed, arranged, performed, and produced by Prince, the album featured six songs included in the popular movie, plus three others: "The Arms of Orion," "Lemon Crush," and "Batdance." "Batdance" became a top pop and R&B hit, and "Partyman" became a major pop hit. In early 1990 Sinead O'Connor scored a top pop hit with Prince's "Nothing Compares 2 U," originally recorded by the Family in 1985. In 1991 Martika achieved a near-smash pop hit with "Love ... Thy Will Be Done," written and produced by Prince.

In 1990 Prince and Morris Day reprised their roles from *Purple Rain* in the film *Graffiti Bridge*. The film was deemed another commercial and artistic failure, but the soundtrack album included Prince's top R&B and smash pop hit "Thieves in the Temple"; Tevin Campbell's near-smash pop hit "Round and Round" (written and produced by Prince); Mavis Staples's "Melody Cool"; the George Clinton—Prince duet "We Can Funk"; and four songs by the reunited Time. Prince subsequently formed the New Power Generation with Levi Seacer Jr., keyboardists Tommy Barbarella and Rosie Gaines, and rapper Tony M., among others. Prince and the New Power Generation's debut album, *Diamonds and Pearls*, yielded five pop hits, including the top pop hit "Cream," the top R&B and smash pop hit "Diamonds and Pearls," and two major pop hits, "Gett Off" and "Money Don't Matter 2 Night."

In 1992 Prince renewed his contract with Warner Bros. Records in a deal reportedly worth $100 million. His next album was issued with a combined male-female symbol as its title and yielded four hits but only one major pop hit, the smash "7," which "sampled" the 1960s soul song "Tramp." Often referred to as Prince's "symbol" album or *TAFKAP* (for "the artist formerly known as Prince"), the album was primarily recorded with the New Power Generation and emphasized elements of rap music. Prince toured briefly in early 1993, but on April 27 he announced his "retirement" from recording and his intention to fulfill his contractual obligation to Warner Bros. with previously recorded material. Two months later, on his 35th birthday, he changed his name to the symbol used on his 1992 album and announced his separation from the New Power Generation. During the year, the renowned Joffrey Ballet utilized his music for its full-length rock ballet *Billboards*. He had never composed the music he had originally intended for the ballet.

Prince opened several Glam Slam nightclubs in 1993 and New Power Generation retail establishments in 1994. *Come*, his last album recorded with the New Power Generation and his last recorded before the name change, was issued in 1994, yielding a major R&B and moderate pop hit with "Letitgo." Dissolving Paisley Park Records, Prince subsequently recorded for NPG/Bellmark and a label using his symbol. "The Most Beautiful Girl in the World" became a smash R&B and pop and major easy-listening hit on NPG/Bellmark, and *The Beautiful Experience* contained seven different mixes of the song.

DISC.: EARLY PRINCE: *P. for You* (19780); *P.* (1979); *Dirty Mind* (1980); *Controversy* (1981); *1999* (1982). THE TIME: *The Time* (1981); *What Time Is It?* (1982); *Ice Cream Castle* (1984); *Pandemonium* (1990). JESSE JOHNSON: *Jesse Johnson's Revue* (1985); *Shockadelic* (1986); *Every Shade of Love* (1988). MORRIS DAY: *Color of Success* (1985); *Daydreaming* (1988); *Guaranteed* (1992). PRINCE: *Sign o' the Times* (1987); *Lovesexy* (1988); *Batman* (soundtrack; 1989); *Graffiti Bridge* (soundtrack; 1990); *The Hits 1* (1993); *The Hits 2* (1993); *The Hits/ The B-Sides* (1993); *The Black Album* (1994); *The Gold Experience* (1995); *The Beautiful Experience (mini)* (1994). PRINCE AND THE REVOLUTION: *Purple Rain* (soundtrack; 1984); *Around the World in a Day* (1985); *Parade* (1986). PRINCE AND THE NEW POWER GENERATION: *Diamonds and Pearls* (1991); *("TAFKAP")* (1992); *Come* (1994).

BIBL.: B. Hoskyns, *P.: Imp of the Perverse* (London, 1988). D. Hill, *P.: A Pop Life* (London, 1989); P. Nilsen, *P.: A Documentary* (London, 1990).—**BH**

Pringsheim, Klaus, German conductor and composer; b. Feldafing, near Munich, July 24, 1883; d. Tokyo, Dec. 7, 1972. A scion of a highly cultured family, he studied mathematics with his father, a prof. at the Univ. of Munich, and physics with Röntgen, the discoverer of X-rays. His twin sister, Katherine, was married to Thomas Mann. In Munich, Pringsheim took piano lessons with Stavenhagen and composition with Thuille. In 1906 he went to Vienna and was engaged as asst. conductor of the Court Opera, under the tutelage of Mahler, who took him as a pupil in conducting and composition, a relationship that developed into profound friendship. Mahler recommended him to the management of the German Opera in Prague; Pringsheim conducted there from 1909 to 1914; then was engaged as conductor and stage director at the Bremen Opera (1915–18) and music director of the Max Reinhardt theaters in Berlin (1918–25). In 1923–24 he conducted in Berlin a Mahler cycle of 8 concerts, featuring all of Mahler's syms. and songs with orch. In 1927 he became the music critic of the socialist newspaper *Vorwärts*. A turning point in Pringsheim's life came in 1931 with an invitation to teach music at the Imperial Academy of Music in Tokyo, where he taught until 1937; several of his Japanese students became prominent composers. From 1937 to 1939 Pringsheim served as music adviser to the Royal Dept. of Fine Arts in Bangkok, Thailand. In 1939 he returned to Japan; was briefly interned in 1944 as an opponent of the Axis policies. In 1946 he went to Calif.; after some intermittent activities, he returned to Japan in 1951; was appointed director of the Musashino Academy of Music in Tokyo; continued to conduct; also wrote music reviews for English-language Tokyo newspapers. As a composer, Pringsheim followed the neo-Romantic trends, deeply influenced by Mahler. His compositions include a *Concerto for Orchestra* (Tokyo, Oct. 13, 1935); *Yamada Nagasama*, Japanese radio opera (1953); Concertino for Xylophone and Orch. (1962); *Theme, Variations, and Fugue* for Wind Orch. (his last composition, 1971–72); and a curious album of 36 2-part canons for Piano (1959). A chapter from his theoretical work *Pythagoras, die Atonalität und wir* was publ. in *Schweizerische Musikzeitung* (1957). His reminiscences, "Mahler, My Friend," were publ. posthumously in the periodical *Composer* (1973–74). Pringsheim was a signatory of a letter of protest by surviving friends of Mahler against the film *Death in Venice*, after a novel of Thomas Mann, in which the central character, a famous writer who suffers a homosexual crisis, was made to resemble Mahler.—**NS/LK/DM**

Prinner, Johann Jacob, Austrian organist, music theorist, and composer; b. probably in Münzbach, 1624; d. Vienna, March 18, 1694. He studied in Siena in 1651. After serving as Kapellmeister at the court of Prince Eggenburg in Graz, he was chamberlain to Archduchess Maria Antonia in Vienna (1680–85), where he remained in the imperial court service for the rest of his life. He wrote the treatise *Musicalischer Schlissl* (1677). Among his extant works are 47 arias for Soprano and Basso Continuo (c. 1680–85) and some suites.—**LK/DM**

Printz, Wolfgang Caspar, significant German music theorist and historian; b. Waldthurn, Upper Palatinate, Oct. 10, 1641; d. Sorau, Lower Lusatia, Oct. 13, 1717. He studied in Waldthurn and at the Vohenstrauss Lateinschule, where he received instruction in music from Kilian Hammer and acquired proficiency in violin and keyboard playing. After further studies in Weiden (1654–59), he became a theological student at the Univ.

of Altdorf; also continued musical training. He became a Lutheran minister in 1661, but soon turned decisively to music and served as a tenor at the Heidelberg court chapel; then entered the service of a Dutch nobleman, whom he accompanied to Italy; there he devoted himself to the study of music theory. Returning to Germany, he served as court composer and music director to Count Leopold of Promnitz in Sorau until 1664; then was Kantor in Triebel (1664–65) before taking up that position in Sorau (1665); was also made music director to Count Balthasar Erdmann of Promnitz (1682). Printz's writings on music theory and history provide a valuable source for the study of 17th-century music; they greatly influenced Mattheson and Walther. He was also a composer, but his large output seems to be entirely lost. His valuable music library was destroyed in the devastating Sorau fire of 1684.

WRITINGS: *Compendium musicae in quo...explicantur...omnia ea quae ad Oden artificiose componendam requiruntur* (Guben, 1668); *Anweisung zur Singe-Kunst oder Kurtzer Bericht wie man einen Kanben...könne singen lehren* (Guben, 1672); *Phrynis Mitilenaeus, oder Satyrischer Componist* (3 vols., Quedlinburg, 1676–79); *Musica modulatoria vocalis oder Manierliche und zierliche Sing-Kunst* (Schweidnitz, 1678); *Declaration oder Weitere Erklärung der Refutation des Satyrischen Componistens* (1679); *Compendium musicae signatoriae et modulatoriae vocalis, das ist Kurtzer Begriff aller derjenigen Sachen, so einem, der die Vocal-Music lernen will, zu wissen von nöthen seyn* (Dresden, 1689; 2nd ed., 1714); *Exercitationes musicae theoretico-practicae curiosae de concordantiis singulis, das ist Musicalische Wissenschaft und Kunst-Übungen* (8 parts, Dresden, 1687–89); *Historische Beschreibung der edelen Sing- und Kling- Kunst* (Dresden, 1690).

BIBL.: H. Heckmann, *W.C. P. und seine Rhythmuslehre* (diss., Univ. of Freiburg, 1952).—**NS/LK/DM**

Prioris, Johannes, Franco-Netherlands composer; b. probably in Brabant, c. 1460; d. c. 1514. He served as maître de chapelle to King Louis XII of France. Among his extant works are 6 masses, including a Requiem Mass, motets, and chansons.

BIBL.: T. Keahey, *The Masses of J. P.* (diss., Univ. of Tex., 1968); C. Douglas, *The Motets of J. P. with a Prefatory Bio-bibliographical Study* (diss., Univ. of Ill., 1969); R. Wexler, *The Complete Works of J. P.* (diss., N.Y.U., 1974).—**LK/DM**

Pritchard, Sir John (Michael), distinguished English conductor; b. London, Feb. 5, 1921; d. Daly City, Calif., Dec. 5, 1989. He studied violin with his father, and then continued his musical training in Italy, returning to England to serve in the British army during World War II. In 1947 he joined the staff of the Glyndebourne Festival Opera as a répétiteur; became chorus master and assistant to Fritz Busch in 1948; conducted there regularly from 1951, serving as its music director (1969–77). He made his first appearance at London's Covent Garden in 1952. He was principal conductor of the Royal Liverpool Phil. (1957–63) and the London Phil. (1962–66), touring widely abroad with the latter. In 1963 he made his U.S. debut as a guest conductor with the Pittsburgh Sym. Orch.; also conducted at the Chicago Lyric Opera (1969) and the San Francisco Opera (1970). On Oct. 25, 1971, he made his Metropolitan Opera debut in N.Y. conducting *Così fan tutte*. As a guest conductor, he appeared with many of the world's leading opera houses and orchs. He was chief conductor of the Cologne Opera (1978–89). In 1979 he became chief guest conductor of the BBC Sym. Orch. in London, and subsequently was made its chief conductor in 1982. He was also joint music director of the Opera National in Brussels (1981–89), and served as the first music director of the San Francisco Opera (1986–89). In 1962 he was made a Commander of the Order of the British Empire, and was knighted in 1983. Pritchard was esteemed for his unpretentious but assured command of a vast operatic and symphonic repertory, extending from the Baroque masters to the leading composers of the present era.

BIBL.: H. Conway, *Sir J. P.: His Life in Music* (London, 1993). —**NS/LK/DM**

Priuli, Giovanni, Italian organist and composer; b. Venice, c. 1575; d. Vienna, 1629. He was a pupil of Giovanni Gabrieli in Venice, for whom he served as substitute organist at San Marco. From about 1614 to 1619 he was Hofkapellmeister to Archduke Ferdinand in Graz, a position he continued to hold when his patron became Emperor Ferdinand II in 1619. He served the emperor until 1622. His sacred vocal music owes much to the influence of Gabrieli, and comprises 5 vols. (Venice, 1618–24). He also brought out 5 vols. of secular vocal music (Venice, 1604–25).—**LK/DM**

Proch, Heinrich, Austrian conductor and composer; b. Bohmisch-Leipa, July 22, 1809; d. Vienna, Dec. 18, 1878. He studied law and at the same time took violin lessons. He became conductor of the Josephstadt Theater in Vienna in 1837, and from 1840 to 1870, conducted at the Vienna Court Opera. He wrote many songs that were popular for a time; his set of variations for coloratura soprano, with flute obbligato, was particularly well known; he also brought out in Vienna a comic opera, *Ring und Maske* (Dec. 4, 1844), and 3 one-act operas: *Die Blutrache* (Dec. 5, 1846), *Zweiter und dritter Stock* (Oct. 5, 1847), and *Der gefährliche Sprung* (Jan. 5, 1849).—**NS/LK/DM**

Procol Harum, progressive rock kings who hit it big with "A Whiter Shade of Pale." **MEMBERSHIP:** Gary Brooker, pno., voc. (b. London, England, May 29, 1945); Keith Reid, lyrics (b. London, England, Oct. 10, 1946); Matthew Fisher, org. (b. London, England, March 7, 1946); Ray Royer, gtr. (b. Oct. 8, 1945); Dave Knights, bs. (b. Islington, London, England, June 28, 1945; Bobby Harrison, drm. (b. East Ham, London, England, June 28, 1943). After their first single, Royer and Harrison left, to be replaced by guitarist Robin Trower (b. London, England, March 9, 1945) and drummer Barry J. "B. J." Wilson (b. Middlesex, England, March 18, 1947; d. Ore., 1989). Knights and Fisher left the group in 1969, to be replaced by organist-bassist Chris Copping (b. Southend, Essex, England, Aug. 29, 1945). Trower departed in 1971. Procol Harum disbanded in 1977 and reunited in 1991 with Brooker, Reid, Fisher, and Trower.

Procol Harum began their evolution as The Paramounts, a rhythm-and-blues group formed in Essex,

England, around 1961. The group comprised pianist Gary Brooker, guitarist Robin Trower, and bassist Chris Copping, later joined by drummer B. J. Wilson in 1963. Recording a series of unsuccessful British R&B singles, The Paramounts persevered until 1966, when Brooker formed a songwriting team with lyricist Keith Reid. Procol Harum was formed in April 1967, with Brooker, Reid, organist Matthew Fisher, guitarist Rob Royer, bassist Dave Knights, and drummer Bobby Harrison. Their debut single on Deram, "A Whiter Shade of Pale," featured Reid's mythic and surreal lyrics and the ominous organ playing of Fisher. It became a smash British and American hit and launched Procol Harum into international prominence. However, both Royer and Harrison soon departed, and Brooker recruited former Paramounts Robin Trower and B. J. Wilson for the completion of their debut album. *Procol Harum* served as an excellent first release, containing nine Brooker-Reid collaborations including "A Whiter Shade of Pale," the foreboding "Something Following Me," the raunchy "Mabel," "Conquistador," and the powerful five-minute tour de force, "(Outside the Gates of) Cerdes." Intellectually as well as emotionally stimulating, the album demonstrated that rock music could be intelligent and challenging.

Touring the U.S. for the first time in 1967 and 1968 as "Homburg" was becoming a moderate American hit single, Procol Harum next recorded *Shine on Brightly*. Issued in the U.S. on A&M Records, the album included "Skip Softly (My Moonbeams)," "Rambling On," and the title song, yet featured the 18-minute "In Held Twas in I," which depicted a stunning musical and lyrical journey from the depths of self-pity and depression to regal affirmation and renewed faith. Their next album, *A Salty Dog*, was their masterpiece, exploring a number of musical avenues enhanced by various dubbed-in sounds. It was filled with excellent songs, all with lyrics by Reid, such as the title song, "The Milk of Human Kindness," "Too Much between Us," "All This and More," "Pilgrim's Progress," and the amusing but fateful "Boredom."

However, after producing *A Salty Dog*, Matthew Fisher left Procol Harum to become a producer and pursue a neglected solo career. Dave Knights also departed, and he and Fisher were replaced by a single new member, bassist-organist Chris Copping, another former member of The Paramounts. Reduced to a performing quartet, Procol Harum emphasized the forceful guitar playing of Robin Trower on *Home* and *Broken Barricades*. *Home* included two Trower-Reid collaborations, "Whisky Train" and "About to Die," as well as Brooker-Reid compositions such as "Still There'll Be More" and "Your Own Choice." *Broken Barricades* contained three more melodies provided by Trower, most significantly the tribute to Jimi Hendrix, "Song for a Dreamer," in addition to Brooker and Reid's "Simple Sister," "Power Failure," and the lurid "Luskus Delph."

In July 1971, Robin Trower departed Procol Harum. The group realigned with Brooker, Wilson, Copping (who switched to organ), guitarist Dave Ball, and bassist Alan Cartwright. While touring North America in late 1971, Procol Harum was invited to record with the Edmonton Symphony Orch. in Canada. Live recordings of the concert became an instant surprise success, garnering the group critical acclaim and an expanded audience. The album, which compiled several of the group's early songs and the "In Held Twas in I" suite in full orchestral and choral treatment, yielded the group's third and final hit, "Conquistador," originally included on their debut album. Procol Harum then switched to Chrysalis Records for *Grand Hotel*. However, their fortunes began to fade with *Exotic Birds and Fruit*, a decidedly "hard rock" effort. *Procol's Ninth*, produced by legendary producers Jerry Leiber and Mike Stoller, included the favorite "Pandora's Box," but *Something Magic* fared poorly and Procol Harum disbanded in 1977. Gary Brooker subsequently recorded several solo albums before becoming a regular member of Eric Clapton's touring band in the late 1980s.

Upon leaving Procol Harum, Robin Trower formed the short-lived group Jude with Scottish vocalist Frankie Miller, former Stone the Crows bassist Jim Dewar, and former Jethro Tull drummer Clive Bunker. Trower next formed his own powerhouse trio with Dewar (who performed vocals) and drummer Reg Isidore. Their debut album for Chrysalis, *Twice Removed from Yesterday*, sold marginally despite the stunning Jimi Hendrix–derived guitar playing of Trower on songs such as "Hannah" and "Man of the World." *Bridge of Sighs* became a best-seller, at least in the U.S., where Trower consciously concentrated his efforts. Former Sly and The Family Stone drummer Bill Lordan replaced Isidore for the *For Earth Below* album. Subsequent Robin Trower albums through 1980 sold well, with *Long Misty Days* yielding Trower's only (minor) hit, "Caledonia." Dewar left in 1980 and Trower formed B.L.T. with Lordan and former Cream bassist Jack Bruce in 1981. Trower soon recorded *Truce* with Bruce before reforming his own band with Dewar for his final Chrysalis album *Back It Up*. In 1986, he recorded the independently released *Passion* and resumed touring, later switching to Atlantic Records.

In 1991, Procol Harum reunited with Gary Brooker, Keith Reid, Matthew Fisher, and Robin Trower for *The Prodigal Stranger* and a new round of touring, with Tim Renwick substituting for Trower. In 1993, Windsong U.K. issued the live BBC Radio One concert *Robin Trower* and, in 1995, Brooker, Fisher, and Trower recorded *The Long Goodbye* with the London Symphony Orch. for RCA.

DISC.: *Procol Harum* (1967); *Shine on Brightly* (1968); *A Salty Dog* (1969); *Home* (1970); *Broken Barricades* (1971); *Live with the Edmonton Symphony Orchestra* (1972); *Grand Hotel* (1973); *Exotic Birds and Fruit* (1974); *Procol's Ninth* (1975); *Something Magic* (1977); *The Chrysalis Years (1973–1977)* (1989); *The Prodigal Stranger* (1991).—**BH**

Procope, Russell, jazz alto saxophonist, clarinetist, violinist, long associated with Duke Ellington; b. N.Y., Aug. 11, 1908; d. there, Jan. 21, 1981. He can be heard on countless Ellington dates from 1946 to 1974. His brother, Bill, played violin, sax, and clarinet; their father was a violinist, their mother a pianist. At six, he started on violin, then began doubling on clarinet, studying with Lt. Eugene Mikell and playing in the 369th Cadet Band. He played with Willie Freeman's Band in 1926 and during the same year also did a spell with drummer Jimmy Campbell's Band in Albany on saxophone and violin. He had a residency at the 116th Street Dancing School in N.Y., then worked with Henri Saparo at Bamboo Inn, with Charlie Skeete (1927), and trombonist Billy Kate (1927–28). Procope played with Jelly Roll Morton at Rose Danceland (summer 1928), with Benny Carter's Band at Arcadia Ballroom (1929), then with Chick Webb (1929–31). After performing with Fletcher Henderson (spring 1931–34), he worked with Tiny Bradshaw (1934–35) in N.Y. and Chicago, then played in Teddy Hill's Band (1936–37), including a tour of Europe. He worked with Willie Bryant, then with John Kirby Sextet until he was called up for service in U.S. Army in late 1943. He played in shows while stationed in N.Y. during his tour of army duty. After he was demobilized in late 1945, he rejoined John Kirby (December 1945), then played with Duke Ellington (spring 1946). After a temporary absence due to illness, he returned to tour Europe with Ellington (autumn 1971), and remained with the band until Duke's death in 1974. He then performed with the Brooks Kerr Trio, including work in the musical "Ain't Misbehavin'" and freelancing.

DISC.: *Persuasive Sax of Russell Procope* (1956).—**JC/LP**

Procter, (Mary) Norma, English contralto; b. Cleethorpes, Feb. 15, 1928. She studied voice with Roy Henderson and Alec Redshaw. She made her debut in Handel's *Messiah* at Southwark Cathedral in 1948, and soon established herself as an outstanding concert singer. In 1961 she made her operatic debut at London's Covent Garden as Gluck's Orpheus.—**NS/LK/DM**

Prod'homme, J(acques)-G(abriel), industrious French librarian and music critic; b. Paris, Nov. 28, 1871; d. Neuilly-sur- Seine, near Paris, June 18, 1956. He studied philology and music history at the Paris École des Hautes Études Sociales (1890–94), then became a writer on musical and other subjects in the socialist publications, among them *La Revue Socialiste, Droits de l'Homme,* and *Messidor.* An ardent believer in the cause of peace, he ed. in Munich the *Deutsche-französische Rundschau,* dedicated to the friendship between the French and German peoples (1899–1902). His hopes for peace were shattered by 2 devastating world wars within his lifetime. Back in Paris, he founded, with Dauriac and Écorcheville, the French section of the IMS (1902), serving as its secretary (1903–13). With La Laurencie, he founded the French Musicological Society (1917), serving as its secretary (1917–20) and vice-president (1929–36). He was curator of the library and archivist of the museum at the Paris Opéra (1931–40); was also librarian at the Paris Cons. (1934–40). He was made a Chevalier of the Légion d'honneur (1928). With others, he tr. Wagner's prose works (13 vols., 1907–25); also Wagner's music dramas (1922–27) and Beethoven's conversation books (1946).

WRITINGS (all publ. in Paris): *Le Cycle Berlioz,* in 2 vols.: *La Damnation de Faust* (1896) and *L'Enfance du Christ* (1899); with C.

Bertrand, *Guides analytiques de l'Anneau du Nibelung. Crépuscule des dieux* (1902); *Hector Berlioz 1803–1869: Sa vie et ses oeuvres* (1905; 2nd ed., rev., 1913); *Les Symphonies de Beethoven (1800–1827)* (1906; 15th ed., 1938); *Paganini* (1907; 2nd ed., 1927; Eng. tr., 1911); *Franz Liszt* (1910); with A. Dandelot, *Gounod 1818–93: Sa vie et ses oeuvres d'après des documents inédits* (2 vols., 1911); *Ecrits de musiciens (XVe-XVIIIe siècles)* (1912); *Richard Wagner et la France* (1921); *La jeunesse de Beethoven, 1770–1800* (1921; 2nd ed., 1927); *L'Opéra, 1669–1925* (1925); *Pensées sur la musique et les musiciens* (1926); *Beethoven raconté par ceux qui l'ont vu* (1927); *Mozart raconté par ceux qui l'ont vu 1756–1791* (1928); *Schubert raconté par ceux qui l'ont vu* (1928); with E. Crauzat, *Paris qui disparaît: Les Menus plaisirs du roi; L'Ecole royale et le Conservatoire de Paris* (1929); *Wagner raconté par ceux qui l'ont vu* (1929); *Les Sonates pour piano de Beethoven, 1782–1823* (1937; 2nd ed., rev., 1950); *L'Immortelle bien-aimée de Beethoven* (1946); *Gluck* (1948); *François-Joseph Gossec, 1734–1829* (1949).—**NS/LK/DM**

Profe, Ambrosius, German organist, music editor, and composer; b. Breslau, Feb. 12, 1589; d. there, Dec. 27, 1661. He studied theology at Wittenburg, then was Kantor and schoolmaster in Jauer, Silesia (1617–29). From 1633 to 1649 he was a church organist in Breslau. He ed. important collections of German sacred music: *Geistliche Concerte und Harmonien* for 1 to 7 Voices (4 vols., 1641–46), *Corollarium geistlicher Collectaneorum* (a suppl. to the previous vol.; 1649), and a collection of Christmas pieces, *Cunis solennibus Jesuli recens-nati sacra genethliaca* (1646). He also brought out Heinrich Albert's *Arien* (1657).—**NS/LK/DM**

Profeta, Laurenţiu, Romanian composer; b. Bucharest, Jan. 12, 1925. He studied with Constantinescu and Mendelsohn (harmony, counterpoint, and composition) at the Bucharest Cons. (1945–49) and with Messner (composition) at the Moscow Cons. (1954–56). In 1945 he was awarded the Enesco Prize. He pursued his career in Bucharest, where he was asst. director of the Romanian Radio (1948–52). From 1952 to 1960 he was director of the music dept. of the Ministry of Culture. He was secretary of the Romanian National Committee of the International Music Council from 1960 to 1970. From 1968 he was also secretary of the Union of Composers and Musicologists, serving as a member of its directory council from 1990. It awarded him its prize 8 times (1968, 1969, 1976, 1979, 1980, 1986, 1990, 1993). In his music, Profeta has followed in the path of neo-Classicism while utilizing various contemporary elements in his scores.

WORKS: DRAMATIC: *The Captain's Wife,* ballet (1946); *The Prince and the Pauper,* ballet (Bucharest, Sept. 15, 1967); *The Wistful Mariner,* ballet (1976); *The Hours of the Sea,* ballet (1979); *The Triumph of Love,* ballet (1983); *Peter Pan's Story,* children's comic opera (Bucharest, Dec. 20, 1984); *Rica,* ballet (1986); *Hershale,* musical (1989); *The Loosers,* musical (Bucharest, Oct. 22, 1990); *Of the Carnival,* ballet (1991); *Eva Now,* musical (1993); *Kadar's Legacy,* musical (1999); *Childhood Remembrances,* radio musical (1999); film scores. ORCH.: *A Suite for Marionettes* for Chamber Orch. (1945); *Days of Vac,* suite (1956); *The Prince and the Pauper,* suite after the ballet (1975). VOCAL: *The Happening in the Garden,* oratorio for Soloists, Reciter, Children's Chorus, and Orch. (1958); *6 Humorous Pieces* for Soloists, Children's Chorus, Small Orch., and Tape (1966); *The Poem of the Forest* for

Children's Chorus, Electric Organ, and Tape (1968); *Romanian Christmas Carols* for Children's Chorus and Orch. (1994); *Sholem Aleichem's Musical World*, Jewish songs (1996); *Gypsy Songs* for Soloist and Orch. (2000). **OTHER:** *Symphonic Pop Music* for Synthesizer (1994).—**NS/LK/DM**

Prohaska, Carl, Austrian composer, father of **Felix Prohaska;** b. Mödling, near Vienna, April 25, 1869; d. Vienna, March 28, 1927. He studied piano with Anna Assmayr in Vienna and with d'Albert in Berlin and composition with Franz Krenn and musicology with Mandyczewski in Vienna. In 1908 he joined the faculty of the Vienna Academy of Music, where he taught piano and theory. He wrote an opera, *Madeleine Guinard*, an oratorio, *Frühlingsfeier* (1913), String Quartet, Piano Trio, Quintet for 2 Violins, Viola, Cello, and Double Bass, and a group of piano pieces.—**NS/LK/DM**

Prohaska, Felix, Austrian conductor, son of **Carl Prohaska;** b. Vienna, May 16, 1912; d. there, March 29, 1987. He received his primary music education at home with his father; then studied piano with Steuermann, and theory with Kornauth, Gál et al. He served as répétiteur at the Graz Opera (1936–39); conducted opera in Duisburg (1939–41) and in Strasbourg (1941–43); then was first conductor of the Vienna State Opera (1945–55) and the Frankfurt am Main Opera (1955–61). He again conducted at the Vienna State Opera (1964–67); conducted at the opera in Hannover (1965–74), and also served as director of the Hochschule für Musik there (1961–75).—**NS/LK/DM**

Prohaska, Jaro(slav), Austrian bass-baritone; b. Vienna, Jan. 24, 1891; d. Munich, Sept. 28, 1965. He sang in the Wiener Sängerknaben, and studied voice with Otto Müller in Vienna. He made his operatic debut in Lübeck in 1922, then sang in Nuremberg (1925–31). In 1932 he joined the Berlin State Opera, remaining on its roster until 1953; also made many appearances at the Bayreuth Festivals (1933–44), where he excelled in such roles as Hans Sachs, Wotan, and the Dutchman. He was director of the West Berlin Hochschule für Musik (1947–59), where he also directed its opera school (1952–59).—**NS/LK/DM**

Prokina, Elena, Russian soprano; b. Odessa, Jan. 16, 1964. Following training in Odessa, she studied at the Theater Inst. and at the Cons. in Leningrad. In 1988 she became a member of the Kirov Opera in Leningrad, with which she appeared in many Russian roles both at home and on tours abroad. In 1994 she made her first appearance at London's Covent Garden as Kát'a Kabanová, and also sang Tatiana at the Glyndebourne Festival and in Monte Carlo, and Donna Anna in Los Angeles. In 1995 she returned to Covent Garden as Desdemona and to Los Angeles as Lina in *Steffelio*, and also appeared as Amelia Boccanegra in Zürich. She sang in recital at London's Wigmore Hall in 1997. In 1998 she was engaged as Kát'a Kabanová in Dallas and as Violetta in Zürich.—**NS/LK/DM**

Prokofiev, Sergei (Sergeievich), great Russian composer of modern times, creator of new and original formulas of rhythmic, melodic, and harmonic combinations that became the recognized style of his music; b. Sontsovka, near Ekaterinoslav, April 27, 1891; d. Moscow, March 5, 1953. His mother was born a serf in 1859, 2 years before the emancipation of Russian serfdom, and she assumed (as was the custom) the name of the estate where she was born, Sontsov. Prokofiev was born on that estate on April 27, 1891, although he himself erroneously believed that the date was April 23; the correct date was established with the discovery of his birth certificate. He received his first piano lessons from his mother, who was an amateur pianist; he improvised several pieces, and then composed a children's opera, *The Giant* (1900), which was performed in a domestic version. Following his bent for the theater, he put together 2 other operas, *On Desert Islands* (1902) and *Ondine* (1904–07); fantastic subjects obviously possessed his childish imagination. He was 11 years old when he met the great Russian master, Taneyev, who arranged for him to take systematic private lessons with Glière, who became his tutor at Sontsovka during the summers of 1903 and 1904 and by correspondence during the intervening winter. Under Glière's knowledgeable guidance in theory and harmony, Prokofiev composed a sym. in piano version and still another opera, *Plague*, based upon a poem by Pushkin. Finally, in 1904, at the age of 13, he enrolled in the St. Petersburg Cons., where he studied composition with Liadov and piano with Alexander Winkler; later he was accepted by no less a master than Rimsky-Korsakov, who instructed him in orchestration. He also studied conducting with Nikolai Tcherepnin, and form with Wihtol. Further, he entered the piano class of Anna Essipova. During the summers, he returned to Sontsovka or traveled in the Caucasus and continued to compose, already in quite an advanced style; the Moscow publisher Jurgenson accepted his first work, a piano sonata, for publication; it was premiered in Moscow on March 6, 1910. It was then that Prokofiev made his first visit to Paris, London, and Switzerland (1913); in 1914 he graduated from the St. Petersburg Cons., receiving the Anton Rubinstein Prize (a grand piano) as a pianist-composer with his Piano Concerto No. 1, which he performed publicly at the graduation concert. Because of audacious innovations in his piano music (he wrote one piece in which the right and left hands played in different keys), he was described in the press as a "futurist," and because of his addiction to dissonant and powerful harmonic combinations, some critics dismissed his works as "football music." This idiom was explicitly demonstrated in his *Sarcasms* and *Visions fugitives*, percussive and sharp, yet not lacking in lyric charm. Grotesquerie and irony animated his early works; he also developed a strong attraction toward subjects of primitive character. His important orch. work, the *Scythian Suite* (arr. from music written for a ballet, *Ala and Lolly*, 1915), draws upon a legend of ancient Russian sun-worship rituals. While a parallel with Stravinsky's *Le Sacre du printemps* may be drawn, there is no similarity between the styles of the 2 works. The original performance of the *Scythian Suite*, scheduled at a Koussevitzky concert in Moscow, was canceled on account of the disruption caused by war, which did not prevent the otherwise intelligent Russian music critic Sabaneyev, blissfully unaware that the announced premiere had been canceled, from delivering a blast of the work as a farrago of atrocious noises. (Sabaneyev was forced to resign his position after this episode.) Another Prokofiev score, primitivistic in its inspiration, was the cantata *Seven, They Are Seven*, based upon incantations from an old Sumerian religious ritual. During the same period, Prokofiev wrote his famous *Classical Symphony* (1916–17), in which he adopted with remarkable acuity the formal style of Haydn's music. While the structure of the work was indeed classical, the sudden modulatory shifts and subtle elements of grotesquerie revealed decisively a new modern art.

After conducting the premiere of his *Classical Symphony* in Petrograd on April 21, 1918, Prokofiev left Russia by way of Siberia and Japan for the U.S. (the continuing war in Europe prevented him from traveling westward). He gave concerts of his music in Japan and later in the U.S., playing his first solo concert in N.Y. on Oct. 29, 1918. Some American critics greeted his appearance as the reflection of the chaotic events of Russia in revolution, and Prokofiev himself was described as a "ribald and Bolshevist innovator and musical agitator." "Every rule in the realm of traditional music writing was broken by Prokofiev," one N.Y. writer complained. "Dissonance followed dissonance in a fashion inconceivable to ears accustomed to melody and harmonic laws." Prokofiev's genteel *Classical Symphony* struck some critics as "an orgy of dissonant sound, an exposition of the unhappy state of chaos from which Russia suffers." One N.Y. critic indulged in the following: "Crashing Siberians, volcano hell, Krakatoa, sea-bottom crawlers. Incomprehensible? So is Prokofiev." But another critic issued a word of caution, suggesting that "Prokofiev might be the legitimate successor of Borodin, Mussorgsky, and Rimsky-Korsakov." The critic was unintentionally right; Prokofiev is firmly enthroned in the pantheon of Russian music.

In 1920 Prokofiev settled in Paris, where he established an association with Diaghilev's Ballets Russes, which produced his ballets *Chout* (a French transliteration of the Russian word for buffoon), *Le Pas d'acier* (descriptive of the industrial development in Soviet Russia), and *L'Enfant prodigue*. In 1921 Prokofiev again visited the U.S. for the production of the opera commissioned by the Chicago Opera Co., *The Love for 3 Oranges*. In 1927 he was invited to be the pianist for a series of his own works in Russia. He gave a number of concerts in Russia again in 1929, and eventually decided to remain there. In Russia he wrote some of his most popular works, including the symphonic fairy tale *Peter and the Wolf*, staged by a children's theater in Moscow, the historical cantata *Alexander Nevsky*, the ballet *Romeo and Juliet*, and the opera *War and Peace*.

Unexpectedly, Prokofiev became the target of the so-called proletarian group of Soviet musicians who accused him of decadence, a major sin in Soviet Russia at the time. His name was included in the official denunciation of modern Soviet composers issued by reactionary Soviet politicians in 1948. He meekly confessed that he had been occasionally interested in atonal and polytonal devices during his stay in Paris, but insisted that he had never abandoned the ideals of classical Russian music. Indeed, when he composed his 7th Sym., he described it specifically as a youth sym., reflecting the energy and ideals of new Russia. There were also significant changes in his personal life. He separated from his Spanish-born wife, the singer Lina Llubera, the mother of his 2 sons, and established a companionship with Myra Mendelson, a member of the Young Communist League. She was a writer and assisted him on the libretto of his *War and Peace*. He made one final attempt to gain favor with the Soviet establishment by writing an opera based on a heroic exploit of a Soviet pilot during the war against the Nazis. But this, too, was damned by the servile Communist press as lacking in true patriotic spirit, and the opera was quickly removed from the repertory. Prokofiev died of heart failure on March 5, 1953, a few hours before the death of Stalin. Curiously enough, the anniversary of Prokofiev's death is duly commemorated, while that of his once powerful nemesis is officially allowed to be forgotten. O. Prokofiev tr. and ed. his *Soviet Diary, 1927, and Other Writings* (London, 1991).

WORKS: DRAMATIC: O p e r a : *Maddalena* (1912–13, piano score only; orchestrated by Edward Downes, 1978; BBC Radio, March 25, 1979; 1st stage perf., Graz, Nov. 28, 1981; U.S. premiere, St. Louis, June 9, 1982); *The Gambler*, after Dostoyevsky (1915–16; rev. 1927; Brussels, April 29, 1929); *The Love for 3 Oranges*, after Gozzi (1919; Chicago, Dec. 30, 1921); *The Fiery Angel* (1919; 2 fragments perf., Paris, June 14, 1928; 1st complete concert perf., Paris, Nov. 25, 1954; 1st stage perf., Venice, Sept. 14, 1955); *Semyon Kotko* (1939; Moscow, June 23, 1940); *Betrothal in a Convent*, after Sheridan's *Duenna* (1940; Leningrad, Nov. 3, 1946); *War and Peace*, after Tolstoy (1941–52; concert perf. of 8 of the original 11 scenes, Ensemble of Soviet Opera of the All-Union Theatrical Society, Oct. 16, 1944; concert perf. of 9 of the original 11 scenes with scenes 6 and 8 omitted, Moscow Phil., June 7, 1945; stage perf. of Part I [*Peace*] with new Scene 2, Maly Theater, Leningrad, June 12, 1946; "final" version of 11 scenes, Prague, June 25, 1948; another "complete" version, Leningrad, March 31, 1955; rev. version in 13 scenes with cuts, Moscow, Nov. 8, 1957; 13 scenes with a choral epigraph, Moscow, Dec. 15, 1959); *A Tale about a Real Man* (1947–48; private perf., Leningrad, Dec. 3, 1948; severely censured by Soviet critics and not produced in public until given at the Bolshoi Theater, Moscow, Oct. 8, 1960). **B a l l e t :** *Buffoon* (1920; Paris, May 17, 1921); *Trapeze* (1924; music used in his Quintet); *Le Pas d'acier* (1924; Paris, June 7, 1927); *L'Enfant prodigue* (1928; Paris, May 21, 1929); *Sur le Borysthène* (1930; Paris, Dec. 16, 1932); *Romeo and Juliet* (1935–36; Brno, Dec. 30, 1938); *Cinderella* (1940–44; Moscow, Nov. 21, 1945); *A Tale of the Stone Flower* (1948–50; Moscow, Feb. 12, 1954). **I n c i d e n t a l M u s i c T o :** *Egyptian Nights* (1933); *Boris Godunov* (1936); *Eugene Onegin* (1936); *Hamlet* (1937–38; Leningrad, May 15, 1938). **F i l m :** *Lt. Kijé* (1933); *The Queen of Spades* (1936); *Alexander Nevsky* (1938); *Lermontov* (1941); *Tonya* (1942); *Kotovsky* (1942); *Partisans in the Ukrainian Steppes* (1942); *Ivan the Terrible* (1942–45). **ORCH.:** *Rêves*, symphonic tableau (St. Petersburg, Dec. 5, 1910); *Autumn*, symphonic tableau (Moscow, Aug. 1, 1911); 5 piano concertos: No. 1 (Moscow, Aug. 7, 1912, composer soloist), No. 2 (Pavlovsk, Sept. 5, 1913, composer soloist), No. 3 (1917–21; Chicago, Dec. 16, 1921, composer soloist), No. 4, for the Left Hand (1931; Berlin, Sept. 5, 1956), and No. 5 (Berlin, Oct. 31, 1932, composer soloist); Sinfonietta

(1914; Petrograd, Nov. 6, 1915; rev. 1929; Moscow, Nov. 18, 1930); *Scythian Suite* (1914; Petrograd, Jan. 29, 1916); 2 violin concertos: No. 1 (1916–17; Paris, Oct. 18, 1923) and No. 2 (Madrid, Dec. 1, 1935); 7 syms.: No. 1, *Classical* (1916–17; Petrograd, April 21, 1918, composer conducting), No. 2 (1924; Paris, June 6, 1925; 2nd version not completed), No. 3 (1928; Paris, May 17, 1929), No. 4 (Boston, Nov. 11, 1930; radically rev. version, 1947), No. 5 (1944; Moscow, Jan. 13, 1945), No. 6 (1945–47; Leningrad, Oct. 11, 1947), and No. 7 (1951–52; Moscow, Oct. 11, 1952); *Buffoon*, suite from the ballet (1923; Brussels, Jan. 15, 1924); *The Love for 3 Oranges*, suite from the opera (Paris, Nov. 29, 1925); *Divertissement* (1925–29; Paris, Dec. 22, 1929); *Le Pas d'acier*, suite from the ballet (1926; Moscow, May 27, 1928); *American Overture* for Chamber Orch. (Moscow, Feb. 7, 1927; also for Orch., 1928; Paris, Dec. 18, 1930); *L'Enfant prodigue*, suite from the ballet (1929; Paris, March 7, 1931); *4 Portraits*, suite from the opera *The Gambler* (1931; Paris, March 12, 1932); *On the Dnieper*, suite from the ballet (1933); 2 cello concertos: No. 1 (1933–38; Moscow, Nov. 26, 1938, Lev Berezovsky soloist) and No. 2 (rev. version of No. 1; Moscow, Feb. 18, 1952, M. Rostropovich soloist; further rev. as *Sinfonia Concertante*, Copenhagen, Dec. 9, 1954, Rostropovich soloist); *Symphonic Song* (Moscow, April 14, 1934); *Lt. Kijé*, suite from the film music (1934; Paris, Feb. 20, 1937); *Egyptian Nights*, suite from the incidental music (Radio Moscow, Dec. 21, 1934); *Romeo and Juliet*, 3 suites from the ballet (No. 1, Moscow, Nov. 24, 1936, No. 2, Leningrad, April 15, 1937, and No. 3, Moscow, March 8, 1946); *Peter and the Wolf*, symphonic fairy tale (Moscow, May 2, 1936); *Semyon Kotko*, suite from the opera (1940); *A Summer Day*, children's suite for Chamber Orch. (1941); *Symphonic March* (1941); *The Year 1941* (1941; Sverdlovsk, Jan. 21, 1943); *Ivan the Terrible*, suite from the film music (1942–45); March for Military Orch. (Moscow, April 30, 1944); *Ode on the End of the War* for 8 Harps, 4 Pianos, Military Band, Percussion Ensemble, and Double Basses (Moscow, Nov. 12, 1945); *Cinderella*, 3 suites from the ballet (No. 1, Moscow, Nov. 12, 1946, No. 2, 1946, and No. 3, Radio Moscow, Sept. 3, 1947); *Waltzes*, suite (1946; Moscow, May 13, 1947); *Festive Poem* (Moscow, Oct. 3, 1947); *Pushkin Waltzes* (1949); *Summer Night*, suite from the opera *Betrothal in a Convent* (1950); *Wedding Scene*, suite from the ballet *A Tale of the Stone Flower* (Moscow, Dec. 12, 1951); *Gypsy Fantasy* from the ballet *A Tale of the Stone Flower* (Moscow, Nov. 18, 1951); *Ural Rhapsody* from the ballet *A Tale of the Stone Flower* (1951); *The Mistress of the Copper Mountain*, suite from the ballet *A Tale of the Stone Flower* (1951; unfinished); *The Meeting of the Volga with the Don River*, for the completion of the Volga-Don Canal (1951; Moscow, Feb. 22, 1952); Cello Concertino (1952; unfinished; completed by M. Rostropovich and D. Kabalevsky); Concerto for 2 Pianos and Strings (1952; unfinished). **CHAMBER:** *Humorous Scherzo* for 4 Bassoons (1912; London, Sept. 2, 1916); *Ballade* for Cello and Piano (1912; Moscow, Feb. 5, 1914); *Overture on Hebrew Themes* for Clarinet, 2 Violins, Viola, Cello, and Piano (N.Y., Jan. 26, 1920); Quintet for Oboe, Clarinet, Violin, Viola, and Double Bass (1924; Moscow, March 6, 1927); 2 string quartets: No. 1 (Washington, D.C., April 25, 1931) and No. 2 (1941; Moscow, Sept. 5, 1942); Sonata for 2 Violins (Moscow, Nov. 27, 1932); 2 violin sonatas: No. 1 (1938–46; BBC, London, Aug. 25, 1946) and No. 2 (Moscow, June 17, 1944; transcribed from the Flute Sonata); Flute Sonata (Moscow, Dec. 7, 1943); Sonata for Solo Violin (1947; Moscow, March 10, 1960); Cello Sonata (1949; Moscow, March 1, 1950). **Piano:** 10 sonatas (1909; 1912; 1917; 1917; 1923; 1940; 1942; 1944; 1947; 1953, unfinished); 4 Etudes (1909); 4 Pieces (1911); 4 Pieces (1912); Toccata (1912); *Sarcasms*, suite of 5 pieces (1912–14); 10

Pieces (1913); *Visions fugitives*, suite of 20 pieces (1915–17); *Tales of an Old Grandmother*, 4 pieces (1918); *March and Scherzo* from the opera *The Love for 3 Oranges* (1922); *Things in Themselves* (1928); 6 Pieces (1930–31); 2 sonatinas (1931–32); 3 Pieces (1934); *Pensées* (1933–34); *Children's Music*, 12 easy pieces (1935); *Romeo and Juliet*, 10 pieces from the ballet (1937); 3 pieces from the ballet *Cinderella* (1942); 3 Pieces (1941–42); 10 pieces from the ballet *Cinderella* (1943); 6 pieces from the ballet *Cinderella* (1944). **VOCAL: Choral:** 2 poems for Women's Chorus and Orch: *The White Swan* and *The Wave* (1909); *Seven, They Are Seven*, cantata for Tenor, Chorus, and Orch. (1917–18; Paris, May 29, 1924); Cantata for the 20th anniversary of the October Revolution, for 2 Choruses, Military Band, Accordions, and Percussion, to texts by Marx, Lenin, and Stalin (1937; perf. in Moscow, April 5, 1966, but not in its entirety; the section which used a text from Stalin was eliminated); *Songs of Our Days*, suite for Solo Voices, Chorus, and Orch. (Moscow, Jan. 5, 1938); *Alexander Nevsky*, cantata for Mezzo-soprano, Chorus, and Orch. (Moscow, May 17, 1939); *Zdravitsa: Hail to Stalin*, cantata for Chorus and Orch., for Stalin's 60th birthday (Moscow, Dec. 21, 1939); *Ballad of an Unknown Boy*, cantata for Soprano, Tenor, Chorus, and Orch. (Moscow, Feb. 21, 1944); *Hymn to the Soviet Union* (1943; submitted to the competition for a new Soviet anthem but failed to win; a song by Alexander Alexandrov was selected); *Flourish, Powerful Land*, cantata for the 30th anniversary of the October Revolution (Moscow, Nov. 12, 1947); *Winter Bonfire*, suite for Narrators, Boys' Chorus, and Orch. (Moscow, Dec. 19, 1950); *On Guard for Peace*, oratorio for Mezzo-soprano, Narrators, Chorus, Boys' Chorus, and Orch. (Moscow, Dec. 19, 1950). **Songs:** 2 Poems (1911); *The Ugly Duckling*, after Hans Christian Andersen (1914); 5 Poems (1915); 5 Poems (1916); 5 Songs without Words (1920; also for Violin and Piano); 5 Poems (1921); 6 Songs (1935); 3 Children's Songs (1936); 3 Poems (1936); 3 songs from the film *Alexander Nevsky* (1939); 7 Songs (1939); 7 Mass Songs (1941–42); 12 transcriptions of folk songs (1944); 2 duets (1945); *Soldiers' March Song* (1950).

BIBL.: I. Nestyev, *S. P.* (Moscow, 1946; Eng. tr., N.Y., 1946; enl. Russian ed., Moscow, 1957; Eng. tr. with a foreword by N. Slonimsky, Stanford, Calif., 1961); M. Sabinina, *S. P.* (Moscow, 1958); M. Hofmann, *P.* (Paris, 1963); H. Brockhaus, *S. P.* (Leipzig, 1964); L. and E. Hanson, *P., The Prodigal Son* (London, 1964); M. Rayment, *P.* (London, 1965); S. Schlifstein, ed., *P.* (Moscow, 1965); L. Danko, *S.S. P.* (Moscow, 1966); M. Brown, *The Symphonies of P.* (diss., Fla. State Univ., 1967); S. Morozov, *P.* (Moscow, 1967); V. Serov, *S. P., A Soviet Tragedy* (N.Y., 1968); R. McAllister, *The Operas of S. P.* (diss., Cambridge Univ., 1970); I. Martynov, *P.* (Moscow, 1974); D. Appel, ed., and G. Daniels, tr., *P. by P.: A Composer's Memoir* (Garden City, N.Y., 1979); V. Blok, ed., *S. P.: Materials, Articles, Interviews* (London, 1980); H. Robinson, *The Operas of S. P. and Their Russian Literary Sources* (diss., Univ. of Calif., Berkeley, 1980); M. Nesteyeva, *S.S. P.* (Moscow, 1981); N. Savkina, *S.S. P.* (Moscow, 1982; Eng. tr., Neptune City, N.J., 1984); D. Gutman, *P.* (London, 1988); S. Fiess, *The Piano Works of S. P.* (Metuchen, N.J., 1994); C. Samuel, *P.* (Paris, 1995); M. Biesold, *S. P.: Komponist im Schatten Stalins: Eine Biographie* (Berlin, 1996); N. Minturn, *The Music of S. P.* (New Haven, 1997); H. Robinson, tr. and ed., *Selected Letters of S. P.* (Boston, 1998).—NS/LK/DM

Propiac, (Catherine Joseph Ferdinand) Girard de,

French composer; b. Dijon, 1759; d. Paris, Oct. 31, 1823. After writing several works for the Paris stage, he left France to serve in Condé's anti-Revolutionary army (1791–99). In 1799 he returned to Paris and was archivist to the Prefecture of State until 1802. Thereafter he devoted himself to belles lettres.

WORKS: DRAMATIC (all 1st perf. in Paris): *Isabelle et Rosalvo*, comédie (June 18, 1787); *Les deux morts*, opéra-comique (June 20, 1787); *Les trois déesses rivales, ou Le double jugement de Paris*, comédie lyrique (July 28, 1788); *La fausse paysanne, ou L'heureuse inconséquence*, comédie (March 26, 1789); *Les savoyards, ou La continence de Bayard*, comédie (May 30, 1789); *La double apothéose*, opéra-comique (1800); *La pension des jeunes garçons*, opéra-comique (1801). **OTHER:** Numerous romances. —LK/DM

Prosdocimus de Beldemandis or Prosdocimo de' Beldomandi,

Italian music theorist; b. probably in Padua, date unknown; d. there, 1428. He was educated at the Univ. of Bologna, and at the Univ. of Padua (doctor in artibus, 1409; doctor in medicine, 1411), where he joined its faculty. In addition to his studies in music, he pursued studies in mathematics and astronomy. In his *Tractatus musicae speculative* (1425), he attacked Marchetto da Padova's division of the whole tone into 5 equal parts. His writings are an important source in the study of Italian music of the early 15th century.

WRITINGS: *Exposiciones tractatus pratice cantus mensurabilis magistri Johannis de Muris* (1404; 2nd version, c. 1411; ed. by F. Gallo, Bologna, 1966; rewritten, 1408, as *Tractatus pratice cantus mensurabilis*; 2nd version, c. 1411); *Brevis summula proporcionum quantum ad musican pertinet* (1409); *Contrapunctus* (1412; ed. and tr. by J. Herlinger, Lincoln, Nebr., 1984); *Tractatus plane musice* (1412); *Tractatus pratice cantus mensurabilis ad modum ytalicorum* (1412); *Parvus tractatulus de modo monocordum dividendi* (1413; ed. and tr. by J. Herlinger, Lincoln, Nebr., 1987); *Tractatus musicae speculative* (1425).—LK/DM

Proske, Carl,

noted German music scholar and editor; b. Gröbnig, Feb. 11, 1794; d. Regensburg, Dec. 20, 1861. He was a medical student, and served in the medical corps during the war of 1813–15. He took the degree of M.D. at Halle Univ. in 1817, and practiced at Oberglogau and Oppeln. In 1823 he renounced medicine for theology, and studied at Regensburg. He was ordained in 1826, and became vicar-choral in 1827 and canon and Kapellmeister of the Church of Our Lady at Regensburg in 1830. After diligent research in Germany and Italy, he began his lifework, the publ. of sacred classics, the first being Palestrina's *Missa Papae Marcelli* (Palestrina's original version, and arrangements by Anerio *a* 4 and Suriano *a* 8), followed by the famous collection *Musica divina*, containing chiefly Italian masterworks of the 16th–17th centuries: Vol. I, 12 masses *a* 4 (1853), Vol. II, motets for the entire church year (1855), Vol. III, fauxbourdons, Psalms, Magnificats, hymns, and antiphons (1859), and Vol. IV, Passions, Lamentations, responses, Te Deums, litanies (1863; ed. by Wesselack; its publication was continued by Schrems and Haberl. Proske also publ. *Selectus novus missarum a* 4–8 (1855–59). His valuable library passed into the care of the Regensburg bishopric.

BIBL.: Dom Mettenleiter, *C. P.* (Regensburg, 1868; 2nd ed., 1895); K. Weinmann, *C. P., der Restaurator der katholischen Kirchenmusik* (Regensburg, 1909).—NS/LK/DM

Prot, Félix-Jean,

French violinist, violist, and composer; b. Senlis, Oise, 1747; d. Paris, 1823. He studied with Desmarets (violin) and Gianotti (composition). He was only 14 when he collaborated with Favart on the opéra-comique *Le bal bourgeos* (Paris, Aug. 1761), which proved tremendously successful. His initial success as a composer for the stage was not sustained, however, and he was active as a violist in the orch. of the Comédie Française in Paris from 1775 to 1822. His other stage works, all premiered in Paris, included *Les rêveries renouvelées des grecs* (June 26, 1779), *Le printemps* (May 19, 1781), and *L'amour à l'épreuve* (Aug. 13, 1784). He also wrote a Simphonie concertante for 2 Violas and Orch. (1786), several simphonies en trio, and chamber music. —LK/DM

Prota, family of Italian musicians:

(1) Ignazio Prota, composer; b. Naples, Sept. 15, 1690; d. there, Jan. 1748. He spent his entire life in Naples, where he studied with his uncle, Filippo Prota, a priest and maestro di cappella at S. Giorgio Maggiore, and with Gaetano Veneziano and Giuliano Perugino at the Cons. S. Maria di Loreto. From 1722 he was maestro at the Cons. S. Onofrio a Capuana. Prota wrote the first opera buffa in the Neapolitan dialect, *La fenta fattucchiera* (Naples, 1721; not extant). He had 2 sons who were musicians:

(2) Tommaso Prota, composer; b. Naples, date unknown; d. after 1768. He studied at the Cons. S. Maria di Loreto in Naples, and then was active in various Italian cities. He wrote 3 stage works (all lost), some instrumental pieces, and various vocal scores.

(3) Giuseppe Prota, oboist and teacher; b. Naples, Dec. 3, 1737; d. there, July 21, 1807. His career was centered on Naples, where he studied at the Cons. S. Maria di Loreto with Cherubino Corona. In 1762 he succeeded his teacher there as an instructor in oboe, bassoon, and flute. From 1778 he was oboist in the royal chapel and from 1779 an instructor in wind instruments at the Cons. della Pietà dei Turchini.

(4) Gabriele Porta, composer, grandson of **(1) Ignazio Prota**; b. Naples, May 19, 1755; d. there, June 22, 1843. He was maestro of the Ss. Annunziata church in Naples in 1780, and then at the monastery church of S. Chiara. His marriage to the Parisian Rosalie Laurent led him to embrace her Jacobin sentiments. After the Republican uprising in 1799, they were both arrested. When Joseph Buonaparte took the throne of Naples in 1806, he made Rosalie director of the music school for women, where Gabriele served as maestro di cappella and a singing teacher. He wrote *Ezio*, opera seria (Perugia, Carnival 1784), *La furberie*, opera buffa (Naples, Carnival 1793), *Le donne dispettose*, opera buffa (Naples, Carnival 1793), *Gli studenti*, opera buffa (Naples, May 1796), and several sacred vocal pieces. His son was also a musician:

(5) Givoanni Prota, pedagogue and composer; b. Naples, c. 1786; d. there, June 13?, 1843. He pursued his career in Naples, where he was a voice teacher and maestro e compositore at the Real Casa d'Educazione Miracoli, the Regina Isabella Borone school for young Neapolitan noblewomen, from about 1820. For Naples, he composed *Il servo furbo*, opera buffa (Carnival 1803), *Amor dal naufragio*, opera buffa (Jan. 1810), and *Il cimento felice*, opera semiseria (1815). Among his other works were instrumental pieces and much sacred vocal music. —**LK/DM**

Prota-Giurleo, Ulisse, distinguished Italian musicologist; b. Naples, March 13, 1886; d. Perugia, Feb. 9, 1966. He studied with Salvatore di Giacomo in Naples; then devoted himself to the study of Neapolitan music and theater. In addition to his valuable books, he contributed important articles to various journals, including "Breve storia del teatro di corte e della musica a Napoli nei secoli XVII e XVIII," in *Il teatro di corte del Palazzo reale di Napoli* (Naples, 1952).

WRITINGS (all publ. in Naples unless otherwise given): *Musicisti napoletani in Russia* (1923); *La prima calcofragia musicale a Napoli* (1923); *Musicisti napoletani alla corte di Portogallo* (1924); *Alessandro Scarlatti "il Palermitano"* (1926); *La grande orchestra del Teatro San Carlo nel '700* (1927); *Nicola Logroscino "il dio dell'opera buffa"* (1927); *Francesco Cirillo e l'introduzione del melodramma a Napoli* (Grumo Nevano, 1952); *Francesco Durante nel 27 centenario della sua morte* (Frattamaggiore, 1955); *La famiglia napoletana dei Prota nella storia della musica* (Milan, 1957); *Miserere, tradotto in dialetto napoletano da Nicola Valletta* (1960); *I teatri di Napoli nel '600: La commedia e le maschere* (1962); *Gian Leonardo dell'Arpa nella storia della musica* (1964); with A. Giovine, *Giacomo Insanguine detto Monopoli, musicista monopolitano: Cenno biografici, elenco di rappresentazioni, bibliografia, indice vari e iconografia* (Bari, 1969).

BIBL.: A. Giovine, *U. P.-G.: Ricordo di un mio maestro* (Bari, 1968).—**NS/LK/DM**

Protopopov, Sergei, Russian choral conductor, teacher, and composer; b. Moscow, April 2, 1893; d. there, Dec. 14, 1954. He studied medicine at the Univ. of Moscow (1913–17) and composition with Yavorsky at the Kiev Cons. (1918–21). He was active as a choral conductor and later taught at the Moscow Cons. (1938–43). His piano sonatas reflect the influence of Yavrosky's theory of model rhythms and are dissonant in the vein of the Lourié, Roslavetz, and Mossolov piano pieces of the period. His compositions included an opera, *Suite of 6 Folk Pieces* for Orch. (1945), *Poem* for Cello and Piano (1935), *3 Poems* for Cello and Piano (1938), piano pieces, including 3 sonatas (1920–22; 1924; *Sonata Terza*, 1924–28) and *3 Preludes* (1938), and and numerous songs.—**NS/LK/DM**

Protschka, Josef, Czech-born German tenor; b. Prague, Feb. 5, 1944. He studied philology and philosophy at the Univ. of Tübingen and the Univ. of Bonn, and pursued vocal instruction with Erika Köth and Peter Witsch at the Cologne Hochschule für Musik. In 1977 he made his operatic debut in Giessen, and then sang in Saarbrücken (1978–80). From 1980 to 1987 he was a leading member of the Cologne Opera. In 1985 he sang Pisandro in the Monteverdi-Henze version of *Il ritorno d'Ulisse* at the Salzburg Festival, and he also appeared at the Vienna State Opera. Following engagements at Milan's La Scala and in Dresden in 1986, and Florence and Zürich in 1987, he sang the title role in Schubert's

Fierrabras at the Vienna Festival in 1988. In 1989 he sang Florestan at the Hamburg State Opera, which role he also chose for his debut at London's Covent Garden in 1990. He made his U.S. debut in 1991 as soloist in *Das Lied von der Erde* with the Houston Sym. Orch. In subsequent seasons, he appeared with many of the world's major opera houses, festivals, and orchs., and also toured as a lieder artist. He served as a prof. at the Cologne Hochschule für Musik's Aachen division and at the Royal Cons. of Music in Copenhagen. In addition to the critical accolades he has won for his roles in operas by Mozart and Wagner, he is much esteemed for his interpretations of the lieder of Schubert and Mendelssohn.—**NS/LK/DM**

Prout, Ebenezer, eminent English music theorist and teacher; b. Oundle, Northamptonshire, March 1, 1835; d. Hackney, Dec. 5, 1909. Excepting some piano lessons as a boy, and later a course with Charles Salaman, he was wholly self-taught. His father had him trained to be a schoolteacher, and he took the degree of B.A. at London Univ. in 1854. However, in 1859 he went over definitely to music. He was organist at Union Chapel in Islington from 1861 to 1873, a prof. of piano at the Crystal Palace School of Art from 1861 to 1885, a prof. of harmony and composition at the National Training School for Music (1876–82), and taught at the Royal Academy of Music (1879–1909). He held the non-resident position of prof. of music at Trinity Coll. in Dublin (from 1894), and also conducted the Hackney Choral Assn. (1876–90). He was the first ed. of the *Monthly Musical Record* (1871–75), and also music critic of *The Academy* (1874–79) and *The Athenaeum* (1879–89). In 1895 both Dublin and Edinburgh univs. conferred on him the degree of Mus.Doc. honoris causa. His theoretical works included *Instrumentation* (1876; 3rd ed., 1904), *Harmony, Its Theory and Practice* (1889; 20th ed., entirely rewritten, 1903), *Counterpoint, Strict and Free* (1890), *Double Counterpoint and Canon* (1891), *Fugue* (1891), *Fugal Analysis* (1892), *Musical Form* (1893), and *Applied Forms* (1895), all of which have passed through many eds. He also publ. *The Orchestra* (2 vols., 1898–99; in Ger., 1905–06) and *Some Notes on Bach's Church-Cantatas* (1907). He was a competent composer of useless works, among them 4 syms., 2 overtures, 2 organ concertos, a Piano Quintet, 2 string quartets, 2 piano quartets, Clarinet Sonata, the cantatas *Hereward, Alfred*, and *The Red Cross Knight*, a considerable amount of church music, and organ arrangements.—**NS/LK/DM**

Provenzale, Francesco, noted Italian composer and teacher; b. Naples, c. 1626; d. there, Sept. 6, 1704. By the early 1650s he was active as a composer of operas in Naples, and thus became the first major figure of the so-called Neapolitan school. In 1663 he began teaching at the Cons. S. Maria di Loreto; that same year was made its chief maestro, a position he retained until 1675. He then was director of the music staff at the cons. of S. Maria della Pietà dei Turchini from 1675 to 1701. He also served as maestro di cappella to the city of Naples from 1665; held a similar post to the treasury of S. Gennaro from 1686 to 1699. In 1680 he was named maestro onorario, without pay, to the viceregal court under its maestro di cappella P.A., Ziani. After Ziani's death in 1684, A. Scarlatti was named his successor, and Provenzale resigned in protest at being passed over by the court authorities. He returned briefly to court service in 1688 as maestro di cappella di camera. Finally, in 1690, he was renamed maestro onorario with a salary of 19 ducats a month.

WORKS: DRAMATIC: Opera: *Il Ciro* (Naples, 1653); *Il Theseo, o vero L'incostanza trionfante* (Naples, 1658); *Il Schiavo di sua moglie* (Naples, 1671); *La colomba ferita*, sacred opera (Naples, Sept. 18, 1672); *La Fenice d'Avila Teresa di Giesù*, sacred opera (Naples, Nov. 6, 1672); *La Stellidaura vendicata* (Naples, Sept. 2, 1674; also known as *Difendere l'offensore, ovvero La Stellidaura vendicata*). The opera *Il martirio di S. Gennaro* (Naples, Nov. 6, 1664) may be by Provenzale. The operas *Xerse* (Naples, 1655?) and *Artemisia* (Naples, 1657?), often listed as original works by Provenzale, may be adaptations by Cavalli. VOCAL: Cantatas; motets; other works.—NS/LK/DM

Prowo, Pierre, German organist and composer; b. Altona, April 8, 1697; d. there, Nov. 8, 1757. He served as organist at the Altona Reformierten Kirche from 1738. Among his works were a Concerto for Flute, 2 Violins, and Basso Continuo, 6 concertos for 3 Oboes and 2 Bassoons, 6 concertos for 2 Recorders, 2 Oboes, 2 Bassoons, and Basso Continuo, 13 sonatas for 2 Recorders and Basso Continuo, 12 sonatas for Flute and Basso Continuo, and 7 sonatas for Flute, Violin, and Basso Continuo.—LK/DM

Prudent, Emile (Racine Gauthier), French pianist, teacher, and composer; b. Angoulême, Feb. 3, 1817; d. Paris, May 13, 1863. Early orphaned, he was adopted by a piano tuner. He studied at the Paris Cons. with Zimmerman (piano; premier prix, 1833) and Laurent (harmony; 2nd prix, 1834). He made tours as a pianist in France, Belgium, England, and Germany; then settled in Paris, where he was greatly esteemed as a teacher. He wrote a number of piano works, contemporary critics ranking him between Thalberg and Döhler. His paraphrase of *Lucia di Lammermoor* enjoyed considerable success.—NS/LK/DM

Pruett, James W(orrell), prominent American music librarian and musicologist; b. Mount Airy, N.C., Dec. 23, 1932. He studied music and comparative literature at the Univ. of N.C. in Chapel Hill (B.A., 1955; M.A., 1957; Ph.D., 1962), where he was a member of its library staff (1955–61), serving as music librarian (1961–76). In 1963 he joined its music dept., serving as prof. of music (1974–87) and chairman of the dept. (1976–86); also was president of the Music Library Assn. (1973–75) and ed. of its journal *Notes* (1974–77). He was chief of the music division of the Library of Congress in Washington, D.C. (from 1987). He ed. *Studies in Musicology: Essays in the History, Style, and Bibliography of Music in Memory of Glen Haydon* (Chapel Hill, 1969), and, with T. Stevens, publ. *Research Guide to Musicology* (Chicago, 1985).
—NS/LK/DM

Prumier, Antoine, French harpist, teacher, and composer; b. Paris, July 2, 1794; d. there, Jan. 20, 1868.

He studied at the Paris Cons. He played the harp in the orch. of the Opéra-Comique (1835–40), and succeeded Nadermann as prof. of harp at the Cons. (1835–67). He composed about 100 fantasies, rondos, and airs with variations for harp. His son, Ange-Conrad Prumier (b. Paris, Jan. 5, 1820; d. there, April 3, 1884), was also a harpist, teacher, and composer. He studied with his father at the Cons., then succeeded him at the Opéra-Comique (1840); was also a prof. at the Cons. (from 1870). He publ. études for harp, nocturnes for harp and horn, and sacred songs.—NS/LK/DM

Prunières, Henry, eminent French musicologist; b. Paris, May 24, 1886; d. Nanterre, April 11, 1942. He studied music history with Rolland at the Sorbonne (1906–13), receiving his doctorat ès lettres from the Univ. of Paris in 1913 with the diss. *L'Opéra italien en France avant Lulli* (publ. in Paris, 1913); also wrote a supplementary diss. in 1913, *La Ballet de cour en France avant Benserade et Lully*, publ. in Paris in 1914. From 1909 to 1914, was an instructor at the École des Hautes Études Sociales in Paris; in 1920, founded the important journal *La Revue Musicale*, of which he was ed.-in-chief until 1939; was head of the French section of the ISCM. He was general editor of a complete ed. of Lully's works (10 vols., Paris, 1930–39).

WRITINGS (all publ. in Paris): *Lully* (1910; 2nd ed., 1927); *La Musique de la chambre et de l'écurie* (1912); *La Vie et l'oeuvre de Claudio Monteverdi* (1924; Eng. tr., 1926; 2nd French ed., 1931); *La Vie illustre et libertine de Jean-Baptiste Lully* (1929); *Cavalli et l'opéra vénitien au XVIIᵉ siècle* (1931); *Nouvelle histoire de la musique* (2 vols., 1934, 1936; Eng. tr., 1943).—NS/LK/DM

Pruslin, Stephen (Lawrence), American pianist, writer on music, and composer; b. N.Y., April 16, 1940. He studied at Brandeis Univ. (B.A., 1961) and Princeton Univ. (M.F.A., 1963), and also studied piano with Luise Vosgerchian and Steuermann. He received a Hertz Memorial Scholarship from the Univ. of Calif. (1964), which enabled him to go to Europe. He settled in London, where he made his recital debut (1970); that same year he became a founding member of the Fires of London with Peter Maxwell Davies, and subsequently appeared with it frequently; also toured widely as a soloist. He became especially known as an interpreter of and a writer on contemporary music. He ed. *Peter Maxwell Davies: Studies from Two Decades* (1979), and also composed scores for the theater, films, and television.
—NS/LK/DM

Prüwer, Julius, Austrian conductor; b. Vienna, Feb. 20, 1874; d. N.Y., July 8, 1943. He studied piano with Friedheim and Moriz Rosenthal, and theory with R. Fuchs and Krenn; also profited greatly by his friendly association with Brahms. He studied conducting with Hans Richter. Prüwer began his career as a conductor in Bielitz; then conducted at the Cologne Opera (1894–96) and at the Breslau Opera (1896–1923), where he distinguished himself by conducting numerous new works. From 1924 to 1933 he conducted popular concerts of the Berlin Phil. In 1933 he was compelled to leave Germany owing to the barbarous racial laws of the Nazi regime; he conducted in Russia and in Austria; eventually reached N.Y., where he remained until his death. **—NS/LK/DM**

Pryor, Arthur (Willard), American trombonist, conductor, and composer; b. St. Joseph, Mo., Sept. 22, 1870; d. Long Branch, N.J., June 18, 1942. He began his professional career in 1889 as a performer on the slide trombone. When Sousa formed his own band in 1892, he hired Pryor as his trombone soloist; from 1895 until he left to form his own band in 1903, Pryor was asst. conductor for Sousa. Pryor's Band gave its first major concert at the Majestic Theatre in N.Y. on Nov. 15, 1903, but beginning in 1904 it initiated series of summer outdoor concerts at Asbury Park, Coney Island, and other amusement parks. From 1903 to 1909 it made six coast-to-coast tours. Unlike Sousa, who had little to do with "canned music," Pryor was quick to take advantage of the developing recording industry; he made some 1,000 acoustic recordings before 1930. He also entered upon a series of commercial radio broadcasts. He composed about 300 works, including operettas, ragtime and cakewalk tunes, and novelties such as *The Whistler and His Dog,* Pryor's best-known work. He was a charter member of ASCAP in 1914 and of the American Bandmasters Assn. in 1929. In 1933 he retired to Long Branch.

BIBL.: D. Frizane, *A. P. (1870–1942) American Trombonist, Bandmaster, Composer* (diss., Univ. of Kans., 1984).**—NS/LK/DM**

Prysock, Arthur "Red", R&B/jazz singer; b. Spartanburg, S.C., Jan. 2, 1929; d. at the King Edward Hospital, Bermuda, June 21, 1997. His attention-getting baritone voice, often compared with that of Billy Eckstine's, was featured on recordings in all genres and on television and radio commercials. He became famous in Buddy Johnson's band (1944–52), having 16 big R&B hits. From then on, he toured internationally from a base in Long Island, N.Y. He gained even more notoriety as a romantic ballad specialist in the 1950s and 1960s. During the 1970s, Prysock mainly played club dates, but resurfaced as a recording artist in 1985 with "Rockin' Good Way." In 1987, he received a Grammy nomination for "Teach Me Tonight'" with singer Betty Joplin. The following year, he was nominated for best jazz vocal performance for "This Guy's in Love with You." He died after a prolonged illness; the cause of death was not released.

DISC.: *Like Who? Like Basie* (1959); *Paul Quinichette* (1960); *Arthur Prysock Sings Only for You* (1961); *For Basie* (1962); *Coast to Coast* (1962); *Basie Reunion* (1962); *Arthur Prysock/Count Basie* (1965); *Arthur Prysock and Count Basie* (1965); *To Love or Not to Love* (1967); *Portrait of Arthur Prysock* (1967); *Mister Prysock* (1967); *This Is My Beloved* (1968); *I Must Be Doing Something Right* (1968); *Rockin' Good Way* (1985); *This Guy's in Love with You* (1986); *Jazz 'Round Midnight* (1995).**—MM/LP**

Przybylski, Bronisław Kazimierz, Polish composer and teacher; b. Łódź, Dec. 11, 1941. He was a student of Franciszek Wesolowski (theory diploma, 1964) and Tomasz Kiesewetter (composition diploma,

1969) at the Łódź State Coll. of Music, of Szabelski in Katowice, and of Haubenstock-Ramati at the Vienna Hochschule für Musik (1975–76). From 1964 he taught at the Łódź State Coll. of Music.

WORKS: DRAMATIC: *Miriam,* ballet (1985); *The Strange Adventures of Mr. Hare,* musical fairy tale (1985); *Wawelski Smok,* ballet (1987); *3 Cheers for the Elephant,* musical fairy tale (1989). **ORCH.:** *Quattro studi* (1970); *Suite of Polish Dances* (1971); *In honorem Nicolai Copernici* (1972); *Scherzi musicali* for Strings (1973); *Memento* (1973); *4 Kurpian Nocturnes* for Harp or Guitar and Strings (1973, 1975); *Concerto Polacco* for Accordion and Orch. (1973); *Guernica: Pablo Picasso in memoriam* (1974); 5 syms.: *Sinfonia Polacca* (1974–78), *Sinfonia da Requiem* (1976), *Sinfonia-Corale* (1981), *Sinfonia-Affresco* (1982), and *Jubiläums-Sinfonie* (1983, 1995); *Radogoszca,* funeral music for Chamber Orch. (1975); *Drammatico* (1976); *Animato e Festivo* (1978); *Cottbuser Ouvertüre* (1980); *A Varsovie* (1981); *Program S,* hommage à Karol Szymanowski for Piano and Strings (1982); Concerto for Harpsichord and Strings (1983); *Folklore,* suite for Strings (1983); *Return,* quasi symphonic poem (1984); *Midnight Echoes Music* for Strings (1985); *Concerto Classico* for Accordion and Orch. or Strings (1986); *Scherzi* for Violin and Chamber Orch. (1990; also for Cello and Symphonic Band); *Lacrimosa 2000* for Strings (1991). **CHAMBER:** Wind Quintet (1967); String Quartet, *Quartetto di Tritone* (1969); *La Follia* for Accordion (1974); *The 4 Seasons* for Accordion (1976); *Arnold Schönberg in memoriam* for String Quartet (1977); *The Royal Tournament* for Wind Quintet (1977); *Asteroedides I-V* for Accordion Quintet (1978); *Quasi un sonata* for Violin and Piano (1980); 3 accordion sonatinas (1983); *Metamorphosen* for Accordion and String Quartet (1985); Trio for Violin, Cello, and Accordion (1986); *Modal Piece I-II* for Accordion Quintet (1986); *Bimodal Piece* for 2 Accordion Quintets (1986); *Musica concertante* for Organ and Percussion (1986); *Folklore II* for Guitar and Harpsichord (1986); *Double Play* for 2 Accordions (1987); *A.B. Sonata* for Accordion (1988); *Night Music* for Flute, Guitar, and Accordion (1988); *Spring Sonata* for Accordion (1989); *Concerto della morte e della vita* for Chamber Group (1991); *Scherzo-Trio* for Violin, Cello, and Piano (1992); *Autumn Multiplay* for 6 Instruments (1994); *A Sleeping Bear* for Accordion (1995); *A Porcelain Dancer* for Accordion (1995). **VOCAL:** *A Tale of the Life and Death of Karol Walter-Swierczewskiego,* cantata for Tenor, Bass, Reciter, and Men's Chorus or Mixed Chorus and Orch. (1969); *Midnight,* monodrama for Actor and Chamber Ensemble (1973); *Voices* for 3 Actors and Chamber Ensemble (1974); *Requiem* for Soprano, 2 Reciters, Boy's Chorus, and Orch. (1976); *Jagsagen* for Speaker and Brass Quintet (1978); *Mazowsze* for Reciter, 4 Optional Melodic Instruments, and Percussion (1979); *The City of Hope,* cantata for Bass, Chorus, and 2 Orchs. (1979); *In Memoriam,* 4 songs for Voice and Chamber Ensemble (1982); *Portrait of a Lady* for Voices and Chamber Ensemble (1982); *Basnie,* fairy tales for Voices and Chamber Ensemble (1982); choruses; solo songs.**—NS/LK/DM**

Ptaszyńska, Marta, Polish composer, percussionist, and teacher; b. Warsaw, July 29, 1943. She was a student in composition of Tadeusz Paciorkiewicz at the State Higher School of Music in Warsaw, where she also studied theory. She studied percussion with Jerzy Zgodziński at the State Higher School of Music in Poznań. In 1969–70 she pursued postgraduate studies in composition with Nadia Boulanger and at Centre Bourdan in Paris. In 1972 she settled in the U.S. and received her Artist Diploma in percussion performance from the Cleveland Inst. of Music in 1974. While pursuing a career as a percussionist, she also taught at Bennington (Vt.) Coll., the Univ. of Calif. at Berkeley and at Santa Barbara, Ind. Univ., the Univ. of Cincinnati Coll.-Cons. of Music, and Northwestern Univ. In 1991 she became deputy director of the American Soc. for Polish Music. Her compositions have won various prizes, including the Polish Radio and TV Competition in 1972 and the Percussive Arts Soc. Competition of the U.S. in 1972 and 1976. In 1986 she took 2nd prize at the International Rostrum of Composers in Paris. She was awarded the Polish Composers' Union Medal in 1988, the Officer's Cross of Merit in 1995, and the Alfred Jurzykowski Foundation Prize of N.Y. in 1997.

WORKS: DRAMATIC: *Oscar z Alway* (Oscar of Alva), television opera (1972); *Pan Marimba* (Mister Marimba), children's opera (1993–95; Warsaw, May 1998). **ORCH.:** *Improwizacje* (Improvisations; 1968; Kraków, March 26, 1971); *Crystallites* (1973; Bydgoszcz, Jan. 24, 1975); *Spectri sonori* (1973; Cleveland, Jan. 22, 1974); Percussion Quartet Concerto (Bennington, Vt., Oct. 20, 1974); *La Novella d'inverno* for Strings (1983–84; Lisbon, May 5, 1985); Marimba Concerto (1984–85); Alto Saxophone Concerto, *Charlie's Dream* (1988); *Ode to Praise All Famous Women* (1992); *Fanfare for Peace* (Cincinnati, Nov. 18, 1994); Concerto grosso for 2 Violins and Chamber Orch. (1996; Warsaw, Jan. 26, 1997). **CHAMBER:** 4 Preludes for Vibraphone and Piano (1965); *Scherzo* for Xylophone and Piano (1967); *Wariacje* (Variations) for Flute (Warsaw, April 2, 1968); *Recitativo, arioso e toccata* for Violin (1968–75); *Jeu-parti* for Harp and Vibraphone (Paris, April 19, 1970); *Mała fantazja meksykańska* (Little Mexican Fantasy) for Percussion and Piano (1971); *Madrigals "Canticum Sonarum" in memoriam Igor Strawiński* for String Quartet, Woodwind Quartet, Trumpet, Trombone, and Gong (1971; Warsaw, May 18, 1972); *Stress* for Percussion and Tape (1971; Cleveland, April 29, 1973); *Space Model* for Percussion and Tape (Warsaw, May 20, 1971); *Arabeska* (Arabesque) for Harp (1972); *Cadenza* for Flute and Percussion (1972; Cleveland, April 1, 1974); *Two Poems* for Tuba (Cleveland, March 1973); *Siderals* for 2 Percussion Quintets and Light Projection (Urbana, Ill., Nov. 21, 1974); *Mobile* for 2 Percussionists (1975); *Classical Variations* for Timpani and String Quartet (1976); *Quodlibet* for Double Bass and Tape (1976); *Melodie z różnych stron* (Tunes from Many Countries of the World) for Percussion Ensemble (1977); *Synchromy* for Percussion Trio (1978; Warsaw, April 22, 1979); *Dream Lands, Magic Spaces* for Violin, Piano, and 6 Percussionists (1978–79; San Jose, Nov. 13, 1980); *Muzyka pięciu stopni* (Music of Five Steps) for 2 Flutes and Percussion Ensemble (1979; Warsaw, July 12, 1980); 6 Bagatelles for Harp (1979); *Scintilla* for 2 Marimbaphones (1983); *Kwiaty księżyca* (Moon Flowers) for Cello and Piano (Warsaw, Sept. 27, 1986); *Graffito* for Marimba (1988); *Ajikan-Unfolding Light* for Flute and Percussion (Southampton, Sept. 10, 1989); *Poetic Impressions* for Wind Quintet and Piano (1991); *Spider Walk* for Percussion (1993); *Four Portraits* for String Quartet (N.Y., April 22, 1994); *Mancala* for 2 Violins (N.Y., April 15, 1997); *Scherzo di fantasia* for Euphonium and Piano (St. Louis, June 29, 1997). **KEYBOARD: Piano:** *Farewell Souvenir* (1975); *Podróże w kosmos* (Journeys into Space; 1978); *Miniatury* (Miniatures; 1982); *Four Seasons* for Piano, 4-Hands (1984); *Music Alphabet* for 2 Pianos (1985–86); *Hommage à I.J. Paderewski* (1992). **Harpsichord:** *Touracou* (Cleveland, April 21, 1974). **VOCAL:** *Bajka o słowikach* (A Tale of Nightingales) for Baritone, Flute, Oboe, Clarinet, Bassoon, Harp, Vibraphone, and Marimba (1968; Warsaw, Jan. 12, 1969); *Vocalise* for Soprano and Vibraphone (Breukelen, July 18, 1971); *Epigrams* for Women's Chorus, Flute,

Harp, Piano, and Percussion (1976–77; Santa Barbara, May 8, 1977); *Un grand sommeil noir* for Soprano, Flute, and Harp (1977); *Dwa sonety do Orfeusza* (Two Sonnets to Orpheus) for Middle Voice and Chamber Orch. (1980–81; Warsaw, Oct. 3, 1989); *Ave Maria* for 4 Men's Voices, Brass Ensemble, Percussion, and Organ (Boston, Oct. 10, 1982; also for Men's Chorus and Chamber Orch., 1987); *Listy polskie* (Polish Letters), cantata (1988; Warsaw, July 15, 1989); *Songs of Despair and Loneliness* for Mezzo-soprano and Piano (1988–89; Warsaw, Oct. 3, 1989); *Holocaust Memorial Cantata* (Schleswig-Holstein, Aug. 16, 1993); *Cantiones Jubilationis: In Praise of Peace* for Women's Chorus and Percussion (Chicago, March 19, 1995); *Silver Echoes of Distant Bells* for Mezzo-soprano and String Quartet (N.Y., Dec. 10, 1995). **OTHER:** *Soirée snobe chez la Princesse*, instrumental theater (1979); children's pieces.—**NS/LK/DM**

Ptolemy (in Latin **Claudius Ptolemaeus**), great Greek astronomer, geographer, mathematician, and music theorist; b. probably in Ptolemais Hermii, Egypt, c.83; d. c. 161. He wrote the foremost treatise on music theory of antiquity, the 3-vol. *Harmonika* (Harmonics; J. Wallis, ed., *Klaudiou Ptolemaiou Harmonikōn biblia gamma* (Oxford, 1682) and I. Düring, ed., *Die Harmonielehre des Klaudios Ptolemaios* (Göteborg, 1930), *Porphyrios Kommentar zur Harmonielehre des Ptolemaios* (Göteborg, 1932), and *Ptolemaios und Porphyrios über die Musik* (Göteborg, 1934).

BIBL.: F. Boll, *Studien über Claudius Ptolemäus: Ein Beitrag zur Geschichte der griechischen Philosophie und Astrologie* (Leipzig, 1894); L. Schönberger, *Studien zum 1. Buch der Harmonik des Cl. Ptolemäus* (Augsburg, 1914); B. Alexanderson, *Textual Remarks on Ptolemy's Harmonica and Porphyry's Commentary* (Göteborg, 1969).—**NS/LK/DM**

Public Enemy, controversial rap group. **MEMBERSHIP:** Chuck D (Carlton Ridenhauer) (b. N.Y.C., Aug. 1, 1960); MC Flavor Flav (William Drayton) (b. N.Y.C., March 16, 1959); Professor Griff (Richard Griffin); Terminator X (Norman Lee Rogers) (b. N.Y.C., Aug. 25, 1966). Richard Griffin left in late 1989.

One of the first rap groups to expand the music's concerns to that of self-education, self-determination, and black pride, Public Enemy broke through with 1990's *Fear of a Black Planet*, which included the controversial "Welcome to the Terrordome" and the anthemic "Fight the Power" and "Power to the People." Public Enemy stirred another round of controversy with "By the Time I Get to Arizona" from *Apocalypse 91*, perhaps their best-selling album.

The evolution of Public Enemy began in 1982 at Adelphi Univ. on Long Island, when Chuck D and Hank Stocklee produced a collection of rap tracks, including "Public Enemy No. 1." Formed on Long Island, N.Y., in the mid-1980s, Public Enemy was comprised of Chuck D, Flavor Flav, Professor Griff, and disc jockey Terminator X. Signed to Rick Rubin's Def Jam label, with distribution by Columbia, the group's debut album, which included "Megablast" and "You're Gonna Get Yours," sold only modestly. However, their second, *It Takes a Nation of Millions to Hold Us Back*, remained on the album charts for nearly a year and proclaimed them "Prophets of Rage." The album featured "Bring the

Noise," "Countdown to Armageddon," "Louder than a Bomb," "Party for Your Right to Fight," and "Don't Believe the Hype," in which they expressed their distrust of the media. In 1989 Professor Griff, as the group's Minister of Information, made anti- Semitic remarks that nearly broke up the group and led to his dismissal by year's end.

Public Enemy broke through as an album group with 1990's *Fear of a Black Planet*. Avoiding at least in part the sexism of some of the songs from their first two albums, *Fear of a Black Planet* contained "Brothers Gonna Work It Out," "Power to the People," "Revolutionary Generation," "Fight the Power" (featured in Spike Lee's film, *Do the Right Thing*), "Burn Hollywood Burn," and "Welcome to the Terrordome." *Apocalypse 91* became perhaps their best-selling and most controversial album. "By the Time I Get to Arizona" threatened violence against the state that refused to honor Martin Luther King Jr.'s nationally proclaimed holiday, and "How to Kill a Radio Consultant" denounced radio stations that refused to play rap songs. The album produced a minor pop hit with "Can't Truss It" and included a collaboration with the white thrash metal band Anthrax on "Bring the Noise." In 1992 *Greatest Misses* compiled many of their earlier favorites, and 1994's *Muse Sick-n-Hour Mess Age* produced a moderate pop and R&B hit with "Give It Up."

DISC.: *Yo! Bum Rush the Show* (1987); *It Takes a Nation of Millions to Hold Us Back* (1988); *Fear of a Black Planet* (1990); *Apocalypse 91 … The Enemy Strikes Black* (1991); *Greatest Misses* (1992); *Muse Sick-n-Hour Mess Age* (1994).—**BH**

Puccini, family of Italian musicians:

(1) Giacomo Puccini, composer; b. Celle di Val di Roggia, Lucca (baptized), Jan. 26, 1712; d. Lucca, May 16, 1781. He studied with Caretti in Bologna, then pursued his career in Lucca, where he was organist at S. Martino (1739–72) and director of the Cappella Palatina (1739–81). He became a member of Bologna's Accademia Filarmonica (1743). He was a talented composer of vocal music; also wrote a number of dramatic pieces for the Lucca municipal elections.

(2) Antonio (Benedetto Maria) Puccini, composer, son of the preceding; b. Lucca, July 30, 1747; d. there, Feb. 10, 1832. He received financial assistance from the Lucca authorities to study in Bologna with Caretti and Zanardi; while there, he married the organist Caterina Tesei, then returned to Lucca, where he was substitute organist for his father at S. Martino (from 1772). He was his father's successor as director of the Cappella Palatina (1781–1805); became a member of Bologna's Accademia Filarmonica (1771). His output reveals a composer of solid technique and expressivity in vocal writing.

(3) Domenico (Vencenzo Maria) Puccini, composer, son of the preceding; b. 1772; d. Lucca, May 25, 1815. After musical training with his parents, he studied with Mattei in Bologna and Paisiello in Naples. He then returned to Lucca as director of the Cappella di Camera (1806–09) and of the municipal chapel (1811–15). He was notably successful as a composer of comic operas.

WORKS: DRAMATIC: Opera: *Le frecce d'amore*, opera pastorale (c. 1800); *L'Ortolanella, o La Moglie capricciosa*, farsa buffa (Lucca, 1800); *Il Quinto Fabio*, opera seria (Livorno, 1810); *La scuola dei tutori*, farsa (Lucca, 1813); *Il Ciarlatano, ossia I finti savoiardi*, atto buffo (Lucca, 1815).

(4) Michele Puccini, teacher and composer, son of the preceding; b. Lucca, Nov. 27, 1813; d. there, Jan. 23, 1864. He studied with his grandfather Antonio Puccini and others in Lucca, and completed his training with Pillotti in Bologna and Donizetti and Mercadante in Naples. He then returned to Lucca as a teacher at the Istituto Musicale Pacini, serving as its director (from 1862); was also organist at S. Martino. He became well known as a teacher. Among his works are 2 operas, *Antonio Foscarini* (n.d.) and *Giambattista Cattani, o La rivoluzione degli Straccioni* (Lucca, 1844).

(5) Giacomo (Antonio Domenico Michele Secondo Maria) Puccini, celebrated composer, son of the preceding; b. Lucca, Dec. 22, 1858; d. Brussels, Nov. 29, 1924. He was the 5th of 7 children of Michele Puccini, who died when Giacomo was only 5; his musical training was thus entrusted to his uncle, Fortunato Magi, a pupil of his father; however, Giacomo showed neither inclination nor talent for music. His mother, determined to continue the family tradition, sent him to the local Istituto Musicale Pacini, where Carlo Angeloni—its director, who had also studied with Michele Puccini—became his teacher. After Angeloni's untiring patience had aroused interest, and then enthusiasm, in his pupil, progress was rapid and he soon became a proficient pianist and organist. He began serving as a church organist in Lucca and environs when he was 14, and began composing when he was 17. After hearing *Aida* in Pisa in 1876, he resolved to win laurels as a dramatic composer. Having written mainly sacred music, it was self-evident that he needed further training after graduating from the Istituto (1880). With financial support from his granduncle, Dr. Nicolao Ceru, and a stipend from Queen Margherita, he pursued his studies with Antonio Bazzini and Amilcare Ponchielli at the Milan Cons. (1880–83). For his graduation, he wrote a *Capriccio sinfonico*, which was conducted by Faccio at a Cons. concert, eliciting unstinting praise from the critics. In the same year, Ponchielli introduced Puccini to the librettist Fontana, who furnished him the text of a 1-act opera; in a few weeks the score was finished and sent to the Sonzongo competition. It did not win the prize, but on May 31, 1884, *Le villi* was produced at the Teatro dal Verme in Milan, with gratifying success. Ricordi, who was present, considered the work sufficiently meritorious to commission the young composer to write a new opera for him; but 5 years elapsed before this work, *Edgar* (3 acts; text by Fontana), was produced at La Scala in Milan (April 21, 1889), scoring only a moderate success. By this time Puccini had become convinced that, in order to write a really effective opera, he needed a better libretto than Fontana had provided. Accordingly, he commissioned Domenico Oliva to write the text of *Manon Lescaut*; during the composition, however, Puccini and Ricordi practically rewrote the entire book, and in the publ. score Oliva's name is not mentioned. With *Manon Lescaut* (4 acts), first produced at the Teatro Regio in Turin on Feb. 1, 1893, Puccini won a veritable triumph, which was even surpassed by his next work, *La Bohème* (4 acts; text by Illica and Giacosa), produced at the same theater on Feb. 1, 1896. These 2 works not only carried their composer's name throughout the world, but also have found and maintained their place in the repertoire of every opera house. With fame came wealth, and in 1900 he built at Torre del Lago, where he had been living since 1891, a magnificent villa. His next opera, *Tosca* (3 acts; text by Illica and Giacosa), produced at the Teatro Costanzi in Rome on Jan. 14, 1900, is Puccini's most dramatic work; it has become a fixture of the standard repertoire, and contains some of his best-known arias. At its premiere at La Scala on Feb. 17, 1904, *Madama Butterfly* (2 acts; text by Illica and Giacosa) was hissed. Puccini thereupon withdrew the score and made some slight changes (division into 3 acts, and addition of the tenor aria in the last scene). This revised version was greeted with frenzied applause in Brescia on May 28 of the same year. Puccini was now the acknowledged ruler of the Italian operatic stage, his works rivaling those of Verdi in the number of performances. The first performance of *Madama Butterfly* at the Metropolitan Opera in N.Y. (Feb. 11, 1907) took place in the presence of the composer, whom the management had invited especially for the occasion. It was then suggested that he write an opera on an American subject, the premiere to take place at the Metropolitan. He found his subject when he witnessed a performance of Belasco's *The Girl of the Golden West*; he commissioned C. Zangarini and G. Civinini to write the libretto, and in the presence of the composer the world premiere of *La Fanciulla del West* occurred, amid much enthusiasm, at the Metropolitan on Dec. 10, 1910; while it never equaled the success of his *Tosca* or *Madama Butterfly*, it had various revivals over the years. Puccini then brought out *La Rondine* (3 acts; Monte Carlo, March 27, 1917) and the 3 1-act operas *Il Tabarro* (after Didier Gold's *La Houppelande*), *Suor Angelica*, and *Gianni Schicchi* (all 1st perf. at the Metropolitan Opera, Dec. 14, 1918). His last opera, *Turandot* (after Gozzi), was left unfinished; the final scene was completed by Franco Alfano and performed at La Scala on April 25, 1926.

BIBL.: A. Bruggemann, *Madama Butterfly e l'arte di G. P.* (Milan, 1904); W. Dry, *G. P.* (London, 1906); F. Torrefranca, *G. P. e l'opera internazionale* (Turin, 1912); A. Weismann, *G. P.* (Munich, 1922); A. Bonaventura, *G. P.: L'Uomo, l'artista* (Livorno, 1924); A. Coeuroy, *La Tosca* (Paris, 1924); A. Fraccaroli, *La vita di G. P.* (Milan, 1925); G. Marotti and F. Pagni, *G. P. intimo* (Florence, 1926); G. Adami, *Epistolario di G. P.* (Milan, 1928; Eng. tr., London, 1931); A. Neisser, *P.* (Leipzig, 1928); F. Salerno, *Le Donne pucciniane* (Palermo, 1928); R. Merlin, *P.* (Milan, 1930); R. Specht, *P.* (Berlin, 1931; Eng. tr., N.Y., 1933); W. Maisch, *P.s musikalische Formgebung* (Neustadt, 1934); G. Adami, *P.* (Milan, 1935; Ger. tr., 1943); K. Fellerer, *G. P.* (Potsdam, 1937); V. Seligman, *P. among Friends* (correspondence; N.Y., 1938); F. Thiess, *P.: Versuch einer Psychologie seiner Musik* (Berlin, 1947); A. Bonaccorsi, *G. P. e i suoi antenati musicali* (Milan, 1950); G. Marek, *P.: A Biography* (N.Y., 1951); D. del Fiorentino, *Immortal Bohemian: An Intimate Memoir of G. P.* (N.Y., 1952); A. Machard, *Une Vie d'amour: P.* (Paris, 1954); L. Ricci, *P. interprete di se stesso* (Milan, 1954); V. Terenzio, *Ritratto di P.* (Bergamo, 1954); M. Carner, *P.* (London, 1958; 2nd ed., rev., 1974); E. Greenfield, *P.: Keeper of the Seal* (London, 1958); C. Sartori, *P.* (Milan, 1958); C.

Paladini, *G. P.* (Florence, 1961); W. Ashbrook, *The Operas of P.* (N.Y., 1968; 2nd ed., rev., 1985); D. Amy, *G. P.* (Paris, 1970); A. Monnosi, *P. a tu per tu* (Pisa, 1970); G. Tarozzi, *P.: La fine del bel canto* (Milan, 1972); N. Galli, *P. e la sua terra* (Lucca, 1974); G. Magri, *P. e le sue rime* (Milan, 1974); I. Lombardi, *P., ancora da scoprire* (Lucca, 1976); E. Siciliani, *P.* (Milan, 1976); W. Weaver, *P.: The Man and His Music* (N.Y., 1977); C. Casini, *G. P.* (Turin, 1978); L. Pinzauti, *P.* (Milan, 1978); H. Greenfield, *P.* (N.Y., 1980); C. Osborne, *The Complete Operas of P.* (London, 1981); A. Bottero, *Le Donne di P.* (Lucca, 1984); M. Carner, *Tosca* (Cambridge, 1985); E. Krause, *P.* (Leipzig, 1985); D. Martino, *Metamorfosi del femminino nei libretti per P.* (Turin, 1985); A. Groos and R. Parker, *G. P.: "La Bohème"* (Cambridge, 1986); J. DiGaetani, *P. the Thinker: The Composer's Intellectual and Dramatic Development* (Bern and N.Y., 1987); M. Kaye, *The Unknown P.: A Historical Perspective on the Songs, including Little-Known Music from "Edgar" and 'La Rondine,"* with Complete Music for Violin and Piano* (Oxford, 1987); G. Musco, *Musica e teatro in G. P.* (vol. I, Cortona, 1989); K. Berg, *G. P.s Opern: Music and Dramaturgie* (Kassel, 1991); R. Giazotto, *P. in Casa P.* (Lucca, 1992); G. Magri, *L'uomo P.* (Milan, 1992); P. Korfmacher, *Exotismus in G. P.s Turandot* (Cologne, 1993); W. Volpers, *G. P.s "Turandot: " Untersuchungen zum Text und zur musikalischen Dramaturgie* (Laaber, 1994); W. Weaver and S. Puccini, eds., *The P. Companion* (N.Y., 1994); M. Girardi, *G. P.: L'arte internazionale di un musicista italiano* (Venice, 1995); G. Ravenni and C. Gianturco, eds., *Convegno internazionale di studi su G. P. nel 70 anniversari della morte* (It. and Eng., Lucca, 1997); C. Wilson, *G. P.* (London, 1997); L. Fairtile, *G. P.: A Guide to Research* (Levittown, N.Y., 1998).—NS/LK/DM

Pucitta, Vincenzo, Italian composer; b. Civitavecchia, near Rome, 1778; d. Milan, Dec. 20, 1861. He studied at the Cons. della Pietà dei Turchini in Naples. After composing various operas for Milan and Venice, he served as music director of the Italian Opera in Amsterdam, and then at the King's Theatre in London from 1809 to 1814, where he wrote several operas for and acted as accompanist to Catalani. During Catalani's directorship of the Théâtre-Italien in Paris, he served as her house composer (1814–17). In 1819 Pucitta toured Austria and Germany with his pupil Elizabeth Ferron, but soon after he abandoned his career as a composer for the stage. In all, he wrote some 35 operas.—LK/DM

Puente, Giuseppe Del, Italian baritone; b. Naples, Jan. 30, 1841; d. Philadelphia, May 25, 1900. He first studied cello at the Naples Cons. but later began to cultivate his voice, making his operatic debut at Iasi. He was then engaged for the Teatro San Carlo in Naples, and for appearances in France, Germany, Russia, Spain, and England (made his Covent Garden debut in 1873, and became very popular there). His first American engagement was under Strakosch at the N.Y. Academy of Music in 1873–74; he became a member of the first Metropolitan Opera season in N.Y. and sang the role of Valentin in the inaugural performance of *Faust* on Oct. 22, 1883; remained on its roster for the seasons of 1883–84, 1891–92, and 1894–95. In 1885 he returned to the N.Y. Academy of Music under Mapleson's management, taking part in the American premiere of *Manon* on Dec. 23 of that year; he was also a member of the opera troupes of Patti and Hinrichs; with the latter's company, he sang in the American premiere of *Cavalleria rusticana* (Philadelphia, Sept. 9, 1891). He married the mezzo-soprano Helen Dudley Campbell.—**NS/LK/DM**

Puente, Tito, multitalented Latin-jazz percussionist, vibraphonist, timbalist, saxophonist, pianist, conga and bongos player; b. N.Y., April 20, 1923; d. there, May 31, 2000. When the rock group Santana recorded "Oye Como Va," a classic Latin hit that Tito Puente had written and recorded, the composer was slightly outraged that such a band would dare sully his music. As soon as the royalty check came (based on massive sales of Santana's first album), Puente discovered the up side of having other people perform his songs. He prefaced the playing of "Oye Como Va" with that little story many times and came to realize that his music did as much to promote Latin jazz for current audiences as Machito's did for an earlier generation. Puente's musical career began with Latin groups such as the Cuarteto Caney and, after World War II, Xavier Cugat.

In the mid-1940s, after serving in the United States Navy during World War II, Puente came back to New York where Noro Morales and Machito gave the budding percussionist work. By the early 1950s, he had formed his own ensemble, The Piccadilly Boys, and played the Palladium, New York's cultural Mecca for Latin bands. His band meanwhile had mutated into The Tito Puente Orchestra and, with lead vocalist Vincentico Valdes, proceeded to change the face of Latin music. Puente took the Cuban charanga form (with its flutes and violins) and arranged them in more of a jazz big band context, punching up the brass and reeds for a more powerful sound. He also started using a lot of non-Latin jazz artists like Doc Severinsen within his bands and playing arrangements of jazz standards with a Latin beat. During the 1960s and 1970s Puente recorded albums for GNP, Tico, and Fania with large bands and small groups, continuing the heavy schedule of touring he had developed in the 1950s. By the 1980s Puente's popularity was even stronger than it was in the early 1950s due to a base of fans that included not only the hard-core Latin music lovers, but a fair number of jazz musicians and fans as well.

It was in 1983 that the multi-talented Puente (timbales, drums, marimba, vibraphone, percussion, vocalist, arranger) won the first of his many Grammy Awards, for the album *Tito Puente and His Latin Ensemble on Broadway*. With over 100 albums to his credit, Puente recorded with most of the major names in Latin music and become a major force in the Latinization of jazz during the last half of the 20th century.

DISC.: *Puente Goes Jazz* (1956); *Let's Cha Cha with Puente* (1957); *Top Percussion* (1957); *Night Beat* (1957); *New Cha Cha/Mambo Herd* (1958); *Cha Cha at El Morocco* (1958); *Dance Mania* (1958); *Puente in Love* (1959); *Mambo with Me* (1959); *Dancing under Latin Skies* (1959); *The Exciting Tito Puente Band in Hollywood* (1961); *In Puerto Rico* (1963); *More Dance Mania* (1963); *My Fair Lady Goes Latin* (1964); *Latin World of Tito Puente* (1964); *Tito Puente and His Latin Ensemble on Broadway* (1982); *Puente Now! The Exciting Tito Puente* (1984); *El Rey* (1984); *Mambo Diablo* (1985); *Un Poco Loco* (1987); *Sensacion* (1987); *Salsa Meets Jazz* (1988); *Out of This World* (1990); *Mambo of the Times* (1991); *The*

Mambo King: His 100th Album (1991); *Live at the Village Gate* (1992); *Tito Puente & His Latin Jazz All Stars* (1993); *Royal T* (1993); *Tambo* (1993); *Master Timabelero* (1993); *Tito Swings...* (1994); *Tito Puente & His Concert Orchestra* (1995); *Bossa Nova by Puente* (1995); *Mambos by Tito* (1995); *Jazzin'* (1995); *Tito's Idea* (1995); *Special delivery* (1996); *Tito Meets Machito: Mambo Kings* (1997); *Dance Mania '98: Live at Birdland* (1998); *Mambo Birdland* (1999); *Por Fin* (2000).

Puget, Loïsa (actually, **Louise-Françoise**), French singer and composer; b. Paris, Feb. 11, 1810; d. Pau, 1889. Her mother, a singer, gave her initial training in music, and she later pursued studies with Adolphe Adam. She became best known via her more than 300 romances, which she introduced to various Parisian salons as a singer (1832–42). Many of these were set to texts by Gustave Lemoine, whom she married in 1842. She also composed the stage works *La mauvais oeil* (Paris, Oct. 1, 1836) and *La veilleuse, ou Les nuits de milady* (Paris, Sept. 27, 1869).—**LK/DM**

Pugliese, Michael (Gabriel), American percussionist and composer; b. Buffalo, N.Y., Sept. 26, 1956; d. N.Y., Nov. 3, 1997. He studied with Jan Williams at the State Univ. of N.Y. at Buffalo (B.F.A., 1979) and at the Manhattan School of Music (M.M., 1981), then pursued a career as an avant-garde percussionist. In 1982 he produced a 12-hour marathon of the music of John Cage at Cooper Union in N.Y.; also gave premiere performances of Cage's *Etudes Boreales, Ryoanji*, and *Three²*, and received their dedications. He was a core member of the Bowery Ensemble and the New Music Consort, and founder of the Talking Drums, an experimental percussion trio. In 1985 he joined the Merce Cunningham Dance Co., with which he subsequently toured throughout the U.S., South America, Europe, and Asia. His compositions for Cunningham are *Peace Talks* (Berkeley, Calif., Sept. 22, 1989) for a Variety of Ethnic Percussion Instruments and Sitar, inspired by the concept of global union of socially and politically troubled nations, *Mixed Signals* for Four Marimbulas and Tape (Paris, 1991), and *Ice Breeze* for Frame Drums, Waterphones, and Chant (London, 1992). Other compositions included *June 22, 1978* for Percussion Quintet, 2 Narrators, and Tape (1978), *Not Jinxed* for 4 Marimbas, 4 Berimbaus, and Digital Delay (1991), *Traditions I* and *II* for Rocks, Glass, Metal, and MOOG Synthesizer (1995), and *Sound Scripts I* and *II* for Bottle Caps and Electronics (1995). Pugliese also appeared as a rock drummer, and made numerous rock arrangements, including one of Henry Mancini's *Peter Gunn* for Percussion Quartet. —**NS/LK/DM**

Pugnani, (Giulio) Gaetano (Gerolamo), celebrated Italian violinist and composer; b. Turin, Nov. 27, 1731; d. there, July 15, 1798. He studied violin with G.B. Somis. When he was 10, he was allowed to play in the last chair of the 2nd violins in the orch. of Turin's Teatro Regio; he officially became a member of the orch. on April 19, 1748. In 1749, on a royal stipend, he went to Rome to study with Ciampi, and later toured in Europe as a concert violinist. Pugnani was particularly successful in London, where he played concerts with J.C. Bach; from 1767 to 1769 he also served as conductor at the King's Theatre, where he brought out his successful opera *Nanetta e Lubino* (April 8, 1769). He then returned to Turin, where he was appointed concertmaster of the King's Music and of the orch. of the Teatro Regio in 1770. He was named general director of instrumental music in 1776; in 1786 he served as supervisor of military music. He made, from 1780 to 1782, a concert tour of Europe, which included a visit to Russia. He was also active as a teacher of the violin. His students included Viotti, Conforti, Bruni, and Polledro. His style of composition approximated that of Tartini. Fritz Kreisler publ. an arrangement for violin and piano of a piece, purportedly by Pugnani, titled *Preludio e Allegro e Tempo di Minuetto*, but this proved to be by Kreisler himself.

WORKS: DRAMATIC: *Nanetta e Lubino*, opera buffa (London, April 8, 1769); *Issea*, favola pastorale (Turin, 1771); *Tamas Kouli-Kan nell'India*, dramma per musica (Turin, Feb. 1, 1772; not extant); *Aurora*, festa per musica (Turin, 1775; not extant); *Adone e Venere*, opera seria (Naples, Nov. 1784); *Achille in Sciro*, dramma per musica (Turin, Jan. 15, 1785); *Demofoonte*, dramma per musica (Turin, Dec. 26, 1787); *Demetrio a Rodi*, festa per musica (Turin, 1789); also *Correso e Calliroe*, balleto eroico (1792; not extant), ballet music to Gluck's *Orfeo* (not extant), and an oratorio, *Betulia liberata*. **OTHER:** Violin Concerto; sinfonias; overtures; 40 trio sonatas; 6 string quartets; Violin Sonatas; duets for 2 Violins; about 20 sonatas for Violin and Basso Continuo.

BIBL.: G. Rangoni, *Essai sur le goût de la musique ... Saggio sul gusto della musica col carattere de' tre celebri sonatori di violino i signori Nardini, Lolli, e P.* (Livorno, 1790); F. Fayolle, *Notices sur Corelli, Tartini, Gaviniès, P. et Viotti* (Paris, 1810); A. Bertolotti, *G. P. e altri musici alla corte di Torino nel secolo XVIII* (Milan, 1892); A. Della Corte, *Notizie di G. P.* (Turin, 1931); E. von Zschinsky-Troxler, *G. P.* (Berlin, 1939).—**NS/LK/DM**

Pugni, Cesare, Italian composer; b. Genoa, May 31, 1802; d. St. Petersburg, Jan. 26, 1870. He studied violin with Alessandro Rolla and composition with Asioli at the Milan Cons. He began his career as a composer for the stage with the ballet *Elerz e Zulmida* (Milan, May 6, 1826) and the opera *Il Disertore svizzero, o La nostaligia* (Milan, May 28, 1831), followed by several other operas: *La vendetta* (Milan, Feb. 11, 1832), *Ricciarda di Edimburgo* (Trieste, Sept. 29, 1832), *Il Contrabbandiere* (Milan, June 13, 1833), and *Un episodio di S. Michele* (Milan, June 14, 1834). He also wrote an ingenious *Sinfonia a canone* for 2 orchs. playing the same music, but with the second orch. coming in one measure later than the first (this musical legerdemain amused Meyerbeer). He then lived in Paris, where he struck up a rewarding collaborative relationship with the choreographer Jules Perrot and produced some 30 ballets, many of which were premiered at Her Majesty's Theatre in London; among the most successful were *Ondine, ou La naiade* (June 22, 1843) and *La Esmeralda* (March 9, 1844). In 1851 he was appointed ballet composer for the imperial theaters in St. Petersburg, where he produced such successful ballets as *Konyok gorbunyok, ili Tsar-devista* (The Little Hump-backed Horse, or the Czar's Daughter; Dec. 15, 1864).—**NS/LK/DM**

Pugno, (Stéphane) Raoul, celebrated French pianist and teacher; b. Montrouge, near Paris (of an Italian father), June 23, 1852; d. (while on a concert tour) Moscow, Jan. 3, 1914. He studied at the Paris Cons. with G. Mathias (piano) and Ambroise Thomas (composition). He became music director of the Paris Opéra in 1871, then served as organist (1872–92) and choirmaster (1878–92) at the church of St.-Eugène. He then taught harmony at the Paris Cons. (1892–96), and subsequently was a prof. of piano there (1896–1901). In the meantime he gave numerous recitals, and gradually rose to the rank of a great virtuoso; he appeared in England in 1894, and in America in 1897–98. He was equally remarkable as an ensemble player; his sonata recitals with Ysaÿe became world famous. Pugno was also a composer, numbering several operas among his works: *Ninetta* (Paris, Dec. 23, 1882), *Le Sosie* (Oct. 7, 1887), *Le Valet de coeur* (April 19, 1888), *Le Retour d'Ulysse* (Paris, Feb. 1, 1889), *La Vocation de Marius* (March 29, 1890), etc. Other works include a ballet, *La Danseuse de corde* (Paris, Feb. 5, 1892), piano pieces, and songs. His score for *La Ville morte* (after Gabriele d'Annunzio), left incomplete at his death, was finished by Nadia Boulanger. —**NS/LK/DM**

Puig, Bernardo Calvo, Spanish organist and composer; b. Vich, Feb. 22, 1819; d. Barcelona, 1880. He was a choirboy at Vich Cathedral, where he studied with José Gallés. He succeeded his teacher as organist there, and later became its asst. maestro de capilla. After further training in Barcelona, he became organist at the church of Nuestra Señora del Pino, and later was maestro de capilla at Barcelona Cathedral. In 1853 he was made director of the Escolania de la Merced. He wrote 2 operas, zarzuelas, and many sacred works. —**LK/DM**

Puig-Roget, Henriette, French organist, pianist, teacher, and composer; b. Bastia, Jan 9, 1910; d. Paris, Nov. 24, 1992. She studied with Philipp (piano), Dupré (organ), J. Gallon (harmony), Tournemire (chamber music), Emmanuel (music history), and Büsser (composition) at the Paris Cons., winning premiers prix in 1926 and 1930. In 1933 she won the Premier 2nd Prix de Rome. From 1934 to 1979 she was organist at l'Oratoire du Louvre in Paris. She also pursued an active career as a pianist until 1975. She was "chef de chant" at the Paris Opéra (1937–40; 1946–57) and then was prof. of piano accompaniment and score reading at the Paris Cons. (1957–79). She wrote many piano books for children.

WORKS: DRAMATIC: B a l l e t : *Cathérinettes* (1937). **ORCH.:** *Montanyas del Rosello* for Organ and Orch. (Paris, April 6, 1933, composer soloist); *3 ballades françaises* (1935; Paris, Jan. 11, 1936); *Sinfonia andorrana* (1936); *Rythmes* (1936; Paris, Jan. 23, 1937); *Concerto sicilien* for Piano and Orch. (1943); *Concerto classique* for Cello and Orch. (1944); *Symphonie pour rire* (1947). **OTHER:** Organ pieces.—**NS/LK/DM**

Pujol, Juan (Pablo), Catalan composer and organist; b. Barcelona, c. 1573; d. there, May 1626. From 1593 to 1595 he was maestro de canto at Tarragona Cathedral, and from 1596 to 1612 he was organist at

Nuestra Señora del Pilar in Saragossa; then at the Barcelona Cathedral until his death. His masses, motets, Passions, Psalms, and villancicos are preserved in MS. A selected ed. of Pujol's works was undertaken by H. Anglès, of which 2 vols. appeared (1926, 1932). —NS/LK/DM

Puliaschi, Giovanni Domenico, Italian singer, chitarrone player, and composer who flourished in the early 17th century. He was a native of Rome, where he became a tenor and chaplain in the papal chapel in 1612. He also was a canon at S. Maria in Cosmedin in Rome. His vocal range made it possible for him to sing both alto and bass roles, as well as tenor. He publ. the collection *Gemma musicale* (Rome, 1618; corrected ed., 1618, as *Musiche varie*), which includes pieces for voice and continuo and an essay on singing.—LK/DM

Puliti, Gabriello, Italian organist and composer; b. Montepulciano, near Arezzo, c. 1575; d. Istria, between 1641 and 1644. He was a member of the Franciscan order, and was active as organist in several monasteries. He composed a vast amount of sacred and secular music, much of which was publ.—LK/DM

Pullaer, Louis van, Flemish composer; b. Cambrai, c. 1475; d. there, Sept. 21, 1528. He became an enfant de choeur at Cambrai Cathedral in 1485, and continued to sing there until 1494. After serving as director of the children's choir at St. Denis in Liège (1495–1503), he was director of the cathedral choirs in Cambrai (1503–07) and Notre Dame in Paris (1507–27). He then was made a canon at Cambrai Cathedral. His best known work is the *Missa Christe resurgens* for 4 Voices.—LK/DM

Pullen, Don (Gabriel), avant-garde jazz pianist, organist, composer; b. Roanoke, Va., Dec. 25, 1941; d. N.Y., April 23, 1995. He began playing at 10. He studied with Muhal Richard Abrams and Giuseppe Logan, before making his recording debut with Logan in 1964. He had his own groups and also worked with Milford Graves in a duo. He composed and arranged for King, and led his own R&B organ group. He worked for a year with Nina Simone (1970–71), with saxophonist Charles Williams, and briefly with Art Blakey (1974). But it was his stint with Charles Mingus (1973–75) that got him substantial attention for his vibrant style and expressive use of clusters of notes over tonal grooves. He and Mingus bandmate George Adams began co-leading a group in 1979, following several European tours Pullen had made with his own bands. The Pullen/Adams group was a staple on the 1980s jazz scene until they disbanded when Adams died. Pullen's quintet in 1985 featured Olu Dara, Donald Harrison, Fred Hopkins, and Bobby Battle on drums. He also gave solo concerts. Pullen died of cancer.

DISC.: *Nommo* (1966); *Solo Piano Album* (1975); *Jazz a confonto* (1975); *Capricorn Rising* (1975); *Tomorrow's Promises* (1976); *Healing Force* (1976); *Montreux Concert* (1977); *Warriors* (1978); *Magic Triangle* (1979); *Earth Beams with George Adams Quartet* (1980); *Evidence of Things Unseen* (1983); *Plays Monk* (1984); *Decisions* (1984); *Well Kept Secret* (1985); *Sixth Sense* (1985); *Breakthrough* (1986); *Song Everlasting* (1987); *Live at the Village Vanguard, V* (1987); *New Beginnings* (1988); *N.Y. Duets* (1989); *Random Thoughts* (1990); *Kele Mou Bana* (1991); *Ode to Life* (1993); *Live...Again* (1995).—LP/MM

Pulli, Pietro, Italian composer; b. Naples, c. 1710; d. after 1759. He was active as a composer of operas for various Italian theaters.

WORKS: DRAMATIC: O p e r a : *Li zitelle de lo vòmmero* (Naples, 1731); *La marina de chiaja* (Naples, 1734); *Il carnevale e la pazzia* (Modena, Carnival 1739–40); *Le nozze del Piacere e dell'Allegria* (Modena, Carnival 1739–40); *Caio Marzio Coriolano* (Reggio Emilia, 1741); *Zenobia* (Milan, Dec. 26, 1748); *Il Demetrio* (Milan, Carnival 1749); *Vologeso re dei Parti* (Modena, Carnival 1750); *Olimpiade* (Modena, Jan. 1751). **OTHER:** Sinfonias, 4 sonatas for Flute and Bass, and arias.—LK/DM

Pullois, Jean or **Johannes,** Flemish composer; b. probably in Antwerp, c. 1420; d. Aug. 23, 1478. He was a singer at the Antwerp Cathedral (1442–47), and then sang in the papal chapel (until 1459). After serving as a member of the Burgundian court chapel, he returned to Antwerp in 1463. He composed both liturgical and secular vocal music. His complete works were ed. by P. Gülke in Corpus Mensurabilis Musicae, XLI (1967). —LK/DM

Punto, Giovanni
See **Stich, Johann Wenzel**

Puppo, Giuseppe, Italian violinist, teacher, and composer; b. Lucca, June 12, 1749; d. Florence, April 19, 1827. He studied at Naples's Cons. di S. Onofrio di Loreto. He was a successful violin virtuoso at an early age. He traveled in Spain, was in England from 1777 until 1783, and then settled in Paris, where he was a fashionable teacher. In 1811 he abandoned his family in Paris and went to Naples, and then to Florence, where he died in poverty. He publ. 2 violin concertos, 8 études for violin, and 6 piano fantasias.—NS/LK/DM

Purcell, Daniel, English organist and composer, brother of **Henry Purcell**; b. London, c. 1660; d. there (buried), Nov. 26, 1717. He became organist of Magdalen Coll., Oxford, in 1688; took his brother's place as a dramatic composer in 1695, and was organist of St. Andrew's, Holborn, from 1713. He supplied scores of incidental music to over 40 plays, and also wrote many other secular vocal works and various instrumental pieces.—NS/LK/DM

Purcell, Henry, great English composer, brother of **Daniel Purcell**; b. London, 1659; d. Dean's Yard, Westminster, Nov. 21, 1695. His parentage remains a matter of dispute, since documentary evidence is lacking. His father may have been Henry Purcell (d. Westminster, Aug. 11, 1664), a singer, who was named a "singing-man" and Master of the Choristers at Westminster Abbey (1661) and a Gentleman of the Chapel Royal (1661), where he became a musician-in-ordinary for the lutes and voices (1662). It is possible that his father was

Thomas Purcell (d. Westminster, July 31, 1682), a singer and composer, who most likely was the brother of the elder Henry Purcell; Thomas became a Gentleman of the Chapel Royal (1661), where he was admitted to the private music for lutes, viols, and voices (1662); with Pelham Humfrey, he served as composer for the violins (from 1672); that same year he was made marshal of the Corp. of Music and a musician-in-ordinary in the King's Private Musick. Whatever the case, the young Henry Purcell became a chorister of the Chapel Royal under Cooke and Humfrey (1669), and also received instruction from Blow; when his voice broke (1673), he was appointed Assistant Keeper of the Instruments; was named composer-in-ordinary for the violins (1677). He became Blow's successor as organist of Westminster Abbey (1679) and one of the 3 organists of the Chapel Royal (1682); was named organ maker and keeper of the king's instruments (1683). His first printed work was a song in Playford's *Choice Ayres* (vol. I, 1675); vol. II (1679) contains other songs and an elegy on the death of Matthew Locke. In 1680 he publ. one of his finest instrumental works, the *Fantasias* for Strings; in that same year he began writing odes and welcome songs; although their texts are almost invariably stupid or bombastic, he succeeded in clothing them in some of his finest music; his incidental music for the stage also dates from that year. He wrote the anthem *My Heart is Inditing* for the coronation of King James II (1685). With *Dido and Aeneas* (1689) he produced the first great English opera. In the remaining years of his life he devoted much time to composition for the theater; he also wrote some outstanding sacred music.

Purcell lies in the north aisle of Westminster Abbey, and his burial tablet well expresses contemporary estimation of his worth: "Here lyes Henry Purcell, Esq.; who left this life, and is gone to that blessed place where only his harmony can be exceeded." His church music shows him to be an original melodist, and a master of form, harmony, and all contrapuntal devices; his music for the stage is equally rich in invention, dramatic instinct, and power of characterization; his chamber works surpass those of his predecessors and contemporaries. A complete ed. of Purcell's works was issued by the Purcell Soc. (London, 1878–1965; 2nd ed., rev., 1974–81).

WORKS: DRAMATIC: Opera: *Dido and Aeneas* (London, 1689). **Semi-opera**: *The Prophetess, or The History of Dioclesian* (London, 1690); *King Arthur, or The British Worthy* (London, 1691); *The Fairy Queen* (London, 1692); *The Indian Queen* (London, 1695; final masque by D. Purcell); *The Tempest, or The Enchanted Island* (c.1695). **Incidental Music To**: N. Lee's *Theodosius, or The Force of Love* (1680); T. D'Urfey's *Sir Barnaby Whigg, or No Wit Like a Woman's* (1681); Tate's *The History of King Richard II (The Sicilian Usurper)*, after Shakespeare (1681); Beaumont and Fletcher's *The Double Marriage* (c.1682–85); Lee's *Sophonisba, or Hannibal's Overthrow* (c.1685); D'Urfey's *A Fool's Preferment, or The 3 Dukes of Dunstable*, after Fletcher's *Noble Gentleman* (1688); Dryden's *Amphitryon, or The Two Sosias* (1690); E. Settle's *Distressed Innocence, or The Princess of Persia* (1690); T. Southerne's *Sir Anthony Love, or The Rambling Lady* (1690); Lee's *The Massacre of Paris* (1690); C. D'Avenant's *Circe* (c.1690); *The Gordian Knot Unty'd* (1691); Dryden and R. Howard's *The Indian Emperor, or The Conquest of Mexico* (1691); Southerne's *The Wives' Excuse, or Cuckolds Make Themselves* (1691); Dryden's *Cleomenes, the Spartan Hero* (1692); W. Mountfort and J. Bancroft's *Henry the 2nd, King of England* (1692); J. Crowne's *Regulus* (1692); Dryden's *Aureng-Zebe* (c.1692); Dryden and Lee's *Oedipus* (c.1692); T. Shadwell's *The Libertine* (c.1692); D'Urfey's *The Marriage-Hater Match'd* (1692); Shadwell's *Epsom Wells* (1693); W. Congreve's *The Double Dealer* (1693); Fletcher's *Rule a Wife and Have a Wife* (1693); T. Wright's *The Female Vertuosos*, after Molière's *Les Femmes savantes* (1693); Southerne's *The Maid's Last Prayer, or Any Rather than Fail* (1693); Congreve's *The Old Bachelor* (1693); D'Urfey's *The Richmond Heiress, or A Woman Once in the Right* (1693); Dryden's *Love Triumphant, or Nature Will Prevail* (1694); E. Ravenscroft's *The Canterbury Guests, or A Bargain Broken* (1694); Southerne's *The Fatal Marriage, or The Innocent Adultery* (1694); Crowne's *The Married Beau, or The Curious Impertinent* (1694); Shadwell's *Timon of Athens*, after Shakespeare (1694); Dryden's *Tyrannic Love, or The Royal Martyr* (1694); D'Urfey's *The Virtuous Wife, or Good Luck at Last* (c.1694); Dryden's *The Spanish Friar, or The Double Discovery* (1694–95); D'Urfey's *The Comical History of Don Quixote* (1694–95); A. Behn's *Abdelazer, or The Moor's Marriage* (1695); *Bonduca, or The British Heroine*, after Beaumont and Fletcher (1695); Southerne's *Oroonoko* (1695); Norton's *Pausanias, the Betrayer of His Country* (1695); T. Scott's *The Mock Marriage* (1695); R. Gould's *The Rival Sisters, or The Violence of Love* (1695). **VOCAL**: Numerous anthems and services (c. 1677-c. 1693); Magnificat and Nunc dimitiis (n.d.); Morning and Evening Service (1682); Te Deum and Jubilate (1694); other sacred works; 24 odes and welcome songs; numerous songs for Solo Voice and Continuo; songs for 2 or More Voices and Continuo; catches. **INSTRUMENTAL**: Various pieces for Winds and Strings, including 14 fantasias, 3 overtures, 5 pavans, 24 sonatas, etc.; many harpsichord pieces.

BIBL.: W. Cummings, *P.* (London, 1881; 3rd ed., 1911; abr. ed., 1923); J. Runciman, *P.* (London, 1909); D. Arundell, *H. P.* (London, 1927); H. Dupre, *P.* (Paris, 1927; Eng. tr., 1928); A. Holland, *H. P.: The English Musical Tradition* (London, 1932; 2nd ed., 1948); F. de Quervain, *Der Chorstil H. P.'s* (Bern, 1935); J. Westrup, *P.* (London, 1937; 4th ed., rev., 1980); S. Favre-Lingorow, *Der Instrumentalstil von P.* (Bern, 1950); W. Mainardus, *Die Technik des Basso Ostinato bei H. P.* (diss., Univ. of Cologne, 1950); S. Demarquez, *P.: La Vie, l'oeuvre* (Paris, 1951); G. van Ravenzwaaij, *P.* (Haarlem and Antwerp, 1954); R. Sietz, *H. P.: Zeit, Leben, Werk* (Leipzig, 1956); I. Holst, ed., *H. P. (1659–1695): Essays on His Music* (London, 1959); R. Moore, *H. P. and the Restoration Theatre* (London, 1961); M. Laurie, *P.'s Stage Works* (diss., Cambridge Univ., 1962); D. Schjelderup-Ebbe, *P.'s Cadences* (Oslo, 1962); F. Zimmerman, *H. P., 1659–1695: An Analytical Catalogue of His Music* (London, 1963); idem, *H. P., 1659–1695: His Life and Times* (London, 1967; 2nd ed., rev., 1983); R. Burkart, *The Trumpet in England in the Seventeenth Century with Emphasis on Its Treatment in the Works of H. P.* (diss., Univ. of Wisc., 1972); I. Spink, *English Song: Dowland to P.* (London, 1974); F. Zimmerman, *H. P. 1659–1695: Melodic and Intervallic Indexes to His Complete Works* (Philadelphia, 1975); K. Rohrer, "The Energy of English Words": A Linguistic Approach to H. P.'s Methods of Setting Texts* (diss., Princeton Univ., 1980); A. Hutchings, *P.* (London, 1982); C. Price, *H. P. and the London Stage* (Cambridge, 1984); E. Harris, *H. P.'s Dido and Aeneas* (Oxford, 1987); F. Zimmerman, *H. P.: A Guide to Research* (N.Y., 1988); M. Campbell, *H. P.: Glory of His Age* (London, 1993); M. Burden, ed., *The P. Companion* (London, 1994); M. Duffy, *H. P.* (London, 1994); R. King, *H. P.* (London, 1994); M. Adams, *H. P.: The Origins and Development of his Musical Style* (Cambridge, 1995);

P. Holman, *H. P.* (Oxford, 1995); J. Keates, *P.: A Biography* (London, 1995); C. Price, ed., *P. Studies* (Cambridge, 1995); R. Thompson, *The Glory of the Temple and the Stage: H. P. 1659–1695* (London, 1995); B. Wood, ed., *A P. Anthology* (Oxford, 1995). **—NS/LK/DM**

Purdie, Bernard (Pretty), pop-jazz drummer; b. Elkton, Md., June 11, 1939. One of the most in-demand soul, R&B, funk and pop drummers, Purdie also has jazz credentials. He started playing percussively at three, got a drum set at eight, and began playing with a local big band at 10. He got his first paying gig at 11 or 12. In school, his teachers had him play trumpet, then flute in order to learn reading. He ran a country music trio, Jackie Lee and the Angels, with Lee, a white guitarist, and a Hawaiian bassist, where he drummed, danced and sang. His early jazz influences were Cozy Cole, Joe Marshall, Sticks Evans, Panama Francis, Louis Bellson, Gene Krupa, and Herbie Lovelle. He went to N.Y. to do his first session work in 1958 and 1959 on two versions of "Love Is Strange" with Mickey and Sylvia. In 1960, he decided to stay in N.Y. with his wife and for six months supported himself with a job at Globe Laundry on 49th St. while he was paid to play on demos for Les Cooper, Doris Troy, and others. Soon he was busily recording for Motown and Stax, playing with James Brown, King Curtis, and many others; through Curtis he was very active at Atlantic. He was CTI's house drummer in the late 1960s and early 1970s, and worked with Grover Washington Jr. and George Benson, among others. He toured with Curtis and Aretha Franklin in 1970, and was Franklin's music director until 1975. During his studio days in the early 1970s, he recorded with Louis Armstrong, Nina Simone and Gato Barbieri, along with numerous rock, pop, and soul sessions. He recorded with Gene Ammons in 1969 and Dizzy Gillespie in 1980 at the Montreux Jazz Festival; he toured with Gillespie in 1983. Purdie recorded with Hank Crawford during the early 1980s, and has continued working steadily into the 1990s. He generated a firestorm of reaction in 1993 when he charged it was his uncredited drumming rather than Ringo Starr's on some Beatles tracks. Purdie claimed proof was forthcoming, but none has been presented. He also said he played with The Animals and The Monkees. He taught at the New School in the 1990s.

DISC.: *Purdie Good* (1971); *Soul Is...Pretty Purdie* (1972); *Delights of the Gardens* (1977).**—LP**

Purim, Flora, pop-jazz singer, guitarist, percussionist; b. Rio de Janeiro, Brazil, March 6, 1942. She married fellow Brazilian, Airto Moreira, and the couple moved to the U.S. in 1968. She toured Europe that year with Stan Getz, played with Duke Pearson, recorded with Gil Evans (1971) and worked with Moreira on Chick Corea's *Return to Forever* and *Light As a Feather* albums. In 1973, she formed a band with Moreira, blending jazz with Brazilian and popular music styles. Purim was jailed in 1975 for cocaine possession but was released a year later. She has since worked again with Moreira and also David Sanborn. She has a tremendous vocal range, which at one time was said to be six octaves:

DISC.: *Love Reborn* (1973); *Butterfly Dreams* (1973); *500 Miles High* (1974); *Open Your Eyes* (1976).
BIBL.: E. Bunker and F. Purim, *Freedom Song: The Story of Flora Purim* (N.Y., 1982).**—MM/LP**

Puschmann, Adam (Zacharias), German poet and Meistersinger; b. Görlitz, 1532; d. Breslau, April 4, 1600. He was a pupil of Hans Sachs. He brought out *Gründtlicher Bericht des deutschen Meistergesanges* (1571; 2nd ed., 1596; ed. by R. Jonas, Halle, 1888) and a *Singebuch* (1588; ed. by G. Münzer, Leipzig, 1906), which contains some 350 melodies.**—NS/LK/DM**

Puschmann, Josef, Czech composer; b. near Bezděz, c. 1740; d. Olomouc, Feb. 3?, 1794. After studying violin and other instruments as a child, he was in the service of Baron Skrbenský in Hoštálkovy (c. 1762–67) and Count Ignác Dominik Chronský in Velké Hoštice (1767–77). After further training in Vienna in 1773, he was music director at Olomouc Cathedral from 1778. Among his works were 7 syms. (4 for use as graduals), 5 orch. serenades, a Violin Concerto, a Viola Concerto, 4 partitas for Winds, a Requiem, a Te Deum, and other sacred pieces.**—LK/DM**

Putnam, Ashley (Elizabeth), American soprano; b. N.Y., Aug. 10, 1952. She studied flute at the Univ. of Mich., eventually turning to voice (B.M., 1974; M.M., 1975). After graduating, she was an apprentice with the Santa Fe Opera Co. In 1976 she made her operatic debut in the title role of Donizetti's *Lucia di Lammermoor* with the Va. Opera Assn. in Norfolk. After winning 1st prize in the Metropolitan Opera Auditions and receiving the Weyerhauser Award (1976), she made her European debut as Musetta in Puccini's *La Bohème* at the Glyndebourne Festival (1978). On Sept. 15, 1978, she won accolades as Violetta in her N.Y.C. Opera debut. In 1986 she made her first appearance at London's Covent Garden as Jenůfa. She sang Donna Elvira at her Metropolitan Opera debut in N.Y. in 1990. In 1995 she appeared as Wagner's Eva at the Cleveland Opera. She portrayed Thomson's St. Theresa I at the Houston Grand Opera in 1996. As a concert artist, she appeared with leading U.S. and European orchs., and also gave recitals.**—NS/LK/DM**

Puyana, Rafael, Colombian harpsichordist; b. Bogotá, Oct. 14, 1931. He studied piano at the New England Cons. of Music in Boston, and harpsichord with Wanda Landowska in N.Y.; also had general music training at the Hartt Coll. of Music in Hartford, Conn. He made a tour of Europe (1955); made his first appearances in N.Y. (1957) and London (1966); thereafter toured worldwide. His extensive repertory ranges from early music to contemporary scores.**—NS/LK/DM**

Puzzi, Giovanni, Italian horn player and composer; b. Parma, 1792; d. London, March 1, 1876. He is believed to have been a pupil of Luigi Belloli in Parma. Following a sojourn in Paris (1815–16), he settled in London and made his debut in 1817 performing his own

Concertante. He acquired a notable reputation as a master of the chromatic late hand-horn technique. In addition to playing in various orchs., he also made appearances as a soloist and as a chamber music artist. Besides his Concertante, he also composed pieces for horn and piano.—**LK/DM**

Pyamour, John, English composer; b. place and date unknown; d. 1431. He was a clerk in King Henry V's chapel royal, and was most likely the first to serve as Master of the Chapel Children. In 1427 he entered the service of John, Duke of Bedford. He composed sacred music, including *Quam pulcra es*, a Marian antiphon for 3 Voices.—**LK/DM**

Pycard, English singer and composer who flourished c. 1400. The *Old Hall Manuscript* contains 6 works by him. His contrapuntal skill was out of the ordinary, and he used complicated canonic forms in sections of the Mass.—**NS/LK/DM**

Pygott, Richard, English composer who flourished in the first half of the 16th century. He was Master of the Children in Thomas Wolsey's household chapel by 1516. From 1524 until about 1554 he was a Gentleman of the Chapel Royal. His extant sacred and secular works are distinguished.—**LK/DM**

Pylkkänen, Tauno Kullervo, Finnish composer; b. Helsinki, March 22, 1918; d. there, March 13, 1980. He studied composition with Palmgren, Madetoja, and Ranta at the Helsinki Academy of Music (1937–40), and also studied musicology at the Univ. of Helsinki (M.A., 1941). He worked at the Finnish Broadcasting Co. (1942–61) and was artistic director of the Finnish National Opera (1960–70); lectured on opera history at the Sibelius Academy (from 1967). He was primarily an opera composer; his idiom was basically Romantic, with sporadic excursions into modernity.

WORKS: DRAMATIC: Opera: *Bathsheba Saaren-maalla* (Bathsheba at Saarenmaa; 1940; rev. 1958); *Mare ja hanen poikansa* (Mare and Her Son; 1943); *Simo Hurtta* (1948); *Suden-morsian* (The Wolf's Bride), radio opera (1950); *Varjo* (The Shadow; 1952); *Ikaros* (1956–60); *Opri and Oleksi* (1957); *Vangit* (The Prisoners; 1964); *Tuntematon sotilas* (The Unknown Soldier; 1967). Ballet: *Kaarina Maununtytar* (Kaarina, Maunu's Daughter; 1960). ORCH.: *Introduction and Fugue* (1940); *Lapin kesa* (Summer in Lapland; 1941); *Kullervon sotaanlahto* (Kullervo Leaves for War; 1942); Sinfonietta (1944); Sym. No. 1 (1945); Suite for Oboe and Strings (1946); *Marathon*, overture (1947); *Symphonic Fantasy* (1948); *Ultima Thule* (1949); Cello Concerto (1950); *Symphonic Prelude* (1952). CHAMBER: *Notturno* for Violin and Piano (1943); String Quartet (1945); *Fantasia appassionata* for Cello and Piano (1954); *Trittico* for Clarinet, Violin, Viola, and Cello (1978). VOCAL: Cantatas; songs. —**NS/LK/DM**

Pyne, Louisa (Fanny), English soprano; b. Aug. 27?, 1832; d. London, March 20, 1904. She was a student of G. Smart. At the age of 10, she made her debut with her sister Susannah in London. In 1849 she made her operatic debut as Bellini's Amina in Boulogne. Returning to London, she appeared at the Princess's Theatre that same year. She also sang at the Haymarket and Royal Italian Opera at Covent Garden, garnering critical accolades at the latter in 1851 for her portrayal of the Queen of the Night. In 1854 she sang in opera in N.Y., and then toured the U.S. with her sister and the tenor William Harrison. In 1857 she and Harrison founded the Pyne-Harrison Opera Co. in London. It gave regular performances at Covent Garden (1859–64), with Pyne taking leading roles in premieres of scores by Balfe, Benedict, and Wallace. In 1868 she married the baritone Frank Bodda and subsequently taught voice. —**NS/LK/DM**

Pythagoras, Greek philosopher and mathematician; b. Samos, c.580 B.C.; d. Metapontum, c.500 B.C. His doctrines on the musical ratios are preserved in the writings of his followers, no books by Pythagoras having come down to us. The Pythagoreans (Archytas, Didymos, Eratosthenes, Euclid, Ptolemy, etc.) reckoned only the 5th and octave as pure consonances (the 4th being the 5th below); their system recognized only intervals reached by successive skips of pure 5ths, the major 3rd being the 4th 5th above (ratio 64:81, instead of the modern 64:80, or 4:5), their minor 3rd the 3rd 5th below; etc. Their 3rds and 6ths were, consequently, dissonant intervals.—**NS/LK/DM**

Quadri, Argeo, Italian conductor; b. Como, March 23, 1911. He studied piano, composition, and conducting at the Milan Cons. (graduated, 1933), then conducted opera throughout Italy. In 1956 he became a conductor at Covent Garden in London. He was a regular conductor at the Vienna State Opera (1957–75). —NS/LK/DM

Quagliati, Paolo, Italian organist and composer; b. Chioggia, c. 1555; d. Rome, Nov. 16, 1628. Born into the nobility, he settled in Rome (c. 1574), where he was organist at S. Maria Maggiore. He was also in the service of the Ludovisi family. Upon the elevation of Cardinal Alessandro Ludovisi as Pope Gregory XV (1621), he became apostolic prothonotary and the pope's private chamberlain. He publ. *Il carro di Fedeltà d'Amore con aggiunta di alcune arie dell'istesso autore,* one of the earliest music dramas, containing not only monodies, but ensemble numbers up to 5 voices (Rome, 1611; ed. in Smith Coll. Music Archives, XIII, 1957). Other works include motets and "dialogues" *a* 2–8 (3 vols., 1612, 1620, 1627), etc.—NS/LK/DM

Quaile, Elizabeth, Irish-American piano pedagogue; b. Omagh, Jan. 20, 1874; d. South Kent, Conn., June 30, 1951. She went to N.Y. and studied with Franklin Robinson, then devoted herself to teaching. From 1916 to 1919 she was head of the piano dept. of the David Mannes School; then went to Paris, where she studied piano with Harold Bauer. Returning to N.Y. in 1921, she founded, with Angela Diller, the Diller-Quaile School of Music. She publ. a number of highly successful piano teaching methods, some written by her alone (*First Book of Technical Exercises, A Pre-Czerny Book,* etc.), and some in collaboration with Diller. The books proved to be standard guides for piano students for many years.—NS/LK/DM

Quantz, Johann Joachim, famous German flutist, writer on music, and composer; b. Oberscheden,

Hannover, Jan. 30, 1697; d. Potsdam, July 12, 1773. His father was a village blacksmith. Young Johann revealed a natural gift for music, and played the double bass at village festivals at age 8. His father died when he was 10, and he was apprenticed to his uncle, Justus Quantz, a "Stadtmusikus" in Merseburg, in 1708, and later to J. A. Fleischhack. He received instruction on string and wind instruments, becoming particularly adept on the violin, oboe, and trumpet, and also studied harpsichord with J.F. Kiesewetter. He completed his apprenticeship in 1713, but remained a journeyman under Fleischhack until 1716. He then became a member of the Dresden municipal band. During a 3-month leave of absence (1717), he studied counterpoint with J. D. Zelenka in Vienna. He subsequently became oboist at the Polish chapel of Augustus II (1718), being active in Dresden and Warsaw, but soon turned to the transverse flute, receiving some lessons from P. G. Buffardin. In 1724 he went to Italy in the entourage of the Polish ambassador and sought out F. Gasparini in Rome for further counterpoint training; after a sojourn in Paris (1726–27), he visited England (1727) before returning to Dresden as a flutist in the court Kapelle (also 1727). He made his first visit to Berlin in the entourage of Augustus II (1728), where he was engaged as teacher to Crown Prince Friedrich. He continued to visit Berlin regularly to instruct the Crown Prince while carrying out his duties in Dresden, which included the making of flutes from 1739. Friedrich ascended the throne as King of Prussia in 1740 and the next year called Quantz to Berlin, where it was his special province to oversee the King's private evening concerts; he was granted an annual salary of 2,000 thalers, plus an honorarium for each new composition and flute he produced. Quantz was held in such high esteem by his patron that he was the only individual granted the right to criticize Friedrich's performances as a musician. His extensive output included some 300 concertos for flute, strings, and basso continuo, 7 concertos for 2 flutes, strings, and basso continuo, 2 concertos for horn, strings, and basso continuo

(1 may not be by Quantz), 2 concertos for oboe, strings, and basso continuo, concerto for oboe d'amore, strings, and basso continuo (not extant), about 200 sonatas for flute and basso continuo, some 60 trio sonatas, 12 duets for 2 flutes or other instruments, 12 capriccios for flute, 8 fantasias for flute, 22 hymns, 6 songs, etc. On the whole, these works reveal Quantz as a transitional figure in the movement from the Baroque to the Classical style. He publ. the valuable treatise *Versuch einer Anweisung die Flöte traversiere zu spielen* (Berlin, 1752; 3rd ed., 1789; many subsequent eds. and trs., including an Eng. tr. by E. Reilly, N.Y., 1966; 2nd ed., rev., 1985). He also wrote an autobiography in F. Marpurg's *Historisch-kritische Beyträge zur Aufnahme der Musik*, I (Berlin, 1754; reprint in W. Kahl, *Selbstbiographien deutscher Musiker des XVIII. Jahrhunderts*, Cologne, 1948).

BIBL.: A. Quantz, *Leben und Werke des Flötisten J.J. Q.* (Berlin, 1877); C. Zoeller, *Thematic Catalogue of the Compositions of J.J. Q.* (MS, c. 1886); A. Raskin, *J.J. Q.: Sein Leben und seine Kompositionen* (diss., Univ. of Cologne, 1923); E. Reilly, *Q. and His Versuch: Three Studies* (N.Y., 1971); M. Brink, *Die Flötenkonzerte von J.J. Q.: Untersuchungen zu ihrer Überlieferung und Form* (2 vols., Hildesheim, 1995); H. Augsbach, *J.J. Q.: Thematisch-systematisches Werkverzeichnis (QV)* (Stuttgart, 1997).—NS/LK/DM

Quasthoff, Thomas, German bass-baritone; b. Hildesheim, Nov. 9, 1959. Although born with severe birth defects, his pronounced vocal gifts determined his choice of careers. He received music training from Charlotte Lehmann and Huber-Contwig in Hannover. After capturing 1st prize in the ARD Competition in Munich in 1988, he launched his career as a concert and lieder artist. He appeared as a soloist with the Berlin Phil., the Vienna Phil., the Dresden State Orch., the Bavarian Radio Sym. Orch. in Munich, the Orchestre de Paris, the Royal Concertgebouw Orch. in Amsterdam, the London Sym. Orch., the London Phil., the Chicago Sym. Orch., the N.Y. Phil., and many other orchs. As a recitalist, his engagements took him all over Europe, and he also sang in Japan and the U.S. In 1997 he sang in the Schubert Bicentenary Concert at London's Wigmore Hall, where he returned that year to give a Brahms Centenary Concert. He made his N.Y. recital debut at Lincoln Center for the Performing Arts in 1999. In 1996 he became a prof. of voice at the Detmold Academy of Music. Quasthoff's repertoire includes the works of such masters as Bach, Mozart, Beethoven, Schubert, Berlioz, Schumann, Mahler, Fauré, and Britten.—LK/DM

Quatremère de Quincy, Antoine-Chrysostome, noted French archeologist, aesthetician, art historian, writer on music, and political leader; b. Paris, Oct. 25, 1755; d. there, Dec. 28, 1849. He studied law, then took courses in art and history at the Collège de Louis-le-Grand. From 1776 he made visits to Italy, where he pursued his interest in archeology. He wrote on aesthetics and art in Paris (from 1786), his first important article on music, "De la nature des opéras bouffons italiens et de l'union de la comédie et de la musique dans ces poèmes" for the *Mercure de France* (March 1789). After the French Revolution, he became an advocate for artistic freedom and the inviolability of copyright protection. He was elected a deputy to the Legislative Assembly (1791), but was imprisoned for 2 years and came close to being executed during the Reign of Terror; was again spared from execution (1795). He then was named a member of the Council of the 500 (1797), a member of the Académie des Inscriptions et Belles Lettres (1804), and a member of the Légion d'honneur (1808). He served as secretary of the Institut de France (from 1816), in which capacity he gave the funeral orations and wrote the biographical notices of the deceased members of the Académie.

WRITINGS (all publ. in Paris): *Dissertation sur les opéras bouffons italiens* (1789); *Discours...sur la liberté des théâtres* (1790); *Rapport...sur les réclamations des directeurs de théâtres et la propriété des auteurs dramatiques* (1792); *Dissertation...sur le système imitatif des arts et le genre poétique* (c. 1804); *Institut royal de France-:...funérailles de Paisiello* (1817), *de M. de Monsigny* (1818), *de M. Méhul* (1819), *de M. Gossec* (1829), *de M. Catel* (1820), and *de M. Boieldieu* (1834); *De l'invention et de l'innovation dans les ouvrages des beaux-arts* (c. 1828); *Recueil des notices historiques lues dans les séances publiques de l'Académie royale des Beaux-arts a l'Institut* (1834; notes on Paisiello, Monsigny, and Méhul publ. separately, see above); *Suite du Recueil* (1837; notices on Gossec, Catel, and Boieldieu publ. separately, see above).—NS/LK/DM

Quattrini, Jan Ludwik, Italian conductor; b. Brescia, May 13, 1822; d. Warsaw, April 10, 1893. He received training at the Milan Cons. After working as a bandmaster in Italy and in Berlin (1839–43), he settled in Warsaw and was a conductor at the Opera from 1845 to 1891. He also had his own singing school, and from 1891 was music director of the Piarists's Church.—LK/DM

Quealey, Chelsea, jazz trumpeter; b. Hartford, Conn., 1905; d. Las Vegas, May 6, 1950. Quealey started on sax, then switched to trumpet. He first worked with the Jan Garber Orch. (c. 1925), then with The California Ramblers (1926–27). Quealey sailed to England in December 1927 to join Fred Elizalde, where he recorded and performed, influencing the burgeoning English jazz scene; however, illness forced his sudden return to the U.S. in June 1929. On his return, he worked in N.Y. through 1930 in show bands. He rejoined The California Ramblers in 1931, but Quealey was again sidetracked by illness. After his recovery, he played briefly with Paul Whiteman, and then joined Ben Pollack in Chicago and moved to Calif. with Pollack. He was back in N.Y. by 1934, where he recorded with Mezz Mezzrow and worked with various groups, including Isham Jones' Juniors (early 1935–36), Joe Marsala (summer–autumn 1936), Frankie Trumbauer (January 1937), and the Bob Zurke Big Band (September 1939–early 1940). Quealey left Zurke to join Jack Crawford's Band in Tex. briefly in early 1940 and then returned to N.Y. and played regularly at Nick's with Georg Brunis, Brad Gowans, Miff Mole, and other jazz revivalists. He moved back to Calif. (c. 1946), worked for a while at various day jobs, and then moved on to Las Vegas. In 1950, he died of heart trouble.—JC/LP

Quebec, Ike (Abrams), jazz tenor saxophonist; b. Newark, N.J., Aug. 17, 1918; d. N.Y., Jan. 16, 1963. His nickname was "Jim Dawgs." Quebec gigged on piano as a teenager and also worked as a dancer. His first professional work was with the Barons of Rhythm in 1940. During the 1940s, he played with numerous small bands, usually based in N.Y., including Frankie Newton, Benny Carter, Coleman Hawkins, Kenny Clarke (with whom he co-wrote the song "Mop Mop"), Hot Lips Page, Trummy Young, Lucky Millinder, Roy Eldridge Quintet, etc. His recording "Blue Harlem" (1945) became a huge hit. He worked on and off with Cab Calloway from June 1944 until early 1951. Alfred Lion hired him as Blue Note's A&R man in the late 1940s, after Quebec repeatedly informed him about talented prospective signees. He led his own band in the 1950s, but his career was briefly stalled because of his heroin addiction. Until the late 1950s, he concentrated on recording and finding acts for the label; he signed Thelonious Monk and Bud Powell to Blue Note, among others. Quebec wrote "Suburban Eyes" for Monk's label debut. He began playing again in the late 1950s, working on Blue Note sessions with Sonny Clark, Jimmy Smith, singer Dodo Green, and Stanley Turrentine, plus his own dates. He also worked as a chauffeur from the late 1950s, making his last recordings in 1961 when illness forced him to quit playing. He died of lung cancer.

DISC.: *Tenor Sax Album: The Savoy Sessions* (1945); *Complete Blue Note 45 Sessions* (1959); *It Might As Well Be Spring* (1961); *Heavy Soul* (1961); *Blue and Sentimental* (1961); *With a Song in My Heart* (1962); *Soul Samba* (1962); *Easy Living* (1962); *Congo Lament* (1962).—**JC/MM/LP**

Queen, successful British group of the mid-1970s to the mid-1980s. **MEMBERSHIP:** Freddie Mercury (Frederick Bulsara) lead voc., kybd. (b. Zanzibar, Africa, Sept. 5, 1946; d. Kensington, England, Nov. 24, 1991); Brian May, lead gtr. (b. Twickenham, Middlesex, England, July 19, 1947); John Deacon, bs. (b. Leicester, England, Aug. 19, 1951); Roger Taylor, drm. (b. Kings Lynn, Norfolk, England, July 26, 1949).

Despite critical hostility, Queen were one of the foremost glitter-rock bands of the era, thanks to the outlandish costumes and flamboyant and blatantly sexual onstage behavior of lead singer Freddie Mercury. Eschewing synthesizers until 1980, Queen broke through into international popularity with 1976's near-smash hit single "Bohemian Rhapsody"; its video helped pioneer rock video in the days before MTV. Recording classics such as "We Will Rock You" and "Another One Bites the Dust," Queen suffered declining popularity in the United States after the mid-1980s. Discontinuing touring in 1986, Queen eventually recorded their most personal and emotionally accessible album, *The Miracle*, in 1989. After years of persistent rumors that he had contracted AIDS, Freddie Mercury died one day after acknowledging the fact (the first rock star to do so). A 1992 tribute concert to Mercury, viewed by as many as one billion people, helped publicize the need to find a cure for the disease.

Queen was formed in 1971 by Brian May and Roger Taylor, former members of the group Smile, and Freddie Mercury from the group Wreckage. John Deacon was recruited through an advertisement, and the band rehearsed for 18 months before performing at showcase engagements in 1972, without playing any clubs or other small venues. Quickly signed to EMI Records (Elektra in the United States), Queen's debut album was accompanied by a massive promotional campaign that alienated many critics. It included the anthemic "Keep Yourself Alive" and yielded a major British hit with "Seven Seas of Rhye" yet failed to produce even a minor American hit. In 1973 Mercury covered the Beach Boys' classic "I Can Hear Music" as "Larry Lurex," and following *Queen II* the group toured Great Britain and America, opening for Mott the Hoople.

Queen broke through in 1975 with the major hit "Killer Queen" from *Sheer Heart Attack*. They subsequently toured the world and became international stars with 1976's *A Night at the Opera*. The album stayed on the charts for more than a year and contained Mercury's near- smash hit "Bohemian Rhapsody," Deacon's major hit "You're My Best Friend," and May's overlooked ballad "39." The promotional video for "Bohemian Rhapsody" helped pioneer rock videos long before the advent of MTV. The follow-up, *A Day at the Races*, produced a major hit with Mercury's "Somebody to Love," and their next album, *News of the World*, featured the smash hit "We Are the Champions" (by Mercury) and the classic "We Will Rock You" (by May). The diversified album *Jazz* produced a two-sided hit with the controversial "Bicycle Race"/"Fat Bottomed Girls."

One of the world's most popular touring bands by the late 1970s, Queen recorded *The Game* after the live set *Queen Live Killers*. *The Game* topped the album charts and remained there for nearly a year, producing two top hits with Mercury's rockabilly-style "Crazy Little Thing Called Love" and Deacon's "Another One Bites the Dust," which surprisingly also became a smash R&B hit. The album yielded the moderate hits "Play the Game," which featured the group's first use of the synthesizer, and "Need Your Loving Tonight." Buoyed by the crossover success of "Another One Bites the Dust," Queen subsequently favored a dance-style sound through the mid-1980s. Major hits through 1984 included "Under Pressure," recorded with David Bowie; "Body Language"; and "Radio Ga-Ga," the last for their new label, Capitol.

Subsequent 1980s recordings by Queen fared less well, as their American popularity faded. Nonetheless, their success grew across the world thanks to well-received international tours. During the decade the members of Queen began pursuing projects away from the group. May composed and recorded soundtracks, most notably for the films *Mad Max* and *The Road Warrior* (also known as *Mad Max 2*). He joined Eddie Van Halen and REO Speedwagon's Alan Gratzer for 1983's minialbum *Star Fleet Project*. Roger Taylor recorded two solo albums before forming his own band, the Cross, in 1987. In 1984 Freddie Mercury scored a minor hit with "Love Kills" from the movie *Metropolis*; he later recorded *Mr. Bad Guy* for Columbia Records.

The group's next album was the disjointed *A Kind of Magic*, which produced a moderate hit with the title song in 1986, the year the group stopped touring. In 1987 Freddie Mercury performed with Spanish opera singer Montserrat Caballé in Barcelona; recordings from the engagement were eventually released in 1992. Queen's next album, *The Miracle*, was perhaps the group's best work, with a surprisingly personal and honest tone. It includes "Invisible Man," "Rain Must Fall," "Was It All Worth It," and "I Want It All" (a minor hit). The foreboding *Innuendo*, Queen's final studio album, featured "These Are the Days of Our Lives" and "The Show Must Go On."

Badgered for years about reports that he had contracted AIDS through his legendary sexual exploits, Freddie Mercury maintained his stance of refusing to give interviews. On Nov. 23, 1991, he publicly acknowledged that he did indeed have AIDS, and he died at his Kensington home in west London the next day. In April 1992 a tribute concert to Freddie Mercury was staged at Wembley Stadium in London, with performances by vocalists George Michael, Liza Minnelli, Elton John, and David Bowie backed by the surviving members of Queen, as well as Def Leppard, Metallica, and Guns N' Roses. The show, broadcast to more than 70 nations, reached upwards of one billion people.

Queen was introduced to an entirely new audience when the 1992 hit movie *Wayne's World* featured "Bohemian Rhapsody"; the song returned to MTV and reached #2 on the pop charts. By 1993, with the dissolution of Queen, Brian May had formed his own band to record *Back to the Light* and tour in support of Guns N' Roses.

DISC.: QUEEN: *Q.* (1973); *At the BBC* (rec. 1973; rel. 1995); *Q. II* (1974); *Sheer Heart Attack* (1974); *A Night at the Opera* (1975); *A Day at the Races* (1977); *News of the World* (1977); *Jazz* (1978); *Q. Live Killers* (1979); *The Game* (1980); *Flash Gordon* (soundtrack; 1980); *Greatest Hits* (1981); *Hot Space* (1982); *The Works* (1984); *A Kind of Magic* (1986); *The Miracle* (1989); *Innuendo* (1991); *Live at Wembley* (1992); *Classic Q.* (1992); *Greatest Hits* (1992); *Q. Collection* (1992); *Made in Heaven* (1995); *Greatest Hits, I and II* (1995). **QUEEN AND GEORGE MICHAEL:** *Five Live* (1993). **BRIAN MAY:** *Patrick* (soundtrack; 1980); *Patrick/Roadgames* (soundtracks) (1992); *Mad Max* (soundtrack; 1980); *The Road Warrior* (soundtrack; reissued as *Mad Max 2: The Road Warrior*, 1983); *Death Before Dishonor* (soundtrack; 1988); *The Day After Halloween* (soundtrack; 1981); *The Day After Halloween/Harlequin* (soundtracks) (1992); *Back to the Light* (1993). **BRIAN MAY AND FRIENDS:** *Star Fleet Project* (mini) (1983). **ROGER TAYLOR:** *Fun in Space* (1982); *Strange Frontier* (1984). **THE CROSS:** *Shove It* (1988). **FREDDIE MERCURY:** *Mr. Bad Guy* (1985); *The Great Pretender* (1992). **FREDDIE MERCURY AND MONTSERRAT CABALLÉ:** *Barcelona* (1992).

BIBL.: G. Tremlett, *The Q. Story* (London, 1978); J. Davis, *Q.: An Illustrated Biography* (London, 1981); R. Clarke, *A Kind of Magic: A Tribute to Freddie Mercury* (London, 1992); R. Sky, *The Show Must Go On: The Life of Freddie Mercury* (London, 1992). —BH

Queen Latifah (originally, Owens, Dana Elaine), positive female rapper who espouses feminism and supports African-American issues; b. Newark, N.J., March 18, 1970. The daughter of a high school art

teacher and a Newark police officer, Dana Owens was raised in a middle-class home. Her father taught her karate and how to handle a firearm. Athletic, she played power forward on two state championship basketball teams in high school. She also started working with some friends in a rap group that won several talent contests. They made a few demos which landed in the hands of rap-pioneer-turned-MTV-host, Fab Five Freddy. He passed them along to Tommy Boy Records, who signed Latifah as a solo act. Her 1989 debut, *All Hail the Queen*, featured a who's who of rap, including De La Soul, DJ Mark, the 45 King, Daddy-O from Stetsasonic, and KRS-One. Taking the name Queen Latifah (an Arabic word meaning delicate), she rapped over house-style tracks, reggae, and funk, talking about feminism and Afrocentrism without losing sight of romance. While the album didn't break any hits, it featured her duet with Monie Love on her theme song, "Ladies First," and earned her a Grammy nomination and *Rolling Stone*'s best female rapper honors. Her honest good looks and well-spoken, informed presence made her a press darling in the best sense of the phrase.

Latifah broke to a wider audience via her rap break on David Bowie's remix of his hit "Fame" and a cover of The O'Jays's "For the Love of Money" with Troop and Levert on the *New Jack City* soundtrack that rose to #12 on the R&B charts. She followed this with *Nature of a Sista*, a more subdued project than her debut. It generated the R&B hits "Latifah's Had It up to Here" (#13) and "Fly Girl" (#16), featuring forgettable male vocalists Simple Pleasure.

Her recording career also opened doors for her in the acting world. She made a guest appearance on the Will Smith TV show *Fresh Prince of Bel Air*, and landed a role in Spike Lee's 1991 feature *Jungle Fever*. Her acting career took off, leaving music in the back seat for a while as she took roles in *House Party 2* and played a supporting role in the 1993 drama *My Life*. These roles led to her joining the cast of *Living Single*, and singing the theme to the Fox sitcom. She held the role for four years.

In 1993, Latifah moved to Motown and released her best-selling effort, *Black Reign*. This presented her pop hit "Unity" which rose to #23 pop and #7 R&B. It also had the minor R&B hit "Just Another Day." She dedicated the album to her brother, who had died in a motorcycle accident earlier that year. "Unity" won her a Grammy Award for Best Rap Solo Performance. The album went gold. In 1996, Latifah took on the role of Cleo, a brazen lesbian, in the film *Set It Off*. She took the role to challenge herself, saying that the character was the furthest thing from her own character as she could get. It led to frequent questions about her own sexuality.

Latifah has proven herself as a businesswoman. She invested early income in smaller ventures like a video store, and has since started her own artist management company and record label, named after her old posse, the Flava Unit (source of the Tuff City compilation). She has directed the careers of such notable performers as LL Cool J, Outkast, and Naughty by Nature.

Despite these demanding activities, she managed to release *Order in the Court* in 1998. Featuring guests like Apache, Sisqo, and Next, the album sold moderately well. By the time it was released, however, Latifah was on to her next projects, playing a jazz singer in the film *Living Out Loud*, writing her autobiography *Ladies First: Revelations of a Strong Woman*, and hosting a syndicated talk show.

DISC.: *All Hail the Queen* (1989); *Nature of a Sista* (1991); *Black Reign* (1993); *Queen Latifah & Original Flava Unit* (1996); *Order in the Court* (1998).—**HB**

Queffélec, Anne (Tita), French pianist; b. Paris, Jan. 17, 1948. She was the daughter of Henri and sister of Yann Queffélec, both noted writers. She received her initial training at the Paris Cons. with Lélia Gousseau (premier prix in piano, 1965) and Jean Hubeau (premier prix in chamber music performance, 1966), and subsequently pursued studies with Brendel, Demus, and Badura-Skoda in Vienna. After capturing 1st prize at the Munich International Competition in 1968 and 5th prize at the Leeds International Competition in 1969, she toured widely at home and abroad; was a soloist with major orchs. of the world, and also was active as a recitalist and chamber music player. In addition to the French repertoire, she became particularly known for her performances of works by Mozart and Scarlatti. —**NS/LK/DM**

Queler, Eve (née Rabin), American conductor; b. N.Y., Jan. 1, 1936. She studied in N.Y. with Bamberger at the Mannes Coll. of Music, and took courses at the Hebrew Union School of Education and Sacred Music. After studying with Rosenstock on a Martha Baird Rockefeller Fund grant, she continued her training with Susskind and Slatkin in St. Louis and with Markevitch and Blomstedt in Europe. She made her conducting debut with *Cavalleria rusticana* in Fairlawn, N.J. (1966), then devoted herself mainly to conducting operas in concert with her own Opera Orch. of N.Y. (from 1967). She led performances of rarely heard operas on both sides of the Atlantic, and also gave the U.S. premieres of many works, ranging from Donizetti to Richard Strauss. She also appeared as a guest conductor with several North American orchs. Queler was the first American woman to conduct such esteemed ensembles as the Philadelphia Orch., the Cleveland Orch., and the Montreal Sym. Orch.—**NS/LK/DM**

Quentin, Jean-Baptiste, French violinist and composer who flourished in the first half of the 18th century. He pursued his career in Paris, where he was a violinist in the Opéra orch. Among his works were numerous vols. of solo and trio sonatas (1724–40). His brother, Bertin Quentin (d. c. 1767), was a violinist, cellist, and composer.—**LK/DM**

Queralt, Francisco, Spanish composer; b. Borjas Blancas, 1740; d. Barcelona, Feb. 28, 1825. He spent most of his life as maestro de capilla at Barcelona Cathedral. Among his works were 4 oratorios, a Magnificat, motets, and Psalms.—**LK/DM**

Querol (Gavaldá), Miguel, Spanish musicologist and composer; b. Ulldecona, Tarragona, April 22,

1912. He studied music at the Benedictine Monastery of Monserrat (1926–36) and later in Barcelona with Juan Lamote de Grignon. He continued his training at the univs. of Saragossa (1943), Barcelona (1944–45), and Madrid (Ph.D., 1948, with the diss. *La escuela estética catalana contemporánea*; publ. in Madrid, 1953). He was prof. of musicology at the Univ. of Barcelona (1957–70). He publ. *La música en las obras de Cervantes* (Barcelona, 1948) and *Breve historia de la música* (Madrid, 1955). Among his compositions are sacred music, chamber pieces, and piano works.—**NS/LK/DM**

Quesne, (Louis) Joseph (Marie), French-born Canadian merchant, composer, violinist, dramatist, poet, and actor; b. St.-Malo, Nov. 15, 1746?; d. Montreal, July 3, 1809. He began his career as a sailor. In 1779 he was commander of the corsaire L'Espoir on its voyage to N.Y. with munitions and provisions for the American rebels when his ship was captured by the British and he was taken to Halifax. Following his release by the governor of Quebec, he decided to settle in Canada and became active as a merchant. He also pursued various interests in music and literature. Quesne composed the first Canadian opera, *Colas et Colinette*, which was premiered in Montreal on Jan. 14, 1790. He also wrote another opera, *Lucas et Cécile*, syms., chamber music, and vocal pieces.—**LK/DM**

Quicksilver Messenger Service, psychedelic San Francisco rockers of the late 1960s; **MEMBERSHIP:** John Cipollina, lead gtr., voc. (b. Berkeley, Calif., Aug. 24, 1943; d. Greenbrae, Calif., May 29, 1989); Gary Duncan (Gary Grubb), lead and rhythm gtr., voc. (b. San Diego, Sept. 4, 1946); David Freiberg, bs. (b. Boston, Aug. 24, 1938); Greg Elmore, drm. (b. Coronado, Calif., Sept. 4, 1946). Songwriter-guitarist-vocalist Dino Valenti (b. Chester Powers, Danbury, Conn., Nov. 7, 1943; d. Santa Rosa, Calif., Nov. 16, 1994) was a member from 1970 to 1979.

Formed in late 1964 in San Francisco by guitarist John Cipollina, bassist David Freiberg, and vocalist Jim Murray, The Quicksilver Messenger Service was conceived as a rock vehicle for folk singer Dino Valenti, who had been an important member of the Greenwich Village folk scene in the early 1960s. As Chester Powers, Valenti wrote "Hey Joe" and "Let's Get Together," the classic psychedelic era song of fellowship. The Quicksilver lineup was completed with the June 1965 addition of Gary Duncan and Greg Elmore, but Valenti was imprisoned on drug charges. He eventually recorded a solo album released in 1968.

Debuting professionally in December 1965, The Quicksilver Messenger Service became a huge live attraction around the Bay Area. They performed at the Monterey International Pop Festival in June 1967, with Murray leaving the following October. Eventually signing with Capitol Records in late 1967, their debut album contained Hamilton Camp's "Pride of Man," Valenti's "Dino's Song," and the classic psychedelic instrumentals "The Fool" and "Gold and Silver."

The Quicksilver Messenger Service's second album included Dale Evans's title song "Happy Trails" and featured the side-long "Who Do You Love Suite," from which was extracted the minor hit "Who Do You Love." Gary Duncan left in January 1969 to form The Outlaws with Dino Valenti, but returned to the group in December with Valenti. In the meantime, the group had added British sessions keyboardist Nicky Hopkins for *Shady Grove*. He remained with the group for *Just for Love*, which yielded a moderate hit with "Fresh Air," and *What About Me*. John Cipollina left in October 1970 and formed Copperhead, which recorded one album for Columbia before disbanding in 1973. David Freiberg left in September 1971, to tour and record with The Jefferson Starship from 1973 to 1985.

Largely inactive in 1973 and 1974, Quicksilver reunited in March 1975 with Cipollina, Freiberg, Valenti, Duncan, and Elmore for the dismal *Solid Silver* album. The group remained nominally intact under Dino Valenti through 1979, as Cipollina pursued sessions work and various music projects around the Bay Area, including Thunder and Lightning with Nick Gravenites and the loosely structured Dinosaurs with other Bay Area music veterans. In 1986, Greg Duncan revived the Quicksilver name for the atrocious *Peace by Piece* album. John Cipollina died in Greenbrae, Calif., of emphysema on May 29, 1989, at the age of 45, and Dino Valenti died in Santa Rosa, Calif., on Nov. 16, 1994, after a brief illness, at the age of 51.

DISC.: QUICKSILVER MESSENGER SERVICE: *Quicksilver Messenger Service* (1968); *Happy Trails* (1969); *Shady Grove* (1970); *Just for Love* (1970); *What about Me* (1970); *Quicksilver* (1971); *Comin' Thru* (1972). **DINO VALENTI:** *Dino* (1968). **COPPERHEAD (WITH JOHN CIPOLLINA):** *Copperhead* (1973).—BH

Quilico, Gino, Canadian bartione, son of **Louis Quilico;** b. N.Y., April 29, 1955. He received training from his parents, and then from James Craig and Constance Fischer at the Univ. of Toronto Opera Dept. On June 8, 1977, he made his operatic debut as Mr. Gobineau in *The Medium* with the COMUS Music Theatre in Toronto. In 1978 he sang Papageno in Milwaukee. He first appeared with the Canadian Opera Co. in 1979 singing Escamillo. Following additional studies at the École d'art lyrique of the Paris Opéra (1979–80), he made his debut with the company in Damase's *L'Héritière* in 1980 and sang with it for 3 seasons. In 1982 he made his British debut with the Scottish Opera at the Edinburgh Festival. He made his first appearance at London's Covent Garden as Gounod's Valentin in 1983. That same year he sang Massenet's Lescaut at his debut with the Opéra de Montréal, a role he also chose for his Metropolitan Opera debut in N.Y. in 1987. In 1988 he appeared as Dandini at the Salzburg Festival. He sang Riccardo in *I Puritani* in Rome in 1990. In 1991 he appeared in Corigliano's *The Ghosts of Versailles* at the Metropolitan Opera. In 1994 he was engaged as Gluck's Oreste at the Vienna Festival. He portrayed Iago in Cologne in 1996. Among his other roles are Monteverdi's Orfeo, Don Giovanni, Dr. Malatesta, and Posa.

BIBL.: R. Mercer, *The Q.s: Louis, G. & Lina: An Operatic Family* (Oakville, Ontario, 1991).—NS/LK/DM

Quilico, Louis, notable Canadian baritone and teacher of Italian and French-Canadian descent, father of **Gino Quilico;** b. Montreal, Jan. 14, 1925. He was a solo chorister in the St.-Jacques Church Choir in Montreal and began his vocal studies with Frank Rowe. After training with Teresa Pediconi and Riccardo Stracciani at the Cons. de Santa Cecilia in Rome (1947–48), he returned to Montreal to study at the Cons. (1948–52) with Lina Pizzolongo (b. Montreal, Jan. 25, 1925; d. Toronto, Sept. 21, 1991), who became his wife in 1949, and with Singher. He completed his training at the Mannes Coll. of Music in N.Y. (1952–55) with Singher and Emil Cooper. In 1954 he made his professional operatic stage debut with the Opera Guild of Montreal as Rangoni. In 1955 he won the Metropolitan Opera Auditions of the Air, but made his U.S. debut with the N.Y.C. Opera on Oct. 10, 1955, as Germont. He made his European debut at the Spoleto Festival as Donizetti's Duca d'Alba in 1959. In 1960 he made his first appearance at London's Covent Garden as Germont, and sang there until 1963. In 1962 he sang for the first time at Moscow's Bolshoi Theater as Rigoletto. He made his debut at the Paris Opéra as Verdi's Rodrigo in 1963. In subsequent seasons, he sang regularly in Europe and with the Canadian Opera Co. On Feb. 10, 1972, Quilico made his Metropolitan Opera debut in N.Y. as Golaud, and thereafter sang there regularly. In 1991 he revealed a lighter touch when he sang Tony in *The Most Happy Fella* at the N.Y.C. Opera. That same year he appeared as Rigoletto at the Opéra de Montréal, a role he essayed over 500 times. From 1970 to 1987 he taught at the Univ. of Toronto, and from 1987 to 1990 at the McGill Cons. in Montreal. In 1965 he received the Prix de musique Calixa-Lavallee and in 1974 he was made a Commander of the Order of Canada.

BIBL.: R. Mercer, *The Q.s: L., Gino & Lina: An Operatic Family* (Oakville, Ontario, 1991).—NS/LK/DM

Quilter, Roger, English composer; b. Brighton, Nov. 1, 1877; d. London, Sept. 21, 1953. He received his primary education at Eton Coll., then studied with Iwan Knorr at the Hoch Cons. in Frankfurt am Main. He was particularly noted for his fine settings of Shakespeare's poems.

WORKS: Incidental music for Shakespeare's play *As You Like It* (1922); *The Sailor and His Lass* for Soprano, Baritone, Chorus, and Orch. (1948); numerous song cycles, among them *7 Elizabethan Lyrics, 3 Songs of the Sea, 4 Shakespeare Songs*, etc.; also a light opera, *Julia* (London, Dec. 3, 1936).

BIBL.: T. Hold, *The Walled-in Garden: A Study of the Songs of R. Q.* (Rickmansworth, 1978); M. Pilkington, *Gurney, Ireland, Q. and Warlock* (London, 1989).—NS/LK/DM

Quinault, Jean-Baptiste-Maurice, French sing- er, actor, and composer; b. Verdun, Sept. 9, 1687; d. Gien, Aug. 30, 1745. He was an actor at the Théâtre Francais (1712–28) and at the Comédie Française in Paris until 1734. He set to music about 20 *intermèdes*, ballets, etc., and also produced a grand ballet, *Les Amours des déesses* (Paris, Aug. 9, 1729).—NS/LK/DM

Quinault, Philippe, French dramatist, poet, and librettist; b. Paris, June 3, 1635; d. there, Nov. 26, 1688. He was Lully's librettist from 1671 to 1676.

BIBL.: G. Crapelet, *Notice sur la vie et les ouvrages de Q.* (Paris, 1824); E. Richter, *P. Q.: Sein Leben, seine Tragödien, seine Bedeutung für das Theater Frankreichs und des Auslandes* (Leipzig, 1910); E. Gros, *P. Q.: Sa vie et son oeuvre* (Paris, 1926); J. Buijtendorp, *P. Q.: Sa vie, ses tragédies et ses tragi- comédies* (Amsterdam, 1928).—NS/LK/DM

Quinet, Fernand, Belgian cellist, teacher, conductor, and composer; b. Charleroi, Jan. 29, 1898; d. Liège, Oct. 24, 1971. After training in theory in Charleroi, he studied with Edouard Jacobs (cello) and Léon Dubois (composition) at the Brussels Cons. (1913–15) before completing his training with d'Indy in Paris. In 1921 he won the Belgian Prix de Rome with his cantata *La guerre.* He played in the Pro Arte Quartet (1916–32), was director of the Charleroi Cons. (1924–38), and was prof. of harmony at the Brussels Cons. (1927–38). From 1938 to 1963 he was director of the Liège Cons. In 1948 he founded the Liège Sym. Orch., which he served as music director until 1965.

WORKS: ORCH.: *3 Symphonic Movements* (London, July 28, 1931). **CHAMBER:** Violin Sonata (1923); *Charade* for Piano Trio (1927); Viola Sonata (1928); *L'École buissoniere* for String Quartet (1930); Suite for 3 Clarinets (1930). **VOCAL:** Cantatas, including *La guerre* (1921); *Moralités-non- légendaires* for Voice and 18 Instruments (1930); songs.—**NS/LK/DM**

Quinet, Marcel, Belgian composer and teacher; b. Binche, July 6, 1915; d. Woluwé-St. Lambert, Brussels, Dec. 16, 1986. He studied at the conservatories of Mons and Brussels with Leon Jongen, Raymond Moulaert, and Marcel Maas (1934–43), and also took private composition lessons with Jean Absil (1940–45). In 1945 he won the Belgian Grand Prix de Rome with his cantata *La Vague et le Sillon.* He was on the staff of the Brussels Cons. (1943–79) and also taught at the Chapelle Musicale Reine Elisabeth (1956–59; 1968–71; 1973–74). In 1978 he was made a member of the Academie Royale de Belgique. His music is moderately modernistic in the amiable manner of the French school, with some euphoniously dissonant excrescences.

WORKS: DRAMATIC: *Les 2 Bavards,* chamber opera (1966); *La Nef des fous,* ballet (1969). **ORCH.:** *3 esquisses concertantes* for Violin and Orch. (1946); *Divertissement* (1946); *3 pièces* (1951; Salzburg, June 21, 1952); *Sinfonietta* (1953); *Variations élégiaques sur un thème de Rolland de Lassus* (1955); 3 piano concertos (1955, 1964, 1966); *Variations* (1956); *Serenade* for Strings (1956); *Impressions symphoniques* (1956); *Allegro de concert* (1958); *Divertimento* for Chamber Orch. (1958); *Concertino* for Flute, Celesta, Harp, and Strings (1959); Sym. (1960); *Concertino* for Oboe, Clarinet, Bassoon, and String Orch. (1960); *Ballade* for Clarinet and Strings (1961); Viola Concerto (1962–63); *Concerto grosso* for 4 Clarinets and Strings (1964); *Overture for a Festival* (1967); *Music for Strings and Timpani* (1971); *Mouvements* for Chamber Orch. (1973); *Esquisses symphoniques* (1973); *Gorgone* (1974); *Séquence* (1974); *Dialogues* for 2 Pianos and Orch. (1975); *Diptyque* for Chamber Orch. (1975); *Climats* for Chamber Orch. (1978); *Caractères* (1978; rev. 1983); *Metamorphoses* (1979); *Préludes* (1979); *Chromatismes* (1980); Concerto for Kettle Drums and Orch. (1981); *Concerto grosso* for 4 Saxophones and Orch. (1982); Concerto for 2 Pianos and Orch. (1983). **CHAMBER:** *8 petites pièces* for Wind Quintet (1946); 2 string trios (1948, 1969); Wind Quintet (1949); Violin Sonatina (1952); Piano Quartet

(1957); String Quartet (1958); *Petite Suite* for 4 Clarinets (1959); *Sonate a 3* for Trumpet, Horn, and Trombone (1961); *Ballade* for Violin and Wind Quintet (1962); Wind Quartet (1964); Sonata for 2 Violins and Piano (1964); *Ballatella* for Trumpet or Horn or Trombone and Piano (1966); *Pochades* for 4 Saxophones (1967); Trio for Oboe, Clarinet, and Bassoon (1967); Flute Sonata (1968); *Polyphonies* for 3 Performers on 8 Wind Instruments (1971); *Novelettes* for 2 Pianos (1973); *Sept tankas* for Double or Triple Vocal Quartet and Piano (1978); *Terzetto* for Flute, Violin, and Harpsichord (1981); *Ebauches* for Saxophone Quartet (1984); solo piano pieces. **VOCAL:** 2 cantatas: *La Vague et le Sillon* (1945) and *Lectio pro Feria Sexta* (1973); *Hommage à Ravel* for Woman's Voice, Piano, Flute, and Cello (1985); songs. —**NS/LK/DM**

Quintanar, Héctor, Mexican composer, conductor, and music educator; b. Mexico City, April 15, 1936. He studied with Chávez, Halffter, and Galindo at the National Cons. in Mexico City (1959–64). After working on problems of electronic music in N.Y. (1964), Paris (1967), and Mexico City (1968), he supervised the construction of Mexico's first electronic music studio at the National Univ. in 1970. In 1975 he founded the Music School of the Sociedad de Autores y Compositores de Música (SACM) in Mexico City, and served as its first director until 1984. He was conductor of the Phil. Orch. of the National Autonomous Univ. of Mexico (UNAM) from 1976 to 1980, of the Michoacán Sym. Orch. in 1986–87, and of the Orch. of the Univ. of Guanajuato from 1992 to 1997.

WORKS: ORCH.: 3 numbered syms. (1960, 1962, 1964); *Sinfonía Modal* (1961); *El Viejo y el Mar,* symphonic poem (1963); *Galaxias* (1968); *Sideral II* (1969); *Mezcla* for Tape and Orch. (1972); *Aries* (1974); *Fiestas* (1976); *Canto breve* (1982); *Himno* (1985); *Divertimento* (1989); *Trópico* (1992); *Paisaje* (1994; also for Winds and Percussion, 1986); *Concierto Clasico* for Piano and Orch. (Guanajuato City, Oct. 19, 1997). **CHAMBER:** Double Quartet for String Quartet, Flute, Oboe, Clarinet, and Bassoon (1966); String Trio (1966); Sonata No. 1 for Violin and Piano (1967); Sonata (No. 2) for 3 Trumpets (1967); *Símbolos* for 7 Instruments, Lights, Tape, and Optional Slides (1969); *Llapso* for 7 Instruments (1970); Quintet for Flute, Trumpet, Violin, Double Bass, and Piano (1972); Duo for Percussion and Tape (1975); Piano Trio (1977); *Paisaje* for Winds and Percussion (1986; also for Orch., 1994); *20 pequeños estudios para niños* for Violin and Piano (1995); *20 estudios para principiantes* for Horn and Piano (1996). **KEYBOARD: Piano:** *Sonidos* (1970); *Diálogos* for Piano and Tape (1973); *5 Piezas para Niños* (1990). **VOCAL:** *Fábula* for Chorus and Orch. (1964); *Aclamaciones* for Chorus, Orch., and Tape (1967); *Solutio?* for Soprano and Piano (1968). **Tape:** *Sideral I* (1968) and *III* (1971).—**NS/LK/DM**

Quintavalle, Antonio, Italian organist and composer; b. place and date unknown; d. c. 1724. After serving as chamber organist at the court in Mantua, he was maestro di cappella at Trent Cathedral from 1712. He wrote the operas *L'oracolo in sogno* (Mantua, June 6, 1699; in collaboration with A. Caldara and C. Pollarolo), *Il trionfo d'amore* (Mantua, Dec. 19, 1703), *Paride sull'Ida, ovvero Gli amori di Paride con Enone* (Mantua, 1704), and *Partenope* (Trent, 1713). He also wrote several oratorios. —**LK/DM**

Quittmeyer, Susan, American mezzo-soprano; b. N.Y., Oct. 27, 1953. She studied at the Illinois Wesleyan Univ. School of Music (1971–75) and at the Manhattan School of Music (1975–77). In 1978 she made her operatic debut as Chloe in *The Tree of Chastity* at the Opera Theatre in St. Louis. Her debut as a soloist came in 1981 when she sang in Beethoven's 9th Sym. with the San Francisco Sym. under Slatkin's direction. She made her recital debut at N.Y.'s Carnegie Recital Hall in 1985. On Dec. 21, 1987, she made her Metropolitan Opera debut in N.Y. as Nicklausse in *Les Contes d'Hoffmann*, and continued to make appearances there until 1994. She portrayed Mozart's Annius at the Bavarian State Opera in Munich in 1986, returning there as Cherubino in 1989. After appearing as Handel's Sextus at the Paris Opéra in 1987, she sang Cherubino and Zerlina at the Vienna State Opera in 1989. In 1992 she sang Cherubino at the Opéra de la Bastille in Paris and Marina at the San Francisco Opera. She appeared as Idamante at the Salzburg Festival in 1994. Following an engagement as Fricka in *Das Rheingold* at the Dallas Opera in 1998, she sang Nicklausse at the Florida Grand Opera in Miami in 1999. She also appeared as a soloist with various orchs. In 1987 she married **James Morris.**—NS/LK/DM

Quivar, Florence, American-American mezzo-soprano; b. Philadelphia, March 3, 1944. She studied at the Philadelphia Musical Academy, the Salzburg Mozarteum, and with Luigi Ricci in Rome. She was a member of the Juilliard Opera Theater in N.Y.; subsequently launched a successful concert career, appearing as soloist with the N.Y. Phil., the Cleveland Orch., the Philadelphia Orch., the Chicago Sym. Orch., and the Boston Sym. Orch. She made her Metropolitan Opera debut in N.Y. as Marina in *Boris Godunov* on Oct. 10, 1977; then sang there regularly, appearing in such roles as Jocasta in *Oedipus Rex*, Isabella in *L'Italiana in Algeri*, Fides in *Le Prophète*, Eboli in *Don Carlos*, Marfa in *Khovanshchina*, and Serena in *Porgy and Bess*. In 1983 she made her first appearance at the Salzburg Festival as a soloist in Mahler's 3rd Sym. with Mehta and the Israel Phil. She made her first operatic appearance there in 1989 as Ulrike. In 1991 she was a soloist in the *Gurrelieder* at the Promenade Concerts in London. She appeared at the Metropolitan Opera Gala in 1996.—NS/LK/DM

R

Raabe, Peter, German conductor and writer on music; b. Frankfurt an der Oder, Nov. 27, 1872; d. Weimar, April 12, 1945. He studied with Bargiel at the Berlin Hochschule für Musik and later continued his training at the Univ. of Jena (Ph.D., 1916). In 1894 he began a career as a theater conductor. From 1899 to 1903 he conducted the Netherlands Opera in Amsterdam, and from 1903 to 1907, the Volks-Symphonie-Konzerte in Munich. In 1907 he became court conductor in Weimar, and in 1910 he was appointed curator of the Liszt Museum in Weimar. From 1920 to 1934 he was Generalmusikdirektor in Aachen. In 1935 he became head of the Reichsmusikkammer and the Deutscher Tonkünstlerverein; in these offices he was called upon to perform administrative tasks for the Nazi regime, including the racial restrictions of musicians. His co-workers presented him with *Von deutscher Tonkünst: Festschrift zu Peter Raabes 70. Geburtstag* (Leipzig, 1942; 2nd ed., rev., 1944). Raabe died just before the total collapse of the Third Reich, which he tried to serve so well. He left some scholarly and valuable writings, among them *Grossherzog Carl Alexander und Liszt* (Leipzig, 1918), *Franz Liszt: Leben und Schaffen* (2 vols., Stuttgart, 1931; rev. ed. 1968 by his son Felix), *Die Musik im dritten Reich* (Regensburg, 1935), *Kulturwille im deutschen Musikleben* (Regensburg, 1936), *Deutsche Meister* (Berlin, 1937), *Wege zu Weber* (Regensburg, 1942), *Wege zu Liszt* (Regensburg, 1943), and *Wege zu Bruckner* (Regensburg, 1944).—**NS/LK/DM**

Raaff, Anton, esteemed German tenor; b. Gelsdorf, near Bonn (baptized), May 6, 1714; d. Munich, May 28, 1797. He studied with Ferrandini in Munich and Bernacchi in Bologna. He sang in Italy, then in Bonn, in Vienna, and at various German courts (1742–52), in Lisbon (1752–55), Madrid (1755–59), and Naples, returning in 1770 to Germany, where he was attached to the court of the Elector Karl Theodor at Mannheim. In 1778 he went to Paris with Mozart. From 1779 he was in Munich. Mozart wrote the role of Idomeneo for him, and also the aria *Se al labbro mio non credi*, K. 295.

BIBL.: H. Freiberger, *A. R. (1714–1797): Sein Leben und Wirken* (Cologne, 1929).—**NS/LK/DM**

Raalte, Albert van, Dutch conductor; b. Amsterdam, May 21, 1890; d. there, Nov. 23, 1952. He studied at the Cologne Cons. with Bram Eldering (violin) and Baussnern (theory), and later in Leipzig with Nikisch and Reger. He was a theater conductor in Brussels (1911) and Leipzig (1912; 1914–15), then at the Dutch National Opera in The Hague, where he formed his own opera enterprise. He remained in the Netherlands during the German occupation. He conducted the radio orch. at Hilversum. He was sent to a concentration camp as a person with Jewish associations. After the liberation in 1945, he returned to his post at Hilversum, building the radio orch. to a high degree of efficiency.—**NS/LK/DM**

Raasted, Niels Otto, Danish organist, conductor, and composer; b. Copenhagen, Nov. 26, 1888; d. there, Dec. 31, 1966. He studied at the Copenhagen Cons. (1909–12), then at the Leipzig Cons. with Reger, Straube, and Teichmüller (1913–14). Returning to Denmark, he became organist at Copenhagen Cathedral, and he also conducted the Bach Soc. (1925–46).

WORKS: ORCH.: 3 syms. (1914, 1938, 1944); orch. suites, among them *Pictures from Finland* (1928) and *Hans Christian Andersen Suite* (1940); *Sinfonia da chiesa* (1944). **CHAMBER:** 3 string quartets (1914, 1918, 1920); 5 violin sonatas; 6 organ sonatas. **VOCAL:** *Saul*, oratorio (1923); 3 cantatas (all perf. on Copenhagen Radio): *Sangen om Kbenhavn* (June 27, 1934), *Thylands pris* (May 12, 1941), and *Kong Vaar* (Oct. 20, 1947).—**NS/LK/DM**

Rääts, Jaan, notable Estonian composer and teacher; b. Tartu, Oct. 15, 1932. He received training in piano from Aleksandra Sarv at the Tartu Music School (graduated, 1952), and then in composition from Mart Saar and Heino Eller at the Tallinn Cons. (graduated, 1957). After working as a sound engineer for the Estonian Radio, he was ed.-in-chief in the dept. of music programs for the Estonian TV (1966–74). He taught at the Estonian Academy of Music from 1968 to 1970, and again from 1974. He also served as chairman of the Estonian Composers Union from 1974 to 1993. Rääts has especially distinguished himself as a composer of instrumental music. His output generally follows along neo-Classical lines.

WORKS: ORCH.: 8 syms. (1957, 1959, 1959, 1966, 1967, 1973, 1985, 1989); Concerto for Chamber Orch. (1961); 2 violin concertos (1963, 1979); 2 piano concertos (1968, 1983); Concerto for 2 Pianos and Orch. (1986); *Five Sketches for Requiem* (1996). **CHAMBER:** 6 string quartets (1955, 1958, 1964, 1970, 1974, 1983) and other pieces. **P i a n o :** *24 Estonian Preludes* (1977); *24 Marginalia* for 2 Pianos (1982); several sonatas.—**NS/LK/DM**

Rabaud, Henri (Benjamin), noted French conductor, pedagogue, and composer; b. Paris, Nov. 10, 1873; d. there, Sept. 11, 1949. His father was Hippolyte Rabaud (1839–1900), prof. of cello at the Paris Cons., where Henri studied with Gédalge and Massenet (1893–94), winning the Premier Grand Prix de Rome in 1894 with his cantata *Daphné.* In 1908 he became conductor at the Paris Opéra and at the Opéra-Comique, and from 1914 to 1918 he was director of the Opéra. In 1918–19 he was engaged to conduct the Boston Sym. Orch. He then was appointed director of the Paris Cons. in 1922, holding this post until 1941.

WORKS: DRAMATIC: O p e r a : *La Fille de Roland* (Paris, March 16, 1904); *Le Premier Glaive* (Béziers, 1908); *Marouf, savetier du Caire* (Paris, May 15, 1914); *Antoine et Cléopâtre*, after Shakespeare (1916–17); *L'Appel de la mer* (Paris, April 10, 1924); *Le Miracle des loups* (Paris, Nov. 14, 1924); *Rolande et le mauvais garçon* (1933; Paris, May 28, 1934); *Le Jeu de l'amour et du hasard* (1948; Monte Carlo, 1954). **OTHER:** Incidental music and film scores. **ORCH.:** 2 syms. (1893, 1900); *La Procession nocturne*, symphonic poem (Paris, Jan. 15, 1899); *Divertissement sur des chansons russes* (1899); *Lamento* (1930); *Prelude and Toccata* for Piano and Orch. (1945). **CHAMBER:** String Quartet (1898); Trio for Oboe, Clarinet, and Bassoon (1949); piano pieces. **VOCAL:** *L'Éte* for Soprano, Alto, Chorus, and Orch. (1895); *Job*, oratorio (1900); *Hymne à la France éternelle* for Chorus (1916); songs.

BIBL.: M. d'Ollone, *H. R.: Sa vie et son oeuvre* (Paris, 1958). —**NS/LK/DM**

Rabe, Folke (Alvar Harald Reinhold), Swedish trombonist and composer; b. Stockholm, Oct. 28, 1935. He studied composition with V. Söderholm, B. Wallner, Blomdahl, and Ligeti at the Stockholm Musikhögskolan (1957–64), where he also received training in trombone and music pedagogy. He began his career as a jazz musician while still a teenager; later was a member of the Culture Quartet (1963–73) and the New Culture Quartet (from 1983), which performed contemporary scores. He was on the staff (1968–80) and served as program director (1977–80) of the Inst. for National Concerts; then was a producer with the Swedish Radio. He experimented with multimedia techniques, producing pieces of "vocal theater" with non-semantic texts.

WORKS: DRAMATIC: I n t e r m e d i a S h o w s : *Ship of Fools* (1983); *The World Museum* (1987); *Beloved Little Pig*, musical fairy tale for children (1986); film scores; incidental

music. **ORCH.:** *Hep-Hep*, overture for Small Orch. (1966); *Altiplano* for Wind Orch. (1982); *All the lonely people*, concerto for Trombone and Chamber Orch. (1990). **CHAMBER:** Suite for 2 Clarinets (1957); *Bolos* for 4 Trombones (1962; in collaboration with J. Bark); *Impromptu* for Clarinet, Trombone, Cello, Piano, and Percussion (1962); *Pajazzo* for 8 Jazz Musicians (1964); *Polonaise* for 4 Trombones and Light (1965–66; in collaboration with J. Bark); *From the Myths of Time* for 3 Cellos, Gamelan, and Percussion (1966); *Pipe Lines* for 4 Trombones (1969); *Zug* for 4 Trombones (1970); *Shazam* for Trumpet (1984); *With Love* for Piano (1985); *Escalations* for Brass Quintet (1988). **VOCAL:** *7 Poems by Nils Ferlin* for Chorus (1958); *Notturno* for Mezzosoprano, Flute, Oboe, and Clarinet (1959); *Pièce* for Speaking Chorus (Swedish, German, and Eng. versions, 1961; in collaboration with L. O'Mansson); *Souvenirs* for Reciter, Electric Organ, and Rhythm Section (1963); *Rondes* for Chorus (1964); *O. D.* for Men's Chorus (1965); *Joe's Harp* for Chorus (1970); *Tva Strofer* for Chorus (1980); *to love* for Chorus, after e.e. cummings (1984); songs. **OTHER:** *Eh??* for Electronics (1967); *To the Barbender* for Tape (1982); *New Construction* for Small Children, Electronics, and Various Sound Sources (1984); *Cyclone* for Electronics (1985).—**NS/LK/DM**

Råberg, Bruno (Ingemar), bassist; b. Karlstad, Sweden, July 13, 1954. He received his B.M. from the New England Cons. of Music. He has performed and recorded with Sam Rivers, Mick Goodrick, Jerry Bergonzi, Bob Mintzer, Bob Moses, Billy Hart, Bruce Barth, Greg Osby, Dick Oatts, and Julius Hemphill. His international tours throughout Europe and Japan have included the Pori Jazz Festival, Allandia Jazz Festival, Monterey Jazz Festival, Nord Kalott Jazz Festival, Heidelberg Jazz Tage, Nurnberg Jazz Festival, and Boston Globe Jazz Festival. Råberg has made numerous TV and radio broadcasts. He currently is Associate Professor of Ensemble Faculty, Berklee.

DISC.: *Pentimento* (1992); *Orbis* (1998); *Presence* (2000).—**LP**

Rabin, Michael, gifted American violinist; b. N.Y., May 2, 1936; d. there, Jan. 19, 1972. He was of a musical family; his father was a violinist in the N.Y. Phil., his mother a pianist. He studied with Ivan Galamian in N.Y. and made excellent progress. In his early youth, he appeared as a soloist with a number of American orchs. He made several European tours as a concert violinist, and also played in Australia. His sudden death at the age of 35 was a shock to American music lovers. —**NS/LK/DM**

Rabinof, Benno, esteemed American violinist; b. N.Y., Oct. 11, 1908; d. Brevard, N.C., July 2, 1975. He studied privately with Küzdö, Kneisel, and Auer. He made his debut on Nov. 18, 1927, playing the Tchaikovsky Violin Concerto with members of the N.Y. Phil., conducted by Auer. In 1930 he played Glazunov's Violin Concerto, with Glazunov himself leading the Boston Sym. Orch. as guest conductor. With his wife, the pianist Sylvia Smith-Rabinof, he traveled extensively in Europe and America.—**NS/LK/DM**

Racek, Jan, Czech musicologist; b. Bučovice, June 1, 1905; d. Brno, Dec. 5, 1979. He studied with Helfert at the Univ. of Brno (Ph.D., 1929, with the diss. *Idea vlasti, národa a slávy v díle B. Smetany* [The Idea of the Fatherland, Nation, and Glory in the Works of B. Smetana]; publ. in Brno, 1933; 2nd ed., aug., 1947); later received a D.Sc. degree (1957). He was director of the music archives of the Moravian Regional Museum (1930–48), and also was a lecturer at the Univ. of Brno (from 1939) and prof. and director of the Brno dept. of ethnography and folk music of the Czech Academy of Sciences (1948–70). He served as ed. of the journal *Musikologie* and as general ed. of Musica Antiqua Bohemica.

WRITINGS: *Leoš Janáček* (Olomouc, 1938); *Slohové problémy italské monodie* (Problems of Style in Italian Monody; Prague and Brno, 1938; Ger. tr., 1965); ed. with L. Firkušný, *Janáčkovy feuilletony z Lidové Noviny* (Janáček's Feuilletons in the Lidové Noviny; Brno, 1938; 2nd ed., rev., 1958, as *Leoš Janáček: Fejetony z Lidových Noviny*; Ger. tr., 1962); *Leoš Janáček a součásni moravští skladatelé* (Leoš Janáček and Contemporary Moravian Composers; Brno, 1940); *Česká hudba od nejstarších dob do počátku 19. stoleti* (Czech Music from the Earliest Times to the Beginning of the 19th Century; Prague, 1949; 2nd ed., aug., 1958); *Ruská hudba: Od nejstarších dob az po velkou řijnovou revoluci* (Russian Music from the Earliest Times up to the Great Revolution; Prague, 1953); *Beethoven a české země* (Beethoven in Bohemia and Moravia; Brno, 1964).—**NS/LK/DM**

Racette, Patricia,
American soprano; b. Manchester, N.H., June 23, 1965. She studied jazz and music education at North Tex. State Univ., and in 1987 she was accepted into the Merola Opera Program in San Francisco. She gained experience at the San Francisco Opera, where she scored a fine success as Micaëla in 1991. After appearing as Musetta in Amsterdam in 1992, she sang Poulenc's Blanche in Vancouver and portrayed Micaëla once again in Geneva in 1993. In 1994 she was engaged as Liù at the Welsh National Opera in Cardiff. She returned to Vancouver as Ellen Orford and sang Mimi at the San Diego Opera in 1995. On Dec. 28, 1995, she made her Metropolitan Opera debut in N.Y. as Musetta, and quickly established herself there in such roles as Mimi, Ellen Orford, Violetta, and Antonia. She returned to the San Francisco Opera in the latter role in 1996. On July 27, 1996, she created the title role of Emmeline Mosher in Picker's *Emmeline* at the Santa Fe Opera. In 1998 she was honored with the Richard Tucker Award. She portrayed Micaëla once more in the Metropolitan Opera Pension Fund Gala in 1999. On April 14, 2000, she created the role of Love Simpson in Floyd's *Cold Sassy Tree* at the Houston Grand Opera. Her operatic engagements have also taken her to Paris, London, Vienna, Chicago, and various other cities. As a concert artist, she has sung with many U.S. orchs., and she has given recitals across North America.—**LK/DM**

Rachmaninoff, Sergei (Vassilievich),
greatly renowned Russian- born American pianist, conductor, and composer; b. probably in Oneg, April 1, 1873; d. Beverly Hills, March 28, 1943. He was of a musical family; his grandfather was an amateur pianist, a pupil of John Field, and his father also played the piano; Rachmaninoff's *Polka* was written on a theme improvised by his father; his mother likewise played piano, and it was from her that he received his initial training at their estate, Oneg, near Novgorod. After financial setbacks, the family estate was sold and he was taken to St. Petersburg, where he studied piano with Vladimir Demiansky and harmony with Alexander Rubets at the Cons. (1882–85); acting on the advice of his cousin, Alexander Siloti, he enrolled as a piano student of Nikolai Zverev at the Moscow Cons. (1885); then entered Siloti's piano class and commenced the study of counterpoint with Taneyev and harmony with Arensky (1888). He met Tchaikovsky, who appreciated his talent and gave him friendly advice. He graduated as a pianist (1891) and as a composer (1892), winning the gold medal with his opera *Aleko*, after Pushkin. Then followed his Prelude in C-sharp minor (1892); publ. that same year, it quickly became one of the most celebrated piano pieces in the world. His 1st Sym., given in Moscow (1897), proved a failure, however. Discouraged, Rachmaninoff destroyed the MS, but the orch. parts were preserved; after his death, the score was restored and performed in Moscow (1945). In the meantime, Rachmaninoff launched a career as a piano virtuoso; also took up a career as a conductor, joining the Moscow Private Russian Orch. (1897). He made his London debut in the triple capacity of pianist, conductor, and composer with the Phil. Soc. (1899). Although he attempted to compose after the failure of his 1st Sym., nothing significant came from his pen. Plagued by depression, he underwent treatment by hypnosis with Nikolai Dahl, and then began work on his 2nd Piano Concerto. He played the first complete performance of the score with Siloti conducting in Moscow (Nov. 9, 1901); this concerto became the most celebrated work of its genre written in the 20th century, and its singular charm has never abated since; it is no exaggeration to say that it became a model for piano concertos by a majority of modern Russian composers, and also of semi-popular virtuoso pieces for piano and orch. written in America. On May 12, 1902, Rachmaninoff married his cousin Natalie Satina; they spent some months in Switzerland, then returned to Moscow. After conducting at Moscow's Bolshoi Theater (1904–06), he decided to spend most of his time in Dresden, where he composed his 2nd Sym., one of his most popular works. Having composed another major work, his 3rd Piano Concerto, he took it on his first tour of the U.S. in 1909. His fame was so great that he was offered the conductorship of the Boston Sym. Orch., but he declined; the offer was repeated in 1918, but once again he declined. He lived in Russia from 1910 until after the Bolshevik Revolution of Oct. 1917, at which time he left Russia with his family, never to return. From 1918 until 1939 he made annual tours of Europe as a pianist; also of the U.S. (from 1918 until his death), where he spent much of his time; he also owned a villa in Lucerne (1931–39), and it was there that he composed one of his most enduring scores, the *Rhapsody on a Theme of Paganini* (1934). In 1932 he was awarded the Gold Medal of the Royal Phil. Soc. of London. After the outbreak of World War II (1939), he spent his remaining years in the U.S. He became a naturalized American citizen a few weeks before his death, having made his last appearance as a pianist in Knoxville, Tenn., on Feb. 15, 1943.

Among Russian composers, Rachmaninoff occupies a very important place. The sources of his inspiration lie in the Romantic tradition of 19th-century Russian music; the link with Tchaikovsky's lyrical art is very strong; melancholy moods prevail and minor keys predominate in his compositions, as in Tchaikovsky's; but there is an unmistakable stamp of Rachmaninoff's individuality in the broad, rhapsodic sweep of the melodic line, and particularly in the fully expanded sonorities and fine resonant harmonies of his piano writing; its technical resourcefulness is unexcelled by any composer since Liszt. Despite the fact that Rachmaninoff was an émigré and stood in avowed opposition to the Soviet regime (until the German attack on Russia in 1941 impelled him to modify his stand), his popularity never wavered in Russia; after his death, Russian musicians paid spontaneous tribute to him. Rachmaninoff's music is much less popular in Germany, France, and Italy; on the other hand, in England and America it constitutes a potent factor on the concert stage.

WORKS: DRAMATIC: O p e r a : *Esmeralda* (1888; introduction to Act 1 and fragment of Act 3 only completed); *Aleko*, after Pushkin's *Tsigani* (The Gypsies; 1892; Moscow, May 9, 1893); *The Miserly Knight*, op.24, after Pushkin (1903–05; Moscow, Jan. 24, 1906); *Francesca da Rimini*, op.25, after Dante's *Inferno* (1900; 1904–05; Moscow, Jan. 24, 1906); *Monna Vanna*, after Maeterlinck (1907; piano score of Act 1 and sketches of Act 2 only completed; Act 1 orchestrated by I. Buketoff; concert perf., Saratoga, N.Y., Aug. 11, 1984). ORCH.: *Scherzo* in D minor (1887); Piano Concerto in C minor (1889; sketches only); 4 numbered piano concertos: No. 1 in F-sharp minor, op.1 (1890–91; Moscow, March 17, 1892; rev. 1917), No. 2 in C minor, op.18 (Moscow, Nov. 9, 1901), No. 3 in D minor, op.30 (N.Y., Nov. 28, 1909), and No. 4 in G minor, op.40 (1926; Philadelphia, March 18, 1927; rev. 1927, 1941); *Manfred*, symphonic poem (1890–91; not extant); Sym. (1897; sketches only); 3 numbered syms.: No. 1 in D minor, op.13 (1895; St. Petersburg, March 27, 1897), No. 2 in E minor, op.27 (1906–08; St. Petersburg, Feb. 8, 1908), and No. 3 in A minor, op.44 (Philadelphia, Nov. 6, 1936; rev. 1938); *Prince Rostislav*, symphonic poem (1891); *The Rock*, fantasy (1893; Moscow, March 20, 1896); *Capriccio on Gypsy Themes* or *Capriccio bohémien*, op.12 (1892, 1894); 2 episodes after Byron's *Don Juan* (1894; not extant); *The Isle of the Dead*, symphonic poem, op.29, after Böcklin's painting (Moscow, May 1, 1909); *Rhapsody on a Theme of Paganini* for Piano and Orch., op.43 (Baltimore, Nov. 7, 1934); *Symphonic Dances*, op.45 (1940; Philadelphia, Jan. 3, 1941). CHAMBER: 2 numbered string quartets (1889, 2 movements only; c. 1896, 2 movements only); *Romance* in A minor for Violin and Piano (c. 1880–90); *Romance* in F minor for Cello and Piano (1890); *Melodie* in D major for Cello and Piano (c. 1890; arranged by M. Altschuler, 1947); String Quintet (n.d.; not extant); *Trio élégiaque* in G minor for Piano Trio (1892); 2 pieces for Cello and Piano, op.2 (1892): *Prélude* in F major (revision of a piano piece, 1891) and *Danse orientale* in A minor; *2 Morceaux de salon* for Violin and Piano, op.6 (1893): *Romance* and *Danse hongroise*; *Trio élégiaque* in D minor for Piano Trio, op.9, in memory of Tchaikovsky (1893; rev. 1907, 1917); Cello Sonata in G minor, op.19 (1901). P i a n o : *Song without Words* (c. 1887); *3 Nocturnes* (1887–88); 4 pieces: *Romance, Prélude, Mélodie,* and *Gavotte* (1887); *Canon* (1890–91); 2 pieces for Piano, 6-Hands: *Waltz* (1890) and *Romance* (1891); *Prélude* (1891; rev. as *Prélude* for Cello and Piano, 1892), *Russian*

Rhapsody for 2 Pianos (1891), *Morceaux de fantaisie* (1892; includes the famous *Prélude* in C-sharp minor), and *Romance* for Piano, 4-Hands (c. 1894); *Fantaisie-tableaux: Suite No. 1* for 2 Pianos, op.5 (1893); *Morceaux de salon*, op.10 (1893–94); *Romance* for Piano, 4-Hands (c. 1894); *6 Morceaux* for Piano, 4-Hands, op.11 (1894); *6 Moments musicaux*, op.16 (1896); *Improvisations* (1896; in *4 Improvisations* in collaboration with Arensky, Glazunov, and Taneyev); *Morceaux de fantaisie* (1899); *Fughetta* (1899); *Suite No. 2* for 2 Pianos, op.17 (1900–1901); *Variations on a Theme of Chopin*, op.22 (1902–03); *10 Préludes*, op.23 (1901–03); *Polka italienne* for Piano, 4-Hands (c. 1906); 2 sonatas: No. 1, op.28 (1907) and No. 2, op.36 (1913; rev. 1931); *13 Préludes*, op.32 (1910); *Études-tableaux*, op.33 (1911); *Polka V.R.*, on a theme by the composer's father, Vasily Rachmaninoff (1911); *Études-tableaux*, op.39 (1916–17); *Oriental Sketch* (1917); *Prélude* (1917); *Fragments* in A-flat major (1917); *Variations on a Theme of Corelli*, op.42 (1931). VOCAL: *Deus meus*, motet for 6 Voices (1890); *O Mother of God Vigilantly Praying* for 4 Voices (1893); *Chorus of Spirits* and *Song of the Nightingale* from *Don Juan* (c. 1894); 6 choruses for Women's or Children's Voices, op.15 (1895–96); *Panteley the Healer* (1901); *Spring*, cantata for Baritone, Chorus, and Orch., op.20 (Moscow, March 24, 1902); *Liturgy of St. John Chrysostom*, op.31 (Moscow, Nov. 25, 1910); *The Bells*, choral sym. for Soprano, Tenor, Baritone, Chorus, and Orch., op.35, after Poe (St. Petersburg, Dec. 13, 1913); *All-Night Vigil*, op.37 (1915); *3 Russian Songs* for Chorus and Orch., op.41 (1926; Philadelphia, March 18, 1927); also 82 songs (1890–1916).

BIBL.: I. Lipayev, *S. R.* (Saratov, 1913); V. Belaiev, *S. R.* (Moscow, 1924; Eng. tr. in *Musical Quarterly*, July 1927); O. von Riesemann, *R.'s Recollections* (N.Y., 1934); W. Lyle, *R.: A Biography* (London, 1939); A. Solovtsov, *S. R.* (Moscow, 1947); J. Culshaw, *S. R.* (London, 1949); V. Seroff, *R.* (N.Y., 1950); A. Alexeyev, *S. R.* (Moscow, 1954); Z. Apetian, ed., *S. V. R.: Letters* (Moscow, 1955); S. Bertensson and J. Leyda, *S. R.: A Lifetime in Music* (N.Y., 1956; 2nd ed., 1965); Z. Apetian, ed., *Reminiscences of R.* (Moscow, 1957; 4th ed., aug., 1974); Y. Keldish, *R. and His Time* (Moscow, 1973); R. Threlfall, *S. R., His Life and Music* (London, 1973); P. Piggott, *R. Orchestral Music* (London, 1974); V. Bryantseva, *S.V. R.* (Moscow, 1976); G. Norris, *R.* (London, 1976; 2nd ed., rev., 1993); Z. Apetian, ed., *S. R.: Literary Heritage* (Moscow, 1978–80); R. Walker, *R.: His Life and Times* (Tunbridge Wells, 1980); R. Threlfall and G. Norris, *Catalogue of the Compositions of S. R.* (London, 1982); R. Palmieri, *S. V. R.: A Guide to Research* (London and N.Y., 1985); C. Poivre D'Arvor, *R., ou, La Passion au bout des doigts* (Monaco, 1986); M. Biesold, *S. R., 1873–1943: Zwischen Moskau und New York: Eine Künstlerbiographie* (Weinheim, 1991); B. Nikitin, *S. R.: Dve zhizni* (Moscow, 1993). —NS/LK/DM

Račiūnas, Antanas, significant Lithuanian composer and pedagogue; b. Užliašiai, near Panevėžys, Sept. 17, 1905; d. Kaunas, April 3, 1984. He studied composition with J. Gruodis at the Kaunas Cons. (graduated, 1933) and with Boulanger and Koechlin in Paris (1936–39). He taught at the Kaunas Cons. (1933–36; 1939–49) and the Vilnius Cons. (1949–59). In 1965 he was made a People's Artist of the Lithuanian S.S.R. He wrote and produced the first opera in Lithuanian.

WORKS: DRAMATIC: O p e r a : *3 Talismen* (Kaunas, March 19, 1936); *Amber Shore* (1940); *Marite* (1953); *Sun City* (1965). ORCH.: 9 syms. (1933, 1946, 1951, 1960, 1961, 1966, 1969, 1970, 1974); 4 symphonic poems: *Evening in Vilnius* (1939), *The Secret of Lake Plateliu* (1956), *Jurgenas and Ramune* (1958), and

Mother Pirčiupio (1972); *Scenes of Lithuania,* suite (1955); 3 Pieces (1964); *Prelude and Joke* (1974); Piano Concerto (1976). **CHAM-BER:** *Sonata-Fantasy* for Oboe and Piano (1963); Cello Sonatina (1965); Sonata for 2 Pianos (1967); Cello Sonata (1968); Suite for 2 Pianos and Percussion (1973); *Triptych* for Oboe and Piano (1973); Violin Sonata (1977); solo piano pieces. **VOCAL:** 2 cantatas (1943, 1949); *Liberated Lithuania,* oratorio (1945); many choruses; songs.—**NS/LK/DM**

Racquet, Charles, French organist and composer; b. Paris, 1597; d. there, Jan. 1, 1664. He was made organist at Notre Dame in Paris in 1618, a position he held with the greatest distinction until shortly before his death. He also served as organiste de la musique ordinaire to Marie de Médicis. His extant works comprise *12 versets de psaumes en duo* and a grand *Fantaisie,* all for organ.—**LK/DM**

Radcliffe, Philip (FitzHugh), English writer on music, teacher, and composer; b. Godalming, April 27, 1905; d. near Dunkirk, Sept. 2, 1986. He studied with Moule and Dent at King's Coll., Cambridge (B.A., 1928; B.Mus., 1929), then served as a Fellow there (1931–37; from 1948) and as a lecturer in music at the Univ. of Cambridge (1947–72). Among his compositions were incidental music for Greek dramas, many sacred unaccompanied choral pieces, and numerous songs.

WRITINGS (all publ. in London unless otherwise given): *Mendelssohn* (1954; 2nd ed., 1967); *John Ireland* (1954); *Beethoven's String Quartets* (1965; 2nd ed., 1978); *Schubert Piano Sonatas* (1967); *E. J. Dent: A Centenary Memoir* (Rickmansworth, 1976); *Mozart Piano Concertos* (1978).—**LK/DM**

Radesca di Foggia, Enrico, Italian organist and composer; b. Foggia, date unknown; d. Turin, 1625. He was organist at Turin Cathedral from about 1597 until he became choirmaster there in 1615. From 1605 he was also in the service of Don Amadeo, son of the Duke of Savoy, and later became choirmaster at his court chapel about 1615. He composed both sacred and secular vocal music. He was one of the earliest composers of sacred music for small vocal ensemble and basso continuo (2 vols., Milan, 1604, 1607), but his secular vocal music is more expansive (7 vols., 1599–1617).—**LK/DM**

Radford, Robert, esteemed English bass; b. Nottingham, May 13, 1874; d. London, March 3, 1933. He was educated at London's Royal Academy of Music, taking voice lessons with Alberto Randegger. He made his operatic debut at Covent Garden in London in 1904 as the Commendatore in *Don Giovanni;* later sang Hagen and Hunding in the first English *Ring* cycle under Richter in London (1908). In 1921 he became a founder, with Beecham, of the British National Opera Co.; later became its director. In 1929 he was appointed to the faculty of his alma mater. His fame as an opera singer was great in England; in addition to singing opera, he greatly distinguished himself as a concert artist. His daughter, Winifred Radford (b. London, Oct. 2, 1901; d. Cheltenham, April 15, 1993), was a singer and teacher. She was closely associated with Bernac and Poulenc. —**NS/LK/DM**

Radić, Dušan, Serbian composer; b. Sombor, April 10, 1929. He studied at the Belgrade Academy of Music, then went to Paris, where he had private lessons with Milhaud and Messiaen. His music followed the cosmopolitan modernistic manner, Baroque in formal structure, dissonant in contrapuntal intricacies, and hedonistic in its utilitarian appeal.

WORKS: *Symphoniette* (1954); *Spisak* (Inventory), song cycle for 2 Women's Voices and 11 Instruments (Belgrade, March 17, 1954); *Balada o mesecu lutalici* (Ballad of the Errant Moon), ballet (Belgrade, Oct. 19, 1960); Concertino for Clarinet and Strings (1956); *Sinfonia* (1965–66); Piano Quintet; several cantatas; songs; theater music; film scores.—**NS/LK/DM**

Radica, Ruben, Croatian composer and teacher; b. Split, May 19, 1931. He studied with Kelemen in Zagreb, Frazzi in Siena, and Leibowitz in Paris. In 1963 he was appointed to the faculty of the Zagreb Academy of Music, serving as its dean (1981–85). He belongs to the avant-garde of Slovenian music; in 1961 he adopted the 12-tone method of composition.

WORKS: ORCH.: *Concerto grosso* (1957); *Concerto abbreviato* for Cello and Orch. (1960); *Lyrical Variations* for Strings (1961); *Formacije* (Formations; 1963); *Sustajarnje* (Prostration) for Electric Organ and Orch. (1967); *Composition* for Ondes Martenot and Chamber Orch. (Graz, Sept. 26, 1968); *Extensio* for Piano and Orch. (1973); *Barocchiana* for Trumpet and Strings (1984). **CHAMBER:** *4 Dramatic Epigrams* for Piano and String Quartet (1959); *Per se II* for Wind Quintet (1975); *Ka* for 2 Instrumental Groups and Synthesizer (1977). **VOCAL:** *19 and 10, Interferences* for Narrator, Chorus, and Orch. (1965); *Alla madrigalesca* for Chorus (1979); *Passion* for Baritone and 3 Instrumental Groups (1981).—**NS/LK/DM**

Radicati, Felice Alessandro, Italian violinist, teacher, and composer; b. Turin, 1775; d. when thrown from his carriage in Bologna, March 19, 1820. He was a pupil of Pugnani. He was a violinist in the Turin cappella until 1798. After marying **Teresa Bertinotti** in 1801, the couple toured Germany, Austria, Holland, England, and Portugal. He was again a member of the Turin cappella (1814–15) before settling in Bologna as concertmaster and director of the orch., as maestro di cappella at S. Petronio, and as prof. of violin at the Cons. As a composer of chamber music, he was hailed as the restorer of the string quartet in Italy.

WORKS: DRAMATIC: Opera: *Il sultano generoso* (c. 1805); *Coriolano* (Amsterdam, 1809); *Fedra* (London, March 5, 1811); *L'intrigo fortunato* (1815); *Castore e Polluce* (Bologna, May 27, 1815); *Blondello ossia Riccardo Cuor di Leone* (Turin, 1816); *La lezione singolare ossia Un giorno a Parigi* (c. 1819); *I due prigiorneri* (c. 1820); *Il medico per forza* (c. 1820). **ORCH.:** Sym.; Clarinet Concerto (1816); Violin Concerto (1819). **CHAMBER:** 9 string quartets; 5 string trios; duos and variations for Violin and Piano; *Grande sonate* for Violin and Viola.

BIBL.: C. Pancaldi, *Cenni intorno F. R.* (Bologna, 1828). —**NS/LK/DM**

Radino, Giovanni Maria, Italian organist and composer; b. place and date unknown; d. after 1607. He was in the service of the family of the Count of Frankenburg in Carinthia, and later was organist at the

Cappella Antoniana in Padua by 1592. He publ. *Il primo libro d'intavolatura di balli d'arpicordo* (Venice, 1592; ed. in Corpus of Early Keyboard Music, XXXIII, 1968; arranged for lute as *Intavolatura di balli per sonar al liuto*, 1592), the first such vol. publ. in Italy for harpsichord performance. He also ed. *Madrigali de diversi* for 4 Voices (Venice, 1598). His son, Giulio Radino, was a composer. His *Concerti per sonare et cantare* appeared posthumously (Venice, 1607).—LK/DM

Radnai, Miklós, Hungarian composer; b. Budapest, Jan. 1, 1892; d. there, Nov. 4, 1935. He studied violin, piano, and composition at the Budapest Academy of Music, then continued his composition studies with Mottl in Munich (1911). In 1925 he was appointed director of the Budapest Opera. He wrote a textbook on harmony and contributed critical essays to publications. He composed a ballet, *The Birthday of the Infanta*, after Oscar Wilde (Budapest, April 26, 1918), *Symphony of the Magyars* for Chorus and Orch., a Violin Concerto, and some chamber music.—NS/LK/DM

Radó, Aladár, Hungarian composer; b. Budapest, Dec. 26, 1882; killed in battle near Belgrade, Sept. 7, 1914. He studied in Budapest and Berlin. His works include 2 operas, *The Black Knight* (1911) and *Golem* (1912), Sym. (1909), *Hungarian Concerto* for Cello and Orch. (1909), 2 string quartets, and String Quintet. He also publ. several albums of piano pieces and song cycles.—NS/LK/DM

Radoux, Jean-Théodore, Belgian composer and pedagogue, father of **Charles Radoux-Rogier;** b. Liège, Nov. 9, 1835; d. there, March 20, 1911. He studied composition with Daussoigne-Méhul at the Liège Cons., winning the Belgian Prix de Rome with the cantata *Le Juif errant* (1859); then went to Paris for additional study with Halévy. He was prof. of bassoon at the Liège Cons. (from 1856), serving as its director (from 1872). He wrote monographs on Daussoigne- Méhul (1882) and Vieuxtemps (1891), and also *La Musique et les Ecoles nationales* (1896), all publ. in Brussels.

WORKS: DRAMATIC: Opera: *Le Béarnais* (Liège, March 14, 1866); *La Coupe enchantée* (Brussels, 1872). **OTHER:** *Cain*, oratorio (1877); 2 symphonic poems: *Ahasvère* and *Le Festin de Balthasar*; *Epopée nationale*, patriotic overture; church music.—NS/LK/DM

Radoux-Rogier (real name, **Radoux**), **Charles,** Belgian pedagogue, writer on music, and composer, son of **Jean-Théodore Radoux;** b. Liège, July 30, 1877; d. there, April 30, 1952. He studied with his father at the Liège Cons., winning the Belgian Prix de Rome with his cantata *Geneviève de Brabant* (1907); was made a prof. of harmony there (1905). He wrote music criticism and was active in folk-song research; served as inspector of music education (1930–42). His compositions included 2 operas, *Les Sangliers des Ardennes* (1905) and *Oudelette* (Brussels, April 11, 1912), orch. pieces, chamber music, piano pieces, choral works, and folk song albums.—NS/LK/DM

Radovanović, Vladan, Serbian composer; b. Belgrade, Sept. 5, 1932. He studied at the Belgrade Academy of Music. His early works were set in a neo-Classical style; later he annexed ultramodern techniques, including electronic effects. His *Urklang* for Mezzo-soprano and Chamber Orch. (Belgrade, March 14, 1962) deploys a counterpoint of instrumental colors, with the soloist singing wordlessly. Similarly wordless is his suite *Chorales, Intermezzi e Fuga* for Women's Chorus (Belgrade, May 16, 1962). His experimental period included such innovative works as *Sphaeroon* for 26 vocal parts, singing detached vowels (Belgrade, March 14, 1962), and *Pentaptych*, suite for Voice and 6 Instruments (Belgrade, April 22, 1964). He later composed *Timbral* for Tape (1988).—NS/LK/DM

Radziwill, Prince Anton Heinrich (Antoni Henryk), Polish cellist, guitarist, singer, composer, and music patron; b. near Vilnius, June 13, 1775; d. Berlin, April 7, 1833. He became widely known as a music patron, his Berlin residence becoming a gathering place for musicians. He befriended Beethoven, Goethe, Mendelssohn, Zelter, Chopin, and others; became governor of the Grand Duchy of Posen (1815). Among the works dedicated to him were Beethoven's *Namensfeier* overture, op.115, Mendelssohn's Piano Quartet, op.1, and Chopin's *Introduction and Polonaise* for Piano and Cello, op.3, and Trio in G minor, op.8. His own works include incidental music to Goethe's *Faust* (Berlin, Oct. 25, 1835), piano pieces, and songs.

BIBL.: Z. Jachimecki and W. Pózniak, *Antoni R. i jego muzyka do Fausta* (Kraków, 1957).—LK/DM

Radziwill, Prince Maciej, Polish composer; b. Szydlowiec, c. 1751; d. Nieświez, 1800. He wrote the opera *Wójt osady albianskiej* (The Headman of the Settlers in Alba; Alba, Nov. 4, 1786), as well as librettos for other composers. Among his other compositions were a *Divertimento* for Orch., 6 polonaises for Orch., and a Serenade for String Quartet.—NS/LK/DM

Rae, Allan, Canadian composer; b. Blairmore, Alberta, July 3, 1942. He studied arranging and theory at the Berklee School of Music in Boston (graduated, 1965) and took courses in electronic music at the Royal Cons. of Music of Toronto (1970–73); then was on its faculty (1973–74).

WORKS: DRAMATIC: Music Theater and Multimedia: *An Approach to Improvisation* (n.d.); *Like Gods, Like Gods among Them* for 6 Speaking Voices, Chorus, Dancers, and Orch. (1973); *Mirror Mirror* (1974); *C.3.3.*, chamber opera (1988); incidental music. **ORCH.:** *Trip* (1970); *Wheel of Fortune* for Winds and Strings (1971); 3 syms.: No. 1, *In the Shadow of Atlantis* (1972), No. 2, *Winds of Change* (1978), and No. 3, *Alam-Al-Mithal* (1980); *The Hippopotamus* (1972); *A Crack in the Cosmic Turtle* for Jazz Group and Orch. (1975); *Image* (1975); Sonata for Clarinet and Strings (1976); Harp Concerto (1976); *4 Paintings of Salvador Dali*, concerto for Double Bass and String Orch. (1977); Concerto for Violin and String Orch. (1979); *Mirror of Galadriel* (1982). **CHAMBER:** 2 string quartets (1966, 1967); *A Day in the Life of a Toad* for Brass Quintet (1970); *Impressions* for Wind Quintet (1971); *Sleep Whispering* for Alto Flute, Piano, and

Vibraphone (1971); 4 brass quartets for 2 Trumpets and 2 Trombones (1975); *Improvizations* for String Quartet (1977); *Whispering of the Nagual* for Flute, Clarinet, Trumpet, Trombone, Cello, Piano, and Percussion (1978); *Images No. 1* for Horn and Trumpet (1979), *No. 2* for Flute and Clarinet (1979), *No. 3* for Trumpet, Horn, and Trombone (1979), and *No. 4* for Flute, Clarinet, and Bassoon (1979); *Kiwani Owapi* (Dakota: Awakening of Earth) for Clarinet, 2 Pianos, and Percussion (1981); *Reflections* for Violin, Cello, and Piano (1981); *En passant* for 2 Marimbas (1982).—**NS/LK/DM**

Raff, (Joseph) Joachim, greatly renowned Swiss pedagogue and composer; b. Lachen, near Zürich, May 27, 1822; d. Frankfurt am Main, June 24, 1882. He was educated at the Jesuit Gymnasium in Schwyz. He was a schoolteacher in Rapperswill (1840–44), but pursued an interest in music. He sent some of his piano pieces to Mendelssohn (1843), who recommended them for publication; having met Liszt in Basel (1845), he received his encouragement and assistance in finding employment; later was his assistant in Weimar (1850–56), where he became an ardent propagandist of the new German school of composition, He then went to Wiesbaden as a piano teacher and composer, where he married the actress Doris Genast. He subsequently was director of the Hoch Cons. in Frankfurt (1877–82), where he also taught composition; students flocked from many countries to study with him, including Edward MacDowell. Raff was a composer of prodigious fecundity, and a master of all technical aspects of composition. He wrote 214 opus numbers that were publ., and many more that remained in MS. In spite of his fame, his music fell into lamentable desuetude after his death. He publ. *Die Wagnerfrage: Wagners letzte künstlerische Kundgebung im Lohengrin* (Braunschweig, 1854).

WORKS: DRAMATIC: O p e r a : *König Alfred* (1848–50; Weimar, March 9, 1851; rev. 1852; Weimar, 1853); *Samson* (1853–57); *Die Parole* (1868); *Dame Kobold*, comic opera (1869; Weimar, April 9, 1870); *Benedetto Marcello* (1877–78); *Die Eifersüchtigen*, comic opera (1881–82). ORCH.: *Grosse Symphonie* (1854; not extant); 11 numbered syms.: No. 1, *An das Vaterland* (1859–61), No. 2 (1866), No. 3, *Im Walde* (1869), No. 4 (1871), No. 5, *Leonore* (1872), No. 6 (1873), No. 7, *In den Alpen* (1875), No. 8, *Frühlingsklänge* (1876), No. 9, *Im Sommer* (1878), No. 10, *Zur Herbstzeit* (1879), and No. 11, *Der Winter* (1876; unfinished; completed by M. Erdmannsdörfer); *Fest- Ouvertüre* (1851–52; not extant); *Konzert-Ouvertüre* (1862); *Jubel-Ouvertüre* (1864); *Fest-Ouvertüre* (1864); overtures to Shakespeare's *The Tempest, Macbeth, Romeo and Juliet,* and *Othello* (1879); 2 violin concertos (1870–71; 1877); Piano Concerto (1873); 2 cello concertos (1874, 1876); 4 suites (1863, 1871, 1874, 1877). CHAMBER: 9 string quartets (1849–74); 5 piano trios (1849–70); 5 violin sonatas (1853–68); Piano Quintet (1862); Octet (1872); Sextet (1872); Cello Sonata (1873); *Sinfonietta* for 2 Flutes, 2 Oboes, 2 Clarinets, and 2 Horns (1873); 2 piano quartets. P i a n o : Solo pieces; pieces for Piano, 4-Hands; arrangements. VOCAL: Various choral works with orch. and many unaccompanied choral works.

BIBL.: A. Schäfer, *Chronologisch-systematisches Verzeichnis der Werke J. R.s* (Wiesbaden, 1888); H. Raff, *J. R.: Ein Lebensbild* (Regensburg, 1925); J. Kälin and A. Marty, *Leben und Werk des*

Komponisten J. R. (Zürich, 1972); M. Römer, *J. R. (1822–1882)* (Wiesbaden, 1982); M. Wiegandt, *Vergessene Symphonik?: Studien zu J. R., Carl Reinecke und zum Problem der Epigonalität in der Musik* (Sinzig, 1997).—**NS/LK/DM**

Ragazzi, Angelo, Italian composer; b. c. 1680; d. Vienna, 1750. He studied violin at the Cons. of S. Maria di Loreto in Naples. He was a violinist and later Konzertmeister at the royal chapel in Naples, and then was in the service of Emperor Charles VI in Vienna from 1713 to 1722 and again from 1729 to 1740. He publ. a fine vol. of *Sonate a quattro* (Rome, 1736), which included 12 sonatas for first violin, ripieno first violin, second violin, third violin or viola, violone, and basso continuo. He also wrote several concertos, a concerto grosso, a sinfonia, and sacred music.—**LK/DM**

Ragin, Derek Lee, American countertenor; b. West Point, N.Y., June 17, 1958. He was a student at the Oberlin Coll.-Cons. of Music. In 1983 he made his operatic debut in Innsbruck in Cesti's *Tito*, and in 1984 he made his London recital debut at Wigmore Hall. On Sept. 27, 1988, he made his Metropolitan Opera debut in N.Y. as Nirenus in *Giulio Cesare*. His first appearance in Salzburg took place in 1990 when he sang Gluck's Orfeo. In 1992 he portrayed Britten's Oberon in St. Louis. He appeared in Hasse's *Attilio regolo* in Dresden in 1997. Among his other roles are Handel's Flavio, Saul, and Tamerlano. His engagements as an oratorio singer and recitalist have taken him to many of the world's leading music centers.—**NS/LK/DM**

Ragué, Louis-Charles, French composer and harp teacher; b. c. 1759; d. Moulins, after 1794. He was active in Paris from 1783 until settling in Moulins about 1794. He composed 2 opéras-comiques, *Memnon* (Paris, Aug. 26, 1784) and *L'amour filial* (Paris, March 2, 1786), the ballet *Les muses, ou Le triomphe d'Apollon* (Paris, Dec. 12, 1793), 3 syms. (1778), 2 harp concertos (1785), much chamber music, harp pieces, and an oratorio. He also wrote 2 harp methods.—**LK/DM**

Rahbari, Alexander (actually, Ali), Iranian-born Austrian conductor; b. Varamin, May 26, 1948. After studying violin at the Tehran Cons., he went to Vienna to study conducting and composition at the Academy of Music, his principal mentors being Swarowsky, Osterreicher, and Einem. He was active as a violinist and conductor in Tehran, where he later was chief conductor of the Opera. In 1977 he went to Austria, becoming a naturalized Austrian citizen. After winning the Besançon conducting competition and a medal at the Geneva competition in 1978, he was invited to appear as a guest conductor with the Berlin Phil. in 1979; thereafter appeared as a guest conductor throughout Europe. In 1989 he became chief conductor of the Belgian Radio and TV Phil. in Brussels.—**NS/LK/DM**

Rahn, John, American composer, music theorist, and bassoonist; b. N.Y., Feb. 26, 1944. He studied classics at Pomona Coll. in Claremont, Calif. (B.A., 1967) and bassoon at the Juilliard School of Music in N.Y. (diploma, 1967). He played in a number of ensembles (1960–70). After military service, he studied composition with Babbitt, Boretz, and Randall at Princeton Univ. (M.F.A., 1972; Ph.D., 1974, with the diss. *Lines [Of and About Music]*). He taught at the Univ. of Mich., Ann Arbor (1973–75), then joined the faculty of the Univ. of Wash. in Seattle (1975), where he became a prof. in 1984; in 1994 he became Assoc. Director for Academic Affairs and Advising and Graduate Program Coordinator there. He was associated with the journal *Perspectives of New Music* (from 1972); in 1983, became ed. In addition to his numerous articles on theory and computer applications, his *Basic Atonal Theory* (N.Y., 1980) has the unique distinction of being a lucid introduction to set theory. Among recent works is an in-progress opera, *The New Mother*, as well as an in-progress book, *Music Inside Out: Going Too Far in Musical Essays*.

WORKS: Sonata for Bassoon and Harpsichord (1967; N.Y., May 26, 1968); *Alice* for Tape (1967); *A Lyrical, Linear Basis for Three Double Basses* (1967; in collaboration with S. A. Jones); *Collaboration* for 5 Instruments (1967); *Epithalamium* for Piano (1968); *5 Forms* for Piano (1968); *Games* for Saxophone and String Quartet (1969; N.Y., April 22, 1970); *Progressive Etude* for Bass Trombone (1969); Quintet for Winds (1969); *Reductionist Variations* for Piano (1969); *Deloumenon* for Concert Band (1970; Ann Arbor, Nov. 13, 1974); *3 Titbits* for Clarinet and Cello (1970); *Counterparts* for Trumpet (1970); *Trois Chants de Mère L'Oie* for Soprano and Piano (1971; Princeton, March 30, 1973); *Hos Estin* for Chorus and Ensemble (1971); Trio for Clarinet, Cello, and Piano (Princeton, May 21, 1972); *Peanut Butter Defies Gravity* for Soprano and Piano (Princeton, May 19, 1973); *Breakfast* for Piano (1976; Seattle, May 18, 1977); *Improvisations on a Synclavier of Corn* for Tape (Seattle, Nov. 1, 1978); *Another Lecture* for Tape and Speaker (Seattle, April 26, 1980); *Out of Haydn* for Fortepiano (1981); *IRT 4/23* for Tape (1983); *Kali* for Computer-generated Tape (Seattle, Feb. 26, 1986); *Miranda* for Computer (Seattle, Nov. 1990); *Pledge* for Viola and Vibraphone (Seattle, Nov. 26, 1990); *Superman* for Viola and Snare Drum (Seattle, Nov. 26, 1990); *Jesse* for Viola and Percussion (1989–90); *Dance* for Computer (Seattle, Feb. 19, 1991; in collaboration with J. Coleman, A. Chavasse, and R. Parker); *Another Lecture* (1992); *Sea of Souls 1* (1993) and 2 for Computer (1994).—**NS/LK/DM**

Raichev, Alexander, prominent Bulgarian composer and pedagogue; b. Lom, April 11, 1922. He studied composition with Vladigerov at the Bulgarian State Cons. in Sofia (1943–47), then took courses in composition with Kodály and Viski and in conducting with Ferencsik at the Budapest Academy of Music (1949–50). Returning to Sofia, he taught at the Bulgarian State Cons. (from 1950), where he also served as rector (1972–79). His music makes use of innovative techniques that breathe new life into traditional genres and forms.

WORKS: DRAMATIC: O p e r a : *The Bridge* (Ruse, Oct. 2, 1965); *Your Presence* (Sofia, Sept. 5, 1969); *Alarm* (Sofia, June 14, 1974); *Khan Asparouch* (Ruse, March 9, 1981). **O p e r - e t t a :** *The Nightingale of Orchid* (Sofia, March 7, 1963). **B a l - l e t :** *A Haidouk Epic* (Sofia, Feb. 13, 1953); *The Spring of the White-legged Maiden* (Sofia, Feb. 26, 1978). **ORCH.:** Piano Concerto (1947); 5 syms.: No. 1, *He Does Not Die*, sym.-cantata (1949), No. 2, *The New Prometheus* (1958), No. 3, *Strivings* (1966),

No. 4 for Strings (1972), and No. 5 for Chamber Orch. (1972); *Sonata-Poem* for Violin and Orch. (1955); *Leninist Generations*, symphonic glorification (1970); *Radiant Dawn*, overture (1971); *Leipzig 33* (1972); Concerto (1978); *Balkan Rhapsody* (1983); overtures, including *Jubilee Overture* (1986) and *Levsky* (1988). **OTHER:** Chamber music; piano pieces. **VOCAL: O r a t o - r i o s :** *Friendship* (1954); *Dimitrov Is Alive* (1954); *October 50* (1967); *Bulgaria—White, Green, Red* (1977); *Oratorio Meeting* (1984). **C a n t a t a s :** *My Dear Lassie* (1974); *Varna* (1979); *September Requiem* for Women's Chamber Chorus and Orch. (1973). **O t h e r :** Choral works and songs.—**NS/LK/DM**

Raichl, Miroslav, Czech composer; b. Náchod, Feb. 2, 1930; d. Pardubice, Jan. 11, 1998. He studied composition with Bořkovec at the Prague Academy of Music, graduating in 1953. He subsequently devoted himself mainly to teaching and administrative work in the Union of Czechoslovak Composers.

WORKS: DRAMATIC: O p e r a : *Fuente Ovejuna*, after Lope de Vega (1957; Prague, 1959). **ORCH.:** 2 syms. (1955; 1958–60); Cello Concerto (1955–56); *Revolutionary Overture* (1958); Symfonietta for Chamber Orch. (1976–77); *5 Dance Fantasies* (1981). **CHAMBER:** Piano Sonata No. 2 (1962). **VO-CAL:** *Someone Was Playing on the Oboe* for Women's Chorus (1970); *Farewell Elegy*, concertant aria for Soprano and Chamber Orch. (1981–82); *3 Ends of Love* for Women's Chorus (1982). —**NS/LK/DM**

Raimbaut de Vaqueiras, French troubadour poet and composer; b. Vaqueiras, c. 1155; d. Greece, Sept. 4(?), 1207. His career was centered on Italy, where he was companion-at-arms to Boniface, Marquis of Monferrat. In 1194 he saved his patron's life and was granted a knighthood. In 1203 he joined his patron on the fourth crusade to the Holy Land. Some 35 poems have been attributed to him, 7 of which are extant with music. See J. Linksill, ed., *The Poems of the Troubadour R. d. V.* (The Hague, 1964).

BIBL.: O. Schultz-Gora, *Die Briefe des Trobadors R. d. V. an Bonifaz I von Monferrat* (Halle, 1893).—**LK/DM**

Raimon de Miraval, Provençal troubadour who flourished from 1180 to 1215. He was a member of the lesser nobility and spent much of his time in the circle of aristocratic patrons in the south of France. Some 48 chansons have been attributed to him, 22 of which are extant with melodies.—**LK/DM**

Raimondi, Gianni, Italian tenor; b. Bologna, April 13, 1923. He was a student of Gennaro Barra-Carcacciolo and Ettore Campogalliani. In 1947 he made his operatic debut as the Duke of Mantua in Bologna, and then sang in other Italian opera centers. In 1953 he made appearances at the Stoll Theatre in London, at the Paris Opéra, and in Monte Carlo. In 1955 he joined Milan's La Scala. He made his U.S. debut in San Francisco in 1957. In 1959 he appeared in Vienna. In 1960 he sang in Munich. On Sept. 29, 1965, he made his Metropolitan Opera debut in N.Y. as Rodolfo, remaining on its roster until 1969. From 1969 to 1977 he sang at the Hamburg State Opera. He became well known for his roles in Rossini's operas, and also had success as Alfredo, Cavaradossi, Faust, Pollione, and Edgardo.

BIBL.: D. Rubboli, *G. R..: Felicemente tenore* (Parma, 1992).
—NS/LK/DM

Raimondi, Ignazio, Italian violinist, conductor, and composer; b. Naples, *c.*1735; d. London, Jan. 14, 1813. He studied violin with Emanuele Barbella, then played in the orch. of the Teatro San Carlo in Naples (1759–62). He then was active in Amsterdam as a violinist and conductor. He settled in London (1780). Among his works was the opera *La Muta* (Paris, Nov. 12, 1789), 2 syms., *Les Aventures de Télémaque dans l'isle de Calypso* (Amsterdam, Jan. 15, 1777) and *The Battle* (1785), Sinfonia concertante for 2 Violins and Orch., 6 violin concertos, and much chamber music, including 27 trios and several string quartets.—NS/LK/DM

Raimondi, Pietro, inventive Italian composer; b. Rome, Dec. 20, 1786; d. there, Oct. 30, 1853. He studied with La Barbara and Tritto at the Cons. della Pietà de' Turchini in Naples. In 1807 he brought out an opera buffa, *Le bizzarie d'amore,* at Genoa; it was followed by about 60 other dramatic works and 22 ballets, for whose production he traveled from place to place (Florence, Naples, Rome, Messina, Milan, etc.). He was director of the royal theaters at Naples (1824–32) and a prof. at the Palermo Cons. (1834–52); in 1852 he became maestro di cappella at St. Peter's in Rome. Raimondi was a contrapuntist of remarkable skill, and many of his fugues were designed to be combined with others to form complex musical structures. His most astounding combinatorial feat, however, was the sacred trilogy *Giuseppe (Joseph),* comprising 3 oratorios (*Potifar, Giuseppe, Giacobbe*), performed at the Teatro Argentina in Rome, Aug. 7, 1852, at first separately, and then simultaneously, the ensemble of 400 musicians on the stage and in the orch. presenting a most striking effect and arousing great curiosity among professional musicians.

BIBL.: F. Cicconetti, *Memorie intorno a P. R.* (Rome, 1867).
—NS/LK/DM

Raimondi, Ruggero, notable Italian bass; b. Bologna, Oct. 3, 1941. He was a student of Pediconi (1961–62) and Piervenanzi (1963–65) at the Cons. di Santa Cecilia in Rome. In 1964 he made his operatic debut as Colline in Spoleto, and then sang at the Teatro La Fenice in Venice until 1969. In 1964 he made his first appearance in Rome as Procida. In 1968 he made his debut at Milan's La Scala as Timur in *Turandot,* and his London debut in a concert perf. of Donizetti's *Lucrezia Borgia.* He sang Don Giovanni at the Glyndebourne Festival in 1969. In 1970 he made his first appearance at the Salzburg Festival as a soloist in the Verdi *Requiem.* On Sept. 14, 1970, he made his Metropolitan Opera debut in N.Y. as Silva in *Ernani,* and subsequently made regular appearances there. He made his first appearance at London's Covent Garden as Verdi's Fiesco on Feb. 23, 1972. In 1978 he returned to the Salzburg Festival to make his operatic bow as Philip in *Don Carlos.* He sang at the Paris Opéra in 1979. In 1982 he appeared as Don Quichotte at the Vienna State Opera. In 1987 he sang Mozart's Count Almaviva in Chicago. He appeared in the opening concert at the new Opéra de la Bastille in Paris in 1989. In 1990 he sang Attila at Covent Garden. In 1992 he appeared as Scarpia in Rome. He returned to Covent Garden in 1994 as Rossini's Mosè. In 1996 he sang Iago in Salzburg. Raimondi's vocal resources are ably complemented by his stage deportment. Among his other distinguished roles are Boris Godunov, Méphistophélès, Sparafucile, Oroveso, and Ramfis.
—NS/LK/DM

Rainforth, Elizabeth, English soprano; b. Nov. 23?, 1814; d. Bristol, Sept. 22, 1877. She spent most of her life in London, where she studied with George and Tom Cooke. After making her stage debut at St. James's Theatre as Mandane in Arne's *Artaxerxes* (Oct. 27, 1836), she completed her training with Crivelli. She sang at Covent Garden until 1843, and then at the Drury Lane Theatre, where she created the role of Arline in Balfe's *The Bohemian Girl* (Nov. 27, 1843). She also sang widely in concerts and oratorios. Following her retirement in 1856, she taught voice in Old Windsor until 1871.
—LK/DM

Rainier, Priaulx, South African-born English composer and teacher; b. Howick, Natal, Feb. 3, 1903; d. Bessen-Chandesse, Auvergne, Oct. 10, 1986. After violin training at the South African Coll. of Music in Cape Town (1913–20), she studied violin at the Royal Academy of Music in London, where she also took courses with McEwen; in 1937 she studied with Boulanger in Paris. From 1943 to 1961 she was a prof. of composition at the Royal Academy of Music.

WORKS: ORCH.: *Incantation* for Clarinet and Orch. (1933); *Sinfonia da camera* for Strings (1947; rev. version, London, Feb. 21, 1958); *Ballet Suite* (1950); *Phala-Phala,* dance concerto (1960–61; London, Jan. 17, 1961); Cello Concerto (1963–64; London, Sept. 3, 1964); *Aequora lunae* (1966–67; Cheltenham, July 18, 1967); *Trios and Triads* for 10 Trios and Percussion (1969–73); *Ploërmel* for Winds and Percussion (London, Aug. 13, 1973); Violin Concerto, *Due canti e finale* (1976–77; Edinburgh, Sept. 8, 1977); *Concertante* for Oboe, Clarinet, and Orch. (1977–80; London, Aug. 7, 1981). **CHAMBER:** String Quartet (1939); Suite for Clarinet and Piano (1943); Violin Sonata (1945); *6 Pieces* for Flute, Oboe, Clarinet, Horn, and Bassoon (1954); *Trio-Suite* for Piano Trio (1959); *Pastoral Triptych* for Oboe (1960); *Quanta* for Oboe and String Trio (1961–62); Suite for Cello (1963–65); String Trio (1965–66); *Grand Duo* for Cello and Piano (1980–82; London, May 30, 1983). **KEYBOARD: P i a n o:** *Barbaric Dance Suite* (1949). **H a r p s i c h o r d:** *Quinque* (1971). **O r g a n:** *Gloriana* (1972); *Primordial Canticles* (1974). **VOCAL:** *3 Greek Epigrams* for Soprano and Piano (1937); *Dance of the Rain* for Tenor and Guitar (1948); *Cycle for Declamation* for Soprano, Tenor, or Baritone (1953); *Requiem* for Tenor and Chorus (1955–56); *The Bee Oracles* for Tenor or Baritone, Flute, Oboe, Violin, Cello, and Harpsichord (1969); *Ubunzima* for Tenor or Soprano and Guitar (1973); *Prayers from the Ark* for Tenor and Harp (1974–75).

BIBL.: J. Opie, *Come and Listen to the Stars: P. R.: A Pictorial Biography* (Penzance, 1988).—NS/LK/DM

Rains, Leon, American bass; b. N.Y., Oct. 1, 1870; d. Los Angeles, June 11, 1954. He studied with Saenger in N.Y. (1891–96) and with Bouhy in Paris. He made a concert tour with Melba in the U.S. (1898), and then was a member of the Dresden Court Opera (1899–1917). He made his first appearance with the Metropolitan Opera in N.Y. on Feb. 24, 1909, as Hagen in Gotterdammerung. In 1924 he settled in Los Angeles as a teacher. —NS/LK/DM

Raisa, Rosa (real name, **Raisa** or **Rose Burschstein**), outstanding Polish soprano; b. Bialystok, May 23, 1893; d. Los Angeles, Sept. 28, 1963. In order to escape the horrors of anti-Semitic persecution, she fled to Naples at the age of 14; on Lombardi's advice she entered the Cons. San Pietro a Majella, where she studied under Barbara Marchisio. She made her operatic debut as Leonora in Verdi's *Oberto, Conte di San Bonifacio* in Parma on Sept. 6, 1913; then sang 2 seasons at the Teatro Costanzi in Rome. In 1914 she made her first appearance at Covent Garden in London. She sang with increasing success in Rio de Janeiro, Montevideo, São Paulo, and Milan. In 1920 she married the baritone Giacomo Rimini, with whom she founded a singing school in Chicago in 1937. Raisa was one of the finest dramatic sopranos of her day, excelling in the Italian repertoire; she created the title role in Puccini's *Turandot* at Milan's La Scala (April 25, 1926), her husband taking the role of Ping.—NS/LK/DM

Raison, André, French composer and organist; b. before 1650; d. Paris, 1719. He received instruction at the seminary of the abbey of Ste. Geneviève in Nanterre. He became organist at the royal abbey of Ste. Geneviève in Paris (c. 1666), and later was also organist at the convent and college of the Jacobins de St. Jacques; was the mentor of Clérambault. He publ. 2 books of organ music (Paris, 1688, 1714; ed. by A. Guilmant and A. Pirro in *Archives des maîtres de l'orgue*, Paris, 1899).—NS/LK/DM

Raitio, Pentti, Finnish composer and pedagogue; b. Pieksämäki, June 4, 1930. He studied composition with Kokkonen (1961–63) and Bergman (1963–66) at the Sibelius Academy in Helsinki, receiving his diploma in 1966. He then was director of the Hyvinkää School of Music (from 1967). He was chairman of the Lahti Organ Festival (1981–85) and of the Assn. of Finnish Music Schools (from 1985).

WORKS: ORCH.: *"13"* (1964); *Audiendum* (1967); 5 Pieces for Strings (1975); *Petandrie* (1977); *Noharmus I* (1978) and *II* (1980); *Canzone d'autunno* (1982); Flute Concerto (1983); *Due figure* (1985); *Yoldia arctica* (1987). CHAMBER: Small Pieces for Brass Instruments (1974); Wind Quintet (1975); *Nocturne* for Violin and Piano (1977). VOCAL: *Joki* (The River), 7 songs for Soprano and 7 Instruments (1965); *Kuun tietä* (Along the Moonlit Path), 3 songs for Soprano and 4 Instruments (1965); *Orfilainen kuoro* (Orphean Chorus), 3 songs for Baritone and Men's Chorus (1966); 3 Songs for Baritone and String Quartet (1970); *Eräs kesäilta* (One Summer Evening) for Men's Chorus (1971); *Laulu* (Song) for Men's Chorus (1972); *Lemminkäinen kuokkavieraana Pohjolassa* for 2 Baritones and Men's Chorus (1978); *Katselen jokea* (I'm Looking at the River), 6 songs for Women's or Youth Chorus (1986).—NS/LK/DM

Raitio, Väinö (Eerikki), Finnish composer; b. Sortavala, April 15, 1891; d. Helsinki, Sept. 10, 1945. He studied in Helsinki with Melartin and Furuhjelm and in Moscow with Ilyinsky; also in Berlin (1921) and Paris (1925–26). From 1926 to 1932 he taught at the Viipuri Music Inst. His music is programmatic in the Romantic manner, but there is a more severe strain in his pieces derived from Finnish legends. He was one of the earliest Finnish composers to embrace modern compositional techniques, being mainly influenced by Scriabin, German expressionism, and French Impressionism.

WORKS: DRAMATIC: Opera: *Jephtan tytär* (Jephtha's Daughter; 1929; Helsinki, 1931); *Prinsessa Cecilia* (1933; Helsinki, 1936); *Väinämöinen kosinta* (Väinämöinen's Courtship; 1935); *Lyydian kuningas* (The King of Lydia; 1937; Helsinki, 1955); *Kaksi kuningatarta* (2 Queens; 1937–40; Helsinki, 1945). Ballet: *Vesipatsas* (Waterspout; 1929). ORCH.: Piano Concerto (1915); *Poem* for Cello and Orch. (1915); *Symphonic Ballad* (1916); Sym. (1918–19); *Joutsenet* (The Swans; 1919); *Fantasia estatica*, symphonic poem (1921); *Antigone* (1921–22); *Kuutamo Jupiterissa* (Moonlight on Jupiter), symphonic tableau (1922); *Fantasia poetica*, symphonic poem (1923); *Felis domestica*, scherzo (1935); Concerto for Violin, Cello, and Orch. (1936); *Nocturne* for Violin and Orch. (1938); *Fantasy* for Cello, Harp, and Orch. (1942); *Le Ballet grotesque* (1943). CHAMBER: String Quartet; Piano Quintet; Violin Sonata; piano and organ works. VOCAL: *Pyramid* for Chorus and Orch. (1924–25).—NS/LK/DM

Raitt, Bonnie, one of the most talented female song interpreters and bottleneck-guitar stylists to emerge in the 1970s; b. Burbank, Calif., Nov. 8, 1949. Bonnie Raitt often toured with the black blues artists that influenced her while recording the songs of obscure contemporary songwriters such as John Prine, Eric Kaz, and Karla Bonoff. Recording the definitive version of Kaz and Libby Titus's moving "Love Has No Pride" and Prine's "Angel from Montgomery," Raitt enjoyed modest success during the 1970s. Neglected by her longtime record label Warner Bros., Bonnie Raitt finally broke through into mass popularity on Capitol Records with the 1989 album *Nick of Time*, and sustained that popularity with 1991's *Luck of the Draw* and 1994's *Longing in Their Hearts*, all produced by Don "Was" Fagenson.

The daughter of Broadway singer-actor John Raitt (*Carousel, The Pajama Game*, and *Oklahoma*), Bonnie Raitt moved with her family from N.Y. to Los Angeles in 1957. Between ages 8 and 14 she was exposed to authentic blues and politicized folk music while attending Quaker summer camps in upstate N.Y. She took up guitar at age nine, and later learned piano. By her mid-teens she had mastered the bottleneck or slide-guitar technique that was to characterize her work. In 1967 she moved to Boston to attend Radcliffe Coll. and met Dick Waterman (her manager until 1986), who introduced her to old blues performers such as John Hurt, Fred McDowell, and Sippie Wallace. She played Cambridge folk clubs such as Club 47 and enjoyed success in folk clubs around Boston, Philadelphia, and N.Y. By 1969 she had dropped out of Radcliffe and met bassist Freebo, a former member of the Edison Electric Band, who became a mainstay of her touring band of the 1970s.

Signed to Warner Bros. Records in spring 1971, Bonnie Raitt's debut album contained two Sippie Wallace songs, "Mighty Tight Woman" and "Woman Be

Wise," the originals "Thank You" and "Finest Lovin' Man," and Robert Johnson's "Walking Blues." Her second album, *Give It Up*, became her first album-chart entry and included "Give It Up or Let Me Go," "Love Me like a Man," Sippie Wallace's "You Got to Know How," and the definitive version of Eric Kaz and Libby Titus's "Love Has No Pride." Bonnie Raitt returned to the West Coast to record *Takin' My Time* under producer John Hall of Orleans. The album featured Eric Kaz's "Cry Like a Rainstorm," Chris Smither's "I Feel the Same," and Randy Newman's "Guilty." By 1974 Raitt's modest success had enabled her to assemble a touring band based around Freebo, and she toured tirelessly for years. She began playing electric lead guitar with *Streetlights*, recorded in N.Y. under R&B producer Jerry Ragavoy. It included a stellar rendition of John Prine's "Angel from Montgomery" and the favorite "You Got to Be Ready for Love."

Bonnie Raitt moved to Los Angeles in 1975, where she recorded *Home Plate*, which included "Good Enough" and "Run Like a Thief." Her first major success came with 1977's *Sweet Forgiveness*, which produced a sluggish version of Del Shannon's "Runaway" (a minor hit) and contained Karla Bonoff's "Home" and Paul Siebel's oft-recorded "Louise." In 1979 Raitt became a founding member of MUSE (Musicians United for Safe Energy) with John Hall, Jackson Browne, and Graham Nash; she performed at five MUSE benefit shows staged at Madison Square Garden. *The Glow*, recorded under producer Peter Asher, included her own "Standin' by the Same Old Love" and Robert Palmer's "You're Gonna Get What's Coming," a minor hit. In 1980 Raitt scored a minor country hit with Rusty Wier's "Don't It Make You Wanna Dance" from the film *Urban Cowboy*. After 1982's *Green Light*, recorded with Tex. guitarist Johnny Lee Schell and veteran keyboardist Ian McLagan, Warner Bros. refused to issue her next album, tentatively titled *Tongue and Groove*. She nonetheless continued to tour with a new band based around Schell and bassist James "Hutch" Hutchinson. She appeared at the Farm Aid and Amnesty International concerts and eventually assembled *Nine Lives* for release on Warner Bros. In 1987 Raitt participated in the joint Soviet/American Peace Concert, staged in Moscow.

Under new management, Bonnie Raitt eventually signed with Capitol Records. She recorded *Nick of Time* under producer Don "Was" Fagenson and the album became a surprise best-seller, eventually moving more than four million copies. The album yielded hits with John Hiatt's "Thing Called Love" (the first single and Raitt's first music video), the title track, and Bonnie Hayes's "Have a Heart"; it also included the self-affirming "I Ain't Gonna Let You Break My Heart Again," "I Will Not Be Denied," and her own "The Road's My Middle Name." In 1990 Raitt recorded duets with John Lee Hooker on "I'm in the Mood" and B. B. King on Doctor John's "Right Place Wrong Time." Raitt netted four Grammys in 1990, celebrating her newfound success and long career in the business. In 1991 she recorded *Luck of the Draw* with producer Don Was. The album yielded the smash hit "Something to Talk About," the major hit "I Can't Make You Love Me," and the moderate hit "Not the Only One" and eventually

sold more than five million copies. That same year Raitt cofounded the Rhythm and Blues Foundation, to help aged (and often poverty-stricken) pioneers of that musical genre. Bonnie Raitt's perseverance had finally paid off, and her success continued with 1994's *Longing in Their Hearts*, again under producer Was. The album featured the major hit "Love Sneakin' Up on You," "Feeling of Falling," and Richard Thompson's "Dimming of the Day." In 1995 she scored a minor hit with a remake of Roy Orbison/Jeff Lynne/Tom Petty's "You Got It," which was used as a theme song for the film *Boys on the Side*; she also issued a two-CD live set, *Road Tested*, along with a video. Raitt was honored with a Bonnie Raitt—signature Fender guitar, with profits earmarked to encourage women to learn the instrument.

DISC.: *B. R.* (1971); *Give It Up* (1972); *Takin' My Time* (1973); *Streetlights* (1974); *Home Plate* (1975); *Sweet Forgiveness* (1977); *The Glow* (1979); *Green Light* (1982); *Nine Lives* (1986); *The B. R. Collection* (1990); *Nick of Time* (1989); *Luck of the Draw* (1991); *Longing in Their Hearts* (1994); *Road Tested* (1995).—**BH**

Rajičič, Stanojlo, Serbian composer and pedagogue; b. Belgrade, Dec. 16, 1910. He studied composition (diplomas, 1934 and 1935) with Karel and Suk and piano (diploma, 1935) with Alois Sima at the Prague Cons. He then attended piano master classes of Hoffmeister in Prague and of Walter Kerschbaumer in Vienna. From 1937 to 1977 he was prof. of composition at the Belgrade Academy of Music. In 1950 he was elected a corresponding member and in 1958 a fellow of the Serbian Academy of Sciences and Arts, serving as secretary of its dept. of visual and musical arts (from 1964); also was elected a member of the Slovenian Academy of Sciences and Arts (1975). He received the Serbian State Prize (1968), the Gottfried von Herder Prize of Vienna (1975), and the Vuk Prize (1986). His early compositions are set in a radical idiom of atonal music, verging on dodecaphony, but later he adopted a national style derived from melorhythms of Serbian folk songs.

WORKS: DRAMATIC: Opera: *Simonida* (1956; Sarajevo, May 24, 1957); *Karadjordje* (1973; Belgrade, June 26, 1977); *Dnevnik jednog ludaka* (The Diary of a Madman; 1977; Belgrade, April 4, 1981); *Bele noći* (White Nights; 1983; Belgrade, April 14, 1985). **Ballet:** *Pod zemljom* (Under the Earth; 1940). **ORCH.:** 6 syms. (1935, 1941, 1944, 1946, 1959, 1967); 3 piano concertos (1940, 1942, 1950); 3 violin concertos (1941, 1946, 1950); 2 clarinet concertos (1943, 1962); Cello Concerto (1949); Bassoon Concerto (1969). **CHAMBER:** Piano Trio (1934); 2 string quartets (1938, 1939); piano pieces. **VOCAL:** *Magnovenja* (Moments), song cycle for Mezzo-soprano and Orch. (1964).—**NS/LK/DM**

Rajna, Thomas, Hungarian-born English pianist, teacher, and composer; b. Budapest, Dec. 21, 1928. He studied with Kodály, Veress, and Weiner at the Franz Liszt Academy of Music in Budapest (1944–47) and with Howells at the Royal Coll. of Music in London (graduated, 1952). He taught at the Guildhall School of Music and Drama in London (1963–67) and the Univ. of Surrey (1967–70). In 1970 he became senior lecturer and in 1989 assoc. prof. at the Univ. of Cape Town. As a pianist, Rajna made tours of Europe and South Africa, becoming primarily known for his performances of Liszt, Granados, Scriabin, Stravinsky, and Messiaen. His own works assume a classical mold, with distinctly modern contents in harmony and counterpoint.

WORKS: DRAMATIC: O p e r a : *Amarantha* (1991–95). **ORCH.:** *Rhapsody* for Clarinet and Orch. (1948–50); *Suite* for Strings (1952–54); 2 piano concertos: No. 1 (1960–62; London, March 18, 1966) and No. 2 (1984); *Movements* for Strings (1962); *Cantilenas and Interludes* (London, Feb. 7, 1968); Harp Concerto (1990); *Fantasy* for Violin and Orch. (1996). **CHAMBER:** *Dialogues* for Clarinet and Piano (1947); String Quartet (1948); *Music* for Cello and Piano (1950); *Music* for Violin and Piano (1956–57); *Serenade* for 10 Winds, Percussion, Harpsichord, and Piano (1958); *Suite* for Violin and Harp (1997). **P i a n o :** *Preludes* (1944–49). **VOCAL:** *3 Hebrew Choruses* (1972); *4 Traditional African Lyrics* for High Voice and Piano (1976). **—NS/LK/DM**

Rajter, L'udovít, Slovak conductor and composer; b. Pezinok, July 30, 1906. He went to Bratislava and studied with Alexander Albrecht at the Municipal Music School (1915–20) and received training in theory, piano, and cello at the Academy of Music and Drama (1920–24). After studying composition with Franz Schmidt and Joseph Marx, and conducting with Clemens Krauss and Alexander Wunderer at the Vienna Academy of Music (1924–29), he attended the master course in composition of Ernst von Dohnányi at the Franz Liszt Academy of Music in Budapest (1930–32). From 1933 to 1945 he held the position of first conductor with the Hungarian Radio in Budapest, and he also taught at the Franz Liszt Academy of Music from 1938 to 1945. He then returned to Bratislava, where he was principal conductor of the Czechoslovak Radio Sym. Orch. from 1945 to 1956. In 1949 he co-founded the Slovak Phil., which he served as first conductor (until 1951; again 1961–76) and as artistic director (1951–61). He also taught at the Academy of Music and Drama from 1949 to 1976. In 1968–69 he was principal conductor of the Basel Radio Sym. Orch. From 1968 to 1977 he served as principal conductor of the Czechoslovak Radio Sym. Orch. He was made a prof. at the Academy of Music and Drama in 1991, the same year that he was named honorary principal conductor for life of the Savaria Sym. Orch.

WORKS: DRAMATIC: *May Feast,* ballet suite (1938); incidental music for radio. **ORCH.:** *Divertimento* (1931–32); *Symphonic Suite* (1932–33); *3 Slovak Dances* (1950); *Songs and Dances from Slovenský Grob* (1963); *Student Suite* (1976); *Allegro sinfonico* (1986); *Sinfonietta* (1993); *Impressioni rapsodiche* (1995). **CHAMBER:** 2 string quartets (1929, 1943); 2 wind quintets (1931; 1985–86); Double Bass Sonata (1962–63); 2 suites for Cello (1977–78; 1985); *Serenata da caccia* for 5 Horns (1978); *Quattro invenzioni* for Oboe, Clarinet, and Horn (1985); *Dialoghi* for 2 Flutes (1987); *Suite* for Violin (1988); *Partita* for 8 Cellos (1994); *Musica alternativa* for 8 Cellos (1994); *Variations* for 8 Cellos (1995); *Fantasy on Two Themes by Eugène d'Albert* for Cello (1995); *Fantasy* for Cello (1995). **O r g a n :** *Preludio: In memoriam Franz Schmidt* (1965). **VOCAL:** Several songs (1923–42); *Mass* for Children's Chorus and Organ (1931); *Iustorum animae* for Chorus (1990); *In memoriam* for Small Chorus and Strings or Organ or Piano (1991).**—NS/LK/DM**

Raksin, David, remarkable American composer of film music; b. Philadelphia, Aug. 4, 1912. He studied piano in his childhood and also learned to play woodwind instruments from his father, a performer and conductor; when barely past puberty, he organized his own jazz band. In 1931 he entered the Univ. of Pa., and in 1934–35 he also studied composition privately with Isadore Freed. In 1935 he went to Hollywood to assist Charlie Chaplin with the music for his film *Modern Times* (which he later orchestrated with Edward Powell); this provided Raksin a wonderful companionship with the great comedian, later resulting in a delectable piece of reminiscences, "Life with Charlie" (*Quarterly Journal of the Library of Congress,* Summer 1983). After a period of travel, he returned to work in the Hollywood film studios and to study with Schoenberg. During his time, he served as assistant to Stokowski, who performed Raksin's brief *Montage* with his Phil. Orch., probably the first piece of film music to be played by a major orch. Raksin composed more than 100 film scores, some of which attained great popularity; his greatest success was the film theme song *Laura,* ingratiatingly melodious in its sinuous and convoluted pattern, which generated more than 400 different recordings. Apart from his activities as a composer and conductor, Raksin appeared as an actor and commentator in television programs. Using material from his film music, he composed several symphonic suites, among them *Forever Amber* and *The Bad and the Beautiful.* Other coruscating scores include *Force of Evil, Carrie, The Redeemer,* and *Separate Tables,* all of which are featured in *Wonderful Inventions* (Library of Congress, Washington, D.C., 1985). Raksin is the first member of his profession invited to deposit his film music in the collections of the Library of Congress in Washington, D.C. He also wrote incidental music for the theater, as well as purely symphonic and choral pieces, including a madrigal, *Simple Symmetries.* His orchestral *Toy Concertino* received many performances, and, at the request of Stravinsky, he made the original band instrumentation of *Circus Polka* for George Balanchine's production with the Barnum and Bailey Circus. In 1956 he joined the composition faculty of the Univ. of Southern Calif., where he also served on its faculty of the School of Public Administration (1968–89); he also taught film and television composition at the Univ. of Calif., Los Angeles (1970–92). He wrote, narrated, and conducted interviews for a three-year series of hour-long radio programs, "The Subject is Film Music." Raksin received an Elizabeth Sprague Coolidge Commission from the Library of Congress; the resulting composition, *Oedipus memneitai* (Oedipus Remembers) for Bass-Baritone Narrator/Soloist, 6-part Mixed Chorus, and Chamber Ensemble, text by the composer, was conducted by him at a special Founder's Day Concert, Oct. 30, 1986, in Washington, D.C. Among recent works is *Swing Low, Sweet Clarinet* for Clarinet and String Quartet, to be performed by the virtuoso Eddie Daniels in Santa Fe. Raksin conducted a concert of the music of his colleague Alex North with the Orquesta Sinfonica of Seville in May, 1991. In April, 1992, he received the Golden Soundtrack Award for Career Achievement from AS-CAP, to whose Board of Directors he was subsequently elected; he also served as president of the Composers & Lyricists Guild of America (1962–70) and of the Society for the Preservation of Film Music (1992–95). He was Guest of Honor at the Ecrans Sonores Festival, Biarritz, France, where Nov. 18, 1993 was declared "David Raksin Day." During this period, Raksin completed a survey/study of transcriptions of Mussorgsky's *Pictures at an Exhibition* (to date some 98 versions), compiled for eventual distribution in the CD/ROM medium. In 1995 he was celebrated at the State of the Art Conference in Vienna, and later spent several weeks in residence at the Johannes Brahms house in Baden Baden. In March 1995 he was honored at the Gstaad Festival in Switzerland, and in August of that year he presented his film work at the European Film Coll. in Ebeltoft, Denmark. On Aug. 23, 1995, he conducted the U.S. Marine Band in transcriptions of 3 of his film pieces. In January 1998, he went to Japan to conduct some of his music at the new Tokyo Opera City Concert Hall in a program planned by Takemitsu which also included pieces by Nino Rota and Takemitsu. In March and April of that same year he was in Norway for presentations at Oslo Univ. and the Film School at Bergen. Raksin is featured in the documentary film "The Hollywood Sound," broadcast via PBS throughout the U.S. and Europe.—**NS/LK/DM**

Ralf, Oscar (Georg), Swedish tenor, brother of **Torsten (Ivar) Ralf;** b. Malmö, Oct. 3, 1881; d. Kalmar, April 3, 1964. He studied with Forsell (1902–04) and Gillis Bratt (from 1905), and in Berlin and Munich. He began his career as a singer at Stockholm's Oscarsteatern, an operetta theater (1905–15); completing his studies with Bratt, he made his operatic debut as Siegmund at the Royal Opera in 1918; was a principal member of the company until 1940; also appeared as Siegmund at Bayreuth in 1927. He was best known for his roles in operas by Wagner and Verdi. He publ. an autobiography, *Tenoren han går i Ringen* (The Tenor Goes into the Ring; Stockholm, 1953).—**NS/LK/DM**

Ralf, Richard, German composer; b. Karlsruhe, Sept. 30, 1897; d. Los Angeles, June 22, 1977. He studied piano as a child with his father, the choirmaster at the Karlsruhe Opera, and later attended the Scharwenka Cons. in Berlin, graduating in 1914. Drafted into the German army in World War I, he suffered severe shell shock at the French front; returning to Berlin, he studied composition with Hugo Kaun. In 1946 he emigrated to the U.S., eventually settling in Los Angeles. His music follows the florid and emotional trend of post-Wagnerian Romanticism. Among his compositions were *Transcendental,* ballet (1921), Violin Sonata (1923), String Quartet (1924), Violin Concerto (1925), *Brothers Arise,* cantata (1959), and *Symphonic Songs* for Mezzo-soprano and Orch. (1968).—**NS/LK/DM**

Ralf, Torsten (Ivar), Swedish tenor, brother of **Oscar (Georg) Ralf;** b. Malmö, Jan. 2, 1901; d. Stockholm, April 27, 1954. He studied at the Stockholm Cons. and with Hertha Dehmlow in Berlin. He made his operatic debut as Cavaradossi in Stettin (1930); then sang in Chemnitz (1932–33) and Frankfurt am Main

(1933–35). He was a member of the Dresden State Opera (1935–44), where he created the role of Apollo in Strauss's *Daphne* in 1938; was made a Kammersänger in 1936. He sang at London's Covent Garden (1935–39; 1948) and at the Teatro Colón in Buenos Aires (1946); made his Metropolitan Opera debut in N.Y. as Lohengrin on Nov. 26, 1945, and remained on its roster until 1948. He was best known for such roles as Walther von Stolzing, Tannhäuser, Parsifal, Otello, and Radames. —**NS/LK/DM**

Ramann, Lina, German pedagogue, writer on music, and composer; b. Mainstockheim, near Kitzingen, June 24, 1833; d. Munich, March 30, 1912. She was a pupil of Franz and Frau Brendel at Leipzig, and also briefly of Liszt. She founded (1858) a music seminary for women teachers in Glückstadt, Holstein, which was moved to Nuremberg (1864) and sold to A. Göllerich (1890). She wrote some piano music but became best known for her writings on music.

WRITINGS (all publ. in Leipzig unless otherwise given): *Aus der Gegenwart* (Nuremberg, 1868); *Bach und Händel* (1868); *Die Musik als Gegenstand des Unterrichts* (1868); *Allgemeine musikalische Erziehungs- und Unterrichtslehre* (1870); *Franz Liszts Oratorium Christus* (1874); ed. *Franz Liszt: Gesammelte Schriften* (1880–83); *Franz Liszt als Künstler und Mensch* (1880–94); *Grundriss der Technik des Klavierspiels* (1885); *Liszt als Psalmensänger* (1886); *Liszt-Pädagogium* (1901).

BIBL.: M. Ille-Beeg, *L. R.* (Nuremberg, 1914).—**NS/LK/DM**

Ramboušek, Joseph, Czech double-bass virtuoso and pedagogue; b. Mníšek, Nov. 16, 1845; d. Moscow, March 10, 1901. He studied with Josef Hrabět at the Prague Cons.; went to Moscow, where he was engaged as a double-bass player at the Opera and taught at the Phil. Inst. Among his pupils was Koussevitzky. —**NS/LK/DM**

Rameau, Jean-Philippe, great French composer, organist, and music theorist; b. Dijon (baptized), Sept. 25, 1683; d. Paris, Sept. 12, 1764. His father was organist of St. Étienne in Dijon. He learned to play the harpsichord as a small child, and from age 10 to 14 attended the Jesuit Collège des Godrans in Dijon, where he took up singing and composing instead of concentrating on his academic studies. At 18 his father sent him to Milan, where he stayed for only a brief time before joining the orch. of a traveling French opera troupe as a violinist. In Jan. 1702 he received a temporary appointment as organist at Avignon Cathedral; in May 1702 he became organist at Clermont Cathedral. By 1706 he was in Paris, where he publ. his first *Livre de pièces de clavecin;* was active there as a church organist until 1708. He succeeded his father as organist at Notre Dame Cathedral in Avignon in 1709, and then became organist to the Jacobins in Lyons in July 1713. He was organist at Clermont Cathedral from 1715 to 1723, where he wrote his famous *Traité de l'harmonie* (Paris, 1722). This epoch-making work, though little understood at the time, attracted considerable attention and roused opposition, so that when he settled definitely in Paris (1723) he was by no means unknown. The fact that he failed in 1727 in a competition for the position of organist at St.-Vincent-de-Paul did not injure his reputation, for it was generally known that Marchand (probably out of jealousy) had exerted his powerful influence in favor of Daquin, who was in every respect inferior to Rameau. In 1732 he became organist at Ste.-Croix-de-la-Bretonnerie, and soon was recognized as the foremost organist in France. In 1726 appeared his *Nouveau système de musique théorique*, an introduction to the *Traité*. The leading ideas of his system of harmony are (1) chord-building by thirds; (2) the classification of a chord and all its inversions as one and the same, thus reducing the multiplicity of consonant and dissonant combinations to a fixed and limited number of root chords; and (3) his invention of a fundamental bass (basse fondamentale), which is an imaginary series of root tones forming the real basis of the varied chord progressions employed in a composition. The stir that these novel theories occasioned, and his reputation as the foremost French organist, by no means satisfied Rameau's ambition; his ardent desire was to bring out a dramatic work at the Opéra. He had made a modest beginning with incidental music to Alexis Piron's comedy *L'Endriague* in 1723. After contributing further incidental music to Piron's comedies *L'Enrôlement d'Arlequin* (1726) and *La Robe de dissension, ou Le Faux Prodigue* (1726), he became music master to the wife of the "fermier-général" La Pouplinière; the latter obtained from Voltaire a libretto for *Samson*, which Rameau set to music; but it was rejected on account of its biblical subject. A second libretto, by Abbé Pellegrin, was accepted, and *Hippolyte et Aricie* was produced at the Opéra in 1733; its reception was cool, despite undeniable superiority over the operas of Lully and his following. Rameau considered abandoning composing any further works for the theater, but the persuasions of his friends, who also influenced public opinion in his favor, were effective; in 1735 he brought out the successful opéra-ballet *Les Indes galantes*, and in 1737 his masterpiece, *Castor et Pollux*, a work that for years held its own beside the operas of Gluck. A career of uninterrupted prosperity commenced. Rameau was recognized as the leading theorist of the time, and his instruction was eagerly sought. For the next 30 years his operas dominated the French stage. He was named Compositeur du cabinet du roy in 1745, and was ennobled 4 months before his death.

From the beginning of his dramatic career Rameau roused opposition, and at the same time found ardent admirers. The first war of words was waged between the "Lullistes" and the "Ramistes." This had scarcely been ended by a triumphant revival of *Pygmalion* in 1751 when the production of Pergolesi's *La Serva padrona* (1752) caused a more prolonged and bitter controversy between the adherents of Rameau and the "Encyclopédistes," a struggle known as "La Guerre des Bouffons," in which Rameau participated by writing numerous essays defending his position. Practically the same charges were made against him as would be made a century later against Wagner: unintelligible harmony, lack of melody, preponderance of discords, noisy instrumentation, etc. But when 25 years later the war between Gluckists and Piccinnists was raging, Rameau's works were praised as models of beauty and perfection. It is a

matter for regret that Rameau was indifferent to the quality of his librettos; he relied so much upon his musical inspiration that he never could be brought to a realization of the importance of a good text; hence the inequality of his operas. Nevertheless, his operas mark a decided advance over Lully's in musical characterization, expressive melody, richness of harmony, variety of modulation, and expert and original instrumentation. The so-called complete edition of Rameau's works, ed. by Saint-Saëns and C. Malherbe (after the latter's death continued by M. Emmanuel and M. Teneo), was never completed (18 vols., Paris, 1895–1924). A new critical edition, under the joint auspices of the Association pour la Publication des Oeuvres de Rameau in Paris and the Broude Trust of N.Y., with N. Zaslaw as general ed. and F. Lesure as managing ed., began publishing in 1983. For a complete edition of his writings, see E. Jacobi, ed., *Jean-Philippe Rameau: Complete Theoretical Writings* (Rome, 1967–72).

WRITINGS (all publ. in Paris): *Traité de l'harmonie reduite à ses principes naturels* (1722; Eng. tr., 1737; modern ed. in Eng. tr. by P. Gossett, 1971); *Nouveau système de musique théorique* (1726); *Dissertation sur les différentes méthodes d'accompagnement pour le clavecin ou pour l'orgue* (1732); *Génération harmonique ou Traité de musique théorique et pratique* (1737; modern ed. in Eng. tr. by D. Hayes in *Rameau's "Génération harmonique,"* diss., Stanford Univ., 1974); *Mémoire où l'on expose les fondements du Système de musique théorique et pratique de M. Rameau* (1749); *Démonstration du principe de l'harmonie* (1750); *Nouvelles réflexions de M. Rameau sur sa Démonstration du principe de l'harmonie* (1752); *Observations sur notre instinct pour la musique* (1754); *Erreurs sur la musique dans l'Encyclopédie* (1755–56); *Suite des erreurs sur la musique dans l'Encyclopédie* (1756); *Prospectus, où l'on propose au public, par voye de souscription, un code de musique pratique, composé de sept méthodes* (1757); *Réponse de M. Rameau à MM. les éditeurs de l'Encyclopédie* (1757); *Nouvelles réflexions sur le principe sonore* (1758–59); *Code de musique pratique, ou Méthodes pour apprendre la musique ... avec de nouvelles réflexions sur le principe sonore* (1760); *Lettre à M. d'Alembert sur ses opinions en musique* (1760); *Origine des sciences, suivie d'une controverse sur le même sujet* (1762); also *Vérités intéressantes* (unfinished MS).

WORKS: DRAMATIC (all first perf. at the Paris Opéra unless otherwise given): **O p e r a :** *Samson*, tragédie en musique (1733; not perf.; not extant); *Hippolyte et Aricie*, tragédie en musique (Oct. 1, 1733); *Les Indes galantes*, opéra-ballet (Aug. 23, 1735); *Castor et Pollux*, tragédie en musique (Oct. 24, 1737); *Les Fêtes d'Hébé (Les Talents lyriques)*, opéra-ballet (May 21, 1739); *Dardanus*, tragédie en musique (Nov. 19, 1739); *La Princesse de Navarre*, comédie-ballet (Versailles, Feb. 23, 1745); *Platée (ou Junon jalouse)*, comédie-lyrique (Versailles, March 31, 1745); *Les Fêtes de Polymnie*, opéra-ballet (Oct. 12, 1745); *Le Temple de la gloire*, opéra-ballet (Versailles, Nov. 27, 1745); *Les Fêtes de l'Hymen et de l'Amour, ou Les Dieux d'Egypte*, ballet-héroïque (Versailles, March 15, 1747); *Zaïs*, ballet-héroïque (Feb. 29, 1748); *Pygmalion*, acte de ballet (Aug. 27, 1748); *Les Surprises de l'Amour*, divertissement (Versailles, Nov. 27, 1748); *Naïs*, pastorale- héroïque (April 22, 1749); *Zoroastre*, tragédie en musique (Dec. 5, 1749); *Linus*, tragédie en musique (not perf.; greater portion of music not extant); *La Guirlande, ou Les Fleurs enchantées*, acte de ballet (Sept. 21, 1751); *Acante et Céphise, ou La Sympathie*, pastorale-héroïque (Nov. 18, 1751); *Daphnis et Eglé*, pastorale-héroïque (Fontainebleau, Oct. 30, 1753); *Lysis et Délie*, pastorale (1753; not perf.; music not extant); *Les Sybarites*, acte de ballet (Fontainebleau, Nov. 13, 1753); *La Naissance d'Osiris, ou La Fête Pamilie*, acte de ballet (Fontainebleau, Oct. 12, 1754); *Anacréon*, acte de ballet (Fontainebleau, Oct. 23, 1754; rev. version to different text, May 31, 1757); *Le Procureur dupé sans le savoir*, opéra-comique en vaudevilles (private perf., 1758 or 1759; music not extant); *Les Paladins*, comédie-ballet (Feb. 12, 1760); *Abaris, ou Les Boréades*, tragédie lyrique (first perf. in concert form in London, April 19, 1975; first stage perf. in Aix-en-Provence, July 21, 1982). **B a l l e t :** *Nélée et Myrthis (Les Beaux Jours de l'amour)*, *Zéphyre (Les Nymphes de Diane)*, and *Io* (none publicly performed). **OTHER :** He also contributed music, in collaboration with others, to the following comedies by A. Piron: *L'Endriague* (Feb. 3, 1723); *L'Enrôlement d'Arlequin* (Feb. 1726); *La Robe de dissension, ou Le Faux Prodigue* (Sept. 7, 1726); *Les Jardins de l'Hymen, ou La Rose* (1726; March 5, 1744); *Les Courses de Tempé* (Aug. 30, 1734); also the intermède en musique *Aruéris* (Dec. 15, 1762). **VOCAL : S e c u l a r C a n t a t a s :** *Thétis* (1718); *Aquilon et Orinthie* (1719); *Les Amants trahis* (1721); *Orphée* (1721); *L'Impatience* (1715–21); *Le Berger fidèle* (1728); *Cantate pour la fête de Saint Louis* (c. 1740). **S a c r e d V o c a l :** 4 Psalm settings for Soloists, Chorus, and Instrumental Ensemble: *Deus noster refugium* (c. 1716), *In convertendo* (c. 1718), *Quam dilecta* (c. 1720), and *Laboravi* (publ. in *Traité de l'harmonie*, 1722). **KEYBOARD :** *Premier livre de pièces de clavecin* (1706); *Pièces de clavecin avec une méthode sur la mécanique des doigts* (1724; rev. 1731, as *Pièces de clavecin avec une table pour les agréments*); *Nouvelles suites de pièces de clavecin* (c. 1728); *Cinq pièces pour clavecin seul, extraites des Pièces de clavecin en concerts* (1741); *Pièces de clavecin en concerts* for Harpsichord, Violin or Flute, and Viol or Violin (1741; 2nd ed., 1752).

BIBL.: BIOGRAPHICAL: C. Poisot, *Notice biographique sur J. P. R.* (Paris, 1864); T. Nisard, *Monographie de J. P. R.* (Paris, 1867); R. Garraud, *R.* (Paris, 1876); H. Grigne, *R.* (Dijon, 1876); A. Pougin, *R.* (Paris, 1876); L. de La Laurencie, *R.* (Paris, 1908); L. Laloy, *R.* (Paris, 1908); Y. Tiénot, *J. P. R.: Esquisse biographique, suivie d'un tableau chronologique comprenant une liste complète des oeuvres de R.* (Paris, 1954); H. Charlier, *J. P. R.* (Lyons, 1955); P. Berthier, *Réflexions sur l'art et la vie de J. P. R. (1683–1764)* (Paris, 1957); C. Girdlestone, *J. P. R.: His Life and Work* (London, 1957; 2nd ed., rev., 1969); J. Malignon, *R.* (Paris, 1960); C. Kintzler, *J. P. R.: Splendeur et naufrage de l'esthétique du plaisir à l'age classique* (Paris, 1983). **WORKS:** G. Graf, *J. P. R. in seiner Oper Hippolyte et Aricie: Eine musikkritische Würdigung* (Wädenswil, 1927); P.-M. Masson, *L'Opéra de R.* (Paris, 1930); Z. Klitenic, *The Clavecin Works of J. P. R.* (diss., Univ. of Pa., 1955); E. Ahnell, *The Concept of Tonality in the Operas of J. P. R.* (diss., Univ. of Ill., 1958); G. Seefrid, *Die Airs de danse in den Bühnenwerken von J. P. R.* (Wiesbaden, 1969); M. Terey-Smith, *J. P. R.: "Abaris ou les Boréades": A Critical Edition* (diss., Eastman School of Music, 1971); J. Anthony, *French Baroque Music from Beaujoyeulx to R.* (London, 1973; 2nd ed., rev., 1978); M. Cyrs, *R.'s "Les fêtes d'Hébé"* (diss., Univ. of Calif., Berkeley, 1975); P. Rice, *The Fontainebleau Operas of J. P. R.: A Critical Study* (diss.,Univ. of Victoria, Canada, 1981); R. Klingsporn, *J. P. R.s Opern im äesthetischen Diskurs ihrer Zeit: Opernkomponistion, Musikanschauung und Opernpublikum in Paris 1733–1753* (Stuttgart, 1996); C. Dill, *Monstrous Opera: R. and the Tragic Tradition* (Princeton, 1998). **THEORIES:** P. Estève, *Nouvelle découverte du principe de l'harmonie, avec un examen de ce que M. R. a publié sous le titre de Démonstration de ce principe* (Paris, 1752); J. Le Rond d'Alembert, *Éléments de musique théorique et pratique selon les principes de M. R.* (Paris, 1752; 2nd ed., 1762); F. Marpurg, *Versuch über die musikalische Temperatur, nebst einem Anhang über die R.- und Kirnbergerschen Grundbass* (Breslau, 1776); M. Keane, *The Theo-*

retical Writings of J. P. R. (diss., Catholic Univ. of America, 1961); J. Krehbiel, *Harmonic Principles of J. P. R. and His Contemporaries* (diss., Ind. Univ., 1964); D. Hayes, *R.'s "Génération harmonique ou Traité de musique théorique et pratique"* (diss., Stanford Univ., 1974); E. Verba, *A Hierarchic Interpretation of the Theories and Music of J. P. R.* (diss., Univ. of Chicago, 1979); E. Haeringer, *L'esthétique de l'opéra en France au temps de J. P. R.* (Oxford, 1990); T. Christensen, *R. and Musical Thought in the Enlightenment* (Cambridge, 1993).—**NS/LK/DM**

Ramey, Phillip, American writer on music and composer; b. Elmhurst, Ill., Sept. 12, 1939. He began playing the piano at 7 and composing at 17. After training in composition with A. Tcherepnin at the International Academy of Music in Nice (summer, 1959) and at DePaul Univ. in Chicago (B.A., 1962), he pursued graduate studies with Beeson at Columbia Univ. (M.A., 1965). He contributed numerous articles to magazines and wrote hundreds of notes for recordings. From 1977 to 1993 he was the annotator and program ed. of the N.Y. Phil. As a composer, he explored atonal and serial writing in several of his works. He later pursued a chromatic but generally tonal course marked by complexity of style and form. His music for piano is thoroughly idiomatic.

WORKS: ORCH.: Concert Suite for Piano and Small Orch. (1962; rev. for Piano and Orch., 1983–84; N.Y., March 9, 1984); *Orchestral Discourse* (1967); 3 piano concertos (1969–71; 1976; 1991–94); Concerto for Horn and Strings (1987; rev. 1989; for the 150th anniversary of the N.Y. Phil.; N.Y., April 22, 1993); *Color Etudes* for Piano and Orch. (arr. 1999–2000 from *Color Etudes* for Piano, 1994). **CHAMBER:** 3 Preludes for Horn (1960); Sonata for 3 Timpani (1961); *Capriccio* for Percussion (1966); *Toccata Breva* for Percussion (1966); *Night Music* for Percussion (1967); *Commentaries* for Flute and Piano (1968); Suite for Violin and Piano (1971; Vilnius, Lithuania, March 3, 1992); *La Citadelle*, rhapsody for Oboe and Piano (1975; rev. 1980; N.Y., May 14, 1981; arr. for Horn and Piano, 1994); *Arabesque* for Flute (1977; N.Y., March 6, 1983); *Fanfare-Sonata* for Trumpet (1981); *Phantasm* for Flute and Violin or 2 Violins (1984); *Café of the Ghosts: Fantasy-Trio on a Moroccan Beggar's Song* for Violin, Cello, and Piano (Sacramento, Calif., Nov. 6, 1992); *Rhapsody* for Cello (1992); Trio Concertant for Violin, Horn, and Piano (1993; Sacramento, Calif., Jan. 30, 1994); *Praeludium* for 5 Horns (1994); *Elegy* for Horn and Piano (N.Y., Nov. 6, 1995); *Gargoyles* for Horn (1995); *Nightfall*, aria for Flute and Piano (1996); Concertino for 4 Horns, Timpani, and Percussion (1996); *Sonata-Ballade* for 2 Horns and Piano (1997; Arlington, Mass., March 1, 1998); *Dialogue* for 2 Horns (1997; Arlington, Mass., March 1, 1998); *Effigies* for Viola and Piano (1998; London, May 19, 1999); *Lyric Fragment* for Flute and Harpsichord or Piano (1998). **KEYBOARD: P i a n o :** *Meditation* (Nice, July 30, 1959; rev. 2000); *Three Early Preludes* (1959; Chicago, Nov. 28, 1961; rev. 1996); *Incantations* (1960; rev. 1982); Suite (1960–63; rev. and expanded 1988); 5 sonatas: No. 1 (Chicago, 1961), No. 2 (1966), No. 3 (1968), No. 4 (1987–88, formerly No. 6; Tangier, Morocco, June 22, 1993), and No. 5 for the Left Hand (1989, formerly *Canticle*; N.Y., March 10, 1991); *Diversions* (1966); *Toccata Giocosa* (1966); *2 Short Pieces* (1967); *Epigrams*, I (1967; N.Y., Feb. 19, 1969) and II (1986; N.Y., March 22, 1987); *Harvard Bells* (1968, formerly Piano Sonata No. 4); *Piano Fantasy* (1969–72; N.Y., Feb. 28, 1983); *Leningrad Rag: Mutations on Scott Joplin* (1972); *Night Song* (1973); *Memorial* (N.Y., Oct. 30, 1977); *Autumn Pastorale* (N.Y., Nov. 22, 1980);

Echoes (1981–82; N.Y., April 21, 1982); *Cossack Variations* (1981–85); *Canzona* (1982; N.Y., Sept. 8, 1983); *Capriccio: Improvisation on a Theme from Youth* (1985; N.Y., April 29, 1986); 2 toccatas: No. 1 (1986; Fullerton, Calif., March 5, 1987) and No. 2 (1990; N.Y., Feb. 27, 1991); *Tangier Nocturne* (Chicago, April 25, 1989); *Burlesque-Paraphrase on a Theme of Stephen Foster* (1990; N.Y., March 10, 1991); *Mirage* (Chicago, April 25, 1990); *Cantus Arcanus* (1990; N.Y., Feb. 27, 1991); *Tangier Portraits: 20 Pieces* (1991–2000); *Chromatic Waltz* (1993; Glion-sur-Montreux, Switzerland, Nov. 11, 1995); *Color Etudes* (1994; N.Y., Oct. 28, 1995); *Akashic Prelude on a Theme of Paul Bowles* (Santa Cruz, Calif., June 11, 1995); *Solemn Prelude* (1996); *Phantoms: Ostinato Etude* (1997). **Harpsichord:** Sonata (Yorkshire, England, July 13, 1998). **VOCAL:** *Cat Songs* for Soprano, Flute, and Piano (1962; rev. 1965); *7, They Are 7,* incantation for Bass-baritone and Orch. (1965); *Merlin's Prophecy* for High Voice and Piano (1966); *A William Blake Trilogy* for Soprano and Piano (1980); *Moroccan Songs to Words of Paul Bowles* for High Voice and Piano (1982–86). **OTHER:** Orchestration of Aaron Copland's *Proclamation* for Piano (N.Y., Nov. 14, 1985).—**NS/LK/DM**

Ramey, Samuel (Edward), outstanding American bass; b. Colby, Kans., March 28, 1942. He attended Kans. State Univ., and then studied voice with Arthur Newman at Wichita State Univ. (B.Mus., 1968). After singing with the Grass Roots Opera Co. in Raleigh, N.C. (1968–69), he continued his studies with Armen Boyajian in N.Y. On March 11, 1973, he made his professional operatic debut as Zuniga in *Carmen* at the N.Y.C. Opera, where he rose to prominence as its principal bass. In 1976 he made his first appearance at the Glyndebourne Festival as Mozart's Figaro. Following debuts at the Lyric Opera in Chicago and at the San Francisco Opera as Colline in 1979, he sang for the first time at Milan's La Scala and at the Vienna State Opera as Mozart's Figaro in 1981. From 1981 to 1989 he appeared in various Rossini roles in Pesaro. In 1982 he made his debut at London's Covent Garden as Mozart's Figaro, and then portrayed Mosè at the Paris Opéra in 1983. On Jan. 19, 1984, he made a brilliant debut at the Metropolitan Opera in N.Y. as Argante in Handel's *Rinaldo*. That same year, he sang the role of Mozart's Figaro for the soundtrack recording of the award-winning film *Amadeus*. His first appearance at the Salzburg Festival came in 1987 when he sang Don Giovanni. He returned to the Metropolitan Opera in such roles as Bartók's Bluebeard in 1989, Don Basilio in 1992, and Boris Godunov in 1997. He also returned to the Lyric Opera in Chicago as Boris Godunov in 1994, and as Méphistophélès at the San Francisco Opera in 1995 and at the Vienna State Opera in 1997. In 1999 he portrayed Olin Blitch at the Metropolitan Opera.—**NS/LK/DM**

Ramin, Günther (Werner Hans), distinguished German organist, conductor, composer, and pedagogue; b. Karlsruhe, Oct. 15, 1898; d. Leipzig, Feb. 27, 1956. As a boy he sang in the Thomanerchor in Leipzig. He then studied organ with Straube, piano with Teichmüller, and theory with Krehl at the Leipzig Cons. In 1918 he was appointed organist of the Thomaskirche in Leipzig; he also was organist of the Gewandhaus concerts and a teacher at the Leipzig Cons. During the season 1933–34, he toured the U.S. as

an organ virtuoso. He was also active as a conductor; he led the Lehrergesangverein in Leipzig (1922–35) and the Gewandhaus Choir (1933–34; 1945–51); from 1935 to 1943 he conducted the Phil. Choir in Berlin. In 1940 he became cantor of the Thomaskirche, where he sought to preserve the integrity of the Thomanerchor after the establishment of the German Democratic Republic. His compositions include an *Orgelchoral-Suite* and many other organ pieces, as well as chamber music and songs. He ed. several collections of organ works and publ. the manual *Gedanken zur Klärung des Orgelproblems* (Kassel, 1929; new ed., 1955). A vol. of his essays on Bach was ed. by D. Hellmann (Wiesbaden, 1973).

BIBL.: L. von Koerber, *Der Thomanerchor und sein Kantor* (Hamburg, 1954); E. Hasse, *Erinnerungen an G. R.* (Berlin, 1958); C. Ramin, *G. R.* (Freiburg im Breisgau, 1958); idem, *Weggefährten im Geiste Johann Sebastian Bachs: Karl Straube—G. R.: Zwei Thomaskantoren 1918–1956* (Darmstadt, 1981).—**NS/LK/DM**

Ramírez, Luis Antonio, Puerto Rican composer and teacher; b. San Juan, Feb. 10, 1923. He studied in San Juan and at the Madrid Cons. (composition diploma, 1964). From 1968 he taught at the Puerto Rico Cons. of Music in San Juan.

WORKS: ORCH.: *Tres Homenages* for Strings (1962–65); *Sinfonietta* (1963); *Suite* (1966); *Balada Concierto* for Violin and Orch. (1967); *Fantasía Sobre un Mito Antillano* (1969); *Tres Piezas Breves* (1972); *Fragmentos*, 3 pieces (1973); 6 symphonic poems: No. 1, *Figuraciones* (1974), No. 2, *Rasgos y Perfiles* for Cello and Orch. (1977), No. 3, *Aire y Tierra* (1978), No. 4, *Ciclos* (1979), No. 5, *El Cuarto Rey Mago* (1983), and No. 6, *La Tierra escuchó tu Voz* (1984); *Suite para la Navidad* (1982); *Días sin Alborada* (1986); *Siete Episodios Históricos* (1986); *Elegía* for Strings (1987). **CHAMBER:** *Sonata Elegíaca* for Cello and Piano (1968); *Meditación a la Memoria de Segundo Ruíz Belvis* for Viola and Piano (1972); piano pieces. **VOCAL:** *Nueve Cantos Antillanos* for Soprano and Orch. (1975).—**NS/LK/DM**

Ramirez, Ram (Roger), pianist, organist, songwriter; b. Puerto Rico, Sept. 15, 1913; d. Jan. 11, 1994. Raised in the San Juan Hill section (near Lincoln Center) of N.Y. Began playing piano at the age of eight, and five years later, joined the musicians' union. He worked with the Louisiana Stompers in N.Y. during the early 1930s, briefly accompanying Monette Moore early in 1933. He left the Louisiana Stompers to join Rex Stewart's Band at the Empire Ballroom, N.Y. (summer 1933). He worked with the Spirits of Rhythm in 1934, joining Willie Bryant early in 1935. He went to Europe with Bobby Martin's Band in June 1937, returning to N.Y. in late 1939. He led his own small group for Asbury Park residency, then worked with Ella Fitzgerald and Frankie Newton before spending a year with Charlie Barnet (1942). He rejoined Frankie Newton (1943), and was then with John Kirby's Sextet from early 1944 until joining Sid Catlett's Band at the Downbeat Club, N.Y. (1944). From the late 1940s Ramirez usually worked with own trio in N.Y. area clubs. He played organ extensively from 1953. He again toured Europe in spring 1968 (accompanying T-Bone Walker) and continued to work regularly through the 1980s. He died of kidney failure. He composed "Lover Man," "Mad about You," and others.—JC/LP

Ramones, The, N.Y.C.'s leading proponents of punk rock in the mid-1970s. **MEMBERSHIP:** Joey Ramone (Jeffrey Hyman), voc. (b. Forest Hills, N.Y., May 19, 1952); Johnny Ramone (John Cummings), gtr. (b. Long Island, N.Y., Oct. 8, 1951); Dee Dee Ramone (Douglas Colvin), bs. (b. Vancouver, British Columbia, Canada, Sept. 18, 1952); Tommy Ramone (Tom Erdelyi), drm. (b. Budapest, Hungary, Jan. 29, 1952). Later members include drummers Marky Ramone (Marc Bell) (b. N.Y.C., July 15, 1956); Richie Ramone (Richard Reinhardt, aka Richard Beau); C. J. Ramone (Christopher Joseph Ward), bs. (b. Long Island, N.Y., Oct. 8, 1965).

The Ramones proffered uncomplicated, furious rock featuring sarcastic, implacable, and wryly satirical lyrics that stood in staunch opposition to the overproduced and complacent contemporary musical styles—from progressive rock to disco to pop—then dominating popular music. Their first two albums, *The Ramones* and *The Ramones Leave Home*, became punk classics, and their headline engagements in London in July 1976 inspired a generation of young British musicians, including the Sex Pistols, the Clash, and dozens of other defiant, unconventional groups. However, while other punk groups either self-destructed, disappeared, or adopted more palatable musical textures and lyrical nuances to gain mainstream populariry, the Ramones remained stylistically intransigent and never attained more than a rabid cult following. Nonetheless, they persevered into the 1990s.

The Ramones formed in Forest Hills (Queens), N.Y., in August 1974 with high school dropouts Jeffrey Hyman, John Cummings, and Douglas Colvin. They debuted at N.Y.'s Performance Studio in March 1974; within two months, manager Tom Erdelyi joined on drums as Hyman switched to lead vocals. They began a residency at CBGB's, one of N.Y.C.'s leading punk clubs (along with Max's Kansas City), in August and became one of the city's leading purveyors of frantic, unadorned, straight-ahead rock featuring vituperative, wryly satirical lyrics. Signed to Sire Records in November 1975, the Ramones' debut album contained punk favorites such as "Beat on the Brat," "Blitzkrieg Bop," "Judy Is a Punk," and "Now I Wanna Sniff Some Glue." Touring exhaustively, the group soon recorded *The Ramones Leave Home*, which included "Pinhead," "Commando," the classic "Gimme Gimme Shock Treatment," and their first minor hit, "Sheena Is a Punk Rocker."

The Ramones conducted their first tour of Great Britain in 1976, and their July 4th debut at London's Roadhouse caused a sensation that drew a number of musicians who would later form some of the country's most outrageous and popular punk bands. Their third album in 18 months, *Rocker to Russia*, produced minor hits with "Rockaway Beach" and "Do You Wanna Dance" and contained "Cretin Hop," "Teenage Lobotomy," and their first ballad, "Here Today, Gone Tomorrow." Tommy Ramone left the group in May 1978

to pursue a career in production, to be replaced by former Richard Hell and the Voidoids drummer Marc Bell, who became Marky Ramone. The group's next album, *Road to Ruin*, included the punk classic "I Wanna Be Sedated" as well as "I Just Want to Have Something to Do," the love song "Questioningly," and a cover of Sonny Bono's "Needles and Pins," a major hit for the Searchers in 1964.

In 1979 the Ramones appeared in the teenage movie *Rock 'n' Roll High School* and recorded *End of the Century*, their best-selling album, under legendary producer Phil Spector. The album featured "Rock 'n' Roll High School," the endearing "Do You Remember Rock 'n' Roll Radio?," and a remake of the Ronettes' "Baby I Love You." The group then recorded *Pleasant Dreams* under songwriter-producer Graham Gouldman, an erstwhile member of 10cc, which included "The KKK Took My Baby Away" and "We Want the Airwaves."

Despite the waning of punk's popularity in the 1980s, the Ramones continued to record for Sire Records. However, Marc Bell left in 1983, to be replaced by Richie Ramone (Richard Beau). Bell returned in 1988, but Dee Dee Ramone departed in 1989 to pursue a solo career as Dee Dee King and was replaced by C. J. Ramone (Chris Ward). None of the group's 1980s albums sold particularly well, although they did record occasional gems such as "Psycho Therapy," "Howling at the Moon," "Animal Boy," "My Brain Is Hanging Upside Down (Bonzo Goes to Bitburg)," "I Wanna Live," and "Merry Christmas (I Don't Want to Fight Tonight)." In 1990 the Ramones toured the world as part of the Escape from N.Y. tour with Debbie Harry and the Tom Tom Club. By 1992 the Ramones had switched to the MCA-distributed Radioactive label for *Mondo Bizarro*, which included "Censorshit," "Cabbies on Crack," and "The Job that Ate My Brain." It was followed by an album of cover songs, *Acid Eaters*. In 1995 the band announced their retirement with the release of *Adios Amigos*, which features "I Don't Want to Grow Up," the ironic "Have a Nice Day," and "Born to Die in Berlin."

DISC.: THE RAMONES: *The R.* (1976); *The R. Leave Home* (1977); *Rocket to Russia* (1977); *Road to Ruin* (1978); *Rock 'n' Roll High School* (soundtrack; 1979); *End of the Century* (1980); *Pleasant Dreams* (1981); *Subterranean Jungle* (1983); *Too Tough to Die* (1984); *Animal Boy* (1986); *Halfway to Sanity* (1987); *R. Mania* (1988); *Brain Drain* (1989); *All the Stuff (and More), Vol. I* (1990); *All the Stuff (and More), Vol. II* (1991); *Loco Live* (1992); *Mondo Bizarro* (1992); *Acid Eaters* (1993); *Adios Amigos!* (1995). **DEE DEE KING:** *Standing in the Spotlight* (1989).

BIBL.: J. Bessman, *R.: An American Band* (N.Y., 1993).—BH

Ramón y Rivera, Luis Felipe, Venezuelan ethnomusicologist and composer; b. San Cristóbal, Aug. 23, 1913; d. Oct. 22, 1993. After studying viola pedagogy at the Caracas Escuela Superior de Música (degree, 1934), he returned to his native city to teach at the Escuela de Artes y Oficios de San Cristóbal (1939) and to found and direct the Táchira Music School (1940–50). He studied folklore and ethnomusicology with Carlo Vega at the Inst. of Musicology in Buenos Aires and with **Isabel Aretz**, whom he married, and Augusto Raúl Cortázar at the Colegio Libre de Estudios Superiores

(1945–47). He returned to Caracas as chief of musicology of the Servicio de Investigaciones Folklóricas Nacionales (1947), and then went back to Buenos Aires to direct the Americana Orch. (1948–52). In 1953 he became director of the National Inst. of Folklore of Venezuela in Caracas. He traveled extensively in South America, taught folklore and ethnomusicology at Venezuelan and foreign univs., and was president of the Venezuelan Soc. of Authors and Composers (1972–73). Ramón y Rivera's extensive fieldwork enabled him to make a comparative study of the music of the South American continent; he contributed greatly to the study of Venezuelan indigenous, folk, and popular music.

WRITINGS: *La polifonia popular de Venezuela* (Buenos Aires, 1949); *El joropo, baile nacional de Venezuela* (Caracas, 1953); *Cantos de trabajo del pueblo venezolano* (Caracas, 1955); *La música colonial profana* (Caracas, 1966); *Música indigena, folklórica y popular de Venezuela* (Buenos Aires, 1970); *La música afrovenezolana* (Caracas, 1971); *La música popular de Venezuela* (Caracas, 1976).
—NS/LK/DM

Ramos de Pareia, Bartolomé, significant Spanish music theorist; b. Baeza, c. 1440; d. c. 1491. He studied with Juan de Monte, and after lecturing at the Univ. of Salamanca, he went to Bologna in 1472. He publ. in 1482 his Latin treatise *Musica practica* (modern ed. by G. Vecchi, 1969), one of the important landmarks in the science of harmony. From 1484 he was in Rome. He established the mathematical ratios 4:5 and 5:6 for the intervals of the major and minor third, thus completing the definition of the consonant triad and laying the basis of our harmonic system. He was also the first to set forth the theory of equal temperament, probably based on the practice of the early Spanish guitarists (*vihuelistas*), since the frets on the guitar were placed a semitone apart.—NS/LK/DM

Ramovš, Primož, Slovenian composer; b. Ljubljana, March 20, 1921; d. Jan. 1999. He studied composition with Slavko Osterc at his hometown's Academy of Music (1935–41), with Vito Frazzi in Siena (1941), and privately with Casella and Petrassi in Rome (1941–43). He was a librarian (1945–52) and chief librarian (1952–87) of the Slovenian Academy of Sciences and Art; was also a prof. at the Ljubljana Cons. (1948–52; 1955–64). The framework of his style of composition was neo-Classical, distinguished by great contrapuntal skill and ingenious handling of rich, dissonant sonorities; dodecaphony and aleatorality were sometimes employed.

WORKS: ORCH.: 3 numbered syms. (1940, 1943, 1948); 3 divertimentos (1941, 1942, 1944); Piano Concerto (1946); Concertino for Piano and Strings (1948); Concerto for 2 Pianos and Strings (1949); *Suite* for 2 Violins, Cello, and String Orch. (1950); *Sinfonietta* (1951); *Musique funèbre* (1955); *Chorale and Toccata* (1955); *Adagio* for Cello and String Orch. (1958); *Concerto piccolo* for Bassoon and Strings (1958); Trumpet Concertino (1960); *7 Compositions* for Strings (1960); Concerto for Violin, Viola, and Orch. (1961); *Koncertantza glasba* (Concertante Music) for Percussion and Orch. (1961); *Intrada* (1962); *Profiles* (1964); *Vzporedja* (Parallels) for Piano and Strings (1965); *Odmevi* (Echoes) for Flute and Orch. (1965); *Antiparallels* for Piano and Orch. (1966; Zagreb, May 15, 1967); *Finale* (1966); *Portret* for Harp,

Winds, Strings, and Percussion (1968); *Symphony 68* (Ljubljana, Oct. 27, 1968); *Nasprotja* (Contrasts) for Flute and Orch. (1969); Sym. for Piano and Orch. (1970); Cello Concerto (1974); Double-Bass Concerto (1976); Bassoon Concerto (1978); *Triplum* (1980); Concerto for 2 Pianos and Orch. (1981); Organ Concerto (1983); *Concerto profano* for Organ and Orch. (1984); Trumpet Concerto (1985); *Kolovrat* for Strings (1986); Concerto for Violin, Cello, and Orch. (1988); *Pismo* (Letter; 1989); Triple Concerto for Oboe, Clarinet, Bassoon, and Orch. (1990); *Per aspera ad astra* (1991); *Celeia laboribus suis gaudens* for Strings (1993); *Zvočni svet* (Sonorous World) for 2 Pianos and Orch. (1993); *AS* (1994); *Živio SGŠ!* for Trumpet and Orch. (1994); *Simfonija Pietà* (1995). **CHAMBER:** Quartet for 4 Horns (1939); Wind Trio (1942); Trio for Flute, Trumpet, and Bassoon (1952); *Kontrasti* for Piano Trio (1961); *Eneafonia* for 9 Instruments (1963); *Fluctuations* for Chamber Ensemble (1964); *Prolog* for Flute, Clarinet, and Bassoon (1966); *Nihanja* (Oscillations) for Flute, Harp, Percussion, and Strings (1969); *Siglali* for Piano and 8 Instruments (1973); Quartet for Flute, Violin, Cello, and Harpsichord (1988); *Dilema* for Clarinet and Piano (1991); *Cum jibilo* for Brass Quintet (1992); *Discessus* for 9 Brass Instruments (1993); *Dovolj naj bo* (It must be enough) for Cello and Piano (1995); many compositions for solo instruments; piano pieces. **VOCAL:** Choruses; songs.—NS/LK/DM

Rampal, Jean-Pierre (Louis), celebrated French flutist, conductor, and teacher; b. Marseilles, Jan. 7, 1922; d. Paris, May 20, 2000. He studied flute as a child with his father, first flutist in the Marseilles orch. and a prof. at the Cons., then studied medicine until being drafted for military service by the German occupation authorities in 1943. When he learned that he was to be sent to Germany as a forced laborer, he went AWOL, and subsequently attended flute classes at the Paris Cons., winning the premier prix in 5 months. He played solo flute in the orch. of the Vichy Opera (1946–50); concurrently began to tour, often in duo recitals with the pianist and harpsichordist Robert Veyron-Lacroix. He was solo flutist in the orch. of the Paris Opéra from 1956 to 1962, and also became a popular artist on the Paris Radio. He subsequently toured throughout the world with phenomenal success as a virtuoso, appearing as soloist with all the major orchs. and in innumerable recitals. In later years, he also appeared as a guest conductor. He taught at the Paris Cons., and gave master classes worldwide. His repertoire was vast, ranging from the Baroque masters to jazz, from the music of Japan to that of India, from arrangements to specially commissioned works. Of the last, such composers as Poulenc and Jolivet wrote pieces for him. Through his countless concerts and recordings, he did more than any other flutist of his time to bring his instrument into the mainstream of musical life. He was made a Chevalier of the Légion d'Honneur in 1966 and an Officier des Arts et Lettres in 1971. With D. Wise, he publ. *Music, My Love: An Autobiography* (N.Y., 1989).
—NS/LK/DM

Rampini, Domenico, Italian composer; b. Friuli province, c. 1765; d. Trieste, Dec. 19, 1816. He was harpsichordist at the theater of S. Samuele in Venice in 1791. He then settled in Trieste, where he was harpsichordist at the theater of S. Pietro from 1792 to 1801, and then was maestro di cappella at the Teatro Nuovo from 1801 until about 1813. He also served as maestro di cappella at the Cathedral.

WORKS (all first perf. in Trieste): **DRAMATIC: Opera:** *L'impresario in Smirne* (Feb. 3, 1798); *Pimmalione* (March 6, 1802). **CANTATAS:** *Inno popolare* (Oct. 4, 1798); *Inno* (Oct. 4, 1799); *Trieste rasserenata* (Oct. 12, 1802); *I geni pacificati* (Feb. 12, 1808); *Minerva consolata* (Jan. 28, 1814); *Il sogno di corvo* (Feb. 12, 1814); *La gloria* (Feb. 1814). **OTHER:** Requiem (1808) and other sacred pieces.—**LK/DM**

Rampini, (Giovanni) Giacomo, Italian composer, uncle of **Giacomo Rampini;** b. Padua, 1680; d. there, May 27, 1760. He became a priest and served as maestro di cappella at Padua Cathedral from 1704 until his death.

WORKS: DRAMATIC: Opera: *Armida in Damasco* (Venice, Oct. 17, 1711); *La gloria trionfante d'amore* (Venice, Nov. 16, 1712); *Marco Attilio Regolo* (Verona, 1713); *Ercole sul Termodonte* (Padua, June 1715). **OTHER:** *Concerto a cinque* for Strings and Basso Continuo (Amsterdam, c. 1717; 4 oratorios: *Christo al cenacolo* (Padua, 1707), *L'angelo di Catiglione* (Padua, June 21, 1712), *Il trionfo della costanzo* (Padua?, 1717), and *David pentito* (Padua, 1728); Mass; Requiem.—**LK/DM**

Rampini, Giacomo, Italian and composer, nephew of **(Giovanni) Giacomo Rampini;** b. Rovigo, date unknown; d. Udine, Nov. 1811. He studied with his uncle in Padua and became a priest. He was organist in Latisana before serving as substitute organist (1775–79) and permanent organist (from 1779) at Udine Cathedral. He also was its maestro di cappella from 1799, and was a teacher at the Udine seminary from 1775. He composed sacred works and sonatas for organ or harpsichord.—**LK/DM**

Ramsey, Robert, English organist and composer; b. c. 1595; d. after 1644. He took his B.Mus. at Cambridge in 1616, and was organist of Trinity Coll. (1628–44) and Master of the Children (1637–44). He wrote numerous church services, anthems, and madrigals, which remained in MS until 1962, when an Evening Service and some madrigals were publ. in England. More recently E. Thompson ed. *Robert Ramsey: English Sacred Music,* in Early English Church Music, VII (London, 1967), and *Robert Ramsey: Latin Sacred Music,* I–II, ibid., XX (1978) and XXXI (1986). See also I. Spink, ed., *English Songs 1625–1660,* in Musica Britannica, XXXIII (London, 1971).—**NS/LK/DM**

Ran, Shulamit, Israeli pianist and composer; b. Tel Aviv, Oct. 21, 1949. She studied piano with Miriam Boskovich and Emma Gorochov and composition with Ben-Haim and Boskovich, then was a scholarship student at the America-Israel Cultural Foundation and the Mannes Coll. of Music in N.Y. (graduated, 1967), her mentors being Reisenberg (piano) and Dello Joio (composition). She continued piano studies with Dorothy Taubman and composition training with Ralph Shapey (1976). She made tours of the U.S. and Europe as a pianist. After serving as artist-in-residence at St. Mary's Univ. in Halifax, Nova Scotia (1972–73), she taught at the

the Univ. of Chicago. She held a Guggenheim fellowship (1977), and was a visiting prof. at Princeton Univ. (1987). In 1991 she became composer-in-residence of the Chicago Sym. Orch. Her 1st Sym. won the Pulitzer Prize in Music in 1991 and first prize in the Kennedy Center Friedheim awards in 1992.

WORKS: DRAMATIC: Opera: *Between Two Worlds: The Dybbuk* (1994–95; Chicago, June 20, 1997). **ORCH.:** *Capriccio* for Piano and Orch. (N.Y., Nov. 30, 1963); *Symphonic Poem* for Piano and Orch. (Jerusalem, Oct. 17, 1967); *10 Children's Scenes* (1970; arranged from a piano work); *Concert Piece* for Piano and Orch. (Tel Aviv, July 12, 1971); Piano Concerto (1977); *Concerto for Orchestra* (1986; N.Y., Feb. 1, 1987); Sym. No. 1 (1989–90; Philadelphia, Oct. 19, 1990); *Chicago Skyline* for Brass and Percussion (Chicago, Dec. 12, 1991); *Legends* (1992–93; Chicago, Oct. 7, 1993); *3 Fantasy Movements* for Cello and Orch. (Berkeley, Calif., Oct. 2, 1993; based on *3 Fantasy Pieces* for Cello and Piano, 1971); *Invocation* for Horn, Timpani, and Chimes (1994; Los Angeles, Feb. 15, 1995). **CHAMBER:** Quartet for Flute, Clarinet, Cello, and Piano (1967); *3 Fantasy Pieces* for Cello and Piano (1971; also as *3 Fantasy Movements* for Cello and Orch., 1993); *Double Vision* for Woodwind Quintet, Brass Quintet, and Piano (1976; Chicago, Jan. 21, 1977); *A Prayer* for Clarinet, Bass Clarinet, Bassoon, Horn, and Timpani (1981); 2 string quartets: No. 1 (1984) and No. 2 (1988–89; Chicago, Nov. 17, 1989); *Concerto da camera I* for Woodwind Quintet (1985) and *II* for Clarinet, String Quartet, and Piano (1987); *Mirage* for 5 Players (1990; N.Y., March 7, 1991); *Inscriptions* for Violin (Chicago, June 9, 1991). **Piano:** *Structures* (1968); *Hyperbolae* (1976); *Sonata Waltzer* (1981–82); *Verticals* (1982). **VOCAL:** *Hatzvi Israel Eulogie* for Mezzo-soprano, Flute, Harp, and String Quartet (1968); *7 Japanese Love Poems* for Voice and Piano (1968); *O the Chimneys* for Mezzo-soprano, Ensemble, and Tape (1969); *Ensembles for 17* for Soprano and 16 Instruments (Chicago, April 11, 1975); *Apprehensions* for Voice, Clarinet, and Piano (1979); *Amichai Songs* for Mezzo-soprano, Oboe or English Horn, Viola da Gamba, and Harpsichord (1985); *Adonai Malach* for Cantor, Horn, Piccolo, Oboe, and Clarinet (1985).—**NS/LK/DM**

Ranalow, Frederick (Baring), Irish baritone; b. Dublin, Nov. 7, 1873; d. London, Dec. 8, 1953. He became a chorister at St. Paul's Cathedral in London when he was 10. After training with Randegger at the Royal Academy of Music in London, he pursued a successful career as an oratorio singer. He also appeared with the Beecham Opera Co., winning praise for his Mozart's Figaro. In 1920 he sang Captain Macheath in Austin's revival of *The Beggar's Opera,* a role he sang on some 1,600 occasions.—**NS/LK/DM**

Ranczak, Hildegard, Czech soprano; b. Vitkovice, Dec. 20, 1895; d. Munich, Feb. 19, 1987. She studied at the Vienna Cons. She made her operatic debut in Düsseldorf in 1918, remaining there until 1923. She then sang in Cologne (1923–25) and Stuttgart (1925–27). In 1927 she joined the Bavarian State Opera in Munich, where she appeared until 1944; sang there again from 1946 to 1949, and also at Covent Garden in London, the Paris Opéra, the Rome Opera, and the Berlin State Opera. She created the role of Clairon in Richard Strauss's *Capriccio* in 1942.—**NS/LK/DM**

Randall, J(ames) K(irtland), American composer; b. Cleveland, June 16, 1929. He studied at the

Cleveland Inst. of Music (1934–47), Columbia Univ. (B.A., 1955), Harvard Univ. (M.A., 1956), and Princeton Univ. (M.F.A., 1958), numbering among his teachers Leonard Shure for piano and Elwell, Thad Jones, Sessions, and Babbitt for composition. He taught at Princeton Univ. (from 1958). From 1980 he produced various improvised performance pieces under the general name INTER/PLAY.

WORKS: *Slow Movement* for Piano (1959); *Improvisation on a Poem by e.e. cummings* for Soprano, Clarinet, Saxophone, Trumpet, Guitar, Piano or Soprano, and Piano (1960); *Pitch-derived Rhythm: 7 Demonstrations* for Flute, Clarinet, Piano, and 2 Cellos (1961–64); *Quartets in Pairs* for Computer (1964); *Mudgett: Monologues by a Mass Murderer* for Taped Violin and Computer (1965); *Lyric Variations* for Taped Violin and Computer (1968); *Quartersines* for Computer (1969); *Music for Eakins*, film score for Computer (1972); *...such words as it were vain to close...* for Piano (1974–76); *Troubador Songs* for Voice and Percussion (1977); *Meditation on Rossignol* for Piano (1978); *Soundscroll 2* for Piano (1978); *Greek Nickel I* and *II* for Piano (1979).—NS/LK/DM

Randegger, Alberto Jr., Italian violinist and composer, nephew of **Alberto Randegger Sr.;** b. Trieste, Aug. 3, 1880; d. Milan, Oct. 7, 1918. He accompanied his uncle to London and appeared as a violinist at an orch. concert conducted by the latter. After taking courses at the Royal Cons. of Music, he lived in Milan. He composed a short opera, *L'ombra di Werther* (Trieste, 1899), as well as a Violin Concerto, piano pieces, and songs.
—NS/LK/DM

Randegger, Alberto Sr., Italian conductor, organist, teacher, and composer, uncle of **Alberto Randegger Jr.;** b. Trieste, April 13, 1832; d. London, Dec. 18, 1911. He studied piano and composition in Italy. After working as a music director in Italian theaters, he settled in London (1854) and gained distinction as a conductor, singing teacher, and composer; was also organist at St. Paul's in Regent's Park (1854–70). He conducted at the Wolverhampton (from 1868) and Norwich (1881–1905) festivals, with the Carl Rosa Opera Co. (1879–85), at Drury Lane and Covent Garden (1887–98), and at the Queen's Hall (1895–97); was a prof. of singing at the Royal Academy of Music (from 1868) and later at the Royal Coll. of Music. He publ. the manual *Singing* (London, 1893). His compositions include the operas *Bianca Capello* (Brescia, 1854) and *The Rival Beauties* (Leeds, 1864), a dramatic cantata, *Fridolin* (1873), sacred music, and songs.—NS/LK/DM

Randle, Thomas, American tenor; b. Los Angeles, Dec. 21, 1958. He received vocal training in Los Angeles, and then pursued a career as a soloist with major orchs. in North America and Europe. In 1988 he made his operatic debut as Tamino with the English National Opera in London, and in 1989 he sang in *The Fairy Queen* at the Aix-en-Provence Festival. After appearing as Tamino at the Glyndebourne Festival in 1991, he returned to the English National Opera in 1992 to create the role of Dionysius in Buller's *Bakxai*. In 1994 he sang in the premiere of Schat's *Symposium* with the Nether-

lands Opera in Amsterdam. He was engaged as Idomeneo at the Scottish Opera in Glasgow in 1996. Throughout these years, he continued to appear frequently in concerts.—NS/LK/DM

Randolph, David, American conductor; b. N.Y., Dec. 21, 1914. He studied at City Coll., N.Y. (B.S., 1936) and Teachers Coll., Columbia Univ. (M.A., 1941). From 1943 to 1947 he was asst. director of music of the U.S. Office of War Information. In 1943 he organized the Randolph Singers, which he conducted until 1972. In 1955 he founded the Masterwork Chorus and Orch., which he conducted until 1992; also led the St. Cecilia Chorus and Orch. and, from 1981, the Masterwork Chamber Orch. He taught conducting at the Dalcroze School (1947–50); was a prof. of music at the State Univ. of N.Y. Coll. at New Paltz (1970–72), at Fordham Univ. (1972–73), and at Montclair State Coll. (from 1973). He was also active as a radio music commentator. He publ. the book *This Is Music* (N.Y., 1964), and also ed. The David Randolph Madrigal Series.—NS/LK/DM

Randolph, Irving "Mouse", trumpeter; b. St. Louis, Miss., June 22, 1909; d. N.Y., Dec. 10, 1997. His first professional work was with Fate Marable's Band; he then joined Norman Mason's Carolina Melodists. He was with drummer Floyd Campbell's Orch. (1928), then worked with Alphonse Trent and J, Frank Terry's Band before joining Andy Kirk from 1931–33. He played occasionally for Fletcher Henderson early in 1934, spell with Benny Carter, then became a regular member of Fletcher Henderson's Band from July 1934. Randolph joined Cab Calloway from spring 1935 until late 1939, when he joined Ella Fitzgerald. He played with Don Redman from May 1943, then with the Ed Hall Sextet throughout the late 1940s. He was with the Eddie Barefield Sextet (1950), after which he embarked on a long spell of touring with Marcelino Guerra's Latin American Orch. He played at the Savoy Ballroom with Bobby Medera's Band (1955). From 1958 through the early 1970s he was a regular member of Henry "Chick" Morrison's Orch. in N.Y., meanwhile taking part in freelance recordings, including sessions with Harry Dial's Bluesicians in 1961.—JC/LP

Randolph, Zilner T(renton), jazz trumpeter, arranger; b. Dermott, Ark., Jan. 28, 1899; d. Feb. 2, 1994. He studied at the Biddle Univ. in N.C.; he later spent several years studying music at the Kreuger Cons. in St. Louis and at the Wisc. Cons. in Milwaukee. He played with many bands in and around Milwaukee including almost four years with Bernie Young's Band at Wisc. Roof Ballroom. He moved to Chicago, and was musical director for Louis Armstrong from March 1931–March 1932, and again in 1933 and July–October 1935. He joined Carroll Dickerson and Dave Peyton in 1934. Randolph formed his own big band in Chicago (1936), and continued to lead it through the 1930s; he was also active as an arranger for Earl Hines, Woody Herman, Fletcher Henderson, Duke Ellington, Blanche Calloway, Ted Weems, and others. During the 1940s he led his own quartet in Gary, Ind., and Chicago. From 1949, he worked with his three children in a family musical act (one son was christened Louis Armstrong Randolph). He recorded on piano in 1951. During the 1970s he ran a teaching studio in Englewood, Ill.—JC/LP

Rands, Bernard, remarkable English-born American composer; b. Sheffield, March 2, 1934. He studied piano and organ at home. At the age of 18, he entered the Univ. of Wales in Bangor, majoring in music and English literature. He also developed a passion for Celtic lore; in his student days he became a sort of polyglot, delving into the linguistic mysteries of Welsh, Irish, and Scottish vocables, and on the way acquiring a fluency in French, Italian, and Spanish. He also immersed himself in the hypergrammatical and ultrasyntactic glossolalia of James Joyce. After graduating from the Univ. of Wales (B.Mus., 1956; M.Mus., 1958), he took lessons in musicology with Vlad in Rome and studied composition with Dallapiccola in Florence (1958–60). He also attended seminars in composition and conducting given by Boulez and Maderna at the Darmstadt summer courses in new music, and later consulted with Berio in Milan on problems of electronic music. He was on the faculty of the Univ. of York (1968–75), and then was engaged as a prof. of music at the Univ. of Calif. at San Diego, where he found the musical atmosphere particularly congenial to his innovative ideas. Rands was a visiting prof. at the Calif. Inst. of the Arts in Valencia in 1984–85 while retaining his San Diego post. In 1989 he became prof. of music at Harvard Univ., where he was the Walter Bigelow Rosen Prof. of Music from 1993. He also taught at the Juilliard School in N.Y. In 1982–83 he held a Guggenheim fellowship. In 1983 he became a naturalized American citizen. He was awarded the Pulitzer Prize in Music in 1984 for his *Canti del sole* for Tenor and Orch. From 1989 to 1996 he was composer-in-residence of the Philadelphia Orch. In 1994 he married **Augusta Read Thomas**.

The sources of Rand's music are astonishingly variegated, drawing upon religious, mystical, mathematical, and sonoristic premises. At one time he was preoccupied with Hinduism; these interests are reflected in his work *Aum*, a mantric word (*Om*) interpreted as having 3 sounds representing the triune stasis of Brahma, Vishnu, and Siva. Despite the complex nature of his compositions, he seems to encounter little resistance on the part of performers and audiences; his music possesses the rare quality of immediate communication. Several works reflect the scientific bent of his mind, as exemplified by *Formants*; there are mundane references in the titles of such works as *Memos* (2B and 2D) and *Agenda*; other sets contain references to sports, as in *Wildtrack*. Then there are in his catalog educational pieces, such as *Sound Patterns*, designed to be interpreted by children and professional performers alike. His *Canti lunatici* penetrate the inner recesses of the human mind in a state of turbulence.

WORKS: DRAMATIC: *Memo 2B* for Trombone and Female Dancer (1980); *Memo 2D* for Trombone, String Quartet, and Female Dancer (1980); *Belladonna*, opera (1999). **ORCH.:** *Per esempio* (1968); *Wildtrack 1* (1969) and *2* for Soprano and Orch. (1973); *Agenda* (1969–70); *Mesalliance* for Piano and Orch. (1972); *Aum* for Harp and Orch. (1974); *Madrigali*, after

Monteverdi/Berio (1977); *Le Tambourin*, 2 suites (both 1984); *Ceremonial 1* (1985), *2* (1986), and *3* (N.Y., March 18, 1991); *Requiescant* (1985–86); *Hiraeth* for Cello and Orch. (San Diego, Feb. 19, 1987); *...Body and Shadow...* (1988; Boston, Feb. 22, 1989); *London Serenade* (1988); *Tre canzone senza parole* (Philadelphia, April 22, 1992); *...Where the Murmurs Die...* (N.Y., Dec. 9, 1993); Sym. (Los Angeles, Feb. 24, 1994); *Canzoni* (1995); Cello Concerto No. 1 (1996); Triple Concerto for Piano, Cello, Percussion, and Orch. (1997). **INSTRUMENTAL ENSEMBLE:** *Actions for 6* for Flute, Harp, 2 Percussion, Viola, and Cello (1962–63); *Formants 2—Labyrinthe* for Clarinet, Trombone, Piano, 2 Percussion, Viola, and Cello (1969–70); *Tableau* for Flute, Clarinet, Piano, Percussion, Viola, and Cello (1970); *déjà* for Flute, Clarinet, Piano, Percussion, Viola, and Cello (1972); *"as all get out"* (1972); *Response—Memo 1B* for Double Bass and Tape or 2 Double Basses (1973); *Cuaderno* for String Quartet (1974); *étendre* (1974); *Scherzi* for Clarinet, Piano, Violin, and Cello (1974); *Serenata 75* (1976); *Obbligato—Memo 2C* for Trombone and String Quartet (1980); *Serenata 85* for Flute, Harp, Violin, Viola, and Cello (1986); *...in the receding mist...* for Flute, Harp, Violin, Viola, and Cello (1988); *Ceremonial* for Symphonic Wind Ensemble (1993); String Quartet No. 2 (1994); Concertino for Oboe and Ensemble (1996). **INSTRUMENTAL SOLO:** *Tre espressioni* for Piano (1960); *Formants 1—Les Gestes* for Harp (1965); *Memo 1* for Double Bass (1971), *2* for Trombone (1972), and *5* for Piano (1975). **VOICES AND INSTRUMENTS:** *Sound Patterns 1* for Voices and Hands (1967), *2* for Voices, Percussion, and Instruments (1967), and *3* for Voices (1969); *Ballad 1* for Mezzo-soprano and 5 Instruments (1970), *2* for Voice and Piano (1970), *3* for Soprano, Tape, and Bell (1973), and *4* for Voices and 20 Instruments (1980); *Canti lunatici* for Soprano and Orch. (1981); *Canti del sole* for Tenor and Orch. (1983–84); *Flickering Shadows* for Solo Voices and Instruments (1983–84); *...among the voices...* for Chorus and Harp (Cleveland, April 16, 1988); *Canti dell' Eclisse* for Bass and Orch. (1992); *Interludium* for Chorus and Orch. (1995); *Requiescant* for Soprano, Chorus, and Orch. (1996). —NS/LK/DM

Rangström, (Anders Johan) Ture, prominent Swedish conductor, music critic, and composer; b. Stockholm, Nov. 30, 1884; d. there, May 11, 1947. He studied counterpoint with Johan Lindegren in Stockholm (1903–04), then went to Berlin, where he took courses in singing with Hey and in composition with Pfitzner (1905–06); continued his vocal training with Hey in Munich (1906–08). He was a music critic for Stockholm's *Svenska Dagbladet* (1907–09), the *Stockholms Dagblad* (1910–14; 1927–30), and the *Nya Dagligt Allehanda* (1938–42). He was conductor of the Göteborg Sym. Orch. (1922–25), and thereafter made guest conducting appearances in Scandinavia. His music is permeated with a lyrical sentiment, and his forms are rhapsodic; in his syms. he achieved great intensity by concentrated development of the principal melodic and rhythmic ideas; his songs are also notable.

WORKS: DRAMATIC: Opera: *Kronbruden* (The Crown Bride; 1915–16; first perf. in German as *Die Kronbraut*, Stuttgart, Oct. 21, 1919; first perf. in Swedish, Göteborg, March 25, 1936); *Middelalderlig* or *Medeltida* (1917–18; Göteborg, May 11, 1921); *Gilgamesj* (1943–44; unfinished; completed and orchestrated by J. Fernström; Stockholm, Nov. 20, 1952). **ORCH.:** *Dityramb* (1909); *Ballad* for Piano and Orch. (1909; rev. 1937); *Ett midsommarstycke* (1910); *En höstrång* (1911); *Havet sjunger* (1913); 4 syms.: No. 1, *August Strindberg in memoriam* (1914; Berlin, Jan.

4, 1922), No. 2, *Mitt Land* (My Country; Stockholm, Nov. 20, 1919), No. 3, *Sång under stjärnorna* (Song under the Stars; 1912; Stockholm, Jan. 8, 1930), and No. 4, *Invocatio* (Göteborg, Nov. 20, 1936); *Intermezzo drammatico*, suite for Small Orch. (1916); *Divertimento elegiaco*, suite for Strings (1918); *Partita* for Violin and Orch. (1933); *Vauxhall*, miniature suite (1937); *På nordisk sträng*, prelude (1941); *Värhymn* (1942); *Festpreludium: Tempest, Youth, Poetry, and Song* (1944). **CHAMBER:** *Improvisata: Vårnätterna* for Violin and Piano (1904); *Ver sacrum* for Cello and Piano (1906–07); *String Quartet: Ein Nachtstück (Notturno) in E.T.A. Hoffmanns Manier* (1909); *Suite (No. 1) in modo antico* for Violin and Piano (1912) and *Suite No. 2 in modo barocco* for Violin and Piano (1921–22); piano pieces. **VOCAL:** Choral works; over 250 songs.

BIBL.: A. Helmer and S. Jacobsson, *T. R.: Life and Work* (Stockholm, 1987).—NS/LK/DM

Ránki, Dezső, Hungarian pianist; b. Budapest, Sept. 8, 1951. He studied piano with Klára Máthé at the Bartók Cons. (1964–69) and at the Franz Liszt Academy of Music with Pál Kadosa and Ferenc Rados (1969–73). In 1969 he won the International Schumann Competition in Zwickau, and from that time toured with notable success. His repertoire encompasses the classics and the moderns. He particularly excels in the works of Béla Bartók.—NS/LK/DM

Ránki, György, noted Hungarian composer; b. Budapest, Oct. 30, 1907; d. there, May 22, 1992. He studied composition with Kodály at the Budapest Academy of Music (1926–30) and ethnomusicology with Schaeffner in Paris (1938–39), and then devoted himself to composition. He won the Erkel (1952, 1957) and Kossuth (1954) prizes, and in 1963 was made a Merited Artist by the government; received the Bartók-Pásztory award (1987). He won distinction as a composer of both serious and popular works.

WORKS: DRAMATIC: *King Pomádé's New Clothes*, comic opera (1953–67); *The Tragedy of Man*, "mystery opera" (1970); *The Boatman of the Moon*, "opera-fantasy" (1979); *Terminal*, music drama (1988); also *3 Nights*, musical tragedy (1961), an operetta, much other theater music, and numerous film scores. **ORCH.:** *Aristophanes Suite* for Violin and String Orch. (1947–58); *Sword Dance* (1949); *Hungarian Dances from the 16th Century* (1950); *Don Quijote y Dulcinea*, 2 miniatures for Oboe and Small Orch. (1961); *Fantasy* for Piano and Orch., after woodcuts by Gyula Derkovits (1962); *Aurora tempestuosa*, prelude (1967); *Circus*, symphonic dance drama (1965); *Raga di notte* for Violin and Orch. (1974); 2 syms.: No. 1 (1977) and No. 2, *In Memoriam Zoltán Kodály* (1981); Concertino for Cimbalom, Xylophone, Timpani, Percussion, and String Quintet (1978); Viola Concerto (1979); *Divertimento* for Clarinet and Strings (1986). **CHAMBER:** *Serenata all'antiqua* for Violin and Piano (1956); *Pentaerophonia*, 3 pieces for Wind Quintet (1958); *Serenade of the 7- Headed Dragon* for Brass Septet (1980); String Quartet No. 1: *In Memoriam Béla Bartók* (1985); *The Tales of Father Goose*, musical joke for Brass Septet (1987); also piano pieces, including 3 sonatas (n.d., 1947, 1980). **VOCAL:** *1944*, oratorio for Baritone, Chorus, and Chamber Orch. (1967); *Cantus urbis* for 4 Soloists, Chorus, and Instrumental Ensemble (1972); *Leverkühn's Abschied*, monodrama for Tenor and 10 Instruments (1979); *Overture to the 21st Century* for Chorus and Orch. (1987); choruses; songs.
—NS/LK/DM

Rankin, Nell, American mezzo-soprano; b. Montgomery, Ala., Jan. 3, 1926. She studied voice with Jeanne Lorraine at the Birmingham Cons. of Music, then continued her training with Karin Branzell in N.Y. (1945–49). In 1949 she made her operatic debut as Ortrud in *Lohengrin* at the Zürich Opera, of which she later became an active member. In 1950–51 she sang at the Basel Opera, and in 1951 appeared at La Scala, Milan. In 1951 she won the Metropolitan Opera Auditions of the Air and made her debut with it in N.Y. on Nov. 22, 1951, as Amneris; she then sang at Covent Garden in London (1953–54) and at the San Francisco Opera (1955). Subsequently she appeared at the Teatro Colón in Buenos Aires, in Mexico, and in Europe. Her best roles were Carmen, Azucena, Ortrud, Santuzza, and Maddalena.—NS/LK/DM

Rankl, Karl, Austrian-born English conductor and composer; b. Gaaden, near Vienna, Oct. 1, 1898; d. Salzburg, Sept. 6, 1968. He was a pupil of Schoenberg and Webern in Vienna, and from both acquired a fine understanding of the problems of modern music. He occupied various positions as a chorus master and an opera coach in Vienna; served as assistant to Klemperer at the Kroll Opera in Berlin (1928–31), and then conducted opera in Graz (1932–37) and at the German Theater in Prague (1937–39). At the outbreak of World War II, he went to England and later became a naturalized subject; was music director at Covent Garden in London (1946–51), the Scottish National Orch. in Glasgow (1952–57), and the Elizabethan Opera Trust in Sydney (1958–60). He composed an opera, *Deirdre of the Sorrows* (1951), which won the Festival of Britain prize but was not perf.; also 8 syms.; an oratorio, *Der Mensch*; and many choral works.—NS/LK/DM

Ranta, Sulho, Finnish composer and writer on music; b. Peräseinäjoki, Aug. 15, 1901; d. Helsinki, May 5, 1960. He studied at the Univ. of Helsinki (M.A., 1925) and took courses in composition with Melartin at the Helsinki Cons. (1921–24), and later in Germany, France, and Italy. Returning to Finland, he taught at the Sibelius Academy in Helsinki (1934–56) and was also active as a music critic and theater conductor. He was ed. of a comprehensive biographical dictionary of Finnish composers, *Suomen Säveltäjiä* (Helsinki, 1945), and a general biographical survey of performers, *Sävelten Taitureita* (Helsinki, 1947). As a composer, he excelled in chamber music and songs.

WORKS: ORCH.: 4 syms.: No. 1, *Sinfonia programmatica* (1929–31), No. 2, *Sinfonia piccola* (1931–32), No. 3, *Sinfonia semplice* (1936), and No. 4, *Sinfonia dell'arte* (1947); *Tuntematon maa* (The Unknown Land) for Piano and Orch. (1930); 2 concertinos: No. 1 for Piano and Strings (1932) and No. 2 for Flute, Harp, Viola, and Strings (1934); *Kainuun kuvia* (Images boréales), suite (1933); *Concerto for Orchestra* (1938); *Kansansatu* (Folk Story), symphonic variations (1940). **CHAMBER:** Piano Trio (1923); *Suite symphonique* for Flute, Clarinet, Horn, String Quartet, and Piano (1926–28); Concertino for String Quartet (1935); piano pieces. **VOCAL:** *Sydärnen tie* (The Way of the Heart), cantata (1945–46); *Oratorio volgare* for Soloists, Chorus, and Orch. (1951); *Eksyneitten legioonalaisten rukous* (Prayer of the Lost Legionnaires) for 8 Soloists, Chorus, and Orch. (1956).
—NS/LK/DM

Raoul de Beavais, French trouvère poet and composer who flourished in the 13th century. A few of his chansons are extant.—LK/DM

Raoul de Ferrières, French trouvère who flourished in the early 13th century. He was a member of the Norman nobility. Several of his chansons are extant. —LK/DM

Raoul de Soissons, French trouvère; b. c. 1212; d. c. 1270. He was a son of Count Raoul le Bon of Soissons. In 1232 he became Sire de Coeuvres. He was active in the crusades, and married Queen Alix of Cyprus. He apparently died while in the retinue of the French king on the Second Crusade. A few of his chansons are extant.

BIBL.: E. Winkler, *Die Lieder R.s v S.s* (Halle, 1914). —LK/DM

Rapchak, Lawrence, American conductor and composer; b. Hammond, Ind., May 7, 1951. He studied piano in grade school and learned to read music in his youth. While still in high school, his debut as a composer was made with his *2 Short Pieces* for Orch. (Hammond, Ind., June 3, 1967). In 1969 he entered the Cleveland Inst. of Music, where he studied composition with Marcel Dick and Donald Erb. He also received training in conducting from James Levine. From 1988 to 1993 he was music director of the Chamber Opera of Chicago. In 1995 he became music director of the Chicago Opera Theater. His compositions emphasize contrasting colors with markedly propulsive rhythms with a preference for dividing the orch. into smaller instrumental groupings.

WORKS: DRAMATIC: *The Lifework of Juan Diaz,* chamber opera after Ray Bradbury (Chicago, April 21, 1990, composer conducting). **ORCH.:** *Poem* for Oboe Ensemble (Cleveland, Dec. 15, 1980); *Bifrost* for Cello and Orch. (1981); *Mesazoa* (1985); *La Siesta* (1987); *Mystic Promenade* (St. Louis, Oct. 7, 1987); *Il Concerto Vetrina* for Bass Clarinet and Small Orch. (1988); Violin Concerto (1988); *Chasing the Sunset* (N.Y., March 12, 1989); *Sinfonia Antiqua* (1990; Detroit, Feb. 7, 1991); Concerto for Oboe, English Horn, and Orch. (1991); *Serenata Gioconda* for Saxophone Quartet and Orch. (Long Island, Nov. 7, 1992); *Orloj* (Omaha, Sept. 30, 1993); *Aubade* (1994); *Saetas* (1996; Chicago, Feb. 13, 1997). **CHAMBER:** *Troika* for 11 Instruments (1994; Chicago, Jan. 8, 1995); *Moa* for 6 Instruments (1998). —NS/LK/DM

Rapee, Erno, Hungarian-American conductor, arranger, and composer; b. Budapest, June 4, 1891; d. N.Y., June 26, 1945. He studied at the National Cons. in Budapest (graduated, 1909). After conducting opera in Dresden and Katowice, he toured Mexico and South America as a pianist. In 1912 he settled in N.Y. as conductor of the Hungarian Opera Co. From 1917 he conducted for various film theaters, becoming closely associated with the Roxy (S. L. Rothafel) enterprises. He also was active as an arranger and composer for silent and then sound films. From 1927 he conducted at the new Roxy Theater, where he led weekly radio broadcasts of symphonic music. After a sojourn in Hollywood (1930–31), he returned to N.Y. as music director for NBC. He was music director at Radio City Music Hall from 1932, where he led numerous radio broadcasts. —NS/LK/DM

Rapf, Kurt, Austrian composer; b. Vienna, Feb. 15, 1922. He studied piano, organ, and composition at the Vienna Academy of Music (1936–42). He was founder-conductor of the chamber music ensemble Collegium Musicum Wien (1945–56) and city music director in Innsbruck (1953–60). He was president of the Austrian Composers' Union (1970–83).

WORKS: ORCH.: *Aphorismen* (1968); Violin Concerto (1971); 3 concertos for Chamber Orch.: No. 1, *Imaginations* (1971), No. 2, *Contrasts* (1972), and No. 3, *Remembrances* (1978); Piano Concerto (1973); *Concerto per viaggio* for Chamber Orch. (1975); *4 Orchestral Pieces* (1975); 2 syms. (1976, 1981); Concerto for Violin, Cello, and Orch. (1976); Organ Concerto (1977–84); *Leanda,* fantasy-overture (1979); Concerto for Organ and Strings (1979); *Concerto estivo* (1982); Concerto for Violin, Piano, and Orch. (1982); *Concerto for Orchestra* (1984). **CHAMBER:** 6 *Pieces* for Wind Quintet (1963); *4 Impressions* for 9 Players (1966); Quintet for Harp and 4 Wind Instruments (1968); *Toccata, Adagio, and Finale* for Organ (1972); *3 Episodes* for Cello (1981–84); piano pieces. **VOCAL:** *Wiener Veduten,* 11 songs for Tenor and Orch. (1972); *Passio aeterna,* oratorio (1979). —NS/LK/DM

Raphael, Günter (Albert Rudolf), German composer; b. Berlin, April 30, 1903; d. Herford, Oct. 19, 1960. His father, Georg Raphael, was music director of Berlin's St. Matthäi. He studied with Max Trapp (piano), Walter Fischer (organ), and Robert Kahn (composition) at the Berlin Hochschule für Musik (1922–25). He taught theory and composition at the Leipzig Cons. and at the Kirchenmusikalisches Institut (1926–34); after his works were banned by the Nazis, he lived in Meiningen and then in Sweden. Following the collapse of the 3rd Reich, he taught in Laubach (1945–48); taught theory and composition at the Duisburg Cons. (1949–53); was on the faculty of the Mainz Cons. (1956–58); served as prof. at the Cologne Hochschule für Musik (1957–60). His early works followed in the German Romantic tradition, but he later adopted a more contemporary idiom with excursions into serialism.

WORKS: ORCH.: 5 syms. (1926; 1932; 1942; 1942–47; 1953); *Theme, Variations, and Rondo* (1927); 2 violin concertos (1929, 1960); *Variations on a Scottish Folktune* (1930); Chamber Concerto for Violin and Chamber Orch. (1930); *Divertimento* (1932); Organ Concerto (1936); *Smetana Suite,* after Smetana's dances (1938); *Sinfonietta* (1938); *Symphonische Fantasie* for Violin and Strings (1940); *Jabonah,* ballet suite (1948); *Reger Suite* (1948); *Sinfonia breve* (1949); Concertino for Alto Saxophone and Chamber Orch. (1951); *Die vier Jahreszeiten* for Strings (1953); *Zoologica* (1958). **CHAMBER:** 2 clarinet quintets (1924); trios for Piano, Violin, and Cello (1925), Flute, Cello, and Piano (1938), Flute, Violin, and Viola (1940), 2 Violins and Viola (1941), and Clarinet, Cello, and Piano (1950); sonatas for Viola and Piano (1925, 1926), Flute and Piano (1925), Violin and Piano (1926, 1968), Cello and Piano (1926), Oboe and Piano (1933), and Violin and Organ (1934); 4 string quartets (1926, 1926, 1930, 1945); String Quintet (1927); 9 sonatas for Solo Instruments (1940–46); 6 duo sonatas for Various Instruments (1940–46);

Woodwind Quintet (1945); piano pieces; organ music. **VO-CAL:** Much choral music, including a cantata (1926), *Requiem* (1927–28), *Te Deum* (1930), *Busskantate* (1952), *Judica Kantate* (1955), and motets.

BIBL.: T. Schinköth, *Musik—das Ende aller Illusionen?: G. R. im NS-Staat* (Hamburg, 1996).—NS/LK/DM

Rappold, Marie (née **Winterroth**), English soprano; b. London, c. 1873; d. Los Angeles, May 12, 1957. The family moved to America when she was a child. She studied with Oscar Saenger in N.Y., making her Metropolitan Opera debut there as Sulamith in *Die Königen von Saba* (Nov. 22, 1905). She remained on its roster until 1909, and then went to Europe. She was married to Dr. Julius Rappold, but divorced him and married **Rudolf Berger** in 1913. She had another period of singing at the Metropolitan Opera (1910–20) and later appeared in Chicago (1927–28). She then settled in Los Angeles as a teacher.—NS/LK/DM

Rappoldi, Eduard, Austrian violinist, teacher, and composer; b. Vienna, Feb. 21, 1831; d. Dresden, May 16, 1903. He studied at the Vienna Cons., then played violin in opera orchs. in Vienna, Rotterdam, Lübeck, and Prague. He was second violinist in the Joachim Quartet in Berlin (1871–77) and then concertmaster of the Court Opera in Dresden (1878–98). From 1893 until his death, he was a prof. of violin at the Dresden Cons. He publ. chamber music, piano pieces, and songs. His wife, Laura (née Kahrer) Rappoldi (b. Mistelbach, near Vienna, Jan. 14, 1853; d. Dresden, Aug. 2, 1925), was a pianist and teacher who began her studies when she was 10. She then was a pupil of Dessoff (composition), Bruckner (counterpoint), and J. Dachs (piano) at the Vienna Cons. (1866–69), and later studied with Liszt in Weimar (1870, 1873), with A. Henselt in St. Petersburg (1870–73), and with Bülow (1874). She was active in Dresden (from 1887), teaching at the Cons. (1890–1910). Their son, Adrian Rappoldi (b. Berlin, Sept. 13, 1876; d. Bamberg, Oct. 12, 1948), was a violinist.—NS/LK/DM

Rascarini, Francesco Maria, Italian alto castrato and composer; b. Reggio Emilia, date unknown; d. Turin, July 1706. He appeared in opera in Bologna in 1658 and in Venice in 1659. From 1662 to 1691 he was in the service of the Duke of Savoy. He also sang in opera again in Venice in 1666, and then in Milan in 1670 and in Piacenza and Parma in 1677. In 1697 he reentered the service of the Duke of Savoy.—LK/DM

Rascher, Sigurd (Manfred), German-born American saxophonist; b. Elberfeld, May 15, 1907. He studied at the Stuttgart Cons., and became proficient on the saxophone. In 1939 he went to the U.S., where he developed a fine concert career. He founded the Rascher Saxophone Quartet (1969), which commissioned numerous works for his instrument, including pieces by Glazunov, Ibert, Martin, Milhaud, and Hindemith. —NS/LK/DM

Raselius (Raesel), Andreas, eminent German music theorist and composer; b. Hahnbach, near Am-berg, Upper Palatinate, c. 1563; d. Heidelberg, Jan. 6, 1602. He was the son of a Lutheran preacher, and studied at the Univ. of Heidelberg (M.A., 1584). After teaching at the Heidelberg Academy (1583–84), he was compelled for religious reasons to leave the city and went to Regensburg as asst. master and Kantor at the Gymnasium Poeticum. He then returned to Heidelberg as Hofkapellmeister to the Elector Palatine Friedrich IV (1600). Raselius greatly distinguished himself as a music theorist and composer.

WORKS: *Cantionale* (1587–88); *Psalmen und geistliche Lieder* for 5 Voices (1591); *Teutscher Sprüche auss den sontäglichen Evangeliis durchs gantze Jar* for 5 Voices (Nuremberg, 1594); *Erercitationes musicae...et aliae cantiones* for 4 to 6 and 8 Voices, *festivitatibus nuptialibus amicorum* (1594); *Teutscher Sprüche auff die fürnemsten järlichen Fest und Aposteltage...* for 5, 6, and 8 to 9 Voices, *auff die 12 modos dodecachordi* (Nuremberg, 1598); *Regenspurgischer Kirchenkontrapunkt, allerley...geistlichen Psalmen und Lieder, D. M. Lutheri...also gesetzt, dass jedermann...ungehindert wol mit singen kann* for 5 Voices (Regensburg, 1599); *Cantica sacro pro nova paochia: geistliche Psalmen und Lieder* for 5 Voices (1599); *Lateinische und deutsche Lieder* (1605).

WRITINGS: *Dodechachordi vivi, in quo 12 modorum musicorum exempla duodena* for 4 to 6 Voices (1589); *Hexachordum seu Questiones musicae practicae...in welcehm viva exempla Dodechachordi Glareani in utraque scala gefunden werden* (Nuremberg, 1591).

BIBL.: J. Auer, *M.A. R.* (Leipzig, 1892); L. Roselius, *A. R. als Motettenkomponist* (Berlin, 1924).—NS/LK/DM

Rasi, Francesco, Italian tenor and composer; b. Arezzo, May 14, 1574; d. Mantua, Dec. 9(?), 1621. He was born into the nobility. He received training from Caccini, and appeared as a singer and chitarrone player in his youth at the court in Florence. After winning success in Rome in 1593, he toured throughout Italy with Gesualdo and accompanied the Bishop of Caserta to Poland. In 1598 he entered the service of the Gonzaga family in Mantua, whom he accompanied on their travels in Europe. He sang Amyntas in Peri's *Euridice* and appeared in Caccini's *Il rapimento di Cefalo* in Florence in 1600. In 1607 he created Monteverdi's Orfeo in Mantua. He portrayed Apollo in M. da Gagliano's *Dafne* in Mantua in 1608. After being implicated in a murder in 1610, he was banned from Tuscany until 1620. During the interim, he sang in various north Italian courts. He composed an opera, *Cibele, ed Ati* (1617; music not extant), a dramatic work, *Elvidia rapita* (c. 1618; music not extant), Latin motets, and songs, and also publ. 2 vols. of monodies (Venice, 1608; Florence, 1610).—LK/DM

Raskin, Judith, noted American soprano; b. N.Y., June 21, 1928; d. there, Dec. 21, 1984. She studied at Smith Coll., graduating in 1949, and took private voice lessons with Anna Hamlin in N.Y. Her stage career received an impetus on July 7, 1956, when she sang the title role in Douglas Moore's folk opera *The Ballad of Baby Doe*, premiered in Central City, Colo. In 1957 she became a member of the NBC-TV Opera; in 1959, joined the N.Y.C. Opera. She made her Metropolitan Opera debut in N.Y. on Feb. 23, 1962, as Susanna in *Le nozze di*

Figaro; sang there until 1972. She taught at the Manhattan School of Music and the 92nd Street "Y" School of Music in N.Y. from 1975 and also at the Mannes Coll. of Music there from 1976.—NS/LK/DM

Rasmussen, Karl Aage, Danish composer, conductor, and teacher; b. Kolding, Dec. 13, 1947. He took courses in music history, theory, and composition at the Århus Cons. (graduated, 1971), where his principal mentors were Nrgård and Gudmundsen-Holmgreen. He taught at the Funen Cons. (1970–72). In 1971 he joined the faculty of the Århus Cons. as a lecturer, becoming a docent in 1979 and a prof. in 1988. He also was a docent at the Royal Danish Cons. of Music in Copenhagen (1980–82). From 1973 to 1988 he was active with the Danish Radio. In 1975 he founded a chamber ensemble, the Elsinore Players, and in 1978 the NUMUS Festival, serving as its artistic director until 1985 and again from 1987 to 1990. In 1986 he founded the Danish Piano Theater. From 1987 to 1990 he was chairman of the Danish Arts Foundation. In addition to monographs on composers, he wrote much music criticism and contributed articles on music history to periodicals in his homeland and abroad. His music follows the cosmopolitan trends of pragmatic hedonism within neo-Classical formal structures.

WORKS: DRAMATIC: *Crapp's Last Tape*, opera (1967); *Jephta*, opera (1977); *Majakovskij*, scenic concert piece (1978); *The Story of Jonah*, musical radio play (1981); *Our Hoffmann*, musical play (1986); *The Sinking of the Titanic*, opera (1993; Jutland, May 4, 1994). **ORCH.:** *Symphony for Young Lovers* (1966); *Recapitulations* (1967); *Symphonie classique* (1968); *Anfang und Ende*, sym. (1972; Århus, Feb. 11, 1976); *Contrafactum* for Cello and Orch. (1979); *A Symphony in Time* (1982); *Movements on a Moving Line* (1987); *Sinking Through the Dream- Mirror*, concerto for Violin and 13 Instruments (1993); *3 Friends* (1994–95); *Scherzo with Bells* (1996); *The Lion, the Mouse, the Big Elephant, and Jens Pismyre* for Actor and Orch. (1997); Double Concerto for Harp, Guitar, and Orch. (1998); *Invisible Mirrors* for Guitar and 13 Instruments (1999). **CHAMBER:** *Protocol and Myth* for Accordion, Electric Guitar, and Percussion (1971); *Genklang* (Echo) for 3 Pianos (1 prepared, 1 mistuned) and Celesta (1972); *A Ballad of Game and Dream* for Chamber Ensemble (1974); *Berio Mask* for Chamber Ensemble (1977); *Encore: I (Lonesome)* for Guitar (1977), *II (Join)* for Guitar (1985), *III (Encore for Frances)* for Cello (1982), *IV (Match)* for Cello and Piano (1983), *V (Ich, nur...)* for Voice (1983), *VI (Chains)* for Clarinet (1983–85), *VII (Strain)* for Piano (1984), *VIII (Fugue)* for Clarinet, Vibraphone, and Piano (1983–84), and *IX (Beat)* for Silenced Percussion (1985); *Italian Concerto* for Chamber Ensemble (1981); *A Quartet of 5* for 2 Trumpets, Horn, and 2 Trombones (1982); *Solos and Shadows* for String Quartet (1983); *Surrounded by Scales* for String Quartet (Lerchenborg, Aug. 4, 1985); *Still* for String Quartet (1989); *Continuo* for Flute and Guitar (1991); *Trauergondol* for Violin, Cello, and Piano (1998). **KEYBOARD: Piano:** *Paganini Variations* (1976); *Fugue* (1984); *Encore VII (Strain)* (1984); *13 Etudes and Postludes* (1990); *Contrary Dances* (1992); *Barcarole* (1996). **Organ:** *Antiphony* (1973); *Chorus* (1985). **VOCAL:** *This Moment* for 3 Sopranos, Flute, and Percussion (1966); *Love Is in the World* for Voice, Guitar, and Percussion (1974–75); *Liederkreis* for Soprano, Tenor or Baritone, Flute, Clarinet, Vibraphone, and Piano (1986).—**NS/LK/DM**

Raspberries, 1970s-era Midwest anglophile rock band. **MEMBERSHIP:** Eric Carmen, kybd., gtr., voc. (b. Cleveland, Ohio, Aug. 11, 1949); Wally Bryson, gtr. (b. Gastonia, N.C., July 18, 1949); Jim Bonfanti, drm. (b. Windber, Pa., Dec. 17, 1948); Dave Smalley, gtr., bs. (b. Oil City, Pa., July 10, 1949); Scott McCarl, bs.; Michael McBride, drm. Formed from parts of some of the most popular Midwestern bands of the late 1960s—including unsuccessful recording acts Cyrus Erie and The Choir—the Raspberries were one of the most eclectic pop bands of the early 1970s. Their songs ran from the gentle anglophila of "Go All the Way" to the raucous "I Wanna Be with You," but never seemed to find a center.

Eric Carmen was a minor classical piano prodigy who started playing Beatles songs to attract girls. He joined the group Cyrus Erie, one of several incestuous bands out of the Cleveland area that exchanged personnel on a regular basis and engaged in friendly rivalry. While between bands after the dissolution of Cyrus Erie, Carmen wrote commercials and did some writing and session work for MOR star Oliver ("Good Morning Starshine"). He and drummer Jim Bonfanti (formerly a member of a competing band, The Choir) shared a dislike for the loose psychedelic jams encroaching on their more lyrical sound. They started to gather other high-visibility people from the Cleveland scene to put together the Midwest's answer to The Beatles. They completed the group with guitarist Wally Bryson and bassist Dave Smalley. Jimmy Ienner—a former vocalist turned record producer—took the group under his wing, pitching them to The Beatles' label, Capitol, in 1971. While the group's first single, the treacly "Don't Want to Say Goodbye," only reached the lower part of the chart, their second single, "Go All the Way" went to #5, striking gold. Their self-titled debut album featured a scratch-and-sniff raspberry on the cover.

The band was back with its second album, *Fresh*, within months of the debut. The rocking "I Wanna Be with You" hit #16. They followed it almost five months later with "Let's Pretend," which rose to #35. The album rose to #30. They went on tour, first with The Hollies, then headlining, playing all across America and Europe. Because their two singles were so radically different, radio had begun to think of them as "too slippery to slot." In the meantime, several members of the group felt they were playing "bubblegum" music instead of rock. After the release of their least successful record (on every level) *Side 3*, the internal strife caused Bonfanti and Smalley to leave the group. Bassist Scott McCarl, a long-time fan, joined on guitar and Mike McBride took over the drumming chores. For a while, it became unclear which pair of the original group members would retain the rights to the Raspberries name, but Bryman and Carmen prevailed and the fourth Raspberries album, *Starting Over*, was released in the spring of 1974. The album spawned the hit single "Overnight Sensation (Hit Record)" which rose to #18. By this time, however, Bryson and Carmen had had it with each other and disbanded the group in 1975.

Eric Carmen signed with Arista as a solo artist. His debut featured the overwrought ballad "All by Myself," which harked back to his classical training (it was loosely based on Rachmaninov's *Piano Concerto #2*). It went to #2 pop in 1977, topping the adult charts and going gold. He followed this with another Rachmaninov-based song, "Never Gonna Fall in Love Again," based loosely on the *Second Symphony*. It rose to #11, once again topping the adult chart. "Sunrise" peaked at #34 and the album sold gold, hitting #21. The first single from *Boats Against the Current*, "She Did It," rose to #23. A series of lackluster singles and albums followed, including the disco-ish *Change of Heart* (#19, 1978), leading critic Dave Marsh to lament: "Eric Carmen, a great rocker in the Raspberries, under [Arista President Clive] Davis's tutelage became a bathetic ruffled shirt."

After an absence of seven years, Carmen signed with Geffen in 1985, taking his first single "I Wanna Hear It from Your Lips" to #35. Several years later, Carmen appeared on the soundtrack to *Dirty Dancing* with the song "Hungry Eyes," which rose to #4. Arista released a hits package, for which Carmen recorded the new track "Let Me Lose Control"; it topped the adult-contemporary chart, rising to #3. Meanwhile, early in the 1980s, Wally Bryson joined with ex-Rascals Gene Cornish and Dino Danelli in the band Fotomaker. The band was short-lived, producing three less-than-memorable albums.

While the Raspberries hits (and some misses) were thoroughly anthologized over the course of the 1990s, the musicians themselves effectively dropped off the radar. In 1997, Celine Dion took "All by Myself" back to #5.

DISC.: *Raspberries* (1972); *Fresh* (1972); *Side Three* (1973); *Starting Over* (1974). **ERIC CARMEN:** *Eric Carmen* (1975); *Boats Against the Current* (1977); *All by Myself* (1977); *Change of Heart* (1978); *Tonight You're Mine* (1980); *The Best of Eric Carmen* (1988); *The Definitive Collection* (1997); *Winter Dreams* (1998); *Someone That You Loved Before* (1998); *I Was Born to Love You* (2000). **FOTOMAKER:** *Fotomaker* (1978); *Vis a Vis* (1978); *Transfer Station* (1979).—**HB**

Rasse, François (Adolphe Jean Jules), Belgian violinist, conductor, teacher, and composer; b. Helchin, Jan. 27, 1873; d. Brussels, Jan. 4, 1955. He studied violin with Ysaÿe at the Brussels Cons., winning the Belgian Grand Prix de Rome in 1899. From 1925 to 1938 he was director of the Liège Cons.

WORKS: DRAMATIC: Opera: *Déidamia* (1905); *Soeur Béatrice* (1938). **Ballet:** *Le maître à danser* (1908). **ORCH.:** *Symphonie romantique* (1901); *Symphonie mélodique* (1903); Violin Concerto (1906); *Symphonie rythmique* (1908); 3 tone poems: *Douleur* (1911), *Joie* (1925), and *Aspiration* (1946); *La Dryade* for Clarinet and Orch. (1943); *Lamento* for Cello and Orch. (1952). **CHAMBER:** 3 piano trios (1897, 1911, 1951); 2 string quartets (1906, 1950); Piano Quintet (1914); Piano Quartet (1941); piano pieces. **VOCAL:** Choral music; song cycles. —**NS/LK/DM**

Rastrelli, Joseph, Italian conductor and composer, son of **Vincenzo Rastrelli;** b. Dresden, April 13, 1799; d. there, Nov. 15, 1842. He began his training with his father, and appeared in public as a violinist in Moscow in 1805. After further studies in Dresden with Fiedler,

his father took him to Italy in 1814, where he received training in counterpoint in Bologna from Padre Mattei. He returned to Dresden in 1817 and scored his first success as a composer with his opera *La schiava circassa*, which was premiered at the Court Theater on Feb. 26, 1820. In 1820 he entered the court service as a violinist. He was made deputy music director of the Court Theater in 1829, and in 1830 he was named royal maestro di cappella, sharing his duties with Morlacchi and Reissiger.

WORKS: DRAMATIC (all first perf. in Dresden unless otherwise given): *La distruzione di Gerusalemme* (Ancona, 1816); *La schiava circassa, ossia Imene e Virtù* (Feb. 26, 1820); *Le donne curiose* (April 14, 1821); *Velleda, ossia Il paladino mutolo* (Jan. 15, 1823); *Amina, ovvero L'innocenza perseguitata* (Milan, March 16, 1824); *Salvator Rosa, oder Zwey Nächte in Rom* (July 22, 1832); *Bertha von Bretagne* (Sept. 12, 1835); *Die Neuvermählten* (March 10, 1839); *Il trionfo di Nabucco il Grande, ossia Punizione di Sedacia* (n.d.). **OTHER:** Viola Concerto; sacred music; choruses; songs.—**LK/DM**

Rastrelli, Vincenzo, Italian composer, father of **Joseph Rastrelli;** b. Fano, near Pesaro, 1760; d. Dresden, March 20, 1839. He studied in Fano, and then with Padre Mattei in Bologna, where he was elected to membership in the Società Filarmonica in 1786. After serving as maestro di cappella at Fano Cathedral and maestro al cembalo at Pesaro's Teatro del Sole, he was composer to the court church in Dresden from 1796 to 1802. Following a sojourn in Moscow (1802–06) and Italy (1806–07), he again held his Dresden position (1807–14; 1824–31), where he also was a singing teacher to the royal family (1814–24). In addition to his many sacred works, he also composed an oratorio, *Tobia*, and a Harpsichord Concerto.—**NS/LK/DM**

Rathaus, Karol, Polish-born American pedagogue and composer; b. Tarnopol, Sept. 16, 1895; d. N.Y., Nov. 21, 1954. He studied at the Vienna Academy of Music and the Univ. of Vienna (Ph.D., 1922) and in Berlin (1920–21; 1922–23). In 1932 he went to Paris, and in 1934 to London. In 1938 he settled in the U.S., becoming a naturalized American citizen in 1946. After a brief stay in Hollywood in 1939, during which he wrote some film scores, he settled in N.Y.; in 1940 he was appointed to the faculty of Queens Coll. He was highly respected as a teacher of composition. His own music, however, never attracted large audiences; always noble in purpose and design and masterly in technique, it reveals a profound feeling for European neo-Romanticism. In 1952 he rev. and ed. the orch. score to Mussorgsky's *Boris Godunov* on a commission from the Metropolitan Opera, which gave the new version on March 6, 1953.

WORKS: DRAMATIC: Opera: *Fremde Erde* (Berlin, Dec. 10, 1930; also as a symphonic interlude, 1950). **Ballet:** *Der letzte Pierrot* (1926; Berlin, May 7, 1927); *Le Lion amoureux* (1937). **Incidental Music:** *Uriel Acosta* (1930; orch. suite, 1933; rev. 1947). **Film:** 17 scores, including *The Brothers Karamazov* (1931), *The Dictator* (1934), *Dame de pique* (1937), *Let Us Live* (1939), and *Out of Evil* (1950). **ORCH.:** 3 syms. (1921–22; 1923; 1942–43); *4 Dance Pieces* (1924); Piano Concertino (1925); *Overture* (1927); Suite for Violin and Chamber Orch. or Piano (1929); Suite (Liège, Sept. 6, 1930); *Allegro concertante* for Strings and Trumpet obbligato (1930); *Serenade* (1932); *Symphonic Movement* (1933); *Contrapuntal Triptych* (1934); *Jacob's Dream*, nocturne (1938); Piano Concerto (1939; Berkeley, Calif., Aug. 1, 1942); *Prelude and Gigue* (1939); *Music for Strings* (1941); *Polonaise symphonique* (1943; N.Y., Feb. 26, 1944); *Vision dramatique* (1945; Tel Aviv, April 4, 1948); *Salisbury Cove Overture* (1949); *Sinfonia concertante* (1950–51); *Intermezzo giocoso* for Woodwinds, Brass, and Percussion (1950–51); *Prelude* (1953; Louisville, June 5, 1954). C H A M B E R : 5 string quartets (1921, 1925, 1936, 1946, 1954); 2 violin sonatas (1924, 1938); Clarinet Sonata (1927); *Little Serenade* for Clarinet, Bassoon, Trumpet, Horn, and Piano (1927); Trio for Violin, Clarinet, and Piano (1944); Piano Quintet (1948; unfinished); *Dedication and Allegro* for Violin and Piano (1949); *Rapsodia notturna* for Viola or Cello and Piano (1950); *Trio Serenade* for Piano Trio (1953); *Divertimento* for 10 Woodwinds (1954; unfinished). K E Y B O A R D : P i a n o : Numerous pieces, including 4 sonatas (1920; 1920–24, rev. 1928; 1927; 1946). O r g a n : *Prelude and Toccata* (1933). VOCAL: *Song without Words* and *Fugue*, both for Chorus and Chamber Orch. (1928); *3 Calderon Songs* for Low Voice and Orch. or Piano (1931); *XXIII Psalm* for Tenor, Women's Chorus, and Orch. or Piano (1945); *O Juvenes*, academic cantata (1947); *Lament from "Iphigenia in Aulis" by Euripides* for Chorus and Horn (1947); *Diapason* for Baritone, Chorus, and Orch., after Dryden and Milton (1950); choruses; songs. —NS/LK/DM

Rathburn, Eldon (Davis), Canadian composer; b. Queenstown, New Brunswick, April 21, 1916. He studied composition with Willan, organ with Peaker, and piano with Godden at the Toronto Cons. of Music (1938–39). From 1947 to 1976 he served as staff composer for the National Film Board; also taught film composition at the Univ. of Ottawa (1972–76). Among his film scores for documentaries are *The Romance of Transportation* (1952), *City of Gold* (1957), and *Labyrinth* (1967).

WORKS: O R C H . : *Symphonette* (1943; rev. 1946); *2 Cartoons* (1944, 1946); *Images of Childhood* (1949–50); *Overture to a Hoss Opera* (1952); *Nocturne* for Piano and Small Orch. (1953); *Overture burlesca* (1953); *Milk Maid Polka* (1956); *Gray City* (1960); *City of Gold*, suite from music to the film (1967); *Aspects of Railroads* (1969); *3 Ironies* for Solo Brass Quintet and Orch. (Hamilton, Ontario, Oct. 15, 1975); *Steelhenge*, Steel Band concerto (1975); *The Train to Mariposa* (1986). C H A M B E R : *5 Short Pieces* for differing combinations of Winds, each piece having a separate title (1949–56); *In 3 Rounds* for Guitar and Double Bass (1971); *The Metamorphic 10* for Accordion, Mandolin, Banjo, Guitar, Double Bass, Harp, Piano, Celesta, and 3 Percussionists (1971); *2 Interplays* for Saxophone Quartet (1972); *Rhythmette* for 2 Pianos and Rhythm Band (1973); *The Nomadic 5*, brass quintet (1974); *Turbo* for Brass Quintet (1978); *The Rise and the Fall of the Steam Railroad* for Chamber Ensemble (1983); *Dorion Crossing*, trio for Clarinet, Cello, and Piano (1987); *2 Railoramas* for Woodwind Quintet (1990). P i a n o : *Silhouette* for 2 Pianos (1936); *Black and White* (1970); *The Iron Horses of Delson* (1980); *6 Railroad Preludes* (1987).—NS/LK/DM

Rathgeber, Johann Valentin, German composer; b. Oberelsbach, near Fulda, April 3, 1682; d. Banz, near Coburg, June 2, 1750. He studied with his father, the village organist and schoolmaster, and then pursued theological training at the Univ. of Würzburg. In 1704 he

became organist and schoolmaster at the Juliusspital in Würzburg. In 1707 he entered the Benedictine abbey in Banz. Following his ordination in 1711, he served as its choirmaster for the rest of his life. He was particularly known as a composer of sacred music, which included many Latin mass settings, Vesper psalms, offertories, and other works (20 vols., Augsburg, 1721–39). Among his other works were 24 concerti grossi (1728) and various keyboard pieces (1743). He also ed. and arranged the well-known collection of popular song settings *Ohrenvergnügendes und Gemüth-ergötzendes Tafel-Confect* (3 vols., 1733, 1737, 1746).—LK/DM

Raţiu, Adrian, Romanian composer and musicologist; b. Bucharest, July 28, 1928. He studied at the Bucharest Cons. (1950–56) with Constantinescu (harmony), Negrea (counterpoint), Rogalski (orchestration), and Klepper (composition), and later attended the summer courses in new music in Darmstadt (1969). In 1962 he became a prof. at the Bucharest Cons. From 1968 he also was a member of the executive committee of the Union of Composers and Musicologists in Romania. His various writings on music appeared in many publications. Among his honors were composition prizes of the Union of Composers and Musicologists (1967, 1972, 1973, 1981, 1990, 1993) and the Enesco Prize of the Romanian Academy (1974). In his music, Raţiu combines accessible atonal writing with euphonious dissonance.

WORKS: O R C H . : 2 syms.: No. 1 (1961; Timişoara, Oct. 13, 1962) and No. 2 (1976–77; Timişoara, May 12, 1977); Concerto for Oboe, Bassoon, and Orch. (1962–63; Bucharest, Nov. 27, 1969); *Diptych* (1965; Timişoara, Dec. 10, 1966); *Studi* for Strings (1968; Bucharest, Dec. 15, 1986); *6 Images* (1971; Craiova, Oct. 19, 1974); Piano Concerto (1988; Bucharest, May 30, 1993). C H A M B E R : 2 string quartets (1956; *Convergences II*, 1988); *Noctural Vision* for Viola and Piano (1964); *Partita* for Wind Quintet (1966); *Impressions* for Chamber Ensemble (1969); *Transfigurations*, quintet for Piano, Clarinet, Violin, Viola, and Cello (1974–75); Trio for Flute, Oboe, and Clarinet (1979–80); *Sonata a cinque* for Brass Quintet (1984); Sonata for Solo Violin (1985); *Alternations* for Clarinet and Bass Clarinet (1986); Trio for Piano, Clarinet, and Guitar or Vibraphone (1987); *Echoes* for Vibraphone and Marimba (1989); *Convergences III* for Flute, Oboe, and Bassoon (1991) and *IV* for Piano, Clarinet or Saxophone, and Percussion (1994); Violin Sonata (1991); piano pieces. VOCAL: *3 Madrigals* for Chorus, after Shakespeare (1964); *Fragment of a Triumphal Arch for Beethoven* for Soprano, Clarinet, and Piano (1970); *Hommage à Erik Satie* for Voice and Piano (1994).—NS/LK/DM

Ratner, Leonard G(ilbert), esteemed American musicologist, music theorist, teacher, and composer; b. Minneapolis, July 30, 1916. He learned to play the violin and viola, and received instruction in composition from Frederick Jacobi, Arnold Schoenberg, Ernest Bloch, and Arthur Bliss. He studied musicology under Manfred Bukofzer at the Univ. of Calif. at Berkeley, where he was the first to be awarded a Ph.D. in music (diss. on the harmonic aspects of classic form, 1947). In 1947 he joined the faculty of Stanford Univ., where he was made a prof. in 1957. He retired in 1984. In 1962–63 he held a Guggenheim fellowship. In 1998 he was elected a fellow of the American Academy of Arts and Sciences and was made an honorary member of the American Musicological Soc. Ratner is particularly known for his contributions to the study of 18th and 19th century music.

WRITINGS: *Music: The Listener's Art* (N.Y., 1957; 3rd ed., 1977); *Harmony: Structure and Style* (N.Y., 1962); *Classic Music: Expression, Form, and Style* (N.Y., 1980); *The Musical Experience* (Stanford, 1983); *Romantic Music: Sound and Syntax* (N.Y., 1992); *The Beethoven String Quartets: Compositional Strategies and Rhetoric* (Stanford, 1995).

WORKS: DRAMATIC: *The Trojan Women*, incidental music to Euripides's play (1944); *Jacob*, allegorical dance (1950); *The Oresteia*, incidental music to Aeschylus's play (1951); *Lazarus Laughed*, incidental music to O'Neill's play (1951); *The Necklace*, chamber opera after Maupassant (1960). **ORCH.:** Sym. (1942); Suite for Strings (1946); *Pastorale* (1947); Concertino for Trumpet and Strings (1955); *Harlequin*, overture (1957); *Overture for a Carnival* (1960); *Film Music* (1961). **CHAMBER:** 3 string trios (1939, 1942); 2 violin sonatas (1939, 1952); 2 string quartets (1942, 1953); Oboe Sonatina (1944); *Serenade* for Oboe, Horn, and String Quartet (1950); *Divertissement* for Oboe, Horn, and Bassoon (1950); Cello Sonata (1953); Sonata for Oboe and Clarinet (1954); Piano Sonata (1954). **VOCAL:** 4 Songs, after Oscar Wilde (1953); *Out Upon It*, madrigal for Chorus, after Suckling (1957).

BIBL.: W. Allanbrook, J. Levy, and W. Mahrt, eds., *Convention in Eighteenth- and Nineteenth-Century Music: Essays in Honor of L. G. R.* (Stuyvesant, N.Y., 1992).—NS/LK/DM

Rats, Erwin, Austrian musicologist; b. Graz, Dec. 22, 1898; d. Vienna, Dec. 12, 1973. He studied musicology with Adler at the Univ. of Vienna (1918–22), and also received training in composition from Schoenberg and Webern. In 1945 he became a prof. of theory at the Vienna Academy of Music. He served as president of the International Gustav Mahler Soc. from 1955, and was ed. of the complete critical edition of Mahler's works. He also ed. the critical editions of Beethoven's piano variations and Schubert's piano sonatas.

WRITINGS (all publ. in Vienna unless otherwise given): *Erkenntnis und Erlebnis des musikalischen Kunstwerks* (1950); *Einführung in die musikalische Formenlehre: Über Formprinzipien in den Inventionen und Fugen J.S. Bachs und ihre Bedeutung für die Kompositionstechnik Beethovens* (1951; 3rd ed., 1973); *Die Originalfassung des Streichquartettes op. 130 von Beethoven* (1952); *Zur Chronologie der Klaviersonaten Franz Schuberts* (1955); *Gustav Mahler* (Berlin, 1957); F. Heller, ed., *Gesammelte Aufsätze* (1975). —NS/LK/DM

Rattle, Sir Simon, eminent English conductor; b. Liverpool, Jan. 19, 1955. He began playing percussion and piano in his youth. At age 11, he played percussion with the Merseyside Youth Orch. He also took up conducting, and made his debut with his own orch. in Liverpool when he was only 15. In 1971 he entered the Royal Academy of Music in London on a piano scholarship, but his interest in conducting led him to follow that career choice. While still at the Academy, he won notice as a conductor before completing his studies in 1974. After winning first prize in the John Player International Conducting Competition in 1974, he served as asst. conductor of the Bournemouth Sym. Orch. from 1974 to 1976. In 1975 he made his profes-

sional debut as an opera conductor with *The Rake's Progress* with the Glyndebourne Touring Opera. He made his first appearance with the Philharmonia Orch. in London in 1976 with notable success, and then made his first tour of the U.S. in 1977 conducting the London Schools Sym. Orch. In 1977 he also made his debut at the Glyndebourne Festival conducting *The Cunning Little Vixen*. From 1977 to 1980 he was assoc. conductor of the Royal Liverpool Phil. and asst. conductor of the BBC Scottish Sym. Orch. in Glasgow. He made his first appearance as a guest conductor of a U.S. orch. in 1979 with the Los Angeles Phil. From 1979 to 1984 he was principal conductor of the London Choral Soc. In 1980 he became principal conductor and artistic advisor of the City of Birmingham Sym. Orch., which he proceeded to mold into one of England's leading orchs. He also served as artistic director of the South Bank Music Festival in London from 1981 to 1983, and as principal guest conductor of the Rotterdam Phil. from 1981 to 1984 and of the Los Angeles Phil. from 1981 to 1992. In 1985 he made his debut with the English National Opera in London conducting *Kát'a Kabanová*. He led the City of Birmingham Sym. Orch. on its first tour of the U.S. in 1988, the same year in which he made his U.S. debut as an opera conductor with *Wozzeck* in Los Angeles. In 1990 he made his first appearance at London's Covent Garden conducting *The Cunning Little Vixen*. Rattle was named music director of the City of Birmingham Sym. Orch. in 1990 in recognition of his outstanding contribution to its success. In 1991 he conducted it in the gala opening concert of Birmingham's new Sym. Hall. From 1992 he also was principal guest conductor of the Orch. of the Age of Enlightenment in London. During these years, he appeared as a guest conductor with several of the world's major orchs. In 1998 he concluded his tenure with the City of Birmingham Sym. Orch., and became one of the most sought after guest conductors in the world. In 2002 he was to assume the position of artistic director of the Berlin Phil. During his extensive tenure in Birmingham, Rattle became known for his eclectic programming that paid special regard to the music of the 20th century. He was awarded honorary doctorates from the Univ. of Birmingham (1985), Birmingham Polytechnic (1985), and the Univ. of Oxford (1999). In 1987 he was made a Commander of the Order of the British Empire, and in 1994 he was knighted. He was made an honorary fellow of St. Anne's Coll., Oxford, in 1991. In 1995 he was named a Chevalier de l'Ordre des Arts et des Lettres of France. He received the Albert Medal of the Royal Soc. of Arts in 1997.

BIBL.: N. Kenyon, *S. R.: The Making of a Conductor* (London, 1987).—NS/LK/DM

Rault, Félix, French flutist, teacher, and composer; b. Bordeaux, 1736; d. Paris, c. 1800. He settled in Paris. After studies with Blavet, he became a part-time flutist in the Opéra orch. in 1754. In 1758 he succeeded Blavet as its flutist, a position he held until 1781. He also was a flutist in the orch. of the Concert Spirituel (c. 1765–76) and the royal chapel (1768–92), and then in the orch. of the Théâtre de la Cité (until 1800). Rault was highly influential as a teacher. He composed 2 flute concertos, 3 trios for 2 Flutes and Bassoon, 3 trios for Flute, Violin, and Viola, and some 30 duos in 6 sets.—LK/DM

Raupach, Hermann Friedrich, German harpsichordist, conductor, and composer; b. Stralsund, Dec. 21, 1728; d. St. Petersburg, Dec. 1778. In 1755 he went to St. Petersburg as deputy harpsichordist in the Court Orch., and subsequently served as Kapellmeister and court composer (1758–62); then was active mainly in Hamburg and Paris until 1768. In Paris he met Mozart, who used several movements of his violin sonatas in his own early keyboard concertos (K.37, 39, and 41). Upon his return to St. Petersburg in 1768, Raupach again became deputy harpsichordist in the Court Orch.; in 1770 he was once more named Kapellmeister. His opera *Alcesta* (St. Petersburg, 1758) was one of the first operas on a Russian text. He also wrote the operas *The New Monastery* (1759), *Siroe* (St. Petersburg, 1760), and *The Good Soldiers* (St. Petersburg, Feb. 29, 1780), ballet scenes in operas by Traetta, 6 Sonates for Violin, op.1 (Paris, c. 1762), 4 Sonates for Violin, op.2 (Paris, c. 1765), and 4 Sonates for 2 Violins and Bass, op.3 (Paris, 1770). —NS/LK/DM

Rautavaara, Einojuhani (actually, **Eino Juhani**), eminent Finnish composer and pedagogue; b. Helsinki, Oct. 9, 1928. He learned to play the piano and pursued his education at the Univ. of Helsinki (M.A., 1953). He also studied composition with Merikanto at the Sibelius Academy in Helsinki (1951–53; diploma, 1957). After training in Vienna (1955), he went to the U.S. on a Koussevitzky Foundation grant and studied composition with Persichetti at the Juilliard School of Music in N.Y. (1955–56) and at the Berkshire Music Center in Tanglewood with Sessions (summer, 1955) and Copland (summer, 1956). Following further studies with Vogel in Ascona (1957), he completed his training with Petzold at the Cologne Hochschule für Musik (1958). He was a non- tenured teacher at the Sibelius Academy from 1957 to 1959, and then was music archivist of the Helsinki Phil. from 1959 to 1961. In 1965–66 he was rector of the Käpylä Music Inst. In 1966 he joined the faculty of the Sibelius Academy, where he served as prof. of composition from 1976 to 1990. He also held the Finnish government appointment of Artist Prof. from 1971 to 1976. In 1965 he was awarded the Arnold Bax Composition Medal and the Wihuri Foundation Sibelius Prize. He received the Pro Finlandia Medal in 1968 and was made a Commander in 1985 of the Order of the Lion of Finland. In 1975 he was made a member of the Royal Academy of Music of Sweden in Stockholm. He was awarded an honorary doctorate from the Univ. of Oulu and received the Finnish Government Music Award in 1985. In 1997 he was honored with the Finland Prize. His autobiography, *Omakuva* (Self-Portrait), was publ. in 1989. Until the early 1970s Rautavaara's compositions were marked by a stylistic diversity in which serial techniques played a major role. He then embarked upon a course that led to a remarkable synthesis of tonality and dodecaphony with the tones coming from a row while the harmony remains tonal.

WORKS: DRAMATIC: O p e r a : *Kaivos* (The Mine; 1957–58; rev. version, Finnish TV, April 10, 1963); *Apollo contra Marsyas,* comic opera-musical (1970; Helsinki, Aug. 30, 1973); *Runo 42, "Sammon ryöstö"* (The Myth of Sampo), choral opera (1974; rev. 1981; Helsinki, April 8, 1983); *Thomas* (1984–85; Joensuu, June 21, 1985); *Vincent* (1986–87; Helsinki, May 17, 1990); *Auringon talo* (The House of the Sun), chamber opera (1990; Lappeenranta, April 25, 1991); *Tietäjien lahja* (The Gift of the Maji), chamber opera (1993–94; Finnish TV, Dec. 23, 1996); *Aleksis kivi* (1995–96; Savonlinna, July 8, 1997). **M y s t e r y P l a y :** *Marjatta matala neiti* (Marjatta, the Lowly Maiden; 1975; Espoo, Sept. 3, 1977). **B a l l e t :** *Kiusaukset* (The Temptations; 1969; Helsinki, Feb. 8, 1973). **ORCH.:** Suite for Strings (1952; based on the String Quartet No. 1); *Pelimannit* (The Fiddlers) for Strings (1952; orchestrated 1972; Helsinki, Nov. 11, 1973); *Divertimento* for Strings (1953); *A Requiem in Our Time* (1953; Cincinnati, May 10, 1954); *Epitaph for Béla Bartók* for Strings (1955; rev. 1986; Helsinki, July 27, 1987); 8 syms.: No. 1 (1956; Helsinki, Jan. 22, 1957; rev. 1988; Helsinki, Aug. 24, 1990), No. 2 (Helsinki, Oct. 11, 1957; rev. 1984; Helsinki, Feb. 16, 1985), No. 3 (1961; Helsinki, April 10, 1962), No. 4, *Arabescata* (Helsinki, Feb. 26, 1963), No. 5 (1985–86; Helsinki, May 14, 1986), No. 6, *Vincentiana* (Helsinki, Oct. 29, 1992), No. 7, *Angel of Light* (1994; Bloomington, Ind., April 23, 1995), and No. 8, *The Journey* (1999; Philadelphia, April 27, 2000); *Praevariata* (1957; Strasbourg, June 1958); *Modificata* (1957; Helsinki, April 25, 1958); *Canto I* (1960; Helsinki, March 7, 1967), *II* (1960; Helsinki, Oct. 27, 1961), *III: A Portrait of the Artist at a Certain Moment* (Jyväskylä, June 27, 1972), and *IV* (1992; Kokkola, Oct. 9, 1993) for Strings; *Helsinki Fanfare* (Helsinki, June 12, 1967; rev. version, Helsinki, April 6, 1987); *Lahti Fanfare* (1967; Lahti, Nov. 1, 1968); *Anadyomene* (Helsinki, May 30, 1968); Cello Concerto (1968; Helsinki, Feb. 26, 1969); *A Soldier's Mass* (Helsinki, Nov. 20, 1968); 3 piano concertos: No. 1 (1969; Helsinki, May 29, 1970), No. 2 (Munich, Oct. 19, 1989), and No. 3, *Gift of Dreams* (1998; Tampere, Aug. 18, 1999); *Dithyrambos* for Violin and Orch. (1970); *Helsinki Dancing* (Helsinki, Dec. 5, 1971); *Säännöllisiä Yksikköjaksoja Puolisäännöllisessä Tilanteessa* (Regular Sets of Elements in a Semi-regular Situation; 1971; Helsinki, April 19, 1972); *Cantus Arcticus,* concerto for Birds and Orch. (Oulu, Oct. 18, 1972); *Dances with the Winds,* flute concerto (1973; Stockholm, May 4, 1974); *Ballad* for Harp and Strings (1973; Helsinki, Oct. 19, 1976; rev. version, Helsinki, May 19, 1981); *Annunciations,* concerto for Organ and Symphonic Wind Orch. (1976; Stockholm, Sept. 13, 1977); Violin Concerto (Helsinki, Aug. 23, 1977); *Suomalainen myytti* (A Finnish Myth) for Strings (1977; Jyväskylä, April 29, 1978); *Angels and Visitations* (Helsinki, Nov. 22, 1978); *Fanfare for the Lahti World Skiing Championships 1978* (1978); *Pohjalainen Polska* (Ostrobothnian Polka; Vaasa, April 11, 1980; rev. version for Strings, Kokkola, Oct. 9, 1993); *Angel of Dusk,* double bass concerto (1980; Helsinki, May 6, 1981); *Hommage à Zoltán Kodály* for Strings (Helsinki, Dec. 16, 1982); *Hommage à Ferenc Liszt* for Strings (1989; Helsinki, Aug. 9, 1990); *Lintukoto* (Isle of Bliss; 1995); *Autumn Gardens* (London, July 26, 1999). **CHAMBER:** 4 string quartets (1952; 1958, Helsinki, April 2, 1959; 1965; 1975); *Pöytämusiikki Herttua Juhanalle* (Banqueting Music for Duke Juhana) for 4 Recorders (1954); *2 Preludes and Fugues* for Cello and Piano (1955); Quartet for Oboe and String Trio (1957; rev. 1965); Wind Octet (1962); Bassoon Sonata (1965; rev. 1968); *Sonetto* for Clarinet and Piano (1969); Sonata for Solo Cello (1969); *Dithyrambos* for Violin and Piano (1970); *Ugrilainen Dialogi* for Violin and Cello (1973); *Variétude* for Violin (1974); Sonata for Flutes and Guitar (1975); *Music* for Upright Piano and Amplified Cello (1976); *Tarantará* for Trumpet (1976); *Polska* for 2 Cellos and Piano (1977); *Angel of Dusk,* concerto for Double Bass, 2 Pianos, and Percussionist (1980; rev. 1993); *Playgrounds for Angels* for 4 Trumpets, 4 Trombones, Horn, and Tuba (Helsinki, Sept. 12, 1981); *Serenade in Brass* for Brass (1982); *Fanfare for Emo* for 2 Trumpets and 2 Trombones (1983); Cello Sonata (Helsinki, Sept. 16, 1991); *Fanfare for the 75th Anniversary of Finland's Independence 1992* for 4 Trumpets (Joensuu, June 14, 1992); *Notturno e danza* for Violin and Piano (1993); String Quintet, *Les cieux inconnus* (1997); *Hymnus* for Trumpet and Organ (1998; London, June 23, 1999); *Con spirito di Kuhmo* for Violin and Cello (Helsinki, Feb. 7, 1999); piano pieces, including 2 sonatas (*Christus und die Fischer,* 1969; *The Fire Sermon,* 1970); organ music; guitar pieces. **VOCAL:** *5 Sonette an Orpheus,* song cycle for High, Medium, or Low Voice and Piano (1954–55; also for Medium Voice and Orch., 1960; Helsinki, April 14, 1961); *Die Liebenden,* song cycle for Voice and Piano (1958–59; also for High Voice and String Orch., 1960); *Itsenäisyyskantaatti* (Independence Cantata) for Soloists, Reciter, Chorus, and Orch. (Tampere, June 10, 1967); *True & False Unicorn* for 3 Reciters, Chamber Chorus, Ensemble, and Tape (1971; Århus, March 25, 1974); *Vigilia* (Vigil Commemorating St. John the Baptist) for Soloists and Chorus (1971–72; part 1, Helsinki, Aug. 28, 1971; part 2, Helsinki, Sept. 9, 1972; rev. 1996; Helsinki, Oct. 14, 1997); *Elämän kirja* (A Book of Life), 11 songs for Soloists and Men's Chorus (1972; Helsinki, Feb. 5, 1975); *Lapsimessu* (A Children's Mass) for Children's Chorus and String Orch. (Espoo, Dec. 20, 1973); *Kainuu,* cantata for Chorus, Reciter, and Percussionist (1975); *Odotus* (Waiting), cantata for Chorus, Reciter, and Organ (1978); *Magnificat* for Soloists and Chorus (1979); *Parantaja* (The Healer) for Reciter, Chorus, and Orch. (Helsinki, May 29, 1981); *Katedralen* (The Cathedral) for Soloists and Chorus (1983); *Katso Minun Kansani on Puu* (Behold, My People Are a Tree), independence cantata 1992 for Chorus and Orch. (1991–92; Joensuu, June 14, 1992); *Canción de Nuestro Tiempo* for Chorus (1993); *On the Last Frontier* for Chorus and Orch. (Helsinki, Oct. 8, 1998); *Halavan Himmeän Alla* (In the Shade of the Willow) for Chorus (1998; Minneapolis, March 12, 1999). **TAPE:** *Number 1* and *2* (both 1980); *Heureka Music 1–2* (1989).

BIBL.: K. Aho, *E. R. sinfonikkona* (E. R. as Symphonist; Helsinki, 1988); A. Sivuoja-Gunaratnam, *Narrating With Twelve-Tones: E. R.'s First Serial Period (ca.1957–1965)* (Helsinki, 1997); C. Wellner, *Das musikdramatische Werk von E. R.* (Vienna, 1998).**—NS/LK/DM**

Rautio, Matti, Finnish composer and teacher; b. Helsinki, Feb. 25, 1922; d. Tampere, June 22, 1986. He studied at the Univ. of Helsinki (M.A., 1945), and also took courses in composition and piano at the Sibelius Academy in Helsinki (certificate, 1950), where he served on its faculty as a piano teacher (1947–64), senior theory teacher (from 1956), and director of the school music dept. (1966–70). In his works, he followed a median line of modern music, programmatic and utilitarian in the use of advanced techniques.

WORKS: *Divertimento 1* for Cello and Orch. or Piano (1955) and *2* for Cello and Piano (1972); *Sininen haikara* (The Blue Heron), suite from the ballet (1957); *Tanhumusiikkia* (Folk Dance Music) for Soprano, Baritone, Chorus, and Orch. (1960); Piano Concerto (1968–71).**—NS/LK/DM**

Rautio, Nina, Russian soprano; b. Bryansk, Sept. 21, 1957. She was trained at the Leningrad Cons. From 1981 to 1987 she appeared at the Leningrad State Theater. In 1987 she joined the Bolshoi Theater in Moscow, with which she toured widely in Russia and Eastern Europe. In 1991 she sang Tatiana with the company during its visit to the Metropolitan Opera in N.Y., and also appeared as Oksana in Rimsky-Korsakov's *Christmas Eve* during its engagement at the Edinburgh Festival. During the 1992–93 season, she sang Lisa in *The Queen of Spades* at the Opéra de la Bastille in Paris. She was engaged as Aida at the Berlin State Opera in the 1994–95 season. On Oct. 3, 1995, she made her debut at the Metropolitan Opera in N.Y. as Aida, a role she then sang in Verona in 1996. She made her first appearance at the San Francisco Opera as Elisabeth in *Don Carlos* in 1998.**—NS/LK/DM**

Rauzzini, Venanzio, Italian castrato soprano, harpsichordist, teacher, and composer; b. Camerino, near Rome (baptized), Dec. 19, 1746; d. Bath, April 18, 1810. He studied in Rome, where he made his debut in Piccinni's *Il finto astrologo* (Feb. 7, 1765). He then was in the service of the Elector Max Joseph III in Munich (1766–72), during which period he commenced his career as a composer for the theater; also sang in Venice and Vienna. He was primo uomo in Mozart's *Lucio Silla* (Milan, Dec. 26, 1772) and in Paisiello's *Sismano nel Mogol* (Milan, Jan. 30, 1773); Mozart wrote his famous motet *Exsultate, jubilate* for him (1773). After singing in Venice (1773–74), Padua (1773), and Turin (1774), he went to London as a leading member of the King's Theatre (1774–77); the revised version of his most successful opera, *Piramo e Tisbe,* was produced there on March 16, 1775. He subsequently was active mainly in Bath as a performer, teacher, and concert manager; also made visits to London. Among his most famous pupils were Mrs. Billington, John Braham, Michael Kelly, and Nancy Storace.

WORKS (all first perf. in London unless otherwise given): **DRAMATIC: O p e r a :** *Piramo e Tisbe* (Munich, 1769; rev. version, March 16, 1775); *L'Eroe cinese* (Munich, 1771; rev. version, March 16, 1782); *Le ali d'amore* (Feb. 29, 1776; rev. version, March 13, 1777); *L'omaggio di paesani al signore del contado* (June 5, 1781; only Act 2 by Rauzzini); *Creusa in Delfo* (April 29, 1783); *Alina, o sia La Regina di Golconda* (March 18, 1784); *La Vestale, o sia L'amore protetto dal cielo* (May 1, 1787). **P a s t i c c i o s :** *Armida* (Nov. 19, 1774); *La Sposa fedele* (Oct. 31, 1775); *Didone* (Nov. 11, 1775); *The Duenna or Double Elopement* (Nov. 21, 1775); *Astarto* (Nov. 2, 1776); *Ezio* (Nov. 17, 1781); *The Village Maid* (n.d.). **O t h e r :** Incidental music. **OTHER:** Italian duets and songs and English songs; 15 sonatas for Piano or Harpsichord, and Violin Accompaniment: 6 as op.1 (1777), 6 as op.8 (1781), and 3 as op.15, nos. 1 to 3 (1786); 12 string quartets: op.2 (c. 1777) and op.7 (c. 1778); 6 Quartets for Piano or Harpsichord, 2 Violins, and Cello, op.6 (c. 1778); 4 duets for Piano or Harpsichord, 4-Hands: 3 as op.12 (1783) and 1 as op.15, no. 4 (1786); a Sinfonia; dances; lessons; etc.

BIBL.: J. Reindl, *V. R. als Instrumental-Komponist* (diss., Univ. of Vienna, 1961).**—NS/LK/DM**

Raval, Sebastián, Spanish soldier, friar, and composer; b. Cartagena, c. 1550; d. Palermo, Oct.(?), 1604.

He served in the Spanish army in Flanders and Sicily, and was gravely wounded in the capture of Maastricht in 1579. After serving as a member of the Capuchin order, he entered the order of St. John of Jerusalem (also known as the Knights of Malta) in 1592, and went to Rome to obtain his knighthood. He had the temerity to challenge Nanino and Soriano to a musical competition, in which he suffered an ignominious defeat. In 1595 he went to Palermo as maestro di cappella at the royal chapel of San Pietro. In 1600 he was emboldened to challenge Achille Falcone to a musical competition, which he lost. Raval appealed the adjudicator's decision to the viceroy with the demand for a new examination. Raval won the second competition, most likely due to Spanish favoritism. Falcone in turn appealed to Nanino and Soriano for a third competition to be held in Rome, but he died before the competition could take place. Raval publ. 2 vols. of motets (Rome, 1593–94), a vol. of Lamentations (Rome, 1594), 2 vols. of madrigals (Venice, 1593, 1595), and 2 other vols. of secular music (Venice, 1593; Palermo, 1596).—LK/DM

Ravel, (Joseph) Maurice, great French composer; b. Ciboure, Basses-Pyrénées, March 7, 1875; d. Paris, Dec. 28, 1937. His father was a Swiss engineer, and his mother of Basque origin. The family moved to Paris when he was an infant. He began to study piano at the age of 7 with Henri Ghis and harmony at 12 with Charles-René. After further piano studies with Emile Descombes, he entered the Paris Cons. as a pupil of Eugène Anthiôme in 1889. He won first medal (1891), and passed to the advanced class of Charles de Bériot; also studied harmony with Emile Pessard. He left the Cons. in 1895 and that same year completed work on his song *Un Grand Sommeil noir*, the *Menuet antique* for Piano, and the *Habanera* for 2 Pianos (later included in the *Rapsodie espagnole* for Orch.); these pieces, written at the age of 20, already reveal great originality in the treatment of old modes and of Spanish motifs; however, he continued to study; in 1897 he returned to the Cons. to study with Fauré (composition) and Gédalge (counterpoint and orchestration); his well-known *Pavane pour une infante défunte* for Piano was written during that time (1899). On May 27, 1899, he conducted the premiere of his overture *Shéhérazade* in Paris; some elements of this work were incorporated in his song cycle of the same name (1903). In 1901 he won the 2nd Prix de Rome with the cantata *Myrrha*; but ensuing attempts to win the Grand Prix de Rome were unsuccessful; at his last try (1905) he was eliminated in the preliminaries, and so was not allowed to compete; the age limit then set an end to his further effort to enter. Since 6 prizes all went to pupils of Lenepveu, suspicion of unfair discrimination was aroused; Jean Marnold publ. an article, "Le Scandale du Prix de Rome," in the *Mercure de France* (June 1905) in which he brought the controversy into the open; this precipitated a crisis at the Cons.; its director, Théodore Dubois, resigned, and Fauré took his place. By that time, Ravel had written a number of his most famous compositions, and was regarded by most French critics as a talented disciple of Debussy. No doubt Ravel's method of poetic association of musical ideas paralleled that of Debussy; his employment of

unresolved dissonances and the enhancement of the diatonic style into pandiatonicism were techniques common to Debussy and his followers; but there were important differences: whereas Debussy adopted the scale of whole tones as an integral part of his musical vocabulary, Ravel resorted to it only occasionally; similarly, augmented triads appear much less frequently in Ravel's music than in Debussy's; in his writing for piano, Ravel actually anticipated some of Debussy's usages; in a letter addressed to Pierre Lalo and publ. in *Le Temps* (April 9, 1907), Ravel pointed out that at the time of the publication of his piano piece *Jeux d'eau* (1902) Debussy had brought out only his suite *Pour le piano*, which had contained little that was novel. In Paris, elsewhere in France, and soon in England and other European countries, Ravel's name became well known, but for many years he was still regarded as an ultramodernist. A curious test of audience appreciation was a "Concert des Auteurs Anonymes" presented by the Société Independante de Musique on May 9, 1911; the program included Ravel's *Valses nobles et sentimentales*, a set of piano pieces in the manner of Schubert; yet Ravel was recognized as the author. Inspired evocation of the past was but one aspect of Ravel's creative genius; in this style are his *Pavane pour une infante defunte, Le Tombeau de Couperin*, and *La Valse*; luxuriance of exotic colors marks his ballet *Daphnis et Chloé*, his opera *L'Heure espagnole*, the song cycles *Shéhérazade* and *Chansons madécasses*, and his virtuoso pieces for Piano *Miroirs* and *Gaspard de la nuit*; other works are deliberately austere, even ascetic, in their pointed classicism: the piano concertos, the Piano Sonatina, and some of his songs with piano accompaniment. His association with Diaghilev's Ballets Russes was most fruitful; for Diaghilev he wrote one of his masterpieces, *Daphnis et Chloé*; another ballet, *Boléro*, commissioned by Ida Rubinstein and performed at her dance recital at the Paris Opéra on Nov. 22, 1928, became Ravel's most spectacular success as an orch. piece.

Ravel never married, and lived a life of semi-retirement, devoting most of his time to composition; he accepted virtually no pupils, although he gave friendly advice to Vaughan Williams and to others; he was never on the faculty of any school. As a performer, he was not brilliant; he appeared as a pianist only in his own works, and often accompanied singers in programs of his songs; although he accepted engagements as a conductor, his technique was barely sufficient to secure a perfunctory performance of his music. When World War I broke out in 1914, he was rejected for military service because of his frail physique, but he was anxious to serve; his application for air service was denied, but he was received in the ambulance corps at the front; his health gave way, and in the autumn of 1916 he was compelled to enter a hospital for recuperation. In 1922 he visited Amsterdam and Venice, conducting his music; in 1923 he appeared in London; in 1926 he went to Sweden, England, and Scotland; in 1928 he made an American tour as a conductor and pianist; in the same year he received the degree of D.Mus. honoris causa at the Univ. of Oxford. In 1929 he was honored by his native town by the inauguration of the Quai Maurice Ravel. Shortly afterward, he began to experience difficulties in muscular coordination, and suffered from attacks of aphasia, symptoms indicative of a cerebral malady; he underwent brain surgery on Dec. 19, 1937, but it was not successful; he died 9 days later.

WORKS: DRAMATIC: O p e r a : *L'Heure espagnole,* opera (1907–09; Paris, May 19, 1911); *L'Enfant et les sortilèges,* fantaisie lyrique (1920–25; Monte Carlo, March 21, 1925). **B a l - l e t :** *Ma Mère l'Oye* (1911; Paris, Jan. 21, 1912; based on the piano work with additional material); *Daphnis et Chloé* (1909–12; Paris, June 8, 1912); *Adélaïde, ou Le Langage des fleurs* (Paris, April 22, 1912; based on the *Valses nobles et sentimentales*); *Le Tombeau de Couperin* (Paris, Nov. 8, 1920; based on the piano work); *La Valse* (Paris, Dec. 12, 1920); *Boléro* (Paris, Nov. 22, 1928). **ORCH.:** *Shéhérazade,* ouverture féerique (1898; Paris, May 27, 1899); *Une Barque sur l'océan* (1906; based on the piano work); *Rapsodie espagnole* (Paris, March 15, 1908); *Pavane pour une infante défunte* (Paris, Dec. 25, 1910; based on the piano work); *Daphnis et Chloé,* 2 suites (1911, 1913); *Alborada del gracioso* (Paris, May 17, 1919; based on the piano work); *La Valse,* poème chorégraphique (Paris, Dec. 12, 1920); *Le Tombeau de Couperin* (Paris, Feb. 28, 1920; based on the piano work); *Tzigane,* rapsodie de concert for Violin and Orch. (Paris, Dec. 7, 1924; based on the work for Violin and Piano); *Menuet antique* (1929; based on the piano work); Piano Concerto in D for Left Hand Alone, written for Paul Wittgenstein (1929–30; Vienna, Nov. 27, 1931); Piano Concerto in G major (1929–31; Paris, Jan. 14, 1932). **CHAMBER:** Violin Sonata (1897); String Quartet in F major (1902–03); *Introduction et Allegro* for Harp, Flute, Clarinet, and String Quartet (1905; Paris, Feb. 22, 1907); Piano Trio (1914); *Le Tombeau de Claude Debussy* for Violin and Cello (1920); Sonata for Violin and Cello (1920–22); *Berceuse sur le nom de Gabriel Fauré* for Violin and Piano (1922); Violin Sonata (1923–27); *Tzigane,* rapsodie de concert for Violin and Piano (London, April 26, 1924). **P i a n o :** *Sérénade grotesque* (c. 1893); *Menuet antique* (1895); *Sites auriculaires* for 2 Pianos (1895–97): *Pavane pour une infante défunte* (1899) and *Jeux d'eau* (1901); *Sonatine* (1903–05); *Miroirs* (1904–05); *Gaspard de la nuit* (1908); *Menuet sur le nom d'Haydn* (1909); *Ma Mère l'Oye,* 5 "pièces enfantines" for Piano, 4-Hands (written for Christine Verger, age 6, and Germaine Durant, age 10, and first perf. by them, Paris, April 20, 1910); *Valses nobles et sentimentales* (1911); *Prélude* (1913); *À la manière de...Borodin* (1913); *A la manière de...Chabrier* (1913); *Le Tombeau de Couperin* (1914–17); *Frontispiece* for 2 Pianos, 5-Hands (1918); *La Valse* for 2 Pianos (1921; based on the orch. work); *Boléro* for 2 Pianos (1930; based on the orch. work). **VOCAL:** *Les Bayadères tournent légères* for Soprano, Chorus, and Orch. (1900); 3 cantatas, all for 3 Solo Voices and Orch.: *Myrrha* (1901), *Alcyone* (1902), and *Alyssa* (1903); *Tout est lumière* for Soprano, Chorus, and Orch. (1901); *La Nuit* for Soprano, Chorus, and Orch. (1902); *Matinée de Provence* for Soprano, Chorus, and Orch. (1903); *Manteau de fleurs* for Voice and Orch. (1903; based on the song for Voice and Piano); *Shéhérazade* for Mezzo-soprano and Orch. (1903; Paris, May 17, 1904); *Noël des jouets* for Voice and Orch. (1905; 2nd version, 1913; based on the song for Voice and Piano); *L'Aurore* for Tenor, Chorus, and Orch. (1905); *Chanson de la Mariée* and *Tout gai* for Voice and Orch. (1904–06; based on songs nos. 1 and 5 from the cycle *Cinq mélodies populaires grecques* for Voice and Piano); *Trois poèmes de Stéphane Mallarmé* for Voice, Piccolo, Flute, Clarinet, Bass Clari- net, Piano, and String Quartet (1913; Paris, Jan. 14, 1914); *Trois chansons* for Chorus (1914–15); *Deux mélodies hébraïques* for Voice and Orch. (1919; based on the songs for Voice and Piano); *Chanson hébraïque* for Voice and Orch. (1923–24; based on song

no. 4 from the cycle *Chants populaires* for Voice and Piano); *Chansons madécasses* for Voice, Flute, Piano, and Cello (1925–26); *Don Quichotte à Dulcinée* for Baritone and Orch. (1932–33; Paris, Dec. 1, 1934); *Ronsard à son âme* for Voice and Orch. (1935; based on the song for Voice and Piano). **S o n g s :** *Ballade de la Reine morte d'aimer* (c. 1893); *Un Grand Sommeil noir* (1895); *Sainte* (1896); *Deux épigrammes de Clément Marot* (1896–99); *Chanson du rouet* (1898); *Si morne!* (1898); *Manteau de fleurs* (1903); *Shéhérazade* (1903; based on the work for Mezzo-soprano and Orch.); *Noël des jouets* (1905); *Cinq mélodies populaires grecques* (1904–06); *Histoires naturelles* (1906); *Les Grands Vents venus d'outremer* (1907); *Sur l'herbe* (1907); *Vocalise-étude en forme de habanera* (1907); *Tripatos* (1909); *Chants populaires* (1910); *Trois poèmes de Stéphane Mallarmé* (1913; based on songs for Voice and Various Instruments); *Deux mélodies hébraïques* (1914); *Trois chansons* (1914–15; based on the choral work); *Ronsard à son âme* (1923–24); *Chansons madécasses* (1926; based on the work for Voice, Flute, Piano, and Cello); *Rêves* (1927); *Don Quichotte à Dulcinée* (1932–33; based on the work for Baritone and Orch.). **OTHER:** Various arrangements, including a celebrated ver- sion of Mussorgsky's *Pictures at an Exhibition* for Orch. (Paris, Oct. 19, 1922, Koussevitzky conducting).

BIBL.: Roland-Manuel, *M. R. et son oeuvre* (Paris, 1914; 2nd ed., rev., 1926; Eng. tr., 1941); W.-L. Landowski, *M. R., Sa vie, son oeuvre* (Paris, 1938; 2nd ed., 1950); Roland-Manuel, *À la gloire de R.* (Paris, 1938; 2nd ed., 1948; Eng. tr., 1947); V. Jankélévitch, *M. R.* (Paris, 1939; 2nd ed., 1956; Eng. tr., 2nd ed., 1959); R. Wild, ed., *M. R. par quelques-uns de ses familiers* (Paris, 1939); M. Goss, *Boléro: The Life of M. R.* (N.Y., 1940); K. Akeret, *Studien zum Klavierwerk von M. R.* (Zürich, 1941); H. Jourdan-Morhange, *R. et nous* (Geneva, 1945); N. Demuth, *R.* (London, 1947); A. Machabey, *M. R.* (Paris, 1947); F. Onnen, *M. R.* (Stockholm, 1947); R. Malipiero, *M. R.* (Milan, 1948); L.-P. Fargue, *M. R.* (Paris, 1949); J. Bruyr, *M. R. ou Le Lyrisme et les sortilèges* (Paris, 1950); L. La Pegna, *R.* (Brescia, 1950); W. Tappolet, *M. R.: Leben und Werk* (Olten, 1950); V. Perlemuter and H. Jourdan- Morhange, *R. d'après R.* (Lausanne, 1953; Eng. tr., 1988, as *R. according to R.*); V. Seroff, *M. R.* (N.Y., 1953); M. Gerar and R. Chalupt, eds., *R. au miroir de ses lettres* (Paris, 1956); J. van Ackere, *M. R.* (Brussels, 1957); J. Geraedts, *R.* (Haarlem, 1957); R. de Fragny, *M. R.* (Lyons, 1960); R. Myers, *R.: Life and Works* (London, 1960); H. Stuckenschmidt, *M. R.: Variationen uber Person und Werk* (Frankfurt am Main, 1966; Eng. tr., 1969); A. Orenstein, *R.: Man and Musician* (N.Y., 1975; new ed., 1991); R. Nichols, *R.* (London, 1977); M. Marnat, ed., *M. R.: L'Hommage de La Revue musicale, decembre 1938* (Lyons, 1987); R. Nichols, *R. Remembered* (London and Boston, 1987); M. Rosenthal, *Satie, R., Poulenc: An Intimate Memoir* (Madras and N.Y., 1987); T. Hirs- brunner, *M. R.: Sein Leben, sein Werk* (Laaber, 1989); A. Oren- stein, ed., *R.: Correspondance, écrits et entretiens* (Paris, 1989; Eng. tr., 1989, as *A R. Reader*); R. Beyer, *Organale Satztechniken in den Werken von Claude Debussy und M. R.* (Wiesbaden, 1992); C. Petersen, *Die Lieder von M. R.* (Frankfurt am Main, 1995); M. Rosenthal, *R.: Souvenirs de Manuel Rosenthal* (Paris, 1995); S. Bruhn, *Images and Ideas in Modern French Piano Music: The Extra-Musical Subtext in Piano Works by R., Debussy, and Messiaen* (Stuyvesant, N.Y., 1997); C. Souillard, *R. (1875–1937)* (Paris, 1998).—NS/LK/DM

Ravenscroft, John, English composer; b. London, date unknown; d. c. 1708. In 1695 he was in Rome, where he publ. a set of "sonate a tre" under the

Italianized name Giovanni Ravenscroft. He apparently was a pupil of Corelli, whose style he imitated. Also extant are his 6 da camera sonatas for 2 Violins and Basso Continuo, op. 2 (London, 1708).—NS/LK/DM

Ravenscroft, Thomas, English editor, music theorist, and composer; b. c. 1582; d. c. 1635. He was a chorister at St. Paul's Cathedral in London under Thomas Giles and Edward Pearce, and also studied at Gresham Coll., Cambridge (B.Mus., 1605). He was music master at Christ's Hospital in London (1618–22). Among his works are 8 verse anthems, 3 full anthems, 3 motets, and 4 fantasias for 5 Viols.

WRITINGS: *A Briefe Discourse of the True (but Neglected) Use of Charact'ring the Degrees by their Perfection, Imperfection, and Diminution in Mensurable Musicke: Harmony of four voyces concerning the pleasure of five usuall recreations, 1. Hunting, 2. Hawking, 3. Dancing, 4. Drinking, 5. Enamouring* (London, 1614); *A Treatise of Musick* (MS). **EDITIONS** (all publ. in London): *Pammelia: Musick's Miscellanie: or Mixed Varietie of Pleasant Roundelayes and Delightful Catches of 3–10 Parts in one* (1609; ed. by P. Warlock, 1928); *Deuteromelia...* [14] *Freemens Songs and...*[17] *Catches* for 3 to 4 Voices (1609); *Melismata: Musicall Phansies, fitting the Court, Citie and Countrey Humours* for 3 to 5 Voices (1611); *The Whole Booke of Psalms* (1621; ed. by W. Havergal, 1845).

BIBL.: D. Mateer, *A Critical Study and Transcription of "A Briefe Discourse" by T. R.* (diss., Univ. of London, 1970). —NS/LK/DM

Raver, Leonard, American organist and teacher; b. Wenatchee, Wash., Jan. 8, 1927; d. N.Y., Jan. 29, 1992. He studied organ and piano in Tacoma, where he was active as a church organist. After moving to N.Y., he pursued a career as a recitalist and a teacher. His appearances as a soloist with the N.Y. Phil. led to his appointment as its organist in 1977, which position he retained until his death. While he displayed a fine command of the Baroque repertoire, he had a special flair for contemporary works. Among the composers he championed were Diamond, Persichetti, Rorem, and Read.—NS/LK/DM

Rawls, Lou, leading mainstream pop vocalist; b. Chicago, Dec. 1, 1935. A professional performer for more than five decades, Lou Rawls is unmistakable. His voice trickles through the speakers like molasses—not overly sweet, kind of smoky, strangely compelling. He has performed as a jazz, blues, soul, gospel, and pop singer, and then mixed them all up into a genre all his own.

While living with his grandmother on the south side of Chicago, Rawls began singing gospel at seven years old. In his late teens, he became a member of the legendary gospel ensemble The Pilgrim Travelers, along with his childhood friend, Sam Cooke. He stayed with the group, with a break for military service, until the mid-1950s, when he and Cooke were in an accident that killed the driver of the car, injured Cooke, and put Rawls in a coma for nearly a week. It took him more than a year to fully recover.

By the time Rawls was ready to start out again, The Pilgrim Travelers had broken up. He started singing blues in nightclubs and also began acting with a part in the hit TV show *77 Sunset Strip*. He recorded a duet with Cooke on "Bring It on Home to Me" and "Having a Party" in 1962, about which time he landed his own solo contract with Capitol Records. Rawls recorded regularly and toured through the mid-1960s, achieving a good deal of popularity. However, he really didn't break through to a pop audience until "Love Is a Hurtin' Thing" which went to #13 pop and topped the R&B charts in 1966. The album from which it came, *Soulin'*, went gold and hit #7.

Working in bars, Rawls had developed the habit of talking through the first few minutes of a song. He decided to include a spoken introduction to his recording of "Dead End Street" in 1967. The single went to #29 pop, #3 R&B, and won Rawls his first Grammy Award for Best Rhythm and Blues Solo Vocal Performance, Male. This sent the album *That's Lou* to #29. He didn't chart another record until 1969, when he took "Your Good Thing Is Going to End" to #18. In all, he would record more than 20 albums for Capitol during the 1960s.

Rawls, however, was a popular live attraction and a stalwart on the variety-show circuit, so much so that he earned his own variety program, *Lou Rawls and the Golddiggers* as a summer replacement show in 1969. In 1971, Rawls earned his second Grammy Award, taking the Best R&B Vocal Performance, Male trophy for "A Natural Man," which had reached #17. While he continued to perform and record, hits eluded him until 1976, when he signed with Kenny Gamble and Leon Huff's Philadelphia International Records. The producers backed Rawls's smooth voice with their sophisticated, orchestral dance music, which proved a master stroke. The song "You'll Never Find Another Love Like Mine" topped the R&B charts for two weeks, the adult-contemporary chart for one, hit #2 on the pop charts, and went gold. The album from which it came, *All Things in Time* rose to #7, and went platinum. Rawls hit another hot streak. In 1977, he took a similar setting for the song "Lady Love" to #24 pop. "See You When I Git There" rose to #8 R&B that same year, and his album, *Unmistakably Lou*, won him his third Grammy.

One of the first African-American spokespersons for a major consumer product, Rawls became the voice of Budweiser beer in the mid-1970s. His relationship with Budweiser led the brewery to sponsor Rawls's annual telethons in support of the United Negro Coll. Fund, which have raised close to a quarter of a billion dollars for scholarships.

While Rawls never matched his late 1970s chart success, he continued to be a force in the music business. In the late 1970s, he appeared in a one-man show on Broadway. His 1989 album *At Last* brought him to the Blue Note jazz label, and found him recording with George Benson, Ray Charles, and others. He continued acting, both on the big screen and TV, and giving voice to animated characters, including Garfield (providing his singing voice) and Harvey the Mailman, a character on the Nickelodeon series *Hey Arnold*. In 1999, Rawls spent several months as a member of the cast of the Broadway show *Smokey Joe's Café*.

Disc.: *Black and Blue* (1962); *Stormy Monday* (1962); *Tobacco Road* (1963); *For You My Love* (1964); *Lou Rawls and Strings* (1965); *Merry Christmas Ho! Ho! Ho!* (1965); *Nobody but Lou* (1965); *Carryin' On* (1966); *Soulin'* (1966); *Live!* (1966); *Soul Stirring Gospel Sounds of the Pilgrim...* (1966); *That's Lou* (1967); *Too Much* (1967); *You're Good for Me* (1968); *Feelin' Good* (1968); *The Way It Was: The Way It Is* (1969); *Your Good Thing* (1969); *Natural Man* (1971); *Silk & Soul* (1972); *Live at the Century Plaza* (1973); *All Things in Time* (1976); *Unmistakably Lou* (1977); *When You Hear Lou, You've Heard It All* (1977); *Live* (1978); *Sit Down and Talk to Me* (1980); *Shades of Blue* (1981); *When the Night Comes* (1983); *Love All Your Blues Away* (1986); *At Last* (1989); *It's Supposed to Be Fun* (1990); *Christmas Is the Time* (1993); *Merry Little Christmas* (1995); *Holiday Cheer* (1995); *Love Is a Hurtin' Thing: The Silk & Soul of Lou Rawls* (1997); *The Best of Lou Rawls: Classic Philadelphia Recordings* (1998); *Seasons 4 U* (1998); *Anthology* (2000).—**HB**

Rawsthorne, Alan, important English composer; b. Haslingden, May 2, 1905; d. Cambridge, July 24, 1971. He went to a dentistry school, and did not begin to study music until he was 20, when he entered the Royal Manchester Coll. of Music; later studied piano with Egon Petri in Berlin (1930–31). After returning to England in 1932, he occupied various teaching posts; then devoted himself mainly to composition, and succeeded brilliantly in producing music of agreeable, and to some ears even delectable, music. In 1961 he was made a Commander of the Order of the British Empire. His music is essentially a revival of the contrapuntal style of the past, without much harmonic elaboration; but the rhythms are virile and the melodies fluid, emanating from a focal point of tonality.

Works: DRAMATIC: Ballet: *Madame Chrysantheme* (London, April 1, 1955). **ORCH.:** Concerto for Clarinet and Strings (1936); *Symphonic Studies* (1938; Warsaw, April 21, 1939); 2 piano concertos: No. 1 (originally for Strings and Percussion, 1939; rescored for Full Orch., 1942) and No. 2 (London, June 17, 1951); 2 violin concertos: No. 1 (1940; sketches lost in an air raid; reconstructed 1943–48; Cheltenham, July 1, 1948) and No. 2 (London, Oct. 24, 1956); 4 overtures: *Street Corner* (1944), *Cortèges* (1945), *Hallé*, for the centennial of the Hallé Orch. (1958), and *Overture for Farnham* (1967); Concerto for Oboe and Strings (1947); Concerto for Strings (1949); 3 syms.: No. 1 (London, Nov. 15, 1950), No. 2, *Pastoral*, for Soprano and Orch. (Birmingham, Sept. 29, 1959), and No. 3 (Cheltenham, July 8, 1964); *Concertante pastorale* for Flute, Horn, and Strings (1951); *Improvisations on a Theme of Constant Lambert* (1960); Concerto for 10 Instruments (1962); *Divertimento* for Chamber Orch. (1962); *Elegiac Rhapsody* for Strings (1964); Cello Concerto (London, April 6, 1966); Concerto for 2 Pianos and Orch. (1968); *Theme, Variations and Finale* (1968); *Triptych* (1970). **CHAMBER:** *Concertante* for Violin and Piano (1935–62); Trio for Flute, Oboe, and Piano (1936); *Theme and Variations* for 2 Violins (1937); Viola Sonata (1938); *Theme and Variations* for String Quartet (1939); 3 string quartets (1939, 1954, 1965); Clarinet Quartet (1948); Cello Sonata (1949); Violin Sonata (1959); Piano Trio (1962); Quintet for Piano, Oboe, Clarinet, Horn, and Bassoon (1963); Quintet for Piano and Strings (1968); Oboe Quartet (1970); Suite for Flute, Viola, and Harp (1970); Quintet for Piano, Clarinet, Horn, Violin, and Cello (1971); *Elegy* for Guitar (1971; completed from composer's sketches by Julian Bream). **Piano:** *Bagatelles* (1938); *The Creel* for 2 Pianos (1940); *Sonatina* (1948); *4 Romantic Pieces* (1953); *Ballade* (1967);

Theme with 4 Studies (1971). **VOCAL:** *A Canticle of Man*, chamber cantata for Baritone, Chorus, Flute, and Strings (1952); *Practical Cats*, children's entertainment for Narrator and Orch., after T. S. Eliot (Edinburgh, Aug. 26, 1954); *Medieval Diptych* for Baritone and Orch. (1962); *Carmen Vitale*, cantata (London, Oct. 16, 1963); *Tankas of the 4 Seasons* for Tenor, Oboe, Clarinet, Bassoon, Violin, and Cello (1965); *The God in the Cave* for Chorus and Orch. (1967).

Bibl.: A. Poulton, ed., *A. R.: A Catalogue of His Music* (Kidderminster, 1984); A. Poulton, ed., *A. R.* (3 vols., Hindhead, 1984–86).—**NS/LK/DM**

Raxach, Enrique, Spanish-born Dutch composer; b. Barcelona, Jan. 15, 1932. After studies with Nuri Aymerich, he attended the summer courses in new music in Darmstadt given by Messiaen, Boulez, Maderna, and Stockhausen (1959–66). In 1962 he settled in the Netherlands and in 1969 became a naturalized Dutch citizen. In his music, Raxach utilizes various contemporary modes of expression, including electronics.

Works: DRAMATIC: *Reflections Inside*, electronic ballet music (1992–94). **ORCH.:** *Polifonías* for Strings (1953–56); *6 Mouvements* (1955); *Metamorphose I* (1956), *II* (1958), and *III* for 15 Solo Instruments (1959); *Prometheus*, renamed *Poème* (1957–58); *Fluxión* for 17 Players (1962–63); *Syntagma* (1964–65); *Textures* (1965–66); *Equinoxial* for Winds, Percussion, Hammond Organ, and Double Basses (1967–68); *Inside Out* for Orch. and Tape ad libitum (1969); *Figuren in einer Landschaft* (1972–74); *Ad Marginem*, triple concerto for Flute, Violin, Viola, and Orch. (1974–75); *Erdenlicht* (1975); *Am Ende des Regenbogens* (1980); *Opus Incertum* for Large Chamber Orch. (1985); *Calles y sueños—in memoriam García Lorca* for Chamber Orch. (1986); *Codex Z* for Large Wind Orch. and Bambuso Sonore (Bamboo Organ) ad libitum (1991); Piano Concertino (1994–95); *Chapter Three, Stage 1* (1997). **CHAMBER:** 2 string quartets: No. 1, *Fases* (1961) and No. 2, with live electronics ad libitum (1971); *Imaginary Landscape* for Flute and Percussionist (1968); *Scattertime* for 6 Players (1971); *Chimaera* for Bass Clarinet and Tape (1974); *Aubade* for Percussion Quintet (1978); *The Hunting in Winter* for Horn and Piano (1979); *Careful with that...* for Clarinet and Percussionist (1982); *Chalumeau* for Clarinet Quartet (1982); *Ode* for Flute and String Trio (1982); *Vórtice* for 6 Bass and 3 Contrabass Clarinets (1983); *Antevísperas* for Saxophone Quartet (1986); *Asalto* for Saxophone and Piano (1986); *Obessum* for Bassoon and 9 Accordions (1988); *Danses Pythiques* for Harp (1992); *Decade* for Bass Clarinet and Accordion (1992); *Neumes* for 6 Percussionists (1996). **KEYBOARD: Piano:** *Ricercare* (1976); *12 Preludes* (1993–94). **Organ:** *Tientos* (1964–65); *The Looking Glass* (1967); *Paralipomena* (1996). **VOCAL:** *Pequeña Cantata* for Tenor and Small Ensemble (1952); *Fragmento II* for Soprano, Flute, and 2 Percussionists (1965–66); *Paraphrase* for Mezzo-soprano and 11 Players (1969); *Interface* for Chorus and Orch. (1971–72); *Sine Nomine* for Soprano and Orch. (1973); *Soirée musicale* for Women's Chorus, Bass Clarinet, and Orch. (1978); *...hub of ambiguity* for Soprano and 8 Players (1984); *Nocturno del hueco* for Chorus, Large Ensemble, and Tape (1990). —**NS/LK/DM**

Ray, Don Brandon, American conductor and composer; b. Santa Maria, Calif., June 7, 1926. He studied composition with John Vincent at the Univ. of Calif., Los Angeles (B.A., 1948), and with Ernst Kanitz at the Univ. of Southern Calif., and conducting with Roger Wagner and Richard Lert. He composed orch. pieces; Protestant church services, incidental music to theatrical plays, and *Symrock* (symphonic rock) for Orch. (1978). —NS/LK/DM

Ray, Johnnie (actually, **John Alvin**), melodramatic American singer, pianist, and songwriter; b. Dallas, Ore., Jan. 10, 1927; d. Los Angeles, Calif., Feb. 24, 1990. Ray's emotive singing, influenced by gospel and blues music, marked a change from the calmer singers of classic pop and looked forward to the development of rock 'n' roll. He scored 22 pop hits in the U.S. between 1951 and 1959, the most popular being "Cry," "The Little Cloud That Cried," and "Just Walking in the Rain," and he was even more popular in Great Britain.

Ray's father, Elmer Ray, was a fiddler; his mother, Hazel Simkins Ray, sang and played piano. He began picking out tunes on the piano at a young age. His hearing was injured in an accident when he was 13 and he was forced to wear a hearing aid for the rest of his life. Nevertheless, at 15 he was singing on local radio. In 1949 he moved to Los Angeles to become a singer. He spent a year there playing small clubs, returned home for a while, then tried his luck in the Midwest in 1950. By April 1951 he was at the Flame Showbar in Detroit, where he was spotted by record executive Danny Kessler, who signed him to the Columbia Records R&B subsidiary OKeh Records.

Ray's second single on OKeh was "Cry" (music and lyrics by Churchill Kohlman)/"The Little White Cloud That Cried" (music and lyrics by Johnnie Ray). "Cry" hit #1 in December 1951, becoming the biggest hit of the year, "The Little White Cloud That Cried" made the Top Ten, and the record sold a million copies. "Cry" had also topped the R&B charts, but after the single's success Ray was transferred to Columbia Records proper and promoted more to the pop market. Both sides of his next single, "Please, Mr. Sun" (music by Ray Getzov, lyrics by Sid Frank)/"Here Am I—Broken Hearted" (music by Ray Henderson, lyrics by B. G. De Sylva and Lew Brown), hit the Top Ten in the late winter of 1952, and the record was another million-seller.

Ray's first album, *Johnnie Ray*, entered the charts in April 1952 and hit the Top Ten; that same month he opened at the prestigious Copacabana nightclub in N.Y. His next major hit was a revival of the 1931 song "Walkin' My Baby Back Home" (music and lyrics by Roy Turk and Fred E. Ahlert); it was also his first chart single in Great Britain. His first British Top Ten came with "Faith Can Move Mountains" (music by Guy Wood, lyrics by Ben Raleigh), which entered the U.K. charts in December but was not a hit in the U.S. On May 25, 1952, he married Marilyn (actually Carol Elizabeth) Morrison; they divorced in January 1954.

Ray's recording of the 1918 song "Somebody Stole My Gal" (music and lyrics by Leo Wood) peaked in the Top Ten in May 1953; it also reached the Top Ten in Britain, where "Let's Walk That-a-Way" followed it into the charts in July and also made the Top Ten and "Such a Night" (music and lyrics by Lincoln Chase), a minor U.S. chart entry, hit #1 in April 1954. That December,

Ray made his film debut acting in a supporting role and singing in the movie musical *There's No Business Like Show Business*, but although he occasionally appeared on television and on film in subsequent years, acting never became a significant part of his career.

Ray scored three Top Ten hits in the U.K. in 1955: "If You Believe," "Hey There" (music and lyrics by Richard Adler and Jerry Ross), and "Song of the Dreamer" (music and lyrics by Eddie "Tex" Curtis). He returned to the U.S. Top Ten in October 1956 with "Just Walking in the Rain" (music and lyrics by Johnny Bragg and Robert S. Riley), which went on to sell a million copies; in Britain it topped the charts. Its follow-up, "You Don't Owe Me a Thing" (music and lyrics by Marty Robbins), did slightly better at home, reaching the Top Ten in February 1957; in the U.K. it was that single's B-side, "Look Homeward Angel" (music and lyrics by Wally Gold), that hit the Top Ten. In March, Ray had his second U.S. chart album, *The Big Beat*. His last significant hit came with "Yes Tonight, Josephine" (music and lyrics by Winfield Scott and Dorothy Goodman), which peaked in the U.S. Top 40 in May and hit #1 in Britain in June.

Ray's records continued to reach the charts through 1959, but his career was eclipsed by the rise of rock 'n' roll. Nevertheless, he continued to record and perform over the next 30 years. He died of liver failure at 62 in 1990.

Disc: *Johnnie Ray* (1951); *At the London Palladium* (1954); *I Cry for You* (1955); *Johnnie Ray* (1955); *The Voice of Your Choice* (1955); *Johnnie Ray Sings the Big Beat* (1957); *Johnnie Ray at the Desert Inn in Las Vegas* (1959); *A Sinner Am I* (1959); *'Til Morning* (1959); *Johnnie Ray on the Trail* (1959); *I Cry for You* (1960); *Johnnie Ray* (1962); *Yesterday, Today and Tomorrow* (1980); *Yesterday—The London Sessions 1976* (1993).

Bibl.: C. Roberts, *The Complete Life of J. R.* (N.Y., 1955); R. Sonin, ed., *The J. R. Story* (London, 1955); J. Whiteside, *Cry: The J. R. Story* (N.Y., 1994).—WR

Razaf, Andy (originally, **Razafinkeriefo, Andreamenentania Paul**), American lyricist; b. Washington, D.C., Dec. 15, 1895; d. North Hollywood, Calif., Feb. 3, 1973. Writing primarily for nightclub revues in Harlem, with occasional forays into Tin Pan Alley and Broadway, Razaf, with collaborators such as Fats Waller and Eubie Blake, wrote a series of jazz and pop standards, among them "Ain't Misbehavin'," "Black and Blue," and "Honeysuckle Rose." He also set lyrics to such Swing Era hits as "In the Mood" and "Stompin' at the Savoy."

Razaf's father was a member of the royal family of Madagascar, his mother the daughter of the former U.S. consul to the country. Shortly before his birth, his mother was forced to return to America due to a French invasion; his father was killed in battle. Razaf's family moved to the N.Y. area in 1900; he attended public school until the age of 16, then studied privately while working as an elevator operator in a Tin Pan Alley office building. At 18 he placed his first song in a Broadway revue: "Baltimo'," for which he wrote both music and lyrics, was used in *The Passing Show of 1913* (N.Y., July 24, 1913). This was, however, an isolated success; for the most part his work was rejected, and he was forced to earn a living in a series of menial jobs. He married Annabelle Miller, a housemaid, in April 1915. (The marriage broke up in the 1920s, though the couple never legally divorced; Mrs. Razaf died in 1958.) After World War I, Razaf wrote topical poetry for Harlem newspapers.

Razaf was the lyricist for the Broadway burlesque revue *Joe Hurtig's Social Maids*, writing songs with composer Hughie Woolford. His "He Wasn't B. in Araby" (music by Edgar Dowell) was used in the 1923 *Plantation Revue*. In March 1924 he appeared in *The Creole Follies* at the Club Alabam. The same year he made his radio debut, singing and playing the ukulele, and in 1925 he made his first recordings. He wrote the lyrics to music by J. P. Johnson for the revue *Desires of 1927*, which toured probably from the fall of 1926 into the winter of 1927. During this period Razaf and Waller sold songs outright on Tin Pan Alley without retaining credit. Unproven rumor suggests that among them was the hit "I Can't Give You Anything but Love," credited to Jimmy McHugh and Dorothy Fields.

Razaf's first song to gain attention was the risqué "My Special Friend (Is Back in Town)" (music by Waller, lyrics also by Bob Schafer), recorded by Ethel Waters and interpolated by her as a post-opening addition to the revue *Africana* (N.Y., July 11, 1927). Razaf and Waller then contributed a handful of songs to the musical *Keep Shufflin'* (N.Y., Feb. 27, 1928), including the title song and "Willow Tree." In September 1928, Razaf enjoyed two hit recordings of his songs, both with music by J. C. Johnson: "Louisiana" (lyrics also by Schafer) by Paul Whiteman and His Orch. with a vocal by Bing Crosby, and "Dusky Stevedore" by Nat Shilkret and His Orch.

In February 1929, Razaf and Waller wrote the songs for *Hot Feet*, a revue at the Harlem nightclub Connie's Inn. The club's owners then produced an expanded version of the revue on Broadway under the name *Connie's Hot Chocolates*. Running 219 performances, the show featured "Ain't Misbehavin'," which was recorded by at least half a dozen artists, including Waller, who used it as his theme song, as well as Louis Armstrong, who performed it in the show. But the best-selling version was by Leo Reisman and His Orch. Also included was "Black and Blue," a lament that has been described as the first African-American protest song. Razaf and Waller wrote a few new numbers for a revised version of *Hot Feet* at Connie's Inn, resulting in the revue *Load of Coal*, which featured "Honeysuckle Rose" and "My Fate Is in Your Hands," the latter a hit for Gene Austin at the end of the year.

Razaf wrote other songs during 1929 that became successful at the time or later. "S'posin'" (music by Paul Denniker) was recorded by Rudy Vallée and was a hit in July, and "Gee Baby, Ain't I Good to You?" (music and lyrics by Don Redman) was recorded by McKinney's Cotton Pickers in November, though a hit recording was 15 years away.

In 1930, Razaf collaborated with James P. Johnson on the songs for *Kitchen Mechanic's Revue* at the Harlem nightclub Smalls' Paradise, among them the witty "A Porter's Love Song to a Chambermaid." Later the same year he and composer Eubie Blake wrote the songs for the Broadway revue *Blackbirds of 1930*, which starred Ethel Waters. Louis Armstrong had a hit immediately with "Memories of You," but the show ran only 62 performances, effectively ending Broadway's interest in African-American revues.

Razaf enjoyed two hits in 1932: Louis Armstrong recorded "Keepin' Out of Mischief Now" (music by Waller), a follow-up to "Ain't Misbehavin'," for a hit in June, and Cab Calloway scored with "Reefer Man" (music by J. Russel Robinson) in July. Calloway later performed the song in the film *International House* (1933), but Razaf's first song to be placed in a motion picture was "If It Ain't Love" (music and lyrics by Razaf, Redman, and Waller) in *Okay America* (1932). Razaf continued to write songs for nightclub revues at Connie's Inn.

"Honeysuckle Rose" earned its first hit recording, albeit as an instrumental, in February 1933 in the hands of Fletcher Henderson and His Orch. In 1934, Waller signed a recording contract with RCA Victor as a singer/pianist and began to record prolifically, frequently drawing on his backlog of compositions with Razaf. As a result, "How Can You Face Me?" became a hit in October and "A Porter's Love Song to a Chambermaid" in November. Razaf, meanwhile, was writing revues with Paul Denniker for the Grand Terrace Café in Chicago.

With the advent of the Swing Era in 1935, Razaf was in demand to fit lyrics to popular swing instrumentals. Andy Kirk and His Orch. got into the hit parade in the spring of 1936 with "Christopher Columbus" (music by Leon "Chu" Berry), for which Razaf had written words. Razaf also added lyrics to the swing standard "Stompin' at the Savoy" (music by Benny Goodman, Chick Webb, and Edgar Sampson) and to the radio themes "Make Believe Ballroom" (music by Denniker) and "The Milkman's Matinee" (music and lyrics by Razaf, Denniker, and Joe Davis) in 1936.

Without divorcing his long-estranged first wife, Razaf married Jean Blackwell, a librarian, on July 31, 1939. Later that year he set words to the big-band classic "In the Mood" (music by Joe Garland), though Glen Miller's hit recording was an instrumental. Razaf's lyrics were heard, however, on "A Lover's Lullaby" (music by Frankie Carle and Larry Wagner), which was in the hit parade for Glen Gray and the Casa Loma Orch. in May 1940.

In 1941, Razaf and Blake attempted to mount a Broadway musical, *Tan Manhattan*, but it closed after an out-of-town tryout and an engagement at the Apollo Theatre in Harlem. Razaf enjoyed a couple of hits in the early 1940s, as "I'm Gonna Move to the Outskirts of Town" (music and lyrics by Razaf and William Weldon) scored for Jimmie Lunceford and His Orch. in May 1942 and the King Cole Trio belatedly gave recognition to "Gee Baby, Ain't I Good to You?" in November 1944. But for the most part Razaf lapsed into obscurity. His second marriage ended in divorce, and following his marriage to Dorothy Carpenter on July 16, 1948, he moved to Los Angeles. His career was virtually ended by an attack of tertiary syphilis in January 1951 that rendered him an invalid for the rest of his life. In 1956, after the release of the film biography *The Benny Goodman Story*, "Memories of You" became a Top 40 hit for the Benny Goodman Trio with Rosemary Clooney. After divorcing his third wife, Razaf married Alice Wilson on Valentine's Day, 1963.

Razaf's songs began to turn up more frequently in musicals and movies and on records shortly after his death in 1973, notably a recording of "In the Mood" by Bette Midler that reached the charts in January 1974 and the use of three of his songs in the Broadway revue *Bubbling Brown Sugar* (N.Y., March 2, 1976). But his real popular comeback was launched by the success of *Ain't Misbehavin'*, a revue dedicated to the music of Fats Waller, which ran for 1,604 performances. From then on, Razaf's songs became staples of such similar revues as *Eubie!* (N.Y., Sept. 20, 1978); *One Mo' Time* (N.Y., Oct. 22, 1979); *Blues in the Night* (N.Y., June 2, 1982); and *Black and Blue* (N.Y., Jan. 26, 1989). Razaf's work also became a surprising favorite among country music artists, as Willie Nelson named a movie and album *Honeysuckle Rose* in 1980 and Hank Williams Jr. scored a chart-topping country hit with "Ain't Misbehavin'" in 1986.

WORKS (only works for which Razaf was the primary, credited lyricist are listed; all dates refer to N.Y. openings unless otherwise indicated): **MUSICALS:** *Joe Hurtig's Social Maids* (Sept. 25, 1922); *Connie's Hot Chocolates* (June 20, 1929); *Black-birds of 1930* (Oct. 22, 1930); *Tan Manhattan* (Feb. 7, 1941); *Ain't Misbehavin'* (May 9, 1978). **NIGHTCLUB REVUES:** *Hot Feet* (Connie's Inn; Feb. 28, 1929); *Load of Coal* (Connie's Inn; 1929); *Kitchen Mechanic's Revue* (Smalls' Paradise; March 17, 1930); *Hot Harlem* (Connie's Inn; 1932); *Harlem Hotcha* (Connie's Inn; September 1932); *Rhythm for Sale* (Grand Terrace Café, Chicago; Jan. 31, 1934); *Chicago Rhythm* (Grand Terrace Café, Chicago; 1934); *Connie's Hot Chocolates of 1935* (Connie's Inn; April 1935); *Ubangi Club Follies* (Ubangi Club; 1935); *Round 'n' Round in Rhythm* (Ubangi Club; 1930s); *Ubangi Club Follies* (Ubangi Club; 1941).

BIBL.: B. Singer, *Black and Blue: The Life and Lyrics of A. R.* (N.Y., 1992).—**WR**

Razumovsky, Count, later Prince Andrei,

Russian diplomat and music patron; b. St. Petersburg, Nov. 2, 1752; d. Vienna, Sept. 23, 1836. He was the Russian ambassador at Vienna from 1793 to 1809. He founded the celebrated Razumovsky Quartet (1808; first violin, Schuppanzigh; second violin, Louis Sina, whose part was occasionally taken over by Razumovsky; viola, Weiss; cello, Lincke), later known as the Schuppanzigh Quartet (without Razumovsky). Razumovsky's name was immortalized through the dedication to him of Beethoven's 3 string quartets, op. 59, and (with Prince Lobkowitz) the 5th and 6th Syms. He was a munificent and prodigal patron of art, but after the destruction by fire of his Vienna palace (Dec. 31, 1814) he gave up the quartet, and disappeared from musical history. —**NS/LK/DM**

Rea, John (Rocco),

Canadian composer and teacher; b. Toronto, Jan. 14, 1944. He studied at Wayne State Univ. in Detroit (B.Mus., 1967). Following training in composition with Weinzweig and Ciamaga at the Univ. of Toronto (M.Mus., 1969), he studied with Babbitt and Westergaard at Princeton Univ. (Ph.D., 1978). In 1973 he became a teacher of composition and theory at McGill Univ. in Montreal, where he also was dean of the faculty of music (1986–91). He was composer-in-residence in Mannheim in 1984 and of the Incontri music festival in Terra di Siena in 1991. In his music, Rea has explored various genres and styles, and has utilized both Western and non-Western elements in a number of his scores.

WORKS: DRAMATIC: *The Days/Les Jours*, ballet (1969; suite, Toronto, July 11, 1974); *The Prisoners Play*, opera (Toronto, May 12, 1973); *Com-possession*, "daemonic afterimages in the theatre of transitory states" (1980). **ORCH.:** *Piece* for Chamber Orch. (1967; rev. 1971); *Hommage à Vasarely* (1977); *Vanishing Points* (1983); *Over Time* (1987); *Time and Again* (Montreal, March 1987). **CHAMBER:** *Sestina* for Chamber Ensemble (1968); *Fantaisies and/et Allusions* for Saxophone Quartet and Snare Drum (1969); *Anaphora I–IV* for Various Instruments (1970–74); *Jeux de scène*, fantaisie-hommage à Richard Wagner for Horn, Oboe, Cello, Piccolo, Flute, Piano, Marimba, 3 Glockenspiels, and Blacksmith's Anvil (1976; Vancouver, Feb. 27, 1977); *Les Blues d'Orphée* for Flute, Clarinet, Viola, Cello, and Piano (1981); *Le Dernière Sirène* for Ondes Martenot, Piano, and Percussion (1981); *Médiator "...pincer la musique aujourd'hui..."* for Chamber Ensemble (1981); *Treppenmusik* for Saxophone Quartet, 4 Clarinets, Violin, Viola, Cello, Double Bass, and Tape (1982); *Glide Reflexions* for 2 Clarinets and 2 Cellos (1984); *Les Raisons des forces mouvants* for Flute, Alto Flute, and String Quartet (1984); *Spin* for String Quartet and Piano (1984); *Some Time Later* for Electronic String Quartet (1986); *Big Apple Jam* for Saxophone Quartet and Tape (1987–91; Montreal, March 19, 1991); *Kubla Khan* for Chamber Ensemble (Waterloo, Ontario, May 1989). **Piano:** *What You Will* for Piano, 2- or 4- Hands (1969); *Las Meninas* (1990–91). **VOCAL:** *Prologue, Scene, and Movement* for Soprano, Viola, and 2 Pianos (1968); *Le Petit Livre des "Ravalets"* for 4 Narrators, Early Music Instruments, and Tape (1983); *Litaneia* for Chorus and Orch. (1984); *Offenes Lied* for 2 Sopranos and Clarinet (1986). **TAPE:** *S. P. I. 51* (1969); *STER 1.3* (1969). —**NS/LK/DM**

Read, Daniel,

important American tunebook compiler and composer; b. Attleboro, Mass., Nov. 16, 1757; d. New Haven, Conn., Dec. 4, 1836. He worked on a farm as a youth. He studied mechanics, and was employed as a surveyor at 18; began to compose at 17. He served in the Continental Army as a private, and at 21 settled at New Stratford; later went to New Haven. In 1782–83 he maintained a singing school on the North River. He also was a comb maker. At his death, he left a collection of some 400 tunes by him and other composers. He publ. *The American Singing Book, or a New and Easy Guide to the Art of Psalmody, devised for the use of Singing Schools in America* (New Haven, 1785; subsequent eds., 1786, 1792, 1793, 1795), the *American Musical Magazine* (containing New England church music; compiled with Amos Doolittle; New Haven, 12 numbers, May 1786 to Sept. 1787; reprinted, Scarsdale, N.Y., 1961), *Supplement to The American Singing Book* (New Haven, 1787), *The Columbian Harmonist*, in 3 books: No. 1 (New Haven, 1793), No. 2 (New Haven, 1794; 2nd ed., with numerous additions, 1798; 3rd ed., with further additions, 1801), and No. 3 (New Haven, 1795); all 3 books in 1 vol. (New Haven, 1795; 2nd ed., completely rev.,

Dedham, Mass., 1804; 3rd ed., Boston, 1807; 4th ed., Boston, 1810), and *The New Haven Collection of Sacred Music* (New Haven, 1818).

BIBL.: V. Bushnell, *D. R. of New Haven (1757–1836): The Man and His Musical Activities* (diss., Harvard Univ., 1979). —NS/LK/DM

Read, Gardner, eminent American composer, pedagogue, and writer on music; b. Evanston, Ill., Jan. 2, 1913. He studied at Northwestern Univ. (1930–32), with Hanson and Rogers at the Eastman School of Music in Rochester, N.Y. (B.M., 1936; M.M., 1937), with Pizzetti in Rome on a Cromwell Traveling Fellowship (1938–39), and with Copland at the Berkshire Music Center in Tanglewood (summer, 1941). In 1936 he won first prize in the American Composers' Contest of the N.Y. Phil. for his 1st Sym. and in 1943 he won the Paderewski Prize for his 2nd Sym. After teaching at the St. Louis Inst. of Music (1941–43) and the Kansas City Cons. (1943–45), he was head of the Cleveland Inst. of Music (1944–48). He subsequently was prof. of music and composer-in-residence at the Boston Univ. School for the Arts (1948–78). He publ. *Thesaurus of Orchestral Devices* (1953), *Music Notation: A Manual of Modern Practice* (1964), *Contemporary Instrumental Techniques* (1976), *Modern Rhythmic Notation* (1978), *Style and Orchestration* (1979), *Source Book of Proposed Music Notation Reform* (1987), *20th-Century Microtonal Notation* (1990), *Compendium of Modern Instrumental Techniques* (1993), and *Pictographic Score Notation* (1995). As a composer, Read has produced a substantial body of works notable for their mastery of orchestration and form.

WORKS: DRAMATIC: *Villon,* opera (1965–67); incidental music. **ORCH.:** *The Lotus-Eaters* (Interlochen, Mich., Aug. 12, 1932); *Sketches of the City* (1933; Rochester, N.Y., April 18, 1934); *The Painted Desert* (Interlochen, Mich., July 28, 1935); *Fantasy* for Viola and Orch. (1935); 4 syms.: No. 1 (1936; N.Y., Nov. 4, 1937), No. 2 (1942; Boston, Nov. 26, 1943), No. 3 (1948), and No. 4 (1951–59; Cincinnati, Jan. 30, 1970); *Prelude and Toccata* for Chamber Orch. (1936–37; Rochester, N.Y., April 29, 1937); Suite for Strings (N.Y., Aug. 5, 1937); *Passacaglia and Fugue* (Chicago, June 30, 1938); *Pan e Dafni* (1940); *American Circle* (Evanston, Ill., March 15, 1941); Overture No. 1 (Indianapolis, Nov. 6, 1943); *Night Flight* (Rochester, N.Y., April 27, 1944); Cello Concerto (1945); *Threnody* for Flute and Strings (Rochester, N.Y., Oct. 21, 1946); *Quiet Music* for Strings (1946; Washington, D.C., May 9, 1948; arranged for organ, 1950); *Partita* for Chamber Orch. (1946; Rochester, N.Y., May 4, 1947); *Bell Overture* (Cleveland, Dec. 22, 1946); *Pennsylvaniana* (1946–47; Pittsburgh, Nov. 21, 1947); *The Temptation of St. Anthony,* dance sym. (1947; Chicago, April 9, 1953); *Dance of the Locomotives* (Boston, June 26, 1948); *Arioso elegiaca* for Strings (1951); *Toccata giocosa* (1953; Louisville, March 13, 1954); *Vernal Equinox* (Brockton, Mass., April 12, 1955); *Jeux des timbres* (1963); *Sonoric Fantasia No. 2* for Violin and Chamber Orch. (1965; also for Violin and Piano) and 3 for Wind and Percussion (1971); Piano Concerto (1977); *Astral Nebulae* (1983). **CHAMBER:** 6 *Intimate Moods* for Violin and Piano (1935–37); Suite for String Quartet (1936); Piano Quintet (1945; also as *Music* for Piano and Strings, 1946); *Sonata brevis* for Violin and Piano (1948); *Sound Piece* for Brass and Percussion (1949); *9 by 6* for 6 Winds (1950); *Sonoric Fantasia No. 1* for Celesta, Harp, and Harpsichord (1958) and *No. 4* for Organ and Percussion (1975–76); *Los dioses aztecas* for 6 Percussion (1959); *Petite suite* for Soprano Recorder, Alto Recorder, Piano, and Harpsichord (1963); *Invocation* for Trombone and Organ (1977); *Galactic Notes* for Organ and Percussion (1978); *Diabolic Dialogue* for Double Bass and 4 Timpani (1978–79); *Music for Chamber Winds* for Double Wind Quintet and Percussion (1980); *Phantasmagoria* for Oboe, Oboe d'Amore, English Horn, and Organ (1985–87; rev. 1988); *Fantasy-Toccata* for Harpsichord (1990); *5 Aphorisms* for Violin and Piano (1991). **KEYBOARD: P i a n o :** *3 Satirical Sarcasms* (1934–35); *Driftwood Suite* (1942); *Sonata da chiesa* (1945; also for Organ and Brass Quintet, 1947); *6 Easy Pieces* (1947–48); *Touch Piece* (1949); *5 Polytonal Etudes* (1961–64); *Motives* (1980). **O r g a n :** *Passacaglia and Fugue* (1935–36; also for 2 Pianos, 1938–40); Suite (1949); *14 Preludes on Old Southern Hymns* (1950, 1960); *Variations on a Chromatic Ground* (1964); *And There Appeared Unto Them Tongues as of Fire* (1977). **VOCAL:** *4 Nocturnes* for Alto and Orch. (1934); *A Merry Madrigal* for Women's Voices (1934–35; also for Chorus, 1964); *From a Lute of Jade* for Mezzo-soprano and Chamber Orch. or Piano (1935–36); *The Golden Journey to Samarkand* for Soloists, Chorus, and Orch. (1936–39); *Songs for a Rainy Night* for Baritone and Piano or Orch. (1938–40; also for Chorus and Piano, 1953); *Songs to Children* for Mezzo-soprano and Piano (1947–49); *A Sheaf of Songs* for Mezzo-soprano and Piano (1949–50; also for Chorus and Piano, 1954); *The Prophet,* oratorio (1960; Boston, Feb. 23, 1977); *Haiku Seasons* for 4 Speakers and 5 Instruments (1970); *The Hidden Lute* for Soprano, Alto Flute, Percussion, and Harp (1979); other choral pieces and songs.

BIBL.: M. Dodd and J. Engquist, *G. R.: A Bio-Bibliography* (Westport, Conn., 1996).—NS/LK/DM

Reading, John, English organist and composer, probably the son of **John Reading;** b. c. 1685; d. London, Sept. 2, 1764. He was a chorister of the Chapel Royal under Blow until 1699, organist of Dulwich Coll. from 1700 to 1702, lay vicar at Lincoln Cathedral in 1702, and Master of the Choristers in 1703; later organist in several London churches (1708–64). He compiled 14 autograph vols. of various works, including 3 for organ, which remain a valuable source in English music. His works (all publ. in London) include *A Book of New Songs...with Symphonies* (c. 1710), *A Book of New Anthems...with Proper Ritornels* (c. 1715), and organ and keyboard music. —NS/LK/DM

Reale, Paul, American composer and pianist; b. New Brunswick, N.J., March 2, 1943. He studied with Luening and Chou Wen-chung at Columbia Univ. (B.A., 1963; M.A., 1967) and with Rochberg and Crumb at the Univ. of Pa. (Ph.D., 1970). He joined the faculty of the Univ. of Calif. at Los Angeles in 1969, becoming a prof. in 1980. As a pianist, he toured Europe, South America, and China; from 1970, specialized in playing 20th-century American music. He also performed numerous guest lectures at the piano on 20th-century music and philosophy. Reale's catalog of works is quite extensive, and covers virtually all genres. His works are mostly based in tonality.

WORKS: DRAMATIC: *Pange Lingua* for Baritone and Chamber Orch. (1967); *The Traveler* for Tenor, Flute/Piccolo, and Piano (1969); *Terza Prattica* for Soloists, Chorus, and Orch. (1972); *Mad Ophelia* for Soprano, Chamber Orch., and Tape (1974); *America: A Premature Celebration* for Flute, Violin, Guitar, and Narrator, after e. e. cummings (1975); *The Waltz King* for

Vocal Soloists, 2 Violins, Piano, and Narrator (1976); *The Ballad of the Sleazy Palace Cafe*, opera, after Peter Belfiore (1979); *Uncle Sigmund Goes to the Opera*, opera (1986). **ORCH.:** Concerto for Harpsichord, Vibraphone, Celesta, and 2 String Orchs. (1966); *Oxyrhynchus Fragment* (1973–78); *Concerto "Dies Irae"* for Piano Trio and Winds (1982); Concertino for Guitar and Winds (1984); *Chorales* for Piano and Brass (1986); 2 piano concertos: No. 1 (1986) and No. 2, *Matisse-Jazz* (1992); *Voyages in Memory* for Orch. and Synthesizer (1987; also for Orch. and Mezzo-soprano); Violin Concerto (1990); *Columbus Concerto* for Organ and Wind Ensemble (1991); *Dancer's Dream* for String Orch. (1993; originally for 9 Solo Strings, 1980); Sinfonia Concertante, *"La Folia"* (1995); *'Watchman, Tell us of the Night*, concerto for 3 Trumpets and Wind Ensemble (1997); *Caldera with Ice Cave* for Piano and String Orch. (1999). **Wind Ensemble:** *Screamers* (1980); *Moonrise, a Polonaise, Early Light* (1983; rev. 1985). **CHAMBER:** *Nel Sonno* for Mixed Chamber Ensemble (1966); Concertino for 2 Flutes, 2 Bassoons, and Cello (1967–69); *Late Telophase* for Flute, Clarinet, Cello, Piano, and Percussion Effects (1971); *Joshua's Trumpet* for Piano and Winds (1972); *The Mysterious Death of the Magic Realist* for Viola, Cello, Guitar, and Harpsichord (1972); *2+2/3* for 2 Violins and 2 Pianos (1975); String Quartet (1976); *Eleven Miniatures* for Wind Quintet (1978); Partita for Flute and String Trio (1978); *Music for Open Spaces* for 10 Brass (1982); *Graces and Furies* for Clarinet and String Quartet (1988); *Dvořák, Anyone?* for Saxophone Quartet (1991); *Seraphim and Cherubim* for Flute Choir (1991); *The Wexford Carol* for String Quartet (1992); *Of Chrome and Brass* for 2 Euphoniums and 2 Tubas (1993); *Ceilidh* for String Quartet (1996); Fanfare for Easter, *"Victimae Paschali"* for 2 Trumpets, Horn, 2 Trombones, and Tuba (1999); also numerous works for solo instruments, including several for guitar, as well as duets and trios. **KEYBOARD: Solo Piano:** *Piece for Piano 1967* (1969); Piano Suite (1970); *Finger Teasers* (1974; also for Tape as *Tape Teasers*); *Salon Music* (1975); *Pieces of Seven* (1978); *Bagatrix* (1980); *Hand Of Glory* (1983); *Simple Suite* (1983); *Classy Contemporaries* (2 vols., 1983–84); 8 piano sonatas: No. 1, *First Sonata* (1985), No. 2, *Dance Sonata* (1985), No. 3, *Sonata Brahmsiana* (1985), No. 4, *Sonata Rochbergiana* (1987), No. 5 (1988), No. 6, *The Waste Land* (1992), No. 7, *Veni Creator Spiritus* (1994), and No. 8, *Il Trionfo della Folia* (1997); *Ex Cello and Stride* (1989); *Improvisations* (1993); *Encore* (1996); *Acrobatics* (1998). **2 Pianos:** *Period Piece* (1990); *Serge P* (1993; based on Prokofiev's op.56); *CPE for Two Pianos* (1999); *Drowsey Maggie* (1999); *Waltzes, Old and New* (1999). **Piano, 4-hands:** *Little Screamers* (1981; from *Screamers* for Wind Ensemble, 1980). **Organ:** *Fantasie* (1970); *Intavolatura III* (1978). **Harpsichord:** *Within the Circle of Fifths* (1974); *Suite for Harpsichord* (1977). **VOCAL: Choral:** *Alleluia Sequence* for Solo Women's Voices and Women's Chorus (1973); *Motet: Miserere* for Chorus (1973); *Season for Darkness* for Chorus, 3 Trombones, Celesta, Timpani, and Organ (1973); *Contrafactum* for Men's Choruses and Piano (1975); *Psalm 118* for Chorus (1975); *I Felt a Funeral* for Women's Chorus, 3 Clarinets, and Piano, after Dickinson (1976); *Libera Me* for Solo Men's Voices and Men's Chorus (1976); *Blessings of God* for Chorus (1978); *Spring and Fall* for Chorus, after Hopkins (1978); *Ave Maria* for Chorus (1979); *The Lamb* for Solo Bass and Women's Chorus, after Blake (1981); *We All Loved You, Jenny Jo* for Mezzo-soprano and Chorus (1981); *Ecce Tu Pulcher Es* for Women's Chorus (1982); *What is Life* for Chorus (1985); *Psalm 84* for Chorus and Organ (1995); *On This Stone* for Solo Sopranos, Baritone, Chorus, Flute, 2 Violins, Handbells, and Organ (1998); *Psalm 109* for 2 Sopranos, Chorus, and Organ (2000). **Songs:** *3 Songs from the Chinese* for Mezzo-soprano, Oboe, and Percussion, after Rexroth (1967–68); *Bicinium No. 2* for Tenor and Guitar, after Milarepa (1973); *Regrets of Adolescence* for Soprano, Trumpet, and Bass Clarinet (1978); *Hopkins Songs* for Tenor and Piano (1994); *Serene Words*, 5 songs for Mezzo-soprano and Piano, after Mistral (2000). **TAPE:** *Tape Teasers* (1974; also for Piano as *Finger Teasers*).—NS/LK/DM

Reaney, Gilbert, learned English musicologist; b. Sheffield, Jan. 11, 1924. He took courses in music and French at the Univ. of Sheffield (B.A., 1948; M.A., 1951, with the diss. *The Ballades, Rondeaux and Virelais Set to Music by Guillaume de Machaut*; B.Mus., 1951); also studied at the Sorbonne in Paris on a French government grant (1950–53). He was a research fellow at the univs. of Reading (1953–56) and Birmingham (1956–59), and then a visiting prof. at the Univ. of Hamburg (1959–60); subsequently was assoc. prof. (1960–63) and prof. (from 1963) at the Univ. of Calif. at Los Angeles. He served as asst. ed. of *Musica Disciplina* (1956–93) and was general ed. of the Corpus Scriptorum de Musica series. His contributions to the latter include: with A. Gilles and J. Maillard, *P. de Vitry: Ars nova*, VIII (1964); *Willemus: Breviarium regulare musicae; Anon.: Tractatus de figuris; J. Torkesey: Declaratio trianguli et scuti*, XII (1966); with A. Gilles, *Anon.: Ars musicae mensurabilis secundum Franconem*, XV (1971); with A. Gilles, *Franco of Cologne: Ars cantus mensurabilis*, XVIII (1974); 3 anonymous 14th-century mensural treatises, XXX (1982); the mensural treatises of John Hothby and Thomas Walsingham, XXXI (1983); with H. Ristory, 4 mainly anonymous mensural treatises of the 13th to 14th centuries, XXXIV (1987). He also ed. *Early Fifteenth-Century Music* in the Corpus Mensurabilis Musicae series, XI/1–7 (1955–83). Among his other writings are *Ch. Jones, the Saint Nicholas Liturgy and Its Literary Relationships* (Berkeley and Los Angeles, 1963) and *Guillaume de Machaut* (London, 1971).—NS/LK/DM

Reardon, John, American baritone; b. N.Y., April 8, 1930; d. Santa Fe, N.Mex., April 16, 1988. He studied at Rollins Coll. (B.Mus., 1952); then took voice lessons with Martial Singher and Margaret Harshaw. He made his first appearance with the N.Y.C. Opera on Oct. 16, 1954, as Falke in *Die Fledermaus*. He made his Metropolitan Opera debut in N.Y. on Sept. 28, 1965, as Count Tomsky in Tchaikovsky's *Queen of Spades*, remaining on its roster until 1977. He mastered an extensive repertoire, which included several roles in modern operas.—NS/LK/DM

Rebel, family of French musicians:

(1) Jean Rebel, singer; b. place and date unknown; d. Versailles, before Feb. 29, 1692. He was a tenor in the private chapel of Louis XIV by 1661, singing there until his death; was also a secular singer at the court. He had 2 children who became prominent musicians:

(2) Anne-Renée Rebel, singer; b. Paris (baptized), Dec. 6, 1663; d. Versailles, May 5, 1722. She began singing at the court when she was about 10, and shortly thereafter took solo roles there. She was held in high esteem by the King.

(3) Jean-Féry Rebel (le père), violinist, harpsichordist, conductor, and composer; b. Paris (baptized), April 18, 1666; d. there, Jan. 2, 1747. He began playing the violin at an early age, winning the approbation of the King and Lully when he was only 8. He was first violin at the Académie Royale de Musique (1699–1700), then joined the King's 24 Violons (1705). He gained the right of succession to half of the office of chamber composer to the court (1718), which was held by his brother-in-law, Lalande; was granted the title as well (1726). He also was active at the Academie Royale de Musique in various capacities, being made its maître de musique (1716); conducted at the Concert Spirituel (1734–35). He was held in high regard by his contemporaries.

WORKS: DRAMATIC: Opera: *Ulysse* (Paris, Jan. 23, 1703). **INSTRUMENTAL:** *Pièces...divisées par* [3] *suites de tons* for Violin and Basso Continuo (1705); *Recueil de 12 sonates à II et III parties* for 2 Violins, Bass Viol, and Basso Continuo (1712); (12) *Sonates* for Violin and Basso Continuo...*mellées de plusieurs récits* for Bass Viol (1713); also choreographed "symphonies" for the dancers at the Académie Royale de Musique: *Caprice* for 3 Violins, Cello, and Basso Continuo (1711); *La Boutade* for 2 Violins, Viol, and Basso Continuo (1712); *Les Caractères de la danse,* fantaisie for 2 Violins and Basso Continuo (1715); *Terpsichore,* sonate for Violin, Flute, and Basso Continuo (1720); *Fantaisie* for 5 Flutes, 2 Violins, and Basso Continuo (1729); *Les Plaisirs champêtres* for 2 Violins and Basso Continuo (1734); *Les Élémens,* simphonie nouvelle for 2 Violins, 2 Flutes, and Basso Continuo (1737). **VOCAL:** Songs, chansons, drinking songs, etc.

(4) François Rebel (le fils), violinist, theorbist, conductor, theater director, and composer, son of the preceding; b. Paris, June 19, 1701; d. there, Nov. 7, 1775. He began music studies at an early age, joined the orch. of the Académie Royale de Musique at age 13, and gained the right of succession to his father's position in the King's 24 Violons when he was 16. He soon became a close associate of François Francoeur, who collaborated with him on several stage works. He was royal chamber composer (1727–55) and surintendant and maître of the royal chamber music (1733–75), and inspecteur général (1743–53) and co-director (with Francoeur; 1757–67) of the Académie Royale de Musique, returning as its administrateur général (1772). In all, he wrote 18 stage works with Francoeur. His other works include cantatas, motets, and songs.—**NS/LK/DM**

Rebelo (or Rebello, Rabello, Rabelo), João Soares or João Lourenço, Portuguese composer;
b. Caminha, 1610; d. Apelação (now in Lisbon), Nov. 16, 1661. He was maestro to King John IV of Portugal, who dedicated to Rebelo his *Defensa de la música moderna* (1649). Psalms a 16, Magnificats, Lamentations, and Misereres by Rebelo were publ. in Rome (1657). —**NS/LK/DM**

Reber, (Napoléon-) Henri, French composer; b.
Mulhouse, Oct. 21, 1807; d. Paris, Nov. 24, 1880. He studied with Reicha and Le Sueur at the Paris Cons., becoming a prof. of harmony there in 1851. He succeeded Halévy as prof. of composition in 1862 (being succeeded in turn by Saint-Saëns in 1880), and was also inspector of the branch conservatories from 1871. He publ. *Traité d'harmonie* (Paris, 1862; 2nd ed., 1889, ed. by T. Dubois).

WORKS: DRAMATIC: Comic Opera (all first perf. at the Opéra-Comique, Paris): *La Nuit de Noël* (Feb. 9, 1848); *Le Père Gaillard* (Sept. 7, 1852); *Les Papillotes de Monsieur Benoist* (Dec. 28, 1853); *Les Dames-capitaines* (June 3, 1857). **Ballet:** *Le Diable amoureux* (Sept. 23, 1840; in collaboration with F. Benoist). **OTHER:** 4 syms.; *Suite de morceaux* for Orch.; String Quintet; Piano Quartet; 3 string quartets; 7 piano trios; piano pieces; 55 melodies for Voice and Piano; 18 vocalises for Soprano or Tenor and Piano; etc.

BIBL.: C. Saint-Saëns, *Notice sur N. H. R.* (Paris, 1881). —**NS/LK/DM**

Rebikov, Vladimir (Ivanovich), Russian
composer; b. Krasnoyarsk, Siberia, May 31, 1866; d. Yalta, Aug. 4, 1920. He studied at the Moscow Cons. with Klenovsky, then in Berlin and Vienna. He then went to Odessa, where his first opera, *In the Thunderstorm,* was produced in 1894. In 1898 he moved to Kishinev, Bessarabia, where he organized a branch of the Imperial Russian Musical Soc. In 1901 he settled in Moscow, remaining there until 1919; he spent his last year of life in the Crimea. His early works were under the influence of Tchaikovsky, but beginning with *Esquisses* for Piano he made a decisive turn toward a modern style; he became particularly fond of the whole-tone scale and its concomitant, the augmented triad, claiming priority in this respect over Debussy and other European composers; his piano piece *Les Démons s'amusent* is based entirely on the whole-tone scale. He declared that music is a language of emotion and therefore could not be confined to set forms, or to arbitrarily defined consonances. An entirely new departure is represented by his *Mélomimiques,* short lyric pieces for Piano, in which mimicry and suggestion are used in an impressionistic manner. He also wrote several vocal "melomimics," 3 "rhythmo-declamations" for Piano (op.32), and 20 for Voice and Piano. In these compositions he abandoned cohesive form in favor of a free association of melodic and rhythmic phrases, sparingly harmonized; prevalence of esthetic theories over musical substance made his experiments ephemeral. A melodious waltz from his children's opera, *The Christmas Tree,* is his most popular composition. He publ. numerous articles on musical aesthetics, particularly relating to modern music, and tr. into Russian Gevaert's *Traité d'instrumentation.*

WORKS: DRAMATIC: *In the Thunderstorm,* opera (Odessa, Feb. 27, 1894); *The Christmas Tree,* children's opera (Moscow, Oct. 30, 1903); *Little Snow White,* musico-psychological pantomime (Tiflis, 1909); *Prince Charming,* fairy opera; scenic fables after Krylov: *The Grasshopper and the Ant, A Dinner with a Bear, The Ass and the Nightingale, The Funeral,* and *The Liar* (Moscow, Dec. 27, 1903); several "musico-psychological tableaux": *Slavery and Freedom, Songs of the Harp, The Nightmare,* etc. **Piano:** Numerous pieces (*Scènes bucoliques, Silhouettes, Dans la forêt, Chansons blanches, Idylles, Les Danses, Les Démons s'amusent,* etc.).

BIBL.: W. Dale, *A Study of the Musicopsychological Dramas of V. I. R.* (diss., Univ. of Calif., Los Angeles, 1955); O. Tompakova, *V. I. R.: Ocherki zhizni i tvorchestva* (Moscow, 1989).—**NS/LK/DM**

Rechberger, Herman(n), Austrian-born Finnish recorder player, conductor, and composer; b. Linz, Feb. 14, 1947. He studied classical guitar at the Bruckner Cons. in Linz, and after further training in Zürich and at the Brussels Cons., he settled in Finland in 1970 and became a naturalized citizen (1974). He took courses with Osmo Lindeman (electronic music), Olli Ruottinen (recorder; teacher's diploma, 1973), Ivan Putilin (guitar; teacher's diploma, 1973), and Aulis Sallinen (composition; diploma, 1976) at the Sibelius Academy in Helsinki (1971–77), where he also received instruction in piano, violin, and oboe. He was active as a music teacher (1975–79), then was a producer of contemporary music for and director of the electronic music studio at the Finnish Radio (1979–84). He toured widely as a recorder player, and also appeared as a conductor. In his own music, he employs the full arsenal of contemporary resources, experimenting in multimedia spectacles, with ample use of electronics.

WORKS: DRAMATIC: Multimedia and Radiophonic: *Naula* (The Nail) for Bass-baritone, Actors, Dancers, Slide Projection, and Instruments (1975–76); *Pekka Mikkosen nousu* (The Rise of Jonathan Smith), radiophonic piece for Narrator, Piano, Various Sound Sources, and Nonconventional Instruments (1976–78); *Tree-O* for Stage Equipment, Slide Projection, 3 Actors, and Lute (1976); *Publico concertante* for 6 to 30 Different Instruments, Audience, and Slides (1977); *Zin Kibaru*, multimedia piece for Young Performers (1977); *...i$mo*, multimedia piece for Sound Objects, Actor, Slide Projectors, Light Organ, Flute, Clarinet, Violin, Cello, Videotape, and Kinetic Wall (1982); *Magnus Cordius—Entries in a Diary*, radiophonic piece for Actors, Orch., Chorus, Early Instruments, Vocal Ensemble, and Tapes (1985); *Die Nonnen* (The Nuns), chamber opera (1987). **Other:** Music for plays and television. **ORCH.:** Concerto for Guitar and Strings (1971); *Kaamos* for Strings and Timpani (1973); *Music for Underdeveloped Film* (1973); *Loitsut* (Charms) for High Soprano and Chamber Orch. (1974); *La macchina capricciosa* for Double Bassoon, Chamber Orch., and Optional Slides (1974–75); *Consort Music 1* for Recorders, Chamber Orch., and Tape (1974–76), *2* for Renaissance Instruments and Chamber Orch. (1977), and *5* (1985–86); *Himojen Puutarha* (The Garden of Delights; 1976–77); *Venezia, visioni per grande orchestra, diversi soli e nastro* (1985). **CHAMBER:** *Ylistyslaulu höyryveturille* (Ode to a Steam Locomotive) for Flute, Clarinet, Viola, and Cello (1971); *Mayenzeit one neidt* for Flute, Violin, Cello, Double Bass, Metronome, and Live Electronics (1974); *Meccanismo* for Flute, Clarinet, Violin, Cello, and Metronomes (1978); *Fragebogen* for Double Bassoon and Pedal Sounds (1979); *Consort Music 3* for 4 Trumpets, 4 Trombones, and Tuba (1980–81); *Almost 4 Seasons* for String Quartet (1981); *Consort on an Egg* for Renaissance Instruments (1985); *NCG 7293* for 2 to 4 Instrumentalists (1986); *tympanon* for 2X5 Tambourins and Cowbells (1987); works for solo instruments. **OTHER:** Choral music; pieces for solo tape and for tape and instruments; text scores; musical graphics. —NS/LK/DM

Reda, Siegfried, German organist, pedagogue, and composer; b. Bochum, July 27, 1916; d. Mülheim, Dec. 13, 1968. He studied in Dortmund, and then with Pepping and Distler in Berlin. In 1946 he became director of the Essen Folkwang-Hochschule, where he also was prof. of organ and composition. From 1953 he also served as director of church music in Mülheim.

Reda was an influential figure in progressive Protestant church music circles in Germany after World War II. In addition to his masterpiece, the Requiem for Soloists, Chorus, and Orch. (1963), he composed much other sacred choral music, as well as various liturgical organ works.

BIBL.: R. Webb, *S. R. (1916–1968)* (diss., Univ. of Cincinnati, 1974).—NS/LK/DM

Redding, Otis, the single most important and influential male soul artist of the 1960s, Redding was one of the first black artists to broaden his appeal to white audiences with a raw, spontaneous style that bore a stark contrast to the smooth, sophisticated music of Motown; b. Dawson, Ga., Sept. 9, 1941; d. near Madison, Wisc., Dec. 10, 1967.

Raised in Macon, Ga., Otis Redding began singing in a local church choir. He dropped out of high school in the tenth grade and began touring the South with Johnny Jenkins and The Pinetoppers. With the group, he made his first recording in 1960 as Otis and The Shooters. He later recorded "Shout Bamalama" in a vocal style reminiscent of Little Richard, and the song was released nationally on the Bethlehem label.

In 1962, Otis Redding was allowed to record his own "These Arms of Mine" at a Johnny Jenkins session at the Stax studio in Memphis that was completed early. The song became a major rhythm-and-blues and minor pop hit in early 1963 on the newly formed Volt subsidiary of Stax Records, to which he was quickly signed. Recording thereafter in Memphis with the Stax house band of Booker T. and The MGs and The Memphis Horns (often augmented by keyboardist Isaac Hayes), Redding scored a number of modest crossover hits for Volt through 1964, including "That's What My Heart Needs," "Pain in My Heart," and "Chained and Bound." He managed his first moderate pop hit with the uptempo "Mr. Pitiful" (backed by "That's How Strong My Love Is") in early 1965. Redding toured regularly through 1967, accompanied by either Booker T. and The MGs or The Bar-Kays, developing a greater initial following for his raw, powerful music in Europe than at home.

In the spring of 1965, Otis Redding broke through into the pop market with the classic "I've Been Loving You Too Long (to Stop Now)," cowritten with Jerry Butler, and his emphatic "Respect." His outstanding *Otis Blue* album included the two hits Sam Cooke's "Shake" and "A Change Is Gonna Come," and The Rolling Stones' "Satisfaction," which later became a crossover hit. Redding's "I Can't Turn You Loose"/"Just One More Day" became a major two-sided rhythm-and-blues hit at the end of 1965, and his *Dictionary of Soul* album yielded crossover hits with "My Lover's Prayer" (by Redding), "Fa-Fa-Fa-Fa-Fa (Sad Song)" (cowritten by Redding and The MGs' Steve Cropper), and the classic "Try a Little Tenderness."

In 1967, Arthur Conley scored a smash crossover hit with the Conley-Redding composition "Sweet Soul Music" and Aretha Franklin had a top pop and R&B hit with Redding's "Respect." Otis Redding recorded *King and Queen* with Carla Thomas and the album yielded smash R&B and major pop hits with Lowell Fulsom's "Tramp" and Eddie Floyd's "Knock on Wood."

Appearing as the only soul act at the June 1967 Monterey International Pop Festival, Otis Redding attained widespread recognition with his incendiary performance and began establishing himself with pop audiences. However, while touring, Redding's airplane crashed into Lake Monona near Madison, Wisc., on Dec. 10, 1967, killing him and four members of The Bar-Kays, James King, Ronald Caldwell, Phalon Jones, and Carl Cunningham. In early 1968, Redding's recording of "(Sittin' on) the Dock of the Bay," cowritten with Steve Cropper, became a top pop and rhythm-and-blues hit. Posthumous crossover hits continued into 1969 with "The Happy Song (Dum Dum)," "Amen," "I've Got Dreams to Remember," "Papa's Got a Brand New Bag" and "Love Man." Redding's recording legacy was largely ignored in the 1970s and 1980s, but virtually all his albums were reissued in CD form by Rhino Records in the early 1990s. Otis Redding was inducted into the Rock and Roll Hall of Fame in 1989.

In the late 1970s, Otis Redding's sons Dexter and Otis III formed The Reddings with cousin Mark Locket for recordings on the Believe in a Dream label, distributed by Columbia. They scored a rhythm-and-blues smash with "Remote Control" in 1980 and eventually switched to Polydor Records in the late 1980s.

DISC.: OTIS REDDING: *Pain in My Heart* (1964); *The Great Otis Redding Sings Soul Ballads* (1965); *Otis Blue/Otis Redding Sings* (1965); *The Soul Album* (1966); *Dictionary of Soul* (1966); *Live in Europe* (1967); *Dock of the Bay* (1968); *The Immortal Otis Redding* (1968); *In Person at the Whiskey a-Go-Go* (1968); *Love Man* (1969); *Tell the Truth* (1970); *Good to Me: Live at the Whiskey a-Go-Go, Vol. 2* (1993). **OTIS REDDING AND CARLA THOMAS:** *King and Queen* (1967). **OTIS REDDING/JIMI HENDRIX EXPERIENCE:** *Historic Performances at the Monterey International Pop Festival* (1970). **OTIS REDDING AND LITTLE JOE CURTIS:** *Here Comes Soul* (1968). **THE REDDINGS:** *The Awakening* (1980); *Class* (1981); *Steamin' Hot* (1982); *If Looks Could Kill* (1985); *The Reddings* (1988).

BIBL.: J. Schiesel, *The Otis Redding Story* (Garden City, N.Y., 1973).—**BH**

Reddy, Helen,

hit maker of the 1970s best remembered for the feminist anthem "I Am Woman"; b. Melbourne, Australia, Oct. 25, 1942. Born into a family of Australian vaudevillians, Helen Reddy performed professionally from the age of four. By her 20s, she had her own television show. At 24, she won a talent contest that sent her to N.Y. for an audition with record company executives. Unfortunately, when she arrived they told her that they were sorry she wasn't a band of four guys her age rather than a passé pop singer. Despite the disappointment, Reddy stayed in the States. She waited tables and did other odd jobs, auditioning at every opportunity, first in N.Y. and by the late 1960s in Los Angeles. Her perseverance paid off in 1971, and she landed a contract with Capitol.

Reddy's sandy alto first came to the attention of American pop fans through a version of "I Don't Know How to Love Him" from the show *Jesus Christ Superstar*. It landed at #13 on the pop charts in 1971, beginning a six-year run of 15 Top 40 hits for the singer. She co-wrote her next hit with fellow Aussie expatriate Peter Allen.

That song, the anthemic "I Am Woman," landed in the film *Stand up and Be Counted*, and became a chart-topping gold record in the fall of 1972. The *I Am Woman* album hit #14 and went platinum. Reddy won a Grammy for Best Female Vocal Performance. Accepting the award she said, "I want to thank God because she makes everything possible."

Reddy's follow-up single, "Peaceful," only reached #12, but by the summer of 1993, Reddy was back atop both the pop and adult-contemporary charts, going gold with the country ballad "Delta Dawn." She also topped the adult charts with the follow-up, "Leave Me Alone (Ruby Red Dress)," a disturbing ballad that went to #3 pop, and gold as well. It propelled he album *Long Hard Climb* to #8 and gold as well. She picked up the pace a little for "Keep on Singing," which topped the adult-contemporary charts but only hit #15 pop. Her follow-up, "You and Me Against the World," could be viewed as tender or treacly, depending how cynical you felt at the moment; it also topped the adult-contemporary chart and went to #9 pop. These came from the *Love Song for Jeffery* album. The Jeffery in question was her husband and manager Jeff Wald; when the couple later filed for divorce, Reddy charged him with abuse. The album rose to #11 and went gold.

Reddy next topped the pop and adult-contemporary charts with the gold single "Angie Baby." The follow-up, "Emotion," rose to the top of the adult-contemporary charts but only hit #22 pop. The album *Free and Easy* rose to #8 and went gold. She next attempted Leon Russell's "Bluebird," only getting it to #35. However, she followed it with another adult-contemporary chart topper, "Ain't No Way to Treat a Lady," which hit #8 pop. It was the title track to her album, which went to #11 and went gold.

Through the 1970s, Reddy started to diversify. She hosted the late-night music program *The Midnight Special* throughout the late 1970s. She also played a singing nun in the film *Airport 75* and starred in Disney's semi-animated *Pete's Dragon*. She also had a role in the bomb film version of *Sgt. Pepper's Lonely Hearts Club Band*. While she never earned critical plaudits, she did help several noted songwriters early in their careers. Her last gold album, *Music Music*, featured a song by Holly Near, later a well-known feminist singer/songwriter. She took a more upbeat approach to "I Can't Hear You No More" which rose to the top of the adult contemporary chart, hitting #29 pop. Her last pop hit was a cover of Cilia Black's "You're My World" (a far cry from "I Am Woman"), which hit #18 in 1977.

Reddy performed sporadically through the 1980s and 1990s, spending more time behind the scenes producing videos, films, and television specials. In the latter part of the 1990s, she started to self-release recordings of her cabaret performances. She made her Broadway debut in 1995 in *Blood Brothers*, taking over the role from Carole King. She also performed on stage in the musicals *Anything Goes*, *Call Me Madam* and *The Mystery of Edwin Drood*. She took on a non-musical role, touring in *Shirley Valentine*. She also found time to serve as Commissioner of Parks and Recreation for the State of Calif.

DISC.: *I Don't Know How to Love Him* (1971); *Helen Reddy* (1971); *I Am Woman* (1972); *Long Hard Climb* (1973); *Love Song for Jeffrey* (1974); *Free and Easy* (1974); *Ain't No Way to Treat a Lady* (1975); *Music, Music* (1976); *Ear Candy* (1977); *Live in London* (1978); *We'll Sing in the Sunshine* (1978); *Reddy* (1979); *Take What You Find* (1980); *Imagination* (1983); *Lust for Life* (1984); *When I Dream* (1996); *Center Stage* (1998); *The Essential Helen Reddy Collection* (1998).—**HB**

Redel, Kurt, German flutist and conductor; b. Breslau, Oct. 8, 1918. He studied at the Breslau Cons.; also conducting with C. Krauss. In 1939 he became a member of the Salzburg Mozarteum Orch.; in 1941 he joined the orch. of the Bavarian State Opera in Munich. From 1946 to 1953 he taught at the North West German Music Academy in Detmold. In 1953 he founded the Pro Arte Orch. of Munich, with which he toured widely. —**NS/LK/DM**

Redford, John, English organist, composer, and poet; b. c. 1485; d. London, 1547. He was one of the vicars-choral, an almoner, and Master of the Choristers at St. Paul's Cathedral in London. His works are found in D. Stevens, ed., *The Mulliner Book,* in Musica Britannica, I (1951), J. Caldwell, ed., *Early Tudor Organ Music I: Music for the Office,* in Early English Church Music, VI (1966), and D. Stevens, ed., *Early Tudor Organ Music II: Music for the Mass,* in Early English Church Music, X (1969).

BIBL.: C. Pfatteicher, *J. R.* (Kassel, 1934).—**NS/LK/DM**

Red Hot Chili Peppers, preeminent white funk band of the late 1980s. **MEMBERSHIP:** Anthony Kiedis, voc. (b. Grand Rapids, Mich., Nov. 1, 1962); Flea (real name, Michael Balzary), bs. (b. Melbourne, Australia, Oct. 16, 1962); Jack Irons, drm. (b. Los Angeles, July 18, 1962); Hillel Slovak, gtr. (b. Haifa, Israel, April 13, 1962; d. Los Angeles, June 25, 1988); John Frusciante, gtr. (b. N.Y.C., March 5, 1970); Dave Navarro, gtr. (b. Santa Monica, Calif., June 7, 1967).

The four original Chili Peppers—Flea, Slovak, Irons, and Kiedis—met while attending Los Angeles' Fairfax H.S. Kiedis's father was an actor and Kiedis himself had played Sylvester Stallone's son in the 1976 movie *Fist.* They started working as Anthem School until Flea left to join the punk band Fear (and also to accept an acting role in the film *Suburbia*) in 1983. Irons and Slovak formed What Is This?, leaving Kiedis groupless. However, Flea soon left Fear, and the band began performing again. Unfortunately, Slovak and Irons were already signed for What Is This? and could not participate on the group's debut album in 1984. Cliff Martinez and Jack Sherman replaced them on an album produced by Gang of Four drummer Andy Gill. Both the What Is This? project and the Chili Peppers's debut didn't do especially well. Irons and Slovak returned to the group in time to tour. Often, the band went on stage wearing nothing but sweat-sock codpieces. Their music was, and continues to be, an amalgam of funk, hip-hop, skatecore metal, and punk.

The next year they went into the studio with George Clinton to make *Freaky Styley.* Clinton brought along members of his P-funk mob, particularly his Horny Horns (Fred Wesley and Maceo Parker). The album was more cohesive, and certainly funkier, than their first outing, but again failed to chart. Their next album finally cracked the charts, but just barely; *The Uplift Mofo Party Plan* reached #148, its sales mostly a tribute to the band's relentless touring and the inclusion of the frat anthem "Party on Your Pussy."

Before they could celebrate, disaster struck. In 1988, Slovak died of a heroin overdose; Kiedis was also having serious problems with opiates; Irons left the band. Rather than disband, Flea and Kiedis initially toured with P-Funk guitarist Blackbyrd McKnight and Dead Kennedys drummer D. H. Peligro, but the combination didn't work. John Frusciante was a fan and guitarist they knew and asked to join. They wound up auditioning drummers, hiring Chad Smith. With the new players, the band went into the studio and recorded 1989's *Mother's Milk,* the band's breakthrough album. Videos for a cover of Stevie Wonder's "Higher Ground" and the single "Knock Me Down" were intriguing enough to get serious play on MTV. The group's popularity increased when they appeared in spring 1990 as part of MTV's Spring Break festivities. However, during their performance, Flea and Smith entered the crowd, grabbing a comely coed, whom Smith proceeded to spank. Flea was found guilty of committing an unnatural act, battery, and disorderly conduct; Smith got off with a battery charge. This only increased the band's standing among its fans.

The band signed with Warner Brothers and retreated to the Sharon Tate mansion with producer Rick Rubin, living there together for the months that it took to make their next album, *BloodSugarSexMagik.* The album broke the band pop, with the single "Under the Bridge," an uncharacteristic ballad, zooming to #2 on the charts, going gold. The album rose to #3 on its way to triple platinum. The band suddenly was a star attraction, headlining the 1992 Lollapalooza festival.

The band's lifestyle proved a little too much for Frusciante. The guitarist had hardly had a drink and never did drugs before he joined the band, but teetering on the verge of rock stardom, he found himself with a drug problem. He left the band and after a series of guitarists who didn't make the grade, former Jane's Addiction guitarist Dave Navarro replaced him. Over the course of the next four years, the group released a greatest hits album, aptly titled *What Hits?,* which went platinum. They contributed the song "Soul to Squeeze" to the *Coneheads* soundtrack, which rose to #22. Flea and Kiedis acted in the movie *The Chase* together and, respectively, in *Private Idaho* and *Point Break.* When they finally got back to music, they cut 1995's *One Hot Minute.* With the rock hit "My Friends" the album went platinum, but that was considered a major comedown after the success of *BloodSugarSexMagik.*

Another long hiatus followed. Flea and Navarro joined with Navarro's old bandmates Perry Farrell and Stephen Perkins for the grueling Jane's Relapse tour. It proved to be too much roadwork for Navarro, who left both Jane's and the Chili Peppers to put together his own project. The Chili Peppers brought back a clean, sober Frusciante, and cut the 1999 opus *Californication*. The album rose to #3 on the charts, going double platinum based largely on the single "Scar Tissue," which won the band a Grammy Award for Best Rock Song.

DISC.: *Red Hot Chili Peppers* (1984); *Freaky Styley* (1985); *The Uplift Mofo Party Plan* (1987); *Mother's Milk* (1989); *BloodSugarSexMagik* (1991); *Out in L.A.* (1994); *One Hot Minute* (1995); *Californication* (1999).—**HB**

Redlich, Hans F(erdinand),

Austrian-born English conductor, musicologist, and composer; b. Vienna, Feb. 11, 1903; d. Manchester, Nov. 27, 1968. He studied piano and composition, but devoted his energies mainly to writing biographical and analytical books on composers; he was only 16 when he publ. an essay on Mahler. After taking courses at the univs. of Vienna and Munich, he obtained his Ph.D. at the Univ. of Frankfurt am Main with the diss. *Das Problem des Stilwandels in Monteverdis Madrigalwerk* (publ. in Berlin, 1931; 2nd ed., aug., 1932, as *Claudio Monteverdi: I. Das Madrigalwerk*). He conducted opera in Mainz (1925–29); then lived in Mannheim. In 1939 he emigrated to England and in 1947 became a naturalized British subject. From 1941 to 1955 he conducted the Choral and Orch. Soc. in Letchworth and also was a lecturer for the extramural depts. of the univs. of Cambridge and Birmingham. From 1955 to 1962 he was a lecturer at the Reid School of Music at the Univ. of Edinburgh; then was at the Univ. of Manchester (1962–68).

WRITINGS: *Gustav Mahler: Eine Erkenntnis* (Nuremberg, 1919); *Richard Wagner: Tristan und Isolde, Lohengrin, Parsifal* (London, 1948; 3rd ed., 1951); *Claudio Monteverdi: Leben und Werk* (Olten, 1949; Eng. tr., 1952); *Bruckner and Mahler* (London, 1955; 2nd ed., rev., 1963); *Alban Berg: Versuch einer Würdigung* (Vienna, 1957; condensed Eng. version, 1957, as *Alban Berg: The Man and His Music*).—**NS/LK/DM**

Redman, Don(ald Matthew),

groundbreaking swing-era composer, arranger, leader, alto and soprano saxophonist; b. Piedmont, W. Va., July 29, 1900; d. N.Y., Nov. 30, 1964. He was an important early jazz arranger, though certainly not, as often claimed, the first or the only of his era. However, he was writing for a band with great soloists and wisely left them room to improvise, mixing ensemble passages with solos, incorporating clever breaks, and call-and-response patterns between sections or individual players. Don's brother, Lewis, led a band in Cumberland, Md., for many years, their father was a noted music-teacher. A prodigy, he began playing trumpet at the age of three, and before he was 12 could play proficiently on all wind instruments including oboe. As a high school senior he was already writing arrangements. After intensive musical studies at Harper's Ferry and the Chicago and Boston conservatories, he graduated from Storer Coll. at 20 with a music degree. He worked in Piedmont for a year, then worked with Billy Paige's Broadway Syncopators, a Pittsburgh band. He went to N.Y. with them in March 1923. Later that year he began recording with Fletcher Henderson and subsequently joined the band early in 1924. He was with Henderson on sax and worked as staff arranger

until June 1927. He moved to Detroit to take an appointment as musical director for McKinney's Cotton Pickers, a position he held until summer 1931. During this period he arranged and recorded with Louis Armstrong studio groups in Chicago. In October 1931 his first band was formed by combining a nucleus of ex-McKinney members with several musicians from Horace Henderson's Band. The band began their first long residency at Connie's Inn in 1932 and subsequently worked regularly throughout the 1930s until disbanding in January 1940. Nobody objected to the title of his instrumental theme, a whole-tone based theme called "Chant of the Weed," though it was obviously a paean to marijuana. The band consolidated its considerable success by appearing on many important radio shows; he was the first black bandleader to have his own radio show. They also appeared in one short film made by National in 1935. Throughout the 1930s Redman also arranged for Paul Whiteman, Ben Pollack, Isham Jones, Nat Shilkret, and others., and also produced specially commissioned orchestrations for Bing Crosby. After his original band broke up in January 1940, he concentrated on freelance arranging, then re-formed again in December 1940. In February 1941 he toured briefly fronting the Snookum Russell Band, then returned to N.Y. to become staff arranger for Bobby Byrne. He returned to freelance arranging, scoring for many name bands; he provided Jimmy Dorsey with the arrangement of his big hit "Deep Purple." He reformed a big band for residency at The Zanzibar, N.Y. (1943), then resumed full-time arranging for Count Basie, Harry James, NBC studio bands, and others. He formed a band for a European tour commencing September 1946, then remained in Europe after the band broke up; he returned to the U.S. in August 1947. He had his own series on CBS television in autumn 1949. From 1951 worked as musical director for singer Pearl Bailey. Redman rarely played in public during the last few years of his life, but recorded on alto, soprano, and piano in 1958–59. He played piano at Georgia Minstrels concert in June 1962 and soprano sax for the Sissle–Blake Grass Roots concert in September 1964. During his later life, he worked on several extended compositions, which, so far, have not been publicly performed.

DISC.: *Shakin' the African* (1931); *Doin' the New Low Down* (1932); *For Europeans Only* (1946); *Don Redman's Park Ave. Patter* (1957); *Dixieland in High Society* (1959).—**JC/LP**

Redman, Joshua,

jazz tenor, soprano and alto saxophonist, son of Dewey Redman; b. Berkeley, Calif., Feb. 1, 1969. His parents were not married, and he was raised by his mother, a dancer, who he credits with nurturing him as a person and as a musician. However, when he became a full-time musician he took his father's surname. The valedictorian of his high school class, he graduated summa cum laude from Harvard in 1991 and was accepted into Yale Law School. In early 1992, Redman decided to become a musician instead of continuing his schooling. The tenor saxophonist had won first prize at the 1991 Thelonious Monk Inst. of Jazz Saxophone Competition. He recorded his debut album in 1993 and was voted the best saxophonist of 1993 in a *Down Beat* critics' poll. Redman's album *Wish* was voted

1994's best jazz album in *Down Beat*'s readers' poll; he also won as jazz musician of the year. Gavin Report proclaimed him artist of the year and *MoodSwing* album of the year. In 1997, he toured in a trio with Christian McBride and his longtime colleague Brian Blade. He is an exciting, inspired, and logical improviser with great passion and exceptional clarity of ideas and execution.

DISC.: *Wish* (1993); *Joshua Redman* (1993); *MoodSwing* (1994); *Spirit of the Moment: Live at the Village Vanguard* (1995); *Freedom in the Groove* (1996); *Timeless Tales (for Changing Times)* (1998); *Beyond* (2000).—LP

Redman, (Walter) Dewey, jazz tenor and alto saxophonist, musette player, father of Joshua Redman; b. Fort Worth, Tex., May 17, 1931. He began playing clarinet at 13, performing in church and at Sam Houston Coll. In high school, he played in marching band with Ornette Coleman, and in another group with Richard Williams and Leo Wright. From 1949–53, he studied and taught in Austin, Tex., and performed with R&B groups. He moved to Los Angeles in 1960 and played with Joe Gordon, Jimmy Woods, and Billy Higgins. He spent seven years in San Francisco, leading his own jazz groups, including the Monte Waters–Dewey Redman Quintet (November 1961), and working gigs with T-Bone Walker, The Five Royales, Pee Wee Crayton, Lowell Fulsom, and Bay Area Quintet. He played sessions or gigs with Pharoah Sanders and Wes Montgomery. He moved to N.Y. in 1967 and joined Coleman, performing and recording with him for seven years; during that time, he also worked with Keith Jarrett, Charlie Haden's Liberation Music Orch., Carla Bley, Roswell Rudd, JCOA, Don Cherry, and his own group. He formed the quartet Old and New Dreams with Haden, Cherry and Ed Blackwell. He recorded with Pat Metheny. He also did a duet record with his son and remains an active performer.

DISC.: *Look for the Black Star* (1966); *Tarik* (1969); *Ear of the Behearer* (1974); *Coincide* (1974); *Soundsigns* (1978); *Musics* (1978); *Redman and Blackwell in Willisau* (1980); *Struggle Continues* (1982); *Living on the Edge* (1989); *Choices* (1992); *African Venus* (1992).—LP

Reed, H(erbert) Owen, American composer and music educator; b. Odessa, Mo., June 17, 1910. He was educated at the Univ. of Mo. (theory and composition, 1929–33), La. State Univ. (B.M. in theory, 1934; M.M. in composition, 1936; B.A. in French, 1937), and at the Eastman School of Music in Rochester, N.Y. (Ph.D. in composition, 1939), where his mentors included Hanson, Rogers, and McHose. He pursued further studies at the Berkshire Music Center in Tanglewood (summer, 1942) with Martinů, Copland, and Bernstein and in Colorado Springs (summer, 1947) with Roy Harris. Subsequently he studied folk music in Mexico (1948–49; 1960), the Caribbean (1976), and Scandinavia (1977), and also native American music in Ariz. In 1939 he joined the faculty of Mich. State Univ., where he was chairman of its theory and composition dept. until 1967; he then was chairman of music composition from 1967 until his retirement as prof. emeritus in 1976. In 1948–49 he held a Guggenheim fellowship and in 1960 a Huntington

Foundation fellowship. His textbooks have been widely used. In his compositions, Reed generally has followed a tonal course with later diversions into nontonal pathways.

WRITINGS: *A Workbook in the Fundamentals of Music* (1947); *Basic Music* (1954); *Basic Music Workbook* (1954); *Composition Analysis Chart* (1958); with P. Harder, *Basic Contrapuntal Technique* (1964); *Basic Contrapuntal Workbook* (1964); with J. Leach, *Scoring for Percussion and the Instruments of the Percussion Section* (1969; rev. ed., 1979); with R. Sidnell, *The Materials of Music Composition* (3 vols., 1978, 1980, in progress).

WORKS: DRAMATIC: *The Masque of the Red Death,* ballet-pantomime (1936); *Michigan Dream,* renamed *Peter Homan's Dream,* folk opera (East Lansing, Mich., May 13, 1955; rev. 1959); *Earth Trapped,* chamber dance opera (1960; East Lansing, Mich., Feb. 24, 1962); *Living Solid Face,* chamber dance opera (1974; Brookings, S. Dak., Nov. 28, 1976); *Butterfly Girl and Mirage Boy,* chamber opera (East Lansing, Mich., May 1980). **ORCH.:** *Evangeline,* symphonic poem (Rochester, N.Y., March 30, 1938); 2 syms.: No. 1 (Rochester, N.Y., April 27, 1939) and No. 2, *La fiesta mexicana,* Mexican folk-song sym. (1968; also for Band, 1949); *Overture* (1940); *Symphonic Dance* (1942); *Cello Concerto* (1949); *Overture for Strings* (1961); *The Turning Mind* (1968); *Ut Re Mi* for Orch. and Taped or Live Men's Voices (1979; also for Wind Ensemble and Taped or Live Men's Voices, 1980). **Band:** *Spiritual* (1947); *La fiesta mexicana,* Mexican folk-song sym. (1949; also for Orch., 1968); *Missouri Shindig* (1951); *Theme and Variations* (1954); *Renascence* (1959); *Che-ba-kun-ah* (Road of Souls) for Wind Ensemble and String Quartet (1959); *The Touch of the Earth* for Concert Band (1971; also for Solo Voices, Chorus, and Concert Band, 1972); *For the Unfortunate* for Concert Band and Tape or Chorus (1975); *Ut Re Mi* for Wind Ensemble and Taped or Live Men's Voices (1980; also for Orch. and Taped or Live Men's Voices, 1979); *The Awakening of the Ents* for Winds and Percussion (1985); *Of Lothlórien* for Winds and Percussion (1987). **CHAMBER:** String Quartet (1937); *Scherzo* for Clarinet and Piano (1947); *Symphonic Dance* for Piano and Woodwind Quintet (1954); *El Muchacho* for 7 Handbells and 3 Percussion (1965); *Fanfare for Remembrance* for 6 Trumpets, Flugelhorn, Percussionist, and Narrator (1986); piano pieces. **VOCAL:** *A Psalm of Praise* for Soprano and 7 Instruments (1937); *Wondrous Love* for Tenor and Woodwind Quintet (1948); *Ripley Ferry* for Women's Voices and Wind Septet (1958); *A Tabernacle for the Sun,* oratorio for Contralto, Chorus, Speaking Men's Chorus, and Orch. (1963); *Rejoice! Rejoice!* for Soloist, Chorus, Taped Chorus, Vibe or Bells, and Double Bass (1977); other choral pieces and songs.—NS/LK/DM

Reed, Jimmy, one of the most influential blues artists of the 1950s; b. Dunleith, Miss., Sept. 6, 1925; d. Oakland, Calif., Aug. 29, 1976. Born on a plantation in Miss., Jimmy Reed was raised from the age of seven with Eddie Taylor, who taught him to play guitar as a youth. Reed moved to Chicago in 1943, but was soon drafted into the U.S. Navy. Following his discharge in 1945, Reed married and moved to Gary, Ind., reuniting with Taylor in 1949 in a musical partnership that lasted through the 1960s. Frequently playing Chicago area clubs, Reed first recorded for the Chance label in 1953 and subsequently failed an audition with Chess Records. He soon signed with the newly formed Chicago-based VeeJay label, for whom he recorded until 1965. Playing simple guitar and harmonica accompanied by guitarist Taylor, Reed scored his first R&B hit (a smash) in 1955 with "You Don't Have to Go." Subsequent R&B smashes included "Ain't That Lovin' You Baby", "You've Got Me Dizzy," and "Little Rain," and, by 1958, Reed was established as Chicago's biggest-drawing blues act.

Jimmy Reed scored his biggest success with 1957's "Honest I Do, " a smash R&B and moderate pop hit, followed by the R&B smash "I'm Gonna Get My Baby." Developing severe problems with unreliability and alcoholism, he was nonetheless consistently in both charts in the early 1960s, beginning with the classic "Baby What You Want Me to Do." Scoring his last R&B and pop crossovers with "Big Boss Man" and "Bright Lights Big City" in 1961, Reed's At Carnegie Hall album was actually a studio re-creation of his live concert.

Jimmy Reed toured Great Britain in 1963, and, with the demise of VeeJay Records in 1965, recorded with little success for Exodus and the BluesWay subsidiary of ABC in the latter half of the 1960s. He toured Europe with the American Folk Blues Festival in 1968 and recorded for a variety of labels in the 1970s. Afflicted with epilepsy since 1957, Reed toured until the mid-1970s, despite the condition and his chronic alcoholism. He died in Oakland, Calif., at the age of 50 on Aug. 29, 1976, of respiratory failure after an epileptic seizure. Jimmy Reed was inducted into the Blues Foundation's Hall of Fame in 1980 and the Rock and Roll Hall of Fame in 1991.

DISC.: *I'm Jimmy Reed* (1958); *Rockin' with Reed* (1959); *Found Love* (1960); *Now Appearing* (1960); *Jimmy Reed at Carnegie Hall* (1961); *Just Jimmy Reed* (1962); *T'Ain't No Big Thing* (1963); *The Twelve String Guitar Blues* (1964); *Jimmy Reed at Soul City* (1964); *The Legend, the Man* (1965); *Jimmy Reed at Carnegie Hall* (1965); *Just Jimmy Reed* (1966); *Sings the Best of the Blues* (1966); *The New Jimmy Reed Album* (1967); *Soulin'* (1967); *Big Boss Man* (1968); *Down in Virginia* (1969); *Jimmy Reed at Carnegie Hall* (1973); *Let the Bossman Speak* (1971). **JIMMY REED AND JOHNNY WINTER:** *Live at Liberty Hall Houston Texas 1972* (1993).—BH

Reed, Lou(is Alan), musically educated American rock singer, guitarist, songwriter, and photographer; b. N.Y., March 2, 1942. He studied piano in his childhood, taking up the guitar in high school. After graduating from Syracuse Univ., he read books, wrote poetry, essayed journalism, vocalized to guitar accompaniment, and finally found his niche improvising variously with such psychedelically inclined groups as The Primitives and The Warlocks. In 1966 he recruited a British musician of a similarly educated background, John Cale, and together they formed a sodality inexplicably named The Velvet Underground, projecting bizarre stage behavior and playing sophisticated numbers in dissonant harmony. They attracted the surrealist artist Andy Warhol, who hired them for his "total environment" show "The Exploding Plastic Inevitable." Under Warhol's nihilistic influence, The Velvet Underground revived the dadaistic, surrealistic type of old European modernism, superadded with the screeching, screaming, sadomasochistic electronic sound to Reed's demoralizing anarchistic lyrics openly extolling the psychedelic advantages of narcotics and totally emancipated sex play in

such songs as "Heroin" and "Venus in Furs." Reed left the group in 1970, and put out such invitations to anarchy as "Walk on the Wild Side," to date and by far his best known song, and "Metal Music Machine," in which electronic bleeps and hisses accompanied the shouted homicidal orders *Live...Take No Prisoners*. His later albums included *Coney Island Baby* (1976), *Street Hassle* (1978), *The Blue Mask* (1982), *New Sensations* (1984), *Mistrial* (1986), *New York* (1989), *Magic and Loss* (1992), and *Set the Twilight Reeling* (1996). Reed has also collaborated with the American theater director Robert Wilson, first on *Time Rocker* (1996), and currently on *Poe-Try* for Hamburg's Thalia Theater, for which he is writing both music and lyrics. Reed's photographic works have been shown at such venues as the Printemps de Cahors in Cahors, France (2000).

BIBL.: D. Clapton, *L. R. and the Velvet Underground* (London, 1982).—NS/LK/DM

Reed, William Henry, English violinist and composer; b. Frome, July 29, 1876; d. Dumfries, July 2, 1942. He studied at the Royal Academy of Music in London. He was a violinist in the London Sym. Orch. at its foundation in 1904, later serving as its concertmaster (1912–35). He taught violin at the Royal Coll. of Music in London. He was a close friend of Elgar, and publ. *Elgar as I Knew Him* (London, 1936) and *Elgar* (London, 1939). His works include the orch. sketches *The Lincoln Imp* (Hereford Festival, 1921) and *Aesop's Fables* (Hereford Festival, 1924), a Violin Concerto, *Rhapsody* for Violin and Orch., 5 string quartets, violin pieces, songs, etc. —NS/LK/DM

Reed, William L(eonard), English composer, lecturer, and editor; b. London, Oct. 16, 1910. He studied at the Guildhall School of Music in London (1917–26), Dulwich Coll., London (1922–29), the Univ. of Oxford (M.A., 1934; B.Mus., 1936; M.Mus., 1939), and with Howells (composition) and Lambert (conducting) at the Royal Coll. of Music in London (1934–36; first Cobbett Prize in composition, 1936). After World War II, he traveled widely in Europe, the U.S., and Asia; in 1961 settled in London, where he served as director of music at the Westminster Theatre Arts Centre (1967–80).

WORKS: DRAMATIC: Musicals: *The Vanishing Island* (Santa Barbara, Calif., 1955; in collaboration with G. Fraser); *Annie* (London, 1967); *High Diplomacy* (London, 1969; in collaboration with G. Fraser); *Love All* (London, 1978). **ORCH.:** *Recitative and Dance* (1934); *Jig* (1935); *Siciliana* (1935); *Pantomime* (1935); *Saraband* (1935); *Idyll* for Small Orch. (1935); *Waltz Fantasy* (1935); *Concert Rhapsody* for Viola and Orch. (1935); *6 Facets* (1936); *A Reflection* for Small Orch. (1936); *Scherzo* (1937); *2 Short Pieces* (1937); *Hornpipe* (1939); *Doctor Johnson's Suite* for Strings (1944); *Country Overture and Scherzo* for Strings (1944); *Mountain House*, suite (1949); *Concert Overture* (1950). **CHAMBER:** *Fantasy* for String Quartet (1936); *Tarantelle fantastique* for Piano and String Quartet (1943); *Waltz* for Piano and String Quartet (1944); 2 suites for Violin and Piano: No. 1 (1945) and No. 2, *On the Road* (1948); *The Top Flat*, suite for Viola and Piano (1947); *Rhapsody on Christmas Carols* for Violin and Piano (1951); piano pieces; organ works. **OTHER:** Vocal music.

WRITINGS (all publ. in London): *The Treasury of Christmas Music* (1950; 7th ed., 1978); *Music of Britain* (1952); *The Treasury of*

Easter Music (1963); with G. Knight, *The Treasury of English Church Music* (5 vols., 1965); *The Second Treasury of Christmas Music* (1967); with E. Smith, *The Treasury of Vocal Music* (4 vols., 1969); *National Anthems of the World* (5th ed. with M. Cartledge, 1978; 6th and 7th eds. with M. Bristow, 1985, 1987).—NS/LK/DM

Reese, Gustave, eminent American musicologist; b. N.Y., Nov. 29, 1899; d. Berkeley, Calif., Sept. 7, 1977. At N.Y.U. he studied jurisprudence (LL.B., 1921) and music (B.Mus., 1930), joining its faculty, teaching there during the periods 1927–33, 1934–37, and 1945–74. He concurrently worked with G. Schirmer, Inc. (1924–45; from 1940 to 1945 as director of publications), and was director of publications for Carl Fischer (1944–55). From 1933 to 1944 he was assoc. ed., and in 1944–45 ed., of the *Musical Quarterly*. In 1934 he was a co-founder of the American Musicological Soc.; was its president from 1950 to 1952, and remained its honorary president until his death. He gave numerous lectures at American univs.; also gave courses at the Juilliard School of Music in N.Y. An entire generation of American music scholars numbered among his students; he was widely regarded as a founder of American musicology as a science. He held a chair at the Graduate School of Arts and Science at N.Y.U., which gave him its "Great Teacher Award" in 1972 and its presidential citation on his retirement from active teaching in 1974; he then became a visiting prof. at the Graduate Center of the City Univ. of N.Y. He died while attending the congress of the International Musicological Soc. in Berkeley. Reese contributed a great number of informative articles to various American and European publications and music encyclopedias, but his most lasting achievement lies in his books, *Music in the Middle Ages* (N.Y., 1940; also in Italian, Florence, 1960) and *Music in the Renaissance* (N.Y., 1954; 2nd ed., rev., 1959), which have become classics of American music scholarship; he also brought out an interesting book that describes selected early writings on music not available in English, *Fourscore Classics of Music Literature* (N.Y., 1957).

BIBL.: J. LaRue, ed., *Aspects of Medieval and Renaissance Music: A Birthday Offering to G. R.* (N.Y., 1966; 2nd ed., 1978).—NS/LK/DM

Reeser, (Hendrik) Eduard, distinguished Dutch musicologist; b. Rotterdam, March 23, 1908. He studied art history with Vogelsang and musicology with Smijers at the Univ. of Utrecht (Ph.D., 1939). He taught music history at the Rotterdam Cons. (1930–37) and musicology at the Univ. of Utrecht (1947–73). He was also president of the Donemus Foundation (1947–57), the Maatschappij tot Bevordering der Toonkünst (1951–69), and the IMS (1972–77). He was made a member of the Royal Dutch Academy of Sciences (1961) and the Royal Academy of Sciences and Arts of Belgium (1973), as well as an honorary member of the Royal Musical Assn. in London (1974).

WRITINGS (all publ. in Amsterdam unless otherwise given): *De musikale handschriften van Alphons Diepenbrock* (1933); *Alphons Diepenbrock* (1935); *De zonen van Bach* (1941; Eng. tr., 1946); *Musiekgeschiedenis in vogelvlucht* (1942; Eng. tr., 1946); *De Vereeniging voor Nederlandsche muziekgeschiedenis 1863–1943:*

Gedenboek (1943); *De geschiedenis van de wals* (1947; Eng. tr., 1947); *Muziek in de gemeenschap der Kunsten* (Rotterdam, 1947); *Een eeuw Nederlandse muziek* (1950); ed. *Verzamelde geschriften van Alphons Diepenbrock* (Utrecht, 1950); *Music in Holland* (1959); ed. *Alphons Diepenbrock: Brieven en documenten* (2 vols., The Hague, 1962, 1967); *Gustav Mahler und Holland* (Vienna, 1980); *Ein Augsburger Musiker in Paris: Johann Gottfried Eckard* (Augsburg, 1985).—NS/LK/DM

Reeve, William, English organist and composer; b. London, 1757; d. there, June 22, 1815. He was a pupil of Richardson. He served as organist at Totness, Devon, from 1781 to 1783, then returned to London, where he composed operettas, pantomimes, and incidental music for plays, for Astley's Circus, and for Covent Garden (1791–1812). In 1792 he became organist of St. Martin's, Ludgate Hill, and from 1802 he was part-proprietor of Sadler's Wells Theatre. Besides music to some 40 plays, Reeve composed glees and songs. His song "I am a friar in orders grey, in the play Merry Sherwood" was very popular.—NS/LK/DM

Reeves, David Wallis, American bandmaster and composer; b. Oswego, N.Y., Feb. 14, 1838; d. Providence, R.I., March 8, 1900. As a boy he began to play cornet in circus and minstrel bands, and later he was in Union Army bands. In 1866 he became the leader of the American Band of Providence, which is said to trace its roots back to the War of 1812. During its 35 years under the direction of Reeves, it became a model of excellence among American municipal bands; Reeves succeeded in standardizing the instrumentation of the ordinary parade and outdoor-concert band. He composed some 80 marches, of which the best is *The 2nd Connecticut Regiment March,* known to have been a favorite of Charles Ives. Reeves was a great friend of Patrick Sarsfield Gilmore, conductor of the band of the N.Y. 22nd Regiment, and it was Gilmore who popularized Reeves's marches. Upon Gilmore's death, Reeves took over the 22nd Regiment Band for the 1892–93 season, but then resumed the conductorship of the American Band. Sousa called Reeves "the father of band music in America."—NS/LK/DM

Reeves, Diane, jazz-pop singer; b. Detroit, Mich., Oct. 23, 1956. As a teenager, she worked with Gene Harris. She was invited to perform at the IAJE Conference in Chicago, December 1974, on the recommendation of John Roberts who had heard her sing with her high school band. She met Clark Terry there, who introduced her to other musicians including then 10-year old Terri Lyne Carrington. Her success was a factor in the IAJE beginning a formal Young Talent program in 1977. Reeves performed with Terry at the Wichita Jazz Festival in 1975, and has returned many times. She attended the Univ. of Colo., worked with Bill Fowler there and attended clinics by Billy Taylor, George Duke, Stanley Clarke, Chick Corea. Upon graduation, she moved to Los Angeles and worked with Sergio Mendes and Harry Belafonte. She earned rave reviews for her mid-1980s appearances at the Monterey Jazz Festival and recordings with Stanley Turrentine and George

Duke. She has also worked with the Colo. Symphony. Reeves has found success working in both jazz and pop fields.

DISC.: *Welcome to My Love* (1987); *Dianne Reeves* (1987); *Better Days* (1987); *I Remember* (1988); *Never Too Far* (1990); *Quiet After the Storm* (1994); *Art & Survival* (1994); *The Grand Encounter* (1996).—**LP**

Reeves, Jim (actually, James Travis), Ameri-

can country-music singer, guitarist, and songwriter; b. Panola County, Tex., Aug. 20, 1923; d. near Nashville, Tenn., July 31, 1964. One of the most successful country-music performers of the 1950s and 1960s, Reeves was an exponent of the pop-styled Nashville Sound that brought crossover success to country music, notably on such hits as "Four Walls" and "He'll Have to Go," though he had begun his recording career with a honky-tonk approach with such hits as "Mexican Joe." For years after his early death, newly unearthed recordings continued to become country hits.

Reeves was the ninth and last child of Tom Reeves, a farmer, and Mary Beulah Adams Reeves. His father died before his first birthday, and his mother and older siblings did farm work to support the family. He took up the guitar as a child and was performing publicly by his adolescence. His primary interest, however, was baseball, and he briefly attended the Univ. of Tex. at Austin in 1942 on a sports scholarship before quitting to volunteer for the military during World War II. After failing his physical he worked in the defense industry, then became a minor-league ballplayer in the St. Louis Cardinals organization in 1944, but by 1947 injuries had ended his sports career. On Sept. 3, 1947, he married Mary Elizabeth White, a schoolteacher.

In the late 1940s and early 1950s, Reeves worked at several radio stations in Tex. as a disc jockey and newscaster while pursuing music on the side. He first recorded for the small Macy's record label in Houston in 1949 or 1950. In 1952 he moved to Shreveport, La., where he worked at KWKH, the station that broadcast the country-music show *Louisiana Hayride*. He was signed to another small label, Abbott Records, and his second release, "Mexican Joe" (music and lyrics by Mitchell Torok), hit #1 in the country charts in May 1953. With that he gave up his radio job and became a full-time performer. His next two singles did not register, but his fifth Abbott record, "Bimbo" (music and lyrics by Rod Morris), topped the country charts in January 1954.

Reeves hit the country Top Ten a second time in 1954 and with two more Abbott singles in the first third of 1955, then switched to the major label RCA Victor Records, continuing his string of hits with his initial RCA single, "Yonder Comes a Sucker" (music and lyrics by Jim Reeves), which reached the country Top Ten in August 1955. With that he was invited to join the *Grand Ole Opry* radio program, debuting on the show on Oct. 19 and moving to Nashville the same month.

Reeves scored two country Top Ten hits in 1956 and another in March 1957; then his career took a giant leap with the release of "Four Walls" (music and lyrics by Marvin Moore and George Campbell), in which he

adopted a lower, more natural singing voice on a slow ballad with a more pop-oriented arrangement that deemphasized country instrumentation and added a prominent vocal chorus. The single topped the country charts in May 1957 and crossed over to the pop Top 40. Its success expanded his touring opportunities and led to a network radio series that ran for 13 weeks beginning in October. He scored a third country Top Ten hit in 1957 and another four in 1958, among them the #1 "Blue Boy" (music and lyrics by Boudleaux Bryant). His three country Top Ten hits of 1959 included the chart-topping "Billy Bayou" and "Home" (both music and lyrics by Roger Miller).

Reeves scored the biggest hit of his career with the million-selling "He'll Have to Go" (music and lyrics by Joe and Audrey Allison), which reached #1 on the country charts in February 1960, made the pop Top Ten, and earned him a Grammy nomination for Best Vocal Performance, Single or Track, Male. It also was his first record to chart in the U.K., reflecting his deliberate cultivation of an international audience, a rarity among country performers. With four more country Top Ten hits in 1960 (two of which also made the pop Top 40), he was the best-selling country artist of the year.

Reeves scored three country Top Ten hits in 1961 and four in 1962, including the chart-topper "I'm Gonna Change Everything" (music and lyrics by Alex Zanetis). In August 1962 he performed in South Africa, helping to expand his international following; he returned to the country in March 1963 and there starred in a film, *Kimberley Jim*, released overseas in 1964 and in the U.S. in 1965. He also performed in Europe in 1963 and 1964. He had another two country Top Ten hits in 1963.

In 1964 he had scored two more country Top Ten hits and reached the Top Ten of the country LP charts for the first time with his album *Good 'n Country* when he crashed a private plane and died at the age of 40 in July. His current single, "I Guess I'm Crazy" (music and lyrics by Werly Fairburn), hit #1 on the country charts in August, and his current album, *Moonlight and Roses*, topped the country charts, as did a quickly released compilation, *The Best of Jim Reeves*, which also made the pop Top Ten and went gold; it earned a Grammy nomination for Best Country & Western Album.

At his death, Reeves left behind a collection of finished, unreleased master recordings as well as numerous demos and live recordings. His estate and RCA carefully issued these tracks, sometimes with elaborate overdubbing to give them a more complete and contemporary sound, over a lengthy period of time and successfully maintained his status as a top-selling country artist. In 1965 he had three Top Ten country hits, including the chart-toppers "This Is It" (music and lyrics by Cindy Walker) and "Is It Really Over?" (music and lyrics by Jim Reeves), the latter earning Grammy nominations for Best Country & Western Single and Best Country & Western Vocal Performance, Male. He also placed three albums in the country Top Ten, including *The Jim Reeves Way*, which earned a Grammy nomination for Best Country & Western Album, and *Up through the Years*, which hit #1. All three of his 1966 singles, "Snow Flake" (music and lyrics by Ned Miller),

"Distant Drums" (music and lyrics by Cindy Walker), and "Blue Side of Lonesome" (music and lyrics by Leon Payne), topped the country charts, while three LPs hit reached the country Top Ten, including the *Distant Drums* album, which hit #1 and went gold. The "Distant Drums" single earned Reeves three Grammy nominations: Best Vocal Performance, Male; Best Country & Western Vocal Performance, Male; and Best Country & Western Recording.

RCA again released three new Reeves singles in 1967, and two made the country Top Ten, including the #1 hit "I Won't Come in While He's There" (music and lyrics by Gene Davis); a *Blue Side of Lonesome* LP also made the country Top Ten. There were two country Top Ten singles in 1968, along with two country Top Ten LPs, another two country Top Ten singles in 1969, and one each in 1970, 1972, and 1973; also, country Top Ten LPs in 1972 and 1973.

By the mid-1970s the stream of previously unreleased Reeves recordings had slowed, but in 1979, RCA electronically added the voice of country singer Deborah Allen to some of his performances, resulting in three country Top Ten hits, the most successful of which was "Oh, How I Miss You Tonight" (music and lyrics by Benny Davis, Joe Burke, and Mark Fisher). In 1981 the gimmick was repeated with Patsy Cline, resulting in the country Top Ten hit "Have You Ever Been Lonely (Have You Ever Been Blue)" (music and lyrics by Peter DeRose and George Brown) and a *Greatest Hits* album featuring separate songs by Reeves and Cline plus the duet that hit the country Top Ten. Meanwhile, Reeves's vintage recordings continued to sell well, a fact confirmed in April 1998 when the 1976 compilation *The Unforgettable Jim Reeves*, consisting of RCA material licensed by Reader's Digest, became his first album to be certified platinum.

DISC.: *Jim Reeves Sings* (1956); *Singing Down the Lane* (1956); *Bimbo* (1957); *Jim Reeves* (1957); *Girls I Have Known* (1958); *God Be With You* (1958); *Songs to Warm the Heart* (1959); *He'll Have to Go* (1960); *According to My Heart* (1960); *The Intimate Jim Reeves* (1960); *Talking to Your Heart* (1961); *Tall Tales and Short Tempers* (1961); *Bimbo* (1963); *The Country Side of Jim Reeves* (1962); *A Touch of Velvet* (1962); *We Thank Thee* (1962); *Good 'N' Country* (1963); *Diamonds in the Sand* (1963); *Gentleman Jim* (1963); *The International Jim Reeves* (1963); *Twelve Songs of Christmas* (1963); *Moonlight and Roses* (1964); *Have I Told You Lately That I Love You?* (1964); *Kimberley Jim* (1964); *The Jim Reeves Way* (1965); *Distant Drums* (1966); *Yours Sincerely, Jim Reeves* (1966); *Blue Side of Lonesome* (1967); *My Cathedral* (1967); *A Touch of Sadness* (1968); *Jim Reeves on Stage* (1968); *Jim Reeves—And Some Friends* (1969); *The Unforgettable Jim Reeves* (1969); *Jim Reeves Writes You a Record* (1971); *Something Special* (1971); *Young and Country* (1971); *My Friend* (1972); *Missing You* (1972); *Something Special* (1972); *Am I That Easy to Forget* (1973); *Great Moments With Jim Reeves* (1973); *I'd Fight the World* (1974); *Songs of Love* (1975); *I Love You Because* (1976); *It's Nothin' to Me* (1977); *Jim Reeves: Nashville '78* (1978); *The Velvet Memories of Jim Reeves: Golden* (1978); *The Best of Jim Reeves, Vol. 4* (1979); *There's Always Me* (1980). *At the Grand Ole Opry* (1987); *Dear Hearts & Gentle People* (1992); *Jim Reeves* (1995). Deborah Allen: *Don't Let Me Cross Over* (1979). **PATSY CLINE:** *Greatest Hits* (1981).

BIBL.: P. Cook, *The Saga of J. R.: Country and Western Singer and Musician* (Los Angeles, 1977); M. Streissguth, *Like a Moth to a Flame: The Jim Reeves Story* (Nashville, 1998).—**WR**

Reeves, (John) Sims, English tenor; b. Shooter's Hill, Kent, Sept. 26, 1818; d. Worthing, London, Oct. 25, 1900. He learned to play several instruments, and had lessons with J. B. Cramer (piano) and W. H. Callcott (harmony). He made his debut as a baritone in *Guy Mannering* in Newcastle upon Tyne (Dec. 14, 1838); also studied further and sang minor tenor roles at London's Drury Lane (1841–43) and studied in Paris under Bordogni and in Milan under Mazzucato, appearing at La Scala in 1846 as Edgardo in *Lucia di Lammermoor*. He sang Faust in the first British performance of Berlioz's *La Damnation de Faust* under the composer's direction (1848), then was a member of Her Majesty's Theatre in London (from 1848); also sang at the leading festivals. He retired in 1891, but reappeared in concerts in 1893. He made a successful tour of South Africa in 1896. He publ. *Sims Reeves; His Life and Recollections Written by Himself* (London, 1888), *My Jubilee, or Fifty Years of Artistic Life* (London, 1889), and *Sims Reeves on the Art of Singing* (London, 1900).

BIBL.: H. Edwards, *The Life and Artistic Career of S. R.* (London, 1881); C. Pearce, *S. R.: Fifty Years of Music in England* (London, 1924).—**NS/LK/DM**

Refardt, Edgar, eminent Swiss musicologist and bibliographer; b. Basel, Aug. 8, 1877; d. there, March 3, 1968. He studied law and obtained the degree of Dr.Jur. in 1901. In 1915 he was appointed librarian and cataloguer of the musical collection of the Municipal Library of Basel. From 1921 to 1948 he was director of the Basel Orch. Society. He publ. valuable bibliographical works on Swiss music as well as essays on various literary and musical subjects.

WRITINGS: *Hans Huber: Beiträge zu einer Biographie* (Leipzig, 1922); *Verzeichnis der Aufsätze zur Musik in den nichtmusikalischen Zeitschriften der Universitätsbibliothek Basel* (Leipzig, 1925); *Historisch-biographisches Musikerlexikon der Schweiz* (Leipzig and Zürich, 1928); *Hans Huber: Leben und Werk eines schweizer Musikers* (Zürich, 1944); *Theodor Fröhlich: Ein schweizer Musiker der Romantik* (Basel, 1947); *Johannes Brahms, Anton Bruckner, Hugh Wolf: Drei Wiener Meister des 19. Jahrhunderts* (Basel, 1949); *Musik in der Schweiz: Ausgewählte Aufsätze* (1952); H. Zehntner, ed., *Thematischer Katalog der Instrumentalmusik des 18. Jahrhunderts in den Handschriften der Universitätsbibliothek Basel* (Bern, 1952).—**NS/LK/DM**

Refice, Licinio, Italian conductor, teacher, and composer; b. Patrica, near Rome, Feb. 12, 1883; d. while conducting his sacred play Santa Cecilia in Rio de Janeiro, Sept. 11, 1954. He studied organ and composition at Rome's Liceo di Santa Cecilia (diploma, 1910). After being ordained (1910), he taught at Rome's Scuola Pontificia Superiore di Musica Sacra (1910–50) and was maestro di cappella at S. Maria Maggiore (1911–47). He also toured Europe and North and South America as a conductor.

WORKS: DRAMATIC: O p e r a : *Cecilia* (1922–23; Rome, 1934); *Margherita da Cortona* (Milan, 1938). **VOCAL:** 4 oratorios: *La Cananea* (1910), *Maria Magdalena* (1914), *Martyrium*

S. Agnetis Virginis (1919), and *Trittico Francescano* (1926); *La vedova di Naim*, cantata (1912); *Stabat Mater* (1917); *Te Deum* (1918); many other sacred works, including over 40 masses; secular songs.

BIBL.: E. Mucci, *L. R.* (Assisi, 1955); T. Onofri and E. Mucci, *Le composizioni di L. R.* (Assisi, 1966).—**NS/LK/DM**

Regamey, Constantin, Swiss pianist and composer; b. Kiev (of a Swiss father and a Russian mother), Jan. 28, 1907; d. Lausanne, Dec. 27, 1982. He went to Poland in 1920 and took piano lessons with Turczyński (1921–25), then turned to linguistics and took courses in Sanskrit at the Univ. of Warsaw and later at L'École des Hautes Études in Paris, graduating in 1936. Returning to Poland, he taught Sanskrit at the Univ. of Warsaw (1937–39); concurrently he ed. periodicals on contemporary music. He was interned by the Germans during World War II, but managed to escape to Switzerland in 1944. He received an appointment to teach Slavic and oriental languages at the Univ. of Lausanne; also gave courses in Indo-European linguistics at the Univ. of Fribourg. However, he did not abandon his musical activities; he served as co-ed. of the *Revue Musicale de Suisse Romande* (1954–62); was president of the Assn. of Swiss Composers (1963–68) and a member of the executive board of the ISCM (1969–73). In 1978 he became partially paralyzed; he dictated the last pages of his last work, *Visions*, to Jean Balissat, a fellow composer, who also orchestrated the work. As a composer, he adopted free serial methods, without a doctrinaire adherence to formal dodecaphony. In 1963 he moderated his modernity and wrote music using free, often composite, techniques.

WORKS: DRAMATIC: *Don Robott*, opera (1970); *Mio, mein Mio*, fairy tale opera, after Bächli and Lindgren (1973). **ORCH.:** *Variazioni e tema* (1948); *Music for Strings* (1953); *Autographe* for Chamber Orch. (1962–66); *4 x 5*, concerto for 4 Quintets (Basel, May 28, 1964); *Lila*, double concerto for Violin, Cello, and Chamber Orch. (1976). **CHAMBER:** Quintet for Clarinet, Bassoon, Violin, Cello, and Piano (1944); String Quartet (1948). **VOCAL:** *7 chansons persanes* for Baritone and Chamber Orch., after Omar Khayyám (1942); *5 études* for Woman's Voice and Orch. (1955–56); *5 poèmes de Jean Tardieu* for Chorus (1962); *Symphonie des Incantations* for Soprano, Baritone, and Orch. (1967); *3 Lieder des Clowns* for Baritone and Orch. (1968; from the opera *Don Robott*); *Unidentity and Infinity* for Silent Narrator, Woman's Voice, and an unidentified number of Instruments (1969); *Alpha*, cantata for Tenor and Orch., to a Hindu text (1970); *Visions* for Baritone, Chorus, Orch., and Organ, after the life of the prophet Daniel (1978–79; orchestrated by J. Balissat).

WRITINGS: *Musique du XXᵉ siècle: Présentation de 80 oeuvres pour orchestre de chambre* (Lausanne and Paris, 1966).

BIBL.: H. Jaccard, *Initiation à la musique contemporaine: Trois compositeurs vaudois: Raffaele d'Alessandro, C. R., Julien-François Zbinden* (Lausanne, 1955).—**NS/LK/DM**

Reger, (Johann Baptist Joseph) Max(imilian), celebrated German composer; b. Brand, Upper Palatinate, Bavaria, March 19, 1873; d. Leipzig, May 11, 1916. His father, a schoolteacher and amateur musician, gave him instruction on the piano, organ, and various string instruments. In 1874 the family moved to Weiden, where he studied organ and theory with Adalbert Lindner; he then attended the teacher-training college; after visiting the Bayreuth Festival in 1888, he decided on a career in music. He went to Sondershausen to study with Riemann in 1890, and continued as his pupil in Wiesbaden (1890–93); was also active as a teacher of piano, organ, and theory (1890–96). Following military service, he returned to Weiden in 1898 and wrote a number of his finest works for organ. He went to Munich in 1901, first gaining general recognition as a pianist, and later as a composer; was prof. of counterpoint at the Königliche Akademie der Tonkünst (1905–06). Prominent compositions from this period included the Piano Quintet, op.64 (1901–02), the Violin Sonata, op.72 (1903), the String Quartet, op.74 (1903–04), the *Variationen und Fuge über ein Thema von J.S. Bach* for Piano, op.81 (1904), and the Sinfonietta, op.90 (1904–05). He went to Leipzig as music director of the Univ. (1907–08) and as prof. of composition at the Cons. (from 1907). His fame as a composer was enhanced by his successful tours as a soloist and conductor in Germany and throughout Europe. While he continued to produce major chamber works and organ pieces, he also wrote such important orch. compositions as the *Variationen und Fuge über ein lustiges Thema von J.A. Hiller*, op.100 (1907), the Violin Concerto, op.101 (1907–08), the *Symphonischer Prolog zu einer Tragödie*, op.108 (1908), the Piano Concerto, op.114 (1910), and the *Variationen und Fuge über ein Thema von Mozart*, op.132 (1914). As a result of having been awarded an honorary Ph.D. from the Univ. of Jena in 1908, he composed his most distinguished sacred work, the *Psalm C*, op.106 (1908–09). He was called to Meiningen as conductor of the Court Orch. in 1911, assuming the title of Hofkapellmeister; was also Generalmusikdirektor (1913–14); settled in Jena in 1915.

Reger was an extraordinarily gifted musician, widely respected as a composer, pianist, organist, conductor, and teacher. A master of polyphonic and harmonic writing, he carried on the hallowed Classical and Romantic schools of composition. Although he wrote major works in nearly every genre, his music has not found a place of permanence in the repertoire.

WRITINGS: *Beiträge zur Modulationslehre* (Leipzig, 1903; 24ᵗʰ ed., 1952).

WORKS: ORCH.: *Heroide*, symphonic movement (1889); *Castra vetera*, incidental music (1889–90); *Symphoniesatz* (1890; Dortmund, 1960); *Lyrisches Andante* for Strings (1898); *Scherzino* for Horn and Strings (1899); *Elegie*, op.26/1 (1899; arranged from a piano work); *2 Romanzen* for Violin and Orch., op.50 (1900); *Variationen und Fuge über ein Thema von Beethoven*, op.86 (1915; arranged from the work for 2 Pianos, 1904); *Sinfonietta*, op.90 (Essen, Oct. 8, 1905); *Suite im alten Stil*, op.93 (1916; arranged from the work for Violin and Piano, 1906); *Serenade*, op.95 (1905–06); *Variationen und Fuge über ein lustiges Thema von J.A. Hiller*, op.100 (Cologne, Oct. 15, 1907); Violin Concerto, op.101 (Leipzig, Oct. 13, 1908); *Aria* for Violin and Chamber Orch., op.103a (1908; arranged from the Suite for Violin and Piano, 1908); *Symphonischer Prolog zu einer Tragödie*, op.108 (1908); Piano Concerto, op.114 (Leipzig, Dec. 15, 1910); *Eine Lustspielouvertüre*, op.120 (1911); *Konzert im alten Stil*, op.123 (1912); *Eine romantische Suite*, op.125 (1912); *4 Tondichtungen* nach Arnold Böcklin, op.128 (Essen, Oct. 12, 1913); *Eine Bal-lettsuite*, op.130 (1913); *Variationen und Fuge über ein Thema von Mozart*, op.132 (1914; Berlin, Feb. 5, 1915; arranged from the work for 2 Pianos, 1914); *Eine vaterländische Ouvertüre*, op.140 (1914); *Sinfonische Rhapsodie* for Violin and Orch., op.147 (unfinished; completed by F. von Reuter). **CHAMBER**: Scherzo for Flute and String Quartet (n.d.); String Quartet (1888–89); Violin Sonata, op.1 (1890); Trio for Violin, Viola, and Piano, op.2 (1891); Violin Sonata, op.3 (1891); Cello Sonata, op.5 (1892); Piano Quintet (1897–98); Cello Sonata, op.28 (1898); Violin Sonata, op.41 (1899); 4 sonatas for Violin, op.42 (1900); 2 clarinet sonatas, op.49 (1900); 2 string quartets, op.54 (1900); *Caprice* for Cello and Piano (1901); Piano Quintet, op.64 (1901–02); *Prelude and Fugue* for Violin (1902); *Romanze* for Violin and Piano (1902); *Petite caprice* for Violin and Piano (1902); *Albumblatt* for Clarinet or Violin, and Piano (1902); *Tarantella* for Clarinet or Violin and Piano (1902); *Allegretto grazioso* for Flute and Piano (1902); Violin Sonata, op.72 (1903); String Quartet, op.74 (1903–04); *Serenade* for Flute, Violin, and Viola, op.77a (1904); String Trio, op.77b (1904); Cello Sonata, op.78 (1904); *Wiegenlied, Capriccio, and Burla* for Violin and Piano, op.79d (1902–04); *Caprice, Kleine Romanze* for Cello and Piano, op.79e (1904); Violin Sonata, op.84 (1905); *Albumblatt, romanze* for Violin and Piano, op.87 (1905); 7 sonatas for Violin, op.91 (1905); *Suite im alten Stil* for Violin and Piano, op.93 (1906; orchestrated 1916); Trio for Violin, Cello, and Piano, op.102 (1907–08); Suite (*6 Vortragstücke*) for Violin and Piano, op.103a (1908); 2 little sonatas for Violin and Piano, op.103b (1909); *12 kleine Stücke nach eigenen Liedern* (from op.76) for Violin and Piano, op.103c (1916); Sonata for Clarinet or Viola and Piano, op.107 (1908–09); String Quartet, op.109 (1909); Piano Quartet, op.113 (1910); Cello Sonata, op.116 (1910); *Preludes and Fugues* for Violin, op.117 (1909–12); Sextet for 2 Violins, 2 Violas, and 2 Cellos, op.118 (1910); String Quartet, op.121 (1911); Violin Sonata, op.122 (1911); *Preludes and Fugues* for Violin, op.131a (1914); *3 Duos (Canons und Fugen) im alten Stil* for 2 Violins, op.131b (1914); 3 suites for Cello, op.131c (1915); 3 suites for Viola, op.131d (1915); Piano Quartet, op.133 (1914); *Allegro* for 2 Violins (1914); Violin Sonata, op.139 (1915); *Serenade* for Flute or Violin, Violin, and Viola, op.141a (1915); String Trio, op.141b (1915); Clarinet Quintet, op.146 (1915); *Prelude* for Violin (1915); numerous pieces for piano and organ works. **VOCAL**: 3 Choruses for Mixed Voices and Piano, op.6 (1892); *Tantum ergo sacramentum* for 5 Voices (1895); *Hymne an den Gesang* for Men's Chorus and Orch. or Piano, op.21 (1898); *Gloriabuntur in te omnes* for 4 Voices (1898); 7 Men's Choruses, op.38 (1899); 3 Choruses, op.39 (1899); *Maria Himmelsfreud!* (1899); 8 settings of *Tantum ergo*, op.61a (1901); 4 settings of *Tantum ergo* for Women's or Men's Voices and Organ, op.61b (1901); 4 settings of *Tantum ergo* for 4 Voices and Organ, op.61c (1901); 8 *Marienlieder*, op.61d (1901); 4 *Marienlieder* for Women's or Men's Voices and Organ, op.61e (1901); 4 *Marienlieder* for 4 Voices and Organ, op.61f (1901); 6 *Trauergesänge*, op.61g (1901); *Palmsonntagmorgen* for 5 Voices (1902); *Gesang der Verklärten* for Mixed Voices and Orch., op.71 (1903); 5 cantatas (1903–05); *10 Gesänge* for Men's Voices, op.83 (1904, 1909); *Weihegesäng* for Chorus and Wind Orch. (1908); *Psalm C* for Chorus, Organ, and Orch., op.106 (1908–09); *Geistliche Gesänge* for 5 Voices, op.110 (1912); *Vater unser* for 12 Voices (1909); 3 *Gesänge* for 4 Women's Voices, op.111b (1909); *Die Nonnen* for Chorus and Orch., op.112 (1909); *Die Weihe der Nacht* for Men's Voices and Orch., op.119 (1911); *Lasset uns den Herren preisen* for 5 Voices (1911); *Römischer Triumphgesang* for Men's Voices and Orch., op.126 (1912); 8 *geistliche Gesänge* for 4 to 8 Voices, op.138 (1914); *Abschiedslied* for 4 Voices (1914); *Requiem* for Soloists, Chorus, and Orch.

(1914; 2nd movement unfinished); 2 *Gesänge*, op.144 (1915); 20 *Responsorien* (1916); works for solo voice.

BIBL.: The *Sämtliche Werke* was publ. in Wiesbaden (38 vols., 1954–86). F. Stein ed. the *Thematisches Verzeichnis der im Druck erschienenen Werke von M. R. einschliesslich seiner Bearbeitungen und Ausgaben* (Leipzig, 1953). H. Rösner ed. a *M.-R.-Bibliographie* (Bonn, 1968). See also the following: R. Braungart, *M. R., Monographien Moderner Musiker*, II (Leipzig, 1907); V. Junk, *M. R. als Orchesterkomponist* (Leipzig, 1910); W. Fischer, *Über die Wiedergabe der Orgelkompositionen M. R.s* (Cologne, 1911); F. Rabich, *R.lieder: Eine Studie* (Langensalza, 1914); R. Eucken, *Persönliche Erinnerungen an M. R.* (Bielefeld, 1916); H. Poppen, *M. R.* (Leipzig, 1918; 3rd ed., 1947); H. Grabner, *R.s Harmonik* (Munich, 1920); R. Würz, ed., *M. R.: Eine Sammlung von Studien* (4 vols., Munich, 1920–23); K. Hasse, *M. R.: Mit R.s Schriften und Aufsätzen* (Leipzig, 1921); A. Lindner, *M. R.: Ein Bild seines Jugendlebens und künstlerischen Werdens* (Stuttgart, 1922; 3rd ed., 1938); G. Bagier, *M. R.* (Stuttgart and Berlin, 1923); E. Gatscher, *Die Fugentechnik M. R.s in ihrer Entwicklung* (Stuttgart, 1925); S. Kallenberg, *M. R.* (Leipzig, 1929); E. Reger, *Mein Leben mit und für M. R.* (Leipzig, 1930); P. Coenen, *M. R.s Variationsschaffen* (diss., Univ. of Berlin, 1935); E. Brand, *M. R. im Elternhaus* (Munich, 1938); F. Stein, *M. R.* (Potsdam, 1939); idem, *M. R.: Sein Leben in Bildern* (Leipzig, 1941; 2nd ed., 1956); A. Kalkoff, *Das Orgelschaffen M. R.s* (Kassel, 1950); special issue of the *Zeitschrift für Musik* (March 1953); G. Wehmeyer, *M. R. als Liederkomponist*, Kölner Beiträge zur Musikforschung, VIII (Regensburg, 1955); E. Otto, *M. R.: Sinnbild einer Epoche* (Wiesbaden, 1957); G. Sievers, *Die Grundlagen Hugo Riemanns bei M. R.* (Wiesbaden, 1967); M. Stein, *Der heitere R.* (Wiesbaden, 1969); H. Wirth, *M. R.* (Hamburg, 1973); K. Röhring, ed., *M. R. 1873–1973: Ein Symposion* (Wiesbaden, 1974); S. Popp and S. Shigihara, eds., *M. R.: Am Wendepunkt zur Moderne: Ein Bildband mit Dokumenten aus den Beständen des M.-R.-Instituts* (Bonn, 1987; Eng. tr., 1988, as *M. R. at the Turning Point to Modernism: An Illustrated Volume with Documents of the M. R. Institute*); W. Grim, *M. R.: A Bio-bibliography* (N.Y., 1988); R. Gadenbach, *M. R. und seine Zeit* (Laaber, 1991); H. Brauss, *M. R.'s Music for Solo Piano* (Edmonton, Alberta, 1994); H. Wilske, *M. R.: Zur Rezeption in seiner Zeit* (Wiesbaden, 1995); P. Zimmermann, *Musik und Text in M. R.s Chorwerken 'grossen Styls'* (Wiesbaden, 1997).
—NS/LK/DM

Regino of Prüm, German music theorist; b. Altrip, near Ludwigshafen, c. 1842; d. Trier, 1915. He studied at the Benedictine abbey of Prüm with Abbot Markward, where he was later made provost (1885) and abbot (1892). In 1899 he became abbot of St. Martin. In addition to the treatise *Epistola de armonica institutione*, he wrote the valuable tonary *Octo toni de musicae artis* (c. 1901), which remains one of the most important extant plainchant sources.

BIBL.: F. Haberl, *Il tonario di R. d. P.* (diss., Pontifico Istituto di Musica Sacra, Rome, 1937); Y. Chartier, *L'Epistola de armonia institutione de R. d. P.* (diss., Univ. of Ottawa, 1965); M. Le Roux, *The "De harmonica institutione" and "Tonarius" of R. of P.* (Ann Arbor, 1970).—LK/DM

Regis, Johannes, Netherlands composer; b. c. 1430; d. probably in Soignies, c. 1485. He was made "magister puerorum" of Cambrai Cathedral (1460), then of Notre Dame in Antwerp (1463). He was secretary to Dufay in Cambrai (1464–74), and finally canon and scholasticus in Soignies (1481–82). He wrote 2 masses on the melody of *L'Homme armé,* a 5-part motet, *O admirabile commercium,* and other vocal pieces. His collected works were publ. in 2 vols. by the American Inst. of Musicology in Rome (1956), under the editorship of C. Lindenburg.

BIBL.: C. Lindenburg, *Het Leven en de werken van J. R.* (Amsterdam, 1939).—NS/LK/DM

Regnart, Jacob, prominent South Netherlandish composer; b. Douai, c. 1540; d. Prague, Oct. 16, 1599. He began his career as a chorister in the Prague Hofkapelle of Maximilian (from 1577), continuing in his service in Vienna when he became the emperor Maximilian. After studies in Italy (1568–70), he became music teacher of the chapel choristers. After Maximilian's death (1576), Emperor Rudolf II appointed Regnart a member of his Hofkapelle, which soon thereafter was removed to Prague, where he became its Vice-Kapellmeister (1579). Regnart was Vice-Kapellmeister (1582–85) and Kapellmeister (1585–96) to Archduke Ferdinand of Innsbruck, then again in Prague as Vice-Kapellmeister (from 1596). He had 4 brothers, all of whom were active as musicians. W. Pass ed. *Jacob Regnart: Opera omnia* in Corpus Mensurabilis Musicae, LXII/4–6 (1972–75).

WORKS: VOCAL: S a c r e d : *Sacrae aliquot cantiones, quas moteta vulgus appellat* for 5 to 6 Voices (Munich, 1575); *Aliquot cantiones, vulgo motecta appellatae, ex veteri atque novo testamento collectae* for 4 Voices (Nuremberg, 1577); *Mariale, hoc est, Opusculum sacrarum cantionum omnibus Beatissimae Virginis Mariae festivitatibus* for 4, 6, and 8 Voices (Innsbruck, 1588); *Missae sacrae ad imitationem selectissimarum cantionum suavissima harmonia* for 5 to 6 and 8 Voices (Frankfurt am Main, 1602); *Continuatio missarum sacrarum, ad imitationem selectissimarum cantionum suavissima harmonia* for 4 to 6, 8, and 10 Voices (Frankfurt am Main, 1603); *Corollarium missarum sacrarum ad imitationem selectissimarum cantionum suavissima harmonia compositarum* (Frankfurt am Main, 1603); *Sacrarum cantionum* for 4 to 8 and 12 Voices (Frankfurt am Main, 1605); *Canticum Mariae* for 5 Voices (Dillingen, 1605); *Missarum flores illustrium numquam hactenus visi* (Frankfurt am Main, 1611); *Magnificat, ad octo modos musicos compositum cum duplici antiphona, Salve regina* for 8 and 10 Voices (Frankfurt am Main, 1614); numerous other works in contemporary collections. **S e c u l a r :** *Il primo libro delle canzone italiane* for 5 Voices (Vienna, 1574); *Kurtzweilige teutsche Lieder, nach Art der Neapolitanen oder welschen Villanellen* for 3 Voices (Nuremberg, 1576; 2nd ed., 1578, as *Der erste Theyl schöner kurtzweiliger teutscher Lieder*); *Der ander Theyl kurtzweiliger teutscher Lieder* for 3 Voices (Nuremberg, 1577); *Der dritter Theyl schöner kurtzweiliger teutscher Lieder* for 3 Voices (Nuremberg, 1579); *Newe kurtzweilige teutsche Lieder* for 5 Voices (Nuremberg, 1580); *Il secundo libro delle canzone italiane* for 5 Voices (Nuremberg, 1581); *Teutsche Lieder...in ein Opus zusamendruckt* for 3 Voices (Munich, 1583); *Tricinia: Kurtzweilige teutsche Lieder* for 3 Voices (Nuremberg, 1584); *Kurtzweilige teutsche Lieder* for 4 Voices (Munich, 1591); other works in contemporary collections.

BIBL.: F. Mossler, *Jakob R.s Messen* (diss., Univ. of Bonn, 1964); W. Pass, *J. R. und seine lateinischen Motetten* (diss., Univ. of Vienna, 1967); idem, *Thematischer Katalog sämtlicher Werke J. R.s,* Tabulae Musicae Austriacae, V (1969).—NS/LK/DM

Regt, Hendrik de, Dutch composer; b. Rotterdam, July 5, 1950. He studied composition with Otto Ketting in The Hague (1968–72).

WORKS: *Canzoni e Scherzi* for Soprano, Flute, and Harp (1972); *Proteus,* music for Flute, Viola, and Harp (1974); *Metamorfosen* for Oboe and English Horn (1974); *Silenus en Bacchanten* for Flute, Oboe, and Guitar (1974); *Pastorale* for Flute and Oboe (1974–75); *Circe* for Clarinet, Violin, and Piano (1975); *4 pezzi* for Clarinet (1978); *Poème* for Flute, Violin, and Viola (1979); Partita for Solo Violin (1979); *Esprit errant* for Baritone and Piano (1981); choruses; about 30 works, each entitled *Musica,* written for different instrumental combinations: for Wind Quintet (1969); Oboe, Cello, Harp, and Percussion (1970); 4 Saxophones (1971); Flute, Percussion, and Narrator (1970–72); Flute, Viola, Cello, Guitar, and Percussion (1972); 2 Trumpets, Horn, and Trombone (1971–72); Flute, Guitar, and Percussion (1972); 4 Clarinets (1972–73); 4 Horns (1974); Solo Violin (1974); Flute, Violin, Viola, and Cello (1974); Flute and Viola (1975); etc. —NS/LK/DM

Rehfuss, Heinz (Julius), German-born Swiss, later American, bass-baritone; b. Frankfurt am Main, May 25, 1917; d. Buffalo, June 27, 1988. He studied with his father, Carl Rehfuss (1885–1946), a singer and teacher, and with his mother, Florentine Rehfuss-Peichert, a contralto. The family moved to Neuchâtel, and Rehfuss became a naturalized Swiss citizen. He made his professional debut in opera at Biel-Solothurn in 1938; then sang with the Lucerne Stadttheater (1938–39) and at the Zürich Opera (1940–52). He subsequently was active mainly in Europe and in America; became a naturalized American citizen; taught voice at the Montreal Cons. in 1961; in 1965 was on the faculty of the State Univ. of N.Y. at Buffalo; in 1970 was a visiting prof. at the Eastman School of Music in Rochester, N.Y. He also toured in Asia, giving vocal recitals in India and Indonesia. He was successful mainly in dramatic roles, such as Don Giovanni and Boris Godunov.—NS/LK/DM

Rehm, Wolfgang, German musicologist; b. Munich, Sept. 3, 1929. He studied with Gurlitt and Zenck at the Univ. of Freiburg im Breisgau (Ph.D., 1952, with the diss. *Das Chansonwerk von Gilles Binchois*), and also studied theory and piano at the Hochschule für Musik in Freiburg im Breisgau. In 1954 he joined the publishing firm of Barenreiter in Kassel, eventually becoming chief ed.; held that position until 1982. In 1960 he was named co-ed. (with Wolfgang Plath) of the *Neue Mozart-Ausgabe,* serving as chief ed. from 1981 to 1994, and then was chief ed. (1981–94).—NS/LK/DM

Reich, Steve (actually, **Stephen Michael**), outstanding American composer; b. N.Y., Oct. 3, 1936. He received training in piano in childhood, and when he was 14 he began to study drumming with the timpanist Roland Kohloff. He also studied philosophy at Cornell Univ. (B.A., 1957), where he received training in music from William Austin. Following private composition lessons with Hall Overton in N.Y. (1957–58), he studied composition with William Bergsma and Vincent Persichetti at the Juilliard School of Music (1958–61), and then pursued postgraduate studies with Darius

Milhaud and Luciana Berio at Mills Coll. in Oakland, Calif. (M.A., 1963). Reich launched his career with the film music for *The Plastic Haircut* (1963). His one-man concert at the San Francisco Tape Music Center in Jan. 1965 featured his *It's Gonna Rain.* In 1966 he returned to N.Y. and founded his own group, Steve Reich and Musicians. His tape piece *Come Out* was first performed at Town Hall in April 1966, and then recorded in 1967. In 1970 Reich studied drumming at the Inst. for African Studies at the Univ. of Ghana in Accra. This sojourn inspired him to write his *Drumming,* which was first performed in N.Y. on Dec. 3, 1971. During the summers of 1973 and 1974 he pursued training in Balinese music in Seattle and Berkeley. With his *Music for Eighteen Musicians,* which was premiered at N.Y.'s Town Hall on April 24, 1976, Reich established himself as a composer of wide appeal. In 1976–77 he studied Hebrew, the Torah, and the traditional forms of cantillation of the Scriptures in N.Y. and Jerusalem. On Feb. 19, 1980, Steve Reich and Musicians gave a sold-out all-Reich concert in N.Y. He was the featured composer at London's Almeida Festival in 1986, and in 1987 his career was highlighted in the PBS film "Steve Reich: A New Musical Language." In 1988 London's South Bank Centre presented a major retrospective of his creative output. His *Different Trains* for String Quartet and Tape (London, Nov. 2, 1988) became a best-selling recording and won a Grammy Award in 1990. In 1991 Steve Reich and Musicians toured Japan for the first time. His documentary video opera *The Cave* was premiered in Vienna on May 16, 1993. Reich was made a member of the American Academy of Arts and Letters in 1994. In 1995 he was in residence at Tanglewood. In 1999 the Lincoln Center Festival in N.Y. presented a series of retrospective concerts in his honor.

In his remarkably varied oeuvre, Reich has pursued an eclectic path in which he has successfully utilized elements of Western Classical music, American vernacular music, most notably jazz, and non-Western music, particularly African and Balinese music. This syncretic approach has won him a diverse and loyal following at home and abroad.

WORKS: *The Plastic Haircut,* film music on tape (1963); *Pitch Charts* for Variable Instrumentation (1963); *Music* for 3 or More Pianos or Piano and Tape (1964); *It's Gonna Rain* for Tape (San Francisco, Jan. 1965); *Oh Dem Watermelons,* film music on tape (1965); *Come Out* for Tape (N.Y., April 1966); *Melodica* for Tape (N.Y., June 1966); *Reed Phase* for Soprano Saxophone and Tape (1966; N.Y., March 17, 1967); *Piano Phase* for 2 Pianos or 2 Marimbas (1967); *Slow Motion Sound for Tape* (1967); *My Name is* for 3 or More Recorders, Performers and Audience (1967); *Violin Phase* for Violin and Tape or 4 Violins (1967); *Pendulum Music* for 3 or More Microphones, Amplifiers, Loudspeakers, and Performers (1968; N.Y., May 27, 1969); *Pulse Music* for Phase Shifting Pulse Gate (N.Y., May 27, 1969); *Four Log Drums* for Phase Shifting Pulse Gate and Log Drums (N.Y., May 27, 1969); *Four Organs* for 4 Electric Organs and Maracas (1970); *Phase Patterns* for 4 Electric Organs (1970); *Drumming* for Percussion, Women's Voices, Whistling, and Piccolo (N.Y., Dec. 3, 1971); *Clapping Music* for 2 Performers Clapping (1972); *Six Pianos* (N.Y., May 16, 1973; as *Six Marimbas,* 1986; N.Y., April 20, 1987); *Music* for Mallet Instruments, Voices, and Organ (N.Y., May 16, 1973); *Music for Pieces of Wood* for 5 Pairs of Tuned Claves (N.Y.,

May 16, 1973); *Music for Eighteen Musicians* for Ensemble and Women's Voices (N.Y., April 24, 1976); *Music for a Large Ensemble* for Ensemble and Women's Voices (1978; Holland Festival, June 1979); Octet for 2 Flutes Doubling Clarinets, 2 Pianos, and String Quartet (Frankfurt am Main, June 21, 1979; rev. as *Eight Lines* for Chamber Orch., N.Y., Dec. 10, 1983); *Variations* for Winds, Strings, and Keyboards (1979; N.Y., Feb. 19, 1980; rev. version, San Francisco, May 14, 1980); *Tehillim* for Voices and Ensemble (1st complete perf., WDR, Cologne, Sept. 20, 1981; also for Voices and Chamber Orch., N.Y., Sept. 16, 1982); *Vermont Counterpoint* for Flute and Tape (N.Y., Oct. 1, 1982; also for 11 Flutes, N.Y., Dec. 10, 1983); *The Desert Music* for Chorus and Orch., after William Carlos Williams (1982–84; WDR, Cologne, March 17, 1984; also for 10 Voices and Orch., Richmond, Va., Jan. 10, 1986); Sextet for Percussion and Keyboards (Paris, Dec. 19, 1984; rev. 1985); *New York Counterpoint* for Clarinet and Tape (1985; N.Y., Jan. 20,1986; also for 11 Clarinets, Tallahassee, June 21, 1987); *Three Movements* for Orch. (St. Louis, April 3, 1986); *Salute* for Orch. (1986; withdrawn); *The Four Sections* for Orch. (San Francisco, Oct. 7, 1987); *Electric Counterpoint* for Guitar and Tape (N.Y., Nov. 5, 1987; also for 13 Guitars, Los Angeles, Feb. 24, 1990); *Different Trains* for String Quartet and tape (London, Nov. 2, 1988); *Typing Music I* for 5 Percussionists, after the documentary video opera *The Cave* (1989); *The Cave,* documentary video opera (1990–93; Vienna, May 16, 1993); *Typing Music (Genesis XII)* for Keyboards and Percussion (N.Y., Feb. 22, 1991); *Duet* for 2 Violins and String Ensemble or String Orch. (1993; Gstaad, Aug. 8, 1995); *Nagoya Marimbas* for 2 Marimbas (Nagoya City, Dec. 21, 1994); *City Life* for Ensemble (Metz, March 7, 1995); *Proverb* for Voices and Ensemble (1995; N.Y., Feb. 10, 1996); *Three Tales,* documentary video opera (1997–2000).

BIBL.: W. Mertens, *American Minimal Music: La Monte Young, Terry Riley, S. R., Philip Glass* (London, 1991). —NS/LK/DM

Reich, Willi, Austrian-born Swiss music critic and musicologist; b. Vienna, May 27, 1898; d. Zürich, May 1, 1980. He studied at the Univ. of Vienna, receiving his Ph.D. (1934) with the diss. *Padre Martini als Theoretiker und Lehrer;* also studied privately with Berg and Webern. He ed. a modern music magazine, *23—Eine Wiener Musikzeitschrift* (1932–37). In 1938 he settled in Switzerland, and in 1948 became music critic of the *Neue Zürcher Zeitung;* in 1961, became a naturalized Swiss citizen. In addition to editing numerous documentary vols., he publ. the studies *Wozzeck: A Guide to the Words and Music of Alban Berg* (N.Y., 1932), *Alban Berg* (Vienna, 1937), *Romantiker der Musik* (Basel, 1947), *Alexander Tscherepnin* (Bonn, 1961; 2nd ed., 1970), *Alban Berg: Leben und Werk* (Zürich, 1963; Eng. tr., 1965), and *Arnold Schonberg oder der konservative Revolutionar* (Vienna, 1968; Eng. tr., 1971, as *Schoenberg: A Critical Biography*). —NS/LK/DM

Reicha (Rejcha), Antoine (-Joseph) (Antonin or **Anton),** distinguished Czech-born French music theorist, pedagogue, and composer; b. Prague, Feb. 26, 1770; d. Paris, May 28, 1836. His father died when he was only 10 months old, and he eventually was adopted by his uncle, who gave him lessons in violin and piano; he also studied flute. The family settled in Bonn in 1785. Antoine played violin and flute there, his fellow musicians including Beethoven and C.G. Neefe. Having acquired a knowledge of composition, he conducted his 1st Sym. in Bonn in 1787. After attending the Univ. there, in the wake of the French invasion, in 1794, he went to Hamburg, where he was active there as a teacher of piano, harmony, and composition; also devoted part of his time to composing. In 1799 he went to Paris to establish himself as a composer for the theater, but found success only with 2 of his syms., an overture, and some scènes italiennes. In 1801 he went to Vienna. He had made the acquaintance of Haydn in Bonn, and the two now became good friends; he received instruction from Albrechtsberger and Salieri. His friendship with Beethoven grew apace, and Prince Lobkowitz commissioned Reicha to write the opera L'Ouragan (c. 1801). The Empress Marie Therese then was moved to commission him to compose the opera Argina, regina di Granata, which was given at the Imperial Palace in a private performance with the Empress taking a prominent role (c. 1802). In 1808 he settled in Paris. Although his operas Cagliostro (Nov. 27, 1810), Natalie (July 13, 1816), and Sapho (Dec. 16, 1822) failed to make an impression, Reicha gained prominence as a music theorist and teacher; in 1818 he was appointed prof. of counterpoint and fugue at the Paris Cons. Among those who studied with him either privately or at the Cons. were Baillot, Habeneck, Rode, Berlioz, Liszt, and Franck. His Cours de composition musicale, ou Traité complet et raisonné d'harmonie pratique (Paris, c. 1817) was adopted by the Cons.; his most significant publication was the Traité de haute composition musicale (Paris, 1824–26). In 1829 he became a naturalized French citizen. He was made Chevalier of the Légion d'Honneur in 1831. In 1835 he succeeded Boieldieu as a member of the Académie. He dictated his autobiography, Notes sur Antoine Reicha, to his student Henri Blanchard about 1824. As a composer, Reicha remains best known for his chamber music. He also wrote a great deal of orch. music, including at least 17 syms. and numerous concertos.

WRITINGS: Practische Beispiele: Ein Beitrag zur Geistescultur des Tonsetzers...begleitet mit philosophisch-practischen Anmerkungen (1803); Sur la musique comme art purement sentimental (c. 1813); Traité de mélodie (Paris, 1814; ed. by C. Czerny as Vollständiges Lehrbuch der musikalischen Composition, II, Vienna, 1832); Petit traité d'harmonie pratique à 2 parties, op.84 (Paris, c. 1814); Cours de composition musicale, ou Traité complet et raisonné d'harmonie pratique (Paris, c. 1817; ed. by C. Czerny as Vollständiges Lehrbuch, I, Vienna, 1832); Traité de haute composition musicale (Paris, 1824–26; ed. by C. Czerny as Vollständiges Lehrbuch, III–IV, Vienna, 1832); À messieurs les membres de l'Académie des beaux-arts à l'Institut de France (Paris, 1831); Art du compositeur dramatique, ou Cours complet de composition vocale (Paris, 1833; ed. by C. Czerny as Die Kunst der dramatischen Composition, Vienna, 1833).

BIBL.: E. Bücken, Anton R.: Sein Leben und seine Kompositionen (Munich, 1912); M. Emmanuel, Antonin R. (Paris, 1937); O. Sotolová, Antonin Rejcha (Prague, 1977; with thematic catalog).—NS/LK/DM

Reichardt, Johann Friedrich, prominent German composer and writer on music, father of **Luise Reichardt;** b. Königsberg, Nov. 25, 1752; d. Giebichen-

stein, near Halle, June 27, 1814. He received his initial musical training from his father, the lutenist Johann Reichardt (c. 1720–80), becoming proficient as a violinist, lutenist, and singer; also studied with J. F. Hartknoch, C. G. Richter, F. A. Veichtner, and others. After attending the Univ. of Königsberg (1768–71), he traveled widely; received some instruction from Kirnberger in Berlin and from Homilius in Dresden; also briefly attended the Univ. of Leipzig. He was active as a government official for a year, and then was appointed Kapellmeister of the Royal Opera in Berlin by Frederick the Great in 1775. In 1783 he founded the Concert Spirituel in Berlin, where he brought out several of his own compositions; traveled widely while retaining his royal appointment. After the death of Frederick the Great in 1786, Reichardt's star rose under the new king, Friedrich Wilhelm II. In collaboration with Goethe, he produced the successful Singspiel Claudine von Villa Bella (Berlin, July 29, 1789). Dissension at the Royal Opera, however, led the King to give Reichardt a leave of absence for 3 years, with full pay, in 1790. He again traveled widely; among the cities he visited was Paris (1792). His sympathies for the French Revolution led his Berlin enemies to persuade Friedrich Wilhelm to dismiss him without pay in 1794. He then settled at his estate in Giebichenstein. In 1796 Friedrich Wilhelm pardoned him and named him director of the Halle salt mines. With the French invasion of 1806, he fled with his family to north Germany; upon his return in 1807, he found that his estate had been destroyed; shortly afterward, Jérôme Bonaparte called him to Kassel as directeur général des théâtres et de son orchestre, but he renewed his travels in 1808. In 1809 he returned to Giebichenstein, where he eked out a living by writing and composing. His most significant contribution as a composer rests upon his more than 1,500 songs. He is generally regarded as the finest lieder composer before Schubert. His stage works are important for their movement away from the opera seria conventions. As a writer on music, he was a pioneering figure in music journalism. His first wife was Juliane (née Benda) Reichardt (b. Potsdam, May 4, 1752; d. there, May 11, 1783), the daughter of Franz Benda; she married Reichardt in 1776; a fine pianist, she also publ. a number of songs.

BIBL.: H. Schletter, J.F. R.: Sein Leben und seine musikalische Tätigkeit (Augsburg, 1865); C. Lange, J.F. R. (Halle, 1902); M. Faller, J.F. R. und die Anfänge der musikalischen Journalistik (Kassel, 1929); P. Sieber, J.F. R. als Musikästhetiker: Seine Anschauungen über Wesen und Wirkung der Musik (Strasbourg, 1930); F. Flössner, Beiträge zur R.-Forschung (Frankfurt am Main, 1933); E. Neuss, Das Giebichensteiner Dichterparadies: J.F. R. und die Herberge der Romantik (Halle, 1949); W. Salmen, J.F. R. (Freiburg, 1963); N. Reich, A Translation and Commentary of Selected Writings of J.F. R. (diss., N.Y.U., 1973); J.F. R. (1752–1814): Komponist und Schriftsteller der Revolutionszeit: Bericht über die Konferenze anlässlich seines 175. Todestages (Halle an der Saale, 1992); D. Fischer-Dieskau, Weil nicht alle Blütenträume reiften: J.F. R., Hofkapellmeister dreier Preussenkönige: Porträt und Selbstporträt (Stuttgart, 1992).—NS/LK/DM

Reichardt, Luise, German singing teacher and composer, daughter of **Johann Friedrich Reichardt;** b.

Berlin, April 11, 1779; d. Hamburg, Nov. 17, 1826. She settled about 1813 in Hamburg, where she was active as a singing teacher; also conducted a women's chorus that became the core of the Hamburg Singverein in 1819. She wrote more than 90 choruses and songs, both sacred and secular. Selections of her works were publ. by G. Rheinhardt (Munich, 1922) and N. Reich (N.Y., 1978).

BIBL.: M. Brandt, *Leben der L. R.* (Karlsruhe, 1858; 2nd ed., 1865).—**NS/LK/DM**

Reicher-Kindermann, Hedwig, esteemed German soprano; b. Munich, July 15, 1853; d. Trieste, June 2, 1883. She was a daughter of the baritone August Kindermann (b. Potsdam, Feb. 6, 1817; d. Munich, March 6, 1891). She began her career as a contralto but later sang soprano. She first sang in the chorus of the Munich Court Opera (1870–71), making her debut at Karlsruhe in 1871. She appeared in Berlin (1874) and Munich (1875), and also sang at the opening of Bayreuth in 1876; then sang in Hamburg (1877) and Vienna (1878). The impresario Neumann engaged her for his Wagner troupe in Leipzig from 1880, and she successfully performed the roles of Fricka, Isolde, Brünnhilde, Waltraute, and Erda. She was married to the playwright Emanuel Reicher, and adopted the hyphenated name Reicher-Kindermann in her professional activities. Her early death was lamented.—**NS/LK/DM**

Reichmann, Theodor, noted German baritone; b. Rostock, March 15, 1849; d. Marbach, May 22, 1903. He studied in Berlin and Prague, and after further training with Lamperti in Milan, made his operatic debut in Magdeburg (1869). Following appearances in Rotterdam, Strasbourg, and Hamburg, he sang in 1874 in Munich, where he became a member of the Court Opera in 1875; also sang at the Bayreuth Festivals (1882–1902), where he was esteemed for his portrayal of Amfortas, which he created. In 1882 he made his London debut as Wotan; his Covent Garden debut followed as Telramund on June 11, 1884. He was a member of the Vienna Court Opera (1883–89). He made his Metropolitan Opera debut in N.Y. as the Dutchman on Nov. 27, 1889, and remained on its roster until 1893; then rejoined the Vienna Court Opera, singing there until his death. He gave his farewell performance in Munich as Hans Sachs on Aug. 11, 1902.—**NS/LK/DM**

Reid (real name, **Robertson**), **General John,** Scottish amateur flutist and composer, and music patron; b. Straloch, Perthshire, Feb. 13, 1721; d. London, Feb. 6, 1807. He studied law at the Univ. of Edinburgh, then entered the army in 1745, attaining the rank of general. He was a talented flutist, numbering some 20 marches, 9 menuets, and several flute sonatas among his works. He left £52,000 to found a chair of music at the Univ. of Edinburgh, also providing that an annual concert of his own compositions should be given. The chair was founded in 1839, and among its occupants were Herbert Oakeley (1865–91) and Donald Tovey (1914–40).—**NS/LK/DM**

Reid, Cornelius L., American voice teacher and music scholar; b. Jersey City, N.J., Feb. 7, 1911. He was a member of the Trinity Church Choir in N.Y. (1920–25), and studied with Frederick Kurzweil and Ruth Kirch-Arndt at the N.Y. Coll. of Music (1945–48). He also studied voice privately with George Mead (1929), Marie Wagner (1929–30), and Douglas Stanley (1934–37), and had coaching from Frieda Hempel (1930) and Povla Frijsh (1932–40). He taught voice privately in N.Y. (from 1934), and at Marymount Coll. (1940–41) and the General Theological Seminary there (1946–49). He conducted various performing groups (1939–45) and gave master classes and lectures throughout the U.S. Reid authored 3 books defining his Functional Vocal training: *Bel Canto: Principles and Practices* (Boston, 1950), *The Free Voice* (N.Y., 1965), and *Voice: Psyche and Soma* (N.Y., 1975); also compiled the important *Dictionary of Vocal Terminology* (N.Y., 1984).—**NS/LK/DM**

Reid, John (Charles), Canadian jazz tenor saxophonist, clarinetist, flutist; b. Toronto, Ontario, Dec. 13, 1951. After playing with local rock bands in Calgary, he joined the 25-piece show group Stratus Faction in 1971, touring North America and performing on TV shows for CTV and CBC networks. He also toured with funk bands in the 1970s before completing his B.M. at the Univ. of Calgary in 1979. He has been leading his own jazz groups since 1974 when he was encouraged by teachers Phil Nimmons and Oscar Peterson to form a quartet to play for Jazz Radio Canda broadcast at the first annual Banff Centre Jazz Workshop. A stint with Alberta Culture took Reid to Edmonton (1980–81), where he played with Tommy Banks, George Blondheim, Bob Stroup and others before returning to Calgary where gigs with the Saturday Pro Band gave him the opportunity to perform with guests Dizzy Gillespie, Paul Horn and Bob Brookmeyer. He has also done gigs behind Harry Connick Jr., Kenny Wheeler, Della Reese, and Lou Rawls; in May 1991, he opened for Mel Torme at the Calgary Centre for Performing Arts. He was a member of the orch. that recorded music for the 1988 Winter Olympic Games. He premiered his "Improvisation No. 1" for solo tenor saxophone for the New Works Calgary Society in September 1991. He is founder and past chairman of the Calgary International Jazz Festival and founding secretary and past president of the Jazz Calgary Society. His quartet is still active in Edmonton, Saskatoon, and Calgary. He began working on his M.A. in Jazz History and Research at Rutgers–Newark in 1998.

DISC.: *Island Shuffle* (1993).—**LP**

Reid, Rufus (L.), jazz bassist, educator; b. Atlanta, Ga., Feb. 10, 1944. Raised in Sacramento, Calif., he began playing trumpet before taking up the double bass while serving in the U.S. Air Force. He played with Buddy Montgomery in Sacramento, and received his A.A. degree from Olympic Coll. in Bremerton, Wash., in 1969. He continued his education at Northwestern Univ., graduating in 1971 with a B.M. He began doing clinics in 1971, adjudicating and performing. His professional career began in Chicago and he played with Sonny Stitt, James Moody, Milt Jackson, Curtis Fuller, and Dizzy Gillespie. He also performed and recorded with Kenny

Dorham, Dexter Gordon, Lee Konitz, and Howard McGhee (all 1970). From the early 1970s, he recorded and made a number of international tours with Bobby Hutcherson's and Harold Land's quintet (1971), Freddie Hubbard and Nancy Wilson (1971), Eddie Harris (1971–74). In 1976 he moved to the N.Y. area, where he played and recorded with the quartet led by Thad Jones and Mel Lewis (1976–77), and toured with Dexter Gordon (1977–79). He has also worked with Booker Ervin, Gene Ammons, Don Byas, Philly Joe Jones, Stan Getz, and more recently with Benny Golson, Art Farmer, Harold Land, Bobby Hutcherson, Freddie Hubbard, Ray Bryant, J.J. Johnson (1992–97), Benny Carter, Joe Henderson, Kenny Burrell, Kenny Barron, and Jimmy Heath. He has appeared on over 200 albums, recording with Konitz (1976), Ricky Ford (1981), and Jack De-Johnette (1982, 1984), Kenny Burrell (1983), Frank Foster and Frank Wess (1983–84), Art Farmer (1984), and Jimmy Heath (1985). From 1980–85, he was on the music panel of the National Foundation for the Advancements in the Arts, specifically for graduating high school students across the nation. Since 1979, he has coached small and large jazz ensembles at William Paterson Coll. in Wayne, N.J., and since the mid-1980s, he has been Director of the Jazz Studies and Performance Program there. He performed and recorded with Andre Previn, Kathleen Battle and the St. Luke's Chamber Orch. in 1992; that same year, he premiered "Two Faces," a concerto for solo double bass and jazz trio, composed by Benny Golson for Reid and the Wayne Chamber Orch. at Alice Tully Hall at Lincoln Center. He joined with Akira Tana in 1990 to form the quintet, TanaReid. They continue to perform and teach around the world. In January 1997, the International Assoc. of Jazz Educators awarded him the Humanitarian Award. *Down Beat* awarded him the 1998 Jazz Educator Achievement Award. His melodicism, fine intonation and technique have made him one of the leading bassists.

DISC.: *Perpetual Stroll* (1980); *Seven Minds* (1984); *Corridor to the Limits* (1989). **TANAREID:** *Yours and Mine* (1990); *Passing Thoughts; Blue Motion* (1993); *Looking Forward* (1995); *Back to Front* (1998); *Double Bass Delights* (1997).

BIBL.: R. Reid, *The Evolving Bassist* (1974).—LP

Reif, Paul, Czech-American composer; b. Prague, March 23, 1910; d. N.Y., July 7, 1978. He played violin as a child, then studied composition in Vienna with Richard Stöhr and Franz Schmidt, and conducting with Franz Schalk and Bruno Walter; also had lessons with Richard Strauss. In 1941 he emigrated to the U.S., and in 1942 joined the U.S. Intelligence Corps; while with the U.S. Army in North Africa, he set to music the soldiers' song *Dirty Gertie from Bizerte*, which was introduced by Josephine Baker in Algiers in April 1943. Upon his discharge in 1945, he was awarded the Croix de Guerre and the Purple Heart. Returning to the U.S., he composed various serious and light scores.

WORKS: *Triple City* for Chorus and Brass Ensemble (N.Y., April 16, 1963); *Requiem to War* for Chorus and Percussion (N.Y., May 20, 1963); *Birches* for Voice and Orch., after Robert Frost (N.Y., Feb. 2, 1965); *Letter from a Birmingham Jail* for Chorus and Piano, after Martin Luther King Jr. (Washington, D.C., March 2, 1965); *Philidor's Defense* for Chamber Orch., inspired by the famous Philidor chess opening: 1. P-K4, P-K4; 2. N-KB3, P-Q3 (N.Y., April 10, 1965); 2 operas: *Mad Hamlet* (1965) and *Portrait in Brownstone* (N.Y., May 15, 1966); *Pentagram* for Piano (1969); *The Artist* (N.Y., April 17, 1972); *The Curse of Mauvais-Air* (N.Y., May 9, 1974); *5 Divertimenti* for 4 Strings (1969); *Episodes* for String Orch. (1972); Quintet for Clarinet, Viola, Piano, Percussion, and Folksinger (1974); *Duo for 3* for Clarinet, Cello, and Mezzo-soprano (1974); *America 1776–1876–1976* for Orch., Solo Guitar, Banjo, Electric Guitar, and Vocal Quartet (N.Y., Jan. 24, 1976).—NS/LK/DM

Reimann, Aribert, German composer, pianist, and teacher; b. Berlin, March 4, 1936. He studied at the Berlin Hochschule für Musik (1955–60) with Otto Rausch (piano), Blacher (composition), and Pepping (counterpoint), and also took courses in musicology at the Univ. of Vienna (1958). In 1963 he received the Prix de Rome and studied at the Villa Massimo in Rome. In 1957 he made his debut as a pianist, becoming particularly known in later years as a sensitive accompanist. From 1971 he was a member of the Berlin Akademie der Künste. He also was a prof. at the Hamburg Hochschule für Musik (1974–83), and later at the Berlin Hochschule der Künste (1983). In 1976 he was made a member of the Bayerische Akademie der Schönen Künste in Munich and in 1985 of the Hamburg Freien Akademie der Künste. In 1986 he won the Prix de la composition musicale of the Prince Pierre Foundation of Monaco. He received the Frankfurt am Main music award in 1991. After adhering to the precepts of the 2nd Viennese School of composition, he abandoned orthodox serialism in favor of a compositional style in which linear elements were occasionally complemented by lyrical effusions.

WORKS: DRAMATIC: O p e r a : *Ein Traumspiel* (1963–64; Kiel, June 20, 1965); *Melusine* (1970; Schwetzingen, April 29, 1971); *Lear* (1976–78; Munich, July 9, 1978); *Die Gespenstersonate* (1983; Berlin, Sept. 25, 1984); *Troades* (1985; Munich, July 7, 1986); *Das Schloss* (1989–91; Berlin, Sept. 2, 1992); *Melusine* (Munich, Oct. 19, 1997). **B a l l e t :** *Stoffreste* (1957; Essen, 1959); *Die Vogelscheuchen* (1969–70; Berlin, Oct. 7, 1970; orch. suite, 1970). **P o é m e V i s u e l :** *Chacun sa chimère* for Tenor and Orch. (1981; Düsseldorf, April 17, 1982). **ORCH.:** *Elegie* (1957; Darmstadt, April 5, 1963); Cello Concerto (1959; Berlin, March 23, 1961); *Monumenta* for Winds and Percussion (1960; Baden-Baden, Nov. 27, 1963); 2 piano concertos: No. 1 (1961; Berlin, Oct. 26, 1962) and No. 2 for Piano and 19 Players (1972; Nuremberg, Jan. 12, 1973); Sym., after the opera *Ein Traumspiel* (1964; Darmstadt, Sept. 12, 1976); *Rondes* for Strings (1967; Cologne, Jan. 25, 1968); *Loqui* (Saarbrücken, Dec. 5, 1969); *Variationen* (1975; Zürich, Jan. 13, 1976); *Sieben Fragmente* (1988); Double Concerto for Violin, Cello, and Orch. (1988–89; Hannover, Nov. 13, 1989); *9 Pieces* (1993; Houston, May 14, 1994); Violin Concerto (1996). **CHAMBER:** *Canzoni e ricercari* for Flute, Viola, and Cello (1961); Cello Sonata (1963); *Nocturnos* for Cello and Harp (1965); *Reflexionen* for 7 Instruments (1966); *Invenzioni* for 12 Players (1979); *Solo* for Cello (1981); String Trio (1987). **KEYBOARD: p i a n o :** Sonata (1957); *Spektren* (1967); *Variationen* (1979); *Auf dem Weg* (Vol. I, 1989–93). **O r g a n :** *Dialogo I* (1963). **VOCAL:** *Ein Totentanz* for Baritone and Chamber Orch. (1960); *Hölderlin- Fragmente* for Soprano and Orch. (1963); *Epitaph* for Tenor and 7 Instruments (1965); *Verrà la morte,* cantata for Soloists, 2 Choruses, and Orch. (1966; Berlin, Feb. 28, 1967); *Nenia* for Speaker and Orch. (1967; Kassel,

June 26, 1968); *Inane*, monologue for Soprano and Orch. (1968); *Fragmente aus Melusine* for Soprano, Baritone, and Orch. (1970); *Zyklus* for Baritone and Orch. (Nuremberg, April 15, 1971); *Lines* for Soprano and Chamber String Orch. (1973); *Wolkenloses Christfest*, requiem for Baritone, Cello, and Orch. (Landau, June 2, 1974); *Fragmente aus Lear* for Baritone and Orch. (1976–78; Zürich, April 29, 1980); *Unrevealed* for Baritone and String Quartet (1980; Berlin, Sept. 3, 1981); *Drei Lieder* for Soprano and Orch. (1980–82; Kiel, June 26, 1982); *Ein apokalyptisches Fragment* for Mezzo-soprano, Piano, and Orch. (Berlin, Sept. 27, 1987); *Sechs Gesänge* for Soprano and String Quartet (1994); *Finite Infinity* for Soprano and Small Orch. (1994–95); *Mignon* for Soprano and Small Orch. (1994–95); *Kumi Ori* for Baritone and Orch. (1999); song cycles and solo songs with piano. —NS/LK/DM

Reimers, Paul, German-American tenor; b. Lunden, Schleswig-Holstein (of Danish parents), March 14, 1878; d. N.Y., April 14, 1942. He studied in Hamburg, where he made his stage debut as Max in *Der Freischütz* (1902). After further training with George Henschel in Scotland, Raimund von Zur Mühlen in London, and Jean Criticos in Paris, he devoted himself to a concert career and sang widely in Europe. In 1913 he went to America. He gave programs of German lieder, and also performed songs of the modern French school. From 1924 he taught at the Juilliard School of Music in N.Y. —NS/LK/DM

Reina, Domenico, Italian tenor; b. Lugano, 1797; d. there, July 29, 1843. He studied with Boile in Milan, making his debut in 1829 at La Scala in Milan as Ilio in Rossini's *Zelmira*. While there, he created Arturo in Bellini's *La Straniera* as well as Tamas in Donizetti's *Gemma di Vergy*. He was greatly admired for his performances of the lyrico-dramatic tenor parts in the operas of Rossini, Bellini, and Donizetti.—NS/LK/DM

Reinagle, Alexander, prominent English-born American pianist, teacher, impresario, and composer; b. Portsmouth (of Austrian parents) (baptized), April 23, 1756; d. Baltimore, Sept. 21, 1809. He studied in Edinburgh with Rayner Taylor, and in London for a time; also visited Lisbon and other continental cities. From his correspondence he appears to have been a close friend of C.P.E. Bach. He went to N.Y. early in 1786, settling in the same year in Philadelphia, where he taught, managed subscription concerts (also in N.Y.), and was active as a singer, pianist, conductor, and composer. In 1787 he introduced 4-hand piano music to America. He was associated, possibly as harpsichordist, with the Old American Co., and took part in its 1788–89 season in N.Y. In 1790 he was engaged as music director of a stock company for the production of plays and comic operas, with Thomas Wignell as general director; also built the New Theatre, which opened on Feb. 2, 1793, with Reinagle acting as composer, singer, and director. He also managed a company in Baltimore (from 1794).

Works: *A Collection of ... Scots Tunes with Variations* for Keyboard (London, c. 1782; 2nd ed., abr., 1787, as *A Selection of the Most Favorite Scots Tunes with Variations*); *6 Sonatas with Accompaniment* for Violin (London, c. 1780); *Miscellaneous Quar-*

tets (Philadelphia, 1791); *Concerto on the Improved Pianoforte with Additional Keys* (1794); *Preludes* (1794); accompaniments and incidental music to *The Sicilian Romance* (1795), *The Witches of the Rock,* pantomime (1796), and various English plays; *Masonic Overture* (1800); 4 piano sonatas (in Library of Congress, Washington, D.C.; Sonata No. 2 publ. in abr. form by J. Howard in *A Program of Early American Piano- Music,* N.Y., 1931; see also S. Duer, *An Annotated Edition of 4 Sonatas by Alexander Reinagle* [Peabody Cons., 1976]); *Collection of Favorite Songs;* music to Milton's *Paradise Lost* (incomplete).

BIBL.: C. Horton, *Serious Art and Concert Music for Piano in America in the 100 Years from A. R. to Edward MacDowell* (diss., Univ. of N.C., 1965).—NS/LK/DM

Reinberger, Jiří, Czech organist, teacher, and composer; b. Brünn, April 14, 1914; d. Prague, May 28, 1977. He was a student of Treglar (organ diploma, 1932) and of Petrželka (composition diploma, 1938) at the Brno Cons., and then of Novák (composition) in Prague (1938–40). He also studied organ with Widermann and in Leipzig with Ramin and Straube. After teaching at the Brno Cons. (1945), he settled in Prague as a teacher at the Cons. From 1951 he taught at the Academy of Musical Arts. He made tours of Europe as a recitalist, winning distinction for his performances of Bach and Czech composers. In 1964 he was made an Artist of Merit by the Czech government. Among his compositions were 2 syms. (1938, 1958), 3 organ concertos (1940, 1956, 1960), and a Cello Concerto (1962).—NS/LK/DM

Reinecke, Carl (Heinrich Carsten), renowned German pianist, composer, conductor, and pedagogue; b. Altona, June 23, 1824; d. Leipzig, March 10, 1910. He was a pupil of his father, a music teacher. His first concert tour was to Denmark and Sweden in 1843. He then went to Leipzig, where he learned much through meetings with Mendelssohn and Schumann. He made a second tour through North Germany, and was from 1846 to 1848 court pianist to Christian VIII at Copenhagen. After spending some years in Paris, he became a teacher at the Cologne Cons. in 1851. He was music director at Barmen (1854–59) and Breslau (1859–60), and (1860–95) conductor of the Gewandhaus Concerts in Leipzig. At the same time, he was a prof. of piano and composition at the Leipzig Cons., where he taught from 1860; was its director from 1897 until his retirement in 1902. An eminent pianist, Reinecke excelled as an interpreter of Mozart. He made concert tours almost yearly, and was enthusiastically welcomed in England, the Netherlands, Scandinavia, Switzerland, and throughout Germany; among his pupils were Grieg, Riemann, Sinding, Arthur Sullivan, Karl Muck, and Cosima Wagner. As a conductor, composer, and teacher of composition, he was the leader in Leipzig for over 35 years. His numerous works, in every genre, are classic in form and of refined workmanship. Altogether he wrote some 300 opus numbers.

Works: DRAMATIC: *König Manfred,* opera (Wiesbaden, July 26, 1867); *Ein Abenteuer Händels oder Die Macht des Liedes,* Singspiel (Schwerin, 1874); *Auf hohen Befehl,* comic opera (Hamburg, Oct. 1, 1886); *Der Gouverneur von Tours,* comic opera (Schwerin, 1891); also 5 musical fairy tales for Soloists, Chorus, and Piano: *Nussknacker und Mausekönig, Schneewittchen, Dorn-*

röschen, Aschenbrödel, and *Die wilden Schwäne*, and the oratorio, *Belsazar*. **ORCH.**: 3 syms.; overtures; smaller works; 4 piano concertos; Violin Concerto; Cello Concerto; Harp Concerto; Flute Concerto. **CHAMBER:** Octet for Wind Instruments; Sextet for Wind Instruments; 5 string quartets; Piano Quintet; 2 piano quartets; 6 piano trios; Trio for Piano, Oboe, and Horn; Trio for Piano, Clarinet, and Horn; Violin Sonata; 3 violin sonatinas; 3 cello sonatas; Sonata for Flute and Piano. **P i - a n o :** Numerous character pieces; Sonata for Piano, Left-Hand; suite, *Biblische Bilder*; 3 sonatas for 2 Pianos. **OTHER:** Cadenzas to 42 movements of piano concertos by Bach, Mozart, Beethoven, and Weber.

WRITINGS: *Was sollen wir spielen?* (1886); *Zur Wiederbelebung der Mozartschen Clavier-Concerto* (1891); *Die Beethovenschen Clavier-Sonaten: Briefe an eine Freundin* (1895; Eng. tr., 1898; 9th Ger. ed., 1924); *Und manche liebe Schatten steigen auf: Gedenkblätter an berühmte Musiker* (1900; 2nd ed., 1910); *Meister der Tonkunst* (1903); *Aus dem Reich der Tone* (1907).

BIBL.: W. von Wasielewski, *C. R.: Ein Künstlerbild* (Leipzig, 1892); E. Segnitz, *C. R.* (Leipzig, 1900); M. Steinitzer, *Das Leipziger Gewandhaus im neuen Heim unter C. R.* (Leipzig, 1924); N. Topusov, *C. R.: Beiträge zu seinem Leben und seiner Symphonik* (Sofia, 1943); M. Wiegandt, *Vergessene Symphonik?: Studien zu Joachim Raff, C. R. und zum Problem der Epigonalität in der Musik* (Sinzig, 1997); K. Seidel, *C. R. und das Leipziger Gewandhaus* (Hamburg, 1998).—NS/LK/DM

Reiner, Fritz (actually, **Frigyes**), eminent Hungarian-born American conductor; b. Budapest, Dec. 19, 1888; d. N.Y., Nov. 15, 1963. He studied piano with Thomán and composition with Koessler at the Royal Academy of Music in Budapest, and concurrently took courses in jurisprudence at the Univ. of Budapest. In 1909 he made his debut in Budapest conducting *Carmen*. In 1910–11 he conducted at the Laibach Landestheater. He was conductor of the Volksoper in Budapest (1911–14) and of the Court (later State) Opera in Dresden (1914–21); also conducted in Hamburg, Berlin, Vienna, Rome, and Barcelona. In 1922 he was engaged as music director of the Cincinnati Sym. Orch.; was naturalized as an American citizen in 1928. In 1931 he became a prof. of conducting at the Curtis Inst. of Music in Philadelphia; among his students were Leonard Bernstein and Lukas Foss. In 1936–37 he made guest appearances at London's Covent Garden; between 1935 and 1938 he was a guest conductor at the San Francisco Opera; from 1938 to 1948 he was music director of the Pittsburgh Sym. Orch.; then was a conductor at the Metropolitan Opera in N.Y. until 1953. He achieved the peak of his success as a conductor with the Chicago Sym. Orch., which he served as music director from 1953 to 1962, and which he brought up to the point of impeccably fine performance in both Classical and modern music. His striving for perfection created for him the reputation of a ruthless master of the orch.; he was given to explosions of temper, but musicians and critics agreed that it was because of his uncompromising drive toward the optimum of orch. playing that the Chicago Sym. Orch. achieved a very high rank among American symphonic organizations.

BIBL.: P. Hart, *F. R.: A Biography* (Evanston, Ill., 1994). —NS/LK/DM

Reiner, Karel, prominent Czech composer and pianist; b. Žatec, June 27, 1910; d. Prague, Oct. 17, 1979. He studied law at the German Univ. in Prague (Dr.Jur., 1933) and musicology at the Univ. of Prague. He also attended Suk's master classes (1931) and A. Hába's courses in microtonal music (1934–35) at the Prague Cons. He was associated with E. Burian's improvisational theater in Prague (1934–38). Unable to leave Central Europe when the Nazis invaded Czechoslovakia, he was detained at Terezín, and later sent to the concentration camps of Dachau and Auschwitz, but survived, and after liberation resumed his activities as a composer and pianist. His earliest works were atonal and athematic; in 1935–36 he wrote a *Suite* and a *Fantasy* for quarter tone piano, and a set of 5 quarter-tone songs; after 1945 he wrote mostly traditional music; then returned to ultramodern techniques.

WORKS: DRAMATIC: O p e r a : *Pohádka o zakleté písen* (Tale of an Enchanted Song; 1949); *Schustermärchen*, fairy tale opera (1972). **B a l l e t :** *Jednota* (Unity; 1933). **ORCH.:** Piano Concerto (1932); Violin Concerto (1937); *Concertante Suite* for Winds and Percussion (1947); *Divertimento* for Clarinet, Harp, Strings, and Percussion (1947); *3 Czech Dances* (1949); *Spring Prelude* (1950); *Motýli tady nežijí* (Butterflies Don't Live Here Anymore), 6 pictures, based on music to the film (1959–60; depicts the fate of Jewish children in the Terezín concentration camp); Sym. (1960); *Symphonic Overture* (1964); Concerto for Bass Clarinet, Strings, and Percussion (1966); *Concertante Suite* (1967); Bassoon Concertino (1969); *Promluvy* (Utterances) for Chamber Orch. (1975); *Music for Strings* (1975); *Introduction and Allegro (Diptych No. 2)* (1976); *Diptych No. 1* (1977); *3 Symphonic Movements* (1978). **CHAMBER:** 3 string quartets (1931, 1947, 1951); *7 Miniatures* for Wind Quintet (1931); *Dvanáct* (The 12), suite for Piano and Wind Quintet (1931); 2 nonets (Concerto, 1933; *Preambule*, 1974); *Sonata brevis* for Cello and Piano (1946); *4 Compositions* for Clarinet and Piano (1954); *3 Compositions* for Oboe and Piano (1955); *Elegie and Capriccio* for Cello and Piano (1957); Double Bass Sonata (1957); Violin Sonata (1959); *Small Suite* for 9 Wind Instruments (1960); *6 Bagatelles* for Trumpet and Piano (1962); *2 Compositions* for Oboe and Harp (1962); *4 Compositions* for Clarinet (1963); *6 Studies* for Flute and Piano (1964); Trio for Flute, Bass Clarinet, and Percussion (1964); Piano Trio (1965); *Suite* for Bassoon and Piano (1965); *Music for 4 Clarinets* (1965); *Črty* (Sketches) for Piano Quartet (1966–67); *Concert Studies* for Cymbalom (1967); *2 Compositions* for Saxophone and Piano (1967); *Concertante Sonata* for Percussion (1967); *Prolegomena* for String Quartet (1968); *4 Abbreviations* for Brass Quintet (1968); *Dua*, 5 compositions for 2 Flutes, 2 Oboes, 2 Clarinets, and 2 Trumpets, in any combination (1969); *Volné listy* (Loose Leaves) for Clarinet, Cello, and Piano (1969); *Formulas* for Trombone and Piano (1970); *Recordings* for Bassoon (1970); *Drawings* for Clarinet, Horn, and Piano (1970); *Maxims* for Flute Quartet (1970); *Tercetti* for Oboe, Clarinet, and Bassoon (1971); *Talks* for Wind Quintet (1971–72); *Akrostichon a Allegro* for Bass Clarinet and Piano (1972); *Duo* for 2 Quarter Tone Clarinets (1972); *Replicas* for Flute, Viola, and Harp (1973); *Sujets* for Guitar (1973); *Overtura ritmica* for Guitar (1974); *Strophes* for Viola and Piano (1975); *Portraits*, suite for String Trio (1977); *Dialogues* for 2 Flutes (1978); *Panels*, sextet for Brasses (1979). **P i a n o :** *9 Merry Improvisations* (1928–29); *5 Jazz Studies* (1930); 3 sonatas (1931, 1942, 1961); *Minda-Minda*, 7 compositions (1937). **VOCAL:** *Bylo jim tisíc let* (It Was a Thousand Years since Then), cantata (1962); *Talks* for Baritone, Saxophone, and Flute (1979); songs.—NS/LK/DM

Reinhard, Kurt, German ethnomusicologist; b. Giessen, Aug. 27, 1914; d. Wetzlar, July 18, 1979. He studied musicology and composition in Cologne (1933–35), and musicology and ethnology at the univs. in Leipzig and Munich under Huber, Ficker, and Ubbelohdé-Doering (1935–36); received a doctorate with a diss. on Burmese music (1938). He worked at the Staatliche Musikinstrumentensammlung in Berlin, then was director of the Berliner Phonogramm-Archiv (1948–68) and head of the dept. of music pedagogy at the Peterson Cons. (1947–52). In 1948 he began teaching at the Free Univ. in Berlin, where he completed a Habilitation on organology (1950); subsequently became prof. and head of the ethnomusicology dept. there (1957). His most important research focused on the folk and art music of Turkey.

WRITINGS: *Die Musik exotischer Völker* (Berlin, 1951); *Chinesische Musik* (Kassel, 1956); *Turkische Musik* (Berlin, 1962); *Einführung in die Musikethnologie* (Wölfenbuttel, 1968). —NS/LK/DM

Reinhardt, Delia, German soprano; b. Elberfeld, April 27, 1892; d. Arlesheim, near Basel, Oct. 3, 1974. She studied with Strakosch and Hedwig Schako at the Hoch Cons. in Frankfurt am Main. She made her operatic debut in Breslau in 1913. In 1916 she joined the Munich Court (later Bavarian State) Opera, where she sang until 1923. She made her debut at the Metropolitan Opera in N.Y. on Jan. 27, 1923, as Sieglinde; then sang at the Berlin State Opera (1924–33); also made guest appearances at Covent Garden in London (1924–27; 1929). She was married to **Gustav Schützendorf,** and later to **Georges Sébastian.** Among her outstanding roles were Desdemona, Elsa, and Eva.—NS/LK/DM

Reinhardt, Django (Jean Baptiste), legendary jazz guitarist; b. Liberchies, Belgium, Jan. 23, 1910; d. Fontainebleau, France, May 16, 1953. He was born of gypsy stock in a caravan, and grew up on the edges of Paris. Though it is usually said that he was totally illiterate, at least one purported autograph survives (from Milan, 1949). His uncle taught him the basics of the banjo, and from the age of 12, he played in bands in local cafes and bars and at dances. He lost the use of two fingers on his left hand, essential for fretting notes, in a fire in 1928; in photographs, the pinky and ring finger appear to be almost welded to the middle finger. He taught himself a completely new method of fingering, and then taught himself to play the guitar using this new technique. From 1928–34, he backed singers on recordings. On his early recordings, there are no solos, just accompaniment and an occasional fill. Introduced to jazz via Louis Armstrong records in 1931, he was also influenced by Eddie Lang; he became the favorite accompanist of popular singer Jean Sablon. He bumped into Stephane Grappelli backstage one day and after jamming on "Dinah," the two organized the Quintette de la Club Hot de France in 1934. The group was unusual in its line up of violin, solo guitar, two rhythm guitars, and bass, but became one of the most admired and adventurous musical collaborations ever. In 1946, he made a brief tour of the U.S. playing electric guitar

with the Duke Ellington band. His many intriguing compositions include "Nuages," "Django's Castle," and "Bolero." His admirers include Charlie Christian, Les Paul, Wes Montgomery, and B.B. King, among many others.

His brother, Joseph (Nin Nin; b. Paris, France, March 1, 1912; d. there, late Feb. 1982) played rhythm guitar with the Quintette. After Django's death in 1953, he led a quintet and made several recordings.

DISC.: *Rare Django* (1928); *Quintette of the Hot Club of France* (1947); *Peche a La Mouche* (1947); *Swing Guitar* (1945); *Paris 1945* (1945); "Swing De Paris" (1947); *Djangology 49* (1949); *At Club St. Germain* (1951); *Nuages (Arcadia Jazz)* (1997); *Djangology* (series).

BIBL.: D. Schulz-Kohn, *Diango Reinhardt: ein Portrat* (Wetzlar, Germany, 1960); R. Spautz, *Diango Reinhardt: Mythos und Realite* (Luxembourg, 1984); P. Williams, *Django Reinhardt* (Montpellier, France, 1991); C. Delaunay, *Django Reinhardt: Souvenirs* (Paris, 1954); Abrams, *The Book of Django* (Los Angeles, 1973); A. Schmitz and P. Maier, *Django Reinhardt: Sein Leben, seine Musik, seine Schallplatten* (Gauting-Buchendorf, 1985). —LP/MM

Reining, Maria, noted Austrian soprano; b. Vienna, Aug. 7, 1903; d. there, March 11, 1991. She studied at a business school, and was employed in the foreign exchange dept. of a Vienna bank before taking up singing. In 1931 she made her debut at the Vienna State Opera, remaining on its roster until 1933; then sang in Darmstadt (1933–35) and at the Bavarian State Opera in Munich (1935–37). In 1937 she rejoined the Vienna State Opera, continuing on its roster, with interruptions, until 1958; also appeared at the Salzburg Festivals (1937–41); Toscanini engaged her to sing Eva in *Die Meistersinger von Nürnberg* in Salzburg under his direction in 1937; she also sang the role of the Marschallin in *Der Rosenkavalier* and the title role in *Arabella* by Richard Strauss. She was equally successful in soubrette roles and as a dramatic soprano. In 1938 she appeared with the Covent Garden Opera in London and with the Chicago Opera; in 1949, as the Marschallin with the N.Y.C. Opera. She also sang at La Scala in Milan, and toured as a concert singer. In 1962 she became a prof. of singing at the Mozarteum in Salzburg.—NS/LK/DM

Reinken (Reincken), Jan Adams, famous organist and composer; b. April 26, 1623; d. Hamburg, Nov. 24, 1722. The place of his birth has not been determined, but it may have been Wilshausen, Alsace, Wildeshausen near Bremen, or in a Dutch village of similar name. By 1654 he was in Hamburg, where he studied with Heinrich Scheidemann, the organist of the Katharinenkirche. In 1657 he became organist of the Berghkercke in Deventer, the Netherlands. In 1658 he returned to Hamburg as asst. organist to Scheidemann at the Katharinenkirche, and in 1663 he succeeded his teacher as organist, a position he held with great distinction for 60 years. Reinken was one of the most celebrated organ virtuosos of his time. In 1720 Bach played at the Katharinenkirche, and Reinken, then 97 years old, was in attendance. He was also a consultant on organ building, and a noted teacher of the organ; his students included Andreas Kneller (later his son-in-law) and G.D. Leiding. He composed several virtuoso organ pieces, and also 6 instrumental suites publ. as *Hortus musicus*. His complete works for keyboard may be found in K. Beckmann, ed., *J.A. Reincken: Sämtliche Orgelwerke* (Wiesbaden, 1974).

WORKS: KEYBOARD: *An den Wasserflüssen Babylon*; *Ballet* in E minor; *Fuga* in G minor; *Partite diverse sopra l'Aria "Schweiget mir von Weiber nehmen," altrimente chiamata "La Meyerin"*; 3 suites, in C major, E minor, and G major; *Toccata* in C major; *Was kann uns kommen an für Noth*. **CHAMBER:** *Hortus musicus*, 6 suites for 2 Violins, Viola da Gamba, and Basso Continuo (Hamburg, 1687; later ed. by J. van Riemsdijk, Amsterdam, 1888). **VOCAL:** *Geistlich Konzert "auf Michael": Und es erhub sich ein Streit* for 4 Voices, 2 Violins, Viola, 2 Trumpets, Timpani, and Basso Continuo.—NS/LK/DM

Reinmar (real name, **Wochinz**), **Hans,** distinguished Austrian baritone; b. Vienna, April 11, 1895; d. Berlin, Feb. 7, 1961. He studied at the Vienna Academy of Music and in Milan. He made his operatic debut in 1919 in Olomouc as Sharpless; then sang in Nuremberg, Zürich, Dresden, and Hamburg; was a member of the Berlin Städtische Oper (1928–45; 1952–61), the Bavarian State Opera in Munich (1945–46; 1950–57), the Berlin State Opera (1948–52), and the Berlin Komische Oper (1952–61); also sang at the festivals in Bayreuth and Salzburg. He excelled in dramatic roles in Italian operas.—NS/LK/DM

Reise, Jay, American composer and teacher; b. N.Y., Feb. 9, 1950. He studied composition with Jimmy Giuffre (1968–70), and pursued his education at Hamilton Coll. (A.B. in English literature, 1972) and the Univ. of Pa. (M.A. in music composition, 1975). He also studied with Messiaen, Davidovsky, Earle Brown, and Schuller at Tanglewood (summers, 1975–77), where he won the Koussevitzky Prize in composition in 1975, and later pursued training in Carnatic (South Indian) rhythm with Adrian L'Armand (1989–92). After teaching at Kirkland Coll. (1976–78) and Hamilton Coll. (1978–80), he joined the faculty of the Univ. of Pa., where he became a prof. of composition. In 1978 and 1984 he held N.E.A. fellowships, in 1980 a Guggenheim fellowship, and in 1998 a Bellagio fellowship. Reise composed the first "operafilm," *Devil in the Flesh* (1998–2000).

WORKS: DRAMATIC: *Rasputin*, opera (N.Y., Sept. 17, 1988); *The Selfish Giant*, choreographic tone poem (London, Dec. 4, 1997); *Devil in the Flesh: The Operafilm* (1998–2000). **ORCH.:** *Hieronymo's Mad Againe* (1976); *Paraphonia* for Chamber Orch. (1978); 3 syms. (*Symphony of Voices*, 1978; 1980; 1983); *Prelude* for Strings (1982); *Rhythms Unto Night* (1994); *Yellowstone Rhythms* for Bassoon and Orch. (1997). **Concert Band:** *Tinicum Rhythms* (1997). **CHAMBER:** *Concerto-Fantasy* for 9 Players (1975); 2 string quartets (1977, 1983); *Nightones* for Trumpet, String Quartet, and Keyboard Percussion (1981); *Fantasy* for Cello and Piano (1983); Sinfonietta for Wind Quintet (1985); *Trio Rhythmikosmos* for Violin, Cello, and Piano (1993); *Duo Rhythmikosmos* for Violin and Piano (1994); *Chesapeake Rhythms* for 11 Players (1995). **VOCAL:** *Movements of Imagination* for Soprano and Chamber Orch. (1974); *Cleopatra* for Soprano and Chamber Ensemble (1979); *Satori* for Soprano and Piano Trio or Piano (1995); *Arcadian Shadows* for Soprano, Clarinet, Cello, and Piano (1996). **OTHER:** Organ music; piano pieces.—NS/LK/DM

Reisenberg, Nadia, Russian-American pianist and pedagogue, sister of **Clara Rockmore;** b. Vilnius, July 14, 1904; d. N.Y., June 10, 1983. She was 9 when she commenced studies with Leonid Nikolayev at the St. Petersburg Cons. In 1920 she left the Soviet Union and toured in Poland, Latvia, Lithuania, and Germany. In 1922 she emigrated to the U.S. and continued her training with Alexander Lambert, and then with Josef Hofmann at the Curtis Inst. of Music in Philadelphia. On Dec. 17, 1922, she made her U.S. debut as soloist in Paderewski's *Fantaisie polonaise* with the N.Y.C. Sym. Orch. with the composer in attendance. On Feb. 6, 1924, she made her N.Y. recital debut. In subsequent years, she toured as a soloist with orchs., as a recitalist, and as a chamber music player. In 1939 she was soloist in all the Mozart concerti on radio with Wallenstein and the WOR Sym. Orch. She devoted much of her time to teaching and served on the faculties of the Curtis Inst. of Music, the Mannes Coll., Queens Coll. of the City Univ. of N.Y., and the Juilliard School. In 1964 she gave her farewell performance in N.Y. as soloist in Liszt's 2nd Piano Concerto. She possessed a fine technique and a lyrical expressivity.

BIBL.: A. and R. Sherman, eds., *N. R.: A Musician's Scrapbook* (College Park, Md., 1985).—NS/LK/DM

Reiser, Alois, Czech-American composer; b. Prague, April 6, 1887; d. Los Angeles, April 4, 1977. He studied composition with Dvořák, and also took cello lessons and toured Europe. He later emigrated to the U.S. and played cello with the Pittsburgh Sym. Orch. and the N.Y. Sym. Orch. From 1918 to 1929 he was engaged as a theater conductor in N.Y. In 1929 he settled in Hollywood, where he worked as a composer and conductor at film studios. His works adhere to the established style of European Romanticism; typical of these are *Slavic Rhapsody*, which he conducted in Los Angeles on March 8, 1931, and *Erewhon*, which he conducted there on Jan. 24, 1936. He composed a Cello Concerto, which he performed in Los Angeles on March 23, 1933; also a considerable amount of chamber music. He wrote an opera, *Gobi*, in which he painted in tones the great Asian desert; it had its first and last performance in N.Y. on July 29, 1923, and even then only in concert excerpts.—NS/LK/DM

Reiss, Albert, German tenor; b. Berlin, Feb. 22, 1870; d. Nice, June 19, 1940. He was an actor before his voice was discovered by Pollini, after which he studied with Wilhelm Vilmar in Berlin, and later with Beno Stolzenburg and Julius Lieban. He made his operatic debut in Königsberg as Ivanov in *Zar und Zimmermann* (Sept. 28, 1897); then sang in various German towns; on Dec. 23, 1901, he made his American debut at the Metropolitan Opera in N.Y. in the minor roles of the Sailor and the Shepherd in *Tristan und Isolde*; remained on its roster until 1920; he won distinction there as David in *Die Meistersinger von Nürnberg* and Mime in the *Ring* cycle. In 1919 he returned to Berlin and sang at the Volksoper (1923–25). In 1938 he retired from the stage and lived in Nice.—NS/LK/DM

Reiss, Józef (Wladyslaw), Polish musicologist; b. Dębica, Aug. 4, 1879; d. Kraków, Feb. 22, 1956. He studied musicology with Adler at the Univ. of Vienna (Ph.D., 1910, with a diss. on the Polish composer Gomólka), and then completed his Habilitation at the Univ. of Kraków (1922), where he then taught until 1939, and again from 1949 to 1953. Among his publications, all in Polish, were *The Problem of Content in Music* (Kraków, 1915; 2nd ed., aug., 1922), *Musical Forms* (Leipzig, 1917; 2nd ed., 1929), *Beethoven* (Warsaw, 1920), *A Concise History of Music* (Warsaw, 1920; 3rd ed., aug., 1931), *Henryk Wieniawski* (Warsaw, 1931; 3rd ed., 1970), *An Almanac of Music in Kraków, 1780–1914* (Kraków, 1939), *Violins and Violinists* (Kraków, 1955), and *Short Encyclopedia of Music* (Warsaw, 1960).—**NS/LK/DM**

Reisserová, Julie, Czech composer; b. Prague, Oct. 9, 1888; d. there, Feb. 25, 1938. She studied with J.B. Foerster and also with Albert Roussel in Paris. Among her works are *Pastorale maritime* for Orch. (1933), *Esquisses* for Piano, and several albums of songs.

BIBL.: J. Vacková, *J. R.* (Prague, 1948).—**NS/LK/DM**

Reissiger, Carl Gottlieb, noted German conductor and composer; b. Belzig, near Wittenberg, Jan. 31, 1798; d. Dresden, Nov. 7, 1859. His father, Christian Gottlieb Reissiger, was the Belzig organist and choirmaster. He studied piano and composition with Schicht at the Leipzig Thomasschule (1811–18), then theory with Salieri in Vienna (1821–22) and voice and composition with Winter in Munich (1822). Weber conducted the premiere of his opera *Didone abbandonata* at the Dresden Court Opera (Jan. 31, 1824). After teaching composition in Berlin (1825–26), he was called to Dresden as director of the Court Opera in 1826; was named Hofkapellmeister in 1828, and was in charge of sacred music and chamber music, as well as the Court Opera, until his death. He was highly esteemed by his contemporaries as a conductor; he built upon the foundation laid by Weber and made the Dresden Court Opera the premiere opera house of Germany. He was a prolific composer, writing with great facility but with little originality. He attained some success with his songs and pieces; his *Danses brillantes pour le pianoforte or Webers letzter Gedanke* (1822) was very popular, as was his melodrama *Yelva* (1827).

BIBL.: W. Neumann, *K.G. R.* (Kassel, 1854); K. Kreiser, *C.G. R.: Sein Leben nebst einigen Beitragen zur Geschichte des Konzertwesens in Dresden* (diss., Univ. of Leipzig, 1918).—**NS/LK/DM**

Reizen, Mark (Osipovich), notable Russian bass; b. Zaytsevo, July 3, 1895; d. Moscow, Nov. 25, 1992. He was a pupil of Bugamelli at the Kharkov Cons. In 1921 he made his operatic debut as Pimen at the Kharkov Opera. After singing at the Kirov Theater in Leningrad (1925–30), he was a principal member of the Bolshoi Theater in Moscow (1930–54). As a guest artist, he sang with the Paris Opéra, the Berlin State Opera, the Dresden State Opera et al.; also toured widely as a concert artist. In 1985 he returned to the Bolshoi Theater to celebrate his 90th birthday, appearing as Gremin in *Evgeny Onegin*. He publ. a vol. of autobiographical notes (Moscow, 1980). Reizen possessed a voice of remarkable

beauty, ably complemented by his assured stage deportment. Among his finest portrayals were Mozart's Don Basilio, Gounod's Méphistophélès, Boris Godunov, Philip II, Dosifey, and Ivan Susanin.—**NS/LK/DM**

Reizenstein, Franz (Theodor), German-born English pianist, teacher, and composer; b. Nuremberg, June 7, 1911; d. London, Oct. 15, 1968. He studied piano with Leonid Kreutzer and composition with Hindemith at the Hochschule für Musik in Berlin (1930–34). With the advent of the anti-Semitic Nazi regime, he went to England, where entered the Royal Coll. of Music in London and studied with Lambert and Vaughan Williams (1934–36); then took private piano lessons with Solomon (1938–40). He was an instructor in piano at the Royal Academy of Music in London (1958–68), and from 1962 until his death, at the Royal Manchester Coll. of Music. He wrote music of fine neo-Romantic quality.

WORKS: DRAMATIC: Radio Opera: *Men against the Sea* (1949); *Anna Kraus* (1952). **ORCH.:** Cello Concerto (1936); *Prologue, Variations and Finale* for Violin and Orch. (1938; originally for Violin and Piano); 2 piano concertos: No. 1 (1941) and No. 2 (1956–61; London, June 7, 1961, composer soloist); *Cyrano de Bergerac*, overture (1951); *Serenade in F* for Wind Ensemble and Double Bass or for Small Orch. (1951); Violin Concerto (1953); Concerto for Strings (1966–67; London, Jan. 17, 1969). **CHAMBER:** Sonata for Solo Cello (1931; rev. 1967); *Theme, Variations and Fugue* for Clarinet Quintet (1932; rev. 1960); Wind Quintet (1934); *Divertimento* for String or Brass Quartet (1936–37); Oboe Sonatina (1937); *Partita* for Flute and String Trio (1938); Violin Sonata (1945); Cello Sonata (1947); Piano Quintet (1948); Trio for Flute, Oboe, and Piano (1949); *Fantasia concertante* for Violin and Piano (1956); Trio for Flute, Clarinet, and Bassoon (1963); *Concert Fantasy* for Viola and Piano (1956); Sonata for Solo Viola (1967); Sonata for Solo Violin (1968); 2 piano sonatas (1944, 1964). **VOCAL:** *Genesis*, oratorio (1958); *Voices of Night*, cantata (1950–51).—**NS/LK/DM**

Rekašius, Antanas, Lithuanian composer; b. Pauvandene, Telsiu, July 24, 1928. He studied composition with Juzeliunas at the Lithuanian State Cons. in Vilnius (1954–59). He taught at the J. Gruodis Music School in Kaunas (1959–69). His music is cast in a highly advanced idiom incorporating aleatory and sonoristic techniques.

WORKS: DRAMATIC: Opera-oratorio: *The Ballad of Light* (1969). **Ballet:** *The Light of Happiness* (1959); *The Smouldering Cross* (1963); *Passions* (1968); *A Little Humming Fly*, children's ballet (1969); *The First Sin* (1992); *The Spider and the Butterfly* (1994). **ORCH.:** *Dramatic Poem* (1958); 9 syms. (1962, 1963, 1969, 1970, 1981, 1982, 1987, 1988, 1991); Concerto for Flute and Chamber Orch. (1971); *Metafonia* for Violin and Orch. (1972); *Diafonia* for Cello and Orch. (1972); *Sonnets* for Chamber Orch. (1974); *Epitaph and Poem* for Strings (1975); *Auto College No. 1* (1977), *No. 2* (1987), and *No. 3* (1995); *Emanations*, concerto for Electric Cello and Chamber Ensemble (1981); *Yet Not Enough*, saxophone concerto (1998). **CHAMBER:** 6 string quartets (1954, 1974, 1976, 1981, 1985, 1991); 6 wind quintets (1974, 1976, 1980, 1981, 1985, 1991); 2 capriccios for Flute and Oboe (1974, 1976); Sonata for Solo Flute (1975); Sonata for Solo Oboe (1976); Sonata for Solo Clarinet (1976); Sonata for Solo Horn (1976). **VOCAL:** Song cycles; children's choruses.—**NS/LK/DM**

Relfe, John, English music theorist and composer; b. Greenwich, 1763; d. London, c. 1837. He was a member of the King's Band in 1810, and also an esteemed teacher of piano and harmony. He composed airs, sonatas, lessons, divertimentos, etc., for harpsichord or piano and songs. He publ. *Guida armonica* (3 parts, 1798; 2nd ed. as *The Principles of Harmony*, 1817), *Remarks on the Present State of Musical Instruction* (1819), and *Lucidus ordo* (1821). He proposed a reformed thoroughbass figuring, marking the root chord *r.*, and the inversions ' and ".—NS/LK/DM

Rellstab, (Heinrich Friedrich) Ludwig, German poet, novelist, and writer on music, son of **Johann Carl Friedrich Rellstab**; b. Berlin, April 13, 1799; d. there, Nov. 27, 1860. He revealed a precocious talent as a keyboard player in childhood, and later received keyboard instruction from L. Berger and training in theory from B. Klein (1816). He was an artillery officer and a teacher of mathematics and history in the Brigade School in Berlin. He retired from the army in 1821, and from 1823 lived as a writer in Berlin; was ed. and music critic of the *Vossische Zeitung* (1826–48). He publ. the satirical pamphlets *Henriette, oder Die schöne Sängerin, Eine Geschichte unserer Tage von Freimund Zuschauer* (Leipzig, 1826; on Henriette Sontag's triumphs) and *Über mein Verhältniss als Critiker zu Herrn Spontini als Componisten und General-Musikdirector in Berlin, nebst einem vergnüglichen Anhang* (Leipzig, 1827; directed against Spohr's truckling to virtuosity in *Agnes von Hohenstaufen*), for each of which he suffered a period of imprisonment, though his opinions were eventually upheld in official circles and by the public. Between 1830 and 1841 he ed. the musical periodical *Iris im Gebiete der Tonkunst*; he also contributed to several other periodicals. His *Gesammelte Schriften* (12 vols., Leipzig, 1843–44; new ed., 24 vols., 1860–61) includes reviews of opera and concerts which came out in the *Vossische Zeitung* between 1826 and 1848. He wrote an autobiography, *Aus meinem Leben* (2 vols., Berlin, 1861).

BIBL.: L. Blengert, *L. R.* (Leipzig, 1918); W. Franke, *Der Theaterkritiker L. R.* (Berlin, 1964).—NS/LK/DM

Rellstab, Johann Carl Friedrich, German music publisher, writer on music, and composer, father of **(Heinrich Friedrich) Ludwig Rellstab**; b. Berlin, Feb. 27, 1759; d. there, Aug. 19, 1813. He was a pupil of Agricola and Fasch. He succeeded his father as head of a printing establishment (1779), adding a music printing and publishing dept. and a circulating library of music. He founded and directed amateur concerts from 1787. After losing his property in the war of 1806, he gave music lessons, lectured on harmony, and wrote criticism for the *Vossische Zeitung*. His compositions, which included a Singspiel, *Die Apotheke*, cantatas, odes, songs, and piano pieces, are unimportant. His daugher, Caroline Rellstab (b. Berlin, April 18, 1793; d. Breslau, Feb. 17, 1813), was a prominent singer. She was a member of the Breslau Opera (from 1811), particularly noted for her portrayal of the Queen of the Night.

WRITINGS: *Versuch über die Vereinigung der musikalischen und oratorischen Declamation, hauptsächlich für Musiker und Com-*

ponisten mit erläuternden Beyspielen (Berlin, 1786); *Anleitung für Clavierspieler, den Gebrauch der Bach'schen Fingersetzung, die Manieren und den Vortrag betreffend* (Berlin, 1790); a polemical pamphlet, *Über die Bemerkungen eines Reisenden die Berlinischen Kirchenmusiken, Concerte, Oper und königliche Kammermusik betreffend* (Berlin, 1789).

BIBL.: O. Guttmann, *J.K.F. R.: Ein Beitrag zur Musikgeschichte Berlins* (Berlin, 1910).—NS/LK/DM

R. E. M., American rock band of the 1980s. **MEMBERSHIP:** Michael Stipe (John Michael Stipe), lead voc. (b. Decatur, Ga., Jan. 4, 1960); Peter Buck, lead gtr., mdln. (b. Berkeley, Calif., Dec. 6, 1956); Michael Mills, bs., kybd., harmony voc. (b. Orange, Calif., Dec. 17, 1958); Bill Berry, drm., harmony voc. (b. Duluth, Minn., July 31, 1958).

The first American rock band of the 1980s to prove the viability of both noncommercial college radio airplay and small, independent-label releases as means of popularizing a contemporary music group, R.E.M. was also an early favorite of rock critics. Maintaining both an anticommercial and anti—pop star stance in achieving their success, R.E.M. challenged listeners to comprehend their intelligent if surreal lyrics, written and initially sung in an almost unintelligible manner by lead vocalist Michael Stipe. Originally favoring a sound derived from 1960s folk-rock, R.E.M. expanded their college following through four years of constant touring, eventually breaking through into the mainstream with *Document* and its near-smash hit single "The One I Love." Unable to extend their success on the I.R.S. label, R.E.M. switched to Warner Bros., scoring their biggest success with 1991's *Out of Time* and the hit single "Losing My Religion." R.E.M. eventually emphasized a harder-edged rock guitar sound with 1994's *Monster* and resumed touring in 1995 after a five-year absence.

R.E.M. was formed in early 1980 in Athens, Ga., by four Univ. of Ga. students. Bassist Michael Mills and drummer Bill Berry had played together in various groups since high school. With Michael Stipe serving as primary lyricist and lead singer and Peter Buck providing guitar, the group gained a local following and subsequently undertook tours of the Southeast. Their first single, "Radio Free Europe," was released on the small Hib-Tone label in 1981 and drew the attention of rock critics and college fans. Signed to the independent I.R.S. label, R.E.M. recorded a five-song EP, *Chronic Town*, in 1981. *Murmur*, their first full-length album, was released in 1982 and sold remarkably well, with A&M handling national distribution of the album. It contained "Radio Free Europe," a minor hit when re-released in 1983, and "Talk About the Passion."

Quickly regarded as one of the more important purveyors of simple and unpretentious but effective and compelling rock music (at a time when the popularity of punk music was fading), R.E.M. conducted their first European tour in 1983 and soon recorded the exciting and engaging album *Reckoning*. It yielded a minor hit with "So. Central Rain (I'm Sorry)" and included the wry "(Don't Go Back To) Rockville." R.E.M. undertook a massive tour to support the rather existential *Fables of the Reconstruction/Reconstruction of the Fables*, recorded in

London with veteran producer Joe Boyd. The album featured "Can't Get There from Here," "Driver 8," and "Feeling Gravity's Pull." They next recorded *Life's Rich Pageant* at John Mellencamp's Ind. studio. It contained "These Days" and "Superman" and produced a minor hit with "Fall on Me." *Dead Letter Office* compiled the *Chronic Town* EP and B-sides from their singles.

R.E.M. broke through into the pop mainstream with 1987's *Document*. Michael Stipe was enunciating more clearly, and the assured, provocative album yielded the near-smash hit "The One I Love" and the minor hit "It's the End of the World as We Know It (And I Feel Fine)"; the album also contained "Disturbance at the Heron House" and "Finest Worksong." In 1988 R.E.M. switched to the major label Warner Bros. Their debut for the label, *Green*, produced a smash hit with "Stand" and a minor hit with "Pop Song 89" and included "Orange Crush" and "World Leader Pretend."

R.E.M. subsequently suspended live performances after the tour in support of *Green*. In 1990 Peter Buck, Mike Mills, and Bill Berry recorded with singer-songwriter Warren Zevon as the Hindu Love Gods. R.E.M. reassembled for 1991's gentle acoustic album *Out of Time*, essentially comprised of love songs. Perhaps the most accessible album of the group's career, the album featured Buck on mandolin as well as a string section. It yielded a smash hit with the poignant "Losing My Religion" and the near-smash "Shiny Happy People" (with vocal backing by Kate Pierson of the B-52's); it also included the country-style "Country Feedback," "Half a World Away," and "Radio Song" (featuring rapper KRS-One). R.E.M. continued in an acoustic vein with the introspective *Automatic for the People*, which produced the three major hits "Drive," "Man on the Moon," and "Everybody Hurts."

R.E.M. returned to a brash, guitar-based rock sound for 1994's *Monster*. Another bestseller, the album featured a wide variety of material, from the sad country song "You" to the psychedelic guitar of the major hit "What's the Frequency, Kenneth?," from the imploring "Let Me In" and the anguished "I Don't Sleep, I Dream" to the raucous guitar duet with Sonic Youth's Thurston Moore on "Circus Envy" and the radio favorite "Bang and Blame." R.E.M. launched their first world tour in five years in 1995, but on March 1 drummer Bill Berry fell ill during a concert in Lausanne, Switzerland. He was operated on for a brain aneurysm and quickly recovered. Not to be outdone, Michael Stipe then underwent a hernia operation. Although their European tour was canceled, R.E.M. resumed their American tour in May.

DISC.: R.E.M.: *Chronic Town (mini)* (1981); *Murmur* (1982); *Reckoning* (1984); *Dead Letter Office* (1987); *Box Set* (1992); *Fables of the Reconstruction/Reconstruction of the Fables* (1985); *Life's Rich Pageant* (1986); *R.E.M. No. 5: Document* (1987); *Eponymous* (1988); *Green* (1988); *Out of Time* (1991); *Automatic for the People* (1992); *Monster* (1994). **TRIBUTE ALBUM:** *Surprise Your Pig: A Tribute to R.E.M.* (1992). **HINDU LOVE GODS:** *Hindu Love Gods* (1990).

BIBL.: M. Gary, *An R.E.M. Companion—It Crawled from the South* (London, 1992).—**BH**

Remedios, Alberto, English tenor; b. Liverpool, Feb. 27, 1935. He studied in Liverpool with Edwin Francis and later in London with Clive Carey at the Royal Coll. of Music. He made his operatic debut as Tinca in *Il tabarro* at the Sadler's Wells Opera in London in 1957; made his first appearance at Covent Garden in London as Dimitri in *Boris Godunov* in 1965; sang at the Frankfurt am Main Opera (1968–70). He made his U.S. debut with the San Francisco Opera in 1973; made his Metropolitan Opera debut in N.Y. as Bacchus in *Ariadne auf Naxos* on March 20, 1976. In 1983 he appeared as Walther von Stolzing at the Scottish Opera in Glasgow. He was engaged as a soloist in Schoenberg's *Gurre-Lieder* in Melbourne in 1988. In 1993 he portrayed Tristan in Nashville. He was highly successful as Lohengrin, Siegfried, and Siegmund; showed fine lyrical talent as Faust in Gounod's opera, and a dramatic flair in Verdi's Otello.—**NS/LK/DM**

Remenkov, Stefan, Bulgarian composer; b. Silistra, April 30, 1923. He studied piano with Nenov and composition with Vladigerov and Stoyanov at the Bulgarian State Cons. in Sofia, graduating in 1950, and later took a course with Khachaturian at the Moscow Cons.

WORKS: DRAMATIC: *The Unvanquished*, ballet (1960); *The Errors Are Ours*, operetta (1966); 2 children's operettas: *Ghanem* (1967) and *The Prince and the Pauper* (1973). **ORCH.:** 2 piano concertos (1953, 1970); *Prelude and Dance* for Strings (1957); 4 syms.: No. 1, *Children's Symphony* (1961), No. 2, *Symphony in the Classical Style* (1962), No. 3 (1965), and No. 4 (1968); Cello Concerto (1964); Concertino for Flute and Strings (1973); *Fantasy* for Violin and Orch. (1974). **CHAMBER:** Violin Sonata (1955); Nonet; 3 piano sonatas (1944, 1948, 1949). —**NS/LK/DM**

Reményi (real name, **Hoffmann**), **Ede (Eduard),** prominent Hungarian violinist; b. Miskolc, Jan. 17, 1828; d. San Francisco, May 15, 1898. He began his training in Eger, and then studied with Böhm at the Vienna Cons. (1842–45). Banished from the Austro-Hungarian realm for his participation in the Hungarian Revolution of 1848, he began the career of a wandering violinist in the U.S. Returning to Europe, he toured Germany with Brahms as his accompanist (1853). After serving as solo violinist to Queen Victoria (1854–59), he returned to Hungary following the amnesty of 1860, and then was made solo violinist to the Austrian court. In 1865 he commenced a brilliant tour, visiting Paris, Germany, Belgium, and the Netherlands. He then proceeded to London in 1877, and to America in 1878, traveling in the U.S., Canada, and Mexico. In 1886 he began a new concert tour around the world, visiting Japan, China, and South Africa. Some notes on his trip to the Far East are in the N.Y. Public Library. His last years were troubled by ill health and a decline in his playing. He was appearing in vaudeville houses by 1898, and collapsed suddenly while playing the pizzicato from the *Sylvia* suite of Delibes at the Orpheum Theater in San Francisco, dying of apoplexy a few hours later. His technique was prodigious; in vigor, passion, and pathos he was unexcelled. He made skillful transcriptions of Chopin's waltzes, polonaises, and mazurkas, and pieces by Bach, Schubert, etc.; these are united under the title *Nouvelle école du violon*. He was also a natural performer of Gypsy music, and Liszt profited much by his help in supplying and arranging authentic Gypsy tunes. He composed a Violin Concerto and some solos for violin. His great-nephew was **Marcel Dick**.

BIBL.: G. Kelly and G. Upton, *Edouard R.: Musician, Littérateur, and Man* (Chicago, 1906); E. Sas, *R.* (Budapest, 1934).—NS/LK/DM

Remington, Emory, American trombonist and pedagogue; b. Rochester, N.Y., Dec. 22, 1891; d. there, Dec. 11, 1971. He was a student of Gardell Simons, Edward Llewellyn, and Ernest Williams. From 1922 until his death he taught at the Eastman School of Music in his native city. He also was first trumpeter in the Rochester Phil. from 1923 to 1949. By adopting the larger-bore trombone with F-valve attachment, Remington proved highly influential as a teacher of the instrument.—NS/LK/DM

Remoortel, Edouard van, Belgian conductor; b. Brussels, May 30, 1926; d. Paris, May 16, 1977. He studied at the Brussels Cons. and at the Geneva Cons.; also took courses in conducting with Guarnieri and Galliera at the Accademia Musicale Chigiana in Siena and privately with Josef Krips. From 1951 he was the principal conductor of the Orchestre National de Belgique in Brussels. In 1958 he was appointed music director of the St. Louis Sym. Orch., retaining this post until 1962. In 1965 he went to Monte Carlo as artistic consultant to the Orchestre National de l'Opera of Monaco, resigning in 1969.—NS/LK/DM

Remy, Alfred, German-American writer on music and editor; b. Elberfeld, March 16, 1870; d. N.Y., Feb. 26, 1937. He emigrated to the U.S. in 1882. He studied at the City Coll. of N.Y. (B.A., 1890), received private instruction in piano, violin, and theory (1890–96), and completed his education at Columbia Univ. (M.A., 1905). He was music critic of *Vogue* and music ed. of *The Lookder-On* (1895–97); taught music and modern languages at various N.Y. institutions (from 1896). He was music ed. of the *New International Encyclopaedia* (1901–30) and ed.-in-chief of the 3rd ed. of *Baker's Biographical Dictionary of Musicians* (1919).—NS/LK/DM

Renaud (real name, **Cronean**), **Maurice (Arnold),** distinguished French baritone; b. Bordeaux, July 24, 1861; d. Paris, Oct. 16, 1933. He studied at the Paris Cons. and the Brussels Cons., then sang at the Théâtre Royal de la Monnaie in Brussels (1883–90) and at the Opéra-Comique in Paris (1890–91). He made his first appearance at the Paris Opéra as Nelusko on July 17, 1891, remaining on its roster until 1902. He then made guest appearances there until 1914, and was also a member of the Monte Carlo Opera (1891–1907). He made his U.S. debut in New Orleans on Jan. 4, 1893; sang at London's Covent Garden (1897–99; 1902–04), at the Manhattan Opera in N.Y. (1906–07; 1909–10), and again in Brussels (1908–14). He made his Metropolitan Opera debut in N.Y. as Rigoletto on Nov. 24, 1910,

remaining on the company's roster until 1912. His finest roles included Athanaël in *Thaïs*, Coppelius, Dapertutto, and Dr. Miracle in *Les Contes d'Hoffmann*, Nevers in *Les Huguenots*, Lescaut in *Manon*, Herod in *Hérodiade*, and Saint- Saëns's *Henry VIII*. His non-French roles included Don Giovanni, Wolfram, Jack Rance, Telramund, and Beckmesser. He was among the most convincing dramatic artists of his era.—NS/LK/DM

Rendall, David, English tenor; b. London, Oct. 11, 1948. He studied at the Royal Academy of Music in London and at the Salzburg Mozarteum. In 1975 he made his operatic debut with the Glyndebourne Touring Opera as Ferrando, and then sang for the first time at London's Covent Garden as the Italian Singer in *Der Rosenkavalier*. In 1976 he made his debut at the Glyndebourne Festival as Ferrando. Following his first appearance at the English National Opera in London in 1976 as Leicester in *Maria Stuarda*, he made regular appearances there until 1992. In 1978 he portrayed Rodolfo at the N.Y.C. Opera and Don Ottavio at the San Francisco Opera. He sang Ernesto in *Don Pasquale* at his Metropolitan Opera debut in N.Y. on Feb. 28, 1980. In 1983 he appeared as Berlioz's Faust in Lyons. He returned to the Glyndebourne Festival as Tom Rakewell in 1989. In 1992 he sang Don Antonio in the first stage production of Gerhard's *The Duenna* in Madrid. In 1996 he was engaged as Hoffmann in Genoa.—NS/LK/DM

Rendall, (Francis) Geoffrey, English organologist and librarian; b. Dulwich, Sept. 20, 1890; d. London, Dec. 3, 1952. He received training in clarinet at Charterhouse School and in classics at Cambridge (M.A., 1914). He was on the staff of the British Museum in London, where he later served as Keeper of Printed Books. Rendall was the author of the valuable study *The Clarinet* (London, 1954; 3rd ed., 1971).—NS/LK/DM

Rendano, Alfonso, Italian pianist, teacher, and composer; b. Carolei, near Cosenza, April 5, 1883; d. Rome, Sept. 10, 1931. He studied in Caserta and then at the Naples Cons. (1863). After making his debut as a pianist in 1864, he pursued training with Thalberg in Naples (1866–67), with Mathias in Paris (1867), and with Reinecke and Richter at the Leipzig Cons. (1868). He successfully toured in Europe. After teaching at the Naples Cons. (1883) and at his own piano school (1883–86), he settled in Rome to teach privately. Rendano was the inventor of the pedale indipendente, which became known as the pedale Rendano. This 3rd pedal was placed between the standard 2 pedals of the piano with the intention of prolonging the vibration of single sounds or chords. He composed an opera, *Consuelo* (Turin, May 25, 1902), a Piano Concerto, a Piano Quintet, many piano pieces, and vocal works.

BIBL.: G. Puccio, *A. R.* (Rome, 1937).—NS/LK/DM

Rener, Adam, South Netherlands composer and singer; b. Liège, c. 1485; d. Altenburg, c. 1520. He was a boy chorister at the court of Emperor Maximilian in 1498. After training in Burgundy (1500–03), he returned to Maximilian's court as a composer. From 1507 to 1517 he was a singer and composer at the court of the Saxon Elector in Torgau. Rener helped to introduce the Netherlands style of composition to Germany. Among his extant works are 9 masses, 8 Magnificats, 4 Proper motet cycles and 18 other motets, and 13 lieder.

BIBL.: J. Kindermann, *Die Messen A. R.s* (diss., Univ. of Kiel, 1962); R. Parker, *The Motets of A. R., c. 1485–c. 1520* (diss., Univ. of Tex. at Austin, 1963).—**LK/DM**

Renié, Henriette, eminent French harpist, pedagogue, and composer; b. Paris, Sept. 18, 1875; d. there, March 1, 1956. She studied with Alphonse Hasselmans at the Paris Cons., receiving the premier prix for harp at the age of 11; then entered the classes of Lenepveu and Dubois in harmony and composition. She performed her own Harp Concerto at the Concerts Lamoureux in Paris on March 24, 1901. She taught at the Paris Cons., numbering among her students Marcel Grandjany. Among her other works were *Pièce symphonique* for Harp and Orch., *Légende et Danse caprice* for Harp and Orch., numerous solo harp pieces, chamber music, and songs.

BIBL.: O. de Montequiou, *H. R. et la harpe* (Paris, 1998). —**NS/LK/DM**

Rennert, Günther, leading German opera producer and administrator; b. Essen, April 1, 1911; d. Salzburg, July 31, 1978. He was educated in Munich, Berlin, and Halle. From 1935 to 1939 he worked in Wuppertal, in Frankfurt am Main (with Walter Felsenstein), and in Mainz; then was chief producer in Königsberg (1939–42), at the Berlin Städtische Oper (1942–44), and at the Bavarian State Opera in Munich (1945). In 1946 he became Intendant of the Hamburg State Opera, a post he held until 1956; then worked as a guest producer with several major opera houses, including La Scala in Milan and the Metropolitan Opera in N.Y. From 1967 to 1976 he was Intendant of the Bavarian State Opera in Munich. Through the consistent successes of his operatic productions in several cities under changing circumstances, Rennert acquired a reputation as one of the most competent members of his profession.

BIBL.: W. Schafer, *G. R.: Regisseur in dieser Zeit* (Bremen, 1962).—**NS/LK/DM**

Renz, Frederick, American harpsichordist and conductor; b. Buffalo, July 27, 1940. He studied at the State Univ. of N.Y. at Fredonia (graduated, 1962) and at Ind. Univ. (M.M. in conducting, 1964; M.M. in harpsichord, 1966), then studied harpsichord with Gustav Leonhardt on a Fulbright fellowship in Amsterdam (1967–69). After performing as a keyboard player with the N.Y. Pro Musica (1969–74), he founded his own Ensemble for Early Music in N.Y. (1974), with which he toured widely. His repertoire extends from the 12th to the early 19th century.—**NS/LK/DM**

REO Speedwagon, 1980s-era Midwestern purveyors of pop power ballads. **MEMBERSHIP:** Neal Doughty, kybd. (b. Evanston, Ill., July 29, 1946); Alan Gratzer, drm. (b. Syracuse, N.Y., Nov. 9, 1948); Barry Lutnell, voc.; Greg Philbin, bs.; Kevin Cronin, gtr., voc. (b. Evanston, Ill., Oct. 6, 1951); Michael Murphy, voc.; Bruce Hall, bs. (b. Champaign, Ill., May 3, 1953); Dave Amato, gtr. (b. March 3, 1953); Bryan Hitt, drm. (b. Jan. 5, 1954); Jesse Harms, kybd. (b. July 6, 1952).

REO Speedwagon began life as a bunch of Univ. of Ill. students playing hard boogie rock. Taking its name from a kind of fire truck, the band became popular in clubs around the Midwest, and came to the attention of manager Irving Azoff, who also handled The Eagles and Steely Dan. The band worked its way up to opening act status and signed with Epic records. REO went through several personnel changes through the early part of the 1970s, replacing vocalist Barry Lutnell with Kevin Cronin, and bassist Greg Philbin with Bruce Hall. Cronin, more folk-oriented than the rest of the hard-rocking band, took a stab at a solo career and was replaced for three albums by Michael Murphy. These recordings were steady, but not big, sellers. Cronin returned for 1976's *REO*, an album that, if anything, sold less than the band's previous efforts.

REO's biggest problem was that their studio albums didn't capture the appeal of their live shows. So, the band put out a live album, *You Get What You Play For*, which went platinum, bringing them new fans. With *You Can Tune a Piano, but You Can't Tuna Fish*, the members started producing themselves, with the band's musical yin and yang—reformed folkie Cronin and unrepentant hard-rock guitarist Richrath—leading the charge. The creative fusion worked and the band started to break through outside the Midwest, even placing a song, "Roll with the Changes," onto the upper reaches of the charts in 1978. The album hit #29 on the charts and went platinum. Continuing to straddle this tenuous creative razor blade, *Nine Lives* went gold, hitting #33.

This set the stage for *High Infidelity*, a theme album about relationships that went over to the pop side of the spectrum. The 1980 chart-topping, platinum hit "Keep on Loving You" introduced the power ballad to pop radio. The band followed this up with the gold #5 "Take It on The Run" and the Top-30 "In Your Letter." Produced with the aural equivalent of a high-gloss finish, full of angelic harmonies and bright guitar work, the album spent 15 weeks at #1, eventually selling more than nine million copies.

Although the next album, *Good Trouble*, went platinum and spawned the #7 1982 hit "Keep the Fire Burnin'" and the #29 "Sweet Time," the group considered it a pretty weak album, done in too big a hurry to capitalize on their success. So the group took a much-needed break, reconvening for *Wheels are Turning* in 1984. The second single released off the album, "Can't Fight This Feeling," confounded everyone who claimed the group was over, topping the pop chart for three weeks and going gold. While the follow-up singles were less-successful, the album eventually went double platinum.

In 1987, the group continued working, landing three more hit singles from the gold *Life As We Know It*: "That' Ain't Love" (#16), "In My Dreams" (#19) and "Here with Me" (#20). In 1990, two founding members, drummer Alan Gratzer and guitarist Gary Richrath, left the band. Richrath eventually resurfaced in his own band. While none of REO Speedwagon's subsequent albums, with former Wang Chung drummer Bryan Hitt and former Ted Nugent guitarist Dave Amato, charted, the band continued to be a live attraction, returning to its original role as a popular live band that sold a few albums.

DISC.: *R E O Speedwagon* (1971); *R.E.O. 2* (1972); *Lost in a Dream* (1974); *Ridin' the Storm Out* (1974); *This Time We Mean It* (1975); *R.E.O* (1976); *Live Again* (1978); *You Can Tune a Piano, but You Can't Tuna Fish* (1978); *Nine Lives* (1979); *Hi-Infidelity* (1980); *Good Trouble* (1982); *Wheels Are Turnin'* (1984); *You Get What You Play For* [live] (1985); *Life As We Know It* (1987); *The Earth, a Small Man, His Dog and a Chicken* (1990); *Second Decade of Rock & Roll* (1991); *Believe in Rock & Roll* (1995); *Building the Bridge* (1996); *The Ballads* (1999).—**HB**

Repin, Vadim, Russian violinist; b. Novosibirsk, Aug. 31, 1971. He was a pupil of Zakhar Bron at the Novosibirsk Cons. When he was 11, he took 1st prize in the junior division of the Wieniawski competition in Poland. At age 13, he appeared with Yevgeny Kissen in the inaugural recital of the 1984 Tchaikovsky competition in Moscow, and subsequently made appearances in his homeland. In 1987 he made his British debut as soloist with the BBC Phil. at the Lichfield Festival. After capturing 1st prize in both the Tibor Varga (1988) and Queen Elisabeth of Belgium (1989) competitions, he toured extensively. During the 1990–91 season, he appeared as soloist with the Minn. Orch., toured Germany with the London Phil., and gave recitals in Paris, London, Frankfurt am Main, and Salzburg. In 1991 he toured the U.S. and Germany with the State Sym. Orch. of Russia, and also made his North American recital debut at the Ravinia Festival in Chicago. In subsequent seasons, his tours took him all over the world. Repin's playing is a tribute to the time-honored Russian tradition of violin virtuosity, most notable for its seemingly effortless technical display and élan.—**NS/LK/DM**

Rescigno, Nicola, American conductor; b. N.Y., May 28, 1916. He studied law in Rome before pursuing a career in music. In 1943 he made his conducting debut at the Brooklyn Academy of Music. In 1954 he co-founded the Lyric Theatre in Chicago, serving as its artistic director until 1956. In 1957 he co-founded the Dallas Civic Opera, where he served as music director until 1981, and of its successor, the Dallas Opera, until 1992. During his long tenure in Dallas, he conducted many premieres. He also was on the roster of the Metropolitan Opera in N.Y. (1978–82), and appeared as a guest conductor of opera companies throughout North and South America and in Europe.—**NS/LK/DM**

Resinarius, Balthasar, significant German composer; b. Tetschen, Bohemia, c. 1485; d. Böhmisch-Leipa, April 12, 1544. He sang and studied under Heinrich Isaac at the court chapel of Emperor Maximilian I. He enrolled at the Univ. of Leipzig (1515). Although he became a Catholic priest in Tetschen (1523), he soon espoused Lutheranism and was made bishop of Leipa.

He was one of the most important early Protestant composers of sacred music. His works were commissioned by Rhau, who included them in his own publications. Among Resinarius's output are 80 responsories and the *St. John Passion* (Wittenberg, 1544), 30 chorale settings (1544), 3 motets (1545), an introit (1545), and 10 hymns.

BIBL.: I.-M. Schröder, *Die Responsorienvertonungen des B. R.* (Kassel, 1954).—**NS/LK/DM**

Resnik, Regina, American soprano, later mezzo-soprano; b. N.Y., Aug. 30, 1922. She studied in N.Y. She made her concert debut at the Brooklyn Academy of Music (Oct. 27, 1942). She sang in opera in Mexico (1943). She won an annual audition at the Metropolitan Opera in N.Y. in 1944, and appeared there as Leonora in *Il Trovatore* (Dec. 6, 1944); continued to sing there regularly, turning to mezzo-soprano roles in 1955. In 1953 she appeared in Bayreuth as Sieglinde; made her Covent Garden debut in London as Carmen in 1957, and sang there until 1972. She remained on the roster of the Metropolitan Opera until 1974. She was active as an opera producer from 1971. Among her finest roles were Mistress Quickly, Marina, Amneris, Herodias, and Clytemnestra. She also created the role of the Countess in Barber's *Vanessa* (1958).—**NS/LK/DM**

Respighi, Ottorino, eminent Italian composer and teacher; b. Bologna, July 9, 1879; d. Rome, April 18, 1936. He studied violin with F. Sarti and composition with L. Torchi and G. Martucci at Bologna's Liceo Musicale (1891–1900). In 1900 he went to Russia, and played 1st viola in the orch. of the Imperial Opera in St. Petersburg; there he took lessons with Rimsky-Korsakov, which proved a decisive influence in Respighi's coloristic orchestration. From 1903 to 1908 he was active as a concert violinist; also played the viola in the Mugellini Quartet of Bologna. In 1913 he was engaged as a prof. of composition at Rome's Liceo (later Conservatorio) di Santa Cecilia; in 1924, was appointed its director, but resigned in 1926, retaining only a class in advanced composition; subsequently devoted himself to composing and conducting. He was elected a member of the Italian Royal Academy on March 23, 1932. In 1925–26 and again in 1932 he made tours of the U.S. as a pianist and a conductor. Respighi's style of composition is a highly successful blend of songful melodies with full and rich harmonies; he was one of the best masters of modern Italian music in orchestration. His power of evocation of the Italian scene and his ability to sustain interest without prolixity is incontestable. Although he wrote several operas, he achieved his greatest success with 2 symphonic poems, *Le fontane di Roma* and *I pini di Roma*, each consisting of 4 tone paintings of the Roman landscape; a great innovation for the time was the insertion of a phonograph recording of a nightingale into the score of *I pini di Roma*. His wife, Elsa Olivieri Sangiacomo Respighi (b. Rome, March 24, 1894), was his pupil; she wrote a fairy opera, *Fior di neve*; the symphonic poem *Serenata di maschere*; and numerous songs; was also a concert singer. She publ. a biography of her husband.

WORKS: DRAMATIC: Opera: *Re Enzo* (Bologna, March 12, 1905); *Semirama*, lyric tragedy (Bologna, Nov. 20, 1910); *Marie-Victoire* (1913–14; not perf.); *La bella dormente nel bosco* or *La bella addormentata nel bosco*, musical fairy tale (1916–21; Rome, April 13, 1922); *Belfagor*, lyric comedy (1921–22; Milan, April 26, 1923); *La campana sommersa*, after Hauptmann's *Die versunkene Glocke* (1923–27; Hamburg, Nov. 18, 1927); *Maria Egiziaca*, mystery play (1929–32; N.Y., March 16, 1932); *La fiamma* (1930–33; Rome, Jan. 23, 1934); a free transcription of Monteverdi's *Orfeo* (Milan, March 16, 1935); *Lucrezia* (1935; Milan, Feb. 24, 1937). Ballet: *La Boutique fantasque*, on themes by Rossini (London, June 5, 1919); *Scherzo veneziano* (Rome, Nov. 27, 1920); *Belkis, Regina di Saba* (1930–31; Milan, Jan. 23, 1932). ORCH.: Piano Concerto (1902); Suite for Organ and Strings (1902–05); *Notturno* (1905); *Sinfonia drammatica* (1913–14); *Le fontane di Roma*, symphonic poem (1914–16; Rome, March 11, 1917); *Antiche arie e danze per liuto*, 3 sets, the 3rd for Strings (1916, 1923, 1931); *Ballata delle gnomidi* (1918–20; Rome, April 11, 1920); *Poema autunnale* for Violin and Orch. (1920–25); *Concerto gregoriano* for Violin and Orch. (1921; Rome, Feb. 5, 1922); *I pini di Roma*, symphonic poem (Rome, Dec. 14, 1924); *Concerto in modo misolidio* for Piano and Orch. (N.Y., Dec. 31, 1925, composer soloist); *Rossiniana*, suite from Rossini's piano pieces (1925); *Vetrate di chiesa*, symphonic impressions (Boston, Feb. 25, 1927); *Impressioni brasiliane*, symphonic suite (1927; São Paulo, June 16, 1928, composer conducting); *Trittico Botticelliano* for Chamber Orch. (1927); *Gli Uccelli*, suite for Small Orch. on themes by Rameau, B. Pasquini, and others (1927); *Toccata* for Piano and Orch. (1928); *Feste romane*, symphonic poem (1928; N.Y., Feb. 21, 1929); *Metamorphosen modi XII* (Boston, Nov. 7, 1930); *Concerto à 5* for Violin, Oboe, Trumpet, Double Bass, Piano, and Strings (1932). Band: *Huntingtower Ballad* (Washington, D.C., April 17, 1932). CHAMBER: 11 pieces for Violin and Piano (1904–07); String Quartet in D major (1907); *Quartetto dorico* for String Quartet (1924); Violin Sonata (1917). VOCAL: *Il tramonto* for Mezzo-soprano and String Quartet, after Shelley (1917); *La Primavera*, cantata for Soloists, Chorus, and Orch. (1918–19; Rome, March 4, 1923); *Lauda per la Natività del Signore* for Soloists, Chorus, and Orch. (1928–30); 45 songs; 3 vocalises; arrangements.

BIBL.: R. de Rensis, *O. R.* (Turin, 1935); E. Respighi, *O. R.: Dati biografici ordinati* (Milan, 1954; abr. Eng. tr., 1962); *O. R.: Catalogo delle opere* (Milan, 1965); E. Battaglia, ed., *O. R.* (Turin, 1985); D. Bryant, ed., *Il Novecento musicale italiano: Tra neoclassicismo e neogoticismo: Atti del convegno di studi promosso dalla Fondazione Giorgio Cini per il 50 anniversario della scomparsa di O. R.* (Florence, 1988).—NS/LK/DM

Reszke, Edouard de
See De Reszke, Edouard

Reszke, Jean de
See De Reszke, Jean

Reszke, Josephine de
See De Reszke, Josephine

Rethberg, Elisabeth (real name, **Lisbeth Sattler**), outstanding German-American soprano; b. Schwarzenberg, Sept. 22, 1894; d. Yorktown Heights, N.Y., June 6, 1976. She studied at the Dresden Cons. and with Otto Watrin. She made her operatic debut as Arsena in *Der Zigeunerbaron* at the Dresden Court Opera (1915); continued to sing there when it became the State Opera in 1918. She then made her U.S. debut as Aida at the Metropolitan Opera in N.Y. on Nov. 22, 1922, remaining one of its most celebrated artists until her farewell performance there in that same role on March 6, 1942. She subsequently embarked on a grand concert tour with Ezio Pinza in the U.S., Europe, and Australia; their close association resulted in a lawsuit for alienation of affection brought by Pinza's wife against her, but the court action was not pursued. Throughout her operatic career, Rethberg sang in many of the major music centers in Italy; also appeared at the Salzburg Festivals and at London's Covent Garden (1925; 1934–39). She excelled in both the German and Italian repertoires; among her memorable roles were Mozart's Countess, Donna Anna, Pamina, Constanze, and Donna Elvira; Verdi's Aida, the 2 Leonoras, Amelia, Desdemona, and Maria Boccanegra; and Wagner's Eva, Elisabeth, Sieglinde, and Elsa; also created the title role in Strauss's *Die ägyptische Helena* (Dresden, June 6, 1928). Rethberg was married twice: first to Ernst Albert Dormann, and then to George Cehanovsky, whom she married in 1956.

BIBL.: H. Henschel and E. Friedrich, *E. R.: Ihr Leben und Künstlertum* (Schwarzenberg, 1928).—NS/LK/DM

Réti, Rudolph (Richard), Hungarian-American music theorist, pianist, and composer; b. Užice, Serbia, Nov. 27, 1885; d. Montclair, N.J., Feb. 7, 1957. He studied at the Vienna Academy of Music and at the Univ. of Vienna. He took an early interest in new music and was one of the founders of the ISCM (Salzburg, 1922). In 1938 he went to the U.S.; in 1943 he married the Canadian pianist Jean Sahlmark; in 1950 they settled in Montclair, N.J. His compositions are marked by precise structure and fine stylistic unity. Among his works are *Symphonia mystica* (1951), *Triptychon* for Orch. (1953), Concertino for Cello and Orch. (1953), 2 piano concertos, Violin Sonata, several choruses and solo songs, and piano pieces. An original music analyst, he wrote several books which contributed to the development of logical theory of modern music: *The Thematic Process in Music* (N.Y., 1952), *Tonality, Atonality, Pantonality* (N.Y., 1958), and *Thematic Patterns in Sonatas of Beethoven* (ed. by D. Cooke, London, 1965).—NS/LK/DM

Rettich, Wilhelm, German-born Dutch composer and conductor; b. Leipzig, July 3, 1892; d. Sinzheim bei Baden-Baden, Dec. 27, 1988. He studied at the Leipzig Cons. with Reger. He was in the German army in World War I and was taken prisoner by the Russians; sent to Siberia, he made his way to China after the Russian Revolution and eventually returned to Leipzig. He occupied various posts as a theater conductor; was music director of the local synagogue until 1933, when the advent of the Nazi regime forced him to leave Germany; he went to the Netherlands and became a naturalized Dutch citizen. In 1964 he returned to Germany and lived in Baden-Baden. As a composer, he excelled in symphonic and chamber music; wrote 3 syms.; Violin Concerto; Piano Concerto; much chamber music for various combinations; choral works; piano pieces and songs.—NS/LK/DM

Return to Forever, influential jazz-rock–new age fusion group. **MEMBERSHIP:** Chick Corea, kybd. (b. Chelsea, Mass., June 12, 1941); Joe Farrell, wdwnds. (b. Chicago Heights, Ill., Dec. 16, 1937; d. Duarte, Calif., Jan. 10, 1986); Flora Purim, voc. (b. Rio de Janeiro, Brazil, March 6, 1942); Stanley Clarke, bs. (b. Philadelphia, Pa., June 30, 1951); Airto Moreira, perc. (b. Itaiopolis, Brazil, Aug. 5, 1941); Lenny White, drm. (b. N.Y.C., Dec. 19, 1949); Al DiMeola, gtr. (b. Jersey City, N.J., July 22, 1954).

Initially, Return to Forever fused Chick Corea's reputation as an improviser—earned with stints in the Latin jazz bands of Willie Bobo and Mongo Santamaria—and the cutting edge groups of Miles Davis and Anthony Braxton. After leaving Braxton's avant-garde group Circle, Corea harked back to his early Latin days, bringing together Brazilian percussionist Airto Moreira and his wife Flora Purim with sax player Joe Farrell and phenomenal young bassist Stanley Clarke. They made two albums, their self-titled debut and *Light As a Feather*, which included one of Corea's best-known compositions, "Spain." Both were moderate successes.

Retaining Clarke, Corea turned the group in a more rock/funk fusion direction, taking on drummer Lenny White—they worked together on Miles Davis's *Bitches Brew*—and running through several guitarists, including Earl Klugh and Bill Connors, before latching onto teen guitar prodigy Al DiMeola. This lineup created fierce, fiery fusion, with DiMeola's astounding dexterity complimenting Clarke and White's funky bottom. The second album featuring this new lineup, *Where Have I Known You Before*, generated enough excitement to reach #32 on the pop album charts in 1974. Their next album, 1975's *No Mystery*, reached #39 (a very respectable performance for a jazz album) and won the Grammy that year for Best Jazz Performance by a Group. A year later, *Romantic Warrior* topped out at #35, and—although it took 14 years—the album eventually went gold. After a couple of live albums (a complete concert recording and an abridged version), the group mutated once again, this time into a 13-piece band that retained Corea and Clarke. This RTF charted at #38 with *Music Magic* in 1977 before Corea retired the subject, though the second lineup got together for a reunion in 1983.

Most members of RTF continued to have remarkable careers in jazz. Clarke produced several albums that eclipsed RTF in popularity, scoring a pop hit with his duo project with George Duke on the #19 "Sweet Baby" in 1981. Clarke went on to work with the group Animal Logic with Police drummer Stewart Copeland, Rite of Strings with Jean-Luc Ponty and DiMeola, and Vertu with Lenny White. He has also scored several award-winning film soundtracks. White, too, continued to record prolifically, both under his own name and as a studio musician. DiMeola began exploring music of the world, working with John McLaughlin and Paco de Lucia on flamenco projects, recording Astor Piazzola

tangos, and forming the group World Sinfonia, dovetailing these eclectic pursuits with his more mainstream work. Corea continued as one of the most respected keyboard players in jazz, both electric and acoustic. He reflected this dual personality by leading two bands in the mid-1990s, the Akoustic and Elektric bands. He became a partner in Stretch Records late in the 1990s.

DISC.: *Light as a Feather* (1972); *Return to Forever* (1972); *Hymn of the Seventh* (1973); *Where Have I Known You Before* (1974); *No Mystery* (1975); *Romantic Warrior* (1976); *The Complete Concert* (1977); *Return to Forever* (live; 1977); *Music Magic* (1977); *Live* (1992).—HB

Reubke, Adolf, German organ builder; b. Halberstadt, Dec. 6, 1805; d. Hausneindorf, near Quedlinburg, March 3, 1875. He founded his firm in Hausneindorf, and built organs for various German cities, including those at Magdeburg Cathedral and at the Leipzig Gewandhaus. His son Emil Reubke (1836–85) became a partner in 1860 and eventually inherited the firm. Another son, (Friedrich) Julius Reubke (b. Hausneindorf, March 23, 1834; d. Pillnitz, near Dresden, June 3, 1858), was a pianist, organist, and composer; he studied with Hermann Bonicke in Quedlinburg, with T. Kullak (piano) and A.B. Marx (composition) at the Berlin Cons., and with Liszt in Weimar (1856). He wrote 2 outstanding sonatas, 1 for piano and 1 for organ (both 1857). Still another son, Otto Reubke (b. Hausneindorf, Nov. 2, 1842; d. Halle, May 18, 1913), was a pianist, conductor, and composer; studied organ with A.G. Ritter in Magdeburg, piano with Bülow and composition with A.B. Marx and Weitzmann at the Berlin Cons., and composition with Hauptmann in Leipzig (1864–67). He subsequently settled in Halle as a pianist, organist, and conductor. He was named Robert Franz's assistant at the Univ. (1877), founded his own choral society (1876), and then served as conductor of the Robert Franz Singakademie (1867–1911). He was named music director (1892) and prof. (1895) at the Univ. Among his works are piano pieces and songs.

BIBL.: D. Chorzempa, *J. R.: Life and Works* (diss., Univ. of Minn., 1971).—NS/LK/DM

Reusner (or **Reussner**), **Esaias,** esteemed German lutenist and composer; b. Löwenberg, Silesia, April 29, 1636; d. Cölln, Berlin, May 1, 1679. A child prodigy, he studied lute with his father, then entered the service of the Swedish general Count Wittenberg in Breslau as a page when he was about 12. After a year in the service of the household of the royal war commissioner Müllner, he became a valet at the Polish court of Princess Radziwill (1651), where he continued his lute training. After returning to Breslau in 1654, he was named lutenist to Georg III, duke of Silesia, in 1655. He then taught lute at the Univ. of Leipzig (1672–73), and subsequently served as a chamber musician at the court of the Elector Friedrich Wilhelm of Brandenburg in Berlin (1674–79). He was a significant figure in the development of the German lute school of composition, being the first German composer to adapt the French lute style. A few of his works have been ed. in Das Erbe Deutscher Musik, 1st series, XII (1939).

BIBL.: G. Sparmann, *E. Reusner und die Lauten-Suite* (diss., Univ. of Berlin, 1926).—NS/LK/DM

Reuss, Allan, jazz guitarist; b. N.Y., June 15, 1915. Did first gig at the age of 12, shortly after taking up banjo. Worked on guitar during the early 1930s and studied with George Van Epps, with Benny Goodman from April–June 1935, then regularly with Goodman (August 1936 until March 1938). Organized own teaching studio in N.Y. and took part in many pick-up recording sessions. With Jack Teagarden from January until June 1939, joined Paul Whiteman autumn 1939. With Ted Weems from spring of 1941 until joining Jimmy Dorsey in March 1942, then did studio work for N.B.C. in Chicago until rejoining Benny Goodman from June 1943 until June 1944. With Harry James until May 1945, led own trio in Los Angeles, then concentrated on freelance session work in Hollywood, also did regular teaching.—JC/LP

Reuss-Belce, Luise, Austrian soprano; b. Vienna, Oct. 24, 1860; d. (found dead in a refugee train) Aibach, Germany, March 5, 1945. She studied voice in Vienna. She made her operatic debut as Elsa in *Lohengrin* in Karlsruhe (1881), and then sang in Bayreuth (1882) and in Wiesbaden (1896–99). Subsequent appearances were at Covent Garden in London (1900) and at the Metropolitan Opera in N.Y., where she made her debut as Brünnhilde in *Die Walküre* (Feb. 11, 1902); then sang in Dresden (1903–11). In 1885 she married Eduard Reuss (b. N.Y., Sept. 16, 1851; d. Dresden, Feb. 18, 1911), a music pedagogue; after his death, she moved to Berlin, where she established a singing school. In 1913 she was appointed stage manager at the festival opera performances in Nuremberg; she was the first woman to occupy such a post in Germany.—NS/LK/DM

Reuter, Rolf, German conductor; b. Leipzig, Oct. 7, 1926. He studied at the Academy for Music and Theater in Dresden. He conducted in Eisenach (1951–55); then was Generalmusikdirektor in Meiningen (1955–61). In 1961 he became a conductor at the Leipzig Opera, and subsequently served as its Generalmusikdirektor (1963–78). He was chief conductor of the Weimar State Orch. (1979–81). From 1981 to 1994 he was chief conductor and music director of the Komische Oper in East Berlin.—NS/LK/DM

Reutter, Georg (von), Austrian organist and composer, father of **(Johann Adam Joseph Karl) Georg von Reutter;** b. Vienna (baptized), Nov. 3, 1656; d. there, Aug. 29, 1738. He may have studied with J.C. Kerll, whom he succeeded as organist of St. Stephen's Cathedral in Vienna in 1686. In 1695 he was in Italy, where he was ennobled by Prince Sforza. Returning to Vienna, he was a continuo player on the theorbo at the Imperial Court Chapel (1697–1703). He was made court organist in 1700, and became Vice- Kapellmeister in 1712 and 1st Kapellmeister in 1715 of the Cathedral, where he remained until 1728; retired as Cathedral organist in 1720 and was succeeded by his son. He wrote a number of toccatas and many *Versetteln* (brief organ preludes); his secular works are lost. A Ricercare, 2 capriccios, and most likely the canzona on *Christ ist erstanden* attributed to him in Denkmäler der Tonkunst in Österreich, XXVII, Jg. XIII/2, are by Strungk.

BIBL.: N. Hofer, *Die beiden R. als Kirchenkomponisten* (diss., Univ. of Vienna, 1915).—NS/LK/DM

Reutter, Hermann, outstanding German composer and pedagogue; b. Stuttgart, June 17, 1900; d. Heidenheim an der Brenz, Jan. 1, 1985. He studied with Franz Dorfmüller (piano), Ludwig Mayer (organ), Karl Erler (voice), and Walter Courvoisier (composition) at the Munich Academy of Music (1920–23). He began his career as a pianist in 1923, and later made numerous concert tours with the singer Sigrid Onegin (1930–35), including 7 separate tours in the U.S. He taught composition at the Stuttgart Hochschule für Musik (1932–36). After serving as director of the Berlin Staatliche Hochschule für Musik (1936–45), he became a teacher of lieder and composition at the Stuttgart Staatliche Hochschule für Musik (1952), serving as its director (1956–66). He then was prof. of music at the Munich Academy of Music. As a composer, Reutter followed the traditional line of German neo-Classicism, in which the basic thematic material, often inspired by German folk music, is arranged along strong contrapuntal lines, wherein a dissonant intervallic fabric does not disrupt the sense of immanent tonality. He excelled particularly in stage music and songs. He brought out an anthology of contemporary art songs, *Das zeitgenössische Lied* (4 vols., Mainz, 1969).

WORKS: DRAMATIC: O p e r a : *Saul* (Baden-Baden, July 15, 1928; rev. version, Hamburg, Dec. 21, 1947); *Der verlorene Sohn* (Stuttgart, March 20, 1929; rev. as *Die Rückkehr des verlorenen Sohnes*, Dortmund, 1952); *Doktor Johannes Faust* (1934–36; Frankfurt am Main, May 26, 1936; rev. version, Stuttgart, 1955); *Odysseus* (1940–42; Frankfurt am Main, Oct. 7, 1942); *Der Weg nach Freundschaft: Ballade der Landstrasse* (Göttingen, Jan. 25, 1948); *Don Juan und Faust* (Stuttgart, June 11, 1950); *Die Witwe von Ephesus* (1953; Cologne, June 23, 1954); *Die Brücke von San Luis Rey* (Frankfurt am Main Radio, June 20, 1954); *Hamlet* (Stuttgart, 1980); also *Der Tod des Empedokles*, scenic concerto (1965; Schwetzingen, May 29, 1966); *Hamlet* (Stuttgart, Dec. 6, 1980). **B a l l e t :** *Die Kirmes von Delft* (1936; Baden-Baden, March 20, 1937); *Topsy* (1950); *Notturno Montmartre* (1951; Stuttgart, Oct. 8, 1952). **ORCH.:** 4 piano concertos (1925; 1928; *Sinfonische Fantasie*, 1938; 1944); Violin Concerto (1932); Piano Concertino (1946); Concerto for 2 Pianos and Orch. (1949); *Concert Variations* for Piano and Orch. (1952); *Prozession* for Cello and Orch. (1956); Sym. for Strings (1960); *Capriccio, Aria, and Finale* for Piano and Orch. (1964); *Figurinen* (1972). **CHAMBER:** Violin Sonata (1925); *Rhapsody* for Violin and Piano (1938); *5 Caprichos sobre Cervantes* for Viola (1968); *Sonata monotematica* for Cello or Bassoon and Piano (1972). **OTHER:** Piano pieces; choral works; about 200 songs.

BIBL.: H. Lindlar, ed., *H. R.: Werk und Wirken: Festschrift der Freunde* (Mainz, 1965).—NS/LK/DM

Reutter, (Johann Adam Joseph Karl) Georg von, Austrian organist and composer, son of **Georg (von) Reutter;** b. Vienna (baptized), April 6, 1708; d. there, March 11, 1772. He began his studies with his father, and then had composition lessons with Caldara. By age 14 he deputized for his father as court organist. After a sojourn in Italy (1729?–31), he returned to Vienna and was made court composer; he brought out many operas and oratorios. He was named 1st Kapellmeister at St. Stephen's Cathedral upon his father's death in 1738, having unofficially carried out those duties since about 1736. While searching for choristers in 1739–40, he recruited the youthful Haydn in Hainburg and took him into his own home in Vienna. Reutter was ennobled in 1740. After L.A. Predieri became 1st Kapellmeister in 1741, he was reduced to serving as a substitute until acquiring the post of 2nd Kapellmeister in 1747. Following Predieri's retirement in 1751, Reutter took over the court Kapelle but did not receive the title of 1st Kapellmeister until Predieri's death in 1769. In 1756 he also obtained the post of 2nd Kapellmeister at the Cathedral. The musical establishment at both the court and the Cathedral declined under his leadership, due in part to inadequate funding. Reutter produced a vast amount of music which is now totally forgotten.

BIBL.: N. Hofer, *Die beiden R. als Kirchenkomponisten* (diss., Univ. of Vienna, 1915).—**NS/LK/DM**

Revelli, William D(onald),

American band director and teacher; b. Spring Gulch, near Aspen, Colo., Feb. 12, 1902. The family moved to southern Ill., near St. Louis, when he was an infant. He began to study the violin at the age of 5, and later was a pupil of Dominic Sarli. After graduating from the Chicago Musical Coll. in 1922, he completed his education at the Columbia School of Music in Chicago (diploma in music education, 1925). In 1925 he became supervisor of music in Hobart, Ind., where he founded the high school band, which he in time built to national prominence, winning the high school band championship for 6 consecutive years. In 1935 he was made director of the Univ. of Mich. Band at Ann Arbor, and was also in charge of its wind instruments dept. Revelli's Symphonic Band toured the country many times and made several trips abroad under State Dept. auspices, most notably a 16-week tour in early 1961 that took it to the Soviet Union, Bulgaria, Turkey, Egypt, and other countries in the Middle East. In 1971 Revelli became director emeritus of the Univ. of Mich. Bands. As an instructor and promoter of bands within the U.S. academic system, Revelli continued the tradition of Fillmore and A.A. Harding. He was active as an ed., adviser, and administrator of various undertakings in the American band field; was also founder of the Coll. Band Directors National Assn. (1941) and was its honorary life president. He received honorary doctoral degrees from 5 American univs.

BIBL.: G. Cavanagh, *W.D. R.: The Hobart Years* (diss., Univ. of Mich., 1971).—**NS/LK/DM**

Revueltas, Silvestre,

remarkable Mexican composer; b. Santiago Papasquiaro, Dec. 31, 1899; d. Mexico City, Oct. 5, 1940. He began violin studies when he was 8 in Colima, then entered the Juárez Inst. in Durango at age 12. After studies with Tello (composition) and

Rocabruna (violin) in Mexico City (1913–16), he took courses at St. Edward Coll. in Austin, Tex. (1916–18), and with Sametini (violin) and Borowski (composition) at the Chicago Musical Coll. (1918–20); returned to Chicago to study violin with Kochanski and Sevčik (1922–26). He was active as a violinist and conductor in Tex. and Ala. (1926–28), and asst. conductor of the Orquesta Sinfónica de Mexico (1929–35); only then did he begin to compose. In 1937 he went to Spain, where he was active in the cultural affairs of the Loyalist government during the Civil War. His health was ruined by exertions and an irregular life-style, and he died of pneumonia. His remains were deposited in the Rotonda de los Hombres Ilustres in Mexico City on March 23, 1976, to the music of his *Redes* and the funeral march from Beethoven's *Eroica*. He possessed an extraordinary natural talent and an intimate understanding of Mexican music; he succeeded in creating works of great originality, melodic charm, and rhythmic vitality.

WORKS (all 1st perf. in Mexico City unless otherwise given): **DRMATIC: B a l l e t :** *El Renacuajo paseador* (1933; Oct. 4, 1940); *La Coronela* (unfinished; completed by Galindo and Huizar; Nov. 20, 1941). **ORCH.:** *Cuauhnahuac* (1931–32; June 2, 1933); *Esquinas* for Small Orch. (Nov. 20, 1931; also for Large Orch., 1933); *Ventanas* (1931; Nov. 4, 1932); *Alcancias* (1932); *Colorines* for Small Orch. (Aug. 30, 1932); *Ocho por Radio* for Small Orch. (Oct. 13, 1933); *Janitzio* (Oct. 13, 1933; rev. 1936); *Caminos* (July 17, 1934); *Planos*, "geometric dance" (Nov. 5, 1934); *Redes*, concert suite from the film score, for Small Orch. (1935; Barcelona, Oct. 7, 1937); *Homenaje a Federico García Lorca* for Small Orch. (1935; Madrid, Sept. 22, 1937); *Sensemayá* (Dec. 15, 1938; also for Voice and Small Orch., 1937); *Música para charlar*, concert suite from the film scores *El Indio* and *Ferrocarriles de Baja California* (Dec. 15, 1938); *La noche de los Mayas*, concert suite from the film score (1939); *Itinerarios* (1939); *Paisajes* (1940); *Troka* (1940). **CHAMBER:** 4 string quartets: No. 1 (1930), No. 2, *Magueyes* (1931), No. 3 (1931; recovered in 1984 and posthumously numbered), and No.4, *Música de feria* (1932; posthumously numbered); *3 Pieces* for Violin and Piano (1932); *Tocata sin fuga* for Violin and 7 Winds (1933); *Canto de guerra de los frentes leales* for 3 Trumpets, 3 Trombones, 2 Tubas, Percussion, and Piano (1938); *3 sonetas* for Chamber Ensemble (1940); *3 Little Serious Pieces* for Piccolo, Oboe, Trumpet, Clarinet, and Saxophone (1940). **VOCAL:** *Sensemayá* for Voice and Small Orch., based on an Afro-Cuban legend (1937; rev. for Large Orch. alone, Dec. 15, 1938); *Hora de junio* for Narrator and Orch. (1938); *Parias* for Soprano, Chorus, and Small Orch. (1940); many songs.

BIBL.: G. Contreras, *S. R.: Genio atormentado* (Mexico City, 1954).—**NS/LK/DM**

Revutsky, Lev(ko Mikolaievich),

Ukrainian composer; b. Irshavetz, near Poltava, Feb. 20, 1889; d. Kiev, March 31, 1977. He went to Kiev and studied with Glière at the Cons. (graduated, 1916). From 1924 to 1941 he taught at the Musico-Dramatic Inst. In 1957 he was elected to the Ukrainian Academy of Sciences. He composed music for the theater, films, and radio, as well as 2 piano concertos (1914, 1934), 2 syms. (1916–21; 1926–27), and choral pieces.—**NS/LK/DM**

Rey, Alvino,

pop-jazz bandleader, guitarist; b. Oakland, Calif., July 1, 1911. Between 1934–39, he played with many bands, including Horace Heidt. Rey formed his own group and took the popular King Sisters vocal group from Heidt. The band worked on a West Coast radio station and he gained respect for his guitar work. Rey formed an excellent new band in 1942, using arrangements by Ray Conniff, Johnny Mandel, Billy May, and Neal Hefti; the band included Al Cohn, Zoot Sims and Herbie Steward at various times. He carried on with smaller lineups through the mid 1960s with the *King Family Show* on TV.

DISC.: *Uncollected Alvino Rey, Vol. 3* (1940).—**LP**

Rey, Cemal Reshid, Turkish pianist, conductor, teacher, and composer; b. Jerusalem, Sept. 24, 1904; d. Istanbul, Oct. 7, 1985. Of a distinguished family (his father was a poet and also served twice as minister of the interior in the Turkish government), he went to Paris at age 9 to study composition with Laparra; then continued his studies at the Geneva Cons. Returning to Paris, he took courses in piano with Long, composition with Fauré, and conducting with Derosse. In 1923 he settled in Constantinople and taught at the Cons.; from 1949 to 1969 he was principal conductor of the Istanbul Radio Orch. His music is imbued with Turkish melorhythms; many of his works are written on Turkish subjects.

WORKS: DRAMATIC: O p e r a : *Yann Marek* (1922); *Sultan Cem* (1923); *Zeybek* (1926); *Tchelebi* (1945); *Benli Hürmüz* (1965). **O p e r e t t a :** *Yaygara* (1969). **ORCH.:** *La Légende du Bebek* (Paris, Dec. 15, 1929); *Karagueuz*, symphonic poem (Paris, Feb. 14, 1932, composer conducting); *Scènes turques* (Paris, March 6, 1932); *Concerto chromatique* for Piano and Orch. (Paris, March 12, 1933, composer soloist); Violin Concerto (1939); 3 syms. (1941, 1950, 1968); *L'Appel*, symphonic poem (Paris, April 3, 1952, composer conducting); *Fatih* (1956); 3 symphonic scherzos (1958); *Colloque instrumental* for Flute, 2 Horns, Harp, and Strings (1957); *Variations on an Istanbul Folksong* for Piano and Orch. (1966). **OTHER:** Numerous arrangements of Turkish folk songs for various instrumental combinations; choruses; piano pieces.

BIBL.: E. İyasoğlu, *C.R. R.: Müzikten ibaret bir dünyada gezintiler* (Istanbul, 1997).—**NS/LK/DM**

Rey, Jean-Baptiste, French conductor and composer, brother of **Louis-Charles-Joseph Rey;** b. Tarn-et-Garonne, Dec. 18, 1734; d. Paris, July 15, 1810. He studied at Toulouse and became a theater conductor in the provinces. In 1776 he settled in Paris as conductor of the Opéra, being named director of its orch. in 1781; was also made master of the musique de chambre to Louis XVI (1779). He conducted at the Concert Spirituel (1781–86), served as prof. of harmony at the Cons. (1799–1801), and was named maître de chapelle to Napoleon in 1804. He taught according to the principles of Rameau and became embroiled in an academic controversy with the followers of the more modern method of Catel. He played an important role in producing operas by Gluck, Grétry. Among his own works was the opera *Diane et Endymion* (Paris, 1791). He also arranged operas by others.—**NS/LK/DM**

Rey, Louis-Charles-Joseph, French composer and cellist, brother of **Jean-Baptiste Rey;** b. Lauzerte,

Oct. 26, 1738; d. Paris, May 12, 1811. He was trained as a cellist, and was in the orch. of the Paris Opéra from 1767 until 1806; also played in the orch. of the royal chapel (from 1772). He composed some stage pieces and chamber music.—**NS/LK/DM**

Reyer (real name, Rey), (Louis-Etienne-) Ernest, French composer; b. Marseilles, Dec. 1, 1823; d. Le Lavandou, near Hyères, Jan. 15, 1909. An ardent admirer of Wagner, he added the German suffix *-er* to his real name. He entered a Marseilles music school when he was 6. He was sent to Algiers in 1839 to work in a government dept. with an uncle, where he composed a Solemn Mass (for the arrival of the French governor in Algiers; perf. 1847) and publ. several songs. He definitely embarked upon a musical career in 1848, studying in Paris with his aunt, **Louise Farrenc.** In 1866 he became librarian at the Opéra, and followed d'Ortigue as music critic of the *Journal des Débats* (1866–98); his collected essays were publ. in 1875 as *Notes de musique;* also in *Quarante ans de musique* (posthumous, 1909). He was elected to David's chair in the Institut in 1876, was made a Chevalier of the Légion d'honneur in 1872, and received the Grande-Croix in 1906. Although Reyer was an avowed admirer of Wagner, his music did not betray specific Wagnerian influences; both in form and in harmonic progressions, Reyer adhered to the Classical French school of composition, with a certain tendency toward exoticism in his choice of librettos. His reputation as a composer for the theater was securely established with his operas *Sigurd* (Brussels, Jan. 7, 1884) and *Salammbô* (Brussels, Feb. 10, 1890).

WORKS: DRAMATIC: *Le Sélam*, "symphonie orientale," but actually an opera (Paris, April 5, 1850); *Maître Wolfram*, opera (Paris, May 20, 1854); *Sacountalâ*, ballet pantomime (Paris, July 14, 1858); *La Statue*, opéra-comique (Paris, April 11, 1861; rev. Paris, Feb. 27, 1903); *Erostrate*, opera (in German, Baden-Baden, Aug. 21, 1862; in French, Paris, Oct. 16, 1871); *Sigurd*, opera (Brussels, Jan. 7, 1884); *Salammbô*, opera (Brussels, Feb. 10, 1890). **VOCAL: S a c r e d :** *Messe pour l'arrivé du Duc d'Aumale à Alger* (1847) and church music; works for men's chorus; piano pieces.

BIBL.: A. Jullien, *E. R.: Sa vie et ses oeuvres* (Paris, 1909); H. Roujon, *Notice sur la vie et les travaux de E. R.* (Paris, 1911); H. de Curzon, *E. R.: Sa vie et ses oeuvres* (Paris, 1923).—**NS/LK/DM**

Reynolds, Anna, English mezzo-soprano; b. Canterbury, Oct. 4, 1931. She studied piano at the Royal Academy of Music in London, and then went to Italy for vocal lessons. She made her operatic debut in Parma in 1960 as Suzuki; subsequently sang in Vicenza (1961), Rome (1964), Spoleto (1966), Trieste (1967), and Venice (1969), and at La Scala in Milan (1973). She made her first appearance in England at Glyndebourne in 1962; sang at Covent Garden in London in 1967; also sang at Bayreuth (1970–76). She made her Metropolitan Opera debut in N.Y. as Flosshilde in *Das Rheingold* on Nov. 22, 1968, and returned there in 1975. She also sang widely as a concert artist and recitalist.—**NS/LK/DM**

Reynolds, Roger (Lee), American composer and teacher; b. Detroit, July 18, 1934. He studied engineering physics (B.S.E., 1957) and was a student of Ross Lee Finney (composition; B.M., 1960; M.M., 1961) at the Univ. of Mich. in Ann Arbor; he was also a co-founder of the ONCE festival there in 1961. He also studied with Roberto Gerhard at the Univ. of Mich. in 1960, following him to the Berkshire Music Center in Tanglewood during the summer of 1961, and winning the Koussevitzky Prize there. In 1962–63 a Fulbright fellowship enabled him to work at the WDR electronic studio in Cologne. He held a Guggenheim fellowship in 1963–64. From 1966 to 1969 he was a fellow of the Inst. of Current World Affairs in Tokyo, where he was co-organizer of the Cross Talk concerts and the Cross Talk festival. He taught at the Univ. of Calif. at San Diego from 1969; he was founder-director of its Center for Music Experiment and Related Research (1971–77), and then chairman of the music dept. (1979–81). As a guest composer and lecturer, he was active in both the U.S. and abroad. In 1982 he was visiting prof. of composition at Yale Univ., and in 1992–93 was the Rothschild composer-in-residence at the Peabody Cons. of Music in Baltimore. In addition to his numerous articles on music, he publ. the studies *Mind Models: New Forms of Musical Experience* (1975), *A Searcher's Path: A Composer's Ways* (1987), and *A Jostled Silence: Contemporary Japanese Musical Thought* (serialized in *Perspectives of New Music*, XXX, 1 and 2, 1992, and XXXI, 2, 1993). In 1971 he received a National Inst. of Arts and Letters award. In 1975, 1978, 1979, and 1986 he held NEA grants. He won the Pulitzer Prize in Music in 1989 for his *Whispers Out of Time* for Strings. In 1990 he received a Suntory Foundation commission. In 1991–92 he received a Koussevitzky Foundation commission. In his music, Reynolds owes much to the examples set by Ives, Varèse, and Cage. He makes use of every resource available to the contemporary composer, from traditional instruments and voices to electronics and computer-generated sounds.

WORKS: DRAMATIC: *The Emperor of Ice Cream*, theater piece for 8 Voices, Piano, Contrabass, and Percussion (1962; concert version, N.Y., March 19, 1965; stage version, Rome, April 27, 1965; rev. 1974); *I/O* for 9 Women Vocalists, 9 Male Mimes, 2 Flutes, Clarinet, Projections, and Live Electronics (1970; Pasadena, Calif., Jan. 24, 1971); *A Merciful Coincidence (VOICESPACE II)*, music theater (Bourges, June 9, 1976); *The Tempest*, incidental music to Shakespeare's play, for Electroacoustic Sound, Voices, and Instruments (Lenox, Mass., July 30, 1980); *Ivanov*, incidental music to Chekhov's play, for Computer-processed Sound (1991; Mito, Japan, Jan. 1992). **ORCH.:** *Graffiti* (1964; Seattle, May 2, 1965); *Threshold* (1967; Tokyo, June 7, 1968); *"...between..."* for Chamber Orch. and Live Electronics (1968; Chicago, March 10, 1970); *Only Now, and Again* for 23 Winds, Piano, and Percussion (Milwaukee, May 6, 1977); *Fiery Wind* (N.Y., Feb. 13, 1978); *Archipelago* for Chamber Orch. and Computer-generated Tape (1982–83; Paris, Feb. 15, 1983); *Transfigured Wind II* for Flute, Orch., and Computer-generated Tape (N.Y., June 4, 1984); *The Dream of the Infinite Rooms* for Cello, Orch., and Computer-generated Tape (1986; Cleveland, March 2, 1987); 3 syms.: *Symphony [Vertigo]* for Orch. and Tape (San Francisco, Dec. 9, 1987), *Symphony [Myths]* (Tokyo, Oct. 25, 1990), and *Symphony [The Stages of Life]* (1991–92; Los Angeles, April 4, 1993); *Whispers Out of Time* for Strings (Amherst, Mass., Dec. 11, 1988); *Dreaming* (1992; N.Y.,

Jan. 10, 1993). **CHAMBER:** *Situations* for Cello and Piano (1960); *Continuum* for Viola and Cello (1960); *Consequent* for Alto Flute, Violin, Bassoon, and Piano (1961); *Wedge* for Chamber Ensemble (1961); *Mosaic* for Flute and Piano (1961); *String Quartet No. 2* (1961); *Quick Are the Mouths of Earth* for Chamber Ensemble (1964–65; N.Y., Nov. 24, 1965); *Gathering* for Woodwind Quintet (1965; Amsterdam, July 12, 1966); *Ambages* for Flute (1965); *Ping* for Piano, Flute, Percussion, Slides, Films, Live Electronics, and Tape (Tokyo, June 5, 1968); *Traces* for Piano, Flute, Cello, Tape, and Live Electronics (N.Y., Dec. 17, 1968); *"...from behind the unreasoning mask"* for Trombone, Percussion, and Tape (Las Vegas, Jan. 20, 1975); *The Promises of Darkness* for Chamber Ensemble (1975; N.Y., Jan. 8, 1976); *Less Than Two* for 2 Pianos, 2 Percussion, and Computer-generated Tape (1977–79; Washington, D.C., Feb. 23, 1979); *Shadowed Narrative* for Chamber Quartet (1977–82; N.Y., March 29, 1982); *"...the serpent-snapping eye"* for Trumpet, Percussion, Piano, and Computer-generated Tape (1978; San Diego, Jan. 31, 1979); *Transfigured Wind I* for Flute (1983), *III* for Flute, Chamber Ensemble, and Computer-generated Tape (Los Angeles, June 22, 1984), and *IV* for Flute and Tape (N.Y., Feb. 10, 1985); *Aether* for Violin and Piano (Washington, D.C., Oct. 29, 1983); *Mistral* for 6 Brass, 6 Strings, and Amplified Harpsichord (1984; N.Y., Feb. 12, 1985); *Summer Island (Islands from Archipelago I)* for Oboe and Computer-generated Tape (1984); *Coconino...a shattered landscape* for String Quartet (London, Nov. 10, 1985); *The Behavior of Mirrors* for Guitar (N.Y., Feb. 9, 1986); *Autumn Island (Islands from Archipelago II)* for Marimba (Washington, D.C., Nov. 7, 1986); *Personae* for Violin, Chamber Ensemble, and Computer-generated Sound (N.Y., March 26, 1990); *Dionysus* for 8 Instruments (Bloomington, Ind., July 1, 1990); *Focus a beam, emptied of thinking, outward...* for Cello (1989; N.Y., Feb. 27, 1992); *Visions* for String Quartet (Tokyo, May 27, 1992); *Kokoro* for Violin (1992); *Ariadne's Thread* for String Quartet and Computer-generated Sound (Radio France, Paris, Dec. 2, 1994). **Piano:** *Fantasy for Pianist* (Warsaw, Sept. 26, 1965); *Variation* (1988; N.Y., Dec. 3, 1991). **VOCAL:** *Sky* for Soprano, Alto Flute, Bassoon, and Harp (1961); *A Portrait of Vanzetti* for Narrator, Instruments, and Tape (1963); *Masks* for Chorus and Orch. (1965); *Blind Men* for Chorus, Brass, Piano, and Percussion (Tanglewood, Aug. 15, 1966); *Again* for 2 Sopranos, 2 Flutes, 2 Contrabasses, 2 Trombones, 2 Percussion, Tape, and Amplification (St.-Paul-de-Vence, France, July 20, 1970); *Compass* for Tenor, Bass, Cello, Contrabass, Projections, and Tape (1972–73; Los Angeles, March 16, 1973); *The Palace (VOICESPACE IV)* for Bass-baritone, Tape, and Staging (1978–80; La Jolla, Calif., Dec. 19, 1980); *Sketchbook (for "The Unbearable Lightness of Being")* for Alto, Piano, and Electronics (N.Y., May 14, 1985); *Not Only Night* for Soprano, Piccolo, Clarinet, Violin, Cello, Piano, and Tape (Los Angeles, Nov. 7, 1988); *Odyssey* for Soprano, Bass-baritone, 16 Instruments, Computer-processed Sound, and Lighting (1989–93; Paris, June 17, 1993); *last things, I think, to think about* for Bass-baritone, Piano, and Computer-processed Sound (N.Y., Nov. 17, 1994). **OTHER:** *Still (VOICESPACE I)* for Electroacoustic Sound (1975); *Eclipse (VOICESPACE III)* FOR Computer-generated and Electroacoustic Sound (1979–80; also as a media piece, 1982); *Vertigo* for Computer-processed Sound (1985; also with synthesized video, 1986); *The Vanity of Words (VOICESPACE V)* for Computer-processed Sound (1986); *Versions/Stages I–IV* for Computer-processed Sound (1988–91) and *V* for Computer-generated Sound (1991).

BIBL.: *R. R.: Portrait of a Composer* (N.Y., 1982). —NS/LK/DM

Reynolds, Verne (Becker), American composer, horn player, and teacher; b. Lyons, Kans., July 18, 1926. He received training in violin, piano, and horn. He was a composition student at the Cincinnati Cons. of Music (B.M., 1950), of Burleigh at the Univ. of Wisc. (M.M., 1951), and of Howells at the Royal Coll. of Music in London. After playing horn in the Cincinnati Sym. Orch. (1947–50), he was 1st horn in the Rochester (N.Y.) Phil. (1959–68). He taught at the Univ. of Wisc. (1950–53), the Ind. Univ. School of Music in Bloomington (1954–59), and the Eastman School of Music in Rochester, N.Y. (1959–95). Reynolds publ. *The Horn Handbook* (Portland, Ore., 1997).

WORKS: ORCH.: Violin Concerto (1951); *Saturday with Venus,* overture (1953); *Celebration Overture* (1960); *Ventures* (1975); *Festival and Memorial Music* (1977); Concerto for Band (1980). **CHAMBER:** *Serenade* for 13 Winds (1958); Flute Sonata (1962); String Quartet (1967); *Concertare I* for Brass Quintet and Percussion (1968), *II* for Trumpet and Strings (1968), *III* for Wind Quintet and Piano (1969), *IV* for Brass Quintet and Piano (1971), and *V* for Chamber Ensemble (1976); Tuba Sonata (1968); Horn Sonata (1970); Violin Sonata (1970); Viola Sonata (1975); *Signals* for Trumpet, Tuba, and Brass (1976); *Events* for Trombone Choir (1977); *Scenes Revisited* for Wind Ensemble (1977); Trio for Horn, Trombone, and Tuba (1978); *Fantasy-Etudes I* for Trumpet and Piano (1979), *II* for Clarinet, Percussion, and Piano (1990), *III* for Euphonium or Tuba and Piano (1991), *IV* for Bassoon and Percussion (1992), and *V* for Horn and Piano (1992); Cello Sonata (1983); Quintet for Piano and Winds (1986); Brass Quintet (1987); Trio for Oboe, Horn, and Piano (1990); Clarinet Sonata (1994); piano pieces. **VOCAL:** *The Hollow Men* for Baritone, Men's Chorus, Brass Choir, and Percussion (1954); *Songs of the Season* for Soprano, Horn, and Piano (1988); *Letter to the World* for Soprano and Percussion (1994).—**NS/LK/DM**

Řezáč, Ivan, Czech composer; b. Řevnice, Nov. 5, 1924; d. Prague, Dec. 26, 1977. He studied piano with Rauch and composition with Šín, Janeček, and Dobiáš at the Prague Academy, graduating in 1953. Later he joined its faculty, becoming its vice-dean in 1961. In his music, he follows the type of optimistic lyricism made popular by Shostakovich.

WORKS: DRAMATIC: Opera: *Pan Theodor Mundstock* (Mr. Theodor Mundstock; 1974). **ORCH.:** 3 piano concertos (1955, 1964, 1972); 2 syms. (1958, 1961); *Návrat* (The Return) for Cello and Orch. (1962); *Quadrature of the Heart* for String Quartet and Orch. (1975); *Vivace* for 67 Musicians (1977); *Montage* (1977). **CHAMBER:** 2 string quartets (1955, 1971); Cello Sonata (1956); Piano Trio (1958); *Nocturnes* for Violin and Piano (1959); *Torso of a Schumann Monument* for Viola and Piano (1963); Duo for Violin and Piano (1965); *6 Tales* for Cello and Guitar (1973); *Musica da camera* for Flute, Oboe, Violin, Viola, and Cello (1973). **Piano:** 2 sonatas (1954, 1957); 2 sonatinas (1959, 1966); *Dry Points* (1962); *Sisyfona Neděle* (Sisyphus Sunday) (1972).—**NS/LK/DM**

Rezniček, Emil Nikolaus von, Austrian conductor, pedagogue, and composer; b. Vienna, May 4, 1860; d. Berlin, Aug. 2, 1945. He studied law at Graz and music with Wilhelm Mayer (W.A. Rémy), and later took a brief course with Reinecke and Jadassohn at the Leipzig Cons. (1884). He was subsequently engaged as a theater conductor in Zürich, Berlin, Mainz, and other cities; was court conductor in Weimar (1896) and Mannheim (1896–99). After a short residence in Wiesbaden, he settled in Berlin, and in 1902 established there a very successful series of concerts for chamber orch., the Orchester-Kammerkonzerte; in 1906 he was appointed prof. at the Scharwenka Cons. in Berlin. He conducted the Warsaw Opera from 1906 to 1909, and then was the conductor of the Komische Oper in Berlin (1909–11); from 1920 to 1926, he taught at the Hochschule für Musik in Berlin. His most successful score was the opera *Donna Diana,* its overture becoming a popular favorite.

WORKS: DRAMATIC: Opera: *Die Jungfrau von Orleans* (Prague, June 19, 1887); *Satanella* (Prague, May 3, 1888); *Emmerich Fortunat* (Prague, Nov. 8, 1889); *Donna Diana* (Prague, Dec. 16, 1894; rev. 1908, 1933); *Till Eulenspiegel* (Karlsruhe, Jan. 12, 1902); *Eros und Psyche* (Breslau, 1917); *Ritter Blaubart* (Darmstadt, Jan. 29, 1920); *Holofernes* (Berlin, Oct. 27, 1923); *Tanzsymphonie* (Leipzig, Jan. 13, 1927); *Satuala* (Leipzig, 1927); *Spiel oder Ernst* (Dresden, Nov. 11, 1930); *Der Gondoliere des Dogen* (Stuttgart, Oct. 29, 1931); *Das Opfer* (1932); *Tenor und Bass* (Stockholm, 1934). **Operetta:** *Die Angst vor der Ehe* (Frankfurt an der Oder, 1914). **ORCH.:** 4 syms.: No. 1, *Tragic* (1904), No. 2, *Ironic* (1905), No. 3 (1918), and No. 4 (1919); *Nachtstück* for Violin or Cello and Orch. (1905); *Serenade* for Strings (1924); *4 Symphonic Dances* (1925); Violin Concerto (Berlin, Feb. 26, 1925); *Raskolnikoff,* overture (1932). **OTHER:** Chamber works, including 3 string quartets (1921, 1923, 1932), piano pieces, and organ music; choral music; songs.

BIBL.: O. Taubmann, *E.N. v.R.* (Leipzig, 1907); M. Chop, *E.N. v.R.: Sein Leben und seine Werke* (Vienna, 1920); R. Specht, *E.N. v.R.: Eine vorläufige Studie* (Leipzig, 1923); F. von Rezniček, *Gegen den Strom* (Vienna, 1960); T. Leibnitz, *Österreichische Spätromantiker: Studien zu E.N. v.R., Joseph Marx, Franz Schmidt, und Egon Kornauth* (Tutzing, 1986).—**NS/LK/DM**

Rhaw or **Rhau, Georg,** German publisher and composer; b. Eisfeld an der Werre, Suhl, 1488; d. Wittenberg, Aug. 6, 1548. He studied at the Univ. of Wittenberg (B.A., 1514), and then was cantor of the Thomaskirche and of the Thomasschule in Leipzig from 1518 to 1520, bringing out the *Missa de Sancto Spirito* (1519) during the disputations between Luther and Eck. He then settled in Eisleben as a schoolmaster, and later taught in Hildburghausen (1521–23). In 1523 he went to Wittenberg, where he established a publishing business, issuing many first eds. of Luther's writings and numerous collections of musical works, mostly Protestant. He wrote *Enchiridion utriusque musicae practicae* (Wittenberg, 1517; 2nd ed., 1518, as *Enchiridion musices ex variis musicorum libris depromptu*; 9th ed., 1558; facsimile ed. by H. Albrecht, Kassel, 1951) and *Enchiridion musicae mensuralis* (Leipzig, 1520; 10th ed., 1553).

BIBL.: W. Wölbing, *Der Drucker und Musikverleger G. Rhaw: Ein Beitrag zur Drucker- und Verlegstätigkeit im Zeitalter der Reformation* (diss., Univ. of Berlin, 1922); V. Mattfeld, *G. Rhaw's Publications for Vespers* (Brooklyn, 1966).—**NS/LK/DM**

Rheinberger, Joseph (Gabriel), eminent German organist, conductor, composer, and pedagogue; b. Vaduz, Liechtenstein, March 17, 1839; d. Munich, Nov. 25, 1901. He played piano and organ as a child, then took regular lessons in organ with J.G. Herzog, piano with J.E. Leonhard, and composition with J.H. Maier at the Munich Cons.; subsequently studied composition with Franz Lachner. From 1864 to 1877 he served as principal conductor of the Munich Choral Soc.; was named Hofkapellmeister in 1877. In 1859 he succeeded his teacher Leonhard as prof. of piano at the Munich Cons., and also taught composition there. His loyalty to the cultural and musical institutions in Munich earned him many honors from the Bavarian government; King Ludwig II made him Knight of St. Michael; in 1894 he was given the rank of "Zivilverdienstorden," the equivalent of nobility; in 1899 he was made Dr.Phil. *honoris causa* by the Univ. of Munich. Rheinberger's reputation as a teacher of organ was without equal during his lifetime; students flocked to him from all parts of the world. As a composer, he created a number of works remarkable for their dignity, formal perfection, and consummate technical mastery, if not their inventive power. His organ sonatas are unquestionably among the finest productions of organ literature. See H.-J. Irmen, *Joseph Rheinberger: Thematisches Verzeichnis seiner Kompositionen* (Regensburg, 1975).

WORKS: DRAMATIC: *Die sieben Raben*, romantic opera (Munich, 1869); *Des Türmers Töchterlein*, comic opera (Munich, 1873); incidental music. **ORCH.:** 2 syms.; 2 organ concertos; Piano Concerto; other orch. works. **CHAMBER:** 3 string quartets; 2 violin sonatas; Cello Sonata; 4 piano sonatas and other piano music. **VOCAL:** Masses; 3 Requiems; cantatas; motets; hymns; sacred songs; secular choral works and songs.

BIBL.: P. Molitor, *J. R. und seine Kompositionen für die Orgel* (Leipzig, 1904); T. Kroyer, *J. R.* (Regensburg, 1916); H. Grace, *The Organ Works of R.* (London, 1925); H.-J. Irmen, *J. R. als Antipode des Cäcilianismus* (Regensburg, 1970); H. Wagner and H.-J. Irmen, eds., *J.G. R.: Briefe und Dokumente seines Leben* (Vaduz, 1982); F.-G. Rössler, *Die ostinaten Werke J. R.s: Studie zur Formkonzeption eines romantischen Klassizisten* (Augsburg, 1994); W. Weyer, *Die Orgelwerke J. R.s: Ein Handbuch für Organisten* (Wilhelmshaven, 1994).—NS/LK/DM

Rhené-Baton (real name, René Baton),

French conductor and composer; b. Courseulles-sur-Mer, Calvados, Sept. 5, 1879; d. Le Mans, Sept. 23, 1940. He studied piano at the Paris Cons. and theory privately with Gédalge. He began his conducting career as a chorus master at the Opéra-Comique in Paris; then conducted various concert groups in Angers and Bordeaux. From 1916 to 1932 he was principal conductor of the Concerts Pasdeloup in Paris. He composed orch. pieces, chamber music, and a number of songs. —NS/LK/DM

Rhodes, Jane (Marie Andrée),

French mezzo-soprano; b. Paris, March 13, 1929. Following vocal studies, she made her debut as Marguerite in *La Damnation de Faust* in Nancy in 1953, which role she also chose for her first appearance at the Paris Opéra in 1958. On Nov. 15, 1960, she made her Metropolitan Opera debut in N.Y. as Carmen, returning to sing Salome in 1962. In 1961 she appeared at the Aix-en-Provence Festival and in 1968 at the Paris Opéra-Comique; also sang in various other French operatic centers, and in Buenos Aires and Tokyo. In 1966 she married **Roberto Benzi**. In addition to her French roles, Rhodes also essayed the roles of Tosca and Renata in Prokofiev's *The Fiery Angel.*—NS/LK/DM

Rhodes, Phillip (Carl),

American composer and teacher; b. Forest City, N.C., June 6, 1940. He studied composition with Klenz and Hamilton at Duke Univ. (B.A., 1962), and then was a student of Martino and Powell (composition) and of Schuller and Perle (theory) at Yale Univ. (M.M., 1966). He served as composer-in-residence in the Cicero (Ill.) Public Schools (1966–68), of the City of Louisville (1969–72), and for the State of Ky. Arts Board (1972–74). In 1974 he joined the faculty of Carleton Coll. in Northfield, Minn., where he was composer-in-residence and the Andrew W. Mellon Prof. of the Humanities.

WORKS: DRAMATIC: Opera: *The Gentle Boy* (1980; rev. 1987); *The Magic Pipe* (1989). **Ballet:** *About Faces* (1970). **ORCH.:** *The Lament of Michal* for Soprano and Orch. (1970); *Divertimento* for Small Orch. (1971); Concerto for Bluegrass Band and Orch. (1974); *Reels and Reveries* (1991). **Wind Ensemble/band:** *Remembrance* for Band (1967); *Three Pieces* for Band (1967); *Ceremonial Fanfare and Chorale* for 2 Brass Choirs (1977); *Cosmic Fantasies* for Band (1984; rev. 1999). **CHAMBER:** Duo for Violin and Cello (1968); *Autumn Setting* for Soprano and String Quartet (1969); *Museum Pieces* for Clarinet and String Quartet (1973); Quartet for Flute, Violin, Cello, and Harp (1975); *Reflections: Eight Fantasies* for Piano (1977); *Partita* for Viola (1978); *Visions of Remembrance* for Soprano, Mezzo-soprano, and 12 Instruments (1979); *Fiddletunes* for Violin and Tape (1996); *Two Appalachian Settings* for String Quartet (2000). **VOCAL: Choral:** *Witticisms and Lamentations From the Graveyard* (1972); *Christmas Cantata: "On the Morning of Christ's Nativity"* for Chorus, Soprano, Tenor, Wind Quartet, and Harp (1976); *Wind Songs* for Treble Choir and Orff Instrumentarium (1979); *Ad Honorem Stravinsky* (1981); *Dancing Songs* for Treble Choir and Orff Instrumentarium (1985); *Nets to Catch the Wind* for Chorus and Percussion (1986); *Chorale and Meditation* for Women's Voices and Organ (1994); *Three Appalachian Settings* for Chorus and Violin (2000). **Oratorio:** *From Paradise Lost* (1972). **Other:** *Five Songs on Children's Poems* for High Voice and Piano (1972); *Mountain Songs* for Soprano and Piano (1976); *Mary's Lullaby* for Soprano, Violin, and Organ (1993).—NS/LK/DM

Rhodes, Todd (Washington),

jazz pianist, arranger; b. Hopkinsville, Ky., Aug. 31, 1900; d. Flint, Mich., Feb. 16, 1963. Family moved to Springfield, Ohio, when Todd was four months old. Studied at the Springfield School of Music (1915–17), then four years at the Erie Cons. in Pa. Moved back to Springfield in 1921 and joined newly organized Synco Septette (which subsequently became McKinney's Cotton Pickers). Remained with the Cotton Pickers until 1934 (working in the latter stages under Cuba Austin's leadership). Gigged with local bands in Detroit until the early 1940s, then did war work in Detroit car factories, continued gigging, mainly as a solo pianist. Formed own quartet in 1946, following year increased to a seven-piece, began recording and playing long residencies in Detroit. Made several successful singles and began widespread touring, playing regular seasons in Fla. He is credited with discovering R&B singer LaVern Baker (who was in his band in 1952) and also giving Johnny Ray his first break.—JC/LP

Rhodes, Willard,

distinguished American music educator and ethnomusicologist; b. Dashler, Ohio, May

12, 1901; d. Sun City, Ariz., May 15, 1992. He earned his A.B. and B.Mus. degrees from Heidelberg Coll. in Tiffin, Ohio, both in 1922, and then studied at the Mannes School of Music in N.Y. (1923–25) and at Columbia Univ. (M.A., 1925); went to Paris, where he took lessons in piano with Cortot and in composition with Boulanger (1925–27). From 1927 to 1935 he served as conductor with the American Opera Co., the Cincinnati Summer Opera Co., and with his own Rhodes Chamber Opera Co. He was director of music in the public schools of Bronxville, N.Y. (1935–37). In 1937 he was appointed to the faculty at Columbia Univ.; became prof. emeritus in 1969. He held the post of music consultant to the U.S. Bureau of Indian Affairs beginning in 1937, and was a founding member (1953) and first president (1956–58) of the Soc. for Ethnomusicology. It was in this connection that he accumulated a most valuable collection of Amerindian folk music, both notated and recorded (many pressings released by the Library of Congress). In 1961 he was elected president of the Soc. for Asian Music, and in 1968 of the International Folk Music Council; also was a Fellow of the African Studies Assn. and numerous other ethnomusicological organizations. He conducted field work in Rhodesia and Nyasaland (1957–58) and in South India (1965–66); was visiting prof. at various institutions.—NS/LK/DM

Riadis (real name, **Khu**), **Emilios,** Greek composer; b. Salonica, May 13, 1885; d. there, July 17, 1935. He studied piano and harmony with Dimitrios Lalas in Salonica, then took courses with Walbrunn, Mayer-Gschrey, Becht, and Stich at the Munich Academy of Music (1908–10). He later studied with Charpentier and Ravel in Paris (1910–15), where he appeared as a composer under the name Riadis, formed from the ending of his mother's maiden name, Elefteriadis (his father's real name was Khu). In 1915 he became a piano teacher at the Salonica Cons. He wrote a number of songs, distinguished by an expressive melodic line, somewhat oriental in its intervallic pattern; his harmonizations are in the French manner. Most of his works for stage, orch., and chamber ensembles were left unfinished.—NS/LK/DM

Ribáry, Antal, Hungarian composer; b. Budapest, Jan. 8, 1924. He studied composition with Rezső Kokai at the Budapest Academy of Music (1943–47), and later took lessons with Ferenc Szabó.

WORKS: DRAMATIC: O p e r a : *Lajos Király Válik* (The Divorce of King Louis; 1959); *Liliom* (1960). B a l l e t : *Fortunio* (1969). ORCH.: *Sinfonietta* (1956); Cello Concerto (1958); 11 syms. (1960–89); *Musica per archi* (1961); *Pantomime* (1962); Violin Concertino (1965); *Dialogues* for Viola and Orch. (1967); 3 piano concertos (1979, 1980, 1985); Violin Concerto (1987); *Funeral Music in Memory of Bohuslav Martinů* (1988). CHAMBER: 4 violin sonatas; 5 string quartets; 2 cello sonatas (1948, rev. 1973; 1968); String Quintet (1956); Viola Sonata (1958); *9 Miniatures* for String Quartet (1966); *5 Miniatures* for Wind Trio (1969); *Chamber Music for 5 Instruments* (1970); *Dialogues* for Flute and Piano (1971); *Fantasia or Fantasia Concertante* for Violin, Viola, and Cello (1973); *Sonata Fantasia* for Cello and Piano (1977–78); *Rhapsodietta* for Flute and Piano

(1982); piano music, including 4 sonatas. VOCAL: Cantatas; *Metamorphosis* for Soprano, 3 Woodwinds, Piano, Vibraphone, 3 Bongos, 3 Gongs, and Strings (1966); *La Paques a New York,* oratorio (1987); songs.—NS/LK/DM

Ribaupierre, André de, Swiss violinist and pedagogue; b. Clarens, May 29, 1893; d. Rochester, N.Y., Jan. 17, 1955. He studied with his brother, Émile, and then with Gorski and Ysaÿe. At 17, he launched his career as a violinist. After teaching a master class at the Lausanne Cons. (1914–19), he went to Cincinnati to study once more with Ysaÿe. From 1921 to 1924 he was head of Ysaÿe's class, and also was a teacher at the Cleveland Inst. of Music from 1923 to 1929. He then returned to Switzerland and was founder-director of the Institut de Ribaupierre. He also was active as a chamber music player. Ribaupierre eventually settled in Rochester, N.Y., as head of the violin dept. at the Eastman School of Music.—NS/LK/DM

Ribera (y Tarragó), Julián, Spanish musicologist; b. Carcagente, near Valencia, Sept. 19, 1858; d. there, May 2, 1934. He was educated at the Univs. of Valencia and Madrid (Ph.D.), and from 1887 taught Arabic at the Univ. of Saragossa and from 1905 Arabian-Spanish literature at the Univ. of Madrid. He brought out the ed. *La música andaluza medieval en las canciones de trovadores, troveros y minnesinger* (3 vols., Madrid, 1923–25).

WRITINGS (all publ. in Madrid): *La música de las cantigas [de Santa María de Alfonso el Sabio]* (1922; 2nd ed., without music transcription, as *Historia de la música árabe medieval y su influencia en la española;* abr. Eng. tr., 1929, as *Music in Ancient Arabia and Spain*); *La música de la jota aragonesa* (1928).—NS/LK/DM

Ribot, Marc, versatile, inventive guitarist, and former member of the Lounge Lizards; b. Newark, N.J., May 21, 1954. This mainstay of the Downtown N.Y. scene, heard frequently and often extensively on albums by Madeleine Peyroux, Medeski, Martin & Wood, Ellery Eskelin, the Klezmatics, John Zorn, David Sanborn, Caetano Veloso, Marisa Monte, Elvis Costello, Tom Waits, Marianne Faithfull, Allen Ginsburg, T-Bone Burnett, and many more. He played in a group called the Real Tones that backed soul singers and other types traveling without a band, people like Wilson Pickett, Solomon Burke (he is on Burke's *Soul Alive!* album), and Chuck Berry. On his own albums, adding many other instruments to his toolbox, he covers an expansive stylistic territory—always in distinctive fashion. Representative of the younger avant-garde that refuses to exclude pop materials he skews familiar tunes and styles into non-Euclidean shapes, and makes avant-garde techniques listener friendly.

DISC.: *Rootless Cosmopolitans* (1990); *Requiem for What's His Name* (1992); *Solo Guitar Works of Frantz Casseus* (1993); *Subsonic 1* (1994); *Shrek* (1994); *Don't Blame Me* (1995); *The Book of Heads* (1995); *Shoe String Symphonettes* (1997).—SH

Ricci, Federico, Italian composer, brother of **Luigi Ricci;** b. Naples, Oct. 22, 1809; d. Conegliano, Dec. 10, 1877. He studied with Zingarelli, Bellini, and his brother

Luigi at the Naples Cons. (1818–29). He gained notable success as a composer for the theater with his opera *La prigione di Edimburgo* (Trieste, March 13, 1838). It was followed by the successful operas *Luigi Rolla* (Florence, March 30, 1841) and *Corrado d'Altamura* (Milan, Nov. 16, 1841); however, having established his reputation, he never again was able to duplicate these successes and in subsequent years devoted himself mainly to composing comic operas. In 1853 he was made maître de chapelle of the imperial theaters in St. Petersburg, but this post only involved supervising the vocal classes at the Cons. In 1869 he went to Paris, where he found success with his opéra bouffe *Une Folie à Rome* (Jan. 30, 1869). He retired to Conegliano in 1876.

BIBL.: F. de Villars, *Notices sur Luigi et F. R., suivies d'une analyse critique de "Crispino e la comare"* (Paris, 1866); L. de Rada, *I fratelli R.* (Florence, 1878).—NS/LK/DM

Ricci, Luigi, Italian composer, brother of **Federico Ricci**; b. probably in Naples, June 8(?), 1805; d. Prague, Dec. 31, 1859. He enrolled at the Naples Cons. when he was 9, his principal teachers being Furno and Zingarelli; also studied privately with Generali. His first opera, *L'Impresario in angustie*, was performed at the Cons. in his 18th year. He scored a major success with his opera *Chiara di Rosembergh* (Milan, Oct. 11, 1831), composed for the diva Giuditta Grisi, and his *Un avventura di Scaramuccia* also proved a popular favorite when premiered there (March 8, 1834). In 1836 he was appointed maestro di cappella in Trieste, where he also became maestro concertatore at the Teatro Grande. After the twins Fanny and Lidia Stolz joined its roster in 1843, Ricci became closely associated with them—indeed, so closely that he began living with them during his tenure as director of the Odessa Opera (1844–45). Returning to Trieste, he finally married Lidia in 1849 but did not abandon his intimacy with Fanny; Lidia bore him a daughter, Adelaide (1850–71), who became a singer at the Paris Théâtre-Italien (1868–69); Fanny bore him a son, also named Luigi (1852–1906), who became a composer. After he produced his last opera, *Il Diavolo a quattro* (Trieste, May 15, 1859), a mental derangement manifested itself, and he was sent to an asylum in Prague, where he spent the remaining months of his life.

BIBL.: V. dal Torso, *L. R.* (Trieste, 1860); F. de Villars, *Notices sur L. et Federico R., suivies d'une analyse critique de "Crispino e la comare"* (Paris, 1866); L. de Rada, *I fratelli R.* (Florence, 1878). —NS/LK/DM

Ricci, Ruggiero, celebrated American violinist; b. San Bruno, Calif., July 24, 1918. His musical education was lovingly fostered by his father, along with that of 6 of his siblings, every one of whom started out as a musician, and 2 of whom, the cellist Giorgio Ricci and the violinist Emma Ricci, achieved the rank of professional performer. Ruggiero studied violin with Louis Persinger, and made a sensational appearance at a public concert in San Francisco on Nov. 15, 1928, when he was 10 years old, with his teacher accompanying him at the piano. On Oct. 20, 1929, he played in N.Y.; he embarked on an international concert tour in 1932. He successfully negotiated the perilous transition from

child prodigy to serious artist. He accumulated a formidable repertoire of about 60 violin concertos, including all the violin works of Paganini; ed. the newly discovered MS of Paganini's early Violin Concerto, presumed to have been composed c. 1815, and gave its first N.Y. perf. with the American Sym. Orch. on Oct. 7, 1977; he also gave the first performances of violin concertos by several modern composers, among them Alberto Ginastera (1963) and Gottfried von Einem (1970). During World War II, he served as "entertainment specialist" with the U.S. Army Air Force. After the end of the war, he returned to the concert stage; made several world tours, which included South America, Australia, Japan, and Russia; he also gave master courses at the N.C. School of the Arts, Ind. Univ., and the Juilliard School of Music in N.Y. He owns a 1734 Guarnerius del Gesù violin. In 1978 he celebrated a "Golden Jubilee," marking half a century of his professional career.—NS/LK/DM

Ricciarelli, Katia, Italian soprano; b. Rovigo, Jan. 18, 1946. She studied at the Venice Cons., making her operatic debut as Mimi in Mantua in 1969. After winning the Giuseppe Verdi Award for Young Singers in Parma (1970) and the New Verdi Voices Contest (1971), she pursued a successful career in the major Italian music centers. She made her U.S. debut as Lucrezia in *I due Foscari* in Chicago (1972); her first appearance at London's Covent Garden was as Mimi (1974), a role she also chose for her Metropolitan Opera debut in N.Y. (April 11, 1975). In 1979 she made her debut in recital at the Salzburg Festival. In 1985 she sang Desdemona in Zeffirelli's film version of Verdi's *Otello*. In 1985–86 she sang Rossini roles in Pesaro, returning there in 1988. She appeared as Desdemona at the Metropolitan Opera and at Covent Garden in 1990. In 1997 she sang Handel's Agrippina in Palermo. Among her other fine roles were Amelia Boccanegra, Suor Angelica, Luisa Miller, and Elisabeth de Valois.—NS/LK/DM

Ricciotti, Carlo, Italian violinist and opera impresario; b. c. 1681; d. The Hague, July 13, 1756. He joined a French opera company in The Hague in 1702, later serving as its director until 1725. Ricciotti publ. *VI concerti armonici a quattro violini obligati, alto viola, violoncello obligato e basso continuo* (The Hague, 1740). Although no composer's name is given on the title page, they were long thought to be by Ricciotti or Pergolesi. They now appear to be the work of Count Unico Wilhelm van Wassenaer.

BIBL.: A. Dunning, *Count Unico Wilhelm van Wassenaer (1692–1766); A Master Unmasked; or, The Pergolesi-R. Puzzle Solved* (Buren, 1980).—LK/DM

Rice, Charlie, jazz drummer; b. Philadelphia, Pa., March 1, 1920. A superb and dynamic player, he was a mainstay of the Philadelphia scene in the 1940s and 1950s. Rice had an extended stay with Jimmy Oliver's house band at the Downbeat opposite visiting stars such as Parker, Gillespie, Bud Powell and Hank Jones during 1945 and probably into 1946 or even 1947. He then led the first house band in Club 421 with Vance Wilson, Red Garland, bassist Bob Bushnell, and trumpeter Johnny

Hughes. Around this time, he rehearsed with Jimmy Heath's big band but he was not available to do gigs with them. He toured the South Pacific with the USO (1951) with J.J. Johnson and Howard McGhee, played with Sonny Stitt and Eddie "Lockjaw" Davis, and Leo Parker. Rice toured and recorded with Chet Baker (1964–65), then left full-time performing to teach music in the public schools.

DISC.: H. McGhee: *South Pacific Jazz* (1952); *Stitt and Jaws at Birdland* (1954). L. Parker: *Let Me Tell You 'Bout it* (1961). C. Baker: *Colpix* (1964).—LP

Rice, Tim, one of the most popular stage and screen lyricists of his generation; b. Buckinghamshire, England Nov. 10, 1944. In his late teens Rice sang with a pop group called The Aardvarks, and then sang with several other groups through the mid-1960s. By 1965, he had started writing songs. That year, he also met Andrew Lloyd Webber by answering an ad Webber had placed for a "with it" lyricist. Coincidentally, both were attending the Royal Coll. of Music in London. They collaborated on the play *The Likes of Us*, which went unproduced.

Taking a cue from one of Lloyd Webber's favorite children's versions of a bible story, the duo wrote *Joseph and the Amazing Technicolor Dream Coat* in 1967. Webber and Rice put their first show on London's West End in 1971 with *Jesus Christ Superstar*. For both of these shows, they raised their initial funding by creating concept albums of the works. The original album version of *Jesus Christ Superstar* topped the album charts for three weeks in 1970. Yvonne Elliman had a #28 hit with "I Don't Know How to Love Him" from that album. Murray Head reached #14 with "Superstar."

The duo split temporarily while Lloyd Webber worked on his next project, a musical based on P. G. Wodehouse's Jeeves books; the play flopped badly. Perhaps seeking to rekindle the old magic, Lloyd Webber returned to Rice. While Lloyd Webber had previously suggested the subject matter for their work, now Rice brought an idea to the table: the story of Argentina's First Lady, Eva Peron. That play, *Evita*, became the pair's biggest box office hit when it opened in 1978, winning two Tony Awards as well as a Grammy Award for Best Original Cast Album. It also changed the balance of power in their relationship and ultimately caused them to stop writing together.

Rice began working with other collaborators. He started a project with Bjorn Ulvaeus and Benny Andersson from the band Abba. Like his earlier works, *Chess* was released as an album before it was staged. Murray Head took the single "One Night in Bangkok" to #3. The play opened in London in 1985, but when it opened on Broadway a year later, it did not do very well. However, 1986 saw Rice collaborating again with Lloyd Webber on an operetta about one of Rice's favorite subjects: cricket. The piece had been commissioned for performance before Queen Elizabeth II.

In 1992, Rice started a new phase in his career. Filling the hole left by the death of lyricist Howard Ashman, he went to work in on new songs for the Disney feature *Aladdin*. Working with Ashman's longtime partner Alan Menken, they came up with the Oscar- and Grammy-winning song "A Whole New World." The album also took home a Grammy for Best Musical Album for Children. Two years later, he collaborated with Elton John on the soundtrack to the Disney film *The Lion King*. He received the Best Original Song Oscar for "Can You Feel Love Tonight?"

After years of rumors and aborted attempts, the film version of *Evita*, starring Madonna, was finally released in 1996. Rice and Lloyd Webber collaborated once again on an original song, "You Must Love Me," for the movie. It earned yet another Best Original Song Oscar.

In 1998, Rice worked again with Elton John, creating a new musical based on the legend of Aida, which opened on Broadway early in the year 2000. Rice also shared another Grammy with John for the Best Musical Show Album for the Broadway version of *The Lion King* in 1999. The duo continued working together, writing the songs for the animated film *The Road to El Dorado*, which opened in the spring of 2000. In addition to his musical activities Rice has co- written a cricket column for the *London Daily Telegraph* since the 1970s. In 1999, he was inducted into the Songwriters Hall of Fame.

DISC.: *I Know Them So Well: The Best of Tim Rice* (1993); *Tim Rice Collection Stage and Screen Classics* (1996). **ANDREW LLOYD WEBBER:** *The Premiere Collection: The Best of Andrew Lloyd Webber* (1988); *The Premiere Collection Encore* (1993).—HB

Rich, Alan, muckraking American music critic; b. Boston, June 17, 1924. He pursued a premed course at Harvard Univ. (A.B., 1945), studied musicology with Bukofzer and Kerman at the Univ. of Calif. at Berkeley (M.A., 1952) and with Deutsch in Vienna (1952–53), and learned the rudiments of conducting from Gmeindl. He was asst. music critic of the *Boston Herald* (1944–45) and the *N.Y. Sun* (1947–48). Rich was a contributor to the *American Record Guide* (1947–61), the *Saturday Review* (1952–53), and *Musical America* (1955–61). After serving as asst. music critic of the *N.Y. Times* (1961–63), he was chief music critic and ed. of the *N.Y. Herald-Tribune* (1963–66). In 1966–67 he was music critic and ed. of the *N.Y. World-Journal-Tribune*, and then was a contributing ed. of *Time* magazine in 1967–68. From 1979 to 1983 he was music and drama critic, as well as arts ed., of *California* magazine, and then served as a contributing ed. to it (1983–85). After holding the post of general ed. of *Newsweek* magazine (1983–87), he was music critic of the *Los Angeles Herald-Examiner* (from 1987). In 1970, 1973, and 1974 he won ASCAP-Deems Taylor awards.

WRITINGS: *Careers and Opportunities in Music* (1964); *Music, mirror of the Arts* (1969); *Simon & Schuster Listeners Guide to Music* (3 vols., 1980); *The Lincoln Center Story* (1984); *American Pioneers: Ives to Cage and Beyond* (London, 1995); *Johann Sebastian Bach: Play by Play* (San Francisco, 1995); *Ludwig van Beethoven: Play by Play* (San Francisco, 1995); *Pyotr Ilich Tchaikovsky: Play by Play* (San Francisco, 1995); *Wolfgang Amadeus Mozart: Play by Play* (San Francisco, 1995).—NS/LK/DM

Rich, Buddy (Bernard), jazz drummer, band leader, singer; b. Brooklyn, N.Y., Sept. 30, 1917; d. Los Angeles, Calif. April 2, 1987. He appeared in his parents' vaudeville act *Wilson and Rich* before he was two years old; he tap-danced and played drums in a Broadway show at age four. His parents dropped out of the act to manage his career and from the age of six, he began touring the U.S. and Australia as a single act, *Baby Traps the Drum Wonder*; at 11, he led his own stage band. Rich began gigging with Art Shapiro (c. 1936) and received his first jazz notice after sitting in with Hot Lips Page's Band in September 1937. He performed with Joe Marsala (October 1937–June 1938), briefly led own band at Piccadilly Roof, N.Y., then worked with Bunny Berigan until joining Harry James in December 1938. After working with Artie Shaw, he joined Tommy Dorsey (November 1939–42). He played in Los Angeles with Benny Carter, and served in the U.S. Marines until June 1944. After being released, Rich rejoined Tommy Dorsey until October 1945; while filming with Dorsey in Hollywood, he played for two weeks with Count Basie at the Club Plantation, Los Angeles. He formed his own band in late 1945, which he continued to lead until January 1947, then in February did first of many tours with Norman Granz's "Jazz at the Philharmonic." With the main exception of Harry James, whom he would join, quit, and rejoin several times, he would alternate between leading his own groups, recording, and touring with "Jazz at the Philharmonic" through the 1950s. During this period, he collaborated with many talented artists, such as Art Tatum, Lester Young, Lionel Hampton, Dizzy Gillespie, Charlie Parker, Oscar Peterson, and Count Basie. He had a bop-oriented band in 1948 which included Warne Marsh, Terry Gibbs and Hal McKusick. The group played at the Hollywood Palladium in June and July (with broadcasts), then went on a three-month cross-country tour, heading first for Northern Calif., with Jimmy Giuffre joining in San Francisco; the tour ended in N.Y. in October. On Dec. 22, Rich fired the whole band for refusing to play what they called "commercial junk." He soon reformed a band, adding a second drummer, Sonny Igoe, which played among other places at Ideal Beach, a resort near Montreal, and on TV shows (1948–49). Rich joined Les Brown in June 1949, but left in September to resume work with J.A.T.P. He led his own band in 1950, performed for the "Josephine Baker" show (1951), then worked in Charlie Ventura's Big Four until November 1951. He worked with Harry James for a year (1953–54), then resumed with Tommy Dorsey until April 1955. He returned to Harry James (1956–57), including a tour of Europe, then formed his own small group; he also acted on TV and worked briefly as a solo vocalist (1959). While on tour with his own quintet in November 1959, he suffered a mild heart attack, but resumed leading a small band in N.Y. (spring 1960) and later toured Asia. He again worked regularly with Harry James (1961–66), reportedly as the world's highest paid sideman; he also did many guest spots on TV shows, concerts, etc. He formed his own big band in 1966, which rapidly achieved international success in clubs, concerts, and college campuses, with albums on the U.S. charts, several overseas tours including "Command Performance" in London (November 1969). He led a small group (1974; with Sonny Fortune and Jack Wilkins) at his own N.Y. club, Buddy's Place, then re-formed his own highly successful big band in the mid-1970s, which continued

to tour through the late 1970s and 1980s. Another stroke in the early 1980s slowed him down for a while, but he made a full and remarkable recovery which he credited to acupuncture. Rich underwent surgery on March 16, 1987 at UCLA Medical Center for a brain tumor and had been undergoing daily treatment before he died.

Among musicians, his work is often criticized as epitomizing cold technique, and as not swinging or being too busy. But his rhythmic style was in keeping with his generation, and he contributed tremendous vitality to any musical occasion. His technique was most evident in solos, where he might fly around the drum set at amazing speed, perform drum rolls and other feats with one hand, or sustain an unbelievably perfect snare drum roll for a minute or more while varying the volume. For such things, drummers often forgave him any shortcomings in musicality. On the other hand, those who were members of his bands are unlikely to forgive him for his truly rude and insulting manner of criticizing them. One band member taped him during such a tirade and circulated this tape as a form of revenge. Many fine musicians passed through his bands, including Warne Marsh, Greg Hopkins, and Steve Marcus. In public, he was very witty, which made him a favorite on the Johnny Carson show, Carson being an amateur drummer.

Disc.: *One Night Stand* (1946); *And His Legendary '47–'48 Orchestra* (1948); *Swinging Count* (1952); *Swingin' Buddy Rich* (1953); *Super Rich* (1953); *Buddy and Sweets* (1955); *This One's for Basie* (1956); *Sings Johnny Mercer* (1956); *Buddy Rich Sings Johnny Mercer* (1956); *Just Sings* (1957); *Buddy Rich Just Sings* (1957); *Rich Versus Roach* (1959); *Buddy Rich vs Max Roach* (1959); *Burnin' Beat* (1962); *Big Swing Face* (1967); *Swingin' New Big Band* (1966); *Swingin' New Band* (1966); *Rich Ala Rahka* (1968); *Mercy, Mercy* (1968); *Rich in London* (1971); *Different Drummer* (1971); *Buddy Rich in London* (1971); *Roar of '74* (1973); *Big Band Machine* (1975); *Speak No Evil* (1976); *Sound of Jazz* (1977); *Lionel Hampton Presents Buddy Rich* (1977); *Europe '77* (1977); *Class of '78* (1977); *Buddy Rich Plays and Plays and Plays* (1977); *Best Band I Ever Had* (1977); *Live at Ronnie Scott's* (1980); *Live at King Street Cafe* (1985). L. Young: "Giants" (1946). C. Parker: *Bird and Diz* (1950). B. Powell: *The Genius of Bud Powell* (1950). A. Blakey: *Drums Ablaze* (1960).

Bibl.: D. J. Cooper, *Buddy Rich Discography* (Lancashire, England, 1974); D. Cooper, *Buddy Rich: A Lifetime of Music* (1989); W. Balliett, *Super Drummer: A Profile of Buddy Rich* (Indianapolis, 1968); D. Meriwether, *The Buddy Rich Orch. and Small Groups* (Spotswood, N.J., 1974); K. Stratemann, *Buddy Rich and Gene Krupa: A Filmo-Discography* (Lubbecke, Germany, 1980); D. Meriwether, *We Don't Play Requests: A Musical Biography/Discography of Buddy Rich* (Chicago, 1984); J. Nesbitt, *Inside Buddy Rich: A Study of the Master Drummer's Style and Technique* (Delevan, N.Y., 1984).—**JC/LP**

Richafort, Jean, eminent Flemish composer; b. probably in Hainaut, c. 1480; d. probably in Bruges, c. 1547. He may have been a pupil of Josquin Des Prez, He was maître de chapelle at St. Rombaud in Mechelen (1507–9), and later was active at the French royal chapel. He excelled as a composer of motets. Among his extant works are 2 masses, a Requiem Mass, 12 Magnificats, many motets, and a number of chansons.

BIBL.: M. Kabis, *The Works of J. R., Renaissance Composer (1480?–1548)* (diss., N.Y.U., 1957).—NS/LK/DM

Richie, Lionel,

composer and performer of romantic ballads; b. Tuskegee, Ala., June 20, 1949. **The Commodores,** popular soul band of the late 1970s. **MEMBERSHIP:** Lionel Richie, voc., kybd., sax.; Thomas McClary, gtr. (b. Oct. 6, 1950); Milan Williams, kybd. (b. March 28, 1949); William King, trpt. (b. Jan. 30, 1949); Ronald LaPread, bs. (b. Sept. 4, 1950); Walter "Clyde" Orange, drm. (b.Dec. 10, 1947). J. D. Nicholas (b. Watford, Hereford, England, April 12, 1952) replaced Lionel Richie in 1982.

Starting out as a funk dance band, The Commodores evolved into a highly popular soul band of the late 1970s, based on Lionel Richie's ingenuous romantic ballads. As Motown Records' first successful self-contained band, The Commodores rivaled the popularity of Stevie Wonder as a company act and Earth, Wind and Fire as a soul band. Beginning solo work in 1981 and leaving the band in 1982, Lionel Richie sustained his reputation as a consummate craftsman of mellow yet compelling love ballads, particularly with the 1983 album *Can't Slow Down.*

Formed in 1968 at Tuskegee Inst. (now Tuskegee Univ.) in Ala. by the merger of The Mystics and The Jays, the Commodores developed a regional reputation as a funk dance band before moving to N.Y. in 1969. Signed to Atlantic Records for one unsuccessful album, the band switched to Motown in 1971 and toured for the next three years as opening act to The Jackson Five. They scored their first major pop and near-smash R&B hit with Milan Williams's instrumental "Machine Gun" in 1974.

After Thomas McClary's funky "Slippery When Wet" hit in 1975, The Commodores began featuring ballads written and sung by Richie, achieving smash pop hits with his "Sweet Love," "Just to Be Close to You," and "Easy." Although their next hits were the funky band compositions "Brick House" and "Too Hot to Handle," they quickly returned to the ballad format and scored the top pop hit "Three Times a Lady" and the smash pop hits "Sail On" and "Still." *In the Pocket* yielded "Lady (You Bring Me Up)" and "Oh No" in 1981, the year Richie began solo work. He wrote the top hit "Lady" and produced *Share Your Love* for Kenny Rogers; he also wrote and sang in duet with Diana Ross the top hit "Endless Love."

Lionel Richie left The Commodores in 1982, and was replaced by J. D. Nicholas. They eventually scored a smash hit with a tribute to Marvin Gaye and Jackie Wilson, "Nightshift," in 1985. Ron La Pread left after the hit, as had Thomas McClary in 1984. By 1986 the Commodores had switched to Polydor Records. In the 1990s, with William King, J. D. Nicholas, and Walter Orange as mainstays, The Commodores recorded for Commodores Records.

In the meantime, Lionel Richie's debut album yielded the three smash hits "Truly," "You Are," and "My Love." His second album, *Can't Slow Down,* included the two top hits "All Night Long (All Night)" and "Hello," plus the smash hits "Running with the Night," "Stuck on You," and "Penny Lover." In early 1985 Richie cowrote with Michael Jackson the "We Are the World" single, recorded by scores of popular artists, which raised more than $50 million for famine relief in Africa. His next album produced *six* hits: the top "Say You, Say Me" (from the movie *White Nights*), the smashes "Dancing on the Ceiling," "Love Will Conquer All," and "Ballerina Girl," plus the major "Deep River Woman" (with the country group Alabama) and "Se La." Beset by personal problems, Richie withdrew from recording and performing in the late 1980s, eventually reemerging with *Back to Front,* the hit "Do It to Me," and a world tour in 1992. However, he failed to produce a follow-up to this album as of 1995.

DISC.: THE COMMODORES: *Machine Gun* (1974); *Caught in the Act* (1975); *Movin' On* (1975); *Hot on the Tracks* (1976); *The Commodores* (1977); *Live!* (1977); *Natural High* (1978); *Greatest Hits* (1978); *Midnight Magic* (1979); *Natural High/Midnight Magic* (1986); *Heroes* (1980); *Heroes/The Commodores* (1986); *In the Pocket* (1981); *All the Great Hits* (1982); *Anthology* (1983); *13* (1983); *Nightshift* (1985); *Best* (1995); *United* (1986); *Rock Solid* (1988). **LIONEL RICHIE:** *L. R.* (1982); *Can't Slow Down* (1983); *Dancing on the Ceiling* (1986); *Back to Front* (1992).

BIBL.: D. Nathan, *L. R.: An Illustrated Biography* (London, 1985).—BH

Richings (originally, Reynoldson), (Mary) Caroline,

English-born American pianist, soprano, impresario, and teacher; b. 1827; d. Richmond, Va., Jan. 14, 1882. She was taken to the U.S. as a child and adopted by the actor Peter Richings. After appearing as a pianist in Philadelphia, she received vocal instruction and made her operatic debut there as Marie in *La Fille du régiment* (Feb. 9, 1852). Her father organized the Richings Grand Opera Co. (1859), and she appeared with it both as a pianist and as a singer; when her father retired (1867), she assumed the position of director. After she married a tenor in the company, Peter Bernard, it was renamed the Richings-Bernard Co.; in 1870 they formed a partnership with Euphrosyne Parepa-Rosa and gave performances as the short-lived Caroline Richings-Bernard Grand Opera Combination. She served as director of her own concert organization, the Old Folks Opera Co. (1874–75), and subsequently settled in Baltimore, singing in light opera and concert; was also active as a voice teacher. She made her farewell stage appearance in her own operetta, *The Duchess* (Baltimore, Aug. 1881).—NS/LK/DM

Richter, Ernst Friedrich (Eduard),

eminent German music theorist, teacher, organist, and composer; b. Gross-Schönau, Oct. 24, 1808; d. Leipzig, April 9, 1879. He studied at the Zittau Gymnasium and then pursued theological studies at the Univ. of Leipzig; received instruction in music from the Kantor Weinlig. When the Leipzig Cons. was founded in 1843, he became Hauptmann's co-adjutor as teacher of harmony. He conducted the Leipzig Singakademie (1843–47), and was organist of the Petrikirche (from 1851) and the Neukirche (from 1862). In 1868 became music director of the Nikolaikirche and cantor of the Thomasschule. He composed several sacred cantatas, masses, Psalms, etc., and also wrote chamber music, piano pieces, and organ compositions. But he became primarily known as the compiler of practical and useful manuals on harmony, counterpoint, and fugue, which went into numerous eds. and trs. into all European languages, among them *Die Grundzüge der musikalischen Formen und ihre Analyse* (Leipzig, 1852), *Lehrbuch der Harmonie* (Leipzig, 1853; 36th ed., 1953; Eng. tr., N.Y., 1867; newly tr. by T. Baker from the 25th Ger. ed., N.Y., 1912; also in Swedish, Russian, Polish, Italian, French, Spanish, and Dutch), *Lehrbuch der Fuge* (Leipzig, 1859; 9th ed., 1921; in Eng., London, 1878; also in Fr.), *Katechismus der Orgel* (Leipzig, 1868; 4th ed., 1896), and *Lehrbuch des einfachen und doppelten Kontrapunkts* (Leipzig, 1872; 15th ed., 1920; Eng. tr., London, 1874, and N.Y., 1884; also in Fr. and Russian). His son, Alfred Richter, brought out an *Aufgabenbuch zu E.F. Richters Harmonielehre* (Leipzig, 1879; 64th ed., 1952).—NS/LK/DM

Richter, Ferdinand Tobias, German-born Austrian organist and composer; b. Würzburg (baptized), July 22, 1651; d. Vienna, Nov. 3, 1711. He was court and chamber organist in Vienna from 1683, and enjoyed a great reputation as a theorist and teacher. Among his compositions were 20 operas, 4 oratorios and other sacred works, music for Jesuit school plays, and various keyboard pieces.—NS/LK/DM

Richter, Franz Xaver, German singer, teacher, and composer of Moravian-Bohemian descent; b. probably in Holleschau, Dec. 1, 1709; d. Strasbourg, Sept. 12, 1789. He applied himself to a thorough study of Fux's *Gradus ad Parnassum*. In 1740 he became Vice-Kapellmeister to the Prince-Abbot Anselm von Reichlin-Meldegg in Kempten, Allgau; by 1749 he was a court musician to the Elector Palatine Carl Theodor in Mannheim, where he was active as a singer and composer; about 1768 he became chamber composer there. From 1768 he was Kapellmeister at Strasbourg Cathedral. Richter wrote a treatise, *Harmonische Belehrung oder gründliche Anweisung zur musikalischen Ton- Kunst oder regulären Composition* (MS; ed. and tr. by C. Kalkbrenner as *Traité d'harmonie et de composition*, Paris, 1804). His extant works include about 80 syms., overtures, 6 harpsichord concertos, 8 flute concertos, Oboe Concerto, 12 sonatas for Harpsichord, and Violin or Flute or Cello, 6 sonatas for 2 Flutes or Violin, 6 solos for Flute or Violin and Basso Continuo, 6 sonatas for 2 Violins, Cello, and Harpsichord, 12 sonatas for 2 Violins, Cello, and Harpsichord, 6 Quartettos for 2 Violins, Viola, and Cello, various keyboard pieces, and much sacred music.

BIBL.: W. Barth, *Die Messenkompositionen F.X. R.s (1709–89)* (diss., Univ. of Munich, 1941); W. Gässler, *Die Sinfonien von F.X. R.* (diss., Univ. of Munich, 1942); R. Pecman, *F.X. R. und seine "harmonische Belehrungen"* (Michaelstein, 1990); J. Reutter, *Studien zur Kirchenmusik F.X. R.s (1709–1789)* (2 vols., Frankfurt am Main, 1993).—NS/LK/DM

Richter, Hans (Johann Baptist Isidor), celebrated Austro- Hungarian conductor; b. Raab, Hungary, April 4, 1843; d. Bayreuth, Dec. 5, 1916. He was born into a musical family; his father, Anton Richter, was a composer and Kapellmeister at Raab Cathedral, and his mother, Josefine (née Czasensky) Richter, was an opera singer and vocal teacher. Richter was blessed with perfect pitch and was only 4 when he began piano lessons with his mother; he soon received instruction in organ and timpani, and also began to sing. In 1854 he was taken to Vienna to pursue academic studies at the Piaristengymnasium; he also was accepted as a chorister in the Imperial Chapel, where he sang until 1858. He then studied at the Cons. of the Gesellschaft der Musikfreunde (1858–62); his principal mentors there were Kleinecke (horn), Heissler (violin), Ramesch (piano), J. Hellmesberger (orchestral training), and Sechter (theory and composition). He continued his training with Kleinecke as an external student until 1865. In addition, he learned to play virtually every instrument in the orch., the harp excepted. While still attending to his studies, he gained experience as a player in various opera orchs. before serving as a horn player in the orch. of Vienna's Kärntnerthortheater (1862–66). In the meantime, he made his professional debut as a conductor in a concert in Raab on Sept. 19, 1865. Upon the recommendation of Heinrich Esser, Wagner invited Richter to Tribschen in 1866 to prepare the fair copy of his score to the opera *Die Meistersinger von Nürnberg*. Wagner was so satisfied with Richter's work that he secured the young musician's appointment as chorus master and répétiteur at the Munich Court Opera. Richter prepared the chorus for the premiere of *Die Meistersinger*, which was conducted by Hans von Bülow on June 21, 1868. Later that year he was appointed court music director in Munich, but was dismissed from his post the following year after a dispute with the royal authorities over aspects of the staging of the premiere of *Das Rheingold*. With Wagner's approval, Richter conducted instead the Brussels premiere (in French) of *Lohengrin* on March 22, 1870, with notable success. In 1871 Richter became conductor of the Opera and Phil. concerts in Budapest, where he won distinction as both an operatic and symphonic conductor. In 1874 he was made the director of the Opera. In 1875 he was called to Vienna to assume the post of 1st Kapellmeister of the Court Opera, a position he retained until 1900. From 1875 to 1882, and again from 1883 to 1898, he was conductor of the Vienna Phil. At Wagner's invitation, he went to Bayreuth in 1876 to conduct the first complete staging of the *Ring* cycle at the opening of the Festival: *Das Rheingold* on Aug. 13, *Die Walküre* on Aug. 14, *Siegfried* on Aug. 16, and *Götterdammerung* on Aug. 17. In May 1877 Wagner invited Richter to share his conducting duties at the Royal Albert Hall in London. That same year Richter was made Vize-Hofkapellmeister of the Court Chapel in Vienna. In 1879 he returned to London to conduct a series of Orchestral Festival Concerts, which he subsequently led as the annual Richter Concerts from 1880 to 1902. In 1882 Richter conducted the first British performances of *Die Meistersinger* (May 30) and *Tristan und Isolde* (June 20) at the Theatre Royal, Drury Lane, London. His debut at London's Covent Garden followed on June 4, 1884, when he conducted *Die Meistersinger*. In 1884 he became conductor of the Gesellschaft der Musikfreunde in Vienna, a post he held until 1890. From 1885 to 1909 he was conductor of the Birmingham Triennial Music

Festival. In 1887 he returned to Bayreuth, and between 1892 and 1912 conducted notable performances at 11 festivals there. In 1893 Richter accepted the conductorship of the Boston Sym. Orch., but was compelled to withdraw his acceptance when he learned from the Viennese authorities that he would lose his pension. Instead, he was made Imperial Hofkapellmeister that year, a title he retained until 1900. In 1895 Richter made his first appearance as a guest conductor with the Hallé Orch. in Manchester, and subsequently served as its conductor from 1899 to 1911. From 1903 to 1910 he conducted seasons of German opera at Covent Garden, and in 1908 conducted the first English-language performances of the *Ring* cycle there. On June 9, 1904, he conducted the inaugural concert of the London Sym. Orch., and then served as its principal conductor until 1911. After making his home in Bayreuth, Richter conducted his farewell performance at the Festival there with *Die Meistersinger* on Aug. 19, 1912. In addition to the honors bestowed upon him in his homeland, he was also honored in England with honorary doctorates in music by the univs. of Oxford (1885) and Manchester (1902), and was made an Honorary Member, 4th class (1904) and Honorary Commander (1907) of the Royal Victorian Order. Richter's unstinting devotion to the composer's intentions, communicated via a flawless conducting technique, resulted in performances of great commitment and authority. He invariably conducted all his scores from memory. While his association with Wagner rendered his performances of the master of Bayreuth's works as authoritative, he also won great renown for his interpretations of Beethoven. He further distinguished himself as an outstanding champion of Mozart, Brahms, Bruckner, Tchaikovsky, Dvořák, and Elgar.

BIBL.: C. Fifield, *True Artist and True Friend: A Biography of H. R.* (Oxford, 1993).—**NS/LK/DM**

Richter, Karl, distinguished German organist, harpsichordist, and conductor; b. Plauen, Oct. 15, 1926; d. Munich, Feb. 15, 1981. He studied organ, harpsichord, and conducting at the Dresden Kreuzschule, then took courses at the Leipzig Cons. with Rudolf Mauersberger, Gunther Ramin, and Karl Straube. In 1946 he became choirmaster of the Christuskirche in Leipzig, and in 1947 he was named organist of Leipzig's Thomaskirche. In 1951 he settled in Munich. He organized the Munich Bach Orch. and Choir, which brought him great acclaim, making many tours and numerous recordings with them; also appeared as a guest conductor in Europe. On April 18, 1965, he made his U.S. debut with them at N.Y.'s Carnegie Hall.—**NS/LK/DM**

Richter, Marga, American composer; b. Reedsburg, Wisc., Oct. 21, 1926. She was prepared for a musical career by her mother, Inez Chandler-Richter, a soprano. She studied at the MacPhail School of Music in Minneapolis, and in 1943 entered the Juilliard School of Music in N.Y., where she studied piano with Tureck and composition with Persichetti and Bergsma, graduating in 1949 (M.S., 1951). She received 30 annual ASCAP awards (1966–95) and 2 grants from the NEA (1977,

1979). Her compositions reflect a pragmatic modern trend without rigid adherence to any particular doctrine or technique; the overriding concern is aural.

WORKS: DRAMATIC: B a l l e t : *Abyss* (1964; Cannes, Feb. 5, 1965); *Bird of Yearning* (1967; as *Der Türm*, Cologne, Oct. 30, 1969; version for Piano, 1976). **ORCH.:** 2 piano concertos: No. 1 (1955) and No. 2, *Landscapes of the Mind I* (1968–74; Tucson, March 19, 1976, Masselos soloist); *Lament* for Strings (1956); *Aria and Toccata* for Viola and String Orch. (1956–57); *Variations on a Sarabande* (1959); *8 Pieces* (1961; originally for Piano); *Fragments* (1976); *Country Auction* for School Band (1976); *Blackberry Vines and Winter Fruit* (North Bennington, Vt., Oct. 17, 1976); *Music for 3 Quintets and Orch.* (1978–80); *Düsseldorf Concerto* for Solo Flute, Solo Viola, Harp, Percussion, and String Ensemble (1981–82; Salzburg, May 20, 1982); *Out of Shadows and Solitude* (1985; Chicago, Dec. 9, 1988); *Quantum Quirks of a Quick Quaint Quark* (1991; Brookville, N.Y., April 25, 1992); *...beside the still waters: Variations and Interludes*, concerto for Piano, Violin, Cello, and Orch. (1992; Greensboro, N.C., July 3, 1993). **CHAMBER:** *1 for 2 and 2 for 3* for Trombone Duet and Trio (1947; rev. 1974); *Clarinet Sonata* (1948); *2 string quartets* (1950, withdrawn; 1958); *Ricercare* for Brass Quartet (1958); *Darkening of the Light* for Viola (1961; version for Cello, 1976); *Suite* for Violin and Piano (1964); *Landscapes of the Mind II* for Violin and Piano (1971) and *III* for Piano Trio (1979); *Pastorale* for 2 Oboes (1975); *Sonora* for 2 Clarinets and Piano (1981); *Seacliff Variations* for Piano, Violin, Viola, and Cello (1984); *Qhanri (Snow Mountain)*, Tibetan variations for Cello and Piano (1988); *Obsessions* for Trombone (1990). **KEYBOARD: P i a n o :** Sonata (1954–55); *Melodrama* for 2 Pianos (1958); *Variations on a Theme by Latimer* for Piano, 4-Hands (1964); *Remembrances* (1971); *Requiem* (1976); *Exequy* (1980); *Quantum Quirks of a Quick Quaint Quark No. 3* (1993). **O r g a n :** *Quantum Quirks of a Quick Quaint Quark No. 2* (1992). **VOCAL:** *Do Not Press My Hands* for Vocal Sextet (1981); *Into My Heart*, 7 poems for Chorus, Oboe, Violin, Brass Sextet, and Percussion (1990); choruses; songs.—**NS/LK/DM**

Richter, Nico (Max), Dutch composer; b. Amsterdam, Dec. 2, 1915; d. there, Aug. 16, 1945. He studied conducting with Scherchen, and directed a student orch. In Feb. 1942 he was arrested by the Nazis as a member of the Dutch Resistance, and spent 3 years in the Dachau concentration camp, which fatally undermined his health; he died shortly after liberation.

WORKS: DRAMATIC: *Amorijs*, chamber opera (1937); *Kannitverstan*, ballet. **ORCH.:** *Serenade*, sinfonietta for Flute, Oboe, Guitar, and Strings (1931–34); *Sinfonia-Divertimento* for Chamber Orch. (1936). **CHAMBER:** Concertino for Clarinet, Horn, Trumpet, Piano, and 2 Violins (1935); Trio for Flute, Viola, and Guitar (1935); *Serenade* for Flute, Violin, and Viola (1945; 2 extant movements reconstructed by Lex van Delden). —**NS/LK/DM**

Richter, Sviatoslav (Teofilovich), legendary Russian pianist; b. Zhitomir, March 20, 1915; d. Moscow, Aug. 1, 1997. He began piano lessons at an early age with his father, a keyboard player and composer. While still a youth, he became active as a piano accompanist. In 1934 he made his formal recital debut at the House of Engineers in Odessa. He entered the Moscow Cons. in 1937, where he studied with Heinrich Neuhaus. Even before completing his formal studies in 1942, he had acquired a notable reputation via various public appearances. After taking the highest honors at the All-Union Competition of Performers in 1945, he pursued a career as a soloist with orchs., as a recitalist, and as a chamber music artist. In 1949 he was awarded the Stalin Prize in recognition of his formidable talent. His career took him to most of the major music centers of his homeland and in Eastern Europe in subsequent years. On Oct. 15, 1960, he made his auspicious American debut as soloist in the Brahms 2nd Piano Concerto with Leinsdorf and the Chicago Sym. Orch. Two days later these forces recorded the work, which was destined to become one of the classic recordings of the century. On Oct. 19, 1960, he made his Carnegie Hall debut in N.Y. to enormous critical acclaim. His London debut followed in 1961. In 1965 and 1970 he made return visits to the U.S. In the later years of his career, Richter limited his engagements, but his many outstanding recordings served to preserve his genius for contemporary and future listeners. He celebrated the 50th anniversary of his formal debut in 1994, and in 1995 he gave his farewell performance. However stupendous his digital mastery, Richter never permitted the mere mechanics of piano virtuosity to obscure his vision of interpretive fidelity to the score. While he naturally was a foremost interpreter of the Russian repertoire, not more so than in Prokofiev, he was also rightly acclaimed the world over as a supreme master of the great Romantic repertoire. Few pianists could hope to equal him in Schubert and Schumann, and none ever surpassed him.—NS/LK/DM

Richter-Haaser, Hans, respected German pianist and teacher; b. Dresden, Jan. 6, 1912; d. Braunschweig, Dec. 13, 1980. At age 13, he became a pupil of Hans Schneider at the Dresden Academy of Music, where he won the Bechstein Prize when he was 18. He made his debut in Dresden (1928), and thereafter performed throughout Germany. After his career was interrupted by World War II, he settled in Detmold and conducted the municipal orch. (1946–47); then was a prof. at the North West German Music Academy there (1947–62); concurrently pursued an international career; made his U.S. debut in N.Y. (1959). He was esteemed for his performances of the Classical and Romantic repertoire, winning high praise for his Beethoven. He also composed 2 piano concertos, chamber music, piano pieces, and songs.—NS/LK/DM

Rickards, Steven, accomplished American countertenor; b. Pottstown, Pa., Sept. 19, 1955. He was a student of Russel Oberlin at Oberlin (Ohio) Coll. (1976), of Elizabeth Mannion and Paul Matthen at Indian Univ. (B.Mus.Ed., 1979; M.M., 1984), of Sir Peter Pears at the Britten-Pears School in Aldeburgh (1981), at the Guildhall School of Music and Drama in London (diplomas in singing, 1982, and opera performance, 1983), and of Roy Delp at Fla. State Univ. in Tallahassee (1989–93). While still a student, he was chosen to create the role of Marat in the premiere of Eaton's *Danton and Robespierre* in Bloomington, Ind., in 1979. He won the countertenor prize at the 's-Hertogenbosch Competition and 2nd prize at the Royal Tunbridge Wells Competition in 1982, and then took 2nd prize at the Oratorio Soc. of

N.Y. Competition in 1985. In 1985 he sang Egeo in the U.S. premiere of Handel's *Teseo* in Boston and created the role of Trinculo in the premiere of Eaton's *The Tempest* at the Santa Fe Opera. From 1985 to 1989 he sang with Chanticleer throughout the U.S. and Europe. He portrayed Apollo in Britten's *Death in Venice* with the Opera Co. of Philadelphia in 1988. After appearing as Medarse in the U.S. premiere of Handel's *Siroe* in N.Y. in 1990, he sang Alcandro in Hasse's *L'Olimpiade* at the Semper Opera in Dresden in 1992. He commissioned and gave the first performance of Ladislav Kubik's *Der Weg* in 1993 in Prague. In 1997 he sang St. Francis Xavier in Zipoli's *San Ignacio de Loyola* in Boston. From 1997 to 1999 he toured with Hillier's Theatre of Voices. In addition to his esteemed interpretations of Buxtehude, Bach, Handel, Purcell, and Dowland, Rickards has won distinction for his performances of scores by contemporary composers, among them Britten and Pärt. —NS/LK/DM

Rickenbacher, Karl Anton, Swiss conductor; b. Basel, May 20, 1940. He received his training at the Berlin Städtisches Cons. (1962–66), his mentors in conducting being Karajan and Boulez. After serving as an asst. conductor at the Zürich Opera (1966–69), he was conductor of the Freiburg im Breisgau Opera (1969–74). From 1976 to 1985 he was Generalmusikdirektor of the Westphalian Sym. Orch. in Recklinghausen. He also served as principal conductor of the BBC Scottish Sym. Orch. in Glasgow from 1977 to 1980. In 1983 he appeared for the first time as a guest conductor with the Berlin Phil. and at the Deutsche Oper in Berlin. In 1987 he made his debuts as a guest conductor with the Royal Phil. and the Philharmonia Orch. in London. After making his first appearances in the U.S. during the 1987–88 season, he was a guest conductor with many European and North American orchs. His repertoire embraces the classical, romantic, and modern repertoires.—NS/LK/DM

Ricketts, Frederick J., English bandmaster and composer who used the pseudonym **Kenneth J. Alford**; b. London, Feb. 21, 1881; d. Reigate, Surrey, May 15, 1945. Trained first as an organist, Ricketts graduated from Kneller Hall, afterward serving his longest stint as bandmaster of the Royal Marines (1928–44). In Feb. 1914 he publ., under his pseudonym "Alford" (not to be confused with the American bandmaster and composer Harry L. Alford), his popular march *Col. Bogey*, epitomizing the steadily swinging and moderately paced English military march. *Col. Bogey* reached its height of fame when it was introduced into the film *The Bridge on the River Kwai* (1958).—NS/LK/DM

Ricordi & Co., G., famous Italian music publishing firm of Milan, founded by Giovanni Ricordi (b. Milan, 1785; d. there, March 15, 1853). As 1st violinist and conductor at the Fiando theater, he also earned small sums as a music copyist, and in 1807 went to Leipzig to learn music engraving in Breitkopf & Härtel's establishment. On returning, he opened a little shop and began publishing in 1808, engraving the first works himself. He was a close friend of Rossini, whose operas he publ.; also recognized Verdi's genius when the latter was still unknown. His son Tito Ricordi (b. Milan, Oct. 29, 1811; d. there, Sept. 7, 1888) succeeded to the business. In 1845 he established the *Gazzetta Musicale,* one of the most important Italian music publications; also introduced the *Edizioni Economiche,* and under his administration the house became the largest music publishing firm in Italy. He was on terms of intimate friendship with Verdi, whose works (especially *Aida*) made a fortune for both publisher and author. Owing to ill health, he withdrew from active management in 1887. His successor was his son Guilio Ricordi (b. Milan, Dec. 19, 1840; d. there, June 6, 1912), a man of extraordinary business ability, who continued the policy of expansion. In 1888 he bought, and consolidated with his own, the important firm of Francesco Lucca. It was he who discovered Puccini. A trained musician, he publ., under the pseudonym of J. Burgmein, much elegant salon music (160 opus numbers). He was ed. of the *Gazzetta Musicale* until his death, upon which the magazine ceased publication. His son Tito (b. May 17, 1865; d. Milan, March 30, 1933), a remarkable pianist, was the subsequent head of the house; he retired in 1919, and control of the firm left the family; it became a limited company in 1952. The catalog contains over 120,000 numbers, and in the archives are the autograph scores of more than 550 operas by the most famous Italian composers. The firm has branches in N.Y., Canada, Australia, and South America.

BIBL.: G. Adami, *G. R. e i suoi musicisti* (Milan, 1933); E. di Valperga, *R.* (Rome, 1943); G. Adami, *G. R., L'Amico dei musicisti italiani* (Milan, 1945); C. Sartori, *Casa R., 1808–1958: Profilo storico* (Milan, 1958).—**NS/LK/DM**

Ridder, Anton de, Dutch tenor; b. Amsterdam, Feb. 13, 1929. He studied voice at the Amsterdam Cons. with Herman Mulder (1947–49) and with Jan Keyzer (1951–56). From 1956 to 1962 he was on the roster of the Karlsruhe Opera; then sang at the Gärtnerplatz State Theater in Munich (1962–66). In 1965 he joined the Komische Oper in West Berlin. In 1969 he took part in the Salzburg Festival; also sang in Vienna and Hamburg. In 1972 he appeared at the Edinburgh Festival. He sang Florestan at the Glyndebourne Festival in 1979. In 1985 he again appeared at the Salzburg Festival. He was equally adept at lyric and dramatic tenor parts. —**NS/LK/DM**

Ridderbusch, Karl, admired German bass; b. Recklinghausen, May 29, 1932; d. Wels, near Linz, June 21, 1997. He was a student of Rudolf Schock at the Duisburg Cons. and of Clemens Kaiser-Breme in Essen. In 1961 he made his operatic debut in Münster. After singing in Essen (1963–65), he appeared with the Deutsche Oper am Rhein in Düsseldorf (from 1965). In 1967 he made his debut at the Bayreuth Festival as Titurel, and sang there regularly until 1976. He appeared for the first time in Paris in 1967. On Nov. 21, 1967, he made his Metropolitan Opera debut in N.Y. as Hunding, and returned there as Hans Sachs in 1976. In 1968 he appeared for the first time in Vienna and at the Salzburg Easter Festival. In 1971 he made his debut at London's

Covent Garden. He also sang with many other leading opera houses and toured widely as a concert singer. He was especially noted for his Wagnerian roles. In addition to those already noted, he excelled as King Marke, Fafner, Hagen, and Daland. Among his esteemed non-Wagnerian roles were Rocco, Boris Godunov, Baron Ochs, and the Doktor in *Wozzeck.*—**NS/LK/DM**

Riddle (Jr.), Nelson (Smock), preeminent American arranger, conductor, and composer; b. Oradell, N.J., June 1, 1921; d. Los Angeles, Calif., Oct. 6, 1985. Riddle was the most successful musical arranger of the 1950s, primarily due to his work with Frank Sinatra. He updated the big-band sound of the Swing Era to support the most significant vocalists of the Sing Era, providing sympathetic orchestrations and conducting the backup orchestras for such performers as Nat "King" Cole, Ella Fitzgerald, and others. He also made his own recordings of instrumentals, notably the hit "Lisbon Antigua," and worked extensively as a composer of scores and conductor for motion pictures and television.

Riddle was the son of Nelson Smock Riddle, a commercial artist who played the trombone, and Marie Albertin Rieber Riddle. He began to study the piano at eight and switched to the trombone at 14. After graduating from high school he became a professional trombonist and arranger for the big bands, starting with Jerry Wald's orchestra in 1940, then moving to Charlie Spivak (1940–43), Alvino Rey (1943), Wald again (1944), and, in May 1944, Tommy Dorsey. In 1945 he entered the army, where he played in a service band. He married Doreen Moran on Oct. 10, 1945; they had six children. Discharged in 1947, he joined Bob Crosby's band and moved to Los Angeles, where he became a staff arranger at NBC radio while studying arranging with Mario Castelnuovo-Tedesco and conducting with Victor Bay. He did his first film work writing, directing, and supervising music for an American version of the 1935 Swedish film *Ocean Breakers,* released in the U.S. in December 1949 as *The Surf.*

In 1950, Riddle left NBC to become a freelance arranger. His chart for "Mona Lisa" (music and lyrics by Jay Livingston and Ray Evans), recorded by Nat "King" Cole, brought the singer a million-selling #1 hit in July 1950. This success was repeated with Riddle's arrangement of "Too Young" (music by Sid Lippman, lyrics by Sylvia Dee), which also hit #1 for Cole in June 1951 and sold a million copies. As a result he was hired by Cole's label, Capitol Records, as a music director. He arranged and conducted the orchestra for Ella Mae Morse's recording of "The Blacksmith Blues" (music and lyrics by Jack Holmes), which hit the Top Ten in April 1952 and sold a million copies; he did the same duties on Nat "King" Cole's "Somewhere along the Way" (music by Kurt Adams, lyrics by Sammy Gallop), which hit the Top Ten in August 1952, and "Pretend" (music and lyrics by Lew Douglas, Cliff Parman, and Frank Lavere), which peaked in the Top Ten in May 1953.

Though Riddle worked with many of the artists on Capitol's roster, including Judy Garland, Peggy Lee, Dean Martin, and Margaret Whiting, his two most successful clients were Cole and Frank Sinatra, who joined the label in 1953. His first session with Sinatra occurred on April 30, 1953, and started with a version of "I've Got the World on a String" (music by Harold Arlen, lyrics by Ted Koehler) that became a chart entry in July. By this time long-playing albums, initially in the ten-inch format, were becoming increasingly important, and Riddle pioneered the development of thematically selected "concept" albums such as Nat "King" Cole's *Two in Love*, which reached the charts in January 1954 and became a Top Ten hit, and Sinatra's *Songs for Young Lovers*, a Top Ten hit that reached the charts in February 1954, and *Swing Easy*, which entered the charts in September and also reached the Top Ten.

Singles continued to have commercial appeal, however, and Riddle arranged and conducted a series of hits for the two singers: "Young-at-Heart" (music by Johnny Richards, lyrics by Carolyn Leigh) for Sinatra, a Top Ten hit in March that sold a million copies; Cole's "Answer Me, My Love" (music by Gerhard Winkler and Fred Rauch, English lyrics by Carl Sigman), which reached the Top Ten in April; Sinatra's "Three Coins in the Fountain" (music by Jule Styne, lyrics by Sammy Cahn), in the Top Ten in July; and Cole's "Smile" (music by Charles Chaplin, lyrics by John Turner and Geoffrey Parson), which reached the Top Ten in October.

Riddle's involvement with Sinatra increased in 1955. He arranged and conducted the singer's first 12-inch LP, *In the Wee Small Hours*, which hit #1 in May, as well as the Top Ten singles "Learnin' the Blues" (music and lyrics by Dolores Vicki Silvers), "Love and Marriage" (music by James Van Heusen, lyrics by Sammy Cahn), and "(Love Is) the Tender Trap" (music by James Van Heusen, lyrics by Sammy Cahn). He did the arrangements for the songs Sinatra sang in the film musical *Guys and Dolls*, released in November. At the same time he branched out on his own, composing the score for the film *Flame of the Islands*, released before the end of the year, and recording the single "Lisbon Antigua" (music by Raul Portela, English lyrics by Harry Dupree), which hit #1 in February 1956 and sold a million copies. He followed it up with a recording of Lionel Newman's "Theme from *The Proud Ones*," taken from a current motion picture, which reached the Top 40 in August.

In addition to his own recordings in 1956, Riddle continued to arrange and conduct for Frank Sinatra, handling his album *Songs for Swingin' Lovers!*, which reached the Top Ten in March and went gold, and the single "Hey! Jealous Lover" (music and lyrics by Sammy Cahn, Kay Twomey, and Bee Walker), which reached the Top Ten in November. In between he did arrangements for Sinatra's appearance in the film *High Society*, released in August, and composed and conducted the music for the first film Sinatra produced as well as starred in, *Johnny Concho*, also released in August, including "Johnny Concho Theme (Wait for Me)" (lyrics by Dick Stanford), which Sinatra recorded for a chart entry. A third film release in August was *Lisbon*, for which Riddle wrote the score. In the fall he took on two television assignments, conducting the orchestras on both *The Nat "King" Cole Show* on network TV and *The Rosemary Clooney Show* in syndication; both programs ran into 1957.

Riddle worked on Sinatra's recordings in the first half of 1957 and his films in the second half. He arranged and conducted the small ensemble that accompanied the singer on the album *Close to You*, which hit the Top Ten in February, as well as the larger group heard on *A Swingin' Affair!*, a Top Ten hit in May. Simultaneous with the release of the latter came Riddle's own album, *Hey...Let Yourself Go!*, which made the charts. Riddle handled the musical arrangements for the Sinatra film *The Joker Is Wild*, released in September; it featured "All the Way" (music by James Van Heusen, lyrics by Sammy Cahn), recorded by Sinatra with an orchestra conducted by Riddle for a Top Ten hit. In October came the film *Pal Joey*, also starring Sinatra, for which Riddle did arrangements; the soundtrack album was a Top Ten hit. The same month marked the premiere of *The Frank Sinatra Show* on network television, for which Riddle served as orchestra leader. The show ran through June 1958. Before the end of 1957, Riddle's next scoring assignment, the film *The Girl Most Likely*, was in theaters.

Riddle opened 1958 by arranging and conducting Frank Sinatra's single "Witchcraft" (music by Cy Coleman, lyrics by Carolyn Leigh), which hit the Top Ten in February and earned him a Grammy nomination for Best Arrangement. That month his own album, *C'mon...Get Happy!* reached the charts. In March came the opening of the film *Merry Andrew*, starring Danny Kaye, with a Riddle score. He worked with Nat "King" Cole on the film *St. Louis Blues*, released in April, and arranged and conducted the album *Frank Sinatra Sings for Only the Lonely*, which hit #1 in October and went gold. And he moonlighted away from Capitol on two projects: his own work, *Cross Country Suite*, for Dot Records, which won the 1958 Grammy for Best Composition, Over 5 Minutes' Duration; and, for Verve Records, arranging and conducting Ella Fitzgerald's acclaimed *George and Ira Gershwin Song Book*, a project that extended into 1959 and ran to five LPs.

Riddle didn't do an album with Frank Sinatra for release in 1959, but he did write the score for the Sinatra film *A Hole in the Head*, released in July. He also composed the theme for the television series *The Untouchables*, which premiered in October, and he contributed music to the film version of the Broadway musical *Li'l Abner*, which opened in December and earned him an Academy Award nomination for best score for his trouble. Taking a leaf from Mitch Miller, his next chart album, in January 1960, was called *Sing Along with Riddle*. In March he arranged and conducted Cole Porter's music and wrote the score for the film *Can-Can*, starring Sinatra, and earned another Oscar nomination. The soundtrack album was a Top Ten hit. He composed the score for Sinatra's next film, *Ocean's 11*, which opened in August. He also arranged and conducted Sinatra's next album, *Nice 'n' Easy*. It hit #1 in October and went gold, and the title track earned a Grammy nomination for Best Arrangement. His album *Untouchables* reached the charts in September; the following month marked the premiere of his TV theme for the series *Route 66*. In December, Nat "King" Cole's album *Wild Is Love*, which he had arranged and conducted, hit the Top Ten.

The year 1961 was transitional for Riddle. *Sinatra's Swingin' Session!!!*, which he had arranged and conducted during recording sessions in August and September 1960, was released in January and reached the Top Ten in February. Sinatra, however, was leaving Capitol Records and launching his own Reprise label, which for a time prevented him from recording with Riddle. Riddle would eventually join Reprise, but in the meantime, preparatory to leaving Capitol, he began doing sessions with artists on other labels. He arranged and conducted Johnny Mathis's Columbia album *I'll Buy You a Star*, which reached the charts in April, and in November cut sessions with Ella Fitzgerald that would result in two Verve releases, *Ella Swings Brightly with Nelson* and *Ella Swings Gently with Nelson*.

In the spring of 1962, when the series had been on the air for two seasons, Capitol released Riddle's "*Route 66* Theme" as a single; it reached the Top 40 in August, and an album, *Route 66 Theme and Other Great TV Themes*, charted in September. The single earned Grammy nominations for Best Instrumental Theme and Best Instrumental Arrangement. Meanwhile, Riddle had co-composed the score for the film *Lolita*, released in June, with Bob Harris. Their theme, "Lolita Ya-Ya," was recorded by The Ventures for a singles chart entry in August, and the soundtrack album reached the charts in September.

In 1963, Riddle went to work at Reprise, where he arranged and conducted albums for label artists such as Rosemary Clooney and Bing Crosby. In January he did a second *Song Book* album with Ella Fitzgerald at Verve, this one devoted to the songs of Jerome Kern. He also returned to work with Sinatra, notably composing and conducting the scores for the June film release *Come Blow Your Horn* and *4 for Texas*, released in December, and arranging and conducting the Top Ten albums *The Concert Sinatra* and the gold-selling *Sinatra's Sinatra*. The latter featured a recording of "Call Me Irresponsible" (music by James Van Heusen, lyrics by Sammy Cahn) that earned a Grammy nomination for Best Background Arrangement.

Riddle arranged and conducted Sinatra's album *Days of Wine and Roses, Moon River, and Other Academy Award Winners*, which reached the charts in April 1964 and made the Top Ten. He scored the film *What a Way to Go!*, released in May, and *Robin and the 7 Hoods*, released in August. The latter produced a charting soundtrack album and earned an Academy Award nomination for Best Score. In October, Riddle cut a third *Song Book* album with Ella Fitzgerald for Verve, this one containing songs by Johnny Mercer. Also at Verve he recorded an album with Oscar Peterson, and the LP, simply called *Oscar Peterson—Nelson Riddle*, earned a Grammy nomination for Best Instrumental Jazz Performance, Large Group or Soloist with Large Group.

In 1965, while continuing to arrange and conduct albums for singers, notably Antonio Carlos Jobim (*The Wonderful World of Antonio Carlos Jobim*) and Jack Jones (*There's Love & There's Love & There's Love*), Riddle devoted much of his time to composing film scores, finishing three, *Harlow, Marriage on the Rocks*, and *A Rage to Live*, all released during the year. In 1966 his music was used in the television series *Batman* that premiered in January, and a soundtrack album reached the charts in April. He arranged and conducted most of the tracks on Frank Sinatra's *Strangers in the Night* LP, which hit #1 in July and sold a million copies.

Riddle returned to a performing role on television with the Feb. 5, 1967, premiere of the variety series *The Smothers Brothers Comedy Hour*, leading the orchestra on the show each week through June 1969. During this period he continued to compose and conduct for motion pictures, scoring *El Dorado* (1967), *The Karate Killers* (1967), and *The Great Bank Robbery* (1969) and leading the orchestra on *How to Succeed in Business without Really Trying* (1967). Upon his departure from the Smothers Brothers show he immediately returned to television in September 1969 with *The Leslie Uggams Show*, which ran only through December, meanwhile scoring the film *Paint Your Wagon*, released in October, which brought him his fourth Academy Award nomination. The soundtrack album was a gold record.

Riddle continued to work primarily as a television conductor in the early 1970s, including stints on *The Tim Conway Comedy Hour* (1970), *CBS Newcomers* (1971), *The Julie Andrews Hour* (1972–73), and *The Helen Reddy Show* (1973). He also took on occasional film assignments, notably arranging and conducting the music for the film *On a Clear Day You Can See Forever* (1970) and scoring *The Great Gatsby* (1974), which produced a soundtrack album that spent several months in the charts and for which he finally won the Academy Award. He also wrote music for television. From 1973 he was semiretired due to poor health, although he took on occasional conducting and scoring assignments for film and television.

In 1983, Riddle arranged and conducted the first of three albums of standards for Linda Ronstadt, *What's New*. The album reached the Top Ten and sold three million copies, and the title track, a Top 40 single, won Riddle a Grammy for Best Instrumental Arrangement Accompanying Vocal(s). The second Ronstadt album, *Lush Life*, released in November 1984, sold a million copies, and the title track won Riddle another Grammy for Best Instrumental Arrangement Accompanying Vocal(s). Riddle completed a third album, *For Sentimental Reasons*, with Ronstadt, and an album with opera singer Kiri Te Kanawa, *Blue Skies*, before his death at 64 from cardiac and kidney failure in 1985. *For Sentimental Reasons* was released in September 1986 and went gold.

WORKS (only works for which Riddle was a primary, credited composer are listed): **FILMS:** *The Surf* (1949); *Flame of the Islands* (1955); *Johnny Concho* (1956); *Lisbon* (1956); *The Girl Most Likely* (1957); *Merry Andrew* (1958); *A Hole in the Head* (1959); *Li'l Abner* (1959); *Can-Can* (1960); *Ocean's 11* (1960); *Lolita* (1962); *Come Blow Your Horn* (1963); *4 for Texas* (1963); *What a Way to Go!* (1964); *Robin and the 7 Hoods* (1964); *Harlow* (1965); *Marriage on the Rocks* (1965); *A Rage to Live* (1965); *El Dorado* (1967); *The Karate Killers* (1967); *The Great Bank Robbery* (1969); *Paint Your Wagon* (1969); *Hell's Bloody Devils* (1970); *The Great Gatsby* (1974); *Harper Valley P.T.A.* (1978); *Rough Cut* (1980). **TELEVISION:** *The Untouchables* (1959); *Route 66* (1960); *Sam Benedict* (1962); *The Rogues* (1964); *Batman* (1966); *The Most Deadly Game* (1970); *Emergency!* (1972).—**WR**

Rider-Kelsey, Corinne (née Rider),

American soprano and teacher; b. near Batavia, N.Y., Feb. 24, 1877; d. Toledo, Ohio, July 10, 1947. She studied with Helen Rice at the Oberlin (Ohio) Coll.-Cons. of Music, and then with L. Torrens in Rockford, Ill., where she made her recital debut (1897); after further training with Toedt and his wife in N.Y., she became successful as a concert singer. She made her debut as a soloist in Handel's *Messiah* in St. Louis (Nov. 24, 1904); made her operatic debut as Micaëla at London's Covent Garden (July 2, 1908), but soon abandoned the opera stage to devote herself to a concert career. In 1926 she married the violinist and composer Lynnel Reed; they settled in Toledo, where she was active as a singer and a teacher.

BIBL.: L. Reed, *Be Not Afraid: Biography of Madame R. K.* (N.Y., 1955).—NS/LK/DM

Řídký, Jaroslav,

eminent Czech composer and teacher; b. Františkov, near Liberec, Aug. 25, 1897; d. Poděbrady, Aug. 14, 1956. He took courses in composition at the Prague Cons. (1919–23) with K. Jirák, J. Křička, and E.B. Foerster, continuing his training in Foerster's master class there (1923–26); also studied harp. He was first harpist in the Czech Phil. (1924–38), and also was conductor of its choir (1925–30). He taught theory at the Prague Cons. (1928–48), and was named a teacher (1946) and a prof. (1955) of composition at the Prague Academy of Music.

WORKS: ORCH.: *Sinfonietta* (1923); 7 syms: No. 1 (1924), No. 2 for Orch. and Cello obbligato (1925), No. 3 (1927), No. 4 for Chorus and Orch. (1928), No. 5 (1930–31), No. 6, *The Year 1938* (1938; unfinished), and No. 7 (1955); Violin Concerto (1926); *Overture* (1928–29); 2 cello concertos (1930, 1940); *Serenade* for Strings (1941); Chamber Sinfonietta (1944–45); Piano Concerto (1952); *Slavonic March* (1954). **CHAMBER:** 2 cello sonatas (1923; 1947–48); Clarinet Quintet (1926); 5 string quartets (1926, 1927, 1931, 1933, 1937); *Serenata appassionata* for Cello and Piano (1929); 2 nonets (1933–34; 1943); Wind Quintet (1945); *Joyous Sonatina* for Violin and Piano (1947); Piano Trio (1950–51); piano pieces. **VOCAL:** 2 cantatas: *A Winter Fairytale* (1936) and *To My Fatherland* (1941); choruses.—NS/LK/DM

Ridout, Godfrey,

Canadian composer, teacher, conductor, and writer on music; b. Toronto, May 6, 1918; d. there, Nov. 24, 1984. He studied at the Toronto Cons. with Charles Peaker (organ and counterpoint), Ettore Mazzoleni (conducting), Weldon Kilburn (piano), and Healey Willan (composition). He served on the faculties of the Toronto Cons. (from 1940) and the Univ. of Toronto (from 1948), retiring in 1982. He also was music director of the Eaton Operatic Soc. (1949–58), director of the Composers, Authors, and Publishers Assn. of Canada (1966–73), and a program annotator for the Toronto Sym. (1973–84). With T. Kenins, he ed. the vol. *Celebration* (Toronto, 1984). In his music, Ridout charted an eclectic path notable for its accessible style.

WORKS: DRAMATIC: *La Prima Ballerina*, ballet (1966; Montreal, Oct. 26, 1967); *The Lost Child*, television opera (1976). **ORCH.:** *Ballade No. 1* (1938; Toronto, May 29, 1939) and *No. 2* (1980) for Viola and Strings; *Festal Overture* (1939); *Comedy Overture* (1941); *Dirge* (1943); *2 Études* for Strings (1946; rev. 1951); *Esther*, dramatic sym. for Soprano, Baritone, Chorus, and

Orch. (1951–52; Toronto, April 29, 1952); *Music for a Young Prince*, suite (1959); *Fall Fair* (N.Y., Oct. 24, 1961); *Overture to Colas et Colinette* (1964); *Partita academica* for Concert Band (1969); *Frivolités canadiennes*, after melodies of Joseph Vézina (1973); *Jubilee* (1973); Concerto Grosso No. 1 for Piano, Violin, and Strings (1974; Toronto, Jan. 18, 1975) and No. 2 for Brass Quintet and Orch. (1980); *George III, His Lament*, variations on an old British tune (1975); *Kid's Stuff* (1978); *No Mean City: Scenes from Childhood* (1983). **CHAMBER:** *Folk Song Fantasy* for Piano Trio (1951); *Introduction and Allegro* for Woodwind Quintet, Violin, and Cello (1968); *2 Dances* for Guitar (1976); *Tafelmusik* for Woodwind Ensemble (1976); *A Birthday Fantasy* for Flute, Clarinet, and Bassoon (1982); piano pieces; organ music. **VOCAL:** *Cantiones Mysticae No. 1* for Soprano and Orch. (N.Y., Oct. 16, 1953), *No. 2, The Ascension*, for Soprano, Trumpet, and Strings (Toronto, Dec. 23, 1962) and *No. 3, The Dream of the Rood*, for Baritone or Tenor, Chorus, Orch., and Organ (1972); *The Dance* for Chorus and Orch. (1960); *Pange lingua* for Chorus and Orch. (1960); *4 Sonnets* for Chorus and Orch. (1964); *In Memoriam Anne Frank* for Soprano and Orch. (Toronto, March 14, 1965); *When Age and Youth Unite* for Voice and/or Chorus and Orch. (1966); *Folk Songs of Eastern Canada* for Soprano and Orch. (1967); *The Seasons* for Tenor and Piano Quintet (1980); *Exile* for Narrator and 9 Instruments (1984).—NS/LK/DM

Riegel (later changed to Rigel), Henri (Heinrich) Joseph,

French composer, father of **Henri-Jean Rigel**; b. Wertheim, Franconia, Feb. 9, 1741; d. Paris, May 2, 1799. He was of German extraction. He studied with F.X. Richter in Mannheim and with Jommelli in Stuttgart. In 1767 he went to Paris, and from 1783 to 1788 he belonged to a group of composers associated with the Concert Spirituel. On the title page of several of his works publ. in Paris his name appears as Rigel, and this gallicized form was adopted by his son Henri-Jean, who was born in Paris. Riegel was one of the earliest composers to write ensemble music with piano, publ. as "symphonies" for 2 Violins, Cello, 2 Horns, and Piano. He was a fairly voluminous composer. He wrote several short operas in the manner of the German Singspiel, all of which were produced in Paris unless otherwise given: *Le Savetier et le financier* (Marly, 1778), *L'Automate* (1781), *Rosanie* (1780), *Blanche et Vermeille* (1781), *Lucas et Babet* (1787), *Les Amours du Gros-Caillou* (1786), and *Alix de Beaucaire* (Montansier, 1791). His other works include 6 syms., keyboard concertos, 6 string quartets, several *Sonates de clavecin en quattuor*, a number of piano sonatas, some with violin obbligato, and 3 *Sonates en symphonies* for Piano. During the revolutionary period in France, he composed various pieces celebrating the events.—NS/LK/DM

Riegel, Kenneth,

American tenor; b. Womelsdorf, Pa., April 29, 1938. He studied at the Manhattan School of Music in N.Y. and also at the Metropolitan Opera Studio. He made his operatic debut as the Alchemist in Henze's opera *König Hirsch* with the Santa Fe Opera in 1965; then sang with the Cincinnati Opera, the Houston Opera, the N.Y.C. Opera, and others. On Oct. 22, 1973, he made his debut with the Metropolitan Opera in N.Y. as Iopas in *Les Troyens*. In 1977 he appeared at the Vienna State Opera, in 1978 at the Paris Opéra, in 1979 at Milan's La Scala, in 1981 at the Hamburg State Opera, in 1983 at the Deutsche Oper in Berlin, and in 1985 at London's Covent Garden. In 1988 he was engaged at the Bavarian State Opera in Munich, in 1992 in Salzburg, and in 1996 in Florence. He also toured as a concert artist.—NS/LK/DM

Rieger, Fritz, German conductor; b. Oberaltstadt, June 28, 1910; d. Bonn, Sept. 29, 1978. He was educated at the Prague Academy of Music, taking courses in piano with Langer, composition with Finke, and conducting with Szell. He conducted at the German Opera Theater in Prague (1931–38), the Bremen Opera (1939–41), and the Mannheim National Theater (1947–49). From 1949 to 1966 he was Generalmusikdirektor of the Munich Phil.; also conducted at the Bavarian State Opera in Munich. In 1972–73 he was chief conductor of the Melbourne Sym. Orch.; he also gave guest performances in Japan. In his programs, he gave considerable prominence to modern music. —NS/LK/DM

Riegger, Wallingford (Constantin), outstanding American composer and teacher; b. Albany, Ga., April 29, 1885; d. N.Y., April 2, 1961. At an early age, he was taken by his family to Indianapolis, where he received his primary musical training at home; his father played violin, and his mother, piano. After his father took the family to N.Y. to pursue his business interests (1900), Wallingford learned to play the cello. He then began serious study with Goetschius (theory) and Schroeder (cello) at the Inst. of Musical Art; after graduating in 1907, he went to Berlin, where he studied cello with Robert Hausmann and Anton Hekking and composition with Max Bruch and Edgar Stillman-Kelley at the Hochschule für Musik (1907–10). In 1910 he made his debut as a conductor with Berlin's Blüthner Orch.; then returned to the U.S. and served as a cellist in the St. Paul (Minn.) Sym. Orch. (1911–14); returning to Germany, he worked as a vocal coach and asst. conductor at the operas in Würzburg (1914–15) and Königsberg (1915–16); then was again conductor of Berlin's Blüthner Orch. (1916–17) before returning to the U.S. He taught theory and cello at Drake Univ., Des Moines (1918–22); in 1922, received the Paderewski Prize for his Piano Trio; in 1924, was awarded the E.S. Coolidge Prize for his setting of Keats's *La Belle Dame sans merci*; in 1925, was given the honorary degree of D.Mus. by the Cincinnati Cons. He taught at the Inst. of Musical Art in N.Y. (1924–25) and at the Ithaca Cons. (1926–28); then settled in N.Y., where he became active as a composer and a participant in various modern music societies; took part in the development of electronic instruments (in association with Theremin), and learned to play an electric cello. His music is of a highly advanced nature; a master craftsman, he wrote in disparate styles with an equal degree of proficiency; used numerous pseudonyms for certain works (William Richards, Walter Scotson, Gerald Wilfring Gore, John H. McCurdy, George Northrup, Robert Sedgwick, Leonard Griegg, Edwin Farell, Edgar Long, etc.). After a long period of neglect on the part of the public and the critics, Riegger began to receive recognition; his 3rd Sym. was the choice of the N.Y. Music Critics' Circle in 1948. He received

further attention in 1957 when he was compelled to appear before the House Un-American Activities Committee to explain his self-proclaimed leftist and pro-Communist sympathies.

WORKS: DRAMATIC: Dance: *Bacchanale* (1930; N.Y., Feb. 2, 1931); *Evocation* (N.Y., April 21, 1932; orchestrated 1948); *Frenetic Rhythms: 3 Dances of Daemoniacal Possession* (N.Y., Nov. 19, 1933); *New Dance* (Bennington, Vt., Aug. 3, 1935; also orch. and chamber versions); *Theater Piece* (1935; N.Y., Jan. 19, 1936); *With My Red Fires* (Bennington, Vt., Aug. 13, 1936); *Chronicle* (N.Y., Dec. 20, 1936); *The Cry* (Bennington, Vt., Aug. 7, 1936); *City Nocturne* (Bennington, Vt., Aug. 7, 1936); *4 Chromatic Eccentricities* (Bennington, Vt., Aug. 7, 1936; based on the *4 Tone Pictures* for Piano, 1932); *Candide* (N.Y., May 6, 1937); *Festive Rhythm* (Bennington, Vt., Aug. 13, 1937); *Trend* (Bennington, Vt., Aug. 13, 1937); *Case History No....* (N.Y., Feb. 28, 1937); *Trojan Incident* (N.Y., April 21, 1938); *Machine Ballet* (Toronto, March 1938); *Fancy Fannie's Judgement Day* (1938; N.Y., Feb. 26, 1939); *Pilgrim's Progress* (N.Y., April 20, 1941). **ORCH.:** *The Beggerman*, overture (1912; St. Paul, Minn., 1913; not extant); *Elegie* for Cello and Orch. (1916; Berlin, Feb. 6, 1917); *Triple Jazz: American Polonaise* (1922; N.Y., July 27, 1923); *Rhapsody: 2nd April* (1924–26; N.Y., Oct. 29, 1931); *Holiday Sketches* for Violin and Orch. (1927); *Study in Sonority* (Ithaca, N.Y., Aug. 11, 1927; orig. *Caprice* for 10 Violins); *Fantasy and Fugue* for Organ and Orch. (1930–31; N.Y., Dec. 5, 1932); *Dichotomy* for Chamber Orch. (Berlin, March 10, 1932); *Scherzo* for Chamber Orch. (1932; N.Y., Jan. 30, 1933; also for 2 Pianos); *Consummation* (1939; withdrawn and utilized in *Music for Orchestra*, 1952); *New Dance* (1940; Pittsburgh, Jan. 30, 1942; also for Band, N.Y., July 7, 1942; also dance and chamber versions); *Canon and Fugue* for Strings (1941; Berkeley, Calif., Aug. 1, 1942; also for Orch., 1941; N.Y., Feb. 14, 1944); *Passacaglia and Fugue* for Band (1942; N.Y., June 16, 1943; also for Orch., 1942; Washington, D.C., March 19, 1944); *Processional: Funeral March* for Band (1943; West Point, N.Y., Jan. 23, 1944; also for Orch., 1943; Moscow, July 3, 1945); 4 syms.: No. 1 (1944; N.Y., April 3, 1949; withdrawn), No. 2 (1945; withdrawn), No. 3 (1946–47; N.Y., May 16, 1948), and No. 4 (1956; Urbana, Ill., April 12, 1957); *Evocation* (Vancouver, British Columbia, Nov. 27, 1948; based on the dance piece, 1932); *Music for Brass Choir* for 10 Trumpets, 8 Horns, 10 Trombones, 2 Tubas, and Percussion (N.Y., April 18, 1949); *Music for Orchestra* (1952; N.Y., March 27, 1955; includes *Consummation* for Orch., 1939); *Prelude and Fugue* for Band (Louisville, May 5, 1953); *Variations* for Piano and Orch. (1952–53; Louisville, Feb. 23, 1954); *Variations* for 2 Pianos and Orch. (1952–54; Fish Creek, Wisc., Aug. 1954); *Suite for Younger Orchestras* (1953; N.Y., April 26, 1954); *Dance Rhythms* (1954; Albany, Ga., March 4, 1955); *Overture* (1955; Cincinnati, Oct. 26, 1956); *Preamble and Fugue* (1955; Oklahoma City, March 18, 1956); *Festival Overture* (Boston, May 4, 1957); *Variations* for Violin and Orch. (1958; Louisville, April 1, 1959); *Quintuple Jazz* (Iowa City, May 20, 1959); *Sinfonietta* (1959); *Introduction, Scherzo, and Fugue* for Cello, Winds, and Timpani (Rochester, N.Y., Sept. 30, 1960; a revision of *Introduction and Fugue* for 4 Cellos, 1957); *Duo* for Piano and Orch. (1960). **CHAMBER:** *Reverie* for Cello and Piano (1918); *Piano Trio* (1919–20); *Whimsy* for Cello or Violin and Piano (1920); *Meditation* for Cello or Violin and Piano (1927); *Suite for Flute* (1928–29); *3 Canons for Woodwinds* for Flute, Oboe, Clarinet, and Bassoon (1931); *Divertissement* for Flute, Cello, and Harp (1933); *New Dance* for 2 Pianos, or Piano, 4-Hands, or Violin and Piano, or Solo Piano (1935; also orch. and band versions, 1940–42); *Music for Voice and Flute* (1936–37); 2 string quartets (1938–39; 1948); *Duos for 3 Woodwinds* for Flute, Oboe, and Clarinet (1943); *Violin*

Sonatina (1947); Piano Quintet (1950–51); Nonet for Brass for 3 Trumpets, 2 Horns, 3 Trombones, and Tuba (1951); *Canon on a Ground Bass of Purcell* for Strings (1951); *Blaserquintett*, woodwind quintet (1952); Concerto for Piano and Woodwind Quintet (1953); *Variations* for Violin and Viola (1957); *Movement* for 2 Trumpets, Trombone, and Piano (1957); *Introduction and Fugue* for 4 Cellos (1957; rev. as *Introduction, Scherzo, and Fugue* for Cello, Winds, and Timpani, 1960); *Cooper Square* for Accordion (1958). **P i a n o :** *Blue Voyage* (1927); *Scherzo* for 2 Pianos (1932; also for Chamber Orch., 1932); *4 Tone Pictures* (1932; dance version as *4 Chromatic Eccentricities*, 1932); *New and Old: 12 Pieces for Piano* (1944); *Variations* for 2 Pianos (1952–53). **V O - C A L :** *La Belle Dame sans merci* for Tenor, Women's Voices, and 7 Instruments (1921–24); *Eternity* for Women's Voices and 4 Instruments (1942); *From Some Far Shore* for 4 Voices and Piano or Organ (1946); *Easter Passacaglia: Ye Watchers and Ye Holy Ones* for 4 Voices and Piano or Organ (1946); *Little Sam: Little Black Sambo* for Narrator and Chamber Orch. (1946); *Who Can Revoke?* for 4 Voices and Piano (1948); *In Certainty of Song*, cantata for 4 Solo Voices, 4 Voices, and Piano or Chamber Orch. (1950); *Non vincit malitia: Evil Shall Not Prevail* for Antiphonal Chorus (1951); *A Child Went Forth* for 4 Voices and Oboe (1953); *A Shakespeare Sonnet* for Baritone, Chorus, and Piano or Chamber Orch. (1956); also solo songs; more than 700 arrangements of carols, anthems, and folk songs. **OTHER:** Several vols. of pedagogical works.

BIBL.: J. Schmoll, *An Analytical Study of the Principal Instrumental Compositions of W. R.* (diss., Northwestern Univ., 1954); P. Freeman, *The Compositional Technique of W. R. as Seen in Seven Major Twelve- tone Works* (diss., Eastman School of Music, 1963); D. Garwood, *W. R.: A Biography and Analysis of Selected Works* (diss., George Peabody Coll. for Teachers, 1970); L. Ott, *An Analysis of the Later Orchestral Style of W. R.* (diss., Mich. State Univ., 1970); N. Savage, *Structure and Cadence in the Music of W. R.* (diss., Stanford Univ., 1972); S. Spackman, *W. R.: Two Essays in Musical Biography* (Brooklyn, N.Y., 1982).—**NS/LK/DM**

Riehl, Wilhelm Heinrich von, German writer on music; b. Biebrich-on-Rhine, May 6, 1823; d. Munich, Nov. 16, 1897. He studied at the Univ. of Munich, where he became (1854) a prof. of political economy and also lectured on music history. He publ. the valuable compendium *Musikalische Charakterköpfe* (3 vols., 1853–61; 6th ed., 1879) and 2 vols. of original songs, *Hausmusik* (1856, 1877). Posthumous publications include *Zur Geschichte der romantischen Oper* (Berlin, 1928) and *Musik im Leben des Volkes*, a collection of articles, ed by J. Müller-Blattau (Kassel, 1936).

BIBL.: H. Simonsfeld, *H. R. als Kulturhistoriker* (Munich, 1899); V. von Geramb, *W.H. R.: Leben und Wirken* (Salzburg, 1954).—**NS/LK/DM**

Riemann, (Karl Wilhelm Julius) Hugo, eminent German musicologist; b. Gross-Mehlra, near Sondershausen, July 18, 1849; d. Leipzig, July 10, 1919. He began his training with his father, Robert Riemann, a landowner and civil servant, who was an amateur musician. He then continued his study of theory in Sondershausen with Heinrich Frankenberger, August Bartel, and Theodor Ratzenberger, and also took courses at the Sondershausen and Arnstadt Gymnasiums. After studying classical languages and literature at the Rossleben Klosterschule (1865–68), he took courses in law and German philology and history at the Univ. of Berlin and in philosophy at the Univ. of Tübingen. He studied harmony with Jadassohn and piano and composition with Reinecke in Leipzig (1871–72), then received his Ph.D. in 1873 from the Univ. of Göttingen with the diss. *Über das musikalische Hören* (publ. in Leipzig, 1874; also publ. as *Musikalische Logik*, Leipzig, 1873). He taught at Bielefeld (1876–78); after qualifying as a lecturer at the Univ. of Leipzig (1878), he taught in Bromberg (1880–81); then taught piano and theoretical courses at the Hamburg Cons. (1881–90); after a brief stay in Sondershausen (1890), he taught at the Wiesbaden Cons. (1890–95). In 1895 he resumed his lectures at the Univ. of Leipzig; was made prof. in 1905, and also director of the Collegium Musicum in 1908 and of the Forschungsinstitut für Musikwissenschaft in 1914. He was honored with a Mus.Doc. from the Univ. of Edinburgh (1899) and with a Festschrift on his 60th birthday.

The mere bulk of Riemann's writings, covering every branch of musical science, constitutes a monument of indefatigable industry, and is proof of enormous concentration and capacity for work. When one takes into consideration that much of this work is the result of painstaking research and of original, often revolutionary, thinking, one must share the great respect and admiration in which Riemann was held by his contemporaries. Although many of his ideas are now seen in a different light, his works treating of harmony were considered to constitute the foundation of modern music theory. His researches in the field of music history have solved a number of vexing problems, and thrown light on others. And, finally, in formulating the new science of musicology, the labors of Riemann were of great significance. His name is indelibly linked to the *Musik-Lexikon* that bears his cognomen. He contributed innumerable articles to various journals, a collection of which was publ. as *Präludien und Studien* (3 vols., 1895, 1900, 1901). He also wrote numerous pedagogical works.

WRITINGS (all publ. in Leipzig unless otherwise given): *Die objektive Existenz der Untertöne in der Schallwelle* (Berlin, 1877); *Studien zur Geschichte der Notenschrift* (1878); *Die Entwickelung unserer Notenschrift*, Sammlung Musikalischer Vorträge, XXVIII (1881); *Musik-Lexikon* (1882; 8th ed., 1916; A. Einstein edited the 9th to 11th eds., 1919, 1922, 1929; W. Gurlitt edited the 12th ed., 3 vols., Mainz, 1959, 1961, 1967; C. Dahlhaus edited a suppl., 2 vols., Mainz, 1972, 1975; Dahlhaus and H. Eggebrecht edited the *Brockhaus-Riemann Musik-Lexikon*, 2 vols., Wiesbaden and Mainz, 1978; suppl., 1989); *Die Natur der Harmonik*, Sammlung Musikalischer Vorträge, XL (1882); *Der Ausdruck in der Musik*, ibid., L (1883); *Musikalische Dynamik und Agogik: Lehrbuch der musikalischen Phrasierung* (Hamburg, 1884); *Opern-Handbuch* (1887; 2nd ed., 1893; reprint with suppl. by F. Stieger, 1979); *Wie hören wir Musik?: Drei Vorträge* (1885; 5th ed., 1921); *Katechismus der Musikinstrumente (Instrumentationslehre)* (1888; 8th ed., 1923, as *Handbuch der Musikinstrumente*; Eng. tr., 1888); *Katechismus der Musikgeschichte* (1888; 5th ed., 1914; Eng. tr., 1892); *Katechismus der Orgel (Orgellehre)* (1888; 2nd ed., 1901; 6th ed., n.d., as *Handbuch der Orgel*); *Katechismus der Musik (Allgemeine Musiklehre)* (1888; 8th ed., 1922; Eng. tr., n.d.); *Grundlinien der Musik-Ästhetik (Wie hören wir Musik?)* (1890; 3rd ed., 1911, as *Katechismus der Musikästhetik*; Eng. tr., 1895); *Präludien und Studien: Gesammelte Aufsätze zur Ästhetik, Theorie und Geschichte der*

Musik (Vol. I, Frankfurt am Main, 1895; Vols. II and III, Leipzig, 1900, 1901); *Geschichte der Musiktheorie im IX.–XIX. Jahrhundert* (1898; 2nd ed., 1921; Eng. tr., 1962); *Die Elemente der musikalischen Ästhetik* (Berlin, 1900); *Geschichte der Musik seit Beethoven (1800–1900)* (Berlin and Stuttgart, 1901); *Beethovens Streichquartette* (Berlin, 1903); *System der musikalischen Rhythmik und Metrik* (1903); *Handbuch der Musikgeschichte* (Vol. i/I, 1904; 2nd ed., 1919; 3rd ed., 1923; Vol. i/2, 1905; 2nd ed., 1920; Vol. ii/I, 1907; 2nd ed., 1920; A. Einstein edited Vol. ii/2, 1912; 3rd ed., 1921; and Vol. ii/3, 1913; 2nd ed., 1922); *Das Problem des harmonischen Dualismus: Ein Beitrag zur Ästhetik der Musik* (1905); *Kleines Handbuch der Musikgeschichte mit Periodisierug nach Stilprinzipien und Formen* (1908; 7th ed., 1947); *Grundriss der Musikwissenschaft* (1908; 4th ed., 1928, by J. Wolf); *Die byzantinische Notenschrift im 10. bis 15. Jahrhundert* (1909); *Musikgeschichte in Beispielen* (3 vols., 1911–12; A. Schering edited the 2nd to 4th eds., 1921–29); *Neue Beiträge zur Lösung der Probleme der byzantinischen Notenschrift* (1915); *Folkloristische Tonalitätsstudien* (1916); *L. van Beethovens sämtliche Klaviersolosonaten: Ästhetische und formaltechnische Analyse* (Berlin, 1918–19; 4th ed., 1920).

BIBL.: *R.-Festschrift* (Leipzig, 1909); H. Grabner, *Die Funktionstheorie H. R.s und ihre Bedeutung für die praktische Analyse* (Munich, 1923); H. Denecke, *Die Kompositionslehre H. R.s* (diss., Univ. of Kiel, 1937); G. Sievers, *Die Grundlagen H. R.s bei Max Reger* (diss., Univ. of Hamburg, 1949); G. Wienke, *Voraussetzungen der "musikalischen Logik" bei H. R.: Studien zur Musikästhetik in der 2. Halfte des 19. Jahrhunderts* (diss., Univ. of Freiburg, 1952); W. Mickelsen, *H. R.'s History of Harmonic Theory with a Translation of Harmonielehre* (diss., Ind. Univ., 1971). **—NS/LK/DM**

Riemenschneider, (Charles) Albert,

American organist, conductor, and educator; b. Berea, Ohio, Aug. 31, 1878; d. Akron, July 20, 1950. He began his musical training with his father, Karl Riemenschneider, president of the Methodist Episcopal Deutsches Wallace Kollegium in Berea, then studied piano, organ, and theory with James Rogers in Cleveland (1896–1902). He also taught piano and organ at his father's school (from 1896), becoming director of its music dept. (1897). Subsequently he studied piano with Hugo Reinhold and composition with R. Fuchs in Vienna (1902–03), organ with Charles Clemens in Cleveland (1903), and organ with Guilmant and composition with Widor in Paris (1904–10). Throughout this period he continued to teach at his father's school, which merged with Baldwin-Wallace Coll. in 1913 to form the Baldwin-Wallace Cons. of Music; thereafter he served as its president until his retirement in 1947; also conducted the Baldwin-Wallace Bach Festival from 1933. He amassed a valuable Bach collection, which was bequeathed to Baldwin-Wallace Coll. in 1951. The Riemenschneider Bach Inst. was founded in 1969; it publishes the journal Bach. He ed. several of Bach's vocal works. **—NS/LK/DM**

Riepel, Joseph,

Austrian violinist, music theorist, and composer; b. Horschlag (baptized), Jan. 22, 1709; d. Regensburg, Oct. 23, 1782. He studied philosophy at the Univ. of Graz, then music in Dresden (1740–45). He was a musician in the chapel of the count of Thurn und Taxis in Regensburg from 1751. His historical importance rests upon his valuable treatises. He composed syms., 3 violin concertos with string quartet accompaniment, divertimentos, canons, etc.

WRITINGS: *Anfangsgründe zur musikalischen Setzkunst, nicht zwar nach altmathematischer Einbildungsart der Zirkel-Harmonisten, sondern durchgehends mit sichtbaren Exemplen abgefasset*, I, *De rhythmopoeia oder Von der Taktordnung* (Regensburg and Vienna, 1752; 2nd ed., 1754); II, *Grundregeln der Tonordnung insgemein* (Frankfurt am Main and Leipzig, 1755); III, *Gründliche Erklärung der Tonordnung insbesondere, zugleich aber für die mehresten Organisten insgemein* (Frankfurt am Main and Leipzig, 1757); IV, *Erläuterung der betrüglichen Tonordnung* (Augsburg, 1765); V, *Unentbehrliche Anmerkungen zum Kontrapunkt* (Regensburg, 1768); *Harmonisches Silbenmass, Dichtern melodischer Werke gewidmet und angehenden Singkomponisten zur Einsicht mit platten Beispielen gesprächweise abgefasst* (2 vols., Regensburg, 1776; vol. 3 in MS); *Basschlüssel, das ist Anleitung für Anfanger und Liebhaber der Setkunst* (ed. by J. Schubarth, Regensburg, 1786).

BIBL.: W. Twittenhoff, *Die musiktheoretischen Schriften J. R.s* (Halle, 1935); E. Schwarzmaier, *Die Takt- und Tonordnung J. R.s* (Wolfenbüttel, 1936); J. Merkl, *J. R. als Komponist* (Kallmünz, 1937); A. Feil, *Satztechnische Fragen in den Kompositionslehren von F.E. Niedt, J. R., und H.Chr. Koch* (Heidelberg, 1955). **—NS/LK/DM**

Ries, Ferdinand,

noted German pianist and composer, son of **Franz (Anton) Ries** and brother of **(Pieter) Hubert Ries**; b. Bonn (baptized), Nov. 28, 1784; d. Frankfurt am Main, Jan. 13, 1838. He studied piano and violin with his father and cello with B.H. Romberg; after further studies with Peter von Winter in Munich (1801), he continued his piano studies with Beethoven in Vienna (1801–04); also had composition lessons with Albrechtsberger. He made his debut in Beethoven's C-minor Concerto in Vienna on Aug. 1, 1804, and later made successful tours in Germany, Scandinavia, and Russia (1809–13); then went to London, where he made his debut at a Phil. Concert on March 14, 1814. He returned to Germany in 1824, settling in Frankfurt am Main in 1827. He was active as a conductor and composer with the Lower Rhine Music Festivals, and also served as conductor of the municipal orch. and Singakademie in Aachen from 1834. His music reflects the spirit and technique, if not the genius, of Beethoven's style. With F. Wegeler, he prepared the vol. *Biographische Notizen über Ludwig van Beethoven* (Koblenz, 1838; Nachtrag by Wegeler, Koblenz, 1845; new ed. by A. Kalischer, Berlin, 1906); although a valuable early source, it must be used with caution, since Ries dictated parts of it to Wegeler late in life.

WORKS: DRAMATIC: Opera: *Die Räuberbraut* (Frankfurt am Main, 1828); *Liska, oder Die Hexe von Gyllensteen* (perf. in London as *The Sorceress*, 1831); *Die Nacht auf dem Libanon* (1834). **Melodrama:** *Die Zigeunerin* (1835). **OTHER:** 2 oratorios; a Requiem; 8 syms.; 5 overtures; chamber music; numerous piano sonatas and other pieces for piano; songs.

BIBL.: C. Hill, *The Music of F. R.: A Thematic Catalogue* (Armidale, New South Wales, 1977).**—NS/LK/DM**

Ries, Franz (Anton),

German violinist, father of **Ferdinand Ries** and **(Pieter) Hubert Ries;** b. Bonn, Nov. 10, 1755; d. Godesberg, Nov. 1, 1846. He studied violin as a child with J.P. Salomon, and entered the Court

Orch. when he was 11. After successful appearances in Vienna as a soloist and chamber music player in 1779, he was given a court appointment by the Elector Maximilian in Bonn that same year; was also active as a teacher, Beethoven being one of his students. Ries lost his court position when the French dissolved the electoral court in 1794, and thereafter eked out a living mainly by teaching.—NS/LK/DM

Ries, Franz, German violinist and music publisher, son of **(Pieter) Hubert Ries;** b. Berlin, April 7, 1846; d. Naumberg, June 20, 1932. He studied violin with his father and later with Massart and Vieuxtemps in Paris. His career as a concert violinist was brief, and in 1875 he entered the music publishing business. From 1881 to 1924 he was director of the firm Ries & Erler in Berlin; in 1924 his son Robert Ries (1889/1942) became the proprietor; after the death of Robert Ries, the firm was taken over by his 2 daughters.—NS/LK/DM

Ries, (Pieter) Hubert, German violinist and composer, brother of **Ferdinand Ries** and son of **Franz (Anton) Ries;** b. Bonn, April 1, 1802; d. Berlin, Sept. 14, 1886. He studied violin with his father, and then with Spohr, and also studied composition with Hauptmann. He settled in Berlin in 1824 as a member of the orch. of the Königstadt Theater. He joined the Court Orch. in 1825, and became director of the Phil. Soc. in 1835, and its concertmaster in 1836; was also active as a teacher until his retirement in 1872. He wrote 2 violin concertos, chamber music, and studies and duets for violin, and also publ. a *Violinschule* (in Eng., 1873).—NS/LK/DM

Rieti, Vittorio, Italian-born American composer and teacher; b. Alexandria, Egypt, Jan. 28, 1898; d. N.Y., Feb. 19, 1994. He studied with Frugatta in Milan, then took courses with Respighi and Casella in Rome, where he lived until 1940, when he emigrated to the U.S.; he became a naturalized American citizen on June 1, 1944. He taught at the Peabody Cons. of Music in Baltimore (1948–49), Chicago Musical Coll. (1950–53), Queens Coll. in N.Y. (1958–60), and N.Y. Coll. of Music (1960–64). His style of composition represents an ingratiating synthesis of cosmopolitan modern tendencies.

WORKS: DRAMATIC: O p e r a : *Orfeo tragedia* (1928; withdrawn); *Teresa nel bosco* (1933; Venice, Sept. 15, 1934); *Don Perlimplin* (1949; Urbana, Ill., March 30, 1952); *Viaggio d'Europa*, radio opera (1954); *The Pet Shop* (1957; N.Y., April 14, 1958); *The Clock* (1959–60); *Maryam the Harlot* (1966). B a l l e t : *L'Arca di Noe* (1923; only orch. suite extant); *Robinson et Vendredi* (1924); *Barabau* (London, Dec. 11, 1925); *Le Bal* (Monte Carlo, May 1929); *David triomphant* (Paris, May 1937); *Hippolyte* (1937); *The Night Shadow* (1941; N.Y., Feb. 1946); *Waltz Academy* (Boston, Oct. 1944); *The Mute Wife* (N.Y., Nov. 1944); *Trionfo di Bacco e Arianna*, ballet-cantata (1946–47; N.Y., Feb. 1948); *Native Dancer* (1959; based on the Sym. No. 5); *Conundrum* (1961); *A Sylvan Dream* (1965; Indianapolis, Oct. 1, 1982); *Scenes Seen* (1975; Indianapolis, March 25, 1976); *Verdiana* (1983; Indianapolis, Feb. 16, 1984); *Indiana* (1984; Indianapolis, Sept. 14, 1985); *Kaleidoscope* (1987; Indianapolis, April 30, 1988). O R C H . : Woodwind Concerto (1923; Prague, May 31, 1924); *Noah's Ark*, symphonic suite (1925); 2 *Pastorali* for Chamber Orch. (1925); 3 piano

concertos (1926; 1930–37; 1955); *Madrigale* for Chamber Orch. (1927); 2 violin concertos: No. 1, *Concerto napoletano* (1928; Paris, May 1930) and No. 2 (1969); 8 syms.: No. 1 (1929; Paris, Jan. 1930), No. 2 (1930; Brussels, April 1931), No. 3, *Sinfonietta* (Paris, May 1932), No 4, *Sinfonia tripartita* (1942; St. Louis, Dec. 16, 1944), No. 5 (1945; Venice, Sept. 1947), No. 6 (1973; N.Y., Dec. 11, 1974), No. 7 (1977), and No. 8, *Sinfonia breve* (Lafayette, Ind., May 2, 1987); *Serenata* for Violin and Chamber Orch. (1931); 2 cello concertos: No. 1 for Cello and Chamber Orch. (1934) and No. 2 (1953); *Concerto du Loup* (1938); Partita for Harpsichord and Chamber Orch. (1946); Concerto for 2 Pianos and Orch. (1951); Harpsichord Concerto (1952–55; rev. 1972); *Introduction e gioco delle ore* (1953); *Dance Variations* for Strings (1956); *La fontaine*, suite (1968; N.Y., Nov. 1, 1969); *Concerto Triplo* for Violin, Viola, Piano, and Orch. (1971; N.Y., Jan. 27, 1973); Concerto for String Quartet and Orch. (1976; N.Y., Feb. 1, 1978); *Concertino pro San Luca* for 10 Instruments (1984); *Concertino Novello* for 10 Instruments (1986); *Congedo* for 12 Instruments (1987); *Enharmonic Variations* for Piano and Chamber Orch. (N.Y., Feb. 4, 1988). CHAMBER: Sonata for Flute, Oboe, Bassoon, and Piano (1924); 5 string quartets (1926, 1941, 1951, 1960, 1988); Woodwind Quintet (1957); Octet for Piano and 7 Instruments (1971); Piano Trio (1972); Piano Quartet (1973); *Allegretto alla croma* for Flute, Oboe, Clarinet, Bassoon, Strings, and Piano (1981); *Romanza lidica* for Clarinet and Piano (1984); Piano Quintet (1989); numerous works for solo piano; pieces for 2 pianos.

BIBL.: F. Ricci, *V. R.* (Naples, 1987).—NS/LK/DM

Rietz, (August Wilhelm) Julius, German cellist, conductor, music editor, and composer; b. Berlin, Dec. 28, 1812; d. Dresden, Sept. 12, 1877. He was of a musical family: his father was a court musician, and his brother was a friend of Mendelssohn. Julius studied cello and played in theater orchs. in Berlin. In 1834 he became 2nd conductor of the Düsseldorf Opera, and from 1847 to 1854 he was chief conductor of the Leipzig Opera; from 1848 to 1860 he served as chief conductor of the Leipzig Gewandhaus Orch. In 1860 he became Hofkapellmeister in Dresden, being named Generalmusikdirektor in 1874; was also artistic director of the Cons. there (from 1870). A scholarly musician and competent conductor, Rietz was also an excellent music editor. He prepared for publication the complete edition of Mendelssohn's works for Breitkopf & Härtel (1874–77), and also ed. Mozart's operas and syms., Beethoven's overtures, etc. As a composer, he followed the musical style of Mendelssohn, numbering among his works 9 syms., a Cello Concerto, incidental music, and songs.

BIBL.: H. Zimmer, *J. R.* (diss., Univ. of Berlin, 1943). —NS/LK/DM

Rifkin, Joshua, American conductor, pianist, harpsichordist, and musicologist; b. N.Y., April 22, 1944. He studied in N.Y. at the H.S. of Music and Art, took courses in theory and composition at the Juilliard Preparatory Division, and received lessons in piano from David Labovitz. He pursued training in composition at the Juilliard School of Music (B.S., 1964), and also attended the composition courses of Stockhausen in Darmstadt (summers, 1961, 1965). His studies in musicology were undertaken at N.Y.U. (1964–66), and he also studied composition with Lutyens in Dartington (summers, 1965–66). After attending the Univ. of Göttingen on a Fulbright scholarship in 1966–67, he completed his training in musicology at Princeton Univ. (M.F.A., 1970). From 1963 to 1975 he was associated with Nonesuch Records in N.Y. In 1970 he joined the faculty of Brandeis Univ. as an instructor, and then served as an asst. (1971–77) and assoc. (1977–82) prof. there. From 1975 to 1982 he was active with L'Ensemble of N.Y. Rifkin founded the Bach Ensemble in 1978, which he led in historically informed performances that were often controversial but always stimulating. He led it on various tours of the U.S. and abroad, making debut appearances in England, Germany, and Italy in 1988, Canada and Belgium in 1992, Austria, France, and Poland in 1993, and Australia in 1997. As a guest conductor, he appeared with the St. Louis Sym. Orch. in 1985, the Victorian State Sym. Orch. in Melbourne, the San Francisco Sym., and the St. Paul (Minn.) Chamber Orch. in 1989, the Los Angeles Chamber Orch. in 1990, the City of London Sinfonia in 1996, the Jerusalem Sym. Orch. and the Prague Chamber Orch. in 1997, and the National Arts Centre Orch. in Ottawa and the Houston Sym. Orch. in 1999, among others. In 1999 he was awarded an honorary doctorate by the Univ. of Dortmund. His articles have appeared in scholarly books and many learned journals. In addition to his espousal of early music, Rifkin's varied repertoire includes scores by the Classical, Romantic, and contemporary masters, as well as rags and tangos.—NS/LK/DM

Rigatti, Giovanni Antonio, Italian composer; b. Venice, 1615; d. there, Oct. 25, 1649. He entered the priesthood and served at San Marco and at S. Maria Formosa in Venice. After holding the position of maestro di cappella at Udine Cathedral (1635–37), he returned to Venice as a chorister at San Marco and as a teaching of singing at the Cons. degli Incurabili. About 1646 he became maestro di cappella to the Patriarch of Venice. Rigatti was a particularly fine composer of church music. Among his extant sacred works are 2 vols. of solo motets, 3 vols. of concertato motets, and 4 vols. of Psalms. Two vols. of his secular vocal music are also extant.—LK/DM

Rigel, Henri-Jean, French pianist, teacher, and composer, son of **Henri (Heinrich) Joseph Riegel;** b. Paris, May 11, 1772; d. Abbeville, Dec. 16, 1852. After receiving lessons in piano and composition from his father, he entered the École Royale de Chant (1784), where he was made a sous-maître de solfège (1785). His works were given at the Concert Spirituel (from 1787). He taught at the Paris Cons. (1795–97), then accompanied Napoleon on his expedition to Egypt (1798), where he served as music director of the new French Theater in Cairo (until 1800). Upon his return to Paris (1800), he became active as a piano teacher and accompanist; Napoleon made him pianiste de la musique particulière de l'Empereur et Roi; he also acquired distinction as a composer. He wrote numerous works, including 2 comic operas, Les Deux Meuniers (Cairo, 1799) and Le

Duel nocturne (Paris, Dec. 23, 1805), many other vocal works, a Sym., 4 piano concertos, other orch. pieces, chamber music, and piano pieces. Many of his works are lost.—NS/LK/DM

Righetti-Giorgi, Geltrude, outstanding Italian contralto; b. Bologna, 1793; d. there, 1862. She studied in Bologna, making her debut there (1814) under the name Righetti. After her marriage to the lawyer Giorgi (1815), she retired from the stage, only to be convinced of her vocal gifts by Rossini. She subsequently distinguished herself in his operas, creating Rosina in his Il Barbiere di Siviglia (1816) and the title role in his La Cenerentola (1817). She continued to sing regularly until 1822, making her last appearance in 1836.—NS/LK/DM

Righini, Vincenzo, Italian tenor, conductor, singing teacher, and composer; b. Bologna, Jan. 22, 1756; d. there, Aug. 19, 1812. He was a choirboy at Bologna's S. Petronio, making his debut in Parma (1775). He then became a member of Bustelli's opera company in Prague (1776), the same year that he wrote for it his first opera, Il Convitato di pietra, which proved successful. He abandoned his singing career and went to Vienna as a singing master to Princess Elisabeth of Württemberg and director of the Italian Opera (1780). From 1787 to 1793 he was Kapellmeister at the Mainz electoral court. In 1788 he married the contralto Anna Maria Lehritter (1762–93). In 1793 he became court Kapellmeister and director of the Italian Opera in Berlin, where he was an influential figure. In 1793 he married the singer Henriette Kneisel (1767–1801); they divorced in 1800. After the Italian Opera was dissolved in the wake of war in 1806, he bided his time until the royal theater was reorganized in 1811, after which he and B.A. Weber shared the duties of Kapellmeister. In 1812 he returned to his homeland. In addition to his operas, Righini wrote a number of successful instrumental works and songs.

Works: DRAMATIC: Il Convitato di pietra, ossia Il Dissoluto punito, dramma tragicomico (Prague, 1776; as Das steinerne Gastmahl, oder Der Ruchlose, Vienna, 1777); La bottega del café, commedia giocosa (Prague, 1778); La Vedova scaltra, dramma giocoso (Prague, 1778); Armida, dramma (Vienna, 1782; rev. Berlin, 1799); L'incontro inaspettato, dramma giocoso (Vienna, 1785; as Die unvermutete Zusammenkunft, Berlin, 1793); Il Demogorgone, ovvero Il Filosofo confuso, opera buffa (Vienna, 1786); Antigono, dramma serio (Mainz, 1788); Alcide al bivio, azione teatrale (Koblenz, 1790; rev. as a cantata, Vienna, 1804); Vasco di Gama, opera (Berlin, 1792; pasticcio in collaboration with others); Enea nel Lazio, dramma eroi- tragico (Berlin, 1793); Il trionfo d'Arianna, dramma (Berlin, 1793); Atalante e Meleagro, festa teatrale (Berlin, 1793); La Gerusalemme liberata, ossia Arminda al campo de' franchi, dramma (Berlin, 1799); Tigrane, dramma eroico (Berlin, 1800); Minerva belebet die Statue des Dädalus, pantomimischer Tanz (Berlin, 1802); La selva incantata, opera (Berlin, 1803); also an oratorio, Der Tod Jesu (1790). **OTHER:** Missa solemnis (1790); Te Deum (1810); masses and other sacred pieces; cantatas and occasional works; many songs; piano pieces; etc.

Bibl.: K.-J. Kleinicke, Das kirchenmusikalische Schaffen von V. R.: Beiträge zur Biographie des Komponisten (Tutzing, 1984); C. Henzel, Die italienische Hofoper in Berlin um 1800: V. R. als preussischer Hofkapellmeister (Stuttgart, 1994).—NS/LK/DM

Righteous Brothers, The, pioneers of the "blue-eyed soul" sound; Bill Medley, bs.-bar. (b. Santa Ana, Calif., Sept. 19, 1940); and Bobby Hatfield, ten. (b. Beaver Dam, Wisc., Aug. 10, 1940).

Bill Medley and Bobby Hatfield formed a vocal duo in 1961 and recorded for Smash Records as The Paramours. They ostensibly received the name The Righteous Brothers from fans attending performances during a six-month engagement at The Black Derby in Santa Ana, Calif. Switching to the small Hollywood label Moonglow, the duo scored their first moderate hit with Medley's "Little Latin Lupe Lu" in 1963. Building a regional following, The Righteous Brothers reached a national audience through regular appearances on television's *Hullabaloo* and *Shindig* shows beginning in 1964.

In June 1964, Medley and Hatfield accepted an offer to record for producer Phil Spector, and, by early 1965, they had scored a top pop and British and smash rhythm-and-blues hit with "You've Lost That Lovin' Feelin,'" written by Spector, Barry Mann, and Cynthia Weil, on Spector's Philles label. A stunning recording featuring layers of orchestration and a near-orgasmic vocal performance by Medley and Hatfield, the single came to be regarded as one of the greatest ever recorded. Under Spector, The Righteous Brothers recorded three more smash crossover hits, "Just Once in My Life," written by Spector, Carole King, and Gerry Goffin; and the Tin Pan Alley standards "Unchained Melody" and "Ebb Tide."

By late 1965, The Righteous Brothers had switched to the Verve subsidiary of MGM Records, where they scored a top pop and major rhythm-and-blues hit with the Spector-styled "(You're My) Soul and Inspiration," written by Barry Mann and Cynthia Weil. After the major hit "He," The Righteous Brothers managed only moderate-to-minor hits through 1967, and, by 1968, the duo had broken up. Medley subsequently pursued a solo recording career on MGM, achieving moderate hits with "Brown Eyed Woman" and "Peace Brother Peace" in 1968. He recorded for MGM through 1970 and then switched to A&M Records. In the meantime, Hatfield recruited Jimmy Walker, a former member of The Knickerbockers (1965's "Lies"), for a sole Righteous Brothers album and recorded a solo album.

The duo reunited in 1974 on Dennis Lambert and Brian Potter's Haven label. Their debut album, *Give It to the People*, surprisingly yielded three hits, a smash hit with the rock-and-roll death song "Rock and Roll Heaven," the major hit title song, and the moderate hit "Dream On." A second album for the label failed miserably, and Medley resumed his solo career in the late 1970s on United Artists. He eventually achieved success in the country field on RCA Records in 1984 with "Till the Memory's Gone," "I Still Do," and "I've Always Got the Heart to Sing the Blues." During the 1980s, Medley opened two successful oldies dance clubs called The Hop in Orange County and, in 1988, joined Paul Revere in opening another, Kicks, in Reno, Nev. In 1987, he scored a top pop and easy-listening hit in duet with Jennifer Warnes on "(I've Had) The Time of My Life" from the hit movie *Dirty Dancing*. The Righteous Brothers' "Unchained Melody" became a major hit from the movie *Ghost* in 1990. In 1991, the duo recorded *Reunion* and Bill Medley recorded *Blue Eyed Singer* for Curb/Warner Brothers Records. They duo has toured regularly during the summer since the mid-1990s.

DISC.: THE RIGHTEOUS BROTHERS: *Right Now!* (1963); *Some Blue-Eyed Soul* (1965); *This Is New* (1965); *Best* (1966); *You've Lost That Lovin' Feelin'* (1965); *Just Once in My Life* (1965); *Back to Back* (1965); *Soul and Inspiration* (1966); *Go Ahead and Cry* (1966); *Sayin' Something* (1967); *Greatest Hits* (1967); *Souled Out* (1967); *Standards* (1968); *One for the Road* (1968); *Greatest Hits, Vol. 2* (1969); *The Righteous Brothers* (1970); *History* (1973); *Give It to the People* (1974); *The Sons of Mrs. Righteous* (1975); *Unchained Melody* (1990); *Reunion* (1991). **JIMMY WALKER AND BOBBY HATFIELD AS THE RIGHTEOUS BROTHERS:** *Re-birth* (1970). **BOBBY HATFIELD:** *Messin' in Muscle* (1971). **BILL MEDLEY:** *100%* (1968); *Soft and Soulful* (1969); *Someone Is Standing Outside* (1970); *Nobody Knows* (1970); *Gone* (1971); *A Song for You* (1971); *Smile* (1973); *Lay a Little Lovin' on Me* (1978); *Sweet Thunder* (1980); *Right Here and Now* (1982); *I Still Do* (1984); *Still Hung Up on You* (1985); *Blue Eyed Singer* (1991).—**BH**

Rignold, Hugo (Henry), English conductor; b. Kingston upon Thames, May 15, 1905; d. London, May 30, 1976. He studied violin in Winnipeg and in 1920 returned to England as a scholarship student at the Royal Academy of Music in London of Hans Wessely (violin), Lionel Tertis (viola), and Leon Goossens (oboe). After working as a violinist and bandleader, he served in the Royal Air Force during World War II, during which time he conducted the Cairo Sym. Orch. (1944). In 1947 he conducted at Sadler's Wells in London. From 1948 to 1954 he was principal conductor of the Liverpool Phil. In 1956, 1971–72, and 1973 he was resident guest conductor of the Cape Town Sym. Orch. He was music director of the Royal Ballet in London (1957–60) and of the City of Birmingham Sym. Orch. (1960–68). —**NS/LK/DM**

Rihm, Wolfgang (Michael), distinguished German composer and teacher; b. Karlsruhe, March 13, 1952. He received training in composition with Eugen Velte at the Karlsruhe Hochschule für Musik (1968–72), with Stockhausen in Cologne (1972–73), and with Klaus Huber in Freiburg im Breisgau (1973–76). He also studied with Fortner and Searle, and received training in musicology with Eggebrecht in Freiburg im Breisgau. From 1970 he attended the summer courses in new music in Darmstadt, and then taught there from 1978. He taught at the Karlsruhe Hochschule für Musik (1973–78). After teaching in Munich (1981), he returned to the Karlsruhe Hochschule für Musik as a prof. (from 1985). In 1997 he won the Prix de Composition Musicale de la Fondation Prince Pierre de Monaco. In his music, Rihm embraces an atonal, post-expressionist path with occasional infusions of tonal writing.

WORKS: DRAMATIC: *Faust und Yorick,* chamber opera (1976; Mannheim, April 29, 1977); *Jakob Lenz,* chamber opera (1977–78; Hamburg, March 8, 1979); *Tutuguri,* ballet (1981–82; Berlin, Nov. 12, 1982); *Die Hamletmaschine,* music theater (1983–86; Mannheim, April 4, 1987); *Oedipus,* music theater (1986–87; Berlin, Oct. 4, 1987); *Die Eroberung von Mexico,* music theater (1987–91; Hamburg, Feb. 9, 1992); *Medea-Spiel,* dance theater (1988–89; Salzburg, April 6, 1989); *Séraphim*, music theater (Frankfurt am Main, Sept. 7, 1994; stage perf., Stuttgart, Nov. 24, 1996). O R C H .: 4 syms.: No. 1 (1969; Hannover, Feb. 5, 1984), No. 2 (1975; Berlin, June 27, 1976), No. 3 for Soprano, Baritone, Chorus, and Orch. (1976–77; Berlin, Nov. 15, 1979), and No. 4, *Symphonie fleuve* (Hamburg, Nov. 6, 1994); *Adagio for Strings* (1969); *Magma* (1973); *Dis-Kontur* (1974; Stuttgart, Oct. 10, 1975); *Sub-Kontur* (1974–75; Donaueschingen, Oct. 26, 1976); *Lichtzwang* for Violin and Orch. "in memoriam Paul Celan" (1975–76; Royan, April 3, 1977); *Cuts and Dissolves* (1976; Paris, March 3, 1977); *Nachtordnung*, 7 pieces for 15 Strings (1976; Berlin, Sept. 19, 1977); *La Musique creuse le ciel* for 2 Pianos annd Orch. (1977–79; Cologne, Nov. 14, 1980); *Abgesangsszene No. 1* (Kassel, Nov. 8, 1979) and *No. 5* (1979; Kiel, Jan. 12, 1981); 3 waltzes: No. 1, *Sehnsuchtswalzer* (1979–81; Stuttgart, Oct. 23, 1981), No. 2, *Drängender Walzer* (1986–87; Frankfurt am Main, Feb. 21, 1987), and No. 3, *Brahmsliebewalzer* (1979–88; Flensburg, July 6, 1988); Viola Concerto (1979–83; Berlin, Nov. 13, 1983); *Doppelgesang No. 1* for Viola, Cello, and Orch. (1980; Baden-Baden, Jan. 18, 1984) and *No. 2* for Clarinet, Cello, and Orch. (1981–83; Hitzacker, Aug. 7, 1983); *Zeichen I* for 2 Soloists and 2 Orchs. (1981–85; Venice, Sept. 29, 1985); *Monodram* for Cello and Orch. (1982–83; Graz, Oct. 9, 1983) *Schattenstück* (1982–84; Karlsruhe, June 24, 1984); *Klangbeschreibung I* for Cello and Orch. (1982–87; Donaueschingen, Oct. 18, 1987) and *III* (1984–87; Donaueschingen, Oct. 18, 1987); *Gebild* for Piccolo Trumpet, 2 Percussionists, and 20 Strings (Zürich, May 15, 1983; rev. version, Lucerne, July 7, 1997); *Chiffre II: Silence to be Beaten* (London, Nov. 30, 1983), *V* (Paris, Dec. 3, 1984), and *VII* (Frankfurt am Main, Sept. 15, 1985); *Spur* (1984–85; Saarbrücken, March 24, 1985); *Umriss* (1985–86; Berlin, May 5, 1986); *Compresenze* (1985–87; Cologne, June 4, 1987); *Unbenannt I* (Munich, May 23, 1986), *II* (Tokyo, Oct. 30, 1987), and *III* (1989–90; WDR, Cologne, March 23, 1990); *Blick* (1987–88; Freiburg im Breisgau, April 25, 1988); *Kein Firmament* for Chamber Orch. (Berlin, Oct. 29, 1988); *Ungemaltes Bild* (1988–90; Stockholm, May 17, 1990); *Ins offene...* (Glasgow, Sept. 22, 1990); *bildos/weglos* (1990–91; *La lugubre gondola/Das Eismeer* for 2 Orch. Groups and Piano "in memoriam Luigi Nono" (1990–92); *et nunc I* and *II* for Wind Orch. (both 1992); *Form/Zwei Formen* (1993–94); *Musik* for Oboe and Orch. (1994); *Ernster Gesang* (Philadelphia, April 25, 1997); *Toccata* for Piano and Orch. (Bremen, May 11, 1998); *Vers une symphonie fleuve IV* (Dresden, Sept. 22, 1998); *Styk und Lethe* for Cello and Orch. (Donaueschingen, Oct. 18, 1998); *Marsyas* for Trumpet, Percussion, and Orch. (Karlsruhe, Nov. 1, 1998); *New work* for Piano, Harp, and Orch. (Berlin, May 22, 1999); *Musik* for Clarinet and Orch. (Munich, Nov. 12, 1999); *Spiegel und Fluss: Nachspiel und Vorspiel* (1999; Hamburg, Jan. 2, 2000). C H A M B E R : Concerto for Piano and 8 Instruments (1969; Karlsruhe, Oct. 3, 1987); 10 string quartets: No. 1 (1970; Hamburg, June 15, 1987), No. 2 (1970), No. 3, *Im Innersten* (1976; Royan, April 3, 1977), No. 4 (1979–81; Badenweiler, Nov. 12, 1983), No. 5, *Ohne Titel* (1981–83; Brussels, Dec. 9, 1983), No. 6, *Blaubuch* (1984; Kassel, Oct. 26, 1985), No. 7, *Veranderungen* (1985; Darmstadt, June 1986), No. 8 (1988; Milan, Jan. 17, 1989), No. 9 (1993); *Music-Hall Suite* for 8 Players (1979; Baden-Baden, April 1980), and No. 10 (Berlin, Sept. 20, 1997); *Chiffre I* for Piano and 7 Instruments (1982; Saarbrücken, April 22, 1983), *III* for 12 Players (Karlsruhe, Dec. 7, 1983), *IV* for Bass Clarinet, Cello, and Piano (1983–84; Hamburg, Feb. 3, 1984), *VI* for 8 Players (Karlsruhe, April 12, 1985), and *VIII* for 8 Players (1985–88; Witten, April 23, 1988); *Musik* for 3 Strings (Darmstadt, July 31, 1978); *Canzona* for 4 Violas (Stuttgart, June 6, 1982); *Fremde Szene I* for Violin, Cello,

and Piano (Salzburg, Aug. 17, 1982), *II* for Violin, Cello, and Piano (1983; Düsseldorf, June 8, 1984), and *III* for Violin, Cello, and Piano (1983; Gelsenkirchen, Nov. 21, 1984); Clarinet Quintet (London, June 29, 1988); *Kalt*, octet (Berlin, Feb. 16, 1991); *Sphere* for Piano, Winds, and Percussion (1992–94); *Antlitz* for Cello and Piano (1993); *Pol.Kolchis.Nucleus* for Chamber Ensemble (Badenweiler, Nov. 13, 1996); *De Coloribus* for Chamber Ensemble (Lucerne, Aug. 23, 1997); *Gedrangte Form* for Chamber Ensemble (Frankfurt am Main, Dec. 1, 1998); *Über die Linie* for Cello (Cologne, April 5, 1999); *Fetzen* for String Quartet (Munich, June 23, 1999); *Trigon: Jagden und Formen* for Chamber Ensemble (Paris, Nov. 18, 1999); piano pieces; organ music. V O C A L : *Konzertarie*, "telepsychogramm" for Mezzo-soprano and Orch. (1975; Rome, June 28, 1989); *Abgesangsszene No. 2* for Medium Voice and Orch. (1979; Karlsruhe, Nov. 5, 1980), *No. 3* for Baritone and Orch. (1979–80; Freiburg im Breisgau, May 18, 1981), *No. 4* for Medium Voice and Orch. (1979; Berlin, Sept. 18, 1983), and *No. 5* for Mezzo-soprano, Baritone, and Orch. (1979–81; Berlin, Sept. 18, 1983); *Lowry-Lieder* for Voice and Orch. (1982–87); *Umsungen* for Baritone and 8 Instruments (1984); *Dies* for Soprano, Alto, Tenor, Baritone, 2 Speakers, Children's Chorus, Speaking Chorus, Mixed Chorus, Organ, and Orch. (1984; Vienna, Nov. 13, 1986); *Andere Schatten*, musical scene for Soprano, Mezzo-soprano, Baritone, Speaker, Chorus, and Orch. (Frankfurt am Main, Sept. 6, 1985); *Klangbeschreibung II* for 4 Voices, 5 Brass, and 6 Percussion (1986–87; Donaueschingen, Oct. 18, 1987); *Mein Tod: Requiem in memoriam Jane S.* for Soprano and Orch. (1988–89; Salzburg, Aug. 16, 1990); *Frau/Stimme* for Soprano and Orch. (Donaueschingen, Oct. 22, 1989); *Geheimer Block* for 4 Soloists, Chorus, and Orch. (Frankfurt am Main, Aug. 27, 1989); *Abschiedsstücke* for Woman's Voice and Small Orch. (1993); *Maximum est unum* for Mezzo-soprano, 2 Choruses, and Orch. (Freiburg im Breisgau, Nov. 17, 1996); *Deutsches Stück mit Hamlet* for 2 Soloists and Orch. (Frankfurt am Main, May 18, 1998); *Drei späte Gedichte von Heiner Müller* for Alto and Orch. (Berlin, May 22, 1999); *In doppelter Tiefe* for Mezzo-soprano, Alto, and Orch. (Berlin, Sept. 29, 1999).

BIBL.: R. Urmetzer, *W. R.* (Stuttgart, 1988).—**NS/LK/DM**

Říhovský, Vojtěch, Czech choirmaster and composer; b. Dub na Moravě, April 21, 1871; d. Prague, Sept. 15, 1950. He was trained in Prague at the Organ School, the Jan Ludvík Singing Inst., and the Arnošt Černý Music Inst. (1887–92). He served as a choirmaster in Dub na Moravě (1892–1902), Chrudim (1902–14), and at St. Ludmila in Prague (1914–36). He composed some 300 sacred works, as well as secular vocal works and instrumental pieces.

BIBL.: C. Russ, *R. als Kirchenkoponist* (Prague, 1913); V. Bathasar, *V. R.* (Prague, 1921); J. Dušek, *V. R. a jeho životní dílo* (*V. R. and His Life's Work*; Prague, 1933).—**NS/LK/DM**

Riisager, Knudåge, prominent Danish composer; b. Port Kunda, Estonia, March 6, 1897; d. Copenhagen, Dec. 26, 1974. He went to Copenhagen and studied theory and composition with Otto Malling and Peder Gram, and violin with Peder Mller (1915–18). He also took courses in political science at the Univ. (1916–21; graduated, 1921) before pursuing musical studies with Roussel and Le Flem in Paris (1921–23), and later with Grabner in Leipzig (1932). He held a civil service position in Denmark (1925–50); was chairman of the

Danish Composers' Union (1937–62) and director of the Royal Danish Cons. (1956–67). A fantastically prolific composer, he wrote music in quaquaversal genres, but preserved a remarkable structural and textural consistency while demonstrating an erudite sense of modern polyphony. He also had a taste for exotic and futuristic subjects. He publ. a collection of essays, *Det usynlige mnster* (The Unseemly Monster; Copenhagen, 1957), and a somewhat self-deprecatory memoir, *Det er sjovt at vaere lille* (It Is Amusing to Be Small; Copenhagen, 1967).

WORKS (all 1st perf. in Copenhagen unless otherwise given): **DRAMATIC: Opera Buffa:** *Susanne* (1948; Jan. 7, 1950). **Ballet:** *Benzin* (1927; Dec. 26, 1930); *Cocktails-Party* (1929); *Tolv med Posten* (12 by the Mail), after H.C. Andersen (1939; Feb. 21, 1942); *Slaraffenland* (Fool's Paradise; 1940; Feb. 21, 1942; originally an orch. piece, 1936); *Qarrtsiluni*, on Eskimo themes (Feb. 21, 1942; originally an orch. piece, 1938); *Fugl fnix* (Phoenix; 1944–45; May 12, 1946); *Étude*, based on Czerny's studies (1947; Jan. 15, 1948); *Månerenen* (The Moon Reindeer; 1956; Nov. 22, 1957); *Stjerner* (1958); *Les Victoires de l'Amour* (1958; March 4, 1962); *Fruen fra havet* (Lady from the Sea; 1959; N.Y., April 20, 1960); *Galla-Variationer* (1966; March 5, 1967); *Ballet Royal* (May 31, 1967); *Svinedrengen* (The Swineherd; Danish TV, March 10, 1969). **ORCH.:** *Erasmus Montanus*, overture (1920; Göteborg, Oct. 15, 1924); *Suite Dionysiaque* for Chamber Orch. (1924); 5 syms.: No. 1 (1925; July 17, 1926), No. 2 (1927; March 5, 1929), No. 3 (Nov. 21, 1935), No. 4, *Sinfonia gaia* (Oct. 24, 1940), and No. 5, *Sinfonia serena* for Strings and Percussion (1949–50; Nov. 21, 1950); *Introduzione di traverso*, overture (1925); *Variations on a Theme of Mezangean* (1926); *T-DOXC*, "poème mécanique" (1926; Sept. 3, 1927); *Klods Hans* (1929); *Fastelavn* (Shrovetide), overture (1929–30); Suite for Small Orch. (1931); *Concerto for Orchestra* (1931; Dec. 7, 1936); Concertino for Trumpet and Strings (1933; March 2, 1934); *Primavera*, overture (1934; Jan. 31, 1935); *Slaraffenland*, 2 suites (1936, 1940; as a ballet, 1940); *Sinfonia concertante* for Strings (1937); *Partita* (1937); *Basta* (1938); *Qarrtsiluni* (1938; as a ballet, 1940); *Torgutisk dans* (1939); *Tivoli-Tivoli!* (Aug. 15, 1943); *Sommer-Rhapsodi* (1943; Jan. 30, 1944); *Bellman-Variationer* for Small Orch. (1945); *Sinfonietta* (Stockholm, Oct. 1, 1947); *Chaconne* (1949); *Archaeopteryx* (1949); *Variations on a Sarabande of Charles, Duke of Orleans, 1415* for Strings (1950); Violin Concerto (1950–51; Oct. 11, 1951); *Toccata* (1952); *Pro fistulis et fidibus* for Woodwinds and Strings (1952; March 2, 1953); *Rondo giocoso* for Violin and Orch. (June 18, 1957); *Burlesk ouverture* (1964); *Entrada-Epilogo* (May 19, 1971); *Bourrée*, ballet-variations (Danish Radio, March 7, 1972); *Trittico* for Woodwinds, Brass, Double Bass, and Percussion (Danish Radio, March 3, 1972); *Apollon* (Nov. 11, 1973). **CHAMBER:** 2 violin sonatas (1917, 1923); 6 string quartets (1918; 1920; 1922; 1925–26; 1932; 1942–43); Sonata for Violin and Viola (1919); Wind Quintet (1921); *Variations* for Clarinet, Viola, and Bassoon (1923); *Sinfonietta* for 8 Wind Instruments (1924); *Divertimento* for String Quartet and Wind Quintet (1925); Sonata for Flute, Violin, Clarinet, and Cello (1927); *Music* for Wind Quintet (1927); *Conversazione* for Oboe, Clarinet, and Bassoon (1932); Concertino for 5 Violins and Piano (1933); *Serenade* for Flute, Violin, and Cello (1936); Quartet for Flute, Oboe, Clarinet, and Bassoon (1941); *Divertimento* for Flute, Oboe, Horn, and Bassoon (1944); Sonatina for Piano Trio (1951); Sonata for 2 Violins (1951); String Trio (1955). **Piano:** 4 *épigrammes* (1921); Sonata (1931); 2 *morceaux* (1933); Sonatina (1950); 4 *Brneklaverstykker* (1964). **VOCAL:** *Dansk Salme* for Chorus and Orch. (1942; April 13, 1943); *Sang til Solen* for Mezzo-soprano, Baritone, Chorus, and Orch. (Sept. 25, 1947); *Sangen om det Uendelige* (*Canto dell'Infinito*) for Chorus and Orch. (1964; Sept. 30, 1965); *Stabat Mater* for Chorus and Orch. (1966; Danish Radio, Nov. 9, 1967); choruses; songs.—NS/LK/DM

Riley, John, jazz drummer; b. Aberdeen, Md., June 11, 1954. He spent his formative years in Scotch Plains, N.J. He got a B.M. from Univ. of North Tex. (1975) and a M.M. from the Manhattan School of Music (1985). He performed with Miles Davis, Dizzy Gillespie, Stan Getz, Milt Jackson, Art Farmer, Ray Brown, Phil Woods, Toots Thielemans, Randy Brecker, and Jack DeJohnette. He toured extensively with the John Scofield Quartet, the Woody Herman Big Band, the Vanguard Jazz Orch., the Carnegie Hall Jazz Band, the Red Rodney Quintet and Bob Mintzer. He also played concerts with Mike Stern and John Abercrombie, Joe Lovano, Dave Liebman, and Bob Berg, among others. He toured with composer/pianists Marvin Hamlisch and Michel LeGrand. Riley has played at all of the world's major jazz festivals. He teaches at Manhattan School of Music, The New School and William Paterson Univ.—LP

Riley, Terry (Mitchell), significant American composer and performer; b. Colfax, Calif., June 24, 1935. He studied piano with Duane Hampton at San Francisco State Coll. (1955–57) and composition with Seymour Shifrin and William Denny at the Univ. of Calif. at Berkeley (M.A., 1961). In 1967 he was a creative assoc. at the Center for Creative and Performing Arts at the State Univ. of N.Y. in Buffalo. From 1971 to 1980 he was assoc. prof. at Mills Coll. in Oakland, Calif. In 1979 he held a Guggenheim fellowship. In 1970 Riley was initiated in San Francisco as a disciple of Pandit Pran Nath, the North Indian singer, and followed him to India. He subsequently appeared frequently with him in concert as tampura, tabla, and vocal accompanist until the master's death in 1996. From 1993 Riley has served as co-director along with Sufi Murshid, Shabda Kahn of the Chisti Sabri India music study tours. From 1989 to 1993 he formed and led the ensemble Khayal; he also performed regularly in solo piano concerts of his works, and appeared often in duo concerts with Indian sitarist Krishna Bhatt, saxophonist George Brooks, and Italian bassist Stefano Scodanibbio. In 1992 he formed a small theater company, The Travelling- Avantt-Gaard, to perform his chamber opera, *The Saint Adolf Ring*, based on the drawings, poetry, writings, and mathematical calculations of Adolf Wölfli, an early 20th century Swiss artist who suffered from schizophrenia and whose entire output was created while he was confined in a mental institution. Riley's contribution to and influence upon the music of the last half of the 20th century is likely incalculable, his *In C* for Variable Ensemble notated in fragments to be played any number of times at will in the spirit of aleatory latitudinarianism, all within the key of C major, with an occasional F sharp providing a trompe l'oreille effect (1964; San Francisco, May 21, 1965) now being *de rigeur* at concerts attempting serious historical overview. His Concerto for String Quartet and Orch., *The Sands* (1991; N.Y., May 3, 1992), was the first-ever new music commission from the Salzburg Festival, his recording of *Cadenza on the Night Plain* for

String Quartet (1983) was critically lauded as one of the best classical albums of the year, and his epic 5-quartet cycle, *Salome Dances for Peace* for String Quartet (1985–87), was nominated for a Grammy Award. In 1990–91 he composed his first orch. work, *Jade Palace*, for the centenary celebration at N.Y.'s Carnegie Hall, which was performed there by Leonard Slatkin and the Saint Louis Sym. Orch. (Feb. 4, 1991). Riley is currently at work on a set of 24 pieces for guitar and guitar ensemble, *The Book of Abbeyozzud*, as well as 2 fairy tales for String Orch. and a new piano concerto to feature himself as pianist with the Paul Dresher Ensemble.

WORKS: DRAMATIC: C h a m b e r O p e r a: *The Saint Adolf Ring* (1992). **TAPE AND INSTRUMENTAL:** Trio for Violin, Clarinet, and Cello (1957); *Spectra* for 3 Winds and 3 Strings (1959); *Concert* for 2 Pianos and Tape (1960); *Earpiece* for 2 Pianos and Tape (1960); String Quartet (1960); String Trio (1961); *I Can't Stop No, Mescalin Mix,* and *She Moves* for Tape (1962–63); *In C* for Variable Ensemble (1964; San Francisco, May 21, 1965); *Tread on the Trail* for Jazz Musicians (1965); *Olson III* for Any Instruments and Voices (1966); *G-Song* for String Quartet (1980); *Sunrise of the Planetary Dream Collector* for String Quartet (1980); *Cadenza on the Night Plain* for String Quartet (1983); *The Medicine Wheel* for String Quartet (1983); *Salome Dances for Peace* for String Quartet (1985–87); *Chanting the Light of Foresight* for Saxophone Quartet (1987); *The Room of Remembrance* for Vibraphone, Marimba, Piano, and Soprano Saxophone (1987); *Chanting the Light of Foresight* for Saxophone Quartet (1987); *The Crows Rosary* for Keyboard and String Quartet (1988); *Cactus Rosary* for Chamber Ensemble (1990); *The Sands,* concerto for String Quartet and Orch. (1991; N.Y., May 3, 1992); *June Buddhas,* concerto for Chorus and Orch., after Jack Kerouac's *Mexico City Blues* (N.Y., Nov. 9, 1991); *Wölfli Portraits* for Flute, Clarinet, Piano, 2 Percussion, Violin, and Cello (1992); *Ascension* for Guitar (1993); *El Hombre,* piano quintet (1993); *Ritmos and Melos* for Violin, Piano, and Percussion (1993); *Night Music* for Piano (1996); *Remember This...*for Voice and 10 Instruments (1997); *DeepChandi* for String Orch., Dancer, and Tape (1998); *MissiGono* for Mixed Instruments (1998); *3 Requiem Quartets* for String Quartet (1998); *Vieux Chateaux* for Piano (1998). **WITH SYNTHESIZERS:** *Poppy Nogoods Phantom Band* (1966); *A Rainbow in Curved Air* (1968); *Genesis '70,* ballet (1970); *Chorale of the Blessed Day* for Voice and 2 Synthesizers or Piano and Sitar (1980); *Eastern Man* for Voice and 2 Synthesizers (1980); *Embroidery* for Voice and 2 Synthesizers or Piano, Synthesizer, Sitar, Tabla, and Alto Saxophone (1980); *Song from the Old Country* for Voice, Piano, Sitar, Tabla, String Quartet, and Synthesizer (1980); *The Ethereal Time Shadow* for Voice and 2 Synthesizers (1982); *Offering to Chief Crazy Horse* for Voice and 2 Synthesizers (1982); *Song of the Emerald Runner* for Voice, Piano, String Quartet, Sitar, Tabla, and Synthesizer (1983); *Jade Palace* for Orch. and Synthesizers (1990–91; N.Y., Feb. 4, 1991); *Diamond Fiddle Language* for Synthesizer and String Bass (1998; in collaboration with S. Scodanibbio); *Shiv-Ji-Ki-Rung* for Synthesizer and String Bass (1998; in collaboration with S. Scodanibbio). **OTHER:** Various improvisational pieces.

BIBL.: W. Mertens, *American Minimal Music: La Monte Young, T. R., Steve Reich, Philip Glass* (London, 1991). **—NS/LK/DM**

Rilling, Helmuth, noted German organist, conductor, and pedagogue; b. Stuttgart, May 29, 1933. He studied at the Hochschule für Musik in Stuttgart (1952–55) and later took a course in organ with Fer-

nando Germani at the Accademia di Santa Cecilia in Rome (1955–57); went to N.Y. to study conducting with Bernstein (1967). He founded the Stuttgart Gachinger Kantorei in 1954, which he conducted on numerous tours. He taught choral conducting and organ at the Kirchenmusikschule in Berlin-Spandau (1963–66); in 1966 he was appointed to the faculty of the Frankfurt am Main Hochschule für Musik. In 1965 he founded the Stuttgart Bach-Collegium, an instrumental ensemble to accompany his Gachinger Kantorei; made his first tour of the U.S. with it in 1968; in 1969 he succeeded Kurt Thomas as conductor of the Frankfurter Kantorei. He was founder-artistic director of the Ore. Bach Festival in Eugene (from 1970). Rilling has acquired a distinguished reputation as both a performing musician and a teacher.

BIBL.: S. Hansen, *H. R.: Conductor, Teacher* (Dayton, 1997). **—NS/LK/DM**

Rimini, Giacomo, Italian baritone and teacher; b. Verona, March 22, 1888; d. Chicago, March 6, 1952. He was trained at the Verona Cons. After making his operatic debut in Verona (1910), he sang in various Italian opera houses. In 1916 he joined the Chicago Opera. He also appeared at London's Covent Garden in 1933. In 1920 he married **Rosa Raisa.** They opened a singing school in Chicago in 1937.**—NS/LK/DM**

Rimmer, John (Francis), New Zealand composer, teacher, and horn player; b. Auckland, Feb. 5, 1939. He studied at the Univ. of New Zealand (B.A., 1961), and with Ronald Tremain at the Univ. of Auckland (M.A., 1963) and with John Weinzweig and Gustav Ciamaga at the Univ. of Toronto (Mus.D., 1972). From 1970 to 1974 he was a lecturer at North Shores Teachers Coll. He was a Mozart Fellow at the Univ. of Otago in 1972. In 1974 he became lecturer, in 1978 a senior lecturer, in 1989 an assoc. prof., and in 1995 was awarded a personal professorial chair in music at the Univ. of Auckland, from which he retired in 1999. In 1983 his *De Aestibus Rerum* won 1st prize in the International Horn Competition and in 1986 his *Fleeting Images* received the International Confederation of Electroacoutic Music Prize in Bourges.

WORKS: DRAMATIC: *The Juggler,* music theater (Hamilton, Oct. 30, 1976); *A Midsummer Night's Dream,* incidental music to Shakespeare's play (Auckland, July 11, 1980); *Sir Gawayne and the Green Knight,* opera (Auckland, Nov. 18, 1981); *Galileo,* chamber opera (Aucland, Sept. 18, 1998). **ORCH.:** 2 syms.: No. 1 (1968; N.Y., Feb. 24, 1970) and No. 2, *The Feeling of Sound* (Auckland, June 1, 1989); *December Nights* for Small Orch. (1970); *Explorations-Discoveries* for Horn and Orch. (1971; Wellington, March 20, 1974); *At the Appointed Time* (Dunedin, Sept. 1, 1973); *The Ring of Fire* for Chamber Orch. (Wellington, Oct. 12, 1976); Viola Concerto (1980; Wellington, Oct. 2, 1982); *Your Piano is My Forte,* concerto for Piano and Chamber Orch. (Auckland, Oct. 13, 1991); *Gossamer* for 12 Solo Strings (1992; Auckland, Feb. 26, 1993); *Vulcan,* fanfare (Auckland, March 11, 1999). **CHAMBER:** *Composition 2* for Wind Quintet and Electronic Sounds (1969; Wellington, Aug. 30, 1971), *5* for Percussion and Electronic Sounds (Cambridge, N.Z., Jan. 10, 1971), and *8* for Violin and Electronic Sounds (Cambridge, N.Z., Jan. 8, 1975); *Refrains, Cadenzas, and Interludes* for String Quartet (1971; Cambridge, N.Z., Jan. 11, 1972); *Interplay* for Harpsichord and Percussion (Auckland, May 7, 1972); *The New Tristan* for Recorders, Synthesizers, and Percussion (Wellington, March 8, 1975); *Where Sea Meets Sky 2* for Chamber Ensemble (Wellington, Nov. 2, 1975); *Extro-Intro* for Horn and Synthesizer (Wellington, Aug. 26, 1977); *Thoughts from Peria* for 8 Instruments (Auckland, April 30, 1978); *De Aestibus Rerum* for Clarinet, Horn, Violin, Cello, and Piano (Auckland, Nov. 27, 1983); *With the Current* for Flute, Cello, Piano, and Percussion (Adelaide, May 6, 1986); *Omarama: Place of Light* for Piano, Violin, and Trumpet (Auckland, April 15, 1987); *Tritones* for Horn and Synthesizer (Wellington, Oct. 31, 1987); *The Revelation of Increasing Complexity* for Clarinet and Percussion (1989; Auckland, July 14, 1990); *Bowed Insights* for String Quartet (Auckland, Sept. 26, 1993); *Merger* for 2 Horns and Tuba (Auckland, March 7, 1999). **OTHER:** *Where Sea Meets Sky 1*, electronic piece (1975; Bourges, June 5, 1976); *De Motu Naturae*, electronic piece (Bourges, June 9, 1985); *Fleeting Images*, computer piece (1985; Vancouver, Feb. 14, 1986); *An Inner Voice*, computer piece (Auckland, Sept. 18, 1991); *A Vocalise for Einstein*, computer piece (1991; Auckland, Aug. 19, 1992); *Pacific Soundscapes With Dancing*, computer piece (Bangkok, Dec. 3, 1995).—**LK/DM**

Rimsky-Korsakov, Andrei (Nikolaievich), Russian musicologist, son of **Nikolai (Andreievich) Rimsky-Korsakov** and uncle of **Georgi (Mikhailovich) Rimsky-Korsakov;** b. St. Petersburg, Oct. 17, 1878; d. there (Leningrad), May 23, 1940. He studied philology at the Univ. of St. Petersburg and later at the univs. of Strasbourg and Heidelberg (Ph.D., 1903). Returning to Russia, he devoted his energies to Russian music history. In 1915 he began the publication of an important magazine, Musikalny Sovremennik (The Musical Contemporary), but the revolutionary events of 1917 forced suspension of its publication. He wrote a major biography of his father (5 vols., Moscow, 1933–46; vol. V ed. by his brother, Vladimir Rimsky-Korsakov); also ed. the 3rd to 5th eds. of his father's autobiography (Moscow, 1926, 1932, 1935) and publ. a study of Maximilian Steinberg (Moscow, 1928). He was married to **Julia Weissberg**. —**NS/LK/DM**

Rimsky-Korsakov, Georgi (Mikhailovich), Russian musicologist and composer, grandson of **Nikolai (Andreievich) Rimsky-Korsakov** and nephew of **Andrei (Nikolaievich) Rimsky-Korsakov;** b. St. Petersburg, Dec. 26, 1901; d. there (Leningrad), Oct. 10, 1965. He was a student of Steinberg, Sokolov, Liapunov, and Nicolai at the St. Petersburg Cons. In 1927 he took his kandidat degree at the Leningrad Inst. of Theater and Music. From 1927 to 1962 he taught at the Leningrad Cons. In 1923 he founded a society for the cultivation of quarter tone music, and wrote some works in that system. He later experimented with electronic instruments, and was co-inventor of the Emeriton in 1930, which was capable of producing a complete series of tones at any pitch and of any chosen or synthetic tone color. He wrote solo pieces for the instrument. His other works include incidental music, film scores, Sym. (1925), Quintet for Clarinet, Horn, and String Trio (1925), 2 string quartets (1926, 1932), Octet for 2 Emeritons, 2 Clarinets, Bassoon, Violin, Viola, and Cello (1932), piano pieces, including 2 sonatas (1924, 1932), and choral music.—**NS/LK/DM**

Rimsky-Korsakov, Nikolai (Andreievich), great Russian composer and teacher, father of **Andrei (Nikolaievich) Rimsky-Korsakov** and grandfather of **Georgi (Mikhailovich) Rimsky-Korsakov;** b. Tikhvin, near Novgorod, March 18, 1844; d. Liubensk, near St. Petersburg, June 21, 1908. He took piano lessons as a child with provincial teachers, and later with a professional musician, Théodore Canillé, who introduced him to Balakirev; he also met Cui and Borodin. In 1856 he entered the St. Petersburg Naval School, graduating in 1862. In 1862 he was sent on the clipper Almaz on a voyage that lasted 2 1/2 years; returning to Russia in the summer of 1865, he settled in St. Petersburg, where he remained most of his life. During his travels he maintained contact with Balakirev, and continued to report to him the progress of his musical composition. He completed his 1st Sym., and it was performed under Balakirev's direction on Dec. 31, 1865, at a concert of the Free Music School in St. Petersburg. In 1871 Rimsky-Korsakov was engaged as a prof. of composition and orchestration at the St. Petersburg Cons., even though he was aware of the inadequacy of his own technique. He remained on the faculty until his death, with the exception of a few months in 1905, when he was relieved of his duties as prof. for his public support of the rebellious students during the revolution of that year. As a music educator, Rimsky-Korsakov was of the greatest importance to the development and maintenance of the traditions of the Russian national school; among his students were Glazunov, Liadov, Arensky, Ippolitov-Ivanov, Gretchaninov, Nikolai Tcherepnin, Maximilian Steinberg, Gnessin, and Miaskovsky. Igor Stravinsky studied privately with him from 1903.

In 1873 Rimsky-Korsakov abandoned his naval career, but was appointed to the post of inspector of the military orchs. of the Russian navy, until it was abolished in 1884. From 1883 to 1894 he was also asst. director of the Court Chapel and led the chorus and the orch. there. Although he was not a gifted conductor, he gave many performances of his own orch. works. He made his debut at a charity concert for the victims of the Volga famine, in St. Petersburg, March 2, 1874; the program included the first performance of his 3rd Sym. From 1886 until 1900 he conducted the annual Russian Sym. concerts organized by the publisher Belaieff; in June 1889 he conducted 2 concerts of Russian music at the World Exposition in Paris, and in 1890 he conducted a concert of Russian music in Brussels; led a similar concert there in 1900. His last appearance abroad was in the spring of 1907, when he conducted in Paris 2 Russian historic concerts arranged by Diaghilev; in the same year, he was elected corresponding member of the French Academy, to succeed Grieg. These activities, however, did not distract him from his central purpose as a national Russian composer. His name was grouped with those of Cui, Borodin, Balakirev, and Mussorgsky as the "Mighty 5," and he maintained a close friendship with most of them; at Mussorgsky's death he collected his MSS and prepared them for publication; he also revised Mussorgsky's opera *Boris Godunov*; it was in Rimsky-Korsakov's version that the opera became famous. He had decisive influence in the affairs of the Belaieff publishing firm and helped publish a great number of works by Russian composers of the St. Petersburg group; only a small part of these sumptuously printed scores represents the best in Russian music, but culturally Rimsky-Korsakov's solicitude was of great importance. Although he was far from being a revolutionary, he freely expressed his disgust at the bungling administration of Czarist Russia; he was particularly indignant about the attempts of the authorities to alter Pushkin's lines in his own last opera, *The Golden Cockerel*, and refused to compromise; he died, of angina pectoris, with the situation still unresolved; the opera was produced posthumously, with the censor's changes; the original text was not restored until the revolution of 1917.

Rimsky-Korsakov was one of the greatest masters of Russian music. His source of inspiration was Glinka's operatic style; he made use of both the purely Russian idiom and coloristic oriental melodic patterns; such works as his symphonic suite *Scheherazade* and *The Golden Cockerel* represent Russian orientalism at its best; in the purely Russian style, the opera *Snow Maiden* and the *Russian Easter Overture* are outstanding examples. In the art of orchestration Rimsky-Korsakov had few equals; his treatment of instruments, in solo passages and in ensemble, was invariably idiomatic. In his treatise on orchestration, he selected only passages from his own works to demonstrate the principles of practical and effective application of registers and tone colors. Although an academician in his general aesthetics, he experimented boldly with melodic progressions and ingenious harmonies that pointed toward modern usages. He especially favored the major scale with the lowered submediant and the scale of alternating whole tones and semi-tones (which in Russian reference works came to be termed as "Rimsky-Korsakov's scale"; in the score of his opera-ballet *Mlada* there is an ocarina part tuned in this scale); in *The Golden Cockerel* and *Kashchei the Immortal* he applied dissonant harmonies in unusual superpositions; but he set for himself a definite limit in innovation, and severely criticized Richard Strauss, Debussy, and d'Indy for their modernistic practices.

WORKS: DRAMATIC: *Pskovityanka* (The Maid of Pskov), opera (1868–72; St. Petersburg, Jan. 13, 1873; 2nd version, 1876–77, further rev., Moscow, Oct. 23, 1901; 3rd version, 1891–92; St. Petersburg, April 18, 1895); *Mlada*, opera-ballet (1872; in collaboration with Borodin, Cui, Mussorgsky, and Minkus; unfinished; 2nd version entirely by Rimsky-Korsakov as a magical opera-ballet, 1889–90; St. Petersburg, Nov. 1, 1892); *Mayskaya noch* (May Night), comic opera after Gogal (1878–79; St. Petersburg, Jan. 21, 1880); *Snegurochka* (The Snow Maiden), opera after Ostrovsky (1880–81; St. Petersburg, Feb. 10, 1882; 2nd version, c. 1895); *Noch pered rozhdestvom* (Christmas Eve), opera after Gogol (1894–95; St. Petersburg, Dec. 10, 1895); *Sadko*, opera (1895–96; Moscow, Jan. 7, 1898); *Bagdadskiy borodobrey* (The Barber of Baghdad), opera (1895; unfinished); *Motsart i Salyeri* (Mozart and Salieri), opera after Pushkin (1897; Moscow, Dec. 7, 1898); *Boyarïnya Vera Sheloga* (The Noblewoman Vera Sheloga), prologue to the 2nd version of *Pskovityanka* (Moscow, Dec. 27, 1898); *Tsarskaya nevesta* (The Czar's Bride), opera (1898–99; Moscow, Nov. 3, 1899); *Skazka o Tsare Saltane, o sïne ego slavnom i moguchem bogatïre knyaze Gvidone Saltanoviche i o prekrasnoy Tsarevne Lebedi* (The Tale of Czar Saltan, of his Son the Renowned and Mighty Bogatïr Prince Guidon Saltanovich, and

of the Beautiful Swan Princess), opera after Pushkin (1899–1900; Moscow, Nov. 3, 1900); *Servilia*, opera (1900–01; St. Petersburg, Oct. 14, 1902); *Kashchey bessmertniy* (Kashchei the Immortal), opera (1901–02; Moscow, Dec. 25, 1902; rev. 1906); *Pan Voyevoda* (The Commander), opera (1902–03; St. Petersburg, Oct. 16, 1904); *Skazaniye o nevidimom grade Kitezhe i deve Fevronii* (The Legend of the Invisible City of Kitezh and the Maiden Fevronii), opera (1903–04; St. Petersburg, Feb. 20, 1907); *Zolotoy petushok* (The Golden Cockerel), opera after Pushkin (1906–07; Moscow, Oct. 7, 1909). **ORCH.:** Sym. No. 1, op.1 (1st version in E-flat minor, 1861–65; St. Petersburg, Dec. 31, 1865; 2nd version in E minor; 1884); *Overture on 3 Russian Themes*, op.28 (1866; 2nd version, 1879–80); *Fantasia on Serbian Themes*, op.6 (1867; 2nd version, 1886–87); *Sadko*, op.5 (1867; 2nd version, 1869; 3rd version, 1892); Sym. No. 2, op.9, *Antar* (1868; 2nd version, 1875; 3rd version, 1897); Sym. No. 3, op.32 (1866–73; St. Petersburg, March 2, 1874; 2nd version, 1886); Concerto for Trombone and Military Band (1877); *Variations* for Oboe and Military Band (1878); *Concertstück* for Clarinet and Military Band (1878); *Legend*, op.29 (original title, *Baba–Yaga*; 1879–80); *Sinfonietta on Russian Themes*, op.31 (1880–84; based on the String Quartet of 1878–79); Piano Concerto in C-sharp minor, op.30 (1882–83); *Fantasia on 2 Russian Themes* for Violin and Orch., op.33 (1886–87); *Capriccio espagnol*, op.34 (1887); *Scheherazade*, symphonic suite, op.35 (St. Petersburg, Nov. 3, 1888); *Souvenir de trois chants polonais* for Violin and Orch. (1888); *Russian Easter Overture*, op.36 (1888); *Serenade* for Cello and Orch., op.37 (1903; arranged from the *Serenade* for Cello and Piano, 1893); *The Tale of Tsar Saltan*, suite from the opera, op.57 (1903); *The Commander*, suite from the opera, op.59 (1903); *Mlada*, suite from the opera (1903); *Night before Christmas*, suite from the opera (1903); *At the Grave* (1904; in memory of Belaieff); *The Little Oak Stick*, op.62 (1905; 2nd version with Chorus ad libitum, 1906); *Greeting* (1906); *The Golden Cockerel*, symphonic arrangement of the introduction and wedding march from the opera (1907). **CHAMBER:** String Quartet in F major, op.12 (1875); Sextet in A major for 2 Violins, 2 Violas, and 2 Cellos (1876); Quintet in B-flat major for Flute, Clarinet, Horn, Bassoon, and Piano (1876); *String Quartet on Russian Themes* (1878–79); 4 variations on a chorale in G minor for String Quartet (1885); *String Quartet on B-la- f* (Belaieff; 1886; other movements by Liadov, Borodin, and Glazunov); String Quartet *Jour de fête* (1887; finale only; other movements by Glazunov and Liadov); Nocturne in F major for 4 Horns (c. 1888); 2 duets in F major for 2 Horns (c. 1893–94); *Canzonetta and Tarantella* for 2 Clarinets (c. 1883–94); *Serenade* for Cello and Piano (1893; also for Cello and Orch., 1903); String Quartet in G major (1897); Theme and Variation No. 4 in G major for String Quartet (1898; in collaboration with others); Allegro in B-flat major for String Quartet (1899; in collaboration with others). **Piano:** Allegro in D minor (1859–60); *Variations on a Russian Theme* (1859–60); Nocturne in D minor (1860); *Funeral March* in D minor (1860); Scherzo in C minor for Piano, 4-Hands (1860); 6 fugues, op.17 (1875); 3 pieces, op.15 (1875–76); 4 pieces, op.11 (1876–77); *6 Variations on B-A-C-H*, op.10 (1878); *Variations on a Theme by Misha* for Piano, 4-Hands (1878–79); Prelude-Impromptu: Mazurka, op.38 (1894); Allegretto in C major (1895); Prelude in G major (1896); Fugal Intermezzo for Piano, 4-Hands (1897); etc. **VOCAL: Choral with Orch.:** *Poem about Alexis, the Man of God*, op.20 (1878); *Glory*, op.21 (1879–80); *Svitezyanka*, cantata for Soprano, Tenor, Chorus, and Orch., op.44 (1897); *Poem of Oleg the Wise* for Tenor, Bass, Men's Chorus, and Orch., op.58 (1899); *From Homer*, prelude-cantata for Soprano, Mezzo-soprano,

Alto, Women's Chorus, and Orch., op.60 (1901). **A C a p - p e l l a :** 2 choruses, op.13 (1875); op.14 (1875); 6 choruses, op.16 (1875–76); 2 choruses, op.18 (1876); 4 choruses, op.23 (1876); 15 Russian folk songs, op.19 (1879); etc.; also 83 solo songs; 4 duets. **ARRANGEMENTS AND EDITIONS:** He ed. a collection of 100 Russian folk songs, op.24 (1876); harmonized 40 folk songs. After Dargomyzhsky's death, he orchestrated his posthumous opera *Kamennyi gost* (The Stone Guest); also orchestrated Borodin's *Prince Igor*; his greatest task of musical reorganization was the preparation for publication and performance of Mussorgsky's works; he reharmonized the cycle *Songs and Dances of Death* and the symphonic picture *Night on Bald Mountain*; orchestrated the opera *Khovanshchina*; rev. *Boris Godunov* (in melody and harmony, as well as in orchestration).

WRITINGS: His most important pedagogical books were studies on harmony (St. Petersburg, 1884; Eng. tr., 1930) and on orchestration (2 vols., St. Petersburg, 1913). He also wrote a valuable autobiography (St. Petersburg, 1909; Eng. tr., 1924). A. Rimsky-Korsakov et al. edited a complete edition of his works (Moscow, 1946 et seq.).

BIBL.: N. van Gilse van der Pals, *R.-K.* (Leipzig, 1914); M. Montagu-Nathan, *R.-K.* (London, 1916); N. van Gilse van der Pals, *R.-K.s Opernschaffen* (Leipzig, 1929); A. Rimsky-Korsakov, *R.-K.* (5 fascicles, Moscow, 1933, 1935, 1936, 1937, 1946; last vol. ed. by V. Rimsky-Korsakov); I. Markevitch, *R.-K.* (Paris, 1935); A. Solovtzov, *R.-K.* (Moscow, 1948; 2nd ed., 1957); G. Abraham, *R.-K.; A Short Biography* (London, 1949); I. Kunin, *R.-K.* (Moscow, 1964); ibid., *N.A. R.-K.* (Moscow, 1979); G. Seaman, *N.A. R.-K.: A Guide to Research* (N.Y., 1988).—**NS/LK/DM**

Rinaldo di (da) Capua,

Italian composer; b. Capua or Rome, c. 1705; d. probably in Rome, c. 1780. He came from the vicinity of Naples and seems to have been active chiefly in Rome, where Burney knew him in 1770, and where most of his operas were given (others were produced in Florence, Venice, London, and Paris). His career as a dramatic composer probably began in 1737. Thereafter he produced about 30 theatrical works with varying success, among them *Ciro riconosciuto* (Rome, Jan. 19, 1737), *Vologeso re de' Parti* (Rome, Carnival 1739), and *La Zingara* (Paris, June 19, 1753; his best work). He also composed 5 syms. and many overtures which reveal an adept hand at orch. writing, numerous oratorios, cantatas, and other works.

BIBL.: R. Bostian, *The Works of R. d.C.* (diss., Univ. of N.C., 1961).—**NS/LK/DM**

Rinck, Johann Christian Heinrich,

famous German organist, teacher, and composer; b. Elgersburg, Thuringia, Feb. 18, 1770; d. Darmstadt, Aug. 7, 1846. He studied under Kittel in Erfurt (1786–89). He was town organist at Giessen (1790–1805) before settling in Darmstadt, where he was organist and teacher at the music school (from 1805); became court organist there in 1813, and chamber musician in 1817. One of the foremost players of the time, he made frequent concert tours. In addition to much music for organ, he wrote masses, cantatas, and motets. He publ. an autobiography (Breslau, 1833).

BIBL.: M. Folsing, *Zuge aus dem Leben und Wirken des Dr. C.H. R.* (Erfurt, 1848); F. Donat, *C.H. R. und die Orgelmusik seiner Zeit* (Bad Oeynhausen, 1933).—**NS/LK/DM**

Ringbom, Nils-Eric,

Finnish violinist, music critic, music administrator, and composer; b. Turku, Dec. 27, 1907; d. Korpoström, Feb. 13, 1988. He studied at the Turku Academy (M.A., 1933) and at the Univ. of Helsinki (D.Mus., 1955, with the diss. *Über die Deutbarkeit der Tonkunst*; publ. in Helsinki and Wiesbaden, 1955); among his teachers were O. Andersson and L. Funtek. He played violin in the Turku Sym. Orch. (1927–28; 1930–33), and was music critic of the *Svenska Pressen* (1933–44) and the *Nya Pressen* (1945–70). He was asst. manager (1938–42) and manager (1942–70) of the Helsinki Phil., and also served as artistic director of the Sibelius Festival (1951–60) and as chairman of the Helsinki Festival (1966–70).

WRITINGS: *Helsingfors orkesterföretag 1882–1932* (Helsinki, 1932); *Säveltaide* (The Art of Music; Helsinki, 1945); *Sibelius* (Stockholm, 1948; Ger. tr., 1950; Eng. tr., 1954); *Musik utan normer* (Music without Norms; 1972); *Orkesterhovdingar* (1981).

WORKS: ORCH.: *Little Suite* (1933; rev. 1946); 5 syms. (1938–39; 1943–44; 1948; 1962; 1970). **CHAMBER:** Duo for Violin and Viola (1945); Wind Sextet (1951); String Quartet (1952); piano pieces. **VOCAL:** *Till livet* (To Life) for Chorus and String Orch. (1936); *Vandrerska* (The Wanderer) for Soprano and Orch. (1942); *Hymn till Helsingfors* for Chorus and Orch. (1949); songs.—**NS/LK/DM**

Ringer, Alexander L(othar),

American musicologist; b. Berlin (of Dutch parents), Feb. 3, 1921. He attended the Hollander Cons. in Berlin. In 1939 went to Amsterdam, where he studied composition with Henk Badings. In 1946 he emigrated to the U.S., and continued his education at the New School for Social Research in N.Y. (M.A., 1949) and at Columbia Univ. (Ph.D., 1955). He taught at the City Coll. of N.Y. (1948–52), the Univ. of Pa. (1952–55), the Univ. of Calif., Berkeley (1955–56), and the Univ. of Okla. (1956–58). In 1958 he was appointed to the faculty of the Univ. of Ill. in Urbana; also was a regular guest lecturer at the Hebrew Univ. in Jerusalem. He contributed many articles to the *Musical Quarterly*; also publ. the study *Arnold Schoenberg: The Composer as Jew* (Oxford, 1990).—**NS/LK/DM**

Rinuccini, Ottavio,

great Italian poet and librettist; b. Florence, Jan. 20, 1562; d. there, March 28, 1621. He was born into a family of the nobility and became a prominent courtier. He commenced writing verses for court entertainments about 1579, and was also active in the Accademia Fiorentina and the Accademia degli Alterati, taking the name "Il Sonnacchioso" ("the somnolent one"). He collaborated with Bardi in preparing intermedi for the wedding of the Grand Duke Ferdinando I (1589). Corsi and Peri then set his pastoral *Dafne* to music, which work is generally recognized as the first opera in the monodic style (Florence, 1598). Rinuccini's *Euridice*, with music by Peri, was performed in 1600, and another setting, by Caccini, in 1602. He also wrote the libretto of Monteverdi's *Arianna* (1608). These texts were republ. by A. Solerti in vol. II of *Gli albori del melodramma* (Milan, 1905) and by A. Della Corte, *Drammi per musica dal Rinuccini allo Zeno* (Turin, 1958).

BIBL.: F. Meda, *O. R.* (Milan, 1894); A. Civita, *O. R. ed il sorgere del melodramma in Italia* (Mantua, 1900); F. Raccamadoro-

Ramelli, *O. R.: Studio biografico e critico* (Fabriano, 1900); A. Solerti, *Le origini del melodramma* (Turin, 1903); A. Della Corte, *O. R. librettista* (Turin, 1925); M. Schild, *Die Musikdramen O. R.s* (Würzburg, 1933).—**NS/LK/DM**

Rios, Waldo de los, Argentine composer, conductor, arranger, and pianist; b. Buenos Aires, Sept. 7, 1934; d. (of a self-inflicted gunshot wound) Madrid, March 29, 1977. He studied in Argentina with his mother, Martha de los Rios, a prominent Argentine folksinger, then had piano, composition, and conducting lessons at the National Academy of Music (graduated, 1954). He served in the Argentine military; concurrently made his first folk recordings with Columbia Records (1955). This and subsequent recordings of indigenous folk tunes arranged for sym. orch. were not well received, since Argentina was experiencing renewed interest in its folk music and was intent upon authenticity. In 1962 he emigrated to Spain, where he subsequently made it his mission to popularize the classics for the enlightenment of the masses; this he accomplished by selecting outstanding movements from large-scale, well-known works and, after condensing them to 3–5 minutes, arranging them for symphonic forces augmented by pop ensembles which included saxophone, drums, and Spanish and/or Latin percussion instruments. His rendition of Mozart's Sym. No. 40 became particularly popular. During the 1970s he was conductor-director of the Manuel de Falla Orch. and Chorus, with which he made numerous recordings, including *Sinfonias* (1971), *Operas* (1974), *Sinfonias for the 70's* (1975), *Concertos for the 70's* (1976), and *Corales* (1978). Among his legitimately original works was *South American Suite* (1957), based upon primitive melodies and rhythms of Paraguay, Argentina, Uruguay, and Peru, and scored for orch. augmented by guitars, Indian harp, and various native wind and percussion instruments.—**NS/LK/DM**

Riotte, Philipp Jakob, German conductor and composer; b. St. Wendel, Saar, Aug. 16, 1776; d. Vienna, Aug. 20, 1856. He studied with André in Offenbach. In 1808 he settled in Vienna, where he conducted at the Theater an der Wien and produced there 48 works of his own, including operas, ballets, and minor pieces; also a Sym., 9 piano sonatas, 6 violin sonatas, etc. He was the author of the "tone picture" *Die Schlacht bei Leipzig* for Piano, which achieved extraordinary popularity in Germany.

BIBL.: G. Spengler, *Der Komponist P.J. R.* (diss., Univ. of Saarbrücken, 1973).—**NS/LK/DM**

Ripa, Alberto da, Italian lutenist and composer, known as **Alberto da Mantovano;** b. Mantua, c. 1500; d. Paris, 1551. He was in the service of Ercole Gonzaga, Cardinal of Mantua, and in 1529 entered the service of François I of France, becoming valet de chambre du roi in 1533. His *Tablature de luth* was brought out posthumously by his pupil Guillaume Morlaye (6 books, Paris, 1552–58). See J.-M. Vaccaro, ed., *Alberto da Rippe: OEuvres, in Le Choeur des Muses, Corpus des Luthistes Francais* (1972–75).—**NS/LK/DM**

Ripa (y Blanque), Antonio, Spanish composer; b. Tarazona, c. 1720; d. Seville, Nov. 3, 1795. He was a choirboy at Tarazona Cathedral, where he was named maestro de capilla when he was only 17. After studying at the diocesan seminary and entering the priesthood, he served as maestro de capilla at the Carmelite nuns' church in Saragossa, then at Cuenca Cathedral, and finally at Seville Cathedral (from 1768). He wrote a distinguished canon of sacred music, including 10 masses, 39 vesper psalms, 11 Lamentations, 140 villancicos, and many other scores.—**LK/DM**

Risler, Edouard, Alsatian pianist; b. Baden-Baden, Feb. 23, 1873; d. Paris, July 22, 1929. He studied piano with Diémer at the Paris Cons. and continued his studies with Klindworth, Stavenhagen, and Eugène d'Albert in Germany. In 1923 he was appointed prof. at the Paris Cons. He gave concert recitals all over Europe and acquired a high reputation as a fine musician as well as a virtuoso pianist; he made a specialty of presenting cycles of one composer's works; he played Beethoven's 32 sonatas, Chopin's complete piano works, and both books of Bach's *Well- tempered Clavier.*—**NS/LK/DM**

Rist, Johann, German poet and composer; b. Ottensen, near Hamburg, March 8, 1607; d. Wedel-on-Elbe, Aug. 31, 1667. He studied theology, law, and poetry at the Univs. of Rinteln and Rostock, and was pastor in Wedel (from 1635). In 1644 he was made poet laureate by the Emperor, and in 1653 was elevated to the rank of nobleman. He organized in Hamburg a Liederschule, for which he secured the cooperation of many important composers of the day, among them Schiedemann and Thomas Selle. He has been described as the "organizer of the German Parnassus," and indeed his role in the development of a purely national type of secular song, of German folk inspiration, was historically significant. He also wrote a number of sacred songs—*O Ewigkeit, du Donnerwort; O Traurigkeit; O Herzeleid; Werde munter, mein Gemüte*; etc.—which are still sung in Lutheran churches in Germany. He compiled valuable collections of German sacred songs. A modern ed. was brought out by E. Mannack, *J. Rist: Sämtliche Werke* (Berlin, 1967 et seq.).

BIBL.: T. Hansen, *J. R. und seine Zeit* (Halle, 1872; reprint, Leipzig, 1973); W. Krabbe, *J. R. und das deutsche Lied* (Bonn, 1910); O. Kern, *J. R. als weltlicher Lyriker* (Marburg, 1919); O. Heins, *J. R. und das niederdeutsche Drama des 17. Jahrhunderts* (1930).—**NS/LK/DM**

Ristenpart, Karl, German conductor; b. Kiel, Jan. 26, 1900; d. Lisbon, Dec. 24, 1967. He studied at the Stern Cons. in Berlin and Vienna. In 1932 he became conductor of the Berlin Chamber Orch.; also led concerts with the Radio Orch. in Berlin. In 1946 he was named conductor of the Chamber Orch. of RIAS (Radio in the American Sector of Berlin). In 1953 he became conductor of the Chamber Orch. of the Saar, a noted ensemble of the Saarland Radio in Saarbrucken; made many tours and recordings with this group.—**NS/LK/DM**

Ristić, Milan, Serbian composer; b. Belgrade, Aug. 31, 1908; d. there, Dec. 20, 1982. He studied in Belgrade with Slavenski and in Prague with Alois Hába. A prolific composer, he wrote mostly instrumental music; his style ranged from neo-Romantic grandiosity to economic neo-Classicism, from epically declamatory diatonicism to expressionistically atonal melos. Some of his works were written in an explicit dodecaphonic technique; in some, he made use of quarter tones.

WORKS: ORCH.: 7 syms. (1941, 1951, 1961, 1966, 1967, 1968, 1972); Violin Concerto (1944); Piano Concerto (1954); *Suite giocosa* (1956); *Symphonic Variations* (1957); *Burleska* (1957); *7 Bagatelles* (1959); *Concerto for Orchestra* (1963); Clarinet Concerto (1964); *4 Movements* for Strings (1971). **CHAMBER:** 2 string quartets; Wind Quintet; Septet; Violin Sonata; Viola Sonata; 24 fugues for various instrumental combinations; Suite for 4 Trombones in quarter- tones.—**NS/LK/DM**

Ristori, Giovanni Alberto, Italian composer; b. probably in Bologna, 1692; d. Dresden, Feb. 7, 1753. He received his education from his father, a violinist in an Italian opera company, with whom he went to Dresden (1715) and obtained the post of director of the Polish chapel in Warsaw. He then was appointed chamber organist to the court of Saxony (1733), church composer (1746), and asst. conductor (1750). He wrote a number of operas for the Italian Opera in Dresden. His *Calandro*, staged at Pillnitz, near Dresden, on Sept. 2, 1726, was one of the earliest Italian comic operas produced in Germany, and so possesses historical significance beyond its intrinsic worth. Other operas produced in Dresden and in court theaters near Dresden were *Cleonice* (Aug. 15, 1718), *Un pazzo ne fà cento, ovvero Don Chisciotte* (Feb. 2, 1727), *Arianna* (Aug. 7, 1736), *Le Fate* (Aug. 10, 1736), etc. He also wrote oratorios, cantatas, and masses, and some instrumental music. Many of his MSS were destroyed during the siege of Dresden (1760) and the bombing of the city in World War II.

BIBL.: C. Mengelberg, *G.A.R.* (Leipzig, 1916). —**NS/LK/DM**

Ritchie, Margaret (Willard), English soprano; b. Grimsby, June 7, 1903; d. Ewelme, Oxfordshire, Feb. 7, 1969. She studied at the Royal Coll. of Music in London and with Plunket Greene, Agnes Wood, and Henry Wood. She established herself as a prominent concert artist early in her career, and also was the principal soprano of Frederick Woodhouse's Intimate Opera Co. Later she sang with the Sadler's Wells Opera in London (1944–47), at the Glyndebourne Festivals (1946–47), with the English Opera Group (from 1947), and at Covent Garden in London. From 1960 she taught voice in Oxford. She created the roles of Lucia in *The Rape of Lucretia* (1946) and of Miss Wordsworth in *Albert Herring* (1947). As a concert artist, she was much admired for her Schubert lieder recitals.—**NS/LK/DM**

Ritchie, Stanley (John), Australian violinist and teacher; b. Yenda, New South Wales, April 21, 1935. He studied violin with Florent Hoogstoel at the New South Wales State Conservatorium of Music in Sydney (diploma, 1956). After receiving instruction in violin and chamber music from Jean Fournier and Sandor Vegh in Paris (1958–59), he went to the U.S. and continued his training with Joseph Fuchs at Yale Univ. (1959–60), Oscar Shumsky, and Samuel Kissell. He served as concertmaster of the N.Y.C. Opera orch. (1963–65) and assoc. concertmaster of the Metropolitan Opera orch. (1965–70); was a member of the N.Y. Chamber Soloists (1970–73), founder of the early music ensemble Aston Magna (1974), and 1st violin in the Philadelphia String Quartet (1975–81). With his wife, harpsichordist and fortepianist Elizabeth Wright, he performed in the Duo Geminiani (from 1974); was prof. of violin and director of the Baroque orch. at Ind. Univ. (from 1982) and a prof. at the Juilliard School in N.Y. (from 1984). He has championed the performance of early music on period instruments.—**NS/LK/DM**

Ritter, Alexander, German violinist, conductor, composer, and poet; b. Narva, Estonia (of German parents), June 27, 1833; d. Munich, April 12, 1896. He was taken to Dresden in 1841, where he studied violin with Franz Schubert (namesake of the great composer), concertmaster of the Dresden Opera; then studied at the Leipzig Cons. (1849–51) with Ferdinand David (violin) and E.F. Richter (theory). In 1854 he married Wagner's niece Franziska Wagner and settled in Weimar, where he entered into a close association with Liszt, Bülow, Cornelius, Raff, and others; was 2nd Konzertmeister in the orch. there (until 1856). He was conductor at the opera in Stettin (1856–58), where his wife was engaged as a soprano; he then lived in Dresden (1858–60), Schwerin (1860–62), and Würzburg (1863–82). When Bülow became conductor at the Hofkapelle in Meiningen (1882), Ritter followed him there and was made 2nd Konzertmeister of the orch.; after Bülow's departure from Meiningen in 1886, Ritter moved to Munich. He wrote 2 operas, *Der faule Hans* (Munich, Oct. 15, 1885) and *Wem die Krone?* (Weimar, June 8, 1890), to his own librettos, several symphonic poems in an intensely Romantic manner (*Seraphische Phantasie, Erotische Legende, Karfreitag und Frohnleichnam*, and *Kaiser Rudolfs Ritt zum Grabe*), a String Quartet, about 60 songs, and piano pieces.. Ritter's significance derives, however, not from his well-made but ephemeral compositions, but from his profound influence on young Richard Strauss; it was Ritter who encouraged Strauss in the creation of a new type of philosophical tone poem along the lines of "Musik als Ausdruck" (music as expression), a modern development of the art of Liszt, Wagner, and Berlioz. Ritter wrote the poem printed in the score of *Tod und Verklärung*.—**NS/LK/DM**

Ritter, Christian, German organist and composer; b. c. 1647; d. after 1717. He was a chamber organist in Halle by 1666. By 1672 he was a court musician there, and subsequently served as court organist as well. By 1681 he was court organist in Stockholm, and soon thereafter was given the additional position of vice-Kapellmeister. After serving as court organist and vice-Kapellmeister in Dresden (1683–88), he returned to Stockholm as a court musician, remaining there until at least 1699. Ritter distinguished himself as a composer of Protestant church music, and numbering among his extant works are 22 motets, a keyboard suite, and an organ sonatina.—**LK/DM**

Ritter, Georg Wenzel, German bassoonist and composer, uncle of **Peter Ritter;** b. Mannheim, April 7, 1748; d. Berlin, June 16, 1808. He joined the Mannheim Court Orch. when he was 16. After it removed to Munich in 1778, he served as 2nd bassoonist in the orch. there until 1788 when he joined the Berlin Court Orch. Ritter was highly regarded as a bassoon virtuoso. Mozart met him in 1777 and wrote the bassoon part of his Sinfonia concertante, K.Anh. 9; 297B for Ritter. Among Ritter's own works are 2 bassoon concertos and 6 quartets for Bassoon and Strings.—**LK/DM**

Ritter, Hermann, German violist, inventor, teacher, writer on music, and composer; b. Wismar, Sept. 16, 1849; d. Würzburg, Jan. 22, 1926. He studied at the Hochschule für Musik in Berlin, and attended courses at the Univ. of Heidelberg. Turning his attention to musical instruments, he began a series of experiments for the purpose of improving the muffled tone of the ordinary viola. Profiting by some practical hints in A. Bagatella's book *Regole per la costruzione di violini* (Padua, 1786), he constructed a slightly larger model possessed of better resonance and a more brilliant tone. Exhibiting this new "viola alta" in 1876, he attracted the attention of Wagner, who invited his cooperation for the Bayreuth Festival. After that engagement he made successful tours of all Europe as a viola virtuoso, and from 1879 was a prof. of viola and music history at the Musikschule in Würzburg. In 1905 he founded the "Ritterquartett" (violin, W. Schulze-Prisca; viola alta, Ritter; viola tenore, E. Cahnbley; viola bassa, H. Knöchel). He publ. numerous compositions and transcriptions for viola and piano, and *Elementartechnik der Viola alta.*

WRITINGS: *Die Geschichte der Viola alta und die Grundsätze ihres Baues* (Leipzig, 1876; 2nd ed., 1877; reprinted, Wiesbaden, 1969); *Repetitorium der Musikgeschichte* (1880); *Aus der Harmonielehre meines Lebens* (1883); *Elementartheorie der Musik* (1885); *Ästhetik der Tonkunst* (1886); *Studien und Skizzen aus Musik- und Kulturgeschichte, sowie Musikästhetik* (Dresden, 1892); *Katechismus der Musikasthetik* (2nd ed., 1894); *Katechismus der Musikinstrumente* (1894); *Volksgesang in alter und neuer Zeit* (1896); *Schubert* (1896); *Haydn, Mozart, Beethoven* (1897); *Die fünfsaitige Geige und die Weiterentwicklung der Streichinstrumente* (1898); *Allgemeine illustrierte Encyklopädie der Musikgeschichte* (6 vols., 1901–02).

BIBL.: G. Adema, *H. R. und seine Viola alta* (Würzburg, 1881; 2nd ed., 1894).—**NS/LK/DM**

Ritter, Peter, German cellist, conductor, and composer, nephew of **Georg Wenzel Ritter;** b. Mannheim, July 2, 1763; d. there, Aug. 1, 1846. His career was centered on Mannheim, where he studied composition with G.J. Vogler. In 1783 he became a cellist in the orch. of the National Theater, becoming its Konzertmeister in 1801. In 1803 he also became Kapellmeister of the orch. of the Grand Duchy of Baden, and made tours as a concert artist. He retired in 1823. Ritter wrote several stage works, the most successful being his Singspiel *Der Zitherschläger* (Stuttgart, 1810). He also wrote the well-known hymn *Grosser Gott wir loben dich* (1792).

WORKS: DRAMATIC (all 1st perf. in Mannheim unless otherwise given): *Der Eremit auf Formentara* (Dec. 14, 1788); *Der*

Sklavenhändler (April 11, 1790); *Die Weihe* (1792); *Die lustigen Weiber von Windsor* (Nov. 4, 1794); *Dilara, oder Die schwarze Zauberin* (1798); *Das neue Jahr in Famagusta* (1804); *Salomons Urteil* (1808); *Marie von Mantalban* (Frankfurt am Main, 1810); *Der Zitherschläger* (Stuttgart, 1810); *Alexander in Indien* (1811); *Feodore* (1811); *Das Tal von Barzelonetta, oder Die beiden Ermiten* (1811); *Das Kind des Herkules* (1812); *Alfred* (1820); *Der Mandarin, oder Die gefoppten Chinesen* (Karlsrue, 1821); *Hoang-Puff, oder Das dreifache Horoskop* (1822); *Bianca* (1824); *Der Talisman* (1824); *Das Grubenlicht* (1833). **OTHER:** Piano Concerto; Cello Concerto; chamber music; *Das verlorne Paradies*, oratorio (1819); *Die Geburt Jesu*, cantata (1832).

BIBL.: W. Schulze, *P. R.* (Berlin, 1895); G. Schmidt, *P. R.* (diss., Univ. of Munich, 1924).—**NS/LK/DM**

Rivé-King, Julie, American pianist, teacher, and composer; b. Cincinnati, Oct. 30, 1854; d. Indianapolis, July 24, 1937. She received her primary instruction from her mother, then studied in N.Y. with William Mason and in Leipzig with Reinecke; also was for a time a pupil of Liszt. She played Liszt's Piano Concerto No. 1 at her American debut, with the N.Y. Phil. (April 24, 1875), marking the beginning of an active career; she gave about 4,000 concerts in the U.S., retiring only a year before her death. In 1876 she married Frank King of Milwaukee. From 1905 to 1936 she was a piano instructor at the Bush Cons. in Chicago. She wrote some attractive piano pieces (*Impromptu, Polonaise héroïque, Bubbling Spring,* etc.).

BIBL.: M. Petteys, *J. R.-K., American Pianist* (diss., Univ. of Mo., 1987).—**NS/LK/DM**

Rivers, Johnny (originally, **Ramistella, John**), 1960s pop crooner; b. N.Y., Nov. 7, 1942. At the age of three, Johnny Rivers moved with his family to Baton Rouge, La., where he grew up. He took up guitar at age eight and formed his first music group at 14. In 1957, he met disc jockey Alan Freed, who suggested the name change to Johnny Rivers. Rivers made his first recordings, in a rockabilly style, in N.Y. in 1958 and moved to Nashville at the age of 17 to record demonstration records. In 1960, he moved to Los Angeles, where he recorded for a number of small labels through 1964. He also briefly performed at Nev. casinos as a member of Louis Prima's band. Playing regularly at Los Angeles discotheques, he began a long-running engagement at the newly opened Whiskey A-Go-Go in 1964. Signed to Imperial Records, Rivers recorded live albums at the club that sparked the discotheque craze and produced a number of cover hits beginning in 1964 with the smash hit "Memphis," written by Chuck Berry. In 1966, he scored a smash hit with P. F. Sloan and Steve Barri's television theme song "Secret Agent Man" and a top hit with "Poor Side of Town," cowritten with producer Lou Adler.

During 1966, Johnny Rivers formed Rivers Music, signing songwriter Jimmy Webb, and Soul City Records, signing The Fifth Dimension. The group scored a number of hits for the label through 1969, including the smash hits "Up, Up and Away" (by Webb), "Stoned Soul Picnic," and "Wedding Bell Blues" (by Laura Nyro), and the medley "Aquarius/Let the Sun Shine In" from the rock musical *Hair*. In 1968, Al Wilson had a major pop hit on Soul City with "The Snake." In 1967, Johnny Rivers performed at the Monterey International Pop Festival and successfully covered several Motown classics, achieving his final major hit for five years with James Hendricks's "Summer Rain." By the end of 1969, he had divested himself of interest in Soul City and ceased personal appearances. His biggest album success came with 1968's *Realization* on Imperial Records. He subsequently recorded for several different labels, scoring his final major hit in 1977 with "Swayin' to the Music (Slow Dancin')" on Big Tree Records. In the early 1980s, he recorded the gospel album *Not a Through Street* for Priority Records and essentially retired from the music business.

DISC.: JOHNNY RIVERS: *The Early Years* (1969); *The Sensational Johnny Rivers* (1964); *Go, Johnny, Go!* (1964); *At the Whiskey A-Go-Go* (1964); *Here We A-Go-Go Again!* (1964); *In Action!* (1965); *Meanwhile, Back at the Whiskey A-Go-Go* (1965); *Rocks the Folk* (1965); *And I Know You Wanna Dance* (1966); *Changes* (1966); *Rewind* (1967); *Realization* (1968); *Slim Slo Slider* (1970); *Home Grown* (1971); *L. A. Reggae* (1972); *Blue Suede Shoes* (1973); *Wild Night* (1976); *Road* (1974); *Last Boogie in Paris* (1974); *New Lovers and Old Friends* (1975); *Outside Help* (1977); *Borrowed Time* (1981); *Not a Through Street* (1983); *Greatest Hits* (rerecordings; 1985); *Totally Live at the Whiskey A-Go-Go* (1995).—**BH**

Rivers, Sam(uel Carthorne), jazz tenor and soprano saxophonist, flutist, pianist, composer; b. El Reno, Okla., Sept. 25, 1930. He came from a musical family; his grandfather, a minister and musician, published *A Collection of Revival Hymns and Plantation Melodies* (1882); his father, a Fisk Univ. graduate, sang with the Fisk Jubilee Singers and Silverstone Quartet while his mother accompanied them on piano. Sam studied violin and sang in church at age five. He studied piano, switched to trombone at 11 while living in North Little Rock, Ark., then took up saxophone at 13 and moved to Tex. to continue studies. After spending three years in the Navy, Rivers played his first professional gig in Vallejo with Jimmy Witherspoon. In 1947 he went to the Boston Cons., remaining there five years, and then studying at Boston Univ. During this time, he played with several Boston-based musicians, including Jaki Byard, Quincy Jones, Gigi Gryce, and Alan Dawson. From 1955–57, he lived in Fla., but was back in Boston in 1958 to join the Herb Pomeroy big band; at the same time, he led his own quartet with 13-year-old Tony Williams on drums. He also worked backing visiting R&B artists, including Maxine Brown, Wilson Pickett, Jerry Butler, B.B. King, and others, then toured with T-Bone Walker. He replaced George Coleman with Miles Davis for six months, including a visit to Japan (1964), and then moved to Calif. to form his first group in 1965; he was back in N.Y. by 1967. He worked with Cecil Taylor (1968–73), including a period as Artist-in-Residence at Antioch Coll., Ohio; he played briefly with M. Tyner in 1970. With his wife, Rivers opened Studio Rivbea in 1971 in lower Manhattan as center for experimental music; he worked with his own groups, Harlem Ensemble, and Winds of Manhattan. He was Composer-in-Residence for the Harlem Opera Society. In 1975, he was guest soloist with the San Francisco Symphony

Orch., and his music was presented at Carnegie Hall for the 1978 Newport in N.Y. festival. A year later, his composition for 32 musicians was presented at N.Y.'s Public Theater. In the early 1990s, he moved to Orlando, Fla., becoming a vital part of the scene there and working with local musicians Anthony Cole and Doug Mathews.

DISC.: *Fuschia Swing Song* (1964); *Contours* (1965); *New Conception* (1966); *Involution* (1966); *Dimensions and Extensions* (1967); *Hues* (1971); *Streams: Live at Montreux* (1973); *Crystals* (1974); *Sizzle* (1975); *Capricorn Rising* (1975); *Quest* (1976); *Sam Rivers/Dave Holland, Vol. 2* (1976); *Sam Rivers, Vol. 2* (1976); *Sam Rivers and Dave Holland* (1976); *Paragon* (1977); *Waves* (1978); *Live Trio Sessions* (1979); *Contrasts* (1979); *Jazzbuhne Berlin '82* (1982); *Colours* (1982); *Lazuli* (1989); *Concept* (1996). M. Davis: *In Tokyo* (1964).—**LP**

Rivier, Jean, French composer and pedagogue; b. Villemonble, July 21, 1896; d. La Penne sur Huveaune, Nov. 6, 1987. His early musical training was interrupted by his enlistment in the French army during World War I. His health was severely damaged as a result of mustard gas, and it was only after a long recuperation that he was able to enter the Paris Cons. in 1922 to study with Emmanuel (music history), J. Gallon (harmony), and Caussade (counterpoint and fugue; premier prix, 1926). He also studied cello with Bazelaire. In subsequent years, he was active with various contemporary music societies in Paris, including Triton, of which he was president (1936–40). From 1948 to 1966 he taught composition at the Paris Cons. In 1970 he was awarded the Grand Prix for music of the City of Paris. He formed a style of composition in which he effectively combined elements of French Classicism and Impressionism.

WORKS: DRAMATIC: Opera: *Vénitienne* (Paris, July 8, 1937). **ORCH.:** Cello Concerto (1927); *Chant funèbre*, symphonic poem (1927); *Danse* (1928); *3 Pastorales* (1928; Paris, Feb. 7, 1929); *Ouverture pour un Don Quichotte* (1929); *Burlesque* for Violin and Orch. (1929); *Adagio* for Strings (1930; Paris, March 1, 1931); *Ouverture pour une opérette imaginaire* (1930); *5 Mouvements brefs* (1931); *Le Livre d'Urien* (1931); 8 syms.: No. 1 (1931; Paris, Jan. 29, 1933), No. 2 for Strings (1937), No. 3 for Strings (1937; Paris, Nov. 25, 1940), No. 4 for Strings (1947), No. 5 (1950; Strasbourg, June 24, 1951), No. 6, *Les Présages* (Paris, Dec. 11, 1958), No. 7, *Les Contrastes* (1961; Paris, Jan. 9, 1962), and No. 8 for Strings (1978); Viola or Alto Saxophone Concertino (1935; Paris, Feb. 15, 1936); *Musiques nocturnes* (1936); *Paysage pour une Jeanne d'Arc à Domrémy*, symphonic tableau (1936; Paris, Jan. 31, 1937); 2 piano concertos: No. 1 (1940) and No. 2, *Concerto breve*, for Piano and Strings (1953); Violin Concerto (1942); *Rapsodie provençale* (Aix-en-Provence, July 22, 1949); *Ouverture pour un drame* (1952); Concerto for Alto Saxophone, Trumpet, and Strings (1954); Concerto for Flute and Strings (Strasbourg, June 1956); *Musique pour un ballet* (1957); *Le Déjeuner sur l'herbe* (1958); Concerto for Clarinet and Strings (1958); Concerto for Bassoon and Strings (1963); Concerto for Brass, Timpani, and Strings (1963); *Drames*, symphonic movement (1966); *Résonances* (1966); *Triade* for Strings (1967); Concerto for Oboe and Strings (1967); Concerto for Trumpet and Strings (1970); *Lento doloroso* for Strings (1981). **CHAMBER:** 2 string quartets (1924, 1940); String Trio (1933); *Grave et presto* for Saxophone Quartet (1938); Duo for Flute and Clarinet (1968); *Climats* for Celesta, Vibraphone, Xylophone, Piano, and Strings (1968); *Capriccio* for Wind Quintet (1972); *Brilliances* for Brass

Septet (1972); *Comme une tendre berceuse* for Flute and Piano (1984); *3 Movements for Clarinet and Piano* (1985). **P i a n o :** *Quatre Fantasmes* (1967); Sonata (1969); *Contrasts* (1981); *Stèle* (1982). **V O C A L :** *Psaume LVI* for Soprano, Chorus, and Orch. (1937); *Ballade des amants désespérés* for Chorus and Orch. (1945); *Requiem* for Mezzo-soprano, Bass, Chorus, and Orch. (1953); *Christus Rex*, oratorio for Contralto, Chorus, and Orch. (1966); *Dolor* for Chorus and Orch. (1973); choruses; songs. —NS/LK/DM

Rizzi, Carlo, Italian conductor; b. Milan, July 19, 1960. He took courses in piano, conducting, and composition at the Milan Cons., and then studied conducting with Delman in Bologna (1984) and Ferrara at the Accademia Musicale Chigiana in Siena (1985). In 1982 he made his debut conducting Donizetti's *L'Ajo nell'imbarazzo, o Don Gregorio* at Milan's Angelicum. In 1985 he was 1st prize winner in the new Toscanini conducting competition in Parma, where he then conducted *Falstaff*; subsequently conducted throughout Italy. In 1988 he made his British debut at the Buxton Festival conducting *Torquato Tasso*, and in 1989 conducted *Il Barbiere di Siviglia* at the Australian Opera in Sydney and *Don Pasquale* at the Netherlands Opera in Amsterdam. He conducted *La Cenerentola* at London's Covent Garden in 1990. He was chosen to conduct *Il Trovatore* at the opening of the restored Teatro Carlo Felice in Genoa in 1991. In 1992 he made his first appearance at the Deutsche Oper in Berlin conducting *L'Italiana in Algeri*. Rizzi served as music director of the Welsh National Opera in Cardiff from 1992. In 1993 he made his first appearance in the U.S. as a guest conductor of the Chicago Sym. Orch. at the Ravinia Festival in Chicago. On Oct. 29, 1993, he made his Metropolitan Opera debut in N.Y. conducting *La Bohème*.—NS/LK/DM

Roach, Max(well Lemuel), remarkable black American jazz drummer and composer; b. Elizabeth City, N.C., Jan. 10, 1924. He was taken to N.Y. as a child, and after playing in a church drum-and-bugle corps, he was a drummer in his high school band; also sat in on jam sessions in various jazz haunts around the city. He began his professional career as a member of Dizzy Gillespie's quintet, becoming immersed in the bebop movement. After a stint with Benny Carter's band (1944–45), he joined Charlie Parker's quintet (1947) and became widely recognized as one of the most innovative drummers of his era. He also studied composition with John Lewis at the Manhattan School of Music. He then led his own groups (from 1949), perfecting his "hard-bop" style. With the trumpeter Clifford Brown, he was co- leader of an outstanding quintet (1953–56). In subsequent years he led various groups, including M'Boom Re, a percussion ensemble (from 1970). With his own quartet, he played throughout the U.S., Europe, and Japan (1976–77). He became a prof. of music at the Univ. of Mass. in Amherst (1972), where he instituted a jazz studies program. As a composer, he became best known for his *Freedom Now Suite* (1960), an expression of his solidarity with the U.S. civil rights movement. He also wrote and recorded the avant-garde scores *Force*

(1976; dedicated to Mao Tse-tung) and *1 in 2—2 in 1* (1978). He was awarded an honorary Mus.D. degree from the New England Cons. of Music in Boston in 1982.—NS/LK/DM

Robbin, Catherine, Canadian mezzo-soprano; b. Toronto, Sept. 28, 1950. She studied at the Royal Cons. of Music in Toronto (B.A., 1977), and with Jacob Hamm and Phyliss Mailing in Vancouver, Audrey Langford in London, Ré Koster in Canada, and Sir Peter Pears in England. In 1972 she made her professional debut as a soloist in *Messiah* with the St. Catharines Sym. Orch. In 1978 she won the Caplet Award at the Concours international de chant in Paris and the Silver Medal at the Concours international in Geneva, and in 1979 the Gold Award in the Benson & Hedges International Competition for Concert Singers. In 1979 she sang Britten's Lucretia at the Aldeburgh Festival and in 1981 she made her N.Y. recital debut. She subsequently devoted herself principally to a career as a concert and oratorio singer with engagements in leading North American and European music centers. Her later operatic appearances included Tchaikovsky's Olga at the Lyons Opera (1984), and various Handelian roles, among them Cleone in Washington, D.C., and N.Y. (1985), Orlando at the London Promenade Concerts (1989), and Rinaldo in Blackheath (1996). While her concert and oratorio performances have been especially successful in the Baroque repertoire, she has also won acclaim for her Mahler and Elgar.—NS/LK/DM

Robbins, Marty (originally, **Robinson, Martin David**), American country singer, songwriter, and guitarist; b. near Glendale, Ariz., Sept. 26, 1925; d. Nashville, Tenn., Dec. 8, 1982. A major country singer of the 1950s and 1960s, Robbins crossed over to the pop charts with some of his biggest hits, including "Singing the Blues," "Don't Worry," and "A White Sport Coat (and a Pink Carnation)." Though accomplished in many styles, he was best known for his ballads about the Old West, especially "El Paso." He reached the country charts 94 times between 1952 and 1983.

Robbins, the son of John and Emma Heckle Robinson, grew up in a large, poor family in the Ariz. desert. When he was 12 his parents divorced, and he moved with his mother to Glendale. During World War II he served with the navy in the Pacific, meanwhile learning to play the guitar. After the war he returned to Ariz., where he gradually built up a career as a singer and guitarist in clubs and on local radio and television. On Sept. 27, 1948, he married Marizona Baldwin, with whom he had two children, the first being Ronald Carson Robinson (b. Phoenix, July 16, 1949), who would become a country singer under the name Ronny Robbins.

Robbins made his debut as a guest on the *Grand Ole Opry* radio show in Nashville in 1948, but his real break didn't come until 1951, when country singer "Little" Jimmy Dickens, a Columbia Records recording artist, appeared on his TV show, *Western Caravan*, and then recommended that Columbia sign him. He made his recording debut with the label in November 1951. His records were not immediately successful, but in January 1953, "I'll Go on Alone" (music and lyrics by Marty Robbins) hit #1 in the country charts. He joined the *Grand Ole Opry* on Jan. 19, 1953, and moved to Nashville.

Robbins had additional country hits in 1953–55, but he didn't top the charts again until he cut "Singing the Blues" (music and lyrics by Melvin Endsley), which went to #1 in November 1956. Guy Mitchell scored the #1 pop hit with the song, but Robbins's recording crossed over to the pop chart and made the Top 40. He did even better with "A White Sport Coat (and a Pink Carnation)" (music and lyrics by Marty Robbins), which hit #1 in the country charts in May 1957, made the pop Top Ten, and sold a million copies.

For the next five years Robbins recorded a series of country #1 hits that also made the Top 40 of the pop charts. They were: "The Story of My Life" (music by Burt Bacharach, lyrics by Hal David) in January 1958; "Just Married" (music and lyrics by Al Allen and Barry DeVorzon) in May 1958; "El Paso" (music and lyrics by Marty Robbins) in December 1959; "Don't Worry" (music and lyrics by Marty Robbins) in February 1961; "Devil Woman" (music and lyrics by Marty Robbins) in September 1962; and "Ruby Ann" (music and lyrics by Roberta Bellamy) in January 1963. Of these, the most significant was the story-song "El Paso," which also topped the pop charts in January 1960, winning a Grammy for Best Country & Western Performance and being featured on the million-selling album *Gunfighter Ballads and Trail Songs*; "Devil Woman" earned Robbins a Grammy nomination for Best Country & Western Recording.

Though his records did not cross over as successfully after 1963, Robbins continued to score hits on the country charts through the rest of the 1960s, notably reaching #1 with "Begging to You" (music and lyrics by Marty Robbins) in February 1964, "Ribbon of Darkness" (music and lyrics by Gordon Lightfoot) in June 1965, "Tonight Carmen" (music and lyrics by Marty Robbins) in July 1967, and "I Walk Alone" (music and lyrics by Herbert Wilson) in November 1968. He began to suffer health problems, suffering a first heart attack in October 1968 and a second in August 1969, and undergoing triple-bypass surgery in January 1970. Nevertheless, he continued to work steadily; in 1969, Frankie Laine scored a Top 40 pop hit and Johnny Bush a Top Ten country hit with his composition "You Gave Me a Mountain," which was nominated for a Grammy for Best Country Song and became a regular part of Elvis Presley's repertoire.

Robbins returned to the top of the country charts and had his biggest pop hit in seven years with "My Woman, My Woman, My Wife" (music and lyrics by Marty Robbins) in May 1970; it won him his second Grammy, for Best Country Song. The conclusion of his Columbia contract was marked by the release of the gold-selling compilations *Marty Robbins' Greatest Hits, Vol. III* (April 1971) and *Marty Robbins' All-Time Greatest Hits* (August 1972), after which he switched to the Decca label, which soon was absorbed into MCA Records. He charted consistently but less successfully with the label

and returned to Columbia in 1976, beginning with "El Paso City" (music and lyrics by Marty Robbins), which hit the top of the country charts, as did a similarly titled album. A revival of the 1927 song "Among My Souvenirs" (music by Horatio Nicholls, lyrics by Edgar Leslie) was also a country #1 in 1976.

Robbins continued to reach the country charts for the rest of his life, though less successfully after 1978. He suffered a third heart attack in January 1981 and a fourth and final one in December 1982, dying after surgery at the age of 57. A compilation of his *Biggest Hits* reached the charts and went gold just after his death.

In addition to his songwriting, recording, and performing, Robbins also acted in more than a dozen low-budget films, mostly Westerns. Among them were *Raiders of Old California* (1957), *The Badge of Marshall Brennan* (1957), *Road to Nashville* (1967), *From Nashville with Music* (1969), and *Guns of a Stranger* (1973). His final film appearance was a cameo in Clint Eastwood's *Honky Tonk Man* (1982), released shortly after his death; his recording of the title song became his final country Top Ten hit. He also had three syndicated television series: the Western drama *The Drifter* (1965), the musical-variety program *The Marty Robbins Show* (1969), and *Marty Robbins' Spotlight* (1977–78), a country music version of *This Is Your Life*.

WRITINGS: *The Small Man: A Novel of the Old West* (Nashville, 1960).

DISC.: *Song of Robbins* (1957); *Gunfighter Ballads and Trail Songs* (1959); *More Gunfighter Ballads and Trail Songs* (1960); *The Essential* (rec. 1951–82; rel. 1992).

BIBL.: Barbara J. Pruett, *Marty Robbins Fast Cars and Country Music* (London, 1991).—**WR**

Robbins Landon, H(oward) C(handler) *See* **Landon, H(oward) C(handler) Robbins**

Robert, Pierre, French composer; b. Louvres, near Paris, c. 1618; d. Paris (buried), Dec. 30, 1699. He spent most of his career in Paris, where he studied at the Notre Dame choir school. About 1637 he became a priest. He was maître de chapelle at Senlis Cathedral (1648–50), in Chartres (1650–52), and at Notre Dame (1653–63). In 1653 he was made one of the four sous-maîtres of the royal chapel, serving with Du Mont, Gobert, and Expills. After the latter two retired in 1669, Robert shared the duties with Du Mont. They also served jointly as Compositeur de la musique de la chapelle et de la chambre du roi from 1672 to 1683. In 1684 Robert left the royal service. He also served as abbot of Chambon, Poitiers diocese (1671–99), and of St. Pierre-de-Melun (1678–99). He publ. *Motets pour la chapelle Roy* for 5 to 6 Voices and Basso Continuo (Paris, 1684), 24 grands motets in the style of Lully. Also extant are 10 petits motets for 2 to 4 Voices (1688).—**LK/DM**

Robert de Handlo, English music theorist who flourished in the early 14th century. He wrote *Regule cum maximis Magistri Franconis cum additionibus aliorum mu-*

sicorum compilate a Roberto de Handlo (1326; ed. by L. Dittmer, Brooklyn, 1959, and by P. Lefferts, Lincoln, Nebr., 1990), a detailed exposition of late ars antiqua developments in notation.—**LK/DM**

Roberts, Marcus (Marthaniel), prodigious young pianist, composer; b. Jacksonville, Fla., Aug. 7, 1963. Blind from birth, he was a winner in the IAJE Young Talent Program in January 1982. He won the Jacksonville piano competition in 1984 and his set was televised. He distinguished himself in Wynton Marsalis's unit when he replaced Kenny Kirkland in 1985. Roberts has immersed himself in the 1920s music of George Gershwin; his 1995 live versions of "Rhapsody in Blue" included freely improvised cadenzas and additions, and the released album gave solo space to everyone. Though he is also influenced by James P. Johnson and the solo recordings of Thelonious Monk, he seems most free when he plays his own material, which involves unusual phrasing and changing meters. He has led his own trio since the late 1990s. He won the Helen Keller Achievement Award in 1998.

DISC.: *Truth Is Spoken Here* (1988); *Deep in the Shed* (1989); *Alone with Three Giants* (1990); *Prayer for Peace* (1991); *As Serenity Approaches* (1991); *If I Could Be with You* (1993); *Gershwin for Lovers* (1994); *Marcus Roberts Plays Ellington* (1995); *Time and Circumstance* (1996); *Blues for the New Millennium* (1997); *The Joy of Joplin* (1998); *The Collected Marcus Roberts* (1998); *In Honor of Duke* (1999).—**LP**

Roberts, Megan, American composer; b. Hempstead, N.Y., Oct. 12, 1952. She was taken to Calif. as a babe in arms, and flourished there, taking lessons with Robert Ashley at Mills Coll. in Oakland, and with Emma Lou Diemer at the Univ. of Calif., Santa Barbara. She experimented with unimedia arts of audio, video, dance, and theater; then switched to rock 'n' roll. Her most mind-boggling contribution to the unichoreovideoelectrobiosonic *School of California Calisthenics is Suite for a Small Chamber* (1976), in which the movements of dancers trigger electronic devices and tape-loop playback machines. In her video piece *Factory* (1976), she utilizes the technique of strobosonic photophonoscopy. On Jan. 14, 1977, she presented in San Francisco a multimedia study in violence free of moral redeeming value. Her major work, *I Could Sit Here All Day* (1976), is scored for birds, drums, and disembodied human voices, and tends to represent the ante-human and anti-human predecessors of rock 'n' roll.—**NS/LK/DM**

Robertson, Alec (actually, Alexander Thomas Paul), English writer on music and broadcaster; b. Southsea, June 3, 1892; d. Midhurst, Jan. 18, 1982. After studies at Bradfield Coll. and the Royal Academy of Music in London (1910–13), he was active with the Gramophone Co. (1920–30); then entered the Collegio Beda in Rome (1930) and was ordained a priest (1934). After serving at Westminster Cathedral, he joined the Gramophone Dept. of the BBC (1940), where he was chief producer of music talks on the Home and Third Programmes, a position he held until 1952. He was also a reviewer (from 1932) and music ed. (1952–72) for the

journal *Gramophone*. His autobiography was publ. as *More than Music* (London, 1961).

WRITINGS (all publ. in London unless otherwise given): *The Interpretation of Plainchant* (1937); *Brahms* (1939; 2nd ed., 1974); *Dvořák* (1945; 2nd ed., 1964); *Contrasts: The Arts and Religion* (1947); *How to Listen to Music* (1948); *Sacred Music* (1950); ed. *Chamber Music* (Harmondsworth, 1956; 4th ed., 1967); ed. with D. Stevens, *Pelican History of Music* (Harmondsworth, 1960–68); *Christian Music* (N.Y., 1961); *Music of the Catholic Church* (1961); ed. *G.B. S. on Music* (1962); *Requiem: Music of Mourning and Consolation* (1967); *Church Cantatas of J.S. Bach* (1972).—**NS/LK/DM**

Robertson, David, American conductor and composer; b. Santa Monica, Calif., July 19, 1958. He received training in horn, viola, conducting, and composition. In 1976 he became a student at the Royal Academy of Music in London, and he also attended the Hilversum conducting courses in 1979 and 1980, and concurrently studied privately with Kondrashin before attending the master class given by Kubelik in Lucerne in 1981. In 1980 he took 2nd prize at the Nicolai Malko Competition in Copenhagen, and then was an assistant at the Deutsche Oper am Rhein in Düsseldorf in 1981. He was a resident conductor of the Jerusalem Sym. Orch. from 1985 to 1987. In 1992 he became music director of the Ensemble InterContemporain in Paris. He became music director of the Orchestre National de Lyon in 2000. In addition to conducting contemporary scores in Paris, Robertson appeared as a guest conductor of the traditional repertoire with various European and American orchs. and in various opera houses. His compositions include Quartet for 4 Trombones (1978–79); *Ricercar I* for Harpsichord and Strings (1981), *II* for Brass Quintet (1983–84), and *III* for Trombone and Marimba (1984–86); an unfinished operatic trilogy: part 1, *Dangerous Children* (1989–90).—**NS/LK/DM**

Robertson, Herb, jazz trumpeter, fluegelhornist, cornetist, pocket trumpeter, bugler, valve trombonist; b. Plainfield, N.J., Feb. 21, 1951. He began playing trumpet at 10. He studied at Berklee (1969–72) with Charlie Mariano, Herb Pomeroy and Phil Wilson and became interested in free jazz, falling under the influence of Booker Little, Don Cherry and Don Ellis; he also studied for nearly ten years with a copper specialist, Donald S. Reinhardt. In 1972, he met Mark Helias in N.J. and they formed a quartet; then he toured the U.S. and Canada in various dance and rock bands, after which he worked with Dewey Redman, Paul Motian, Ray Anderson, Rashied Ali, Tim Berne (many times since 1983), Ratzo Harris, Charlie Haden's Liberation Music Orch., and played in a group accompanying the Merce Cunningham dance company. Robertson toured Europe with a quintet (1987); he worked with saxophonist Andy Laster (1988), Charlie Elgart's big band and Marc Ducret (1991). He moved to Berlin, Germany in the early 1990s.

DISC.: *Transparency* (1985); *Little Trumpet* (1986); *X-cerpts: Live at Willisau* (1988); *Shades of Bud Powell* (1988); *Certified* (1991).—**LP**

Robertson, Leroy, American composer and teacher; b. Fountain Green, Utah, Dec. 21, 1896; d. Salt

Lake City, July 25, 1971. He studied in Provo, then in Boston with Chadwick and Converse at the New England Cons. of Music (diploma, 1923); subsequently went to Europe, where he took courses with Bloch in Switzerland, Leichtentritt in Berlin, and Toch. Returning to America, he studied at the Univ. of Utah (M.A., 1932) and later at the Univ. of Southern Calif. in Los Angeles (Ph.D., 1954). He was a prof. and chairman of the music dept. at Brigham Young Univ. in Provo (1925–48); then was chairman of the music dept. at the Univ. of Utah (1948–63). In 1947 his symphonic work *Trilogy* received the 1st prize of $25,000 in a contest sponsored by Henry H. Reichhold of Detroit; it was performed by the Detroit Sym. Orch. on Dec. 11, 1947, but despite the attendant publicity, the work was not successful, and there were few subsequent performances. Other works include *The Book of Mormon*, oratorio (Salt Lake City, Feb. 18, 1953), *Prelude, Scherzo, Ricercare* for Orch. (1940), *Rhapsody* for Piano and Orch. (1944), *Punch and Judy Overture* (1945), Violin Concerto (1948), Piano Concerto (Salt Lake City, Nov. 30, 1966), Cello Concerto (1966), Piano Quintet (1933), String Quartet (1940; N.Y. Music Critics' Circle Award, 1944), *American Serenade* for String Quartet (1944), other chamber music, piano pieces, and songs.

BIBL.: M. Wilson, *H. R.: Music Giant From the Rockies* (Salt Lake City, 1996).—**NS/LK/DM**

Robertson, Rae, Scottish pianist; b. Ardersier, Inverness, Nov. 29, 1893; d. Los Angeles, Nov. 4, 1956. He studied with F. Niecks at the Univ. of Edinburgh; then at the Royal Academy of Music in London with Matthay and F. Corder. He married **Ethel Bartlett**, with whom he gave numerous concerts in Europe and America as duo-pianists (from 1928). With her he ed. an Oxford Univ. Press series of works for 2 pianos.—**NS/LK/DM**

Robertson, Stewart (John), Scottish conductor and pianist; b. Glasgow, May 22, 1948. He studied at the Royal Scottish Academy of Music in Glasgow (1965–69), the Univ. of Bristol (1969–70), the Vienna Academy of Music (1975), and the Salzburg Mozarteum (1977). His conducting mentors were Suitner and Swarowsky; also studied piano with Denis Matthews. In 1968–69 he was asst. chorus master of Glasgow's Scottish Opera and of the Edinburgh Festival. After serving as chorus master of the London City Singers (1970–72), he conducted at the Cologne Opera (1972–75). In 1975–76 he was music director of the Tanz Forum at the Zürich Opera, and then of the Scottish Opera Touring Co. (1976–79). From 1979 to 1982 he was music director of the Hidden Valley Chamber Orch. in Calif. From 1980 to 1988 he was assoc. conductor and director of the apprentice artists program of the Des Moines Metro Opera. In 1984–85 he was music director of the Mid-Columbia Sym. Orch., and in 1985–86 asst. conductor of the Oakland (Calif.) Sym. Orch. He subsequently was music director of the Santa Fe (N.Mex.) Sym. Orch. (from 1986), the Glimmerglass Opera in N.Y. (from 1987), and the Fla. Grand Opera (from 1998).—**NS/LK/DM**

Robertson, Zue (C. Alvin), early jazz trombonist; b. New Orleans, March 7, 1891; d. Watts, Calif., 1943.

He played piano at age five, switched to trombone at 13, receiving tuition from his cousin, Baptiste Delisle. He did his first jobs with the Cherry Blossom Band led by drummer Cornelius Tillman. He went on tour (c. 1910), playing in a band accompanying the Kit Carson Wild West Show. He played at the opening of Pete Lala's Cafe in New Orleans (c. 1912): during the following year he traveled to Chicago with a road show, then returned to play in New Orleans. He joined the Olympia Band, replacing Ed Vinson, and worked on trombone with Manuel Perez, and also with Richard M. Jones at George Fewclothes's Club. He did occasional work with John Robichaux on trombone and with the P. G. Loral Band on euphonium. He moved to Chicago in 1917 to work at De Lure Cafe, with Jelly Roll Morton in 1923 and to tour with King Oliver in 1924. After extensive touring with W. C. Handy, he returned to Chicago to join Dave Peyton at the Grand Theatre before further touring in the "Drake and Walker Show." Robertson settled in N.Y. from spring 1929 and worked mostly on piano and organ (at the Lincoln and Lafayette Theaters), but gave up trombone entirely in 1930. He moved to Calif. (c. 1932), working on piano and string bass throughout the 1930s. In 1943, he collapsed and died after suffering a pulmonary hemorrhage. It has been suggested that his correct nickname was Zoo, gained while Robertson was working with traveling circuses.—**JC/LP**

Robeson, Paul (Leroy Bustill), American singer, actor, and political activist; b. Princeton, N.J., April 9, 1898; d. Philadelphia, Pa., Jan. 23, 1976. Possessing a deep, resonant voice and a commanding presence, Robeson simultaneously pursued careers as a concert artist and as a stage and film actor. His performance of "Ol' Man River" (music by Jerome Kern, lyrics by Oscar Hammerstein II) is especially memorable due to his several recordings and his appearance in the 1936 film *Show Boat*. His 1940 recording of "Ballad for Americans" (music by Earl Robinson, lyrics by John Latouche), later inducted into the NARAS Hall of Fame, remains a stirring statement. But he was equally effective acting in plays by Eugene O'Neill and as the first African-American to portray *Othello* on Broadway. His career was effectively stifled from the late 1940s due to his outspoken political views. Since his death he has been widely recognized as a forerunner in the pursuit of racial equality.

Robeson's father, William Drew Robeson (originally Roberson), was a former slave who became a minister. His mother, Maria Louisa Bustill Robeson, was a teacher. Robeson displayed early ability as a scholar and athlete; in 1915 he won an academic scholarship to Rutgers, where he earned varsity letters in several sports and was twice chosen All-American in football. He graduated Phi Beta Kappa as class valedictorian, then attended Columbia Univ. Law School. On Aug. 17, 1921, he married hospital chemist Eslanda Cardozo Goode; they had a son, Paul Robeson Jr.

In 1920, Robeson starred in an amateur production of the play *Simon the Cyrenian* at the Harlem YMCA. He made his professional debut in April 1922 in *Taboo*, a short-lived play. Shortly after, he joined the singing group the Four Harmony Kings in the long-running revue *Shuffle Along*. He went to England and toured with *Taboo*, retitled *Voodoo*, making his British debut at Blackpool on July 20, 1922.

In 1923, Robeson appeared in the chorus of *The Plantation Revue*. Meanwhile, he continued to attend Columbia Law, from which he graduated that February. Though he never took the bar examination, he worked briefly in a law office. In 1924 he joined the theatrical troupe the Provincetown Players and starred in a revival of O'Neill's *The Emperor Jones*, followed by the playwright's controversial new work *All God's Chillun Got Wings* (N.Y., May 15, 1924), which concerned an interracial marriage. That fall he made his movie debut in the silent film *Body and Soul*.

On April 19, 1925, the Provincetown Players sponsored Robeson's concert debut in a recital of spirituals at the Greenwich Village Theatre; in the wake of its success he acquired a booking agent for concert work and signed a recording contract with Victor. He made his London acting debut in *The Emperor Jones* on Sept. 10. In December he scored his first record hit with the spiritual "Steal Away." He undertook a U.S. concert tour in the first quarter of 1926, then returned to Broadway, where he appeared in the play *Black Boy* (N.Y., Oct. 6, 1926).

Robeson toured Europe in the fall of 1927. He enjoyed a second record hit with "Deep River," another spiritual, in October. In March and April 1928 he appeared on Broadway in the play *Porgy* (based on the Du Bose Heyward novel that later was the source for the George Gershwin opera *Porgy and Bess*).

Robeson had been the original choice to play Joe in *Show Boat* on Broadway, but he had become unavailable when the musical was delayed. After it opened on Broadway, on Dec. 27, 1927, he was cast in the London production, which opened on May 3, 1928. On March 1 he had recorded "Ol' Man River" backed by Paul Whiteman and His Orch.; the recording became the biggest hit of his career.

Robeson focused primarily on Europe over the next few years. He toured Central Europe in the spring of 1929 and again in the winter of 1930, made a second silent film, *Borderline*, in Switzerland in March 1930, and appeared in London in *Othello* in May 1930 and in O'Neill's *The Hairy Ape* in May 1931. He returned to Broadway for a revival of *Show Boat* (N.Y., May 19, 1932) and, with other members of the cast, including Helen Morgan, recorded songs from the musical for an album of 78-rpm records on Brunswick (later Columbia), one of the first cast albums ever made; it was inducted into the NARAS Hall of Fame in 1991.

In 1933, Robeson starred in a movie version of *The Emperor Jones*, his first appearance in a sound film. As in most of his films, he sang several songs. He traveled to the Soviet Union in 1934, where he was impressed by the absence of racism and became an advocate of the communist regime.

In the mid-1930s, while living in England, Robeson alternated stage appearances with performances in the British films *Sanders of the River* (1935), *Song of Freedom* (1936), *King Solomon's Mines* (1937), *Big Fella* (1937), and

Jericho (released in the U.S. as *Dark Sands*;1938), though he later expressed dissatisfaction with their colonialist themes and racial stereotypes. His only Hollywood film of the period was *Show Boat*. He also traveled widely in Europe, returning to the Soviet Union and singing for the Loyalist forces in the Spanish civil war.

In 1939, Robeson found a film more to his liking, playing a mineworker in the British movie *The Proud Valley* (1940), but it was his last starring role on film. (His last movie appearance was in *Tales of Manhattan* in 1942.) He returned to live in the U.S. in the fall of 1939. In November his live radio performance of "Ballad for Americans" was a sensation, and the subsequent recording, spread across both sides of two 78s, sold well. *John Henry* (N.Y., Jan. 10, 1940) was an unsuccessful musical, running only 47 performances, but Robeson scored a triumph with *Othello* (N.Y., Oct. 19, 1943), which ran 296 performances on Broadway and toured the U.S. into 1945. From 1945 to 1947 he also undertook an extensive American concert tour.

In the anticommunist fervor of the post–World War II era in America, Robeson became a target. Though he denied to a Congressional committee that he was a communist in 1946, he was closely allied with left-wing causes, including the 1948 presidential campaign of Henry A. Wallace, of whose Progressive Party Robeson was a founder. After giving a speech in Paris in April 1949 in which he suggested that blacks would refuse to fight a war against the Soviet Union, he was vilified. A concert he gave in Peekskill, N.Y., in the fall turned into a riot when attendees were attacked by right-wing fanatics. Robeson's passport was revoked in 1950 and, dropped by his booking agency, he had to arrange his own concert appearances on a much more modest scale. He was also forced to make his own records through his Othello Recording Co. It was not until 1958 that the Supreme Court restored his right to travel.

As the McCarthy era gave way, he gave a comeback concert at Carnegie Hall in May 1958, which was recorded and released by Vanguard Records, then left for England, where he appeared in *Othello* with the Royal Shakespeare Co. at Stratford-on-Avon in April 1959. Robeson returned to the U.S. in 1963 and lived in retirement until his death following a stroke at the age of 77.

WRITINGS: *Here I Stand* (N.Y., 1958); P. Foner, ed., *P. R. Speaks: Writings, Speeches, Interviews, 1918–74* (N.Y., 1978).

BIBL.: E. Robeson (his wife), *Paul Robeson, Negro* (N.Y., 1930); S. Graham, *Paul Robeson: Citizen of the World* (N.Y., 1946); M. Seton, *Paul Robeson* (London, 1958); E. Hoyt, *Paul Robeson: The American Othello* (Cleveland, Ohio, 1967); E. Greenfield, *Paul Robeson* (1975); C. Wright, *Robeson, Labor's Forgotten Champion* (Detroit, 1975); R. Dent, et al., eds., *Paul Robeson: Tributes and Selected Writings* (N.Y., 1976); D. Gilliam, *Paul Robeson, All-American* (Washington, D.C., 1976); Editors of Freedomways, *Paul Robeson, The Great Forerunner* (N.Y., 1978); S. Robeson, *The Whole World in His Hands: A Pictorial Biography of Paul Robeson* (N.Y., 1981); L. Davis, *A Paul Robeson Research Guide* (Westport, Conn., 1983); C. Bell, *Paul Robeson's Last Days in Philadelphia* (Bryn Mawr, Pa., 1986); R. Ramdin, *Paul Robeson: The Man and His Mission* (London, 1987); M. Duberman *Paul*

Robeson (N.Y., 1988); S. Erlich, *Paul Robeson* (1988); P. and F. McKissack, *Paul Robeson: A Voice to Remember* (1992); L. Brown, *The Young Paul Robeson: On My Journey Now* (Boulder, Colo., 1997).—WR

Robin, Mado, French soprano; b. Yseures-sur-Creuse, near Tours, Dec. 29, 1918; d. Paris, Dec. 10, 1960. She studied voice with Giuseppe Podestà. She then began her career as a concert artist, making her operatic debut in 1945 as Gilda at the Paris Opéra. She also sang at the Opéra-Comique, and made guest appearances in Brussels, Liège, and San Francisco. She was best known for her performances in the roles of Lakmé and Lucia. —NS/LK/DM

Robinson, Anastasia, English soprano, later contralto; b. in Italy, c. 1692; d. Southampton, April 1755. She was the daughter of the portrait painter Thomas Robinson. After studying music with Croft and singing with Sandoni and Lindelheim, she began her career singing in private concerts at her father's home in London. Handel wrote the soprano part of his *Ode for Queen Anne's Birthday* (1714) for her and she made her operatic debut with his company in London in the pasticcio *Creso* on Jan. 27, 1714. She subsequently sang in several of Handel's operas, creating the role of Oriana in his *Amadigi di Gaula* on May 25, 1715. After his company was disbanded in 1717, she turned to contralto roles and appeared at London's Drury Lane in 1719–20. She then was a member of Handel's Royal Academy of Music (1720–24), where she created the roles of Elmira in *Floridante* (Dec. 9, 1721), Matilda in *Ottone, Rè di Germania* (Jan. 12, 1723), Teodata in *Flavio, Rè di Longobardi* (May 14, 1723), and Cornelia in *Giulio Cesare in Egitto* (Feb. 20, 1724). In 1724 she retired from the stage and married the Earl of Peterborough, who did not publicly acknowledge their marriage until 1735. —NS/LK/DM

Robinson, Earl (Hawley), American composer; b. Seattle, July 2, 1910; d. in an automobile accident there, July 20, 1991. He studied with George McKay at the Univ. of Wash. (B.M. and teaching diploma, 1933), and then went to N.Y. (1934), where he completed his training with Copland and Eisler; was also active with the Workers Laboratory Theater and the Composers Collective of the Pierre Degeyter Club; it was during this period that he first gained notice via his topical songs. He won a Guggenheim fellowship (1942); was active in Hollywood as a composer for films until he was blacklisted during the McCarthy era; then returned to N.Y. and served as head of the music dept. at Elisabeth Irwin H.S. (1958–65). The film *The House I Live In* (1946) was inspired by his song of that title (1942), which won him an Academy Award in 1947. His autobiography appeared posthumously as *Ballad of an American* (Lanham, Md., 1998).

WORKS: DRAMATIC: Music Drama: *Song of Atlantis* (1983). **Folk Opera:** *Sandhog* (1951–54); *David of Sassoon* (1978). **Musicals:** *Processional* (1938); *Sing for Your Supper* (1939); *1 Foot in America* (1962); *Earl Robinson's America* (1976); *Listen for the Dolphin*, children's musical (1981). **Bal-** let: *Bouquet for Molly* (1949). **Other:** Film scores. **ORCH.:** *Good Morning* (1949); *A Country They Call Puget Sound*, tone poem for Tenor and Orch. (1956; rev. 1961); Banjo Concerto (1966–67); *The New Human*, piano concerto (1973); *To the Northwest Indians* for Narrator, Folk Instruments, and Orch. (1974). **VOCAL:** Cantatas; songs.—NS/LK/DM

Robinson, Faye, prominent black American soprano; b. Houston, Nov. 2, 1943. She studied at Bennett Coll. in Greensboro, N.C., Tex. Southern Univ. in Houston, and North Tex. State Univ. in Denton. After winning 1st prize in the San Francisco Opera Auditions, she made her debut as Micaëla in *Carmen* at the N.Y.C. Opera on Sept. 2, 1972; was on its roster until 1979. She appeared with opera companies in Houston, Philadelphia, Pittsburgh, San Diego, and Washington, D.C.; also sang widely in Europe and appeared frequently at the Aix-en-Provence Festival from 1974; was a guest artist with the Paris Opéra, the Vienna State Opera, the Hamburg State Opera, the Frankfurt am Main Opera, the Bavarian State Opera in Munich, and others. She was also active as a concert artist. Her operatic roles include Donna Anna, Pamina, Constanze, Elvira in *I Puritani*, Gilda, Liù, Violetta, the 4 principal soprano roles in *Les Contes d'Hoffmann*, and Gounod's Juliette; also sang in the premiere of Tippett's *The Mask of Time* (Boston, April 5, 1984).—NS/LK/DM

Robinson, J(oseph) Russel, early jazz writer, pianist; b. Indianapolis, Ind., July 8, 1892; d. Palmdaie, Calif., Sept. 30, 1963. At 14, he formed a piano and drum act with his brother, they toured (mostly through the South) until 1914; during this time he had sold his first composition "Sapho Rag" and composed "Eccentric." He played solo piano in Ind. before moving to Chicago to play with the New Orleans Jazz Band led by Henry and Merritt Brunies. He moved to N.Y., joining the Original Dixieland Jazz Band in January 1919. He left the O.D.J.B. during their stay in London and returned to N.Y. in October 1919. He worked as W. C. Handy's professional manager; rejoined O.D.J.B. for their residency at the Folies Bergere in N.Y. (September 1920). From the spring of 1921 Robinson worked as an accompanist for various singers including Marion Harris, Lucille Hegamin, and Lizzie Miles, then quit professional playing to work as a full-time composer. He took part in the revived O.D.J.B. in 1936, then moved back to the West Coast to resume composing. One of his most famous tunes is "Margie," he also wrote the lyrics for "Memphis Blues" and "Ole Miss."—JC/LP

Robinson, Michael, American composer; b. N.Y., March 11, 1956. He began piano lessons as a child, and also studied trumpet. His first significant teacher was Barney Bragin, who encouraged his interest in jazz and improvisation. In high school he began to study the saxophone and also composed his first work, *Promenade des Tortues* for Clarinet and Piano. He then studied at the State Univ. of N.Y. at Potsdam, pursuing a classical degree in saxophone while continuing his interest in jazz through private study with Lee Konitz. He left school and began playing in N.Y. and soon made a decided shift away from improvisation to composition. He returned to the State Univ. of N.Y. at Potsdam to complete his degree, then studied briefly with Mel Powell, Subotnick, and Leonard Stein while taking courses at the Calif. Inst. of the Arts. Returning once again to N.Y., and influenced by exposure to the music of Morton Feldman, he began composing slow moving, transcendental pieces of some duration. In 1984 he began experimenting with computers, and gradually began composing directly for the computer/synthesizer, turning out works of considerable energy and polyphony. He gave his first concert of works at St. Peter's Church in N.Y. (1985), and subsequently composed works to be performed exclusively by the computer or sequenced in real time, without live intervention or overdubbing. In 1989 he moved to Maui, where he acquired a MIDI system, which expanded his range of compositional possibilities. Returning to the mainland U.S. in 1990, he settled in Beverly Hills, where he released his first CD, *Trembling Flowers* (1991). In 1992 he began composing extremely contrapuntal, multi-movement pieces, subsequently released on the recording *Fire Monkey* (1993). In 1994 he also began working with exotic instrumental timbres and tunings, becoming particularly interested in North Indian classical music; the resulting early compositions so influenced comprise his CD *Hamoa* (1995). From 1996 Robinson began producing his own CDs, visually distinct for their lavish Japanese rice paper covers and autographed inner gold label; these include *Adorned With Pearl* (1996), *Chinese Legend* (1997), *Luminous Realms* (1998), *Lunar Mansions* (1998), *Sagarmatha* (1998), *Astral Palace* (1999), *Jaunpuri* (1999), *Monsoon Clouds* (1999), and *Snow Leopard Meadow* (1999).—**LK/DM**

Robinson, Michael Finlay, English musicologist; b. Gloucester, March 3, 1933. He was educated at the Univ. of Oxford (B.A., 1956; B.Mus., 1957; M.A., 1960; Ph.D., 1963, with the diss. *Neapolitan Opera, 1700–1780)*. He taught at the Royal Scottish Academy of Music in Glasgow (1960–61), the Univ. of Durham (1961–65), and McGill Univ. in Montreal (1965–70). In 1970 he joined the faculty of the Univ. of Wales Coll. in Cardiff, where he was senior lecturer (1975–91) and prof. (1991–94), and head of the music dept. (1987–94). He publ. *Opera Before Mozart* (1966), *Naples and Neapolitan Opera* (1972), and a thematic catalog of the works of Paisiello (2 vols., 1990, 1993).—**NS/LK/DM**

Robinson, Perry (Morris), jazz clarinetist; b. N.Y., Sept. 17, 1938. His father, **Earl Robinson,** composed "Joe Hill," "The House I Live In," "Black and White" (a hit for the rock band Three Dog Night), and "Ballad for Americans." His family moved to Los Angeles when he was five, and he started on clarinet at nine, studying with Kalman Bloch of the Los Angeles Phil.; his father took him to jazz concerts and he became interested in Benny Goodman. He returned to N.Y. at age 12 and attended the H.S. of Music and Art (1952–56), where he played saxophone and clarinet and jammed with Pete LaRoca, George Braith, and others. He first heard Buddy DeFranco and became influenced by Tony Scott (with whom he would later informally study), Pee Wee Russell, Sonny Rollins, and Charlie Parker. He went to the Manhattan School of Music for a year after high school, and studied with Ernie Simon of the Mannes School of Music. Through the 1960s, he played with Archie Shepp, Roswell Rudd, and Gunter Hampel's Galaxie Dream Band, Carla Bley, and Charlie Haden's first Liberation Orch. In 1973–75, Robinson was involved in the Darius Brubeck group, which came to be engulfed in the larger "Two Generations of Brubeck" ensemble with Dave, Chris and Dan Brubeck as well. During the 1980s, he led the Pipe Dreams band, which featured two vocalists, clarinet, and guitar. His mid-1990s ensemble is known as the Space-Time Swing Band, which originally included Mark Whitecage and swing drummer/singer Frankie Fame and later featured Steve Swell and drummer Lou Grassi. He also joined a klezmer band in Amsterdam, Klezmokum, headed by Burton Greene which performed at the Knitting Factory in N.Y. in 1998. A clarinet concerto written for Robinson was premiered in 1985 with the composer, Gary Schneider, leading the Hoboken Chamber Orch. (now the Hudson Chamber Orch.); it has subsequently been performed several times.

DISC.: *Funk Dumpling* (1962); *The Traveler* (1977); *Kundalini* (1978); *Nightmare Island* (1988); *Call to the Stars* (1990). **H. GRIMES:** *The Call* (1965). **A. SHEPP:** *Mama Too Tight* (1966). **C. HADEN:** *Liberation Music Orch.* (1970). **JAZZ COMPOSERS ORCH.:** *Escalator Over the Hill* (1971); *Spirits* (1971); *Angel* (1972); *Broadway/Folksong* (1972); *I Love Being with You* (1972); *European Concert* (c. 1973); *Out from Under* (1974); *Journey to the Song Within* (1974); *Celebrations* (1974); *Cosmic Dancer* (c. 1975); *Enfant Terrible* (1975); *Transformation* (1976); *Birdfree* (1976); *That Came Down on Me* (1978); *All Is Real* (1978); *All the Things You Could Be If Charles Mingus Was Your Daddy* (1980); *Life on This Planet* (1981); *Jubilation* (1983); *Fresh Heat* (1985); *Celestial Glory* (1991); *Brubecks: Two Generations of Brubeck* (1973); *Brother, the Great Spirit Made Us All* (1974); *INTERface: Poum!* (c. 1974); *Live at Environ* (1977). **CLARINET SUMMIT:** *You Better Fly Away* (1979). **J. FISCHER AND P. ROBINSON:** *Live in Eastern Europe* (1981); *Licorice Factory* (1985). **E. ROBINSON:** *Alive and Well* (c. 1986). **R. ANDERSON:** *It Just So Happens* (1987). **GERMAN CLARINET DUO:** *Materialized Perception* (1991). **KLEZMOKUM:** *Jew-azzic Park* (1994).—**MF**

Robinson, (Peter) Forbes, English bass; b. Macclesfield, May 21, 1926; d. London, May 13, 1987. He studied at Loughborough Coll., then went to Italy and took courses at the La Scala Opera School in Milan. He made his professional debut as Monterone at Covent Garden in London in 1954; later sang at the Aldeburgh Festival and the Edinburgh Festival, and with the English Opera Group, the English National Opera, the Teatro Colón in Buenos Aires, and the Zürich Opera. He had an extensive repertoire; his roles included Figaro, Boris Godunov, Don Giovanni, King Philip, Claggart in *Billy Budd*, and Tippett's King Priam, which role he created in 1962; also appeared widely as a concert artist. —**NS/LK/DM**

Robinson, Prince, early jazz tenor saxophonist, clarinetist; b. Portsmouth, Va., June 7, 1902; d. N.Y., July 23, 1960. He began playing clarinet at age of 14, mostly self-taught. He first worked in Lilian Jones's Jazz Hounds (1919–21), then with pianist Quentin Redd's Band in Atlantic City (1922). In 1923, he went to N.Y. to join Lionel Howard's Musical Aces. He spent the next two years mainly with Elmer Snowden, occasionally with June Clark, then worked with Duke Ellington from spring 1925. He left Ellington in summer 1926, and worked with a few other bands, before joining McKinney's Cotton Pickers, with whom he played for about seven years (1928–summer 1931; 1932–35). He spent the balance of the 1930s with Blanche Calloway's Band (summer 1935 until early 1937), Willie Bryant (April 1937–October 1938), and then Roy Eldridge (November 1938–40). In the early 1940s, he worked for two years with Louis Armstrong's Big Band (1940–42), and a year with Lucky Millinder (1942–43), and then began to freelance around N.Y. In 1945 began working regularly with Claude Hopkins, an association that lasted on and off until 1952. He toured with Henry "Red" Allen in 1954. During the second half of the 1950s, he played regular dates with Freddie Washington's Dixiecrats in Bayside, Long Island, until summer of 1959. He took part in the Fletcher Henderson reunion band in July 1958. Robinson was hospitalized with cancer for the last few months of his life.—JC/LP

Robinson, Ray, American writer on music and choral conductor; b. San Jose, Calif., Dec. 26, 1932. He learned to play the viola, and studied at San Jose State Coll. (B.A., 1956) and at Ind. Univ. in Bloomington (M.M., 1958; D.Mus.Ed., 1969, with the diss. *A History of the Peabody Conservatory*). He was an assoc. prof. of music and chairman of the division of fine arts at Cascade Coll. in Portland, Ore. (1959–63). From 1963 to 1966 he was dean of the Peabody Cons. of Music in Baltimore; then was its assoc. director (1966–69). From 1969 to 1987 he was president of Westminster Choir Coll. in Princeton, N.J. His books include *The Choral Experience* (with A. Winold; 1976), *Choral Music: A Norton Historical Anthology* (1978), *Krzysztof Penderecki: A Guide to His Works* (1983), *A Study of the Penderecki St. Luke Passion* (with A. Winold; 1983), and *John Finley Williamson: A Centennial Appreciation* (1987).—NS/LK/DM

Robinson, Sharon, American cellist; b. Houston, Dec. 2, 1949. She studied at the N.C. School of the Arts in Winston-Salem (graduated, 1968), the Univ. of Southern Calif. in Los Angeles (1968–70), and the Peabody Cons. of Music in Baltimore (B.M., 1974). In 1974 she made her formal debut in N.Y., and subsequently appeared as a solo artist and chamber music player. In 1975 she won the Levintritt Award. She married the violinist **Jaime Laredo** in 1976, with whom she joined that year with the pianist Joseph Kalichstein to form the Kalichstein-Laredo-Robinson Trio. They subsequently toured extensively in North America and Europe. —NS/LK/DM

Robison, Paula (Judith), gifted American flutist; b. Nashville, Tenn., June 8, 1941. Her family went to Los Angeles when she was a child, where she studied piano, but then turned to the flute. After attending the Univ. of Southern Calif., she studied flute with Julius Baker at the Juilliard School of Music in N.Y. (graduated, 1963); continued her studies with Marcel Moyse at the Marlboro (Vt.) Festival and in N.Y., where she made her recital debut (1961). After sharing 1st prize in the Munich Competition (1964), she became the first American to capture the 1st prize for flute in the Geneva International Competition (1966). She became a member of the Chamber Music Soc. of Lincoln Center in 1969. With her husband, the violist Scott Nickrenz, she was made co-artistic director of chamber music at the Spoleto Festival of Two Worlds in Italy and Charleston, S.C. (1977), and at the Spoleto/Melbourne (Australia) Festival of Three Worlds (1986). She was also active as a teacher. She commissioned and gave the premieres of works by Leon Kirchner, Robert Beaser, Toru Takemitsu, and Oliver Knussen.—NS/LK/DM

Robles, Marisa, Spanish harpist, teacher, and composer; b. Madrid, May 4, 1937. She was educated at the Madrid Cons., graduating in 1953. In 1954 she made her formal debut as soloist with the Orquesta Nacional de España in Madrid. In 1958 she joined the faculty of the Madrid Cons. After making her home in England in 1959, she became well known via television appearances. In 1963 she made her London concert debut, and subsequently appeared as a soloist with orchs. and as a recitalist throughout the world. From 1971 she also was a prof. of harp at the Royal Coll. of Music in London. In 1991 and 1994 she was artistic director of the World Harp Festival.—NS/LK/DM

Robson, Christopher, Scottish countertenor; b. Falkirk, Dec. 9, 1953. He attended the Cambridge Coll. of Arts and Technology (1970–72) and the Trinity Coll. of Music in London (1972–73), and also received vocal instruction from Paul Esswood and Helga Moth. He was a member of various groups, among them the London Oratory Choir (1974–80), the Monteverdi Choir (1974–84), the Westminster Cathedral Choir (1980–85), the King's Consort (1981–86), and the New London Consort (from 1986). In 1976 he made his formal debut in a concert performance of Handel's *Samson* in London, and in 1979 his stage debut as Argones in Handel's *Sosarme* in Birmingham. He made his first appearance at London's Covent Garden as Athamas in Handel's *Semele* in 1988. During the 1992–93 season, he sang Tolomeo in Handel's *Giulio Cesare* with the Scottish Opera in Glasgow. In the 1993–94 season, he appeared as Arsamenes in Handel's *Xerxes* at the English National Opera in London, which role he reprised during the 1995–96 season at the Lyric Opera in Chicago. He was engaged as Prince Orlovsky at the Bavarian State Opera in Munich in the 1997–98 season.—NS/LK/DM

Rocca, Lodovico, Italian composer; b. Turin, Nov. 29, 1895; d. there, June 25, 1986. He studied with Orefice at the Milan Cons., and also attended the Univ. of Turin. From 1940 to 1966 he was director of the Turin Cons.

WORKS: DRAMATIC: O p e r a : *La morte di Frine* (1917–20; Milan, April 24, 1937); *In terra di leggenda* (1922–23; Milan, Sept. 28, 1933); *Il Dibuk* (1928–30; Milan, March 24, 1934);

Monte Ivnor (1936–38; Rome, Dec. 23, 1939); *L'uragano* (1942–51 Milan, Feb. 8, 1952). **ORCH.:** *Contrasti* (1919); *Aurora di morte* (1920); *La foresta delle samodive* (1921); *L'alba del malato* (1922); *Le luci* (1923); *La cella azzurra* (1925); *Interludio epico* (1928). **VO-CAL:** *Biribù, Occhi di rana* for Voice and String Quartet (1937); *Schizzi francescani* for Tenor and 8 Instruments (1942); *Antiche iscrizioni* for Soloists, Chorus, and Orch. (1952; Rome, Feb. 6, 1953); songs.

BIBL.: M. Bruni, *L. R.* (Milan, 1963).—**NS/LK/DM**

Rochberg, George, significant American composer and teacher; b. Paterson, N.J., July 5, 1918. He took courses in counterpoint and composition with Weisse, Szell, and Mannes at the Mannes Coll. of Music in N.Y. (1939–42). After military service during World War II, he took courses in counterpoint and composition with Scalero and Menotti at the Curtis Inst. of Music in Philadelphia (B.Mus., 1948). He also studied at the Univ. of Phil. (M.A., 1949). He taught at the Curtis Inst. of Music (1948–54). He was in Rome on Fulbright and American Academy fellowships (1950). In 1951 he became music ed. of the Theodore Presser Co. in Philadelphia, and soon after was made its director of publications. In 1960 he joined the faculty of the Univ. of Pa. as chairman of the music dept., a position he held until 1968, then continued on its faculty as a prof. of music, serving as Annenberg Prof. of the Humanities from 1979 until his retirement in 1983. He held 2 Guggenheim fellowships (1956–57; 1966–67), was elected to membership in the American Academy of Arts and Letters (1985), and was made a fellow of the American Academy of Arts and Sciences (1986); was awarded honorary doctorates from the Univ. of Phil. (1985) and the Curtis Inst. of Music (1988). He publ. the study *The Hexachord and Its Relation to the Twelve-Tone Row* (Bryn Mawr, Pa., 1955). A collection of his writings was ed. by W. Bolcom as *The Aesthetics of Survival: A Composer's View of Twentieth-century Music* (Ann Arbor, 1984). In his style of composition, Rochberg pursues the ideal of tonal order and logically justifiable musical structures; the most profound influence he experienced was that of Schoenberg and Webern; many of his early works follow the organization in 12 different notes; more recently, he does not deny himself the treasures of the past. In his works, recognizable fragments from music by composers as mutually unrelated as Schütz, Bach, Mahler, and Ives are commented upon via quotation, juxtaposition, and polarity.

WORKS: DRAMATIC: *The Confidence Man*, opera, after Melville (Santa Fe, July 31, 1982); *Phaedra*, monodrama for Mezzo-soprano and Orch. (1974–75; Syracuse, N.Y., Jan. 9, 1976); incidental music to Ben Jonson's play *The Alchemist* (1965; N.Y., Oct. 13, 1968). **ORCH.:** *Night Music* (1948; N.Y., April 23, 1953; orig. the 2nd movement of the Sym. No. 1); *Capriccio* (1949; rev. 1957; orig. the 3rd movement of the Sym. No. 1); 6 syms: No. 1 (1st version in 3 movements, 1948–57; Philadelphia, March 28, 1958; 2nd version in 5 movements, including *Night Music* and *Capriccio*, 1971–77), No. 2 (1955–56; Cleveland, Feb. 26, 1959), No. 3 for Solo Voices, Chamber Chorus, Double Chorus, and Orch. (1966–69; N.Y., Nov. 24, 1970), No. 4 (Seattle, Nov. 15, 1976), No. 5 (1984; Chicago, March 13, 1986), and No. 6 (Pittsburgh, Oct. 16, 1987); *Cantio sacra* for Small Orch. (1954); *Cheltenham Concerto* for Flute, Oboe, Clarinet, Bassoon, Horn,

Trumpet, Trombone, and Strings (1958); *Time-Span I* (St. Louis, Oct. 22, 1960; withdrawn) and *II* (1962; Buffalo, Jan. 19, 1964); *Apocalyptica* for Wind Ensemble (1964; Montclair, N.J., May 19, 1965); *Black Sounds* for 17 Winds (1965); *Zodiac* (Cincinnati, May 8, 1965; orch. version of the *12 Bagatelles* for Piano, 1952); *Music for the Magic Theater* for 15 Instruments (1965); *Fanfares for Brass* (Philadelphia, March 17, 1968); *Imago mundi* (1973; Baltimore, May 8, 1974); Violin Concerto (1974; Pittsburgh, April 4, 1975); *Transcendental Variations* for Strings (1975; based on the String Quartet No. 3, 1972); Oboe Concerto (1983; N.Y., Dec. 13, 1984); Clarinet Concerto (1994–95); *Eden: Out of Time and Out of Space*, concerto for Guitar and Chamber Ensemble (1997). **CHAMBER:** 7 string quartets: No. 1 (1952; N.Y., Jan. 10, 1953), No. 2, with Soprano (1959–61; Philadelphia, April 30, 1962), No. 3 (N.Y., May 15, 1972), No. 4 (1977; Philadelphia, Jan. 20, 1979), No. 5 (1978; Philadelphia, Jan. 20, 1979), No. 6 (1978; Philadelphia, Jan. 20, 1979), and No. 7, with Baritone (1979; Ann Arbor, Jan. 27, 1980); Chamber Sym. for 9 Instruments (1953); *Serenate d'estate* for Flute, Harp, Guitar, and String Trio (1955); 3 piano trios (1963; 1985; *Summer 1990*, 1990); *Contra mortem et tempus* for Flute, Clarinet, Piano, and Violin (1965; N.Y., May 15, 1972); Quintet for Piano and String Quartet (1975; N.Y., March 15, 1976); *Octet: A Grand Fantasia* for Flute, Clarinet, Horn, Piano, Violin, Viola, Cello, and Double Bass (N.Y., April 25, 1980); Trio for Clarinet, Horn, and Piano (1980); String Quintet (Philadelphia, Jan. 6, 1982); Quartet for Piano, Violin, Viola, and Cello (1983; Washington, D.C., June 18, 1985); *To the Dark Wood* for Woodwind Quintet (1985; Armidale, Australia, Oct. 3, 1986); Trio for Piano, Violin, and Cello (1985; Washington, D.C., Feb. 27, 1986); Violin Sonata (1988; Pasadena, Calif., April 10, 1989); *Ora Pro Nobis* for Flute and Guitar (1989–90); *Muse of Fire* for Flute and Guitar (1990; N.Y., Feb. 1991); *Summer 1990*, trio for Violin, Cello, and Piano (1990; Philadelphia, March 23, 1992); *American Bouquet, Versions of American Popular Song* for Guitar (1991); *Sonata-Aria* for Cello and Piano (1992; Houston, Jan. 25, 1993). **Piano:** *Book of Contrapuntal Pieces* (1940–77); *Variations on an Original Theme* (1941); *3 Elegiac Pieces* (1945–98); *Sonata Seria* (1948–98); *12 Bagatelles* (1952; also as *Zodiac* for Orch., 1965); *Sonata-fantasia* (1956); *Bartókiana* (1959); *Nach Bach* (1966; also for Harpsichord); *Carnival Music* (1969); *Partita-variations* (1976); *4 Short Sonatas* (1984); *Circles of Fire* for 2 Pianos (1996–97). **VOCAL:** *David, the Psalmist* for Tenor and Orch. (1954); *Blake Songs* for Soprano and 8 Instruments (1961); *Passions according to the 20th Century* for Solo Voices, Chorus, Jazz Quintet, Brass Ensemble, Percussion, Piano, and Tape (1967; withdrawn); *Tableaux* for Soprano, 2 Actors, Small Men's Chorus, and 12 Instruments (1968); *Sacred Song of Reconciliation* for Bass-baritone and Chamber Orch. (1970); also a cappella choruses; songs.

BIBL.: J. Buccheri, *An Approach to Twelve-tone Music: Articulation of Serial Pitch Units in Piano Works of Schoenberg, Webern, Krenek, Dallapiccola, and R.* (diss., Univ. of Rochester, 1975); C. Sams, *Solo Vocal Writing in Selected Works of Berio, Crumb, and R.* (diss., Univ. of Wash., 1975); J. Smith, *The String Quartets of G. R.* (diss., Eastman School of Music, 1976); J. Dixon, *G. R.: A Bio-Bibliographic Guide to His Life and Works* (Stuyvesant, N.Y., 1991).—**NS/LK/DM**

Roche, Jerome (Lawrence Alexander), English musicologist; b. Cairo, May 22, 1942; d. Durham, June 2, 1994. He studied at St. John's Coll., Cambridge (B.A., 1962; Mus.B., 1963), and received his Ph.D. from the Univ. of Cambridge in 1968 with the diss. *North Italian Liturgical Music in the Early 17th Century*. In 1967 he became a lecturer at the Univ. of Durham. He publ. the books *Palestrina* (London, 1972) and *The Madrigal* (London, 1972; 2nd ed., 1990); with his wife, Elizabeth, he brought out a useful reference source, *A Dictionary of Early Music from the Troubadours to Monteverdi* (London, 1981); also publ. *Lassus* (Oxford, 1982) and *North Italian Church Music in the Age of Monteverdi* (Oxford, 1984). —NS/LK/DM

Rocherolle, Eugénie, American composer; b. New Orleans, Aug. 24, 1936. After piano studies in childhood, she pursued training in piano and composition at Sophie Newcomb Coll. of Tulane Univ. She also received training from Boulanger in Paris. In addition to composing, she was also active as a pianist, teacher, and lyricist. Her compositions are unabashedly Romantic in nature. Among her works are *America, My Home* for Chorus and Concert Band (1976), for the U.S. Bicentennial, *The New Colossus* for Chorus and Concert Band (1986), for the 100th anniversary of the Statue of Liberty, various choral pieces, and much piano music. —NS/LK/DM

Rochlitz, (Johann) Friedrich, German writer on music; b. Leipzig, Feb. 12, 1769; d. there, Dec. 16, 1842. A pupil of Doles at the Leipzig Thomasschule, he entered the Univ. of Leipzig as a theological student; publ. some novels and sketches. His 2 pamphlets, *Blicke in das Gebiet der Künste under der praktischen Philosophie* (Gotha, 1796) and *Einige Ideen uber die Anwendung des guten Geschmacks auf die religiosen Versammlungshäuser der Christen* (Leipzig, 1796), treat in part of music. In 1798 he founded the *Allgemeine Musikalische Zeitung*, which he ed. until 1818 and contributed to until 1835. From 1805 he was a director of the Leipzig Gewandhaus Concerts. His best-known work is *Für Freunde der Tonkunst* (4 vols., Leipzig, 1824–32; 3rd ed., 1868), which contains biographies, essays, analyses of compositions, etc.; vol. IV has an outline, *Geschichte der Gesangmusik*, which Rochlitz supplemented by a *Sammlung vorzüglicher Gesang-Stücke* in 3 vols., from Dufay to Vallotti. J. Müller-Blattau compiled Rochlitz's essays on Bach under the title *Wege zu Bach* (1926). Rochlitz composed songs for men's chorus and a setting of the 23rd Psalm. He also wrote texts for operas, oratorios, cantatas, etc.

BIBL.: H. Ehinger, *F. R. als Musikschriftsteller* (Leipzig, 1929).—NS/LK/DM

Rockefeller, Martha Baird, American pianist and music patroness; b. Madera, Calif., March 15, 1895; d. N.Y., Jan. 24, 1971. She studied at Occidental Coll. in Los Angeles and the New England Cons. of Music in Boston (graduated, 1917); received instruction in piano from Schnabel in Berlin. After touring with Dame Nellie Melba (1918), she appeared as a soloist with leading orchs. and as a recitalist until her retirement in 1931. In later years she devoted herself to musical philanthropy; after the death of her 3rd husband, John D. Rockefeller Jr., she organized the Martha Baird Rockefeller Fund for Music (1962); by the time it was dissolved in 1982, it had dispensed grants of some $9,000,000 to individuals and organizations.—NS/LK/DM

Rockmore, Clara, Russian-born American theremin player, sister of **Nadia Reisenberg;** b. Vilnius, March 9, 1911. She received piano lessons as a small child, and at the age of 4 entered the Imperial Cons. of Music in St. Petersburg (1915–17); subsequently settled in N.Y., where she studied violin with Auer (1925–28) and theremin with Leon Theremin, its inventor (1932–34). She thereafter devoted herself to a career as a theremin player; gave a public demonstration of the instrument (which, incidentally, plays without being touched) in a concert at N.Y.'s Town Hall on Oct. 30, 1934, which included a rendition of Franck's formidable Violin Sonata. She subsequently appeared as a soloist with major orchs. and as a recitalist. In 1977 Rockmore made a historically significant recording, *The Art of the Theremin—Clara Rockmore*. With the rekindling of interest in the instrument in the 1980s, she became something of a celebrity; at the instigation of filmmaker and theremin enthusiast Steve Martin, her ancient instrument was repaired by Robert Moog and subsequently appeared as the subject of a CBS-TV documentary program entitled *The Art of the Theremin*.—NS/LK/DM

Rockpile, principals of pub rock. **MEMBERSHIP:** Dave Edmunds, gtr., kybd., voc. (b. Cardiff, Wales, April 15, 1944); Nick Lowe, bs., voc. (b. Woolbridge, Suffolk, England, March 25, 1949); Billy Bremner, gtr., voc. (b. Scotland, 1947); Terry Williams, drm. (b. Hollywood, Calif., June 6, 1947).

First working together in Brinsley Schwarz, one of the best-known London pub-rock bands of the mid-1970s, Dave Edmunds and Nick Lowe were two of the most important British producers of the late 1970s and 1980s. With both favoring the sound of music from the 1950s and early 1960s (in stark contrast to the vapid, overproduced progressive-rock and pop bands then so popular), Edmunds and Lowe formed Rockpile in 1977 for recordings and tours under each of their names before recording a sole album in 1980 as Rockpile. Dave Edmunds enjoyed considerable success on his own, particularly in the early 1980s, but he largely withdrew from touring in 1987. Nick Lowe persevered with less acclaim, receiving a modicum of recognition in Little Village (with John Hiatt, Ry Cooder, and Jim Keltner) in 1992.

Dave Edmunds played in Welsh bands in the 1960s and formed the trio Love Sculpture in 1967. The group scored a smash British hit with a frantic instrumental version of Khatchaturian's "Sabre Dance" in late 1968. After the group disbanded in 1969, Edmunds returned to rural Wales to build his own recording studio, Rockfield, where he developed and refined his talent for re-creating the sound and feel of music from the 1950s and 1960s—from sparse rockabilly and country to elaborate Phil Spector–styled epics. He performed all vocal and instrumental duties for his smash 1971 British and American hit, a remake of Smiley Lewis's 1955 R&B hit "I Hear You Knocking." He recorded his debut album, *Rockpile*, in 1972 and achieved smash British hits with remakes of the Ronettes' "Baby I Love You" and the Chordettes' "Born to Be with You" in 1973. He also produced albums by Shakin' Stevens and Ducks Deluxe in the early 1970s and appeared in the 1974 David Essex film *Stardust*, writing several songs for the soundtrack.

Nick Lowe formed his first band, Sound 4 Plus 1, with guitarist Brinsley Schwarz at age 14, and later helped form Kippington Lodge with Schwarz in 1965. By late 1969 the group had evolved into Brinsley Schwarz, with Schwarz, Lowe, keyboardist Bob Andrews, and drummer Bill Rankin. Signed to British Liberty/United Artists (with early releases on Capitol in the United States), Brinsley Schwarz debuted at the Fillmore East, but their credibility was immediately brought into question when a planeload of British journalists were flown to N.Y. to witness the event.

The group adopted an unobtrusive stance on the London pub and club circuit and developed a modest following as principals of so-called pub rock. Following their first two albums, the group added second guitarist Ian Gomm for *Silver Pistol*, generally regarded as their most consistent work. After *Nervous on the Road*, which included Lowe's "(What's So Funny 'Bout) Peace, Love and Understanding," Dave Edmunds produced their final British-only album *New Favourites*, but the group broke up in early 1975. Brinsley Schwarz and Bill Rankin joined the pub-rock band Ducks Deluxe in their final days, and Schwarz and Bob Andrews later manned the Rumour, Graham Parker's backup band through 1980. The Rumour issued two albums of their own in the late 1970s, while Ian Gomm pursued a solo career that produced a major hit with "Hold On" in 1979.

Nick Lowe began hanging around Stiff Records, a small independent label based in London, and assisted Dave Edmunds in the recording of *Subtle as a Flying Mallet*, issued on RCA Records in late 1975. Lowe produced Graham Parker and the Rumour's first and third albums, *Howlin Wind* and *Stick to Me*, while Edmunds produced the Flamin' Groovies' *Shake Some Action*. In 1977 Lowe and Edmunds formed the ad hoc group Rockpile with guitarist-vocalist Billy Bremner and drummer Terry Williams to accompany their solo recordings and tours. As one of the few signings to Led Zeppelin's Swan Song label, Edmunds recorded *Get It* with the group, augmented by Bob Andrews. The album featured Lowe's "I Knew the Bride," Edmunds and Lowe's "Here Comes the Weekend," Edmunds's country-style "Worn Out Shoes, Brand New Pockets," and Graham Parker's "Back to School Days." During 1977 Lowe produced the Damned's debut British album and Elvis Costello's stunning debut, *My Aim Is True*. Lowe and Edmunds took part in the first tour of Stiff artists before Lowe left the label to become an independent producer.

In 1978 both Dave Edmunds and Nick Lowe were busy with a variety of projects. Lowe recorded his solo debut, *Pure Pop for Now People* (titled *Jesus of Cool* in Great Britain), which included his own "Marie Provost," "Heart of the City," and "So It Goes" as well as the collaborative "(I Love the Sound of) Breaking Glass," a smash British hit. Edmunds recorded *Tracks on Wax 4*, which contained "Trouble Boys," Lowe's "Television," Lowe and Edmunds's "What Looks Best on You," and Lowe and Rockpile's "Never Been in Love." During the same year Edmunds produced the Flamin'

Groovies' *Now* and Lowe produced Elvis Costello's *This Year's Model* and *Armed Forces*, which included a potent version of Lowe's "(What's So Funny 'Bout) Peace, Love and Understanding."

In 1979 Lowe produced the Pretenders' first single, "Stop Your Sobbing," and recorded *Labour of Lust*, his best-selling album. It included "Switchboard Susan," his own "Cracking Up," and the major pop hit "Cruel to Be Kind," written by Lowe and Ian Gomm. Lowe married Carlene Carter in August and later produced her albums *Musical Shapes* and *Blue Nun*. In the meantime, Edmunds recorded *Repeat When Necessary*, which featured Hank DeVito's "Sweet Little Lisa" and "Queen of Hearts," Graham Parker's "Crawling from the Wreckage," and Elvis Costello's "Girls Talk," a minor hit.

In 1980 Rockpile finally recorded an album under their own name, *Seconds of Pleasure*. It was dominated by songs written by Lowe, such as "Play That Fast Thing (One More Time)," "Pet You and Hold You," and "When I Write the Book," and yielded a moderate hit with "Teacher Teacher." Rockpile subsequently dissolved, and Terry Williams played with Dire Straits from 1983 to 1987. Dave Edmunds recorded *Twangin'*, which yielded a minor hit with John Fogerty's "Almost Saturday Night"; he also produced the Stray Cats hits "Rock This Town" and "Stray Cut Strut" as well as their albums *The Stray Cats* and *Rant and Rave*. In the meantime, Nick Lowe recorded *Nick the Knife* and *The Abominable Showman* and produced Paul Carrack's *Suburban Voodoo*, the Fabulous Thunderbirds' *T-Bird Rhythm*, and one side of John Hiatt's *Riding with the King*.

Dave Edmunds switched to Columbia Records for *D.E. 7th*, which featured "Me and the Boys" (by Terry Adams of NRBQ), Bruce Springsteen's "From Small Things (Big Things One Day Come)," and the country-style "Warmed Over Kisses (Left Over Love)." He later recorded *Information* under producer Jeff Lynne and scored a moderate hit with Lynne's "Slipping Away." During the mid-1980s Edmunds produced the Everly Brothers' two comeback albums, *EB '84* and *Born Yesterday*, as well as the Fabulous Thunderbirds' *Tuff Enuff* and k. d. lang's debut *Angel with a Lariat*. Nick Lowe assembled his Cowboy Outfit with Paul Carrack and Martin Belmont for two albums. Their eponymous debut included Lowe's "Half a Boy and Half a Man," whereas *The Rose of England* included John Hiatt's "She Don't Love Nobody," Elvis Costello's "Indoor Fireworks," and a minor-hit version of "I Knew the Bride (When She Used to Rock and Roll)."

In 1987 Dave Edmunds toured in support of the live set *I Hear You Rockin'*, often regarded as his finest later album. It reprised his most popular recordings yet failed to sell in significant quantities. He subsequently withdrew from touring, although he served as concertmaster for the two-month 1990 tour by Graham Parker and Dion, whose comeback album *Yo Frankie* he produced; he also played with Ringo Starr's All-Starr Band in 1992. Edmunds recorded *Closer to the Flame*, which featured Al Anderson's "Never Take the Place of You" and John Hiatt and Anderson's "I Got Your Number," for Capitol in 1990.

In 1987 Nick Lowe, Ry Cooder, and Jim Keltner backed John Hiatt for the recording of Hiatt's breakthrough album *Bring the Family*. Dave Edmunds produced Nick Lowe's 1990 Warner Bros. album *Party of One*. In 1992 Lowe rejoined Hiatt, Cooder, and Keltner in the short-lived supergroup Little Village. In 1994 Lowe released *The Impossible Bird*, a collection of country-style songs that won critical praise though few sales; it was followed by a live album.

DISC.: LOVE SCULPTURE: *Blues Helping* (1970); *Forms and Feelings* (1970). BRINSLEY SCHWARZ: *Brinsley Schwarz* (1970); *Despite It All* (1971); *Silver Pistol* (1972); *Nervous on the Road* (1972); *Brinsley Schwarz* (1978); *Brinsley Schwarz* (1995). THE RUMOUR: *Max* (1977); *Frogs, Sprouts, Clogs, and Krauts* (1979). IAN GOMM: *Gomm with the Wind* (1979); *What a Blow* (1980). ROCKPILE: *Seconds of Pleasure* (1980). DAVE EDMUNDS: *R.* (1972); *Subtle as a Flying Mallet* (1975); *Get It* (1977); *Tracks on Wax 4* (1978); *Repeat When Necessary* (1979); *Twangin'* (1981); *Best* (1981); *D.E. 7th* (1982); *Information* (1983); *Riff Raff* (1984); *I Hear You Rockin'* (1987); *Closer to the Flame* (1990); *Anthology (1968–1990)* (1993). NICK LOWE: *Pure Pop for Now People* (1978); *Labour of Lust* (1979); *Nick the Knife* (1982); *The Abominable Showman* (1983); *Nick Lowe and His Cowboy Outfit* (1984); *The Rose of England* (1985); *Basher: The Best of Nick Lowe* (1989); *Sixteen All-Time Lowes* (1986); *Party of One* (1990); *The Impossible Bird* (1994); *Nick Lowe and the Impossible Birds: Live! on the Battlefield* (1995). LITTLE VILLAGE: *Little Village* (1992).
—BH

Rockstro (real name, **Rackstraw**), **William (Smith)**,

English pianist, organist, teacher, writer on music, and composer; b. North Cheam, Surrey, Jan. 5, 1823; d. London, July 2, 1895. He studied at the Leipzig Cons. under Mendelssohn, Plaidy, and Hauptmann. Returning to London, he taught piano and singing. Rockstro wrote a popular ballad, *Queen and Huntress*, and also publ. piano arrangements of numerous operas. He devoted himself to a close study of ecclesiastical music, and became an acknowledged authority on plainchant. In 1876 he became a Roman Catholic.

WRITINGS (all publ. in London): *A History of Music for Young Students* (1879); *A Key to Practical Harmony* (1881); *The Rules of Counterpoint* (1882); *The Life of G.F. Handel* (1883); *Mendelssohn* (1884); *A General History of Music* (1886; 3rd ed., 1897); with H. Holland, *Jenny Lind the Artist* (1891); *Jenny Lind: A Record and Analysis of Jenny Lind-Goldschmidt* (1891).
—NS/LK/DM

Rodan (real name, **Rosenblum**), **Mendi**,

Romanian-born Israeli conductor; b. Iaşi, April 17, 1929. He studied in Bucharest at the Academy of Music (1945–47) and the Arts Inst. (1947–49), then conducted various ensembles in Romania. He settled in Israel (1960) and became a naturalized citizen (1961). Rodan was chief conductor of the Israel Broadcasting (later Jerusalem) Sym. Orch. (1963–72) and founder-conductor of the Jerusalem Chamber Orch. (1965–69), with which he toured Europe, the U.S., and the Far East. He was also made a teacher (1962) and a prof. (1973) at Jerusalem's Rubin Academy of Music, where he later was director. (1985–94). He was music director of the Israel Sinfonietta in Beersheba (1977–91) and chief conductor of the Orchestre National de Belgique in Brussels (1983–89). From 1993 to 1997 he was co-conductor of the Israel Phil. in Tel Aviv. From 1997 he was music director of the Israel Sym. Orch.—NS/LK/DM

Rode, (Jacques-) Pierre (Joseph),

renowned French violinist and composer; b. Bordeaux, Feb. 16, 1774; d. Château de Bourbon, near Damazan, Nov. 25, 1830. He studied violin with André-Joseph Fauvel (1780–88), making his first public appearance at age 12 in Bordeaux. He then was taken to Paris by Fauvel and became a pupil of Viotti (1787). He made his first appearance there as soloist in Viotti's 13th Concerto (1790), and introduced Viotti's 17th and 18th concertos to the Parisian public (1792); was a violinist in the orch. of the Théâtre de Monsieur (1789–92). In 1795 he was appointed prof. of violin at the Paris Cons., but immediately embarked on a tour of Holland and Germany; also appeared in London, but was exiled (along with Viotti) for political reasons in 1798. He returned to Paris in 1799 and resumed his duties at the Cons.; also served as solo violin at the Opéra. He became solo violinist to Napoleon in 1800, and brought out his extraordinarily successful 7th Violin Concerto. While on his way to Russia in 1803, he played throughout Germany; served as solo violinist to Czar Alexander I in St. Petersburg (1804–08). He scored an enormous success in Russia, but after his return to Paris his playing declined. In 1811–12 he toured Europe, and while in Vienna he performed Beethoven's Violin Sonata, op.96—a score written expressly for him—with Archduke Rudolph (Dec. 29, 1812). He returned to France in 1819, but made only a few unsuccessful appearances in subsequent seasons; a disastrous appearance in Paris in 1828 caused him to abandon the concert stage. At the apex of his career, Rode was acclaimed as the foremost representative of the French violin school. He was also esteemed as a composer. In addition to 13 notable violin concertos, he composed 12 string quartets (quatuors brilliants), 24 duos for 2 Violins, 24 caprices, airs variés, etc. With Baillot and Kreutzer, he wrote the violin method for the Cons. (1803).—NS/LK/DM

Rode, Wilhelm,

German bass-baritone; b. Hannover, Feb. 17, 1887; d. Icking, near Munich, Sept. 2, 1959. He studied in Hannover. He made his operatic debut in 1908 as the Herald in *Lohengrin* in Erfurt, then sang in Bremerhaven (1912–14), Breslau (1914–21), and Stuttgart (1921–22). He was a leading member of the Bavarian State Opera in Munich (1922–30), the Vienna State Opera (1930–32), and the Deutsches Opernhaus in Berlin (1932–45), where he also served as Intendant (1935–45); also appeared at London's Covent Garden and in other European opera houses. A member of the Nazi party, he was compelled to give up his career at the close of World War II. He became best known for his roles in Wagner's operas.—NS/LK/DM

Rodeheaver, Homer A(lvan),

American composer of gospel hymns and music publisher; b. Union Furnace, Ohio, Oct. 4, 1880; d. Winona Lake, Ind., Dec. 18, 1955. Taken to Jellicoe, Tenn., as a child, he grew up helping in his father's lumber business and learning to play the trombone from a local musician. During the Spanish-American War, he enlisted as trombonist in the 4th Tenn. Regimental Band. After the war, he became interested in gospel songs and evangelism; accompanied the evangelist Billy Sunday on his tours (1910–30), leading the singing with his trombone. With Bentley DeForrest Ackley, he founded the Rodeheaver-Ackley publishing firm in Chicago in 1910; it became the Rodeheaver Co. in 1911 and the Rodeheaver Hall-Mack Co. in 1936. After he removed the firm to Winona Lake, Ind., in 1941, it once again became the Rodeheaver Co. He composed the music for many gospel songs, of which the best known is *Then Jesus Came*. His theme song was *Brighten the Corner*, composed by Charles H. Gabriel. Besides editing some 80 gospel song collections, he publ. *Song Stories of the Sawdust Trail* (N.Y., 1917), *20 Years with Billy Sunday* (Nashville, 1936), and *Letter from a Missionary in Africa* (Chicago, 1936). Rodeheaver was one of the most influential figures in American musical evangelism of his day.

BIBL.: T. Porter, *H.A. R. (1880–1955): Evangelistic Musician and Publisher* (diss., New Orleans Baptist Theological Seminary, 1981).—NS/LK/DM

Rodgers, Jimmie (actually, James Charles),

American country singer, songwriter, and guitarist; b. Meridian, Miss., Sept. 8, 1897; d. N.Y., May 26, 1933. Rodgers was the first major country-music performer and a profound influence whose writing and performing styles served to define the genre. His music mixed folk, blues, jazz, and pop, and his frequently sentimental lyrics usually had a regional focus. He was also a distinctive singer, his style characterized by his "blue yodel." Such successors as Roy Acuff, Bob Wills, and Bill Monroe showed his immediate influence in the 1930s and 1940s and often performed his songs. But his impact was just as strong on a later generation of performers including Hank Snow, Webb Pierce, and Hank Williams in the 1940s and 1950s and in turn on their successors, Lefty Frizzell, Johnny Cash, and Merle Haggard in the 1950s and 1960s. Among his many compositions, "T for Texas," "Mule Skinner Blues," and "In the Jailhouse Now" are the best remembered.

Rodgers's father, Aaron Woodberry Rodgers (originally Rogers), was a railroad worker. His mother, Eliza Bozeman Rodgers, died in 1903, and he was raised largely by an aunt. He left school in 1911 and, after a flirtation with performing, followed his father on the railroad. He married Stella Kelly on May 1, 1917, but the marriage was short-lived; though a daughter was born, the couple divorced in November 1919. On April 7, 1920, Rodgers married Carrie Williamson, with whom he had two more daughters, one of whom died in infancy. After suffering a lung hemorrhage in 1924, Rodgers was diagnosed with tuberculosis; thereafter he worked less frequently for the railroad, stopping completely in 1926. He returned to performing, sometimes working as a blackface banjo player in a medicine show.

Moving to Asheville, N.C., Rodgers performed on the radio in the spring of 1927. His breakthrough came when he was recorded by Ralph Peer for Victor Records in Bristol, Tenn., in August 1927. His first record, "Sleep, Baby, Sleep"/"The Soldier's Sweetheart," released in October, sold well, and Peer conducted another recording session in November that produced "Blue Yodel" (or, "T for Texas"), released in April 1928, which sold a million copies.

Over the next five years Rodgers recorded more than a hundred sides for Victor. His biggest hits were "In the Jailhouse Now" (released in April 1928); "The Brakeman's Blues" (May 1928); "Blue Yodel No. 3" (September 1928); "Waiting for a Train" (February 1929); "Anniversary Yodel (Blue Yodel No. 7)" (music and lyrics also by Elsie McWilliams, Rodgers's sister-in-law; November 1929); and "Roll Along, Kentucky Moon" (music and lyrics by Bill Halley; March 1932), though each of his releases sold in the hundreds of thousands, at least until the onset of the Depression. (Biographer Nolan Porterfield estimated that Rodgers had sold 12 million records in the U.S. by the late 1940s.)

Rodgers recorded in a variety of styles, from solo performances with his own guitar accompaniment to arrangements for Hawaiian and jazz bands. On "Blue Yodel No. 9" in 1930 he was accompanied by Louis Armstrong on trumpet; in 1931 he recorded with the Carter Family. Rodgers also performed extensively, touring throughout the South and Southwest. He settled in Kerrville, Tex., later moving to San Antonio as his health deteriorated.

Though the Depression cut into his record sales, Rodgers continued to record. He died of tuberculosis within days of completing a series of new sides for Victor in N.Y.

Rodgers's recordings sold consistently after his death. *Jimmie Rodgers Memorial*, a retrospective album, reached the Top Ten in 1949, the same year that Tommy Duncan and His Western All Stars enjoyed a hit on the country charts with Rodgers's "Gambling Polka Dot Blues" (music and lyrics also by Raymond Hall). Rodgers's songs continued to provide hits for country performers in the 1950s, including Lefty Frizzell's 1951 recording of "Travellin' Blues" (music and lyrics also by Shelly Lee Alley) and Webb Pierce's massively popular 1955 version of "In the Jailhouse Now" and 1956 recording of "Any Old Time." In 1955, RCA Victor scored a Top Ten country hit with an overdubbed version of "In the Jailhouse Now No. 2" (originally recorded in 1930), credited to Jimmie Rodgers and the Rainbow Ranch Boys. The label began to reissue Rodgers's recordings on LP with *Never No Mo' Blues* in August 1956.

Notable recordings of Rodgers's songs in the 1960s included the Fendermen's Top Ten pop hit with "Mule Skinner Blues (Blue Yodel No. 9)" (music and lyrics also by George Vaughn) in 1960, Johnny Cash's "In the Jailhouse Now" and Grandpa Jones's "T for Texas" in 1962, and Merle Haggard's tribute album, *Same Train, Different Time*, in 1969. Dolly Parton had a country hit with "Mule Skinner Blues" in 1970, and Tompall and His Outlaw Band charted with "T for Texas" in 1976.

Not surprisingly, Rodgers was among the first entrants to the Country Music Hall of Fame in 1961. Twenty-five years later he was admitted to the Rock &

Roll Hall of Fame, an acknowledgment of the influence he had on a broader range of popular music. That influence was further demonstrated by the 1997 release of *The Songs of Jimmie Rodgers—A Tribute Album*, a centennial anniversary recording supervised by Bob Dylan and featuring such disparate performers as Bono from U2, Mary Chapin Carpenter, Willie Nelson, John Mellencamp, Van Morrison, and Jerry Garcia.

Rodgers's complete recordings were reissued on eight compact discs by Rounder Records in 1991.

BIBL.: C. Rodgers, *My Husband J. R.* (San Antonio, 1935); M. Paris and C. Comber, *J. The Kid: The Life of J. R.* (London, 1977); C. Bond, *The Recordings of J. R.* (Los Angeles, 1978); R. Krishef, *J. R.* (1978); N. Porterfield, *J. R.: The Life and Times of America's Blue Yodeler* (Urbana, Ill., 1979; rev. ed., 1992).—**WR**

Rodgers, Joan, English soprano; b. Whitehaven, Nov. 4, 1956. After pursuing studies in Russian at the Univ. of Liverpool, she studied music at the Royal Northern Coll. of Music in Manchester. In 1981 she was awarded the Kathleen Ferrier Memorial Scholarship, and then made her professional operatic debut at the Aix-en-Provence Festival in 1982 as Pamina. In 1983 she made first appearances in London with the English National Opera as the Wood Nymph in *Rusalka* and at Covent Garden as the Princess in *L'Enfant et les sortilèges*. She made her debut at the Glyndebourne Festival in 1989 as Mozart's Susanna, and then was soloist in Mahler's 4th Sym. at the Promenade Concerts in London. Her first appearance in Salzburg followed in 1991 when she sang at a Mozart Matinée. In 1992 she sang Handel's Cleopatra at the Scottish Opera in Glasgow, and also appeared as Mozart's Susanna in Florence. In 1995 she sang Mélisande with Opera North in Leeds. She returned to the Glyndebourne Festival in 1997 to sing Handel's Theodora. In 1999 she appeared as Poulenc's Blanche at the English National Opera. As a recitalist and a soloist with orchs., her engagements took her to the principal music centers of Europe. In 1988 she married **Paul Daniel.**—**NS/LK/DM**

Rodgers, Richard (Charles), reliable American composer, lyricist, and theatrical producer; b. Hammels Station, N.Y., June 28, 1902; d. N.Y., Dec. 30, 1979. Rodgers was the most successful theatrical composer of the 20th century. Between 1919 and 1979 he was the primary composer for 43 musicals and revues that played on Broadway and in the West End; he wrote 28 of those shows with lyricist Lorenz Hart and nine with Oscar Hammerstein II. With Hart, Rodgers's work is best remembered for its individual songs, including such standards as "Blue Moon," "My Funny Valentine," and "The Lady Is a Tramp." With Hammerstein, the musicals themselves are better remembered, and they include *Oklahoma!, South Pacific, The King and I,* and *The Sound of Music,* each of which ran for more than a thousand performances in their initial Broadway productions. While consistently inventive and risk-taking, Rodgers adapted his musical approach to his collaborators, creating melodic miniatures to match Hart's witty words and lush, expansive accompaniments to Hammerstein's operettalike librettos and lyrics. Rodgers

differed from many of his peers in that he spent relatively little time writing outside the theater. Though he enjoyed many popular hits, he contributed virtually no independent songs to Tin Pin Alley. Nineteen of his musicals were adapted into films (albeit sometimes unrecognizably), and he wrote ten original film scores; but most of his work for the movies was concentrated into a few years in the 1930s. He also wrote occasionally for television. His work brought him Academy, Emmy, Grammy, and Tony awards, and he twice won the Pulitzer Prize. But his greatest achievement was to transform the American musical theatre from a vehicle for bringing light entertainment to New Yorkers, to an art form capable of the most ambitious and serious expression, reaching audiences worldwide.

Rodgers's father, William Abraham Rodgers, was a medical doctor. After Rodgers began to pick out melodies at the piano at age four, his mother, Mamie Levy Rodgers, gave him his first lessons. Rodgers began to write music at nine. In May 1915 his older brother Mortimer, a student at Columbia Coll., took him to see the college variety show *On Your Way.* Hammerstein, then a 19-year-old Columbia undergraduate, was in the cast, and the 12-year-old Rodgers met him that night.

Rodgers composed his first song, "Campfire Days," at age 14 in 1916. Mortimer Rodgers belonged to an athletic group, The Akron Club, which planned a charity revue in 1917. Mortimer suggested his brother as the show's composer, and Rodgers wrote the songs for *One Minute Please,* given one performance at the Plaza Hotel on Dec. 29.

Rodgers wrote the songs for a second Akron Club charity revue, *Up Stage and Down,* given one performance at the Waldorf-Astoria Hotel on March 8, 1919. He wrote most of the lyrics himself, although three songs had lyrics by Hammerstein. Already embarked on a professional career, Hammerstein was not available as a regular collaborator, however, and Rodgers was introduced to Lorenz Hart by a member of the Akron Club. Hart directed the second and final performance of *Up Stage and Down,* retitled *Twinkling Eyes,* at the 44th Street Theatre in May, marking Rodgers's professional debut.

Rodgers and Hart immediately began to write songs together, and they auditioned some of their material for actor/producer Lew Fields, who chose "Any Old Place with You" for interpolation into his currently running musical, *A Lonely Romeo* (N.Y., June 10, 1919); it was performed shortly before the show closed, in August 1919, and also became Rodgers's first song to be professionally published.

Rodgers began to attend Columbia in September 1919, primarily to work on the varsity shows. He wrote a third Akron Club show, *You'd Be Surprised,* which played a single performance at the Plaza Hotel on March 6, 1920, as well as the 1920 Columbia varsity show *Fly with Me,* performed four times at the Astor Hotel starting on March 24. Lew Fields, whose son Herbert Fields choreographed the show, attended one of the performances and hired Rodgers and Hart to write the songs for his next musical production, *Poor Little Ritz Girl.* But after the Boston tryout he threw out half of their score and replaced it with songs by Sigmund Romberg and Alex Gerber; the show had a profitable run of 93 performances.

Though the professional accomplishments of the 18-year-old Rodgers augured well for the future, he and Hart next spent a frustrating five years doing amateur shows. After writing a fourth Akron Club musical, *Say Mama!* (Feb. 10, 1921) and a second Columbia varsity show, *You'll Never Know* (April 20, 1921), Rodgers transferred to the Inst. of Musical Art (now Juilliard), where he studied harmony with Percy Goetschius, ear-training with George Wedge, music history with Henry Krehbiel, and music theory with Franklin W. Robinson. He wrote the institute's annual shows, *Say It with Jazz* (June 1, 1921) and *Jazz à la Carte* (June 2, 1922).

Also in 1922, Rodgers and Hart worked on a musical called *Winkle Town*, which, though unproduced, is notable for its librettists, Herbert Fields and Oscar Hammerstein II, both of whom Rodgers would work with again, and for its score, which included several songs that turned up in later shows, among them an early version of "Manhattan."

After writing a third show, *A Danish Yankee in King Tut's Court* (May 31, 1923), at the Inst. of Musical Art, Rodgers left the school in June 1923. In 1924, Rodgers, Hart, and Herbert Fields, using the pseudonym Herbert Richard Lorenz, wrote a play, *The Melody Man*, which ran for 61 performances on Broadway. But by 1925, Rodgers was ready to give up composing.

After he accepted a job as a salesman of children's underwear, he and Hart were offered yet another amateur show, writing songs for a benefit for the Theatre Guild, which they accepted reluctantly on the grounds that it was being performed in a Broadway theater and was likely to be seen by the critics. *The Garrick Gaieties* gave two performances on May 17, 1925; it was so popular that it was repeated several times and finally began a regular run on June 8, eventually racking up 231 performances. Ben Selvin and His Orch., recording under the name "Knickerbockers," scored a double-sided best-selling record with two songs from the show, "Manhattan" and "Sentimental Me," in the fall.

The success of *The Garrick Gaieties* enabled Rodgers and Hart to mount their already-written musical *Dearest Enemy*. With a book by Herbert Fields, who would be the librettist on most of their shows of the 1920s, it was another hit, running 286 performances and featuring "Here in My Arms," a hit for Leo Reisman and His Orch. in May 1926.

Five Rodgers and Hart shows opened on Broadway and in the West End in 1926, and four of them were successful. *The Girl Friend*, their second book musical with Herbert Fields, ran 301 performances and featured the title song, which George Olsen and His Orch. recorded for a hit in August, and "The Blue Room," a hit for the Revelers in October. The second edition of *The Garrick Gaieties* ran 174 performances; its hit song was "Mountain Greenery," recorded by Roger Wolfe Kahn and His Orch. *Lido Lady*, Rodgers and Hart's first British musical, ran 259 performances. *Peggy-Ann* was their third Broadway musical with Herbert Fields, and their most successful yet, running 354 performances and

spawning two hits, "Where's That Rainbow?" for George Olsen and "A Tree in the Park" for Helen Morgan. Their only misstep of the year was agreeing to write songs for producer Florenz Ziegfeld's flop *Betsy*, their first setback after six straight hits.

Rodgers and Hart wrote only two shows in 1927, and both were successful. *One Dam Thing after Another*, a British revue, ran 237 performances. Its most memorable song was "My Heart Stood Still," which the songwriters interpolated into their Broadway musical *A Connecticut Yankee*, another collaboration with Herbert Fields. George Olsen had the most popular of several recordings of the song, while Ben Selvin scored a hit with "Thou Swell." *A Connecticut Yankee* ran 421 performances, Rodgers and Hart's biggest hit yet, and their last success on Broadway until 1936.

Several of the shows Rodgers and Hart wrote during this period produced hit songs, however. *Present Arms* (1928) contained "You Took Advantage of Me," recorded by Paul Whiteman and His Orch., and "Do I Hear You Saying 'I Love You'?" recorded by Vaughn Deleath and Irving Kaufman (under the pseudonym Frank Harris). "With a Song in My Heart" from *Spring Is Here* (1929) became a hit for Leo Reisman. *Simple Simon* (1930) contained "Ten Cents a Dance," a hit for Ruth Etting, who sang it onstage. And the London musical *Ever Green* (1930), the songwriters' only successful show of the early 1930s, featured "Dancing on the Ceiling," which took a while to cross the Atlantic but finally became a U.S. hit for British bandleader Jack Hylton in February 1932.

Rodgers married Dorothy Feiner, whom he had known since childhood, on March 5, 1930. They had two daughters, one of whom, Mary Rodgers, became a Broadway composer best known for the 1959 musical *Once upon a Mattress*.

Rodgers and Hart had their first songs used in a motion picture and made their movie debut in the Paramount short *Makers of Melody* in 1929. The first motion picture for which they wrote songs was Paramount's adaptation of B. G. De Sylva, Lew Brown, and Ray Henderson's musical *Follow Thru*, released in September 1930. Hollywood also began to option Rodgers and Hart musicals, and movie versions of *Spring Is Here*, *Present Arms* (retitled *Leathernecking*), and *Heads Up!* (without the exclamation mark) appeared in 1930. In July the songwriters signed a three-picture deal with Warner Bros. and went west to write songs for *The Hot Heiress*. Before the film was released they returned to N.Y. and to their partnership with Herbert Fields and wrote *America's Sweetheart*, a musical that satirized Hollywood. Opening in February 1931, the show had a modest run of 135 performances and featured a minor hit in "I've Got Five Dollars," recorded by Emil Coleman and His Orch. *The Hot Heiress*, released the following month, was a failure, causing Warner Bros. to buy the songwriters out of their contract.

Rodgers and Hart returned to Hollywood in November 1931 with a one-picture deal at Paramount; ultimately, they wrote songs for three films during the year they spent with the studio. The most successful was *Love Me Tonight*, a vehicle for Maurice Chevalier and

Jeanette MacDonald released in August 1932. The score produced four hits: the title song for George Olsen; "Mimi" for Chevalier; "Isn't It Romantic?" for Harold Stern and His Orch.; and "Lover" for Paul Whiteman. *The Phantom President*, starring George M. Cohan and released in October, was a failure, as was *Hallelujah, I'm a Bum*, released in February 1933 and starring Al Jolson, who made a minor hit out of the title song.

Rodgers and Hart moved over to MGM in late 1932, where their efforts were largely wasted, at least from the studio's point of view. Their two major assignments were *I Married an Angel*, which was not produced at the time, though the songwriters later took the idea and some of the music back to N.Y. with them, and a film initially called *Hollywood Revue of 1933* that was released in May 1934 as *Hollywood Party* with only a few of the many songs they wrote for it.

One of the discards, intended for Jean Harlow, was called "Prayer." Hart wrote a new lyric and came up with a title song for *Manhattan Melodrama*. This too was dropped, and a third lyric was added to create "The Bad in Every Man," which was used in the picture when it was released in May 1934. Hart then wrote a fourth lyric to create "Blue Moon," one of the few Richard Rodgers melodies ever published independent of a movie or musical and the biggest hit ever written by Rodgers and Hart. The most successful of the first recordings of the song was the one by Glen Gray and the Casa Loma Orch. that became a best-seller in January 1935.

Leaving MGM in the spring of 1934, Rodgers and Hart moved back to N.Y. but were unable to secure work and returned to Hollywood, where they wrote the songs for *Mississippi*, a film starring Bing Crosby at Paramount. Upon the film's release in April 1935, three of the songs became hits for Crosby, "Down by the River," "It's Easy to Remember," and "Soon," the latter two becoming best-sellers.

Rodgers and Hart finally found a berth on Broadway, albeit an unorthodox one, in *Jumbo*, a cross between a musical and a circus that played at the cavernous Hippodrome starting in November 1935. At 221 performances, *Jumbo* had the second-longest run of any musical of the 1935–36 season, but its enormous production cost made it a financial failure.

The show with the longest run of the season was Rodgers and Hart's theatrical comeback, *On Your Toes*, for which they wrote the songs and collaborated on the libretto with codirector George Abbott. It ran 318 performances, and "There's a Small Hotel" spent ten weeks in the hit parade in a recording by the Hal Kemp Orch., while the score also included "Glad to Be Unhappy" and the ballet "Slaughter on Tenth Avenue."

On Your Toes began a run of eight successful Rodgers and Hart shows between 1936 and 1942, with only one failure. Their next musical, *Babes in Arms* (1937), was their first for which they alone wrote both the songs and the libretto. It ran 289 performances, and though none of its songs became hits at the time, four have gone on to become standards: "I Wish I Were in Love Again," "The Lady Is a Tramp," "My Funny Valentine," and "Where or When." Another 289-performance run was enjoyed by the political satire *I'd Rather Be Right* (1937), in which

George M. Cohan portrayed President Franklin Roosevelt. *I Married an Angel* (1938), rescued from Hollywood, ran 338 performances, and the title song spent seven weeks in the hit parade for the Larry Clinton Orch. The Benny Goodman Orch. took "This Can't Be Love" from *The Boys from Syracuse* (1938) into the hit parade for ten weeks; the show ran for 235 performances.

Goodman had seven weeks in the hit parade with "I Didn't Know What Time It Was" from *Too Many Girls* (1939), which enjoyed a 249-performance run. *Pal Joey* ran 374 performances, and though it produced no hits during its initial run (probably due to the radio ban that kept ASCAP compositions off the air during 1941), it contained "Bewitched (Bothered and Bewildered)," which later became one of Rodgers and Hart's most successful songs. At 427 performances *By Jupiter* (1942) was the team's most successful musical. In this case the lack of hits drawn from the score seems due to the recording ban that began two months after the show opened.

Rodgers became more ambitious during the late 1930s and early 1940s. He began to compose occasional instrumental works and studied piano with Herman Wasserman. He coproduced the 1941 musical *Best Foot Forward* as well as *By Jupiter*. But as his career expanded, his partner's contracted. As early as 1938, Lorenz Hart's alcoholism and erratic behavior began to threaten his work. Due to Hart's absence, Rodgers was forced to complete the lyrics to *Too Many Girls* himself; the songwriters failed to produce a show in 1941 because of Hart's problems; and much of *By Jupiter* was written in a hospital where Hart was undergoing detoxification. In September 1941, Rodgers contacted Oscar Hammerstein II to inquire whether he would be willing to replace Hart if necessary. After *By Jupiter*, the Theatre Guild offered Rodgers the chance to write a musical version of the Lynn Riggs play *Green Grow the Lilacs*; when Hart refused the project, Rodgers turned to Hammerstein.

The result was *Oklahoma!*, a landmark in the history of the American musical theatre and of popular music for several reasons. If it was not the first musical to closely integrate book, music, and dance, it established such integration as a standard for the musicals that followed, if only because, at a run of 2,248 performances (five years and nine weeks), it was the longest-running musical in Broadway history up to its time. It also won Rodgers a special Pulitzer Prize.

When *Oklahoma!* opened, the recording ban was still in place, but several artists recorded a cappella versions of its songs, notably Bing Crosby in a duet with Trudy Erwin and backed by the Sportsman Glee Club, who recorded "People Will Say We're in Love" and "Oh, What a Beautiful Mornin'," both of which became Top Ten hits. When Decca Records settled with the musicians' union, label president Jack Kapp took the unusual step of recording the Broadway cast for a 78-rpm album. Released in December 1943, it became a Top Ten hit, eventually selling several million copies; drawn from the album, Alfred Drake's recording of "The Surrey with the Fringe on Top" became a chart single. This success, coupled with the introduction of the 33-

1/3–rpm LP in 1949, established the cast album as a popular form.

Rodgers returned to his partnership with Lorenz Hart for a final time, writing several new songs for a revival of *A Connecticut Yankee* (N.Y., Nov. 17, 1943), but Hart died five days after the show opened.

The long run of *Oklahoma!* allowed Rodgers and Hammerstein to take their time in preparing their next show. In the meantime they formed their own publishing company, Williamson Music, Inc. (both were the sons of fathers named William), and they began a series of outside productions with the hit play *I Remember Mama* (N.Y., Oct. 19, 1944).

Rodgers and Hammerstein's second musical, *Carousel*, opened in April 1945. With an unusually dark plot and such challenging music as the extended "Soliloquy," it nevertheless ran 890 performances, and the cast album hit #1. The score also produced three Top Ten hits: "If You Loved Me" by Perry Como (three other recordings of the song also reached the Top Ten); "June Is Bustin' Out All Over" by Hildegarde with Guy Lombardo and His Royal Canadians; and "You'll Never Walk Alone" for Frank Sinatra.

State Fair, the only movie musical for which Rodgers and Hammerstein wrote an original score, followed in August 1945. It contained two Top Ten hits: "That's for Me," recorded by Jo Stafford, and "It Might As Well Be Spring," by Sammy Kaye, which won the 1945 Academy Award for Best Song. (Dick Haymes, who starred in the film, also recorded Top Ten versions of both songs.)

After producing Irving Berlin's long-running musical *Annie Get Your Gun* in 1946, Rodgers and Hammerstein mounted their third show, *Allegro*, in 1947. Their first work not to be based on an earlier play, it was also their first failure, though it ran 315 performances and Frank Sinatra scored a Top Ten hit with "So Far."

Rodgers and Hart were given a successful (if fictionalized) film biography, *Words and Music*, in late 1948, and the soundtrack album was a #1 hit. A single version of "Slaughter on Tenth Avenue" by Lenny Hayton and the M-G-M Orch. was drawn from the soundtrack and became a minor hit, while Perry Como, who sang "The Blue Room" in the film, revived it on record, also for a minor hit.

South Pacific (1949), Rodgers and Hammerstein's fourth musical, became the second longest running show of their career, piling up 1,925 performances on Broadway. Recipient of the Tony Award for Best Musical and the Pulitzer Prize for Drama, the show produced a cast album that topped the charts for more than a year and sold several million copies, while three of its songs became hits. Perry Como topped the charts with "Some Enchanted Evening," beating out five other Top Ten versions, including one by the show's star, Ezio Pinza. Como also had the most successful of several versions of "Bali Ha'i," another Top Ten hit. And Margaret Whiting had the best-selling version of "A Wonderful Guy."

Meanwhile, Rodgers and Hart's catalog continued to produce hits. The Ames Brothers revived "Sentimental

Me" and went to #1 with it in June 1950. That same month Bill Snyder and His Orch. peaked in the Top Ten with "Bewitched (Bothered and Bewildered)," the most successful of nine chart recordings of the song. The song's renewed popularity led Columbia Records to record the score of *Pal Joey* as an album, and this in turn led to a Broadway revival opening Jan. 3, 1952, that ran 542 performances, making it the longest-running revival in Broadway history up to that time.

Rodgers and Hammerstein's next musical, *The King and I* (1951), was the third of their massive hits, running 1,246 performances and winning the Tony Award for Best Musical. The original cast album reached the Top Ten and stayed in the charts over a year; there was also a studio cast version featuring Dinah Shore that reached the Top Ten, while Frank Sinatra had a minor hit with "We Kiss in a Shadow."

Peggy Lee and Gordon Jenkins and His Chorus and Orch. revived Rodgers and Hart's "Lover" in 1952, peaking in the Top Ten in July. That same month Ray Anthony scored a minor hit with a revival of "Slaughter on Tenth Avenue." Rodgers's major work of the year was to write the musical score to a 13-hour television documentary, *Victory at Sea*, broadcast as 26 half-hour episodes starting on Oct. 26, prior to which he premiered an excerpt, "Guadalcanal March," at a Rodgers and Hammerstein concert at Lewisohn Stadium in N.Y. on Aug. 3. A feature-film version of *Victory at Sea* opened in July 1954. There were also three volumes of soundtrack albums, each of which reached the Top Ten.

Me and Juliet (1953), Rodgers and Hammerstein's sixth Broadway show, was a backstage musical with an original book by Hammerstein. With a run of 358 performances, it turned a modest profit; its cast album reached the Top Ten, and Perry Como had a #1 hit with "No Other Love."

After avoiding film treatments of their frequently revived musicals, Rodgers and Hammerstein saw three adaptations of their shows released within a year. *Oklahoma!* opened in movie theaters in October 1955 and was one of the biggest box office hits of the year. Its soundtrack album hit #1 and stayed in the charts for more than five years, selling more than two million copies. *Carousel*, released in February 1956, was a flop at the box office, but its soundtrack album hit the Top Ten and sold a million copies. *The King and I*, released in June 1956, was among the year's biggest moneymakers, and the soundtrack album topped the charts, where it remained for more than five years, and sold a million copies.

Rodgers and Hammerstein's seventh musical, *Pipe Dream* (1955), was a failure, though it spawned two Top 40 hits, "All at Once You Love Her" for Perry Como, and "Everybody's Got a Home but Me" for Eddie Fisher, as well as chart singles for Carmen McRae ("The Next Time It Happens") and, in 1962, Johnny Mathis ("Sweet Thursday").

Rodgers and Hammerstein turned to television in March 1957, preparing a new musical version of *Cinderella*, starring Julie Andrews. The soundtrack album reached the charts, and Vic Damone had a chart single with "Do I Love You (Because You're Beautiful)?" In

November a film adaptation of *Pal Joey* appeared, starring Frank Sinatra and featuring several Rodgers and Hart standards interpolated into the score. The soundtrack album was a Top Ten hit, and "The Lady Is a Tramp" became a signature song for Sinatra.

South Pacific, the fourth film adaptation of a Rodgers and Hammerstein musical, was the biggest box office hit of 1958. The soundtrack album was the best-selling LP of the year, and it stayed in the charts almost five years, reportedly selling eight million copies worldwide. Rodgers and Hammerstein also returned to Broadway in 1958, with *Flower Drum Song*; its 600 performances made it a solid hit, if not a smash on the scale of some of the team's other shows. The cast album hit the top of the charts and stayed in them nearly three years, earning a gold record.

The Sound of Music, Rodgers and Hammerstein's last musical, was the biggest hit of the 1959–60 Broadway season and among the songwriters' most successful shows, with a run of 1,443 performances; it tied for the Tony Award for Best Musical. The cast album went to #1, stayed in the charts more than five years, and sold two million copies; it won the 1960 Grammy Award for Best Show Album, Original Cast. The score included several songs that became chart singles, including the title song (for Patti Page), "Climb Ev'ry Mountain" (for Tony Bennett), and "Do-Re-Mi" (for Mitch Miller and His Orch. and Chorus), while "My Favorite Things" became one of Rodgers's few songs written with Hammerstein to become popular among jazz musicians, notably John Coltrane, who recorded it and named an album after it. By late 1968, when Herb Alpert and the Tijuana Brass had a chart single with it, it had become a Christmas standard. Meanwhile, Rodgers and Hart's songs proved amenable to doo-wop singing: Dion and the Belmonts reached the Top Ten with "Where or When" in 1960, and the Marcels topped the charts with "Blue Moon" in 1961.

Oscar Hammerstein's death on Aug. 23, 1960, put an end to Rodgers's second major songwriting partnership; he did not find a third, and initially decided to write his own lyrics. His first project after Hammerstein's death was writing background music for the documentary television series *Winston Churchill—The Valiant Years*, for which he won an Emmy Award.

A movie version of *Flower Drum Song* was released in November 1961; the soundtrack album spent more than six months in the charts. A second screen version of *State Fair*, starring Pat Boone and Bobby Darin, was released in April 1962. It contained several new songs written by Rodgers alone; the film was unsuccessful, but the soundtrack album reached the charts. *Billy Rose's Jumbo*, starring Doris Day and released in December 1962, was another box office flop with a charting soundtrack; its score was augmented by Rodgers and Hart standards from other shows.

Rodgers's only musical for which he wrote both music and lyrics was *No Strings* (1962). It was a success on Broadway, running 580 performances. Its cast album reached the Top Ten and stayed in the charts more than a year; it was the Grammy Award–winner for Best Original Cast Show Album, and "The Sweetest Sounds"

earned a nomination for Song of the Year. Nevertheless, Rodgers turned to lyricist Alan Jay Lerner for his next project, a musical tentatively titled *I Picked a Daisy*. But the partnership did not take, and Lerner went on to do the show with Burton Lane as *On a Clear Day You Can See Forever*.

Rodgers became president of the Music Theater of Lincoln Center in 1964, and the organization mounted many low-priced revivals of his shows, starting with *The King and I* on July 6. In 1965 there was a second version of the television musical *Cinderella*, which unlike the first was on videotape and thus was replayed many times. (A third version, featuring Whitney Houston, was broadcast in 1997.) Rodgers songs continued to enjoy chart revivals during the 1960s, notably including Top 40 recordings of "You'll Never Walk Alone" by Patti Labelle and Her Blue Belles (1964) and by the Brooklyn Bridge (1969); "If I Loved You" by Chad and Jeremy (1965); "Some Enchanted Evening" by Jay and the Americans (1965); and "Glad to Be Unhappy" by the Mamas and the Papas (1967).

Rodgers teamed with Stephen Sondheim for his next musical, *Do I Hear a Waltz?* (1965), which ran 220 performances—not enough to turn a profit, but it produced a charting cast album. March 1965 saw the release of the film version of *The Sound of Music* starring Julie Andrews. Rodgers wrote music and lyrics for two new songs for the movie, which outdistanced *Gone with the Wind* to become the biggest box office success in history up to that time. The soundtrack album hit #1 and stayed in the charts more than four years, selling a reported seven million copies worldwide.

Rodgers wrote music and lyrics for the songs for a television musical based on George Bernard Shaw's *Androcles and the Lion* in 1967. He left his post at Lincoln Center after the summer revival of *Oklahoma!* (June 23, 1969; the sixth Broadway revival) and following a heart attack in July. His next new musical was *Two by Two* (1970), with lyrics by Martin Charnin; it ran 343 performances and turned a profit. Though increasingly incapacitated by ill health, Rodgers continued to work, producing *Rex* (1976) with Sheldon Harnick and a musical adaptation of *I Remember Mama* (1979) with Charnin, neither of which was successful. Rodgers died in 1979 at the age of 77.

Rodgers's works have been revived frequently on Broadway, especially *On Your Toes* and *Pal Joey*, among those written with Lorenz Hart, and *Oklahoma!*, *Carousel*, *South Pacific*, and *The King and I*, among those with Oscar Hammerstein II. *State Fair* was mounted as a stage musical in 1995 and came to Broadway in 1996. That season the most recent revival of *The King and I* (N.Y., April 11, 1996) won the Tony Award for Best Revival.

WORKS (only works for which Rodgers was a primary, credited composer are listed): **MUSICALS/REVUES/ PLAYS** (dates refer to N.Y. openings unless otherwise noted): *Twinkling Eyes* (May 18, 1919); *Poor Little Ritz Girl* (July 27, 1920); *The Melody Man* (May 13, 1924); *The Garrick Gaieties* (May 17, 1925); *Dearest Enemy* (Sept. 18, 1925); *The Girl Friend* (March 17, 1926); *The Garrick Gaieties* (May 10, 1926); *Lido Lady* (London, Dec. 1, 1926); *Peggy-Ann* (Dec. 27, 1926); *Betsy* (Dec. 28, 1926);

One Dam Thing after Another (London, May 19, 1927); *A Connecticut Yankee* (Nov. 3, 1927); *She's My Baby* (Jan. 3, 1928); *Present Arms* (April 26, 1928); *Chee-Chee* (Sept. 25, 1928); *Spring Is Here* (March 11, 1929); *Heads Up!* (Nov. 11, 1929); *Simple Simon* (Feb. 18, 1930); *Ever Green* (London, Dec. 3, 1930); *America's Sweetheart* (Feb. 10, 1931); *Jumbo* (Nov. 16, 1935); *On Your Toes* (April 11, 1936); *Babes in Arms* (April 14, 1937); *I'd Rather Be Right* (Nov. 2, 1937); *I Married an Angel* (May 11, 1938); *The Boys from Syracuse* (Nov. 23, 1938); *Too Many Girls* (Oct. 18, 1939); *Higher and Higher* (April 4, 1940); *Pal Joey* (Dec. 25, 1940); *By Jupiter* (June 3, 1942); *Oklahoma!* (March 31, 1943); *Carousel* (April 19, 1945); *Allegro* (Oct. 10, 1947); *South Pacific* (April 7, 1949); *The King and I* (March 29, 1951); *Me and Juliet* (May 28, 1953); *Pipe Dream* (Nov. 30, 1955); *Flower Drum Song* (Dec. 1, 1958); *The Sound of Music* (Nov. 16, 1959); *No Strings* (March 15, 1962); *Do I Hear a Waltz?* (March 18, 1965); *Two by Two* (Nov. 10, 1970); *Rodgers and Hart* (May 13, 1975); *Rex* (April 25, 1976); *I Remember Mama* (May 31, 1979); *State Fair* (Des Moines, Aug. 12, 1995; N.Y., March 27, 1996). **FILMS:** *Spring Is Here* (1930); *Heads Up* (1930); *The Hot Heiress*1931); *ove Me Tonight* (1932); *The Phantom President* (1932); *Hallelujah, I'm a Bum* (1933); *Hollywood Party* (1934); *Mississippi* (1935); *Dancing Pirate* (1936); *Fools for Scandal* (1938); *Babes in Arms* (1939); *The Boys from Syracuse* (1940); *Too Many Girls* (1940); *They Met in Argentina* (1941); *State Fair* (1945); *Words and Music* (1948); *Victory at Sea* (1954); *Oklahoma!* (1955); *Carousel* (1956); *The King and I* (1956); *Pal Joey* (1957); *South Pacific* (1958); *Flower Drum Song* (1961); *State Fair* (1962); *Billy Rose's Jumbo* (1962); *The Sound of Music* (1965). **TELEVISION:** *Victory at Sea* (1952–53); *Cinderella* (March 31, 1957); *Winston Churchill— The Valiant Years* (Nov. 27, 1960–June 1961); *Cinderella* (Feb. 22, 1965); *Androcles and the Lion* (Nov. 15, 1967); *Cinderella* (Nov. 2, 1997). **RADIO:** *Let's Have Fun* (Oct. 22, 1935). **MISCELLANEOUS:** *All Points West* (symphonic narrative with text by Hart; Academy of Music, Philadelphia, Nov. 27, 1936, Philadelphia Orch. under Paul Whiteman, with Ray Middleton); *Nursery Ballet* (suite for piano; Carnegie Hall, N.Y., Dec. 25, 1938, Paul Whiteman and His Orch.); *Ghost Town* (ballet; Metropolitan Opera House, N.Y., Nov. 12, 1939, Ballet Russe de Monte Carlo).

WRITINGS: Ed., *The R. and Hart Song Book* (N.Y., 1951); H. Simon, ed., *The R. and Hammerstein Song Book* (N.Y., 1958; 2nd ed. rev., 1968); *Musical Stages: An Autobiography* (N.Y., 1975).

BIBL.: D. Taylor, *Some Enchanted Evenings: The Story of R. and Hammerstein* (N.Y., 1953); D. Ewen, *R. R.* (N.Y., 1957; 2nd ed. rev., 1963, as *With a Song in His Heart*); S. Green, *The R. and Hammerstein Story* (N.Y., 1958); *The R. R. Fact Book* (N.Y., 1965; new ed. with supplement, 1968); S. Marx and J. Clayton, *R. and Hart* (1976); F. Nolan, *The Sound of Their Music: The Story of R. and Hammerstein* (N.Y., 1978); S. Green, *R. and Hammerstein Fact Book* (1980); S. Green, *The R. and Hammerstein Story* (1980); S. Suskin, *Berlin, Kern, R., Hart, and Hammerstein: A Complete Song Catalogue* (Jefferson, N.C., 1990); E. Mordden, *R. and Hammerstein* (N.Y., 1992); W. Hyland, *R. R.* (New Haven, Conn., 1998). **—WR**

Rodio, Rocco, Italian music theorist and composer; b. Bari, Apulia, c. 1535; d. Naples, after 1615. He was in the service of Sigismund August of Poland, then was active in Naples (from 1575). He publ. *Regole di musica Rocco Rodio...tutti i canoni sopra il canto fermo* (Naples, 1600). His works include *Missarum decem liber primus* for 4 to 6 Voices (Rome, 1562), *Libro di ricercate a 4* (Naples, 1575), and 17 madrigals for 4 Voices.

BIBL.: M. Kastner, *Note critiche ed illustrative di R. R., cinque ricercate, una fantasia* (Padua, 1958).**—NS/LK/DM**

Rodolphe, Jean Joseph (actually, **Johann Joseph Rudolph**), Alsatian horn player, violinist, and composer; b. Strasbourg, Oct. 14, 1730; d. Paris, Aug. 12?, 1812. He studied horn with his father, Theodor Peter Rudolph, and took violin lessons with J.M. Leclair (*c.*1745); was also a violinist in Bordeaux and Montpellier. He was in Parma as a violinist in the ducal orch. by 1754, where he received instruction in counterpoint from Traetta (from 1758). As a chamber virtuoso, became a member of the Stuttgart Court Orch. (*c.*1760), where he completed his studies with Jommelli. With the choreographer J.G. Noverre, he brought out several ballets. He appeared in Paris as a horn virtuoso at the Concert Spirituel in 1764, but continued to work in Stuttgart until returning to Paris in 1767 as a member of Prince Conti's orch.; became a violinist and hornist in the Opéra orch. and later was active at the royal chapel. He befriended the young Mozart during the latter's visit to Paris in 1778. From 1784 until the Revolution, Rodolphe taught composition at the École Royale de Chant et de Déclamation; later was prof. of solfège at the Paris Cons. (1798–1802). He publ. *Solfège ou Nouvelle méthode de musique* (Paris, 1784; 2nd ed., rev., 1790) and *Théorie d'accompagnement et de composition* (Paris, c. 1785).

WORKS: **DRAMATIC: O p e r a :** *Le Mariage par capitulation*, opéra-comique (Paris, Dec. 3, 1764); *L'Aveugle de Palmire*, opéra-comique (Paris, March 5, 1767); *Isménor*, opéra-ballet (Versailles, Nov. 17, 1773). **B a l l e t :** *Renaud et Armide* (Stuttgart, Feb. 11, 1761); *Psyche et l'Amour* (Stuttgart, Feb. 11, 1762); *Médée et Jason* (Ludwigsburg, Feb. 11, 1763; rev. by Noverre, Paris, Jan. 30, 1780); *Apollon et Daphne* (Kassel, *c.*1764; in collaboration with Deller); *Télèphe et Isménie ou La Mort d'Eurite* (Kassel, 1768; in collaboration with Deller); *Apelle et Campaspe* (Paris, Oct. 1, 1776). **INSTRUMENTAL:** 2 horn concertos; 24 fanfares for 3 Horns; 3 sets of violin duos; 2 sets of violin études. **—NS/LK/DM**

Rodrigo, Joaquín, eminent Spanish composer and teacher; b. Sagunto, Nov. 22, 1901; d. Madrid, July 6, 1999. He contracted diphtheria and went totally blind at the age of 4. He studied harmony and composition with Francisco Antich (1917–22), and also received advice from Enrique Gomá and Eduardo López Chavarri. In 1927 he went to Paris, where he studied with Dukas at the École Normale de Musique. In 1928 he was befriended by Falla. In 1932 he returned to Spain. He was awarded the Conde de Catagena Scholarship in 1934 and returned to Paris to pursue training in music history and musicology with Emmanuel at the Cons. and with Pirro at the Sorbonne. In 1939 he settled in Madrid, and in 1940 he was appointed to a provisional chair at the Real Cons. Superior de Música. Rodrígo was awarded the Premio Nacional de Música in 1942. In 1947 he was appointed to the Manuel de Falla Chair in Music as a prof. in the faculty of philosophy and arts at Madrid Complutense Univ. He was elected a full member of the Real Academia de Bellas Artes de San Fernando of Madrid in 1950. The French government bestowed upon him the order of Officier de l'Ordre des arts et des Lettres in 1960, and in 1963 the order of Chevalier de la Légion d'honneur. King Juan Carlos I of Spain conferred the title of Marques de los Jardines de Aranjuez upon him in 1991, the same year that the Cons. Superior de Música in Valencia was named in his honor. His 95th birthday was the occasion of various tributes, including concerts and the Príncipe de Asturias Prize for the Arts. Rodrígo's music is expertly crafted and is reflective of the colors and melorhythms of Spain. His most celebrated score is the *Concierto de Aranjuez* for Guitar and Orch. (1939; Barcelona, Nov. 9, 1940), which became a classic during his own lifetime. Among his later concertos, the *Fantasía para un gentilhombre* for Guitar and Orch. (1954), the *Concierto madrigal* for 2 Guitars and Orch. (1966), and the *Concierto Andaluz* for 4 Guitars and Orch. (1967) also won favor. In addition to his many fine solo guitar pieces, he also composed a number of effective solo piano pieces.

WORKS: DRAMATIC: *El duende azul*, operetta (Madrid, May 22, 1946); *Pavana Real*, ballet (Barcelona, Dec. 19, 1955); *El hijo fingido*, zarzuela (1955–60; Madrid, Dec. 5, 1964); *La bella durmiente*, ballet (Television Española, Madrid, June 1962); incidental music. **ORCH.:** *Cançoneta* for Strings (Valencia, 1923); *Juglares* (1923; Valencia, 1924); *Cinco piezas infantiles* (1924; Valencia, Feb. 16, 1927); *Preludio para un poema a la Alhambra* (1928; Paris, May 5, 1930); *Dos miniaturas andaluzas* for Strings (1929); *Tres viejos aires de danza* (1929; Valencia, Jan. 20, 1930); *Zarabanda lejana y villancico* for Strings (1930; Paris, March 9, 1931); *Per la flor del Lliri Blau*, symphonic poem (Valencia, July 26, 1934; also for Band); *Concierto do Aranjuez* for Guitar and Orch. (1939; Barcelona, Nov. 9, 1940; also for Harp and Orch., San Sebastián, Aug. 24, 1974); *Homenage a la Tempranica* (Zaragossa, Nov. 3, 1939); *Concierto heroico* for Piano and Orch. (1942; Lisbon, April 3, 1943); *Concierto de estío* for Violin and Orch. (1943; Lisbon, April 16, 1944); *Dos piezas caballeerescas* for Orch. of Cellos (Madrid, May 27, 1945); *Concerto in modo galante* for Cello and Orch. (Madrid, Nov. 4, 1949); *Concierto serenata* for Harp and Orch. (1952; Madrid, Nov. 9, 1956); *Soleriana* (Berlin, Aug. 22, 1953); *Fantasía para un gentilhombre* for Guitar and Orch. (1954; San Francisco, March 5, 1958; also for Flute and Orch., 1978); *Música para un jardín* (1957; Valencia, Feb. 23, 1958); *Sones en lar Giralda* for Harp and Orch. (Madrid, Dec. 23, 1963; also for Guitar and Orch.); *Adagio para instrumentos de viento* (Pittsburgh, June 1966); *Concierto madrigal* for 2 Guitars and Orch. (1966; Los Angeles, July 30, 1970); *Dos danzas españolas* for Castanets and Orch. (Las Palmas, June 22, 1966); *Concierto andaluz* for 4 Guitars and Orch. (San Antonio, Nov. 18, 1967); *A la busca del más allá* (1976; Houston, March 27, 1978); *Concierto pastoral* for Flute and Orch. (London, Oct. 17, 1978); *Concierto como un divertimento* for Cello and Orch. (1981; London, April 15, 1982); *Concierto para una fiesta* for Guitar and Orch. (1982; Fort Worth, Tex., March 5, 1983); *Palillos y panderetas (Música para una tonadilla imaginaria)* (Madrid, Nov. 30, 1982); *Rincones de España*, guitar concerto (1990; N.Y., March 7, 1991). **CHAMBER:** *Dos esbozos* for Violin and Piano (1923; Paris, Nov. 18, 1928); *Siciliana* for Cello and Piano (1929; Paris, March 9, 1930); *Rumaniana* for Violin and Piano (1943); *Aria antigua* for Flute and Piano (Madrid, June 10, 1959; also for Flute and Guitar, Madrid, Dec. 18, 1994, and for Flute and Percussion, Madrid, Feb. 21, 1996); *Sonata pimpante* for Violin and Piano (Brussels, Feb. 26, 1966); *Sonata a la breve* for Cello and Piano (Barcelona, May 11, 1977); *Serenaata al alba del día* for Flute or Violin and Guitar (1982; Los Angeles, Dec. 7, 1983); *Set cancons*

valencianes for Violin and Piano (1982). **Piano:** Suite (1923); *Canción y danza* (1925); *Bagatela* (1926); *Preludio al gallo mañanero* (1926; Paris, March 14, 1928); *Serenata española* (1931); *Sonada de adíos (Homenaje a Paul Dukas)* (1935); *Cuatro piezas* (1938; Paris, March 9, 1939); *Cinco piezas del siglo XVI* (1938); *Gran marcha de los subsecretarios* for Piano, 4-Hands (1941); *Tres danzas de España* (1941); *A l'ombre de Torre Bermeja* (1945); *Cuatro estampas andaluzas* (1946–52; Valencia, April 8, 1952); *El álbum de Cecilia* (1948; Madrid, May 15, 1952); *Sonatas de Castilla (con toccata a modo de pregón)* (1950–51; Madrid, Nov. 18, 1951); *Danza de la amapola* (1972); *Atardecer* for Piano, 4-Hands (1975; Aranjuez, Jan. 28, 1988); *Sonatina para dos muñecas* for Piano, 4-Hands (1977); *Tres evocaciones (Homenaje a Joaquín Turina)* (1981; Seville, Jan. 19, 1983); *Preludio de añoranza* (1987; Madrid, March 21, 1988). **Guitar:** *En los trigales* (1938); *Tiento antiguo* (1942); *Bajando de la meseta* (1954); *Tres piezas españolas* (1954); *Entre olivares* (1956); *Juto al Generalife* (1959); *Tonadilla* for 2 Guitars (1959); *En tierras de Jerez* (1960); *Sonata giocosa* (1960); *Invocación y danza (Homenaje a Manuel de Falla)* (1961; Brède, France, May 12, 1962); *Tres pequeñas piezas* (1963); *Sonata a la española* (Rome, May 30, 1969); *Elogio de la guitarra* (1971); *Pájaros de primavera* (1972); *Dos preludios* (1977); *Tríptico* (1978); *Un tiempo fue Itálica famosa* (1981); *¡ Qué buen caminito! (Pequeña fantasía)* (Seville, Oct. 10, 1987). **VOCAL:** *Quatre cançons en llengua catalana* for Soprano and Orch. (Barcelona, Oct. 17, 1946); *Tríptic de Mosén Cinto* for Soprano and Orch. (Barcelona, Oct. 17, 1946); *Cuatro madrigales amatorios* for Soprano and Piano (1947; Madrid, Feb. 4, 1948; also for Soprano and Orch.); *Romance del Comendador de Ocaña* for Soprano and Orch. (1947; Madrid, April 5, 1948); *Ausencias de Dulcinea* for Bass-baritone, 4 Sopranos, and Orch. (Madrid, April 19, 1948); *Doce canciones españolas* for Voice and Piano (1951; Madrid, May 3, 1952); *Villancicos y canciones de Navidad* for Soprano, Baritone, Chorus, and Orch. (1952; León, Dec. 22, 1970); *Música para un códice salmantino*, cantata for Bass, Chorus, and Orch. (Salamanca, Oct. 12, 1953); *Cánticos nupciales* for 3 Sopranos and Organ (Madrid, April 6, 1963); *Cantos de amor y de guerre* for Soprano and Orch. (1965; Madrid, March 15, 1968); *Himnos de los neófitos de Qumrán* for 3 Sopranos, Men's Chorus, and Orch. (Cuenca, April 15, 1965; rev. version, Cuenca, March 25, 1975); *Rosaliana* for Soprano and Orch. (La Coruña, July 29, 1965); *Con Antonio Machado* for Voice and Piano (Seville, Oct. 4, 1971); *Cántico de San Francisco de Asís* for Chorus and Orch. (1982; London, March 15, 1986). **OTHER:** Arrangements by Rodrígo and others of many of his works.

BIBL.: F. Sopeña, *J. R.* (Madrid, 1946); idem, *J. R.* (Madrid, 1970); V. Vayá Pla, *J. R., su vida y su obra* (Madrid, 1977); G. Wade, *J. R.: Concierto de Aranjuez* (Leeds, 1985); V. Kamhi, *De la mano de J. R.: Historia de nuestro vida* (Madrid, 1986; Eng. tr., 1992, as *Hand in Hand with J. R.: My Life at the Maestro's Side*); J. Arnau Amo, *La obra J. R.* (Valencia, 1992); L. Newcomb, *J. R. and Spanish Nationalism* (Gainesvilles, Fla., 1995); G. Wade, *Distant Sarabandes: The Solo Guitar Music of J. R.* (York, 1996); A. González Lapuente, *J. R.* (Madrid, 1997).—NS/LK/DM

Rodrígues de Ledesma, Mariano, Spanish composer; b. Saragossa, Dec. 14, 1779; d. Madrid, March 28, 1848. He was a choirboy at Saragossa Cathedral, being a pupil of F.J. García and José Gil Palomar. He conducted at the Seville Opera (1800–05), then at Madrid's Los Caños del Peral theater; became a supernumerary tenor at the royal chapel (1807). In 1811 he emigrated to London for political reasons; there he gained distinction as a singing teacher. He returned to Spain in 1814 and became 1st tenor of the royal chapel and singing master to the Princess Luisa Carlota. In 1823 he again went to London for political reasons, and taught singing at the Royal Academy of Music. After returning to Spain in 1831, he once more served as 1st tenor (until 1836) and choirmaster (1836–47) of the royal chapel. He wrote both sacred and secular music, and is recognized as one of Spain's earliest Romanticists.

BIBL.: R. Mitjana, *El maestro R.d.L. y sus Lamentaciones de Semana Santa: Estudio crítico-biográfico* (Malaga, 1909). —**NS/LK/DM**

Rodriguez, Felipe, Spanish composer; b. Madrid, May 1, 1759; d. there, May 1814. He was a member of the Monserrat School, and in 1778 he was ordained priest; served as organist in Madrid. He wrote organ pieces, some of which are printed in *Música instrumental*, ed. by D. Pujol (vol. 2, Montserrat, 1946), and church music. His Rondo for Piano is printed by J. Nín in the collection *17 sonates et pièces anciennes d'auteurs espagnols* (Paris, 1929).—**NS/LK/DM**

Rodriguez, Robert Xavier, American composer; b. San Antonio, June 28, 1946. He studied with Hunter Johnson and Kent Kennan at the Univ. of Tex. in Austin (B.M., 1967; M.M., 1969), Stevens and Dahl at the Univ. of Southern Calif. in Los Angeles (D.M.A., 1975), Druckman at the Berkshire Music Center in Tanglewood, and Boulanger in Paris; also attended master classes given by Maderna and Carter. He taught at the Univ. of Southern Calif. (1973–75) and at the Univ. of Tex. in Dallas (from 1975); held a Guggenheim fellowship (1976); was composer-in-residence of the Dallas Sym. Orch. (1982–85).

WORKS: DRAMATIC: O p e r a : *Le Diable amoureux* (1978; orch. suite, 1978); *Suor Isabella* (1982; Boston, May 3, 1984); *Tango*, chamber opera (1985); *Monkey See, Monkey Do*, children's opera (1986); *Frida* (1990); *The Old Majestic* (1991). **B a l l e t :** *Estampie* (1980); *Meta-4* (1993). **ORCH.:** *Adagio* for 7 Winds and Strings (1967); 3 piano concertos (1968; 1972; 1973–74); *Lyric Variations* for Oboe, 2 Horns, and Strings (1970); *Sinfonia concertante* for Saxophone, Harpsichord, and Chamber Orch. (1974); *Favola concertante* for Violin, Cello, and Strings (1975); *Frammenti musicali* for Flute or Violin and Strings (1978); *Favola Boccaccesca* (1979); *Oktoechoes*, concerto for Octet and Orch. (1983; Dallas, May 4, 1984); *Trunks: A Circus Story* for Narrator and Orch. (1983); *7 Deadly Sins* for Wind Ensemble and Percussion (1984); *A Colorful Symphony* for Narrator, Orch., and Optional Visual Effects, for children (1987; Indianapolis, May 3, 1988); *Invocation of Orpheus*, trumpet concerto (1989); *A Gathering of Angels*, bolero (1989); *Ursa: 4 Seasons* for Double Bass and Strings (San Antonio, Nov. 29, 1990); *Piñata* (1990); *Máscaras* for Cello and Orch. (1994). **CHAMBER:** 2 piano trios (1970, 1971); Sonata for Soprano Saxophone or Clarinet and Piano (1972); *Toccata* for Guitar Quartet (1975); *Variations* for Violin and Piano (1975); *Quodlibet on Medieval Tunes* for Instruments (1978); *Semi-suite* for Violin and Piano (1980–81; originally for Piano, 4-Hands; also for Violin and Orch., or Violin, Clarinet, Piano, and Percussion, 1984); *Les Niais Amoureux* for Quartet (1989); 3 Lullabies for Guitar (1993). **P i a n o :** *For Piano I–II* (1972); *Serbelloni Birthday Rag* (1976; arranged for Orch., 1977); *Fantasia Lussuriosa* (1989). **VOCAL:** Cantata for Soprano, Chorus, and Orch. (1972); *Canto*, cantata for Soprano, Tenor, Piano, Cello, and Orch. (1973); *Transfigurationis mysteria* for 3 Solo Voices, Narrator, Chorus, and Orch. (1978); *Praline and Fudge* for Baritone and Piano, to texts from cookbooks (1979); *Adoración Ambulante*, folk mass for Tenor, Bass, Chorus, Children's Chorus, Mariachi Band, Dancers, Puppets, Slides, Fireworks, Orch., and Audience Participation (1994); *Scrooge*, concert scene from "A Christmas Carol" for Bass-baritone, Chorus, and Orch. (El Paso, Tex., Dec. 9, 1994).—**NS/LK/DM**

Rodriguez, Santiago, talented Cuban-American pianist; b. Cardenas, Feb. 16, 1952. He settled in the U.S. when he was 8 and pursued training in New Orleans, at the Univ. of Tex., and at the Juilliard School in N.Y. He made his debut at age 9 with the New Orleans Phil.; in 1975 he won 1st prize at the Univ. of Md. Piano Competition, and in 1981 shared 2nd prize at the Van Cliburn Piano Competition. In 1982 he was awarded an Avery Fisher Career Grant, and in 1986 was honored as the first recipient of the Shura Cherkassky Recital Award of N.Y.'s 92nd St. Y. Rodriguez has appeared widely as a soloist with orchs. and as a recitalist, both in the U.S. and abroad. He also taught at the Univ. of Md. at Coll. Park. He is a versatile virtuoso whose expansive and intriguing repertoire includes not only standard works but works by Busoni, Mrs. H.H.A. Beach, Castelnuovo-Tedesco, Hanson, Ginastera, Shchedrin, and others.—**NS/LK/DM**

Rodriguez, Vicente, Spanish organist and composer; b. Onteniente, near Valencia, c. 1685; d. Valencia (buried), Dec. 16, 1760. He was a cleric, and served as interim organist (1713–15) and organist (1715–60) at Valencia Cathedral. He wrote several masses and also keyboard music.—**NS/LK/DM**

Rodriguez de Hita, Antonio, Spanish composer; b. c. 1724; d. Madrid, Feb. 21, 1787. From 1740 to 1757 he was maestro de capilla at Palencia Cathedral, where he publ. a book of advice to his pupils, *Consejos que a sus discípulos da don Antonio Rodriguez de Hita*. Then he held that title at the Convent of the Incarnation in Madrid. From 1768 he collaborated with the dramatist Ramón de la Cruz in a series of notable stage works impregnated with Spanish atmosphere; the best are the zarzuelas *Las segadoras de Vallecas* (Madrid, Sept. 13, 1768) and *Las labradoras de Murcia* (Madrid, Sept. 16, 1769). He also composed the Spanish opera *La Briseida* (Madrid, July 10, 1768) and various sacred and secular choral works.—**NS/LK/DM**

Rodwin, David, American composer; b. New Rochelle, N.Y., Oct. 22, 1970. He studied politics (A.B., 1992) and also took music courses with Steven Mackey at Princeton Univ., then took courses at the Juilliard School of Music in N.Y. (1993). He also studied with Amnon Wolman and Michael Pisaro at Northwestern Univ. (M.M., 1995), and attended a professional film scoring workshop at the Univ. of Calif. at Los Angeles (1996); also studied dance and clowning. He has also directed a number of plays, including Peter Shaffer's *Amadeus* (1991) and Eric Bentley's *Are You Now or Have You Ever Been* (1992) at Princeton Univ., where he also directed the men's a cappella group, The Princeton

Tigertones. Rodwin composes most effectively for the theater, and often performs in his own works. In 1996 he settled in Los Angeles, where he became active with ASK Theatre Project's first Composer/Playwright Studio.

WORKS: DRAMATIC: O p e r a : *Ecstatic Journey*, multimedia opera (1995); TUNAFISH! for 3 Voices and Percussion, micro-opera (1995); *"Untitled no. 576"* (1995); *Virtual Motion*, 1-man "hyper-opera" (1997–98). **M u s i c a l s :** *Stargazers*, political musical drama (1992); *Star Drek!: A Musical Parody* (1994); *Hook, Rod & Pipe: A Musical Overture* (1997); *WARNING!: eXplicit Material* (2000). **O t h e r :** Incidental music; works for dance, including *Dis/Family Function* for Tenor Saxophone (1995) and *Stripping* for Electronic Media (1998); film scores. **ORCH.:** *Strangeland* (1997); *tR/Averse* (1995). **CHAMBER:** *Challah* for String Quartet (1995); *Chain Fence* for Baritone Saxophone, Piano, and Percussion (1995); *F-L-O-W-E-R* for 2 Violas (1995); *Untitled* for Violin and Piano (1993); *Wave* for Clarinet and Piano (1993); *Jud's Oak Desk/Lonely Room #2* for Cello (1991); *Like Clockwork* for Piano (1998). **VOCAL:** *Sister I'm Here* for Baritone, Bass, and Symphonic Band (1991).—**LK/DM**

Rodzinski, Artur, eminent Polish-born American conductor; b. Spalato, Dalmatia, Jan. 1, 1892; d. Boston, Nov. 27, 1958. He studied jurisprudence at the Univ. of Vienna, and at the same time took lessons in piano with Sauer, composition with Schreker, and conducting with Schalk. He made his conducting debut in Lwów in 1920; subsequently conducted at the Warsaw Opera. In 1926 he was appointed asst. conductor to Stokowski with the Philadelphia Orch.; concurrently he was head of the opera and orch. depts. at the Curtis Inst. of Music. In 1929 he was appointed conductor of the Los Angeles Phil.; after 4 seasons there, he was engaged as conductor of the Cleveland Orch., where he introduced the novel custom of presenting operas in concert form; on Jan. 31, 1935, he conducted the American premiere of Shostakovich's controversial opera *Lady Macbeth of the District of Mtzensk*. He became a naturalized American citizen in 1932. In 1943 he received his most prestigious appointment as conductor of the N.Y. Phil., but his independent character and temperamental ways of dealing with the management forced him to resign amid raging controversy in the middle of his 4th season (Feb. 3, 1947); almost immediately he was engaged as conductor of the Chicago Sym. Orch., but there, too, a conflict rapidly developed, and the management announced after a few months of the engagement that his contract would not be renewed, stating as a reason that his operatic ventures using the orch. were too costly. After these distressing American experiences, Rodzinski conducted mainly in Europe; in the autumn of 1958 he received an invitation to conduct at the Lyric Opera in Chicago, but after 3 performances of *Tristan und Isolde* (Nov. 1, 7, and 10), a heart ailment forced him to cancel his remaining appearances; he died in a Boston hospital.

BIBL.: H. Rodzinski, *Our Two Lives* (N.Y., 1976). —**NS/LK/DM**

Roesgen-Champion, Marguerite, Swiss harpsichordist and composer; b. Geneva, Jan. 25, 1894; d. Paris, June 30, 1976. She studied composition with Bloch and Jaques-Dalcroze at the Geneva Cons., but devoted herself mainly to harpsichord playing, giving numerous recitals in Europe. Her own works, couched in the neo-Romantic vein, include *Faunesques* for Orch. (Paris, 1929), *Concerto moderne* for Harpsichord and Orch. (Paris, Nov. 15, 1931, composer soloist), *Aquarelles*, symphonic suite (Paris, Nov. 26, 1933), Harp Concerto (Paris, March 28, 1954), 5 harpsichord concertos (1931–59), including No. 1, *Concerto moderne* (Paris, Nov. 15, 1931, composer soloist), *Concerto romantique* for Piano and Orch. (1961), a number of pieces for flute in combination with the harpsichord and other instruments, and a curious piece for Piano, 4-Hands, entitled *Spoutnik* (1971).—**NS/LK/DM**

Rogalski, Theodor, Romanian conductor, teacher, and composer; b. Bucharest, April 11, 1901; d. Zürich, Feb. 2, 1954. He was a student of Gheorghe Cucu (theory), Castaldi (composition), and Cuclin (music history) at the Bucharest Cons. (1919–20), of Karg-Elert (conducting and composition) at the Leipzig Cons. (1920–23), and of d'Indy (composition) and Ravel (orchestration) in Paris (1924). Returning to Bucharest, he was conductor of the Radio Sym. Orch. (1930–51), and then of the Phil.: he also was prof. of orchestration at the Cons. (from 1950). In 1923 and 1926 he was awarded the Enesco Prize for composition. In 1953 he was made a Merited Artist by the Romanian government. His music was permeated by the spirit of Romanian folk melos, while his harmony and orchestration revealed coloristic infusions.

WORKS: DRAMATIC: B a l l e t : *Fresque antique* (1923). **ORCH.:** Rondo (1921); *2 Dansuri româneşti* (1926; Bucharest, Jan. 20, 1927); *2 Symphonic Sketches* (1929; Bucharest, May 11, 1930); *2 Capricii* (1932); *3 Dansuri româneşti* (1950; Bucharest, May 27, 1951). **CHAMBER:** *Crépuscule* for Violin and Piano (1922); *Frühlingsnacht* for 2 Violins and Viola (1922); String Quartet (1923); *Esquisse* for Violin and Piano (1923); *Sonet* for Violin and Piano (1924); *Porumbel* for Violin (1925); *La chef* for String Quartet (1928); piano pieces, including a Sonata (1919). **VOCAL:** Many songs with orch. or piano. —**NS/LK/DM**

Rogatis, Pascual de
See **De Rogatis, Pascual**

Rogé, Pascal, French pianist; b. Paris, April 6, 1951. He entered the Paris Cons. at age 11 and made his debut as a soloist at the same age in Paris; his principal teacher was L. Descaves, and he graduated with premiers prix in piano and chamber music (1966); then studied with Julius Katchen (1966–69). In 1969 he made his London debut; after winning joint 1st prize in the Long-Thibaud Competition in Paris in 1971, he pursued a successful international career.—**NS/LK/DM**

Rogel, Jose, Spanish composer; b. Orihuela, Alicante, Dec. 24, 1829; d. Cartagena, Feb. 25, 1901. At a very early age he was taught music by the organist J. Cascales, and at 10 composed a Mass, which he conducted himself. After he finished his law studies in Valencia, he studied counterpoint with Pascual Perez Cascon; subsequently conducted at various theaters in

Madrid, and in 1854 began his unusually successful career as a composer of zarzuelas, of which he wrote 81 (some in collaboration). Among the best are El Joven Telemaco, Las Amazones del Tormes, El Rey Midas, Los Infiernos de Madrid, Genoveva de Brabante, and Pablo y Virginia.—NS/LK/DM

Roger, Gustave-Hippolyte, famous French tenor; b. La Chapelle St.-Denis, near Paris, Dec. 17, 1815; d. Paris, Sept. 12, 1879. He was a pupil of Blès Martin at the Paris Cons., making his debut as Georges in Halévy's *L'Éclair* at the Paris Opéra- Comique in 1838. He then was at the Paris Opéra (from 1848), where he created the role of the Prophète in Meyerbeer's opera (1849); later toured in Germany. While he was hunting in the fall of 1859, the accidental discharge of his gun injured his right arm so severely that it had to be amputated. An artificial arm proved ineffective, and he was obliged to retire from the stage in 1861. From 1868 until his death he was a prof. of singing at the Paris Cons. He publ. his memoirs as *Le Carnet d'un ténor* (Paris, 1880).

BIBL.: A. Laget, *G.-H. R.: Notice biographique* (Paris, 1865). —NS/LK/DM

Roger, Victor, French composer and music critic; b. Montpellier, July 22, 1853; d. Paris, Dec. 2, 1903. He studied at the École Niedermeyer in Paris. He wrote light music, composing some 30 operettas, of which the following were brought out in Paris with considerable success: *Joséphine vendue par ses soeurs* (March 20, 1886), *Oscarine* (Oct. 15, 1888), *Le Fétiche* (March 13, 1890), *Samsonnet* (Nov. 26, 1890), *Miss Nicol-Nick* (Jan. 23, 1895), *Sa Majesté l'Amour* (Dec. 24, 1896), *L'Auberge du Tohu-Bohu* (Feb. 10, 1897), *Les Fêtards* (Oct. 28, 1897), *L'Agence Crook et Cie* (Jan. 22, 1898), *La Petite Tâche* (March 26, 1898), and *Le Jockey malgré lui* (Dec. 4, 1902). After his death, 3 completely finished scores were found: *La Fille de Fra Diavolo*, *La Princesse de Babylone*, and *Adélaïde*. —NS/LK/DM

Roger-Ducasse, Jean (-Jules Aimable), French composer and teacher; b. Bordeaux, April 18, 1873; d. Le-Taillan-Médoc, near Bordeaux, July 19, 1954. He studied at the Paris Cons. with Fauré (composition), Pessard (harmony), Gédalge (counterpoint), and de Bériot. In 1902 he won the 2nd Prix de Rome for the cantata *Alcyone*. In 1909 he was appointed inspector of singing in the Paris schools; subsequently was a prof. of ensemble at the Paris Cons.; from 1935 to 1940, taught composition there; then retired to Bordeaux. His first work to be played in public was a *Petite suite* for Orch. (Paris, March 5, 1898). He adopted a pleasing style of Impressionism; his symphonic pieces enjoyed considerable success, without setting a mark for originality. His autobiography was publ. in *L'Écran des musiciens* (1930).

WORKS: DRAMATIC: *Orphée*, mimodrama (1913; St. Petersburg, Jan. 31, 1914); *Cantegril*, comic opera (1930; Paris, Feb. 9, 1931). **ORCH.:** *Variations plaisantes sur un thème grave* (Paris, Jan. 24, 1909); *Suite française* (1909); *Prélude d'un ballet* (1910); *Le Joli Jeu de furet*, scherzo (1911); *Nocturne de printemps* (Paris, Feb. 14, 1920); *Symphonie sur la Cathédrale de Reims*

(unfinished); *Le Petit Faune* (Bordeaux, May 22, 1954). **CHAMBER:** Piano Quartet (1899–1912); String Quartet (1900–1909). **VOCAL:** *Au Jardin de Marguerite* for Soloists, Chorus, and Orch. (1901–05); *Sarabande* for Voices and Orch. (1911); *Sur quelques vers de Virgile* for Chorus and Orch.; songs. **OTHER:** Pedagogical works.

BIBL.: L. Ceillier, *R.-D.* (Paris, 1920); *Catalogue de l'oeuvre de R.-D.* (Bordeaux, 1955).—NS/LK/DM

Rogers, Bernard, distinguished American composer and pedagogue; b. N.Y., Feb. 4, 1893; d. Rochester, N.Y., May 24, 1968. He began piano lessons when he was 12, and after leaving school at 15, he was employed in an architectural firm while training in architecture at Columbia Univ. He subsequently received instruction in theory from Hans van den Berg, composition from Farwell, and harmony and composition from Bloch in Cleveland; returning to N.Y., he continued his studies with Goetschius at the Inst. of Musical Art (1921). Later he held a Guggenheim fellowship (1927–29), which made it possible for him to train with Bridge in England and Boulanger in Paris. He first won recognition as a composer with his orch. work *To the Fallen* (1918; N.Y., Nov. 13, 1919), on the strength of which he received a Pulitzer Traveling Scholarship. He taught at the Cleveland Inst. of Music (1922–23), the Hartt School of Music in Hartford, Conn. (1926–27), and the Eastman School of Music in Rochester, N.Y. (1929–67), where he also served as chairman of the composition dept. In 1947 he was elected to membership in the National Inst. of Arts and Letters. He publ. a valuable manual, *The Art of Orchestration* (N.Y., 1951).

WORKS (all 1st perf. in Rochester, N.Y., unless otherwise given): **DRAMATIC: Opera:** *Deirdre* (1922); *The Marriage of Aude* (May 22, 1931); *The Warrior* (1944; N.Y., Jan. 11, 1947); *The Veil* (Bloomington, Ind., May 18, 1950); *The Nightingale* (1954). **ORCH.:** *To the Fallen* (1918; N.Y., Nov. 13, 1919); *The Faithful*, overture (1922); *Soliloquy No. 1* for Flute and Strings (1922) and *No. 2* for Bassoon and Strings (Oct. 18, 1938); *In the Gold Room* (1924); *Pastorale* for 11 Instruments (1924); *Fuji in the Sunset Glow* (1925); *Hamlet*, prelude (1925); 5 syms.: No. 1, *Adonais* (1926; April 29, 1927), No. 2 (1928; Oct. 24, 1930), No. 3, *On a Thanksgiving Song* (1936; Oct. 27, 1937), No. 4 (1940; May 4, 1948), and No. 5, *Africa* (1958; Cincinnati, Jan. 30, 1959); *3 Japanese Dances* (1933; May 3, 1934); *2 American Frescoes* (1934); *Once upon a Time*, 5 fairy tales for Small Orch. (April 4, 1935); *The Supper at Emmaus* (April 29, 1937); *Fantasy* for Flute, Viola, and Strings (1937; April 25, 1938); *The Song of the Nightingale*, suite (1939; Cincinnati, March 21, 1940); *The Colors of War* (Oct. 25, 1939); *The Dance of Salome* (April 25, 1940); *The Plains* for Small Orch. (1940; N.Y., May 3, 1941); *Invasion* (N.Y., Oct. 17, 1943); *Anzacs* (1944); *Elegy in Memory of Franklin D. Roosevelt* (1945; N.Y., April 11, 1946); *Characters from Hans Christian Andersen* for Small Orch. (April 28, 1945); *Amphitryon Overture* (1946; N.Y., March 10, 1947); *Elegy* for Small Orch. (1947); *The Silver World* for Small Orch. (1949); *The Colors of Youth* (1951); *Portrait* for Violin and Orch. (1952); *Fantasy* for Horn, Timpani, and Strings (1952; Feb. 20, 1955); *Dance Scenes* (Louisville, Oct. 28, 1953); *Variations on a Song by Mussorgsky* (1960); *New Japanese Dances* (1961); *Allegory* for Small Orch. (1961); *Apparitions* (1967). **CHAMBER:** *Mood* for Piano Trio (1918); 2 string quartets (1918, 1925); *The Silver World* for Flute, Oboe, and Strings (1950); String Trio (1953); *Ballade* for Bassoon, Viola, and Piano (1959); Violin Sonata (1962). **VOCAL: Chorus and Orch.:**

The Raising of Lazarus (1928); *The Exodus* (1931); *The Passion*, oratorio (1942; Cincinnati, May 12, 1944); *A Letter from Pete*, cantata (1947); *The Prophet Isaiah*, cantata (1950); *The Light of Man*, oratorio (1964). **S o l o   V o i c e   a n d   O r c h .** : *Arab Love Songs* for Soprano and Orch. (1927); *Horse Opera* for Narrator and Orch. (1948); *Leaves from the Tale of Pinocchio* for Narrator and Orch. (1951); *Psalm LXVIII* for Baritone and Orch. (1951); *The Musicians of Bremen* for Narrator and 13 Instruments (1958); *Aladdin* for Narrator and Wind Ensemble (1965). **O t h e r** : *Psalm XCIX* for Chorus and Organ (1945); *Response to Silent Prayer* for Chorus (1945); *Hear My Prayer, O Lord* for Soprano, Chorus, and Organ (1955); *Psalm XVIII* for Men's Voices and Piano (1963); *Psalm LXXXIX* for Baritone, Chorus, and Piano (1963); *Faery Song* for Women's Voices (1965); *Dirge for 2 Veterans* for Chorus and Piano (1967); *Psalm CXIV* for Chorus and Piano (1968).

BIBL.: S. Dershan, *Orchestration in the Orchestral Works of B. R.* (diss., Univ. of Rochester, 1975); D. Intili, *Text-Music Relationships in the Large Choral Works of B. R.* (diss., Case Western Reserve Univ., 1977); F. Koch, *Reflections on Composing: Four American Composers: Elwell, Shepherd, R., Cowell* (Pittsburgh, 1983).—NS/LK/DM

Rogers, Clara Kathleen (née **Barnett**), English-born American soprano, teacher, and composer; b. Cheltenham, Jan. 14, 1844; d. Boston, March 8, 1931. She was the daughter of the composer John Barnett. She studied at the Leipzig Cons. with Moscheles and Plaidy (piano), Papperitz and Richter (theory), and David and Rietz (ensemble playing), then singing with Goetz in Berlin and with Sangiovanni in Milan. She made her debut in Turin (1863) as Isabella in *Robert le Diable* (stage name, "Clara Doria"). She went to America in 1871 with the Parepa-Rosa Co., making her debut in N.Y. in *The Bohemian Girl* (Oct. 4, 1871). Having married a Boston lawyer, Henry M. Rogers, in 1878, she later settled in Boston as a teacher; from 1902, was a prof. of singing at the New England Cons. of Music. She publ. *The Philosophy of Singing* (1893), *Dreaming True* (1899), *My Voice and I* (1910), *English Diction in Song and Speech* (1912), *The Voice in Speech* (1915), and *Memories of a Musical Career* (Boston, 1919) and its sequel, *The Story of Two Lives* (Norwood, Mass., 1932). She composed a String Quartet (1866), a Violin Sonata (1903), a Cello Sonata, and many songs.—NS/LK/DM

Rogers, Nigel (David), English tenor, conductor, and teacher; b. Wellington, Shropshire, March 21, 1935. He studied at King's Coll., Cambridge (1953–56), in Rome (1957), in Milan (1958–59), and with Hüsch at the Munich Hochschule für Musik (1959–64). He became a singer with the Studio der frühen Musik in Munich in 1961 and later acquired a fine reputation as an interpreter of Baroque music. He was a prof. of singing at the Royal Coll. of Music in London (from 1978) and founded the vocal ensemble Chiaroscuro for the performance of Italian Baroque music (1979).—NS/LK/DM

Roget, Henriette, French composer and organist; b. Bastia, Corsica, Jan. 9, 1910. She studied organ with Marcel Dupré and composition with Henru Busser at the Paris Cons., receiving the Premier 2nd Prix de Rome

in 1933. She was director in charge of voice training at the Paris Opéra until 1959; she also served as organist at the Oratoire du Louvre and prof. of piano accompanying and score reading at the Paris Cons. She wrote a great number of piano books for children, among them *Adroits petits doigts* (1957), *Abécédaire* (1958), and *Méthode* (1970).

WORKS: DRAMATIC: B a l l e t : *Cathérinettes* (1937). **ORCH.**: *Montanyas del Rosello* for Organ and Orch. (Paris, April 6, 1933, composer soloist); *Sinfonia andorrana* (1936); *3 ballades françaises* (Paris, Jan. 11, 1936); *Rythmes* (Paris, Jan. 23, 1937); *Concerto sicilien* for Piano and Orch. (1943); *Concerto classique* for Cello and Orch. (1944); *Symphonique pour rire* (1947). **O r g a n** : Various effective pieces.—NS/LK/DM

Rogg, Lionel, eminent Swiss organist, harpsichordist, pedagogue, and composer; b. Geneva, April 21, 1936. He studied at the Geneva Cons. with Charles Chaix (harmony, counterpoint, and composition), Pierre Segond (organ; 1st prize, 1956), and André Perret and Nikita Magaloff (piano; 1st prize, 1957), and then with André Marchal in Paris. From 1960 he was a prof. at the Geneva Cons. After performing all of Bach's organ works in a series of recitals at Victoria Hall in Geneva in 1961, he toured throughout the world as an organ and harpsichord virtuoso. He also gave master classes in keyboard interpretation and publ. a course on organ improvisation. Rogg's exhaustive repertoire ranges from Bach and Buxtehude to Hindemith and Ligeti. He is especially known as a master of improvisation. Among his compositions are an Organ Concerto (1992) and numerous solo organ pieces, piano music, and vocal scores, including a Missa Breves for Chorus and Orch. and a cantata.—NS/LK/DM

Rogier, Philippe, Flemish composer; b. Arras, c. 1561; d. Madrid, Feb. 29, 1596. He became a boy treble at the court of King Philip II in Madrid in 1572. He later entered the priesthood and served as a chaplain of the royal chapel. After serving as vice-maestro de capilla (1584–86), he was maestro de capilla (from 1586) at the court. He also held several non-residential benefices. Rogier was highly regarded by his contemporaries, and composed some 250 works. Among his extant compositions are several masses, motets, and chansons.

BIBL.: P. Becquart, *Musiciens néerlandais à la cour de Madrid: P. R. et son école* (Brussels, 1967).—LK/DM

Rogister, Jean (François Toussaint), Belgian violist, pedagogue, and composer; b. Liège, Oct. 25, 1879; d. there, March 20, 1964. He studied violin, viola, horn, and composition at the Liège Cons., where he was head of the viola classes there (1900–45); also was head of the viola classes at the Brussels Cons. (1945–48). He played in various orchs., and was also founder of the Liège Quartet (1925), with which he toured extensively. His style of composition followed the precepts of Cesar Franck, but upon occasion he introduced into his music some modernistic impressionistic sonorities.

WORKS: DRAMATIC: L y r i c   D r a m a : *Lorsque minuit sonna* (1930). **ORCH.**: *Fantaisie concertante* for Viola and Orch. (1910); Viola Concerto (1914); Cello Concerto (1917);

Trombone Concerto (1919); *Destin* (1919); *La Fiancée du lutin* (1920); *Poème* for Violin and Orch. (1920); *Nuit d'Avril* (1921); *Paysage* (1923); 3 syms.: No. 1 (1927), No. 2, *Symphonie wallonne* (1931–32), and No. 3 for String Quartet and Orch. (1942–43); *Fantaisie burlesque sur un thème populaire* (1928); *La Lune et les peupliers* (1932); *Impression de mai* for Violin and Orch. (1935); Suite for Flute and Chamber Orch. (1949); *Jeux symphoniques* (1952); *Hommage à César Franck* (1955); *Adagio* for 2 String Ensembles (1960). **CHAMBER:** 8 string quartets (1902, 1914, 1921, 1926, 1927, 1928, 1931, 1940); *Symphonie intime* for String Quartet, Double Bass, Flute, Clarinet, and Bassoon (1929); Quintet for Harpsichrod, 2 Quintons, Viola d'Amore, and Viola da Gamba (1934); *Esquisse dramatique* for String Quartet (1935); Wind Quintet (1947). **VOCAL:** *The Bells*, oratorio for Soprano and 8 Instruments, after Edgar Allan Poe (1924); *Requiem for* Chorus and Orch. (1944; Liège, March 24, 1946); choruses; songs.

BIBL.: J. Servais, *J. R.: Un Musicien du coeur* (1972). —NS/LK/DM

Rögner, Heinz, German conductor; b. Leipzig, Jan. 16, 1929. He studied piano with Hugo Steuer, viola with Gutschlicht, and conducting with Egon Bölsche at the Hochschule für Musik in Leipzig. He was a conductor at the German National Theater in Weimar (1951–54); then led the opera school at the Hochschule für Musik in Leipzig (1954–58). From 1958 to 1962 he was chief conductor of the Great Radio Orch. in Leipzig; from 1962 to 1973 he was Generalmusikdirektor of the State Opera in East Berlin. In 1973 he became chief conductor of the (East) Berlin Radio Sym. Orch.; also appeared as a guest conductor in Europe. He served as music director of the Yomiuri Nippon Sym. Orch. in Tokyo (1985–91).—NS/LK/DM

Rogowski, Ludomir (Michal), Polish composer and conductor; b. Lublin, Oct. 3, 1881; d. Dubrovnik, March 14, 1954. He was a student of Noskowski (composition) and Mlynarski (conducting) at the Warsaw Cons., and then of Nikisch and Riemann in Leipzig. In 1909 he went to Vilnius as director of the Organ School. He also founded the Vilnius Sym. Orch. in 1910. From 1912 to 1914 he was a theater conductor in Warsaw. In 1926 he settled in Dubrovnik. In 1938 he was awarded the Polish State Music Prize.

WORKS: DRAMATIC: O p e r a : *Tamara* (1918); *Un Grand Chagrin de la petite Ondine* (1919); *La Sérénade inutile* (1921); *Królewicz Marko* (1930). **B a l l e t :** *Bajka* (1922); *Kupala* (1925). **ORCH.:** *Images ensoleillees* (1918); *Villafranca* (1919); 7 syms. (1921, 1936, 1940, 1943, 1947, 1949, 1951); *Les Saisons* (1933); *Les Sourires* (1933); *Poème du travail* (1936); *Fantômes* (1937); 4 rhapsodies on Slavonic themes (1945); *Dubrovnik Impressions* (1950). **OTHER:** 2 string quartets; choral arrangements of Slavonic songs.—NS/LK/DM

Roguski, Gustav, Polish composer and pedagogue; b. Warsaw, May 12, 1839; d. there, April 5, 1921. He studied in Germany with Kiel, then went to Paris, where he became a pupil of Berlioz. Returning to Warsaw in 1873, he was appointed prof. at the Cons. He wrote a Sym., 2 string quartets, a Quintet for Wind Instruments and Piano, many piano pieces, choruses, and songs. He also publ. a manual of harmony (with L. Zelenski). Roguski was greatly esteemed as a teacher of composition, numbering Paderewski among his pupils. —NS/LK/DM

Rojo Olalla, Casiano, Spanish organist, choirmaster, and writer on music; b. Hacinas, Aug. 5, 1877; d. Burgos, Dec. 4, 1931. He studied at the Santo Domingo de Silos monastery in Burgos, where he became a Benedictine monk (1896), and later pursued studies with Pothier in Belgium. He was active as an organist and choirmaster, and became an authority on Gregorian chant. He publ. a valuable manual, *Método de canto gregoriano* (Valladolid, 1906), as well as *Manual de canto gregoriano* (Silos, 1908), *Cantus Lamentationum* (Bilbao, 1917), *Antiphonarium Mozarabicum de la Catedral de León* (with G. Prado; León, 1928), and *El Canto mozárabe* (with G. Prado; Barcelona, 1929).—NS/LK/DM

Rokitansky, Hans, Freiherr von, Austrian bass; b. Vienna, March 8, 1835; d. Schloss Laubegg, Styria, Nov. 2, 1909. He received his training in Bologna and Milan. After making his concert debut in London in 1856, he made his operatic debut at the Théâtre-Italien in Paris in 1857 as Oroveso. He sang in Prague from 1862 to 1864. From 1864 to 1893 he was a member of the Vienna Court Opera, and then taught at the Vienna Cons. from 1894. Among his finest roles were Sarastro, Leporello, Caspar, Heinrich, and the Landgrave. His brother, Victor, Freiherr von Rokitansky (b. Vienna, July 9, 1836; d. there, July 17, 1896), was a singer and composer of songs who taught at the Vienna Cons. (1871–80).—NS/LK/DM

Rokseth, Yvonne (née Rihouët), eminent French musicologist; b. Maisons–Laffitte, near Paris, July 17, 1890; d. Strasbourg, Aug. 23, 1948. She studied at the Paris Cons., with d'Indy and Roussel at the Schola Cantorum, and with Pirro at the Sorbonne, receiving her doctorat és lettres in 1930 with the diss. *La Musique d'orgue au XVe siècle et au début du XVIe* (publ. in Paris, 1930). She was a librarian at the Cons. and the Bibliothèque Nationale (1934–37); then was made maître de conférences at the Univ. of Strasbourg (1937); after serving in the Resistance during World War II, she rejoined its faculty as prof. of musicology. She ed. the valuable *Polyphonies du XIIIe siècle: Le Manuscrit H 196 de la Faculté de médecine de Montpellier* (4 vols., Paris, 1935–39); also publ. a biography of Grieg (Paris, 1933) and other vols.—NS/LK/DM

Roland, Claude-Robert, Belgian composer, organist, conductor, and teacher; b. Pont-de-Loup, Dec. 19, 1935. He studied composition at the Music Academy in Châtelet and at the conservatories of Mons, Liège, Paris, and Brussels with Froidebise, C. Schmit, R. Bernier, Messiaen, and Defossez; also took a course in conducting with Scherchen. He was an organist in churches in various Belgian cities (1955–67); was director of the Music Academy at Montignies-le-Tilleul (1966–75); in 1972, was appointed to the staff of the Brussels Cons.

WORKS: ORCH.: *Recherche* (1956); *Indicatif 1* for 12 Strings (1957); *Sinfonia scolastica pour les bouffons de la Reine* (1961); *Serenade* for Chamber Orch. (1961); Organ Concerto (1963); *Rossignolet du bois* (1971). CHAMBER: *Sonance* for String Quartet (1956); *2 sonances* for Piano (1956, 1960); *Sonance* for Clavichord (1959); *Chansons et reveries* for Violin and Piano (1962); *Ballade* for Violin and Piano (1966); *Prélude, Fugue et Rondo a 5* for Wind Quintet (1967); *Sonancelle* for Guitar (1967); *Prelude, Fugue et Commentaires* for 4 Clarinets (1971); *Faits-divers* for Horn and Piano (1981); *Thriller* for Trumpet and Piano (1985); *De profundis* for Tuba and Piano (1985).—NS/LK/DM

Rolandi, Gianna, gifted American soprano; b. N.Y., Aug. 16, 1952. Her first contact with opera came through her mother, herself a singer, and by the age of 15 she had already become acquainted with much of the operatic repertoire. She then enrolled at the Curtis Inst. of Music in Philadelphia (B.M., 1975). While still a student there, she was contracted to sing at the N.Y.C. Opera, with which she made an impressive debut as Olympia in *Les Contes d'Hoffmann* (Sept. 11, 1975). On Dec. 26, 1979, she made her Metropolitan Opera debut in N.Y. as Sophie in *Der Rosenkavalier*. In 1981 she made her European debut at the Glyndebourne Festival singing Zerbinetta. In 1982 she sang the title role in a televised production of *Lucia di Lammermoor* with the N.Y.C. Opera, receiving flattering notices from the press. She scored an outstanding success as Bianca in Rossini's *Bianca e Falliero* at its U.S. premiere at the Greater Miami Opera in 1987. In 1989 she appeared as Cimarosa's Curiazio at the Rome Opera. In 1993 she sang Despina in Chicago. In 1996 she toured the U.S. as a soloist with the BBC Sym. Orch. of London. She was married to **Andrew Davis**.—NS/LK/DM

Roland-Manuel (real name, **Roland Alexis Manuel Lévy**), French composer and writer on music; b. Paris, March 22, 1891; d. there, Nov. 1, 1966. He was a pupil of Roussel and d'Indy, and also studied privately with Ravel. In 1947 he became a prof. at the Paris Cons. In his compositions, he adopted the French neo-Classical style, close to Roussel's manner; however, he became best known as a perspicacious critic, publishing, in Paris, 3 vols. on Ravel: *Maurice Ravel et son oeuvre* (1914; 2nd ed., rev., 1926; Eng. tr., 1941), *Maurice Ravel et son oeuvre dramatique* (1928), and *À la gloire Maurice Ravel* (1938; 2nd ed., 1948; Eng. tr., 1947); also monographs on Satie (1916), Honegger (1925) and Falla (1930).

WORKS: DRAMATIC: *Isabelle et Pantalon*, opéra-bouffe (Paris, Dec. 11, 1922); *Le Diable amoureux*, light opera (1929); *L'Écran des jeunes filles*, ballet (Paris, May 16, 1929); *Elvire*, ballet on themes of Scarlatti (Paris, Feb. 8, 1937). OTHER: *Jeanne d'Arc*, oratorio (1937); Piano Concerto (1938); *Cantique de la sagesse* for Chorus and Orch. (1951).—NS/LK/DM

Roldán, Amadeo, Cuban violinist, conductor, and composer; b. Paris (of Cuban parents), July 12, 1900; d. Havana, March 2, 1939. He studied violin at the Madrid Cons. with Fernández Bordas, graduating in 1916. He won the Sarasate Violin Prize, and subsequently studied composition with Conrado del Campo in Madrid and

with Pedro Sanjuán. In 1921 he settled in Havana, and in 1924 he became concertmaster of the Orquesta Filarmónica; in 1925, asst. conductor; in 1932, conductor. He was prof. of composition at the Cons. (from 1935). In his works, he employed with signal success the melorhythms of Afro-Cuban popular music; as a mulatto, he had an innate understanding of these elements.

WORKS: DRAMATIC: Ballet: *La Rebambaramba*, employing a number of Cuban percussion instruments (1927–28; suite, Havana, Aug. 12, 1928). ORCH.: *Obertura sobre témas cubanos* (Havana, Nov. 29, 1925); *El Milagro de Anaquillé* (Havana, Sept. 22, 1929); *3 Toques* for Chamber Orch. (1931). CHAMBER: *Rítmica* Nos. 1–4 for Piano and Wind Quintet, and Nos. 5 and 6 for Percussion Ensemble. VOCAL: *Danza negra* for Voice and 7 Instruments (1929); *Motivos de son* for Voice and 9 Instruments (1930).—NS/LK/DM

Rolfe Johnson, Anthony, English tenor and conductor; b. Tackley, Nov. 5, 1940. He was a student of Ellis Keeler at the Guildhall School of Music in London, and later of Vera Rozsa. He gained experience singing in the chorus and appearing in small roles at the Glyndebourne Festivals between 1972 and 1976. In 1973 he made his formal operatic debut with the English Opera Group in *Iolanta*. In 1978 he made his first appearance with the English National Opera in London as Don Ottavio. He sang Tamino with the Welsh National Opera in Cardiff in 1979. In 1983 he appeared as Aschenbach at Glasgow's Scottish Opera. In 1987 he made his first appearance at the Salzburg Festival in Schmidt's *Das Buch mit sieben Siegeln*. On Dec. 22, 1988, he made his debut at London's Covent Garden as Jupiter in Handel's *Semele*. In 1990 he returned to the Salzburg Festival to sing his first operatic role there, Monteverdi's Orfeo. From 1990 he served as director of singing at the Britten-Pears School in Snape, but also continued his singing career. In 1994 he appeared as Peter Grimes in the reopening of the Glyndebourne Festival and sang Aschenbach at the Metropolitan Opera in N.Y. As a concert artist, he received many engagements with leading orchs. in Europe and North America. In 1997 he made his debut as a conductor with *Orfeo* in St. Louis.—NS/LK/DM

Roll, Michael, English pianist; b. Leeds, July 17, 1946. He received his training from Fanny Waterman. In 1958 he made his formal debut as soloist in the Schumann Concerto under Sir Malcolm Sargent's direction at London's Royal Festival Hall. After winning 1st prize in the Leeds competition in 1963, he made regular appearances as soloist with the principal British orchs.; later toured with British orchs. in Europe and the Far East. In 1974 he made his U.S. debut with Colin Davis and the Boston Sym. Orch. In subsequent years, he appeared not only as a soloist with various orchs. but as a recitalist. In 1992 he made his N.Y. recital debut. He was married to **Juliana Markova**.—NS/LK/DM

Rolla, Alessandro, Italian violinist, violist, teacher, and composer, father of **Giuseppe Antonio Rolla;** b. Pavia, April 6, 1757; d. Milan, Sept. 15, 1841. He was 1st violist (1782–92) and 1st violinist (1792–1803) in the

Parma ducal orch., then 1st violinist and director of Milan's La Scala orch. (1803–33) and 1st prof. of violin and viola at the Milan Cons. (1808–35). Paganini was sent to Parma in 1795 to study with Rolla, but upon his arrival Rolla is reported to have told him that there was nothing left to teach him.

WORKS: DRAMATIC: B a l l e t : *Adelasia* (Milan, 1779); *Iserbeck* (Padua, 1802); *Eloisa e Roberto* or *Il Conte d'Essex* (Rome, 1805); *Pizzarro* (Milan, 1807); *Abdul* (Vienna, 1808); *Achilles auf Skyros* (Vienna, 1808). ORCH.: Syms.; 10 violin concertos; 15 viola concertos; other works. CHAMBER: Many pieces.

BIBL.: G. Zampieri, *L'epoca e l'arte di A. R.* (Pavia, 1941); L. Inzaghi, *A. R.: Vita e opera del grande musicista, maestro di Niccoló Paganini* (Milan, 1984).—**NS/LK/DM**

Rolla, Giuseppe Antonio, Italian violinist and composer, son of **Alessandro Rolla;** b. Parma, April 18, 1798; d. Dresden, May 19, 1837. He studied with his father. He was concertmaster of the orch. of the Italian Opera Co. in Dresden (1823–35). He composed a Violin Concerto and pieces for violin and viola.—**NS/LK/DM**

Rolland, Romain, famous French author and musicologist; b. Clamecy, Nièvre, Jan. 29, 1866; d. Vézelay, Yonne, Dec. 30, 1944. He was educated in Paris at the École Normale Supérieure (1886–89), the École de Rome (1889–91), and the Sorbonne (doctorat és lettres, 1895, with the diss. *Les Origines du théâtre lyrique moderne: L'Histoire de l'opéra en Europe avant Lully et Scarlatti*; publ. in Paris, 1895; 4th ed., 1936). He then was a prof. of music history at the École Normale Supérieure until becoming the first prof. of music history at the Sorbonne (1903); was also director of the École des Hautes Sociales (1903–09). In 1900 he organized the first international congress for the history of music in Paris, and read a paper on *Les Musiciens italiens en France sous Mazarin et "l'Orfeo" de Luigi Rossi* (publ. 1901); with J. Combarieu, he ed. the transactions and the papers read as *Documents, mémoires et voeux* (1901). In 1901 he founded, with J. Combarieu (ed.), P. Aubry, M. Emmanuel, L. Laloy, and himself as principal contributors, the fortnightly *Revue d'Histoire et Critique Musicales*. From 1913 he resided in Switzerland, but in 1938 returned to France and took up his residence at Vézelay.

Rolland's writings exhibit sound scholarship, broad sympathy, keen analytical power, well-balanced judgment, and intimate acquaintance with the musical milieu of his time. The book by which he is most widely known is *Jean-Christophe*, a musical novel remarkable for its blending of historical accuracy, psychological and aesthetic speculation, subtle psychological analysis, and romantic interest; it won him the Nobel Prize in literature (1915). The first vol. was publ. in 1905, the last (10th) in 1912 (Eng. tr., N.Y., 1910–13). Rolland's other works include *Paris als Musikstadt* (1904; in Strauss's series *Die Musik*; rewritten and publ. in French as *Le Renouveau in Musiciens d'aujourd'hui*); *Beethoven* (Paris, 1903; 3rd ed., 1927, as *La Vie de Beethoven*; Eng. tr., 1969); *La Vie de Haendel* (Paris, 1906; 2nd ed., 1910; Eng. tr., 1916; rev. and enl. by F. Raugel, 1974); *Voyage musical au pays du passé* (1920; Eng. tr., 1922); *Beethoven: Les Grandes Époques*

créatrices (4 vols., Paris, 1928–45; Eng. tr., 1964); *Goethe et Beethoven* (1930; Eng. tr., 1931); *Beethoven: Le Chant de la Résurrection* (1937; on the *Missa solemnis* and the last sonatas); essays in various journals he collected and publ. in 2 vols. as *Musiciens d'autrefois* (1908; 6th ed., 1919; Eng. tr., 1915) and *Musiciens d'aujourd'hui* (1908; 8th ed., 1947; Eng. tr., 1914); D. Ewen, ed., *Essays on Music* (a selection from some of the above books; N.Y., 1948).

BIBL.: P. Seippel, *R. R.: L'Homme et l'oeuvre* (Paris, 1913); S. Zweig, *R. R.: Der Mann und das Werk* (Frankfurt am Main, 1921; Eng. tr., N.Y., 1921); J. Bonnerot, *R. R., Sa vie, son oeuvre* (Paris, 1921); E. Lerch, *R. R. und die Erneuerung der Gesinnung* (Munich, 1926); M. Lob, *Un Grand Bourguignon, R. R.* (Auxerre, 1927); C. Sénéchal, *R. R.* (Paris, 1933); M. Doisy, *R. R.* (Brussels, 1945); R. Argos, *R. R.* (Paris, 1950); W. Starr, *A Critical Bibliography of the Published Writings of R. R.* (Evanston, Ill., 1950); J. Robichez, *R. R.* (Paris, 1961); E. Bondeville, *R. R. à la recherche de l'homme dans la création artistique* (Paris, 1966).—**NS/LK/DM**

Rolle, Johann Heinrich, German organist, violinist, violist, and composer; b. Quedlinburg, Dec. 23, 1716; d. Magdeburg, Dec. 29, 1785. He studied with his father, the Kantor and composer Christian Friedrich Rolle (b. Halle, April 14, 1681; d. Magdeburg, Aug. 25, 1751). He was an organist in Magdeburg (1732–36), and later played violin and later viola in the Berlin Court Orch. (1741–47). He then returned to Magdeburg as organist at the Johanniskirche, and in 1751 became his father's successor. He wrote numerous oratorios, many choral works, orch. pieces, chamber music, keyboard pieces, songs, etc.

BIBL.: W. Kawerau, *J.H. R.: Ein musikalisches Characterbild* (Magdeburg, 1885); R. Kaestner, *J.H. R.: Untersuchungen zu Leben und Werk* (Kassel, 1932).—**NS/LK/DM**

Roller, Alfred, influential Austrian stage designer and painter; b. Vienna, Oct. 2, 1864; d. there, June 21, 1935. He studied painting at the Vienna Academy. Roller became closely associated with Mahler at the Vienna Court Opera. With Gustav Klimt, Egon Schiele, Oskar Kokoschka et al., he founded the Vienna Sezession, a group of artists whose ideals were at variance with the established orthodoxy of the day. His ideal as a stage designer was to integrate the elements of space, color, and light in an effort to harmonize stage decors with the music and stage action. His slogan, "space, not pictures," embodied his attempt to discard naturalism in opera productions in favor of a new symbolism. In his production of *Tristan und Isolde* (1903), which inaugurated his 30-year tenure as chief designer at the Vienna Opera, he allowed a different color to symbolize the mood of each act. The subtle lighting effects he achieved prompted one reviewer to declare "here is the conception of the music of light." His Wagner productions, which continued with the first 2 parts of the *Ring* cycle, set new standards throughout Europe. They also had a strong influence on later productions at Bayreuth. In his production of *Don Giovanni* (1905), he introduced his "Roller towers," focal points in a stylized stage picture which, remaining on stage throughout the opera, served different purposes as the action progressed. He was also active in Berlin, Salzburg, and Bayrueth. He designed the Dresden premiere productions of *Elektra*

(1909) and *Der Rosenkavalier* (1911). His subtle and harmonious use of color was also in evidence for the premiere production of *Die Frau ohne Schatten* (Vienna, 1919). Roller taught at the Vienna School of Arts and Crafts for 25 years.—**NS/LK/DM**

Röllig, Carl Leopold, German glass-harmonica player, inventor, and composer; b. Hamburg, c. 1735; d. Vienna, March 4, 1804. He was music director of Ackermann's theater company in Hamburg (1764–69; 1771–72). After taking up the glass harmonica about 1780, he toured widely. He invented the Orphika (c. 1795) and the Xänorphika (1801), pianos with bows instead of hammers. In 1791 he settled in Vienna (1791). He wrote a comic opera, *Clarisse* (Hamburg, Oct. 10, 1771), and various pieces for glass harmonica, including 4 concertos. He publ. *Über die Harmonika* (Berlin, 1787), *Versuch einer musikalischen Intervallentabelle* (Leipzig, 1789), *Orphica, ein musikalisches Instrument erfunden von C.L. Röllig* (Vienna, 1795), and *Versuch einer Anleitung zur musikalischen Modulation durch mechanische Vortheile* (Vienna, 1799); his *Miscellanea, figurierter Kontrapunkt* remains in MS.—**NS/LK/DM**

Rollin, Jean, French composer; b. Paris, Aug. 3, 1906; d. Bayeux, Calvados, Aug. 30, 1977. He studied composition at the Paris Cons. with N. Gallon, and musicology with Pirro and Masson. His works included Concerto for Piano and Strings (1947), Violin Concerto (1950), Double Bass Concerto (1951), 2 syms. (1953, 1958), *Gringoue*, opera (1965), chamber music, and songs.—**NS/LK/DM**

Rolling Stones, The, bad boys of rock and roll, and one of the longest-lived (and financially successful) pop groups of all time. **MEMBERSHIP:** Michael "Mick" Jagger, lead voc., har. (b. Dartford, Kent, England, July 26, 1943); Keith Richards, rhythm gtr. (b. Dartford, Kent, England, Dec. 18, 1943); Brian Jones, gtr., sitar, dulcimer, voc. (b. Lewis Brian Hopkin-Jones, Cheltenham, Gloucestershire, England, Feb. 28, 1942; d. Sussex, England, July 3, 1969); Bill Wyman, bs. (b. William Perks, Plumstead, London, England, Oct. 24, 1936); Charlie Watts, drm. (b. Islington, London, June 2, 1941); Ian Stewart, pno. (b. Pittenweem, Fife, Scotland, July 18, 1938; d. London, England, Dec. 12, 1985). Stewart was phased out of the band in 1963, although he continued to tour and record with the group, becoming known as the "sixth Rolling Stone." Brian Jones left the group in June 1969, to be replaced by guitarist Michael "Mick" Taylor (b. Welwyn Garden City, Hertfordshire, England, Jan. 17, 1949). Taylor left in 1974 and was replaced by guitarist Ron Wood (b. Hillingdon, Middlesex, England, June 1, 1947). Bill Wyman left the group in 1992.

Mick Jagger and Keith Richards first met in primary school and encountered each other again in 1960. Jagger, a student at the London School of Economics, was playing with mutual friend Dick Taylor in Little Blues and The Blue Boys, who subsequently added Richards. Brian Jones had been playing as a jazz saxophonist before briefly joining Alexis Korner's Blues Incorporated, which included Charlie Watts. Wanting to form

his own rhythm-and-blues band, Jones recruited pianist Ian Stewart and guitarist Jeff Bradford, among others. Jones first met Jagger, Richards, and Taylor at the Ealing Jazz club, where Blues Incorporated held residency. Jagger and Richards were soon jamming there with Charlie Watts and harmonica player Cyril Davies. By 1961, Jagger was rehearsing with Jones, Bradford, and Stewart, to soon be joined by Richards and Taylor, as Bradford became the first departure. Jagger began singing with Blues Incorporated in late 1961, joining as permanent singer in early 1962, by which time the band had graduated to the Marquee club in London. Jagger, Jones, and Richards began sharing an apartment and recorded a demonstration tape that was rejected by EMI Records. Taylor became the next departure, later to form The Pretty Things.

After debuting at the Marquee club in July 1962 as Brian Jones and Mick Jagger and The Rolling Stones, the group added bassist Bill Wyman through auditions in December 1962 and attempted to persuade drummer Charlie Watts also to join. He did join in January 1963 and the group (Jagger, Richards, Jones, Stewart, Watts, and Wyman) subsequently played the rhythm-and-blues club circuit and secured a residency at the Crawdaddy Club in Richmond, where they attracted a burgeoning following. In May, Andrew "Loog" Oldham became their manager and signed the group with Decca Records (London in the U.S.). He began cultivating a rebellious image for the group and demoted Ian Stewart, who continued to record and play with the band, eventually becoming their tour manager.

The Rolling Stones' first single, Chuck Berry's "Come On," became a minor British hit in June 1963. They conducted their first British tour in support of The Everly Brothers and Little Richard in September, scoring their first major British hit in December with "I Wanna Be Your Man," provided by Beatles songwriters John Lennon and Paul McCartney. Gene Pitney managed a minor American hit with Jagger and Richards "That Girl Belongs to Yesterday" at the beginning of 1964 and The Rolling Stones soon achieved a smash British hit with Buddy Holly's "Not Fade Away," the group's first moderate American hit. Their debut American album was pervaded with American rhythm-and-blues songs such as "Walking the Dog," "I Just Want to Make Love to You," "Can I Get a Witness," and "Tell Me" (their first major American hit). The group first toured the U.S. in June, returning in October. The Rolling Stones' *12 X 5* included the top British and major American hit "It's All Over Now" (originally recorded by Bobby Womack's Valentinos) and the smash American hit "Time Is on My Side" (previously recorded by Irma Thomas). By year's end, Marianne Faithfull had scored a major American and near-smash British hit with Jagger and Richards's "As Tears Go By."

With *Now!* Jagger and Richards began writing songs for the group. The album produced a major American hit with their "Heart of Stone" in early 1965. *Out of Our Heads*, recorded primarily in Chicago, finally established The Rolling Stones in the U.S. The album yielded a near-smash with Jagger and Richards's "The Last Time" (backed with "Play with Fire") and a top hit with their classic "(I Can't Get No) Satisfaction" (both top British hits). The album also included "The Spider and the Fly" and the satirical "Under Assistant West Coast Promotion Man." The Rolling Stones toured the U.S. twice in 1965, achieving a top British and American hit with "Get Off My Cloud" and a smash American hit with their version of "As Tears Go By" from *December's Children*. The psychedelic "19th Nervous Breakdown" became a smash British and American hit and the group conducted their last tour of America for three years in 1966. Otis Redding scored a moderate pop and smash rhythm-and-blues hit with "Satisfaction" in early 1966 and Chris Farlowe scored a top British hit with Jagger and Richards's "Out of Time" that summer.

Aftermath, the first Rolling Stones' album consisting entirely of Jagger-Richards compositions, established the group as an album band. While including the top British and American hit "Paint It Black" (on which Brian Jones played sitar), the album contained the major American hit "Lady Jane" (Jones on dulcimer), the chauvinistic "Stupid Girl" and "Under My Thumb," and the 11-minute "Goin' Home." During July, "Mother's Little Helper," backed by "Lady Jane," became a near-smash American hit, while "Have You Seen Your Mother, Baby, Standing in the Shadows," one of their most ambitious productions to date, proved a smash British and American hit in November.

After the live album *Got Live, If You Want It*, The Rolling Stones issued *Between the Buttons*, Andrew Oldham's final production for the group. It included the top American and smash British hit "Ruby Tuesday"/"Let's Spend the Night Together," as well as the overlooked "Yesterday's Papers," "Amanda Jones," and "Something Happened to Me Yesterday." Appearing on CBS-television's *Ed Sullivan Show* in January 1967, the group performed "Let's Spend the Night Together" as "Let's Spend Some Time Together." Later Jagger and Richards, then Jones, were charged in the first big drug arrests in British rock, in response to which the stately *London Times* came to their defense. Their next album, *Flowers*, featured a number of their recent hits plus "Out of Time" and the country-styled "Back Street Girl" and "Sittin' on a Fence."

The Rolling Stones next attempted to capitalize on psychedelia and the success of The Beatles' *Sgt. Pepper's Lonely Hearts Club Band*. "Dandelion"/"We Love You" became a major British and American hit, but the self-produced *Their Satanic Majesties Request* was not well received critically, yet yielded a major American hit with "She's a Rainbow." During 1967, Brian Jones had ostensibly played very little on the recordings of The Rolling Stones, becoming estranged from the rest of the group and even requiring hospitalization in December. He was arrested again in May 1968, shortly before the release of "Jumpin' Jack Flash," often regarded as the group's most potent single since "Satisfaction" and their first top British and American hit in two years.

The much-delayed *Beggar's Banquet*, undoubtedly The Rolling Stones' finest and most coherent album, included the classic "Sympathy for the Devil," the anthemic "Salt of the Earth," the country-styled "No Expectations," and "Stray Cat Blues" and "Jigsaw

Puzzle," as well as "Street Fighting Man," oddly only a minor hit as a single. After participating in the legendary never-to-be-seen (until 1996) television special "Rock and Roll Circus," Brian Jones quit the group in early July 1969, to be replaced by guitarist Mick Taylor from John Mayall's band. On July 3, Jones was found dead in the swimming pool of his Sussex home at the age of 25, leading to later speculation that he was murdered. Two days later, Taylor debuted with The Rolling Stones at a free concert at London's Hyde Park, attended by 250,000 fans. Mick Jagger soon left for Australia to perform the title role in the movie *Ned Kelly*, released in 1970.

During the summer of 1969, another classic Rolling Stones single, "Honky Tonk Women," recorded with Mick Taylor, became a top British and American hit. The group subsequently embarked on an American tour in November. Concluding the tour, the group announced plans for a free concert in northern Calif., but the concert site was changed several times and eventually took place at Altamont Speedway. Held on Dec. 6, the concert was a highly publicized tragedy. With the Hells Angels providing security in exchange for beer, the show was staged without adequate food services and health facilities and The Stones, demonstrating their aloofness from the audience, delayed more than an hour before appearing on the stage. Once they took the stage, the group worked the crowd into hysteria with unfortunate results. During "Under My Thumb," a fan near the front was stabbed to death (as graphically captured in the film *Gimme Shelter*) and the concert devolved into ugly chaos. Charges and counter charges by participants were later aired, and the leftist press denounced the event as the "death" of rock 'n' roll and the "Woodstock spirit."

Also in late 1969, The Rolling Stones released *Let It Bleed*, which contained Robert Johnson's "Love in Vain," "Gimme Shelter" (ironic in the light of Altamont), the classic "You Can't Always Get What You Want," and the menacing "Midnight Rambler," as well as the title song. A period of inactivity ensued for the group, as Jagger appeared as the ambisexual star of Nicholas Roeg's *Performance* film. The soundtrack album included a memorable Jagger solo single, "Memo from Turner." In March 1971, The Rolling Stones announced they were leaving England for tax purposes, yet they conducted their first British tour in five years, augmented by keyboardist Nicky Hopkins and saxophonist Bobby Keys. In April, they issued the sexist and racist "Brown Sugar" (a top American and smash British hit) on their newly formed record label, Rolling Stones Records, distributed by Atlantic in the U.S. Their debut album for the label, *Sticky Fingers*, contained "Brown Sugar," the countrified "Wild Horses" (a major hit), "Dead Flowers," the jam-style "Can't You Hear Me Knocking," and "Sister Morphine," the latter coauthored (without credit) by Marianne Faithfull.

By the early 1970s, concerts by The Rolling Stones were attended more as cultural events than as musical performances. Mick Jagger, in particular, was adopted by the so-called "jet set," especially after his much-publicized marriage to Bianca de Macias in May 1971.

The double-record set *Exile on Main Street* was released to coincide with their massive 1972 tour accompanied by Nicky Hopkins and Bobby Keys. The album included "Rocks Off," "Rip This Joint," and "Sweet Virginia," and produced a near-smash British and American hit with "Tumbling Dice" and a major American hit with "Happy."

Conducting immensely successful tours of America and Europe in 1973, The Rolling Stones' next two albums, *Goat's Head Soup*, recorded in Jamaica, and *It's Only Rock 'n' Roll*, were considered minor works compared to previous albums, yet each contained several exceptional songs. *Goat's Head Soup* yielded a top American and smash British hit with the ballad "Angie" and a minor hit with "Doo Doo Doo Doo Doo (Heartbreaker)," while containing the notorious "Star Star," perhaps better known as "Starfucker." *It's Only Rock 'n' Roll*, the first Stones album produced by Jagger and Richards as "The Glimmer Twins," featured the major international hits "It's Only Rock 'n' Roll" and "Ain't Too Proud to Beg" (originally a hit for The Temptations), while including "Dance Little Sister" and "Time Waits for No One." In 1974, the in-concert film *Ladies and Gentlemen: The Rolling Stones*, filmed in Tex. during the 1972 tour, was released.

During 1975, The Rolling Stones again mounted a huge, lavishly staged, and lucrative American tour, augmented by Billy Preston. Mick Taylor had quit the group the previous December, to be replaced by "guest artist" Ron Wood, guitarist for The Faces, for the grandiose tour. Their next album, *Black and Blue*, eventually appeared in 1976 to critical disapproval. The album's sexist promotional campaign later inspired a boycott by Women Against Violence Against Women (WAVAW) against the entire organization responsible for distribution of Rolling Stones Records, Warner Communications. The album yielded only one major hit, "Fool to Cry." Ron Wood finally became an official member of the group in June 1977. In the meantime, Bill Wyman had recorded two solo albums, and Mick Taylor had worked with The Jack Bruce Band and Gong before recording a solo album for Columbia Records in 1979 and touring and recording with Bob Dylan in the early 1980s.

The Rolling Stones again toured the U.S. in 1978, this time without the elaborate staging and massive props of the 1975 tour, accompanied by keyboardists Ian McLagan (formerly of The Faces) and Ian Stewart. Performing at small and medium-sized halls as well as at huge outdoor concerts, the group broke the rock concert attendance record in July at the New Orleans Superdome, where more than 80,000 fans were present. *Some Girls* became the group's best-selling nonanthology album on the strength of the top American and smash British disco-style hit single "Miss You," the near-smash American hit "Beast of Burden," and the moderate American hit "Shattered." The album also contained "When the Whip Comes Down," "Far Away Eyes," and Richards's "Before They Make Me Run."

In February 1977, Keith Richards was arrested in Toronto on charges of possession of heroin for sale, yet he got off lightly in October 1978, being required to continue drug rehabilitation and perform a benefit concert. For the concert, performed in April 1979, Richards and Ron Wood assembled The New Barbarians with keyboardist Ian McLagan, saxophonist Bobby Keys, jazz bassist Stanley Clarke, and Meters drummer Joe Modeliste. The concert and subsequent American tour neatly coincided with the release of Wood's third solo album, *Gimme Some Neck*, which included eight originals by Wood and Bob Dylan's "Seven Days." During 1979, The Rolling Stones were the subject of controversy as the result of former associate Tony Sanchez's ghastly and lurid account of his eight-year tenure with The Rolling Stones, *Up and Down with The Rolling Stones*. Their reputation had also been tarnished by a film made by Robert Franks during the group's 1972 tour, *Cocksucker Blues*. The movie, completed in 1973 and shown several times during 1975 and 1976, was legally suppressed by the group and ultimately withdrawn from public viewing in 1988.

Finally, in 1980, another much-delayed Rolling Stones album was issued, *Emotional Rescue*, but it did little to dispel the allegation that the group was no longer the "world's greatest rock 'n' roll band." The album produced a smash British and American hit with the title song and a major American hit with "She's So Cold." In 1981, The Rolling Stones redeemed themselves with the unaffected *Tattoo You* album, the smash international hit "Start Me Up" and the major American hits "Waiting on a Friend" and "Hang Fire," and a massively successful tour conducted in the final four months of the year. However, despite signing a new distribution deal with Columbia Records in August 1983, the group recorded only two studio albums, 1983's *Undercover* and 1986's *Dirty Work*, over the next seven years. During that time, they scored a mere five hits, highlighted by the smash American and major British hits "Undercover of the Night" and "Harlem Shuffle," the latter a cover version of Bob and Earl's 1964 hit.

Much of the 1980s was taken up by individual efforts by the members of The Rolling Stones, as Jagger and Richards became estranged from each other. In 1983, Bill Wyman and Charlie Watts toured as part of Ronnie Lane's brief benefit tour for Appeal for Actions Research into Multiple Sclerosis. Mick Jagger shared lead vocals with Michael Jackson on The Jacksons' smash 1984 pop and R&B and major British hit "State of Shock." He recorded two lackluster solo albums, *She's the Boss* and *Primitive Cool*, managing major hits with "Just Another Night" and "Dancing in the Street" (recorded with David Bowie). In 1988, he became the first member of The Rolling Stones to tour solo and to tour Japan. Longtime associate Ian Stewart, who had recorded an album with his blues band Rocket 88 in 1980, died in London of a heart attack on Dec. 12, 1985, at the age of 47. Charlie Watts began performing with large bands in late 1985 and assembled the British jazz band The Charlie Watts Orch. for one 1987 American album, *Live at Fulham Town Hall*, and two brief American tours. Ron Wood toured with Bo Diddley as The Gunslingers in 1987 and 1988.

In 1986, Keith Richards served as music director for the Chuck Berry concert film *Hail! Hail! Rock 'n' Roll* and produced Aretha Franklin's version of "Jumpin' Jack Flash," a major pop and R&B hit from the movie of the same name. Two years later, he assembled a group that came to be known as The X-Pensive Winos, with drummer and songwriting partner Steve Jordan, guitarist Waddy Wachtel, keyboardist Ivan Neville, and bassist Charlie Drayton. They recorded *Talk Comes Cheap*, which featured the bitter indictment of Jagger, "You Don't Move Me Anymore," and toured America in late 1988, with their Dec. 15 show eventually being released as *Live at the Hollywood Palladium*. In May 1989, Bill Wyman opened the restaurant Sticky Fingers Cafe in the fashionable Kensington district of London.

Inducted into the Rock and Roll Hall of Fame in 1989, The Rolling Stones finally assembled that year to record the diverse *Steel Wheels* album and conduct a world tour, their first tour in eight years. The album sold more than two million copies, producing American hits with "Mixed Emotions" (a smash) and "Rock and a Hard Place," and the tour was the highest- grossing rock tour to date. In 1990, they toured about a dozen European cities with their "Urban Jungle" tour. "Highwire," which castigated international arms dealers, became a minor hit and was one of two studio cuts from the otherwise live *Flashpoint* album. In late 1991, The Rolling Stones signed a new record deal with Virgin Records that was to commence in 1993, but Bill Wyman soon quit the group.

Mick Jagger appeared in the 1992 science fiction thriller *Freejack* and later recorded his third solo album *Wandering Spirit*. In 1992, Ron Wood issued his solo album, *Slide on This*, and Keith Richards recorded a second solo album, *Main Offender*, and toured with The X-Pensive Winos into 1993. Bill Wyman and Charlie Watts recorded solo albums, released in Japan and Great Britain, respectively.

The Rolling Stones' debut album on Virgin Records, *Voodoo Lounge*, was issued shortly before the group conducted a three-month tour of American stadiums. Recorded with bassist Darryl Jones, the album produced only minor hits with "Love Is Strong" and "Out of Tears," yet it sold more than two million copies and seemed to reestablish the group after a five-year lapse. The well-received American tour grossed more than $120 million and continued in Central and South America and Australia in 1995. The tour ultimately grossed more than $300 million and appeared to confirm the group's reputation as the "world's greatest rock 'n' roll band," at least in live performance.

The Rolling Stones' 1995 live acoustic album *Stripped* yielded a major British hit with Bob Dylan's "Like a Rolling Stone." In September 1997, the group launched a year-long world tour in support of *Bridges to Babylon*, which featured "Anybody Seen My Baby?" and "Already Over Me." This tour produced 1998's live set *No Security*, used as the name of their 1999 world tour.

DISC.: STUDIO ALBUMS BY THE ROLLING STONES: *The Rolling Stones* (1964); *12 X 5* (1964); *Now!* (1965); *Out of Our Heads* (1965); *December's Children (and Everybody's)* (1965); *Aftermath* (1966); *Between the Buttons* (1967); *Their Satanic Majesties Request* (1967); *Beggar's Banquet* (1968); *Let It Bleed* (1969); *Sticky Fingers* (1971); *Exile on Main Street* (1972); *Goat's Head Soup* (1973); *It's Only Rock 'n' Roll* (1974); *Black and Blue* (1976); *Some Girls* (1978); *Emotional Rescue* (1980); *Tattoo You* (1981); *Undercover* (1983); *Dirty Work* (1986); *Steel Wheels* (1989); *Voodoo Lounge* (1994); *Bridges to Babylon* (1997). **"LIVE" ALBUMS BY THE ROLLING STONES:** *Got Live If You Want It* (1966); *Get Yer Ya-Ya's Out* (rec. November 1969; rel. 1970); *Love You Live* (rec. 1975–77; rel. 1977); *Still Life* (American concert 1981; rel. 1982); *Flashpoint* (rec. 1989–90; rel. 1991); *Stripped* (1995); *Rock and Roll Circus* (filmed and recorded December 1968; rel. 1996); *No Security* (1998). **BRIAN JONES:** *Brian Jones Presents the Pipes of Pan at Joujouka* (1971). **WYMAN, WATTS, JAGGER, RY COODER, AND NICKY HOPKINS:** *Jammin' with Edward* (1972). **BILL WYMAN:** *Monkey Grip* (1974); *Stone Alone* (1976); *Drinkin' TNT 'n' Smokin' Dynamite* (1982). **MICK TAYLOR:** *Mick Taylor* (1979/1992); *Coastin' Home* (1996). **MICK TAYLOR AND CARLA OLSON:** *Too Hot for Snakes* (1991). **RON WOOD:** *I've Got My Own Album to Do* (1974); *Now Look* (1975); *Gimme Some Neck* (1979); *1234* (1981); *Slide on This* (1992); *Slide on Live* (1998). **RON WOOD AND RONNIE LANE:** *Mahoney's Last Chance* (soundtrack; 1976). **ROCKET 88 (WITH IAN STEWART):** *Rocket 88* (1981). **MICK JAGGER:** *Performance* (soundtrack; 1970); *Ned Kelly* (soundtrack; 1970); *She's the Boss* (1985); *Primitive Cool* (1987); *Wandering Spirit* (1993). **KEITH RICHARDS:** *Talk Is Cheap* (1988); *Keith Richards and The X-Pensive Winos at the Hollywood Palladium* (rec. December 1988; rel. 1991); *Main Offender* (1992). **CHARLIE WATTS:** *Long Ago and Far Away* (1996).

BIBL.: P. Goodman, *Our Own Story by The R. S.* (N.Y., 1965); D. Dalton, *R. S.: An Unauthorized Biography in Words, Pictures and Music* (N.Y., 1972); M. L. Dimmick, *The R. S.: An Annotated Bibliography* (Pittsburgh, Pa., 1972, 1979); R. M. Elman, *Uptight with The Stones: A Novelist's Report* (N.Y., 1973); J. Marks-Highwater, *Mick Jagger: The Singer, Not the Song* (N.Y., 1973); R. Greenfield, *A Journey Through America with The R. S.* (N.Y., 1974); A. Scaduto, *Mick Jagger: Everybody's Lucifer* (N.Y., 1974); G. Tremlett, *The R. S.* (N.Y., 1974); *Rolling Stone, The R. S.* (San Francisco, Calif., 1975); R. Carr, *R. S.: An Illustrated Record* (N.Y., 1976); T. Jasper, *The R. S.* (London, 1976); J. J. Pascall, *The R. S.* (London, N.Y., 1977); B. Charone, *Keith Richards: Life As a Rolling Stone* (London, 1979); T. Sanchez, *Up and Down with The R. S.: The Inside Story* (N.Y., 1979); D. Dalton, *R. S.* (N.Y., 1979); D. Dalton, *The R. S.: The First Twenty Years* (N.Y., 1981); M. Aftel, *Death of a Rolling Stone: The Brian Jones Story* (N.Y., 1982); T. Dowley, *The R. S.* (N.Y., 1983); R. Palmer, *The R. S.* (Garden City, N.Y., 1983); S. Weiner and L. Howard, *The R. S. A to Z* (N.Y., 1983); S. Booth, *Dance with the Devil: The R. S. and Their Time* (N.Y., 1984); P. Norman, *Symphony for the Devil: The Rolling Stone Story* (N.Y., 1984); S. Booth, *The True Adventures of The R. S.* (London, 1985); F. Aeppli, *Heart of Stone: The Definitive R. S. Discography, 1962–83* (Ann Arbor, Mich., 1985); N. Fitzgerald, *Brian Jones: The Inside Story of the Original Rolling Stone* (N.Y., 1985); C. Flippo, *On the Road with The R. S.: 20 Years of Lipstick, Handcuffs, and Chemicals* (Garden City, N.Y., 1985). H. W. McPhail, *Yesterday's Paper: The R. S. in Print, 1963–84* (Ann Arbor, Mich., 1986); M. Elliott, *The R. S.: Complete Recording Sessions 1963–89* (N.Y., 1989); P. Norman, *The Life and Good Times of The R. S.* (N.Y., 1989); M. Bonanno, *The R. S. Chronicle: The First Thirty Years* (N.Y., 1990); A. E. Hotchner, *Blown Away: The R. S. and the Death of the Sixties* (N.Y., 1990); B. Wyman and R. Coleman, *Stone Alone: The Story of a Rock 'n' Roll Band* (N.Y., 1990); V. Bockriss, *Keith Richards: The Biography* (N.Y., 1992); C. Andersen, *Jagger Unauthorized* (N.Y., 1993); G. Giuliano, *The R. S. Album: Thirty Years of Music and Memorabilia* (N.Y., 1993); L.

Jackson, *Golden Stone: The Untold Life and Tragic Death of Brian Jones* (N.Y., 1993); D. Seay, *Mick Jagger: The Story Behind The R. S.* (Secaucus, N.J., 1993); C. Sandford, *Mick Jagger: Primitive Cool* (N.Y., 1994); S. Booth, *Keith* (N.Y., 1995); J. Karnbach and C. Bernson, *It's Only Rock 'n' Roll: The Ultimate Guide to The R. S.* (N.Y., 1997); D. Loewenstein, ed., *The R. S.: A Life on the Road* (N.Y., 1998).—**BH**

Rollini, Adrian, jazz bass saxophonist, vibraphonist, brother of Arthur Rollini; b. N.Y., June 28, 1904; d. Homestead, Fla., May 15, 1956. He was a child prodigy on piano; at four, he gave a Chopin recital at the Waldorf Astoria Hotel, N.Y. At 14 he led his own band in N.Y., doubling on piano and xylophone. He worked with the California Ramblers in the early 1920s; while with this band he bought his first bass sax, specializing on the instrument for several years thereafter. He went to London in December 1927 to join Fred Elizalde at the Savoy Hotel; other than two brief vacations in the U.S. (spring 1928 and winter 1928) he remained in London until December 1929. Returning to N.Y., he joined Bert Lown's Orch. and remained until spring 1931. He did a short spell playing in a re-formed California Ramblers in 1931, then was mostly active on freelance recording sessions. Throughout the 1920s and early 1930s Rollini participated in countless pick-up recording groups, mostly on bass sax, sometimes on "hot fountain pen." In 1935 he organized his own club, Adrian's Tap Room, at the Hotel President, N.Y. From this time onwards Rollini specialized on vibraphone, but did some recordings on piano and drums. He doubled with Richard Himber's Orch. in mid-1930s, but continued to lead his own small groups for long residencies at various hotels in N.Y. and Chicago. In the early 1950s, he moved to Fla. where he opened his own hotel. There, he continued to play various residencies in Miami; last working at the Eden Roc Hotel in September 1955. He died of pneumonia and complications following a liver ailment.

Disc.: "Swing Low" (1934); *Adrian Rollini His Quintet* (1938); *Chopsticks* (1953); *Battle of Jazz* (1953).—**JC/LP**

Rollins, Sonny (Theodore Walter), one of the greatest and most respected tenor (and soprano) saxophonists, often called the greatest living jazz musician; b. N.Y., Sept. 7, 1930. He used a 1929 birth year for many years in order to join the union when he was underaged. His mother was from the Virgin Islands. He began on piano, but after hearing his aunt's collections of Louis Jordan records, he decided to take up the saxophone. Though his mother was supportive of his decision to be a musician, his father and grandmother were initially against it. As a teen, he would visit such players as Coleman Hawkins and Eddie Lockjaw Davis after school to get pointers on the saxophone. He first recorded in 1948 with Babs Gonzales, then in 1949 with Bud Powell and Fats Navarro; he then went to Chicago, where he studied with Ike Day. Rollins was featured in a Chicago concert with Bruz Freeman in 1950 and won the Metronome award that year. He also worked with Miles Davis, recording his now-standard "Oleo" and "Airegin" (1954), and Thelonious Monk in the early 1950s. He considered Monk an especially important mentor. The album *Tenor Madness* (1956) has both Roll-

ins and Coltrane on the title track, the only recording of them together. Rollins took a break from performing in (September 1955 in Chicago through late 1956) to rid himself of his heroin habit at a Chicago clinic, then joined the Clifford Brown–Max Roach quintet in December 1955 until autumn 1957. He has led his own groups ever since to almost instant acclaim. His "St. Thomas," recorded in 1956, has become a standard and was the first of several calypsos he has recorded. He first met Ornette Coleman in Los Angeles in 1957, whose new, freer style of playing would have a great impact on Rollins's style in the early 1960s. He rejoined Monk briefly at the Five Spot in September 1958, after Griffin had quit, demanding more money. He toured Europe in May 1959 with his regular trio of Pete LaRoca and Henry Grimes. Rollins took another sabbatical (around June 1959) to work on ideas about the new free-jazz and about composition; he lived in Greenwich Village, N.Y. and sometimes practiced on the walkway of the Wiliamsburg Bridge, in order not to bother his neighbors. He said he was preparing to unveil a new direction in jazz in the fall of 1960, but did not do so until November 1961 when he opened at the Village Vanguard with Jim Hall. (Many musicians have drawn inspiration from his work of the 1960s.) Rollins toured the U.S. and Europe (1962–63) with Ornette Coleman's colleagues Don Cherry and Billy Higgins, and also that year recorded *What's New*, an album of Brazilian and Latin performances that featured some of the most astounding improvisations ever recorded. He toured Japan in 1963 with Paul Bley, another Coleman associate. He wrote/improvised solo saxophone music for parts of the film score to *Alfie* (1966), including "Alfie's Theme" (not the Bacharach-David title song). However, his behavior in the 1960s was unpredictable; during 1963, he appeared with a Mohawk haircut; for a Boston TV appearance, he let the rhythm section walk for most of the first number, playing only a few notes here and there; at Lincoln Center's famous *Titans of the Tenor* concert on February 1966, he played a set of only a few minutes, announced he'd be back, but never returned. In 1968, he began another period of retirement by spending three months at an ashram near Bombay to study the holy Hindu books, the Gita and Vedantas. Later his guru revealed that he was a highly spiritual person, gifted with special attributes. He continued to work on personal health, yoga, and new ideas about fusion, and returned to performing in 1972, showing some fusion influences on his albums but for the most part playing acoustic jazz in concert at first. He appeared at Carnegie Hall as part of the 1972 Newport in N.Y. Festival with Al Dailey, and also was awarded a Guggenheim Fellowship that year. Rollins toured Tokyo and was videotaped there in 1973. He continued to tour through the 1970s and 1980s; in the early 1980s, he played a series of concerts with younger musicians in N.Y., including a famous appearance with Wynton Marsalis in April 1983 at Town Hall, during which he collapsed from exhaustion while playing; by June of that year, he was working again. His concerto for Saxophone and Orch. was premiered in Japan in 1986. Gradually, over the next decade, he cut back on performing, eliminating club work altogether, and playing only about 40–50 major concerts a year. Since the mid-1990s, he has toured with Clifton Anderson, Bob Cranshaw, and various drummers, guitarists or keyboardists. His bands often lack cohesion and his own performances, while always played with a hoarse, passionate sound, range from crowd-pleasing repetition to some of the most ecstatic flights that jazz has ever known.

DISC.: *Sonny and the Stars* (1951); *Sonny Rollins with the Modern Jazz Quartet* (1951); *Sonny Rollins Quartet* (1951); *Sonny Rollins Quintet* (1954); *Moving Out* (1954); *Work Time* (1955); *Three Giants* (1956); *Tenor Madness* (1956); *Sonny Rollins, Vol. 1* (1956); *Sonny Rollins Plus 4* (1956); *Saxophone Colossus* (1956); *Plays for Bird* (1956); *Way Out West* (1957); *Sound of Sonny* (1957); *Sonny Rollins, Vol. 2* (1957); *Night at the Village Vanguard* (1957); *More from the Vanguard* (1957); *Newk's Time* (1957); *Brass & Trio* (1958); *Modern Jazz Quartet with Sonny Rollins* (1958); *Freedom Suite* (1958); *Sonny Rollins and the Contemporary Leaders* (1958); *Sonny Rollins and the Big Brass* (1958); *In Stockholm* (1959); *Aix-En-Provence* (1959); *Complete RCA Victor Recordings* (rec. 1962–64; rel.1997); *What's New?* (1962); *Our Man in Jazz* (1962); *The Bridge* (1962); *Stuttgart* (1963); *Sonny Meets Hawk!* (1963); *Live in Paris* (1963); *All the Things You Are* (1963); *Three in Jazz* (1964); *Standard Sonny Rollins* (1964); *Sonny Rollins & Co.* (1964); *Now's the Time* (1964); *There Will Never Be Another You* (1965); *Sonny Rollins on Impulse!* (1965); *Live in Europe* (1965); *East Broadway Run Down* (1966); *Alfie* (1966); *Next Album* (1972); *In Japan* (1973); *Horn Culture* (1973); *Cutting Edge* (1974); *Nucleus* (1975); *Way I Feel* (1976); *Easy Living* (1977); *Milestone Jazzstars in Concert* (1978); *Don't Stop the Carnival* (1978); *Don't Ask* (1979); *Solo Album* (1985); *G-Man* (1986); *Dancing in the Dark* (1988); *Fallin' in Love with Jazz* (1989); *Old Flames* (1993); *Plus 3* (1996).

BIBL.: T. Sjorgren, *Sonny Rollins Discography* (Copenhagen); D. Baker, *The Jazz Style of S. R.* (Lebanon, Ind., 1980); C. Blancq, S. R., *The Journey of a Jazzman* (Boston, 1983); C. Gerard, *Jazz Masters: Sonny Rollins* (N.Y. 1980); E. Nisenson, *Open Sky: Sonny Rollins's World of Improvisation* (St. Martin's Press, 2000). —LP

Rolnick, Neil (Burton), American composer and teacher; b. Dallas, Oct. 22, 1947. After studying English literature at Harvard Univ. (B.A., 1969), he studied composition with Adams and Imbrie at the San Francisco Cons. of Music (1973–74) and with Felciano and Wilson at the Univ. of Calif. at Berkeley (M.A., 1976; Ph.D., 1980); he also studied with Milhaud at the Aspen (Colo.) Music School and received training in computer music from Chowning at Stanford Univ. (summer, 1976). He pursued research at IRCAM in Paris (1977–79). Rolnick has performed with various ensembles, including Dogs of Desire, a "multimedia orch. of the future," which he co-founded, in 1994, with David Alan Miller. He has received numerous awards, grants, and fellowships, including a Fulbright fellowship (1989) for travel to Yugoslavia and a Rockefeller Foundation grant (1994) for extended residence at the Bellagio Center in Italy; in 1995 he worked in Japan on a fellowship from the Asian Cultural Council. From 1981 he taught at the Rensselaer Polytechnic Inst. in Troy, N.Y. In 1994, with Paul Lansky and Joel Chadabe, he founded the Electronic Music Foundation in Albany, N.Y. In 1995 Rolnick began a collaborative effort with Joel Chadabe called 2 Places @ Once, now an ongoing project which exploits the possibilities of teleconferenced musical and video performance. The first performance took place at The Kitchen in N.Y. and the Electronic Cafe International in Santa Monica, Calif., on March 8, 1998. In 1996 he also began performing with 6 other musicians as Fish Love That, a band committed to the exploration of "the landscape between composition and multi-images improvisation." In addition to the works listed below, Rolnick collaborated on a video with John Sturgeon, *Melting Pot* (1985).

WORKS: *Massachusetts F* for String Quartet, Percussion, and Piano (1974); *Empty Mirror* for Tape (1975); *Hell's Bells* for Tape (1975); *Newsical Muse*, live electronic music for radio (Berkeley, KPFA-FM Radio, June 4, 1975); *SF Hack* for Tape and Percussion (1975; in collaboration with M. Haller; also for Video); *Memory* for Tape (1976); *Thank You, Thelonius* for Trumpet, Trombone, Cello, Marimba, and Cimbalom (1976); *Video Songs* for Tape (1976); *A Po-sy, a Po-sy* for Tenor, Violin, Double Bass, Percussion, and Tape, to texts by Charles Olson (1976; rev. 1981); *Blue Monday* for Soprano, Flute, Clarinet, Saxophone, Violin, Cello, and Percussion (1977; rev. for 13 Instruments and Synthesizer, 1983); *Ever-livin' Rhythm* for Percussion and Tape (1977); *Wondrous Love* for Trombone and Tape (1979); *Blowing* for Flute (1980); *No Strings* for 12 Winds, 2 Pianos, 4 Percussion, and Organ (1980); *Lao Tzu's Blues* for Tenor and Piano (1981); *Loopy* for Synthesizer (1982); *Real Time* for Synthesizer and 13 Instruments (1983); *The Original Child Bomb Song* for Soprano and Synthesizer (1983); *A La Mode* for 8 Instruments and Synthesizer (1985); *The Master Speed* for Chorus, Instruments, and Synthesizer (1985); *What Is The Use?*, film music (1985); *A Robert Johnson Sampler* for Computer (1987); *Melting Pot*, video work (1987; in collaboration with J. Sturgeon); *Vocal Chords* for Jazz Singer, Digital Delay, and Sampler (1988); *Drones and Dances* for Chamber Orch. and Synthesizer (1988); *Balkanization* for Computer (1988); *I Like It* for 2 Singers and Computer (1989); *ReRebong* for Gamelan and Computer (1989); *Macedonian Air Drumming* for Computer with Air Drum MIDI Controllers (1990); *Sanctus*, electronic film score (1990); *ElectriCity* for Flute, Clarinet, Violin, Cello, Synthesizer, Sampler, and Digital Processing (1991); *Nerve Us* for Computer (1992); *Requiem Songs for the Victims of Nationalism* for 2 Singers, Percussion, and Computer (1993); *Heat: The Rise and Fall of Isabella Rico* for 2 Singers, Amplified Chamber Orch., and Video (1994); *An Irish Peace* for Variable Instruments (1994); *HomeGame* for 2 Actos, 5 Instruments, Interactive Video, and Computer-mediated Story Generation (1994–95); *The Rico Songs and Interludes* (1997–98); *The Rise & Fall of Isabella Rico*, musical (1999–2000).—NS/LK/DM

Rolón, José, Mexican composer and teacher; b. Ciudad Guzmán, July 21, 1876; d. Mexico City, Feb. 3, 1945. He studied with Moszkowski and Gédalge in Paris. In 1911 he founded a music school in Guadalajara, which he headed until 1927. He then completed his training with Boulanger and Dukas at the École Normale de Musique in Paris (1927–29). In 1930 he joined the faculty of the Cons. Nacional de Música in Mexico City, where he taught until his death. Rolón's first works were influenced by German Romanticism. Mexican nationalism came to dominate his later works and, after 1924, a modern French influence became discernible. His Piano Concerto is a classic in the virtuoso tradition.

WORKS: DRAMATIC: Ballet: *El Festín de los Enanos* (1925). **ORCH.:** Sym. (1918–19); *Obertura de Concierto* (1920); *Scherzo Sinfonico* (1928); Piano Concerto (1928–35;

Mexico City, Sept. 4, 1942); *Cuauhtémoc* (1929); *Zapotlán: 1895,* symphonic suite (1929; Mexico City, Nov. 4, 1932); *Baile Michoacano* (1930). C H A M B E R: Piano Quartet (1914); String Quartet (1935). P i a n o : *Tres Danzas indígenas Jalisenais* (1929). V O - C A L: Songs.—NS/LK/DM

Roman, Johan Helmich, significant Swedish composer; b. Stockholm, Oct. 26, 1694; d. Haraldsmala, near Kalmar, Nov. 20, 1758. He was of Swedish-German descent. He mastered the violin and oboe in childhood, and by 1711 he was a member of the royal chapel, where his father, Johan Roman, was also a member. With the permission of King Charles XII, he pursued his training in England (c. 1715–21), where he may have received lessons from Pepusch; was also associated with Ariosti, G.B. Bononcini, Geminiani, and Handel. He returned to Stockholm in 1721, where he was deputy master (1721–27) and chief master (1727–45) of the royal chapel. He was compelled to retire as a result of deafness and ill health, and subsequently served as hovintendent (court steward). In 1731 he organized the first public concerts given in Stockholm. He was elected a member of the Royal Academy of Science in 1740. Roman was the first Swedish composer to write instrumental and choral music that could compare favorably with German and Italian works, and was for that reason called "the father of Swedish music." His style shows the influence of Handel. Some 400 extant works are attributed to him, the majority of MSS being housed at the Royal Swedish Academy of Music in Stockholm. His most celebrated work is the orch. suite *Bilägers musiquen* (Royal Wedding Music) or *Drottningholmsmusiquen* (1744; ed. by C. Genetay, Stockholm, 1958). He also wrote 6 suites, at least 17 sinfonias, 4 overtures, 4 violin concertos, 12 sonate for Flute, Violone, and Harpsichord, 13 trio sonatas for 2 Violins and Basso Continuo, at least 11 harpsichord sonatas, violin pieces, and sacred and secular vocal works. A collected ed. of his works began appearing in 1965 in the series Monumenta Musicae Svecicae. See I. Bengtsson, ed., *Mr. Roman's Spuriosity Shop: A Thematic Catalogue of 503 Works (1213 Incipits and Other Excerpts) from ca. 1680–1750 by More Than Sixty Composers* (Stockholm, 1976).

BIBL.: A. Sahlstedt, *Äreminne öfwer hofintendenten kongl. capellmastaren...J.H. R.* (Stockholm, 1767); P. Vretblad, *J.H. R. 1694–1758; Svenska musikens fader* (2 vols., Stockholm, 1914); I. Bengtsson, *J.H. R. och hans Instrumentalmusik: Käll-och stilkritiska studier* (Uppsala, 1955); I. Bengtsson and R. Danielson, *Handstilar och notpikturer i Kungl. musikaliska akademiens R.-samling* (Uppsala, 1955); G. Carleberg, *Buxtehude, Telemann och R.* (Stockholm, 1965); E. Helenius- Öberg, *J.H. R.: Liv och verk genom samtida ögon: Dokumentens vittnesbörd* (Stockholm, 1994). —NS/LK/DM

Roman, Stella (real name, **Florica Vierica Alma Stela Blasu**), Romanian-American soprano; b. Cluj, March 25, 1904; d. N.Y., Feb. 12, 1992. She was a student of Pfeiffer in Cluj, Cosma, Vulpescu, and Pessione in Bucharest, Narducci and Poli-Randaccio in Milan, and Baldassare- Tedeschi and Ricci in Rome. In 1932 she made her operatic debut in Piacenza. In 1940 she made her first appearance at Milan's La Scala as the Empress in *Die Frau ohne Schatten.* On Jan. 1, 1941, she made her Metropolitan Opera debut in N.Y. as Aida. She remained on its roster until 1950, becoming best known for such roles as Gioconda, Amelia, Leonora in *Il Trovatore,* Desdemona, and Tosca.—NS/LK/DM

Romani, Carlo, Italian composer, nephew of **Pietro Romani;** b. Avelino, May 24, 1824; d. Florence, March 4, 1875. He studied with Palafuti (piano) and Picchianti (composition), then completed his studies under his uncle. He set to music the recitatives of *Der Freischütz* for its first Italian performance (Florence, Feb. 3, 1843). He also composed operas (all produced in Florence) *Tutti amanti* (1847), *Il Mantello* (1852; successful), *I Baccanali di Roma* (1854), and *Ermellina ossia Le Gemme della corona* (1865), an oratorio, *San Sebastiano* (1864), and various patriotic songs.—NS/LK/DM

Romani, Felice, renowned Italian librettist; b. Genoa, Jan. 31, 1788; d. Moneglia, Jan. 28, 1865. He was educated at the Univ. of Pisa. He wrote about 100 librettos for Mayr, Winter, Vaccai, Rossini, Bellini, Donizetti, Pacini, Ricci, etc.

BIBL.: F. Regli, *Elogio a F. R.* (Turin, 1865); L. Lianovosani, *Saggio bibliografico relativo ai melodrammi di F. R.* (Milan, 1878); E. Branca (R.'s wife), *F. R. ed i piu riputati maestri di musica del suo tempo* (Turin, 1882); C. Paschetto, *F. R.* (Turin, 1907); M. Rinaldi, *F. R.* (Rome, 1965).—NS/LK/DM

Romani, Pietro, Italian conductor, teacher, and composer, uncle of **Carlo Romani;** b. Rome, May 29, 1791; d. Florence, Jan. 11, 1877. He studied with Fenaroli. He became conductor at the Teatro della Pergola in Florence, where he also taught singing at the Istituto Musicale. He wrote 2 operas, *Il Qui pro quo* (Rome, 1817) and *Carlo Magno* (Florence, 1823), and ballet music, but he is remembered chiefly for his aria *Manca un foglio, for Bartolo in Il Barbiere de Siviglia,* which he wrote for the production of the opera in Florence in 1816 as a substitute for Rossini's original aria *A un dottor della mia sorte,* which presented some vocal difficulties. Romani's aria was long retained in many productions of the opera. —NS/LK/DM

Romberg, Andreas Jakob, German violinist and composer, cousin of **Bernhard Heinrich Romberg;** b. Vechta, near Münster, April 27, 1767; d. Gotha, Nov. 10, 1821. He was the son of the clarinetist and violinist Gerhard Heinrich Romberg (b. Aug. 8, 1745; d. Nov. 14, 1819). He studied with his father, then made his debut at age 7 in Münster with his cousin. The two subsequently toured (with their fathers) to Frankfurt am Main (1782) and Paris (1784, 1785); they played in the Bonn electoral orch. from 1790 until the French invasion of 1793 compelled them to flee to Hamburg. After playing in the opera orch. at the Ackermann Theater, they set out on a tour of Italy (1795–96); they also visited Vienna in 1796 and were befriended by Haydn; then returned to Italy. After another sojourn in Paris (1801), Andreas Romberg settled in Hamburg and devoted himself mainly to composition; he was then called to Gotha as court Kapellmeister (1815). He had 2 sons: Heinrich Maria (b.

Paris, April 4, 1802; d. Hamburg, May 2, 1859) became concertmaster of the St. Petersburg Imperial Opera orch. (1827) and later served as its music director; Ciprian Friedrich (b. Hamburg, Oct. 28, 1807; d. there, Oct. 14, 1865) was first cellist of the St. Petersburg German Opera orch. (1835–45).

WORKS: DRAMATIC: O p e r a : *Der blaue Ungeheuer* (1790–93; not perf.); *Die Macht der Musik* (1791; not perf.); *Die Nebelkappen* (1793; unfinished); *Der Rabe* (Hamburg, April 7, 1794); *Don Mendoza* (Paris, 1802; in collaboration with B.H. Romberg); *Point de bruit* (Paris, 1810); *Die Ruinen zu Paluzzi* (Hamburg, Dec. 27, 1811); *Die Grossmut des Scipio* (Gotha, 1816). **ORCH.:** 10 syms.; 20 violin concertos; 2 concertos for Violin and Cello; 2 concertos for 2 Violins; Concerto for Clarinet and Violin. **CHAMBER:** Many works, including 19 string quartets; Octet for Strings; Clarinet Quintet; 8 flute quartets; String Quintet; Piano Quartet; 3 violin sonatas. **VOCAL:** Various sacred vocal works; many secular choral pieces, including the popular *Lied von der Glocke* (1809); part-songs; lieder.

BIBL.: K. Stephenson, *A. R.: Ein Beitrag zur Hamburger Musikgeschichte* (Hamburg, 1938).—**NS/LK/DM**

Romberg, Bernhard Heinrich,

German cellist and composer, cousin of **Andreas Jakob Romberg;** b. Dinklage, Nov. 11, 1767; d. Hamburg, Aug. 13, 1841. He was the son of the bassoonist and cellist Bernhard Anton Romberg (b. Munster, March 6, 1742; d. there, Dec. 14, 1814), who played in the orch. of the Prince-Bishop of Münster (1776–1803). Bernhard Heinrich began his career in Münster when he appeared with his cousin at age 7; they toured with their fathers thereafter, making visits to Frankfurt am Main (1782) and Paris (1784, 1785). After playing in the Bonn electoral orch. (1790–93), they fled in the face of the French invasion and went to Hamburg, where they were members of the opera orch. at the Ackermann Theater; they then toured Italy (1795–96) and visited Vienna (1796), where they became friends of Haydn. After further travels in Italy and another visit to Paris (1801), the cousins pursued separate careers. Bernhard Heinrich visited Spain in 1801, served as prof. of cello at the Paris Cons. (1801–03), and then joined the Berlin Royal Court Orch. (1805). He visited Russia in 1807 and England in 1814; was Berlin Hofkapellmeister (1816–19). In 1820 he went to Hamburg, which he made his home with the exception of another Berlin sojourn (1826–31); also made extensive tours as a virtuoso. He publ. *Méthode de violoncelle* (Berlin, 1840). He had 2 children who pursued musical careers: Bernhardine (b. Hamburg, Dec. 14, 1803; d. there, April 26, 1878), a concert singer, and Karl (b. Moscow, Jan. 16, 1811; d. Hamburg, Feb. 6, 1897), a cellist in the St. Petersburg German Opera orch. (1830–42).

WORKS: DRAMATIC: *Der Schiffbruch*, operetta (1791; not perf.); *Die wiedergefundene Statue*, opera (c. 1792; not perf.); *Don Mendoza*, opera (Paris, 1802; in collaboration with A. Romberg); *Ulisse und Circe*, opera (Berlin, July 27, 1807); *Rittertreue*, opera (Berlin, Jan. 31, 1817); *Daphne und Agathokles*, ballet (Berlin, 1818); *Alma*, opera (Copenhagen, May 15, 1824); incidental music. **ORCH.:** 5 syms.; *Symphonie burlesque* for Children's Instruments and Orch.; 2 overtures; 10 cello concertos; Concertino for 2 Horns and Orch.; Double Concerto for Violin, Cello, and Orch.; many pieces for cello and orch. **CHAMBER:** 11 string quartets; cello studies; piano pieces; songs.

BIBL.: H. Schafer, *B. R.: Sein Leben und Wirken* (diss., Univ. of Bonn, 1931).—**NS/LK/DM**

Romberg, Sigmund,

versatile Hungarian-born American operetta composer, conductor, and pianist; b. Nagykanizsa, Hungary, July 29, 1887; d. N.Y., Nov. 9, 1951. Perhaps the most prolific Broadway composer of the 1910s and among the most successful of the 1920s, Romberg resurrected the Viennese operetta style of musical theater pioneered by Victor Herbert in the long-running (and frequently revived) shows *The Student Prince, The Desert Song,* and *The New Moon,* which contained such standards as "Softly, as in a Morning Sunrise," "Lover, Come Back to Me," and "Stouthearted Men." But he also was able to adapt to the different demands of Hollywood and the hit parade in a string of film scores and in such pop hits as "When I Grow Too Old to Dream" and "Close as Pages in a Book."

Romberg was the son of Adam and Clara Romberg. His mother was a novelist who wrote under the name Clara Berg. His father, who worked in a chemical factory, was an amateur pianist and gave him his first piano lessons; he also took violin lessons from the age of seven. He graduated from the Univ. of Bucharest and studied civil engineering at the Polytechnische Hochschule in Vienna from 1904 to 1907. At the same time he was assistant manager of the city's leading opera house, the Theater-an-der-Wien, and he studied music with Richard Heuberger for three years. He left school in 1907 to join the army, serving in the 19th Hungarian Infantry Regiment for 18 months.

Romberg moved to London, then immigrated to the U.S. in 1909, later becoming an American citizen. Initially he worked at the Eagle Pencil Co. in N.Y., then played background music in Hungarian restaurants. In 1912 he formed an orchestra to play at Bustanoby's Restaurant, which became a popular night spot. He began to publish songs in 1913 and had his first song interpolated into a musical with the mounting of the German show *Die Mitternachtsmadel,* later presented in English as *The Midnight Girl* (N.Y., Feb. 23, 1914). This led him to a job as staff composer for the Shubert Organization and his first Broadway show, the revue *The Whirl of the World.*

During the next six years Romberg wrote or cowrote 25 Broadway shows for the Shuberts (and had interpolations into several more), including the 1914, 1916, 1917, 1918, and 1919 editions of *The Passing Show* revue and the Al Jolson vehicles *Dancing Around, Robinson Crusoe Jr.,* and *Sinbad.* His major successes of this period were both adaptations of Viennese operettas: *The Blue Paradise,* based on *Ein Tag im Paradies,* which featured "Auf Wiedersehen" (lyrics by Herbert Reynolds), a record hit for Harry Macdonough and Alice Green (Olive Kline) in November 1915, ran more than 350 performances; and *Maytime,* based on *Wie Einst im Mai,* which featured "Will You Remember?" (also known as "Sweetheart"; lyrics by Rida Johnson Young), a record hit for Alice Green and Raymond Dixon (Kline and Lambert Murphy) in January 1918, ran for nearly 500 performances. *Maytime* was made into a film in 1937, which led to a hit revival of "Will You Remember?" by Victor Young and His Orch.

After serving in the U.S. Army during World War I, Romberg left the Shuberts to form his own production company with Max Wilner. Their productions included Romberg's next two musicals, *The Magic Melody* and *Love Birds*, but these and the team's other efforts were only modestly successful, and Romberg returned to his job with the Shuberts, writing another 21 shows for them during the next seven years. (In 1924 he began to work with other producers as well as the Shuberts.) As before, these included annual editions of *The Passing Show* in 1923 and 1924 as well as Al Jolson's *Bombo*. But Romberg's first assignment was *Blossom Time*, based on the Viennese operetta *Das Drei Mädelhaus*, a stage biography of Franz Schubert. Romberg adapted Schubert's music to Broadway, resulting in the longest running musical of the 1921–22 season and the hit "Song of Love" (lyrics by Dorothy Donnelly; based on a theme in the first movement of the *Unfinished Symphony*), most successfully recorded by Lucy Isabelle Marsh and Royal Dadmun, though there were also popular records by Edwin Dale and Prince's Orch. (A perennial touring success, *Blossom Time* returned to Broadway in 1931, 1938, and 1943.)

In addition to the three shows he wrote for the Shuberts in 1922, Romberg found the time to compose the score for his first film, *Foolish Wives*, and to contribute interpolated songs to another Shubert production, *The Lady in Ermine* (N.Y., Oct. 2, 1922), including "When Hearts Are Young" (lyrics by Cyrus Wood, music also by Alfred Goodman), which spawned hit records for the orchestras of Paul Specht and Paul Whiteman in March 1923.

Romberg's next major success, his longest-running show and frequently cited as his single greatest work, was *The Student Prince*, based on the play *Old Heidelberg*. The hit of the show was "Deep in My Heart, Dear" (lyrics by Donnelly), which became a popular instrumental for Benny Krueger and His Orch. in July 1924 and a vocal hit Franklyn Baur in November, both recordings preceding the show's N.Y. opening. In addition to its two-year run in N.Y., *The Student Prince* became a continual touring success, and it was brought back to Broadway in 1931 and 1943, finally being added to the repertoire of the N.Y.C. Opera in 1980. There was also a film version that used Romberg's music in 1954, leading to a Top 40 hit recording of "Drink, Drink, Drink" (lyrics by Donnelly) for Mario Lanza, who dubbed the song onscreen.

Romberg married Lillian Harris in March 1925. He composed two modestly successful shows that year, then produced *The Desert Song*, with a libretto by Oscar Hammerstein II, Otto Harbach, and Frank Mandel, lyrics by Hammerstein and Harbach. A long-running success, the show produced the hits "One Alone," "The Riff Song," and the title song (also known as "Blue Heaven"), all recorded by Nat Shilkret. Another touring warhorse, *The Student Prince*, returned to Broadway in 1946 and 1973 and was filmed three times, in 1929, 1943, and 1953.

My Maryland, based on the Civil War play *Barbara Fritchie*, was one of the stage hits of the 1927–28 season, and it brought Whiteman a two- sided record hit with

the songs "Your Land and My Land" and "Silver Moon" (both lyrics by Donnelly). During the same season *The New Moon* (lyrics by Hammerstein) began an extended tryout run in Philadelphia, leading to a N.Y. opening the following year, when it became the biggest musical hit of the 1928–29 season. It was also Romberg's most successful score as far as record covers went—five songs became hits. "Softly, as in a Morning Sunrise" and "One Kiss" made up the two sides of a disk by Shilkret that sold well in January 1929; "Marianne" was a hit for the Arden-Ohman Orch.; "Stout-Hearted Men" was a hit for Perry Askam; and the show's biggest hit, "Lover, Come Back to Me," its melody partially drawn from Tchaikovsky's *June Barcarolle* for piano, was recorded most successfully by Whiteman, though the Arden-Ohman Orch., Rudy Vallée and His Connecticut Yankees, and Askam all did well with it, too. The show returned to Broadway in 1942 and 1944 and was first performed by the N.Y. State Opera in 1986. There were film versions in 1930 and 1940, and Nat "King" Cole revived "Lover, Come Back to Me" in 1953 for a Top 40 hit.

Romberg moved to Hollywood in 1930 and thereafter divided his time between writing for the theater and the screen, following the modestly successful show *Nina Rosa* with the films *Viennese Nights* and *Children of Dreams*, then returning to Broadway for the less successful *East Wind* and *Melody*. In 1933 he went to Paris for the specially commissioned musical *Rose de France*, which was produced by the Société Anonyme Française Chappell. In 1934 he began doing radio shows for Swift and Co.

The Night Is Young, on which Romberg collaborated with Hammerstein, was a flop at the box office, but its songs were successful in the record stores. The title track was a hit for Glen Gray and the Casa Loma Orch. and for Smith Ballew and His Orch.; "When I Grow Too Old to Dream" was on the hit parade in April and May 1935 for Gray and was also a hit for Nelson Eddy. Later that year *May Wine* became Romberg's biggest Broadway hit since *The New Moon*, its standout song being "I Built a Dream One Day" (lyrics by Hammerstein), which became a hit for Ray Noble and His Orch. in January 1936.

Romberg continued to balance Broadway and Hollywood projects, following with another show, *Forbidden Melody*, then the films *They Gave Him a Gun* and *The Girl of the Golden West*, then the stage musical *Sunny River*. The failure of his last two shows may have convinced him that his operetta approach had lost favor in N.Y., since in 1942 he launched a new career as an orchestra leader, taking a 50-piece ensemble on tour for up to 100 concerts a year for the rest of his life and making recordings of his own work and that of other composers for RCA Victor. The records sold, and the concerts played to audiences in the tens of thousands.

In 1945 he brought "An Evening with Romberg" to radio. He also demonstrated that he was able to compete with the new generation on Broadway by writing *Up in Central Park*, which had the second-longest N.Y. run of any of his shows, generating the hit "Close as Pages in a Book" (lyrics by Dorothy Fields), which charted for Benny Goodman and His Orch. in May 1945.

The show was revived in 1947 and made into a film the following year.

Romberg composed "Zing Zing-Zoom Zoom" (lyrics by Charles Tobias) for his 1950 Christmas card, which led to a recording on which his orchestra backed Perry Como. When the song was released on the flip side of Como's chart-topping single "If," it also became a chart hit, Romberg's last in his lifetime. *The Girl in Pink Tights*, mounted more than two years after his death, was only a modest success onstage, but it produced "Lost in Loveliness" (lyrics by Leo Robin), which generated chart records for Billy Eckstine and Dolores Gray. *Deep in My Heart* was a screen biography.

WORKS (only shows for which Romberg was credited or cocredited as composer are listed): **MUSICALS/REVUES/ OPERETTAS** (openings are in N.Y. unless noted otherwise): *The Whirl of the World* (Jan. 10, 1914); *The Passing Show of 1914* (June 10, 1914); with Harry Carroll, *Dancing Around* (Oct. 10, 1914); with Harry Carroll, *Maid in America* (Feb. 18, 1915); *Hands Up* (July 22, 1915); with Edmund Eysler, *The Blue Paradise* (Aug. 5, 1915); *A World of Pleasure* (Oct. 14, 1915); *Ruggles of Red Gap* (Dec. 25, 1915); with James F. Hanley, *Robinson Crusoe Jr.* (Feb. 17, 1916); with Otto Motzan, *The Passing Show of 1916* (June 22, 1916); with Robert Winterberg, *The Girl from Brazil* (Aug. 30, 1916); with Otto Motzan and Herman Timberg, *The Show of Wonders* (Oct. 26, 1916); *Follow Me* (Nov. 29, 1916); with Emmerich Kalman, *Her Soldier Boy* (Dec. 6, 1916); with Otto Motzan, *The Passing Show of 1917* (April 26, 1917); with Oscar Straus, *My Lady's Glove* (June 18, 1917); *Maytime* (Aug. 16, 1917); with Herman Timberg, *Doing Our Bit* (Oct. 18, 1917); with Herman Timberg, *Over the Top* (Nov. 28, 1917); *Sinbad* (Feb. 14, 1918); with Zoel Parenteau, *Follow the Girl* (March 2, 1918); with Jean Schwartz, *The Passing Show of 1918* (July 25, 1918); *The Melting of Molly* (Dec. 30, 1918); with Jean Schwartz, *Monte Cristo Jr.* (Feb. 12, 1919); with Jean Schwartz, *The Passing Show of 1919* (Oct. 23, 1919); *The Magic Melody* (Nov. 11, 1919); *Love Birds* (March 15, 1921); *Blossom Time* (Sept. 28, 1921); *Bombo* (Oct. 6, 1921); *The Blushing Bride* (Feb. 6, 1922); with Leo Fall, *The Rose of Stamboul* (March 7, 1922); *Springtime of Youth* (Oct. 26, 1922); *The Dancing Girl* (Jan. 24, 1923); with Jean Schwartz, *The Passing Show of 1923* (June 14, 1923); with Jean Schwartz, *Innocent Eyes* (May 20, 1924); with Herbert Stothart, *Marjorie* (Aug. 11, 1924); with Jean Schwartz, *The Passing Show of 1924* (Sept. 3, 1924); *Artists and Models* (Oct., 15, 1924); with Harry Tierney, *Annie Dear* (Nov. 4, 1924); *The Student Prince* (Dec. 2, 1924); *Louie the 14th* (March 3, 1925); *Princess Flavia* (Nov. 2, 1925); *he Desert Song* (Nov. 30, 1926); *Cherry Blossoms* (March 28, 1927); *My Maryland* (Sept. 12, 1927); *My Princess* (Oct. 6, 1927); *The Love Call* (Oct. 24, 1927); *The New Moon* (Philadelphia, Dec. 22, 1927; N.Y., Sept. 19, 1928); *Nina Rosa* (Sept. 20, 1930); *East Wind* (Oct. 27, 1931); *Melody* (Feb. 14, 1933); *Rose de France* (Paris, Oct. 23, 1933); *May Wine* (Dec. 5, 1935); *Forbidden Melody* (Nov. 2, 1936); *Sunny River* (Dec. 4, 1941); *Up in Central Park* (Jan. 27, 1945); *My Romance* (Oct. 29, 1948); *The Girl in Pink Tights* (March 5, 1954). **FILMS:** *Foolish Wives* (1922); *The Desert Song* (1929); *Viennese Nights* (1930); *New Moon* (1930); *Children of Dreams* (1931); *The Night Is Young* (1935); *Maytime* (1937); *They Gave Him a Gun* (1937); *The Girl of the Golden West* (1938); *New Moon* (1940); *The Desert Song* (1943); *Up in Central Park* (1948); *The Desert Song* (1953); *The Student Prince* (1954); *Deep in My Heart* (1954).

BIBL.: E. Arnold, *Deep in My Heart: A Story Based on the Life of S. R.* (N.Y., 1949); J. Koegel, *The Film Operettas of S. R.* (thesis, Calif. State Univ., 1984).—**WR**

Rome, Harold (Jacob), American composer and lyricist; b. Hartford, Conn., May 27, 1908; d. N.Y., Oct. 26, 1993. Rome entered the musical theater of the 1930s with the topical, socially conscious revue *Pins and Needles* and continued to work in a left-wing political vein until after World War II, when he began to write more conventional musical comedies. His songs always gave voice to the yearnings of the lower middle class, however. His other most successful shows were *Fanny* and *Call Me Mister*. His most popular songs were "(All of a Sudden) My Heart Sings," "South America, Take It Away," and "Wish You Were Here."

Rome was the son of Louis and Ida Aronson Rome; his father was president of the Conn. Coal Co. He attended Trinity Coll. in Hartford from 1924 to 1926, then transferred to Yale, earning a B.A. degree in 1929. He attended Yale Law School for a year, 1929–30, then transferred to the Yale School of Architecture and received a B.F.A. in 1934. He studied music with Lehman Engel and John Colman, and composition with Reuven Kosakoff, Tom Timoth, and Joseph Schillinger, and he played piano in dance bands to help pay for his education. After graduating he got a job in an architectural firm in N.Y. but continued to augment his income playing piano.

Rome gave up his architectural job in 1935 to become musical director at the Green Mansions resort in Warrensburg, N.Y. There he produced musical revues during the summers of 1935, 1936, and 1937. After his first year he was commissioned by the International Ladies Garment Workers Union to write songs for an amateur revue to be performed by union members. The first performance of the revue, *Pins and Needles*, took place on June 14, 1936, but it did not open in a Broadway theater until nearly a year and a half later. It then became a phenomenal success, running 1,108 performances and being constantly updated to maintain its topicality. "Sunday in the Park" from the score reached the hit parade in April 1938 for the Hudson-DeLange Orch.

With *Pins and Needles* still running, Rome was hired to write the songs for another revue, *Sing Out the News*, in 1938. The show, for which he also cowrote the libretto, ran 105 performances and spawned a hit in "F.D.R. Jones," recorded by Ella Fitzgerald.

Rome married radio advertising writer Florence M. Miles on Feb. 3, 1939; they had two children. He joined the army in 1943 and spent the rest of the war years writing songs for military shows including *Stars and Gripes* and *Lunchtime Follies*, which were performed at U.S. bases and defense facilities, and *Skirts*, which ran in London. He had a rare song not from a stage show in "(All of a Sudden) My Heart Sings" (adapted from "Ma Mie," music by Henri Herpin, original French lyrics by Jean Marie Blanvillain), which became a Top Ten hit for Johnnie Johnston in March 1945 and was used in the movie musical *Anchors Aweigh*, released in July.

Rome's next Broadway revue, *Call Me Mister* (1946), touched on the topical subject of returning servicemen. It ran 734 performances and generated two outside hits, both of which were released before the opening date. "South America, Take It Away" was a Top Ten, million-selling record for Bing Crosby and the Andrews Sisters, and "Along with Me" made the charts for Margaret Whiting. A movie version released in early 1951 retained only three songs from the stage show.

Rome succeeded with a book musical in the summer of 1952 with *Wish You Were Here*, which ran 598 performances and generated a chart-topping single by Eddie Fisher with the title song and a Top Ten cast album. An even longer run—888 performances—was enjoyed by 1954's *Fanny*, which also spawned a Top Ten cast album. A 1961 nonmusical movie version retained Rome's songs largely as background music, but the soundtrack album spent nearly three months in the charts.

Paul Anka scored a Top 40 hit with his revival of "(All of a Sudden) My Heart Sings" in December 1958, a feat repeated by Mel Carter seven years later. Rome returned to Broadway in April 1959 with *Destry Rides Again*, which ran 472 performances. Three years later came *I Can Get It for You Wholesale*, which ran 300 performances and is best remembered as the Broadway debut of Barbra Streisand in a minor role. *The Zulu and the Zayda*, which ran for 179 performances starting in November 1965, was billed as a play with music, but it contained as many songs as the average musical.

Rome was commissioned to write the songs for a musical adaptation of *Gone with the Wind* in Japan, resulting in the three-month run of *Scarlett* in Tokyo at the start of 1970. A revised version of the show, retitled *Gone with the Wind*, had a run of 397 performances in London starting in May 1972 and played a U.S. tour starting Aug. 28, 1973, in Los Angeles, but never reached Broadway. Rome died of a stroke at 85 in 1993.

WORKS (only works for which Rome was a primary, credited composer and/or lyricist are listed): **MUSICALS/ REVUES/PLAYS** (dates refer to N.Y. openings unless otherwise noted): *Pins and Needles* (Nov. 27, 1937); *Sing Out the News* (Sept. 24, 1938); *Let Freedom Ring* (Oct. 5, 1942); *Call Me Mister* (April 18, 1946); *Alive and Kicking* (Jan. 17, 1950); *Bless You All* (Dec. 14, 1950); *Wish You Were Here* (June 25, 1952); *Fanny* (Nov. 4, 1954); *Destry Rides Again* (April 23, 1959); *I Can Get It for You Wholesale* (March 22, 1962); *The Zulu and the Zayda* (Nov. 10, 1965); *La Grosse Valise* (Dec. 14, 1965); *Scarlett* (Tokyo, Jan. 3, 1970); *Gone with the Wind* (revised version of *Scarlett*; London, May 3, 1972; Los Angeles, Aug. 28, 1973). **FILMS:** *Call Me Mister* (1951); *Fanny* (1961).

BIBL.: F. Rome (his wife), *The Scarlett Letters* (N.Y., 1971). —WR

Romero, family of famous Spanish-American guitarists constituting a quartet known as Los Romeros:

Celedonio Romero (b. Málaga, March 2, 1918) pursued a career as a soloist in Spain; he served as mentor to each of his 3 sons, **Celin Romero** (b. Málaga, Nov. 23, 1940), **Pepe Romero** (b. Málaga, March 8, 1944), and **Angel Romero** (b. Málaga, Aug. 17, 1946); they eventually appeared together as a guitar quartet, playing engagements throughout Spain. The family emigrated to the U.S. in 1958 and made their first tour of the country in 1961; billed as "the royal family of the guitar," they toured with great success worldwide. In addition to making their own arrangements and transcriptions, they commissioned works from various composers, including Joaquín Rodrigo and Federico Moreno Torroba.—NS/LK/DM

Romero, Mateo (real name, **Mathieu Rosmarin**), Netherlands-born Spanish composer; b. Liège, 1575 or 1576; d. Madrid, May 10, 1647. He was a soldier and was often called "El Maestro Capitan." After serving with the Spanish army in Flanders, he became cantor of the Flemish chapel in Madrid (1593), and was maestro de from 1598 to 1634; in 1609 he was ordained a priest. In 1638 he went to Portugal as emissary to the Duke of Braganza (the future Emperor João IV). He enjoyed a reputation as one of the finest composers of both sacred and secular music of his time. Many of his works are lost; 22 secular compositions are found in J. Aroca, ed., *Cancionero musical y poético del siglo XVII, recogido por Claudio de la Sablonara* (Madrid, 1916).

BIBL.: R. Pelinski, *Die weltliche Vokalmusik Spaniens am Anfang des 17. Jahrhunderts, der Cancionero de la Sablonara* (Tutzing, 1971).—NS/LK/DM

Römhild or **Römhildt, Johann Theodor,** German organist and composer; b. Salzungen, Sept. 23, 1684; d. Merseburg, Oct. 26, 1756. He studied with Johann Jakob Bach in Ruhla, and in 1697 entered the Thomasschule in Leipzig, where he was a pupil of Schelle and Kuhnau; later studied at the Univ. of Leipzig (1705–8). He was Kantor at Spremberg and Freystadt. In 1731 he was appointed court musician in Merseburg, and in 1735 Cathedral organist there. He composed over 250 sacred cantatas, 19 secular cantatas, 2 oratorios, 2 masses, a *St. Matthew Passion* (publ. in Leipzig, 1921), motets, and some instrumental works. —NS/LK/DM

Ronald, Sir Landon (real name, **Landon Ronald Russell**), English pianist, conductor, and composer, son of **Henry Russell** and brother of **Henry Russell**; b. London, June 7, 1873; d. there, Aug. 14, 1938. He entered the Royal Coll. of Music in London, where he studied composition with Parry and also attended the classes of Stanford and Parratt. He first embarked on a concert career as a pianist, but soon turned to conducting light opera and summer sym. concerts; was conductor of the New Sym. Orch. of London (1909–14) and of the Scottish Orch. in Glasgow (1916–20). He served as principal of the Guildhall School of Music and Drama in London (1910–38). He was knighted in 1922. He composed an operetta, *A Capital Joke*; a ballet, *Britannia's Realm* (1902; for the coronation of King Edward VII); and a scenic spectacle, *Entente cordiale* (1904; to celebrate the triple alliance of Russia, France, and England); about 300 songs. He publ. 2 autobiographical books: *Variations on a Personal Theme* (London, 1922) and *Myself and Others* (London, 1931).—NS/LK/DM

Ronconi, family of Italian musicians:

(1) Domenico Ronconi, tenor and singing teacher; b. Lendinara, near Rovigo, July 11, 1772; d. Milan, April 13, 1839. He made his debut in Venice (1797). After singing in St. Petersburg (1801–5), he returned to Italy and appeared at Milan's La Scala (1808), where he was chosen to create roles in operas by Mosca, Orlandi, and Lamberti; then sang at the Italian Opera in Vienna (1809) and in Paris (1810). After further appearances in Italy, he was a member of the Munich Hof- und Nationaltheater (1819–29). He then returned to his homeland and opened his own singing school in Milan. He had 3 sons who became musicians:

(2) Giorgio Ronconi, baritone; b. Milan, Aug. 6, 1810; d. Madrid, Jan. 8, 1890. He studied with his father, and made his debut as Valdeburgo in *La Straniera in Pavia* (1831). He then went to Rome, where he sang in the premieres of Donizetti's *Il Furioso all'isola di San Domingo* and *Torquato Tasso* in 1833; subsequently sang in the premieres of that composer's *Il campanello* in Naples (1836), *Pia de' Tolomei* in Venice (1837), *Maria di Rudez* in Venice (1838), *Maria Padilla* in Milan (1841), and *Maria di Rohan* in Vienna (1843). From 1839 he sang at Milan's La Scala, where he was chosen by Verdi to create the title role in his *Nabucco* (1842). In 1842 he made his London debut at Her Majesty's Theatre, and later made frequent appearances at Covent Garden (1847–66); also sang in St. Petersburg (1850–60). After a sojourn in N.Y. (1866–72), he went to Granada and founded his own singing school; then was prof. of singing at the Madrid Cons. (from 1874). Although his voice was mediocre, he won distinction for his dramatic abilities.

(3) Felice Ronconi singing teacher; b. Venice, 1811; d. St. Petersburg, Sept. 10, 1875. He received music training from his father, and then was active as a singing teacher in Würzburg, Frankfurt am Main, Milan, and St. Petersburg. He wrote a method on the teaching of singing, and also composed some songs.

(4) Sebastiano Ronconi, baritone; b. Venice, May 1814; d. Milan, Feb. 6, 1900. He studied with his father. He made his debut as Torquato Tasso in Lucca (1836), and later sang throughout Europe and the U.S. He spent his last years teaching voice in Milan.—**NS/LK/DM**

Ronettes, The, the best remembered of the early 1960s "girl groups". **MEMBERSHIP:** Veronica "Ronnie" Bennett (b. N.Y., Aug. 10, 1943); Estelle Bennett (b. N.Y., July 22, 1944); Nedra Talley (b. N.Y., Jan. 27, 1946).

Formed in N.Y. in 1958 as the dance act The Dolly Sisters, the group comprised sisters Estelle and Veronica "Ronnie" Bennett and cousin Nedra Talley. Performing as resident dancers at the Peppermint Lounge in N.Y. in 1961, the group signed with Don Kirshner's Colpix label, initially recording as Ronnie and The Relatives. Becoming The Ronettes in 1962, they recorded several singles and an album's worth of material released in 1965. They attracted the attention of producer Phil Spector, who signed them to his Philles label. In 1963, they scored a smash pop, R&B and British hit with "Be My Baby," written by Spector, Jeff Barry, and Ellie Greenwich. Through 1964 they achieved major pop hits with "Baby, I Love You," written by Spector, Barry and Greenwich, and "Walking in the Rain," written by Barry Mann and Cynthia Weil, and moderate pop hits with "Do I Love You?" and "(The Best Part Of) Breaking Up." They achieved their last (minor) hit in late 1966 as The

Ronettes Featuring Veronica with "I Can Hear Music," a major hit for The Beach Boys in 1969.

The Ronettes continued to record for Philles Records with only minor success through 1966, when they broke up. In 1968, Ronnie Bennett married Phil Spector and she spent the next four years with him ensconced in his Beverly Hills mansion. In 1969, he unsuccessfully attempted to revive The Ronettes' career on A&M Records with "You Came, You Saw, You Conquered." On her own, Ronnie Spector managed a minor hit with George Harrison's "Try Some, Buy Some" on Apple Records in 1971. In 1973, she separated from Spector and formed a new edition of The Ronettes that lasted three years and recorded two unsuccessful singles for Buddah Records. Late 1970s releases for Ronnie Spector included 1976's "Paradise," written by Phil Spector and Harry Nilsson and produced by Spector, and 1977's "Say Goodbye to Hollywood," written by Billy Joel and produced by "Miami" Steven Van Zandt. In 1980, she recorded *Siren* for Genya Ravan's N.Y.–based Polish Records, and the album included The Ramones' "Here Today, Gone Tomorrow" and "Happy Birthday, Rock and Roll," dedicated to Phil Spector. In 1986 she sang the lead line from "Be My Baby" behind Eddie Money's smash pop hit "Take Me Home Tonight." Ronnie Spector recorded *Unfinished Business* for Columbia Records in 1987, and Harmony Books published her book *Be My Baby* in 1990.

DISC.: THE RONETTES: *Presenting the Fabulous Ronettes* (1964); *The Ronettes Featuring Veronica* (1965); *The Early Years, 1961–62* (1965). **RONNIE SPECTOR:** *Siren* (1980); *Unfinished Business* (1987).

BIBL.: R. Spector with V. Waldron, *Be My Baby: How I Survived Mascara, Miniskirts and Madness, Or My Life as a Fabulous Ronette* (N.Y., 1990).—**BH**

Roney, Wallace, talented trumpeter; b. Philadelphia, Pa., May 25, 1960. Wallace Roney spent a large part of his artistically impressionable years as a child prodigy in Washington, D.C., where he attended the Duke Ellington School for the Arts and Howard Univ. before briefly enrolling in Boston's Berklee School of Music. His first major gigs were with Abdullah Ibrahim, Chico Freeman, Art Blakey's Jazz Messengers (where he played alongside Wynton Marsalis), and the Tony Williams Quintet. His use of the muted trumpet and his lean style of playing have caused some critics to draw easy (if somewhat misguided) comparisons with Miles Davis. The appearance of a more substantive relationship was furthered when he played in the big band that backed up Davis at the 1991 Montreux Jazz Festival, an event at which the master presented the young man with one of his trumpets. He also toured with Tony Williams, Herbie Hancock, and Ron Carter in a Davis tribute band.

DISC.: *Verses* (1987); *According to Mr. Roney* (1987–92); *Intuition* (1988); *The Standard Bearer* (1990); *Obsession* (1991); *Seth Air* (1992); *Misterios* (1994); *Crunchin'* (1993); *Munchin'* (1995); *The Wallace Roney Quintet* (1996); *Village* (1997).—**GM**

Ronga, Luigi, eminent Italian musicologist; b. Turin, June 19, 1901; d. Rome, Sept. 11, 1993. After obtaining an arts degree from the Univ. of Turin, he went to Dresden to pursue his training in musicology. In 1930 he received his libera docenza. In 1926 he became a prof. at the Palermo Cons. In 1930 he settled in Rome, where he was a teacher at the Accademia di Santa Cecilia and at the Pontifico Istituto di Musica Sacra. He then was a lecturer (1938–50) and subsequently a prof. (1950–71) at the Univ. of Rome. He was ed. of *Rassegna musicale* (1928–29) and *Rivista musicale italiana* (1954–55).

WRITINGS: *Per la critica wagneriana* (Turin, 1928); *Gerolamo Frescobaldi, organista vaticano, nella storia della musica strumentale* (Turin, 1930); *Lezioni di storia della musica* (2 vols., Rome, 1933, 1935; new ed., 1991); *Rossini* (Florence, 1939); *Lineamenti del romanticismo musicale* (Rome, 1943); *La musica nell'antichità* (Rome, 1945); *Claude Debussy e l'impressionismo musicale* (Rome, 1946); *Il dramma musicale di Richard Wagner* (Rome, 1947); *Arte e gusto nella musica, dell'ars nova a Debussy* (Milan, 1956); *Bach, Mozart, Beethoven: Tre problemi critici* (Venice, 1956); *The Meeting of Poetry and Music* (N.Y., 1956); *La musica nell'età barocca* (Rome, 1959); *Il linguaggio musicale romantico* (Rome, 1960); *L'esperienza storica della musica* (Bari, 1960); *Introduzione a "La Diana schernita" di Cornacchioli* (Rome, 1961); *La musica europa nella seconda meta dell'Ottocento* (Rome, 1961); *Storia della musica* (2 vols., Rome, 1962–63).

BIBL.: *Scritti in onore di L. R.* (Milan and Naples, 1973). —NS/LK/DM

Ronnefeld, Peter,

German conductor and composer; b. Dresden, Jan. 26, 1935; d. Kiel, Aug. 6, 1965. He studied with Blacher in Berlin and Messiaen in Paris. After winning the Hilversum conducting competition in 1955, he was asst. conductor at the Vienna State Opera (1958–61); served as chief conductor at the Theater der Stadt Bonn (1961–63); then was Generalmusikdirektor in Kiel from 1963 until his death. As a conductor, he specialized in modern music, but he also excelled in the Romantic repertoire; his own opera, *Die Ameise* (Düsseldorf, Oct. 21, 1961), had a fine reception. He also wrote a chamber opera, *Nachtausgabe* (Salzburg, 1956), 2 ballets, *Peter Schlemihl* (1955–56) and *Die Spirale* (1961), Concertino for Flute, Clarinet, Horn, Bassoon, and Strings (1950), *Sinfonie '52* (1952), *Rondo* for Orch. (1954), *2 Episodes* for Chamber Orch. (1956), a cantata, *Quartar* (1958), chamber music, and songs.—NS/LK/DM

Ronstadt, Linda,

popular female rock vocalist; b. Tucson, Ariz., July 15, 1946. Linda Ronstadt combined folk, rock, and country music, along with the best material by young singer–songwriters and astutely chosen remakes of earlier pop hits, to become one of the most popular female rock vocalists of the second half of the 1970s. Always an eclectic singer, she spent her second decade on the pop scene exploring various musical genres, including reviving earlier pop standards with noted arranger Nelson Riddle to surprising success and exploring her own Mexican-American heritage.

Raised in Tucson, Linda Ronstadt was inspired to sing by a musically talented father. By age 14 she was singing with brother Pete and sister Suzi in local pizza parlors and clubs, occasionally accompanied by bassist-guitarist Bob Kimmel. After one semester at the Univ. of Ariz., she joined Kimmel in Los Angeles, where the two formed the Stone Poneys with local guitarist Kenny Edwards. Playing the region's club circuit, the group signed with Capitol Records in 1966 and recorded two albums largely comprised of material written by Kimmel and Edwards, although their only major hit was Mike Nesmith's "Different Drum." After a third album, recorded with studio musicians, Ronstadt pursued a solo career, initially as a country singer. In 1970 she achieved a major hit with "Long, Long Time." In 1971 her touring band coalesced around future Eagles Glenn Frey, Don Henley, and Randy Meisner, who accompanied her on her self-titled solo album from that year, which produced a minor hit with Jackson Browne's "Rock Me on the Water."

Touring with Neil Young in early 1973, Linda Ronstadt reenlisted Kenny Edwards, who recruited songwriter-guitarist Andrew Gold for her new backup band. She recorded *Don't Cry Now* with three different producers. The album included three songs written by John David Souther—the title song, "I Can Almost See It," and "The Fast One"—and yielded minor hits with Eric Kaz and Libby Titus's "Love Has No Pride" and "Silver Threads and Golden Needles," a major hit for the Springfields in 1962. One of the album's producers, Peter Asher, became Ronstadt's sole producer and manager through the 1970s; he produced the breakthrough *Heart Like a Wheel*, her final effort for Capitol Records. The album was an instant best-seller, yielding a top pop hit with "You're No Good" (a minor hit for Betty Everett in 1963), a smash country hit with Hank Williams's "I Can't Help It (If I'm Still in Love with You)," and a smash country and pop hit with Phil Everly's "When Will I Be Loved." The album also contained Souther's "Faithless Love," Anna McGarrigle's title song, and the Lowell George favorite "Willin'."

Linda Ronstadt's next album, *Prisoner in Disguise*, produced pop hits with covers of the Motown standards "Heat Wave" and "Tracks of My Tears" and a smash country hit with Neil Young's "Love Is a Rose"; it also included Lowell George's "Roll Um Easy" and Dolly Parton's "I Will Always Love You." *Hasten Down the Wind* contained the major pop hit "That'll Be the Day" (Buddy Holly's biggest hit), the smash country hit "Crazy" (Patsy Cline's biggest hit), and three compositions by Karla Bonoff, including the minor hits "Someone to Lay Down Beside Me" and "Lose Again." After completing a six-month tour of Europe and America in December 1976 and singing at President Carter's inaugural the following January, Linda Ronstadt recorded *Simple Dreams*. The album sold more than three million copies and produced five hit singles: "I Never Will Marry" (a near-smash country hit), Roy Orbison's "Blue Bayou" (a smash pop and country hit), Buddy Holly's "It's So Easy" (a smash pop hit), Warren Zevon's "Poor Poor Pitiful Me," and the Rolling Stones' "Tumblin' Dice."

During 1978 Linda Ronstadt attempted to record a trio album with Emmylou Harris and Dolly Parton, but the hastily made recordings proved unsatisfactory for release. Ronstadt's formula for success continued with *Living in the U.S.A.*, which produced hits with cover versions of "Back in the U.S.A." (Chuck Berry), "Ooh

Baby Baby" (The Miracles), and "Just One Look" (Doris Troy). The album also contained J. D. Souther's "White Rhythm and Blues" and Elvis Costello's "Alison," Ronstadt's concession to the burgeoning New Wave movement. *Mad Love* was Ronstadt's attempt to record in a more contemporary vein; she included three songs by Costello and three by Mark Goldenburg of the Los Angeles-based Cretones, but the hits were "How Do I Make You" and covers of "Hurt So Bad" (Little Anthony and the Imperials) and "I Can't Let Go" (The Hollies). Her first album of new material in nearly 10 years to *not* sell a million copies, *Get Closer*, yielded moderate pop hits with the title cut and "I Knew You When," and a major country hit with "Sometimes You Just Can't Win."

Linda Ronstadt abandoned rock music for the rest of the 1980s to pursue projects that helped establish her as an all-around entertainer. She appeared as Mabel in the Broadway production of Gilbert and Sullivan's *The Pirates of Penzance* and the subsequent movie version, in 1980 and 1983, respectively. In 1983, against the advice of then-boyfriend and former governor of Calif. Jerry Brown, Ronstadt performed at the Sun City resort in South Africa. Later in the year, in a daring career move that defied conventional music-industry wisdom, she recorded an entire album of Tin Pan Alley ballads, *What's New*, with arranger-conductor Nelson Riddle, best known for his 1950s work with Nat "King" Cole and Frank Sinatra, and his 46- piece orchestra. Although the album yielded only a minor pop hit, the title song, it eventually sold more than two million copies and encouraged Ronstadt to record two more albums with Riddle, *Lush Life* and *For Sentimental Reasons*. She made her big-band debut at Radio City Music Hall in N.Y. with mixed results, and later played Las Vegas with the entire retinue. In late 1984 Linda Ronstadt performed the role of Mimi in a small-scale version of Puccini's opera *La Bohème* at the Public Theater in N.Y. Despite the improved power and discipline of her voice, the performance was judged lackluster and disappointing by critics. In late 1986 Ronstadt scored a smash pop hit with James Ingram on "Somewhere Out There" from the animated movie *An American Tail*.

Finally, in 1987 Linda Ronstadt's long-anticipated collaboration with Emmylou Harris and Dolly Parton was released on Warner Bros. Over the next year, *Trio* produced smash country hits with "To Know Him Is to Love Him" (a top pop hit for the Teddy Bears in 1958), "Those Memories of You," Linda Thompson's "Telling Me Lies," and Parton's "Wildflowers." Lauded for its rich harmonies, exquisite lead vocals, and sympathetic arrangements, the album sold more than a million copies. Ronstadt next pursued a reawakened fascination with traditional Mexican music, mariachi music in particular, performing in Luis Valdez's *Corridos! Tales of Passion and Revolution* for PBS television and recording the poignant *Canciones de Mi Padre* (Songs of My Father) for Elektra Records. The album sold astoundingly well for a foreign-language recording and inspired her to tour with mariachi bands in 1988 and 1992. The 1988 tour produced an award-winning PBS television show. She recorded two more albums of Mexican music, *Mas Canciones* (More Songs) and *Frenesi* (Frenzy), in the early 1990s.

Linda Ronstadt returned to contemporary music with 1989's *Cry Like a Rainstorm—Howl Like the Wind*. The album included four songs written by Jimmy Webb and four duets with New Orleans vocalist Aaron Neville. Three of the duets became hits: the pop smash "Don't Know Much" and the near-smash "All My Life," both top easy-listening hits; and "When Something Is Wrong with My Baby." After nearly 40 years in the music business, Neville finally received widespread recognition as a result of the best-selling album. In the late-1980s and 1990s Ronstadt became recognized as a producer by supervising albums by David Lindley, Neville, and Jimmy Webb. She returned to her country-rock sound with 1995's *Feels Like Home*, which featured Randy Newman's title song, Neil Young's "After the Goldrush," and Tom Petty's "The Waiting."

DISC.: THE STONE PONEYS: *The Stone Poneys* (1967; reissued as *Beginnings*, 1975); *Evergreen, Vol. 2* (1967); *Stone Poneys and Friends, Vol. III* (1968); *Different Drum* (1974); *Stoney End* (1972). **LINDA RONSTADT:** *Hand Sown … Home Grown* (1969); *Silk Purse* (1970); *L. R.* (1971); *Heart Like a Wheel* (1974); *A Retrospective* (1977); *Rockfile (early Capitol material)* (1986); *Don't Cry Now* (1973); *Prisoner in Disguise* (1975); *Hasten Down the Wind* (1976); *Greatest Hits, Vol. 1* (1976); *Simple Dreams* (1977); *Living in the U.S.A.* (1978); *Mad Love* (1980); *Greatest Hits, Vol. 2* (1980); *Keeping Out of Mischief* (1981); *Get Closer* (1982); *What's New* (1983); *Lush Life* (1984); *For Sentimental Reasons* (1986); *'Round Midnight: The Nelson Riddle Sessions* (1986); *Prime of Life* (1986); *Canciones de Mi Padre* (1987); *Cry Like a Rainstorm—Howl Like the Wind* (1989); *Mas Canciones* (1991); *Frenesi* (1992); *Winter Light* (1993); *Feels Like Home* (1995). **THE PIRATES OF PENZANCE:** *Broadway Cast Album* (1981). **LINDA RONSTADT, DOLLY PARTON, AND EMMYLOU HARRIS:** *Trio* (1987).

BIBL.: R. Kanakaris, *L. R.: A Portrait* (Los Angeles, 1977); V. Claire, *L. R.* (N.Y., 1978); M. Moore, *The L. R. Scrapbook* (N.Y., 1978); C. Berman, *L. R.* (Carson City, 1980).—**BH**

Röntgen, Julius, German-born Dutch pianist, conductor, pedagogue, and composer; b. Leipzig, May 9, 1855; d. Bilthoven, near Utrecht, Sept. 13, 1932. He studied music with his father, Engelbert Rontgen (1829–97), and later with Plaidy and Reinecke in Leipzig and F. Lachner in Munich. From 1877 to 1925 he taught in Amsterdam. He was conductor of the Soc. for the Promotion of Music (1886–98) and also a co-founder (1884) of the Amsterdam Cons., which he served as director from 1912 to 1924. He was a friend of Brahms and Grieg, and ed. the letters of Brahms to T. Engelmann (1918); publ. a biography of Grieg (1930). An astonishingly industrious composer, he wrote an enormous amount of music in every genre, cast in an expansive Romantic style: 21 syms., 7 piano concertos, 2 violin concertos, 2 cello concertos, 3 operas (*Agnete, Samum,* and *Der lachende Kavalier*), much chamber music, etc.—**NS/LK/DM**

Ronzi de Begnis (originally, **Ronzi**), **Giuseppina,** notable Italian soprano; b. Milan, Jan. 11, 1800; d. Florence, June 7, 1853. She married **Giuseppe de Begnis** in 1816, and that same year made her operatic debut in Bologna. She then appeared in Genoa, Florence, and Bergamo. In 1818 she sang Ninetta in *La gazza ladra* in Pesaro under Rossini's direction, and soon acquired a fine reputation for her performances in his operas. In 1819 she went to Paris with her husband, where she sang Rosina opposite his Don Basilio in the first production there of Rossini's *Il Barbiere di Siviglia* at the Théâtre-Italien on Oct. 26 of that year. She and her husband continued to appear in Paris until 1821, when they proceeded to London. She made her debut there at the King's Theatre on May 19, 1821, singing Fiorilla opposite her husband's Don Geronio in Rossini's *Il turco in Italia*. She continued to sing with her husband until they were separated in 1825, and she subsequently pursued her career in Naples, where she created roles in Mercadante's *Zaira* (1831) and Donizetti's *Fausta* (1832), *Sancia di Castiglia* (1832), *Buondelmonte* (1834), and *Roberto Devereux* (1837). Donizetti also chose her to create the title role in his *Gemma di Vergy* at Milan's La Scala on Dec. 26, 1834. In 1843 she returned to London to sing Norma in an English-language staging at Covent Garden. In addition to her Italian portrayals, she had marked success in Mozartian roles.—NS/LK/DM

Roocroft, Amanda,

English soprano; b. Coppull, Feb. 9, 1966. She was a student of Barbara Robotham at the Royal Northern Coll. of Music in Manchester. After winning the Kathleen Ferrier Prize in 1988, she made her formal operatic debut in 1990 as Sophie at the Welsh National Opera in Cardiff, and then appeared as Pamina with the Glyndebourne Touring Opera. In 1991 she made her first appearance at London's Covent Garden as Pamina, and also was engaged as Fiordiligi at the Glyndebourne Festival. She portrayed the latter role in Paris, Amsterdam, and Lisbon in 1992, and then at the Bavarian State Opera in Munich in 1993. In 1993 she also appeared as Ginevra in *Ariodante* at the English National Opera in London, and then returned to the Glyndebourne Festival as Donna Anna and to Munich as Amelia Boccanegra in 1994. She sang Fiordiligi upon her return to Covent Garden in 1995. After singing in recital at London's Wigmore Hall in 1997, she once again returned to the Glyndebourne Festival as Kát'a Kabanová in 1998.—NS/LK/DM

Rooley, Anthony,

English lutenist and teacher; b. Leeds, June 10, 1944. He received training in guitar at the Royal Academy of Music in London (1965–68), but was self-taught as a lutenist. From 1969 to 1971 he taught at the Royal Academy of Music, and later gave courses in Japan, Italy, and Switzerland as well as in England. With James Tyler, he founded the Consort of Musicke in 1969, an ensemble devoted to the performance of Renaissance music. From 1972 he was its sole director, and led it on many tours of Europe, the Middle East, and North America. In later years, he also was active as a stage director of early music and was co-director of the early music recording label Musica Oscura. He publ. the vols. *A New Varietie of Lute Lessons* (1975), *The Penguin Book of Early Music* (1976), and *Performance: Revealing the Orpheus Within* (1990). —NS/LK/DM

Roos, Robert de,

Dutch composer; b. The Hague, March 10, 1907; d. there, March 18, 1976. He was a student of Wagenaar (composition) at the Royal Cons. of Music in The Hague. After further studies in Paris (1926–34) with Koechlin, Roland-Manuel, and Milhaud (composition), Philipp (piano), and Monteux (conducting), he completed his training in his homeland with Dresden. He was a cultural attaché at the Dutch embassy in Paris (1947–56), and then was first secretary for press and cultural affairs for the Dutch embassies in Caracas (1957–62), London (1962–67), and Buenos Aires (1967).

WORKS: DRAMATIC: *Kaartspel* (Card Game), ballet (1930); *Landelijke Comedie* (Pastoral Comedy), dance pantomime (1937–39); incidental music. **ORCH.:** *5 Etudes* for Piano and Small Orch. (1929); *Mouvement symphonique* (1930); Violin Concertino (1939); *Danses* for Flute and Small Orch. (1940); Viola Concerto (1941–42); *Sinfonietta* (1943); 3 sinfonias: No. 1, *Sinfonia romantica: Museum-Symphonie* for Chamber Orch. (1943), No. 2 (1952), and No. 3, *Sinfonia in 2 moti* for Strings (1968); Piano Concerto (1943–44); *Quo Vadis*, suite (1947); *Variations sérieuses sur un thème ingénu* (1947); 2 violin concertos (1949–50; 1956–58); *Suggestioni* (1961); *Composizioni* (1962); *Musica* for Violins, Cellos, and Double Basses (1971); *Rapsodie e Danza* for 2 Flutes and Orch. (1972–73). **CHAMBER:** Sextet for Piano and Winds (1935); 7 string quartets (1941; 1942; 1944–45; 1945–49; 1951; 1969–70; *Quartettino*, 1970); Sonata for Solo Violin (1943); *Introduction, Adagio, and Allegro* for 2 Violins (1945); Violin Sonata (1946); *Capriccio* for Clarinet and Piano (1952); *Distrazioni* for Violin and Piano (1953); *3 pezzi senza nome* for Piano Quartet (1958); Trio for 2 Violins and Cello (1965); *4 per 2* for Oboe and Viola (1966); *Incontri* for Wind Quintet (1966); *Incidenze* for Flute, Cello or Viola da Gamba, and Harpsichord (1966–67); Piano Trio (1968); *2 moti lenti* for 2 Violins and Cello (1970); *4 pezzi* for Wind Trio (1970–71). **VOCAL:** Chamber oratorio (1928); *Lyrische suite* for Chorus and Small Orch. (1938); *Adam in ballingschap* for 2 Narrators, 2 Flutes, 2 Horns, and Strings (1944); *De getemde Mars* for Chorus and Orch. (1948); *Postrema Verba*, cantata for Baritone, Chorus, and 25 Instruments (1969); *2 Songs* for Baritone and Instruments (1971); *3 Romantic Songs* for Soprano and Orch. (1975).—NS/LK/DM

Roosenschoon, Hans,

Dutch-born South African composer; b. The Hague, Dec. 17, 1952. He was taken in infancy to Pretoria, where he studied at the Cons. (1969–71; 1974–75). Following further training with Paul Patterson at the Royal Academy of Music in London (1977–78), he returned to South Africa and pursued studies at the univs. of Stellenbosch (M.Mus., 1989) and Cape Town (D.Mus., 1991). In 1976 he joined the staff of the South African Broadcasting Corp. in Johannesburg, later serving it in Cape Town as production manager for music from 1980 to 1995. In his output, Roosenschoon has demonstrated an adept handling of various styles, both traditional and contemporary. In some of his works, he explores the use of African elements and electronics.

WORKS: ORCH.: *Tablo* (1976); *Sinfonietta* (1976); *Katutura* (1977); *Palette* for Strings (1977; Johannesburg, April 24, 1978); *'n Saaier het uitgegaan om te saai...* (1978); *Mosaiek* (1978); *Ghomma* (1980; Johannesburg, July 2, 1983); *Ikonografie* (1983; Cape Town, Nov. 2, 1989); *Anagram* (1983; Cape Town, May 29, 1984); *Timbila* for Chopi Xylophone Ensemble and Orch. (Grahamstown, July 12, 1985); *Architectura* (Johannesburg, Oct. 8, 1986); *Horizon, Night-Sky, and Landscape* for Strings (Bloemfontein, June 18, 1987); *Chronicles* (Grahamstown, July 10, 1987); *Clouds Clearing* for Strings (1987; Cape Town, July 16, 1994); *Mantis*, ballet suite (Johannesburg, Oct. 22, 1988); *Circle of Light* (Cape Town, March 9, 1989); *Die Sonnevanger* (1990; Cape Town, Sept. 11, 1992); *The Magic Marimba* (Cape Town, Oct. 10, 1991); *do-re-mi-fabriek* (Johannesburg, Nov. 29, 1992); Trombone Concerto (1994–95). **CHAMBER:** Suite for Oboe and Piano (1973); *Bepeinsing* for Cello and Piano (1973); *Toccatino* for Piano Quartet (1973); *Makietie* for Brass Quintet (London, Dec. 1, 1978); String Quartet (1995). **KEYBOARD: P i a n o :** *Drie Klavierstuck* (1972); *Goggaboek* (1972); Sonatina (1974; Johannesburg, May 13, 1977); *Credo* (1975; Johannesburg, May 13, 1977); *Fingerprints* (Johannesburg, Nov. 1, 1989). **O r g a n :** Double Fugue (1975); Chorale Prelude (1978; Durban, Aug. 5, 1979); Chorale Prelude (1978; Durban, Aug. 5, 1979). **VOCAL:** *Ekstase* for Chorus and Orch. (1975); *Cantata on Psalm 8* for Chorus and Orch. (1976; Johannesburg, July 7, 1977); *Ars Poetica* for Baritone, Double Chorus, and Orch. (Johannesburg, Oct. 9, 1979); *Psalm 23* for Chorus (1979); *Firebowl* for Chorus (1980; Windhoek, May 21, 1986); *Does the noise in my head bother you?* for 2 Choruses, Pop Group, and Orch. (Cape Town, July 29, 1988); *Prayer of St. Richard: Thanks be to Thee* for Chorus (Johannesburg, Nov. 18, 1990); *Miserere* for Men's Chorus (1991); *Ko, lat ons sing* for Double Chorus (Stellenbosch, June 18, 1993); *Mbira* for Chorus (1994). **ELECTRONIC:** *Kataklisme* (1980; Johannesburg, July 4, 1983); *Helios* (1984; Grahamstown, July 6, 1985); *If Music Be* (1984; Cape Town, Nov. 21, 1985); *Narcissus* (1985). —NS/LK/DM

Roosevelt, J(oseph) Willard, American composer, pianist, and teacher; b. Madrid, Jan. 16, 1918. He was the grandson of President Theodore Roosevelt. He studied at Harvard Coll. (1936–38), at the Longy School of Music in Cambridge, Mass. (1936–38; 1940–41), with Boulanger in Paris and Gargenville (1938–39), at the N.Y. Coll. of Music (composition and piano diplomas, 1947), and at the Hartt Coll. of Music in Hartford, Conn. (B.Mus., 1959; M.Mus., 1960). In addition to his appearances as a pianist, he lectured on music at Columbia Univ. (1961), Fairleigh-Dickinson Univ. (1964–67), and the N.Y. Coll. of Music (1967–68).

WORKS: DRAMATIC: O p e r a : *And the Walls Came Tumbling Down* (1974–76). **ORCH.:** Piano Concerto (1948; rev. 1983); Cello Concerto (1963); *Amistad, homenaje al gran Morel-Campos*, overture (1965). **B a n d :** *The Twinkle in His Eye*, in memory of the composer's father, Kermit Roosevelt (1979; rev. 1993). **CHAMBER:** *Song and Dance Suite* for Oboe, Clarinet, and Viola (1991); Suite for Viola (1992); *Fanfare for Sagamore Hill* for Brass Quintet (Oyster Bay, N.Y., July 4, 1993); Trio for Clarinet, Cello, and Piano (1993). **P i a n o :** *Theme and Variations* (1948; rev. version, Long Island, N.Y., March 28, 1995, composer pianist). **VOCAL:** *War is Kind* for Soloists and Small Orch. (1976; rev. for Soprano, Narrator, Oboe, String Quartet, and Piano, 1992; N.Y., Jan. 1993); *Hopkins Suite* for Baritone, Speaker, and Piano, after Gerard Manley Hopkins (1991); solo songs.—NS/LK/DM

Root, Frederick W(oodman), American organist, singing teacher, writer on music, and composer, son of **George Frederick Root;** b. Boston, June 13, 1846; d. Chicago, Nov. 8, 1916. He was taught by his father, then by B.C. Blodgett and William Mason in N.Y. In 1863 he became organist of the 3rd Presbyterian Church in Chicago, and in 1865 of the Swedenborgian Church. In

1869–70 he traveled in Europe, studying singing with Vannuccini in Florence. He publ. singing manuals and vocal collections, and composed anthems, cantatas, songs.—NS/LK/DM

Root, George Frederick, American music educator, music publisher, and composer, father of **Frederick W(oodman) Root;** b. Sheffield, Mass., Aug. 30, 1820; d. Bailey's Island, Maine, Aug. 6, 1895. He was a pupil of George J. Webb in Boston, then lived in N.Y. He was organist of the Church of the Strangers. Going to Chicago in 1859, he joined the music publishing firm of Root and Cady, established in 1858 by his elder brother, Ebenezer Towner Root, and Chauncey Marvin Cady; it was dissolved in 1871. He wrote many popular songs (*Battlecry of Freedom; Tramp, tramp, tramp; Just before the battle, Mother*) and publ. numerous collections of church music and school songs. For some of his earlier compositions he used the German tr. of his name, Friedrich Wurzel, as a pseudonym. He wrote an autobiography, *The Story of a Musical Life* (Cincinnati, 1891).

BIBL.: P. Carder, *G.F. R., Pioneer Music Educator: His Contributions to Mass Instruction in Music* (diss., Univ. of Md., 1971). —NS/LK/DM

Rootering, Jan-Hendrik, German bass; b. Wedingfeld, March 18, 1950. He first studied with his father, a voice teacher, and then at the Hamburg Hochschule für Musik. In 1980 he made his operatic debut as Colline at the Hamburg State Opera, and then sang there regularly. He also appeared at the Bavarian State Opera in Munich from 1982, and was made a Bavarian Kammersänger in 1989. In 1983 he portrayed King Marke in Frankfurt am Main. On Jan. 15, 1987, he made his Metropolitan Opera debut in N.Y. as the Landgrave, and subsequently sang such roles there as Claggart, Sparafucile, and Pogner (1993). In 1987 he was engaged as Orestes in Geneva, Sarastro at London's Covent Garden, and Marcel in *Les Huguenots* at the Deutsche Oper in Berlin. He sang Gurnemanz at the Opéra de la Bastille in Paris in 1997. In 1999 he portrayed Hans Sachs at the Lyric Opera of Chicago. He also sang as a soloist with orchs. and as a recitalist. Among his other roles were Fasolt, Falstaff, and Baron Ochs.—NS/LK/DM

Rootham, Cyril (Bradley), English organist, teacher, and composer; b. Bristol, Oct. 5, 1875; d. Cambridge, March 18, 1938. He studied music with his father, Daniel Rootham (1837–1922). He won classical and musical scholarships at St. John's Coll., Cambridge (B.A., 1897; Mus.B., 1900; M.A., 1901; Mus.Doc., 1910), and finished at the Royal Coll. of Music in London under Stanford, Parratt, and Barton. He was organist (from 1901) and a lecturer (from 1913) at St. John's Coll., Cambridge; also conductor of the Univ. Musical Soc. there (1912–36). His career as a composer was very much bound to the musical life of Cambridge. He brought out his opera, *The 2 Sisters*, there on Feb. 14, 1922; also wrote *For the Fallen* for Chorus and Orch. (1919) and *Brown Earth* (London, March 14, 1923). His 2nd Sym., *Revelation* (with a choral ending), was performed posthumously by the BBC, March 17, 1939.

Other works include *Pan*, rhapsody for Orch. (1912), String Quintet (1909), String Quartet (1914), Septet for Viola, Flute, Oboe, Clarinet, Bassoon, Horn, and Harp (1930), and Piano Trio (1931).—**NS/LK/DM**

Ropartz, (Joseph) Guy (Marie), French conductor, teacher, and composer; b. Guingamp, Côtes-du-Nord, June 15, 1864; d. Lanloup-par-Plouha, Côtes-du-Nord, Nov. 22, 1955. He entered the Paris Cons. as a pupil of Dubois and Massenet, and then took lessons in organ and composition from Franck, who remained his chief influence in composition. From 1894 to 1919 he was director of the Cons. and conductor of the sym. concerts at Nancy. From 1919 to 1929 he conducted the Municipal Orch. and was director of the Cons. in Strasbourg. In 1949 he was elected a member of the Institut de France.

WORKS: DRAMATIC: O p e r a : *Le Pays* (1910; Nancy, Feb. 1, 1912). **B a l l e t :** *Prélude dominical et 6 pièces à donner pour chaque jour de la semaine* (1929); *L'Indiscret* (1931). **I n c i - d e n t a l   M u s i c   T o :** *Le Pêcheur d'Islande* (1891); *Le Mystère de saint Nicolas* (1905); *Oedipe à Colonne* (1914). **ORCH.:** *La Cloche des morts* (1887); *Les Landes* (1888); *Marche de fête* (1888); *5 pièces bréves* (1889); *Carnaval* (1889); *Sérénade* (1892); *Dimanche breton* (1893); 5 syms.: No. 1 (1894), No. 2 (1900), No. 3 for Chorus and Orch. (1905), No. 4 (1910), and No. 5 (1944); *À Marie endormie* (1912); *La Chasse du prince Arthur* (1912); *Soir sur les Chaumes* (1913); *Divertissement* (1915); *Romanza e Scherzino* for Violin and Orch. (1926); *Rapsodie* for Cello and Orch. (Paris, Nov. 3, 1928); *Concerto for Orchestra* (1930); *Sérénade champêtre* (1932; Paris, Feb. 24, 1934); *Bourrées bourbonnaises* (1939); *Petite symphonie* for Chamber Orch. (1943); *Divertimento* (1947). **CHAMBER:** 6 string quartets (1893, 1912, 1925, 1934, 1940, 1951); 2 cello sonatas (1904, 1918); 3 violin sonatas (1907, 1917, 1927); Piano Trio (1918); String Trio (1935). **P i a n o :** *Dans l'ombre de la montagne* (1913); *Musiques au jardin* (1917); *Croquis d'été* (1918); *Croquis d'automne* (1929); *Jeunes filles* (1929). **VO- CAL:** 5 motets (1900); *Requiem* for Soloists, Chorus, and Orch. (1938; Paris, April 7, 1939); *De Profundis* for Solo Voice, Chorus, and Orch. (1942); masses; songs.

BIBL.: F. Lamy, *J.-G. R.: L'homme et l'oeuvre* (Paris, 1948); L. Kornprobst, *J.-G. R.* (Strasbourg, 1949); *Livre du centenaire de J. G. R.* (Paris, 1966).—**NS/LK/DM**

Roppolo, Leon (Joseph), New Orleans clarinetist, composer; b. Lutcher, La., March 16, 1902; d. La., Oct. 5, 1943. He had his first music lessons from his father, who was a clarinetist, also learned guitar which he played occasionally throughout his career. His cousin Feno was also a clarinetist. He did early gigs at Bucktown, Lake Pontchartrain, with Georg Brunis, later working with pianist Eddie Shields and with Santo Pecora in various clubs in New Orleans, and played residency at Tore's Club (c. 1917). He left New Orleans in a band accompanying vocalist Bea Palmer; subsequently worked with Carlisle Evans's Band on riverboats and played residencies in Davenport, Iowa. Roppolo moved to Chicago with boyhood friends Georg Brunis and Paul Mares to join the Friars' Inn Society Orch. (c. 1921), later named The New Orleans Rhythm Kings. After 18 months he traveled to N.Y. with Paul Mares and joined Al Siegal's Orch. at Mills Caprice in Greenwich Village. He moved to Tex. and joined Peck

Kelley's Bad Boys (summer 1924), then rejoined Carlisle Evans in St. Paul, was taken ill at Marigold Gardens, Minn., and returned to New Orleans. After playing in a revived New Orleans Rhythm Kings (with Paul Mares) in New Orleans (spring 1925), Roppolo subsequently suffered severe breakdown and was committed to a La. mental home. Despite his breakdown, he continued to play regularly, mainly on tenor sax; he organized a band in the mental institution. He was temporarily released in the early 1940s; returned home to New Orleans, played two nights for Santo Pecora on the S. S. Capitol and sat in with Abbie Brunies on tenor sax. He was an inventive player, and also took composer/co-composer credits, "Farewell Blues," "Milenberg Joys," and "Tin Roof Blues."—**LP**

Rore, Cipriano de, celebrated Flemish composer; b. 1515 or 1516; d. Parma, Sept. 1565. He may have been born in Machelen (near Ghent), Mechelen, or Antwerp, and he appears to have spent his youth in Machelen before setting out for Italy. He went to Venice, where he may have been a pupil of Willaert, the maestro di cappella at San Marco; publ. his first book of madrigals in 1542. He may have entered the service of the Duke of Ferrara, Ercole II, as maestro di cappella as early as 1545, although records do not list him until 1547. After the death of Ercole II in 1559, Rore entered the service of Margaret of Parma, the governor of the Netherlands, at her court at Brussels. By 1561 he was in the service of her husband, Ottavio Farnese, in Parma. In 1563 he was elected Willaert's successor as maestro di cappella at San Marco. Because of problems in the cappella, he quit his post in 1564 and returned to Parma. Rore was one of the great masters of the madrigal. He was a major influence on such composers as Lasso, Monte, and Monteverdi. He also wrote a number of outstanding sacred works. The complete works, ed. by B. Meier, in Corpus Mensurabilis Musicae, commenced publication in 1959.

WORKS: VOCAL: S a c r e d : *Motectorum liber primus* for 5 Voices (Venice, 1544); *Motetta* for 5 Voices (Venice, 1545); *Il terzo libro di motetti* for 5 Voices (Venice, 1549); *Passio...secundum Joannem* for 2 to 6 Voices (Paris, 1557); *Motetta* for 4 Voices (Venice, 1563); *Sacrae cantiones* for 5 to 7 Voices (Venice, 1595). **M a d r i g a l s :** *I madrigali* for 5 Voices (Venice, 1542; 2nd ed., enl., 1544, as *Il primo libro de madregali cromatici*); *Il secondo libro de madregali* for 5 Voices (Venice, 1544); *Il terzo libro di madrigali* for 5 Voices (Venice, 1548); *Musica...sopra le stanze del Petrarcha...libro terzo* for 5 Voices (Venice, 1548); *Il primo libro de madrigali* for 4 Voices (Ferrara, 1550); *Il quarto libro de'i madrigali* for 5 Voices (Venice, 1557); *Il secondo libro de madregali* for 4 Voices (Venice, 1557); *Li madrigali libro quarto* for 5 Voices (Venice, 1562); *Le vive fiamme de' vaghi e dilettevoli madrigali* for 4 to 5 Voices (Venice, 1565); *Il quinto libro de madrigali* for 5 Voices (Venice, 1566). **C h a n s o n s :** *Il primo libro de madrigali* for 4 Voices (Ferrara, 1550). **S e c u l a r   L a t i n   M o t e t s :** *Motetta* for 5 Voices (Venice, 1545); *Le vive fiamme de' vaghi e dilettevoli madrigali* for 4 and 5 Voices (Venice, 1565); *Il quinto libro de madrigali* for 5 Voices (Venice, 1566).

BIBL.: U. Rossi, *Sei lettere di C. d.R., con cenni biografici* (Reggio Emilia, 1888); R. van Aerde, *Notice sur la vie et les oeuvres de C. d.R.* (Mechelen, 1909); J. Musiol, *Cyprian d.R., ein Meister der venezianischen Schule* (Breslau, 1933).—**NS/LK/DM**

Rorem, Ned, brilliant American composer, pianist, and writer; b. Richmond, Ind., Oct. 23, 1923. His father, C. Rufus Rorem, was a medical economist, and his mother, Gladys Miller Rorem, was a civil rights activist. Following piano lessons with Margaret Bonds as a youth, he entered the American Cons. in Chicago in 1938 to study harmony with Sowerby. After further training with Nolte at Northwestern Univ. (1940–42) and Scalero at the Curtis Inst. of Music in Philadelphia (1942–44), he went to N.Y. and received private lessons in orchestration from Virgil Thomson (1944) and then pursued training in composition with Wagenaar at the Juilliard School of Music (B.S., 1946; M.S., 1948). During the summers of 1946 and 1947, he studied with Copland at the Berkshire Music Center in Tanglewood. In 1949 he went to Paris, where he rapidly absorbed French musical culture and mastered the French language. After a sojourn in Morocco (1949–51), he lived in Paris until 1957, where he found a patroness in the Vicomtesse Noailles and moved in the circle of modern French intelligentsia. In 1951 he received a Fulbright fellowship and in 1957 a Guggenheim fellowship. From 1959 to 1961 he was composer-in-residence at the State Univ. of N.Y. at Buffalo. In 1965 he became a prof. of composition at the Univ. of Utah, where he later was composer-in-residence (until 1967). He received an award from the National Inst. of Arts and Letters in 1968. In 1971 and 1975 he received ASCAP-Deems Taylor awards for his outstanding achievements as a writer. In 1976 he won the Pulitzer Prize in Music for his *Air Music* for Orch. In 1978 he received a 2nd Guggenheim fellowship. In 1980 he became a teacher of composition at the Curtis Inst. of Music. In 1980, 1982, 1985, and 1990 he served as composer-in-residence at the Santa Fe Chamber Music Festival. In 2000 he became president of the American Academy of Arts and Letters. Rorem is one of America's most distinguished and original compositional craftsmen. A born linguist, he has a natural feeling for vocal line and for prosody of text. He is without question one of the finest composers of art songs America has produced. An elegant stylist in French as well as in English, he has publ. 14 books recounting with gracious insouciance his encounters in Paris and N.Y., as well as collections of essays on matters strictly musical.

WORKS: DRAMATIC: O p e r a : *Cain and Abel* (1946); *A Childhood Miracle* (1952; N.Y., May 10, 1955); *The Robbers* (1956; N.Y., April 14, 1958); *Miss Julie* (N.Y., Nov. 4, 1965; rev. 1978; N.Y., April 5, 1979); *3 Sisters Who Are Not Sisters* (1968; Philadelphia, July 24, 1971); *Bertha* (1968; N.Y., Nov. 26, 1973); *Fables*, 5 short operas (1970; Martin, Tenn., May 21, 1971); *Hearing* (1976; N.Y., March 15, 1977; arranged from a song cycle, 1966). **M u s i c a l C o m e d y :** *The Ticklish Acrobat* (1958). **B a l l e t :** *Lost in Fear* (1945); *Death of the Black Knight* (1948); *Ballet for Jerry* (1951); *Melos* (1951); *Dorian Gray* (1952); *Early Voyagers* (1959); *Excursions* (1965). Also incidental music. **ORCH.:** *Overture for G.I.'s* for Band (1944); 3 piano concertos: No. 1 (1948; withdrawn), No. 2 (1950), and No. 3, *Piano Concerto in 6 Movements* (1969; Pittsburgh, Dec. 3, 1970); Overture (1949); 3 syms.: No. 1 (1950), No. 2 (La Jolla, Calif., Aug. 5, 1956), and No. 3 (1958; N.Y., April 16, 1959); *Design* (1953; Louisville, May 29, 1955); *Sinfonia* for Wind Orch. (Pittsburgh, July 14, 1957); *Eagles* (1958; Philadelphia, Oct. 23, 1959); *Pilgrims* for Strings (1958; N.Y., Jan. 30, 1959); *Ideas* (1961); *Lions (A Dream)* (1963; N.Y., Oct.

28, 1965); *Water Music* for Clarinet, Violin, and Orch. (1966; Oakland, Calif., April 9, 1967); *Air Music* (1974; Cincinnati, Dec. 5, 1975); *Assembly and Fall* (Raleigh, N.C., Oct. 11, 1975); *Sunday Morning* (1977; Saratoga, N.Y., Aug. 25, 1978); *Remembering Tommy* for Cello, Piano, and Orch. (1979; Cincinnati, Nov. 13, 1981); Organ Concerto (Portland, Maine, March 19, 1985); String Sym. (Atlanta, Oct. 31, 1985); Violin Concerto (Springfield, Mass., March 30, 1985); *Frolic*, fanfare (Houston, April 12, 1986); *A Quaker Reader* for Chamber Orch. (N.Y., Oct. 9, 1988; orchestration of 8 of 11 pieces from the organ works, 1976); *Fantasy and Polka* (1988; Evian, France, May 20, 1989); Concerto for Piano, Left-hand, and Orch. (1991; Philadelphia, Feb. 4, 1993); English Horn Concerto (1992; N.Y., Jan. 27, 1994); *Triptych*, 3 pieces for Chamber Orch. (Bexley, Ohio, Oct. 4, 1993); Double Concerto for Violin, Cello, and Orch. (Indianapolis, Oct. 15, 1998). **CHAMBER:** *Concertino da Camera* for Harpsichord and 7 Instruments (1947; Minneapolis, Oct. 10, 1993); 3 string quartets (1947, withdrawn; 1950; 1991); *Mountain Song* for Flute and Piano (1949); Violin Sonata (1949); *3 Slow Pieces* for Cello and Piano (1950, 1959, 1970; N.Y., Oct. 8, 1977); *11 Studies* for 11 Players (Buffalo, May 17, 1960); Trio for Flute, Cello, and Piano (1960); *Lovers* for Harpsichord, Oboe, Celli, and Percussion (N.Y., Dec. 15, 1964); *Day Music* for Violin and Piano (1971; Ames, Iowa, Oct. 15, 1972); *Night Music* for Violin and Piano (1972; Washington, D.C., Jan. 12, 1973); *Solemn Prelude*, fanfare for Brass (N.Y., May 1973); *Book of Hours* for Flute and Harp (1975; N.Y., Feb. 29, 1976); *Sky Music* for Harp (Albuquerque, June 1976); *Romeo and Juliet* for Flute and Guitar (1977; N.Y., March 1, 1978); *After Reading Shakespeare* for Cello (1980; N.Y., March 15, 1981); Suite for Guitar (Cuyahoga Falls, Ohio, July 25, 1980); *Winter Pages*, quintet for Clarinet, Bassoon, Violin, Cello, and Piano (1981; N.Y., Feb. 14, 1982); *Dances* for Cello and Piano (1983; Detroit, May 5, 1984); *Picnic on the Marne*, 7 waltzes for Alto Saxophone and Piano (N.Y., Feb. 14, 1984); *The End of Summer* for Clarinet, Violin, and Piano (1985; Bombay, March 26, 1986); *Scenes from Childhood*, septet for Oboe, Horn, Piano, and String Quartet (Santa Fe, Aug. 11, 1985); *Bright Music* for Flute, 2 Violins, Cello, and Piano (1987; Bridgehampton, N.Y., Aug. 6, 1988); *Fanfare and Flourish* for 2 Trumpets, 2 Trombones, and Organ (N.Y., Oct. 16, 1988); *Diversions* for Brass Quintet (1989; Nantucket, Mass., July 11, 1990); *Spring Music* for Violin, Cello, and Piano (1990; N.Y., Feb. 8, 1991). **KEYBOARD: P i a n o :** Sonata for Piano, 4-Hands (1943); 3 sonatas (1948, 1949, 1954); *A Quiet Afternoon* (1948); *Toccata* (1948); *Barcarolles* (1949); Suite for 2 Pianos (1949); *Sicilienne* for 2 Pianos (1950); *Burlesque* (1955); *Slow Waltz* (1958); *8 Etudes* (1975; Washington, D.C., March 13, 1976); *Song and Dance* (1986; College Park, Md., July 12, 1987); *For Shirley* for Piano, 4-Hands (1989). **O r g a n :** *Fantasy and Toccata* (1946); *Pastorale* (1950); *A Quaker Reader* (1976; N.Y., Feb. 2, 1977; 8 movements orchestrated for Chamber Orch., 1988); *Views from the Oldest House* (1981; Washington, D.C., June 29, 1982); *Organbook I* (N.Y., Oct. 30, 1989), *II* (1989; Nantucket, Mass., July 7, 1990) and *III* (1989; Nantucket, Mass., July 7, 1990). **H a r p s i c h o r d :** *Spiders* (1968; Waterloo, Ontario, July 23, 1969). **VOCAL:** *The 70th Psalm* for Chorus and Wind Ensemble (Washington, D.C., Aug. 1943); *The Long Home* for Chorus and Orch. (1946); *Mourning Scene from Samuel* for Voice and String Quartet (1947); *A Sermon on Miracles* for Voice, Chorus, and Strings (Boston, Nov. 30, 1947); *6 Irish Poems* for Voice and Orch. (1950); *The Poet's Requiem* for Soprano, Chorus, and Orch. (1955; N.Y., Feb. 15, 1957); *Miracles of Christmas* for Chorus and Organ or Piano (1959); *King Midas*, cantata for Voice(s) and Piano (1961; N.Y., March 11, 1962); *2 Psalms and a Proverb* for Chorus and 5 Strings (1962); *Lift Up*

Your Heads (The Ascension) for Chorus, Wind Ensemble, and Timpani (1963; Washington, D.C., May 7, 1964); *Laudemus Tempus Actum* for Chorus and Orch. or Piano (1964); *Letters from Paris* for Chorus and Small Orch. (1966; Ann Arbor, April 25, 1969); *Prosper for the Votive Mass of the Holy Spirit* for Chorus and Organ (1966); *Sun* for Soprano and Orch. (1966; N.Y., July 1, 1967); *Praises for the Nativity* for 4 Soloists, Chorus, and Organ (1970); *Ariel* for Soprano, Clarinet, and Piano (Washington, D.C., Nov. 26, 1971); *Little Prayers* for Soprano, Baritone, Chorus, and Orch. (1973; Sioux City, Iowa, April 20, 1974); *Missa Brevis* for 4 Soloists and Chorus (1973; Cleveland, June 17, 1974); *Serenade on 5English Poems* for Voice, Violin, Viola, and Piano (1975; Akron, May 23, 1976); *The Santa Fe Songs* for Medium Voice, Violin, Viola, Cello, and Piano (Santa Fe, July 27, 1980); *After Long Silence* for Voice, Oboe, and String Orch. (Miami, June 11, 1982); *A Whitman Cantata* for Men's Chorus, 12 Brass, and Timpani (N.Y., Sept. 11, 1983); *An American Oratorio* for Tenor, Chorus, and Orch. (1984; Pittsburgh, Jan. 4, 1985); *Pilgrim Strangers* for 6 Men's Voices (N.Y., Nov. 16, 1984); *Homer*, 3 scenes from *The Iliad*, for Chorus and 8 Instruments (1986; Lancaster, Pa., April 12, 1987); *The Death of Moses* for Chorus and Organ (1987; N.Y., Jan. 29, 1988); *The Schuyler Songs* for Voice and Orch. (1987; Fargo, N.Dak., April 23, 1988); *Te Deum* for Chorus, 2 Trumpets, 2 Trombones, and Organ (Indianapolis, July 19, 1987); *Goodbye My Fancy*, oratorio for Alto, Baritone, Chorus, and Orch. (1988; Chicago, Nov. 8, 1990); *The Auden Poems* for Voice, Violin, Cello, and Piano (1989; Santa Fe, July 29, 1990); *Swords and Plowshares* for 4 Soloists and Orch. (1990; Boston, Nov. 14, 1991); *Songs of Sadness* for Voice, Guitar, Cello, and Clarinet (N.Y., Oct. 30, 1994); *Present Laughter* for Chorus, 4 Brasses, and Piano (1995); *Evidence of Things Not Seen*, 36 songs for 4 Voices and Piano (1996); numerous other choral pieces, both sacred and secular; song cycles; some 200 solo songs.

WRITINGS (all publ. in N.Y.): *The Paris Diary of Ned Rorem* (1966; reprint, 1983, with *The New York Diary*, as *The Paris and New York Diaries*); *The New York Diary* (1967; reprint, 1983, with *The Paris Diary of Ned Rorem*, as *The Paris and New York Diaries*); *Music from the Inside Out* (1967); *Music and People* (1968); *Critical Affairs: A Composer's Journal* (1970); *Pure Contraption: A Composer's Essays* (1973); *The Final Diary, 1961–1972* (1974; reprint, 1983, as *The Later Diaries of Ned Rorem*); *An Absolute Gift: A New Diary* (1977); *Setting the Tone: Essays and a Diary* (1983); *The Nantucket Diary of Ned Rorem, 1973–1985* (1987); *Settling the Score: Essays on Music* (1988); *Knowing When to Stop: A Memoir* (1994); *Other Entertainment: Collected Pieces* (1996).

BIBL.: A. McDonald, *N. R.: A Bio-Bibliography* (Westport, Conn., 1989).—NS/LK/DM

Rosa, Carl (real name, **Karl August Nikolaus Rose**), German violinist, conductor, and opera impresario; b. Hamburg, March 22, 1842; d. Paris, April 30, 1889. At 12 he made tours as a violinist in England, Denmark, and Germany; studied further in the conservatories of Leipzig (1859) and Paris. He was concertmaster at Hamburg (1863–65), and gave a concert at the Crystal Palace in London (March 10, 1866). He toured in the U.S. with Bateman, meeting Euphrosyne Parepa and marrying her in N.Y. in 1867. They organized an English opera company and toured America until 1871, then returned to London. After his wife's death in 1874, he produced opera in English in various London theaters, forming the Carl Rosa Opera Co. (1875), which gave regular performances at the Theatre Royal at Drury Lane (from 1883). Following Rosa's death, the company became notably successful as a touring enterprise, being granted the title of the Royal Carl Rosa Opera Co. by Queen Victoria in 1893. It remained active until 1958.—NS/LK/DM

Rosa, Salvator(e), Italian painter, poet, and musician; b. Arenella, near Naples, June 21, 1615; d. Rome, March 15, 1673. He studied music and became an expert lute player. From 1635 to 1640 he divided his time between Rome and Naples, and from 1640 to 1649 was court painter to the Medici at Florence; then lived in Rome. The pieces credited to Rosa by Burney and others have been proved to be spurious; it is doubtful whether Rosa ever composed music. His satire, *La musica*, written about 1640 and containing sharp criticism of Italian church music of his day, was publ. posthumously in 1695, and was reprinted several times. Mattheson attacked Rosa's views in his *Mithridat, wider den Gift einer welschen Satyre des Salvator Rosa* (1749).

BIBL.: D. Battesti, *Saggio sulla vita e le satire di S. R.* (Bourges, 1913); F. Gerra, *S. R. e la sua vita romana dal 1650 al 1672...* (a summary of 200 letters written by Rosa; Rome, 1937). —NS/LK/DM

Rosand, Aaron, gifted American violinist and pedagogue; b. Hammond, Ind., March 15, 1927. A child prodigy, he made his formal debut at age 9 in a recital at Chicago's Civic Opera House, sharing the occasion with Jan Peerce, who was also making his Chicago debut. After studies with P. Marinus Paulsen (1935–39) and Leon Sametini (1940–44), he completed his training with Zimbalist at the Curtis Inst. of Music in Philadelphia (1944–48). He made his N.Y. debut in a Town Hall recital (1948); following his European debut in Copenhagen (1955), he pursued an international career as a virtuoso. He taught at the Curtis Inst. of Music (from 1981). A charismatic performer, blessed with a singing tone supported by an extraordinary technique, he established himself as a champion of the Romantic repertoire. In addition to the standard literature, he has consistently sought out rarely heard compositions by Spohr, Godard, Wieniawski, Lalo, Vieuxtemps, and many others for performance at his concerts.—NS/LK/DM

Rosbaud, Hans, eminent Austrian conductor; b. Graz, July 22, 1895; d. Lugano, Dec. 29, 1962. He studied at the Hoch Cons. in Frankfurt am Main. He was director of the Hochschule für Musik in Mainz (1921–30); also conducted the City Orch. there; served as 1st Kapellmeister of the Frankfurt am Main Radio and of the Museumgesellschaft concerts (1928–37); then was Generalmusikdirektor in Munster (1937–41) and in Strasbourg (1941–44); subsequently was appointed Generalmusikdirektor of the Munich Phil. (1945). In 1948 he became chief conductor of the Sym. Orch. of the Southwest Radio in Baden–Baden, and in 1957, music director of the Tonhalle Orch. in Zürich. He particularly distinguished himself as a conductor of modern works. He conducted the first performance of Schoenberg's *Moses und Aron* (concert perf., Hamburg, 1954); also conducted its first stage performance (Zürich, 1957).

BIBL.: J. Evans, *H. R.: A Bio-Bibliography* (N.Y., 1992). —NS/LK/DM

Rosé, Arnold (Josef), distinguished Austrian violinist and pedagogue; b. Iaşi, Oct. 24, 1863; d. London, Aug. 25, 1946. He studied under Karl Heissler at the Vienna Cons., and made his professional debut at the Gewandhaus in Leipzig, Oct. 30, 1879. In 1881 he was appointed concertmaster of the Vienna Phil. and Opera orch., a post he held for 57 years. He also founded the Rosé quartet in 1882, which won a high reputation throughout Europe; the quartet made its American debut at the Library of Congress in Washington, D.C., on April 28, 1928. Rosé taught at the Vienna Academy of Music (1893–1924). In the face of the Nazi Anschluss, he fled in 1938 to London, where he made his last public appearance in 1945. In 1902 Rosé married Justine Mahler, a sister of Gustav Mahler.—**NS/LK/DM**

Rose, Bernard (William George), English organist, conductor, musicologist, and composer; b. Little Hallingbury, Hertfordshire, May 9, 1916. He studied with Alcock at the Royal Coll. of Music in London (1933–35), and subsequently was an organ scholar at St. Catharine's Coll., Cambridge, where his principal mentors were Middleton and Dent (B.A., 1938; Mus.B., 1939). He then was organist (1939–57), teacher (1946–55), and lecturer (1955–81) at Queen's Coll., Oxford; was also made a supernumerary Fellow (1949) and an official Fellow (1954) there, obtaining his D.Mus. (1955). He served as organist, Informator choristarum, and Fellow at Magdalen Coll., Oxford (1957–81), where he also was vice-president (1973–75). Throughout his career he was active as a conductor, being mainly known for his choral performances. He was president of the Royal Coll. of Organists (1974–76). In 1980 he was made an Officer of the Order of the British Empire. He prepared numerous eds. of English works ranging from the 16th to the 18th century, and also composed a number of sacred works.—**NS/LK/DM**

Rose, Jerome, noted American pianist and teacher; b. Los Angeles, Aug. 12, 1938. He was a pupil of Adolf Baller at the San Francisco Cons. (1952–56), making his debut at the age of 15 with the San Francisco Sym. Orch. He studied piano and chamber music with Shure at the Mannes Coll. of Music in N.Y. (B.S., 1960; M.S., 1961), and also with Serkin at the Marlboro (Vt.) School of Music (1956, 1965). In 1961 he captured 1st prize at the Busoni Competition in Bolzano, and then pursued an international career. In 1981 he organized the International Festival of the Romantics in London. In 1986 he organized the Franz Liszt Celebration in Washington, D.C., and was also awarded the Franz Liszt Medal by the Hungarian government. He was artist-in-residence at Bowling Green (Ohio) State Univ. (from 1963); also visiting artist-in-residence at the Univ. of Mich. in Ann Arbor (1984–85). Rose has won special praise for his performances of the Romantic repertoire; in addition to his compelling readings of Liszt, he gives fine interpretations of Beethoven, Schubert, Schumann, and Chopin. He is pianist-author of the film *For the Young Virtuoso: A Piano Master class with Jerome Rose* (1987).—**NS/LK/DM**

Rose, Leonard (Joseph), eminent American cellist and pedagogue; b. Washington, D.C., July 27, 1918; d. White Plains, N.Y., Nov. 16, 1984. He began to study the cello at age 10, and enrolled at the Miami Cons. when he was 11, continuing his training with Walter Grossman. He then went to N.Y. to study with his cousin, Frank Miller, and subsequently received a scholarship to the Curtis Inst. of Music in Philadelphia, where he completed his studies with Felix Salmond (1934–38). He was asst. 1st cellist of the NBC Sym. Orch. in N.Y. (1938–39), then 1st cellist of the Cleveland Orch. (1939–43). He also served as head of the cello depts. at the Cleveland Inst. of Music and the Oberlin (Ohio) Cons. In 1943 he became 1st cellist of the N.Y. Phil.; appeared at his concerto debut with it at Carnegie Hall on Jan. 29, 1944; resigned his post in 1951 and embarked upon a brilliant career as a virtuoso of the first rank in appearances as a soloist with the world's great orchs.; also gave recitals and appeared in numerous chamber music settings, later serving as a member of the renowned Istomin-Stern- Rose Trio (from 1961). He taught at the Juilliard School of Music in N.Y. (1947–51; 1962–84) and at the Curtis Inst. of Music (1951–62). Among his notable pupils were Stephen Kates, Lynn Harrell, and Yo-Yo Ma.—**NS/LK/DM**

Roseingrave, family of English musicians:

(1) Daniel Roseingrave, organist and composer; b. 1650; d. Dublin, May 1727. He was organist at Gloucester (1679–81), Winchester (1682–92), and Salisbury (1692–98) cathedrals. After settling in Dublin, he was organist and stipendiary at Christ Church Cathedral from 1698. From 1698 to 1719 he was also organist and lay vicar at St. Patrick's Cathedral. He composed several sacred works. He had 2 sons who became musicians:

(2) Thomas Roseingrave, organist, teacher, and composer; b. Winchester, 1688; d. Dunleary, June 23, 1766. He was taken to Dublin by his father, who was his first teacher. He attended Trinity Coll. and then was sent to Italy for further music study in 1709. During his Italian sojourn, he was befriended by Alessandro and Domenico Scarlatti. Returning to England about 1714, he was active in London. He promoted the music of Domenico Scarlatti, and presented the composer's opera *Amor d'un'ombra e Gelosea d'un'aura* under the title *Narciso* in 1720, for which he himself wrote 2 arias and 2 duets. He also publ. an edition of 42 of Scarlatti's sonatas in 1739. In 1725 he became organist at St. George's, Hanover Square. Ill health restricted his activities from 1744, and about 1749 he returned to Dublin. He was particularly known as a composer of keyboard pieces.

WORKS: *Phaedra and Hippolitus,* opera (Dublin, March 6, 1753); Harpsichord Concerto; *A Celebrated Concerto* for Harpsichord, and other harpsichord pieces; organ music; 12 Italian cantatas (London, 1735); anthems; songs.

(3) Ralph Roseingrave, organist and composer; b. Salisbury, c. 1695; d. Dublin, 1747. He studied with his father, whom he succeeded as organist at St. Patrick's Cathedral in 1719, a post he officially assumed in 1726. At his father's death in 1727, he also became his successor at Christ Church Cathedral. He composed sacred music and organ pieces.—**LK/DM**

Rösel, Peter, outstanding German pianist and teacher; b. Dresden, Feb. 2, 1945. He began training in his youth. In 1963 he won 2nd prize in the International Schumann Competition in Zwickau. He was then chosen by the German Democratic Republic's Ministry of Culture for further training at the Moscow Cons., where he studied with Dmitri Bashkirov and Lev Oborin, graduating in 1969. In 1978 he made a highly successful tour of the U.S. as piano soloist with the Gewandhaus Orch. of Leipzig. He became a prof. at the Dresden Hochschule für Musik in 1985. Apart from a brilliant technique, Rosel has a Romantic sensitivity characteristic of the Russian mode of instrumental playing; his repertoire is comprehensive, ranging from Mozart to Prokofiev.

BIBL.: H.-P. Müller, *P. R.: Für Sie porträtiert* (Leipzig, 1986). —NS/LK/DM

Rosell, Lars-Erik, Swedish composer, teacher, and organist; b. Nybro, Aug. 9, 1944. He studied organ (1962–68) and was a composition student of Ingvar Lidholm at the Stockholm Musikhögskolan (1968–72). He then taught counterpoint there (from 1973). He was also active as an organist, becoming well known for his advocacy of contemporary scores. In his music, he often requires improvisation from performers.

WORKS: *Moments of a Changing Sonority* for Harpsichord, Hammond Organ, and Strings (1969); *Terry Riley* for 3 Pianos (1970); *Twilight* for Chamber Ensemble (1970); *Dorian Mode* for Piano, Vibraphone, Clarinet, Cello, and Trombone (1971); *3 Psaltarpsalmer* for Chorus and Instruments (1971); *Poem in the Dark* for Mezzo-soprano, Flute, Trombone, Double Bass, and Percussion, after Sachs (1972); *Efter syndafallet*, dramatic scene for Soprano, Alto, Baritone, and Instrumental Ensemble, after Arthur Miller's play *After the Fall* (Stockholm, Feb. 15, 1973); *Nattesang*, chamber opera (Copenhagen, Dec. 15, 1974); *Visiones prophetae*, biblical scene for Soloists, 3 Choruses, Wind Orch., Harp, Organ, and 2 Double Basses (Lund, June 27, 1974); *Musik* for Cello and String Orch. (Stockholm, March 4, 1975); *Expando* for Orch. (1976); *Reflections* for Trombone and Organ (1979); *Ordens kalla*, scenic cantata (Stockholm, Nov. 7, 1980); *Stages* for 7 Instruments (1980); *Tillfallig avbrott*, chamber opera (Stockholm, Dec. 12, 1981); Organ Concerto (Stockholm, Nov. 25, 1982); *Amedee*, chamber opera (1983–85); 2 string quartets (1989; 1994–98); Viola Sonata (1989); *Fantasie concertante* for Cello and Orch. (1992); Overture for Organ (1993); *Musica dolce* for Flute (1994); *Fem preludier* for Organ (1996); *Vaggsång* for Mezzo-soprano and Piano (1996).—**NS/LK/DM**

Rosen, Charles (Welles), erudite American pianist, teacher, and writer on music; b. N.Y., May 5, 1927. He began piano studies when he was only 4. Between the ages of 7 and 11 he studied at the Juilliard School of Music in N.Y., and then took piano lessons with Moriz Rosenthal and Hedwig Kanner-Rosenthal (1938–44). He continued his training with the latter (1944–52) and also received lessons in theory and composition from Karl Wiegl. He concurrently studied music history at Princeton Univ. (B.A., 1947; M.A., 1949), where he took his Ph.D. in Romance languages in 1951. In 1951 he made his debut in N.Y., and subsequently appeared as a soloist with major orchs. and as a recitalist. He was asst. prof. of modern languages at the Mass. Inst. of Technol-

ogy (1953–55). In 1971 he became prof. of music at the State Univ. of N.Y. at Stony Brook. In 1976–77 he also was the Ernest Bloch Prof. of Music at the Univ. of Calif. at Berkeley. As a pianist, Rosen has garnered notable distinction for his insightful interpretations of Bach, Beethoven, and Debussy, and for his traversal of such 20th–century composers as Schoenberg, Webern, Boulez, and Carter. He has contributed brilliant articles on various subjects to various publications. In 1972 he received the National Book Award for his distinguished vol. *The Classical Style: Haydn, Mozart, Beethoven* (N.Y., 1971). His subsequent books included *Arnold Schoenberg* (N.Y., 1975), *Sonata Forms* (N.Y., 1980; 2nd ed., rev., 1988), *Frontiers of Meaning: Three Informal Lectures on Music* (N.Y., 1994), and *The Romantic Generation* (Cambridge, Mass., 1995).—**NS/LK/DM**

Rosen, Jerome (William), American clarinetist, teacher, and composer; b. Boston, July 23, 1921. He studied at N.Mex. State Univ. in Las Cruces, and with William Denny and Sessions at the Univ. of Calif. at Berkeley (M.A., 1949). Then, as recipient of a Ladd Prix de Paris, he went to Paris, where he continued his studies with Milhaud and also obtained a diploma as a clarinetist (1950). Upon his return to the U.S., he became a teacher at the Univ. of Calif. at Davis (1952). He was subsequently made an assoc. prof. (1957), and a prof. (1963), and also served as director of its electronic music studio; was made prof. emeritus (1988).

WORKS: DRAMATIC: O p e r a : *Emperor Norton of the U.S.A.* (1990). **C h a m b e r O p e r a :** *Calisto and Melibea* (1978; Davis, Calif., May 31, 1979). **M u s i c a l P l a y :** *Emperor Norton Lives!* (1976). **D a n c e S a t i r e s :** *Search* (1953); *Life Cycle* (1954). **O R C H.:** Saxophone Concerto (1957; Sacramento, Calif., Jan. 24, 1958); *5 Pieces* for Band (1960); *Sounds and Movements* (1963); Concerto for Clarinet, Trombone, and Band (1964); *Synket Concerto* (1968); *3 Pieces* for 2 Recorders and Orch. (1972); Clarinet Concerto (1973; Sacramento, Calif., Dec. 4, 1976); *3 Waltzes* for Saxophone and Band (1995). **C H A M B E R :** Woodwind Quintet (1949); Sonata for Clarinet and Cello (1950); 2 string quartets (1953, 1965); Clarinet Quintet (1959); *Serenade* for Clarinet and Percussion (1967); Quintet for Saxophone and String Quartet (1974); *Serenade* for Clarinet and Violin (1977); *Play Time I* for Clarinet and Double Bass (1981) and *II* for Clarinet and String Quartet (1981). **VOCAL:** *13 Ways of Looking at a Blackbird*, song cycle for Soprano and Piano (1951); *Serenade* for Soprano and Saxophone (1964); *Chamber Music* for Women's Voices and Harp (1975); *Campus Doorways* for Chorus and Orch. (1978); *White-Haired Lover*, song cycle for Baritone, Flute, Clarinet, String Quartet, and Piano (1985); *Love Poems*, song cycle for Man's and Woman's Speaking Voices, Flute, Clarinet, String Quartet, and Piano (1988).—**NS/LK/DM**

Rosen, Nathaniel (Kent), American cellist and teacher; b. Altadena, Calif., June 9, 1948. He studied at Pasadena City Coll. (1965–67) and with Piatigorsky at the Univ. of Southern Calif. in Los Angeles (Mus.B., 1971). He made his debut as a soloist with the Los Angeles Phil. in 1969, and in 1970 won the Piatigorsky Award of the Violoncello Soc. of N.Y., which led to his N.Y. debut at Carnegie Recital Hall. He was an asst. prof. at Calif. State Univ. at Northridge (1970–76); also was principal cellist of the Los Angeles Chamber Orch.

(1970–76) and of the Pittsburgh Sym. Orch. (1977–79). In 1978 he became the first American cellist to capture the Gold Medal at the Tchaikovsky Competition in Moscow; subsequently toured throughout the globe as a soloist, as a recitalist, and as a chamber music artist; taught at the Manhattan School of Music (from 1982).
—NS/LK/DM

Rosenberg, Hilding (Constantin), important Swedish composer and teacher; b. Bosjökloster, Ringsjön, Skåne, June 21, 1892; d. Stockholm, May 19, 1985. He studied piano and organ in his youth, and then was active as an organist. He went to Stockholm in 1914 to study piano with Andersson; then studied composition with Ellberg at the Stockholm Cons. (1915–16), and later took a conducting course there. He made trips abroad from 1920; then studied composition with Stenhammar and conducting with Scherchen. He was a répétiteur and asst. conductor at the Royal Opera in Stockholm (1932–34); also appeared as a guest conductor in Scandinavia and later in the U.S. (1948), leading performances of his own works; likewise was active as a teacher, numbering Bäck, Blomdahl, and Lidholm among his students. Rosenberg was the foremost Swedish composer of his era. He greatly influenced Swedish music by his experimentation and stylistic diversity, which led to a masterful style marked by originality, superb craftsmanship, and refinement.

WORKS: DRAMATIC: O p e r a : *Resa till Amerika* (Journey to America; Stockholm, Nov. 24, 1932; orch. suite, Stockholm, Sept. 29, 1935); *Spelet om St. Örjan*, children's opera (1937; rev. 1941); *Marionetter* (1938; Stockholm, Feb. 14, 1939; 2 suites for Small Orch., 1926; overture and dance suite, 1938); *De två konungadöttrarna* (The 2 Princesses), children's opera (Swedish Radio, Stockholm, Sept. 19, 1940); *Lycksalighetens o* (The Isle of Bliss; 1943; Stockholm, Feb. 1, 1945; *Vindarnas musik* for Orch. from the opera, 1943); *Josef och hans bröder* (Joseph and His Brothers), opera-oratorio, after Thomas Mann (1946–48; Swedish Radio, Stockholm: part 1, May 30, 1946; part 2, Dec. 19, 1946; part 3, Sept. 9, 1947; part 4, Jan. 23, 1948; *Partita* for Orch. from the opera-oratorio, 1948); *Kaspers fettisdag* (Kasper's Shrove Tuesday), chamber opera (1953; Swedish Radio, Stockholm, Feb. 28, 1954); *Porträtett* (The Portrait), radio opera after Gogol (1955; Swedish Radio, Stockholm, March 22, 1956; rev. 1963); *Hus med dubbel ingång* (The House with 2 Doors), lyric comedy after Calderón (1969; Stockholm, May 24, 1970). B a l l e t : *Eden* (1946; based on the Concerto No. 1 for Strings, 1946); *Salome* (1963; Stockholm, Feb. 28, 1964; based on the *Metamorfosi sinfoniche Nos. 1* and 2, 1963); *Sönerna* (The Sons; Swedish TV, Stockholm, Dec. 6, 1964; based on the *Metamorfosi sinfoniche No. 3*, 1964); *Babels torn* (The Tower of Babel; 1966; Swedish TV, Stockholm, Jan. 8, 1968; based on the Sym. for Wind and Percussion, 1966). P a n t o m i m e : *Yttersta domen* (The Last Judgment; 1929; not perf.; 2 preludes and 2 suites for Orch. from the pantomime, 1929). M e l o d r a m a s : *Prometheus och Ahasverus* (Swedish Radio, Stockholm, April 27, 1941); *Djufars visa* (Djufar's Song; Swedish Radio, Stockholm, Dec. 18, 1942; suite for Orch. from the melodrama, 1942). I n c i d e n t a l M u s i c T o : Plays and films. ORCH.: *Adagio* (1915); Syms.: No. 1 (1917; rev. 1919; Göteborg, April 5, 1921; rev. 1922–71; Stockholm, May 18, 1974), No. 2, *Sinfonia grave* (1928–35; Göteborg, March 27, 1935), No. 3 (Swedish Radio, Stockholm, Dec. 11, 1939; orig. subtitled *De frya tidsåldrarna* [The 4 Ages of Man], with text from Rolland's novel *Jean Christoph*;

rev. 1952), No. 4, *Johannes uppenbarelse* (The Revelation of St. John), for Baritone, Chorus, and Orch. (Swedish Radio, Stockholm, Dec. 6, 1940), No. 5, *Hortulanus* or *Örtagårdsmästaren* (The Keeper of the Garden), for Alto, Chorus, and Orch. (Swedish Radio, Stockholm, Oct. 17, 1944), No. 6, *Sinfonia semplice* (1951; Gavle, Jan. 24, 1952), Sym. for Wind and Percussion (1966; Göteborg, Oct. 27, 1972; music also used in the ballet *Babels torn*, 1966), No. 7 (Swedish Radio, Stockholm, Sept. 29, 1968), and No. 8, *In candidum*, for Chorus and Orch. (1974; Malmö, Jan. 24, 1975); *3 fantasistycken* (1918; Göteborg, 1919); *Sinfonia da chiesa No. 1* (1923; Stockholm, Jan. 16, 1925; rev. 1950) and *No. 2* (1924; Stockholm, Jan. 20, 1926); 2 violin concertos: No. 1 (1924; Stockholm, May 8, 1927) and No. 2 (1951; Stockholm, March 25, 1952); *Suite on Swedish Folk Tunes* for Strings (Swedish Radio, Stockholm, Sept. 13, 1927); Threnody for Stenhammar *(Sorgemusik)* (1927); Trumpet Concerto (1928; Stockholm, Jan. 16, 1929); *Overtura piccola* (1934); *Symphonie Concertante* for Violin, Viola, Oboe, Bassoon, and Orch. (1935; Göteborg, Jan. 1936); 2 cello concertos: No. 1 (1939) and No. 2 (1953; Swedish Radio, Stockholm, April 25, 1954); *Adagio funèbre* (1940); *I bergakungens sal* (In the Hall of the Mountain King), suite (1940); Viola Concerto (1942; Swedish Radio, Stockholm, Feb. 11, 1943); 4 concertos for Strings: No. 1 (1946; Swedish Radio, Stockholm, July 6, 1947; music used in the ballet *Eden*, 1946), No. 2 (n.d.), No. 3 (n.d.), and No. 4 (1966; Stockholm, Sept. 14, 1968); *Overtura bianca-nera* (1946); Concerto No. 2 (1949; Malmö, Jan. 12, 1950) and No. 3, *Louisville* (1954; Louisville, March 12, 1955; rev. 1968) for Orch.; Piano Concerto (1950; Göteborg, March 14, 1951); *Ingresso solenne del premio Nobel* (1952); *Variations on a Sarabande* (1953); *Riflessioni* No. 1 (1959; Swedish Radio, Stockholm, April 24, 1965), No. 2 (1960; Swedish Radio, Stockholm, March 2, 1962), and No. 3 (1960) for Strings; *Dagdrivaren (The Sluggard)* for Baritone and Orch. (1962; Stockholm, Oct. 28, 1964); *Metamorfosi sinfoniche Nos. 1 to 3* (1963–64; music from Nos. 1 and 2 used in the ballet *Salome*, 1963; music from No. 3 used in the ballet *Sönerna*, 1964); various suites, preludes, partitas, etc. CHAMBER: String quartets: No. 1 (1920; Stockholm, March 6, 1923), No. 2 (1924; Stockholm, March 6, 1925), No. 3, *Quartetto pastorale* (1926; Göteborg, April 3, 1932), No. 4 (1939; Stockholm, Nov. 2, 1942), No. 5 (1949; Stockholm, May 23, 1950), No. 6 (Stockholm, May 25, 1954), No. 7 (1956; Swedish Radio, Stockholm, Nov. 13, 1958), No. 8 (1956; Swedish Radio, Stockholm, Dec. 20, 1958), No. 9 (1956; Swedish Radio, Stockholm, March 17, 1959), No. 10 (1956; Swedish Radio, Stockholm, May 12, 1959), No. 11 (1956; Swedish Radio, Stockholm, Oct. 23, 1959), and No. 12, *Quartetto riepilogo* (1956; Swedish Radio, Stockholm, Dec. 11, 1959); Trio for Flute, Violin, and Viola (1921); 3 sonatas for Solo Violin (1921; 1953; 1963, rev. 1967); 2 violins sonatas (1926, 1940); Trio for Oboe, Clarinet, and Bassoon (1927); *Taffelmusik* for Piano Trio or Chamber Orch. (1939); Wind Quintet (1959); Sonata for Solo Flute (1959); Sonata for Solo Clarinet (1960); numerous piano works. VOCAL: O r a t o r i o s : *Den heliga natten* (The Holy Night; Swedish Radio, Stockholm, Dec. 27, 1936); *Perserna* (The Persians; 1937; not perf.); *Huvudskalleplats* (Calvary), for Good Friday (Swedish Radio, Stockholm, April 15, 1938; rev. 1964–65); *Svensk lagsaga* (Swedish Radio, Stockholm, Feb. 24, 1942); *Hymnus* (1965; Swedish Radio, Stockholm, July 24, 1966). C a n t a t a s : *Julhymn av Romanus* (Swedish Radio, Stockholm, Dec. 25, 1941); Cantata for the National Museum (1942; Swedish Radio, Stockholm, June 1, 1943); *Lyrisk svit* (Göteborg, Oct. 2, 1954); *Hymn to a University* (1967; Lund, June 13, 1968). Also choruses and songs.

BIBL.: M. Pergament, *H. R., a Giant of Modern Swedish Music* (Stockholm, 1956); P. Lyne, *H. R.: Catalogue of Works* (Stockholm, 1970).—NS/LK/DM

Rosenblum, Mathew, American composer; b. N.Y., March 19, 1954. He studied at the New England Cons. of Music in Boston (B.M., 1977; M.M., 1979) and Princeton Univ. (M.F.A., 1981). In 1980 he won the Rockefeller Foundation Contemporary American Chamber Works award; also received grants and awards from BMI (1978), the N.J. State Council on the Arts (1981), the Inst. of Contemporary American Music (1981), the American Composers Alliance (1987), and the N.Y. Foundation for the Arts (1989); was artist-in-residence at the MacDowell Colony, the Djerassi Foundation, and Yaddo. His recent works use hybrid tuning systems that combine both just- and equal-tempered intervals.

WORKS: *Harp Quartet* for Alto Flute/Flute, Bass Clarinet/Clarinet, Viola, and Harp (N.Y., Dec. 8, 1980); *Cascades* for Violin (1982; Glassboro, N.J., April 30, 1983); *Le Jon Ra* for 2 Cellos (1983; N.Y., April 24, 1987); *Continental Drift* for Horn, Percussion, and 2 Keyboards (San Francisco, Sept. 26, 1988); *Circadian Rhythms* for Cello, Percussion, and 2 Keyboards (N.Y., June 6, 1989; also for Clarinet, Harp, Synthesizer, and 2 Percussion; Oslo, Sept. 24, 1990).—NS/LK/DM

Rosenboom, David (Charles), American composer, performer, and teacher; b. Fairfield, Iowa, Sept. 9, 1947. He took courses in composition and electronic and computer music at the Univ. of Ill. at Urbana, where his principal mentors were Gordon Binkerd, Salvatore Martirano, Kenneth Gaburo, and Lejaren Hiller, and also studied theory, conducting, physics, computer science, and experimental psychology. In 1967–68 he was a creative assoc. at the Center for Creative and Performing Arts at the State Univ. of N.Y. at Buffalo and artistic coordinator of the Electric Circus in N.Y.; also in N.Y. he was co-founder and president of the Neurona Co., a research and development firm for electronics in the arts (1969–71). From 1972 to 1979 he taught at York Univ. in Toronto, and concurrently served as director of the Laboratory of Experimental Aesthetics at the Aesthetic Research Center of Canada, where he pursued studies in information processing as it relates to aesthetics; his studies resulted in several musical works. With D. Buchla, he developed the Touché, a computerized keyboard instrument, during his period as a software developer with Buchla's firm in Berkeley, Calif. (1979–80). In 1979 he joined the faculty of Mills Coll. in Oakland, Calif., where he was assoc. prof. of music and director of the Center for Contemporary Music (from 1983). He also was head of the music dept. (from 1984), holder of the Darius Milhaud Chair in Music (from 1988), and prof. of music (1989–90) there. From 1981 to 1984 he also taught at the San Francisco Art Inst. In 1990 he became dean of music at the Calif. Inst. of the Arts. In 1995 he was the George A. Miller Visiting Prof. at the Univ. of Ill. He wrote a number of articles on contemporary music for various journals and publications; ed. the book *Biofeedback and the Arts: Results of Early Experiments* (1975) and brought out the vol. *Selected Articles 1968–1982* (1984); also publ. a monograph, *Extended Musical Interface with the Human Nervous System: Assessment and Prospectus* (1990). Rosenboom has pursued a special interest in interdisciplinary work with the goal of combining the arts, sciences, and humanities. His music is generally experimental in nature, explorative of unique notation systems, improvisation, and extended instrumental techniques. He designed and co-developed H(ierarchical) M(usic) S(pecification) L(anguage), a widely used programmimg language for interactive computer music systems (1987).

WORKS: *Contrasts* for Violin and Orch. (1963); *Caliban upon Setebos* for Orch. (1966); *The Brandy of the Damned*, theater piece, with Electronic Tape (1967); *How Much Better if Plymouth Rock Had Landed on the Pilgrims* for Variable Ensembles, Electronics, and Outdoor Environments (1969–72); *On Being Invisible* for Soloist, with Computer- assisted Brain Signal Analysis and Electronic Music System, Touch Sensors, and Small Acoustic Sources (1976–77); *In the Beginning: I (Electronic)* for Soloist, with Computer-assisted Electronic Music System (1978), *II (Quartet)* for 2 or 4 Cellos and 2 Violas, Trombone, and Percussion (1979), *III (Quintet)* for Woodwind Quintet (1979), *Etude I (Trombones)* for any number of Trombones (1979), *IV (Electronic)* for Soloist, with Computer-assisted Electronic Music System (1980), *Etude II* (Keyboards/Mallets/Harps) for 2, 4, 6, or 8 Players (1980), *Etude III (Piano and 2 Oranges)* for Piano (1980), and *V (The Story)* for Chamber Orch., Film or Video, and Synthetic Speech (1980); *Future Travel* for Piano, Violin, and Computer Music System (1982; rev. 1987); *Champ Vital (Life Field)*, trio for Violin, Piano, and Percussion (1987); *Systems of Judgment*, tape collage (1987); *2 Lines*, duets for Melodic Instruments (1989); *Predictions, Confirmations, and Disconfirmations* for Piano, Computer Software, and Automatically Responding Instruments (1991); *Extended Trio* for Improvising Trio, Computer Software, and Computer Music Systems (1992; in collaboration with C. Haden and T. Sankaran); *It Is About To...Sound*, interactive computer media installation utilizing the music of John Cage and 36 other composers (1993; in collaboration with M. Coniglio and S. Mosko); *On Being Invisible II: Hypatia Speaks to Jefferson in a Dream*, multimedia performance piece (1994–95); *Brave New World: Music for the Play* for Computer Music System (1995); *Bell Solaris* for Piano (1997–98); *Seeing the Small in the Large* for Orch. (1998–99); also film music; improvisational pieces; sound sculptures; many other works.—NS/LK/DM

Rosenfeld, Paul (Leopold), American author and music critic; b. N.Y., May 4, 1890; d. there, July 21, 1946. He studied at Yale Univ. (B.A., 1912) and at Columbia Univ. School of Journalism (Litt.B., 1913). He then associated himself with progressive circles in literature and music; wrote music criticism for *The Dial* (1920–27); contributed also to other literary and music magazines. Although not a musician by training, Rosenfeld possessed a penetrating insight into musical values; he championed the cause of modern American music. He collected the most significant of his articles in book form: *Musical Portraits* (on 20 modern composers; 1920); *Musical Chronicle*, covering the N.Y. seasons 1917–23 (1923); *An Hour with American Music* (1929); *Discoveries of a Music Critic* (1936). Analects from his articles were publ. as *Musical Impressions* (N.Y., 1969).

BIBL.: J. Mellquist and L. Wiese, eds., *P. R., Voyager in the Arts* (N.Y., 1948); B. Mueser, *The Criticism of New Music in N.Y.: 1919–1929* (City Univ. of N.Y., 1975); C. Silet, *The Writings of P. R.: An Annotated Bibliography* (N.Y., 1981).—NS/LK/DM

Rosenhain, Jacob (Jakob or Jacques), German pianist and composer; b. Mannheim, Dec. 2, 1813; d. Baden-Baden, March 21, 1894. He was a child prodigy, making his debut in Frankfurt am Main when he was 8. He studied with Kalliwoda, Jakob Schmitt, and Schnyder von Wartensee. In 1837 he went to Paris and London, continuing his travels until 1870, when he settled as a teacher in Baden-Baden. His brother Eduard Rosenhain (b. Mannheim, Nov. 16, 1818; d. Frankfurt am Main, Sept. 6, 1861) was also a noteworthy pianist and teacher. He wrote a Serenade for Cello and Piano and piano pieces.

WORKS: DRAMATIC: O p e r a : *Der Besuch im Irrenhause* (Frankfurt am Main, Dec. 29, 1834); *Le Démon de la nuit* (Paris, March 17, 1851); *Le Volage et jaloux* (Baden-Baden, Aug. 3, 1863). **ORCH.:** 3 syms.; Piano Concerto. **CHAMBER:** 4 piano trios; 3 string quartets; 2 cello sonatas; piano pieces.

BIBL.: E. Kratt-Harveng, *Jacques R., Komponist und Pianist: Ein Lebensbild* (Baden-Baden, 1891).—**NS/LK/DM**

Rosenman, Leonard, American composer; b. N.Y., Sept. 7, 1924. He studied with local teachers, and later took courses with Sessions, Dallapiccola, and briefly with Schoenberg. His main mundane occupation is that of a movie composer; he wrote the scores for such commercially notable films as *East of Eden, Rebel without a Cause,* and *The Chapman Report;* also compiled music for television programs, among them *The Defenders* and *Marcus Welby, M.D.* But he is also the composer of a number of highly respectable musical works, among them a Violin Concerto and the challenging score *Foci* for 3 Orchs. His *Threnody on a Song of K. R.* (written to the memory of his wife, Kay Rosenman), a set of orch. variations on her original melody, was performed by the Los Angeles Phil., under the composer's direction, May 6, 1971. Among his later compositions are *Foci I* for Orch. (1981; rev. 1983) and *Chamber Music 5* for Piano and 6 Players (1979).—**NS/LK/DM**

Rosenmüller, Johann, significant German composer; b. Ölsnitz, near Zwickau, c. 1619; d. Wolfenbüttel (buried), Sept. 12, 1684. He studied music at the Ölsnitz Lateinschule and theology at the Univ. of Leipzig (1640). He was made an assistant at the Leipzig Thomasschule to teach music in 1642, being made first assistant in 1650; was also named organist of the Nicolaikirche in 1651 and music director in absentia of the Altenburg court in 1654. However, he lost these posts when he and several of the schoolboys were arrested and incarcerated as homosexuals in 1655. Rosenmüller escaped and eventually made his way to Venice, where he became a trombonist at San Marco in 1658. He secured a position as a composer there by 1660, and later was composer at the Ospedale della Pietà (1678–82). He then returned to Germany to serve as Kapellmeister at the Wolfenbüttel court. He was a distinguished composer of both sacred vocal works and instrumental music. His compositions were well known in Germany and helped to advance the acceptance of the northern Italian styles.

WORKS: SACRED VOCAL: *Kern-Sprüche mehrentheils aus heiliger Schrifft Altes und Neues Testaments* for 1 to 5 Voices, Strings, and Basso Continuo (Leipzig, 1648; some ed. by D.

Krüger, Hohenheim, near Stuttgart, 1960–68); *Andere Kern–Sprüche* for 1 to 5 Voices, Strings, and Basso Continuo (Leipzig, 1652–53; some ed. by A. Tunger, Hohenheim, near Stuttgart, 1960–63); 8 Funeral Songs for 5 Voices (Leipzig, 1649–54; ed. by F. Hamel in *Acht Begräbnisgesange zu fünf Stimmen,* Wolfenbüttel, 1930); *Magnificat* for 8 Voices, 5 Strings, Brass, and Basso Continuo; *Dies irae* for 4 Voices, 6 Strings, and Basso Continuo; *Gloria in excelsis Deo* for 8 Voices, 3 Strings, Brass, and Basso Continuo; *Lamentationes Jeremiae* for Voice and Basso Continuo (ed. by F. Hamel in Nagels Musikarchiv, XXVII–XXVIII); *Missa* for 4 Voices and Basso Continuo; *Missa brevis* for 5 Voices, 5 Strings, Brass, and Basso Continuo; *Nunc dimittis* for Voice, 3 Strings, and Basso Continuo; *Nunc dimittis* for 4 Voices, 5 Strings, and Basso Continuo; numerous other works to Latin or German texts. **INSTRUMENTAL:** *Paduanen, Alemanden, Couranten, Balletten, Sarabanden, a 3* and Basso Continuo (Organ) (Leipzig, 1645); *Studenten-Music* for 3 and 5 Strings and Basso Continuo (Leipzig, 1654; ed. by F. Hamel in Nagels Musikarchiv, LXI, 1929); 11 *Sonate da camera* for 5 Strings and Other Instruments (Venice, 1667; ed. by K. Nef in Denkmäler Deutscher Tonkunst, XVIII, 1904); 12 *Sonate* for 2 to 5 Strings and Other Instruments and Basso Continuo (Nuremberg, 1682; ed. by E. Pätzold, Berlin, 1954–56); various other sonatas, canons, dances, and other pieces in MS collections.

BIBL.: A. Horneffer, *J. R. (c. 1619–1684)* (Charlottenburg, 1898); F. Hamel, *Die Psalmkompositionen J. R.s* (Strasbourg, 1933); A. Lehmann, *Die Instrumentalwerke von J. R.* (diss., Univ. of Leipzig, 1965); K. Snyder, *J. R.'s Music for Solo Voice* (diss., Yale Univ., 1970).—**NS/LK/DM**

Rosenshein, Neil, American tenor; b. N.Y., Nov. 27, 1947. He studied at Wilkes Coll. in Wilkes-Barre, Pa. (1967), and with Jennie Tourel and others at N.Y.'s Juilliard School (1969). He made his operatic debut as Count Almaviva in *Il Barbiere di Siviglia* in Cocoa Beach, Fla. (1972); his first appearance in Europe was as Tom Rakewell in *The Rake's Progress* with the Netherlands Opera in Amsterdam (1982). He made frequent appearances with the major U.S. and European opera houses thereafter, and also sang with the leading orchs. On June 2, 1986, he made his Covent Garden debut in London as Lensky in *Eugene Onegin.* He made his Metropolitan Opera debut in N.Y. as Alfredo in *La Traviata* on Nov. 19, 1987. In 1988 he sang in the premiere of Argento's *The Aspern Papers* in Dallas. On Dec. 19, 1991, he created the role of Leon in Corigliano's *The Ghosts of Versailles* at the Metropolitan Opera. In 1994 he appeared in Santa Fe as Cavaradossi. Among his other roles are Belmonte in *Die Entführung aus dem Serail,* Tamino in *Die Zauberflöte,* Oberon, Werther, Alfred in *Die Fledermaus,* Alfonso in Korngold's *Violanta,* and the title role in Stravinsky's *Oedipus Rex.*—**NS/LK/DM**

Rosenstock, Joseph, Polish-born American conductor; b. Kraków, Jan. 27, 1895; d. N.Y., Oct. 17, 1985. He studied in Kraków and at the Vienna Cons., and also received instruction from Franz Schreker. He was asst. conductor at the Stuttgart Opera (1919–20), a conductor (1920–22) and Generalmusikdirektor (1922–25) at the Darmstadt Opera, and Generalmusikdirektor at the Wiesbaden Opera (1927–29). On Oct. 30, 1929, he made his Metropolitan Opera debut in N.Y. conducting *Die Meistersinger von Nürnberg;* returning to Germany, he became Generalmusikdirektor at the Mannheim National Theater in 1930. As a Jew, he was removed from his post by the Nazis in 1933; he then conducted the Judisches Kulturbund in Berlin until 1936. He went to Tokyo to become conductor of the Nippon Phil. (1936); as an alien, he lost his post and was removed to Karuizawa with the Japanese attack on Pearl Harbor in 1941; after his liberation in 1945, he returned to Tokyo to help reorganize musical life under the U.S. occupation forces. In 1946 he settled in the U.S.; became a naturalized citizen in 1949. He became a conductor at the N.Y.C. Opera in 1948, and subsequently was its general director (1952–56); after serving as music director of the Cologne Opera (1958–60), he conducted at the Metropolitan Opera in N.Y. (1960–69). His wife was **Herta Glaz.**—NS/LK/DM

Rosenthal, Harold (David), English music editor and critic; b. London, Sept. 30, 1917; d. there, March 19, 1987. He received his B.A. degree from Univ. Coll., London, in 1940. In 1950 he launched, with the Earl of Harewood, the magazine *Opera* and was its ed. (1953–86). He was archivist of the Royal Opera House in London (1950–56). Rosenthal contributed to many European and American music journals, and also wrote numerous biographical entries on singers for *The New Grove Dictionary of Music and Musicians* (1980). In 1983 he was made an Officer of the Order of the British Empire. His publications, all publ. in London, included *Sopranos of Today* (1956), *Two Centuries of Opera at Covent Garden* (1958), ed. with J. Warrack, *The Concise Oxford Dictionary of Opera* (1964; 2nd ed., rev., 1979), and *Covent Garden: A Short History* (1967). He ed. *The Opera Bedside Book* (1965) and *The Mapleson Memoirs* (1966); also wrote an autobiography, *My Mad World of Opera* (1982).
—NS/LK/DM

Rosenthal, Manuel, French conductor and composer; b. Paris, June 18, 1904. He studied solfège and violin at the Paris Cons., and composition with Ravel. In 1928 he made his conducting debut with the Concerts Pasdeloup in Paris. From 1934 until his mobilization as an infantryman at the outbreak of World War II in 1939, he was co-conductor of the Orchestre National de la Radiodiffusion in Paris. After being held as a prisoner-of-war in Germany (1940–41), he was released and returned to France and became active in the Résistance. From 1944 to 1947 he was chief conductor of the French Radio orch. in Paris. In 1948 he became a teacher at the Coll. of Puget Sound in Tacoma, Wash. He became conductor of the Seattle Sym. Orch. in 1949. In 1951 he was summarily dismissed for moral turpitude after it was learned that the soprano he has engaged as soloist with the orch. as Mme. Rosenthal was not his legal wife. In 1962 he became prof. of conducting at the Paris Cons. From 1964 to 1967 he was conductor of the Liège Sym. Orch. He made his belated Metropolitan Opera debut in N.Y. on Feb. 20, 1981, conducting a triple bill of Ravel's *L'Enfant et les sortilèges,* Poulenc's *Les Mamelles de Tirésias,* and Satie's *Parade.* He continued to conduct there until 1988. In 1986 he conducted the *Ring* cycle at the Seattle Opera. Rosenthal publ. the books *Satie, Ravel, Poulenc: An Intimate Memoir* (Madras and N.Y., 1987),

Musique dorable (Paris, 1994), and *Ravel: Souvenirs de Manuel Rosenthal* (Paris, 1995). In 1992 he received the Grand Prix for music of the City of Paris. He also was honored as a Commandeur dans l'Ordre de la Légion d'honneur.

WORKS: DRAMATIC: *Rayon des soieries,* comic opera (1926–28; Paris, June 2, 1930); *Un baiser pour rien* or *La Folle du Logis,* ballet (1928–29; Paris, June 15, 1936); *Les Bootleggers,* musical comedy (1932; Paris, April 1933); *La Poule Noire,* musical comedy (1934–37; Paris, May 31, 1937); *Gaieté Parisienne,* ballet after Offenbach (Monte Carlo, April 5, 1938); *Que le diable l'emporte,* ballet (1948); *Les Femmes au Tombeau,* lyric drama (1956; Paris, May 29, 1957); *Hop, Signor!,* lyric drama (1957–61; Toulouse, March 24, 1962). **ORCH.:** *Sérénade* (1927); *Les Petits Métiers* (1933); *Jeanne d'Arc* (1934–36); *Saint François d'Assise,* suite (1936–39); *Musique de Table* (1941); *Noce Villageoise* (1941); *Symphonie de Noël* (1947); *Aesopi Convivium* for Violin, Piano, and Orch. (1947–48); *Magic Manhattan* (1948); Sym. (1949; Paris, June 12, 1950); *Offenbachiana* (1953); *Rondes Françaises* (1955); *Aeolus* for Wind Quintet and Strings (1968); *Deux Etudes en Camïeu* for Strings and Percussion (1969); *Le Temple de Mémoire* (1975; Paris, Oct. 1976). **CHAMBER:** Sonatine for 2 Violins and Piano (1923); *Saxophone-Marmelade* for Alto Saxophone and Piano (1929); *Trois Pièces* for Harp and 6 Instruments (1937); *Les Soirées du Petit Juas* for String Quartet (1942); *Juventas* for Clarinet, 2 Violins, Viola, and Cello (1988). **PIANO:** *Valse des Pêcheurs à la Ligne* (1927); *Huit Bagatelles* (1924); *Six Caprices* (1926); *La Belle Zélie* for 2 Pianos (1948). **VOCAL:** *Cinq Chanons Juives* for Soprano or Tenor and Orch. (1925); *Chansons d'Monsieur Bleu* for Mezzo-soprano and Orch. (1932–34); *Trois Mélodies* for Mezzo-soprano or Tenor and Orch. (1933); *Saint François d'Assise,* oratorio for Reciter, Chorus, and Orch. (1936–39; Paris, Nov. 1, 1944); *Trois Burlesques* for Chorus and Orch. (1941); *Trois Chansons d'Amour* for Soprano and Orch. (1941); *Trois Précieuses* for Soprano and Orch. (1941); *Deux Prières pour les Temps Malheureux* for Baritone and Orch. (1942; Paris, June 10, 1963); *Six Chansons d'Outre-Mer* for Mezzo-soprano and Orch. (1942); *Trois Chants de Femmes Berbères* for Soprano, Contralto, and Orch. (1943–44); *Le Pietà d'Avignon* for 4 Soloists, String Orch., and Trumpet (1943); *Cantata pour le Temps de la Nativité* for Soprano, Chorus, and Orch. (1942); *Deux Sonnets de Jean Cassou* for Soprano and Orch. (1944); *Trois Pièces Liturgiques* for Voice or Chorus and Orch. (1944); *A Choeur Vaillant* for Chorus (1952–53); *Missa Deo Gratias* for Soprano, Mezzo-soprano, Tenor, Bass, Chorus, and Orch. (1953; Paris, Jan. 1955); many songs for Voice and Piano.

BIBL.: D. Saudinos, *M. R.: Une vie* (Paris, 1992).
—NS/LK/DM

Rosenthal, Moriz, famous Austrian pianist; b. Lemberg, Dec. 17, 1862; d. N.Y., Sept. 3, 1946. He studied piano at the Lemberg Cons. with Karol Mikuli, who was a pupil of Chopin; in 1872, when he was 10 years old, he played Chopin's Rondo in C for 2 Pianos with his teacher in Lemberg. The family moved to Vienna in 1875, and Rosenthal became the pupil of Joseffy, who inculcated in him a passion for virtuoso piano playing, which he taught according to Tausig's method. Liszt accepted Rosenthal as a student during his stay in Weimar and Rome (1876–78). After a hiatus of some years, during which Rosenthal studied philosophy at the Univ. of Vienna, he returned to his concert career in 1884, and established for himself a reputation as one of the world's greatest virtuosos; was nicknamed (because of his small stature and great pianistic power) "little giant of the piano." Beginning in 1888 he made 12 tours of the U.S., where he became a permanent resident in 1938. He publ. (with L. Schytte) a *Schule des höheren Klavierspiels* (Berlin, 1892). He was married to **Hedwig Kanner-Rosenthal.**—NS/LK/DM

Rosenthal, Ted, jazz pianist, composer; b. Great Neck, Long Island, N.Y., Nov. 15, 1959. He received his Bachelors and Masters degrees from the Manhattan School of Music and continued private studies with Phillip Kawin. He won first prize at the 1988 Thelonious Monk International Jazz Piano Competition. He toured internationally with Gerry Mulligan from about mid-1992 through Mulligan's death in January 1996. During the late 1990s, he was a regular at the Blue Note's Sunday jazz brunch with Jay Leonhart. He has also performed with Art Farmer, James Moody, Jon Faddis, Benny Golson, the Lincoln Center Jazz Orch., Jim Hall, Lee Konitz, and Michael Brecker. He played with David Sanborn on the NBC TV show *Night Music* in the late 1980s. He has won three NEA grants for performance, one of which supported his premiere of "Round for a Plague Year" and "Blues for Arnie" at the Greenwich House, N.Y. (January 1995). In early 1995, he performed in seven African countries. He has been teaching at the New School/Mannes Coll. of Music since 1990, presents clinics while on tour, and publishes regularly.

DISC.: *New Tunes New Traditions* (1989); *Images of Monk* (1992); *Calling You* (1992); *Maybeck Recital Hall Series* (1994); *Rosenthology* (1995); *Ted Rosenthal at Maybeck* (1995).—LP

Rosetti (real name, **Rösler**), **(Francesco) Antonio** (actually, **Franz Anton** or **František Antonin**), Bohemian composer; b. Leitmeritz, c. 1750; d. Ludwigslust, June 30, 1792. For many years Rosetti was confused with a Bohemian cobbler named Franz Anton Rösler, who was born in Niemes in 1746 and whose date of birth was erroneously listed as that of Rosetti; by adopting the name of Antonio Rosetti, he created further problems by being confused with 5 contemporary musicians with that name. He was a theological student. He was engaged as a string player in court orchs., and in 1789 became Kapellmeister to the Duke of Mecklenburg-Schwerin. He was a prodigiously fertile composer who wrote in the manner of Haydn and Boccherini, and was even dubbed "a German Boccherini." He wrote 3 Requiems, one of which was composed in memory of Mozart; it was performed in Prague shortly after Mozart's death in 1791; its score is unfortunately lost. His other works include *Das Winterfest der Hirten*, drama with Orch. (Ludwigslust, Dec. 10, 1789), over 40 publ. syms., 5 piano concertos, 7 violin concertos, 4 clarinet concertos, about 10 flute concertos, 15 horn concertos, 6 concertos for 2 Horns, 8 bassoon concertos, etc. He also composed works for wind instruments and numerous other chamber works, as well as songs.

BIBL.: H. Kaul, *Anton Rosetti: Sein Leben und seine Werke* (diss., Univ. of Munich, 1911); S. Murray, *The Music of A. R. (Anton Rösler) c. 1750–1792: A Thematic Catalog* (Warren, Mich., 1996).—NS/LK/DM

Rosewoman, Michele, pianist of lightning reflexes and considerable imagination; b. Oakland, Calif., 1953. She is best known for her quintet, Quintessence, the personnel of which is different on each of its three albums. Her occasional vocals are never better than adequate, however; but they are significant in that they show her contemporary pop leanings—on her live album, *Spirit*, she sings the Earth, Wind & Fire song of that title. Her style is a mix of post-bop, Latin jazz, some slight African influences, touches of the avant-garde, and—mostly with Quintessence—the akimbo rhythmic accents of the M-Base school.

She started playing at age six, and from age 17 studied with pianist Ed Kelly, an Oakland hometown hero who has recorded with Pharoah Sanders. She also had lessons in percussion with Marcus Gordon, in Cuban folkloric music with Orlando "Puntilla" Rios, and in voice with Joyce Bryant. Her association with members of the Black Artists Group and the Association for the Advancement of Creative Music prompted her to move to N.Y. in 1978; her N.Y. debut came with Oliver Lake at Carnegie Recital Hall. She has recorded with Billy Bang (the *Rainbow Gladiator* album), Ralph Peterson (*Art*), and Greg Osby (*Greg Osby and Sound Theatre*). Her big band, New Yor-Uba, to which she has devoted considerable time, has not yet been recorded.

DISC.: *The Source* (1984); *Quintessence* (1989); *Contrast High* (1989); *Occasion to Rise* (1993); *Harvest* (1993); *Spirit* (1996). —SH/NAL

Rosier, Carl, Flemish violinist and composer; b. Liège, Dec. 26, 1640; d. Cologne, before Dec. 12, 1725. He became a violinist at the Bonn electoral court about 1664, and subsequently was Vice-Kapellmeister. He went to Cologne in 1675, but was also active as a violinist in Holland from about 1683 to 1699; was appointed Kapellmeister of the Cologne Cathedral in 1699 and also of the city in 1701. He was an accomplished composer of instrumental music.

BIBL.: U. Niemöller, *C. R. (1640–1725), Kölner Dom- und Ratskapellmeister, Beiträge zur rheinischen Musikgeschichte*, XXIII (Cologne, 1957).—NS/LK/DM

Rosing, Vladimir, Russian-American tenor and opera director; b. St. Petersburg, Jan. 23, 1890; d. Los Angeles, Nov. 24, 1963. He studied voice with Jean de Reszke. He made his operatic debut in St. Petersburg in 1912, then gave a successful series of recitals in programs of Russian songs in London between 1913 and 1921. In 1923 he was appointed director of the opera dept. at the Eastman School of Music in Rochester, N.Y.; founded an American Opera Co., which he directed in a series of operatic productions in the English language. In 1939 he went to Los Angeles as organizer and artistic director of the Southern Calif. Opera Assn.

BIBL.: R. Rosing, *V. R.: Musical Genius, an Intimate Biography* (Manhattan, Kans., 1993).—NS/LK/DM

Roslavetz, Nikolai (Andreievich), remarkable Russian composer; b. Suray, Jan. 4, 1881; d. Moscow, Aug. 23, 1944. He received training in violin from his uncle and in theory from A.M. Abaza in Kursk. In 1902 he entered the Moscow Cons., where he studied violin with J. Hřimalý and composition with Ilyinsky and Vassilenko (graduated, 1912; Silver Medal for the cantata *Heaven and Earth*). In 1921–22 he was director of the Kharkov Cons. From 1923 to 1929 he was a board member of the Assn. for Contemporary Music, and in 1924 he edited the forward-looking but short-lived journal *Muzykalnaya Kultura*. He also taught at the Moscow Music Polytechnical School (1928–30). A composer of advanced tendencies even in his student years, Roslavetz's early works were undeniably influenced by Scriabin, but by 1913 he had publ. an atonal violin sonata (No. 1), the first of its kind by a Russian composer. His fully mature Third String Quartet of 1920 exhibits his "new system of sound organization," an individualized application of multi-tone chords, producing dodecaphonic effects. Roslavetz became a prominent figure of the cadre of advanced Soviet musicians of the 1920s, but with a change of Soviet cultural policy and the adoption of "socialist realism" and nationalism in the late 1920s, he was subjected to severe criticism in the press for persevering in his aberrant ways. By 1930 he had become a musical persona non grata and his name was expunged from musical writings and programs. It was assumed for decades that Roslavetz had disappeared into the black hole of Stalin's gulags but this was not the case. He failed in his attempt to conciliate the authorities by composing operettas, but was given an opportunity to redeem himself by removing to remote Tashkent to compose ballets on Uzbek folk songs and serve as music director of the Uzbek State Music Theater (1931–33). He then returned to Moscow, where he taught at the Music Polytechnical School (until 1935). From 1936 to 1938 he was repertoire advisor of the All-Union Radio Committee. He also wrote music criticism until the first of several crippling strokes disabled him in 1940. His death went unnoticed in a war-torn world, and later the bulk of his works was assumed irretrievably lost. However, interest in his music was initiated by the German musicologist D. Gojowy in the 1970s. In the 1980s and 1990s the Central State Archives for Literature and Art in Moscow discovered many of Roslavetz's "lost" works, albeit often incomplete and mostly in short or piano score. Several works were then completed and edited for performance by several Russian composers and musicologists, most notably A. Raskatov and M. Lobanova.

WORKS: DRAMATIC: Ballet: *Pakhta* (1933). **ORCH.:** *In the Hours of the New Moon*, tone poem (c. 1912–13; ed. by M. Lobanova; Saarbrücken Radio, June 14, 1990); *Man and the Sea*, symphonic poem (1921); *End of the World*, symphonic poem (1922); 2 syms.: No. 1 (1922) and No. 2 (not extant); 2 chamber syms.: No. 1 (c. 1922; completed and orchestrated by A. Raskatov) and No. 2 (c. 1938); 2 violin concertos: No. 1 (1925; piano reduction, Moscow, May 29, 1929; full score recovered in 1988 and 1st perf. in Moscow, Nov. 18, 1989) and No. 2 (late 1930s). **CHAMBER:** *Nocturne* for Oboe, Harp, 2 Violas, and Cello (1913); 6 violin sonatas: No. 1 (1913), No. 2 (1917), No. 3 (not extant), No. 4 (1920), No. 5 (1922–23; not extant), and No. 6 (c. 1940); 5 string quartets: No. 1 (1913), No. 2 (not extant), No. 3 (1920), No. 4 (not extant), and No. 5 (1941); *Poem* for Violin and Piano (1915); *Music for String Quartet*

(1916; extant adagio and scherzo movements of a string quartet edited and titled by A. Raskatov); 5 piano trios: No. 1 (not extant), No. 2 (1920; edited by M. Lobanova), No. 3 (1920), No. 4 (1927; edited by M. Lobanova), and No. 5 (not extant); Cello Sonata (1921); *Meditation* for Cello and Piano (1921); *3 Dances* for Violin and Piano (1921); 2 viola sonatas (1925, 1926, both reconstructed by A. Raskatov); *Legend* for Violin and Piano (1940–41); *24 Preludes* for Violin and Piano (1941–42). **Piano:** 3 Pieces (1914); 3 Etudes (1914); 6 sonatas: No. 1 (1914), No. 2 (1916; reconstructed by Eduard Babasjan), No. 3 (not extant), No. 4 (1923; not extant), No. 5 (1923), and No. 6 (only sketches extant); 2 Pieces (1915); *Quasi Poeme* (1915); *Quasi Prelude* (1915); *Prelude* (1915); 5 Preludes (1919–22); 2 Poemes (1920). **VOCAL:** *Heaven and Earth*, cantata after Byron (1912); 3 Pieces for Voice and Piano (1913); *Melancholy Landscapes* for Voice and Piano (1913); *October*, cantata (1926); *Komsomolija* for Chorus and Orch. (Moscow, Sept. 30, 1928).—**NS/LK/DM**

Rösler or **Rössler, Johann Joseph** (actually, **Jan Josef**), Bohemian pianist and composer; b. Banska Stiavnica, Aug. 22, 1771; d. Prague, Jan. 28, 1813. He studied music with his father, then was a composer for Prague's Nostitz Theater, where he brought out the opera *Elisene, Prinzessin von Bulgarien* (Oct. 18, 1807), the first original stage work to be produced there. He went to Vienna (1805) and was active at the Court Theater; was also in the service of Countess Lobkowitz. His other works include keyboard sonatas, piano pieces, and the *Cantate auf Mozart's Tod* (1798). A movement from one of his piano concertos was erroneously attributed to Beethoven.—**NS/LK/DM**

Rösler, Endre, Hungarian tenor; b. Budapest, Nov. 27, 1904; d. there, Dec. 13, 1963. He studied in Budapest and with De Lucia and Garbin in Italy. In 1927 he made his operatic debut as Alfredo at the Budapest Opera, where he was a principal member for some 30 years. Subsequently he sang comprimario roles there. At the apex of his career, he appeared as a guest artist with other European opera houses and also pursued a concert career. From 1953 until his death he taught at the Budapest Academy of Music. He was especially esteemed for his roles in Mozart's operas.

BIBL.: P. Varnai, *R. E.* (Budapest, 1969).—**NS/LK/DM**

Ros-Marbá, Antoni, Spanish conductor; b. Barcelona, April 2, 1937. He studied at the Barcelona Cons., and later with Celibidache at the Accademia Musicale Chigiana in Siena and Martinon in Düsseldorf. After making his debut in Barcelona (1962), he conducted in Europe, the U.S., Mexico, and Israel. He was conductor of the Orquesta Sinfónica de Radio Televisión Española in Madrid (1966–68) and of the Orquesta Ciudad de Barcelona (1967–78). He was chief conductor of the Orquesta Nacional de España in Madrid (1979–81); served as principal conductor of the Netherlands Chamber Orch. (1979–85) and again as conductor of the Orquesta Ciudad de Barcelona (1981–86). In 1989 he became music director of the Teatro Real in Madrid. —**NS/LK/DM**

Rosner, Arnold, American composer and teacher; b. N.Y., Nov. 8, 1945. He studied mathematics at N.Y.U., and theory and composition with Leo Smit, Allen Sapp, and Lejaren Hiller at the State Univ. of N.Y. at Buffalo (Ph.D., 1972). From 1983 he taught at Kingsborough Community Coll. His music is couched formally in a neo-Classical idiom, but he freely admits melodic, harmonic, and contrapuntal methods of contemporary usage.

WORKS: DRAMATIC: O p e r a : *The Chronicle of Nine* (1984); *Bontsche Schweig* (1994). **ORCH.:** 6 syms. (1961, 1961, 1963, 1964, 1973, 1976); *5 Meditations* (1967); *6 Pastoral Dances* (1968); *A Gentle Musicke* for Flute and Strings (1969); *A Mylai Elegy* (1971); 2 concerti grossi (1974, 1979); *5 Ko-ans* (1976); *Responses, Hosanna, and Fugue* for Harp and Strings (1977); *Nocturne* (1978); *From the Diaries of Adam Czerniakow* for Narrator and Orch. (1986); *Gematria* (1991); *A Sephardic Rhapsody* (1992); *Variations on a Theme by Frank Martin* (1996); Concerto for 2 Trumpets, Strings, and Timpani (1997); *Tempus Perfectum* (1998); *A Millennium Overture* (1999). **B a n d :** *Trinity* (1988); *Lovely Joan* (1990); *De Profundis* (1991); *Eclipse* (1994); *Dances of Initiation* (1993); *RAGA!* (1995). **CHAMBER:** 5 string quartets (1962, 1963, 1965, 1972, 1975); Sonata for Flute and Cello (1962); Violin Sonata (1963); Woodwind Quintet (1964); Concertino for Harp, Harpsichord, Celesta, and Piano (1968; rev. 1988); 2 cello sonatas (1968, 1989); Sonata for Oboe or Violin and Piano (1972); Brass Quintet (1978); Horn Sonata (1979); *A Plaintive Harmony* for Horn (1988); Trombone Sonata (1997); *Serpentine* for Clarinet and Piano (1998). **KEYBOARD: P i a n o :** 3 sonatas (1963, 1970, 1978); *Of Numbers and Bells* for 2 Pianos (1983). **H a r p s i c h o r d :** *Musique de clavecin* (1974); *Sonatine d'amour* (1987). **VOCAL: C h o r a l :** 3 Masses (1967, 1971, 1974); *Requiem* (1973); *Magnificat* (1979); *Let Them Praise* for Boy's Chorus (1984). **S o n g s :** *3 Elegiac Songs* (1973); *Nightstone* (1979); *Besos sin Cuento* for Low Voice, Flute, Viola, and Harp (1989); *Songs of Lightness and Angels* for Voice, Horn, and Piano (1990); *The Parable of the Law* for Baritone and Orch., after Kafka (1993); *Of Songs and Sonnets* for Countertenor and Harpsichord, after Milton (1997).—NS/LK/DM

Rosnes, Renee (Irene Louise), jazz pianist, composer; b. Regina, Saskatchewan, Canada, March 24, 1962. The youngest of three adopted girls, she grew up in Vancouver. Her father and mother are Canadian Indians. Her oldest sister played piano and violin; the middle sister played piano and cello. Renee began piano at three, then took up violin a few years later. In elementary school, she began learning pop tunes from the radio. She played classical violin in youth orchestras from age 8 to 18. An astute grade school music director brought her into the jazz band and encouraged her interest. She studied music at the Royal Cons. of Music (Toronto), then returned to Vancouver, where she performed. In 1986, she came to N.Y. on a grant from the Canada Council of the Arts; she decided to stay after working with Joe Henderson at the Village Vanguard. From 1987–89, she played with the Blue Note records house group, Out of the Blue. She married drummer Billy Drummond in 1990. During the late 1980s and 1990s, she toured with J.J. Johnson, and also worked with James Moody, Jon Faddis, Bobby Hutcherson, and Wayne Shorter. Since 1991, she has led her own trio. In spring 1996, she led a group at a tribute to Mary Lou Williams at the Kennedy Center, D.C. and for a week at Sweet Basil (N.Y.), and in May performed in an Ellington tribute at Lincoln Center. She has been the pianist

for the Carnegie Hall Jazz Band since the early 1990s She has worked with Ralph Moore and her husband in the group Native Colors; in the mid-1990s, Moore left to play in the Tonight Show band and she was also offered a place, but declined. Her compositions include "Malaga Moon," which was recorded by J.J. Johnson and performed by the Carnegie Hall Jazz Band, and "Abstraction Blues (For Georgia O'Keefe)," commissioned and premiered by Jazz at Lincoln Center. She has won numerous Canadian Juno awards and readers polls.

DISC.: *Renee Rosnes* (1989); *Face to Face* (c. 1989); *For the Moment* (1990); *Without Words* (1992); *Ancestors* (1995); *Live in Toronto* (1996); *As We Are Now* (1997). J. Henderson: *Punjab* (1986). G. Thomas: *Seventh Quadrant* (1987); *While the Gate Is Open* (1990). Out of the Blue: *Spiral Staircase* (1989). J. Faddis: *Into the Faddisphere* (1989); *Hornucopia* (c. 1991). B. Drummond: *Native Colours* (1991); *The Gift* (1993). J.J. Johnson: *Let's Hang Out* (1992).

BIBL.: R. Rosnes, *North of the Border* (Second Floor Music/Hal Leonard).—LP

Rosolino, Frank, jazz trombonist; b. Detroit, Mich., Aug. 20, 1926; d. Los Angeles, Nov. 26, 1978. He was born in a musical family, and first played guitar at age 10; he switched to trombone in high school. From 1944–45, he was in an Army band; on his discharge, he settled in Los Angeles and played with a number of bands, leading up to two years with Gene Krupa (1948–49), where his humorous scat singing was highlighted. In the early 1950s, he was back in Detroit leading his own band, but by 1952 had joined with Stan Kenton, remaining with him for two years. He played at the famous Lighthouse sessions in the late 1950s, and also worked as a session musician for recordings and films through the 1960s. In 1970s, he toured with the Supersax ensemble. A fluid and engaging player, known for his extroverted sense of humor, he shocked the jazz world by murdering his wife and two children before turning the gun on himself in 1978.

DISC.: *Frank Rosolino Quartet* (1952). Kenton Presents Jazz: *Frank Rosolino* (1954); *Howard Rumsey's Lighthouse All* (1955); *Frankly Speaking* (1955); *I Play Trombone* (1956); *Legend of Frank Rosolino* (1957); *Frank Rosolino Quintet* (1957); *Free for All* (1958); *Turn Me Loose* (1961); *Thinking About You* (1976); *In Denmark* (1978); *Frank Rosolino Sextet* (1983); *Rosolino Connection* (1984).

BIBL.: R. Machado, *Basic Discography of Frank Rosolino* (Fortaleza, Brazil, 1988).—LP

Rosowsky, Solomon, Latvian music scholar and composer; b. Riga, March 27, 1878; d. N.Y., July 30, 1962. He studied law at the Univ. of Kiev, and composition at the St. Petersburg Cons. with Liadov, Rimsky-Korsakov, and Glazunov. He was a co-founder of the Soc. for Jewish Folk Music in St. Petersburg in 1909. In 1920 he went back to Riga, and organized the first Jewish Cons. of Music. In 1925 he emigrated to Palestine, then settled in N.Y. in 1947, devoting himself mainly to the music of biblical times, culminating in the publication of an important vol., *The Cantillation of the Bible* (N.Y., 1957). His compositions include a Piano Trio (1909) and several scores of incidental music for plays in Yiddish. —NS/LK/DM

Ross, Hugh (Cuthbert Melville), English-born American organist, choral conductor, and teacher; b. Langport, Aug. 21, 1898; d. N.Y., Jan. 20, 1990. He studied at the Royal Coll. of Music in London and at New Coll., Oxford (D.Mus.), his principal mentors being Mengelberg and Vaughan Williams. In 1921 he went to Winnipeg as conductor of its Male Voice Choir; in 1922 he founded that city's Phil. Choir, and in 1923 its Orchestral Club, which later became the Winnipeg Sym. Orch. In 1927 he settled in N.Y. as conductor of the Schola Cantorum, which post he held until 1971; also appeared as a guest conductor throughout North America. He taught at the Manhattan School of Music (from 1930); was also chairman of the choral dept. at the Berkshire Music Center at Tanglewood (1941–62). In 1949 he became a naturalized American citizen. He championed contemporary works.—NS/LK/DM

Ross, Scott, American harpsichordist and organist; b. Pittsburgh, March 1, 1951; d. Assas, France, June 14, 1989. He went to France in his youth and entered the Nice Cons. in 1965 to study organ with René Saorgin and harpsichord with Huguette Grémy-Chauliac, taking the premier prix on the latter instrument in 1968. In 1969 he entered the Paris Cons. and studied harpsichord with Robert Veyron-Lacroix. Upon completing his training there in 1971, he pursued further studies in harpsichord with Kenneth Gilbert and was awarded a diplôme supérieur in 1972. In 1971 he captured 1st prize in the Bruges competition. In 1973 he became a prof. at Laval Univ. in Quebec, remaining primarily active in France as a harpsichordist and organist. Ross was held in high regard for his insightful interpretations of 17th- and 18th-century music, especially the works of Bach, Scarlatti, and composers of the French school. —NS/LK/DM

Ross, Walter (Beghtol), American composer and teacher; b. Lincoln, Nebr., Oct. 3, 1936. He studied at the Univ. of Nebr. (M.Mus., 1962), with Ginastera at the Instituto Torcuato di Tella in Buenos Aries (1965), and with Robert Palmer (composition) and Husa (conducting) at Cornell Univ. (D.M.A., 1966). In 1967 he was appointed to the music faculty of the Univ. of Va. Much of his music is inspired by American themes.

WORKS: DRAMATIC: O p e r a : *In the Penal Colony* (1972). ORCH.: Concerto for Brass Quintet and Orch. (1966); 2 trombone concertos (1970, 1982); 2 syms.: No. 1, *A Jefferson Symphony*, for Tenor, Chorus, and Orch. (Charlottesville, Va., April 13, 1976) and No. 2 for Strings (1994); Concerto for Wind Quintet and String Orch. (1977); *Nocturne* for Strings (1980); Concerto for Bassoon and Strings (1983); Concerto for Oboe, Harp, and Strings (1984); *Overture to the Virginian Voyage* (1986); Concerto for Flute, Guitar, and Orch. (1987); *Sinfonietta Concertante* for Strings (1987); Concerto for Euphonium, Symphonic Brass, and Timpani (1988); *Fantastic Dances* for Strings (1990); *Mosaics*, piano concerto (1991); *Scherzo Festivo* (1992); *A Celebration of Dances* (1993); Clarinet Concerto (1994); Double Bass Concerto (1995); Violin Concerto (1996); Concerto for Oboe d'Amore and Strings (1998). B a n d : Many works. CHAMBER: *Cryptical Triptych* for Trombone and Piano (1968); *5 Dream Sequences* for Percussion Quartet and Piano (1968); *Canzona I* (1969) and *II* (1979) for 4 Trumpets, 4 Horns, 4

Trombones, 2 Euphoniums, 2 Tubas, and 3 Percussion, *III* for 12 Horns (1986), and *IV* for 4 Trumpets, 4 Horns, 4 Trombones, 2 Tubas, Timpani, and 2 Percussion (1989); 3 wind quintets (1974, 1985, 1989); String Trio (1978); Violin Sonata (1981); Suite No. 1 for Chamber Ensemble (1983); 4 brass trios (1985; 1986; 1986; *Shapes of Klee*, 1995); Brass Quintet No. 1 (1987); *Oil of Dog* for Brass Quintet and Actor (1988); *Shapes in Bronze* for 2 Euphoniums and 2 Tubas (1992); *Summer Dances* for Oboe and Marimba (1992); *Contrasts!* for 12 Euphoniums (1992); *Harlequinade* for Flute, Oboe, Clarinet, Horn, Bassoon, and Piano (1994); *Shortened Suite* for Trumpet and Bassoon (1996); *Trio Fantastico* for Oboe d'Amore, Bassoon, and Piano (1998); *A Suite of Klee* for Oboe, Clarinet, and Bassoon (1999). VOCAL: Numerous pieces, including *The Pleasure's in Walking Through*, cantata for Soprano, Chorus, and Orch. (1997).—NS/LK/DM

Rosseau, Norbert (Oscar Claude), Belgian composer; b. Ghent, Dec. 11, 1907; d. there, Nov. 1, 1975. He played violin as a child. His family emigrated to Italy in 1921, and he studied piano with Silvestri and composition with Respighi at the Accademia di Santa Cecilia in Rome (1925–28). His early works are cast in a traditional style of European modernism; later he halfheartedly experimented with dodecaphony and electronics.

WORKS: DRAMATIC: O p e r a : *Sicilenne* (1947); *Les Violons du prince* (1954). B a l l e t : *Juventa* (1957). ORCH.: *Suite Agreste* (1936); *H2O*, symphonic poem (1938; Liège, June 24, 1939); 2 concertos (1948, 1963); 2 syms.: No. 1 (1953) and No. 2, *Sinfonia sacra*, for Soloists, Chorus, and Orch. (1960–63); *Suite concertante* for String Quintet, Winds, Harpsichord, and Timpani (1959); Concerto for Wind Quintet and Orch. (1961); *Variations* (1963); Viola Concerto (1964); *Sonata a 4* for 4 Violins and Strings (1966); Horn Concerto (1967). CHAMBER: Violin Sonatina (1949); *3 jouets* for Oboe, Clarinet, and Bassoon (1955); Wind Quintet (1955); Clarinet Sonatina (1956); String Quartet (1956); Trio for Flute, Cello, and Piano (1956); *Rapsodie* for Flute, Bassoon, and Piano (1958); *Serenade à Syrinx* for Flute, Violin, Cello, and Harp (1959); Concertino for Piano, Double String Quartet, and Double Bass (1963); *Pentafonium* for Viola, Cello, Flute, Oboe, and Harpsichord (1964); *Diptique* for String Quartet (1971); *Dialogue* for Flute, Oboe, Viola, and Piano (1971); Piano Quartet (1975). VOCAL: *Inferno*, oratorio after Dante (1940); *L'An mille*, dramatic ode (1946); *Incantations*, cantata (1951); *Maria van den Kerselare*, Flemish oratorio (1952); *Zeepbellen*, chamber cantata, with Children's Chorus (1958); *Il Paradiso terrestre*, oratorio after Dante (1968).—NS/LK/DM

Rossellini, Renzo, Italian composer and teacher; b. Rome, Feb. 2, 1908; d. Monte Carlo, May 14, 1982. He studied composition in Rome with Setaccioli and Sallustio, and also took courses in orchestration with Molinari. In 1940 he was appointed prof. of composition at the Rome Cons., and in 1956 at the Accademia di Santa Cecilia in Rome. In 1973 he was named artistic director at the Opera at Monte Carlo. He publ. 2 books of autobiographical content, *Pagine di un musicista* (Bologna, 1964) and *Addio del passato* (Milan, 1968).

WORKS: DRAMATIC: O p e r a : *Alcassino e Nicoletta* (1928–30); *La guerra* (Rome, Feb. 25, 1956); *Il vortice* (Naples, Feb. 8, 1958); *Uno sguardo del ponte* (Rome, March 11, 1961); *L'Avventuriere* (Monte Carlo, Feb. 2, 1968); *La Reine morte* (Monte Carlo, 1973). B a l l e t : *La danza di Dassine* (San Remo, Feb. 24, 1935); *Poemetti pagani* (Monte Carlo, 1963); *Il Ragazzo e la sua ombra* (Venice, 1966). **O t h e r :** Film music. **ORCH.:** *Suite in 3 tempi* (1931); *Stornelli della Roma bassa* (1946); *Ut unum sint* (Miami, Oct. 20, 1963).—**NS/LK/DM**

Rosseter, Philip, English lutenist and composer; b. 1567 or 1568; d. London, May 5, 1623. He became a lutenist to King James I in 1603. From 1609 to 1617 he was active as a manager of theater companies, and oversaw productions at both the court and in public theaters. He was active with Campion, with whom he publ. a vol. of lute songs (1621). Among his other works were *A Booke of Ayres, set foorth to be song to the Lute, Orpharian, and Bass Violl* (London, 1601; ed. by E. Fellowes and rev. by T. Dart in The English Lute-Songs, series I, VIII, and IX, London, 2nd ed., 1966) and *Lessons for Consort* (London, 1609), as well as many lute pieces in contemporary collections.

BIBL.: J. Jeffreys, *The Life and Works of P. R.* (Wendover, 1990).—**LK/DM**

Rossi, Abbate Francesco, Italian composer; b. Bari, c. 1645; d. date unknown. He was a canon in Bari in 1680. He composed the operas *Bianca di Castiglia* (Milan, 1674), *Il Sejano moserno della Tracia* (Venice, 1680), *La pena degli occhi and La Clorilda* (both Venice, 1688), and *Mitrane* (Venice, 1689); also an oratorio, *La Caduta degli angeli*, Requiem, Psalms, etc.—**NS/LK/DM**

Rossi, Giovanni (Gaetano), Italian composer; b. Borgo S. Donnino, Parma, Aug. 5, 1828; d. Genoa, March 30, 1886. He studied at the Milan Cons., and from 1852 was maestro concertatore at the Teatro Regio in Parma. He was also organist at the court chapel and deputy singing master at the Cons., becoming deputy composition master (1853), composition master and vice-director (1856), and director (1864) of the Cons. He then was director of the Teatro Carlo Felice in Genoa (1874–86), and also of the Genoa Liceo Musicale (1874–86). Among his compositions were the operas *Elena di Taranto* (Parma, 1852), *Giovanni Giscala* (Parma, 1855), *Nicolò de Lapi* (Parma, 1865), and *La Contessa d'Altenberg* (Borgo S. Donnino, 1871); also an oratorio, *Le sette parole*, an overture, *Saulo*, a Requiem, 3 masses, etc. —**NS/LK/DM**

Rossi, Giulio, Italian bass; b. Rome, Oct. 27, 1865; d. Milan, Oct. 9, 1931. He had a tenor voice until he was 19, when an unintentional plunge into the Tiber in Dec. induced an illness, after which his voice lowered to the range of basso profondo. He then began vocal study under Oreste Tomassoni, making his debut at Parma, Oct. 20, 1887. In 1889 he toured South America with Adelina Patti, and made 2 tours of Mexico and Calif. with Luisa Tetrazzini. He made his Metropolitan Opera debut in N.Y. as the King in *Aida* on Nov. 16, 1908, remaining on its roster until 1919.—**NS/LK/DM**

Rossi, Lauro, Italian composer; b. Macerata, Feb. 19, 1810; d. Cremona, May 5, 1885. He was a pupil of Furno, Zingarelli, and Crescentini at Naples, bringing out a comic opera, *Le Contesse villane*, there (1829) with

fair success. He was asst. director at the Teatro Valle in Rome (1831–33). With his 10th opera, *La casa disabitata o I falsi monetari*, produced at La Scala, Milan, Aug. 11, 1834, he won a veritable triumph; it made the rounds of Italy and was given in Paris. In 1835 he went to Mexico as conductor and composer to an Italian opera troupe; when it folded, he set up his own opera company, becoming its director in 1837, and going to Havana (1840) and New Orleans (1842), returning to Italy in 1843. He brought out a new opera, *Il Borgomastro di Schiedam* (Milan, June 1, 1844), with indifferent success; his opera *Il Domino nero* (Milan, Sept. 1, 1849) fared a little better. His most successful opera was *La Contessa di Mons* (Turin, Jan. 31, 1874). He wrote 29 operas in all. In 1850 he was given the post of director of the Milan Cons., and in 1870 he succeeded Mercadante as director of the Naples Cons. He resigned in 1878, and retired to Cremona in 1880.—**NS/LK/DM**

Rossi, Luigi, eminent Italian lutenist, keyboard player, singing teacher, and composer; b. Torremaggiore, Foggia, c. 1597; d. Rome, Feb. 19, 1653. He studied in Naples with G. de Macque, then went to Rome, where his opera *Il palazzo incantato, overo La guerriera amante* was produced (Feb. 22, 1642). In 1646 he was called by Cardinal Mazarin to Paris with 20 other singers, and there staged his most important opera, *Orfeo* (March 2, 1647), the first Italian opera expressly written for a Paris production. He also composed the oratorio *Giuseppe* and some 300 chamber cantatas.

BIBL.: A. Wotquenne, *Étude bibliographique sur le compositeur napolitain L. R.* (Brussels, 1909); A. Ghislanzoni, *L. R.: Biografia e analisi delle composizioni* (Milan, 1954); E. Caluori, *The Cantatas of L. R.* (diss., Brandeis Univ., 1972).—**NS/LK/DM**

Rossi, Mario, eminent Italian conductor; b. Rome, March 29, 1902; d. there, June 29, 1992. He studied at the Rome Cons. (graduated, 1925). He was deputy conductor of the Augusteo Orch. in Rome (1926–36) and resident conductor of the Maggio Musicale Orch. in Florence (1936–44); subsequently was chief conductor of the RAI Orch. in Turin (1946–69); also appeared as a guest conductor in Europe. He became especially well known for his performances of contemporary music. —**NS/LK/DM**

Rossi, Michel Angelo, esteemed Italian violinist, organist, and composer, known as **Michel Angelo del Violino;** b. Genoa, 1601 or 1602; d. Rome (buried), July 7, 1656. His uncle, Lelio Rossi, was a Servite friar and principal organist at the cathedral of S. Lorenzo in Genoa; Michel Angelo served as his assistant until his own departure to Rome about 1624. There he entered the service of Cardinal Maurizio of Savoy. After studies with Frescobaldi, he won the patronage of the Barberini family in 1630. He entered the service of the Este family in Modena in 1638, and also served the Sforza family in Ferrara; eventually returned to Rome. Rossi won special recognition as a violinist. His importance as a composer rests upon his output for keyboard, which included *Toccate e correnti* for Organ or Harpsichord (Rome, c. 1640; 2nd ed., 1657; ed. in Corpus of Early Keyboard

Music, XV, 1966). He also composed 2 operas: *Erminia sul Giordano* (Rome, Feb. 2, 1633) and *Andromeda* (Ferrara, 1638).

BIBL.: J. Peterson, *The Keyboard Works of M. R.* (diss., Univ. of Ill., 1975); C. Moore, *The Composer M. R.: A "Diligent Fantasy Maker" in Seventeenth-Century Rome* (N.Y., 1993).—NS/LK/DM

Rossi, Salamone (also Salomone, Salamon de', or Shlomo),

distinguished Italian composer of Jewish descent; b. probably in Mantua, Aug. 19, 1570; d. probably there, c. 1630. He was closely associated with the Mantuan court for a number of years, being granted the privilege of not having to conform to the Mantuan law of wearing a yellow badge to acknowledge his Jewish heritage; the privilege was accorded him by Duke Vincenzo Gonzaga in 1606, and was renewed by Duke Francesco II upon his accession in 1612. In later years he devoted much time to a Jewish theatrical troupe, but continued to be associated with musical events at the court. He was a leading figure in the development of the trio sonata and the chamber duet. Among his instrumental works are *Il primo libro delle sinfonie e gagliarde...per sonar* for 2 Violas or Cornetts and Chitarrone or Other Instruments (1607), *Il secondo libro delle sinfonie e gagliarde, a 3, per sonar...con alcune delle dette a 4, 5, ed alcune canzoni per sonar, a 4, nel fine* for Violas and Chitarrone (1608), *Il terzo libro de varie sonate, sinfonie, gagliarde, brandi e corrente* for 2 Violas da Braccio and Chitarrone or Other Instruments, op.12 (1623), and *Il quarto libro de varie sonate, sinfonie, gagliarde, brandi e corrente* for 2 Violins and Chitarrone (1622). He also wrote sacred and secular vocal pieces.

BIBL.: S. Naumbourg, *Essai sur la vie et les oeuvres de Salamon R.* (Paris, 1877); E. Birnbaum, *Jüdische Musiker am Hofe zu Mantua von 1542–1628* (Vienna, 1893; Eng. tr., rev. and aug., 1978); J. Newman, *The Madrigals of Salamon de' R.* (diss., Columbia Univ., 1962); J. Newman and F. Rikko, *A Thematic Index to the Works of Salamon R.* (Hackensack, N.J., 1972). —NS/LK/DM

Rossi, Tino,

popular French chansonnier; b. Ajaccio, Corsica, April 29, 1907; d. Neuilly, Seine, Sept. 26, 1983. His father, a tailor, wanted him to continue in the same profession, but Rossi apprenticed himself in a church choir. He never studied voice formally, but rather devoted himself to singing popular ballads, accompanying himself on the guitar. He filled engagements in the provinces until 1934, when he was engaged as a featured singer at the Casino de Paris. A combination of good looks and natural talent made him a "vedette" overnight; the women of Paris flocked to hear him, and some of them he married. He died peacefully in his sleep of cancer of the pancreas.—NS/LK/DM

Rossi-Lemeni, Nicola,

Italian bass; b. Constantinople (of an Italian father and a Russian mother), Nov. 6, 1920, d. Bloomington, Ind., March 12, 1991. He was educated in Italy; studied law and planned a diplomatic career. In 1943 he decided to become a professional singer, but World War II interfered with his plans, and his debut as Varlaam in Venice did not take place until May 1, 1946. He first sang in the U.S. as Boris Godunov with the San Francisco Opera (Oct. 2, 1951); sang at the Metropolitan Opera in N.Y. in 1953–54. In 1980 he joined the faculty of Ind. Univ. in Bloomington. He married **Virginia Zeani** in 1958. Besides the regular operatic repertoire, he sang a number of roles in modern works, such as Wozzeck.—NS/LK/DM

Rossini, Gioachino (Antonio),

great Italian opera composer possessing an equal genius for shattering melodrama in tragedy and for devastating humor in comedy; b. Pesaro, Feb. 29, 1792; d. Paris, Nov. 13, 1868. He came from a musical family; his father served as town trumpeter in Lugo and Pesaro and played brass instruments in provincial theaters and his mother sang opera as seconda donna. When his parents traveled, he was usually boarded in Bologna. After the family moved to Lugo, his father taught him to play the horn; he also had a chance to study singing with a local canon. Later the family moved to Bologna, where he studied singing, harpsichord, and music theory with Padre Tesei; also learned to play the violin and viola. Soon he acquired enough technical ability to serve as maestro al cembalo in local churches and at occasional opera productions. He studied voice with Matteo Babbini. In 1806 he was accepted as a student at the Liceo Musicale in Bologna, where he studied singing and solfeggio with Gibelli, cello with Cavedagna, piano with Zanotti, and counterpoint with Padre Mattei. He also began composing. On Aug. 11, 1808, his cantata *Il pianto d'Armonia sulla morte d'Orfeo* was performed at the Liceo Musicale in Bologna and received a prize. About the same time he wrote his first opera, *Demetrio e Polibio* (Rome, May 18, 1812). In 1810 he was commissioned to write a work for the Teatro San Moise in Venice; he submitted his opera *La cambiale di matrimonio*, which won considerable acclaim at its premiere (Nov. 3, 1801). His next work was *L'equivoco stravagante*, premiered in Bologna on Oct. 26, 1811. There followed a number of other operas: *L'inganno felice* (Venice, Jan. 8, 1812), *Ciro in Babilonia* (Ferrara, March 1812), and *La scala di seta* (Venice, May 9, 1812). In 1812 he obtained a commission from La Scala of Milan; the resulting work, *La pietra del paragone*, was a fine success at its first performance (Sept. 2, 1812). In 1813 he brought out 3 operas for Venice: *Il Signor Bruschino* (Jan.), *Tancredi* (Feb. 6), and *L'Italiana in Algeri* (May 22), the last becoming a perennial favorite. The next 3 operas, *Aureliano in Palmira* (Milan, Dec. 26, 1813), *Il Turco in Italia* (Milan, Aug. 14, 1814), and *Sigismondo* (Venice, Dec. 26, 1814), were unsuccessful. By that time Rossini, still a very young man, had been approached by the impresario Barbaja, the manager of the Teatro San Carlo and the Teatro Fondo in Naples, with an offer for an exclusive contract, under the terms of which Rossini was to supply 2 operas annually for Barbaja. The first opera Rossini wrote for him was *Elisabetta, regina d'Inghilterra*, premiered at the Teatro San Carlo in Naples on Oct. 4, 1815; the title role was entrusted to Isabella Colbran, who was Barbaja's favorite mistress. An important innovation in the score was Rossini's use of *recitativo stromentato* in place of the usual *recitativo secco*. His next opera, *Torvaldo e Dorliska*, premiered in Rome on Dec. 26., 1815, was an unfortunate failure. Rossini now determined to try his skill in composing an opera buffa, based on the famous play by Beaumarchais *Le Barbier de Seville*; it was an audacious decision on Rossini's part, since an Italian opera on the same subject by Paisiello, *Il Barbiere di Siviglia*, first performed in 1782, was still playing with undiminished success. To avoid confusion, Rossini's opera on this subject was performed at the Teatro Argentina in Rome under a different title, *Almaviva, ossia L'inutile precauzione*. Rossini was only 23 years old when he completed the score, which proved to be his greatest accomplishment and a standard opera buffa in the repertoire of theaters all over the world. Rossini conducted its first performance in Rome on Feb. 20, 1816, but if contemporary reports and gossip can be trusted, the occasion was marred by various stage accidents which moved the unruly Italian audience to interrupt the spectacle with vociferous outcries of derision; however, the next performance scored a brilliant success. For later productions he used the title *Il Barbiere di Siviglia*. Strangely enough, the operas he wrote immediately afterward were not uniformly successful: *La Gazzetta*, premiered in Naples on Sept. 26, 1816, passed unnoticed; the next opera, *Otello*, also premiered in Naples on Dec. 4, 1816, had some initial success but was not retained in the repertoire after a few sporadic performances. There followed *La Cenerentola* (Rome, Jan. 25, 1817) and *La gazza ladra* (Milan, May 31, 1817), which fared much better. But the following 7 operas, *Armida, Mosè in Egitto, Ricciardo e Zoraide, Ermione, La Donna del lago, Maometto II,* and *Zelmira*, premiered in Naples between 1817 and 1822, were soon forgotten; only the famous *Prayer* in *Mosè in Egitto* saved the opera from oblivion. The prima donna assoluta in all these operas was Isabella Colbran; after a long association with Barbaja, she went to live with Rossini, who finally married her on March 16, 1822. This event, however, did not result in a break between the impresario and the composer; Barbaja even made arrangements for a festival of Rossini's works in Vienna at the Kärnthnertortheater, of which he became a director. In Vienna Rossini met Beethoven. Returning to Italy, he brought out a fairly successful mythological opera, *Semiramide* (Venice, Feb. 3, 1823), with Colbran in the title role. Rossini then signed a contract for a season in London with Giovanni Benelli, director of the Italian opera at the King's Theatre. Rossini arrived in London late in 1823 and was received by King George IV. He conducted several of his operas, and was also a guest at the homes of the British nobility, where he played piano as an accompanist to singers, at very large fees. In 1824 he settled in Paris, where he became director of the Théâtre-Italien. For the coronation of King Charles X he composed *Il viaggio a Reims*, which was performed in Paris under his direction on June 19, 1825. He used parts of this *pièce d'occasion* in his opera *Le Comte Ory*. In Paris he met Meyerbeer, with whom he established an excellent relationship. After the expiration of his contract with the Théâtre-Italien, he was given the nominal titles of "Premier Compositeur du Roi" and "Inspecteur Général du Chant en France" at an annual salary of 25,000 francs. He was now free to compose for the Paris Opéra; there, on Oct. 9, 1826, he brought out *Le Siège de Corinthe*, a revised French version of *Maometto II*. Later he also

revised the score of *Mosè in Egitto*, which was first performed at the Paris Opéra in French as *Moïse et Pharaon* on March 26, 1827. There followed *Le Comte Ory* (Aug. 20, 1828). In May 1829 Rossini was able to obtain an agreement with the government of King Charles X guaranteeing him a lifetime annuity of 6,000 francs. In return, he promised to write more works for the Paris Opéra. On Aug. 3, 1829, his *Guillaume Tell* was given its premiere at the Opéra; it became immensely popular.

At the age of 37, Rossini stopped writing operas. The French revolution of July 1830, which dethroned King Charles X, invalidated his contract with the French government. Rossini sued the government of King Louis Philippe, the successor to the throne of Charles X, for the continuation of his annuity; the incipient litigation was settled in 1835. In 1832 Rossini met Olympe Pélissier, who became his mistress; in 1837 Rossini legally separated from Colbran. She died in 1845, and on Aug. 16, 1846, Rossini married Pélissier. From 1836 to 1848 they lived in Bologna, where Rossini served as consultant to the Liceo Musicale. In 1848 they moved to Florence; in 1855 he decided to return to Paris, where he was to remain for the rest of his life. His home in the suburb of Passy became the magnet of the artistic world. Rossini was a charming, affable, and gregarious host; he entertained lavishly; he was a great gourmet, and invented recipes for Italian food that were enthusiastically adopted by French chefs. His wit was fabulous, and his sayings were eagerly reported in the French journals. He did not abandon composition entirely during his last years of life; in 1867 he wrote a *Petite messe solennelle*; as a token of gratitude to the government of the 2nd Empire he composed a *Hymne à Napoleon III et à son vaillant peuple*; of great interest are the numerous piano pieces, songs, and instrumental works which he called *Péchés de vieillesse*, a collection containing over 150 pieces.

What were the reasons for Rossini's decision to stop writing operas? Rumors flew around Paris that he was unhappy about the cavalier treatment he received from the management of the Paris Opéra, and he spoke disdainfully of yielding the operatic field to "the Jews" (Meyerbeer and Halévy), whose operas captivated the Paris audiences. The report does not bear the stamp of truth, for Rossini was friendly with Meyerbeer until Meyerbeer's death in 1864. Besides, he was not in the habit of complaining; he enjoyed life too well. He was called "Le Cygne de Pesaro" ("The Swan of Pesaro," his birthplace). The story went that a delegation arrived from Pesaro with a project of building a monument to Rossini; the town authorities had enough money to pay for the pedestal, but not for the statue itself. Would Rossini contribute 10,000 francs for the completion of the project? "For 10,000 francs," Rossini was supposed to have replied, "I would stand on the pedestal myself." *Se non è vero è ben trovato.* He had a healthy sense of self-appreciation, but he invariably put it in a comic context. While his mother was still living, he addressed his letters to her as "Mother of the Great Maestro."

The circumstance that Rossini was born on a leap-year day was the cause of many a bon mot on his part. On Feb. 29, 1868, he decided to celebrate his 19th birthday, for indeed, there had been then only 19 leap years since his birth. He was superstitious; like many Italians, he stood in fear of Friday the 13th. He died on Nov. 13, 1868, which was a Friday. In 1887 his remains were taken to Florence for entombment in the Church of Santa Croce.

Rossini's melodies have been used by many composers as themes for various works: Respighi utilized Rossini's *Quelques riens* in his ballet *La Boutique fantasque*, and other themes in his orch. suite *Rossiniana*. An opera entitled *Rossini in Neapel* was written by Bernhard Paumgartner. Britten made use of Rossini's music in his orch. suites *Soirées musicales* and *Matinées musicales*. The most famous arrangement of any of Rossini's compositions is the aforementioned *Prayer* from *Mosè in Egitto*, transcribed for violin by Paganini.

A complete ed. of the works of Rossini, the *Quaderni rossiniani, a cura della Fondazione Rossini*, began publication in Pesaro in 1954.

WORKS: DRAMATIC: O p e r a : *Demetrio e Polibio*, opera seria (1808; Teatro Valle, Rome, May 18, 1812); *La cambiale di matrimonio*, farsa (Teatro San Moisè, Venice, Nov. 3, 1810); *L'equivoco stravagante*, opera buffa (Teatro del Corso, Bologna, Oct. 26, 1811); *L'inganno felice*, farsa (1811; Teatro San Moisè, Venice, Jan. 8, 1812); *Ciro in Babilonia, ossia La caduta di Baldassare*, dramma con cori or oratorio (Teatro Municipale, Ferrara, March 1812); *La scala di seta*, farsa (Teatro San Moisè, Venice, May 9, 1812); *La pietra del paragone*, melodramma giocoso or opera buffa (Teatro alla Scala, Milan, Sept. 26, 1812); *L'occasione fa il ladro, ossia Il cambio della valigia*, burletta per musica (Teatro San Moisè, Venice, Nov. 24, 1812); *Il Signor Bruschino, ossia Il Figlio per azzardo*, farsa giocosa (1812; Teatro San Moise, Venice, Jan. 1813); *Tancredi*, opera seria or melodramma eroico (1812–13; Teatro La Fenice, Venice, Feb. 6, 1813); *L'Italiana in Algeri*, melodramma giocoso (Teatro San Benedetto, Venice, May 22, 1813); *Aureliano in Palmira*, opera seria or dramma serio (Teatro alla Scala, Milan, Dec. 26, 1813); *Il Turco in Italia*, opera buffa or dramma buffo (Teatro alla Scala, Milan, Aug. 14, 1814); *Sigismondo*, opera seria or dramma (Teatro La Fenice, Venice, Dec. 26, 1814); *Elisabetta, regina d'Inghilterra*, dramma (Teatro San Carlo, Naples, Oct. 4, 1815); *Torvaldo e Dorliska*, dramma semiserio (Teatro Valle, Rome, Dec. 26, 1815); *Il Barbiere di Siviglia*, opera buffa or commedia (1st perf. as *Almaviva, ossia L'inutile precauzione*, Teatro Argentina, Rome, Feb. 20, 1816); *La Gazzetta, ossia Il matrimonio per concorso* (subtitle does not appear in the first printed libretto), opera buffa (Teatro dei Fiorentini, Naples, Sept. 26, 1816); *Otello, ossia Il Moro di Venezia*, opera seria or dramma (Teatro del Fondo, Naples, Dec. 4, 1816); *La Cenerentola, ossia La bontà in trionfo*, dramma giocoso (1816–17; Teatro Valle, Rome, Jan. 25, 1817); *La gazza ladra*, melodramma or opera semiseria (Teatro alla Scala, Milan, May 31, 1817); *Armida*, opera seria or dramma (Teatro San Carlo, Naples, Nov. 11, 1817); *Adelaide di Borgogna, ossia Ottone, re d'Italia*, dramma (Teatro Argentina, Rome, Dec. 27, 1817); *Mosè in Egitto*, azione tragico-sacra or oratorio (Teatro San Carlo, Naples, March 5, 1818); *Adina, o Il Califfo di Bagdad*, farsa (1818; Teatro São Carlos, Lisbon, June 22, 1826); *Ricciardo e Zoraide*, dramma, opera seria, or opera semiseria (Teatro San Carlo, Naples, Dec. 3, 1818); *Ermione*, azione tragica (Teatro San Carlo, Naples, March 27, 1819); *Eduardo* [later *Edoardo*] *e Cristina*, dramma (Teatro San Benedetto, Venice, April 24, 1819); *La Donna del lago*, melodramma or opera seria (Teatro San Carlo, Naples, Sept. 24, 1819); *Bianca e Falliero, ossia Il consiglio dei tre*, opera seria (Teatro alla Scala, Milan, Dec. 26, 1819); *Maometto II*, dramma or opera seria (Teatro San Carlo, Naples, Dec. 3, 1820); *Matilde Shabran* [later *Matilde di Shabran*], *ossia Bellezza e Cuor di Ferro*, opera semiseria (1820–21; Teatro Apollo, Rome, Feb. 24, 1821); *Zelmira*, dramma or opera seria (1821–22; Teatro San Carlo, Naples, Feb. 16, 1822); *Semiramide*, melodramma tragico or opera seria (1822–23; Teatro La Fenice, Venice, Feb. 3, 1823); *Il viaggio a Reims, ossia L'albergo del Giglio d'Oro*, cantata scenica (Théâtre-Italien, Paris, June 19, 1825); *Le Siège de Corinthe*, grand opera (rev. of *Maometto II*; Opéra, Paris, Oct. 9, 1826); *Moise et Pharaon, ou Le Passage de la Mer Rouge*, grand opera (rev. of *Mosè in Egitto*; Opéra, Paris, March 26, 1827); *Le Comte Ory*, opera-comique (utilizing numbers from *Il viaggio a Reims*; Opéra, Paris, Aug. 20, 1828); *Guillaume Tell*, grand opera (1828–29; Opéra, Paris, Aug. 3, 1829). **ORCH.:** Overture in D major (1808); 3 sinfonias: D major (1808); E-flat major (1809; later rev. for use as the overture to *La cambiale di matrimonio*); A major (discovered by P. Ingerslev-Jenson and called the "Odense"); *Variazioni in fa maggiore per piu strumenti obbligati con accompagnamento di orchestra* (1809); *Variazioni in do maggiore per clarinetto obbligato con accompagnamento di orchestra* (1810); marches. **CHAMBER:** 6 *sonate a quattro* (1804); 5 string quartets (1806–08); 5 duets (1806); *Tema con variazione per quattro strumenti a fiato* for Flute, Clarinet, Horn, and Bassoon (1812); *Rondeau fantastique* for Horn and Piano (1856). **VOCAL: C a n t a t a s :** *Il pianto d'Armonia sulla morte d'Orfeo* (Bologna, Aug. 11, 1808); *La morte di Didone* (1811; Venice, May 2, 1818); *Dalle quete e pallid'ombre* (1812); *Egle ed Irene* (1814); *L'Aurora* (Rome, Nov. 1815); *Le nozze di Teti e di Peleo* (Naples, April 24, 1816); *Cantata con cori* ("*Omaggio Umiliato...*"; also known as *Corifea, Partenope*, or *Igea*; Naples, Feb. 20, 1819); *Cantata a tre voci con cori* ("*Cantata...9 Maggio 1819*"; Naples, May 9, 1819); *La riconoscenza* (Naples, Dec. 27, 1821); *L'augurio felice* (1822); *La Santa Alleanza* (Verona, Nov. 24, 1822); *Il vero omaggio* (Verona, Dec. 3, 1822); *Il Bardo* (1822); *Omaggio pastorale* (Treviso, April 1, 1823); *Il pianto delle muse in morte di Lord Byron* (London, June 9, 1824); *Cantata per il battesimo del figlio del banchiere Aguado* (Paris, July 16, 1827); *Giovanna d'Arco* (1832; rev. 1852); *Cantata ad Onore del Sommo Pontefice Pio IX* (Bologna, Aug. 16, 1846). **O t h e r :** 3 early masses (the first contains 3 sections only by Rossini for a composite score composed by students of the Liceo Musicale in 1808 and perf. in Bologna, June 2, 1808; 1808; 1809); *Messa solenne* (Naples, March 19, 1820); *Tantum ergo* (1824); *Soirées musicales* (1830–35); *Stabat Mater* (1st version, 1831–32; orch. version, 1841; Paris, Jan. 7, 1842); *Tantum ergo* (Bologna, Nov. 28, 1847); *O salutaris Hostia* (1857); *Laus Deo* (1861); *Petite messe solennelle* (1863; Paris, March 14, 1864; orch. version, 1867; Paris, Feb. 24, 1869).

BIBL.: A valuable source is the *Bollettino del Centro R.ano di Studi* (Pesaro, 1955–60; 1967 et seq.). See also G. Righetti-Giorgi, *Cenni di una donna già cantante sopra il maestro R.* (Bologna, 1823); G. Carpani, *Le Rossiniane, ossia Lettere musico-teatrali* (Padua, 1824); Stendhal, *Vie de R.* (Paris, 1824; many subsequent eds. and trs.; Eng. tr. as *Life of R.*, tr. and ed. by R. Coe, London and N.Y., 1956; 2nd ed., 1970); J.A. Wendt, *R.'s Leben und Treiben* (Leipzig, 1824); J.-L. d'Ortigue, *De la guerre des dilettanti, ou De la Révolution opérée par R. dans l'opéra français, et des rapports qui existent entre la musique, la littérature et les arts* (Paris, 1830); A. Zanolini, *Biografia di G. R.* (Paris, 1836; also later eds.); L. and M. Escudier, *R.: Sa vie et ses oeuvres* (Paris, 1854); E. de Mirecourt, *R.* (Paris, 1855); A. Aulagnier, *G. R.: Sa vie et ses oeuvres* (Paris, 1864); A.-J. Azevedo, *G. R.: Sa vie ses oeuvres* (Paris, 1864); F. Hiller, *Plaudereien mit R.*, Vol. II of *Aus dem Tonleben unserer Zeit* (Leipzig, 1868); H. Edwards, *Life of R.* (London, 1869; reissued in a condensed version as *R. and His School*, London, 1881); C. Montrond, *R.: Étude biographique* (Lille, 1870); F. Mordani, *Della vita privata di G. R.: Memorie inedite* (Imola, 1871); A. Pougin, *R.: Notes, impressions, souvenirs, commentaires* (Paris, 1871); G. Vanzolini, *Della vera patria di G. R.* (Pesaro, 1873); L. Silvestri, *Della vita e delle opere di G. R. ...* (Milan, 1874); C. Magnico, *R. e Wagner, o La musica italiana e la musica tedesca* (Genoa, 1875); G. de Sanctis, *G. R.: Appunti di viaggio* (Rome, 1878); J. Sittard, *G.A. R.* (Leipzig, 1882); C. Thrane, *R. og operaen* (Copenhagen, 1885); V. Camaiti, *G. R.: Notizie biografiche, artistiche e aneddotiche* (Florence, 1887); R. Gandolfi, *G. R.* (Florence, 1887); G. Mazzatinti, *Lettere inedite di G. R.* (Imola, 1890); A. Allmäyer, *Undici lettere di G. R. pubblicate per la prima volta ...* (Siena, 1892); A. Kohut, *R.* (Leipzig, 1892); G. Mazzatinti, *Lettere inedite e rare di G. R.* (Imola, 1892); E. Michotte, *Souvenirs: Une Soirée chez R. à Beau-Sejour (Passy) 1858 ...* (Brussels, n.d. [after 1893]; Eng. tr. by H. Weinstock, Chicago, 1968); E. Checchi, *R.* (Florence, 1898); A. Maffei, *R.* (Florence, 1898); G. Mazzatinti and F. and G. Manis, *Lettere di G. R.* (Florence, 1902); L. Dauriac, *R.: Biographie critique* (Paris, 1906); E. Michotte, *Souvenirs: La Visite de R. Wagner à R. (Paris, 1860): Détails inédits et commentaires* (Paris, 1906; Eng. tr. by H. Weinstock, Chicago, 1968); E. Corradi, *G. R.* (Rome, 1909); F. Cowen, *R.* (London and N.Y., 1912); G. Fara, *Genio e ingegno musicale: G. R.* (Turin, 1915); N. Morini, *La casa di R. in Bologna* (Bologna, 1916); L. Neretti, *I due inni patriottici di G. R.* (Florence, 1918); F. Vatielli, *R. e Bologna* (Bologna, 1918); H. de Curzon, *R.* (Paris, 1920; 2nd ed., 1930); R. Fauchois, *R.* (Lyons, 1922); G. Radiciotti, *Il Barbiere di Siviglia: Guida attraverso la commedia e la musica* (Milan, 1923); G. Gatti, *Le "Barbier de Séville" de R.* (Paris, 1926); G. Biamonti, *Guglielmo Tell* (Rome, 1929); G. Radiciotti, *G. R.: Vita documenta, opere ed influenza su l'arte* (3 vols., Tivoli, 1927–29); idem, *Aneddoti rossiniani autentici* (Rome, 1929); H. de Curzon, *Une Heure avec R.* (Paris, 1930); A. Bonaventura, *R.* (Florence, 1934); G. Derwent, *R. and Some Forgotten Nightingales* (London, 1934); H. Gerigk, *R.* (Potsdam, 1934); F. Toye, *R.: A Study in Tragi-Comedy* (London and N.Y., 1934); H. Faller, *Die Gesangskoloratur in R.s Opern und ihre Ausführung* (Berlin, 1935); G. Monaldi, *Gli Uomini illustri: G. R. nell'arte, nella vita, negli aneddoti* (Milan, n.d. [1936]); L. D'Amico, *R.* (Turin, 1939); R. Bacchelli, *G. R.* (Turin, 1941; 2nd ed., 1945); F. Bonavia, *R.* (London, 1941); A. Fraccaroli, *R.* (Milan, 1941; 4th ed., 1944); G. Roncaglia, *R. l'olimpico* (Milan, 1946; 2nd ed., 1953); G. Brigante Colonna, *Vita di R.* (Florence, 1947); K. Pfister, *Das Leben R.s: Gesetz und Triumph der Oper* (Vienna and Berlin, 1948); C. van Berkel, *G. R.* (Haarlem, 1950); F. Bonafé, *R. et son oeuvre* (Le-Puy-en-Velay, 1955); U. Gozzano, *R.: Il romanzo dell'opera* (Turin, 1955); L. Rognoni, *R., con un'appendice comprendente lettere, documenti, testimonianze* (Parma, 1956; 3rd ed., 1977); R. Bacchelli, *R. e esperienze rossiniane* (Milan, 1959); P. Ingerslev-Jensen, *R.* (Copenhagen, 1959); F. Schlitzer, *Un piccolo carteggio inedito di R. con un impresario italiano a Vienna* (Florence, 1959); V. Viviani, ed., *I libretti di R.* (Milan, 1965); A. Bonaccorsi, ed., *G. R.* (Florence, 1968); F. d'Amico, *L'opera teatrale di G. R.* (Rome, 1968); H. Weinstock, *R.: A Biography* (N.Y., 1968); P. Gossett, *The Operas of R.: Problems of Textual Criticism in Nineteenth-Century Opera* (diss., Princeton Univ., 1970); N. Till, *R.: His Life and Times* (Tunbridge Wells, 1983); A. Camosci, *G. R. dai ritratti e dalle scritture* (Rome, 1985); P. Mioli, *Invito all'ascolto di G. R.* (Milan, 1986); R. Osborne, *R.* (London, 1986; rev. ed., 1993); R. Bacchelli, *Vita di R.* (Florence, 1987); M. Beghelli and N. Gallino, eds., *Tutti i libretti di R.* (Milan, 1991); A Bassi, *G. R.* (Padua, 1992); B. Cagli and S. Ragni, eds., *G. R.: Lettere e documenti* (Pesaro, 1992 et seq.); A. Kendall, *G. R.: The Reluctant Hero* (London, 1992); P. Fabbri, ed., *G. R., 1792–1992, il testo e la scena: Convegno internazionale di studi, Pesaro, 25–28 giugno 1992* (Pesaro, 1994); C. Osborne, *The Bel Canto Operas of R., Donizetti, and Bellini* (Portland, Ore., 1994); M. Grempler, *R. e la patria: Studien zu Leben und Werk G. R.s vor dem Hintergrund des Risorgimento* (Kassel, 1996); D. Tortora, *Drammaturgia del R. serio: Le opere della maturità: Da Tancredi a Semiramide* (Rome, 1996); M. Emanuele, *L'ultima stagione italiana: Le forme dell'opera seria di R. da Napoli a Venezia* (Florence and Turin, 1997); U. Teske-Spellerberg, *Die Klaviermusik von G. R.* (Tutzing, 1998).—**NS/LK/DM**

Rössl-Majdan, Hildegard, Austrian contralto; b. Moosbierbaum, Jan. 21, 1921. She was educated at the Vienna Academy of Music. In 1946 she launched her career as a concert singer; also appeared at the Vienna State Opera, Milan's La Scala, London's Covent Garden, and other European opera houses; sang at the festivals in Salzburg, Edinburgh, and Aix-en-Provence; later was active as a voice teacher.—**NS/LK/DM**

Rossum, Frederik (Leon Hendrik) van, Belgian composer and teacher of Dutch descent; b. Elsene, Brussels, Dec. 5, 1939. He took Belgian citizenship when he was 18, and studied composition with Souris and Quinet at the Brussels Cons. (1956–62), winning a Premier Grand Prix de Rome for his *Cantate de la Haute Mer* (1965). He taught piano at the Brussels Cons. (1965–68), then became prof. of counterpoint at the Liège Cons. (1968). He served as prof. of analysis at the Brussels Cons. (from 1971), and also was director of the Watermael-Bosvoorde Academy of Music.

WORKS: *Petite pièce* for Clarinet and Piano (1961); Piano Sonata (1963); *Capriccio* for Wind Quintet (1963); Sinfonietta (1964); *Cantata sacrée* for Chorus, Strings, and Harpsichord (1966); *12 Miniatures* for Piano or Orch. (1967); *Divertimento* for Strings (1967); *Sinfonie concertante* for Horn, Piano, Percussion, and Orch. (1968); *Graffiti* for Violin and Piano (1968); *Duetto* for Cello and Piano (1968); *Pyrogravures* for Wind Quintet (1968); *Threni* for Mezzo-soprano and Orch. (1969); *Der Blaue Reiter* for Orch., in homage to German expressionistic painters (1971); *Epitaph* for Strings (1972); Piano Quintet (1972); *Rétrospection* for Soprano, Contralto, Chorus, 2 Pianos, and Percussion (1973); *Réquisitoire* for Brass and Percussion (1973); Piano Concerto (1975); *Petite suite réactionnaire* for Orch. (1975); *De soldaat Johan*, television opera (1975–76); 2 violin concertos (1979; 1985–89); *Polyptyque* for Orch. (1986); piano pieces.—**NS/LK/DM**

Rostal, Max, Austrian-born English violinist and pedagogue; b. Teschen, Silesia, Aug. 7, 1905; d. Bern, Aug. 6, 1991. He studied violin with Arnold Rosé in Vienna and with Carl Flesch in Berlin, where he also took courses in composition with Emil Bohnke and Mátyás Seiber at the Hochschule für Musik; then was a prof. there (1930–33). In 1934 he left Nazi Germany; eventually went to London and became a naturalized British subject. He was a prof. at the Guildhall School of Music (1944–58), the Cologne Cons. (1957), and the Bern Cons. (1958). In 1977 he was made a Commander of the Order of the British Empire. He was especially noted for his performances of contemporary music.—**NS/LK/DM**

Rostropovich, Leopold, Russian cellist and teacher, father of **Mstislav (Leopoldovich) Rostropov-**

ich; b. Voronezh, March 9, 1892; d. Orenburg, July 31, 1942. He studied cello with his father, Vitold Rostropovich. In addition to giving concerts, he served as a prof. at the Azerbaijan Cons. (1925–31). He then lived in Moscow, but after the outbreak of the Nazi-Soviet war in 1941, he moved to Orenburg.—NS/LK/DM

Rostropovich, Mstislav (Leopoldovich), famous Russian cellist and conductor, son of **Leopold Rostropovich;** b. Baku, March 27, 1927. A precocious child, he began cello studies with his father at an early age; also had piano lessons from his mother. In 1931 the family moved to Moscow, where he made his debut when he was 8; continued his training at the Central Music School (1939–41); then studied cello with Kozolupov and composition with Shebalin and Shostakovich at the Moscow Cons. (1943–48); subsequently studied privately with Prokofiev. He won the International Competition for Cellists in Prague in 1950, and the next year made his first appearance in the West in Florence. A phenomenally successful career ensued. He made his U.S. debut at N.Y.'s Carnegie Hall in 1956, winning extraordinary critical acclaim. He became a teacher (1953) and a prof. (1956) at the Moscow Cons., and also a prof. at the Leningrad Cons. (1961). A talented pianist, he frequently appeared as accompanist to his wife, **Galina Vishnevskaya,** whom he married in 1955. In 1961 he made his first appearance as a conductor. As his fame increased, he received various honors, including the Lenin Prize in 1963 and the Gold Medal of the Royal Phil. Soc. of London in 1970. In spite of his eminence and official honors, however, he encountered difficulties with the Soviet authorities, owing chiefly to his spirit of uncompromising independence. He let the dissident author Aleksandr Solzhenitsyn stay at his dacha near Moscow, protesting the Soviet government's treatment of the Nobel prize winner for literature in a letter to *Pravda* in 1969. Although the letter went unpubl. in his homeland, it was widely disseminated in the West. As a result, Rostropovich found himself increasingly hampered in his career by the Soviet Ministry of Culture. His concerts were canceled without explanation, as were his wife's engagements at the Bolshoi Theater. Foreign tours were forbidden, as were appearances on radio, television, and recordings. In 1974 he and his wife obtained permission to go abroad, and were accompanied by their 2 daughters. He made a brilliant debut as a guest conductor with the National Sym. Orch. in Washington, D.C. (March 5, 1975); his success led to his appointment as its music director in 1977. Free from the bureaucratic annoyances of the U.S.S.R., he and his wife publicized stories of their previous difficulties at home in Russia. Annoyed by such independent activities, the Moscow authorities finally stripped them both of their Soviet citizenship as "ideological renegades." The Soviet establishment even went so far as to remove the dedication to Rostropovich of Shostakovich's 2nd Cello Concerto. The whole disgraceful episode ended when the Soviet government, chastened by perestroika, restored Rostropovich's citizenship in Jan. 1990, and invited him to take the National Sym. Orch. to the U.S.S.R. Besides conducting the American orch. there, Rostropovich appeared as soloist in Dvořák's Cello Concerto.

His return to Russia was welcomed by the populace as a vindication of his principles of liberty. A symbolic linguistic note: the difficult-to-pronounce first name of Rostropovich, which means "avenged glory," is usually rendered by his friends and admirers as simply Slava, that is, "glory." In 1993 he took the National Sym. Orch. on another visit to Russia and on Sept. 26 conducted it in a special concert in Moscow's Red Square in commemoration of the 100th anniversary of the death of Tchaikovsky. In 1994 he stepped down as the orch.'s music director and was named life-time conductor laureate.

Rostropovich is duly recognized as one of the greatest cellists of the century, a master interpreter of both the standard and the contemporary literature. To enhance the repertoire for his instrument, he commissioned and premiered numerous scores, including works by Prokofiev, Shostakovich, Britten, Piston, and Foss. As a conductor, he proved himself an impassioned and authoritative interpreter of the music of the Russian national and Soviet schools of composition. He organized the 1st Rostropovich International Cello Competition in Paris in 1981 and the Rostropovich Festival in Snape, England, in 1983. He was made an Officer of the French Légion d'honneur in 1982, and received an honorary knighthood from Queen Elizabeth II of England in 1987. In 1993 he was awarded the Japanese Praemium Imperiale. He received the Polar Music Prize of Sweden in 1995.

BIBL.: T. Gaidamovich, *M. R.* (Moscow, 1969); J. Roy, *R., Gainsbourg et Dieu* (Paris, 1992); S. Khentova, *R.* (St. Petersburg, 1993); C. Samuel, *M. R. and Galina Vishnevskaya: Russia, Music, and Liberty: Conversations with Claude Samuel* (Portland, Ore., 1995); T. Grum-Grzhimako, *R. i ego sovremenniki: V legendakh, byliakh i dialogakh* (Moscow, 1997).—NS/LK/DM

Rosvaenge (real name, **Rosenving-Hansen**), **Helge,** esteemed German tenor; b. Copenhagen (of German parents), Aug. 29, 1897; d. Munich, June 19, 1972. He studied in Copenhagen and Berlin. He made his operatic debut as Don José in Neustrelitz in 1921; then sang in Altenburg (1922–24), Basel (1924–26), and Cologne (1926–29). He distinguished himself as a member of the Berlin State Opera (1929–44); also sang in Vienna and Munich. He appeared at the Salzburg (1933, 1937) and Bayreuth (1934, 1936) festivals; made his debut at London's Covent Garden as Florestan in 1938. After World War II, he again sang in Berlin and Vienna; made a concert tour of the U.S. in 1962. In his prime, he was compared to Caruso as a practitioner of bel canto. He excelled in the operas of Mozart; was also noted for his portrayals of Radamès, Manrico, Huon, and Calaf. He publ. the autobiographical booklets *Skratta Pajazza* (*Ridi, Pagliaccio*; Copenhagen, 1945); *Mach es besser, mein Sohn* (Leipzig, 1962); and *Leitfaden für Gesangsbeflissene* (Munich, 1964).

BIBL.: F. Tassie, *H. R.* (Augsburg, 1975).—NS/LK/DM

Rota (real name, **Rinaldi**), **Nino,** brilliant Italian composer; b. Milan, Dec. 3, 1911; d. Rome, April 10, 1979. He was a precocious musician. At the age of 11 he wrote an oratorio that had a public performance, and at 13 he composed a lyric comedy in 3 acts, *Il Principe porcaro*, after Hans Christian Andersen. He entered the Milan Cons. in 1923, and took courses with Delachi, Orefici, and Bas. After private studies with Pizzetti (1925–26), he studied composition with Casella at the Accademia di Santa Cecilia in Rome, graduating in 1930, and then pursued training at the Curtis Inst. of Music in Philadelphia, studying composition with Scalero and conducting with Reiner (1931–32). Returning to Italy, he entered the Univ. of Milan to study literature, gaining a degree in 1937. He taught at the Taranto music school (1937–38), and then was a teacher (from 1939) and director (1950–78) at the Bari Liceo Musicale. His musical style demonstrates a great facility, and even felicity, with occasional daring excursions into the forbidding territory of dodecaphony. However, his most durable compositions are related to his music for the cinema; he composed the sound tracks of a great number of films of the Italian director Federico Fellini covering the period from 1950 to 1979.

WORKS: DRAMATIC: O p e r a : *Il Principe porcaro* (1925); *Ariodante* (Parma, Nov. 5, 1942); *Torquemada* (1943; rev. version, Naples, Jan. 24, 1976); *I 2 timidi*, radio opera (Italian Radio, 1950; stage version, London, March 17, 1952); *Il cappello di paglia di Firenzi* (1946; Palermo, April 2, 1955) *La scuola di guida* (Spoleto, 1959); *Lo scoiattolo in gamba* (Venice, Sept. 16, 1959); *La notte di un nevrastenico*, opera buffa (concert version, Turin, July 9, 1959; stage version, Milan, Feb. 8, 1960); *Aladino e la lampada magica* (Naples, Jan. 14, 1968); *La visita meravigliosa*, after H.G. Wells (Palermo, Feb. 6, 1970); *Napoli milionaria* (Spoleto, June 22, 1977). **B a l l e t :** *La rappresentazione di Adamo ed Eva* (Perugia, Oct. 5, 1957); *La strada* (after the 1954 Fellini film of the same name; Milan, 1965; rev. 1978); *La Molière imaginaire* (Paris, 1976). **F i l m :** Scores for films by Fellini, including *Lo sceicco bianco* (*The White Sheik*; 1950); *I vitelloni* (1953); *La strada* (1954); *Il bidone* (1955); *Notti di Cabiria* (1957); *La dolce vita* (1959); part of *Boccaccio 70* (1962); *Otto de mezza* (*8 1/2*; 1963); *Giulietta degli spiriti* (*Juliet of the Spirits*; 1965); *Satyricon* (1969); *The Clowns* (1971); *Fellini Roma* (1972); *Amarcord* (1974); *Casanova* (1977); *Orchestra Rehearsal* (1979). His scores for other directors include Cass's *The Glass Mountain* (1950); De Filippo's *Napoli milionaria* (1950); Vidor's *War and Peace* (1956); Visconti's *Le notti bianche* (1957), *Rocco e i suoi fratelli* (1960), and *Il gattopardo* (*The Leopard*; 1963); Zeffirelli's *The Taming of the Shrew* (1966) and *Romeo e Giulietta* (1968); Bondarchuk's *Waterloo* (1969); Coppola's *The Godfather I* (1972) and *II* (1974); Harvey's *The Abdication* (1974); Wertmuller's *Love and Anarchy* (1974); Guillermin's *Death on the Nile* (1978); Monicelli's *Caro Michele* (1978); and Troell's *Hurricane* (1979). **ORCH.:** *Balli* (1932); *Serenata* (1932); 3 syms. (1936–39; 1937–41, rev. 1975; 1957); *Sinfonia sopra una canzone d'amore* (1947–72); Harp Concerto (1948); *Variazioni sopra un tema gioviale* (1954); *Concerto festivo* (1958); 2 piano concertos (1960; *Piccolo mondo antico*, 1979); *Concerto soirée* for Piano and Orch.; *Fantasia sopra 12-note del "Don Giovanni" di Mozart* for Piano and Orch. (1961); Concerto for Strings (1964); Trombone Concerto (1968); *Divertimento concertante* for Double Bass and Orch. (1968–69); 2 cello concertos (1972, 1973); *Castel del Monte* for Horn and Orch. (1975–76); Bassoon Concerto (1974–77); *The Godfather Suite* (from the films; Buffalo, Nov. 5, 1976). **CHAMBER:** *Invenzioni* for String Quartet (1933); Viola Sonata (1934); *Canzona* for 11 Instruments (1935); Quintet for Flute, Oboe, Viola, Cello, and Harp (1935); Violin Sonata (1937); Sonata for Flute and Harp (1937); String Quartet (1948–54); Trio for Flute, Violin, and Piano (1958); Nonet (1958); *Elegy* for Oboe and Piano (1959); Sonata for Organ and Brass (1968); Trio for Clarinet, Cello, and Piano (1973). **KEYBOARD: P i a n o :** *Variazioni e fuga sul nome B-A-C-H* (1950); *15 Preludes* (1964). **O r g a n :** Sonata (1965). **VOCAL: O r a t o r i o s :** *L'infanzia di S. Giovanni Battista* (1923); *Mysterium Catholicum* (1962); *La vita di Maria* (1970); *Roma capomunni* (1972); *Rabelaisiana* (1978). **O t h e r :** 3 masses (1960–62); songs.—**NS/LK/DM**

Roth, Daniel, distinguished French organist, pedagogue, and composer; b. Mulhouse, Oct. 31, 1942. He went to Paris, where he studied with Marie-Claire Alain and Maurice Duruflé at the Cons. At the age of 20, he made his recital debut at the organ of the Basilique Sacré-Coeur. In 1963 he became its asst. organist, and then was its titular organist from 1972 to 1985. He won the Grand Prix de Chartres in 1971. After teaching at the Marseilles Cons. in 1973–74, he served as artist-in-residence of the National Shrine of the Immaculate Conception and as chairman of the organ dept. at the Catholic Univ. of America in Washington, D.C., from 1974 to 1976. He then taught again at the Marseilles Cons. from 1976 to 1979. From 1977 he made regular tours of the U.S. and Canada while pursuing an active career as a recitalist in Europe and Japan. He taught at the Strasbourg Cons. from 1979 to 1988. In 1985 he became titular organist at St.-Sulpice in Paris. He also taught at the Saarbrücken Hochschule für Musik from 1988 to 1995, and then was prof. of organ at the Frankfurt am Main Hochschule für Musik. In 1986 he was made a Chevalier de l'ordre des Arts et des Lettres. As a virtuoso, Roth is especially known for his mastery of improvisations, which he regularly includes in his recitals. He has composed many organ pieces and several transcriptions. Among his other works are a number of choral pieces, including *Dignare me O Jesu* for Soloists, Chorus, and Orch. (1990), and *Ain Karïm*, a fantasy for Flute and Organ (1995).—**NS/LK/DM**

Roth, Feri, Hungarian-American violinist and teacher; b. Zvolen, Czechoslovakia, July 18, 1899; d. Los Angeles, May 7, 1969. He studied at the Royal Academy of Music in Budapest. He organized the Budapest String Quartet (1923), with which he toured Europe; then emigrated to the U.S. and formed the Roth Quartet (1928; with Jenö Antal, Ferenc Molnar, and Janos Scholz), which made an American debut at the Pittsfield Music Festival, Sept. 21, 1928. In 1946 he was appointed prof. of violin and chamber ensemble at the Univ. of Calif. at Los Angeles, a post he held until his death. —**NS/LK/DM**

Rothenberg, Ned, virtuoso wind player; b. Boston, Mass., Sept. 15, 1956. Ned Rothenberg's playing successfully bridges the worlds of twentieth-century avant-garde composition and jazz-based improvisation via a highly personalized, idiosyncratic approach to reeds and shakuhachi (Japanese end-blown flute). This is not music for the casual listener; with its focus on microscopic detail and extended technique, his music is cerebral in the best sense of the word—challenging, provocative, and ear-expanding—and amply rewards attentive listening.

He honed his skills in the late 1970s with Anthony Braxton, appearing on the monumental *Creative Orch.* Moving to N.Y., he became involved with the downtown jazz/new music/no wave crossover scene, notably as a member of the trio Semantics with drummer Samm Bennett and multi-instrumentalist Elliott Sharp. Since then he has worked with a host of collaborators from the fields of jazz, free improvisation, modern classical, and world music, establishing himself as one of the foremost practitioners of his instruments. Rothenberg's explorations of microtones and the extreme ranges of his instruments are foregrounded in intimate settings, such as his duets with Tuvan overtone singer Sainkho and his New Winds trio with fellow innovators Robert Dick and J. D. Parran. His compositional acumen is showcased in larger ensembles like the all-star nonet Powerlines and the Ned Rothenberg Double Band, the latter of which finds him in unusually funky territory reminiscent of the work of Brooklyn's M-Base players.

DISC.: *The Cliff* (1989); *Traction* (1991); *Opposites Attract* (1991); *The Crux* (1993); *Overlays* (1993); *Antonyms* (1994); *Digging It Harder from Afar* (1994); *Powerlines* (1995); *Real and Imagined Time* (1995); *Amulet* (1996); *Potion* (1998).—DR/SH

Rothenberger, Anneliese, esteemed German soprano; b. Mannheim, June 19, 1924. After vocal study in with Erika Müller at the Mannheim Hochschule für Musik, she made her operatic debut in Koblenz in 1943. From 1946 to 1957 and again from 1958 to 1973 she was a member of the Hamburg State Opera; also had engagements in Düsseldorf, Salzburg, Edinburgh, and Aix-en- Provence. In 1958 she joined the Vienna State Opera; also sang at La Scala in Milan and in Munich. On Nov. 18, 1960, she made a notable debut at the Metropolitan Opera in N.Y. as Zdenka in *Arabella*, and remained on its roster until 1966. She was one of the most versatile singers of her generation, capable of giving congenial renditions of soprano roles in operas of Mozart and Verdi. She also gave excellent performances of the challenging role of Marie in Berg's *Wozzeck*. She further distinguished herself in the even more demanding role of Lulu in Berg's opera. She publ. an autobiography, *Melodie meines Lebens* (Munich, 1972). —NS/LK/DM

Rother, Artur (Martin), German conductor; b. Stettin, Oct. 12, 1885; d. Aschau, Sept. 22, 1972. He studied piano and organ with his father, and also attended the univs. of Tübingen and Berlin. In 1906 he became a répétiteur at the Wiesbaden Opera. He was an assistant at the Bayreuth Festivals (1907–14), and from 1927 to 1934 he was Generalmusikdirektor in Dessau. In 1938 he went to Berlin as a conductor at the Deutsches Opernhaus, where he remained until 1958. He was also chief conductor of the Berlin Radio (1946–49). —NS/LK/DM

Rothier, Léon, French bass and teacher; b. Rheims, Dec. 26, 1874; d. N.Y., Dec. 6, 1951. He studied at the Paris Cons. with Crosti (singing), Lherie (opéra comique), and Melchissedec (opera), winning 1st prizes in all 3 classes upon graduation. He made his operatic debut as Jupiter in Gounod's *Philemon et Baucis* at the Opéra-Comique in Paris in 1899, remaining there until 1903; then was active in Marseilles (1903–07), Nice (1907–09), and Lyons (1909–10). On Dec. 10, 1910, he made his American debut at the Metropolitan Opera in N.Y. as Méphistophélès; remained on its roster until 1939 and then devoted himself to recitals. He taught at the Volpe Inst. in N.Y. (from 1916); also privately after his retirement from the stage.—NS/LK/DM

Rothmüller, (Aron) Marko, Croatian baritone and teacher; b. Trnjani, Dec. 31, 1908; d. Bloomington, Ind., Jan. 20, 1993. He studied in Zagreb, then took lessons in singing with Franz Steiner in Vienna, and also had lessons in composition with Alban Berg. He made his operatic debut as Ottokar in *Der Freischütz* at the Schiller Theater in Hamburg-Altona in 1932. He was a member of the opera in Zagreb (1932–34) and Zürich (1935–47), and also with the Covent Garden Opera in London (1939; 1948–55). He sang with the N.Y.C. Opera (1948–52); also at the Glyndebourne and Edinburgh festivals (1949–52); made his debut at the Metropolitan Opera in N.Y. on Jan. 22, 1959, as Kothner in *Die Meistersinger von Nürnberg*; appeared there again in 1960 and 1964. He taught at the Ind. Univ. School of Music in Bloomington from 1955 to 1979. He was distinguished in Wagnerian roles; also sang leading roles in modern works, including Wozzeck in Berg's opera. He wrote some chamber music and songs. Rothmüller publ. an interesting vol., *Die Musik der Juden* (Zürich, 1951; Eng. tr., London, 1953; 2nd ed., rev., 1967).—NS/LK/DM

Rothwell, Evelyn, English oboist; b. Wallingford, Jan. 24, 1911. She studied at the Royal Coll. of Music in London with Leon Goossens, and in 1931 joined the Covent Garden Opera touring orch. She then was a member of the Scottish Orch. in Glasgow (1933–36) and of the London Sym. Orch. (1935–39); also played in the Glyndebourne Festival Orch. (1934–39). In 1939 she married **John Barbirolli**. In 1971 she became a prof. of oboe at the Royal Academy of Music in London. She was made an Officer of the Order of the British Empire in 1984.

BIBL.: H. Atkins and P. Cotes, *The Barbirollis: A Musical Marriage* (London, 1983).—NS/LK/DM

Rothwell, Walter Henry, English-American conductor; b. London, Sept. 22, 1872; d. Santa Monica, Calif., March 12, 1927. He studied at the Vienna Cons. with J. Epstein (piano), R. Fuchs (theory), and Bruckner (composition), and then took further courses in Munich with Thuille and Schillings. In 1895 he became asst. conductor to Mahler at the Hamburg Opera, and then conducted the German opera in Amsterdam (1903–04) and the Savage Opera Co. in the U.S. (1904–08). He was conductor of the St. Paul Sym. Orch. (1908–14). In 1919 he was engaged to organize and conduct the Los Angeles Phil. Orch., which he led until his death. —NS/LK/DM

Rott, Hans (actually, **Johann Carl Maria**), talented Austrian composer; b. Vienna, Aug. 1, 1858; d. there, June 25, 1884. He studied organ and composition with Bruckner at the Vienna Cons. (1874–77), where he also took courses with L. Landskron (piano), H. Grädener (harmony), and F. Krenn (counterpoint and composition). He then was organist at the Piarist Church in Vienna (until 1878). Rott became insane in 1880 and spent the last 4 years of his short life in the psychiatric clinic of Vienna's General Hospital. Bruckner admired his talent, as did Mahler. His works include a Sym. for Strings (1874–75), Sym. in E major (1878–80), *Pastorales Vorspiel* for orch. (1880), String Quartet, String Quintet, and songs. A century after Rott's death, interest in his music led to belated premieres of his Sym. in E major (Cincinnati, March 4, 1989) and his *Pastorales Vorspiel* (Vienna, Feb. 8, 2000). His extant compositions are housed in Vienna's Österreichische Nationalbibliothek.—NS/LK/DM

Rottenberg, Ludwig, Austrian conductor and composer; b. Czernowitz, Bukovina, Oct. 11, 1864; d. Frankfurt am Main, May 6, 1932. He studied with A. Hřimalý, R. Fuchs, and E. Mandyczewski in Vienna; was Kapellmeister at the Stadttheater in Brünn (1891–92) and at the Frankfurt am Main opera (1893–1926). In 1910 and 1913 he conducted at Covent Garden in London. He publ. a collection of 30 songs, a Violin Sonata, and piano variations; his opera, *Die Geschwister*, was produced in Frankfurt am Main on Nov. 30, 1915. Rottenberg was the father-in-law of **Paul Hindemith.**—NS/LK/DM

Röttger, Heinz, German conductor and composer; b. Herford, Westphalia, Nov. 6, 1909; d. Dessau, Aug. 26, 1977. He studied in Munich at the Academy of Music (1928–31) and took courses in musicology at the Univ. (Ph.D., 1937, with the diss. *Das Formproblem bei Richard Strauss;* publ. in Berlin, 1937). He served as music director of the Stralsund City Theater (1948–51), Generalmusikdirektor in Rostock (1951–54), and chief conductor of the Dessau Landestheater (from 1954).

WORKS: DRAMATIC: O p e r a : *Bellmann* (1946); *Phaëton* (1957); *Der Heiratsantrag* (1959); *Die Frauen von Troja* (1961); *Der Weg nach Palermo* (1965); *Spanisches Capriccio* (1976). B a l l e t : *...und heller wurde jeder Tag* (1964); *Der Kreis* (1964). ORCH.: 2 syms. (1939; *Dessauer Sinfonie,* 1966–67); 2 violin concertos (1942, 1970); Piano Concerto (1950); Cello Concerto (1962); Viola Concerto (1966). OTHER: Chamber music; piano pieces.—NS/LK/DM

Rotzsch, Hans-Joachim, German tenor and choral conductor; b. Leipzig, April 25, 1929. He studied at the Leipzig Hochschule für Musik, where his principal teachers were Günther Ramin, Amadeus Webersinke, and Johannes Weyrauch. He also studied voice with Fritz Polster. In 1961 he joined the faculty of the Leipzig Hochschule für Musik, and in 1963 he became director of the choral program at the Univ. of Leipzig. He was named cantor of the Thomaskirche of Leipzig in 1972, which position he held with distinction until 1991. He also conducted the Neues Bachisches Collegium Musicum. He distinguished himself as a soloist in Bach's passions, oratorios, and cantatas as well as in the capacity of choral conductor. During the 1984–85 and

1985–86 seasons, he conducted a series of performances of Bach's works at Leipzig's Thomaskirche and Gewandhaus in commemoration of the 300th anniversary of the master's birth.—NS/LK/DM

Rouget, Gilbert, French ethnomusicologist; b. Paris, July 9, 1916. He studied at the Sorbonne in Paris under André Schaeffner and Constantin Brăiloiu (1935–42). He joined the ethnomusicology dept. at the Musée de l'Homme in 1941, succeeding Schaeffner as director in 1965; also became director of research at CNRS in 1972. During expeditions to equatorial and western Africa (1946–70), he made 3 films in collaboration with J. Rouch: *Sortie des novices de Sakpata; Batteries dogon: Éléments pour une étude des rhythmes;* and *Danses des reines a Porto-Novo.* His field of study focuses on the music of Africa, particularly that of southern Benin; he has collected many recordings and written a number of articles, the originality and scholarship of which have made substantial contributions to African ethnomusicology.—NS/LK/DM

Rouget de l'Isle or **Lisle, Claude-Joseph,** French poet and composer; b. Lons-le-Saunier, Jura, May 10, 1760; d. Choisy-le-Roy, June 27, 1836. He composed the music to the *Chant de guerre pour l'armée du Rhin* in 1792, while stationed in Strasbourg as a military engineer; it was known for a time as the *Marseillais' Hymn* and finally acquired the popular designation of the *Marseillaise,* having been taken up by the Marseilles soldiers marching toward Paris. Rouget de l'Isle was not a revolutionary; he was in fact imprisoned for refusing to take the oath against the crown. After his release, he rejoined the army. The *Marseillaise* was then authorized as the national song in 1795. However, it fell out of favor during the years of the Empire and the Restoration. Rouget de l'Isle spent many years in poverty until the *Marseillaise* regained its place during the July Revolution of 1830 and he was granted a pension by Louis-Philippe. In 1879 it became the official French national anthem. Rouget de l'Isle was honored with reburial in the Invalides in Paris on Bastille Day (July 14, 1915). He also composed a *Hymne dithyrambique sur la conjuration de Robespierre* (1794), *Chant des vengeances* (1798), and a *Chant du combat* for the army in Egypt (1800). He publ. 50 *Chants français* in 1825, and also wrote several opera librettos.

BIBL.: J. Tiersot, *R. d. l'Isle: Son oeuvre, sa vie* (Paris, 1892); A. Köckert, *R. d. l'Isle* (Leipzig, 1898); A. Lanier, *R. d. l'Isle* (Besançon, 1907); J. Tiersot, *Histoire de la Marseillaise* (Paris, 1915); R. Brancour, *La Marseillaise et le Chant du départ* (1916); A. Becker, *La Marseillaise* (Braunschweig, 1930); G. de Froidcourt, *Grétry, R. d. Lisle et la Marseillaise* (Liège, 1945).—NS/LK/DM

Rouleau, Joseph (Alfred Pierre), admired Canadian bass and teacher; b. Matane, Quebec, Feb. 28, 1929. He went to Montreal and studied with Édouard Woolley and Albert Cornellier, and then at the Cons. with Martial Singher (1949–52). In 1951 he made a concert tour of eastern Canada. After further training with Mario Basiola and Antonio Narducci in Milan (1952–54), he made his first major appearance in opera as Colline at the New Orleans Opera in 1955. In 1956 he sang Verdi's King Philip II in Montreal. On April 23, 1957, he made his debut at London's Covent Garden as Colline, and continued to make appearances there for some 20 seasons. He made his first appearance at the Paris Opéra as Raimondo in 1960. In 1965–66 he toured Australia with Joan Sutherland's operatic enterprise. In 1967 he sang Basilio with the Canadian Opera Co., and returned there as Ramfis in 1968. In the latter year, he also made his debut at the N.Y.C. Opera as Méphistophélès. In subsequent years, he sang with various North American and European opera companies. He also was engaged as a soloist with leading orchs. on both sides of the Atlantic. On April 13, 1984, he made his Metropolitan Opera debut in N.Y. as the Grand Inquisitor. His esteemed portrayal of Boris Godunov in Montreal in Feb. 1988 was telecast by the CBC. From 1980 he taught at the Montreal Cons. In 1967 he won the Prix de musique Calixa-Lavallée. He was made an Officer of the Order of Canada in 1977. In 1990 he was awarded the Prix Denise-Pelletier.—NS/LK/DM

Rouse, Charlie, tenor saxophonist for Thelonious Monk; b. Washington, D.C., April 6, 1924; d. Seattle, Wash., Nov. 30, 1988. For more than a decade, he augmented Monk's tricky tunes with a brand of bop that both understated and expanded what the iconoclastic composer was trying to say; and yet he remained his own man, recording frequently before, during, and after his time with Monk and owing only a little stylistically to his longtime employer.

He started out in his early 20s with stints in Billy Eckstine's and Dizzy Gillespie's bands, which gave him a healthy dose of the classic bebop style, which he further explored while working with Tadd Dameron and Fats Navarro. However, a few years later he went in a whole other direction when he was hired to replace his idol, Ben Webster, in Duke Ellington's band in 1949. A missing birth certificate, however, prevented him from acquiring a passport to tour Europe, thus ending his Ellington gig. He easily found other work, though, playing with Count Basie, Clifford Brown, Bennie Green, and Oscar Pettiford. During the late 1950s he teamed up with French horn player Julius Watkins to form the group Les Jazz Modes. They were picked up by Atlantic Records in 1957 after a few releases on the small independent Dawn label. His next major project would be long-lasting and an absolute musical classic: serving as second-hand man in Monk's quartet. He took to Monk's music so readily because it allowed him to use both his bop and Ellington experience at the same time, mixing improvisational wit with unusually tuneful melodies. Their collaboration lasted from 1959 to 1970, including many essential recordings for both Riverside and Columbia. Beginning in 1960, he would occasionally make his own records, many of which feature neither Monk compositions nor even Monkish playing; consequently, these recordings clearly demonstrate his own identifiable style. Yet, it is initially shocking to hear him play with a more traditional pianist. Ultimately, it is his connection with Monk for which he will be forever remembered, and he was always eager to celebrate the man he played with for so

many years. In 1980, along with Kenny Barron, Buster Williams, and former Monk drummer Ben Riley, he formed the group Sphere, initially as a Monk tribute band, although they eventually included originals and other standards in their repertoire, including an album's worth of Charlie Parker tunes. And three of his final projects exemplify the connection he had with Monk's music: first, a duet with the ultimate Monk cheerleader, Steve Lacy, on "Ask Me Now," included as part of producer Hal Willner's 1984 Monk tribute collection *That's the Way I Feel Now*, second, his participation on Carmen McRae's beautiful 1988 set *Carmen Sings Monk*, and finally, performing as guest of honor at a posthumous Monk birthday celebration (released on CD as *Epistrophy*) just weeks before his own death from lung cancer in 1988.

He played a derivation of hard bop that featured a restraint unusual for most tenor players at the time. Never relying on speed, he soloed with patience and deliberation, careful to never lose sight of the melody. He was fully capable of cooking on the up-tempo tunes, as well as offering up breathy, rich sounds on ballads. All of these traits, along with a rhythmic savviness and overall consistency, made him such a valuable contributor to Monk's quartets.

DISC.: *Unsung Hero* (1960); *Takin' Care of Business* (1960); *Thelonious Monk: Criss-Cross* (1963); *Two Is One* (1974); *Cinnamon Flower* (1977); *Moment's Notice* (1978); *The Upper Manhattan Jazz Society* (1981); *Four in One* (1982); *Flight Path* (1983); *Social Call* (1984); *Pumpkins Delight* (1986); *Sphere* (1987); *On Tour* (1987); *Live at the Umbria Jazz* (1988); *Sphere: Bird Songs* (1988); *Epistrophy* (1989); *Four for All* (1990); *Les Jazz Modes* (1995).—EJL

Rouse, Christopher (Chapman), prominent American composer and teacher; b. Baltimore, Feb. 15, 1949. He studied with Richard Hoffmann at the Oberlin (Ohio) Coll. Cons. of Music (B.Mus., 1971). After private lessons with George Crumb (1971–73), he completed his training with Karel Husa at Cornell Univ. (D.M.A., 1977). He taught at the Univ. of Mich. (1978–81) and at the Eastman School of Music in Rochester, N.Y. (from 1981), where he was a prof. (from 1991). While retaining his latter position, he also taught at the Juilliard School in N.Y. (from 1997). In 1985–86 he was composer-in-residence of the Indianapolis Sym. Orch., and then of the Baltimore Sym. Orch. from 1986 to 1989. In 1990 he held a Guggenheim fellowship. In 1993 he was awarded the Pulitzer Prize in Music for his Trombone Concerto, and also was awarded the American Academy of Arts and Letters Award in Music. Rouse first attracted notice in the 1970s with works of a bold and often raucous disposition. By the mid-1980s his works became more introspective in nature and revealed Rouse's penchant for more traditional forms and harmonies.

WORKS: ORCH.: *The Infernal Machine* (1980; Evian, France, May 9, 1981); *Gorgon* (Rochester, N.Y., Nov. 15, 1984); Double Bass Concerto (1985; Buffalo, Feb. 25, 1988); *Phantasmata* (1985; St. Louis, Oct. 25, 1986); *Phaethon* (1986; Philadelphia, Jan. 8, 1987); 2 syms.: No. 1 (1986; Baltimore, Jan. 21, 1988) and No. 2 (1994; Houston, March 2, 1995); *Jagannath* (1987; Houston, Sept. 22, 1990); *Iscariot* for Chamber Orch. (St. Paul, Minn., Oct. 28, 1989); *Concerto per Corde* for Strings (N.Y., Nov. 28, 1990); Trombone Concerto (1991; N.Y., Dec. 30, 1992); Violin Concerto

(1991; Aspen, July 12, 1992); Cello Concerto (1992; Los Angeles, Jan. 23, 1994); Flute Concerto (Detroit, Oct. 27, 1994); *Envoi* (1995; Atlanta, May 9, 1996); *Der gerettete Alberich* for Percussion and Orch. (1997; Cleveland, Jan. 15, 1998); *Seeing* for Piano and Orch. (1998; N.Y., May 6, 1999); *Concert de Gaudi* for Guitar and Orch. (1999; Hamburg, Jan. 2, 2000); *Rapture* (1999; Pittsburgh, May 5, 2000). **CHAMBER**: *Liber Daemonum* for Organ (1980); 2 string quartets (1982; Aspen, Colo., July 23, 1988); *Rotae Passionis* for Chamber Ensemble (1982; Boston, April 8, 1983); *Compline* for Chamber Ensemble (N.Y., Dec. 6, 1996). **VOCAL**: *Mitternachtlieder* for Baritone and Chamber Ensemble (1979); *Karolju* for Chorus and Orch. (1990; Baltimore, Nov. 7, 1991); *Kabir Padavali* for Soprano and Orch. (1997; Minneapolis, Jan. 8, 1999).—NS/LK/DM

Rouse, Mikel (actually, **Michael Joseph**), formidably original American composer; b. St. Louis, Mo., Jan. 26, 1957. His father was a state trooper and his mother a social (case) worker. He attended the Kansas City Art Inst. where he studied music, art, and filmmaking (graduated 1977), and the Cons. of Music at the Univ. of Mo. at Kansas City. He moved to N.Y. in 1979, where he further studied African and other world musics, as well as the Schillinger method of composition. He formed his own contemporary chamber ensemble, Mikel Rouse Broken Consort, consisting of keyboard, electric guitar/bass, woodwinds, and percussion, with which he produced numerous recordings, including *Jade Tiger* (1984), *A Walk In The Woods* (1985), *A Lincoln Portrait* (1988), and *Soul Menu* (1993). Rouse has become most widely known for his trilogy of operas, beginning with *Failing Kansas* (1994), inspired by Truman Capote's *In Cold Blood*, which explores his technique of counterpoetry (a rhythmically strict counterpoint of unpitched/pitched and spoken/sung voices). Other works that explore this technique include *Living Inside Design* (1994; a collection of extended spoken songs) and *Autorequiem* (1994) for Strings, Percussion, and Soice. The second in the trilogy is the critically acclaimed *Dennis Cleveland* (1996), the first-ever talk-show opera. The third and final work is the in-progress *The End of Cinematics*, in collaboration with John Jesurun, based upon four "retro-songs" and involving the use of real-time film. Composers are usually elevated by terms applied to their work that manage to enter common musical parlance. Rouse has not one but two: the above-mentioned counterpoetry (of his own devising) and totalism (coined by the N.Y. critic Kyle Gann). His *Quorum* (1984), the first piece of its kind for drum sequencer, was used by Ulysses Dove in his choreographic work, *Vespers*, presented by the Alvin Ailey Dance American Theater in 1987.

WORKS: DRAMATIC: Opera: *Balboa*, video opera (1982); *Glass Bead Game*, after Hermann Hesse (1989); Trilogy, comprising *Failing Kansas*, after Truman Capote's *In Cold Blood* (N.Y., Feb. 2, 1995), *Dennis Cleveland* (N.Y., Oct. 28, 1996), and *The End of Cinematics* (1999). **OTHER**: *Living Inside Design* for Voice, Taped Accompaniment, and Video Images (1994; also for Voice and Ensemble); *cameraworld*, digital multi-media project (1999). **ORCH.**: *Autumn in New York* (1982); *Shield 81* for Chamber Orch. (1982); *A Walk in the Woods* for Chamber Orch. (1984); *Red 20* (1984); *American Nova* (1985). **CHAMBER**: *Quartet* for 3 Violins and Double Bass (1981); *Jade Tiger* for Chamber Ensemble (1982); *Colorado Suite* for Violin and Elec-

tronics (1984); *Quorum* for 18 Percussionists (1984; also for Electronic Drum Sequencer); *Book One*, book of 9 string quartets (1986; N.Y., July 3, 1989); *A Lincoln Portrait* for Chamber Ensemble (1987); *Hope Chest* for Chamber Quartet (1991; N.Y., April 21, 1992); *Copperhead* for Electric Quartet of Woodwinds, Electronics, Keyboard, Bass, and Percussion (N.Y., April 21, 1992); *Soul Menu* for Chamber Ensemble (1993; N.Y., Jan. 16, 1994). **Piano**: *Two Paradoxes Resolved* (1989). **VOCAL**: *Etudes* for Voice and Ensemble (1981); *Set the Timer/Uptight* for Voice and Ensemble (1986); *Social Responsibility* for Voice and Ensemble (1987); *Against All Flags* for Voice and Ensemble (1988); *Left in My Life* for Voices and Electronics (1993; Poitiers, France, Nov. 19, 1994); *Kiss Him Goodbye* for Voices and Electronics (1993; N.Y., May 21, 1994); *Living Inside Design* for Voice and Ensemble (Rome, April 27, 1994; also for Voice, Taped Accompaniment, and Video Images); *Autorequiem* for Voices and Orch. (Minn., May 7, 1994); *return*, a collection of songs constructed around samples from *Book One*, for Voice and Ensemble (1999). **ELECTRONIC**: *Untitled* (1982); *Quorum* for Electronic Drum Sequencer (1984; also for 18 Percussionists).—LK/DM

Rouse, (Robert) Steve(n), accomplished American composer; b. Moss Point, Miss., July 9, 1953. He began composing and improvising as a young child, and subsequently studied piano, bassoon, and saxophone. At 13 he became a bassoonist with the Gulf Coast Sym. Orch. and also began performing with his own rhythm and blues group. He studied with Luigi Zaninelli at the Univ. of Southern Miss. (B.M., 1977) and with Leslie Bassett and William Albright at the Univ. of Mich. (M.M., 1982; D.M.A., 1987); while at the latter he also served as music director and accompanist for the dance dept. of Eastern Mich. Univ. and started a successful jingle production company partnership. In 1988 Rouse joined the faculty of the Univ. of Louisville School of Music, and from 1990 to 1998 served as the univ.'s principal coordinator for the New Dimension Series, a series of new music concerts produced collaboratively with the Louisville Orch. In 1999 he was a visiting prof. at of composition at Ind. Univ. As composer-in-residence for Meet The Composer Louisville Residence from 1995 to 1998, Rouse wrote music for all levels of public school music ensembles and also worked extensively with students, teachers, and administrators to develop and implement a variety of music outreach programs. From 1989 he served as a first-round juror for the Grawemeyer International Composition Award, and from 1991 he served as a National Advisory Board member for the League of Composers/International Soc. for Contemporary Music. In addition to various commissions and grants, he won the Prix de Rome (1987) and received the Research and Creative Achievement Award from the Univ. of Louisville (1999).

WORKS: CHAMBER Opera: *The Mousewife* (1996). **ORCH.**: *Freedom's Ring* (1978); 2 syms.: No. 1, *Symphony: Light Descending* (1987) and No. 2, *Symphony 2* (1999–2000); *Ribbons* for Strings (1988; rev. 1991); *Short Stories* (1990); *Into the Light* (1991); *Enigma-Release* for Flügelhorn, Percussion, and Strings (1994); *Light Fantastic* (1994); *Kick!* for Young String Orch. (1996; also for Band); *Pegasus* for Young Orch. (1998; also for Band). **CHAMBER**: *Wiggly Lines* for Clarinet and Bassoon (1975); *Ju Jubes* for Flute and Piano (1976); *Quicksilver* for Brass Quintet (1981); *Crosswinds* for Organ and Ensemble (1984); *Flash Point* for Woodwind Quartet (1984); *For Igor* for Violin and Piano (1984); *Diamonds* for Violin (1989); *The Avatar* for Trumpet and Piano (1991); Violin Sonata (1992); *'Bone To Be Wild* for Trombone and Piano (1993); *A Flying Leap!* for 7 Trumpets (1994); *Enigma-Release* for Alto Saxophone and Piano (1994; also for Flügelhorn, Percussion, and Strings); *More Light* for Trumpet and Piano (1995); *Shadow Rounds* for Trumpet Ensemble (2000). **KEYBOARD:** Piano Sonata (1983); *Crop Circles* for Piano (1995); *One Presence* for Organ and Piano (1998). **VOCAL:** *Dense Pack* for Chorus (1983); *Psalm 70* for Chorus and Piano (1992); *Psalm 23* for Chorus or Chorus and Piano (1993); *She'll Be Comin' Round* for High Voice and Piano (1995); *Waiting for Daylight* for Soprano and Orch. (1997); *Lines for Valentines* for Voice and Piano (1998). **OTHER:** Various works for young ensembles.—LK/DM

Roussakis, Nicolas, Greek-born American composer and teacher; b. Athens, June 10, 1934; d. N.Y., Oct. 23, 1994. He emigrated to the U.S. in 1949 and became a naturalized citizen in 1956; attended Columbia Univ. (B.A., 1956; M.A., 1960; D.M.A., 1975), where he studied with Luening, Beeson, Cowell, Weber, Shapey, and Jarnach. He received a Fulbright grant for study in Germany (1961–63); attended seminars of Boulez, Berio, Ligeti, and Stockhausen in Darmstadt. Upon his return to the U.S., he became active with contemporary music groups. He taught at Columbia Univ. (1968–77) and at Rutgers, the State Univ. of N.J. (from 1977). His works are marked by an aggressive modernity of idiom, but are satisfyingly playable and surprisingly pleasurable even to untutored ears. They include *Night Speech* for Chorus and Percussion (1968), *Short Pieces* for 2 Flutes (1969), Concertino for Percussion and Woodwinds (1973), *Ode and Cataclysm* for Orch. (1975), *Ephemeris* for String Quartet (1979), *Fire and Earth and Water and Air* for Orch. (1980–83), *Pas de deux* for Violin and Piano (1985), *Trigono* for Trombone, Vibraphone, and Drums (1986), *The God Abandons Antony*, cantata for Narrator, Chorus, and Orch. (1987), *Hymn to Apollo* for Small Orch. (1989), *To Demeter*, for Orch. (1994; N.Y., Oct. 29, 1995), piano pieces, and choruses.—NS/LK/DM

Rousseau, Eugene, noted American saxophonist and pedagogue; b. Blue Island, Ill., Aug. 23, 1932. He studied clarinet at the Chicago Musical Coll. (B.M.B., 1953), oboe at Northwestern Univ. (M.M., 1954), and saxophone at the Paris Cons. (1960–61), and then completed his academic training at the Univ. of Iowa (Ph.D., 1962, with the diss. *Clarinet Instructional Materials from 1732 to circa 1825*). In 1965 he made his Carnegie Recital Hall debut in N.Y. He was the first saxophonist to give solo recitals in London, Amsterdam, Vienna, and Berlin (1967) and in Paris (1968), and also appeared as a soloist with orchs. in the U.S., Europe, and the Far East. In 1969 he was co-founder of the World Saxophone Congress. He taught at Luther Coll. in Iowa (1956–59), Central Mo. State Univ. (1962–64), and the Univ. of Iowa (1964); in 1964 he joined the faculty of the Ind. Univ. School of Music, where he was chairman of the woodwind dept. (1966–73), a prof. (1972–88), and Distinguished Prof. (from 1988). He was also a guest prof. at the Vienna Hochschule für Musik (1981–82), Ariz. State Univ. (1984), and the Prague Cons. (1985). He publ. a *Method for Saxophone* (2 vols., 1973, 1977).—NS/LK/DM

Rousseau, Jean-Jacques, great Swiss-born French philosopher and author; b. Geneva, June 28, 1712; d. Ermenonville, near Paris, July 2, 1778. Without other musical training besides desultory self-instruction, Rousseau made his debut as a music scholar at the age of 29, reading a paper before the Académie in Paris (1724), which was received and publ. as a *Dissertation sur la musique moderne* (1743). His opera *Les Muses galantes* had only 1 private representation, at the house of La Pouplinière in 1745; his revision of the intermezzo *La Reine de Navarre* (by Voltaire and Rameau) was a failure in Paris; but his opera *Le Devin du village* (Fontainebleau, Oct. 18, 1752; Paris Opéra, March 1, 1753) was very successful and remained in the repertoire for 75 years. In the meantime, his musical articles for the *Encyclopédie* had evoked scathing criticism from Rameau and others; improved by revision and augmentation, they were republ. as his *Dictionnaire de musique* (Geneva, 1767; the existence of this ed. cannot be proved; 1st known ed., Paris, 1768). In 1752 commenced the dispute, known as the "guerre des bouffons," between the partisans of French and Italian opera; Rousseau sided with the latter, publ. a *Lettre à M. Grimm au sujet des remarques ajoutées à sa lettre sur Omphale* (1752), followed by the caustic *Lettre sur la musique française* (1753; to which the members of the Opéra responded by burning him in effigy and excluding him from the theater) and *Lettre d'un symphoniste de l'Académie royale de musique à ses camarades* (1753). He wrote 2 numbers for the melodrama *Pygmalion* (1770; Paris, Oct. 30, 1775). Publ. posthumously were 6 new arias for *Le Devin du village*, and a collection of about 100 romances and duets, *Les Consolations des misères de ma vie* (1781), and fragments of an opera, *Daphnis et Chloé* (1780). His writings on music are included in the *Oeuvres complètes de Jean-Jacques Rousseau* (4 vols., 1959–69); for his letters, see R. Leigh, ed., *Correspondance complète Jean-Jacques Rousseau* (18 vols., 1965–73).

BIBL.: A. Jensen, *J.-J. R.: Fragments inédits, recherches biographiques* (Paris, 1882); A. Jansen, *J.-J. R. als Musiker* (Berlin, 1884); A. Pougin, *J.-J. R., Musicien* (Paris, 1901); E. Istel, *J.-J. R. als Komponist seiner lyrischen Szene "Pygmalion"* (Leipzig, 1901); E. Schütte, *J.-J. R.: Seine Persönlichkeit und sein Stil* (Leipzig, 1910); J. Tiersot, *J.-J. R.* (Paris, 1912); E. Faguet, *R. artiste* (Paris, 1913); A. Sells, *The Early Life of R.: 1712–40* (London, 1929); R. Gerin, *J.-J. R.* (Paris, 1930); M. Moffat, *R. et le théâtre* (Paris, 1930); A. Pochon, *J.-J. R., musiciens et le critique* (Montreux, 1940); J. Senelier, *Bibliographie générale des oeuvres de J.-J. R.* (Paris, 1949); P. Gülke, *R. und die Musik, oder, Von der Zuständigkeit des Dilettanten* (Wilhelmshaven, 1984); M. O'Dea, *J.-J. R.: Music, Illusion, and Desire* (N.Y., 1995).—NS/LK/DM

Rousseau, Marcel (-Auguste-Louis), French composer, son of **Samuel-Alexandre Rousseau;** b. Paris, Aug. 18, 1882; d. there, June 11, 1955. He studied with his father, then entered the Paris Cons. as a student of Lenepveu; won the Deuxième Premier Grand Prix de Rome with the cantata *Maia* (1905); later added his father's first name to his own, and produced his works as Samuel-Rousseau. In 1947 he was elected to the Académie des Beaux-Arts.

WORKS: DRAMATIC: O p e r a (all 1st perf. in Paris): *Tarass Boulba* (Nov. 22, 1919); *Le Hulla* (March 9, 1923); *Le Bon Roi*

Dagobert (Dec. 5, 1927); *Kerkeb* (April 6, 1951). **B a l l e t :** *Promenade dans Rome* (Paris, Dec. 7, 1936); *Entre 2 rondes* (Paris, April 27, 1940). **O R C H . :** *Tableaux: Solitude triste* and *Impression dolente;* etc.—NS/LK/DM

Rousseau, Samuel-Alexandre, French conductor, teacher, and composer, father of **Marcel (-Auguste-Louis) Rousseau;** b. Neuve-Maison, Aisne, June 11, 1853; d. Paris, Oct. 1, 1904. He studied at the Paris Cons. with Franck (organ) and Bazin (composition), winning the Grand Prix de Rome with the cantata *La Fille de Jephté* (1878) and the Prix Cressent with the comic opera *Dianora* (Paris, Opéra-Comique, Dec. 22, 1879). His opera *Mérowig* was awarded the Prize of the City of Paris, and was performed in concert form at the Grand Théâtre there on Dec. 12, 1892. In 1892 he was appointed conductor at the Théâtre-Lyrique in Paris. He was for 10 years chorus master at the Société des Concerts du Cons., and also taught harmony at the Paris Cons. On June 8, 1898, his lyric drama *La Cloche du Rhin* was staged at the Paris Opéra with considerable success, but had only 9 performances in all; this was followed by the music dramas *Milia* (Opéra-Comique, 1904) and *Léone* (Opéra-Comique, March 7, 1910).
—NS/LK/DM

Roussel, Albert (Charles Paul Marie), outstanding French composer and teacher; b. Tourcoing, Département du Nord, April 5, 1869; d. Royan, Aug. 23, 1937. Orphaned as a child, he was educated by his grandfather, mayor of his native town, and after the grandfather's death, by his aunt. He studied academic subjects at the Coll. Stanislas in Paris and music with the organist Stoltz; then studied mathematics in preparation for entering the Naval Academy; at the age of 18, he began his training in the navy; from 1889 to Aug. 1890 he was a member of the crew of the frigate *Iphigénie,* sailing to Indochina. This voyage was of great importance to Roussel, since it opened for him a world of oriental culture and art, which became one of the chief sources of his musical inspiration. He later sailed on the cruiser *Dévastation;* received a leave of absence for reasons of health, and spent some time in Tunis; was then stationed in Cherbourg, and began to compose there. In 1893 he was sent once more to Indochina. He resigned from the navy in 1894 and went to Paris, where he began to study music seriously with Gigout. In 1898 he entered the Schola Cantorum in Paris as a pupil of d'Indy; continued this study until 1907, when he was already 38 years old, but at the same time he was entrusted with a class in counterpoint, which he conducted at the Schola Cantorum from 1902 to 1914; among his students were Satie, Golestan, Le Flem, Roland-Manuel, Lioncourt, and Varèse. In 1909 Roussel and his wife, Blanche Preisach-Roussel, undertook a voyage to India, where he became acquainted with the legend of the queen Padmavati, which he selected as a subject for his famous opera-ballet. His choral sym. *Les Evocations* was also inspired by this tour. At the outbreak of World War I in 1914, Roussel applied for active service in the navy but was rejected, and volunteered as an ambulance driver. After the Armistice of 1918, he settled in Normandy and devoted himself to composi-

tion. In the autumn of 1930 he visited the U.S.

Roussel began his work under the influence of French Impressionism, with its dependence on exotic moods and poetic association. However, the sense of formal design asserted itself in his symphonic works; his Suite (1926) signalizes a transition toward neo-Classicism; the thematic development is vigorous, and the rhythms are clearly delineated, despite some asymmetrical progressions; the orchestration, too, is in the Classical tradition. Roussel possessed a keen sense of the theater; he was capable of fine characterization of exotic or mythological subjects, but also knew how to depict humorous situations in lighter works.

WORKS (all 1st perf. in Paris unless otherwise given): **D R A M A T I C :** *Le marchand de sable qui passe,* incidental music (Le Havre, Dec. 16, 1908); *Le festin de l'araignée,* ballet- pantomime (1912; April 3, 1913); *Padmâvati,* opera-ballet (1914–18; June 1, 1923); *La naissance de la lyre,* lyric opera (1923–24, July 1, 1925); *Sarabande,* ballet music (June 16, 1927); *Bacchus et Ariane,* ballet (1930; May 22, 1931; 2 orch. suites: No. 1, April 2, 1933; No. 2, Feb. 2, 1934); *Le testament de la tante Caroline,* opera-bouffe (1932–33; Olomouc, Nov. 14, 1936); *Aenéas,* ballet (Brussels, July 31, 1935); Prelude to Act 2 of *Le quatorze juillet,* incidental music (July 14, 1936); *Elpénor* for Flute and String Quartet, radio music (n.d.). **O R C H . :** *Marche nuptiale* (1893); *Résurrection,* symphonic prélude (May 17, 1904); *Vendanges* (1904; April 18, 1905; not extant); 4 syms.: No. 1, *Le poème de la forêt* (1904–06; 1st complete perf., Brussels, March 22, 1908), No. 2 (1919–21; March 4, 1922), No. 3 (1929–30; Boston, Oct. 24, 1930), and No. 4 (1934; Oct. 19, 1935); *Evocations* (1910–11; May 18, 1912); *Pour une fête de printemps,* symphonic poem (1920; Oct. 29, 1921); Suite (1926; Boston, Jan. 21, 1927); Concerto for Small Orch. (1926–27; May 5, 1927); Piano Concerto (1927; June 7, 1928); *Little Suite* (April 11, 1929); *A Glorious Day* for Military Band (1932; July 1933); *Sinfonietta* for Strings (Nov. 19, 1934); *Rapsodie flamande* (Brussels, Dec. 12, 1936); Cello Concertino (1936; Feb. 6, 1937). **C H A M B E R :** *Fantaisie* for Violin and Piano (1892; not extant); *Andante* for Violin, Viola, Cello, and Organ (1892; not extant); Horn Quintet (Feb. 2, 1901); 1 unnumbered violin sonata (May 5, 1902); 2 numbered violin sonatas: No. 1 (1907–08; Oct. 9, 1908; rev. 1931) and No. 2 (1924; Oct. 15, 1925); Piano Trio (1902; April 14, 1904; rev. 1927); *Divertissement* for Wind Quintet and Piano (April 10, 1906); *Impromptu* for Harp (April 6, 1919); *Fanfare pour un sacre païen* for Brass and Drums (1921; April 25, 1929); *Joueurs de flûte* for Flute and Piano (1924; Jan. 17, 1928); *Ségovia* for Guitar (Madrid, April 25, 1925); *Sérénade* for Flute, Violin, Viola, Cello, and Harp (Oct. 15, 1925); Duo for Bassoon and Cello or Double Bass (1925; Dec. 23, 1940); Trio for Flute, Viola, and Cello (Oct. 29, 1929); String Quartet (1931–32; Brussels, Dec. 9, 1932); *Andante and Scherzo* for Flute and Piano (Milan, Dec. 17, 1934); *Pipe* for Flageolet and Piano (1934); String Trio (1937); *Andante* for Oboe, Clarinet, and Bassoon (Nov. 30, 1937). **K E Y B O A R D : P i a n o :** *Des heures passant* (1898); *Conte à la poupée* (1904); *Rustiques* (1904–06; Feb. 17, 1906); Suite (1909–10; Jan. 28, 1911); Sonatine (1912; Jan. 18, 1913); *Petit canon perpetuel* (1913); *Doute* (1919; May 5, 1920); *L'accueil des muses* (in memoriam Debussy) (1920; Jan. 24, 1921); *Prélude and Fugue* (1932–34; Feb. 23, 1935); 3 pieces (1933; April 14, 1934). **O r g a n :** *Prélude and Fughetta* (1929; May 18, 1930). **V O C A L :** 2 madrigals for Chorus (1897; May 3, 1898); *Deux mélodies* for Voice and Piano or Orch. (1919; orch. version, Dec. 9, 1928); *Madrigal aux muses* for Women's Voices (1923; Feb. 6, 1924); *Deux poèmes de Ronsard* for Voice and Flute (No. 1, May 15, 1924; No. 2, May 28, 1924); *Le bardit de francs* for Men's Voices, Brass, and Percussion ad libitum (1926; Strasbourg, April 21, 1928); *Psalm LXXX for Tenor, Chorus, and Orch.* (1928; April 25, 1929); many songs for Voice and Piano. N. Labelle ed. a *Catalogue raisonné de l'oeuvre d'Albert Roussel* (Louvain-la-Neuve, 1992).

BIBL.: L. Vuillemin, *A. R. et son oeuvre* (Paris, 1924); A. Hoérée, *A. R.* (Paris, 1938); N. Demuth, *A. R.: A Study* (London, 1947); R. Bernard, *A. R.: Sa vie, son oeuvre* (Paris, 1948); M. Pincherle, *A. R.* (Geneva, 1957); B. Deane, *A. R.* (London, 1961); J. Eddins, *The Symphonic Music of A. R.* (diss., Fla. State Univ., 1967); A. Surchamp, *A. R.* (Paris, 1967); R. Follet, *A. R.: A Bio-Bibliography* (Westport, Conn., 1988); M. Kelkel and M. Cusin, *Colloque international A. R., 1869–1937 (1987): Lyon, France and Saint- Etienne, Loire, France* (Paris, 1989).—NS/LK/DM

Rousselière, Charles, French tenor; b. St. Nazaire, Jan. 17, 1875; d. Joue-les-Tours, May 11, 1950. He studied at the Paris Cons. He made his operatic debut in 1900 as Samson at the Paris Opéra, where he sang until 1912; also sang with the Monte Carlo Opera (1905–14), creating roles in Mascagni's *Amica*, Saint-Saëns's *L'Ancêtre*, and Fauré's *Pénélope*; also sang the role of Julien in Charpentier's opera at its first performance at the Opéra-Comique in Paris. He made his debut at the Metropolitan Opera in N.Y. as Romeo on Nov. 26, 1906, but remained on its roster for only 1 season. He made guest appearances at La Scala in Milan, the Teatro Colón in Buenos Aires, in Palermo, etc. —NS/LK/DM

Rousset, Christophe, remarkable French harpsichordist and esteemed conductor; b. Avignon, April 12, 1961. Following training with André Raynaud and Huguette Dreyfus at the Schola Cantorum in Paris, he was a student of Kenneth Gilbert before completing his studies with Bob van Asperen (harpsichord), the Kuijken brothers and Lucy van Dael (chamber music), and Leonhardt (interpretation) at the Royal Cons. of Music at The Hague (soloist diploma, 1983). In 1983 he took 1st prize in the Bruges harpsichord competition, and then launched a global career. From 1992 he also was active with his own Les Talens Lyriques ensemble. In 1999 he was a guest conductor of the N.Y. Collegium Vocal Ensemble and Orch. Rousset has won critical accolades for his extraordinary command of the harpsichord repertory. He particularly excells in the music of the French school, giving particularly outstanding performances of Couperin and Rameau.—NS/LK/DM

Roussier, Abbé Pierre-Joseph, French writer on music; b. Marseilles, 1716; d. Ecouis, Normandy, Aug. 18, 1792. He served as canon in Ecouis.

WRITINGS: *Observations sur différents points d'harmonie* (1765); *Traité des accords, et de leur succession* (1764; supplemented by *L'Harmonie pratique*, 1775); *Mémoire sur la musique des anciens* (1770); *Notes et observations sur le mémoire du P. Amiot concernant la musique des chinois* (1779); *Mémoire sur la nouvelle harpe de M. Cousineau* (1782); *Mémoire sur le clavecin chromatique* (1782); *Lettre sur l'acceptation des mots "basse fondamentale"* (1783; *Journal Encyclopédique,* vol. I); etc.

BIBL.: R. Osborne, *The Theoretical Writings of Abbé P.- J. R.* (diss., Ohio State Univ., 1966).—NS/LK/DM

Routh, Francis (John), English pianist, organist, conductor, writer on music, and composer; b. Kidder-

minster, Jan. 15, 1927. He studied at King's Coll., Cambridge (1948–51), at the Royal Academy of Music in London (1951–53), and with Seiber. He was founder and artistic director of the Redcliffe Concerts (from 1964), with which he presented works by British composers of the past and present. From 1980 to 1987 he was editor of the magazine *Composer.* In 1980 he became a contributor to *The Annual Register.*

WORKS: ORCH (all 1st perf. in London unless otherwise given): Violin Concerto (1965; April 25, 1968); *Dialogue* for Violin and Orch. (May 20, 1969); Double Concerto for Violin, Cello, and Orch. (May 11, 1970); Sym. (1973; Dublin, July 22, 1975); Cello Concerto (1973; May 20, 1974); Piano Concerto (1976; Sept. 26, 1977); *Scenes I* (1978) and *II* (1999); Oboe Concerto (Dec. 11, 1986) *Poème fantastique* (Jan. 31, 1989); *Romance* (1989); Suite for Strings (March 11, 1993); *Capriccio* (1995); *Triumphal March* (1997). **CHAMBER:** Duo for Violin and Piano (Dec. 3, 1967); *Dance Suite* for String Quartet (Nov. 28, 1968); Sonata for Solo Cello (Oct. 10, 1971); Piano Quartet (Oct. 10, 1971); *Serenade* for String Trio (1972); 2 cello sonatas: No. 1 (Nov. 10, 1975) and No. 2 (1999); *Mosaics* for 2 Violins (Nov. 27, 1977); Oboe Quartet (Oct. 19, 1977); *Fantasy* for Violin and Piano (July 23, 1980); Concerto I (Feb. 28, 1982), II (Nov. 20, 1985), III (July 27, 1991), and IV (Oct. 10, 1997) for Ensemble; *Tragic Interludes* for Oboe (Feb. 24, 1983); *Dance Interludes* for Flute and Guitar (Sept. 4, 1987); *Diversions* for Violin (June 22, 1987); *Fantasy Duo* for Violin and Piano (Jan. 14, 1991); Sonata for Solo Violin (May 11, 1994); Clarinet Quintet (Aug. 7, 1995); *Divertimento* for String Quartet (June 14, 1998). **KEYBOARD: Piano:** *Little Suite* (March 27, 1974); *Ballade* (1982); *Celebration* (Sept. 27, 1984); *Elegy* (May 28, 1986); *Scenes for Piano I* (April 14, 1991), *II, Touraine* (April 17, 1994), *III, Angels of Albion* (1995), *IV, Bretagne* (May 14, 1999), and *V, Sonata Festiva* (1999). **Organ:** *Fantasia I* (Oct. 10, 1958) and *II* (June 10, 1971); Sonatina (Dec. 8, 1965); *A Sacred Tetralogy, I, The Manger Throne* (May 28, 1960), *II, Lumen Christi* (Jan. 18, 1970), *III, Aeterne Rex Altissime* (June 6, 1971), and *IV, Gloria tibi Trinitas* (June 9, 1974); *Four Marian Antiphons, I, Alma Redemptoris Mater* (May 20, 1990), *II, Ave Regina Coelorum* (Nov. 9, 1998), *III, Regina Coeli Laetare* (Feb. 18, 1995), and *IV, Salve Regina* (Nov. 6, 1988); *Exultet Coelum laudibus* (Feb. 11, 1996). **VOCAL:** *Balulalow* (1955); *Ode to the Evening Star* for Chorus (April 28, 1967); *Spring Night,* concert aria for Mezzo-soprano and Orch. (March 13, 1972); *On a Deserted Shore* for Soprano, Chorus, 2 Pianos, and Percussion (Dec. 8, 1975); *The Death of Iphigenia* for Soprano and 13 Instruments (Dec. 13, 1978); *Vocalise for Soprano, Clarinet, Violin, Cello, and Piano* (July 12, 1979); *Love's Fool* for Soprano, Flute, and Guitar (Oct. 24, 1983); *Woefully Arranged* for Soprano, Baritone, Chorus, Boy's Chorus, and Orch. (Jan. 17, 1993); *Cantate Domino* for Soprano, Clarinet, and Strings (June 26, 1994). **Songs For High Voice and Piano:** *A Woman Young and Old* (1962); *Shakespeare Songs* (1963, 1992); *Songs of Farewell* (1965); *Songs of Lawrence Durrell* (1966); *Songs of Sir Walter Scott* (1980); *Songs of Dachine Rainer* (1980); *Ripeness is All* (1990).

WRITINGS: *The Organ* (1958); *Contemporary Music: An Introduction* (1968); *Contemporary British Music* (1972); *Early English Organ Music* (1973); with others, *Patronage of the Creative Artist* (1974); *Stravinsky* (1975).—NS/LK/DM

Routley, Erik (Reginald), English clergyman, organist, teacher, writer on music, and composer; b. Brighton, Oct. 31, 1917; d. Nashville, Tenn., Oct. 8, 1982. He studied classics at Magdalen Coll., Oxford (1936–40; B.A., 1940) and theology at Mansfield Coll., Oxford

(1940–43). In 1943 he was made a minister in the Congregational Church of England and Wales, and then pursued his education at Oxford (B.D., 1946; Ph.D., 1952, with the diss. *An Historical Study of Christian Hymnology: Its Development and Discipline*; publ. as *The Music of Christian Hymnody*, London, 1957). In 1948 he became director of music at Mansfield Coll. After serving as a minister in Edinburgh (1959–67) and Newcastle upon Tyne (1967–75), he was prof. of church music at Westminster Choir Coll. in Princeton, N.J. (from 1975). He also appeared as an organ recitalist. From 1964 he was ed. of the Studies in Church Music series. Routley was a composer mainly of sacred music.

WRITINGS (all publ. in London unless otherwise given): *The Church and Music: An Enquiry into the History, the Nature and the Scope of Christian Judgment of Music* (1950; 2nd ed., rev., 1967); with K. Parry, *Companion to Congregational Praise* (1953); *The English Carol* (1958); *Ecumenical Hymnody* (1959); *Hymns Today and Tomorrow* (N.Y., 1964); *Twentieth Century Church Music* (1964); *Words, Music and the Church* (Nashville, Tenn., 1968); *The Musical Wesleys* (1969).

BIBL.: R. Leaver, ed., *Duty and Delight: R. Remembered. A Memorial Tribute to E. R. (1917–1982)* (1985).—NS/LK/DM

Rovelli, Pietro, Italian violinist and composer; b. Bergamo, Feb. 6, 1793; d. there, Sept. 8, 1838. He studied with R. Kreutzer, then played in Italy. He was concertmaster of the Court Orch. in Munich (1815–19), after which he taught and conducted in Bergamo. He publ. excellent études and caprices for Violin as well as *Variazioni* for Violin and Orch.—NS/LK/DM

Rovere, Agostino, Italian bass; b. Monza, 1804; d. N.Y., Dec. 10, 1865. He studied in Milan, making his debut in 1826 in Pavia. He was a leading singer at La Scala in Milan (1831–44; 1846–47; 1856–57), and also appeared in Vienna (1839; 1842–45), where he created the role of Boisfleury in Donizetti's *Linda di Chamounix*; also sang at Covent Garden in London (1847–48). He was most famous for his buffo roles, excelling as Leporello, Bartolo, and Dulcamara.—NS/LK/DM

Rovetta, Giovanni, Italian composer; b. Venice, c. 1595; d. there, Oct. 23, 1668. He pursued his career in Venice, where his life was centered on San Marco. After serving as a boy treble there, he was an instrumentalist (1615–17). In 1623 he became a bass singer there, and soon entered the priesthood. After serving as an asst. maestro di cappella (1627–44), he succeeded Monteverdi as maestro di cappella in 1644, a position he retained until his death. Rovetta distinguished himself as a composer of both sacred and secular music, and was one of the principal composers in the concertato style. He publ. 8 vols. of sacred music (Venice, 1626–62) and 4 vols. of madrigals (Venice, 1629–45). He also composed the operas *Ercole in Lidia* (1645) and *Argiope* (1649), but they are not extant.—NS/LK/DM

Rowen, Ruth Halle, American music educator; b. N.Y., April 5, 1918. She studied at Barnard Coll. (B.A., 1939) and with Mitchell, Lang, Hertzmann, and Moore at Columbia Univ. (M.A., 1941; Ph.D., 1948). She was director of the education dept. of Carl Fischer, Inc. (1954–63), then taught at the City Coll. of N.Y. (1963–67) and at the graduate school of the City Univ. of N.Y. (from 1967). She wrote *Early Chamber Music* (N.Y., 1949; new ed., 1974) and *Music through Sources and Documents* (Englewood Cliffs, N.J., 1978).—NS/LK/DM

Rowicki, Witold, Polish conductor and composer; b. Taganrog, Russia, Feb. 26, 1914; d. Warsaw, Oct. 1, 1989. He studied violin with Malawski and composition with Piotrowski and Wallek-Walewski at the Kraków Cons. (graduated as a violinist, 1938); then studied with Rudolf Hindemith, the brother of Paul Hindemith (1942–44). Although he made his conducting debut in 1933, he pursued a career as a violinist until the end of World War II. In 1945 he helped organize the Polish Radio Sym. Orch. in Katowice, which he conducted until 1950; then in 1950 he reorganized the Warsaw Phil., which he conducted until 1955, at which time he opened the orch.'s new home and oversaw the renaming of the orch. as the National Phil. before resigning his post. From 1958 to 1977 he was again the conductor of the National Phil.; then was chief conductor of the Bamberg Sym. Orch. (1982–85). He became widely known for his promotion of contemporary Polish music. He wrote syms., other orch. works, chamber music, and songs.

BIBL.: L. Terpilowski, *W. R.* (Kraków, 1961).—NS/LK/DM

Rowley, Alec, English pianist, teacher, and composer; b. London, March 13, 1892; d. Weybridge, Jan. 11, 1958. He was a pupil of Corder at the Royal Academy of Music in London. From 1920 he taught at London's Trinity Coll. of Music. He also was active as a recitalist. He composed a *Rhapsody* for Viola and Orch. (1936), 2 piano concertos (both 1938), an Oboe Concerto, 2 trios for Flute, Oboe and Piano (1930), a String Quartet (1932), numerous piano pieces, and some vocal music.—NS/LK/DM

Roxburgh, Edwin, English composer, oboist, conductor, and teacher; b. Liverpool, Nov. 6, 1937. He studied composition with Howells at the Royal Coll. of Music in London, with Nono and Dallapiccola in Italy, and with Boulanger in France; completed his education at St. John's Coll., Cambridge. He was principal oboist in the Sadler's Wells Opera orch. in London (1964–67), then prof. of composition and founder-director of the 20th-century performance studies dept. at the Royal Coll. of Music (from 1967); also appeared as an oboist and was conductor of the 20th Century Ensemble of London. With L. Goossens, he publ. *The Oboe* (London, 1976). He composed a number of finely crafted orch., chamber, and vocal works, his idiomatic writing for woodwinds being particularly admirable.

WORKS: DRAMATIC: *Abelard*, opera; *The Tower*, ballet (1964). ORCH.: *Variations* (1963); *Montage* (1977); *7 Tableaux*, trumpet concerto (1979); *Prelude* (1981); *Saturn* (1982); *Serenata* for Strings (1983); *Tamesis* for Chamber Orch. (1983). CHAMBER: *Movements* for String Quartet (1961); Quartet for Flute, Clarinet, Violin, and Cello (1964); *Music 3* for String Trio (1966);

Dithyramb I for Clarinet and Percussion (1972) and *II* for Piano and 3 Percussion (1972); *Nebula I* for Clarinet Choir (1974) and *II* for Wind Quintet (1974); *At the Still Point of the Turning World* for Amplified Oboe and Electronics (1978); *Hexham Tropes* for Oboe, Oboe d'Amore, Bassoon, and Harpsichord (1979); *Wind Quintet No. 2* (1983); *Quartet for Flute, Violin, Viola, and Cello* (1984); *Voyager* for 3 Oboes, 3 English Horns, and 3 Bassoons (1989); piano pieces. **VOCAL:** *Recitative after Blake* for Contralto and String Quintet or String Orch. (1961); *Night Music* for Soprano and Orch. (1969); *How Pleasant to Know Mr. Lear* for Narrator and Chamber Orch. (1971); *A Scottish Fantasy* for Soprano, Violin, and String Orch. (1973); *A Portrait of e e cummings* for 2 Narrators, Violin, and Orch. (1974); *The Rock*, oratorio for Soloists, Chorus, Children's Chorus, and Orch. (1979); *et vitam venturi saeculi* for Chorus (1983); other choruses; songs.—NS/LK/DM

Roxy Music, one of the most experimental and provocative bands to emerge from the early 1970s British school of progressive rock. **MEMBERSHIP:** Bryan Ferry, lead voc., pno. (b. Washington, County Durham, England, Sept. 26, 1945); Brian Eno (Brian Peter George St. John le Baptiste de la Salle Eno), synth. (b. Woodbridge, Suffolk, England, May 15, 1948); Phil Manzanera (Philip Targett-Adams), lead gtr. (b. London, England, Jan. 31, 1951); Andy Mackay, sax., oboe (b. London, England, July 23, 1946); Graham Simpson, bs.; Paul Thompson, drm. (b. Jarrow, Northumberland, England, May 13, 1951). Graham Simpson left in 1972, to be replaced by a quick succession of other bassists; Brian Eno left in 1973 and was replaced by Eddie Jobson (b. Birmingham, England, April 28, 1955) on violin and synthesizer. The band was inactive from late 1976 to 1978, then regrouped with Ferry, Manzanera, Thompson, Mackay, and various supporting musicians; Paul Thompson left in 1980 and the band itself ended in 1983.

Roxy Music won immediate acceptance in Great Britain and Europe yet never achieved more than cult status in the United States. Roxy Music featured two of the most influential British musicians of the era, lead guitarist Phil Manzanera and synthesizer player Brian Eno, as well as lead vocalist Bryan Ferry, who supplied the group's decadent, romantically nostalgic, and vaguely existentialist lyrics sung in a mechanical, colorless voice. Moving through a variety of eccentric images based in part on dress, Roxy Music dropped their initial glitter-rock stance and adopted a more musical approach with the departure of Brian Eno in 1973. Recording perhaps the finest album of their career with 1982's *Avalon*, Roxy Music endured until 1983, by which time their mechanistic, fashion-conscious, and synthesizer-based musical style had been adopted by Talking Heads, Blondie, Devo, and Duran Duran.

Bryan Ferry manned his first band, The Banshees, in summer 1964 and subsequently attended Newcastle Univ., from which he received a Fine Arts degree in 1968. During college he was a member of the white soul band Gas Board with bassist Graham Simpson. In November 1970 Ferry and Simpson formed Roxy Music with guitarist Roger Bunn, added saxophonist Andy Mackay the following January, and later enlisted keyboardist Brian Eno and drummer Dexter Lloyd. Eno had studied avant-garde music in England and Italy prior to his induction into the group by Mackay. Drummer Paul Thompson, a former member of Newcastle's Smokestack, replaced Lloyd in June 1971, and with the September departure of Bunn, former Nice guitarist David O'List manned Roxy Music through September 1972. Playing their first engagement in late 1971, Roxy Music added guitarist Phil Manzanera, a former member of Quiet Sun, when O'List left.

Signed to Island Records (Warner Bros./Reprise in the United States) and given early exposure through a *Melody Maker* article, Roxy Music recorded their debut album in spring 1972 with King Crimson lyricist Peter Sinfield as producer before embarking on their first tour of Great Britain that August. The album sold quite well in Great Britain and yielded a smash British hit with "Virginia Plain." First touring America in late 1972 and Europe in spring 1973, Roxy Music scored near-smash British hits with "Pyjamarama" and "Street Life" in 1973. Their album *For Your Pleasure*, also released in 1973, included the dance parody "Do the Strand," "Editions of You," and "In Every Dream Home a Heartache."

With Brian Eno's July 1973 departure, Bryan Ferry dropped his glitter garb in favor of white tuxedo and bow tie and adopted a more traditional approach to his music; the earlier complex arrangements were replaced by more straightforward rock and roll. Roxy Music's debut for their new label Atco, *Stranded*, included the British hit "Street Life" as well as "Song for Europe" and "Mother of Pearl."The group began to make inroads in the United States with several American tours between 1974 and 1976. *Country Life*, their best-selling album in America, included "All I Want Is You," "Out of the Blue," and "Thrill of It All." Their next, *Siren*, contained "Both Ends Burning" and "Sentimental Fool" and yielded their first moderate American hit with "Love Is the Drug."

Bryan Ferry launched his own parallel solo recording career in 1974 on Atlantic Records. He achieved his first minor American hit at the end of 1976 with "Heart on My Sleeve" from *Let's Stick Together*. By then Roxy Music had disbanded, with Phil Manzanera and Brian Eno recording with 801 and Ferry touring with his own band. The group reconvened in August 1978 with Ferry, Manzanera, Andy Mackay, and Paul Thompson, plus keyboardist Paul Carrack (Ace) and bassist Gary Tibbs. *Manifesto* yielded a moderate hit with "Dance Away," and the reunited group toured America in spring 1979 and recorded *Flesh and Blood* (and its minor hit "Over You") with Ferry, Manzanera, and Mackay as mainstays. The album yielded British hits with "Oh Yeah" and the title cut, a minor American hit. Following 1982's *Avalon*, often regarded as their masterpiece, Roxy Music disbanded.

Phil Manzanera subsequently recorded with Andy Mackay in the Explorers and later recorded several solo albums as well as albums with John Wetton and Sergio Dias. Ferry continued to pursue his modest solo career, scoring a moderate hit with "Kiss and Tell," from *Bete Noire* in 1988, the year he conducted his first American tour. In 1989 Reprise issued *Street Life*, comprised of Roxy Music hits and six solo hits by Ferry. Following an album of cover songs, *Taxi*, Ferry recorded perhaps the finest album of his career, *Mamouna*, with Robin Trower as coproducer; once again he toured the United States, with Trower as guest guitarist.

Between 1973 and 1977, Brian Eno recorded four albums for Island Records with which he demonstrated the concept of the recording studio as a compositional tool. Generally regarded as his most important solo works, these four albums—*Here Come the Warm Jets*, *Taking Tiger Mountain (By Strategy)*, *Another Green World*, and *Before and After Science*—were excerpted as *More Blank than Frank* in 1986. He also recorded two intriguing, highly influential all-instrumental albums with guitar synthesizer master Robert Fripp in the mid-1970s. Eno pursued his interest in the keyboard synthesizer through a series of albums in the 1970s and 1980s; he also recorded two albums with Phil Manzanera and others as 801 in 1976–1977.

Eno worked with David Bowie on his late-1970s electronic-music album *Low*, the song "Heroes," and *Lodger*, and produced the debut albums of Ultravox and Devo in 1977 and 1980, respectively. He produced three Talking Heads albums between 1978 and 1980, cowriting songs and singing on *Remain in Light*, and recorded *My Life in the Bush of Ghosts* with David Byrne in 1981. Later, with Canadian producer/engineer David Lanois, Eno pursuing an interest in multimedia video installations, and he opened an art gallery in 1987. His video-audio-sculpture show *Latest Flame: Light and Sound Structures by Brian Eno* ran for two months at San Francisco's Exploratorium in 1988. In 1990 Eno released his first album of songs in 13 years, *Wrong Way Up*, with John Cale. Several other instrumental projects followed. In 1995 he collaborated again with David Bowie.

DISC.: ROXY MUSIC: *R. M.* (1972); *For Your Pleasure* (1973); *Stranded* (1974); *Country Life* (1974); *Siren* (1975); *Viva! R. M.* (1976); *Greatest Hits* (1977); *Manifesto* (1979); *Flesh and Blood* (1980); *The Atlantic Years, 1973–1980* (1983); *Avalon* (1982); *The High Road (mini)* (1983); *Street Life: 20 Great Hits* (1989); *Heart Still Beating* (1990). **BRIAN ENO:** *Here Come the Warm Jets* (1974); *Taking Tiger Mountain (By Strategy)* (1975); *Another Green World* (1976); *Before and After Science* (1978); *Discreet Music* (1977); *Music for Films* (1979); *Music for Airports* (1979); *On Land* (1982); *Apollo* (1983); *Thursday Afternoon* (1985); *More Blank Than Frank* (1986); *Desert Island Selection* (1987); *My Squelchy Life* (1991); *The Shutov Assembly* (1992); *Nerve Net* (1992); *Neroli* (1993); *Brian Eno I* (1994); *Brian Eno II* (1994). **BRIAN ENO AND ROBERT FRIPP:** *No Pussyfooting* (1975); *Evening Star* (1976); *The Essential Fripp and Eno* (1994). **801:** *801 Live* (1976); *Listen Now!* (1977). **BRIAN ENO AND DAVID BYRNEMY LIFE IN THE BUSH OF GHOSTS** (1981). **BRIAN ENO AND JOHN CALE:** *Wrong Way Up* (1990). **BRYAN FERRY:** *These Foolish Things* (1974); *Another Time, Another Place* (1974); *Let's Stick Together* (1976); *In Your Mind* (1977); *The Bride Stripped Bare* (1978); *Boys and Girls* (1985); *Bete Noire* (1987); *Taxi* (1993); *Mamouna* (1994). **PHIL MANZANERA:** *Diamond Head* (1975); *K-Scope* (1979); *Guitarissimo* (1987); *Primitive Guitars* (1987); *Southern Cross* (1991). **QUIET SUN:** *Mainstream* (1976). **THE EXPLORERS:** *The Explorers* (1985). **PHIL MANZANERA AND JOHN WETTON:** *Wetton/Manzanera* (1987). **PHIL MANZANERA AND SERGIO DIAS:** *Mato Grosso* (1991).

BIBL.: B. Lazell and D. Rees, *B. F. and R. M.* (London, 1982).—BH

Roy, Klaus George, Austrian-born American composer, writer, and program annotator; b. Vienna, Jan. 24, 1924. He went to the U.S. in 1940 and became a naturalized American citizen in 1944. He studied at Boston Univ. with Geiringer (B.Mus., 1947) and at Harvard Univ. with Davison, Kinkeldey, Merritt, and Piston (M.A., 1949). In 1945–46 he served as an officer in education and information with U.S. Army General Headquarters in Tokyo. From 1948 to 1957 he was employed as a librarian and instructor at Boston Univ. He also wrote music criticism for the *Christian Science Monitor* (1950–57). From 1958 to 1988 he was program annotator and ed. of the Cleveland Orch. He also taught at the Cleveland Inst. of Art (1975–87) and served as adjunct prof. at the Cleveland Inst. of Music (1986–94), which bestowed upon him an honorary doctorate in music (1987). A perspicacious collection of his writings appeared as *Not Responsible for Lost Articles: Thoughts and Second Thoughts from Severance Hall 1958–1988* (Cleveland, 1993). He writes compositions in a variety of genres, all extremely pleasing to the ear.

WORKS: DRAMATIC: *Sterlingman*, chamber opera (WGBH-TV, Boston, April 18, 1957); *Zoopera: The Enchanted Garden* (Cleveland, Sept. 2, 1983). **ORCH.:** *Chorale-Variants on an Appalachian Ballad* (1965; Cleveland, April 3, 1966). **CHAMBER:** Duo for Flute and Clarinet (1947); Trombone Sonata (1950–51); *Christopher-Suite* for Piano or Harpsichord (1953); *Nostalgicon*, 9 retrospective pieces for Piano (1964–65); *Inaugural Fantasia* for Organ (1965); *Serenade* for Cello (Cleveland, May 15, 1968); *Retrospective '15-'50* for Violin and Piano (1974; rev. 1983); *Cheaper by the Dozen*, 12 flute duets (1985). **VOCAL:** *St. Francis' Canticle of the Sun* for Chorus and Viola (Boston, Nov. 5, 1951); *The Clean Dispatch of Dying*, song cycle for Soprano and Piano (1951); *Lie Still, Sleep Becalmed* for Chorus (1954); *Lunar Modulations* for Children's Chorus and Percussion (Cuyahoga Falls, Ohio, July 19, 1969); *7 Brief Sermons on Love* for Soprano and Organ (1972); *A New Song* for Chorus, Speaking Chorus, and Organ (1973); *Winter Death Songs*, 7 haiku for Low Voice and Piano (1982); *Songs of Alexias* for Low Voice and Piano (1982); *Miracles Are Not Ceased*, scena for Soprano and Oboe (1985); *The Illuminated Fountain* for Soprano and Oboe (1993); *To Seek a Newer World* for Men's Chorus, Brass, and Percussion (1993).—NS/LK/DM

Royal, Marshal (Walton), alto saxophonist, clarinetist, brother of Ernie Royal; b. Sapulpa, Okla., Dec. 5, 1912. He was raised in Los Angeles; his father was a music teacher and bandleader and his mother played piano. Royal started on violin, then guitar and clarinet before taking up alto sax. He played in local bands from the age of 13, with Curtis Mosby from 1929–31, then joined Les Hite, working in Hite's band until 1939. After a brief stint with Cee Pee Johnson's Band, he joined Lionel Hampton's Band from October 1940 until September 1942 (occasionally doubling on violin). Then he joined the U.S. Navy and led his own service band. After the war, he was briefly with Eddie Heywood in N.Y. (spring 1946), but then returned to Calif. He did studio work for five years and gigged with various bands in Los Angeles. In spring of 1951, he joined Count Basie's Septet on clarinet (replacing Buddy De Franco); Royal remained with Basie when he reformed his big band (playing lead alto), until early 1970. During the 1970s and 1980s, he was an active freelancer, touring Europe and the U.S. During the 1980s, he played in the Concord Superband and also cut his own albums with Jake Hanna and Monty Alexander.

DISC.: *First Chair* (1978); *Royal Blue* (1980).—**JC/LP**

Royer, Joseph-Nicolas-Pancrace, French composer; b. Turin, c. 1705; d. Paris, Jan. 11, 1755. He was a native of Burgundy, and settled in Paris in 1725. He was maître de musique at the Opéra (1730–33), and then maître de musique des enfans de France (1734), serving with Matho; obtained the latter's reversion as chantre de la musique de la chambre du roi (1735). In 1748 he became director of the Concert Spirituel; in 1753, obtained the reversion of maître de musique de la chambre du roi from Rebel and Bury; that same year was named director and composer at the Opéra.

WORKS: DRAMATIC (all 1st perf. in Paris unless otherwise given): *Le Fâcheux Veuvage*, opéra-comique (Aug. 1725); *Crédit est mort*, opéra-comique (Feb. 19, 1726); *Pyrrhus*, tragédie-lyrique (Oct. 26, 1730); *Zaïde, reine de Granade*, opéra-ballet (Sept. 3, 1739); *Le Pouvoir de l'amour*, opéra-ballet (April 23, 1743); *Almasis* (Versailles, Feb. 26, 1748); *Myrtil et Zélie*, pastorale-héroïque (Versailles, June 20, 1750); *Prométhée et Pandore*, opera (n.d.; not perf.). **OTHER:** Vocal pieces and *Pièces de clavecin 1er livre* (Paris, 1746).—**NS/LK/DM**

Rozanov, Sergei (Vasilievich), Russian clarinetist and pedagogue; b. Ryazan, July 5, 1870; d. Moscow, Aug. 31, 1937. He settled in Moscow and studied with Zimmermann at the Cons. (1886–90). After playing in several opera orchs. (1891–94), he was a member (1894–97) and then first clarinetist (1897–1929) in the orch. of the Bolshoi Theater. He also pursued a solo career. From 1916 until his death he taught at the Cons. He wrote studies on the schools of clarinet playing (Moscow, 1947; 7th ed., 1968) and the principles of teaching wind instruments (Moscow, 1955). He also prepared transcriptions of various works for clarinet. —**NS/LK/DM**

Rôze, Marie (real name Hippolyte Ponsin), French soprano and pedagogue, mother of Raymond Rôze; b. Paris, March 2, 1846; d. there, June 21, 1926. She studied at the Paris Cons. with Mocker and later with Auber, winning 2 prizes in 1865. She made her debut at the Opéra-Comique in the title role of Hérold's *Marie* (Aug. 16, 1865), singing there for 3 seasons. She then appeared at the Paris Opéra as Marguerite in Gounod's *Faust* (Jan. 2, 1879). She made her London debut as Marguerite (1872), and continued to sing in England for many years. She visited America twice, in 1877–78 and 1880–81. In 1874 she married an American bass, Julius E. Perkins, who died the following year. In 1890 she settled in Paris as a teacher. —**NS/LK/DM**

Rôze, Raymond, English composer, son of Marie Rôze; b. London, 1875; d. there, March 31, 1920. He

studied at the Brussels Cons., where he won 1st prize. He wrote overtures and incidental music to many plays. In 1913 he organized at Covent Garden a season of opera in English, during which he conducted his own opera *Joan of Arc* (Oct. 31, 1913); another opera, *Arabesque*, was produced at the Coliseum in London in 1916.—**NS/LK/DM**

Rozhdestvensky, Gennadi (Nikolaievich), eminent Russian conductor, son of Nikolai Anosov; b. Moscow, May 4, 1931. He studied piano with Oborin and conducting with his father at the Moscow Cons., graduating in 1954. From 1951 to 1961 he served as asst. conductor at the Bolshoi Theater in Moscow, and from 1964 to 1970 was its principal conductor. From 1961 to 1974 he was chief conductor of the All-Union Radio and TV Sym. Orch. in Moscow; also was chief conductor of the Stockholm Phil. (1975–77), the BBC Sym. Orch. in London (1978–81), and the Vienna Sym. Orch. (1981–83). In 1982 he founded and became chief conductor of the State Symphonic Orch. of the Soviet Ministry of Culture in Moscow. In 1991 he renamed it the Soviet Phil., and then later that year the State Symphonic Kapelle of Moscow. He conducted it at its U.S. debut in N.Y. on Feb. 4, 1992. From 1991 he also served as chief conductor of the Royal Stockholm Phil. He married Viktoria Postnikova in 1969. He is distinguished by his encompassing interest in new music; he conducted notable performances of works by Soviet composers, particularly Prokofiev and Shostakovich, as well as by Stravinsky, Schoenberg, Berg, Milhaud, Honegger, and Poulenc. Rozhdestvensky publ. a technical treatise on conducting (Leningrad, 1974) and a collection of essays on his thoughts on music (Moscow, 1975).—**NS/LK/DM**

Rozkošný, Josef Richard, Czech composer; b. Prague, Sept. 21, 1833; d. there, June 3, 1913. He studied painting and music in Prague, his teachers being Tomaschek (piano) and Kittl (composition). His songs and choruses became popular, and he successfully attempted the composition of operas to Czech librettos; 8 operas were produced in Prague, among them *Svatojanské proudy* (The Rapids of St. John; Oct. 3, 1871), *Popelka* (Cinderella; May 31, 1885), and *Černé jezero* (The Black Lake; Jan. 6, 1906). He also publ. a number of piano pieces.—**NS/LK/DM**

Rózsa, Miklós, brilliant Hungarian-American composer; b. Budapest, April 18, 1907; d. Los Angeles, July 27, 1995. He studied violin in childhood with Lajos Berkovits. After training at the Leipzig Cons. with Straube and Grabner, he went to Paris in 1931 and established himself as a composer. In 1935 he went to London. In 1940 he emigrated to the U.S., and settled in Hollywood; was on the staff of MGM (1948–62); also taught at the Univ. of Southern Calif. in Los Angeles (1945–65). His autobiography was publ. as *Double Life* (London, 1982). His orch. and chamber music is cast in the advanced modern idiom in vogue in Europe between the 2 world wars; neo-Classical in general content, it is strong in polyphony and incisive rhythm;

for his film music, he employs a more Romantic and diffuse style, relying on a Wagnerian type of grandiloquence. He won Oscars for his film scores to *Spellbound* (1945), *A Double Life* (1947), and *Ben-Hur* (1959).

WORKS: DRAMATIC: Film: *Knight without Armour* (1937); *The Four Feathers* (1939); *The Thief of Bagdad* (1940); *Lydia* (1941); *That Hamilton Woman* (1941); *Jacare* (1942); *Jungle Book* (1942); *5 Graves to Cairo* (1943); *Double Indemnity* (1944); *The Lost Weekend* (1945); *Spellbound* (1945); *The Killers* (1946); *The Strange Love of Martha Ivers* (1946); *Brute Force* (1947); *A Double Life* (1947); *The Naked City* (1948); *The Secret beyond the Door* (1948); *Madame Bovary* (1949); *The Asphalt Jungle* (1950); *Quo vadis?* (1951); *Ivanhoe* (1952); *Plymouth Adventure* (1952); *Julius Caesar* (1953); *The Story of Three Loves* (1953); *Knights of the Round Table* (1954); *Lust for Life* (1956); *A Time to Love and a Time to Die* (1958); *Ben-Hur* (1959); *El Cid* (1961); *King of Kings* (1961); *The V.I.P.s* (1963); *The Green Berets* (1968); *The Private Life of Sherlock Holmes* (1970); *The Golden Voyage of Sinbad* (1974); *Providence* (1977); *Time after Time* (1979); *Eye of the Needle* (1981); *Dead Men Don't Wear Plaid* (1982). **ORCH.:** *Rhapsody* for Cello and Orch. (1929); *Variations on a Hungarian Peasant Song* for Violin and Orch. (1929; also for Violin and Piano); *North Hungarian Peasant Songs and Dances* for Violin and Orch. (1929; also for Violin and Piano); *Symphony in 3 Movements* (1930; rev. 1993); *Scherzo* (1930; originally a movement of the preceding); *Serenade* for Small Orch. (1932; rev. 1946 as *Hungarian Serenade*); *Theme, Variations, and Finale* (1933; rev. 1943); Concerto for Strings (1943; Los Angeles, Dec. 28, 1944; rev. 1957); *The Vintner's Daughter*, 12 variations on a French Folk Song (1955; also for Piano, 1953); Violin Concerto (Dallas, Jan. 5, 1956; Jascha Heifetz soloist); *Overture to a Symphony Concert* (1957); *Notturno ungherese* (1964); *Sinfonia concertante* for Violin, Cello, and Orch. (1966); Piano Concerto (1966; Los Angeles, April 6, 1967); Cello Concerto (1969); *Tripartita* (1973); Viola Concerto (1979; Pittsburgh, May 4, 1984; Pinchas Zukerman, soloist). **CHAMBER:** Trio-Serenade for Violin, Viola, and Cello (1927); Piano Quintet (1928); Duo for Violin and Piano (1931); Duo for Cello and Piano (1931); Sonata for 2 Violins (1933; rev. 1973); 2 string quartets (1950, 1981); Flute Sonata (1983); Sonata for Solo Clarinet (N.Y., Jan. 14, 1987); various works for piano. **VOCAL:** Choral works; songs.

BIBL.: C. Palmer, *M. R.: A Sketch of His Life and Work* (N.Y., 1975).—NS/LK/DM

Rozsnyai, Zoltán,

Hungarian-born American conductor; b. Budapest, Jan. 29, 1927; d. San Diego, Sept. 10, 1990. He was educated in Budapest, where he studied with Bartók, Kodály, and Dohnányi at the Franz Liszt Academy of Music, and took courses at the Technical Univ. and the Pazmany Peter Univ., before completing his studies at the Univ. of Vienna. He was conductor of the Miskolc Phil. (1948–50) and the Debrecen Opera (1950–53). After the abortive Hungarian revolution in 1956, he settled in the U.S. In 1957 he founded the Philharmonia Hungarica, with which he toured in 1958. In 1962–63 he was an asst. conductor of the N.Y. Phil. He was music director of the Cleveland Phil. (1965–68) and the San Diego Sym. Orch. (1967–71). In 1976 he became music director of the Golden State Opera Co. in Los Angeles. He was music director of the Knoxville (Tenn.) Sym. Orch. from 1978 to 1985.—NS/LK/DM

Różycki, Ludomir,

Polish composer and pedagogue; b. Warsaw, Nov. 6, 1884; d. Katowice, Jan. 1, 1953. He was a student of his father and Zawirski (piano), and of Noskowski (composition) at the Warsaw Cons., graduating with honors in 1903; then completed his training with Humperdinck in Berlin (1905–08). In 1908 went to Lemberg as conductor at the Opera and as a piano teacher at the Cons. After another Berlin sojourn (1914–20), he went to Warsaw as conductor of the Opera. In 1926 he helped to found the Polish Composers Union and served as its first president. From 1930 to 1945 he was a prof. at the Warsaw Cons., and then from 1945 at the Katowice Cons. He was highly regarded in Poland as a national composer of stature; his style of composition was a successful blend of German, Russian, and Italian ingredients, yet the Polish characteristics were not obscured by the cosmopolitan harmonic and orch. dress.

WORKS: DRAMATIC: Opera: *Boleslaw Śmialy* (Boleslaw the Bold; 1908; Lemberg, Feb. 11, 1909); *Meduza* (1911; Warsaw, Oct. 22, 1912); *Eros i Psyche* (1916; in German, Breslau, March 10, 1917); *Casanova* (1922; Warsaw, June 8, 1923); *Beatrix Cenci* (1926; Warsaw, Jan. 30, 1927); *Mlyn diabelski* (The Devilish Mill; 1930; Poznań, Feb. 21, 1931). **Operetta:** *Lili chce śpiewac* (Lile Wants to Sing; 1932; Poznań, March 7, 1933). **Ballet:** *Pan Twardowski* (1920; Warsaw, May 9, 1921); *Apollo i dziewczyna* (Apollo and the Maiden; 1937). **ORCH.:** *Stańczyk*, symphonic scherzo (1903); symphonic poems: *Boleslaw Smialy* (1906); *Pan Twordowski* (1906); *Anhelli* (1909); *Król Koftua* (1910); *Mona Lisa Gioconda* (1911); *Pietà* (1942); *Warszawa wyzwolona* (Warsaw Liberated; 1950); 2 piano concertos (1918, 1942); Violin Concerto (1944). **CHAMBER:** Violin Sonata (1903); Cello Sonata (1906); Piano Quintet (1913); String Quartet (1916); piano pieces. **VOCAL:** Choral music; song cycles.

BIBL.: A. Wieniawski, *L. R.* (Warsaw, 1928); M. Kaminski, *L. R.* (Katowice, 1951); J. Kański, *L. R.* (Kraków, 1955).—NS/LK/DM

Rubalcaba, Gonzalo,

Cuban jazz pianist; b. Havana, Cuba, May 27, 1963. His father, Guillermo, was an acclaimed Cuban pianist who played with the orch. of innovator Enrique Jorrin; his grandfather, Jacobo, penned some of the most beloved danzones of Cuban ballroom society. Despite the U.S. embargo, friends used to smuggle records in and he heard American radio. While he studied classical music at the Amadeo Roldan Cons. in Havana, at home he listened to Art Tatum, Count Basie, Charlie Parker, and Dizzy Gillespie. By the time he was a teenager, he and friends had formed a jazz-oriented band. He eventually performed in Europe and South America. In 1985, Dizzy Gillespie heard Rubalcaba in Havana and pronounced him the greatest jazz pianist he had encountered in more than a decade. Gillespie tried to bring him to N.Y., but the State Department denied his visa. Wynton Marsalis, Charlie Haden and others lobbied in his favor, but several years passed. He played the Montreal Jazz Festival in 1992. When Gillespie died in January 1993, he was invited by Lorraine, Gillespie's widow, to attend the funeral as one of the pallbearers, and was allowed a visa to attend the funeral. Later that year, he played a concert at Lincoln Center to great critical acclaim. His move to the Dominican Republic in the mid-1990s made it possible for him to get paid for working in the U.S. (since he was a non-resident of Cuba). The fact that he has clung to his

Cuban citizenship and refused to seek asylum in the U.S. has drawn vitriol from some reporters, audiences, anti-Castro lobbyists, and many Cuban émigrés. He moved his family to Fla. with the permission of the Cuban government. He made his Chicago-area debut 1997 at Ravinia.

DISC.: *Mi Gran Pasion* (1987); *Live in Havana* (1989); *Giraldilla* (1990); *Discovery: Live at Montreux* (1990); *Images: Live at Mt. Fuji* (1991); *Blessing* (1991); *Suite 4 Y 20* (1992); *Rapsodia* (1992); *Diz* (1993).—**LP**

Rubbra, (Charles) Edmund, notable English composer and teacher; b. Northampton, May 23, 1901; d. Gerard's Cross, Feb. 13, 1986. His parents were musical, and he was taught to play the piano by his mother. He left school when he was 14 and was employed in various factories; at the same time, he continued to study music by himself, and attempted some composition; received a scholarship to study composition at Reading Univ. in 1920, and then entered the Royal Coll. of Music in London in 1921, taking courses with Holst (composition), R.O. Morris (harmony and counterpoint), and Evlyn and Howard Jones (piano); also received some instruction from Vaughan Williams there before completing his studies in 1925. He taught at the Univ. of Oxford (1947–68) and at the Guildhall School of Music and Drama in London (from 1961). In 1960 he was made a Commander of the Order of the British Empire. He compensated for a late beginning in composition by an extremely energetic application to steady improvement of his technique; finally elaborated a style of his own, marked by sustained lyricism and dynamic Romanticism; his harmonic language often verged on polytonality. He publ. the books *Holst: A Monograph* (Monaco, 1947), *Counterpoint: A Survey* (London, 1960), and *Casella* (London, 1964).

WORKS: DRAMATIC: *Bee-Bee-Bei*, opera (1933); *Prism*, ballet (1938). **ORCH.:** *Double Fugue* (1924); *Triple Fugue* (1929); *Sinfonia concertante* for Piano and Orch. (1934; London, Aug. 10, 1943); *Rhapsody* for Violin and Orch. (1934); 11 syms.: No. 1 (1935–37; London, April 30, 1937), No. 2 (1937; London, Dec. 16, 1938; rev. 1951), No. 3 (1939; Manchester, Dec. 15, 1940), No. 4 (1941; London, Aug. 14, 1942), No. 5 (1947–48; London, Jan. 26, 1949), No. 6 (London, Nov. 17, 1954), No. 7 (Birmingham, Oct. 1, 1957), No. 8, *Hommage à Teilhard de Chardin* (1966–68; London, Jan. 5, 1971), No. 9, *Sinfonia sacra, the Resurrection*, for Soprano, Alto, Baritone, Chorus, and Orch. (1971–72), No. 10, *Sinfonia da camera* (1974; Middlesborough, Jan. 8, 1975), and No. 11 (1978–79; London, Aug. 20, 1980); *Soliloquy* for Cello and Orch. (London, Jan. 1, 1945); Viola Concerto (London, April 15, 1953); Piano Concerto (1956); Violin Concerto (1959). **CHAMBER:** *Fantasy* for 2 Violins and Piano (1925); 3 violin sonatas (1925, 1931, 1967); *Lyric Movement* for String Quartet and Piano (1929); 4 string quartets (1933, rev. 1956; 1952; 1962–63; 1976–77); Cello Sonata (1946); *The Buddha*, suite for Flute, Oboe, Violin, Viola, and Cello (1947); 2 piano trios (1950, 1970); Oboe Sonata (1958); various piano pieces. **VOCAL:** Many choral works; songs.

BIBL.: R. Grover, *The Music of E. R.* (Aldershot, 1993). —**NS/LK/DM**

Rubenson, Albert, admirable Swedish composer; b. Stockholm, Dec. 20, 1826; d. there, March 2, 1901. He received training in violin from Peter Elwers in Stockholm, and then studied with Ferdinand David (violin), Moritz Hauptmann (harmony and counterpoint), and Niels Gade (composition) at the Leipzig Cons. (1844–48). After completing his training with Gade in Copenhagen, he returned to Stockholm in 1850. From 1853 to 1857 he wrote music criticism for the *Ny tidning för musik*. With Ludvig Norman and Frans Hedberg, he founded and wrote for the *Tidning för Theater och Musik* in 1859. He then devoted himself mainly to composition until becoming inspector of the Cons. in 1872, where he was given the title of director in 1888. While Rubenson's works reflect the influence of the German Romanticists, they also project his own individual voice. His most important work is his Sym. in C major (1847; rev. 1851; Stockholm, March 3, 1857). Among his other orch. scores, the *Symphonic Intermezzo* (1860) and the *Trois Pièces symphoniques* (1871) are particularly appealing.

WORKS: DRAMATIC: *En natt bland, fjällen* (A Night in the Mountains), operetta (1858); *Halte Hulda*, incidental music to Bjørnson's play (1865). **ORCH.:** Sym. in C major (1847; rev. 1851; Stockholm, March 3, 1857); Suite (1850–51); *Sorgespels-Ouverture* (Overture to a Tragedy; 1858); *Julius Caesar*, overture after Shakespeare (1859); *Drapa* (Ode; c. 1860); *Festival March* (1878). **OTHER:** String Quartet (c. 1850); *Korsfarersang* (Crusading Song) for Men's Chorus; numerous songs, including settings of Heine (1848), Robert Burns, and Bjørnson; many piano pieces.—**NS/LK/DM**

Rubin, Marcel, Austrian composer; b. Vienna, July 7, 1905; d. there, May 12, 1995. He studied piano with Richard Robert, theory of composition with Richard Stöhr, and counterpoint and fugue with Franz Schmidt at the Vienna Academy of Music; simultaneously attended courses in law. In 1925 he went to Paris, where he took private lessons with Milhaud. He was back in Vienna in 1931 to complete his studies in law, and in 1933 received his degree of Dr.Juris. After the Nazi Anschluss of Austria in 1938, Rubin, being a non-Aryan, fled to Paris, but was interned as an enemy alien; after France fell in 1940, he made his way to Marseilles. Convinced that only the Communists could efficiently oppose fascism, he became a member of the illegal Austrian Communist party in exile; in 1942 he went to Mexico and remained there until 1946; returned to Vienna in 1947. His music followed the modernistic models of Parisianized Russians and Russianized Frenchmen, with a mandatory hedonism in "new simplicity." Although he studied works of Schoenberg, Berg, and Webern with great assiduity and wrote articles about them, he never adopted the method of composition with 12 tones in his own music.

WORKS: DRAMATIC: *Die Stadt*, dance piece (1932; rev. 1980); *Kleider machen Leute*, comic opera (1966–69; Vienna, Dec. 14, 1973). **ORCH.:** 10 syms. (1927, rev. 1957; 1937, rev. 1974; 1939, rev. 1962; 1943–45, rev. 1971; 1964–65; 1973–74, rev. 1983; 1977; 1980; 1984; 1986); *Ballade* (1948); *Rondo-Burleske* (1960); *Drei Komodianten*, little suite (1963); *Sonatine* (1965); *Sinfonietta* for Strings (1966); *Pastorale* for Strings (1970); Double Bass Concerto (1970); Trumpet Concerto (1971–72); Bassoon Concerto (1976; Vienna, Aug. 23, 1977); *Hymnen an die Nacht* (1982; Vienna, April 18, 1985). **CHAMBER:** String Quartet No. 1 (1926; rev. 1961); Trio for Strings (1927; rev. 1962); *Sonatine* for Oboe and Piano (1927); Cello Sonata (1928); *Divertimento* for

Piano Trio (1966–67); *Serenade* for 5 Brass (1971); Violin Sonata (1974); Clarinet Quintet (1985). **P i a n o :** 3 sonatas (1925, rev. 1974; 1926–27; 1928). **VOCAL:** *Ein Heiligenstädter Psalm* for Baritone, Chorus, and Orch., after Beethoven's Heiligenstädt Testament (1977; Vienna, March 7, 1978); *Licht über Damaskus,* oratorio for 4 Soloists, Chorus, Organ, and Orch. (1987–88).

BIBL.: H. Krones, *M. R.* (Vienna, 1975).—NS/LK/DM

Rubin, Vanessa,

pop/jazz singer who performed with Cleveland and N.Y. jazz groups; b. Cleveland, Ohio, 1958. Like many of the pop/jazz singers who dominated the charts in the late 1940s and early 1950s, Vanessa Rubin is blessed with a beautiful, rich voice and she can swing effectively, but tends to stick close to a song's melody rather than improvise. At times her sound is reminiscent of a young Ernestine Anderson, though without as deep a feeling for the blues. Her first training was in the Western classical tradition and she later started working in jazz settings, singing at Cleveland nightspots with the Blackshaw Brothers organ combo and the Cleveland Jazz All-Stars, featuring Kenny Davis and Ernie Krivda. She moved to N.Y. in 1982 and worked with top-flight pianists such as Kenny Barron, John Hicks, Stanley Cowell, Harold Mabern, and Norman Simmons, and performed with the big bands of Lionel Hampton and Mercer Ellington and Frank Foster's Loud Minority. She has recorded a number of fine albums for Novus.

DISC.: *Soul Eyes* (1992); *Pastiche* (1993); *I'm Glad There Is You* (1994); *Vanessa Rubin Sings* (1995); *New Horizons* (1997). —AG

Rubini, Giovanni Battista,

celebrated Italian tenor; b. Romano, near Bergamo, April 7, 1794; d. there, March 3, 1854. His teacher was Rosio of Bergamo. After an auspicious debut in Pavia (1814), he appeared in Naples (1815–25), where he profited from further study with Nozzari. On Oct. 6, 1825, he sang in Paris, where he scored his first triumphs in Rossini's operas at the Théâtre-Italien. His performances of the leading parts in the operas of Bellini and Donizetti were also very successful, and there is reason to believe that Rubini's interpretations greatly contributed to the rising fame of both of those composers. Between 1831 and 1843 he sang in Paris and London; in 1843 he undertook a tour with Liszt, traveling with him in the Netherlands and Germany; in the same year he sang in Russia with tremendous acclaim; visited Russia again in 1844, then returned to Italy, where he bought an estate near his native town, and remained there until his death; for some years he gave singing lessons. He publ. *12 lezioni di canto moderno per tenore o soprano* and an album of 6 songs, *L'addio.*

BIBL.: C. Traini, *Il cigno di Romano: G.B. R.* (Romano, 1954). —NS/LK/DM

Rubinstein, Anton (Grigorievich),

renowned Russian pianist, conductor, composer, and pedagogue, brother of **Nikolai (Grigorievich) Rubinstein;** b. Vykhvatinetz, Podolia, Nov. 28, 1829; d. Peterhof, near St. Petersburg, Nov. 20, 1894. He was of a family of Jewish merchants who became baptized in Berdichev in July 1831. His mother gave him his first lessons in piano; the family moved to Moscow, where his father opened a small pencil factory. A well-known Moscow piano teacher, Alexandre Villoing, was entrusted with Rubinstein's musical education, and was in fact his only piano teacher. In 1839 Villoing took him to Paris, where Rubinstein played before Chopin and Liszt. He remained there until 1841, then made a concert tour in the Netherlands, Germany, Austria, England, Norway, and Sweden, returning to Russia in 1843. Since Anton's brother Nikolai evinced a talent for composition, the brothers were taken in 1844 to Berlin, where, on Meyerbeer's recommendation, Anton studied composition with Dehn. He subsequently made a tour through Hungary with the flutist Heindl. He returned to Russia in 1848 and settled in St. Petersburg. There he enjoyed the enlightened patronage of the Grand Duchess Helen, and wrote 3 Russian operas: *Dmitri Donskoy* (1852), *The Siberian Hunters* (1853), and *Thomas the Fool* (1853). In 1854, with the assistance of the Grand Duchess, Rubinstein undertook another tour in western Europe. He found publishers in Berlin, and gave concerts of his own works in London and Paris, exciting admiration as both composer and pianist; on his return in 1858, he was appointed court pianist and conductor of the court concerts. He assumed the direction of the Russian Musical Soc. in 1859, and in 1862 founded the Imperial Cons. in St. Petersburg, remaining its director until 1867. For 20 years thereafter he held no official position; from 1867 until 1870 he gave concerts in Europe, winning fame as a pianist second only to Liszt. During the season of 1872–73, he made a triumphant American tour, playing in 215 concerts, for which he was paid lavishly; appeared as a soloist and jointly with the violinist Wieniawski. He produced a sensation by playing without the score, a novel procedure at the time. Returning to Europe, he elaborated a cycle of historical concerts, in programs ranging from Bach to Chopin; he usually devoted the last concert of a cycle to Russian composers. In 1887 he resumed the directorship of the St. Petersburg Cons., resigning again in 1891, when he went to Dresden. He returned to Russia the year of his death.

In 1890 he established the Rubinstein Prize, an international competition open to young men between 20 and 26 years of age. Two prizes of 5,000 francs each were offered, 1 for composition, the other for piano. Quinquennial competitions were held in St. Petersburg, Berlin, Vienna, and Paris.

Rubinstein's role in Russian musical culture was of the greatest importance. He introduced European methods into education, and established high standards of artistic performance. He was the first Russian musician who was equally prominent as composer and interpreter. According to contemporary reports, his playing possessed extraordinary power (his octave passages were famous) and insight, revealed particularly in his performance of Beethoven's sonatas. His renown as a composer was scarcely less. His *Ocean Symphony* was one of the most frequently performed orch. works in Europe and America; his piano concertos were part of the standard repertoire; his pieces for Piano Solo, *Melody in F, Romance,* and *Kamennoi Ostrow,* became perennial favorites. After his death, his orch. works all but vanished from concert programs, as did his operas, with the exception of *The Demon*, which is still perf. in Russia. His Piano Concerto No. 4, in D minor, is occasionally heard.

WORKS: DRAMATIC: Opera: *Dmitri Donskoy* (1849–50; St. Petersburg, April 30, 1852); *The Siberian Hunters* (1852; Weimar, 1854); *Stenka Razin* (1852; unfinished); *Hadji-Abrek* (1852–53; 1st perf. as *Revenge*, St. Petersburg, 1858); *Thomas the Fool* (St. Petersburg, May 23, 1853); *Das verlorene Paradies* (1856; Düsseldorf, 1875); *Die Kinder der Heide* (1860; Vienna, Feb. 23, 1861); *Feramors* (1862; Dresden, Feb. 24, 1863); *Der Thurm zu Babel* (1869; Königsberg, 1870); *The Demon* (1871; St. Petersburg, Jan. 25, 1875); *Die Makkabäer* (1874; Berlin, April 17, 1875); *Nero* (1875–76; Hamburg, Nov. 1, 1879); *The Merchant Kalashnikov* (1877–79; St. Petersburg, March 5, 1880); *Sulamith* (1882–83; Hamburg, Nov. 8, 1883); *Unter Räubern* (Hamburg, Nov. 8, 1883); *Der Papagei* (Hamburg, Nov. 11, 1884); *The Careworn One* (1888; St. Petersburg, Dec. 3, 1889); *Moses* (1885–91; Prague, 1892); *Christus* (1887–93; Bremen, 1895). **Ballet:** *The Vine* (1882). **ORCH.:** 7 piano concertos: 2 unnumbered (1847; 1849, rev. as the Octet in D major, 1856), No. 1, op.25 (1850), No. 2, op.35 (1851), No. 3, op.45 (1853–54), No. 4, op.70 (1864), and No. 5, op.94 (1874); 6 syms.: No. 1, op.40 (1850), No. 2, op.42, *Ocean* (1st version, 1851; 2nd version, 1863; 3rd version, 1880), No. 3, op.56 (1854–55; originally designated as Sym. No. 4), No. 4, op.95, *Dramatic* (1874), No. 5, op.107 (1880), and No. 6, op.111 (1886); Concert Overture, op.60 (1853); *Triumphal Overture*, op.43 (1855); Violin Concerto, op.46 (1857); *Faust*, symphonic picture, op.68 (1864); 2 cello concertos: No. 1, op.65 (1864) and No. 2, op.96 (1874); *Ivan the Terrible*, symphonic picture, op.79 (1869); *Fantasia* for Piano and Orch., op.84 (1869); *Romance and Caprice* for Violin and Orch., op.86 (1870); *Russia* (1882); *Fantasia eroica*, op.110 (1884); *Concertstück* for Piano and Orch., op.113 (1889); *Antony and Cleopatra*, overture, op.116 (1890); Suite, op.119 (1894); Overture (1894). **CHAMBER:** Octet, op.9 (1849; originally the Piano Concerto, 1849); 3 violin sonatas: No. 1, op.13 (1856), No. 2, op.19 (1853), and No. 3, op.98 (1876); 5 piano trios: No. 1, op.15 (1851), No. 2, op.15 (1851), and 3 unnumbered: op.52 (1857), op.85 (1870), and op.108 (1883); 10 string quartets (1852–80); 2 cello sonatas: No. 1, op.18 (1852) and No. 2, op.39 (1857); Viola Sonata, op.49 (1855); Quintet for Winds and Piano, op.55 (1855; rev. 1860); String Quintet, op.59 (1859); Piano Quartet, op.66 (1864); String Sextet, op.97 (1876); Piano Quintet, op.99 (1876); also many piano pieces. **VOCAL:** Choral works; numerous songs.

WRITINGS: *Memoirs* (St. Petersburg, 1889; Eng. tr. as *Autobiography of Anton Rubinstein*, Boston, 1890); *Music and Its Representatives* (Moscow, 1891; Eng. tr., N.Y., 1892; also publ. as *A Conversation on Music*); *Leitfaden zum richtigen Gebrauch des Pianoforte-Pedals* (Leipzig, 1896; French tr., Brussels, 1899); *Gedankenkorb, Litterarischer Nachlass* (Stuttgart, 1896); *Die Meister des Klaviers* (Berlin, 1899).

BIBL.: A. McArthur, *A. R.* (London, 1889); E. Zabel, *A. R.* (Leipzig, 1892); L. Martinov, *Episodes de la vie de R.* (Brussels, 1895); A. Soubies, *A. R.* (Paris, 1895); E. Wessel, *Some Explanations, Hints and Remarks of A. R. from His Lessons in the St. Petersburg Cons.* (St. Petersburg, 1901; Ger. tr., Leipzig, 1904); N. Findeisen, *A. R.* (Moscow, 1907); La Mara, *A. R., Musikalische Studienkopfe* (vol. 3, 7th ed., Leipzig, 1909; separately, Leipzig, 1911); N. Bernstein, *A. R.* (Leipzig, 1911); A. Hervey, *A. R.* (London, 1913); K. Preiss, *A. R.s pianistische Bedeutung* (Leipzig, 1914); I. Glebov, *A. R. in His Musical Activities and Opinions of His Contemporaries* (Moscow, 1929); C. Bowen, *"Free Artist": The Story of A. and Nicholas R.* (N.Y., 1939; fictionalized account, but accurate; with a complete list of works and a detailed bibliography, compiled by O. Albrecht); L. Barenboym, *A.G. R.*, vol. I (Moscow, 1957); L. Sitsky, *A. R.: An Annotated Catalog of Piano Works and Biography* (Westport, Conn., 1998).—**NS/LK/DM**

Rubinstein, Arthur (actually, **Artur**), celebrated Polish-born American pianist; b. Łódź, Jan. 28, 1887; d. Geneva, Dec. 20, 1982. He was a product of a merchant family with many children, of whom he alone exhibited musical propensities. He became emotionally attached to the piano as soon as he saw and heard the instrument. At the age of 7, on Dec. 14, 1894, he played pieces by Mozart, Schubert, and Mendelssohn at a charity concert in Łódź. His first regular piano teacher was one Adolf Prechner. He was later taken to Warsaw, where he had piano lessons with Alexander Różycki; then went to Berlin in 1897 to study with Heinrich Barth; also received instruction in theory from Robert Kahn and Max Bruch. In 1900 he appeared as soloist in Mozart's A major Concerto, K.488, in Potsdam; he repeated his success that same year when he played the work again in Berlin under Joachim's direction; then toured in Germany and Poland. After further studies with Paderewski in Switzerland (1903), he went to Paris (1904), where he played with the Lamoureux Orch. and met Ravel, Dukas, and Thibaud. He also played the G minor Piano Concerto by Saint-Saëns in the presence of the composer, who commended him. The ultimate plum of artistic success came when Rubinstein received an American contract. He made his debut at Carnegie Hall in N.Y. on Jan. 8, 1906, as soloist with the Philadelphia Orch. in his favorite Saint-Saëns concerto. His American tour was not altogether successful, and he returned to Europe for further study. In 1915 he appeared as soloist with the London Sym. Orch. During the season 1916–17, he gave numerous recitals in Spain, a country in which he was to become extremely successful; from Spain he went to South America, where he also became a great favorite; he developed a flair for Spanish and Latin American music, and his renditions of the piano works of Albéniz and Falla were models of authentic Hispanic modality. Villa-Lobos dedicated to Rubinstein his *Rudepoema*, regarded as one of the most difficult piano pieces ever written. Symbolic of his cosmopolitan career was the fact that he maintained apartments in N.Y., Beverly Hills, Paris, and Geneva. He was married to Aniela Mlynarska in 1932. Of his 4 children, 1 was born in Buenos Aires, 1 in Warsaw, and 2 in the U.S. In 1946 he became a naturalized American citizen. On June 11, 1958, Rubinstein gave his first postwar concert in Poland; in 1964 he played in Moscow, Leningrad, and Kiev. In Poland and in Russia he was received with tremendous emotional acclaim. But he forswore any appearances in Germany as a result of the Nazi extermination of the members of his family during World War II. On April 30, 1976, at the age of 89, he gave his farewell recital in London.

Rubinstein was one of the finest interpreters of Chopin's music, to which his fiery temperament and poetic lyricism were particularly congenial. His style of playing tended toward bravura in Classical compositions, but he rarely indulged in mannerisms; his performances of Mozart, Beethoven, Schumann, and Brahms were particularly inspiring. In his characteristic spirit of robust humor, he made jokes about the multitude of notes he claimed to have dropped, but asserted that a worse transgression against music would be pedantic inflexibility in tempo and dynamics. He was a bon vivant, an indefatigable host at parties, and a fluent, though not always grammatical, speaker in most European languages, including Russian and his native Polish. In Hollywood, he played on the sound tracks for the films *I've Always Loved You* (1946), *Song of Love* (1947), and *Night Song* (1947). He also appeared as a pianist, representing himself, in the films *Carnegie Hall* (1947) and *Of Men and Music* (1951). A film documentary entitled *Artur Rubinstein, Love of Life* was produced in 1975; a 90-minute television special, *Rubinstein at 90*, was broadcast to mark his entry into that nonagenarian age in 1977; he spoke philosophically about the inevitability of dying. He was the recipient of numerous international honors: a membership in the French Académie des Beaux Arts and the Légion d'Honneur, and the Order of Polonia Restituta of Poland; he held the Gold Medal of the Royal Phil. Soc. of London and several honorary doctorates from American institutions of learning. He was a passionate supporter of Israel, which he visited several times. In 1974 an international piano competition bearing his name was inaugurated in Jerusalem. On April 1, 1976, he received the U.S. Medal of Freedom, presented by President Ford. During the last years of his life, he was afflicted with retinitis pigmentosa, which led to his total blindness; but even then he never lost his joie de vivre. He once said that the slogan "wine, women, and song" as applied to him was 80% women and only 20% wine and song. And in a widely publicized interview he gave at the age of 95 he declared his ardent love for Annabelle Whitestone, the Englishwoman who was assigned by his publisher to help him organize and edit his autobiography, which appeared as *My Young Years* (N.Y., 1973) and *My Many Years* (N.Y., 1980). He slid gently into death in his Geneva apartment, as in a pianissimo ending of a Chopin nocturne, ritardando, morendo...Rubinstein had expressed a wish to be buried in Israel; his body was cremated in Switzerland; the ashes were flown to Jerusalem to be interred in a separate emplacement at the cemetery, since the Jewish law does not permit cremation.

BIBL.: B. Gavoty, *A. R.* (Geneva, 1955; Eng. tr., 1956); H. Sachs, *R.: A Life* (N.Y., 1995).—**NS/LK/DM**

Rubinstein, Beryl, American pianist, teacher, and composer; b. Athens, Ga., Oct. 26, 1898; d. Cleveland, Dec. 29, 1952. He studied piano with his father and Alexander Lambert; toured the U.S. as a child (1905–11), then went to Berlin to study with Busoni and Vianna da Motta. He was appointed to the faculty of the Cleveland Inst. of Music in 1921, and became its director in 1932. He wrote an opera, *The Sleeping Beauty*, to a libretto by John Erskine (Juilliard School of Music, N.Y., Jan. 19, 1938); 32 piano studies; 3 dances for Piano; transcriptions from Gershwin's *Porgy and Bess*. He conducted his orch. *Scherzo* with the Cleveland Orch. on March 17, 1927; performed his Piano Concerto with the same orch. on Nov. 12, 1936.—**NS/LK/DM**

Rubinstein, Nikolai (Grigorievich), prominent Russian pianist, conductor, teacher, and composer, brother of **Anton (Grigorievich) Rubinstein;** b. Moscow, June 14, 1835; d. Paris, March 23, 1881. He began to study piano with his mother at the age of 4, when his brother, 6 years older than he, was already on the road to fame as a child prodigy; was taken to Berlin with his brother in 1844, studying with T. Kullak (piano) and Dehn (harmony and counterpoint). The brothers met Mendelssohn and Meyerbeer; returning to Moscow in 1846, Nikolai began to take lessons with A. Villoing. He also studied law, and received a degree from the Univ. of Moscow (1855); subsequently was a minor functionary in the government; earned his living by giving private lessons. In 1858 he began his concert career; appeared in Russia, and also in London. In 1859 he became head of the Moscow branch of the Russian Musical Soc.; in 1866 this society opened the Moscow Cons., of which he was director until his death. From 1860 he was the regular conductor of the Moscow concerts of the Imperial Russian Musical Soc. In 1878 he conducted 4 Russian concerts at the Paris Exposition; at the first and the fourth of the series he performed Tchaikovsky's Piano Concerto No. 1 (which he had criticized sharply when Tchaikovsky first submitted it to him in 1874). Anton Rubinstein declared that Nikolai was a better pianist than himself, but this generous appreciation was not accepted by the public. As an educator, however, Nikolai played perhaps a greater role than his famous brother. Among his pupils were S. Taneyev, Siloti, and Emil Sauer.

BIBL.: C. Bowen, *"Free Artist": The Story of Anton and N. R.* (N.Y., 1939).—**NS/LK/DM**

Rubio (Calzón), Samuel, Spanish musicologist; b. Posada de Omano, Oct. 20, 1912; d. Madrid, March 15, 1986. He entered the Augustinian order and was active in various monasteries. He received instruction in philosophy, theology, Gregorian chant, and other subjects, and later went to Rome to study sacred music and musicology at the Pontificio Instituto di Musica Sacra (1952–55) and musicology with Anglès at the Univ. (Ph.D., 1967, with the diss. *Cristóbal de Morales*; publ. in El Escorial, 1969). After serving as organist and choirmaster at the Escorial (1939–59; 1971–72), he was prof. of musicology at the Madrid Cons. (from 1972). He was the ed. of the collected works of Juan de Anchieta and Juan Navarro.

WRITINGS: *In XVI centenario nativitatis Sancti Patris Augustini: XXIV cantica sacra in honorem S. P. Augustini ex auctoribus antiquis et hodiernis* (Bilbao, 1954); *La politonía clásica* (El Escorial, 1956; Eng. tr., 1972); *Catalogo del archivo de música del monasteria de San Lorenzo el Real de El Escorial* (Cuenca, 1976); *Antonio Soler: Catálogo Crítico* (Cuenca, 1980).—**NS/LK/DM**

Rúbner, (Peter Martin) Cornelius
See **Rybner, (Peter Martin) Cornelius**

Rübsam, Wolfgang, German organist and teacher; b. Giessen, Oct. 16, 1946. He studied at Southern Methodist Univ. in Dallas (M.Mus., 1970), and took lessons with Helmut Walcha at the Frankfurt am Main

Staatliche Hochschule für Musik, where he graduated with an artist diploma in 1971; he subsequently studied with Marie-Claire Alain in Paris (1971–74). In 1974 he joined the faculty of Northwestern Univ. He made extensive tours as an organ virtuoso.—NS/LK/DM

Rubsamen, Walter (Howard), renowned American musicologist; b. N.Y., July 21, 1911; d. Los Angeles, June 19, 1973. He studied flute with Barrère in N.Y. and musicology at Columbia Univ. with Lang (B.A., 1933), then attended classes of Ursprung and Ficker at the Univ. of Munich, receiving his doctorate with the diss. *Pierre de la Rue als Messenkomponist* (1937). Returning to the U.S., he was appointed to the music faculty at the Univ. of Calif., Los Angeles, obtaining a full professorship in 1955; was chairman of the music dept. (1965–73). He ed. the *Opera omnia* of Pierre de La Rue for the American Inst. of Musicology and brought out a German 16ᵗʰ-century *Magnificat on Christmas Carols* (N.Y., 1971); contributed a number of informative articles on ballad opera in England and on Renaissance composers to various American and European publications.

WRITINGS: *Literary Sources of Secular Music in Italy c. 1500* (Berkeley, Calif., 1943); with D. Heartz and H.M. Brown, *Chanson and Madrigal, 1480–1530* (Cambridge, Mass., 1964). —NS/LK/DM

Ruby, Harry (originally, **Rubenstein, Harold**), American songwriter, librettist, and screenwriter; b. N.Y., Jan. 27, 1895; d. Los Angeles, Calif., Feb. 23, 1974. Ruby was primarily a composer, though on occasion he also wrote lyrics, and he frequently collaborated with his long-time partner, lyricist Bert Kalmar, on the librettos to their stage musicals and the screenplays to their film musicals. Ruby's hits included "Three Little Words," "I Wanna Be Loved by You," "Who's Sorry Now?" and "A Kiss to Build a Dream On." He and Kalmar generally worked alone, but their other collaborators included Jerome Kern, Irving Berlin, and Oscar Hammerstein II.

Ruby had no formal music training. He began his career playing piano in cafés and in vaudeville, then became a song plugger for a succession of N.Y. music publishers, meeting Kalmar, a vaudeville magician, along the way. (Unless otherwise noted, Kalmar wrote the lyrics to Ruby's music for all the songs discussed below.) His first songwriting recognition came when two of his songs, "If You Hadn't Answered No" (lyrics by Kalmar and Edgar Leslie) and "It's All Right If You Love (One Another)" (lyrics by Leslie), were used in the Broadway revue *Words and Music* (N.Y., Nov. 24, 1917). He wrote several songs for the *Ziegfeld Follies of 1918* (N.Y., June 18, 1918), among them "Come On, Papa" (lyrics by Leslie), which became a hit for the Avon Comedy Four in April 1919. Vaudeville star George Jessel introduced and popularized "And He'd Say Oo-La-La! Wee Wee!" (lyrics by Jessel), but it was recorded for a hit in October by Billy Murray.

For the *Ziegfeld Follies of 1920* (N.Y., June 22, 1920), Ruby and Kalmar collaborated with Irving Berlin on "I'm a Vamp from East Broadway," introduced by

Fanny Brice. The songwriters themselves introduced "So Long, Oo Long" on the stage of the Palace Theatre in N.Y., donning false beards to appear with the King of David Band. Frank Crumit recorded the song for a hit in August. British actress Beatrice Lillie popularized "Snoops, the Lawyer," but the hit recording in October was by Eddie Cantor. "Timbuctoo" was a hit for Crumit with the Paul Biese Trio in April 1921, and "My Sunny Tennessee," interpolated by Cantor into the revue *The Midnight Rounders of 1921* (N.Y. Feb. 7, 1921), was a hit for the Peerless Quartet in January 1922.

Up to 1922, Ruby and Kalmar had placed only individual songs in vaudeville, revues, and on records. The first revue for which they received primary credit was *Arabian Nights*, written for the Marigold Gardens in Chicago and opening on April 3, 1922. The following year brought their first musical to reach Broadway, *Helen of Troy, N.Y.*, which ran for 193 performances but produced no hits. At the same time, however, they scored two independent hits: "I Gave You Up Just Before You Threw Me Down" (music also by Fred E. Ahlert) for Billy Murray and Gladys Rice (under the pseudonym Rachel Grant) in May 1923, and "Who's Sorry Now?" (music by Ted Snyder, lyrics by Ruby and Kalmar), a sheet-music million-seller introduced by vaudeville stars Van and Schenck that had its most popular recording by Isham Jones and His Orch. in August.

Ruby and Kalmar's second musical, *No Other Girl*, had a long, troubled tryout on the road during 1924 before arriving in N.Y. for a 56-performance run. The team finished the year writing the libretto for Irving Berlin's *Music Box Revue* (N.Y., Dec. 1, 1924). They also wrote the libretto for the American musical version of the German play *Frühling im Herbst*, retitled *Holka-Polka* (N.Y., Oct. 14, 1925). They were finally able to mount their third musical, *The Ramblers*, in 1926, writing the songs and cowriting the libretto with Guy Bolton. It ran 291 performances and launched "All Alone Monday," recorded for a hit by Nat Shilkret and the Victor Orch. in January 1927.

Ruby and Kalmar collaborated with composer Jerome Kern and lyricist/librettist Otto Harbach on their next show, *Lucky*, which ran only 71 performances but included two hits, "Dancing the Devil Away" (lyrics also by Harbach), recorded by Dan Voorhees and His Earl Carroll Vanities Orch., and "The Same Old Moon" (lyrics also by Harbach), recorded by Carl Fenton and His Orch. *The Five O'Clock Girl* was more successful onstage, running 278 performances, and it too had two hits, which appeared on either side of a record by Nat Shilkret—"Thinking of You" and "Up in the Clouds."

Ruby and Kalmar worked on three musicals that opened in 1928. The first was *She's My Baby* (N.Y., Jan. 3, 1928), for which they cowrote the libretto with Guy Bolton; the songs were handled by Richard Rodgers and Lorenz Hart. For *Good Boy*, Herbert Stothart was brought in as a cocomposer with Ruby. The show ran 253 performances and was memorable for Helen Kane's performance of "I Wanna Be Loved by You," which she recreated in a hit recording in November. Her tag phrase, "Boop-boop-a-doop," became her trademark and inspired the Betty Boop cartoon character. Ruby and Kalmar's third show of the year was *Animal Crackers*. Their talent for writing comic songs stood them in good stead as they provided material for the Marx Brothers, and "Hooray for Captain Spaulding" became Groucho Marx's signature song. The show ran for 213 performances.

Ruby and Kalmar's last Broadway show for nearly 12 years was *Top Speed*, which they coproduced and cowrote the libretto for with Guy Bolton. Running 102 performances, it was a relative disappointment and may have hastened the team's decision to move to Hollywood in 1930. There they worked on film adaptations of three of their shows, all released in 1930: *The Cuckoos*, based on *The Ramblers*; *Animal Crackers*; and *Top Speed*. For *The Cuckoos* they wrote "I Love You So Much," which became a hit for Bob Haring and His Orch. in August. They also wrote the screenplay and two songs for *Check and Double Check* (1930), one of which was "Three Little Words," performed in the film and recorded by Duke Ellington and His Famous Orch. with vocals by the Rhythm Boys, a trio including Bing Crosby. The record became a best-seller in November.

The flood of movie musicals in 1930 was followed by a drought in 1931. But Ruby and Kalmar scored an independent hit in June with "Nevertheless (I'm in Love with You)," recorded by Jack Denny and His Orch. Things started to pick up in the second half of 1932, when Ruby and Kalmar had two films in release. They cowrote the Marx Brothers film *Horse Feathers* with S. J. Perelman and wrote the incidental songs including "Everyone Says 'I Love You,'" which became a hit for Isham Jones in September. Then they cowrote the Eddie Cantor film *The Kid from Spain* with William Anthony McGuire, also writing four songs, among them "What a Perfect Combination" (music also by Harry Akst, lyrics also by Irving Caesar), which Cantor made into a hit in November.

Ruby and Kalmar were back with the Marx Brothers for *Duck Soup*, cowriting the script with Nat Perrin and Arthur Sheekman. Probably signing to RKO in 1934, they wrote *Hips Hips Hooray* with Edward Kaufman and contributed the songs. Next came *Kentucky Kernals*, for which they wrote the script with Fred Guiol, as well as the songs. In 1935 they wrote the screenplay and one song for *Bright Lights* at Warner Bros. Back at RKO they collaborated with Viola Brothers Shore on the screenplay for *Walking on Air*; Sid Silvers cowrote the song lyrics. Ruby, Kalmar, and Shore also wrote *The Life of the Party* (1937). The late 1930s were less active for the team, though they wrote songs for MGM's *Everybody Sing* (1938) and RKO's *The Story of Vernon and Irene Castle* (1939), starring Fred Astaire and Ginger Rogers.

Ruby and Kalmar returned to Broadway in 1941, writing the songs for *High Kickers* and collaborating on the libretto with the show's star, George Jessel. It ran 171 performances. After five years of inactivity, Ruby returned with the title song for *Do You Love Me?* (1946), for which he wrote both music and lyrics. In the film, Harry James and His Orch. backed Dick Haymes in his performance of the song; on records, James used singer Ginnie Powell for a hit in July, the month after he had

scored a hit revival of "Who's Sorry Now?" Ruby wrote lyrics to Rube Bloom's music for the two songs in *Wake Up and Dream*, including "Give Me the Simple Life," which became a hit for Benny Goodman and His Orch. in March 1946. Ruby wrote most of the English lyrics to the songs by Ernesto Lecuona for the film *Carnival in Costa Rica* (1947). He and Kalmar had their last new song in a film with "Go West Young Man," used in the Groucho Marx movie *Copacabana* (1947). Kalmar died on Sept. 18, 1947.

Ruby wrote lyrics to Johnnie Scott's music for "Maybe It's Because," which was used in the Broadway revue *Along Fifth Avenue* (N.Y., Jan. 13, 1949). Dick Haymes recorded it for a Top Ten hit in August 1949. Ruby and Kalmar's story, "Life of Marilyn Miller," was the source material for the Miller film biography *Look for the Silver Lining* (1949), and Ruby again worked solely as a lyricist, this time for composer Alfred Newman, on "Blue (With or Without You)," written for the film *Pinky* (1949), though the lyric was used only for promotional purposes.

In July 1950, MGM released *Three Little Words*, a film biography of Ruby and Kalmar in which Red Skelton played the former and Fred Astaire the latter. Ruby himself had a cameo as a baseball player. The film stimulated the team's song catalog, leading to Top Ten revivals of "Thinking of You," which earned three chart covers, the most popular being the one by Don Cherry, and "Nevertheless (I'm in Love with You)," which produced six new chart recordings, with Paul Weston and His Orch. having the most successful one.

In the 1930s, Ruby and Kalmar had written a song called "Moonlight on the Meadow," which was not a success. Oscar Hammerstein II revised the lyric to produce "A Kiss to Build a Dream On" for the 1935 Marx Brothers film *A Night at the Opera*, but the song was not used. Finally it was used in the 1951 film *The Strip*, resulting in two chart recordings, the more popular of which was the one by Hugo Winterhalter and His Orch. and Chorus, which reached the Top Ten in February 1952, though the one by Louis Armstrong, who appeared in the film, had a longer life, later being used prominently in the 1993 film *Sleepless in Seattle*. The song was Ruby's only one to earn an Academy Award nomination.

Ruby's last film credit came when he cowrote the screenplay to *Lovely to Look At*, the 1952 remake of *Roberta*, the stage and movie musical by Kern and Harbach. Ruby reached television in 1957, writing the theme song for the long-running series *The Real McCoys*. The same year, his music entered the rock 'n' roll era, as Connie Francis enjoyed her first hit with a cover of "Who's Sorry Now?" that reached the Top Ten in March 1958 and sold a million copies.

WORKS (only works for which Ruby was one of the primary, credited songwriters are listed): **MUSICALS/REVUES** (dates refer to N.Y. openings): *Helen of Troy, N.Y.* (Sept. 4, 1923); *No Other Girl* (Aug. 13, 1924); *The Ramblers* (Sept. 20, 1926); *Lucky* (March 22, 1927); *The Five O'Clock Girl* (Oct. 10, 1927); *Good Boy* (Sept. 5, 1928); *Animal Crackers* (Oct. 23, 1928);

Top Speed (Dec. 25, 1929); *High Kickers* (Oct. 31, 1941). FILMS: *The Cuckoos* (1930); *Animal Crackers* (1930); *The Kid from Spain* (1932); *Horse Feathers* (1932); *Duck Soup* (1933); *Hips Hips Hooray* (1934); *Kentucky Kernels* (1934); *Walking on Air* (1936); *Wake Up and Dream* (1946).—**WR**

Ruckers, celebrated family of Flemish harpsichord makers. **Hans Ruckers,** "the elder" (b. Mechelen, c. 1545; d. Antwerp, 1598), was the first instrument maker in the family. His second son, **Johannes Ruckers,** also known as **Hans** or **Jan Ruckers** (b. Antwerp [baptized], Jan. 15, 1578; d. there, April 24, 1643), was greatly esteemed by his contemporaries. **Andreas or Andries Ruckers, "the elder"** (b. Antwerp [baptized], Aug. 15, 1579; d. after 1645), built harpsichords between 1601 and 1644. **Andreas or Andries Ruckers, "the younger"** (b. Antwerp [baptized], March 31, 1607; d. there, before 1667), son of the elder Andreas, made instruments from 1637.

BIBL.: A. Pols, *De R.s en de klavierbouw in Vlaanderen* (Antwerp, 1942); J. Lambrechts-Douillez and M.-J. Basschaerts-Eykens, *H. en J. R.s* (Antwerp, 1983); G. O'Brien, *R.: A Harpsichord and Virginal Building Tradition* (Cambridge, 1990) —**NS/LK/DM**

Rudd, Roswell (Hopkins, Jr.), avant-garde jazz trombonist; b. Sharon, Conn., Nov. 17, 1935. Both his parents were musicians. He studied voice and French horn at Yale Univ. (1954–58). He began his jazz career playing in New Orleans revival-styled bands in the late 1950s and early 1960s; he also co-led a group with Steve Lacy (1963) to play all Monk tunes. He then did a stylistic turnabout; influenced by Albert Ayler, his playing became very free and radical. He formed N.Y. Art Quartet with John Tchicai, playing Scandinavia in 1965. He worked with Archie Shepp in the late 1960s–70s. After a long period of inactivity, he re-emerged on the N.Y. scene in the mid-1990s. In 1999, he played with re-formed N.Y. Art Quartet at a much publicized and well-received gig at 1999 Bell Atlantic Jazz Fest, N.Y. and recorded album with them for DIW label.

DISC.: *Roswell Rudd* (1965); *Everywhere* (1966); *Numatik Swing Band* (1973); *Flexible Flyer* (1974); *Maxine* (1976); *Inside Job* (1976); *Definitive* (1979); *Regeneration* (1983).—**LP**

Rudel, Julius, prominent Austrian-born American conductor; b. Vienna, March 6, 1921. Following training at the Vienna Academy of Music, he emigrated to the U.S. in 1938 and became a naturalized American citizen in 1944. He completed his studies at the Mannes School of Music in N.Y. In 1943 he joined the staff of the N.Y.C. Opera as a répétiteur. On Nov. 25, 1944, he made his conducting debut there with *Der Zigeunerbaron,* and subsequently remained closely associated with it. From 1957 to 1979 he served as its music director. During his innovative tenure, he programmed an extensive repertoire of standard, non-standard, and contemporary operas. He made a special effort to program operas by American composers. He also was music director of the Caramoor Festival in Katonah, N.Y., and the Wolf Trap Farm Park for the Performing Arts in Vienna, Va. He

was the first music director of the Kennedy Center in Washington, D.C. (1971–74). On. Oct. 7, 1978, he made his Metropolitan Opera debut in N.Y. conducting *Werther,* and continued to make occasional appearances there in subsequent years. He also appeared as a guest conductor of operas in San Francisco, Chicago, London, Paris, Berlin, Munich, Milan, Hamburg, and Buenos Aires. After serving as music director of the Buffalo Phil. from 1979 to 1985, he concentrated on a career as a guest conductor around the world. In 1969 the Julius Rudel Award for young conductors was established in his honor.—**NS/LK/DM**

Ruders, Poul, Danish composer; b. Ringsted, March 27, 1949. He began piano and organ lessons in childhood, and later pursued training in organ at the Royal Danish Cons. of Music in Copenhagen (graduated, 1975). Although he had a few orchestration lessons there, he was mainly autodidact as a composer. From 1975 he was active as a Lutheran church organist and choirmaster. Later he devoted much time to composition and guest lecturing. In 1991 he was a guest lecturer at Yale Univ. He received the Charles Heidseick Award of the Royal Phil. Soc. of London in 1991. In his music, Ruders has been particularly cognizant of all styles of music, from the Baroque to the popular genres. His works are notable for their startling juxtapositions and superimpositions of various styles and techniques.

WORKS: DRAMATIC: Opera: *Tycho* (1985–86; Århus, May 16, 1987); *Tjenerindens Fortaelling* (The Handmaid's Tale), after Margaret Atwood (1997–98; Copenhagen, March 6, 2000). ORCH.: *Pavane* (1971); *Capriccio pian'e forte* (1978); 2 syms.: No. 1, *Himmelhoch Jauchzend-zum Tode betrübt'* (1989) and No. 2, *Symphony and Transformation* (1995–96); 2 violin concertos: No. 1 (1981; Copenhagen, Oct. 16, 1982) and No. 2 (1990–91); *Manhattan Abstraction* (1982); *Thus Saw St. John* (1984); Concerto for Clarinet and Twin Orch. (1985); *Jubileephony* (1986); *Drama Trilogy I: Dramaphonia* for Piano and Orch. (1987), *II: Monodrama* for Percussionist and Orch. (1988), and *III: Polydrama* for Cello and Orch. (1988); *Psalmodies* for Guitar and Orch. (1989); *Tundra* (1990); *The Second Night Shade* (1991); *Solar Trilogy I, Gong* (1992), *II, Zenith* (1992–93), and *III, Corona* (1995); Cello Concerto No. 2, *Anima* (1993); *The Return of the Light* (1994); Viola Concerto (1994); Piano Concerto (1994); *Concerto in Pieces: Purcell Variations* (1994–95); *Credo* for Clarinet, 2 Violins, and Small String Orch. (1996). CHAMBER: 3 string quartets (1972; 1979; *Motet,* 1979); *Bravour-Studien* for Cello (1976); *Wind-Drumming* for Wind Quintet and 4 Percussionists (1979); *4 Compositions* for 9 Instruments (1980); *Diferencias* for 7 Instruments (1980); *Carnival* for Electric Alto Flute and Foot Bongos (1980); *Cha Cha Cha* for Percussion (1981); *Greeting Concertino* for 8 Instruments (1982); *4 Dances in 1 Movement* for Chamber Ensemble (1983); *Vox im Rama* for Clarinet, Electric Violin, and Piano (1983); *Alarm* for Percussion (1983); *Tattoo for 1* for Clarinet (1984); *Tattoo for 3* for Clarinet, Cello, and Piano (1984); *Corpus cum Figuris* for Chamber Ensemble (1985); *Break-Dance* for Piano, 2 Trumpets, and 3 Trombones (1985); *Cembal d'Amore* for Harpsichord and Piano (1986); *Nightshade* for Chamber Ensemble (1987); *Throne* for Clarinet and Piano (1988); *Variations* for Violin (1989); *De Profundis* for 2 Pianos and Percussion (1990); *Towards the Precipice* for Percussion (1990); *Second Set of Changes* for 4 Viols (1994); *Chaconne* for Guitar (1996); Horn Trio (1999). KEYBOARD: Piano: *3 Letters From the Unknown Soldier* (1967); 2 sonatas (*Dante,* 1970; 1982); 7

Recitatives (1977); *13 Postludes* (1988); *Star-Prelude and Love Fugue* (1990). O r g a n : *Requiem* (1968). VOCAL: *Stabat Mater* for Chorus, Piano, and Organ (1973); *Pestilence Songs* for Soprano, Guitar, and Saloon Piano (1975); *glOriA* for Chorus and 12 Brasses (1981); *3 motets* for Chorus (1981, 1985, 1988); *The City in the Sea* for Contralto and Orch. (1990); *The Bells* for Soprano and Chamber Ensemble, after Poe (1993).—NS/LK/DM

Rudhyar, Dane (real name, Daniel Chennevière),

French-born American composer, painter, and mystical philosopher; b. Paris, March 23, 1895; d. San Francisco, Sept. 13, 1985. He changed his name in 1917 to Rudhyar, derived from an old Sanskrit root conveying the sense of dynamic action and the color red, astrologically related to the zodiacal sign of his birth and the planet Mars. He studied philosophy at the Sorbonne in Paris (baccalaureat, 1911), and took music courses at the Paris Cons. In composition he was largely self-taught; he also achieved a certain degree of proficiency as a pianist; developed a technique which he called "orchestral pianism." In 1913 the publisher Durand commissioned him to write a short book on Debussy, with whom he briefly corresponded. At the same time, he joined the modern artistic circles in Paris. In 1916 he went to America; became a naturalized American citizen in 1926. His "dance poems" for Orch., *Poèmes ironiques* and *Vision végétale*, were performed at the Metropolitan Opera in N.Y. (April 4, 1917). In 1918 he visited Canada; in Montreal he met the pianist Alfred Laliberté, who was closely associated with Scriabin, and through him Rudhyar became acquainted with Scriabin's theosophic ideas. In Canada he also publ. a collection of French poems, *Rapsodies* (Toronto, 1918). In 1920 he went to Hollywood to write scenic music for *Pilgrimage Play, The Life of Christ*, and also acted the part of Christ in the prologue of the silent film version of *The Ten Commandments* produced by Cecil B. DeMille. In Hollywood he initiated the project of "Introfilms," depicting inner psychological states on the screen through a series of images, but it failed to receive support and was abandoned. Between 1922 and 1930 he lived in Hollywood and N.Y.; was one of the founding members of the International Composers Guild in N.Y. In 1922 his orch. tone poem *Soul Fire* won the $1,000 prize of the Los Angeles Phil.; in 1928 his book *The Rebirth of Hindu Music* was publ. in Madras, India. After 1930 Rudhyar devoted most of his time to astrology. His first book on the subject, *The Astrology of Personality* (1936), became a standard text in the field; it was described by Paul Clancy, the pioneer in the publication of popular astrological magazines, as "the greatest step forward in astrology since the time of Ptolemy." A new development in Rudhyar's creative activities took place in 1938 when he began to paint, along nonrepresentational symbolistic lines; the titles of his paintings (*Mystic Tiara, Cosmic Seeds, Soul and Ego, Avatar,* etc.) reflect theosophic themes. His preoccupations with astrology left him little time for music; about 1965 he undertook a radical revision of some early compositions, and wrote several new ones; was also active as a lecturer.

The natural medium for Rudhyar's musical expression was the piano; his few symphonic works were mostly orchestrations of original piano compositions. In his writing for piano he built sonorous chordal formations supported by resonant pedal points, occasionally verging on polytonality; a kinship with Scriabin's piano music was clearly felt, but Rudhyar's harmonic idiom was free from Scriabin's Wagnerian antecedents. Despite his study of oriental religions and music, Rudhyar did not attempt to make use of Eastern modalities in his own music. He lived his last years in Palo Alto, Calif., and kept active connections with the world of theosophy; he also orchestrated his early piano works. Before his death his wife asked him whom he expected to meet beyond the mortal frame; he replied, "Myself."

WORKS: ORCH.: *3 poèmes ironiques* (1914); *Vision végétale* (1914); *The Warrior*, symphonic poem for Piano and Orch. (1921; Palo Alto, Dec. 10, 1976); *Sinfonietta* (1927); *Syntonies* in 4 sections: *To the Real* (1920), *The Surge of Fire* (1921), *Ouranos* (1927), and *The Human Way* (1927); *Tripthong* for Piano and Orch. (1948; rev. 1977); *Thresholds* (1954); *Dialogues* for Chamber Orch. (1977; San Francisco, May 23, 1982); *Cosmic Cycle* (1981). CHAMBER: *3 Melodies* for Flute, Cello, and Piano (1919); *3 Poems* for Violin and Piano (1920); *Solitude* for String Quartet (1950); *Piano Quintet* (1950); *Barcarolle* for Violin and Piano (1955); *Alleluia* for Carillon (1976); *Nostalgia* for Flute, Piano, and Strings (1977); *2 string quartets* (*Advent*, 1978; *Crisis and Overcoming*, 1979). P i a n o : *3 poèmes* (1913); *Mosaics*, tone cycle in 8 movements on the life of Christ (1918); *Syntony* (1919–34; rev. 1967); *9 Tetragrams* (1920–67)); *Pentagrams* (1924–26); *3 Paeans* (1925); *Granites* (1929); *Transmutation* (1976); *Theurgy* (1976); *Autumn and 3 Cantos* (1977); *Epic Poem* (1979); *Rite of Transcendence* (1981). S o n g s : *3 chansons de Bilitis* (1919); *3 poèmes tragiques* (1918); *3 invocations* (1939).

WRITINGS: *Claude Debussy et son oeuvre* (Paris, 1913); *Art as Release of Power* (N.Y., 1930); *The Astrology of Personality* (N.Y., 1936; 2nd ed., 1979); *The Practice of Astrology* (Amsterdam, 1967; N.Y., 1970); *The Planetarization of Consciousness* (Amsterdam, 1970; N.Y., 1972); *The Astrological Houses* (N.Y., 1972); *Culture, Crisis and Creativity* (Wheaton, Ill., 1977); *The Astrology of Transformation* (Wheaton, 1980); *The Magic of Tone and the Art of Music* (Boulder, Colo., 1982); *The Rhythm of Wholeness* (Wheaton, 1983).

BIBL.: A. Morang, *D. R., Pioneer in Creative Synthesis* (N.Y., 1939); *D. R.: A Brief Biography* (Berkeley, Calif., 1972).—NS/LK/DM

Rüdinger, Gottfried,

German composer; b. Lindau, Aug. 23, 1886; d. Gauting, near Munich, Jan. 17, 1946. He was a student in theology, and also took courses in composition with Reger at the Leipzig Cons. (1907–09). In 1910 he settled in Munich and began teaching privately; taught at the Academy of Music there from 1920. He composed industriously in many genres; brought out a "peasant play-opera," *Die Tegernseer im Himmel*, and several children's operas, including *Benchtesgadener Sagenspiel, Musikantenkomodie*, and *König Folkwart*; also 2 syms.; 2 violin concertos; Cello Concerto; much choral and chamber music, and a number of instructive piano pieces. His pieces for small brass ensembles, in the style of old town piper music, are especially attractive.—NS/LK/DM

Rudnytsky, Antin,

Polish-American pianist, conductor, and composer; b. Luka, Galicia, Feb. 7, 1902; d. Toms River, N.J., Nov. 30, 1975. He studied piano with

Schnabel and Petri, composition with Schreker, and musicology with Curt Sachs in Berlin; received his Ph.D. at the Univ. of Berlin in 1926. In 1927 he went to Russia, where he conducted opera in Kharkov and Kiev; then was conductor of the Lwów Opera (1932–37). In 1937 he emigrated to the U.S.; toured with his wife, the singer Maris Sokil, as her piano accompanist. He composed 3 syms. (1936, 1941, 1942); a Cello Concerto (1942); an opera, *Dovbush* (1937); some ballet music; miscellaneous pieces for instrumental ensembles; piano works.
—NS/LK/DM

Rudolf, Max, eminent German-born American conductor and teacher; b. Frankfurt am Main, June 15, 1902; d. Philadelphia, Feb. 28, 1995. He began his musical training when he was 7. He studied cello with Maurits Frank, piano with Eduard Jung, and composition with Bernhard Sekles, and also learned to play the organ and the trumpet. In 1921–22 he attended the Univ. of Frankfurt am Main. In 1922 he became a répétiteur at the Freiburg im Breisgau Opera, where he made his conducting debut in 1923. After working as a répétiteur at the Darmstadt Opera (1923–25), he returned there to hold its post of 1st conductor from 1927 to 1929. From 1929 to 1935 he conducted at the German Theater in Prague. In 1929–30 he appeared as a guest conductor of the Berlin Phil. In 1935 he went to Göteborg, where he made appearances as a conductor with both the radio orch. and the orch. society. In 1940 he emigrated to the U.S. and in 1945 became a naturalized American citizen. He conducted the New Opera Co. in N.Y. before joining the staff of the Metropolitan Opera in N.Y. in 1945. On Jan. 13, 1946, he made his first appearance as a conductor at the Metropolitan Opera in a Sunday night concert. His formal debut followed on March 2, 1946, when he conducted *Der Rosenkavalier*. From 1950 to 1958 he served as artistic administrator of the Metropolitan Opera, and also was active as a conductor there. In 1958 he became music director of the Cincinnati Sym. Orch., a position he retained with distinction until 1969. In 1966 he led it on a world tour and in 1969 on a major tour of Europe. He also served as music director of the Cincinnati May Festival in 1963 and again from 1967 to 1970. From 1970 to 1973 he was head of the opera and conducting depts. at the Curtis Inst. of Music in Philadelphia. In 1973–74 he was principal conductor of the Dallas Sym. Orch., and he also returned to the Metropolitan Opera as a conductor during this time. In 1976–77 he was music advisor of the N.J. Sym. Orch. In subsequent years, he made occasional appearances as a guest conductor with American orchs. From 1983 he again taught at the Curtis Inst. of Music. In 1988 he received the first Theodore Thomas Award for his services to music. He publ. the widely used vol. *The Grammar of Conducting: A Comprehensive Guide to Baton Technique and Interpretation* (N.Y., 1950; 3rd ed., 1994, with the assistance of Michael Stern). As was to be expected, Rudolf displayed a mastery of baton technique. In his interpretations, he excelled in unmannered performances of the great Austro-German masterpieces.
—NS/LK/DM

Rudorff, Ernst (Friedrich Karl), German pianist, teacher, and composer; b. Berlin, Jan. 18, 1840; d.

there, Dec. 31, 1916. He studied with Bargiel in Berlin and with Moscheles, Plaidy, and Reinecke in Leipzig. After teaching in Cologne (1865–69), he was head of the piano dept. at the Hochschule für Musik in Berlin (1869–1910). He was a friend of Brahms. He composed 3 syms., a *Romantische Ouvertüre*, *Variations on an Original Theme* for Orch., a String Sextet, choral works, duets, songs, and piano pieces.—NS/LK/DM

Rudy, Mikhail, notable Russian-born French pianist; b. Tashkent, April 3, 1953. He studied at the Moscow Cons. (1969–75), where he was a student of Yakov Flier. In 1972 he was a prizewinner in the Bach Competition in Leipzig, and in 1975 he captured 1st prize in the Long-Thibaud Competition in Paris. In 1977 he made his debut in the West as a soloist in Beethoven's Triple Concerto in Paris. Rudy became a naturalized French citizen in 1980. In 1981 he made his U.S. debut as a soloist with the Cleveland Orch. under Maazel's direction. In 1987 he made his first appearance at the Salzburg Easter Festival under Karajan's baton. His London debut followed in 1988 when he was engaged as a soloist with the London Sym. Orch. conducted by Tilson Thomas. Rudy returned to Russia for the first time in 12 years of exile in 1989, and was the first soloist to record with the St. Petersburg Phil. in 30 years with Jansons conducting. Their collaboration in all of the Rachmaninoff concertos won them the Grand Prix de Disque. In 1994 he appeared as a soloist with the Berlin Phil. with Jansons conducting. He appeared in recital at London's Wigmore Hall in 1997. As a soloist, he also played with many other orchs., among them the Concertgebouw Orch. in Amsterdam, the Residentie Orch. in The Hague, the Rotterdam Phil., the Munich Phil., the Dresden State Orch., the London Phil., the Philharmonia Orch. in London, the Philadelphia Orch., the Boston Sym. Orch., the Pittsburgh Sym. Orch., the Houston Sym. Orch., the St. Louis Sym. Orch., the Montreal Sym. Orch., and the Indianapolis Sym. Orch. His festival engagements have taken him to the Edinburgh Festival, the Aldeburgh Festival, the Berlin Festival, the Vienna Festival, the Salzburg Festival, and the Schleswig-Holstein Festival. His expansive repertoire ranges from Bach to the moderns. While he is especially admired for his performances of such Russian masters as Scriabin, Rachmaninoff, Stravinsky, Prokofiev, and Shostakovich, he has won distinction for his interpretations of the Austro-German masters of the 18th and 19th centuries as well as of such other notable composers as Chopin, Debussy, Ravel, Bartók, and Messiaen. Rudy has made a transcription for piano of Stravinsky's complete *Petrouchka*.—LK/DM

Rudziński, Witold, Polish composer and pedagogue; b. Sebezh, Lithuania, March 14, 1913. He studied composition with Tadeusz Szeligowski and piano with Stanisław Szpinalski at the Cons., and Slavonic philology at the Stefan Batory Univ. (graduated, 1936) in Vilnius. In 1938–39 he completed his training in composition with Nadia Boulanger and Charles Koechlin in Paris, where he also studied Dom André Mocquereau's theory of rhythm at the Gregorian Inst. From 1939 to 1942 he was prof. of theory at the Vilnius Cons. After residing in Warsaw (1943–45), he was a prof. at the Łódź Cons. (1945–47). He then returned to Warsaw and served as director of the music dept. of the Ministry of Culture and Art (1947–48) and of the State Phil. and Central Opera (1948–49). In 1957 he became a lecturer in composition and theory at the State Higher School of Music, where he also was vice-rector (1967–69). In 1965 he won 1st prize in the Grieg Competition for Composers in Bergen. He received various Polish state honors and was awarded an honorary doctorate by the Warsaw Academy of Music in 1998. Among his important writings are a monograph on Moniuszko (Kraków, 1954), *Warsztat kompozytorski Beli Bartóka* (The Composing Technique of Béla Bartók; Kraków, 1964), and *Nauka o rytmie muzycznym* (The Study of Musical Rhythm; Kraków, 1987).

WORKS: DRAMATIC: *Janko muzykant* (Janko the Fiddler), opera (1951; Bytom, June 20, 1953); *Komendant Paryża (Jarosław Dąbrowski)* (The Commandant of Paris [Jarosław Dąbrowski]), opera (1958; Poznań, March 27, 1960); *Odprawa posłów greckich* (The Dismissal of the Greek Envoys), opera (1962; Kraków, Nov. 14, 1966); *Sulamita*, opera (1964); *Żółta szlafmyca* (The Yellow Nightcap), comic opera (1969; Gdynia, Jan. 25, 1970); *Chłopi* (The Peasants), opera (1972; Warsaw, June 30, 1974); *Pierścień i róża* (The Ring and the Rose), children's opera (1982; Wrocław, Oct. 13, 1984); *Jakub i Rachel* (Jacob and Rachel), ballet (1991). **ORCH.:** Piano Concerto (1936; rev. 1947); 2 syms. (1938, 1944); *Divertimento* for Strings (1940); *Parady* (Parades), suite (1958); *Muzyka koncertująca* (Musique concertante) for Piano and Chamber Orch. (1958; Warsaw, Sept. 20, 1961); *Obrazy Świętokrzyskie* (Pictures from the Holy Cross Mountains; 1965); *Moniuszkiana*, suite (1965); Concerto Grosso for Percussion and 2 String Orchs. (1970; also for Percussion and 2 Pianos, 1992); *Uwertura góralska* (Highlander Overture; 1970); *Capriccio-Impromptu-Hommage à Bizet* for Violin and Small Orch. (1986; also for Violin and Piano, 1980). **CHAMBER:** lute Sonatina (1934); Viola Sonata (1946); Nonet (Prague, May 1947); Quintet with Flute (1954; Warsaw, Feb. 1955); *Wariacje i fuga* (Variations and Fugue) for Percussion (1966); *Preludia* for Clarinet, Viola, Harp, and Percussion (1967; Warsaw, May 26, 1969); *Largo, aria e toccata* for Harp (1968; Warsaw, May 26, 1969); *Burleska* for Clarinet and Piano (1969); *Polonaise-rapsodie* for Cello and Piano (1969; Warsaw, April 29, 1970); *Fantazja góralska* (Highlander Fantasia) for Guitar (1970); *Sonata pastorale* for Violin and Piano (1978); *Capriccio-Impromptu-Hommage à Bizet* for Violin and Piano (1980; also for Violin and Small Orch., 1986); *Ricercar sopra "Roman Lasocki"* for Violin (1981; Barcelona, Dec. 9, 1982); *Pobudka* (Reveille) for 4 Violins (1985); *Dialog*, alto saxophone sonata (1987); *Plejady* (Pleiades), clarinet sonata (1987; Warsaw, March 9, 1988); *Kasjopea* (Cassiope), violin sonata (1987); Concerto grosso for Percussion and 2 Pianos (1992; also for Percussion and 2 String Orchs., 1970); *Serenata* for Violin, Viola, and Cello (1993); *Etude-Fantaisie* for Flute and Piano (1994); *Capriccio* for Clarinet (1995); *Passacaglia* for Violin (1996). **KEYBOARD: Piano:** *Suita polska* (Polish Suite; 1950); *Quasi una sonata* (1975). **Harpsichord:** Sonata (1977–78). **Clavichord:** *Proverbia latina* (1974). **VOCAL:** *Ballada o Janosiku* (Ballad of Janosik) for Voice and Piano (1941; also for Chorus and Small Orch., 1955); *Pięć lat* (Five Years) for Chorus (1945); 7 Folk Songs for Chorus (1945); *Pieśni kurpiowskie* (Songs from Kurpie) for Chorus or 2 Solo Voices and Small Orch. (1947); *Chłopska droga* (Peasants's Road), cantata for Soprano, Tenor, Baritone, Chorus, and Orch. (1952; Bydoszcz, May 1, 1953); *Przewodnik liryczny po Warszawie* (A Lyrical Guide

to Warsaw) for Soprano and Piano (Warsaw, Nov. 1953); *Deux portraits des femmes* for Soprano and String Quartet (1960; Warsaw, May 1961); *Dach świata* (The Roof of the World) for Reciter and Orch. (1960; Warsaw, May 1961); *Gaude Mater Polonia* for Reciter, Soprano, Alto, Tenor, Chorus, and Orch. (Warsaw, Oct. 7, 1966); *Lipce* for Chorus and Orch. (1968); *Do obywatela Johna Browna* (To the Citizen John Brown), concertino for Soprano, Flute, Horn, Cello, Piano, and Percussion (1972); *Gdziekolwiek ziemia jest snem* (Wherever the Earth is a Dream) for Soprano and Piano (1975); *Chleba powszedniego* (Our Daily Bread), motet for Man's Voice, Chorus, and Organ (1987); *Trzy pieśni starohebrajskie* (Three Old Hebrew Songs) for Voice and Piano (1987); *W kręgu psalmów* (The Circle of Psalms) for Soprano, Tenor, Baritone, Boy's Chorus, 2 Mixed Choruses, and 6 Percussion Groups (1987; Wrocław, Sept. 3, 1990); *Trzy liturgie etiopskie* (Three Ethiopian Liturgies) for 6 Men's Voices (Warsaw, July 1988); *Gadanki-piewanki* (Speaking-Singing) for Speaking Chorus (1989); *Madonna*, 5 songs for Soprano, Flute or Clarinet ad libitum, and Piano (1991); *Psalmus VI "Domine, ne in furore tuo arguas me"* for 5 Voices or Chorus and Organ (1992); *Słowa Panny Maryji* (The Words of the Virgin Mary) for Chorus and Small Orch. (1992); *Litania Ostrobramska* (Litany to the Holy Virgin of Ostra Brama) for Soprano, 2 Trumpets, 4 Timpani, and Organ (1994).

BIBL.: L. Bielawski and H. Kowalczyk, eds., *W. R. w 80-lecie urodzin* (Studies Presented to W. R. on the Occasion of his 80th Birthday; Warsaw, 1993).—NS/LK/DM

Rudziński, Zbigniew, Polish composer and teacher; b. Czechowice, Oct. 23, 1935. He went to Warsaw and studied at the State Music School (1949–56), pursued training in English philology at the Univ. (1952–53), and was a composition student of Piotr Perkowski at the State Higher School of Music (1956–60; graduated, 1962). In 1965–66 he held a French government scholarship to study with Nadia Boulanger in Paris, and later held a Dutch government scholarship in the Netherlands in 1970–71. In 1973 he joined the faculty of the State Higher School of Music (later Academy of Music) in Warsaw as a composition teacher, becoming an assoc. prof. in 1975 and a prof. in 1989. From 1981 to 1984 he was also its vice-rector. In 1981–82 he was president and in 1985–86 general secretary of the Polish Composers' Union, from which he received its Award in 1991.

WORKS: DRAMATIC: Opera: *Manekiny* (The Mannequins; Wrocław, Oct. 29, 1981). **ORCH.:** *Contra fidem* (1963–64; Warsaw, Sept. 22, 1964); *Moments musicaux I* (Warsaw, Sept. 30, 1965), *II* (Warsaw, Sept. 16, 1967), and *III* (Warsaw, March 22, 1968); Sym. for Men's Chorus and Orch. (Warsaw, Sept. 20, 1969); *Muzyka nocą* (Music at Night) for Small Orch. (Warsaw, Sept. 23, 1970); *Campanella* for Percussion Ensemble (Copenhagen, June 8, 1977); *Trytony* (Tritons) for Percussion Ensemble (1979–80; Warsaw, Sept. 22, 1980). **CHAMBER:** Trio for 2 Clarinets and Bassoon (1958; Warsaw, March 14, 1959); Clarinet Sonata (1959); Sonata for 2 String Quartets, Piano, and Percussion (1960; Katowice, June 1962); String Trio (Warsaw, June 25, 1964); *Impromptu* for 2 Pianos, 3 Cellos, and Percussion (Warsaw, Sept. 19, 1966); Quartet for 2 Pianos and Percussion (Baden-Baden, Oct. 5, 1969); *Trzy portrety romantyczne* (Three Romantic Portraits) for 12 Saxophones (1991). **Piano:** Sonata (1975; Hiram, Ohio, June 18, 1976). **VOCAL:** 4 Folk Songs for Soprano and Piano (1955; Warsaw, June 11, 1956); 4 Songs for Baritone and Chamber Ensemble (1960–61; Warsaw, Oct. 25,

1961); *Epigrams* for 2 Women's Choruses, Flute, and Percussion (1962; Warsaw, March 1, 1963); 3 Songs for Tenor and 2 Pianos (1968); *Requiem ofiarom wojen* (Requiem for the Victims of Wars) for Reciter, Chorus, and Orch. (Kassel, April 9, 1971; also for Chorus and Orch., Warsaw, Sept. 23, 1973); *Tutti e solo* for Soprano, Flute, Horn, and Piano (Brussels, March 26, 1973); *Struny na ziemi* (Strings in the Earth) for Soprano and String Orch. (Warsaw, Dec. 15, 1982); *Księga godzin* (The Book of Hours) for Mezzo-soprano and Piano Trio (Abbeville, Nov. 18, 1983); *To nie są sny* (These are not Dreams) for Mezzo-soprano and Piano (Schweinfurt, Aug. 8, 1987); *Suita polska* (Polish Suite) for 8 Women's Voices or Women's Chorus and Piano (Warsaw, June 1990); *Posłuchaj...* (Listen...) for Soprano and Piano (1993). **OTHER:** *Studium na c* (Study for C) for Ensemble ad libitum (Warsaw, Jan. 23, 1964).—**NS/LK/DM**

Rufer, Josef (Leopold), Austrian music scholar; b. Vienna, Dec. 18, 1893; d. Berlin, Nov. 7, 1985. He studied composition with Zemlinsky, and then with Schoenberg in Vienna (1919–22). He was assistant to Schoenberg at the Prussian Academy of Arts in Berlin (1925–33); from 1928, was also active as a music critic. From 1947 to 1950 he ed. (with Stuckenschmidt) the monthly music magazine *Stimmen;* then taught at the Free Univ. (from 1950) and at the Hochschule für Musik (1956–69) in Berlin. He publ. *Die Komposition mit zwölf Tönen* (Berlin, 1952; Eng. tr., 1954, as *Composition with 12 Notes Related Only to One Another*), *Musiker über Musik* (Darmstadt, 1955), *Das Werk Arnold Schönbergs* (Kassel, 1959; Eng. tr., 1962, as *The Works of Arnold Schoenberg*), and *Technische Aspekte der Polyphonie in der 1. Hälfte des 20. Jahrhunderts* (Ghent, 1969).—**NS/LK/DM**

Ruff, Willie (Henry, Jr.), French hornist, bassist; b. Sheffield, Ala., Sept. 1, 1931. He was in the army band in the late 1940s. He studied at Yale Univ. (M.M., 1954); he formed a duo with pianist Dwike Mitchell and played a series of successful nightclub engagements. In 1959, they gave a series of jazz concerts in Russia, triumphantly overriding Soviet scruples regarding the allegedly decadent nature of jazz. They were equally triumphant as part of President Johnson's goodwill entourage to Mexico in 1966; in 1979, the duo performed in China. During the 1970s, he later taught at Yale Univ. —**NS/LP**

Ruffo, Titta (real name, **Ruffo Cafiero Titta),** famous Italian baritone; b. Pisa, June 9, 1877; d. Florence, July 5, 1953. He found it convenient to transpose his first and last names for professional purposes. He studied with Persichini at the Accademia di Santa Cecilia in Rome, then with Casini in Milan. He made his operatic debut in Rome as the Herald in *Lohengrin* (1898); then sang in South America; returning to Italy, he appeared in all the principal theaters; also sang in Vienna, Paris, and London. He made his American debut in Philadelphia as Rigoletto (Nov. 4, 1912) with the combined Philadelphia-Chicago Opera Co., and then sang in Chicago (1912–14; 1919–27); his first appearance with the Metropolitan Opera was as Figaro in *Il Barbiere di Siviglia* (N.Y., Jan. 19, 1922). He left the Metropolitan in 1929 and returned to Rome. In 1937 he was briefly under arrest for opposing the Mussolini regime; then went to Florence, where he remained until his death. His memoirs appeared as *La mia parabola* (Milan, 1937; rev. 1977, by his son). A renowned dramatic artist, he excelled in roles from Verdi's operas; was also an outstanding Figaro, Hamlet, Tonio, and Scarpia.

BIBL.: M. Barrenechea, *T. R.: Notas de psicología artística* (Buenos Aires, 1911); A. Farkas, ed., *T. R.: An Anthology* (Westport, Conn., 1984); D. Liburdi, *T. R.: I costumi teatrali* (Pisa, 1993). —**NS/LK/DM**

Ruffo, Vincenzo, Italian composer; b. Verona, c. 1508; d. Sacile, Feb. 9, 1587. He received training at the Scuola degli Accoliti at Verona Cathedral (1520–34). From about 1542 to 1546 he was musico to Alfonso d'Alvalos, Marquis of Vasto and governor general of Milan. In 1544 he was made maestro di cappella at Verona Cathedral, and also maestro di musica of the Accademia Filarmonica in Verona in 1551. From 1563 to 1572 he was maestro di cappella at Milan Cathedral. He later was active at Pistoia Cathedral (1573–77), again in Verona (1578–80), and finally in Sacile. Ruffo was a prolific composer, producing both sacred and secular works of great discernment. He publ. at least 14 vols. of sacred music (1542–92) and 10 vols. of secular music (1545–64), including in the latter some 260 madrigals.

BIBL.: W. Wtorczyk, *Die Madrigale V. R.s* (diss., Free Univ. of Berlin, 1955); L. Lockwood, *The Counter-Reformation and the Masses of V. R.* (Venice, 1970).—**NS/LK/DM**

Rufus, a Chicago-based multiracial funk and dance group of the 1970s. **MEMBERSHIP:** Chaka Khan (Yvette Marie Stevens), voc. (b. Great Lakes, Ill., March 23, 1953); Kevin Murphy, kybd.; Nate Morgan, kybd.; Tony Maiden, gtr.; Bobby Watson, bs.; John Robinson, drm. Nate Morgan was replaced by David Wolinski in 1977.

Rufus scored a series of pop and R&B hits between 1974 and 1983. Featuring the powerful voice and erratic stage presence of Chaka Khan, Rufus achieved their first crossover smash with Stevie Wonder's "Tell Me Something Good" and persevered through 1983's "Ain't Nobody." Chaka Khan began a parallel solo career in 1978, and left Rufus for good in 1983, but she has enjoyed limited success.

Rufus evolved out of the American Breed (1968's "Bend Me, Shape Me") in the person of keyboardist Kevin Murphy. He formed Smoke, later known as Ask Rufus, with a variety of players. With the departure of vocalist Paulette McWilliams, Murphy recruited black vocalist Chaka Khan in 1972. Born Yvette Stevens, she had formed her first vocal group at age 11 and quit school to work with Chicago groups such as Lyfe and the Babysitters, changing her name to Chaka Khan in 1970. Signed to ABC Records, Rufus' debut album sold poorly. By 1974 the group was comprised of Khan, Murphy, keyboardist Nate Morgan, guitarist Tony Maiden, bassist Bobby Watson, and drummer John Robinson. During sessions for their second album, the group encountered Stevie Wonder, who offered his "Tell Me Something Good." The song became a smash pop and R&B hit in 1974, and the album, *Rags to Rufus,* later yielded crossover smashes with "You Got the Love" and "Once You Get Started," effectively launching the group's career.

Featuring infectious driving rhythms and the strong vocals of Chaka Khan, Rufus achieved smash R& and moderate pop hits with "Please Pardon Me (You Remind Me of a Friend)," "Sweet Thing" (a pop smash), and "Dance Wit Me" from *Rufus Featuring Chaka Khan*, as well as "At Midnight (My Love Will Lift You Up)" and "Hollywood" from *Ask Rufus*. David Wolinski replaced Nate Morgan in 1977, and the crossover hits continued with "Stay," "Do You Love What You Feel," and "Sharing the Love" through 1981. Rufus recorded *Numbers* and *Party 'Til You're Broke* without Chaka Khan, but neither album sold well or produced a hit single. Chaka Khan's final two albums with Rufus, *Camouflage* and the live set *Stompin' at the Savoy*, produced Rufus' final R& smashes with "Sharing the Love" and "Ain't Nobody" (a major pop hit), respectively.

Chaka Khan initiated her solo career in 1978, scoring an R& smash and major pop hit with Nicholas Ashford and Valerie Simpson's "I'm Every Woman," and the R& smashes "Clouds" and "What Cha' Gonna Do for Me." She next recorded an album of jazz standards, *Echoes of an Era*, with Chick Corea, Freddie Hubbard, Joe Henderson, and Lenny White, and the jazz-style *Chaka Khan*. Khan later scored the R& smash "Got to Be There" and the top R& and smash pop hit "I Feel for You," written by Prince and recorded with Grandmaster Mel and Stevie Wonder, but subsequent singles were essentially restricted to the R& field. She managed a major pop hit in 1989 with "I'll Be Good for You," recorded with Quincy Jones and Ray Charles, from Jones's album *Back on the Block*, but 1993's "Feels Like Heaven," recorded with Peter Cetera, proved to be only a minor pop hit. She appeared on the video and recording of Whitney Houston's 1993 remake of "I'm Every Woman."

DISC.: RUFUS: *R.* (1973); *Rags to R.* (1974); *Rufusized* (1974); *R. Featuring Chaka Khan* (1975); *Ask Rufus* (1977); *Street Player* (1978); *Numbers* (1978); *Masterjam* (1979); *Party 'Til You're Broke* (1981); *Camouflage* (1981); *Very Best* (1982); *Soul in Red* (1983); *Live—Stompin' at the Savoy* (1983). **CHAKA KHAN:** *Chaka* (1978); *Naughty* (1980); *What Cha' Gonna Do for Me* (1981); *Chaka Khan* (1982); *I Feel for You* (1984); *Destiny* (1986); *C.K.* (1988); *Life Is a Dance/The Remix Project* (1989); *The Woman I Am* (1992). **CHAKA KHAN/CHICK COREA/FREDDIE HUBBARD/JOE HENDERSON/LENNY WHITE:** *Echoes of an Era* (1982).—**BH**

Ruggi, Francesco, Italian composer; b. Naples, Oct. 21, 1767; d. there, Jan. 23, 1845. He studied at the Cons. di S. Loreto in Naples under Fenaroli, and became a prof. of composition at the Cons. di San Pietro a Majella. He wrote the operas *L'ombra di Nino* (Naples, 1795), *La Guerra aperta* (Naples, 1796), and *Sofi tripponi* (Milan, 1804), and much sacred music.—**NS/LK/DM**

Ruggles, Carl (actually, **Charles Sprague**), remarkable American composer; b. Marion, Mass., March 11, 1876; d. Bennington, Vt., Oct. 24, 1971. He learned to play violin as a child, then went to Boston, where he took violin lessons with Felix Winternitz and theory with Josef Claus; later enrolled as a special student at Harvard Univ., where he attended composition classes of John Knowles Paine. Impressed with the widely assumed supremacy of the German school of composition (of which Paine was a notable representative), Ruggles Germanized his given name from Charles to Carl. In 1907 he went to Minn., where he organized and conducted the Winona Sym. Orch. (1908–12). In 1917 he went to N.Y., where he became active in the promotion of modern music; was a member of the International Composers Guild and of the Pan American Assn. of Composers. He later taught composition at the Univ. of Miami (1938–43). Ruggles wrote relatively few works, which he constantly revised and rearranged, and they were mostly in small forms. He did not follow any particular modern method of composition, but instinctively avoided needless repetition of thematic notes, which made his melodic progressions atonal; his use of dissonances, at times quite strident, derived from the linear proceedings of chromatically inflected counterpoint. A certain similarity with the 12-tone method of composition of Schoenberg resulted from this process, but Ruggles never adopted it explicitly. In his sources of inspiration, he reached for spiritual exaltation with mystic connotations, scaling the heights and plumbing the depths of musical expression. Such music could not attract large groups of listeners and repelled some critics; one of them remarked that the title of Ruggles's *Sun-Treader* ought to be changed to *Latrine-Treader*. Unable and unwilling to withstand the prevailing musical mores, Ruggles removed himself from the musical scene; he went to live on his farm in Arlington, Vt., and devoted himself mainly to his avocation, painting; his pictures, mostly in the manner of Abstract Expressionism, were occasionally exhibited in N.Y. galleries. In 1966 he moved to a nursing home in Bennington, where he died at the age of 95. A striking revival of interest in his music took place during the last years of his life, and his name began to appear with increasing frequency on the programs of American orchs. and chamber music groups. His MSS were recovered and publ.; virtually all of his compositions have been recorded.

WORKS: *Mood* for Violin and Piano (c. 1918); *Toys* for Voice and Piano (1919); *Men and Angels* (*Men* for Orch., 1920–21; *Angels* for 6 Muted Trumpets, 1920–21; perf. as *Men and Angels*, N.Y., Dec. 17, 1922; *Angels* rev. for 4 Trumpets and 3 Trombones, 1938, and perf. in Miami, April 24, 1939); *Vox clamans in deserto* for Soprano and Chamber Orch. (1923; N.Y., Jan. 13, 1924); *Men and Mountains* for Chamber Orch. (N.Y., Dec. 7, 1924; rev. for Large Orch., N.Y., March 19, 1936; rev. 1941); *Portals* for 13 Strings (1925; N.Y., Jan. 24, 1926; rev. for String Orch., 1929; rev. 1941 and 1952–53); *Sun-Treader* for Large Orch. (1926–31; Paris, Feb. 25, 1932, N. Slonimsky conducting); *Evocations*, 4 chants for Piano (1937, 1943; N.Y., Jan. 9, 1943; rev. 1954; orch. version, N.Y., Feb. 3, 1971); *Organum* for Large Orch. (1944–47; N.Y., Nov. 24, 1949; also arranged for 2 Pianos, 1946–47); *Exaltation*, hymn tune for "congregation in unison" and Organ (1958); also several unfinished works.

BIBL.: L. Harrison, *About C. R.* (Yonkers, N.Y., 1946); T. Peterson, *The Music of C. R.* (diss., Univ. of Wash., 1967); N.

Archabal, *C. R.: Composer and Painter* (diss., Univ. of Minn., 1975); M. Ziffrin, *C. R.: Composer, Painter, and Storyteller* (Urbana, Ill., 1994); J. Green, *C. R.: A Bio-Bibliography* (Westport, Conn., 1995).—NS/LK/DM

Rühlmann, (Adolf) Julius, German trombonist, pedagogue, and writer on music; b. Dresden, Feb. 28, 1816; d. there, Oct. 27, 1877. He played the trombone in the Court Orch. of Dresden. He founded the Dresden Tonkunstlerverein (1855), and also taught piano and music history at the Dresden Cons. He prepared a valuable *Geschichte der Bogeninstrumente*, which was publ. posthumously by his son, Richard Rühlmann (1882), and *Die Urform der Bogeninstrumente* (1874). —NS/LK/DM

Ruhnke, Martin, German musicologist; b. Köslin, June 14, 1921. He studied with Blume at the Univ. of Kiel (Ph.D., 1954, with the diss. *Joachim Burmeister: Ein Beitrag zur Musiklehre um 1600*; publ. in Kassel, 1955). After serving as an asst. lecturer at the Free Univ. in Berlin (1954–60), he completed his Habilitation there in 1961 with his *Beiträge zu einer Geschichte der deutschen Hofmusikkollegien im 16. Jahrhundert* (publ. in Berlin, 1963). In 1964 he became prof. of musicology at the Univ. of Erlangen. As an authority on Telemann, he served as general ed. of the complete critical edition of that composer's works (from 1960) and as ed. of *Georg Philipp Telemann: Thematisch-Systematisches Verzeichnis seiner Werke: Instrumentalwerke* (2 vols., Kassel, 1984, 1992). From 1968 to 1974 he was president of the Gesellschaft für Musikforschung. He was president of the Internationalen Telemann-Gesellschaft from 1991.

BIBL.: W. Hirschmann et al., eds., *Festschrift M. R.: Zum 65. Geburtstag* (Stuttgart, 1986); W. Hirschmann, W. Hobohm, and C. Lange, eds., *Auf der gezeigten Spur: Beiträge zur Telemannforschung: Festgabe M. R. zum 70. Geburtstag am 14. Juni 1991* (Oschersleben, 1994).—NS/LK/DM

Ruiter, Wim de, Dutch composer, organist, and teacher; b. Heemstede, Aug. 11, 1943. He studied organ with Piet Kee in Amsterdam (1963–69) and composition with Ton de Leeuw there (1968–74). He taught at the Zwolle Cons. (1973–77) and the Amsterdam Cons. (from 1973). He was also active as a concert organist.

WORKS: CHAMBER Opera: *Een Job van onze tijd* (1991). **ORCH.:** *Re* (Utrecht, Sept. 14, 1975); *3 Pieces* (1977); *Spectrum* (1978); *Allegro, adagio en variaties* (1980); *Theme, Variations, and Finale* (1985); Accordion Concerto (1987; rev. 1988). **CHAMBER:** *Solo* for Flute (1969); *Music* for 2 Double Basses (1969); Quartet for 2 Violas and 2 Cellos (1970); Quartet for Flute, Bass Clarinet, Vibraphone, and Piano (1970); *2 Quartets Together* (1970; a joining together of the previous 2 quartets); 3 string quartets (1972, 1974, 1984); *Thick & Thin* for Organ, 4-Hands, 4-Feet (1975); *Tall & Small* for Treble Recorder (1975); *Off & On* for 4 Bass Clarinets (1976); *To Be or Not to Be* for 12 Wind Instruments and Vibraphone (1976); Quintet for 5 Flutes and Tape (1976; in collaboration with Jacques Bank); Quartet for Recorders (1977); String Quartet (1984); Flute Quartet No. 2 (1986); *Time* for Flute, Bass Clarinet, Piano, Tape, and Video (1986); Sonata for Bass Clarinet, Piano, and 2 Percussionists (1987); *Variaties* for Bass Clarinet and Vibraphone (1988); Trio

for Viola, Cello, and Double Bass (1988); *Pastorale* for Bass Clarinet and Tape (1994); *Oks* for 3 Trumpets, 2 Trombones, Percussion, and Organ (1994); *I/oon* for Bassoon, Accordion, and Percussion (1995); Sonata for Wind Ensemble and String Quintet (1996); *Whim* for Violin and Organ (1997); *Hop* for 2 Percussionists (1998). **VOCAL:** *Situations* for 16 Voices (1970); *Hoplopoia* for Chorus and Orch. (1973); choral works; songs. —NS/LK/DM

Ruiz, Hilton, likes to call himself the original bebop Latin pianist, although he is much more; b. N.Y., May 29, 1952. Hilton Ruiz was something of a child prodigy, appearing on a local N.Y. television show, performing at Carnegie Recital Hall at the age of eight, and playing in an accordion symphony at nine. He studied classical piano as well as Latin, and received jazz guidance from the late Mary Lou Williams and Cedar Walton. By his early teens he was working with a variety of Latin soul bands and, at age 14, recorded with a group called Ray Jay and the East Siders. Before he was 20, he had worked with Frank Foster, Joe Newman, Cal Massey, Freddie Hubbard, and Joe Henderson—an impressive list for an established player, a truly remarkable list for a relative newcomer. As an adult, he has also worked and recorded with Rahsaan Roland Kirk, Pharoah Sanders, and Charles Mingus. His own recordings have touched all bases—from straight-ahead funk to Latin soul—in part reflecting a peripatetic lifestyle that has taken him on tours to virtually every part of the world.

DISC.: *Manhattan Mambo* (1992); *Heroes* (1994); *Hands on Percussion* (1995); *Piano Man* (1995); *Island Eyes* (1997).—BP

Rummel, family of German musicians:

(1) Christian (Franz Ludwig Friedrich Alexander) Rummel, pianist, conductor, and composer; b. Brichsenstadt, Bavaria, Nov. 27, 1787; d. Wiesbaden, Feb. 13, 1849. He went to Mannheim and studied violin with Heinrich Ritter and composition with Karl Jakob Wagner; also received advice from the Abbé Vogler. He began his career as a military bandmaster in 1806. He served during the Peninsular War (1808–13) and was made a prisoner of war, and later fought at the Battle of Waterloo. He settled in Wiesbaden as a teacher, and then organized and conducted the Court Orch. from 1815; after it was dissolved in 1842, it was absorbed into the theater orch., with Rummel serving as conductor; he also toured widely in Europe as a pianist. He wrote pieces for piano and orch., a Clarinet Concerto, military-band music, chamber works, numerous pieces for solo piano, and various transcriptions for piano. Several of his children became musicians, including the following:

(2) Josephine Rummel, pianist; b. Manzanares, Spain, May 12, 1812; d. Wiesbaden, Dec. 19, 1877. She studied piano with her father, then made tours of Europe. She also served as court pianist in Wiesbaden.

(3) Joseph Rummel, pianist, clarinetist, and composer; b. Wiesbaden, Oct. 6, 1818; d. London, March 25, 1880. He studied piano and clarinet with his father, then was in the service of the Duke of Oldenberg in Wiesbaden; was active in Paris (1847–70) and then in London. He wrote a vast amount of music, mainly for piano.

(4) August Rummel, pianist; b. Wiesbaden, Jan. 14, 1824; d. London, Dec. 14, 1886. He studied with his father, then settled in London, where he became well known as a pianist. Other members of the family were as follows:

(5) Franz Rummel, pianist, son of **(3) Joseph Rummel;** b. London, Jan. 11, 1853; d. Berlin, May 2, 1901. He studied with Louis Brassin at the Brussels Cons., winning first prize in 1872; toured in America 4 times (1878, 1886, 1890, 1898). He married a daughter of S. F. B. Morse, inventor of the telegraph.

(6) Walter Morse Rummel, distinguished pianist, son of **(5) Franz Rummel;** b. Berlin, July 19, 1887; d. Bordeaux, May 2, 1953. He studied piano with Leopold Godowsky and composition with Hugo Kaun. In 1908 he went to Paris, where he became acquainted with Debussy, and devoted himself to promoting his piano works, of which he became a foremost interpreter. He was married to the pianist Thérèse Chaigneau, with whom he appeared in duo-piano recitals (later divorced), and to Sarah Harrington (also divorced). His grandfather was S. F. B. Morse, inventor of the telegraph
—NS/LK/DM

Rundgren, Todd, American studio genius; b. Upper Darby, Pa., June 22, 1948. First recognized as the leader of the late-1960s Philadelphia group The Nazz, Todd Rundgren quickly established himself as one of America's studio geniuses with productions for The Band, Grand Funk Railroad, and The New York Dolls. Mastering a variety of instruments and musical styles, Rundgren performed all the musical chores on a number of his own albums. A compelling songwriter, he composed melodically and harmonically rich and demanding songs that were at once personal and intelligent. Playing and singing virtually all parts on 1972's *Something/Anything?* album, his biggest commercial and artistic success and generally regarded as his masterpiece, Rundgren formed Utopia in 1974 to explore new electronic musical devices and advanced technology on songs often cosmically obscure. He enjoyed modest success both on his own and with Utopia during the 1970s, while producing albums for a variety of artists, including Hall and Oates, the Patti Smith Group, and Meatloaf (his multi-million-selling debut *Bat Out of Hell*). Rundgren began programming computers in the late 1970s, an avocation that later led to pioneering efforts in video production and computer technology. Along with Thomas Dolby, Todd Rundgren was at the forefront of multimedia technology, issuing his 1993 *No World Order* as the first interactive music-only compact disc.

Growing up in the suburbs of Philadelphia, Todd Rundgren experimented with both guitar and flute during his high school years, joining the local blues band Woody's Truck-stop after graduation. He left the group in 1967 to form the Nazz with vocalist Robert Antoni. Under the influence of the British groups of the mid-1960s, the Nazz concentrated on a careful mix of vocal harmonies and Rundgren's guitar playing, signing with Screen Gems/Columbia in 1968. With Rundgren writing most of the material and arranging

the music, they managed a minor pop hit with "Hello It's Me" and recorded two overlooked albums before Rundgren's departure in 1970. He was replaced by Rick Nielsen and Tom Petersson, later members of Cheap Trick.

In the meantime, Todd Rundgren had learned engineering and production. He worked with the short-lived Ampex label, producing Ian and Sylvia's *Great Speckled Bird*, engineering Jesse Winchester's debut album, and performing all technical and musical chores save bass and drums for his own album *Runt*, which yielded a major hit with "We Gotta Get You a Woman." Word of his reputation as a studio master spread after he engineered the Band's *Stage Fright*, and in the next two years he engineered the Butterfield Blues Band's *Live* and coproduced Badfinger's *Straight Up* with George Harrison.

After *Runt*, Todd Rundgren switched to Albert Grossman's Bearsville label for the double record set *Something/Anything?*, his best-selling album. Largely played and sung by Rundgren on his own, the album demonstrated a diversity of styles. It included the favorites "It Wouldn't Have Made Any Difference" and "Black Maria" and yielded a major hit with "I Saw the Light," a minor hit with "Couldn't I Just Tell You," and a smash hit with a remake of "Hello It's Me." In contrast to the highly melodic and well-crafted songs of his previous albums, *A Wizard/A True Star* was rather esoteric and featured bold and loud synthesizer and guitar work. Essentially a creature of the studio, Rundgren produced Fanny's *Mother's Pride*, Grand Funk Railroad's best-selling *We're an American Band*, the debut album by The New York Dolls, and Daryl Hall and John Oates's experimental *War Babies* album.

By 1974 Todd Rundgren had formed Utopia with synthesizer player Roger Powell and drummer John "Willie" Wilcox to experiment with new technologies and sounds. Their debut album sold modestly as Rundgren developed a devoted following in Great Britain and the United States. On his own, Rundgren recorded favorites such as "Just One Victory," "Sometimes I Don't Know What to Feel," "The Dream Goes on Forever," "Real Man," and "Love in Action." *Faithful* contained precise renditions of songs by Jimi Hendrix, the Beatles, and the Beach Boys and included "Love of the Common Man." Utopia's lineup stabilized with Powell, Wilcox, and bassist Kasim Sulton by 1977. Their *Oops! Wrong Planet* featured "Love Is the Answer," and *Adventures in Utopia*, their best-selling album, produced hits with "Set Me Free" and "The Very Last Time." Rundgren's *Hermit of Mink Hollow*, which he wrote, arranged, produced, played, and sang in its entirety, yielded a major hit with "Can We Still Be Friends?" and helped establish him with the mainstream-rock audience.

In the late 1970s Todd Rundgren continued to be active in the studio. He produced Meatloaf's debut album, *Bat Out of Hell* (which sold more than 26 million copies worldwide), the Tubes' *Remote Control*, and the Patti Smith Group's *Wave*. He also began a career-long study of computer and multimedia technology, producing Holst's *The Planets* as RCA's first videodisc and creating the second video to be played on MTV, for

3091

"Time Heals." Utopia recorded its last albums in the early to mid-1980s, while Rundgren cut the all-solo effort *The Ever Popular Tortured Artist Effect*. He followed this with *A Cappella*, a curious album comprised entirely of synthesized vocal recordings.

During the 1980s Todd Rundgren produced albums for What Is This?, XTC, and the Pursuit of Happiness. He moved to the San Francisco Bay Area in the mid-1980s and eventually released *Nearly Human* in 1989, the year Rhino Records issued anthology sets for both Utopia and Rundgren. In 1992 Rhino issued a set of his production efforts, and in 1993 Rundgren released *No World Order* as the first interactive compact disc, allowing listeners to choose from nearly a thousand four-bar music segments in various forms, directions, moods, tempos, and mixes. In 1995 Todd Rundgren announced his intention to become the first CD-ROM–only artist, signing with the interactive CD label ION. As TR-1 he has been an active voice on the Internet.

DISC.: THE NAZZ: *Introducing The Nazz* (1968); *(reissued as) The Nazz* (1983); *Nazz Nazz* (1969); *Nazz III* (1971); *Best* (1984). TODD RUNDGREN: *Runt* (1970); *The Ballad of T. R.* (1971); *Something/Anything?* (1972); *A Wizard/A True Star* (1973); *Todd* (1973); *Initiation* (1975); *Faithful* (1976); *Hermit of Mink Hollow* (1978); *Back to the Bars* (1978); *Healing* (1981); *The Ever Popular Tortured Artist Effect* (1983); *A Cappella* (1985); *Anthology (1968–1985)* (1989); *Undercover* (soundtrack; 1987); *Nearly Human* (1989); *2nd Wind* (1991); *No World Order* (1993); *Best* (1994); *No World Order Lite* (1994). TODD RUNDGREN PRODUCTIONS: *An Elpee's Worth of Productions* (1992). UTOPIA: *Todd Rundgren's Utopia* (1974); *T. R.'s Utopia: Another Live* (1975); *RA* (1977); *Oops! Wrong Planet* (1977); *Adventures in Utopia* (1980); *Deface the Music* (1980); *Swing to the Right* (1982); *Utopia* (1982); *Oblivion* (1984); *POV* (1985); *Anthology (1974–1985)* (1989); *Redux '92: Live in Japan* (1993). ROGER POWELL: *Cosmic Furnace* (1973); *Air Pocket* (1980). KASIM SULTON: *Kasim* (1982).—BH

Run-D.M.C., first mainstream successful rap group.

MEMBERSHIP: Joseph "Run" Simmons (b. Queens, N.Y., Nov. 14, 1964); Darryl "D.M.C." McDaniels (b. Queens, N.Y., May 31, 1964); Jason "Jam Master Jay" Mizell (b. Queens, N.Y., Jan. 21, 1965).

The first rap group to enjoy mainstream pop success, thanks in large part to 1986's smash pop hit and video "Walk This Way," Run-D.M.C. was also the first rap group to have a video screened on MTV, to make the cover of *Rolling Stone*, and to perform on *American Bandstand* as well as the *only* rap group to appear at 1985's Live Aid concert. Although Run-D.M.C. projected a violent gangster image, their music concerned itself with peaceful messages advocating the avoidance of drugs and gangs. Nonetheless, their concerts, particularly those in 1986 in support of *Raising Hell*, were often accompanied by violence, drawing attention to the paradox between their good intentions and the violent outcome of their live music.

Joseph "Run" Simmons's brother Russell was instrumental in establishing rap artists such as Kurtis Blow and Grandmaster Flash and the Furious Five—pioneering rap acts—by booking them into Harlem clubs; he cofounded the pioneering rap label Def Jam, with Rick Rubin, and encouraged his younger brother to pursue a performing career. Joseph Simmons began composing and performing raps with Kurtis Blow in the late 1970s and began collaborating with Darryl McDaniels in the early 1980s to form Run-D.M.C. with disc jockey Jason Mizell. Scoring their first major R&B hit in 1983 with "It's Like That" on the small, independent label Profile, Run-D.M.C. continued to achieve major R&B hits through 1985 with "Hard Times," "Rock Box," and "30 Days" from their debut album; the title track and "You Talk Too Much" from *King of Rock*, regarded as one of rap's landmark albums; and "You Can't Rock It Like This" from the film *Krush Groove*. In 1985 they appeared at the Live Aid concert and later contributed to the recording of "Sun City" by Artists United Against Apartheid.

Run-D.M.C. scored an R&B smash with "My Adidas" in 1986 and soon established themselves with a larger audience with the pop and R&B smash "Walk This Way," featuring Aerosmith's Steve Tyler and Joe Perry (the song also revived Aerosmith's career). Both songs were included on their *Raising Hell* album, as was "You Be Illin'" (a major crossover hit) and "It's Tricky" (a major R&B hit); the album sold more than three million copies. They conducted a four-month, 62-city tour that year, but a number of their concerts were marred by violence. Their next album, *Tougher Than Leather*, sold quite well but not spectacularly and produced a major R&B hit with "Run's House." However, 1990's *Back from Hell* sold modestly at best; Simmons and McDaniels both admitted to drug and alcohol problems, and Simmons also had to defend himself against a charge of rape, later dropped. Run-D.M.C. did not score another major pop hit until 1993's "Down with the King." In 1992 MCA Music Entertainment, the distributor of Run-D.M.C.'s NewYork-based record label JDK Records, withdrew the misogynist "No Head, No Backstage Pass" by the group FU2 in the wake of the "Cop Killer" controversy that embroiled Ice-T.

DISC.: RUN-D.M.C.: *R.-D.M.C.* (1984); *King of Rock* (1985); *Raising Hell* (1986); *Tougher Than Leather* (1988); *Back from Hell* (1990); *Together Forever: Greatest Hits 1983–1991* (1991); *Down with the King* (1993).—BH

Rung, Frederik, Danish conductor, teacher, and composer, son of **Henrik Rung;** b. Copenhagen, June 14, 1854; d. there, Jan. 22, 1914. He studied with his father, succeeding him as conductor of the Cecilia Soc. (1871). He founded its Madrigalkoret (1887), which won considerable renown, and was also 2nd conductor (1884–1908) and chief conductor (from 1908) at the Royal Theater in Copenhagen. He taught at the Copenhagen Cons. (1881–93).

WORKS: DRAMATIC: O p e r a : *Det hemmelige Selskab* (The Secret Party; Copenhagen, Feb. 9, 1888); *Den trekantede Hat* (The 3-cornered Hat; Copenhagen, Nov. 7, 1894). ORCH.: 2 syms.; Rhapsody; *Danse des papillons*. CHAMBER: Serenade for 9 Instruments; Piano Quintet; 2 string quartets; Violin Sonata; piano pieces; songs.—NS/LK/DM

Rung, Henrik, Danish conductor and composer, father of **Frederik Rung;** b. Copenhagen, March 3, 1807;

d. there, Dec. 13, 1871. He founded the Cecilia Soc. (1851). He wrote a number of choral works and popular songs.

BIBL.: C. Thrane, *Caeciliaföreningen og dens Stifter* (Copenhagen, 1901).—NS/LK/DM

Rungenhagen, Carl Friedrich, German conductor and composer; b. Berlin, Sept. 27, 1778; d. there, Dec. 21, 1851. He was a pupil of Benda. In 1815 he became 2nd conductor of the Singakademie, succeeding Zelter in 1833 as 1st conductor. He was a member of the Berlin Academy, and a teacher in the School of Composition. He composed 4 operas, 3 oratorios, a Te Deum, 30 motets, 30 4-part songs, over 100 sacred and 1,000 secular songs, syms., quartets, etc.—NS/LK/DM

Runnicles, Donald, Scottish conductor; b. Edinburgh, Nov. 16, 1954. He was educated at the univs. of Edinburgh and Cambridge, and also studied at the London Opera Centre. In 1980 he became a répétiteur at the Mannheim National Theater, where he then was a conductor (1984–87). He then was conductor in Hannover (1987–89). From 1989 to 1992 he was Generalmusikdirektor in Freiburg im Breisgau. He also conducted at the Metropolitan Opera in N.Y. (from 1988), the San Francisco Opera (from 1990), the Vienna State Opera (from 1990), and the Glyndebourne Festival (from 1991). In 1992 he became music director of the San Francisco Opera. In 1994 he scored an outstanding success at the Edinburgh Festival conducting Mahler's 8th Sym. On Sept. 5, 1997, he conducted the gala reopening performance at the renovated San Francisco Opera house. In 2000 he became principal guest conductor of the Atlanta Sym. Orch. while retaining his position with the San Francisco Opera. Runnicles conducts left-handed.—NS/LK/DM

Rúnólfsson, Karl Ottó, Icelandic trumpeter, teacher, and composer; b. Reykjavík, Oct. 24, 1900; d. there, Nov. 29, 1970. He studied in Copenhagen (1926–27) and with Mixa and Urbancic at the Reykjavík Coll. of Music (1934–39). He was active with brass bands; played 1st trumpet in the Icelandic Sym. Orch. (1950–55); taught at the Reykjavík Coll. of Music (1939–64). He wrote a set of Icelandic songs for Voice and Orch. (1938), *Esja*, sym. (1968), choral works on Icelandic themes, Trumpet Sonata, and Violin Sonata. —NS/LK/DM

Rupnik, Ivan, Serbian composer; b. Belgrade, Aug. 29, 1911. He studied in Ljubljana; later in Vienna with Berg. His early works are in a neo-Romantic vein, with expressionistic overtones; later he abjured modern devices and began writing music for the masses, in conformity with socialist ideology. His cantata, *Song of the Dead Proletarians,* which he conducted in Belgrade on Dec. 14, 1947, is an epitome of programmatic realism. He also wrote 2 syms., several overtures (*Romantic Overture; Youth Overture*), ethnic symphonic works (*Musical Impressions from Istria; A Peasant Evening Party*), and a *Hymn of Peace.*—NS/LK/DM

Rupp, Franz, German-American pianist and teacher; b. Schongau, Feb. 24, 1901; d. N.Y., May 27, 1992. He received his training at the Munich Akademie der Tonkunst. In 1920 he made his first tour of the U.S. with Willy Burmester, and subsequently acquired a distinguished reputation as an accompanist to Fritz Kreisler. In 1938 he settled in the U.S. and was accompanist to Marian Anderson until her retirement in 1965. He continued to perform regularly until his farewell appearance at the Lockenhaus Festival in Austria in 1985. He was also active as a teacher at the Curtis Inst. of Music in Philadelphia.—NS/LK/DM

Rusca, Francesco, Italian composer who flourished in the 2nd half of the 17th century. He was maestro di cappella at Como Cathedral from 1659 until 1699. He wrote about 100 masses, Psalms, cantatas, etc., in a highly developed polyphonic style, containing as many as 16 independent vocal and instrumental parts. His 5 keyboard toccatas are included in vol. III of *I classici* (Como, 1961).—NS/LK/DM

Rusconi, Gerardo, Italian composer; b. Milan, Feb. 1, 1922; d. there, Dec. 23, 1974. He studied at the Parma Cons., and began his career as a composer by writing light music for the stage, radio, and the films; then undertook more serious genres of music. He composed *La moglie di Lot* for Soprano, Horn, and Piano (1962), *Concerto breve* for Horn and Strings (1965), *3 musiche* for Flute and Piano (1967), *Moments* for Orch. in memory of Martin Luther King (1968), *L'appuntamento,* opera (1971), and numerous transcriptions and harmonizations of popular songs.—NS/LK/DM

Rush, 1980s progressive rockers. **MEMBERSHIP:** Geddy Lee (real name, Gary Lee Winery), voc., bs., kybd. (b. Toronto, Canada, July 29, 1953); Alex Lifeson (real name, Zivojinovich), gtr. (b. British Columbia, Canada, Aug. 27, 1953); John Rutsey, drm.; Neal Peart, drm. (b. Hamilton, Ontario, Sept. 12, 1952).

Rush started off as a power trio, playing Led Zeppelin–like hard boogie and blues in Toronto-area bars. They cut a self-released single in 1973, a cover of Buddy Holly's "Not Fade Away." A year later, their self-titled debut album also came out on their own label, although London Records distributed it. While that first record didn't sell especially well, it received enough recognition to land them opening slots on tours with The New York Dolls and ZZ Top.

Between its first and second albums, the band was transformed thanks to two major changes. First, Rush changed drummers, bringing on Neal Peart. In addition to his virtuoso playing ability, Peart proved to be a very skilled lyricist. Second, the band signed to Mercury Records. Their next two albums found Rush playing pedestrian hard rock, though the level of musicianship and Lee's castrato voice gave the band the beginnings of a distinctive sound. They became popular live attraction, and their 1976 live album, *All the World's a Stage,* even made the U.S. Top 40, going gold at the time and platinum four years later. This marked a turning point in the band's career. Not only did this begin their string of gold records; it also saw them taking their musicianship in a more progressive direction.

In 1976 Rush released the concept album *2112*. Based on the writings of Ayn Rand, album combined her philosophy of self-determination with the band's audacious hard-rock chops. It transformed the group into the thinking person's hard rockers. With a title track that ran around 20 minutes long, the album went gold on its release, eventually going triple platinum. The follow-up album, *A Farewell to Kings*, also sold platinum, rising to #33 on the charts. While *Hemispheres* didn't crack the Top 40, it also went gold shortly after its release and eventually went platinum. Clearly the band was developing a substantial cult following.

The release of *Permanent Waves* in 1980 demonstrated just how substantial a cult Rush had built, while expanding on it. The lead-off track, "Spirit of Radio" became a hit on album radio and even went Top 20 in England. The album went to #4 on the charts, again going gold shortly after its release and eventually reaching platinum. The band continued to transform its sound, moving increasingly from its hard-rock roots into a more progressive, radio-friendly style. Rush added synthesizers to their sound, with Lifeson softening his guitar sound with the sort of shimmering effects that permeated 1980s music. These sonic changes informed their next album, 1981's *Moving Pictures*. Again, the lead track, "Tom Sawyer," became a massive album rock hit, and the instrumental "YYZ" and the rock star rumination "Limelight" also earned airplay. The album rose to #3, going platinum shortly after it came out. It eventually sold more than four million copies. Rush followed this with a live album, *Exit, Stage Left*, which captured the band's style in transition, but still reached the Top Ten and went gold.

Back in the studio, however, they captured lightning in a bottle again with 1982's *Signals*. This album gave Rush something no one (including the band) would have thought possible: a Top 40 hit. The song "New World Man" actually rose to #21; it did not really affect the sales of the album, however. Its profile was almost identical to its predecessor: #10 pop and gold, eventually rising to platinum, as did the next two albums, *Grace Under Pressure* and *Power Windows*. With each subsequent album, Rush moved further from hard rock and deeper into synthesizers and effects.

By the 1987 release of *Hold Your Fire*, Rush's core of fans started to dwindle slightly; the album reached #13, but has yet to break gold status. With the live album *Show of Hands*, the band completed its obligation to Mercury. Moving to Atlantic, Rush hoped that the change of venue might energize them. Their first album for the new company, 1989's *Presto*, showcased many of the band's virtues, including the sinew and immediacy that much of their later 1980s output lacked. It sold gold and hit #16. They followed this two years later with the dark *Roll the Bones*, which tied *Moving Pictures* as the band's highest-charting album at #3, but managed to sell only gold. *Counterparts* (1993) found the band eschewing some of the effects and synths, but in service of songs that even the band concedes were weak.

The group took some time to recharge. Lifeson recorded *Victor*, an album more informed by Pearl Jam than Rush. Peart, always a drummer with the technique of a surgeon, took swing lessons, putting them to work on his *Burning for Buddy* project, a tribute to big-band drummer Buddy Rich. Lee took some time out for fatherhood. When Rush reconvened to cut 1996's *Test for Echo*, it showed the influence of their side projects in a positive way: Lee let go a little, Lifeson rocked a little harder, and Peart swung. The album rocketed into the charts at #5, going gold. Then Peart suffered tragedy: first, his 19-year-old daughter was killed in an automobile accident in the fall of 1997; less than a year later, his wife died of cancer. Rush released a three-CD live set dedicated to Peart's late family members, then Lee and Lifeson went about other business. As of the beginning of the year 2000, the band's future continued to be up in the air.

DISC.: RUSH: *Rush* (1974); *Caress of Steel* (1975); *Fly by Night* (1975); *All the World's a Stage* (1976); *2112* (1976); *A Farewell to Kings* (1977); *Hemispheres* (1978); *Permanent Waves* (1980); *Moving Pictures* (1981); *Exit...Stage Left* (1981); *Signals* (1982); *Grace Under Pressure* (1984); *Power Windows* (1985); *Hold Your Fire* (1987); *A Show of Hands* (1988); *Presto* (1989); *Roll the Bones* (1991); *Counterparts* (1993); *Test for Echo* (1996). **ALEX LIFESON:** *Victor* (1995). **NEAL PEART:** *Burning for Buddy* (1994).—HB

Rush, Loren, American composer; b. Fullerton, Calif., Aug. 23, 1935. He studied piano, bassoon, and double bass, and played bassoon in the Oakland Sym. Orch. and double bass in the Richmond Sym. Orch.; also was a drummer. He studied composition with Erickson at San Francisco State Coll. (B.A., 1957); upon graduation, organized the Loren Rush Jazz Quartet; enrolled at the Univ. of Calif. at Berkeley, studying composition with Imbrie, Shifrin, Denny, and Cushing (M.A., 1960), and completed his training at Stanford Univ. (D.M.A., 1960). He was active in various new-music ventures; was chairman of the composition dept. at the San Francisco Cons. (1967–69); taught at Stanford Univ. (from 1967), where he served as assoc. director of the Center for Computer Research in Music and Acoustics (from 1975). In his works, he applies a whole spectrum of modern techniques, including serialism, spatial distribution, controlled improvisation, and pointillistic exoticism. He is married to **Janis Mattox**.

WORKS: *5 Japanese Poems* for Soprano, Flute, Clarinet, Viola, and Piano (1959); *Serenade* for Violin and Viola (1960); *String Quartet* (1960–61); *Mandala Music*, improvisation for a group, inspired by the oriental geometrization of the cosmos and an important symbol in Jungian psychology (1962); *Hexahedron* for Piano, notated on all 6 surfaces of a large cube (1964); *Nexus 16* for Chamber Orch. (1964); *Dans le sable* for Soprano, Narrator, 4 Altos, and Chamber Orch. (1967–68; also for Large Orch., 1970); *Soft Music, Hard Music* for 3 Amplified Pianos (1969–70); *The Cloud Messenger* for Orch. (1966–70); *Oh, Susanna* for Piano (1970); *A Little Traveling Music* for Amplified Piano and 4-track Tape (1971–73); *I'll See You in My Dreams* for Amplified Orch. and Tape (1973); *Song and Dance* for Orch. and 4-track Tape (1975); *The Digital Domain* for Tape (1983; in collaboration with J. Mattox).—NS/LK/DM

Rushton, Julian (Gordon), English musicologist; b. Cambridge, May 22, 1941. He studied at the Guildhall School of Music and Drama in London (1959–60), Trinity Coll., Cambridge (B.A., 1963; B.M., 1965; M.A., 1967), and at Magdalen Coll., Oxford (Ph.D., 1969, with the diss. *Music and Drama at the Académie Royale de Musique, Paris, 1774–1789*). He was a lecturer at the Univ. of East Anglia (1968–74) and at the Univ. of Cambridge (1974–81). In 1982 he became West Riding Prof. of Music at the Univ. of Leeds. In 1979 he became a member of the editorial committee of Musica Britannica, serving as chairman from 1993. In 1991 he became general ed. of the Cambridge Music Handbooks series. From 1994 to 1999 he was president of the Royal Musical Assn. Rushton has contributed articles to various scholarly and reference books, as well as to learned journals.

WRITINGS: *W.A. Mozart: Don Giovanni* (Cambridge, 1981); *The Musical Language of Berlioz* (Cambridge, 1983); *Classical Music: A Concise History* (London, 1986); *W.A. Mozart: Idomeneo* (Cambridge, 1993); *Berlioz: Roméo et Juliette* (Cambridge, 1994); *Elgar: Enigma Variations* (Cambridge, 1999).—**NS/LK/DM**

Russell, George (Allan), jazz composer, pianist, drummer and brilliant theorist, lecturer, and educator; b. Cincinnati, Ohio, June 23, 1923. His biological father taught music at Oberlin Coll.; his mother was a black student there who gave him up for adoption at birth. He never knew them, and his "real" parents were Bessie Sledge, a nurse, and Joseph Russell, a chef on the B&O Railroad. He played drums in a Boy Scout drum and bugle corps. He received a scholarship to Wilberforce Univ. H.S. program in Ohio, where he played in the Collegians with Ernie Wilkins. He was hospitalized in Chicago at 19 (c. 1942) for tuberculosis; he learned arranging from a fellow patient, bassist Harold Gaston. He played drums with Benny Carter but was soon replaced by Max Roach and began to concentrate on writing. Russell wrote for Earl Hines in the mid-1940s; he sold his first big-band compositions to Benny Carter and Dizzy Gillespie in 1945. Inspired by hearing Monk's "Round Midnight," in 1945 he moved to N.Y., where he became friends with Gil Evans. He then had an offer from Charlie Parker to tour as his drummer, but fell ill again with tuberculosis. While in the hospital (September 1945–December 1946), he began work on his textbook on the use of modes in jazz music, inspired by his friend Miles Davis, with whom he would sit at the piano and trade chords. Russell's early compositions included "Cubana-Be-Cubana-Bop," written with Gillespie for a Gillespie Carnegie Hall Concert in September 1947. He studied privately with classical theorist Stefan Wolpe in N.Y., 1949. He became a widely published composer in the late 1940s and 1950s and his songs were performed or recorded by Buddy DeFranco ("A Bird in Igor's Yard," 1949), Hal McKusick ("Concerto for Billy the Kid," 1955), Charlie Ventura ("West of Bengazi" and "Caravan"), Artie Shaw ("Poinciana"), and Lee Konitz ("Ezz-thetic," a striking variation on "Love for Sale," also recorded by Max Roach). His book, *The Lydian Chromatic Concept of Tonal Organization*, was first published in 1959. In the mid-1950s, he began a rehearsal group, his "Smalltet," with Art Farmer and Bill Evans, Hal McKusick, Barry Galbraith, Joe Harris, and either Milt Hinton or Teddy Kotick on bass. After teaching at the Lenox School of Jazz (1958–59), he became active as a pianist in his own sextet (1960–65). The sextet briefly included Eric Dolphy in 1960, and at times Don Ellis, Chuck Israels, and Steve Swallow. He played at the landmark 1962 Washington D.C. Jazz Festival, toured the Midwest and played the Newport Festival in 1964. In 1964, he toured Europe, and then settled in Sweden. Swedish Radio's jazz director, Bosse Broberg afforded Russell numerous recording opportunities and new commissions. Russell taught at Lund Univ. in Sweden, the Vaskilde Summer School in Denmark, and in Norway, and toured Europe with a sextet of Scandinavians. He performed with the radio orchestras of Oslo and Copenhagen. He returned to the Boston area and has been a faculty member at the New England Cons. of Music since 1969, where he directs the Living Time Orch. This 19-piece band spent six weeks at the Village Vanguard in 1978, and since then has toured throughout Europe and Japan, including frequent appearances at the Bottom Line, N.Y. He made his first tour of the U.K. in early 1986. He was a 1989 MacArthur Fellow; he was named a 1990 Jazz Master by the NEA and a 1996 Jazz Master by the New England Foundation for the Arts. He has received six fellowships from the NEA, two Guggenheim Fellowships (including the first one ever received by a jazz artist, in 1969), and two Grammy nominations. He wrote the three hour "Time Line," for orch., jazz musicians, choirs, rock groups and dancers for the NEC in 1992.

Russell's method is based around the priority of the Lydian mode over the major (or Aeolian), which he contends is proven by the harmonic overtone series; it encourages musicians to find alternate scales to use over chords, and even to superimpose one scale on another to create polytonality or what he calls pantonality. Many musicians, including Coltrane, Dolphy, Bill Evans, and Miles Davis have learned about modes from him. Art Farmer, David Baker, Jan Garbarek, Terje Rypdal, Palle Mikkelborg, and Carla Bley studied directly with him.

DISC.: *George Russell Octets* (1955); *N.Y., N.Y.* (1958); *Stratusphunk* (1960); *Jazz in the Space Age* (1960); *George Russell at the Five Spot* (1960); *George Russell in Kansas City* (1961); *Ezz-Thetic* (1961); *Stratus Seekers* (1962); *Outer View* (1962); *Sextet at Beethoven Hall* (1965); *Listen to the Silence* (1971); *Vertical Form VI* (1977); *N.Y. Big Band* (1978); *Electronic Sonata for Souls Loved by Nature* (1979); *American Time Spiral* (1980); *Live in an American Time Spiral* (1982); *So What* (1983); *African Game* (1983); *London Concert, Vols. 1 & 2* (1989). D. Gillespie: "Cubana Be," "Cubana Bop" (1947). L. Tristano: "Crosscurrents" (1949). L. Konitz: *Odjenar* (1951); *Ezz-thetic* (1951). T. Charles: *The Teddy Charles Tentet* (1956). H. McKusick: *Jazz Workshop* (1956); *Brandeis Jazz Festival: Modern Jazz Concert* (1957). B. Evans: *Living Time* (1972).

WRITINGS: *The Lydian Chromatic Concept of Tonal Organization for Improvisation* (N.Y., 1953).—**LP**

Russell, (George) Alexander, American organist and composer; b. Franklin, Tenn., Oct. 2, 1880; d. Dewitt, N.Y., Nov. 24, 1953. The son of a Presbyterian minister, he studied at home; his mother, Felicia Putnam Russell (a direct descendant of General Israel Putnam of Revolution fame), taught him piano. The family moved to Tex., where he studied academic subjects. He then entered the Coll. of Fine Arts of Syracuse Univ., studying organ with George A. Parker and composition with William Berwald, where he took his B.Mus. in 1901; subsequently studied in Europe with Leopold Godowsky and Harold Bauer (piano), and with Widor (organ). Returning to America in 1908, he toured as accompanist to various artists. From 1910 to 1952, was associated with the Auditorium concerts at Wanamaker's department store in N.Y.; was also director of music at Princeton Univ. (1917–35). He wrote a number of organ works, piano pieces, songs, and partsongs.

BIBL.: J. Howard, *Studies of Contemporary American Composers: A. R.* (N.Y., 1925).—NS/LK/DM

Russell, Henry, English impresario, son of **Henry Russell** and brother of **Sir Landon Ronald;** b. London, Nov. 14, 1871; d. there, Oct. 11, 1937. He studied singing at the Royal Coll. of Music, and devised an original method of vocal instruction, which attracted the attention of Melba, who sent him a number of her good pupils. Owing to his wide acquaintance with singers, he was invited in 1904 to manage a season of opera at Covent Garden. In 1905 he took his company to the U.S., where Boston was the principal field of his operations; his success resulted, in 1909, in the formation of the Boston Opera Co., of which he was general manager until its dissolution in 1914. Just before the outbreak of World War I, he had taken the entire Boston troupe to Paris, where he gave a successful spring season at the Théâtre des Champs-Elysees. He then lived mostly in London. He publ. a book of memoirs, *The Passing Show* (London, 1926).—NS/LK/DM

Russell, Leon (Hank Wilson), gospel-style piano player with raspy mumbling vocals and compelling songwriting; b. Lawton, Okla., April 2, 1941. Leon Russell established himself as one of rock's most unique figures. Initially a well-known session player and producer in Los Angeles during the mid-1960s, Russell first came to the public's attention in the late 1960s with the Asylum Choir, in collaboration with songwriter-guitarist Marc Benno. He subsequently came to prominence as organizer and mastermind behind Joe Cocker's 1970 Mad Dogs and Englishmen tour, who later pursued a modestly successful solo recording career in the 1970s. His popularity faded after the mid-1970s, although he made a remarkable comeback in the country field with his 1979 duet album with Willie Nelson. Continuing to tour in the 1980s and 1990s, Leon Russell returned to recording in 1992 after nearly a decade's absence.

Leon Russell started 10 years of classical piano lessons at age three and took up trumpet at 14, soon forming his first band. He later played briefly with Ronnie Hawkins and the Hawks and toured with Jerry Lee Lewis for six months. After moving to Los Angeles in 1959, he learned guitar from James Burton and became a session musician. He played on most of Phil Spector's hit productions through 1966, and on isolated hits by the Byrds, Herb Alpert, and Bob Lind. Russell also recorded with an astounding variety of artists, from Frank Sinatra to Gary Lewis and the Playboys, from Bobby Darin to Paul Revere and the Raiders.

In 1966 Leon Russell met songwriter-guitarist Marc Benno (b. July 1, 1947, Dallas, Tex). By 1967 Russell had withdrawn from the studio scene to build his own elaborate home studio, although he occasionally appeared with friends Delaney and Bonnie Bramlett and played on infrequent sessions. Working briefly with the Bramletts, guitarist Don Preston, bassist Carl Radle, and others in the New Electric Horn Band, Russell formed the Asylum Choir with Benno in 1968, signing with theSmash subsidiary of Mercury Records. Their debut album sold poorly and their second, recorded in 1969, wasn't issued until the end of 1971, on Shelter Records. It included Russell's "Hello Little Friend" and Benno and Russell's "Sweet Home Chicago" and "Tryin' to Stay Alive."

In 1969 Leon Russell assisted Delaney and Bonnie on their album *Original—Accept No Substitute*, along with organist Bobby Whitlock, bassist Carl Radle, and vocalist Rita Coolidge. Later in the year he worked on Joe Cocker's second album, which contained Russell's "Delta Lady," written for Rita Coolidge. By the beginning of 1970, Russell and English producer Denny Cordell had formed Shelter Records, which soon released Russell's debut album. Recorded with Eric Clapton, George Harrison, and Stevie Winwood, among others, the modest-selling album included three classic Russell compositions, "Delta Lady," "Hummingbird," and "A Song for You," as well as two excellent collaborations, "Prince of Peace" and "Roll Away the Stone."

In a single day in March 1970 Leon Russell assembled the nucleus of the Mad Dogs and Englishmen aggregation for a two-month tour backing Joe Cocker. Consisting of more than 40 people, the entourage included Carl Radle, guitarists Chris Stainton and Don Preston, and backup singers Rita Coolidge and Claudia Lennear. The tour proved enormously successful, as did the subsequent live album and movie, but much to Cocker's chagrin, the spotlight frequently fell on Russell or Coolidge, who regularly performed Russell and Bonnie Bramlett's "Superstar." Shortly after the tour's conclusion in May, Russell assisted Eric Clapton with his debut solo album, coauthoring "Blues Power."

Leon Russell's next album, *Leon Russell and the Shelter People,* was recorded with four sets of accompanying musicians: The Shelter People, The Tulsa Tops, The Muscle Shoals Swampers, and Friends from England. The album included two Bob Dylan songs and excellent originals such as "Sweet Emily," "She Smiles Like a River," "The Ballad of Mad Dogs and Englishmen," and Russell and Don Preston's "Stranger in a Strange Land." In 1971 Russell produced the Bob Dylan singles "Watching the River Flow" and "George Jackson" and appeared at George Harrison's August Concert for Bangladesh. Finally, in 1972 Russell scored his first major hit with "Tight Rope" from *Carney,* his best-selling album; it also contained his own "If the Shoe Fits …," "Magic Mirror," the minor hit "Queen of the Roller Derby," and the engaging "This Masquerade," a smash pop and R&B hit for George Benson in 1976.

Following *Leon Live*, Leon Russell confounded critics with the unexpected album of country standards, *Hank-Wilson's Back*, which yielded the minor hit "Roll in My Sweet Baby's Arms." In 1974 Russell ceased touring, appeared in the film biography *A Poem Is a Naked Person*, and issued *Stop All That Jazz*. His next album, *Will o' the Wisp*, produced a major hit with "Lady Blue" and a minor hit with "Back to the Island."

Russell subsequently severed his relationship with Shelter Records and recorded for his own label, Paradise, distributed by Warner Bros. In spring 1976 he announced his secret marriage the previous June tovocalist Mary McCreary, who had already recorded two solo albums and provided background vocals to Russell's *Will o' the Wisp*. The couple launched the Paradise label with the appropriately titled *Wedding Album*, which yielded the minor hit "Rainbow in Your Eyes," Russell's last. Subsequent albums by Mary alone, Leon alone, and the couple together fared poorly.

Russell bounced back with 1979's *One for the Road*, recorded with Willie Nelson, which included the top country hit "Heartbreak Hotel." He later recorded with the bluegrass-style New Grass Revival. Russell returned to touring in the mid-1980s, gigging with Edgar Winter in 1987 and 1989. In 1992 Leon Russell recorded *Anything Can Happen* for Virgin Records, and later played sessions for George Jones, Bela Fleck, and the Tractors.

Marc Benno briefly returned to Tex. after the demise of Asylum Choir, but he was back in Los Angeles by 1969, where he signed with A&M Records as a solo act. Although he never rose from obscurity, he did write a number of excellent songs, including "Family Full of Soul," "Don't Let the Sun Go Down," and "Either Way It Happens." Benno traveled with Rita Coolidge's Dixie Flyers during her 1971 European tour, and contributed a number of songs to her first three albums, including "(I Always Called Them) Mountains," "Second Story Window," "Nice Feelin'," and "Inside of Me." After years off the concert and recording scene, Benno re-emerged in 1979 with *Lost in Austin*, ably assisted by Eric Clapton. In the late 1980s he composed "Rock 'n' Roll Me Again" for the best-selling *Beverly Hills Cop* soundtrack and moved to the San Francisco Bay Area. Marc Benno returned to recording with 1993's *Take It Back to Texas* on the Sky Ranch label.

DISC.: THE ASYLUM CHOIR: *Look Inside the Asylum Choir* (1968); *Asylum Choir II* (1971). **MARC BENNO:** *Marc Benno* (1970); *Minnows* (1971); *Ambush* (1972); *Lost in Austin* (1979); *Take It Back to Texas* (1993). **LEON RUSSELL:** *Looking Back* (1974); *L. R.* (1970); *L. R. and the Shelter People* (1971); *Carney* (1972); *Leon Live* (1973); *Hank Wilson's Back* (1973); *Stop All That Jazz* (1974); *Will o' the Wisp* (1975); *Best* (1976); *Americana* (1978); *Live and Love* (1979); *Solid State* (1984); *Hank Wilson, Vol. II* (1984); *Anything Can Happen* (1992). **MARY MCCREARY:** *Butterflies in Heaven* (1973); *Jezebel* (1974); *Heart of Fire* (1979). **LEON AND MARY RUSSELL:** *Wedding Album* (1976); *Make Love to the Music* (1977). **LEON RUSSELL AND WILLIE NELSON:** *One for the Road* (1979). **LEON RUSSELL AND THE NEW GRASS REVIVAL:** *Live Album* (1981).—**BH**

Russell, Lillian (real name, **Helen Louise Leonard**), colorful American soprano and actress; b. Clinton, Iowa, Dec. 4, 1861; d. Pittsburgh, June 6, 1922. She studied with L. Damrosch in N.Y., where she sang in the chorus for a production of *H.M.S. Pinafore* in 1879. In the following year she was engaged by the entertainer and manager Tony Pastor for the vaudeville circuit, assuming the stage name of Lillian Russell. Her first success came in 1881, when she starred in *The Grand Mogul* (also known as *The Snake Charmer*) in N.Y.; she subsequently starred in *Polly, or The Pet of the Regiment* (1885), *Pepita, or The Girl with the Glass Eyes* (1886), *The Queen's Mate* (1888), *Poor Jonathan* (1890), *La Cigale* (1891), *Princess Nicotine* (1893), *An American Beauty* (1896), and *Whirl-i-gig* (1899). She toured England and the U.S. in a burlesque company with Joe Weber and Lew Fields (1899–1904); after her last stage appearance, in *Hokey-pokey* (1912), she remained in the limelight by writing a syndicated newspaper column and lecturing on the vaudeville circuit.

BIBL.: P. Morell, *L. R.: The Era of Plush* (N.Y., 1940); J. Burke, *Duet in Diamonds: The Flamboyant Saga of L. R. and Diamond Jim Brady in America's Gilded Age* (N.Y., 1972).—**NS/LK/DM**

Russell, Luis (Carl), Panamanian-born jazz band leader, arranger, pianist; b. Careening Clay, Aug. 6, 1902; d. N.Y., Dec. 11, 1963. His father, Felix Alexander Russell, was a pianist, organist, and music teacher. Luis studied guitar, violin, organ, and piano. He first worked accompanying silent films in a Panama cinema (1917), then played in the Casino Club, Colon, Panama. In 1919 he won $3,000 in a lottery and moved with his mother and sister to New Orleans. He gigged in various clubs and took lessons from Steve Lewis, and then joined Arnold Du Pas Orch. (late 1921–22). Beginning in 1923, he worked at Tom Anderson's Cabaret in Albert Nicholas's Band (1923); when Nicholas left, Luis Russell became the band's leader until late 1924 when he accepted an offer to join Doc Cooke in Chicago; while waiting for union clearance he gigged with King Oliver. Russell worked with Doc Cooke for several months (on piano and organ), then joined King Oliver (1925) with whom he remained until summer 1927 when the band was resident in N.Y. Russell joined drummer George Howe's Band at the Nest Club, N.Y; in October 1927: he was appointed leader of the band and they remained resident there for a year. In 1929 the band also accompanied Louis Armstrong for several months. By this time his ten-piece band (which included several former Oliver sidemen) boasted major soloists in Red Allen, J. C. Higginbotham, Charlie Holmes, and Albert Nicholas; the rhythm section included New Orleanians Pops Foster and Paul Barbarin. During the early 1930s the band continued to play long residencies in N.Y., and also did extensive touring. They backed Louis Armstrong for two days at the Savoy in September 1935 after which Armstrong's manager, Joe Glaser, hired them as the regular accompanying unit for Louis Armstrong; from then on, it was billed as Louis Armstrong's Orch. During the late 1930s, Luis Russell occasionally doubled on trombone. Though most of the original Russell Band had left by 1940, Luis continued working for Louis Armstrong until 1943. He then formed his own big band which did widespread touring as well as residencies in N.Y. He left full-time music in 1948 and opened a small stationery store. He occasionally gigged with his own small bands and continued to teach piano and organ. In 1959 he made his first return visit to Panama (after an absence of almost 40 years); while in Bocas del Tore he gave a classical piano recital. During the early 1960s he worked as a chauffeur, but continued teaching until shortly before his death. He died of cancer.

DISC.: "Savoy Shout" (1929); "Call of the Freaks" (1929).—JC/LP

Russell, William (real name, Russell William Wagner),

American composer; b. Canton, Mo., Feb. 26, 1905; d. New Orleans, Aug. 9, 1992. When he began to study music he eliminated his patronymic as possibly invidious, and placed his first Christian name as a surname. He was fascinated with the sounds of drums, and wrote music almost exclusively for percussion instruments; his first important work in this category was the *Fugue for 8 Percussion Instruments* (1932). Another work of importance was *3 Dance Movements* (N.Y., Nov. 22, 1933); the scoring is for tone clusters and piano strings activated with a fork, and a cymbal sounded by drawing the teeth of a saw across its edge; the ensemble also includes a bottle which must be broken at the climax. His other percussion works include *Ogou Badagri* (1933; based on Voodoo rites); *3 Cuban Pieces* (1935); *Made in America* (1936; the scoring calls for firecrackers); *March Suite* (1936); Concerto for Trumpet and Percussion (1937). Giving up composition, he moved to New Orleans in 1940, and from 1944 to 1957 he recorded historic jazz on his own label; from 1958 he was the jazz-archive curator at Tulane Univ. As late as age 85 he continued playing violin with the New Orleans Ragtime Orch. For a retrospective concert of his works in N.Y. on Feb. 24, 1990, he broke his compositional silence by writing a percussion *Tango* to accompany his *3 Dance Movements*; the concert included the premiere performances of his Trumpet Concerto and *Ogou Badagri*.—NS/LK/DM

Russo, William (Joseph),

American composer and teacher; b. Chicago, June 25, 1928. He studied privately with Lennie Tristano (composition and improvisation, 1943–46), John J. Becker (composition, 1953–55), and Karel B. Jirák (composition and conducting, 1955–57). He was a trombonist and chief composer-arranger with the Stan Kenton Orch. (1950–54); then worked with his own groups in N.Y. and London. He taught at the School of Jazz in Lenox, Mass. (summers, 1956–57), and at the Manhattan School of Music (1958–61). In 1965 he joined the faculty of Columbia Coll. in Chicago; also was a Distinguished Visiting Prof. of Composition at the Peabody Inst. in Baltimore (1969–71), a teacher at Antioch Coll. (1971–72), and composer- in-residence of the city and county of San Francisco (1975–76). He publ. *Composing for the Jazz Orchestra* (Chicago, 1961; 2nd ed., 1973), *Jazz: Composition and Orchestration* (Chicago, 1968; 2nd ed., 1974), and *Composing Music: A New Approach* (Chicago, 1988). Russo's expertise as a composer-arranger has led him to create a number of remarkable third-stream scores.

WORKS: DRAMATIC: Opera: *John Hooton* (1961; BBC, London, Jan. 1963); *The Island* (1963); *Land of Milk and Honey* (1964); *Antigone* (1967); *Aesop's Fables*, rock opera (N.Y., Aug. 17, 1972); *A General Opera* (1976); *The Payoff*, cabaret opera (Chicago, Feb. 16, 1984); *A Cabaret Opera* (1985; alternate forms as *The Alice B. Toklas Hashish Fudge Review*, N.Y., Dec. 8, 1977; *Paris Lights*, N.Y., Jan. 24, 1980, and *The Shepherds' Christmas*, Chicago, Dec. 1979); *Dubrovsky* (1988); *The Sacrifice* (1990). **Ballet:** *The World of Alcina* (1954; rev. 1962); *Les Deux Errants* (Monte Carlo, April 1956); *The Golden Bird* (Chicago, Feb. 17, 1984). **Other:** Other stage pieces; film music. **ORCH.:** *Allegro* for Concert Band (1957; N.Y., July 18, 1961); 2 syms.: No. 1 (1957) and No. 2, *Titans* (1958; N.Y., April 16, 1959); *Newport Suite* (Newport, R.I., July 4, 1958; rev. for Jazz Orch., 1960); *Concerto grosso* for Saxophone Quartet and Concert Band (N.Y., July 29, 1960); Cello Concerto (1962); *3 Pieces* for Blues Band and Orch. (Ravinia Festival, July 7, 1968); *Street Music: A Blues Concerto* (1975; San Francisco, May 19, 1976); *Urban Trilogy* (1981; Los Angeles, March 13, 1982). **Jazz Orch.:** *Solitaire*, with Strings (1949); 2 suites: No. 1 (1952; rev. 1962) and No. 2 (1951–54; rev. 1962); *4 Pieces* (1953–54); *The 7 Deadly Sins* (1960); *Variations on an American Theme* (1960; Kansas City, Mo., Feb. 4, 1961); *The English Concerto*, with Violin (Bath, June 11, 1963); *America 1966* (Ravinia Festival, Aug. 3, 1966); *The New Age Suite* (1984); *For My Friend* (1991); *The Horn Blower* (1991); *The Garden of Virtue* (1993). **CHAMBER:** *21 Etudes* for Brass Instruments (1959); Violin Sonata (1986); *Memphis* for Alto Saxophone and 9 Instruments (Memphis, Tenn., April 21, 1988); *Women* for Harmonica, Piano, and String Quartet (1990); piano pieces. **VOCAL: Rock Cantatas:** *The Civil War* (1968); *David* (1968); *Liberation* (1969); *Joan of Arc* (1970); *The Bacchae* (1972); *Song of Songs* (1972). **Other Cantatas:** *Im Memoriam* for Jazz Orch. (Los Angeles, March 7, 1966); *Songs of Celebration* for 5 Solo Voices, Chorus, and Orch. (1971; Baltimore, Feb. 21, 1973; rev. version, San Francisco, May 18, 1975); *The Touro Cantata* (N.Y., April 4, 1988). **Other Vocal:** *Talking to the Sun*, song cycle theater piece (Chicago, March 5, 1989); *Listen Beneath* for Soprano, Jazz Contralto, and Orch. (1992); *In Memoriam, Hermann Conaway* for Mezzo-soprano, Tenor, Baritone, and 11 Instruments (1994); choruses; songs.—NS/LK/DM

Russolo, Luigi,

Italian inventor, painter, and composer; b. Portogruaro, April 30, 1885; d. Cerro di Laveno, Varese, Feb. 4, 1947. In 1909 he joined the futurist movement of Marinetti, and formulated the principles of "art of noises" in his book, *L'arte dei rumori* (Milan, 1916). He constructed a battery of noise-making instruments ("intonarumori"), with which he gave concerts in Milan (April 21, 1914) and Paris (June 18, 1921), creating such a commotion in the concert hall that on one occasion a group of outraged concertgoers mounted the stage and physically attacked Russolo and his fellow noisemakers. The titles of his works sing the glory of the machine and of urban living: *Convegno dell'automobili e dell'aeroplani*, *Il Risveglio di una citta*, and *Si pranza sulla terrazza dell'Hotel*. In his "futurist manifesto" of 1913, the noises are divided into 6 categories, including shrieks, groans, clashes, explosions, etc. In 1929 he constructed a noise instrument which he called "Russolophone." Soon the novelty of machine music wore out, the erstwhile marvels of automobiles and airplanes became commonplace, and the future of the futurists turned into a yawning past; Russolo gradually retreated from cultivation of noise and devoted himself to the most silent of all arts, painting. His pictures, influenced by the modern French school, and remarkable for their vivid colors, had several successful exhibitions in Paris and N.Y. The text of Russolo's manifesto is reproduced, in an Eng. tr., in N. Slonimsky's *Music since 1900* (N.Y., 1937; 5th ed., rev., 1994).

BIBL.: M. Zanovello Russolo, *R.: L'uomo, l'artista* (Milan, 1958); R. Payton, *The Futurist Musicians: Francesco Balilla Pratella and L. R.* (diss., Univ. of Chicago, 1974); G. Maffina, *L. R. e l'arte dei rumori* (Turin, 1978).—**NS/LK/DM**

Rust, family of German musicians:

(1) Friedrich Wilhelm Rust, violinist, pianist, and composer; b. Wörlitz, near Dessau, July 6, 1739; d. Dessau, Feb. 28, 1796. He was a child prodigy. He studied law in Halle (1758–62), where he also received instruction in music from W. F. Bach. He then found a patron in Prince Leopold III of Anhalt-Dessau and continued his studies with G. F. Müller (violin and keyboard); also studied with Karl Höckh in Zerbst; during a sojourn in Potsdam (1763–64), he took courses in violin with Franz Benda and in composition with C. P. E. Bach. After traveling in Italy with his patron (1765), he returned to Dessau to serve the prince; was his court music director (from 1775). He was esteemed as a composer of instrumental music. See R. Czach, ed., *F. W. Rust: Werke für Klavier und Streichinstrumente*, Das Erbe Deutscher Musik, 2nd series, Mitteldeutschland, I (1939).

BIBL.: F. Hosaeus, *F. W. R. und das Dessauer Musikleben 1766–1796* (Dessau, 1882); E. Prieger, *F. W. R.: Ein Vorganger Beethovens* (Cologne, 1894); R. Czach, *F. W. R.* (Essen, 1927).

(2) Wilhelm Karl Rust, pianist, organist, and teacher, son of the preceding; b. Dessau, April 29, 1787; d. there, April 18, 1855. A child prodigy, he studied with his father, then went to Halle to study philosophy (1805), where he continued his music training with Turk. He subsequently went to Vienna (1807) and won the praise of Beethoven for his expertise as a keyboard artist. After serving as organist of the Protestant church (1819–27), he returned to Dessau as a teacher.

(3) Wilhelm Rust, organist, pianist, teacher, editor, and composer, grandson of **(1) Friedrich Wilhelm Rust;** b. Dessau, Aug. 15, 1822; d. Leipzig, May 2, 1892. He studied piano and organ with his uncle, **(2) Wilhelm Karl Rust,** then composition with F. Schneider (1840–43). He went to Berlin in 1849 as a teacher; joined the Singakademie and the Bach Soc., serving as director of the latter (1862–75); was also made the Berlin representative of the Leipzig Bach-Gesellschaft (1853) and was editor in chief of the complete works of Bach publ. under its auspices (from 1858). He served as organist at the church of St. Luke (from 1861) and taught composition at the Stern Cons. (from 1870). In 1878 he settled in Leipzig as organist of the Thomaskirche and a teacher at the Cons.; was named Kantor of the Thomasschule in 1880. He wrote some choral pieces, sacred songs, and keyboard music.—**NS/LK/DM**

Rust, Giacomo, Italian composer; b. Rome, 1741; d. Barcelona, 1786. He studied at the Turchini Cons. in Naples and with Rinaldo di Capua in Rome. In 1763 he composed his first opera for Venice, where many of his subsequent operas were premiered. In 1777 he was called to Salzburg as court Kapellmeister, but ill health compelled him to give up his post within a few months and he returned to Italy to continue his productive career as an opera composer. In 1783 he became maestro di cappella at the Barcelona Cathedral, but continued to compose until his death. In all, he wrote some 30 dramatic scores.—**NS/LK/DM**

Rutini, Ferdinando, Italian composer, son of **Giovanni Marco Rutini;** b. c. 1764; d. Terracina, Nov. 13, 1827. He studied in Florence, and later served as maestro di cappella in Ancona (1802–12), Macerata (1812–16), Aquapendente (1820–25), and Terracina (from 1825). Among his works were some 35 operas, a Harpsichord Concerto, and chamber pieces.—**LK/DM**

Rutini, Giovanni Marco, Italian composer, father of **Ferdinando Rutini;** b. Florence, April 25, 1723; d. there, Dec. 22, 1797. He was a student of Leo (composition), N. Fago (harpsichord), and Pagliarulo (violin) at the Cons. della Pietà dei Turchini in Naples (1739–44). In 1748 he went to Prague, where he found a patroness in Maria Antonia Walpurgis, the Electress of Saxony. He went to St. Petersburg in 1758 and served as harpsichord teacher to the future Empress Catherine II and as conductor of the private orch. of Count Peter Sheremetev. In 1761 he returned to his homeland and in 1762 he was made a member of the Accademia Filarmonica of Bologna. While spending most of his time in Florence, he also held the title of maestro di cappella to the Duke of Modena from 1769. Rutini was especially successful as a composer for the theater. However, his historical significance rests chiefly upon his harpsichord sonatas which played a major role in the development of the Classical style, and which greatly influenced Haydn and Mozart.

WORKS: DRAMATIC (all 1st perf. in Florence unless otherwise given): *Alessandro nell'Indie* (Prague, Carnival 1750); *Semiramide* (Prgue, 1752; rev. version, Dresden, 1780); *Il retiro degli dei* (St. Petersburg, Dec. 13, 1757); *Il negligente* (St. Petersburg, 1758); *Il caffè di campagna* (Bologna, Carnival 1762); *I matrimoni in maschera* (Cremona, Jan. 1763); *Ezio* (Jan. 30, 1763); *L'olandese in Italia* (1765); *L'amore industrioso* (Venice, 1765); *Il contadino incivilito* (March 31, 1766); *Le contese domestiche* (Dec. 26, 1766); *L'amor tra l'armi* (Siena, July 3, 1768); *Faloppa mercante* (Dec. 26, 1769); *La Nitteti* (Modena, Carnival 1770); *L'amor per rigiro* (Poggio a Caiano, Oct. 5, 1773); *Vologeso re de' Parti* (Jan. 22, 1775); *Sicotencal* (Turin, Carnival 1776; rev. as *Zulima*, Florence, Jan. 25, 1777); *Il finto amante* (Pistoia, 1776). **KEYBOARD:** Over 80 harpsichord sonatas (1748–86); *12 divertimenti facili e brevi* for Harpsichord, 4–Hands or Harp and Harpsichord (1793); *Rondò* for Piano and Orch. ad libitum (1797). **VOCAL:** Oratorios, cantatas, and sacred pieces.

BIBL.: G. Balducci, *La figura e l'opera di G.M. R.* (diss., Univ. of Florence, 1964); F. Meinero, *Le sonate di G.M. R.* (diss., Univ. of Turin, 1975).—**NS/LK/DM**

Rutkowski, Bronislaw, Polish organist, teacher, and composer; b. Komaje, near Vilnius, Feb. 27, 1898; d.

Leipzig, June 1, 1964. He studied organ with Handschin and theory with Kalafati and Vitols at the St. Petersburg Cons. After further training with Surzyński (organ), Rytel and Statkowski (theory), and Melcer (conducting) at the Warsaw Cons. (graduated, 1924), he completed his studies in paris (1924–26) with Vierne (organ) and Pirro (aesthetics). From 1926 to 1939 he taught at the Warsaw Cons., and then at the Kraków Cons. from 1946, where he was rector from 1955 until his death. He made tours as a recitalist throughout Europe. Among his works were choral pieces and organ music.—NS/LK/DM

Rutter, John (Milford), distinguished English conductor and composer; b. London, Sept. 24, 1945. He was educated at Clare Coll., Cambridge (B.A., 1967; Mus.B., 1968; M.A., 1970), where he was later director of music (1975–79). Among his teachers was David Willcocks, with whom he co-edited several choral collections, including 3 in the Carols for Choirs series (Oxford, 1970–80). He also taught through the Open Univ. (1975–88). In 1981 he founded the Cambridge Singers, subsequently conducting them in an extensive repertoire. In 1990 he conducted their Carnegie Hall debut in N.Y. In 1984 he established Collegium Records, a label dedicated to their performances. He established his own publishing imprint, the Collegium Choral Series, in 1994. In 1995 he launched the Oxford Choral Classics series of anthologies. He was awarded a Lambeth Doctorate of music for services to church music in 1996. His compositions and arrangements are numerous and accessible, and feature an extensive catalog of choral works that are frequently performed in Britain and the U.S.

WORKS: *The Falcon* for Chorus and Orch. (1969); *Fancies* for Chorus and Chamber Orch. (1972); *Partita* for Orch. (1973); *Gloria* for Chorus, Brass Ensemble, Percussion, and Organ (1974; for Orch., 1988); *Bang!,* children's opera (1975); *Canticles of America* for Chorus and Orch. (1976); *Beatles' Concerto* for 2 Pianos and Orch. (1977); *The Reluctant Dragon* for Voices and Chamber Orch. (1978); *Suite antique* for Flute, Harpsichord, and Strings (1979); *Reflections* for Piano and Orch. (1979); *The Piper of Hamelin,* children's opera (1980); *The Wind in the Willows* for Voices and Chamber Orch. (1981); *Requiem* for Soprano and Chorus (1985); *Te Deum* for Chorus and Various Accompaniments (1988); *Magnificat* for Soprano, Chorus, and Ensemble (1990); *Psalmfest* for Soloists, Chorus, and Orch. (1993); *Birthday Madrigals* for Chorus, String Bass, and Piano (1995); *Come down, O love divine* for Double Chorus (1998).—NS/LK/DM

Rütti, Carl, Swiss pianist, organist, teacher, and composer; b. Fribourg, March 24, 1949. He received training in piano and organ at the Zürich Cons., taking diplomas in both subjects in 1975, and then completed his piano studies with Kendall Taylor at the Royal Coll. of Music in London in 1976. In 1972 he became a teacher at the Zürich Cons. and in 1980 organist in Oberägeri. He toured East Germany as a pianist in 1987, and also appeared in Copenhagen. In 1991–92 he again made appearances in Germany. In 1994 he was an organ recitalist in Manchester and a piano recitalist in London. He gave a piano recital in Indianapolis in 1998. Rütti has devoted much of his compositional effort to choral music. Among his most important works are *Buch der*

Bilder, 7 motets after Rilke (1982), *O magnum mysterium* (Austrian TV Christmas broadcast, 1992), *Veni, Creator Spiritus* (1997), *Gloria* (1998), *Stabat Mater* (1998), and *Alpha et Omega* (1999).—LK/DM

Ruwet, Nicolas, French linguist and musical analyst; b. Saive, Belgium, Dec. 31, 1932. He studied Romance philology at the Univ. of Liège, with Lévi-Strauss and Benveniste at the École Pratique des Hautes Études in Paris, and with Jakobson and Chomsky at the Mass. Inst. of Technology; also studied music privately. In 1968 he became prof. of linguistics at the Univ. of Paris at Vincennes. Although not primarily a musician, he has been a fundamental thinker in the semiology of music, contributing important articles which were reprinted in his *Langage, musique, poésie* (Paris, 1972). His multileveled system for analyzing musical syntax, "distributional analysis," has been a central influence in the work of Nattiez and his followers.—NS/LK/DM

Ruyneman, Daniel, Dutch composer; b. Amsterdam, Aug. 8, 1886; d. there, July 25, 1963. He began his study of music relatively late. He received training in piano from De John and in composition from Zweers at the Amsterdam Cons. (1913–16). In 1918 he was a co-founder of the Nederlansche Vereeniging voor Moderne Scheppende Toonkunst, which became the Dutch section of the ISCM in 1922. In 1930 he organized the Netherlands Soc. for Contemporary Music, serving as president until 1962; ed. its journal, *Maandblad voor Hedendaagse Muziek* (1930–40), until it was suppressed during the Nazi occupation of the Netherlands; was general secretary of the ISCM (1947–51). Ruyneman made a special study of Javanese instruments and introduced them in some of his works. He was naturally attracted to exotic subjects with mystic connotations and coloristic effects; also worked on restoration of early music. In 1930 he orchestrated fragments of Mussorgsky's unfinished opera *The Marriage,* and added his own music for the missing acts of the score.

WORKS: DRAMATIC: O p e r a : *De gebroeders Karamasoff* (1928); *Le Mariage* (1930). I n c i d e n t a l M u s i c : *De Clown,* "psycho-symbolic" play (1915). ORCH.: 2 syms.: No. 1, *Symphonie brève* (1927), and No. 2, *Symphony 1953* (1953; Utrecht, March 14, 1956); *Musica per orchestra per una festa Olandese* (1936); *Concerto for Orchestra* (1937); Piano Concerto (1939); Violin Concerto (1940; Amsterdam, Feb. 23, 1943); *Partita* for Strings (1943); *Amphitryon,* overture (1943); *Amatarasu* (Ode to the Sun Goddess), on a Japanese melody, for Chamber Ensemble (1953); *Gilgamesj,* Babylonian epos (1962). CHAM-BER: 3 violin sonatas (No. 2, 1914; No. 3, 1956); *Klaaglied van een Slaaf* for Violin and Piano (1917); *Hiëroglyphs* for 3 Flutes, Celesta, Harp, Cup-bells, Piano, 2 Mandolins, and 2 Guitars (1918; the unique cup-bells, which some claim were cast by J. Taylor & Co., Loughborough, England, and which others claim were found by the composer in a London junk shop, were destroyed in a Rotterdam air raid in 1940, and perfs. of the work since then have substituted a vibraphone); Violin Sonata (1925); *Divertimento* for Flute, Clarinet, Horn, Violin, and Piano (1927); Clarinet Sonata (1936); *4 tempi* for 4 Cellos (1937); *Sonatina in modo antiquo* for Cello and Piano (1939); *Sonata da camera* for Flute and Piano (1942); String Quartet (1946); *Nightingale Quintet* for Winds (1949); *4 chansons Bengalies* for Flute and Piano (1950); Sonatina for Flute and Piano or Harpsichord (1951); Oboe Sonatina (1952); *Reflexions II* for Flute, Viola, and Guitar (1959), *III* for Flute, Violin, Viola, Cello, and Piano or Harpsichord (1960–61; reconstructed by R. du Bois), and *IV* for Wind Quintet (1961); 3 *Fantasies* for Cello and Piano or Harpsichord (1960). **P i a n o :** 3 *Pathematologieën* (1915); 2 sonatinas (1917, 1954); Sonata (1931); *Kleine Sonata* (1938); 5 *sonatines mélodiques pour l'enseignement moderne du piano* (1947). **VOCAL:** *Sous le pont Mirabeau* for Women's Chorus, Flute, Harp, and String Quartet (1917); *De Roep* (The Call), a color spectrum of wordless vowel sounds for Chorus (1918); *Sonata*, on wordless vowel sounds, for Chamber Chorus (1931); 4 *Liederen* for Tenor and Small Orch. (1937); *Die Weise von Liebe und Tod des Kornets Christoph Rilke* for Narrator and Piano (1946; orchestrated 1951); *Ancient Greek Songs* for Baritone or Bass, Flute, Oboe, Cello, and Harp (1954); 5 *Melodies* for Voice and Piano (1957); 3 *chansons de Maquisards condamnes* for Alto or Baritone, and Orch. (1957); *Reflexions I* for Soprano, Flute, Guitar, Viola, Vibraphone, Xylophone, and Percussion (1958–59).

BIBL.: A. Petronio, *D. R. et son oeuvre* (Liège, 1922). —NS/LK/DM

Ruzicka, Peter, German composer and Intendant; b. Düsseldorf, July 3, 1948. Following training in piano, oboe, and composition at the Hamburg Cons. (1963–68), he studied law and musicology in Munich, Hamburg, and Berlin (Ph.D., 1977). He was Intendant of the (West) Berlin Radio Sym. Orch. from 1979 to 1987. From 1988 to 1997 he was Intendant of the Hamburg State Opera and State Phil. Orch. He also taught at the Hamburg Hochschule für Musik from 1990. In 1996 he became artistic director of the Munich Biennale. He served as artistic advisor of the Royal Concertgebouw Orch. in Amsterdam in 1997. In 1999 he became president of the Bavarian Theater Academy. He also was artistic director of the Salzburg Festival from 2001. He was made a fellow of the Bavarian Academy of Fine Arts in Munich in 1985 and of the Free Academy of Arts in Hamburg in 1987. In his compositions, Ruzicka has followed a determined contemporary path that is reflected in his capable handling of various avant-garde techniques in whatever genre he chooses to explore.

WORKS: DRAMATIC: *Outside-Inside*, radiophonic piece (Radio Bremen/Bavarian Radio, June 10, 1972; also as an expanded music theater piece, Augsburg, Aug. 18, 1972). **ORCH.:** *Antifone-Strofe* for 25 Solo Strings and Percussion (Göttingen, Oct. 23, 1970); *Sinfonia* for 25 Solo Strings, 16 Vocalists, and Percussion (1970–71; Stuttgart, Sept. 25, 1971; rev. version, Berlin, Nov. 20, 1974); *Versuch*, 7 pieces for Strings (1970–74; Stuttgart, Oct. 11, 1975); *Metastrofe* for 87 Instrumentalists (Berlin, May 4, 1971); *In processo di tempo* for 26 Instrumentalists and Cello (1971; Hilversum, Sept. 11, 1972); *Feed Back* for 4 Orch. Groups (Donaueschingen, Oct. 21, 1972); *Torso* (Cologne, Dec. 7, 1973); *Einblendungen* (1973–77; Hannover, Dec. 1, 1977); *Befragung*, 5 pieces (1974; Paris, Oct. 30, 1975); *Emanazione*, variations for Flute and 4 Orch. Groups (1975; Berlin, Jan. 13, 1976); *Abbrüche* (1977–78; Düsseldorf, April 20, 1978); *Annäherung und Stille*, 4 fragments after Schumann for Piano and 42 Strings (Interlaken, Aug. 23, 1981); *...den Impuls zum Weitersprechen erst empfinge* for Viola and Orch. (1981; Saarbrücken, June 1, 1982); *Satyagraha* (1984; Hamburg, Oct. 16, 1985); *Fünf Bruchstücke* (1984–87; Berlin, Feb. 15, 1988); *Metamorphosen über ein Klangfeld von Joseph Haydn* (Cologne, Oct. 5, 1990); *...das Gesegnete, das Verfluchte*, 4 sketches (1991; Munich, Nov. 27,

1992); *Tallis* (Kiel, Aug. 11, 1993); *...Inseln, randlos...*for Violin, Chamber Chorus, and Orch. (1994–95; Frankfurt am Main, April 27, 1977); *Nachtstück* (1997; Berlin, April 22, 1998); *...Vorgefühle...* (1998). **CHAMBER:** *Drei Szenen* for Clarinet (1967; Hamburg, Feb. 27, 1970); *Ausgeweidet die Zeit...*, 3 night pieces for Piano (1969; Spoleto, July 1, 1971); Sonata for Solo Cello (1969; Hamburg, Feb. 27, 1970); 4 string quartets: No. 1 (1969–70; Hamburg, Feb. 27, 1970; rev. version, Kiel, Nov. 20, 1970), No. 2, *...fragment...* (1970; Stuttgart, June 18, 1974), No. 3, *...über ein Verschwinden* (1992; Cologne, April 5, 1993), and No. 4, *...Sich Verlierend*, for String Quartet and Speaker (1996; Cologne, Oct. 14, 1977); *Movimenti* for Harpsichord (1969–70; Hamburg, June 12, 1974); *Stress* for 8 Percussion Groups (Munich, April 13, 1972); *Zeit* for Organ (Kassel, April 3, 1975); *Z–Zeit* for Organ (1975; Bremen, May 13, 1976); *Stille* for Cello (Erlangen, Nov. 28, 1976); *Seboniana* for 3 Flutes, 1 Player (Marktbreit, Sept. 29, 1979); *Préludes* for Piano (Neumünster, Aug. 16, 1987); *Klangschatten* for String Quartet (Vienna, Nov. 18, 1991). **VOCAL:** *Esta Noche*, funeral music for the victims of the Vietnam War, for Alto or Tenor, Flute, English Horn, Viola, and Cello (1967; Hamburg, April 18, 1968); *Todesfuge* for Alto, Speaker, Chamber Ensemble, and Tape (1968–69; Hamburg, Feb. 27, 1970); *Elis* for Mezzo-soprano, Oboe or Oboe d'amore, and Orch. (1969; Leverkusen, April 9, 1970); *Gestalt und Abbruch* for Voices (Donaueschingen, Oct. 21, 1979); *...der die Gesänge zerschlug* for Baritone and Chamber Ensemble (Berlin, Sept. 3, 1985); *Vier Gesänge nach Fragmenten von Nietzsche* for Mezzo-soprano and Piano (1992; Savonlinna, July 13, 1993); *Sechs Gesänge nach Fragmenten von Nietzsche* for Mezzo-soprano and Orch. (1997; Stuttgart, Feb. 7, 1998). **OTHER:** *DE.../MUSAC* for Variable Ensemble (1971); *Bewegung* for Tape (1972).—NS/LK/DM

Růžička, Rudolf, Czech composer and pedagogue; b. Brno, April 25, 1941. After attending the Brno Cons. (1958–62), he studied composition with Theodor Schaefer and Miloslav Ištvan (1962–67) and Miloslav Kabeláč (1967–69) at the Janáček Academy of Music and Dramatic Arts (1967–69). In 1969 he joined the faculty of the latter, where he taught courses in electroacoustic and computer composition. As a prominent figure in avant-garde circles, Růžička became suspect in the eyes of the rigid Communist regime. All the same, he persevered in his activities with various avant-garde groups at home and abroad. In 1970 his *Gurges* won 1st prize in the Musica Nova competition in Brno and in 1984 his *Tibia I* received 1st prize in the Marcel Josse competition in Paris. Following the collapse of the Communist regime in 1989, Růžička assumed an even greater prominence among the avant-garde of his homeland and abroad. While he has composed various works in the traditional genres, he has become best known for his use of computers in producing innovations in the forms and structures of his works.

WORKS: ORCH.: *Suite of Ancient Dances* (1964); *Cosmic Symphony* for Organ and Orch. (1971); Concertante Sym. for Chamber String Orch. (1972); *Symphonic Concerto* for Violin and Orch. (1972); *Festive Overture* (1973); Sym. No. 4 (1974); Concerto for Double Bass and Strings (1978); Double Concerto for Oboe, Trumpet, and Orch. (1981); *Festive Music* for Brass Ensemble (1985). **CHAMBER:** *Divertimento* for 2 Flutes and Piano (1960); *Miniatures* for Flute and Piano (1962); Trio for Flute, Viola, and Harp (1963); *Sonata aleatoria* for Organ, Piano, and Percussion (1963); *Sonata nuova* for Cello and Piano (1967); *Contaminationi* for Bass Clarinet and Piano (1968); *Sonata triste* for Trombone and Piano (1972); String Quartet No. 2 (1972); *Sonata bravura* for Violin or Viola or Cello and Piano (1973); Sextet No. 2 for Flute, Oboe, and String Quartet (1975); Wind Quintet No. 2 (1975); *Divertimento* for 4 Horns (1979); Suite No. 3 for Clarinet (1980); *Nomos I* for Flute and Guitar (1981), *II* for English Horn or Flute or Oboe or Clarinet or Saxophone (1982), and *III* for Harp (1983); Quartet for 4 Saxophones (1986); *Musica giocosa* for Chamber Ensemble (1987); Chamber Concerto No. 1 for Oboe or Clarinet and Brass Quintet (1988) and No. 2 for Flute and Viola Ensemble (1988); *Fulmen* for Percussion (1991). **VOCAL:** *Morning Song*, cantata for Chorus and Orch. (1958); *Anna* for Reciter, Alto, Flute, and Harp (1966); *Cantilena Ae Ae Ae* for Chorus (1970); *Homage to Apollo* for Soprano, Alto, Chamber Chorus, Flute, Oboe and Harp (1974); *Olympic Songs* for Reciter, Bass-baritone, Chamber Chorus, and Chamber Orch. (1976); *Eirene* for Mixed or Men's or Children's Chorus (1977); *Auletike* for Chorus and Oboe or Flute (1977); *Femis* for Medium Voice and Instruments (1979); *Ode to Aphrodite* for Soprano and Harp (1982); *The Aeolian Harp* for Medium Voice, Harp, and Percussion (1989). **OTHER:** *Electronia A* for Alto, Chamber Orch., and Electronics (1964), *B* for Chamber Chorus, Chamber Orch., and Electronics (1965), and *C* for Electronics (1966); *Timbri* for Wind Quintet and Electroacoustics (1967); *Deliciae* for Double Bass and Electroacoustics (1968); *Gurges* for Spatial Electroacoustics (1968); *Anthroporea* for Spatial Electroacoustics (1969); *Aphorisms* for Reciter and Electroacoustics (1969); *Mavors* for Electroacoustics (1970); *Discordia* for Electronics (1970); *Cantata Ai Ai A* for Mezzo-soprano, Bass-Baritone, Chamber Chorus, Chamber Orch., and Electroacoustics (1971); *Tibia* for Flute and Electroacoustics (1972); Concertino for Harp and Electroacoustics (1973); *Arcanum* for Electroacoustics (1974); *Malefica* for Mezzo-soprano, Flute, Clarinet, Viola, Harpsichord or Piano, and Electroacoustics (1974); *Paean* for Trombone and Electroacoustics (1976); *Tibia I* for Saxophone and Electroacoustics (1984); *Rota* for Piano or Harpsichord and Electroacoustics (1985); Suite No. 6 for Synthesizer (1986); *Celula* for Electroacoustics (1986); *Bucina* for Trumpet and Electroacoustics (1988); *Parabola* for Synthesizer (1989); *Rosa sepulcreti* for Baritone and Electroacoustics (1989); Chamber Concerto No. 3 for Synthesizer and Chamber Orch. (1990); *Crucifixion I* for Computer (1992); *Aves* for Electroacoustics and Computer (1994).—**NS/LK/DM**

Růžičková, Zuzana, Czech harpsichordist and teacher; b. Plzeň, Jan. 14, 1928. She studied at the Prague Academy of Music. In 1956 she won the Munich International Competition. She was a member of the Prague Chamber Soloists (1962–67), which she co-founded with the conductor Vaclav Neumann. In 1962 she joined the faculty of the Prague Academy of Music. She appeared in duo recitals with Josef Suk from 1963. In 1969 she was named an Artist of Merit. In 1952 she married **Viktor Kalabis.**
BIBL.: B. Berkovec, *Z. R.* (Prague, 1972).—**NS/LK/DM**

Ryan, Thomas, Irish-American violist, clarinetist, and composer; b. in Ireland, 1827; d. New Bedford, Mass., March 5, 1903. He received instruction in violin and wind instruments in Ireland before emigrating to the U.S. in 1844. He settled in 1845 in Boston, where he founded the Mendelssohn Quintette Club, playing the viola (and upon occasion the clarinet), with August Fries (1st violin), Francis Riha (2nd violin), Eduard

Lehmann (viola and flute), and Wulf Fries (cello); traveled all over the U.S. with it until it was dissolved in 1895, doing missionary work in bringing good music to remote communities; he also acted as its manager; arranged Classical sonatas and other works for it; after half a century, Ryan was the sole remaining original member of the organization. He publ. his memoirs, *Recollections of an Old Musician* (N.Y., 1899).—**NS/LK/DM**

Ryba, Jakub (Šimon) Jan, Czech choirmaster, teacher, writer on music, and composer; b. Přeštice, Oct. 26, 1765; d. (suicide) Rožmitál pod Třemšinem, April 8, 1815. He studied academic subjects in Prague, and in 1788 became school- and choirmaster in Rožmitál. He wrote about 90 masses, the most famous being *Hej, mistre* (Hail, Master!; 1796); he also composed various other sacred works, including 7 Requiems, numerous motets, over 50 pastorellas, arias, and choruses. His secular works include 6 stage pieces and songs. He was also a prolific composer of instrumental music, but little of it is extant.
BIBL.: J. Němeček, *Světskě skladby J.J. R.* (Secular Works; diss., Univ. of Prague, 1945); idem, *J.J. R.: Zivot a dilo* (Life and Works; Prague, 1963).—**NS/LK/DM**

Rybner (real name, Růbner), (Peter Martin) Cornelius, Danish pianist, conductor, teacher, and composer; b. Copenhagen, Oct. 26, 1855; d. N.Y., Jan. 21, 1929. He studied at the Copenhagen Cons. with Gade and J.P. Hartmann, and then at the Leipzig Cons. with Ferdinand David (violin) and Reinecke (piano); finished his pianistic studies under Hans von Bülow and Anton Rubinstein. After a series of concerts in Europe as pianist, he settled in Karlsruhe. He succeeded Mottl in 1892 as conductor of the Phil. Soc., and held this position until 1904, when he emigrated to the U.S., succeeding MacDowell as head of the music dept. at Columbia Univ. (1904–19). About 1920 he changed his name to Rybner. His works include a ballet, *Prinz Ador* (Munich, 1902), a symphonic poem, *Friede, Kampf und Sieg,* a Violin Concerto, numerous choruses, piano pieces, songs, and some chamber music.—**NS/LK/DM**

Rychlík, Jan, Czech composer; b. Prague, April 27, 1916; d. there, Jan. 20, 1964. He studied with Řídký at the Prague Cons. (1939–45) and in his master classes there (1945–46). A practical musician, he played in dance orchs., experimented with modern techniques, and was active as a music critic. He wrote a book on jazz and one on valveless brass instruments.
WORKS: *Symphonic Overture* (1944); *Suite* for Wind Quintet (1946); *Concert Overture* (1947); *Partita giocosa* for Wind Orch. (1947); Trio for Clarinet, Trumpet, and Bassoon (1948); *Divertimento* for 3 Double Basses (1951); *Études* for English Horn and Piano (1953); String Trio (1953); *4 Partitas* for Flute (1954); *Chamber Suite* for String Quartet (1954); *Arabesques* for Violin and Piano (1955); *Burlesque Suite* for Clarinet (1956); *Serenade* for Wind Octet (1957); Wind Quintet (1960); *Hommagi gravicembalistici* for Harpsichord (1960); *African Cycle I–V* for 8 Winds and Piano (1961; Prague, June 29, 1962); *Relazioni* for Alto Flute, English Horn, and Bassoon (1964); music for films and plays. —**NS/LK/DM**

Rychlik, Józef, Polish composer and teacher; b. Kraków, May 12, 1946. He was a student of composition and theory of Bogusław Schaeffer at the State Higher School of Music in Kraków (1965–70), and later held a French government scholarship to study in Paris (1978). In 1972 he joined the faculty of the State Higher School of Music in Kraków.

WORKS: ORCH.: *Sekwencje przestrzenne* (Spatial Sequences) for Chamber Orch. (1971); *Szkice* (Sketches) for Organ and Orch. (1972); *Plenitudo temporis* (1974). **CHAMBER:** String Quartet (1968); *Muzyka symfoniczna* (Symphonic Music) *I* for 2 Pianos and 2 String Quartets (1969–70) and *II* for Chamber Ensemble (1969–70; Warsaw, Sept. 26, 1971); *à 2* for Percussion (1970); *Ametrio* for Flute, Violin, and Cello (1971); *Wielokropek* (Ellipsis) for Piano, Wind Instrument, and Any 4 Instruments (1972; Kraków, March 7, 1974); *Invocazioni intorno* for Horn and Percussion (Kraków, May 21, 1997). **O r g a n :** *Grave-ap* (1973). **VOCAL:** *Nokturn* for Soprano, Flute, Piano, and 3 Cymbals (1966); *Musica per gliss* for 2 Sopranos, Violin, Vibraphone, and Piano (1970); *VO-TO* for Chorus (1973); *Podtytuł-Sen Eurydyki II* (Subtitle-Euridice's Dream II) for Soprano and Tape (1982). **TAPE:** *Muzyka ścienna* (Wall Music; 1975); *Musinelle* (Kraków, Nov. 27, 1975); *Podtytuł-Sen Eurydyki* (Subtitle-Euridice's Dream; 1978); *Aura I* (1992); *Logo III* (1996). **OTHER:** *Peut- être,* graphic piece for any Solo Instrument or Voice or Chamber Ensemble or Ballet Group with Tape ad libitum (1974). **—NS/LK/DM**

Rydl, Kurt, Austrian bass; b. Vienna, Oct. 8, 1947. He received vocal training in Vienna and Moscow. In 1973 he made his operatic debut as Wagner's Daland in Stuttgart. He became a member of the Vienna State Opera in 1976, where he sang such roles as Osmin, Rocco, King Marke, the Landgrave, Hagen, Méphistophélès, Zaccaria, and King Philip II. As a guest artist, he sang at the Salzburg Festival (1985; 1987–90), Barelona (1990), Milan's La Scala (1990–91; 1998), Florence (1992), London's Covent Garden (1995, 1997), and Trieste (1998).**—NS/LK/DM**

Rydman, Kari, Finnish composer; b. Helsinki, Oct. 15, 1936. He studied musicology at the Univ. of Helsinki, and was autodidact as a composer. He developed energetic activities as a composer, music critic, and schoolteacher. In his music he reveals himself as a blithe spirit, writing ultramodern pieces, but also turning out some fetching Finnish pop tunes.

WORKS: 5 string quartets (1959, 1963, 1964, 1964, 1966); Piano Quintet (1960); Trio for Violin, Cello, and Percussion (1961); *Sonata 1* for 3 Violins, Viola, Cello, Piano, and Percussion (1962), *2* for Violin, Viola, Guitar, and Percussion (1962), *4* for Violin, Clarinet, Guitar, and Percussion (1963), *6* for Cello and Percussion (1964), *8* for Viola and Harpsichord (1967), and *9* for Small Orch. (1969); *Khoros 1* for 3 Flutes, Oboe, Percussion, Harp, Violin, Viola, Cello, and Double Bass (1964) and *2* for Orch. (1966); *Rondeaux des nuits blanches d'été* for Orch. (1966); *Symphony of the Modern Worlds,* which contains blues, beat rhythms, political songs, and the Chinese Communist anthem, *Dong Fang Hong* (The East Is Red) (1968); *DNA* for Orch. and Electronic Organ (1970); *Suite* for Narrator and Orch. (1971). **—NS/LK/DM**

Ryelandt, Joseph, Belgian composer and teacher; b. Bruges, April 7, 1870; d. there, June 29, 1965. He studied composition with Edgar Tinel. Thanks to a personal fortune (he was a baron), he did not have to earn a living by his music. He was director of the Bruges Cons. (1924–45) and a teacher at the Ghent Cons. (1929–39). He lived a very long life (*obiit aet. 95*) and composed much music.

WORKS: DRAMATIC: *La Parabole des vierges,* spiritual drama (1894); *Sainte Cecile,* lyrical drama (1902). **ORCH.:** 5 syms. (1897, 1904, 1908, 1913, 1934); *Gethsemani,* symphonic poem (1908); *Patria,* overture (1917). **CHAMBER:** 7 violin sonatas; 4 string quartets; 3 cellos sonatas; 2 piano quintets; 2 piano trios; Viola Sonata; Horn Sonata; 11 piano sonatas; organ music. **VOCAL:** 5 oratorios: *Purgatorium* (1904), *De Komst des Heren* (1906–07), *Maria* (1910), *Agnus Dei* (1913–15), and *Christus Rex* (1921–22); *Te Deum* for Soloists, Chorus, and Orch. (1927); 7 cantatas; songs.**—NS/LK/DM**

Rypdal, Terje, Norwegian composer and jazz and rock guitarist; b. Oslo, Aug. 23, 1947. He took up the piano at age 5 and the guitar at 13, and subsequently studied musicology at the Univ. of Oslo and was a composition student of Mortensen at the Oslo Cons. (1970–72) and of George Russell, who introduced him to his Lydian Concept of tonal organization. Rypdal was active as a performer with his own pop band, the Vanguards, and later with his group, Dreams. He also worked with Russell's sextet and big band. In 1969 he became a member of the Jan Garbarek Quartet. His long association with jazz and rock had significant impact upon his approach to composition. Whether composing in a serial or tonal mode, Rypdal's music relfects a penchant for utilizing late romantic, jazz, and avant-garde elements.

WORKS: DRAMATIC: *Orfeus,* opera (1971); *Freden,* opera (1976); incidental music. **ORCH.:** *Capriccio* for Strings (1970); Double Bass Concerto (1973); 5 syms. (1973, 1977, 1981, 1986, 1992); *Tumulter* for Percussion and Orch. (1973); *Krystaller* for Alto Flute and Orch. (1973); Horn Concerto (1977); *Julemusikk* for Strings (1978); Piano Concerto (1979); *In Autumn* for Electric Guitar, Trumpet, and Orch. (1979); *Undisonus* for Violin and Orch. (1979–81); *Shadows* for Oboe, 4 Trombones, Percussion, and Strings (1980); *Hulter til Bulter* for Percussion and Orch. (1980); *Modulation* for Harmonica and Orch. (1980); *A.B.C. or Adventure-Bedtime Story-Celebration* for Accordion and Orch. (1981); *Labyrint* (1982); *Vilanden,* symphonic poem (1982); *Telegram* for Chamber Orch. (1982); *Imagi* for Cello and Big Band (1983–84); *Patina* for Cello and Orch. (1984); *Buldur og Brak* for Symphonic Band (1986); *Lirum Larum* for Electric Guitar, 2 Rock Bands, Symphonic Band, Chorus, and Orch. (1987); *Det blå Folket* (1987); *Over Fjorden* for Symphonic Band (1989); *The Vanguardian* for Jazz Guitar and Orch. (1989); *Soleis* for Pan Flute and Orch. (1990); *Q.E.D.* (1991); *Hip som Happ* (1991); *Déja-vu* for Soprano Saxophone, Bass Clarinet, Baritone Saxophone, and Strings (1991); *Adagio von Mozart* (1991); Double Concerto for 2 Electric Guitars and Orch. (1992); *Sinfonietta* (1995); *Zoom* for Symphonic Band (1995); *That's the Beauty of It* for Electric Guitar and Orch. (1996); Concerto for Electric Guitar, Electric Bass or Contrabass, Drums or Percussion, Sculpture, and Wind Orch. (1997); *But the Melody Lingers On...and On* (1997). **CHAMBER:** String Quartet (1970); Wind Quintet (1973); *Whenever I Seem to Be Far Away* for Electric Guitar, Strings, Oboe, and Clarinet (1974); *Unfinished Highballs* for Jazz Quartet (1976); *Concerto ECM* for Electric Guitar, 8 Cellos, Keyboards, and Percussion (1982); *Enigma* for 2 Trumpets, Horn, Trombone, and Tuba (1982); *10 X 10* for Improvisation Ensemble (1983); *Vidare* for Acoustic or Electric Violin (1984); *Crooner Songs* for Clarinet, Trumpet, Violin, Keyboards, and Percussion (1986); *Troll* for Electric Guitar, Flute, Clarinet, Violin, Cello, and Keyboards (1986); *Passion* for Harpsichord or Synthesizer, Vibraphone, and Fretless Electric Bass Guitar (1987); *The Illuminator* for Electric Guitar, Percussion, Winds, Brass, Double Bass, and Keyboards (1987); *Drømmespinn* for Oboe, 2 Violins, Viola, Cello, and Double Bass (1988); *Arktik* for Electric Guitar or Alto Flute, Trumpet, Synthesizer, Double Bass, and Percussion (1988); *Sesam* for Clarinet, Trombone, and Piano or Synthesizer (1989); *Inntil Vidare* for Violin, Trumpet, Electric Guitar, Bass Guitar, and Percussion (1990); *Largo* for Electric Guitar, Strings, and Percussion (1991); *Détente* for Flute, Clarinet, 2 Violins, Viola, Cello, and 2 Synthesizers (1992); *Fire* for Violin, Oboe, Viola, and Cello (1992); *The Big Bang II* for Oboe or English Horn, Cello, Double or Electric Bass, Synthesizer, Percussion, and Electric Guitar (1992); *Time* for English Horn, Cello, Double Bass, Synthesizer, Percussion, and Guitar (1993); Sonata for Violin and Keyboards (1998); *Two of a Kind* for Violin and Cello (1999). **VOCAL:** *Eternal Circulation* for Soprano, Chorus, and Orch. (1970); *Spegling* for Mezzo-soprano and Orch. (1981); *Ineo* for Chorus, Electric Guitar, and Orch. (1983); *Vardøger* for Men's Chorus (1984); *Metamorphosis* for Women's Chorus (1984); *The Big Bang* for Women's Chorus and Chamber Ensemble (1990); *Voices of the Wind* for Chorus, Children's Chorus, and Orch. (1997); *Il Canzonière* for Chorus, Instruments, and Synthesizer (1998).—NS/LK/DM

Rysanek, Leonie, distinguished Austrian soprano; b. Vienna, Nov. 14, 1926; d. there, March 7, 1998. She studied at the Vienna Cons. with Rudolf Grossmann, whom she later married. She made her operatic debut as Agathe in *Der Freischütz* in Innsbruck in 1949; then sang at Saarbrücken (1950–52). She first attracted notice when she appeared as Sieglinde at the Bayreuth Festival in 1951; became a member of the Bavarian State Opera in Munich in 1952, and went with it to London's Covent Garden in 1953, where she sang Danae; in 1954 she joined the Vienna State Opera; also sang in various other major European opera houses. On Sept. 18, 1956, she made her U.S. debut as Senta at the San Francisco Opera; later made a spectacular appearance at the Metropolitan Opera in N.Y. on Feb. 5, 1959, when she replaced Maria Callas in the role of Lady Macbeth in Verdi's opera on short notice; she continued to sing there with notable distinction for some 35 years. She received the Lotte Lehmann Ring from the Vienna State Opera in 1979. In 1984 she toured Japan with the Hamburg State Opera. In 1986 she appeared as Kostelnička in *Jenůfa* in San Francisco. She sang Kabanicha in *Kat'á Kabanová* in Los Angeles in 1988. In 1990 she appeared as Herodias at the Deutsche Oper in Berlin. In 1992 she sang the Countess in *The Queen of Spades* in Barcelona, a role she repeated for her farewell appearance at the Metropolitan Opera on Jan. 2, 1996. Her younger sister Lotte Rysanek (b. Vienna, March 18, 1928) attained a fine reputation in Vienna as a lyric soprano.

BIBL.: P. Dusek and P. Schmidt, *L. R.: 40 Jahre Operngeschichte* (Hamburg, 1990).—NS/LK/DM

Rytel, Piotr, Polish composer and teacher; b. Vilnius, Sept. 20, 1884; d. Warsaw, Jan. 2, 1970. He studied with Michalowski and Noskowski at the Warsaw Cons. In 1911, was appointed a prof. of piano, and in 1918 a prof. of harmony there. He was director of the Sopot State Coll. of Music (1956–61).

WORKS: DRAMATIC: O p e r a : *Ijola* (1927; Warsaw, Dec. 14, 1929); *Koniec Mesjasza* (1935–36); *Krzyzowcy* (1940–41); *Andrzej z Chelmna* (1942–43). **B a l l e t :** *Faun i Psyche* (1931); *Śląski pierścień* (The Silesian Ring; 1956). **ORCH.:** Piano Concerto (1907); 5 symphonic poems: *Grazyna* (1908; rev. 1954), *Poemat* (1910), *Korsarz*, after Byron (The Corsair; 1911), *Sen Dantego* (The Dream of Dante; 1911), and *Legenda o sw. Jerzym* (The Legend of St. George; 1918); 3 syms.: No. 1 (1909), No. 2, *Mickiewiczowska* (in honor of the Polish poet Mickiewicz) for Tenor, Chorus, and Orch. (1949), and No. 3 for Tenor and Orch. (1950–51); Violin Concerto (1950); *Sinfonia concertante* for Flute, Clarinet, Horn, Harp, and Orch. (1960). **CHAMBER:** *Romance* for Clarinet and Piano (1948); *Variations* for Clarinet and Piano (1957).—NS/LK/DM

Ryterband, Roman, Polish-born American pianist and composer; b. Łódź, Aug. 2, 1914; d. Palm Springs, Calif., Nov. 17, 1979. After a period of study in Poland, he lived mostly in Switzerland; eventually settled in America, becoming a naturalized citizen in 1964. His works reflect Polish motifs; his harmonic idiom is mildly modernistic. His works include an "opera grotesque," *Fantomes rebelles*, a music drama, *A Border Incident*, Sonata for 2 Flutes and Harp, Quintet for 2 Flutes, Viola, Cello, and Harpsichord, *Russian Rhapsody* for Orch., *Suite polonaise* for Piano, and assorted pieces for various instrumental combinations.
—NS/LK/DM

Rzewski, Frederic (Anthony), American pianist, teacher, and avant-garde composer; b. Westfield, Mass., April 13, 1938. He studied counterpoint with Thompson and orchestration with Piston at Harvard Univ. (B.A., 1958) and continued his studies with Sessions and Babbitt at Princeton Univ. (M.F.A., 1960); then received instruction from Dallapiccola in Florence on a Fulbright scholarship (1960–61) and from Carter in Berlin on a Ford Foundation grant (1963–65). With Curran and Teitelbaum, other similarly futuroscopic musicians, he founded the M.E.V. (Musica Elettronica Viva) in Rome in 1966; was active as a pianist in various avant-garde settings; played concerts with the topless cellist Charlotte Moorman; also devoted much time to teaching. In 1977 he became prof. of composition at the Liège Cons. As a composer, he pursues the shimmering distant vision of optimistic, positivistic anti-music. He is furthermore a granitically overpowering piano technician, capable of depositing huge boulders of sonoristic material across the keyboard without actually wrecking the instrument.

WORKS: ORCH.: *Nature morte* for 25 Instruments (1965); *A Long Time Man* for Piano and Orch. (1979); *The Price of Oil* for 2 Speakers, Winds, and Percussion (1980); *Satyrica* for Jazz Band (River Falls, Wisc., April 27, 1983); *Una breve storia d'estate* for 3 Flutes and Small Orch. (1983). **INSTRUMENTAL:** Octet for Flute, Clarinet, Trumpet, Trombone, Piano, Harp, Violin, and Double Bass (1961–62); *For Violin* (1962); *Speculum Dianae* for 8 Instruments (1964); *Les Moutons de Panurge* for Variable Ensemble (1969); *Last Judgement* for 1 or More Trombones (1969);

Attica for Narrator and Variable Ensemble (1972); *Coming Together* for Narrator and Variable Ensemble (1972); *What Is Freedom?* for 6 Instruments (1974); *13 Instrumental Studies* (1977); *Song and Dance* for Flute, Bass Clarinet, Vibraphone, and Electric Bass (1977); *Whang Doodles,* trio for Violin, Piano, and Percussion (Chicago, Aug. 20, 1990); *Crusoe* for 4 to 12 Performers (1993). **P i a n o :** *Preludes* (1957); *Poem* (1959); Sonata for 2 Pianos (1960); *Study I* (1960) and *II* (1961); *Falling Music* for Amplified Piano and Tape (1971); *Variations on No Place to Go but Around* (1974); *The People United Will Never Be Defeated,* 36 variations on the Chilean song *El pueblo unido jamas sera vencido!* (1975); *4 pieces* (1977); *4 North American Ballads* (1978–79); *Squares* (1979); *Winnsboro Cotton Mill Blues* for 2 Pianos (1980); *A Machine* for 2 Pianos (1984); Sonata (1991). **O T H E R :** *Spacecraft* (his magnum opus; 1967; "plan for spacecraft" publ. in *Source,* 3, 1968); *Impersonation,* audiodrama (1967); *Requiem* (1968); *Symphony for Several Performers* (1968).—**NS/LK/DM**

S

Saar, Mart, Estonian composer; b. Vastemõisa, Livonia, Sept. 16, 1882; d. Tallinn, Oct. 28, 1963. He was a pupil of Louis Homilius, Rimsky-Korsakov, and Liadov at the St. Petersburg Cons. (1901–11). He was active as a folk-song collector, critic, and teacher in Dorpat, Reval (Tallinn), and Hüpassare; also taught composition at the Tallinn Cons. (1943–56). He was one of Estonia's leading composers, composing orch. music, choral works, including cantatas and many songs, and much piano music.

BIBL.: K. Leichter, *M. S.* (Tallinn, 1964); V. Rumessen, ed., *M. S. sõnas ja pildis* (M. S. in Words and Pictures; Tallinn, 1973). —NS/LK/DM

Saariaho, Kaija (Anneli), significant Finnish composer; b. Helsinki, Oct. 14, 1952. She was a student of Heininen at the Sibelius Academy in Helsinki (1976–81), and also attended the Univ. of Industrial Arts in Helsinki. She pursued training with Ferneyhough and Huber at the Freiberg im Breisgau Hochschule für Musik (diploma, 1983), and also attended the summer courses in new music in Darmstadt (1980, 1982) and worked in computer music at IRCAM in Paris (1982). From 1983 to 1986, and again from 1988 to 1992, she held a Finnish government artist's grant. In 1986 she won the Kranichstein Prize in Darmstadt. She received the Prix Italia in 1988. In 1988–89 she held a composition fellowship at the Univ. of Calif. at San Diego. In 1989 she received the Austrian TV's Ars Electronica. Saariaho has followed an advanced compositional path in which she makes use of tape, live electronics, and computers. Her *Lonh* for Soprano and Electronics (Vienna, Oct. 20, 1996) won the Nordic Council's Music Prize in 2000. Her works are often of striking individuality and communicative power.

WORKS: DRAMATIC: *Maa,* ballet (Helsinki, Oct. 31, 1991); *Clémence,* opera after Amin Maalouf (1999–2000; Salzburg, Aug. 15, 2000); several tape music scores for theater. **ORCH.:** *Verblendungen* for Orch. and Tape (1982–84; Helsinki, April 10, 1984); *Du Cristal* (1989–90; Helsinki, Sept. 5, 1990); *...à la Fumée* (1990; Helsinki, March 20, 1991); *Graal Théâtre* for Violin and Orch. (1994; London, Aug. 29, 1995; also for Violin and Chamber Orch., Helsinki, Sept. 14, 1997); *Forty Heartbreaks* (1998). **CHAMBER:** *Canvas* for Flute (1978); *Yellows* for Horn and Percussion (1980); *Im Traume* for Cello and Piano (1980); *Laconisme de l'aile* for Flute (1982; Freiburg im Breisgau, March 1, 1983); *Jardin Secret II* for Harpsichord and Tape (1984; Savonlinna, July 12, 1986) and *III: Nymphéa* for String Quartet and Live Electronics (N.Y., May 20, 1987); *Lichtbogen* for Chamber Ensemble and Live Electronics (1985–86; Paris, May 13, 1986); *Io* for Chamber Ensemble, Tape, and Live Electronics (1986–87; Paris, July 27, 1987); *Petals* for Cello and Optional Electronics (Bremen, May 20, 1988); *Oi kuu* for Bass Clarinet and Cello (Warsaw, Sept. 15, 1990; also for Bass Flute and Cello); *Amers* for Cello, Chamber Ensemble, and Live Electronics (London, Dec. 8, 1992); *NoaNoa* for Flute and Electronics (Darmstadt, July 23, 1992); *Près* for Cello and Electronics (Strasbourg, Nov. 10, 1992); *6 Japanese Gardens* for Percussion and Electronics (1993); *Solar* for Chamber Ensemble (Antwerp, Oct. 26, 1993); *Nocturne* for Violin (Helsinki, Feb. 16, 1994); *Trois Rivières* for Percussion Quartet and Electronics (Strasbourg, Sept. 25, 1994); *Folia* for Double Bass and Electronics (Lyons, March 23, 1995); *Mirrors* for Cello and Flute (Siegen, June 18, 1997); *Spins and Spells* for Cello (1997); *Neiges* for Cello Octet (Beauvais, May 9, 1998); *Cendres* for Alto Flute, Cello, and Piano (Essen, Sept. 30, 1998); *Couleurs du Vent* for Flute (1998; Kuhmo, July 26, 1999; also for Alto Flute, Lemi-Lappeenranta Festival, Aug. 4, 1999). **VOCAL:** *Bruden* (The Bride), song cycle for Soprano, 2 Flutes, and Percussion (1977); *Jing* for Soprano and Cello (1979); *Nej och inte* (No and not), 3 songs for Women's Quartet or Chorus (1979); *Suomenkielinen sekakuorokappale* (A Piece for Mixed Chorus in the Finnish Language; 1979); *Preludi-Tunnustus-Postludi* (Prelude-Confession-Postlude) for Soprano and Prepared Grand Piano (1980); *Study for Life* for Woman's Voice, Dancer, Tape, and Light (1980); *Kolme Preludia* (3 Preludes) for Soprano and Organ (1980); *...sah den Vögeln* for Soprano, Flute, Oboe, Cello, and Prepared Piano (1981); *Ju lägre solen* for Soprano, Flute, and Guitar (1982; Freiburg im Breisgau, March 1, 1983; rev. 1985 as *Adjö*); *Piipää* for 2 Singers, Tape, and Live Electronics (1987); *Grammaire des Rêves* for Soprano, Alto, 2 Flutes, Harp, Viola, and Cello (1988; Paris, March 20, 1989);

From the grammar of dreams for 2 Sopranos (Huddersfield, Nov. 24, 1988); *Nuits, adieux* for 4 Voices and Live Electronics (Witten, May 11, 1991; also for Chorus, 1996; Paris, March 20, 1997); *Caliban's Dream* for Baritone, Guitar, Mandolin, Harp, and Double Bass (Brussels, March 13, 1993); *Château de l'âme* for Soprano and Orch. (Salzburg, Aug. 9, 1996); *Lonh* for Soprano and Electronics (Vienna, Oct. 20, 1996); *Die Aussicht* for Soprano, Flute, Guitar, Violin, and Cello (1996; Manta, Italy, July 6, 1997; also for Soprano, Flute, Piano, and Cello, 1998); *Miranda's Lament* for Soprano, Clarinet, Harp, Violin, and Contrabass (1997; Järvenpää, Jan. 13, 1998); *Oltra mar* for Chorus and Orch., after Amin Maalouf and Abou Saîd (1998–99; N.Y., Nov. 11, 1999). **ELECTRONIC:** *Stilleben* (1987–88).—**NS/LK/DM**

Sabaneyev, Leonid (Leonidovich), Russian writer on music and composer; b. Moscow, Oct. 1, 1881; d. Antibes, May 3, 1968. He studied with Taneyev at the Moscow Cons., and also took a course in mathematics at the Univ. of Moscow. In 1920 he joined the board of the newly organized Moscow Inst. of Musical Science. In 1926 he left Russia and eventually settled in France. He was an energetic promoter of modern music, and a friend of Scriabin, about whom he wrote a monograph, which would have been important if his account of Scriabin's life and ideology could be trusted; he compromised himself when he wrote a devastating review of Prokofiev's *Scythian Suite* at a concert that never took place. His books in Eng. comprised *Modern Russian Composers* (N.Y., 1927) and *Music for the Films* (London, 1935). His compositions included the ballet, *L'Aviatrice* (Paris, 1928), *Flots d'azur*, symphonic poem (1936), *The Revelation*, oratorio (1940), 2 piano trios (1907, 1924), Violin Sonata (1924), piano pieces, and songs.
—**NS/LK/DM**

Sabata, Victor de
See **De Sabata, Victor**

Sabbatini, Galeazzo, Italian composer and music theorist; b. probably in Pesaro, 1597; d. there, Dec. 6, 1662. He studied with Vincenzo Pellegrini, canon of Pesaro Cathedral. Sabbatini was subsequently canon there (1626–30), then was maestro di cappella to the Duke of Mirandola (1630–39); again served as canon at Pesaro Cathedral (from 1641). He publ. the theoretical vol. *Regola facile e breve per sonare sopra il basso continuo nell'organo, manacordo o altro simile stromento* (Venice, 1628). He publ. 5 books of madrigals *a 2–5* (Venice, 1625–36) and various sacred works.—**LK/DM**

Sabbatini, Giuseppe, Italian tenor; b. Rome, May 11, 1957. He studied double bass at the Cons. di Santa Cecilia in Rome and received private vocal instruction from Silvana Ferraro. After making his operatic debut in Spoleto as Edgardo in 1987, he appeared in such major Italian music centers as Trieste, Naples, Rome, Turin, Florence, Bologna, and Milan. In 1991 he made his first appearance at London's Covent Garden as Lensky, where he sang Des Grieux in 1994. In 1993 he portrayed Rodolfo and Alfredo at the Lyric Opera in Chicago. He was engaged as Faust in Tokyo and Geneva in 1995, and also sang Donizetti's Riccardo Percy at the

San Francisco Opera. In 1997 he appeared as Massenet's Nicias in Nice and as Donizetti's Roberto Devereux in Monte Carlo. He portrayed Rossini's Arnold at the Vienna State Opera in 1998. In addition to his operatic career, he has also appeared in concert settings.
—**NS/LK/DM**

Sabbatini, Luigi Antonio, Italian music theorist and composer; b. Albano Laziale, near Rome, Oct. 24, 1732; d. Padua, Jan. 29, 1809. He studied in Padua and with Padre Martini in Bologna, where he also entered the St. Francis monastery. He was maestro di cappella at the basilica of S. Barnaba in Marino (1767–72). In 1772 he was appointed to the Franciscan basilica of the 12 Holy Apostles in Rome, and in 1786 he took over the duties of maestro di cappella at the Antonius Basilica, succeeding Agostino Ricci, who was in turn the successor of Vallotti. He composed a number of sacred vocal works but his significance rests upon his work as a music theorist. Among his publications were *Notizie sopra la vita e le opere del rev. P.F.A. Vallotti* (Padua, 1780), *Elementi teorici della musica colla pratica dei medesimi, in duetti e terzetti a canone accompagnati dal basso* (Rome, 1789–90), *La vera idea delle musicali numeriche segnature diretta al giovane studioso dell'armonia* (Venice, 1799), and *Trattato sopra le fughe musicali di L.A. Sabbatini corredato da copiosi saggi del suo antecessore F.A. Vallotti* (Venice, 1802).—**NS/LK/DM**

Sacchini, Antonio (Maria Gasparo Gioacchino), prominent Italian composer; b. Florence, June 14, 1730; d. Paris, Oct. 6, 1786. He entered the Cons. of Santa Maria di Loreto at Naples as a violin pupil of Nicola Fiorenza; also received instruction in singing from Gennaro Manna and in harpsichord, organ, and composition from Francesco Durante. His intermezzo *Fra Donato* was performed at the Cons. in 1756; his comic opera *Olimpia* was given at the Teatro dei Fiorentini in 1758, the same year in which he became maestro di cappella straordinario at the Cons.; he was made secondo maestro in 1761. His opera seria, *Olimpiade*, scored a remarkable success at its Padua premiere on July 9, 1763; it subsequently was performed throughout Italy. During a stay in Rome, he produced several comic operas, including *Il finto pazzo per amore* (1765), *La Contadina in corte* (1766), and *L'isola d'amore* (1766). In 1768 he was named director of the Cons. dell'Ospedaletto in Venice; also made a visit to Germany, where he brought out the operas *Scipione in Cartagena* (Munich, Jan. 8, 1770), *Calliroe* (Stuttgart, Feb. 11, 1770), and *L'Eroe cinese* (Munich, April 27, 1770). In 1772 he went to London, where he acquired a notable reputation; among the operas produced there were *Tamerlano* (May 6, 1773), *Montezuma* (Feb. 7, 1775), *Erifile* (Feb. 7, 1778), *L'Amore soldato* (May 4, 1778), *L'Avaro deluso, o Don Calandrino* (Nov. 24, 1778), and *Enea e Lavinia* (March 25, 1779). In 1781 he received an invitation from Marie Antoinette, through the "intendant des menus-plaisirs," to go to Paris. His name was already known in France, since his opera *L'isola d'amore*, arranged as *La Colonie* ("comic opera imitated from the Italian"), had been produced in Paris on Aug. 16, 1775; upon his arrival he was forthwith commissioned to write 3 works at a fee of 10,000 francs each. For this purpose he adapted his Italian opera *Armida e Rinaldo* (Milan, 1772) to a French text as *Renaud*, "tragédie lyrique" in 3 acts (produced at the Académie Royale de Musique, Feb. 25, 1783), and his opera *Il Cidde* (Rome, 1764) as *Chimène* (Fontainebleau, Nov. 18, 1783); the third opera, *Dardanus*, was a new work; it was staged at the Trianon at Versailles, Sept. 18, 1784, in the presence of Louis XVI and Marie Antoinette. In Paris Sacchini found himself in unintended rivalry with Piccinni as a representative of Italian music in the famous artistic war against the proponents of the French operas of Gluck; Sacchini's most successful opera, however, was to the French text *Œdipe à Colonne*, first presented at Versailles (Jan. 4, 1786) and produced at the Paris Opéra (Feb. 1, 1787) after Sacchini's death. It held the stage for half a century, and there were sporadic revivals later on. His last opera, also to a French libretto, *Arvire et Evelina*, was left unfinished, and was produced posth. (Paris Opéra, April 29, 1788; third act added by J.B. Rey). Sacchini found his métier as a composer of serious operas, but his works were nonetheless typical products of the Italian operatic art of his time, possessing melodious grace but lacking in dramatic development. Among his other compositions were 8 oratorios, masses, mass movements, motets, Psalms, arias, 2 syms. (1767), 6 Trio Sonatas, op.1 (London, c. 1775), 6 String Quartets, op.2 (London, 1778), 6 Sonatas for Harpsichord or Piano and Violin, op.3 (London, 1779), and *A Second Set of 6 Favorite Lessons* for Harpsichord or Piano and Violin, op.4 (London, c. 1780).

BIBL.: U. Prota-Giurleo, *S. non nacque a Pozzuoli* (Naples, 1952); F. Schlitzer, *A. S.: Schede e appunti per una sua storia teatrale* (Siena, 1955); U. Prota-Giurleo, *S. a Napoli* (Naples, 1956); idem, *S. fra Piccinisti e Gluckisti* (Naples, 1957); E. Thierstein, *Five French Operas of S.* (diss., Univ. of Cincinnati, 1974). —NS/LK/DM

Sacco, P(atrick) Peter, American composer, tenor, and teacher; b. Albion, N.Y., Oct. 25, 1928. He was born into a musical family and began touring as a child pianist and boy soprano at an early age. Following studies at the Eastman Preparatory School in Rochester, N.Y. (1941–44), he pursued training with Vivian Major and William Willett at the State Univ. of N.Y. at Fredonia (B.M., 1950). During military service, he continued his studies with Wolfgang Niederste-Schee in Frankfurt am Main (1950–52). After his discharge, he completed his training with Barlow, Rogers, and Hanson at the Eastman School of Music in Rochester, N.Y. (M.M., 1954; D.Mus., 1958). From 1959 until his retirement in 1980 he taught at San Francisco State Univ. He also pursued an active career as a concert artist. In his music, Sacco adhered to traditional harmony but developed an ingenious chromatic method of expression.

WORKS: CHAMBER Opera: *Mr. Vinegar* (1966–67; Redding, Calif., May 12, 1967). **ORCH.:** 3 syms.: No. 1 (1955; Oklahoma City, Dec. 17, 1958), No. 2, *Symphony of Thanksgiving* (1965–76; San Francisco, March 23, 1976), and No. 3, *Convocation Symphony* (Redding, Calif., June 1, 1968); 4 *Sketches on Emerson Essays* for Wind Ensemble (1963); Piano Concerto (1964; San Francisco, April 4, 1968); Violin Concerto (1969–74; Walnut Creek, Calif., April 24, 1974); band music. **CHAMBER:** Clari-

net Quintet (1956); String Quartet (1966). **P i a n o :** 2 sonatas (1951, 1965); 4 sonatinas (1962–63); *Variations on Schubert's "An die Musik"* for Piano, 4-Hands (1981). **VOCAL:** 3 oratorios: *Jesu* (Grand Rapids, Mich., Dec. 3, 1956), *Midsummer Dream Night* (San Francisco, June 15, 1961), and *Solomon* (San Francisco, Dec. 12, 1976); cantatas; choruses; anthems; many solo songs.—NS/LK/DM

Sacher, Paul, respected Swiss conductor and philanthropist; b. Basel, April 28, 1906; d. near there, May 26, 1999. He studied with Weingartner (conducting) at the Basel Cons. and with Karl Nef (musicology) at the Univ. of Basel. In 1926 he founded the Basel Chamber Orch., which specialized in playing works from the pre-Classical and contemporary periods. In 1928 he also organized the Basel Chamber Choir. In 1933 he founded the Schola Cantorum Basiliensis, and was also director of the Collegium Musicum in Zürich from 1941. His Schola Cantorum Basiliensis was amalgamated with Basel's Cons. and Musikschule to form the Musikakademie der Stadt Basel, which he directed from 1954 to 1969. He appeared as a guest conductor in many European cities. He made his U.S. debut as a guest conductor with the Collegiate Chorale in N.Y. (April 3, 1955). In 1934 he married Maja Stehlin, widow of Emmanuel Hoffmann, whose father founded the Hoffmann-La Roche pharmaceutical firm, makers of the drugs Valium and Librium. Through his wife's fortune, Sacher was able to pursue his goal of commissioning works from the leading composers of the 20th century; in all, he commissioned over 200 works, including scores by Stravinsky, Bartók, Strauss, Honegger, Hindemith, Martin, Britten, Henze, and Boulez, many of which received their premieres under his direction. In 1983 he purchased the entire Stravinsky archive in N.Y. for $5,250,000. In 1986 the Paul Sacher Foundation building was opened in Basel; it houses the archives of Stravinsky, Webern, Martin, and Maderna, as well as of Sacher.

BIBL.: E. Lichtenhahn and T. Seebass, eds., *Musik Handschriften aus der Sammlung P. S.: Festschrift zu P. S.s siebzigstem Geburtstag* (Basel, 1976); M. Rostropovich, ed., *Dank an P. S.* (Zürich, 1976).—NS/LK/DM

Sachs, Curt, eminent German musicologist; b. Berlin, June 29, 1881; d. N.Y., Feb. 5, 1959. While attending the Gymnasium in Berlin, he studied piano and composition with L. Schrattenholz and clarinet with Rausch. He entered the Univ. there, where he studied music history with Oskar Fleischer, and also art history (Ph.D., 1904). He was active as an art historian until 1909 while receiving instruction in musicology from Kretzschmar and Wolf; then devoted himself to musicology, specializing in the history of musical instruments. In 1919 he became director of Berlin's Staatliche Instrumenten Sammlung; also taught at the Univ. of Berlin, the Staatliche Hochschule für Musik, and the Akademie für Kirchen- und Schulmusik. In 1933 he was compelled to leave Germany; went to Paris as chargé de mission at the Musée de l'Homme; was a visiting prof. at the Sorbonne. In 1937 he settled in the U.S.; was a prof. of music at N.Y.U. (1937–53); also was consultant to the

N.Y. Public Library (1937–52), adjunct prof. at Columbia Univ. (from 1953), and president of the American Musicological Soc. (1949–50).

WRITINGS: *Musikgeschichte der Stadt Berlin bis zum Jahre 1800* (1908); *Musik und Oper am kurbrandenburgischen Hof* (1910); *Reallexikon der Musikinstrumente* (1913); *Handbuch der Musikinstrumentenkunde* (1920; second ed., 1930); *Die Musikinstrumente des alten Ägyptens* (1921); *Katalog der Staatlichen Instrumentensammlung* (1922); *Das Klavier* (1923); *Die modernen Musikinstrumente* (1923); *Geist und Werden der Musikinstrumente* (1929); *Vergleichende Musikwissenschaft in ihren Grundzügen* (1930); *Eine Weltgeschichte des Tanzes* (1933; Eng. tr., 1937); *Les Instruments de musique de Madagascar* (1938); *The History of Musical Instruments* (1940); *The Rise of Music in the Ancient World* (1943); ed. *The Evolution of Piano Music* (1944); *The Commonwealth of Art* (1946); *Our Musical Heritage* (1948; second ed., 1955); *Rhythm and Tempo: A Study in Music History* (1953).

BIBL.: G. Reese and R. Brandel, eds., *The Commonwealth of Music, in Honor of C. S.* (N.Y., 1965).—NS/LK/DM

Sachs, Hans, famous German poet and Meistersinger; b. Nuremberg, Nov. 5, 1494; d. there, Jan. 19, 1576. He was educated at the Nuremberg grammar school (1501–09). After serving his apprenticeship (1511–16), he returned to Nuremberg as a master shoemaker in 1520; joined the Meistersinger guild about 1509, where he received instruction from Linhard Nunnenbeck. Under Sachs, the Meistergesang was an active force in the Reformation movement from 1520. He wrote over 6,000 poetic works, ranging from Meisterlieder to dramatic pieces; he also wrote 13 Meistertone. For his musical works, see E. Goetze and C. Drescher, eds., *Hans Sachs: Sämtliche Fabeln und Schwänke* (Halle, 1893–1913) and F. Ellis, ed., *The Early Meisterlieder of Hans Sachs* (Bloomington, Ind., 1974). Sachs is the central figure in Wagner's opera *Die Meistersinger von Nürnberg*.

BIBL.: C. Schweitzer, *Un Poète allemand au XVIe siècle: Étude sur la vie et les oeuvres de H. S.* (Nancy, 1889); K. Drescher, *Studien zu H. S.* (Marburg, 1891); R. Genée, *H. S. und seine Zeit* (Leipzig, 1894; second ed., 1901); B. Suphan, *H. S.: Humanitätszeit und Gegenwart* (Weimar, 1895); H. Holzschuher, *H. S. in seiner Bedeutung für unsere Zeit* (Berlin, 1906); H. Nutzhorn, *Meistersangeren H. S.* (Copenhagen, 1911); F. Ellis, *H. S. Studies* (Bloomington, Ind., 1941); B. Könneker, *H. S.* (Stuttgart, 1971); H. Brunner, G. Hirschmann, and F. Schnelbogl, eds., *H. S. und Nürnberg: H. S. zum 400. Todestag* (Nuremberg, 1976); N. Holzberg, *H.-S.-Bibliographie* (Nuremberg, 1976); K. Wedler, *H. S.* (Leipzig, 1976).—NS/LK/DM

Sachs, Joel, American pianist, conductor, and musicologist; b. New Haven, Conn., Dec. 19, 1939. He studied piano with Ray Lev and theory with Sam DiBonaventura and David Kraehenbuehl. In 1957 he entered Harvard Coll., majoring in chemistry and physics, but eventually turned to music, studying with Piston, Thompson, Pirotta, and Ward; also took piano lessons with Miklos Schwalb in Boston and with Rosina Lhévinne in N.Y. In 1961 he received a fellowship for travel in Europe; after appearances as a pianist in London in 1963, he returned to the U.S. to study musicology at Columbia Univ., completing his Ph.D. in composition in 1968. He joined similarly inclined musicians and scholars to form Continuum, a group devoted

to the exploration of new music; gave concerts with it in the U.S. and Europe, attaining a considerable reputation for excellence. He also taught and was active as coordinator of contemporary music (from 1985) at the Juilliard School in N.Y. Through the years he gave several hundred concerts and lectures dealing with 20th-century music; also directed radio performances in Europe dedicated to the works of Ives and Webern. In purely musicological pursuits, particularly valuable are his detailed writings on the works of J.N. Hummel, for which he had the cooperation of Hummel's descendants.—NS/LK/DM

Sachse, Leopold, German-American bass, opera producer, and administrator; b. Berlin, Jan. 5, 1880; d. Englewood, N.J., April 3, 1961. He studied at the Cologne Cons., then in Vienna. In 1902 he joined the Strasbourg Opera as a baritone. He then was Intendant in Münster (1907), Halle (1914–19), and at the Hamburg Opera (1922–33), where he produced a number of contemporary works. He was forced to leave his homeland by the Nazis and settled in the U.S. He was a producer at the Metropolitan Opera in N.Y. (1935–55), and also taught stage technique at the Juilliard Graduate School in N.Y. (1936–43); was a stage director at the N.Y.C. Opera (from 1945). He founded his own Opera in English Co. (1951).—NS/LK/DM

Sack (real name, Weber), Erna, German soprano; b. Berlin, Feb. 6, 1898; d. Mainz, March 2, 1972. She studied in Prague and with O. Daniel in Berlin. She made her operatic debut as a contralto at the Berlin Städtische Oper (1925), then turned to coloratura soprano roles and sang in Bielefeld (1930–32), Wiesbaden (1932–34), and Breslau (1934–35); subsequently, in 1935, joined the Dresden State Opera, where she was chosen to create the role of Isotta in Strauss's *Die schweigsame Frau*; appeared with the company as Zerbinetta under Strauss's direction during its visit to London's Covent Garden in 1936. In 1937 she sang opera in Chicago and made a concert tour of the U.S.; also appeared in opera in Milan, Paris, Vienna, Salzburg, and other major European music centers. After World War II, she made an extensive world tour as a concert singer (1947–52); again gave concerts in the U.S. (1954–55). In 1966 she settled in Wiesbaden.—NS/LK/DM

Sacrati, Francesco, Italian composer; b. Parma (baptized), Sept. 17, 1605; d. probably in Modena, May 20, 1650. He was one of the earliest composers for the opera theaters that opened in Venice after 1637; was also a pioneer of opera buffa before the rise of the Neapolitan school. He wrote an opera, *La Delia*, for the opening of the Teatro Crimani dei Santi Giovanni e Paolo in Venice (Jan. 20, 1639); there followed *La finta pazza* (Teatro Novissimo, Venice, Jan. 14, 1641), also one of the earliest Italian operas performed in Paris (Salle du Petit Bourbon, Dec. 14, 1645). Other operas by Sacrati were *Bellerofonte* (Venice, 1642), *L'Ulisse errante* (Venice, 1644), and *L'isola d'Alcina* (Bologna, 1648). All of his operas are lost. In 1649 he became maestro di cappella to the

Modena court. Research by A. Curtis suggests that Sacrati played a major role in preparing the final form of Monteverdi's last opera, *L'incoronazione di Poppea*. —NS/LK/DM

Sade (actually, **Helen Folsade Adu**), pop's enigmatic, sultry, sophisticated chanteuse; b. Ibadan, Nigeria, Jan. 16, 1959. The daughter of a Nigerian teacher and an English nurse, Helen Folsade Adu left her birth country of Nigeria when her parents separated. Her mother moved back to London, where Sade (a nickname based on her middle name) eventually studied fashion design. Some of her creations went on tour with Spandau Ballet in the late 1970s. She also sang with a jazz funk band called Pride. Eventually, she took sax player and guitarist Stuart Matthewman, keyboard player Andrew Hale and bassist Paul Spencer Denman and formed her own band. The simple yet elegant song "Your Love Is King" brought them to the Top Ten throughout Europe. In 1985, she released her debut album *Diamond Life*. Launched with the internationally successful (#5 pop, #1 adult contemporary in the U.S.) "Smooth Operator," the album also went to #5, sold quadruple platinum, and earned her a Best New Artist Grammy. Followed less than a year later by the chart topping, *Promise* she stayed on the pop charts with the #5 hit "The Sweetest Taboo," which also topped the adult charts, and the #20 "Never As Good As the First Time." She spent close to a year on the road supporting the two records. *Promise* eventually sold triple platinum.

Sade took a break, relocating to Madrid. She came back in 1988 with the self-produced album *Stronger Than Pride*, a pun on her earlier band. More raw than her first two records, it launched the hit "Paradise" which topped the R&B charts, and peaked at #16 pop. She spent over a year on the road with the album, which peaked at #7 and went triple platinum. It was another four years before she re-emerged with 1992's *Love Deluxe*. In between, she was married to Spanish filmmaker Carlos Scola, and divorced a year later. Even more stripped down than *Stronger Than Pride*, *Love Deluxe* generated only a modest hit in the #28 "No Ordinary Love" but topped out at #3 and sold quadruple platinum anyway. Since the release of a greatest hits album in 1994, Sade has stayed out of the media spotlight.

DISC.: *Diamond Life* (1984); *Promise* (1985); *Stronger Than Pride* (1988); *Love Deluxe* (1992); *Best of* (1994).—HB

Sadie, Julie Anne (née **McCormack**), American cellist and musicologist; b. Eugene, Ore., Jan. 26, 1948. She was educated at the Univ. of Ore. (B.Mus., 1970), Cornell Univ. (M.A., 1973; Ph.D., 1978), and City Univ. (M.A., 1993). She was active as a cellist and viola da gambist, and later as a player on the Baroque cello. From 1974 to 1976 she taught at the Eastman School of Music in Rochester, N.Y. In 1978 she married **Stanley Sadie** and settled in London, where she has lectured at King's Coll., Univ. of London (1982) and at the Royal Coll. of Music (1986–88). From 1993 to 1998 she was involved in efforts to save and establish a museum in the house where Handel composed *Messiah*. In addition to articles and reviews in various journals, she publ. the vols. *The Bass Viol in French Baroque Chamber Music* (1980), *Everyman Companion to Baroque Music* (1991), and, with R. Samuel, *The New Grove Dictionary of Women Composers* (1994).—NS/LK/DM

Sadie, Stanley (John), eminent English musicologist and lexicographer; b. London, Oct. 30, 1930. He studied music privately with Bernard Stevens (1947–50) and then with Dart, Hadley, and Cudworth at Cambridge (B.A. and Mus.B., 1953; M.A., 1957; Ph.D., 1958, with the diss. *British Chamber Music, 1720–1790*). He was on the staff of Trinity Coll. of Music in London from 1957 to 1965. From 1964 to 1981 he was a music critic on the staff of the *Times* of London. In 1967 he became the ed. of the *Musical Times*, which position he retained until 1987. A distinguished scholar, he wrote the following monographs (all publ. in London): *Handel* (1962), *Mozart* (1966), *Beethoven* (1967; second ed., 1974), *Handel* (1968), *Handel Concertos* (1972), and *Mozart Symphonies* (1986). He also publ. numerous articles in British and American music journals. With Arthur Jacobs, he ed. *The Pan Book of Opera* (London, 1964; rev. ed. as *Opera: A Modern Guide*, N.Y., 1972; new ed., 1984). In 1969 Sadie was entrusted with the formidable task of preparing for publication, as ed.-in-chief, a completely new ed. of *Grove's Dictionary of Music and Musicians*; after 11 years of labor, *The New Grove Dictionary of Music and Musicians* was publ. in London in 1980; this sixth ed., in 20 vols., reflected the contributions of more than 2,400 scholars throughout the world, and was accorded a premier place of honor among the major reference sources of its kind. He also supervised the planning and the early stages of editing of the rev., 28-vol. edition (2000–01). He likewise ed. *The New Grove Dictionary of Musical Instruments* (1984) and was co-ed., with H. Wiley Hitchcock, of *The New Grove Dictionary of American Music* (4 vols., 1986). With A. Hicks, he ed. the vol. *Handel Tercentenary Collection* (Ann Arbor, 1988). He also ed. *The Grove Concise Dictionary of Music* (1988; U.S. ed., 1988, as *The Norton/Grove Concise Encyclopedia of Music*) and *The New Grove Dictionary of Opera* (4 vols., 1992). He likewise ed. *Wolfgang Amadè Mozart: Essays on His Life and His Music* (Oxford, 1995). He served as ed. of the Master Musicians series from 1976. In 1981 he received the honorary degree of D.Litt. from the Univ. of Leicester and was made an honorary member of the Royal Academy of Music in London, and in 1997 an honorary Fellow of the Royal Coll. of Music in London. In 1982 he was made a Commander of the Order of the British Empire. In 1978 he married **Julie Anne Sadie**, with whom he is writing a guide to European composer museums to be publ. in 2001.—NS/LK/DM

Sadra, I Wayan, significant Indonesian composer, performer, and writer on music; b. Denpasar, Bali, Aug. 1, 1953. He attended the local high school cons., Konservatori Karawitan (KOKAR; graduated, 1972), where he specialized in traditional Balinese music, particularly *gender wayang* (music for the Balinese shadow play). In 1973–74 he worked with the well-known experimental Indonesian choreographer Sardono W. Kusumo; after touring with his group in Europe and the Middle East,

Sadra settled in Jakarta, where he studied painting and taught Balinese gamelan at Institut Kesenian Jakarta (IKJ, Jakarta Fine Arts Inst.; 1975–78); also taught Balinese music at the Indonesian Univ. (1978–80), and experimental composition, Balinese gamelan, and music criticism at Sekolah Tinggi Seni Indonesia Surakarta (STSI, National Coll. of the Arts; from 1983), where he earned a degree in composition (1988); concurrently wrote new-music criticism for various Indonesian newspapers, including *Suara Karya* and *Bali Post*. He appeared widely as a performer with traditional Indonesian ensembles; performed throughout Indonesia and Europe, and in Singapore, Japan, Hong Kong, Australia, and Seoul. In 1988 he was keynote speaker at the national Pekan Komponis (Composers' Festival) in Jakarta; in 1989, appeared in Calif. at the Pacific Rim Festival; in 1990, was a featured participant at Composer-to-Composer in Telluride, Colo. Concurrent with the development of Indonesia's national identity has come an increase of national new-music festivals, increased interaction among artists from different regions, and the greater degree of individual freedom to create autonomous music; all have contributed to the emergence of a distinct Indonesian aesthetic and a contemporary art music. Sadra is one of the outstanding young composers to emerge from this period, and his works have contributed much to the development of "musik kontemporer," "komposisi," and "kreasi baru" ("new creations"). He is also concerned with the social context of performance, considering audience development as important as the development of new works. His compositions are often scored for unusual combinations of instruments. In an experimental piece performed at the Telluride Inst., raw eggs were thrown at a heated black panel; as the eggs cooked and sizzled, they provided both a visual and sonic element for the closing of the piece. He also proposed to the mayor of Solo, Central Java, a new work entitled *Sebuah Kota Yang Bermain Musik* (A City That Plays Music), wherein the entire population of the city would make sounds together for a specified 5 minutes; the proposal was not accepted, but Sadra hopes for its realization in the future.

WORKS: *Nadir* for Gong Kebyar (1977); *Lanyad* for Gong Kebyar (1978); *Lad-Lud-an* for Knobbed Gongs from Reong and Terompong, 4 Kempul, Gong, 8 Kendang, 2 Suling, Gentorak, Ceng-Ceng, and Rebab (1981); *Gender* for Javanese Gender, 2 Balinese Gender, and Visual Elements, including Shadow Puppets (1982); *Sekitar 12–14 Menit* for Javanese Gamelan (1987); *Karya spontan* (Spontaneous Creation), accompaniment for Theater Perampok, for Saluang (Sumatran end-blown flute), Gender, Bumbung, and Kenong (1988); *Stay a Maverick* for Javanese Gamelan, Balinese Suling, and Sunda nese Kecapi (1989); *Terus dan Terus* (On and On) for Balinese Drum, Javanese Drum, and Drone Instruments (1989). **DANCE ACCOMPANIMENT:** *Kicaka* for Gender Wayang, Suling Gambuh, Reong, Terompong, and Kendang (1976); *Gatotkaca-Sraya* for Gong Kebyar (1980); *Mecanda* (for children's improvised dance) for Genggong, Ceng-Ceng Kopyak, Tambur, and Gong Kebyar (1981); *Kusalawa* (1984); *Drebah* (1987); *Buhin*, collaborative improvisation for Triplex (Masonite board), Milk Cans Suling Gambuh,

Balinese Drums, Gentorak, Knobbed Gongs, Rebab, and Slentem (1983); *O-A-E-O* for Voices, Flexotone, Kemanak, Suling, Rebab, Kendang, and Javanese Gamelan (1988); *Aku* for Street Musicians, Suling, Singers, and Drums (1990).—NS/LK/DM

Saenz, Pedro, Argentine composer; b. Buenos Aires, May 4, 1915; d. 1995. He studied piano with Alberto Williams and theory with Arturo Palma. In 1948 he went to Paris, where he took lessons with Honegger, Milhaud, and Rivier. Returning to Buenos Aires, he occupied numerous teaching and administrative posts in educational institutions. Among his compositions were *Movimientos sinfónicos* for Orch. (1963); Piano Quintet (1942); String Trio (1955); *Divertimento* for Oboe and Clarinet (1959); *Capriccio* for Harpsichord and String Quartet (1966); numerous piano pieces and songs.—NS/LK/DM

Saeverud, Harald (Sigurd Johan), prominent Norwegian composer, father of **Ketil Hvoslef** (real name, **Saeverud**); b. Bergen, April 17, 1897; d. Siljustl, March 27, 1992. He studied theory at the Bergen Music Academy with B. Holmsen (1915–20) and with F.E. Koch at the Hochschule für Musik in Berlin (1920–21); took a course in conducting with Clemens Krauss in Berlin (1935). In 1953 he received the Norwegian State Salary of Art (a government life pension for outstanding artistic achievement). He began to compose very early, and on Dec. 12, 1912, at the age of 15, conducted in Bergen a program of his own symphonic pieces. His music was permeated with characteristically lyrical Scandinavian Romanticism, with Norwegian folk melos as its foundation; his symphonic compositions are polyphonic in nature and tonal in essence, with euphonious dissonant textures imparting a peculiarly somber character.

WORKS: DRAMATIC: *The Rape of Lucretia*, incidental music to Shakespeare's play (1935; also a *Lucretia Suite* for Orch., 1936); *Peer Gynt*, incidental music to Ibsen's play (1947; Oslo, March 2, 1948; also as 2 orch. suites and a piano suite); *Olav og Kari*, dance scene (1948); *Ridder Blåskjeggs mareritt* (Bluebeard's Nightmare), ballet (Oslo, Oct. 4, 1960). **ORCH.:** 9 syms.: No. 1, in 2 symphonic fantasias (1916–20; Bergen, 1923), No. 2 (1922; Bergen, Nov. 22, 1923; rev. 1934; Oslo, April 1, 1935), No. 3 (1925–26; Bergen, Feb. 25, 1932), No. 4 (Oslo, Dec. 9, 1937), No. 5, *Quasi una fantasia* (Bergen, March 6, 1941), No. 6, *Sinfonia dolorosa* (1942; Bergen, May 27, 1943), No. 7, *Salme* (Psalm; Bergen, Sept. 1, 1945), No. 8, *Minnesota* (Minneapolis, Oct. 18, 1958), and No. 9 (Bergen, June 12, 1966); *Ouverture Appassionata* (1920; retitled second fantasia of his Sym. No. 1); *50 Small Variations* (1931); Oboe Concerto (1938); *Divertimento No. 1* for Flute and Strings (1939); *Syljetone* (The Bride's Heirloom Brooch) for Chamber Orch. or Piano (1939); *Rondo amoroso* for Chamber Orch. or Piano (1939); *Gjaetlevise-Variasjoner* (Shepherd's Tune Variations) for Chamber Orch. (1941); *Siljuslåtten* (Countryside Festival Dance; 1942; also for Piano); *Galdreslåtten* (The Sorcerer's Dance; 1942); *Romanza* for Violin and Orch. or Piano (1942); *Kjempeviseslåtten* (Ballad of Revolt; 1943; also for Piano); Piano Concerto (1948–50); Violin Concerto (1956); *Allegria (Sinfonia concertante)* (1957); Bassoon Concerto (1963); *Mozart-Motto- Sinfonietta* (1971). **CHAMBER:** *20 Small Duets* for Violins (1951); 3 string quartets (1970, 1975, 1978); *Pastorale* (Indian Summer) for Cello (1978). **P i a n o :** *5 Capricci* (1918–19); Sonata (1921); *Tunes and Dances from Siljustl*

(5 vols., 1943–46); 6 sonatinas (1948–50); *Fabula gratulatorum* (1973).

BIBL.: C. Baden, *H. S. 80 år* (Oslo, 1977); L. Reitan, *H. S. (1897–1992): Mannen, musikken og mytene* (Oslo, 1997). **—NS/LK/DM**

Saeverud, Ketil
See **Hvoslef, Ketil**

Safonov, Vasili (Ilich),

eminent Russian pianist, conductor, and pedagogue; b. Ishcherskaya, Caucasus, Feb. 6, 1852; d. Kislovodsk, Feb. 27, 1918. He went to St. Petersburg to study piano with Leschetizky, and entered the Cons. in 1879. He took courses in piano with Brassin and in theory with Zaremba, graduating with a gold medal. After making his debut as pianist with the Imperial Russian Music Society in St. Petersburg on Nov. 22, 1880, he taught piano at the St. Petersburg Cons. (1881–85). In 1885 he was appointed to the piano faculty of the Moscow Cons., and in 1889 became its director, resigning in 1905; among his pupils were Scriabin and Medtner. He conducted the sym. concerts of the Imperial Russian Music Society in Moscow (1889–1905; 1909–11). Safonov was the first modern conductor to dispense with the baton. He achieved international fame as a forceful and impassioned interpreter of Russian music, and conducted in almost all the capitals of Europe. On March 5, 1904, he made his debut as a guest conductor with the N.Y. Phil., obtaining sensational success; as a consequence, he was invited to serve as its conductor (1906–09); at the same time, he was also director of the National Cons. in N.Y. He publ. *A New Formula for the Piano Teacher and Piano Student* (Moscow, 1916; in Eng.).

BIBL.: Y. Ravicher, *V.I. S.* (Moscow, 1959).**—NS/LK/DM**

Sagaev, Dimiter,

Bulgarian composer and teacher; b. Plovdiv, Feb. 27, 1915. He was a student of Stoyanov and Vladigerov at the Bulgarian State Cons. in Sofia (graduated, 1940), where he then taught. His music is Romantic in essence and national in its thematic resources.

WORKS: DRAMATIC: O p e r a : *Under the Yoke* (1965); *Samouil* (1975). **B a l l e t :** *The Madara Horseman* (1960); *Orpheus* (1978). **OTHER:** Incidental music. **ORCH.:** *Youth Suite* (1952); *Sofia,* symphonic poem (1954); *3 Bulgarian Symphonic Dances* (1956); 2 violin concertos (1963, 1964); Viola Concerto (1963); 2 oboe concertos (1964, 1991); 7 syms. (1964, 1977, 1979, 1980, 1981, 1982, 1987); Flute Concerto (1974); Cello Concerto (1977); Concerto for Wind Orch. (1981); Clarinet Concerto (1983); Horn Concerto (1986); Trumpet Concerto (1989); Piano Concerto (1992). **CHAMBER:** 7 string quartets (1945, 1962, 1962, 1963, 1966, 1967, 1968); 2 wind quintets (1961, 1962); Trio for Flute, Violin, and Piano (1974); Quartet for Flute, Viola, Harp, and Piano (1975); Clarinet Sonata No. 3 (1989). **VOCAL:** *In the Name of Freedom,* oratorio (1969); *The Shipka Epic* (1977); *The Artist,* oratorio (1987); songs.**—NS/LK/DM**

Sahl, Michael,

American composer; b. Boston, Sept. 2, 1934. He studied at Amherst Coll. (B.A., 1955), with Sessions and Babbitt at Princeton Univ. (M.F.A.,

1957), with Dallapiccola on a Fulbright fellowship in Florence (1957), and with Citkowitz, Foss, and Copland. From 1963 he wrote various film scores. After serving as a creative associate at the State Univ. of N.Y. at Buffalo (1965), he was pianist and music director for Judy Collins (1968–69), and then music director of WBAI-FM in N.Y. (1972–73). He collaborated with Eric Salzman on a number of music theater pieces, including the opera *Civilizations and its Discontents* (1977), which won the Prix Italia in 1980. They also wrote the book *Making Changes: A Practical Guide to Vernacular Harmony* (1977). In his output, he developed a populist style in which elements of art music and popular music combine to produce a refreshing synergy.

WORKS: DRAMATIC: *Biograffiti* (N.Y., Dec. 14, 1974; in collaboration with E. Salzman); *The Conjuror* (N.Y., June 1, 1975; in collaboration with E. Salzman); *Stauf* (N.Y., May 25, 1976; final version, Philadelphia, Sept. 20, 1987; in collaboration with E. Salzman); *Civilization and its Discontents* (N.Y., May 19, 1977; rev. as a radio opera, 1980; in collaboration with E. Salzman); *An Old-Fashioned Girl* (N.Y., May 19, 1977); *Noah* (N.Y., Feb. 10, 1978; in collaboration with E. Salzman); *The Passion of Simple Simon* (N.Y., Feb. 1, 1979; rev. as a radio opera, 1980; in collaboration with E. Salzman); *Boxes* (1982–83; in collaboration with E. Salzman); *Dream Beach* (N.Y., March 20, 1988); *Body Language* (1995–96). **ORCH.:** 5 syms. (1971, 1973, 1978, 1982, 1983); Violin Concerto (1974). **CHAMBER:** String Quartet (1969); Piano Sonata (1972); *Doina* for Violin, Piano, Double Bass, and Drums (1979); *In the Woods* for Clarinet, Violin, Piano, and Double Bass (1984); *Jungles* for Electric Violin, Electric Guitar, Piano, Double Bass, and Drums (1992); Trio for Violin, Cello, and Piano (1997). **OTHER:** Vocal music; tape pieces. **—NS/LK/DM**

Sahm, Doug,

vocalist, guitarist; b. San Antonio, Tex., Nov. 6, 1941; d. Taos, N.M., Nov. 18, 1999. **The Sir Douglas Quintet,** Tex.-based British-sounding group. **MEMBERSHIP:** Doug Sahm, gtr., fdl., voc.; Augie Meyer, org. (b. San Antonio, Tex., May 31, 1940); Francisco "Frank" Morin, horns (b. Aug. 13, 1946); Harvey Kagan, bs. (b. April 18, 1946); John Perez, drm. (b. Nov. 8, 1942).

In one of the stranger odysseys in the history of rock music, Doug Sahm started his career as a country-music prodigy at age six, switched to rock and roll during the mid-1950s with The Knights, and eventually formed the British- sounding Sir Douglas Quintet in 1964 with organist Augie Meyer, hitting with "She's About a Mover" in 1965. He later introduced Tex-Mex accordionist Flaco Jimenez to rock audiences, and he eventually formed The Texas Tornados in 1989 with Jimenez, vocalist Freddy Fender, and Augie Meyer. Along with Los Lobos, The Texas Tornados helped popularize Tex-Mex music in the 1990s, but Sahm left the group in 1994 to re-form The Sir Douglas Quintet with two of his sons.

Doug Sahm began singing at age five and took up pedal steel guitar at six. He soon began making personal appearances with Webb Pierce and Faron Young, becoming a featured player on the *Louisiana Hayride* country radio program by age eight. Making his first recordings around age 11, he switched to rock and roll in 1955 when he formed The Knights. The group achieved several local hits through 1962.

In late 1964 Doug Sahm assembled The Sir Douglas Quintet with organist Augie Meyer. Traveling to Houston to record for Huey Meaux, the group scored a major hit with Sahm's "She's About a Mover" in 1965, followed by the moderate hit "The Rains Came" and the oddly titled debut album *The Best of the Sir Douglas Quintet*. Meaux hoped to mask their Tex. identities by giving them a British-sounding name and obscuring their faces in a dimly lit cover shot for the album. The band subsequently moved to San Francisco without Meyer, recording *Honkey Blues* for Smash Records. Rejoined by Meyer, they recorded *Mendocino* for Smash, hitting with Sahm's title song. They then recorded two eclectic albums of country, Tex-Mex, blues, and rock songs before Sahm disbanded the group and returned to San Antonio.

Moving to Austin in late 1972, Doug Sahm switched to Atlantic Records for *Doug Sahm and His Band* and *Texas Tornado*. Recorded with stellar backing musicians, including Bob Dylan, Dr. John, and Tex-Mex accordionist Flaco Jimenez, the sessions featured Sahm's "Texas Tornado," Dylan's "Wallflower," and "(Is Anybody Going to) San Antone," released as a single. Sahm switched to Warner Bros. for 1974's *Groover's Paradise*, recorded with Stu Cook and Doug Clifford of Creedence Clearwater Revival. Sahm reunited The Sir Douglas Quintet in 1977 to record *Live Love* for Meyer's Texas Re-Cord label, and he eventually joined John Fahey's Takoma label at the beginning of the 1980s. Sahm toured through the decade both as a solo act and with various backup bands, often reviving the name of the Quintet, even if no other original members were on board.

In 1989 Doug Sahm toured with blues singer Angela Strehli as Antone's Texas R&B Revue, with Flaco Jimenez as special guest. Later in the year he performed in San Francisco with Jimenez, Augie Meyer, and country singer Freddy Fender. Fender, although Mexican-American by birth, had scored top country and smash pop hits with "Before the Next Teardrop Falls" and "Wasted Days and Wasted Nights" in 1975 before his career faded. Jimenez had been playing Tex-Mex music on accordion for nearly 35 years. As The Texas Tornados, the group signed with Reprise Records and recorded three albums that sold quite well and helped popularize Tex-Mex music. However, in 1994 Doug Sahm re-formed The Sir Douglas Quintet with sons Shawn and Shandon to record *Day Dreaming at Midnight*.

DISC.: SIR DOUGLAS QUINTET: *The Best of the Sir Douglas Quintet* (1966); *Honkey Blues* (1968); *Mendocino* (1969); *Together After Five* (1970); *1 + 1 + 1 = 4* (1970); *Rough Edges* (1973); *Texas Tornado* (1973); *Live Love* (1978); *Best* (1980); *Border Wave* (1981); *Quintessence* (1983); *Day Dreaming at Midnight* (1994). **DOUG SAHM:** *The Return of Doug Saldana* (1971); *D. S. and His Band* (1973); *The Best of D. S.'s Atlantic Sessions19* (1992); *Groover's Paradise* (1974); *The Best of D. S. and the Sir Douglas Quintes (1968–1975)* (1990); *Hell of a Spell* (1980); *Juke Box Music* (1989). **THE TEXAS TORNADOS:** *The Texas Tornados* (1990); *Los Texas Tornados* (1991); *Zone of Our Own* (1991); *Hangin' by a Thread* (1992); *Best* (1994).—**BH**

Saikkola, Lauri, Finnish violinist and composer; b. Vyborg, March 31, 1906; d. Helsinki, Sept. 24, 1995. He studied violin at the local music school (1919–28) and composition privately with Akimov and Funtek (1930–34). He was a violinist in the Viipuri (Vyborg) Phil. (1923–34) and the Helsinki Phil. (1934–65). His extensive compositional output followed along traditional lines.

WORKS: DRAMATIC: O p e r a : *Taivaaseen menija*, radio opera (1950); *Ristin* (1957–58). **ORCH.:** *1500m.* (1933); *Lasten maailmasta* for Strings (1933); 10 syms. (1938, 1946, 1949, 1951, 1958, 1982, 1984, 1984, 1985, 1989); *Pieni elegia* for Strings (1939); *Kuvia Karjalasta* (1940–46); *Pieni sävelmä* for Strings (1946); *Canzone* for Strings (1948); *Overtura del dramma* (1949); *Music* for Strings (1950); Violin Concerto (1952); *Concerto da camera* for Piano and Chamber Orch. (1957); *Musica sinfonica* (1966); Concertino for Clarinet and Strings (1968); *Raasepori* (1971); *Concerto miniaturo* for Viola and Strings (1979); 12 sinfoniettas (1983–90); *Tripartita* for Strings (1984). **CHAMBER:** 5 string quartets (1931, 1938, 1983, 1984, 1985); *Divertimento* for Wind Quartet (1968); Wind Quintet (1968); *Notturno* for Violin and Piano (1977); piano pieces. **VOCAL:** *Laulusarja* for Soprano and Orch. (1946); *Kevät merellä* for Tenor or Soprano and Orch. (1977); *Unen kaivo* for Voice and Orch. (1985); many mixed and men's choral pieces; numerous pieces for Voice and Piano.—**NS/LK/DM**

Sainte-Colombe, Sieur de or Monsieur de (real name, August Dautrecourt),

important French bass violist, lutenist, teacher, and composer who flourished in the second half of the 17th century. He was born into the minor nobility, and received training from Nicolas Hotman. After a period in Lyons, he settled in Paris in 1660 and acquired fame as a performer and teacher under the name Monsieur de Sainte-Colombe. Among his notable pupils were Danoville, Marais, Jean Rousseau, and Milton. He was also a notable composer of music for the bass viol, leaving a collection of 67 *Concerts à deux violes esgales* in MS (ed. in Publications de la Société française de musicologie, i/20, 1973).—**LK/DM**

Sainte-Marie, Buffy,

Native American singer, songwriter, artist, activist and mom; b. Piapot Reserve, Saskatchewan, Canada, Feb. 20, 1941. Born on a Cree Reservation in Canada, Sainte-Marie was adopted by a white couple in New England after her mother died in an accident in Edmonton. She was not even aware of her Native-American heritage until her mid-teens. Her memories of her adoptive family seem less than pleasant.

While in college during the early 1960s, Sainte-Marie started to make a name for herself on the folkie coffeehouse circuit with her dark good looks and distinctive, dusky, vibrato-laden alto. Although her voice made her a difficult sell for radio, she showed remarkable ability as a songwriter. During this period, she wrote genuinely touching love songs like "Until It's Time for You to Go" (a Top 40 hit for Elvis) and (later) the Grammy and Oscar winning "Up Where We Belong," and powerful protest songs like "Universal Soldier" (covered by Donovan). Her songs have been performed by artists ranging from Neil Diamond, Barbra Streisand, and Janis Joplin to noted songwriters in their own right like Tracy Chapman. She described her goal as a songwriter as trying "to write the kind of songs that would make as much sense in ancient Rome as they would today."

Signed to Vanguard records (along with many other fellow folkies) in the mid-1960s, Sainte-Marie never experienced a great deal of record company support, but they also let her experiment. She recorded songs with orchestrations by Peter (PDQ Bach) Shickele, covered tunes by dark horses like Leonard Cohen and explored genres from country to flat-out rock. Her future husband Jack Nitzsche produced the *She Used to Wanna Be a Ballerina* album, which featured Ry Cooder and Crazy Horse. Her one Top 40 hit as an artist, "Mister Can't You See" (#38, 1972) came from the *Moon Shot* album which featured soul stalwarts, the Memphis Horns.

In 1976 Sainte-Marie retired from active touring and recording to be a mother, although she and her son Dakota Wolfchild Starblanket appeared for five years as regulars on *Sesame Street*, exposing the young viewers to Native American culture. She became very active within the American Indian Movement. During that time, she earned a Ph.D. in fine art, experimenting with digital images on her computer. She also has degrees in education and Oriental philosophy. She wrote a children's book, *Nokosis and the Magic Hat*, in the mid-1980s. In her home studio, she also began working on creating music digitally, creating the score for a Canadian documentary about strippers.

In 1993, with her high school senior son in the band, Sainte-Marie released and toured to support her first album in a decade and a half, *Coincidence and Likely Stories*. Her 1996 album *Up Where We Belong* found her playing favorite songs, both her own and others, on her new equipment. She claims to sing better in her 50s than when she started, noting in *The London Times*, "When I was just out of college, I couldn't sing my way out of a hat." She also has created the Cradleboard Teaching Project, a multimedia curriculum used throughout the country to teach students in grades 3–12 about the indigenous people of the Americas.

Disc.: *It's My Way!* (1964); *Many a Mile* (1965); *Little Wheel Spin & Spin* (1966); *Fire & Fleet & Candlelight* (1967); *I'm Gonna Be a Country Girl Again* (1968); *Illuminations* (1970); *She Used to Wanna Be a Ballerina* (1971); *Moon Shot* (1972); *Quiet Places* (1973); *Native North American Child: An Odyssey* (1974); *Buffy* (1974); *Changing Woman* (1975); *Sweet America* (1976); *Spotlight on Buffy Sainte-Marie* (1981); *Coincidence & Likely Stories* (1992); *Up Where We Belong* (1996).—**HB**

Saint-Foix, (Marie-Olivier-) Georges (du Parc Poulain), Comte de, eminent French musicologist; b. Paris, March 2, 1874; d. Aix-en-Provence, May 26, 1954. He studied law at the Sorbonne and concurrently attended classes in theory with d'Indy and had violin lessons (diploma, 1906) at the Schola Cantorum in Paris. His principal, and most important, publ. was *Wolfgang-Amédée Mozart, sa vie musicale et son oeuvre, de l'enfance à la pleine maturité* (5 vols., Paris, 1912–46; vols. 1–2 with T. de Wyzewa); also publ. *Les Symphonies de Mozart* (Paris, 1932; second ed., 1948; Eng. tr., London, 1947).—**NS/LK/DM**

Saint-George, ᵗGeorge, noted English viola d'amore player; b. Leipzig (of English parents), Nov. 6, 1841; d. London, Jan. 5, 1924. He studied piano, violin, and theory in Dresden and Prague. His violin teacher, Moritz Mildner of Prague, had a fine viola d'amore, which he lent to Saint-George for practicing; he made such progress on this little-used instrument that he decided to adopt it as a specialty. About 1862 he settled in London and became a manufacturer of string instruments; gave performances on the Welsh crwth for the "Hon. Soc. Cymmrodorion"; also played the viola d'amore in duos with his son, Henry Saint-George (b. London, Sept. 26, 1866; d. there, Jan. 30, 1917), who assisted him on the viola da gamba.—**NS/LK/DM**

Saint-George, Henry, English instrumentalist and writer on music, son of George Saint-George; b. London, Sept. 26, 1866; d. there, Jan. 30, 1917. He studied the violin with his father, with whom he subsequently gave concerts, playing works for early instruments. He was ed. of *The Strad*. He publ. *The Bow: Its History, Manufacture and Use* (1895; third ed., 1922), *The Place of Science in Music* (1905), and *Fiddles: Their Selection, Preservation and Betterment* (1910).—**NS/LK/DM**

Saint-Georges, Joseph Boulogne, Chevalier de, noted West Indian violinist and composer; b. near Basse Terre, Guadeloupe, c. 1739; d. Paris, June 9?, 1799. He was the son of a wealthy Frenchman and a black slave, and was reared in Santo Domingo. He went to Paris with his father in 1749 (his mother joined them in 1760); as a youth he studied boxing and fencing, and became one of the leading fencers of Europe; he also studied music with Jean-Marie Leclair *l'aîné* and with François Gossec (1763–66); the latter dedicated his op.9 string trios to him. In 1769 he became a violinist in the orch. of the Concert des Amateurs, becoming its director in 1773; after it was disbanded in 1781, he founded his own Concert de la Loge Olympique, for which Haydn composed his set of Paris syms.; it was disbanded in 1789. He also continued his activities as a fencer, and visited London in this capacity in 1785 and 1789. In 1791 he became a captain in the National Guard in Lille and soon was charged with organizing a black regiment, the Legion Nationale des Américains et du Midi (among his 1,000 troops was the father of Dumas *père*); when the venture proved of little success, he was relieved of his duties and later imprisoned for 18 months; after living on St. Dominique, he returned to Paris about 1797.

Works: DRAMATIC: O p e r a (all first perf. in Paris): *Ernestine* (July 19, 1777); *La Chasse* (Oct. 12, 1778); *L'Amant anonyme* (March 8, 1780); *Le Droit du seigneur* (n.d.); *La Fille garçon* (Aug. 18, 1787); *Le Marchand de marrons* (1788); *Guillaume tout coeur* (1790). OTHER: 9 symphonies concertantes; 15 violin concertos; chamber music; songs.

Bibl.: E. Derr, *J. B., C. de S.-G.: Black Musician and Athlete in Galant Paris* (Ann Arbor, 1972).—**NS/LK/DM**

Saint-Huberty, Mme. de (real name, Antoinette Cécile Clavel), French soprano; b. Strasbourg, Dec. 15, 1756; d. (murdered) London, July 22, 1812. She studied with J.B. Lemoyne in Warsaw. After

singing in Strasbourg, she went to Paris and appeared as Melissa in Gluck's *Armide* (1777); was a leading singer at the Opéra (1781–90), where she sang in the premiere of Piccinni's *Didon* (1783); also created Hypermnestra in Salieri's *Les Danaïdes* (1784) and the title roles in Edelmann's *Ariane dans l'isle de Naxos* (1782), Sacchini's *Chimène* (1783), and Lemoyne's *Phédre* (1786). With the coming of the Revolution, she left France in the company of the Count of Antraigues; they were married in 1790. When her husband was imprisoned by Napoleon in Italy in 1797, she assisted in his rescue; they finally settled in London, where they were both murdered by a servant.

BIBL.: E. de Goncourt, *Mme. S.-H.* (1885).—NS/LK/DM

Saint-Marcoux, Micheline Coulombe,

Canadian composer and teacher; b. Notre-Dame-de-la-Doré, Quebec, Aug. 9, 1938; d. Montreal, Feb. 2, 1985. After training with François Brassard (piano and harmony) in Jonquière, Quebec (1956–58), she went to Montreal and pursued studies with Yvonne Hubert (piano), Françoise Aubut (theory), and Claude Champagne (composition) at the École Vincent-d'Indy (B.Mus., 1962). She continued her training with Tremblay and Pépin at the Montreal Cons., taking the premier prix in composition in 1967. That same year, she won the Prix d'Europe for her orch. score *Modulaire*. In 1968 she went to Paris and studied electronic music with the Groupe de recherches musicales of the ORTF and received training from Schaeffer at the Cons. She also studied privately with Amy and Guézec. In 1969 she was a founder of the Groupe international de musique electroacoustique de Paris. In 1971 she returned to Montreal and helped organize the Ensemble Polycousmie, which was dedicated to experimenting with electronic techniques in combination with percussion and dance. From 1971 to 1984 she taught at the Montreal Cons. In a number of her works, she applied serial techniques.

WORKS: DRAMATIC: *Tel qu'en Lemieux*, film score (1973); *Comment Wang-Fô fut sauvé*, incidental music (1983); *Transit*, musical theater (1984). **ORCH.:** *Modulaire* for Orch. and Ondes Martenot (1967; Montreal, March 31, 1968); *Hétéromorphie* (1969; Montreal, April 14, 1970); *Luminance* (1978). **CHAMBER:** *Évocations dorances* for Piccolo, 3 Flutes, Oboe, and Clarinet (1964); Flute Sonata (1964); String Quartet (1966); *Équation I* for 2 Guitars (1968); *Séquences* for 2 Ondes Martenot and Percussion (1968; rev. 1973); *Trakadie* for Percussion and Tape (1970); *Épisode II* for 3 Percussion (1972); *Genesis* for Wind Quintet (1975); *Miroirs* for Harpsichord and Tape (1975); *Regards* for 3 Winds, Harp, Piano, Percussion, 3 Strings, and Tape (1978); *Mandala I* for Flute, Oboe, Cello, Piano, and Percussion (1980); *Intégration I* for Cello (1980) and *II* for Violin (1980); *Composition I* for Horn (1981); *Horizon I* for Flute (1981) and *II* for Oboe (1981); *Étreinte* for 3 Ondes Martenot (1984). **P i a n o :** *Suite Doréane* (1961); *Variations* (1963); *Kaleidoscope* (1964); *Assemblages* (1969); *Mandala II* (1980). **VOCAL:** *Chanson d'automne* for Soprano or Tenor, Flute, Violin and Piano (1963; rev. 1966); *Wing Tra La* for Chorus and 6 Performers (1964); *Makazoti* for 8 Voices, 4 Winds, 2 Strings, and Percussion (1971); *Alchera* for Mezzo-soprano, 8 Instruments, Tape, and Lights (1973); *Ishuma* for Soprano and 9 Instruments (1974); *Moments* for Soprano, Flute, Viola, and Cello (1977); *Gésode I* for Soprano

and Piano (1981) and *II* for Tenor and Piano (1981). **ELEC-TROACOUSTIC:** *Bernavir* (1970); *Arksalalartôq* (Paris, Feb. 26, 1971); *Contrastances* (1971); *Moustieres* (1971); *Zones* (1972); *Constellation I* (1980).—NS/LK/DM

Sainton, Prosper (Philippe Cathérine),

French violinist and composer; b. Toulouse, June 5, 1813; d. London, Oct. 17, 1890. He was a pupil of Habeneck at the Paris Cons., winning first prize for violin in 1834. After making a successful tour of Europe, he was a prof. at the Toulouse Cons. (1840–44). He settled in England in 1844, where he was a prof. at the Royal Academy of Music (from 1845) and concertmaster of the orchs. of the Phil. Society (1846–54), the Royal Italian Opera at Covent Garden (1847–71), the Sacred Harmonic Society (from 1848), and at Her Majesty's Theatre (1871–80); served as conductor of the state band and as violin soloist to the Queen (1848–55). He wrote 2 violin concertos and several violin solos. In 1860 he married Charlotte (Helen, née Dolby) Sainton-Dolby (b. London, May 17, 1821; d. there, Feb. 18, 1885), a contralto, teacher, and composer. She prepared a singing manual and also composed cantatas and numerous songs. —NS/LK/DM

Saint-Saëns, (Charles-) Camille,

celebrated French composer; b. Paris, Oct. 9, 1835; d. Algiers, Dec. 16, 1921. His widowed mother sent him to his great-aunt, Charlotte Masson, who taught him to play piano. He proved exceptionally gifted, and gave a performance in a Paris salon before he was 5; at 6, he began to compose; at 7, he became a private pupil of Stamaty; so rapid was his progress that he made his pianistic debut at the Salle Pleyel on May 6, 1846, playing a Mozart concerto and a movement from Beethoven's C minor Concerto, with Orch. After studying harmony with Pierre Maleden, he entered the Paris Cons., where his teachers were Benoist (organ) and Halévy (composition). He won the second prize for organ in 1849, and the first prize in 1851. In 1852 he competed unsuccessfully for the Grand Prix de Rome, and failed again in a second attempt in 1864, when he was already a composer of some stature. His *Ode à Sainte Cécile* for Voice and Orch. was awarded the first prize of the Société Sainte- Cécile (1852). On Dec. 11, 1853, his first numbered sym. was performed; Gounod wrote him a letter of praise, containing a prophetic phrase regarding the "obligation de devenir un grand maitre." From 1853 to 1857 Saint- Saëns was organist at the church of Saint-Merry in Paris; in 1857 he succeeded Léfebure-Wély as organist at the Madeleine. This important position he filled with distinction, and soon acquired a great reputation as virtuoso on the organ and a master of improvisation. He resigned in 1876, and devoted himself mainly to composition and conducting; also continued to appear as a pianist and organist. From 1861 to 1865 he taught piano at the École Niedermeyer; among his pupils were André Messager and Gabriel Fauré. Saint-Saëns was one of the founders of the Société Nationale de Musique (1871), established for the encouragement of French composers, but withdrew in 1886 when d'Indy proposed to include works by foreign composers in its program. In 1875 he married Marie Truffot; their 2 sons died in infancy; they separated in 1881, but were never legally divorced; Madame Saint-Saëns died in Bordeaux on Jan. 30, 1950, at the age of 95. In 1891 Saint-Saëns established a museum in Dieppe (his father's birthplace), to which he gave his MSS and his collection of paintings and other art objects. On Oct. 27, 1907, he witnessed the unveiling of his own statue (by Marqueste) in the court foyer of the opera house in Dieppe. He received many honors: in 1868 he was made a Chevalier of the Legion of Honor; in 1884, Officer; in 1900, Grand-Officer; in 1913, Grand-Croix (the highest rank). In 1881 he was elected to the Institut de France; he was also a member of many foreign organizations; received an honorary Mus.D. degree at the Univ. of Cambridge. He visited the U.S. for the first time in 1906; was a representative of the French government at the Panama-Pacific Exposition in 1915 and conducted his choral work *Hail California* (San Francisco, June 19, 1915), written for the occasion. In 1916, at the age of 81, he made his first tour of South America; continued to appear in public as conductor of his own works almost to the time of his death. He took part as conductor and pianist in a festival of his works in Athens in May 1920. He played a program of his piano pieces at the Saint-Saëns museum in Dieppe on Aug. 6, 1921. For the winter he went to Algiers, where he died.

The position of Saint-Saëns in French music was very important. His abilities as a performer were extraordinary; he aroused the admiration of Wagner during the latter's stay in Paris (1860–61) by playing at sight the entire scores of Wagner's operas; curiously, Saint-Saëns achieved greater recognition in Germany than in France during the initial stages of his career. His most famous opera, *Samson et Dalila*, was produced in Weimar (1877) under the direction of Eduard Lassen, to whom the work was suggested by Liszt; it was not performed in France until nearly 13 years later, in Rouen. He played his first and third piano concertos for the first time at the Gewandhaus in Leipzig. Solidity of contrapuntal fabric, instrumental elaboration, fullness of sonority in orchestration, and a certain harmonic saturation are the chief characteristics of his music, qualities that were not yet fully exploited by French composers at the time, the French public preferring the lighter type of music. However, Saint-Saëns overcame this initial opposition, and toward the end of his life was regarded as an embodiment of French traditionalism. The shock of the German invasion of France in World War I made him abandon his former predilection for German music, and he wrote virulent articles against German art. He was unalterably opposed to modern music, and looked askance at Debussy; he regarded later manifestations of musical modernism as outrages, and was outspoken in his opinions. That Saint-Saëns possessed a fine sense of musical characterization, and true Gallic wit, is demonstrated by his ingenious suite *Carnival of the Animals*, which he wrote in 1886 but did not allow to be publ. during his lifetime. He also publ. a book of elegant verse (1890). For a complete list of his works, see the Durand *Catalogue général et thématique des oeuvres de Saint-Saëns* (Paris, 1897; rev. ed., 1909).

WORKS: DRAMATIC (all first perf. in Paris unless otherwise given): **O p e r a :** *La Princesse jaune* (June 12, 1872); *Le Timbre d'argent* (Feb. 23, 1877); *Samson et Dalila* (Weimar, Dec. 2, 1877); *Étienne Marcel* (Lyons, Feb. 8, 1879); *Henry VIII* (March 5, 1883); *Proserpine* (March 16, 1887); *Ascanio* (March 21, 1890); *Phryné* (May 24, 1893); *Frédégonde* (Dec. 18, 1895); *Les Barbares* (Oct. 23, 1901); *Hélène* (Monte Carlo, Feb. 18, 1904); *L'Ancêtre* (Monte Carlo, Feb. 24, 1906); *Déjanire* (Monte Carlo, March 14, 1911). **B a l l e t :** *Javotte* (Lyons, Dec. 3, 1896). **I n c i d e n - t a l M u s i c T o :** *Antigone* (Nov. 21, 1893); *Parysatis* (Béziers, Aug. 17, 1902); *Andromaque* (Feb. 7, 1903); *La Foi* (Monte Carlo, April 10, 1909); *On ne badine pas avec l'amour* (Feb. 8, 1917). **F i l m :** *L'Assassinat du Duc de Guise* (Nov. 16, 1908). **ORCH.:** Overture to a comic opera (c. 1850); *Scherzo* for Small Orch. (c. 1850); 5 syms.: A major (c. 1850), No. 1 in E-flat major, op.2 (Paris, Dec. 18, 1853), F major, *Urbs Roma* (1856; Paris, Feb. 15, 1857), No. 2 in A minor, op.55 (Leipzig, Feb. 20, 1859), and No. 3, *Organ*, in C minor, op.78 (London, May 19, 1886); *Ouverture d'un opéra comique inachevé*, op.140 (1854); *Tarantelle* for Flute, Clarinet, and Orch., op.6 (1857); 5 piano concertos (all first perf. with the composer as soloist): No. 1, op.17 (1858; Leipzig, Oct. 26, 1865), No. 2, op.22 (Paris, May 6, 1868), No. 3, op.29 (Leipzig, Nov. 25, 1869), No. 4, op.44 (Paris, Oct. 31, 1875), and No. 5, *Egyptian*, op.103 (Paris, June 3, 1896); 3 violin concertos: No. 1, op.20 (1859; Paris, April 4, 1867), No. 2, op.58 (1858; Paris, Feb. 13, 1880), and No. 3, op.61 (1880; Paris, Jan. 2, 1881); *Introduction and Rondo capriccioso* for Violin and Orch., op.28 (1863); *Suite*, op.49 (1863); *Spartacus Overture* (1863); *Marche héroïque*, op.34 (1871); *Romance* for Flute or Violin and Orch., op.37 (1871); *Le Rouet d'Omphale*, op.31 (Paris, Jan. 9, 1872); 2 cello concertos: No. 1, op.33 (1872; Paris, Jan. 19, 1873) and No. 2, op.119 (1902; Paris, Feb. 5, 1905); *Phaéton*, op.39 (Paris, Dec. 7, 1873); *Romance* for Horn or Cello and Orch., op.36 (1874); *Romance* for Violin and Orch., op.48 (1874); *Danse macabre*, op.40 (1874; Paris, Jan. 24, 1875); *La Jeunesse d'Hercule*, op.50 (Paris, Jan. 28, 1877); *Suite algérienne*, op.60 (Paris, Dec. 19, 1880); *Morceau de concert* for Violin and Orch., op.62 (1880); *Une Nuit à Lisbonne*, op.63 (1880; Paris, Jan. 23, 1881); *Jota aragonese*, op.64 (1880); *Rapsodie d'Auvergne*, op.73 (1884); *Wedding Cake* for Piano and Orch., op.76 (1885); *Le Carnaval des animaux* (1886; Paris, Feb. 26, 1922); *Havanaise* for Violin and Orch., op.83 (1887); *Morceau de concert* for Horn and Orch., op.94 (1887); *Rapsodie bretonne*, op.7 bis (1891); *Africa* for Piano and Orch., op.89 (Paris, Oct. 25, 1891); *Sarabande et Rigaudon*, op.93 (1892); *Marche du couronnement*, op.117 (c. 1902); *Caprice andalous* for Violin and Orch., op.122 (1904); *Trois tableaux symphoniques d'après La foi*, op.130 (1908); *Morceau de concert* for Harp and Orch., op.154 (1918); *Cyprès et Lauriers* for Organ and Orch., op.156 (1919); *Odelette* for Flute and Orch., op.162 (1920); also works for Band. **CHAMBER:** 2 piano quartets (1853, 1875); Piano Quintet, op.14 (1855); *Caprice brillant* for Piano and Violin (1859); Suite for Piano and Cello, op.16 (1862); 2 piano trios, opp. 18 and 92 (1863, 1892); *Sérénade* for Piano, Organ, Violin, and Viola or Cello, op.15 (1866; also for Orch.); *Romance* for Piano, Organ, and Violin, op.27 (1868); *Les Odeurs de Paris* for 2 Trumpets, Harp, Piano, and Strings (c. 1870); *Berceuse* for Piano and Violin, op.38 (1871); 2 cello sonatas, opp. 32 and 123 (1872, 1905); *Allegro appassionato* for Cello and Piano, op.43 (1875; also for Cello and Orch.); *Romance* for Piano and Cello, op.51 (1877); Septet for Piano, Trumpet, and Strings, op.65 (1881); *Romance* for Piano and Horn, op.67 (1885); 2 violin sonatas, opp. 75 and 102 (1885, 1896); *Caprice sur des airs danois et russes* for Piano, Flute, Oboe, and Clarinet, op.79 (1887); *Chant saphique* for Piano and Cello, op.91 (1892); *Fantaisie* for Harp, op.95 (1893); *Barca-*

rolle for Violin, Cello, Organ, and Piano, op.108 (1897); 2 string quartets, opp. 112 and 153 (1899, 1918); *Fantaisie* for Violin and Harp, op.124 (1907); *La Muse et le poète* for Violin, Cello, and Piano, op.132 (1910; also for Violin, Cello, and Orch.); *Triptyque* for Piano and Violin, op.136 (1912); *Élégie* for Piano and Violin, op.143 (1915); *Cavatine* for Piano and Trombone, op.144 (1915); *L'Air de la pendule* for Piano and Violin (c. 1918); *Prière* for Organ and Violin or Cello, op.158 (1919); *Élégie* for Piano and Violin, op.160 (1920); Oboe Sonata, op.166 (1921); Clarinet Sonata, op.167 (1921); Bassoon Sonata, op.168 (1921); piano pieces. **VOCAL:** Sacred pieces, including *Oratorio de Noël* for Solo Voices, Chorus, String Quartet, Harp, and Organ, op.12 (1858), *Veni Creator* for Chorus and Organ ad libitum (1858), and *Le Déluge*, oratorio for Solo Voices, Chorus, and Orch., op.45 (1875; Paris, March 5, 1876); secular choral works; song cycles (*Mélodies persanes* [1870], *La Cendre rouge* [1914], etc.); about 100 solo songs; also cadenzas to Mozart's piano concertos K.482 and 491, and to Beethoven's fourth Piano Concerto and Violin Concerto; made various transcriptions and arrangements.

WRITINGS (all publ. in Paris unless otherwise given): *Notice sur Henri Reber* (1881); *Harmonie et mélodie* (1885; ninth ed., 1923); *Charles Gounod et le "Don Juan" de Mozart* (1893); *Problèmes et mystères* (1894; rev. ed., aug., 1922, as *Divagations sérieuses*); *Portraits et souvenirs* (1899; third ed., 1909); *Essai sur les lyres et cithares antiques* (1902); *Quelques mots sur "Proserpine"* (Alexandria, 1902); *École buissonnière: Notes et souvenirs* (1913; abr. Eng. tr., 1919); *Notice sur Le Timbre d'argent* (Brussels, 1914); H. Bowie, ed., *On the Execution of Music, and Principally of Ancient Music* (San Francisco, 1915); *Au courant de la vie* (1916); *Germanophile* (1916); *Les idées de M. Vincent d'Indy* (1919); F. Rothwell, tr., *Outspoken Essays on Music* (London and N.Y., 1922).

BIBL.: C. Bellaigue, *M. C. S.-S.* (Paris, 1889); C. Kit and P. Loanda, *Musique savante. Sur la musique de M. S.-S.* (Lille, 1889); Blondel, *C. S.-S. et son cinquantenaire artistique* (Paris, 1896); O. Neitzel, *C. S.-S.* (Berlin, 1899); E. Solenière, *C. S.-S.* (Paris, 1899); special S.-S. issue of *Le Monde Musical* (Oct. 31, 1901); E. Baumann, *Les Grandes Formes de la musique: L'Oeuvre de S.-S.* (Paris, 1905; new ed., 1923); L. Auge de Lassus, *S.-S.* (Paris, 1914); J. Bonnerot, *C. S.-S.* (Paris, 1914; second ed., 1922); J. Montargis, *C. S.-S.* (Paris, 1919); *Funerailles de S.-S.* (collection of speeches, Paris, 1921); J. Chantavoine, *L'Oeuvre dramatique de C. S.-S.* (Paris, 1921); A. Hervey, *S.-S.* (London, 1921); W. Lyle, *C. S.-S., His Life and Art* (London, 1923); G. Servières, *S.-S.* (Paris, 1923; second ed., 1930); A. Dandelot, *S.-S.* (Paris, 1930); J. Handschin, *C. S.-S.* (Zürich, 1930); J. Normand, *S.-S.* (1930); L. Schneider, *Une Heure avec S.-S.* (1930); J. Langlois, *C. S.-S.* (Moulins, 1934); R. Dumanine, *Les Origines normandes de C. S.-S.* (Rouen, 1937); R. Fauchois, *La Vie et l'oeuvre prodigieuse de C. S.-S.* (Paris, 1938); J. Chantavoine, *C. S.-S.* (Paris, 1947); J. Harding, *S.-S. and His Circle* (London, 1965); S. Ratner, *The Piano Works of C. S.-S.* (diss., Univ. of Mich., 1972); D. Fallon, *The Symphonies and Symphonic Poems of C. S.-S.* (diss., Yale Univ., 1973); E. Harkins, *The Chamber Music of S.-S.* (diss., N.Y.U., 1976); M. Stegemann, *C. S.-S. und das franzosische Solokonzert von 1850 bis 1920* (Mainz, 1984; Eng. tr., 1991); R. Smith, *S.-S. and the Organ* (Stuyvesant, N.Y., 1992).—**NS/LK/DM**

Saito, Hideo, Japanese cellist, conductor, and music educator; b. Tokyo, May 23, 1902; d. there, Sept. 18, 1974. He was a cello student of Julius Klengel in Leipzig (1923–27) and of Feuermann in Berlin (1930). Returning to Japan, he played cello in the Nihon Sym. Orch., and studied conducting with Rosenstock. He was a co-founder of the Toho Music School in Tokyo, where he taught cello, conducting, and academic music courses. Among his students was Seiji Ozawa, who came to regard Saito's influence as a major factor in his own career.—**NS/LK/DM**

Sakač, Branimir, Croatian composer and teacher; b. Zagreb, June 5, 1918; d. there, Dec. 29, 1979. He received training at the Zagreb Academy of Music (graduated, 1941), and later taught there. He adopted a purely structural method of composition, using highly dissonant contrapuntal combinations within strict neo-Classical forms.

WORKS: DRAMATIC: *Songelu* for Light Projections, Actor, and Ensemble (1972);. **ORCH.:** *Serenade* for String Orch. (1947); *Simfonija o mrtvom vojniku* (Sym. of the Dead Soldiers; 1951); Chamber Sym. (1953); *Episode* for Orch. and Tape (1963); *Prostori* (Spaces) for Orch. and Tape (1965); *Syndrome* for Chamber Orch. (1966); *Solo I* for Violin and Chamber Orch. (1968); *Turm-Musik* (Tower Music; 1970). **CHAMBER:** Sonata for Solo Violin (1953); *Study I* for Piano and Percussion (1963); *Structure I* for Chamber Ensemble (1965); *Doppio* for String Quartet (1968); *Attitudes* for Cello and Piano (1969–70); *Scena* for Chamber Ensemble (1971); *A Play* for Chamber Ensemble (1973). **VOCAL:** *Omaggio—Canto della Commedia* for 7 Soloists, Chorus, Violin, and Percussion (1969); *Bellatrix-Alleluia*, cycle of 5 pieces; *Bellatrix-Alleluia* for Voices and Ensemble, *Sial* for Chamber Ensemble and Folk Instruments, *Umbrana* for 12 Voices, *Synthana* for Tape, and *Matrix- Symphony* for 3 Voices and Orch. (1970–73); *Barasou* (Ballad of Rats and Mice) for Voice and Chamber Ensemble (1971). **Piano:** *Aleatory Prélude* for Piano and Tape (1961); *Study II* (1964); *Ad litteram* (1970); *Ariel* (1979).—**NS/LK/DM**

Sala, Nicola, Italian teacher, music theorist, and composer; b. Tocco-Gaudio, near Benevento, April 7, 1713; d. Naples, Aug. 31, 1801. He was a pupil of Fago, Abos, and Leo at the Cons. della Pietà de' Turchini in Naples (1732–40), and apparently taught there for many years, serving as secondo maestro (1787–93) and primo maestro (1793–99). He publ. the celebrated theoretical work *Regole del contrappunto prattico* (3 vols., 1794; reprinted by Choron in Paris, 1808, as *Principii di composizione delle scuole d'Italia*). He brought out several operas: *Vologeso* (Rome, 1737), *La Zenobia* (Naples, Jan. 12, 1761), *Demetrio* (Naples, Dec. 12, 1762), *Merope* (Naples, Aug. 13, 1769), an oratorio, *Giuditta* (1780), masses, litanies, and other religious works.—**NS/LK/DM**

Salabert, Francis, French music publisher; b. Paris, July 27, 1884; d. in an airplane accident at Shannon, Ireland, Dec. 28, 1946. The Editions Salabert was founded by his father, Edouard Salabert (b. London, Dec. 1, 1838; d. Paris, Sept. 8, 1903), in 1896; Francis took over from his ailing father in 1901. A professional musician and composer in his own right, he made a series of practical arrangements for small orch. of numerous classical and modern works, which were widely used. Editions Salabert expanded greatly through the purchase of the stock of orch. and other music of the firms Gaudet (1927), Mathot (1930), Senart (1941), Rouart-Lerolle (1942), and Deiss (1946). On the death of Francis Salabert, his widow assumed the directorship. —**NS/LK/DM**

Salas y Castro, Esteban, Cuban composer; b. Havana, Dec. 25, 1725; d. Santiago de Cuba, July 14, 1803. He studied organ and theology. In 1764 became maestro de capilla in Santiago de Cuba and was also active as a conductor of a chamber ensemble. He became a priest in 1790, and subsequently taught philosophy, theology, and ethics. He wrote mainly villancicos.

BIBL.: P. Hernández Balaguer, *Obras de E. S.* (Santiago de Cuba, 1960).—**NS/LK/DM**

Salazar, Adolfo, eminent Spanish musicologist; b. Madrid, March 6, 1890; d. Mexico City, Sept. 27, 1958. He studied with Falla and Perez Casas, then went to Paris, where he completed his training with Ravel. He was ed.-in-chief of the *Revista Musical Hispano-Americana* (1914–18) and music critic of Madrid's *El Sol* (1918–36); was founder and later secretary of the Sociedad Nacional de Música (1915–22). During the final period of the Spanish Civil War, he was cultural attaché at the Spanish embassy in Washington, D.C. (1938–39); then settled in Mexico City as a writer and teacher, serving on the faculties of the Colegio de México (from 1939) and the National Cons. (from 1946). Salazar was also a composer, numbering 3 symphonic works, *Paisajes, Estampas,* and *Don Juan de los Infernos,* songs to words by Verlaine, and piano pieces among his works.

WRITINGS: *Música y músicos de hoy* (Madrid, 1928); *Sinfonía y ballet* (Madrid, 1929); *La música contemporánea en España* (Madrid, 1930); *La música actual en Europa y sus problemas* (Madrid, 1935); *El siglo romántico* (Madrid, 1935; new ed., 1955, as *Los grandes compositores de la época romántica*); *La música en el siglo XX* (Madrid, 1936); *Música y sociedad en el siglo XX* (Mexico City, 1939); *Las grandes estructuras de la música* (Mexico City, 1940); *La rosa de los vientos en la música europea* (Mexico City, 1940; reissued in 1954 as *Conceptos fondamentales en la historia de la música*); *Forma y expresión en la música: Ensayo sobre la formación de los géneros en la música instrumental* (Mexico City, 1941); *Introducción en la música actual* (Mexico City, 1941); *Los grandes periodos en la historia de la música* (Mexico City, 1941); *Poesía y música en lengua vulgar y sus antecedentes en la edad media* (Mexico City, 1943); *La música en la sociedad europea* (4 vols., Mexico City, 1942–46); *La música moderna* (Buenos Aires, 1944; Eng. tr., 1946, as *Music in Our Time*); *Música, instrumentos y danzas en las obras de Cervantes* (Mexico City, 1948); *La danza y el ballet* (Mexico City, 1949); *La música, como proceso histórico de su invención* (Mexico City, 1950); *J.S. Bach* (Mexico City, 1951); *La música de España* (Buenos Aires, 1953).—**NS/LK/DM**

Salazar, Manuel, Costa Rican tenor; b. San José, Jan. 3, 1887; d. there, Aug. 6, 1950. He was trained in Italy and N.Y. In 1913 he made his operatic debut in Vicenza as Edgardo, and then sang in various Italian opera houses. After appearing in Havana (1917), he toured North America with the San Carlo Opera Co. On Dec. 31, 1921, he made his Metropolitan Opera debut in N.Y. as Alvaro, and remained on its roster until 1923. Among his other roles were Radames, Andrea Chénier, and Canio.—**NS/LK/DM**

Saldoni, Baltasar, Spanish composer and lexicographer; b. Barcelona, Jan. 4, 1807; d. Madrid, Dec. 3,

1889. He was a pupil of Mateo Ferrer in Montserrat and of Francisco Queralt in Barcelona, then completed his studies with Carnicer in Madrid (1829). In 1830 he became prof. of voice training and singing at the Madrid Cons. In 1826 he produced in Madrid his light opera *El triunfo del amor* and the Italian operas *Saladino e Clotilde* (1833), *Ipermestra* (Jan. 20, 1838), and *Cleonice regina di Siria* (Jan. 24, 1840); he also wrote the zarzuelas *La corte de Mónaco* (Feb. 16, 1857) and *Los maridos en las mascaras* (Barcelona, Aug. 26, 1864). His magnum opus as a scholar was the *Diccionario biográfico-bibliográfico de efemérides de músicos españoles,* in 4 vols. (Madrid, 1868–81), to which was added a supplementary vol. in the form of a chronology of births and deaths of Spanish musicians, with exhaustive biographical notes. This monumental compilation, upon which Saldoni worked nearly 40 years, contains (inevitably) a number of errors, but in the absence of other musicographical works on Spanish musicians, it still retains considerable documentary value.—**NS/LK/DM**

Salerno-Sonnenberg, Nadja, gifted American violinist of Russian-Italian descent; b. Rome, Jan. 10, 1961. After violin lessons with Antonio Marchetti, her mother took her to the U.S., where she continued her training with Jascha Brodsky at the Curtis Inst. of Music in Philadelphia (1969–75). In 1975 she went to N.Y. to pursue studies with Dorothy DeLay at the Juilliard School. After winning the Naumburg Competition in 1981, she dropped out of Juilliard sans diploma to launch an independent career. On Feb. 6, 1982, she made her N.Y. recital debut at Alice Tully Hall. In 1983 she was awarded an Avery Fisher Career Grant. Her nonconformist persona, highlighted by her impassioned stage deportment and disdain for conventional attire, made her a popular media figure. All the same, she revealed a genuine talent in her virtuosic performances of the violin literature. Her later career was hampered by personal problems, including an accident to one of her hands and an attempted suicide. However, she persevered and obtained engagements with leading orchs. and as a recitalist. In 1999 she was awarded the Avery Fisher Prize. Her life was the subject of the film *Speaking in Strings* (1999).—**NS/LK/DM**

Sales, Franz, Netherlands composer; b. Namur, c. 1550; d. Prague, July 15, 1599. After serving at the courts in Hechingen and Munich (1580), he was a tenor at the Innsbruck court chapel (1580–87). He then was Kapellmeister at the collegiate foundation for the ladies of families of the nobility in Hall in the Tirol (1587–91), and subsequently a tenor at the Prague imperial court (from 1591). He excelled as a composer of Mass Propers for 5 to 6 Voices (3 vols., Prague, 1596). His brother, Nikolaus Sales (b. probably in Namur, before 1550; d. Stuttgart, April 5, 1606), was a composer who sang at the Stuttgart court chapel (from 1565).—**NS/LK/DM**

Sales, Pablo Hernández
  See **Hernández Sales, Pablo**

Sales (de Sala), Pietro Pompeo, esteemed Italian composer; b. Brescia, c. 1729; d. Hanau, Nov. 21,

1797. After attending the Univ. of Innsbruck, he began his career as a conductor of an Italian opera company; traveled with it in various European cities. He served as director of the court chapel of Prince-Bishop Joseph, Landgrave of Hessen-Darmstadt, in Augsburg and Dillingen an der Donau (1756–68), then was director of the court chapel of the Trier Elector Clemens Wenzeslaus, Prince-Bishop of Augsburg, in Ehrenbreitstein am Rhein (1768–86); subsequently was active at the elector's court in Koblenz, which was disrupted twice during the French Revolutionary wars; he fled the French for the third time in 1797 and made his way to Hanau, dying shortly afterward. He was a distinguished representative of the Italian style.

WORKS: DRAMATIC: O p e r a : *Le nozze di Amore e di Norizia* (Munich, 1765); *Antigona in Tebe* (Padua, 1767); *L'Antigono* (Munich, 1769); *Achille in Sciro* (Munich, 1774); *Il Re pastore* (n.d.). **S i n g s p i e l :** *L'isola disabitata* (Augsburg, 1758); also *Massanissa, oder Die obsiegende Treu*, Jesuit drama (Innsbruck, 1752), and *Le Cinesi*, componimento drammatico (Augsburg, 1757). **O r a t o r i o s :** *Oratorio per la festa del Santo Natale* (Augsburg, 1756); *Giefte* (Mannheim, 1762); *Passion* (Ehrenbreitstein, 1772); *Giuseppe riconosciuto* (Ehrenbreitstein, 1780); *Gioas re di Giuda* (Ehrenbreitstein, 1781); *La Betulia liberata* (Ehrenbreitstein, 1783); *Affectus amantis* (Ehrenbreitstein, 1784); *Sant'Elena* (Koblenz, 1791). **OTHER:** Sacred vocal pieces; 3 syms.; several concertos; etc.

BIBL.: F. Collignon, *P.P. S.* (diss., Univ. of Bonn, 1923). —NS/LK/DM

Saléza, Albert, French tenor; b. Bruges, near Bayonne, Oct. 18, 1867; d. Paris, Nov. 26, 1916. He studied with Bax and Obin at the Paris Cons., making his debut as Mylio in *Le Roi d'Ys* at the Paris Opéra-Comique on July 19, 1888. After appearances in Rouen, Bordeaux, and Nice, he returned to Paris to make his debut at the Opéra as Mathôs in Reyer's *Salammbô* on May 16, 1892. He sang in the posthumous premiere of Franck's *Hulda* in Monte Carlo (March 4, 1894), and then in the premiere of Lefebvre's *Djelma* at the Paris Opéra (May 25, 1894). He made his first appearance at London's Covent Garden as Gounod's Roméo on May 10, 1898, and continued to sing there until 1902; made his Metropolitan Opera debut in N.Y. in the same role on Dec. 2, 1898; was on its roster until 1901, and again in 1904–05; also sang regularly in Paris until 1911, when he joined the faculty of the Cons. He was especially noted for such roles as Gounod's Faust, John of Leyden, Raoul in *Les Huguenots*, Edgardo in *Lucia di Lammermoor*, the Duke of Mantua, Rigoletto, Tannhäuser, Don José, Siegmund, and Otello.—NS/LK/DM

Salieri, Antonio, famous Italian composer and teacher; b. Legnago, near Verona, Aug. 18, 1750; d. Vienna, May 7, 1825. He studied violin and harpsichord with his brother, Francesco, then continued violin studies with the local organist, Giuseppe Simoni. He was orphaned in 1765; subsequently was taken to Venice, where he studied thoroughbass with Giovanni Pescetti, deputy maestro di cappella of San Marco, and singing with Ferdinando Pacini, a tenor there. Florian Gassmann took Salieri to Vienna in 1766 and provided for his musical training and a thorough education in the liberal arts; there he came into contact with Metastasio and Gluck, the latter becoming his patron and friend. His first known opera, *La Vestale* (not extant), was premiered in Vienna in 1768. His comic opera, *Le Donne letterate*, was successfully performed at the Burgtheater in Jan. 1770. The influence of Gluck is revealed in his first major production for the stage, *Armida* (June 2, 1771). Upon the death of Gassmann in 1774, Salieri was appointed his successor as court composer and conductor of the Italian Opera. After Gluck was unable to fulfill the commission for an opera to open the Teatro alla Scala in Milan, the authorities turned to Salieri; his *L'Europa riconosciuta* inaugurated the great opera house on Aug. 3, 1778. While in Italy, he also composed operas for Venice and Rome. He then returned to Vienna, where he brought out his Lustspiel, *Der Rauchfangkehrer* (April 30, 1781). With Gluck's encouragement, Salieri set his sights on Paris. In an effort to provide him with a respectful hearing, Gluck and the directors of the Paris Opéra advertised Salieri's *Les Danaides* (April 26, 1784) as a work from Gluck's pen; following a number of performances, it was finally acknowledged as Salieri's creation. Returning to Vienna, he composed 3 more stage works, including the successful *La grotta di Trofonio* (Oct. 12, 1785). His French opera *Les Horaces* (Paris, Dec. 7, 1786) proved a failure. However, his next French opera, *Tarare* (Paris Opera, June 8, 1787), was a triumphant success. After Da Ponte revised and tr. Beaumarchais's French libretto into Italian and Salieri thoroughly recomposed the score, it was given as *Axur, re d'Ormus* (Vienna, Jan. 8, 1788), and then performed throughout Europe to great acclaim. Salieri was appointed court Kapellmeister in Vienna in 1788, and held that position until 1824; however, he did not conduct operatic performances after 1790. He continued to compose for the stage until 1804, his last major success being *Palmira, regina di Persia* (Oct. 14, 1795).

Salieri's influence on the musical life of Vienna was considerable. From 1788 to 1795 he was president of the Tonkunstler-Sozietat, the benevolent society for musicians founded by Gassmann in 1771; he was its vice-president from 1795; he was also a founder of the Gesellschaft der Musikfreunde. He was widely celebrated as a pedagogue, his pupils including Beethoven, Hummel, Schubert, Czerny, and Liszt. He was the recipient of numerous honors, including the Gold Medallion and Chain of the City of Vienna; he was also a Chevalier of the Légion d'honneur and a member of the French Institut. Salieri's eminence and positions in Vienna earned him a reputation for intrigue; many unfounded stories circulated about him, culminating in the fantastic tale that he poisoned Mozart; this tale prompted Pushkin to write his drama *Mozart and Salieri*, which subsequently was set to music by Rimsky-Korsakov; a contemporary dramatization of the Mozart-Salieri rivalry, Peter Shaffer's *Amadeus*, was successfully produced in London in 1979 and in N.Y. in 1980; it later obtained even wider circulation through the award-winning film version of 1984. Salieri was a worthy representative of the traditional Italian school of operatic composition. He was a master of harmony and orchestration. His many operas are noteworthy for their expressive melodic writing and sensitive vocal treatment. All the same, few held the stage for long, and all have disappeared from the active repertoire. He also composed numerous sacred works, secular works, including cantatas, choruses, and songs, and instrumental pieces.

BIBL.: I. von Mosel, *Über das Leben und die Werke des A. S.* (Vienna, 1827); W. Neumann, *A. S.* (Kassel, 1855); R. Nützlader, *S. als Kirchenmusiker* (diss., Univ. of Vienna, 1924); G. Magnani, *A. S.: Musicista legnaghese* (Legnago, 1934); A. Della Corte, *Un Italiano all'estero: A. S.* (Turin and Milan, 1937); R. Angermüller, *A. S.: Sein Leben und seine weltlichen Werke unter besonderer Berücksichtigung seiner "grossen" Opern* (diss., Univ. of Salzburg, 1970; publ. in 3 vols., Munich, 1971–74); V. Braunbehrens, *S.: Ein Musiker im Schatten Mozarts* (Munich, 1989; Eng. tr., 1992, as *Maligned Master: The Real Story of A. S.*); V. Della Croce and F. Blanchetti, *Il caso S.* (Turin, 1994); J. Rice, *A. S. and Viennese Opera, 1770–1800* (Chicago, 1998).—NS/LK/DM

Salignac, Thomas (real name, **Eustace Thomas**), French tenor, opera director, and teacher; b. Générac, near Nîmes, March 19, 1867; d. Paris, 1945. He studied in Marseilles and with Duvernoy at the Paris Cons. In 1893 he became a member of the Paris Opéra-Comique. On Dec. 11, 1896, he made his debut at the Metropolitan Opera in N.Y. as Don José, remaining on its roster for that season and again from 1898 to 1903. He also sang at London's Covent Garden (1897–99; 1901–04) and again at the Paris Opéra-Comique (1905–14). He sang in the premieres of operas by Laparra, Leroux, Milhaud, and Widor, and in the private premiere of Falla's *El retablo de Maese Pedro* (1923). In 1913–14 he was director of the Nice Opera, and later of an opéra comique company which toured North America in 1926. He was founder-ed. of the journal *Lyrica* (1922–39), and a teacher at the American Cons. in Fontainebleau (1922–23) and at the Paris Cons. (from 1924).—NS/LK/DM

Salimbeni, Felice, Italian castrato soprano; b. Milan, c. 1712; d. Ljubljana, Aug. 1751. He was a student of Porpora. Following his operatic debut in Hasse's *Caio Fabrizio* (Rome, 1731), he sang widely in Italy. He also sang in Vienna, was a court singer in Berlin (1745–50), and won particular success in Hasse's operas in Dresden.—NS/LK/DM

Salinas, Francisco de, eminent Spanish organist and music theorist; b. Burgos, March 1, 1513; d. Salamanca, Jan. 13, 1590. He became blind at the age of 10. He was taught organ, and studied languages at the Univ. of Salamanca. In 1538 he was taken to Rome by Cardinal Pedro Sarmiento de Salinas, where he was made a priest and was granted an annual pension by Pope Paul III. From 1553 to 1558, he was organist at the vice-regal chapel in Naples, and in 1559 he became organist at Sigüenza Cathedral; later was organist at Léon Cathedral. From 1567 he was prof. of music at the Univ. of Salamanca. He wrote the theoretical treatise *De musica libri septem* (Salamanca, 1577), chiefly valuable for the examples of Spanish folk music it contains. It was to Salinas that Luis de Léon dedicated his famous *Odas a Salinas*.

BIBL.: A. Daniels, *The De musica libri VII of Franciscus d.S.* (diss., Univ. of Southern Calif., 1962).—NS/LK/DM

Sallinen, Aulis, prominent Finnish composer; b. Salmi, April 9, 1935. He studied under Merikanto and Kokkonen at the Sibelius Academy in Helsinki (1955–60). He was managing director of the Finnish Radio Sym. Orch. in Helsinki (1960–70) and also taught at the Sibelius Academy (1963–76). Sallinen held the government-bestowed title of Professor of Arts for Life (from 1981), the first such appointment. In 1979 he was made a member of the Royal Swedish Academy of Music in Stockholm. With Penderecki, he was awarded the Withuri International Sibelius Prize in 1983. In his music, he uses modern techniques, with a prevalence of euphonious dissonance and an occasional application of serialism.

WORKS: DRAMATIC: Opera: *Ratsumies* (The Horseman; 1973–74; Savonlinna, July 17, 1975); *Punainen viiva* (The Red Line; 1976–78; Helsinki, Nov. 30, 1978); *Kuningas lähtee Ranskaan* (The King Goes Forth to France; 1983; Savonlinna, July 7, 1984; in Eng., Santa Fe, July 29, 1986); *Kullervo* (1986–88; Los Angeles, Feb. 25, 1992); *Palatsi* (The Palace; 1991–93; Savonlinna, July 26, 1995); *King Lear* (1999–2000). **Ballet:** *Variations sur Mallarmé* (1967; Helsinki, 1968); *Midsommernatten* (Atlanta, March 29, 1984; based on the Sym. No. 3); *Himlens hemlighet* (Secret of Heavens; Swedish TV, Oct. 20, 1986; based on the syms. Nos. 1, 3, and 4). **ORCH.:** 2 *Mythical Scenes* (1956); Concerto for Chamber Orch. (1959–60); *Variations* (1963); *Mauermusik* (1962); *14 Juventas Variations* (1963); *Metamorphoses* for Piano and Chamber Orch. (1964); Violin Concerto (1968); *Chorali* for 32 Wind Instruments, 2 Percussion, Harp, and Celesta (1970); 7 syms.: No. 1 (Helsinki, Dec. 2, 1971), No. 2, *Symphonic Dialogue,* for Percussion and Orch. (1972; Norrköping, Feb. 25, 1973), No. 3 (Helsinki, April 8, 1975), No. 4 (Turku, Aug. 9, 1979), No. 5, *Washington Mosaics* (Washington, D.C., Oct. 10, 1985), No. 6, *From a New Zealand Diary* (1989–90; Napier, New Zealand, Sept. 6, 1990), and No. 7, *The Dreams of Gandalf* (Göteborg, Nov. 27, 1996); *Chamber Music I* for Strings (1975), *II* for Alto Flute and Strings (1975–76; Helsinki, Oct. 1976), and *III: The Nocturnal Dances of Don Juanquixote* for Cello and String Orch. (Naantali, June 15, 1986); Cello Concerto (1976; Lucerne, Aug. 1977); *Shadows,* prelude (Washington, D.C., Nov. 30, 1982); *Fanfare* for Brass and Percussion (Houston, May 17, 1986); *Sunrise Serenade* for 2 Trumpets, Piano, and Strings (Helsinki, Oct. 12, 1989); Flute Concerto (Helsinki, March 8, 1995); *Palace Rhapsody,* after the opera (1996; Cheltenham, July 6, 1997); *A Solemn Overture* (Monte Carlo, Oct. 12, 1997). **CHAMBER:** 5 string quartets: No. 1 (1958), No. 2, *Canzona* (1960), No. 3, *Some Aspects of Peltoniemi Hintrik's Funeral March* (1969; also for String Orch.), No. 4, *Quiet Songs* (1971), and No. 5, *Pieces of Mosaic* (1983; Kuhmo, July 18, 1984); *Elegy for Sebastian Knight* for Cello (1964); *Quattro per quattro* for Oboe or Flute or Clarinet, Violin, Cello, and Harpsichord (1964–65); *Cadenze* for Violin (1965); *Notturno* for Piano (1966); *Quatre études* for Violin and Piano (1970); *Chaconne* for Organ (1970); Sonata for Solo Cello (1971); *Metamorfora* for Cello and Piano (1974); *Canto and Ritornello* for Violin (1975); *Echoes from a Play* for Oboe and String Quartet (1990; Chicago, July 30, 1991); *From a Swan Song* for Cello and Piano (1991). **VOCAL:** *Suite grammaticale* for Children's Chorus and Chamber Orch. (1971); *4 Dream Songs* for Soprano and Orch. (1972); *Songs from the Sea* for Children's Chorus (1974); *Dies Irae* for Soprano, Bass, Men's Chorus, and Orch. (1978; Budapest, Oct. 15, 1979); *Song around*

a Song for Children's Chorus (1980; Wiesbaden, May 16, 1981); *The Iron Age: Suite* for Soprano, Children's Chorus, Mixed Chorus, and Orch. (1983; Helsinki, March 20, 1985); *The Beaufort Scale,* humoresque for Chorus (1984); *Anthem for Ants* for Women's Chorus (Tapiola, April 16, 1988); *Elaman ja Kuoleman Lauluja* (Songs of Life and Death) for Baritone or Mezzo-soprano, Chorus, and Orch. (1994–95; Helsinki, Jan. 18, 1995); *Hold Fast Your Dreams* for Women's Chorus and Children's Chorus (1996; also for Boy's Chorus or Mixed Chorus).
—NS/LK/DM

Salmanov, Vadim (Nikolaievich), Russian composer and teacher; b. St. Petersburg, Nov. 4, 1912; d. there (Leningrad), Feb. 27, 1978. He studied piano with his father and theory with Akimenko. He studied composition with Gnessin at the Leningrad Cons. (1936–41), where he later was head of its composition dept. (1947–51), a teacher (1951–65), and a prof. (from 1965). His early works are marked by broad Russian melodism, with the harmonic structure following the models of Prokofiev and Shostakovich; after 1960 he adopted more advanced techniques, including dodeca-phony.

WORKS: DRAMATIC: B a l l e t : *The Man* (1960). **ORCH.:** *Little Symphony* for Strings (1941); *The Forest,* symphonic picture (1948); *Russian Capriccio* (1950); *Slavic Dance* (1952); *Poetic Pictures,* symphonic suite (1952); 4 syms. (1952, 1959, 1963, 1976); Sonata for Piano and Strings (1961); *Children's Symphony* (1962); 2 violin concertos (1964, 1974); *Nights in the Big City* for Violin and Chamber Orch. (1969); *Monologue* for Cello and Chamber Orch. (1972). **CHAMBER:** 6 string quartets (1945; 1947, rev. 1958; 1961; 1963; 1968; 1971); 2 violin sonatas (1945, 1962); 2 piano trios (1946, 1949); Piano Quartet (1947). **VOCAL:** *Soja,* symphonic poem for Voice and Orch. (1951); *The 12,* oratorio, after Alexander Blok (1957); 2 cantatas: *Ode to Lenin* (1970) and *The Scythians,* after Alexander Blok (1973); choruses; songs, including *Spain Is in My Heart* for Mezzo-soprano and Piano (1962).

BIBL.: M. Aranovsky, *V.N. S.* (Leningrad, 1961).
—NS/LK/DM

Salmen, Walter, respected German musicologist; b. Paderborn, Sept. 20, 1926. He began musicological training with Besseler at the Univ. of Heidelberg and also took organ and composition lessons with Poppen, Fortner, and Petersen. He continued musicological study at the Univ. of Münster (Ph.D., 1949, with the diss. *Das deutsche Tenorlied bis zum Lochamer Liederbuch*) and completed his Habilitation at the Univ. of Saarbrücken in 1958 with his *Der fahrende Musiker im europäischen Mittelalter* (Kassel, 1960). He became a research asst. at the Deutsches Volksliedarchiv in Freiburg im Breisgau in 1950, and then was made prof. (1963) and research fellow (1964) at the Univ. of Saarbrücken; after serving as prof. and director of the musicological inst. at the Univ. of Kiel (1966–73), he was engaged as prof. and director of the musicological inst. at the Univ. of Innsbruck, positions he held until 1993. He ed. the Müller-Blattau Festschrift (Saarbrücken, 1960), *Beiträge zur Musikanschauung im 19. Jahrhundert* (Regensburg, 1965), *Kieler Schriften zur Musikwissenschaft* (Kassel, 1967–74), *Der Sozialstatus des Berufsmusikers vom 17. bis 19. Jahrhundert* (Kassel, 1971), *Innsbrucker Beitrage zur Musikwis-*senschaft (Innsbruck, 1977–97), *The Social Status of the Professional Musician from the Middle Ages to the 19th Century* (N.Y., 1983), and *Der musikalische Satz* (Innsbruck, 1987).

WRITINGS: *Das Lochamer Liederbuch* (Leipzig, 1951); *Die Schichtung der mittelalterlichen Musikkultur in der ostdeutschen Grenzlage* (Kassel, 1954); *Das Erbe des ostdeutschen Volksgesanges: Geschichte und Verzeichnis seiner Quellen und Sammlungen* (Würzburg, 1956); *Johann Friedrich Reichardt* (Freiburg im Breisgau, 1963); *Geschichte der Musik in Westfalen* (Kassel, 1963–67); *Geschichte der Rhapsodie* (Freiburg im Breisgau, 1966); *Haus- und Kammermusik: Privates Musizieren im gesellschaftlichen Wandel zwischen 1600 und 1900* (Leipzig, 1969); *Musikgeschichte Schleswig-Holsteins von der Frühzeit bis zur Reformation* (Neumünster, 1972); *Musikleben im 16. Jahrhundert* (Leipzig, 1976); *Bilder zur Geschichte der Musik in Österreich* (Innsbruck, 1983); *Musiker im Porträt* (Munich, 1983); *Der Spielmann im Mittelalter* (Innsbruck, 1983); *Das Konzert: Eine Kulturgeschichte* (Munich, 1988); *Tanz im 17. und 18. Jahrhundert* (Leipzig, 1988); *Tanz im 19. Jahrhundert* (Leipzig, 1989); *Jüdische Musikanten und Tänzer vom 13. bis 20. Jahrhundert: "—denn die Fiedel macht das Fest"* (Innsbruck, 1991); *"Critiques Musicaux d'Artiste": Künstler und Gelehrte schreiben über Musik* (Freiburg im Breisgau, 1993); *König David: Eine Symbolfigur in der Musik* (Fribourg, 1995); *Beruf: Musiker—Verachtet, Vergöttert, Vermarktet—Eine Sozialgeschichte in Bildern* (Kassel, 1997); *Der Tanzmeister: Geschichte und Profile eines Berufes vom 14. bis 19. Jahrhundert* (Hildesheim, 1997); *Tanz und Tanzen im Mittelalter und in der Renaissance* (Hildesheim, 1999).

BIBL.: M. Fink, R. Gstrein, and G. Mössmer, eds., *Musica Privata: Festschrift für W. S. zum 65. Geburtstag* (Innsbruck, 1992).
—NS/LK/DM

Salmenhaara, Erkki (Olavi), Finnish composer and musicologist; b. Helsinki, March 12, 1941. He studied composition with Kokkonen at the Sibelius Academy in Helsinki (diploma, 1963). Following further training from Ligeti in Vienna (1963), he studied musicology with Tawaststjerna at the Univ. of Helsinki (Ph.D., 1970, with a diss. on the music of Ligeti). In 1963 he joined the faculty there, serving as prof. of musicology from 1975 until 1999. From 1963 to 1973 he was a music critic for the Finnish daily *Helsingin Sanomat*. He served as chairman of the Soc. of Finnish Composers from 1974 to 1976 and of the Assn. of Finnish Sym. Orchs. from 1974 to 1978. Salmenhaara has publ. or ed. some 20 books on music theory and history, including monographs on Ligeti and the Brahms syms., and biographies of Sibelius and Madetoja. He also wrote the survey on the era from Romanticism to World War II in the 4-vol. history of Finnish music (1995–96). After a radical avant-garde period in the early 1960s, Salmenhaara turned toward a neo-tonal style of composition.

WORKS: DRAMATIC: O p e r a : *Portugalin nainen* (The Portuguese Woman; 1970–72; Helsinki, Feb. 4, 1976). **ORCH.:** 5 syms.: No. 1, *Crescendi* (1962; Helsinki, Jan. 11, 1963; rev. 1963), No. 2 (1963; Helsinki, Jan. 17, 1964; rev. 1966), No. 3 (Turku, Dec. 5, 1963; rev. 1964), No. 4, *Nel mezzo del cammin di nostra vita* (1971–72; Helsinki, Oct. 13, 1972), and No. 5, "*Lintukoto*" (Isle of Bliss) for Soprano, Baritone, Chorus, and Orch., after Aleksis Kivi (1989; Helsinki, March 24, 1990); *Le bateau livre* (Helsinki, June 1, 1965; rev. 1966); *Suomi—Finland* (1966; Helsinki, Oct. 31, 1967); *La fille en mini-jupe* (1967; Helsinki, Feb. 13,

1968); *Canzonetta per archi* (1971; Savonlinna, July 10, 1972); *Illuminations* (1971); Horn Concerto (1973; Oslo, Oct. 3, 1974); *Canzona per piccola orchestra* (Kuopio, July 26, 1974); *Poema* for Violin or Viola or Cello and String Orch. (1975; Graz, May 28, 1976); *Introduction and Chorale* for Organ and Orch. (1978; Helsinki, Dec. 1, 1979); *Lamento per orchestra d'archi* (Kokkola, Aug. 26, 1979); Concerto for 2 Violins and Orch. (1980; Finnish Radio, Jan. 18, 1988); *Adagio* for Oboe and Strings (1981; Porvoo, June 13, 1982; also for Oboe and Piano or Organ); *Adagietto* (1981; Finnish Radio, Dec. 23, 1982); Cello Concerto (1983–87; Lahti, March 24, 1988); *Sinfonietta per archi* (1985; Kokkola, Feb. 16, 1986); *Elegy V* for Strings (Paris, Dec. 13, 1995). **CHAMBER:** *Adagio* for Violin or Cello and Piano (Helsinki, May 1960; from the first Cello Sonata); 2 cello sonatas: No. 1 (Helsinki, May 1960; rev. 1969) and No. 2 (1982; Helsinki, June 26, 1986); *Elegy I* for 3 Flutes, 2 Trumpets, and Double Bass (1963; Finnish TV, May 23, 1964), *II* for 2 String Quartets (1963; Helsinki, May 8, 1964), *III* for Cello (1965; Helsinki, Feb. 20, 1966), and *IV* for Viola (Helsinki, Nov. 1, 1967); Wind Quintet (Hässelby, Sweden, Aug. 28, 1964); *Prelude, Pop Tune and Fugue* for Flute (1967; Stockholm, March 31, 1968); *Trois scènes de nuit* for Violin and Piano (Stockholm, April 11, 1970); *And the Fire and the Rose are One* for 2 Violins (1971; London, Jan. 17, 1972); *Leggenda* for Harp (1971; Helsinki, March 5, 1972); Quartet for Flute, Violin, Viola, and Cello (1971; Copenhagen, Feb. 1972); Sonatine for 2 Violins (1972; Amsterdam, Jan. 31, 1973); String Quartet No. 1 (1977; Jyväskylä, June 29, 1978); Sonatine for Flute and Guitar (1981; Helsinki, May 26, 1986); *Ballade* for Harp or Kantele (1981; first perf. on 2 kanteles, Helsinki, May 14, 1983); *Inventio* for Kantele or Harp (1981); Violin Sonata (1982; Finnish Radio, Sept. 11, 1983); Suite for Accordion (Ikaalinen, June 12, 1983); *Introduction and Allegro* for Clarinet or Viola, Cello, and Piano (1985; Turku, Oct. 12, 1990); 2 bagatelles: No. 1 for Flute and Harp (1989; Helsinki, Nov. 13, 1990) and No. 2 for Flute and Harp or Piano (Helsinki, Dec. 8, 1991); *Sarja puhaltimille* (Suite for Winds) for Flute, Oboe, Clarinet, and Bassoon (1995). **KEYBOARD: Piano:** *17 Small Pieces* (1957–60); 4 sonatas: No. 1 (1965–66), No. 2 (Hässelby, Sweden, Sept. 30, 1973), No. 3 (1975; Helsinki, Oct. 13, 1976), and No. 4 (1980; Finnish Radio, July 13, 1982); *Kocab* (Helsinki, Nov. 5, 1972); *Thème and variations sur le nom Erik Tawaststjerna* (1976; Kuopio, Feb. 11, 1977); Sonatine (Helsinki, Oct. 22, 1979); *Little Suite* (1980). **Organ:** *Toccata* (Weimar, Oct. 21, 1965); *Prelude—Interlude—Postlude* (1969); *Ricercata* (1971; Lahti, Aug. 9, 1977); *Introduction and Toccata* (1985; Helsinki, April 9, 1986). **Harpsichord:** *Etude* (Helsinki, Feb. 16, 1969). **VOCAL:** *3 Japanese Songs* for Voice and Piano (1960; rev. 1964; Helsinki, May 21, 1966); *Lenore*, song cycle for Mezzo-soprano or Baritone and Piano (1962–64; Helsinki, March 21, 1965); *Kuun kasvot* (The Face of the Moon), song cycle for Chorus (1964); *Requiem profanum* for Soprano, Alto, Baritone, Organ, Piano, and String Orch. (1968–69; Helsinki, May 24, 1969); *Syyskuu Romaniassa* (Autumn in Romania), song cycle for Mezzo-soprano and Piano (Helsinki, Sept. 21, 1970); *Satumaisessa metsässä* (In a Fairytale Forest), song cycle for Soprano and Piano (Helsinki, Oct. 27, 1974); *Missa profana* for Chorus (Tampere, June 3, 1977); *Selene*, song cycle for Baritone and Piano (1977; Finnish Radio, Oct. 25, 1978); *Ruususolmu* (The Rose Knot) for Chorus (1988; Joensuu, March 30, 1989); *Senteniae Trimalchionis* for Chorus (1991; Helsinki, May 9, 1992); *Neljä Mustapään laulua* (Four Songs to Words by Mustapää) for Soprano and Piano (1995; Finnish Radio, May 17, 1996); other choral pieces and songs.—**NS/LK/DM**

Salmhofer, Franz, Austrian conductor, operas administrator, and composer; b. Vienna, Jan. 22, 1900; d. there, Sept. 22, 1975. He studied composition with Schreker and Schmidt at the Vienna Academy of Music and musicology with Guido Adler at the Univ. of Vienna. In 1929 he became conductor at the Vienna Burgtheater, for which he composed incidental music, ballets, and operas; he resigned in 1939; from 1945 to 1955, was director at the Vienna State Opera; then was director of the Vienna Volksoper (1955–63). In 1923 he married the pianist Margit Gál.

WORKS: DRAMATIC: Opera: *Dame im Traum* (Vienna, Dec. 26, 1935); *Iwan Sergejewitsch Tarassenko* (Vienna, March 9, 1938); *Das Werbekleid* (Salzburg, Dec. 5, 1943); *Dreikönig* (1945; Vienna, 1970). **Ballet:** *Das lockende Phantom* (1927); *Der Taugenichts in Wien* (1930); *Österreichische Bauernhochzeit* (1933); *Weihnachtsmarchen* (1933). Also incidental music to about 300 plays.—**NS/LK/DM**

Salminen, Matti, notable Finnish bass; b. Turku, July 7, 1945. He studied at the Sibelius Academy in Helsinki and with Luigi Rossi in Rome. In 1966 he joined the Finnish National Opera in Helsinki, where he sang his first major role, Verdi's Philip II, in 1969. From 1972 to 1979 he was principal bass of the Cologne Opera. In 1973 he sang Fafner at Milan's La Scala and Glinka's Ivan Susanin in Wexford. He made his first appearance at London's Covent Garden as Fasolt in 1974. From 1975 he sang at the Savonlinna Festival. In 1976 he made his debut at the Bayreuth Festival as Hunding. On Jan. 9, 1981, he made his Metropolitan Opera debut in N.Y. as King Marke. He appeared as Boris Godunov in Zürich in 1985. In 1990 he sang Hunding at the Metropolitan Opera, a role he repeated in 1997 to great acclaim. During the 1992–93 season, he was engaged as King Philip at the Deutsche Oper in Berlin. After singing Fasolt at the Lyric Opera in Chicago in 1996, he portrayed Fafner at the Metropolitan Opera in 1997. In 1999 he appeared as King Marke at the Salzburg Easter Festival and as Hagen at the Finnish National Opera. His performances in operas by Mozart, Wagner, and Verdi have been much admired.

BIBL.: P. Tuomi-Nikula, *Kuningasbasso: M. S.* (Porvoo, 1994).—**NS/LK/DM**

Salmond, Felix (Adrian Norman), distinguished English cellist and pedagogue; b. London, Nov. 19, 1888; d. N.Y., Feb. 19, 1952. He studied at the Royal Coll. of Music in London with W.E. Whitehouse, and in Brussels with Edouard Jacobs. He made his debut in London (1909), accompanied at the piano by his mother, Mrs. Norman Salmond. He was the soloist in the premiere of Elgar's Cello Concerto, under Elgar's direction, in London on Oct. 27, 1919; after a European tour, he settled in America (debut, N.Y., March 29, 1922); was head of the cello dept. at the Curtis Inst. of Music in Philadelphia (1925–42) and taught at the Juilliard Graduate School of Music in N.Y. (from 1924). He enjoyed a reputation as a fine chamber music player and an excellent teacher; was the mentor of Orlando Cole, Leonard Rose, Bernard Greenhouse, and many other cellists of distinction.—**NS/LK/DM**

Salò, Gasparo de
  See **Gasparo da Salò**

Salomon, Johann Peter, German violinist, impresario, and composer; b. Bonn (baptized), Feb. 20, 1745; d. London, Nov. 25, 1815. He was a member of the Electoral orch. at Bonn (1758–62); after a successful concert tour he was engaged as concertmaster and composer to Prince Heinrich of Prussia at Rheinsberg (1764). When the orch. was disbanded (c. 1780), Salomon went to Paris and then to London, where he settled in 1781. He made his debut at Covent Garden on March 23 of that year; began promoting concerts in 1783, introducing syms. by Haydn and Mozart in 1786. In 1790 he went to Italy to engage singers for the Italian Opera in London, and from there went to Vienna, where he saw Haydn and persuaded him to accept an engagement in London. At Salomon's behest Haydn wrote the works familiarly known as his "Salomon Symphonies"; it is through his association with Haydn's 2 visits to England, in 1790–91 and 1794–95, that Salomon's name remains in the annals of music. He was a founder of the Phil. Soc. in London (1813), conducting its first concert on March 8, 1813. His own works are of merely antiquarian interest and include the operas *Les Recruteurs* (Rheinsberg, 1771), *Le Séjour du bonheur* (Berlin, March 5, 1773), *Titus* (Rheinsberg, 1774), *La Reine de Golconde* (Rheinsberg, 1776), and *Windsor Castle, or The Fair Maid of Kent* (Covent Garden, London, April 6, 1795; in collaboration with R. Spofforth). He also wrote an oratorio, *Hiskias* (1779) and other vocal works, several violin concertos, string trios, string quartets, sonatas for violin and cello, etc.—**NS/LK/DM**

Salomon, (Naphtali) Siegfried, Danish cellist and composer; b. Copenhagen, Aug. 3, 1885; d. there, Oct. 29, 1962. He studied with Rudinger, Malling, and Bondesen at the Copenhagen Cons. (1899–1902), Klengel in Leipzig, and Le Flem in Paris. Returning to Copenhagen, he was principal cellist in the Tivoli Orch. (from 1903) and a cellist in the Royal Orch. (1907–56). He also pursued a solo career. He wrote an opera, *Leonora Christina* (1926); 2 syms. (1916, 1920); Violin Concerto (1916); 2 cello concertos (1922, 1958); Piano Concerto (1947); 6 string quartets and other chamber music; piano pieces; songs.—**NS/LK/DM**

Salonen, Esa-Pekka, spirited Finnish conductor and composer; b. Helsinki, June 30, 1958. He entered the Sibelius Academy in Helsinki as a horn pupil of Holgar Fransman in 1973, taking his diploma in 1977. He then studied composition with Rautavaara and conducting with Panula, and subsequently studied with Donatoni in Siena, attended the Darmstadt summer course, and finally received instruction from Castiglioni in Milan (1980–81). After appearances as a horn soloist, he took up conducting and was a guest conductor throughout Scandinavia, and later extended his activities to include Europe. In 1984 he made his U.S. debut as a guest conductor with the Los Angeles Phil. He became principal conductor of the Swedish Radio Sym. Orch. in Stockholm in 1984, and led it on a tour of the U.S. in

1987. He also served as principal guest conductor of the Oslo Phil. (from 1984) and the Philharmonia Orch. in London (from 1985). In 1989 he was appointed music director of the Los Angeles Phil., which tenure began in 1992. In his music, Salonen tends toward pragmatic aural accessibility, employing fairly modern techniques while preserving the formal centrality of traditional tonality.

WORKS: ORCH.: *Apokalyptische Phantasie* for Brass Band and Tape (1978); *Boutade* for Violin, Cello, Piano, and Orch. (1979); *...auf den ersten Blick und ohne zu wissen,* alto saxophone concerto (1980–81; Helsinki, Sept. 22, 1981; rev. 1983); *Giro* (1982; rev. version, Porvoo, June 29, 1997); *Mimo II* for Oboe and Orch. (Helsinki, Dec. 14, 1992); *L.A. Variations* (1996; Los Angeles, Jan. 16, 1997); *Gambit* (Holland Festival, June 6, 1998). **CHAMBER:** *Horn Music I* for Horn and Piano (1976) and *II* for 6 Horns, Percussion, and Tape (1979); Cello Sonata (1976–77); *Nachtlieder* for Clarinet and Piano (1978); *Sets* for Brass Quintet (1978); *Prologue* for Oboe, Violin, Cello, and Percussion (1979); *Goodbye* for Violin and Guitar (1979–80); Wind Quintet (1982); *Meeting* for Clarinet and Harpsichord (Helsinki, Dec. 14, 1982); *Yta I* for Alto Flute (Kemijarvi, Nov. 17, 1982), *II* for Piano (Helsinki, Sept. 26, 1985; also for Harpsichord, March 11, 1987), and *III* for Cello (1986; Viitasaari, July 23, 1987); *Second Meeting* for Oboe and Piano (Stockholm, Feb. 23, 1992). **VOCAL:** *Aubades* for Flute, Soprano, and Strings (1977–78); *Floof* for Soprano and Instrumental Ensemble (1982; Helsinki, Aug. 27, 1988; rev. 1990); *5 Images After Sappho,* song cycle for Soprano and Orch. (Ojai, Calif., June 4, 1999). **TAPE:** *Baalal* (Finnish Radio, Helsinki, July 7, 1982).—**NS/LK/DM**

Salonen, Sulo (Nikolai), Finnish organist and composer; b. Pyhtää, Jan. 27, 1899; d. Porvoo, May 21, 1976. He was a pupil of Furuhjelm and Palmgren at the Helsinki Cons. (1917–22; 1926–29). He then was organist in Jacobstad (1929–48) and Sibbo (1952–64).

WORKS: *Passion Cantata* (1942); *Viisauden ylistys* (In Praise of Wisdom) for Narrator, Voices, and Instruments (1961); *Requiem* (1962); Wind Quintet (1962); String Trio (1971); 2 string quartets (1971, 1972); *Cum jubilo* for Chorus, Organ, and Percussion (Helsinki, Jan. 24, 1974); about 50 motets; numerous organ pieces.—**NS/LK/DM**

Salter, Lionel (Paul), English conductor, pianist, harpsichordist, and writer on music; b. London, Sept. 8, 1914. He studied at the Royal Coll. of Music in London and at the Univ. of Cambridge with Dent and Ord (B.A., 1935; B.Mus., 1936), then returned to the Royal Coll. of Music, where he studied conducting with Lambert and piano with Benjamin. He began his career working in radio and television in London, and in 1945 he became asst. conductor of the BBC Theatre Orch. From 1948 he held administrative posts with the BBC, retiring in 1974. His books include *Going to a Concert* (London, 1950), *Going to the Opera* (London, 1955), *The Musician and His World* (London, 1963), and *Music and the 20th-Century Media* (with J. Bornoff; Florence, 1972); he also compiled a useful *Gramophone Guide to Classical Music and Recordings.*—**NS/LK/DM**

Salt-N-Pepa, one of the first, most important, and longest running of all woman acts in rap. **MEMBERSHIP:** Salt (real name, Cheryl James), rapper (b. Brooklyn, N.Y., March 8, 1963); Pepa (real name, Sandy

Denton), rapper (b. Kingston, Jamaica, Nov. 9, 1969); Pamela Green, DJ. Later Spinderella (real name, Deidre Roper), DJ (b. N.Y.C., Aug. 3) replaced Green. In the early 1980s, Cheryl James and Sandy Denton were both nursing students at Queens Borough Comm. Coll., supporting themselves by working in the telephone sales department at Sears, with Kid n Play and Martin Lawrence as workmates. Another fellow worker was Hurby "Luv Bug" Azor (not to be confused with Bronx rap pioneer Herbie "Luv Bug" Starsky), also a college student at N.Y.C.'s Center for Media Arts. As a final project, Azor wanted to produce a rap record, and asked James and Denton if they would be his "talent." They went into the studio and cut "The Show Stopper," an answer record to Doug E. Fresh and Slick Rick's hit "The Show." Azor got an A, but more important the record was released under the name Supernature, where it rose to #46 on the R&B chart in 1985. This launched Azor's production career and the "Salt n Pepper MCs" (as they called themselves on the record—a reference to James's slightly lighter complexion) getting signed to a larger rap- oriented independent record company, Next Plateau. Azor remained with them as their manager, producer, alleged songwriter, and James's boyfriend.

James and Denton entered the studio with Azor and a new deejay, Pamela Green. Their Next Plateau debut, 1986's *Hot, Cool and Vicious*, started off as a moderate success, with three mid-level R&B hits: "Chick on the Side," "My Mike Sounds Nice," and a reworking of the Otis Redding/Carla Thomas hit "Tramp." A San Francisco deejay liked the flip side of the latter cut better and created a remix of the frankly sexy "Push It." It rose to #19 pop, going platinum and taking the album to platinum and #26.

Before they went in to record *A Salt with a Deadly Pepa*, Green left the group and was replaced by Diedre "DJ Spinderella LaToya" Roper. The record produced a couple of moderate hits, including a reworking of the Isley Brothers' "It's Your Thing," which they recorded as "Shake Your Thing" with the Washington D.C. go-go band EU. That tune went to the R&B Top Ten, the album reached #38 pop and went gold in 1988.

Striking while the iron was still at least lukewarm, they released a remix package, *A Blitz of Salt n Pepa Hits*, an ironic title as it turned out, because their greatest music and success was yet to come. During the three years between *A Salt...* and their next release, *Black's Magic*, the group became more active in their direction and started to shoulder Azor out of the way, with good results. With each of the trio co-producing, along with the help of Steevee-O, 1990's *Black Magic* was a breakthrough, bringing a level of conscious Afro-centricity to the pop image the group had put forward on its first two albums, without losing the sexy fun of its more pop side. The first single, "Expression," went high in the R&B charts before running up to #26 on the pop charts and going platinum. "Do You Want Me" reached #21 pop and went gold. The anthemic "Let's Talk about Sex," aided by an amazing video, went to #13 pop and also sold gold. They later turned it into an even more important project, recutting it as "Let's Talk about AIDS," an extended public service announcement for safe sex. The album reached #38 and platinum status.

Over the next two years, the group separated from Azor. In 1993, Salt-N-Pepa released their fourth album, *Very Necessary*. The new album brought a sheen of sophistication to their previously jejune sexuality, which went over in a very big way. The first single, "Shoop" rose to #4 and went gold. The follow-up, a reworking of an obscure single by Stax artist Linda Lyndell's "What a Man" recorded with vocal group En Vogue, reached #3 and went platinum. The third single, "None of Your Business," only reached #32, but came out in time to be eligible for the 1995 Grammy Awards, winning for Best Rap Performance. They went on tour with R. Kelly.

Another three-year hiatus followed, with the group recording a tune here and there for soundtracks and appearing in the film *Who's Da Man*. They headlined the 1995 fundraising project, "Ain't Nothing But a She Thing," with their contribution hitting #38 on the pop charts. During the fall of 1997, the group put out *Brand New*. Despite an eclectic line-up of guest artists, including Kirk Franklin, Sheryl Crow, and Queen Latifa, the album didn't perform as well as expected, despite going gold. Denton married Treach from Naughty By Nature. James had already married and had a couple of children. Roper made a solo album (with an appearance by Salt-n-Pepa) and opened a Queens-based day spa. Denton opened a clothing boutique in Atlanta. Another greatest hit package was planned for release in 2000.

DISC.: *Hot, Cool & Vicious* (1986); *A Salt with a Deadly Pepa* (1988); *Black's Magic* (1990); *Very Necessary* (1993); *Brand New* (1997).—**HB**

Saltzmann-Stevens, Minnie, American soprano; b. Bloomington, Ill., March 17, 1874; d. Milan, Jan. 25, 1950. She studied voice with Jean De Reszke in Paris. She made her operatic debut as Brünnhilde in the English version of the *Ring* at London's Covent Garden in 1909; she continued to sing there until 1913; also appeared at the Bayreuth Festivals of 1911 and 1913. From 1911 to 1914 she sang with the Chicago Grand Opera. Her other roles included Kundry, Isolde, and Sieglinde.—**NS/LK/DM**

Salva, Tadeáš, Slovak composer; b. Lúčky, near Ružonberok, Oct. 22, 1937; d. Bratislava, Jan. 3, 1995. Following early training with Viliam Kostka, he studied cello, accordion, and piano at the Žilina Cons. (1953–58). During this time, he also took composition lessons with Zimmer in Bratislava. He continued his composition studies with Moyzes and Cikker at the Bratislava Academy of Music and Drama (1958–60). Subsequently he completed his composition training with Szabelski in Katowice and Lutosławski in Warsaw. From 1965 to 1968 he was head of the music dept. of the Czech Radio in Košice. He then was a dramaturg for the Czech TV in Bratislava (1965–77) and the Slovak Folk Artistic Ensemble (1977–88). In his music, Salva embraced sonorism with occasional excursions into aleatory procedures.

WORKS: DRAMATIC: *Margita a Besná*, television opera (1971); *The Weeping*, radio opera (1977); *Reminiscor*, ballet-opera (1982). **ORCH.:** Cello Concerto (1966); *Burlesca*, concerto for Violin and Chamber Ensemble (1970); *Étude* (1972); Concertante

Sym. (1978); *Musica in memoriam Arthur Honegger* for Trumpet, Bass, Organ, and Strings (1978); *Rhapsody* for Violin and Orch. (1981); *Symfonia pastoralis* (1983); *12 Symphonic Préludes* (1987); *Ballad Symphony* (1989); *Liturgical Chamber Symphony* (1989); *Slovak Concerto Grosso No. 5* for Violin, English Horn, Bass Clarinet, Organ, and Strings (1989); *Slovak Liturgical Concerto Grosso* for Strings (1994). **CHAMBER:** 4 string quartets (1959, 1962, 1973, 1988); *Ballad* for Violin (1974); *Musica...Musica* for Brass and Winds (1979); *Fairy Tales about Magic Violins Playing Themselves* for Violin, Piano, and Percussion (1979); *Variations in memoriam J. Ježek* for Flute, Clarinet, Double Bass, Piano, and Percussion (1982); *Slovak Rhapsody No. 1* for Clarinet, Trumpet, Cimbalom, and Percussion (1984); *Impressions* for Horn and Piano (1986); *Étude* for 3 Violins and Tape (1987); *Slovak Concerto Grosso No. 3* for Clarinet, Cello, and Organ (1988) and *No. 4* for Flute, Clarinet, Violin, Cello, and Piano (1988); *Saxofoniada* for 4 Saxophones (1988); *3 Arias* for Cello and Piano (1990); piano pieces; organ music. **VOCAL:** Concerto for Reciter, 4 Men's Voices, Clarinet, and Percussion (1964); *Requiem aeternam* (1967); *Ballad-Fantasia* for Soprano, Piano, and Orch. (1971); *Wedding Ballad* for Soprano, Alto, Chorus, Bass Clarinet, Viola, Double Bass, and Flute (1972); *Elegies* for Soprano, Reciter, Chorus, and Chamber Ensemble (1972); *Good Morning, My Deceased Ones* for Soprano and Men's Chorus (1973); *Slovak Concerto Grosso No. 1* for Alto, Baritone, and Folk Instruments (1978) and *No. 2* for Soprano, Bass, and Chamber Ensemble (1981); *Aria* for Soprano, Alto, Tenor, Bass, and Piano (1980); *Mechúrik-Koúrik and his Friends* for Soloists, Women's Chorus, and Orch. (1983); *The Purest Love*, cantata (1984); *Slovak Song of Songs*, oratorio for Soprano, Bass, Chorus, Organ, and Orch. (1987); *Slovak Vocal Concerto Grosso* for Soprano, Alto, Tenor, Bass, and Chorus (1993).—**NS/LK/DM**

Salvador, Sal (Sergio), jazz guitarist; b. Monson, Mass., Nov. 21, 1925; d. Sept. 22, 1999. His father gave him his first guitar; after hearing Charlie Christian, he took up electric guitar and studied with Oscar Moore, Hy White, and Eddie Smith. He played with local groups in Springfield, Mass., then moved to N.Y. in 1949; on the recommendation of his friend Mundell Lowe, he got a job at Radio City Music Hall in 1951. Salvador then worked at NBC studios and toured with Terry Gibbs, Eddie Bert, and the Dardanelles. He returned to N.Y., formed a quartet with Lowe, and became a studio musician for Columbia, backing up Tony Bennett, Julie London, Rosemary Clooney, and Marlene Dietrich. He played with Stan Kenton (summer 1952–December 1953), led a quartet with Eddie Costa (1954), and played at the Newport Jazz festival (1958), a performance that was captured in the film, *Jazz on a Summer's Day.* He formed the group Colors in Sound, then moved to the West Coast, where he played occasionally in duets with guitarist Alan Hanlon during the 1970s. Salvador led a big band during the 1980s and was also head of the guitar department at the Univ. of Bridgeport during this time. Since 1989, he has led the quintet Crystal Image.

DISC.: *Sal Salvador Quintet* (1953); *Kenton Presents Jazz: Sal Salvador* (1954); *Frivolous Sal* (1956); *Shades of Sal Salvador* (1956); *A Tribute to the Greats* (1957); *Colors in Sound* (1958); *Beat for This Generation* (1959); *Sal Salvador Quartet* (1961); *You Ain't Heard Nothin Yet* (1963); *Music to Stop Smoking By* (1964); *Starfingers* (1978); *Juicy Lucy* (1978); *Parallelogram* (1978); *In Our Own Sweet Way* (1982); *World's Greatest Jazz Standards* (1983); *Plays Gerry Mulligan* (1984); *Sal Salvador and Crystal Image* (1989); *Way of the Wind* (1994); *Lorinda's Kitchen* (1995); *Second Time Around* (1996).—**LP**

Salvayre, Gaston (actually, **Gervais-Bernard**), French composer; b. Toulouse, June 24, 1847; d. St. Ague, near Toulouse, May 17, 1916. He was a pupil at the Toulouse Cons., then entered the Paris Cons., studying organ with Benoist and composition with Ambroise Thomas. After failing to win the Prix de Rome for 5 consecutive years, he finally obtained it in 1872 with the cantata *Calypso.* He subsequently devoted himself mainly to composition and also wrote music criticism for *Gil Blas.* He was made a Chevalier of the Légion d'honneur in 1880.

WORKS: DRAMATIC: O p e r a : *Le Bravo* (Paris, April 18, 1877); *Richard III* (in Italian as *Riccardo III*, St. Petersburg, Dec. 21, 1883; in French, Nice, Jan. 29, 1891); *La Dame de Monsoreau* (Paris, Jan. 30, 1888); *Solange* (Paris, March 10, 1909); *Egmont* (Paris, Dec. 6, 1886). **B a l l e t :** *Le Fandango* (Paris, Nov. 26, 1877); *La Fontaine des fées* (Paris, 1899); *L'Odalisque* (Paris, 1905); also *Calypso*, dramatic scene (1872). **ORCH.:** *Le Jugement dernier* (Paris, Dec. 3, 1876; also known as *La Résurrection* and *La Vallee de Josaphat*); *Ouverture symphonique* (Paris, March 22, 1874); *Air et Variations* for String Orch. (1877). —**NS/LK/DM**

Salvi, Lorenzo, Italian tenor; b. Ancona, May 4, 1810; d. Bologna, Jan. 16, 1879. He made his debut at the Teatro San Carlo in Naples in 1830, then sang at La Scala in Milan (1839–42); during his tenure there, he created the title role in Verdi's *Oberto*; also the role of Riccardo in *Giorno di regno.* He made guest appearances at Covent Garden in London (1847–50) and in N.Y. He became particularly known for his roles in operas by Bellini and Donizetti.—**NS/LK/DM**

Salvini-Donatelli, Fanny (real name, **Francesca Lucchi**), Italian soprano; b. Florence, 1815; d. Milan, June 1891. She made her debut at the Teatro Apollo in Venice as Rosina in 1839, then sang throughout Italy. She also appeared in Vienna (1842) and in London at Drury Lane (1858), and likewise appeared in various other European music centers. She retired from the stage in 1859 but briefly resumed her career in 1865. She created the role of Violetta in *La Traviata* in 1853 in Venice and distinguished herself in other Verdi operas. —**NS/LK/DM**

Salviucci, Giovanni, Italian composer; b. Rome, Oct. 26, 1907; d. there, Sept. 4, 1937. He studied with Respighi and Casella, and also took courses in law at the Univ. of Rome. He then taught at the Istituto Muzio Clementi in Rome and wrote music criticism for the *Rassegna Nazionale.* He developed a fine style of instrumental writing; his works were performed by Italian orchs. with increasing frequency, but his early death cut short his promising career. His Overture in C-sharp minor (1932) received a national prize.

WORKS: ORCH.: *La Tentazione e la preghiera*, symphonic poem (1931); *Sinfonia italiana* (1932; Rome, Feb. 25, 1934);

Overture in C-sharp minor (1932); Sinfonia da camera (1933); Introduzione, Passacaglia e Finale (1934). **CHAMBER:** String Quartet (1932); *Serenata* for 9 Instruments (1937). **VOCAL:** *Psalm of David* for Soprano and Chamber Orch. (Rome, 1935); *Alcesti* for Chorus and Orch., after Euripides (1937); songs.

BIBL.: G. Arledler, *Prospettive critiche su G. S.* (diss., Univ. of Bologna, 1974).—**NS/LK/DM**

Salzedo (actually, Salzédo), (Léon) Carlos,

eminent French-born American harpist, pedagogue, and composer; b. Arcachon, April 6, 1885; d. Waterville, Maine, Aug. 17, 1961. He studied at the Bordeaux Cons. (1891–94), winning the premier prix in piano; then entered the Paris Cons., where his father, Gaston Salzedo, was a prof. of singing; studied with Charles de Bériot (piano), gaining the premier prix in 1901, and with Hasselmans (harp), also receiving the premier prix. He began his career as a concert harpist upon graduation; traveled all over Europe (1901–05); was solo harpist of the Association des Premiers Prix de Paris in Monte Carlo (1905–09). In 1909 he settled in N.Y.; was first harpist in the orch. of the Metropolitan Opera (1909–13). In 1913 he formed the Trio de Lutèce (from Lutetia, the ancient name for Paris), with Georges Barrère (flute) and Paul Kéfer (cello). In 1921 he was co-founder, with Edgard Varèse, of the International Composers' Guild in N.Y., with the aim of promoting modern music; this organization presented many important contemporary works; in the same year, he founded a modern music magazine, *Eolian Review*, later renamed *Eolus* (discontinued in 1933). He became a naturalized American citizen in 1923. He taught at the Inst. of Musical Art in N.Y., and the Juilliard Graduate School of Music; organized and headed the harp dept. at the Curtis Inst. of Music in Philadelphia. In 1931 he established the Salzedo Harp Colony at Camden, Maine, for teaching and performing during the summer months. Salzedo introduced a number of special effects, and publ. special studies for his new techniques; designed a "Salzedo Model" harp, capable of rendering novel sonorities (Eolian flux, Eolian chords, gushing chords, percussion, etc.). His own compositions are rhythmically intricate and contrapuntally elaborate and require a virtuoso technique. He publ. *Modern Study of the Harp* (N.Y., 1921; second ed., 1948), *Method for the Harp* (N.Y., 1929), and *The Art of Modulating* (with L. Lawrence; N.Y., 1950).

WORKS: 3 *morceaux* for Harp (1913); *Terres enchantées* or *The Enchanted Isle*, symphonic poem for Harp and Orch. (1918; Chicago, Nov. 28, 1919, composer soloist); 5 *Poetical Studies* for Harp (1918); 3 *Poems* for Soprano, 6 Harps, and 3 Wind Instruments (1919); *Bolmimerie* for 7 Harps (1919); 4 *Preludes to the Afternoon of a Telephone* for 2 Harps (1921); Harp Sonata (1922); 3 *Poems by Mallarmé* for Soprano, Harp, and Piano (1924); 2 harp concertos: No. 1 for Harp and 7 Wind Instruments (1925–26; N.Y., April 17, 1927, composer soloist) and No. 2 (n.d.; orchestration completed by R.R. Bennett); *Pentacle*, 5 pieces for 2 Harps (1928); *Préambule et Jeux* for Harp, 4 Wind Instruments, and 5 String Instruments (Paris, 1929); *Scintillation* for Harp (1936); *Panorama*, suite for Harp (1937); *Suite* for Harp (1943); 10 *Wedding Presents* for Harp (1946–52); *Prélude fatidique* for Harp (1954); various other works; many transcriptions for Harp.

BIBL.: S. Archambo, *C. S. (1885–1961): The Harp in Transition* (diss., Univ. of Kans., 1984).—**NS/LK/DM**

Salzer, Felix, distinguished Austrian-born American music theorist and pedagogue; b. Vienna, June 13, 1904; d. N.Y., Aug. 12, 1986. He studied musicology with Guido Adler at the Univ. of Vienna (Ph.D., 1926, with the diss. *Die Sonatenform bei Schubert*), and concurrently studied theory and analysis with Weise and Schenker; later received a conducting diploma from the Vienna Academy of Music (1935). With O. Jonas, he was founder-ed. of the journal *Der Dreiklang* (1937–39). He emigrated to the U.S. in 1939 and became a naturalized American citizen in 1945; taught at N.Y.'s Mannes Coll. of Music (1940–56), serving as its executive director (1948–55); was again a teacher there (1962–81); was also a prof. of music at Queens Coll. of the City Univ. of N.Y. (from 1963). He was a leading "Schenkerian" theorist and was instrumental in bringing the views of his teacher to the attention of American musicians; his own contribution was in the expansion and application of Schenker's concepts (previously restricted to a narrow range of tonal music) to Renaissance, medieval, and some 20th-century music. He publ. a number of important books on music theory: *Sinn und Wesen der abendländischen Mehrstimmigkeit* (Vienna, 1935), *Structural Hearing* (2 vols., N.Y., 1952; new ed., N.Y., 1962), and *Counterpoint in Composition: The Study of Voice Leading* (with C. Schachter; N.Y., 1969), and also ed. (with William Mitchell) *Music Forum* (N.Y., from 1967), a hardcover periodical.—**NS/LK/DM**

Salzman, Eric, versatile American composer, writer on music, editor, teacher, and pioneer of new music theater; b. N.Y., Sept. 8, 1933. His maternal grandfather, Louis Klenetzky, was a song-and-dance performer in the Yiddish theater and his mother, Frances Klennett Salzman, a founder-director of a children's music-theater company. He studied composition and theory in N.Y. with Mark Lawner while still in high school; then studied composition at Columbia Univ. with Luening, Ussachevsky, Mitchell, and Beeson (B.A., 1954) and at Princeton Univ. with Sessions, Babbitt, Kim, and Cone (M.F.A., 1956); in addition, he took courses in musicology with Strunk, Mendel, and Pirotta. In 1956–58 he was in Rome on a Fulbright fellowship for study with Petrassi at the Accademia di Santa Cecilia; also attended courses of Stockhausen, Scherchen, Maderna, and Nono at Darmstadt (summer, 1957). Returning to the U.S., he was a music critic for the *N.Y. Times* (1958–62) and the *N.Y. Herald Tribune* (1964–67); from 1984 to 1991 he was ed. of the *Musical Quarterly* and from 1962 to 1964 and again from 1968 to 1972 music director of the Pacifica Radio station WBAI-FM in N.Y., where he founded the Free Music Store. He taught at Queens Coll. of the City Univ. of N.Y. (1967–68); also lectured at N.Y.U., Yale Univ., Brooklyn Coll., Hunter Coll., Instituto Torquato di Tella in Buenos Aires, the Banff Centre for the Arts et al. Salzman has long been active in creating new music theater for contemporary performing arts; he founded and was artistic director, in N.Y., of the Electric Ear (at Electric Circus; 1967–68), New Image of Sound (1968–71), Quog Music Theater

(1970–82), and Music Theater/N.Y. (from 1993); also was founder and artistic director of the American Music Theater in Philadelphia (1982–93); his works for Quog Music Theater include *Ecolog*, music theater work for television (1971; in collaboration with J. Cassen), *Helix* for Voice, Percussion, Clarinet, and Guitar (1972), *Voices*, a capella radio opera (1972), *Saying Something* (1972–73), and *Biograffiti* (1972–73). From 1975 to 1990 he produced and directed some 2 dozen recordings (2 receiving Grammy Award nominations, a Prix Italia, and an Armstrong Award), featuring works by Weill, Partch, and Bolcom et al., as well as his own music; also produced numerous programs for public radio. He is the composer, author, and/or adaptor of more than 24 music-theater works; in all capacities, he merges the most advanced techniques in mixed media with ideas and forms derived from popular music and theater. He made a significant reconstruction and adaptation for the American Music Theater Festival of the long-unperformed Gershwin/Kaufman *Strike Up the Band* (1984) and the Kurt Weill/Alan Jay Lerner *Love Life* (1990), and a translation/adaptation of a French music-theater piece, *Jumelles*, by James Giroudon, Pierre Alain Jaffrennou, and Michel Rostain (as *The Silent Twins*, London Opera Festival, June 17, 1992). In 1994 he commenced work on a new music theater piece commissioned by the National Theater in Quimper, France. His writings include *Twentieth Century Music: An Introduction* (Englewood Cliffs, N.J., 1967; third ed., rev., 1988; tr. into Spanish, Portuguese, Hungarian, and Japanese), *Making Changes: A Practical Guide to Vernacular Harmony* (with M. Sahl; N.Y., 1977), and *The New Music Theater* (Oxford, 1998). Salzman is also a seasoned and enthusiastic ornithologist and has contributed writings on natural history to various publs. He is married to the environmentalist Lorna Salzman, with whom he has twin daughters, Eva, a poet resident in England, and Stephanie, a music-theater and pop song lyricist and composer.

WORKS: String Quartet (1955); Flute Sonata (1956); *Night Dance* for Orch. (1957); Songs for Voice and Piano, after Whitman (1955–57); *Cummings Set* for Voice and Piano (1958; also for Orch., 1962); *Partita* for Violin (1958); *Inventions* for Orch. (1957–58); *In Praise of the Owl and the Cuckoo* for Soprano, Guitar, Violin, and Viola (1963–64); *Larynx Music*, verses for Soprano, Guitar, and 4-track Tape (1966–67); *Verses* for Guitar (1967); *Foxes and Hedgehogs*, verses and cantos for 4 Voices and 2 Instrumental Groups with Sound Systems, after John Ashbery (N.Y., Nov. 30, 1967); *Queens Collage*, academic festival overture for Tape (1966); *The Peloponnesian War*, mime- dance theater piece (1967–68; in collaboration with D. Nagrin); *Wiretap* for Tape (1968); *Feedback*, multi-media participatory environmental work for Live Performers, Visuals, and Tape (1968; in collaboration with S. Vanderbeek); *The Nude Paper Sermon* for Actor, Renaissance Consort, Chorus, and Electronics, after Stephen Wade and John Ashbery (1968–69); *Can Man Survive?*, environmental multi-media piece for the centennial of the American Museum of Natural History (1969–71); *Strophe/Antistrophe* for Keyboard and Tape (1969; rev. 1971); *The 10 Qualities* and 3 Madrigals for Chorus (1970–71); *Fantasy on Lazarus* for String Orch. (1974); *The Conjurer*, music theater work (1975; in collaboration with M. Sahl); *Accord*, music theater piece for Accordion (1975); *Stauf*, music theater piece, after *Faust* (1976; rev. 1987; in

collaboration with M. Sahl); *Civilization and Its Discontents*, music theater comedy (1977; in collaboration with M. Sahl); *Noah*, music theater miracle (N.Y., Feb. 10, 1978; in collaboration with M. Sahl); *The Passion of Simple Simon* (1979; in collaboration with M. Sahl); *Boxes*, music theater piece (1982–83; in collaboration with M. Sahl); *Variations on Sacred Harp Hymn Tunes* for Harpsichord (1982); *Big Jim & the Small- time Investors*, music theater piece, after N. Jackson (1985–86; rev. 1990); *Toward a New American Opera*, mixed-media piece (1985); *Birdwalk* for Tape and Optional Keyboard (1986); *Signals*, structure for conducted improvisation for Any Number of Vocal or Instrumental Performers (1988); *The Last Words of Dutch Schultz* (1995–96; in collaboration with V. Vasilevski); *Body Language* for Singers, Dancers, Violin, Piano, and Accordion (1995–96; in collaboration with M. Sahl).—**NS/LK/DM**

Sam and Dave, Sam Moore (b. Miami, Fla., Oct. 12, 1935) and Dave Prater (b. Ocilla, Ga., May 9, 1937; d. near Sycamore, Ga., April 9, 1988).

One of the most exciting live soul acts of the 1960s and soul music's most popular duo, Sam and Dave scored a series of hits from 1966 to 1968, highlighted by the classics "Hold On! I'm Comin'" and "Soul Man." Working with producer-songwriters Isaac Hayes and Dave Porter and recording at the Stax studio in Memphis, Sam and Dave provided a raw, dynamic sound that contrasted sharply with the smoother sound of Motown. Sam and Dave broke up in 1969 and reunited twice between 1972 and 1981, enjoying renewed popularity as a result of The Blues Brothers' 1978 hit recording of "Soul Man." Sam and Dave were inducted into the Rock and Roll Hall of Fame in 1992.

Sam Moore and Dave Prater, veterans of the gospel groups The Melionaires and The Sensational Hummingbirds, respectively, met at the King of Hearts club in Miami in 1961. They teamed up as a duet and recorded for Roulette Records in the early 1960s with little success. Signed to Atlantic Records by Jerry Wexler in 1965, with singles and albums issued on the Stax label, the duo recorded at the Stax studio in Memphis under songwriter-producers Isaac Hayes and Dave Porter, who wrote virtually all their hits. Usually recording with Hayes on piano and backed by Booker T. and The MGs and the raw-sounding Memphis Horns, Sam and Dave scored a smash rhythm-and-blues hit with "You Don't Know Like I Know" at the beginning of 1966. Their classic "Hold On! I'm Comin'" became a top R&B and major pop hit, followed by the rhythm-and-blues smashes "Said I Wasn't Gonna Tell Nobody," "You Got Me Hummin'," and "When Something Is Wrong with My Baby." They later scored pop and rhythm-and-blues smashes with the classic "Soul Man" and "I Thank You."

In 1968, Sam and Dave's recording contract reverted to Atlantic Records when Stax Records was sold to Gulf-Western. Their subsequent success was largely restricted to the rhythm-and-blues field, most notably with "You Don't Know What You Mean to Me" and "Soul Sister, Brown Sugar." Disbanding for solo careers in late 1969, Sam and Dave reunited from 1972 to 1975, recording *Back at 'Cha* for United Artists. They again separated, reactivating the duo after the success of The Blues Brothers' late 1978 recording of "Soul Man" to tour through 1981. In 1986, Sam Moore re-recorded "Soul Man" with Lou Reed for the film of the same name. Dave Prater was killed in an automobile accident near Sycamore, Ga., on April 9, 1988. Sam Moore appeared with Junior Walker in the 1988 movie *Tapeheads* and enjoyed a renewed solo career in 1994 when his duet with Conway Twitty on "Rainy Night in Georgia" appeared on the smash crossover album *Rhythm, Country and Blues*. Sam and Dave were inducted into the Rock and Roll Hall of Fame in 1992.

WRITINGS: S. Moore, *S. and D.: An Oral History* (N.Y., 1998).

DISC.: *Hold On! I'm Comin'* (1966); *Sam and Dave* (1967); *Double Dynamite* (1967); *Soul Men* (1967); *I Thank You* (1968); *Best* (1969); *Back at 'Cha* (1975); *The Best Soul* (1991); *Soothe Me* (1993); *Sweat 'n' Soul: Anthology* (1993); *Greatest Songs* (1995); *Very Best* (1995); *Soul Man* (1996); *The Soul of Sam and Dave* (1989); *Sweet and Funky Gold* (1988).

Sam the Sham & the Pharaohs,

the original Tex-Mex hitmakers. **MEMBERSHIP:** Domingo "Sam" Samudio, voc., org. (b. Dallas, Tex., 1940); Ray Stinnet, gtr.; David Martin, bs.; Butch Gibson, sax.; Jerry Patterson, drm. Creating a visual identity with his turban, and a musical identity with his organ-fueled Tex-Mex rock and roll, Domingo Samudio earned a warm place in the heart of bar-band musicians everywhere. As Sam the Sham (a bit of self-deprecating humor about his vocal ability), he set the charts on fire with 1965's "Wooly Bully," a tune about his cat. He has spent the rest of his career trying to live that tune down.

Formed in Dallas in the early 1960s, the group went to Memphis to record some of Samudio's humorous tunes. Early songs like "Haunted House" didn't find an audience, but his next song, "Wooly Bully" caught on to the extent that MGM leased it and bought the group out of their independent record contract with Memphis-based Pen records. The rollicking Tejano song rose to #2 in the spring of 1965, going gold. They followed this with several equally novel, equally rollicking songs, "JuJu Hand," which hit #26, and "Ring Dang Doo," which peaked at #33. But by early 1966, the group appeared to be washed up. However, a novelty mixture of Tex Mex and doo wop, "Li'l Red Riding Hood," saved the day, again rising to #2 and going gold. Similar novelties followed, including "The Hair on My Chinny Chin Chin" getting to #22 and "How Do You Catch a Girl" topping out at #27.

After this, the band stopped selling and morphed from Sam the Sham and the Pharaohs to the Sam the Sham revue before breaking up altogether in the late 1960s. Samudio cut a solo album, *Sam Hard and Heavy*, for Atlantic, featuring tunes by Boz Scaggs and Doc Pomus and players including Duane Allman and the Memphis Horns. Despite all of this musical firepower, it didn't sell, although Samudio did earn a Grammy Award for Best Liner Notes! By the mid-1970s, plagued by drugs and taxes, Samudio dropped out of the music business and went to work as a deckhand and on the oil rigs in the Gulf of Mexico. In 1982 Ry Cooder convinced Samudio to play on the soundtrack for *The Border*, luring him out of "retirement."

After making the soundtrack, Samudio returned to Memphis to run a street ministry providing food and care to prisoners and indigent people in the South and Mexico, partly with revenue from his old tunes as they got placed in films and collections. He occasionally makes tapes of his own gospel compositions and will still perform his old songs as part of a program of his gospel music.

DISC.: *Wooly Bully* (1965); *Li'l Red Riding Hood* (1966); *Sam, Hard & Heavy* (1970); *Sam the Sham & Pharaohs* (1996).—**HB**

Samara, Spiro

(actually, **Spyridon Filiskos**), Greek composer; b. Corfu, Nov. 29, 1861; d. Athens, March 25, 1917. He was a pupil of Enrico Stancampiano in Athens, and later of Delibes at the Paris Cons. He won considerable success with his first opera, *Flora mirabilis* (Milan, May 16, 1886), and devoted himself almost exclusively to dramatic composition. Other operas were *Medgè* (Rome, 1888), *Lionella* (Milan, 1891), *La Martyre* (Naples, May 23, 1894), *La furia domata* (Milan, 1895), *Istoria* (Milan, 1903); as *La biondinetta*, Gotha, 1906), *Mademoiselle de Belle-Isle* (Genoa, Nov. 9, 1905), *Rhea* (Florence, April 11, 1908), and *La guerra in tempo di guerra* (Athens, 1914). He publ. *Scènes orientales*, suite for Piano, 4-Hands, many pieces for piano duo, and songs.—**NS/LK/DM**

Samaroff, Olga

(née **Hickenlooper**), American pianist and educator; b. San Antonio, Aug. 8, 1882; d. N.Y., May 17, 1948. She studied as a child with her mother and grandmother (Mrs. L. Grünewald, a former concert pianist), and subsequently studied in Paris (with Delaborde), Baltimore (with Ernest Hutcheson), and Berlin (with Ernst Jedliczka). She made her concert debut in N.Y. (Jan. 18, 1905) with the N.Y. Sym. Soc.; appeared with other orchs. in the U.S. and Europe; gave joint recitals with Kreisler, Zimbalist, and other violinists. She was music critic for the *N.Y. Evening Post* (1927–29); was on the faculties of the Philadelphia Cons. and the Juilliard School of Music in N.Y. (1924–48); among her outstanding students were Eugene List, Rosalyn Tureck, William Kapell, and Alexis Weissenberg. In 1911 she married **Leopold Stokowski;** they divorced in 1923. Her autobiography was publ. as *An American Musician's Story* (N.Y., 1939). She also publ. *The Layman's Music Book* (N.Y., 1935; second ed., rev., 1947, as *The Listener's Music Book*), *The Magic World of Music* (N.Y., 1936), and *A Music Manual* (N.Y., 1937).

BIBL.: D. Pucciani, *O. S. (1882–1948), American Musician and Educator* (diss., N.Y.U., 1979).—**NS/LK/DM**

Samazeuilh, Gustave (Marie Victor Fernand),

French writer on music and composer; b. Bordeaux, June 2, 1877; d. Paris, Aug. 4, 1967. He studied music with Chausson, at the Paris Schola Cantorum with d'Indy, and also took some lessons from Dukas. In his music, he absorbed the distinct style of French Impressionism, but despite the fine craftsmanship of his work, performances were few and far between. He publ. the studies *Paul Dukas* (Paris, 1913; second ed., 1936) and *Ernest Chausson: Musicien de mon temps* (Paris, 1947), and also ed. *Écrits de Paul Dukas sur la musique* (Paris, 1948).

WORKS: ORCH.: *Étude symphonique* (1906); *Nuit* (Paris, March 15, 1925); *Naiades au soir* (Paris, Oct. 18, 1925); *Sérénade* (1926); *Gitanes* (1931); *L'Appel de la danse* (1946). **CHAMBER:** Violin Sonata (1903); String Quartet (1911); *Esquisse d'Espagne* for Flute and Piano (1914); *Luciole* for Clarinet and Piano (1934); *Suite en trio* for Strings (1938); *Cantabile e capriccio* for String Quartet (1948); many transcriptions for piano of orch. works by d'Indy, Debussy, Franck, and Fauré. **CHORUS AND ORCH.:** *Le Sommeil de Canope* (1908); *Chant d'Espagne* (Paris, Jan. 10, 1926); *Le Cercle des heures* (Paris, Feb. 17, 1934).

BIBL.: J. Poupard, *Entretiens avec G. S.* (Paris, 1962). **—NS/LK/DM**

Saminsky, Lazare, Russian-American composer, conductor, and writer on music; b. Valegotsulova, near Odessa, Nov. 8, 1882; d. Port Chester, N.Y., June 30, 1959. He studied mathematics and philosophy at the Univ. of St. Petersburg, and composition with Rimsky-Korsakov and Liadov and conducting with N. Tcherepnin at the St. Petersburg Cons. (graduated, 1910). He emigrated to the U.S. in 1920, settling in N.Y.; in 1923 he was a co-founder of the League of Composers; served as music director of Temple Emanu-El in N.Y. (1924–56), where he founded the annual Three Choirs Festival (1926). He was married to an American writer, Lillian Morgan Buck, who died in 1945; in 1948 he married the American pianist Jennifer Gandar. He wrote an autobiography, *Third Leonardo* (MS, 1959). In his compositions, he followed the Romantic tradition; Hebrew subjects and styles play an important part in some of his music.

WORKS: DRAMATIC: *The Gagliarda of a Merry Plague*, opera ballet (1924; N.Y., Feb. 22, 1925); *The Daughter of Jephta*, opera ballet (1928); *Julian, the Apostate Caesar*, opera (1933–38). **ORCH.:** *Vigiliae*, symphonic triptych (1912; Moscow, Feb. 20, 1913, composer conducting); 5 syms.: No. 1, *Of the Great Rivers*, in "E-Frimoll" (free minor mode) (1914; Petrograd, Feb. 25, 1917, composer conducting), No. 2, *Symphonie des sommets* (1918; Amsterdam, Nov. 16, 1922), No. 3, *Symphony of the Seas* (1924; Paris, June 1925, composer conducting), No. 4 (1926; Berlin, April 19, 1929, composer conducting), and No. 5, *Jerusalem, City of Solomon and Christ*, for Chorus and Orch. (1929–30; N.Y., April 29, 1958); *Lament of Rachel*, ballet suite (Boston, March 3, 1922); *Venice*, "poem-serenade" for Chamber Orch. (Berlin, May 9, 1928); *Ausonia*, suite (1930; Florence, Feb. 24, 1935); *To a New World* (1932; N.Y., April 16, 1951); *3 Shadows* (1935; N.Y., Feb. 6, 1936); *Pueblo, A Moon Epic* (1936; Washington, D.C., Feb. 17, 1937); *Stilled Pageant* (1937; Zürich, Aug. 1938); *East and West*, suite for Violin and Orch. (1943). **VOCAL:** *Litanies of Women* for Voice and Chamber Orch. (1925; Paris, May 21, 1926); *Eon Hours*, suite of 4 rondos for 4 Voices and 4 Instruments (1935; N.Y., Nov. 28, 1939); *Requiem*, in memory of Lillian M. Saminsky (N.Y., May 20, 1946); *A Sonnet of Petrarch* for 3 Voices and 3 Instruments (1947); several Hebrew services. **OTHER:** Piano pieces.

WRITINGS: *Music of Our Day* (N.Y., 1932; second ed., rev. and aug., 1939); *Music of the Ghetto and the Bible* (N.Y., 1934); *Living Music of the Americas* (N.Y., 1949); *Physics and Metaphysics of Music and Essays on the Philosophy of Mathematics* (The Hague, 1957); *Essentials of Conducting* (N.Y., 1958).

BIBL.: D. de Paoli et al., *L. S.: Composer and Civic Worker* (N.Y., 1930).**—NS/LK/DM**

Sammarco, (Giuseppe) Mario, Italian baritone; b. Palermo, Dec. 13, 1868; d. Milan, Jan. 24, 1930.

He studied singing with Antonio Cantelli, making a successful debut as Valentine in Faust in Palermo (1888); then sang in Brescia, Madrid, Lisbon, Brussels, Moscow, Warsaw, Berlin, and Vienna. After his London appearance as Scarpia in Tosca at Covent Garden in 1904, he sang there every season until the outbreak of World War I in 1914. He made his American debut as Tonio (Feb. 1, 1908) at the Manhattan Opera House in N.Y.; from 1910 to 1913 he sang with the Chicago Grand Opera; retired from the operatic stage in 1919 and later settled in Milan as a teacher. He was one of the finest verismo singers of his time.**—NS/LK/DM**

Sammartini, Giovanni Battista, significant Italian composer and pedagogue, brother of **Giuseppe (Francesco Gaspare Melchiorre Baldassare) Sammartini;** b. probably in Milan, 1700 or 1701; d. there, Jan. 15, 1775. It is likely that he studied music with his father, Alexis Saint-Martin, a French oboist who settled in Italy. In 1728 he became maestro di cappella of the Congregation of the SS. Entierro in Milan, which met at the Jesuit church of S. Fedele; he held this position most of his life. He also held similar positions with various other churches in Milan, and was active as a composer of sacred music and as an organist. In 1768 he became maestro di cappella to the ducal chapel at S. Gottardo; was a founder-member of Milan's philharmonic society. A noted teacher, he taught at the Collegio de' Nobili from 1730. His most famous pupil was Gluck, who studied with him from about 1737 to 1741. Sammartini's historical importance rests upon his contribution to the development of the Classical style; his large body of syms. (68 in all), concertos, and other works for orch. are noteworthy for their extensive thematic development and evolution of sonata form. The earliest known dated syms., in 3-movement form, are credited to him. However, the claim that he composed a 4-movement sym. in 1734 lacks confirmation. See B. Churgin, ed., *The Symphonies of G.B. S.* (Cambridge, Mass., 1968–). Additional works for orch. include 6 violin concertos, a Concerto for 2 Violins, 2 flute concertos, a Concerto for 2 Violins and 2 Oboes, 7 orch. concertinos, etc. His chamber music includes 21 quartets, 6 quintets, about 200 trios, many sonatas and duets, etc. He also composed the following works for the theater: *Memet*, opera (Lodi, 1732), *L'ambizione superata dalla virtù*, opera (Milan, Dec. 26, 1734), *L'Agrippina, moglie di Tiberio*, opera (Milan, Jan. 1743), *La gara dei geni*, introduzione e festa da ballo (Milan, May 28, 1747), and *Il trionfo d'amore*, ballet (Milan, 1773). He also composed a number of arias and secular cantatas, as well as sacred cantatas and other religious works, including the oratorio *Gesù bambino adorato dalli pastori* (Milan, Jan. 11, 1726). Many other works attributed to him are doubtful or spurious.

BIBL.: B. Churgin, *The Symphonies of G.B. S.* (diss., Harvard Univ., 1963); N. Jenkins and B. Churgin, *Thematic Catalogue of the Works of G.B. S.: Orchestral and Vocal Music* (Cambridge, Mass., 1976); M. Marley, *The Sacred Cantatas of G.B. S.* (diss., Univ. of Cincinnati, 1978); A. Gehann, *G.B. S.: Die Konzerte* (Frankfurt am Main, 1995).**—NS/LK/DM**

Sammartini, Giuseppe (Francesco Gaspare Melchiorre Baldassare), Italian oboist and composer, brother of **Giovanni Battista Sammar-**

tini, called "il Londinese" after settling in London; b. Milan, Jan. 6, 1695; d. London, Nov. 1750. He most likely studied oboe with his father, Alexis Saint-Martin, who settled in Italy. By 1720 he was a member of the orch. of the Teatro Regio Ducal in Milan. In 1728 he went to London, where he established himself as a virtuoso oboist; also played in the opera orch. at the King's Theatre. From 1736 until his death he also was music master to the wife and children of the Prince of Wales. He composed a considerable number of instrumental works, including 12 concerti grossi, 16 overtures, concertos for various instruments, many sonatas, duets, etc. His vocal music includes 9 cantatas, an aria and a sinfonia for the oratorio *La calunnia delusa* (Milan, 1724), and a pasticcio by several Italian composers. He may also have composed the masque *The Judgement of Paris* (c. 1740), which is usually attributed to Arne. See R. Fiske, "A Cliveden Setting," *Music & Letters*, XLVII (1966).—**NS/LK/DM**

Sammons, Albert (Edward), esteemed English violinist and pedagogue; b. London, Feb. 23, 1886; d. Southdean, Sussex, Aug. 24, 1957. He received some instruction from his father and others in London, but was mainly autodidact. He began his professional career at age 11, making his solo debut at 20. He was first violinist of the London String Quartet (1907–16); was also concertmaster of Beecham's Orch. (1908–13), Diaghilev's Ballets Russes orch. (from 1911), and the orch. of the Phil. Soc. (from 1913). In subsequent years, he appeared as a soloist with various orchs. in England, becoming well known as a champion of the Elgar Violin Concerto; Delius dedicated his Violin Concerto to Sammons, who ed. its violin part and was soloist in its premiere (London, Jan. 30, 1919). For a quarter of a century he gave duo recitals with the pianist William Murdoch, often playing premieres of British scores. He served as a prof. at the Royal Coll. of Music in London. In 1944 he was made a Commander of the Order of the British Empire. He also composed; his *Phantasy Quartet* for Strings was awarded the Cobbett Prize. He publ. *The Secret of Technique in Violin Playing* (London, 1916) and *Violin Exercises for Improving the Bowing Technique by Means of the Tone Perfecter* (London, 1930).—**NS/LK/DM**

Samosud, Samuil (Abramovich), prominent Russian conductor and teacher; b. Tiflis, May 14, 1884; d. Moscow, Nov. 6, 1964. He studied cello at the Tiflis Cons. (graduated, 1906). After playing cello in various orchs., he went to St. Petersburg, where he was a conductor at the Maryinsky Theater (1917–19) and artistic director of the Maly Theater (1918–36). He then settled in Moscow and was artistic director of the Bolshoi Theater (1936–43), the Stanislavsky-Nemirovich-Danchenko Music Theater (1943–50), and the Moscow Phil. and the All-Union Radio orch. (1953–57); also taught conducting at the Leningrad Cons. (1929–36), being made a prof. in 1934. In 1937 he was made a People's Artist of the U.S.S.R. He conducted premieres of a number of works by Soviet composers, including Shostakovich's opera *The Nose* (1930) and Prokofiev's 7th Sym. (1952).—**NS/LK/DM**

Sampson, Edgar (Melvin; aka The Lamb), jazz saxophonist, violinist, composer, arranger; b. N.Y., Aug. 31, 1907; d. Englewood, N.J., Jan. 16, 1973. Sampson began on violin at the age of six and doubled alto sax from his early teens. He led his own high school band, then began working with pianist Joe Coleman in N.Y. in 1924. Sampson played a season with Duke Ellington at the Kentucky Club, then played with Bingie Madison and Billy Fowler (1926) before playing at the Savoy Ballroom with Arthur Gibbs. Sampson was with the Charlie Johnson Band from 1928–30, and briefly with Alex Jackson (c. 1930), then joined Fletcher Henderson (1931–32). His most important gig was with Chick Webb (1934–July 1936); while with Chick he composed many tunes that were to become jazz standards. He left the band to become a freelance arranger, scoring for Artie Shaw, Red Norvo, Teddy Hill, Benny Goodman, Teddy Wilson, and many other groups. Sampson made a few brief returns to full-time playing. He recorded with Lionel Hampton in 1938, worked as musical director of the Ella Fitzgerald Band from July–November 1939, and playing alto/baritone with Al Sears (1943). Sampson resumed regular playing in the late 1940s, and led his own band in N.Y. (1949–51), playing mostly tenor sax. He spent most of the 1950s arranging for, and playing with, several Latin- American jazz-flavored bands, including Marcellino Guerra, Tito Puente, and Tito Rodriguez. He returned to leading his own small band through the late 1950s and early 1960s, and also gigged regularly with Harry Dial's Bluesicians. In the late 1960s, Sampson retired from making music due to complications from diabetes. The disease eventually led to the amputation of one of his legs and to his death in the early 1970s.

Sampson is best remembered for the songs "Stompin' at the Savoy," "Don't Be That Way," "Blue Minor," "If Dreams Come True," "Blue Lou," and "Lullaby in Rhythm." They were written originally for Chick Webb but later became big hits for Benny Goodman. Many have become standards for swing-styled jazz bands. His daughter, Gladys, is a successful composer.

DISC.: *Sampson Swings Again* (1956); *Swing Softly Sweet Sampson* (1957).—**JC/MM/LP**

Sams, Eric, English writer on music; b. London, May 3, 1926. He was educated at Corpus Christi Coll., Cambridge (1947–50; B.A., 1950), and later was awarded his Ph.D. (1972). He worked in Army cryptanalysis (1947–50), and then was in the British civil service (1950–78). In 1976–77 he was a visiting prof. at McMaster Univ. in Hamilton, Ontario, Canada. Sams is an expert in codes and ciphers. His work was detailed in the television film *Code and Cipher in Music* (1989). He contributed articles and reviews to various publications. His valuable books comprise *The Songs of Hugo Wolf* (London, 1961; third ed., rev. and enl., 1993), *The Songs of Robert Schumann* (London, 1969; third ed., rev. and enl., 1993), and *Brahms Songs* (London, 1972). He also publ. *The Real Shakespeare* (London, 1995).—**NS/LK/DM**

Samuel, Adolphe (-Abraham), Belgian composer and teacher, father of **Eugène Samuel-Holeman;**

b. Liège, July 11, 1824; d. Ghent, Sept. 11, 1898. He was educated at the Liège Cons. and the Brussels Cons., winning the Belgian Grand Prix de Rome (1845). He taught harmony at the Brussels Cons. (1850–70), and in 1871 was appointed director of the Ghent Cons. He publ. *Cours d'accompagnement de la basse chiffrée* (Brussels, 1849), *Cours d'harmonie pratique* (Brussels, 1861), and *Livre de lecture musicale* (Paris, 1886). Among his works are 5 operas: *Il a rêvé* (1845), *Giovanni da Procida* (1848), *Madeleine* (1849), *Les Deux Prétendants* (1851), and *L'Heure de la retraite* (1852), as well as 7 syms., overtures, string quartets, and piano pieces.

BIBL.: E. Mathieu, *Notice sur A. S.* (Brussels, 1922). —NS/LK/DM

Samuel, Gerhard, German-born American conductor, composer, and pedagogue; b. Bonn, April 20, 1924. He studied violin in his youth. In 1939 he emigrated to the U.S. and in 1943 became a naturalized American citizen. He studied conducting with Hermann Genhart at the Eastman School of Music in Rochester, N.Y. (B.S., 1945), composition with Hindemith at Yale Univ. (M.M., 1947), and conducting with Koussevitzky at the Berkshire Music Center at Tanglewood (summers, 1946–47). After playing violin in the Rochester Phil. (1941–45) and conducting on Broadway (1948–49), he was a violinist and assoc. conductor with the Minneapolis Sym. Orch. (1949–59). He also was music director of the Collegium Musicum and the Minneapolis Civic Opera (1949–59). From 1959 to 1971 he was music director of the Oakland (Calif.) Sym. Orch. He also was music director of the San Francisco Ballet (1960–70), as well as the Oakland Chamber Orch. and the Cabrillo Festival (1962–66). From 1970 to 1973 he was assoc. conductor of the Los Angeles Phil. He also was on the faculty of the Calif. Inst. of the Arts in Valencia from 1972 to 1976. In 1976 he became director of orchestral activities at the Univ. of Cincinnati Coll.-Cons. of Music, where he was music director of its Philharmonia Orch. until 1997. He also was music director of the Cincinnati Chamber Orch. from 1983 to 1991. In 1997 he became music director of the Cosmopolitan Orch. in N.Y. As a guest conductor, he appeared with orchs. throughout North America and abroad. In 1994 he won the Alice M. Ditson Award. In his compositions, Samuel has pursued a contemporary path.

WORKS: DRAMATIC: *Agam,* ballet music (1982); *Nicholas and Conception,* ballet (1987). **ORCH.:** *Looking at Orpheus Looking* (1971); *Into Flight From* (1972); *Requiem for Survivors* (1974); *Cold When the Drum Sounds for Dawn* (1975); *On a Dream* for Viola and Orch. (1977); *Out of Time,* short sym. (1978); *Chamber Concerto in the Shape of a Summer* for Flute, 3 Percussion, and Strings (1981); Double Concerto for Viola, Violin, and Orch. (1983); *Before Webern* (1983); *Lucille's Wave* (1984); *As Imperceptibly as Grief* (1987); *Apollo and Hyacinth* (1989); Soprano Saxophone Concerto (1990); *Outcries and Consolations* (1990); *Auguri* (1993); *Tragic Scene* (1994); *Transformations* for Violin and Strings (1994); *In Search of Words* (1995). **CHAMBER:** *3 Hymns to Apollo* for Cello and 7 Instrumentalists (1973); *Beyond McBean* for Violin and 13 Instrumentalists (1975); *Au Revoir to Lady R* for Clarinet, Cello, and Percussion (1976); 2 string quartets (1978, 1981); *Pezzo Serioso* for 2 Tubas and Percussion (1978); *Circles* for 3 Percussion (1979); *Put Up My Lute* for Cello and 3 Percussion

(1979); *Aftermath* for Clarinet and 3 Percussion (1983); *Nocturne on an Impossible Dream* for Violin, Clarinet, Piano, 2 Percussion, Violin, Viola, Cello, and Bass (1986); *The Naumburg Cadenza* for Violin (1990); *Dirge for John Cage* for Bassoon and Percussion (1992); *Left-Over Mirrors* for 3 Flutes, 3 Horns, and 3 Percussion (1992); *Music for 4* for Violin, Clarinet, Cello, and Piano (1992); *After a Dirge* for Flute, Bassoon, and 3 Percussion (1993). **VOCAL:** *12 on Death and No* for Tenor, Chorus, and Orch. (1968); *The Relativity of Icarus* for Contralto or Baritone and 8 Instrumentalists (1970); *To an End* for Chorus and Orch. (1972); *And Marsyas* for Mezzo-soprano and 10 Instrumentalists (1974; rev. 1989); *Sun-Like* for Soprano and Chamber Ensemble (1975); *Fortieth Day* for Soprano, Narrator, and 7 Instrumentalists (1976); *Paul Blake—Ikon Maker* for Soprano and 8 Instrumentalists (1979); *What of My Music* for Soprano, 3 Percussion, and String Bass Ensemble (1979); *The Emperor and the Nightingale* for Soprano, Bass-baritone, String Bass, and 3 Percussion (1980); *On the Beach at Night Alone* for Chorus, Clarinet, and Strings or Organ (1980); *3 Minor Desperations* for Mezzo-soprano and Orch. (1980); *Traumbild* for Soprano, Tenor, and Orch. (1983); *Mid-Autumn Moon* for Mezzo-soprano or Baritone and 5 Instrumentalists (1988); *This Heart That Broke So Long...* for Soprano or Tenor and Piano (1991).—NS/LK/DM

Samuel, Harold, distinguished English pianist and pedagogue; b. London, May 23, 1879; d. there, Jan. 15, 1937. He studied at the Royal Coll. of Music in London with Dannreuther (piano) and Stanford (composition), and later was on its faculty. He was particularly distinguished as an interpreter of Bach. In 1921 he gave 6 successive Bach recitals in London and a similar cycle in N.Y.; toured the U.S. regularly from 1924. He wrote a musical comedy, *Hon'ble Phil*, songs, and piano pieces.—NS/LK/DM

Samuel, Léopold, Belgian composer; b. Brussels, May 5, 1883; d. there, March 10, 1975. He studied with Edgar Tinel at the Brussels Cons. and took courses in Berlin, winning the Belgian Prix de Rome with his cantata *Tycho-Brahé* (1911). He later served as inspector of music education in Belgium (1920–45) and was made a member of the Belgian Royal Academy (1958). His works follow in a late Romantic style, with pronounced impressionistic elements.

WORKS: DRAMATIC: Opera: *Ilka* (1919); *La Sirène au pays des hommes* (1937). **ORCH.:** *Morceaux de concert* for Cello and Orch. (1908); *Petite suite fantasque* (1945). **CHAMBER:** String Quintet (1909); Piano Trio (1920); 3 string quartets (1941, 1942, 1948); *Pièce à 5* for Flute, String Trio, and Harp (1954); *Invocation* for Cello and Piano (1959). **VOCAL:** Songs. —NS/LK/DM

Samuel-Holeman, Eugène, Belgian pianist, conductor, and composer, son of **Adolphe (-Abraham) Samuel;** b. Brussels, Nov. 3, 1863; d. there, Jan. 25, 1942. After studying piano and theory at the Ghent Cons., he was active as a pianist and conductor, pursuing his career primarily in France. He wrote an opera, *Un vendredi saint en Zélande*, a monodrama, *La jeune fille à la fenêtre* (1904), Sym., Harp Concerto, chamber music, and songs.—NS/LK/DM

Samuel-Rousseau
See **Rousseau, Marcel (-Auguste-Louis)**

Sanabria, Bobby (actually, **Robert D.**), jazz percussionist who greatly influenced the Afro-Cuban and jazz fields; b. South Bronx, N.Y, June 2, 1957. He grew up listening to Puerto Rican, Cuban, and Brazilian music, as well as jazz, funk, rock, and R&B. Inspired and encouraged by Tito Puente, he attended Berklee (1975–79), where he received his B.M.; while at Berklee, he received the Faculty Association Award for his work as an instrumentalist. After graduation, he became a major player in the Afro-Cuban and jazz fields. He recorded or performed with Mongo Santamaria, Tito Puente, Dizzy Gillespie, Paquito D'Rivera, Michael Gibbs, Chico Freeman, Luis "Perico Ortiz," Chico O'Farrill, Celia Cruz, Henry Threadgill, and Mario Bauza. In 1983, Sanabria was awarded a NEA grant. Since the mid-1980s, he has performed for and lectured to thousands of N.Y. public school students, teachers, and families as part of the Arts Connection and Arts Exposure Program. He has conducted clinics, and lectures worldwide, and seminars on the Afro-Cuban jazz tradition. His group Ascension has performed in major clubs and festivals in the U.S. and abroad. He is currently on the faculty of the Drummer's Collective and the New School/Mannes Coll. of Music. He has composed for Off-Broadway theater, big band, and chamber ensembles as well as for his own group, and has had works commissioned by *Meet the Composer*. Sanabria has been featured on numerous Grammy-nominated records, among them *The Mambo Kings* movie soundtrack and numerous TV and radio jingles. He is the author of the three-part video instructional series *Getting Started on Congas*. He writes musician profiles for his web site, *Clave Chronicles*, and has published numerous articles in various publications such as *Modern Drummer* magazine and *Latin Percussion Inc.*

DISC.: *N.Y.C. ACH!* (1993).—**LP**

Sanborn, David, hit-making jazz-fusion saxophonist of the 1980s; b. Tampa, Fla., July 30, 1945. Although born in Fla., David Sanborn grew up in St. Louis. Despite an early bout with polio as a child (that causes him to lean to one side when he plays), he developed a powerful, biting sound on his alto saxophone. By the age of 15, he was sitting in with local bluesmen such as Little Milton and Albert King. In the later 1960s, he became a member of the Paul Butterfield Blues Band, playing with them at Woodstock. During the 1970s, he became an in-demand session player working with artists ranging from Stevie Wonder, Paul Simon, and Bruce Springsteen to Gil Evans. He played the sax on David Bowie's hit "Young Americans."

While he still continues to work as a session musician, since 1975 Sanborn has earned kudos for his solo work. He started releasing rhythm and blues- flavored dance music with jazzy improvisation, earning the Best R&B Instrumental Performance Grammy in 1981 for "All I Need Is You." His 1985 record *Straight to the Heart* won him the Best Jazz Fusion Performance or Instru-

mental Grammy in 1985. He took the same award home a year later for his work with Bob James on *Double Vision*. A year after that, he took Best R&B Instrumental Performance, Orch., Group or Soloist for "Chicago Song," taking the same award home the next year for *Close-up*, with its rollicking cover of "You Are Everything." During this period of recording success, Sanborn also hosted the weekly late night variety show *Night Music*, which generally hosted an eclectic group of musicians and gave them the opportunity to play together. He also hosted a show for National Public Radio.

By 1991, Sanborn felt comfortable enough with his success to emphasize his love of jazz over his more pop-oriented hits. *Upfront* marked the first release Sanborn considered jazz. Even his follow-up, the more earthy, blues- oriented *Another Hand* included a cover of Ornette Coleman's "Ramblin'." However, by the middle of the decade, he returned to more mainstream work. 1995's *Pearls* found him playing ballads with an orchestra arranged and conducted by Johnny Mandel. He earned his sixth Grammy in 1999, taking the trophy for Best Contemporary Jazz Performance for his *Inside* album.

DISC.: *Taking Off* (1975); *Love Songs* (1976); *Sanborn* (1976); *Promise Me the Moon* (1977); *Heart to Heart* (1978); *Hideaway* (1979); *Voyeur* (1980); *As We Speak* (1981); *Backstreet* (1982); *Straight to the Heart* (1984); *A Change of Heart* (1987); *Close-Up* (1988); *Another Hand* (1991); *Upfront* (1992); *Hearsay* (1994); *Pearls* (1995); *Songs from the Night Before* (1996); *Inside* (1999).—**HB**

Sances, Giovanni Felice, Italian singer, teacher, and composer; b. Rome, c. 1600; d. Vienna (buried), Nov. 12, 1679. After serving several patrons, he was called to Vienna as a singer in the court chapel in 1636; in 1649 he was named asst. Kapellmeister, and subsequently was Kapellmeister (1669–76). He played a significant role in the cultivation of Italian dramatic music at the Viennese court. He composed the operas *Ermiona* (Padua, April 11, 1636), *I trionfi d'Amore* (Prague, July 2, 1648), *La Roselmina fatta canara* (Vienna, Feb. 1662), *Mercurio esploratore* (Vienna, Feb. 21, 1662), *Apollo deluso* (Vienna, June 9, 1669), and *Aristomene Messenio* (Vienna, Dec. 22, 1670). Other works include 6 sepolchri (1669–70), about 600 sacred works, and various secular vocal chamber pieces.

BIBL.: P. Webhofer, *G.F. S. (ca. 1600–1679): Biographisch-bibliographische Untersuchung und Studie über sein Motettenwerk* (Innsbruck, 1965).—**NS/LK/DM**

Sánchez de Fuentes, Eduardo, important Cuban composer and educator; b. Havana, April 3, 1874; d. there, Sept. 7, 1944. He studied music with Ignacio Cervantes and Carlos Anckermann. He occupied an influential position in the artistic affairs of Cuba. He wrote 5 operas and many other works, but is known outside Cuba chiefly by his popular song *Tú*, which he publ. at the age of 18.

WORKS: DRAMATIC: O p e r a (all first perf. in Havana): *El náufrago*, after Tennyson's *Enoch Arden* (1900; Jan. 31,

1901); *La dolorosa* (April 23, 1910); *Doreya* (1917; Feb. 7, 1918); *El caminante* (1921); *Kabelia*, after a Hindu legend (June 22, 1942). ORCH.: *Temas del patio*, symphonic prelude; *Anacaona*, symphonic poem (1928). VOCAL: *Bocetos cubanos* for Soprano, Women's Chorus, and Orch. (1922); songs. OTHER: Piano pieces.

WRITINGS (all publ. in Havana): *El folklore en la música cubana* (1923); *Folklorismo* (1928); *Viejos ritmos cubanos* (1937).

BIBL.: M. Guiral, *Un gran musicógrafo y compositor cubano: E. S.d.F.* (Havana, 1944); O. Martínez, *E. S.d.F.: In Memoriam* (Havana, 1944).—NS/LK/DM

Sandberg, Mordecai, Romanian-born American composer and music theorist; b. in Romania, Feb. 4, 1897; d. Toronto, Dec. 28, 1973. As a child, he studied violin with a Gypsy violinist-conductor, composing the overture *Demosthenes* while still in his teens. He pursued training in music in Vienna while attending the Univ. there as a medical student (M.D., 1921). From 1922 to 1938 he was active as both a physician and a composer in Jerusalem, where he founded the local branch of the ISCM and the Inst. of New Music; in 1930 he served as contributing ed. of the Hebrew monthly music journal *Hallel*. In 1929–30 he pursued research on acoustics in Germany; also lectured at the Berlin Hochschule für Musik and publ. an essay on his music theories as *Die Musik der Menschheit: Die Tondifferenzierung und ihre Bedeutung*. In 1938 he lectured on microtones at the Congress of Music and Life in London. He went to the U.S. in 1939 and later settled in N.Y., where several of his works were premiered, including *Ezkerah* (I Remember; 1952), an oratorio "dedicated to the memory of all victims of persecution, oppression, and hatred." From 1970 until his death he taught at York Univ. in Toronto. Sandberg was an original and prolific composer. He was one of the earliest explorers of microtonal music, originating his own "Universal Tonal System" using microtones based on a synthesis of Oriental and Western scales. To facilitate the writing and performance of microtonal music, he designed a refined notational system and several instruments, including 2 harmoniums—one bichromatic with quarter tones (1926) and one with 12th and 16th tones (1929), both built by Straube. He composed orch. works, including 5 syms., a Concerto for Clarinet and Strings, and a Concerto for Oboe, Viola, and Orch.; much chamber music, including sextets, quintets, quartets, and sonatas for cello, piano, violin, viola, and organ; numerous sacred and secular vocal works, including 15 oratorios, among them *Ruth* (N.Y., May 22, 1949) and *Ezkerah* (N.Y., April 22, 1952); *Shelomoh*, symphonic tetralogy for Soloists, Chorus, and Orch.; *Jerusalem*, cantata (N.Y., Nov. 10, 1943); *Hebrew Spirituals and Prayer for Peace* (N.Y., Jan. 16, 1946). His major achievement was his *Symphonic Psalms*, settings of the entire book of Psalms, among them *Pilgrim Songs* (Psalms 128, 130, and 134; N.Y., Jan. 16, 1946), *Songs of Ascent* (Psalms 126, 131, and 132; N.Y., June 17, 1947), and *Psalm 51* (N.Y., May 30, 1987).—NS/LK/DM

Sandberger, Adolf, eminent German musicologist; b. Würzburg, Dec. 19, 1864; d. Munich, Jan. 14, 1943. He studied composition in Würzburg and Munich (1881–87) and musicology in Munich and Berlin (1883–87), and obtained his Ph.D. in 1887 at the Univ. of Würzburg with the diss. *Peter Cornelius* (publ. in Leipzig, 1887) and completed his Habilitation in 1894 at the Univ. of Munich with his *Beiträge zur Geschichte der Bayerischen Hofkapelle unter Orlando di Lasso* (Vols. 1 and 3 publ. in Leipzig, 1894–95; Vol. 2 not publ.). In 1889 he was appointed head of the music dept. at the Bavarian Hofbibliothek in Munich; also was a reader (1900–1904) and a prof. (1904–30) at the Univ. of Munich. He was ed. of Denkmaler der Tonkunst in Bayern (1900–1931) and the *Neues Beethoven-Jahrbuch* (1924–42); with F. Haberl, he also ed. Breitkopf & Härtel's monumental edition of the complete works of Lassus (1894–1927). Sandberger was one of the most important teachers of musicology in Germany; he formulated the basic principles of 20th-century musical bibliography. Among his writings were *Emmanuel Chabriers Gwendoline* (Munich, 1898), *Über zwei ehedem Wolfgang Mozart zugeschriebene Messen* (Munich, 1907), and *Ausgewählte Aufsätze zur Musikgeschichte* (Munich, 1921–24). He was also a composer; wrote 2 operas, choral pieces, chamber works, songs, etc.

BIBL.: T. Kroyer, ed., *Festschrift zum 50. Geburtstag A. S.* (Munich, 1918).—NS/LK/DM

Sandburg (Sandberg), Carl (August), plainspoken American author, folksinger, and guitarist; b. Galesburg, Ill., Jan. 6, 1878; d. Flat Rock, N.C., July 22, 1967. Sandburg was more folklorist than folkie, an award- winning poet and biographer who also carried an acoustic guitar on the lecture circuit and sang traditional material, helping to spread folk music to generations of college students and to transform it into a contemporary form.

Sandburg's parents, August and Clara Anderson Sandberg, were Swedish immigrants. His father was a blacksmith's helper. In grade school he and two of his siblings altered the spelling of their name to Americanize it. (He also called himself Charles from the age of eight, not returning to his real first name until 1910.) Though a good student he was forced to leave school at 14 to help support his large family. For the next five years he held various menial jobs, most often driving a milk wagon. During this period he learned to play the banjo and to sing minstrel songs. He left home in June 1897 to find work in Kans. harvesting wheat among other odd jobs, but he also became a tramp, living in hobo jungles and riding the rails, learning songs like "Hallelujah, I'm a Bum" along the way. He returned to Galesburg in October and went back to driving a milk wagon, later becoming a painter's apprentice.

When the U.S. declared war on Spain in April 1898, Sandburg enlisted in the army and was stationed in Cuba and Puerto Rico, returning to the U.S. after the war ended in August. His veteran status entitled him to free tuition at Lombard Coll. in Galesburg, and he enrolled in October, though he also had to work at a firehouse to help support himself and his family. He left without a degree in 1902 (though he would be awarded an honorary one in 1923). Late in the year the magazine

The Thistle was the first to published one of his poems, "The Falling Leaves." *In Reckless Ecstasy*, a book of poetry and essays, was locally published.

From 1902 through 1909, Sandburg worked primarily as a traveling salesman of stereoscopic photographs while struggling to establish himself as a writer and lecturer. In the fall of 1907 he became a district organizer for the Wisc. Social-Democratic Party, a post he held through the spring of 1909. He married Anna Maria Elizabeth ("Lilian," or, as he called her, "Paula") Steichen (1883–1977), sister of the noted photographer Edward Steichen (whose biography he would write), on June 15, 1908. They had three daughters, Margaret, Janet, and Mary Ellen (called Helga, who also became a writer). In June 1909 he moved to Milwaukee and embarked upon a career in journalism, working for various newspapers in the city. In the spring of 1910 he campaigned for Emil Seidel, the Social-Democratic candidate for mayor, and was rewarded with the job of private secretary to the mayor when Seidel won. He held the post until November, resigning to return to newspaper work.

Sandburg moved to Chicago in mid-1912, working initially for the *Chicago Evening World*, then, in 1913, for *The Day Book*. In March 1914, *Poetry: A Magazine of Verse* published nine of his poems, and in November, one of them, "Chicago," won the Levinson Prize. This launched his career as a poet. His first major book of poetry, *Chicago Poems*, followed.

After *The Day Book* ceased publication in July 1917, Sandburg moved to the *Chicago Daily News*, reporting and writing editorials. In the fall of 1918 he joined the Newspaper Enterprise Association, a news syndicate, initially serving as Stockholm correspondent during the closing days of World War I. He returned to the *Chicago Daily News* in June 1919. *Cornhuskers*, his second book of poetry, shared the Poetry Society of America Prize in 1919. (He would share the prize again for his third book of poetry, *Smoke and Steel*, in 1921.) In December 1919 he returned to the lecture circuit, reading his poems and singing folk songs while playing guitar. This became a regular occupation, and for the next half century he spent a considerable part of his time on the road performing, which enabled him to collect more folk songs.

In 1920, Sandburg became the *Daily News* film critic, a post he held for seven years. (For his last five years at the paper he was a columnist; he resigned in 1932.) *Rootabaga Stories* was the first of a series of children's books. *Pictorial Review*'s 1925 serialization of excerpts from his biography *Abraham Lincoln: The Prairie Years* brought him financial security for the first time, and the book itself became a best- seller, with 48,000 two-volume, $10 sets purchased within a year. Unconventional in approach, it was considered more a work of literature than of history.

Sandburg's recitals led to a contract with Victor Records in 1925, and his recording of "The Boll Weevil" on March 3, 1926, was among the earliest commercial record releases of folk music. His musical interest was also expressed in *The American Songbag*, an anthology of 280 songs that was the first folk songbook intended for a general audience.

Sandburg spent most of the 1930s working on the second part of his Lincoln biography, *Abraham Lincoln: The War Years*, which eventually appeared as a four-volume set and won the Pulitzer Prize in History in 1940. From 1941 to 1943 he wrote a weekly news column for the Chicago Times Syndicate, later collected in *Home Front Memo*. During World War II he was active in a variety of ways, including writing and narrating radio programs and films in support of the war effort. *Remembrance Rock*, his only novel (initially commissioned by the MGM movie studio, though never made into a film), was a critical failure but a popular success. *Complete Poems* won him a second Pulitzer Prize in 1951 and was followed by *Always the Young Strangers*, a memoir of his youth, which was published on his 75th birthday.

On Feb. 12, 1959, the 150th anniversary of Lincoln's birth, Sandburg addressed a Joint Session of Congress, the first private citizen to do so since 1874. He won the 1959 Grammy Award for Best Documentary or Spoken Word Recording for his album *A Lincoln Portrait* and was nominated in the same category in 1962 for *Carl Sandburg Reading His Poetry*. *The World of Carl Sandburg*, a theatrical revue drawn from his work and including songs from *The American Songbag*, ran on Broadway in 1960. He was a consultant on the Biblical film *The Greatest Story Ever Told* (1965).

Sandburg's writings reflected an expansive populism frequently compared to that of Walt Whitman, crystallized in his belief in the People. This infused his biographical work and his poetry and was also reflected in his efforts to collect and proliferate American folk songs. Though he was not known primarily as a musician, many of his poems were set to music, notably by Earl Robinson, Jacques Wolfe, Richard Donovan, and Ruth Crawford Seeger. The songs he collected, performed, and published in *The American Songbag*— among them "The Foggy, Foggy Dew," "The Buffalo Skinners," "I Ride an Old Paint," "The John B. Sails," and "Frankie and Johnny"—helped to extend the popularity of folk music to a larger audience. For example, "Wanderin'," a Minn. folk song discovered by Sandburg, became a Top Ten hit for Sammy Kaye and His Orch. in 1950.

As a poet-performer who celebrated the common man in a vernacular style, Sandburg, influenced by Whitman, in turn influenced Allen Ginsberg and Bob Dylan, who made a point of visiting him a few years before his death.

WRITINGS: *In Reckless Ecstasy* (Galesburg, Ill., 1904); *Incidentals* (Galesburg, Ill., 1907); *The Plaint of a Rose* (Galesburg, Ill., 1908); *You and Your Job* (Chicago, 1908); *Chicago Poems* (N.Y., 1916); *Cornhuskers* (N.Y., 1918); *The Chicago Race Riots: July, 1919* (N.Y., 1919); *Smoke and Steel* (N.Y., 1920); *Rootabaga Stories* (N.Y., 1922); *Slabs of the Sunburnt West* (N.Y., 1922); *Rootabaga Pigeons* (N.Y., 1923); *Abraham Lincoln: The Prairie Years* (N.Y., 1926); R. West, ed., *Selected Poems* (N.Y., 1926); *The American Songbag* (N.Y., 1927); *Good Morning, America* (N.Y., 1928); *Abe Lincoln Grows Up* (N.Y., 1928); *Steichen the Photographer* (N.Y., 1929); *Potato Face* (N.Y., 1930); *Early Moon* (N.Y., 1930); with P. Angle, *Mary Lincoln: Wife and Widow* (N.Y., 1932); *The People, Yes* (N.Y., 1936); *Abraham Lincoln—The War Years* (N.Y., 1939); *Storm over the Land* (N.Y., 1942); *Home Front Memo* (N.Y., 1943); with F. Meserve, *The Photographs of Abraham Lincoln* (N.Y., 1944); *Re-*

membrance Rock (N.Y., 1948); Lincoln Collector: The Story of the Oliver R. Barrett Lincoln Collection (N.Y., 1949); Complete Poems (N.Y., 1950, rev., exp., 1970); New American Songbag (N.Y., 1950); Always the Young Strangers (N.Y., 1953); Abraham Lincoln: The Prairie Years and the War Years (one-volume edition; N.Y., 1954); Prairie-Town Boy (N.Y., 1955); The S. Range (N.Y., 1957); Harvest Poems, 1910–60 (N.Y., 1960); Wind Song (N.Y., 1960); Honey and Salt (N.Y., 1963); The Wedding Procession of the Rag Doll and the Broom Handle and Who Was in It (N.Y., 1967); H. Mitgang, ed., The Letters of C. S. (N.Y., 1968); The S. Treasury (N.Y., 1970); M. Sandburg (his daughter), ed., Breathing Tokens (N.Y., 1978); Rainbows Are Made (N.Y., 1982); Ever the Winds of Chance (Urbana, Ill., 1983); D. and D. Fetherling, ed., C. S. at the Movies: A Poet in the Silent Era, 1920–27 (Metuchen, N. J., 1985); G. Hendrick, ed., Fables, Foibles, and Foobles (Urbana, Ill., 1988), G. and W. Hendrick, ed., Billy Sunday and Other Poems (N.Y., 1993); G. Hendrick and W. Hendrick, eds., Selected Poems (N.Y., 1996).

BIBL.: K. Detzer, C. S.: A Study in Personality and Background (N.Y., 1941); N. Corwin, The World of C. S. (N.Y., 1961); H. Golden, C. S. (Cleveland, 1961); H. Sandburg (his daughter), Sweet Music (N.Y., 1963); R. Crowder, C. S. (N.Y., 1964); H. Durnell, The America of C. S. (Washington, D.C., 1965); J. Haas, C. S.: A Pictorial Biography (N.Y., 1967); M. Van Doren, C. S. (Washington, D.C., 1969); N. Callahan, C. S., Lincoln of Our Literature (N.Y., 1970); W. Rogers, C. S., Yes (N.Y., 1970); G. Allen, C. S. (Minneapolis, 1972); H. Sandburg, A Great and Glorious Romance: The Story of C. S. and Lilian Steichen (N.Y., 1978); W. Sutton, C. S. Remembered (Metuchen, N. J., 1979); J. Hacker, C. S. (N.Y., 1984); G. d'Alessio, Old Troubadour—C. S. with His Guitar Friends (N.Y., 1987); N. Callahan, C. S.: His Life and Works (University Park, Pa., 1987); H. Sandburg, "...Where Love Begins" (N.Y., 1989); P. Niven, C. S.: A Biography (N.Y., 1991).—**WR**

Sandby, Hermann, Danish cellist and composer; b. Kundby, March 21, 1881; d. Copenhagen, Dec. 14, 1965. After training in Copenhagen, he was a student of Hugo Becker (cello) and Iwan Knorr (composition) in Frankfurt am Main (1895–1900). He gave concerts in Europe before playing in the Philadelphia Orch. (1912–16). After living in N.Y. (1916–30), he returned to Denmark.

WORKS: DRAMATIC: Stage music. **ORCH.:** Cello Concerto (1915; Philadelphia, Feb. 5, 1916); 5 syms. (1930–54); Pastorale d'automne (1937); Serenade for Strings (1940); Nordische Rhapsodie (1954); Violin Concerto; Triple Concerto for Violin, Viola, Piano, and Orch. **CHAMBER:** 4 string quartets (1907–36); String Quintet (1936); Piano Quintet (1938); Piano Trio (1940); piano pieces. **VOCAL:** Songs.—**NS/LK/DM**

Sanderling, Kurt, eminent German conductor, father of **Thomas Sanderling;** b. Arys, Sept. 9, 1912. He received a private education. In 1931 he became a répétiteur at the Berlin Städtische Oper. Being Jewish, he left Nazi Germany for the Soviet Union in 1936. After serving as a conductor with the Moscow Radio Orch. (1936–41), he was a conductor with the Leningrad Phil. (1941–60). From 1960 to 1977 he was chief conductor of the (East) Berlin Sym. Orch., and also of the Dresden State Orch. from 1964 to 1967. In 1965 he made his first appearance at the Salzburg Festival. He made his London debut in 1970 with the Gewandhaus Orch. of Leipzig. From 1972 he made appearances as a guest conductor of the New Philharmonia Orch. (later the Philharmonia Orch.) of London. He also was engaged as a guest conductor throughout Europe, North America, and Japan. Sanderling acquired a distinguished reputation as an interpreter of the Austro-German repertoire, especially of Beethoven, Brahms, and Mahler. He also was an outstanding interpreter of the music of Shostakovich.

BIBL.: H. Bitterlich, K. S.: Für Sie portratiert (Leipzig, 1987). —**NS/LK/DM**

Sanderling, Thomas, German conductor, son of **Kurt Sanderling;** b. Novosibirsk, Russia, Oct. 2, 1942. He studied at the Leningrad Cons. and at the Hanns Eisler Hochschule für Musik in East Berlin. In 1962 he made his conducting debut with the (East) Berlin Sym. Orch. After serving as music director in Sondershausen (1963–64) and Reichenbach (1964–66), he was music director in Halle (from 1966). In 1978 he became permanent guest conductor of the (East) Berlin State Opera. In 1979 he made a highly successful debut at the Vienna State Opera conducting Die Zauberflöte, and subsequently was engaged by many major opera houses and orchs. in Europe and abroad. From 1984 to 1986 he was artistic director of the Amsterdam Phil. He was music director of the Osaka Sym. Orch. from 1992.—**NS/LK/DM**

Sanders, Joe (actually, **Joseph L.**), jazz pianist, singer, leader, arranger; b. Thayer, Kans., Oct. 15, 1896; d. Kansas City, Mo., May 14, 1965. Nicknamed "The Old Left Hander," Sanders shared leadership of Coon-Sanders Night Hawks with drummer Carleton A, Coon. After serving in the U.S. Army during World War I, he and Coon formed a small band that operated in Kansas City. After their broadcasting debut in 1921, they began gradually to augment their membership. In 1924, they secured their first club residencies in Chicago; beginning in 1926, they appeared regularly at the Blackhawk, Chicago, also toured extensively during the summer months. In May 1932, co-leader Carleton Coon died, and Sanders continued to lead the band, then billed as Joe Sanders Original Nighthawks. The band had a long residency at the Blackhawk Cafe through the 1930s. During the 1940s, Sanders did extensive studio work in Hollywood; he also led the band at the Trianon Ballroom while still making appearances at the Blackhawk. During the 1950s, he was a regular member of the Kansas City Opera Company. After suffering for many years with eyesight problems, he had a stroke in 1964 and died soon after.—**JC/LP**

Sanders, Pharoah (Farrell), influential avantgarde jazz tenor and alto saxophonist, flutist, percussionist; b. Little Rock, Ark., Oct. 13, 1940. He received piano lessons from his grandfather and studied drums and clarinet; he also played whistles and cigar tubes and sang. He took up the saxophone and flute at age 16 and played R&B locally, sitting in with visiting artists, including Bobby "Blue" Bland. In 1959, Sanders won a music scholarship to a junior college in Oakland, Calif. While there, he played with Dewey Redman, Monty Waters, and Philly Joe Jones, among other jazz musicians, and performed in blues and R&B groups. Around

1960–61, he met John Coltrane in Calif., and they spent a day trying out mouthpieces together in pawn shops. Sanders moved to N.Y. at the end of 1962 and met Coltrane again when the quartet was playing at the Half Note in 1963. From late-1964 to mid-1965, he studied and worked with Sun Ra, while saxophonist John Gilmore was with Art Blakey. He seems to have recorded with Ra and with the Latin Jazz Quintet during this time, and played with a group led by Don Cherry–Billy Higgins group. Sanders moved back to Calif., and when he saw Coltrane at the Jazz Workshop in San Francisco in September 1965, Coltrane asked him to join the group; he played on some significant recordings and toured Japan with Coltrane in the summer of 1966. With Coltrane, he played free solos composed of shrieks and moans. By October 1966, he had formed his own group with Sonny Sharrock; with Coltrane's support, they recorded in November 1966. The more accessible modal vamp of "The Creator Has a Master Plan" from *Karma* (1969) was something of a hit. He began incorporating influences and instruments from Africa and Asia. During this period, he also worked with Don Cherry and recorded with the Jazz Composer's Orch. During the 1980s, he mainly performed outside of the U.S., and recordings showed him developing what is considered an astounding mastery of standards, including a ballad performance of "It's Easy to Remember" that favorably recalled Coltrane. *Blues for Coltrane*, an LP on which he played, won the Grammy for Best Jazz Album in 1989. He worked with musicians from Gnawa, and journeyed to Africa in 1994. During the 1990s, he continued to incorporate world-music influences in his group and compositions; his touring group included a traditional Moroccan musician.

DISC.: *Pharoah* (1965); *Tauhid* (1966); *Karma* (1969); *Jewels of Thought* (1969); *Thembi* (1970); *Live at the East* (1971); *Black Unity* (1971); *Journey to the One* (1980); *Live* (1982); *Africa* (1987); *Oh Lord, Let Me Do No Wrong* (1987); *Message from Home* (1994). **J. COLTRANE:** *Ascension* (1965); *Live in Seattle* (1965); *Live at the Village Vanguard Again* (1966); *Concert in Japan* (1966).—**LP**

Sanders, Samuel, American pianist and teacher; b. N.Y., June 27, 1937; d. there, July 9, 1999. Although he suffered from a congenital heart condition and had to undergo surgery when he was 9, he pursued his education at Hunter Coll. (B.A., 1959) and was a student of Sergius Kagen (accompaniment) and Irwin Freundlich (piano) at the Juilliard School of Music (M.S., 1961) in N.Y. He also studied with Martin Canin and Boulanger. When he was 12 he made his debut as a recitalist at N.Y.'s Town Hall. After winning a special citation as an accompanist at the Tchaikovsky Competition in Moscow in 1966, he pursued a notably successful career as an accompanist to many of the major musicians of the day, among them Itzhak Perlman, Mstislav Rostropovich, Pinchas Zukerman, Leonard Rose, Yo-Yo Ma, Lynn Harrell, Beverly Sills, Jessye Norman, and Håkan Hagegård. He also was active as a chamber music player and, in 1980, he founded the Cape and Islands Chamber Music Festival on Cape Cod. In 1963 he joined the faculty of the Juilliard School of Music, where he was instrumental in establishing its master's degree program in accompaniment. From 1972 to 1979 he also

was a prof. at the State Univ. of N.Y. in Purchase. In later years, his career was hampered with recurrent heart problems, which led to open heart surgery, followed by heart transplants in both 1990 and 1998.—NS/LK/DM

Sanderson, Sibyl, American soprano; b. Sacramento, Calif., Dec. 7, 1865; d. Paris, May 15, 1903. She was educated in San Francisco, where her musical talent attracted attention; taken to Paris by her mother at the age 19, she studied at the Cons. with Massenet, Sbriglia, and Mathilde Marchesi. Massenet was charmed with her voice and her person and wrote the leading part in *Esclarmonde* for her; she created it at the Opéra-Comique, on May 14, 1889. The role of Thais (Paris Opera, March 16, 1889) was also written by Massenet for her. Other French composers were equally enchanted with her; Saint-Saëns wrote *Phryné* for her (1893). She made her American debut at the Metropolitan Opera in N.Y. as Manon (Jan. 16, 1895), but had little success with the American public. In 1897 she married a wealthy Cuban, Antonio Terry, who died in 1899. —NS/LK/DM

Sandi, Luis, Mexican conductor, teacher, and composer; b. Mexico City, Feb. 22, 1905. He studied violin with Rocabruna (1923–30) and composition with Campa and Mejía (1925–31) at the National Cons. of Mexico City. He conducted a chorus at the Cons. (1922–35); in 1937 he founded the Coro de Madrigalistas and conducted it until 1965. He was a prof. of music in primary schools (1924–32) and chief of the Music Section of the Secretariat of Public Education (1933–65). He publ. *Introducción al estudio de la música: Curso completo* (Mexico City, 1923; second ed., 1956) and a collection of articles as *De música y otras cosas* (Mexico City, 1969).

WORKS: DRAMATIC: O p e r a : *Carlota* (Mexico City, Oct. 23, 1948); *La señora en su balcón* (1964). **B a l l e t :** *Día de difuntos* (1938); *Bonampak* (1948; Mexico City, Nov. 2, 1951); *Coatlicue* (1949). **ORCH.:** *El venado* (1932; Mexico City, Oct. 28, 1938); *Sonora* (1933); *Suite banal* for Small Orch. (1936); *Norte* (Mexico City, Aug. 15, 1941); Flute Concertino (1944); *Tema y Variaciones* (1944); *Esbozos sinfónicos* (1951); *4 Miniatures* (1952); *América*, symphonic poem (1965); Sym. No. 2 (1979). **CHAMBER:** String Quartet (1938); *La hoja de plata* for Instruments (1939); *Fátima*, suite for Guitar (1948); *Cuatro momentos* for String Quartet (1950); *Hoja de album* for Cello and Piano (1956); Cello Sonatina (1958); Quintet (1960); Sonatina for Solo Violin (1967); Violin Sonata (1969); *4 piezas* for Recorders (1977); piano pieces. **VOCAL:** *Las troyanas* for Chorus and Instruments (1936); *Gloria a los héroes*, cantata (1940); *La suave patria*, cantata (1951); choruses; songs.—NS/LK/DM

Sandole, Dennis, jazz educator, composer, guitarist; b. Philadelphia, Pa., Sept. 29, 1913. He was self-taught and toured as a guitarist and arranger in the bands of Ray McKinley (c. July–December 1942), Tommy Dorsey (February 1943–May 1944), Boyd Raeburn (May and June 1944), and Charlie Barnet (c. April–August 1946); Barnet recorded Sandole's composition "Dark Bayou." In the early and mid-1940s, he also did studio work, including film soundtracks in Hollywood. During his Hollywood days, he began to develop original concepts for teaching guitar that became his unpublished method Guitar Lore. Around the fall of 1946, just after leaving Barnet, he began to devote himself to teaching at a Philadelphia school and then at nearby Granoff Studios. He still performed on occasion, including gigs on 52nd Street in N.Y. During much of the 1950s, Sandole was involved in a writers' workshop along with James Moody, Benny Golson, Thad Jones, Art Farmer, and Al "Tootie" Heath, musicians would get together to play and discuss each other's compositions. During this period, Art Farmer and James Moody recorded his pieces. Sandole and his younger brother Adolphe (1918–c. 1981), a composer who played reed instruments and piano, recorded an album entitled *Modern Music from Philadelphia*. From the 1960s through the 1990s, he continued to run a private studio in Philadelphia.

DISC.: *Modern Music from Philadelphia* (1956).—**LP**

Sándor, Arpád, Hungarian-born American pianist, cousin of **György Sándor;** b. Budapest, June 5, 1896; d. there, Feb. 10, 1972. He studied with Bartók and Kodály at the Royal Academy of Music in Budapest, graduating in 1914. He toured the U.S. as an accompanist in 1922, and also wrote art and music criticism for the *Berliner Tageblatt* (1926–33). He then settled in the U.S. and became a naturalized American citizen (1943); toured widely as an accompanist to leading artists, including Jascha Heifetz and Lily Pons.—**NS/LK/DM**

Sándor, György, admired Hungarian-born American pianist and teacher, cousin of **Arpád Sándor;** b. Budapest, Sept. 21, 1912. He studied at the Royal Academy of Music in Budapest with Bartók (piano) and Kodály (composition). After making his debut in Budapest (1930), he toured in Europe before settling in the U.S. (1939); became a naturalized American citizen (1943). After World War II, he played in major music centers of the world. He also taught at Southern Methodist Univ. in Dallas (1956–61); then was director of graduate studies in piano at the Univ. of Mich. in Ann Arbor (1961–81); subsequently taught at the Juilliard School in N.Y. (from 1982). He won particular distinction as an interpreter of the music of Bartók, Kodály, and Prokofiev; was soloist in the premiere of Bartók's third Piano Concerto (Philadelphia, Feb. 8, 1946). He made brilliant transcriptions of Dukas's *L'Apprenti sorcier* and Shostakovich's *Danse russe.* He publ. *On Piano Playing: Motion, Sound, and Expression* (N.Y., 1981). —**NS/LK/DM**

Sandoval, Arturo, Latin-jazz trumpeter, pianist, composer; b. Artemisa, Cuba, Nov. 6, 1949. He was a member of the Cuban pop-jazz group Irakere, which performed in 1977 during a State Department-sponsored jazz concert in Cuba; it was here that he caught the eye of Dizzy Gillespie. Sandoval later traveled internationally with Irakere, and recorded overseas with Gillespie by special arrangement with the Cuban government. He eventually came to the U.S. in July 1990, after he defected while on tour with Gillespie, who called the State Department on his behalf. During the 1990s, he performed at inaugural balls and Super Bowls, toured in 50 countries, won three Grammy Awards, soloed at the Academy Awards, and performed for President Clinton five times. However, he was denied U.S. citizenship in April 1997 due to his previous membership in the Cuban Communist party. He said that he joined Cuba's Communist Party three months before he defected specifically so that he could take his wife and 20-year-old son with him on tour; then the whole family could escape. The rejection of Sandoval's citizenship application caused an uproar from his colleagues in the arts and from the National Academy of Recording Arts and Sciences. Individuals and arts organization sent a flurry of faxes and letters to the White House vouching for Sandoval's anti-Castro credentials and his moral character. Finally, he was granted citizenship in 1999. Since 1992, he has taught music at Fla. International Univ.

DISC.: *To a Finland Station* (1982); *Breaking the Sound Barrier* (1983); *Tumbaito* (1986); *No Problem* (1986); *Flight to Freedom* (1991); *I Remember Clifford* (1992); *Arturo Sandoval & the Latin Tradition* (1995).—**LP**

Sandström, Sven-David, Swedish composer and teacher; b. Borensberg, Oct. 30, 1942. He studied art history and musicology at the Univ. of Stockholm (1963–67) and attended composition classes with Lidholm at the Stockholm Musikhögskolan (1967–72). He also took special courses in advanced techniques of composition with Norgard and Ligeti. In 1981 he joined the faculty of the Stockholm Musikhögskolan. In 1983 he served as chairman of the Swedish section of the ISCM. He became a prof. at the Ind. Univ. School of Music in Bloomington in 1999. In his early works he made use of quarter-tone tuning. Later he turned to tonal and modal writing.

WORKS: DRAMATIC: *Stark såsom döden* (Strong like Death), church opera (Stockholm, April 18, 1978); *Hasta o älskade brud* (Hasta, O Beloved Bride), chamber opera (1978); *Kejsaren Jones* (Emperor Jones), after O'Neill (1980); *Ett drömspel* (The Dreamplay), incidental music to Strindberg's play (1980); *Amos,* church opera (1981); *Slottet det vita,* opera (1981–82; Stockholm, Feb. 12, 1987); *Admorica,* ballet (1985); *Den elfte gryningen,* ballet (Stockholm, Nov. 4, 1988); ballet music (1991); *Staden,* opera (1996; Stockholm, Sept. 12, 1997). **ORCH.:** *Bilder* (Pictures) for Percussion and Orch. (Norrköping, April 17, 1969); *Intrada* for Wind Instruments, Strings, and Percussion (1969); *17 Bildkombinationen* (17 Picture Combinations) for Wind Instruments, Percussion, and Strings (1969); *In the Meantime* for Chamber Orch. (1970); *Sounds* for 14 Strings (1970); *To You* (Arvika, Aug. 15, 1970); *Around a Line* for Wind Instruments, Piano, Percussion, and Strings (1971); *Through and Through* (1972; Stockholm, Feb. 1, 1974); *Con tutta forza* for 41 Wind Instruments and 6 Percussionists (Stockholm, Oct. 28, 1976); *Culminations* (Swedish Radio, Feb. 22, 1977); *Agitato* for Piano and Orch. (1978); *The Rest Is Dross* for Strings (1979); Flute Concerto (1980; Stockholm, Oct. 24, 1983); *Lonesome,* guitar concerto (1982–83; Malmö, May 18, 1983); Concerto for Violin and String Orch. (1985; Orebro, Jan. 18, 1986); *A Day—The Days* (1987); Overture (Stockholm, June 18, 1987); *Invigningsfanfar* for the 50th anniversary of the Swedish Radio (Swedish Radio, Oct. 14, 1988); Cello Concerto (1989; Stockholm, March 2, 1990); Piano Concerto (1990; Helsingborg, Jan. 31, 1991); *Pieces of Pieces* (1992); *Vattenmusik 1* and *2* for

Wind Band (1992); Percussion Concerto (1993); *First-pieces*, overture (1994); *Symphonic Piece* for Orch. and Men's Chorus (1994); *Young Pieces* (1995); Sym. (1999). **CHAMBER:** *Music for 5 String Instruments* (1968); *Sonata for Solo Flute* (1968); *Combinations* for Clarinet (1960); *Concertato* for Clarinet, Trombone, Cello, and Percussion (1969); *String Quartet* (1969); *Disturbances* for 6 Brasses (1970); *Disjointing* for Trombone (1970); *Jumping Excursions* for Clarinet, Cello, Trombone, and Cymbal (1970); *Mosaic* for String Trio (1970); *Under the Surface* for 6 Trombones (1971); *Concentration* for 8 Wind Instruments and 4 Double Basses (1971); *Closeness* for Clarinet (1973); *...And All the Flavors Around*, 6 pieces for Violin, Piano, Clarinet, and Flute (1973); *6 Character Pieces* for Flute, Oboe, Bassoon, 2 Violins, Double Bass, and Percussion (1973); *Convergence* for Bassoon (1973); *Inside* for Bass Trombone and Piano (1974); *Metal, Metal* for 4 Percussionists (1974); *In the Shadow of...* for Piano, Cello, and Percussion (1974); *Ratio* for Tuba and Bass Drum (1974); *Utmost* for Wind Quintet, Trumpet, Trombone, Tuba, and Percussion (London, Nov. 10, 1975); *Effort* for Cello (1977); *Break This Heavy Chain That Does Freeze My Bones Around* for 2 Bassoons (1979); *Within* for 8 Trombones and Percussion ad libitum (1979); *Drums* for Timpani and 4 Percussionists (1980); *Behind* for String Quartet (1981); *The Last Fight* for Percussion (1984); *Sax Music* for Saxophone Quartet (1985); *Chained* for Percussion Ensemble (1986); *The Slumberous Mass* for 4 Trombones (1987); *Dance III* for 3 Cellos (1988); *Pieces of Wood* for 6 Percussionists (1992). **KEYBOARD: P i a n o :** *Concentration II* for 2 Pianos (1972); *High Above* (1972); *5 Duets* for Piano (1973); *Introduction—Out of Memories—Finish* for 2 Pianos (1981). **O r g a n :** *The Way* (1973); *Openings* (1975); *Libera me* (1980). **VOCAL:** *Invention* for 16 Voices (1969); *Lamento* for 3 Choral Groups and 4 Trombones (1971); *Visst?* for Soprano, 2 Choruses, Wind Instruments, Pop Orch., and Violin Group (1971; Mellerud, April 23, 1972); *Just a Bit* for Soprano, Bassoon, Violin, and Harp (1972); *Birgitta-Music I* for Speaking and Singing Groups, Orch., Renaissance Ensemble, Organ, and Folk Musicians and Dancers (Vadstena, June 23, 1973); *Dilecte mi (Canticum canticorum)*, motet for Men's and Women's Choruses (1974); *Expression* for Amplified Mezzo-soprano, Cello, Piano, 4- Hands, and Tape (1976); *A Cradle Song/The Tyger*, 2 poems for Chorus, after William Blake (1978); *Spring—Introduction—Earth's Answer*, 3 poems for Chorus, after William Blake (1978); *Tystnaden* (Silence) for Tenor, Narrator, and 14 String Instruments (1979); *Requiem: De ur alla minnen fallna* (Requiem: Mute the Bereaved Memories Speak) for 4 Soloists, Mixed Chorus, Children's Chorus, Orch., and Tape (1979; Stockholm, Feb. 19, 1982); *Agnus Dei* for Chorus (1980); *Our Peace*, motet for 3 Choruses and 3 Organs (1983); *Missa brevis* for Chorus (1984); *Ut över slätten med en doft av hav*, cantata for Soloists, Chorus, and Orch. (1984); *Convivere* for 5 Singers and 6 Instrumentalists (1985); *Kantat till Filharmonin* for Soloists, Chorus, and Orch. (1985); *Stille etter Gud* for 3 Choruses (1986); *24 romantiska etyder* for Chorus (1988); *Mass and Psaltery Psalm* for Soloists, Chorus, Brass Quintet, and 2 Organs (1992); *High Mass* for Chorus, Organ, and Orch. (1993–94); *Nobelmusik* for Chorus, Brass Quintet, and Organ (1994); *Se, öarna* for Mezzo-soprano and Wind Quintet (1998).—**NS/LK/DM**

Sandt, Maximilian van de, Dutch pianist, teacher, and composer; b. Rotterdam, Oct. 18, 1863; d. Cologne, July 14, 1934. He was a pupil of Liszt in the last year of the master's life. He toured in Europe with conspicuous success. From 1896 to 1906 he was on the faculty of the Cologne Cons., and from 1910 he taught at Bonn. He composed many brilliant piano pieces in a Romantic vein.—**NS/LK/DM**

Sandunova, Elizaveta Semyonovna, prominent Russian mezzo-soprano who was known as **Uranova**; b. St. Petersburg, c. 1772; d. Moscow, Dec. 3, 1826. She was a student of Martín y Soler, Paisiello, and Sarti in St. Petersburg. In 1790 she made her operatic debut in Martín y Soler's *Arbore di Diana* in St. Petersburg, and then sang at the imperial theaters there from 1791 to 1794. She took the professional name of Uranova by order of Catherine II in honor of the discovery of the planet Uranus. After marrying the actor Sila Sandunov in 1794, they appeared together at the Petrovsky Theater in Moscow. They were divorced in 1810 and in 1813 Uranova returned to St. Petersburg, where she made frequent appearances until her retirement from the stage in 1823.—**NS/LK/DM**

Sandvik, Ole Mrk, respected Norwegian musicologist; b. Hedemarken, May 9, 1875; d. Holmenkollen, near Oslo, Aug. 5, 1976. He received training for careers in teaching (1895) and theology (graduated, 1902), and also studied music with his father and Gudbrand Bhn, and in Germany (1913); took his Ph.D. in 1922 at the Univ. of Christiania. He taught at Christiania's (Oslo's) Hegdehaugen School (1913–45) and gave courses in church music at the Seminary for Practical Theology at the Univ. of Christiania (Oslo; 1916–45). He was founder of the Norwegian Musicological Soc., serving as ed. of its yearbook (1937–72).

WRITINGS: *Norsk kirkenmusikk og densilder* (Christiania, 1918); *Folkemusik i Gudbrandsdalen* (Christiania, 1919; second ed., 1948); *Norsk folkemusik: Saerlig stlandsmusikken* (Christiania, 1921); with G. Schjelderup, *Norges musikhistorie* (Christiania, 1921–22); ed. with H. Panum and W. Behrend, *Illustreret musiklexsikon* (Copenhagen, 1924–26; new ed., 1940); *Graduale for den norske kirke* (Oslo, 1925; second ed., 1957); with J. Gleditsch et al., *Koralbok for den norske kirke* (Oslo, 1926); *Liturgisk musikk til minnegudstjenester på 900-års- jubileet Olsok 1930* (Oslo, 1930); *Norsk koralhistorie* (Oslo, 1930); *Kingotona* (Oslo, 1941); *Vesperale for den norske kirke* (Oslo, 1941); *Gregoriansk sang* (Oslo, 1945); *Ludwig M. Lindeman og folkemelodien: Ein kilderstudie* (Oslo, 1950); *Setesdalsmelodier* (Oslo, 1952); *Norske religiose folketoner* (Oslo, 1960–64); *"Springleiker" i norske bygdier* (Oslo, 1967); ed. with O. Gaukstad, *David Monrad Johansen i skrift og tale* (Oslo, 1968).

BIBL.: *Festschrift til O.M. S.s, 70 års dagen 1875–9. Mai 1945* (Oslo, 1945).—**NS/LK/DM**

Sandvold, Arild (Edvin), eminent Norwegian organist, choral conductor, teacher, and composer; b. Christiania, June 2, 1895; d. there (Oslo), Aug. 15, 1984. He studied at the Christiania Cons. and with Straube in Leipzig. He made Christiania the center of his activities, where he was active as an organist from 1914, later serving as cathedral organist and subsequently canon at Var Frelsers Church (1933–66). From 1917 to 1969 he taught organ at the Cons. He was conductor of the Caecilia Choral Soc. from 1928 to 1957. In 1956 the

Norwegian government awarded him an annual stipend. He composed mainly sacred works, including cantatas. His most ambitious score was his *Misjonskantate* (Mission Cantata; 1942; orchestrated 1967). He also wrote many organ pieces. Sandvold greatly influenced the course of 20th- century Norwegian sacred music. —NS/LK/DM

Sangiovanni, Antonio, celebrated Italian singing teacher; b. Bergamo, Sept. 14, 1831; d. Milan, Jan. 6, 1892. He studied at the Milan Cons. where, in 1854, he was appointed prof. of singing. Two generations of Italian and foreign singers were his pupils.—NS/LK/DM

Sanjuán, Pedro, Spanish-born American conductor, teacher, and composer; b. San Sebastián, Nov. 15, 1886; d. Washington, D.C., Oct. 18, 1976. He studied composition with Turina. After conducting in Europe, he went to Havana, where he organized the Havana Phil. (1926); was also a teacher of composition there, numbering Roldán, Caturla, and other Cuban composers among his pupils. After a sojourn in Madrid (1932–36), he again conducted the Havana Phil. (1939–42); in 1942 he was appointed prof. of composition at Converse Coll. in Spartanburg, S.C. In 1947 he became a naturalized American citizen.

WORKS: ORCH.: *Rondo fantástico* (Havana, Nov. 29, 1926); *Castilla,* suite (Havana, June 12, 1927); *Sones de Castilla* for Small Orch.; *La Macumba,* "ritual sym." (St. Louis, Dec. 14, 1951, composer conducting); *Antillean Poem* for Band (N.Y., Aug. 11, 1958, composer conducting); *Symphonic Suite* (Washington, D.C., May 9, 1965). OTHER: Choral works; piano pieces. —NS/LK/DM

Sanjust, Filippo, Italian stage designer and opera director; b. Rome, Sept. 9, 1925; d. there, Nov. 29, 1992. He studied architecture in Rome and at Princeton Univ. before turning to stage design. In 1958 Visconti chose him as designer for his staging of *Don Carlos* at London's Covent Garden, and thereafter they collaborated successfully on various productions, including *Il Trovatore* at Covent Garden (1964) and *Le nozze di Figaro* in Rome (1964) and at the Metropolitan Opera in N.Y. (1968). Henze chose Sanjust as designer for the premieres of his *Der junge Lord* in Berlin in 1965 and for his *The Bassarids* at the Salzburg Festival in 1966. From 1969 Sanjust combined work as a stage designer with opera directing. Among his most distinguished productions were *Ariadne auf Naxos* (1976) and *Falstaff* (1980) in Vienna, *L'incoronazione di Poppea* (1979) in Brussels, and *Simon Boccanega* (1980) at Covent Garden.—NS/LK/DM

Sankey, Ira D(avid), noted American evangelistic singer, gospel hymn composer, and hymnbook compiler; b. Edinburgh, Pa., Aug. 28, 1840; d. N.Y., Aug. 13, 1908. As a youth of 17, he became choir leader in the Methodist Church of New Castle, Pa.; served for a year with the N.Y. 12th Infantry Regiment at the time of the Civil War. In 1870 he was a delegate to the YMCA convention at Indianapolis, where his forceful singing attracted the attention of the evangelist preacher Dwight L. Moody. He joined Moody as music director

and remained at this post for some 30 years, until approaching blindness forced his retirement in 1903. Of his many gospel tunes, the most popular has proved to be *The Ninety and Nine* (1874), which he improvised at a moment's notice during a service in Edinburgh, Scotland. His chief publications were *Sacred Songs and Solos* (London, 1873) and 6 vols. of *Gospel Hymns and Sacred Songs* (1875–91). As president of the publ. firm of Biglow & Main (1895–1903), he brought out numerous works, including many of his own. He also publ. *My Life and the Story of the Gospel Hymns and of the Sacred Songs and Solos* (Philadelphia, 1906). He is not to be confused with another gospel song writer, Ira Allan Sankey, a lesser light than Ira D(avid) Sankey.

BIBL.: E. Goodspeed, *A Full History of the Wonderful Career of Moody and S.,* in Great Britain and America (N.Y., 1876); *The I.D. S. Centenary: Proceedings of the Centenary Celebration...with Some Hitherto Unpublished Correspondence* (New Castle, Pa., 1941); C. Ludwig, *S. Still Sings* (Anderson, Ind., 1947).—NS/LK/DM

Sanromá, Jesús Maria, brilliant Puerto Rican pianist; b. Carolina (of Catalonian parents), Nov. 7, 1902; d. San Juan, Oct. 12, 1984. At the age of 14, he was sent to the U.S. by the governor of Puerto Rico. He he studied piano with Antoinette Szumowska at the New England Cons. of Music in Boston, and in 1920 won the Mason & Hamlin piano prize; then studied with Cortot (in Paris) and Schnabel (in Berlin). From 1926 to 1944 he was pianist of the Boston Sym. Orch. He taught at the New England Cons. of Music (1930–41), and gave annual concerts in the U.S., Canada, and South America; also played in Europe. In 1951 he was appointed chairman of the music dept. at the Univ. of Puerto Rico; he was head of the piano dept. at the Puerto Rico Cons. of Music (1959–80). He excelled particularly as an interpreter of contemporary music; gave the premieres of Piston's Concertino (1937) and Hindemith's Concerto (1947).

BIBL.: E. Belava, *El niño S.: Biografia mínima* (San Juan, 1952; second ed., 1962).—NS/LK/DM

Santa Cruz (Wilson), Domingo, eminent Chilean composer and music educator; b. La Cruz, near Quillota, July 5, 1899; d. Santiago, Jan. 6, 1987. He studied jurisprudence at the Univ. of Chile, then entered diplomatic service, and was second secretary of the Chilean legation in Spain (1921–24). He received his musical training with Enrique Soro in Santiago and with Conrado del Campo in Madrid. Returning to Chile, he devoted himself to musical administration, teaching, and composition. From 1928 to 1953 he served as a prof. at the National Cons. in Santiago; was acting dean (1932–33) and dean (1933–51; 1962–68) of the faculty of fine arts at the Univ. of Chile. His role in the promotion of musical culture in Chile was of great importance. In his works, he followed the cosmopolitan traditions of neo-Classical music; made use of identifiable Chilean melodies in but a few of his compositions.

WORKS (all first perf. in Santiago unless otherwise given): ORCH.: *5 piezas breves* for Strings (May 31, 1937); *Variaciones* for Piano and Orch. (June 25, 1943); *Sinfonia concertante* for Flute, Piano, and Strings (Nov. 29, 1945); 4 syms.: No. 1 for

Strings, Celesta, and Percussion (1945–46; May 28, 1948; rev. 1970), No. 2 for Strings (Nov. 26, 1948), No. 3 for Contralto and Orch. (Washington, D.C., May 9, 1965), and No. 4 (1968). **CHAMBER**: 3 string quartets (1930; 1946–47; 1959); piano pieces. **VOCAL**: *Cantata de los ríos de Chile* for Chorus and Orch. (1941; Nov. 27, 1942); *Egloga* for Soprano, Chorus, and Orch. (1949; Nov. 24, 1950); *Cantares de la pascua* for Women's Voices (1949; Dec. 7, 1950); *Canciones del mar*, song cycle (1955); *Endechas* for Tenor and 8 Instruments (1957); *Oratio Ieremiae prophetae* for Chorus and Orch. (1970).—**NS/LK/DM**

Santa Maria, Fráy Tomas de, important Spanish organist and composer; b. Madrid, c. 1510; d. Ribadavia, 1570. He publ. *Libro llamado Arte de tañer fantasía* (Valladolid, 1565), a treatise on playing fantasias on keyboard instruments and on the guitar or lute (Ger. tr., with critical and biographical introduction, by E. Harich-Schneider and R. Boadella, Leipzig, 1937).

BIBL.: W. Hultberg, *Sancta Maria's "Libro llamado Arte de tañer fantasía": A Critical Evaluation* (diss., Univ. of Southern Calif., 1964).—**NS/LK/DM**

Santana, innovative rock group led by Latin-rock/jazz guitarist and bandleader, Carlos Santana; Carlos Santana, lead gtr., voc. (b. Autlan de Navarro, Mexico, July 20, 1947); Gregg Rolie, kybd., voc. (b. Seattle, Wash., June 17, 1947); David Brown, bs. (b. N.Y., Feb. 15, 1947); Mike Carabello, congas, perc. (b. San Francisco, Calif., Nov. 18, 1947); Jose "Chepito" Areas, timbales, perc.n; and Michael Shrieve, drm. (b. San Francisco, Calif., July 6, 1949). Later members included guitarist-vocalist Neal Schon (b. San Mateo, Calif., Feb. 27, 1954); lead vocalists Leon Patillo, Greg Walker, Alex Ligertwood, and Buddy Miles; percussionists Coke Escovedo, Armando Peraza (timbales), and Raul Rekow (conga); keyboardists Tom Coster and Chester Thompson; bassists Alphonso Johnson and Benny Reitveld; and drummers Leon "Ndugu" Chancler and Graham Lear. Gregg Rolie and Neal Schon departed in 1972 and formed Journey in 1973.

As one of the few unknown acts to appear at the Woodstock Festival in August 1969, Santana electrified the crowd with a stunning extended performance of the band's "Soul Sacrifice," featuring one of the most famous drum solos in the history of rock by Michael Shrieve. Signed to Columbia Records, Santana's debut album came out barely a month after Woodstock. It featured layers of exotic percussion and Carlos Santana's passionate lead guitar playing (replete with his signature sustained-note style) and became an instant success, staying on the album charts for more than two years. The album included "Soul Sacrifice," a minor hit version of Olatunji's "Jingo," and the near-smash hit "Evil Ways." *Abraxas*, usually regarded as their finest work, yielded a smash hit with Peter Green's "Black Magic Woman" and a major hit with Tito Puente's "Oye Como Va," while containing Carlos's own "Samba Pa Ti." For their third album, variously referred to as *New Album* and *Santana III*, the group added guitarist Neal Schon and percussionist Coke Escovedo. The album produced a major hit with "Everybody's Everything" and a moderate hit with "No One to Depend On."

Internal disputes within Santana had become rife in 1971, and the group disbanded for a time in 1972. In the meantime, Carlos Santana recorded a best- selling live album with powerhouse drummer-vocalist Buddy Miles from The Electric Flag. Santana formed a new edition of the group in the fall of 1972, by which time he had embraced the teachings of guru Sri Chinmoy and taken on the spiritual name "Devadip." The new group's lineup included holdovers Neal Schon, Gregg Rolie, Chepito Areas, and Michael Shrieve plus keyboardist Tom Coster and aging Latin percussionist Armando Peraza, among others. Shrieve had introduced Carlos Santana to the music of Miles Davis and John Coltrane, and this aggregation recorded Santana's first departure from Latin-style rock, *Caravanserai*, which revealed a decided jazz orientation. Gregg Rolie and Neal Schon subsequently departed to form Journey with bassist Ross Valory in 1973.

In 1973, Carlos Santana toured and recorded *Love, Devotion, Surrender* with guitarist "Mahavishnu" John McLaughlin, the man who had introduced him to the philosophy of Sri Chinmoy. Santana later recorded *Illuminations* with fellow devotee "Turiya" Alice Coltrane, the keyboard and harp-playing widow of jazz saxophonist John Coltrane. The Santana group's next album, *Welcome*, recorded with jazz vocalist Leon Thomas, continued to exhibit the group leader's spiritual bent and jazz orientation. Yet another edition of the band, with vocalist Leon Patillo and drummers Michael Shrieve and Leon "Ndugu" Chancler (Shrieve's subsequent replacement), recorded *Borboletta*. During 1975, Santana, rejoined by original bassist David Brown, toured the U.S. with Eric Clapton and, at mid-year, impresario Bill Graham became the group's manager.

Eventually, in 1976, Santana returned to its Latin-style sound with the highly acclaimed *Amigos* album, which featured "Europa," "Dance, Sister, Dance," and "Gitaro." The members included Tom Coster (utilizing synthesizer for the first time), vocalist Greg Walker, Armando Peraza, and Leon Chancler. Walker, Peraza, and Chancler left before the release of *Festival*, but Walker and Chepito Areas returned for the double-record set *Moonflower*, along with newcomers Raul Rekow (congas) and Graham Lear (drums). The live album yielded a major hit with a cover version of The Zombie's "She's Not There," whereas *Inner Secrets* provided hits with cover versions of Buddy Holly's "Well All Right" and The Classics IV's "Stormy." In 1979, Carlos Santana issued the mostly instrumental solo album *Oneness: Silver Dreams–Golden Reality*. *Marathon* featured new vocalist Alex Ligertwood and yielded a moderate hit with "You Know That I Love You." By early 1980, Santana included Ligertwood, Armando Peraza, Graham Lear, and Raul Rekow, among others. During the year, Carlos Santana recorded *The Swing of Delight* with jazz musicians Herbie Hancock, Wayne Shorter, and Ron Carter.

The group scored a major hit with Russ Ballard's "Winning" and a minor hit with J. J. Cale's "The Sensitive Kind" from *Zebop!*, the band's last best-selling album. They managed their final major hit in 1982 with "Hold On" from *Shango*. Carlos next recorded the diverse solo album *Havana Moon* with Booker T. Jones, The Fabulous Thunderbirds, and Willie Nelson, who sang lead vocals on "They All Went to Mexico." Santana began playing Nev. casinos in 1984, by which time the group included vocalists Greg Walker and Alex Ligertwood, drummer Graham Lear, and later-day mainstays Chester Thompson (kybd.) and Alphonso Johnson (bs.). The group toured with Bob Dylan in 1985 and added Buddy Miles for the *Freedom* album and tour. After the *Blues for Salvador* album and tour, Carlos Santana toured the U.S. and Europe with jazz saxophonist Wayne Shorter.

During 1988, Santana reunited with Carlos Santana, Gregg Rolie, Chepito Areas, and Michael Shrieve, joined by Armando Peraza, Chester Thompson, and Alphonso Johnson, for a tour, but a promised reunion album was never recorded, and the veterans soon went their separate ways. In 1989, Carlos Santana formed his own record label, Guts and Grace Records. The Santana group recorded two more albums for Columbia before switching to Polydor Records in 1992. In 1993, they toured with Bob Dylan and recorded *Sacred Fire*, for which the group added Carlos's guitar-playing brother Jorge, a veteran of the 1970s Latin rock group Malo (1972's major hit "Suavecito"). In 1994, Santana performed at the Woodstock II Festival and Island Records issued *The Santana Brothers*, recorded by Carlos and Jorge Santana with their nephew Carlos Hernandez. Carlos Santana toured with Jeff Beck in 1995. In 1998, Gregg Rolie, Neal Schon, Mike Shrieve, Mike Carabello, and Chepito Areas reunited to record *Abraxas Pool* for Miramar Records, eventually released in 1997. Santana was inducted into the Rock and Roll Hall of Fame in 1998. Carlos Santana made a surprise "comeback" with his album *Supernatural* in 1999, featuring Santana accompanying various recent rock stars.

DISC.: SANTANA: *Santana* (1969); *Abraxas* (1970/1985); *Santana III* (1971); *Caravanserai* (1972); *Welcome* (1973); *Borboletta* (1974); *Amigos* (1976); *Festival* (1976); *Moonflower* (1977); *Inner Secrets* (1978); *Marathon* (1979); *Zebop!* (1981/1984); *Shango* (1982); *Beyond Appearances* (1985); *Freedom* (1987); *Spirits Dancing in the Flesh* (1990); *Lotus* (rec. 1973 in Japan; rel.1991); *Milagro* (1992); *Sacred Fire: Live in South America* (1993). **CARLOS SANTANA AND BUDDY MILES:** *Live!* (1972). **CARLOS SANTANA AND JOHN MCLAUGHLIN:** *Love, Devotion, Surrender* (1973). **DEVADIP CARLOS SANTANA AND TURIYA ALICE COLTRANE:** *Illuminations* (1974). **CARLOS SANTANA:** *Oneness/Silver Dreams— Golden Reality* (1979); *The Swing of Delight* (1980); *Havana Moon* (1983); *Blues for Salvador* (1987); *Supernatural* (1999). **THE SANTANA BROTHERS:** *Brothers* (1994). **ABRAXAS POOL (WITH GREGG ROLIE, NEAL SCHON, MICHAEL SHRIEVE, MIKE CARABELLO, AND CHEPITO AREAS):** *Abraxas Pool* (1997).

Santi, Nello, Italian conductor; b. Adria, Sept. 22, 1931. He studied at the Padua Liceo Musicale and with Coltro and Pedrollo. In 1951 he made his debut conducting *Rigoletto* in Padua, and then conducted in various Italian opera houses. From 1958 he was a regular conductor at the Zürich Opera. In 1960 he made his first appearance at London's Covent Garden conducting *La Traviata*. That same year he made his debuts at the Vienna State Opera and the Salzburg Festival. He made his Metropolitan Opera debut in N.Y. on Jan. 25, 1962, conducting *Un ballo in maschera*. He remained on its roster until 1965, and then conducted there regularly from 1976. As a guest conductor, he led operatic performances in Milan, Paris, Berlin, Munich, Florence, Naples, Geneva, and other European music centers. He also appeared as a guest conductor with many European orchs. In 1986 he became chief conductor of the Basel Radio Sym. Orch. In 1988 he conducted *Aida* in the first arena production in London at Earl's Court. He has won particular distinction for his performances of the Italian operatic repertoire.—NS/LK/DM

Santini, Abbate Fortunato, Italian music scholar and composer; b. Rome, Jan. 5, 1778; d. there, Sept. 14, 1861. He studied counterpoint with Jannacconi and at the Collegio Salviati, and later organ with Guidi; was ordained a priest in 1801. He devoted much time to acquiring a valuable library, which included about 4,500 MSS and 1,100 printed items; its holdings were enumerated in his *Catalogo della musica esistente presso Fortunato Santini in Roma nel palazzo de' principi Odescalchi incontro la chiesa de' SS. XII. Apostoli* (Rome, 1820). His original compositions include a Requiem, a Stabat Mater, and many motets.

BIBL.: V. Stassov, *L'Abbé S. et sa collection musicale à Rome* (Florence, 1854); J. Killing, *Kirchenmusikalische Schätze der Bibliothek des Abbate F. S.* (Düsseldorf, 1910).—NS/LK/DM

Santini, Gabriele, Italian conductor; b. Perugia, Jan. 20, 1886; d. Rome, Nov. 13, 1964. After studies in Perugia and Bologna, he conducted opera in Rio de Janeiro, Buenos Aires, N.Y., and Chicago. From 1925 to 1929 he was Toscanini's assistant at La Scala in Milan; then was a conductor (1929–33) and artistic director (1944–47) at the Rome Opera.—NS/LK/DM

Santley, Sir Charles, noted English baritone; b. Liverpool, Feb. 28, 1834; d. Hove, near London, Sept. 22, 1922. He studied with Nava in Milan, making his operatic debut as Dr. Grenville in *La Traviata* in Pavia (1857); then continued his training with García in London, where he sang for the first time as Adam in Haydn's *Creation* on Nov. 16, 1857. His British operatic debut followed as Hoël in *Dinorah* at Covent Garden in a production mounted by the Pyne-Harrison Co. (Oct. 1, 1859); he continued to sing with the company until 1863, creating many roles in English operas under its auspices. In 1862 he appeared with the Royal Italian Opera at Covent Garden; that same year he became a member of Mapleson's company at Her Majesty's Theatre, winning renown for his portrayal of Valentine in 1863; he left the company in 1870. After singing at the Gaiety Theatre and touring in the U.S. as a concert artist (1871), he sang with the Carl Rosa Opera Co. (1875–77); subsequently devoted himself to oratorio and concert appearances. He sang in Australia (1889–90) and again in the U.S. (1891). On May 23, 1911, he made his farewell appearance at Covent Garden but came out of retirement in 1915 to sing at a concert for Belgian war refugees. In 1887 he was made a Commander of the

Order of St. Gregory by Pope Leo XIII, and in 1907 he was knighted by King Edward VII. His publ. some songs under the pseudonym Ralph Betterton; he also publ. *Student and Singer* (London, 1892; reminiscences), *The Singing Master* (2 parts, London, 1900), *The Art of Singing and Vocal Declamation* (London, 1908), and *Reminiscences of My Life* (London, 1909).

BIBL.: J. Levien, *Sir C. S.* (London, 1930).—NS/LK/DM

Santoliquido, Francesco, Italian composer; b. San Giorgio a Cremano, Naples, Aug. 6, 1883; d. Anacapri, Aug. 26, 1971. He studied at the Liceo di Santa Cecilia in Rome, graduating in 1908. In 1912 he went to live in Hammamet, a village in Tunisia, spending part of each year in Rome; in 1933 he made his home in Anacapri. Many of his compositions contain melodic inflections of Arabian popular music. He publ. *Il Dopo-Wagner, Claudio Debussy e Richard Strauss* (Rome, 1909; second ed., 1922); also books of verse; wrote short stories in Eng. His third wife was the pianist and teacher Ornella (née Puliti) Santoliquido (b. Florence, Sept. 4, 1906; d. there, Nov. 11, 1977). She studied with Brugnoli, and, after receiving her diploma at the Florence Cons., she continued her training with Casella in Rome and Cortot in Paris. She was a teacher at the Rome Cons. (1939–71); played in chamber-music concerts; became an advocate of contemporary music.

WORKS: DRAMATIC: O p e r a : *La Favola di Helga* (Milan, Nov. 23, 1910); *Ferhuda* (Tunis, Jan. 30, 1919); *L'Ignota* (1921; not perf.); *La porta verde*, musical tragedy (Bergamo, Oct. 15, 1953). **B a l l e t :** *La Bajadera dalla maschera gialla* (1917). **ORCH.:** *Crepuscolo sul mare* (Nuremberg, Jan. 19, 1909, composer conducting); *Acquarelli* (1914; Rome, April 11, 1923); *Il profumo delle oasi sahariane* (1915; Tunis, April 17, 1918); 2 syms. (1916; c. 1927); *La sagra dei morti*, heroic elegy for the victims of World War I (1920); *Grotte di Capri* (1925; rev. 1943); *Preludio e Burlesca* for Strings (1938); *Alba di gloria sul passo Uarièu*, symphonic prelude (1939; Rome, Nov. 13, 1940); *Santuari asiatici*, symphonic sketches (1952). **CHAMBER:** Violin Sonata (1924); String Quartet (1931); *Aria antica* for Cello and Piano; *Chiarita lunare* for Violin and Piano; *2 pezzi* for 5 Wind Instruments. **P i a n o :** *Piccola ballata; 2 acquaforti tunisine.* **VOCAL:** Song cycle after P. Louÿs; *Messa facile* for Chorus.—NS/LK/DM

Santoro, Claudio, distinguished Brazilian composer, conductor, and teacher; b. Manáos, Nov. 23, 1919; d. Brasília, March 27, 1989. He studied at the Rio de Janeiro Cons. and received training from Guerra and Koellreutter. In 1946 he held a Guggenheim fellowship. In 1947 he received a French scholarship and pursued his studies in Paris with Boulanger and Eugène Bigot. He was awarded the Lili Boulanger Prize in 1948. In 1965 he held a Ford Foundation scholarship and was active in Berlin. From 1970 to 1978 he taught at the Univ. of Heidelberg-Mannheim. In 1979 he settled in Brasília, where he was a conductor at the Univ. and of the orch. of the National Theater until his death. He also appeared as a guest conductor in South America and Europe. In his earliest works, he composed mainly in the 12-tone manner. After a period in which he wrote in an accessible style, he returned to advanced techniques, including aleatory.

WORKS: DRAMATIC: B a l l e t : *A fábrica* (1947); *Anticocos* (1951); *O café* (1953); *Icamiabas* (1959); *Zuimaaluti* (1960); *Prelúdios* (1962). **ORCH.:** 14 syms.: No. 1 (1940), No. 2 (1945), No. 3 (Rio de Janeiro, Dec. 20, 1949), No. 4, *Da paz* (Rio de Janeiro, Oct. 30, 1945), No. 5 (Rio de Janeiro, March 28, 1956), No. 6 (Paris, May 1, 1963), No. 7, *Brasília* (1960), No. 8 (1963), No. 9 (1982), No. 10 (1982), No. 11 (1984), No. 12 (1985), No. 13 (1986), and No. 14 (1987); *Variations on a 12- tone Row* (1945); *Ponteio* for Strings (Rio de Janeiro, June 19, 1945); 2 violin concertos (1951, 1958); *Chôro* for Saxophone and Orch. (Rio de Janeiro, June 20, 1952); 3 piano concertos (1953, 1959, 1960); *Abertura tragica* (1958); Cello Concerto (1961; Washington, D.C., May 12, 1965); *Asymptotic Interactions* (1969). **CHAMBER:** 5 violin sonatas (1940–57); String Trio (1941); Flute Sonata (1941); 7 string quartets (1943–65); 4 cello sonatas (1943–63); Oboe Sonata (1943); Trumpet Sonata (1946); *Diagrammas cíclicos* for Piano and Percussion (1966); *Mutations I-VI* for Various Instruments (1968–72); *Antistruktur* for Harp and Cello (1970). **P i a n o :** 25 preludes (1957–63). **VOCAL:** *Ode to Stalingrad* for Chorus and Orch. (1947); *Berlin, 13 de agôsto* for Narrator, Chorus, and Orch. (1962); *Agrupamento a 10* for Voice and Chamber Orch. (1966).

BIBL.: V. Mariz, *C. S.* (Rio de Janeiro, 1994).—NS/LK/DM

Santos, (José Manuel) Joly Braga, Portuguese conductor and composer; b. Lisbon, May 14, 1924; d. there, July 18, 1988. He studied composition with Luis de Freitas Branco at the Lisbon Cons. (1934–43), conducting with Scherchen at the Venice Cons. (1948), electronic music at the Gavessano (Switzerland) Acoustic Experimental Studio (1957–58), and composition with Mortari at the Rome Cons. (1959–60). He conducted the Oporto Radio Sym. Orch. (1955–59); subsequently was active as a guest conductor. His music represents a felicitous fusion of Portuguese Renaissance modalities and folk rhythms.

WORKS: DRAMATIC: O p e r a : *Viver ou morrer* (To Live or to Die), radio opera (1952); *Mérope* (Lisbon, May 15, 1959); *Trilogia das Barcas* (1969; Lisbon, May, 1970). **B a l l e t :** *Alfama* (1956); *A nau Catrineta* (1959); *Encruzilhada* (1968). **ORCH.:** 3 symphonic overtures (1945, 1947, 1954); 6 syms.: No. 1 (1946), No. 2 (1948), No. 3 (1949), No. 4 (1950), No. 5, *Virtus Lusitaniae* (1966), and No. 6 for Soprano, Chorus, and Orch. (1972); *Nocturno* for Strings (1947); Concerto for Strings (1951); *Variações sinfónicas sobre un theme de l'Alentejano* (1952); Viola Concerto (1960); *Divertimento* for Chamber Orch. (1961); *3 esboços sinfónicos* (3 Symphonic Sketches; 1962); *Sinfonietta* for Strings (1963); Double Concerto for Violin, Cello, String Orch., and Harp (1965); *Variações concertantes* for Harp and Strings (1967); Piano Concerto (1973); *Variações* (1976). **CHAMBER:** *Nocturno* for Violin and Piano (1942); 2 string quartets (1944, 1956); Violin Sonata (1945); Piano Quartet (1957). **VOCAL:** *Requiem à memória de Pedro de Freitas Branco* for Soloists, Chorus, and Orch. (1964); *Ode à música* for Chorus and Orch. (1965); choruses.—NS/LK/DM

Santucci, Marco, Italian composer; b. Camajore, Tuscany, July 4, 1762; d. Lucca, Nov. 29, 1843. He studied at the Cons. di Loreto in Naples. He went to Lucca in 1790 and was ordained a priest in 1794. After serving as maestro di cappella at Rome's S. Giovanni in Laterano (1797–1808), he returned to Lucca as canon at the Cathedral. A motet *a 16* for 4 choirs received a prize from the Accademia Napoleone in 1806 because of the "entirely new and original" combination of voices. Baini publ. an energetic protest against this award, pointing out that such polyphonic writing was common in works by Italian composers of the 16th and 17th centuries. Santucci also wrote masses, motets, Psalms, canons in up to 7 parts, syms., organ sonatas, etc. He publ. the treatise *Sulla melodia, sull'armonia e sul metro* (Lucca, 1828).

BIBL.: G. Rinuccini, *Biografia di M. S.* (Milan, 1851). —NS/LK/DM

Sanz, Gaspar, Spanish priest, guitarist, and composer who flourished from the mid-17th century to the early 18th century. A native of Calanda, Aragón, he received the Bachelor of Theology degree at the Univ. of Salamanca. After studying music with Cristofor Caresana, Orazio Benevoli, P.A. Ziani, and Lelio Colista in Italy, he returned to Spain to pursue his career. He wrote the significant treatise *Instrucción de música sobre la guitarra española y método de sus primeros rudimentos hasta tañerla con destreza* (Saragossa, 1674; 8th ed., 1697; facsimile eds., Madrid, 1951 and Saragossa, 1966), which he dedicated to his pupil, Don Juan of Austria; it contains examples of contemporary Spanish dance music and folk songs.—NS/LK/DM

Sanzogno, Nino, Italian conductor and composer; b. Venice, April 13, 1911; d. Milan, May 4, 1983. He studied at the Venice Cons. (graduated, 1932), pursuing his training with Malipiero (composition) in Venice and Scherchen (conducting) in Brussels. He began his career as a violinist in the Guarneri Quartet. In 1937 he became conductor at the Teatro La Fenice in Venice, and he also conducted the Gruppo Strumentale Italiano (1938–39). In 1939 he made his first appearance at Milan's La Scala, returning there as a conductor in subsequent years. In 1955 he conducted Cimarosa's *Il Matrimonio segreto* at the first performance given at Milan's Piccola Scala. He took the company to the Edinburgh Festival in 1957. As a guest conductor, he appeared with principal Italian, European, and North and South American opera houses. In addition to his performances of works from the standard repertoire, he became particularly known for his advocacy of contemporary composers, among them Petrassi, Malipiero, Milhaud, Berio, Hartmann, and Poulenc.—NS/LK/DM

Saperton, David, American pianist and teacher; b. Pittsburgh, Oct. 29, 1889; d. Baltimore, July 5, 1970. He received his first instruction on the piano from his grandfather, a former tenor at the Brünn Opera, while his father, a physician and former concert bass, superintended his theoretical studies. At the age of 10, he made his first public appearance with an orch. in Pittsburgh; in 1905 he gave a recital in N.Y.; from 1910 to 1912 he toured Germany, Austria, Hungary, Italy, Russia, and Scandinavia. In 1924 he joined the piano faculty of the Curtis Inst. of Music in Philadelphia.—NS/LK/DM

Saporiti (real name, **Codecasa**), **Teresa,** Italian soprano; b. c. 1763; d. Milan, March 17, 1869. She joined Pasquale Bondini's Italian company in 1782 and appeared with it in Leipzig, Dresden, and Prague, often being obliged to appear in male costume and take on castrati roles. The success of Bondini's production of *Le nozze di Figaro* in Prague in 1786 prompted him to request an opera from Mozart for the following year; the part of Donna Anna in *Don Giovanni* was written with Saporiti's voice in mind: the taxing coloratura in her aria in the second act indicates that Mozart had a high opinion of her ability. She then appeared in Venice (1788–89) and at Milan's La Scala (1789); later in Bologna, Parma, and Modena. By 1795 she was prima buffa assoluta in Gennaro Astarita's company in St. Petersburg; sang in Astarita's own comic operas, as well as in revivals of Cimarosa's *Italiana in Londra* and Paisiello's *Il Barbiere di Siviglia*. She then fell into total oblivion. If the dates of her life can be verified, she lived to about the age of 105.—NS/LK/DM

Sapp, Allen Dwight, Jr., American composer and pedagogue; b. Philadelphia, Dec. 10, 1922; d. Cincinnati, Jan. 4, 1999. He studied composition with Piston and Thompson and music history with Davison at Harvard Univ. (B.A., 1942), and then pursued private training in composition with Copland and Boulanger. Following military service during World War II, he returned to Harvard Univ. to complete his education (M.A., 1949). He was on the staff of Harvard Univ. (1948–58), and then taught at Wellesley Coll. (1958–61). From 1961 to 1975 he was on the faculty of the Univ. of Buffalo (later the State Univ. of N.Y. at Buffalo). He was a faculty member at Fla. State Univ. from 1975 to 1978. He served as dean (1978–80) and as prof. of composition (1978–93) at the Univ. of Cincinnati Coll.-Cons. of Music. In his early compositions, Sapp wrote in a neo-Classical vein. From 1949 he experimented with serial techniques but within tonal frames of reference.

WORKS: ORCH.: *Andante* (1941; N.Y., April 18, 1942); Concertino for Piano and Chamber Orch. (1942); 2 suites: No. 1 (1949) and No. 2 (1952–56; Buffalo, Dec. 8, 1968); *The Double Image* (1957; Buffalo, May 28, 1967); *The Women of Trachis,* overture (Boston, Nov. 27, 1960); *June* for Wind Quintet and Strings (Boston, June 14, 1961); *Colloquies I* for Piano and Strings (1963; Buffalo, Feb. 23, 1964); *Imaginary Creatures: A Bestiary for the Credulous* for Harpsichord and Chamber Orch. (1981; Cincinnati, March 21, 1982); *Xenón Ciborium* (1982–85; Cincinnati, Oct. 11, 1986); *The Cheektowaga and Tonawanda Divisions* for Wind Orch. (1983; first complete perf., Cincinnati, March 7, 1984); *The 4 Winds* for Wind Orch. (1984; Boulder, Colo., Feb. 27, 1985); *Cincinnati Morality and Consolation* for Wind Orch. (1985; Cincinnati, May 21, 1986); *The Four Reasons,* concerto for Chamber Orch. (1993; Cincinnati, March 20, 1994); Concerto for Clarinets and Orch. (1996–97; Cincinnati, March 4, 1997). **CHAMBER:** Cello Sonata (1941–42); 4 violin sonatas: No. 1 (1942–43; N.Y., June 21, 1945), No. 2 (1948), No. 3 (1960), and No. 4 (1981; Buffalo, Dec. 10, 1982); Viola Sonata (1948; rev. version, Cincinnati, Oct. 29, 1986); Piano Trio (1949); 4 string quartets (1951, 1981, 1981, 1981); *Chaconne* for Violin and Organ (1953); *6 Ricercare* for Viols (1956); String Trio (1957); *6 Variations on the Hymn Tune Durant* for Flute, Oboe, English Horn, and Bassoon (1960); *Variations on A solis ortus cardine* for Oboe, Horn, 2 Violins, Viola, Cello, and Contrabass (Buffalo, Dec. 9, 1962); *Irregular Polygon* for String Quartet (1973); *Nocturne* for Cello (1978); *Colloquies II* for Piano, Flute, and Viola (1978; rev. 1982),

III for Piano and 10 Winds (1981; Cincinnati, April 25, 1982), *IV: The Lament of Adonis* for Cello and Piano (1984; Cincinnati, May 14, 1985), *V: The Cage of All Bright Knocks* for Alto Flute and Piano (Cincinnati, Nov. 14, 1986), and *VI: Socrates and Phaedrus Speak of Love by the Banks of the Ilissus* for Oboe and Piano (1988; Cincinnati, Jan. 10, 1990); *Taylor's 9* for Percussion Ensemble (Cincinnati, Oct. 9, 1981); *Sirius: Stella Canis; The Companion of Sirius: The Serious Companion* for Tuba and Piano (1984); *A Garland for Anna* for Violin (1984); *13 Anti-Strophes* for Cello and Piano (1985); *Romance* for Violin (1985); *Fantasia* for Violin and Piano (1986; Cincinnati, Feb. 20, 1987); *To Be Played Softly...* for Violin, Viola, and Cello (Cincinnati, June 13, 1987); *Inscriptions and Commentaries* for Oboe, Violin, Viola, and Cello (Cincinnati, Nov. 1, 1991); *Polyhedra* for Woodwind Quintet (1992; Dodge City, Kans., Feb. 20, 1993). **KEYBOARD: P i a n o :** 10 sonatas (1941; 1954–56, rev. 1957; 1957; 1957; 1980; 1980; 1980; 1985, rev. 1986; 1989; 1989); 3 sonatas for Piano, 4-Hands (1944, 1981, 1981); 2 sonatinas (1945, 1957); Suite (1949); *4 Dialogues* for 2 Pianos (1954–55); *7 Bagatelles* (1956); *4 Impromptus* (1957); *Up in the Sky* (1983–84); *Eaux-Fortes* for Piano Duet (1984); *Aquarelles* for Piano Duet (1984); *A Bestiary*, 25 preludes (1989). **O r g a n :** *Epithalamium* (1986). **VOCAL:** *The Marriage Song* for Chorus and Chamber Orch. (1948); *5 Landscapes* for Chorus (1950); *The Lady and the Lute* for Soprano and Piano (1952); *7 Epigrams (Both Sweet and Sour)* for Bass and Piano (1952; Cambridge, Mass., April 25, 1958); *The Little Boy Lost* for Chorus and Instrumental Ensemble (1953); *A Maiden's Complaint in Springtime* for Chorus, Winds, and Strings (1959–60; Wellesley, Mass., April 17, 1960); *7 Songs of Carew* for High Voice and Piano (1961, 1982; Cincinnati, April 24, 1985); *Canticum Novum Pro Pace* for Men's Chorus and Wind Quintet (1962; Buffalo, March 31, 1963); *Crennelations* for Tenor and Orch. (1982; Cincinnati, Feb. 26, 1983); *Moral Maxims: 30 Songs for 30 Years* for High Voice and Piano (1982; Cincinnati, May 5, 1987); *Illusions and Affirmations* for Bass and String Orch. (1982); *Affliction* for Mezzo-soprano and Piano (1983); *A Set of 12 Canons* for 2 Sopranos, Tenor, and Chamber Group (Cincinnati, Dec. 10, 1987); *Anoia* for Soprano, Flute, Clarinet, Violin, and Cello (Cincinnati, Feb. 13, 1988); *Dix chansons sphériqies* for Soprano and Piano (Cincinnati, Oct. 28, 1989). **BIBL.:** A. Green, *A. S.: A Bio-Bibliography* (Westport, Conn., 1996).—NS/LK/DM

Sarabia, Guillermo, Mexican baritone; b. Mazatlán, Aug. 30, 1936; d. Amsterdam, Sept. 19, 1985. He studied with Herbert Graf, Ria Ginster, Dusolina Giannini, and Carl Ebert in Zürich at the Opera Studio and Cons. After making his operatic debut as Doktor Faust in Detmold (1965), he sang in various German opera houses. On May 5, 1973, he made his Metropolitan Opera debut in N.Y. as Amonasro. In 1976 he made his first appearance at the N.Y.C. Opera as the Dutchman. His guest appearances took him to Vienna, Berlin, London, Paris, and Milan. He made his last appearance in the U.S. as Falstaff with Solti and the Chicago Sym. Orch. in 1985, shortly before his death. Among his other roles were Pizzaro, Rigoletto, Scarpia, and Wozzeck. —NS/LK/DM

Saracini, Claudio, significant Italian composer, known as **Il Palusi**; b. Siena, July 1, 1586; d. probably there, after 1649. He was born into a noble and musical family, and learned to sing and play the lute. His travels took him all over Europe. Saracini is recognized as an outstanding monodist of his era, the equal of Sigismondo d'India. He publ. 6 vols. of *Musiche* (Venice, 1614–24), which includes 129 solo songs, duets, trios, and theorbo pieces.

BIBL.: E. Pintér, *C. S.: Leben und Werk* (2 vols., Frankfurt am Main, 1992; includes complete works).—LK/DM

Saradzhev, Konstantin, Armenian conductor and pedagogue; b. Derbent, Oct. 8, 1877; d. Yerevan, July 22, 1954. He studied violin with Hřimalý at the Moscow Cons. (graduated, 1898). After further training with Ševčík in Prague (1900), he studied conducting with Nikisch in Leipzig (1904–08). He began his conducting career in Moscow, where he championed the cause of Soviet composers. From 1922 to 1935 he also was prof. of conducting at the Cons. He then settled in Yerevan, where he was artistic director of the Opera and Ballet Theater. He also was director of the Cons. (from 1939) and principal conductor of the Phil. (1941–44). In 1946 he was made a People's Artist of the Armenian S.S.R.—NS/LK/DM

Sárai, Tibor, Hungarian composer and teacher; b. Budapest, May 10, 1919. He studied composition with Kadosa and violin with Sándor at the Franz Liszt Academy of Music in Budapest (diploma, 1942). In 1948 he became secretary general of the Union of Hungarian Musicians; after serving as head of the music dept. of the Hungarian Ministry of Culture (1949–50), he held that position with the Hungarian Radio (1950–53). From 1953 to 1959 he taught at the Béla Bartók Cons. in Budapest; then was a prof. at the Franz Liszt Academy of Music (1959–80). He was also secretary general of the Assn. of Hungarian Musicians (1959–78); likewise was vice-president (1975–77) and secretary general (1980–82) of the International Music Council of UNESCO. In 1959 he was awarded the Erkel Prize and in 1975 the Kossuth Prize. In 1988 he was made a Merited Artist by the Hungarian government. In his compositions, he adheres to the national Hungarian tradition, enhanced by a free use of euphonious dissonances.

WORKS: O R C H .: *Serenade* for Strings (1946); *Tavaszi concerto* (Spring Concerto) for Flute, Viola, Cello, and String Orch. (1955); *6 Scenes* from the dance play *János vitéz* (1956–57); 3 syms. (1965–67; 1972–73; 1987); *Musica* for 45 Strings (1970–71); *Epitaph in Memory of Ferenc Szabó* (1974); *Notturno* (1977–78); *Autumn Concerto* for Violin, Cello, Horn, Trumpet, and Orch. (1984). **CHAMBER:** 3 string quartets (1958; 1971; 1980–82); *Lassu es friss* for Violin and Piano (1958); Quartet for Flute, Violin, Viola, and Cello (1961–62); *Studio* for Flute and Piano (1964); Sonata for Solo Violin (1990); piano pieces. **VOCAL:** *Variations on a Theme of Peace*, oratorio for Soloists, Chorus, and Orch. (1961–64); *De profundis*, cantata for Tenor and Wind Quintet (1968); *Diagnosis '69* for Tenor and Orch. (1969); *Future Questioning* for Alto, Baritone, Men's Chorus, and Orch. (1971); *Christ or Barabbas* for Tenor, Baritone, Bass, Chorus, and Orch. (1976–77); *Scena* for Soprano and Bassoon (1980); songs. —NS/LK/DM

Sarasate (y Navascuéz), Pablo (Martin Melitón) de, celebrated Spanish violinist and composer; b. Pamplona, March 10, 1844; d. Biarritz, Sept. 20,

1908. He commenced playing the violin when he was 5, and after making his public debut at age 8, he was granted a private scholarship to study with M. Sáez in Madrid. With the assistance of Queen Isabella, he pursued his studies with Alard at the Paris Cons. (from 1856), where he took premiers prix in violin and solfège (1857) and in harmony (1859). He launched his career as a virtuoso with a major concert tour when he was 15. In 1866 he acquired a Stradivarius violin. His playing was noted for its extraordinary beauty of tone, impeccable purity of intonation, perfection of technique, and grace of manner. In the early years of his career, his repertoire consisted almost exclusively of fantasies on operatic airs, most of which he arranged himself. He later turned to the masterpieces of the violin literature. His tours, extending through all of Europe, North and South America, South Africa, and the Orient, were an uninterrupted succession of triumphs. He bequeathed to his native city the gifts that had been showered upon him by admirers throughout the world; the collection was placed in a special museum. Among the works written for him were Bruch's second Concerto and *Scottish Fantasy*, Lalo's Concerto and *Symphonie espagnole*, Saint-Saëns's first and third concertos and *Introduction et Rondo capriccioso*, and Wieniawski's second Concerto. Sarasate's compositions, pleasing and effective, include his *Zigeunerweisen* (1878), *Spanische Tänze* (4 books, 1878–82), and *Carmen* fantasy (1883).

BIBL.: L. Zarate, *S.* (Barcelona, 1945); A. Sagardia, *P. S.* (Palencia, 1956); L. Iberni, *P. S.* (Madrid, 1994).—**NS/LK/DM**

Saraste, Jukka-Pekka, Finnish conductor; b. Helsinki, April 22, 1956. He studied violin and conducting at the Sibelius Academy in Helsinki, obtaining diplomas in both subjects in 1979; then made his debut as a conductor with the Helsinki Phil. in 1980. After winning the Nordic conducting competition in 1981, he appeared as a guest conductor throughout Scandinavia. In 1983 he made his first tour of the U.S. as co-conductor (with Okko Kamu) of the Helsinki Phil.; his British debut followed in 1984, when he appeared as a guest conductor of the London Sym. Orch. at a Promenade concert in London; he also made his German debut as a guest conductor with the Munich Phil. In 1985 he was named principal guest conductor of the Finnish Radio Sym. Orch. in Helsinki. He toured Australia in 1986. In 1987 he took the Finnish Radio Sym. Orch. to England, during which tour he conducted all the Sibelius syms. at the Brighton Festival; that same year, he was promoted to chief conductor of the orch. and became principal conductor of the Scottish Chamber Orch. in Glasgow. In 1994 he became music director of the Toronto Sym. —**NS/LK/DM**

Sargeant, Winthrop, prominent American music critic; b. San Francisco, Dec. 10, 1903; d. Salisbury, Conn., Aug. 15, 1986. He studied violin in San Francisco with Arthur Argiewicz and with Lucien Capet in Paris; took composition lessons with Albert Elkus in San Francisco and with Carl Prohaska in Vienna. He played the violin in the San Francisco Sym. Orch. (1922–24), the N.Y. Sym. Orch. (1926–28), and the N.Y. Phil. (1928–30).

He then devoted himself to musical journalism. He was on the editorial staff of *Musical America* (1931–34), music critic of the *Brooklyn Daily Eagle* (1934–36), and served as music ed. of *Time* magazine (1937–39). He also wrote essays on various subjects for *Time* (1939–45), and subsequently was roving correspondent for *Life* magazine (1945–49) and music critic for the *New Yorker* (1947–72), continuing as a contributor to the latter until his death. He evolved a highly distinctive manner of writing: professionally solid, stylistically brilliant, and ideologically opinionated; he especially inveighed against the extreme practices of the cosmopolitan avant-garde. He publ. *Jazz: Hot and Hybrid* (N.Y., 1938; third ed., N.Y., 1975), *Geniuses, Goddesses, and People* (N.Y., 1949), *Listening to Music* (N.Y., 1958), *In Spite of Myself: A Personal Memoir* (N.Y., 1970), and *Divas: Impressions of Today's Sopranos* (N.Y., 1973).—**NS/LK/DM**

Sargent, Sir (Harold) Malcolm (Watts), eminent English conductor; b. Stamford, Lincolnshire, April 29, 1895; d. London, Oct. 3, 1967. He studied organ at the Royal Coll. of Organists in London, then was articled to Keeton, organist of Peterborough Cathedral (1912–14); subsequently served in the infantry during World War I. He made his first major conducting appearance on Feb. 3, 1921, in Leicester, leading the Queen's Hall Orch. of London in his own composition, *Allegro impetuoso: An Impression on a Windy Day*. He then went to London, where he conducted the D'Oyly Carte Opera Co. and Diaghilev's Ballets Russes; from 1928 he was conductor-in-chief of the Royal Choral Soc. From 1929 to 1940 he was conductor of the Courtauld-Sargent Concerts in London. He toured Australia in 1936, 1938, and 1939, and Palestine in 1937. He was conductor-in-chief and musical adviser of the Hallé Orch. of Manchester (1939–42); then was principal conductor of the Liverpool Phil. (1942–48). In 1945 he made his American debut with the NBC Sym. Orch. in N.Y.; then made appearances in Europe, Australia, and Japan. He was knighted in 1947. From 1950 to 1957 he was chief conductor of the BBC Sym. Orch. in London; led this ensemble on several European tours. From 1948 to 1966 he also served as chief conductor of the London Promenade Concerts. He took the London Phil. on an extensive Far Eastern tour in 1962; also led the Royal Phil. to the Soviet Union and the U.S. in 1963. His performances of the standard repertoire were distinguished for their precision and brilliance; he championed the music of Elgar, Vaughan Williams, Walton, and other English composers throughout his career. A commemorative stamp with his portrait was issued by the Post Office of Great Britain on Sept. 1, 1980.

BIBL.: C. Reid, *M. S.: A Biography* (London, 1968). —**NS/LK/DM**

Sargon, Simon, Indian-born American pianist and composer; b. Bombay (of Sephardic, Russian-Jewish, and Indian descent), April 6, 1938. He took private piano lessons with Horszowski, studied theory at Brandeis Univ. (B.A., 1959) and composition with Persichetti at the Juilliard School of Music in N.Y. (M.S., 1962), and took a course with Milhaud at the Aspen (Colo.) School of Music. He was a teacher at Sarah Lawrence Coll. in Bronxville, N.Y. (1965–68), at the Rubin Academy of Music in Jerusalem (1971–74), where he served as head of the voice dept., and at Hebrew Univ. in Jerusalem (1973–74). In 1974 he was appointed music director at Temple Emanu-El in Dallas.

WORKS: DRAMATIC: *Thirst,* chamber opera, after Eugene O'Neill (Jerusalem, Dec. 17, 1972); *A Voice Still and Small,* children's musical play (Dallas, Dec. 6, 1981); *Saul, King of Israel,* opera (1990). **ORCH.:** Sym., *Holocaust,* for Baritone, Men's Chorus, and Orch. (1985); *Questings,* horn concerto (1987). **VOCAL:** 3 cantatas: *Elul: Midnight* (Dallas, Sept. 17, 1976), *Flame of the Lord* (Dallas, May 31, 1977), and *Visions of Micah* (Dallas, April 30, 1980); *Not by Might,* oratorio, after the Books of the Maccabees (Dallas, Dec. 16, 1979); temple services; songs. —NS/LK/DM

Sari, Ada (real name, Jadwiga Szajerowa),

Polish soprano; b. Wadowice, near Kraków, June 29, 1886; d. Ciechocinek, July 12, 1968. She studied in Milan. After appearances in Rome, Naples, Trieste, and Parma, she joined the Warsaw Opera; made extensive tours in Europe, South America, and the U.S.; later taught voice in Warsaw.—NS/LK/DM

Sárközy, István, Hungarian composer and teach-

er; b. Erzsébetfalva, Nov. 26, 1920. He was a student of Farkas and Szatmári, and of Kodály and Viski at the Budapest Academy of Music. From 1957 to 1960 he was ed.-in-chief for music with Editio Musica Budapest. In 1959 he became a teacher of theory at the Budapest Academy of Music.

WORKS: DRAMATIC: *Az új traktorállomás* (The New Tractor Station), ballet (1949); *Liliomfi,* musical play (1950); *Szelistyei asszonyok* (The Women of Szelistye), opera (1951); folk dance plays; incidental music. **ORCH.:** Concerto grosso (1943; rev. 1969 as *Ricordanze I*); *To Youth* (1953); Sinfonia concertante for Clarinet and 24 Strings (1963; also for Clarinet, 24 Strings, and 12 Winds, 1964); *Concerto semplice: Ricordanze II* for Violin and Orch. (1973); *Confessioni* for Piano and Orch. (1979). **CHAMBER:** *Sonata da camera* for Flute and Piano (1964); *Ciaccona* for Cello (1967); Chamber Sonata for Clarinet and Piano (1969); *Psaume et jeu,* wind quartet (1970); *Ricordanze III,* string quartet (1977). **Piano:** *12 Variations* (1945); Sonatina for 2 Pianos (1950). **VOCAL:** *A walesi bárdok* (The Bards of Wales) for Baritone and Orch. (1942–43); *Munkások* (Workers) for Bass and Orch. (1947); *Vörös Rébék* for Mezzo-soprano and Orch. (1947); *12 Balkan Folksongs* for Soprano and Chamber Orch. (1949); *Óda Sztálinhoz* (Ode to Stalin), cantata for Chorus and Orch. (1949); *Ifjúság,* suite for Chorus and Orch. (1952); *Júlia énekek* (Julia Songs), chamber cantata for Tenor, Chorus, and 4 Instruments (1958); *Reng már a föld...* (The Earthquake Approaches), cantata for Baritone, Chorus, and Orch. (1967); *Aki szegény...* (He Who is Poor) for Soprano, Chorus, and Orch. (1967); *Ypsilon háború* ("Y" War), comedy oratorio for 10 Solo Singers, Vocal Quintet, Flute, Clarinet, String Quintet, and Harpsichord (1971); choruses; solo songs.—NS/LK/DM

Sarly, Henry, Belgian composer; b. Tirlemont, Dec.

28, 1883; d. Brussels, Dec. 3, 1954. He studied with his father and with Huberti, Tinel, Gilson, and Du Bois at the Brussels Cons.; in 1921 he became inspector of musical education in Belgian schools. He composed a number of attractive pieces, among them *Scènes brabançonnes* for Orch., Piano Quintet, *Poème* for Piano Trio, Violin Sonata, numerous piano pieces, and songs. He also publ. a manual, *Cours théorique et pratique d'harmonie.*—NS/LK/DM

Saro, J. Heinrich, German bandmaster and com-

poser; b. Jessen, Jan. 4, 1827; d. Berlin, Nov. 27, 1891. In 1859 he became a bandmaster in Berlin, and in 1867 his band won the international competition at the Paris Exposition; in 1872 he was awarded a gold medal for his performance at the Boston Jubilee. He wrote a number of brilliant pieces of military music, and also some symphonic works. He publ. *Lehre vom musikalischen Wohlklang und Tonsatz und Instrumentationslehre für Militärmusik.*—NS/LK/DM

Sárosi, Bálint, Hungarian ethnomusicologist; b.

Csikrákos, Jan. 1, 1925. He was educated in Csolszereda, and took a doctorate in Hungarian and Romanian philology in Budapest (1948); also received diplomas in musicology (1956) and composition (1958) at the Budapest Academy of Music, where his teachers included Kodály. He worked in Kodály's group for folk-music research at the Hungarian Academy of Sciences in 1958; in 1974 he became director of the folk-music dept. of the Academy's Inst. for Musicology. His fieldwork includes trips to Ethiopia (1965) and Armenia (1972); his most important research is in the field of instrumental folk music.

WRITINGS: *Die Volksmusikinstrumente Ungarns* (Leipzig, 1967); *Cigányzene* (Gypsy Music; Budapest, 1971; Eng. tr., 1978); *Zenei anyanyelvünk* (Our Own Musical Vernacular; Budapest, 1973).—NS/LK/DM

Sarrette, Bernard, French bandmaster and peda-

gogue; b. Bordeaux, Nov. 27, 1765; d. Paris, April 11, 1858. A captain in the national guard at Paris, he brought together, after July 13, 1789, 45 musicians to form the nucleus of the Parisian band of the national guard. In 1790 the City of Paris assumed the expenses of this band, which was increased to 70 members, among them artists of distinction. In 1792 the financial embarrassments of the Commune led to the suspension of payment, but Sarrette held the band together and, with the aid of the municipality, established a free school of music employing all the members as teachers. From this school came the musicians employed in the 14 armies of the Republic. Its energetic principal had it converted into a national Inst. of Music, in a decree of Nov. 8, 1793; it was organized as the Paris Cons. in a decree of Aug. 3, 1795. Sarrette, having gained his end, assumed the captaincy of the 103rd Regiment; but the board of directors (5 inspectors and 4 profs.) proved so incompetent that he was recalled to the directorship of the Cons. in 1796. By introducing advanced methods of instruction and establishing the school of declamation, the concert hall, the grand library, etc., he raised the Cons. to an institution of the first rank. At the Restoration in 1814 he was deprived of his position; nor would he accept it after the revolution of 1830, not wishing to oust his friend Cherubini.

BIBL.: P. Constant, *B. S. et les origines du Conservatoire national de musique et de déclamation* (Paris, 1895).—NS/LK/DM

Sarro (or Sarri), Domenico Natale, Italian

composer; b. Trani, Apulia, Dec. 24, 1679; d. Naples, Jan. 25, 1744. He settled in Naples and studied at the Cons. di S. Onofrio. From 1704 to 1707 he was vicemaestro di cappella at the court; in 1725, became its vice-maestro, and in 1735, assumed the duties of maestro di cappella when Mancini fell ill; upon Mancini's death in 1737, Sarro formally assumed the post. From 1728 he was also maestro di cappella of the city. Sarro was one of the principal Neapolitan composers of his day. His output includes 28 secular operas, several sacred operas and oratorios, serenatas, cantatas, and a Flute Concerto.

BIBL.: G. Brandenburg, *Zur Geschichte der weltlichen Solokantate in Neapel im frühen Settecento: Die Solokantaten von D. S. (1679–1744)* (Frankfurt am Main, 1991).—NS/LK/DM

Sarti, Giuseppe, noted Italian composer, nick-

named "Il Domenichino"; b. Faenza (baptized), Dec. 1, 1729; d. Berlin, July 28, 1802. He took music lessons in Padua with Valotti; when he was 10, he went to Bologna to continue his studies with Padre Martini. Returning to Faenza, he was organist at the Cathedral (1748–52); in 1752 he was appointed director of the theater in Faenza; that same year his first opera, *Pompeo in Armenia*, was performed. His next opera, *Il Re pastore*, was staged in Venice in 1753 with great success. Toward the end of 1753 he went to Copenhagen as a conductor of Pietro Mingotti's opera troupe. His work impressed the King of Denmark, Frederik V, and in 1755 he was named court Kapellmeister. He subsequently was made director of the Italian Opera, but it was closed in 1763; he then was appointed director of court music. In 1765 he was sent by the King to Italy to engage singers for the reopening of the Opera, but Frederik's death aborted the project. Sarti remained in Italy, where he served as maestro di coro at the Pietà Cons. in Venice (1766–67). In 1768 he returned to Copenhagen, where he resumed his duties as director of the royal chapel; from 1770 to 1775 he was conductor of the court theater. He then returned to Italy with his wife, the singer Camilla Passi, whom he had married in Copenhagen. He became director of the Cons. dell'Ospedaletto in Venice in 1775. In 1779 he entered the competition for the position of maestro di cappella at Milan Cathedral, winning it against a number of competitors, including Paisiello. By this time his prestige as a composer and as a teacher was very high. Among his numerous pupils was Cherubini. In 1784 he was engaged by Catherine the Great as director of the Imperial chapel in St. Petersburg. On his way to Russia, he passed through Vienna, where he was received with honors by the Emperor Joseph II; he also met Mozart, who quoted a melody from Sarti's opera *Fra i due litiganti* in *Don Giovanni*. His greatest success in St. Petersburg was *Armida e Rinaldo* (Jan. 26, 1786), remodeled from an earlier opera, *Armida abbandonata*, originally performed in Copenhagen in 1759; the leading role was sung by the celebrated Portuguese mezzo-soprano Luiza Todi, but she developed a dislike of Sarti, and used her powerful influence with Catherine the Great to prevent his reengagement. However, he was immedi-

ately engaged by Prince Potemkin, and followed him to southern Russia and Moldavia during the military campaign against Turkey; on the taking of Ochakov, Sarti wrote an ode to the Russian liturgical text of thanksgiving, and it was performed in Jan. 1789 at Jassy, Bessarabia, with the accompaniment of cannon shots and church bells. Potemkin offered him a sinecure as head of a singing school in Ekaterinoslav, but Sarti did not actually teach there. After Potemkin's death in 1791, his arrangements with Sarti were honored by the court of St. Petersburg; in 1793 he was reinstated as court composer and was named director of a conservatory. Sarti's operas enjoyed considerable success during his lifetime but sank into oblivion after his death. He was an adept contrapuntist, and excelled in polyphonic writing; his *Fuga a otto voci* on the text of a Kyrie is notable. He was also astute in his adaptation to political realities. In Denmark he wrote Singspiels in Danish, and in Russia he composed a Requiem in memory of Louis XVI in response to the great lamentation at the Russian Imperial Court at the execution of the French king (1793). He also composed an offering to the Emperor Paul, whose daughters studied music with Sarti. After Paul's violent death at the hands of the palace guard, Sarti decided to leave Russia, but died in Berlin on his way to Italy. In 1796 Sarti presented to the Russian Academy of Sciences an apparatus to measure pitch (the so-called St. Petersburg tuning fork).

WORKS: DRAMATIC: *Pompeo in Armenia*, dramma per musica (Faenza, Carnival 1752); *Il Re pastore*, dramma per musica (Venice, Carnival 1753); *Vologeso*, dramma per musica (Copenhagen, Carnival 1754); *Antigono*, dramma per musica (Copenhagen, Oct. 14, 1754; some arias by other composers); *Ciro riconosciuto*, dramma per musica (Copenhagen, Dec. 21, 1754); *Arianna e Teseo*, dramma per musica (Copenhagen, Carnival 1756); *Anagilda*, dramma per musica (Copenhagen, Fall 1758); *Armida abbandonata*, dramma per musica (Copenhagen, 1759; later version as *Armida e Rinaldo*, St. Petersburg, Jan. 26, 1786); *Achille in Sciro*, dramma per musica (Copenhagen, 1759); *Andromaca*, dramma per musica (Copenhagen, 1759?); *Filindo*, pastorale eroica (Copenhagen, 1760); *Astrea placata*, festa teatrale (Copenhagen, Oct. 17, 1760); *La Nitteti*, dramma per musica (Copenhagen, Oct. 12, 1760); *Issipile*, dramma per musica (Copenhagen, 1760?); *Alessandro nell'Indie*, dramma per musica (Copenhagen, 1761); *Semiramide*, dramma per musica (Copenhagen, Fall 1762); *Didone abbandonata*, dramma per musica (Copenhagen, Winter 1762); *Narciso*, dramma pastorale (Copenhagen, Carnival 1763); *Cesare in Egitto*, dramma per musica (Copenhagen, Fall 1763); *Il naufragio di Cipro*, dramma pastorale (Copenhagen, 1764); *Il gran Tamerlano*, tragedia per musica (Copenhagen, 1764); *Ipermestra*, dramma per musica (Rome, Carnival 1766); *La Giardiniera brillante*, intermezzo (Rome, Jan. 3, 1768); *L'Asile de l'amour*, dramatic cantata (Copenhagen, July 22, 1769); *La Double Méprise, ou, Carlile et Fany*, comédie mêlée d'ariettes (Copenhagen, July 22, 1769); *Soliman den Anden*, Singspiel (Copenhagen, Oct. 8, 1770); *Le Bal*, opéra-comique (Copenhagen, 1770); *Il tempio d'eternità*, festa teatrale (Copenhagen, 1771); *Demofoonte*, dramma per musica (Copenhagen, Jan. 30, 1771); *Tronfølgen i Sidon*, lyrisk tragicomedia (Copenhagen, April 4, 1771); *Il Re pastore*, dramma per musica (Copenhagen, 1771; a different score from the one of 1753); *La clemenza di Tito*, dramma per musica (Padua, June 1771); *Deucalion og Pyrrha*, Singspiel (Copenhagen, March 19,

1772); *Aglae, eller Støtten*, Singspiel (Copenhagen, Feb. 16, 1774); *Kierlighedsbrevene*, Singspiel (Copenhagen, March 22, 1775); *Farnace*, dramma per musica (Venice, 1776); *Le gelosie villane (Il Feudatario)*, dramma giocoso (Venice, Nov. 1776); *Ifigenia*, dramma per musica (Rome, Carnival 1777); *Medonte re di Epiro*, dramma per musica (Florence, Sept. 8, 1777); *Il Militare bizzarro*, dramma giocoso (Venice, Dec. 27, 1777); *Olimpiade*, dramma per musica (Florence, 1778); *Scipione*, dramma per musica (Mestre, Fall 1778); *I contratempi*, dramma giocoso (Venice, Nov. 1778); *Adriano in Siria*, dramma per musica (Rome, Dec. 26, 1778); *L'ambizione delusa*, intermezzo (Rome, Feb. 1779); *Mitridate a Sinope*, dramma per musica (Florence, Fall 1779); *Achille in Sciro*, dramma per musica (Florence, Fall 1779); *Siroe*, dramma per musica (Turin, Dec. 26, 1779); *Giulio Sabino*, dramma per musica (Venice, Jan. 1781); *Demofoonte*, dramma per musica (Rome, Carnival 1782; a different score from the one of 1771); *Didone abbandonata*, dramma per musica (Padua, June 1782; a different score from the one of 1762); *Alessandro e Timoteo*, dramma per musica (Parma, April 6, 1782); *Fra i due litiganti il terzo gode*, dramma giocoso (Milan, Sept. 14, 1782; subsequently perf. under various titles); *Attalo re di Bitinia*, dramma per musica (Venice, Dec. 26, 1782); *Idalide*, dramma per musica (Milan, Jan. 8, 1783); *Erifile*, dramma per musica (Pavia, Carnival 1783); *Il trionfo della pace*, dramma per musica (Mantua, May 10, 1783); *Olimpiade*, dramma per musica (Rome, 1783; a different score from the one of 1778); *Gli Amanti consolati*, dramma giocoso (St. Petersburg, 1784); *I finti eredi*, opera comica (St. Petersburg, Oct. 30, 1785); *Armida e Rinaldo*, dramma per musica (St. Petersburg, Jan. 26, 1786; based upon *Armida abbandonata* of 1759); *Castore e Polluce*, dramma per musica (St. Petersburg, Oct. 3, 1786); *Zenoclea*, azione teatrale (1786; not performed); *Alessandro nell'Indie*, dramma per musica (Palermo, Winter 1787; a different score from the one of 1761); *Cleomene*, dramma per musica (Bologna, Dec. 27, 1788); *The Early Reign of Oleg*, Russian opera to a libretto by Catherine the Great (St. Petersburg, Oct. 22, 1790; in collaboration with V. Pashkevich); *Il trionfo d'Atalanta* (1791; not performed); *Andromeda*, dramma per musica (St. Petersburg, Nov. 4, 1798); *Enea nel Lazio*, dramma per musica (St. Petersburg, Oct. 26, 1799); *La Famille indienne en Angleterre*, opera (St. Petersburg, 1799); *Les Amours de Flore et de Zéphire*, ballet anacréontique (Gatchina, Sept. 19, 1800). **OTHER:** Several secular cantatas, masses, Requiems, Te Deums, etc.; instrumental works, including syms. and chamber works.

BIBL.: G. Pasolini, *G. S.* (Faenza, 1883); C. Rivalta, *G. S.: Musicista faentino del secolo XVIII* (Faenza, 1928); F. Samory, *A G. S. nel 2 centenario di sua nascita* (Faenza, 1929); R. Jones, *A Performing Edition and Discussion of G. S.'s Te Deum in D* (diss., Stanford Univ., 1966).—NS/LK/DM

Sartori, Claudio,

eminent Italian music scholar and bibliographer; b. Brescia, April 1, 1913; d. Milan, March 11, 1994. He received an arts degree in 1934 from the Univ. of Pavia with a thesis in music history, then studied with Gerold at the Univ. of Strasbourg and with Vittadini at the Pavia Cons. He served as an asst. librarian at the Bologna Cons. (1938–42), where in 1943 he was appointed prof. of Italian literature; in 1967 he assumed a similar professorship at the Milan Cons. He founded and became director of the Ufficio Ricerche Musicali in 1965; its aim was to conduct a thorough codification of Italian musical sources, providing information on all MSS and publ. music in Italy before 1900, on all publ. librettos in Italy down to 1800, and on all literature on music in Italy. In addition to this invaluable compilation, he also served as ed.-in-chief of *Dizionario Ricordi della musica e dei musicisti* (Milan, 1959). In 1983 he was made a corresponding member of the American Musicological Soc.

WRITINGS: *Il R. Conservatorio di Musica G.B. Martini di Bologna* (Florence, 1942); *Bibliografia delle opere musicali stampate da Ottaviano Petrucci* (Florence, 1948; later continued as "Nuove conclusive aggiunte alla 'Bibliografia del Petrucci'," Collectanea Historiae Musicae, I, 1953); *Bibliografia della musica strumentale italiana stampata in Italia fino al 1700* (2 vols., Florence, 1952 and 1968); *Monteverdi* (Brescia, 1953); *Catalogo delle musiche della Cappella del Duomo di Milano* (Milan, 1957); *Riccardo Malipiero* (Milan, 1957); *Casa Ricordi 1808–1958* (Milan, 1958); *Dizionario degli editori musicali italiani* (Florence, 1958); *Giacomo Puccini a Monza* (Monza, 1958); *Puccini* (Milan, 1958); ed. *Puccini Symposium* (Milan, 1959); *Assisi: La Cappella della Basilica di S. Francesco: Catalogo del fondo musicale nella Biblioteca comunale di Assisi* (Milan, 1962); ed. *L'enciclopedia della musica* (Milan, 1963–64); *Commemorazione di Ottaviano de' Petrucci* (Fossombrone, 1966); *Giacomo Carissimi: Catalogo delle opere attribuite* (Milan, 1975); ed., with F. Lesure, *Bibliografia della musica italiana vocale profana pubblicata dal 1500 al 1700* (Geneva, 1978).

BIBL.: M. Donà and F. Lesure, eds., *Scritti in memoria di C. S.* (It., Fr., and Eng.; Lucca, 1997).—NS/LK/DM

Sartorio, Antonio,

important Italian composer; b. Venice, 1630; d. there, Dec. 30, 1680. His first opera, *Gl' amori infruttuosi di Pirro*, was performed in Venice on Jan. 4, 1661; his second opera, *Seleuco* (Venice, Jan. 16, 1666), established his reputation. In 1666 he went to Germany to take up the post of Kapellmeister to Duke Johann Friedrich of Braunschweig-Lüneburg, who maintained his court in Hannover. He held this post until 1675, but continued to make regular visits to Venice to oversee productions of his operas. It was in Venice that he brought out his most famous opera, *L'Adelaide*, on Feb. 19, 1672. He returned to Venice permanently in 1675; in 1676 he was appointed vice-maestro di cappella at San Marco, a position he held until his death. Sartorio was a leading representative of the Venetian school of opera; his operas are notable for their arias, which he composed in a varied and effective manner.

WORKS: DRAMATIC: O p e r a (all first perf. in Venice unless otherwise given): *Gl'amori infruttuosi di Pirro* (Jan. 4, 1661); *Seleuco* (Jan. 16, 1666); *La prosperità d'Elio Seiano* (Jan. 15, 1667); *La caduta d'Elio Seiano* (Feb. 3, 1667); *L'Ermengarda regina de' Longobardi* (Dec. 26, 1669); *L'Adelaide* (Feb. 19, 1672); *L'Orfeo* (Dec. 14, 1672); *Massenzio* (Jan. 25, 1673); *Alcina* (c. 1674; not perf.); *Giulio Cesare in Egitto* (Dec. 17, 1676); *Antonino e Pompeiano* (1677); *L'Anacreonte tiranno* (1677); *Ercole su'l Termodonte* (1678); *I duo tiranni al soglio* (Jan. 15, 1679); *La Flora* (music completed by M.A. Ziani; Carnival 1681). **OTHER:** A number of cantatas and sacred vocal works;. *23 Salmi a due chori ma accomodati all' uso della serenissima cappella ducale di S. Marco* for 8 Voices (Venice, 1680).—NS/LK/DM

Sartorius (real name, Schneider), Paul,

German organist and composer; b. Nuremberg (baptized), Nov. 16, 1569; d. Innsbruck, Feb. 28, 1609. He studied with Lechner in Nuremberg, then went to Rome for further study. He was organist at the court chapel of Archduke Maximilian II of Austria in Mergentheim, Franconia (1594–1602) and in Innsbruck (1602–09).

WORKS: *Missae tres* for 8 Voices (Munich, 1599); *Madrigali libro primo* for 5 Voices (1600); *Neue teutsche Liedlein, nach Art der welschen Canzonette* for 4 Voices (Nuremberg, 1601): *Sonetti spirituali* for 6 Voices (Nuremberg, 1601); *Sacrae cantiones sive motecta* for 6 to 8, 10, and 12 Voices (Nuremberg, 1602); other works in contemporary collections.—NS/LK/DM

Sáry, László, Hungarian composer; b. Győr, Jan. 1, 1940. He studied at the Budapest Academy of Music with Szervánszky, and after graduation in 1966, he helped to found the Budapest New Music Studio (1970). His works represent various contemporary trends, ranging from the music of Christian Wolff to the American minimalists.

WORKS: ORCH.: *Canzone solenne* (1970); *Immaginario No. 1* (1971); *Diana búcsúja* (Diana's Farewell) for Chamber Orch. (1976); *Music for 24 Strings and 24 Winds: Hommage à Szervánszky* (1977); *Párhuzamos mozgások* (Parallel Movements) for Chamber Orch. (1981); *In memoriam Igor Stravinsky* for 24 Wind Instruments (1981); *Hyperion sorsdala* (Hyperion's Song of Destiny) for 24 String Instruments (1985–86); *Tükörképek* (Mirror Images) for 24 Strings and 24 Winds (1986); *Polyphonie* for 18 Strings and 10 Winds (1986); *7 Movements* for Saxophone, Harp, Percussion, and 14 Strings (Budapest, Nov. 19, 1994). **CHAMBER ENSEMBLE:** *Polyrhythmia* for 100 Bells and 10 Players (1979); *Discussions* (1980); *Pentagram* for 5 Percussion Groups and Prepared Piano (1982); *Előjáték és hat miniat&ubdlac;r* (Prelude and Six Miniatures) for 5 Percussion Groups (1982); *Hölderlin tornya* (Hölderlin's Tower; 1985); *Az ismétlődő ötös* (Fives Repeated; 1985). **CHAMBER:** *Variazioni* for Clarinet and Piano (1965); *Catacoustics* for 2 Pianos (1967); *Pezzo concertato* for Flute and Piano (1967); *Fluttuazioni* for Violin and Piano (1967); *Incanto* for 5 Saxophones (1969); *Versetti* for Organ and Percussion (1970); *Sonanti No. 2* for Flute and Percussion (1970); *Image* for Clarinet, Cello, and Piano (1972); *Az ég virágai* (Flowers of Heaven) for 1 to 4 Pianos (1973); *Oda egy feketerigó halálára* (Ode on the Death of a Blackbird) for Brass Quintet (1982); *Egy akkordsor forgatókönyve* (Scenario of a Series of Chords) for Piano(s) and Flute(s) (1982); *Kettős végtelen* (Double Infinity) for 2 Cimbaloms (1986); *String Quartet in 4 Movements with Piano in the fourth movement* (1986); *In All Eternity* for String Quartet (1986); *Az elhagyott kert éneke* (Song of the Deserted Garden) for String Quartet and Alto Flute (1986); *és a Nap?* (and the Sun?) for String Quartet (1986); *Variations* for String Quartet (1986–88); also works for Solo Instruments; pieces for Unspecified Instruments. **VOCAL:** *Lamento* for 5 Voices (1965); *Három madrigál* (3 Madrigals) for 5 Voices or Chamber Chorus (1966); *Quartetto* for Soprano, Flute, Violin, and Cimbalom (1968); *Incanto* for 5 Voices (1969); *Cantata No. 1* for Soprano, Chamber Chorus, and Instrumental Ensemble (1969); *Hommage aux ancêtres* for 6 Voices, 3 Trumpets, and 3 Trombones (1970); *Psalmus* for Soprano and Melody Instrument (1972); *In sol* for 4-part Vocal Ensemble (1975); *Lied in lyd* for Alto, Bass, and Chamber Chorus (1975); *Hangok fehérben* (Voices in White) for Chamber Chorus (1975); *Variáciok 14 hang fölött* (Variations on 14 Pitches) for Soprano and Piano (1975); *Dob és tánc* (Drum and Dance) for 24-part Women's Chorus (1975); *A hangzök változásai* (Mutations of the Sounds of Speech) for Soloists, Chorus, and Strings (1979); *Socrates utolsó tanítása* (Socrates's Last Teaching) for Soprano and Piano (1980); *Imitatio homophona* for Soprano and 3 Identical Instruments (1982); *Hold-ének* (Moon-Song) for Soprano, Bass, and Chorus (1982); *Kánon a felkelő naphoz* (Canon to the Rising Sun) for 4- or 6-part Chorus of Equal Voices or Instrumental Ensemble (1982);

Magnificat for Soprano and Melody Instrument (1982; rev. 1986). **OTHER:** Collaborative works, including *Hommage à Dohnányi* for Chamber Ensemble (1979; with Z. Jeney, B. Dukay, and L. Vidovszky).—NS/LK/DM

Sás (Orchassal), Andrés, French-born Peruvian composer; b. Paris, April 6, 1900; d. Lima, July 25, 1967. He went to Brussels, where he studied harmony at the Anderlecht Academy, violin with Marchot, chamber music with Miry, and music history with Closson at the Cons., and counterpoint and fugue privately with Imbert. In 1924 he was engaged by the Peruvian government to teach violin at the National Academy of Music in Lima; in 1928 he returned temporarily to Belgium; the following year, he settled in Lima permanently. He married the Peruvian pianist Lily Rosay, and with her established the Sás-Rosay Academy of Music. He became profoundly interested in Peruvian folk music, and collected folk melodies; made use of many of them in his own compositions.

WORKS: DRAMATIC: Ballet: *La señora del pueblo* (Viña del Mar, Chile, Jan. 20, 1946); *El hijo pródigo* (1948). **Incidental Music To:** Molière's *Le Malade imaginaire* (1943). **ORCH.:** *Canción india* (1927); *3 estampas del Perú* (1936); *Poema indio* (1941); *Sueño de Zamba* (1943); *Danza gitana* (1944); *La patrona del pueblo* (1945); *La parihuana* (1946); *Las seis edades de la Tía Conchita* (1947); *La leyenda de la Isla de San Lorenzo* (1949); *Fantasía romántica* for Trumpet and Orch. (1950). **CHAMBER:** *Recuerdos* for Violin and Piano (also for Orch.; 1927); *Rapsodia peruana* for Violin and Piano (also for Orch.; 1928); *Sonata- Fantasia* for Flute and Piano (1934); *String Quartet* (1938); *Cantos del Peru* for Violin and Piano (1941). **Piano:** *Aires y Danzas del Peru* (2 albums, 1930 and 1945); *Suite peruana* (1931); *Himno y Danza* (1935); *Sonatina peruana* (1946). **VOCAL:** Numerous choruses and songs.—NS/LK/DM

Sass, Marie Constance, Belgian soprano; b. Oudenaarde, Jan. 26, 1834; d. Auteuil, near Paris, Nov. 8, 1907. She studied with Gevaert in Ghent, Ugalde in Paris, and Lamperti in Italy, making her operatic debut as Gilda in Venice (1852). She then went to Paris, where she sang at the Théâtre-Lyrique (1859) and at the Opéra (from 1860), where she was the first Paris Elisabeth in the controversial mounting of *Tannhäuser* (1861) and where she created the roles of Selika in *L'Africaine* (1865) and Elisabeth de Valois in *Don Carlos* (1867); subsequently appeared at Milan's La Scala (1869–70). During her Paris years, she made appearances under the name Marie Sax until a lawsuit was brought against her by Adolphe Sax; thereafter she reverted to her real name, also using the name Sasse. She was married to **Castelmary** (1864–67). After retiring from the stage in 1877, she taught voice. Sass died in abject poverty. —NS/LK/DM

Sass, Sylvia, Hungarian soprano; b. Budapest, July 21, 1951. She was a student of Olga Revghegyi at the Budapest Academy of Music, and later in her career received some lessons from Callas. In 1971 she made her operatic debut as Frasquita at the Hungarian State Opera in Budapest, where she subsequently sang many major roles. In 1972 she appeared as Violetta at the

Bulgarian State Opera in Sofia. She made her first appearance at the Hamburg State Opera as Fiodiligi in 1975, the same year she made her debut at Glasgow's Scottish Opera as Desdemona. In 1976 she sang Giselda at her debut at London's Covent Garden and appeared as Violetta in Aix-en-Provence. On March 12, 1977, she made her Metropolitan Opera debut in N.Y. as Tosca. In 1979 she appeared in recital at London's Wigmore Hall. In subsequent years, she sang in opera and concert in many major music centers. Among her other operatic roles were Donna Elvira, Countess Almaviva, Donna Anna, Lady Macbeth, Turandot, Salome, and Bartók's Judith. Her concert repertoire extended from Bach to Messiaen.—NS/LK/DM

Satie, Erik (Alfred-Leslie), celebrated French composer who elevated his eccentricities and verbal virtuosity to the plane of high art; b. Honfleur, May 17, 1866; d. Paris, July 1, 1925. He received his early music training from a local organist, Vinot, who was a pupil of Niedermeyer. At 13 he went to Paris, where his father was a music publisher, and received instruction in harmony from Taudou and in piano from Mathias; however, his attendance at the Cons. was only sporadic between 1879 and 1886. He played in various cabarets in Montmartre, and in 1884 publ. a piano piece which he numbered, with malice aforethought, op.62. His whimsical ways and Bohemian manner of life attracted many artists and musicians; he met Debussy in 1891; joined the Rosicrucian Society in Paris in 1892 and began to produce short piano pieces with eccentric titles intended to ridicule modernistic fancies and Classical pedantries alike. Debussy thought highly enough of him to orchestrate 2 numbers from his piano suite Gymnopédies (1888). Satie was almost 40 when he decided to pursue serious studies at the Paris Schola Cantorum, taking courses in counterpoint, fugue, and orchestration with d'Indy and Roussel (1905–8). In 1898 he had moved to Arcueil, a suburb of Paris; there he held court for poets, singers, dancers, and musicians, among whom he had ardent admirers. Milhaud, Sauguet, and Désormière organized a group, which they called only half-facetiously "École d'Arcueil," in honor of Satie as master and leader. But Satie's eccentricities were not merely those of a Parisian poseur; rather, they were adjuncts to his aesthetic creed, which he enunciated with boldness and total disregard for professional amenities (he was once brought to court for sending an insulting letter to a music critic). Interestingly enough, he attacked modernistic aberrations just as assiduously as reactionary pedantry, publishing "manifestos" in prose and poetry. Although he was dismissed by most serious musicians as an uneducated person who tried to conceal his ignorance of music with persiflage, he exercised a profound influence on the young French composers of the first quarter of the 20th century; moreover, his stature as an innovator in the modern idiom grew after his death, so that the avant-garde musicians of the later day accepted him as inspiration for their own experiments; thus "space music" could be traced back to Satie's musique d'ameublement, in which players were stationed at different parts of a hall playing different pieces in different tempi. The instruction in his piano piece Vexations, to play it 840 times in succession, was carried out literally in N.Y. on Sept. 9, 1963, by a group of 5 pianists working in relays overnight, thus setting a world's record for duration of any musical composition. When critics accused Satie of having no idea of form, he publ. Trois Morceaux en forme de poire, the eponymous pear being reproduced in color on the cover; other pieces bore self-contradictory titles, such as Heures séculaires et instantanées and Crépuscule matinal de midi; other titles were Pièces froides, Embryons desséchés, Prélude en tapisserie, Préludes flasques (pour un chien), Descriptions automatiques, etc. In his ballets, he introduced jazz for the first time in Paris; at the performance of his ballet Relâche (Nov. 29, 1924), the curtain bore the legend "Erik Satie is the greatest musician in the world; whoever disagrees with this notion will please leave the hall." He publ. a facetious autobiographical notice as Mémoires d'un amnésique (1912); N. Wilkins tr. and ed. The Writings of Erik Satie (London, 1980).

WORKS: DRAMATIC: Geneviève de Brabant, marionette opera (1899); Le Piège de Méduse, lyric comedy (1913); Parade, ballet (Paris, May 18, 1917); Mercure, ballet (Paris, June 15, 1924); Relâche, ballet (Paris, Nov. 29, 1924). Also incidental music to Le Fils de étoiles (1891; prelude reorchestrated by Ravel, 1913), Le Prince de Byzance (1891), Le Nazaréen (1892), La Porte heroïque du ciel (1893), and Pousse l'Amour (1905). **ORCH.:** Jack in the Box (1900; orchestrated by Milhaud, 1920); En habit de cheval (1911); Cinq Grimaces (1914); Trois petites pièces montées (1919; also for Piano, 4-Hands, 1920); La belle excentrique (1920). **CHAMBER:** Choses vues à droite et à gauche (sans lunettes) for Violin and Piano (1914). **Piano:** 3 Sarabandes (1887–88; orchestrated by Caby); Trois Gymnopédies (1888; Nos. 1 and 3 orchestrated by Debussy, 1896; No. 2 orchestrated by H. Murrill and by Roland-Manuel); Trois Gnossiennes (1890; orchestrated by Lanchbery; No. 3 orchestrated by Poulenc, 1939); Trois Préludes from Le Fils des étoiles (1891; orchestrated by Roland-Manuel); 9 Danses gothiques (1893); Quatre Préludes (1893; Nos. 1 and 3 orchestrated by Poulenc, 1939); Prélude de la Porte héroïque du ciel (1894; orchestrated by Roland-Manuel, 1912); 2 Pièces froides (1897); Valse, Je te veux (c. 1900; arranged for Violin and Orch.; also arranged for Orch. by C. Lambert); 3 Nouvelles Pièces froides (n.d.); Le Poisson rêveur (1901; arranged for Piano and Orch. by Caby); Trois Morceaux en forme de poire for Piano, 4-Hands (1903; orchestrated by Désormière); Douze Petits Chorals (c. 1906); Passacaille (1906); Prélude en tapisserie (1906); Aperçus désagréables for Piano, 4-Hands (1908–12); Deux Rêveries nocturnes (1910–11); En habit de cheval for Piano, 4-Hands (1911); Trois Véritables Préludes flasques (pour un chien) (1912); 3 Descriptions automatiques (1913); 3 Embryons desséchés (1913); 3 Croquis et agaceries d'un gros bonhomme en bois (1913); 3 Chapitres tournés en tous sens (1913); 3 Vieux Séquins et vieilles cuirasses (1913); Enfantines (1913); 6 Pièces de la période 1906–13; 21 Sports et divertissements (1914); Heures séculaires et instantanées (1914); Trois Valses du precieux degoûté (1914; orchestrated by Greenbaum); Avant-dernières pensées (1915); Parade, suite for Piano, 4-Hands, after the ballet (1917); Sonatine bureaucratique (1917); 5 Nocturnes (1919); Premier Menuet (1920). **VOCAL:** Trois Mélodies de 1886 for Voice and Piano (1886); Messe des Pauvres for Chorus and Organ or Piano (1895; orchestrated by D. Diamond, 1960); Trois Poèmes d'amour for Voice and Piano (1914); Trois Mélodies for Voice and Piano (1916); Socrate for 4 Sopranos and Chamber Orch. (1918; Paris, Feb. 14, 1920); Ludions, 5 songs for Voice and Piano (1923).

BIBL.: P.-D. Templier, *E. S.* (Paris, 1932); R. Myers, *E. S.* (London, 1948); A. Rey, *E. S.* (Paris, 1974; rev. and aug., 1995); G. Wehmeyer, *E. S.* (Berlin, 1974); M. Brendel, *E. S.* (1982); V. Lajoinie, *E. S.* (Lausanne, 1985); J.-J. Barbier, *Au piano avec E. S.* (Paris, 1986); M. Rosenthal, *S., Ravel, Poulenc: An Intimate Memoir* (Madras and N.Y., 1987); A. Gillmor, *E. S.* (Boston, 1988); R. Orledge, *S. the Composer* (Cambridge, 1990); N. Perloff, *Art and the Everyday: Popular Entertainment and the Circle of E. S.* (Oxford, 1991); O. Volta, *S. et la danse* (Paris, 1992); G. Wehmeyer, *E. S.: Bilder und Dokumente* (Munich, 1992); R. Orledge, *S. Remembered* (Portland, Ore., 1995); L. Striegel, *Schlaffe Präludien und verdorrte Embryos: Klavierspielen mit E. S.* (Fernwald, 1997); G. Wehmeyer, *E. S.* (Reinbek bei Hamburg, 1998).—**NS/LK/DM**

Satoh, Sômei, Japanese composer; b. Sendai, Jan. 19, 1947. Born into a musical family, he was self-educated in composition. In the late 1960s he began experimenting in music, producing multimedia scores. In 1983–84 he lived in N.Y. on a Rockefeller Foundation scholarship. His music, ethereally static and subtly metered in the non-Western tradition, seeks to reproduce the inner voices of elements and beings.

WORKS: *Litania* for 1 or 2 Pianos and Tape or Digital Delay (1973); *Hymn for the Sun* for 2 Pianos and Digital Dlay (1975); *Cosmic Womb* for 1 or 2 Pianos and Tape or Digital Delay (1975); *Incarnation I* for Piano, Marimba, and Harp (1977) and *II* for Piano and Digital Delay (1978); *The Heavenly Spheres Are Illuminated by Light* for Soprano, Piano, and Percussion (1979); *Birds in Warped Time I* for Shakuhachi, Sangen, and 20-String Koto (1980) and *II* for Violin and Piano (1980); *Lyra* for 2 Harps, Percussion, and Strings (1980); *Sumeru I* for Percussion and Strings (1982) and *II* for Tubular Bells, Piano, and Strings (1985); *A Journey Through Sacred Time* for Shō, 2 Harps, Percussion, and Strings (1983); *Naohi* for Piano (1983); *Hikari* (Light) for Trumpet and Piano (1986); *Shirasagi* (A White Heron) for String Quartet (1987); *Stabat Mater*, operatic oratorio for Soprano and Chorus (1987); *Uzu* (Vortex) for Flute, Clarinet, Piano, Harp, and Percussion (1988); *Toki No Mon* (A Gate into Infinity) for Violin, Piano, and Percussion (1988); *Homa* for Soprano and String Quartet or String Orch. (1988); *Ruika* (Miserere) for Cello and String Orch. (1990); *Toward the Night* for String Quartet or String Orch. (1991); *Kami No Miuri* (Gods Sells His Own Body) for Mezzo-soprano and 7 Instruments (1991); *Recitative* for Accordion (1991); *Burning Meditation* for Baritone, Harp, Tubular Bells, and String Quartet (1993; rev. version, N.Y., Dec. 19, 1995); *Lanzarote* for Soprano Saxophone and Piano (1993); pieces for Japanese instrumental ensembles; tape music.—**NS/LK/DM**

Satoh, Toyohiko, Japanese lutenist, teacher, and composer; b. Fukuyama, Nov. 4, 1943. He received training in guitar from Kazuhito Osawa (1963–66) and in composition from Taijiro Goh (1963–68) in Tokyo, where he also was a student at the Rikkyo Univ. of Tatsuo Minagawa (1963–67). In 1966 he made his recital debut as a guitarist in Tokyo. In 1968 he entered the Schola Cantorium Basiliensis in Basel, where he studied with Eugen Dombois until 1972. He made his recital debut as a lutenist in Tokyo in 1970, and then his European debut in a lute recital in Basel in 1972. In 1973 he played in Amsterdam and became prof. of lute at the Royal Cons. of Music at The Hague. In subsequent years, he also gave master classes in Europe, North America, and Japan. In 1978 he made his debut as a soloist with orch. when he played the Vivaldi Lute Concerto with the Amsterdam Baroque Orch. conducted by Ton Koopman. On Oct. 14, 1982, he made his formal N.Y. recital debut at Carnegie Recital Hall. Thereafter, his engagements took him all over the world as a master of the Baroque lute repertoire. Among the many composers he has championed are J.S. Bach, Sylvius Leopold Weiss, Robert de Visée, John Dowland, Charles Mouton, Pierre Gautier, and Giovanni Girolamo Kapsberger. With his own Alba Musica Kyo ensemble, he has not only programmed works of the Medieval, Renaissance, and Baroque eras, but contemporary ones as well, including several of his own.—**LK/DM**

Satter, Gustav, Austrian pianist and composer; b. Rann, Slovenia, Feb. 12, 1832; d. place and date unknown. He studied in Vienna and Paris. He undertook a pianistic tour in the U.S. and Brazil (1854–60) with surprising success; went back to Paris, where Berlioz warmly praised his music. He then lived in Vienna, Dresden, Hannover, and Stockholm.

WORKS: *Olanthe*, opera; 3 overtures: *Lorelei, Julius Caesar*, and *An die Freude*; 2 syms.; *George Washington*, symphonic poem; much chamber music; 3 sonatas, studies, waltzes, etc., for piano; about 160 opus numbers in all.

BIBL.: Anonymous (most likely Satter), *The Life and Works of G. S.* (Macon, Ga., 1879).—**NS/LK/DM**

Sauer, Emil (Georg Konrad) von, eminent German pianist and pedagogue; b. Hamburg, Oct. 8, 1862; d. Vienna, April 27, 1942. He was a student of Nikolai Rubinstein in Moscow (1879–91) and of Liszt in Weimar (1884–85). On Jan. 13, 1885, he made his formal debut in Berlin. In 1894 he toured England for the first time. He made his U.S. debut as soloist in both the Beethoven *Emperor* and Henselt concertos at the Metropolitan Opera House in N.Y. with Emil Paur conducting on Jan. 10, 1899. From 1901 to 1907, and again from 1915, he was a prof. at the Meisterschule für Klavierspiel at the Vienna Cons. He also continued to appear as a virtuoso until 1936. In 1917 he was ennobled for his services to music. Sauer was especially known for his interpretations of the Romantic repertoire. He also was a composer and wrote 2 piano concertos, 2 piano sonatas, and many piano etudes. He also edited an edition of the piano music of Brahms. His autobiography was publ. as *Meine Welt* (Stuttgart, 1901). —**NS/LK/DM**

Sauguet, Henri (real name, **Jean Pierre Poupard**), French composer; b. Bordeaux, May 18, 1901; d. Paris, June 22, 1989. He assumed his mother's maiden name as his own. He was a pupil of Vaubourgois in Bordeaux and of Canteloube in Montauban. In 1922 he went to Paris, where he studied with Koechlin; became associated with Satie, and formed a group designated as the École d'Arcueil (from the locality near Paris where Satie lived). In conformity with the principles of utilitarian music, he wrote sophisticated works in an outwardly simple manner; his first conspicuous success was the production of his ballet *La Chatte* by Diaghilev in 1927. He was elected a member of the

Académie des Beaux Arts in 1976. He was the author of *La Musique, ma vie* (Paris, 1990).

WORKS: DRAMATIC: O p e r a : *Le Plumet du colonel* (Paris, April 24, 1924); *La Chartreuse de Parme* (1927–36; Paris, March 16, 1939; rev. 1968); *La Contrebasse* (1930; Paris, 1932); *La Gageure imprévue* (1942; Paris, July 4, 1944); *Les Caprices de Marianne* (Aix-en-Provence, July 20, 1954); *Le Pain des autres* (1967–74); *Boule de suif* (Lyons, 1978); *Tistou les pouces verts* (Paris, 1980). B a l l e t : *La Chatte* (Monte Carlo, April 30, 1927); *Paul et Virginie* (Paris, April 15, 1943); *Les Mirages* (Paris, Dec. 15, 1947); *Cordelia* (Paris, May 7, 1952); *L'As de coeur* (1960); *Paris* (1964); *L'Imposteur ou Le Prince et le mendiant* (1965). ORCH.: 3 piano concertos (1934; 1948; 1961–63); 4 syms.: No. 1, *Expiatoire*, in memory of innocent war victims (1945; Paris, Feb. 8, 1948), No. 2, *Allégorique* (1949), No. 3, *INR* (1955), and No. 4, *Du troisième âge* (1971); *Orphée* for Violin and Orch. (Aix-en-Provence, July 26, 1953); *Mélodie concertante* for Cello and Orch. (1963); *The Garden Concerto* for Harmonica and Orch. (1970); *Reflets sur feuilles* for Harp, Piano, Percussion, and Orch. (1979). CHAMBER: 3 string quartets (1926, 1948, 1979); *Divertissement de chambre* for Flute, Clarinet, Viola, Cello, and Piano (1931); Suite for Clarinet and Piano (1935); *Golden Suite* for Brass (1963); *Sonatine bucolique* for Alto Saxophone and Piano (1964); *Sonatine aux bois* for Oboe and Piano (1971); *Oraisons* for Organ and 4 Saxophones (1976); *Alentours saxophoniques* for Alto Saxophone, Winds, and Piano (1976); *Ne moriatur in aeternum "in memoriam André Jolivet"* for Trumpet and Organ (1979); *Sonate d'église* for Organ and String Quintet (1985); *Musique pour Cendrars* for Piano and String Quintet (1986); piano pieces. VOCAL: *La Voyante*, cantata for Woman's Voice and 11 Instruments (1932); *Petite Messe pastorale* for 2 Voices and Organ (1934); *Le Cornette*, ballade for Bass and Orch. (1951); *Plus loin que la nuit et le jour*, cantata for Chorus (1960); *L'oiseau a vu tout cela*, cantata for Baritone and String Orch. (1960); *Chant pour une ville meurtrie*, oratorio (1967); *Messe jubilatoire* for Tenor, Bass, and String Quartet (1983); songs.

BIBL.: M. Schneider, *H. S.* (Paris, 1959); F.-Y. Bril, *H. S.* (Paris, 1967); D. Austin, *H. S.: A Bio-Bibliography* (N.Y., 1991).—NS/LK/DM

Saunders, Arlene, American soprano and teacher; b. Cleveland, Oct. 5, 1935. She studied at Baldwin-Wallace Coll. and in N.Y. She made her operatic debut as Rosalinde with the National Opera Co. in 1958, and in 1961 she won the Vercelli Vocal Competition and made her European debut as Mimi at Milan's Teatro Nuovo. That same year, she appeared as Giorgetta in *Il Tabarro* at the N.Y.C. Opera. In 1964 she joined the Hamburg State Opera, where she subsequently sang regularly and was made a Kammersängerin in 1967; also appeared as Pamina at the Glyndebourne Festival (1966), as Louise at the San Francisco Opera (1967), as the creator of the title role in Ginastera's *Beatrice Cenci* at the Opera Soc. in Washington, D.C. (Sept. 10, 1971), as Eva in her Metropolitan Opera debut in N.Y. (April 2, 1976), and as Minnie at London's Covent Garden (1980); in 1985 she made her farewell appearance in opera as the Marschallin at the Teatro Colón in Buenos Aires. She taught at Rutgers, the State Univ. of N.J. (from 1987), and at the Abraham Goodman School in N.Y. (from 1987). Among her other roles were Sieglinde, Nedda, Desdemona, Tosca, and Santuzza.—NS/LK/DM

Saunders, Red (Theodore), jazz drummer, vibraphonist, timpanist, leader; b. Memphis, Tenn., March 2, 1912; d. Chicago, Ill., March 5, 1981. Saunders began playing drums while attending school in Milwaukee. He played locally and then moved to Chicago in the early 1930s. There he joined pianist Stomp King, and then worked with Tiny Parham at the Savoy Ballroom (c. 1934). In 1937, Saunders began leading his own band at the Club DeLisa, Chicago, for an 18-year residency. During this period, he also subbed with the Louis Armstrong All-Stars, Duke Ellington, Woody Herman, and many others. Saunders led a band at the Regal, Chicago, from 1960 until 1967. He continued to play during the late 1960s, appearing with Art Hodes at the New Orleans Jazz Festival in 1968 and working with Little Brother Montgomery in 1969. Saunders continued to work through the 1970s, occasionally reviving his big band.—JC/LP

Saunders, Russell, eminent American organ pedagogue; b. Montezuma, Iowa, Oct. 24, 1921; d. Rochester, N.Y., Dec. 6, 1992. He was a student of Frank Jordan at Drake Univ., where he received the degrees of B.Mus.Ed. (1948), M.M. in organ (1949), and an honorary D.Mus. (1977); also studied organ with Arthur Foister at Syracuse Univ. and on a Fulbright grant in Germany with Helmut Walcha (1953–54). From 1948 to 1967 he taught organ and church music at Drake Univ., and then at the Eastman School of Music in Rochester, N.Y., from 1967 until his death. Early in his Eastman years, Saunders gave up public performance and devoted himself to the study of historical performance practices. He became an acknowledged authority and appeared frequently as a lecturer and master teacher at workshops and conferences.

BIBL.: K. Snyder, ed., *The Organist as Scholar: Essays in Memory of R. S.* (Stuyvesant, N.Y., 1994).—NS/LK/DM

Sauret, Emile, French violinist, pedagogue, and composer; b. Dun-le-Roi, Cher, May 22, 1852; d. London, Feb. 12, 1920. A child prodigy, he appears to have studied with Bériot at the Brussels Cons.; he also claimed to have been a pupil of Vieuxtemps and Wieniawski. He made his London debut at the age of 14, and toured the U.S. in 1872, 1874, 1876, 1877, and 1895. After teaching at the Royal Academy of Music in London (1890–1903), he was on the faculty of the Chicago Musical Coll. (1903–06). Following a sojourn in Geneva and Berlin, he returned to London as a prof. at Trinity Coll. of Music in 1908. In 1873 he married **Teresa Carreño** (divorced in 1876). Sauret was a typical representative of the French school of violin playing, distinguished by grace, elegance, and excellent taste. He publ. a method, *Gradus ad Parnassum du violoniste*.

WORKS: VIOLIN AND ORCH.: *Souvenir de Moscou, Rapsodie russe, Rapsodie suédoise, Farfalla,* and *Elégie et Rondo*. VIOLIN AND PIANO: *Feuilles d'album, Pensées fugitives, Scènes champêtres, 20 grandes études, 12 études artistiques, 24 études-caprices.* OTHER: About 25 transcriptions.—NS/LK/DM

Saury, Maxim, jazz clarinetist, leader; b. Enghien-les-Bains, France, Feb. 27, 1928. His father, a violinist, did not encourage him to study music, and when his mother began teaching him violin, he was not enthusiastic about playing. At age 15, he heard clarinetist Hubert Rostaing play with Django Reinhardt and became excited. Saury took enough clarinet lessons to be able to join Christian Azzi's amateur band in 1946. In 1947, he was hired by Claude Bolling and won a prize as best amateur clarinetist at a Brussels festival. He recorded and performed with Bolling during 1948–53 while also gigging with others and leading his own small bands. From 1954–67, he played traditional jazz in Paris with his band the New Orleans Sound. His band performed with visiting American jazzmen Sidney Bechet, Albert Nicholas, Barney Bigard, Bill Coleman, and Peanuts Holland. He also recorded with Holland, Mezz Mezzrow, and Sammy Price. During the 1960s, Saury undertook many tours around the world and played at major European jazz festivals; however, he cut back on his club work. He played in the U.S. with Barney Bigard (1968), with Claude Luter to celebrate Louis Armstrong (1970), and for the American bicentennial (1976).

DISC.: *Mezzrow Meets Saury* (1955); *Rendez- vous a la Nouvelle-Orl[00e9]ans* (1961); *Slow Time* (1963); *Maxi, Maxim, Maximum* (1968).—**LP**

Sauter, Eddie (actually, **Edward Ernest**), jazz arranger, composer, trumpeter; b. Brooklyn, N.Y., Dec. 2, 1914; d. Nyack, N.Y., April 21, 1981. Sauter originally played drums, studied at Columbia Univ., and played and arranged for the Columbia Blue Lions. He next played trumpet with bands that worked on Atlantic liners. He traveled extensively throughout Europe, then settled in N.Y. He worked with Archie Bleyer in 1932 and also for a brief spell with Charlie Barnet, while he continued studying arranging and composition at the Juilliard School of Music. Sauter played trumpet and, occasionally, mellophone with Red Norvo in late 1935, but he was active mainly as Red's staff arranger until June 1939; at this point, he began arranging regularly for Benny Goodman. Sauter scored for many big bands during the 1940s, including Woody Herman and Tommy Dorsey; he also worked briefly as staff arranger for Ray McKinley. After three long spells in the hospital (suffering from a lung ailment), he joined with pianist-arranger Bill Finegan to form the Sauter-Finegan Orch. in 1952. The band was originally a studio unit, but later did tours and residencies before disbanding in 1957 (Finegan revived the band in N.Y. in 1987). Sauter then worked in Germany as musical director for Sudwest-funk radio until autumn 1958. During the 1960s, he continued composing and arranging, including the striking album *Focus*, which set improvising by Stan Getz and Roy Haynes against written string parts; he scored the film *Mickey One* (1965), also with Getz. Sauter was less active in the 1970s, and he died in 1981.

DISC.: *Sound of Sauter-Finegan* (1952); *New Directions in Music* (1952); *Inside Sauter-Finegan* (1953); *Sons of Sauter-Finegan* (1954); *Concert Jazz* (1954); *Under Analysis* (1956); *Adventure in Time* (1956); *Straight Down the Middle* (1957); *Inside Sauter-Finegan Revisited* (1961).—**JC/LP**

Sauveur, Joseph, French acoustician; b. La Fleche, March 24, 1653; d. Paris, July 9, 1716. A deaf-mute, learning to speak in his seventh year, he became a remarkable investigator in the realm of acoustics. In 1696 he became a member of the Académie. He was the first to calculate absolute vibration numbers, and to explain scientifically the phenomenon of overtones.

WRITINGS (all publ. in the *Mémoires of the Académie*): *Principes d'acoustique et de musique* (1700–01); *Application des sons harmoniques à la composition des jeux d'orgue* (1702); *Méthode générale pour former des systèmes tempérés...* (1707); *Table générale des systèmes tempérés* (1711); *Rapports des sons des cordes d'instruments de musique aux flèches des cordes* (1713).—**NS/LK/DM**

Savage, Henry W(ilson), American impresario; b. New Durham, N.H., March 21, 1859; d. Boston, Nov. 29, 1927. He started in business as a real estate operator in Boston, where he took control of the Castle Square Opera House by default in 1894. He founded his own company there to present opera in English in 1895, and subsequently gave performances in Chicago, N.Y., and other cities; with Maurice Grau, he produced opera in English at the Metropolitan Opera in N.Y. (1900). His Henry Savage Grand Opera Co. toured throughout the U.S. with an English-language production of Parsifal in 1904–05; subsequently made successful tours with Puccini's *Madama Butterfly* (1906) and *La fanciulla del West* (1911) and Lehár's *Die lustige Witwe* (1907).—**NS/LK/DM**

Savall, Jordi, outstanding Spanish viol player, conductor, and music scholar; b. Barcelona, Aug. 1, 1941. He began his training at the Barcelona Cons. After studying with August Wenzinger at the Schola Cantorum Basiliensis in Basel (1966–70), he joined its faculty in 1973. In 1974 he founded Hespèrion XX, which he developed into one of the world's foremost early music chamber ensembles and which he led on numerous tours and in many recordings. He also led La Capella Reial de Catalunya and Le Concert des Nations. As a soloist, he has attained renown as a master of viol playing. In his research, he has combed various archives and has amassed a voluminous library of early music MSS on microfilm. Savall and his musicians play from these MSS and eschew the practice of rewriting scores into modern notation. Thus their programs remain as true to the original music as possible while brining a refreshing spontaneity to their performances. Savall's repertoire generally embraces music from the 10th to 18th centuries, but he has also explored works through the late Classical era in his role as a conductor.—**LK/DM**

Saville, Frances, American soprano; b. San Francisco, Jan. 6, 1863; d. Burlingame, Calif., Nov. 8, 1935. She went early to Australia, where she made her debut in oratorio; continued her studies in Paris with Marchesi. In 1892 she made her operatic debut in Brussels; also appeared with the Carl Rosa Co. in England, at the Opéra-Comique in Paris, and in Vienna, Berlin, St. Petersburg, Warsaw, etc. On Nov. 18, 1895, she made her debut as Juliette at the Metropolitan Opera in N.Y., on whose roster she remained through that season and again in 1899–1900. She also sang with the Vienna Court Opera (1899–1903).—**NS/LK/DM**

Savín, Francisco, Mexican conductor and composer; b. Mexico City, Nov. 18, 1929. He studied piano in Mexico City with José Velásquez (1944–53) and took conducting lessons with Scherchen and composition with Rodolfo Halffter (1955–56); continued his studies at the Prague Academy of Music, and also had composition lessons with Janeček (1957–59). He was an asst. conductor of the Mexican National Sym. Orch. (1959–62) and principal conductor of the Xalapa Sym. Orch. (1963–67). He was then director of the National Cons. of Music in Mexico City (1967–70), where he led conducting workshops (from 1973).

WORKS: ORCH.: *Metamorfosis* (1962); *Concreción* for Electronic Organ and Orch. (1969). **CHAMBER:** *2 formas plásticas* for Wind Quintet (1964, 1965); *Quasar 1* for Electronic Organ, Tape, and Percussion (1970). **VOCAL:** *Quetzalcoátl,* symphonic poem for 2 Narrators and Orch. (1957); *3 líricas* for Mezzo-soprano, Flute, Clarinet, Viola, Percussion, and Piano (1966); *Monología de las Delicias* for 4 Women's Voices and Orch. (1969).—NS/LK/DM

Sawallisch, Wolfgang, eminent German conductor; b. Munich, Aug. 26, 1923. He began piano study when he was 5, and later pursued private musical training with Ruoff, Haas, and Sachse in Munich before entering military service during World War II (1942); then completed his musical studies at the Munich Hochschule für Musik. In 1947 he became répétiteur at the Augsburg Opera, making his conducting debut there in 1950. He then was Generalmusikdirektor of the opera houses in Aachen (1953–58), Wiesbaden (1958–60), and Cologne (1960–63); also conducted at the Bayreuth Festivals (1957–61). From 1960 to 1970 he was chief conductor of the Vienna Sym. Orch., making his first appearance in the U.S. with that ensemble in 1964; also was Generalmusikdirektor of the Hamburg State Phil. (1961–73). From 1970 to 1980 he was chief conductor of the Orchestre de la Suisse Romande in Geneva, and from 1971 he also served as Generalmusikdirektor of the Bavarian State Opera in Munich, where he was named Staatsoperndirektor in 1982. In 1990 he was named music director of the Philadelphia Orch., which position he assumed in 1993. That same year, he took it on an acclaimed tour of China. He appeared as a guest conductor with a number of the world's major orchs. and opera houses. A distinguished representative of the revered Austro-German tradition, he has earned great respect for his unostentatious performances; he has also made appearances as a sensitive piano accompanist to leading singers of the day. His autobiography appeared as *Im Interesse der Deutlichkeit: Mein Leben mit der Musik* (Hamburg, 1988). He also publ. *Kontrapunkt—Herausforderung Musik* (Hamburg, 1993).

BIBL.: H. Krellmann, ed., *Stationen eines Dirigenten, W. S.* (Munich, 1983).—NS/LK/DM

Sax, Adolphe (actually, **Antoine-Joseph**), Belgian inventor of the saxophone, son of **Charles-Joseph Sax;** b. Dinant, Nov. 6, 1814; d. Paris, Feb. 4, 1894. He acquired great skill in manipulating instruments from his early youth, and his practical and imaginative ideas led him to undertake improvements of the clarinet and other wind instruments. He studied the flute and clarinet at the Brussels Cons., and in 1842 went to Paris with a wind instrument of his invention, which he called the "saxophone," made of metal, with a single-reed mouthpiece and conical bore. He exhibited brass and woodwind instruments at the Paris Exposition of 1844, winning a silver medal. His father joined him in Paris, and together they continued the manufacture of new instruments. They evolved the saxhorn (improved over the bugle-horn and ophicleide by replacing the keys with a valve mechanism) and the saxo-tromba, a hybrid instrument producing a tone midway between the bugle and the trumpet. Conservative critics and rival instrument makers ridiculed Sax's innovations, but Berlioz and others warmly supported him; he also won praise from Rossini. His instruments were gradually adopted by French military bands. Sax won a gold medal at the Paris Industrial Exposition of 1849. Financially, however, he was unsuccessful, and was compelled to go into bankruptcy in 1856 and again in 1873. He taught the saxophone at the Paris Cons. from 1858 to 1871, and also publ. a method for his instrument. He exhibited his instruments in London (1862) and received the Grand Prix in Paris (1867) for his improved instruments. Although Wieprecht, Červený, and others disputed the originality and priority of his inventions, legal decisions gave the rights to Sax; the saxophone became a standard instrument, and many serious composers made use of it in their scores. The instrument fell into desuetude after Sax's death, but about 1918 a spectacular revival of the saxophone took place, when it was adopted in jazz bands. Its popularity became worldwide, numerous methods were publ. and special schools established, and there appeared saxophone virtuosos for whom many composers wrote concertos.

BIBL.: T. Lajarte, *Instruments S. et fanfares civiles* (Paris, 1876); J. Kool, *Das Saxophone* (Leipzig, 1931); A. Remy, *La Vie tourmentée d'A. S.* (Brussels, 1939); L. Kochnitzky, *A. S. and His Saxophone* (N.Y., 1949); M. Perrin, *Le Saxophone, Son histoire, sa technique et son utilisation dans l'orchestre* (Paris, 1955); J. Londeix, *125 ans de musique pour saxophone* (Paris, 1971); M. Haine, *A. S.: Sa vie, son oeuvre, ses instruments de musique* (Brussels, 1980); W. Horwood, *A. S., 1814–1894: Life and Legacy* (Baldock, 1983; rev. ed., 1992).—NS/LK/DM

Sax, Charles-Joseph, Belgian instrument maker, father of **Adolphe (Antoine-Joseph) Sax;** b. Dinant-sur-Meuse, Feb. 1, 1791; d. Paris, April 26, 1865. He began his career by manufacturing brass and woodwind instruments in Dinant-sur-Meuse, then established an instrument factory at Brussels in 1815, manufacturing not only wind instruments, but also pianos, harps, and guitars; his specialty, however, was brass instruments. He joined his son in Paris, and helped him to launch his revolutionary inventions.—NS/LK/DM

Saxton, Robert (Louis Alfred), English composer and teacher; b. London, Oct. 8, 1953. He was a student of Elisabeth Lutyens (1970–74), of Robin Holloway at St. Catherine's Coll., Cambridge (1972–75; B.A.), of Robert Sherlaw Johnson at Worcester Coll., Oxford (1975–76; B.Mus.), and of Luciano Berio (1976–77). In

1979 he became a teacher at the Guildhall School of Music and Drama in London, where he headed its composition dept. from 1990. His music reveals fine craftsmanship and harmonic invention.

WORKS: DRAMATIC: O p e r a : *Caritas* (1990–91). **ORCH.:** *Reflections of Narziss and Goldmund* (1975; Royan, April 8, 1977); *Choruses to Apollo* (1980; London, Jan. 28, 1981); *Traumstadt* (Harrogate, Aug. 12, 1980); *Ring of Eternity* (1982–83; London, Aug. 24, 1983); *Concerto for Orchestra* (London, Aug. 13, 1984); *The Circles of Light*, chamber sym. (1985–86; London, March 5, 1986); Viola Concerto (Cheltenham, July 9, 1986); *Variation on "Sumer is icumen in"* (Aldeburgh, June 13, 1987); *Fanfare* (Porvoo, Finland, June 18, 1987); *In the Beginning* (1987; London, Jan. 30, 1988); *Birthday Music for Sir William Glock* (BBC Radio 3, London, May 3, 1988); *Elijah's Violin* (1988; London, Feb. 13, 1989); *Music to Celebrate the Resurrection of Christ* (1988; BBC 2 TV, London, March 26, 1989); Violin Concerto (1989; Leeds, June 22, 1990); *Psalm—A Song of Ascents* for Trumpet and Orch. (1992; London, Jan. 23, 1993); Cello Concerto (1992; London, March 18, 1993); *Ring, Time* for Symphonic Wind Ensemble (1994; London, Feb. 9, 1995); *Carmen Natale* for Strings (Bristol, Nov. 15, 1996); *A Yardstick to the Stars* for Chamber Orch. (1998; also for Piano and String Quartet, Durham, Feb. 28, 1995). **CHAMBER:** *Krystallen* for Flute and Piano (1973; BBC Radio 3, London, Jan. 28, 1975); *Echoes of the Glass Bead Game* for Wind Quintet (1975; London, June 28, 1977); *Arias* for Oboe and Piano (1977; London, April 6, 1978); *Toccata* for Cello (Norfolk, Aug. 19, 1978); *Canzona—in memoriam Igor Stravinsky* for Chamber Ensemble (1978; Newcastle upon Tyne, Feb. 23, 1979); *Processions and Dances* for Chamber Ensemble (London, July 6, 1981); *Piccola musica per Luigi Dallapiccola* for Chamber Ensemble (Montepulciano, Aug. 5, 1981); *Chiaroscuro* for Percussion (1981; Keele, Jan. 21, 1982); *Fantasiestück* for Accordion (1982); *The Sentinel of the Rainbow* for Chamber Ensemble (London, Oct. 24, 1984); *Birthday Piece for RRB* (Richard Rodney Bennett)for Chamber Ensemble (London, March 20, 1986); *Night Dance* for Guitar (1986–87; London, April 5, 1987); *Paraphrase on Mozart's "Idomeneo"* for Wind Octet (Glyndebourne, June 15, 1991); *Invocation, Dance, and Meditation* for Viola and Piano (Lichfield, July 6, 1991); *Fantazia* for String Quartet (1993; London, April 5, 1994); *A Yardstick to the Stars* for Piano and String Quartet (Durham, Feb. 28, 1995; also for Chamber Orch., 1998); *Songs, Dances, and Ellipses* for String Quartet (London, Nov. 5, 1997). **P i a n o :** *Ritornelli and Intermezzi* (London, Nov. 1972); *2 Pieces* (1976); *Sonatas for 2 Pianos* (London, Dec. 1, 1977); *Sonata "in Memory of Béla Bartók"* (Cambridge, Aug. 19, 1981); *Chacony* for Piano, Left-Hand (Aldeburgh, June 20, 1988); *Fantazia on the Notes E, Eb, C, B, and A* (London, Dec. 11, 1996). **VOCAL:** *La Promenade d'Automne* for Soprano and 6 Players (1972); *Where Are You Going to My Pretty Maid?* for Soprano and 6 Players (1973); *What Does the Song Hope For?* for Soprano, Chamber Ensemble, and Tape, after Auden (1974; Hildersum, Sept. 1975); *Brise Marine* for Soprano, Piano, and Tape (1976); *Cantata [No. 1] on Poems of Hölderlin* for Tenor, Countertenor, and Piano (London, Oct. 6, 1979), No. 2 for Tenor, Oboe, and Piano (London, July 14, 1980), and No. 3 for 2 Sopranos and Tape Delay (London, Dec. 12, 1981); *Eloge* for Soprano, Flute, Oboe, Clarinet, Horn, Piano, and String Quartet (London, Nov. 26, 1980); *Chaconne* for Double Chorus (London, July 13, 1981); *Child of Light* for Women's Voices and Organ (1984); *I Will Awake the Dawn* for Double Chorus (1986–87; London, Sept. 10, 1987); *Rex Gloriae* for Women's Voices and Organ (Gloucester, July 8, 1988); *At the Round Earth's Imagined Corners* for Chorus (London, July 5, 1992); *Prayer to a Child* for Soprano and 2 Clarinets (Birmingham, Sept. 20, 1992); *O Sing Unto the Lord a New Song* for Chorus and Organ (London, Nov. 24, 1993); *Canticum Luminis* for Soprano, Chorus, and Orch. (1994; Cambridge, March 11, 1995); *Prayer Before Sleep* for Soprano, Cello, and Piano (London, Dec. 8, 1997).—NS/LK/DM

Sayão, Bidú (actually, **Balduina de Oliveira**), noted Brazilian soprano; b. Niteroi, near Rio de Janeiro, May 11, 1902; d. Rockport, Maine, March 12, 1999. She studied with Elena Teodorini in Rio de Janeiro, and then with Jean de Reszke in Vichy and Nice. Returning to Brazil, she gave her first professional concert in Rio de Janeiro in 1925; in 1926 she sang the role of Rosina in *Il Barbiere di Siviglia* at the Teatro Municipal there. She made her American debut on Dec. 29, 1935, in a recital in N.Y. On Feb. 13, 1937, she sang Manon at her Metropolitan Opera debut in N.Y., earning enthusiastic reviews; remained on its roster until 1952. She retired in 1958. Her finest performances were in lyric roles in bel canto operas; especially memorable were her interpretations of Violetta, Gilda, and Mimi. She also showed her versatility in coloratura parts, such as Lakme; in France, she was described as "a Brazilian nightingale." She also sang vocal parts in several works of her great compatriot Villa-Lobos. She was a recipient of numerous honors from European royalty, and of the Palmes Academiques from the French government; in 1972 she was decorated a Commandante by the Brazilian government.—NS/LK/DM

Sayer, Leo (Gerard Hugh), 1970s hitmaker; b. Shoreham-by-Sea, England, May 21, 1948. Although his manager's wife nicknamed him "Leo" because of his mane of hair, that was his only leonine characteristic. Leo Sayer was downright petite, standing 5' 4" and weighing in at a bit over 100 pounds. His mother was a nurse, his father an engineer, and he grew up on the hospital grounds, which was convenient since he was a frequent target for bullies.

While attending art school in the late 1960s, he played harmonica in the Terraplane Blues Band. After graduating, he got a job in London converting photographs into record covers for Island and Trojan records. He earned some extra cash busking and playing pick-up gigs on the harmonica, but the workload led to a nervous breakdown in 1968. He returned home to Shoreham-by-Sea, living on a friend's houseboat, and started writing songs as part of his therapy. He started playing in the bands Jester and Patches. Patches caught the ear of David Courtney. Formerly a drummer for English Elvis wannabe Adam Faith (who had a Top 40 hit in the U.S. with "It's Alright" in 1965), Courtney now worked as a talent scout. He brought Patches to Faith, who offered to manage Sayer and obtain a record deal for him.

Sayer and Courtney also started writing together. They recorded some demos at Roger Daltrey's studio, and Daltrey liked the Sayer-Courtney songs so much, he recorded nine of them for his 1973 solo debut album. "Giving It All Away" became a substantial hit in England and on rock radio in the U.S. Daltrey offered Sayer some tips on stagecraft and even loaned him a PA system.

When Sayer's debut, *Silverbird*, came out in 1974, it spawned the European hit "One Man Band." Sayer toured the continent with Roxy Music; dressed in white-face and a clown costume, he got noticed. Sayer's second album contained several more of the songs from the Daltrey album, including his version of "Giving It All Away" from which the title *Just a Boy* came. That album spawned a huge worldwide hit, the rollicking "Long Tall Glasses," which rose to #9 in the U.S., propelling the album to #16. His third album, produced by former Supertramp bassist Frank Farrell, yielded yet another European hit, "Moonlighting," in 1975.

Later in 1975, Sayer fell under the sway of producer Richard Perry, who knew how to create pop hits and how to ride a trend. He recorded *Endless Flight* with Sayer, taking him to the top of the charts worldwide with the ballad "When I Need You" and the disco-light tune "You Make Me Feel like Dancing," which won Sayer a Grammy award for Best Rhythm and Blues Song of 1976. Both singles went gold. A third single, "How Much Love" rose to #17. The album hit #10 and went platinum.

A year later, Sayer's second foray with Perry, *Thunder in My Heart*, was somewhat less successful. It spawned two singles that barely scratched the Top 40, the title track and "Easy to Love." The album also barely made the Top 40, sneaking in at #37. Despite a plethora of musicians from Fleetwood Mac, Toto, Elton John's band, and other big-name session players, his 1978 album *Leo Sayer* stiffed, although "I Can't Stop Loving You (Though I Try)" became a hit in Europe. His next album, *Here*, paired him with most of Booker T and the MGs and Al Kooper, but also failed to set the charts afire.

In 1980 he came back with a new producer and a leaner sound on *Living in a Fantasy*. The ballad "More than I Can Say" propelled Sayer to #2, topping the adult contemporary charts and going gold. The title track rose to #23, but the album barely made the Top 40, stalling at #36. Sayer next hosted a BBC TV show, spent some time in the U.S., and unable to convert anything from 1982's *World Radio* into a hit, started playing Vegas-style showrooms. Not happy with this, he fired his management, but it was too little too late. After 1984's *Have You Ever Been in Love*, he dropped off the pop music radar.

During the late 1990s, Sayer experienced something of a renaissance when the Prodigy's Keith Flint mentioned he was a fan of Sayer's. Sayer started making appearances on British TV again, and even went out for his first full-fledged tour of the continent in over a decade.

DISC.: *Silverbird* (1974); *Just a Boy* (1974); *Another Year* (1975); *Endless Flight* (1976); *Thunder in My Heart* (1977); *Leo Sayer* (1978); *Here* (1979); *Living in a Fantasy* (1980); *World Radio* (1982); *Have You Ever Been in Love* (1984); *Love Songs* (1997).—**HB**

Saygun, Ahmed Adnan, Turkish teacher and composer; b. Izmir, Sept. 7, 1907; d. Istanbul, Jan. 6, 1991. He studied composition in Paris with Borrel at the Cons. and with Le Flem and d'Indy at the Schola Cantorum. Returning to Turkey in 1931, he taught at the Istanbul Cons. (1936–39); accompanied Bartók on a music-ethnological trip through Anatolia (1936). From 1964 he taught composition at the State Cons. in Ankara and from 1972 at the Istanbul State Cons. He wrote operas, including *Tasbebek* (Ankara, Dec. 27, 1934) and *Kerem* (1947; Ankara, March 1, 1953), as well as the oratorio *Yunus Emre* (Ankara, May 25, 1946), 4 syms. (1953, 1955, 1961, 1973), a Piano Concerto (1956), a Violin Concerto (1967), and chamber pieces.
—**NS/LK/DM**

Sayles, Emanuel (Rene; aka Manny), early jazz banjoist, guitarist, singer; Donaldsonville, La., Jan. 31, 1907; d. New Orleans, Oct. 5, 1986. His father, George (c. 1880–c. 1955), was a guitarist with New Orleans's Silver Leaf Orch. (1898–1918) but then retired from music making except for occasional gigs in the 1920s. Emmanuel first studied violin and viola with Dave Perkins, then taught himself banjo and guitar. Sayles attended high school in Pensacola, Fla., for two years, then moved to New Orleans, where he joined William Ridgley's Tuxedo Orch. During 1928, he worked with Fate Marable on the riverboat S.S. *Capitol*, recorded with the Jones-Collins Astoria Hot Eight (1929), and then returned to riverboat work with Armand Piron and Sidney Desvigne. Sayles moved to Chicago in 1933, where he led his own small group and played for many leaders, including bassist John Lindsey; Sayles also recorded with Roosevelt Sykes. He returned to New Orleans in 1949, where he continued to play regularly. In the 1960s, he worked in Cleveland with Punch Miller (1960), then joined George Lewis and toured Japan with him (1963–64). In 1964 he toured with pianist Sweet Emma Barrett. In 1965, Sayles returned to Chicago to work as house musician at Bill Reinhardt's Jazz Ltd. Club. Three years later, he was back in New Orleans, where he played regularly at Preservation Hall as well as at other local clubs. He undertook several tours from the late 1960s on, including trips to Australia (1971) and Russia (1979), both with the Preservation Hall Jazz Band; he also toured Europe in the early 1980s. He remained active in New Orleans until his death.
—**JC/LP**

Saylor, Bruce (Stuart), American composer and teacher; b. Philadelphia, April 24, 1946. He studied composition with Weisgall and Sessions at the Juilliard School of Music in N.Y. (B.Mus., 1968; M.S., 1969). In 1969–70 he held a Fulbright grant and pursued his training with Petrassi at the Accademia di Santa Cecilia in Rome. In 1970 he entered the Graduate School of the City Univ. of N.Y. and studied composition with Perle and theory with Salzer, taking his Ph.D. in 1978. He taught at Queens Coll. of the City Univ. of N.Y. (1970–76) and at N.Y.U. (1976–79). In 1979 he returned to Queens Coll., where he became a prof. at the Aaron Copland School of Music. He also served on the faculty of the Graduate School of the City Univ. of N.Y. from 1983. From 1992 to 1994 he was composer-in-residence of the Lyric Opera of Chicago, which gave the premiere of his opera *Orpheus Descending* on June 10, 1994. He received grants from the NEA (1976, 1978), the Ives scholarship (1976) and an award (1983) from the American Academy and Inst. of Arts and Letters, a Guggenheim fellowship (1982–83), and the Ingram Merrill Foundation Award (1991). He is married to the mezzo-soprano Constance Beavon, who has performed many of his vocal works.

WORKS: DRAMATIC: *My Kinsman, Major Molineux,* opera (Pittsburgh, Aug. 28, 1976); *Cycle,* dance piece (Chilmark, Mass., July 27, 1978; rev. version, Chilmark, Mass., July 24, 1980); *Inner World Out,* dance piece (Chilmark, Mass., Aug. 30, 1978); *Wildfire,* dance piece (Chilmark, Mass., Aug. 29, 1979; rev. version as *Wildfire II,* N.Y., April 2, 1985); *The Waves,* 3 dramatic monologues for Mezzo-soprano and 5 Instruments (Chilmark, Mass., Aug. 27, 1981; rev. version, Paris, Nov. 18, 1985); *Spill,* dance piece (N.Y., May 10, 1984); *Voices from Sandover,* incidental music (N.Y., May 23, 1989); *Orpheus Descending,* opera (Chicago, June 10, 1994). **ORCH.:** *Cantilena* for Strings (N.Y., May 1965); *Notturno* for Piano and Orch. (1969); *Turns and Mordents,* flute concerto (New Haven, Conn., March 6, 1977); *Symphony in 2 Parts* (1980; Houston, Feb. 6, 1981); *Archangel* for Antiphonal Brass Quartet and Orch. (San Francisco, May 20, 1990); *Supernova* for Concert Band (Lancaster, Pa., Nov. 6, 1992). **CHAMBER:** Woodwind Quintet (1965; Sunnyside, N.Y., March 21, 1992); Suite for Viola (1967); Duo for Violin and Viola (Rome, May 12, 1970); *Conductus* for 3 Winds, 3 Strings, and Percussion (Rome, May 1970); *Firescreen* for Flute, Cello, and Piano (N.Y., Nov. 1, 1979); *St. Ulmo's Fire* for Flute and Harp (N.Y., March 16, 1980); *Fire-Flaught* for Flute, Bassoon, and Harp (1982); *State Trumpets* for Organ and Brass (Lattingtown, N.Y., Sept. 23, 1982; also for Organ); *Carillon Te Deum* for Bells (Ithaca, N.Y., June 29, 1983); Fanfare for Double Brass Quintet (N.Y., Nov. 14, 1983); *Soggetti I* for Flute (Paris, Nov. 18, 1985) and *II* for Flute and Harpsichord (N.Y., May 11, 1986); *Electra: A translation* for Viola, Contrabass, and Piano (Minneapolis, May 11, 1986); Trio for Clarinet, Viola, and Piano (Washington, D.C., June 20, 1989); *Fanfares and Echoes* for Horn and String Trio (Paris, Nov. 28, 1992). **KEYBOARD: Piano:** *5 Short Pieces* (1965–67; N.Y., April 16, 1969); *Saltarello* (Paris, Nov. 18, 1981); *Quattro Passi* (1991; N.Y., Sept. 16, 1992). **Organ:** *Ricercare and Sinfonia* (1965, 1969; N.Y., Aug. 22, 1971); *State Trumpets* (Rome, May 22, 1983; also for Organ and Brass). **VOCAL:** *5 Songs from "Whispers of Heav'nly Death"* for Soprano and String Quartet (1965–67); *To Winter* and *To Autumn* for Soloists, Chorus, and Orch. (1968); *3 Collects* for Mezzo-soprano and Organ (1968); *Benedictus es* for Chorus and Organ (1969); *2 Yiddish Folksongs* for Tenor, Chorus, and Piano, 4-Hands (1969); *Lyrics* for Soprano and Violin (1970; N.Y., Nov. 13, 1971); *Loveplay* for Mezzo-soprano, Flute, and Viola (N.Y., Nov. 18, 1975; also for Voice, Flute, and Cello, N.Y., Jan. 30, 1977); *4 Psalms* for Voice and Flute (1976–78); *Songs from Water Street* for Mezzo-soprano, Viola, and Piano (Washington, D.C., May 10, 1980); *Swimming by Night* for Mezzo-soprano, Viola, and Piano (1980; N.Y., Jan. 25, 1982); *Te Deum* for Chorus and Organ (N.Y., Oct. 23, 1982); *5 Old Favorites* for Voice, Flute, and Piano (1983; N.Y., Jan. 22, 1984); *It Had Wings* for Voice and Piano (Rome, April 12, 1984; also for Voice and Orch., N.Y., Nov. 3, 1991); *Psalm 23* for Voice and Oboe (McLean, Va., Aug. 17, 1985; also for Chorus and Instruments obbligato (N.Y., Nov. 15, 1987); *See You in the Morning* for Soprano and 6 Instruments (N.Y., Feb. 22, 1987); *Mass of the Holy Trinity* for Congregation, Chorus, Organ, and Brass (Paris, June 14, 1987); *Jubilate Fantasy* for Soprano, Chorus, and Orch. (Paris, Dec. 19, 1990); *Behold that Star* for Soprano and String Quartet (Paris, Dec. 19, 1990); *Star of Wonder,* Christmas cantata for Soprano, Children's Chorus, String Quartet, and Harp (Paris, Dec. 19, 1990); *3 Spirituals* for Soprano and Chorus (Paris, Dec. 19, 1990); *The Star Song* for Mezzo-soprano, Chorus, and Orch. (Rome, Sept. 25, 1992); *Honor, Honor,* spiritual for Soprano and Chorus (N.Y., May 3, 1993; also for Voice and Piano, Chicago, Aug. 11, 1993); *Angels* for Mezzo-soprano, Flute, Cello, and Piano (N.Y., May 11, 1993); *Canticle of Blessing* for Chorus, Brass, Percussion, and Organ (Flushing, N.Y., May 17, 1994); *In Praise of Jerusalem* for Chorus, 3 Brass Ensembles, and Organ (1994); *Song of Ascent* for Chorus, 3 Trumpets, and Organ (1994; Chicago, Jan. 29, 1995); *Magnificat* for Voice, Flute, and Guitar (Chicago, Feb. 13, 1995); *By the Power of Your Love* for 3 Women's Voices and Chorus (Chicago, March 12, 1995).—NS/LK/DM

Sayve, Lambert de, Flemish composer; b. Sayve, near Liège, 1548 or 1549; d. Linz, between Feb. 16 and 28, 1614. As a youth he went to Vienna, where he became a singer in the imperial chapel in 1562. In 1569 he became choirmaster at the monastery of Melk, near Linz, a post he retained until 1577 (made a trip to Spain in 1570–71). He was a tutor to the choirboys in the chapel of Archduke Karl in Graz (1577–82). He was named choirmaster of the chapel of Archduke Matthias of Austria in 1583, and returned to Vienna; became master of the imperial chapel in 1612. He publ. *Sacrae symphoniae* for 4 to 13 and 15 to 16 Voices (Klosterbruck, 1612) and wrote several motets, masses, and other sacred works. He also publ. *Primo libro delle* [24] *canzoni a la napolitana* for 5 Voices (Vienna, 1582) and (22) *Teutsche Liedlein* for 4 Voices (1602).

BIBL.: R. Bragard, *L. d.S.: Étude biographique et bibliographique* (Liège, 1934); G. Rebscher, *L. d.S. als Motettenkomponist* (diss., Univ. of Frankfurt am Main, 1959).—NS/LK/DM

Sbriglia, Giovanni, Italian tenor and singing teacher; b. Naples, June 23, 1829; d. Paris, Feb. 20, 1916. He made his debut at the Teatro San Carlo in Naples in 1853. He was heard in Italy by Maretzek, the impresario, who engaged him for a season at the Academy of Music in N.Y., where Sbriglia appeared with Adelina Patti (1860). He then made a grand tour of the U.S. with Parodi and Adelaide Phillipps, and also sang in Mexico and Havana. He returned to Europe in 1875 and settled in Paris, where he became a highly successful vocal teacher. Jean, Joséphine, and Edouard de Reszke studied with him when they were already professional artists; he trained the baritone voice of Jean de Reszke, enabling him to sing tenor roles. Pol Plançon, Nordica, and Sibyl Sanderson were among his pupils. —NS/LK/DM

Scacchi, Marco, eminent Italian choirmaster, pedagogue, writer on music, and composer; b. Gallese, near Viterbo, c. 1600; d. there, c. 1684. After studies with Giovanni Francesco Anerio, he went to Warsaw and was made a royal musician in 1626; then served as choirmaster at the court from 1628 until ill health compelled him in 1649 to retire to Gallese, where he devoted himself to teaching. He composed 10 operas for Warsaw (1628–49) and also wrote masses, sacred concertos, and madrigals. For his works, see J. Mattheson, *Der vollkommene Capellmeister* (Hamburg, 1739). Scacchi was a distinguished writer on music and effectively defended modern music against the polemics of Paul Siefert. His most significant writings are *Cribrum musicum ad triticum Syferticum, seu Examinatio succinta psalmorum* (Venice, 1643), *Lettera per maggiore informatione a chi leggera il mio "Cribrum"* (Venice, 1644), *Epistola ad Excellentissimum Dn. CS. Wernerum* (c. 1648), *Judicium cribri musici* (Warsaw, c. 1649), and *Breve discorso sopra la musica moderna* (Warsaw, 1649).

BIBL.: P. Syfert (Seifert), *Anticribratio musica ad avenam S.anam* (Danzig, 1645).—**NS/LK/DM**

Scacciati, Bianca, Italian soprano; b. Florence, July 3, 1894; d. Brescia, Oct. 15, 1948. She studied in Milan. She made her operatic debut there as Marguerite in *Faust* in 1917. She rapidly asserted herself as one of the most impressive dramatic sopranos in Italy; sang for many seasons at La Scala in Milan; also made successful appearances at Covent Garden in London, at the Paris Opéra, and at the Teatro Colón in Buenos Aires. She was particularly noted for her interpretation of the title role of Puccini's *Turandot*.—**NS/LK/DM**

Scaggs, Boz (actually, **Scaggs, William Royce**), guitarist, vocalist; b. Ohio, June 8, 1944. Gaining his first recognition as guitarist and vocalist on Steve Miller's first two late–1960s albums, Boz Scaggs debuted solo in 1969 with his self-titled album, an overlooked blues classic recorded in Muscle Shoals, Ala., with Duane Allman. Becoming a major star in his adopted hometown of San Francisco in the early 1970s, Scaggs broke through as an album artist with 1974's *Slow Dancer*. Adopting a sophisticated soul-style sound, he was established nationally with 1976's *Silk Degrees* album and its four hit singles. Scoring four major hits again in 1980, Scaggs withdrew from recording and touring in 1981. Scaggs eventually issued new, modest-selling albums, in 1988 and 1994.

William "Boz" Scaggs grew up in Okla. and Tex., met Steve Miller at age 15 in a Dallas-area high school, and soon accepted Miller's offer to join his band, The Marksmen, as vocalist. He learned rhythm guitar from Miller, who moved to Wisc. to attend the Univ. of Wisc. at Madison, a year before Scaggs's graduation. Scaggs followed Miller to the university the following year and joined Miller's band, The Ardells, before returning to Tex. in 1963, where he formed his own band, The Wigs. In 1964 Scaggs traveled to England and decided to stay in Europe, singing on the streets of European cities and eventually establishing Stockholm as his base. Around 1966 he recorded a blues and folkstyle album, *Boz*, that was issued in Europe only. Summoned by Steve Miller in 1967, Scaggs moved to San Francisco, where he joined Miller's band during the heyday of psychedelia and appeared on *Children of the Future* and *Sailor*, two of Miller's most highly regarded albums, before departing in August 1968.

Signed to Atlantic Records, Boz Scaggs's solo debut was arguably his finest work. Produced with engineer Marlin Greene and *Rolling Stone* editor Jann Wenner, the album was recorded in Muscle Shoals, Ala., with the able assistance of keyboardist Barry Beckett and guitarist Duane Allman. It featured the 13-minute "Loan Me a Dime" and included "I'll Be Long Gone," "Sweet Release," and early country artist Jimmie Rodgers's "Waiting for a Train." After returning to San Francisco permanently in 1970, Scaggs switched to Columbia Records for recordings in a less bluesy, more pop-oriented vein. *Moments*, recorded in San Francisco, yielded two minor hits with "We Were Always Sweethearts" and "Near You," but the follow-up, *Boz Scaggs and Band*, largely recorded in London, failed to produce a hit, although it did contain the favorite "Runnin' Blue." *My Time*, partially recorded in Muscle Shoals, produced the minor hit "Dinah Flo," but Scaggs was not to register another hit for four years.

Employing veteran Motown producer Johnny Bristol and utilizing studio musicians exclusively, Boz Scaggs recorded *Slow Dancer* in an orchestrated soul style. The album, often regarded as his finest later effort, includes "Angel Lady," "You Make It So Hard (To Say No)," and Bristol's "I've Got Your Number." Scaggs debuted the album in March 1974 at Oakland's Paramount Theater in a first-of-its-kind "black tie optional" setting, lavishly staging the event with a 27-piece orchestra and formally attired rock band, which included guitarist Les Dudek. Scaggs retained the format for Bay Area New Year's Eve shows in 1974, 1975, and 1976.

Boz Scaggs fully embraced a sophisticated soul and disco-tinged style for 1976's *Silk Degrees*. The album finally established him nationally, yielding the moderate hits "It's Over" and "What Can I Say" as well as the smash hit "Lowdown" and the near-smash "Lido Shuffle." It also included Scaggs's "We're All Alone Now," a top easy-listening and smash pop hit for Rita Coolidge in 1977. However, the album's phenomenal success overshadowed Scaggs's subsequent work. The equivocal *Down Two, Then Left* produced minor hits with "Hard Times" and "Hollywood," whereas *Middle Man* yielded major hits with "Breakdown Dead Ahead" and "Jojo," both cowritten with producer David Foster. In 1980 Scaggs scored major hits with "Look What You've Done to Me," from the movie *Urban Cowboy*, and "Miss Sun."

In 1981 Boz Scaggs ceased recording and began limiting live performances to Bay Area benefits and Japan, where his records had sold spectacularly. In 1984 he opened the restaurant Blue Light Cafe in San Francisco, later opening one of San Francisco's most daring and prominent nightclubs, Slim's, in 1988. He also released his first album of new material in eight years, but the sophisticated *Other Roads* produced only a moderate hit with the ballad "Heart of Mine." With the expiration of his Columbia contract, Boz Scaggs switched to Virgin Records for the rather sparse album *Some Change* in 1994, and conducted his first American concert tour in 14 years.

DISC.: *B. S.* (1969); *Moments* (1971); *B. S. and Band* (1971); *My Time* (1972); *Slow Dancer* (1974); *Silk Degrees* (1976); *Silk Degrees/Slow Dancer* (1986); *Down Two, Then Left* (1977); *Middle Man* (1980); *Hits!* (1980); *Other Roads* (1988); *Some Change* (1994). —**BH**

Scala, Francis (Maria), Italian-American bandmaster and composer; b. Naples, 1819 or 1820; d.

Washington, D.C., April 18, 1903. Beginning his musical career on the clarinet, he enlisted in the U.S. Navy as a musician third-class on the frigate Brandywine when it was anchored at Naples in 1841. Following the ship's return to Washington, D.C., Scala left the navy for the Marine Corps, and in 1843 was designated fife-major of the fife corps associated with Marine Corps headquarters. On Sept. 9, 1855, he became de facto the leader of the Marine Band; in 1861 he was made "Principal Musician," and on Sept. 4, 1868, was referred to, for the first time, as "Leader of the Band," a position he retained until 1871. John Philip Sousa was one of his apprentice bandsmen. In 1945 his son Norman P. Scala made the first of several gifts to the Library of Congress honoring his father; these materials contain a large amount of MSS and printed music, chiefly band arrangements made by or for Scala, that represent in essence the library of the Marine Band during the Civil War; included is a note in the hand of President Abraham Lincoln, then Scala's Commander-in-Chief.

BIBL.: D. Ingalls, *F. S., Leader of the Marine Band from 1855–1871* (thesis, Catholic Univ. of America, 1955). —NS/LK/DM

Scalchi, Sofia, celebrated Italian mezzo-soprano; b. Turin, Nov. 29, 1850; d. Rome, Aug. 22, 1922. She studied with Boccabadati, making her debut at Mantua in 1866 as Ulrica in Verdi's *Un ballo in maschera*. She then sang throughout Italy. She appeared in concert in London (Sept. 16, 1868) and at Covent Garden (Nov. 5, 1868) as Azucena, obtaining enormous success; continued to appear there regularly until 1889, and also sang in St. Petersburg (1872–81; 1889–90). On Dec. 20, 1882, she made her U.S. debut as Arsaces in *Semiramide* at N.Y.'s Academy of Music; then was engaged for the first performance at the Metropolitan Opera, where she sang Siebel in *Faust* on Oct. 22, 1883; was again on its roster in 1891–92 and from 1893 to 1896, and then retired from the operatic stage. Her voice had a range of 2 1/2 octaves; it was essentially a contralto voice, but with so powerful a high register that she successfully performed soprano parts. Among her other roles were Fidès, Ortrud, Amneris, Emilia, and Mistress Quickly. —NS/LK/DM

Scalero, Rosario, eminent Italian pedagogue and composer; b. Moncalieri, near Turin, Dec. 24, 1870; d. Settimo Vittone, near Turin, Dec. 25, 1954. After training at the Turin Liceo Musicale, he studied violin with Sivori in Genoa and Wilhelmj in London; subsequently studied general subjects with Mandyczewski in Vienna. He taught violin in Lyons (1896–1908); then went to Rome as a teacher of theory at the Accademia di Santa Cecilia; was also founder-director of the Società del Quartetto (1913–16) and a high commissioner for examinations at the conservatories of Naples, Rome, and Parma. From 1919 to 1928 he was chairman of the theory and composition dept. at N.Y.'s David Mannes School; also taught at the Curtis Inst. of Music in Philadelphia (1924–33; 1935–46), where his students included Samuel Barber, Gian Carlo Menotti, and Lukas Foss. He wrote a Violin Concerto, *Neapolitan Dances* for Violin and Piano, chamber music, sacred songs, etc.—NS/LK/DM

Scalzi, Carlo, Italian castrato soprano who flourished from 1719 to 1738. He sang in Venice (1719–21; 1724–25), Reggio and Modena (1720), Genoa (1722–23; 1733), Parma (1725), Naples (1726–27; 1730), where he created Hasse's *Ezio*, and Rome (1728–29; 1731–32). Handel then called him to London, where he made his first appearance in the pasticcio *Semiramide riconosciuta* (Oct. 30, 1733). Handel composed the role of Alceste in *Arianna in Creta* (Jan. 26, 1734) for him, and he also appeared in other works by that composer until the end of 1734. In 1737–38 he again sang in Venice.—NS/LK/DM

Scandello, Antonio, distinguished Italian instrumentalist and composer; b. Bergamo, Jan. 17, 1517; d. Dresden, Jan. 15, 1580. He was born into a family of the nobility, and studied in his native city and played cornett at S. Maria Maggiore there. After serving Cardinal Christoph Madruzzi in Trent (1547–49), he was called to Dresden by the Elector Moritz of Saxony as an instrumentalist in the court chapel; later became a Protestant and in 1562 was made a citizen of Dresden. When the Kapellmeister Le Maistre became ill in 1566, Scandello assumed most of his responsibilities, and upon Le Maistre's retirement in 1568, Scandello was made his successor. Under his leadership, the Dresden court chapel attained notable distinction. Scandello was a particularly fine composer of sacred music. His *St. John Passion* (1561) was the first work of its kind in Germany to combine the chorale and motet styles. His other works include masses, motets, and Italian and German secular songs.—NS/LK/DM

Scarabelli, Diamante Maria, Italian soprano who flourished from 1695 to 1718. She was born in Bologna, where she first gained distinction (1696–97; 1699; 1700; 1708–09; 1718). She also made many appearances in Venice (1695; 1703; 1707–12; 1714–16), and sang in Milan (1699), Pavia and Genoa (1705), Ferrara (1715), and Padua (1718). She was in the service of the Duke of Mantua (1697–1708), Cardinal Grimani, Viceroy of Naples (1709), and the Duke of Modena (1715). Scarabelli was greatly esteemed for her roles in operas by Caldara, Handel, Lotti, Orlandini, and C.F. Pollarolo. —NS/LK/DM

Scaria, Emil, outstanding Austrian bass; b. Graz, Sept. 18, 1838; d. Blasewitz, near Dresden, July 22, 1886. He studied with Netzer in Graz and Lewy in Vienna, making his debut as St. Bris in *Les Huguenots* in Pest (1860); following additional training with García in London, he sang in Dessau (1862–63), Leipzig (1863–65), and Dresden (from 1865), where he won notable distinction by singing both bass and baritone roles. After appearing as a guest artist at the Vienna Court Opera (1872–73), he sang there regularly as one of its leading artists until his death. He also sang with Angelo Neumann's company; while appearing in *Die Walküre* with the company in London in May 1882, he suffered a mental breakdown; however, he appeared in public 2 days later in *Siegfried*, and then sang Gurnemanz in the first mounting of *Parsifal* at the Bayreuth Festival on July 26, 1882. He continued to make tours with Neumann's

company, returned to Bayreuth in 1883, and made a concert tour of the U.S. in 1884. In early 1886 he suffered a relapse and shortly thereafter died insane. He was hailed as one of the greatest Wagnerians of his time. —NS/LK/DM

Scarlatti, (Giuseppe) Domenico, famous Italian composer, harpsichordist, and teacher, son of **(Pietro) Alessandro (Gaspare) Scarlatti** and uncle of **Giuseppe Scarlatti;** b. Naples, Oct. 26, 1685; d. Madrid, July 23, 1757. Nothing is known about his musical training. On Sept. 13, 1701, he was appointed organist and composer at the Royal Chapel in Naples, where his father was maestro di cappella. The 2 were granted a leave of absence in June 1702, and they went to Florence; later that year Domenico returned to Naples without his father, and resumed his duties. His first opera, *Ottavia ristituita al trono*, was performed in Naples in 1703. He was sent to Venice by his father in 1705, but nothing is known of his activities there. In 1708 he went to Rome, where he entered the service of Queen Maria Casimira of Poland; he remained in her service until 1714, and composed a number of operas and several other works for her private palace theater. He became assistant to Bai, the maestro di cappella at the Vatican, in 1713; upon Bai's death the next year, he was appointed his successor; he also became maestro di cappella to the Portuguese ambassador to the Holy See in 1714. During his years in Rome, he met such eminent musicians as Corelli and Handel. Mainwaring relates the unconfirmed story that Scarlatti and Handel engaged in a friendly contest, Scarlatti being judged the superior on the harpsichord and Handel on the organ. He resigned his positions in 1719; by 1724 he was in Lisbon, where he took up the post of mestre at the patriarchal chapel. His duties included teaching the Infanta Maria Barbara, daughter of King John V, and the King's younger brother, Don Antonio. In 1728 Maria Barbara married the Spanish Crown Prince Fernando, and moved to Madrid. Scarlatti accompanied her, remaining in Madrid for the rest of his life. In 1724 he visited Rome, where he met Quantz; in 1725 he saw his father for the last time in Naples; in 1728 he was in Rome, where he married his first wife, Maria Caterina Gentili. In 1738 he was made a Knight of the Order of Santiago. When Maria Barbara became queen in 1746, he was appointed her maestro de cámera. His last years were spent quietly in Madrid; from 1752 until 1756, Antonio Soler studied with him. So closely did he become associated with Spain that his name eventually appeared as Domingo Escarlatti.

Scarlatti composed over 500 single-movement sonatas for solo keyboard. Although these works were long believed to have been written for the harpsichord, the fact that Maria Barbara used pianos in her residences suggests that some of these works were written for that instrument as well; at least 3 were written for the organ. His sonatas reveal his gifts as one of the foremost composers in the "free style" (a homophonic style with graceful ornamentation, in contrast to the former contrapuntal style). He also obtained striking effects by the frequent crossing of hands, tones repeated by rapidly changing fingers, etc. During his lifetime the following collections of keyboard works were publ.: *Essercizi per gravicembalo* (London, 1738), *XLII Suites de pièces pour le clavecin* (London, 1739), and *Pièces pour le clavecin* (3 vols., Paris, 1742–46). The principal MS sources are found in the library of the Arrigo Boito Conservatorio in Parma and the Biblioteca Marciana in Venice. Alessandro Longo, Ralph Kirkpatrick, and Giorgio Pestelli prepared chronological catalogues of his sonatas. The one by Kirkpatrick is the most widely accepted. The following editions of his sonatas should be consulted: A. Longo, ed., *Opere complete per clavicembalo di D. S.* (11 vols., Milan, 1906–08), R. Kirkpatrick, *D. S.: Sixty Sonatas* (N.Y., 1953), K. Gilbert, ed., *D. S.: Sonates*, in Le Pupitre (Paris, 1971–85), R. Kirkpatrick, ed., *D. S.: Complete Keyboard Works in Facsimile* (N.Y., 1971 et seq.), and E. Fadini, ed., *D. S.: Sonate per clavicembalo* (Milan, 1978 et seq.).

WORKS: DRAMATIC: O p e r a : *Ottavia ristituita al trono*, melodramma (Naples, Carnival 1703); *Giustino*, dramma per musica (Naples, Dec. 19, 1703; in collaboration with Legrenzi); *Irene*, dramma per musica (Naples, Carnival 1704; a complete revision of the opera by Pollarolo); *Silvia*, dramma pastorale (Rome, Jan. 27, 1710); *Tolomeo e Alessandro, ovvero La corona disprezzata*, dramma per musica (Rome, Jan. 19, 1711); *Orlando, ovvero La gelosa pazzia*, dramma (Rome, Carnival 1711); *Tetide in Sciro*, dramma per musica (Rome, Jan. 10, 1712); *Ifigenia in Aulide*, dramma per musica (Rome, Jan. 11, 1713); *Ifigenia in Tauri*, dramma per musica (Rome, Feb. 15, 1713); *Amor d'un ombra e gelosia d'un'aura*, dramma per musica (Rome, Jan. 20, 1714; rev. version as *Narciso*, London, May 30, 1720); *Ambleto*, dramma per musica (Rome, Carnival 1715); *La Dirindina*, farsetta per musica (1715; intermezzo for the preceding work; not perf.); *Intermedi pastorali*, intermezzo in Ambleto (Rome, Carnival 1715); *Berenice, regina d'Egitto, ovvero Le gare d'amore e di politica*, dramma per musica (Rome, Carnival 1718; in collaboration with Porpora). OTHER: Oratorios; cantatas; Stabat Mater; Salve Regina for Soprano and Strings; other sacred works.

BIBL.: A. Longo, *D. S. e la sua figura nella storia della musica* (Naples, 1913); W. Gerstenberg, *Die Klavier-Kompositionen D. S.s* (Regensburg, 1933); S. Sitwell, *A Background for D. S.* (London, 1935); C. Valabrega, *Il Clavicembalista D. S., il suo secolo, la sua opera* (Modena, 1937; second ed., rev., 1955); S. Luciani, *D. S.* (Turin, 1939); R. Kirkpatrick, *D. S.* (Princeton and London, 1953; third ed., rev., 1968); M. Bogianckino, *L'arte clavicembalista di D. S.* (Rome, 1956); A. Basso, *La formazione storica ed estetica della storia di D. S.* (diss., Univ. of Turin, 1957); H. Keller, *D. S., ein Meister des Klaviers* (Leipzig, 1957); G. Pestelli, *Le sonate di D. S.: Proposta di un ordinamento cronologico* (Turin, 1967); J. Sheveloff, *The Keyboard Music of D. S.: A Reevaluation of the Present State of Knowledge in the Light of the Sources* (diss., Brandeis Univ., 1970); S. Choi, *Newly Found 18th-century Manuscripts of D. S.'s Sonatas and Their Relationship to Other 18th and Early 19th-century Sources* (diss., Univ. of Wisc., Madison, 1974); B. Ife, *D. S.* (Sevenoaks, England, 1985); R. Pagano, *S.: Alessandro e D.: Due vite in una* (Milan, 1985); P. Williams, ed., *Bach, Handel, and S.: Tercentenary Essays* (Cambridge, 1985); M. Boyd, *D. S.: Master of Music* (London, 1986); C. Vidali, *A. and D. S.: A Guide to Research* (N.Y., 1993).—NS/LK/DM

Scarlatti, Giuseppe, Italian composer, grandson of **(Pietro) Alessandro (Gaspare) Scarlatti** and nephew of **(Giuseppe) Domenico Scarlatti;** b. Naples, c. 1718; d. Vienna, Aug. 17, 1777. He was in Rome in 1739, and later in Lucca, where he married Barbara Stabili, a singer (1747); went to Vienna in 1757. He wrote 31 operas, produced in Rome, Florence, Lucca, Turin, Venice, Naples, Milan, and Vienna, of which the most successful was *L'isola disabitata* (Venice, Nov. 20, 1757). Another Giuseppe Scarlatti (a nephew of Alessandro Scarlatti), whose name appears in some reference works, was not a musician.—NS/LK/DM

Scarlatti, (Pietro) Alessandro (Gaspare),

important Italian composer, father of **(Giuseppe) Domenico Scarlatti** and grandfather of **Giuseppe Scarlatti**; b. Palermo, May 2, 1660; d. Naples, Oct. 22, 1725. Nothing is known concerning his musical training. When he was 12, he went with his 2 sisters to Rome, where he found patrons who enabled him to pursue a career in music. His first known opera, *Gli equivoci nel sembiante*, was performed there in 1679. By 1680 he was maestro di cappella to Queen Christina of Sweden, whose palace in Rome served as an important center for the arts. He also found patrons in 2 cardinals, Benedetto Pamphili and Pietro Ottoboni, and served as maestro di cappella at S. Gerolamo della Carità. From 1684 to 1702 he was maestro di cappella to the Viceroy at Naples. During these years he composed prolifically, bringing out numerous operas and oratorios. In addition, he served as director of the Teatro San Bartolomeo, where he conducted many of his works. His fame as a composer for the theater soon spread, and many of his works were performed in the leading music centers of Italy; one of his most popular operas, *Il Pirro e Demetrio* (Naples, Jan. 28, 1694), was even performed in London. His only confirmed teaching position dates from this period, when he served for 2 months in the spring of 1689 as a faculty member of the Cons. di Santa Maria di Loreto. Tiring of his exhaustive labors, he was granted a leave of absence and set out for Florence in June 1702; Prince Ferdinando de' Medici had been one of his patrons for some years in Florence, and Scarlatti hoped he could find permanent employment there. When this did not materialize, he settled in Rome and became asst. maestro di cappella at S. Maria Maggiore in 1703; he was promoted to maestro di cappella in 1707. One of his finest operas, *Il Mitridate Eupatore*, was performed in Venice in 1707. Since the Roman theaters had been closed from 1700, he devoted much of his time to composing serenatas, cantatas, and oratorios. In late 1708 he was again appointed maestro di cappella to the Viceroy at Naples. His most celebrated opera from these years, *Il Tigrane*, was given in Naples on Feb. 16, 1715. His only full-fledged comic opera, *Il trionfo dell'onore*, was performed in Naples on Nov. 26, 1718. Scarlatti's interest in purely instrumental music dates from this period, and he composed a number of conservative orch. and chamber music pieces. Having again obtained a leave of absence from his duties, he went to Rome to oversee the premiere of his opera *Telemaco* (1718). His last known opera, *La Griselda*, was given there in Jan. 1721. From 1722 until his death he lived in retirement in Naples, producing only a handful of works. Scarlatti was the foremost Neapolitan composer of the late Baroque era in Italy. A complete edition of his operas began to appear in the Harvard Publications in Music

series in 1974. An edition of his oratorios commenced publication in Rome in 1964.

WORKS: DRAMATIC: O p e r a (all are drammas and were first perf. in Naples unless otherwise given): *Gli equivoci nel sembiante* (first perf. publicly, Rome, Feb. 5, 1679; later perf. as *L'errore innocente*, Bologna, 1679, and as *L'amor non vuole inganni*, Linz, Carnival 1681); *L'honestà negli amori* (Rome, Feb. 6, 1680); *Tutto il mal non vien per nuocere*, commedia (Rome, 1681; later perf. as *Dal male il bene*, Naples, 1687); *Il Pompeo* (Rome, Jan. 25, 1683); *La Guerriera costante* (Rome, Carnival 1683); *L'Aldimiro o vero Favor per favore* (Nov. 6, 1683); *La Psiche o vero Amore innamorato* (Dec. 21, 1683); *Olimpia vendicata* (Dec. 23, 1685); *La Rosmene o vero L'infedeltà fedele*, melodramma (Rome, Carnival 1686); *Clearco in Negroponte* (Dec. 21, 1686); *La Santa Dinna*, commedia (Rome, Carnival 1687; only Act 3 by Scarlatti); *Il Flavio* (Nov. 14?, 1688); *L'Anacreonte tiranno*, melodramma (Feb. 9, 1689); *L'Amazzone corsara [guerriera] o vero L'Alvilda* (Nov. 6, 1689); *La Statira* (Rome, Jan. 5, 1690); *Gli equivoci in amore o vero La Rosaura*, melodramma (Rome, Dec. 1690); *L'humanità nelle fiere o vero Il Lucullo* (Feb. 25, 1691); *La Teodora Augusta* (Nov. 6, 1692); *Gerone tiranno di Siracusa* (Dec. 22, 1692); *L'Amante doppio o vero Il Ceccobimbi*, melodramma (April 1693); *Il Pirro e Demetrio* (Jan. 28, 1694; later perf. as *La forza della fedeltà*, Florence, 1712); *Il Bassiano o vero Il maggior impossibile*, melodramma (1694); *La santa Genuinda, o vero L'innocenza difesa dall'inganno*, dramma sacro (Rome, 1694; only Act 2 by Scarlatti); *Le nozze con l'inimico o vero L'Analinda*, melodramma (1695; later perf. as *L'Analinda overo Le nozze col nemico*, Florence, Carnival 1702); *Nerone fatto Cesare*, melodramma (Nov. 6, 1695); *Massimo Puppieno*, melodramma (Dec. 26, 1695); *Penelope la casta* (Feb. 23?, 1696); *La Didone delirante*, opera drammatica (May 28, 1696); *Comodo Antonino* (Nov. 18, 1696); *L'Emireno o vero Il consiglio dell'ombra*, opera drammatica (Feb. 2, 1697); *La caduta de' Decemviri* (Dec. 15, 1697); *La Donna ancora è fedele* (1698); *Il Prigioniero fortunato* (Dec. 14, 1698); *Gli'inganni felici* (Nov. 6, 1699; later perf. as *L'Agarista ovvero Gl'inganni felici*, with the intermezzo *Brenno e Tisbe*, Florence, Carnival 1706); *L'Eraclea* (Jan. 30, 1700); *Odoardo*, with the intermezzo *Adolfo e Lesbina* (May 5, 1700); *Dafni*, favola boschereccia (Aug. 5, 1700; later perf. as *L'amore non viene dal caso*, Jesi, Carnival 1715); *Laodicea e Berenice* (April 1701); *Il pastor[e] di Corinto*, favola boschereccia (Aug. 5, 1701); *Tito Sempronio Gracco*, with the intermezzo *Bireno e Dorilla* (Carnival? 1702); *Tiberio imperatore d'Oriente* (May 8, 1702); *Il Flavio Cuniberto* (Pratolino, Sept.? 1702); *Arminio* (Pratolino, Sept. 1703); *Turno Aricino* (Pratolino, Sept. 1704); *Lucio Manlio l'imperioso* (Pratolino, Sept. 1705); *Il gran Tamerlano* (Pratolino, Sept. 1706); *Il Mitridate Eupatore*, tragedia (Venice, Carnival 1707); *Il trionfo della libertà*, tragedia (Venice, Carnival 1707); *Il Teodosio* (Jan. 27, 1709); *L'amor volubile e tiranno* (May 25, 1709; later perf. as *La Dorisbe o L'amor volubile e tiranno*, Rome, Carnival 1711, and as *La Dorisbe*, Genoa, 1713); *La Principessa fedele* (Feb. 8, 1710); *La fede riconosciuta*, dramma pastorale (Oct. 14, 1710); *Giunio Bruto o vero La caduta dei Tarquini* (1711; not perf.; only Act 3 by Scarlatti); *Il Ciro* (Rome, Carnival 1712); *Scipione nelle Spagne*, with the intermezzo *Pericca e Varrone* (Jan. 21, 1714); *L'amor generoso*, with the intermezzo *Despina e Niso* (Oct. 1, 1714); *Il Tigrane o vero L'egual impegno d'amore e di fede* (Feb. 16, 1715); *Carlo re d'Allemagna* (Jan. 30, 1716); *La virtù trionfante dell'odio e dell'amore* (May 3, 1716); *Telemaco* (Rome, Carnival 1718); *Il trionfo dell'onore*, commedia (Nov. 26, 1718); *Il Cambise* (Feb. 4, 1719); *Marco Attilio Regolo*, with the intermezzo *Leonzio e Eurilla* (Rome, Carnival 1719); *La Griselda* (Rome, Jan. 1721). Several operas attributed to him are now considered doubtful. **SERENATAS:** *Diana ed Endimione* (c. 1680–85); *Serenata in honor of James II of England* (Rome, 1688); *Il genio di Partenope, la gloria del Sebeto, il piacere di Mergellina* (Naples, Jan. 1696); *Venere, Adone e Amore* (Naples, July 15, 1696); *Il trionfo delle stagioni* (Naples, July 26, 1696); *Venere ed Amore* (c. 1695–1700); *Clori, Lidia e Filli* (c. 1700); *Clori, Dorino e Amore* (Naples, May 2, 1702); *Venere e Adone: Il giardino d'amore* (c. 1702–5); *Endimione e Cintia* (Rome, 1705); *Amore e Virtù ossia Il trionfo della virtù* (Rome, 1706); *Clori e Zeffiro* (Rome, 1706?); *Fileno, Niso e Doralbo: Serenata a Filli* (Rome, 1706?); *Sole, Urania e Clio: Le Muse Urania e Clio lodano le bellezze di Filli* (Rome, 1706?); *Venere, Amore e Ragione: Il ballo delle ninfe: Venere, havendo perso Amore, lo ritrova fra le ninfe e i pastori dei Sette Colli* (Rome, 1706); *Cupido e Onestà: Il trionfo dell'Onestà* (Rome, Sept. 1709); *Le glorie della Bellezza del Corpo e dell'Anima* (Naples, Aug. 28, 1709); *Pace, Amore e Provvidenza* (Naples, Nov. 4, 1711); *Il genio austriaco* (Naples, June 21, 1712); *Il genio austriaco: Zefiro, Flora, il Sole, Partenope e il Sebeto* (Naples, Aug. 28, 1713); *Serenata in honor of the Vicereine, Donna Barbara d'Erbenstein* (Naples, Dec. 4, 1715); *La gloria di Primavera: Primavera, Estate, Autunno, Inverno e Giove* (Vienna, April 1716?); *Partenope, Teti, Nettuno, Proteo e Glauco* (Naples, 1716); *Filli, Clori e Tirsi* (Naples, 1718?); *La virtù negli amori: La Notte, il Sole, Lanso, Lisa, Toante e Agave* (Rome, Nov. 16, 1721); *Erminia, Tancredi, Polidoro e Pastore* (Naples, June 13, 1723); *Diana, Amore, Venere* (undated). **ORATORIOS AND OTHER SACRED:** Oratorio (Rome, Feb. 24, 1679); Oratorio (Rome, April 12, 1680); *Passio Domini Nostri Jesu Christi secundum Joannem* (c. 1680); Oratorio (Rome, Feb. 20, 1682); *Agar et Ismaele esiliati* (Rome, 1683); *Il trionfo della gratia* (Rome, 1685); *Il martirio di S. Teodosia* (Modena, 1685); *I dolori di Maria sempre vergine* (Naples, 1693); *La Giuditta* (Naples, 1693); *Samson vindicatus* (Rome, March 25, 1695); *Cantata...per la notte di Natale* (Rome, Dec. 24, 1695); *Il martirio di S. Orsola* (c. 1695–1700); *Davidis pugna et victoria* (Rome, March 5, 1700); *La Giuditta* (1700); *L'assunzione della Beata Vergine Maria* (Rome, 1703); *S. Michaelis Arcangelis cum Lucifer pugna et victoria* (Rome, April 3, 1705); *S. Casimiro, re di Polonia* (Florence, 1705); *S. Maria Maddalena de' pazzi* (Rome, 1705); *S. Filippo Neri* (Rome, 1705); *Qual di lieti concenti* (Rome, 1705?); *Il Sedecia, re di Gerusalemme* (Urbino, 1705?); *Abramo il tuo sembiante*, Christmas cantata (Rome, Dec. 24, 1705); *Il trionfo della Ss. Vergine assunta in cielo* (Florence, 1706); *S. Francesco di Paolo* (Urbino, 1706); *Humanità e Lucifero* (1706?); *Il martirio di S. Susanna* (Florence, 1706); *Alcene, ove per queste*, Christmas cantata (Rome, Dec. 24, 1706); *Cain overo Il primo omicidio* (Venice, Lent 1707); *Il giardino di rose: La Ss. Vergine del Rosario* (Rome, April 24, 1707); *Il martirio di S. Cecilia* (Rome, Lent 1708); *La Ss. Annunziata* (Rome, March 25, 1708); *Oratorio per la Passione di Nostro Signore Gesù Cristo* (Rome, April 4, 1708); *La vittoria della fede* (Rome, Sept. 12, 1708); *Il trionfo del valore* (Naples, March 19, 1709); *La Ss. Trinità* (Naples, May 1715); *La Vergine addolorata* (Rome, 1717); *La gloriosa gara tra la Santità e la Sapienza* (Rome, June 13, 1720). **OTHER:** Over 600 cantatas, a number of masses and mass movements, motets, and madrigals; instrumental music, including 12 sinfonie di concerto grosso, toccatas for Keyboard, sonatas, suites, etc.

BIBL.: E. Dent, *A. S.: His Life and Works* (London, 1905; second ed., rev., 1960, by F. Walker); C. van den Borren, *A. S. et l'esthétique de l'opéra napolitain* (Brussels and Paris, 1921); P. Struver, *Die Cantata da camera A. S.s* (diss., Univ. of Munich, 1923); U. Prota-Giurleo, *A. S. "il Palermitano"* (Naples, 1926); A. Lorenz, *A. S.s Jugendoper* (Augsburg, 1927); O. Tilby, *La Famiglia S.: Nuove ricerche e documenti* (Rome, 1947); P. Taylor Lee, *The Keyboard Style of A. S.* (diss., Yale Univ., 1959); M. Fabbri, *A. S.*

e il Principe Ferdinando de' Medici (Florence, 1961); E. Hanley, *A. S.'s Cantate da Camera: A Bibliographical Study* (diss., Yale Univ., 1963); O. Henry, *The Doctrine of Affections in Selected Solo Cantatas of A. S.* (diss., Ohio State Univ., 1963); C. Morey, *The Late Operas of A. S.* (diss., Ind. Univ., 1965); D. Poultney, *The Oratorios of A. S.: Their Lineage, Milieu, and Style* (diss., Univ. of Mich., 1968); P. Brandvik, *Selected Motets of A. S.* (diss., Univ. of Ill., 1969); J. Shaffer, *The Cantus Firmus in A. S.'s Motets* (diss., George Peabody Coll. of Teachers, 1970); P. Piersall, *The Bass Cantatas of A. S.* (diss., Univ. of Ore., 1971); R. Pagano, *L. Bianchi, and G. Rostirolla, A. S.* (Turin, 1972); M. Inkeles, *A Study, Realization, and Performance of Unpublished Cantatas for Soprano and Basso Continuo ca. 1690–1706 of A. S.* (diss., Columbia Univ. Teachers Coll., 1977); D. Grout, *A. S.: An Introduction to His Operas* (Berkeley, 1979); W. Osthoff and J. Ruile-Dronke, eds., *Colloquium A. S.* (Tutzing, 1979); W. Holmes, *La Statira by Pietro Ottoboni and A. S.: The Textual Sources, with a Documentary Postscript* (N.Y., 1983); F. D'Accone, *The History of a Baroque Opera: A. S.'s "Gli equivoci nel sembiante"* (N.Y., 1985); R. Pagano, *S.: A. e Domenico: Due vite in una* (Milan, 1985); U. Schachet-Pape, *Das Messenschaffen von A. S.* (Frankfurt am Main and N.Y., 1993); C. Vidali, *A. and D. S.: A Guide to Research* (N.Y., 1993); M. Lutolf, ed., *A. S. und seine Zeit* (Bern, 1995).—**NS/LK/DM**

Scarpini, Pietro, Italian pianist, teacher, and composer; b. Rome, April 6, 1911. He studied at the Accademia di Santa Cecilia in Rome. He made his concert debut in 1936, and then gave recitals in Europe and in the U.S. From 1940 to 1967 he taught at the Florence Cons., and in 1967 he joined the faculty of the Milan Cons. He specialized in the modern repertoire of piano music. Among his works are a Piano Concerto and a Piano Quintet. He also made an arrangement for two pianos of Mahler's 10th Sym.—**NS/LK/DM**

Scelsi, Giacinto (actually, **Conte Giacinto Scelsi di Valva**), remarkable Italian composer; b. La Spezia, Jan. 8, 1905; d. Rome, Aug. 9, 1988. He was descended from a family of the nobility. He received some guidance in harmony from Giacinto Sallustio; after studies with Egon Koehler in Geneva, he completed his formal training with Walter Klein in Vienna (1935–36), where he became interested in the Schoenbergian method of writing music outside the bounds of traditional tonality; at the same time, he became deeply immersed in the study of the musical philosophy of the East, in which the scales and rhythms are perceived as functional elements of the human psyche. As a result of these multifarious absorptions of ostensibly incompatible ingredients, Scelsi formulated a style of composition that is synthetic in its sources and pragmatic in its artistic materialization. His works began to have a considerable number of performances in Italy and elsewhere, most particularly in the U.S. A curious polemical development arose after his death, when an Italian musician named Vieri Tosatti publ. a sensational article in the *Giornale della Musica*, declaring "I was Giacinto Scelsi." He claimed that Scelsi used to send him thematic sections of unfinished compositions, usually in the 12-tone system, for development and completion, using him as a ghostwriter. So many of such "improvisations" did Scelsi send to Tosatti that the latter had 2 other musicians to serve as secondary "ghosts," who, in turn, confirmed their participation in this peculiar transaction. The matter finally got to the court of public opinion, where it was decided that the works were genuine compositions by Scelsi, who improvised them on his electric piano, and merely ed. for better effect by secondary arrangers.

WORKS: ORCH.: *Rotative* for 3 Pianos, Winds, and Percussion (1930); *Rapsodia romantica* (1931); *Sinfonietta* (1932); *Preludio e fuga* (1938); *Ballata* for Cello and Orch. (1945); *Quattro pezzi (su una nota sola)* for Chamber Orch. (1959); *Hurqualia* (1960); *Aiôn* (1961); *Chukrum* for Strings (1963); *Hymnos* for Organ and 2 Orchs. (1963); *Anagamin* for 12 Strings (1965); *Anahit* for Violin and 18 Instruments (1965); *Ohoi* for 16 Strings (1966); *Natura renovatur* for 11 Strings (1967). **CHAMBER:** 4 string quartets (1944, 1961, 1963, 1964); 5 divertimenti for Violin (1952, 1954, 1955, 1955, 1956); Suite for Flute and Clarinet (1953); *Preghiera per un' ombra* for Clarinet (1954); *Pwyll* for Flute (1954); *Tre studi* for Clarinet (1954); *Coelocanth* for Viola (1955); *Hykos* for Flute and Percussion (1955); *Ixor* for Clarinet or Soprano Saxophone (1956); *Quattro pezzi* for Horn (1956); *Quattro pezzi* for Trumpet (1956); *Tre pezzi* for Soprano Saxophone or Bass Trumpet (1956); *Rucke di Guck* for Piccolo and Oboe (1957); *Tre pezzi* for Trombone (1957); *Trilogy* for Cello (1957–65); *Elegia per Ty* for Viola and Double Bass (1958); *I presagi* for 10 Instruments (1958); Trio for Violin, Viola, and Cello (1958); *Kya* for Clarinet and 7 Instruments (1959); *Xnoybis* for Violin (1964); Duo for Violin and Cello (1965); *Ko-Lho* for Flute and Clarinet (1966); *Ko-Tha* for Guitar and Percussion (1967); *Okanagon* for Harp, Tam-tam, and Double Bass (1968); *Praham II* for 9 Instruments (1973); *En maintenant, c'est à vous de jouer* for Cello and Double Bass (1974); *Voyages* for Cello (1974); *Dharana* for Double Bass and Cello (1975); *Kshara* for 2 Double Basses (1975). **Piano:** 11 suites (c. 1929–56); *6 pièces* (1930–40); *4 poems* (1936–39); *24 Préludes* (1936–40); *Hispania* (1939); 4 sonatas (n.d., 1939, 1939, 1941); *Quattro illustrazioni* (1953); *Cinque incantesimi* (1953); *Action music* (1955); *Aitsi* for Amplified Piano (1974). **VOCAL:** *Perdus* for Woman's Voice and Piano (1937); *La Nascita del verbo* for Chorus and Orch. (1948; Brussels, June 28, 1950); *Yamaon* for Bass and 5 Instruments (1954–58); *Tre canti popolari* for Chorus (1958); *Tre canti sacri* for Chorus (1958); *Hô* for Soprano (1960); *Wo-Ma* for Bass (1960); *Khoom* for Soprano and 6 Instruments (1962); *Lilitu* for Woman's Voice (1962); *Taiagarù* for Soprano (1962); *Yliam* for Women's Chorus (1964); *Uaxuctum* for Chorus and Orch. (1966); *TKRDG* for 6 Men's Voices, Amplified Guitar, and 2 Percussionists (1968); *Konx-om-pax* for Chorus and Orch. (1969); *Ogloudoglou* for Voice and Percussion (1969); *3 Latin Prayers* for Man's or Woman's Voice or Chorus (1970); *Pranam I* for Voice and 12 Instruments (1972); *Canti del capricorno* for Woman's Voice, Another Voice, and Instruments (1972–73); *Sauh I and II* for 2 Women's Voices or Voice and Tape (1973); *Manto per quattro* for Voice, Flute, Trombone, and Cello (1974); *Pfhat* for Chorus and Orch. (1974); *Litanie* for 2 Women's Voices or Woman's Voice and Tape (1975); *Maknongan* for Bass (1976).

BIBL.: A. Cremonese, *G. S.: Prassi compositiva e riflessione teorica fino alla metà anni '40* (Palermo, 1992); K. Angermann, ed., *Symposium G. S.* (Hofheim, 1993).—**NS/LK/DM**

Schacht, Matthias Henriksen, Danish scholar, writer on music, and composer; b. Visby, Gotland, April 29, 1660; d. Kerteminde, Fyn, Aug. 8, 1700. He studied at the Univ. of Copenhagen and at univs. in Germany. He was a schoolmaster in Visby (1682–83), Kantor of the Odense grammar school (1683–86), and rector at the Kerteminde school (from 1686), where he was also active as a town musician. He wrote widely on scholarly subjects, and also wrote the vol. *Musicus danicus eller Danske sagmester*, which includes a biographical dictionary of musicians; he completed the MS in 1687, but it was not publ., even though Gerber utilized it for his own *Lexikon* (1790–92); it was finally ed. and publ. by G. Skjerne in Copenhagen in 1928. His compositions are not extant.—**NS/LK/DM**

Schacht, Theodor, Freiherr von, German pianist, composer, and conductor; b. Strasbourg, 1748; d. Regensburg, June 20, 1823. He studied piano with Küffner and harmony with Riepel in Regensburg (1756–66), then took lessons in composition with Jommelli in Stuttgart (1766–71). Returning to Regensburg in 1771, he became Hofkavalier; in 1773 he was appointed court music Intendant, serving as director of its Italian opera from 1774 to 1778 and again from 1784 to 1786. From 1786 to 1805 he was music director of the court orch. He then went to Vienna; in 1812 he returned to Germany. He was a prolific musician; wrote a number of operas and theater pieces to German and Italian texts, as well as competently crafted syms., concertos, and chamber music. He was a minor master of contrapuntal arts; his series of 84 canons, dedicated to members of "the fair sex," quite amusing and even daring for his time, was publ. in Baden in 1811 under the title *Divertimento del bel sesso nel soggiorno di Baden*.—**NS/LK/DM**

Schack, Benedikt (Emanuel), Bohemian-born Austrian tenor and composer; b. Mirotitz (baptized), Feb. 7, 1758; d. Munich, Dec. 10, 1826. He began his training with his father, a school teacher; after further studies in Staré Sedlo and Svatá Hora, he continued his training as a chorister at the Prague Cathedral (1773–75); then went to Vienna, where he received lessons in singing from Karl Frieberth, and also studied medicine and philosophy. He became Kapellmeister to Prince Heinrich von Schönaich-Carolath in Silesia in 1780; became a member of Schikaneder's traveling theater troupe in 1786, and went with it to Vienna, where he was its principal tenor at the Freihaus-Theater auf der Wieden (from 1789). He was a close friend of Mozart, who wrote the role of Tamino for him; his wife, Elisabeth (née Weinhold) Schack, appeared as the third Lady in the first perf. of *Die Zauberflöte*. If contemporary accounts are to be trusted, it was Schack who sang passages from the Mozart Requiem for the dying composer. After a sojourn in Graz (1793–96), he went to Munich as a member of the Hoftheater; having lost his voice, he was pensioned about 1814. Mozart wrote piano variations (K. 613) on an aria from Schack's opera *Die verdeckten Sachen*. Among Schack's theatrical pieces, the following were performed in Vienna: *Der dumme Gärtner aus dem Gebirge* (July 12, 1789), *Die wiener Zeitung* (Jan. 12, 1791), *Die Antwort auf die Frage* (Dec. 16, 1792), and *Die beiden Nannerin* (July 26, 1794).
—**NS/LK/DM**

Schadewitz, Carl, German choral conductor, teacher, and composer; b. St. Ingbert, Jan. 23, 1887; d.

Reppendorf, near Kitzingen, March 27, 1945. He studied in Würzburg, where he was active for most of his life as a choral conductor and teacher. He was a prolific composer, his works including a musical fairy tale, *Johannisnacht*, a "Romantic" oratorio, *Kreislers Heimkehr*, an opera, *Laurenca*, a tone poem, *Heldengedenken* (1943), a number of songs, of which the cycle *Die Heimat* (1934) is outstanding, much chamber music, and choruses.

BIBL.: A. Maxsein, *C. S.* (Würzburg, 1954).—NS/LK/DM

Schaefer, Theodor, Czech composer and teacher; b. Telč, Jan. 23, 1904; d. Brno, March 19, 1969. He studied with Kvapil at the Brno Cons. (1922–26) and with Novák at the Prague Cons. (1926–29). Upon graduation, he taught at the Palacký Univ. at Olomouc, the Brno Cons. (1948–59), and at the Janáček Academy of Music in Brno (1959–69). He was an advocate of a so-called diathematic principle of constructing themes using fragments of preceding thematic units.

WORKS: DRAMATIC: *Maugli*, children's opera (1932); *Legenda o štěstí* (Legend of Happiness), ballet (1952). **ORCH.:** 2 unnumbered syms. (1926; 1955–61); Violin Concerto (1932–33); *Wallachian Serenade* (1936); Piano Concerto (1937–43); *Jánošík*, balladic overture (1939); *Diathema* for Viola and Orch. (1955–56); *The Barbarian and the Rose* for Piano and Orch. (1957–58); *Diathema* (1957–58); *Rhapsodic Reportage* (1960). **CHAMBER:** 3 string quartets (1929; 1941; 1944–45); Wind Quintet (1935–36); *Divertimento mesto* for Wind Quintet and String Trio (1946); *Cikánovy housle* (Gypsy Violin), 4 movements for Violin and Piano (1960). **P i a n o :** *Etudes* (1936–37); *Theme with Variations* (1936). **VOCAL:** *Milostné balady* (Love Ballads) for Voice and Piano, commemorating the destruction of Lidice by the Nazis (1943); *Winter Cantata* for Soprano, Chorus, and Orch. (1943–45); *Bithematikon* for Baritone and Piano (1967).—NS/LK/DM

Schaeffer, Bogusław (Julien), outstanding Polish composer, pianist, pedagogue, writer on music, stage manager, and playwright; b. Lwów, June 6, 1929. He studied violin in Opole, and then went to Kraków, where he took courses in composition with Malawski at the State Higher School of Music and in musicology with Jachimecki at the Jagiellonian Univ. (1949–53). He later received instruction in advanced techniques from Nono (1959). In 1963 he became prof. of composition at the State Higher School of Music in Kraków Cons., and he also served as prof. of composition at the Salzburg Mozarteum (from 1986). In 1967 he founded the periodical *Forum Musicum*, devoted to new music; in addition to his writings on music, he was active as a playwright from 1955; he was the most widely performed playwright in Poland from 1987 to 1995, winning an award at the Wrocław Festival of Contemporary plays in 1987 and in 5 subsequent years. All of his plays were publ. in 3 vols. and were translated into 16 languages. As a composer, he received many awards, and numerous concerts of his works were presented in Poland and abroad. In 1995 he was made an honorary member of the Polish Soc. of Contemporary Music. In 1999 the Jagiellonian Univ. held an international conference in his honor, which was devoted to his compositions, plays, and graphics. He is married to **Mieczysława Janina Hanuszewska-Schaeffer.** Their son, Piotr (Mikołaj) Schaeffer (b. Kraków, Oct. 1, 1958), is a

music journalist. Schaeffer's earliest compositions (*19 Mazurkas* for Piano, 1949) were inspired by the melorhythms of Polish folk songs, but he made a decisive turn in 1953 with his *Music for Strings: Nocturne*, which became the first serial work by a Polish composer; he devised a graphic and polychromatic optical notation indicating intensity of sound, proportional lengths of duration, and position of notes in melodic and contrapuntal lines, with the components arranged in binary code; he also wrote music in the "third stream" style, combining jazz with classical procedures. In 1960 he invented topophonical music in a tone-color passacaglia form in his *Topofonica* for 40 Instruments. In 1966 he created so-called idiomatic music by using various stylistic categories, including early jazz, neo-Classicism, entertainment music, and indeterminate music (e.g. *Howl*). In 1967 he introduced his own rhythmic system, built on metric-tempo proportions. In 1970 he began using synthesizers and computers. Many of his chamber scores, such as *Quartet 2+2*, utilize indeterminacy. He experimented by introducing ideas of philosophers such as Heraclitus, Spinoza, Bergson, and Heidegger in his music called *Heraklitiana*, *Spinoziana* et al. In his music for and with actors, he uses mixed media procedures. With his *Missa elettronica* (1975), he charted a bold course in sacred music. Schaeffer is regarded as one of the foremost composers of microtonal scores. *Three Short Pieces* for Orch. (1951) and *Music for String Quartet* (1954) are notable examples of his early microtonal works in which he uses a 24-tone row with 23 different microtonal intervals. In 1979 he introduced a new kind of instrumentation in which the disposition of instruments totally changes many times, thus utilizing various changing orchs.; in his Organ Concerto the disposition of instruments changes 53 times. Each of his orch. works and concertos follows this new disposition, sometimes very specifically, as in his *Musica ipsa* (1962). In his orch. works, he utilizes precisely calculated textures. Many of his works are inspired by paintings and literature. There are great influences of his theatrical praxis on his music. He uses electronic and computer media in a free and poetic manner.

WORKS: DRAMATIC: *TIS-MW–2*, metamusical audiovisual spectacle for Actor, Mime, Ballerina, and 5 Musicians (1962–63; Kraków, April 25, 1964); *TIS GK*, stage work (1963); *Audiences I–V* for Actors (1964); *Howl*, monodrama for Narrator, 2 Actors, Ensemble of Instrumentalists, and Ensemble of Performers, after Alan Ginsberg (1966; Warsaw, March 1, 1971); *Kwartet* (Quartet) for 4 Actors (1966; Lódź, March 8, 1976); *Hommage à Czyżewski* for Ensemble of Stage and Musical Performers (1972); *Vaniniana* for 2 Actors, Soprano, Piano, Cello, and Electronic Sources (1978; Lecce, Oct. 24, 1985); *Teatrino fantastico* for Actor, Violin, and Piano, with Multimedia and Tape (Brussels, Nov. 17, 1983); *Liebesbliecke*, opera (1990). **Plays (WITH Original Music):** *Anton Webern* (1955); *Eskimos' Paradise* (1964; the same as his *Audience III*); *Scenario* for 3 Actors (1970); *Mroki* (Darknesses; 1979); *Zorza* (Dawn; 1981); *Grzechy starosci* (Sins of Old Age; 1985); *Kaczo* for 2 Actors and an Actress (1987); *Ranek* (Daybreak; 1988). **ORCH.:** 4 piano concertos (*Quattro movimenti*, 1957, Wrocław, Jan. 18, 1968; 1967; 1988–90; 1999); *Tertium datur* for Harpsichord and Chamber Orch. (1958; Warsaw, Sept. 18, 1960);

Concerto breve for Cello and Orch. (1959); *Equivalenze sonore,* concerto for Percussion Chamber Orch. (1959; Warsaw, March 1, 1971); *Mała symfonia (Scultura)* (Little Symphony [Scultura]) (1960; Warsaw, Sept. 29, 1965); *Konstrukcje łączne* (Joint Constructions) for Strings (1960); *Concerto per sei e tre* for Changing Solo Instrument (Clarinet, Saxophone, Violin, Cello, Percussion, and Piano) and 3 Orchs. (1960; Katowice, Sept. 7, 1962); *Topofonica* for 40 Instruments (1960; Kielce, Feb. 22, 1985); *Kody* (Codes) for Chamber Orch. (Warsaw, Sept. 19, 1961); *Musica* for Harpsichord and Orch. (Venice, April 25, 1961); Violin Concerto (1961–63); *Course "j"* for Jazz Ensemble and Chamber Sym. Orch. (Warsaw, Oct. 28, 1962); *Musica ipsa* (Warsaw, Sept. 20, 1962); *S'alto* for Saxophone and Chamber Orch. (Zagreb, May 13, 1963); *Collage and Form* for 8 Jazz Musicians and Orch. (1963; Urbana, Ill., March 19, 1967); *Collage* for Chamber Orch. (1964; Warsaw, April 18, 1985); *Symfonia: Muzyka orkiestrowa* (Symphony: Orchestral Music; 1967); *Koncert jassowy* (Jazz Concerto) for Jazz Ensemble and Orch. (1969; Boston, Oct. 30, 1976); *Teksty* (Texts; 1971); *Experimenta* for Pianist on 2 Pianos and Orch. (1971; Poznań, April 26, 1972); *Konfrontacje* (Confrontations) for Solo Instrument and Orch. (1972); Sym. in 9 Movements for 6 Solo Instruments and Orch. (1973; Wrocław, Sept. 18, 1978); *Tentative music* for 159 Instruments (1973; also for 1, 5, 9, 15, 19, and 59 Instruments); *Uwertura Warsawska* (Warsaw Overture; Warsaw, Sept. 10, 1975); *Romuald Traugutt* (1976; Warsaw, Sept. 20, 1977); *Gravesono* for Winds and Percussion (1977); *Kesukaan I* (1978; Rzeszów, April 8, 1983) and *II* (1991) for 13 Strings; *Jangwa* for Double Bass and Orch. (1979; La Jolla, Dec. 14, 1990); *Maah* for Orch. and Tape (1979; Kraków, Feb. 14, 1989); *Entertainment Music* for Winds and Percussion (1981); *Five Introductions and an Epilogue* for Small Chamber Orch. (1981); Guitar Concerto (Rzeszów, March 9, 1984); Accordion Concerto (1984); Concerto for Organ, Violin, and Orch. (1984; Nuremberg, July 5, 1985); Concerto for Flute, Harp, and Orch. (1986); Saxophone Concerto (1986); Concerto for Violin, Gasab-Violin, 2 Oboes, English Horn, and Orch. (1986); Double Concerto for 2 Violins and Orch. (1988; Warsaw, March 21, 1995); Concerto for Jazz Percussion, Piano, and Orch. (1988; Kraków, June 23, 1993); Concerto for 2 Pianos, 8-Hands, and Orch. (1988); *Sinfonia* (1988; Opole, March 19, 1993); *blueS No. 5* for Piano and Orch. (1992; Warsaw, March 21, 1995); Sym. No. 6 (1993); *Love Song* for Strings (1994); *Leopolis* for Violin and Orch. (1994); *Orchestral and Electronic Changes* for Amplified Instruments and Orch. (1994); Clarinet Concerto (Kraków, April 3, 1995); Flute Concerto (1996); Concerto for Violin, Piano, and Orch. (1997); Sym. No. 7 (1997); Viola Concerto (1997); *Monophonie I* for 16 Flutes (1997), *II* for 13 Violas (1997), *III* for 12 Oboes (1998), *IV* for 8 English Horns (1998), *V* for 12 Cellos (1999), *VI* for 12 Trumpets (1999), and *VII* for 17 Saxophones (1999); *Enigma* (1997); *Musica dell' Avvenire* for Percussion Orch. (1997); *Concerto da camera* for 18 Instruments (1997); Bassoon Concerto (1998); *Mikrosonate* for Chamber Orch. (1999). **CHAMBER:** *Muzyka* (Music) for String Quartet (1954); Sonata for Solo Violin (1955; Warsaw, April 24, 1983); *Permutacje* (Permutations) for 10 Instruments (1956; Paris, March 30, 1965); *Ekstrema* (Extremes) for 10 Instruments (1957; Warsaw, Nov. 22, 1988); 9 string quartets: No. 1 (1957; Salzburg, June 26, 1990), No. 2 (1964; Palermo, Dec. 28, 1968), No. 3 (1971; Kraków, Dec. 18, 1985), No. 4 (1973), No. 5 (1986), No. 6 (1993), No. 7 (1997), No. 8 (1998), and No. 9 (1999); Concerto for String Quartet (1959; Innsbruck, June 28, 1990); *Monosonata* for 6 String Quartets (1959; Vienna, June 19, 1961); *Montaggio* for 6 Players (1960; Kraków, Jan. 24, 1963); *Azione a due* for Piano and 11 Instruments (1961; Stuttgart, Dec. 4, 1970); *Imago musicae* for Violin and 9 Instruments (1961; Hannover,

May 27, 1966); 4 Pieces for String Trio (1962); Quartet for 2 Pianists and 2 Optional Performers (instrumental version, Warsaw, Feb. 18, 1965; instrumental-vocal version, Warsaw, May 3, 1966); *Przesłanie* (Transmissions) for Cello and 2 Pianos (1965; Geneva, Dec. 13, 1966); Quartet for Oboe and String Trio (1966; Kraków, May 3, 1977); Trio for Flute, Harp, Viola, and Tape (1966; Siena, March 28, 1967); Trio for Piano, Violin, and Cello (1969; Baalbek, March 26, 1974); *Heraklitiana* for 12 Solo Instruments and Tape (1970); *Estratto* for String Trio (1971; Kraków, April 7, 1987); *Mare concertino* for Piano and 9 Instruments (1971; Poznań, April 27, 1972); *Warianty* (Variants) for Wind Quintet (1971); *Sgraffito* for Flute, Cello, Harpsichord, and 2 Pianos (1971; Kraków, Jan. 29, 1973); *Sny o Schaefferze* (Dreams of Schaeffer) for Performers (1972; Kraków, April 14, 1975); *blueS No. 2* for Instrumental Ensemble (1972); *Free Form No. 1* for 5 Instruments (1972; Zagreb, May 17, 1973), *No. 2, (Evocazioni)* for Double Bass (1972; Cologne, Oct. 17, 1974), and *No. 3* for Double Bass and Piano (1987); *Heideggeriana* for 11 Instruments (1979; Warsaw, Nov. 22, 1988); Concerto for Saxophone Quartet (1980); Octet for Winds and Double Bass (1980); *Addolorato* for Violin and Tape (1981; Kraków, Feb. 22, 1988); *Gasab* for Gasab Violin and Piano (Brussels, Nov. 16, 1983); *Schpass* for 3 Oboes (1986; Kraków, Feb. 22, 1988); *Kwaiwa* for Violin and Computer (1986; Kraków, Feb. 22, 1988); *Mały koncert* (Little Concerto) for Violin and 3 Oboes (1987; Kraków, Feb. 22, 1988); *Bewegnung* for Oboe, Piano, and Percussion (1994); Septet for Oboe, Bass Clarinet, Cello, and Percussion (1995); *Hommage à Guillaume Schaeffer* for 2 Cellos and Piano (1995); Trio for Flute, Viola, and Guitar (1995); *OSCENOI* for Clarinet, Soprano, and Instruments (1995); Concerto for Clarinet and 5 Instruments (1996); *Hommage à Barbara Buczek* for 2 Saxophones (1996); Quartet for Piano, Violin, Viola, and Cello (1997); *Max Ernst Variations* for Saxophone, Accordion, Piano, and Computer (1998); 6 Etudes for String Quartet (1999). **KEYBOARD: P i a n o:** *Model I* (1956; Kraków, Sept. 29, 1961), *II* (1957; Kraków, May 19, 1962), *III* (1961; Warsaw, Sept. 21, 1964), *IV* (1963; Paris, March 10, 1968), *V* (1965; Utrecht, Sept. 3, 1967), *VI* (1970), *VII* (1971; Ann Arbor, Nov. 26, 1974), *VIII* (1972; Vienna, May 7, 1975), *IX* (1976), *X* (1977), *XI* (1981), *XII* (1984), *XIII* (1986), *XIV* (1988), *XV* (1988), and *XVI* (1991); *blueS No. 1* for 2 Pianos and Tape (1972; Wrocław, April 21, 1977), *No. 3* for 2 Pianos (1978), *and No. 4* for 2 Pianos and Tape (1988); *Open Music No. 2* (1975; Brussels, Nov. 16, 1983), *No. 3* (1975; Częstochowa, March 16, 1984), and *No. 4* (1983) for Piano and Tape; *Acontecimiento* for 3 Pianos and Computer (1988); *Megasonata* (1994); *Sexternus* for 6 Pianos (1998). **O r g a n:** 4 sonatas: No. 1, *Wiosna* (Spring; 1985), No. 2, *Lato* (Summer; 1985), No. 3, *Jesien* (Autumn; 1986), and No. 4, *Zima* (Winter; 1986). **VOCAL:** *Aspekty ekspresyjne* (Expressive Aspects) for Soprano and Flute (1963; Kraków, June 21, 1969); *Music for MI* for Voice, Vibraphone, 6 Narrators, Jazz Ensemble, and Orch. (Warsaw, Oct. 25, 1963); *Media* for Voices and Instruments (1967); *Bergsoniana* for Soprano, Flute, Piano, Horn, Double Bass, and Tape (1972; Brussels, March 26, 1973); *Missa elettronica* for Boy's Chorus and Tape (1975; Warsaw, Sept. 23, 1976; also for Chorus and Tape); *Miserere* for Soprano, Chorus, Orch., and Tape (1978); *Te Deum* for Solo Voices, Vocal Ensemble, and Orch. (1979); *Stabat Mater* for Soprano, Alto, Chorus, Strings, and Organ (1983; Kraków, Feb. 20, 1990); *Missa sinfonica* for Soprano, Violin, Soprano Saxophone, and Orch. (Katowice, April 25, 1986); *Liturgische Sätze* for Solo Voices, Chorus, and Orch. (1991); *4 Psalms* for Chorus and Orch. (1999); *Das Leben einer Stadt* for 3 Sopranos, Orch., and Electronic Media (1999). **O T H E R:** *Symfonia: Muzyka elektroniczna* (Symphony: Electronic Music) for Tape (1964; Warsaw, June 16,

1966); Concerto for Tape (1968; San Benedetto del Tronto, July 6, 1969); *Berlin '80/I* (Berlin, Oct. 2, 1980) and *II* (Berlin, Oct. 3, 1980) for Piano, Syn-lab, Electronic Media, and Tape.

WRITINGS: *Mały informator muzyki XX wieku* (Little Lexicon of Music of the 20th Century; Kraków, 1958; new ed., 1987); *Nowa muzyka: Problemy współczesnej techniki kompozytorskiej* (New Music: Problems of Contemporary Technique in Composing; Kraków, 1958; new ed., 1969); *Klasycy dodekafonii* (Classics of Dodecaphonic Music; 2 vols., Kraków, 1961, 1964); *Leksykon kompozytorów XX wieku* (Lexicon of 20th-century Composers; 2 vols., Kraków, 1963, 1965); *W kręgu nowej muzyki* (In the Sphere of New Music; Kraków, 1967); *Dźwięki i znaki* (Sounds and Signs: Introduction to Contemporary Composition; Warsaw, 1969); *Muzyka XX wieku, Tworcy i problemy* (Music of the 20th Century, Composers and Problems; Kraków, 1975); *Wstęp do kompozycji* (Introduction to Composition; in Polish and Eng.; Kraków, 1976); *Dzieje muzyki* (History of Music; Warsaw, 1983); *Dzieje kultury muzycznej* (History of Music Culture; Warsaw, 1987); *Kompozytorzy XX wieku* (Composers of the 20th Century; 2 vols., Kraków, 1988, 1990).

BIBL.: J. Hodor and B. Pociej, *B. S. and His Music* (Glasgow, 1975); L. Stawowy, *B. S.: Leben, Werk, Bedeutung* (Innsbruck, 1991); J. Zając, *Muzyka, teatr i filozofia B. S.* (The Music, Theater and Philosophy of B. S.; Salzburg, 1992).—**NS/LK/DM**

Schaeffer, Pierre, French acoustician, composer, and novelist; b. Nancy, Aug. 14, 1910; d. Aix-en-Provence, Aug. 19, 1995. Working in a radio studio in Paris, he conceived the idea of arranging a musical montage of random sounds, including outside noises. On April 15, 1948, he formulated the theory of *musique concrète*, which was to define such random assemblages of sounds. When the magnetic tape was perfected, Schaeffer made use of it by rhythmic acceleration and deceleration, changing the pitch and dynamics and modifying the nature of the instrumental timbre. He made several collages of elements of "concrete music," among them *Concert de bruits* (1948) and (with P. Henry) *Symphonie pour un homme seul* (1950); he also created an experimental opera, *Orphée 53* (1953). He incorporated his findings and ideas in the publ. *A la recherche de la musique concrète* (Paris, 1952) and in *Traité des objects sonores* (Paris, 1966). Eventually he abandoned his acoustical experimentations and turned to literature. He publ. both fictional and quasi-scientific novels, among them *Traité des objets musicaux* (1966); *Le Gardien de volcan* (1969); *Excusez-moi si je meurs* (1981); *Prélude, Chorale et Fugue* (1983).

BIBL.: M. Pierret, *Entretiens avec P. S.* (Paris, 1969); S. Brunet, *P. S.* (Paris, 1970).—**NS/LK/DM**

Schaeffner, André, French musicologist and ethnomusicologist; b. Paris, Feb. 7, 1895; d. there, Aug. 11, 1980. He studied composition with d'Indy at the Schola Cantorum (1921–24), ethnology with M. Mauss at the Institut d'Ethnologie (1932–33), religious science at the École Pratique des Hautes Études (1934–37; diploma, 1940), and archeology with S. Reinach at the École du Louvre in Paris. In 1929 he founded the ethnological dept. at the Musée de l'Homme in Paris, which he headed until 1965. Between 1931 and 1958 he led 6 scientific excursions in Africa. From 1958 to 1961 he was president of the Société Française de Musicologie. He

also took great interest in modern music and in lexicography; in addition to editing the French edition of Riemann's *Musiklexikon* (*Dictionnaire de musique*, Paris, 1931), he brought out the books *Le jazz* (with A. Coeuroy; Paris, 1926), a monograph on Stravinsky (Paris, 1931), *Origines des instruments de musique* (Paris, 1936; new ed., 1994), *Les Kissi: une Société noire et ses instruments de musique* (Paris, 1951), and *Segalen et Claude Debussy* (with A. Joly-Segalen; Monaco, 1961). His *Le sistre et le hochet: Musique, théâtre et danse dans las sociétés africaines* was publ. posthumously (Paris, 1990). A Festschrift was publ. in his memory in 1982.
—**NS/LK/DM**

Schäfer, Dirk, eminent Dutch composer, pianist, and pedagogue; b. Rotterdam, Nov. 23, 1873; d. Amsterdam, Feb. 16, 1931. He studied in Rotterdm and Cologne. After a European concert tour, he settled in Amsterdam, where he was active as a pianist and teacher. I. Schäfer-Dumstorff ed. his *Het klavier* (Amsterdam, 1942).

WORKS: ORCH.: *Suite pastorle* (1903); *Rhapsodie javanaise* (1904). **CHAMBER:** Piano Quintet (1901); 4 violin sonatas (1901–09); Cello Sonata (1909); String Quartet (1922); many piano pieces. **VOCAL:** Songs.—**NS/LK/DM**

Schafer, R(aymond) Murray, Canadian composer, writer, and educator; b. Sarnia, Ontario, July 18, 1933. After obtaining his Licentiate from the Royal Schools of Music (1952), he studied with Alberto Guerrero (piano), Greta Kraus (harpsichord), Arnold Walter (musicology), and John Weinzweig (composition) at the Royal Cons. of Music of Toronto (1952–55). He pursued studies in languages, literature, and philosophy on his own, and then lived in Vienna (1956–57). After receiving some lessons from Peter Racine Fricker in England, he returned to Toronto in 1961 and served as director of the Ten Centuries Concerts. From 1963 to 1965 he was artist-in-residence at Memorial Univ., and from 1965 to 1975 taught at Simon Fraser Univ. In 1972 he founded the World Soundscape Project for the purpose of exploring the relationship between people and their acoustic world. As the self-styled "father of acoustic ecology," he campaigned against the "sonic sewers" of modern urban life caused by noise pollution. In 1974 he held a Guggenheim fellowship and in 1987 received the Glenn Gould Award. In addition to his many books on music, he also wrote literary works and was active as a visual artist. Over the years, Schafer has utilized various contemporary techniques in his compositions. His explorations into ancient and modern languages, literature, and philosophy are reflected in many of his works. In his later scores, he made use of Eastern philosophy and religion.

WRITINGS: *British Composers in Interview* (London, 1963); *The Composer in the Classroom* (Toronto, 1965); *Ear Cleaning: Notes for an Experimental Music Course* (Toronto, 1967); *The New Soundscape* (Toronto, 1969); *The Book of Noise* (Vancouver, 1970); *When Words Sing* (Scarborough, Ontario, 1970); *The Public of the Music Theatre: Louis Riel—A Case Study* (Vienna, 1972); *The Rhinoceros in the Classroom* (London, 1975); *E.T.A. Hoffmann and Music* (Toronto, 1975); *Creative Music Education* (N.Y., 1976); ed.

and commentator, *Ezra Pound and Music: The Complete Criticism* (N.Y., 1977); *On Canadian Music* (Bancroft, Ontario, 1984); *Dicamus et Labyrinthos: A Philologist's Notebook* (Bancroft, Ontario, 1984); *The Thinking Ear: Complete Writings on Music Education* (Toronto, 1986); *Patria and the Theatre of Confluence* (Indian River, Ontario, 1991).

WORKS: DRAMATIC: *Loving* or *Toi*, opera (1963–65; first complete perf., Toronto, March 11, 1978); *Patria*, cycle of 12 musical/theatrical pieces (1966-in progress); *Jonah*, theater piece (1979); *Apocalypsis*, musical/theatrical pageant (London, Oct. 28, 1980). ORCH.: *In Memoriam: Alberto Guerrero* for Strings (1959); *Partita* for Strings (1961); *Canzoni for Prisoners* (1962); Untitled Composition No. 1 for Small Orch. (1963) and No. 2 for Full Orch. (1963); *Statement in Blue* for Youth Orch. (1964); *Son of Heldenleben* for Orch. and Tape (Montreal, Nov. 13, 1968); *No Longer Than Ten (10) Minutes* (1970; rev. 1972); *East* for Small Orch. (1972); *North/White* for Orch. and Snowmobile (Vancouver, Aug. 17, 1973); *Train* for Youth Orch. (1976); *Cortège* for Small Orch. (1977); Flute Concerto (Montreal, Oct. 8, 1984); *Ko wo kiku* (Listen to the Incense; 1985); *Dream Rainbow Dream Thunder* (1986); Concerto for Harp, Orch., and Tape (1987); Concerto for Guitar and Small Orch. (1989); *Scorpius* (1990; Toronto, March 25, 1991); *The Darkly Splendid Earth: The Lonely Traveller* for Violin and Orch. (Toronto, April 17, 1991). CHAMBER: Concerto for Harpsichord and 8 Winds (1954); Sonatina for Flute and Harpsichord or Piano (1958); *Minimusic* for Any Combination of Instruments or Voices (1967); 6 string quartets (1970; *Waves*, 1976; 1981; 1989; *Rosalind*, 1989; 1993); *Music for Wilderness Lake* for 12 Trombones and Small Rural Lake (1979); *Theseus* for Harp and String Quartet (1983); *Le Cri de Merlin* for Guitar and Tape (1987). VOCAL: *Minnelieder* for Mezzo-soprano and Woodwind Quintet (1956; also for Mezzo-soprano and Orch., 1987); *Protest and Incarceration* for Mezzo-soprano and Orch. (1960); *Brébeuf*, cantata for Baritone and Orch. (1961); *5 Studies on Texts by Prudentius* for Soprano and 4 Flutes (1962); *Threnody* for Chorus, Orch., and Tape (1966; rev. 1967); *Lustro*, part 1: *Divan i Shams i Tabriz* for 6 Solo Voices, Orch., and Tape (1969; rev. 1970), 2: *Music for the Morning of the World* for Voice and Tape (1970), and 3: *Beyond the Great Gate of Light* for 6 Solo Voices, Orch., and Tape (1972); *Enchantress* for Voice, Exotic Flute, and 8 Cellos (1971); *In Search of Zoroaster* for Man's Voice, Chorus, Percussion, and Organ (1971); *Miniwanka or the Moments of Water* for Women's Voices or Chorus (1971); *Adieu Robert Schumann* for Alto and Orch. (1976); *The Garden of the Heart (The Thousand and One Nights)* for Alto and Orch. (1980); *Snowforms* for Women's Voices (1981; rev. 1983); *A Garden of Bells* for Chorus (1983); *Letters from Mignon* for Mezzo-soprano and Orch. (1987); *The Death of the Buddha* for Chorus, Gongs, and Bell Tree (1989); *Gitanjali* for Soprano and Small Orch. (1990; Ottawa, May 14, 1992). OTHER: *Kaleidoscope* for Tape (1967); *Harbour Symphony* for Fog Horns (1983).—NS/LK/DM

Schaffrath, Christoph, German harpsichordist, teacher, and composer; b. Hohenstein-on-Elbe, near Chemnitz, 1709; d. Berlin, Feb. 17, 1763. He was harpsichordist to the king and Polish Prince Sangusko (from 1730). He entered the service of Crown Prince Freidrich (later Friedrich the Great) in Ruppin in 1734, following his patron to Rheinsberg in 1736; when Friedrich became king in 1740, Schaffrath went to Berlin as harpsichordist in the court Kapelle; was named musician to Princess Amalie, the king's sister, in 1741. He wrote some 13 syms., 6 overtures, a Flute Concerto, 2 violin concertos, 13 keyboard concertos, 2 concertos for 2 Keyboards and Strings, much chamber music, etc. —NS/LK/DM

Schalk, Franz, noted Austrian conductor, brother of **Josef Schalk;** b. Vienna, May 27, 1863; d. Edlach, Sept. 2, 1931. He studied with Bruckner at the Vienna Cons. After making his debut in Liberec (1886), he conducted in Reichenbach (1888–89), Graz (1889–95), and Prague (1895–98), and at the Berlin Royal Opera (1899–1900). He subsequently concentrated his activities in Vienna, where he conducted at the Court Opera (from 1900); when it became the State Opera in 1918, he was named its director; after sharing that position with R. Strauss (1919–24), he was sole director until 1929. He was a regular conductor with the Vienna Phil. from 1901 until his death; also was conductor of the Gesellschaft der Musikfreunde (1904–21). On Dec. 14, 1898, he made his Metropolitan Opera debut in N.Y. conducting *Die Walküre*, but remained on the roster for only that season. He also conducted *Ring* cycles at London's Covent Garden in 1898, 1907, and 1911; likewise conducted at the Salzburg Festivals. He devoted part of his time to teaching conducting in Vienna. A champion of Bruckner, he ed. several of his syms., even recomposing his 5th Sym. While Schalk's eds. were well-intentioned efforts to obtain public performances of Bruckner's scores, they are now totally discredited. L. Schalk ed. his *Briefe und Betrachtungen* (Vienna, 1935).—NS/LK/DM

Schalk, Josef, Austrian pianist, teacher, and writer on music, brother of **Franz Schalk;** b. Vienna, March 24, 1857; d. there, Nov. 7, 1900. He studied with Bruckner and Epstein. He was a piano teacher at the Vienna Cons. His arrangements of the Bruckner syms. for Piano, 4-Hands, did much to make these works known, and his book, *Anton Bruckner und die moderne Musikwelt* (1885), effectively upheld Bruckner's music. He was also a friend of Hugo Wolf, whom he championed. —NS/LK/DM

Schall, Claus Nielsen, Danish violinist and composer; b. Copenhagen, April 28, 1757; d. there, Aug. 9, 1835. He became a dancer at the Royal Theater in 1772, was made a member of the court chapel in 1775, and became répétiteur and director of the ballet at the Royal Theater in 1776. After touring in Europe, he returned to Copenhagen as Konzertmeister of the Opera in 1792; was made composer to the Royal Ballet in 1795; served as music director of the Opera (1818–34). He wrote 6 Singspiels, of which the following (all first perf. in Copenhagen) were the most successful: *Claudine af Villa Bella* (Jan. 29, 1787), *Kinafarerne* (March 2, 1792), *Domherren i Milano* (March 16, 1802), and *De tre Galninger* (March 19, 1816). He also wrote some 20 ballets, various orch. pieces, chamber music, and songs.

BIBL.: J. Friedrich, *C. S. als dramatischer Komponist* (diss., Univ. of Breslau, 1930).—NS/LK/DM

Schall, Richard, German musicologist; b. Dortmund, Dec. 3, 1922. He studied at the Univ. of Marburg

(Ph.D., 1946, with the diss. *Hugo Kaun: Leben und Werk, 1863–1932: Ein Beitrag zur Musik der Jahrhundertwende;* publ. in Regensburg, 1948); also received instruction in theory from H. Gebhard-Elsass and in conducting from H. von Waltershausen, and later attended the library school of the Bavarian State Library in Munich, where he took the senior librarian's examination (1956). From 1962 to 1986 he was musicological adviser to the Bavarian Radio, for which he prepared various publications. He contributed numerous articles to *Die Musik in Geschichte und Gegenwart;* also served as ed. of the *Quellenkataloge zur Musikgeschichte* (Wilhelmshaven, from 1966), the *Taschenbücher zur Musikwissenschaft* (Wilhelmshaven, from 1969), *Veröffentlichungen zur Musikforschung* (Wilhelmshaven, from 1972), and *Paperbacks on Musicology* (N.Y., from 1980). His writings are of value for the bibliography of German musicology.—NS/LK/DM

Scharrer, August, German composer and conductor; b. Strasbourg, Aug. 18, 1866; d. Weiherhof, near Furth, Oct. 24, 1936. After studies in Strasbourg and Berlin, he was a theater conductor in Karlsruhe (1897–98) and Regensburg (1898–1900); from 1914 to 1931 he conducted the Phil. Soc. of Nuremberg. He wrote an opera, *Die Erlösung* (Strasbourg, Nov. 21, 1895), overtures, chamber music, choruses, and songs. —NS/LK/DM

Scharrer, Irene, English pianist and teacher; b. London, Feb. 2, 1888; d. there, Jan. 11, 1971. She studied with Matthay at the Royal Academy of Music in London. After making her London debut in 1904, she toured throughout England and Europe; made her first visit to the U.S. in 1925. In addition to appearing as a soloist with orchs., recitalist, and chamber-music artist, she gave duo recitals with her cousin, **Dame Myra Hess,** with whom she gave her farewell perf. in London in 1958. She also engaged in teaching.—NS/LK/DM

Scharwenka, (Franz) Xaver, Polish-German pianist, composer, and pedagogue, brother of **(Ludwig) Philipp Scharwenka;** b. Samter, Posen, Jan. 6, 1850; d. Berlin, Dec. 8, 1924. He studied with Kullak and Wuerst at the Kullak Academy of Music in Berlin, graduating in 1868, then joined its faculty. He made his debut in Berlin in 1869, then made regular tours from 1874; also presented chamber music concerts in Berlin from 1881. With his brother, he founded the Scharwenka Cons. in Berlin in 1881. In 1891 he went to the U.S. and opened a N.Y. branch of his Cons.; appeared as soloist in his own Piano Concerto (N.Y., Jan. 24, 1891). Returning to Berlin in 1898, he became co-director of the newly amalgamated (1893) Klindworth-Scharwenka Cons.; in 1914 he established his own course of master classes for piano. As a composer, he was undoubtedly superior to his brother, although both were faithful imitators of Schumann and other German Romantics. He wrote an opera, *Mataswintha* (Weimar, Oct. 4, 1896), a Sym. (1885), 4 piano concertos, chamber music, and numerous effective piano pieces, of which his *Polish Dances* became favorites with American piano teachers and students. He also publ. technical studies for piano, *Beiträge zur*

Fingerbildung; Studien im Oktavenspiel, a collection of famous études, arranged according to progressive difficulty, under the title *Meisterschule des Klavierspiels, Methodik des Klavierspiels* (1907; with A. Spanuth), and a book of memoirs, *Klänge aus meinem Leben: Erinnerungen eines Musikers* (Leipzig, 1922).—NS/LK/DM

Scharwenka, (Ludwig) Philipp, Polish-German composer and pedagogue, brother of **(Franz) Xaver Scharwenka;** b. Samter, Posen, Feb. 16, 1847; d. Bad Nauheim, July 16, 1917. He studied with Wuerst and Dorn at the Kullak Academy of Music in Berlin, and in 1868 was appointed teacher of composition there. With his brother he founded in 1881 the Scharwenka Cons. in Berlin. Together they made an American trip in 1891. In 1893 the Scharwenka Cons. was amalgamated with the Klindworth Cons.; the resulting Klindworth- Scharwenka Cons. acquired an excellent reputation for its teaching standards. He was an accomplished composer, numbering among his works 2 syms., overtures, *Arkadische Suite* for Orch. (1887), a Violin Concerto (1895), *Frühlingswogen,* symphonic poem (1891), *Dramatische Fantasie* for Orch. (1900), choral works, chamber music, piano pieces, and songs.—NS/LK/DM

Schat, Peter, significant Dutch composer; b. Utrecht, June 5, 1935. He was a student of Baaren at the Utrecht Cons. (1952–58), of Seiber in London (1959), and of Boulez in Basel (1960–62). Settling in Amsterdam, he was active with the Studio for Electro-Instrumental Music (from 1967), and with the Amsterdam Electric Circus (from 1973). After teaching at the Royal Cons. of Music in The Hague (1974–83), he devoted himself fully to composition. In his early works, he followed a diligent serialist path. Later he combined serial and tonal elements in his works. Finally, he experimented with a method of 12 tonalities related only to each other as formulated in his "tone clock" (1982). In his "tone clock", Schat distinguishes between 12 trichords, one being the natural trichord, which are interrelated through their steering principle. This expansive harmonic and melodic method points the way to a new tonal system. He explained his system in the book *De Toonklok, Essays en gesprekken over muziek* (Amsterdam, 1984; Eng. tr., 1993).

WORKS: DRAMATIC: *Labyrint,* a kind of opera (1964; Amsterdam, June 23, 1966); *Reconstructie,* a morality (Amsterdam, June 29, 1969; in collaboration with L. Andriessen, R. de Leeuw, M. Mengelberg, and J. van Vlijmen); *Het vijde seizoen* (The 5th Season), music theater (1973); *Houdini,* circus opera (1974–76; Amsterdam, Sept. 29, 1977); *I am Houdini,* ballet (1976); *Aap verslaat de knekelgeest* (Monkey Subdues the White-Bone Demon), strip opera (1980); *Symposion,* opera (1989). **ORCH.:** *Mozaïeken* (Mosaics; 1959); *Concerto da camera* (1960); *Entelechie I* for 5 Instrumental Groups (1960–61); *Dansen uit het Labyrint* (Dances from the Labyrinth; 1963); *Clockwise and anti-clockwise* for 16 Winds (1967); *On Escalation* for 6 Percussionists and Orch. (1968); *Thema* for Oboe and Orch. (1970); 2 syms.: No. 1 (1978; rev. 1979) and No. 2 (1983; rev. 1984); *Serenade* for 12 Strings (1984); *De hemet* (The Heavens; 1990); *Opening* (1991); *Études* for Piano and Orch. (1992); *Préludes* for Flute and Small Orch. (1993); *Arch Music for St. Louis* (1997). **CHAMBER:** *Introduction and Adagio* for String Quartet (1954); Septet for Flute, Oboe, Bass Clarinet, Horn, Cello, Piano, and Percussion

(1956); Octet for Flute, Oboe, Clarinet, Bassoon, Horn, 2 Trumpets, and Trombone (1958); *2 Pieces* for Flute, Violin, Trumpet, and Percussion (1959); *Improvisations and Symphonies* for Wind Quintet (1960); *Signalement* for 6 Percussionists and 3 Double Basses (1961); *Hypothema* for Recorders (1969); *Diapason* for Ensemble (1996). **KEYBOARD: P i a n o :** *Inscripties* (1959); *Anathema* (1969); *Polonaise* (1981). **O r g a n :** *Passacaglia and Fugue* (1954). **VOCAL:** *Cryptogamen*, 5 songs for Baritone and Orch. (1959); *The Fall* for 16 Voices (1960); *Entelechie II* for Mezzo-soprano and 10 Instruments (1961); *Stemmen uit het Labyrint* (Voices from the Labyrinth) for Alto, Tenor, Basso Profondo, and Orch. (1963); *Koren uit het Labyrint* (Choruses from the Labyrinth) for Chorus and Orch. (1964); *Scènes uit het Labyrint* (Scenes from the Labyrinth) for Reciter, Alto, Tenor, Bass, Chorus, and Orch. (1964); *Improvisaties uit het Labyrint* (Improvisations from the Labyrinth) for 3 Singers and 4 Instrumentalists (1964); *To You* for Mezzo-soprano, Amplified Instruments, and Electronics (1972); *Het vijde seizoen* (The 5th Season), cantata for Soprano and Chamber Ensemble (1973); *Canto General*, "in memoriam Salvador Allende," for Mezzo-soprano, Violin, and Piano (1974); *Mei '75, een lied van bevrijding* (May '75, a Song of Liberation) for Mezzo-soprano, Baritone, Chorus, and Orch. (1975); *Houdini Symphony* for Soprano, Mezzo-soprano, Tenor, Baritone, Chorus, and Orch. (1976); *De briefscène* (The Letter Scene) for Soprano, Tenor, and Orch. or Piano (1976); *Kind en kraai* (Child and Crow), song cycle for Soprano and Piano (1977); *Adem* (Breath) for Chamber Chorus (1984); *For Lenny* for Tenor and Piano (for Leonard Bernstein's 70th birthday; 1988); *De Trein* (The Train) for 5 Men's Voices and Orch. (1989); *Een Indisch Requiem* for Tenor, Chorus, and Orch. (1995); *The Food of Love* for Mezzo-soprano, Tenor, and Chamber Orch. (1997). **OTHER:** *Banden uit het Labyrint* (Tapes from the Labyrinth), electronic music (1965); *The Aleph*, electronic music (1965); *The Tone Clock* for Mechanical Clock (1987); *Alarm for Carillon and Ringing Bells ad libitum* (1994).—**NS/LK/DM**

Schaub, Hans (actually, **Siegmund Ferdinand**), German music critic, teacher, and composer; b. Frankfurt am Main, Sept. 22, 1880; d. Hanstedt, near Marburg, Nov. 12, 1965. He studied at the Frankfurt am Main Hoch Cons. with Iwan Knorr (theory) and Carl Friedberg (piano), with Arnold Mendelssohn in Darmstadt, and with Humperdinck in Berlin; also took lessons with Richard Strauss. He taught at the Breslau Cons. (1903–06); was on the faculty of Benda's Cons. and served as ed. of the *Deutsche Musikerzeitung* in Berlin (1906–16). After working as a music critic and pedagogue in Hamburg (1916–51), he settled in Hanstedt. Among his compositions were *Passacaglia* for Orch. (1928); *3 Intermezzi* for Small Orch.; *Capriccio* for Violin and Piano; *Den Gefallenen*, cantata (1940); *Deutsches Te Deum*, oratorio (1942).—**NS/LK/DM**

Schech, Marianne, German soprano; b. Geitau, Jan. 18, 1914; d. May 22, 1999. She was educated in Munich. She made her operatic debut in Koblenz in 1937, and then sang in Munich (1939–41), Düsseldorf (1941–44), and at the Dresden State Opera (1944–51); also sang with the Bavarian State Opera in Munich. In 1956 she was named a Kammersängerin. On Jan. 22, 1957, she made her debut at the Metropolitan Opera in

N.Y. as Sieglinde in *Die Walküre*; also made guest appearances in London, Vienna, and Hamburg. She retired from the stage in 1970 and devoted herself mainly to teaching.—**NS/LK/DM**

Scheel, Fritz, German conductor; b. Lübeck, Nov. 7, 1852; d. Philadelphia, March 13, 1907. His grandfather and father were orch. conductors, and at 9 the boy played the violin in his father's orch.; from 1864 to 1867 he was a pupil of F. David in Leipzig. At 17 he began his career as a concertmaster and conductor at Bremerhaven. In 1873 he was solo violinist and conductor of the summer concerts in Schwerin, and in 1884 he became conductor of the Chemnitz municipal orch.; from 1890 to 1893 he was conductor of orch. concerts in Hamburg. He went to the U.S. in 1893, and after conducting the Trocadero concerts at the World's Columbian Exposition in Chicago (1894), he served as founder-conductor of the San Francisco Sym. Society (1895–99); subsequently was the first conductor of the Philadelphia Orch. (1900–07).—**NS/LK/DM**

Scheff, Fritzi, famous Austrian soprano; b. Vienna, Aug. 30, 1879; d. N.Y., April 8, 1954. She studied with her mother, the singer Anna Jäger, and after further training with Schröder-Hanfstängl in Munich, she completed her studies at the Frankfurt am Main Cons. She made her operatic debut as Martha in Frankfurt am Main (1896), and soon adopted her mother's maiden name of Scheff for professional purposes. After singing at the Munich Court Opera (1897–1900), she made her Metropolitan Opera debut in N.Y. as Marzellina in *Fidelio* (Dec. 28, 1900), and remained on its roster until 1903; concurrently sang at London's Covent Garden. She later shifted to light opera, and it was in this field that she became famous. She created the role of Fifi in Victor Herbert's operetta *Mlle. Modiste* (Trenton, N.J., Oct. 7, 1905); her singing of Fifi's waltz song *Kiss Me Again* became a hallmark of her career. She also found success as a dramatic actress, becoming particularly well known for her appearance in Arsenic and Old Lace. Her 3 marriages (to Baron Fritz von Bardeleben, the American writer John Fox Jr., and the singer George Anderson) ended in divorce.—**NS/LK/DM**

Scheibe, Johann Adolf, German music theorist and composer; b. Leipzig, May 3, 1708; d. Copenhagen, April 22, 1776. He was the son of the organ builder Johann Scheibe (b. Saxony, c. 1680; d. Leipzig, Sept. 3, 1748), in whose workshop he lost his right eye when he was 8. He commenced the study of keyboard instruments at age 6; after attending the school of the Nicolaikirche, he entered the Univ. of Leipzig as a law student in 1725, but was compelled to give up his studies when the family's financial condition changed for the worse. He subsequently devoted himself to music, being mainly autodidact; failing to obtain organ posts at the Nicolaikirche in Leipzig (1729; Bach was one of the adjudicators), in Prague and Gotha (1735), and in Sondershausen and Wolfenbüttel (1736), he went to Hamburg as a music critic and composer (1736); brought out his *Der critische Musikus*, which includes his famous attack on Bach (No. 6, 1737). After serving as Kapellmeister to Margrave Friedrich Ernst of Brandenburg-Culmbach, the governor of Holstein (1739–40), he was made Kapellmeister at the court of King Christian VI in Copenhagen in 1740; with the accession of King Frederik V in 1747, Scheibe was pensioned and settled in Sønderborg, where he devoted himself to running a music school for children. In 1766 he once again resumed a relationship with the Danish court, serving as a composer for it until his death. The major portion of his compositional output, which includes the Singspiel *Thusnelde* (libretto publ. in Leipzig and Copenhagen, 1749), 150 flute concertos, and some 30 violin concertos, is not extant. He is therefore primarily known as an important music theorist of his era.

WRITINGS: *Compendium musices theoretico-practicum, das ist Kurzer Begriff derer nötigsten Compositions-Regeln* (c. 1730; publ. by P. Benary in *Die deutsche Kompositionslehre des 18. Jahrhunderts*, Leipzig, 1961); *Der critische Musikus* (vol. I, Hamburg, 1738; vol. II, Hamburg, 1740; complete ed., Leipzig, 1745); *Beantwortung der unparteiischen Anmerkungen über eine bedenkliche Stelle in dem sechsten Stücke des critischen Musicus* (Hamburg, 1738; reprint in *Der critische Musikus*, Leipzig, 1745); *Eine Abhandlung von den musicalischen Intervallen und Geschlechtern* (Hamburg, 1739); *Thusnelde, ein Singspiel in vier Aufzügen, mit einem Vorbericht von der Möglichkeit und Beschaffenheit guter Singspiele begleitet* (Leipzig and Copenhagen, 1749); *Abhandlung vom Ursprunge und Alter der Musik, insonderheit der Vokalmusik* (Altona and Flensburg, 1754); *Über die musikalische Composition, erster Theil: Die Theorie der Melodie und Harmonie* (Leipzig, 1773).

BIBL.: K. Storch, *S.s Anschauungen von der musikalische Historie, Wissenschaft und Kunst* (diss., Univ. of Leipzig, 1923); E. Rosenkaimer, *J.A. S. als Verfasser des Critischen Musikus* (Bonn, 1929); I. Willheim, *J.A. S.: German Musical Thought in Transition* (diss., Univ. of Ill., 1963); G. Skapski, *The Recitative in J.A. S.'s Literary and Musical Work* (diss., Univ. of Tex., 19 63).—NS/LK/DM

Scheibler, Johann Heinrich, German inventor and writer on music; b. Montjoie, near Aachen, Nov. 11, 1777; d. Krefeld, Nov. 20, 1837. He studied with J.N. Wolff. A silk manufacturer at Krefeld, he became interested in acoustic phenomena and invented an apparatus, consisting of 56 tuning forks, for tuning fixed-tone instruments according to the equally tempered scale. At the Stuttgart Congress of physicists in 1834, Scheibler proposed the pitch of $a^1 = 440$ (vibrations) at 69 F, which was adopted (hence called the "Stuttgart pitch"). His system is more clearly explained by Töpfer (1842), Vincent (1849), and Lecomte (1856).

WRITINGS: *Der physikalische und musikalische Tonmesser* (Essen, 1834); *Anleitung, die Orgel vermittelst der Stösse (vulgo Schwebungen) und des Metronoms correct gleichschwebend zu stimmen* (Krefeld, 1834); *Über mathematische Stimmung, Temperaturen und Orgelbaustimmung nach Vibrationsdifferenzen oder Stossen* (Krefeld, 1835); *Mitteilung über das Wesentliche des musikalischen und physikalischen Tonmessers* (Krefeld, 1836).

BIBL.: J. Löhr, *Über die S.'sche Erfindung überhaupt und dessen Pianoforte- und Orgel-Stimmung insbesondere* (Krefeld, 1836).—NS/LK/DM

Scheidemann, Heinrich, important German organist, pedagogue, and composer; b. Wöhrden, Hol-

stein, c. 1595; d. Hamburg, 1663. He studied with Sweelinck in Amsterdam (1611–14), and in 1629 succeeded his father as organist at the Katharinenkirche in Hamburg, holding that post until his death. Among his students was J.A. Reinken, who became his assistant in 1658 and his successor at his death. Scheidemann excelled especially as a composer of organ music. See G. Fock and W. Breig, eds., *Heinrich Scheidemann: Orgelwerke* (1967–71).—NS/LK/DM

Scheidemantel, Karl, noted German baritone; b. Weimar, Jan. 21, 1859; d. there, June 26, 1923. He was a pupil of Bodo Borchers, and sang at the court theater in Weimar (1878–86); also studied voice with Julius Stockhausen in the summers of 1881–83. He was a member of the Dresden Court Opera from 1886 to 1911; also sang at the Munich Court Opera (1882), London's Covent Garden (debut as Wolfram, June 14, 1884), the Vienna Court Opera (1890), and Milan's La Scala (1892). From 1911 to 1920 he was a prof. at the Grossherzogliche Musikschule in Weimar; from 1920 to 1922 he was director of the Landestheater in Dresden. He publ. *Stimmbildung* (1907; fourth ed. as *Gesangsbildung*, 1913; in Eng., 1910); also ed. a collection of songs, *Meisterweisen* (1914). Among his finest roles were Hans Sachs, Kurwenal, Amfortas, Klingsor, Telramund, Pizarro, and Scarpia; he also created the roles of Kunrad in *Feuersnot* (Dresden, Nov. 21, 1901) and Faninal in *Der Rosenkavalier* (Dresden, Jan. 26 1911).

BIBL.: P. Trede, *K. S.* (Dresden, 1911).—NS/LK/DM

Scheidl, Theodor, Austrian baritone and teacher; b. Vienna, Aug. 3, 1880; d. Tübingen, April 22, 1959. He was trained in Vienna. After making his debut there at the Volksoper in *Lohengrin* (1910), he sang in Olmütz (1911–12) and Augsburg (1913). He was a member of the Stuttgart Opera (1913–21) and of the Berlin State Opera (1921–32). He also appeared at the Bayreuth Festivals, most notably as Klingsor (1914), Amfortas (1924–25), and Kurwenal (1927). In 1932 he joined the German Theater in Prague. In 1937 he became a prof. of voice at the Munich Hochschule für Musik. He settled in Tübingen as a teacher in 1944.—NS/LK/DM

Scheidt, family of German singers, all siblings:

(1) **Selma vom Scheidt,** soprano; b. Bremen, Sept. 26, 1874; d. Weimar, Feb. 19, 1959. She was a pupil of Heinrich Böllhoff in Hamburg, and later of Theodor Bertram. In 1891 she made her operatic debut as Agathe in Elberfeld. After singing in Essen (1892–94) and Düsseldorf (1894–95), she appeared in Aachen, Bonn, and Berlin. In 1900 she joined the Weimar Opera, where she sang for some 25 years.

(2) **Julius vom Scheidt,** baritone; b. Bremen, March 29, 1877; d. Hamburg, Dec. 10, 1948. He made his operatic debut in Cologne in 1899, and sang there until 1916. After appearing at the Berlin Deutsches Opernhaus (1916–24), he sang at the Hamburg Opera (1924–30). He subsequently taught voice.

(3) **Robert vom Scheidt,** baritone; b. Bremen, April 16, 1879; d. Frankfurt am Main, April 10, 1964. He

studied at the Cologne Cons. In 1897 he made his operatic debut at the Cologne Opera, singing there until 1903. From 1903 to 1912 he sang at the Hamburg Opera, and in 1904 at the Bayreuth Festival. He was a member of the Frankfurt am Main Opera from 1912 to 1940, singing in the premieres of Schreker's *Die Gezeichneten* (1918) and *Der Schatzgräber* (1920), and of Egk's *Die Zaubergeige* (1935).—NS/LK/DM

Scheidt, Samuel, important German organist, teacher, and composer; b. Halle (baptized), Nov. 3, 1587; d. there, March 24, 1654. He studied at the Halle Gymnasium. From c. 1603 to 1608 he was organist at the Moritzkirche in Halle, and then went to Amsterdam to study with Sweelinck. He returned to Halle in 1609, and was appointed court organist to Margrave Christian Wilhelm of Brandenburg; in 1619 he also assumed the post of court Kapellmeister. When the margrave left for Denmark in 1625 to support the Protestant cause in the Thirty Years' War, Scheidt retained his post even though without emolument, eking out a modest living by teaching. In 1628 he was named music director of the Marktkirche, the principal church in Halle, continuing in this employment until 1630. In 1638 he resumed his post as court Kapellmeister and served until his death. Scheidt was highly esteemed as an organist, was consulted on the building of organs as an inspector, and was also a noted organ teacher. As a composer, he excelled in both keyboard and sacred vocal works. A collected ed. of his works was begun by G. Harms and continued by others (16 vols., 1923–83).

WORKS: KEYBOARD: *Tabulatura nova continens variationes aliquot psalmorum, fantasiarum, cantilenarum, passamezzo et canones* (Hamburg, 1624); *Pars secunda tabulaturae continens fugarum, psalmorum, cantionum et echus, tocatae, variationes varias omnimodas pro quorumvis organistarum captu et modulo* (Hamburg, 1624); *III. et ultima pars tabulaturae continens Kyrie Dominicale, Credo in unum Deum, Psalmum de Coena Domini sub communione, hymnos praecipuorum festorum totius anni, Magnificat...& Benedicamus* (Hamburg, 1624); *Tabulatur-Buch hundert geistlicher Lieder und Psalmen* (Görlitz, 1650); additional instrumental works include *Paduana, galliarda, courante, alemande, intrada, canzonetto, ut vocant, in gratiam musices studiosorum, potissimum violistarum, a* 4, 5, and Basso Continuo (Hamburg, 1621); *Ludorum musicorum secunda pars continens paduan, galliard, alemand, canzon, et intrad, a* 4, 5, 7, and Basso Continuo (Hamburg, 1622); *Ludorum musicorum tertia pars continens paduanas, cour. et canzon., a* 3, 4, 7, 8, and Basso Continuo (Hamburg, 1624; not extant); *Ludorum musicorum quarta pars, a* 3, 4, and Basso Continuo (Hamburg, 1627); *LXX Symphonien auff Concerten manir: Vornemlich auff Violinen zu gebrauchen durch die gewohnliche Tonos, und die 7 Claves, a* 2 and Basso Continuo (Leipzig, 1644); also canons in *Tabulatura nova continens variationes aliquot psalmorum, fantasiarum, cantilenarum, passamezzo et canones* (Hamburg, 1624). **VOCAL: Church Music:** *Cantiones sacrae* for 8 Voices (Hamburg, 1620); *Pars prima concertuum sacrorum, adiectis symphoniis et choris instrumentalibus* for 2 to 5, 8, and 12 Voices and Basso Continuo (Hamburg, 1622); *Newe geistliche Concerten...prima pars* for 2 and 3 Voices and Basso Continuo (Halle, 1631); *Geistlicher Concerten...ander Theil* for 2 to 6 Voices and Basso Continuo (Halle, 1634); *Geistlicher Concerten...dritter Theil* for 2 to 6 Voices and Basso Continuo (Halle, 1635); *Liebliche Krafft-Blumlein aus des Heyligen Geistes Lustgarten abgebrochen und zum Vorschmack dess ewigen Lebens im zweystim-* *michten Himmels-Chor versetzet* for 2 Voices and Basso Continuo (Halle, 1635); *Geistlicher Concerten...vierter Theil* for 2 to 6 Voices and Basso Continuo (Halle, 1640).

BIBL.: C. Mahrenholz, *S. S.: Sein Leben und sein Werk* (Leipzig, 1924); R. Hünicken, *S. S.: Ein althallischer Musikus* (Halle, 1934); W. Serauky, *S. S. in seinen Briefen* (Halle, 1937); a Festschrift in honor of his 350th birthday (Wolfenbüttel, 1937); E. Gessner, *S. S.s geistliche Konzerte: Ein Beitrag zur Geschichte der Gattung* (Berlin, 1961).—NS/LK/DM

Schein, Ann, American pianist; b. White Plains, N.Y., Nov. 10, 1939. She studied with Glenn Gunn in Washington, D.C., Mieczyslaw Munz at the Peabody Cons. of Music in Baltimore, Artur Rubinstein (1961–63), and Dame Myra Hess (1961–65). She made her London debut in a recital in 1958; after appearing as a soloist with the N.Y. Phil. and making her Carnegie Hall recital debut in 1962, she toured widely. In 1968 she organized the People-to-People Music Committee in an effort to encourage amicable relations between nations via the art of music. She taught at the Peabody Cons. (from 1980) and the Aspen (Colo.) School of Music (from 1984). Her husband is the violinist Earl Carlyss. In addition to her performances of Chopin, she has won accolades for her interpretations of works by contemporary composers.—NS/LK/DM

Schein, Johann Hermann, important German composer; b. Grunhain, near Annaberg, Jan. 20, 1586; d. Leipzig, Nov. 19, 1630. His father was a pastor; upon his death, Schein moved to Dresden, where he entered the Hofkapelle of the Elector of Saxony as a boy soprano. He received instruction from the Kapellmeister, Rogier Michael, then continued his studies in music at Pforta, an electoral school near Naumburg (1603–07), where his teachers were Bartholomaus Scheer and Martin Roth. In 1607 he returned to Dresden, and in 1608 received an electoral scholarship to study jurisprudence and liberal arts at the Univ. of Leipzig, where he remained until 1612. In 1613 he became Hausmusikmeister to Gottfried von Wolffersdorff in Weissenfels, and also served as praeceptor to his children. In 1615 he was appointed Kapellmeister to Duke Johann Ernst the Younger in Weimar. In 1616 he was named cantor at the Thomasschule in Leipzig, as successor to Calvisius. His duties in Leipzig inlcuded directing the choral music at the Thomaskirche and the Nicolaikirche, and teaching singing and Latin grammar and syntax at the Thomasschule. Schein was one of the earliest German composers to introduce into Lutheran church music the Italian techniques of madrigal, monody, and concerto. In the alliterative parlance of learned German writers, Schein became known as the chronologically second of the glorious trio of near-contemporaneous German masters, Schütz (b. 1585), Schein (b. 1586), and Scheidt (b. 1587). But Schütz, the oldest of them, outlived Schein by 42 years; he visited him at his deathbed and brought him, as a friendly offering, a 6-part motet of his composition on Schein's favorite passage from the New Testament. A collected ed. of his works, edited by A. Prufer, was publ. by Breitkopf und Härtel (7 vols., Leipzig, 1901–23). The *Neue Ausgabe sämtlicher Werke*, ed. by A. Adrio, began publ. in Kassel in 1963 by Bärenreiter.

WORKS: VOCAL: S a c r e d : *Cymbalum Sionium sive Cantiones sacrae*, for 5 to 12 Voices (Leipzig, 1615); *Opella nova, geistlicher Concerten...auff italiänische Invention componirt* for 3 to 5 Voices and Basso Continuo (Leipzig, 1618; second ed., 1626); *Fontana d'Israel, Israelis Brünlein, auserlesener Krafft-Sprüchlin altes und Newen Testaments...aufeiner...Italian madrigalische Manier* for 5 and 6 Voices and Basso Continuo (Leipzig, 1623; second ed., 1651); *Opella nova, ander Theil, geistlicher Concerten* for 3 to 6 Voices, Instruments, and Basso Continuo (Leipzig, 1626); *Cantional oder Gesangbuch Augspurgischer Confession* for 4 to 6 Voices (Leipzig, 1627; second ed., enl., 1645). **S e c u l a r :** Texts by Schein: *Venus Kräntzlein...oder Newe weltliche Lieder* for 5 Voices, *neben etzlichen Intraden, Gagliarden und Canzonen* (Wittenberg, 1609); *Musica boscareccia, oder Wald-Liederlein auff italian-villanellische Invention...mit lebendiger Stimm...auch auff musicalischen Instrumenten zu spielen* for 3 Voices (Leipzig, 1621; 6th ed., 1643; *Ander Theil* [Leipzig, 1628; 6th ed., 1641] *Dritter Theil* [Leipzig, 1628; 5th ed., 1643]; also publ. with rev. text as *Musica boscareccia sacra* [3 vols., Erfurt, 1644–51]); *Diletti pastorali, Hirten Lust* for 5 Voices and Basso Continuo, *auff Madrigal-Manier componirt* (Leipzig, 1624); *Studenten-Schmauss a 5: Einer löblischen Compagni de la Vinobiera* (Leipzig, 1626). **I N S T R U M E N - TAL :** *Banchetto musicale newer...Padouanen, Gagliarden, Couren-ten und Allemanden a 5, auff allerley Instrumenten* (Leipzig, 1617); other works are found in several of his vocal collections. **BIBL.:** A. Prüfer, *J.H. S.* (Leipzig, 1895); A. Prüfer, *J.H. S. und das weltliche deutsche Lied des 17. Jahrhunderts* (Leipzig, 1908); I. Hueck, *Die künstlerische Entwicklung J.H. S.s, dargestellt an seinen geistlichen Werken* (diss., Univ. of Freiburg, 1945); A. Adrio, *J.H. S.* (Berlin, 1959); H. Rauhe, *Dichtung und Musik im weltlichen Vokalwerk J.H. S.s* (diss., Univ. of Hamburg, 1959); W. Reckziegel, *Das Cantional von J.H. S.: Seine geschichtlichen Grundlagen* (Berlin, 1963); F. Peterson, *J.H. S.'s Cymbalum Sionium: A Liturgico-musical Study* (diss., Harvard Univ., 1966). **—NS/LK/DM**

Scheinpflug, Paul, German violinist, conductor, and composer; b. Loschwitz, near Dresden, Sept. 10, 1875; d. Memel, March 11, 1937. He studied violin with Rappoldi and composition with Draeseke at the Dresden Cons. In 1898 he went to Bremen as concertmaster of the Phil. and conductor of the Liederkranz, and then was conductor of the Königsberg Musikverein (1909–14). After conducting the Blüthner Orch. in Berlin (1914–19), Scheinpflug was music director in Duisburg (1920–28) and of the Dresden Phil. (1929–33).

WORKS: DRAMATIC: O p e r a : *Das Hofkonzert* (1922). **ORCH.:** *Frühlung* (1906); *Lustspiel-Ouvertüre* (1909); *Bundes-Ouverture* (1918); *Serenade* for Cello, English Horn or Viola, Harp, and Strings (1937); *Ein Sommertagebuch* (1937); *Nokturno* (1937). **CHAMBER:** Piano Quartet (1903); Violin Sonata (1908); String Quartet (1912); String Trio (1912). **V O - CAL :** Men's choruses; songs.**—NS/LK/DM**

Schelble, Johann Nepomuk, German singer, conductor, pedagogue, and composer; b. Hüfingen, May 16, 1789; d. there, Aug. 6, 1837. He studied with Weisse in Donaueschingen, Volger in Darmstadt, and Krebs in Stuttgart, where he then sang as a tenor and baritone at the court and opera (1808–14); also was a teacher at the Royal Musical Inst. (from 1812). From 1814 to 1816 he was in Vienna and became a close friend of Beethoven; settled in Frankfurt am Main, where he founded the Cäcilien-Verein (1818), and sang at the Frankfurt am Main theater (1817–19). His methods for teaching the musical rudiments and training the sense of absolute pitch were much admired; he enjoyed the esteem of many musicians of his time; Mendelssohn paid tribute to him in his correspondence. In addition to various didactic works, he also composed vocal and chamber music.

BIBL.: K. Lang, *Die Gehörsentwicklungs-Methode von S.* (Braunschweig, 1873); O. Bormann, *J.N. S. 1789–1837* (diss., Univ. of Frankfurt am Main, 1926).**—NS/LK/DM**

Schelle, Johann, significant German composer; b. Geising, Thuringia (baptized), Sept. 6, 1648; d. Leipzig, March 10, 1701. He received his early musical training from his father, a schoolmaster, and in 1655 was sent to Dresden to sing in the choir of the electoral chapel, which was directed by Schütz. In 1657 he went to Wolfenbüttel, where he sang in the choir of the ducal court. In 1665 he became a student at the Thomasschule in Leipzig under Knüpfer; subsequently studied at the Univ. of Leipzig, becoming cantor in Eilenburg in 1670. In 1677 he succeeded Knüpfer as cantor of the Thomaskirche in Leipzig; also served as director chori musici for the city, and acted as director of music for the Nicolaikirche. He taught music at the Thomasschule, being succeeded by his cousin, **Johann Kuhnau.** Schelle's importance as a composer rests upon his settings of the sacred Gospel cantata to German texts (in place of the traditional Latin texts) for Protestant liturgical use in Leipzig. He extended this practice to the chorale cantata as well. See A. Schering's ed. in the Denkmäler Deutscher Tonkunst, LVIII-LIX (1918).

BIBL.: F. Graupner, *Das Werk des Thomaskantors J. S.* (Berlin, 1929); R. Murray, *The German Church Music of J. S.* (diss., Univ. of Mich., 1971).**—NS/LK/DM**

Schelle, Michael, American composer, teacher, and writer on music; b. Philadelphia, Jan. 22, 1950. He studied theater at Villanova Univ. (B.A., 1971), then pursued musical training at Butler Univ. (B.M., 1974), at the Hartt School of Music of the Univ. of Hartford (M.M., 1976), with Copland (1976–77), and with Argento at the Univ. of Minn. (Ph.D., 1980). From 1979 he taught at Butler Univ., where he also was composer-in-residence from 1981. He received grants from the NEA, the Rockefeller Foundation, BMI, ASCAP et al., and in 1989 was named distinguished composer of the year by the Music Teachers National Assn. Many major American orchs. have commissioned and premiered his scores, including those of Indianapolis, Detroit, Buffalo, Cleveland, Seattle, Milwaukee, Cincinnati, Kansas City, Chicago, and Springfield. He was also a guest composer at Capital Univ. in Columbus, Ohio (1991), the Univ. of Southern Calif. in Los Angeles (1994), and Sam Houston State Univ. in Huntsville, Tex. (1995), among others. Schelle publ. *The Score: Interviews with Film Composers* (Los Angeles, 1999).

WORKS: DRAMATIC: *The Great Soap Opera*, chamber opera (1988; Indianapolis, June 9, 1989); *Aesop Rules!*, children's musical (1996). **ORCH.:** *Lancaster Variations* (1976); *El Medico* (1977); *Masque—A Story of Puppets, Poets, Kings, and Clowns*

(1979); *Pygmies I* for Youth Orch. and Tape (1982) and *II* for Youth Orch. and Speaker (1983); Oboe Concerto (1983; Indianapolis, Jan. 6, 1984); *Swashbuckler!* (1984); Concerto for 2 Pianos and Orch. (1987; Indianapolis, Jan. 14, 1988); *The Big Night* (1989); *Rapscallion* for Chamber Orch. (1990); *Blast!* (1992); *Spirits* (1993); *Centennimania I* for the 100th anniversary of the Cincinnati Sym. Orch. (1994); *Giant* (1994); *Mayday!* for Percussion and Orch. (1995); *Spider Baby* for Chamber Orch. (1996); *Ear Infection* for Orch. and 1,000 Kazoos in the Audience (1998); *Samurai (In Memoriam Akira Kurosawa)* (1998). S y m p h o n i c B a n d / l a r g e W i n d E n s e m b l e: *King Ubu* (1980); *Cliff Hanger March* (1984); *7 Steps from Hell* (1985); *Contraband* (1990); *Guttersnipe* (1994); *Centennimania II: When Hell Freezes Over* for the 100th anniversary of the Butler Univ. School of Music (Indianapolis, Oct. 6, 1995); *When Hell Freezes Over II*, double concerto for Bass Clarinet, Baritone Saxophone, and Symphonic Wind Ensemble or Concert Band (1995). **CHAMBER:** *Song without Words* for Piano Trio (1977); Chamber Concerto for Violin and 3 Players (1978); *Music for the Last Days of Strindberg* for 9 Players (1979); Double Quartet for 8 Winds (1980); *Cry Wolf!* for Piano, Cello, and 5 Percussionists (1981); *Rattlesnake!* for Percussionist and Auxiliary Percussionists (1983); *Blue Plate Special* for Tuba and Auxiliary Percussion (1983); *Music for the Alabama Kid* for 8 Players (1984); *Play Us Chastity on Your Violin*, chamber concerto for Violin and 13 Players (1984); *Howl!* for Clarinet and 4 Players (1986); *Daydream* for 6 Players or Actors (1988); *Musica Magnetizzare* for Piano and 4 Players (1988); *Racing with Rabbits!* for Percussionist (1988); *Buckeye Zombies* for 5 Players (1995); *Subwoofer* for Flute (1996); *Godzilla Brillante* for Chamber Ensemble (1997). P i a n o: 3 sonatas (n.d.; 1976; *Janus*, 1998); *Hammerstein* (1994). **VOCAL:** *The Wife Wrapt in Wether's Skin* for Men's Chorus (1974); *Cantus Matrimonium* for Chorus, Organ, and Instruments (1976); *Katzenmusik* for Baritone and 6 Players, after T.S. Eliot's *Old Possum's Book of Practical Cats* (1976); *Caroleluia* for Chorus (1978); *Swanwhite—Letters to Strindberg from Harriet Bosse*, song cycle for Soprano and Piano (1981); *Golden Bells* for Chorus and Orch. (1983; completion of an unfinished work by N. Dinerstein); *Dei Angelis* for Chorus and Organ (1987); *Kidspeace* for Voices and Orch. (1987); *Oboe Darkness* for Youth Chorus, Oboe, and Percussion (1987); *6 Seasonal Anthems* for Chorus and Organ (1987); *The Misadventures of Struwwelpeter*, song cycle for Tenor and Piano (1991).—**NS/LK/DM**

Schelling, Ernest (Henry), American conductor, composer, and pianist; b. Belvidere, N.J., July 26, 1876; d. N.Y., Dec. 8, 1939. He first appeared in public as a child prodigy, playing the piano at the age of 4 1/2 at the Academy of Music in Philadelphia. He was then sent to Paris in 1882, where he studied at the Cons. with Mathias until 1885; later received instruction from Moszkowski, Leschetizky, H. Huber, K. Barth, and finally Paderewski in Morges, Switzerland (1898–1902). Extended tours in Europe (from Russia to Spain) followed; he also toured in South America. Returning to the U.S. in 1905, he devoted most of his energies to conducting and composing. He conducted the N.Y. Phil. young people's concerts (1924–39); was conductor of the Baltimore Sym. Orch. (1936–38); also made frequent appearances as a conductor in Europe. He was elected a member of the National Inst. of Arts and Letters in 1913.

WORKS: ORCH.: Sym. (n.d.); *Légende symphonique* (1904; Philadelphia, Oct. 31, 1913); *Suite fantastique* for Piano and Orch. (1905; Amsterdam, Oct. 10, 1907); *Impressions from an Artist's Life*, symphonic variations for Piano and Orch. (1913; Boston, Dec. 31, 1915, composer soloist); Violin Concerto (Providence, R.I., Oct. 17, 1916, Fritz Kreisler soloist); *A Victory Ball*, symphonic poem after Noyes (Philadelphia, Feb. 23, 1923); *Morocco*, symphonic tableau (N.Y., Dec. 19, 1927, composer conducting). **CHAMBER:** Violin Sonata (n.d.); *Divertimenti* for Piano Quintet (1925); piano pieces.

BIBL.: T. Hill, *E. S. (1876–1939): His Life and Contributions to Music Education through Educational Concerts* (diss., Catholic Univ. of America, 1970).—**NS/LK/DM**

Schemelli, Georg Christian, German musician; b. Herzberg, c. 1676; d. Zeitz, March 5, 1762. He sang in the Dresden court Kapelle, then was at the Leipzig Thomasschule (1695–1700), Kantor in Treuenbrietzen (1707–17), and court Kantor in Zeitz (1727–58). He publ. a vol. of 954 hymns as *Musicalisches Gesangbuch* (Leipzig, 1736), to which J.S. Bach contributed (see C. Terry, *The Four-part Chorales of J.S. Bach*; London, 1929; second ed., 1964).—**NS/LK/DM**

Schenck, Andrew (Craig), American conductor; b. Honolulu, Jan. 7, 1941; d. Baltimore, Feb. 19, 1992. He was educated at Harvard Univ. (B.A., 1962) and Ind. Univ. (Mus.M., 1968), and then pursued training in conducting with Bernstein at the Berkshire Music Center in Tanglewood, Monteux in Hancock, Maine, and in Germany on a Fulbright scholarship (1962–63), subsequently winning first prize in the Besançon conducting competition. He was asst. conductor of the Honolulu Sym. Orch. (1970–73) and the Baltimore Sym. Orch. (1973–80), and then founder-music director of the Baltimore Chamber Opera (1980–84). After serving as a resident conductor of the San Antonio Sym. Orch. (1986–88), he was music director of the Nassau (N.Y.) Sym. Orch. and the Atlantic Sinfonietta of N.Y. Schenck made a special effort to program American music at his concerts, both with his own orchs. and as a guest conductor with the Pittsburgh Sym. Orch., the Chicago Sym. Orch., the London Sym. Orch. et al.—**NS/LK/DM**

Schenck, Johannes, esteemed Dutch-born German viola da gambist and composer; b. Amsterdam (baptized), June 3, 1660; d. c. 1712. He entered the service of the Elector Palatine Johann Wilhelm I of Düsseldorf about 1696, and was granted the post of Kammerdiener, and later was court chamber councillor (c. 1710–12). Among his instrumental works were *Uitgevondene tyd en konstoeffeningen* for Viola da Gamba and Basso Continuo, op.2 (c. 1668), *Il giardino armonico* for 2 Violins, Viola da Gamba, and Basso Continuo, op.3 (1691), *Scherzi musicali* for Viola da Gamba and Basso Continuo ad libitum, op.6 (n.d.; ed. by H. Leichtentritt, Leipzig, 1906), (18) *Suonate* for Violin and Violone or Harpsichord, op.7 (n.d.), and *L'echo du Danube*, 6 sonatas for Viola da Gamba, op.9 (c. 1705); also vocal works, including (27) *Eegine gesangen, uit de opera von Bacchus, Ceres en Venus* for Voice and Basso Continuo, op.1 (1687), *C. van Eekes koninklyke harpliederen* for 2 Voices, 2 Viola da Gambas, and Basso Continuo, op.4 (c. 1693), and (63) *Zangswyze uitbreiding over 't Hooglied van Salomen* for Voice and Basso Continuo, op.5 (1697).—**NS/LK/DM**

Schenk, Erich, eminent Austrian musicologist; b. Salzburg, May 5, 1902; d. Vienna, Oct. 11, 1974. He studied theory and piano at the Salzburg Mozarteum and musicology with Sandberger at the Univ. of Munich (Ph.D., 1925, with the diss. *Giuseppe Antonio Paganelli: Sein Leben und seine Werke*; publ. in Salzburg, 1928), and completed his Habilitation at the Univ. of Rostock in 1929 with his *Studien zur Triosonate in Deutschland nach Corelli,* where he subsequently founded its musicology dept. (1936). From 1940 until his retirement in 1971 he was a prof. of musicology at the Univ. of Vienna. He was particularly esteemed for his studies of Baroque and Classical music. In 1947 he revived the Denkmäler der Tonkunst in Österreich series, overseeing its progress until 1972. In 1955 he also took over the valuable *Studien zur Musikwissenschaft.* Festschrifts honored him on his 60th (Vienna, 1962) and 70th (Kassel, 1975) birthdays.

WRITINGS: *Johann Strauss* (Potsdam, 1940); *Musik in Kärnten* (Vienna, 1941); *Beethoven zwischen den Zeiten* (Bonn, 1944); *950 Jahre österreichische Musik* (Vienna, 1946); *Kleine wiener Musikgeschichte* (Vienna, 1946); *W.A. Mozart: Eine Biographie* (Vienna, 1955; Eng. tr., 1960, as *Mozart and His Time*; second Ger. ed., aug., 1975, as *Mozart: Sein Leben, seine Welt*); *Ausgewählte Aufsätze: Reden und Vorträge* (Vienna, 1967); ed. *Beethoven-Studien* (Vienna, 1970).—**NS/LK/DM**

Schenk, Johann Baptist, Austrian composer and teacher; b. Wiener-Neustadt, Nov. 30, 1753; d. Vienna, Dec. 29, 1836. He received elementary instruction in music as a small child, and then studied with the Baden choirmaster Anton Stoll; learned to play violin and keyboard instruments, and began composing in his youth. In 1773 he went to Vienna, where he took courses in counterpoint and composition with Wagenseil. In 1778 he established his reputation with the performance of a Mass, and in 1780 he began composing for the theater, winning notable success with his *Der Dorfbarbier.* In 1793 Beethoven took surreptitious lessons from him while studying formally with Haydn.

WORKS: DRAMATIC (all Singspiels and first perf. in Vienna unless otherwise given): *Der Schatzgräber,* opera (1780; not perf.); *Der Dorfbarbier,* comedy (June 18, 1785; as a Singspiel, Oct. 30, 1796); *Die Weinlese* (Oct. 12, 1785); *Die Weihnacht auf dem Lande* (Dec. 14, 1786); *Im Finstern ist nicht gut tappen* (Oct. 12, 1787); *Das unvermutete Seefest* (Dec. 9, 1789); *Das Singspiel ohne Titel,* operetta (Nov. 4, 1790); *Der Erntekranz* (July 9, 1791); *Achmet und Almanzine* (July 17, 1795); *Die Jagd* (May 7, 1799); *Der Fassbinder* (Dec. 17, 1802). **OTHER:** 5 cantatas; various sacred pieces; 10 syms.; several concertos; chamber music; choruses; songs.

BIBL.: F. Staub, *J. S. Eine Skizze seines Lebens* (Wiener-Neustadt, 1901); E. Rosenfeld (-Roemer), *J.B. S. als Opernkomponist* (diss., Univ. of Vienna, 1921); F. Rieger, *J. S.: Ein Altmeister des deutschen Singspiels* (St. Pölten, 1944).—**NS/LK/DM**

Schenk, Otto, Austrian opera producer and actor; b. Vienna, June 12, 1930. He studied at the Reinhardt Seminar and at the Univ. of Vienna. In 1952 he began his career as an actor, and in later years became particularly known for his portrayal of the jailer Frosch in *Die Fledermaus.* In 1957 he produced his first opera, *Die Zauberflöte,* at the Salzburg Landestheater. His productions of *Dantons Tod* and *Lulu* at the Vienna Festival in 1962 secured his reputation, and in 1963 he conquered audiences at the Salzburg Festival with *Die Zauberflöte.* In 1964 he oversaw a production of *Jenůfa* at the Vienna State Opera, where he was made resident producer in 1965. In 1968 he staged *Tosca* for his first production at the Metropolitan Opera in N.Y., and subsequently produced there *Fidelio* (1970), *Tannhäuser* (1977), *Les Contes d'Hoffmann* (1981), *Arabella* (1982), and the *Ring* cycle (1986–91). His other productions included *Le nozze di Figaro* at Milan's La Scala (1974) and *Un ballo in maschera* at London's Covent Garden (1975). His productions followed along traditional lines with a preference for naturalistic settings.—**NS/LK/DM**

Schenker, Heinrich, outstanding Austrian music theorist; b. Wisniowczyki, Galicia, June 19, 1868; d. Vienna, Jan. 13, 1935. He studied jurisprudence at the Univ. of Vienna (Dr.Jur., 1890), and concurrently took courses with Bruckner at the Vienna Cons. He composed some songs and piano pieces; Brahms liked them sufficiently to recommend Schenker to his publisher Simrock. For a while Schenker served as accompanist of the baritone Johannes Messchaert. He then returned to Vienna and devoted himself entirely to the development of his theoretical research. Schenker gathered around himself a group of enthusiastic disciples who accepted his novel theories, among them Otto Vrieslander, Hermann Roth, Hans Weisse, Anthony van Hoboken, Oswald Jonas, Felix Salzer, and John Petrie Dunn. He endeavored to derive the basic laws of musical composition from a thoroughgoing analysis of the standard masterworks. The result was the contention that each composition represents a horizontal integration, through various stages, of differential triadic units derived from the overtone series. By a dialectical manipulation of the thematic elements and linear progressions of a given work, Schenker succeeded in preparing a formidable system in which the melody is the "Urlinie" (basic line), the bass is "Grundbrechung" (broken ground), and the ultimate formation is the "Ursatz" (background). The result seems as self-consistent as the Ptolemaic planetary theory of epicycles. Arbitrary as the Schenker system is, it proved remarkably durable in academia; some theorists even attempted to apply it to modern works lacking in the triadic content essential to Schenker's theories.

WRITINGS: *Ein Beitrag zur Ornamentik als Einführung zu Ph.E. Bachs Klavierwerke* (Vienna, 1904; second ed., rev., 1908; Eng. tr. in *Music Forum,* IV, 1976); *Neue musikalische Theorien und Fantasien:* I. *Harmonierlehre* (Stuttgart, 1906; Eng. tr., ed. by O. Jonas, Chicago, 1954); II. *Kontrapunkt* in 2 vols., *Cantus Firmus und zweistimmiger Satz* (Vienna, 1910), and *Drei- und mehrstimmiger Satz, Übergänge zum freien Satz* (Vienna, 1922); Eng. tr. of both vols. by J. Thymn, N.Y., 1987; III. *Der freie Satz* (Vienna, 1935; new ed. by O. Jonas, 1956; Eng. tr. by E. Oster, 1979); *Beethovens Neunte Sinfonie* (Vienna, 1912; Eng. tr., ed. by J. Rothgeb, New Haven, 1992); *Der Tonwille* (a periodical, 1921–24); *Beethovens Fünfte Sinfonie* (Vienna, 1925); *Das Meisterwerk in der Musik* (3 vols., Vienna, 1925, 1926, 1930); *Fünf Urlinie-Tafeln* (Vienna, 1932; second ed., rev., 1969 as *Five Graphic Music Analyses by F. Salzer*); *Johannes Brahms: Oktaven und Quinten* (Vienna, 1933).

BIBL.: O. Jonas, *Das Wesen des musikalischen Künstwerks*

(Vienna, 1934; second ed., rev., 1973 as *Einführung in die Lehre H. S.s*; Eng. tr., 1982); A. Katz, *Challenge to Musical Tradition* (N.Y., 1945); F. Salzer, *Structural Hearing* (N.Y., 1952; second ed., 1962); F. Salzer and C. Schachter, *Counterpoint in Composition: The Study of Voice Leading* (N.Y., 1969): L. Laskowski, ed., *H. S.: An Annotated Index to His Analyses of Musical Works* (N.Y., 1978); A. Forte and S. Gilbert, *An Introduction to S.ian Analysis* (London, 1982); F.-E. von Cube, *The Book of the Musical Artwork: An Interpretation of the Musical Theories of H. S.* (Lewiston, N.Y., 1988); H. Siegel, ed., *S. Studies* (Cambridge, 1989); A. Cadwallader, ed., *Trends in S.ian Research* (N.Y., 1990); H. Federhofer, ed., *H. S. als Essayist und Kritiker: Gesammelte Aufsätze, Rezensionen und kleinere Berichte aus den Jahren 1891–1901* (Hildesheim, 1990); D. Neumeyer and S. Tepping, *A Guide to S.ian Analysis* (Englewood Cliffs, N.J., 1992); M. Eybl, *Ideologie und Methode: Zum ideengeschichtlichen Kontext von S.s Musiktheorie* (Tutzing, 1995); L. Balsius, *S.'s Argument and the Claims of Music Theory* (Cambridge, 1996); R. Snarrenberg, *S.'s Interpretive Practice* (N.Y., 1997); C. Schachter and H. Siegel, eds., *S. Studies 2* (Cambridge, 1999).—NS/LK/DM

Scherchen, Hermann, eminent German conductor, father of **Tona Scherchen;** b. Berlin, June 21, 1891; d. Florence, June 12, 1966. He was mainly self-taught in music. He learned to play the viola and joined the Blüthner Orch. in Berlin at age 16, then was a member of the Berlin Phil. (1907–10). He worked with Schoenberg (1910–12), and toured as a conductor (1911–12); became conductor of the Riga Sym. Orch. in 1914, but with the outbreak of World War I that same year, he was interned in Russia. After the Armistice, he returned to Berlin and founded the Neue Musikgesellschaft in 1918; also ed. the periodical *Melos* (1920–21). He was conductor of the Frankfurt am Main Museumgesellschaft concerts (1922–28) and Generalmusikdirektor in Königsberg (1928–33); also conducted at many contemporary-music festivals. With the advent of the Nazi regime in 1933, he settled in Switzerland, where he had conducted the concerts of the Winterthur Musikkollegium from 1922; continued in this capacity until 1947. He also conducted the Zürich Radio Orch. (from 1933), serving as its director (1944–50). He was ed. of the Brussels periodical *Musica Viva* (1933–36). Scherchen founded the Ars Viva Orch. (1939) and that same year an annual summer school for conductors. After World War II, he resumed his extensive European guest conducting engagements. On Oct. 30, 1964, he made his long-awaited U.S. debut, as a guest conductor with the Philadelphia Orch. He distinguished himself as a scholarly exponent of modern music; conducted many premieres of ultramodern works; publ. a valuable manual, *Lehrbuch des Dirigierens* (Leipzig, 1929; Eng. tr., 1933, as *Handbook of Conducting;* 6th ed., 1949); also publ. *Vom Wesen der Musik* (Zürich, 1946; Eng. tr., 1947, as *The Nature of Music*); *Musik für Jedermann* (Winterthur, 1950). J. Lucchesi ed. his *Werke und Briefe* (Berlin, 1991 et seq.).

BIBL.: M. Kreikle, *H. S. 1891–1966: Phonographie: Deutsche Rundfunkproduktionen, Industrietonträger, Eigenaufnahmen* (Frankfurt am Main, 1992).—NS/LK/DM

Scherchen, Tona, Swiss-born French composer, daughter of **Hermann Scherchen;** b. Neuchatel, March 12, 1938. She was taken to China at age 12 by her mother, the Chinese composer Hsia Shu-sien, who was her first mentor in theory, composition, and classical Chinese music (from 1952). She studied basic Western theory and the Chinese instrument P'i p'a at the conservatories in Shanghai and Peking (1957–60). Upon returning to Europe, she studied composition with Henze at the Salzburg Mozarteum (1961–63). She continued her training in Paris with Pierre Schaeffer at the Centre de Recherche Musicale (1963), and also received instruction in analysis from Messiaen at the Cons. (1963–64), where she won a premier prix; then had private lessons with Ligeti in Vienna (1966–67). In 1972 she settled in France and later became a naturalized French citizen. In 1991 she was awarded the Prix Italia. In addition to works for traditional instruments, she has produced electronic and multimedia scores. In all her works, her Eastern heritage has remained a powerful resource and inspiration.

WORKS: DRAMATIC: *Tzan-Shen,* ballet (1970–71; version of *Shen* for Percussion, 1968); *Éclats obscurs,* radiophonic piece, after St.-John Perse (1982). **Multimedia:** *Between* (1978–86); *Cancer, solstice '83* (1983–87); *Fuite?* (1987); *Le Jeu de Pogo,* radiophonique film piece (1989–91). **ORCH.:** *Tzang* for Chamber Orch. (1966); *Khouang* (1966–68); *Tao* for Viola and Orch. (1971); *Vague-T'ao* (1974–75); *"S..."* for Chamber Orch. (1975); *Oeil de chat* (1976–77); *L'Invitation au voyage* for Chamber Orch. (1977); *Lô* for Trombone and 12 Strings (1978–79); *L'Illégitime* for Orch. and Tape (1985–86). **CHAMBER:** *In, Sin,* 2 pieces for Flute (1965); *Hsun* for 6 Instruments (1968); *Shen* for 6 Percussionists or Percussion Orch. (1968; ballet version as *Tzan-Shen,* 1970–71); *Tzoue,* trio for Clarinet or Flute, Cello or Double Bass, and Harpsichord (1970; also as a multimedia piece, 1980); *Yun-Yu* for Violin or Viola and Vibraphone (1972); *Bien* for 12 Instruments (1972–73); *Tjao-Houen* for 9 Instruments (1973); *Ziguidor* for Wind Quintet (1977); *Tzing* for Brass Quintet (1979); *Tarots* for Harpsichord and 7 Instruments (1981–82); *Lustucru* for Variable Ensemble (1983). **VOCAL:** *Wai* for Mezzo-soprano and String Quartet (1966–67); *Tzi* for 16-voice Chorus (1969–70); *La Larme de crocodile* for Voice (1977).
—NS/LK/DM

Schering, Arnold, eminent German music historian; b. Breslau, April 2, 1877; d. Berlin, March 7, 1941. His father was a merchant. The family moved to Dresden, where Schering began to take violin lessons with Blumner. In 1896 he went to Berlin, where he studied violin with Joachim, hoping to start a concert career; he organized a tour with the pianist Hinze-Reinhold, but soon gave up virtuoso aspirations, and in 1898 entered classes in musicology with Fleischer and Stumpf at the Univ. of Berlin; then took courses with Sandberger at the Univ. of Munich and with Kretzschmar at the Univ. of Leipzig, obtaining his Ph.D. in 1902 with the diss. *Geschichte des Instrumental- (Violin-) Konzerts bis A. Vivaldi* (publ. in Leipzig, 1905; second ed., 1927); subsequently completed his Habilitation there in 1907 with his *Die Anfänge des Oratoriums* (publ. in an aug. ed. as *Geschichte des Oratoriums,* Leipzig, 1911). He devoted himself to teaching and musical journalism; from 1904 to 1939 he was ed. of the *Bach-Jahrbuch.* From 1909 to 1923 he taught at the Leipzig Cons.; from 1915 to 1920 he was prof. of the history and aesthetics of music at the Univ. of Leipzig; then was prof. of music at the Univ. of

Halle (1920–28); subsequently was prof. of musicology at the Univ. of Berlin (1928–41). In 1928 he became president of the Deutsche Gesellschaft für Musikwissenschaft. In his voluminous publications, he strove to erect an infallible system of aesthetic principles derived from musical symbolism and based on psychological intuition, ignoring any contradictions that ensued from his axiomatic constructions. In his book *Beethoven in neuer Deutung*, publ. in 1934 at the early dawn of the Nazi era, he even attempted to interpret Beethoven's music in terms of racial German superiority, alienating many of his admirers. But in his irrepressible desire to establish an immutable sequence of historic necessity, he compiled an original and highly informative historical tabulation of musical chronology, *Tabellen zur Musikgeschichte*, which was publ. in 1914 and went through several eds.

WRITINGS: *Musikalische Bildung und Erziehung zum musikalischen Hören* (Leipzig, 1911; fourth ed., 1924); *Tabellen zur Musikgeschichte* (Leipzig, 1914; fourth ed., 1934; fifth ed., 1962, by H.J. Moser); *Aufführungspraxis alter Musik* (Berlin, 1931); *Geschichte der Musik in Beispielen* (Leipzig, 1931; second ed., 1954; Eng. tr., 1950); *Beethoven in neuer Deutung* (Berlin, 1934); *Beethoven und die Dichtung* (Berlin, 1936); *Johann Sebastian Bachs Leipziger Kirchenmusik* (Leipzig, 1936; second ed., 1954); *Von grossen Meistern der Musik* (Leipzig, 1940); *Das Symbol in der Musik* (ed. by W. Gurlitt; Berlin, 1941); *Über Kantaten J.S. Bachs* (ed. by F. Blume; Berlin, 1942; second ed., 1950); *Vom musikalischen Künstwerk* (ed. by F. Blume; Berlin, 1949; second ed., 1951); *Humor, Heldentum, Tragik bei Beethoven* (Strasbourg, 1955).

BIBL.: H. Osthoff, ed., *Festschrift A. S. zum 60. Geburtstag* (Berlin, 1937).—NS/LK/DM

Scherman, Thomas (Kielty), American conductor; b. N.Y., Feb. 12, 1917; d. there, May 14, 1979. He was a son of Harry Scherman, founder and president of the Book-of-the-Month Club. He attended Columbia Univ. (B.A., 1937), and then studied piano with Vengerova, theory with Weisse, and conducting with Bamberger, Rudolf, and Klemperer, whose assistant he became in conducting a chamber orch. composed of European refugees at the New School for Social Research in N.Y. (1939–41). He subsequently served in the U.S. Army (1941–45), reaching the rank of captain in the Signal Corps. In 1947 he became asst. conductor of the National Opera in Mexico City; that same year, he organized in N.Y. the Little Orch. Society for the purposes of presenting new works, some of them specially commissioned, and of reviving forgotten music of the past; he also gave performances of operas in concert versions. He terminated the seasons of the Little Orch. Soc. in 1975, but organized the New Little Orch. Soc. to present children's concerts, which he led until his death.
—NS/LK/DM

Schermerhorn, Kenneth (de Witt), American conductor; b. Schenectady, N.Y., Nov. 20, 1929. He studied conducting with Richard Burgin at the New England Cons. of Music in Boston (graduated, 1950), and also took courses at the Berkshire Music Center at Tanglewood, where he won the Koussevitzky Prize. His first important engagement was as conductor of the American Ballet Theater in N.Y. (1957–67); also was asst.

conductor of the N.Y. Phil. (1960–61). He was music director of the N.J. Sym. Orch. in Newark (1963–68) and the Milwaukee Sym. Orch. (1968–80); then was general music director of the American Ballet Theater in N.Y. (from 1982) and also music director of the Nashville (Tenn.) Sym. Orch. (from 1983) and the Hong Kong Phil. (1984–88). In 1975 he married **Carol Neblett**.
—NS/LK/DM

Schetky, Johann Georg Christoph, German cellist and composer; b. Darmstadt, Aug. 19, 1737; d. Edinburgh, Nov. 29, 1824. The original family name was Von Teschky, and Schetky's ancestors were from Transylvania. His father was a court official and musician in Hessen-Darmstadt. He became principal cellist in the Darmstadt court orch. in 1758, receiving instruction in composition from the court Vice-Kapellmeister Endler and in cello from Anton Filtz of Mannheim. After a sojourn in Hamburg (1768–69), he went to London in 1772, then settled in Edinburgh, where he was principal cellist of its Musical Society. He married Maria Anna Teresa Reinagle, sister of Alexander Reinagle. He played a prominent role in Edinburgh musical life, winning distinction as a composer for his chamber music, which included 6 string quartets, 6 string trios, 6 duos for Violin and Cello, 6 sonatas for Cello and Bass, harpsichord sonatas, and songs. He also composed syms., cello concertos, and vocal pieces. His son J(ohn) George Schetky (b. Edinburgh, June 1, 1776; d. Philadelphia, Dec. 11, 1831) was the second of 11 children; he emigrated to America in 1787; was naturalized in Philadelphia on Nov. 19, 1806. He appeared as a cellist in Philadelphia, and in c. 1800 entered into partnership with Benjamin Carr in the music publ. business; was a co-founder of the Musical Fund Society in Philadelphia. His arrangement for military band of Koczwara's Battle of Prague was much played.

BIBL.: L. Schetky, *The S. Family; A Compilation of Letters, Memoirs and Historical Data* (Portland, Ore., 1942).—NS/LK/DM

Schibler, Armin, Swiss composer; b. Breuzlingen, Nov. 20, 1920; d. Zürich, Sept. 7, 1986. He went to Zürich and studied with Frey and Müller, and then with Burkhard (1942–45). After further training in England (1946), he attended the summer courses in new music in Darmstadt (1949–53) and profited from studies with Fortner, Krenek, Leibowitz, and Adorno. He taught music at the Zürich Real- und Literargymnasium from 1944. His music represented an eclectic synthesis of various 20th-century compositional techniques.

WORKS: DRAMATIC: *Der spanische Rosenstock*, opera (1947–50; Bern, April 9, 1950); *Der Teufel im Winterpalais*, opera (1950–53); *Das Bergwerk von Falun*, opera (1953); *Die späte Sühne*, chamber opera (1953–54); *Die Füsse im Feuer*, opera (Zürich, April 25, 1955); *Blackwood & Co.*, musical burlesque (1955–58; Zürich, June 3, 1962); *La Folie de Tristan*, music theater (1980); *Antonie und die Trompete*, chamber musical (1981); *Amadeus und der graue Bote*, chamber opera (1982–85); *Königinnen von Frankreich*, musical chamber-comedy (1982–85); *Schlafwagen Pegasus*, chamber opera (1982–85); *Sansibar oder Die Rettung*, music theater (1984–86). **Ballet:** *Der Raub des Feuers* (1954); *Die Gefangene*, chamber ballet (1957); *Ein Lebenslauf*, chamber ballet (1958); *Selene und Endymion* (1959–60); *Die Legende von der drei*

Liebespfändern (1975–76); *La Naissance d'Eros* (1985). **R a d i o P i e c e s :** *Das kleine Mädchen mit den Schwefelhölzchen*, melodrama (1955; rev. 1965); *Orpheus: Die Unwiederbringlichkeit des Verlorenen* (1967–68); *The Point of Return* (1971–72); *...später als du denkst* (1973); *...der da geht...* (1974); *Epitaph auf einen Mächtigen* (1974–75). **O R C H .:** Concertino for Piano and Chamber Orch. (1943); *Fantasy* for Viola and Small Orch. (1945); *Fantasy* for Oboe, Harp, and Small Orch. (1946); 4 syms.: No. 1 (1946), No. 2 (1952–53), No. 3 (Winterthur, Nov. 13, 1957), and No. 4, *Sechs Orchesterstücke* (1968); *Symphonic Variations* (1950); *Concertante fantasie* for Cello and Orch. (1951); Horn Concerto (1956); Trombone Concerto (1957); *Concerto breve* for Cello and Strings (1958–59); Violin Concerto (1959–60); 2 percussion concertos (1959–60; 1962–63); Trumpet Concerto (1960–61); *Metamorphoses ebrietatis* (1962–63); Piano Concerto (1962–68); Bassoon Concerto (1966–67); *Concerto 77* for Orch., Big Band, Jazz-Rock Group, and Tape (1976–77); *Konzertante Fantasie*, alto saxophone concerto (1978); *Dialogues concertants*, harp concerto (1985). **C H A M B E R :** Sonata for Solo Flute (1944); 5 string quartets (1945; 1951; 1958; 1961–62; 1975); *Konzertantes Duo* for Violin and Piano (1949–51); *Kaleidoskop* for Wind Quintet (1954); *Ballade* for Viola and Piano (1957); *Epitaph, Furioso und Epilog* for Flute, Violin, Viola, and Cello (1958); *Recitativi e Danze* for 2 Violins, Viola, and 2 Cellos (1962–64); *Fantaisie concertante* for Harp (1964); *Pantomimes solitaires* for Violin and Piano (1964); *Anspielungen* for Clarinet and Piano (1972); *Quatuor sonore pour un quatuor de corps*, saxophone quartet (1980); piano pieces; organ music. **V O C A L :** 5 oratorios: *Media in vita* for 4 Soloists, Mixed Chorus, Men's Chorus, and Orch. (1958–59), *Der Tod Enkidus* for Choruses and Orch. (1970–72), *Der Tod des Einsiedlers* for Soloists, Chorus, and Chamber Ensemble (1975), *Messe für die gegenwärtige Zeit* for 2 Soloists, Youth Chorus, 2 Pianos, and Jazz-rock Group (1979–80), and *De Misterio* for Speaking Voice, Man's Voice, and Orch. (1982); *Huttens letzte Tage* for Voice and Orch. (1966–67); *Iter Montanum* for Voice, Piano, and String Orch. (1983–84). **BIBL.:** K. Wörner, *A. S.: Werk und Persönlichkeit* (Amriswil, 1953); H.-R. Metzger, *A. S., 1920–1986* (2 vols., Zürich, 1990–91). **—NS/LK/DM**

Schicht, Johann Gottfried, German keyboard player, conductor, and composer; b. Reichenau, Saxony, Sept. 29, 1753; d. Leipzig, Feb. 16, 1823. In 1776, already well trained as an organist and pianist, he matriculated at the Univ. of Leipzig as a law student; he concurrently played in Hiller's "Grosses Concert." Giving up the law, he played in Hiller's Musikubende Gesellschaft. In 1781 he became a violinist in the Gewandhaus concerts, succeeding Hiller as their conductor in 1785. He was founder-conductor of the Singakademie (1802–07), then music director of the Univ. (from 1808) and Kantor of the Thomasschule (from 1810). He publ. *Grundregeln der Harmonie nach dem Verwechslungssystem* (Leipzig, 1812).

WORKS: VOCAL: O r a t o r i o s : *Die Feier der Christen auf Golgotha; Moses auf Sinai; Das Ende des Gerechten.* **O t h e r :** Masses; motets; Te Deums; the 100th Psalm; several chorale-motets (*Nach einer Prüfung kurzer Tage, Jesus meine Zuversicht, Herzlich lieb hab' ich dich, o Herr*, etc.); 9 settings of Leo's *Miserere a 4–8*; an excellent book of chorales (1819; of 1,285 melodies, 306 are original). **P i a n o :** Concerto; sonatas; caprices; etc.**—NS/LK/DM**

Schick, George, Czech-American conductor; b. Prague, April 5, 1908; d. N.Y., March 7, 1985. He studied at the Prague Cons. He was asst. conductor at the Prague National Theater from 1927 until 1938. He settled in the U.S. in 1939. He was conductor of the San Carlo Opera (1943), from 1948 to 1950 of the Little Sym. of Montreal, and from 1950 to 1956 assoc. conductor of the Chicago Sym. Orch. He was a conductor at the Metropolitan Opera in N.Y. (1958–69), and then served as president of the Manhattan School of Music in N.Y. (1969–76).**—NS/LK/DM**

Schick, Margarete (Luise née Hamel), noted German soprano; b. Mainz, April 26, 1773; d. Berlin, April 29, 1809. Her father was the bassoonist J.N. Hamel. After keyboard and vocal training, the elector of Mainz ennabled her to continue her vocal studies with Domonicus Steffani in Würzburg; returning to Mainz, she sang at the electoral court while pursuing further studies with Righini; made her stage debut there in 1791. She settled in Berlin in 1793 as a court chamber and theater singer; also sang at the National Theater (from 1794). She especially excelled in operas by Gluck and Mozart; her most celebrated role was Gluck's Iphigenia, but she also was admired for Mozart's Susanna and Zerlina. Her contemporaries regarded her as the equal of the famous Mara. In 1791 she married the violinist Ernst Schick.

BIBL.: K. von Levezow, *Leben und Kunst der Frau M.L. S., geboren Hamel* (Berlin, 1809).**—NS/LK/DM**

Schickele, Peter, American composer and musical humorist; b. Ames, Iowa, July 17, 1935. He was educated at Swarthmore Coll. (B.A., 1957) and studied composition with Harris in Pittsburgh (1954), Milhaud at the Aspen (Colo.) School of Music (1959), and Persichetti and Bergsma at the Juilliard School of Music in N.Y. (M.S., 1960). After serving as composer-in-residence to the Los Angeles public schools (1960–61), he taught at Swarthmore Coll. (1961–62) and at the Juilliard School of Music (from 1962). He rocketed to fame at N.Y.'s Town Hall on April 24, 1965, in the rollicking role of the roly-poly character P.D.Q. Bach, the mythical composer of such outrageous travesties as *The Civilian Barber, Gross Concerto for Divers Flutes* (featuring a Nose Flute and a Wiener Whistle to be eaten during the perf.), *Concerto for Piano vs. Orchestra, Iphigenia in Brooklyn, The Seasonings, Pervertimento for Bagpipes, Bicycles & Balloons, No-No Nonette, Schleptet, Fuga Meshuga, Missa Hilarious, Sanka Cantata, Fantasie-Shtick*, and the opera *The Abduction of Figaro* (Minneapolis, April 24, 1984). He publ. *The Definitive Biography of P.D.Q. Bach (1807–1742?)* (N.Y., 1976). In 1967 he organized a chamber-rock-jazz trio known as Open Window, which frequently presented his serious compositions; among these are several orch. works, vocal pieces, film and television scores, and chamber music. In later years, he was host of his own radio program, "Schickele Mix."**—NS/LK/DM**

Schidlowsky, León, Chilean composer and teacher; b. Santiago, July 21, 1931. He studied in Santiago at the National Cons. (1940–47), and also took courses in philosophy and psychology at the Univ. of Chile (1948–52), and had private lessons in composition with Focke and in harmony with Allende-Blin. He then went to Germany for further studies (1952–55). Returning to Chile, he organized the avant-garde group Agrupación Tonus for the propagation of new techniques of composition. He taught at the Santiago Music Inst. (1955–63) and served as prof. of composition at the Univ. of Chile (1962–68), then held a Guggenheim fellowship (1968). In 1969 he emigrated to Israel, where he was appointed to the faculty of the Rubin Academy of Music. In his music, he adopts a serial technique, extending it into fields of rhythms and intensities; beginning in 1964, he superadded aleatory elements, using graphic notation.

WORKS: DRAMATIC: O p e r a : *Die Menschen* (1970). **ORCH.:** *Tríptico* (1959); *Eróstrato* for Percussion Orch. (1963); *Nueva York*, dedicated to "my brothers in Harlem" (Washington, D.C., May 9, 1965); *Kadish* for Cello and Orch. (1967); *Epitaph for Hermann Scherchen* (1967); *Babi Yar* for Strings, Piano, and Percussion (1970); *Serenata* for Chamber Orch. (1970); *Arcanas* (1971); *Constellation II* for Strings (1971); *Prelude to a Drama* (1976); *Images* for Strings (1976); *Lux in Tenebris* (1977); *Tel Aviv* (1978–83); *Trilogy* (1986); *Ballade* for Violin and Orch. (1986); *Elegy* (1988); *Laudatio* (1988); *Kaleidoscope* (1989); *Prelude* (1990); *Polyphony IV* (1991); *Exhortatio* (1991); *I Will Lay Mind Hand Upon My Mouth* (1994); *Absalom* (1996); *Dark Night* for Strings (1997); *De Profundis* for Strings (1997); *Mahnmal* (Memorial; 1999). **CHAMBER:** *Elegía* for Clarinet and String Quartet (1952); Trio for Flute, Cello, and Piano (1955); *Cuarteto mixto* for Flute, Clarinet, Violin, and Cello (1956); Concerto for 6 Instruments (1957); *In memoriam* for Clarinet and Percussion (1957); *4 Miniatures* for Flute, Oboe, Clarinet, and Bassoon (1957); *Soliloquios* for 8 Instruments (1961); *Visiones* for 12 Strings (1967); String Quartet (1967); Wind Quintet (1968); *Eclosión* for 9 Instruments (1967); *6 Hexáforos* for 6 Percussionists (1968); Sextet (1970); *Kolot* for Harp (1971); *Meshulash* (Triangle) for Piano Trio (1971); *Voices* for Harp (1972); *Invention* for Flute and Piano (1975); Piano Quartet (1988); String Quartet (1988); *Shadows II* for Chamber Ensemble (1990); *Trio-in Memoriam Luigi Nono* for Viola, Cello, and Double Bass (1990); *Sealed Room* for 12 Instruments (1991); *Threnos* for Flute, Viola, and Percussion (1996). **P i a n o :** *6 Miniatures*, after paintings by Klee (1952); *8 Structures* (1955); *5 Pieces* (1956); *Actus* (1972); *Trilogy* for 2 Pianos (1990); *Toccata* (1990). **VOCAL:** *Requiem* for Soprano and Chamber Orch. (1954); *Caupolicán*, epic narrative for Narrator, Chorus, 2 Pianos, Celesta, and Percussion Orch. (1958); *Oda a la tierra* for 2 Narrators and Orch. (1958–60); *La Noche de Cristal*, sym. for Tenor, Men's Chorus, and Orch., commemorating the martyrdom of Jews on the Nazi "crystal night" (1961); *Invocación* for Soprano, Narrator, Percussion, and String Orch. (1964); *Amereida* (consisting of *Memento, Llaqui*, and *Ecce Homo*) for Narrator and Orch. (1965–72); *Jeremias* for 8 Mixed Voices and String Orch. (1966); *Rabbi Akiba*, scenic fantasy for Narrator, 3 Soloists, Children's and Mixed Choruses, and Orch. (1972); *Hommage à Neruda* for Chorus and Orch. (1975); *Adieu* for Mezzo-soprano and Chamber Orch. (1982); *Amerindia*, a pentology: *I: Prologue* for Orch. (1982), *II: Los Heraldos Negros* for Narrator, Harp, Piano, Percussion, and String Orch. (1983), *III: Sacsahuaman* for Winds and Percussion (1983), *IV: Yo Vengo a Hablar* for Narrator and Orch. (1983), and *V: Era e Crepusculo de la Iguana* for Narrator and Orch. (1985); *Missa in nomine Bach* for Chorus and 8 Instruments (1984); *Laude* for Chorus and Orch. (1984); *Missa-dona nobis pacem* for Chorus (1987); *Chanson* for Voice and Tam-tam (1988); *Carrera* for Narrator and Orch. (1991); *Silvestre Revueltas*, oratorio for Narrator, 9 Voices, and

Chamber Orch. (1994); *Am Grab Kafka's* for Woman Singer Playing Crotales (1994); *Si muero* (If I Die) for Narrator, Flute, Harp, and Organ (1998); *The Sacrifice of Isaac* for Narrator, Tenor, Bass, Chorus, and Orch. (1999); *Der schwarze Gott* for Voice, Flute, and Percussion (1999).

BIBL.: W. Elias, *L. S.* (Tel Aviv, 1978).—NS/LK/DM

Schiedermair, Ludwig, eminent German musicologist; b. Regensburg, Dec. 7, 1876; d. Bensberg, near Cologne, April 30, 1957. He studied in Munich with Sandberger and Beer-Walbrunn, and received his Ph.D. at the Univ. of Erlangen in 1901 with the diss. *Die Künstlerische Bestrebungen am Hofe des Kurfürsten Ferdinand Maria von Bayern*; studied further with Riemann at the Univ. of Leipzig and with Kretzschmar at the Univ. of Berlin; completed his Habilitation in 1906 at the Univ. of Marburg with his *Simon Mayr: Beiträge zur Geschichte der Oper um die Wende des 18. und 19. Jahrhunderts* (publ. in Leipzig, 1907–10), where he then taught (1906–11); then went to the Univ. of Bonn (1911), where he was a reader (1915–20) and a prof. (1920–45). He was founder-director of the Beethoven Archives in Bonn; was made president of the Deutsche Gesellschaft für Musikwissenschaft (1937) and chairman of the music section of the Deutsche Akademie (1940). A Festschrift was publ. in honor of his 60th (Berlin, 1937) and 80th (Cologne, 1956) birthdays.

WRITINGS: *Gustav Mahler* (Leipzig, 1901); *Bayreuther Festspiele im Zeitalter des Absolutismus* (Leipzig, 1908); *Die Briefe Mozarts und seiner Familie* (5 vols., Munich, 1914; vol. 5 is an iconography); *W.A. Mozarts Handschrift* (Bückeburg, 1919; facsimiles); *Einführung in das Studium der Musikgeschichte* (Munich, 1918; new ed., Bonn, 1947); *Mozart* (Munich, 1922; second ed., Bonn, 1948); *Der junge Beethoven* (Leipzig, 1925; fourth ed., 1970); *Beethoven: Beiträge zum Leben und Schaffen* (Leipzig, 1930; third ed., 1943); *Die deutsche Oper* (Leipzig, 1930); *Die Gestaltung weltanschaulicher Ideen in der Vokalmusik Beethovens* (Leipzig, 1934); *Musik am Rheinstron* (Cologne, 1947); *Musikalische Begegnungen; Erlebnis und Erinnerung* (Cologne, 1948); *Deutsche Musik im Europäischen Raum* (Münster, 1954).—NS/LK/DM

Schiedermayer, Johann Baptist, German organist and composer; b. Pfaffenmünster, Bavaria, June 23, 1779; d. Linz, Jan. 6, 1840. He served as Linz Cathedral organist. He wrote *Theoretisch-praktische Chorallehre zum Gebrauch beim katholischen Kirchenritus* (1828). He composed the Singspiels *Wellmanns Eichenstämme* (Linz, 1815), *Das Glück ist kugelrund* (Linz, 1816), and *Die Rückkehr ins Vaterhaus* (Linz, 1816), as well as 16 masses and much other sacred music, syms., string trios, organ pieces, etc.—NS/LK/DM

Schiedmayer, the name of 2 well-known German firms of piano makers in Stuttgart: Schiedmayer & Söhne and Schiedmayer Pianofortefabrik. Balthasar Schiedmayer (1711–81) began manufacturing musical instruments in Erlangen c. 1740; at his death, his son Johann David Schiedmayer (1753–1805) assumed the management; he was succeeded by his 19-year-old son, Johann Lorenz Schiedmayer (1786–1860), with whom he had moved (c. 1800) from Erlangen to Nuremberg. Johann Lorenz ended the business at Nuremberg after 2 years, and went to Vienna for a brief time; in 1809 he was in Stuttgart, where he set up business in partnership with a young piano maker, Carl Dieudonné (d. 1825); from 1825, he carried on the business alone, until 1845, when his eldest sons, Adolf Schiedmayer (1819–90) and Hermann Schiedmayer (1820–61), entered the firm, which was then called J.L. Schiedmayer & Sohne. In 1853 Johann Lorenz Schiedmayer provided his 2 younger sons, Julius Schiedmayer (1822–78) and Paul Schiedmayer (1829–90), with their own separate factory, producing harmoniums. After their father's death, they turned to piano making, and their business became known as Schiedmayer Pianofortefabrik. Upon Paul Schiedmayer's death, his son, Max Julius Schiedmayer, became head of the firm.

BIBL.: A. Eisenmann, *S. und Söhne* (Stuttgart, 1909); *150 Jahre S. und Söhne* (Stuttgart, 1959).—NS/LK/DM

Schieferdecker, Johann Christian, German organist and composer; b. Teuchern, near Weissenfels, Nov. 10, 1679; d. Lübeck, April 5, 1732. He studied at the Thomasschule (1692–97) and Univ. (1697–1702) in Leipzig. In 1706 he became Buxtehude's deputy at Lübeck's St. Marienkirche. On Jan. 23, 1707, he succeeded Buxtehude as organist and parish clerk; as the successful applicant, he was required to marry Buxtehude's daughter, Anna Margareta (Sept. 5, 1707), a requirement declined by Mattheson and Handel. The Abendmusiken, which had achieved wide respect under Tunder and Buxtehude, were continued under his supervision until 1730. His works for these concerts are lost. He also wrote several operas, other church music, and organ pieces.—NS/LK/DM

Schierbeck, Poul (Julius Ouscher), distinguished Danish organist, pedagogue, and composer; b. Copenhagen, June 8, 1888; d. there, Feb. 9, 1949. He studied composition with Nielsen and Laub, and also received instruction from Paul Hellmuth, Henrik Knudsen, and Frank van der Stucken. He was organist at Copenhagen's Skovshoved Church (1916–49) and a teacher of composition and instrumentation at the Royal Danish Cons. of Music (1931–49). In 1947 he was made a member of the Royal Swedish Academy of Music in Stockholm.

WORKS: DRAMATIC: Opera: *Fête galante* (1923–30; Copenhagen, Sept. 1, 1931). **ORCH.:** Sym. (1916–21; Göteborg, Feb. 15, 1922, Nielsen conducting); *Natten* (The Night), symphonic scene for Piano and Orch. (1938); *Andante doloroso* for Strings (1942). **VOCAL:** Many cantatas; numerous choral works; songs, including the sets *Nakjaelen* (1921) and *Alverden gaar omkring* (The World Goes Round; 1938). **OTHER:** Chamber music; organ chorales.

BIBL.: O. Mathisen, *P. S.* (diss., Univ. of Copenhagen, 1972).—NS/LK/DM

Schiff, András, distinguished Hungarian-born Austrian pianist; b. Budapest, Dec. 21, 1953. He studied piano as a child with Elizabeth Vadasz in Budapest, where he made his debut at 9. He then entered the Franz Liszt Academy of Music at 14, continuing his studies with Kadosa, and also studied with George Malcolm in

London. After winning prizes at the TchaikovskyCompetition in Moscow in 1974 and at the Leeds Competition in 1975, he embarked upon aninternational career. He made his U.S. debut at N.Y.'s Carnegie Hall as soloist with thevisiting Franz Liszt Chamber Orch. of Budapest in 1978; then settled in the West (1979). He firstgained recognition for his insightful and intellectually stimulating interpretations of the music of Bach. He later acquired distinction as an interpreter of Mozart, Beethoven, Schubert, Schumann, and Chopin. On Oct. 19, 1989, he made his Carnegie Hall recital debut in N.Y. In 1993 he played a cycle of the complete piano sonatas of Schubert as part of the Schubertiade at N.Y.'s 92nd Street Y. In 1997 he was awarded the Leónie Sonning Music Prize of Denmark.—NS/LK/DM

Schiff, Heinrich, Austrian cellist and conductor; b. Gmunden, Nov. 18, 1951. He studied cello with Tobias Kühne in Vienna and André Navarra in Detmold. After winning prizes in competitions in Geneva, Vienna, and Warsaw, he appeared as a soloist with many leading European orchs. On Aug. 21, 1981, he made his U.S. debut as soloist in the Dvořák Concerto with the Cleveland Orch. at the Blossom Music Center under Sir Colin Davis's direction. While continuing to pursue his career as a cello virtuoso, he also took up conducting. From 1990 to 1996 he was artistic director of the Northern Sinfonia in Newcastle upon Tyne. In 1995 he became music director of the Winterthur Stadtorchester. He also appeared as a guest conductor with various European orchs. As a cello virtuoso, he maintains a repertoire ranging from Vivaldi to the contemporary era, including a concerto written for him by Henze. He also performs rarely heard scores, including 2 concertos by Vieuxtemps, which he discovered.—NS/LK/DM

Schifrin, Lalo (Boris), Argentine-American pianist, conductor, and composer; b. Buenos Aires, June 21, 1932. He studied music at home with his father, the concertmaster of the Teatro Colón orch.; subsequently studied harmony with Juan Carlos Paz; won a scholarship to the Paris Cons. in 1950, where he received guidance from Koechlin, and took courses with Messiaen. He became interested in jazz, and represented Argentina at the International Jazz Festival in Paris in 1955; returning to Buenos Aires, he formed his own jazz band, adopting the bebop style. In 1958 he went to N.Y., and later was pianist with Dizzy Gillespie's band (1960–62); composed for it several exotic pieces, such as *Manteca, Con Alma*, and *Tunisian Fantasy*, based on Gillespie's *Night in Tunisia*. In 1963 he wrote a ballet, *Jazz Faust*. In 1964 he went to Hollywood, where he rapidly found his métier as composer for the films and television; among his scores are *The Liquidator* (1966), *Cool Hand Luke* (1967), *The Fox* (1967), *The Amityville Horror* (1978), *The Sting II* (1983), and *Bad Medicine* (1985). He also experimented with applying the jazz idiom to religious texts, as, for instance, in his *Jazz Suite on Mass Texts* (1965). He achieved his greatest popular success with the theme-motto for the television series *Mission: Impossible* (1966–73), in 5/4 time, for which he received 2 Grammy awards. His adaptation of modern techniques into mass media placed him in the enviable position of being praised by professional musicians. His oratorio *The Rise and Fall of the Third Reich*, featuring realistic excerpts and incorporating an actual recording of Hitler's speech in electronic amplification, was brought out at the Hollywood Bowl on Aug. 3, 1967. His other works include a Suite for Trumpet and Brass Orch. (1961), *The Ritual of Sound* for 15 Instruments (1962), *Pulsations* for Electronic Keyboard, Jazz Band, and Orch. (Los Angeles, Jan. 21, 1971), *Madrigals for the Space Age*, in 10 parts, for Narrator and Chorus (Los Angeles, Jan. 15, 1976), *Capriccio* for Clarinet and Strings (Los Angeles, Nov. 5, 1981), Guitar Concerto (1984), *Songs of the Aztecs* for Soloist and Orch. (Teotihuacan, Mexico, Oct. 29, 1988), and 2 pianos concertos, including No. 2, *Concerto of the Americas* (Washington, D.C., June 11, 1992). He served as music director of the newly organized Paris Phil from 1988.—NS/LK/DM

Schikaneder, Emanuel (actually, **Johannes Joseph**), prominent Austrian actor, singer, dramatist, theater director, and composer; b. Straubing, Sept. 1, 1751; d. Vienna, Sept. 21, 1812. He studied at Regensburg's Jesuit Gymnasium, where he was a chorister at the cathedral. He became an actor with F.J. Moser's troupe about 1773, then its director (1778); met Mozart in Salzburg in 1780. In 1783 he became lessee of Vienna's Kärnthnertortheater until 1784; was a member of the National Theater (1785–86), then organized his own theater company. Following a sojourn as director of the Regensburg Court Theater (1787–89), he returned to Vienna to assume the directorship of the Freihaus-Theater; gave up his management duties in 1799, but remained the theater's artistic director until it closed in 1801. He persuaded Mozart to set his play *Die Zauberflöte* to music; with Schikaneder as Papageno, it was first performed on Sept. 30, 1791. In 1801 he opened the Theater an der Wien, but then sold it in 1806; after a period as director of the Brünn theater, he returned to Vienna. He suffered several financial setbacks over the years and died insane. He wrote roughly 100 plays and librettos.

BIBL.: E. von Komorzynski, *E. S.: Ein Beitrag zur Geschichte des deutschen Theaters* (Berlin, 1901; second ed., rev., 1951); idem, *Der Vater der Zauberflöte: E. S.s Leben* (Vienna, 1948; second ed., 1990).—NS/LK/DM

Schiler, Victor, Danish pianist and conductor; b. Copenhagen, April 7, 1899; d. there, Feb. 17, 1967. He studied with his mother, Augusta Schiler (1868–1946), then with Ignaz Friedman and Artur Schnabel. He made his debut in 1914; from 1919, toured in Europe; made his first American tour in 1948–49. He was also active as a conductor in Denmark.—NS/LK/DM

Schiller, (Johann Christian) Friedrich von, great German man of letters; b. Marbach, Nov. 10, 1759; d. Weimar, May 9, 1805. Many musicians have turned to his works for inspiration.

BIBL.: M. Berendt, *S. bis Wagner* (Berlin, 1901); J. Baltz, *Beethoven und S.* (Arnsberg, 1905); A. Kohut, *F. S. in seinen Beziehungen zur Musik* (Stuttgart, 1905); H. Knudsen, *S. und die Musik* (diss., Univ. of Greifswald, 1908); G. Adler, *S. und Schubert* (Vienna, 1910).—NS/LK/DM

Schiller, Madeline, gifted English pianist; b. London, 1845; d. N.Y., July 3, 1911. She studied piano in London with Benjamin Isaacs, Benedict, and Halle, and later with Moscheles in Leipzig, making her debut there with the Gewandhaus Orch. on Jan. 23, 1862, in Mendelssohn's first Piano Concerto. She became known for her extraordinary ability to learn a new work in a short time; she demonstrated this talent by learning a piano concerto by Raff in a week and repeating this feat with the fourth Piano Concerto of Saint-Saëns. She engaged in an active career as a concert pianist in Europe, Australia, and the U.S. In 1872 she married an American, Marcus Elmer Bennett, but was widowed in 1876. On Nov. 12, 1881, Schiller made history when she gave the world premiere of Tchaikovsky's second Piano Concerto with the N.Y. Phil., anticipating its first Moscow performance by 6 months. She continued to perform as a soloist and with orchs. until 1900, when an injury forced her to retire. She died of a cerebral hemorrhage during an intense heat wave in N.Y. —NS/LK/DM

Schilling, Gustav, German musical lexicographer; b. Schwiegershausen, near Hannover, Nov. 3, 1805; d. Crete, Nebr., March 1880. He studied theology and music in Göttingen and Halle, then was active as a writer on theology, music, and politics. When he was prosecuted for debt in 1857, he fled to the U.S. and later settled in Nebr. His most important work was the *Enzyklopädie der gesammten musikalischen Wissenschaften oder Universal-Lexikon der Tonkunst* (6 vols., 1835–38; second ed., 7 vols., 1840–42); also pub. *Versuch einer Philosophie des Schönen in der Musik* (1838), *Lehrbuch der allgemeinen Musikwissenschaft* (1840), *Geschichte der heutigen oder modernen Musik* (1841), *Die musikalische Europa* (1842), *Musikalische Dynamik; oder, Die Lehre vom Vortrage in der Musik* (1843), *Der Pianist* (1843), *Franz Liszt* (1844), *Sicher Schlüssel zur Klaviervirtuosität* (1844), *Die schöne Kunst der Töne* (1847), *Musikalische Didaktik* (1851), *Allgemeine Volksmusiklehre* (1852), and *Akustik oder die Lehre vom Klange* (second ed., 1856).—NS/LK/DM

Schillinger, Joseph (Moiseievich), Russian-born American music theorist and composer; b. Kharkov, Aug. 31, 1895; d. N.Y., March 23, 1943. He studied at the St. Petersburg Cons. with Tcherepnin, Wihtol, and others. He was active as a teacher, conductor, and administrator in Kharkov (1918–22), Moscow, and Leningrad (1922–28). In 1928 he emigrated to the U.S. and became a naturalized American citizen in 1936; settled in N.Y. as a teacher of music, mathematics, and art history as well as his own system of composition based on rigid mathematical principles; taught at the New School for Social Research, N.Y.U., and Columbia Univ. Teachers Coll.; also gave private lessons. Among his pupils were Tommy Dorsey, Vernon Duke, George Gershwin, Benny Goodman, Oscar Levant, and Glenn Miller. Schillinger publ. a short vol. of musical patterns, *Kaleidophone: New Resources of Melody and Harmony* (N.Y., 1940). L. Dowling and A. Shaw ed. and publ. his magnum opus, *The Schillinger System of Musical Composition* (2 vols., N.Y., 1941; fourth ed., 1946); this was followed by *The Mathematical Basis of the Arts* (N.Y.,

1948) and *Encyclopedia of Rhythm* (N.Y., 1966). Schillinger was also a composer. His works include *March of the Orient* for Orch. (Leningrad, May 12, 1926), *First Airphonic Suite* for Theremin and Orch. (Cleveland, Nov. 28, 1929; Leo Theremin soloist), *North-Russian Symphony* (1930), *The People and the Prophet*, ballet (1931), piano pieces, songs, etc.

BIBL.: F. Schillinger, *J. S.: A Memoir by His Wife* (N.Y., 1949); D. Augestine, *Four Theories of Music in the United States, 1900–1950: Cowell, Yasser, Partch, S.* (diss., Univ. of Tex., 1979). **—NS/LK/DM**

Schillings, Max von, German composer and conductor; b. Duren, April 19, 1868; d. Berlin, July 24, 1933. While attending the Gymnasium at Bonn, he studied violin with O. von Königslow, and piano and composition with K.J. Brambach. He then entered the Univ. of Munich, where he studied law, philosophy, literature, and art. He became associated with Richard Strauss, and under his influence decided to devote himself entirely to music. In 1892 he was engaged as asst. stage director at the Bayreuth Festival; in 1902 he became chorus master. He went to Stuttgart in 1908 as assistant to the Intendant at the Royal Opera, and then was its Generalmusikdirektor (1911–18); upon the inauguration of its new opera theater, he was ennobled as von Schillings; was Intendant of the Berlin State Opera (1919–25). He made several visits as a conductor to the U.S. In 1923 he married **Barbara Kemp.** As a composer, he trailed in the path of Wagner, barely avoiding direct imitation. J. Beck ed. *Max von Schillings: Gesamtverzeichnis seiner Werke* (Berlin, 1933).

WORKS: DRAMATIC: Opera: *Ingwelde* (Karlsruhe, Nov. 13, 1894); *Der Pfeifertag* (Schwerin, Nov. 26, 1899; rev. 1931); *Moloch* (Dresden, Dec. 8, 1906); *Mona Lisa* (Stuttgart, Sept. 26, 1915). **ORCH.:** 2 Phantasiestücke: *Dem Andenken seiner Mutter* (1883) and *Aus dem Jahre* (1890); 2 symphonische Phantarien: *Meergruss* and *Seemorgen* (1895); *Ein Zwiegespräch*, tone poem for Violin, Cello, and Orch. (1896); *Symphonischer Prolog zu Sophokles Ödipus* (1900); *Musik zu Aeschylos Orestie* (1901); *Musik zu Goethes Faust*, part 1 (1908; rev. and aug., 1915); Violin Concerto (1910); *Festlicher Marsch* for Military Band (1911); *Tanz der Blumen* for Small Orch. (1930). **CHAMBER:** String Quartet (1887; rev. 1906); Improvisation for Violin and Piano (1895); Piano Quintet (1917); piano pieces. **VOCAL:** Choral works and songs.

BIBL.: R. Louis, *M. S.* (Leipzig, 1909); A. Richard, *M. S.* (Munich, 1922); W. Raupp, *M. v.S.: Der Kampf eines deutschen Künstlers* (Hamburg, 1935); J. Geuenich and K. Strahn, eds., *Gedenkschrift M. v.S. zum 100. Geburtstag* (Düren, 1968); C. Detig, *Deutsche Kunst, deutsche Nation der Komponist M.v. S.s.* (Kassel, 1998).**—NS/LK/DM**

Schimon, Adolf, Austrian pianist, singing teacher, and composer; b. Vienna, Feb. 29, 1820; d. Leipzig, June 21, 1887. He studied with Berton, Halévy, and others at the Paris Cons. He studied the Italian method in Florence, bringing out his opera *Stradella* there in 1846. He was maestro al cembalo at Her Majesty's Theatre in London (1850–53), then at the Italian Opera in Paris (1854–59). In 1858 Flotow brought out Schimon's comic opera *List um List at Schwerin*. He taught singing at the Leipzig Cons. (1874–77) and in Munich (1877–86). His other works included Italian and French songs, German lieder, 2 string quartets, a Piano Trio, Violin Sonata, piano music, etc. He married **Anna Schimon-Regan** in 1872.**—NS/LK/DM**

Schimon-Regan, Anna, distinguished German soprano; b. Aich, near Karlsbad, Sept. 18, 1841; d. Munich, April 18, 1902. In 1859 she had her first singing lessons from Mme. Schubert in Karlsbad; the next year her aunt, **Caroline Unger,** took her to Florence and taught her until 1864. She was then engaged at the court opera in Hannover (1864–67); during the winter of 1867–68 she sang in Berlioz's concerts in St. Petersburg. She made her first visit to England in 1869, appearing in concerts with Unger; gave song recitals there every winter until 1875. In 1872 she married **Adolf Schimon** and settled in Munich.**—NS/LK/DM**

Schindelmeisser, Louis (actually, **Ludwig Alexander Balthasar**), German conductor and composer; b. Königsberg, Dec. 8, 1811; d. Darmstadt, March 30, 1864. He studied with Marx and Gährich in Berlin, then with his stepbrother, Heinrich Dorn, in Leipzig (1831), where he was befriended by Wagner. After conducting in Salzburg, Innsbruck, Graz, Berlin (1837), Pest (1838–47), Hamburg, Frankfurt am Main, and Wiesbaden, he was Hofkapellmeister in Darmstadt (from 1853).

WORKS: DRAMATIC: Opera: *Peter von Szapáry* (Budapest, Aug. 8, 1839); *Malwina* (Budapest, 1841); *Der Rächer*, after Corneille's *Le Cid* (Budapest, April 4, 1846); *Melusine* (Darmstadt, 1861). **Ballet:** *Diavolina*. **OTHER:** 2 orch. overtures: *Rule Britannia* and *Loreley*; numerous piano pieces; songs.**—NS/LK/DM**

Schindler, Anton Felix, Moravian violinist, conductor, and writer on music; b. Meedl, Moravia, June 13, 1795; d. Bockenheim, near Frankfurt am Main, Jan. 16, 1864. He studied violin with his father, then went to Vienna in 1813 to study law. In 1814 he met Beethoven, soon becoming his secretary, his social mediator, and, to some extent, his business manager; for some years he held the position of concertmaster of the orch. of the Josephstadttheater. Beethoven's stormy temper created inevitable difficulties; during one such outburst, Beethoven even accused his faithful helper of mishandling the financial receipts from the ticket sales for the premiere of the 9th Sym. However, Schindler had enough modesty and intelligence to disregard such personal misunderstandings, and continued to serve Beethoven. After Beethoven's death, Schindler obtained possession of valuable MSS, documents, papers, and about 400 of the biographically important conversation books, which recorded Beethoven's dialogues with friends and visitors. In a misguided attempt to protect Beethoven's reputation, Schindler apparently destroyed some of these materials, at least the parts that reflected Beethoven's pettiness and complaints. More reprehensible is the indication that some of Beethoven's conversation books, invaluable in their biographical content, were altered by Schindler, as appears from the painstaking handwriting analysis conducted on these books in 1977 by D. Beck and G. Herre. In 1846 Schindler sold most of his Beethoven collection to the Royal Library in Berlin. He served as music director in Münster (1831–35) and Aachen (1835–37). In 1848 he moved to Frankfurt am Main and supported himself mainly by teaching. In 1856 he settled in Bockenheim, where he remained until his death. No matter what criticism can be raised against Schindler as a man of limited endowments unable to grasp the dimension of Beethoven's genius, the fact remains that it was Schindler who became the prime source of information about Beethoven's life, a witness to the musical greatness that Beethoven embodied. His fundamental book, *Biographie von Ludwig van Beethoven*, was publ. in Münster in 1840; the second ed., containing the valuable supplement *Auszuge aus Beethovens Konversationsheften*, appeared in 1845; the English tr. of the original ed., made by Moscheles, was publ. in London in 1841. The third ed. of Schindler's biography appeared in 1860 and was tr. into Eng. by D. MacArdle under the title *Beethoven as I Knew Him* (London, 1966). Of interest are also Schindler's diaries (1841–43), which were ed. by M. Becker (Frankfurt am Main, 1939).

BIBL.: E. Hüffer, *A.F. S., Der Biograph Beethovens* (diss., Univ. of Münster, 1909).—**NS/LK/DM**

Schipa, Tito (actually, **Raffaele Attilio Amadeo**),
famous Italian tenor; b. Lecce, Jan. 2, 1888; d. N.Y., Dec. 16, 1965. He studied with A. Gerunda in Lecce and with E. Piccoli in Milan, and began his career as a composer of piano pieces and songs; then turned to singing, and in 1910 made his operatic debut at Vercelli in *La Traviata*. After numerous appearences in Europe, he was engaged by the Chicago Opera (1919–32). He made his first appearance with the Metropolitan Opera in N.Y. on Nov. 23, 1932, as Nemorino in *L'elisir d'amore*, and continued to sing with the Metropolitan until 1935, then again in 1941. Schipa made extensive tours of Europe and South America, as well as in the U.S. He retired from the operatic stage in 1954, but continued to give concerts until late in life. Among his greatest roles were Des Grieux in *Manon*, the Duke of Mantua, Don Ottavio, and Werther. He wrote an operetta, *La Principessa Liana* (1935), a Mass (1929), and several songs. He also wrote a book, *Si confessi* (Genoa, 1961). His autobiography appeared in 1993.—**NS/LK/DM**

Schipper, Emil (Zacharias),
Austrian bass-baritone; b. Vienna, Aug. 19, 1882; d. there, July 20, 1957. He studied in Vienna and with Guarino in Milan. He made his operatic debut at the German Theater in Prague in 1904 as Telramund; then sang in Linz (1911–12), at the Vienna Volksoper (1912–15), the Bavarian Court (later State) Opera (1916–22), and the Vienna State Opera (1922–28); also made guest appearances at Covent Garden in London (1924–28), in Chicago (1928–29), and in Salzburg (1930; 1935–36). His finest roles were in operas by Wagner and R. Strauss. He was married to **Maria Olczewska**.—**NS/LK/DM**

Schippers, Thomas,
greatly gifted American conductor; b. Kalamazoo, Mich., March 9, 1930; d. N.Y.,

Dec. 16, 1977. He played piano in public at the age of 6, and was a church organist at 14. He studied piano at the Curtis Inst. of Music in Philadelphia (1944–45) and privately with Olga Samaroff (1946–47); subsequently attended Yale Univ., where he took some composition lessons from Hindemith. In 1948 he won second prize in the contest for young conductors organized by the Philadelphia Orch. He then took a job as organist at the Greenwich Village Presbyterian Church in N.Y.; joined a group of young musicians in an enterprise called the Lemonade Opera Co., and conducted this group for several years. On March 15, 1950, he conducted the N.Y. premiere of Menotti's opera *The Consul*; also conducted the television premiere of his *Amahl and the Night Visitors* (N.Y., Dec. 24, 1951). On April 9, 1952, he made his first appearance at the N.Y.C. Opera conducting Menotti's *The Old Maid and the Thief*, remaining on its roster until 1954. On March 26, 1955, he led the N.Y. Phil. as guest conductor. On Dec. 23, 1955, he made his debut at the Metropolitan Opera in N.Y. conducting *Don Pasquale*; conducted there regularly in subsequent seasons. From 1958 to 1976 he was associated with Menotti at the Spoleto Festival of Two Worlds. Other engagements included appearances with the N.Y. Phil., which he accompanied in 1959 to the Soviet Union as an alternate conductor with Leonard Bernstein. In 1962 he conducted at La Scala the premiere of Manuel de Falla's cantata *Atlantida*. In 1964 he conducted at the Bayreuth Festival. He was a favorite conductor for new works at the Metropolitan Opera; conducted the first performance of Menotti's opera *The Last Savage* and the opening of the new home of the Metropolitan with Samuel Barber's *Antony and Cleopatra* (Sept. 16, 1966); he also conducted the first production at the Metropolitan of the original version of Mussorgsky's *Boris Godunov* (1974). In 1970 he was appointed music director of the Cincinnati Sym. Orch., one of the few American-born conductors to occupy a major sym. orch. post; was also a prof. at the Univ. of Cincinnati Coll.-Cons. of Music (from 1972). There was an element of tragedy in his life. Rich, handsome, and articulate, he became a victim of lung cancer, and was unable to open the scheduled season of the Cincinnati Sym. Orch. in the fall of 1977; in a grateful gesture the management gave him the title of conductor laureate; he bequeathed a sum of $5,000,000 to the orch. His wife died of cancer in 1973. When he conducted *La forza del destino* at the Metropolitan Opera on March 4, 1960, the baritone Leonard Warren collapsed and died on the stage.—**NS/LK/DM**

Schirmer,
family of German-American music publishers. The first of the family to be connected with music was **Johann Georg Schirmer**, who settled in Sondershausen. He was a cabinet and instrument maker. His son, **Ernst Ludwig Rudolf Schirmer** (b. Sondershausen, May 8, 1784), emigrated to N.Y. with his wife and children in 1840. His son **(Friedrich) Gustav (Emil) Schirmer** (b. Königsee, Thuringia, Sept. 19, 1829; d. Eisenach, Aug. 5, 1893) found employment in the music store of Scharfenberg & Luis, and later entered the employ of Kerksieg & Breusing, music dealers, becoming manager in 1854. In 1861 he took over the business with a partner, and acquired sole control in

1866, establishing the firm that was to become **G. Schirmer, Inc.** He was an enlightened and progressive publisher; entered into personal relations with noted European composers, and was among the original patrons of Wagner's Bayreuth Festival. He was an amateur pianist and had a real love for music. The diary of Tchaikovsky's visit to N.Y. in 1891 makes repeated mention of Schirmer and his family. Schirmer married an American, Mary Fairchild, by whom he had 5 daughters and 2 sons. The younger of these sons, **Gustave Schirmer** (b. N.Y., Feb. 18, 1864; d. Boston, July 15, 1907), organized in 1885 the Boston Music Co., which gained prominence especially through the publ. of Ethelbert Nevin's music. Shortly afterward, with his brother **Rudolph Edward Schirmer** (b. N.Y., July 22, 1859; d. Santa Barbara, Calif., Aug. 19, 1919), he became a partner in the firm founded by their father in N.Y., and after the latter's death in 1893, he managed the business jointly with his brother, retaining independent control of the Boston Music Co. Rudolph was educated in N.Y. public schools, and lived in Weimar with his mother, brother, and 4 sisters (1873–75). He studied violin and piano with Helene Stahl and came in contact with the Liszt circle; in 1876 he entered the Coll. of N.J. (later Princeton Univ.), and after graduation in 1880 studied law for 4 years at Columbia Coll., being admitted to the bar in 1884. In 1885 he took the place of his brother Gustave in his father's music publ. business. Later he was rejoined by Gustave, and upon their father's death in 1893, Rudolph became president of the firm, assuming sole control from 1907. In 1915 he founded the *Musical Quarterly*. **Gustave Schirmer, third** (b. Boston, Dec. 29, 1890; d. Palm Beach, Fla., May 28, 1965), son of Gustave Schirmer and grandson of the founder of G. Schirmer, Inc., inherited the Boston Music Co. from his father and acquired the Willis Music Co. of Cincinnati. He was president of G. Schirmer, Inc. from 1919 to 1921 and from 1944 to 1957. Rudolph E. Schirmer's son, also named **Rudolph Edward Schirmer** (b. Santa Barbara, Calif., June 8, 1919), was vice-president from 1949 to 1965 and chairman of the board from 1965 to 1979 of G. Schirmer, Inc.—NS/LK/DM

Schirmer, Ernest Charles, American music publisher; b. Mt. Vernon, N.Y., March 15, 1865; d. Waban, Mass., Feb. 15, 1958. After serving as business manager (1891–1902) and partner (1902–17) of the Boston Music Co., he founded the E.C. Schirmer Music Co. in 1921. It published the Concord Series, the Choral Repertory of the Harvard Univ. Glee Club, Radcliffe, Vassar, and Wellesley Coll. Choral Music, the Polyphonic and "A Cappella" Libraries, the St. Dunstan Edition of Sacred Music, and treatises on harmonic analysis, musical theory, and music appreciation. The firm enjoyed a world market for its publications, with agencies in London and Hamburg.—NS/LK/DM

Schirmer, G., Inc., American music publishing firm. It was an outgrowth of the business founded in N.Y. in 1848 by Kerksieg & Breusing, of which Gustav Schirmer became manager in 1854. With another employee, Bernard Beer, he took over the business in 1861, and the firm became known as "Beer & Schirmer." In

1866 he became the sole owner, establishing the house of "G. Schirmer, Music Publishers, Importers and Dealers." After his death in 1893, the firm was incorporated under the management of his sons, Rudolph Edward Schirmer and Gustave Schirmer. Rudolph Schirmer died in 1919, and was succeeded by his nephew Gustave Schirmer, third, who was president until 1921. W. Rodman Fay was president (1921–29). Carl Engel served as president from 1929 to 1944, with the exception of 1933, when Hermann Irion held the office. Gustave Schirmer, third, was again president from 1944 until 1957. In 1969 G. Schirmer, Inc. was acquired by Macmillan, Inc., and in 1973 Schirmer Books was founded as a division of Macmillan Publ. Co., Inc., taking over the publication of books on music for college, trade, and professional/reference markets, while G. Schirmer continued publication of musical works. In 1986 the latter was sold to Music Sales Corp. of N.Y. After several subsequent changes in ownership, Schirmer Books became an imprint of the Gale Group in 1999.

In 1892 the firm began publ. of the Library of Musical Classics, notable for careful editing and general typographical excellence; with its didactic Latin motto, "Musica laborum dulce lenimen," it became a familiar part of musical homes. In the same year was launched the Collection of Operas, a series of vocal scores with original text and Eng. tr.; another series, The Golden Treasury, was begun in 1905. Schirmer's Scholastic Series, containing pedagogical works, began publ. in 1917. Among other laudable initiatives was the American Folk-Song Series, offering authentic folk material. The firm entered the field of musical lexicography in 1900 when it publ. *Baker's Biographical Dictionary of Musicians*, ed. by Theodore Baker. A second ed. appeared in 1905. Alfred Remy was ed. of the third edition (1919). The fourth edition was ed. by Carl Engel (1940). Nicolas Slonimsky brought out a Supplement in 1949, and then ed. the 5th edition (1958) and the Supplements of 1965 and 1971; he subsequently ed. the 6th (1978), 7th (1984), and 8th (1992) editions. The exhaustively rev. and expanded 9th "Centennial" edition, was publ. in 2000. Theodore Baker also compiled and ed. *A Dictionary of Musical Terms* (G. Schirmer, N.Y., 1895; many reprints) and *Pronouncing Pocket-Manual of Musical Terms* (1905; more than a million copies sold). In 1915 the *Musical Quarterly* was founded under the editorship of O.G. Sonneck; its subsequent editors have been Carl Engel (1929–44), Gustave Reese (1944–45), Paul Henry Lang (1945–72), Christopher Hatch (1972–77), Joan Peyser (1977–84), Eric Salzman (1984–91), and Leon Botstein (from 1992). It has publ. articles by the foremost scholars of Europe and the U.S.; beginning in 1989, it was publ. by the Oxford Univ. Press. The music catalog of G. Schirmer, Inc. comprises tens of thousands of publs., ranging from solo songs to full orch. scores. Particularly meritorious is the endeavor of the publishers to promote American music; the firm has publ. works by Ernest Bloch, Charles Loeffler, Charles Griffes, Walter Piston, Roy Harris, William Schuman, Samuel Barber, Gian Carlo Menotti, Paul Creston, Leonard Bernstein, Elliott Carter, Henry Cowell, Norman Dello Joio, Morton Gould, Virgil Thomson, Milton Babbitt, Gunther

Schuller, and many others; it also took over some works of Charles Ives. Among European composers, the works of Arnold Schoenberg, Gustav Holst, and Benjamin Britten are included in the Schirmer catalogue, as well as a number of works by modern Russian composers.—NS/LK/DM

Schirmer, Ulf, German conductor; b. Eschenhausen, near Bremen, Jan. 8, 1959. He received training in composition from Ligeti and in conducting from Horst Stein and Dohnányi. After working as a répétiteur at the Mannheim National Theater (1980), he was named to that position at the Vienna State Opera (1981). He was assistant to Maazel (1982) and Stein (1983) at the Bayreuth Festival, and then conducted at the Vienna State Opera (1984–86), where he subsequently served as first conductor (1986–88). From 1988 to 1991 he was Generalmusikdirektor in Wiesbaden. He appeared as a guest conductor at the Salzburg Festival (1989), with the Vienna Phil. (1992), at Milan's La Scala (1993), and with the Berlin Phil. (1993), among others. From 1995 to 1999 he was chief conductor of the Danish National Radio Sym. Orch. in Copenhagen.—NS/LK/DM

Schirring, Nils, Danish musicologist; b. Copenhagen, April 8, 1910. He studied musicology with Abrahamsen and Larsen at the Univ. of Copenhagen (M.A., 1933), and concurrently took lessons in cello from L. Jensen. He completed his musicological training at the Univ. of Copenhagen (Ph.D., 1950, with the diss. *Det 16. og 17. århundredes verdslige danske visesang*; publ. in Copenhagen, 1950). He worked at the Copenhagen Music History Museum (1932–53); also wrote music criticism and served as ed. of *Dansk musiktidsskrift* (1943–45) and *Dansk årbog for musikforskning* (with S. Sorensen; from 1961). In 1950 he joined the faculty of the Univ. of Copenhagen, retiring in 1980.

WRITINGS (all publ. in Copenhagen): *Billeder fra 125 aars musikliv (1827–1952)* (1952); *Selma Nielsens Viser* (1956); *Allemande og fransk ouverture* (1957); *Musikkens vije* (1959; second ed., 1964); ed. with S. Kragh-Jacobsen, *August Bournonville: Lettres à la maison de son enfance* (1969–70); with N. Jensen, *Deutschdänische Begegnungen um 1800: Künst, Dichtung, Musik* (1974); *Musikkens Historie i Danmark* (1978).—NS/LK/DM

Schiske, Karl (Hubert Rudolf), distinguished Austrian composer and pedagogue; b. Raab, Feb. 12, 1916; d. Vienna, June 16, 1969. He studied at the New Vienna Cons. (1932–38) and received training in piano with Roderich Bass and Julius Varga, and in harmony and counterpoint with Ernst Kanitz. After taking diplomas in composition (1939) and piano (1940) at the Vienna Academy of Music, he pursued his academic training at the Univ. of Vienna (Ph.D., 1942, with the diss. *Zur Dissonanzanwendung in den Symphonien Anton Bruckners*). In 1952 he became a teacher of composition at the Vienna Academy of Music, and was granted the title of prof. in 1954. In 1966–67 he also was a visiting prof. at the Univ. of Calif. at Riverside. Among his honors were the music prize of the City of Vienna (1950), the Austrian State Prize (1952), and the Great Austrian State Prize (1967). Schiske was highly influential as a teacher. His compositional technique was curiously synthetic, and yet invariably logical, containing elements of early polyphony and contemporary serialism.

WORKS: ORCH.: *Vorspiel* (1937–38); Piano Concerto (1938–39); 2 concertos for Strings (1940–41; 1945); Trumpet Concerto (1939–40); 5 syms. (1941–42; 1947–48; 1950–51; 1955; 1965); *Tanzrondo* (1942); *Kammerkonzert* (1949); Violin Concerto (1952); *Synthese* (1958); *Divertimento* for Chamber Orch. (1963; also for 10 Instruments). CHAMBER: 2 string quartets (1936–37; 1945); Sextet for Clarinet, String Quartet, and Piano (1937); 3 suites for 2 Recorders (1941, 1945, 1949); Violin Sonata (1943–44); Quintet for Flute, Oboe, Clarinet, Horn, and Bassoon (1945); *Musik* for Clarinet, Trumpet, and Viola (1947–48); *Drei Stücke für Gloria* for Violin (1951); Sonatine for Violin, Cello, and Piano (1951–52); Trio Sonata for 3 Melody Instruments or Organ (1954); *Dialog* for Cello and Piano (1967). KEYBOARD: P i - a n o : *Kleine Suite* (1935); *Thema, 8 Variationen und Doppelfuge* (1935–36); Sonata (1936); *Rhapsodie* (1945); *Tanzsuite* (1945); Sonata for Piano, 4-Hands (1949); *Drei Stücke nach Volksweisen* (1951); *Étudensuite* (1951); Sonatine (1953). O r g a n : *Variationen über ein eigenes Thema* (1938); *Toccata* (1951–52); Choral-Partita (1957). VOCAL: *Reitjagd*, cantata for Baritone, Chorus, and Orch. (1938); *Vom Tode*, oratorio for Soprano, Alto, Tenor, Bass, Chorus, Orch., and Organ (1946); *Candada* for Soprano, Chorus, and Orch. (1956); *Missa: Cunctipotens genitor Deus* for Chorus and Organ ad libitum (1954); choruses; songs.—NS/LK/DM

Schitz, Aksel (Hauch), famous Danish tenor, baritone, and pedagogue; b. Roskilde, Sept. 1, 1906; d. Copenhagen, April 19, 1975. His father was an architect, and he urged Schitz to follow an academic career; accordingly, he enrolled at the Univ. of Copenhagen in language studies (M.A., 1929). He also studied singing, first at the Danish Royal Opera School in Copenhagen, and later with John Forsell in Stockholm. He made his concert debut in 1938; his operatic debut followed in 1939 as Ferrando in *Così fan tutte* at the Royal Danish Theater in Copenhagen, and he soon gained wide recognition as a Mozartian and as a lieder artist. In 1946 he made appearances in England; in 1948 he visited the U.S. His career was tragically halted when he developed a brain tumor in 1950, which led to an impairment of his speech; however, he regained his capacities as a singer and gave concerts as a baritone. From 1955 to 1958 he taught voice at the Univ. of Minn.; from 1958 to 1961, was a prof. of voice at the Royal Cons. of Music and the Univ. of Toronto; from 1961 to 1968, at the Univ. of Colo.; and from 1968, at the Royal Danish School of Educational Studies in Copenhagen. In 1977 a memorial fund was formed in the U.S. to preserve his memory by granting scholarships in art songs. He publ. *The Singer and His Art* (N.Y., 1969).

BIBL.: G. Schitz, *Kunst og Kamp: Gerd og A. S.* (Copenhagen, 1951).—NS/LK/DM

Schjelderup, Gerhard (Rosenkrone), Norwegian composer and writer on music; b. Christiansand, Nov. 17, 1859; d. Benediktbeuren, Bavaria, July 29, 1933. He went to Paris in 1878, and studied with Franchomme (cello) and Massenet and Savard (composition); in 1888 he settled in Germany. He wrote music influenced partly by Wagner, partly by Grieg.

WORKS: DRAMATIC: O p e r a : *Østenfor sol og vesten-for mane* (East of the Sun and West of the Moon; 1889–90); *Sampo Lappelill* (1890; not perf.); *Sonntagsmorgen* (1891–92; Munich, May 9, 1893); *Norwegische Hochzeit* (1894; Prague, March 17, 1900); *En hellig aften* (A Holy Evening; 1895; Christiania, 1915); *Et folk i nød* (A People in Need; n.d., not perf.); *Frühlingsnacht* (1906–07; Dresden, May 1, 1908; later perf. as *Vaarnat* [Spring Night] and *Stjernenaltter* [Starry Nights]); *Opal* (Dresden, 1915); *Die scharlachrote Blume* (n.d.; not perf.); *Sturmvögel* (Schwerin, Sept. 19, 1926). **B a l l e t :** *Wunderhorn* (Christiania, 1905). **O t h e r :** Incidental music. **ORCH.:** 2 syms. (1887, 1924); *In Baldurs Hain* (In Baldur's Grove) for Violin and Orch. (1904); 2 symphonic poems: *Eine Sommernacht auf dem Fjord* and *Brand*. **OTHER:** Choral works; chamber music; songs; etc.

WRITINGS: *Edvard Grieg og hans verker* (Copenhagen, 1903; second ed., 1908, with Niemann); *Richard Wagner: Hans liv og verker* (Copenhagen, 1907; second ed., 1923); with S. Sandvik, *Norges musikhistorie* (Christiania, 1921).—**NS/LK/DM**

Schlegel, Leander, Dutch pianist, teacher, and composer; b. Oegstgeest, near Leiden, Feb. 2, 1844; d. Overveen, near Haarlem, Oct. 20, 1913. He studied at the royal music school in The Hague, then went to Leipzig, where he was a student of Reinecke. After touring with Wilhelmj as his accompanist, he returned to the Netherlands, where he was director of the music school in Haarlem (1870–98); in 1898 he moved to Overveen, where he continued to teach. He was a composer of solid attainments; in his music he tried to emulate Brahms. He wrote a Sym., a Violin Concerto, a Piano Quartet, a String Quartet, a number of piano pieces in a Romantic mood, and many melodious songs. —**NS/LK/DM**

Schlesinger, Adolph Martin, German music publisher, father of **Maurice (Moritz) Adolphe Schlesinger;** b. Sulz, Silesia, Oct. 4, 1769; d. Berlin, Nov. 11, 1838. He was active as a book dealer in Berlin before 1795. He founded his own music publ. firm in 1810, which became Schlesinger'sche Buch- und Musikalien-handlung in 1821. He was one of Beethoven's German publishers. In 1831 his son, Heinrich Schlesinger (b. Berlin, 1810; d. there, Dec. 14, 1879), took charge of the firm; after his father's death, his mother shared control of the business (1838–44); thereafter he resumed sole charge. The firm publ. the influential journal *Echo* (1851–65). In 1864 the business was sold to R. Lienau (1838–1920), whose sons took it over after his death. The firm was further enlarged and enriched by the acquisition of several other music publ. firms, among them Haslinger of Vienna (1875), Krentzlin of Berlin (1919), Vernthal of Berlin (1925), and Köster of Berlin (1928). Schlesinger was the original publisher of *Der Freischütz* by Carl Maria von Weber, Beethoven's opp. 108–11, 132, 135, and also works by Mendelssohn, Chopin, Liszt, and Berlioz.—**NS/LK/DM**

Schlesinger, Maurice (Moritz) Adolphe (baptized **Mora Abraham**), German music publisher, son of **Adolph Martin Schlesinger;** b. Berlin, Oct. 3, 1797; d. Baden-Baden, Feb. 25, 1871. He moved to Paris in 1819, and was at first engaged in book selling. In

1821 he established a music publishing business, and launched the publication of the *Gazette musicale de Paris* (1834–35), which merged with the *Revue musicale* to become the *Revue et gazette musicale* (1835); the latter continued to appear until 1880. He became one of the most important Paris publishers, bringing out scores by Beethoven, Donizetti, Meyerbeer, Berlioz, Liszt, Chopin, and others. In 1846 he sold the catalogue to Brandus and Dufour; later it was acquired by Joubert.—**NS/LK/DM**

Schlesinger, Sebastian Benson, German composer; b. Hamburg, Sept. 24, 1837; d. Nice, Jan. 8, 1917. He went to the U.S. at the age of 13, and studied music in Boston, chiefly under Otto Dresel. He was for 17 years German consul in Boston, lived for a time in London, and during his last years was in Paris. Schlesinger was a gifted composer. He publ. about 120 songs, which received praise from Max Bruch and Robert Franz. He also wrote several piano pieces in a Romantic vein.—**NS/LK/DM**

Schlick, Arnolt, eminent blind German organist and composer; b. probably in Heidelberg, c. 1460; d. probably there, after 1521. He was made organist for life at the Palatine court in Heidelberg in 1509, and also traveled as an organist and a consultant on the organ. He publ. *Spiegel der Orgelmacher und Organisten* (Speyer, 1511; facsimile and Eng. tr. by E. Barber, Buren, 1978). He brought out *Tablaturen etlicher lobgesang und lidlein uff die orgeln un lauten* (Mainz, 1512; ed. by G. Harms, Hamburg, 1924; second ed., 1957).—**NS/LK/DM**

Schlick, Barbara, admired German soprano; b. Würzburg, July 21, 1943. She studied at the Würzburg Hochschule für Musik, with Lohmann in Wiesbaden, and with Wesselmann in Essen. In 1966 she joined Adolf Scherbaum's Baroque ensemble as a soloist, and began to sing widely in Europe. In 1972 she toured North America as soloist with Paul Kuentz and his chamber orch. In subsequent years, she appeared as a concert artist and established a strong reputation as an exponent of early music. From 1979 she also sang in Baroque and classical operas, appearing in Munich, Göttingen, Bern, St. Gallen, and Hamburg. She taught at the Würzburg Hochschule für Musik.—**NS/LK/DM**

Schloezer, Boris de, renowned Russian-French writer on music; b. Vitebsk, Dec. 20, 1881; d. Paris, Oct. 7, 1969. He studied music in Brussels and Paris, and returning to Russia, devoted himself to a profound study of philosophy, aesthetics, and theory. His sister, Tatiana Schloezer, was the second wife of Scriabin, and Schloezer became a close friend of Scriabin, who confided to him his theosophic and musical ideas. In 1920 he emigrated to France, where he continued his literary activities in the Russian emigre press and in French literary magazines. He publ. a monograph on Scriabin in Russian (vol. 1, Berlin, 1923; French tr., Paris, 1975; Eng. tr. by N. Slonimsky, Berkeley and Los Angeles, 1987; vol. II not completed); other books include *Igor Stravinsky* (Paris, 1929) and *Introduction à J.S. Bach* (Paris,

1947). He also wrote a philosophical fantasy, *Mon nom est personne* and *Rapport secret*, depicting a distant planet whose inhabitants achieved immortality and divinity through science.

BIBL.: *B. d.S.* (Paris, 1981).—NS/LK/DM

Schlosser, Max, distinguished German tenor; b. Amberg, Oct. 17, 1835; d. Utting am Ammersee, Sept. 2, 1916. He sang in Zürich, St. Gallen, and Augsburg, but then decided to become a baker. Still, he did not abandon hopes for a stage career. He met Bülow, who entrusted him with the role of David at the premiere of *Die Meistersinger von Nürnberg* in Munich in 1868; he remained a member of the Munich Court Opera until his retirement in 1904. He also sang at Bayreuth and made guest appearances with Neumann's traveling opera company. He was principally known for his fine performances of the Wagnerian repertoire.—NS/LK/DM

Schlusnus, Heinrich, eminent German baritone; b. Braubach am Rhein, Aug. 6, 1888; d. Frankfurt am Main, June 18, 1952. He studied voice in Frankfurt am Main and Berlin. He made his operatic debut as the Herald in *Lohengrin* at the Hamburg Opera on Jan. 1, 1914, and then was on its roster for the 1914–15 season. After singing in Nuremberg (1915–17), he was a leading member of the Berlin Royal (later State) Opera, remaining there until 1945; also appeared in Chicago (1927–28), Bayreuth (1933), and Paris (1937). He was renowned as a lieder artist.

BIBL.: E. von Naso and A. Schlusnus, *H. S.: Mensch und Sänger* (Hamburg, 1957).—NS/LK/DM

Schlüter, Erna, German contralto, later soprano; b. Oldenburg, Feb. 5, 1904; d. Hamburg, Dec. 1, 1969. She made her operatic debut as a contralto in Oldenburg in 1922. Turning to soprano roles, she sang in Mannheim (1925–30) and Düsseldorf (1930–40). From 1940 to 1956 she was a member of the Hamburg State Opera. On Nov. 26, 1947, she made her Metropolitan Opera debut in N.Y. as Isolde, remaining on the roster for one season. In 1948 she appeared at the Salzburg Festival as Beethoven's Leonore. She also made guest appearances at London's Covent Garden, the Vienna State Opera, in Amsterdam, and in Brussels. Her most famous role was Elektra.—NS/LK/DM

Schmedes, Erik, Danish tenor; b. Gentofte, near Copenhagen, Aug. 27, 1868; d. Vienna, March 21, 1931. He studied with Artôt in Paris, Rothmühl in Berlin, and Ress in Vienna, making his operatic debut as a baritone in Wiesbaden (Jan. 11, 1891) as the Herald in *Lohengrin*; then sang tenor roles in Nuremberg (1894) and Dresden (1894–97). After a course of study with A. Iffert in Dresden, he developed a definite tenor voice, and appeared as Siegfried at the Vienna Opera (Feb. 11, 1898); remained on its roster until 1924. He sang at the Bayreuth Festivals (1899–1902; 1906), and made his Metropolitan Opera debut in N.Y. as Siegmund (Nov. 18, 1908), remaining on its roster for only that season. —NS/LK/DM

Schmelzer, Johann Heinrich, eminent Austrian violinist and composer; b. Scheibbs, Lower Austria, c. 1621; d. Prague, between Feb. 20 and March 20, 1680. He settled in Vienna, where he received his music training. He became a violinist in the court chapel (about 1635) and in the Court Orch. (1649); served as Vice-Kapellmeister (1671–79) and as Kapellmeister (1679–80). In 1673 he was ennobled and added "von Ehrenruef" to his name. He died of the plague. Schmelzer was a significant composer of instrumental music, playing a key role in the development of the suite and sonata. He had 3 sons who became musicians: Andreas Anton Schmelzer (b. Vienna [baptized], Nov. 26, 1653; d. there, Oct. 13, 1701) was a violinist and composer; studied with his father; played in the Court Orch. from 1671; succeeded his father as composer of ballet music (1681–93), producing about 65 ballet suites. Georg Joseph Schmelzer (b. Vienna [baptized], April 7, 1655; d. probably there, c. 1700). Peter Clemens (Clement) Schmelzer (b. Vienna [baptized], June 28, 1672; d. there, Sept. 20, 1746) played in the Court Orch. from 1692 until a finger injury ended his active career in 1729; however, he did not officially retire until 1740.

BIBL.: E. Wellesz, *Die Ballett-Suiten von J.H. und A.A. S.* (Vienna, 1914).—NS/LK/DM

Schmelzl, Wolfgang, Austrian singer, teacher, and composer; b. Kennath, c. 1500; d. Steinfeld, c. 1561. He was a Protestant cantor in Amberg, then, c. 1540, he went to Vienna as a teacher; was also a singer at the S. Salvator Chapel. He settled as a Catholic priest at St. Lorenz in Steinfeld. He is known for a collection of 4- to 5-voiced quodlibets and folk songs of the period (1544). —NS/LK/DM

Schmid, Anton, Austrian writer on music; b. Pihl, near Leipa, Bohemia, Jan. 30, 1787; d. Salzburg, July 3, 1857. After studying singing at the monastery of the Calced Augustinians in Leipa, he went to Vienna, where he was employed as a librarian (1819) and custodian (1844) at the court library, where he compiled the collection that became the Austrian National Library.

WRITINGS: *Ottaviano dei Petrucci da Fossombrone, der erste Erfinder des Musiknotendruckes mit beweglichen Metalltypen, und seine Nachfolger im 16. Jahrhundert* (Vienna, 1845); *Joseph Haydn und Niccolò Zingarelli* (Vienna, 1847); *Christoph Willibald Ritter von Gluck: Dessen leben und tonkünstlerisches Wirkens* (Leipzig, 1854).—NS/LK/DM

Schmid, Erich, Swiss conductor and composer; b. Balsthal, Jan. 1, 1907. He began his studies at the Solothurn teachers training college. Following musical instruction from Max Kaempfert and Hermann Suter, he pursued his training at the Hoch Cons. in Frankfurt am Main (1928–30) and won the Frankfurt an Main Mozart Prize. In 1930–31 he completed his studies with Schoenberg at the Prussian Academy of Arts in Berlin. After appearing with the Hessian Radio in Frankfurt am Main (1931–33), he was music director in Glarus (1934–49). From 1949 to 1957 he was chief conductor of the Zürich Tonhalle Orch., and from 1949 to 1975 was conductor of the Gemischter Chor in Zürich. He was chief conductor of the Beromünster Radio Orch. in Zürich from 1957 to 1970. As a guest conductor, he appeared with various European orchs. From 1978 to 1984 he was principal guest conductor of the City of Birmingham Sym. Orch. Schmid was esteemed for his championship of modern music.

WORKS: ORCH.: *3 Stücke* (1930); Suite No. 1 for Wind Orch. and Percussion (1931). **CHAMBER:** 2 sonatinas: No. 1 for Piano and Violin (1929) and No. 2, *Zwei Sätze*, for Violin and Piano (1932–34); String Quartet (1930–31); Trio for Clarinet, Cello, and Piano (1931); *Notturno* for Bass Clarinet, Violin, and Cello (1935); *Rhapsodie* for Clarinet and Piano (1936); *Mura*, trio for Flute, Violin, and Cello (1955). **Piano:** *6 Stücke* (1932); *Widmungen* (1933–35); *5 Bagatellen* (1943). **VOCAL:** Suite for Mezzo-soprano and Chamber Orch. (1929–36); 4 choruses (1930–40); 3 songs (1938–41).—**NS/LK/DM**

Schmid, Ernst Fritz, eminent German musicologist; b. Tübingen, March 7, 1904; d. Augsburg, Jan. 20, 1960. He studied violin, viola, and viola d'amore at the Munich Academy of Music, and also took private lessons in theory and conducting. He then studied musicology at the univs. of Munich (with Sandberger), Freiburg im Breisgau (with Gurlitt), Tübingen (with Hasse), and Vienna (with Haas, Orel et al.); received his Ph.D. from the Univ. of Tübingen in 1929 with the diss. *Carl Philipp Emanuel Bach und seine Kammermusik* (publ. in Kassel, 1931); completed his Habilitation as a Privatdozent in musicology at the Univ. of Graz in 1934 with his *Joseph Haydn: Ein Buch von Vorfahren und Heimat des Meisters* (publ. in Kassel, 1934). He became a prof. at the Univ. of Tübingen in 1935; also founded the Schwabisches Landesmusikarchiv; he left Tübingen in 1937 to devote himself to private research. During World War II, he served in the German army. In 1948 he founded the Mozartgemeinde, and in 1951 the German Mozartgesellschaft. In 1954 he became academic director of the Neue Mozart Ausgabe; from 1955 he oversaw the publ. of the new critical ed. of Mozart's complete works, the *Neue Ausgabe Sämtlicher Werke*. In addition to his valuable research on Mozart, he discovered the private music collection of Emperor Franz II in Graz in 1933; this important collection is now housed in Vienna's Nationalbibliothek.

WRITINGS: *Wolfgang Amadeus Mozart* (Lübeck, 1934; third ed., 1955); *Die Orgeln der Abtei Amorbach* (Buchen, 1938); ed. *Ein schwäbisches Mozartbuch* (Lorch and Stuttgart, 1948); *Musik am Hofe der Fürsten von Löwenstein-Wertheim-Rosenberg, 1720–1750* (Würzburg, 1953); *Musik an den schwäbischen Zollernhöfen der Renaissance* (Kassel, 1962).

BIBL.: W. Fischer et al., eds., *In memoriam E.F. S., 1904–1960: Ein Gedenkblatt für seine Angehörigen und Freunde* (Reckling hausen, 1961).—**NS/LK/DM**

Schmid, Heinrich Kaspar, German composer and teacher; b. Landau an der Isar, Bavaria, Sept. 11, 1874; d. Munich, Jan. 8, 1953. He studied with Thuille and Bussmeyer at the Munich Academy of Music (1899–1903). In 1903 he went to Athens, where he taught music at the Odeon; in 1905 he returned to Munich and was on the faculty of the Academy of Music until 1921; then was director of the Karlsruhe Cons. (1921–24) and

of the Augsburg Cons. (1924–32). His eyesight failed him and he was totally blind during the last years of his life. As a composer, he followed the Romantic tradition of the Bavarian School; he wrote a great number of lieder, and composed Singspiels in a folklike manner, as well as choruses and chamber music.

BIBL.: H. Roth, *H.K. S.* (Munich, 1921).—**NS/LK/DM**

Schmidl, Carlo, Italian music publisher and lexicographer; b. Trieste, Oct. 7, 1859; d. there, Oct. 7, 1943. He was the son and pupil of the Hungarian composer Antonio (actually, Anton) Schmidl (1814–80). In 1872 he entered the employ of the music publisher Vicentini, and in 1889 he established his own business at Trieste; also directed the Leipzig branch of the Ricordi Co. (1901–06). He compiled and publ. an important biographical music dictionary, *Dizionario universale dei musicisti* (Milan, 1887–89; second ed., 1926–29; suppl., 1938; third ed., 1938), containing scrupulously accurate data on Italian musicians, exact dates of performance of major works, and other information testifying to independent research. Schmidl also wrote biographies of Schumann (1890) and G.S. Mayr (1901).—**NS/LK/DM**

Schmidt, Andreas, German baritone; b. Düsseldorf, June 30, 1960. He studied with Ingeborg Reichelt in Düsseldorf and with Fischer-Dieskau in Berlin. In 1984 he made his operatic debut as Dr. Malatesta at the Deutsche Oper in Berlin. After making his first appearance at London's Covent Garden as Valentin in 1986, he returned to Berlin to create the title role in Rihm's *Oedipus* in 1987. In 1990 he created the role of Ryuji in Henze's *Das verratene Meer* in Berlin and sang Olivier in *Capriccio* in Salzburg. He was engaged as Lysiart in *Euryanthe* at the Aix-en-Provence Festival in 1993. On Nov. 18, 1996, he made his N.Y. recital debut. In 1997 he sang in the Brahms centenary concert at London's Wigmore Hall. As a soloist with orchs. and as a lieder artist, he has sung throughout the world. Among his other operatic roles are Mozart's Count, Don Giovanni, Papageno, and Guglielmo, Posa, Amfortas, Wolfram, and Méphistophélès.—**NS/LK/DM**

Schmidt, Annerose, German pianist; b. Wittenberg, Oct. 5, 1936. She studied with her father for 12 years, making her debut in Wittenberg when she was 9; then completed her training with Hugo Steurer at the Leipzig Hochschule für Musik (1953–58). In 1954 she was awarded a diploma at the International Chopin Competition in Warsaw, and in 1956 captured first prize at the International Robert Schumann Competition in Zwickau. She toured in both Eastern and Western Europe, appearing with the Gewandhaus Orch. of Leipzig, the Dresden State Orch., the Royal Phil. of London, the Concertgebouw Orch. of Amsterdam, and the Residentie Orch. of The Hague; also appeared at festivals in Salzburg, the Netherlands, Prague, Edinburgh, Berlin, Dresden, and Warsaw. In 1980 she made her U.S. debut as soloist with Kurt Masur and the Gewandhaus Orch. at Carnegie Hall in N.Y. She became a prof. at the East Berlin Hochschule für Musik in 1986. While best known for her performances of Bach,

Mozart, Beethoven, Schumann, Chopin, and Brahms, Schmidt also plays contemporary works, including those of Siegfried Matthus and Wolfgang Rihm. —NS/LK/DM

Schmidt, Franz, important Austrian composer and pedagogue; b. Pressburg, Dec. 22, 1874; d. Perchtoldsdorf, near Vienna, Feb. 11, 1939. He began his musical training with the Pressburg Cathedral organist, Maher; in 1888 his family settled in Vienna, where he had piano lessons from Leschetizky and also studied composition with Bruckner, theory with Fuchs, and cello with Hellmesberger at the Cons. (from 1890). He was a cellist in the orch. of the Vienna Court Opera (1896–1911); also taught cello at the Cons. of the Gesellschaft der Musikfreunde (1901–08) and was prof. of piano (1914–22) and of counterpoint and composition (from 1922) at the Vienna Staatsakademie; also served as director (1925–27); subsequently was director of the Vienna Hochschule für Musik (1927–31). In 1934 he was awarded an honorary doctorate from the Univ. of Vienna. After his retirement in 1937, Schmidt received the Beethoven Prize of the Prussian Academy in Berlin. His second wife, Margarethe Schmidt, founded the Franz Schmidt-Gemeinde in 1951. Schmidt's music is steeped in Viennese Romanticism; the works of Bruckner and Reger were particularly influential in his development, but he found an original voice in his harmonic writing. Although he is regarded in Austria as a very important symphonic composer, his music is almost totally unknown elsewhere. Outside his homeland, he remains best known for his orch. suite, *Zwischenspiel aus einer unvollständigen romantischen Oper* (Vienna, Dec. 6, 1903), taken from his opera *Notre Dame* (1902–04; Vienna, April 1, 1914). Among his other significant works are 4 syms.: No. 1 (1896–99; Vienna, Jan. 25, 1902), No. 2 (1911–13; Vienna, Dec. 3, 1913), No. 3 (Vienna, Dec. 2, 1928), and No. 4 (1932–33; Vienna, Jan. 10, 1934), a Piano Concerto for Piano, Left-hand and Orch., for Paul Wittgenstein (1923; Vienna, Feb. 2, 1924), and the oratorio *Das Buch mit Sieben Siegeln* (1935–37; Vienna, June 15, 1938). He also composed 2 string quartets (1925, 1929) and other chamber works, 2 piano sonatas, and much organ music.

BIBL.: A. Liess, *F. S.: Sein Leben und Schaffen* (Graz, 1951); C. Nemeth, *F. S.: Ein Meister nach Brahms und Bruckner* (Vienna, 1957); R. Scholz, *F. S. als Orgelkomponist* (Vienna, 1971); N. Tschulik, *F. S.* (Vienna, 1972; Eng. tr., 1980); H. Truscott, *The Music of F. S.*: vol. I, *The Orchestral Music* (London, 1985); T. Leibnitz, *Österreichische Spätromantiker: Studien zu Emil Nikolaus von Reznicek, Joseph Marx, F. S., und Egon Kornauth* (Tutzing, 1986); T. Corfield, *F. S. (1874–1939): A Discussion of his Style with Special Reference to the Four Symphonies and "Das Buch mit sieben Siegeln"* (N.Y. and London, 1989); G. Gruber, *F. S. als Rektor der Fachhochschule für Musik und darstellende Kunst in Wien (1927–1931)* (Vienna, 1989); M. Gailit, *Das Orgelsoloschaffen von F. S. (1874–1939)* (Vienna, 1990); R. Schuhenn, *F. S.s oratorische Werke: Zur Entstehungsgeschichte des "Buches mit sieben Siegeln" und der "Deutschen Auferstehung"* (Vienna, 1990).—NS/LK/DM

Schmidt, Gustav, German conductor and composer; b. Weimar, Sept. 1, 1816; d. Darmstadt, Feb. 11, 1882. He studied with Hummel, Eberwein, and Lobe in Weimar and with Mendelssohn in Leipzig, then conducted opera in Brünn (1841–44), Würzburg (1845), Frankfurt am Main (1846; 1851–61), Wiesbaden (1849), Leipzig (1864–76), and Mainz; was court Kapellmeister in Darmstadt (from 1876). He was a determined champion of Wagner and Berlioz. He wrote the operas *Prinz Eugen* (Frankfurt am Main, 1847), *Weibertreue or Die Weiber von Weinsberg* (Weimar, 1858), *La Réole* (Breslau, 1863), and *Alibi* (Weimar, 1880), as well as songs and choruses.—NS/LK/DM

Schmidt, Johann Christoph, German organist and composer; b. Hohnstein, near Pirna, Aug. 6, 1664; d. Dresden, April 13, 1728. He entered the Dresden court chapel as a chorister in 1676, where he received training from Christoph Bernhard. After serving as an instrumentalist in the Court Orch., he became master of the choristers in 1687 and second organist in 1692. In 1694 he went to Italy to complete his training. Upon his return to Dresden, he was made deputy Kapellmeister and chamber organist (1696). In 1698 he was promoted to principal Kapellmeister, pursuing his duties in Kraków and Warsaw as well as in Dresden, since he was responsible for the music for both the Saxon electoral and Polish courts. He also served as Kapellmeister for the Protestant and Catholic church music at the court, turning over his duties for the Catholic church music to J.D. Heinichen in 1717. Under Schmidt's leadership, the Dresden Court Orch. became one of the most celebrated in Europe. He wrote an opera seria, *Latona in Delo* (n.d.), a divertissement, *Les Quatre Saisons* (Dresden, Sept. 23, 1719), 4 overture-suites, 4 masses, 7 cantatas, and 4 motets.—NS/LK/DM

Schmidt, Johann Philipp Samuel, German composer; b. Königsberg, Sept. 8, 1779; d. Berlin, May 9, 1853. He settled in Berlin, where he studied with J.G. Naumann and then took a government position; also devoted much time to performing, writing on music, and composing. He wrote several operas, including *Das Fischermädchen* (1818), orch. works, chamber music, sacred works, songs, etc.—NS/LK/DM

Schmidt, John Henry (actually, **Johann Heinrich**), German-American organist, singing teacher, and composer who flourished in the late 18th century. He lived in Radevormwald, near Düsseldorf, until 1783, when he went to the Netherlands. He was organist at the Cathedral of St. John in Schiedam (1785–90). He was active as a singing teacher and piano manufacturer in Charleston, S.C., in 1796; that same year, he settled in Philadelphia, where he became organist of St. Peter's Church (1797); also announced concerts in Baltimore (1796) and Albany (1797). He composed a *Sonata for Beginners.*—NS/LK/DM

Schmidt, Joseph, Romanian tenor; b. Bavideni, Bukovina, March 4, 1904; d. Zürich, Nov. 16, 1942. He studied at the Berlin Cons. In 1928 he began his career as a radio singer and won great popularity in Germany. In 1933 he went to Belgium; in 1938 was briefly in America; then settled in Switzerland, where he died in an internment camp. His voice was regarded as of great lyric expressiveness, but being almost a dwarf (he stood only 4 feet, 10 inches in height), he was unable to appear in opera.

BIBL.: A. Fassbind, *J. S.: Ein Lied Geht um die Welt: Spuren einer Legende* (Zürich, 1992).—**NS/LK/DM**

Schmidt, Ole, Danish conductor and composer; b. Copenhagen, July 14, 1928. He studied at the Royal Danish Cons. of Music in Copenhagen (1947–55) and received training in conducting from Albert Wolff, Celibidache, and Kubelik. From 1959 to 1965 he was conductor of the Royal Danish Opera and Ballet in Copenhagen. After serving as chief conductor of the Hamburg Sym. Orch. (1970–71), he was a guest conductor of the Danish Radio Sym. Orch. in Copenhagen (from 1971). He also appeared as a guest conductor throughout Europe. Following his first appearance as a guest conductor of the BBC Sym. Orch. in London in 1977, he appeared as a guest conductor of all the BBC regional orchs. From 1979 to 1985 he was chief conductor of the Århus Sym. Orch. In 1980 he made his U.S. debut as a guest conductor of the Oakland (Calif.) Sym. Orch. From 1986 to 1989 he was chief guest conductor of the Royal Northern Coll. of Music in Manchester, England. In 1989–90 he was interim conductor of the Toledo (Ohio) Sym. Orch.

WORKS: DRAMATIC: *Bag taeppet*, ballet (Copenhagen, Oct. 9, 1954); *Feber*, ballet (Copenhagen, Oct. 8, 1957); *Chopiniana*, ballet (Copenhagen, Feb. 2, 1958); *Ballet* (1959; Copenhagen, April 27, 1961); *Udstilling*, opera (Copenhagen, Dec. 5, 1969); *Jeanne d'Arc*, music for C.T. Dreyer's silent film of 1927 (Los Angeles, May 27, 1983); *Dyrefabler og Fabeldyr*, musical fairy tale (Copenhagen, April 26, 1987); *Harald og Tine*, musical (Århus, Sept. 9, 1988). **ORCH.:** 2 piano concertos: No. 1 for Piano and Chamber Orch. (1951) and No. 2 for Piano and Strings (1954); *Elegi* for Oboe and Strings (1955); Sym. (1956); *Pièce concertante* for Trumpet, Trombone, and Orch. (1957); 2 accordion concertos (*Symphonic Fantasy and Allegro*, 1958; 1962); Suite for Flute and Chamber Orch. (1960); *Briol* (1962); Concerto for Horn and Chamber Orch. (1966); Concert Overture (1966); *2 mobiler* for Winds, Percussion, and Piano (1970); Violin Concerto (1971); Tuba Concerto (1975); *Tango Grosso* (Copenhagen, Sept. 14, 1975); Guitar Concerto (1976); *Dansk-Faerøsk Fanfare* (1977; rev. 1992); Sinfonietta for 3 Quintets (1977); Duo concertante for Flugelhorn, Tuba, and Orch. (1981); *Festouverture* for Wind Orch. (1984); *Hommage a Stravinsky* for Wind Orch. (Århus, May 23, 1985); Concerto for Flute and Strings (Århus, Nov. 27, 1985); *Renaessancedans* (1986); *Rapsodi* for Violin and Orch. (1988); *Pneumafonikon* (1992); *Øresundssymfoni* (1994; collaborative piece). **CHAMBER:** 5 string quartets (1954, 1963, 1965, 1969, 1977); Quartet for 2 Trumpets, Trombone, and Tuba (1955); *Divertimento* for Violin, Cello, Viola, and Piano (1956); Octet for Flute, Oboe, Clarinet, Bassoon, 2 Violins, Viola, and Cello (1960); 2 accordion toccatas (1960, 1963); *Fanfare, Intrada, and Gigue* for 7 Players (1967); *Festmusik* for Organ, 3 Trumpets, 3 Trombones, and 2 Timpani (1975); *Raxallo*, quintet for 2 Trumpets, Horn, Trombone, and Tuba (1976); Tuba Sonata (1976); *Fragmenter og samtaler* for 2 Trumpets, Horn, Trombone, and Tuba (1976); 2 accordion dialogues (1977, 1992); *Tube and Bones* for 3 Trombones and Tuba (1982); *Blå strå* for Flute, Violin,

Viola, and Cello (1986); *Jahreszeiten* for Oboe and Organ (1989); *Karnak* for Trombone and Piano (1990); Wind Quintet (1991); Trio Sonata for 2 Trumpets and Organ (1992); Viola Sonata (1992–93); piano pieces.—**NS/LK/DM**

Schmidt, Trudeliese, German mezzo-soprano; b. Saarbrücken, Nov. 7, 1941. She received her training in Saarbrücken and Rome. In 1965 she made her operatic debut as Hansel in Saarbrücken. In 1969 she became a member of the Deutsche Oper am Rhein in Düsseldorf. From 1971 she appeared in various German music centers, and in 1974 toured Japan with the Bavarian State Opera of Munich. She sang Dorabella at the Glyndebourne Festival in 1976. In subsequent years, she appeared in leading European music centers. In 1985 she was a soloist in Mozart's *Coronation Mass* with Karajan and the Vienna Phil. at a special concert at the Vatican in Rome for Pope John Paul II. She was engaged as Fatima in *Oberon* at Milan's La Scala in 1989. In 1990 she sang Strauss's Composer in Barcelona. She appeared at the Munich Festival in 1997. In 1999 she celebrated her 30th anniversary with the Deutsche Oper am Rheim. Among her prominent roles are Cherubino, Rossini's Isabella, Weber's Fatima, and Strauss's Octavian and Composer.—**NS/LK/DM**

Schmidt, Wolfgang, German tenor; b. Kassel, Aug. 19, 1956. He was a student of Martin Gründler at the Frankfurt am Main Hochschule für Musik. After appearances with the Pocket Opera in Nuremberg, he sang at the Court Theater in Bayreuth (1982–84), in Kiel (1984–86), and in Dortmund (1986–89). In 1989 he sang Wagner's Erik at the Bregenz Festival, and that same year he joined the Deutsche Oper am Rhein in Düsseldorf. In 1991 he was engaged by the Salzburg Festival and the Vienna State Opera. He portrayed Tannhäuser at the Bayreuth Festival in 1992. On April 22, 1993, he made his Metropolitan Opera debut in N.Y. as Siegfried, a role he reprised at Bayreuth in 1994 and at Milan's La Scala in 1997. After singing Tristan at the San Francisco Opera in 1998, he returned there as Siegfried in 1999. He also appeared widely as a concert artist.—**NS/LK/DM**

Schmidt-Görg, Joseph, eminent German musicologist; b. Rüdinghausen, near Dortmund, March 19, 1897; d. Bonn, April 3, 1981. He studied musicology with Schiedermair and Schmitz at the Univ. of Bonn (Ph.D., 1926, with the diss. *Die Messen des Clemens non Papa*; completed his Habilitation there in 1930 with his *Die Mitteltontemperatur*). He became Schiedermair's assistant in the Beethoven Archives in Bonn in 1927; later served as director of the archives (1946–72); concurrently lectured on musicology at the Univ. of Bonn (1930–65). On his 70th birthday, he was presented with a Festschrift under the friendly Latin title *Colloquium amicorum* (Bonn, 1967), containing a catalogue of his writings. His publs. include *Unbekannte Manuskripte zu Beethovens weltlicher und geistlicher Gesangsmusik* (Bonn, 1928), *Katalog der Handschriften des Beethoven-Hauses und Beethoven-Archivs Bonn* (Bonn, 1935), *Nicolas Gombert: Leben und Werk* (Bonn, 1938), and *Ludwig van Beethoven* (with H. Schmidt; Bonn, 1969; Eng. tr., N.Y., 1970). —**NS/LK/DM**

Schmidt-Isserstedt, Hans, respected German conductor; b. Berlin, May 5, 1900; d. Holm-Holstein, near Hamburg, May 28, 1973. He studied composition with Schreker at the Berlin Hochschule für Musik; also took courses at the univs. of Berlin, Heidelberg, and Münster. In 1923 he became a répétiteur at the Wuppertal Opera; after conducting opera in Rostock (1928–31) and Darmstadt (1931–33), he held the post of first conductor at the Hamburg State Opera (1935–43); then joined the Deutsche Oper in Berlin, where he was made Generalmusikdirektor in 1944. In 1945 he was mandated by the British occupation authorities with the direction of the music section of the Hamburg Radio; he organized the North German Radio Sym. Orch., which he led with notable distinction until his retirement in 1971; was also chief conductor of the Stockholm Phil. (1955–64). He appeared widely as a guest conductor; also conducted at Covent Garden in London and at the Bavarian State Opera in Munich. He was especially admired for his cultured performances of the Austro-German repertoire.—NS/LK/DM

Schmieder, Wolfgang, noted German music librarian; b. Bromberg, May 29, 1901; d. Fürstenfeldbruck, Nov. 8, 1990. He studied musicology with Kroyer and Moser, German philology and literature with F. Panzer and F. von Waldberg, and art history with C. Neumann at the Univ. of Heidelberg (Ph.D., 1927, with the diss. *Zur Melodiebildung in Liedern von Neidhart von Reuental*). He then was an asst. lecturer in its musicology dept. (1927–30); subsequently studied library science with M. Bollert at the Sachsischen Landesbibliothek in Dresden and with O. Glauning at the Univ. of Leipzig Library. He was librarian of the Technische Hochschule in Dresden (1931–33); then went to Leipzig as head of the archives of Breitkopf & Härtel (1933–42). In 1946 he founded the music dept. of the City and Univ. Library in Frankfurt am Main, which he headed until 1963. He was presented a Festschrift on his 70th birthday in 1971, *Quellenstudien zur Musik*, ed. by K. Dorfmuller and G. von Dadelsen. Of his numerous publications, of fundamental importance is his exhaustive *Thematisch- systematisches Verzeichnis der musikalischen Werke von Johann Sebastian Bach: Bach-Werke-Verzeichnis* (Leipzig, 1950; 5th ed., rev., 1990); also valuable is *Musikalische alte Drücke bis etwa 1750* (with G. Hartweig; 2 vols., Wolfenbüttel, 1967).—NS/LK/DM

Schmitt, Aloys, German pianist and composer, brother of **Jacob Schmitt** and father of **Georg Aloys Schmitt;** b. Erlenbach, Aug. 26, 1788; d. Frankfurt am Main, July 25, 1866. He studied composition with André at Offenbach, and in 1816 went to Frankfurt am Main, where he remained all his life with the exception of short stays in Berlin and Hannover (1825–29). He composed 4 operas, *Der Doppelgänger* (Hannover, 1827), *Valeria* (Mannheim, 1832), *Das Osterfest zu Paderborn* (Frankfurt am Main, 1843), and *Die Tochter der Wüste* (Frankfurt am Main, 1845), 2 oratorios, *Moses* and *Ruth*, church music, etc., but he is principally known and appreciated for his numerous piano compositions, including 4 piano concertos, several piano quartets, piano trios, a number of attractive character pieces for piano,

and studies for school.

BIBL.: H. Henkel, *Leben und Wirken von Dr. Aloys Schmitt* (Frankfurt am Main, 1873).—NS/LK/DM

Schmitt, Camille, Belgian organist, pedagogue, and composer; b. Aubange, March 30, 1908; d. Limelette, May 11, 1976. He studied at the Brussels Cons. (1928–37). He was an organist in France and Belgium (1923–29; 1940–48), a prof. at the Liège Cons. (1947–66), and director of the French Section of the Brussels Cons. (1966–73). In 1961 he married **Jacqueline Fontyn.**

WORKS: ORCH.: *Triptyque angevin* (1941); *Psaume* (1942); Sinfonietta (1943); *Rapsodie* (1944); *Préludes joyeux* (1945; Copenhagen, June 2, 1946); Piano Concerto (1955); *Métamorphoses* (1963); *Contrepoints* (1965); *Polyphonies* (1966); *Alternances* (1970). **CHAMBER:** Wind Quintet (1943); Trio for Oboe, Clarinet, and Bassoon (1945); String Quartet (1948); *Prélude* for Clarinet and Piano (1952); *Dialogue* for Violin and Piano (1953); *Métamorphoses* for Cello and Piano (1961); Quartet for 4 Clarinets (1964); *Burlesques* for Flute, Oboe, Clarinet, and Bassoon (1965); *Contrepoints* for Wind Quintet (1965); *Polyphonies* for Wind Quintet (1969); *Polyphonies* for Saxophone Quartet (1970). **P i a n o :** *Polyphonies* (1966); *Histoire pour Pierre* (1970). **VOCAL:** *Psautier* for Alto, Piano, Oboe, Clarinet, and Bassoon (1946); *La Halte des heures*, cantata for Voice and Piano (1959); choruses. —NS/LK/DM

Schmitt, Florent, outstanding French composer; b. Blâmont, Meurthe-et-Moselle, Sept. 28, 1870; d. Neuilly-sur-Seine, near Paris, Aug. 17, 1958. He studied piano with H. Hess and harmony with G. Sandré at the Nancy Cons. (1887–89), then entered the Paris Cons., where he took courses in harmony with Dubois and Lavignac, fugue with Gédalge, and composition with Massenet and Fauré. He won the second Prix de Rome with his cantata *Frédégonde* (1897) and the Grand Prix de Rome with his cantata *Sémiramis* (1900). He spent the years 1901–04 in the Villa Medicis in Rome, sending to the Académie several important instrumental and choral works; then traveled in Germany, Austria, Hungary, and Turkey. In 1906 he returned to Paris, where he served as a member of the executive committee of the Société Musicale Indépendante from its foundation in 1909; was also a member of the Société Nationale de Musique. He became an influential music critic, writing regularly for *Le Temps* (1919–39); was also director of the Lyons Cons. (1922–24). In 1936 he was elected to Dukas's place in the Institut; also became a Commander of the Légion d'honneur. Schmitt spent his formative years in the ambience of French symbolism in poetry and Impressionism in music, and he followed these directions in his programmatically conceived orch. music; he nonetheless developed a strong, distinctive style of his own, mainly by elaborating the contrapuntal fabric of his works and extending the rhythmic design to intricate, asymmetrical combinations; he also exploited effects of primitivistic percussion, in many respects anticipating the developments of modern Russian music. The catalogue of his works is very long; he continued to compose until his death at the age of 87.

WORKS: DRAMATIC: B a l l e t : *La Tragédie de Salomé* (Paris, Nov. 9, 1907; orch. suite, Paris, Jan. 8, 1911); *Le Petit Elfe*

Ferme-l'oeil, after Hans Christian Andersen (Paris, Feb. 29, 1924); *Oriane la sans-égale* (Paris, Jan. 7, 1938). **I n c i d e n t a l M u s i c T o :** *Antoine et Cléopâtre*, after Shakespeare (Paris, June 14, 1920); *Reflets* (Paris, May 20, 1932). **ORCH.:** *En été* (1894); *Musiques de plein-air* (1897–99); *Le Palais hanté*, after Poe (1900–1904); *3 rapsodies* (1903–04); *Scherzo vif* for Violin and Orch. (1903–10); *Feuillets de voyage* (1903–13); *Reflets de l'Allemagne*, suite (1905); *Sélamlik*, symphonic poem for Military Band (1906); *Puppazzi*, suite (1907); *Légende* for Viola or Saxophone and Orch. (1918); *Mirages: Tristesse de Pan, La Tragique Chevauchée* (1921); *Fonctionnaire MCMXII: Inaction en musique* (1924; Paris, Jan. 16, 1927); *Danse d'Abisag* (1925); *Salammbô*, after Flaubert (1925); *Ronde burlesque* (1927; Paris, Jan. 12, 1930); *Çhançunik* (humorous phonetic spelling of *Sens unique*, i.e., "one-way street"; Paris, Feb. 15, 1930); *Symphonie concertante* for Piano and Orch. (Boston, Nov. 25, 1932, composer soloist); *Suite sans esprit de suite* (1937; Paris, Jan. 29, 1938); *Branle de sortie* (1938; Paris, Jan. 21, 1939); *Janiana*: Sym. for Strings (score entitled Sym. No. 2; 1941; Paris, May 1, 1942); *Habeyssée* for Violin and Orch. (phonetic representation of "ABC," as pronounced in French; Paris, March 14, 1947); Sym. (1957; Strasbourg, June 15, 1958). **CHAMBER:** *Scherzo-pastorale* for Flute and Piano (1889); *4 pièces* for Violin and Piano (1901); Piano Quintet (1901–08); *Andante et Scherzo* for Harp and String Quartet (1906); *Lied et Scherzo* for Double Wind Quintet (1910); *Sonate libre en deux parties enchaînées* for Violin and Piano (1919); *Suite en rocaille* for Flute, Violin, Viola, Cello, and Harp (1934); *Sonatine en trio* for Flute, Clarinet, and Harpsichord (1935); *Minorités* for Flute, Violin, and Piano (1938); *Hasards* for Violin, Viola, Cello, and Piano (1939); *A tours d'anches* for Flute, Clarinet, Bassoon, and Piano (1939); Quartet for Saxophones (1941); String Trio (1944); Quartet for Flutes (1944); String Quartet (1945–48). **P i a n o :** *Musiques intimes* (2 sets, 1890–1900 and 1898–1904); *Soirs*, 10 preludes (n.d.); *Ballade de la neige* (1896); *Pièces romantiques* (1900–1908); *Nuits romaines* (1901); *3 danses* (1935; also for Orch.); *Clavecin obtempérant*, suite (1945). **VOCAL:** *Tristesse au Jardin* for Voice and Orch. (1897–1908); *Musique sur l'eau* for Voice and Orch. (1898); *Danse des Devadasis* for Voice, Chorus, and Orch. (1900–1908); *Psaume XLVII* for Soprano, Chorus, Orch., and Organ (1904; Paris, Dec. 27, 1906); *Chant de guerre* for Tenor, Men's Chorus, and Orch. (1914); *Kerob-Shal* for Tenor and Orch. (1920–24); *Fête de la lumière* for Soprano, Chorus, and Orch. (1937); *L'Arbre entre tous* for Chorus and Orch. (1939); *A contre-voix* for Chorus (1943); other choruses; motets; solo songs. **BIBL.:** P. Ferroud, *Autour de F. S.* (Paris, 1927); Y. Hucher, *F. S., L'homme et l'artiste* (Paris, 1953); Y. Hucher and M. Raveau, *L'Oeuvre de F. S.* (Paris, 1960).—**NS/LK/DM**

Schmitt, Georg Aloys, German pianist, conductor, and composer, son of **Aloys Schmitt** and nephew of **Jacob Schmitt;** b. Hannover, Feb. 2, 1827; d. during a rehearsal in Dresden, Oct. 15, 1902. He studied with his father, and after theory training from Vollweiler in Heidelberg, toured Europe as a pianist. He subsequently devoted himself mainly to theatrical conducting. He was court conductor at Schwerin (1857–92), and in 1893 was appointed director of the Mozartverein in Dresden, which had a multitudinous choral ensemble (some 1,400 members) and its own orch. He wrote 3 operas, orch. works, chamber music, piano pieces, songs, etc., and also ed. and completed Mozart's Mass in C minor (1901).—**NS/LK/DM**

Schmitt, Jacob, German pianist, teacher, and composer, brother of **Aloys Schmitt** and uncle of **George Aloys Schmitt;** b. Obernburg, Bavaria, Nov. 2, 1803; d. Hamburg, May 24, 1853. He studied with his brother, becoming a reputable piano teacher. He wrote about 370 piano pieces, including sonatinas for 2- and 4-hands, numerous studies, rondos, and nocturnes. Especially useful is his *Musikalisches Schatzkästlein*, a collection of 133 short piano pieces.—**NS/LK/DM**

Schmitt-Walter, Karl, German baritone; b. Gernersheim am Rhein, Dec. 23, 1900; d. Kreuth, Oberbayern, Jan. 14, 1985. He studied in Nuremberg and Munich. He made his operatic debut in 1921 in Oberhausen; then sang in Nuremberg, Saarbrücken, and Dortmund. He was a member of the Wiesbaden Opera (1929–34), the Berlin Deutsche Oper (1934–50), and the Bavarian State Opera in Munich (1950–61); also sang at Bayreuth and Salzburg. In 1957 he became a prof. of voice at the Munich Academy of Music.—**NS/LK/DM**

Schmitz, Elie Robert, eminent French pianist and pedagogue; b. Paris, Feb. 8, 1889; d. San Francisco, Sept. 5, 1949. He studied at the Paris Cons. with Diémer, winning the premier prix. In 1908 he toured as accompanist of Slezak, Emma Eames, and other celebrated singers. In 1912 he organized in Paris the Assn. des Concerts Schmitz, which he led until 1914. In 1919 he toured the U.S. as a pianist; in 1920 he founded the Franco-American Music Soc. in N.Y. (incorporated in 1923 as Pro Musica), of which he was president from its inception; toured again in the U.S. and Europe (1921–29), and in the Orient (1929–30; 1932–33); eventually settled in San Francisco as a teacher. He publ. a book on his system of piano study, *The Capture of Inspiration* (N.Y., 1935; second ed., 1944), and a valuable technical analysis with commentary, *The Piano Works of Claude Debussy* (N.Y., 1950).—**NS/LK/DM**

Schmitz, Eugen, German musicologist; b. Neuburg an der Donau, Bavaria, July 12, 1882; d. Leipzig, July 10, 1959. He studied musicology with Sandberger and Kroyer at the Univ. of Munich (Ph.D., 1905, with the diss. *Der Nürnberger Organist Johann Staden: Beiträge zur Würdigung seiner musikgeschichtlichen Stellung*; extracts publ. in Leipzig, 1906), then completed his Habilitation there in 1909 with his *Beiträge zur Geschichte der italienischen Kammerkantate im 17. Jahrhundert* (publ. in Leipzig, 1914, as *Geschichte der Kantate und des geistlichen Konzerts I. Theil: Geschichte der weltlichen Solokantate*; second ed., 1955, as *Geschichte der weltlichen Solokantate*). He wrote music criticism in Dresden, and also taught music at the Dresden Technische Hochschule (1916–39). From 1939 to 1953 he was director of the Musikbibliothek Peters in Leipzig.

WRITINGS: *Hugo Wolf* (Leipzig, 1906); *Richard Strauss als Musikdramatiker: eine ästhetische-kritische Studie* (Munich, 1907); *Richard Wagner* (Leipzig, 1909; second ed., 1918); *Harmonielehre als Theorie: Aesthetik und Geschichte der musikalischen Harmonik* (Munich, 1911); *Palestrina* (Leipzig, 1914; second ed., 1954); *Musikästhetik* (Leipzig, 1915; second ed., 1925); *Orlando di Lasso* (Leipzig, 1915; second ed., 1954); *Klavier, Klaviermusik und*

Klavierspiel (Leipzig, 1919); *Richard Wagner: Wie wir ihn heute sehen* (Dresden, 1937); *Schuberts Auswirkung auf die deutsche Musik bis zu Hugo Wolf und Bruckner* (Leipzig, 1954); *Unverwelkter Volksliedstil: J.A.P. Schulz und seine "Lieder im Volkston"* (Leipzig, 1956).—**NS/LK/DM**

Schmitz, (Franz) Arnold,

German musicologist; b. Sablon, near Metz, July 11, 1893; d. Mainz, Nov. 1, 1980. He took courses in musicology, history, and philosophy at the univs. of Bonn, Munich, and Berlin; his principal mentors were Friedlaender, Kroyer, Sandberger, Schiedermair, and Wolf; received his Ph.D. in 1919 from the Univ. of Bonn with the diss. *Untersuchungen über des jungen Schumann Anschauungen vom musikalischen Schaffen*; completed his Habilitation there in 1921. He taught there (1921–28) and at the Dortmund Cons. (1925–29), then at the univs. of Breslau (1929–39) and Mainz (1947–61); he served as rector at the latter (1953–54; 1960–61); later taught at the Univ. of Basel (1965–67).

WRITINGS: *Beethovens "zwei Prinzipe"* (Berlin, 1923); *Beethoven: unbekannte Skizzen und Entwürfe* (Bonn, 1924); *Das romantische Beethovenbild* (Berlin, 1927); *Die Bildlichkeit der wortgebundenen Musik J.S. Bachs* (Mainz, 1950).—**NS/LK/DM**

Schmöhe, Georg,

German conductor; b. Gummersbach, Feb. 16, 1939. He studied at the Berlin Hochschule für Musik and the Milan Cons., and also received training from Karajan, Celibidache, Ferrara, and Blacher. He was a conductor in Bern (1964–65), Essen (1965–67), Wuppertal (1967–70), Kiel (1970–73), and Düsseldorf (1973–74). From 1974 to 1980 he was Generalmusikdirektor in Bielefeld, and from 1978 to 1982 he was chief conductor of the Caracas Sym. Orch. He was chief conductor of the Nüremberg Sym. Orch. from 1989 to 1992. From 1992 he was Generalmusikdirektor of the Kassel State Theater. He also was a guest conductor with opera houses and orchs. in Europe.—**NS/LK/DM**

Schnabel, Artur,

celebrated Austrian-born American pianist and pedagogue, father of **Karl Ulrich Schnabel;** b. Lipnik, April 17, 1882; d. Axenstein, Switzerland, Aug. 15, 1951. He first studied with Hans Schmitt and made his debut at 8, and then studied with Leschetizky in Vienna (1891–97). He went to Berlin in 1900; there he married the contralto Therese Behr (1905), with whom he frequently appeared in recitals; he also played in recitals with leading musicians of the day, including Flesch, Casals, Feuermann, Huberman, Primrose, and Szigeti. He likewise gave solo recitals in Europe and the U.S., presenting acclaimed cycles of the Beethoven sonatas; taught at the Berlin Hochschule für Musik (from 1925). After the advent of the Nazi regime in 1933, he left Germany and settled in Switzerland; taught master classes at Lake Como and recorded the first complete set of the Beethoven sonatas. With the outbreak of World War II in 1939, he went to the U.S., becoming a naturalized American citizen in 1944. After teaching at the Univ. of Mich. (1940–45), he returned to Switzerland. Schnabel was one of the greatest pianists and pedagogues in the history of keyboard playing; eschewing the role of the virtuoso, he concentrated

upon the masterworks of the Austro-German repertoire with an intellectual penetration and interpretive discernment of the highest order; he was renowned for his performances of Beethoven and Schubert; prepared an edition of the Beethoven piano sonatas. He was also a composer. A renewed interest in his music led to the recording of several of his compositions in the 1980s. In his works, he pursued an uncompromisingly modernistic idiom, thriving on dissonance and tracing melodic patterns along atonal lines.

WORKS: ORCH.: Piano Concerto (1901); 3 syms.: No. 1 (1937–38; Minneapolis, Dec. 13, 1946), No. 2 (1941–42; London recording studio, July 18–20, 1988), and No. 3 (1948); *Rhapsody* (1946; Cleveland, April 15, 1948). **CHAMBER:** Piano Quintet (1916); 5 string quartets (1918; 1921; 1923–24; 1924; 1940); Sonata for Solo Violin (1919); String Trio (1925); Sonata for Solo Cello (1931); Violin Sonata (1935); Piano Trio (1945); *Duodecimet* for Wind Quintet, Bass Clarinet, Trumpet, String Trio, Double Bass, and Percussion (1950; unfinished; completed and orchestrated by R. Leibowitz). **P i a n o :** *3 Pieces* (1896); *3 Pieces* (1906); *Dance Suite* (1921); Sonata (1922); *Piano Piece in 7 Movements* (1936); *7 Pieces* (1947). **VOCAL:** *Aussöhnung* for Voice and Piano (1902); *Notturno* for Voice and Piano (1914); *2 Pieces* for Chorus and Orch. (1943).

WRITINGS: *Reflections on Music* (Manchester, 1933; N.Y., 1934); *Music and the Line of Most Resistance* (Princeton, N.J., 1942); *My Life and Music* (London, 1961).

BIBL.: C. Saerchinger, *A. S.* (London, 1957); K. Wolff, *The Teaching of A. S.* (London, 1972).—**NS/LK/DM**

Schnabel, Joseph Ignaz,

German organist, violinist, teacher, and composer; b. Naumburg am Queiss, Silesia, May 24, 1767; d. Breslau, June 16, 1831. He settled in Breslau in 1797, where he became organist at St. Clara and a violinist at the Vincentiuskirche and in the theater orch. He was appointed Kapellmeister of the Cathedral in 1804, and from 1812 he taught at the Roman Catholic Seminary and was director of the Royal Inst. for Church Music. He wrote many sacred works, including masses, graduals, offertories, and hymns; also a Clarinet Concerto, marches for military band, vocal works, and chamber music. His brother, Michael Schnabel (b. Naumburg, Sept. 23, 1775; d. Breslau, Nov. 6, 1842), founded a piano factory in Breslau (1814); his son, Karl Schnabel (b. Breslau, Nov. 2, 1809; d. there, May 12, 1881), an excellent pianist and composer of operas and piano music, carried on the business.

BIBL.: A. Schirdewahn, *Dommkapellmeister J. S. und sein Sohn August als Lehrer am Breslauer Schullehrer-Seminar* (Breslau, 1935).—**NS/LK/DM**

Schnabel, Karl Ulrich,

German-American pianist, teacher, and composer, son of **Artur Schnabel;** b. Berlin, Aug. 6, 1909. He was a student of Leonid Kreutzer (piano) and Paul Juon (composition) at the Prussian State Academy of Music in Berlin (1922–26). After making his debut in Berlin in 1926, he toured in Europe. From 1935 to 1940 he made duo appearances with his father. On Feb. 23, 1937, he made his U.S. debut in N.Y., where he settled in 1939. With his wife, Helen (née Fogel) Schnabel, he toured extensively in duo recitals from 1940 until her death in 1974. From 1980 he appeared in duo recitals with Joan Rowland. In addition to his many tours around the globe, he devoted much time to teaching. He was the author of *Modern Technique of the Pedal* (N.Y., 1950). He also composed pieces for Piano, 4-Hands.—NS/LK/DM

Schnebel, Dieter, eminent German composer; b. Lahr, March 14, 1930. At 10, he began piano lessons with Wilhelm Siebler. After further piano instruction from Wilhelm Resch in Villingen (1945–49), he studied theory and music history with Erich Doflein at the Freiburg im Breisgau Hochschule für Musik (1949–52). He also attended the summer courses in new music in Darmstadt beginning in 1950. He completed his studies at the Univ. of Tübingen (1952–56), where he took courses in theology, philosophy, and musicology, receiving his doctorate with a thesis on Schoenberg's dynamics. From 1963 to 1970 he taught religion in Frankfurt am Main, and then religion and music in Munich from 1970 to 1976. He also devoted increasing attention to his career as a composer. In 1976 he was a prof. of experimental music and musicology at the Berlin Hochschule für Musik. In 1991 he was made a member of the Berlin Akademie der Künste. The complex construction of his early works gave way in 1968 he simpler forms intended for wider audiences; in 1984 he began a "third period" of major forms as collections of traditions and innovation, first the mass (*Miss [Dahlemer Messe]*), then the symphony (*Sinfonie X*) and opera (*Majakovskis Tod*; Venice, Sept. 1996). Among his writings are *Mauricio Kagel: Musik, Theater, Film* (1970), *Denkbare Musik: Schriften 1952–72* (1972), *MO-NO: Musik zum Lesen* (1973), and *Anschläge-Ausschläge: Texte zur Neuen Musik* (1994). In his music, Schnebel follows a conceptually sophisticated and highly avant-garde course in which he makes use of such unusual materials as vocal noise, breath, and graphics.

WORKS: DRAMATIC: Music Theater: *ki-no (Räume 1)* (1963–67; Munich, July 10, 1967); *Maulwerke* (1968–74; Donaueschingen, Oct. 20, 1974); *Körper-Sprache* (1979–80; Metz, Nov. 20, 1980); *Jowaegerli (Tradition IV, 1)* (1982–83; Baden-Baden, June 26, 1983); *Zeichen-Sprache* (1987–89; Berlin, April 12, 1989); *Chili (Tradition IV, 2)* (1989–91; Hamburg, May 12, 1991). **ORCH.:** *Versuche I-IV* (1953–56; rev. 1964; first complete perf., Stuttgart, Sept. 14, 1973); *Webern-Variationen (Re- Visionen I, 3)* for Chamber Orch. (1972; Paris, Oct. 20, 1973); *Canones* (1975–77; rev. 1993–94; Ludwigshafen, March 6, 1995); *Orchestra* (1974–77; Cologne, Jan. 20, 1978); *Schubert-Phantasie (Re-Visionen I, 5)* (1978; Frankfurt am Main, March 16, 1979; rev. 1989); *Thanatos-Eros (Tradition III, 1)* (1979–82; Graz, Nov. 5, 1982; rev. version, Berlin, April 12, 1985); *Sinfonie-Stücke* (1984–85; Hamburg, June 23, 1985); *Mahler-Moment (Re-Visionen II, 4)* for Strings (1985; Zürich, April 4, 1986); *Sinfonie X* for Orch., Alto, and Tape (1987–92; Donaueschingen, Oct. 18, 1992); *Mozart-Moment (Re-Visionen II, 3)* for Small Orch. (1988–89; Frankfurt am Main, June 16, 1989); *Verdi-Moment (Re-Visionen II, 5)* (Frankfurt am Main, June 16, 1989); *Janáček-Moment (Re-Visionen II, 1)* (1991–92; Hamburg, May 22, 1992); *inter* for Small Orch. (Frankfurt am Main, Sept. 3, 1994). **CHAMBER:** *Analysis (Versuche I)* for String Instrument and Percussion (1953; Brussels, Dec. 12, 1964); *Stücke* for String Quartet (1954–55; Rome, June 1968); *anschläge-ausschläge (Modelle No. 5)* for Flute, Cello, and Harpsichord (1965–66; Zürich, Jan. 5, 1970); *In motu proprio (Tradition I)* for 7 Cellos or 7 Clarinets (Paris, Oct. 24, 1975); *Drei-Klänge*

(Räume 4) for Chamber Ensemble (1976–77; Bremen, Dec. 12, 1977); *B-Dur-Quintett (Tradition II, 1)* for 2 Violins, Viola, Cello, and Piano (1976–77; Darmstadt, April 17, 1978); *Handwerke-Blaswerke I* for Wind Player, String Player, and Percussionist (1977; Frankfurt am Main, April 16, 1978); *Rhythmen (aus Schulmusik)* for Percussion (1977; Munich, June 20, 1978); *Pan* for Flute and Cello (1978; Zürich, Jan. 25, 1980; rev. version, Lahr, April 21, 1988); *Beethoven-Symphonie (Re-Visionen I, 2)* for Chamber Ensemble (1985; Essen, April 14, 1988); *5 Inventionen* for Cello (1987; Stuttgart, May 3, 1988); *Marsyas* for Bass Clarinet and Percussion (Munich, Nov. 22, 1987); *Circe* for Harp (San Felice, June 1988); *Sisyphos* for 2 Winds (Leipzig, Nov. 26, 1990); *4 Stücke* for Violin and Piano (Frankfurt am Main, Sept. 24, 1991); *Languido* for Bass Flute and Live Electronics (1992–93; Graz, Oct. 9, 1993). **KEYBOARD: Piano:** *espressivo (Modelle No. 2)* (1961–63; Munich, April 16, 1964); *concert sans orchestre (Modelle No. 3)* (1964; Zürich, June 13, 1970); *Bagatellen* (1986; Bonn, Jan. 17, 1987); *Monotonien* for Piano and Live Electronics (1988–89; Munich, Oct. 28, 1993). **Organ:** *Zwischenfugen (Tradition V, 1)* (1979–82; Essen, April 26, 1986). **VOCAL:** *Für Stimmen (...missa est)* for Chorus (1956–69); *Das Urteil* for Chorus, Orch., and Tape (1959; rev. version, Hannover, Aug. 31, 1990); *Glossolalie 6 (Projekte IV)* for 3 to 4 Speakers and for 3 to 4 Instrumentalists (1960–61; Paris, Oct. 21, 1966); *Bach-Contrapuncti (Re-Visionen I, 1)* for Chorus (1972–76); *Wagner-Idyll (Re-Visionen I, 4)* for Voice and Chamber Ensemble (Berlin, Sept. 9, 1980); *Lieder ohne Worte (Tradition III, 3)* for Voice and 2 Instruments (1980–86; Münster, Feb. 14, 1987); *5 Geistliche Lieder von Bach* for Voice and Small Orch. (1984; Cologne, Oct. 12, 1985); *Missa (Dahlemer Messe)* for 4 Soloists, Chorus, Orch., and Organ (1984–87; Berlin, Nov. 11, 1988); *Metamorphosenmusik* for Voice and Chamber Ensemble (1986–87; Aachen, Jan. 10, 1990); *Schumann-Moment (Re-Visionen II, 2)* for Voices, Harp, and Percussion (Frankfurt am Main, June 16, 1989); *Chili* for 3 Speakers, 4 Singers, and Chamber Ensemble (1989–91); *Lamento di Guerra* for Mezzo-soprano and Organ or Synthesizer (Berlin, Sept. 29, 1991); *Mit diesen Händen* for Voice and Cello (Cologne, Dec. 14, 1992); *Kaschnitz-Gedichte* for Speaker and Piano (Tutzing, Nov. 25, 1994). **OTHER:** Tape pieces; graphic and conceptual works.

BIBL.: W. Grünzweig, G. Schröder, and M. Supper, eds., *S. 60.* (Hofheim, 1990); H.-K. Metzger and R. Riehn, eds., *D. S.* (Munich, 1980); C. Henius, *S., Nono, Schönberg, oder, Die wirkliche und die erdachte Musik: Essays und Autobiographisches* (Hamburg, 1993).—NS/LK/DM

Schneerson, Grigori, eminent Russian musicologist; b. Eniseisk, Siberia, March 13, 1901; d. Moscow, Feb. 6, 1982. He was the son of a political exile under the tsarist regime; went to Moscow as a youth, and studied piano at the Cons. with Medtner and Igumnov. From 1939 to 1948 he was in charge of the music dept. of the Society for Cultural Relations with Foreign Nations; from 1948 to 1961, was head of the foreign section of the monthly *Sovietskaya Muzyka*, and from 1954 to 1966, ed. the bibliographic series Foreign Literature of Music. A remarkably gifted linguist, he mastered several European languages and undertook a study of Chinese. In his polemical writings he displayed wit and sarcasm in attacking the extreme manifestations of Western modernism, but preserved scholarly impartiality in analyzing the music of all genres and styles. He was a Member Correspondent of the Academy of the Arts of the German Democratic Republic (1968), Honorary Member of the Accademia di Scienze, Lettere, Arti (1976), and a recipient of the Bernier Prize of the Académie des Beaux-Arts, Paris (1976). Among his writings, all publ. in Moscow, were monographs on Khachaturian (1957; Eng. tr., 1959) and Ernst Busch (1962; rev. 1964), a study of French music in the 20th century (1964; rev. 1970), and a vol. of articles on foreign music (1974). He also ed. a vol. on Shostakovich (1976).—NS/LK/DM

Schnéevoigt, Georg (Lennart), prominent Finnish conductor; b. Vyborg, Nov. 8, 1872; d. Malmö, Nov. 28, 1947. He received training in cello in Helsinki, with Karl Schröder in Sondershausen, and with Julius Klengel in Leipzig. He then continued his musical studies in Brussels, Dresden, and with Robert Fuchs in Vienna. Returning to Helsinki, he served as principal cellist in the Phil. (1895–98; 1899–1903) and as a cello teacher at the Music Inst. In 1901 he launched his conducting career in Riga. From 1904 to 1908 he was conductor of the Kaim Orch. in Munich. After conducting the Kiev Sym. Orch. (1908–09), he was conductor of the Riga Sym. Orch. (1912–14). He also conducted the Helsinki Sym. Orch. (1912–14); in 1914 it merged with Kajanus' Helsinki Phil. to form the Helsinki City Orch. with Schnéevoigt as co-conductor (1916–32). From 1932 to 1941 Schnéevoigt was its sole conductor. He also was conductor of the Stockholm Konsertförening (1915–21), founder-conductor of the Christiania (later Oslo) Phil. (1919–27), conductor in Düsseldorf (1924–26), of the Los Angeles Phil. (1927–29), and of the Riga Opera (1929–32). Subsequently he conducted in Malmö. In 1907 he married the pianist and teacher Sigrid Ingeborg Sundgren (b. Helsinki, June 17, 1878; d. Stockholm, Sept. 14, 1953). She studied at the Helsinki Music Inst. (1886–94) and with Busoni in Berlin (1894–97). From 1901 she taught at the Helsinki Music Inst. She also appeared as a soloist with orchs., often under the direction of her husband, and as a recitalist.—NS/LK/DM

Schneider, family of German musicians:

(1) Johann (Gottlob) Schneider, organist, teacher, and composer; b. Alt-Waltersdorf, Saxony, Aug. 1, 1753; d. Gersdorf, May 3, 1840. He studied music with his father, and also took law courses at the Univ. of Leipzig, becoming its church organist in 1812. He had 3 sons who became musicians:

(2) (Johann Christian) Friedrich Schneider, organist, conductor, teacher, and composer; b. Alt-Waltersdorf, Saxony, Jan. 3, 1786; d. Dessau, Nov. 23, 1853. He commenced music studies with his father, then received training from Schönfelder and Unger in Zittau. He began composing as a youth and publ. 3 piano sonatas in 1804. In 1805 he entered the Univ. of Leipzig and became its organist in 1807; was also organist at Leipzig's Thomaskirche (from 1812) and music director of the city theater (from 1817). He brought out the extremely successful oratorio *Das Weltgericht* (1819), and then was called to Anhalt-Dessau as court Kapellmeister in 1821; was founder- director of a celebrated music school (1829–53). His son, Theodor Schneider (b. Dessau, May 14, 1827; d. Zittau, June 15, 1909), was a cellist and conductor; studied with his father and with Drech-

sler; became a cellist in the Anhalt-Dessau Court Orch. (1845); was made Kantor and choirmaster at Dessau's Schlosskirche (1853); served as Kantor and music director of Chemnitz's Jakobikirche (1860–96), and was also conductor of the Singakademie and of the Männergesangverein.

WORKS: DRAMATIC: O r a t o r i o s : *Die Höllenfahrt* (1810); *Das Weltgericht* (1819); *Totenfeier* (1821); *Die Sündflut* (1823); *Das verlorene Paradies* (1824); *Jesu Geburt* (1825); *Pharao* (1828); *Christus das Kind* (1828–29); *Gideon* (1829); *Absalon* (1831); *Das befreite Jerusalem* (1835); *Salomonis Tempelbau* (1836); *Bonifazius* (1837); *Christus der Erloser* (1838); *Gethesemane und Golgotha* (1838). **OTHER:** 14 masses, 25 cantatas, and other sacred works; 7 operas; 23 syms.; 7 piano concertos; 20 overtures; much chamber music; about 400 part-songs for Men's Voices; about 200 lieder.

WRITINGS: *Elementarbuch der Harmonie und Tonsetzkunst* (1820; Eng. tr., 1828); *Vorschule der Musik* (1827); *Handbuch des Organisten* (1829–30).

BIBL.: W. Neumann, *F. S.: Eine Biographie* (Kassel, 1854); F. Kempe, *F. S. als Mensch und Künstler* (Dessau, 1859; second ed. Berlin, 1864); A. Fast, *F. S. in seinen Sinfonien und Ouvertüren* (diss., Univ. of Halle, 1924); K. Hoede, *F. S. und die Zerbster Liedertafel zur Hundertjahrfeier 1927* (Zerbst, 1927); H. Lomnitzer, *Das musikalische Werk F. S.s (1786–1853), insbesondere die Oratorien* (diss., Univ. of Marburg, 1961).

(3) Johann Schneider, organist, pedagogue, and composer; b. Alt-Gersdorf, near Zittau, Oct. 28, 1789; d. Dresden, April 13, 1864. He studied jurisprudence and organ, and in 1812 became a church organist at Görlitz, and in 1825 was appointed court organist at Dresden. He was praised by Mendelssohn as one of the finest organ virtuosos of the period; was also greatly renowned as a teacher. He composed a number of organ pieces and songs with organ obbligato.

(4) (Johann) Gottlieb Schneider, organist and composer; b. Alt-Gersdorf, near Zittau, July 19, 1797; d. Hirschberg, Aug. 4, 1856. He studied with his father and at the Univ. of Leipzig, and from 1825 was organist at Hirschberg's Kreuzkirche. He wrote organ works and piano pieces.—NS/LK/DM

Schneider, (Abraham) Alexander, Russianborn American violinist, conductor, and teacher; b. Vilnius, Oct. 21, 1908; d. N.Y., Feb. 2, 1993. He enrolled in the Vilnius Cons. at 10 and in the Frankfurt an Main Hochschule für Musik at 16; at the latter he studied violin with Adolf Rebner; later took lessons with Carl Flesch in Berlin. While still in his teens, he became concertmaster of the Frankfurt am Main Museumgesellschaft Orch.; was also active in Saarbrücken and Hamburg. In 1932 he became second violinist in the Budapest Quartet, with which he toured widely. He settled in the U.S. in 1938, and remained with the Budapest Quartet until 1944; then played in the Albeneri Trio and the N.Y. Quartet, and also conducted chamber orch. concerts. In 1945 he received the Elizabeth Sprague Coolidge Medal for eminent services to chamber music. In 1950 he persuaded Casals to come out of retirement and honor the 200th anniversary of Bach's death with a festival in Prades; he continued to work with Casals in subsequent years, organizing the Casals Festival in San

Juan, Puerto Rico, in 1957. He founded his own quartet in 1952, and was again a member of the Budapest Quartet from 1955 until it disbanded in 1967. In later years he gave increasing attention to conducting, leading both chamber groups and major orchs.; he was also active as a teacher. In 1988 he received a Kennedy Center Honor for his services to music.—NS/LK/DM

Schneider, Georg Abraham, German horn player, oboist, conductor, and composer; b. Darmstadt, April 19, 1770; d. Berlin, Jan. 19, 1839. He studied with J.W. Magnold in Darmstadt, where he became a member of the court chapel in 1787; later took courses in theory and composition with J.G. Portmann. In 1795 he joined the Rheinsberg Court Orch., then settled in Berlin and became a member of the royal chapel in 1803. He founded a series of subscription concerts in 1807 and the Musikalische Übungsakademie zur Bildung der Liebhaber in 1818; also was conductor of the Reval theater (1813–16). He was made music director of Berlin's royal theater in 1820 and then its Kapellmeister in 1825. He taught at the music school of the royal theater and at the Prussian Academy of Arts.

WORKS: DRAMATIC: Operetta: *Die Orakelspruch; Aucassin und Nicolette; Die Verschworenen; Der Traum; Der Währwolf.* Other Dramatic: 13 ballets; music to numerous plays; melodramas; etc. OTHER: 2 oratorios; cantatas; orch. masses; 54 entr'actes for Orch.; overtures; concertos for Horn, Flute, Oboe, English Horn, Bassoon, etc.; quintets, quartets, and other chamber music.

BIBL.: A. Meyer-Hanno, *G.A. S. und seine Stellung im Musikleben Berlins* (Berlin, 1965).—NS/LK/DM

Schneider, Hortense (Caroline-Jeanne), French soprano; b. Bordeaux, April 30, 1833; d. Paris, May 6, 1920. Following her debut as Inès in *La favorite* in Agen (May 15, 1853), she went to Paris and joined the Bouffes-Parisiens in 1855. She sang at the Variétés (1856–58) and the Palais-Royal (1858–64), and then scored a remarkable success when Offenbach chose her to create the title role in his *La belle Hélène* (Dec. 17, 1864). Her popularity increased when she created the title roles in his *La Grande Duchessse de Gérolstein* (April 12, 1867) and *La Périchole* (Oct. 6, 1868). She then appeared in London (1868–69) and St. Petersburg (1872). Her career off the stage was a colorful one, more than a match for the roles she played on stage.

BIBL.: M. Rouff and T. Casevitz, *H. S.: La vie de fête sous le Second Empire* (Paris, 1931).—NS/LK/DM

Schneider, Julius, German organist, teacher, and composer; b. Berlin, July 6, 1805; d. there, April 3, 1885. He studied composition with Bernhard Klein, and organ and piano with various teachers in Berlin. In 1829 he became organist of the Friedrichwerder church in Berlin, and in 1854 was appointed teacher of organ at the Berlin Inst. of Church Music. He composed a variety of organ pieces, a Piano Concerto, and some chamber music.—NS/LK/DM

Schneider, Maria, jazz composer, leader; b. Windom, Minn., Nov. 27, 1960. She began on piano, then played clarinet and violin. Her piano teacher played stride. Schneider first heard modern jazz in the mid-1970s at the Univ. of Minn. Her music theory teachers in college suggested that she pursue composition, so she started writing for the college big band; she also studied Brazilian music with Manfredo Fest. She went to graduate school at the Eastman School of Music, and married fellow student John Fedchock; they moved to N.Y. in 1985. After about a month, she got work copying and transcribing for Gil Evans. When Evans started working with Laurent Cugny and the Orchestre National de Jazz in France, Schneider did some re-orchestrations of his pieces for this smaller band. She worked for Evans until his death in 1988. In the early 1990s, she and Fedchock started a big band with some of his former colleagues from Woody Herman's band. This band has been playing a regular weekly engagement in N.Y. since 1993. When she and Fedchock divorced in 1995, Schneider became the band's sole leader. During the later 1990s, she worked in France and Holland, presenting her own works while continuing to champion Gil Evans's music. She teaches at the New School and at the Manhattan School of Music.

DISC.: *Evanescence* (1992); *Coming About* (1996).—LP

Schneider, Marius, distinguished German musicologist; b. Hagenau, July 1, 1903; d. Marquartstein, July 10, 1982. He studied philology and musicology at the univs. of Strasbourg and Paris, then trained with Wolf at the Univ. of Berlin (Ph.D., 1930, with the diss. *Die Ars nova des XIV. Jahrhunderts in Frankreich und Italien;* publ. in Wolfenbüttel, 1931); his Habilitation was rejected there after Nazi intervention in 1937, but was subsequently accepted by the Univ. of Cologne after the collapse of the Third Reich (1955). He was Hornbostel's assistant at the Berlin Phonogramm-Archiv (1932–34), and then was its director. After serving in the armed forces during World War II, he went to Barcelona in 1944 as founder-director of the ethnomusicology dept. at the Spanish Inst. of Musicology. He taught at the Consejo Superior de Investigaciones Cientificas at the Univ. of Barcelona (1947–55); then taught comparative musicology and ethnomusicology at the Univ. of Cologne (1955–68); subsequently was on the faculty of the Univ. of Amsterdam (1968–70). He made valuable contributions to musicology, the philosophy of music, and the history of musical structures. A Festschrift was publ. in his honor (Regensburg, 1977).

WRITINGS: *Geschichte der Mehrstimmigkeit: Historische und phänomenologische Studien:* I, *Die Naturvölker;* II, *Die Anfänge in Europa* (Berlin, 1934–35; second ed., 1968, with vol. III, *Die Kompositionsprinzipien und ihre Verbreitung*); *El origen musical de los animales-simbolos en la mitología y la escultura antiguas: Ensayo histórico-etnográfico sobre la subestructura totemística y megalítica de las altas culturas y su supervivencia en el folklore español* (Barcelona, 1946); *La danza de espadas y la tarantela: Ensayo musicológico, etnográfico y arqueológico sobre los ritos medicinales* (Barcelona, 1948); *Singende Steine: Rhythmus-Studien an drei kalantanischen Kreuzgängen romanischen Stils* (Kassel, 1955); *Die Natur des Lobgesangs* (Basel, 1964); ed. *Aussereuropäische Folklore und Kunstmusik* (Cologne, 1972); ed. *Studien zur Mittelmeermusik:* I, *Die tunesische Nuba ed Dhil* (Regensburg, n.d.).—NS/LK/DM

Schneider, Max, eminent German musicologist; b. Eisleben, July 20, 1875; d. Halle, May 5, 1967. He studied musicology at the Univ. of Leipzig with Riemann and Kretzschmar, and harmony and composition with Jadassohn. He continued his musicological training at the Univ. of Berlin (Ph.D., 1917), where he was a librarian (1904–07), then was asst. librarian at the Royal Library (1907–14). He conducted in Halle (1897–1901), and also taught at the Church Music Inst. in Berlin; then was a prof. at the univs. of Breslau (1915–28) and Halle (1928–60). He publ. *Beiträge zu einer Anleitung Clavichord und Cembalo zu spielen* (Strasbourg, 1934) and *Beiträge zur Musikforschung* (vol. I, Halle, 1935). He did useful work in compiling miscellaneous bio-bibliographical materials in music; ed. numerous important bibliographical surveys; also ed. the works of Heinrich Schutz. He enjoyed a well-merited reputation in Germany as a thorough scholar. He was honored 3 times by Festschrifts: H. Zingel, ed., *Festschrift Max Schneider zum 60. Geburtstag* (Halle, 1935), W. Vetter, ed., *Festschrift Max Schneider zum 80. Geburtstag* (Leipzig, 1955), and W. Siegmund-Schulze, ed., *Festschrift Max Schneider zum 85. Geburtstag* (Leipzig, 1960).—**NS/LK/DM**

Schneider, Peter, Austrian conductor; b. Vienna, March 26, 1939. He received training in conducting from Swarowsky at the Vienna Academy of Music. In 1959 he made his debut conducting Handel's *Giulio Cesare* at the Salzburg Landestheater. He was named to the position of first conductor at the Heidelberg Theater in 1961, and at the Deutsche Oper am Rhein in Düsseldorf in 1968. From 1978 to 1985 he was Generalmusikdirektor in Bremen. He conducted at the Bayreuth Festival for the first time in 1981, and led a *Ring* cycle there in 1987. From 1985 to 1987 he was Generalmusikdirektor of the Mannheim National Theater. He was a conductor with the Vienna State Opera during its visit to London's Covent Garden and Tokyo in 1986. From 1993 to 1998 he was Generalmusikdirektor of the Bavarian State Opera in Munich. As a guest conductor, he appeared with various opera companies in Europe and the U.S. —**NS/LK/DM**

Schneiderhan, Wolfgang (Eduard), noted Austrian violinist and pedagogue; b. Vienna, May 28, 1915. He studied violin mainly in Prague with Ševčik and Pisek, and later with Julius Winkler in Vienna. He was concertmaster of the Vienna Sym. Orch. (1933–37), then of the Vienna Phil. (1937–51); concurrently was first violinist in his own Scheiderhan Quartet. From 1951 he made tours of Europe as a soloist with the major orchs. He taught at the Salzburg Mozarteum (1938–56) and at the Vienna Academy of Music (1939–50); was on the faculty of the Lucerne Cons. (from 1949). With Rudolf Baumgartner, he helped to found the Lucerne Festival Strings in 1956. He married **Irmgard Seefried** in 1948. He was best known for his performances of the Viennese classics and contemporary music.

BIBL.: F. Fassbind, *W. S., Irmgard Seefried: Eine Künstler- und Lebensgemeinschaft* (Bern, 1960); *W. S. zum 60. Geburtstag* (Wiesbaden, 1975).—**NS/LK/DM**

Schneider-Trnavský, Mikuláš, Slovak choral conductor and composer; b. Trnava, May 24, 1881; d. Bratislava, May 28, 1958. He studied in Budapest, Vienna, and Prague. He was choirmaster of the cathedral of St. Mikuláš in Trnava (1909–58); was named a National Artist in 1956. He publ. several valuable collections of Slovak folk songs, arranged with piano accompaniment: *Sbierka slovenských ludových piesní* (2 vols., 1905–10), *Sbierka slovenských národných piesní* (5 sections, Bratislava, 1930; new ed., Prague, 1935–40), and *50 Slovakische Volkslieder* (Bratislava, 1943). He also publ. a book of memoirs, *Usmevy a slzy* (Smiles and Tears; Bratislava, 1959).

WORKS: *Bellarosa*, operetta (1941); *Dumka and Dance* for Orch. (1905); *Comedy Overture* (1930–31); *Symphony of Recollections* (1956); Violin Sonata (1905); Slovak Sonatina for Piano (1938); church music, including several masses; songs.

BIBL.: J. Samko, *M. S.-T.-phol'ad na život a dielo* (Bratislava, 1965).—**NS/LK/DM**

Schneidt, Hanns-Martin, German conductor and pedagogue; b. Kitzingen am Main, Dec. 6, 1930. He became a member of the Thomanerchor in Leipzig in 1941, where he studied under Günther Ramin. In 1949 he went to Munich to study conducting, composition, organ, and musicology. In 1955 he became director of the Berlin Church Music School, and also founder-director of the Berlin Bach Collegium and Choir. Following his debut as a conductor with the Berlin Phil. in 1960, he appeared in Germany and abroad as a conductor with orchs. and opera houses. From 1963 to 1985 he was Generalmusikdirektor of Wuppertal. He also was a prof. at the Hamburg Staatlichen Hochschule für Musik from 1971 to 1978. In 1985 he became artistic director of the Munich Bach Choir and Orch., as well as prof. of conducting and church music at the Munich Staatlichen Hochschule für Musik, in 1995 artistic director of the German Music School Orch., and in 1997 music director of the Schneidt-Bach Choir and Orch. in Tokyo. His all-embracing repertoire extends from Monteverdi to composers of the present day.—**NS/LK/DM**

Schneitzhoeffer, Jean, French composer; b. Toulouse, Oct. 13, 1785; d. Paris, Oct. 4, 1852. He studied with Catel at the Paris Cons. After serving as timpanist at the Paris Opéra (1815–23), he was appointed chef du chant there; from 1831 to 1850 he was in charge of choral classes at the Paris Cons. He composed several ballet scores for the Paris Opéra, of which *La Sylphide* (1832), which he wrote for the famous dancer Maria Taglioni, became a perennial favorite. His other ballets are *Proserpine* (1818), *Zémire et Azor* (1824), and *Mars et Venus*. He also composed several concert overtures and a Requiem.—**NS/LK/DM**

Schnitger, Arp, esteemed German organ builder; b. Schmalenfleth, Golzwarden, Oldenburg, July 2, 1648; d. Neuenfelde, July 24, 1719. He was apprenticed to his cousin, Berendt Huess, in Glückstadt, Holstein, whom he assisted in building the organ for St. Cosmae in Stade (1669–73), which he later augmented; his finest instrument is at St. Nicolai in Hamburg (1682–87). Two of his sons followed in his profession: Johann Georg (Jürgen) Schnitger (b. [baptized] Sept. 4, 1690; d. after 1733) and

Franz Caspar Schnitger (b. [baptized] Oct. 15, 1693; d. in the Netherlands, 1729). They completed their father's work at the Grote Kerk in Zwolle, and also rebuilt the large organ at St. Laurents in Alkmaar.

BIBL.: P. Rubardt, *A. S.* (Freiberg, 1928); G. Fock, *S. und seine Schule* (Kiel, 1931); G. Fock, *A. S. und seine Schule* (Kassel, 1975).—NS/LK/DM

Schnitter, David (Bertram),

jazz tenor saxophonist; b. Newark, N.J., March 19, 1948. He attended Jersey City State Coll. (B.A., 1970). From 1970–74, he taught private students and performed around the N.Y. area. From 1975–80, he performed and recorded with Art Blakey, touring Europe, Japan, Brazil, and the U.S. During this time, he also recorded four albums as a leader and more than 30 records as a sideperson with Blakey, Red Rodney, Richard "Groove" Holmes, Charles Earland, and Johnny Lytle, among others. From 1980–82, he performed and recorded with Freddie Hubbard, touring the U.S. and Europe; he also performed in major European festivals and clubs as a leader. From 1982–90, he resided in Spain, teaching in seminars and performing with Johnny Griffin, Slide Hampton, Gary Bartz, Sal Nistico, Tete Montolieu, and Bobby Hutcherson. From 1991 to the present, he has performed in the N.Y. area with the Mickey Bass Quartet and the Jimmy Madison Quintet. He currently teaches Theory Performance and saxophone at the New School.

DISC.: *Invitation* (1976); *Goliath* (1977); *Thundering* (1978); *Glowing* (1981).—LP

Schnittke, Alfred (Garrievich),

prominent Russian composer of German descent; b. Engels, near Saratov, Nov. 24, 1934; d. Hamburg, Aug. 3, 1998. He studied piano in Vienna (1946–48), where his father was a correspondent of a German-language Soviet newspaper; then took courses in composition with Golubev and in instrumentation with Rakov at the Moscow Cons. (1953–58); after serving on its faculty (1962–72), he devoted himself fully to composition. He pursued many trips abroad, and in 1981 was a guest lecturer at the Vienna Hochschule für Musik und Darstellende Künst. In 1981 he was elected a member of the Bayerische Akademie der Schönen Künste. In 1985 he survived a serious heart attack. In 1988 and again in 1991 he suffered debilitating strokes. After writing in a conventional manner, he became acutely interested in the new Western techniques, particularly in serialism and "sonorism," in which dynamic gradations assume thematic significance. He soon became known as one of the boldest experimenters in modernistic composition in Soviet Russia.

WORKS: DRAMATIC: **Opera:** *Odinnadtsataya Zapoved* (The 11th Commandment; 1962; unfinished); *Historia von D. Johann Fausten* (1989–93; Hamburg, June 22, 1995); *Zhizn's idiotom* (Life With an Idiot; 1990–91; Amsterdam, April 13, 1992); *Gesualdo* (1993–94; Vienna, May 26, 1995). **Ballet:** *Labirintï* (Labyrinths; 1971; Leningrad, June 7, 1978); *Zhyoltïy zvuk* (Yellow Sound), after Kandinsky (Saint Bomme, France, 1974); *Sketches*, after Gogol (1984; Moscow, Jan. 16, 1985; in collaboration with E. Denisov, S. Gubaidulina, and G. Rozhdestvensky); *Peer Gynt*, after Ibsen (1986; Hamburg, Jan. 1989).

Also incidental music to plays and many film scores. ORCH.: 4 violin concertos: No. 1 (1957; rev. 1962; Moscow, Nov. 29, 1963), No. 2 for Violin and Chamber Orch. (1966; Leningrad, Feb. 20, 1968), No. 3 for Violin and Chamber Orch. (1978; Moscow, Jan. 29, 1979), and No. 4 (1982; West Berlin, Sept. 11, 1984); Piano Concerto (1960); *Poem about Cosmos* (1961); *Music for Chamber Orch.* (1964); *Music* for Piano and Chamber Orch. (1964); *...pianissimo...* (1967–68; Donaueschingen, Oct. 19, 1969); Sonata for Violin and Chamber Orch. (1968; Moscow, Feb. 5, 1986; chamber orch. version of Sonata No. 1 for Violin and Piano); Double Concerto for Oboe, Harp, and Strings (1970–71; Zagreb, May 1972); 9 syms.: No. 1 (1969–72; Gorky, Feb. 9, 1974), No. 2, *St. Florian*, for Chamber Chorus and Orch. (1979; London, April 23, 1980), No. 3 (Leipzig, Nov. 5, 1981), No. 4 for Tenor, Alto, Chorus, and Orch. or Chamber Orch. (Moscow, April 12, 1984), No. 5, *Concerto Grosso No. 4/Symphony No. 5* (1987–88; Amsterdam, Nov. 10, 1988), No. 6 for Chamber Orch. (1991–92), No. 7 (1993; N.Y., Feb. 10, 1994), No. 8 (1993–94; Stockholm, Nov. 11, 1994), and No. 9 (1997–98; rev. by G. Rozhdestvensky following the composer's instruction, 1998; Hamburg, Feb. 14, 1999); *In memoriam* (1972–78; Moscow, Dec. 20, 1979; orch. version of Piano Quintet); 6 concerti grossi: No. 1 for 2 Violins, Prepared Piano, Harpsichord, and Strings (Leningrad, March 21, 1977), No. 2 for Violin, Cello, and Orch. (West Berlin, Sept. 11, 1982), No. 3 for 2 Violins and Chamber Orch. (Moscow, April 20, 1985), No. 4, *Concerto Grosso No. 4/Symphony No. 5* (1987–88; Amsterdam, Nov. 10, 1988), No. 5 for Violin, Piano, and Orch. (1990–91; N.Y., May 2, 1991), and No. 6 for Piano and Orch. (1993); Concerto for Piano and Strings (Leningrad, Dec. 10, 1979); *Passacaglia* (1979–80; Baden-Baden, Nov. 8, 1981); *Gogol Suite* (from incidental music to *The Dead Souls Register*; London, Dec. 5, 1980); *Ritual* (Novosibirsk, March 15, 1985); *(K)ein Sommernachstraum* ([Not] A Midsummer Night's Dream; Salzburg, Aug. 12, 1985); Viola Concerto (1985; Amsterdam, Jan. 6, 1986); 2 cello concertos: No. 1 (Munich, May 7, 1986) and No. 2 (1989); *Quasi una Sonata* for Violin and Chamber Orch. (1987; chamber orch. version of Sonata No. 2 for Violin and Piano); Trio Sonata for Chamber Orch. (1987; chamber orch. version of String Trio); *4 Aphorisms* (West Berlin, Sept. 18, 1988); *Monologue* for Viola and String Orch. (Bonn, June 4, 1989); Concerto for Piano, 4-Hands, and Chamber Orch. (1989; Moscow, April 27, 1990); *Für Liverpool* (1994); *Concerto for Three* for Violin, Viola, Cello, and Strings with Piano (1994); *5 Fragments on Pictures by Hieronymus Bosch* (London, Nov. 11, 1994). CHAMBER: 3 violin sonatas: No. 1 (1963), No. 2, *Quasi una Sonata* (1968), and No. 3 (1994); *Dialogue* for Cello and 7 Instruments (1965); 4 string quartets (1966, 1980, 1983, 1989); *Serenade* for Violin, Clarinet, Double Bass, Piano, and Percussion (1968); *Canon in memoriam Igor Stravinsky* for String Quartet (1971); *Suite in Old Style* for Violin and Piano or Harpsichord (1972); Piano Quintet (1972–76; orchestrated as *In memoriam*); *Hymnus I* for Cello, Harp, and Timpani (1974), *II* for Cello and Double Bass (1974), *III* for Cello, Bassoon, Harpsichord, and Bells or Timpani (1975), and *IV* for Cello, Double Bass, Bassoon, Harpsichord, Harp, Timpani, and Bells (1976; all first perf. Moscow, May 26, 1979); *Praeludium in memoriam Dmitri Shostakovich* for 2 Violins or 1 Violin and Tape (1975); *Cantus Perpetuus* for Keyboards and Percussion (1975); *Moz-Art* for 2 Violins (1976); *Mozart à la Haydn* for 2 Violins, 2 Small String Ensembles, Double Bass, and Conductor (1977); 2 cello sonatas (1978, 1994); *Stille Musik* for Violin and Cello (1979); *Polyphonic Tango* for Ensemble (1979); *Moz-Art* for Oboe, Harpsichord, Harp, Violin, Cello, and Double Bass (1980); Septet (1981–82); *Lebenslauf* for 4 Metronomes, 3 Percussionists, and Piano (1982);

A Paganini for Violin (1982); *Schall und Hall* for Trombone and Organ (1983); String Trio (1985; new version for Chamber Orch. as Trio-Sonata; rev. as a Piano Trio, 1992); Piano Quartet (1988); *Klingende buchstaben* for Cello (1988); *3 x 7* for Clarinet, Horn, Trombone, Harpsichord, Violin, Cello, and Double Bass (1989); *Moz-Art à la Mozart* for 8 Flutes and Harpsichord (1990); Quartet for 4 Percussionists (1994). **P i a n o :** *Prelude and Fugue* (1963); *Improvisation and Fugue* (1965); *Variations on a Chord* (1965); *4 Pieces* (1971); *Dedication to Stravinsky, Prokofiev, and Shostakovich* for Piano, 6-Hands (1979); 2 sonatas (1987–88; 1990). **VOCAL:** *Nagasaki*, oratorio for Mezzo-soprano, Chorus, and Orch. (1958); *Songs of War and Peace*, cantata for Soprano, Chorus, and Orch. (1959); *3 Poems* for Mezzo-soprano and Piano (1965); *Voices of Nature* for 10 Women's Voices and Vibraphone (1972); *Requiem* for 3 Sopranos, Alto, Tenor, Chorus, and 8 Instrumentalists, after stage music to Schiller's *Don Carlos* (1975; Budapest, Oct. 8, 1977); *Der Sonnengesang des Franz von Assisi* for 2 Choruses and 6 Instruments (1976); *3 Madrigals* for Soprano and 5 Instruments (Moscow, Nov. 10, 1980); *3 Scenes* for Soprano and Instrumental Ensemble (1980); *Minnesang* for 52 Voices (1980–81; Graz, Oct. 21, 1981); *Seid nüchtern und wachet...*, cantata for 4 Soloists, Chorus, and Orch. (first perf. as *Faust Cantata*, Vienna, June 19, 1983); Concerto for Chorus (1984–85); *Busslieder* for Chorus (Moscow, Dec. 26, 1988); *Eroffnungsvers zum ersten Festspielsonntag* for Chorus (Lockenhaus, July 2, 1989).

BIBL.: T. Burde, *Zum Leben und Schaffen des Komponisten A. S.* (Kludenbach, 1993); D. Shulgin, *Gody neizvestnosti A. S.: Besedy s kompozitorom* (Moscow, 1993); *A. S. zum 60. Geburtstag: Eine Festschrift* (Hamburg, 1994).—**NS/LK/DM**

Schnoor, Hans, distinguished German writer on music; b. Neumünster, Oct. 4, 1893; d. Bielefeld, Jan. 15, 1976. He studied with Riemann and Schering at the Univ. of Leipzig, where he received his Ph.D. with the diss. *Das Buxheimer Orgelbuch* in 1919. He was a music critic in Dresden and Leipzig (1922–26), and then music ed. of the *Dresdner Anzeiger* (1926–45). He was an authority on the life and music of Weber.

WRITINGS: *Musik der germanischen Völker im XIX. und XX. Jahrhundert* (Breslau, 1926); with G. Kinsky and R. Haas, *Geschichte der Musik in Bildern* (Leipzig, 1929; Eng. tr., 1930); *Weber auf dem Welttheater* (Dresden, 1942; fourth ed., 1963); *Weber: Ein Lebensbild aus Dresdner Sicht* (Dresden, 1947); *400 Jahre deutscher Musikkultur: Zum Jubiläum der Staatskapelle und zur Geschichte der Dresdner Oper* (Dresden, 1948); *Geschichte der Musik* (1953); *Weber: Gestalt und Schöpfung* (Dresden, 1953; second ed., rev., 1974); *Oper, Operette, Konzert: Ein praktisches Nachschlagsbuch* (Gutersloh, 1955); ed. *Bilderatlas zur Musikgeschichte* (Brussels, 1960; second ed., 1963); *Harmonie und Chaos* (Munich, 1962); *Musik und Theater ohne eigene Dach* (Hagen, 1969); *Die Stunde des Rosenkavalier* (Munich, 1969).—**NS/LK/DM**

Schnorr von Carolsfeld, Ludwig, greatly admired German tenor; b. Munich, July 2, 1836; d. Dresden, July 21, 1865. He was the son of the noted painter Julius Schnorr von Carolsfeld. After studies with J. Otto in Dresden and at the Leipzig Cons., he was engaged by Eduard Devrient for the Karlsruhe Opera in 1854; became its principal tenor in 1858, then was the leading tenor at the Dresden Court Opera (from 1860). Wagner chose him to create the role of Tristan in *Tristan und Isolde* (Munich, June 10, 1865); his wife, **Malvina**

Schnorr von Carolsfeld (née Garrigues), sang Isolde. He was also an outstanding Tannhäuser, and won accolades as an oratorio and lieder artist as well. His death at the age of 29 was widely lamented.

BIBL.: C. Garrigues, *Ein ideales Sängerpaar: L. S.v.C. und Malvina Schnorr von Carolsfeld* (Copenhagen, 1937).—**NS/LK/DM**

Schnorr von Carolsfeld, Malvina (née Garrigues), esteemed German soprano; b. Copenhagen, Dec. 7, 1825; d. Karlsruhe, Feb. 8, 1904. She studied with García in Paris, making her operatic debut in *Robert le diable* in Breslau (1841), and singing there until 1849. After appearances in Coburg, Gotha, and Hamburg, she joined the Karlsruhe Opera in 1854. Wagner chose her to create the role of Isolde in *Tristan und Isolde* (Munich, June 10, 1865), with her husband, **Ludwig Schnorr von Carolsfeld,** singing Tristan. Following his untimely death at the age of 29, she quit the operatic stage and became a convert to spiritualism. She publ. a vol. of poems by her husband and herself in 1867.

BIBL.: C. Garrigues, *Ein ideales Sängerpaar: Ludwig Schnorr von Carolsfeld und M. S.v.C.* (Copenhagen, 1937).—**NS/LK/DM**

Schnyder von Wartensee, (Franz) Xaver, significant Swiss composer; b. Lucerne, April 18, 1786; d. Frankfurt am Main, Aug. 27, 1868. He had piano lessons at age 16 with P. Heggli, then taught himself to play the double bass, cello, clarinet, viola, and timpani; in 1811 he went to Vienna, where he met Beethoven and studied composition with J.C. Kienlen. After teaching at Pestalozzi's Inst. in Yverdun (1816–17), he settled in Frankfurt am Main. He played recitals on the glass harmonica and piano, taught, composed, and founded the Liederkranz (1828). He founded the Schnyder von Wartensee Foundation in 1847, which sponsored competitions in the sciences and assisted in the publ. of scientific and artistic works.

WORKS: DRAMATIC: *Ubaldo,* opera (1811–12; only 1 chorus extant); *Heimweh und Heimkehr,* operetta (1854; Zürich, Dec. 14, 1855). **ORCH:** 5 syms., including No. 2, *Erinnerung an Joseph Haydn* (Frankfurt am Main, Oct. 20, 1837), and No. 3, *Militärsymphonie* (Frankfurt am Main, Jan. 18, 1850); other orch. works; chamber music; much choral music; songs; piano music.

BIBL.: *Lebenserinnerungen von X. S.v.W.* (Zürich, 1887; new ed. by W. Schuh, Berlin, 1940).—**NS/LK/DM**

Schoberlechner, Franz, Austrian pianist and composer; b. Vienna, July 21, 1797; d. Berlin, Jan. 7, 1843. He studied with Hummel in Vienna, making his debut in Hummel's second Concerto (1809), written for him; then continued his training with E.A. Förster. On a pianistic tour to Italy, he produced his opera *I Virtuosi teatrali* at Florence (1814), and the next year became maestro di cappella to the Duchess of Lucca, producing there a second opera, *Gli Arabi nelle Gallie* (1816); in 1820 returned to Vienna, where he brought out an opera in German, *Der junge Onkel* (Jan. 14, 1823). He made a trip to Russia in 1823, and there married the singer Sophie dall'Occa (1807–63), with whom he made further tours to Italy and Vienna. He purchased a villa in Florence in 1831, and retired to it some years later. Besides his operas, he composed overtures, string quartets, a Piano Trio, and many piano pieces.—NS/LK/DM

Schobert, Johann, important composer; b. probably in Silesia, c. 1735; d. Paris, Aug. 28, 1767 (with his entire family, except 1 child, from eating poisonous mushrooms). About 1760 he settled in Paris, where he entered the service of the Prince de Conti. His works show the general characteristics of the Mannheim School, although it cannot be proved that he ever was in that city. Mozart was significantly influenced by him, and reworked and incorporated movements of his scores into his own sonatas and piano concertos. See H. Riemann, ed., *Johann Schobert: Ausgewählte Werke*, Denkmäler Deutscher Tonkunst, XXXIX (1909).

WORKS: *Le Garde-chasse et le braconnier*, opéra- comique (Paris, Jan. 18, 1766); the following were publ. in Paris (1761–67), and many appeared in later eds. with different op. nos.: (2) Sonates for Harpsichord and Violin ad libitum, op.1; 2 Sonates for Harpsichord and Violin ad libitum, op.2; 2 Sonates for Harpsichord and Violin ad libitum, op.3; (2) Sonates for Harpsichord, op.4; (2) Sonates for Harpsichord and Violin ad libitum, op.5; (3) Sonates en trio for Harpsichord and Violin and Cello ad libitum, op.6; (3) Sonates en quatuor for Harpsichord and 2 Violins and Cello ad libitum, op.7; 2 Sonates for Harpsichord and Violin, op.8; (3) Sinfonies for Harpsichord and Violin and Horns ad libitum, op.9; (3) Sinfonies for Harpsichord and Violin and Horns ad libitum, op.10; Concerto I for Harpsichord, 2 Violins, Viola, Cello, and 2 Horns ad libitum, op.11; Concerto II for Harpsichord, 2 Violins, Viola, Cello, 2 Oboes, and 2 Horns ad libitum, op.12; Concerto III pastorale for Harpsichord, 2 Violins, 2 Horns ad libitum, Viola, and Cello, op.13; 6 Sonates for Harpsichord and Violin ad libitum, op.14; Concerto IV for Harpsichord, 2 Violins, 2 Horns ad libitum, Viola, and Cello, op.15; 4 Sonates for Harpsichord, Violin, and Cello, op.16; 4 Sonates for Harpsichord and Violin, op.17; Concerto V for Harpsichord, 2 Violins, and Cello, op.18; 2 Sonates for Harpsichord or Piano, and Violin, op.19 (may be spurious); 3 Sonates for Harpsichord and Violin, op.20 (probably by T. Giordani); *Morceau de musique curieux...menuet qui peut s'exécuter de différentes façon* for Harpsichord, Violin, and Cello.

BIBL.: H. David, *J. S. als Sonatenkomponist* (Leipzig, 1928); H. Turrentine, *J. S. and French Clavier Music from 1700 to the Revolution* (diss., Univ. of Iowa, 1962).—NS/LK/DM

Schock, Rudolf (Johann), German tenor; b. Duisburg, Sept. 4, 1915; d. Duren-Gürzenich, Nov. 13, 1986. He studied in Cologne, Hannover, and with Robert von der Linde and Laurenz Hofer in Berlin. At the age of 18, he joined the chorus of the Duisburg Opera. In 1937 he made his operatic debut in Braunschweig, where he sang until 1940. After singing in Hannover (1945) and at the Berlin State Opera (1946), he was a member of the Hamburg State Opera (1947–56), with which company he visited the Edinburgh Festival (1952). In 1948 he made his first appearance at the Salzburg Festival as Idomeneo and in 1951 his debut at the Vienna State Opera. In 1959 he made his Bayreuth Festival debut as Walther von Stolzing. He also appeared in operetta.

Among his other roles were Tamino, Florestan, Max in *Der Freischütz*, and Bacchus in *Ariadne auf Naxos*. His autobiography was publ. as *Ach ich hab' in meinerm Herzen* (Berlin and Munich, 1985).—NS/LK/DM

Schoebel, Elmer, jazz arranger, composer, pianist; b. East St. Louis, Ill., Sept. 8, 1896; d. St. Petersburg, Fla., Dec. 14, 1970. At age 14, he began playing piano accompaniment in a silent-movie house in Champaign, Ill., then toured for a long time accompanying various variety acts. In 1920, he played in Chicago with the 20th Century Jazz Band. From 1922 until 1923, Schoebel played regularly in the Friars' Society Orch. (the New Orleans Rhythm Kings), then formed his own band for residency at Midway Gardens, Chicago. He travelled to N.Y. with Isham Jones in 1925, but then returned to Chicago, where he led his own band and, through the late 1920s, played for various leaders, including Louis Panico and Art Kassel. During this period, he also did regular arranging and transcribing for the Melrose Publishing House. Schoebel achieved great success as a composer ("Nobody's Sweetheart," "Farewell Blues," and many others). He worked mainly at arranging and composing through the 1930s until becoming chief musical arranger for Warner Brothers' N.Y. publishing company. He played regularly in N.Y. from the late 1940s through the 1950s. In 1958, he moved to Fla., where he worked with local bands until his death. —JC/LP

Schoeck, Othmar, eminent Swiss pianist, conductor, and composer; b. Brunnen, Sept. 1, 1886; d. Zürich, March 8, 1957. He was the son of the painter Alfred Schoeck. He went to Zürich, where he took courses at the Industrial Coll. before pursuing musical training with Attenhofer, Freund, Hegar, and Kempter at the Cons. (from 1905); after further studies with Reger in Leipzig (1907–08), he returned to Zürich and conducted the Aussersihl Men's Chorus (1909–15), the Harmonie Men's Chorus (1910–11), and the Teachers' Chorus (1911–17); then was conductor of the St. Gallen sym. concerts (1917–44). Schoeck was one of the most significant Swiss composers of his era; he won his greatest renown as a masterful composer of songs, of which he wrote about 400. He also was highly regarded as a piano accompanist and a conductor. Among his many honors were an honorary doctorate from the Univ. of Zürich (1928), the first composer's prize of the Schweizerische Tonkunstlerverein (1945), and the Grand Cross of Merit and Order of Merit of the Federal Republic of Germany (1956). In 1959 the Othmar Schoeck Gesellschaft was founded to promote the performance of his works.

WORKS: DRAMATIC: O p e r a : *Don Ranudo de Colibrados*, op.27 (1917–18; Zürich, April 16, 1919); *Venus*, op.32 (1919–20; Zürich, May 10, 1922); *Penthesilea*, op.39 (1924–25; Dresden, Jan. 8, 1927); *Massimilla Doni*, op.50 (1934–35; Dresden, March 2, 1937); *Das Schloss Dürande*, op.53 (1938–39; Berlin, April 1, 1943); other stage works. ORCH.: *Serenade* for Small Orch., op.1 (1906–07); *Eine Ratcliff-Ouvertüre* (1907); *Concerto quasi una fantasia* for Violin and Orch., op.21 (1911–12); *Praeludium*, op.48 (1932); *Sommernacht* for Strings, op.58 (1945); *Suite* for Strings, op.59 (1949); Cello Concerto, op.61 (1947); *Festlicher Hymnus*, op.64 (1951); Horn Concerto, op.65 (1951). CHAM-

BER: 3 violin sonatas (1908, 1909, 1931); 2 string quartets (1912–13; 1923); 2 clarinet sonatas (1916; 1927–28); piano pieces. VOCAL: C h o r a l : 's Seeli for Men's Chorus (1906–07); 5 Lieder (1906–15); Sehnsucht for Men's Chorus (1909); Der Postillon for Tenor, Men's Chorus, and Piano or Orch., op.18 (1909); Dithyrambe for Double Chorus and Orch., op.22 (1911); Wegelied for Men's Chorus, and Piano or Orch., op.24 (1913); Trommelschläge for Chorus and Orch., op.26 (1915); Die Drei for Men's Chorus (1930); Cantata for Baritone, Men's Chorus, and Instruments, op.49 (1933); Für ein Gesangfest im Frühling for Men's Chorus and Orch., op.54 (1942); Nachruf (1943); Zimmerspruch for Men's Chorus (1947); Vision for Men's Chorus, Brass, Percussion, and Strings, op.63 (1950); Maschinenschlacht for Men's Chorus, op.67a (1953); Gestutze Eiche for Men's Chorus, op.67b (1953). O t h e r : Numerous works for Solo Voice with instrumental accompaniment; about 400 songs, including cycles.

BIBL.: H. Corrodi, ed., O. S.: Festgabe...zum 50. Geburtstag (Erlenbach and Zürich, 1936); W. Vogel, Wesenszüge von O. S.s Liedkunst (Zürich, 1950); idem, Thematisches Verzeichnis der Werke von O. S. (Zürich, 1956); F. Kienberger, O. S.: Eine Studie (Zürich, 1975); S. Tiltmann-Fuchs, O. S.s Liederzyklen für Singstimme und Orchester (Regensburg, 1976); D. Puffet, The Song Cycles of O. S. (Stuttgart and Bern, 1982); B. Föllmi, Praktisches Verzeichnis der Werke O. S.s (Zürich, 1997).—NS/LK/DM

Schoelcher, Victor,

French statesman and writer on music; b. Paris, July 21, 1804; d. Houilles, Dec. 24, 1893. He was educated at the Collège Louis le Grand. As a radical republican, he was expelled from France upon the accession of Napoleon II. He lived in England until his return to Paris in 1870; was elected a member of the National Assembly in 1871 and was made a life senator in 1875. He collected musical instruments, scores, and rare books; also pursued an intensive study of the life of Handel. With the assistance of Rophino Lacy, he wrote the valuable work Haendel et son temps, which was publ. in an Eng. tr. by J. Lowe as The Life of Handel (London, 1857); the first 4 chapters of the French MS were publ. in La France Musicale (1860–62), and the entire MS was purchased by the Paris Cons. in 1881. In 1873 he gave his extensive private library to the Paris Cons. He also publ. La Modernité de la musique (Paris, 1881). —NS/LK/DM

Schoemaker, Maurice,

Belgian composer; b. Anderlecht, near Brussels, Dec. 27, 1890; d. Brussels, Aug. 24, 1964. He studied harmony with Théo Ysaÿe, counterpoint with Michel Brusselmans, fugue with Martin Lunssens, and composition and orchestration with Paul Gilson. He was one of 8 Gilson pupils to form, in 1925, the Groupe des Synthétistes, whose aim was to promote modern music. He held administrative posts in various Belgian musical organizations.

WORKS: DRAMATIC: O p e r a : Swane (1933); Arc-enciel (1937); De Toverviool (1954). **R a d i o P l a y s :** Sire Halewijn (1935); Médée la magicienne (1936); Philoctetes (1942). **B a l l e t :** Breughel-Suite (1928); Pan (1937). **ORCH.:** Le Facétieux Voyage (1914); Récit, Aria et Final for Violin and Orch. (1920); Pan, prelude (1921); Feu d'artifice for Wind Orch. (1922); 2 fantasques (1924); Sinfonia da camera (1929); Légende de Sire Halewijn, symphonic poem (1930); Rapsodie flamande (1931); Variations on a Popular Song (1937); Sinfonia breve (1938); Pièce

concertante for Trombone and Orch. (1939); Variazioni for Horn and Orch. (1941); Mouvement symphonique (1942); Scènes espagnoles (1943); 2 danses flamandes (1944); Sym. (1946); Bassoon Concerto (1947); Ouverture romane (1947); Marillac l'Epée, dramatic prologue (1949). **CHAMBER:** Piano Trio (1934); Piano Sonata (1934); Sonata for Solo Cello (1940); Suite champêtre for Oboe, Clarinet, and Bassoon (1940); String Quartet (1945); Variations miniatures for String Trio (1949); Morceau de concert for Trombone and Piano (1949); Tombeau de Chopin for 2 Pianos (1949); Sonata du souvenir for Cello and Piano (1953); La Cage des oiseaux for 4 Clarinets (1961).—NS/LK/DM

Schoenberg (originally, Schönberg), Arnold (Franz Walter),

great Austrian-born American composer whose new method of musical organization in 12 different tones related only to one another profoundly influenced the entire development of modern techniques of composition; b. Vienna, Sept. 13, 1874; d. Los Angeles, July 13, 1951. He studied at the Realschule in Vienna; learned to play the cello, and also became proficient on the violin. His father died when Schoenberg was 16; he took a job as a bank clerk to earn a living; an additional source of income was arranging popular songs and orchestrating operetta scores. Schoenberg's first original work was a group of 3 piano pieces, which he wrote in 1894; it was also about that time that he began to take lessons in counterpoint from Alexander Zemlinsky, whose sister he married in 1901. He also played cello in Zemlinsky's instrumental group, Polyhymnia. In 1897 Schoenberg wrote his first String Quartet, in D major, which achieved public performance in Vienna on March 17, 1898. About the same time, he wrote 2 songs with piano accompaniment which he designated as op.1. In 1899 he wrote his first true masterpiece, Verklärte Nacht, set for string sextet, which was first performed in Vienna by the Rosé Quartet and members of the Vienna Phil. on March 18, 1902. It is a fine work, deeply imbued with the spirit of Romantic poetry, with its harmonic idiom stemming from Wagner's modulatory procedures; it remains Schoenberg's most frequently performed composition, known principally through its arrangement for string orch. About 1900 he was engaged as conductor of several amateur choral groups in Vienna and its suburbs; this increased his interest in vocal music. He then began work on a choral composition, Gurre-Lieder, of monumental proportions, to the translated text of a poem by the Danish writer Jens Peter Jacobsen. For grandeur and opulence of orchestral sonority, it surpassed even the most formidable creations of Mahler or Richard Strauss; it calls for 5 solo voices, a speaker, 3 men's choruses, an 8-part mixed chorus, and a very large orch. Special music paper of 48 staves had to be ordered for the MS. He completed the first 2 parts of Gurre-Lieder in the spring of 1901, but the composition of the remaining section was delayed by 10 years; it was not until Feb. 23, 1913, that Franz Schreker was able to arrange its complete performance with the Vienna Phil. and its choral forces.

In 1901 Schoenberg moved to Berlin, where he joined E. von Wolzogen, F. Wedekind, and O. Bierbaum in launching an artistic cabaret, which they called Überbrettl. He composed a theme song for it with trumpet obbligato, and conducted several shows. He met Richard Strauss, who helped him to obtain the Liszt Stipendium and a position as a teacher at the Stern Cons. He returned to Vienna in 1903 and formed friendly relations with Gustav Mahler, who became a sincere supporter of his activities; Mahler's power in Vienna was then at its height, and he was able to help him in his career as a composer. In March 1904 Schoenberg organized with Alexander Zemlinsky the Vereinigung Schaffender Tonkünstler for the purpose of encouraging performances of new music. Under its auspices he conducted on Jan. 26, 1905, the first performance of his symphonic poem *Pelleas und Melisande*; in this score occurs the first use of a trombone glissando. There followed a performance on Feb. 8, 1907, of Schoenberg's *Kammersymphonie*, op.9, with the participation of the Rosé Quartet and the wind instrumentalists of the Vienna Phil.; the work produced much consternation in the audience and among critics because of its departure from traditional tonal harmony, with chords built on fourths and nominal dissonances used without immediate resolution. About the same time, he turned to painting, which became his principal avocation. In his art, as in his music, he adopted the tenets of Expressionism, that is, freedom of personal expression within a self-defined program. Schoenberg's reputation as an independent musical thinker attracted to him such progressive-minded young musicians as Alban Berg, Anton von Webern, and Egon Wellesz, who followed Schoenberg in their own development. His second String Quartet, composed in 1908, which included a soprano solo, was his last work that carried a definite key signature, if exception is made for his *Suite* for Strings, ostentatiously marked as in G major, which he wrote for school use in America in 1934. On Feb. 19, 1909, Schoenberg completed his piano piece op.11, no. 1, which became the first musical composition to dispense with all reference to tonality. In 1910 he was appointed to the faculty of the Vienna Academy of Music; in 1911 he completed his important theory book *Harmonielehre*, dedicated to the memory of Mahler; it comprises a traditional exposition of chords and progressions, but also offers illuminating indications of possible new musical developments, including fractional tones and melodies formed by the change of timbre on the same note. In 1911 he went again to Berlin, where he became an instructor at the Stern Cons. and taught composition privately. His *5 Orchesterstücke*, first perf. in London on Sept. 3, 1912, under Sir Henry Wood's direction, attracted a great deal of attention; the critical reception was that of incomprehension, with a considerable measure of curiosity. The score was indeed revolutionary in nature, each movement representing an experiment in musical organization. In the same year, Schoenberg produced another innovative work, a cycle of 21 songs with instrumental accompaniment, entitled *Pierrot Lunaire*, and consisting of 21 "melodramas," to German texts translated from verses by the Belgian poet Albert Giraud. Here he made systematic use of *Sprechstimme*, with a gliding speech-song replacing precise pitch (not an entire innovation, for Engelbert Humperdinck had applied it in his incidental music to Rosmer's play *Königskinder* in 1897). The work was given, after some 40 rehearsals, in Berlin on Oct. 16, 1912, and the reaction was startling, the purblind critics drawing upon the strongest invective in their vocabulary to condemn the music.

Meanwhile, Schoenberg made appearances as conductor of his works in various European cities (Amsterdam, 1911; St. Petersburg, 1912; London, 1914). During World War I, he was sporadically enlisted in military service; after the Armistice, he settled in Mödling, near Vienna. Discouraged by his inability to secure performances for himself and his associates in the new music movement, he organized in Vienna, in Nov. 1918, the Verein für Musikalische Privataufführungen (Society for Private Musical Performances), from which critics were demonstratively excluded, and which ruled out any vocal expression of approval or disapproval. The organization disbanded in 1922. About that time, Schoenberg began work on his *Suite* for Piano, op.25, which was to be the first true 12-tone piece consciously composed in that idiom. In 1925 he was appointed prof. of a master class at the Prussian Academy of Arts in Berlin. With the advent of the beastly Nazi regime, the German Ministry of Education dismissed him from his post as a Jew. As a matter of record, Schoenberg had abandoned his Jewish faith in Vienna on March 25, 1898, by being baptized in the Protestant Dorotheer Community (Augsburger Konfession); 35 years later, horrified by the hideous persecution of Jews at the hands of the Nazis, he was moved to return to his ancestral faith and was reconverted to Judaism in Paris on July 24, 1933. With the rebirth of his hereditary consciousness, he turned to specific Jewish themes in works such as *Survivor from Warsaw* and *Moses und Aron*. Although Schoenberg was well known in the musical world, he had difficulty obtaining a teaching position; he finally accepted the invitation of Joseph Malkin, founder of the Malkin Cons. of Boston, to join its faculty. He arrived in the U.S. on Oct. 31, 1933. After teaching in Boston for a season, he moved to Hollywood. In 1935 he became a prof. of music at the Univ. of Southern Calif. in Los Angeles, and in 1936 accepted a similar position at the Univ. of Calif. at Los Angeles, where he taught until 1944, when he reached the mandatory retirement age of 70. On April 11, 1941, he became a naturalized American citizen. In 1947 he received the Award of Merit for Distinguished Achievements from the National Inst. of Arts and Letters. In the U.S. he changed the original spelling of his name from Schönberg to Schoenberg.

In 1924 Schoenberg's creative evolution reached the all-important point at which he found it necessary to establish a new governing principle of tonal relationship, which he called the "method of composing with 12 different notes related entirely to one another." This method was adumbrated in his music as early as 1914, and is used partially in his *5 Klavierstücke*, op.23, and in his *Serenade*, op.24; it was employed for the first time in its integral form in the piano *Suite*, op.25 (1924); in it, the thematic material is based on a group of 12 different notes arrayed in a certain pre-arranged order; such a tone row was henceforth Schoenberg's mainspring of thematic invention; development was provided by the devices of inversion, retrograde, and retrograde inversion of the basic series; allowing for transposition, 48 forms were obtainable in all, with counterpoint and harmony, as well as melody, derived from the basic tone row. Immediate repetition of thematic notes was admitted; the realm of rhythm remained free. As with most historic innovations, the 12-tone technique was not the creation of Schoenberg alone but was, rather, a logical development of many currents of musical thought. Josef Matthias Hauer rather unconvincingly claimed priority in laying the foundations of the 12-tone method; among others who had elaborated similar ideas at about the same time with Schoenberg was Jef Golyscheff, a Russian émigré who expounded his theory in a publication entitled "12 Tondauer-Musik." Instances of themes consisting of 12 different notes are found in the *Faust Symphony* of Liszt and in the tone poem *Also sprach Zarathustra* of Richard Strauss in the section on Science. Schoenberg's great achievement was the establishment of the basic 12-tone row and its changing forms as foundations of a new musical language; using this idiom, he was able to write music of great expressive power. In general usage, the 12-tone method is often termed "dodecaphony," from Greek dodeca, "12," and phone, "sound." The tonal composition of the basic row is devoid of tonality; an analysis of Schoenberg's works shows that he avoided using major triads in any of their inversions, and allowed the use of only the second inversion of a minor triad. He deprecated the term "atonality" that was commonly applied to his music. He suggested, only half in jest, the term "atonicality," i.e., absence of the dominating tonic. The most explicit work of Schoenberg couched in the 12-tone idiom was his *Klavierstück*, op.33a, written in 1928–29, which exemplifies the clearest use of the tone row in chordal combinations. Other works that present a classical use of dodecaphony are *Begleitungsmusik zu einer Lichtspielszene*, op.34 (1929–30); Violin Concerto (1934–36); and Piano Concerto (1942). Schoenberg's disciples Berg and Webern followed his 12-tone method in general outlines but with some personal deviations; thus, Berg accepted the occasional use of triadic harmonies, and Webern built tone rows in symmetric groups. Other composers who made systematic use of the 12-tone method were Egon Wellesz, Ernst Krenek, René Leibowitz, Roberto Gerhard, Humphrey Searle, and Luigi Dallapiccola. As time went on, dodecaphony became a lingua franca of universal currency; even in Russia, where Schoenberg's theories were for many years unacceptable on ideological grounds, several composers, including Shostakovich in his last works, made use of 12-tone themes, albeit without integral development. Ernest Bloch used 12-tone subjects in his last string quartets, but he refrained from applying inversions and retrograde forms of his tone rows. Stravinsky, in his old age, turned to the 12-tone method of composition in its total form, with retrograde, inversion, and retrograde inversion; his conversion was the greatest artistic vindication for Schoenberg, who regarded Stravinsky as his most powerful antagonist, but Schoenberg was dead when Stravinsky saw the light of dodecaphony.

Schoenberg's personality was both heroic and egocentric; he made great sacrifices to sustain his artistic convictions, but he was also capable of engaging in bitter polemics when he felt that his integrity was under attack. He strongly opposed the claims of Hauer and others for the priority of the 12-tone method of composition, and he vehemently criticized in the public press the implication he saw in Thomas Mann's novel *Doktor Faustus*, in which the protagonist was described as the inventor of the 12-tone method of composition; future historians, Schoenberg argued, might confuse fiction with facts, and credit the figment of Mann's imagination with Schoenberg's own discovery. He was also subject to superstition in the form of triskaidecaphobia, the fear of the number 13; he seriously believed that there was something fateful in the circumstance of his birth on the 13th of the month. Noticing that the title of his work *Moses und Aaron* contained 13 letters, he crossed out the second "a" in Aaron to make it 12. When he turned 76 and someone remarked facetiously that the sum of the digits of his age was 13, he seemed genuinely upset, and during his last illness in July 1951, he expressed his fear of not surviving July 13; indeed, he died on that date. Schoenberg placed his MSS in the Music Division of the Library of Congress in Washington, D.C.; the remaining materials were deposited after his death at the Schoenberg Inst. at the Univ. of Southern Calif. in Los Angeles. Schoenberg's centennial in 1974 was commemorated worldwide. A Journal of the Schoenberg Inst. began publ. in 1976, under the editorship of Leonard Stein.

Schoenberg's personality, which combined elements of decisive affirmation and profound self-negation, still awaits a thorough analysis. When he was drafted into the Austrian armed forces during World War I (he never served in action, however) and was asked by the examiner whether he was the "notorious" modernist composer, he answered "someone had to be, and I was the one." He could not understand why his works were not widely performed. He asked a former secretary to Serge Koussevitzky why the Boston Sym. Orch. programs never included any of his advanced works; when the secretary said that Koussevitzky simply could not understand them, Schoenberg was genuinely perplexed. "Aber, er spielt doch Brahms!" he said. To Schoenberg, his works were the natural continuation of German classical music. Schoenberg lived in Los Angeles for several years during the period when Stravinsky was also there, but the two never made artistic contact. Indeed, they met only once, in a downtown food market, where they greeted each other, in English, with a formal handshake. Schoenberg wrote a satirical canon, *Herr Modernsky*, obviously aimed at Stravinsky, whose neo-Classical works ("ganz wie Papa Bach") Schoenberg lampooned. But when Schoenberg was dead, Stravinsky said he forgave him in appreciation of his expertise in canonic writing.

In his private life, Schoenberg had many interests; he was a fairly good tennis player, and also liked to play chess. In his early years in Vienna, he launched several theoretical inventions to augment his income, but none of them ever went into practice; he also designed a set of playing cards. The MSS of arrangements of Viennese operettas and waltzes he had made in Vienna to augment his meager income were eventually sold for large sums of money after his death. That Schoenberg needed money but was not offered any by an official musical benefactor was a shame. After Schoenberg relocated to Los Angeles, which was to be his final destination, he obtained successful appointments as a prof. at the Univ. of Southern Calif. and eventually at the Univ. of Calif., Los Angeles. But there awaited him the peculiar rule of age limitation for teachers, and he was mandatorily retired when he reached his seventieth year. His pension from the Univ. of Calif., Los Angeles, amounted to $38 a month. His difficulty in supporting a family with growing children became acute and eventually reached the press. He applied for a grant from the munificent Guggenheim Foundation, pointing out that since several of his own students had received such awards, he was now applying for similar consideration, but the rule of age limitation defeated him there as well. It was only after the Schoenberg case and its repercussions in the music world that the Guggenheim Foundation cancelled its offensive rule. Schoenberg managed to square his finances with the aid of his publishing income, however, and, in the meantime, his children grew up. His son Ronald (an anagram of Arnold) eventually became a city judge, an extraordinary development for a Schoenberg!

WORKS: DRAMATIC: *Erwartung*, monodrama, op.17 (1909; Prague, June 6, 1924, Gutheil-Schoder mezzo-soprano, Zemlinsky conducting); *Die glückliche Hand*, drama with music, to Schoenberg's own libretto, op.18 (1910–13; Vienna, Oct. 14, 1924, Stiedry conducting); *Von Heute auf Morgen*, opera, op.32 (1928–29; Frankfurt am Main, Feb. 1, 1930, W. Steinberg conducting); *Moses und Aron*, biblical drama, to Schoenberg's own libretto (2 acts composed 1930–32; third act begun in 1951, but not completed; radio perf. of Acts 1 and 2, Hamburg, March 12, 1954, Rosbaud conducting; stage perf., Zürich, June 6, 1957, Rosbaud conducting). **ORCH.:** *Frülings Tod*, symphonic poem (fragment, 1898; Berlin, March 18, 1984, R. Chailly conducting); *Pelleas und Melisande*, symphonic poem, after Maeterlinck, op.5 (1902–03; Vienna, Jan. 26, 1905, composer conducting); *Kammersymphonie No. 1* for 15 Instruments, op.9 (1906; Vienna, Feb. 8, 1907; arranged for Orch., 1922; new version for Orch., op.9b, 1935); *5 Orchester-Stücke*, op.16 (1909; London, Sept. 3, 1912, Sir Henry Wood conducting; rev. 1922 and 1949); *3 Little Pieces* for Chamber Orch. (1911; Berlin, Oct. 10, 1957); *Variations*, op.31 (1926–28; Berlin, Dec. 2, 1928, Furtwängler conducting); *Begleitungsmusik zu einer Lichtspielszene*, op.34 (1929–30; Berlin, Nov. 6, 1930, Klemperer conducting); *Suite* in G major for Strings (1934; Los Angeles, May 18, 1935, Klemperer conducting); Violin Concerto, op.36 (1934–36; Philadelphia, Dec. 6, 1940, Krasner soloist, Stokowski conducting); second Chamber Sym., op.38a (1906–16; 1939; N.Y., Dec. 15, 1940, Stiedry conducting; op.38b is an arrangement for 2 Pianos, 1941–42); Piano Concerto, op.42 (1942; N.Y., Feb. 6, 1944, Steuermann pianist, Stokowski conducting); *Theme and Variations* for Wind Band, op.43a (1943; arranged for Orch., op.43b, Boston, Oct. 20, 1944, Koussevitzky conducting). **CHAMBER:** 1 unnumbered string quartet in D major (1897; Vienna, March 17, 1898); 4 numbered string quartets: No. 1, in D minor, op.7 (1904–05; Vienna, Feb. 5, 1907), No. 2, in F-sharp minor, op.10, with Voice (Vienna, Dec. 21, 1908, Rosé Quartet, Gutheil Schoder mezzo-soprano; arranged for String Orch., 1929), No. 3, op.30 (Vienna, Sept. 19, 1927, Kolisch Quartet), and No. 4, op.37 (1936; Los Angeles, Jan. 9, 1937, Kolisch Quartet); *Verklärte Nacht*, sextet for Strings, op.4 (1899; Vienna, March 18, 1902; arranged for String Orch., 1917; rev. 1943; perf. as the ballet *The Pillar of Fire*, N.Y., April 8, 1942); *Ein Stelldichein* for Oboe, Clarinet, Violin, Cello, and Piano (1905); *Die eiserne Brigade*, march for String Quartet and Piano (1916); *Weihnachtsmusik* for 2 Violins, Cello, Harmonium, and Piano (1921); *Serenade* for Clarinet, Bass Clarinet, Mandolin, Guitar, Violin, Viola, and Cello, op.24 (fourth movement with a sonnet by Petrarch for Baritone; 1920–23; Donaueschingen, July 20, 1924); Quintet for Flute, Oboe, Clarinet, Horn, and Bassoon, op.26 (Vienna, Sept. 13, 1924); *Suite* for 2 Clarinets, Bass Clarinet, Violin, Viola, Cello, and Piano, op.29 (1925–26; Paris, Dec. 15, 1927); *Ode to Napoleon* for String Quartet, Piano, and Reciter, after Byron (1942; also a version with String Orch., N.Y., Nov. 23, 1944, Rodzinski conducting); String Trio, op.45 (1946; Cambridge, Mass., May 1, 1947); *Phantasy* for Violin, with Piano Accompaniment (Los Angeles, Sept. 13, 1949). **KEYBOARD: Piano:** *3 Klavierstücke*, op.11 (1909; Vienna, Jan. 14, 1910; rev. 1924); *6 kleine Klavierstücke*, op.19 (1911; Berlin, Feb. 4, 1912); *5 Klavierstücke*, op.23 (1920–23); *Suite*, op.25 (1921–23); *Klavierstück*, op.33a (1928–29; Hamburg, Jan. 30, 1931); *Klavierstück*, op.33b (1931). **Organ:** *Variations on a Recitative*, op.40 (1941; N.Y., April 10, 1944). **VOCAL: Choral:** *Gurre-Lieder* for Soloists, Chorus, and Orch. (1900–03; 1910–11; Vienna, Feb. 23, 1913, Schreker conducting); *Friede auf Erden*, op.13 (1907; Vienna, Dec. 9, 1911, Schreker conducting); 4 pieces for Chorus, op.27 (1925); *3 Satires*, op.28 (1925); 3 German folk songs (Vienna, Nov. 1929); 6 pieces for Men's Chorus, op.35 (1929–30; Frankfurt am Main, Nov. 29, 1931, F. Schmidt conducting); *Kol Nidre* for Speaker, Chorus, and Orch., op.39 (Los Angeles, Oct. 4, 1938, composer conducting); *Genesis*, prelude for Orch. and Chorus (Los Angeles, Jan. 11, 1945); *A Survivor from Warsaw* for Narrator, Chorus, and Orch., op.46 (1947; Albuquerque, Nov. 4, 1948); 3 German folk songs for Chorus, op.49 (1948); *Dreimal tausend Jahre* for Chorus, op.50a (Fylkingen, Sweden, Oct. 29, 1949); *De Profundis* for Chorus, after a Hebrew text, op.50b (1950; Cologne, Jan. 29, 1954); *Modern Psalm* for Chorus, Speaker, and Chorus, after the composer (unfinished; Cologne, May 29, 1956, Sanzogno conducting). The oratorio *Die Jakobsleiter*, begun in 1917, was left unfinished; a performing version was prepared by Winfried Zillig, and given for the first time in Vienna on June 16, 1961. **Songs:** 2 songs, op.1 (1898); 4 songs, op.2 (1899); 7 Chansons, *Bretll-Lieder* (1901); *Nachtwandler* for Soprano, Piccolo, Trumpet, Side Drum, and Piano (1901); 6 songs, op.3 (1899–1903); 8 songs, op.6 (1903–05); 6 songs, op.8 (nos. 2, 5, and 6 for Orch., Prague, Jan. 29, 1914, Zemlinsky conducting); 2 ballads, op.12 (1907); 2 songs, op.14 (1907–08); cycle of 15 poems after Stefan George's *Das Buch der hängenden Gärten* (1908–09; Vienna, Jan. 14, 1910); *Herzgewächse* for Soprano, Celesta, Harmonium, and Harp, after Maeterlinck, op.20 (1911); *Pierrot Lunaire*, 21 poems for Sprechstimme, Piano, Flute/Piccolo, Clarinet/Bass Clarinet, Violin/Viola, and Cello, after Albert Giraud, op.21 (Berlin, Oct. 16, 1912, A. Zehme soloist, composer conducting); 4 songs, op.22 (with Orch.; 1913–16; Frankfurt am Main, Feb. 21, 1932, Rosbaud conducting); *Lied der Waldtaube* for Mezzo-soprano and Chamber Ensemble (1922; arranged from *Gurre-Lieder*); 3 songs, op.48 (1933; London, June 5, 1952). **ARRANGEMENTS AND TRANSCRIPTIONS:** 2 chorale preludes by Bach, for Large Orch.: No. 1, *Komm, Gott, Schöpfer, Heiliger Geist*, and No. 2, *Schmucke dich, O liebe Seele* (N.Y., Dec. 12, 1922); *Prelude and Fugue* in E-flat major for Organ by Bach, for Large Orch. (1928; Vienna, Nov. 10, 1929, Webern conducting); Piano Quartet No. 1, in G minor, op.25, by Brahms, for Orch. (1937; Los Angeles, May 7, 1938, Klemperer conducting); also a Cello Concerto, transcribed from a Harpsichord Concerto by G.M. Monn (1932–33; London, Dec. 7, 1935, Feuermann soloist); Concerto for String Quartet and Orch. after Handel's Concerto Grosso, op.6, No. 7 (1933; Prague, Sept. 26, 1934, Kolisch Quartet); etc.

WRITINGS: *Harmonielehre* (Vienna, 1911; third ed., rev., 1922; abr. Eng. tr., 1947, as *Theory of Harmony*; complete Eng. tr., 1978); *Models for Beginners in Composition* (N.Y., 1942; third ed., rev., 1972, by L. Stein); *Style and Idea* (N.Y., 1950; enl. ed. by L. Stein, London, 1975); *Structural Functions of Harmony* (N.Y., 1954; second ed., rev., 1969, by L. Stein); *Preliminary Exercises in Counterpoint*, ed. by L. Stein (London, 1963); *Fundamentals of Musical Composition*, ed. by L. Stein (London, 1967); also numerous essays in German and American publs.

BIBL.: COLLECTED WORKS, SOURCE MATE-RIAL: J. Rufer and his successors are preparing a complete ed. of his works, *A. S.: Sämtliche Werke* (Mainz, 1966 et seq.). Rufer also compiled an annotated catalogue, *Das Werk A. S.s* (Kassel, 1959; Eng. tr., 1962; second Ger. ed., rev., 1975). I. Vojtch ed. Vol. I of the *Gesammelte Schriften* (Frankfurt am Main, 1976). See also the following: *A. S.: Mit Beiträgen von Alban Berg, Paris von Gutersloh...* (Munich, 1912); E. Wellesz, *A. S.* (Leipzig, 1921; Eng. tr., rev., London, 1925); E. Stein, *Praktischer Leitfaden zu S.s Harmonielehre* (Vienna, 1923); P. Stefan, *A. S.: Wandlung, Legende, Erscheinung, Bedeutung* (Vienna, 1924); *A. S. zum 60. Geburtstag* (Vienna, 1934); H. Wind, *Die Endkrise der bürgerlichen Musik und die Rolle A. S.s* (Vienna, 1935); M. Armitage, ed., *A. S.* (N.Y., 1937); R. Leibowitz, *S. et son école* (Paris, 1947; Eng. tr., 1949); D. Newlin, *Bruckner, Mahler, S.* (N.Y., 1947; rev. ed., 1978); H. Stuckenschmidt, *A. S.* (Zürich, 1951; second ed., rev., 1957; Eng. tr., 1959); J. Rufer, *Die Komposition mit zwölf Tönen* (Berlin, 1952; Eng. tr., 1954, as *Composition with 12 Notes Related to One Another*); L. Rognoni, *Espressionismo e dodecafonia* (Turin, 1954; second ed., rev., 1966, as *La scuola musicale di Vienna*); K. Wörner, *Gotteswort und Magie* (Heidelberg, 1959; Eng. tr., rev., 1963, as *S.'s "Moses and Aron"*); M. Kassler, *The Decision of A. S.'s Twelve-Note-Class-System and Related Systems* (Princeton, 1961); G. Perle, *Serial Composition and Atonality: An Introduction to the Music of S., Berg and Webern* (Berkeley, 1962; fifth ed., rev., 1982); W. Rogge, *Das Klavierwerke A. S.s* (Regensburg, 1964); J. Meyerowitz, *A. S.* (Berlin, 1967); B. Boretz and E. Cone, eds., *Perspectives on S. and Stravinsky* (Princeton, 1968); G. Krieger, *S.s Werke für Klavier* (Göttingen, 1968); A. Payne, *S.* (London, 1968); W. Reich, *A. S., oder Der konservative Revolutionär* (Vienna, 1968; Eng. tr., 1971); R. Brinkmann, *A. S.: Drei Klavierstücke Op.11* (Wiesbaden, 1969); R. Leibowitz, *S.* (Paris, 1969); D. Rexroth, *A. S. als Theoretiker der tonalen Harmonik* (Bonn, 1971); J. Maegaard, *Studien zur Entwicklung des dodekaphonen Satzes bei A. S.* (Copenhagen, 1972); A. Whittall, *S. Chamber Music* (London, 1972); E. Freitag, *A. S. in Selbstzeugnissen und Bilddokumenten* (Reinbek, 1973); H. Stuckenschmidt, *S.: Leben, Umwelt, Werk* (Zürich, 1974; Eng. tr., 1976, as *S.: His Life, World and Work*); G. Manzoni, *A. S.: L'uomo, l'opera, i testi musicati* (Milan, 1975; rev. ed., 1997); C. Rosen, *A. S.* (N.Y., 1975); G. Schubert, *S.s frühe Instrumentation* (Baden-Baden, 1975); M. Macdonald, *S.* (London, 1976); D. Newlin, *S. Remembered: Diaries and Recollections (1938–76)* (N.Y., 1980); W. Bailey, *Programmatic Elements in the Works of A. S.* (Ann Arbor, 1983); W. Jakobik, *A. S.: die Verräumlichte Zeit* (Regensburg, 1983); J. Hahl-Koch, ed., *A. S./Wassily Kandinsky: Letters, Pictures and Documents* (London, 1984); P. Franklin, *The Idea of Music: S. and Others* (London, 1985); G. Bauer, *A Contextual Approach to S.'s Atonal Works: Self Expression, Religion, and Music Theory* (diss., Wash. Univ., 1986); J. Brand, C. Hailey, and D. Harris, eds., *The Berg-S. Correspondence* (N.Y., 1986); E. Smaldone, *Linear Analysis of Selected Posttonal Works of A. S.: Toward an Application of Schenkerian Concepts to Music of the Posttonal Era* (diss., City Univ. of N.Y., 1986); J. Smith, *S. and His Circle: A Viennese Portrait* (N.Y., 1986); M. Mäckelmann, *S.: Fünf Orchesterstücke op.16* (Munich, 1987); J. and J. Christensen, *From A. S.'s*

Literary Legacy: A Catalog of Neglected Items (Warren, Mich., 1988); G. Beinhorn, *Das Groteske in der Musik: A. S.s Pierrot Lunaire* (Pfaffenweiler, 1989); G. Biringer, *Registral and Temporal Influences on Segmentation and Form in S.'s Twelve-Tone Music* (diss., Yale Univ., 1989); R. Boestfleisch, *A. S.s frühe Kammermusik: Studien unter besonderer Berücksichtigung der ersten beiden Streichquartette* (Frankfurt am Main, 1990); E. Haimo, *S.'s Serial Odyssey: The Evolution of his Twelve-Tone Method, 1914–1928* (Oxford, 1990); A. Ringer, *A. S.: The Composer as Jew* (Oxford, 1990); M. Sichardt, *Die Entstehung der Zwölftonmethode A. S.s* (Mainz, 1990); A. Trenkamp and J. Suess, eds., *Studies in the S.ian Movement in Vienna and the United States: Essays in Honor of Marcel Dick* (Lewiston, N.Y., 1990); W. Thomson, *S.'s Error* (Philadelphia, 1991); J. Dunsby, *S.: Pierrot lunaire* (Cambridge, 1992); B. Meier, *Feschichtliche Signaturen der Musik bei Mahler, Strauss und S.* (Hamburg, 1992); S. Milstein, *A. S.: Notes, Sets, Forms* (Cambridge, 1992); N. Nono-Schoenberg, ed., *A. S., 1874–1951: Lebensgeschichte in Begegnungen* (Klagenfurt, 1992); W. Frisch, *The Early Works of A. S., 1893–1908* (Berkeley, 1993); C. Sterne, *A. S.: The Composer as Numerologist* (Lewiston, N.Y., 1993); C.-S. Mahnkopf, *Gestalt und Stil: S.s Erste Kammersymphonie und ihr Umfeld* (Kassel, 1994); S. Litwin and K. Velten, eds., *Stil oder Gedanke?: Zur S.-Rezeption in Amerika und Europe* (Saarbrücken, 1995); B. Kienscherf, *Das Auge hört mit: Die Idee der Farblichtmusik und ihre Problematik—beispielhaft dargestellt zu Werken von Alexander Skrjabin und A. S.* (Frankfurt am Main, 1996); B. von Thülen, *A. S.: Eine Kunstanschauung der Moderne* (Würzburg, 1996); P. Barbaud, *S.* (Nice, 1997); J. Brand and C. Hailey, eds., *Constructive Dissonance: A. S. and the Transformations of Twentieth-Century Culture* (Berkeley, 1997); F. Nicolas, *La singularité S.: Trois conférences à l'IRCAM (25 novembre 1996, 9 decembre 1996 et 6 janvier 1997)* (Paris, 1997); W. Bailey, ed., *The A. S. Companion* (Westport, Conn., 1998); P. Gradenwitz, *A. S. und seine Meisterschule: Berlin 1925–1933* (Vienna, 1998); W. Sinkovicz, *Mehr als zwölf Töne: A. S.* (Vienna, 1998); C. Cross and R. Berman, eds., *Political and Religious Ideas in the Works of A. S.* (Levittown, N.Y., 1999); B. Simms, ed., *S., Berg, and Webern: A Companion to the Second Viennese School* (Westport, Conn., 1999).
—NS/LK/DM

Schoenberg, Loren, jazz tenor saxophonist, bandleader, author, pianist, radio host; b. Paterson, N.J., July 23, 1958. He began broadcasting in 1972 on WBAI. He entered the Manhattan School of Music as a Music Theory major, piano minor (1976–80). In the interim, he had begun playing the tenor saxophone, and worked in Eddie Durham's quartet throughout his college years. This association led to work with other leaders, including Al Casey, Jo Jones, Sammy Price, Jabbo Smith, Panama Francis, and the Buck Clayton Orch. (1986–89). In 1979, he produced a tribute to Charlie Parker and Lester Young at Carnegie Recital Hall. The next year, he formed his own big band in N.Y. and began an association with Benny Goodman, first as an archivist and later as his personal manager. After Goodman's death in 1986, Schoenberg appraised for and was then appointed curator of the Goodman Archives at Yale Univ.; in 1989, he produced a tribute to Goodman at Carnegie Hall. Since 1984, he has been a co-host of *Jazz the Archives*, a radio program on the NPR station WBGO in Newark, N.J. From 1986–92, he was a member of the American Jazz Orch., and was its musical director and conductor for its final two seasons. Since 1985, his own band has performed frequently for the N.Y. Swing Dance Society as well as at many other venues in and around N.Y.; his band toured the country in 1989. He was the musical director for the International Duke Ellington Conference in 1993 and is an artistic consultant to "Jazz at Lincoln Center." He has taught at the Manhattan School of Music since 1996 and at the New School since 1992.

DISC.: *That's the Way It Goes* (1984); *Time Waits for No One* (1987); *Solid Ground* (1988); *S'posin'* (1990); *Just A-Settin' and A-Rockin'* (1990); *Manhattan Work Song* (1992); *Out of this World* (1997).—**LP**

Schoen-René, Anna, German-American singing teacher; b. Koblenz, Jan. 12, 1864; d. N.Y., Nov. 13, 1942. She studied singing with Pauline Viardot-García. She appeared in opera before settling in the U.S., where she taught in Minneapolis and then at the Juilliard School of Music in N.Y. She publ. a book of memoirs, *America's Musical Heritage* (N.Y., 1941).—**NS/LK/DM**

Schöffler, Paul, distinguished German bass-baritone; b. Dresden, Sept. 15, 1897; d. Amersham, Buckinghamshire, Nov. 21, 1977. He studied in Dresden, Berlin, and Milan. In 1925 he made his operatic debut at the Dresden State Opera as the Herald in *Lohengrin*; continued on its roster until 1938, then was a member of the Vienna State Opera until 1965. He also sang at London's Covent Garden (1934–39; 1949–53), the Bayreuth Festivals (1943–44; 1956), and the Salzburg Festivals (1938–41; 1947; 1949–65). He made his Metropolitan Opera debut in N.Y. on Jan. 26, 1950, as Jochanaan in *Salome*; continued to sing there, with interruptions, until 1956, returning there in 1963 to sing one of his finest roles, Hans Sachs; remained on its roster until 1965, when he went to England. His other notable roles included Figaro, Don Giovanni, the Dutchman, Kurwenal, Scarpia, and Hindemith's Cardillac and Mathis der Maler; he also created the role of Jupiter in the first stage perf. of Strauss's *Die Liebe der Danae* (1952) and Einem's *Danton* (1947).

BIBL.: H. Christian, *P. S.: Versuch einer Würdigung* (Vienna, 1967).—**NS/LK/DM**

Scholes, Percy (Alfred), eminent English writer on music; b. Leeds, July 24, 1877; d. Vevey, Switzerland, July 31, 1958. (He pronounced his name "Skoles.") He took his B.Mus. at the Univ. of Oxford in 1908, and his doctorat ès lettres from the Univ. of Lausanne (1934) for his study of Puritans and music. He began his career as a church organist; in 1907, founded the Home Music Study Union, and until 1921 ed. its *Music Student* (later *Music Teacher*); also wrote for the *Evening Standard* (1913–20), *Observer* (1920–27), and the *Radio Times* (1923–29). He lived in Switzerland (1928–40); then made his home in England (1940–57) until returning to Switzerland. He received many honors, including the degrees of D.Mus. (1943) and D.Litt. (1950) from the Univ. of Oxford, and D.Litt. (1953) from the Univ. of Leeds; was made an Officer of the Order of the British Empire in 1957. A writer of great literary attainments and stylistic grace, he succeeded in presenting music "appreciation" in a manner informative and stimulating to the layman and professional alike.

WRITINGS: *Everyman and His Music* (1917); *An Introduction to British Music* (1918); *The Listener's Guide to Music* (1919; 10th ed., 1942); *Music Appreciation: Why and How?* (1920; fourth ed., 1925); *The Book of the Great Musicians* (3 vols., 1920); *New Works by Modern British Composers* (2 series, 1921, 1924); *The Beginner's Guide to Harmony* (1922); *The Listener's History of Music* (3 vols., 1923–28; fourth ed., 1933); *Crotchets* (1924); *Learning to Listen by Means of the Gramophone* (1925); *Everybody's Guide to Broadcast Music* (1925); *The Appreciation of Music by Means of the Pianola and Duo Art* (1925); *A Miniature History of Music* (1928); *The Columbia History of Music through Eye and Ear* (5 albums of records with accompanying booklets; 1930–39; eds. in Japanese and Braille); *Music and Puritanism* (Vevey, 1934); *The Puritans and Music in England and New England* (London, 1934); *Music: The Child and the Masterpiece* (1935; American ed., *Music Appreciation: Its History and Technics*); *Radio Times Music Handbook* (1935; third ed., 1936; American ed. as *The Scholes Music Handbook*, 1935); *The Oxford Companion to Music* (1938; 9th ed., rev., 1955; rev. and aug. by D. Arnold as *The New Oxford Companion to Music*, 2 vols., 1983); *God Save the King: Its History and Romance* (1942; new ed. as *God Save the Queen! The History and Romance of the World's First National Anthem*, 1954); *The Mirror of Music, 1844–1944, A Century of Musical Life in Britain as Reflected in the Pages of the "Musical Times"* (1947); *The Great Dr. Burney* (2 vols., 1948); *Sir John Hawkins: Musician, Magistrate, and Friend of Johnson* (1952); *The Concise Oxford Dictionary of Music* (1952; third ed., rev., 1980 by M. Kennedy; rev. and aug. ed., 1985 by Kennedy as *The Oxford Dictionary of Music*; second ed., rev., 1994); *The Oxford Junior Companion to Music* (1954; second ed., rev., 1979).—**NS/LK/DM**

Scholl, Andreas, remarkable German countertenor; b. Eltville, near Wiesbaden, Nov. 10, 1967. He became a member of the Kiedricher Chorbuben in Eltville when he was 7. He pursued vocal training with René Jacobs at the Scholar Cantorum Basilienses (1987–93), and was active as a soloist in oratorio and cantata performances. In 1992 he scored a notable success as a recitalist when he substituted on short notice for Jacobs in Paris. Thereafter he was engaged to sing with the principal early music orchs. and at leading festivals. In 1996 he appeared with the Collegium Vocale at the London Promenade Concerts. In 1997 he made his Wigmore Hall debut in London, the same year he was engaged to sing in Handel's *Solomon* at the Barbican in London. In 1998 he made an auspicious stage debut as Bertarido in Handel's *Rodelinda* at the Glyndebourne Festival. In addition to his outstanding interpretations of Handel, he has won notable distinction for his Bach and Vivaldi.—**NS/LK/DM**

Schollum, Robert, Austrian composer, writer on music, and teacher; b. Vienna, Aug. 22, 1913; d. there, Sept. 30, 1987. He was a student at the Vienna Academy of Music and at the New Vienna Cons. He also received training from Marx and Lustgarten (theory and composition), Lafite (piano and organ), and Nilius (conducting). From 1959 to 1982 he taught voice at the Vienna Academy of Music. He was president of the Austrian Composers Union from 1965 to 1970, and again in 1983. In 1961 he was awarded the Austrian State Prize for composition and in 1971 the prize of the City of Vienna. After World War II, the influence of impressionism on his music was replaced by dodecaphony, aleatory, and timbre display.

WRITINGS (all publ. in Vienna unless otherwise given): *Musik in der Volksbildung* (1962); *Egon Wellesz* (1964); *Die Wiener Schule: Entwicklung und Ergebnis* (1969); with J. Fritz et al., *Das kleine Wiener Jazzbuch* (Salzburg, 1970); *Singen als menschliche Kundgebung: Einführung in die Arbeit mit den "Singblättern zur Musikerziehung"* (1970); *Das Österreichische Lied des 20. Jahrhunderts* (Tutzing, 1977); *Vokale Aufführungspraxis* (1983).

WORKS: DRAMATIC: *Der Tote Mann*, musical comedy (1936–38); *Mirandolina*, musical comedy (1950); *Der Biedermann Elend*, opera (1962). **ORCH.:** *Dance Suite* (1933); *17 Intermezzi on Folk Songs* (1934–35); *Romance* for Violin and Orch. (1942); *Festive Capriccio* (1943); 3 violin concertos: No. 1 (1944), No. 2 (1961; Vienna, Feb. 1, 1963), and No. 3 (1979–81; Vienna, Feb. 26, 1982); *Admonter Dance* (1945); Clarinet Concerto (1948); *Sonata* (1949); *Serenade* (1949–52); Piano Concerto (1950); Cello Concerto (1953–55); 6 syms.: No. 1 (1954–55; Vienna, March 26, 1976), No. 2 (1955–59; Linz, Oct. 28, 1963), No. 3 (1962; Vienna, May 6, 1966), No. 4 (1966–67; Vienna, Jan. 26, 1968), No. 5, *Venetianische Ergebnisse* (1969; Vienna, Jan. 23, 1970), and No. 6 (1986; Vienna, Feb. 12, 1987); *Toccata* (1957); *Dialogue* for Horn and Strings (1958); *Contures* for Strings (1958); *Game* (1970–71); *Exclamation* (1973); *Seestück* for Piano and Orch. (1974–79; Vienna, May 23, 1980); *Epitaph for Hingerichtete* (1976); *Konzertstück, Fanfares* (Linz, Sept. 8, 1984). **CHAMBER:** Bassoon Sonata (1949); Viola d'Amore Sonata (1949); 2 string quartets (1949; 1966–67); Viola Sonata (1950); Trio for Flute, Bassoon or Cello, and Piano (1951); Violin Sonata (1953); *Chaconne* for Viola and Piano (1955); Octet (1959); Suite for Trumpet and Piano (1964); Trio for Oboe, Clarinet, and Piano (1965); *2 Pieces* for Clarinet and Piano (1966); Alto Flute Sonata (1968); Oboe Sonata (1970); *5 Pieces* for Wind Quintet (1970–71); *Die Ameisen* for Cello and Piano (1973–74); Wind Quintet (1975); *Adagio* for Cello and Piano (1981); several sonatinas and Konzertstücken; piano pieces; organ music. **VOCAL:** Choral pieces; songs. —NS/LK/DM

Scholtz, Herrmann, German pianist, teacher, and composer; b. Breslau, June 9, 1845; d. Dresden, July 13, 1918. He studied in Breslau, with Plaidy in Leipzig, and with Hans von Bülow and Rheinberger in Munich. He taught at the Munich Hochschule fur Musik (1870–75), then went to Dresden. He was an accomplished pianist and a fine teacher. Among his works were a number of piano pieces in a fashionable style: *Albumblätter, Mädchenlieder, Lyrische Blätter, Stimmungsbilder, Ballade*, etc. —NS/LK/DM

Scholz, Bernhard E., German conductor, pedagogue, and composer; b. Mainz, March 30, 1835; d. Munich, Dec. 26, 1916. He studied with H. Esser and H. Pauer in Mainz, S. Dehn in Berlin, and A. Sangiovanni in Milan. After teaching in Munich and conducting in Zürich and Nuremberg, he was asst. court Kapellmeister in Hannover (1859–65); then conducted the Cherubini Soc. in Florence (1865–66), led the concerts of the Breslau Orch. Society (1871–82), and in 1883 succeeded Raff as director of the Hoch Cons. in Frankfurt am Main. He retired in 1908.

WORKS: DRAMATIC: Opera: *Carlo Rosa* (Munich, 1858); *Ziethen'sche Husaren* (Breslau, 1869); *Morgiane* (Munich, 1870); *Golo* (Nuremberg, 1875); *Der Trompeter von Sakkingen* (Wiesbaden, 1877); *Die vornehmen Wirte* (Leipzig, 1883); *Ingo* (Frankfurt am Main, 1898); *Anno 1757* (Berlin, 1903); *Mirandolina* (Darmstadt, 1907). **OTHER:** A great many choral works, with orch.; 2 syms.; Piano Concerto; 2 string quartets; String Quintet; Piano Quartet; 2 piano trios; 3 violin sonatas; 5 cello sonatas; numerous piano pieces and songs.

WRITINGS: Ed. *S.W. Dehns Lehre vom Contrapunkt, dem Canon und der Fuge* (Berlin, second ed., 1883); *Wohin treiben wir?* (Frankfurt am Main, 1897); *Musikalisches und Persönliches* (Stuttgart, 1899); *Die Lehre vom Kontrapunkt und der Nachahmung* (Leipzig, 1904); *Verklungene Weisen* (Mainz, 1911).—NS/LK/DM

Schönbach, Dieter, German composer; b. Stolp-Pommern, Feb. 18, 1931. He studied at the Freiburg im Briesgau Hochschule für Musik with Bialas and Fortner (1949–59). He was music director of the Bochum theater (1959–73). His style of composition is quaquaversal. He wrote the first genuine multimedia opera, *Wenn die Kälte in die Hütten tritt, um sich bei den Frierenden zu wärmen, weiss einer "Die Geschichte von einem Feuer"* (Kiel, 1968); his other works include *Farben und Klänge*, in memory of Kandinsky, for Orch. (1958), Piano Concerto (1958), *Canticum Psalmi Resurrectionis* (Rome, June 13, 1959), *Kammermusik* for 14 Instruments (1964), *Hoquetus* for 8 Wind Instruments (1964), 4 chamber music pieces, each titled *Canzona da sonar* (1966–67), *Atemmusik* for Fifes, Whistles, and some other "breath" Instruments (1969), *Hymnus 2*, multimedia show (Munich, 1972), and *Come S. Francesco II*, chamber spectacle for Speaker, Dancer, Chamber Orch., and Multivision (1979).—NS/LK/DM

Schönberg, Arnold (Franz Walter
See Schoenberg, Arnold (Franz Walter)

Schonberg, Harold C(harles), eminent American music critic; b. N.Y., Nov. 29, 1915. He studied at Brooklyn Coll. (B.A., 1937) and at N.Y.U. (M.A., 1938). He served in the army (1942–46); then was on the staff of the *N.Y. Sun* (1946–50); he was appointed to the music staff of the *N.Y. Times* in 1950; was senior music critic from 1960 until 1980. In 1971 he was the first music critic to be honored with the Pulitzer Prize in criticism. In his concert reviews and feature articles, he reveals a profound knowledge of music and displays a fine journalistic flair without assuming a posture of snobbish aloofness or descending to colloquial vulgarity. His intellectual horizon is exceptionally wide; he is well-versed in art, and can draw and paint; he is a chess aficionado and covered knowledgeably the Spassky-Fischer match in Reykjavík in 1972 for the *N.Y. Times*. He publ. in N.Y.: *Chamber and Solo Instrument Music* (1955); *The Collector's Chopin and Schumann* (1959); *The Great Pianists* (1963; second ed., rev., 1987); *The Great Conductors* (1967); *Lives of the Great Composers* (1970; second ed., 1981; third ed., 1997); *Facing the Music* (1981); *The Glorious Ones: Classical Music's Legendary Performers* (1985); *Horowitz: His Life and Music* (1992). —NS/LK/DM

Schönberg, Stig Gustav, Swedish organist and composer; b. Västra Husby, May 13, 1933. He studied at the Stockholm Musikhögskolan (1953–60), where he graduated with diplomas as a music teacher, organist, and choirmaster. His composition mentors were Larsson and Blomdahl, and he also studied theory with Erland von Koch and Valdemar Söderholm. He received training in organ with Flors Peeters in Belgium. He was active as a church organist and toured as a recitalist.

WORKS: DRAMATIC: B a l l e t : *Madeleine och Conrad* (1967; rev. 1972). ORCH.: *Intermezzo* (1958); *Introduktion och Allegro* for Strings (1958–59); Concerto for Organ and Strings (1962); *Sinfonia aperta* (1965); 3 concertinos for Strings (1966); *Fantasia* for Strings (1967); *Concitato* (1968); *Impromptu visionario* (1972); Concerto for 2 Flutes and Strings (1976); Sym. No. 2 (1977); Concerto for Organ and Orch. (1982); Concerto for Organ and Brass Orch. (1986–87); Bassoon Concerto (1992); Concerto for Trombone and Small Orch. (1994); Concerto for Double Bass and Small Orch. (1997); *Ouvertora concerto* (1997). CHAMBER: 7 string quartets (1961–84); *Madrigaler* for 2 Trumpets and 2 Trombones (1962); *Intrada* for 2 Trumpets, 2 Trombones, and Organ (1963); Sonata for Flute and Organ (1963); Trio for Flute, Violin, and Cello (1967); 2 violin sonatas (1964, 1967); *Vad Ijus over griften*, intrada for Organ and Brass Ensemble (1971); *Liten fantasi* for 2 Trumpets (1973); Flute Sonata (1974); *Pastoral* for Horn and Organ (1979); *Air* for Viola and Organ (1982); Sonata for Cello and Organ (1984); *Poème memorial* for Viola, and Piano or Organ or Harpsichord (1985); *Sonata all ricercata* for Violin and Organ (1989); Sonata for Saxophone and Organ (1996–97); piano pieces and organ music. VOCAL: Various works for Soloists, Chorus, and Instrument(s), including *Regina coeli* (1973), *Cantata gloriae* (1975), *Missa coralis* (1983), *Missa da pacem* (1985), and *Missa brevis* (1994); also a *Te Deum* for Chorus and String Orch. (1993), choruses, and songs.—NS/LK/DM

Schöne, Lotte (real name, **Charlotte Bodenstein**), admired Austrian-born French soprano; b. Vienna, Dec. 15, 1891; d. Paris, Dec. 22, 1977. She studied in Vienna. She made her debut at the Vienna Volksoper in 1912, and continued to appear there until 1917, then sang at the Vienna Court (later State) Opera (1917–26). She also appeared at the Berlin Städtische Oper (1926–33), and made many appearances at the Salzburg Festivals (1922–35). After leaving Germany in 1933, she went to Paris, became a naturalized French citizen, and made guest appearances at the Opéra and the Opéra-Comique; she was compelled to go into hiding during the Nazi occupation, but resumed her career after the liberation, and sang in Berlin in 1948; she retired in 1953. Among her many notable roles were Cherubino, Papagena, Susanna, Despina, Pamina, Zerlina, Sophie, Mimi, Liù, and Mélisande.—NS/LK/DM

Schöne, Wolfgang, German baritone; b. Bad Gandersheim, Feb. 9, 1940. He received his vocal training at the Hochschules für Musik in Hannover and Hamburg (diploma, 1969), his principal teacher being Naan Pöld. He took prizes in competitions in Berlin, Bordeaux, 's-Hertogenbosch, and Rio de Janeiro, and was active as a concert artist. In 1970 he launched his operatic career with engagements at the Württemberg State Opera in Stuttgart, the Hamburg State Opera, and the Vienna State Opera. In 1973 he became a member of the Württemberg State Opera, where he was honored as a

Kammersänger. In 1984 he sang Don Giovanni at the reopening of the Stuttgart Opera. In 1990 he was engaged as the Count in *Capriccio* at the Salzburg Festival. He portrayed Dr. Schön at the Théâtre du Châtelet in Paris in 1992. In 1997 he appeared as Amfortas at the Opéra de la Bastille in Paris. As a concert singer, he garnered extensive engagements in Europe and the Americas, appearing with many notable orchs. and as a recitalist. Among his operatic roles are Don Giovanni, Guglielmo, Count Almaviva, Eugene Onegin, Wolfram, Amfortas, Golaud, Mandryka, and Tom in Henze's *The English Cat*, which role he created at the Schwetzingen Festival in 1983.—NS/LK/DM

Schönherr, Max, Austrian conductor, musicologist, and composer; b. Marburg an der Drau, Nov. 23, 1903; d. Mödling, near Vienna, Dec. 13, 1984. He studied with Hermann Frisch in Marburg and Roderich von Mojsisovics at the Graz Cons., and later studied musicology at the Univ. of Vienna (Ph.D., 1970). After conducting at the Graz Landestheater (1924–28), he settled in Vienna as a conductor with the Theater an der Wien and Stadttheater (1929–33), the Volksoper (1933–38), and the Austrian Radio (1931–68), where he won distinction for his idiomatic readings of light Viennese scores. He composed much light music in a stylish manner, and also made effective arrangements of scores by the Viennese Strausses et al. He publ. *Carl Michael Ziehrer: Sein Werk, sein Leben, seine Zeit* (Vienna, 1974), *Lanner, Strauss, Ziehrer: Synoptic Handbook of the Dances and Marches* (Vienna, 1982), and with E. Brixel, *Karl Komzák: Vater, Sohn, Enkel: Ein Beitrag zur Rezeptionsgeschichte der Österreichischen Popularmusik* (Vienna, 1989). A Lamb ed. the vol. *Unterhaltungsmusik aus Österreich: Max Schönherr in seinen Erinnerungen und Schriften (Light Music from Austria: Reminiscences and Writings of Max Schönherr)* (in Ger. and Eng., N.Y., 1992). —NS/LK/DM

Schöning, Klaus, German radio producer and writer on music; b. Rastenburg, Feb. 24, 1936. After univ. studies in Munich, Göttingen, and Berlin, he worked in the theater. In 1961 he began a lengthy association with the Westdeutscher Rundfunk (WDR) of Cologne, where he is producer, director, and chief ed. of the WDR Studio for Acoustic Art, an international workshop for audio art and research that he established. He commissioned and produced over 1,000 radio broadcasts for the WDR and other international radio stations; was a pioneer in the reorientation of the German Horspiel in the late 1960s, his main programs being "New Hörspiel," "Composers as Hörspielmakers," and "Ars Acustica." Among the composers from whom he has commissioned works are John Cage, Alvin Curran, Pauline Oliveros, Alison Knowles, Charles Amirkhanian, Jackson Mac Low, and Joan La Barbara. With support from the WDR and the Goethe Inst., he also developed a transcontinental link for acoustic art, Acustica International; in 1985 he was artistic director of the first Acustica International Festival (Cologne), and, in 1990, of the Sound Art Festival and second Acustica International Festival (N.Y. and Montreal). He was the producer of the first Satellite Soundsculptures with *Ear-*

bridge Köln -San Francisco (1987) and *Soundbridge Köln -Kyoto* (1993) by Bill Fontana. In 1993 he was curator of sound installation with radio compositions by John Cage at the Venice Biennale and in 1993–94 at the Museum of Contemporary Art in San Francisco and the Guggenheim Museum in N.Y. He has won numerous awards for his productions, including the Prix Italia, Prix Futura, Karl-Sczuka-Preis, Hörspielpreis der Kriegsblinden, and Premio Ondas; in 1983 he received the Berliner Kunstpreis for Film/Radio/TV and in 1993 the Medienkunstpreis of the Zentrum für Kunst- und Medientechnologie in Karlsruhe. He also lectured extensively in Germany, France, and the U.S.; was curator of the exhibition "American Audio Art on WDR" at the Whitney Museum of Art in N.Y. (1990). Among his numerous publications are *John Cage: Roaratorio: Ein irischer Circus über Finnegans Wake* (1982), *Geschichte und Typologie des Hörspiels* (7 vols., 1988–90), and *1. Acustica International: Komponisten als Hörspielmacher* (1990); he also produced the CD-anthology *Ars Acustica* (1992). —NS/LK/DM

Schønwandt, Michael, Danish conductor; b. Copenhagen, Sept. 10, 1953. After training in musicology at the Univ. of Copenhagen (B.Mus., 1975), he studied conducting and composition at the Royal Academy of Music in London (1975–77). In 1977 he made his conducting debut in Copenhagen, and subsequently appeared as a guest conductor with various European orchs. After conducting opera at the Royal Danish Theater in 1979, he appeared as a guest conductor at London's Covent Garden, the Paris Opéra, and the Stuttgart Opera. In 1981 he became music director of the Collegium Musicum in Copenhagen. He was also principal guest conductor of the Théâtre Royal de la Monnaie in Brussels (1984–87), the Nice Opera (1987–91), and the Danish Radio Sym. Orch. in Copenhagen (from 1989). From 1992 to 1998 he was chief conductor of the Berlin Sym. Orch. In 1999 he became music director of the Royal Theater and Royal Danish Orch. in Copenhagen.—NS/LK/DM

Schönzeler, Hans-Hubert, German conductor and musicologist; b. Leipzig, June 22, 1925; d. London, 1997. He went to Australia as a youth, and studied conducting with Goossens at the New South Wales Conservatorium of Music in Sydney; later traveled in Europe, where he received further instruction in conducting with Kubelik, with Zecchi in Hilversum, and with Kempen in Siena. He eventually made his home in London, where he led the 20th-Century Ensemble (1957–62). In 1967 he was appointed deputy chief conductor of the West Australian Sym. Orch. in Perth, while continuing his appearances as a guest conductor in Europe. He publ. *Bruckner* (London and N.Y., 1970; rev. ed., 1978), *Dvořák* (London, 1984), *Furtwängler* (London, 1987), and *Zu Bruckners IX. Symphonie: die Krakauer Skizzen/Bruckner's 9th Symphony: the Cracow Sketches* (Vienna, 1987).—NS/LK/DM

Schop, Johann, German instrumentalist and composer; b. place and date unknown; d. Hamburg, 1667.

He learned to play the violin, lute, cornett, and trombone. He was a probationary musician (1614–15) and a regular musician (1615) in the Wolfenbüttel Hofkapelle. After serving at the Copenhagen court (1615–19), he became a municipal violinist in Hamburg in 1621. Schop acquired a fine reputation as both an instrumentalist and a composer. He excelled in the composition of both instrumental and vocal works. He had 2 sons who were musicians: Johann Schop (b. Hamburg [baptized], Oct. 5, 1626; d. after 1670), was a violist and composer, and Albert Schop (b. Hamburg [baptized], July 6, 1632; d. after 1667), was an organist and composer.

BIBL.: K. Stephenson, *J. S.: Sein Leben und Wirken* (diss., Univ. of Halle, 1924).—LK/DM

Schopenhauer, Arthur, great German philosopher; b. Danzig, Feb. 22, 1788; d. Frankfurt am Main, Sept. 21, 1860. Although his excursions into the realm of music are neither remarkable nor very valuable, they are stimulating, and have inspired a number of valuable contributions by modern investigators, especially in the field of musical esthetics. Wagner was influenced to a considerable extent by Schopenhauer's philosophical system.

BIBL.: F. von Hausegger, *Richard Wagner und A. S.* (Leipzig, 1878; second ed., 1892); M. Seydel, *A. S.s Metaphysik der Musik* (Leipzig, 1895); E. Zoccoli, *L'estetica di S.* (Milan, 1901); G. Melli, *La filosofia di S.* (Florence, 1905); T. Lessing, *S., Wagner, Nietzsche* (Munich, 1906); F. Wagner, *Beiträge zur Würdigung der Musiktheorie S.s* (diss., Univ. of Bonn, 1910); A. von Gottschalk, *Beethoven und S.* (Blanckenburg, 1912); A. Huebscher, *S.: Gestern-Heute-Morgen* (1973).—NS/LK/DM

Schorr, Friedrich, renowned Hungarian-American bass-baritone; b. Nagyvárad, Sept. 2, 1888; d. Farmington, Conn., Aug. 14, 1953. He studied law at the Univ. of Vienna, and also took private lessons in singing. He appeared with the Chicago Grand Opera (1912), then was a member of the opera companies in Graz (1912–16), Prague (1916–18), Cologne (1918–23), and of the Berlin State Opera (1923–31); also sang Wotan at Bayreuth (1925–31), and appeared at London's Covent Garden (1925–33). He made his Metropolitan Opera debut in N.Y. as Wolfram on Feb. 14, 1924, and continued as a member until his farewell performance as the Wanderer in *Siegfried* on March 2, 1943. Schorr is generally recognized as the foremost Wagnerian bass-baritone of his era; he also sang roles in operas by Beethoven, Strauss, Verdi, and Puccini, and appeared in the U.S. premieres of Krenek's *Jonny Spielt Auf* (Daniello; 1929) and Weinberger's *Schwanda* (title role; 1931) at the Metropolitan Opera.—NS/LK/DM

Schott, Anton, German tenor; b. Schloss Staufeneck, June 24, 1846; d. Stuttgart, Jan. 6, 1913. He was in the Prussian army. After the Franco-Prussian War, he sang at the Munich Opera (1871) and the Berlin Opera (1872–75), then in London and in Italy. He made his U.S. debut at the Metropolitan Opera in N.Y. as Tannhäuser (Nov. 17, 1884), and was on its roster until 1885, and again in 1886–87. He excelled as an interpreter of Wagnerian roles. He publ. a polemical brochure, *Hie Welf, hie Waibling* (1904).—NS/LK/DM

Schott, Bernhard, prominent German music publisher; b. Eltville, Aug. 10, 1748; d. Sandholf, near Heidesheim, April 26, 1809. He studied at the Univ. of Mainz, graduating as magister artium in 1771. He was granted a privilegium exclusivum and the title of music engraver to the elector in 1780. At his death, his sons, Johann Andreas (1781–1840) and Johann Joseph (1782–1855), carried on the business as B. Schotts Söhne. The 2 sons of Johann Andreas, Franz Philipp (b. July 30, 1811; d. May 8, 1874) and Peter (d. Paris, Sept. 20, 1894), continued the business; Peter was manager of the Paris and Brussels branches, and Franz Philipp was sole owner of the Mainz firm (from 1855). Peter Schott Jr. eventually became director, together with Franz von Landwehr and Ludwig Strecker (1853–1943); the latter's sons, Ludwig Strecker (1883–1978) and Willy Strecker (1884–1958), became partners in the firm in 1920. The Schott catalogue is one of the richest in the world, publishing works by the great masters as well as by leading contemporary composers; among its critical editions are the complete works of Wagner, Schoenberg, and Hindemith. It also publ. the journals *Cacilia* (1824–48), *Suddeutsche Musikzeitung* (1852–69), and *Melos* (1920–34; 1946–74); the last was combined with the *Neue Zeitschrift für Musik* in 1974. The firm likewise publ. the famous *Riemann Musik- Lexikon.*

BIBL.: *Der Musikverlag B. S.* (Mainz, 1954); H.-C. Müller, *B. S., Hofmusikstecher in Mainz: Die Frühgeschichte seines Musikverlages bis 1797, mit einem Verzeichnis der Verlagswerke 1779–1797* (Mainz, 1977).—NS/LK/DM

Schouwman, Hans, Dutch pianist, singer, and composer; b. Gorinchem, Aug. 8, 1902; d. The Hague, April 8, 1967. After training from Peter van Anrooy, he was active as a recitalist accompanying himself at the piano. He also devoted much time to composition.

WORKS: ORCH.: *5 Sketches* for Clarinet and Small Orch. (1942); *Suite* for Amateur Orch. (1958); *De Prinses op de erwt* (1965). **CHAMBER:** 2 oboe sonatinas (1940, 1944); *Aubade en Barcarolle* for Clarinet and Piano (1944); Trio for Clarinet, Bassoon, and Piano (1944); *Romance en Humoreske* for Bassoon and Piano (1944); *4 Pieces* for Flute and Piano (1944); *2 Legends* for Horn and Piano (1944); *Nederlandse suite* for Wind Quintet (1953); *3 Preludes* for Piano, Left-hand (1959). **VOCAL:** *3 danswijzen* (3 Dance Tunes) for Voice, 2 Flutes, Strings, and Percussion (1938); *Friesland*, 4 songs for Voice and Orch. (1945); *Memento mori* for Alto, Chorus, and Small Orch. (1947); *Notturno* for Mezzo-soprano, Cello, and Piano (1949); *Om de kribbe* for Soprano, Contralto, Women's Chorus, and Piano (1952); vocal duets; solo songs; arrangements.—NS/LK/DM

Schrade, Leo, eminent German musicologist; b. Allenstein, Dec. 13, 1903; d. Spéracédès, Alpes-Maritimes, Sept. 21, 1964. He studied with Hermann Halbig at the Univ. of Heidelberg (1923–27), with Sandberger at the Univ. of Munich, and with Kroyer at the Univ. of Leipzig (Ph.D., 1927, with the diss. *Die ältesten Denkmäler der Orgelmusik als Beitrag zu einer Geschichte der Toccata*; publ. in Münster, 1928); completed his Habilitation in 1929 at the Univ. of Königsberg. He taught at the univs. of Königsberg (1928–32) and Bonn (from 1932). In 1937 he emigrated to the U.S.; was on the faculty of Yale Univ. (1938–58), where he taught music

history; in 1958 he was appointed to the music faculty of the Univ. of Basel. He was also the Charles Eliot Norton Lecturer at Harvard Univ. in 1962–63. He was founder-ed. of the Yale Studies in the History of Music and the Yale Collegium Musicum series (1947–58); was co-ed. of the *Journal of Renaissance and Baroque Music* (1946–47), *Annales musicologiques* (1953–64), and the *Archiv für Musikwissenschaft* (1958–64); served as an ed. of the series Polyphonic Music in the Fourteenth Century (vols. 1–3, 1956; vol. 4, 1958).

WRITINGS: *Beethoven in France: The Growth of an Idea* (New Haven, 1942); *Monteverdi: Creator of Modern Music* (N.Y., 1950; second ed., 1964); *Bach: The Conflict Between the Sacred and the Secular* (N.Y., 1954); *W.A. Mozart* (Bern and Munich, 1964); *Tragedy in the Art of Music* (Cambridge, Mass., 1964).

BIBL.: *Musik und Geschichte: L. S. zum sechzigsten Geburtstag* (Cologne, 1963; Eng. tr., 1965, as *Music and History: L. S. on the Occasion of His 60th Birthday*); *L. S. in memoriam* (Bern and Munich, 1966); E. Lichtenhahn, ed., *L. S.: De scientia musicae studia atque orationes* (Bern and Stuttgart, 1967); W. Arlt et al., eds., *Gattungen der Musik in Einzeldarstellungen: Gedenkschrift für L. S.* (Bern and Munich, 1973).—NS/LK/DM

Schrader, Barry, American composer; b. Johnstown, Pa., June 26, 1945. He received degrees at the Univ. of Pittsburgh in English literature (B.A., 1967) and in musicology (M.A., 1970); also served as an organist at Heinz Chapel. In 1969–70 he studied electroacoustic techniques with Subotnick. In 1970 he moved to Los Angeles and attended the Calif. Inst. of the Arts (M.F.A. in composition, 1971); later joined its faculty. From 1975 to 1978 he also taught at Calif. State Univ. at Los Angeles. He organized a series of electroacoustic music programs under the name "Currents," held in Los Angeles from 1973 to 1979; also participated in many electronic music festivals in other countries. In 1984 he became the first president of the Soc. for Electro-Acoustic Music in the U.S. He publ. *Introduction to Electro-Acoustical Music* (Englewood Cliffs, N.J., 1982). Most of his music is for electronic sound; in his *Bestiary* (1972–74), Schrader explored the potentialities of synthesizing new timbres; in his *Trinity* (1976), he transmuted given timbres to more complex sonorities; in his *Lost Atlantis*, he essayed a programmatic use of electronic sound. He also experimented in combining live music with electronic resources, as in his work *Moon-Whales and other Moon Songs* (1982–83).

WORKS: *Signature for Tempo* for Soprano and Piano (1966); *Serenade* for Tape (1969); *Incantation* for Tape (1970); *Sky Ballet* for Sound Environment (1970); *Elysium* for Harp, Dancers, Tape, and Projections (1971); *Besitary* for Tape (1972–74); *Trinity* for Tape (1976); *Lost Atlantis* for Tape (1977); *Moon-whales and Other Moon Songs* for Soprano and Tape (1982–83); *Electronic Music Box I* for Sound Installation (1983), *II* (1983), and *III* (1984); *TWO: Square Flowers Red: SONGS* (1990); also many film scores, including *Death of the Red Planet* (1973), *Heavy Light* (1973), *Exploratorium* (1975), *Mobiles* (1978), *Along the Way* (1980), and *Galaxy of Terror* (1981).—NS/LK/DM

Schramm, Hermann, German tenor; b. Berlin, Feb. 7, 1871; d. Frankfurt am Main, Dec. 14, 1951. He made his operatic debut in Breslau in 1895 as Gomez in Kreutzer's *Die Nachtlager von Granada*. From 1896 to

1900 he sang at the Cologne Opera. In 1899 he appeared at London's Covent Garden and at the Bayreuth Festival (debut as David). From 1900 to 1933 he was a member of the Frankfurt am Main Opera, where he created the role of the chancellor in Schreker's *Der Schatsgräber* (1920). Schramm was hailed as the finest David and Mime of his era.—**NS/LK/DM**

Schramm, Margit, German soprano; b. Dortmund, July 21, 1935; d. Munich, May 12, 1996. She was educated at the Dortmund Cons., and made her debut at Saarbrücken in 1956. She sang in Koblenz (1957–58), in Munich at the Gärtnerplatz State Theater (1959–64), in Berlin at the Theater des Westens (1965–66), and in the municipal theaters in Dortmund (1967). In 1968 she joined the ensemble of the State Theater in Wiesbaden. Her repertoire of German and Austrian operettas was vast and impressive.—**NS/LK/DM**

Schramm, Melchior, esteemed German organist and composer; b. Munsterberg, Silesia, c. 1553; d. Offenburg, Baden, Sept. 6, 1619. After serving as a chorister in the Hofkapelle of Archduke Ferdinand of the Tirol, he was awarded a scholarship to study with the Innsbruck court organist, Servatius Rorif. In 1571–72 he was organist at a Halle convent; after serving as organist (1574–1605) and Kapellmeister (1574–94) at the Sigmarigen court, he was civic organist at Offenburg's Heilig Kreuz Kirche (from 1605). His works include 3 vols. of motets (1576, 1606, 1612) and a vol. of German madrigals (1579).—**NS/LK/DM**

Schrammel, Johann, Austrian violinist and composer; b. Neulerchenfeld, near Vienna, May 22, 1850; d. Vienna, June 17, 1893. He studied violin with Ernst Melzer before pursuing training at the Vienna Cons. (1862–66) with Heissler and Hellmesberger. After playing in the Harmonie and Josephstadt theater orchs. and in Margold's salon orch. in Vienna, he founded the Schrammel Trio there in 1878, which became a quartet in 1886. Schrammel wrote many popular dances, marches, and songs. His march *Wien bleibt Wien* (1887) has remained a favorite in the Viennese repertory. His brother, Joseph Schrammel (b. Ottakring, near Vienna, March 3, 1852; d. Vienna, Nov. 24, 1895), was also a violinist and composer. After studies with Hellmesberger (1865–67), he played in his brother's trio.

BIBL.: H. Mailler, *S.-Quartett* (Vienna, 1943); R. Moissl, *Die S.-Dynastie* (St. Pölten, 1943).—**LK/DM**

Schreiber, Frederick (actually, **Friedrich**), Austrian-American organist, choirmaster, and composer; b. Vienna, Jan. 13, 1895; d. N.Y., Jan. 15, 1985. He studied piano, cello, and composition in Vienna. After teaching at the Cons. there (1927–38), he emigrated to N.Y. and was organist and choirmaster of the Reformed Protestant Church (1939–58). Among his orch. works are 7 syms. (1927–57); *The Beatitudes,* symphonic trilogy for Orch. and Chorus (1950); *Christmas Suite* (1967); *Images* (1971); *Contrasts* (1972); 2 piano concertos; Cello Concerto; 2 violin concertos; *Variations on a German Folksong* (1974); numerous choral pieces; chamber music, including 2 string quintets, 7 string quartets, Piano Quartet, and 3 piano trios; much organ music.—**NS/LK/DM**

Schreier, Peter (Max), esteemed German tenor and conductor; b. Meissen, July 29, 1935. He sang in the Dresdner Kreuzchor. He gained a taste for the theater when he appeared as one of the 3 boys in *Die Zauberflöte* at Dresden's Semper Opera House (1944). He received private vocal lessons from Polster in Leipzig (1954–56), and then with Winkler in Dresden; also took courses at the Hochschule für Musik there (1956–59); concurrently worked at the studio of the Dresden State Opera, where he appeared as Paolino in *Il Matrimonio segreto* (1957); made his official debut there as the first Prisoner in *Fidelio* (1959), and went on to become a regular member of the company in 1961. In 1963 he joined the Berlin State Opera, and became one of its principal artists; he also made guest appearances with opera houses throughout Eastern Europe and the Soviet Union; likewise sang in London (debut as Ferrando with the visiting Hamburg State Opera, 1966) and at the Salzburg Festivals (from 1967), the Vienna State Opera (from 1967), the Metropolitan Opera in N.Y. (debut as Tamino, Dec. 25, 1967), La Scala in Milan (1969), and the Teatro Colón in Buenos Aires (1969). His roles in Mozart's operas brought him critical acclaim; he was also a distinguished oratorio and lieder artist, excelling in a repertoire that ranged from Bach to Orff. In 1970 he launched a second, equally successful career as a conductor. In 1964 he was honored with the title of Kammersänger. He publ. the book *Aus meiner Sicht: Gedanken und Erinnerungen* (ed. by M. Meier; Vienna, 1983).

BIBL.: G. Schmiedel, *P. S.: Für Sie portratiert* (Leipzig, 1976); W.-E. von Lewinski, *P. S.: Interviews, Tatsachen, Meinungen* (Munich, 1992).—**NS/LK/DM**

Schreker, Franz, eminent Austrian conductor, pedagogue, and composer; b. Monaco (of Austrian parents), March 23, 1878; d. Berlin, March 21, 1934. His father, the court photographer, died when he was 10. The family went to Vienna, where he studied with Arnold Rosé; also received instruction in composition from Robert Fuchs at the Cons. (1892–1900). He first gained notice as a composer with his pantomime *Der Geburtstag der Infantin* (Vienna, Aug. 1908); that same year he founded the Phil. Chorus, serving as its conductor until 1920. He won great distinction with his opera *Der ferne Klang* (Frankfurt am Main, Aug. 18, 1912); outstanding among his later operas were *Die Gezeichneten* (Frankfurt am Main, April 25, 1918) and *Der Schatzgräber* (Frankfurt am Main, Jan. 21, 1920). After teaching composition at the Vienna Academy of Music (1912–20), he settled in Berlin as director of the Hochschule für Musik. Being of Jewish birth, he became a target of the rising Nazi movement; in 1931 he withdrew from performance his opera *Christophorus* in the face of Nazi threats; his last opera, *Der Schmied von Gent,* was premiered in Berlin on Oct. 29, 1932, in spite of Nazi demonstrations. Schreker was pressured into resigning his position at the Hochschule für Musik in 1932, but that same year he was given charge of a master class in composition at the Prussian Academy of Arts; he lost this position when the Nazis came to power in 1933. Shortly afterward, he suffered a major heart attack, and spent the remaining months of his life in poor health and reduced circumstances. As a composer, Schreker led the neo-Romantic movement in the direction of Expressionism, emphasizing psychological conflicts in his operas; in his harmonies, he expanded the basically Wagnerian sonorities to include many devices associated with Impressionism. He exercised considerable influence on the German and Viennese schools of his time, but with the change of direction in modern music toward economy of means and away from mystical and psychological trends, Schreker's music suffered a decline after his death.

WORKS: DRAMATIC: Opera (all but the first to his own librettos): *Flammen* (c. 1900; concert perf., Vienna, April 24, 1902); *Der ferne Klang* (1901–10; Frankfurt am Main, Aug. 18, 1912); *Das Spielwerk und die Prinzessin* (1909–12; Frankfurt am Main and Vienna, March 15, 1913; rev. as *Das Spielwerk*, 1916; Munich, Oct. 30, 1920); *Die Gezeichneten* (1913–15; Frankfurt am Main, April 25, 1918); *Der Schatzgräber* (1915–18; Frankfurt am Main, Jan. 21, 1920); *Irrelohe* (1919–23; Cologne, March 27, 1924); *Christophorus, oder Die Vision einer Oper* (1924–27; Freiburg im Breisgau, Oct. 1, 1978); *Der singende Teufel* (1924–28; Berlin, Dec. 10, 1928); *Der Schmied von Gent* (1929–32; Berlin, Oct. 29, 1932). **Pantomime**: *Der Geburtstag der Infantin* for Strings (Vienna, Aug. 1908; rev. as *Spanisches Fest* for Orch., 1923). **Dance Allegory**: *Der Wind* for Clarinet and Piano Quartet (1908). **Ballet**: *Rokoko* (1908; rev. as *Ein Tanzspiel*, 1920). **ORCH.:** *Love Song* for Strings and Harp (1895; not extant); *Intermezzo* for Strings (1900; included in the *Romantische Suite*, 1902); *Romantische Suite* (1902; includes the *Intermezzo for Strings*, 1900); *Ekkehard*, overture (1902); *Phantastische Ouverture* (1902); *Festwalzer und Walzerintermezzo* (1908); *Vorspiel zu einem Drama* (1913; used as a prelude to his opera *Die Gezeichneten*); *Kammersymphonie* for 23 Solo Instruments (1916; Vienna, March 12, 1917); *Kleine Suite* for Chamber Orch. (1928; Breslau, Jan. 17, 1929); *4 Little Pieces* (1930); *Vorspiel zu einer grossen Oper* (1933; Baden-Baden, March 11, 1958; symphonic fragments from an unfinished opera, *Memnon*). **CHAMBER:** Violin Sonata (1897); piano pieces. **VOCAL:** *Der Holdstein* for Soprano, Bass, Chorus, and Orch. (c. 1898); *Psalm CXVI* for Women's Chorus, Orch., and Organ (1900); *Schwanengesang* for Chorus and Orch. (1902); *Fünf Gesänge* for Alto or Bass and Orch. (c. 1921; based on the song cycle, 1909); *Vom ewigen Leben* for Voice and Orch. (1927; based on *Zwei lyrische Gesänge*, 1924); some unaccompanied choral pieces; songs.

BIBL.: P. Bekker, *F. S.: Studie zur Kritik der modernen Oper* (Berlin, 1919; second ed., 1983); R. Hoffmann, *F. S.* (Leipzig and Vienna, 1921); J. Kapp, *F. S.: Der Mann und sein Werk* (Munich, 1921); F. Bayerl, *F. S.s Opernwerk* (Erlangen, 1928); *S.-Heft* (Berlin, 1959); G. Neuwirth, *F. S.* (Vienna, 1959); H. Bures-Schreker, *El caso S.* (Buenos Aires, 1969; rev. Ger. tr. with H. Stuckenschmidt and W. Oehlmann as *F. S.*, Vienna, 1970); G. Neuwirth, *Die Harmonik in der Oper "Der ferne Klang" von F. S.* (Regensburg, 1972); F. Heller, ed., *Arnold Schönberg—F. S.: Briefwechsel* (Tutzing, 1974); O. Kolleritsch, ed., *F. S. am Beginn der neuen Musik, Studien zur Wertungsforschung*, XI (Graz, 1978); R. Ermen, ed., *F. S. (1878–1934) zum 50. Todestag* (Aachen, 1984); M. Brzoska, *F. S.s Oper "Der Schatzgräber"* (Stuttgart, 1988); C. Hailey, *F. S.: His Life, Times, and Music* (Cambridge, 1993). —NS/LK/DM

Schröder, family of German musicians:

(1) Karl Schröder, violinist and violist; b. Oberbosa, Thuringia, March 17, 1816; d. Berlin, April 21, 1890. He studied with G. Siebeck and A.B. Marx in Eisleben. After serving as a town musician in Quedlinburg, he was music director in Neuhaldensleben. He also played in a family quartet with his sons:

(2) Hermann Schröder, violinist, teacher, and composer; b. Quedlinburg, July 28, 1843; d. Berlin, Jan. 30, 1909. He studied with his father, and with W. Sommer and A.G. Ritter in Magdeburg, then settled in Berlin, where he was director of his own music school (from 1873). He also taught at the Institut für Kirchenmusik (from 1885), where he later was asst. director. He publ. *Untersuchung über die sympathischen Klänge der Geigeninstrumente* (1891), *Die symmetrische Umkehrung in der Musik* (1902), and *Ton und Farbe* (1906), as well as a violin method, *Die Kunst des Violinspiels* (1887). Among his compositions were chamber music for instructive purposes: *6 instruktive Quartette, 3 kleine Trios*, etc.

(3) Karl Schröder, cellist, conductor, teacher, and composer; b. Quedlinburg, Dec. 18, 1848; d. Bremen, Sept. 22, 1935. He studied with his father, becoming a member of the Sondershausen Hofkapelle when he was 14; also received instruction from Drechsler and Kiel. He played in the family quartet until it was dissolved in 1873, and was Kapellmeister at Berlin's Kroll Opera (1872–73). After serving in the Braunschweig Hofkapelle (1873–74), he was solo cellist in the Gewandhaus Orch. in Leipzig (1874–81), where he also taught at the Cons. In 1881 he returned to Sondershausen as Hofkapellmeister, and also was director of his own music school until 1886. He then was conductor of the German Opera in Rotterdam (1886–87), in Berlin (1887–88), and in Hamburg (1888–90). In 1890 he once more returned to Sondershausen as director of the Cons. (until 1909), and then taught cello at Berlin's Stern Cons. (1911–24). He wrote 2 operas, *Aspasia* (1892), and *Asket* (1893), 3 syms., 6 cello concertos, and chamber music. He compiled 3 pedagogical manuals: *Katechismus der Dirigierens und Taktierens* (1889), *Katechismus des Violinspiels* (1889), and *Katechismus des Violoncellspiels* (1890), all of which were publ. in Eng. trs. (1893, 1895, 1896). His collections of Classical works for the cello, especially *Vortragstudien* (60 pieces), are of value.

(4) Alwin Schröder, violist, cellist, and teacher; b. Neuhaldensleben, June 15, 1855; d. Boston, Oct. 17, 1928. He studied piano with his father and violin with his brother Hermann, and then continued violin studies with De Ahna and Tappert at the Berlin Hochschule für Musik. He was 11 when he took his father's place as violist in the family quartet. He was a violinist (1872–75) and a cellist (from 1875) in Karl Liebig's orch., and in 1880 became deputy to his brother Karl in Leipzig's Gewandhaus Orch., and then was joint principal with J. Klengel (from 1881); also taught at the Cons. In 1891 he emigrated to the U.S. and later became a naturalized citizen. He played in the Boston Sym. Orch. (1891–1925), and also was a member of the Kneisel Quartet. He wrote some manuals and prepared transcriptions for cello. —NS/LK/DM

Schröder, Hanning, German composer; b. Rostock, July 4, 1896; d. Berlin, Oct. 16, 1987. He was a medical student, and concurrently he took violin lessons with Havemann in Berlin and composition with

Weismann in Freiburg im Breisgau; then took a course in musicology with W. Gurlitt. In 1929 he married the musicologist Cornelia Auerbach (b. Breslau, Aug. 24, 1900); they remained in Germany under the Nazi regime, but were barred from professional work for their act of human charity in giving shelter to a Jewish couple in their Berlin apartment. After the fall of the Third Reich, they resumed their careers.

WORKS: *Hänsel und Gretel*, children's Singspiel (Berlin, Dec. 23, 1952); *Musik* for Recorder (1954), and similar solo works for Viola, Cello, Violin, and Bassoon; *Divertimento* for 5 Wind Instruments (1957); *Divertimento* for Viola and Cello (1963); *Metronome 80* for Violin (1969); Nonet for Wind Quintet, Violin, Viola, Cello, and Double Bass (1970); *Varianten* for Flute and Orch. (1971).

BIBL.: N. Schüler, *H. S.: Dokumente: Kritisches Werkverzeichnis* (Hamburg, 1996).—**NS/LK/DM**

Schröder, Jaap, distinguished Dutch violinist, conductor, and pedagogue; b. Amsterdam, Dec. 31, 1925. He was a student of Jos de Clerck at the Sweelinck Cons. in Amsterdam (soloist diploma, 1947). He then went to Paris and studied with Fournier at the École Jacques Thibaud (premier prix, 1948), with Masson (musicology) at the Sorbonne (1947–49), and with Jean Pasquier (1948–49). In 1950 he made his professional debut as a violinist in Mozart's A major Concerto, K.219, in Maastricht. From 1950 to 1963 he was concertmaster of the Radio Chamber Orch. in Hilversum, and from 1960 to 1973 he was concertmaster and conductor of Concerto Amsterdam. He was a member of the Netherlands String Quartet from 1952 to 1969 and of Quadro Amsterdam from 1960 to 1966. From 1963 to 1991 he was prof. of violin at the Sweelinck Cons. and at the Schola Cantorum Basiliensis in Basel from 1974 to 1991. In 1973 he organized the Quartetto Esterhazy with the purpose of performing the Classical string quartet repertoire along historically informed lines, and remained active with it until 1981. From 1973 to 1981 he also was concertmaster of the Aston Magna Ensemble in the U.S. He was concertmaster of the Academy of Ancient Music in London from 1980 to 1984, and also was principal guest conductor of the Smithsonian Chamber Orch. in Washington, D.C., from 1981 to 1990. In 1982 he founded the Smithson String Quartet in the latter city, with which he was active until 1996. In 1989 he founded the Atlantis Ensemble for the purpose of performing Classical and Romantic works on period instruments. He also was a member of the Arcadia Players, a Baroque trio, from 1991 to 1995. As a guest conductor, he has appeared with both period and modern instrument orchs. He was a visiting lecturer at the Juilliard School in N.Y. (1982, 1984) and at Yale Univ. (1982–96), a guest prof. at the Edsburg Music Inst. in Stockholm (from 1986), the Luxembourg Cons. (1994–97), and the Sibelius Academy in Helsinki (1996–99), and a teacher of master classes on both sides of the Atlantic. To mark the 250th anniversary of Bach's death in 2000, he wrote a study on the Leipzig master's Sonatas for Solo Violin. Schröder has won notable distinction for his performances of the violin literature of the 17th and 18th centuries. He has also performed much music from the Classical and Romantic eras.—**NS/LK/DM**

Schrøder, Jens, Danish conductor; b. Bielsko, Poland, Nov. 6, 1909; d. Ålborg, Aug. 10, 1991. He studied at the Prague Academy of Music. After conducting in various Danish cities, he was chief conductor of the Municipal Theater (1942–75) and the Sym. Orch. (1942–80) in Ålborg; he also was a guest conductor with the Danish Radio Sym. Orch. and the Royal Danish Orch. in Copenhagen. In 1980 he was made a Knight of the Dannebrog Order (first Grade) for his services to Danish music.—**NS/LK/DM**

Schröder-Devrient, Wilhelmine, celebrated German soprano; b. Hamburg, Dec. 6, 1804; d. Coburg, Jan. 26, 1860. She received early training for the stage from her father, Friedrich Schröder (1744–1816), a baritone, and from her mother, Antoinette Sophie Bürger, a well-known actress; she herself played children's parts and was an actress until her 17th year. After the death of her father, she followed her mother to Vienna, where she studied with Mozatti. She made her operatic debut at the Kärnthnertortheater in Vienna on Jan. 20, 1821, as Pamina, then sang Agathe in *Der Freischütz* under Weber's direction (Vienna, March 7, 1822). When *Fidelio* was revived in Vienna in 1822, she sang Leonore in the presence of Beethoven (Nov. 3, 1822). In 1822 she sang in Dresden, and then was a member of its court opera from 1823 to 1847, where she received additional training from the chorus master, Aloys Mieksch. She also made guest appearances in Berlin (1828), Paris (1830–32), and London (1832–33; 1837); likewise won renown as a concert artist, continuing to make appearances in this capacity in Germany until 1856. She was one of the great singing actresses of her era, numbering among her many fine roles Donna Anna, Euryanthe, Norma, Rossini's Desdemona, Amina, and Lady Macbeth. Wagner held her in high esteem and chose her to create the roles of Adriano Colonna in *Rienzi* (Dresden, Oct. 20, 1842), Senta in *Der fliegende Holländer* (Dresden, Jan. 2, 1843), and Venus in *Tannhäuser* (Dresden, Oct. 19, 1845). She was married 3 times: her first husband was the actor Karl Devrient, whom she divorced in 1828; her second husband, a Saxon officer named Von Doring, cheated her out of her earnings, and she likewise divorced him; her third husband was the Livonian baron Von Bock, whom she married in 1850. A purported autobiography, publ. anonymously in many eds. since about 1870 as *Aus den Memoiren einer Sängerin or Memoires d'une chanteuse allemande*, is in fact a pornographic fantasy whose real author is unknown. A novel based on her life by Eva von Baudissin, *Wilhelmine Schröder-Devrient: Der Schicksalsweg einer grossen Künstlerin*, was publ. in Berlin in 1937.

BIBL.: C. von Glümer, *Erinnerungen an W. S.-D.* (Leipzig, 1862); A. von Wolzogen, *W. S.-D.* (Leipzig, 1863); C. Hagemann, *W. S.-D.* (Berlin, 1904; second ed., 1947); J. Bab, *Die D.s* (Berlin, 1932).—**NS/LK/DM**

Schröder-Feinen, Ursula, German soprano; b. Gelsenkirchen, July 21, 1936. She studied voice with Maria Helm in Gelsenkirchen, and took courses at the Essen Folkwangschule. She sang in the chorus of the Gelsenkirchen Opera (1958), where she made her operatic debut as Aida in 1961, and remained on its roster until 1968; then sang with the Deutsche Oper am Rhein in Düsseldorf (1968–72). On Dec. 4, 1970, she made her Metropolitan Opera debut in N.Y. as Chrysothemis in *Elektra*; also sang at Bayreuth, Salzburg, Milan, and Berlin. She retired in 1979. Schröder-Feinen was a versatile singer whose repertoire included major dramatic roles in German and Italian opera.—NS/LK/DM

Schröter, family of German musicians:

(1) Johann Friedrich Schröter, oboist and teacher; b. Eilenburg, 1724; d. Kassel, 1811. He began his career as an oboist in Count Brühl's regiment. In 1766 he went to Leipzig, where he nurtured his children's musical careers; also took them on tours of Germany, the Netherlands, and England (1771–c. 1773). He later was a court musician and teacher in Hanau (1779–86) and Kassel. His four children were:

(2) Corona (Elisabeth Wilhelmine) Schröter, soprano, actress, and composer; b. Guben, Jan. 14, 1751; d. Ilmenau, Aug. 23, 1802. She began her musical training with her father, becoming proficient as a keyboard player, guitarist, and singer; continued her studies with Hiller in Leipzig, where she sang in his Grand Concerts from 1765; later became active as an actress in amateur productions there. She won the admiration of Goethe, who arranged for her to be made a Kammersängerin to the Duchess Anna Amalia in Weimar in 1776; she also appeared as an actress at the amateur court theater, frequently taking roles opposite Goethe in his own dramas. When the court theater became a professional ensemble in 1783, she devoted herself to singing, teaching, poetry, drawing, and painting. Her association with the court ended about 1788. She settled in Ilmenau about 1801. She created the title role in and wrote music for Goethe's Singspiel *Die Fischerin* (1782); also wrote other stage music and publ. *25 Lieder in Musik gesetzt* for Voice and Piano (Weimar, 1786; includes one of the earliest settings of Goethe's *Der Erlkönig* from *Die Fischerin*) and (16) *Gesänge* for Voice and Piano (Weimar, 1794).

BIBL.: H. Düntzer, *Charlotte von Stein und C. S.: Eine Vertheidigung* (Stuttgart, 1876); P. Pasig, *Goethe und Ilmenau mit einer Beigabe: Goethe und C. S.* (Ilmenau, 1902); H. Stümcke, *C. S.* (Bielefeld, 1904; second ed., 1926).

(3) Johann Samuel Schroeter, pianist and composer; b. probably in Guben, c. 1752; d. London, Nov. 1, 1788. He commenced musical studies with his father, and about 1763 became a pupil of Hiller in Leipzig, where he sang in Hiller's concerts and later was active as a pianist (from 1767). He went to London with his family, then settled there; was organist at the German Chapel before being made music master to Queen Charlotte in 1782 in succession to J.S. Bach. He eventually entered the service of the Prince of Wales (later King George IV). He publ. 12 concertos for Keyboard and Strings (London, 6 c. 1774 and 6 c. 1777), various sonatas and other chamber pieces, and some vocal music. His widow became attached to Haydn during Haydn's stay in London (1790–91), and sent him many impassioned letters, of which copies made by Haydn are extant.

(4) (Johann) Heinrich Schröter, violinist and composer; b. Warsaw, c. 1760; d. probably in Paris, after 1782. He first made an impression as a soloist in a Dittersdorf violin concerto in Leipzig (1770). After appearing in concerts with his family in London, he went with his father to Hanau in 1779; gave concerts with his sister Marie in Frankfurt am Main (1780) and in Leipzig (1782) before disappearing from the musical scene. His extant works comprise 6 violin duets (London, c. 1772), *6 Duo concertans* for 2 Violins (Paris, c. 1785), and 6 string trios (London and Paris, c. 1786).

(5) Marie Henriette Schröter, singer; b. Leipzig, 1766; d. probably in Karlsruhe, after 1804. She studied with her father and gave concerts in Leipzig; went with her father to Hanau, where she became a court music teacher when she was only 13. She was a Kammersängerin at the Darmstadt court until 1804.—NS/LK/DM

Schröter, Christoph Gottlieb, German organist, music theorist, and composer; b. Hohnstein, near Schandau, Saxony, Aug. 10, 1699; d. Nordhausen, May 20, 1782. He began his music studies with his father, and in 1706 was sent to Dresden, where he became a soprano in the royal chapel and received instruction in keyboard instruments from the Kapellmeister; was made Ratsdiskantist in 1710, and later took instruction in organ and fugue at the Kreuzschule. After theological training in Leipzig (1717–18), he returned to Dresden as music copyist to Antonio Lotti; in 1719 he was made a secretary to a baron, in which capacity he traveled throughout Germany, the Netherlands, and England. He was a lecturer on music at the Univ. of Jena (1724–26), then was organist at the principal church in Minden (1726–32) and in Nordhausen (1732–82). In 1739 he became a member of Mizler's Societät der Musikalischen Wissenschaften of Leipzig. During the French occupation of Nordhausen in 1761, his home was ransacked and his library destroyed. He composed 5 cantata cycles, 4 Passions, a *Sieben Worte Jesu*, and various instrumental works, including serenades, concertos, sonatas, organ pieces, etc., almost all of which are lost. Schröter claimed priority for the invention of a hammer action for keyed string instruments, anticipating Cristofori's invention of the pianoforte; his argument is expounded with polemical passion in his paper "Umständliche Beschreibung eines neuerfundenen Clavierinstruments, auf welchem man in unterschiedenen Graden stark und schwach spielen kann," which was publ. in 1763 in Marpurg's *Kritische Briefe*; however, music historians rejected his arguments as chronologically invalid. In the field of music theory, he publ. an important paper, *Deutliche Anweisung zum General-Bass, in beständiger Veränderung des uns angebohrnen harmonischen Dreyklanges* (Halberstadt, 1772), in which he expounded the thesis that the major and minor triads are the sole fundamental chords in harmony. He also publ. *Christoph Gottlieb Schröters...Letzte Beschäftigung mit musicalischen Dinge, nebst sechs Temperatur-Plänen und einer Noten-Tafel* (Nordhausen, 1782) and other works in an egotistically assertive vein.—NS/LK/DM

Schröter, Leonhart, German composer; b. Torgau, c. 1532; d. Magdeburg, c. 1601. He was educated in

Torgau, Annaberg, and Meissen; was town Kantor in Saalfeld (1561–71; 1573–76) and librarian at the Wolfenbüttel court (1571–73); then Kantor at Magdeburg's Alstadt Lateinschule (1576–95). His works include *55 geistliche Lieder* for 4 Voices (Wittenberg, 1562), *Der 12. und 124. Psalm Davids* for 4 Voices (Magdeburg, 1577), *Canticum sanctorum Ambrosii et Augustini Te Deum laudamus* for 8 Voices (Magdeburg, 1584), and *Epithalamii cantilena...in honorem nuptiarum ... Melchioris Papae* for 10 Voices (Magdeburg, 1587).

BIBL.: G. Hofmann, *L. S.: Ein lutherischer Kantor zu Magdeburg* (diss., Univ. of Freiburg, 1932); H. Hasse, *Der erste herzogliche Bibliothekar: Ein Musiker: Bemerkungen uber den Kantor und Komponisten L. S.* (Frankfurt am Main, 1972).—**NS/LK/DM**

Schub, André-Michel, French-born American pianist; b. Paris, Dec. 26, 1952. He was taken to N.Y. as an infant and was taught piano by his mother; then became a pupil of Jascha Zayde. After attending Princeton Univ. (1968–69), he studied with Rudolf Serkin at the Curtis Inst. of Music in Philadelphia (1970–73). In 1974 he won first prize in the Naumburg competition and in 1977 the Avery Fisher Prize; after winning first prize in the Van Cliburn competition in 1981, he pursued an international career. His brilliant virtuoso technique is matched by a sensitive temperament; he shines in the Classic and Romantic repertoire.—**NS/LK/DM**

Schubart, Christian Friedrich Daniel, prominent German instrumentalist, poet, journalist, writer on music, and composer; b. Obersontheim, Swabia, March 24, 1739; d. Stuttgart, Oct. 10, 1791. He revealed musical and literary gifts as a child, but his parents insisted that he pursue theological studies; he took courses in Nördlingen and Nuremberg, and also received some instruction in music from his father and G.W. Gruber; then was a student at the Univ. of Erlangen (1758–60), where he proved a contentious pupil. He served as organist and preceptor in Geisslingen (1763–69); was made court organist in Ludwigsburg in 1769, and also was harpsichordist at the opera and a music teacher before being banished for dissolute conduct in 1773. He then went to Augsburg, where he brought out the periodical *Deutsche Chronik* in 1774, continuing its publication in Ulm until 1777. His journal was devoted to politics, literature, and music; his political writings won him many enemies, and in 1777 he was imprisoned by Duke Carl Eugen of Württemberg in the Hohenasperg fortress. During his imprisonment, he wrote extensively and also composed. He won particular distinction as a keyboardist and writer. As a composer, he was most successful with songs, most of which he set to his own texts. They are historically important for their contribution to the creation of the German lied of the folk type. A number of composers set his poems to music: Schubert's settings of his *Die Forelle* and *An mein Klavier* became famous.

WRITINGS: *Ideen zu einer Ästhetik der Tonkunst* (1784–85; ed. by his son, Ludwig Schubart, Vienna, 1806); *Leben und Gesinnungen, von ihm selbst im Kerker aufgesetzt* (2 vols., Stuttgart, 1791–93)

BIBL.: L. Schubart, *S.s Karakter* (Erlangen, 1798); idem, ed., *C.F.D. S.: Gesammelte Schriften und Schicksale* (Stuttgart,

1839–40); G. Hauff, *S. in seinen Leben und seinen Werken* (Stuttgart, 1885); E. Holzer, *S. als Musiker* (Stuttgart, 1905); D. Ossenkop, *C.F.D. S.'s Writings on Music* (diss., Columbia Univ., 1960).—**NS/LK/DM**

Schubaur, Johann Lukas, German physician and composer; b. Lechfeld (baptized), Dec. 23, 1749; d. Munich, Nov. 15, 1815. He was the son of the painter Ignatius Schubaur. He was orphaned quite young and then reared in the Zwiefalten monastery. After attending school in Augsburg, he studied at the Neuburg an der Donau theological seminary, where he received a thorough grounding in music. He then went to Vienna and studied music while earning his livelihood by giving piano lessons and composing short pieces; took his medical degree in Ingolstadt, and then began his practice at the Barmherzige Brüder hospital in Neuburg an der Donau in 1775; shortly thereafter, he settled in Munich, where he became court physician and president of the medical commission. A dilettante composer, he won notable success with only one score, his Singspiel *Die Dorfdeputierten* (Munich, May 8, 1783). His other Singspiels, all produced in Munich, were *Melide oder Der Schiffer* (Sept. 24, 1782), *Das Lustlager* (1784), and *Die treuen Köhler* (Sept. 29, 1786).

BIBL.: E. Reipschläger, *S., Danzi und Poissl als Opernkomponisten* (diss., Univ. of Rostock, 1911).—**NS/LK/DM**

Schubel, Max, American composer; b. N.Y., April 11, 1932. He was educated at N.Y.U. (graduated, 1953), his composition teachers being Charles Haubiel in N.Y. and Frank Martin. In 1960 he formed OPUS ONE, an independent recording company dedicated to producing non-commercial concert and electronic music; in 1982 its headquarters was moved to a small cabin he built on a remote mountain in the Catskills. From 1954 Schubel spent much of his time on his small island in Moosehead Lake, Maine, where he became interested in environmental protection and self-sufficient living; developed skills in recycling, composting, raising chickens, and developing non-electrical sources of power and water. As a composer, he received 2 NEA awards (1974, 1982) and a Ford Foundation Recording Grant (1971); also was in residence at the MacDowell Colony, the Wurlitzer Foundation, Ossabaw Island, and Wolf Trap.

WORKS: ORCH.: *Fracture* (1969); *Divertimento* for Piano, Trumpet, and Chamber Orch. (1980; rev. 1987); *Guale* (1984); *Punch and Judie* for Chamber Orch. (1980); *Scherzo* (1987); *SuperScherzo* for Chamber Orch. (1988–89). **CHAMBER:** *Insected Surfaces*, concerto for Clarinet, Cello, Bass, Harpsichord, and Piano (1965); *Exotica* for Cello and Harpsichord (1967); 2 string quartets (1968, 1980); *Zing and ZipZap* for Chamber Ensemble (1986); *The Spoors of Time* for Viola and Piano (1986); Septet (1988); *Dragondust* for Clarinet and Piano (1988); String Quintet (1989); Trio for Violin, Cello, and Piano (1989). **PIANO:** *Everybody's Favourite Rag* (1979); *Miraplex* (1979); *B Natural* for Prepared Piano (1980); *Stable Turner* (1981); *Klish Klash* for Prepared Piano (1982); *Dragonseed* (1986).—**NS/LK/DM**

Schubert, family of German musicians:

(1) Anton Schubert, double-bass player; b. Dresden, June 28, 1766; d. there, Oct. 12, 1853. He was a member of the Dresden Court Orch. from 1790 until he retired in 1840.

(2) **Franz Anton Schubert**, double-bass player and composer, brother of the preceding; b. Dresden, July 20, 1768; d. there, March 5, 1827. He was named director of the Italian Opera in 1808 and royal church composer in 1814 in Dresden. He composed much church music.

(3) **Franz Schubert**, violinist and composer, son of the preceding; b. Dresden, July 22, 1808; d. there, April 12, 1878. He studied with his father, Rottmeier, and L. Haase; after further training with C.P. Lafont in Paris, he returned to Dresden as a member of the Court Orch. in 1823, becoming its concertmaster in 1861. With F.A. Kummer, he wrote some duos for cello; also composed 12 bagatelles, *Die Biene* being the most successful in his day. His wife was the soprano Maschinka Schubert (b. Reval, Aug. 25, 1815; d. Dresden, Sept. 20, 1882), the daughter of the Kapellmeister Georg Abraham Schneider (1770–1839) and the singer Caroline Portmann; she was a pupil of her mother and of Giulio Bordogni; made her debut in London (1832), and later was a leading singer at the Dresden Court Opera. Their daughter was the soprano Georgine Schubert (b. Dresden, Oct. 28, 1840; d. Strelitz, Dec. 26, 1878); she studied with her mother, and later with Jenny Lind and Manuel García; made her operatic debut in *La Sonnambula* in Hamburg (1839), and then sang widely in both opera and concert.—NS/LK/DM

Schubert, Ferdinand (Lukas),

Austrian teacher and composer, brother of **Franz (Peter) Schubert**; b. Lichtenthal, near Vienna, Oct. 18, 1794; d. Vienna, Feb. 26, 1859. He began his music training with his father, and after taking instruction at Vienna's Normalhauptschule (1807–08), he taught at his father's school. He was an asst. teacher (1810–16) and a teacher (1816–24) at the Alsergrund orphanage, then headmaster (1824–51) and director (1851–59) of the Normalhauptschule. He was devoted to his brother and took charge of his MSS after his death. He wrote two Singspiels and much sacred music, including four masses and a Requiem. —NS/LK/DM

Schubert, Franz (Peter),

great Austrian composer, a supreme melodist and an inspired master of lieder, brother of **Ferdinand (Lukas) Schubert**; b. Vienna, Jan. 31, 1797; d. there, Nov. 19, 1828. He studied violin with his father, a schoolmaster, and received instruction on the piano from his brother Ignaz; in addition, he took lessons in piano, organ, singing, and theory with Holzer, the choirmaster. In 1808 he became a member of the Vienna Imperial Court chapel choir, and also entered the Stadtkonvict, a training school for court singers, where he studied music with the Imperial Court organist Wenzel Ruzicka and with the famous court composer Salieri. He played violin in the school orch. and conducted it whenever an occasion called for it. He began composing in school, and wrote a *Fantasie* for Piano, 4-Hands, several chamber pieces, orch. overtures, and the unfinished Singspiel *Der Spiegelritter*. His first song, *Hagars Klage*, is dated March 30, 1811. In 1813 he left the Stadtkonvict, but Salieri, evidently impressed by his talent, continued to give him instruction. He further attended a training college for teachers in Vienna, and then became an instructor at his father's school. Although very young, he began writing works in large forms; between 1813 and 1816 he composed 5 syms., 4 masses, several string quartets, and also some stage music. He also wrote his first opera, *Des Teufels Lustschloss*. It was then that he wrote some of his most famous lieder. He was only 17 when he wrote *Gretchen am Spinnrade*, and only 18 when he composed the overpowering dramatic song *Erlkönig*. The prodigious facility that Schubert displayed is without equal; during the year 1815 he composed about 140 songs; on a single day, Oct. 15, he wrote 8 lieder. He became friendly with the poets Johann Mayrhofer and Franz von Schober, and set a number of their poems to music. In 1817 he lodged with Schober and his widowed mother, arranging to pay for his keep from his meager resources. It was then that he met the noted baritone Johann Michael Vogl, who put many of Schubert's songs on his concert programs. Outstanding lieder from this period include the 3 *Harfenspieler*, *Der Wanderer*, *Der Tod und das Mädchen*, *Ganymed*, *An die Musik*, and *Die Forelle*. During the summer of 1818, he served as music tutor to the family of Count Esterházy at Zélesz in Hungary. On March 1, 1818, his Overture in C major, "in the Italian style," became his first orch. work to be accorded a public performance in Vienna. On June 14, 1820, his Singspiel *Die Zwillingsbrüder* was performed at the Kärnthnertortheater in Vienna. On Aug. 19, 1820, a score of his incidental music for the play *Die Zauberharfe* was heard at the Theater an der Wien; this score contains an overture that became subsequently popular in concert performances under the name *Rosamunde Overture*, although it was not composed for the score to the play *Rosamunde, Fürstin von Zypern*, which was produced at the Theater an der Wien more than 3 years later, on Dec. 20, 1823. Although Schubert still had difficulties in earning a living, he formed a circle of influential friends in Vienna, and appeared as a pianist at private gatherings; sometimes he sang his songs, accompanying himself at the keyboard; he was also able to publ. some of his songs. A mystery is attached to his most famous work, begun in 1822, the Sym. in B minor, known popularly as the "Unfinished" Sym. Only 2 movements are known to exist, with portions of the third, a Scherzo, in sketches. What prevented him from finishing it? Speculations are as rife as they are worthless, particularly since he was usually careful in completing a work before embarking on another composition. In 1823 he completed his masterly song cycle *Die schöne Müllerin*; in 1824 he once again spent the summer as a private tutor in Count Esterházy's employ in Zélesz. In 1827 he wrote another remarkable song cycle, *Die Winterreise*. On March 26, 1828, he presented in Vienna a public concert of his works. From that year, which proved to be his last, date several masterpieces, including the 2 books of songs collectively known as the *Schwanengesang*. His health was frail, and he moved to the lodgings of his brother Ferdinand. On the afternoon of Nov. 19, 1828, Schubert died, at the age of 31. For a thorough account of his illness, see E. Sams's "Schubert's Illness Reexamined," *Musical Times* (Jan. 1980). There is no incontrovertible evidence that Schubert died of syphilis.

Schubert is often described as the creator of the genre of strophic lieder; this summary description is chronologically untenable, since Zelter wrote strophic lieder a generation before him. Goethe, whose poems were set to music by Zelter, Beethoven, and Schubert, favored Zelter's settings. What Schubert truly created was an incomparably beautiful florilegium of lieder typifying the era of German Romantic sentiment and conveying deeply felt emotions, ranging from peaceful joy to enlightened melancholy, from philosophic meditation to throbbing drama; the poems he selected for his settings were expressive of such passing moods. He set to music 72 poems by Goethe, 47 by Mayrhofer, 46 by Schiller, 44 by Wilhelm Müller, 28 by Matthison, 23 by Hölty, 22 by Kosegarten, 13 by Körtner, 12 by Schober, and 6 by Heine.

In a sense, Schubert's *Moments musicaux, Impromptus,* and other piano works are songs without texts. On several occasions, he used musical material from his songs for instrumental works, as in the great *Wanderer Fantasia* for Piano, based on his song *Der Wanderer,* and the "Forellen" Piano Quintet, in which the fourth movement is a set of variations on the song *Die Forelle.* His String Quartet in D minor includes a set of variations on his song *Der Tod und das Mädchen* in its second movement. But Schubert was not given to large theater works and oratorios. Even his extended works in sonata form are not conceived on a grand scale but, rather, are constructed according to the symmetry of recapitulations; his music captivates the listeners not by recurring variety but by the recalled felicities; time and again in his MSS, he simply indicates the repetition of a group of bars by number. Therein lies the immense difference between Schubert and Schumann, both Romantic poets of music: where Schubert was satisfied with reminding the listener of a passage already heard, Schumann variegates. Schubert was indeed the most symmetrical composer in the era of free-flowing musical prose and musical poetry.

Much confusion exists in the numbering of Schubert's syms., the last being listed in most catalogues as No. 9; the missing uncounted sym. is No. 7, which exists as a full draft, in 4 movements, of which the first 110 bars are fully scored; several "completions" exist, the first by John Francis Barnett, made in 1883, the second by Felix Weingartner, manufactured in 1934, and the third, and perhaps the most Schubertomorphic, constructed with artful imitation of Schubert's ways and means, by Brian Newbould, in 1977. The "Unfinished" Sym. is then No. 8. There remains the "Gmunden" or "Gastein" Sym., so named because Schubert was supposed to have written it in Gastein, in the Tirol, in 1825. It was long regarded as irretrievably lost, but was eventually identified with No. 9, the great C major Sym. Incredibly, as late as 1978 there came to light in a somehow overlooked pile of music in the archives of the Vienna Stadtsbibliothek a sketch of still another Schubert sym., composed during the last months of his life; this insubstantial but magically tempting waft of Schubert's genius was completed by Brian Newbould; it is numbered as his 10th.

The recognition of Schubert's greatness was astonishingly slow. Fully 40 years elapsed before the discovery of the MS of the "Unfinished" Sym. Posthumous performances were the rule for his sym. premieres, and the publication of his syms. was exceedingly tardy. Schumann, ever sensitive to great talent, was eager to salute the kindred genius in Schubert's syms., about whose "Heavenly length" he so admiringly complained. But it took half a century for Schubert to become firmly established in music history as one of the great Sch's (with Chopin phonetically counted in).

WORKS: In the list of Schubert's works given below, the D. numbers are those established by O. Deutsch (with D. Wakeling) in his *Schubert: Thematic Catalogue of All His Works in Chronological Order* (London, 1951; in Ger. as *Franz Schubert: Thematisches Verzeichnis seiner Werke in chronologischer Folge ...* , publ. in the *Neue Ausgabe sämtlicher Werke* of Schubert in a rev. ed. in 1978). **DRAMATIC:** *Der Spiegelritter,* D.11, Singspiel (1811–12; unfinished; only the Overture and Act I completed; Swiss Radio, Dec. 11, 1949); *Des Teufels Lustschloss,* D.84, opera (1813–15; 2 versions; Vienna, Dec. 12, 1879); *Adrast,* D.137, opera (1817–19; unfinished; Vienna, Dec. 13, 1868); *Der vierjährige Posten,* D.190, Singspiel (1815; Dresden, Sept. 23, 1896); *Fernando,* D.220, Singspiel (1815; Vienna, April 13, 1907); *Claudine von Villa Bella,* D.239, Singspiel (1815; unfinished; only the Overture and Act I completed; Vienna, April 26, 1913); *Die Freunde von Salamanka,* D.326, Singspiel (1815; Halle, May 6, 1928); *Die Bürgschaft,* D.435, opera (1816; unfinished; only Acts I and II completed; Vienna, March 7, 1908); *Die Zauberharfe,* D.644, melodrama (Theater an der Wien, Vienna, Aug. 19, 1820); *Die Zwillingsbrüder,* D.647, Singspiel (1819; Kärnthnertortheater, Vienna, June 14, 1820); *Sakuntala,* D.701, opera (1820; only sketches for Acts I and II; Vienna, June 12, 1971); Duet and Aria for Hérold's *Das Zauberglöckchen (La Clochette),* D.723 (Vienna, June 20, 1821); *Alfonso und Estrella,* D.732, opera (1821–22; Weimar, June 24, 1854); *Die Verschworenen (Der häusliche Krieg),* D.787, Singspiel (1823; Vienna, March 1, 1861); *Rüdiger,* D.791, opera (1823; sketches only; Vienna, Jan. 5, 1868); *Fierabras,* D.796, opera (1823; Karlsruhe, Feb. 9, 1897); *Rosamunde, Fürstin von Zypern,* D.797, incidental music to the play by H. von Chézy (Theater an der Wien, Vienna, Dec. 20, 1823); *Der Graf von Gleichen,* D.918, opera (1827; sketches only); *Der Minnesänger,* D.981, Singspiel (date unknown; unfinished; not extant). **ORCH.:** Overture in D major, D.2a (originally D.996; 1811?; fragment only); Sym. in D major, D.2b (originally D.997; 1811?; fragment of first movement only); Overture in D major, to Albrecht's comedy *Der Teufel als Hydraulicus,* D.4 (1812?); Overture in D major, D.12 (1811?); Overture in D major, D.26 (1812); 3 minuets and trios, D.39a (1813; not extant); orch. fragment in D major, D.71c (originally D.966a; 1813); Sym. No. 1, in D major, D.82 (1813); orch. fragment in B-flat major, D.94a (1814?); Sym. No. 2, in B-flat major, D.125 (1814–15); Sym. No. 3, in D major, D.200 (1815); Concerto (Concertstück) in D major for Violin and Orch., D.345 (1816); Sym. No. 4, in C minor, D.417, "Tragic" (1816); Rondo in A major for Violin and Strings, D.438 (1816); Overture in B-flat major, D.470 (1816); Sym. No. 5, in B-flat major, D.485 (1816); Overture in D major, D.556 (1817); Polonaise in B-flat major for Violin and Orch., D.580 (1817); Sym. No. 6, in C major, D.589 (1817–18); Overture in D major, D.590, "im italienischen Stile" (1817); Overture in C major, D.591, "im italienischen Stile" (1817); Sym. in D major, D.615 (piano sketches for 2 movements only; 1818); Overture in E minor, D.648 (1819); Sym. in D major, D.708a (sketches only; 1821); Sym. (No. 7) in E minor/major, D.729 (1821; sketched in score; performing version realized by R.F. Barnett, Felix Wein-gartner, and Brian Newbould); Sym. No. 8, in B minor, D.759, "Unfinished" (1822; 2 movements and an unfinished scherzo); "Gmunden" or "Gastein" Sym., D.849 (identical with D.944); Sym. (No. 10) in D major, D.936a (1828; sketches only; performing versions realized by Brian Newbould and by Peter Gülke); Sym. No. 9, in C major, D.944, "Great" (1825–26). **CHAMBER:** String Quartet, D.2c (originally D.998; 1811?; fragment only); 6 minuets, D.2d (originally D.995; 1811); sketch for a trio of a minuet, in C major, D.2f (1811); String Quartet in C major, D.3 (1812; fragment only); Overture in C minor, D.8 (1811); Overture in C minor, D.8a (an arrangement of D.8; 1811); String Quartet in G minor/B-flat major, D.18 (1810?); String Quartet, D.19 (1810?; not extant); String Quartet, D.19a (1810?; not extant); Overture in B-flat major, D.20 (1812; not extant); Trio (Sonata in one movement) in B-flat major, D.28 (1812); String Quartet in C major, D.32 (1812); String Quartet in B-flat major, D.36 (1812–13); String Quartet in C major, D.46 (1813); String Quartet in B-flat major, D.68 (1813; 2 movements only); Wind Octet in F major, D.72 (1813); Allegro in F major, D.72a (1813; unfinished); String Quartet in D major, D.74 (1813); Wind Nonet in E-flat minor, D.79, "Franz Schuberts Begräbnis-Feyer" (*Eine kleine Trauermusik*) (1813); Minuet in D major, D.86 (1813); String Quartet in E-flat major, D.87 (1813); Andante in C major, D.87a (1813); 5 minuets and 6 trios, D.89 (1813); 5 Deutsche and 7 trios, with coda, D.90 (1813); String Quartet in D major, D.94 (1811?); 5 minuets and 6 Deutsche, with trios, D.94b (1814; not extant); Trio in G major, for Schubert's arrangement of Matiegka's *Notturno*, op.21, D.96 (1814); String Quartet in C minor, D.103 (1814; fragments, Grave, and Allegro extant); String Trio in B-flat major, D.111a (1814; not extant); String Quartet in B-flat major, D.112 (1814); String Quartet in G minor, D.173 (1815); String Quartet in E major, D.353 (1816); 4 komische Ländler in D major, D.354 (1816); 8 Ländler in F-sharp minor, D.355 (1816); 9 Ländler in D major, D.370 (1816); 11 Ländler in B-flat major, D.374 (1816); Sonata (Sonatina) in D major, D.384 (1816); Sonata (Sonatina) in A minor, D.385 (1816); Sonata (Sonatina) in G minor, D.408 (1816); String Trio in B-flat major, D.471 (1816; unfinished); Adagio and Rondo concertante in F major, D.487 (1816); Sonata (Duo) in A major, D.574 (1817); String Trio in B-flat major, D.581 (1817); Variations in A major, D.597a (1817; not extant); Overture in B-flat major, D.601 (an arrangement of the D.470 overture; 1816?; fragment only); Piano Quintet in A major, D.667, "Die Forelle" (1819); String Quartet in C minor, D.703 (*Quartettsatz*) (1820); Introduction and variations on *Trockne Blumen* from *Die schöne Müllerin*, in E minor/E major, D.802 (1824); Octet in F major, D.803 (1824); String Quartet in A minor, D.804 (1824); String Quartet in D minor, D.810, "Der Tod und das Mädchen" (1824); Sonata in A minor, D.821, "Arpeggione" (1824); String Quartet in G major, D.887 (1826); Rondo in B minor (*Rondo brillant*), D.895 (1826); Piano Trio movement in E-flat major, D.897, "Notturno" (1828?); Piano Trio in B-flat major, D.898 (1828?); Piano Trio in E-flat major, D.929 (1827); Fantasy in C major, D.934 (1827); String Quintet in C major, D.956 (1828); Fugue in C major, D.A1/3 (1812;?) fragment only). **Piano Solo:** Fantasie in C minor, D.2e (originally D.993; 1811); Fugue in D minor, D.13 (1812?); Overture, D.14 (1812?; sketch only; not extant); 6 variations in E-flat major, D.21 (1812; not extant); 7 variations in F major, D.24 (1812; fragment only; not extant); Fugue in C major, D.24a (1812); Fugue in G major, D.24b (1812); Fugue in D minor, D.24c (1812); Fugue in C major, D.24d (1812; fragment only); Fugue in F major, D.25c (1812; fragment only); Andante in C major, D.29 (1812); fugal sketches in B-flat major, D.37a (originally D.967; 1813?); Fugue in E

minor, D.41a (1813; fragment only); Fugue in E minor, D.71b (1813; fragment only); Allegro in E major, D.154 (sketch of D.157; 1815); 10 variations in F major, D.156 (1815); Sonata in E major, D.157 (1815; unfinished); Adagio in G major, D.178 (1815); Sonata in C major, D.279 (1815); Allegretto in C major, D.346 (1816?; fragment only); Allegretto moderato in C major, D.347 (1813?; fragment only); Andantino in C major, D.348 (1816; fragment only); Adagio in C major, D.349 (1816?; fragment only); Sonata in F major, D.459 (1816; fragment only); *5 Klavierstücke*, D.459a (first 2 from preceding work; 1816?); Adagio in D-flat major, D.505 (original slow movement of D.625; 1818); Rondo in E major, D.506 (1817); Sonata in A minor, D.537 (1817); Sonata in A-flat major, D.557 (1817); Sonata in E minor, D.566 (1817); Sonata in D-flat major, D.567 (unfinished; first version of D.568; 1817); Sonata in E-flat major, D.568 (1826?); Scherzo in D major and Allegro in F-sharp minor, D.570 (unfinished; 1817); Sonata in F-sharp minor, D.571 (1817; fragment only); Sonata in B major, D.575 (1817); 13 variations on a theme by Anselm Hüttenbrenner, in A minor, D.576 (1817); 2 scherzos, in B-flat major and D-flat major, D.593 (1817); Andante in A major, D.604 (1816?); Fantasia in C major, D.605 (1821–23; fragment only); Fantasy in C major, D.605a, "Grazer Fantasie" (1818?); March in E major, D.606 (1818?); Adagio in E major, D.612 (1818); Sonata in C major, D.613 (2 movements; 1818); Sonata in F minor, D.625 (2 movements; 1818); Sonata in C-sharp minor, D.655 (1819; fragment only); Sonata in A major, D.664 (1819?); Variations on a Waltz by Diabelli, in C minor, D.718 (1821); Overture to *Alfonso und Estrella*, in D major, D.759a (an arrangement of the D.732 overture; 1822); Fantasy in C major, D.760, "Wanderfantasie" (1822); Sonata in E minor, D.769a (originally D.994; 1823?; fragment only); 6 *Momens musicals* [sic], in C major, A-flat major, F minor, C-sharp minor, F minor, A-flat major, D.780 (1823–28); Sonata in A minor, D.784 (1823); *Ungarische Melodie* in B minor, D.817 (1824); Sonata in C major, D.840, *Reliquie* (unfinished; 1825); Sonata in A minor, D.845 (1825); Sonata in D major, D.850 (1825); Sonata in G major, D.894 (originally known as the *Fantasie, Andante, Menuetto und Allegretto*; 1826); 4 impromptus, in C minor, E-flat major, G-flat major, and A-flat major, D.899 (1827); Allegretto in C minor, D.900 (1820?; fragment only); Allegretto in C minor, D.915 (1827); sketch for a piano piece in C major, D.916b (1827); sketch for a piano piece in C minor, D.916c (1827); 4 impromptus, in F minor, A-flat major, B-flat major, and F minor, D.935 (1827); 3 Klavierstücke, in E-flat minor, E-flat major, and C major, D.946 (1828); Sonata in C minor, D.958 (1828); Sonata in A major, D.959 (1828); Sonata in B-flat major, D.960 (1828); March in G major, D.980f (date unknown). **4-hands:** Fantasie in G major, D.1 (1810); Fantasie in G major, D.1b (1810?; fragment only); Sonata in F major, D.1c (1810; unfinished); Fantasie in G minor, D.9 (1811); Fantasie in C minor, D.48, "Grande sonate" (2 versions; 1813); Overture in D major, D.592, "im italienischen Stile" (an arrangement of D.590; 1817); Overture in C major, D.597, "im italienischen Stile" (an arrangement of D.591; 1817); 4 polonaises, in D minor, B-flat major, E major, and F major, D.599 (1818); *3 marches héroïques*, in B minor, C major, and D major, D.602 (1818?); Rondo in D major, D.608 (2 versions; 1818); Sonata in B-flat major, D.617 (1818); Deutscher in G major, with 2 trios and 2 Ländler, in E major, D.618 (1818); Polonaise and Trio, D.618a (sketch only; 1818; orch. by Raymond Leppard; Indianapolis, Nov. 8, 1990, Leppard conducting); 8 variations on a French song, in E minor, D.624 (1818); Overture in G minor, D.668 (1819); Overture in F major, D.675 (1819); *3 marches militaires*, in D major, G major, and E-flat major, D.733 (1818); Overture to *Alfonso und Estrella*, D.773 (an arrangement of the D.732 overture; 1823); Overture to *Fierabras*, D.798 (an arrangement of the D.796 overture; 1823); Sonata in C major, D.812, "Grand duo" (1824; orchestrated by Raymond Leppard; Indianapolis, Nov. 8, 1990, Leppard conducting); 8 variations on an original theme, in A-flat major, D.813 (1824); 4 Ländler, in E-flat major, A-flat major, C minor, and C major, D.814 (1824); *Divertissement a l'hongroise* in G minor, D.818 (1824); 6 *grandes marches*, in E- flat major, G minor, B minor, D major, E-flat minor, and E major, D.819 (1824); *Divertissement sur des motifs originaux français* in E minor, D.823: 1, *Marche brillante*; 2, *Andantino varié*; 3, *Rondeau brillant* (1825?); 6 polonaises, in D minor, F major, B-flat major, D major, A major, and E major, D.824 (1826); *Grande marche funèbre* in C minor, D.859 (on the death of Alexander I of Russia; 1825); *Grande marche héroïque* in A minor, D.885 (for the coronation of Nicholas I of Russia; 1826); 8 variations on a theme from Hérold's *Marie*, in C major, D.908 (1827); March in G major, D.928, "Kindermarsch" (1827); Fantasie in F minor, D.940 (1828); Allegro in A minor, D.947, Lebensstürme (1828); Rondo in A major, D.947 (1828); Fugue in E minor, D.952 (1828); Allegro moderato in C major and Andante in A minor (Sonatine), D.968 (1818?); Introduction, 4 variations on an original theme, and Finale, in B-flat major, D.968a (originally D.603; 1824?); 2 *marches caractéristiques* in C major, D.968b (originally D.886; 1826?). **D a n c e s F o r P i a n o :** Waltzes and March, D.19b (1812?; not extant); 12 minuets with trios, D.22 (1812; not extant); 30 minuets with trios, D.41 (1813; 10 not extant); 2 minuets, in D major and A major, both with 2 trios, D.91 (1813; 2 other minuets lost); 12 Wiener Deutsche, D.128 (1812?); Deutscher in E major, with trio, D.135 (1815); Deutscher in C-sharp minor, with trio, D.139 (1815); 12 waltzes, 17 Ländler, and 9 écossaises, D.145 (1815–21); 20 waltzes (*Letzte Walzer*), D.146 (Nos. 1 and 3–11, 1815; Nos. 2 and 12–20, 1823); Écossaise in D minor/F major, D.158 (1815); Minuet in A minor, with trio, D.277a (1815); 12 écossaises, D.299 (1815); Minuet in A major, with trio, D.334 (1815?); Minuet in E major, with 2 trios, D.335 (1813?); 36 Originaltänze (*Erste Walzer*), D.365 (1816–21); 17 Ländler, D.366 (1816–24); 8 Ländler, D.378 (1816); 3 minuets, in E major, A major, and C major, each with 2 trios, D.380 (1816); 12 Deutsche, D.420 (1816); 6 écossaises, D.421 (1816); Écossaise in E-flat major, D.511 (1817?); 8 écossaises, D.529 (1817); Minuet in C-sharp minor, D.600 (1814?); Trio in E major, D.610 (1818); Deutscher in C-sharp minor and Écossaise in D-flat major, D.643 (1819); 12 Ländler, D.681 (1815?; Nos. 1–4 not extant); 6 écossaises, D.697 (1820); Deutscher in G-flat major, D.722 (1821); 16 Ländler and 2 écossaises (*Wiener-Damen Ländler*), D.734 (1822?); Galop and 8 écossaises, D.735 (1822?); 2 Deutsche, in A major and D major, D.769 (No. 1, 1824; No. 2, 1823); 34 *Valses sentimentales*, D.779 (1823?); 12 écossaises, D.781 (1823); Écossaise in D major, D.782 (1823?); 16 Deutsche and 2 écossaises, D.783 (1823–24); 12 Deutsche (Ländler), D.790 (1823); 3 écossaises, D.816 (1824); 6 Deutsche, D.820 (1824); 2 Deutsche, in F major and G major, D.841 (1825); Waltz in G major (*Albumblatt*), D.844 (1825); 12 Grazer Walzer, D.924 (1827); Grazer Galopp in C major, D.925 (1827); Deutscher, D.944a (1828; not extant); 12 waltzes (*Valses nobles*), D.969 (1826); 6 Ländler, D.970 (date unknown); 3 Deutsche, in A minor, A major, and E major, D.971 (1822); 3 Deutsche, in D-flat major, A-flat major, and A major, D.972 (date unknown); 3 Deutsche, in E major, E major, and A-flat major, D.973 (date unknown); 2 Deutsche, both in D-flat major, D.974 (date unknown); Deutscher in D major, D.975 (date unknown); Cotillon in E-flat major, D.976 (1825); 8 écossaises, D.977 (date unknown); Waltz in A-flat major, D.978 (1825); Waltz in G major, D.979 (1826); 2 waltzes, in G major and B minor, D.980 (1826); 2 dance sketches, in A major and E major, D.980a (originally D.640; date unknown); 2 Ländler, both in E-flat major, D.980b (originally D.679; date unknown); 2 Ländler, both in D-flat major, D.980c (originally D.680; fragment only; date unknown); Waltz in C major, D.980d (1827); 2 dance sketches, in G minor and F major, D.980c (date unknown). **VOCAL: C h u r c h :** *Salve Regina* in F major for Soprano, Organ, and Orch., D.27 (1812); Kyrie in D minor for Soprano, Tenor, Chorus, Organ, and Orch., D.31 (1812); Kyrie in B-flat major for Chorus, D.45 (1813); Kyrie in D minor for Soprano, Alto, Tenor, Bass, Chorus, and Orch., D.49 (1813); Kyrie in F major for Chorus, Organ, and Orch., D.66 (1813); Mass No. 1, in F major, for 2 Sopranos, Alto, 2 Tenors, Bass, Chorus, Organ, and Orch., D.105 (1814); *Salve Regina* in B-flat major for Tenor, Organ, and Orch., D.106 (1814); *Totus in corde langueo*, offertory in C major for Soprano or Tenor, Clarinet or Violin, Organ, and Orch., D.136 (1815); Mass No. 2, in G. major, for Soprano, Tenor, Bass, Chorus, Organ, and Strings, D.167 (1815); *Stabat Mater* in G minor for Chorus, Organ, and Orch., D.175 (1815); *Tres sunt*, offertory in A minor for Chorus, Organ, and Orch., D.181 (1815); *Benedictus es, Domine*, gradual in C major for Chorus, Organ, and Orch., D.184 (1815); *Dona nobis pacem* in F major for Bass, Chorus, Organ, and Orch., D.185 (alternative movement for D.105; 1815); *Salve Regina* (offertorium) in F major for Soprano, Organ, and Orch., D.223 (2 versions, 1815 and 1823); Mass No. 3, in B-flat major, for Soprano, Alto, Tenor, Bass, Chorus, Organ, and Orch., D.324 (1815); *Deutsches Salve Regina (Hymne an die heilige Mutter Gottes)* in F major for Chorus and Organ, D.379 (1816); *Stabat Mater* (oratorio) in F major/F minor for Soprano, Tenor, Bass, Chorus, and Orch., D.383 (1816); *Salve Regina* in B-flat major for Chorus, D.386 (1816); Mass No. 4, in C major, for Soprano, Alto, Tenor, Bass, Chorus, Organ, and Orch., D.452 (1816); *Tantum ergo* in C major for Soprano, Chorus, Organ, and Orch., D.460 (1816); *Tantum ergo* in C major for Soprano, Alto, Tenor, Bass, Chorus, and Orch., D.461 (1816); Magnificat in C major for Soprano, Alto, Tenor, Bass, Chorus, Organ, and Orch., D.486 (1815); *Auguste jam coelestium* in G major for Soprano, Tenor, and Orch., D.488 (1816); *Deutsches Requiem (Deutsche Trauermesse)* in G minor for Soprano, Alto, Tenor, Bass, Chorus, and Organ, D.621 (1818); *Salve Regina* (offertorium) in A major for Soprano and Strings, D.676 (1819); Mass No. 5, in A-flat major, for Soprano, Alto, Tenor, Bass, Chorus, Organ, and Orch., D.678 (2 versions, 1819–22); *Tantum ergo* in B-flat major for Soprano, Alto, Tenor, Bass, Chorus, Organ, and Orch., D.730 (1821); *Tantum ergo* in C major for Chorus, Organ, and Orch., D.739 (1814); *Tantum ergo* in D major for Chorus, Organ, and Orch., D.750 (1822); *Salve Regina* in C major for 2 Tenors and 2 Basses, D.811 (1824); *Deutsche Messe* for Chorus and Organ, or Chorus, Organ, and Orch., D.872 (1827); Mass No. 6, in E-flat major, for Soprano, Alto, Tenor, Bass, Chorus, and Orch., D.950 (1828); Benedictus in A minor for Soprano, Alto, Tenor, Bass, Chorus, Organ, and Orch., D.961 (alternative movement for D.452; 1828); *Tantum ergo* in E- flat major for Soprano, Alto, Tenor, Bass, Chorus, and Orch., D.962 (1828); *Intende voci,* offertory in B-flat major for Tenor, Chorus, and Orch., D.963 (1828); etc. **O t h e r V o c a l :** *Quell' innocente figlio,* D.17 (many versions, 1812); *Entra l'uomo allor che nasce,* D.33 (many versions, 1812); *Te solo adoro* for Soprano, Alto, Tenor, and Bass, D.34 (1812); *Serbate, o dei custodi,* D.35 (2 versions, 1812); *Die Advokaten* for Men's Voices and Piano, D.37 (1812); *Totengräber- lied* for Men's Voices, D.38 (1813); *Dreifach ist der Schritt der Zeit* for Men's Voices, D.43 (1813); *Dithyrambe,* D.47 (1813; fragment only); *Unendliche Freude* for Men's Voices, D.51 (1813); *Vorüber die stöhnende Klage* for Men's Voices, D.53 (1813); *Unendliche*

Freude, canon for Men's Voices, D.54 (1813); *Selig durch die Liebe* for Men's Voices, D.55 (1813); *Hier strecket der wallende Pilger* for Men's Voices, D.57 (1813); *Dessen Fahne Donnerstürme wallte* for Men's Voices, D.58 (1813); *Hier umarmen sich getreue Gatten* for Men's Voices, D.60 (1813); *Ein jugendlicher Maienschwung*, D.61 (1813); *Thronend auf erhabnem Sitz* for Men's Voices, D.62 (1813); *Wer die steile Sternenbahn* for Men's Voices, D.63 (1813); *Majestätsche Sonnenrosse* for Men's Voices, D.64 (1813); *Schmerz verzerret ihr Gesicht*, canon, D.65 (1813; sketch only); *Frisch atmet des Morgens lebendiger Hauch* for Men's Voices, D.67 (1813); *Dreifach ist der Schritt der Zeit*, D.69 (1813); *Dreifach ist der Schritt der Zeit (Ewig still steht die Vergangenheit)*, canon for Men's Voices, D.70 (1813); *Die zwei Tugendwege* for Men's Voices, D.71 (1813); *Trinklied (Freunde, sammelt euch im Kreise)* for Bass, Men's Voices, and Piano, D.75 (1813); *Zur Namensfeier meines Vaters* for Men's Voices and Guitar, D.80 (1813); *Verschwunden sind die Schmerzen*, canon for Men's Voices, D.88 (1813); *Wer ist gross?* for Bass, Men's Voices, and Orch., D.110 (1814); *Mailied (Grüner wird die Au)* for Men's Voices, D.129 (1815); *Der Schnee zerrinnt*, canon, D.130 (1815); *Lacrimoso son io*, canon, D.131 (2 versions, 1815); *Lied beim Rundetanz*, D.132 (1815?); *Lied im Freien*, D.133 (1815?); *Klage um Ali Bey* for Men's Voices, D.140 (1815); *Bardengesang* for Men's Voices, D.147 (1816); *Trinklied (Brüder! unser Erdenwallen)* for Tenor, Men's Voices, and Piano, D.148 (1815); *Nun lasst uns den Leib begraben (Begrabnislied)* for Chorus and Piano, D.168 (1815); *Osterlied* for Chorus and Piano, D.168a (originally D.987; 1815); *Trinklied vor der Schlacht* for 2 Unison Choruses and Piano, D.169 (1815); *Schwertlied* for Voice, Unison Chorus, and Piano, D.170 (1815); *Trinklied (Ihr Freunde und du gold'ner Wein)* for Voice, Unison Chorus, and Piano, D.183 (1815); *An die Freude* for Voice, Unison Chorus, and Piano, D.189 (1815); *Mailied (Grüner wird die Au)* for 2 Voices, D.199 (1815); *Mailied (Der Schnee zerrinnt)* for 2 Voices, D.202 (1815); *Der Morgenstern* for 2 Voices, D.203 (1815); *Jägerlied* for 2 Voices, D.204 (1815); *Lützows wilde Jagd* for 2 Voices, D.205 (1815); *Hymne an den Unendlichen* for Chorus and Piano, D.232 (1815); *Das Abendrot* for Men's Voices and Piano, D.236 (1815); *Trinklied im Winter* for Men's Voices, D.242 (1815); *Frühlingslied (Die Luft ist blau)* for Men's Voices, D.243 (1815); *Willkommen, lieber schöner Mai*, canon for 3 Voices, D.244 (2 versions, 1815); *Punschlied: Im Norden zu singen* for 2 Voices, D.253 (1815); *Trinklied (Auf! jeder sei nun froh)* for Men's Voices and Piano, D.267 (1815); *Bergknappenlied* for Men's Voices and Piano, D.268 (1815); *Das Leben*, D.269 (2 versions, 1815); *Punschlied (Vier Elemente, innig gesellt)* for Men's Voices and Piano, D.277 (1815); *Namensfeier für Franz Michael Vierthaler (Gratulations Kantate)* for Soprano, Tenor, Bass, Chorus, and Orch., D.294 (1815); *Das Grab*, D.329a (1815; sketch only); *Das Grab* for 4 Voices and Piano, D.330 (1815); *Der Entfernten* for Men's Voices, D.331 (1816?); *Die Einsiedelei* for Men's Voices, D.337 (1816?); *An den Frühling* for Men's Voices, D.338 (1816?); *Amors Macht*, D.339 (1816?); *Badelied*, D.340 (1816?); *Sylphen*, D.341 (1816?); *Trinklied (Funkelnd im Becher)* for Men's Voices, D.356 (1816); *Gold'ner Schein*, canon for 3 Voices, D.357 (1816); *Fischerlied* for Men's Voices, D.364 (1816?); *Das Grab* for Men's Voices and Piano, D.377 (1816); *Die Schlacht*, D.387 (1816; sketch only); *Beitrag zur fünfzig jährigen Jubelfeier des Herrn Salieri* for Tenor, Men's Voices, and Piano, D.407 (1816); *Naturgenuss* for Men's Voices and Piano, D.422 (1822?); *Andenken (Ich denke dein, wenn durch den Hain)* for Men's Voices, D.423 (1816); *Erinnerungen (Am Seegestad)* for Men's Voices, D.424 (1816); *Lebensbild* for Men's Voices, D.425 (1816; not extant); *Trinklied (Herr Bacchus ist ein braver Mann)* for Men's Voices, D.426 (1816; not extant); *Trinklied im Mai* for Men's Voices, D.427 (1816); *Widerhall (Auf ewig dein)* for Men's Voices, D.428 (1816); *An die Sonne* for Chorus and Piano, D.439 (1816); *Chor der Engel* for Chorus, D.440 (1816); *Das grosse Halleluja* for Chorus and Piano, D.442 (1816); *Schlachtlied* for Chorus and Piano, D.443 (1816); *Prometheus*, cantata for Soprano, Bass, Chorus, and Orch., D.451 (1816; not extant); *Kantate zu Ehren von Josef Spendou* for 2 Sopranos, Bass, Chorus, and Orch., D.472 (1816); *Der Geistertanz* for Men's Voices, D.494 (1816); *La pastorella al prato* for Men's Voices and Piano, D.513 (1817?); *Jagdlied* for Unison Voices and Piano, D.521 (1817); *Gesang der Geister über den Wassern* for Men's Voices, D.538 (1817); *Das Grab* for Unison Voices and Piano, D.569 (1817); *Lied im Freien* for Men's Voices, D.572 (1817); *Das Dörfchen*, D.598 (originally D.641; 1817; sketch only); *Die Geselligkeit (Lebenslust)* for Chorus and Piano, D.609 (1818); *Leise, leise lasst uns singen* for Men's Voices, D.635 (1819?); *Viel tausend Sterne prangen* for Chorus and Piano, D.642 (1812?); *Das Grab* for Chorus, D.643a (1819); *Sehnsucht (Nur wer die Sehnsucht kennt)* for Men's Voices, D.656 (1819); *Ruhe, schönstes Gluck der Erde* for Men's Voices, D.657 (1819); *Kantate zum Geburtstag des Sängers Johann Michael Vogl (Der Frühlingsmorgen)* for Women's and Men's Voices and Piano, D.666 (1819); *Lazarus, oder Die Feier der Auferstehung*, oratorio for 3 Sopranos, 2 Tenors, Bass, Chorus, and Orch., D.689 (1820; unfinished); *Der 23. Psalm* for Women's Voices and Piano, D.706 (1820); *Frühlingsgesang* for Men's Voices, D.709 (1822); *Im Gegenwärtigen Vergangenes* for Men's Voices and Piano, D.710 (1821); *Gesang der Geister über den Wassern* for Men's Voices, 2 Violas, 2 Cellos, and 2 Double Basses, D.714 (originally D.704 as a sketch; 1820–21); *Die Nachtigall* for Men's Voices and Piano, D.724 (1821); *Frühlingsgesang* for Men's Voices and Piano, D.740 (1822); *Geist der Liebe (Der Abend schleiert Flur und Hain)* for Men's Voices and Piano, D.747 (1822); *Am Geburtstag des Kaisers*, cantata for Soprano, Alto, Tenor, Bass, Chorus, and Orch., D.748 (1822); *Gott in der Natur* for Women's Voices and Piano, D.757 (1822); *Des Tages Weihe* for Chorus and Piano, D.763 (1822); *Ich hab' in mich gesogen*, D.778b (1823?; sketch only); *Gondelfahrer* for Men's Voices and Piano, D.809 (1824); *Gebet* for Chorus and Piano, D.815 (1824); *Lied eines Kriegers* for Bass, Unison Voices, and Piano, D.822 (1824); *Wehmut* for Men's Voices, D.825 (1826); *Ewige Liebe* for Men's Voices, D.825a (1826); *Flucht* for Men's Voices, D.825b (1825); *Der Tanz* for Chorus and Piano, D.826 (1828); *Bootgesang* for Men's Voices and Piano, D.835 (1825); *Coronach (Totengesang der Frauen und Mädchen)* for Women's Voices and Piano, D.836 (1825); *Trinklied aus dem 16. Jahrhundert* for Men's Voices, D.847 (1825); *Nachtmusik* for Men's Voices, D.848 (1825); *Widerspruch* for Men's Voices and Piano, D.865 (1826?); Canon for 6 Voices, D.873 (1826?; sketch only); *Nachklänge* for Men's Voices, D.873a (1826?; sketch only); *Die Allmacht* for Chorus and Piano, D.875a (1826; sketch only); *Mondenschein* for Men's Voices and Piano, D.875 (1826); *Nachthelle* for Tenor, Men's Voices, and Piano, D.892 (1826); *Grab und Mond* for Men's Voices, D.893 (1826); *Wein und Liebe* for Men's Voices, D.901 (1827); *Zur guten Nacht* for Baritone, Men's Voices, and Piano, D.903 (1827); *Schlachtlied* for Men's Voices, D.912 (1827); *Nachtgesang im Walde* for Men's Voices and 4 Horns, D.913 (1827); *Frühlingslied* for Men's Voices, D.914 (1827); *Das stille Lied* for Men's Voices, D.916 (1827; sketch only); *Ständchen*, D.920 (originally D.921; 2 versions, 1827); *Der Hochzeitsbraten* for Soprano, Tenor, Bass, and Piano, D.930 (1827); *Kantate für Irene Kiesewetter* for 2 Tenors, 2 Basses, Chorus, and Piano, 4-Hands, D.936 (1827); *Hymnus an den Heiligen Geist*, D.941 (now listed as D.948; 2 versions, 1828); *Mirjams Siegesgesang* for Soprano, Chorus, and Piano, D.942 (1828); *Der 92. Psalm: Lied für den Sabbath* for Soprano, Alto, Tenor, Baritone, Bass, and Chorus, D.953 (1828); *Glaube, Hoff-*

nung und Liebe for 2 Tenors, 2 Basses, Chorus, and Wind Instruments or Piano, D.954 (1828); *Gott im Ungewitter* for Chorus and Piano, D.985 (1827?); *Gott der Weltschopfer* for Chorus and Piano, D.986 (1827?); *Liebe säuseln die Blätter*, canon for 3 Voices, D.988 (1815?). **S o n g s :** Sketch for a song, D.1a (no text; 1810?); *Hagars Klage*, D.5 (Schücking; 1811); *Des Mädchens Klage*, D.6 (Schiller; 1811?); *Leichenfantasie*, D.7 (Schiller; 1811?); *Der Vatermörder*, D.10 (Pfeffel; 1811); *Der Geistertanz*, D.15 and 15a (fragments only; Matthisson; 1812?); *Quell'innocente figlio*, D.17 (Metastasio; 1812); *Klaglied*, D.23 (Rochlitz; 1812); *Der Jüngling am Bache*, D.30 (Schiller; 1812); *Entra l'uomo allor che nasce*, D.33 (Metastasio; 1812); *Serbate, o dei custodi*, D.35 (Metastasio; 1812); *Lebenstraum*, D.39 (Baumberg; 1810?); *Misero pargoletto*, D.42 (several versions; Metastasio; 1813?); *Totengräberlied*, D.44 (Hölty; 1813); *Die Schatten*, D.50 (Matthisson; 1813); *Sehnsucht*, D.52 (Schiller; 1813); *Verklärung*, D.59 (Pope; Herder, tr.; 1813); *Thekla: Eine Geisterstimme*, D.73 (Schiller; 1813); *Pensa, che questo istante*, D.76 (2 versions; Metastasio; 1813); *Der Taucher*, D.77 (2 versions; second version originally D.111; Schiller; first version, 1813–14; second version, 1815); *Son fra l'onde*, D.78 (Metastasio; 1813); *Auf den Sieg der Deutschen*, D.81, with 2 Violins and Cello (Schubert?; 1813); *Zur Namensfeier des Herrn Andreas Siller*, D.83, with Violin and Harp (1813); *Don Gayseros*, D.93 (3 versions: *Don Gayseros, Don Gayseros; Nächtens klang die süsse Laute; An dem jungen Morgenhimmel*; F. de la Motte Fouqué; 1815?); *Adelaide*, D.95 (Matthisson; 1814); *Trost: An Elisa*, D.97 (Matthisson; 1814); *Erinnerungen*, D.98 (2 versions; Matthisson; 1814); *Andenken*, D.99 (Matthisson; 1814); *Geisternähe*, D.100 (Matthisson; 1814); *Erinnerung*, D.101 (Matthisson; 1814); *Die Betende*, D.102 (Matthisson; 1814); *Die Befreier Europas in Paris*, D.104 (3 versions; Mikan; 1814); *Lied aus der Ferne*, D.107 (2 versions; Matthisson; 1814); *Der Abend*, D.108 (Matthisson; 1814); *Lied der Liebe*, D.109 (Matthisson; 1814); *An Emma*, D.113 (3 versions; Schiller; 1814); *Romanze*, D.114 (2 versions; Matthisson; 1814); *An Laura, als sie Klopstocks Auferstehungslied sang*, D.115 (Matthisson; 1814); *Der Geistertanz*, D.116 (Matthisson; 1814); *Das Mädchen aus der Fremde*, D.117 (Schiller; 1814); *Gretchen am Spinnrade*, D.118 (Goethe; 1814); *Nachtgesang*, D.119 (Goethe; 1814); *Trost in Tränen*, D.120 (Goethe; 1814); *Schäfers Klagelied*, D.121 (2 versions; Goethe; 1814); *Ammenlied*, D.122 (Lubi; 1814); *Sehnsucht*, D.123 (Goethe; 1814); *Am See*, D.124 (2 versions; Mayrhofer; 1814); *Szene aus Goethes Faust*, D.126, with 4 Voices (2 versions; Goethe; 1814); *Ballade*, D.134 (Kenner; 1815?); *Rastlose Liebe*, D.138 (2 versions; Goethe; first version, 1815; second version, 1821); *Der Mondabend*, D.141 (Kumpf; 1815); *Geistes-Gruss*, D.142 (6 versions; Goethe; 1815?); *Genügsamkeit*, D.143 (Schober; 1815); *Romanze*, D.144 (unfinished; F. Graf zu Stolberg- Stolberg; 1816); *Der Sänger*, D.149 (2 versions; Goethe; 1815); *Lodas Gespenst*, D.150 (Ossian; E. Baron de Harold, tr.; 1816); *Auf einen Kirchhof*, D.151 (Schlechta; 1815); *Minona*, D.152 (Bertrand; 1815); *Als ich sie erröten sah*, D.153 (Ehrlich; 1815); *Das Bild*, D.155 (1815); *Die Erwartung*, D.159 (2 versions; Schiller; 1816); *Am Flusse*, D.160 (Goethe; 1815); *An Mignon*, D.161 (2 versions; Goethe; 1815); *Nähe des Geliebten*, D.162 (2 versions; Goethe; 1815); *Sängers Morgenlied*, D.163 (Körner; 1815); *Liebesrausch*, D.164 (fragment only; Körner; 1815); *Sängers Morgenlied*, D.165 (Körner; 1815); *Amphiaraos*, D.166 (Körner; 1815); *Trinklied vor der Schlacht*, D.169, for 2 Unison Choruses (Körner; 1815); *Schwertlied*, D.170, with Unison Chorus (Körner; 1815); *Gebet während der Schlacht*, D.171 (Körner; 1815); *Der Morgenstern*, D.172 (fragment only; Körner; 1815); *Das war ich*, D.174 (2 versions; Körner; first version, 1815; second version, 1816); *Die Sterne*, D.176 (Fellinger; 1815); *Vergebliche Liebe*, D.177 (Bernard;

1815); *Liebesrausch*, D.179 (Körner; 1815); *Sehnsucht der Liebe*, D.180 (2 versions; Körner; 1815; second version not extant); *Die erste Liebe*, D.182 (Fellinger; 1815); *Trinklied*, D.183, with Unison Chorus (Zettler; 1815); *Die Sterbende*, D.186 (Matthisson; 1815); *Stimme der Liebe*, D.187 (Matthisson; 1815); *Naturgenuss*, D.188 (Matthisson; 1815); *An die Freude*, D.189, with Unison Chorus (Schiller; 1815); *Des Mädchens Klage*, D.191 (2 versions; Schiller; 1815); *Der Jüngling am Bache*, D.192 (Schiller; 1815); *An den Mond*, D.193 (Hölty; 1815); *Die Mainacht*, D.194 (Hölty; 1815); *Amalia*, D.195 (Schiller; 1815); *An die Nachtigall*, D.196 (Hölty; 1815); *An die Apfelbäume, wo ich Julien erblickte*, D.197 (Hölty; 1815); *Seufzer*, D.198 (Hölty; 1815); *Auf den Tod einer Nachtigall*, D.201 (fragment only; Hölty; 1815); *Das Traumbild*, D.204a (Hölty; 1815; not extant); *Liebeständelei*, D.206 (Körner; 1815); *Der Liebende*, D.207 (Hölty; 1815); *Die Nonne*, D.208 (2 versions; Hölty; first version, fragment only, 1815; second version, originally D.212, 1815); *Der Liedler*, D.209 (Kenner; 1815); *Die Liebe (Klärchens Lied)*, D.210 (Goethe; 1815); *Adelwold und Emma*, D.211 (Bertrand; 1815); *Der Traum*, D.213 (Hölty; 1815); *Die Laube*, D.214 (Hölty; 1815); *Jägers Abendlied*, D.215 (Goethe; 1815); *Meerestille*, D.215a (Goethe; 1815); *Meerestille*, D.216 (Goethe; 1815); *Kolmas Klage*, D.217 (Ossian; 1815); *Grablied*, D.218 (Kenner; 1815); *Das Finden*, D.219 (Kosegarten; 1815); *Der Abend*, D.221 (Kosegarten; 1815); *Lieb Minna*, D.222 (Stadler; 1815); *Wandrers Nachtlied*, D.224 (Goethe; 1815); *Der Fischer*, D.225 (Goethe; 1815); *Erster Verlust*, D.226 (Goethe; 1815); *Idens Nachtgesang*, D.227 (Kosegarten; 1815); *Von Ida*, D.228 (Kosegarten; 1815); *Die Erscheinung*, D.229 (Kosegarten; 1815); *Die Täuschung*, D.230 (Kosegarten; 1815); *Das Sehnen*, D.231 (Kosegarten; 1815); *Geist der Liebe*, D.233 (Kosegarten; 1815); *Tischlied*, D.234 (Goethe; 1815); *Abends unter der Linde*, D.235 (Kosegarten; 1815); *Abends unter der Linde*, D.237 (Kosegarten; 1815); *Die Mondnacht*, D.238 (Kosegarten; 1815); *Huldigung*, D.240 (Kosegarten; 1815); *Alles um Liebe*, D.241 (Kosegarten; 1815); *Die Bürgschaft*, D.246 (Schiller; 1815); *Die Spinnerin*, D.247 (Goethe; 1815); *Lob des Tokayers*, D.248 (Baumberg; 1815); *Die Schlacht*, D.249 (Schiller; 1815; fragment only); *Das Geheimnis*, D.250 (Schiller; 1815); *Hoffnung*, D.251 (Schiller; 1815); *Das Mädchen aus der Fremde*, D.252 (Schiller; 1815); *Punschlied: Im Norden zu singen*, D.253 (Schiller; 1815); *Der Gott und die Bajadere*, D.254 (Goethe; 1815); *Der Rattenfänger*, D.255 (Goethe; 1815); *Der Schatzgräber*, D.256 (Goethe; 1815); *Heidenröslein*, D.257 (Goethe; 1815); *Bundeslied*, D.258 (Goethe; 1815); *An den Mond*, D.259 (Goethe; 1815); *Wonne der Wehmut*, D.260 (Goethe; 1815); *Wer kauft Liebesgötter?*, D.261 (Goethe; 1815); *Die Fröhlichkeit*, D.262 (Prandstetter; 1815); *Cora an die Sonne*, D.263 (Baumberg; 1815); *Der Morgenkuss*, D.264 (2 versions; Baumberg; 1815); *Abendständchen: An Lina*, D.265 (Baumberg; 1815); *Morgenlied*, D.266 (Stolberg; 1815); *An die Sonne*, D.270 (Baumberg; 1815); *Der Weiberfreund*, D.271 (Cowley; Ratschky, tr.; 1815); *An die Sonne*, D.272 (Tiedge; 1815); *Lilla an die Morgenröte*, D.273 (1815); *Tischlerlied*, D.274 (1815); *Totenkranz für ein Kind*, D.275 (Matthisson; 1815); *Abendlied*, D.276 (Stolberg; 1815); *Ossians Lied nach dem Falle Nathos*, D.278 (2 versions; Ossian; Harold, tr.; 1815); *Das Rosenband*, D.280 (Klopstock; 1815); *Das Mädchen von Inistore*, D.281 (Ossian; Harold, tr.; 1815); *Cronnan*, D.282 (Ossian; Harold, tr.; 1815); *An den Frühling*, D.283 (Schiller; 1815); *Lied*, D.284 (Schiller?; 1815); *Furcht der Geliebten (An Cidli)*, D.285 (2 versions; Klopstock; 1815); *Selma und Selmar*, D.286 (2 versions; Klopstock; 1815); *Vaterlandslied*, D.287 (2 versions; Klopstock; 1815); *An sie*, D.288 (Klopstock; 1815); *Die Sommernacht*, D.289 (2 versions; Klopstock; 1815); *Die frühen Gräber*, D.290 (Klopstock; 1815); *Dem Unendlichen*, D.291 (3 versions; Klopstock; 1815); *Shilric und Vinvela*, D.293 (Ossian; Harold, tr.; 1815); *Hoffnung*, D.295 (2 versions; Goethe; 1816?); *An den Mond*, D.296 (Goethe; 1816?); *Augenlied*, D.297 (2 versions; Mayrhofer; 1817?); *Liane*, D.298 (Mayrhofer; 1815); *Der Jüngling an der Quelle*, D.300 (Salis-Seewis; 1817?); *Lambertine*, D.301 (Stoll; 1815); *Labetrank der Liebe*, D.302 (Stoll; 1815); *An die Geliebte*, D.303 (Stoll; 1815); *Wiegenlied*, D.304 (Körner; 1815); *Mein Gruss an den Mai*, D.305 (Kumpf; 1815); *Skolie*, D.306 (Deinhardstein; 1815); *Die Sternewelten*, D.307 (Jarnik; Fellinger, tr.; 1815); *Die Macht der Liebe*, D.308 (Kalchberg; 1815); *Das gestörte Glück*, D.309 (Körner; 1815); *Sehnsucht*, D.310 (2 versions; Goethe; 1815); *An den Mond*, D.311 (1815; fragment only); *Hektors Abschied*, D.312 (2 versions; Schiller; 1815); *Die Sterne*, D.313 (Kosegarten; 1815); *Nachtgesang*, D.314 (Kosegarten; 1815); *An Rosa*, D.315 (Kosegarten; 1815); *An Rosa*, D.316 (2 versions; Kosegarten; 1815); *Idens Schwanenlied*, D.317 (2 versions; Kosegarten; 1815); *Schwangesang*, D.318 (Kosegarten; 1815); *Luisens Antwort*, D.319 (Kosegarten; 1815); *Der Zufriedene*, D.320 (Reissig; 1815); *Mignon*, D.321 (Goethe; 1815); *Hermann und Thusnelda*, D.322 (Klopstock; 1815); *Klage der Ceres*, D.323 (Schiller; 1815–16); *Harfenspieler*, D.325 (Goethe; 1815); *Lorma*, D.327 (Ossian; Harold, tr.; 1815; fragment only); *Erlkönig*, D.328 (4 versions; Goethe; 1815); *Die drei Sänger*, D.329 (Bobrik; 1815; fragment only); *Das Grab*, D.330 (Salis-Seewis; 1815); *An mein Klavier*, D.342 (Schubart; 1816?); *Am Tage aller Seelen (Litanei auf das Fest aller Seelen)*, D.343 (2 versions; Jacobi; 1816); *Am ersten Maimorgen*, D.344 (Claudius; 1816?); *Der Entfernten*, D.350 (Salis-Seewis; 1816?); *Fischerlied*, D.351 (Salis-Seewis; 1816); *Licht und Liebe (Nachtgesang)* D.352, for Soprano and Tenor (Collin; 1816?); *Die Nacht*, D.358 (Uz; 1816); *Sehnsucht*, D.359 (Goethe; 1816); *Lied eines Schiffers an die Dioskuren*, D.360 (Mayrhofer; 1816); *Am Bach im Frühlinge*, D.361 (Schober; 1816); *Zufriedenheit*, D.362 (Claudius; 1816?); *An Chloen*, D.363 (Uz; 1816; fragment only); *Der König in Thule*, D.367 (Goethe; 1816); *Jägers Abendlied*, D.368 (Goethe; 1816); *An Schwager Kronos*, D.369 (Goethe; 1816); *Klage*, D.371 (1816); *An die Natur*, D.372 (Stolberg-Stolberg; 1816); *Lied*, D.373 (Fouqué; 1816); *Der Tod Oskars*, D.375 (Ossian; Harold, tr.; 1816); *Lorma*, D.376 (Ossian; Harold, tr.; 1816; fragment only); *Morgenlied*, D.381 (1816); *Abendlied*, D.382 (1816); *Laura am Klavier*, D.388 (2 versions; Schiller; 1816); *Des Mädchens Klage*, D.389 (Schiller; 1816); *Entzuckung an Laura*, D.390 (Schiller; 1816); *Die vier Weltalter*, D.391 (Schiller; 1816); *Pflügerlied*, D.392 (Salis-Seewis; 1816); *Die Einsiedelei*, D.393 (Salis-Seewis; 1816); *An die Harmonie*, D.394 (Salis-Seewis; 1816); *Lebensmelodien*, D.395 (Schlegel; 1816); *Gruppe aus dem Tartarus*, D.396 (Schiller; 1816; fragment only); *Ritter Toggenburg*, D.397 (Schiller; 1816); *Frühlingslied*, D.398 (Hölty; 1816); *Auf den Tod einer Nachtigall*, D.399 (Hölty; 1816); *Die Knabenzeit*, D.400 (Hölty; 1816); *Winterlied*, D.401 (Hölty; 1816); *Der Flüchtling*, D.402 (Schiller; 1816); *Lied*, D.403 (4 versions; Salis-Seewis; 1816); *Die Herbstnacht*, D.404 (Salis-Seewis; 1816); *Der Herbstabend*, D.405 (2 versions; Salis- Seewis; 1816); *Abschied von der Harfe*, D.406 (Salis-Seewis; 1816); *Die verfehlteStunde*, D.409 (Schlegel; 1816); *Sprache der Liebe*, D.410 (Schlegel; 1816); *Daphne am Bach*, D.411 (Stolberg-Stolberg; 1816); *Stimme der Liebe*, D.412 (2 versions; Stolberg-Stolberg; 1816); *Entzückung*, D.413 (Matthisson; 1816); *Geist der Liebe*, D.414 (Matthisson; 1816); *Klage*, D.415 (Matthisson; 1816); *Lied in der Abwesenheit*, D.416 (Stolberg-Stolberg; 1816; fragment only); *Stimme der Liebe*, D.418 (Matthisson; 1816); *Julius an Theone*, D.419 (Matthisson; 1816); *Minnelied*, D.429 (Hölty; 1816); *Die frühe Liebe*, D.430 (2 versions; Hölty; 1816; second version not extant); *Blumenlied*, D.431 (Hölty; 1816); *Der Leidende*, D.432 (2 versions; 1816); *Seligkeit*, D.433 (Hölty; 1816); *Erntelied*, D.434 (Hölty; 1816); *Klage*, D.436 (2 versions; Hölty; 1816; second version originally D.437); *Das grosse Halleluja*, D.442 (Klopstock;

1816); *Schlachtlied*, D.443 (Klopstock; 1816); *Die Gestirne*, D.444 (Klopstock; 1816); *Edone*, D.445 (Klopstock; 1816); *Die Liebesgötter*, D.446 (Uz; 1816); *An den Schlaf*, D.447 (1816); *Gott im Frühlinge*, D.448 (2 versions; Uz; 1816); *Der gute Hirt*, D.449 (Uz; 1816); *Fragment aus dem Aeschylus*, D.450 (2 versions; Aeschylus; Mayrhofer, tr.; 1816); *Grablied auf einen Soldaten*, D.454 (Schubart; 1816); *Freude der Kinderjahre*, D.455 (Köpken; 1816); *Das Heimweh*, D.456 (Winkler; 1816); *An die untergehende Sonne*, D.457 (Kosegarten; 1816–17); *Aus Diego Manazares (Ilmerine)*, D.458 (Schlechta; 1816); *An Chloen*, D.462 (Jacobi; 1816); *Hochzeit-Lied*, D.463 (Jacobi; 1816); *In der Mitternacht*, D.464 (Jacobi; 1816); *Trauer der Liebe*, D.465 (2 versions; Jacobi; 1816); *Die Perle*, D.466 (Jacobi; 1816); *Pflicht und Liebe*, D.467 (Gotter; 1816); *An den Mond*, D.468 (Hölty; 1816); *Mignon*, D.469 (Goethe; 1816; fragments only); *Liedesend*, D.473 (2 versions; Mayrhofer; 1816); *Lied des Orpheus, als er in die Hölle ging*, D.474 (2 versions; Jacobi; 1816; first version unfinished); *Abschied (nach einer Wallfahrtsarie)*, D.475 (Mayrhofer; 1816); *Rückweg*, D.476 (Mayrhofer; 1816); *Alte Liebe rostet nie*, D.477 (Mayrhofer; 1816); *Harfenspieler I (Gesänge des Harfners No. 1)*, D.478 (2 versions; Goethe; first version, 1816; second version, 1822); *Harfenspieler II (Gesänge des Harfners No. 3)*, D.479 (2 versions; Goethe; first version, 1816; second version, 1822); *Harfenspieler III (Gesänge des Harfners No. 2)*, D.480 (3 versions; Goethe; first and second versions, 1816; third version, 1822); *Sehnsucht*, D.481 (Goethe; 1816); *Der Sänger am Felsen*, D.482 (Pichler; 1816); *Lied*, D.483 (Pichler; 1816); *Gesang der Geister über den Wassern*, D.484 (Goethe; 1816; fragment only); *Der Wanderer*, D.489 (3 versions; Lübeck; 1816; second version originally D.493b; third version originally D.493a); *Der Hirt*, D.490 (Mayrhofer; 1816); *Geheimnis*, D.491 (Mayrhofer; 1816); *Zum Punsche*, D.492 (Mayrhofer; 1816); *Abendlied der Fürstin*, D.495 (Mayrhofer; 1816); *Bei dem Grabe meines Vaters*, D.496 (Claudius; 1816); *Klage um Ali Bey*, D.496a (Claudius; 1816); *An die Nachtigall*, D.497 (Claudius; 1816); *Wiegenlied*, D.498 (1816); *Abendlied*, D.499 (Claudius; 1816); *Phidile*, D.500 (Claudius; 1816); *Zufriedenheit*, D.501 (2 versions; Claudius; 1816); *Herbstlied*, D.502 (Salis-Seewis; 1816); *Mailied*, D.503 (Hölty; 1816); *Am Grabe Anselmos*, D.504 (2 versions; Claudius; 1816); *Skolie*, D.507 (Matthisson; 1816); *Lebenslied*, D.508 (Matthisson; 1816); *Leiden der Trennung*, D.509 (2 versions; Metastasio; Collin, tr.; 1816; first version, fragment only); *Vedi quanto adoro*, D.510 (Metastasio; 1816); *Nur wer die Liebe kennt*, D.513a (Werner; 1817?; sketch only); *Die abgeblühte Linde*, D.514 (Széchényi; 1817?); *Der Flug der Zeit*, D.515 (Széchényi; 1817?); *Sehnsucht*, D.516 (Mayrhofer; 1816?); *Der Schäfer und der Reiter*, D.517 (2 versions; Fouqué; 1817); *An den Tod*, D.518 (Schubart; 1817?); *Die Blumensprache*, D.519 (Platner?; 1817?); *Frohsinn*, D.520 (2 versions; Castelli; 1817); *Jagdlied*, D.521 (Werner; 1817); *Die Liebe*, D.522 (Leon; 1817); *Trost*, D.523 (1817); *Der Alpenjäger*, D.524 (3 versions; Mayrhofer; 1817); *Wie Ulfru fischt*, D.525 (2 versions; Mayrhofer; 1817); *Fahrt zum Hades*, D.526 (Mayrhofer; 1817); *Schlaflied (Abendlied; Schlummerlied)*, D.527 (2 versions; Mayrhofer; 1817); *La pastorella al prato*, D.528 (Goldoni; 1817); *An eine Quelle*, D.530 (Claudius; 1817); *Der Tod und das Mädchen*, D.531 (Claudius; 1817); *Das Lied vom Reifen*, D.532 (Claudius; 1817; fragment only); *Täglich zu singen*, D.533 (Claudius; 1817); *Die Nacht*, D.534 (Ossian; Harold, tr.; 1817); *Lied*, D.535, with Small Orch. (1817); *Der Schiffer*, D.536 (2 versions; Mayrhofer; 1817); *Am Strome*, D.539 (Mayrhofer; 1817); *Philoket*, D.540 (Mayrhofer; 1817); *Memnon*, D.541 (Mayrhofer; 1817); *Antigone und Oedip*, D.542 (Mayrhofer; 1817); *Auf dem See*, D.543 (2 versions; Goethe; 1817); *Ganymed*, D.544 (Goethe; 1817); *Der Jüngling und der Tod*, D.545 (2 versions; Spaun; 1817); *Trost im Liede*, D.546 (Schober; 1817); *An die Musik*, D.547 (2 versions;

Schober; 1817); *Orest auf Tauris*, D.548 (Mayrhofer; 1817); *Mahomets Gesang*, D.549 (Goethe; 1817; fragment only); *Die Forelle*, D.550 (5 versions; Schubart; 1817?–21); *Pax vobiscum*, D.551 (Schober; 1817); *Hänflings Liebeswerbung*, D.552 (2 versions; Kind; 1817); *Auf der Donau*, D.553 (Mayrhofer; 1817); *Uraniens Flucht*, D.554 (Mayrhofer; 1817); sketch for a song, D.555 (no text; 1817); *Liebhaber in allen Gestalten*, D.558 (Goethe; 1817); *Schweizerlied*, D.559 (Goethe; 1817); *Der Goldschmiedsgesell*, D.560 (Goethe; 1817); *Nach einem Gewitter*, D.561 (Mayrhofer; 1817); *Fischerlied*, D.562 (Salis-Seewis; 1817); *Die Einsiedelei*, D.563 (Salis-Seewis; 1817); *Gretchen im Zwinger (Gretchen; Gretchens Bitte)*, D.564 (Goethe; 1817; fragment only); *Der Strom*, D.565 (1817); *Das Grab*, D.569, for Unison Chorus (Salis-Seewis; 1817); *Iphigenia*, D.573 (Mayrhofer; 1817); *Entzückung an Laura*, D.577 (2 versions; Schiller; 1817; fragments only); *Abschied*, D.578 (Schubert; 1817); *Der Knabe in der Wiege (Wiegenlied)*, D.579 (2 versions; Ottenwalt; 1817; second version, fragment only); *Vollendung*, D.579a (originally D.989; Matthisson; 1817); *Die Erde*, D.579b (originally D.989a; Matthisson; 1817); *Gruppe aus dem Tartarus*, D.583 (Schiller; 1817); *Elysium*, D.584 (Schiller; 1817); *Atys*, D.585 (Mayrhofer; 1817); *Erlafsee*, D.586 (Mayrhofer; 1817); *An den Frühling*, D.587 (2 versions; Schiller; 1817; second version originally D.245); *Der Alpenjäger*, D.588 (2 versions; Schiller; 1817; first version, fragment only); *Der Kampf*, D.594 (Schiller; 1817); *Thekla: Eine Geisterstimme*, D.595 (2 versions; Schiller; 1817); *Lied eines Kindes*, D.596 (1817; fragment only); *Auf der Riesenkoppe*, D.611 (Korner; 1818); *An den Mond in einer Herbstnacht*, D.614 (Schreiber; 1818); *Grablied für die Mutter*, D.616 (1818); a vocal exercise for 2 Voices and Figured Bass, D.619 (no text; 1818); *Einsamkeit*, D.620 (Mayrhofer; 1818); *Der Blumenbrief*, D.622 (Schreiber; 1818); *Das Marienbild*, D.623 (Schreiber; 1818); *Blondel zu Marien*, D.626 (1818); *Das Abendrot*, D.627 (Schreiber; 1818); *Sonett I*, D.628 (Petrarch; Schlegel, tr.; 1818); *Sonett II*, D.629 (Petrarch; Schlegel, tr.; 1818); *Sonett III*, D.630 (Petrarch; Gries, tr.; 1818); *Blanka (Das Mädchen)*, D.631 (Schlegel; 1818); *Vom Mitleiden Mariä*, D.632 (Schlegel; 1818); *Der Schmetterling*, D.633 (Schlegel; 1819?); *Die Berge*, D.634 (Schlegel; 1821?); *Sehnsucht*, D.636 (3 versions; Schiller; 1821?); *Hoffnung*, D.637 (Schiller; 1819?); *Der Jüngling am Bache*, D.638 (2 versions; Schiller; 1819); *Widerschein*, D.639 (2 versions; Schlechta; 1819?; second version originally D.949); *Abend*, D.645 (Tieck; 1819; fragment only); *Die Gebüsche*, D.646 (Schlegel; 1819); *Der Wanderer*, D.649 (Schlegel; 1819); *Abendbilder*, D.650 (Silbert; 1819); *Himmelsfunken*, D.651 (Silbert; 1819); *Das Mädchen*, D.652 (2 versions; Schlegel; 1819); *Bertas Lied in der Nacht*, D.653 (Grillparzer; 1819); *An die Freunde*, D.654 (Mayrhofer; 1819); *Marie*, D.658 (Novalis; 1819); *Hymne I*, D.659 (Novalis; 1819); *Hymne II*, D.660 (Novalis; 1819); *Hymne III*, D.661 (Novalis; 1819); *Hymne IV*, D.662 (Novalis; 1819); *Der 13. Psalm*, D.663 (M. Mendelssohn, tr.; 1819; fragment only); *Beim Winde*, D.669 (Mayrhofer; 1819); *Die Sternennächte*, D.670 (Mayrhofer; 1819); *Trost*, D.671 (Mayrhofer; 1819); *Nachtstück*, D.672 (2 versions; Mayrhofer; 1819); *Die Liebende schreibt*, D.673 (Goethe; 1819); *Prometheus*, D.674 (Goethe; 1819); *Strophe aus Die Götter Griechenlands*, D.677 (2 versions; Schiller; 1819); *Über allen Zauber Liebe*, D.682 (Mayrhofer; 1820?; fragment only); *Die Sterne*, D.684 (Schlegel; 1820); *Morgenlied*, D.685 (Werner; 1820); *Frühlingsglaube*, D.686 (3 versions; Uhland; first and second versions, 1820; third version, 1822); *Nachthymne*, D.687 (Novalis; 1820); *4 Canzonen: Non t'accostar all'urna* (Vitorelli), *Guarda, che bianca luna* (Vitorelli), *Da quel sembiante appresi* (Metastasio), *Mio ben ricordati* (Metastasio), D.688 (all 1820); *Abendröte*, D.690 (Schlegel; 1823); *Die Vögel*, D.691 (Schlegel; 1820); *Der Knabe*, D.692 (Schlegel; 1820); *Der Fluss*, D.693 (Schlegel; 1820); *Der Schiffer*, D.694 (Schlegel; 1820); *Namenstagslied*, D.695 (Stadler; 1820); *Des Fräuleins Liebeslauschen (Liebeslauschen)*, D.698 (Schlechta; 1820); *Der entsühnte Orest*, D.699 (Mayrhofer; 1820); *Freiwilliges Versinken*, D.700 (Mayrhofer; 1820); *Der Jüngling auf dem Hügel*, D.702 (Hüttenbrenner; 1820); *Der zürnenden Diana*, D.707 (2 versions; Mayrhofer; 1820); *Im Walde (Waldesnacht)*, D.708 (Schlegel; 1820); *Lob der Tränen*, D.711 (2 versions; Schlegel; 1818); *Die gefangenen Sänger*, D.712 (Schlegel; 1821); *Der Unglückliche*, D.713 (2 versions; Pichler; 1821); *Versunken*, D.715 (Goethe; 1821); *Grenzen der Menschheit*, D.716 (Goethe; 1821); *Suleika*, D.717 (1821?); *Geheimes*, D.719 (Goethe; 1821); *Suleika*, D.720 (2 versions; 1821); *Mahomets Gesang*, D.721 (Goethe; 1821; fragment only); *Linde Lüfte wehen*, D.725 (1821; fragment only); *Mignon*, D.726 (Goethe; 1821); *Mignon*, D.727 (Goethe; 1821); *Johanna Sebus*, D.728 (Goethe; 1821; fragment only); *Der Blumen Schmerz*, D.731 (Mayláth; 1821); *Ihr Grab*, D.736 (Engelhardt; 1822?); *An die Leier*, D.737 (Bruchmann; 1822?); *Im Haine*, D.738 (Bruchmann; 1822?); *Sei mir gegrüsst*, D.741 (Rückert; 1821?); *Der Wachtelschlag*, D.742 (Sauter; 1822); *Selige Welt*, D.743 (Senn; 1822); *Schwanengesang*, D.744 (Senn; 1822); *Die Rose*, D.745 (2 versions; Schlegel; 1822); *Am See*, D.746 (Bruchmann; 1822?); *Herrn Josef Spaun, Assessor in Linz (Sendschreiben an den Assessor Spaun in Linz)*, D.749 (Collin; 1822); *Die Liebe hat gelogen*, D.751 (Platen-Hallermünde; 1822); *Nachtviolen*, D.752 (Mayrhofer; 1822); *Heliopolis*, D.753 (Mayrhofer; 1822); *Heliopolis*, D.754 (Mayrhofer; 1822); *Du liebst mich nicht*, D.756 (2 versions; Platen-Hallermünde; 1822); *Todesmusik*, D.758 (Schober; 1822); *Schatzgräbers Begehr*, D.761 (2 versions; Schober; 1822); *Schwestergruss*, D.762 (Bruchmann; 1822); *Der Musensohn*, D.764 (2 versions; Goethe; 1822); *An die Entfernte*, D.765 (Goethe; 1822); *Am Flusse*, D.766 (Goethe; 1822); *Willkommen und Abschied*, D.767 (2 versions; Goethe; 1822); *Wandrers Nachtlied*, D.768 (Goethe; 1824); *Drang in die Ferne*, D.770 (Leitner; 1823); *Der Zwerg*, D.771 (Collin; 1822?); *Wehmut*, D.772 (Collin; 1822?); *Auf dem Wasser zu singen*, D.774 (Stolberg-Stolberg; 1823); *Dass sie hier gewesen*, D.775 (Rückert; 1823?); *Du bist die Ruh*, D.776 (Rückert; 1823); *Lachen und Weinen*, D.777 (Rückert; 1823?); *Greisengesang*, D.778 (2 versions; Rückert; 1823); *Die Wallfahrt*, D.778a (Rückert; 1823?); *Der zürnende Barde*, D.785 (Bruchmann; 1823); *Viola*, D.786 (Schober; 1823); *Lied (Die Mutter Erde)*, D.788 (Stolberg-Stolberg; 1823); *Pilgerweise*, D.789 (Schober; 1823); *Vergissmeinnicht*, D.792 (Schober; 1823); *Das Geheimnis*, D.793 (Schiller; 1823); *Der Pilgrim*, D.794 (2 versions; Schiller; 1823); *Die schöne Müllerin*, song cycle, D.795 (Müller; 1823; 1, *Das Wandern*; 2, *Wohin?*; 3, *Halt!*; 4, *Danksagung an den Bach*; 5, *Am Feierabend*; 6, *Der Neugierige*; 7, *Ungeduld*; 8, *Morgengruss*; 9, *Des Müllers Blumen*; 10, *Tränenregen*; 11, *Mein!*; 12, *Pause*; 13, *Mit dem grünen Lautenbande*; 14, *Der Jäger*; 15, *Eifersucht und Stolz*; 16, *Die liebe Farbe*; 17, *Die böse Farbe*; 18, *Trockne Blumen*; 19, *Der Müller und der Bach*; 20, *Des Baches Wiegenlied*); *Romanze zum Drama Rosamunde*, D.797 (Chézy; 1823); *Im Abendrot*, D.799 (Lappe; 1824?); *Der Einsame*, D.800 (2 versions; Lappe; 1825); *Dithyrambe*, D.801 (Schiller; 1826); *Der Sieg*, D.805 (Mayrhofer; 1824); *Abendstern*, D.806 (Mayrhofer; 1824); *Auflösung*, D.807 (Mayrhofer; 1824); *Gondelfahrer*, D.808 (Mayrhofer; 1824); *Lied eines Kriegers*, D.822, with Unison Chorus (1824); *Nacht und Träume*, D.827 (2 versions; Collin; 1823); *Die junge Nonne*, D.828 (Craigher de Jachelutta; 1825); *Abschied*, D.829 (Pratobevera; 1826); *Lied der Anne Lyle*, D.830 (MacDonald; 1825); *Gesang der Norna*, D.831 (Scott; Spiker, tr.; 1825); *Des Sängers Habe*, D.832 (Schlechta; 1825); *Der blinde Knabe*, D.833 (2 versions; Cibber; Craigher, tr.; 1825); *Im Walde*, D.834 (2 versions; Schulze; 1825); *Ellens Gesang*, D.837 (Scott; Storck, tr.; 1825); *Ellens Gesang*, D.838 (Scott; Storck, tr.; 1825); *Ellens Gesang (Hymne an die*

Jungfrau), D.839 (Scott; Storck, tr.; 1825); *Totengräbers Heimwehe*, D.842 (Craigher; 1825); *Lied des gefangenen Jägers*, D.843 (Scott; Storck, tr.; 1825); *Normans Gesang*, D.846 (Scott; Storck, tr.; 1825); *Das Heimweh*, D.851 (2 versions; Felsö-Eör; 1825); *Die Allmacht*, D.852 (2 versions; Pyrker; 1825); *Auf der Bruck*, D.853 (2 versions; Schulze; 1825); *Fülle der Liebe*, D.854 (Schlegel; 1825); *Wiedersehn*, D.855 (Schlegel; 1825); *Abendlied für die Entfernte*, D.856 (Schlegel; 1825); *2 Szenen aus dem Schauspiel Lacrimas*, D.857: 1, *Lied der Delphine*; 2, *Lied des Florio* (Schütz; 1825); *An mein Herz*, D.860 (Schulze; 1825); *Der liebliche Stern*, D.861 (Schulze; 1825); *Um Mitternacht*, D.862 (2 versions; Schulze; first version, 1825; second version, 1826); *An Gott*, D.863 (Hohlfeld; 1827; not extant); *Das Totenhemdchen*, D.864 (Bauernfeld; 1824; not extant); *Widerspruch*, D.865 (Seidl; 1826?); *4 Refrainlieder*, D.866 (Seidl; 1828): 1, *Die Unterscheidung*; 2, *Bei dir allein*; 3, *Die Männer sind méchant*; 4, *Irdisches Glück*; *Wiegenlied*, D.867 (Seidl; 1826?); *Totengräber-Weise*, D.869 (Schlechta; 1826); *Der Wanderer an den Mond*, D.870 (Seidl; 1826); *Das Zügenglöcklein*, D.871 (2 versions; Seidl; 1826); *O Quell, was strömst du rasch und wild*, D.874 (Schulze; 1826; fragment only); *Im Jänner 1817 (Tiefes Leid)*, D.876 (Schulze; 1826); *Gesänge aus Wilhelm Meister*, D.877: 1, *Mignon und der Harfner*; 2, 3, and 4, *Lied der Mignon* (Goethe; 1826); *Am Fenster*, D.878 (Seidl; 1826); *Sehnsucht*, D.879 (Seidl; 1826); *Im Freien*, D.880 (Seidl; 1826); *Fischerweise*, D.881 (2 versions; Schlechta; 1826); *Im Frühling*, D.882 (Schulze; 1826); *Lebensmut*, D.883 (Schulze; 1826); *Über Wildemann*, D.884 (Schulze; 1826); *Trinklied (Come, thou monarch of the vine)*, D.888 (Shakespeare; Grünbühel and Bauernfeld, tr.; 1826); *Ständchen (Hark, hark the lark)*, D.889 (Shakespeare; Schlegel, tr.; 1826); *Hippolits Lied*, D.890 (Gerstenberg; 1826); *Gesang (An Sylvia; Who Is Sylvia?)*, D.891 (Shakespeare; Bauernfeld, tr.; 1826); *Fröhliches Scheiden*, D.896 (Leitner; 1827–28; sketch only); *Sie in jedem Liede*, D.896a (Leitner; 1827–28; sketch only); *Wolke und Quelle*, D.896b (Leitner; 1827–28; sketch only); *3 Gesänge*, D.902 (1827): 1, *L'incanto degli occhi (Die Macht der Augen)*; 2, *Il Traditor deluso (Der getäuschte Verräter)*; 3, *Il modo di prender moglie (Die Art, ein Weib zu nehmen)*; *Alinde*, D.904 (Rochlitz; 1827); *An die Laute*, D.905 (Rochlitz; 1827); *Der Vater mit dem Kind*, D.906 (Bauernfeld; 1827); *Romanze des Richard Löwenherz*, D.907 (2 versions; Scott; Müller, tr.; 1826); *Jägers Liebeslied*, D.909 (Schober; 1827); *Schiffers Scheidelied*, D.910 (Schober; 1827); *Die Winterreise*, song cycle, D.911 (Müller; 1827; Book I: 1, *Gute Nacht*; 2, *Die Wetterfahne*; 3, *Gefrorne Tränen*; 4, *Erstarrung*; 5, *Der Lindenbaum*; 6, *Wasserflut* [2 versions]; 7, *Auf dem Flusse*; 8, *Rückblick*; 9, *Irrlicht*; 10, *Rast* [2 versions]; 11, *Frühlingstraum*; 12, *Einsamkeit* [2 versions]; Book II: 13, *Die Post*; 14, *Der greise Kopf*; 15, *Die Krähe*; 16, *Letzte Hoffnung*; 17, *Im Dorfe*; 18, *Der stürmische Morgen*; 19, *Täuschung*; 20, *Der Wegweiser*; 21, *Das Wirthaus*; 22, *Mut* [2 versions]; 23, *Die Nebensonnen* [2 versions]; 24, *Der Leiermann* [2 versions]); sketch for a song, D.916a (no text; 1827); *Das Lied im Grünen*, D.917 (Reil; 1827); *Frühlingslied*, D.919 (Pollak; 1827); *Heimliches Lieben*, D.922 (2 versions; 1827); *Eine altschottische Ballade*, D.923 (3 versions; first and third for 2 Voices; Eng. author unknown; Herder, tr.; 1827); *Das Weinen*, D.926 (Leitner; 1827–28); *Vor meiner Wiege*, D.927 (Leitner; 1827–28); *Der Wallensteiner Lanzknecht beim Trunk*, D.931 (Leitner; 1827); *Der Kreuzzug*, D.932 (Leitner; 1827); *Des Fischers Liebesglück*, D.933 (Leitner; 1827); *Lebensmut*, D.937 (Rellstab; 1828; fragment only); *Der Winterabend*, D.938 (Leitner; 1828); *Die Sterne*, D.939 (Leitner; 1828); *Auf dem Strom*, D.943, with Horn or Cello obbligato (Rellstab; 1828); *Herbst*, D.945 (Rellstab; 1828); *Glaube, Hoffnung und Liebe*, D.955 (Kuffner; 1828); *Schwanengesang*, D.957 (1828; Book I: 1, *Liebesbotschaft* [Rellstab]; 2, *Kriegers Ahnung* [Rellstab]; 3, *Frühlingssehnsucht* [Rellstab]; 4, *Ständchen*

[Rellstab]; 5, *Aufenthalt* [Rellstab]; 6, *In der Ferne* [Rellstab]; Book II: 7, *Abschied* [Rellstab]; 8, *Der Atlas* [Heine]; 9, *Ihr Bild* [Heine]; 10, *Das Fischermädchen* [Heine]; 11, *Die Stadt* [Heine]; 12, *Am Meer* [Heine]; 13, *Der Doppelgänger* [Heine]; 14, *Die Taubenpost* [Seidl]); *Der Hirt auf dem Felsen*, D.965, with Clarinet obbligato (Müller; 1828); *Der Graf von Habsburg*, D.990 (Schiller; 1815?); *Kaiser Maximilian auf der Martinswand*, D.990a (Collin; 1815?); *Augenblicke in Elysium*, D.990b (originally D.582; Schober; not extant); *Das Echo*, D.990c (originally D.868; Castelli); *Die Schiffende*, D.990d (Holty; not extant); *L'incanto degli occhi*, D.990e (Metastasio); *Il Traditor deluso*, D.990f (Metastasio; not extant); *Mein Frieden*, D.AI/30 (Heine; 1815?).

BIBL.: COLLECTED EDITIONS, SOURCE MATE-RIAL: The first complete critical edition of his works, *F. S.s Werke: Kritisch durchgesehene Gesamtausgabe*, edited by E. Mandyczewski (assisted by Brahms, Brüll, Hellmesberger, J.N. Fuchs et al.), was publ. by Breitkopf & Härtel (40 vols. in 21 series, Leipzig, 1884–97). A new and exhaustive critical edition, *F. S.: Neue Ausgabe sämtlicher Werke*, ed. by W. Durr, A. Feil, C. Landon et al., is being publ. under the sponsorship of the Internationalen Schubert-Gesellschaft (Kassel, 1964 et seq.). The standard thematic catalogue is by O. Deutsch and D. Wakeling, *S.: Thematic Catalogue of All His Works in Chronological Order* (London, 1951; in Ger. as *F. S.: Thematisches Verzeichnis seiner Werke in chronologischer Folge...*, publ. in the *Neue Ausgabe sämtlicher Werke* of Schubert in a rev. ed. in 1978; new ed. as *The S. Thematic Catalog*, 1995). Other sources include the following: O. Deutsch, ed., *F. S.s Briefe und Schriften* (Munich, 1919; Eng. tr., 1928; fourth Ger. ed., 1954); *Bericht über den Internationalen Kongress für S.forschung: Wien 1928* (Augsburg, 1929); O. Deutsch, ed., *F. S.s Tagebuch* (facsimile and transcription; Vienna, 1928; Eng. tr., 1928); W. Kahl, *Verzeichnis des Schrifttums über F. S.: 1828–1928* (Regensburg, 1938); H. Werlé, ed., *F. S. in seinen Briefen und Aufzeichnungen* (Leipzig, 1948; fourth ed., 1955); R. Klein, *S.- Stätten* (Vienna, 1972); E. Hilmar, *Verzeichnis der S.-Handschriften in der Musiksammlung der Wiener Stadt- und Landesbibliothek* (Kassel, 1978); W. Thomas, *S.-Studien* (Frankfurt am Main, 1990); F. Dieckmann, *F. S.: Eine Annäherung* (Frankfurt am Main, 1996); M. Stegemann, *S.- Almanach: Eine musikalisch-historische Chronik* (Munich, 1996); W. Dürr and A. Krause, eds., *S.-Handbuch* (Kassel, 1997); R. Erickson, ed., *S.'s Vienna* (New Haven, 1997); C. Gibbs, ed., *The Cambridge Companion to S.* (Cambridge, 1997); E. Hackenbracht, ed., *1797–1997: Der Flug der Zeit: F. S.: Ein Lesebuch* (Tutzing, 1997); B. Newbould, ed., *S. Studies* (Aldershot, 1998). **BIOGRAPHICAL:** H. Kreissle von Hellborn, *F. S.: Eine biographische Skizze* (Vienna, 1861; second ed., greatly enl. as *F. S.*, 1865; Eng. tr., London, 1866); A. Reissmann, *F. S.: Sein Leben und seine Werke* (Berlin, 1873); H. Frost, *F. S.* (London, 1881; second ed., 1923); M. Friedlaender, *Beiträge zur Biographie F. S.s* (Berlin, 1887; new ed. as *F. S.: Skizze seines Lebens und Wirken*, Leipzig, 1928); A. Niggli, *S.* (Leipzig, 1890); H. Ritter, *F. S.* (Bamberg, 1896); R. Heuberger, *F. S.* (Berlin, 1902; third ed., rev., 1920, by H. von der Pforten); M. Zenger, *F. S.s Wirken und Erdenwallen* (Langensalza, 1902); O. Deutsch, *S.-Brevier* (Berlin, 1905); W. Klatte, *S.* (Berlin, 1907); L.-A. Bourgault-Ducoudray, *S.* (Paris, 1908; new ed., 1926); H. Antcliffe, *S.* (London, 1910); W. Dahms, *S.* (Berlin, 1912); O. Deutsch, ed., *F. S.: Die Dokumente seines Lebens und Schaffens* (in collaboration, first with L. Scheibler, then with W. Kahl and G. Kinsky; it was planned as a comprehensive work in 3 vols. containing all known documents, pictures, and other materials, arranged in chronological order, with a thematic catalogue; only 2 vols. publ.: Vol. III, *Sein Leben in Bildern*, Munich, 1913; Vol. II, part 1, *Die Dokumente seines Lebens*, Munich, 1914, which appeared in an Eng. tr. by Eric Blom as *S.: A Documentary Biography*, London, 1946, and in an American ed. as *The S. Reader: A Life of F. S. in Letters and Documents*, N.Y., 1947; a second Ger. ed., enl., was publ. in the *Neue Ausgabe sämtlicher Werke* of Schubert in 1964; new ed., 1996); K. Kobald, *S. und Schwind* (Zürich, 1921); O. Bie, *F. S.: Sein Leben und sein Werk* (Berlin, 1925; Eng. tr., 1928); E. Bethge, *F. S.* (Leipzig, 1928); H. Eulenberg, *S. und die Frauen* (Hellerau, 1928); N. Flower, *F. S.* (London and N.Y., 1928; new ed., 1949); A. Glazunov, *S.* (Leningrad, 1928); K. Kobald, *F. S. und seine Zeit* (Zürich, 1928; Eng. tr., 1928; new Ger. ed., 1948); G. Kruse, *F. S.* (Bielefeld, 1928); P. Landormy, *La Vie de S.* (Paris, 1928); J.-G. Prod'homme, *S.* (Paris, 1928); idem, *S. raconté par ceux qui l'ont vu* (Paris, 1928); P. Stefan, *F. S.* (Berlin, 1928; new ed., Vienna, 1947); A. Weiss, *F. S.* (Vienna, 1928); R. Bates, *F. S.* (London, 1934); W. Vetter, *F. S.* (Potsdam, 1934); G. Schünemann, *Erinnerungen an S.* (Berlin, 1936); A. Orel, *Der junge S.* (Vienna, 1940); A. Kolb, *F. S.: Sein Leben* (Stockholm, 1941); K. Höcker, *Wege zu S.* (Regensburg, 1942); B. Paumgartner, *F. S.* (Zürich, 1943; second ed., 1947); R. Tenschert, *Du holde Kunst: Ein kleiner S.-Spiegel* (Vienna, 1943); A. Hutchings, *S.* (London, 1945; fourth ed., rev., 1973); W. and P. Rehberg, *F. S.* (Zürich, 1946); C. Weingartner, *F. S.* (Alten, 1947); R. Schauffler, *F. S.: The Ariel of Music* (N.Y., 1949); A. Einstein, *S.: A Musical Portrait* (N.Y., 1951; Ger. ed., 1952); H. Rutz, *S.: Dokumente seines Lebens und Schaffens* (Munich, 1952); H. Goldschmidt, *F. S.* (Berlin, 1954; fifth ed., 1964); P. Mies, *F. S.* (Leipzig, 1954); O. Deutsch, ed., *S.: Die Erinnerungen seiner Freunde* (Leipzig, 1957; Eng. tr. as *S.: Memoirs by His Friends*, N.Y., 1958; third Ger. ed., 1974); M.J.E. Brown, *S.: A Critical Biography* (London, 1958; second ed., 1961); F. Hug, *F. S.: Leben und Werk eines Frühvollendeten* (Frankfurt am Main, 1958); L. Kusche, *F. S.: Dichtung und Wahrheit* (Munich, 1962); K. Kobald, *F. S.* (Vienna, 1963); A. Kolb, *S.* (Gütersloh, 1964); J. Bruyr, *F. S.: L'Homme et son oeuvre* (Paris, 1965); F. de Eaubonne and M.-R. Hofmann, *La Vie de S.* (Paris, 1965); W. Marggraf, *F. S.* (Leipzig, 1967); J. Reed, *S.: The Final Years* (London, 1972); J. Wechsberg, *S.* (N.Y., 1977); H. Fröhlich, *S.* (Munich, 1978); H. Osterheld, *F. S.: Schicksal und Persönlichkeit* (Stuttgart, 1978); P. Gammond, *S.* (London, 1982); E. Hilmar, *F. S. in seiner Zeit* (Vienna, 1985); G. Marek, *S.* (N.Y., 1985); C. Osborne, *S. and his Vienna* (London, 1985); J. Reed, *S.* (London, 1987); F. Hilmar, *S.* (Graz, 1989); E. Krenek, *F. S.: Ein Porträt* (Tutzing, 1990); P. Gülke, *F. S. und seine Zeit* (Laaber, 1991); M. Schneider, *S.* (Paris, 1994); E. McKay, *F. S.: A Biography* (Oxford, 1996); M. Wagner, *F. S.: Sein Werk, sein Leben* (Vienna, 1996); W. Bodendorff, *Wer war F. S.?: Eine Biographie* (Augsburg, 1997); E. Hilmar, *F. S.* (Reinbek, 1997); H. Knaus, *F. S.: Vom Vorstadtkind zum Compositeur* (Vienna, 1997); B. Newbould, *S.: The Music and the Man* (Berkeley, 1997). **CRITICAL, ANALYTICAL:** J. Rissé, *F. S. in seinen Liedern* (2 vols., Hannover, 1872); H. de Curzon, *Les Lieder de F. S.* (Brussels, 1899); M. Gallet, *S. et le Lied* (Paris, 1907); O. Wissig, *F. S.s Messen* (Leipzig, 1909); M. Bauer, *Die Lieder F. S.s* (Leipzig, 1915); H. von der Pfordten, *S. und das deutsche Lied* (Leipzig, 1916; second ed., 1920); R. Krott, *Die Singspiele S.s* (diss., Univ. of Vienna, 1921); O. Deutsch, *Die Originalausgaben von S.s Goethe-Liedern* (Vienna, 1926); H. Költzsch, *F. S. in seinen Klaviersonaten* (Leipzig, 1927); F. von Kraus, *Beiträge zur Erforschung des malenden und poetisierenden Wesens in der Begleitung von F. S.s Liedern* (Mainz, 1927); R. Capell, *S.'s Songs* (London, 1928; third ed., rev., 1973, by M. Cooper); F. Damian, *F. S.s Liederkreis, Die schöne Müllerin* (Leipzig, 1928); F. Günther, *S.s Lied* (Stuttgart, 1928); K. Huschke, *Das 7 Gestirn der grossen S. 'schen Kammermusikwerke* (Pritzwalk, 1928); K. Kobald, *Der Meister des deutschen Liedes, F. S.* (Vienna and Leipzig, 1928); C. Lafite, *Das S.lied und seine*

Sänger (Vienna, 1928); P. Mies, *S., Der Meister des Liedes* (Berlin, 1928); F. Weingartner, *S. und sein Kreis* (Zürich, 1928); H. Biehle, *S.s Lieder als Gesangsproblem* (Langensalza, 1929); H. Bosch, *Die Entwicklung des Romantischen in S.s Liedern* (Leipzig, 1930); H. Therstappen, *Die Entwicklung der Form bei S.* (Leipzig, 1931); E. Laaff, *F. S.s Sinfonien* (Wiesbaden, 1933); E. Porter, *The Songs of S.* (London, 1937); G. Abraham, ed., *The Music of S.* (N.Y., 1947); W. Vetter, *Der Klassiker S.* (2 vols., Leipzig, 1953); E. Schmitz, *S.s Auswirkung auf die deutsche Musik bis zu Hugo Wolf und Bruckner* (Leipzig, 1954); H. Haas, *Über die Bedeutung der Harmonik in den Liedern F. S.s* (Bonn, 1957); H.-M. Sachse, *F. S.s Streichquartette* (Munich, 1958); M. Chusid, *The Chamber Music of F. S.* (diss., Univ. of Calif., Berkeley, 1961); E. Porter, *S.'s Song-technique* (London, 1961); E. Norman-McKay, *The Stage-works of S., Considered in the Framework of Austrian Biedermeier Society* (diss., Univ. of Oxford, 1962–63); A. Bell, *The Songs of S.* (Lowestoft, 1964); R. Stringham, *The Masses of F. S.* (diss., Cornell Univ., 1964); S. Kunze, *F. S.: Sinfonie h-moll: Unvollendete* (Munich, 1965); M.J.E. Brown, *Essays on S.* (London, 1966); idem, *S. Songs* (London, 1967); T. Georgiades, *S.: Musik und Lyrik* (Göttingen, 1967); P. Radcliffe, *S. Piano Sonatas* (London, 1967); D. Weekley, *The One-piano, Four-hand Compositions of F. S.: Historical and Interpretative Analysis* (diss., Ind. Univ., 1968); J. Westrup, *S. Chamber Music* (London, 1969); M. Brown, *S. Symphonies* (London, 1970); H. Gál, *F. S. oder Die Melodie* (Frankfurt am Main, 1970; Eng. tr. as *F. S. and the Essence of Melody*, London, 1974); M. Citron, *S.'s Seven Complete Operas: A Musico-dramatic Study* (diss., Univ. of N.C., 1971); D. Fischer-Dieskau, *Auf den Spuren der S.-Lieder: Werden-Wesen-Wir* (Wiesbaden, 1971; Eng. tr. as *S.: A Biographical Study of His Songs*, London, 1976); R. Weber, *Die Sinfonien F. S.s im Versuch einer Strukturwissenschaftlichen Darstellung und Untersuchungen* (diss., Univ. of Münster, 1971); G. Cunningham, *F. S. als Theaterkomponist* (diss., Univ. of Freiburg, 1974); G. Moore, *The S. Song Cycles, with Thoughts on Performance* (London, 1975); E. Badura-Skoda and P. Branscombe, eds., *S. Studies: Problems of Style and Chronology* (Cambridge, 1982); L. Minchin, *S. in English* (London, 1982); J. Reed, *The S. Song Companion* (Manchester, 1984); W. Maser, *Armer S.!: Fälschungen und Manipulationen: Marginalien zu F. S.s Sinfonie von 1825* (Stuttgart, 1985); R. Schulz-Storck, *Tempobezeichnungen in F. S.s Liedern* (1985); W. Frisch, *S.: Critical and Analytical Studies* (Lincoln, Nebr., 1986); H. Jaskulsky, *Die lateinischen Messen F. S.s* (Mainz, 1986); E. McKay, *The Impact of the New Pianofortes on Classical Keyboard Style: Mozart, Beethoven, and S.* (West Hagley, West Midlands, 1987); B. Eckle, *Studien zu F. S.s Orchestersatz: Das obligate Accompagnement in den Sinfonien* (Stuttgart, 1988); E. Partsch, ed., *F. S.—Der Fortschrittliche? Analysen—Perspektiven—Fakten* (Tutzing, 1989); H. Utz, *Untersuchungen zur Syntax der Lieder F. S.s* (Munich, 1989); E. McKay, *F. S.'s Music for the Theatre* (Tutzing, 1990); M.-A. Dittrich, *Harmonik und Sprachvertonung in S.s Liedern* (Hamburg, 1991); W. Dürr and A. Feil, *F. S.: Unter Mitarbeit von Walburga Litschauer* (Stuttgart, 1991); T. Waidelich, *F. S., Alfonso und Estrella: Eine frühe durchkomponierte deutsche Oper: Geschichte und Analyse* (Tutzing, 1991); S. Youens, *Retracing a Winter's Journey: S.'s Winterreise* (Ithaca, 1991); A. Krause, *Die Klaviersonaten F. S.s: Form, Gattung, Ästhetik* (Kassel, 1992); B. Newbould, *S. and the Symphony: A New Perspective* (Surbiton, 1992); S. Youens, *S.: Die schöne Müllerin* (Cambridge, 1992); K. Bangerter, *F. S.: Grosse Sinfonie in C-Dur, D.944* (Munich, 1993); M. Hirsch, *S.'s Dramatic Lieder* (Cambridge, 1993); J. Stüber, *S.s Quartett "Der Tod und das Mädchen": Anleitung zur Intonationsanalyse* (Bonn, 1993); H.-J. Hinrichsen, *Untersuchungen zur Entwicklung der Sonatenform in der Instrumentalmusik F. S.s* (Tutzing, 1994); R. Kramer, *Distant Cycles: S. and the Conceiving of Song* (Chicago, 1994); H. Well, *Frühwerk und Innovation: Studien zu den "Jugendsinfonien" F. S.s* (Kassel, 1995); W. Bodendorff, *F. S.s Frauenbild* (Augsburg, 1996); D. Fischer-Dieskau, *S. und seine Lieder* (Stuttgart, 1996); S. Näher, *Das S.-Lied und seine Interpreten* (Stuttgart, 1996); S. Saathen, *Wanderfantasie: Ein S.-buch* (Vienna, 1996); M. Stegemann, *"Ich bin zu Ende mit allen Träumen": F. S.* (Munich, 1996); W. Bodendorff, *Die kleineren Kirchenwerke F. S.s* (Augsburg, 1997); S. Youens, *S., Müller, and Die schöne Müllerin* (Cambridge, 1997); L. Kramer, *F. S.: Sexuality, Subjectivity, Song* (Cambridge, 1998); M. Chusid, *A Companion to S.'s "Schwanengesang"* (New Haven, 2000). ICONOGRAPHY: O. Deutsch, *Die historischen Bildnisse F. S.s in getreuen Nachbildungen* (Vienna, 1922); A. Orel, *F. S., 1797–1828: Sein Leben in Bildern* (Leipzig, 1939); R. Petzoldt, *F. S.: Sein Leben in Bildern* (Leipzig, 1953); E. Hilmar and O. Brusatti, eds., *F. S.* (exhibition catalogue; Vienna, 1978).—NS/LK/DM

Schubert, Richard, German tenor; b. Dessau, Dec. 15, 1885; d. Oberstaufen, Oct. 12, 1959. He studied with Rudolf von Milde. In 1909 he made his operatic debut as a baritone in Strasbourg. Following further training from Milde and Hans Nietan in Dresden, he turned to tenor roles and sang in Nuremberg (1911–13) and Wiesbaden (1913–17). From 1917 to 1935 he was a member of the Hamburg Opera, where he became well known for his Wagnerian roles. He also created the role of Paul in Korngold's *Die tote Stadt* there in 1920. As a guest artist, he sang at the Vienna State Opera (1920–29) and in Chicago (1921–22).—NS/LK/DM

Schuberth, family of German musicians and music publishers:

(1) Gottlob Schuberth, clarinetist and oboist; b. Karsdorf, Aug. 11, 1778; d. Hamburg, Feb. 18, 1846. He studied in Jena and received violin lessons from Stamitz. He was active as a clarinetist and oboist in Magdeburg (from 1804), settling in Hamburg in 1833. He had 4 sons:

(2) Julius (Ferdinand Georg) Schuberth, music publisher; b. Magdeburg, July 14, 1804; d. Leipzig, June 9, 1875. He learned the music publishing business in Magdeburg, and founded his own business in Hamburg in 1826. As proprietor of J. Schuberth & Co., he opened branches in Leipzig (1832) and in N.Y. (1850); his brother, Friedrich Schuberth, took over the Hamburg firm in 1853 under the name of Fritz Schuberth. Julius Schuberth ed. a *Musikalisches Fremdwörterbuch* (Hamburg, 1840; 8th ed., 1870), the *Kleine Hamburger Musik Zeitung* (1840–50), a *Musikalisches Conversationslexicon* (Leipzig, 1850; 10th ed., 1877; Eng. tr., 1895), the *New Yorker Musikzeitung* (1867), and *Schuberths kleine Musikzeitung* (1871–72). After his death, his widow and nephew ran the firm until it was sold to Felix Siegel in 1891. In 1943 the entire stock of the business was destroyed in an air raid; after World War II, it was reestablished in Wiesbaden.

(3) Ludwig Schuberth, conductor and composer; b. Magdeburg, April 18, 1806; d. St. Petersburg, May 1850. He studied with his father and Carl Maria von Weber, and was only 16 when he was made music director at the Magdeburg theater. Later he was Hofkapellmeister in Oldenburg, and then subsequently settled in St.

Petersburg as conductor of the German Opera (1845). He wrote operas, syms., and chamber music.

(4) Carl Schuberth, cellist, conductor, and composer; b. Magdeburg, Feb. 25, 1811; d. Zürich, July 22, 1863. He studied piano with his father and cello with L. Hesse. After touring (1828–29), he became first cellist in the Magdeburg theater orch. He then toured widely in Europe before settling in St. Petersburg as solo cellist at the court (1835); was also music director of the Univ. and conductor of the imperial court orch. In 1855 he settled in Switzerland. He publ. 2 cello concertos, Variations for Cello and Orch., String Octet, 2 string quintets, 4 string quartets, and a Cello Sonata.

(5) Friedrich (Wilhelm August) Schuberth, music publisher; b. Magdeburg, Oct. 27, 1817; d. after 1890. In 1853 he took over the Hamburg firm established by his brother Julius Schuberth, under the name Fritz Schuberth.—NS/LK/DM

Schuch, Ernst von, eminent Austrian conductor; b. Graz, Nov. 23, 1846; d. Kötzschenbroda, near Dresden, May 10, 1914. He studied law in Graz, where he also received instruction in music from Eduard Stolz, and served as director of the Musikverein; then went to Vienna, where he completed his training in law at the Univ. and also continued his musical studies with Otto Dessoff. He began his career as a violinist. After serving as music director of Lobe's theater in Breslau (1867–68), he conducted in Würzburg (1868–70), Graz (1870–71), and Basel (1871). In 1872 he was called to Dresden as conductor of Pollini's Italian Opera; that same year he was named Royal Music Director at the Court Opera, and then Royal Kapellmeister in 1873, sharing his duties with Julius Rietz until 1879 and with Franz Wüllner until 1882, when he became sole Royal Kapellmeister. In addition to his exemplary performances at the Court Opera, he also distinguished himself as conductor of the concerts of the Königliche Kapelle from 1877. In 1889 he was named Dresden's Generalmusikdirektor, and in 1897 was ennobled by Emperor Franz Joseph of Austria-Hungary. He appeared widely as a guest conductor in Europe; his only visit to the U.S. was in 1900, when he led concerts in N.Y. During his long tenure, Schuch conducted 51 world premieres at the Dresden Court Opera, including Strauss's *Feuersnot* (Nov. 21, 1901), *Salome* (Dec. 9, 1905), *Elektra* (Jan. 25, 1909), and *Der Rosenkavalier* (Jan. 26, 1911); was also the first conductor to perform Puccini's operas and Mascagni's *Cavalleria rusticana* in Germany. In his concert programs, he likewise conducted many works by contemporary composers. In 1875 he married the Hungarian soprano Clementine Procházka (b. Odenburg, Feb. 12, 1850; d. Kötzschenbroda, June 8, 1932); she studied with Mathilde Marchesi at the Vienna Cons., then was principal coloratura soprano at the Dresden Court Opera (1873–1904), where she took the name Schuch-Proska after her marriage. On June 4, 1884, she made her debut at London's Covent Garden as Eva in *Die Meistersinger von Nürnberg*; also sang in Vienna and Munich. Her other notable roles included Blondchen, Zerlina, Amina, Aennchen, and Violetta. Their daughter Liesel von Schuch (b. Dresden, Dec. 12, 1891; d. there, Jan. 10, 1990) was also a coloratura soprano at the Dresden Court (later State) Opera (1914–35); then taught voice at the Dresden Hochschule für Musik (until 1967).

BIBL.: P. Sakolowski, *E. v.S.* (Leipzig, 1901); F. von Schuch, *Richard Strauss, E. v.S. und Dresdens Oper* (Dresden, 1952; second ed., 1953).—**NS/LK/DM**

Schüchter, Wilhelm,
German conductor; b. Bonn, Dec. 15, 1911; d. Dortmund, May 27, 1974. He studied conducting with Abendroth and composition with Jarnach at the Cologne Hochschule für Musik. He then conducted opera at Würzburg (1937–40), and served as assistant to Karajan in Aachen (1940–42); also conducted at the Berlin Städtische Opera (1942–43). In 1947 he was appointed to the post of first conductor of the North German Radio Sym. Orch. in Hamburg. After serving as principal guest conductor of the NHK Sym. Orch. in Tokyo (1958–61), he settled in Dortmund as Generalmusikdirektor in 1962; was named artistic director of its Städtische Oper in 1965, and conducted the inaugural production at its new opera house in 1966. He acquired a fine reputation as a Wagnerian interpreter. —**NS/LK/DM**

Schudel, Thomas (Michael),
American-born Canadian composer and teacher; b. Defiance, Ohio, Sept. 8, 1937. He studied composition with Marshall Barnes and bassoon with George Wilson at Ohio State Univ. (B.S., 1959; M.A., 1961), and then composition with Leslie Bassett and Ross Lee Finney at the Univ. of Mich. (D.M.A., 1971). He was principal bassoonist in the Regina Sym. Orch. in Saskatchewan from 1964 to 1967, and again from 1968 to 1974. In 1964 he joined the faculty of the Univ. of Saskatchewan, Regina campus (later the Univ. of Regina), where he was made an asst. prof. in 1966, an assoc. prof. in 1972, and a prof. in 1977. He became a naturalized Canadian citizen in 1974. In 1972 his first Sym. won first prize in the City of Trieste Competition for symphonic composition.

WORKS: DRAMATIC: *Oresteia*, incidental music (1981); *The Enchanted Cat*, children's operetta (1992; Prairie Opera, March 21, 1993). **ORCH.:** 2 syms.: No. 1 (1971; Trieste, Oct. 20, 1972) and No. 2 (1983; Regina, Feb. 1985); *Variations* (1977); *Winterpiece* for Chamber Orch. and Dancers (1979); *Elegy and Exaltation* for Concert Band (1984); Concerto for Piccolo, Strings, and Percussion (1988; Regina, Feb. 5, 1989); Concerto for Alto Trombone and Chamber Orch. (Regina, Nov. 24, 1990); *A Tangled Web* for Chamber Orch. (Regina, May 2, 1993); *Sinfonia Concertante* for Saxophone Quartet and Wind Ensemble (Winnipeg, Feb. 10, 1994). **CHAMBER:** Set No. 2 for Wind and Brass Quintets (1963); Violin Sonata (1966); *String Quartet 1967* (1967); *Chanson and Minuet* for Flute and Piano (1977); Trio for 3 Percussionists (1977); *Triptych* for Chamber Wind Ensemble (1978); *Richter 7.8* for 12 Tubas or Low Brass (1979); *Etchings* for Horn and Piano (1985); *Incantations* for Double Bass and Percussion (1986); *Dialogues* for Trombone and Percussion (1987); *Pentagram* for Saxophone Quartet and Percussion (1987); *5 Pastels* for Oboe and Percussion (1990); *Trigon* for 2 Saxophones and Percussion (1992); *3 Dimensions* for Oboe and String Quartet (1995). **VOCAL: Choral:** *Psalm 23* (1968); *A Dream Within a Dream, Ale*, and *Eldorado*, after Poe (1985); *Pick Up the Earth, Gold and Rose*, and *Another Love Poem*, after Anne Campbell (1994). **Other:** *Queer Cornered Cap* for Mezzosoprano, Flute, and Marimba, after Anne Campbell (1982);

A.C.T.S. for Narrator, Flute, Oboe, Clarinet, Double Bass, and Percussion, after Anne Campbell (1986); *Edging Out* for Soprano, Flute, Oboe, and Vibraphone, after Anne Campbell (1987); *An Emily Dickinson Folio* for Soprano, Flute, Clarinet, Viola, Vibraphone, and Piano (1991); *A Christina Rossetti Folio* for Soprano, Alto Saxophone, and Marimba (1999); various songs.—**NS/LK/DM**

Schuh, Willi,
eminent Swiss music critic and musicologist; b. Basel, Nov. 12, 1900; d. Zürich, Oct. 4, 1986. He studied music in Aarau with Kutschera and Wehrli, in Bern with Papst, and in Munich with Courvoisier and Beer-Walbrunn. He took courses in art history and musicology in Munich with Sandberger and in Bern with Kurth; in 1927 he received his Ph.D. from the Univ. of Bern with the diss. *Formprobleme bei Heinrich Schütz* (publ. in Leipzig, 1928). In 1928 he was engaged as music critic of the *Neue Zurcher Zeitung*; was its music ed. from 1944 until 1965; was also ed.-in-chief of the *Schweizerische Musikzeitung* (1941–68). He also taught music history and harmony in Winterthur, in St. Gall, and at the Zürich Cons. He was made an honorary member of the Schweizerischer Tonkünstlerverein in 1969 and of the Schweizerische Musikforschende Gesellschaft in 1971. He was an ed. of the *Schweizer Musikerlexikon* (Zürich, 1964). Several of his writings were republished in *Kritiken und Essays* (4 vols.: vol. 1, *Über Opern von Richard Strauss*, Zürich, 1947; vol. 2, *Zeitgenössische Musik*, Zürich, 1947; vol. 3, *Schweizer Musik der Gegenwart*, Zürich, 1948; vol. 4, *Von neuer Musik*, Zürich, 1955); also *Umgang mit Musik: Über Komponisten, Libretti und Bilder* (Zürich, 1970; second ed., 1971). He was the ed. of *Die Briefe Richard Wagners an Judith Gautier* (Zürich, 1936), *Ferruccio Busoni: Briefe an seine Frau* (Zürich, 1936), *Hugo von Hofmannsthal's Beethoven* (Vienna, 1937; second ed., 1949), with H. Ehinger and E. Refardt, *Schweizer Musikbuch* (Zürich, 1939), *Richard Strauss: Betrachtungen und Erinnerungen* (Zürich, 1949; Eng. tr., 1955; second Swiss ed., rev., 1957), *Hugo von Hofmannsthal: Briefwechsel* (Zürich, 1952; Eng. tr., 1961; fourth Swiss ed., rev., 1970), *Richard Strauss: Briefe an die Eltern* (Zürich, 1954), *Igor Strawinsky: Leben und Werk, von ihm selbst* (Zürich and Mainz, 1957), *Richard Strauss und Stefan Zweig: Briefwechsel* (Frankfurt am Main, 1957; Eng. tr., 1977, as *A Confidential Matter: The Letters of Richard Strauss and Stefan Zweig 1931–1935*), with G. Kende, *Richard Strauss und Clemens Krauss: Briefwechsel* (Munich, 1963; second ed., 1964), and *Richard Strauss und Willi Schuh: Briefwechsel* (Zürich, 1969). His publ. writings include *Othmar Schoeck* (Zürich, 1934), *In memoriam Richard Strauss* (Zürich, 1949), *Danae oder Die Vernunftheirat* (Frankfurt am Main, 1952), *Renoir und Wagner* (Zürich, 1959), *Ein paar Erinnerungen an Richard Strauss* (Zürich, 1964), *Hugo von Hofmannsthal und Richard Strauss: Legende und Wirklichkeit* (Munich, 1964), *Der Rosenkavalier: Vier Studien* (Olten, 1968), and *Richard Strauss: Jugend und frühe Meisterjahre: Lebenschronik 1864–98* (the authorized biography; Zürich, 1976; Eng. tr., 1982, as *Richard Strauss: A Chronicle of the Early Years 1864–98*).

BIBL.: A. Briner, *W. S., 1900–1986: Musikwissenschafter, NZZ-Redaktor, Schoeck-Pionier und Strauss-Biograph* (Zürich, 1998).—**NS/LK/DM**

Schüler, Johannes, German conductor; b. Vietz, Neumark, June 21, 1894; d. Berlin, Oct. 3, 1966. He received his training at the Berlin Hochschule für Musik. After conducting opera in Gleiwitz (1920–22), Königsberg (1922–24), and Hannover (1924–28), he was music director in Oldenburg (1928–32) and Essen (1933–36). From 1936 to 1949 he conducted at the Berlin State Opera, where he was granted the titles of Staatskapellmeister and Generalmusikdirektor. He then was Generalmusikdirektor in Hannover from 1949 to 1960, where he conducted a number of contemporary operas.—NS/LK/DM

Schulhoff, Ervín, Czech composer and pianist, great-grandnephew of **Julius Schulhoff;** b. Prague, June 8, 1894; d. in the concentration camp in Wülzburg, Bavaria, Aug. 18, 1942. He was a student of Kaan at the Prague Cons. (1904–06), of Thern in Vienna, and of Reger at the Leipzig Cons. (1908–10) before completing his training at the Cologne Cons. (1911–14). In 1913 he won the Mendelssohn Prize for piano and in 1918 for composition. Following military service during World War I, he was active in Germany (1919–23), where he became involved in left-wing avant-garde circles. During this period, he was attracted to Dadaism and jazz. His music of this period also reveals the influence of Schoenberg and Stravinsky. Upon returning to Prague, he taught piano privately and later was on the faculty of the Cons. (1929–31). As a pianist, he was a champion of the quarter tone music of Alois Hába and his disciples. After composing works along expressionist and neo-Classical lines, Schulhoff embraced the tenets of proletarian art in the early 1930s. He also became a member of the Communist Party, a decision that placed him in peril after the Nazi occupation in 1939. When the Nazis attacked the Soviet Union in 1941, Schulhoff was arrested and imprisoned in Prague. Later that year he was sent to the concentration camp in Wülzburg, where he died of tuberculosis.

WORKS: DRAMATIC: *Ogelala,* ballet (1922–24; Dessau, Nov. 21, 1925); *Námĕsíčná* (The Sleepwalker), dance grotesque (1925; Oxford, July 24, 1931); *Le bourgeois gentilhomme,* music for Molière's play (1926); *Plameny* (Flames), tragicomedy (1927–29; Brno, Jan. 27, 1932). **ORCH.:** 2 piano concertos (1913, 1923); *Joyful Overture* (1913); *32 Variations on an Original 8-bar Theme* (1919); Suite for Chamber Orch. (1921); 8 syms.: No. 1 (1925), No. 2 (1932; Prague, April 24, 1935), No. 3 (1935), No. 4, *Spanish,* for Baritone and Orch. (1936–37), No. 5 (1938), No. 6, *Symphony of Freedom,* for Chorus and Orch. (1940–41; Prague, May 5, 1946), No. 7, *Eroica* (1941; unfinished), and No. 8 (1942; unfinished); Double Concerto for Flute, Piano, and Orch. (1927); *Festive Overture* (1929); Concerto for String Quartet and Wind Orch. (1930; Prague, Nov. 9, 1932). **CHAMBER:** 2 violin sonatas (1913, 1927); Cello Sonata (1914); Sextet for 2 Violins, 2 Violas, and 2 Cellos (1920–24); *Bass Nightingale* for Contrabassoon (1922); *5 Pieces* for String Quartet (1923); 2 string quartets (1924, 1925); Duo for Violin and Cello (1925); Concertino for Flute, Viola, and Double Bass (1925); *Divertissement* for Oboe, Clarinet, and Bassoon (1926); Sonata for Solo Violin (1927); Flute Sonata (1927); *Hot Sonata* for Alto Saxophone and Piano (1930). **P i a n o :** *Variations on an Original Theme* (1913); *9 Little Round Dances* (1914); *10 Variations on "Ah vous dirais-je, Maman"* (1914); *5 Grotesques* (1917); 1 unnumbered sonata (1918); 3 numbered sonatas (1924, 1926, 1927); *5 Burlesques* (1918); *3 Waltzes* (1918); *5 Humoresques* (1919); *5 Arabesques* (1919); *5 Pictures* (1919); *10 Themes* (1920); *Ironies,* 6 pieces for Piano, 4-Hands (1920); *Partita* (1920); *11 Inventions* (1921); *Rag Music* (1922); *6 Family Matters* (1923); 2 suites (1925, 1926); *Esquisses de Jazz* (1927); *Hot Music* (1928); *Suite dansante en jazz* (1931); *Studien,* 2 pieces (1936). **VOCAL:** *3 Songs* for Alto and Piano (1914); *Krajiny* (Landscapes), 5 songs for Mezzo-soprano and Orch. (1918–19); *Menschheit* for Alto and Orch. (1919); *Serious Songs* for Baritone, 4 Winds, and Percussion (1922); *H.M.S. Royal Oak,* jazz oratorio for Reciter, Jazz Singer, Chorus, and Symphonic Jazz Orch. (1930; Brno Radio, Feb. 12, 1935); *Manifest,* cantata after *The Communist Manifesto* of Marx and Engels, for 4 Soloists, Double Chorus, Children's Chorus, and Wind Orch. (1932–33; Prague, April 5, 1962); *1917,* song cycle for Voice and Piano (1933).

BIBL.: V. Stará, *E. S.: Vzpomínky, studie a dokumenty* (E. S.: Recollections, Studies and Documents; Prague, 1958); O. Pukl, *Konstanty, dominanty a varianty S.ova skladebného stylu* (The Constants, Dominants and Variants of S.'s Compositional Style; Prague, 1986); J. Bek, *E. S.: Leben und Werk* (Hamburg, 1994); T. Widmaier, ed., *E. S.-Kolloquium* (Hamburg, 1996).—NS/LK/DM

Schulhoff, Julius, noted Bohemian pianist, teacher, and composer, great-granduncle of **Ervin Schulhoff;** b. Prague, Aug. 2, 1825; d. Berlin, March 13, 1898. He studied in Prague, then proceeded to Paris, where he gave concerts under the patronage of Chopin, to whom he dedicated his first composition, an *Allegro brillant.* After a long tour through Austria, England, Spain, and Southern Russia, he returned to Paris, where he was a successful teacher. After the outbreak of the Franco-Prussian War (1870), he settled in Dresden; moved to Berlin shortly before his death. He publ. excellent salon music for piano, his *Galop di bravura* and *Impromptu Polka* being particular favorites.—NS/LK/DM

Schuller, George, jazz drummer, composer, producer, son of **Gunther Schuller,** brother of **Ed Schuller;** b. N.Y., Dec. 29, 1958. His family moved to Boston in 1967 where he was raised and educated. In 1982, he received a bachelor's degree in Jazz Performance from the New England Cons. of Music. For the next 12 years, he performed around Boston with Herb Pomeroy, Jaki Byard, Jerry Bergonzi, George Garzone, Mick Goodrick, Ran Blake, Billy Pierce, and John LaPorta. In 1984, he co-founded the 12-piece ensemble Orange Then Blue, which has toured extensively in the U.S., Canada, Middle East, and Europe. He has also performed or recorded with Joe Wilder, Mose Allison, Lee Konitz, Danilo Perez, Joey Calderazzo, Kenny Werner, Tom Harrell, Fred Hersch, Attila Zoller, and the Smithsonian Jazz Masterworks Orch. He has appeared at jazz festivals in Detroit, Munich, Sandpoint, Boston, Montreal, Vancouver, Toronto, and across Canada. He received a Mass. Artist Foundation Fellowship for Music Composition (1987) and a NEA Composition Grant (1995). During the 1990s, he has freelanced with Tom Varner, Matt Darriau, and Tom Beckham while also leading his own groups, including Schulldogs with George Garzone, Ruckus, and Orange Then Blue.

DISC.: *Lookin' Up from Down Below* (1988); *Jumpin' in the Future* (1988). **ORANGE THEN BLUE:** *Orange Then Blue* (1986); *Where Were You?* (1987); *Funkallero* (1989); *While You Were Out...* (1992).—**LP**

Schuller, Gunther (Alexander), significant American composer, conductor, and music educator; b. N.Y., Nov. 22, 1925. He was of a musical family; his paternal grandfather was a bandmaster in Germany before emigrating to America; his father was a violinist with the N.Y. Phil. He was sent to Germany as a child for a thorough academic training; returning to N.Y., he studied at the St. Thomas Choir School (1938–44). He also received private instruction in theory, flute, and horn. He played in the N.Y.C. Ballet orch. (1943), and then was first horn in the Cincinnati Sym. Orch. (1943–45) and the Metropolitan Opera orch. in N.Y. (1945–49). At the same time, he became fascinated with jazz; he played the horn in a combo conducted by Miles Davis; also began to compose jazz pieces. He taught at the Manhattan School of Music in N.Y. (1950–63), the Yale Univ. School of Music (1964–67), and the New England Cons. of Music in Boston, where he greatly distinguished himself as president (1967–77). He was also active at the Berkshire Music Center at Tanglewood as a teacher of composition (1963–84), head of contemporary-music activities (1965–84), artistic co-director (1969–74), and director (1974–84). In 1984–85 he was interim music director of the Spokane (Wash.) Sym. Orch.; then was director of its Sandpoint (Idaho) Festival. In 1986 he founded the Boston Composers' Orch. In 1988 he was awarded the first Elise L. Stoeger Composer's Chair of the Chamber Music Soc. of Lincoln Center in N.Y. In 1975 he organized Margun Music to make available unpubl. American music. He founded GunMar Music in 1979. In 1980 he organized GM Recordings. He publ. the manual *Horn Technique* (N.Y., 1962; second ed., 1992) and the very valuable study *Early Jazz: Its Roots and Musical Development* (3 vols., N.Y., 1968 et seq.). A vol. of his writings appeared as *Musings* (N.Y., 1985). He also publ. *The Compleat Conductor* (N.Y., 1997). In his multiple activities, he tried to form a link between serious music and jazz; he popularized the style of "cool jazz" (recorded as Birth of the Cool). In 1957 he launched the slogan "third stream" to designate the combination of classical forms with improvisatory elements of jazz as a synthesis of disparate, but not necessarily incompatible, entities, and wrote fanciful pieces in this synthetic style; in many of these, he worked in close cooperation with John Lewis of the Modern Jazz Quartet. As part of his investigation of the roots of jazz, he became interested in early ragtime and formed, in 1972, the New England Cons. Ragtime Ensemble; its recordings of Scott Joplin's piano rags in band arrangement were instrumental in bringing about the "ragtime revival." In his own works he freely applied serial methods, even when his general style was dominated by jazz. He received honorary doctorates in music from Northwestern Univ. (1967), the Univ. of Ill. (1968), Williams Coll. (1975), the New England Cons. of Music (1978), and Rutgers Univ. (1980). In 1967 he was elected to membership in the National Inst. of Arts and Letters, and in 1980 to the American Academy and Inst.

of Arts and Letters. In 1989 he received the William Schuman Award of Columbia Univ. In 1991 he was awarded a MacArthur Foundation grant. In 1994 he won the Pulitzer Prize in Music for his orch. work, *Of Reminiscences and Reflections* (1993), composed in memory of his wife who died in 1992. He received the Gold Medal of the American Academy of Arts and Letters in 1997.

WORKS: DRAMATIC: O p e r a : *The Visitation* (Hamburg, Oct. 12, 1966); *The Fisherman and His Wife*, children's opera (Boston, May 7, 1970); *A Question of Taste* (Cooperstown, N.Y., June 24, 1989). **B a l l e t :** *Variants* for Jazz Quartet and Orch. (1960; N.Y., Jan. 4, 1961). **F i l m :** *Automation* (1962); *Journey to the Stars* (1962); *Yesterday in Fact* (1963). **T e l e v i s i o n :** *Tear Drop* (1966); *The 5 Senses*, ballet (1967). **ORCH.:** 2 horn concertos: No. 1 (1944; Cincinnati, April 6, 1945, composer soloist) and No. 2 (1976; Budapest, June 19, 1978); Cello Concerto (1945; rev. 1985); *Suite* for Chamber Orch. (1945); *Vertige d'Eros* (1945; Madison, Wisc., Oct. 15, 1967); *Symphonic Study* (1947–48; Cincinnati, May 1949); *Dramatic Overture* (1951; Darmstadt, Aug. 1954); *Recitative and Rondo* for Violin and Orch. (1953; Chicago, July 16, 1967; also for Violin and Piano); *Symphonic Tribute to Duke Ellington* (1955; Lenox, Mass., Aug. 19, 1976); *Little Fantasy* (Englewood, N.J., April 7, 1957); *Contours* for Chamber Orch. (1958; Cincinnati, Dec. 31, 1959); *Spectra* (1958; N.Y., Jan. 14, 1960); Concertino for Jazz Quartet and Orch. (1959; Baltimore, Jan. 2, 1960); *7 Studies on Themes of Paul Klee* (Minneapolis, Nov. 27, 1959); *Capriccio* for Tuba and Orch. (1960); *Contrasts* for Wind Quintet and Orch. (1960; Donaueschingen, Oct. 22, 1961); *Journey to the Stars* (Toledo, Ohio, Dec. 1, 1962); *Movements* for Flute and Strings (Dortmund, May 29, 1962); 2 piano concertos: No. 1 (Cincinnati, Oct. 29, 1962) and No. 2 (1981; Mainz, Nov. 24, 1982); *Composition in 3 Parts* (Minneapolis, March 29, 1963); *Diptych* for Brass Quintet and Band (1963; also for Brass Quintet and Orch.; Ithaca, N.Y., March 22, 1964); *Meditation* for Band (Greensboro, N.C., March 7, 1963); *Threnos* for Oboe and Orch. (Cologne, Nov. 29, 1963); *5 Bagatelles* (Fargo, N.Dak., March 22, 1964); *American Triptych: 3 Studies in Textures* (New Orleans, March 9, 1965); Sym. (Dallas, Feb. 8, 1965); 2 concertos: No. 1, *Gala Music* (Chicago, Jan. 20, 1966) and No. 2 (Washington, D.C., Oct. 12, 1976); *5 Etudes* (1966; New Haven, March 19, 1967); *Triplum I* (N.Y., June 28, 1967) and *II* (Baltimore, Feb. 26, 1975); *Colloquy* for 2 Pianos and Orch. (Berlin, June 6, 1968); Double Bass Concerto (N.Y., Jan. 27, 1968); *Fanfare for St. Louis* (St. Louis, Jan. 24, 1968); *Shapes and Designs* (Hartford, April 26, 1969); *Consequents* (New Haven, Dec. 16, 1969); *Museum Piece* for Renaissance Instruments and Orch. (Boston, Dec. 11, 1970); *Concerto da camera* for Chamber Orch. (1971; Rochester, N.Y., April 24, 1972); *Capriccio stravagante* (San Francisco, Dec. 6, 1972); *3 Nocturnes* (Interlochen, July 15, 1973); *4 Soundscapes—Hudson Valley Reminiscences* (1974; Poughkeepsie, N.Y., March 7, 1975); 2 violin concertos: No. 1 (Lucerne, Aug. 25, 1976) and No. 2 (1991); *Deai—Encounters* for 7 Voices and 3 Orchs. (Tokyo, March 17, 1978); Contrabassoon Concerto (1978; Washington, D.C., Jan. 16, 1979); Trumpet Concerto (Jefferson, N.H., Aug. 25, 1979); *Eine kleine Posaunenmusik* for Trombone and Orch. (Norfolk, Conn., July 18, 1980); *Music for a Celebration* for Chorus, Audience, and Orch. (Springfield, Mass., Sept. 26, 1980); *In Praise of Winds* for Large Wind Orch. (Ann Arbor, Feb. 13, 1981); Alto Saxophone Concerto (1983; Pittsburgh, Jan. 18, 1984); *Concerto quarternio* for Violin, Flute, Oboe, Trumpet, and Orch. (N.Y., Nov. 21, 1984); *Concerto festivo* for Brass Quintet and Orch. (Trier, Nov. 29, 1984); *Jubilee Musik* (Dayton, March 7, 1984); Bassoon Concerto, *Eine kleine*

Fagottmusik (Washington, D.C., May 17, 1985); *Farbenspiel*, concerto (Berlin, May 8, 1985); Viola Concerto (New Orleans, Dec. 17, 1985); Concerto for String Quartet and Orch. (Madison, Wisc., Feb. 20, 1988); Flute Concerto (Chicago, Oct. 13, 1988); *On Winged Flight*, divertimento for Band (Tallahassee, Fla., March 4, 1989); *Chamber Symphony* (Cleveland, April 16, 1989); Concerto for Piano, 3-Hands (2 Pianos) and Chamber Orch. (1989; Springfield, Ill., Jan. 19, 1990); *Ritmica Melodia Armonia* (1992); *Of Reminiscences and Reflections* (Louisville, Dec. 2, 1993); *The Past is Present* (1993; Cincinnati, March 25, 1994); Organ Concerto (Calgary, Oct. 14, 1994); *Blue Dawn Into White Heat* for Concert Band (1995). CHAMBER: *Romantic Sonata* for Clarinet, Horn, and Piano (1941; rev. 1983); *Suite* for Woodwind Quintet (1945); *3 hommages* for Horn or 2 Horns and Piano (1942–46); *Fantasia concertante No. 1* for 3 Oboes and Piano (1947) and *No. 2* for 3 Trombones and Piano (1947); Quartet for 4 Double Basses (1947); *Perpetuum mobile* for 4 Horns, and Bassoon or Tuba (1948); Trio for Oboe, Horn, and Viola (1948); Oboe Sonata (1948–51); *Duo Sonata* for Clarinet and Bass Clarinet (1948–49); *Fantasy* for Cello (1951); *5 Pieces* for 5 Horns (1952); *Recitative and Rondo* for Violin and Piano (1953; also for Violin and Orch.); 3 string quartets (1957, 1965, 1986); Woodwind Quintet (1958); *Fantasy Quartet* for 4 Cellos (1959); *Fantasy* for Harp (1959); *Lines and Contrasts* for 16 Horns (1960); *Double Quintet* for Wind and Brass Quintets (1961); *Music* for Brass Quintet (1961); *Fanfare* for 4 Trumpets and 4 Trombones (1962); *Music* for Carillon (1962; also arranged for other instruments); *Studies* for Horn (1962); *Little Brass Music* for Trumpet, Horn, Trombone, and Tuba (1963); *Episodes* for Clarinet (1964); *Aphorisms* for Flute and String Trio (1967); *5 Moods* for 4 Tubas (1973); *Sonata serenata* for Clarinet, Violin, Cello, and Piano (1978); Octet (1979); Piano Trio (1983); *On Light Wings* for Piano Quartet (1984); Sextet for Bassoon, Piano, and String Quartet (1986); *The Sandpoint Rag* for Ragtime Ensemble (1986; also for Brass Sextet); *Chimeric Images* for Chamber Group (1988); *A Bouquet for Collage* for Clarinet, Flute, Violin, Cello, Piano, and Percussion (1988); Horn Sonata (1988); *5 Impromptus* for English Horn and String Quartet (1989); *Hommage à Rayechla* for 8 Cellos or Multiples Thereof (1990); *A Trio Setting* for Clarinet, Violin, and Piano (1990); Brass Quintet No. 2 (1993); Sextet for Piano, Left-Hand, and Woodwind Quintet (1994). Piano: *Sonata/Fantasia* (Boston, March 28, 1993). VOCAL: *O Lamb of God* for Chorus and Optional Organ (1941); *O Spirit of the Living God* for Chorus and Optional Organ (1942); *6 Renaissance Lyrics* for Tenor and 7 Instruments (1962); *Journey into Jazz* for Narrator, Jazz Quintet, and Orch. (Washington, D.C., May 30, 1962); *5 Shakespearean Songs* for Baritone and Orch. (1964); *Sacred Cantata* for Chorus and Chamber Orch. (1966); *The Power within Us*, oratorio for Baritone, Narrator, Chorus, and Orch. (1971); *Poems of Time and Eternity* for Chorus and 9 Instruments (1972); *Thou Art the Son of God*, cantata for Chorus and Chamber Ensemble (1987); songs. **BIBL.:** N. Carnovale, *G. S.: A Bio-Bibliography* (Westport, Conn., 1987).—NS/LK/DM

Schulthess, Walter, Swiss conductor and composer; b. Zürich, July 24, 1894; d. there, June 23, 1971. He studied with Andreae in Zürich, Courvoisier in Munich, and Ansorge in Berlin, and in 1918 settled in Zürich. As a composer, he excelled in lyric songs, in a style resembling Othmar Schoeck's. He also wrote a Violin Concertino (1921), *Serenade* for Orch. (1921), *Symphonische Variationen* for Cello and Orch. (1926), and various chamber works, including a String Quartet (1921), 2 violin sonatas (1921, 1922), and *3 Capricen nach Paganini* for Violin and Piano (1923), as well as piano pieces, choruses, and lieder. He married **Stefi Geyer** in 1919. —NS/LK/DM

Schultz, Svend (Simon), Danish composer, pianist, and conductor; b. Nykøbing Falster, Dec. 30, 1913; d. Klampenborg, June 6, 1998. He received training in piano and composition at the Copenhagen Cons. (1933–38), where his principal mentor was Schierbeck. After serving as music critic for *Politiken* (1942–49), he was a choral conductor with the Danish Radio in Copenhagen (from 1949). He also appeared as a pianist and conductor of his own works throughout Europe. His music is neo-Classical in style and is characterized by simplicity of form and a cumulative rhythmic drive.

WORKS: DRAMATIC: O p e r a : *Bag kulisserne* (Behind the Scenes; 1946; Copenhagen, May 26, 1949); *Solbadet* (The Sunbath; 1947; Århus, Nov. 26, 1949); *Kaffehuset* (The Coffee House; 1948); *Høst* (Harvest; 1950); *Bryllupsrejsen* (The Honeymoon; 1951); *Hyrdinden og skorstensfejeren* (The Shepherdess and the Chimney Sweep), puppet opera (1953); *Tordenvejret* (The Thunderstorm; 1954); *Hosekraemmeren* (The Stocking Peddler; 1955; rev. 1985; Århus, May 4, 1990); *The Marionettes*, puppet opera (1957); *Dommer Lynch* (Judge Lynch; 1959); *Konen i muddergrøften* (The Woman in the Muddy Ditch), comic television opera (1964; Danish TV, April 18, 1965); *Lykken og forstanden*, children's opera (1973). C h a m b e r O p e r e t t a : *Den kåde Donna* (Copenhagen, Aug. 30, 1957). M u s i c a l C h u r c h P l a y : *Eva* (1968). ORCH.: *Serenade* for Strings (1940); 7 syms. (1941, 1949, 1955, 1957, 1960, 1962, 1973); Piano Concerto (1943); *Storstrømsbroen* (The Storstroem Bridge; 1951); *Introduction and Rondo* for Piano and Orch. (Danish Radio, Nov. 8, 1964); *2 Variations: Nocturne and Aubade* (1965); *Northern Overture* (1975); *Pale make* (1981); Concertino for Clarinet and Strings (1982); Harp Concertino (1986); *Hommage à Rossini* (1986); *Garde-Gratulation* for Wind Orch. (1992). CHAMBER: 6 string quartets (1939, 1940, 1940, 1961, 1962, 1975); 2 piano trios (1942, 1963); Flute Quartet (1961); *Romantic Trio* for Piano Trio (1961); Quartet for Flute, Violin, Viola, and Cello (1962); Clarinet Quintet (1965); *Music for Wind Players* for Flute, Trumpet, Clarinet, Percussion, Vibraphone, and Piano (1966); *Quintetto per Nefertite* for Flute, Violin, Viola, Cello, and Piano (1985). P i a n o : Sonata (1931); 2 sonatinas (1940, 1950). VOCAL: *Job*, oratorio (1945); *Sankt Hans Nat* for Soloists, Chorus, and Orch. (1953); *Hymn* for Chorus and Orch. (Copenhagen, March 13, 1957); *Hr. Mortens klosterrov* (Morten's Pillage of the Monastery) for Soloists, Chorus, and Chamber Orch. (1958; Copenhagen, Oct. 13, 1960); *3 Pastorales* for Soloists, Chorus, and Orch. (Danish Radio, May 28, 1962); *The 4 Temperaments* for Women's Chorus, Men's Chorus, and Orch. (Hillerød, Nov. 15, 1974); *Jul*, cantata (1981); *It Is Perfectly True*, scene for Soloists, Chorus, and Clarinet (1982); *Davids salme 130* for Chorus and Organ (1994).—NS/LK/DM

Schultze, Norbert, German composer; b. Braunschweig, Jan. 26, 1911. He studied piano, conducting, and composition at the Cologne Staatliche Hochschule für Musik, and after studying theatrical arts in Cologne and Munich (1931), he was active as an actor and composer in a student cabaret, *Vier Nachrichter*, in Munich (1931–32). He then conducted opera in Heidelberg (1932–33) and Darmstadt (1933–34), and later was

a composer for stage, films, and television; was head of his own music publishing business (from 1953). He wrote the operas *Schwarzer Peter* (Hamburg, 1936) and *Das kalte Herz* (Leipzig, 1943), television opera, *Peter der dritte* (1964), operetta, *Regen in Paris* (Nuremberg, 1957), and 3 pantomimes: *Struwwelpeter* (Hamburg, 1937), *Max und Moritz* (Hamburg, 1938), and *Maria im Walde* (Vienna, 1940). However, his chief claim to fame was a sentimental song, *Lili Marleen* (1938), which became immensely popular during World War II among both German and Allied soldiers after it was broadcast from the German-occupied Belgrade in 1941; it was tr. into 27 languages. For some of his works he used the names Frank Norbert, Peter Kornfeld, and Henri Iversen.
—NS/LK/DM

Schulz, Johann Abraham Peter, esteemed German conductor and composer; b. Lüneburg, March 31, 1747; d. Schwedt an der Oder, June 10, 1800. He studied with J.C. Schmügel in Lüneburg and Kirnberger in Berlin (1765–68). From 1768 to 1773 he was accompanist and music teacher to Princess Sapieha Woiwodin von Smolensk of Poland, with whom he traveled throughout Europe. He returned to Berlin as music director of the new French theater in 1776 and of the private theater of the Prussian crown princess Friederike Luise in 1778. From 1780 to 1787 he was court composer to Prince Heinrich, the brother of the king, in Rheinsberg. In 1787 he went to Copenhagen as Hofkapellmeister and director of the Royal Danish Theater, positions he held with distinction until tuberculosis compelled him to step down in 1795. He spent his last years in Berlin and Rheinsberg, visiting Schwedt an der Oder intermittently for his health. He was known primarily for his marked ability as a lieder composer.

WORKS: DRAMATIC: *Das Opfer der Nymphen* (for the birthday of Friedrich the Great; 1774); *Clarissa, oder Das unbekannte Dienstmädchen* (Berlin, 1775); *Musique de l'impromptu* (c. 1779); *La Fée Urgèle, ou Ce qui plaît aux dames* (1780–81; Rheinsberg, 1782; rev. version in Ger., Berlin, 1789); *La Vérité* (Rheinsberg, 1785); *Panomphée* (c. 1785); *Athalie* (Rheinsberg, 1785; rev. version, Berlin, 1786); *Minona oder Die Angelsachsen* (Hamburg, 1786); *Aline, reine de Golconde* (Rheinsberg, 1787); *Indtoget* (1789–90; Copenhagen, Feb. 26, 1793); *Høstgildet* (Copenhagen, Sept. 16, 1790); *Peters bryllup* (Copenhagen, Dec. 12, 1793). **VOCAL: O r a t o r i o s :** *Maria og Johannes* (1787–88); *Christi død* (Christiansborg, 1792); *Frelserens sidste Stund* (Copenhagen, March 1794). **C a n t a t a s :** *Vater, bester lebe* for Voice and Orch. (Berlin, 1774); *Universitiets-kantata til død af H. v. Stampe* (Copenhagen, 1789); *Kantata til Kronprinds Fredericks formoeling* (Copenhagen, 1790); *Sorge-sange da Prindsesse Sophie Frederike bisattes* (Roskilde, Dec. 28, 1794); *Jesu Minde* (1794). **O t h e r :** Motets, hymns, and other sacred works, and lieder, including (25) *Gesänge am Clavier* (Berlin and Leipzig, 1779), (48) *Lieder im Volkston* (3 vols., Berlin, 1782–85), *Johann Peter Uzens lyrische Gedichte religiösen Inhalts* (Hamburg, 1784; second ed., 1794), and *Gedichte von Friederike Brun, geboren Münter* (Zürich, 1795). **OTHER:** Chamber music.

WRITINGS: With J. Kirnberger, *Die wahren Grundsätze zum Gebrauche der Harmonie...als Zusatz zu der Kunst des reinen Satzes in der Musik* (Berlin and Königsberg, 1773; second ed., 1793; publ. as Kirnberger's); *Entwurf einer neuen und leichtverständlichen Musiktablatur* (Berlin, 1786); *Gedanken über den Einfluss der*

Musik auf die Bildung eines Volks (Copenhagen, 1790; Danish tr., 1790); *Über den Choral und die ältere Literatur desselben* (second ed., Erfurt, 1872).

BIBL.: C. Klunger, *J.S.P. S. in seinen volkstümlichen Liedern* (Leipzig, 1909); O. Riess, *J.A.P. S.' Leben* (Leipzig, 1913); E. Schmitz, *Unverwelkter Volkslied-Stil J.A.P. S. und J.H. Voss* (Kassel and Basel, 1960); F. Jekutsch, J. Kremer, and A. Schnoor, eds., *Christian Flor (1626–1697), J.A.P. S. (1747–1800): Texte und Dokumente zur Musikgeschichte Lüneburgs* (Hamburg, 1997).
—NS/LK/DM

Schulz, Johann Philipp Christian, German conductor and composer; b. Langensalza, Feb. 1, 1773; d. Leipzig, Jan. 30, 1827. He studied with Engel and Schicht in Leipzig, and from 1810 was conductor of the Gewandhaus concerts and the Singakademie there. In 1818 he became music director of the Univ. of Leipzig. He wrote an overture to Klingemann's *Faust* and other orch. works, stage music, a *Salvum fac regem* for Chorus and Orch., partsongs, and lieder.—NS/LK/DM

Schulz-Beuthen, Heinrich, German composer; b. Beuthen, June 19, 1838; d. Dresden, March 12, 1915. He was destined for a career as a civil engineer, and while a student at the Univ. of Breslau, he learned to play the piano and attempted composition; produced a Singspiel, *Fridolin* (Breslau, 1862); then went to study at the Leipzig Cons. with Moscheles (piano) and Hauptmann (composition). In 1866 he went to Zürich, where he remained until 1880. He then lived in Dresden (1880–93) and Vienna (1893–95), finally settling in Dresden, where he became a prof. at the Cons. He was an ardent disciple of Liszt and Wagner; during his lifetime he was regarded as a significant composer.

WORKS: 5 operas, including *Aschenbrödel* (Zürich, 1879); 8 syms.: No. 1, *Dem Andenken Haydns*, No. 2, *Frühlingsfeier*, No. 3, *Sinfonia maestosa*, No. 4, *Schön Elsbeth*, No. 5, *Reformationssymphonie* (with Organ), No. 6, *Konig Lear* (with Men's Chorus), No. 7 (expanded from a string quartet), and No. 8, *Siegessymphonie*; symphonic poems: *Mittelalterliche Volksszene, Des Meeres und der Liebe Wellen, Beethoven- Hymnus, Ein Pharaonenbegräbnis, Wilhelm Tell,* and *Sturmesmythe*; overtures; orch. suites; *Symphonisches Konzert* for Piano and Orch.; String Quintet; Wind Octet; String Trio; etc.; sacred choral music; piano pieces.

BIBL.: K. Mey, *H. S.-B.* (Leipzig, 1909); A. Zosel, *H. S.-B.* (Würzburg, 1931).—NS/LK/DM

Schulze, Christian Andreas, German composer; b. Dresden, c. 1660; d. Meissen, Sept. 11, 1699. He was a pupil at the Dresden Kreuzschule and the Univ. of Leipzig. In 1678 he settled in Meissen as Kantor of the municipal church and the Franciscaneum, the municipal Lateinschule; he later became Kantor of the Cathedral as well. He was a notable composer of sacred music, numbering among his works a *Historia resurrectionis* (1686), sacred concertos, and Protestant church cantatas.—NS/LK/DM

Schulze, Hans-Joachim, distinguished German musicologist; b. Leipzig, Dec. 3, 1934. He studied musicology in Leipzig at the Hochschule für Musik (1952–54) and with Serauky, Eller, and Besseler at the

Karl Marx Univ. (1954–57), and completed his education at the Univ. of Rostock (Ph.D., 1979, with the diss. *Studien zur Bach-Überlieferung im 18. Jahrhundert*; publ. in Leipzig, 1984). In 1957 he became a research assistant at the Leipzig Bach Archive, where he later served as deputy director (1974–79). With C. Wolff, he was co-ed. of the *Bach-Jahrbuch* (from 1975). He was made head research fellow of the Nationale Forschungs- und Gedenkstatten Johann Sebastian Bach in Leipzig in 1979, and was appointed director of the Leipzig Bach Archive in 1986. He was a lecturer at the Martin Luther Univ. in Halle-Wittenberg (1987–88), and has lectured as a visiting prof. in univs. in Europe and the U.S. A devoted scholar of Bach, Schulze is a respected authority in his field.

WRITINGS: Ed. with W. Neumann, *Schriftstücke von der Hand Johann Sebastian Bachs, Bach-Dokumente*, I (Leipzig, 1963); ed. *Fremdschriftliche und gedruckte Dokumente zur Lebensgeschichte Johann Sebastian Bachs 1685–1750, Bach-Dokumente*, II (Leipzig, 1969); ed. *Dokumente zum Nachwirken Johann Sebastian Bachs 1750–1800, Bach- Dokumente*, III (Leipzig, 1972); *Johann Sebastian Bach: Leben und Werk in Dokumenten* (Leipzig, 1975); ed. with C. Wolff, *Bach Compendium: Analytisch-bibliographisches Repertorium der Werke Johann Sebastian Bachs* (7 vols., Leipzig and Dresden, 1986–89).—NS/LK/DM

Schulz-Evler, Andrei, Polish pianist, teacher, and composer; b. Radom, Dec. 12, 1852; d. Warsaw, May 15, 1905. He studied at the Warsaw Cons., and later with Tausig in Berlin. He was a prof. of piano at the Kharkov Music School (1888–1904). He publ. 52 piano pieces and songs; his transcription of the *Blue Danube Waltz* was very popular with pianists for a time.—NS/LK/DM

Schuman, Patricia, American soprano; b. Los Angeles, Feb. 4, 1954. She studied at the Univ. of Calif. at Santa Cruz. After appearances in San Francisco, Houston, N.Y., Paris, Venice, and Washington, D.C., she sang Dorabella and Zerlina at the Théâtre Royal de la Monnaie in Brussels in 1983. In 1986 she sang in the U.S. premiere of *Il viaggio a Reims* in St. Louis. She was engaged to sing Poppea at the Théâtre du Châtelet in Paris in 1989. On Sept. 27, 1990, she made her debut at the Metropolitan Opera in N.Y. as Donna Elvira. That same year, she also appeared as Blanche in Poulenc's *Dialogues des Carmélites* in Seattle. In 1992 she portrayed Donna Elvira at her debut at London's Covent Garden. She sang in *La clemenza di Tito* at the Salzburg Festival in 1997.—NS/LK/DM

Schuman, William (Howard), eminent American composer, music educator, and administrator; b. N.Y., Aug. 4, 1910; d. there, Feb. 15, 1992. He began composing at 16, turning out a number of popular songs, and also played in jazz groups. He took courses at N.Y.U.'s School of Commerce (1928–30) before turning decisively to music and taking private lessons in harmony with Max Persin and in counterpoint with Charles Haubiel (1931) in N.Y. After attending summer courses with Wagenaar and Schmid at N.Y.'s Juilliard School (1932–33), he pursued his education at Teacher's Coll. of Columbia Univ. (B.S., 1935; M.A., 1937); also

studied conducting at the Salzburg Mozarteum (summer, 1935) and composition with Harris, both at the Juilliard School (summer, 1936) and privately (1936–38). He came to the attention of Koussevitzky, who conducted the premieres of his *American Festival Overture* (1939), third Sym. (1941; received the first N.Y. Music Critics' Circle Award), *A Free Song* (1943; received the first Pulitzer Prize in Music), and the Sym. for Strings (1943); Rodzinski conducted the premiere of his fourth Sym. (1942). After teaching at Sarah Lawrence Coll. (1935–45), he served as director of publications of G. Schirmer, Inc. (1945–52) and as president of the Juilliard School of Music (1945–62), where he acquired a notable reputation as a music educator; he subsequently was president of Lincoln Center for the Performing Arts in N.Y. (1962–69). He was chairman of the MacDowell Colony (from 1973) and the first chairman of the Norlin Foundation (1975–85). The recipient of numerous honors, he held 2 Guggenheim fellowships (1939–41), was elected a member of the National Inst. of Arts and Letters (1946) and the American Academy of Arts and Letters (1973), was awarded the gold medal of the American Academy and Inst. of Arts and Letters (1982), won a second, special Pulitzer Prize (1985), and received the National Medal of Arts (1987) and a Kennedy Center Honor (1989). Columbia Univ. established the William Schuman Award in 1981, a prize of $50,000 given to a composer for lifetime achievement; fittingly, Schuman was its first recipient. His music is characterized by great emotional tension, which is maintained by powerful asymmetric rhythms; the contrapuntal structures in his works reach a great degree of complexity and are saturated with dissonance without, however, losing the essential tonal references. In several of his works, he employs American melorhythms, but his general style of composition is cosmopolitan, exploring all viable techniques of modern composition.

WORKS: DRAMATIC: O p e r a : *The Mighty Casey* (1951–53; Hartford, Conn., May 4, 1953; rev. as the cantata *Casey at the Bat*, Washington, D.C., April 6, 1976). **B a l l e t :** *Undertow* (N.Y., April 10, 1945); *Night Journey* (Cambridge, Mass., May 3, 1947); *Judith* (1949; Louisville, Jan. 4, 1950); *Voyage for a Theater* (N.Y., May 17, 1953; withdrawn); *The Witch of Endor* (N.Y., Nov. 2, 1965; withdrawn). **F i l m :** *Steeltown* (1941); *The Earth Is Born* (1959). **ORCH.:** *Potpourri* (1932; withdrawn); 10 syms.: No. 1 for 18 Instruments (1935; N.Y., Oct. 21, 1936; withdrawn), No. 2 (1937; N.Y., May 25, 1938; withdrawn), No. 3 (Boston, Oct. 17, 1941), No. 4 (1941; Cleveland, Jan. 22, 1942), No. 5, Sym. for Strings (Boston, Nov. 12, 1943), No. 6 (1948; Dallas, Feb. 27, 1949), No. 7 (Boston, Oct. 21, 1960), No. 8 (N.Y., Oct. 4, 1962), No. 9, *Le fosse ardeatine* (1968; Philadelphia, Jan. 10, 1969), and No. 10, *American Muse* (1975; Washington, D.C., April 6, 1976); Piano Concerto (1938; rev. 1942; N.Y., Jan. 13, 1943); *American Festival Overture* (Boston, Oct. 6, 1939); *Newsreel*, in 5 Shots for Concert Band (1941; also for Orch., N.Y., July 15, 1942); *Prayer in Time of War* (Pittsburgh, Feb. 26, 1943); *William Billings Overture* (1943; N.Y., Feb. 17, 1944; withdrawn); *Variations on a Theme by Eugene Goossens* (No. 5 of 10 variations, each by a different composer; 1944; Cincinnati, March 23, 1945); *Circus Overture: Side Show* (1944; for Small Orch., Philadelphia, July 20, 1944; for Full Orch., Pittsburgh, Jan. 7, 1945); *Undertow*, choreographic episodes from the ballet (Los Angeles, Nov. 29, 1945); Violin Concerto (1947; Boston, Feb. 10, 1950; rev. 1954;

N.Y., Feb. 26, 1956; rev. 1958–59; Aspen, Colo., Aug. 9, 1959); *George Washington Bridge* for Concert Band (Interlochen, Mich., July 30, 1950); *Credendum, Article of Faith* (Cincinnati, Nov. 4, 1955); *New England Triptych* (Miami, Oct. 28, 1956); *Chester Overture* for Concert Band from *New England Triptych* (1956); *When Jesus Wept* for Concert Band from *New England Triptych* (1958); *A Song of Orpheus* for Cello and Orch. (1961; Indianapolis, Feb. 17, 1962; arranged for Cello and Chamber Orch. in collaboration with J. Goldberg, 1978); *Variations on "America"* after the organ work by Ives (1963; N.Y., May 20, 1964; also for Band, 1968); *The Orchestra Song* (1963; N.Y., April 11, 1964; also for Band as *The Band Song*); *Philharmonic Fanfare* for Concert Band (N.Y., Aug. 10, 1965; withdrawn); *Dedication Fanfare* for Concert Band (St. Louis, July 4, 1968); *To Thee Old Cause* for Oboe, Brass, Timpani, Piano, and Strings (N.Y., Oct. 3, 1968); *In Praise of Shahn*, canticle (1969; N.Y., Jan. 29, 1970); *Anniversary Fanfare* for Brass and Percussion (1969; N.Y., April 13, 1970); *Voyage for Orchestra* (Rochester, N.Y., Oct. 27, 1972); *Prelude for a Great Occasion* for Brass and Percussion (Washington, D.C., Oct. 1, 1974); *Be Glad Then, America* for Concert Band from *New England Triptych* (1975); *3 Colloquies* for Horn and Orch. (1979; N.Y., Jan. 24, 1980); *American Hymn* (1980; St. Louis, Dec. 24, 1982; also for Band). **CHAMBER:** *Canon and Fugue* for Piano Trio (1934; withdrawn); 2 pastorales: No. 1 for Alto and Clarinet, or 2 Violas, or Violin and Cello (1934), and No. 2 for Flute, Oboe, and Clarinet; or Flute, Violin, and Clarinet (1934; withdrawn); 5 string quartets: No. 1 (N.Y., Oct. 21, 1936; withdrawn), No. 2 (1937), No. 3 (1939; N.Y., Feb. 27, 1940), No. 4 (Washington, D.C., Oct. 28, 1950), and No. 5 (1987; N.Y., June 21, 1988); *Quartettino* for 4 Bassoons (1939); *Amaryllis*, variations for String Trio (Washington, D.C., Oct. 31, 1964; also for String Orch.); *XXV Opera Snatches* for Trumpet (1978; N.Y., Jan. 10, 1979); *Night Journey* for Various Instruments, after the ballet (1980; Albany, N.Y., Feb. 27, 1981); *American Hymn* for Brass Quintet (1980; N.Y., March 30, 1981); *Dances* for Wind Quintet and Percussion (1984; N.Y., Oct. 1, 1985). **P i a n o :** *3-score Set* (1943); *Voyage* (1953); *3 Piano Moods* (1958). **VOCAL** (all for a cappella Mixed Chorus unless otherwise given): *God's World* for Voice and Piano (1932); *4 Canonic Choruses* (1932–33; N.Y., May 3, 1935); *Pioneers!* for 8-part Chorus (1937; Princeton, N.J., May 23, 1938; withdrawn); *Choral Etude* (1937; N.Y., March 16, 1938); *Prologue* for Chorus and Orch. (N.Y., May 7, 1939); *Prelude* for Soprano and Women's or Mixed Chorus (1939; N.Y., April 24, 1940); *This Is Our Time*, secular cantata No. 1 for Chorus and Orch. (N.Y., July 4, 1940); *Requiescat* for Women's or Mixed Chorus and Piano (N.Y., April 4, 1942); *Holiday Song* for Women's Voices or Mixed Chorus and Piano (1942; N.Y., Jan. 13, 1943; also for Voice and Piano); *A Free Song*, secular cantata No. 2 for Chorus and Orch. (1942; Boston, March 26, 1943); *Orpheus and His Lute* for Voice and Piano (1944; also for Cello and Orch. as *A Song of Orpheus*, 1961); *Te Deum* (1944; Cambridge, Mass., April 1945); *Truth Shall Deliver* for Men's Chorus (New Haven, Conn., Dec. 7, 1946); *The Lord Has a Child* for Mixed or Women's Chorus or Voice and Piano (1956); *5 Rounds on Famous Words* (Nos. 1–4, 1956; No. 5, 1969); *Carols of Death* (1958; Canton, N.Y., March 20, 1959); *Deo ac veritati* for Men's Chorus (Hamilton, N.Y., April 19, 1963); *Declaration Chorale* (1971; N.Y., April 30, 1972); *Mail Order Madrigals* (1971; Ames, Iowa, March 12, 1972); *To Thy Love*, choral fantasy on old English rounds for 3-part Women's Chorus (1973); *Concerto on Old English Rounds* for Viola, Women's Chorus, and Orch. (Boston, Nov. 29, 1974); *The Young Dead Soldiers* for Soprano, Horn, Woodwinds, and Strings (1975; Washington, D.C., April 6, 1976); *Casey at the Bat*, cantata for Soprano, Baritone, Chorus, and Orch. (Washington, D.C.,

April 6, 1976; revision of the opera *The Mighty Casey*); *In Sweet Music* for Mezzo-soprano, Flute, Viola, and Harp (N.Y., Oct. 29, 1978; based on the song *Orpheus and His Lute*, 1944); *Time to the Old* for Voice and Piano (1979); *Esses: Short Suite for Singers on Words Beginning with S* (Ithaca, N.Y., Nov. 13, 1982); *Perceptions* (1982; Greenwich, Conn., Jan. 9, 1983); *On Freedom's Ground: An American Cantata* for Baritone, Chorus, and Orch., for the rededication of the Statue of Liberty (1985; N.Y., Oct. 28, 1986).

BIBL.: F. Schreiber and V. Persichetti, *W. S.* (N.Y., 1954); C. Rouse, *W. S.: Documentary* (N.Y., 1980).—**NS/LK/DM**

Schumann, Camillo, German organist and composer, brother of **Georg (Alfred) Schumann;** b. Königstein, March 10, 1872; d. Gottleuba, Dec. 29, 1946. He learned the rudiments of music from his father; then studied with Jadassohn and Reinecke at the Leipzig Cons. After further study with Adolf Bargiel in Berlin (1894–96), he became organist at the Eisenach church. For some years before his death, he lived in retirement at Gottleuba. He was a prolific composer, especially noted for his organ works; he also wrote 6 cantatas, 3 piano trios, 5 cello sonatas, 2 clarinet sonatas, 2 violin sonatas, and 30 albums of piano pieces.—**NS/LK/DM**

Schumann, Clara (Josephine) (née **Wieck**), famous German pianist, teacher, and composer, daughter of **Friedrich Wieck** and wife of **Robert (Alexander) Schumann;** b. Leipzig, Sept. 13, 1819; d. Frankfurt am Main, May 20, 1896. She was only 5 when she began musical training with her father. She made her debut at the Leipzig Gewandhaus on Oct. 20, 1828, where she gave her first complete recital on Nov. 8, 1830. Her father then took her on her first major concert tour in 1831–32, which included a visit to Paris. Upon her return to Leipzig, she pursued additional piano training as well as studies in voice, violin, instrumentation, score reading, counterpoint, and composition; she also publ. several works for piano. In 1838 she was named kk. Kammervirtuosin to the Austrian court. Schumann entered Clara's life in 1830 when he became a lodger in the Wieck home; in 1837 he asked her to marry him, a request which set off a contentious battle between the couple and Clara's father; the issue was only settled after the couple went to court, and they were finally married on Sept. 12, 1840. They went to Dresden, and then to Düsseldorf (1850). In spite of her responsibilities in rearing a large family, she continued to pursue a concert career. She also became active as a teacher, serving on the faculty of the Leipzig Cons. and teaching privately. After her husband's death in 1856, she went to Berlin in 1857; after a sojourn in Baden-Baden (1863–73), she lived intermittently in Berlin (1873–78). Throughout these years, she toured widely as a pianist; made regular appearances in England from 1856; toured Russia in 1864. In 1878 she settled in Frankfurt am Main as a teacher at the Hoch Cons., a position she retained with distinction until 1892. She made her last public appearance as a pianist in 1891. As a pianist, she was a masterly and authoritative interpreter of Schumann's compositions; later she became an equally admirable interpreter of Brahms, her lifelong friend. She was completely free of all mannerisms, and impressed her audiences chiefly by the earnestness of her regard for the music she played. A remarkable teacher, she attracted students from many countries. As a composer, she revealed a genuine talent especially in her numerous character pieces for piano. She wrote a Piano Concerto (1836), a Piano Trio (1847), a Piano Concertino (1847), *Drei Romanzen* for Violin and Piano (1853), and some songs. Schumann made use of her melodies in several of his works. She wrote cadenzas to Beethoven's concertos in C minor and G major; ed. the Breitkopf & Härtel edition of Schumann's works, and some of his early correspondence; also ed. finger exercises from Czerny's piano method.

BIBL.: A. von Meichsner, *Friedrich Wieck und seine leiden Töchter C. S., geb. Wieck, und Marie Wieck* (Leipzig, 1875); La Mara, *C. S.,* in Vol. V of *Musikalische Studienköpfe* (Leipzig, 1882; third ed., 1902); B. Litzmann, *C. S.: Ein Kunstlerleben nach Tagebüchern und Briefen* (3 vols., Leipzig, 1902–8; Eng. tr. in 2 vols., abr., London, 1913); W. Kleefeld, *C. S.* (Bielefeld, 1910); F. May, *The Girlhood of C. S.* (London, 1912); E. Schumann, *Erinnerungen* (1925; Eng. tr., 1927); B. Litzmann, ed., *C. S.-Johannes Brahms: Briefe aus den Jahren 1853–1896* (2 vols., Leipzig, 1927; Eng. tr., n.d.); K. Höcker, *C. S.* (1938); J. Burk, *C. S.: A Romantic Biography* (N.Y., 1940); L. Henning, *Die Freundschaft C. S.s mit Johannes Brahms* (Zürich, 1952); W. Quednau, *C. S.* (Berlin, 1955); M. and J. Alley, *A Passionate Friendship: C. S. and Brahms* (London, 1956); R. Pitron, *C. S.* (Paris, 1961); K. Stephenson, *C. S.: 1819–1896* (Bonn, 1969); J. Chissell, *C. S.* (London, 1983); N. Reich, *C. S.: The Artist and the Woman* (London, 1985); U. Fischer-Schmidt, *C. S., 1819–1896: Für kritische Hörer und Leser: Ein kommentiertes Auswahlverzeichnis* (Berlin, 1987); C. Lépront, *C. S.: La vie a quatre mains* (Paris, 1988); J. Klassen, *C. W.-S.: Die Virtuosin als Komponisten: Studien zu ihrem Werk* (Kassel, 1990); E. Weissweiler, *C. S.: Eine Biographie* (Hamburg, 1990); B. Borchard, *C. S.: Ihr Leben* (Frankfurt am Main, 1991); P.-A. Koch, *C. W.-S.: (1819–1896): Kompositionen: Eine Zusammenstellung der Werke, Literatur und Schallplatten* (Frankfurt am Main, 1991); G. Nauhaus, *The Marriage Diaries of Robert and C. S.: From Their Wedding Through the Russian Trip* (Boston, 1993); C. de Vries, *Die Pianistin C. W.-S.: Interpretation im Spannungsfeld von Tradition und Individualität* (Mainz, 1996); R. Hofmann, *C. S.s Briefe an Theodor Kirchner* (Tutzing, 1996); E. Ostleitner und U. Simek, eds., *Ich fahre in mein liebes Wien: C. S., Fakten, Bilder, Projektionen* (Vienna, 1996); V. Beci, *Die andere C. S.* (Düsseldorf, 1997); W. Held, *Manches geht in Nacht verloren: Die Geschichte von C. und Robert Schumann* (Hamburg, 1998).—**NS/LK/DM**

Schumann, Elisabeth, celebrated German-born American soprano; b. Merseburg, June 13, 1888; d. N.Y., April 23, 1952. She studied in Dresden, Berlin, and Hamburg. She made her operatic debut at the Hamburg Opera on Sept. 2, 1909, as the Shepherd in *Tannhäuser*; remained on its roster until 1919. In the meantime, she made her American debut at the Metropolitan Opera in N.Y. on Nov. 20, 1914, as Sophie in *Der Rosenkavalier*, one of her most famous roles; sang there only one season (1914–15). From 1919 to 1938 she was a principal member of the Vienna State Opera. In 1921 she made a concert tour of the U.S. with Richard Strauss. After the Anschluss in 1938, she settled in the U.S. and taught at the Curtis Inst. of Music in Philadelphia. She became a naturalized American citizen in 1944. She publ. *German Song* (London, 1948). Among her finest roles were Blondchen, Zerlina, Susanna, Adele, and Sophie; she also was renowned as an incomparable lieder artist.

BIBL.: G. Puritz, *E. S.: A Biography* (London, 1993).—**NS/LK/DM**

Schumann, Georg (Alfred), German conductor and composer, brother of **Camillo Schumann;** b. Königstein, Oct. 25, 1866; d. Berlin, May 23, 1952. He studied with his father, the town music director, and with his grandfather, a cantor, then took courses in Dresden and at the Leipzig Cons. with Reinecke and Jadassohn; received the Beethoven Prize in 1887. He conducted a choral society in Danzig (1890–96) and the Bremen Phil. (1896–99). In 1900 he settled in Berlin, where he was made conductor of the Singakademie; was made a member of the Akademie der Künste in 1907, teaching a master class in composition (1913–45); was elected its president in 1934.

WORKS: *Zur Karnevalszeit,* orch. suite; *Liebesfrühling,* overture; *Lebensfreude,* overture; 2 syms.; 2 violin sonatas; 2 piano quintets; Cello Sonata; Piano Trio; Piano Quartet; *Ruth,* oratorio (1909); other choral works, with Orch.: *Amor und Psyche, Totenklage, Sehnsucht,* and *Das Tranenkrüglein*; numerous songs; piano pieces.

BIBL.: P. Hielscher, *G. S.* (Leipzig, 1906); H. Biehle, *G. S.* (Münster, 1925).—**NS/LK/DM**

Schumann, Robert (Alexander), great German composer of surpassing imaginative power whose music expressed the deepest spirit of the Romantic era, husband of **Clara (Josephine) Schumann** (née **Wieck**); b. Zwickau, June 8, 1810; d. Endenich, near Bonn, July 29, 1856. He was the fifth and youngest child of a Saxon bookseller, who encouraged his musical inclinations. At about the age of 7, he began taking piano lessons from J.G. Kuntzsch, organist at the Zwickau Marienkirche. In 1828 he enrolled at the Univ. of Leipzig as studiosus juris, although he gave more attention to philosophical lectures than to law. In Leipzig he became a piano student of Friedrich Wieck, his future father-in-law. In 1829 he went to Heidelberg, where he applied himself seriously to music. In 1830 he returned to Leipzig and lodged in Wieck's home. He also took a course in composition with Heinrich Dorn. His family life was unhappy; his father died at the age of 53 of a nervous disease not distinctly diagnosed, and his sister Emily at the age of 19, most likely a suicide. Of his 3 brothers, only one reached late middle age. Schumann became absorbed in the Romantic malaise of *Weltschmerz*; his idols included the writers and poets Jean Paul, Novalis, Kleist, Byron, Lenau, and Hölderin. Schumann wrote plays and poems in the Romantic tradition and at the same time practiced his piano playing in the hope of becoming a virtuoso pianist. He never succeeded in this ambition; ironically, it was to be his beloved bride, Clara (Josephine) Schumann (née Wieck), who would become a famous concert pianist, with Schumann himself often introduced to the public at large as merely her husband. His own piano study was halted when he developed an ailment in the index and middle fingers of his right hand. He tried all the fashionable remedies of the period, allopathy, homeopathy, and electrophysical therapy; in addition, he used a mechanical device to lift the middle finger of his right hand, but it only caused him harm. His damaged fingers exempted him from military service; the medical certificate issued in 1842 stated that the index and middle fingers of his right hand were affected so that he was unable to pull the trigger of a rifle. Schumann had a handsome appearance; he liked the company of young women, and enjoyed beer, wine, and strong cigars; this was in sharp contrast with his inner disquiet. As a youth, he confided to his diary a fear of madness. He had auditory hallucinations which caused insomnia, and he also suffered from acrophobia. When he was 23 years old, he noted sudden onsets of inexpressible angst, momentary loss of consciousness, and difficulty in breathing. He called his sickness a pervasive melancholy, a popular malaise of the time. He thought of killing himself. What maintained his spirits then was his great love for Clara, 9 years his junior; he did not hesitate to confess his psychological perturbations to her. Her father must have surmised the unstable character of Schumann, and resisted any thought of allowing Clara to become engaged to him; the young couple had to go to court to overcome Wieck's objections, and were finally married on Sept. 12, 1840, the day before Clara turned 21. In 1843, when Schumann and Clara already had 2 daughters, Wieck approached him with an offer of reconciliation. Schumann gladly accepted the offer, but the relationship remained only formal.

Whatever inner torment disturbed Schumann's mind, it did not affect the flowering of his genius as a composer. As a young man he wrote music full of natural beauty, harmonious and melodious in its flow. His very first opus number was a set of variations on the notes A, B, E, G, G, which spelled the name of Countess Meta von Abegg, to whom he was also poetically attached. And, incidentally, it was Ernestine's adoptive father, an amateur flutist, who gave him the theme for his remarkable set of variations for Piano titled *Etudes symphoniques*.

As Schumann's talent for music grew and he became recognized as an important composer, he continued his literary activities. In 1834 he founded, with J. Knorr, L. Schunke, and Wieck, a progressive journal, the *Neue Zeitschrift für Musik*, in which he militated against the vapid mannerisms of fashionable salon music and other aspects of musical stagnation. He wrote essays, signing them with the imaginary names of Florestan, Eusebius, or Meister Raro. (Eusebius was the name of 3 Christian saints; etymologically, it is a compound of the Greek components *eu*, "good," and *sebiai*, "to worship." *Florestan* is obviously "one in a state of flowering"; *Raro* is "rare"; he also noticed that the juxtaposition of the names Clara and Robert would result in the formation of Raro: ClaRARObert.) As early as 1831, Schumann, in the guise of Eusebius, hailed the genius of Chopin in an article in the *Allgemeine Musikalische Zeitung*; it was signed only by his initials, and in an editorial note, he was identified merely as a young student of Prof. Wieck; but the winged phrase became a favorite quotation of biographers of both Chopin and Schumann, cited as Schumann's discovery of Chopin's talent. Actually, Chopin was a few months older than Schumann, and had already started on a brilliant concert career, while

Schumann was an unknown. One of the most fanciful inventions of Schumann was the formation of an intimate company of friends, which he named Davidsbündler to describe the sodality of David, dedicated to the mortal struggle against Philistines in art and to the passionate support of all that was new and imaginative. He immortalized this society in his brilliant piano work *Davidsbündlertänze*. Another characteristically Romantic trait was Schumann's attachment to nocturnal moods, nature scenes, and fantasies; the titles of his piano pieces are typical: *Nachtstücke*, *Waldszenen*, and *Fantasiestücke*, the last including the poetic *Warum?* and the explosive *Aufschwung*. A child at heart himself, he created in his piano set of exquisite miniatures, *Kinderszenen*, a marvelous musical masterpiece which included the beautifully sentimental dream piece *Traumerei*. Parallel with his piano works, Schumann produced some of his finest lieder, including the song cycles to poems by Heine (op.24) and Eichendorff (op.39), *Die Frauenliebe und Leben* (op.42), and *Dichterliebe*, to Heine's words (op.48). In 1841, in only 4 days, he sketched out his First Sym., in B-flat major, born, as he himself said, in a single "fiery hour." He named it the *Spring* sym. It was followed in rapid succession by 3 string quartets (op.41), the Piano Quintet (op.44), and the Piano Quartet (op.47). To the same period belongs also his impassioned *Das Paradies und die Peri* for Soloists, Chorus, and Orch. Three more syms. followed the *Spring* sym. within the next decade, and also a Piano Concerto, a masterpiece of a coalition between the percussive gaiety of the solo part and songful paragraphs in the orch.; an arresting hocketus occurs in the finale, in which duple meters come into a striking conflict with the triple rhythm of the solo part.

In 1843 Schumann was asked by Mendelssohn to join him as a teacher of piano, composition, and score reading at the newly founded Cons. in Leipzig. In 1844 he and Clara undertook a concert tour to Russia. In the autumn of 1844 they moved to Dresden, remaining there until 1850. To this period belong his great C major Sym. (1846), the Piano Trio (1847), and the opera *Genoveva* (1848). In 1847 he assumed the conducting post of the Liedertafel, and in 1848 organized the Chorgesang-Verein in Dresden. In 1850 he became municipal music director in Düsseldorf, but his disturbed condition manifested itself in such alarming ways that he had to resign the post in 1853, though he continued to compose. In the latter year, Schumann completed his expansive setting of *Szenen aus Goethes Faust* for Soloists, Chorus, and Orch. In 1853 he also completed a Violin Concerto. Joachim, in whose care Schumann left the work, thought it was not worthy of his genius, and ruled that it should not be performed until the centennial of Schumann's death. The concerto was first performed in Berlin on Nov. 26, 1937.

Schumann's condition continued to deteriorate. On Feb. 27, 1854, he threw himself into the Rhine, but was rescued. On March 4, 1854, he was placed, at his own request, in a sanatorium at Endenich, near Bonn, remaining there until the end of his life. Strangely, he did not want to see Clara, and there were months when he did not even inquire about her and the children. But Brahms was a welcome visitor, and Schumann enjoyed his company during his not infrequent periods of lucidity. According to Schumann's own account during his confinement in Endenich in 1855, he contracted syphilis in 1831 and was treated with arsenic. See F. Franken, "Robert Schumann in der Irrenanstalt Endenich," *Robert Schumanns letzte Lebensjahre: Protokoll einer Krankheit, Archiv Blätter 1* (Berlin, March 1994).

As both man and musician, Schumann is recognized as the quintessential artist of the Romantic era in German music. He was a master of lyric expression and dramatic power, perhaps best revealed in his outstanding piano music and songs. His syms., by turns compelling and poetic, have acquired repertoire status, as have several of his chamber works. Only his large dramatic vocal scores, still largely neglected, remain to be discovered via recordings to reveal the full genius of Schumann's creative vision.

WORKS: DRAMATIC: *Der Corsar*, opera (1844; unfinished; only a chorus and sketch for an air completed); *Genoveva*, opera, op.81 (1847–49; Leipzig, June 25, 1850); *Manfred*, incidental music to Byron's play, op.115 (1848–49; Leipzig, June 13, 1852). **ORCH.:** Piano Concerto in E-flat major (1828; unfinished); Piano Concerto in F major (1829–31; unfinished); *Introduction and Variations on a Theme of Paganini* (1831); Sym. in G minor (1832–33; first movement perf. Zwickau, Nov. 18, 1832; first complete perf., Schneeberg, Feb. 12, 1833; 3 movements only with a sketch for a fourth movement); Piano Concerto in D minor (1839; one movement only); Sym. in C minor (1840–41; sketches for 4 movements; some of the music used in Sym. No. 2, in C major, op.61); Sym. No. 1, in B-flat major, op.38, *Spring* (Leipzig, March 31, 1841); *Ouvertüre, Scherzo, und Finale* in E major, op.52 (Leipzig, Dec. 6, 1841; rev. 1845); Piano Concerto in A minor, op.54 (first movement composed as the *Fantasie* for Piano and Orch., 1841; movements 2–3, 1845; Leipzig, Jan. 1, 1846); Sym. No. 2, in C major, op.61 (1845–46; Leipzig, Nov. 5, 1846); *Conzertstück* in F major for 4 Horns and Orch., op.86 (1849; Leipzig, Feb. 25, 1850); *Introduction and Allegro Appassionato, Conzertstück*, op.92 (1849; Leipzig, Feb. 14, 1850); Sym. No. 3, in E- flat major, op.97, *Rhenish* (1850; Düsseldorf, Feb. 6, 1851); *Die Braut von Messina*, overture in C minor, to Schiller's play, op.100 (1850–51; Düsseldorf, March 13, 1851); Sym. No. 4, in D minor, op.120 (originally Sym. No. 2; Leipzig, Dec. 6, 1841; rev. as Sym. No. 4, 1851; Düsseldorf, Dec. 30, 1852); *Julius Cäsar*, overture in F minor, to Shakespeare's play, op.128 (1851; Düsseldorf, Aug. 3, 1852); Cello Concerto in A minor, op.129 (1850; Leipzig, June 9, 1860); *Fantasie* in C major for Violin and Orch., op.131 (1853; Hannover, Jan. 1854); *Introduction and Allegro* in D minor/D major for Piano and Orch., op.134 (Utrecht, Nov. 26, 1853); *Hermann und Dorothea*, overture in B minor, to Goethe's poem, op.136 (1851); Violin Concerto in D minor (1853; Berlin, Nov. 26, 1937). **CHAMBER:** Quartet in C minor for Violin, Viola, Cello, and Piano (1828–30); Quartet in F minor (1829); Quartet in B major for Violin, Viola, Cello, and Piano (1831–32; unfinished); Quartet (1838; not extant); sketches for 2 string quartets: D major and E-flat major (1839); 3 string quartets, op.41: A minor, F major, A major (1842); Quintet in E-flat major for 2 Violins, Viola, Cello, and Piano, op.44 (1842); Quartet in E-flat major for Violin, Viola, Cello, and Piano, op.47 (1842); *Andante and Variations* for 2 Pianos, 2 Cellos, and Horn (1843; original version of op.46); Trio No. 1, in D minor, for Violin, Cello, and Piano, op.63 (1847); *Adagio and Allegro* for Horn and Piano, with Violin or Cello ad libitum, in A-flat major, op.70 (1849); *Phantasiestücke* for Clarinet and Piano, with Violin or Cello ad libitum, op.73 (1849); Trio No. 2, in F major, for Violin, Cello, and Piano, op.80 (1847); *Phantasiestücke* for Violin,

Cello, and Piano, op.88 (1842); *3 Romanzen* for Oboe and Piano, with Violin or Clarinet ad libitum, op.94 (1849); *5 Stücke im Volkston* for Cello and Piano, with Violin ad libitum, op.102 (1849); Sonata No. 1, in A minor, for Violin and Piano, op.105 (1851); Trio No. 3, in G minor, for Violin, Cello, and Piano, op.110 (1851); *Märchenbilder* for Viola and Piano, with Violin ad libitum, op.113 (1851); Sonata No. 2, in D minor, for Violin and Piano, op.121 (1851); *Märchenerzählungen* for Clarinet, Viola, and Piano, with Violin ad libitum, op.132 (1853); Sonata for Violin and Piano, *F. A. E.* [based on the thematic motto of Joachim, *Frei aber einsam*] (1853; second and fourth movements by Schumann; first movement by Dietrich; third movement by Brahms); Sonata No. 3, in A minor, for Violin and Piano (1853; incorporates Schumann's 2 movements composed for the *F. A. E.* sonata); *5 Romanzen* for Cello and Piano (1853; not extant). **P i a n o :** 8 polonaises for Piano, 4-Hands (1828); *Variations on a Theme of Prince Louis Ferdinand of Prussia* for Piano, 4-Hands (1828); *Romanze* in F minor (1829; unfinished); *6 Walzer* (1829–30); *Thème sur le nom Abegg varié pour le pianoforte*, op.1 (1829–30); *Variations on a Theme of Weber*, from *Preziosa* (1831); *Valse* in E-flat major (1831; unfinished); *Valse per Friedrich Wieck* (1831–32; unfinished); Sonata in A-flat major (1831–32; first movement and Adagio); *Andante with Variations on an Original Theme* in G major (1831–32); *Prelude and Fugue* (1832); *Papillons*, op.2 (1829–31); *6 Studien nach Capricen von Paganini*, op.3, I (1832; formerly op.2); *6 Intermezzos*, op.4 (1832; formerly known as *Pièces phantastiques*, op.3); *Phantasie satyrique* (1832; fragments only); *Fandango* in F-sharp minor (1832); *Exercice fantastique* (1832; formerly op.5; not extant); *Rondo* in B-flat major (1832; unfinished); *12 Burlesken* (1832); *Fugue* in D minor (1832); *Fugue No. 3* (1832); 5 pieces (1832–33; 1, 4, and 5 unfinished); *Sehnsuchts-walzer Variationen: Scènes musicales sur un thème connu* (1832–33); 10 *Impromptus über ein Thema von Clara Wieck*, op.5 (1833); *Etüden in Form freier Variationen über ein Beethovensches Thema* (1833); *Variations sur un nocturne de Chopin* (1834); movement for a Sonata, in B-flat major (1836); Sonata No. 4, in F minor (1836–37; unfinished); *Davidsbündlertänze*, 18 character pieces, op.6 (1837); *Toccata* in C major, op.7 (1829–32; formerly op.6); *Allegro* in B minor, op.8 (1831); *Carnaval: Scènes mignonnes sur quatre notes*, op.9 (1833–35); *6 Konzert-Etüden nach Capricen von Paganini*, op.10, II (1833); Sonata No. 1, in F-sharp minor, op.11 (1832–35); *Phantasiestücke*, op.12 (1832?–37); *Symphonische Etüden*, op.13 (1834–37); *Concert sans orchestre*, in F minor, op.14 (1835–36; rev. as Sonata No. 3, 1853); *Scherzo* (1836; from op.14); *Kinderszenen*, op.15 (1838); *Kreisleriana*, op.16 (1838; rev. 1850); *Phantasie* in C major, op.17 (1836–38); *Arabeske* in C major, op.18 (1838); *Blumenstück* in D-flat major, op.19 (1839); *Humoreske* in B-flat major, op.20 (1838); 8 *Novelletten*, op.21 (1838); Sonata No. 2, in G minor, op.22 (1833–38; new finale, 1838); *Nachtstücke*, 4 pieces, op.23 (1839); *Allegro* in C minor (1839; not extant); *Faschingsschwank aus Wien: Phantasiebilder*, op.26 (1839–40); 3 *Romanzen*, op.28: B-flat minor, F-sharp major, B major (1839); *Klavierstücke*, op.32 (1838–39); Sonatina in B-flat major (1840; not extant); *Andante and Variations* in B- flat major, op.46, for 2 Pianos (1843); *Studien für den Pedal-Flügel*, op.56 (1845); *4 Skizzen für den Pedal-Flügel*, op.58 (1845); *6 Fugues on B-A-C-H*, op.60, for Pedal Piano or Organ (1845); *Bilder aus Osten: 6 Impromptus*, op.66, for Piano, 4-Hands (1848); *Album für die Jugend*, op.68 (1848); *4 Fugues*, op.72: D minor, D minor, F minor, F major (1845); *4 Marches*, op.76: E-flat major, G minor, B-flat major (Lager-Scene), E-flat major (1849); *Waldszenen*, op.82 (1848–49); *12 vierhändige Klavierstücke für kleine und grosse Kinder*, op.85 (1849); *Bunte Blätter*, op.99 (1838–49); *Ballszenen*, op.109, for Piano, 4-Hands (1851); *Phantasiestücke*, 3 pieces, op.111: C minor, A-flat major, C minor (1851); *3 Clavier-Sonaten für die Jugend*, op.118: G major, D major, C major (1853); *Albumblätter*, op.124 (1854); *7 Klavierstücke in Fughettenform*, op.126 (1853); *Kinderball*, op.130, for Piano, 4- Hands (1853); *5 Gesänge der Frühe*, op.133 (1853); *Canon on F. Himmel's An Alexis send ich dich*, in A-flat major (1854); *Thema in E-flat major* (1854); *Variations on an Original Theme* (1854). **VOCAL: V a r i o u s V o i c e s :** *Psalm CL* for Soprano, Alto, Piano, and Orch. (1822); Overture and chorus (*Chor von Landleuten*), with Orch. (1822); 6 Lieder for Men's Voices, op.33 (1840): 1, *Der träumende See* (Mosen); 2, *Die Minnesänger* (Heine); 3, *Die Lotosblume* (Heine); 4, *Der Zecher als Doktrinär* (Mosen); 5, *Rastlose Liebe* (Goethe); 6, *Frühlingsglocken* (Reinick); *Tragödie* for Chorus and Orch. (Heine; 1841); *Das Paradies und die Peri* for Solo Voices, Chorus, and Orch., op.50 (adaptation of Moore's *Lalla Rookh*; Leipzig, Dec. 4, 1843); *Szenen aus Goethes Faust* for Solo Voices, Chorus, and Orch. (Goethe; 1844–53; Cologne, Jan. 13, 1862); *5 Lieder* for Mixed Voices, op.55 (R. Burns; 1846): 1, *Das Hochlandmädchen*; 2, *Zahnweh*; 3, *Mich zieht es nach dem Dörfchen hin*; 4, *Die alte, gute Zeit*; 5, *Hochlandbursch*; *4 Gesänge* for Mixed Voices, op.59 (1846): 1, *Nord oder Süd!* (K. Lappe); 2, *Am Bodensee* (Platen); 3, *Jägerlied* (Mörike); 4, *Gute Nacht* (Rückert); also a fifth song added later, *Hirtenknaben-Gesang* (Droste-Hulshoff); *3 Gesänge* for Men's Voices, op.62 (1847): 1, *Der Eidgenossen Nachtwache* (Eichendorff); 2, *Freiheitslied* (Rückert); 3, *Schlachtgesang* (Klopstock); *Ritornelle in canonischen Weisen* for Men's Voices, op.65 (Rückert; 1847): 1, *Die Rose stand im Tau*; 2, *Lasst Lautenspiel und Becherklang*; 3, *Blüt' oder Schnee!*; 4, *Gebt mir zu trinken!*; 5, *Zürne nicht des Herbstes Wind*; 6, *In Sommertagen rüste den Schlitten*; 7, *In Meeres Mitten ist ein offener Laden*; 8, *Hätte zu einem Traubenkerne*; *Beim Abschied zu singen* for Chorus and Wind Instruments, op.84 (Feuchtersleben; 1847); *Zum Anfang* for Men's Voices (Rückert; 1847); *3 Freiheitsgesänge* for Men's Voices, with Wind Instruments ad libitum (1848): 1, *Zu den Waffen* (Ullrich); 2, *Schwarz- Rot-Gold* (Freiligrath); 3, *Deutscher Freiheitsgesang* (Furst); *Romanzen und Balladen* for Mixed Voices, op.67, I (1849): 1, *Der König von Thule* (Goethe); 2, *Schön-Rohtraut* (Mörike); 3, *Heidenröslein* (Goethe); 4, *Ungewitter* (Chamisso); 5, *John Anderson* (Burns); *Romanzen und Balladen* for Mixed Voices, op.75, II (1849): 1, *Schnitter Tod* (*Des Knaben Wunderhorn*; Brentano); 2, *Im Walde* (Eichendorff); 3, *Der traurige Jäger* (Eichendorff); 4, *Der Rekrut* (Burns); 5, *Vom verwundeten Knaben* (Herder's *Volkslieder*); *Romanzen* for Women's Voices and Piano ad libitum, op.69, I (1849): 1, *Tamburinschlägerin* (Alvaro de Ameida; Eichendorff, tr.); 2, *Waldmädchen* (Eichendorff); 3, *Klosterfräulein* (Kerner); 4, *Soldatenbraut* (Mörike); 5, *Meerfey* (Eichendorff); 6, *Die Kapelle* (Uhland); *Romanzen* for Women's Voices and Piano ad libitum, op.91, II (1849): 1, *Rosmarien* (*Des Knaben Wunderhorn*); 2, *Jäger Wohlgemut* (*Des Knaben Wunderhorn*); 3, *Der Wassermann* (Kerner); 4, *Das verlassene Mägdelein* (Mörike); 5, *Der Bleicherin Nachtlied* (Reinick); 6, *In Meeres Mitten* (Rückert); *Verzweifle nicht im Schmerzenstal*, motet for Double Chorus and Organ ad libitum, op.93 (Rückert; 1852; orchestrated 1852); *Requiem für Mignon* for Solo Voices, Chorus, and Orch., op.98b (Goethe; 1849; Düsseldorf, Nov. 21, 1850); *5 Gesänge aus H. Laubes Jagdbrevier* for Men's Voices and Piano, 4-Hands, ad libitum, op.137 (Laube; 1849): 1, *Zur hohen Jagd*; 2, *Habet acht!*; 3, *Jagdmorgen*; 4, *Frühe*; 5, *Bei der Flasche*; *4 doppelchörige Gesänge* for Mixed Voices, op.141 (1849): 1, *An die Sterne* (Rückert); 2, *Ungewisses Licht* (Zedlitz); 3, *Zuversicht* (Zedlitz); 4, *Talismane* (Goethe); *Romanzen und Balladen* for Mixed Voices, op.145, III (1849–51): 1, *Der Schmidt* (Uhland); 2, *Die Nonne* (anonymous); 3, *Der Sänger* (Uhland); 4, *John Anderson* (Burns); 5, *Romanze vom Gänsebuben* (Malsburg); *Romanzen*

und Balladen for Mixed Voices, op.146, IV (1849–51): 1, *Brautgesang* (Uhland); 2, *Der Bänkelsänger Willie* (Burns); 3, *Der Traum* (Uhland); 4, *Sommerlied* (Rückert); *Das Schifflein*, with Flute and Horn (Uhland); *Nachtlied* for Chorus and Orch., op.108 (Hebbel; 1849; Düsseldorf, March 13, 1851); *Der Rose Pilgerfahrt* for Solo Voices, Chorus, and Orch., op.112 (Horn; 1851; Düsseldorf, Feb. 5, 1852); *Der Königssohn* for Solo Voices, Chorus, and Orch., op.116 (Uhland; 1851); *Des Glockentürmers Töchterlein* for Mixed Voices (Rückert; 1851); *Fest-Ouvertüre* for Tenor, Chorus, and Orch., op.123 (Müller and Claudius; 1852–53; Düsseldorf, May 17, 1853); *Des Sängers Fluch* for Solo Voices, Chorus, and Orch., op.139 (Pohl, after Uhland; 1852); *Vom Pagen und der Königstochter* for Solo Voices, Chorus, and Orch., op.140 (Geibel; 1852); *Das Glück von Edenhall* for Solo Voices, Chorus, and Orch., op.143 (Hasenclever, after Uhland; 1853); *Bei Schenkung eines Flügels* for Mixed Voices and Piano (Schumann; 1853); *Neujahrslied* for Chorus and Orch., op.144 (Rückert; 1849–50; Düsseldorf, Jan. 11, 1851); *Mass* for Chorus and Orch., op.147 (1852–53); *Requiem* for Chorus and Orch., op.148 (1852). **S o n g s :** *Verwandlung* (Schulze; 1827); *Lied* (Schumann; 1827); *Sehnsucht* (Schumann; 1827); *Die Weinende* (Byron; 1827); *Erinnerung* (Jacobi; 1828); *Kurzes Erwachen* (Kerner; 1828); *Gesanges Erwachen* (Kerner; 1828); *An Anna*, I (Kerner; 1828); *An Anna*, II (Kerner; 1828); *Im Herbste* (Kerner; 1828); *Hirtenknabe* (Schumann; 1828); *Der Fischer* (Goethe; 1828); *Klage* (Jacobi; 1828; not extant); *Vom Reitersmann* (date unknown); *Maultreiberlied* (1838; not extant); *Ein Gedanke* (Ferrand; 1840); *Patriotisches Lied* for Voice, Chorus, and Piano (N. Becker; 1840); *Der Reiter und der Bodensee* (Schwab; 1840; fragment only); *Die nächtliche Heerschau* (Zedlitz; 1840; fragment only); *Liederkreis*, op.24 (Heine; 1840): 1, *Morgens steh ich auf und frage*; 2, *Es treibt mich hin*; 3, *Ich wandelte unter den Bäumen*; 4, *Lieb Liebchen*; 5, *Schöne Wiege meiner Leiden*; 6, *Warte, warte, wilder Schiffmann*; 7, *Berg und Burgen schaun herunter*; 8, *Anfangs wolit ich fast verzagen*; 9, *Mit Myrten und Rosen*; *Myrthen*, op.25 (1840): 1, *Widmung* (Rückert); 2, *Freisinn* (Goethe); 3, *Der Nussbaum* (Mosen); 4, *Jemand* (Burns); 5, *Lieder aus dem Schenkenbuch im Divan*, I (Goethe); 6, *Lieder aus dem Schenkenbuch im Divan*, II (Goethe); 7, *Die Lotosblume* (Heine); 8, *Talismane* (Goethe); 9, *Lied der Suleika* (Goethe; attributed to Marianne von Willemer); 10, *Die Hochländer- Witwe* (Burns); 11, *Lieder der Braut aus dem Liebesfrühling*, I (Rückert); 12, *Lieder der Braut aus dem Liebesfrühling*, II (Rückert); 13, *Hochländers Abschied* (Burns); 14, *Hochländisches Wiegenlied* (Burns); 15, *Aus den hebräischen Gesängen* (Byron); 16, *Rätsel* (C. Fanshawe); 17, *2 Venetianische Lieder*, I (Moore); 18, *2 Venetianische Lieder*, II (Moore); 19, *Hauptmanns Weib* (Burns); 20, *Weit, weit* (Burns); 21, *Was will die einsame Träne?* (Heine); 22, *Niemand* (Burns); 23, *Im Westen* (Burns); 24, *Du bist wie eine Blume* (Heine); 25, *Aus den östlichen Rosen* (Rückert); 26, *Zum Schluss* (Rückert); *Lieder und Gesänge*, op.27, I (1840): 1, *Sag an, o lieber Vogel* (Hebbel); 2, *Dem roten Röslein* (Burns); 3, *Was soll ich sagen?* (Chamisso); 4, *Jasminenstrauch* (Rückert); 5, *Nur ein lächelnder Blick* (G.W. Zimmermann); *3 Gedichte*, op.29 (Geibel; 1840): 1, *Ländliches Lied* for 2 Sopranos; 2, *Lied* for 3 Sopranos; 3, *Zigeunerleben* for Soprano, Alto, Tenor, and Bass, and Triangle and Tambourine ad libitum; *3 Gedichte*, op.30 (Geibel; 1840): 1, *Der Knabe mit dem Wunderhorn*; 2, *Der Page*; 3, *Der Hidalgo*; *3 Gesänge*, op.31 (1840): 1, *Die Löwenbraut* (Chamisso); 2, *Die Kartenlegerin* (Chamisso, after Béranger); 3, *Die rote Hanne*, with Chorus ad libitum (Chamisso, after Béranger); *4 Duette* for Soprano and Tenor, op.34 (1840): 1, *Liebesgarten* (Reinick); 2, *Liebhabers Ständchen* (Burns); 3, *Unterm Fenster* (Burns); 4, *Familien-Gemälde* (A. Grün); *12 Gedichte*, op.35 (Kerner; 1840): 1, *Lust der Sturmnacht*; 2, *Stirb, Lieb und Freud!*; 3, *Wanderlied*; 4, *Erstes Grün*; 5, *Sehnsucht* nach der Waldgegend; 6, *Auf das Trinkglas eines verstorbenen Freundes*; 7, *Wanderung*; 8, *Stille Liebe*; 9, *Frage*; 10, *Stille Tränen*; 11, *Wer machte dich so krank?*; *6 Gedichte*, op.36 (Reinick; 1840): 1, *Sonntags am Rhein*; 2, *Ständchen*; 3, *Nichts schöneres*; 4, *An den Sonnenschein*; 5, *Dichters Genesung*; 6, *Liebesbotschaft*; *12 Gedichte aus "Liebesfrühling,"* op.37 (Rückert; 1840; Nos. 2, 4, and 11 by Clara Schumann): 1, *Der Himmel hat ein' Träne geweint*; 3, *O ihr Herren*; 5, *Ich hab in mich gesogen*; 6, *Liebste, was kann denn uns scheiden?* for Soprano and Tenor; 7, *Schön ist das Fest des Lenzes* for Soprano and Tenor; 8, *Flügel! Flügel! um zu fliegen*; 9, *Rose, Meer und Sonne*; 10, *O Sonn, o Meer, o Rose*; 12, *So wahr die Sonne scheinet* for Soprano and Tenor; *Liederkreis*, op.39 (Eichendorff; 1840): 1, *In der Fremde*; 2, *Intermezzo*; 3, *Waldesgespräch*; 4, *Die Stille*; 5, *Mondnacht*; 6, *Schöne Fremde*; 7, *Auf einer Burg*; 8, *In der Fremde*; 9, *Wehmut*; 10, *Zwielicht*; 11, *Im Walde*; 12, *Frühlingsnacht*; *5 Lieder*, op.40 (1840): 1, *Märzveilchen* (H.C. Andersen); 2, *Muttertraum* (Andersen); 3, *Der Soldat* (Andersen); 4, *Der Spielmann* (Andersen); 5, *Verratene Liebe* (Chamisso); *Frauenliebe und -leben*, op.42 (Chamisso; 1840): 1, *Seit ich ihn gesehen*; 2, *Er, der Herrlichste von allen*; 3, *Ich kann's nicht fassen, nicht glauben*; 4, *Du Ring an meinem Finger*; 5, *Helft mir, ihr Schwestern*; 6, *Süsser Freund, du blickest*; 7, *An meinem Herzen, an meiner Brust*; 8, *Nun hast du mir den ersten Schmerz getan*; *3 zweistimmige Lieder*, op.43 (1840): 1, *Wenn ich ein Vöglein wär* (Das Knaben Wunderhorn); 2, *Herbstlied* (S.A. Mahlmann); 3, *Schön Blümelein* (Reinick); *Romanzen und Balladen*, op.45, I (1840): 1, *Der Schatzgräber* (Eichendorff); 2, *Frühlingsfahrt* (Eichendorff); 3, *Abends am Strand* (Heine); *Dichterliebe*, op.48 (Heine; 1840): 1, *Im wunderschönen Monat Mai*; 2, *Aus meinen Tränen spriessen*; 3, *Die Rose, die Lilie, die Taube, die Sonne*; 4, *Wenn ich in deine Augen seh*; 5, *Ich will meine Seele tauchen*; 6, *Im Rhein, im heiligen Strome*; 7, *Ich grolle nicht*; 8, *Und wüssten's die Blumen, die kleinen*; 9, *Das ist ein Flöten und Geigen*; 10, *Hör' ich das Liedchen klingen*; 11, *Ein Jüngling liebt ein Mädchen*; 12, *Am leuchtenden Sommermorgen*; 13, *Ich hab' im Traum geweinet*; 14, *Allnächtlich im Traume*; 15, *Aus alten Märchen*; 16, *Die alten, bösen Lieder*; *Romanzen und Balladen*, op.49, II (1840): 1, *Die beiden Grenadiere* (Heine); 2, *Die feindlichen Brüder* (Heine); 3, *Die Nonne* (A. Fröhlich); *Lieder und Gesänge*, op.51, II: 1, *Sehnsucht* (Geibel; 1840); 2, *Volksliedchen* (Rückert; 1840); 3, *Ich wandre nicht* (C. Christern; 1840); 4, *Auf dem Rhein* (K. Immermann; 1846); 5, *Liebeslied* (Goethe; 1850); *Romanzen und Balladen*, op.53, III (1840): 1, *Blondels Lied* (Seidl); 2, *Loreley* (W. Lorenz); 3, *Der arme Peter* (Heine); *Belsatzar*, op.57 (Heine; 1840); *Romanzen und Balladen*, op.64, IV: 1, *Die Soldatenbraut* (Mörike; 1847); 2, *Das verlassne Mägdelein* (Mörike; 1847); 3, *Tragödie* (Heine; 1841); *Spanisches Liederspiel*, op.74 (Geibel, after Spanish poets; 1849): 1, *Erste Begegnung* for Soprano and Alto; 2, *Intermezzo* for Tenor and Bass; 3, *Liebesgram* for Soprano and Alto; 4, *In der Nacht* for Soprano and Tenor; 5, *Es ist verraten* for Soprano, Alto, Tenor, and Bass; 6, *Melancholie* for Soprano; 7, *Geständnis* for Tenor; 8, *Botschaft* for Soprano and Alto; 9, *Ich bin geliebt* for Soprano, Alto, Tenor, and Bass; 10, *Der Kontrabandiste* for Baritone; *Lieder und Gesänge*, op.77, III: 1, *Der frohe Wandersmann* (Eichendorff; 1840); 2, *Mein Garten* (Hoffmann von Fallersleben; 1850); 3, *Geisternähe* (Halm; 1850); 4, *Stiller Vorwurf* (O. Wolff?; 1840); 5, *Aufträge* (C. L'Egru; 1850); *Soldatenlied* (Hoffmann von Fallersleben; 1844); *Das Schwert* (Uhland; 1848); *Der weisse Hirsch* (Uhland; 1848; sketches only); *Die Ammenuhr* (Des Knaben Wunderhorn; 1848); *4 Duette* for Soprano and Tenor, op.78 (1849): 1, *Tanzlied* (Rückert); 2, *Er und Sie* (Kerner); 3, *Ich denke dein* (Goethe); 4, *Wiegenlied* (Hebbel); *Sommerruh*, duet (C. Schad; 1849); *Lieder-Album für die Jugend*, op.79 (1849): 1, *Der Abendstern* (Hoffmann von Fallersleben); 2, *Schmetterling* (von Fallersle-

ben); 3, *Frühlingsbotschaft* (Hoffmann von Fallersleben); 4, *Frühlingsgruss* (von Fallersleben); 5, *Vom Schlaraffenland* (von Fallersleben); 6, *Sonntag* (von Fallersleben); 7, *Zigeunerliedchen* (Geibel); 8, *Des Knaben Berglied* (Uhland); 9, *Mailied*, duet ad libitum (C. Overbeck); 10, *Das Käuzlein* (Des Knaben Wunderhorn); 11, *Hinaus ins Freie!* (von Fallersleben); 12, *Der Sandmann* (Kletke); 13, *Marienwürmchen* (Des Knaben Wunderhorn); 14, *Die Waise* (von Fallersleben); 15, *Das Glück*, duet (Hebbel); 16, *Weihnachtslied* (Andersen); 17, *Die wandelnde Glocke* (Goethe); 18, *Frühlingslied*, duet ad libitum (von Fallersleben); 19, *Frühlings Ankunft* (von Fallersleben); 20, *Die Schwalben*, duet (Des Knaben Wunderhorn); 21, *Kinderwacht* (anonymous); 22, *Des Sennen Abschied* (Schiller); 23, *Er ist's* (Mörike); *Spinnelied*, trio ad libitum (anonymous); *Des Buben Schützenlied* (Schiller); 26, *Schneeglöckchen* (Rückert); 27, *Lied Lynceus des Türmers* (Goethe); 28, *Mignon* (Goethe); *3 Gesänge*, op.83 (1850): 1, *Resignation* (Buddeus); 2, *Die Blume der Ergebung* (Rückert); 3, *Der Einsiedler* (Eichendorff); *Der Handschuh*, op.87 (Schiller; 1850); *6 Gesänge*, op.89 (W. von der Neun; 1850): 1, *Es stürmet am Abendhimmel*; 2, *Heimliches Verschwinden*; 3, *Herbstlied*; 4, *Abschied vom Walde*; 5, *Ins Freie*; 6, *Röselein, Röselein!*; *7 Gedichte*, op.90 (Lenau; 1850): 1, *Lied eines Schmiedes*; 2, *Meine Rose*; 3, *Kommen und Scheiden*; 4, *Die Sennin*; 5, *Einsamkeit*; 6, *Der schwere Abend*; 7, *Requiem*; *3 Gesänge*, op.95 (Byron; 1849): 1, *Die Tochter Jephthas*; 2, *An den Mond*; 3, *Dem Helden*; *Lieder und Gesänge*, op.96, IV (1850): 1, *Nachtlied* (Goethe); 2, *Schneeglöckchen* (anonymous); 3, *Ihre Stimme* (Platen); 4, *Gesungen!* (Neun; Schöpff); 5, *Himmel und Erde* (Neun; Schöpff); *Lieder und Gesänge aus Wilhelm Meister*, op.98a (Goethe; 1849): 1, *Kennst du das Land*; 2, *Ballade des Harfners*; 3, *Nur wer die Sehnsucht kennt*; 4, *Wer nie sein Brot mit Tränen ass*; 5, *Heiss mich nicht reden*; 6, *Wer sich der Einsamkeit ergibt*; 7, *Singet nicht in Trauertönen*; 8, *An die Türen will ich schleichen*; 9, *So lasst mich scheinen*; *Minnespiel*, op.101 (Rückert; 1849): 1, *Meine Töne still und heiter* for Tenor; 2, *Liebster, deine Worte stehlen* for Soprano; 3, *Ich bin dein Baum* for Alto and Bass; 4, *Mein schöner Stern!* for Tenor; 5, *Schön ist das Fest des Lenzes* for Soprano, Alto, Tenor, and Bass; 6, *O Freund, mein Schirm, mein Schutz!* for Alto or Soprano; 7, *Die tausend Grüsse* for Soprano and Tenor; 8, *So wahr die Sonne scheinet* for Soprano, Alto, Tenor, and Bass; *Mädchenlieder* for Soprano and Alto or 2 Sopranos, op.103 (Kulmann; 1851): 1, *Mailied*; 2, *Frühlingslied*; 3, *An die Nachtigall*; 4, *An den Abendstern*; *7 Lieder*, op.104 (Kulmann; 1851): 1, *Mond, meiner Seele Liebling*; 2, *Viel Glück zur Reise, Schwalben!*; 3, *Du nennst mich armes Mädchen*; 4, *Der Zeisig*; 5, *Reich mir die Hand, o Wolke*; 6, *Die letzten Blumen starben*; 7, *Gekämpft hat meine Barke*; *Schön Hedwig*, declamation, op.106 (Hebbel; 1849); *6 Gesänge*, op.107 (1851–52): 1, *Herzeleid* (Ullrich); 2, *Die Fensterscheibe* (Ullrich); 3, *Der Gärtner* (Mörike); 4, *Die Spinnerin* (Heyse); 5, *Im Wald* (Müller); 6, *Abendlied* (Kinkel); *3 Lieder* for 3 Women's Voices, op.114 (1853): 1, *Nänie* (Bechstein); 2, *Triolett* (L'Egru); 3, *Spruch* (Rückert); *4 Husarenlieder* for Baritone, op.117 (Lenau; 1851): 1, *Der Husar, trara!*; 2, *Der leidige Frieden*; 3, *Den grünen Zeigern*; 4, *Da liegt der Feinde gestreckte Schar*; *3 Gedichte*, op.119 (G. Pfarrius; 1851): 1, *Die Hütte*; 2, *Warnung*; 3, *Der Bräutigam und die Birke*; *2 Balladen*, declamations, op.122 (1852–53): 1, *Ballade vom Haideknaben* (Hebbel); 2, *Die Flüchtlinge* (Shelley); *5 heitere Gesänge*, op.125 (1850–51): 1, *Die Meerfee* (Buddeus); 2, *Husarenabzug* (C. Candidus); 3, *Jung Volkers Lied* (Mörike); 4, *Frühlingslied* (Braun); 5, *Frühlingslust* (Heyse); *5 Lieder und Gesänge*, op.127: 1, *Sängers Trost* (Kerner; 1840); 2, *Dein Angesicht* (Heine; 1840); 3, *Es leuchtet meine Liebe* (Heine; 1840); 4, *Mein altes Ross* (Moritz, Graf von Strachwitz; 1850); 5, *Schlusslied des Narren* (Shakespeare; 1840); *Frühlingsgrusse* (Lenau; 1851); *Gedichte der Königin Maria Stuart*, op.135

(1852): 1, *Abschied von Frankreich*; 2, *Nach der Geburt ihres Sohnes*; 3, *An die Königin Elisabeth*; 4, *Abschied von der Welt*; 5, *Gebet*; *Spanische Liebeslieder*, op.138 (Geibel; 1849): 1, *Vorspiel* for Piano, 4-Hands; 2, *Tief im Herzen trag ich Pein* for Soprano; 3, *O wie lieblich ist das Mädchen* for Tenor; 4, *Bedeckt mich mit Blumen* for Soprano and Alto; 5, *Flutenreicher Ebro* for Baritone; 6, *Intermezzo* for Piano, 4-Hands; 7, *Weh, wie zornig ist das Mädchen* for Tenor; 8, *Hoch, hoch sind die Berge* for Alto; 9, *Blaue Augen hat das Mädchen* for Tenor and Bass; 10, *Dunkler Lichtglanz* for Soprano, Alto, Tenor, and Bass; from *Des Sängers Fluch*, op.139 (Pohl, after Uhland; 1852): 4, *Provenzalisches Lied*; 7, *Ballade*; *4 Gesänge*, op.142 (1840): 1, *Trost im Gesang* (Kerner); 2, *Lehn deine Wang* (Heine); 3, *Mädchen-Schwermut* (Bernhard); 4, *Mein Wagen rollet langsam* (Heine); *Mailied*, duet (1851); *Liedchen von Marie und Papa*, duet (Schumann; 1852); *Glockentürmers Töchterlein* (Rückert); *Das Käuzlein* (*Des Knaben Wunderhorn*); *Deutscher Blumengarten*, duet (Rückert).

BIBL.: COLLECTED WORKS, SOURCE MATERIAL: A complete edition of his works, *R. S.: Werke*, was ed. by Clara Schumann et al. and publ. by Breitkopf & Härtel (34 vols., Leipzig, 1881–93; suppl. ed. by Brahms, 1893). His *Gesammelte Schriften über Musik und Musiker* is a collection of his articles from the *Neue Zeitschrift für Musik* (4 vols., Leipzig, 1854; Eng. tr., London, 1877; 5th Ger. ed., rev. by M. Kreisig, 1914). A judicious selection from the complete writings, ed. by H. Simon, was publ. under the same title as the original edition (3 vols., Leipzig, 1888–89). A selection of Schumann's critical reviews, tr. into Eng. by P. Rosenfeld, was publ. in N.Y. in 1946. A new critical ed. of his complete works, *R. S.: Neue Ausgabe sämmtlicher Werke*, ed. by A. Mayeda and K. Niemöller, began publ. in Mainz in 1991. See also H. Drinker, *Texts of the Vocal Works of R. S. in English Translation* (N.Y., 1947), and L. Minchin, *S. in English: Four Famous Song-Cycles in Singable English Verse* (London, 1981). A thematic catalogue was prepared by A. Dörffel, *Thematisches Verzeichniss sämmtlicher in Druck erschienenen Werke R. S.s* (Leipzig, 1860; fourth ed., 1868). See also K. Hofmann, *Die Erstdrucke der Werke von R. S.* (Tutzing, 1979). Other sources include: F. Kerst, *S.-Brevier* (Berlin, 1905); A. Schumann, ed., *Der junge S.: Dichtungen und Briefe* (Leipzig, 1910); W. Boetticher, *R. S. in seinen Schriften und Briefen* (Berlin, 1942); G. Eismann, *R. S.: Ein Quellenwerk über sein Leben und Schaffen* (2 vols., Leipzig, 1956); R. Münnich, *Aus R. S.s Briefen und Schriften* (Weimar, 1956); F. Munte, *Verzeichnis des deutschsprachigen Schrifttums über R. S. 1856–1970* (Hamburg, 1972); G. Nauhaus, *R. S.: Haushaltbücher* (2 vols., Leipzig, 1982). **CORRESPONDENCE AND DIARIES:** C. Schumann, ed., *S.s Jugendbriefe: Nach den Originalen mitgeteilt* (Leipzig, 1885; Eng. tr., London, 1888; fourth Ger. ed., 1910); F. Jansen, ed., *R. S.s Briefe: Neue Folge* (Leipzig, 1886; Eng. tr., London, 1890; second Ger. ed., aug., 1904); H. Erler, *R. S.s Leben: Aus seinen Briefen geschildert* (2 vols., Berlin, 1886–87; third ed., 1927); G. Eismann, ed., *R. S.: Tagebücher, Vol. I* (1827–38) (Leipzig, 1971); E. Weissweiler, ed., *Clara Schumann und R. S.: Briefwechsel: Kritische Gesamtausgabe* (Basel, 1984 et seq.); G. Nauhaus, *The Marriage Diaries of R. and Clara S.: From Their Wedding Through the Russian Trip* (Boston, 1993). **BIOGRAPHICAL:** W. von Wasielewski, *R. S.* (Dresden, 1858; Eng. tr., Boston, 1871; aug. Ger. ed., 1906); A. Reissmann, *R. S.: Sein Leben und seine Werke* (Berlin, 1865; third ed., 1879; Eng. tr., London, 1886); A. Niggli, *R. S.* (Basel, 1879); P. Spitta, *Ein Lebensbild R. S.s* (Leipzig, 1882); W. von Wasielewski, *S.iana* (Bonn, 1883); J. Fuller Maitland, *S.* (London, 1884; new ed., 1913); H. Reimann, *R. S.s Leben und Werke* (Leipzig, 1887); R. Batka, *S.* (Leipzig, 1893); H. Abert, *R. S.* (Berlin, 1903; third ed., 1918); A. Paterson, *S.* (London, 1903;

rev. ed., 1934); L. Schneider and M. Mareschal, *S.: Sa vie et ses oeuvres* (Paris, 1905); C. Mauclair, *S.* (Paris, 1906); P. Möbius, *Über R. S.s Krankheit* (Halle, 1906); M.D. Calvocoressi, *S.* (Paris, 1912); M. Wieck, *Aus dem Kreise Wieck-S.* (Dresden, 1912; second ed., 1914); W. Dahms, *S.* (Berlin, 1916); F. Nussbaum, *Der Streit um R. S.s Krankheit* (diss., Univ. of Cologne, 1923); F. Niecks, *R. S.: A Supplementary and Corrective Biography* (London, 1925); R. Pitrou, *La Vie intérieure de R. S.* (Paris, 1925); E. Schumann, *Erinnerungen* (Stuttgart, 1925; Eng. tr., London, 1927); V. Basch, *S.* (Paris, 1926); idem, *La Vie douloureuse de S.* (Paris, 1928; Eng. tr., N.Y., 1931); H. Tessmer, *R. S.* (Stuttgart, 1930); E. Schumann, *R. S.: Ein Lebensbild meines Vaters* (Leipzig, 1931); M. Beaufils, *S.* (Paris, 1932); C. Valabrega, *S.* (Modena, 1934); W. Gertler, *R. S.* (Leipzig, 1936); W. Korte, *R. S.* (Potsdam, 1937); E. Bücken, *R. S.* (Cologne, 1940); W. Boetticher, *R. S.: Einführung in Persönlichkeit und Werk* (Berlin, 1941); H. Kleinebreil, *Der kranke S.: Untersuchungen über Krankheit und Todesursache* (diss., Univ. of Jena, 1943); R. Schauffler, *Florestan: The Life and Work of R. S.* (N.Y., 1945); J. Chissell, *S.* (London, 1948; 5th ed., rev., 1989); R. Sutermeister, *R. S.: Sein Leben nach Briefen, Tagebüchern und Erinnerungen des Meisters und seiner Gattin* (Zürich, 1949); K. Wörner, *R. S.* (Zürich, 1949); A. Coeuroy, *R. S.* (Paris, 1950); E. Müller, *R. S.* (Olten, 1950); M. Brion, *S. et l'âme romantique* (Paris, 1954; Eng. tr. as *S. and the Romantic Age*, London, 1956); P. and W. Rehberg, *R. S.: Sein Leben und sein Werk* (Zürich, 1954); A. Boucourechliev, *S.* (Paris, 1956; new ed., 1995; Eng. tr., 1959); G. Eismann, *R. W.: Eine Biographie in Wort und Bild* (Leipzig, 1956; second ed., aug., 1964; Eng. tr., 1964); H. Moser and E. Rebling, eds., *R. S.: Aus Anlass seines 100. Todestages* (Leipzig, 1956); R. Petzold and E. Crass, *R. S.: Sein Leben in Bildern* (Leipzig, 1956); P. Young, *Tragic Muse: The Life and Works of R. S.* (London, 1957; second ed., enl., 1961); K. Laux, *R. S.* (Leipzig, 1972); T. Dowley, *S.: His Life and Times* (Tunbridge Wells, 1982); P. Sutermeister, *R. S.: Eine Biographie nach Briefen, Tagebuchern und Erinnerungen von R. und Clara S.* (Tübingen, 1982); R. Taylor, *R. S.: His Life and Work* (London, 1982); H. Köhler, *R. S.: Sein Leben und Wirken in den Leipziger Jahren* (Leipzig, 1986); U. Rauchfleisch, *R. S., Leben und Werk: Eine Psychobiographie* (Stuttgart, 1990); B. Meier, *R. S.* (Reinbek bei Hamburg, 1995); J. Daverio, *R. S.: Herald of a "New Poetic Age"* (N.Y., 1997); G. Spies, *R. S.* (Stuttgart, 1997); E. Burger, *R. S.: Eine Lebenschronik in Bildern und Dokumenten* (Mainz, 1998); W. Held, *Manches geht in Nacht verloren: Die Geschichte von Clara und R. S.* (Hamburg, 1998). **CRITICAL, ANALYTICAL:** L. Mesnard, *Un Successeur de Beethoven: Étude sur R. S.* (Paris, 1876); F. Jansen, *Die Davidsbündler: Aus R. S.s Sturm- und Drangperiode* (Leipzig, 1883); B. Vogel, *R. S.s Klaviertonpoesie* (Leipzig, 1886); M. Friedlaender, *Textrevision zu R. S.s Liedern* (Leipzig, 1887); V. Joss, *Friedrich Wieck und sein Verhältniss zu R. S.* (Dresden, 1900); M. Katz, *Die Schilderung des musikalischen Eindrucks bei S.* (Giessen, 1910); I. Hirschberg, *R. S.s Tondichtungen balladischen Charakters* (Langensalza, 1913); E. Wolff, *R. S. Lieder in ersten und späteren Fassungen* (Leipzig, 1914); O. Karsten, *Die Instrumentation R. S.s* (diss., Univ. of Vienna, 1922); F. Schnapp, *Heinrich Heine und R. S.* (Hamburg, 1924); P. Frenzel, *R. S. und Goethe* (Leipzig, 1926); G. Minotti, *Die Enträtselung des Schumannschen Sphinx-Geheimnisses* (Leipzig, 1926); J. Fuller Maitland, *S.'s Pianoforte Works* (London, 1927); M. Cohen, *Studien zur Sonataform bei R. S.* (diss., Univ. of Vienna, 1928); K. Wagner, *R. S. als Schüler und Abiturient* (Zwickau, 1928); J. Fuller Maitland, *S.'s Concerted Chamber Music* (London, 1929); M. Ninck, *S. und die Romantik in der Musik* (Heidelberg, 1929); R. Goldenberg, *Der Klaviersatz bei S.* (diss., Univ. of Vienna, 1930); H. Rosenwald, *Geschichte des deutschen Liedes zwischen Schubert und S.* (Berlin, 1930); W. Gertler, *R. S. in seinen* *früheren Klavierwerken* (Wolfenbüttel, 1931); M. Schweiger, *Die Harmonik in den Klavierwerken R. S.s* (diss., Univ. of Vienna, 1931); W. Schwarz, *S. und die Variation: Mit besonderer Berücksichtigung der Klavierwerke* (Kassel, 1932); H. Kötz, *Der Einfluss Jean Pauls auf R. S.* (Weimar, 1933); G. Wilcke, *Tonalität und Modulation im Streichquartett Mendelssohns und S.s* (Leipzig, 1933); G. Minotti, *Die Geheimdokumente der Davidsbündler* (Leipzig, 1934); P. Kehm, *Die "Neue Zeitschrift für Musik" unter S.s Redaktion: 1834–44* (diss., Univ. of Munich, 1943); I. Forger, *R. S. als Kritiker: Ein Beitrag zur Geschichte der musikalischen Kritik und zum S.-Problem* (diss., Univ. of Münster, 1948); W. Edelmann, *Über Text und Musik in R. S.s Sololieder* (diss., Univ. of Münster, 1950); G. Abraham, ed., *S.: A Symposium* (London, 1952); H. Homeyer, *Grundbegriffe der Musikanschauung R. S.s: Ihr Wesen, ihre Bedeutung und Funktion in seinem literarischen Gesamtwerk* (diss., Univ. of Münster, 1956); H. Pleasants, *The Musical World of R. S.* (N.Y., 1965); L. Plantinga, *S. As Critic* (New Haven, 1967); T. Brown, *The Aesthetics of R. S.* (N.Y., 1968); A. Gebhardt, *R. S. als Symphoniker* (Regensburg, 1968); E. Sams, *The Songs of R. S.* (London, 1969; second ed., rev., 1975); S. Walsh, *The Lieder of S.* (London, 1971); J. Chissel, *S. Piano Music* (London, 1972); A. Desmond, *S. Songs* (London, 1972); A. Walker, ed., *R. S.: The Man and His Music* (London, 1972; second ed., rev., 1976); W. Boetticher, *R. S.s Klavierwerke: Entstehung, Urtext, Gestalt: Untersuchungen anhand unveröffentlicher Skizzen und biographischer Dokumente* (Wilhelmshaven, 1976 et seq.); R. Hallmark, *The Genesis of S.'s "Dichterliebe": A Source Study* (Ann Arbor, 1979); D. Fischer-Dieskau, *R. S., Wort und Musik: Das Vokalwerk* (Stuttgart, 1981; Eng. tr., 1988, as *R. S., Words and Music: The Vocal Compositions*); G. Moore, *"Poet's Lore" and Other S. Cycles and Songs* (London, 1981); A. Gerstmeier, *Die Lieder S.s: zur Musik des frühen 19. Jahrhunderts* (Tutzing, 1982); H.-P. Fricker, *Die musikkritischen Schriften R. S.s: Versuch eines literaturwissenschaftlichen Zugangs* (Bern, 1983); J. Finson and R. Todd, eds., *Mendelssohn and S.: Essays on their Music and its Context* (Durham, N.C., 1984); R. Kapp, *Studien zum Spätwerk R. S.s* (Tutzing, 1984); F. Otto, *R. S. als Jean-Paul-Leser* (Frankfurt am Main, 1984); B. Borchard, *R. S. und Clara Wieck: Bedingungen künstlerischer Arbeit in der ersten Halfte des 19. Jahrhunderts* (Weinheim, 1985); D. Fischer-Dieskau, *R. S.: Das Vokalwerk* (Munich, 1985); B. Meissner, *Geschichtsrezeption als Schaffenskorrelat: Studien zum Musikgeschichtsbild R. S.s* (Bern, 1985); P. Ostwald, *S.: Music and Madness* (London, 1985); J. Finson, *R. S. and the Study of Orchestral Composition: The Genesis of the First Symphony* (Oxford, 1989); M. Waldura, *Monomotivik, Sequenz und Sonatenform in Werk R. S.s* (Saarbrücken, 1990); B. Appel and I. Hermsträwer, eds., *R. S. und die Dichter* (Düsseldorf, 1991); N. Marston, *S.: Fantasie, op.17* (Cambridge, 1992); A. Mayeda, *R. S.s Weg zur Symphonie* (Zürich, 1992); M. Gleiss, ed., *R. S.s letzte Lebensjahre: Protokoll einer Krankheit* (Berlin, 1994); D. Hoffmann-Axthelm, *R. S.: "Glücklichsein und tiefe Einsamkeit": Eine Essay* (Stuttgart, 1994); R. Todd, *S. and His World* (Princeton, 1994); K. Leven-Keesen, *R. S.s "Szenen aus Goethes Faust" (Wo0): Studien zu Frühfassungen anhand des Autographs Wiede 11/3* (Berlin, 1996); C. Westphal, *R. S.: Liederkreis von H. Heine, op.24* (Munich, 1996); A. Herrmann, *R. S. als Pädagoge in seiner Zeit* (Berlin, 1997); W. Frobenius et al., eds., *R. S.: Philologische, analytische, sozial- und rezeptionsgeschichtliche Aspekte* (Saarbrücken, 1998); L. Hotaki, *R. S.s Mottosammlung: Übertragung, Kommentar, Einführung* (Freiburg in Breisgau, 1998).—NS/LK/DM

Schumann-Heink, Ernestine (née **Rössler**), famous Austrian-born American contralto and mezzo-soprano; b. Lieben, near Prague, June 15, 1861; d. Los Angeles, Nov. 17, 1936. Her father was an officer in the Austrian army; her mother, an Italian amateur singer. In 1872 she was sent to the Ursuline Convent in Prague, where she sang in the church choir; after lessons from Marietta von Leclair in Graz, she made her first public appearance there as soloist in Beethoven's 9th Sym. (1876); made her operatic debut at the Dresden Court Opera (Oct. 15, 1878) as Azucena, where she sang until 1882; also continued her studies with Karl Krebs, Franz Wüllner, and others. From 1883 to 1897 she was a member of the Hamburg Opera; appeared with the company on its visit to London's Covent Garden in 1892, where she sang Erda, Fricka, and Brangäne. She was a regular singer at the Bayreuth Festivals from 1896 to 1914; appeared at Covent Garden (1897–1901); also sang with the Berlin Royal Opera. She made her U.S. debut as Ortrud in Chicago on Nov. 7, 1898, a role she chose for her Metropolitan Opera debut in N.Y. on Jan. 9, 1899; canceled her contract with the Berlin Royal Opera in order to remain a member of the Metropolitan Opera (until 1903; then appeared intermittently until 1932); created the role of Clytemnestra in *Elektra* (Dresden, Jan. 25, 1909); made her last operatic appearance as Erda at the Metropolitan on March 11, 1932. She became a naturalized American citizen in 1908. During the last years of her life, she was active mainly as a teacher. Her operatic repertoire included about 150 parts; her voice, of an even quality in all registers, possessed great power, making it peculiarly suitable to Wagnerian roles. She was married in 1882 to Ernst Heink of Dresden, from whom she was later divorced; in 1893 she married the actor Paul Schumann in Hamburg; he died in 1904; she assumed the names of both Schumann and Heink. Her third husband was a Chicago lawyer, William Rapp Jr., whom she married in 1905 and then subsequently divorced (1914).

BIBL.: M. Lawton, *S.-H., The Last of the Titans* (N.Y., 1928); J. Howard, *Madame E. S.-H.: Her Life and Times* (Sebastopol, Calif., 1990).—NS/LK/DM

Schünemann, Georg, eminent German musicologist and music educator; b. Berlin, March 13, 1884; d. there (suicide), Jan. 2, 1945. He studied at the Stern Cons. in Berlin; played flute in various orchs. in Berlin, then took courses in musicology with Kretzschmar, Friedlaender, Wolf, and others at the Univ. of Berlin; also studied German literature and philosophy there, receiving his Ph.D. in 1907 with the diss. *Geschichte des Dirigierens* (publ. in Leipzig, 1913). In 1919 he joined the faculty of the Univ. of Berlin. He was appointed deputy director of the Berlin Hochschule für Musik in 1920, and director in 1932; later held the post of director of the State Musical Instrument Collections. In 1935 he was appointed director of the music division of the Prussian State Library. He took his own life during the darkest stages of World War II.

WRITINGS: *Das Lied der deutschen Kolonisten in Russland* (Berlin, 1923); *Die Musica des Listhenius* (Berlin, 1927); *Geschichte der deutschen Schulmusik* (Leipzig, 1928; second ed., 1931); *Die Musikerziehung*, I: *Die Musik in Kindheit und Jugend, Schule und Volk* (Leipzig, 1930); *C.F. Zelter, der Begründer der preussischen Musikpflege* (Berlin, 1932); *Führer durch die deutsche Chorliteratur* (2 vols., Wolfenbüttel, 1935–36); ed. *Musiker-Handschriften von*

Bach bis Schumann (facsimile ed., Berlin, 1936; rev. and publ. in an Eng. tr. by W. Gerstenberg and M. Hürimann, 1968); *C.F. Zelter, Der Mensch und sein Werk* (Berlin, 1937); *Die Violine* (Hamburg, 1940); *Geschichte der Klaviermusik* (Hamburg, 1940; second ed., rev. by H. Gerigk, 1953; third ed., 1956); *Die Singakademie zu Berlin* (Regensburg, 1941); ed. *Ludwig van Beethovens Konversationshefte* (not complete; 3 vols., Berlin, 1941–43).—**NS/LK/DM**

Schunk, Robert, German tenor; b. Neu-Isenburg, Jan. 5, 1948. He was a pupil of Martin Grundler at the Frankfurt Hochschule für Musik. In 1973 he made his operatic debut as Jack in *The Midsummer Marriage* in Karlsruhe, where he sang until 1975; then appeared in Bonn (1975–77), Dortmund (1977–79), and at the Bayreuth Festivals (from 1977), where he was heard as Siegmund, Melot, Erik, and Walther in *Tannhäuser*. As a guest artist, he appeared in operas in Hamburg, Munich, Vienna, Cologne, Berlin, Geneva, Chicago, and San Francisco. He made his debut at the Metropolitan Opera in N.Y. as Florestan on Dec. 10, 1986. In 1987 he sang for the first time at London's Covent Garden as the Emperor in *Die Frau ohne Schatten*. His other roles include Don Carlos, Weber's Max, Hoffmann, Walther von Stolzing, and Parsifal.—**NS/LK/DM**

Schunke, Karl, German pianist, teacher, and composer, cousin of **Ludwig Schunke;** b. Magdeburg, 1801; d. (suicide) Paris, Dec. 16, 1839. He studied music with his father, the horn player Michael Schunke (1778–1821), then took some lessons with Ferdinand Ries, whom he accompanied to London. In 1828 he went to Paris, where he became a fashionable piano teacher; nevertheless, he suffered from some sort of malaise and killed himself. He composed a number of brilliant salon pieces a la mode and transcriptions of operatic arias for piano. —**NS/LK/DM**

Schunke, Ludwig, German pianist and composer, cousin of **Karl Schunke;** b. Kassel, Dec. 21, 1810; d. Leipzig, Dec. 7, 1834. He studied with his father, Gottfried Schunke (1777–1861), who was a horn player, then went to Paris, where he studied piano with Kalkbrenner and Reicha. He settled in Leipzig in 1833 and became a close friend of Schumann, of whom he was an exact contemporary, and with whom he became associated in founding the *Neue Zeitschrift für Musik*. His early death was greatly mourned, for his piano pieces were full of promise; among them were a Sonata, a set of variations, 2 *Caprices*, and a set of *Charakterstücke*. Schumann wrote a heartfelt appreciation of Schunke's talent, which was reprinted in his *Gesammelte Schriften*.—**NS/LK/DM**

Schuppanzigh, Ignaz, esteemed Austrian violinist; b. Vienna, Nov. 20, 1776; d. there, March 2, 1830. After learning to play the viola, he took up the violin about 1793. He became first violinist in a string quartet with Kraft, Sina, and Weiss that appeared weekly at Prince Lichnowsky's residence; among the prince's guests was Beethoven, who befriended Schuppanzigh. In 1795 he became concertmaster of the Augarten orch. concerts, and about 1798, manager. During the 1804–05 season, he organized with Kraft, Mayseder, and Schreiber his own string quartet, which gave subscription concerts. In 1808 he founded the private string quartet of Count Razumovsky with Linke and Weiss; when the count did not play, Sina took his place as second violinist. After a fire destroyed Razumovsky's palace in 1814, the quartet was dissolved. In 1816 Schuppanzigh went to St. Petersburg, where he proved a determined champion of the music of Beethoven. In 1823 he returned to Vienna and became a member of the court chapel and later director of the Court Opera; also continued to be active as a quartet player. In addition to playing in premieres of works by Beethoven, he also played in premieres of works by Schubert. Although his friendship with Beethoven was frequently tested by Beethoven's moods, Schuppanzigh never wavered in his respect. He also composed, his works including a *Solo brillant* for Violin and String Quartet, solo variations on a Russian theme, and 9 variations for 2 Violins. —**NS/LK/DM**

Schürer, Johann Georg, prominent German composer; b. probably in Raudnitz, Bohemia, c. 1720; d. Dresden, Feb. 16, 1786. He settled in Dresden about 1746, where he first gained notice as composer and music director of an opera troupe at the Zwinger; in 1748 he was made Kirchencompositeur to the court, a position he held with distinction until his retirement in 1780. His mastery of contrapuntal writing is revealed in his numerous sacred compositions, which include the oratorios *Il Figliuol Prodigo* (1747), *Isacco figura del Redentore* (1748), and *La Passione di Jesu Christo* (n.d.), and various masses and Psalms. He also wrote the operas *Astrea placata ovvero La felicità della terra* (Warsaw, Oct. 7, 1746), *La Galatea* (Dresden, Nov. 8, 1746), *L'Ercole sul Termodonte* (Dresden, Jan. 9, 1747), *Doris* (Dresden, Feb. 13, 1747), and *Calandro* (Dresden, Jan. 20, 1748), and 7 cantatas.

BIBL.: R. Haas, *J.G. S. (1720–1786): Ein Beitrag zur Geschichte der Musik in Dresden* (Dresden, 1915).—**NS/LK/DM**

Schuricht, Carl, distinguished German conductor; b. Danzig, July 3, 1880; d. Corseaux-sur-Vevey, Switzerland, Jan. 7, 1967. He studied at home, his father being an organ manufacturer and his mother a pianist. He then took lessons with Humperdinck at the Hochschule für Musik in Berlin, and later in Leipzig with Reger. He began his career conducting in various provincial theaters. In 1911 he became music director in Wiesbaden, and in 1942 principal guest conductor of the Dresden Phil. He made numerous guest conducting appearances in various European music centers, and also conducted in the U.S. for the first time in 1927. After falling out of favor with the Nazis in 1944, he fled to Switzerland, which remained his home until his death. In 1946 he reopened the Salzburg Festival; continued to conduct there and in France. In 1956 he took the Vienna Phil. on its first U.S. tour, sharing his duties with André Cluytens. In 1957 he conducted at the Ravinia Festival with the Chicago Sym. Orch. and at the Tanglewood Festival with the Boston Sym. Orch.; in subsequent years, he regularly conducted the Berlin and Vienna

Phils.; also was a frequent guest conductor of the Stuttgart Radio Sym. Orch. He also composed, wrote orch. music, piano pieces, and songs. As a conductor, Schuricht was one of the last representatives of the Austro-German tradition. After concentrating on contemporary music in his early years, he turned to the great masterworks of the Austro-German repertory, his interpretations being noted for their freedom and beauty of expression.

BIBL.: B. Gavoty, *C. S.* (Geneva, 1955).—NS/LK/DM

Schurmann (Schürmann), (Eduard) Gerard,

pianist, conductor, and composer of Dutch and Hungarian descent; b. Kertosono, Dutch East Indies, Jan. 19, 1924. His father was an employee at a sugar factory in Java, and his mother was a pianist who had studied with Bartók at the Budapest Academy of Music. As war clouds gathered over Southeastern Asia, Schurmann was sent to England in 1937; he went to school in London, and after matriculation joined the Royal Air Force, serving in aircrews on active flying duty. While still in uniform, he gave piano recitals; studied piano with Kathleen Long and composition with Alan Rawsthorne. During his travels in Italy, he took lessons in conducting with Ferrara. The government of the Netherlands offered him the position of cultural attaché at the Dutch Embassy in London; being fluent in the Dutch language, which was his mother tongue in the Dutch East Indies, he accepted. Later, he moved to the Netherlands, where he was active with the radio in Hilversum. He developed a successful career in London as a pianist, conductor, and composer. In 1981 he settled in Hollywood, where he became active as a film composer; also traveled widely as a guest conductor, presenting a comprehensive repertory ranging from Haydn to contemporary composers, including his own works. The structure of Schurmann's music is asymptotic toward tonality; melodic progressions are linear, with the fundamental tonic and dominant often encasing the freely atonal configurations, while dodecaphony assumes the adumbrative decaphonic lines, with 2 notes missing in the tone row. The harmonic texture is acrid, acerbic, and astringent; the styptic tendency is revealed in his predilection for dissonant minor seconds and major sevenths treated as compound units; yet after the needed tension is achieved, the triadic forms are introduced as a sonic emollient. Thanks to this versatility of application, Schurmann achieves a natural felicity in dealing with exotic subjects; his proximity to gamelan-like pentatonicism during his adolescence lends authentic flavor to his use of pentatonic scales; remarkable in his congenial treatment is the set *Chuench'i*, to Eng. trs. of 7 Chinese poems. On the other hand, his intimate knowledge of Eng. music and history enables him to impart a true archaic sentiment to his opera-cantata based on the medieval poem *Piers Plowman*. Schurmann is self-critical in regard to works of his that he deems imperfect; thus, he destroyed his Piano Concerto, which he had played under prestigious auspices with the London Sym. Orch. conducted by Sir Adrian Boult in Cambridge in April 1944.

WORKS: DRAMATIC: Opera: *Piers Plowman*, opera-cantata after William Langland (Gloucester Cathedral,

Aug. 22, 1980). **ORCH.:** *6 Studies of Francis Bacon*, comprising *Figures in a Landscape, Popes, Isabel, Crucifixion, George and the Bicycle*, and *Self-Portrait* (1968; Dublin, Jan. 7, 1969); *Variants* (1970; Guildford, March 8, 1971); *Attack and Celebration* (1971); Piano Concerto (1972–73; Portsmouth, Nov. 21, 1973); Violin Concerto (1975–78; Liverpool, Sept. 26, 1978); *The Garden of Exile*, cello concerto (1989–90). **CHAMBER:** Violin Sonata (1943); 2 string quartets (1943, 1946); *Duo* for 2 Violins (1950); Wind Quintet (1964; rev. 1976); *Fantasia* (1968); Flute Sonatina (1968); *Serenade* for Violin (1969); *Duo* for Violin and Piano (1984); Quartet for Piano and Strings (1986). **P i a n o :** Sonata (1943); *Rotterdam*, suite for 2 Pianos (1944); *Bagatelles* (1945); *Contrasts* (1973); *Leotaurus* (1975); *2 Ballades* (1981–83). **VOCAL:** *Pacific*, 3 songs (1943); *5 Facets* (London, Jan. 20, 1946, Peter Pears tenor, Benjamin Britten pianist); *9 poems of William Blake* (1956); *Chuench'i*, cycle of 7 songs from the Chinese for Voice and Orch. (1966; Harrogate, Aug. 10, 1969); *Summer Is Coming*, madrigal (1970); *The Double Heart*, cantata for Voices (1976); *9 Slovak Folk Songs* for High Voice and Piano or Orch. (1988).—NS/LK/DM

Schürmann, Georg Caspar,

eminent German composer; b. Idensen, near Hannover, 1672 or 1673; d. Wolfenbüttel, Feb. 25, 1751. He went to Hamburg, where he became a male alto at the Opera and in various churches when he was 20; after appearing with the Hamburg Opera at the Braunschweig court of Duke Anton Ulrich of Braunschweig-Lüneburg in 1697, the duke engaged him as solo alto to the court; was also active as a conductor at the Opera and at the court church. After the duke sent him to Italy for further training (1701–2?), he was loaned to the Meiningen court as Kapellmeister and composer; in 1707 he resumed his association with the Braunschweig-Wolfenbüttel court, where he was active as a composer and conductor for the remainder of his life. Schurmann was a leading opera composer during the Baroque era. He wrote over 40 operas, only 3 of which survived in their entirety after their Braunschweig premieres: *Heinrich der Vogler* (part I, Aug. 1, 1718; part II, Jan. 11, 1721), *Die getreue Alceste* (1719), and *Ludovicus Pius, oder Ludewig der Fromme* (1726). He was also a noted composer of sacred music.

BIBL.: G. Schmid, *Die frühdeutsche Oper und die musikdramatische Kunst G.C. S.s* (2 vols., Regensburg, 1933–34). —NS/LK/DM

Schuster, Joseph,

distinguished German conductor and composer; b. Dresden, Aug. 11, 1748; d. there, July 24, 1812. After initial training with his father, a Dresden court musician, and J.G. Schürer, he pursued studies on a scholarship in Italy with Girolamo Pera (1765–68). After serving as a church composer in Dresden (1772–74), he returned to Italy and completed his studies with Padre Martini in Bologna; wrote operas for Venice and Naples, and was named honorary maestro di cappella to the King of Naples. Settling in Dresden in 1781, he was active as a conductor at the court church and theater; with Seydelmann, he shared the duties of Kapellmeister to the elector from 1787. Schuster assumed a leading position at the Dresden court, both as a conductor and as a composer. Of his some 20 works for the stage, the Singspiel *Der Alchymist oder Der*

Liebesteufel (Dresden, March 1778) won great popularity in Germany. He was an admired composer of orch. works, sacred music, chamber music, and pieces for the fortepiano. His Padua String Quartet in C major (1780) was formerly attributed to Mozart.—**NS/LK/DM**

Schütz, Gabriel, German violist, cornet player, teacher, and composer; b. Lübeck, Feb. 1, 1633; d. Nuremberg, Aug. 9, 1710. He was a student of Nicolaus Bleyer in Lübeck. In 1656 he went to Nuremberg, where he won distinction as an instrumentalist and teacher. In 1658 he was made a probationary and in 1666 a permanent town musician. He composed various pieces for gamba.—**LK/DM**

Schütz, Heinrich (also **Henrich**), great German composer; b. Köstritz, Oct. 8, 1585; d. Dresden, Nov. 6, 1672. He was born into a prosperous family of innkeepers; in 1590 the family settled in Weissenfels, where his father became burgomaster. He was trained in music by Heinrich Colander, the town organist. In 1599 he became a choirboy in the court chapel of Landgrave Moritz of Hessen-Kassel; in Kassel he pursued his academic studies with Georg Otto, the court Kapellmeister. On Sept. 27, 1608, he entered the Univ. of Marburg to study law; an opportunity to continue his musical education came in 1609 when Landgrave Moritz offered to send him to Venice to take lessons with Giovanni Gabrieli. Under Gabrieli's tutelage, he received a thorough training in composition, and he also learned to play the organ. In 1611 he brought out a book of 5-voice madrigals, which he dedicated to his benefactor, Landgrave Moritz. After Gabrieli's death in 1612 Schütz returned to Kassel, serving as second organist at the court chapel. In 1615 the Elector invited him to Dresden as Saxon Kapellmeister; Praetorius was also active at the Dresden court for special occasions at this time. In 1616 Landgrave Moritz asked the Elector to allow Schütz to return to Kassel, but the Elector declined; in 1617 Schütz assumed fully his duties as Saxon Kapellmeister, being granted an annual salary of 400 florins from 1618. In addition to providing music for court occasions, he was responsible for overseeing the functions of the court chapel. In 1619 he publ. his first collection of sacred music, the *Psalmen Davids sampt etlichen Moteten und Concerten*. On June 1, 1619, he married Magdalena Wildeck, the daughter of a court official in Dresden. They had 2 daughters. His wife died on Sept. 6, 1625, and Schütz remained a widower for the rest of his life. During a court visit to Torgau, Schütz composed the first German opera, *Dafne*, set to Opitz's translation and adaptation of Rinuccini's libretto for Peri's opera; it was presented at Hartenfels Castle on April 13, 1627, to celebrate the wedding of the Princess Sophia Eleonora of Saxony to Landgrave Georg II of Hesse-Darmstadt. In 1628 he was granted a leave of absence, and went to Italy. There he had an occasion to study the new operatic style of Monteverdi; he adopted this new style in his *Symphoniae sacrae* (publ. in Venice, 1629). He returned to his post in Dresden in 1629. When Saxony entered the Thirty Years' War in 1631, conditions at the Dresden court chapel became difficult. In 1633 Schütz accepted an invitation to go to Copenhagen,

where he obtained the post of Kapellmeister to King Christian IV. In June 1634 he returned to Dresden. His *Musicalische Exequien*, composed for the interment of Prince Heinrich Posthumus, appeared in 1636. He also publ. 2 vols. of *Kleine geistliche Concerte* (1636 and 1639). He composed the music for the opera-ballet *Orpheus und Euridice*, which was performed in Dresden on Nov. 20, 1638, to celebrate the marriage of Prince Johann Georg of Saxony and Princess Magdalena Sybilla of Brandenburg. In late 1639 Schütz obtained another leave of absence to serve as Kapellmeister to Georg of Calenberg, who resided in Hildesheim. After a year's stay in Dresden, in 1641–42, he set out once more for Copenhagen, where he again served as Kapellmeister, until April 1644. Returning to Germany, he lived mostly in Braunschweig (1644–45), and was active at the court of nearby Wolfenbüttel. In 1645 he returned to Dresden; the Elector declined his request for retirement but did allow him to live a part of each year in Weissenfels. Schütz continued to compose industriously during these years. The second book of his *Symphoniae sacrae* appeared in 1647, followed by his *Geistliche Chor-Music* in 1648. In succeeding years, Schütz repeatedly asked to be pensioned, but his requests were ignored. Finally, when Johann Georg II became Elector in 1657, Schütz was allowed to retire on a pension with the title of Chief Kapellmeister. His Passions *St. Luke*, *St. John*, and *St. Matthew* all date from these last years, as does his *Christmas Oratorio*. About 1670 he returned to Dresden to settle his affairs and await his end, which came peacefully in 1672, in his 87th year.

The importance of Schütz in music history resides in his astute adaptation of the new Italian styles to German music. He was extraordinarily productive, but not all of his works survived; the majority of his extant compositions are vocal works of a sacred nature. The most important collection of Schütz's MSS is housed in the Hessische Landesbibliothek in Kassel. The first major edition of his works, edited by Philipp Spitta, was publ. by Breitkopf & Härtel (16 vols., Leipzig, 1885–94; suppl. vols. were publ. in 1909 and 1927). A second edition of his works, *Neuen Schütz-Gesellschaft*, began to appear in 1955 in Kassel. A third ed., *Stuttgarter Schütz-Ausgabe*, began publication in 1971. A catalogue of his works, ed. by W. Bittinger, is found in his *Schütz-Werke-Verzeichnis (SWV): Kleine Ausgabe* (Kassel, 1960).

WORKS: *Il primo libro de madrigali* (Venice, 1611); *Die Wort Jesus Syrach...auff hochzeitlichen Ehrentag des...Herrn Josephi Avenarii* (perf. in Dresden, April 21, 1618; publ. in Dresden, 1618); *Concert mit 11 Stimmen: Auff des...Herrn Michael Thomae-...hochzeitlichen Ehren Tag* (perf. in Leipzig, June 15, 1618; publ. in Dresden, 1618); *Psalmen Davids sampt etlichen Moteten und Concerten* (Dresden, 1619); *Der 133. Psalm...auff die hochzeitliche Ehrenfrewde Herrn Georgii Schützen* (perf. in Leipzig, Aug. 9, 1619; publ. in Leipzig, 1619; not extant); *Syncharma musicum* (perf. in Breslau, Nov. 3, 1621; publ. in Breslau, 1621; not extant); *Historia der frölichen und siegreichen Aufferstehung unsers einigen Erlösers und Seligmachers Jesu Christi* (Dresden, 1623); *Kläglicher Abschied von der churfürstlichen Grufft zu Freybergk* (perf. in Freiberg, Jan. 28, 1623; publ. in Freiberg, 1623); *Cantiones sacrae* (Freiberg, 1625); *De vitae fugacitate: Aria...bey Occasion des...Todesfalles der...Jungfrawen Anna Marien Wildeckin* (perf. in Dresden, Aug. 15, 1625; publ. in Freiberg, 1625); *Ultima* verba psalmi 23...super...obitu...Jacobi Schultes (perf. in Leipzig, July 19, 1625; publ. in Leipzig, 1625); *Psalmen Davids, hiebevorn in teutzsche Reimen gebracht, durch D. Cornelium Beckern, und an jetzo mit ein hundert und drey eigenen Melodeyen...gestellet* (Freiberg, 1628; second ed., 1640; third ed., rev. and enl., Dresden, 1661); *Symphoniae sacrae* (Venice, 1629); *Verba D. Pauli...beatis manibus Dn. Johannis-Hermanni Scheinii...consecrata* (perf. in Leipzig, Nov. 19, 1630; publ. in Dresden, 1631; not extant); *An hoch printzlicher Durchläuchtigkeit zu Dennenmarck-...Beylager: Gesang der Venus-Kinder in der Invention genennet Thronus Veneris* (perf. in Copenhagen, Oct. 1634; publ. in Copenhagen, 1634); *Musicalische Exequien...dess...Herrn Heinrichen dess Jüngern und Eltisten Reussen* (perf. in Gera, Feb. 4, 1636; publ. in Dresden, 1636; not extant); *Erster Theil kleiner geistlichen Concerten* (Leipzig, 1636); *Anderer Theil kleiner geistlichen Concerten* (Dresden, 1639); *Symphoniarum sacrarum secunda pars* (Dresden, 1647); *Danck-Lied: Für die hocherwiesene fürstl. Gnade in Weymar* (perf. in Weimar, Feb. 12, 1647; publ. in Gotha, 1647); *Musicalia ad chorum sacrum, das ist: Geistliche Chor-Music...erster Theil* (Dresden, 1648); *Symphoniarum sacrarum tertia pars* (Dresden, 1650); *Zwölff geistliche Gesänge* (Dresden, 1657); *Canticum B. Simeonis...nach dem hochseligsten Hintritt...Johann Georgen* (perf. in Dresden, Oct. 8, 1657; publ. in Dresden, 1657); *Historia, der freuden- und gnadenreichen Geburth Gottes und Marien Sohnes, Jesu Christi* (Dresden, 1664; includes the Christmas Oratorio, which was lost until discovered by Schering, 1908); *Die sieben Wortte unsers lieben Erlösers und Seeligmachers Jesu Christi* (date not determined); *Historia des Leidens und Sterbens unsers Herrn und Heylandes Jesu Christi nach dem Evangelisten S. Matheum* (perf. in Dresden, April 1, 1666); *Historia des Leidens und Sterbens...Jesu Christi nach dem Evangelisten St. Lucam* (perf. in Dresden, April 8, 1666); *Historia des Leidens und Sterbens...Jesu Christi nach dem Evangelisten St. Johannem* (perf. in Dresden, April 13, 1666); *Königs und Propheten Davids hundert und neunzehender Psalm...nebenst dem Anhange des 100. Psalms...und eines deutschen Magnificats* (Dresden, 1671).

BIBL.: *H. S.: Autobiographie (Memorial 1651)* (facsimile ed., Leipzig, 1972); M. Geier, *Kurtze Beschreibung des...Herrn H. S.ens...Lebens-Lauff* (Dresden, 1672; reprint, 1935); J. Mattheson, *Grundlage einer Ehren-Pforte...* (Hamburg, 1740; new ed. by M. Schneider, Berlin, 1910); M. Fürstenau, *Beiträge zur Geschichte der königlich sächsischen musikalischen Kapelle* (Dresden, 1849); ibid., *Zur Geschichte der Musik und des Theaters am Hofe zu Dresden* (Vol. I, Dresden, 1861); F. Spitta, *Die Passionen nach den vier Evangelisten von H. S.* (Leipzig, 1886); P. Spitta, *Die Passionsmusiken von Sebastian Bach und H. S.* (Hamburg, 1893); A. Pirro, *S.* (Paris, 1913; second ed., 1924); E. Müller von Asow, *H. S.: Leben und Werke* (Berlin and Dresden, 1922); J. Müller-Blattau, ed., *Die Kompositionslehre H. S.ens in der Fassung seines Schülers Christoph Bernhard* (Leipzig, 1926; second ed., 1963); H. Spitta, *H. S.' Orchester- und unveröffentlichte Werke* (diss., Univ. of Göttingen, 1927); W. Schuh, *Formprobleme bei H. S.* (Leipzig, 1928); R. Gerber, *Das Passionsrezitativ bei H. S. und seine stilgeschichtlichen Grundlagen* (Gütersloh, 1929); E. Müller von Asow, ed., *H. S.: Gesammelte Briefe und Schriften* (Regensburg, 1931); A. Heller, *Der Deutsche H. S. in seinen italienischen Madrigalen* (diss., Univ. of Prague, 1934); W. Kreidler, *H. S. und der Stile concitato von Claudio Monteverdi* (Kassel, 1934); A. Abert, *Die stilistischen Voraussetzungen der "Cantiones sacrae" von H. S.* (Wolfenbüttel and Berlin, 1935); K. Gudewill, *Das sprachliche Urbild bei H. S.* (Kassel, 1936); H. Moser, *H. S.: Sein Leben und Werk* (Kassel, 1936; second ed., rev., 1954; Eng. tr. as *H. S.: His Life and Work* by C. Pfatteicher, St. Louis, 1959); L. Reitter, *Doppelchortechnik bei H. S.* (Derendingen, 1937); H. Hoffmann, *H. S. und Johann Sebastian Bach: Zwei Tonsprachen und ihre Bedeutung für die Aufführungspraxis* (Kassel, 1940); H. Moser, *Kleines H.-S.-Buch* (Kassel, 1940; third ed., 1952; Eng. tr., 1967); C. Roskowski, *Die "Kleinen geistlichen Konzerte" von H. S.* (diss., Univ. of Münster, 1947); J. Piersig, *Das Weltbild des H. S.* (Kassel, 1949); G. Toussaint, *Die Anwendung der musikalisch-rhetorischen Figuren in den Werken von H. S.* (diss., Univ. of Mainz, 1949); G. Weizsäcker, *H. S.: Lobgesang eines Lebens* (Stuttgart, 1952; second ed., 1956); C. Agey, *A Study of the "Kleine geistliche Konzerte" and "Geistliche Chormusik" of H. S.* (diss., Fla. State Univ., 1955); J. Heinrich, *Stilkritische Untersuchungen zur "Geistlichen Chormusik" von H. S.* (diss., Univ. of Göttingen, 1956); H. Eggebrecht, *H. S.: Musicus poeticus* (Göttingen, 1959); G. Kirchner, *Der Generalbass bei H. S.* (Kassel, 1960); W. Haacke, *H. S.: Eine Schilderung seines Lebens und Wirkens* (Königstein, 1960); W. Huber, *Motivsymbolik bei H. S.* (Basel, 1961); L. Schrade, *Das musikalische Werk von H. S. in der protestantischen Liturgie* (Basel, 1961); H. Wichmann-Zemke, *Untersuchungen zur Harmonik in den Werken von H. S.* (diss., Univ. of Kiel, 1967); R. Tellart, *H. S.: L'Homme et son oeuvre* (Paris, 1968); H. Drude, *H. S. als Musiker der evangelischen Kirche* (diss., Univ. of Göttingen, 1969); H. Eggebrecht, *S. und Gottesdienst: Versuch über das Selbstverständliche* (Stuttgart, 1969); O. Brodde, *H. S.: Weg und Werk* (Kassel, 1972); R. Petzoldt and D. Berke, *H. S. und seine Zeit in Bildern* (Kassel, 1972); W. Siegmund-Schultze, ed., *H. S. 1585–1672: Festtage 1972* (Gera, 1972); R. Grunow, ed., *Begegnungen mit H. S.: Erzählungen über Leben und Werk* (Berlin, 1974); A. Skei, *H. S.: A Guide to Research* (N.Y. and London, 1981); M. Gregor-Dellin, *H. S.: Sein Leben, sein Werk, seine Zeit* (Munich, 1984); H. Krause-Graumnitz, *H. S.: Ein Leben im Wert und in den Dokumenten seiner Zeit* (Leipzig, 1985); B. Smallman, *The Music of H. S.* (Leeds, 1985); D. Miller and A. Highsmith, eds., *H. S.: A Bibliography of the Collected Works and Performing Editions* (N.Y., 1986); G. Spagnoli, ed., *The Letters and Documents of H. S., 1656–1672: An Annotated Translation* (Ann Arbor, 1990); I. Bossuyt, *H. S. (1585–1672) en de historia* (Leuven, 1991); M. Heinemann, *H. S. und seine Zeit* (Laaber, 1993); idem, *H. S.* (Reinbek bei Hamburg, 1994).—NS/LK/DM

Schützendorf, family of German musicians, all brothers:

(1) Guido Schützendorf, bass; b. Vught, near 's-Hertogenbosch, the Netherlands, April 22, 1880; d. in Germany, April 1967. He studied at the Cologne Cons. He sang with the German Opera Co., with which he toured the U.S. (1929–30); also sang under the name **Schützendorf an der Mayr.**

(2) Alfons Schützendorf, bass-baritone; b. Vught, May 25, 1882; d. Weimar, Aug. 1946. He studied in Cologne and with Borgatti in Milan. He sang at the Bayreuth Festivals (1910–12) and at London's Covent Garden (1910); taught at the Essen Folkwangschule (1927–31) and in Berlin (from 1932). He was esteemed for such roles as Wotan, Klingsor, and Telramund.

(3) Gustav Schützendorf, baritone; b. Cologne, 1883; d. Berlin, April 27, 1937. He studied at the Cologne Cons. and in Milan. He made his operatic debut as Don Giovanni in Düsseldorf (1905); after singing in Berlin, Wiesbaden, and Basel, he was a member of the Bavarian Court Opera (later State Opera) in Munich (1914–20) and the Berlin State Opera (1920–22); made his Metropolitan Opera debut in N.Y. as Faninal on Nov. 17, 1922, and remained on its roster until 1935. He married **Grete**

Stückgold in 1929.

(4) Leo Schützendorf, bass-baritone; b. Cologne, May 7, 1886; d. Berlin, Dec. 31, 1931. He studied with D'Arnals in Cologne. He made his operatic debut in Düsseldorf (1908); sang in Krefeld (1909–12), Darmstadt (1913–17), Wiesbaden (1917–19), and Vienna (1919–20) and at the Berlin State Opera (1920–29), where he created the role of Wozzeck (Dec. 14, 1925); among his other roles were Faninal, Beckmesser, and Boris Godunov.—**NS/LK/DM**

Schuur, Diane, jazz/pop/blues pianist and vocalist; b. Seattle, Wash., 1953. A self-professed disciple of Dinah Washington, Diane Schuur has spent the past several years veering from Brazilian to adult-contemporary pop to blues in hopes of escaping the daunting "next Ella" pigeonhole that set her up for unfair and unrealistic expectations. Blinded after birth in a hospital accident, Schuur got her big break in 1979 when she was invited to sing with Dizzy Gillespie at the Monterey Jazz Festival. She became one of the first acts signed to Dave Grusin and Larry Rosen's GRP label in 1984 after they spotted her singing with Stan Getz on a PBS-televised White House concert. Her Grammy-winning 1987 collaboration with The Count Basie Orchestra showcased the roof-raising power of her voice and endeared her to the burgeoning audience of new jazz listeners enticed by the sonic clout of the then-fledgling compact disc. But conquering the contemporary jazz market so early in her career left Schuur searching for material to challenge her formidable vocal skills. In recent years she's done numerous conceptual jazz-vocal projects, but hasn't been able to rekindle the gospel and R&B roots she celebrated on 1988's underrated *Talkin' 'Bout You*

DISC.: *Deedles* (1984); *Schuur Thing* (1985); *Timeless* (1986); *Diane Schuur and the Count Basie Orchestra* (1987); *Talkin' 'Bout You* (1988); *Pure Schuur* (1991); *In Tribute* (1992); *Love Songs* (1993); *Heart to Heart* (with B. B. King; 1994); *Love Walked In* (1996); *Blues for Schuur* (1997); *Music Is My Life* (1999); *Friends for Schuur* (2000).—**DO**

Schuyler, Philippa Duke, black American pianist and composer; b. N.Y., Aug. 2, 1931; d. in a helicopter crash in Da Nang Bay, Vietnam, May 9, 1967. By the age of 12, she had written the whimsical *Cockroach Ballet* for Piano and had become the youngest member of ASCAP; at the age of 14, she appeared as piano soloist with the N.Y. Phil. at Lewisohn Stadium in a program that included the scherzo from her "fairy-tale symphony," *Rumpelstiltskin* (July 13, 1946); made her Town Hall debut in N.Y. on May 12, 1953. She traveled to Africa, Europe, South America, and Asia under the auspices of the State Dept., playing command performances for such leaders as Emperor Haile Selassie of Ethiopia and the Queen of Malaya. A product of miscegenation (her mother was from a wealthy white Tex. family; her father, George Schuyler, was the black novelist and newspaper ed.), she was a founder of the Amerasian Foundation to aid children fathered by American soldiers in Vietnam. Most of her more than 60 compositions were for solo piano, many with humorous

titles, some inspired by her travels; few were publ. Her last completed composition, *Nile Fantasia* for Piano and Orch., was performed posthumously (N.Y., Sept. 24, 1967). She wrote 5 books about her life and travels: *Adventures in Black and White* (N.Y., 1960), *Who Killed the Congo* (N.Y., 1963), *Jungle Saints: Africa's Heroic Catholic Missionaries* (Rome, 1962), *Kingdom of Dreams* (with her mother, Josephine Schuyler; N.Y., 1966), and *Good Men Die* (N.Y., 1969). Her funeral at St. Patrick's Cathedral in N.Y. received extensive press coverage. In recognition of her musical and literary precocity, Mayor Fiorello LaGuardia declared June 19, 1940, Philippa Schuyler Day at the N.Y. World's Fair.

BIBL.: J. Schuyler, *Philippa the Beautiful American: The Travelled History of a Troubadour* (N.Y., 1969).—**NS/LK/DM**

Schuyt (Schuijt), Cornelis (Floriszoon), eminent Netherlands organist and composer; b. Leiden, 1557; d. there, June 9, 1616. With the exception of a visit to Italy as a young man, he spent his entire life in his native city. He was named asst. town organist to his father in 1593, and was active at the Pieterskerk and the Hooglandsche Kerk; after his father's death in 1601, he was appointed his successor as first organist at the Pieterskerk. The influence of Italian music is revealed in his masterful madrigals.

WORKS (all publ. in Leiden): *Il primo libro de madrigali* for 5 Voices (1600); *Hollandsche madrigalen* for 5 to 6 and 8 Voices (1603); *12 padovante et altretante gagliarde...con 2 canzone alla francese, a 6* (1611); *Hymneo, overo Madrigali nuptiali et altri amorosi* for 6 Voices, *con un echo doppio* for 12 Voices (1611).

BIBL.: A. Annegarn, *Floris en C. Schuyt: Muziek in Leiden van de vijftiende tot het begin van de zeventiende eeuw* (Utrecht, 1973).—**NS/LK/DM**

Schuyt, Nico(laas), Dutch composer; b. Alkmaar, Jan. 2, 1922; d. Amsterdam, Jan. 25, 1992. He received training from Jacob van Domselaer (piano and harmony), Eberhard Rebling (piano), and Willem Hijstek (theory) before completing his studies with Bertus van Lier (composition; 1949–52). From 1964 he was active with Donemus in Amsterdam.

WORKS: ORCH.: Concerto for Youth Orch. (1952–53); *Réveil* (1955); *Corteggio* (1958); *Sinfonia divertente* for Small Orch. (1958); Sonatina for Youth Chamber Orch. (1961); Sonata (1964); *Discorsi capricciosi* for Small Orch. (1965); *Hymnus* for Small Orch. (1966); *Greetings from Holland* for Small Orch. (1970); *Quasi in modo di valzer* (1973); *Discorsi, discorsi...* for Wind Orch. (1979); *Festa seria* (1980); *Down to the Shades* (1985; rev. 1986); *Discorsi ariosi* for Wind Orch. (1988). **CHAMBER:** *Sonata a tre* for Oboe, Bassoon, and Piano (1953–54); *5 Dramatic Nocturnes* for Flute and Piano (1954); *Quatuor de ballet* for Clarinet, Trumpet, Percussion, and Piano (1962); *De belevenissen van Strip-Thijs* for Clarinet, Trumpet, Percussion, and Piano (1962); *Allegro and Passacaglia* for Violin and Piano (1965); *Alla notturna* for 2 Oboes, Oboe d'Amore, and English Horn (1971); *Furies for 4* for Piano Quartet (1975); *Atalanta* for Flute, Violin, Cello, and Harp (1986); piano music. **VOCAL:** *Arkadia* for Mezzo-soprano, Viola, and Cello (1966); *Naar de maan* (To the Moon) for Women's Chorus, Mixed Chorus, and Orch. (1967–68). —**NS/LK/DM**

Schwanenberg, Johann Gottfried, German keyboard player, music theorist, and composer; b. probably in Wolfenbüttel, c. 1740; d. Braunschweig, March 29, 1804. He studied with G.C. Schurmann and Ignazio Fiorillo in Wolfenbüttel; after continuing his training in Venice on a court stipend with Hasse, Gaetano Latilla, and Giuseppe Saratelli (1756–61), he returned to the Braunschweig court as Kapellmeister (1762–1802). He was praised by his contemporaries as both a keyboard virtuoso and as a composer. In one of his theoretical papers, he argues for the deletion of H from the German musical scale. He produced 14 operas to Italian librettos, all first perf. in Braunschweig, including *Adriano in Siria* (Aug. 1762), *Solimano* (Nov. 4, 1762), and *Antigono* (Feb. 2, 1768); also various sacred vocal works, 23 syms., 4 harpsichord concertos, 25 harpsichord sonatas, etc. —NS/LK/DM

Schwann, William (Joseph), pioneering American discographer; b. Salem, Ill., May 13, 1913; d. Burlington, Vt., June 7, 1998. He began his career as an organist and choir director in Louisville (Ky.) churches (1930–35). He studied at the Univ. of Louisville (B.A., 1935), Boston Univ. (1935–37), and Harvard Univ. (1937–39), where his teachers included E.B. Hill, Hugo Leichtentritt, A.T. Merritt, Walter Piston, and G. Wallace Woodworth. He also received private organ instruction from E. Power Biggs. He was a music critic for the *Boston Herald* (1937–41), and also ran his own record shop in Cambridge (1939–53). In 1949 he launched his *Schwann Record Catalog,* the first monthly compilation of available recordings in the world. An invaluable source, it expanded over the years to include not only long-playing records but also tapes and compact discs; special compilations were also issued from time to time. In 1976 his firm, W. Schwann, Inc., was acquired by ABC Publishing Co. Among Schwann's numerous accolades are honorary D.Mus. degrees from the Univ. of Louisville (1969) and the New England Cons. of Music in Boston (1982).—NS/LK/DM

Schwantner, Joseph, American composer and teacher; b. Chicago, March 22, 1943. He studied classical guitar and composed jazz pieces in his youth before pursuing his training with Bernard Dieter at the American Cons. of Music in Chicago (B.M., 1964) and with Donato and Stout at Northwestern Univ. (M.M., 1966; D.M., 1968). In 1965, 1966, and 1968 he received BMI Student Composer awards. In 1970 he won the first Charles Ives Scholarship of the American Academy of Arts and Letters. He taught at the Eastman School of Music in Rochester, N.Y. (from 1970), where he then was a prof. of composition (from 1980). He also was composer-in-residence of the St. Louis Sym. Orch. (1982–85), the Cabrillo Music Festival (1992), and the Sonoklect New Music Festival (1993). In 1974, 1977, 1979, and 1988 he received NEA composer fellowship grants. He held a Guggenheim fellowship in 1978. In 1979 he won the Pulitzer Prize in Music for his orch. score *Aftertones of Infinity.* In 1981 he received a first-prize Kennedy Center Freidheim Award. His early works followed the dictates of serialism, but he eventually developed an eclectic style, incorporating tonal materials into harmonically complex works. Interested in new colors, textures, and timbres, he often employs tonalities produced by a wide spectrum of musical instruments.

WORKS: DRAMATIC: Ballet: *Through Interior Worlds* (Seattle, Oct. 9, 1992; concert version, Nashville, Tenn., Oct. 7, 1994). **ORCH.:** *Modus Caelestis* (1973); *And the Mountains Rising Nowhere* (1977); *Aftertones of Infinity* (1978; N.Y., Jan. 29, 1979); *From a Dark Millennium* (1981); *Distant Runes and Incantations* for Piano and Chamber Orch. (Pasadena, Calif., June 1, 1984); *Someday Memories* (1984; St. Louis, May 16, 1985); *A Sudden Rainbow* (1984; St. Louis, Jan. 31, 1986); *Toward Light* (1986; Canton, Ohio, March 15, 1987); *From Afar,* fantasy for Guitar and Orch. (1987; N.Y., Jan. 8, 1988); Piano Concerto (N.Y., July 8, 1988); *Freeflight* (1989); *A Play of Shadows,* fantasy for Flute and Orch. (N.Y., April 16, 1990); Percussion Concerto (1991; N.Y., Jan. 6, 1995). **CHAMBER:** *Diaphonia Intervallum* for Alto Saxophone and Chamber Ensemble (1965); *Chronicon* for Bassoon and Piano (1968); *Consortium I* for Flute, Clarinet, Violin, Viola, and Cello (1970) and *II* for Flute, Clarinet, Violin, Cello, Piano, and Percussion (1971); *Elixir* for Flute and 5 Players (1974); *Autumn Canticles* for Violin, Cello, and Piano (1974); *In Aeternum* for Cello and 4 Players (1975); *Canticle of the Evening Bells* for Flute and 12 Players (1976); *Wind Willow, Whisper* for Chamber Ensemble (1980); *Through Interior Worlds* for Chamber Ensemble (1981); *Music of Amber* for Flute, Clarinet, Violin, Cello, Percussion, and Piano (1981); *Velocities* for Marimba (1990). **VOCAL:** *Wild Angels of the Open Hills,* song cycle for Soprano, Flute, Harp, and Chamber Ensemble (1977); *Sparrows* for Soprano and Chamber Ensemble (1979); *2 Poems of Agueda Pizarro* for Voice and Piano (1981); *New Morning for the World: Daybreak of Freedom* for Speaker and Orch., after Martin Luther King Jr. (1982); *Magabunda (Witchnomad),* song cycle for Soprano and Orch. (1983); *Dreamcaller,* song cycle for Soprano, Violin, and Chamber Orch. (St. Paul, Minn., May 11, 1984). —NS/LK/DM

Schwartz, Arthur, American composer; b. N.Y., Nov. 25, 1900; d. Kintnersville, Pa., Sept. 4, 1984. Schwartz wrote the music for 22 stage and 11 movie musicals between 1927 and 1963. His most successful shows were small-scale revues; in fact, none of his book musicals on Broadway turned a profit. Collaborating most frequently with lyricist Howard Dietz, he scored numerous song hits and standards, including "I Guess I'll Have to Change My Plan," "Dancing in the Dark," and "That's Entertainment," and he also worked with some of the top lyricists of his time, among them Otto Harbach, E. Y. Harburg, Ira Gershwin, Dorothy Fields, Oscar Hammerstein II, Johnny Mercer, Frank Loesser, and Sammy Cahn.

Schwartz was the son of a lawyer who encouraged him to take up the legal profession. He learned to play piano and was working as an accompanist to silent films at the age of 14. While attending N.Y.U., 1916–20, he wrote football songs. Graduating with a B.A., he earned a masters degree in English literature at Columbia Univ. in 1921, then attended Columbia Law School.

Schwartz published his first song, "Baltimore, Md., You're the Only Doctor for Me" (lyrics by Eli Dawson), in 1923. He graduated from law school in the spring of 1924 and took a job as a counselor at a summer camp because lyricist Lorenz Hart was also a counselor there. The two wrote songs for camp shows, and though Hart maintained his partnership with Richard Rodgers, he encouraged Schwartz to pursue a career as a composer.

Schwartz was admitted to the bar and set up a law practice. After Howard Dietz collaborated with Jerome Kern on the unsuccessful *Dear Sir* (N.Y., Sept. 23, 1924), Schwartz tried to convince Dietz to work with him; Dietz initially demurred.

Schwartz broke into writing theater music by composing three songs for the third edition of the Off-Broadway revue *The Grand Street Follies* (N.Y., June 15, 1926). He made it to Broadway the following year, writing half the songs for the revue *The New Yorkers*, which ran 52 performances. After placing songs in two more shows by the end of the year, Schwartz quit his law practice to write music full-time. He also convinced Dietz (who maintained his own full-time job as director of publicity and advertising for MGM) to work with him.

Schwartz and Dietz's first effort was the appropriately titled revue *The Little Show*, which played 321 performances in Broadway's smallest theater, the Music Box. Schwartz did not write the show's hit song, "Moanin' Low," but among his contributions was "I Guess I'll Have to Change My Plan," which had actually been written five years earlier in his summer camp days and given a Lorenz Hart lyric as "I Love to Lie Awake in Bed." More than three years after *The Little Show* opened, "I Guess I'll Have to Change My Plan," popularly known as "The Blue Pajama Song" because of a line in the lyric, finally became a hit in August 1932 in a recording by Rudy Vallée.

In 1930, Schwartz contributed to a remarkable six shows—three each in London and N.Y.—and three motion pictures. His most notable success in the West End was *Here Comes the Bride*, "a musical farcical comedy" with lyrics mostly by Desmond Carter, which ran 175 performances. On Broadway, *The Second Little Show* and *Princess Charming* were disappointments, but *Three's a Crowd*, a revue that featured the same cast as *The Little Show*, was a hit, running 271 performances; one of the cast members, Libby Holman, made a hit out of "Something to Remember You By" (lyrics by Dietz) in December. "I'm Afraid of You" (lyrics by Ralph Rainger and Edward Eliscu) marked Schwartz's entry into films when it was used in Paramount's *Queen High*, which was released in August.

Dietz and Schwartz's fourth revue, *The Band Wagon* (1931), is considered their best work. Starring Fred and Adele Astaire in their final appearance as a duo, the show ran 260 performances and included four song hits. "Dancing in the Dark," the most successful song of Schwartz's career, was recorded by several artists, the most popular versions being issued by Bing Crosby and Fred Waring's Pennsylvanians. Leo Reisman and His Orch. employed Fred Astaire as vocalist for a disc featuring "I Love Louisa" and "New Sun in the Sky." And though "High and Low" (lyrics also by Desmond Carter) had been used previously in *Here Comes the Bride* and in the 1930 film *The Lottery Bride*, it took exposure in *The Band Wagon* (and placement as the B-side of "Dancing in the Dark") to make it a hit for Fred Waring.

Flying Colors could not match its predecessor, but it ran a profitable 188 performances and featured three hits: Leo Reisman scored with "Alone Together" in November 1932, following it with "Louisiana Hayride," which featured Schwartz himself on vocals; the orchestra of Roger Wolfe Kahn had a hit with "A Shine on Your Shoes."

Apart from Dietz in 1933, Schwartz wrote an independent hit, "Trouble in Paradise," which scored for Glen Gray and the Casa Loma Orch. in July, and he wrote the music for a London musical, *Nice Goings On*, which had a run of 221 performances. His only effort for Broadway was a couple of songs used in the straight play *She Loves Me Not* (N.Y., Nov. 20, 1933).

In 1934, Schwartz and Dietz reunited to write songs for the radio serial *The Gibson Family*, which ran for a full 39-week season. They also found time to pen "Born to Be Kissed" for the Jean Harlow film *Girl from Missouri*, which became a hit for Freddy Martin and His Orch. in July. Schwartz also collaborated with E. Y. Harburg on the independent song "Then I'll Be Tired of You," a hit for Fats Waller in September. The first book musical by Schwartz and Dietz was *Revenge with Music*, which ran 158 performances. Both of the songs to emerge as hits from the show had been written for *The Gibson Family*: "You and the Night and the Music," recorded by Libby Holman, star of *Revenge with Music*, and "If There Is Someone Lovelier than You," recorded by Enric Madriguera and His Orch.

Schwartz married musical comedy star Katherine Carrington, who had appeared in Irving Berlin's *Face the Music* and Jerome Kern's *Music in the Air*, in 1934. Carrington went on to star in Kurt Weill's *The Eternal Road* in 1937; she died on April 2, 1953.

Schwartz and Dietz returned to the revue format for *At Home Abroad* (1935), which ran 198 performances. The London success *Follow the Sun* (1936) drew songs from earlier American shows and added Desmond Carter on lyrics; it ran 204 performances. Before the year was out Schwartz had written songs for two motion pictures, *Under Your Spell* with Dietz, and *That Girl from Paris* with Edward Heyman.

Schwartz suffered two flops with book musicals in 1937, though *Virginia*, which he wrote with Al Stillman, contained "You and I Know," a hit parade entry for the Glenn Miller Orch. in November, and *Beat the Devil*, written with Dietz, contained "I See Your Face Before Me," a hit for Guy Lombardo and His Royal Canadians in March 1938. The failure of *Beat the Devil* led to the temporary suspension of the team of Schwartz and Dietz, and Schwartz teamed up with Dorothy Fields for his next show, 1939's *Stars in Your Eyes*, which starred Ethel Merman and ran 127 performances. Tommy Dorsey and His Orch. made a hit out of "This Is It" from the score.

Schwartz collaborated with Oscar Hammerstein II on songs for the patriotic show *American Jubilee* that was part of the N.Y. World's Fair in the summer of 1940. He then left for Hollywood to write songs for the movies. In March 1941, Artie Shaw and His Orch. scored a Top Ten revival with an instrumental treatment of "Dancing in the Dark."

Schwartz made his most substantial mark as a Hollywood composer with the all-star feature *Thank Your Lucky Stars*, released in the fall of 1943. Among the 12 songs he and Frank Loesser wrote for the film were three hits: "The Dreamer" and "How Sweet You Are," both given Top Ten recordings by Kay Armen and the Baladiers, and the war-themed novelty tune "They're Either Too Young or Too Old" by Jimmy Dorsey and His Orch. with a vocal by Kitty Kallen, which was nominated for an Academy Award.

Schwartz turned to movie producing in 1944 with *Cover Girl*, for which he hired Jerome Kern and Ira Gershwin to write the songs. He also produced the Cole Porter film biography *Night and Day*, released in July 1946. His final Hollywood effort before returning to Broadway was *The Time, the Place and the Girl*, released in December 1946, for which he wrote the songs with Leo Robin. Three of them became hits: "A Gal in Calico" for Johnny Mercer (with three competing Top Ten renditions); "Oh, But I Do" by Margaret Whiting; and "Rainy Night in Rio" by Sam Donohue. "A Gal in Calico" earned Schwartz his second Oscar nomination.

After failing with the book musical *Park Avenue*, written with Ira Gershwin, Schwartz returned to the revue format and to Howard Dietz for *Inside U.S.A.*, which he also produced. It was his last major success on Broadway, running 399 performances and featuring "Haunted Heart," a chart record for Perry Como in June 1948. The musical *A Tree Grows in Brooklyn*, for which Schwartz wrote songs with Dorothy Fields, had a run of 270 performances, but that was not enough to turn a profit. Though no individual songs emerged from the score as hits, such songs as "He Had Refinement" and "Make the Man Love Me" remain memorable, and the cast album reached the Top Ten in the spring of 1951.

MGM mounted a lavish film treatment of *The Band Wagon* in 1953. The movie shared only its title, some of its songs, and Fred Astaire with the original Broadway revue; with many songs interpolated from other Schwartz-Dietz shows and with the addition of the newly written "That's Entertainment," it was virtually an Arthur Schwartz anthology film, and it is remembered as one of the best movie musicals of the 1950s. Like *A Tree Grows in Brooklyn*, Schwartz's next Broadway musical, *By the Beautiful Sea* (1954), featured lyrics by Dorothy Fields and a part for comic actress Shirley Booth. And like its predecessor, the show ran a respectable but not-quite-profitable 270 performances.

Schwartz wrote songs with Sammy Cahn for a Dean Martin/Jerry Lewis film, *You're Never Too Young*, in 1955, and in 1956 he scored two television musicals, *High Tor*, which had a book and lyrics by Maxwell Anderson and featured Bing Crosby and Julie Andrews, and *A Bell for Adano*, with lyrics by Howard Dietz.

In the early 1960s, Schwartz and Dietz returned to Broadway with two musicals, *The Gay Life*, featuring Barbara Cook, and *Jennie*, starring Mary Martin, neither of which was a success. These were Schwartz's last Broadway productions, though he continued to work on shows and try to get them mounted, notably *Nickleby and Me*, based on the Charles Dickens novel *Nicholas Nickleby*, for which he wrote both music and lyrics.

Schwartz died of a stroke at the age of 83, survived by his wife Mary, two sons—one of whom was disc jockey, singer, and fiction writer Jonathan Schwartz—and one grandchild.

WORKS (only works for which Schwartz was a primary, credited composer are listed): **MUSICALS/REVUES** (all dates refer to N.Y. openings unless otherwise noted): *The New Yorkers* (March 10, 1927); *The Little Show* (April 30, 1929); *Here Comes the Bride* (London, Feb. 20, 1930); *The Co-Optimists of 1930* (London, April 4, 1930); *The Second Little Show* (Sept. 2, 1930); *Princess Charming* (Oct. 13, 1930); *Three's a Crowd* (Oct. 15, 1930); *The Band Wagon* (June 3, 1931); *Flying Colors* (Sept. 15, 1932); *Nice Goings On* (London, Sept. 13, 1933); *Revenge with Music* (Nov. 28, 1934); *At Home Abroad* (Sept. 19, 1935); *Follow the Sun* (London, Feb. 4, 1936); *Virginia* (Sept. 2, 1937); *Between the Devil* (Dec. 22, 1937); *Stars in Your Eyes* (Feb. 9, 1939); *Park Avenue* (Nov. 4, 1946); *Inside U.S.A.* (April 30, 1948); *A Tree Grows in Brooklyn* (April 19, 1951); *By the Beautiful Sea* (April 8, 1954); *The Gay Life* (Nov. 18, 1961); *Jennie* (Oct. 17, 1963). **FILMS:** *Under Your Spell* (1936); *That Girl from Paris* (1936); *Navy Blues* (1941); *All Through the Night* (1942); *Cairo* (1942); *Thank Your Lucky Stars* (1943); *The Time, the Place and the Girl* (1946); *Excuse My Dust* (1951); *Dangerous When Wet* (1953); *The Band Wagon* (MGM 1953); *You're Never Too Young* (1955). **TELEVISION:** *High Tor* (CBS, March 10, 1956); *A Bell for Adano* (CBS, June 2, 1956). —WR

Schwartz, Elliott (Shelling), American composer, teacher, and writer on music; b. N.Y., Jan. 19, 1936. He studied composition with Luening and Beeson at Columbia Univ. (A.B., 1957; M.A., 1958; Ed.D., 1962), and also had private instruction in piano from Alton Jones and in composition from Creston. He likewise studied composition at the Bennington (Vt.) Composers Conference (summers, 1961–66). After teaching at the Univ. of Mass. in Amherst (1960–64), he joined the faculty of Bowdoin Coll. in Brunswick, Maine (1964). Schwartz was assoc. prof. (1970–75) and then prof. (from 1975) and chairman of its music dept. (1975–87). He also held appointments as Distinguished Univ. Visiting Prof. (1985–86) and part-time prof. of composition (1989–92) at Ohio State Univ., and as visiting Bye fellow at Robinson Coll., Cambridge, England (1993, 1999). He was vice president of the American Music Center (1982–88), chairman of the American Soc. of Univ. Composers (1984–88), and president of the Coll. Music Soc. (1989–90). In 1995 he was co-founder and first president of the Maine Composers Forum. He became a member of the board of directors of the American Composers Alliance in 1996. Schwartz's compositions are marked by an integration of different stylistic elements—including tonality, atonality, triadic modality, the use of chance operations, improvisation, and serial procedures—into a textural collage.

WRITINGS: *The Symphonies of Ralph Vaughan Williams* (Amherst, Mass., 1964); ed. with B. Childs, *Contemporary Composers on Contemporary Music* (N.Y., 1967; rev. 1998); *Electronic Music: A Listener's Guide* (N.Y., 1973; second ed., rev., 1976); *Music: Ways of Listening* (N.Y., 1982); with D. Godfrey, *Music Since 1945: Issues, Materials, and Literature* (N.Y., 1993).

WORKS: DRAMATIC: *Elevator Music* for Any Instruments (1967); *Areas* for Flute, Clarinet, Violin, Cello, Trombone, Piano, and 2 to 4 Dancers (1968); *Gibson Hall* for Keyboards and

Synthesizer (1969); Music for Soloist and Audience (1970); *Telly* for 5 Woodwind or Brass, 4 Percussion, 3 Television Sets, and Tape (1972); *A Dream of Beats and Bells* for Piano and Audience (1977); *California Games* for 4 to 6 Players, Tape, and Audience (1978); *Radio Games*, duet for Performers in a Radio Studio and Audience (1980). **O R C H .**: *Music* for Orch. and Tape (1965); *Texture* for Chamber Orch. (1966); *Magic Music* for Piano and Orch. (1968); *Island* (1970); *Dream Overture* (1972); *The Harmony of Maine* for Synthesizer and Orch. (1974); *Eclipse III* for Chamber Orch. (1975); *Janus* for Piano and Orch. (1976); *Chamber Concerto I* for Double Bass and 15 Instruments (1977) and *III* for Piano and Small Orch. (1977); *Zebra* for Youth Orch. and Tape (1981); *Celebrations/Reflections: A Time Warp* (1985); *4 Ohio Portraits* (Columbus, Ohio, April 12, 1986); *Timepiece 1794* for Chamber Orch. (1994); *Equinox: Concerto for Orchestra* (1994); *Chiaroscuro: Zebra Variations* for Symphonic Wind Ensemble (1995); *Rainbow* (1996). **C H A M B E R :** Oboe Quartet (1963); Trio for Flute, Cello, and Piano (1964); *Music for Napoleon and Beethoven* for Trumpet, Piano, and 2 Tapes (1969); Septet for Voice, Piano, and 5 Instruments (1969); *Eclipse I* for 10 Instruments (1971); Octet (1972); *Echo Music II* for Wind Quartet and Tape (1974); *A Bowdoin Anthology* for Narrator, Instruments, and Tape (1976); *Chamber Concerto II* for Clarinet and 9 Instruments (1977), *IV* for Saxophone and 10 Instruments (1981), and *V* for Bassoon, Strings, and Piano (1992); *Bellagio Variations* for String Quartet (1980); *Octagon* for 8 Percussion (1984); *Purple Transformation* for Wind Ensemble (1987); *Memorial in 2 Parts* for Violin and Piano (1988); *Northern Pines* for 2 Oboes, Clarinet, 2 Horns, and Piano (1988); *Palindromes* for Cello and Percussion (1989); *A Garden for RKB* for Violin, Clarinet, and Piano (1990); *Elan* for Flute, Clarinet, Violin, Cello, and Piano (1991); *Rows Garden* for Woodwind Quintet (1993); *Spaces* for Piano and Percussion (1995); *Reflections* for 6 Bassoons (1995); *Tapestry* for Violin, Piano, and Cello (1997); *Vienna Dreams* for Viola, Clarinet, and Piano (1998); *Kaleidoscope* for Violin, Contrabassoon, and Piano (1999).—**NS/LK/DM**

Schwarz, Boris, distinguished Russian-born American violinist, teacher, and musicologist; b. St. Petersburg, March 26, 1906; d. N.Y., Dec. 31, 1983. He went to Berlin as a youth; at the age of 14, made his debut as a violinist in Hannover, accompanied at the piano by his father, Joseph Schwarz. He took violin lessons with Flesch in Berlin (1922–25) and Thibaud and Capet in Paris (1925–26); subsequently took courses in musicology with Sachs, Schering, and Wolf at the Univ. of Berlin (1930–36). In 1936 he emigrated to the U.S., becoming a naturalized American citizen in 1943. He completed his musicological studies with Lang at Columbia Univ. (Ph.D., 1950, with the diss. *French Instrumental Music Between the Revolutions, 1789–1830*; publ. in N.Y., 1950; second ed., rev., 1983). After serving as concertmaster of the Indianapolis Sym. Orch. (1937–38) and playing in the NBC Sym. Orch. in N.Y. (1938–39), he was a prof. of music at Queens Coll. of the City Univ. of N.Y. (1941–76), where he founded (1945) the Queens Coll. Orch. Soc., conducting annual concerts of symphonic and choral music; also was chairman of its music dept. (1948–51; 1952–55). In 1959–60 he held a Guggenheim fellowship. A trilingual writer, he was fluent in Russian, German, and English; contributed numerous articles, mostly on Russian music, to *The New Grove Dictionary of Music and Musicians* (1980) and to various music journals. His valuable study, *Music and Musical Life in Soviet Russia, 1917–1970* (N.Y., 1972; second ed., rev., 1983), was highly critical of certain aspects of the musical situation in Russia; it won an award from ASCAP as the best book on music criticism. His second book, *Great Masters of the Violin* (N.Y., 1983), is valuable for its accuracy of documentation.

BIBL.: M. Brown, ed., *Russian and Soviet Music: Essays for B. S.* (Ann Arbor, 1984).—**NS/LK/DM**

Schwarz, Gerard (Ralph), esteemed American conductor; b. Weehawken, N.J., Aug. 19, 1947. He commenced trumpet lessons when he was 8, and after attending the National Music Camp in Interlochen, Mich. (summers, 1958–60), he studied at N.Y.'s H.S. of Performing Arts; also received trumpet instruction from William Vacchiano (1962–68), and completed his training at the Juilliard School (B.S., 1972). He played in the American Brass Quintet (1965–73) and the American Sym. Orch. in N.Y. (1966–72); also made appearances as a conductor. After serving as co-principal trumpet of the N.Y. Phil. (1972–75), he pursued a conducting career. He was music director of the Waterloo Festival in Stanhope, N.J., and of its music school at Fairleigh Dickinson Univ. (from 1975), of the 92nd St. Y Chamber Sym. (later N.Y. Chamber Sym.) in N.Y. (from 1977), and of the Los Angeles Chamber Orch. (1978–86). He also appeared widely as a guest conductor; one such engagement, at the Mostly Mozart Festival in N.Y. in 1980, led to his appointment as its music adviser in 1982; he then served as its music director from 1984 to 2001, and subsequently was its conductor emeritus. He also was music adviser (1983–85) and principal conductor (from 1985) of the Seattle Sym. Orch. In 1989 he received the Alice M. Ditson Award for Conductors. In 1993 he stepped down as music director of the Waterloo Festival. From 1993 to 1996 he was artistic advisor of the Tokyu Bunkamura, a Tokyo cultural center. In 2001 he became principal conductor of the Royal Liverpool Phil., a position he was to hold concurrently with his music directorship of the Seattle Sym. Orch. Schwarz is duly recognized as one of America's outstanding conductors, and a musician of uncommon attainments. He has won especial critical accolades for his discerning and innovative programs; his vast repertoire ranges from early music to the contemporary era.—**NS/LK/DM**

Schwarz, Hanna, German mezzo-soprano; b. Hamburg, Aug. 15, 1943. She studied in Hamburg, Hannover, and Essen. In 1970 she made her operatic debut as Maddalena in *Rigoletto* in Hannover. In 1973 she became a member of the Hamburg State Opera. She sang with the Bavarian State Opera in Munich for the first time in 1974. In 1975 she made her debut at the Bayreuth Festival as Flosshilde in *Das Rheingold*, and continued to sing there during the next decade. In 1977 she made her U.S. debut as Fricka in *Das Rheingold* at the San Francisco Opera, and also appeared as Preziosilla at the Paris Opéra. In 1978 she sang Cherubino at the Deutsche Oper in Berlin. On Feb. 24, 1979, she appeared as Countess Geschwitz in the first complete performance of *Lulu* at the Paris Opéra. That same year she also made her debut at the Salzburg Festival as a soloist in Beethoven's 9th Sym. In 1980 she sang for the first time at London's Covent Garden as Waltraute and returned to the Salzburg Festival to sing Juana in a concert performance of Krenek's *Karl V*. In 1992 she made her first operatic stage appearance at the Salzburg Festival when she sang Herodias. She was engaged as Fricka and Waltraute at the Bayreuth Festival in 1995, and that same year she sang in the premiere of Schnittke's *Historia von D. Johann Fausten* in Hamburg. In 1996 she appeared as Herodias and Fricka at the Metropolitan Opera in N.Y. As a concert artist, she sang widely in Europe and North America.—NS/LK/DM

Schwarz, Joseph, German baritone; b. Riga, Oct. 10, 1880; d. Berlin, Nov. 10, 1926. He studied in Berlin with Alexander Heinemann, and then continued his training at the Vienna Cons. In 1900 he made his operatic debut in *Aida* in Linz. Following engagements in Riga, Graz, and St. Petersburg, he sang in Vienna, principally at the Volksoper and then at the Court Opera (1909–15). From 1915 he was a principal member of the Berlin Royal (later State) Opera. He also sang at the Chicago Opera (1921–25) and at London's Covent Garden as Rigoletto (1924).—NS/LK/DM

Schwarz, Paul, Austrian tenor; b. Vienna, June 30, 1887; d. Hamburg, Dec. 24, 1980. He sang in Bielitz and Vienna (1909–12). From 1923 to 1933 he was a member of the Hamburg Opera, where he gained success in buffo roles. He made guest appearances in Berlin, Paris, Amsterdam, and London (Covent Garden debut as Monostatos, 1936). During World War II, he lived in the U.S. After the War, he resumed his career in Europe, singing until 1949.—NS/LK/DM

Schwarz, Rudolf, Austrian-born English conductor; b. Vienna, April 29, 1905; d. London, Jan. 30, 1994. He studied violin. He joined the Düsseldorf Opera as a répétiteur (1923), and then made his conducting debut there (1924); subsequently was a conductor at the Karlsruhe Opera (1927) until being removed in 1933 by the Nazis as a Jew. After serving as music director of the Judischer Kulturbund in Berlin (1936–39), he was imprisoned (1939–40), and then interred at the Belsen concentration camp (1943–45). Following his liberation, he settled in England, becoming a naturalized British subject in 1952. He was conductor of the Bournemouth Municipal Orch. (1947–51) and music director of the City of Birmingham Sym. Orch. (1951–57); after serving as chief conductor of the BBC Sym. Orch. in London (1957–62), he was principal conductor (1964–67) and artistic director (1967–73) of the Northern Sinfonia in Newcastle upon Tyne. He was made a Commander of the Order of the British Empire in 1973.—NS/LK/DM

Schwarz, Vera, Austrian soprano; b. Zagreb, July 10, 1889; d. Vienna, Dec. 4, 1964. She studied voice and piano in Vienna, where she appeared in operettas. She went to Hamburg in 1914 and to Berlin in 1917; toured in South America. In 1939 she went to Hollywood, where she became a vocal instructor. In 1948 she returned to Austria; gave courses at the Mozarteum in Salzburg. Her best roles were Carmen and Tosca. —NS/LK/DM

Schwarzkopf, Dame (Olga Maria) Elisabeth (Friederike), celebrated German-born English soprano; b. Jarotschin, near Posen, Dec. 9, 1915. She studied with Lula Mysz-Gmeiner at the Berlin Hochschule für Musik. She made her operatic debut as a Flower Maiden in Parsifal at the Berlin Städtische Oper (April 17, 1938), and then studied with Maria Ivogün while continuing on its roster, appearing in more important roles from 1941. In 1942 she made her debut as a lieder artist in Vienna, and also sang for the first time at the State Opera there as Zerbinetta, remaining on its roster until the Nazis closed the theater in 1944. Having registered as a member of the German Nazi Party in 1940, Schwarzkopf had to be de-Nazified by the Allies after the end of World War II. In 1946 she rejoined the Vienna State Opera and appeared as Donna Elvira during its visit to London's Covent Garden in 1947; subsequently sang at Covent Garden regularly until 1951. In 1947 she made her first appearance at the Salzburg Festival as Susanna; also sang regularly at Milan's La Scala (1948–63). Furtwängler invited her to sing in his performance of the Beethoven 9th Sym. at the reopening celebrations of the Bayreuth Festival in 1951. She then created the role of Anne Trulove in Stravinsky's *The Rake's Progress* in Venice on Sept. 11, 1951. On Oct. 25, 1953, she gave her first recital at N.Y.'s Carnegie Hall; made her U.S. operatic debut as the Marschallin with the San Francisco Opera on Sept. 20, 1955. On Oct. 13, 1964, she made her belated Metropolitan Opera debut in N.Y. in the same role, continuing on its roster until 1966. In 1975 she made a farewell tour of the U.S. as a concert singer. She married **Walter Legge** in 1953 and became a naturalized British subject. She ed. his memoir, *On and Off the Record* (N.Y., 1982; second ed., 1988). In 1992 she was made a Dame Commander of the Order of the British Empire. In addition to her acclaimed Mozart and Strauss roles, she was also admired in Viennese operetta. As an interpreter of lieder, she was incomparable.

BIBL.: A. Jefferson, *E. S.* (London, 1995); A. Sanders and J. Steane, *E. S.: A Career on Record* (Portland, Ore., 1996). —NS/LK/DM

Schweinitz, Wolfgang von, German composer; b. Hamburg, Feb. 7, 1953. After studies with Esther Ballou at the American Univ. in Washington, D.C. (1968–69), he pursued his training with Ernst Klussmann (1971–73) and György Ligeti (1973–75) at the Hamburg Hochschule für Musik. In 1975–76 he worked at the Center for Computer Research in Music and Acoustics at Stanford Univ. in Calif. He was a resident at the German Academy in Rome in 1978–79. In 1986 he won the first annual Schneider-Schott prize for young German composers. In 1988 he received the Plöner Hindemith- Preis. Schweinitz established his name as a composer with his song cycle *Papiersterne* (1980–81), which premiered at the Berlin Festival on Sept. 22, 1981. His most ambitious score is the "azione musicale" *Patmos* (1986–89), a complete setting of the book of *Revelation*. It was first performed in Munich on April 28, 1990.

WORKS: DRAMATIC: *Patmos,* "azione musicale" (1986–89; Munich, April 28, 1990). **ORCH.:** 2 syms. (1973,

1974); *Mozart-Variationen* (1976); Piano Concerto (1979); Konzertouvertüre (1979–80; Darmstadt, July 5, 1980); *...wir aber singen*, symphonic cycle for Cello and Orch. (I, Kiel, Sept. 6, 1992; II, Hagen, Sept. 5, 1995; III, 1996). **CHAMBER:** String Quartet (1977); *Adagio* for English Horn, Basset Horn, Horn, and Bassoon (1983); *Englische Serenade* for 2 Clarinets, 2 Bassoons, and 2 Horns (1984; Hamburg, March 27, 1985); *Musik* for 4 Saxophones (1985; Witten, April 27, 1986); *Morgenlied* for Flute (1990); *Franz [Schubert] and Morton [Feldman] Singing Together in Harmony (With the Lord Himself Enjoying His Bells*, 12 stanzas for Violin, Cello, and Piano (1993–94). **KEYBOARD: P i a n o :** *3 Etudien* (1983–84; Hamburg, Feb. 24, 1984). **O r g a n :** *7 Patmos Souvenirs* (1990). **VOCAL:** *Die Brücke* for Tenor, Baritone, and Small Orch. (1978); *Papiersterne*, song cycle for Mezzo-soprano and Piano (1980–81; Berlin, Sept. 22, 1981); *Mass* for Soloists, Chorus, and Orch. (1981–83; Berlin, July 8, 1984); *6 Alte Lieder* for Children's Chorus, 2 Soprano Recorders, 2 Alto Recorders, 2 Trumpets, and Percussion (1984).
—NS/LK/DM

Schweitzer, Albert, famous Alsatian theologian, philosopher, medical missionary, organist, and music scholar; b. Kaysersberg, Jan. 14, 1875; d. Lambaréné, Gabon, Sept. 4, 1965. He studied piano as a child with his father, a Lutheran pastor, then began organ studies at 8, his principal mentors being Eugen Munch in Mulhouse, Ernst Munch in Strasbourg, and Widor in Paris. He pursued training in philosophy (Ph.D., 1899) and theology (Ph.D., 1900) at the Univ. of Strasbourg; also received instruction in theory from Jacobsthal in Strasbourg and in piano from Philipp and M. Jäell in Paris. In 1896 he became organist of the Bach Concerts in Strasbourg; also joined the faculty of the Univ. there in 1902, where he also completed his full medical course (M.D., 1912); concurrently was organist of the Bach Soc. in Paris (1905–13). In 1913 he went to Lambaréné in the Gabon province of French Equatorial Africa, and set up a jungle hospital, which subsequently occupied most of his time and energy. However, he continued to pursue his interest in music, theology, and philosophy, making occasional concert tours as an organist in Europe to raise funds for his hospital work among the African natives. In 1952 he was awarded the Nobel Peace Prize, the only professional musician to hold this prestigious award. His philosophical and theological writings had established his reputation as one of the foremost thinkers of his time. In the field of music he distinguished himself as the author of one of the most important books on Bach, greatly influencing the interpretation of Bach's music, and contributing to the understanding of Bach's symbolic treatment of various musical devices. He ed. *J.S. Bach: Complete Organ Works: A Critico-practical Edition* (N.Y.; vols. I-V, 1912–14, with C. Widor; vols. VI-VIII, 1954–67, with E. Nies-Berger).

WRITINGS: *Eugène Munch, 1857–1898* (Mulhouse, 1898); *J.S. Bach, le musicien-poète* (Paris, 1905; aug. Ger. eds., 1908, 1915; Eng. tr. by E. Newman, 2 vols., Leipzig, 1911); *Deutsche und französische Orgelbaukunst und Orgelkunst* (Leipzig, 1906; second ed., 1927); *Aus meiner Kindheit und Jugendzeit* (Bern and Munich, 1924; Eng. tr., 1924, as *Memoirs of Childhood and Youth*); *Aus meinem Leben und Denken* (Leipzig, 1931; Eng. tr., 1933); also various theological and philosophical books. A complete German ed. of his writings was ed. by R. Grabs (5 vols., Munich, 1974).

BIBL.: C. Campion, *A. S.: Philosopher, Theologian, Musician, Doctor* (N.Y., 1928); J. Regester, *A. S.: The Man and His Work* (N.Y., 1931); M. Ratter, *A. S.* (London, 1935; rev. ed., 1950); A. Roback, ed., *The A. S. Jubilee Book* (Cambridge, Mass., 1946); H. Hagedorn, *Prophet in the Wilderness: The Story of A. S.* (N.Y., 1947); O. Kraus, *A. S.: His Work and His Philosophy* (N.Y., 1947); G. Seaver, *A. S.: The Man and His Mind* (London, 1947); R. Grabs, *A. S.: Weg und Werk eines Menschenfreundes* (Berlin, 1953); R. Sonner, *S. und die Orgelbewegung* (Colmar, 1955); W. Picht, *The Life and Thought of A. S.* (N.Y., 1965); E. Jacobi, *A. S. und die Musik* (Wiesbaden, 1975); S. Hanheide, *Johann Sebastian Bach im Verständis A. S.s* (Munich, 1990); K. and A. Bergel, eds., *A. S. and Alice Ehlers: A Friendship in Letters* (Lanham, Md., 1991); H. Schützeichel, *Die Konzerttätigkeit A. S.s* (Bern, 1991); idem, *Die Orgel im Leben und Denken A. S.s* (Kleinblittersdorf, 1991); M. Murray, *A. S., Musician* (Aldershot, 1994).—**NS/LK/DM**

Schweitzer, Anton, German composer; b. Coburg (baptized), June 6, 1735; d. Gotha, Nov. 23, 1787. He was a chorister, and later played viola in Hildburghausen. After study with J.F. Kleinknecht in Bayreuth, he returned to Hildburghausen as Kammermusicus, and following further training in Italy (1764–66), he returned once more to Hildburghausen as court Kapellmeister. In 1769 he became conductor of Seyler's opera troupe, which was engaged by the Weimar court in 1771. He produced his successful Singspiel *Die Dorfgala* there (June 30, 1772), which was followed by the successful *Alkeste* (May 28, 1773), the first through-composed grand opera to a German libretto, the text being by C.M. Wieland. After fire destroyed the Weimar theater in 1774, he accompanied Seyler's troupe to Gotha, where he subsequently was director of the ducal chapel from 1778 until his death. Among his other stage works were *Rosamunde*, Singspiel (Mannheim, Jan. 20, 1780), *Die Wahl des Herkules*, lyric drama (Weimar, Sept. 4, 1773), and the melodrama *Pygmalion*, after Rousseau (Weimar, May 13, 1772; not extant). He also wrote many ballets, syms., and piano pieces.

BIBL.: J. Maurer, *A. S. als dramatischer Komponist* (Leipzig, 1912).—**NS/LK/DM**

Schwemmer, Heinrich, German composer and teacher; b. Gumpertshausen bei Hallburg, March 28, 1621; d. Nuremberg (buried), May 31, 1696. He settled in Nuremberg in 1641. After studies with Kindermann, he taught school (from 1650) and served as Director cori musici (from c. 1656),sharing the latter position with Paul Hainlein. He composed a number of cantatas and choral concertos.—**LK/DM**

Schwencke, family of German musicians:

(1) Johann Gottlieb Schwencke, bassoonist and composer; b. Breitenau, Saxony, Aug. 11, 1744; d. Hamburg, Dec. 7, 1823. He was greatly esteemed as a bassoonist, serving as a town musician in Hamburg, where he was also active as a piano teacher.

(2) Christian Fredrich Gottlieb Schwencke, pianist and composer, son of the preceding; b. Wachenhausen, Harz, Aug. 30, 1767; d. Hamburg, Oct. 27, 1822. He began piano study as a child, performing one of his father's piano concertos in Hamburg in 1779. He went to Berlin in 1782 to study with Marpurg and Kirnberger; after attending the Univs. of Leipzig and Halle (1787–88), he was in 1788 named C.P.E. Bach's successor as Hamburg Stadtkantor, a position he retained until his death. Schwenke was also a contributor to the *Allgemeine Musikalische Zeitung* (from 1799), ran his own music business (from 1801), and was director of a music academy for private performances (from 1805). He wrote incidental music, oratorios, cantatas, 2 piano concertos, an Oboe Concerto, 3 piano sonatas, 3 violin sonatas, 6 organ fugues, and songs. He also ed. rescored versions of Handel's *Messiah* and *Alexander's Feast*, Bach's Mass in B minor and *Magnificat*, and Hasse's *Te Deum*. He had 2 sons who became musicians:

(3) **Johann Friedrich Schwencke,** organist, cellist, clarinetist, and composer; b. Hamburg, April 30, 1792; d. there, Sept. 28, 1852. He received instruction in theory and composition from his father, being made organist of Hamburg's Nikolaikirche in 1829. He wrote numerous cantatas, over 500 chorale preludes and postludes for organ, and a Septet for 5 Cellos, Double Bass, and Kettledrums, and harmonized about 1,000 chorales and 73 Russian folk songs. He also publ. the popular *Choralbuch zum Hamburgischen Gesangbuch* (1832), made many transcriptions, and orchestrated Beethoven's *Adelaide* and various works by other composers. His son, Friedrich Gottlieb Schwencke (b. Hamburg, Dec. 15, 1823; d. there, June 11, 1896), was a pianist, organist, and composer who studied with his father, whom he succeeded as organist at the Nikolaikirche in 1852; also made tours as a pianist and organist, including a successful visit to Paris (1855). He wrote 2 fantasies for Organ, Trumpet, Trombones, and Timpani, sacred songs for Women's Voices and Organ, chorale preludes, and songs. He also brought out an augmented ed. of his father's chorales (1886).

(4) **Karl Schwencke,** pianist and composer; b. Hamburg, March 7, 1797; d. probably in Nussdorf, near Vienna, Jan. 7, 1870. He traveled widely; in Vienna in 1824 he met Beethoven, who composed the canon *Schwenke dich* for him. His own works include a Sym. in D major (Paris, 1843), a Mass, a Violin Sonata, 3 sonatas for Piano Duet, and solo piano pieces.—NS/LK/DM

Schwertsik, Kurt, Austrian composer, horn player, and teacher; b. Vienna, June 25, 1935. He studied composition with Marx and Schiske at the Vienna Academy of Music (1949–57), where he also received training in horn. From 1955 to 1959 he played horn in the Niederösterreichisches Tonkünstler-Orch. in Vienna. With Cerha, he founded the new music ensemble die reihe in Vienna in 1958. He continued his training with Stockhausen in Darmstadt and Cologne (1959–62), and held a bursary with the Austrian Cultural Inst. in Rome (1960–61). From 1962 to 1968 he again played horn in the Niederösterreichisches Tonkünstler-Orch. He also studied analysis with Polnauer (1964–65). While serving as a visiting teacher of composition at the Univ. of Calif. at Riverside (1966), he pursued his studies in analysis with Jonas. In 1968 he became a horn player in the Vienna Sym. Orch. He also taught composition at the

Vienna Cons. from 1979. A skillful and imaginative composer, he explores in his works many new paths in synthesizing the traditional with the contemporary.

WORKS: **DRAMATIC:** *Der lange Weg zur grossen Mauer,* opera (1974; Ulm, May 13, 1975); *Walzerträume (...als das Tanzen noch geholfen hat),* ballet (1976; Cologne, Feb. 16, 1977); also as the ballet or set of 3 orch. suites, *Wiener Chronik 1848,* 1976–77); *Ur-Faust,* music to Goethe's play (1976; Mattersburg, Feb. 2, 1977); *Kaiser Joseph und die Bahnwärters-Tochter,* music to Herzmanovsky-Orlando's play (1977); *Das Märchen von Fanferlieschen Schönefusschen,* opera (1982; Stuttgart, Nov. 24, 1983); *Macbeth,* dance theater (Heidelberg, Feb. 10, 1988); *Die verlorene Wut,* Singspiel (ORF, Dec. 26, 1989); *Das Friedensbankett,* operetta (1990); *Frida Kahlo,* ballet (1991; Bremen, Feb. 8, 1992); *Ulrichslegende,* music for an opera (1992); *Café Museum oder die Erleuchtung,* opera (Deutschlandsberg, Oct. 9, 1993); *Nietzsche,* ballet (1994); *Der ewige Frieden,* operetta (1994; Bonn, Jan. 8, 1995); *Die Welt der Mongolen,* opera (1996; Linz, Feb. 2, 1997). **ORCH.:** 4 syms.: No. 1, *...für Audifax und Abachum* (1963–70), No. 2, *Draculas Haus- und Hofmusik: Eine transsylvanische Symphonie* for Strings (1968), No. 3, *Symphonie im Mob-Stil* (1971), and No. 4, *Irdische Klänge* (Vienna, April 16, 1980); Alphorn Concerto "in the Celtic manner" (1975; Vienna, May 15, 1977); Violin Concerto (Graz, Oct. 9, 1977); *Epilog zu Rosamunde* (Vienna, May 31, 1978); *Tag- und Nachtweisen* (Salzburg, Aug. 25, 1978); Concerto for Guitar and Small Orch. (1979); *Instant Music for Flute and Wind Orch.* (1981; Vienna, Nov. 28, 1982; rev. 1983); *Der irdischen Klänge 2. Teil, nämlich Fünf Naturstücke* (1984; Vienna, Dec. 4, 1985); Timpani Concerto, *Irdische Klänge 4* (1987–88; Vienna, July 5, 1988); Double Bass Concerto, *ein emfindsames Konzert* (Heidelberg, April 29, 1989); *Mit den Riesenstiefeln, Irdische Klänge 5* (1991; Vienna, April 24, 1992); *Uluru (in mitten der Irdischen Klänge)* (Vienna, Nov. 19, 1992); *Baumgesänge* (Vienna, Nov. 16, 1992); *Sinfonia- Sinfonietta* (1996); *Unter Messing Baumen* (1998); *Schrumpf- Symphonie* (Salzburg, Dec. 31, 1999). **CHAMBER:** Horn Sonata (1952); *Duo and Double* for Violin and Piano (1957); Trio for Violin, Horn, and Piano (1960); String Quartet (1961); *Salotto romano* for 12 Bass Instruments (1961); *Liebesträume* for 7 Instruments (1963); *Eichendorff Quintet* for Winds (1964); *Proviant* for Wind Sextet (1965); *5 Nocturnes* for Cello and Piano (1966); *Querschnitt durch eine Operette* for Wind Quintet (1966); *Österreichisches Quodlibet* for Chamber Ensemble (Montreal, April 28, 1967); *Musik vom Mutterland Mu* for 11 Instruments (1974); *Skizzen und Entwürfe* for String Quartet (Hamburg, Sept. 13, 1974); *Twilight Music: A Celtic Serenade* for Octet (1976; Hall, Aug. 25, 1977); *Kleine Blaumusik* for 2 Trumpets and 2 Trombones (Graz, Oct. 16, 1977); *Bagatellen* for Piano Trio (Vienna, Dec. 12, 1979); *Sotto Voce: Gedämpfte Unterhaltung* for Flute, Violin, Cello, and Guitar (South German Radio, Stuttgart, Oct. 3, 1980); *Blechpartie im neuesten Geschmack* for Brass Quintet (Innsbruck, Nov. 8, 1982; rev. 1986); *Fantasy Piece* for Trumpet and Piano (1982); *Hornpostille,* 4 pieces for 4 Horns (Vienna, Sept. 1983); *Neues von Eu-Sirius* for 2 Violins and Viola (Vienna, Oct. 2, 1988); *Am Ende Steht ein Marsch* for Wind Octet (Vienna, March 4, 1991); *3 späte Liebeslieder* for Cello and Piano (Vienna, Oct. 17, 1992); *Möbelmusik-Klassich* for 2 Violins, Viola, and Double Bass (1993); *Wake* for String Quartet (1994). **VOCAL:** *Shâl-i-mâr,* 7 songs for Baritone and Orch. (1962–72; rev. version, Vienna, Oct. 24, 1992); *Stückwerk* for Soprano and Chamber Orch. (1966; Vienna, Jan. 30, 1967); *Kurt Schwertsiks lichte Momente* for Singers and Instrumentalists (1971); *Brautigan Songbook* for Voice and Piano (1971); *Manchmal vertrödelt Christa S. den Tag* for Voice and Instrumentalists (1975); *Ich sein Blumenbein,* 11 songs for Voice and Piano (Vienna, June 1980; also for Voice, Guitar, and Keyboards); *Starckdeutsche Lieder und Tänze* for Baritone and Orch. (1980–82; Vienna, Feb. 13, 1986); *Kurze Geschichte der Bourgeoise* for Chorus (1981); *...& was ist dann Friede?*, 6 songs for Voice and Guitar (1983); *Starker Tobak*, cantata for Soprano and 7 Instruments (Vienna, Sept. 13, 1983); *Iba di gaunz oaman Fraun*, 8 songs for Soprano, Piano, Bass, and Drums (1983; Vienna, Jan. 1984); *Cinq chansons cryptiques* for Voice and Piano (1985; Vienna, June 1986); *Gute Nacht, Guten Morgen*, 8 songs for Voice and Piano (1985; Vienna, Oct. 26, 1986); *Das Leben*, 8 songs for Mezzo-soprano and Celtic Naturehorn (Bregrenz, Aug. 21, 1986); *Gedichte an Ljuba*, 5 songs for Voice and Piano (1986; Vienna, Feb. 5, 1987); *Es friert zuweilen auch den Geist* for Voice and Piano (1991); *Human Existence* for Soprano and Ensemble (Dartington, Aug. 17, 1992); *Singt meine Schwäne* for Soprano and Ensemble (Dartington, Aug. 17, 1992); *Der Herr weis was der Wil* for Soprano and Ensemble (Dartington, Aug. 17, 1992); *The Fox and the Magpie* for Tenor, Baritone, Soprano Saxophone, Horn, Bassoon, and Piano (Sydney, July 18, 1994); *Roald Dahl's "Goldilocks"* for Narrators and Orch. (1997).—**NS/LK/DM**

Schwieger, Hans,

German-born American conductor; b. Cologne, June 15, 1906. He studied in Cologne. He was asst. conductor at the Berlin State Opera (1927–30), at the Kassel Opera (1930–31), in Mainz (1932–33), and in Danzig (1936–37). In 1937 he went to Japan, where he conducted the Tokyo Sym. Orch. In 1938 he settled in the U.S.; became a naturalized American citizen in 1944. He organized and conducted the Southern Sym. Orch. in Columbia, S.C. (1938–41), and then was conductor of the Fort Wayne Phil. (1944–48). From 1948 to 1971 he was conductor of the Kansas City (Mo.) Phil. He then filled engagements as a guest conductor in Europe.—**NS/LK/DM**

Schwindl, Friedrich,

violinist and composer; b. May 3, 1737; d. Karlsruhe, Aug. 7, 1786. He was Konzertmeister to the Margrave of Wied- Runkel and virtuoso di camera to the Count of Colloredo before going to The Hague (about 1770), where he was active as a teacher and as first violinist to Prince William V of Orange. After a sojourn in Switzerland, he was made Konzertmeister to the Margrave of Bad Durlach in Karlsruhe in 1780. Throughout his career, he traveled widely as a virtuoso. He was greatly admired as a composer of instrumental music, which was played in Europe and even in America during his lifetime. His output includes more than 30 syms., much chamber music, and vocal pieces.

BIBL.: A. Downs, *The Symphonies of F. S.* (diss., N.Y.U., 1973).—**NS/LK/DM**

Schytte, Ludvig (Theodor),

Danish pianist, teacher, and composer; b. Århus, April 28, 1848; d. Berlin, Nov. 10, 1909. He was a pharmacist as a young man, then began to study piano with Anton Rée and composition with Gade, finishing under Taubert in Berlin and Liszt in Weimar. He settled in Vienna in 1887 as a teacher, then moved to Berlin in 1907, where he taught at the Stern Cons. A master of the miniature forms, he wrote a number of attractive piano pieces, some of which became extremely popular; about 200 were publ.

WORKS: KEYBOARD: P i a n o   S o l o : *Promenades musicale; Rapsodie norvégienne; Aus froher Kinderzeit; Spanische Nächte; Valse piquante; Waldbilder; Aus der Heimat und Fremde;* numerous piano studies (*6 brillante Vortragsetüden, Melodische Spezialetüden, Studien in Ornamentik und Dynamik*). **4 - h a n d s :** *Bajaderntänze; Kindersymphonie; Musikalische Wandelbilder; Reiseblätter; Kindersuite;* etc. **OTHER:** *Hero*, opera (Copenhagen, Sept. 25, 1898); *Der Mameluk*, operetta (Vienna, Dec. 22, 1903); Piano Concerto; chamber music; *Die Verlassene*, song cycle.—**NS/LK/DM**

Sciammarella, Valdo,

Argentine composer; b. Buenos Aires, Jan. 20, 1924. He studied composition with Julián Bautista, and subsequently engaged in pedagogy. In 1965 he was appointed head of the music dept. at the National School of Fine Arts in Buenos Aires. He wrote a lyric comedy, *Marianita Limena* (Buenos Aires, Nov. 11, 1957), *Variaciones concertantes* for Piano and Orch. (1952), *Scherzino* for Oboe, Clarinet, and Bassoon (1956), *Galeria humana*, chamber ballet (1962), and piano pieces.—**NS/LK/DM**

Sciarrino, Salvatore,

Italian composer; b. Palermo, April 4, 1947. He was 12 when he began to compose under the tutelage of Antonino Titione; also received some guidance from Evangelisti. After studies with Turi Belfiore (1964), he attended Evangelisti's electronic music sessions at the Accademia di Santa Cecilia in Rome (1969). He taught at the Milan Cons. (from 1974); also served as artistic director of the Teatro Comunale in Bologna (1977–80). His music reveals an innovative approach to traditional forms; in some works he utilizes aleatoric procedures.

WORKS: DRAMATIC: O p e r a : *Amore e Psiche* (Milan, March 2, 1973); *Aspern* (Florence, June 8, 1978); *Cailles en sarchophage* (Venice, Sept. 26, 1979); *Vanitas* (Milan, Dec. 11, 1981); *Lohengrin* (Milan, Jan. 15, 1983); *Perseo e Andromeda* (1990; Stoccardo, Jan. 27, 1991). **ORCH.:** *Berceuse* (1967; Venice, Sept. 13, 1969); *Da a da da* (Venice, Sept. 12, 1970); *Sonata da camera* (Rome, Oct. 31, 1971); *Grande sonata da camera* (1971; Paris, Feb. 21, 1972); *Rondo* for Flute and Orch. (1972; Naples, April 6, 1973); *Romanza* for Viola d'Amore and Orch. (Florence, Oct. 20, 1973); *Variazioni* for Cello and Orch. (Saarbrücken, May 23, 1974); *Clair de lune* for Piano and Orch. (Milan, Feb. 12, 1976); *Il paese senz'alba* (Naples, June 19, 1977); *Che sai guardiano, della notte?* for Clarinet and Small Orch. (Paris, June 19, 1979); *Autoritratto nella notte* (Lugano, March 17, 1983); Violin Concerto, *Allegoria della notte* (Rome, Oct. 1, 1985); *Sul poemi concentrici I, II,* and *III* (RAI, Turin, April 8, 1988); *Lettura da lontano* for Double Bass and Orch. (Milan, Oct. 21, 1989). **CHAMBER:** *Quartetto II* for String Quartet (1967); *...Da un divertimento* for 10 Instruments (1970); *Arabesque* for 2 Organs (1971); *2 Studies* for Cello (1974); 2 piano trios (1975, 1986); 2 quintets (1976, 1977); *Ai limiti della notte* for Viola (1979; also for Cello); *Fauno che fischia a un merlo* for Flute and Harp (1980); *Introduzione all'oscuro* for Instruments (1981); *Nox apud Orpheum* for 2 Organs and Instruments (1982); *Codex purpureus I* for String Trio (1983); *Codex purpureus II* for 2 Violins, Viola, Cello, and Piano (1984); *La canzone di ringraziamento* for Flute (1985); *Esplorazione del bianco III* for Jazz Ensemble (1986); *Il motivo degli oggetti di vetro* for 2 Flutes and Piano (1987); *Il silenzio degli oracoli* for Wind Quintet (1989); also piano pieces, including 3 sonatas (1976, 1983, 1986). **VOCAL:** *Aka aka to I, II,* and *III* for Soprano and 12 Instruments (1968); *Il paese senza tramonto* for Soprano and Orch. (Montepulciano, Aug. 14, 1977); *12 canzoni da battello* for Soprano and Instruments (1977); *Kindertotenlied* for Soprano, Tenor, and Small Orch. (1978; Venice, Oct. 7, 1979); *Un'immagine di Arpocrate* for Chorus, Piano, and Orch. (Donaueschingen, Oct. 19, 1979); *Flos florum* for Chorus and Orch. (Turin, April 30, 1981); *Efebo con radio* for Voice and Orch. (Florence, May 28, 1981); *Rose, Liz* for Voice and 5 Instruments (1984); *Morte di Borromini* for Narrator and Orch. (Milan, Oct. 18, 1988); *Due Arie marine* for Mezzo-soprano and Electronics (Turin, Oct. 27, 1990).—**NS/LK/DM**

Scimone, Claudio, Italian conductor, musicologist, and music educator; b. Padua, Dec. 23, 1934. He studied conducting with Zecchi, Mitropoulos, and Ferrara. In 1959 he founded the noted chamber orch. I Solisti Veneti (in Padua), and made numerous tours with it, presenting works from the Baroque to the avant-garde. He also acquired a fine reputation as a scholar specializing in Italian music; supervised a modern ed. of the works of Giuseppe Tartini, and prepared a complete edition of Rossini. He taught at the Venice Cons. (1961–67) and the Verona Cons. (1967–74); then was a teacher and director of the Padua Cons. (1974–83). In addition to numerous articles for various music journals, he publ. *Segno, Significato, Interpretazione* (1970).—**NS/LK/DM**

Scio, Julie-Angélique, French soprano; b. Lille, 1768; d. Paris, July 14, 1807. She launched her career in 1786 under the name Mlle. Grécy. After appearances in Montpellier, Avignon, and Marseilles, she married the violinist Etienne Scio (1766–1796) and settled with him in Paris. In 1792 she made her first appearance at the Opéra-Comique, and then became a principal member of the Opéra, where she created the title role in Cherubini's *Médée* (March 13, 1797) and the role of Constance in his *Les Deux journées* (March 14, 1800). She also won distinction in operas by Berton, Dalayrac, and Le Sueur. —**NS/LK/DM**

Sciutti, Graziella, Italian soprano, opera producer, and teacher; b. Turin, April 17, 1927. She received her training at the Accademia di Santa Cecilia in Rome. In 1951 she made her debut as Lucy in Menotti's *The Telephone* at the Aix-en-Provence Festival. In 1954 she sang for the first time at the Glyndebourne Festival as Rosina, and she returned there until 1959. She sang Carolina in *Il Matrimonio segreto* at the opening of the Piccola Scala in Milan in 1955. From 1956 she appeared at La Scala in Milan. She made her debut at London's Covent Garden in 1956 as Oscar, and made appearances there until 1962. In 1958 she made her first appearance at the Salzburg Festival as Despina, and continued to sing there until 1966. In 1961 she made her U.S. debut as Susanna at the San Francisco Opera. After her career as a soubrette exponent ended, she devoted herself to producing opera in Glyndebourne, at Covent Garden, in N.Y., Chicago, and other opera centers. From 1986 she also ran her own music academy in Florence. —**NS/LK/DM**

Scobey, Bob (actually, **Robert Alexander Jr.**), jazz trumpeter; b. Tucumcari, N.Mex., Dec. 9, 1916; d. Montreal, Quebec, Canada, June 12, 1963. His family moved to Stockton, Calif. in 1918. He started playing cornet at age 9, trumpet at 14. He studied at Berklee Coll. and began playing professionally when he was 20. Scobey worked in pit bands, dance orchestras, and clubs during the 1930s. In 1938 he met Lu Watters. He co-founded Lu Watters's Yerba Buena Band in the late 1930s, playing cornet alongside Watters until 1949, except for the period 1942–46 when he was in the Army performing with its band. During the 1950s, he led his own band in Calif.; his group made many recordings, were headliners at most traditional jazz festivals, and had a three-year residency at two clubs in Oakland. He opened his own club in Chicago in 1959 while making regular trips with his group to N.Y., Las Vegas, and San Francisco. In 1962, he toured Europe as part of the Harlem Globetrotters' package. He continued to play dates with his band until weeks before he died of cancer. His widow, Jan, wrote his biography.

DISC.: *Bob Scobey's Frisco Band, Vol. 1* (1950); *Vocals by Clancy Hayes* (1955); *Scobey and Clancy* (1955); *Direct from San Francisco* (1956); *Swingin' on the Golden Gate* (1957); *College "Classics"* (1957); *Rompin' and Stompin'* (1958).

BIBL.: J. Goggin, *B. S.: A Bibliography & Discography*; J. Scobey, *Jan Scobey Presents He Rambled! 'til Cancer Cut Him Down: B. S., Dixieland Jazz Musician and Bandleader, 1916–63* (Northridge, Calif., 1976).—**JC/LP**

Scofield, John, influential avant-garde jazz guitarist; b. Dayton, Ohio, Dec. 26, 1951. He was raised in Wilton, Conn. He picked up his first guitar at age 11 and started out playing rock, but soon turned to jazz. He attended Berklee (1971) with Joe Lovano, Bill Frisell, George Garzone, Billy Pierce, Billy Drewes, and Jamey Haddad but left when he started to get gigs. In the early 1970s, he played or recorded with Charles Mingus, Jack DeJohnette, and Gerry Mulligan. During this time, Gil Evans, a friend and neighbor, was his role model for composition. He toured with the George Duke-Billy Cobham band in the mid-1970s, sometimes on the same bill with Weather Report. He became even better known through a three-year stint in Miles Davis's band from 1984–87. Scofield went on to record an award-winning series of albums for Blue Note, three of which reached #1 on the Billboard jazz chart. Since about 1987, he has played once a year with Palle Danielsson, Knut Riisnes, and Jon Christensen at the Molde Jazz Festival in Norway. In 1993, he toured with Joe Henderson in a Miles Davis tribute. In addition to leading his own band since 1985, Scofield has guested with McCoy Tyner, Gary Burton, Chet Baker, and Herbie Hancock. He continues to tour with his band about half of each year. During the 1990s, he won numerous Readers' Polls and awards for his recordings and performances.

DISC.: *John Scofield Live* (1977); *East Meets West* (1977); *Bar Talk* (1980); *Shinola* (1981); *Loud Jazz* (1987); *Live Three Ways* (1990); *Hand Jive* (1993); *Groove Elation* (1995); *Quiet* (1996); *A Go Go* (1997); *Bump* (2000); *Steady Groovin': The Blue Note Groove Sides* (2000).

WRITINGS: *J. S.: Guitar Transcriptions* (Winona, Minn., 1987); with K. Chipkin *Time on My Hands* (Miami, 1991).—**LP**

Scontrino, Antonio, prominent Italian double bass player, teacher, and composer; b. Trapani, May 17, 1850; d. Florence, Jan. 7, 1922. He studied at the Palermo Cons., becoming a virtuoso on the double bass and giving concerts. He went to Munich for a special study of German music at the Musikschule (1872–74). After various engagements as an orch. player and teacher, he settled in Florence in 1892, and taught composition at the Reale Istituto Musicale.

WORKS: DRAMATIC: O p e r a : *Matelda* (Milan, June 19, 1879); *Il Progettista* (Rome, Feb. 8, 1882); *Il sortilegio* (Turin, June 21, 1882); *Gringoire* (Milan, May 24, 1890); *La Cortigiana* (Milan, Jan. 30, 1896). OTHER: Incidental music to Gabriele d'Annunzio's *Francesca da Rimini* (Rome, Dec. 12, 1901). ORCH.: *Sinfonia marinaresca* (Florence, Feb. 12, 1897); Double Bass Concerto (Hamburg, Oct. 18, 1908); *Sinfonia romantica* (Berlin, March 9, 1914); *Preludio Religioso* (1919); Bassoon Concerto (Florence, Dec. 20, 1920); Piano Concerto. CHAMBER: 4 string quartets (1901, 1903, 1905, 1918); pieces for Violin and Piano; piano pieces. VOCAL: Choral music; songs.

BIBL.: *A. S. nella vita e nell'arte* (Trapani, 1935). —NS/LK/DM

Scott, Bobby, jazz-pop pianist, songwriter, composer, singer; b. N.Y., Jan. 29, 1937; d. there, Nov. 5, 1990. He studied music with Edvard Moritz, then worked with Louis Prima, Tony Scott, and Gene Krupa, with whom he toured in JATP in 1955. In the 1950s and 1960s, Scott recorded trio, combo, and big band albums. A number he composed for the play *A Taste of Honey* (1961), became a hit for several artists in the 1960s. He continued composing, arranging, producing, and performing into the 1970s and 1980s. He also recorded chamber music works in the 1970s.

DISC.: *Great Scott* (1954); *Compositions of Bobby Scott, Vol. 1* (1954); *Scott Free* (1955); *Bobby Scott and Two Horns* (1956); *Complete Musician* (1960); *I Had a Ball* (1964); *Robert William Scott* (1971); *Forecast: Rain with Sunny Skies* (1978).—LP

Scott, Bud (Arthur Jr.), jazz guitarist, banjoist, singer, violinist; b. New Orleans, La., Jan. 11, c. 1890; d. Los Angeles, Calif., July 2, 1949. He played guitar and violin from early childhood. Professionally active from the turn of the century, he worked with John Robichaux's Orch. (c. 1904), and also played briefly in Freddie Keppard's Olympia Orch. Scott left New Orleans in January 1913 as the featured violinist with a traveling show. By 1915, he was in N.Y., where he played in various theater orchestras; he remained there through 1921, except for a period in 1917 when he was in Baltimore as banjoist with Bob Young's Band. In N.Y., he had many engagements as vocalist with the Clef Club Orch., including a famous appearance at Carnegie Hall in 1919. Scott then joined Will Marion Cook's Orch. in 1921. Late in 1923, he moved to Chicago; during the next three years, he would work on and off with King Oliver in Chicago and Kid Ory on the West Coast. In 1926, he began working with Erskine Tate in Chicago before joining Dave Peyton in late 1926. He continued to work with Peyton (on violin) for over two years, but also worked as manager (and banjoist) at the Cafe de Paris, Chicago, in 1927 before making a brief return to

Erskine Tate. Scott then worked with Jimmie Noone at the Apex Club (1928). During this period, Scott also did extensive freelance recordings, including sessions with Jelly Roll Morton. After working with Fess Williams (January 1929) and again with Peyton (summer 1929), Scott left Chicago in September 1929 to make his home in Los Angeles, where he worked with various bands and also led his own trio for several years. In 1944, he rejoined Kid Ory and continued to work with him until late 1948 when ill health forced him to quit regular playing. He appeared in the film *New Orleans*.—JC/LP

Scott, Cecil (Xavier) Jr., jazz clarinetist, tenor and baritone saxophonist; b. Springfield, Ohio, Nov. 22, 1905; d. N.Y., Jan. 5, 1964. His father, Cecil Sr., was a violinist. In 1919, while in high school, Cecil Jr. formed a trio with his brother Lloyd (a drummer) and pianist Don Frye. By 1922 they were operating as a seven-piece band, Scott's Symphonic Syncopators. They toured around Ohio until early 1924, then played at the Royal Gardens, Pittsburgh, prior to residency at Herman's Inn, N.Y., from June–October l924. The band alternated dates in their home state with residencies in N.Y. (1926–early 1927) and road dates through Pittsburgh, Buffalo, and Canada. In December 1927, they began a long residency at N.Y.'s Savoy Ballroom while continuing to make occasional road trips. In June 1929, Cecil became the leader of the band, and his Bright Boys toured (and played at many N.Y. residencies) until the early 1930s. However, Cecil suffered a serious accident, badly damaging his ankle in a fall; the resultant complications caused the amputation of a leg and he was forced to disband. After his recovery, he did extensive recording work for Clarence Williams. He also did occasional work with Fletcher Henderson and played regularly with Vernon Andrade's Orch. during the mid-1930s. Scott played with Teddy Hill in 1936 and 1937 (in N.Y. and on tour). He then played for a long period with a band led by Alberto Socarras until he formed his own band for a residency at the Ubangi Club starting in 1942. During the mid-1940s, he worked with Hot Lips Page in Chicago (c. 1944), then played regularly with Art Hodes's small groups while continuing regular freelance recording work. During the 1950s and early 1960s, Scott led his own small groups in N.Y. He also worked with Henry "Chick" Morrison's Band in 1950–52, and with Jimmy McPartland's Band (c. 1953–54). In August 1959, he played in Canada with Willie "The Lion" Smith.—JC/LP

Scott, Cyril (Meir), remarkable English composer; b. Oxton, Cheshire, Sept. 27, 1879; d. Eastbourne, Dec. 31, 1970. He was a scion of a cultural family; his father was a classical scholar, his mother a fine amateur musician. Having displayed a natural penchant for music as a child, he was sent to Frankfurt am Main at age 12 to study with Uzielli and Humperdinck, remaining there for a year and a half before returning to England; he once again went to Frankfurt am Main in 1895 to study piano and theory with Iwan Knorr. In 1898 he went to Liverpool as a teacher. In 1900 Hans Richter conducted Scott's *Heroic Suite*, in Liverpool and Manchester; also in 1900, his first Sym. was played in

Darmstadt; his overture *Pelléas and Mélisande* was performed in Frankfurt am Main. His second Sym. (1902) was given at a Promenade Concert in London on Aug. 25, 1903. (It was later converted into *3 Symphonic Dances*.) His setting of Keats's *La Belle Dame sans merci* for Baritone, Chorus, and Orch. was premiered in London in 1916. His opera *The Alchemist* (1917), for which he wrote his own libretto, was premiered in Essen on May 28, 1925. In 1920 Scott traveled to the U.S. and played his first Piano Concerto with the Philadelphia Orch. under Stokowski (Nov. 5, 1920). However, Scott acquired fame mainly as a composer of some exotically flavored piano pieces, of which *Lotus Land* became a perennial favorite; Fritz Kreisler arranged it for violin and piano, and played it repeatedly at his concerts. Other popular piano pieces were *Danse negre, Chinese Serenade, Russian Dance, Sphinx, Autumn Idyll, Berceuse, Little Russian Suite, Indian Suite, Spanish Dance,* and most particularly the ingratiating suite *Impressions of the Jungle Book,* after Kipling. He also wrote over 100 songs. In all these pieces, Scott showed himself a master of musical miniature; he wrote in a distinctly modern idiom, very much in the style of French Impressionism; employed sonorous parallel progressions of unresolved dissonant chords; made frequent use of the whole-tone scale. His writing for piano is ingratiating in its idiomatic mastery; his harmonious modalities exude an aura of perfumed euphony. Among his other works are 2 more operas, *The Saint of the Mountain* (1925) and *Maureen O'Mara* (1946), 3 ballets, *The Incompetent Apothecary* (1923), *Karma* (1926), and *The Masque of the Red Death* (1932), *Christmas Overture* (London, Nov. 13, 1906), *La Princesse Maleine,* symphonic poem (London, Aug. 22, 1907), 3 violin concertos (1927, c. 1935, c. 1935), Cello Concerto (1931), Harpsichord Concerto (1937), Sym. No. 3, *The Muses* (1939), Oboe Concerto (1946), *Sinfonietta* for Strings, Organ, and Harp (1954), *Neapolitan Rhapsody* for Orch. (1960), *Sinfonietta* for Strings (1962), numerous overtures and suites, *Nativity Hymn* for Chorus and Orch. (1913), *The Ballad of Fair Helen of Kirkconnel* for Baritone and Orch. (1925), *Rima's Call to the Birds* for Soprano and Orch. (1933), *Let Us Now Praise Famous Men* for Chorus and Orch. (1935), *Ode to Great Men* for Tenor and Orch. (1936), *Hymn of Unity* for Solo Voices, Chorus, and Orch. (1946), more than 100 songs, Piano Quartet (1900), 4 string quartets (1920, 1958, 1960, 1968), 3 piano trios (1920, 1950, 1957), 2 piano quintets (1924, 1952), 2 string trios (1931, 1949), Cello Sonata (1950), Clarinet Quintet (1953), Flute Sonata (1961), 3 piano sonatas (1910, 1932, 1956), and 160 other piano pieces. From his early youth, Scott was attracted to occult sciences, and was a believer in the reality of the supernatural; he publ. books and essays on music as a divinely inspired art, and inveighed violently against jazz as the work of Satan. Among his books, all publ. in London, are *The Philosophy of Modernism in Its Connection with Music* (1917), *The Initiate Trilogy* (1920, 1927, 1935), *My Years of Indiscretion* (1924), *The Influence of Music on History and Morals: A Vindication of Plato* (1928), *Music: Its Secret Influence through the Ages* (1933; aug. ed., 1958), *An Outline of Modern Occultism* (1935), *The Christian Paradox* (1942), an autobiographical vol., *Bone of Contention* (1969), and 2 books on medical matters, *Medicine,*

Rational and Irrational (1946) and *Cancer Prevention* (1968).

BIBL.: A. Hull, *C. S.: Composer, Poet and Philosopher* (London, 1918; third ed., 1921); I. Parrott, *C. S. and his Piano Music* (London, 1992).—NS/LK/DM

Scott, Francis George, Scottish composer; b. Hawick, Roxburghshire, Jan. 25, 1880; d. Glasgow, Nov. 6, 1958. He studied humanities at the Univ. of Edinburgh, Moray House Coll. of Education in Edinburgh, and the Univ. of Durham (B.M., 1909); also took theory lessons with a local organist, and later pursued training with Roger-Ducasse. After a period as a school teacher, he was a lecturer in music at Jordanhill Coll. in Glasgow (1925–46). Scott was at his best as a composer of songs; publ. *Scottish Lyrics* for Voice and Piano (5 vols., London and Glasgow, 1922–39) and *35 Scottish Lyrics and Other Poems* (Glasgow, 1949); also wrote *The Ballad of Kynd Kittok* for Baritone and Orch. (1934), *Renaissance,* overture (1937; Glasgow, Jan. 14, 1939), *The Seven Deadly Sinnes,* dance suite for Orch. (1941), and *Lament for the Heroes* for String Orch. (1941). Scott had a number of ardent admirers in England, among them the poet Hugh MacDiarmid and the composer Kaikhosru Sorabji, who in their exuberant encomiums place him in the ranks of Schubert and Schumann as a songwriter.

BIBL.: H. MacDiarmid, *F.G. S.: An Essay on his 75th Birthday* (Edinburgh, 1955).—NS/LK/DM

Scott, Hazel (Dorothy), jazz pianist, singer; b. Port of Spain, Trinidad, June 11, 1920; d. N.Y., Oct. 2, 1981. She was taken to the U.S. as a child and was musically nurtured by her mother, who led an all-female band. Hazel enrolled in the Juilliard School of Music in N.Y. but soon abandoned all academic ambitions and began playing in nightclubs. In 1938, she sang in the Broadway show *Sing Out the News;* she also appeared in several films, including *Broadway Rhythm* and *Rhapsody in Blue.* From 1939–45, she performed at Cafe Society Downtown, a Greenwich Village club in N.Y. In 1945, she married Adam Clayton Powell Jr., an African-American congressman from Harlem; they divorced in 1960 when he became embroiled in messy political, financial, and personal troubles. She moved to Paris and became popular at nightclubs there. She returned to N.Y. in 1967, remaining active as a performer until a few weeks before her death of pancreatic cancer.

DISC.: *Late Show* (1952); *Hazel Scott* (1952); *Relaxed Piano Moods* (1955); *Afterthoughts* (1980).—NS/LP

Scott, James (Sylvester), significant black American ragtime pianist and composer; b. Neosoho, Mo., Feb. 12, 1885; d. Kansas City, Kans., Aug. 30, 1938. He received music lessons from John Coleman in Neosoho. After the family went to Carthage, Mo., he became active as a pianist in various local haunts. In 1902 he began working for the Dumars Music Co., which publ. his first rags; he gained his first success with his *Frog Legs Rag* (1906); his finest rag, *Grace and Beauty,* was publ. in 1909. About 1920, after travels as a ragtime pianist, he settled in Kansas City, where he was active as a teacher, theater musician, and bandleader. Although relatively unknown in his day, Scott is now recognized as one of the leading ragtime composers of his era.—**NS/LK/DM**

Scott, Leon, jazz trumpeter; b. Demopolis, Ala., Aug. 15, 1904; d. Chicago, Ill., Jan. 2, 1974. His father played baritone horn. Leon began on trumpet, was taught by John Whatley in Birmingham, Ala., and then moved to Chicago, where he studied music with Major N. Clark-Smith. He worked with a series of bands, including Lester Boone (1925), John Morrisett (1926), Tiny Parham (1927), Sammy Stewart (1928–29), and Walter Barnes (late 1929). In 1930–31 he toured France and Belgium with Earl Moss. Scott worked with Lucky Millinder in Chicago and N.Y. (1931), prior to a brief return to Tiny Parham's Band. He worked often with Carroll Dickerson during the 1930s and then with Jimmie Noone (1937–39); he also worked with Earl Hines (1938). From 1941–late 1945 he worked in Hawaii, and then moved to Los Angeles in 1946 where he worked with Benny Carter and Eddie Heywood before moving back to Chicago in the late 1940s. Scott freelanced around Chicago during the 1950s and 1960s; beginning in 1965, he began to play many dates with Franz Jackson (including overseas tours). Ill health caused an end to regular playing during the early 1970s. Leon's daughter Julie L. Scott plays French horn and piano.—**JC/LP**

Scott, Raymond (originally, **Warnow, Harry**), jazz leader, pianist; b. Brooklyn, N.Y., Sept. 10, 1910; d. Feb. 8, 1994. Scott studied at N.Y.'s Inst. of Musical Art during the early 1930s, then began working at CBS studios in N.Y. During the mid-1930s, he led a studio novelty quintet. He was well known for clever novelty arrangements such as "An Eighteenth-Century Drawing Room," "Dinner Music for a Pack of Hungry Cannibals," and "When Cootie Left the Duke." After leading on the West Coast and scoring for and appearing in several films, he formed his own big band in 1939. The band toured regularly and also played several residencies, including the Blackhawk, Chicago, in 1940. He returned to the CBS staff in 1942 and August of that year began directing an all-star studio group, which at various times included Charlie Shavers, Cozy Cole, Ben Webster, Emmett Berry, Johnny Guarneri, George Johnson, and Jerry Jerome. While he was a staff musician, Scott also was music director for the radio and TV versions of *Our Hit Parade*; he married Dorothy Collins, a regular on the show that he discovered when she was a teenager. During the 1950s and 1960s, he was mainly active as an arranger-composer and musical director. In the early 1970s, he moved to Van Nuys, Calif., where he retired. In the 1990s, his music was re-recorded by Don Byron. Scott has become a favorite among N.Y.'s downtown avant-garde jazz scene.

DISC.: *Reckless Nights and Turkish Twilights* (1937); *Powerhouse, Vol. 1* (1949); D. Byron: *Bug Music* (1996).—**JC/LP**

Scott, Ronnie, famed British jazz tenor and soprano saxophonist, leader; b. London, England, Jan. 28, 1927; d. there, Dec. 23, 1996. His father, Joseph "Jock" Scott (1903–58), was a saxophonist and bandleader; his uncle was violinist Dave Scott. Ronnie took tenor sax lessons at age 15; when he was 16, he began playing with various leaders. He played on several trips aboard the *Queen Mary* ocean lines in 1947 and 1950; he is said to have studied jazz in N.Y. after the boat stopped there. He organized his first band in 1952, and worked with various lineups through the 1950s. Scott first visited the U.S. with his sextet in 1957; he opened his first jazz club in London in 1959. From the early 1960s through the 1990s, he led groups of various sizes. He led big band tours with Scott Walker (1968), Ella Fitzgerald (1969), Jack Jones (1972), and Nancy Wilson (1973). He was also featured in the Kenny Clarke-Francy Boland Big Band (1962–72) and was featured as a soloist at many international festivals and in a brief season in Portugal with Mike Carr (1970). From the 1970s through the mid-1990s, he was frequently on the road, primarily in Europe, while he continued to perform regularly at his London-based club. He was awarded the OBE (Order of the British Empire) in 1981. He was temporarily out of action due to dental surgery during 1995–96. He committed suicide at his London home late in 1996.

Scott is best known as co-operator (with Peter King) of one of the most famous jazz clubs in the world—a club that has been in existence for almost 30 years.

DISC.: *Battle Royal* (1951); *Scott at Ronnie's* (1973); *Serious Gold* (1977); *Never Pat a Burning Dog* (1990); *The Band: Live at Ronnie Scott's* (1968).

BIBL.: R. Scott and M. Hennessey, *Some of My Best Friends Are Blues* (London, 1979); K. Grime, *Jazz at Ronnie Scott's by Kitty Grime* (London, 1979); J. Fordham, *Let's Join Hands and Contact the Living: Ronnie Scott and His Club* (London, 1986); J. Fordham, *Jazz Man—The Amazing Story of Ronnie Scott and his Club* (London, 1995).—**JC-B/MM/LP**

Scott, Shirley, R&B/jazz organist, pianist; b. Philadelphia, Pa., March 14, 1934. Called the "Queen of the Hammond Organ," Scott has led her group, usually comprised of organ, saxophone and drums, since the late 1950s. She is also a pianist of great technical skill. In 1955, she worked with Bill Carney and John Coltrane. She came to prominence playing in Eddie "Lockjaw" Davis's trio (1955). Scott began recording on her own in 1958. Beginning in 1961, she started a long series of recordings with Stanley Turrentine, whom she later married. Many of these sessions are under Turrentine's name. After they broke up in the early 1970s, she recorded less frequently, but Scott continues to work with her band; in 1982, she recorded with Dexter Gordon. She led the band on Bill Cosby's ill-fated revival of the game show *You Bet Your Life* in 1992. Scott spent a period in the hospital following abuse of diet pills from 1997–98, but then returned to performing.

DISC.: *Great Scott!* (1958); *Shirley Scott Plays Horace Silver* (1961); *Blue Seven* (1961); *For Members Only* (1963); *Great Live Sessions* (1964); *Girl Talk* (1967); *One for Me* (1974); *Oasis* (1989); *Blues Everywhere* (1991); *Skylark* (1995).—**MM/LP**

Scott, Stephen, American composer and performer; b. Corvallis, Ore., Oct. 10, 1944. He studied with

Homer Keller at the Univ. of Ore. (B.A., 1967) and with Paul Nelson at Brown Univ. (M.A., 1969); also studied African music in Ghana, Tanzania, and Zimbabwe (1970). In 1969 he began teaching at Colo. Coll. in Colorado Springs, where he founded the Pearson Electronic Sound Studio (1969), the New Music Ensemble (1972), and, after developing a unique bowed piano technique, the Bowed Piano Ensemble (1977). Scott's most significant works are scored for bowed piano strings, which, as Ingram Marshall aptly wrote, "...must be included with the prepared piano work of John Cage in the '40s and '50s, as well as the player piano machinations Conlon Nancarrow in the '60s and '70s as examples of startlingly unique artistic vision." Among his awards are the New England Cons./Rockefeller Foundation Chamber Music Prize (1980) and an NEA Composer's Fellowship (1985–86). His *Tears of Niobe* (1990) was elected to represent the U.S. at the 1991 International Rostrum of Composers in Paris. The Bowed Piano Ensemble of Colo. Coll. was featured on his 1990 CD release, *Vikings of the Sunrise*. Two concert films have been made of his works: Peter Savage's *Vikings of the Sunrise* and Tom Sanny and Amy Scott's *Entrada*.

WORKS: *Music I* (1977), *II* (1978), and *III* for Bowed Strings (1977–79); *Arcs* (1980); *Rainbows* (1981); *Minerva's Web* (1985); *The Tears of Niobe* (1986); *Bowed Rosary* (1990; in collaboration with T. Riley); *Thirteen* (1991); *Music* for Bowed Piano and Chamber Orch. (1993); *Vikings of the Sunrise* (1995); *Baltic Sketches* (1997); *Double Variations* (1999); *Entrada* (1999). —**NS/LK/DM**

Scott, Tom (actually, Thomas Jefferson),

American folksinger and composer; b. Campbellsburg, Ky., May 28, 1912; d. N.Y., Aug. 12, 1961. He studied violin with an uncle. He played in dance bands and also wrote songs; then went to Hollywood, where he took theory lessons with Antheil; subsequently studied with Harrison Kerr and Riegger.

WORKS: DRAMATIC: O p e r a : *The Fisherman* (1956). **ORCH.:** *Song with Dance* (1932); *Plymouth Rock* (1938); *Hornpipe and Chantey* (1944); Sym. No. 1 (Rochester, N.Y., Oct. 22, 1946); *From the Sacred Harp* (1946); *Johnny Appleseed* (N.Y., March 1, 1948); *Lento* for Saxophone and Strings (1953). **CHAMBER:** 2 string quartets (1944, 1956); *Emily Dickinson Suite* for Violin and Harp (1955). **VOCAL:** *Ballad of the Harp Weaver* for Narrator, Harp, Chorus, and String Quartet (N.Y., Feb. 22, 1947); also chanteys for chorus; solo songs; arrangements of folk songs.—**NS/LK/DM**

Scott, Tony (originally, Sciacca, Anthony),

jazz clarinetist, saxophonist, flutist, pianist, guitarist; b. Morristown, N.J., June 17, 1921. His father was a barber; both parents enjoyed playing the violin. He studied clarinet and piano at Juilliard from 1940–42, and started jamming at Minton's in 1941; he caused some antagonism among the other musicians by his habit of jumping up on stage without asking permission. Scott spent three years in army bands (1942–45) and, after leaving the service, worked with Tommy Dorsey, Charlie Ventura, Claude Thornhill, and Earl Bostic, among others. He was befriended by Ben Webster, who influenced his big sound and was an early fan of Charlie Parker's. In the early 1950s, Scott led a quartet at Minton's and the Metropole; in 1953 he was voted the *Down Beat* Critics' Poll "New Star" on clarinet, and he began to record more as a leader. He took lessons with composer Stefan Wolpe, the fruits of which are heard on his compositions "Portrait of Anne Frank" and "Piece for Stefan Wolpe" (1959). During this period, he worked with Billie Holiday (1954, 1956), Carmen McRae, and Sarah Vaughan (1946, 1950) and spent a month in Ellington's orch. He became Harry Belafonte's pianist and musical director (1955), touring the world with him in 1957. He was an early booster of pianist Bill Evans, using him on a number of recordings beginning in 1956. In late 1959, he went to Japan, and then studied Eastern musics for several years, visiting Bali (where he played with a traditional orch.), Malaysia, Thailand (where he played with the king, a noted jazz patron and saxophonist), and India. In 1964, he recorded *Music for Zen Meditation* with a koto and shakuhachi player in Tokyo, an album that became a cult favorite. In July 1965 he returned to N.Y. and began a 15-month residency at the Dom, an East Village club. He left for Europe in 1968. He has been based in Rome since the early 1970s and occasionally performs at European festivals. He has recorded with Indonesian groups, on an album paying homage to Africa, and on several more meditation albums.

DISC.: *Music After Midnight* (1953); *Tony Scott Quartet* (1954); *Jazz for GIs: Tony Scott and Mat Mathews* (1954); *Tony Scott* (1955); *Scott's Fling* (1955); *That's How I'm Living* (1955); *Both Sides of Tony Scott* (1956); *Touch of Tony Scott* (1956); *In Concert* (1957); *The Modern Art of Jazz* (1957); *Tony Scott in Hi Fi* (1957); *Dedications* (1957); *South Pacific Jazz* (1958); *52nd Street Scene* (1958); *Free Blown Jazz* (1959); *I'll Remember* (1959); *Sung Heroes* (1959); *Hi Fi Land of Jazz* (1959); *Golden Moments* (1959); *Gypsy* (1959); *My Kind of Jazz* (1960); *Music for Zen Meditation & Other Joys* (1964); *Music for Yoga Meditation and Other Joys* (1967); *Homage to Lord Krishna* (1969); *Prism* (1977); *African Bird: Come Back! Mother Africa* (1981); *Meditation* (1984); *Astral Meditation* (1988); *Clarinet Album* (1994); *Dialog with Myself: Like a Child's Whisper* (1995); *In Africa* (1997); *Homage to Billie Holiday: Body & Soul* (1998); *Homage to a Lady* (1998); *Poets of Jazz* (1998); *At Last* (1999).—**MS/LP**

Scott-Heron, Gil,

jazz singer, songwriter, poet; b. Chicago, Ill., April 1, 1949. Raised in Jackson, Tenn., by his grandmother, Scott-Heron wrote novels and poetry before forming a partnership with keyboard player Brian Jackson in the early 1970s. Their music was initially percussion accompanying Scott-Heron's spoken poetry, but the arrangements steadily grew jazzier and more complex. His reputation for provocative thought also grew, and he began to reach an audience even beyond the U.S. In 1974, the album *Winter In America*, which included "The Bottle," made its creator a surprise dance floor star; a year later "Johannesburg" also was a hit. The 1970s and early 1980s were his most successful years. He had a mini-revival in the mid-1980s, when an experiment with Bill Laswell led to the song "Re-Ron." In the mid-1990s, he made another brief comeback.

DISC.: *Small Talk at 125th & Lenox Ave.* (1970); *Pieces of a Man* (1971); *Free Will* (1972); *Winter in America* (1974); *The*

Revolution Will Not Be Televised (1974); *The First Minute of a New Day* (1974); *The Midnight Band* (1975); *From South Africa to South Carolina* (1975); *It's Your World* (1976); *Bridges* (1977); *Secrets* (1978); *The Mind of Gil Scott-Heron* (1979); *1980* (1980); *Real Eyes* (1980); *Reflections* (1981); *Moving Target* (1982); *The Best of Gil Scott-Heron* (1984); *Tales of Gil Scott-Heron and His Amnesia Express* (1990); *Glory—The Gil Scott-Heron Collection* (1990); *Minister of Information* (1994); *Spirits* (1994).—**MM/LP**

Scotti, Antonio, celebrated Italian baritone; b. Naples, Jan. 25, 1866; d. there, Feb. 26, 1936. He studied with Ester Trifari- Paganini in Naples. He made his operatic debut in Naples (March 1889) as Cinna in Spontini's *La Vestale,* then sang elsewhere in Italy, Russia, Spain, and South America. He made his London debut at Covent Garden on June 8, 1899, as Don Giovanni, and appeared in the same role with the Metropolitan Opera in N.Y. (Dec. 27, 1899). He remained with the Metropolitan for 33 years; made his farewell appearance on Jan. 20, 1933. He also toured in America with his own company. He possessed great histrionic ability, and was especially noted for his dramatic roles (Scarpia, Rigoletto, Falstaff, Don Giovanni, and Iago).—**NS/LK/DM**

Scotto, Renata, famous Italian soprano; b. Savona, Feb. 24, 1933. She commenced music study in Savona at age 14, and when she was 16, she went to Milan for vocal training with Emilio Ghirardini, then with Merlini, and finally with Mercedes Llopart. She made her debut as Violetta in Savona in 1952. After winning a national vocal competition in 1953, she made her formal debut as Violetta at Milan's Teatro Nuovo; then joined Milan's La Scala, where she sang secondary roles until being called upon to replace Maria Callas as Amina during the company's visit to the Edinburgh Festival in 1957. She made her U.S. debut at the Chicago Lyric Opera on Nov. 2, 1960, as Mimi, a role she also chose for her Metropolitan Opera debut in N.Y. on Oct. 13, 1965. She scored a brilliant success with her portrayal of Mimi in the Metropolitan Opera production of *La Bohème* in the "Live from Lincoln Center" telecast on PBS (March 15, 1977), and continued to make appearances there until her final engagement as Cio-Cio-San in 1987. She also toured widely as a recitalist. In later years, she was active as an opera director. In 1995 she sang the Marshallin at the Spoleto Festival U.S.A. in Charleston, S.C. In 1999 she portrayed Madame Flora in *La Voix Humaine* and Menotti's Medium in a double bill staging in Turin. Among her other fine roles were Lucia, Gilda, Elena in I Vespri Siciliani, Norma, Manon Lescaut, and Luisa Miller. She publ. the book *Scotto: More than a Diva* (with O. Riva; N.Y., 1984).

BIBL.: B. Tosi, *R. S.: Voce di due mondi* (Venice, 1990).
—**NS/LK/DM**

Scotus Erigena, John
See **Erigena, John Scotus**

Scovotti, Jeanette, American soprano; b. N.Y., Dec. 5, 1936. She received her training in N.Y. at the H.S. of Music and Art, and at the Juilliard School of Music. She began her career singing in concerts. In 1960 she appeared as Despina with the New England Opera Theater in Boston. After singing at the Santa Fe Opera, she appeared as Blondchen at the San Francisco Opera. On Nov. 15, 1962, she made her Metropolitan Opera debut in N.Y. as Adele, and remained on its roster until 1966. She also appeared at the Teatro Colón in Buenos Aires (1963–65). From 1966 to 1977 she sang with the Hamburg State Opera. In 1977 she appeared in the U.S. premiere of Glinka's *Ruslan and Ludmila* in Boston. Among her other roles of note were Zerlina, Rosina, Gilda, Lucia, Aminta in *Die schweigsmae Frau,* the Italian Singer in *Capriccio,* and the title role in Krenek's *Sardakai.*—**NS/LK/DM**

Scriabin, Alexander (Nikolaievich), remarkable Russian composer whose solitary genius had no predecessors and left no disciples, father of **Marina Scriabine;** b. Moscow, Jan. 6, 1872; d. there, April 27, 1915. His father was a lawyer; his mother, Lyubov Petrovna (née Shchetinina), was a talented pianist who had studied with Leschetizky at the St. Petersburg Cons.; his mother died of tuberculosis when he was an infant, and his father remarried and spent the rest of his life in the diplomatic service abroad. Scriabin was reared by an aunt, who gave him initial instruction in music, including piano; at 11 he began regular piano lessons with Georgi Conus, and at 16 became a pupil of Zverev; in 1885 he commenced the study of theory with Taneyev. When he entered the Moscow Cons. in 1888, he continued his studies with Taneyev, and also received instruction in piano with Safonov. He practiced assiduously, but never became a virtuoso pianist; at his piano recitals, he performed mostly his own works. Graduating with a gold medal from Safonov's class, Scriabin remained at the Moscow Cons. to study fugue with Arensky, but failed to pass the required test and never received a diploma for composition. Upon leaving the Cons. in 1892, he launched a career as a concert pianist. By that time he had already written several piano pieces in the manner of Chopin; the publisher Jurgenson brought out his opp. 1, 2, 3, 5, and 7 in 1893. In 1894 Belaieff became his publisher and champion, financing his first European tour in 1895; on Jan. 15, 1896, Scriabin gave a concert of his own music in Paris. Returning to Russia, he completed his first major work, a Piano Concerto, and was soloist in its first performance on Oct. 23, 1897, in Odessa. In the same year, he married the pianist Vera Isakovich. They spent some time abroad; on Jan. 31, 1898, they gave a joint recital in Paris in a program of Scriabin's works. From 1898 to 1903 Scriabin taught piano at the Moscow Cons. His first orch. work, *Rêverie,* was conducted in Moscow by Safonov on March 24, 1899; he also conducted the first performance of Scriabin's first Sym. (March 29, 1901). Scriabin's second Sym. was brought out by Liadov in St. Petersburg (Jan. 25, 1902). After the death of Belaieff in 1904, Scriabin received an annual grant of 2,400 rubles from the wealthy Moscow merchant Morosov, and went to Switzerland, where he began work on his third Sym., *Le Poème divin*; it had its first performance in Paris on May 29, 1905, under the direction of Arthur Nikisch. At that time Scriabin separated from Vera Isakovich and established a household with Tatiana Schloezer, sister of the music critic Boris de Schloezer, who subsequently became Scriabin's close friend and biographer. In Dec. 1906 he appeared as a soloist with Modest Altschuler and the Russian Sym. Soc. in N.Y.; also gave recitals of his works there and in other U.S. music centers. Tatiana Schloezer joined him in N.Y. in Jan. 1907, but they were warned by friends familiar with American mores of the time that charges of moral turpitude might be brought against them, since Scriabin had never obtained a legal divorce from his first wife and Tatiana Schloezer was his common-law wife. There was no evidence that such charges were actually contemplated, but to safeguard themselves against such a contretemps, they went to Paris in March 1907. Altschuler continued to champion Scriabin's music, and on Dec. 10, 1908, gave the world premiere with his Russian Sym. Orch. of Scriabin's great work *Le poème de l'extase*; the first Russian performance followed in St. Petersburg (Feb. 1, 1909). In the spring of 1908, Scriabin met Serge Koussevitzky, who became one of his most ardent supporters, both as a conductor and as a publisher. He gave Scriabin a 5-year contract with his newly established publishing firm Editions Russes, with a generous guarantee of 5,000 rubles annually. In the summer of 1910, Koussevitzky engaged Scriabin as soloist on a tour in a chartered steamer down the Volga River, with stopovers and concerts at all cities and towns of any size along the route. Scriabin wrote for Koussevitzky his most ambitious work, *Promethée*, or *Poème du feu*, with an important piano part, which featured the composer as soloist at its premiere in Moscow (March 15, 1911). The score also included a color keyboard (*clavier à lumière* or, in Italian, *luce*) intended to project changing colors according to the scale of the spectrum, which Scriabin devised (for at that time he was deeply immersed in the speculation about parallelism of all arts in their visual and auditory aspects). The construction of such a color organ was, however, entirely unfeasible at the time, and the premiere of the work was given without luce. A performance with colored lights thrown on a screen was attempted by Altschuler at Carnegie Hall in N.Y. on March 20, 1915, but it was a total failure. Another attempt was made in Moscow by Safonov after Scriabin's death, but that, too, was completely unsuccessful. The crux of the problem was that the actual notes written on a special staff in the score had to be translated into a color spectrum according to Scriabin's visualization of corresponding colors and keys (C major was red, F-sharp major was bright blue, etc.). Perhaps the nearest approximation to Scriabin's scheme was the performance of *Promethée* by the Univ. of Iowa Sym. Orch. on Sept. 24, 1975, under the direction of James Dixon, with a laser apparatus constructed by Lowell Cross; previously, the pianist Hilde Somer made use of the laser to accompany her solo piano recitals of Scriabin's works, without attempting to follow the parallelism of sounds and colors envisioned by Scriabin, but nonetheless conveying the idea underlying the scheme. The unique collaboration between Scriabin and Koussevitzky came to an unfortunate end soon after the production of *Promethée*; Scriabin regarded Koussev-

itzky as the chief apostle of his messianic epiphany, while Koussevitzky believed that it was due principally to his promotion that Scriabin reached the heights in musical celebrity; to this collision of 2 mighty egotisms was added a trivial disagreement about financial matters. Scriabin left Koussevitzky's publishing firm, and in 1912 signed a contract with Jurgenson, who guaranteed him 6,000 rubles annually. In 1914 Scriabin visited London and was soloist in his Piano Concerto and in *Prometheus* at a concert led by Sir Henry Wood (March 14, 1914); he also gave a recital of his own works there (March 20, 1914). His last public appearance was in a recital in Petrograd on April 15, 1915; upon his return to Moscow, an abscess developed in his lip, leading to blood poisoning; he died after a few days' illness. His 3 children (of the union with Tatiana Schloezer) were legitimized at his death. His son Julian, an exceptionally gifted boy, was accidentally drowned at the age of 11 in the Dnieper River at Kiev (June 22, 1919); Julian's 2 piano preludes, written in the style of the last works of his father, were publ. in a Scriabin memorial vol. (Moscow, 1940).

Scriabin was a genuine innovator in harmony. After an early period of strongly felt influences (Chopin, Liszt, and Wagner), he gradually evolved in his own melodic and harmonic style, marked by extreme chromaticism; in his piano piece *Désir*, op.57 (1908), the threshold of polytonality and atonality is reached; the key signature is dispensed with in his subsequent works; chromatic alterations and compound appoggiaturas create a harmonic web of such complexity that all distinction between consonance and dissonance vanishes. Building chords by fourths rather than by thirds, Scriabin constructed his "mystic chord" of 6 notes (C, F-sharp, B-flat, E, A, and D), which is the harmonic foundation of *Promethée*. In his seventh Piano Sonata (1913) appears a chordal structure of 25 notes (D-flat, F-flat, G, A, and C, repeated in 5 octaves), which was dubbed "a 5-story chord." These harmonic extensions were associated in Scriabin's mind with theosophic doctrines; he aspired to a universal art in which the impressions of the senses were to unite with religious experience. He made plans for the writing of a "Mysterium," which was to accomplish such a synthesis, but only the text of a preliminary poem (*L'Acte préalable*) was completed at his death. Scriabin dreamed of having the "Mysterium" performed as a sacred action in the Himalayas, and actually made plans for going to India; the outbreak of World War I in 1914 put an end to such a project. Scriabin's fragmentary sketches for *L'Acte préalable* were arranged in 1973 by the Russian musician Alexander Nemtin, who supplemented this material with excerpts from Scriabin's 8th Piano Sonata, *Guirlandes*, and Piano Preludes, op.74; the resulting synthetic score was performed in Moscow on March 16, 1973, under the title *Universe*; a species of color keyboard was used at the performance, projecting colors according to Scriabin's musical spectrum.

WORKS: ORCH.: Piano Concerto, op.20 (1896; Odessa, Oct. 23, 1897, composer soloist); Symphonic Poem (1896–97); *Rêverie*, op.24 (1898; Moscow, March 24, 1899); *Andante* for Strings (1899); 3 syms.: No. 1, op.26 (1899–1900; Moscow, March 29, 1901), No. 2, op.29 (1901; St. Petersburg, Jan. 25, 1902), and

No. 3, op.43, *Le divin poème* (1902–04; Paris, May 29, 1905); *Le poème de l'extase*, op.54 (1905–08; N.Y., Dec. 10, 1908); *Promethée, or Poème du feu*, op.60 (1908–10; Moscow, March 15, 1911, composer soloist). **CHAMBER:** *Romance* for Horn and Piano (1890); second Variation for *Variations on a Russian Theme* for String Quartet (1899; in collaboration with 9 other composers). **P i a n o :** *Canon* (1883); *Nocturne* in A-flat major (1884); *Valse* in F minor, op.1 (1885); *Sonate-fantaisie* (1886); *Valse* in G-sharp minor (1886); *Valse* in D-flat major (1886); *Variations on a Theme by Mlle. Egorova* (1887); 11 sonatas: in E-flat major (1887–89), op.6 (1892), op.19, *Sonata-Fantasy* (1892–97), op.23 (1897–98), op.30 (1903), op.53 (1907), op.62 (1911), op.64, *Messe blanche* (1911), op.66 (1913), op.68, *Messe noire* (1913), and op.70 (1913); *3 Pieces*, op.2 (1887–89); *Feuillet d'album* in A-flat major (1889); *10 Mazurkas*, op.3 (1889); *Mazurka* in F major (1889?); *Mazurka* in B minor (1889?); *Fantasy* for 2 Pianos (1889?); *Allegro appassionato*, op.4 (1892; based on the first movement of the Sonata in E-flat major); *2 Nocturnes*, op.5 (1890); *Deux impromptus à la Mazur*, op.7 (1892); *Douze études*, op.8 (1894); *2 Pieces for Piano, Left-Hand*, op.9 (1894); *2 Impromptus*, op.10 (1894); *24 Préludes*, op.11 (1888–96); *2 Impromptus*, op.12 (1895); *6 Préludes*, op.13 (1895); *2 Impromptus*, op.14 (1895); *5 Préludes*, op.15 (1895–96); *5 Préludes*, op.16 (1894–95); *7 Prüludes*, op.17 (1895–96); *Allegro de concert*, op.18 (1896); *Polonaise*, op.21 (1897); *4 Préludes*, op.22 (1897); *9 Mazurkas*, op.25 (1899); *2 Préludes*, op.27 (1900); *Fantaisie*, op.28 (1900); *4 Préludes*, op.31 (1903); *Deux poèmes*, op.32 (1903); *4 Préludes*, op.33 (1903); *Poème tragique*, op.34 (1903); *3 Préludes*, op.35 (1903); *Poème satanique*, op.36 (1903); *4 Préludes*, op.37 (1903); *Valse*, op.38 (1903); *4 Préludes*, op.39 (1903); *2 Mazurkas*, op.40 (1902–03); *Poème*, op.41 (1903); *Huit études*, op.42 (1903); *Deux poèmes*, op.44 (1905); *3 Pièces*, op.45 (1904–05); *Scherzo*, op.46 (1905); *Quasi-valse*, op.47 (1905); *4 Préludes*, op.48 (1905); *3 Pièces*, op.49 (1905); *Feuille d'album* (1905); *4 Pieces*, op.51 (1906); *3 Pieces*, op.52 (1906); *4 Pieces*, op.56 (1907); *2 Pieces*, op.57 (1907); *Feuillet d'album*, op.58 (1910); *2 Pieces*, op.59 (1910); *Poème-nocturne*, op.61 (1911); *Deux poèmes*, op.63 (1911); *Trois études*, op.65 (1912); *2 Préludes*, op.67 (1912–13); *Deux poèmes*, op.69 (1913); *Deux poèmes*, op.71 (1914); *Vers la flamme*, op.72 (1914); *Deux danses*, op.73 (1914); *5 Préludes*, op.74 (1914).

BIBL.: I. Lipayev, *A.N. S.* (Moscow, 1913); E. Gunst, *S. and His Work* (Moscow, 1915); V. Karatigin, *S.* (Petrograd, 1915); A. Hull, *A Great Russian Tone-poet: S.* (London, 1916; second ed., 1927); A. Koptyayev, *A.N. S.* (Petrograd, 1916); L. Sabaneyev, *S.* (Moscow, 1916; second ed., 1923); M. Montagu-Nathan, *Handbook to the Piano Works of A. S.* (London, 1917; second ed., 1922); I. Glebov, *S.* (Petrograd, 1921); I. Lapshin, *S.'s Intimate Thoughts* (Petrograd, 1922); L. Sabaneyev, *A.N. S.* (Moscow, 1922; second ed., 1923); B. Asafiev, *S. 1871–1915* (Petrograd, 1923); L. Sabaneyev, ed., *Pisma A.N. S.a* (letters; Moscow,1923); B. de Schloezer, *A. S. lichnost mysteriya* (A. S., Character of Mystery; Vol. I, Berlin, 1923; Fr. tr., Paris, 1975; Eng. tr., by N. Slonimsky, Berkeley and Los Angeles, 1987; Vol. II not completed); A. Swan, *S.* (London, 1923); V. Yakovlev, *A.N. S.* (Moscow, 1925); P. Dickenmann, *Die Entwicklung der Harmonik bei A. S.* (Bern and Leipzig, 1935); M. Metshik, *A. S.* (Moscow, 1935); A. Nikolayev, *A. S.* (Moscow, 1940); L. Danilevich, *A.N. S.* (Moscow, 1953); H. Boegner, *Die Harmonik der späten Klavierwerke S.s* (diss., Univ. of Munich, 1955); D. Blagoy, *Etyudi S.a* (Moscow, 1963); C. von Gleich, *Die sinfonischen Werke von A. S.* (Bilthoven, 1963); H. Forster, *Die Form in den symphonischen Werken von A.N. S.* (diss., Univ. of Leipzig, 1964); M. Mikhailov, *A.N. S.* (Moscow, 1966); V. Dernova, *S.'s Harmony* (Leningrad, 1968; Eng. tr. and commentary by R. Guenther, diss., Catholic Univ. of America, 1979); F.

Bowers, S.: *A Biography of the Russian Composer* (2 vols., Palo Alto, 1969); V. Delson, *S.* (Moscow, 1971); W. Evrard, *S.* (Paris, 1972); E. Kaufman, *The Evolution of Form and Technique in the Late Works of S.* (diss., Yale Univ., 1972); H. Steger, *Der Weg der Klaviersonaten bei A. S.* (Munich, 1972); F. Bowers, *The New S.: Enigma and Answers* (N.Y., 1973); S. Pavchinsky and V. Zuckerman, eds., *A.N. S.* (Moscow, 1973); H. Steger, *Materialstrukturen in den fünf späten Klaviersonaten A. S.s* (Regensburg, 1977); G. Eberle, *Zwischen Tonalität und Atonalität: Studien zur Harmonik A. S.s* (Munich, 1978); M. Kelkel, *A. S., sa vie, l'ésotérisme et la langage musical dans son oeuvre* (Paris, 1978); H. Macdonald, *S.* (London, 1978); E. Rudakova and A. Kandinsky, *A.N. S.* (Moscow, 1979); O. Kolleritsch, ed., *A. S.* (Graz, 1980); I. Belza, *A.N. S.* (Moscow, 1983); H. Metzger and R. Riehn, eds., *A. S. und die S.isten, Musik Konzepte*, Nos. 32–33 (Munich, 1983) and Nos. 37–38 (Munich, 1984); S. Schibli, *A. S. und seine Musik: Grenzuberschreitungen eines prometheschen Geistes* (Munich, 1983); J. Baker, *The Music of A. S.* (New Haven, 1986); A. Pople, *S. and Stravinsky 1908–1914: Studies in Theory and Analysis* (N.Y. and London, 1989); M. Schmidt, *Ekstase als musikalisches Symbol in den Klavierpoèmes A. S.s* (Pfaffenweiler, 1989); L. Verdi, *A. S., tra musica e filosofia* (Florence, 1991); B. Kienscherf, *Das Auge hört mit: Die Idee der Farblichtmusik und ihre Problematik—beispielhaft dargestellt zu Werken von A. S. und Arnold Schönberg* (Frankfurt am Main, 1996); M. Helkel, *A. S.: Un musicien à la recherche de l'absolu* (Paris, 1999).—**NS/LK/DM**

Scriabine, Marina, Russian-French music scholar and composer, daughter of **Alexander (Nikolaievich) Scriabin**; b. Moscow, Jan. 30, 1911. After her father's death, she lived with her mother in Kiev and Moscow; when her mother died, she went to Belgium to live with her maternal grandmother; in 1927 she settled in Paris. She studied at the École Nationale des Arts Décoratifs and designed art posters; studied theory with Leibowitz. In 1950 she joined the Radiodiffusion Française and worked in electronic techniques; composed a *Suite radiophonique* (1951); also a ballet, *Bayalett* (1952), and some chamber music. In 1967 she received a doctorate in aesthetics for her thesis *Réprésentation du temps et de l'intemporalité dans les arts plastiques figuratifs*. She publ. *Problèmes de la musique moderne* (in collaboration with her uncle, Boris de Schloezer; Paris, 1959; also in Spanish, 1960), *Le Langage musical* (Paris, 1963), and *Le Miroir du temps* (Paris, 1973). She contributed the biographical entry on Scriabin for the *Encyclopédie de la musique* (Paris, 1961), and also wrote an introduction to Schloezer's book on Scriabin, in French (Paris, 1975). —**NS/LK/DM**

Scribe, (Augustin) Eugène, famous French dramatist and librettist; b. Paris, Dec. 24, 1791; d. there, Feb. 20, 1861. He was a scholarship student at the Collège Ste.-Barbe in Paris. After training in the law, he turned to the theater, being made a member of the Académie Française (1836). He was closely associated as a librettist with Meyerbeer, but also wrote librettos for Auber, Bellini, Donizetti, Gounod, Halévy, Offenbach, Verdi, and others. See *Eugène Scribe: Oeuvres completes* (76 vols., Paris, 1874–85).

BIBL.: N. Arvin, *E. S.* (N.Y., 1924); K. Pendle, *E. S. and French Opera of the 19th Century* (Ann Arbor, 1979).—**NS/LK/DM**

Scribner, Norman (Orville), American organist, conductor, and composer; b. Washington, D.C., Feb. 25, 1936. He studied organ with Paul Callaway and theory with Walter Spencer Huffman at the Peabody Cons. of Music in Baltimore (B.Mus., 1961). In 1960 he was appointed director of music of St. Alban's Episcopal Church in Washington, D.C.; was also a staff keyboard artist with the National Sym. Orch. (1963–67). In 1965 he founded the all-volunteer Choral Arts Soc. of Washington, D.C.; in 1971 he founded the Norman Scribner Choir. He served on the faculties of American Univ. (1960–63) and George Washington Univ. (1963–69). He composed a Sextet for Winds and Piano (1975), *The Nativity,* choral cantata (1975), *The Tide Pool,* song cycle for Mezzo-soprano and Orch. (1977), *Laudate Dominum,* choral cantata (1979), *I Hear America Singing,* choral suite (1979), and *Nicholas,* musical show (1980).—NS/LK/DM

Scudo, P(ietro), Italian-born French writer on music and composer; b. Venice, June 8, 1806; d. Blois, Oct. 14, 1864. He was reared in Germany, then went to Paris, where he studied at Choron's Institution Royale de Musique Classique et Religieuse (c. 1824–30). He was for a time an opera singer and also played clarinet in military bands, then turned to journalism. He publ. several political pamphlets, and also became music critic of the influential *Revue des Deux Mondes.* A writer of considerable talent, he held reactionary views and violently attacked Berlioz, Liszt, and Wagner. He became deranged and died in an insane asylum. He was the composer of several songs, and also wrote a musical novel, *Le Chevalier Sarti* (1857; not connected with the composer Giuseppe Sarti), the sequel to which, *Frédérique,* was publ. in the *Revue des Deux Mondes.*

WRITINGS (all publ. in Paris): *Critique et littérature musicales* (Vol. I, 1850; third ed., enl., 1856; Vol. II, 1859); *L'art ancienne et l'art moderne: nouveaux mélanges de critique et de littérature musicales* (1854); *L'année musicale, ou Revue annuelle des théâtres lyriques et des concerts* (1860–62); *La musique en l'année 1862* (1863).—NS/LK/DM

Sculthorpe, Peter (Joshua), eminent Australian composer and teacher; b. Launceston, Tansmania, April 29, 1929. He studied at the Univ. of Melbourne Conservatorium of Music (B.Mus., 1951) and with Wellesz and Rubbra at Wadham Coll., Oxford (1958–60). In 1963 he joined the faculty of the Univ. of Sydney, where he later served as prof. of composition. He also was composer-in-residence at Yale Univ. while on a Harkness Fellowship (1966–67) and a visiting prof. at the Univ. of Sussex (1972–73). In 1970 he was made a Member and in 1977 an Officer of the Order of the British Empire. He was awarded the Silver Jubilee Medal in 1977. In 1980 he received an honorary doctor of letters degree from the Univ. of Tasmania, and in 1989 he received the same from the Univ. of Sussex; that same year he also received an honorary doctor of music degree from the Univ. of Melbourne. He was elected a fellow of the Australian Academy of the Humanities in 1991. In 1994 he received the Sir Bernard Heinze Award for his contributions to Australian music. He was awarded the R.M. Johnston Medal from the Royal Soc. of Tasmania in 1997. His 70th birthday was marked by many concerts in 1999 devoted to his music. His memoirs appeared as *Sun Music: Journeys and Reflections From a Composer's Life* (1999). Schulthorpe rejected such modern compositional methods as atonality and serialism to pursue an independent course. He has found inspiration in aboriginal Australian music, as well as in the music of Asia, particularly Japanese and Balinese music. In all of his music, one finds a discerning musicianship, mastery of resources, and inventiveness.

WORKS: DRAMATIC: *Sun Music,* ballet (Sydney, Aug. 2, 1968; based on the *Sun Music* series); *Rites of Passage,* theater piece (1972–73); *Quiros,* television opera (ABC National TV, July 1, 1982). **ORCH.:** *Irkanda IV* for Violin, Percussion, and Strings (Melbourne, Aug. 5, 1961); *Small Town* (Hobart, Dec. 13, 1963; rev. 1976); *Sun Music I* (London, Sept. 30, 1965), *II: Ketjak* (1966; rev. version, Sydney, Feb. 22, 1969), *III: Anniversary Music* (1967), and *IV* (Melbourne, May 29, 1967); *From Tabuh Tabuhan* (1968); *Music for Japan* (Melbourne, May 25, 1970); *Overture for a Happy Occasion* (Launceston, Nov. 16, 1970); *Lament* for Strings (Wollongong, May 26, 1976; also for Cello and Strings, Sydney, Sept. 22, 1991); *Port Essington* for String Trio and String Orch. (Sydney, Aug. 18, 1977); *Mangrove* (Sydney, April 27, 1979); *Cantares* for Chamber Orch. (1979; Sydney, Jan. 17, 1980); Piano Concerto (1983); 3 sonatas for Strings: No. 1 (1983), No. 2 (Brighton, May 19, 1988), and No. 3, *Jabiru Dreaming* (1994); *Little Suite* for Strings (Sydney, Sept. 22, 1983); *Sun Song* (Perth, Oct. 20, 1984); *Earth Cry* (Adelaide, Aug. 22, 1986); *Autumn Song* for Strings (1986; also for Chorus, 1968); *Kakadu* (Aspen, Colo., July 24, 1988); *Nourlangie,* concerto for Guitar, Percussion, and Strings (Brisbane, Oct. 24, 1989); *Little Nourlangie* for Organ and Orch. (Sydney, June 6, 1990); *From Uluru* (1991); *Nangaloar* (Aspen, Colo., July 14, 1991); *Awake Glad Heart!* for 2 Trumpets, Cello, and Strings (1992; arranged from *The Birthday of Thy King* for Chorus, 1988); *Memento mori* (1992–93; Perth, July 2, 1993); *Darwin Marching* (Darwin, Feb. 18, 1995); *Little Requiem* for Koto and Strings (Sydney, June 20, 1996); *Port Arthur in Memoriam* for Trumpet or Oboe and Strings (1996); *Love-Song* for Guitar and Strings (Darwin, July 12, 1997); *Cello Dreaming* for Cello, Strings, and Percussion (Manchester, England, April 29, 1998); *Great Sandy Island* (Tokyo, Oct. 13, 1998); *Rockpool Dreaming* for Soprano Saxophone and Strings (Newcastle, New South Wales, Feb. 7, 1999); *My Country Childhood* (Adelaide, Sept. 23, 1999); *Gondwana- Land* (Malvern, England, Oct. 22, 1999). **Band:** *Burke and Willis Suite* for Symphonic Band (Melbourne, Nov. 11, 1985; also for Brass Band, Adelaide, March 3, 1986). **CHAMBER:** 15 string quartets: No. 1 (1947), No. 2 (1948), No. 3 (1949), No. 4 (1950), No. 5, *Irkanda II* (1959), No. 6 (1964–65; Sydney, April 1, 1965), No. 7, *Red Landscape* (Norfolk, Va., July 29, 1966; rev. 1994), No. 8, *String Quartet Music* (1968; London, Jan. 15, 1970), No. 9 (Sydney, Oct. 17, 1975), No. 10 (San Francisco, April 8, 1983), No. 11, *Jabiru Dreaming* (Adelaide, March 10, 1990), No. 12 (London, July 19, 1994), No. 13, *Island Dreaming,* with mezzo-soprano (Paris, Dec. 3, 1996), No. 14 (Launceston, March 5, 1998), and No. 15 (Melbourne, July 10, 1999); *The Loneliness of Bunjil* for String Trio (1954; London, Nov. 30, 1960; rev. 1964); *Irkanda I* for Violin (Melbourne, June 30, 1955) and *III* for Piano Trio (1961); Sonata for Viola and Percussion (Attingham Park, July 1960); *Tabuh Tabuhan* for Wind Quintet and Percussion (Adelaide, March 20, 1968); *Dream* for Any Instruments and Any Number of Players (Sydney, Sept. 22, 1970); *How the Stars Were Made* for 4 Percussionists (Canberra, Oct. 4, 1971); *Alone* for Violin (1976); *Landscape II* for Amplified Piano and String Trio (Sydney, April 27, 1978); *Little Serenade* for String Quartet (1978); *Requiem* for Cello (Mittagong, April 14,

1979); *Tailitnama Song* for 5 Players (1981); *Dhilile* for 4 Percussionists (1981; Adelaide, March 7, 1990); *Songs of Sea and Sky* for Clarinet and Piano (New Haven, Conn., Oct. 15, 1987; also for Flute and Piano); *Sun Song* for 4 Percussionists (Paris, June 1, 1989); *Threnody (In memoriam Stuart Challender)* for Cello (Sydney, Feb. 20, 1991); *Tropic* for 6 Players (Brighton, May 23, 1992); *Dream Tracks* for Clarinet, Violin, and Piano (San Diego, Oct. 31, 1992); *From Saibai* for Violin and Piano (N.Y., May 10, 1993); *Into the Dreaming* for Guitar (London, March 15, 1994; also for Harp); *Chorale* for 8 Cellos (Glamorgan, Wales, Aug. 28, 1994); *Simori* for Flute and Guitar (Darwin, July 7, 1995). **P i a n o :** *2 Easy Pieces* (1958, 1968); *Callabonna* (1963; Melbourne, July 30, 1989); *Landscape I* for Amplified Piano and Tape (Perth, Feb. 28, 1971); *Night Pieces* (Perth, Feb. 28, 1971); *Koto Music I* and *II* for Amplified Piano and Tape (1976); *4 Pieces* for Piano Duet (Sydney, April 28, 1979); *Mountains* (1980; Sydney, July 4, 1981); *Nocturnal* (1983); *A Little Book of Hours* (1998). **VOCAL:** *Sun Music* for Chorus, Piano, and Percussion (Adelaide, March 13, 1966); *Morning Song for the Christ Child*, carol for Chorus (1966); *Sea Chant* for Unison Voices and Orch. (1968; Melbourne, June 1975); *Autumn Song* for Chorus (1968; also for String Orch., 1986); *Love 200* for 2 Singers, Rock Band, and Orch. (Sydney, Feb. 14, 1970); *The Song of Tailitnama* for High Voice, 6 Cellos, and Percussion (1974; also for Medium Voice and Piano, 1984; Sydney, Sept. 9, 1986); *Child of Australia* for Soprano, Speaker, Chorus, and Orch. (Sydney, Jan. 26, 1988); *The Birthday of Thy King*, carol for Chorus (Cambridge, Dec. 24, 1988; also arranged as *Awake Glad Heart!* for 2 Trumpets, Cello, and Strings, 1992); *It's You* for Chorus (Sydney, May 6, 1989); *Psalm 150* for Treble Voices and Optional Voices and/or Instruments (Launceston, Oct. 27, 1996); *Maranoa Lullaby* for Mezzo- soprano and String Quartet (Sydney, Nov. 26, 1996); *Love Thoughts* for Soprano, 2 Speakers, and Chamber Group (1998).

BIBL.: M. Hannan, *P. S.: His Music and Ideas 1929–1979* (Brisbane, 1982); D. Hayes, *P. S.: A Bio-Bibliography* (Westport, Conn., 1993).—**NS/LK/DM**

Seagle, Oscar, American baritone and singing teacher; b. Chattanooga, Tenn., Oct. 31, 1877; d. Dallas, Dec. 19, 1945. He sang in concerts in the U.S. from 1896 until 1905, then went to Paris for further study with Jean de Reszke. He made his Paris debut in 1907, and also sang in England. He returned to America at the outbreak of World War I in 1914, and settled in N.Y. as a singing teacher.—**NS/LK/DM**

Seal (originally, **Samuel, Sealhenry**), singer who blends pop, rock, soul, dance and alternative into something uniquely his own; b. Paddington, England, Feb. 19, 1963. The child of a Brazilian father and a Nigerian mother, his early childhood was marked by his mother's forced expulsion from England, leaving him to live with an abusive father, and his own bout with the disease lupus, which left the tell-tale scars on his face. He left home at 15.

During the mid-to-late 1980s, Seal spent several years on public assistance, augmenting this by passing out handbills. He befriended club music producer Adamsky, who used him as the singer on the house music tune "Killer" in 1990. The song topped the charts. This landed him a deal with ZZT Records. He went into the studio with producer Trevor Horn (formerly of the Buggles) and musicians including Wendy and Lisa,

former members of Prince's New Power Revolution, to cut his eponymous 1991 debut. In addition to "Killer," the album contained the hit "Crazy" which became an international hit, rising to #7 in the U.S. The album went platinum and rose to #24.

Seal moved to the U.S. A bout with double pneumonia followed by a severe car accident which in turn was followed by a bout of post-viral fatigue kept the artist sidelined for a couple of years. He finally re-emerged with his eponymous sophomore effort in 1994. Once again produced by Horn and featuring Wendy and Lisa, the album also had guest appearances by Jeff Beck and Joni Mitchell. The single "Prayer for the Dying," a melancholy ballad, rose to #21. The song "Kiss from a Rose," one of the closest things pop music has seen to a madrigal since "Scarborough Fair," was featured on the soundtrack of the film *Batman Forever*, topped the pop charts, and spent 12 weeks atop the adult contemporary charts. It took home three Grammy awards: Song of the Year, Record of the Year, and Best Male Pop Vocal Performance. The album went to #20 and quadruple platinum.

Seal's 1998 album *Human Being* featured musicians ranging from synthesizer wiz William Orbit to former E Street Band keyboard player David Sancious. While the artistry remained intact, perhaps he stayed away too long, because the album only went gold.

DISC.: *Seal* (1991); *Seal* (1994); *Human Being* (1998).—**HB**

Seals and Crofts, middle of the road hitmakers of the early 1970s. **MEMBERSHIP:** Jim Seals, voc., gtr., vln., sax. (b. Sidney, Tex., Oct. 17, 1941); Dash (real name, Darrell) Crofts, voc., drm., mdln., kybd., gtr. (b. Cisco, Tex., Aug. 14, 1940).

Although they started recording hit records together during the 1970s under their own names, Seals and Crofts had worked together for many years before they became a successful pop duo. Seals comes from a family rife with musical talent. His brother Dan Seals started out as England Dan, part of the duo England Dan and John Ford Coley, before pursuing his solo country career. Cousins include country singer Johnny Duncan, Brady Seals of Little Texas, Troy Seals who wrote for George Jones and Ronnie Milsap, and Chuck Seals who wrote the Ray Price hit "Crazy Arms." By junior high, Seals had already won a state fiddle championship. Around that time, Croft and Seals started playing together in the group Dean Beard and the Crew Cuts. They also started doing session work, recording with artists including Gene Vincent. In the late 1950s, Beard became a member of the Champs. In the wake of their chart-topping hit "Tequila," cut with session musicians, he needed musicians to form a touring band. He called Seals and Croft, and they moved from Tex. to Los Angeles. In Los Angeles, they also became session musicians, playing with Jerry Butler, Buck Owens, the Monkees, and others. They also joined the Knickerbockers, contributing songs to the *Lies* album.

In the mid-1960s, Seals and Croft formed a band called the Dawnbreakers, beginning a long relationship with guitarist Louie Shelton. The duo became interested in the Bahai faith, which helped shape their music. By

1969, they signed with Bell and recorded their eponymous debut as Seals and Crofts, a heavily orchestrated affair. That album and the follow-up, *Down Home*—a more stripped-down album reflecting the folkier side of the duo—didn't sell especially well. They went over to Warner, but their label debut *Year of Sundays* also didn't make much of an impression. They continued to do session work, with Crofts playing mandolin on James Taylor's *One Man Dog*.

The duo finally broke in a big way with their fourth album, 1972's *Summer Breeze*, largely on the strength of the #6 title track. The single "Hummingbird" hit #20, and the album went gold, reaching #7. In 1973 they released *Diamond Girl*. Again, the title track rose to #6 and the second single, "We May Never Pass This Way Again," hit #21 and was a theme song at high school proms for years after. The album went gold and rose to #4.

The usually mild-mannered duo thrust themselves into controversy with the title track from their next album, *Unborn Child*. Written in the wake of *Roe v. Wade* (the court decision legalizing abortion), the song became a rallying point for the pro-life movement and was banned by many radio stations. Not surprisingly, the album went gold, and hit #14 on the charts. Their subsequent album, 1975's *I'll Play for You*, while still selling gold, only hit #30 on the charts, with the title track only getting as high as #18. That year, however, they released a greatest hits collection that went double platinum, peaking at #11. In the wake of that success, they scored a Top Ten single with the title track from their next album, *Get Closer*. The album brushed into the Top 40 and went gold.

Seals and Croft's career began to lose momentum in the later 1970s. They scored a #28 single with "My Fair Share," recorded for the soundtrack to the film *One on One*; this was one of their first hits that they didn't write. Their 1978 album *Takin' It Easy*, released at the height of disco, featured a minor dance hit "You're the Love." By 1979, they were doing commercials for McDonalds. They also recorded the theme song "The First Year" for the TV series *The Paper Chase*. They recorded their final album, *The Longest Road*, in 1980.

Although they have embarked on a couple of reunion tours, the end of the early 1980s found the duo largely retired. Seals moved to Costa Rica, where he owns a coffee plantation. Crofts still plays occasional session and tours with Bahai musicians as part of choral concerts. He released a solo album in the late 1990s, and both appeared on an album by Louie Shelton around the same time.

DISC.: *Seals and Crofts* (1970); *Down Home* (1970); *Year of Sundays* (1972); *Summer Breeze* (1972); *Diamond Girl* (1973); *Unborn Child* (1974); *Year of Sundays / Summer Breeze* (1974); *S. & C. 1 & 2* (1974); *I'll Play for You* (1975); *Get Closer* (1976); *Sudan Village* (1976); *One on One* (1977); *Takin' It Easy* (1978); *Longest Road* (1980).—**HB**

Seaman, Christopher, English conductor; b. Faversham, Kent, March 7, 1942. He studied at King's Coll., Cambridge (M.A., 1963) and received training in conducting at the Guildhall School of Music in London.

In 1964 he became principal timpanist of the London Phil. In 1968 he was made asst. conductor of the BBC Scottish Sym. Orch. in Glasgow, and then was its principal conductor from 1971 to 1977. From 1973 to 1979 he was also principal conductor of the Northern Sinfonia in Newcastle upon Tyne. In 1978 he became principal conductor of the Robert Mayer children's concerts in London. From 1979 to 1983 he was chief guest conductor of the Utrecht Sym. Orch. In 1987 he became conductor-in-residence of the Baltimore Sym. Orch. In 1993 he became music director of the Naples (Fla.) Phil.—**NS/LK/DM**

Searchers, The, British pop hitmakers of the mid-1960s. **MEMBERSHIP:** John McNally, voc., gtr. (b. Liverpool, England, Aug. 30, 1941); Mike Pender (real name, Michael Pendergast), voc., gtr. (b. Liverpool, England, March 3, 1942); Tony Jackson, voc., bs. (b. Liverpool, England, July 16, 1940); Chris Curtis (real name, Crummy), drm., voc. (b. Oldham, England, Aug. 26, 1942); Frank Allen, bs., voc. (b. Hayes, England, Dec. 14, 1943); Spencer James, voc., gtr. (b. Hayes, England, 1953); John Blunt, drm. (b. London, England, March 28, 1947); Billy Adamson, drm., voc.; Eddie Rothe (real name, Walter Edgar Rothe), drm. (b. Buckingham, England).

For over 40 years, the Searchers have remained popular, playing their older hits while continuing to create new music. Like the Beatles, the group's members began their careers playing in a variety of skiffle groups that eventually coalesced around guitarist John McNally. They first worked as a backing band for vocalist Johnny Sandon. When Sandon left, they carried on as a quartet, taking their name from a John Wayne film (the same one that inspired Buddy Holly's "That'll Be the Day"). The Searchers played the haunts around Liverpool that became legendary in The Beatles' story—The Cavern and the Iron Door—and the clubs on Hamburg's Reeperbaum like the Star. All members had vocal ability, leading to some impressive harmonies, along with the distinctive sound of Pender's 12- string guitar.

In 1963 the Searchers started recording, larding the English hit parade with a series of singles including "Sweets for My Sweet," which knocked the Beatles out of the #1 slot, and "Sugar and Spice." They started off 1964 topping the U.K. charts with the Sonny Bono/Jack Nitzche composition "Needles and Pins." This broke the band in the U.S., rising to #13. They followed this at roughly three-month intervals with "Don't Throw Your Love Away" (#16), "Some Day We're Gonna Love Again" (#34), and Jackie DeShannon's "When You Walk in the Room" (#35). The Searchers had their biggest hit with a cover of "Love Potion Number Nine" that carried them into 1965, rising to #3. Over the course of that year, they charted with a rocked up version of Malvina Reynolds ecofolk anthem "What Have They Done to the Rain" (#29) and "Bumble Bee" (#21).

While they never hit the U.S. Top 40 again after that, the Searchers continued to chart often in Europe. The band went through several personnel changes over the years, but continued to record new material, despite frequently being relegated to the oldies circuit. In the late 1970s, they were signed to Sire records and issued two much-ballyhooed but commercially unsuccessful albums. Mike Pender split and formed his own version of the Searchers in 1985. He was replaced by former First Class ("Beach Baby") guitarist Spencer James, who added his synthesizer guitar to the band's sound. In 1989 the group played to over 75,000 people at London's Wembley Stadium, opening for another British rock survivor, Cliff Richard. They continued to go strong, playing hundreds of shows a year into the new millennium.

DISC.: *Meet the Searchers* (1963); *Sugar & Spice* (1963); *Twist at the Star Club Hamburg* (live; 1963); *Ain't Gonna Kiss You* (1963); *Sweets for My Sweet* (1963); *Hear! Hear!* (1964); *It's the Searchers* (1964); *When You Walk in the Room* (1964); *Hungry for Love* (1964); *The New Searchers* (1965); *The Searchers No. 4* (1965); *Take Me for What I'm Worth* (1965); *Sounds Like the Searchers* (1965); *Bumble Bee* (1965); *Searchers '65* (1965); *Four by Four* (1966); *Second Take* (1972); *The Searchers File* (1977); *Rock Music from Britain* (1979); *The Searchers* (1979); *Play for Today* (1981); *Love Melodies* (1981); *The Silver Searchers* (1984); *Live at the Star Club* (1994).—**HB**

Searle, Humphrey, distinguished English composer, teacher, and writer on music; b. Oxford, Aug. 26, 1915; d. London, May 12, 1982. He studied classical literature at Oxford (1933–37) and music at the Royal Coll. of Music in London (1937), where his teachers were John Ireland and R.O. Morris. In 1937 he went to Vienna, where he took private lessons with Webern; this study proved to be a decisive influence in Searle's own compositions, which are imbued with the subtle coloristic processes peculiar to the second Viennese School of composition. He served in the British army during World War II, and was stationed in Germany in 1946. Returning to London, he engaged in various organizations promoting the cause of modern music. He was honorary secretary of the Liszt Society (1950–62); was an adviser on music for the Sadler's Wells Ballet (1951–57). In 1964–65 he was composer-in-residence at Stanford Univ. in Calif.; after serving as a prof. at the Royal Coll. of Music in London (1965–76), he was composer-in-residence at the Univ. of Southern Calif. in Los Angeles (1976–77). In 1968 he was made a Commander of the Order of the British Empire. Although Searle's method of composing included some aspects of the 12-tone method, he did not renounce tonal procedures, and sometimes applied purely national English melodic patterns. As a writer, he became particularly well known for his writings on Liszt.

WORKS: DRAMATIC: O p e r a : *The Diary of a Madman* (Berlin, Oct. 3, 1958); *The Photo of the Colonel* (Frankfurt am Main, June 3, 1964); *Hamlet* (1964–68; Hamburg, March 5, 1968). **B a l l e t :** *Noctambules* (1956); *The Great Peacock* (1957–58); *Dualities* (1963). **ORCH.:** 2 suites for Strings (1942, 1943); 2 piano concertos (1944, 1955); *Fuga giocosa* (1948); 5 syms.: No. 1 (1953), No. 2 (1956–58), No. 3 (1958–60; Edinburgh, Sept. 3, 1960), No. 4 (Birmingham, Nov. 8, 1962), and No. 5 (Manchester, Oct. 7, 1964); *Scherzi* for Small Orch. (1964); *Sinfonietta* (1968–69); *Zodiac Variations* for Small Orch. (1970); *Labyrinth* (1971); *Tamesis* (1979). **CHAMBER:** Bassoon Quintet (1945); *Intermezzo* for 11 Instruments (1946); Quartet for Clarinet, Bassoon, Violin, and Viola (1948); *Passacaglietta in nomine Arnold*

Schoenberg for String Quartet (1949); *Gondoliera* for English Horn and Piano (1950); *Suite* for Clarinet and Piano (1956); *3 Movements* for String Quartet (1959); *Il penseroso e L'allegro* for Cello and Piano (1975). **VOCAL:** *Gold Coast Customs* for Speaker, Men's Chorus, and Orch. (1947–49); *The Shadow of Cain* for Speakers, Men's Chorus, and Orch. (1951); *Jerusalem* for Speakers, Tenor, Chorus, and Orch. (1970); *Kubla Khan* for Tenor, Chorus, and Orch. (1973); *Rhyme Rude to My Pride* for Men's Voices (1974); *My Beloved Spake* for Chorus and Organ (1976); *Dr. Faustus* for Solo Voices, Chorus, and Orch. (1977).

WRITINGS (all publ. in London): *The Music of Liszt* (1954; second ed., 1966); *Twentieth Century Counterpoint* (1954); *Ballet Music: An Introduction* (1958; second ed., rev., 1973); with R. Layton, *Twentieth-Century Composers 3: Britain, Scandinavia and the Netherlands* (1972).—**NS/LK/DM**

Sears, Al(bert Omega), jazz tenor saxophonist; b. Macomb, Ill., Feb. 21, 1910; d. N.Y., March 23, 1990. Brother of sax-playing leader Marion Sears. Al originally specialized on alto and baritone saxes. He first worked professionally in Buffalo with various bands before moving to N.Y. to replace Johnny Hodges in Chick Webb's Band in 1928. Before joining Elmer Snowden in N.Y. (1931), Sears toured in the "Keep Shulflin'" revue and then led his own band while also working as a sideman with others. In spring 1932 he was forced to leave Snowden because of a bad case of pneumonia; Sears returned to Buffalo and reformed his own band. He toured with Bud Harris and his Rhythm Rascals in early 1933, then led his own band for several years in various cities in the 1930s; he also left music temporarily in 1935 to study business management. Sears joined Andy Kirk from February 1941 until summer 1942, then reformed his own band, which played in N.Y. and did a long U.S.O. tour in 1943; Lester Young was a sideperson. Sears joined Lionel Hampton for four months beginning in December 1943, then worked with Duke Ellington from May 1944 until September 1949 (brief absence in early 1949). Sears then played in Johnny Hodges's small band from March 1951 until October 1952. After the success of his composition "Castle Rock," he formed his own music publishing company which became his major occupation. Sears continued to record through the 1950s, and also played occasionally with Duke Ellington's Orch.

DISC.: *Dance Music with a Swing Beat* (1959); *Swing's the Thing* (1960).—**JC/LP**

Seashore, Carl Emil, Swedish-American psychologist; b. Morlunda, Jan. 28, 1866; d. Lewiston, Idaho, Oct. 16, 1949. He was taken to the U.S. as a child. He studied at Gustavus Adolphus Coll. in Minn. (B.A., 1891), and pursued the study of psychology at Yale Univ. (Ph.D., 1895), where he was an assistant in its psychological laboratory (1895–97). He joined the faculty of the Univ. of Iowa in 1902, where he was head of its psychology dept. and its psychological laboratory (from 1905). He devised a widely used method for measuring musical talent ("Seashore Test") through special measurements of his own invention (audiometer, tonoscope, chronograph, etc.).

WRITINGS: *Measures of Musical Talent* (N.Y., 1919; second ed., rev., 1939 with D. Lewis and J. Saetveit as *Seashore Measures* *of Musical Talents*; third ed., rev., 1960); ed. *Psychology of the Vibrato in Voice and Instrument* (Iowa City, 1936); *Psychology of Music* (N.Y., 1938); *In Search of Beauty in Music: A Scientific Approach to Musical Aesthetics* (N.Y., 1947).—NS/LK/DM

Sébastian, Georges (real name, **György Sebestyén**), Hungarian-born French conductor; b. Budapest, Aug. 17, 1903; d. Le Hauteville, Yvelines, April 12, 1989. He studied with Bartók, Kodály, and Weiner at the Budapest Academy of Music (graduated, 1921), then received instruction in conducting from Walter in Munich (1922–23). He conducted at the Hamburg Opera (1924–25) and with the Leipzig Gewandhaus Orch. (1925–27). After serving as principal conductor at Berlin's Städtische Oper (1927–31), he went to Moscow as music director of the Radio and as a conductor with the Phil. In 1938 he went to the U.S.; was conductor of the Scranton (Pa.) Phil. (1940–45); also conducted in South America. In 1946 he settled in Paris, where he conducted at the Opéra and the Opéra-Comique; also appeared with the Orchestre National de France. Sébastian became well known for his championship of the Romantic repertoire. He conducted complete cycles of the Brucker and Mahler syms. in France. —NS/LK/DM

Sebastiani, Johann, German composer; b. near Weimar, Sept. 30, 1622; d. Königsberg, 1683. He settled in Königsberg about 1650, and was made Kantor at the Cathedral in 1661 and court Kapellmeister to the Elector of Brandenburg in 1663; was pensioned in 1679. He wrote a Passion, *Das Leyden und Sterben unsers Herrn und Heylandes Jesu Christi nach dem heiligen Matthaeo* for 5 Voices, 6 Instruments, and Basso Continuo (Konigsberg, 1672; ed. in Denkmäler Deutscher Tonkunst, XVII, 1904), which is noteworthy for the devotional chorales therein introduced. He also wrote *Erster Theil der Parnass-Blumen oder* [60] *geist- und weltliche Lieder* (Hamburg and Wolfenbüttel, 1672), *Ander Theil der Parnass-Blumen* (Hamburg, 1675), various funeral songs (1663–80), and many occasional pieces.—NS/LK/DM

Sebestyén, János, esteemed Hungarian harpsichordist, organist, and pedagogue; b. Budapest, March 2, 1931. He was an organ pupil of Ferenc Gergely at the Budapest Academy of Music (graduated, 1956). He toured as a harpsichord and organ virtuoso in Europe, the U.S., and the Far East. He was founder-director of the harpsichord dept. at the Budapest Academy of Music (from 1970). In 1982 he was made a Merited Artist by the Hungarian government. In 1983, 1988, and 1993 he served as president of the jury of the Liszt International Organ Competition in Budapest.—NS/LK/DM

Sebök, György, Hungarian-born American pianist and pedagogue; b. Szeged, Nov. 2, 1922; d. Bloomington, Ind., Nov. 14, 1999. He began his training in Szeged at age 5, and made his first public appearance as a pianist in 1936. At 16, he entered the Franz Liszt Academy of Music in Budapest, where he graduated in 1942. In 1949 he became a prof. of piano at the Béla Bartók Cons. in Budapest. He was soloist in the first Bartók Memorial Concert in Budapest in 1950. In 1951 he won the Berlin Prize and in 1952 the Liszt Prize in Budapest. He toured in Eastern and Central Europe, as well as in Russia. When the Hungarian Revolution failed in 1956, he went to Paris. In 1962 he became a prof. at the Ind. Univ. School of Music in Bloomington, where he was made a Distinguished Prof. in 1985. He became a naturalized American citizen in 1970. Sebök's engagements took him all over the world as a soloist with orchs., as a recitalist, and as a chamber music artist. He also gave master classes in the U.S. and abroad. In 1993 he received the Cross of Merit from the Hungarian Republic for his services to music, in 1995 he was awarded the Gold Medal of the City of Paris, and in 1996 he was named a Chevalier de l'Ordre des Arts et des Lettres of France.—NS/LK/DM

Sechter, Simon, famous Austrian organist, pedagogue, and composer; b. Friedberg, Bohemia, Oct. 11, 1788; d. Vienna, Sept. 10, 1867. In 1804 he went to Vienna, where he studied with L. Koželuh and Hartmann; then was a piano and singing teacher at the Inst. for the Blind (1810–25). He also was assist. (1824–25) and principal (from 1825) Hoforganist, and likewise served as prof. of thoroughbass and counterpoint at the Cons. (1851–63). He won his greatest renown as a teacher, numbering among his best-known pupils Henselt, Bruckner, Vieuxtemps, and Thalberg; Schubert took a lesson from him (Nov. 4, 1828) shortly before his untimely death. Although he was a master contrapuntist, his output is unknown outside his homeland. Among his more than 8,000 works were 3 operas, *Ezzeline, die unglückliche Gegangene aus Deli-Katesse* (1843; not perf.), *Ali Hitsch-Hatsch* (1843; Vienna, Nov. 12, 1844), and *Melusine* (1851; not perf.), 2 oratorios, *Die Offenbarung Johannes* (1838–45) and *Sodoms Untergang* (1840), 35 masses, 2 Requiems, many other sacred works, choral pieces, orch. music, and chamber pieces.

WRITINGS: *Die Grundsätze der musikalischen Komposition*: I, *Die richtige Folge der Grundharmonien* (Leipzig, 1853), II, *Von den Gesetzen des Taktes in der Musik; Vom einstimmigen Satz; Die Kunst, zu einer gegebenen Melodie die Harmonie zu finden* (Leipzig, 1853), and III, *Vom drei- und zweistimmigen Satze; Rhythmische Entwürfe; Vom strengen Satze, mit Kurzen Andeutungen des freien Satzes; Vom doppelten Contrapunkte* (Leipzig, 1854).

BIBL.: C. Pohl, *S. S.* (Vienna, 1868); J. Markus, *S. S.: Biographisches Denkmal* (Vienna, 1888); G. Capellen, *Ist das System S. S.s ein geeigneter Ausgangspunkt für die theoretische Wagnerforschung?* (Leipzig, 1902); E. Tittel, *S. S. als Kirchenkomponist* (diss., Univ. of Vienna, 1935).—NS/LK/DM

Seckendorff, Karl Siegmund, Freiherr von, German writer and composer; b. Erlangen, Nov. 26, 1744; d. Ansbach, April 26, 1785. He studied literature and jurisprudence at the Univ. of Erlangen. He was an officer in the Austrian army (1761–74), then in the diplomatic service in Weimar (1776–84); shortly before his death, he was appointed Prussian ambassador in Ansbach (1784). At Weimar he was on close terms with Goethe, who allowed him to write music for a number of his poems before their publ. (*Der Fischer, Der König in Thule*, etc.); in these songs, Seckendorff caught the characteristic inflections of folk melodies.

WORKS: DRAMATIC: *Lila*, Liederspiel (Weimar, 1776); *Le marché (La foire) du village*, ballet-comique (1776); *Proserpina*, monodrama (Weimar, 1778); *Die Laune des Verliebten* (Weimar, May 20, 1779; not extant); *Jery und Bätely*, Singspiel (Weimar, July 12, 1780; not extant); *Der Geist der Jugend*, comédie-ballet (Weimar, Jan. 30, 1782; not extant); *Der Blumenraub*, operetta (1784); *Die Empfindsamkeit* (n.d.). **OTHER:** Chamber music; *Volks- und andere Lieder* for Voice and Piano (3 vols., Weimar, 1779–82) and other lieder in contemporary collections; keyboard music, including 2 sonatas for 3 Pianos.

BIBL.: V. Knab, *K.S. v.S. (1774–1785): Ein Beitrag zur Geschichte des deutschen volkstümlichen Liedes und der Musik am weimarischen Hof im 18. Jahrhundert* (diss., Univ. of Bonn, 1914). —NS/LK/DM

Secunda, Sholom, Russian-born American composer; b. Alexandria, near Kherson, Sept. 4, 1894; d. N.Y., June 13, 1974. His family went to the U.S. in 1907. He took music lessons with Goetschius and Bloch at the Inst. of Musical Art in N.Y., graduating in 1917. He became a naturalized American citizen in 1923. In 1932 he became a founder of the Society of Jewish Composers, Publishers and Songwriters, which was absorbed by Broadcast Music, Inc. in 1940. From 1916 to 1973 he was associated with the Yiddish Theater in N.Y., for which he wrote over 40 operettas; most of these hardly made any impression outside ethnic circles, but one song, *Bei mir bist du schön*, from the operetta *I Would if I Could* (1933), made an unexpected splash even among gentiles, and was sung, in the original Yiddish, by the Andrews Sisters, Rudy Vallee, July Garland, and Kate Smith, becoming one of the most popular songs worldwide. Secunda sold the copyright in 1937 for $30; he regained it in 1961, but never made any appreciable sum of money from it; a legal hassle with the author of the lyrics, Jacob Jacobs, further depleted Secunda's income. Other songs from his operettas were often taken as traditional; among these, *Dona, Dona, Dona*, from the operetta *Esterke* (1940), was recorded by Joan Baez. He also wrote some Jewish service music.

BIBL.: V. Secunda, *Bei Mir Bist Du Schön: The Story of S. S.* (N.Y., 1982).—NS/LK/DM

Secunde, Nadine, American soprano; b. Independence, Ohio, Dec. 21, 1953. She studied at the Oberlin Coll.-Cons. of Music, with Margaret Harshaw at the Ind. Univ. School of Music in Bloomington, and in Germany as a Fulbright scholar. From 1980 to 1985 she was a member of the Wiesbaden State Theater. In 1985 she made her debut as Kát'a Kabanová at the Cologne Opera, where she remained as a principal member. She sang Elsa at the Bayreuth Festival in 1987, and returned there in 1988 as Sieglinde in the *Ring* cycle. In 1988 she appeared as Elsa at London's Covent Garden and as Elisabeth at the Lyric Opera in Chicago. She portrayed Berlioz's Cassandre in Los Angeles in 1991. In 1994 she sang Elisabeth in Munich, returning there in 1997 to sing in the premiere of Henze's *Venus und Adonis*. Her other roles include Agathe, Chrysothemis, and Ariadne. —NS/LK/DM

Sedaka, Neil, B. Brooklyn, N.Y., March 13, 1939. Coming from a doo-wop background, yet classically trained, Neil Sedaka composed more than 1,000 tunes, including a dozen major pop hits he recorded between 1959 and 1963 that were co-authored with Howard Greenfield, his lyricist until 1972. Toiling at N.Y.'s famed Brill Building under Don Kirshner, the team achieved their first success as authors of Connie Francis's "Stupid Cupid." Sedaka's own hits included "Oh! Carol," written for fellow songwriter Carole King, and "Breaking Up Is Hard to Do," perhaps his finest song. Sedaka ceased performing and recording after his popularity faded with the advent of the British Invasion, yet he continued to write songs. In the early 1970s, encouraged by the enormous success of Carole King's *Tapestry*, Sedaka successfully attempted a comeback, first in Great Britain and then in the U.S. Signing with Elton John's Rocket label, he scored top pop hits with "Laughter in the Rain" and "Bad Blood." Although his careful mixture of early and recent material worked well on television and the cabaret circuit, Neil Sedaka has not had a major hit since 1980's "Should've Never Let You Go," recorded with his daughter Dara.

Extensively trained in the classics on piano from the age of nine, Neil Sedaka wrote his first song with 16-year-old Brooklyn buddy Howard "Howie" Greenfield when he was 13. Sedaka joined the high school vocal group The Tokens with Hank Medress in 1955, recording two Sedaka- Greenfield songs. Medress later realigned the group in the 1960s, scoring a top hit with "The Lion Sleeps Tonight." In 1957 Sedaka won a piano scholarship to the famed Juilliard School of Music, where he studied for two years.

In 1958, through songwriters Doc Pomus and Mort Shuman, Sedaka and Greenfield were signed as professional songwriters to Al Nevins and Don Kirshner's Aldon Publishing Company, housed in N.Y.'s Brill Building, where Carole King, Gerry Goffin, Barry Mann, and Cynthia Weil also worked. Sedaka and Greenfield's first songwriting success came in the summer of 1958 when Connie Francis had a major hit with their "Stupid Cupid." They later provided her with "Where the Boys Are," and Greenfield also co- authored her hits "Everybody's Somebody's Fool," "My Heart Has a Mind of Its Own," and "Breakin' in a Brand New Heart," as well as The Shirelles' "Foolish Little Girl."

Neil Sedaka signed his own recording deal with RCA Records and soon achieved a major pop and R&B hit with "The Diary" at the end of 1958. In 1959 he toured Great Britain for the first time and played piano on Bobby Darin's smash pop and R&B hit "Dream Lover." Over the next four years, he regularly scored major pop hits with Greenfield collaborations such as "Oh! Carol," written for Carole King, "Stairway to Heaven" and "Calendar Girl" (both near-smash hits), the classic "Breaking Up Is Hard to Do" (a top hit), and "Next Door to an Angel," all of which became major R&B hits. "Little Devil" and "Happy Birthday, Sweet Sixteen," one of their most enduring compositions, were near-smash pop-only hits, and Sedaka achieved his last moderate hits for more than ten years with "Alice in Wonderland," "Let's Go Steady Again" and "Bad Girl" in 1963. In early 1962 The Everly Brothers scored a near-smash pop hit with "Crying in the Rain," co-written by Howie Greenfield and Carole King.

In 1966, after three years of relative failure, Neil Sedaka ceased recording and live performances to concentrate on his songwriting with Greenfield. In 1969–70 their songs "Working on a Groovy Thing" and "Puppet Man" became major pop hits for The Fifth Dimension. Buoyed by the 1971 success of Carole King's *Tapestry*, Sedaka attempted a comeback on mentor Don Kirshner's Kirshner label with *Emergence*, which he regarded as his best album. The 1971 album failed to sell in the U.S., but he nonetheless encountered success in Great Britain, returning to live performance at London's Royal Albert Hall. In 1972 Sedaka moved to London, where he teamed with new lyricist Phil Cody, effectively ending his partnership with Greenfield. Howie Greenfield died in Los Angeles on March 4, 1986, at the age of 49.

Neil Sedaka produced his second Kirshner album, *Solitaire*, and recorded it and the British-only album *The Tra-La Days Are Over* with a group called Hot Legs, which later became 10 cc. He subsequently recorded two more British albums and, in 1974, was signed by Elton John to his newly formed Rocket label. Sedaka's first Rocket album, *Sedaka's Back*, compiled songs from his three British albums and produced three American pop hits, the top hit "Laughter in the Rain," written with Phil Cody, and the major hits "The Immigrant" (dedicated to John Lennon) and "That's When the Music Takes Me." In 1975 The Captain and Tenille scored a top hit with Neil Sedaka and Howie Greenfield's "Love Will Keep Us Together," and The Carpenters achieved a major hit with Sedaka and Phil Cody's "Solitaire." Sedaka's *The Hungry Years* yielded a top hit with "Bad Blood," recorded with Elton John and co-written with Cody, and a near-smash with an engaging, slowed-down version of "Breaking Up Is Hard to Do." Sedaka subsequently scored a major hit with "Love in the Shadows" and a moderate hit with "Steppin' Out" on Rocket and performed his first American television special on NBC in 1976.

Neil Sedaka switched to Elektra Records in 1977 and managed his last (major) hit in 1980 with "Should've Never Let You Go," recorded with his daughter Dara. *My Friend* compiled recordings he made between 1974 and 1980. In 1982 Putnam published Sedaka's autobiography *Laughter in the Rain*. In the mid-1990s, Neil Sedaka enjoyed European success with recordings of his own lyrics put to the classical melodies of Chopin, Tchaikovsky and Rachmaninoff, among others.

WRITINGS: *Laughter in the Rain: My Own Story* (N.Y., 1982).

DISC. *Rock with Sedaka* (1959); *Circulate* (1960); *Little Devil and His Other Hits* (1961); *Sings His Greatest Hits* (1962); *Italiano* (1964); *Live in Australia* (1976); *Emergence* (1971); *Solitaire* (1972); *Sedaka's Back* (1974); *The Hungry Years* (1975); *Oh! Carol and Other Hits* (1975); *Let's Go Steady Again* (1975); *Steppin' Out* (1976); *Pure Gold* (1976); *Stupid Cupid* (1976); *Breaking Up Is Hard to Do—The Original Hits* (1976); *Greatest Hits* (1977); *1950s and 1960s* (1977); *A Song* (1977); *All You Need Is Music* (1978); *Many Sides* (1978); *In the Pocket* (1980); *Now* (1981); *Superbird* (1982); *Come See about Me* (1984); *Tuneweaver* (1995); *All Time Greatest Hits* (1988); *All Time Greatest Hits, Vol. 2* (1991); *My Friend* (1986); *Singer, Songwriter, Melody Maker* (1981); *Neil Sedaka's Diary* (1991); *Greatest Hits Live* (1992); *Laughter in the Rain: The Best of Neil Sedaka* (1994).—**BH**

Sedric, Gene (actually, **Eugene Hall**; aka **"Honey Bear"**), jazz tenor saxophonist, clarinetist; b. St. Louis, Mo., June 17, 1907; d. N.Y., April 3, 1963. His delightful work was a highlight of many Fats Waller recordings. Sedric gained his nickname in the 1930s; at the time, he wore an exotic camel-hair overcoat. His father, Paul 'Con Con' Sedric, was a professional ragtime pianist. As a boy, he played in the local Knights of Pythias Band. In the early 1920s, he worked with Charlie Creath, Fate Marable, Dewey Jackson, Ed Allen (late 1922–fall 1923), and then, in September 1923, he joined Julian Arthur's Band, accompanying Jimmy Cooper's "Black and White Revue." During 1924–early 1925, he gigged in N.Y. until joining Sam Wooding. Sedric sailed to Europe with Wooding in May 1925, and remained with Wooding until October 1931 when the band temporarily disbanded. He returned to N.Y. and played again with Wooding in the summer of 1932. After a brief spell with Fletcher Henderson, Sedric performed with Fats Waller from 1934–42. During Fats Waller's solo tours, Sedric worked with various bands, including Mezz Mezzrow's Disciples of Swing (November 1937) and Don Redman (1938–39). From the mid-1940s to the early 1950s, he led his own small groups in N.Y. and on the road, except for a period in mid-1943 when he was sidetracked by illness, and brief periods in late 1944 when he performed with the Phil Moore Four and with the Hazel Scott Show in late 1945. In the spring of 1951 he toured with Bobby Hackett's Band, then after a spell with Jimmy McPartland, he sailed to Europe in February 1953 to tour with Mezz Mezzrow. From August 1953, he worked regularly in a band led by Conrad Janis in N.Y., and did many freelance recording sessions. Illness forced him to give up playing for the last 18 months of his life.—**JC/LP**

Seedo (Sidow or Sydow), German composer; b. c. 1700; d. probably in Prussia, c. 1754. He was active at London's Drury Lane (1731–34), where he contributed music to several stage pieces. About 1736 he went to Potsdam to work with the Royal Band.—**NS/LK/DM**

Seefried, Irmgard, outstanding German soprano; b. Köngetried, Bavaria, Oct. 9, 1919; d. Vienna, Nov. 24, 1988. She received her early musical instruction from her father, then studied voice at the Augsburg Cons., graduating in 1939. She made her professional operatic debut as the Priestess in *Aida* at the Aachen Stadttheater (Nov. 8, 1940); her first appearance at the Vienna State Opera followed as Eva in *Die Meistersinger von Nürnberg* (May 2, 1943); Richard Strauss chose her for the role of the Composer in *Ariadne auf Naxos* at his 80th-birthday celebration there (1944). She subsequently sang in Salzburg, Edinburgh, Berlin, Paris, London, and Buenos Aires. On Nov. 20, 1953, she made her Metropolitan Opera debut in N.Y. as Susanna in *Le nozze di Figaro*. She was made a Kammersängerin of the Vienna State Opera in 1947; was named an honorary member in 1969. In 1948 she married **Wolfgang Schneiderhan.**

BIBL.: F. Fassbind, *Wolfgang Schneiderhan, I. S.: Eine Künstler- und Lebensgemeinschaft* (Bern, 1960).—**NS/LK/DM**

Seeger, Charles (Louis), eminent American musicologist, ethnomusicologist, teacher, and composer, father of **Pete(r) Seeger;** b. Mexico City (of American parents), Dec. 14, 1886; d. Bridgewater, Conn., Feb. 7, 1979. He was educated at Harvard Univ. (graduated, 1908). After conducting at the Cologne Opera (1910–11), he returned to the U.S. as chairman of the music dept. of the Univ. of Calif. at Berkeley (1912–19), where he gave the first classes in musicology in the U.S. (1916); then taught at N.Y.'s Inst. of Musical Art (1921–33) and the New School for Social Research (1931–35); at the latter, he gave the first classes (with Henry Cowell) in ethnomusicology in the U.S. (1932); was also active in contemporary music circles, as a composer and a music critic. He served as a technical adviser on music to the Resettlement Administration (1935–38), as deputy director of the Federal Music Project of the Works Progress Administration (1938–41), and as chief of the music division of the Pan-American Union (1941–53) in Washington, D.C.; was also a visiting prof. at Yale Univ. (1949–50). He subsequently was a research musicologist at the Inst. of Ethnomusicology at the Univ. of Calif. at Los Angeles (1960–70), and then taught at Harvard Univ. (from 1972). He was a founder and chairman (1930–34) of the N.Y. Musicological Soc., which he helped to reorganize as the American Musicological Soc. in 1934; was its president (1945–46) and also president of the American Soc. for Comparative Musicology (1935) and the Soc. for Ethnomusicology (1960–61; honorary president from 1972). Seeger also was instrumental (with Cowell and Joseph Schafer) in the formation of the N.Y. Composers' Collective (1932); since he was profoundly interested in proletarian music throughout the 1930s, he wrote on the need for a revolutionary spirit in music for such publications as *The Daily Worker;* he also contributed songs under the name Carl Sands to *The Workers Song Books* (1934 and 1935). Two of his essays are of especial historical interest: "On Proletarian Music" (*Modern Music,* XI/3 [1934]), which lamented the dearth of folk songs in the work of professional musicians, and "Grassroots for American Composers" (*Modern Music,* XVI [1938–40]), which, by shedding earlier Marxist rhetoric, had wide influence on the folk movement in the 1950s. Since many of his compositions were destroyed by fire at Berkeley in 1926, his extraordinary contribution to American music rests upon his work as a scholar whose uniquely universalist vision for the unification of the field of musicology as a whole continues to challenge the various, sometimes contentious contributing factions of musicology, ethnomusicology, and comparative musicology. He was also a noted teacher; one of his most gifted students, **Ruth (Porter) Crawford,** became his second wife. In addition to Pete(r) Seeger, 2 other of his children became musicians: Mike (Michael) Seeger (b. N.Y., Aug. 15, 1933) was a folksinger and instrumentalist; after learning to play various folk instruments on his own, he became active in promoting the cause of authentic folk music of the American Southeast; became widely known for his expertise as a banjo player; with John Cohen and Tom Paley, he organized the New Lost City Ramblers in 1958; then founded the Strange Creek Singers in 1968. Peggy (actually, Margaret) Seeger (b. N.Y., June 17, 1935) was a folksinger, songwriter, and song collector; studied both classical and folk music; after further training at Radcliffe Coll., she became active as a performer; settled in England in 1956, becoming a naturalized subject in 1959; became a leading figure in the folk-music revival.

WRITINGS: With E. Stricklen, *Harmonic Structure and Elementary Composition* (Berkeley, 1916); *Music as Recreation* (Washington, D.C., 1940); with R. Crawford Seeger, J. Lomax, and A. Lomax, *Folk Song: USA* (N.Y., 1947; second ed., rev., 1975); *Music and Society: Some New World Evidence of Their Relationship* (Washington, D.C., 1953); *Studies in Musicology, 1935–1975* (Berkeley, 1977); ed. *Essays for a Humanist: An Offering to Klaus Wachsmann* (N.Y., 1977); A. Pascarella, ed., *Studies in Musicology II, 1929–1979* (Berkeley, 1994).

BIBL.: A. Pescatello, *C. S.: A Life in American Music* (Pittsburgh, 1992); T. Greer, *A Question of Balance: C. S.'s Philosophy of Music* (Berkeley, 1998).—**NS/LK/DM**

Seeger, Horst, German musicologist; b. Erkner, near Berlin, Nov. 6, 1926; d. Dresden, Jan. 2, 1999. He began his training at the Berlin Hochschule für Musik (1950–55), and studied musicology at Humboldt Univ. in Berlin, where he received his Ph.D. in 1958 with the diss. *Komponist und Folklore in der Musik des 20. Jahrhunderts.* He was chief dramaturg of the (East) Berlin Komische Oper (1960–73). From 1973 to 1983 he served as Intendant of the Dresden State Opera. His books include *Wolfgang Amadeus Mozart* (Leipzig, 1956); *Kleines Musiklexikon* (Berlin, 1958); *Joseph Haydn* (Leipzig, 1961); *Der kritische Musikus: Musikkritiken aus zwei Jahrhunderten* (Leipzig, 1963); *Musiklexikon* (Leipzig, 1966); *Wir und die Musik* (Berlin, 1968); *Opern-Lexikon* (Berlin, 1978; third ed., rev., 1987).—**NS/LK/DM**

Seeger, Mike, folk-revivalist, multi-instrumentalist, folklorist, and record producer, son of ethnomusicologist **Charles Seeger** and composer **Ruth Crawford Seeger,** and half-brother of folk revivalist **Pete Seeger;** b. N.Y., Aug. 15, 1933. Seeger has played a seminal role in the preservation and popularization of old-time country music for nearly 40 years. He began performing as a bluegrass-styled banjo player in the Washington, D.C., area in the mid-1950s. He produced for Folkways Records one of the first albums of bluegrass music in 1957, an important anthology because Folkways catered to a Northern, urban audience who were unfamiliar (at that time) with the diversity of bluegrass styles. About the same time, he formed The New Lost City Ramblers with Tom Paley and John Cohen, a band dedicated to performing the old-time music of the 1920s and 1930s in almost literal, note-for-note recreations.

Seeger made his first solo LP in 1962 (*Old-Time Country Music,* Folkways). By using an Ampex multi-track tape machine, he was able to play all of the parts, creating in effect his own stringband. The sound of the album was not much different from the style of the Ramblers at that time. Perhaps most interesting was his recreation of both Monroe Brothers on the tune "Rollin' On."

In this same period, he began making a series of field trips to the South. One of the first artists he "discovered" was blues guitarist Elizabeth "Libba" Cotten, who had worked as a maid for the Seeger family. It turned out that she was a talented guitar player in the country-blues style, as well as a skilled songwriter. (Her "Freight Train" became one of the hits of the folk revival.) Seeger also sought out performers of the 1920s and 1930s who had stopped recording; one of his most important finds was banjoist Doc Boggs. He was also a champion of the autoharp, introducing the country-picking of Maybelle Carter and other important autoharp players to a new audience. His anthology *Mountain Music on the Autoharp* introduced several fine players, including Kilby Snow.

Seeger recorded a second solo album in 1965 for Vanguard, a more low-keyed affair than his first, while continuing to perform with the Ramblers through 1968. Although the Ramblers never officially "disbanded," they were less active from 1968 onwards. Seeger made two excellent solo albums for Mercury in the mid-1970s, *Music from True Vine*, featuring the charming autoharp song "I Rambled This Country from Early to Late," and *The Second Annual Farewell Reunion*, that featured Seeger performing with traditional performers and revivalists; the most interesting cut on this was his eery recreation of "The Train that Carried My Girl from Town" by Frank Hutchinson, featuring Seeger on fiddle, harmonica, and vocals along with the slide guitar of Ry Cooder.

In the early 1970s, Seeger formed with Ramblers bandsmate Tracy Schwartz, then-wife Alice Gerrard, Hazel Dickens, and bluegrass banjo player Lamar Grier a bluegrass-country group called The Strange Creek Singers. This short-lived band played an amalgam of country and bluegrass sounds. Seeger also performed as a duo with Alice Gerrard, and the pair recorded an album for Greenhays Records, and with his sister Peggy Seeger. (The two made a 1968 duo recording for British Argo records, and also performed songs from their mother's collections of children's songs for Rounder Records.)

Through the 1980s and early 1990s, Seeger continues to perform as a soloist and sometimes member of The New Lost City Ramblers. He also was the main force behind the old-time music "exercise" record, A-Robics and the Exertions (Flying Fish). He continued his field work, producing the videotape *Talkin' Feet* in the late 1980s, a documentary on traditional flat-foot dancing of the upper South.

DISC.: *Old Time Country Music* (1962); *Mike Seeger* (1965); *Peggy 'n' Mike* (with Peggy Seeger; 1968); *Music from True Vine* (1972); *Second Annual Farewell Reunion* (1973); *American Folk Songs for Children* (with Peggy Seeger; 1988); *Third Annual Farewell Reunion* (1997); *Fresh Old-Time Stringband Music* (1988); *Southern Banjo Styles* (1999); *Retrograss* (with David Grissman and John Hartford; 1999). **FIELD RECORDINGS BY MIKE SEEGER:** *Close to Home Old Time Music from Mike Seeger's Collection 1952–67* (1998).—RC

Seeger, Pete(r) R., influential American folksinger, songwriter, and banjoist; son of **Charles Seeger,**

stepson of **Ruth Crawford Seeger,** and half-brother of **Mike Seeger;** b. N.Y., May 3, 1919. Seeger popularized American and international folk songs, drawing from the influence of such peers and predecessors as Lead Belly and Woody Guthrie and helping to spark the folk music revival of the late 1950s and early 1960s as personified by such descendants as Bob Dylan, Joan Baez, and Peter, Paul and Mary. Despite political persecution due to his left-wing views, he gained considerable popularity in his two early groups, The Almanac Singers and the Weavers, and in a solo career lasting more than 50 years. Though best known for his engaging concert performances of stirring folk songs that he adapted and introduced, such as "We Shall Overcome," he also wrote several songs that became hits for others, notably "If I Had a Hammer," "Where Have All the Flowers Gone?" and "Turn! Turn! Turn!" And he developed and popularized the five-string banjo, writing a widely used instruction manual for the instrument.

Seeger's father, musicologist Dr. Charles Louis Seeger Jr., was unemployed at the time of his birth, having been dismissed from his position as music professor at the Univ. of Calif. at Berkeley the previous year because he was a conscientious objector to World War I. Seeger's mother, Constance de Clyver Edson Seeger, was a violin teacher. During his childhood his parents became instructors at the Juilliard School of Music. He grew up at the home of his paternal grandparents in Patterson, N.Y., but attended boarding schools from the age of four. Though he scorned formal music instruction, he began to play the ukulele and the autoharp about the age of eight, and at the start of his teens he obtained a four-string banjo. Probably in the summer of 1936, his father took him to a folk music festival in Asheville, N. C., where he first heard the five-string banjo and became interested in it.

Seeger intended to become a journalist and entered Harvard in 1936 majoring in sociology. He dropped out in 1938 and sought work in journalism in N.Y., but became increasingly involved in folk music instead, meeting Aunt Molly Jackson and Lead Belly, who taught him to play the guitar. From 1939 to 1940 he worked as an assistant to Alan Lomax at the Archive of Folk Song in the Library of Congress. In May 1940 he met Woody Guthrie, whom he accompanied on a trip around the U.S. that summer. The two worked on a songbook, *Hard Hitting Songs for Hard Hit People*, not formally published until more than a quarter-century later. In the fall Seeger met Lee Hays, who also was working on a songbook, and with Hays's roommate, writer Millard Lampell, formed the politically oriented Almanac Singers, a group eventually joined by Guthrie and many other performers over the two years of its existence.

Seeger left The Almanac Singers when he was inducted into the army in July 1942. On July 20, 1943, he married Toshi Aline Ohta, with whom he had four children. Assigned to the Special Services division as an entertainer, he was stationed on Saipan during World War II. After his return from the war, in December 1945 he became the national director of People's Songs Inc., an organization formed to expand the popularity of topical folk music. Booking performers and publishing a monthly journal, *People's Songs Bulletin*, to which Seeger contributed, it existed until March 1949, when it went bankrupt. Seeger launched a solo career during this period, appearing at the Village Vanguard nightclub in N.Y. in December 1946.

Seeger campaigned for and traveled with third-party presidential candidate Henry Wallace in 1948. Shortly after the end of the campaign, he teamed up with former Almanac Singer Lee Hays to form The Weavers, also featuring Ronnie Gilbert and Fred Hellerman. Early in 1949 he wrote music to Hays's lyrics for "The Hammer Song" (aka "If I Had a Hammer"), recorded by The Weavers in December for a single released on Hootenanny Records. A phrase from the song, "Sing out," was used as the name of a new folk-music magazine that began publishing in 1950, and the song's sheet music was printed on the cover of the first issue. Seeger became a regular contributor to *Sing Out!*

The Weavers struggled until Seeger got them booked into the Village Vanguard in December 1949 for the same fee he could have received performing alone. They went on to enormous success, beginning with the million-selling single "Tzena Tzena Tzena" (music by Issachor Miron [real name Michrovsky], revised by Julius Grossman, English lyrics by Mitchell Parish)/"Goodnight Irene" (music and lyrics by Lead Belly) on Decca Records in the summer of 1950. Also in 1950 the newly formed independent Folkways label released Seeger's first solo album, *Darling Corey*, some of it recorded three years earlier.

The Weavers scored a second million-seller in the spring of 1951 with "On Top of Old Smoky." (Though it was a traditional American folk song, "On Top of Old Smoky" was copyrighted as having new lyrics and arrangement by Seeger. He later denied the credit.) That summer they reached the charts with "Kisses Sweeter Than Wine" (music by "Joel Newman" [Lead Belly], adapted from the Irish folk song "Drimmer's Cow," lyrics by "Paul Campbell" [The Weavers]), and in February 1952 they charted with "Wimoweh" (music and lyrics by "Paul Campbell" [The Weavers], adapted from "Mbube," music and lyrics by Solomon Linda). But they were forced to disband in early 1953 due to red-baiting.

Though the group had been associated with left-wing causes, only Seeger had actually been a member of the Communist party during the 1940s. In the anti-Communist hysteria of the early 1950s he was forced to sustain his career performing primarily at schools, colleges, and summer camps and recording dozens of albums of traditional folk music for Folkways. On Aug. 16, 1955, he appeared as an unfriendly witness before the House Committee on Un-American Activities, declining either to answer questions or to take the Fifth Amendment. As a result he was cited for ten counts of contempt of Congress in 1956 and indicted in 1957, though his case did not come to trial for four years.

The Weavers reunited for a concert at Carnegie Hall on Christmas Eve, 1955, and thereafter went back to performing and recording for the independent Vanguard label. Pop singer Jimmie Rodgers revived "Kisses Sweeter Than Wine" for a Top Ten hit in December 1957. Seeger left The Weavers in 1958 and returned to solo work. On his recordings for Folkways he began to mix in contemporary topical songs, notably on *Gazette*, released in 1958, as well as some of his own compositions. *The Rainbow Quest*, released in July 1960, featured "Where Have All the Flowers Gone?" Seeger adapted the melody from the folk song "Drill Ye Tarriers Drill" and based the lyrics on a Ukrainian folk song quoted in Mikhail Sholokov's novel *And Quiet Flows the Don*. He earned his first Grammy nomination in 1960 for Best Album Created for Children for *Folk Songs for Young People*.

Late in 1960, Seeger signed to Columbia Records, a major label. In March 1961 he finally went on trial for the contempt charges. He was found guilty and sentenced to a year in prison, but his conviction was overturned by the U.S. Court of Appeals in May 1962. On April 30, 1961, he recorded his first Columbia album, *Story Songs*, live at the Village Gate coffeehouse in Greenwich Village; it was released in October. In December the Tokens hit #1 with the million-selling "The Lion Sleeps Tonight" (music and lyrics by Hugo Peretti, Luigi Creatore, George David Weiss, and Albert Stanton), technically based on "Mbube" but in fact an adaptation of "Wimoweh." In March 1962 The Kingston Trio reached the Top 40 with a version of "Where Have All the Flowers Gone?" that included added verses by Joe Hickerson. In October, Peter, Paul and Mary took "If I Had a Hammer" into the Top Ten.

Seeger released his second Columbia album, *The Bitter and the Sweet*, in November 1962. Another live album, recorded at the Bitter End club in Greenwich Village on July 23, 1962, included "Turn! Turn! Turn! (To Everything There Is a Season)," its lyrics adapted by Seeger from the Book of Ecclesiastes. In January 1963, Columbia released *Children's Concert at Town Hall*, recorded the previous April, and it earned a Grammy nomination for Best Recording for Children.

Seeger appeared twice in the spring of 1963 at Carnegie Hall, first on May 2–3 for reunion concerts with The Weavers that were taped and released on two albums, then on June 8 for a solo performance recorded by Columbia. In August, as Trini Lopez's version of "If I Had a Hammer" reached the Top Ten, Seeger and his family embarked on a trip around the world that lasted ten months.

The Carnegie Hall concert was released on a Columbia album in October as *We Shall Overcome*. The title song was based on the Reverend Charles Tindley's 1903 composition "I'll Overcome Some Day" and the traditional gospel hymn "I'll Be All Right," and adapted by Seeger, Zilphia Horton, Frank Hamilton, and Guy Carawan. It had already become an anthem of the civil rights movement, and Joan Baez's recording of it reached the charts in November. The album also contained "Guantanamera," Seeger and Hector Angulo's musical setting of a poem by Cuban writer José Marti. But it was Seeger's version of Malvina Reynolds's satiric "Little Boxes" that Columbia released as a single and which reached the charts, becoming his only chart single as a solo performer.

We Shall Overcome, which was nominated for a Grammy for Best Folk Recording, became his only charting album, though this may have had less to do with his actual popularity than with the glut of his recordings on the market. A clause in his Columbia contract allowed him to continue to record for Folkways, which also possessed a backlog of unreleased material from the 1950s, and other labels licensed or acquired older recordings, resulting in several Seeger album releases each year until the late 1960s. The singer, meanwhile, was unavailable to follow up the success of *We Shall Overcome* for Columbia. By the time he returned to the U.S. in June 1964, the British Invasion led by The Beatles had changed the record market drastically.

Seeger continued to release acoustic live albums on Columbia, *I Can See a New Day* in November 1964 and *Strangers and Cousins* in June 1965. The latter earned a Grammy nomination for Best Folk Recording. Though he opposed the development of topical folk music into popular folk-rock in 1965, as exemplified by Bob Dylan's appearance with a rock band at the Newport Folk Festival in July 1965, Seeger saw his songs adapted into folk-rock hits. Johnny Rivers reached the Top 40 in October 1965 with a revival of "Where Have All the Flowers Gone?" and The Byrds hit #1 in December with "Turn! Turn! Turn! (To Everything There Is a Season)."

In January 1966, Columbia released Seeger's first studio recording for the label, *God Bless the Grass*, a concept album that signaled his growing interest in environmentalism. Living beside the Hudson River in Beacon, N.Y., he had begun to raise money to build a sloop to sail the river and raise concerns about pollution. The album was another Grammy nominee for Best Folk Recording.

In the winter of 1965–66, Seeger, who had been blacklisted from network television since the early 1950s, hosted the series *Rainbow Quest* on a local N.Y. station. In September 1966 The Sandpipers scored a Top Ten hit with their version of "Guantanamera." In November, backed by the rock group the Blues Project, Seeger recorded the Columbia album *Waist Deep in the Big Muddy and Other Love Songs*. Released in July 1967, it featured a Seeger-written title song that was a bitter allegory expressing opposition to the Vietnam War. "Waist Deep in the Big Muddy" was released as a single, and Seeger was engaged to sing it on the network television series *The Smothers Brothers Comedy Hour*. But though his appearance on the show in September broke his decades-long blacklist, the song was censored by the network. An uproar followed, and Seeger was allowed to sing the song on a return appearance in February 1968, by which time it had been nominated for a Grammy for Best Folk Performance.

The sloop *Clearwater* was launched in June 1969, and it marked Seeger's increasing involvement in community issues and lowered national profile thereafter. He played himself in *Alice's Restaurant*, the film based on Arlo Guthrie's song, in August 1969, and sang his song "Old Devil Time" in the film *Tell Me That You Love Me, Junie Moon*, released in May 1970. His album *Young vs. Old*, released in August 1969, earned a Grammy nomination for Best Folk Performance. In November, Judy Collins reached the charts with a revival of "Turn! Turn! Turn! (To Everything There Is a Season)." Seeger had begun to record less frequently, and *Rainbow Race*, released in June 1971, on which he wrote eight of the ten songs himself, was his last album for Columbia. Robert John revived "The Lion Sleeps Tonight" for a million-selling Top Ten hit in February 1972.

Seeger returned to recording for Folkways with *Banks of Marble and Other Songs* at the end of 1974. He had begun touring with Arlo Guthrie, and the two released the double live album *Together in Concert*, which reached the charts in the spring of 1975. They followed it with two similar collections, *Precious Friend* in 1982 and *More Together Again in Concert* in 1994. Seeger returned to solo record-making with *Circles & Seasons*, released by Warner Bros. Records in July 1979. On Jan. 11, 1980, he performed a concert at Sanders Theatre in Cambridge, Mass., that was recorded by Folkways for the double album *Sing Along*. On Nov. 28–29, 1980, he participated in a final reunion of The Weavers at Carnegie Hall that was taped for an album, *Together Again* (1981), and filmed for a documentary on the group, *The Weavers: Wasn't That a Time!* (1982). In September 1984 he and Arlo Guthrie joined Ronnie Gilbert and Holly Near for a concert tour chronicled on the album *HARP* (1985). He earned another Grammy nomination for Best Traditional Folk Recording in 1986 for his participation in the New Lost City Ramblers' album *20th Anniversary Concert*.

With the rise of compact discs and the sale of Folkways Records to the Smithsonian Institution in 1987, Seeger's recordings began to be reissued extensively. In April 1996, Living Music released *Pete*, his first newly recorded studio album in 17 years, consisting mostly of familiar songs on which he was accompanied by choruses. It won a Grammy for Best Traditional Folk Album. Seeger became less active in his late seventies, but he still made occasional appearances, and he recorded new performances for both *Where Have All the Flowers Gone: The Songs of Pete Seeger*, a tribute album released in March 1998, and *If I Had a Hammer: Songs of Hope & Struggle*, a Smithsonian/Folkways compilation released in May 1998.

WRITINGS: BOOKS: *The Steel Drums of Kim Loy Wong* (N.Y., 1961); *How to Play the 5-String Banjo* (N.Y., 1948; 2nd rev. ed., 1954; 3rd rev. ed., 1962); with J. Lester, *The Twelve-String Guitar as Played by Leadbelly* (N.Y., 1965); J. Schwartz, ed., *The Incompleat Folksinger* (N.Y., 1972); *Henscratches and Flyspecks: How to Read Melodies from Songbooks in Twelve Confusing Lessons* (N.Y., 1973); with B. Reiser, *Everybody Says Freedom* (N.Y., 1990); Reiser, *Carry It On: The Story of American's Working People in Song and Picture* (Bethlehem, Pa., 1991); *Where Have All the Flowers Gone: A Singer's Stories, Songs, Seeds, Robberies* (Bethlehem, Pa., 1993). **SONGBOOKS:** Ed., with W. Guthrie, *The People's Songbook* (N.Y., 1948); with R. Gilbert, F. Hellerman, and L Hays, *The Weavers Sing* (N.Y., 1951); ed. with The Weavers, *The Carolers' Songbag* (N.Y., 1952); ed., *American Favorite Ballads* (N.Y., 1961); *The Goofing Off Suite* (N.Y., 1961); ed., *Woody Guthrie Folk Songs* (N.Y., 1963); *The Bells of Rhymney* (N.Y., 1964); *Bits and Pieces* (N.Y., 1965); ed. with J. Marris and C. Metzler, *Songs for Peace* (N.Y., 1966); ed. with A. Lomax and W. Guthrie, *Hard*

Hitting Songs for Hard Hit People (N.Y., 1967); *Oh, Had I a Golden Thread* (N.Y., 1968); *P. S. on Record* (N.Y., 1971).

DISC.: *Darling Corey* (1950); *Songs to Grow On—Vol. 2* (1951); *Songs to Grow On—Vol. 3* (1951); *American Folk Songs for Children* (1953); *Pete Seeger Sampler* (1954); *Sing Out! Hootenanny* (1959); *German Folk Songs* (1954); *Goofing Off Suite* (1954); *Frontier Ballads Vols. I and II* (1954); *Birds, Beasts, Bugs and Little Fishes* (1954); *Hootenanny Tonight!* (1954); *How to Play the Five String Banjo* (1954); *The Folksinger's Guitar Guide* (1955); *Folksongs of Four Continents* (1955); *Camp Songs* (1955;) *Country Dance Music Washboard Band* (1956); *With Voices We Sing Together* (1956); *American Industrial Ballads* (1956;) *Love Songs for Friends and Foes* (1956); *Studs Terkel's Weekly Almanac on Folk Music Blues on WFMT with Big Bill Broonzy and Pete Seeger* (1956); *Big Bill Broonzy and Pete Seeger in Concert* (1956); *Sing Out with Pete!* (1956–61); *American Ballads* (1957); *American Favorite Ballads* (December 1957); *Pete Seeger and Sonny Terry* (July 1958); *Gazette with Pete Seeger—Vol. 1* (1958); *Sleep Time* (1958); *Song and Play Time with Pete Seeger* (1958); *Hootenanny at Carnegie Hall* (1958–59); *American Playparties* (1959); *Folk Songs for Young People* (1959); *American Favorite Ballads—Vol. 2* (February 1959); *American Favorite Ballads—Vol. 3* (1959); *Nonesuch* (August 1959); *Indian Summer* (soundtrack; 1959–60); *Highlights of Pete Seeger at the Village Gate with Memphis Slim and Willie Dixon—Vol. 1* (1960); *Pete Seeger at the Village Gate—Vol. 2* (1960); *Songs of the Civil War* (1960); *American History in Ballad and Song—Vols. 1 and 2* (1960–61); *Champlain Valley Songs* (February 1960); *The Rainbow Quest* (July 1960); *American Favorite Ballads—Vol. 4* (1961); *Gazette—Vol. 2* (1961); *Pete Seeger: Story Songs* (April 1961); *American Favorite Ballads—Vol. 5* (1962); *American Game and Activity Songs for Children* (1962); *The 12-String Guitar as Played by Leadbelly* (1962); *The Bitter and the Sweet* (May 1962); *Pete Seeger: Children's Concert at Town Hall* (April 21, 1963); *We Shall Overcome* (June 8, 1963); *Ballads of Sacco and Vanzetti* (1963); *Little Boxes and Other Broadsides* (1963;) *The Nativity* (1963–64); *Strangers and Cousins* (1963–64); *Songs of Struggle and Protest* (January 1965); *I Can See a New Day* (January 1965); *God Bless the Grass* (January 1966); *Dangerous Songs!* (August 1966); *Pete Seeger Sings Woody Guthrie* (1967); *Waist Deep in the Big Muddy* (August 1967); *Traditional Christmas Carols* (1967); *Pete Seeger Sings Leadbelly* (1968); *Pete Seeger Sings and Answers Questions at the Ford Hall Forum in Boston* (1968); *Pete Seeger Now* (1968); *Pete Seeger Young vs. Old* (1971); *Rainbow Race* (1973); *The World of Pete Seeger* (1974); *Banks of Marble* (1974); *Pete Seeger and Brother Kirk Visit Sesame Street* (1974); *Pete Seeger and Arlo Guthrie Together in Concert* (1975); *Fifty Sail on Newburgh Bay* (1976); *Circles and Seasons* (1979); with Arlo Guthrie, *Precious Friend* (1982); *Pete* (1996).

BIBL.: D. Dunaway, *How Can I Keep from Singing: P. S.* (N.Y., 1981; new ed., 1990).—**WR**

Seeger, Ruth (Porter) Crawford, gifted American composer, folk music researcher, and teacher; b. East Liverpool, Ohio, July 3, 1901; d. Chevy Chase, Md., Nov. 18, 1953. She studied at the School of Musical Art in Jacksonville, Fla., where she then served on its faculty as a piano teacher (1918–21). In 1921 she enrolled at the American Cons. in Chicago, where she received training in piano from Heniot Lévy and Louise Robyn, and in theory and composition from John Palmer and Adolf Weidig. After additional piano studies with Djane Lavoie-Herz, as well as teaching posts at the American Cons. (1925–29) and the Elmhurst (Ill.) Coll. of Music (1926–29), she went to N.Y. to pursue training in com-

position with **Charles Seeger**, whom she married in 1931. A Guggenheim fellowship in 1930 allowed her to complete her studies in Berlin and Paris. Upon her return to the U.S., she devoted much time to folk music research and to teaching young children. She transcribed, arranged, and ed. hundreds of folk songs from the collection at the Library of Congress in Washington, D.C., and publ. the collections *American Folksongs for Children* (Garden City, N.Y., 1948), *Animal Folksongs for Children* (Garden City, N.Y., 1950), and *American Folk Songs for Christmas* (Garden City, N.Y., 1953). As a composer, Crawford wrote several bold and insightful works in an experimental tonal style. While she anticipated many techniques of the future avant-garde, her last works took on a less dissonant voice and were notably influenced by her folk music research.

WORKS: ORCH.: Suite for Small Orch. (1926); *Rissolty Rossolty* (1939). **CHAMBER:** Violin Sonata (Chicago, May 22, 1926); Suite for 5 Winds and Piano (1927; rev. 1929; Cambridge, Mass., Dec. 14, 1975); Suite No. 2 for Strings and Piano (1929); *4 Diaphonic Suites* for Various Instruments (1930); String Quartet (1931; N.Y., Nov. 13, 1933); Suite for Wind Quintet (Washington, D.C., Dec. 2, 1952). **P i a n o :** 5 preludes (1924–25); 4 preludes (1927–28); *Piano Study in Mixed Accents* (1930). **VOCAL:** *Adventures of Tom Thumb* for Narrator and Piano (1925); 5 songs for Voice and Piano, after Sandburg (1929); 3 chants: No. 1, *To an Unkind God*, for Women's Chorus, No. 2, *To an Angel*, for Soprano and Chorus, and No. 3, for Soprano, Alto, and Women's Chorus (all 1930); 3 songs for Alto, Oboe, Percussion, Piano, and Optional Orch., after Sandburg: No. 1, *Rat Riddles* (N.Y., April 21, 1930), No. 2, *In Tall Grass* (Berlin, March 10, 1932), and No. 3, *Prayers of Steel* (Amsterdam, June 14, 1933); 2 Ricercari for Voice and Piano: No. 1, *Sacco, Vanzetti* and No. 2, *Chinaman, Laundryman* (both 1932).

BIBL.: M. Gaume, *R.C. S.: Memoirs, Memories, Music* (Metuchen, N.J., 1986); J. Straus, *The Music of R.C. S.* (Cambridge, 1995); J. Tick, *R.C. S.: A Composer's Search for American Music* (N.Y., 1997).—**NS/LK/DM**

Segal, Uriel, Israeli conductor; b. Jerusalem, March 7, 1944. He studied violin in childhood. After training at the Rubin Academy of Music in Jerusalem, he studied conducting with Mendi Rodan at the Guildhall School of Music and Drama in London (1966–69). In 1969 he made his conducting debut in Copenhagen, the same year that he won first prize in the Mitropoulos Competition in N.Y. In 1969–70 he was an asst. conductor of the N.Y. Phil. He made his debut as an opera conductor in 1973 with *Der fliegende Holländer* at the Santa Fe Opera. From 1980 to 1983 he was principal conductor of the Bournemouth Sym. Orch., and from 1981 to 1985 he was chief conductor of the Philharmonia Hungarica in Marlkreis Recklinghausen. In 1989 he became music director of the Chautauqua (N.Y.) Sym. Orch. He also was chief conductor of the Century Orch. Osaka in Japan from 1989 to 1998. Segal was principal conductor of the Louisville Orch. from 1995 to 1998, and then served as its music director from 1998.—**NS/LK/DM**

Seger, Bob, nationally recognized guitarist and vocalist; b. Dearborn, Mich., May 6, 1945; **THE SILVER BULLET BAND**, rock group. **MEMBERSHIP:** Bob Seger, gtr., voc.; Andrew "Drew" Abbott, gtr.; Robyn Robbins, kybd.; Alto Reed, sax.; Chris Campbell, bs.; Charlie Allen Martin, drm. Later members include keyboardist Craig Frost and drummers Don Brewer and David Teegarden.

A regional star of the South and Midwest since the late 1960s, Bob Seger labored for nearly a decade before gaining his first national recognition with 1976's *Live Bullet*, sometimes regarded as one of the finest live rock albums ever made. Established nationally with *Night Moves* and its three hit singles, Seger provided songs reflecting and celebrating the working- class American experience and served as model for later populists such as Bruce Springsteen and John Mellencamp, although he never enjoyed Springsteen's status as a critics's favorite. Like Springsteen, Seger remained committed to the idea that rock could function as a force to improve the quality of life. Astutely mixing original high-energy songs in the classic rock-and-roll mode and poignant, intelligent, and personal ballads, Seger's albums from 1976 to 1981 sold millions of copies. As a low-profile rock star, Bob Seger toured infrequently in the 1980s and not at all in the 1990s yet continued to record popular albums that maintained both his integrity and his artistry.

Bob Seger took up ukulele at age five and later learned guitar and piano. At age six he moved with his family to Ann Arbor, Mich., where he grew up. While still in high school he began playing local lounges and teen clubs with the three-piece band the Decibels. After high school, Seger joined the Town Criers and met Eddie Andrews, recording his first single, "East Side Story," for Andrews's Hideout label in 1966. It was a local success, as were its follow-ups, "Persecution Smith" and "Heavy Music," which led to a Capitol Records recording contract in 1968. He assembled the Bob Seger System and scored a major national hit in 1970 with "Ramblin' Gamblin' Man." None of the group's three albums sold particularly well outside the Detroit region, so Seger disbanded the group and recorded the solo album *Brand New Morning* with acoustic instruments.

Subsequently recording for Eddie Andrews's Palladium label (distributed nationally by Reprise), Seger assembled the nucleus of his Silver Bullet Band around guitarist Andrew "Drew" Abbott and bassist Chris Campbell. With Abbott taking over on lead guitar, Seger was able to concentrate on his gruff, raspy style of singing. The album *Seven* revealed his developing talent as a songwriter and yielded a minor hit with the hard-driving "Get Out of Denver." Returning to Capitol Records, Seger and his band toured the nation extensively in 1974 and 1975 and recorded *Beautiful Loser*. The album included the powerful title song as well as the ballad "Jody Girl," "Travelin' Man," and the moderate hit "Katmandu," and sold more copies than the combined total sales of Seger's first seven albums.

Adding saxophonist Alto Reed and new keyboardist Robyn Robbins, Bob Seger and the Silver Bullet Band recorded *Live Bullet* in Detroit. The album included many of his regional hits, such as "Heavy Music" and "Lookin' Back," reprised his national hits "Ramblin' Gamblin' Man," "Get Out of Denver," and "Kat-

mandu," and yielded a minor hit with a remake of Ike and Tina Turner's 1973 hit "Nutbush City Limits." It remained on the album charts for more than three years.

Finally, after 10 years of modest success, Bob Seger became established nationally with 1976's *Night Moves*, hailed as one of the finest albums of the 1970s. The album yielded a smash hit with the title cut, a major hit with "Mainstreet," and a moderate hit with the hard-charging "Rock and Roll Never Forgets." In 1977 drummer David Teegarden, an associate of Seger's from the early 1970s and a former member of Teegarden and Van Winkle, joined the Silver Bullet Band. Recorded with the Muscle Shoals Rhythm Section, *Stranger in Town* contained "Feel Like a Number" and produced a smash hit with "Still the Same" and major hits with "Hollywood Nights," "We've Got Tonite" (a smash pop and top country hit for Kenny Rogers and Sheena Easton in 1983), and "Old Time Rock & Roll." Seger subsequently cowrote the Eagles' top hit "Heartache Tonight" with Don Henley, Glenn Frey, and J. D. Souther. Keyboardist Robyn Robbins left Seger's band in 1979 and was replaced with Craig Frost, a former member of Grand Funk Railroad.

Bob Seger's next album, *Against the Wind*, included the favorite "Betty Lou's Gettin' Out Tonight" and yielded four hits, the smashes "Fire Lake" and the title cut, the major hit "You'll Accomp'ny Me," and the moderate hit "Horizontal Bop." Criticized as commercial, the album was Seger's last album to sell multimillion copies. The band toured extensively in 1980 and the tour produced the live double-record set *Nine Tonight*, producing a smash hit with "Tryin' to Live My Life without You" and a moderate hit with "Feel Like a Number." Their next tour and album did not come until 1983, by which time Seger had dismissed guitarist Drew Abbott and drummer Dave Teegarden, the latter replaced by another former member of Grand Funk Railroad, Don Brewer. *The Distance* contained "Makin' Thunderbirds" and yielded a smash hit with Rodney Crowell's "Shame on the Money" and major hits with "Even Now" and "Roll Me Away."

During another three-year hiatus, Bob Seger scored a moderate hit with his earlier "Old Time Rock & Roll" from the movie *Risky Business* and a major hit with "Understanding" from the movie *Teachers*. *Like a Rock* produced two major hits, "American Storm" and the title track, and two minor hits, "It's You" and "Miami," in 1986. The tour in support of the album was conducted with Don Brewer, band veterans Alto Reed, Craig Frost, and Chris Campbell, and three newcomers, keyboardist Bill Payne (Little Feat) and guitarists Rick Vito and Fred Tackett. The following year Seger achieved a top hit with "Shakedown" from the movie *Beverly Hills Cop II* but then was inactive again for three years. He eventually returned to recording with 1991's *The Fire Inside*, produced by Don Was. The album produced a hit single, "The Real Love," but Bob Seger did not tour after its release and his next output, from 1994, was a greatest hits compilation.

Disc.: THE BOB SEGER SYSTEM: *Ramblin' Gamblin' Man* (1969); *Noah* (1969); *Mongrel* (1970). **BOB SEGER:** *Brand New Morning* (1971); *Smokin' O.P.'s* (1972); *Back in '72*

(1973); *Seven* (1974); *Beautiful Loser* (1975). **BOB SEGER AND THE SILVER BULLET BAND:** *Live Bullet* (1976); *Night Moves* (1976); *Stranger in Town* (1978); *Against the Wind* (1980); *Nine Tonight* (1981); *The Distance* (1983); *Like a Rock* (1986); *The Fire Inside* (1991); *Greatest Hits* (1994).—**BH**

Seger (also **Seeger, Seegr, Segert, Zeckert,** etc.), **Josef (Ferdinand Norbert),** eminent Czech organist, pedagogue, and composer; b. Řepin, near Mělnik (baptized), March 21, 1716; d. Prague, April 22, 1782. He studied organ with Czernohorsky, counterpoint with Jan Zach and František Tuma, and thoroughbass with Felix Benda in Prague, where he also was a graduate in philosophy from the Univ. He was active in Prague as a violinist at St. Martin's and as an organist at the Crusader's Church (1745–82); also served as organist at the church in Tyn (1741?–82). He was greatly esteemed as a teacher of composition, numbering among his most important pupils Josef Jelínek, Karl Kopřiva, J.A. Koželuch, Jan Kuchař, Vincenc Mašek, Josef Mysliveček, and Václav Pichl. He composed many preludes, toccatas, and fugues for organ; D. Türk ed. 8 toccatas and fugues (1793; modern ed. in Musica Antiqua Bohemica); he also wrote sacred music and pedagogical works.—**NS/LK/DM**

Segerstam, Leif (Selim), prominent Finnish conductor and composer; b. Vaasa, March 2, 1944. He studied violin and conducting (diplomas in both, 1963) and also took courses in composition with Fougstedt, Kokkonen, and Englund at the Sibelius Academy in Helsinki. He then was a student of Persinger (violin), Overton and Persichetti (composition), and Morel (conducting) at the Juilliard School of Music in N.Y., where he took his diploma (1964) and postgraduate diploma (1965). In the summer of 1964 he also attended Susskind's conducting course at the Aspen (Colo.) Music School. After conducting at the Finnish National Opera in Helsinki (1965–68), he became a conductor at the Royal Theater in Stockholm in 1968. He was made its principal conductor in 1970 and its music director in 1971. In 1972–73 he held the post of first conductor at the Deutsche Oper in Berlin. In 1973–74 he was general manager of the Finnish National Opera. He was chief conductor of the Austrian Radio Sym. Orch. in Vienna (1975–82) and the Finnish Radio Sym. Orch. in Helsinki (1977–87), and also was Generalmusikdirector of the State Phil. in Rheinland-Pfalz (1983–89). From 1989 to 1995 he was chief conductor of the Danish National Radio Sym. Orch. in Copenhagen. In 1995 he became chief conductor of the Helsinki Phil., and in 1997 prof. of conducting at the Sibelius Academy. In 1999 he was awarded the Nordic Council Music Prize. He was to assume the position of music director of the Finnish National Opera in 2001. Segerstam is one of the most prolific composers of his era. He composes in what he describes as a "freely pulsative" style. Among his works are 8 violin concertos (1967–93), 2 piano concertos (1977, 1981), 19 syms. (1977–94), 8 cello concertos (1981–93), a series of *Thoughts* for Orch. (1987 et seq.), 27 string quartets (1962–90), 4 string trios (1977–91), many other chamber pieces, piano music, organ pieces, and many songs.—**NS/LK/DM**

Segni, Julio, important Italian organist, harpsichordist, and composer, known as **Julio da Modena;** b. Modena, 1498; d. Rome, July 23, 1561. He studied singing with Bidon da Asti in Modena, where he sang plainchant at the Cathedral (1513), and also was a pupil of Giacomo Fogliano (1512–14). He later went to Rome, where his performances at the Vatican were acclaimed. After serving as first organist at San Marco in Venice (1530–32), he entered the service of Guido Ascanio Sforza, Cardinal of S. Fiore, in Rome. Segni was regarded as the foremost organist of his time. A number of his impressive ricercari have been publ. in modern eds. —**NS/LK/DM**

Segovia, Andrés, Marquis of Salobreia, great Spanish guitarist and teacher; b. Linares, near Jaen, Feb. 21, 1893; d. Madrid, June 2, 1987. He took up the guitar at a very early age, and although his parents opposed his choice of instrument and saw to it that he received lessons in piano and cello instead, it was all to no avail. While taking courses at the Granada Inst. of Music, he sought out a guitar teacher; finding none, he taught himself the instrument; later studied briefly with Miguel Llobet. He made his formal debut in Granada at the age of 16, then played in Madrid in 1912, at the Paris Cons. in 1915, and in Barcelona in 1916; toured South America in 1919. He made his formal Paris debut on April 7, 1924 in a program that included a work written especially for him by Roussel, entitled simply *Segovia.* He made his U.S. debut at N.Y.'s Town Hall on Jan. 8, 1928, and subsequently toured all over the world, arousing admiration for his celebrated artistry wherever he went. He did much to reinstate the guitar as a concert instrument capable of a variety of expression; made many transcriptions for the guitar, including one of Bach's *Chaconne* from the Partita No. 2 for Violin. He also commissioned several composers to write works for him, including Ponce, Turina, Castelnuovo-Tedesco, Moreno-Torroba, Villa-Lobos, and Tansman. He continued to give concerts at an advanced age; made appearances in 1984 in celebration of the 75th anniversary of his professional debut. He received many honors during his long career; a commemorative plaque was affixed in 1969 to the house where he was born, honoring him as the "hijo predilecto de la ciudad." In 1981 King Juan Carlos of Spain made him Marquis of Salobreia; that same year the Segovia International Guitar Competition was founded in his honor. In 1985 he was awarded the Gold Medal of the Royal Phil. Society of London. He wrote *Andrés Segovia: An Autobiography of the Years 1893–1920* (N.Y., 1976).

BIBL.: V. Borri, *The S. Technique* (N.Y., 1972); G. Wade, *S.: A Celebration of the Man and His Music* (London, 1983); G. Wade, *Maestro S.* (London, 1986); G. Wade and G. Garno, *A New Look at S., His Life, His Music* (2 vols., Pacific, Mo., 1997). —**NS/LK/DM**

Segurola, Andrés (Perello) de
See **De Segurola, Andrés (Perello)**

Seguin, (Arthur) Edward (Sheldon), English bass of Irish descent; b. London, April 7, 1809; d.

N.Y., Dec. 6, 1852. He studied at the Royal Academy of Music in London, where he first appeared in student operatic performances in 1828. After singing at Covent Garden (1833–34), the King's Theatre, and Drury Lane (1835–38), he made his U.S. debut in N.Y. in Rooke's *Amelie* on Oct. 15, 1838. He then toured North America with his own opera company. His wife, Ann Childe (b. London, c. 1812; d. N.Y., Aug. 1888), was a soprano. After studying at the Royal Academy of Music, she sang with her husband in London and N.Y. Following his death, she taught voice. Their son, Edward Seguin (b. 1837; d. Oct. 9, 1879), was a bass who appeared with the Euphrosyne Parepa-Rosa, Emma Abbott, and American opera companies.—**LK/DM**

Seibel, Klauspeter, German conductor; b. Offenbach, May 7, 1936. He received training in Nuremberg and Munich. Following his conducting debut at Munich's Gärtnerplatz State Theatre in 1957, he conducted opera in Freiburg im Breisgau (1963–65), Lübeck (1965–67), Kassel (1967–71), and Frankfurt am Main (1971–75). In 1975 he became Generalmusikdirektor in Freiburg im Breisgau, a position he retained until 1981. He also served as music director of the Nuremberg Sym. Orch. (from 1975). From 1987 to 1995 he was Generalmusikdirektor in Kiel. In 1995 he became music director of the La. Phil. in New Orleans and in 1997 Generalmusikdirektor of the Frankfurt am Main Opera. —**NS/LK/DM**

Seiber, Mátyás (György), significant Hungarian-born English composer; b. Budapest, May 4, 1905; d. in an automobile accident in Kruger National Park, Johannesburg, South Africa, Sept. 24, 1960. Of a musical family, he learned to play the cello at home; later entered the Budapest Academy of Music, where he studied composition with Kodály (1919–24). During the following years, he traveled as a member of a ship's orch. on a transatlantic liner; visited Russia as a music journalist. From 1928 to 1933 he taught composition at the Frankfurt am Main Hoch Cons.; was the cellist in the Lenzewski Quartet, which specialized in modern music; then was again in Budapest. The catastrophic events in Germany and the growing Nazi influence in Hungary forced him to emigrate to England in 1935, where he quickly acquired a group of loyal disciples; was co-founder of the Society for the Promotion of New Music (1942) and founder-conductor of the Dorian Singers (1945); taught at Morely Coll. (from 1942). His early music followed the national trends of the Hungarian School; later he expanded his melodic resources to include oriental modes and also jazz, treated as folk music; by the time he arrived in England, he had added dodecaphony to his oeuvre, though he used it in a very personal, lyrical manner, as in his cantata *Ulysses* and his third String Quartet. He publ. the books *Schule für Jazz-Schlagzeug* (Mainz, 1929) and *The String Quartets of Béla Bartók* (London, 1945).

WORKS: DRAMATIC: *Eva spielt mit Puppen,* opera (1934); 2 operettas; *The Invitation,* ballet (London, Dec. 30, 1960); over 25 film scores, including Orwell's *Animal Farm.* **ORCH.:** *Besardo Suite* No. 1 (1940) and No. 2 for Strings (1941); *Transylvanian Rhapsody* (1941); *Pastorale and Burlesque* for Flute and Strings (1941–42); *Fantasia concertante* for Violin and String Orch. (1943–44; London, Dec. 3, 1945); *Notturno* for Horn and Strings (1944); Concertino for Clarinet and Strings (1951; London, May 11, 1954); *Elegy* for Viola and Small Orch. (1955); *3 Pieces* for Cello and Orch. (1956); *Improvisations* for Jazz Band and Sym. Orch. (London, June 2, 1959; in collaboration with J. Dankworth). **CHAMBER:** 3 string quartets (1924; 1934–35; *Quartetto Lirico,* 1948–51); *Sarabande and Gigue* for Cello and Piano (1924); *Sonata da camera* for Violin and Cello (1925); *Serenade* for 2 Clarinets, 2 Bassoons, and 2 Horns (1925); *Divertimento* for Clarinet and String Quartet (1928); *2 Jazzolettes* for 2 Saxophones, Trumpet, Trombone, Piano, and Percussion (1929, 1933); *4 Hungarian Folksongs* for 2 Violins (1931); *Fantasy* for Cello and Piano (1940); *Fantasia* for Flute, Horn, and String Quartet (1945); *Andantino and Pastorale* for Clarinet and Piano (1949); *Concert Piece* for Violin and Piano (1953–54); *Improvisation* for Oboe and Piano (1957); *Permutazioni a cinque* for Wind Quintet (1958); Violin Sonata (1960); piano pieces. **VOCAL:** *Ulysses,* cantata for Tenor, Chorus, and Orch., after James Joyce (1946–47; London, May 27, 1949); *4 French Folksongs* for Soprano and Strings (1948); *Faust* for Soprano, Tenor, Chorus, and Orch. (1949); *Cantata secularis* for Chorus and Orch. (1949–51); *3 Fragments from "A Portrait of the Artist as a Young Man,"* chamber cantata for Narrator, Wordless Chorus, and Instrumental Ensemble, after James Joyce (1957); *More Nonsense* for Baritone, Violin, Guitar, Clarinet, and Bass Clarinet, after E. Lear (1957); songs with orch. or instrumental accompaniment; folk song arrangements.—**NS/LK/DM**

Seidel, Friedrich Ludwig, German organist, conductor, and composer; b. Treuenbrietzen, June 1, 1765; d. Charlottenburg, May 5, 1831. He studied with Benda in Berlin, then served as organist of the Marienkirche (from 1792); became asst. conductor at the National Theater in 1801, and was named music director of the royal chapel in 1808 and court Kapellmeister in 1822, being pensioned in 1830. He composed the Singspiel *Claudine von Villa Bella,* several operas, 3 ballets, incidental music and other dramatic works, sacred works, chamber music, and piano pieces.—**NS/LK/DM**

Seidel, Jan, Czech composer; b. Nymburk, Dec. 25, 1908. He was first attracted to architecture and graphic art, and also attended Alois Hába's classes in quartertone composition at the Prague Cons. (1936–40); then took private lessons in theory with J.B. Foerster for a more traditional musical training. He was a composer, conductor, and pianist in E.F. Burian's Theater; acted as artistic adviser to the recording firm Esta (1938–45) and the Gramophone Corp. (1945–53); was chief of the Opera of the National Theater (1958–64); then served as dramatic adviser there. In 1976 he was made a National Artist by the Czech government. His String Quartet No. 2 is in the quarter tone system, but most of his music is based on folk-song tradition according to the doctrine of socialist realism.

WORKS: DRAMATIC: O p e r a : *Tonka Šibenice* (Tonka the Gallows; 1964). **ORCH.:** Sym. No. 1, *Prologue* (1942); 2 oboe concertos (1955); 2 orch. suites from the film *The Piper of Strakonice* (1956, 1958); *Lovecká sinfonietta* (Hunting Sinfonietta) for Horn and Small Orch. (1965–66; Prague, March 14, 1973); Concerto for Flute, Strings, and Piano (1966); *Giocosa* (1972). **CHAMBER:** 4 string quartets: No. 1, with Soprano (1930), No. 2, with Narrator (1940), No. 3, *Chrysanthemums* (1943), and

No. 4 (1944); 2 wind quintets (1941, 1946); Violin Sonata (1950). **VOCAL:** 3 cantatas: *Call to Battle* (1946), *May Prelude* (1952), and *Message to the Living* (1953); also numerous patriotic choruses and songs.—**NS/LK/DM**

Seidl, Anton, famous Hungarian conductor; b. Pest, May 7, 1850; d. N.Y., March 28, 1898. He studied at the Univ. and at the Cons. in Leipzig, then was engaged by Hans Richter as chorus master at the Vienna Court Opera. Richter in turn recommended him to Wagner to assist in preparing the score and parts of the *Ring* tetralogy for the Bayreuth Festival of 1876. Returning to Leipzig, he was first conductor of its Opera (1879–82); in 1882 he was engaged by the impresario Angelo Neumann for a grand tour of Wagner's operas. From 1883 he conducted the Bremen Opera; in 1885 he was engaged to conduct the German opera repertoire at the Metropolitan Opera in N.Y. He made his American debut with *Lohengrin* there (Nov. 23, 1885), then conducted the American premieres of *Die Meistersinger von Nürnberg* (Jan. 4, 1886), *Tristan und Isolde* (Dec. 1, 1886), *Siegfried* (Nov. 9, 1887), and the *Ring* cycle (March 4–11, 1889). In 1891 he was engaged as conductor of the N.Y. Phil., and led it until his death (of ptomaine poisoning). Seidl was an excellent technician of the baton and established a standard of perfection rare in American orch. playing of that time; he introduced many unfamiliar works by German composers and conducted the premiere of Dvořák's *New World Sym.* (N.Y., Dec. 15, 1893). He married the Austrian soprano Auguste Kraus (b. Vienna, Aug. 28, 1853; d. Kingston, N.Y., July 17, 1939); after vocal studies with Marchen, she made her operatic debut at the Vienna Court Opera in 1877, where she sang minor roles; then sang in Leipzig (1881–82), where she subsequently became a member of Neumann's Wagnerian company and married Seidl; sang at Her Majesty's Theatre in London in 1882 and then made her Metropolitan Opera debut in N.Y. as Elisabeth in *Tannhäuser* under her husband's direction, remaining on its roster until 1888. Among her best known roles were Elsa, Eva, Siegliende, and Gutrune.

BIBL.: H. Krehbiel, *A. S.* (N.Y., 1898); H. Finck, ed., *A. S.: A Memorial by His Friends* (N.Y., 1899).—**NS/LK/DM**

Seiffert, Max, eminent German musicologist; b. Beeskow an der Spree, Feb. 9, 1868; d. Schleswig, April 13, 1948. He studied musicology with Philipp Spitta at the Univ. of Berlin (Ph.D., 1891, with the diss. *J.P. Sweelinck und seine direkten deutschen Schüler*; publ. in Leipzig, 1891). He was ed.-in-chief of *Sammelbände der Internationalen Musik- Gesellschaft* (1903–14); with J. Wolf and M. Schneider, he ed. the *Archiv für Musikwissenschaft* (1918–26); also taught at Berlin's Hochschule für Musik and at the Akademie für Kirchen- und Schulmusik (from 1909). He served as provisional director of the Fürstliches Forschungsintitut für Musikwissenschaft in Bückeburg (from 1921); after it became the Staatliches Institut für deutsche Musikforschung in Berlin in 1935, he served as its director until 1942. He publ. *Geschichte der Klaviermusik* (Berlin, 1899–1901), nominally the third ed. of Weitzmann's history, but actually a new and valuable study. He contributed many editions to the Denkmäler Deutscher Tonkunst series (1892–1927); also ed. the works of Sweelinck (12 vols., 1895–1901). Festschrifts were publ. in his honor for his 70th (1938) and 80th (1948) birthdays.—**NS/LK/DM**

Seiffert, Peter, German tenor; b. Düsseldorf, Jan. 4, 1954. He was educated at the Robert Schumann Hochschule für Musik in Düsseldorf. After appearing at the Deutsche Oper am Rhein in Düsseldorf, he sang at the Deutsche Oper in Berlin (from 1982) and at the Bavarian State Opera in Munich (from 1983). In 1984 he first appeared at the Vienna State Opera and at Milan's La Scala. In 1988 he made his debut at London's Covent Garden as Parsifal. He portrayed Strauss's Emperor during the Bavarian State Opera's visit to the new Nagoya Opera House in Japan in 1992. That same year, he was engaged as Narraboth in Salzburg. In 1993 he sang Tamino at the Metropolitan Opera in N.Y. He portrayed Florestan in London in 1995. In 1996 he was engaged as Walther von Stolzing at the Bayreuth Festival. He sang Lohengrin in Munich in 1999. As a concert artist, he sang with various orchs. on both sides of the Atlantic. His other operatic roles include Faust, Lensky, Lohengrin, Erik, and Jenik. In 1986 he married **Lucia Popp.**—**NS/LK/DM**

Seinemeyer, Meta, admired German soprano; b. Berlin, Sept. 5, 1895; d. Dresden, Aug. 19, 1929. She studied with Nikolaus Rothmühl and Ernst Grenzebach in Berlin. She made her operatic debut there in *Orphée aux enfers* at the Deutsches Opernhaus (1918), where she continued to sing until 1925; also toured the U.S. with the German Opera Co. (1923–24); then was a member of the Dresden State Opera (from 1925); also appeared in South America (1926), at the Vienna State Opera (1927), and at London's Covent Garden (1929). She married the conductor Frieder Weissmann on her deathbed. Her voice possessed a silken quality and a natural expressiveness; she was particularly esteemed for her roles in operas by Wagner, Verdi, Puccini, and Strauss. —**NS/LK/DM**

Seixas (real name, Vas), (José Antonio) Carlos de, important Portuguese organist and composer; b. Coimbra, June 11, 1704; d. Lisbon, Aug. 25, 1742. He received his primary musical education from his father, whom he succeeded as organist at Coimbra Cathedral when he was 14; at 16 he was named organist at the royal chapel, a position he retained until his death; was knighted by John V of Portugal in 1738. He wrote a great number of keyboard sonatas (sometimes designated as "toccatas"), of which 88 are preserved. He knew Domenico Scarlatti personally, but was not demonstrably influenced by the Italian style of keyboard composition. Eighty keyboard sonatas by Seixas were ed. by S. Kastner in Portugaliae Musica (Lisbon, 1965); an overture, sinfonia, and Harpsichord Concerto were ed. in the same series (1969).

BIBL.: S. Kastner, *C. S.* (Coimbra, 1947); K. Heimes, *C. S.'s Keyboard Sonatas* (diss., Univ. of South Africa, 1967). —**NS/LK/DM**

Séjan, Nicolas, French organist, teacher, and composer; b. Paris, March 19, 1745; d. there, March 16, 1819.

He studied organ with his uncle, Nicolas-Gilles Forqueray, and harmony and improvisation with Louis Charles Bordier. In 1760 he became organist at St.-André-des-Arts. In 1764 he made his first appearance at the Concert Spirituel, where he earned a reputation as a virtuoso. In 1773 he was named one of the 4 organists at Notre Dame Cathedral. He was also organist at the church of the Cordeliers (1773–76), St. Séverin (from 1782), St. Sulpice (1783–91), and the royal chapel (1790–91); also was the first prof. of organ at the École Royale de Chant (from 1789). He lost all of his posts during the Revolution, but succeeded in preventing the destruction of the organs in his care, and assisted the church musicians during the Reign of Terror. He was prof. of organ at the Paris Cons. from its founding in 1795 until 1802; was made organist at the Dome des Invalides and at St. Sulpice in 1806, and also at the royal chapel in 1814. He publ. 6 sonates for Harpsichord and Violin ad libitum (Paris, c. 1772; violin part not extant), *Recueil de pièces* for Harpsichord and Piano, *dans le genre gracieus ou gay* (Paris, 1784), and 3 sonatas for Harpsichord or Piano (Paris, 1784; Nos. 1 and 3 with Violin and Cello obbligato).—NS/LK/DM

Šejna, Karel, Czech conductor; b. Zálezly, Nov. 1, 1896; d. Prague, Dec. 17, 1982. He studied double bass with F. Cerný at the Prague Cons. (1914–20), and also took private lessons in composition with K.B. Jirák. In 1921 he joined the Czech Phil. in Prague as principal double bass; later appeared as a conductor with it; in 1937 he was appointed its second conductor; was its artistic director in 1949–50; then second conductor again from 1950 until 1965; subsequently appeared with it as a guest conductor. He was particularly esteemed for his congenial interpretations of Czech music. In 1960 he was made an Artist of Merit by the Czech government. —NS/LK/DM

Sekles, Bernhard, German conductor, composer, and teacher; b. Frankfurt am Main, March 20, 1872; d. there, Dec. 8, 1934. He studied with Knorr and Uzielli at the Hoch Cons. in Frankfurt am Main, where he became a prof. of theory in 1896. From 1923 to 1933 he was director of the Cons.

WORKS: DRAMATIC: O p e r a : *Scheherazade* (Mannheim, Nov. 2, 1917); *Die zehn Küsse* (1926). B a l l e t : *Der Zwerg und die Infantin* (1913); *Die Hochzeit des Faun* (1921). ORCH.: *Aus den Garten der Semiramis*, symphonic poem; *Die vier Temperamente*; Sym.; *Sommergedicht*; *Kleine Suite*; *Serenade* for 11 Instruments. CHAMBER: *Passacaglia und Fuge* for String Quartet; Trio for Clarinet, Cello, and Piano; Violin Sonata; piano music. VOCAL: Songs.—NS/LK/DM

Selby, William, English organist and composer; b. in England, c. 1738; d. Boston, Dec. 12, 1798. In 1760 he was appointed organist at Holy Sepulcher Church in London, where from 1765 to 1770 he publ. both sacred and secular music. He settled in the U.S. in 1771, becoming organist at King's Chapel in Boston. In 1773–74 he was organist at Trinity Church in Newport, R.I., and in 1776 he returned to Boston as organist at Trinity Church; from 1778 was organist at the Stone Chapel (formerly King's Chapel). He led an extremely active musical life in Boston as an organist and conductor, giving many concerts of secular music as well as religious, and generally raising the musical standards of the area. He composed and publ. 9 Psalms and hymns for Solo Voice, 8 religious and secular choral works, 6 songs, 9 pieces for Guitar, and 3 pieces for Keyboard. —NS/LK/DM

Selena (Quintanilla Perez), Grammy winning *tejano* star murdered on the brink of her crossover success; b. Lake Jackson, Tex., April 16, 1971; d. Corpus Christi, Tex., March 31, 1995. A few days shy of her 24th birthday when she was shot dead by the president of her fan club, Selena was already a major star in Latin music and about to make her move into the mainstream pop arena. Often referred to as "the Latina Madonna," she was much beloved in the Hispanic community, known for her loyalty to her family and her roots as well as her dedication to anti-drug and AIDS education programs. Ironically, although most of her success came from songs performed in Spanish, she never really mastered the language, learning the songs phonetically.

Her father played with the *tejano* band Los Dinos even before his daughter was born. She once described the music as a blend of country, polka, and jazz. By the time she was 10, Selena was singing with the band, recording for the Latin audience by 1983. Still in her teens, she married Los Dinos guitarist Chris Perez. The rest of the band consisted of her brother Abraham on bass and her sister Suzette on drums. By 1987, Selena earned Female Vocalist of the Year and Performer of the Year honors at the Tejano Music Awards, which led the Latin division of EMI to come calling. Selena and Los Dinos released their EMI debut in 1990. They released two albums a year, winning the 1993 Best Mexican American Performance Grammy for *Selena Live*. Selena invested some of her newfound wealth in manufacturing her own line of clothes, and also opened a Corpus Christi boutique.

In 1994 Selena appeared in the film *Don Juan De-Marco*, playing a singer, and won another Grammy for the title track of her gold *Amor Prohibido* album. By 1995, she had sold out 61,000 seats at the Astrodome for a concert and recorded her first English-language album. However, Selena's time in the spotlight was short-lived. She discovered that the president of her fan club (who also managed the Corpus Christi boutique) had been embezzling money from the club. When Selena fired her, the woman shot the star, who died an hour later. The murderer was convicted and sentenced to a minimum 30 years in jail.

Ironically, Selena became even more popular after death, mirroring the careers of stars from Elvis to Janis Joplin and Jimi Hendrix. The *Dreaming of You* album came out, topped the charts, and went double platinum. A movie made of the star's life also became a hit. The title track rose to #22 pop.

DISC.: *Selena* (1989); *Ven Conmigo* (1990); *Entre a Mi Mundo* (1992); *Live* (1993); *Amor Prohibido* (1994); *Mis Primeras Grabaciones Freddie* (1995); *Las Reinas del Pueblo* (1995); *Dreaming of You* (1995); *Siempre Selena* (1996).—HB

Selig, Robert Leigh, American composer; b. Chicago, Jan. 29, 1939; d. Cambridge, Mass., Jan. 15, 1984. He studied at Northwestern Univ., and later (1966–67) took doctoral courses at Boston Univ., where he studied with Gardner Read. He held Guggenheim fellowships twice, in 1971 and in 1977. In 1968 he was appointed to the faculty at the New England Cons. of Music in Boston.

WORKS: *Mirage* for Trumpet and String Orch. (1967); *Variations* for Brass Quintet (1967); *Islands* for Chorus and Chamber Orch. (1968); Concerto for Rock Group and Orch. (1969); *Rhapsody* for Flute, Violin, and Clarinet (1970); *Orestes: Flight into Fury* for Trumpet and Piano (1970); Quartet for Voice, Flute, Cello, and Percussion (1971); Sym. for Woodwind Quintet (1971); *Chocorua,* opera for Voice, Chorus, and Chamber Orch. (1972); *Pometacomet, 1676* for Band (1974–75); *Survival Fragments* for Soprano and Piano (1976); Sonata, *3 Cryptic Portraits* for Piano (1977); *Music for Brass Instruments* (1977); *Reflections from a Back Window* for Piano (1980); *After the Ice* for Soprano and Piano (1981).—NS/LK/DM

Selika, Marie (née **Smith**), black American soprano; b. Natchez, Miss., c. 1849; d. N.Y., May 19, 1937. She went to Cincinnati as a child and received music lessons at the expense of a wealthy white family. She pursued training with Bianchi in San Francisco, where she made her debut in 1876. After further studies with Farini in Chicago, she went to Boston in 1878 to continue her training. She made appearances as a concert artist, taking the professional name of Selika. In 1882 she went to England to complete her studies. After appearing at a command performance for Queen Victoria in 1882, she toured as a successful concert artist in Europe, the U.S., and the West Indies (1882–85; 1887–92). She married the tenor known as Signor Velosko (real name Sampson Williams), who often appeared in concerts with her. Her rendition of E. Mulder's *Polka Staccato* led to her being dubbed the "Queen of Staccato."—LK/DM

Sellars, Peter, provocative American theater producer; b. Pittsburgh, Sept. 27, 1957. His fascination with the stage began at age 10, when he began working with a puppet theater. He later attended Harvard Univ., where his bold theatrical experiments resulted in his expulsion from student theater groups. He gained wide notice when he produced Gogol's *The Inspector General* for the American Repertory Theater in Cambridge, Mass., in 1980. During the 1981–82 season, he staged a highly controversial mounting of Handel's *Orlando,* in which the protagonist is depicted as an astronaut. In 1983 he became director of the Boston Shakespeare Co. and in 1984 of the American National Theater Co. at the Kennedy Center in Washington, D.C. In 1987, at the Houston Grand Opera, he produced John Adam's opera *Nixon in China,* which he then mounted in other U.S. cities and at the Holland Festival in 1988; that same year, he jolted the Glyndebourne Festival with his staging of Nigel Osborne's *Electrification of the Soviet Union.* He oversaw the Los Angeles Festival in 1990. That same year he became artistic advisor of the Boston Opera Theatre. In 1991 he mounted the premiere of Adams's *The Death of Klinghoffer* in Brussels, and in 1992 Messi-

aen's *St. François d'Assise* at the Salzburg Festival. His staging of *Pelléas et Mélisande* in Amsterdam in 1993 concentrated on the contemporary themes of sex and violence. His *Pelléas et Mélisande* was then mounted at the Los Angeles Opera in 1995. In 1997 he returned to the Salzburg Festival to produce Ligeti's *Le Grand Macabre.* In 1998 he was awarded the Erasmus Prize of the Netherlands.—NS/LK/DM

Selle, Thomas, German composer; b. Zörbig, near Bitterfeld, March 23, 1599; d. Hamburg, July 2, 1663. He was educated in Delitzsch and at the Univ. of Leipzig (matriculated, 1622). He was Kantor in Heide, and then rector in Wesselburen (1625–34). After serving as Kantor in Itzehoe (1634–41), he settled in Hamburg as Kantor at the Johanneum and as civic director of church music (from 1641). Selle wrote a vast amount of vocal music, both sacred and secular, including the *St. John Passion* for 5 to 6 Voices (1641; enl. 1643; ed. in Das Chorwerk, XXVI, 1934), historically important as the first such work to include instrumental interludes. He prepared a collected MS edition of his works, consisting of 16 partbooks and 3 books of tablature; it includes 282 compositions, 193 to German texts and 89 to Latin texts (1646–53).

BIBL.: S. Günther, *Die geistliche Konzertmusik von T. S. nebst einer Biographie* (diss., Univ. of Giessen, 1935); J. Birke, *Die Passionsmusiken von T. S.* (diss., Univ. of Hamburg, 1957). —NS/LK/DM

Sellner, Joseph, German oboist, conductor, teacher, and composer; b. Landau, Bavaria, March 13, 1787; d. Vienna, May 17, 1843. He played the oboe in an Austrian army regiment, then at the German Opera in Prague (1811–17). Subsequently he settled in Vienna, where he played at the Court Opera (from 1817) and taught at the Cons. (from 1821), conducting its student concerts (until 1838). His *Theoretischpraktische Oboen-Schule* is a fine method for oboe. He also publ. a Concerto and 3 concertinos for Oboe and Orch. and a Concerto for 2 Oboes.—NS/LK/DM

Selmer, Johan Peter, Norwegian conductor and composer; b. Christiania, Jan. 20, 1844; d. Venice, July 21, 1910. After studying law in Norway, he took a course under Ambroise Thomas at the Paris Cons. (1869–70); later studied at the Leipzig Cons. with Richter (1871–74). From 1883 to 1886 he conducted Christiania's Musikforeningen. He was greatly influenced by Berlioz, Liszt, and Wagner, and his symphonic pieces bear the imprint of late Romanticism. Like Grieg, he made use of Norwegian folk material. His most important work was *Prometheus,* symphonic poem (Oct. 29, 1898).

WORKS: ORCH. (all first perf. in Christiania): *L'année terrible,* scène funèbre (Sept. 30, 1871); *Alastor* (Oct. 24, 1874); *Karneval i Flandern* (Nov. 8, 1890); *In den bergen,* suite (1892); *Prometheus,* symphonic poem (Oct. 29, 1898). CHORAL WITH ORCH.: *Nordens aand* (The Spirit of the North; 1872); *Hilsen til Nidaros* (Greeting to Nidaros; 1883); *Selvmorderen og pilgrimene* (The Suicide and the Pilgrims; 1888); *Tyrekerne gaar nod Athen* (The Turks Go Towards Athens; c. 1893); various works for Men's Voices and Women's Voices; about 100 songs; etc.

BIBL.: P. Merkel, *Der norwegische Komponist J. S.: Ein Leb-ensbild* (Leipzig, 1904); S. Lind, *J. S. som komponist* (diss., Univ. of Oslo, 1950).—NS/LK/DM

Selva, Blanche, French pianist and teacher; b. Brive, Jan. 29, 1884; d. St. Amand, Tallende, Puy-de-Dome, Dec. 3, 1942. She studied piano at the Paris Cons., and took courses in composition with d'Indy at the Paris Schola Cantorum. She was one of the strongest propagandists of modern French music early in the 20th century. She presented programs of piano works by Debussy, Ravel, and others, and also became a proponent of Czech music. She taught at the Schola Cantorum (1901–22), then at the Strasbourg Cons. and Prague Cons. She publ. several books dealing with piano technique; her compendium, *L'Enseignement musical de la technique du piano* (4 vols., Paris, 1922) is valuable. She also publ. disquisitions on musical form: *La Sonate* (Paris, 1913), *Quelques mots sur la sonate* (Paris, 1914), and *Les Sonates de Beethoven* (Barcelona, 1927), and a monograph on Déodat de Séverac (Paris, 1930).
—NS/LK/DM

Selvin, Ben(jamin B.), American bandleader, violinist, and record executive; b. N.Y., March 14, 1898; d. Manhasset, N.Y., July 15, 1980. Selvin claimed the title of the most prolific recording artist in history, having cut 9,000 sides in 17 years, 1917–34. The discs were recorded under a variety of different names and for various record labels. Selvin's biggest hit was "Dardanella," an instrumental ragtime tune that became the first dance-band record to sell approximately one million copies. But he enjoyed more than a hundred hits, enough to make him second only to Paul Whiteman as the most successful bandleader of the 1920s.

Selvin began as a violinist working for bandleader Charles Strickland, also finding a niche in handling the band's finances. In 1917 he launched his own society dance band, starting a seven-year residency at the Moulin Rouge club in N.Y. Signed to Victor Records, he cut his first hit, "I'm Forever Blowing Bubbles," at his first recording session on July 18, 1919. Credited to "Selvin's Novelty Orch.," the record became a best-seller in October 1919. On Nov. 20, 1919, the orchestra recorded "Dardanella" (music by Felix Bernard and Johnny S. Black, lyrics by Fred Fisher). It became the most popular record of 1920. Selvin's other major hits include "Yes! We Have No Bananas" (October 1923), "Oh, How I Miss You Tonight" (October 1925, as The Cavaliers), Richard Rodgers and Lorenz Hart's "Manhattan" (November 1935, as The Knickerbockers), Irving Berlin's "Blue Skies" (April 1927), "Happy Days Are Here Again" (March 1930), and "When It's Springtime in the Rockies" (May 1930). In all, Selvin recorded under more than a hundred names, though it must be noted that he frequently functioned as a music contractor, assembling groups for recording sessions, rather than as a musician.

Selvin gave up his career as a performer in 1934 and went to work for the newly formed Muzak company as a vice president of recording and programming. He helped the company become the leader in providing instrumental background music in public places. He moved to Columbia Records in 1947 as director of A&R, in which capacity he supervised recording sessions for Frank Sinatra, Doris Day, Dinah Shore, and others. He worked at RCA Victor from 1952 to 1963. When he retired from the company at age 65 he was presented with a gold record for "Dardanella." He then became a consultant to the 3M audiotape manufacturing company. He was also one of the founders of Majestic Records. He died of a heart attack at age 82, survived by a wife and three children.—WR

Sembach (real name, **Semfke**), **Johannes,** German tenor; b. Berlin, March 9, 1881; d. Bremerhaven, June 20, 1944. He studied in Vienna and with Jean de Reszke in Paris. In 1900 he made his operatic debut at the Vienna Court Opera. From 1905 to 1913 he was a member of the Dresden Court Opera, where he appeared as a Wagnerian and also created the role of Aegisthus in Strauss's *Elektra* (1909). On Nov. 26, 1914, he made his Metropolitan Opera debut in N.Y. as Parsifal, remaining on its roster until 1917; was again on its roster during the 1920–22 seasons. His guest engagements also took him to London, Paris, and South America. In 1925 he settled in Berlin as a voice teacher.
—NS/LK/DM

Sembrich, Marcella (real name, **Prakseda Marcelina Kochańska**), famous Polish-American soprano; b. Wisniewczyk, Galicia, Feb. 15, 1858; d. N.Y., Jan. 11, 1935. Sembrich was her mother's maiden name. Her father, Kasimir Kochański, was a village musician. She began studying piano with him when she was 4 and soon thereafter violin as well; at 10 she played both instruments in public, and at 11 she entered the Lemberg Cons., where her principal teacher was Wilhelm Stengel (b. Lemberg, Aug. 7, 1846; d. N.Y., May 15, 1917), whom she later married (May 5, 1877). In 1874 she played and sang for Liszt, who urged her to train her voice. She then studied singing with Viktor Rokitansky in Vienna, and with G.B. Lamperti, the younger, in Milan. She made her operatic debut in Athens on June 3, 1877, as Elvira in Bellini's *I Puritani* under the stage name of Sembrich. Following training in the German repertory from Richard Lewy in Vienna, she sang Lucia di Lammermoor at the Dresden Court Opera in 1878, remaining on its roster until 1880. On June 12, 1880, she chose that role for her first appearance at London's Covent Garden, where she sang for 5 seasons. It was also as Lucia di Lammermoor that she made her U.S. debut at the Metropolitan Opera in N.Y. on Oct. 24, 1883. Thereafter she sang at the principal opera houses of Germany, Austria, France, Spain, Scandinavia, and Russia until 1898, then was a regular member of the Metropolitan Opera from 1898 to 1900, and again from 1901 to 1909. Her farewell appearance in opera was at the Metropolitan on Feb. 6, 1909. In subsequent years she devoted herself to lieder recitals, remaining active until her retirement in 1917. She was also active as a teacher, serving as head of the vocal depts. at both the Curtis Inst. of Music in Philadelphia and at the Inst. of Musical Art in N.Y. Her operatic repertoire included some 40 roles, the most outstanding being Susanna, Zerlina, the Queen of the Night, Rosina, Gilda, Violetta, Eva in *Die Meistersinger von Nürnberg*, Elsa in *Lohengrin*, and Mimi, as well as her incomparable Lucia.

BIBL.: G. Armin, *M. S. und Herr Prof. Julius Hey* (Leipzig, 1898); H. Owen, *A Recollection of M. S.* (N.Y., 1950). **—NS/LK/DM**

Semeonova, Nedyalka, Bulgarian violinist and teacher; b. Khaskovo, Dec. 2, 1901; d. Paris, March 14, 1959. A child prodigy, she studied at a very early age with her father. Following concerts in the U.S. (1913), she pursued training in Dresden with Auer, Rapoldi, and Havemann, and later with Auer in N.Y. (1921–23). Following a successful N.Y. debut in 1923, she toured throughout Europe, the U.S., India, and the Far East. In 1932 she returned to Bulgaria but continued to make tours. From 1946 she also taught violin at the Bulgarian State Cons. in Sofia.**—NS/LK/DM**

Semet, Théophile (-Aimé-Emile), French composer; b. Lille, Sept. 6, 1824; d. Corbeil, near Paris, April 15, 1888. He studied with Halévy in Paris, where he was a percussionist in the Opéra orch. He wrote popular songs before producing the following operas for Paris: *Nuits d'Espagne* (Dec. 30, 1857), *Gil Blas* (March 23, 1860), *Ondine* (Jan. 7, 1863), and *La Petite Fadette* (Sept. 11, 1869).**—NS/LK/DM**

Semkow, Jerzy, prominent Polish conductor; b. Radomsko, Oct. 12, 1928. He studied at the Univ. of Kraków (1946–50) and at the Leningrad Cons. (1951–55). After serving as asst. conductor of the Leningrad Phil. (1954–56), he conducted at Moscow's Bolshoi Theater (1956–58); also continued his training with Kleiber in Prague, Serafin in Rome, and Walter in Vienna. He was artistic director and chief conductor of the Warsaw National Opera (1959–62); then was chief conductor of the Royal Danish Theater in Copenhagen (1966–76). In 1968 he made his U.S. debut as a guest conductor of the Boston Sym. Orch. He served as music director of the St. Louis Sym. Orch. (1976–79), artistic director of the RAI orch. in Rome (1979–83), and music adviser and principal conductor of the Rochester (N.Y.) Phil. (1985–89). His guest conducting engagements took him all over the world. He is especially admired for his performances of Polish and Russian scores, particularly of works from the late Romantic era.**—NS/LK/DM**

Senaillé (also **Senaillié, Senallié,** etc.), **Jean Baptiste,** French violinist and composer; b. Paris, Nov. 23, 1687; d. there, Oct. 15, 1730. Although the spelling "Senaillé" is widely used, he signed his name "Senaillié," as did his father; contemporary eds. of his music invariably used the form "Senaillié." He most likely studied with his father, whom he succeeded in the "24 violons du roi" in 1713. After an Italian sojourn (c. 1717–19), he resumed his position in Paris in 1720; also appeared at the Concert Spirituel (1728–30). His music reflects Italian influences. He publ. 50 violin sonatas (with continuo) in 5 books (1710–27).

BIBL.: A. Kish, *J.B. Senallié: His Life, his Time and his Music* (diss., Bryn Maur Coll., 1964).**—NS/LK/DM**

Sender (Barayón), Ramon, Spanish-born American poet, novelist, writer on music, and composer; b. Madrid, Oct. 29, 1934. He was sent to the U.S. in 1939 as a Spanish Civil War refugee. After studies in piano with Copeland (1948–52) and in composition with Carter, he took courses at the Accademia di Santa Cecilia in Rome (1952–53); also had private lessons with Haieff. Returning to the U.S., he had lessons with Shapero and Cowell; also studied at Brandeis Univ. (1953–54) and at the San Francisco Cons. of Music (B.Mus., 1962). In 1962 he co-founded (with Morton Subotnick) the San Francisco Tape Music Center, which gave important first performances of works by Oliveros, Riley, Reich, and others; while serving as its co-director, he continued his composition studies with Milhaud at Mills Coll. in Oakland, Calif. (M.A., 1965), where the Tape Music Center was moved in 1966. In 1966 Sender moved to Sonoma, Calif., where he undertook research into acoustic vocalizations and comparative religions; also taught hatha-yoga, meditation, and mantric chant at the Morning Star Range, a shelter for Haight-Ashbury youth; in 1969 he became co-music director of Wheeler's Ranch. He wrote a series of essays on the Open Land Movement (*The Open Land Church*, 1971; etc.); also taught courses in electronic music composition at Sonoma State Univ. (1971); traveled to South America and to India, where he studied yoga and Sanskrit. From 1976 to 1980 he served as asst. director of the Occidental Community Choir. In addition to his work as a composer, Sender devoted much time to writing essays, novels, and poetry; among his literary works are *Zero Weather* (1980) and *Death in Zamora, a Son's Search for His Mother* (1984). In 1983 he received an NEA grant for creative prose; from 1981 to 1984 he wrote book and music reviews for the *San Francisco Chronicle*.

WORKS: *Kore* for 2-channel Tape and Liquid Projections (1961); *Balances* for Amplified and Prepared String Trio and String Bass, and Mixer Console (1962); Violin Sonata (1962); *Time Fields*, study in multiple, simultaneous rhythms for Piano, Cello, String Bass, Oboe, Clarinet, and Percussion (1963); *City Scape*, a 6-hour work for approximately 10 Actor-Musicians, House, 2 Parks, and 2 Trucks (1963; in collaboration with A. Martin and K. Dewey); *Information* for 2 Pianos and Narrator (1963); *Transformation*, theater piece (1963; in collaboration with M. Subotnick and R. Levine); *Desert Ambulance* for Accordion, 2-channel Tape, Movie, Slides, and Liquid Projections (1964; in collaboration with A. Martin); *In the Garden* for 2-channel Tape, Viola, Clarinet, and Visual Score (1965; in collaboration with A. Martin); *Loopy Gamelan on C, "O 'C' Can You Say,"* for Children's Chorus and 4 Cassette Recorders loaded with Loopies (1976); *Great[10] Grandpa Lemuel's Death- Rattle Reincarnation Blues* for Amplified Accordion and Dixieland Band with Ampex PR–10 Tape Duplicator (or equivalent) (1981); *Our Mother the Earth* for Chorus, after Tewa Pueblo Indians (1983); *I Have a Dream* for Chorus, after Martin Luther King Jr. (1984).**—NS/LK/DM**

Sendrey, Albert Richard, American composer, son of **Aladár Szendrei;** b. Chicago, Dec. 26, 1911. He studied in Leipzig, Paris, and London. He was an arranger for film companies in Paris (1935–37) and

London (1937–44) before settling in Hollywood in 1944. Among his original works are *Oriental Suite* for Orch. (1935), 3 syms., piano pieces, and cello pieces. —NS/LK/DM

Sendrey, Alfred
See **Szendrei, Aladár**

Sénéchal, Michel, French tenor and teacher; b. Tavery, Feb. 11, 1927. He received training at the Paris Cons. After making his operatic debut in Brussels in 1950, he won the Geneva International Competition in 1952 and subsequently sang regularly at the Opéra and the Opéra-Comique in Paris. In 1966 he made his first appearance at the Glyndebourne Festival as Ravel's Gonzalve. From 1972 to 1988 he sang at the Salzburg Festival. In 1980 he became director of the opera school at the Paris Opéra. He sang the villains in *Les Contes d'Hoffmann* at his Metropolitan Opera debut in N.Y. on March 8, 1982. In 1985 he created the role of Pope Leo X in Boehmer's *Docteur Faustus* at the Paris Opéra. He was best known for his character roles.—NS/LK/DM

Senesino (real name, **Francesco Bernardi**), celebrated Italian castrato alto who took his professional name from his birthplace; b. Siena, c. 1680; d. probably there, c. 1759. He began his career in Venice (1707–08). After singing in Bologna (1709) and Genoa (1709, 1712), he again appeared in Venice (1713–14); then sang in Naples (1715–16). In 1717 he was called to the Dresden court, where he was a prominent singer until he was dismissed for unconscionable behavior during a rehearsal in 1720. Handel heard him during a visit to Dresden, and engaged him for the Royal Academy of Music opera productions in London, where Senesino made his debut at the King's Theatre on Nov. 19, 1720. He remained with the company until 1728, although his arrogance caused bitter disputes with Handel. After singing in Venice (1729), he was reengaged by Handel and Heidegger for the new Academy opera productions in London (1730–33). Senesino's dislike for Handel prompted him to lend his support to the Opera of the Nobility, with which he was associated from 1733 to 1736. After appearances in Florence (1737–39), he retired from the operatic stage (1740). Although Senesino was personally disagreeable to many of his colleagues, there was no denying the greatness of his vocal abilities; indeed, in spite of their disagreements, Handel wrote no fewer than 17 roles for him.—NS/LK/DM

Senff, Bartholf (Wilhelm), German music publisher and editor; b. Friedrichshall, near Coburg, Sept. 2, 1815; d. Badenweiler, June 25, 1900. As a young man he entered Kistner's music publ. house in Leipzig, advancing to the position of managing clerk. He began editing the *Signale für die Musikalische Welt*, a trial number appearing in Dec. 1842; the first regular number was issued on Jan. 1, 1843. This was one of the most important German music periodicals of the 19th century. It includes reports of musical events, special articles, and correspondence from the music centers of the world, with many celebrated musicians contributing to

it. He remained ed. until his death, and publication continued (1917–18 excepted) until 1941. He founded his own publishing business in 1847, his catalogue including original publications of works by Schumann, Liszt, Anton Rubinstein, Raff, et al. His niece, Marie Senff, managed the firm until 1907, when she sold it and the *Signale* to Simrock of Berlin.—NS/LK/DM

Senfl, Ludwig, important Swiss composer; b. probably in Basel, c. 1486; d. Munich, between Dec. 2, 1542 and Aug. 10, 1543. He became a choirboy in Emperor Maximilian I's Hofkapelle in 1496, then went with the Kapelle to Konstanz in 1507, where he was Isaac's copyist. He apparently accompanied the latter to Italy about 1509, but by 1513 he was a member of the Kapelle in Vienna as Isaac's successor; after the emperor's death in 1519, he was dismissed the following year. In 1523 he settled in Munich as composer to the Bavarian Hofkapelle of Duke Wilhelm IV; under his direction, the Hofkapelle was raised to an exalted standard. Senfl was one of the great masters of the motet and lied of his era. He ed. and completed Isaac's *Choralis Constantinus*, and also ed. the historically important *Liber selectarum cantionum* (1520), one of the earliest books with musical notation publ. in Germany. W. Gerstenberg et al. began ed. his complete works (Wolfenbüttel, 1937–61).

WORKS: *5 Salutationes Domini nostri Hiesu Christi*, motets in 4 voices (Nuremberg, 1526); *Varia carminum genera, quibus tum Horatius tum alii egreii poetae harmoniis composita* for 4 Voices (Nuremberg, 1534; 9 odes are in P. Hofhaimer's *Harmonie poeticae*, 1539); *Magnificat octo tonorum* for 4–5 Voices (Nuremberg, 1537); 81 numbers are in *121 newe Lieder* (Nuremberg, 1534), and 64 numbers in *115 guter newer Liedlein* (Nuremberg, 1544); also single compositions in various collections of the period.

BIBL.: T. Kroyer, *L. S. und sein Motettenstil* (Munich, 1902); E. Löhrer, *Die Messen von L. S.* (Lichtensteig, 1938); E. Dreyer, *L. S.s melodische Arbeit und ihre Tradition* (diss., Univ. of Leipzig, 1958); M. Bente, *Neue Wege der Quellenkritik und die Biographie L. S.s* (Wiesbaden, 1968); W. Seidel, *Die Lieder L. S.s* (Bern and Munich, 1969).—NS/LK/DM

Senn, Kurt Wolfgang, Swiss organist, pedagogue, and music editor; b. Szczakow, Poland, March 11, 1905; d. Bern, June 25, 1965. He studied at the Basel Cons. and with Straube in Leipzig (1923–29). He was organist in Elgg and Thalwil (1929–38), and also taught at the Zürich Academy of Music. From 1938 until his death he was organist at the Bern Cathedral. He also taught church music at the Univ. and organ at the Cons. in Bern. As a recitalist, Senn made many tours. He ed. many scores for performance.—NS/LK/DM

Serafin, Tullio, eminent Italian conductor; b. Rottanova de Cavarzere, Venice, Sept. 1, 1878; d. Rome, Feb. 2, 1968. He studied at the Milan Cons. He made his conducting debut in Ferrara in 1898. In 1901 Toscanini engaged him as one of his asst. conductors at La Scala in Milan. He was principal conductor of La Scala (1909–14; 1917–18). From 1924 to 1934 he was a conductor at the Metropolitan Opera in N.Y. In 1934 he became chief conductor and artistic director of the Rome Opera, a post he retained until 1943; then was engaged as artistic director of La Scala (1946–47). From 1956 to 1958 he conducted at the Chicago Lyric Opera; in 1962 he was named artistic adviser of the Rome Opera. He was especially authoritative in the Italian operatic repertoire. As an artistic adviser, he helped launch the careers of Maria Callas and several other noted artists. He publ. (with A. Toni) 2 vols. on the history of Italian opera, *Stile, tradizioni e convenzioni del melodramma italiano del Settecento e del l'Ottocento* (Milan, 1958–64).

BIBL.: T. Celli and G. Pugliese, *T. S.: Il patriarca del melodramma* (Venice, 1985).—NS/LK/DM

Seraphin (also **Serafin, Serafino**), **Sanctus (Santo),** celebrated Italian violin maker; b. Udine, Nov. 1, 1699; d. Venice, c. 1758. He was a pupil of Niccolo Amati, then settled in Venice about 1720; signed his name on the labels as "Sanctus Seraphinus Nicolai Amati Cremonensis Alumnus." His instruments contained elements characteristic of Stainer and Niccolo Amati. His nephew Giorgio Seraphin (Serafino) (b. Venice, c. 1726; d. there, Jan. 25, 1775) worked in Venice in the first half of the 18th century.—NS/LK/DM

Serassi, Giuseppe, Italian organ builder, known as "il Vecchio;" b. Como, 1694; d. Crema, Aug. 1, 1760. He settled in Bergamo about 1730, and built the organs at San Pellegrino, Lodi, and the Santuario di Caraveggio. His son, Andrea Luigi Serassi (b. Bergamo, May 19, 1725; d. there, 1799), carried on the business, and built the cathedral organs in Crema, Fossano, Parma, and Vigevano. His son, Giuseppe Serassi, known as "Il Giovane" (b. Bergamo, Nov. 16, 1750; d. there, Feb. 19, 1817), continued the family tradition and built about 350 organs. He publ. a description of the new organ at Como (1808), with a short history of the organ and good rules for registration; also brought out a pamphlet, *Sugli organi* (Bergamo, 1816). After his death, the family tradition was carried on by his son and grandson; the business was dissolved in 1870.—NS/LK/DM

Serauky, Walter (Karl-August), eminent German musicologist; b. Halle, April 20, 1903; d. there, Aug. 20, 1959. He studied musicology in Halle and with Schering at the Univ. of Leipzig (Ph.D., 1929, with the diss. *Die musikalische Nachahmungsästhetik im Zeitraum von 1700 bis 1850*; publ. in Münster, 1929); completed his Habilitation in 1932 at the Univ. of Halle, where he subsequently served as a prof. (from 1940); then was director of the musicological inst. at the Univ. of Leipzig (from 1949), which post he shared with Besseler (from 1956). He contributed valuable essays to various German publications; also publ. *Samuel Scheidt in seinen Briefen* (Halle, 1937) and *G.F. Händel: Sein Leben, sein Werk* (Kassel and Leipzig, 1956–58).—NS/LK/DM

Șerban, Andrei, Romanian theater and opera producer; b. Bucharest, June 21, 1943. He received training at the Theater Inst. in Bucharest. He began his career as a producer of plays in his homeland, where he attracted notice with his staging of *Ubu Roi* in 1966. In 1970 he went to N.Y. to work with the experimental theater

group La Mama, where his production of *The Cherry Orchard* in 1972 was produced to much critical acclaim. In 1980 he made his debut as an opera producer with *Eugene Onegin* at the Welsh National Opera in Cardiff. He staged *Turandot* in Los Angeles and at London's Covent Garden in 1984, and returned to Covent Garden to produce *Fidelio* in 1985 and *Prince Igor* in 1990. From 1990 to 1993 he was artistic director of the National Theater in Bucharest. He produced *Les Contes d'Hoffmann* at the Vienna State Opera in 1993. After staging *Lucia di Lammermoor* at the Opéra de la Bastille in Paris in 1995, he produced *Thaïs* in Nice in 1997. In 1999 he mounted the *Ring* cycle at the San Francisco Opera. His opera productions reflect his long and successful career in the legitimate theater.—NS/LK/DM

Serebrier, José, Uruguayan-American conductor and composer; b. Montevideo, Dec. 3, 1938. He began to conduct at the age of 12. He went to the U.S. in 1950 and studied composition with Giannini at the Curtis Inst. of Music in Philadelphia (1956–58) and conducting with Dorati in Minneapolis; also took conducting lessons with Monteux at his summer residence in Maine. He subsequently conducted guest engagements in the U.S., South America, and Europe; gave the first performance in Poland of the fourth Sym. of Charles Ives. He was assoc. conductor of the American Sym. Orch. in N.Y. (1962–67), composer-in-residence of the Cleveland Orch. (1968–70), and music director of the Cleveland Phil. (1968–71). He was principal guest conductor of the Adelaide Sym. Orch. (from 1982); was founder and artistic director of the International Festival of the Americas (1984). In 1969 he married **Carole Ann Farley**.

WORKS: Quartet for Saxophones (1955); *Pequeña música* for Wind Quintet (1955); Sym. No. 1 (1956); *Momento psicologico* for String Orch. (1957); *Suite canina* for Wind Trio (1957); Sym. for Percussion (1960); *The Star Wagon* for Chamber Orch. (1967); *Nueve* for Double Bass and Orch. (1970); *Colores mágicos*, variations for Harp and Chamber Orch., with "Synchrona" images (Washington, D.C., May 20, 1971); *Preludio fantastico y danza magica* for 5 Percussion (1973); Violin Concerto (1992); band music.—NS/LK/DM

Sereni, Mario, Italian baritone; b. Perugia, March 25, 1928. He studied at the Accademia di Santa Cecilia in Rome, and also in Siena with Mario Basiola. He made his debut at the Florence May Festival in 1953, and then sang throughout Italy. In 1956 he sang at the Teatro Colón in Buenos Aires. He made his Metropolitan Opera debut in N.Y. on Nov. 9, 1957, as Gérard in *Andrea Chénier*; subsequently sang there for some 2 decades in such roles as Amonasro, Belcore, Germont, Marcello, and Sharpless; also sang in London, Vienna, Milan, Chicago, Houston, Dallas, and other opera centers. —NS/LK/DM

Sérieyx, Auguste (Jean Maria Charles), French teacher, writer on music, and composer; b. Amiens, June 14, 1865; d. Montreux, Feb. 19, 1949. He studied in Paris at the Schola Cantorum with Gédalge and d'Indy, and then taught composition there (1900–14). He collaborated with d'Indy on his monumental

Cours de composition (3 vols., Paris, 1897–1933); publ. *Les Trois Etats de la tonalité* (Paris, 1910) and *Cours de grammaire musicale* (Paris, 1925). His compositions include both sacred and secular vocal works, a Violin Sonata, piano pieces, and songs.

BIBL.: J. Matthey, *Inventaire de fonds musical A. S.* (Lausanne, 1974).—NS/LK/DM

Serini, Giovanni Battista, Italian teacher and composer; b. Cremona, c. 1724; d. place and date unknown. He studied with Galuppi, then was Kapellmeister at the court of Count Wilhelm zu Schaumberg-Lippe in Buckeburg; may have also been in the service of Robert d'Arcy, fourth Earl of Holdernesse (Yorkshire). Among his extant works are sinfonies, 6 harpsichord concertos, 6 sonatas for Flute and Basso Continuo, 3 harpsichord sonatas, and vocal pieces.—NS/LK/DM

Serkin, Peter (Adolf), outstanding American pianist, son of **Rudolf Serkin;** b. N.Y., July 24, 1947. At age 11, he enrolled at the Curtis Inst. of Music in Philadelphia, where he studied with Horszowski, Luvisi, and his father (graduated, 1964). He made his debut as a soloist with Schneider and a chamber orch. at the Marlboro (Vt.) Music Festival (1958); later studied there with the flutist Marcel Moyse, and also received additional piano training from Karl Ulrich Schnabel. He made his N.Y. debut as a soloist with Schneider and his chamber orch. (Nov. 29, 1959); his N.Y. recital debut followed (March 27, 1965). In 1973 he formed the group Tashi ("good fortune" in Tibetan) with clarinetist Richard Stoltzman, violinist Ida Kavafian, and cellist Fred Sherry; the group toured extensively, giving performances of contemporary music in particular. After leaving the group in 1980, Serkin renewed his appearances as a soloist and recitalist. While he championed modern music, he acquired a distinguished reputation as an interpreter of both traditional and contemporary scores. He excels in works by Mozart, Beethoven, Schubert, Brahms, Stravinsky, Schoenberg, Messiaen, Takemitsu, Peter Lieberson, and others. He also made appearances as a fortepianist. In 1983 he was awarded the Premio of the Accademia Musicale Chigiana in Siena. In 1992 he joined the faculty of the Curtis Inst. of Music in Philadelphia.—NS/LK/DM

Serkin, Rudolf, eminent Austrian-born American pianist and pedagogue of Russian descent, father of **Peter (Adolf) Serkin;** b. Eger, March 28, 1903; d. Guilford, Vt., May 8, 1991. He studied piano with Richard Robert and composition with Joseph Marx and Schoenberg in Vienna. He made his debut as a soloist with Oskar Nedbal and the Vienna Sym. Orch. at age 12; his career began in earnest with his Berlin appearance with the Busch Chamber Orch. in 1920; thereafter he performed frequently in joint recitals with Adolf Busch, whose daughter he married in 1935. He made his U.S. debut in a recital with Busch at the Coolidge Festival in Washington, D.C., in 1933; then made a critically acclaimed appearance as a soloist with Toscanini and the N.Y. Phil. (Feb. 20, 1936). In 1939 he became a naturalized U.S. citizen. After World War II, he pursued an international career; appeared as a soloist with all the major orchs. of the world, gave recitals in the leading music centers, and played in numerous chamber music settings. In 1939 he was appointed head of the piano dept. at the Curtis Inst. of Music in Philadelphia; was its director from 1968 to 1976. In 1950 he helped to establish the Marlboro (Vt.) Music Festival and school, and subsequently served as its artistic director. In 1985 he celebrated his 70th anniversary as a concert artist. He received the Presidential Medal of Freedom in 1963; in 1988 he was awarded the National Medal of Arts. The authority and faithfulness of his interpretations of the Viennese classics placed him among the masters of the 20th century.—NS/LK/DM

Serly, Tibor, Hungarian-born American violist, conductor, teacher, music theorist, and composer; b. Losonc, Nov. 25, 1901; d. London, Oct. 8, 1978. His family moved to the U.S. in 1905, and he became a naturalized American citizen in 1911. He received his early musical training from his father, Lajos Serly, founder of the first Hungarian theater in N.Y. and his own Hungarian-German opera company; then returned to Hungary, where he enrolled in the Royal Academy of Music in Budapest; there he took courses with Koessler, Hubay, Bartók, and Kodály (graduated, 1925). Upon his return to the U.S., he was a violist in the Cincinnati Sym. Orch. (1926–27); then was a violinist (1928–35) and asst. conductor (1933–35) with the Philadelphia Orch.; subsequently was a violinist in the NBC Sym. Orch. in N.Y. (1937–38). After studying conducting with Scherchen in Europe (1934), he led various concerts in N.Y.; was primarily active as a private teacher from 1938. When Bartók settled in the U.S. in 1940, Serly became his closest friend and adviser; after Bartók's death in 1945, Serly completed the last 17 measures of Bartók's third Piano Concerto, and totally reconstructed and orchestrated Bartók's Viola Concerto from 13 unnumbered MS pages. In 1948 he devised a system of composition called Modus Lascivus. Although the medieval Modus Lascivus was synonymous with the C-major scale, Serly expanded its connotation to include enharmonic modulation. He wrote the treatises *A Second Look at Harmony* (1965), *Modus Lascivus: The Road to Enharmonicism* (1976), and *The Rhetoric of Melody* (with N. Newton; 1978). Shortly before his death, he made an arrangement of Bartók's Viola Concerto for cello and orch.

WORKS: DRAMATIC: Ballet: *Mischchianza* (1937); *Ex Machina* (1943); *Cast Out* (1973). **ORCH.:** *Transylvania Rhapsody* (1926); Viola Concerto (1929); 2 syms.: No. 1 (1931; Budapest, May 13, 1935, composer conducting) and No. 2 for Winds, Brass, and Percussion (1932); *6 Dance Designs* (1932–33; Budapest, May 13, 1935); *The Pagan City*, symphonic poem (1932–38; in collaboration with J. Klenner); *Transylvanian Suite* for Chamber Orch. (1935); *Sonata concertante* for Strings (1935–36); *Colonial Pageant* and *Alarms and Excursions*, 2 suites (1936–37); *Midnight Madrigal* for Trumpet and Orch. (1939); Concerto for 2 Pianos and Orch. (1943–58); *American Elegy*, based on *Taps* (1945); *Rhapsody* for Viola and Orch. (1946–48; N.Y., Feb. 27, 1948); *Miniature Suite* for 12 Winds and Percussion (1947; revision of a discarded *Rhapsody* of 1927); *American Fantasy of Quodlibets* (1950); Concerto for Trombone and Chamber Orch. (1952–54); *Lament: Homage to Bartók* (1955); Concerto for Violin, Winds, and

Orch. (1953–58; Portland, Ore., Nov. 30, 1978); *Symphonic Variations* for Audience and Orch. (1956); String Sym. (1956–58); *Little Christmas Cantata* for Audience and Orch. (1957); *Symphony in 4 Cycles* for Strings (1960); *Concertino 3 x 3* for Piano and Chamber Orch. (1964–65; Syracuse, N.Y., Jan. 13, 1967); *Canonic Fugue in 10 Voices on 10 Tones* for Strings (1971; Portland, Ore., June 5, 1977); *Music* for 2 Harps and Strings (1976). **CHAMBER:** Violin Sonata (1923); String Quartet (1924); Sonata for Solo Violin (1947); Trio for Clarinet, Violin, and Piano (1949); *Chorale in 3 Harps* (1967); *Rondo Fantasy in Stringometrics* for Violin and Harp (1969); piano pieces, including *40 Piano Études in Modus Lascivus* (1946–60; first complete perf. by his second wife, Miriam Molin, N.Y., May 4, 1977). **VOCAL:** *4 Songs from Chamber Music* for Soprano and Orch., after James Joyce (1926); *Strange Story* for Mezzo-soprano and Orch., after E. Wylie (1927); *Anniversary Cantata on a Quodlibet* for Voices and Small Orch. (1966); *Consovowels 1–5*: No. 1 for Soprano (1968), Nos. 2 and 3 for Soprano and Clarinet (1970, 1971), and Nos. 4 and 5 for Soprano and Violin (both 1974).—**NS/LK/DM**

Sermilä, Jarmo (Kalevi), Finnish trumpeter and composer; b. Hämeenlinna, Aug. 16, 1939. He studied at the Hämeenlinna School of Music, and then received instruction in composition from Marttinen and Kokkonen at the Sibelius Academy in Helsinki (diploma, 1975) and from Kovaříček in Prague, and also pursued studies in musicology at the Univ. of Helsinki (M.A., 1975). In 1973 he co-founded the Finnish Radio's experimental music studio in Helsinki, which he led as artistic director until 1979. From 1977 to 1982 he was composer-in-residence of the city of Hämeenlinna. In 1981 he became vice president of the Finnish Composers' Soc. He also was artistic director of the new music festival Time of Music in Viitasaari from 1987 to 1999, and served as vice president of Teosto, the Finnish performing rights society from 1994 to 1999. As a trumpeter, he performed much contemporary music, including his own works. His compositions, which range from aleatory to jazz settings, employ various techniques.

WORKS: **DRAMATIC:** *The Wolf Bride*, electroacoustic ballet (1980; Helsinki, Feb. 26, 1981); *Merlin's Masquerade*, children's fantasy for Tape, 8 Instruments, 4 Rooms, Optional Dance, etc. (1987; Hämeenlinna, Aug. 8, 1988); *The Doors*, scenic song cycle for 4 Men Singers and 7 Doors (Helsinki, June 2, 1998). **ORCH.:** *Early Music* (1971; Kotka, Sept. 22, 1982); *Pentagram* for Trumpet and Orch. (1972; Turku, Jan. 18, 1973); *Mimesis 2* (1974; Helsinki, Jan. 30, 1976); *Cornologia* for 24 to 44 Horns (1975); *Counterbass* for Double Bass and Strings (1975); *Manifesto* (1977; Turku, April 1, 1982); *Time Mahcine* (1978; Hämeenlinna, Dec. 8, 1979); *A Circle of the Moon* for Oboe and Orch. (1979; Montevideo, Oct. 15, 1980); *LABOR!* (Helsinki, April 15, 1982); *Transformations* for Strings (1984; Stockholm, Sept. 27, 1988); *Quattro rilievi* (1988–89; Nos. 1 and 2, Hämeenlinna, Aug. 24, 1989, and Nos. 3 and 4, Helsinki, Aug. 26, 1989); *Baby Tiger's Broken Thought* (Helsinki, Nov. 21, 1992); *Un'asserzione di una signora* for Horn and Strings (Lieksa, July 29, 1994); *Train of Thoughts* for Flugelhorn and Orch. (Hämeenlinna, Oct. 7, 1999). **CHAMBER:** *Crisis* for Clarinet, 2 Violins, Viola, and Cello (1972; Hämeenlinna, Nov. 28, 1976); *Colors and Contrasts* for Flute, Violin, and Piano (1976; Prague, March 8, 1979); *Thus I Saw This* for Flute, Oboe, Clarinet, Bassoon, and Horn (1977; Helsinki, Oct. 24, 1989); *Dissimilitudes* for 2 Violins, 2 Violas, and 2 Cellos (1980–91; Rovaniemi, Sept. 7, 1995); *The*

Mythic Man for Percussion Quartet (Tampere, Nov. 15, 1982); *Clockwork Etudes* for Bass Clarinet and Marimba or Vibraphone (1983; Hämeenlinna, Nov. 20, 1984); *A Prague Thoroughfare* for Electric Guitar, 2 Violins, Viola, and Cello (1983; Hämeenlinna, Aug. 24, 1989); *...and an elk was formed by Hiisi* for 2 Trombones, 2 Percussion, and Tape (1984; Helsinki, Oct. 1, 1985); *Diary Fragments by Kilgore Trout 1* for Oboe, Violin, Viola, and Cello (1984; Leningrad, Nov. 1, 1986), *2* for 2 Trumpets, Horn, Trombone, and Tuba (1988; Viitasaari, July 9, 1992), and *3* for 2 Violins, Viola, and Cello (1996; St. Gallen, Sept. 11, 1997); *Jean-Eduard en face du fait accompli* for Saxophone Quartet (1986–89; Lüneburg, Nov. 29, 1987); *Movimenti e ritonelli* for 2 Violins, Viola, and Cello (1986–95; Hämeenlinna, Dec. 3, 1995); *Ego 1* for Violin, Cello or Double Bass, and Accordion (Oulu, June 10, 1988) and *2* for Flute, Cello, and Accordion (1989; Helsinki, Oct. 1991); *Trocortro* for Trumpet, Horn, and Trombone (Hämeenlinna, July 12, 1990); *Danza 1* for Harp and Marimba or Vibraphone (1991; Hämeenlinna, June 7, 1992) and *2* for Flute, Guitar, and Tape (1991; Tampere, Feb. 27, 1993); *...tota noin...* for Flute, Oboe, Clarinet, and Percussion (1992); *Mechanical Partnership* for Bass Clarinet and Accordion (1994); *Dramma per due* for Double Bass and Percussion (Oulu, Oct. 15, 1995); *Dragonfly Day* for Recorder(s), Guitar, Violino, and Cello (1995; Ålborg, Jan. 20, 1996); *Quasi come Quasimodo* for Tuba and Percussion (1997); *Il mondo assurdo del Signor B.* for Viola and Tape (1997; Florence, Dec. 19, 1998); *La fille joue aux oiseaux de nuit* for Recorder(s) and Tape (1998; Viitasaari, July 10, 1999); *Weimariana* for Oboe, Cello, and Piano (Weimar, May 13, 1999). **VOCAL:** *Talvipäivän seisaus* (Winter Solstice) for Soprano and Piano (Hämeenlinna, May 18, 1969); *Love-Charm Songs* for Soprano and Chamber Ensemble (Helsinki, Oct. 29, 1976); *The Hard Burden of Night* for Bass and Piano (Hämeenlinna, July 29, 1982); *Lakeus* (The Plains) for Mezzo-soprano and Cello (1986; Helsinki, April 4, 1988); *Hitaat auringot* (The Slow Suns) for Soprano, Clarinet, and Piano (Lahti, Aug. 3, 1989); *Rituaaleja* (Rituals) for Men's Chorus and Percussion (1991); *Puhetta* (Talk) for Chorus (1993; Hämeenlinna, Aug. 14, 1994). **OTHER:** *On the Road: A Concerto of Our Time* for Trumpet, Percussion, and Chorus (Helsinki, Dec. 10, 1993); electroacoustic, jazz, and improvisational pieces.—**NS/LK/DM**

Sermisy, Claudin or **Claude de,** significant French composer; b. c. 1490; d. Paris, Sept. 13, 1562. He served as a cleric at the Saint-Chapelle in Paris in 1508. He also was a singer in the private chapel of Louis XII, and may have traveled abroad with the King's chapel. After serving as a canon at Notre-Dame-de-la-Rotonde in Rouen, he went to the parish church of Cambron in the Amiens diocese in 1524. In 1532 he returned to Paris as sous-maître at the royal chapel, and also held the eleventh canonry of the Saint-Chapelle from 1533. He was an outstanding composer of both sacred and secular music. A number of his chansons, masses, and motets were publ. in contemporary collections. G. Allaire and I. Cazeaux ed. a complete collection of his works in Corpus Mensurabilis Musicae, LXII/1 (1970–74).

BIBL.: G. Allaire, *The Masses of Claudin d.S.* (diss., Boston Univ., 1960); I. Cazeaux, *The Secular Music of Claudin d.S.* (diss., Columbia Univ., 1961).—**NS/LK/DM**

Serocki, Kazimierz, prominent Polish composer; b. Toruń, March 3, 1922; d. Warsaw, Jan. 9, 1981. He studied piano with Szpinalski and composition with Sikorski at the ód Cons. (graduated, 1946), then received further training in composition from Boulanger and in piano from Lévy in Paris (1947–48). He was active as a pianist in Poland (1946–51). With Tadeusz Baird and Jan Krenz, he formed the modernistic Group '49, dedicated to the cause of the avant-garde; in 1956 he was one of the organizers of the audaciously futuristic "Warsaw Autumn" Festivals. In the interim he toured as a concert pianist. In his early music, he fell into the fashionable neo-Classical current strewn with tolerable dissonances and spiked with bristling atonalities; experimented with Webernized dodecaphonies before molding his own style of composition, an amalgam of pragmatic serialism and permissible aleatory procedures, while maintaining an air of well-nigh monastic nominalism in formal strictures and informal structures; in some pieces, he made incursions into the exotic field of American jazz.

WORKS: ORCH.: *Symphonic Scherzo* (1948); *Triptych* for Chamber Orch. (1949); *4 tańce ludowe* (4 People's Dances) for Chamber Orch. (1949); *Romantic Concerto* for Piano and Orch. (1950); 2 syms.: No. 1 (1952) and No. 2, *Symphony of Songs*, for Soprano, Baritone, Chorus, and Orch. (Warsaw, June 11, 1953); Trombone Concerto (1953); Sinfonietta for 2 String Orchs. (1956); *Musica concertante* for Chamber Orch. (1958); *Episodes* for Strings and 3 groups of Percussion (1958–59); *Segmenti* for 12 Winds, 6 Strings, Piano, Celesta, Harpsichord, Guitar, Mandolin, and 58 Percussion Instruments (1960–61); *Symphonic Frescoes* (1963); *Forte e piano* for 2 Pianos and Orch. (1967; Cologne, March 29, 1968); *Dramatic Story* (1968–71; Warsaw, Sept. 23, 1971); *Fantasia elegiaca* for Organ and Orch. (1971–72; Baden-Baden, June 9, 1972); Sonatina for Trombone and Orch. (1972–73; Strasbourg, Dec. 19, 1975); *Concerto alla cadenza* for Recorder and Orch. (1975); *Ad Libitum*, 5 pieces (1976; Hamburg, Sept. 17, 1977); *Pianophonie* for Piano, Electronic Sound Transformation, and Orch. (1976–78; Metz, Nov. 18, 1978). CHAMBER: Suite for 4 Trombones (1953); *Continuum*, sextet for 123 Percussion Instruments manipulated by 6 Multimanual Percussionists (1965–66); *Swinging Music* for Clarinet, Trombone, Cello or Double Bass, and Piano (1970); *Phantasmagoria* for Piano and Percussion (1970–71); *Impromptu fantastique* for 6 Flutes, Mandolins, Guitars, Percussionists, and Piano (1973–74). Piano: Sonatina (1952); Sonata (1955); *A piacere* (1963). VOCAL: *3 melodie Kurpiowskie* (3 Melodies from Kurpie) for 6 Sopranos, 6 Tenors, and Chamber Orch. (1949); 2 cantatas: *Mazowsze* (1950) and *Murarz warszawski* (1951); *Serce nocy* (Heart of the Night), cycle for Baritone and Piano (1956); *Oczy powietrza* (Eyes of the Wind), cycle for Soprano and Orch. or Piano (1957–58); *Niobe* for 2 Narrators, Chorus, and Orch. (1966); *Poezje* (Poems) for Soprano and Chamber Orch. (1968–69). —NS/LK/DM

Seroen, Berthe, Belgian-born Dutch soprano and teacher; b. Mechelen, Nov. 27, 1882; d. Amsterdam, April 17, 1957. She was trained at the Brussels Cons. After giving concerts in Belgium and France, she made her operatic debut in Antwerp in 1908 at the Flemish Opera as Elisabeth in *Tannhäuser*. She later sang at the Théâtre Royal de la Monnaie in Brussels. In 1914 she settled in Holland and pursued a career as a concert artist. She taught at the Rotterdam Cons. (from 1927),

and at the conservatories in Amsterdam and Utrecht (from 1937). Seroen was particularly admired for her performances of contemporary Dutch and French art songs.—NS/LK/DM

Serov, Alexander (Nikolaievich), important Russian music critic and composer; b. St. Petersburg, Jan. 23, 1820; d. there, Feb. 1, 1871. He studied law, and also took cello lessons with Karl Schuberth. He became a functionary in the Ministry of Justice and served in St. Petersburg (1840–45), Simferopol, Crimea (1845–48), and Pskov (1848–51). He never took lessons in composition, except a correspondence course in counterpoint with Joseph Hunke, but achieved a certain mastery in harmony and orchestration by studying the classics. In 1851 he began writing critical articles on music, and soon became an important figure in Russian journalism; in 1856 he became ed. of the *Musical and Theatrical Monitor*. In 1858 he made his first trip abroad, visiting Germany and Bohemia; the following year made another German visit, and also traveled in Austria and Switzerland; during this journey he met Wagner, whose ardent admirer he became and remained to the end of his career; expounded Wagner's ideas in Russian publications and engaged in bitter polemics with those who did not subscribe to his views, including his old friend and schoolmate Vladimir Stasov. Serov started very late in the field of composition. Inspired by the performance of a biblical play, *Judith*, by an Italian troupe at St. Petersburg in 1861, he resolved to write an opera on this subject, essaying an Italian libretto, but later deciding on a Russian text. *Judith* was produced in St. Petersburg on May 28, 1863, with excellent success, but although Serov intended to emulate Wagner in the music, the style of *Judith* was closer to Meyerbeer. Quite different was Serov's second opera, *Rogneda*, written on a Russian subject, in a distinctly national idiom, with plentiful use of Russian folk songs. *Rogneda* was staged in St. Petersburg on Nov. 8, 1865, and won a spectacular success; the Tsar Alexander II attended a subsequent performance and granted Serov an annual stipend of 1,000 rubles for it. He then began the composition of another Russian opera, *Vrazhya sila* (Malevolent Power), but death (as a result of heart failure) overtook him when the fifth act was still incomplete; the opera was finished by N.T. Soloviev and produced in St. Petersburg on May 1, 1871. All 3 operas of Serov retain their popularity in Russia but are unknown elsewhere. Serov wrote further an Ave Maria for Adelina Patti (1868), a Stabat Mater, incidental music to *Nero*, *Plyaska Zaporozhtsev* (Dance of the Zaporozh Cossacks) for Orch. (1867), *Ouverture d'une comédie* for Piano, 4-Hands, and a few other small pieces. A selection from his writings was publ. in 4 vols. (St. Petersburg, 1892–95). In 1863 Serov married a Cons. pupil, Valentina Bergmann (1846–1924), who was the first Russian woman to compose operas: *Uriel Acosta* (Moscow, 1885) and *Ilya Murometz* (Moscow, March 6, 1899; with Chaliapin in the title role). She helped to ed. and publ. Serov's posthumous works, and also wrote essays and publ. a number of piano pieces and a book of memoirs (St. Petersburg, 1914) under the name Valentina Serova.

BIBL.: N. Findeisen, *A.N. S.: His Life and Music* (St. Petersburg, 1900; second ed., 1904); V. Serova, *A.N. S.* (St. Petersburg, 1914); G. Khubov, *The Life of A.N. S.* (Moscow, 1950).
—NS/LK/DM

Serra, Luciana, Italian soprano; b. Genoa, Nov. 4, 1942. She was a student of Michele Casato at the Genoa Cons. In 1966 she made her operatic debut in Cimarosa's *Il Convito* at the Hungarian State Opera in Budapest. From 1969 to 1976 she was a member of the Tehran Opera. In 1980 she made her first appearance at London's Covent Garden as Olympia in *Les Contes d'Hoffmann*. She sang Lucia at the Hamburg State Opera in 1982 and at Milan's La Scala in 1983. Following her U.S. debut as Violetta in Charleston in 1983, she sang Lakmé at the Lyric Opera in Chicago that same year. She portrayed the Queen of the Night at the Vienna State Opera in 1988. In 1992 she was engaged as Zerlina in *Fra Diavolo* at La Scala. She sang Olympia in Genoa in 1996. Among her other roles were Adina, Ophelia, Rosina, Norina, Elvira in *I Puritani*, and Hanna Glawari.
—NS/LK/DM

Serrao, Paolo, Italian pedagogue and composer; b. Filadelfia, Catanzaro, 1830; d. Naples, March 17, 1907. He studied with Mercadante at the Naples Cons., and taught there from 1863. His first opera to be performed was *Pergolesi* (Naples, July 19, 1857), followed by *La duchessa di Guisa* (Naples, Dec. 6, 1865) and *Il figliuol prodigo* (Naples, April 23, 1868). He also composed an oratorio, *Gli Ortonesi in Scio* (1869), *Omaggio a Mercadante*, funeral sym. (1871), *Le tre ore d'agonia*, passion, and much church music.**—NS/LK/DM**

Servais, (Adrien-) François, famous Belgian cellist, teacher, and composer, father of **Joseph Servais;** b. Hal, near Brussels, June 6, 1807; d. there, Nov. 26, 1866. He studied at the Brussels Cons. He played in a Brussels theater orch., then went to Paris, where he gave a concert in 1834 with brilliant success. On May 25, 1835, he played his own Cello Concerto at a Phil. Soc. concert in London; subsequently made a grand tour of Europe, and spent several years in Russia as a concert player, even reaching Siberia. He was appointed prof. at the Brussels Cons. in 1848, and taught many pupils who became distinguished artists. His adopted son was **François (Franz Matheiu) Servais.** He wrote 2 cello concertos, 16 fantasias for Cello and Orch., 6 études and 14 duos for Cello and Piano (with Gregoir), 6 caprices for Cello and Cello ad libitum, 3 duos for Violin and Cello (with Léonard), and a duo for Violin and Cello (with Vieuxtemps).
BIBL.: A Peeters, *A.-F. S. (1807–1866): Biografie, werk en bijdrage tot de ontwikkeling van de 19de-eeuwse colletechniek* (Leuven, 1988).**—NS/LK/DM**

Servais, François (Franz Matheiu), French composer and conductor; b. St. Petersburg, c. 1847; d. Asnieres, near Paris, Jan. 14, 1901. It was claimed for him that he was an illegitimate son of Liszt and Princess Carolyne Sayn-Wittgenstein, but nothing in her voluminous correspondence with Liszt indicates that she was

an expectant mother. However it might be, he was adopted by **(Adrien-) François Servais** and assumed his name. He studied cello with Kufferath at the Brussels Cons., and won the Belgian Prix de Rome in 1873 with the cantata *La mort du Tasse*. He founded the Concerts d'Hiver in Brussels. Servais was a champion of Wagner, several of whose operas he introduced to Brussels. He himself wrote an opera, *L'Apollonide*, later titled *Ion* (Karlsruhe, 1899).
BIBL.: E. Michotte, *Au souvenir de F. S.* (Paris, 1907).
—NS/LK/DM

Servais, Joseph, Belgian cellist, teacher, and composer, son of **(Adrien-) Francois Servais;** b. Hal, near Brussels, Nov. 23, 1850; d. there, Aug. 29, 1885. He was a pupil of his father at the Brussels Cons., where he won a premier prix in cello (1866). He made his debut in a joint recital with him in Warsaw (1867), then went to Weimar, where he played in the court orch. (1868–70). From 1872 he served as a prof. at the Brussels Cons. He wrote a Cello Concerto (unfinished) and a String Quartet.**—NS/LK/DM**

Sessions, Roger (Huntington), eminent American composer and teacher; b. Brooklyn, Dec. 28, 1896; d. Princeton, N.J., March 16, 1985. He studied music at Harvard Univ. (B.A., 1915), and took a course in composition with Parker at the Yale School of Music (B.M., 1917). He then took private lessons with Bloch in Cleveland and N.Y., an association of great importance for Sessions; his early works were strongly influenced by Bloch's rhapsodic style and rich harmonic idiom verging on polytonality. He taught theory at Smith Coll. (1917–21), then was appointed to the faculty of the Cleveland Inst. of Music, first as assistant to Bloch, then as head of the dept. (1921–25). He lived mostly in Europe from 1926 to 1933, supporting himself on 2 Guggenheim fellowships (1926, 1927), an American Academy in Rome fellowship (1928), and a Carnegie Foundation grant (1931); also was active with Copland in presenting the Copland-Sessions Concerts of contemporary music in N.Y. (1928–31), which played an important cultural role at that time. His subsequent teaching posts included Boston Univ. (1933–35), the N.J. Coll. for Women (1935–37), Princeton Univ. (1935–44), and the Univ. of Calif. at Berkeley (1944–53); returned to Princeton as Conant Professor of Music in 1953 and as co-director of the Columbia-Princeton Electronic Music Center in N.Y. in 1959; subsequently taught at the Juilliard School of Music in N.Y. (1965–85); also was Bloch Prof. at Berkeley (1966–67) and Norton Prof. at Harvard Univ. (1968–69). In 1938 he was elected a member of the National Inst. of Arts and Letters, in 1953 of the American Academy of Arts and Letters, and in 1961 of the American Academy of Arts and Sciences. In 1974 he received a special citation of the Pulitzer Award Committee "for his life's work as a distinguished American composer." In 1982 he was awarded a second Pulitzer Prize for his *Concerto for Orchestra* (1979–81). In his compositions, Sessions evolved a remarkably compact polyphonic idiom, rich in unresolvable dissonances and textural density, and yet permeated with true lyricism. In his later works, he adopted a *sui generis* method of serial composition. The music of Sessions is decidedly in advance of his time; the difficulty of his idiom, for both performers and listeners, creates a paradoxical situation in which he is recognized as one of the most important composers of the century, while actual performances of his works are exasperatingly infrequent.

WORKS: DRAMATIC: O p e r a : *Lancelot and Elaine* (1910); *The Fall of the House of Usher* (1925; unfinished); *The Trial of Lucullus* (Berkeley, April 18, 1947); *Montezuma* (1941–63; West Berlin, April 19, 1964). **I n c i d e n t a l M u s i c To :** L. Andreyev's *The Black Maskers* (Northampton, Mass., June 1923; orch suite, 1928; Cincinnati, Dec. 5, 1930); Volkmüller's *Turandot* (Cleveland, May 8, 1925). **ORCH.:** Sym. in D major (1917); 9 numbered syms.: No. 1 (Boston, April 22, 1927), No. 2 (1944–46; San Francisco, Jan. 9, 1947), No. 3 (1955–57; Boston, Dec. 6, 1957), No. 4 (1958; Minneapolis, Jan. 2, 1960), No. 5 (Philadelphia, Feb. 7, 1964), No. 6 (Newark, N.J., Nov. 19, 1966), No. 7 (Ann Arbor, Mich., Oct. 1, 1967), No. 8 (N.Y., May 2, 1968), and No. 9 (1975–78; Syracuse, Jan. 17, 1980); *Nocturne* (1921–22); *3 Dirges* (1933; withdrawn); Violin Concerto (1930–35; Chicago, Jan. 8, 1940); Piano Concerto (N.Y., Feb. 10, 1956); *Divertimento* (1959–60; Honolulu, Jan. 9, 1965); *Rhapsody* (Baltimore, March 18, 1970); Concerto for Violin, Cello, and Orch. (N.Y., Nov. 5, 1971); Concertino for Chamber Orch. (Chicago, April 14, 1972); *Concerto for Orchestra* (1979–81; Boston, Oct. 23, 1981). **CHAM-BER:** Piano Trio (1916); 3 violin sonatas (1916; 1953; 1981, unfinished); *Pastorale* for Flute (1927; not extant); 2 string quartets: No. 1 (1936; Washington, D.C., April 1937) and No. 2 (Madison, Wisc., May 28, 1951); Duo for Violin and Cello (1942); String Quintet (1957–58; N.Y., Nov. 23, 1959); 6 Pieces for Cello (1966; N.Y., March 31, 1968); *Canons (to the Memory of Igor Stravinsky)* for String Quartet (1971); Duo for Violin and Cello (1978; unfinished). **KEYBOARD: P i a n o :** 3 sonatas: No. 1 (1927–30; N.Y., May 6, 1928), No. 2 (1946; N.Y., March 1947), and No. 3 (1964–65; Berkeley, Calif., March 1969); *4 Pieces for Children* (1935–39); *Pages from a Diary*, later titled *From My Diary* (1937–39); *5 Pieces* (1975); *Waltz* (1977–78). **O r g a n :** 3 *Chorale Preludes* (1924–26); *Chorale* (1938). **VOCAL:** *Romauldo's Song* for Soprano and Orch. (Northampton, Mass., June 1923); *On the Beach at Fontana* for Soprano and Piano (1930); *Turn, O Libertad* for Chorus and Piano, 4-Hands or 2 Pianos (N.Y., April 1944); *Idyll of Theocritus* for Soprano and Orch. (1953–54; Louisville, Jan. 14, 1956); *Mass* for Unison Chorus (1955; N.Y., April 1956); *Psalm CXL* for Soprano and Organ (Princeton, N.J., June 1963; also for Soprano and Orch., Boston, Feb. 11, 1966); *When Lilacs Last in the Dooryard Bloom'd*, cantata for Soprano, Alto, Baritone, Chorus, and Orch. (1964–70; Berkeley, Calif., May 23, 1971); *3 Choruses on Biblical Texts* for Chorus and Orch. (1971–72; Amherst, Mass., Feb. 8, 1975).

WRITINGS: *The Musical Experience of Composer, Performer, Listener* (Princeton, N.J., 1950); *Harmonic Practice* (N.Y., 1951); *Reflections on the Music Life in the United States* (N.Y., 1956); *Questions about Music* (Cambridge, Mass., 1970); E. Cone, ed., *Roger Sessions on Music: Collected Essays* (Princeton, N.J., 1979); A. Olmstead, ed., *Correspondence of Roger Sessions* (Ithaca, N.Y., 1992).

BIBL.: E. Schweitzer, *Generation in String Quartets of Carter, S., Kirchner, and Schuller* (diss., Eastman School of Music, 1965); R. Henderson, *Tonality in the Pre-serial Instrumental Music of R. S.* (diss., Eastman School of Music, 1974); M. Campbell, *The Piano Sonatas of R. S.: Sequel to a Tradition* (diss., Peabody Inst., 1982);

S. Kress, *R. S., Composer and Teacher: A Comparative Analysis of R. S.'s Philosophy of Educating Composers and his Approach to Composition in Symphonies Nos. 2 and 8* (diss., Univ. of Fla., 1982); C. Mason, *A Comprehensive Analysis of R. S.'s Opera Montezuma* (diss., Univ. of Ill., Urbana, 1982); F. Prausnitz, *R. S.: A Critical Biography* (London, 1983); R. Meckna, *The Rise of the American Composer-Critic: Aaron Copland, R. S., Virgil Thomson, and Elliott Carter in the Periodical "Modern Music," 1924–1946* (diss., Univ. of Calif., Santa Barbara, 1984); A. Olmstead, *R. S. and his Music* (Ann Arbor, 1985); idem, *Conversations with R. S.* (Boston, 1986). —NS/LK/DM

Šesták, Zdeněk, Czech composer and musicologist; b. Citoliby, near Louny, Dec. 10, 1925. He received training in composition from Hlobil and Krejčí at the Prague Cons. (1945–50) and in musicology at the Charles Univ. in Prague (1945–50). In addition to composing, Šesták devoted much time to researching the musical history of Citoliby and its leading composers of the past, Václav Jan Kopřiva and his son Karel Blažej Kopřiva. Their works, along with other 18th-century composers of the region, are showcased in Šesták's anthology of recordings entitled *Hudba citolibských mistrů 18. století* (Music of the Citoliby Masters of the 18th Century, 1968 and 1985). In his own music, Šesták has followed the path of Czech modernism without straying from accessible modes of expression.

WORKS: ORCH.: 6 syms.: (*Epitaph*, 1961; 1970; 1971; 1973; *Chronos*, 1978; *Eternal Unrest of the Heart*, 1979); *Sonata sinfonica* (1976); *Making the Moment Alive* (1980); 2 violin concertos (*Sursum corda*, 1981; *John the Violinist*, 1985); Viola Concerto, *Socratic Meditations* (1982). **CHAMBER:** 9 string quartets (n.d.; n.d.; *Akroasis*, 1974; *Familiar Voice*, 1975; *Labyrinth of the Soul*, 1976; *Mácha Variations*, 1993; *Soliloquia*, 1994; *Seeking Light*, 1996; *Sisyfos*, 1999); Concertino for Wind Quintet (1964); *Divertimento Concertante* for 5 Winds (1966); *5 Virtuoso Inventions* for Bassoon (1966); Sonata for 2 Clarinets (1967); *3 Metamorphoses* for Flute (1968); *Musica tripartita* for Clarinet (1968); Quintet for 2 Violins, 2 Violas, and 2 Cellos, *Concentus musicus* (1975); *Euterpé* for Oboe and Piano (1977); *Serenade of Congratulation* for Flute, Clarinet, Trumpet, and 2 Bassoons (1978); *Sonata da camera* for 2 Oboes, 2 Clarinets, 2 Horns, and 2 Bassoons (1978); *Serenáda* for 3 Clarinets (1986); *Evocationes paschales* for Trumpet and Organ (1993); Sonata for Trumpet and Organ, *Dies laetitiae* (1994); *Partita capricciosa* for 2 Oboes, 2 English Horns, 2 Horns, and 2 Bassoons (1997); *Nonetto* for 2 Oboes, 2 English Horns, 2 Horns, 2 Bassoons, and Contrabassoon (1997); *Symposium musicum* for Chamber Ensemble (1997); *Musica bizzara* for Bassoon and Piano (1999); *Trois pièces* for Clarinet and Piano (1999). **VOCAL:** *Fatum* for Mezzo-soprano, Bass, Chorus, and Orch., after Sophocles (1983); *Queen Dagmar*, oratorio for Soloists, Chorus, Organ, and Orch. (1989); sacred and secular cantatas; choruses; song cycles; solo songs.—NS/LK/DM

Seter, Mordecai, Russian-born Israeli composer; b. Novorossiysk, Feb. 26, 1916. He went to Palestine in 1926, where he studied with J. Weinberg and R. Burstein-Arber. He then traveled to Paris, where he received instruction in piano from Lévy and in theory from Dandelot (1932–34), completing his training with Dukas (1934–35) and Boulanger (1935–37) at the École Normale de Musique. Returning to Palestine, he taught at the Rubin Academy of Music at the Univ. of Tel Aviv (from 1951); was a prof. there from 1972 until his retirement as prof. emeritus in 1985. In 1962 he received the Prix d'Italie, in 1965 the Israel State Prize, and in 1983 the A.C.U.M. Prize. His works are marked by the eastern Mediterranean style and techniques of composition.

WORKS: DRAMATIC: B a l l e t : *Pas de deux* or *Women in Tent* (ballet version of the *Ricercar*, 1956); *Midnight Vigil, Rhapsody on Yemenite Themes* (1958); *The Legend of Judith* (1962); *Part Real, Part Dream* (ballet version of the *Fantasia concertante*, 1964); *Jephthah's Daughter* (ballet version of sym. score, 1965); *Stone of Destiny* (1974). **R a d i o p h o n i c   O r a t o r i o :** *Midnight Vigil* (1962; concert version of the ballet; Jerusalem, July 16, 1963). **ORCH.:** *Elegy* for Viola or Clarinet and Orch. or Piano (1954); *Ricercar* for Violin, Viola, Cello, and String Ensemble (1956); *Variations* (1959); *Fantasia concertante* for Chamber Orch. (1965); Sinfonietta (1966); *Yemenite Suite* for Chamber Orch., with optional Voice (1966); *Meditation* (1967); *Rounds* for Chamber Orch. (1967–68); *Requiem* for Oboe, Piano, and Strings (1970). **CHAMBER:** *Partita* for Violin and Piano (1951); Sonata for 2 Violins (1952); Sonata for Solo Violin (1953); *Diptyque* for Wind Quintet (1955); *Chamber Music 1970*, 6 works for different instrumental combinations (1970); *Concertante* for Violin, Oboe, Horn, and Piano (1973); 2 piano quartets (1973–81; 1982); Piano Trio (1973); Woodwind Trio (1974); Quintet for Violin, Cello, Flute, Horn, and Piano (1975); *Ensemble* for 6 Instruments (1975); *Solo and Tutti* for Clarinet and String Quartet (1976); 4 string quartets (1976–77); *The Double* for Clarinet and Piano (1986); *Post Scriptum* for String Quartet (1986). **P i a n o :** Sonata (1982); *Triptyque I, II,* and *III* (all 1985); *Contrasts* (1987). **VOCAL:** *Sabbath Cantata* for Soloists, Chorus, and String Orch. (1940); *Jerusalem* for Chorus and Orch. (1966); *Saperi* for Chorus, Percussion, Piano, and Strings (1968). **—NS/LK/DM**

Ševčik, Otakar, noted Czech violinist and pedagogue; b. Horaždowitz, March 22, 1852; d. Písek, Jan. 18, 1934. He studied violin with his father, then at the Prague Cons. with Anton Bennewitz. From 1870 to 1873 he was concertmaster of the Mozarteum in Salzburg, then held a similar post in the Theater an der Wien in Vienna. He was a prof. at the Prague Cons. (1892–1906). After teaching privately in Písek, he was prof. of violin at the Vienna Academy of Music (1909–18), and then taught at the Prague Master School (1919–21); also gave master classes in the U.S. (1920, 1924, 1931), London (1932), and elsewhere. His method, in contradistinction to the usual diatonic system, is founded on chromatic progressions, especially valuable in securing both accuracy and facility. His most famous pupils were Jan Kubelík, Efrem Zimbalist, and Erica Morini. He wrote many pieces for solo violin.

WRITINGS: *Schule der Violine-Technik* (1881); *Schule der Bogentechnik* (1895); *Lagenwechsel und Tonleiter-Vorstudien* (1895); *Triller-Vorstudien und Ausbildung des Finger-Anschlages* (1901); *Doppelgriff-Vorstudien in Terzen, Sexten, Oktaven und Dezimen* (1901); *Violine-Schule für Anfänger* (1904–08).

BIBL.: V. Nopp, *Profesor O. S.: Žvot a dílo* (Professor O. S.: Life and Work; Brno, 1948); O. Ševl and J. Dostál, eds., *O. S.* (Prague, 1953).**—NS/LK/DM**

Séverac, (Marie-Joseph-Alexandre) Déodat de, French composer; b. Saint Félix de Caraman en Lauragais, Haute-Garonne, July 20, 1872; d. Céret,

Pyrénées- Orientales, March 24, 1921. He studied piano with his father, a painter and music lover, then in Toulouse at the Dominican Coll. of Sorèze, at the Univ. (law), and at the Cons. (1893–96); also took courses with d'Indy and Magnard (composition), Blanche Selva and Albéniz (piano), Guilmant (organ), and Bordes (choral conducting) at the Paris Schola Cantorum. After completing his training (1907), he divided his time between Paris and his native town, devoting himself mainly to composition. His works are notable for their Gallic refinement. P. Guillot ed. his *Ecrits sur la musique* (Liège, 1996; includes catalog of works).

WORKS: DRAMATIC: O p e r a : *Le Coeur du moulin* (1903–08; Paris, Dec. 8, 1909); *Héliogabale* (Béziers, Aug. 21, 1910); *La Fille de la terre* (Coursan, July 1913); *Le Roi pinard* (1919). **I n c i d e n t a l   M u s i c   T o :** L. Damard's *Le Mirage* (1905); M. Navarre's *Muguetto* (Tarn, Aug. 13, 1911); E. Verhaeren's *Hélène de Sparthe* (Paris, May 5, 1912). **ORCH.:** 4 symphonic poems: *L'Automne* for Voice and Orch. (1900), *L'Hiver* for Voice and Orch. (1900), *Nymphes au crépuscule* (1901), and *Les Grenouilles qui demandent un roi* (1909–21); *Didon et Enée*, suite (1903); *Tryptique* (1903–04). **CHAMBER:** *Sérénade au clair de lune* for Flute or Oboe, Piano, Harp, and String Quintet (1890; rev. 1919); Piano Quintet (1898); *Les Muses sylvestres*, suite for 5 Woodwinds and String Quartet (1908); *Le Parc aux cerfs* for Oboe, String Quintet, and Piano (1909); piano pieces; organ music. **VOCAL:** Choral works; arrangements of early folk songs.

BIBL.: B. Selva, *D. d.S.* (Paris, 1930); E. Brody, *The Piano Works of D. d.S.: A Stylistic Analysis* (diss., N.Y.U., 1964); *Centenaire D. d.S.* (Paris, 1972).**—NS/LK/DM**

Severinsen, Doc (actually, **Carl Hilding**), American trumpeter, bandleader, conductor, and teacher; b. Arlington, Ore., July 7, 1927. He studied cornet with his father and with Benny Baker. After playing lead trumpet in the big bands of Charlie Barnet, Tommy Dorsey, and Benny Goodman, he joined the staff of NBC in 1949 and appeared regularly on television. He became asst. conductor of Skitch Henderson's orch. on Johnny Carson's *Tonight* television show in 1962, and from 1967 to 1992 was the music director. He also worked with his own groups in concert and nightclub settings, made many recordings, and was active in brass clinics and workshops for young musicians. He likewise appeared as a trumpet virtuoso and conductor with various American orchs. In 1993 he was named principal pops conductor of the Minn. Orch. in Minneapolis. While perhaps best known for his work in popular music, he has not forsaken the performance of more serious music. On Sept. 24, 1992, he was soloist in the premiere of Zwilich's Trumpet Concerto in San Diego. **—NS/LK/DM**

Sevitzky (real name, **Koussevitzky**), **Fabien,** Russian-born American conductor, nephew of **Serge (Alexandrovich) Koussevitzky;** b. Vishny Volochok, Sept. 29, 1891; d. Athens, Feb. 2, 1967. He studied double bass at the St. Petersburg Cons., where he graduated with its gold medal (1911). He then played in orchs., made appearances as a soloist, and began his conducting career. His uncle, who was already a celebrated double bass player himself, suggested that he adopt a truncated form of the last name, and he complied to avoid a family quarrel. In 1922–23 he played in the orch. of the Warsaw Opera and in the Warsaw Phil. With his wife, the Russian singer Maria Koussevitzky, he went to Mexico in 1923; then emigrated to the U.S., becoming a naturalized American citizen in 1928. He played in the Philadelphia Orch. (1923–30); organized the Philadelphia Chamber String Sinfonietta in 1925, and led several ensembles in Boston from 1930. He then was music director of the Indianapolis Sym. Orch. (1937–55), the Univ. of Miami Sym. Orch. (1959–65), and the Greater Miami Phil. (1965–66). He died while on a visit to Athens to conduct the State Orch.—NS/LK/DM

Sex Pistols, The, the archetypal punk rock band.

MEMBERSHIP: Johnny Rotten (John Lydon), voc. (b. London, England, Jan. 30, 1956); Steve Jones, gtr., voc. (b. London, England, May 3, 1955); Glen Matlock, bs. (b. London, England, Aug. 27, 1956); Paul Cook, drm. (b. London, England, July 27, 1956). Glen Matlock was replaced in February 1977 by Sid Vicious (John Simon Ritchie) (b. London, England, May 10, 1957; d. N.Y., Feb. 2, 1979).

The Sex Pistols quickly gained notoriety in Great Britain for their adamantly incompetent playing, cynically vituperative and anticommercial lyrics, and deliberate onstage vulgarity. Reacting to the complacency and blandness of established popular musicians and the policies of the music industry in general, the Sex Pistols intentionally sought to shock and agitate fans out of their musical apathy with tasteless acts of outrage, antagonism, and hostility. They were almost instantly transformed from unknowns to the most publicized and scrutinized rock band in the world in less than a year, without having even released an album. They scored their first recorded successes in Great Britain with "Anarchy in the U.K." and the controversial "God Save the Queen" in 1976–1977. Introducing the shocking, irreverent attitude and style of punk to America, the Sex Pistols essentially disintegrated after their overpublicized debut American tour of early 1978. Nonetheless, Sid Vicious continued to draw massive media attention for the alleged murder of his girlfriend in October 1978 and his drug-overdose death in February 1979, dramatized in the 1986 underground movie classic *Sid and Nancy*. Lead vocalist Johnny Rotten, one of the most acerbic and provocative figures in rock, persevered with Public Image Ltd. (PiL) after the demise of the Sex Pistols, but he never expanded his following beyond that of a cult.

The Sex Pistols were formed by entrepreneur Malcolm McLaren in August 1975 with vocalist Johnny Rotten and three former members of the Swankers, Steve Jones, Glen Matlock, and Paul Cook. They played their first engagement in November and quickly generated outrage and havoc with their cynical and nihilistic songs and tastelessly hostile and abusive performances. The subject of rapidly spreading notoriety, the Sex Pistols signed with EMI Records in October 1976 and soon scored a smash British hit with the widely banned "Anarchy in the U.K.," written by Matlock. However,

they were dropped by EMI in January after swearing on BBC-TV, an incident that won them front-page news coverage.

Disputes between Matlock and Rotten led to Matlock's departure from the Sex Pistols in February 1977, and he was replaced on bass by Sid Vicious, a former member of Siouxsie and the Banshees and Flowers of Romance. Picked up by A&M Records in March, the group was immediately dumped by the label and subsequently signed to Virgin Records in May. Their first release for the label, Matlock's sarcastic "God Save the Queen," became a smash British hit despite its banishment from radio. Their debut album, *Never Mind the Bollocks, Here's the Sex Pistols*, was issued in late 1977 (on Warner Bros. in the United States) and included "Pretty Vacant," "No Feelings," and the vitriolic tribute to their first label, "EMI."

In January 1978 the Sex Pistols made their first American tour, accompanied by media coverage unseen since the advent of the Beatles and the Rolling Stones. After the group's final engagement at Winterland in San Francisco on Jan. 14, 1978, before the largest audience of their career, the Sex Pistols fell into disarray. Sid Vicious, Steve Jones, and Paul Cook later recorded a crude version of Frank Sinatra's theme song, "My Way," and by April Johnny Rotten (now using the name John Lydon) had formed Public Image Ltd. (PiL) with former Clash and Flowers of Romance guitarist Keith Levene. Recording their debut British album in 1978, the group released several albums through the early 1990s. Drummer Martin Atkins joined PiL in 1979 and became a mainstay in the ever-changing group. Rotten published his autobiography in 1994. Steve Jones and Keith Levene later recorded solo albums, and Jones formed Havana 3 A.M. with guitarist Gary Myrick, singer Nigel Dixon, and former Clash bassist Paul Simonon in 1991.

Sid Vicious was charged with the Oct. 21, 1978, stabbing death of his American girlfriend Nancy Spungen at N.Y.'s Chelsea Hotel, but he was found dead of a heroin overdose in a Greenwich Village apartment on Feb. 2, 1979, at age 21, while out on bail. Their "romance" was dramatized in the gritty, raunchy, yet engaging 1986 movie *Sid and Nancy*, cowritten and directed by Alex Cox.

DISC.: **THE SEX PISTOLS:** *Never Mind the Bollocks, Here's the S. P.* (1977); *Live at Chelmsford Top Security Prison* (1990); *The Great Rock 'n' Roll Swindle* (1992). **PUBLIC IMAGE LTD.:** *Second Edition* (1979); *The Flowers of Romance* (1981); *This Is What You Want ... This Is What You Get* (1984); *Public Image Ltd.* (1986); *Happy?* (1987); *9* (1989); *Greatest Hits So Far* (1990); *That What Is Not* (1992). **KEITH LEVENE:** *Violent Opposition* (1989). **STEVE JONES:** *Fire and Gasoline* (1989). **HAVANA 3 A.M.:** *Havana 3 A.M.* (1991).

BIBL.: B. Gruen, *Chaos: The S. P.* (London, 1990); J. Savage, *England's Dreaming: S. P. and Punk Rock* (London, 1991).—**BH**

Seydelmann, Franz, German composer; b. Dresden, Oct. 8, 1748; d. there, Oct. 23, 1806. He was the son of Franciscus Seydelmann, a tenor in the Dresden electoral Kapelle, where he received instruction in music from J.C. Weber, J.G. Schürer, and J.G. Naumann; accompanied Naumann on a study tour of Italy

(1765–68). Returning to Dresden, he was named church composer (1772) and Kapellmeister (1787) at the court. His most successful works for the theater were 2 operas buffa, *Il Mostro ossia Da gratitudine amore* (1785) and *Il Turco in Italia* (1788); thereafter he devoted himself mainly to writing sacred music.

WORKS: DRAMATIC (all first perf. in Dresden unless otherwise given): **O p e r a :** *La Serva scaltra* (1773); *Arsene* or *Die schöne Arsene* (March 3, 1779); *Das tartarische Gesetz* (c. 1779); *Der lahme Husar* (Leipzig, July 17, 1780); *Der Kaufmann von Smyrna* (c. 1780); *Der Soldat* (1783); *Il capriccio corretto* (1783); *La Villanella di Misnía* (1784; in Ger. as *Das sächsische Bauermädchen*, Frankfurt am Main, 1791); *Il Mostro ossia Da gratitudine amore* (1785); *Il Turco in Italia* (1788); *Amore per oro* (1790). **O r a t o - r i o s :** *La Betulia liberata* (1774); *Gioas rè di Giuda* (1776); *La morte d'Abele* (1801). **OTHER:** About 36 masses, 40 Psalms, 37 offertories, 32 antiphons, 15 vespers, etc.; cantatas; songs; 6 sonatas for Harpsichord and Flute (Nos. 1, 2, and 6 as 3 sonates, Dresden, 1785); 3 sonates for Harpsichord or Piano and Violin (Dresden, c. 1786); *6 Sonaten für zwo Personen auf einem Clavier* (Leipzig, 1781); other sonatas for Harpsichord.

BIBL.: R. Cahn-Speyer, *F. S. als dramatischer Komponist* (Leipzig, 1909).—**NS/LK/DM**

Seyfert, Johann Caspar, German violinist, lutenist, and composer, father of **Johann Gottfried Seyfert;** b. probably in Augsburg, c. 1697; d. there, May 26, 1767. He studied with Philipp David Kräuter, the Augsburg Kantor, and with J.G. Pisendel and S.L. Weiss in Dresden. He pursued his career in Augsburg, where he was made choral director of the church of St. Anne in 1723. In 1741 he succeeded Kräuter as Kantor and was made director of Protestant music. Much of his extensive sacred and secular output is not extant, with the exception of his oratorio for the Augustan Confession (Augsburg, 1730) and a *Choralbuch* (1748).—**LK/DM**

Seyfert, Johann Gottfried, German keyboard player and composer, son of **Johann Caspar Seyfert;** b. Augsburg, May 11, 1731; d. there, Dec. 12, 1772. He first studied with his father, and received instruction in keyboard playing from Johann Zach. After studies with Leitdorfer in Bayreuth (1747–50), he studied with Hasse in Dresden before completing his training with C.P.E. Bach in Berlin and G.C. Wagenseil in Vienna. In 1753 he returned to Augsburg, where he worked closely with his father. Upon his father's death in 1767, he was named his successor as Kantor and music director at the church of St. Anne. He composed operas, syms., chamber music, masses, oratorios, cantatas, and other works, but much of his large output is not extant.—**LK/DM**

Seyfried, Ignaz (Xaver), Ritter von, Austrian conductor, teacher, and composer; b. Vienna, Aug. 15, 1776; d. there, Aug. 27, 1841. He was a close friend of Mozart, and had some piano lessons with him; studied also with Koželuh and Albrechtsberger. In 1797 he became conductor at Schikaneder's Freihaus-Theater in Vienna, then was conductor of the Theater an der Wien (1801–27). He was an extremely prolific composer, and some of his Singspiels were very successful; one of them, *Die Ochsenmenuette*, based on Haydn's music

(Vienna, Dec. 31, 1823), gave rise to the well-known anecdote about Haydn's composing an *Ox Minuet* for a butcher and receiving an ox as a gift. Seyfried also wrote the opera *Der Wundermann am Rheinfall* (Vienna, Oct. 26, 1799), which elicited praise from Haydn. He further wrote numerous melodramas, ballets, oratorios, motets, syms., quartets, etc. He publ. *Albrechtsberger's Sämmtliche Schriften* (1826), *Preindl's Wiener Tonschule* (1827), and *Ludwig van Beethoven's Studien im Generalbasse, Contrapuncte und in der Compositions-Lehre* (1832).

BIBL.: A. Schmidt, *Denksteine: Biographien von I.R. v.S...* (Vienna, 1848); B. von Seyfried, *I. Ritter von S.: Thematisch-bibliographisches Verzeichnis: Aspekte der Biographie und des Werkes* (Frankfurt am Main and N.Y., 1990).—**NS/LK/DM**

Seymour, John Laurence, American composer; b. Los Angeles, Jan. 18, 1893; d. San Francisco, Feb. 1, 1986. He studied piano at the Univ. of Calif. at Berkeley (B.A. in music, 1917; M.A. in Slavic languages, 1919), received instruction in piano and theory from Fannie Charles Dillon and in violin from Leila Fagge, and then took courses in composition with Pizzetti and Bohgen in Italy and with d'Indy in Paris (1923–28); later obtained his Ph.D. in English literature in 1940 from the Univ. of Calif. at Berkeley with the diss. *Drama and Libretto*. He lectured there on opera and drama (1928–36), and also served as chairman of the theater dept. of Sacramento Jr. Coll.; later was a librarian at Southern Utah Coll. in Cedar City (1969–85). His opera, *In the Pasha's Garden*, was premiered at the Metropolitan Opera in N.Y. on Jan. 24, 1935, and won the David Bispham Memorial Award.

WORKS: DRAMATIC: O p e r a : *Les précieuses ridicules* (1920); *In the Pasha's Garden* (1934; N.Y., Jan. 24, 1935); *Ramona* (Provo, Utah, Nov. 11, 1970); *Ollanta, el Jefe Kolla* (1977). **O p - e r e t t a :** *Bachelor Belles* (1922); *Hollywood Madness* (1936); *The Devil and Tom Walker* (1942). **M u s i c a l s :** *Ming Toy* (1949); *The Lure and the Promise* (1960). **OTHER:** Piano Concerto; String Quartet; 2 string trios; sonatas for various instruments; piano pieces; songs; etc.—**NS/LK/DM**

Sgambati, Giovanni, celebrated Italian pianist, conductor, teacher, and composer; b. Rome, May 28, 1841; d. there, Dec. 14, 1914. He studied piano with Amerigo Barbieri, and appeared in public at the age of 6. In 1849 he was taken by his family to Trevi, where he studied with Natalucci; returning to Rome in 1860, he received lessons in counterpoint from Giovanni Aldega. In 1862 he became a pupil of Liszt, remaining his lifelong friend and champion. After taking his diploma di socio onorario at the Accademia di Santa Cecelia in Rome (1866), he embarked upon an outstanding career as a pianist, making tours of Europe with enormous success. In Rome he also was active as a conductor. Historically, Sgambati's concerts were important as the first systematic attempt to introduce to the Italian public a varied fare of symphonic music. Sgambati continued to tour as a pianist. After a concert tour in Italy and Germany, he established in 1868 a free piano class annexed to the Accademia di Santa Cecilia in Rome, which in 1877 was formally recognized by the government as the Liceo Musicale; it became the foremost music school in Italy, and Sgambati taught piano there until his death. He was an ardent admirer of Wagner, whom he met in 1876; Wagner recommended Sgambati to Schott of Mainz, who subsequently brought out many of Sgambati's works. As a pianist and teacher, Sgambati enjoyed a very high reputation in Germany and Italy. His own music betrays strong Germanic influence; unlike most Italian composers of his time, he devoted his energies exclusively to instrumental music, avoiding all service to the theater.

WORKS: ORCH.: 2 syms.: No. 1 in D minor (Rome, March 28, 1881) and No. 2 in E-flat major (1883); Piano Concerto (1878–80); *Epitalamio sinfonico* (1887); *Te Deum laudamus* for String Orch. and Organ (1893; also for Large Orch., 1908). OTHER: Sacred music, including a Requiem for Baritone, Voices, and Orch. or Organ (1895–96; rev. 1901); chamber works, including 2 string quartets (1864; c. 1882); String Nonet (1866; not extant); 2 piano quintets (1866; c. 1876); songs; numerous piano pieces; transcriptions for Piano.—NS/LK/DM

Sgouros, Dimitris, gifted Greek pianist; b. Athens, Aug. 30, 1969. He enrolled in the Athens Cons., where he found a mentor in Maria Herogiorgiou-Sigara, and later took lessons with Stewart Gordon in Baltimore and Guy Johnson at the Royal Academy of Music in London; subsequently pursued training in mathematics at the Univ. of Athens. He won the UNICEF Competition in 1980. His musical prowess was evident in his youth: he was only 7 when he made his public debut in Piraeus, and at the age of 12 he appeared as soloist in the Rachmaninoff third Piano Concerto with Rostropovich and the National Sym. Orch. at Carnegie Hall in N.Y. He made his London debut at 13, and subsequently performed as a soloist with many major orchs. and as a recitalist.—NS/LK/DM

Sgrizzi, Luciano, Italian harpsichordist; b. Bologna, Oct. 30, 1910; d. Monaco, Sept. 11, 1994. He learned to play the piano as a child and was awarded a diploma from the Accademia Filarmonica in Bologna. He pursued training in piano and harmony at the Bologna Cons. (1920–21), and also studied organ and composition. Following studies in organ and composition with Ferrari-Trecate at the Parma Cons. (1927–31), he completed his training with Bertelin in Paris. Although he made appearances as a pianist from the days of his youth, he turned to the harpsichord and clavichord in 1948 and subsequently gave numerous recitals. He championed the vast collection of harpsichord sonatas by Domenico Scarlatti. His repertoire embraced numerous works by Italian and French composers. He edited many performing eds., ranging from Monteverdi to Pergolesi.—NS/LK/DM

Shade, Ellen, American soprano; b. N.Y., Feb. 17, 1944. She studied with Talma at Hunter Coll. of the City Univ. of N.Y., and with Tito Capobianco and Cornelius Reid. Following an apprenticeship at the Santa Fe Opera (1968–69), she made her operatic debut as Liù in Frankfurt am Main in 1972. That same year, she made her U.S. operatic debut as Micaëla in Pittsburgh. She then sang in Houston, Dallas, Santa Fe, New Orleans, Milwaukee, and Cincinnati. On April 21, 1976, she made her debut at the Metropolitan Opera in N.Y. as Wagner's Eva. That same year, she sang for the first time at London's Covent Garden as Emma in *Khovanshchina*, and returned there in 1978 to create the role of Eve in Penderecki's *Paradise Lost*. In 1981 she made her debut at the N.Y.C. Opera as Donna Elvira. She first appeared at the Salzburg Festival in Einem's *Der Prozess* in 1988, and also sang Kát'a Kabanová in Geneva that year. In 1992 she portrayed Strauss's Empress in Amsterdam and Salzburg. She was engaged as Arabella at Covent Garden in 1996. As a soloist, she appeared with many orchs. in North America and Europe.—NS/LK/DM

Shafran, Daniel (Borisovich), remarkable Russian cellist; b. Petrograd, Jan. 13, 1923. He studied cello with his father, Boris Shafran, who was an eminent cellist. He received first prize at the 1937 All-Union competition for string players in Moscow, then continued his training with Alexander Stirmer at the Leningrad Cons. (graduated, 1950), winning the Prague International Cello Competition (1950). He played through Russia, and later made tours throughout the world with great success. In 1955 he was made a People's Artist of the R.S.F.S.R.

BIBL.: I. Yampolsky, *D. S.* (Moscow, 1973).—NS/LK/DM

Shaham, Gil, American violinist; b. Urbana, Ill., Feb. 19, 1971. He was taken to Israel as a child by his parents. He began violin training at age 7 with Samuel Bernstein at the Rubin Academy of Music and later was a pupil in Jerusalem of Haim Taub. In 1980 he began working with Dorothy DeLay and Jens Ellerman at the Aspen (Colo.) Music School. He made his debut as soloist in 1981 with Alexander Schneider and the Jerusalem Sym. Orch. After capturing first prize in the Claremont competition in Israel (1982), he continued his training on scholarship at N.Y.'s Juilliard School with DeLay and Hyo Kang. In 1990 he received the Avery Fisher Career Grant. He made his Carnegie Hall recital debut in N.Y. on Jan. 23, 1992. In subsequent seasons, Shaham appeared internationally as a soloist with major orchs. and as a recitalist. His repertoire embraces scores extending from Paganini to Samuel Barber.—NS/LK/DM

Shakespeare, William, English tenor, singing teacher, and composer; b. Croydon, June 16, 1849; d. London, Nov. 1, 1931. He studied at the Royal Academy of Music with Sterndale Bennett in London. He went to Leipzig for study with Reinecke, but soon left for Milan to cultivate his voice under Lamperti's guidance. From 1875 he appeared in England as a tenor; in 1878 he was appointed prof. of singing at the Royal Academy of Music, where he was highly esteemed. His compositions are entirely in the vein of German Romanticism, his model being Mendelssohn. He publ. *The Art of Singing* (3 parts; 1898–99), *Singing for Schools and Colleges* (1907), *Plain Words on Singing* (1924), and *The Speaker's Art* (1931).—NS/LK/DM

Shallon, David, Israeli conductor; b. Tel Aviv, Oct. 15, 1950. He studied composition and conducting with

Sheriff, then completed his conducting studies with Swarowsky at the Vienna Academy of Music (1973–75). He was an assistant to Bernstein in Europe (1974–79), and also made appearances as a guest conductor with major European orchs. and opera houses. Shallon led the premiere of Gottfied von Einem's controversial opera *Jesu Hochzeit* in Vienna in 1980. He made his U.S. debut as a guest conductor with the San Francisco Sym. in 1980. From 1987 to 1993 he was Generalmusikdirektor of the Düsseldorf Sym. Orch.—**NS/LK/DM**

Shamo, Igor, talented Ukrainian composer; b. Kiev, Feb. 21, 1925; d. there, Aug. 17, 1982. He studied medicine in Kiev, and after World War II, studied composition with Liatoshinsky at the Kiev Cons., graduating in 1951. Many of his works, numbering some 200, used native instruments such as the bayan and the bandura, and the lyrics extolled Soviet youth and the Soviet system. In 1975 he received the Shevchenko State Prize of the Ukrainian SSR and became a National Artist of the Ukraine.

WORKS: DRAMATIC: Film scores. **ORCH.:** *Symphonic Dances* (1949); Piano Concerto (1951); *Festival Suite* (1954); *Moldavian Poem—Rad o diya* (1956); 3 syms. (1964, 1968, 1975); *Komsomol Overture* (1967); *Theatrical Kaleidoscope* (1968); *Evening Music* (1971); *Morning Music* (1975); Flute Concerto (1975); Concerto for Bayan and Strings (1980); Sinfonietta-Concerto for Chamber Orch. (1980). **CHAMBER:** Piano Trio (1947); 5 string quartets (1955–80); Piano Quintet (1958); piano pieces. **VOCAL:** *Lenin*, cantata-oratorio (1980); choruses.

BIBL.: L. Efremova, *I. S.* (Moscow, 1958).—**NS/LK/DM**

Sha Na Na, performers of amusing and lively re-creations of the music, dress, and choreography of 1950s rock and roll. **MEMBERSHIP:** John "Bowzer" Bauman, voc. (b. Queens, N.Y., Sept. 14, 1947); Henry Gross, gtr. (b. Brooklyn, N.Y., April 1, 1951); Donald York, kybd., voc.; Lennie Baker, sax. (b. Whitman, Mass., April 18, 1946); Johnny "Jocko" Marcellino, drm. The above are original members. Keyboardist-vocalist "Screamin'" Scott Simon joined in 1969. Guitarist-vocalist Dave "Chico" Ryan joined in early 1970s. Group mainstays since the mid-1980s: York, Baker, Marcellino, Simon, and Ryan.

Sha Na Na were launched into international prominence through their appearance at 1969's Woodstock Festival and the subsequent film. Featured at Ralph Nader's first rock-and-roll revival show several months later, Sha Na Na frequently upstaged the original 1950s acts in concert during the early 1970s. From 1977 to 1981 Sha Na Na appeared on their own syndicated television show that further expanded their audience.

Formed out of Columbia Univ. glee club the Columbus Kingsmen in 1969, the group was initially comprised of John "Bowzer" Bauman, Johnny Contrado, Donald York, Frederick "Denny" Greene, Lennie Baker, Chris "Vinnie Taylor" Donald, Elliot Cahn, Bruce Clarke, Henry Gross, and Johnny "Jocko" Marcellino. Sha Na Na performed only their seventh engagement on Sunday morning, Aug. 17, 1969, at the Woodstock Festival, preceding Jimi Hendrix. Henry Gross soon left to pursue a solo career that peaked with 1976's smash

hit "Shannon," and keyboardist-vocalist "Screamin'" Scott Simon joined shortly after the Woodstock appearance. Signed to Kama Sutra Records, the group recorded a number of albums for the label through 1976, scoring their biggest success with 1973's *The Golden Age of Rock 'n' Roll*. Re-creating the sight and sound of 1950s rock and roll, complete with split-second group choreography, gold lamé costumes, oily ducktail haircuts, and feigned "greaser" hostility, Sha Na Na became a fixture on the rock-and-roll revival circuit of the 1970s. Bassist-vocalist Dave "Chico" Ryan joined the group around 1974.

Retaining a remarkably stable lineup during the 1970s, Sha Na Na had their own syndicated television show that ran from 1977 to 1981. They also appeared in the 1978 movie musical *Grease*, starring John Travolta and Olivia Newton-John. By the mid-1980s John "Bowzer" Bauman, Frederick "Denny" Greene, and Johnny Contrado had left the group, which continued with Donald York, "Screamin'" Scott Simon, Lennie Baker, Dave "Chico" Ryan, and Johnny "Jocko" Marcellino as mainstays. More a musical revue than a rock band, Sha Na Na continue to play around 150 engagements a year at fairs, clubs, and private parties well into the 1990s.

DISC.: SHA NA NA: *Rock 'n' Roll Is Here to Stay* (1969); *S. N. N.* (1971); *The Night Is Still Young* (1972); *The Golden Age of Rock 'n' Roll* (1973); *From the Streets of New York* (1973); *Hot Sox* (1974); *Sha Na Now* (1975); *The Best* (1976); *S. N. N. Is Here to Stay* (1978); *Remember Then* (1981); *Sh-Boom* (1981); *34th and Vine* (1990); *Havin' an Oldies Party* (1991); *25th Anniversary Collection* (1993). **HENRY GROSS:** *Henry Gross* (1972); *Henry Gross* (1974); *Plug Me into Something* (1975); *Release* (1976). **"SCREAMIN'" SCOTT SIMON:** *Transmissions from Space* (1982).—**BH**

Shanet, Howard, American conductor; b. N.Y., Nov. 9, 1918. He studied cello with Evsei Beloussoff, played in the National Orch. Assn., under the direction of Barzin, and later studied conducting with Rudolph Thomas and Stiedry, and at the Berkshire Music Center in Tanglewood with Koussevitzky; also took composition lessons with Weisse, Dessau, Martinů, Lopatnikoff, and Honegger. He completed his academic studies at Columbia Univ. (A.B., 1939; A.M., 1941). He taught at Hunter Coll. in N.Y. (1941–42). After serving in the U.S. Army as a warrant officer and bandleader (1942–46), he again taught at Hunter Coll. (1946–53); also was on the staff at the Berkshire Music Center (summers, 1949–52). In 1953 he was appointed to the faculty of Columbia Univ. and as conductor of the Univ. Orch. and asst. (later full) prof. of music, which led to his designation as Director of Music Performance in 1978; in 1989 he was named Professor Emeritus. He served as asst. conductor of the N.Y.C. Sym. (1947–48), conductor of the Huntington (W.Va.) Sym. Orch. (1951–53), and a guest conductor with the Israel Phil. (1950) and the N.Y. Phil. (1951, 1959). In 1977 he received the presidential citation of the National Federation of Music Clubs and a certificate of distinguished service from the Inst. of International Education; in 1990 he was invited by the Coll. of Physicians and Surgeons of Columbia Univ. to give the Dean's Distinguished Lecture in the Humanities, the first musician to be accorded that honor. He composed

Allegro Giocoso for String Quartet (1942; also for String Orch., 1987), *A War March* for Military Band (1944), *Introduction and Fugue* for Flute, Clarinet, and Bassoon (1947), *2 Canonic Pieces* for 2 Clarinets (1947), and *Variations on a Bizarre Theme* for Orch. (1960), and also arranged and reconstructed the score *Night of the Tropics* by Gottschalk (1955). He publ. an "adult education book," *Learn to Read Music* (N.Y., 1956; tr. into Norwegian, 1972, It., 1975, and Sp., 1981), a fundamental documentary vol., *Philharmonic: A History of New York's Orchestra* (N.Y., 1975), and ed. and wrote a critical introduction for *Early Histories of the New York Philharmonic*, containing reprints of books by Krehbiel, Huneker, and Erskine (N.Y., 1978). He also publ. authoritative articles on such varied subjects as Bach's transpositions, Bizet's suppressed sym., and (in *The New Grove Dictionary of American Music*) the development of orchs. in the U.S.—NS/LK/DM

Shank, Bud (Clifford Everett Jr.),

bop-flavored jazz alto saxophonist, flutist, composer; b. Dayton, Ohio, May 27, 1926. He began playing clarinet at age 10, then switched to saxophone when he was 14; he studied with Shorty Rogers. Shank spent a year with Charlie Barnet, and later played with Stan Kenton (1950–51). He was a featured member of the Lighthouse All-Stars group (1953–56). Shank began making albums as a leader in 1954; that same year, he participated in some of the first Brazilian jazz albums, with Laurindo Almeida. He was among the first bop players to utilize the flute as a legitimate lead instrument. He also did a lot of studio work and was heard on film soundtracks. He made nearly 30 albums as a leader on World Pacific/Pacific Jazz (1954–70). He worked mostly with small group sets, always with excellent sidesmen. His works included albums of pop songs; "Michelle," with Chet Baker on flugelhorn, was a hit in the U.S. In 1974 Shank co-formed the L.A. Four with Shelly Manne, Ray Brown, and Almeida. During the 1970s, he recorded several albums with Bill Mays. He toured Europe several times and played with Frank Morgan and Shorty Rogers, among others, in the 1980s and 1990s.

DISC.: *Compositions of Shorty Rogers* (1954); *Saxophone Artistry of* (1955); *Bud Shank and Bob Brookmeyer* (1955); *Jazz at Cal-Tech* (1956); *Flute 'n Oboe* (1956); *Live at the Haig* (1956); *Jazz Swings Broadway* (1957); *I'll Take Romance* (1958); *Misty Eyes* (1958); *Bud Shank in Africa* (1958); *Holiday in Brazil* (1959); *Bud Shanks Plays Tenor* (1960); *Slippery When Wet* (1960); *Koto and Flute* (1960); *Flute 'n Alto* (1960); *Barefoot Adventure* (1961); *New Groove* (1961); *The Talents of Bud Shanks* (1961); *Bossa Nova Jazz Samba* (1962); *Brasamba! Bossa Nova* (1963); *Bud Shank and His Brazilian Friends* (1965); *Bud Shank and the Sax Section* (1966); *California Dreamin'* (1966); *Flute, Oboe and Strings* (1966); *Brazil! Brazil! Brazil!* (1967); *Magical Mystery* (1968); *Let It Be* (1969); *Sunshine Express* (1976); *Heritage* (1978); *Crystal Comments* (1979); *Explorations* (1980); *This Bud's for You* (1984); *California Concert* (1985); *At Jazz Alley* (1986); *Tomorrow's Rainbow* (1988); *Drifting Timelessly* (1990); *Doctor Is In* (1991); *I Told You So* (1992); *New Gold* (1995); *Plays the Music of Bill Evans* (1996); *Bud Shank Sextet Plays Harold Arlen* (1996); *Jazz in Hollywood* (1997); *Bud Shank and Bill Perkins* (1998); *A Flower Is a Lovesome Thing* (1998). —MM/LP

Shankar, Ravi, famous Indian sitarist, teacher, and composer; b. Varanasi, Uttar Pradesh, April 7, 1920. He revealed a notable talent as a musician and dancer in childhood. After some training from his brother, Uday Shankar, he accompanied him to Paris in 1930 to further his education. Returning to India, he pursued his musical training with Ustad Allauddin Khan in Maihar (1936). After World War II, Shankar became active as a performer. He also served as director of the instrumental ensemble of All-India Radio from 1949 to 1956. In 1956–57 he toured Europe and the U.S., and subsequently performed extensively in both East and West. In 1962 he became founder-director of the Kinnara School of Music in Bombay. His numerous sitar recitals in the West did much to foster an appreciation for Indian music. He publ. a memoir, *My Music, My Life* (N.Y., 1968). E. Barnett ed. *Ravi Shankar: Learning Indian Music, a Systematic Approach* (1981).

WORKS: DRAMATIC: *Ghanashyam* (A Broken Branch), opera-ballet (1989); several ballets; film scores, including the trilogy *Pather Panchali* (1955), *Aparajito* (1956), and *Apur Sansar* (1959); television music. **OTHER:** 2 sitar concertos (1971, 1976); instrumental pieces; songs.—NS/LK/DM

Shankar (Lakshminarayana), Indian singer, composer, arranger, producer, and violinist; b. Madras, April 26, 1950. He first studied voice, violin, and drumming at home with his father, V. Lakshminarayana (d. Dec. 3, 1990), and mother, L. Seethlakshmi; then went to the U.S., where he earned his Ph.D. at Wesleyan Univ. in Middletown, Conn. (1974). With the English-Irish composer Caroline, he formed the pop group the Epidemics in 1980, bringing together in its performances and recordings a variety of genres, including classical Indian, folk, pop, and Western; is also active with his own Indian classical group, Shankar. He invented the Ten String Stereophonic Double Violin, a double-bodied instrument that, when both necks are played simultaneously, is capable of producing all the tones of the orch. string family; when the necks are played separately, the strings of the one not played respond sympathetically. The instrument made its debut in Shankar's *Ragam Tanam Pallavi Ragam Hemmavthi* for Double Violin and South and North Indian Drums (1980), which appeared on the album *Who's to Know*; other albums include *Palghat Mani Tyer* (2 vols.), *Pancha Nadai Pallavi*, and *Eye Catcher*. He also provided film scores for *The Last Temptation of Christ* (1989) and *Jacob's Ladder* (1990). Shankar has appeared widely at festivals promoting a variety of social causes; he performed at the United Nations Peace Day Festival in N.Y. (1987), festivals in support of the Schizophrenia Research Foundation in India (1989–91), and the Tibet Alive for World Peace concert (1991). His other compositions include *Himmalaya* for Vocalists and Double Violin (1981) and the song *Never Take No for an Answer* (1985).—NS/LK/DM

Shannon, Del (originally, **Westover, Charles**), rock and roll singer/songwriter; b. Coopersville, Mich., Dec. 30, 1934; d. Santa Clara, Calif., Feb. 8, 1990. Charles Westover took up guitar and singing as an early teenager and adopted his stage name, Del

Shannon, after graduating from high school. He first performed on the Army's *Get Up and Go* radio show in Germany in 1958 while serving in the Army. Following his discharge in 1959, he returned to Battle Creek, Mich., and performed in local clubs with pianist Max Crook. In 1960, he signed with the Detroit-based Big Top label, achieving his most celebrated hit (a top pop and British hit) with "Runaway," co-written with Crook, in 1961. He followed up with the smash hit "Hats Off to Larry" and the major hit "So Long Baby." First touring Great Britain in the fall of 1962, Shannon met The Beatles and won a devoted following. Touring Great Britain again in the spring of 1963, he performed with The Beatles in May. Scoring smash British hits with "The Swiss Maid" and "Two Kinds of Teardrops," Shannon had a major American hit with "Little Town Flirt" in 1963, followed by the minor hit "From Me to You," the first song written by John Lennon and Paul McCartney to make the American charts.

In late 1962, Del Shannon left Big Top amidst legal disputes with the label and his managers, forming the short-lived label, Berlee, on which he managed a minor hit with "Sue's Gotta Be Mine" in late 1963. Switching to Amy Records in 1964, he scored a major hit with Otis Blackwell's "Handy Man," a near-smash with the classic "Keep Searchin' (We'll Follow the Sun)," and a moderate hit with "Stranger in Town" through 1965. In early 1965, Peter and Gordon had a near-smash American hit with Shannon's "I Go to Pieces." By 1966, he had moved to Los Angeles and signed with Liberty Records. He enjoyed little success with the label and left it in 1969, later arranging The Smith's smash hit "Baby It's You" and producing Brian Hyland's smash hit "Gypsy Woman."

Del Shannon toured Great Britain regularly in the 1960s and 1970s, recording *Live in England* in 1972. He later recorded singles with Jeff Lynne ("Cry Baby Baby Cry") and Dave Edmunds ("And the Music Plays On") in England. He met Tom Petty in 1978 and, over the next three years, recorded *Drop Down and Get Me*, with Petty as producer. The album produced a moderate hit with a remake of Phil Phillips's 1959 smash hit "Sea of Love," but Shannon was unable to sustain a career outside the oldies revival circuit. Del Shannon was nearing completion of a new album with Lynne and Petty (later released as *Rock On*) when he shot himself to death on Feb. 8, 1990. Shannon was inducted into the Rock and Roll Hall of Fame in 1999.

DISC.: *Runaway* (1961); *Little Town Flirt* (1963); *Handy Man* (1964); *Sings Hank Williams* (1965); *1,661 Seconds* (1965); *This Is My Bag* (1966); *Total Commitment* (1966); *Further Adventures of Charles Westover* (1968); *Live in England* (1974); *Drop Down and Get Me* (1981); *Rock On!* (1991).—**BH**

Shapero, Harold (Samuel), American pianist, teacher, and composer; b. Lynn, Mass., April 29, 1920. After piano lessons with Eleanor Kerr, he studied composition with Slonimsky at the Malkin Cons. in Boston (1936–37), Krenek (1937), Piston at Harvard Univ. (1938–41), Hindemith at the Berkshire Music Center at Tanglewood (summers, 1940–41), and Boulanger at the Longy School (1942–43). In 1941 he received the Ameri-

can Prix de Rome for his *9-Minute Overture*. He held Naumburg (1942), Guggenheim (1947, 1948), and Fulbright (1948) fellowships. In addition to his appearances as a pianist, he taught at Brandeis Univ. (from 1952), where he was founder-director of its electronic music studio. In some of his early scores, Shapero employed dodecaphonic techniques. On the whole, his music adhered to an austere Classical pattern, without excluding a highly emotional melodic line. His exceptional mastery of contrapuntal technique secured clarity of intermingled sonorities in his chamber music.

WORKS: ORCH.: *9-Minute Overture* (1940; N.Y., June 8, 1941); *Serenade* for Strings (1945); *Symphony for Classical Orchestra* (1947; Boston, Jan. 30, 1948); *Sinfonia: The Travelers Overture* (1948); *Concerto for Orchestra* (1950); *Credo* (Louisville, Oct. 19, 1955); *Lyric Dances* (1955); *On Green Mountain* for Jazz Ensemble (1957; also for Orch., 1981); *Partita* for Piano and Small Orch. (1960). **CHAMBER:** String Trio (1938); *3 Pieces for 3 Pieces* for Flute, Clarinet, and Bassoon (1939); Trumpet Sonata (1940); String Quartet (1941); Violin Sonata (1942); *3 Improvisations* (1968), *3 Studies* (1969), and *4 Pieces* (1970) for Piano and Synthesizer. **Piano:** Sonata for Piano, 4-Hands (1941); 4 sonatas (1944, 1944, 1944, 1948); *Variations* (1947); *American Variations* (1950). **VOCAL:** *4 Baritone Songs* (1942); *2 Psalms* for Chorus (1952); *Hebrew Cantata* for Soprano, Alto, Tenor, Baritone, Chorus, Flute, Trumpet, Violin, Harp, and Organ (1954); *2 Hebrew Songs* for Tenor and Piano (1970; also for Tenor, Piano, and String Orch., 1980).—**NS/LK/DM**

Shapey, Ralph, American conductor, teacher, and composer; b. Philadelphia, March 12, 1921. He studied violin with Zetlin and composition with Wolpe. He was asst. conductor of the Philadelphia National Youth Administration Sym. Orch. (1938–47). In 1954 he founded and became music director of the Contemporary Chamber Players of the Univ. of Chicago, with which he presented new works. In 1963–64 he taught at the Univ. of Pa., and then was made prof. of music at the Univ. of Chicago in 1964; after serving as Distinguished Prof. of Music at the Aaron Copland School of Music at Queens Coll. of the City Univ. of N.Y. (1985–86), he resumed his duties at the Univ. of Chicago, retiring as prof. emeritus in 1991. Disappointed by repeated rejections of his works by performers and publishers, Shapey announced in 1969 that he would no longer submit his works to anyone for performance or publication. However, in 1976 he had a change of heart and once more gave his blessing to the performance and publication of his works. In 1982 he became a MacArthur Fellow. In 1989 he was elected a member of the American Academy and Inst. of Arts and Letters. On Nov. 21, 1991, he conducted the premiere of his *Concerto Fantastique* with the Chicago Sym. Orch. In 1992 the judges of the Pulitzer Prize in Music awarded him its prize for this score, but then the Pulitzer Prize board rejected its own judges' decision and denied Shapey the honor. The ensuing scandal did little to enhance the reputation of the Pulitzer Prize in Music. In 1993 Shapey was honored with the Paul Fromm Award. In 1994 he was elected a member of the American Academy of Arts and Sciences. His music employs serialistic but uncongested procedures in acrid counterpoint, while formally adhering to neo-Classical paradigms.

WORKS: DRAMATIC: Opera: *The Quatagonists* (1997). **ORCH.:** *Fantasy for Symphony Orchestra* (1951); Sym. No. 1 (1952); Concerto for Clarinet and Chamber Ensemble (1954; Strasbourg, June 9, 1958); *Challenge—The Family of Man* (1955); *Ontogeny* (1958; Buffalo, May 1, 1965); *Invocation,* concerto for Violin and Orch. (1958; N.Y., May 24, 1968); *Rituals* (1959; Chicago, May 12, 1966); Double Concerto for Violin, Cello, and Orch. (1983; N.Y., Jan. 24, 1984); *Groton: 3 Movements* for Young Orchestra (1984); *Symphonie concertante* (1985); Concerto for Piano, Cello, and String Orch. (1986); *Concerto Fantastique* (1989; Chicago, Nov. 21, 1991); *Stony Brook Concerto* (1996); *Gamper Festival Concerto* (1998). **CHAMBER:** 10 string quartets (1946; 1949; 1950–51; 1953; 1957–58; 1963; 1972; 1993; 1995; 1998); Piano Quintet (1946–47); Violin Sonata (1949–50); Oboe Sonata (1951–52); Quartet for Oboe, Violin, Viola, and Cello (1952); Cello Sonata (1953); Piano Trio (1953–55); *De Profundis* for Double Bass, Piccolo or Flute, Oboe or English Horn, Clarinet or Bassoon, and Clarinet or Alto Saxophone (1960); *Movements* for Woodwind Quintet (1960); Chamber Sym. for 10 Instruments (1962); *Convocation* for Chamber Ensemble (1962); Brass Quintet (1963); String Trio (1965; second movement for Solo Violin as Sonata No. 1, 1972); *Partita* for Violin, 11 Instruments, and 2 Percussion (1966); *Partita-Fantasy* for Cello, 14 Instruments, and Percussion (1966); *3 for 6* for Chamber Ensemble (1979); Concerto Grosso for Woodwind Quintet (1981); *Discourse II* for Violin, Clarinet, Cello, and Piano (1983); *Concertante I* for Trumpet and 10 Performers (1984) and *II* for Alto Saxophone and 14 Performers (1987); *Soli* for Solo Percussion (1985); *Kroslish Sonate* for Cello and Piano (1985); *Variations* for Viola and 9 Performers (1987); *Intermezzo* for Dulcimer and Piano or Celesta (1990); Duo for 2 Wind Players (1991); *Movement of Varied Moments for Two* for Flute and Vibraphone (1991); Trio for Violin, Cello, and Piano (1992); Trio Concertante for Violin, Piano, and Percussion (1992); *Inventions* for Clarient and Percussion (1992); *Dinosaur Annex* for Violin and Vibraphone Marimba (1993); *Constellations for Bang on a Can All-Stars* for Chamber Ensemble (1993); *Rhapsody* for Cello and Piano (1993); *Evocation IV* for Violin, Cello, Piano, and Percussion (1994); *Sonata Appassionata* for Cello and Piano (1995); *Interchange* for Percussion Quartet (1996); *Inter Two (Between Two)* for Percussion Duo (1997); *Solo-Duet-Trio* for Cello and Tape (1998; rev. 1999); *Images* for Oboe, Piano, and Percussion (1998). **KEYBOARD:** Piano and organ pieces. **VOCAL:** Cantata for Soprano, Tenor, Bass, Narrator, Chamber Orch., and Percussion (1951; rev. as String Quartet No. 5, 1957–58); *Soliloquy* for Narrator, String Quartet, and Percussion (1959); *Dimensions* for Soprano and 23 Instruments (1960); *Incantations* for Soprano and 10 Instruments (1961); *Praise,* oratorio for Bass-baritone, Double Chorus, and Chamber Ensemble (1962–71; Chicago, Feb. 28, 1976); *Songs of Eros* for Soprano, Orch., and Tape (1975); *The Covenant* for Soprano, Chamber Orch., and Tape (1977); *Song of Songs I-III* for Soprano, Chamber Orch., and Tape (1979–80); *In Memoriam Paul Fromm* for Soprano, Baritone, and 9 Performers (1987); *Centennial Celebration* for Soprano, Mezzo-soprano, Tenor, Baritone, and 12 Players (1991); *Goethe Songs* for Soprano and Piano (1995); *Celebration* for Soprano, Tenor, Baritone, Bass-baritone, Chorus, Dancers, and Orch. (1997); *Ode a la Cuore* for Bass-baritone, Violin, Viola, Cello, and Piano (1998); *The Voice: The Coming of the Second Flood* for Narrator, Soprano, Mezzo-soprano, Tenor, Bass-baritone, and Chamber Orch. (1999).

BIBL.: P. Finley, *A Catalogue of the Works of R. S.* (Stuyvesant, N.Y., 1997).—NS/LK/DM

Shaporin, Yuri (Alexandrovich), significant Russian composer; b. Glukhov, Ukraine, Nov. 8, 1887; d. Moscow, Dec. 9, 1966. He studied law, and graduated from the Univ. of St. Petersburg in 1912; also studied at the St. Petersburg Cons. with Sokolov (composition), graduating in 1918. He wrote theatrical music in Leningrad, then moved to Moscow in 1936, where he served as a prof. at the Cons. (from 1939). His masterpiece is the opera *The Decembrists,* which occupied him for over 30 years.

WORKS: DRAMATIC: *Polina Gyebl,* opera (1925; rev. and enl. as *The Decembrists,* 1925–53; Moscow, June 23, 1953); about 80 theater scores; much film music. **ORCH.:** *The Flea,* comic suite (1928). **VOCAL:** *On the Field of Kolikovo,* sym.-cantata for Solo Voices, Chorus, and Orch. (1918–39; Moscow, Nov. 18, 1939); Sym. for Chorus, Orch., Band, and Piano (1928–33; Moscow, May 11, 1933); *A Tale of the Battle for the Russian Land,* oratorio for Solo Voices, Chorus, and Orch. (Moscow, April 18, 1944); songs. **Piano:** 2 sonatas (1924, 1926).

BIBL.: E. Grosheva, *Y. S.: i evo oratorii* (Moscow, 1947); idem, *Y.A. S.* (Moscow, 1957); I. Martynov, *Y. S.* (Moscow, 1966). —NS/LK/DM

Sharp, Cecil (James), English folk music collector and editor; b. London, Nov. 22, 1859; d. there, June 23, 1924. He studied mathematics and music at Uppingham and Clare Coll., Cambridge. In 1882 he settled in Adelaide, where he worked in a bank and practiced law, becoming assoc. to the Chief Justice of Southern Australia; in 1889 he resigned from the legal profession and took up a musical career. He was asst. organist of the Adelaide Cathedral, and co-director of the Adelaide Coll. of Music. In 1892 he returned to England; was music instructor of Ludgrove School (1893–1910) and principal of the Hampstead Cons. (1896–1905). At the same time, he became deeply interested in English folk songs; publ. a *Book of British Songs for Home and School* (1902); then proceeded to make a systematic survey of English villages with the aim of collecting authentic specimens of English songs. In 1911 he established the English Folk Dance Society; also was director of the School of Folk Song and Dance at Stratford-upon-Avon. During World War I he was in the U.S., collecting folk music in the Appalachian Mountains, with a view to establishing their English origin. In 1923 he received the degree of M.M. honoris causa from the Univ. of Cambridge. In 1930 the "Cecil Sharp House" was opened in London as headquarters of the English Folk Dance Soc. (amalgamated with the Folk Song Soc. in 1932).

WRITINGS (all publ. in London): *English Folk-song: Some Conclusions* (1907; second ed., 1936; fourth ed., 1965, by M. Karpeles); *Folk-singing in Schools* (1912); *Folk-dancing in Elementary and Secondary Schools* (1912); with A. Oppe, *The Dance: An Historical Survey of Dancing in Europe* (1924). **FOLKSONG EDITIONS** (all publ. in London): *Folk Songs from Somerset* (1904–09); with S. Baring-Gould et al., *Songs of the West* (1905); with S. Baring-Gould, *English Folk Songs for Schools* (1905); with H. MacIlwaine and G. Butterworth, *The Morris Book* (1907–13); with G. Butterworth, *Morris Dance Tunes* (1907–24); with G. Butterworth and M. Karpeles, *The Country Dance Book* (1909–22); *Country Dance Tunes* (1909–22); *English Folk-carols* (1911); *The Sword Dances of Northern England* (1911–13; second ed., 1950–51, by M. Karpeles); with O. Campbell, *English Folk-songs from the Southern Appalachians* (1917; second ed., 1932; third ed., 1960, by M. Karpeles); *Folk-songs of English Origin Collected in the Appalachian Mountains* (1919–21); M. Karpeles, ed., *Cecil Sharp's Collection of English Folk Songs* (1973).

BIBL.: A. Fox Strangways and M. Karpeles, *C. S.* (London, 1933; second ed., 1955; rev. by Karpeles as *C. S.: His Life and Work*, 1967).—**NS/LK/DM**

Sharp, Elliott, American electric guitarist and composer; b. Cleveland, March 1, 1951. He studied anthropology at Cornell Univ. (1969–71), then took degrees in music at Bard Coll. (B.A., 1973), where he studied ethnomusicology with Roswell Rudd and composition with Elie Yarden and Boretz, and at the State Univ. of N.Y. at Buffalo (M.A., 1977), where he studied ethnomusicology with Charles Keil and composition with Hiller. In 1980 he formed Carbon, one of N.Y.'s most innovative "downtown" ensembles; in late 1989 its flexible instrumentation included, in addition to electric harp, keyboards, and drums, "slabs"—homemade instruments made of wood and long metal strips that produce both ethereal harmonics and percussive sounds when struck with drumsticks. Since he is well versed in both science and physics, Sharp employs mathematical formulas and relationships in his works; he tends toward micro-rhythms, what he calls "layers of resonating rhythms that groove hard and cause a certain type of turbulence," which led one reviewer to describe his music as "urban rāgas." His musical aims are often political; some works utilize sampled voices of politicians, while Sharp sees the flexible organization and improvisatory performance style of Carbon itself as an implicit expression of his own social and political ideas.

WORKS: *Innosense* for 3 Musicians and Tapes (N.Y., Oct. 22, 1981); *Crowds and Power* for 21 Musicians (N.Y., Oct. 15, 1982); *Haka* for 4 Musicians (Washington, D.C., Oct. 12, 1983); *Marco Polo's Argali* for 10 Musicians (N.Y., March 1, 1985); *Sili/Contemp/Tation* for 3 Musicians (N.Y., April 4, 1986); *Self-Squared Dragon* for 9 Musicians (Zürich, Feb. 5, 1986); *Re/Iterations* for Orch. (N.Y., June 23, 1986); *Tessalation Row* for String Quartet (N.Y., July 11, 1986); *20 Below* for 6 Keyboards (N.Y., April 1, 1987); *Mansereel* for 4 Musicians (Philadelphia, Oct. 2, 1987); *Larynx* for 13 Musicians (N.Y., Nov. 13, 1987); *Hammer Anvil Stirrup* for String Quartet (Pori, Finland, July 15, 1988); *Jump Cut* for 4 Musicians (Troy, N.Y., Dec. 5, 1988); *Ferrous* for 5 Musicians (N.Y., Nov. 30, 1989); *Deception* for 6 Musicians and Film (N.Y., Feb. 8, 1990).—**NS/LK/DM**

Sharrock, Sonny (Warren Harding), avant-garde guitarist; b. Ossining, N.Y., Aug. 27, 1940; d. there, May 26, 1994. He was self-taught on guitar. He studied at Berklee when he was 21, took four months of composition, then left in 1962. He played bebop in Calif., then moved to N.Y. in 1965. He studied with Sun Ra and began playing with Olatunji, after being invited by Pat Patrick and other Sun Ra members who were in the group. Sharrock worked with Byard Lancaster, a Berklee classmate, who came to N.Y. at about the same time. In 1966 Sharrock also worked with Dave Burrell, Frank Wright, and Sunny Murray. Late in the year, he played a Sunday afternoon concert with Lancaster in Philadelphia. Pharoah Sanders sat in, then asked him to

join his band the next night in N.Y. and to record with him later that week. Sharrock achieved his greatest notoriety as a member of various groups led by Herbie Mann from 1967–73. With Mann, he cut a striking figure, wearing a long robe and waving his arms flamboyantly while he soloed. He formed his own group in 1973, and did some tours and recording with his wife Lynda. He joined the group Last Exit in 1985, with whom he toured extensively (including Europe), and then made both avant-garde and rock/R&B releases as a leader. He died of a heart attack while exercising.

Sharrock was extremely influential in jazz/rock circles where he is best known for his work with Sanders and for his remarkable solo albums. It is said that he made the remark that when playing in concert he wanted "the first three rows to bleed from the ears." He also did music for *Space Ghost Coast to Coast* on the Cartoon Network.

His wife Lynda (Linda Chambers) (b. Philadelphia, Pa., April 3, 1947) sang with him in his 1960s-era groups and when he was a member of Herbie Mann's group.

DISC.: *Black Woman* (1969); *Paradise* (1975); *Last Exit* (1986); *Guitar* (1986); *Seize the Rainbow* (1987); *Faith Moves* (1989); *Live in N.Y.* (1989); *Highlife* (1990); *Ask the Ages* (1991). **P. SANDERS:** *Tauhid* (1966).—**LP**

Sharrow, Leonard, noted American bassoonist and pedagogue; b. N.Y., Aug. 4, 1915. He studied at the Inst. of Musical Art in N.Y. (1932–35). He was first bassoonist in the National Sym. Orch. in Washington, D.C. (1935–37), then played in the NBC Sym. Orch. in N.Y. (1937–41); subsequently was first bassoonist in the Buffalo Phil. (1946), Detroit Sym. Orch. (1946–47), NBC Sym. Orch. (1947–51), Chicago Sym. Orch. (1951–64), and Pittsburgh Sym. Orch. (1977–87). He taught at the Juilliard School of Music in N.Y. (1948–51), Roosevelt Coll. in Chicago (1952–55), the Ind. Univ. School of Music in Bloomington (1964–77), the Aspen (Colo.) Music School (from 1967), and the New England Cons. of Music in Boston (1986–89). He also toured as a bassoon virtuoso and chamber music player. As a teacher, he was mentor to several generations of bassoonists. He publ. eds. of works by Corelli, Vivaldi, Handel, Boismortier, Weber, Hummel, J.A. Koželuh et al.—**NS/LK/DM**

Shaughnessy, Ed(win Thomas), jazz drummer, composer; b. Jersey City, N.J., Jan. 29, 1929. In the late 1940s, he used two bass drums with Charlie Ventura's Bop for the People band and also played with Charlie Parker. He worked with Duke Ellington for six weeks while Louis Bellson and Pearl Bailey went on honeymoon and also played with Charles Mingus, Teddy Charles, Booker Little, Gary McFarland, Gil Evans, and Oliver Nelson, among others. In the 1960s, he began doing studio work in N.Y. He was featured for many years in the *Tonight Show* band.

DISC.: *Jazz in the Pocket* (1990).—**LP**

Shavers, Charlie (actually, **Charles James**), bravura jazz trumpeter, arranger, singer, composer; b. N.Y., Aug. 3, 1917; d. there, Aug. 8, 1971. The son of a trumpet player, Shavers was a distant relative of trumpeter Fats Navarro. He began playing piano and banjo, then switched to trumpet. He played occasionally with pianist Willie Gant in N.Y. He also played with Tiny Bradshaw (1936) and Lucky Millinder (early 1937). In November 1937, Shavers joined John Kirby at the Onyx Club (replacing Frankie Newton). He soon became the sextet's principal arranger and, while with the group, composed such hits as "Pastel Blue," which became "Why Begin Again" with words, and "Undecided," a hit (with words by Sid Robin) for Ella Fitzgerald and the Ames Brothers. He finally left John Kirby in 1944, doubling with Raymond Scott at CBS during his last year. In February 1945 Shavers first joined Tommy Dorsey; for the next 11 years he left and rejoined the band many times. During the mid-1940s and 1950s, he occasionally reunited with Kirby for performances and recordings. He also made several tours with Norman Granz's *Jazz at the Philharmonic*, including trips to Europe. Shavers also worked with Benny Goodman for several months beginning in July 1954. He made a notable appearance on the Art Ford TV show in 1958 as director of a jam session featuring Coleman Hawkins and Lester Young.

During the 1960s, Shavers regularly led his own quartet in N.Y. clubs. He worked for years with a Dorsey ghost band fronted by Sam Donahue and visited Europe with this unit in 1964. Beginning in 1965, the ghost band became the Frank Sinatra Jr. touring show. Featured as a vocalist and player, Shavers went on tours to Japan, Vietnam, Hong Kong, Canada, and South America. He also did a wide variety of recorded work. In late 1969 and again during 1970, Shavers toured Europe (including Britain) as a soloist. He continued to perform in N.Y. until a few months before his death from throat cancer.

DISC.: *Like Charlie* (1960); *Excitement Unlimited* (1963); *Live* (1970).—JC/LP

Shaw (real name, Shukotoff), Arnold,

American composer, writer, editor, lecturer, and music executive; b. N.Y., June 28, 1909; d. Las Vegas, Sept. 26, 1989. He was of Russian-Jewish descent. He majored in English literature at the City Coll. of N.Y. (B.S., 1929) and Columbia Univ. (M.A., 1931). In his college years he was a campus radical, active particularly in the Anti-Fascist Assn. of the Staffs of the City Coll. As such, he was listed as "subversive" by some right-wing political organizations. He made a living by composing and teaching music at the New School for Social Research in N.Y., the Univ. of Calif. at Los Angeles, and the Univ. of Nev. in Reno and Las Vegas, where in 1985 he founded the Popular Music Research Center. In order to protect himself against would-be political factions, he changed his name from the Russian-sounding Shukotoff to the more common name Shaw. Among the various positions he occupied was that of music executive with the Dutchess Music Corp. (1950–53), Hill and Range Songs (1953–55), and the Edward B. Marks Music Corp. (1955–66); at these companies he promoted such popular singers as Rod McKuen, Burt Bacharach, and Elvis Presley. He wrote numerous articles and books, and

received the ASCAP- Deems Taylor Award (1968, 1979). He ed., with L. Dowling, *The Schillinger System of Musical Composition* (N.Y., 1941; fourth ed., 1946), and publ. a novel, *The Money Song* (N.Y., 1953). His compositions include the musical *They Had a Dream* (1976), some snappy piano pieces, and songs.

WRITINGS (all publ. in N.Y.): Ed. with L. Dowling, *The Schillinger System of Musical Composition* (1941; fourth ed., 1946); *Lingo of Tin Pan Alley* (1950) *Belafonte: An Unauthorized Biography* (1960); *Sinatra: Twentieth-Century Romantic* (1968); *The Rock Revolution* (1969); *The World of Soul: Black America's Contribution to the Pop Music Scene* (1970); *The Street That Never Slept: New York's Fabled 52nd Street* (1971; reprint, 1977, as *52nd Street, the Street of Jazz*); *The Rockin' 50s: The Decade That Transformed the Pop Music Scene* (1974); *Honkers and Shouters: The Golden Years of Rhythm and Blues* (1978); *Dictionary of American Pop Rock: From Blue Suede Shoes to Blondie* (1982); *Sinatra, the Entertainer* (1982). —NS/LK/DM

Shaw, Artie (originally, Arshawsky, Arthur Jacob),

American bandleader, clarinetist, and songwriter; b. N.Y., May 23, 1910. Shaw was among the most successful bandleaders of the Swing Era as well as an accomplished clarinetist. Musically restless and temperamentally unsuited to the demands of being an entertainer, he formed and dissolved orchestras frequently, then retired permanently less than 20 years after his debut as a leader. But in the late 1930s and 1940s he repeatedly placed among the top recording and performing artists in the U.S., his major hits including "Begin the Beguine," "Frenesi," and "Star Dust."

Shaw's father, Harry Arshawsky, was a photographer; his mother, Sarah Strauss Arshawsky, was a seamstress. The family moved to New Haven, Conn., in 1916, and Shaw took up the ukulele at age ten, changing to saxophone by the age of 12. At 15 he dropped out of high school to play professionally and by the summer of 1925 was in a band led by Johnny Cavallaro that toured as far south as Fla. By 1926 he had switched to clarinet and moved to Cleveland, where he worked in the band led by violinist Austin Wylie. After three years he joined Irving Aaronson's Commanders, then moved to N.Y., where he established himself during the early 1930s as a successful studio musician.

As early as the mid-1930s, Shaw doubted that he wanted to pursue a permanent career as a musician, also considering farming and writing as professions. But in May 1936 he made a sensational appearance at a Swing concert at the Imperial Theater in N.Y., leading a band that featured a string quartet, and he was offered the financial backing to form his own orchestra. This he did, and Art Shaw and His New Music, including the string section, made its first recordings for Brunswick on June 11, 1936, and appeared at the Lexington Hotel in N.Y.

The band struggled until March 1937, when Shaw broke it up and, in April, formed a more conventional 14-piece Swing band on the formula of more successful rivals such as Benny Goodman and Tommy Dorsey. It took a while even for this unit to catch on, but Shaw reached the hit parade for nine weeks starting in February 1938 with "Goodnight, Angel" (music by Allie

Wrubel, lyrics by Herb Magidson). Though it did not reach the hit parade, Shaw's debut single for RCA Victor's Bluebird label, "Begin the Beguine" (music and lyrics by Cole Porter)/"Indian Love Call" (music by Rudolf Friml, lyrics by Otto Harbach and Oscar Hammerstein II), recorded July 24 and released in August, became a massive hit, one of the first million-selling records since the onset of the Depression.

Shaw's increasing prominence led to a major N.Y. booking at the Hotel Lincoln, beginning Oct. 26, and a feature on the nationally broadcast radio series *Melody and Madness*, beginning Nov. 20. In December, "Deep in a Dream" (music by James Van Heusen, lyrics by Eddie DeLange) began a 14-week run in the hit parade, followed by "They Say" (music by Paul Mann and Stephan Weiss, lyrics by Edward Heyman) and "Thanks for Everything" (music by Harry Revel, lyrics by Al Dubin), both of which entered the chart in January 1939. "I Poured My Heart into a Song" (music and lyrics by Irving Berlin) had nine weeks in the hit parade starting in July; "Comes Love" (music and lyrics by Sam H. Stept, Charles Tobias, and Lew Brown) was listed for seven weeks starting in August; and "Melancholy Mood" (music and lyrics by Vick Knight) was in the listings in October. November saw the release of the first film featuring Shaw and his band, *Dancing Co-Ed*, for which he wrote the music.

Shaw was absent from the bandstand periodically due to illness during 1939, and on Nov. 18 he suddenly walked out on the band, his radio program, and an engagement at the Pennsylvania Hotel in N.Y., moving to Mexico for a couple of months. By January 1940, however, he was in Hollywood filming another motion picture, *Second Chorus*. Shaw had been married twice by this time. His first marriage, to Jane Carns, was annulled; his second, to Margaret Allen, a nurse, ended in divorce. On Feb. 13, 1940, he married film actress Lana (Julia Jean Mildred Frances) Turner; they divorced on Sept. 12, 1941.

Shaw returned to recording with a studio orchestra in March, and on July 1 began accompanying comedians George Burns and Gracie Allen on their radio show. He organized a new touring band again using strings and debuted with it in San Francisco on Sept. 12. By then his March recording of a song he had heard in Mexico, "Frenesi" (music by Alberto Dominguez), was in release; it topped the charts in December, becoming the second-biggest hit of 1940, outdistanced only by Glenn Miller's "In the Mood." In January *Second Chorus* was released, and from its score "The Love of My Life" (lyrics by Johnny Mercer) earned Shaw an Academy Award nomination. That same month his instrumental recording of "Star Dust" (music by Hoagy Carmichael, lyrics by Mitchell Parish) entered the Top Ten on its way to selling a million copies, followed in February by another million-seller, "Summit Ridge Drive" (music by Shaw), on which Shaw was accompanied by his small group, The Gramercy 5, and the Top Ten hit "Concerto for Clarinet" (music by Shaw) from *Second Chorus*. In March he made the Top Ten with the hit instrumental "Dancing in the Dark" (music by Arthur Schwartz, lyrics by Howard Dietz).

Notwithstanding this success, Shaw again disbanded and moved to N.Y., where he studied orchestration with Hans Burns. By September, however, he had again reorganized and launched Artie Shaw and His Symphonic Swing, scoring a Top Ten hit in January 1942 with "Blues in the Night" (music by Harold Arlen, lyrics by Johnny Mercer). With U.S. entry into World War II, Shaw disbanded and enlisted in the navy, organizing a service band that played in the Pacific combat zone. Discharged in 1944, he married Elizabeth Kern, daughter of composer Jerome Kern; they had a son but divorced in 1945.

Shaw reorganized his band in the fall of 1944 and scored Top Ten hits with "It Had to Be You" (music by Isham Jones, lyrics by Gus Kahn; a reissue of his 1938 recording) in November and "Ac-Cent-Tchu-Ate the Positive" (music by Harold Arlen, lyrics by Johnny Mercer) in February 1945. His album *Artie Shaw* was a Top Ten hit in July.

Shaw married film actress Ava Gardner on Oct. 17, 1945. Upon their divorce in October 1946 he married novelist Kathleen Windsor, author of *Forever Amber*; this marriage ended in divorce in 1949. Leaving RCA Victor, Shaw recorded for Musicraft Records in 1946 with a band that featured vocalist Mel Tormé, but he again disbanded and was inactive in music until the spring of 1949, when he formed a new band that leaned toward bebop. By September he was leading a more conventional big band again, but it proved short-lived. Signed to Decca Records, he scored two Top Ten records in 1950, one co-billed with singer Dick Haymes, "Count Every Star" (music by Bruno Coquatrix, lyrics by Sammy Gallop) in August, the other co-billed with orchestra leader Gordon Jenkins, "I'm Forever Blowing Bubbles" (music by John W. Kellette, lyrics by Jean Kenbrovin), in October.

In May 1952, Shaw published *The Trouble with Cinderella*, a ponderous autobiography that detailed his ambivalence about the music business and popular success. On June 12 he married for the seventh time, to Doris Dowling; they had a son and divorced in 1956. He re-formed the Gramercy 5 in October 1953 and toured with it into 1954 before breaking it up to run a dairy farm. He returned to perform with a big band briefly in 1955, then left music for good, moving to Gerona, Spain. In 1956 he married film actress Evelyn Keyes; they formally divorced in the early 1980s, having separated long before.

Shaw returned to the U.S. in 1960. He owned a gun manufacturing company, ran a film distribution and production company, lectured at universities, attempted to produce a stage adaptation of F. Scott Fitzgerald's novel *The Great Gatsby*, and wrote fiction. In 1983 he allowed an Artie Shaw Orch. to be formed under the direction of Dick Johnson and made appearances with the band, though he did not play.

WRITINGS: *Three Variations on a Theme, A Clarinet Method; The Trouble with Cinderella (An Outline of Identity)* (autobiography; N.Y., 1952); *I Love You, I Hate You, Drop Dead!* (fiction; 1965); *The Best of Intentions and Other Stories* (fiction; Santa Barbara, 1989).

BIBL.: E. Blandford, *A. S.: A Bio-Discography* (Hastings, England, 1974); B. Korst and C. Garrod, *A. S. and His Orch.* (Spotswood, N. J., 1974; rev. ed. Zephyrhills, Fla., 1986).—WR

Shaw, Charles "Bobo", free-jazz drummer, leader; b. Pope, Miss., Sept. 15, 1947. He studied drums with Joe Charles, Ben Thigpen Sr., Lige Shaw, Charles Payne, and Rich O'Donnell. He played trombone briefly, and played bass with Frank Mokuss. He played drums with Oliver Sain, Julius Hemphill, Ike and Tina Turner, Oliver Lake, Roland Hanna, Ron Carter, Elvin Jones, Albert King, Reggie Workman, Art Blakey, and the St. Louis Symphony Orch. He co-founded the Black Artists' Group (BAG), toured Europe with them for a year in the late 1960s, and played free jazz in Paris for a year with Anthony Braxton, Steve Lacy, Frank Wright, Alan Silva, and Michel Portal. Shaw returned to St. Louis in the 1970s and recorded there with Oliver Lake (1971). He led the Red, Black & Green Solidarity Unit and Human Arts Ensemble in the mid-1970s, recording with Lester and Joseph Bowie, Julius Hemphill, Lake and others. After touring with the Human Arts Ensemble in Europe during the late 1970s, Shaw recorded with Billy Bang in the mid-1980s.

DISC.: *Bugle Boy Bop* (1977); *P'nkj'zz* (1981); *Junk Trap* (1997). **HUMAN ARTS ENSEMBLE:** *Whisper of Dharma* (1972); *Under the Sun* (1973).—LP

Shaw, Geoffrey (Turton), English organist, music educator, and composer, brother of **Martin (Edward Fallas) Shaw;** b. London, Nov. 14, 1879; d. there, April 14, 1943. He was a chorister at St. Paul's Cathedral in London and studied at Gonville and Caius Coll., Cambridge (B.A., 1901; Mus.B., 1902). From 1902 to 1910 he was music master at Gresham's School, Holt. In 1920 he was named his brother's successor as organist at St. Mary's, Primrose Hill, London. He also served as inspector of music to the Board of Education from 1928 until his retirement in 1942. In 1932 he was awarded the honorary Lambeth degree of D.Mus. In 1947 the Geoffrey Shaw Memorial Fund was established to assist musically talented children. He composed a ballet, *All at Sea*, orch. works, and chamber pieces.—NS/LK/DM

Shaw, George Bernard, famous Irish dramatist; b. Dublin, July 26, 1856; d. Ayot St. Lawrence, England, Nov. 2, 1950. Before winning fame as a playwright, he was active as a music critic in London, writing for the *Star* under the name of "Corno di Bassetto" (1888–89) and for the *World* (1890–94). In 1899 he publ. *The Perfect Wagnerite*, a highly individual socialistic interpretation of the *Ring of the Nibelung*. His criticisms from the *World* were reprinted as *Music in London* (3 vols., 1932; new ed., 1950); those from the *Star* as *London Music in 1888–89* (London and N.Y., 1937); selected criticisms were ed. by E. Bentley (N.Y., 1954). Shaw's play *Arms and the Man* was made into an operetta, *The Chocolate Soldier*, by Oskar Straus (1908); his *Pygmalion* was converted into a highly successful musical comedy under the title *My Fair Lady*, with a musical score by Frederick Loewe (1956).—NS/LK/DM

Shaw, (Harold) Watkins, English musicologist and teacher; b. Bradford, April 3, 1911. He studied history at Wadham Coll., Oxford (B.A., 1932), then took courses in musicology with Colles and R.O. Morris at the Royal Coll. of Music in London (1932–33); received the D.Litt in the faculty of music from the Univ. of Oxford (1967). In 1949 he was appointed lecturer at the Worcester Coll. of Education; from 1971 until his retirement in 1980, he served as keeper of the Parry Room Library at the Royal Coll. of Music. In 1985 he was made an Officer of the Order of the British Empire. Among his publs. are *The Three Choirs Festival, c. 1713–1953* (1954), *The Story of Handel's "Messiah," 1741–1784* (London, 1963), *A Textual and Historical Companion to Handel's "Messiah"* (London, 1965), *The Organists and Organs of Hereford Cathedral* (Hereford, 1976), and *The Succession of Organists of the Chapel Royal and the Cathedrals of England and Wales from c. 1538: Also of the Organists of the Collegiate Churches of Westminster and Windsor, Certain Academic Choral Foundations, and the Cathedrals of Armagh and Dublin* (Oxford, 1991). He also ed. *Sir Frederick Ouseley and St Michael's, Tenbury* (Birmingham, 1988). —NS/LK/DM

Shaw, Lige (Elijah W.), jazz drummer, percussionist; b. Jackson, Tenn., Sept. 9, 1900; d. St. Louis, Mo., 1982. He worked as a tap dancer at age 11; moved to Memphis in 1914, worked at mechanical dentistry, and began gigging on drums. From fall 1917 through mid-1921, he toured with various "minstrel" troups as a band member; from 1922, he worked mostly in St. Louis, including five years as a house musician at a local theater from 1924–29. He was working out of Miss. for two years beginning in 1929, and then returned to St. Louis. He worked with various local bands, including trumpeter Walter 'Crack' Stanley (1932) and Charlie Creath (1933–34). Shaw continued to work in St. Louis regularly throughout the late 1930s, and served a long term as president of the local musicians' union. He recommended touring in 1941 with the Ringling Brothers' Circus Band, but was back in St. Louis two years later, where he worked clubs and resumed his duties in the musicians' union (remaining its president until 1957). During the 1950s, he worked regularly with Singleton Palmer in clubs and on recording. He also opened his own piano tuning and repair service, and worked on local riverboats.—JC/LP

Shaw, Martin (Edward Fallas), English organist and composer, brother of **Geoffrey (Turton) Shaw;** b. London, March 9, 1875; d. Southwold, Sussex, Oct. 24, 1958. He was a pupil at the Royal Coll. of Music in London, and played organ in various churches in London. In 1900 he founded the Purcell Operatic Society in London. He was made an Officer of the Order of the British Empire in 1955. He composed the operas *Mr. Pepys* (London, Feb. 11, 1926) and *The Thorn of Avalon* (1931); also incidental music; sacred works; some 100 songs; etc. He publ. *The Principles of English Church Music Composition* (London, 1921) and *Up to Now* (autobiography; London, 1929). Among his eds., all publ. in London, are *Songs of Britain* (with F. Kidson; 1913), *The English Carol Book* (with P. Dearmer; 1913–19), *The League of Nations Song Book* (with P. Dearmer; 1921), *Songs of Praise* (with P. Dearmer and R. Vaughan Williams; 1925;

second ed., aug., 1931), and *The Oxford Book of Carols* (1928; 25th ed., rev., 1964).

BIBL.: E. Routley, *M. S.: A Centenary Appreciation* (London, 1975).—NS/LK/DM

Shaw, Mary (née **Postans**), English contralto; b. Lea, Kent, 1814; d. Hadleigh Hall, Suffolk, Sept. 9, 1876. She studied at the Royal Academy of Music in London (1828–31), and then with Sir George Smart. Under the name Mary Postans, she made a successful debut in London (1834); the next year she married the painter Alfred Shaw and thereafter appeared as Mary Shaw. In 1838 she sang with the Leipzig Gewandhaus Orch. under Mendelssohn's direction; her operatic debut followed as Imelda in the premiere of Verdi's first opera, *Oberto, conte di San Bonifacio*, at Milan's La Scala (Nov. 17, 1839); in 1842 she sang at London's Covent Garden and at Drury Lane. In 1844, at the height of her success, her husband went insane; the shock affected her vocal cords, so that she was unable to sing. Some time later she remarried and went to live in the country. —NS/LK/DM

Shaw, Oliver, blind American organist, tenor, teacher, and composer; b. Middleboro, Mass., March 13, 1779; d. Providence, R.I., Dec. 31, 1848. He lost his eyesight in an accident. About 1800 he began taking music lessons with John Berkenhead, Gottlieb Graupner, and Thomas Granger. After teaching piano and organ in Dedham, Mass. (1805–07), he settled in Providence. He was organist at the First Congregational Church (1809–32), and a founder of the Psallonian Society in 1809, remaining its director until it was disbanded in 1833. He was a composer of popular psalm tunes and ballads, including *Mary's Tears, The Inspiration, Sweet Little Ann,* and *The Death of Perry.* He publ. the manuals *A Plain Introduction to the Art of Playing the Pianoforte* (1811) and *O. Shaw's Instructions for the Pianoforte* (1831).

BIBL.: T. Williams, *A Discourse on the Life and Death of O. S.* (Boston, 1851); F. Denison, A. Stanley, and E. Glezen, eds., *Memorial of O. S.* (Providence, R.I., 1884); B. Degen, *O. S.: His Music and Contribution to American Society* (diss., Univ. of Rochester, 1971).—NS/LK/DM

Shaw, Robert (Lawson), renowned American conductor; b. Red Bluff, Calif., April 30, 1916; d. New Haven, Conn., Jan. 25, 1999. He came from a clerical family; his father and his grandfather were clergymen; his mother sang in church choirs. He studied at Pomona Coll. (1934–38), where he conducted its Glee Club. In 1938 Fred Waring asked him to help organize the Fred Waring Glee Club, and Shaw conducted it until 1945. In 1941 he founded his own Collegiate Chorale in N.Y., which he led in diversified programs of choral music, old and new, until 1954. In 1944 he was awarded a Guggenheim fellowship. He taught choral conducting at the Berkshire Music Center at Tanglewood (summers, 1946–48), and concurrently at the Juilliard School of Music in N.Y. In 1946 he made his debut as a sym. conductor with the Naumburg Orch. in N.Y. In 1948 he founded the Robert Shaw Chorale, which he conducted

with notable success for 20 seasons. Eager to acquire more experience as an orch. conductor, he studied conducting with Monteux in San Francisco and Rodzinski in N.Y. in 1950. From 1953 to 1958 he conducted summer concerts of the San Diego Sym. Orch. In 1956 he led the Robert Shaw Chorale through a tour of 15 countries of Europe, including Russia, and the Middle East, under the auspices of the State Dept. In 1964 the Robert Shaw Chorale gave concerts in South America. For his Chorale, Shaw commissioned several choral works from contemporary composers, including Bartók, Milhaud, Britten, Barber, and Copland. Beginning in 1956 he was co-director of the Alaska Festival of Music in Anchorage. From 1956 to 1967 he served as assoc. conductor with Szell and the Cleveland Orch. In 1967 he became music director of the Atlanta Sym. Orch., and by dint of talent and perseverance brought it to a high degree of excellence. In 1977 he conducted it at the gala concert for President Carter's inauguration in Washington, D.C., and in 1988 he took it to Europe. After retiring from his post in 1988, he was accorded the titles of music director emeritus and conductor laureate. He then was active as director of the new inst. named in his honor at Emory Univ. In 1991 he received a Kennedy Center Honor. In 1992 President Bush awarded him the National Medal of Arts. He received the Theodore Thomas Award of the Conductors' Guild in 1993. In 1995 he took part as both conductor and reciter in the 50th anniversary concert of the Atlanta Sym. Orch. in a program later telecast to the nation by PBS. While Shaw eventually won respect as a sym. conductor, it was as a master of the choral repertoire that he attained international distinction. For more than half a century he was America's preeminent choral conductor. His 13 Grammy Awards and numerous honorary doctorates attest to the unbounded esteem and admiration he was accorded during his remarkable career.

BIBL.: J. Mussulman, *Dear People...R. S.: A Biography* (Bloomington, Ind. and London, 1979).—NS/LK/DM

Shaw, Woody (Herman II), well-known jazz trumpeter, flugelhornist, composer; b. Laurinburg, N.C., Dec. 24, 1944; d. N.Y. May 10, 1989. He was raised in Newark, N.J. from his early years, where his father led a gospel group. His first big gig was at the Club Coronet in Brooklyn with Willie Bobo's band, which included Chick Corea and Joe Farrell. He met Eric Dolphy there and made his first recordings with him in 1963, already expressing a striking voice as a player and writer. He spent time in Europe, where he played with Bud Powell, Johnny Griffin, and Kenny Clarke, among others. When he returned, he performed with Horace Silver, Corea, and for a short time with Art Blakey. Shaw's heroin addiction led to health problems; complications from diabetes made him nearly blind (he always wore thick glasses). He finally lost his sight to degenerative eye disease and fell from a subway platform into a train's path on Feb. 27, 1989. He lost an arm and was in a coma at Bellevue Hospital until he died.

DISC.: *In the Beginning...* (1965); *Blackstone Legacy* (1970); *Song of Songs* (1972); *Moontrane* (1974); *Love Dance* (1975); *Red's Fantasy* (1976); *Cassandranite* (1976); *Rosewood* (1977); *Iron Men* (1977); *Complete CBS Studio Recordings* (1977); *Woody III* (1978);

Stepping Stones (1978); *United* (1981); *Night Music* (1982); *Master of the Art* (1982); *Lotus Flower* (1982); *Time Is Right* (1983); *Setting Standards* (1983); *Solid* (1986); *Double Take* (1986).

BIBL.: D. Carley, *W. S.: Jazz Trumpet Solos* (Winona, Minn., 1989).—**LP**

Shawe-Taylor, Desmond (Christopher),

eminent Irish music critic; b. Dublin, May 29, 1907; d. Long Crichel, Dorset, Nov. 1, 1995. He was educated at Oriel Coll., Oxford (1926–30). Through the years he contributed literary and musical criticism to various newspapers and periodicals. After service in World War II, he was engaged as music critic of the New Statesman in 1945, retaining his post until 1958; from 1950 to 1958 he also served as phonograph record reviewer for the *Observer*. In 1958 he was named music critic of the *Sunday Times*; he retired in 1983; also was a guest critic for the *New Yorker* (1973–74). He was made a Commander of the Order of the British Empire in 1965. His writings are notable for their unostentatious display of wide learning. He publ. the vol. *Covent Garden for the World of Music Series* (London, 1948); also, with Edward Sackville-West, *The Record Guide* (London, 1951, and later rev. eds.). He contributed a number of insightful biographies of singers to *The New Grove Dictionary of Music and Musicians* (1980).—**NS/LK/DM**

Shchedrin, Rodion (Konstantinovich), bril-

liant Russian composer; b. Moscow, Dec. 16, 1932. His father was a music theorist and writer. After piano lessons in childhood, he attended the music and then choral schools (1948–51) attached to the Moscow Cons. He subsequently took courses in piano with Yakov Flier and composition with Yuri Shaporin at the Cons. (1951–55), where he subsequently taught (1965–69). Following graduation, he achieved great recognition within the accepted Soviet establishment. He also wrote about current trends in Soviet music in official publications, and held several significant posts within the Composer's Union, including chairman of the Russian Federation section (from 1974). Shchedrin received many awards, and was made a People's Artist of the U.S.S.R. (1981). In 1989 he was elected to membership in the Akademie der Künste in Berlin. His music has wide appeal, artfully employing numerous pseudo-modernistic devices; particularly interesting among his compositions are the aleatoric second Sym., the prepared encore for the first Piano Concerto, and his ballets *Anna Karenina* and *Carmen Suite*, which incorporate music by earlier composers (Tchaikovsky and Bizet, respectively). He was married to the ballerina Maya Plisetskaya, for whom he wrote several ballets.

WORKS (all first perf. in Moscow unless otherwise given): **DRAMATIC: O p e r a :** *Not for Love Alone* (Dec. 25, 1961; also for Chamber Orch., 1971); *Dead Souls*, after Gogol (1976; June 7, 1977); *Lolita* (1994). **B a l l e t :** *The Little Humpback Horse* (1955; March 4, 1960); *Carmen Suite* (April 20, 1967); *Anna Karenina* (1971; June 10, 1972); *The Seagull* (1979; rev. 1980). **OTHER:** Incidental music to plays; film scores. **ORCH.:** 5 piano concertos: No. 1 (Nov. 7, 1954; rev. version, May 5, 1974), No. 2 (1966; Jan. 5, 1967), No. 3, *Theme and Variations* (1973; May 5, 1974), No. 4, *Sharp Keys* (1991; Washington, D.C., June 11,

1992), and No. 5 (Los Angeles, Oct. 21, 1999); 2 suites from *The Little Humpback Horse* (1955, 1965); 2 syms.: No. 1 (Dec. 6, 1958) and No. 2, *25 Preludes* (April 11, 1965); 5 concertos: No. 1, *Naughty Limericks* (Nov. 17, 1963), No. 2, *The Chimes* (1968; Leningrad, Dec. 24, 1973), No. 3, *Old Russian Circus Music* (1988; Chicago, Oct. 25, 1990), No. 4, *Khorovody* (Round Dances; Tokyo, Nov. 2, 1989), and No. 5, *Four Russian Songs* (1998); Suite from *Not for Love Alone* (1964); *Symphonic Fanfares*, festive overture (Nov. 6, 1967); *Anna Karenina*, Romantic music (Oct. 24, 1972); *The Nursery*, transcription of Mussorgsky's song cycle (Stockholm, March 5, 1972); *Solemn Overture* (Dec. 1982); *Self-Portrait* (1984); *Music for the Town of Kothen* for Chamber Orch. (1985); *Music* for Strings, Oboes, Horns, and Celesta (1986); *Geometry of Sound* for 18 Soloists (Cologne, April 28, 1987); *Sotte voce*, cello concerto (London, Nov. 8, 1994); *Kristallene Gusli* (Nov. 21, 1994); *Concerto cantabile* for Violin and Strings (1998). **CHAMBER:** 2 string quartets (1951, 1954); Suite for Clarinet and Piano (1951); Piano Quintet (1952); Chamber Suite for 20 Violins, Harp, Accordion, and 2 Double Basses (1961); *The Frescoes of Dionysus* for Nonet (1981); *Musical Offering* for Organ, 3 Flutes, 3 Bassoons, and 3 Trombones (Oct. 21, 1983); *Musical Offering* for Organ and Wind Instruments (1985); *Echo Sonata* for Solo Violin (Cologne, April 28, 1987); *Russian Tunes* for Cello (1990); *Menuhin Sonata* for Violin and Piano (1999). **P i a n o :** 2 Études (1949); *Festivity on a Collective Farm* (1951); 9 Pieces (1952–61); *Variations on a Theme of Glinka* (1957); *Toccatina* (1958); Sonata (1962); *24 Preludes and Fugues* (1970); *Polyphonic Book* (1972); *Notebook for Youth* (1982); *Hommage à Chopin* for 4 Pianos (1983); numerous other solo pieces. **VOCAL:** *Ukrainian Night Is Quiet* (1950); 13 Russian Folk Songs (1950); 12 Choruses (1950–70); *Song and Ditties of Varvara* (1961); *Bureaucratiade*, cantata based upon rules of a boarding house (1963; Feb. 24, 1965); 3 Solfège Exercises (1965); 2 Laments (1965); *Poetica= Poetoria*, concerto for Narrator, Woman Soloist, Chorus, and Orch. (Feb. 24, 1968); *Lenin Lives in the People's Heart* (1969; Feb. 6, 1970); *The Song of Pugachev* (1981); 6 Stanzas from *Eugene Onegin* (1981); Concertino for Chorus (1982); *Prayer* for Chorus and Orch. (March 7, 1991); *Long Life* for Chorus, Piano, and 3 Percussionists (1991).—**NS/LK/DM**

Shchelokov, Viacheslav (Ivanovich), Rus-

sian trumpet pedagogue and composer; b. Sloboda Elan, near Tzaritzin, Dec. 11, 1904; d. Sverdlovsk, Jan. 4, 1975. He studied trumpet with Mikhail Tabakov and composition with Alexander Alexandrov and Anatoly Alexandrov at the Moscow Cons. (graduated, 1931). In 1931 he became a teacher of trumpet at the Tchaikovsky Music School in Sverdlovsk. He was a teacher (1935–47) and a prof. (1947–75) of trumpet at the Cons. of the Urals, where he also served as director (1951–53) and chairman of the wind instrument dept. (1954–75).

WORKS: ORCH.: 10 trumpet concertos (1928, 1945, 1945, 1947, 1955, 1958, 1967, 1967, 1968, 1974); *Poem Captain Gastello* (1942); *Victory March* (1945); *Festival of Victory* (1951); *Children's Concerto* for Trumpet and Orch. (1967). **CHAMBER:** *Comical Procession* for Trumpet and Piano (1947); *Pioneer Suite* for Trumpet and Piano (1954); *Poem* for Trumpet and Piano (1958); *Study Etudes* for Trumpet (3 vols., 1964–65); other trumpet pieces.

BIBL.: B. Manzhora, *V.I. S.* (Sverdlovsk, 1968). —**NS/LK/DM**

Shcherbachev, Vladimir (Vladimirovich), Russian composer; b. Warsaw, Jan. 24, 1889; d. Leningrad, March 5, 1952. He studied at the St. Petersburg Cons. with Maximilian Steinberg and Liadov, graduating in 1914. From 1924 to 1931 he was a prof. of composition at the Leningrad Cons. He wrote an opera, *Anna Kolosova* (1939), 5 syms.: No. 1 (1913; Petrograd, Nov. 5, 1916), No. 2 (1922–24; Leningrad, Dec. 14, 1924), No. 3 (1926–31; Leningrad, Feb. 4, 1932, composer conducting), No. 4, *History of the Izhorsky Factory* (1932–34; partial perf., Leningrad, May 28, 1934; first complete perf., Radio Leningrad, Dec. 23, 1935; first public perf., Leningrad, Jan. 21, 1936), and No. 5, *Russkaya* (1942–48; Leningrad, Dec. 21, 1948; rev. version, Kiev, Oct. 21, 1950), and music for films, the orch. suite from one, *The Thunderstorm*, becoming popular in Russia. He further wrote *A Fairy Tale* for Orch. (Petrograd, Dec. 20, 1915), Nonet (1917), numerous piano works, and songs.

BIBL.: G. Orlov, *V.V. S.* (Leningrad, 1959).—**NS/LK/DM**

Shearing, George (Albert), famed pop/jazz pianist and composer; b. Battersea, London, England, Aug. 13, 1919. He was blind from birth. He played piano and accordion from early childhood. He learned to read music with Braille notation; he studied classical piano at a school for the blind during the early 1930s; during 1937, he played in a band for blind students led by Claude Bampton. Shearing appeared at hotels and did radio work; his first solo broadcast was in February 1939. He worked with various British jazz leaders as well as French violinist Stephane Grappelli, then a resident of Britain, between the late 1930s and 1947; he first visited the U.S. in late 1946, and emigrated a year later. In the early 1940s, he had played in the swing style of the time. In the late 1940s, influenced by the innovations of bebop, he developed a new style, characterized by surprising, extended harmonies, and a pianistic technique whereby both hands play thick chords in parallel motion ("locked-hands style"). In 1949, he formed his first quintet of piano, guitar, vibes, bass, and drums; he has been one of the most popular jazz musicians in the world ever since. His extremely successful group recorded until 1967. Shearing composed several famous tunes, among them "Lullaby of Birdland" (1952) and one favored by Miles Davis and Bill Evans, "Conception" (greatly rearranged by Davis as "Deception"). Since 1967, Shearing has led trios and duos and even a big band, and has recorded with Carmen McRae and Mel Torme. In 1978, he formally ended his quintet, although he revived it again during the 1990s for recording and touring. He has also guested with several major symphony orchestras. He appeared in the video *Lullaby of Birdland* (1992).

DISC.: *London Years 1939–1943* (1943); *So Rare* (1947); *Piano Solo* (1947); *Lullaby of Birdland* (1949); *George Shearing Quintet* (1949); *George Shearing Goes Hollywood* (1949); *You're Hearing the George Shearing Quartet* (1950); *Souvenirs* (1951); *Touch of Genius* (1951); *An Evening with the George Shearing Quintet* (1951); *I Hear Music* (1952); *The Shearing Spell* (1955); *Shearing Caravan* (1955); *Shearing in Hi Fi* (1955); *Latin Escapade* (1956); *Shearing Piano* (1956); *White Satin & Black Satin* (1956); *Velvet Carpet* (1956); *In the Night* (1957); *Shearing on Stage* (1957); *Latin lace* (1958); *Burnished Brass* (1958); *On the Sunny Side of the Strip* (1959); *Satin Brass* (1959) *White Satin* (1960); *Swinging's Mutual* (1960); *Nat King Cole Sings/George Shearing Plays* (1961); *And the Montgomery Brothers* (1961); *Satin Affair* (1961); *Jazz Moments* (1962); *Old Gold and Ivory* (1963); *Rare Form* (1963); *Out of the Woods* (1964); *Music Is to Hear: Joe Williams* (1971); *The George Shearing Quartet* (1972); *Gas* (1973); *My Ship* (1974); *Reunion* (1976); *500 Miles* (1977); *Getting in the Swing of Things* (1979); *Two for the Raod* (1980); *On a Clear day* (1980); *Alone Together* (1981); *Evening with George Shearing and Mel Torme* (1982); *Top Drawer* (1983); *Live at the Café Carlyle* (1984); *Grand Piano* (1985); *Plays Music of Cole Porter* (1986); *More Grand Piano* (1986); *Breakin' Out* (1987); *Dexterity* (1987); *Perfect Match* (1988); *George Shearing in Dixieland* (1989); *Walkin'—Live at the Blue Note* (1992); *That Shearing Sound* (1994); *Paper Moon: Songs of Nat King Cole* (1995); *Christmas with George Shearing Quintet* (1998).—**JC/JC-B/LP/NS/MM**

Shebalin, Vissarion (Yakovlevich), Russian composer; b. Omsk, June 11, 1902; d. Moscow, May 28, 1963. He studied at the Moscow Cons. with Miaskovsky (1923–28), then began teaching there; in 1935, was appointed prof. of composition there, and from 1942 to 1948 he was its director. On Feb. 10, 1948, by resolution of the Central Committee of the Communist Party, he was condemned (along with Shostakovich, Prokofiev, Miaskovsky, and others) for adhering to a "decadent formalism" in composition; but these strictures were removed in a corrective declaration of May 28, 1958, "restoring the dignity and integrity of Soviet composers." In addition to his original compositions, Shebalin also completed Mussorgsky's unfinished opera *The Fair at Sorotchintsy,* using only Mussorgsky's own material (Leningrad, Dec. 21, 1931; version with supplementary materials, Moscow, March 19, 1952).

WORKS: DRAMATIC: Opera: *The Taming of the Shrew,* after Shakespeare (concert version, Oct. 1, 1955; stage version, Kuibishev, May 25, 1957); *Sun over the Steppe* (Moscow, June 9, 1958). **Ballet:** *Festival* (1958; unfinished); *Reminiscences of a Bygone Day* (1961). **Musical Comedy:** *Bridegroom from the Embassy* (Sverdlovsk, Aug. 1, 1942). **ORCH.:** 5 syms.: No. 1 (1925; Leningrad, Nov. 13, 1926), No. 2 (1929), No. 3 (1934; Moscow, Feb. 11, 1944), No. 4 (1935; Moscow, Feb. 27, 1936), and No. 5 (Moscow, Oct. 9, 1962); *Overture on Mari Themes* (1926); Horn Concertino (1930; rev. 1959); Violin Concertino (1931); 3 suites (1935; 1935, rev. 1961; 1963); *Variations on Russian Folk Songs* (1940); Violin Concerto (Leningrad, Oct. 29, 1940); *Russian Overture* (1941); Sinfonietta (1949); Cello Concerto (1950). **CHAMBER:** 9 string quartets (1923, 1934, 1939, 1940, 1942, 1943, 1947, 1960, 1963); Piano Trio (1924); Viola Sonata (1954); Violin Sonata (1958); Cello Sonata (1960); Guitar Sonatina (1963); also several piano sonatas. **VOCAL:** *Lenin,* symphonic poem for Soloists, Chorus, and Orch. (1931; Leningrad, Jan. 21, 1934; rev. 1959); *Moscow,* cantata (Moscow, Dec. 14, 1946); songs.

BIBL.: I. Boelza, *V. S.* (Moscow, 1945); I. Boelza and V. Protopopov, eds., *V.Y. S.: Articles, Reminiscences, Materials* (Moscow, 1970); V. Protopopov, ed., *V.Y. S.: Literary Heritage* (Moscow, 1975).—**NS/LK/DM**

Sheila E(scovedo), hereditary percussionist who became a big star as a singer; b. Oakland, Calif., Dec. 12 1957. The oldest child of former Santana percussionist Pete Escovedo, Sheila E comes from a musical dynasty.

In addition to her father, her uncle Coke Escovedo also worked with Santana and a host of others, including the "family band" Azteca. Her brother was in the band Con Funk Shun. Her uncle Alejandro has half a dozen solo albums in addition to his punk rock days with the Nuns and True Believers.

Although Sheila began performing on percussion with the family group Azteca at the age of five, during her teens she wanted to be an Olympic athlete. She broke many track records at Oakland H.S., but found the lure of the stage too great. At her father's suggestion, she studied violin for several years, but had a natural penchant for percussion. During the 1970s, she cut two albums with her father for Fantasy as Pete and Sheila (both were reissued in 1999). During the latter part of the decade, she became an in-demand percussionist, touring with George Duke, Lionel Richie, Marvin Gaye, and others.

In 1984 Sheila got sucked into Prince's Minneapolis funk Mafia, first appearing on Prince's "Erotic City," the B-side of the chart topper "Let's Go Crazy," as a vocalist. Later that same year, she released her solo debut, *The Glamorous Life*. Based on the same sounds and rhythms that made her mentor so famous, she landed a #7 single with the title track and followed that with the #34 "The Belle of St. Mark." The album hit #28 and went gold. Her 1985 album *Romance 1600* benefitted from the single "A Love Bizarre," which appeared in the film *Krush Groove*. The song went to #11 and catapulted the album to gold.

After leaving Prince behind, her records have leaned more heavily on her percussive abilities. She may have found them more artistically satisfying, particularly 1989's *Latina Familia* set, an all-star Latin percussion workout for Verve/CTI, but they didn't sell nearly as well. In the early 1990s, Sheila went on tour with Prince, playing trap drums for the first time. She also can play trombone, bass, piano, trumpet and saxophone. In the late 1990s, she became the first female bandleader on a late night talk show, playing the tunes for Magic Johnson's short-lived program. She has appeared playing drums in a soft-drink commercial and continues to be an in-demand session player.

DISC.: *The Glamorous Life* (1984); *Romance 1600* (1985); *Sheila E* (1987); *Sex Cymbal* (1991); *Writes of Passage* (1998). Pete Escovedo and Tito Puente: *Latina Familia* (1989).—**HB**

Sheinfeld, David, American composer and violinist; b. St. Louis, Sept. 20, 1906. He began violin training as a child, then studied harmony and counterpoint in Chicago; subsequently was a student of Respighi in Rome (1929–31). After pursuing his career in Chicago (1931–44), he studied conducting with Monteux; then played in the Pittsburgh Sym. Orch. (1944–45) and the San Francisco Sym. Orch. (1945–71). In 1993 he received an award from the American Academy of Arts and Letters. He received a Koussevitzky Foundation commission in 1996. In 1998 he was awarded a Heller Foundation grant. In his compositions from 1962, Sheinfeld combined tonal and atonal writing.

WORKS: ORCH.: *Adagio and Allegro* (1946; San Francisco, March 14, 1947); *Concerto for Orchestra* (1949; San Francisco, Feb.

20, 1951); *Fantasia* for Trumpet, Piano, Percussion, and Strings (1951); Violin Concerto (1955; Philadelphia, April 23, 1965); Concerto for Woodwinds and Chamber Orch. (1957; San Francisco, Jan. 14, 1958); *Etudes* (1959; Pittsburgh, Nov. 18, 1960); *Dialogues* for Chamber Orch. (Philadelphia, Oct. 26, 1966); *Confrontations* for Electric Guitar, Electric Violin, Saxophone, and Orch. (1969; Oakland, Calif., Jan. 20, 1970); *Time Warp* for Electric Instruments and Orch. (1972; San Francisco, Jan. 24, 1973); *Dreams and Fantasies* (1981; San Francisco, May 5, 1982); 2 syms.: No. 1, *Polarities* (1991) and No. 2 (1995); $E=MC^2$ for String Quartet and Orch. (1998). **CHAMBER:** Sonata for Solo Violin (1950); *Serenade* for 6 Instruments (1961); *Patterns* for Harp (1962); *4 Pieces* for Cello (1964); *Duo* for Viola and Harp (1965); *Memories of Yesterday and Tomorrow* for 3 Players (1971); *Elegiac Sonorities* for Organ (1973); *Dualities* for Harp (1976); 2 string quartets (1978, 1994); *Threnody* for Violin (1981). **VOCAL:** *The Earth Is a Sounding Board* for Small Chorus and Orch. (1978); *Dear Theo* for Baritone and 9 Instruments (1996). —**NS/LK/DM**

Shekhter, Boris (Semyonovich), Russian composer and teacher; b. Odessa, Jan. 20, 1900; d. Moscow, Dec. 16, 1961. After studies at the Odessa Cons. (graduated, 1922), he entered the Moscow Cons., studying composition with Vasilenko and Miaskovsky (graduated, 1929). In 1940 he became a prof. at the Ashkhabad Cons.

WORKS: DRAMATIC: Opera: *1905 god* (The Year 1905; 1935; rev. 1955; in collaboration with A. Davidenko); *Yusup i Akhmet* (1941; Ashkhabad, June 12, 1942; in collaboration with A. Kuliyev); *Pushkin v Mikhailovskom* (1955). **ORCH.:** 5 syms. (1929; 1943; 1944–45; 1947; 1951, rev. 1952–53); *Turkmenia*, suite based on Central Asian themes (1932; Florence, April 4, 1934); Piano Concerto (1932); *Rhapsody* (1935). **OTHER:** Cantatas; choruses; piano pieces; songs.—**NS/LK/DM**

Shelley, Howard (Gordon), English pianist and conductor; b. London, March 9, 1950. He studied piano in childhood and was only 10 when he appeared on British television. He subsequently studied at the Royal Coll. of Music in London (1967–71), his principal mentors being Harold Craxton, Kendall Taylor, Lamar Crowson, and Ilona Kabos. In 1971 he received the Dannreuther Concerto Prize and the Silver Medal of the Worshipful Company of Musicians, and also made his formal debut at London's Wigmore Hall. In 1972 he made his first appearance at London's Promenade Concerts, a televised event that launched his international career. After marrying the pianist Hilary Macnamara in 1975, he made duo appearances with her as well as continuing his solo career. In 1983 he played all the solo piano works of Rachmaninoff for the first time in a cycle at Wigmore Hall. After making his debut as a conductor with the London Sym. Orch. in 1985, he pursued a dual career as pianist and conductor. From 1990 to 1992 he was assoc. conductor of the London Mozart Players, and then served as its principal guest conductor from 1992 to 1998. In addition to such masters as Mozart, Schubert, Chopin, Schumann, Rachmaninoff, Vaughan Williams, and Hindemith, Shelley has championed the piano music of contemporary composers, including Sir Michael Tippett, Howard Ferguson, Peter Dickinson, and Edward Cowie.—**NS/LK/DM**

Shelton, Lucy (Alden), American soprano; b. Pomona, Calif., Feb. 25, 1944. She studied at Pomona Coll. (B.A., 1965) and with Gladys Miller at the New England Cons. of Music in Boston (M.M., 1968); completed her training with DeGaetani at the Aspen (Colo.) School of Music. While a member of the Jubal Trio, she shared in winning the Naumburg Competition in 1977, and then won it on her own in 1980. She sang with the Waverly Consort, the N.Y. Pro Musica, and the 20th Century Consort of the Smithsonian Institution, and also pursued a career as a touring solo artist. In 1989 she sang the role of Jenifer in the Thames TV production of Tippett's *Midsummer Marriage* in England. While she has become closely associated with the performance of contemporary music, her repertoire ranges across the entire spectrum of music.—NS/LK/DM

Sheng, Bright, remarkable Chinese composer; b. Shanghai, Dec. 6, 1955. He began piano lessons when he was 5; after graduating from high school, he worked as a pianist and timpanist in a dance company in Chinhai, near Tibet, where he began to study Chinese folk music. After China's Cultural Revolution, he entered the Shanghai Cons. (1976), where he earned an undergraduate degree in composition. In 1982 he followed his parents to the U.S., where he attended Queens Coll. at the City Univ. of N.Y. and Columbia Univ.; his teachers included Chou-Wen Chung, Davidovsky, Perle, and Weisgall. Sheng received numerous awards, both in China and the U.S., including NEA grants, a Guggenheim fellowship, and awards from the American Academy and Inst. of Arts and Letters. His works have been championed by such eminent artists as Peter Serkin, who commissioned his *My Song* (1988), and Gerard Schwarz, who has given many premiere performances of his orch. pieces. His *H'un (Lacerations): In Memoriam 1966–1976* was the first runner-up for the 1989 Pulitzer Prize in Music. In 1993 it was performed by Masur and the N.Y. Phil. in 6 cities during its European tour and in 1994 it was a featured work by Poland's National Phil. at the Warsaw Autumn Festival. Sheng appeared throughout the U.S. as a lecturer. After serving as composer-in-residence of the Chicago Lyric Opera, for which he wrote the opera *The Song of Majnun* (April 9, 1992) with a libretto by Andrew Porter on an Islamic legend, he held that post with the Seattle Sym. Orch. (1992–94). He also orchestrated Leonard Bernstein's *Arias and Barcarolles*, which received its premiere performance under the direction of Leonard Slatkin in N.Y. on Dec. 6, 1990. In 1994–95 he was artist-in-residence of the Univ. of Washington. Like so many refugees of China's cultural upheaval, Sheng strives to find the personal means to integrate the disparate musical styles of China and the West.

WORKS: DRAMATIC: O p e r a : *The Song of Majnun* (Chicago, April 9, 1992); *may i feel, said he,* after e.e. cummings (1996). **T h e a t e r P i e c e :** *The Silver River,* after D.H. Hwang (1997). **ORCH.:** *3 Pieces* (1981; Shanghai, July 1, 1982); *Adagio* for Chamber Orch. (N.Y., March 7, 1987); *H'un (Lacerations): In Memoriam 1966–1976* (1987; N.Y., April 16, 1988); *Fanfare* (from *China Dreams;* 1992); *Prelude* (from *China Dreams;* Houston, Nov. 1994); *China Dreams* (1995); *Postcards* (1997); *Spring Dreams* for Cello and Traditional Chinese Orch. (1997); *Two Poems* for Cello and Orch. (1998); *Flute Moon* (Houston, May 22, 1999); *Nanking Nanking* (1999); *Red Silk Dance* (1999); Piano Concerto (2000). **CHAMBER:** Trio for Flute, Harp, and Cello (1982); *3 Etudes* for Flute (1982; N.Y., Nov. 8, 1985; rev. 1988); *5 Pieces* for Oboe and Cello (1983; N.Y., Feb. 20, 1986); 3 string quartets: No. 1 (1984; N.Y., Nov. 11, 1985), No. 2 (1984; Tanglewood, Aug. 21, 1985), and No. 3 (1993); *Shao* for Oboe, Violin, Cello, and Piano (N.Y., April 1986); *3 Pieces* for Viola and Piano (1986; N.Y., Jan. 15, 1987); The Stream Flows for Viola (1988); *4 Movements* for Piano Trio (N.Y., April 24, 1990); *The Stream Flows—Two Pieces* for Violin (1990); *Concertino* for Clarinet and String Quartet (1993); *Seven Short Yadhtrib Variations* for Bassoon (1994); *Seven Tunes Heard in China* for Cello (1995); *Three Songs* for Pipa and Cello (1999). **P i a n o :** *Suite* (Aspen, Aug. 23, 1984); *My Song* (N.Y., Nov. 11, 1989). **VOCAL:** *3 Chinese Poems* for Mezzo-soprano and Piano (1982–92); *4 Poems from the Tang Dynasty* for Mezzo-soprano and Piano (1984; Tanglewood, Aug. 23, 1985); *5 Chinese Folk Songs* for Tenor and Piano (N.Y., Sept. 21, 1985); *2 Poems from the Sung Dynasty* for Soprano and Chamber Orch. (1985; N.Y., March 26, 1986); *3 Chinese Love Songs* for Soprano, Viola, and Piano (Tanglewood, Aug. 26, 1988); *2 Folk Songs from Qinghai* for Chorus, 2 Pianos, and 2 Percussion or Chorus and Orch. (Boston, Oct. 28, 1989); *Fragments from "The Song of Magnun"* for Soprano, Tenor, Large and Small Choruses, and Orch. (1992); *may i feel, said he* for Soprano, Tenor, and Piano, 4-Hands (1996).—NS/LK/DM

Shepherd, Arthur, eminent American composer and pedagogue; b. Paris, Idaho, Feb. 19, 1880; d. Cleveland, Jan. 12, 1958. He studied with G. Haessel, and in 1892 entered the New England Cons. of Music in Boston, where he studied piano with Dennee and Carl Faelten, and composition with Goetschius and Chadwick. In 1897 he went to Salt Lake City, where he was active as a teacher and as conductor of the Salt Lake Sym. Orch. He returned to Boston in 1908, and became a prof. of harmony and counterpoint at the New England Cons. of Music (until 1917; again in 1919–20). In 1917 he joined the U.S. Army, and was bandmaster of the 303rd Field Artillery in France. He settled in Cleveland, where he was asst. conductor (1920–26) and program annotator (1920–30) of its orch., prof. at Western Reserve Univ. (1927–50), and music critic of the *Cleveland Press* (1928–31). In 1938 he was elected to membership in the National Inst. of Arts and Letters. A composer of national tendencies, Shepherd wrote in a grand Romantic manner, derived from an intense feeling for American melos. He publ. a valuable handbook, *The String Quartets of Beethoven* (Cleveland, 1937).

WORKS: ORCH.: 3 overtures: *The Nuptials of Attila, Ouverture joyeuse* (1902), *The Festival of Youth* (1915), and *Overture to a Drama* (1919; Cleveland, March 27, 1924); *Fantaisie humoresque* for Piano and Orch. (Boston, Feb. 8, 1918); 2 syms.: No. 1, *Horizons* (Cleveland, Dec. 15, 1927) and No. 2 (1939; Cleveland, March 7, 1940); *Choreographic Suite* (Cleveland, Oct. 22, 1931); *Fantasy on Down East Spirituals* (Indianapolis, Nov. 2, 1946); Violin Concerto (1946–47); *Theme and Variations* (Cleveland, April 9, 1953). **B a n d :** *Hilaritas,* overture (1942). **CHAMBER:** 2 violin sonatas (1914, 1927); 5 string quartets (1926, 1933, 1936, 1944, 1955); Piano Quintet (1940); *Praeludium salutatorium* for Flute, Oboe, Horn, Bassoon, Violin, Viola, and Cello (1942); *Divertissement* for Flute, Oboe, Clarinet, Bassoon, and Horn (1943). **P i a n o :** 2 sonatas in F minor (1907, 1929).

VOCAL: *The City in the Sea* for Baritone, Double Chorus, and Orch. (1913); *Song of the Sea Wind* for Women's Voices and Piano (1915); *He Came All So Still* for Women's Voices (1915); *Deck Thyself My Soul* for Chorus and Organ (1918); *Triptych* for Voice and String Quartet (1926); *Song of the Pilgrims* for Tenor, Double Chorus, and Orch. (1932); *Ballad of Trees and the Master* for Chorus (1935); *Invitation to the Dance* for Chorus and Orch. or 2 Pianos (1936); *Grace for Gardens* for Chorus (1938); *Build Thee More Stately Mansions* for Women's Voices (1938); *Psalm XLII* for Chorus and Orch. (1944); *Drive On* for Baritone and Chorus (1946); *A Psalm of the Mountains* for Chorus and Orch. or Piano (1956); songs.

BIBL.: R. Loucks, *A. S.: American Composer* (Provo, Utah, 1980).—**NS/LK/DM**

Shepp, Archie (Vernon),

famed avant-garde jazz saxophonist, playwright, poet, educator; b. Fort Lauderdale, Fla., May 24, 1937. He studied clarinet and alto saxophone as a child in Philadelphia before switching to tenor and soprano saxophone. As a teen, he played in R&B bands. During this time, he met Lee Morgan, Cal Massey, Jimmy Heath, and John Coltrane. He majored in theater at Goddard Coll. (1955–59), then moved to N.Y., where he performed with Cecil Taylor, and on stage in Jack Gelber's *The Connection*. He co-led a group with B. Dixon, and formed the New York Contemporary Five with him, John Tchicai, and later, Don Cherry. Shepp worked and recorded with John Coltrane on several occasions (approximately late 1964–66); he believes that Coltrane helped him to get his recording contract with Impulse. During his performance of "Mama Rose" at Newport (1966), there was an audience outburst at the word "vagina" intoned during the poem. Shepp recorded frequently in late 1960s, featuring most of the young N.Y.–based musicians, in particular Grachan Moncur III, B. Harris, D. Burrell, and Roswell Rudd. Shepp toured extensively in Europe in the 1970s. Since the mid-1970s, he has been active as a professor in the Department of African American Music at Amherst, Mass. He has also written plays, including *The Communist* and *Junebug Graduates Tonight*; in collaboration with Cal Massey, he wrote the music for *Lady Day: A Musical Tragedy* by Aishah Rahman. In the 1970s and 1980s, Shepp began to perform standards.

DISC.: *Archie Shepp–Bill Dixon Quartet* (1962); *N.Y. Contemporary Five in Europe* (1963); *Archie Shepp in Europe* (1963); *And the N.Y. Contemporary Five* (1963); *Four for Trane* (1964); *On This Night* (1965); *Fire Music* (1965); *Three for a Quarter: One for a Dime* (1966); *Mama Too Tight* (1966); *Live in San Francisco* (1966); *Magic of Ju-Ju* (1967); *Yasmina: A Black Woman* (1969); *Blase* (1969); *Things Have Got to Change* (1971); *For Losers* (1971); *Archie Shepp and Philly Joe Jones* (1971); *Cry of My People* (1972); *Attica Blues* (1972); *There's a Trumpet in My Soul* (1975); *Montreux, Vols. 1 & 2* (1975); *Ballads for Trane* (1977); *Duet with Dollar Brand* (1978); *Attica Big Band* (1979); *I Know About the Life* (1981); *Archie Shepp and Jeanne Lee* (1984); *Live on Broadway* (1985); *Splashes* (Tribute to Wilbur Little; 1987); *En Concert a Banlieues Bleues* (1989); *I Didn't Know About You* (1990).

BIBL.: G. Cerutti, *Discographie A. S.* (Sierre, Switzerland 1982).—**LP**

Sheppard, John,

English composer; b. c. 1515; d. c. 1559. He became Informator choristarum at Magdalen Coll., Oxford, in 1543, and by 1552 he was a Gentleman of the Chapel Royal. His distinguished output of sacred music includes Latin masses, Mass sections, Magnificats, motets, English service music, and anthems.

BIBL.: H. Lamont, *J. S.: His Life and Music* (diss., Univ. of Southern Calif., 1963).—**NS/LK/DM**

Shere, Charles,

American writer on music and composer; b. Berkeley, Calif., Aug. 20, 1935. He was reared on a small farm in Sonoma County, where he attended high school and learned to play wind instruments; after graduating from the Univ. of Calif. at Berkeley with a degree in English (1960), he studied composition with Erickson privately and at the San Francisco Cons. of Music, and also studied conducting with Samuel (1961–64); also studied art, on which he later wrote and lectured extensively. From 1964 to 1967 he was music director of Berkeley's KPFA-FM; also was active at San Francisco's KQED-TV (1967–73), an instructor at Mills Coll. in Oakland (1973–84), and art and music critic for the Oakland *Tribune* (1972–88). He was co-founder, publisher, ed., and a major contributor to *EAR*, a monthly new-music tabloid magazine. He is married to Lindsey Remolif Shere, the famed pastry chef of Chez Panisse in Berkeley. Shere describes his early compositions, many notated in open form and scored for unspecified or variable ensembles, as "rural and contemplative rather than urban and assertive in nature"; his later works utilize more conventional notation, his shift from pen-and-ink to computer-generated notation coinciding with a greater use of rhythmic conventions, as in the ostinatos in the finales of his *Symphony in 3 Movements* (1988), Concerto for Violin with Harp, Percussion, and Small Orchestra (1985), and *Sonata: Bachelor Machine* (1989).

WORKS: DRAMATIC: O p e r a : *The Box of 1914* (1980; San Francisco, Jan. 29, 1981); *The Bride Stripped Bare by Her Bachelors, Even* (partial perf., Oakland, Dec. 1, 1984); *Ladies Voices*, chamber opera for 3 Sopranos and 6 Instruments (Berkeley, Oct. 30, 1987). **ORCH.:** Small Concerto for Piano and Orch. (1964; Aptos, Calif., Aug. 22, 1965); *Nightmusic* for Diminished Orch. (1967; Oakland, Jan. 24, 1982, K. Nagano conducting); *Soigneur de gravité (de l'orgue pour orchestre)* (1972); *Music for Orchestra (Symphony)* (Kensington, Calif., Oct. 28, 1976, composer conducting); *Tongues for Poet* (speaking in tongues), Chamber Orch., and Tape (San Francisco, May 6, 1978); Concerto for Violin, Harp, Percussion, and Small Orchestra (1985; Aptos, Calif., July 21, 1990); *Symphony in 3 Movements* (1988; Berkeley, April 28, 1989, K. Nagano conducting). **CHAMBER:** *Fratture* for 7 Instruments (1962; Osaka, Dec. 23, 1963); *Ces désirs du quatuor* for any 4 Musicians (1965); Quartet No. 2 for 3 to 5 or 6 Musicians (1966); *Screen*, Quartet No. 3 for 4 to 6 Strings (1969); Quartet No. 7, *Like a piece of silvered glass*, for Flute, English Horn, Clarinet, and Bassoon (1970); *Handler of Gravity* for Organ and Optional Chimes (1971); *Parergon to Woodwind Quintet* for English Horn, Bass Clarinet, and Bassoon (1974); String Quartet No. 1 (Oakland, Calif., May 10, 1980). **P i a n o :** *Sonata: Bachelor Machine* (1989; San Francisco, July 25, 1990). **VOCAL:** *Certain Phenomena of Sound* for Soprano and Violin (1983; San Francisco, Feb. 11, 1984); *Requiem with Oboe* for 8 Voices or Double Chorus and Oboe (San Francisco, June 11, 1985); *I Like It to Be a Play* for Tenor, Baritone, Bass, and String Quartet (San Francisco, Feb. 6, 1989). **TAPE:** *Ces désirs du vent des gregoriens* for Tape (1967).

WRITINGS: Among his publications are *Even Recently Cultural History, Five Lectures for the 1980s* (Lebanon, N.H., 1995); *Thinking Sound Music: The Life and Work of Robert Erickson* (1995); *Everbest Ever: Letters from Virgil* (1995).—**NS/LK/DM**

Sheremetiev, Count Alexander, Russian nobleman and amateur musician; b. St. Petersburg, March 12, 1859; d. Ste.-Geneviève-des-Bois, near Paris, May 18, 1931. The private choir maintained by his father, Dmitri, attained wide celebrity in St. Petersburg. In 1882 Count Alexander founded a sym. orch. in his own name, and in 1884 a church choir under the direction of Archangelsky. In 1898 he instituted in St. Petersburg a series of sym. concerts at popular prices, conducted by himself and others. Thanks to his inherited wealth, he was able to engage excellent musicians; presented programs of Russian composers, thus contributing to the cause of national music. He also wrote some pieces himself (*Pathetische Fantasie* for Orch., chamber music, etc.). After the Revolution of 1917 he went to Paris, and died in poverty, in a Russian charity institution near Paris.—**NS/LK/DM**

Sheridan, Margaret, Irish soprano; b. Castlebar, County Mayo, Oct. 15, 1889; d. Dublin, April 16, 1958. She was a student of William Shakespeare at the Royal Academy of Music in London (1909–11) and of Alfredo Martino in Italy. In 1918 she made her operatic debut in *La Bohème* in Rome. She sang at London's Covent Garden (1919; 1925–26; 1928–30) but pursued her career principally in Italy. In 1931 she settled in Dublin as a singing teacher. She was esteemed for her roles in Puccini's operas.—**NS/LK/DM**

Sheriff, Noam, Israeli conductor, composer, and pedagogue; b. Tel Aviv, Jan. 7, 1935. He studied composition with Ben-Haim (1949–57), conducting with Markevitch at the Salzburg Mozarteum (1955), philosophy at the Hebrew Univ. in Jerusalem (1955–59), and composition with Blacher at the Berlin Hochschule für Musik (1960–62). In 1955 he won the first Josef Krips prize of the Israel Phil. conducting competition. He returned there in 1959 and won the conducting competition outright. In the meantime, he was founder-conductor of the Hebrew Univ. Sym. Orch. (1955–59). From 1963 to 1983 he taught composition, orchestration, and conducting at the Rubin Academies of Music in Jerusalem and Tel Aviv. He was music director of the Kibbutz Chamber Orch. from 1970 to 1982, and also was assoc. conductor of the Israel Chamber Orch. (1971–73). From 1983 to 1986 he taught orchestration at the Cologne Hochschule für Musik, and then was on the faculty of the Rubin Academy of Music in Jerusalem (1986–88). In 1989 he became music director of the Israel Sym. Orch., Rishon LeZion. He also was a prof. at the Univ. of Tel Aviv's Rubin Academy of Music from 1991, where he was head of the orch. conducting dept. In 1998 he became director of the Rubin Academy of Music. In his music, Sheriff has adroitly fused Western and Eastern elements in scores made notable by their command of orchestration and form.

WORKS: DRAMATIC: *Destination 5,* ballet music (1961); *Psalms of Jerusalem,* ballet (1982); *The Sorrows of Job,* opera (1990);

Gesualdo, chamber opera (1996). **ORCH.:** *Festival Prelude* (1957); *Song of Degrees* (1959); *Music* for Chamber Orch. (1961); *Heptaprisms* (1965); *Metamorphoses on a Galliard* for Chamber Orch. (1967); *Chaconne* (1968); *2 Epigrams* for Chamber Orch. (1968); *Sonata* for Chamber Orch. (1973); *Essay* for Strings (1977); *Prayers* for Strings (1983); Violin Concerto (1984); *La Folia Variations* (1984); *Mechaye Hametim* (Revival of the Dead), sym. for Soloists, Choruses, and Orch. (1985); *A Vision of David* for Narrator and Orch. (1986); Concerto for Cello and Chamber Orch. (1987; rev. 1996); *Scarlattiana,* piano concerto (1994); *Hassid's Reward* for Bass Clarinet and Strings (1997); *Akeda (The Sacrifice of Isaac)* (1997). **CHAMBER:** Piano Sonata (1961); *Confession* for Cello (1966); *Invention* for Flute (1966); 2 string quartets (1969–82; *Rosendorf,* 1996); *Mai Ko Mashma Lan* for Harp and String Quartet (1976); *Trey-Assar,* dodekalog for 12 Cellos (1978); *Meeting for 6* for 6 Cellos (1985–86); *Sonata à 3* for Flute, Alto Flute, and Piccolo (1998). **VOCAL:** *Adhrei* for Alto and Chamber Group (1961); *Sephardic Passion* for Soloists and Orch. (1992); *Psalms of Jerusalem* for Tenor, Bass, 4 Choruses, and Orch. (1995); *Bereshit (Genesis)* for Soloists, Children's Chorus, and Orch. (1998); songs.—**NS/LK/DM**

Sherman, Jimmy (actually, **James Benjamin**), jazz pianist, arranger; b. Williamsport, Pa., Aug. 17, 1908; d. Philadelphia, Pa., Oct. 11, 1975. He was originally taught piano by his sister, then studied with private teachers. He did his first gigs for local high school dances, then played occasionally with Jimmy Gorham's Band. Sherman's first professional work was with Alphonse Trent on a Great Lakes steamer (1930), then with Peanuts Holland (1931), Al Sears (1932), Stuff Smith (1933–34), and Lil Armstrong's Big Band (1935), and then he rejoined Stuff Smith in N.Y. (1936). In 1936 and 1937 Sherman also recorded with Putney Dandridge, Lil Armstrong, Mildred Bailey, and Billie Holiday. From 1938 until 1952, he worked as accompanist-arranger for the vocal group the Charioteers (including a tour of Europe in 1948), then returned to Pa. He played for three years at the Tally Ho motel near Valley Forge, then in 1960 began long residency at Miss Jeanne's Crossroad Tavern, where he played regularly through 1969.—**JC/LP**

Sherman, Norman (Morris), American bassoonist, teacher, and composer; b. Boston, Feb. 25, 1926. He studied composition with Roslyn Brogue Henning and at Boston Univ. (1946–50), where he also received instruction in bassoon from Ernst Panenka, and subsequently attended Messiaen's analysis class at the Paris Cons. (1950). He was principal bassoonist with the Winnipeg Sym. Orch. (1957–61), the Residentie Orch. in The Hague (1961–69), the National Arts Centre Orch. in Ottawa (1969–73), the Israel Radio Orch. (1973–74), and the Kingston (Ont.) Sym. Orch. (1974–91). He also taught composition, bassoon, and chamber music at the Queen's Univ. in Kingston (from 1974).

WORKS: DRAMATIC: Ballet: *The Red Seed* (1950). **ORCH.:** *Sinfonia concertante* for Bassoon and Strings (1950; Winnipeg, Jan. 19, 1961; *2 Pieces* (1952–62); *Through the Rainbow and/or Across the Valley* (1966–67; Rotterdam, April 25, 1968); *Thesis* (Kingston, March 23, 1975); *Canadian Summer* (1976); *The 2-Bit Dance Hall* (1980); *Garden of Love* for Strings, Brass, and Percussion (1988). **Band:** *The Pioneers* (1982). **CHAMBER:**

Concerto for Flute, Clarinet, Horn, Bassoon, and Piano (1948); *Traditions* for Flute, Oboe, Clarinet, and Bassoon (1948); *The Reunion* for Flute, Violin, Viola, and Cello (1971; CBC, Feb. 4, 1979); *Quadron* for String Quartet (Kingston, July 15, 1976); *Quintessant* for Flute, Oboe, Clarinet, Horn, and Bassoon (Kingston, May 11, 1977); *Bouquet* for Piano or Celesta, Clarinet, and 3 Percussion (1978); *Icthyon* for 13 Strings (1979); *Entretien* for Flute and Bassoon (1981); *Euphoria* for Flute, Clarinet, Horn, Bassoon, and Percussion (1983); *Tango* for Flute, Horn, Viola, and Cello (1984); *La Bodega* for Flute and Guitar (1987); *Retort* for Accordion and Percussion (1993); *Et cetera* for Guitar Quartet (1995); *Tutti Flutti* for 9 Flutes (1997); *The National Anthem of the Moon* for Trumpet, Horn, and Trombone (1999); piano pieces. **VOCAL:** *The Events of November 10, 1812* for Narrator and Orch. (1978).—**NS/LK/DM**

Sherman, Russell, American pianist and pedagogue; b. N.Y., March 25, 1930. He took instruction in piano with Steuermann (1941–55), and earned a degree in humanities at Columbia Univ. (B.A., 1949). On Nov. 17, 1945, he made his formal debut in a recital in N.Y., and then pursued a modest concert career while devoting himself mainly to teaching. In 1967 he became chairman of the piano dept. of the New England Cons. of Music in Boston. He was active in promoting contemporary music in chamber ensembles in the Boston area. His performances won praise for their discernment and spontaneity. In 1975 a N.Y. recital attracted attention and quickened interest in his career; in 1978 he performed in Paris and London, and was a soloist with the leading orchs. of Europe. In 1986 he joined the faculty of the Juilliard School in N.Y. On March 28, 1993, he played the premiere of Gunther Schuller's *Sonata/Fantasia* in Boston. Sherman publ. the vol. *Piano Pieces* (N.Y., 1996).—**NS/LK/DM**

Sherock, Shorty (originally, **Cherock, Clarence Francis**), jazz trumpeter; b. Minneapolis, Minn., Nov. 17, 1915; d. North Ridge, Calif., Feb. 19, 1980. Sherock began playing cornet as a child, and did local gigs while attending high school in Gary, Ind. He attended Ill. Military Academy in Abington. He worked with Charlie Pierce and Dell Coon before joining Ben Pollack in 1936. Sherock worked briefly with a series of leaders before joining Jimmy Dorsey (1937–39). He then worked with Bob Crosby (summer 1939 to January 1940), Gene Krupa (January 1940 to March 1941), Tommy Dorsey (April–July 1941), Raymond Scott (summer 1941), Bud Freeman (late 1941), Bob Strong (early 1942), Alvino Rey (July 1942), and Horace Heidt (late 1942–March 1945). He led his own band until June 1946, disbanded but reformed again in 1948. In the late 1940s, Sherock settled in Calif., rejoined Jimmy Dorsey for a brief spell in 1950, then worked as a freelance studio musician in Hollywood. He worked with George Auld in 1954 in Los Angeles, but during the 1950s and 1960s was mainly active as a studio musician.—**JC/LP**

Sherry, Fred (Richard), American cellist and conductor; b. Montrose, N.Y., Oct. 27, 1948. He studied cello with Leonard Rose and Channing Roberts, and chamber music with Felix Galimir at the Juilliard School

of Music in N.Y. (1965–69). In 1968 he won the Young Concert Artist competition, which led to his solo debut at N.Y.'s Carnegie Recital Hall in 1969. With Richard Fritz, he organized the new-music group Speculum Musicae in 1971, remaining with it until 1978; was also a founding member of the chamber group Tashi in 1973. In 1989 he became artistic director of the Chamber Music Soc. of Lincoln Center in N.Y., which position he resigned in 1991.—**NS/LK/DM**

Shibata, Minao, Japanese composer; b. Tokyo, Sept. 29, 1916. He studied science at the Univ. of Tokyo (graduated, 1939) and music with Saburo Moroi (1940–43). From 1959 to 1969 he taught at the Tokyo National Univ. of Fine Arts and Music.

WORKS: DRAMATIC: Opera: *Strada a Roma*, radio opera (1961); *Forgotten Boys* (1990). **ORCH.:** Sinfonia (Tokyo, Dec. 12, 1960); *Consort* for Orch. and Tape (1972–73); *Metaphor* for 27 Japanese Instruments (1975); *Yūgaku* for Orch. and Tape (1977); *Diaphonia* for Orch. and Tape (1979); *U235 and the Peace of Mankind* (1983); *Metafonia* (1984); *Antifonia* (1989). **CHAMBER:** 2 string quartets (1943, 1947); *Classical Suite* for Violin and Piano (1953); *Essay* for 3 Trumpets and 3 Trombones (1965); *Imagery* for Marimba (1969); *Display '70 I* (1969) and *II* (1970) for Ryûteki, Marimba, Percussion, and Tape; *Concerto for 8* for 8 Flutes (1971); *Trimurti* for Flute, Violin, Keyboard, and Electronics (1973–74); *Ashirai* for 6 Percussionists (1980). **KEYBOARD: Piano:** Sonata (1943); 2 *Improvisations* (1957, 1968); *Generation* (1981). **Organ:** *Diferencias* (1983). **VOCAL:** *Symbology* for Soprano and Chamber Orch. (1953); *Black Portrait* for Soprano and Chamber Orch. (1954); *3 Poems on Katsue Kitazono* for Soprano and Chamber Orch. (1954–58); *Black Distance* for Soprano and Chamber Orch. (1958); *The Street* for Chorus and 4 Percussion (1960); *Poem Recited in the Night* for Soprano and Chamber Orch. (1963); *L'Oiseau noir en soliel Levant* for Narrator, 6 Soloists, Piano, Percussion, and Synthesizer (1986). **OTHER:** *Musique concrète* for Tape (1955); *Improvisation* for Electronic Sound (1968).—**NS/LK/DM**

Shicoff, Neil, American tenor; b. N.Y., June 2, 1949. He began vocal training with his father, a cantor, and then studied at the Juilliard School in N.Y. After singing Narroboth in Salome in Washington, D.C., he appeared as Ernani at the Cincinnati May Festival in 1975. On Oct. 15, 1976, he made his Metropolitan Opera debut in N.Y. as Rinuccio in *Gianni Schicchi*, returning there in subsequent seasons as the Duke in *Rigoletto*, Rodolfo, Werther, Hoffmann, Romeo, Massenet's *Des Grieux*, and Lensky. He also sang at London's Covent Garden (debut as Pinkerton, 1978), the Chicago Lyric Opera (debut as Rodolfo, 1979), the San Francisco Opera (debut as Edgardo, 1981), and the Paris Opéra (debut as Romeo, 1981). In 1988 he sang Macduff in the BBC production of *Macbeth*. In 1990 he made his debut in Barcelona as Hoffmann. In 1993 he appeared at Covent Garden as Pinkerton. In 1997 he returned to the Metropolitan Opera as Lensky. He portrayed Don Carlos at the Opéra de la Bastille in Paris in 1998, the same year that he sang Ernani at the Vienna State Opera. He also toured as a concert artist. In 1978 he married the soprano Judith Haddon.—**NS/LK/DM**

Shield, William, English violinist and composer; b. Swalwell, County Durham, March 5, 1748; d. Brightling, Sussex, Jan. 25, 1829. He was taught by his father, a singing master, on whose death he was apprenticed to a shipbuilder; then took lessons in music with Charles Avison at Newcastle upon Tyne. He played violin in various small theaters in the neighborhood, and in 1772 settled in London as violinist at the King's Theatre; from 1773 to 1791 he played the viola there. He produced his first comic opera, *A Flitch of Bacon*, at the Haymarket Theatre on Aug. 17, 1778; it was followed by a great number of theatrical pieces. After holding the post of composer to Covent Garden from 1778 to 1791, he traveled in France and Italy, returning to Covent Garden in 1792; he retained this position until 1797. He was appointed Master of the King's Music in 1817, and was the last to compose court odes in 1818. He wrote about 40 light operas, pantomines, musical farces, ballad operas, etc., as well as 6 string quartets, 6 string trios, 6 duets for 2 Violins, and other instrumental pieces. He publ. *An Introduction to Harmony* (1800) and *The Rudiments of Thoroughbass* (1815). Shield had some original ideas, and was not averse to experimentation; e.g., he wrote movements in 5/4 time.—**NS/LK/DM**

Shifrin, David, American clarinetist and teacher; b. N.Y., Jan. 2, 1950. He studied at the H.S. of Performing Arts in N.Y. (1964–65), the Interlochen (Mich.) Arts Academy (1965–67), and the Curtis Inst. of Music in Philadelphia (artist diploma, 1971; B.M., 1973). He played clarinet in the Cleveland Orch., the Los Angeles Chamber Orch., the Dallas Sym. Orch., the Honolulu Sym. Orch., and the American Sym. Orch. in N.Y. As a soloist, he appeared with various orchs. in the U.S. and abroad, and was also very active as a recitalist and chamber music artist. He was artistic director of Chamber Music Northwest in Portland, Ore. (from 1980). In 1987 he was awarded an Avery Fisher Career Grant. He was then a member (from 1989) and artistic director (from 1992) of the Chamber Music Soc. of Lincoln Center in N.Y. He taught at the Cleveland Inst. of Music (1974–76), the Univ. of Mich. (1976–82), the Univ. of Southern Calif. in Los Angeles (1982–87), the Juilliard School in N.Y. (1987–90), and at the Yale Univ. School of Music (from 1987). In addition to his performances of the standard clarinet literature, Shifrin has commissioned scores from several American composers, among them Stephen Albert and Ezra Laderman.—**NS/LK/DM**

Shifrin, Seymour, American composer and teacher; b. N.Y., Feb. 28, 1926; d. Boston, Sept. 26, 1979. After studies at N.Y.'s H.S. of Music and Art, he received private instruction from Schuman (1942–45). He continued his training at Columbia Univ. (B.A., 1947), where he completed his graduate study in composition with Luening (M.A., 1949), and then pursued additional training with Milhaud in Paris on a Fulbright scholarship (1951–52). He held 2 Guggenheim fellowships (1956, 1960). Shifrin taught at Columbia Univ. (1949–50), City Coll. of the City Univ. of N.Y. (1950–51), the Univ. of Calif. at Berkeley (1952–66), and at Brandeis Univ. (1966–79). He wrote music of high chromatic consistency, with finely delineated contrapuntal lines often resulting in sharp dissonance.

WORKS: ORCH.: *Music for Orchestra* (1948); *Chamber Symphony* (1952–53); *3 Pieces* (1958; Minneapolis, Jan. 8, 1960). **CHAMBER:** Cello Sonata (1948); 5 string quartets (1949; 1962; 1965–66; 1966–67; 1971–72); *Serenade* for Oboe, Clarinet, Horn, Viola, and Piano (1954); *Concert Piece* for Violin (1959); *In eius memoriam* for Flute, Clarinet, Violin, Cello, and Piano (1967–68); *Duo* for Violin and Piano (1969); Piano Trio (1974); *The Nick of Time* for Flute, Clarinet, Percussion, Piano Trio, and Double Bass (1978). **Piano:** *4 Cantos* (1948); *Composition* (1950); *Trauermusik* (1956); *The Modern Temper* for Piano, 4-Hands (1959); *Fantasy* (1961); *Responses* (1973); *Waltz* (1977). **VOCAL:** *Cantata to Sophoclean Choruses* for Chorus and Orch. (1957–58; Boston, May 2, 1984); *Odes of Chang* for Chorus, Piano, and Percussion (1963); *Satires of Circumstance* for Mezzo-soprano, Flute, Clarinet, Violin, Cello, Double Bass, and Piano (1964); *Chronicles* for 3 Male Soloists, Chorus, and Orch. (1970; Boston, Oct. 27, 1976); *A Renaissance Garland* for Soprano, Tenor, Recorders, Viols, Lute, and Percussion (1975); *Five Last Songs* for Soprano and Piano (1979; also for Soprano and Chamber Orch. as completed by M. Boykan).—**NS/LK/DM**

Shilkret, Nat(haniel), American conductor, arranger, and composer; b. N.Y., Dec. 25, 1889; d. Franklin Square, Long Island, N.Y., Feb. 18, 1982. He studied composition with Pietro Floridia. He played the clarinet in the Russian Sym. Orch. in N.Y., the N.Y. Phil., the N.Y. Sym. Orch., and the Metropolitan Opera orch., as well as in bands led by Sousa, Pryor, and E.F. Goldman. In 1916 he became music director of the Victor Talking Machine Co., and created the Victor Salon Orch. in 1924, for which he made numerous arrangements, recordings, and radio broadcasts. In 1935 he went to Hollywood, where he became active as a film score arranger and composer. He wrote a symphonic poem, *Skyward* (1928), a Trombone Concerto (1942), various descriptive pieces for orch., chamber music, and numerous songs; also commissioned Schoenberg, Stravinsky, Toch, Milhaud, Castelnuovo-Tedesco, and Tansman to write a movement each for a biblical cantata, *Genesis* (1947), to which he himself contributed a movement.—**NS/LK/DM**

Shiloah, Amnon, Israeli ethnomusicologist; b. Lanus, Argentina (of Syrian parents), Sept. 28, 1928. He went to Israel in 1941 to study flute with Uri Toeplitz at the Rubin Academy of Music in Jerusalem; later studied flute at the Paris Cons. (1954–58), and also took courses with Corbin and Chailley at the Sorbonne Inst. of Musicology. He returned to Israel as flutist of the Israel Broadcasting Sym. Orch. (1959–60); studied Hebrew and Arab literature at Hebrew Univ. in Jerusalem (M.A., 1960); subsequently earned his Ph.D. at the Sorbonne (1963, with the diss. *La Perfection des connaissances musicales*, a study of Arab theory; publ. in Paris, 1972). As head of the folklore dept. of the Israel Broadcasting Authority, Shiloah undertook extensive fieldwork in Jewish and Arab music (1965–69); also directed the Jewish music center at Hebrew Univ. (1967–71), where he was head of the musicology dept. (1970–75) and a prof. (from 1973). He co-edited the periodical *Yuval*; also produced records of Jewish and Eastern Christian music. His research focuses on the literature of Arab and Hebrew theory in addition to contemporary musics of both cultures.

WRITINGS: *Caractéristiques de l'art vocale arabe du Moyen-Âge* (Tel Aviv, 1963); *Kit'ey ham-musika baz-zohar* (Musical Passages in the Zohar; Jerusalem, 1977); *The Epistle on Music of the Ikhwan al-Safa* (Tel Aviv, 1978).—NS/LK/DM

Shim, Kunsu, innovative Korean composer; b. Pusan, South Korea, Sept. 25, 1958. He studied composition with Inyong La at the Yonsei Univ. in Seoul (1979–83), and from 1983 to 1986 attended composition master classes with Sukhi Kang. In 1987 he went to Germany, where in he studied composition with Helmut Lachenmann at the Musikhochschule in Stuttgart (1987–88) and with Nicolaus Huber at the Folkwang Musikhochschule in Essen (1989–92). He won numerous prizes for his compositions in Seoul (1981–83), and in 1992 lectured at the Yonsei Univ., Kyemynug Univ., and Yongnam Univ. in Korea and in Lisbon. From 1993 he also gave workshops and lectures in the U.S., and was an artist-in-residence at the Djerassi Foundation in Woodside, Calif. (1993); in 2000 he made a lecture tour in Hong Kong and Korea. In 1998 he received a grant from the Akademie der Künste in Berlin.

WORKS: *A Lasting Song for Geha* for Piano (1990); *Orchester in Stereo mit fünf sinustönen* for 2 Orchs. (1990); *Music for 4 Violins and 1 or 3 Players* (1990; rev. 1992); *...vague sensations of something vanishing* for String Quartet and Double Bass (1992); *...floating, song, feminine...* for Marimba Player (1992); *Peripatetic Exercise* for 3 Tenor Recorder Players (1992); *Peripatetic Exercise* for Piano (1992); *birds, stones, wind, in silences..., for Martha* for Violin (1992); *secret garden,* 3 pieces for Piano, 7 Drums, and Cassette Recorder (1993); *Marimba, Bow, Stone, Player* for 1 Marimba Player with 2 Bows and Stones (1993); *tree, voice...to move* for 12 Vocalists (1993); *(untitled)* for Piano and Orch. (1993); *(untitled)* for Flute and Orch. (1993); *für Wasser, fünf Glas-Flaschen, Steinchen und drei Spieler* (Books 1 & 2, 1994); *expanding space in limited time* for Violin (1994); *(untitled)* for Flute and String Quartet (1994); *positive spaces—for Lee Ufan I* for Soprano, Flute, Clarinet, Violin, and Cello (1994), *II* for Saxophone, Trumpet, Violin, Piano, and 2 Percussionists (1994), *III* for Bass Flute, Violin, Piano, and Dancer (1994), and *IV* for Any Instruments in Any Number (1994); *three poems—for T. L.* for Percussion Player (1994); *(untitled)* for Flute (1994); *(untitled)* for Piano (1994); *man lässt Dinge fallen und beobachtet sie—eine Herbstmusik* for Any Number of Players (1994); *waiting moments/silences* for 4 Voices (1994); *eine Weile lang mit einem Violinisten,* music for an individual listener (1994); *silence, time, beginning* for Flute, Clarinet, Voice, Violin, Viola, and Cello (1994–95).—LK/DM

Shimizu, Osamu, Japanese composer; b. Osaka, Nov. 4, 1911; d. Tokyo, Oct. 29, 1986. He studied traditional Japanese instruments, and also took courses in theory and composition with Hashimoto and Hosokawa at the Tokyo Music School (1936–39). He was active in the music dept. of Tokyo Radio, and also wrote articles on music.

WORKS: **DRAMATIC: O p e r a :** *The Tale of the Mask-Maker Shuzenji* (Osaka, Nov. 4, 1954); *The Charcoal Princess* (Osaka, Nov. 1, 1956); *The Man Who Shoots at the Blue Sky* (Osaka, Nov. 26, 1956); *Gauche, the Violoncellist* (Osaka, Oct. 11, 1957); *The Singing Skeleton* (Osaka, March 15, 1962); *Shunkan, the Exile* (Osaka, Nov. 18, 1964); *The Merciful Poet,* operetta (1965); *Muko Erabi* (The Marriage Contest), comic opera (Los Angeles,

Oct. 3, 1968); *Daibutsu- Kaigen* (The Great Image of Buddha), historic opera on the inauguration of the bronze statue of Buddha on April 9, A.D. 752 (Tokyo, Oct. 2, 1970); *Ikuta Gawa* (The River Ikuta; Tokyo, Nov. 10, 1971). **B a l l e t :** *The Sun* (1955); *The Crane* (1956); *The Earth* (1957); *Araginu* (1958); *Fire in the Field* (1962); *Love Poems* (1966). **ORCH.:** *Ballad* for Violin and Orch. (1941); *Dance Suite on the Themes of Flowers* (1944); *Poème* for Flute and Orch. (1950); *4 Movements on Indian Melodies* (1950); 3 syms.: No. 1 (Tokyo, Dec. 8, 1951), No. 2 (1957), and No. 3 (1961); Suite (1953); *Taiheiraku* (1971). **CHAMBER:** String Quartet (1940); *Ballad* for Flute and Piano (1940); Quartet for Flute, Oboe, Clarinet, and Bassoon (1958). **VOCAL:** *Olympic Hymn,* for the opening of the Olympic Games (Tokyo, Oct. 10, 1964); numerous cantatas, including *Ren-nyo* (Tokyo, April 8, 1948), *La Paix* (Tokyo, April 22, 1949), and *Hymn to Dengyo-Daishi* (1966); much choral music; many songs.—NS/LK/DM

Shimoyama, Hifumi, Japanese composer; b. Aomoriken, June 21, 1930. He studied with Y. Matsudaira. In his music, he followed a determined contemporary path.

WORKS: **DRAMATIC:** *Halley's Comet (Fulfillment of a 76-Year Vow),* radiophonic piece (1981). **ORCH.:** *Reflections* for 3 Groups of Strings (1967; Hamburg, June 27, 1969); *Zone* for 16 Strings (1970); *Fümon* for Chamber Orch. and Tape (1974); *Saikyo* (1981); Cello Concerto (1984); *Yugenism I* (1988) and *II* for Clarinet, Strings, and Percussion (1998); *Ritorno* for Strings and Percussion (1994); *Doubridge* for String Orch. or String Ensemble (1995–96); Cello Concerto (1996); *Wave* for Cello, Strings, Harp, Piano, and Percussion (1996). **CHAMBER:** Violin Sonata (1956); String Quartet (1959); *Structure* for 4 Players (1961); *Dialog* for Cello and Piano (1962) and *1 to 3* for 2 Guitarists (1963, 1971, 1984); *2 Ceremonies* for Cello (1969, 1971); *Exorcism* for 5 Strings (1970); *MSP* for Violin and Piano (1972); *Wave* for Cello, Strings, Harp, Piano, and Percussion (1972); *Transmigration I* for Percussion and Double Bass (1973) and *II* for Shakuhachi, Cello, and Harp (1984); *Poem* for Cello, Piano, and Tape (1974); *Kaisho* for Organ and Percussion (1982); *Meditation* for Cello and Piano (1983); *Fümon IV* for Percussion and Tape (1984) and *V* for Clarinet, Horn, Trombone, Cello, Double Bass, Percussion, and Tape (1992); *Cube* for 8 Cellos and Timpani (1985); *The Da I* (1985) and *II* (1991) for 4 Percussionists; *Emanation* for Alto Saxophone and Percussion (1986); *Mirage* for Cello and Percussion (1989); *Ichigo no Tsukikage* for Koto, Cello, and Tape (1989–90); *Aira* for Cello (1990); *Gamma* for Guitar and String Trio (1990); *Solo* for Cello (1993); *3 Visions* for Wind Quintet and Percussion (1993); *Keikyo* for Clarinet, Double Bass, Percussion, and Tape (1994); *4 Landcapes for HET* for Flute, Bass Clarinet, Piano, and Percussion (1994); *The DA* for Marimba and 3 Percussionists (1995); *Zone* for 16 Strings (1996); *Fantasy for Kaguya-hime* for Shakuhachi, Piano, Percussion, and String Quartet (1998); *Exorcism* for String Quartet (1998). **VOCAL:** *Breath* for Chorus, Percussion, Piano, and 3 Horns (1971; Tokyo, Nov. 9, 1972); *Voices* for 3 Soloists and 2 Percussionists (1985); *Catalysis III* for Soprano and Tuba (1991).—NS/LK/DM

Shinohara, Makota, Japanese composer and teacher; b. Osaka, Dec. 10, 1931. He was a student of Ikenouchi at the Tokyo National Univ. of Fine Arts and Music (1952–54), of Messiaen at the Paris Cons. (1954–59), of Zimmermann at the Cologne Hochschule für Musik (1962–64), and of Stockhausen in Cologne (1962–65). He then worked at the Univ. of Utrecht electronic music studio (1965–66) and at the Columbia-Princeton Electronic Music Studio in N.Y. (1971–72). After serving as a prof. of Japanese music at McGill Univ. in Montreal (1978), he settled in the Netherlands in 1979 as a composer and teacher.

WORKS: ORCH.: *Solitude* (1961); *Visione II* (1970); *Egalisation* (1975); *Liberation* for Strings (1977); *Cooperation* for 8 Japanese and 8 Western Instrumentalists (1990; rev. version, Zürich, Sept. 16, 1991). **CHAMBER:** Violin Sonata (1958); *8 pièces concertante* for Trumpet and Piano (1959); *Obsession* for Oboe and Piano (1960); *Alternance* for 6 Percussionists (1961–62); *Consonance* for Flute, Horn, Cello, Harp, Vibraphone, and Marimba (1967); *Reflexion* for Oboe (1970); *Rencontre* for Percussion and Tape (1972); *Tayutai* for Koto, Percussion, and Voice (1972); *Kyudo* for Shakuhachi and Harp (1973); *Passage* for Stereophonically Amplified Bass Flute (1980; rev. 1986); *Play* for 9 Winds (1982; rev. 1985); *Turns* for Chamber Ensemble (1984); *Evolution* for Cello (1986); *Situations* for Saxophone and 2 Digital Electric Keyboards (1993). **PIANO:** *Undulation A* for 1 Piano (1996) and *B* for 2 Pianos (1997). **VOCAL:** *Personnage* for Man's Voice, Tape, and Optional Pantomime and Color Lighting (1968); *Ways of Dreams* for Chorus, Japanese Instruments, and Chamber Orch. (1992). **OTHER:** Tape pieces. **—NS/LK/DM**

Shira, Francesco, Italian conductor, singing teacher, and composer; b. Malta, Aug. 21, 1808; d. London, Oct. 15, 1883. He studied at the Milan Cons. with Basili. He brought out his first opera, *Elena e Malvina*, at La Scala in Milan (Nov. 17, 1832), on the strength of which he was engaged as conductor of the Teatro São Carlos in Lisbon (1833–42); also taught at the Lisbon Cons. In 1842, after a brief sojourn in Paris, he became conductor for the English Opera at the Princess's Theatre in London; then conducted at Drury Lane in London (1844–47); in 1848 he went over to Covent Garden; returned to Drury Lane in 1852. In later years he made a high reputation as a singing teacher, without abandoning composition. He wrote the operas *Niccolò de' Lapi* (London, 1863), *Selvaggia* (Venice, Feb. 20, 1875), and *Lia* (Venice, 1876).**—NS/LK/DM**

Shirai, Mitsuko, notable Japanese soprano, mezzo-soprano, and teacher; b. Nagano, May 28, 1947. She studied in Japan before settling in Germany, where she completed her vocal studies with Schwarzkopf. She won first prizes in vocal competitions in Vienna, Zwickau, 's-Hertogenbosch, Athens, and Munich (1973–76). With her husband **Hartmut Höll** she began to tour widely as a lieder artist in 1973. In addition to appearances throughout Germany and Europe, they also toured North and South America, Japan, Israel, and Africa. In 1987 she made her stage debut as Despina at the Frankfurt am Main Opera. In 1989 she made her N.Y. debut at Carnegie Hall in Ravel's *Shéhérazade*. She taught at the Karlsruhe Hochschule für Musik, and also gave master classes. In 1997 she and her husband were the recipients of the ABC International Music Award. Shirai's extraordinary vocal range allows her enormous scope in the choice of repertoire. In addition to the great masters of the Austro-German lied, she has championed

scores by Berlioz, Lili Boulanger, Loeffler, Schoeck, Hindemith, Prokofiev, Malipiero, Carillo, and many others. Her operatic roles include works by Mozart, Wagner, Hugo Wolf, and Dukas.**—NS/LK/DM**

Shirelles, The, pioneering girl group of the 1960s; Shirley Owens (b. June 10, 1941), Beverly Lee (b. Aug. 3, 1941), Doris Coley (b. Aug. 2, 1941; d. Sacramento, Calif. Feb. 4, 2000), and Addie "Micki" Harris (b. Jan. 22, 1940; d. Atlanta, Ga. June 10, 1982), all born in Passaic, N. J.

Formed in 1957 while Shirley Owens, Beverly Lee, Doris Coley, and Addie "Micki" Harris were in high school in Passaic, N. J., The Shirelles were convinced to record for Florence Greenberg's tiny Tiara label. Their first recording, "I Met Him on a Sunday (Ronde, Ronde)," written by the four, became a moderate pop hit when leased to Decca Records in 1958. Florence Greenberg and songwriter Luther Dixon subsequently formed Scepter Records. With Greenberg as manager and Dixon as producer, The Shirelles scored a minor hit in 1959 with "Dedicated to the One I Love," written by Lowman Pauling of The Five Royales. In 1960, "Tonight's the Night," cowritten by Owens and Dixon, became a moderate pop and major rhythm-and-blues hit. Their next single included as its B-side "Boys," later recorded by The Beatles, and their subsequent single, "Will You Love Me Tomorrow," written by Carole King and Gerry Goffin, became a top pop and smash R&B hit. The song's success established the Scepter label and made The Shirelles one of the most popular girl groups of the early 1960s.

In 1961, The Shirelles scored pop and rhythm-and-blues smashes with "Dedicated to the One I Love" (upon re-release) and "Mama Said," coauthored by Dixon. After the major pop hit "Big John" (a smash R&B hit), the group achieved smash crossover hits with "Baby It's You," written by Burt Bacharach, Hal David, and Bernie Williams, and the maudlin "Soldier Boy," co-written by Dixon and Greenberg. "Welcome Home Baby" and "Everybody Loves a Lover" became major pop and R&B hits, and were followed by the crossover smash "Foolish Little Girl," coauthored by Neil Sedaka's songwriting partner Howie Greenfield. After their final major pop hit, "Don't Say Goodnight and Mean Goodbye," The Shirelles worked on the movie *It's a Mad, Mad, Mad, Mad World*. Their minor 1964 crossover hit "Sha-La-La" soon became a major hit for England's Manfred Mann.

Luther Dixon subsequently left Scepter for Capitol Records and The Shirelles never again scored a major hit. Doris Coley, by then Doris Kenner, left the group in 1968 and the remaining three attempted a comeback on RCA Records in the early 1970s. In 1975, Kenner returned, as Shirley Owens, by then Shirley Alston, left for a solo career. Micki Harris, Beverly Lee, and Doris Kenner toured as The Shirelles in the early 1980s, but, on June 10, 1982, Harris died of a heart attack at the age of 42 after a performance in Atlanta. The three surviving original members subsequently agreed that each could assemble groups using The Shirelles' name. The Shirelles were given the Heritage award by the Rhythm and Blues Foundation in 1994 and inducted into the Rock and Roll Hall of Fame in 1996. Kenner died of breast cancer in early 2000.

DISC.: THE SHIRELLES: *Tonight's the Night* (1960); *Sing to Trumpets and Strings* (1961); *Baby It's You* (1962); *Foolish Little Girl* (1963); *Sing Their Songs in the Great Movie "It's a Mad, Mad, Mad, Mad World" and Others* (1963); *Sing Golden Oldies* (1964); *Spontaneous Combustion* (1967); *Happy and in Love* (1971); *The Shirelles* (1972). THE SHIRELLES AND KING CURTIS: *Give a Twist Party* (1962); *Eternally Soul* (1968). SHIRLEY ALSTON: *Shirley Alston* (1976). LADY ROSE (SHIRLEY ALSTON): *Lady Rose* (1977); *Sings The Shirelles' Greatest Hits* (1977).—BH

Shirinsky, Vasili (Petrovich), Russian violinist, conductor, teacher, and composer; b. Ekaterinodar, Jan. 17, 1901; d. Mamontovka, near Moscow, Aug. 16, 1965. He studied violin with D. Krein and composition with Miaskovsky at the Moscow Cons., then played in orchs.; in 1923 he joined the Moscow Cons. Quartet as second violin. Concurrently, he was active as conductor with the Moscow Radio Orch. (1930–32) and the Opera Theater Orch. (1932–36); was a teacher (1939–49) and a prof. (1949–65) at the Moscow Cons. In 1944 he was made a People's Artist of the R.S.F.S.R. He wrote 2 operas, *Pyer i Lyus* (1943–46) and *Ivan the Terrible* (1951–54), Violin Concerto (1921), 2 syms. (1936, 1938), Harp Concerto (1957), 6 string quartets (1923, 1925, 1929, 1940, 1953, 1958), piano pieces, including a Sonata (1929), 98 fugues (1937–63), and 24 preludes (1962), incidental music for theatrical plays, film scores, and choruses. His music adheres to the principles of socialist conservatism, emphasizing playability and tonal coherence; it was met with appreciation by the Soviet critics, but its performances were few and far between. His brother, Sergei Shirinsky (b. Ekaterinodar, July 18, 1903; d. Moscow, Oct. 18, 1974), was a cellist, who promoted in his programs the cause of Soviet music; he also made arrangements of various works by Classical and Romantic composers.—NS/LK/DM

Shirley, George (Irving), black American tenor and teacher; b. Indianapolis, April 18, 1934. He was educated at Wayne State Univ. in Detroit, and then received vocal training from Thelmy Georgi in Washington, D.C. and Cornelius Reid in N.Y. He made his operatic debut as Eisenstein in *Die Fledermaus* with the Turnau Opera Players in Woodstock, N.Y. (1959). In 1960 he won the American Opera Auditions and in 1961 the Metropolitan Opera Auditions; following appearances in Europe, he made his Metropolitan Opera debut in N.Y. as Ferrando on Oct. 24, 1961, and continued to sing there until 1973, as well as with other U.S. opera companies; in addition, he sang at Glyndebourne, Covent Garden in London, and La Scala in Milan. He created the role of Romilayu in Kirchner's *Lily* (N.Y., April 14, 1977). In 1992 he was made the Joseph Edgar Maddy Distinguished Univ. Prof. of Music at the Univ. of Mich. In 1993 he appeared as Edrisi in Szymanowski's *King Roger* in Buffalo. He portrayed Strauss's Herod in Detroit in 1996.—NS/LK/DM

Shirley, Jimmy (actually, **James Arthur**), jazz guitar, electric bass; b. Union, S.C., May 31, 1913; d. N.Y., Dec. 3, 1989. Shirley spent his childhood in Cleve-

land, Ohio, and was originally taught music by his father. He worked with J. Frank Terry's Band and with Hal Draper in Cincinnati (1934–36), then led his own quartet in Cleveland before moving to N.Y.; he also worked with Clarence Profit 1937–41, then spent two years accompanying Ella Fitzgerald. Shirley joined Herman Chittison's Trio in 1944 and for the next ten years played for long spells with Chittison. From the mid-1940s, Shirley also led his own small group in N.Y. clubs. He temporarily used a "vibrola" attachment on his guitar. During the mid-1940s and 1950s, Shirley also worked with Phil Moore, pianist Oliver "Toy" Wilson, Vin Strong, Billy Williams, and the Four Keys, among others. From the early 1960s, he regularly doubled on Fender Bass with George James's Band in 1963 and with Buddy Tate in 1967 and continued to work through the 1970s, mainly in N.Y.—JC/LP

Shirley-Quirk, John (Stanton), distinguished English baritone; b. Liverpool, Aug. 28, 1931. He studied voice with Roy Henderson, and at the same time took courses in chemistry and physics at the Univ. of Liverpool. He made his operatic debut as the Doctor in *Pelléas et Mélisande* at the Glyndebourne Festival (1961); then was a leading member of the English Opera Group (1964–76), where he became well known for his roles in Britten's operas; created all 7 baritone roles in Britten's *Death in Venice* (June 16, 1973). In 1973 he sang at London's Covent Garden; then made his Metropolitan Opera debut in N.Y. as the Traveler in *Death in Venice* on Oct. 18, 1974. On July 7, 1977, he created the role of Lev in Tippett's *The Ice Break* at Covent Garden. He also toured widely as a concert artist. In 1975 he was made a Commander of the Order of the British Empire. —NS/LK/DM

Shmueli, Herzl, Israeli musicologist; b. Constantinople, Nov. 8, 1920. He began studying violin at 7 and piano at 10. In 1933 he went to Palestine, where he studied violin with P. Ginzburg (until 1934). He later attended the Tel Aviv Cons. (1944–48) while studying theory and composition with Boskovich; subsequently studied musicology with Cherbuliez, composition and history with Hindemith at the Univ. of Zürich, and acoustics at the Zürich Eidgenössische Technische Hochschule für Musik (1949–53); received his Ph.D. from the Univ. of Zürich (1953, with the diss. *Higgajon Bechinnor: Betrachtungen zum Leierspiel des Jehudaa Ben-Arie Mosscato, Rabbi zu Mantua*; publ. in Tel Aviv, 1954). He returned to Tel Aviv to teach at the Music Teachers' Seminary (from 1953), where he served as director (1955–66); concurrently taught at the Tel Aviv Academy of Music. When the dept. of musicology of the Univ. of Tel Aviv was founded in 1966, he joined its faculty, subsequently becoming a prof. and dept. chairman (1971); also was chairman of the Israeli Musicological Soc. (1968–71). Shmueli directed a series of programs on music for Israeli Instructional TV, and spoke throughout Israel before many non-academic audiences; his research centers on Israeli song and art music, in addition to music of the early Romantics and of England in the

17th and 19th centuries. His writings, all publ. in Tel Aviv, include *Umanut harmusica* (Musical Craft; 1955), *Toldot hamak'hela* (History of the Choir; 1963), and *Hazemer hayisraeli* (Israeli Song; 1971).—**NS/LK/DM**

Shoemaker, Carolie J., American composer and multidisciplinary performance artist; b. Kennewick, Wash., April 9, 1963. She studied composition with William O. Smith and Diane Thome, and voice with Montserrat Alavedra at the Univ. of Wash. (B.F.A., 1989). She conducted lifelong studies in violin, voice, drama, dance, literary arts, linguistics, electronic music, and composition. Her work emphasizes the interaction of language and music and brings together such aural and visual elements as speech, narration, movement, tape, electronics, and live music into a synergistic whole. Many of her compositions are scored for variable ensemble and involve structured improvisation.

WORKS: *The Elephant's Child* for Narrator and Brass Quintet (1987); *Stitch in Time* for Voice and Tape (1988); *Classified Info* for Mixed Instruments and Newspaper (1989); *Crackdown* for Tape with Optional Live Sung/Spoken Performance (1989); *Extended Forcast* for Voice, String Quartet, and Bass Viol (1989); *Lagan Tide* for Tape, Mixed Instruments, and Voice (1989); *Bedtime Stories* for Voice over Variable Solo, or Group Ensemble with Electronics (1990); *Yo(u) Tarzan* for Voice, Sequenced Electronics, and Tape (1990).—**NS/LK/DM**

Shoffner, Bob (actually, **Robert Lee**), early jazz trumpeter; b. Bessie, Tenn., April 30, 1900; d: Chicago, Ill., March 5, 1983. His family moved to St. Louis in 1902, and at age nine, he began playing the drums, then bugle, in the local Knights of Phythias Band. He did summer tours in this boys' band, then switched to trumpet in 1911, taught by "Professor" Blue; Shoffner also began playing piano. He enlisted in the U.S. Army and spent two years with the l0th Cavalry in Ariz., eventually playing trumpet in the division band. After his release in 1919, he worked in St. Louis and on the riverboats with Charlie Creath, then toured with Tommy Parker's Band. In 1921, Shoffner visited Chicago and decided to stay there, working with various bands, before returning to St. Louis to play a season with Charlie Creath in 1922. He then settled in Chicago; from June 1924–February 1927, he worked with King Oliver, except for a brief period in early 1925. Lip problems led him to return to St. Louis in early 1927 for an operation; but he was soon back in Chicago, working with various groups through the end of the decade. In early 1931, he toured with McKinney's Cotton Pickers but, due to union restrictions, was unable to work with them in Detroit, so he returned to Chicago. He worked with various leaders there through late 1934, then relocated to N.Y., where he continued to freelance. He was back in Chicago by early 1938, and in late 1940, left full-time music to work in the administrative offices of the State of Ill. He kept this job for many years, although he continued gigging until the mid-1940s. Shoffner recommenced full-time playing in 1957. He did regular local gigs, then joined Franz Jackson's Original Jazz All-Stars;

he also organized his own concert brass band. Shoffner was forced by illness to quit regular playing in 1963, although he played occasionally in the mid-1960s. —**JC/LP**

Shore, Dinah (Frances Rose), American singer, television personality, and actress; b. Winchester, Tenn., March 1, 1917; d. Los Angeles, Feb. 24, 1994. Shore was the most successful solo female recording artist of the 1940s, while also maintaining a constant presence on radio. In the 1950s and early 1960s she hosted her own musical variety series on television, and she returned to TV as a talk show host in the 1970s. Her Southern background was reflected in her warm manner and engaging singing style. Among her 69 singles that reached the charts between 1940 and 1957, the most popular were "I'll Walk Alone," "The Gypsy," and "Buttons and Bows."

The daughter of S. A. and Anna Stein Shore, Shore grew up in Nashville, where she sang in her church choir. During her college years she took singing and acting lessons and sang on the local radio station. She made a first attempt to launch a career as a singer in N.Y. in 1937 before returning home to graduate from Vanderbilt Univ. with a B. A. in sociology in 1938. Then she headed back to N.Y. Early in her career she adopted the 1925 song "Dinah" (music by Harry Akst, lyrics by Sam M. Lewis and Joe Young) as her theme song; she also adopted the title as her first name.

In N.Y., Shore sang without pay on WNEW, a local station, where her vocal coach was Jimmy Rich. She sang with Leo Reisman and His Orch. at the Strand Theatre in N.Y. in January 1939 and in March began performing on the network radio series *Ben Bernie, the Old Maestro*. In August she launched her own network radio series, *The Dinah Shore Show*, a 15-minute weekly broadcast on Sunday evenings that ran through January 1940. She made her first recordings in 1939 as a featured vocalist with Xavier Cugat and His Orch.

Shore became a regular on the musical satire program *Chamber Music Society of Lower Basin Street* in February 1940. Her own show returned to the air in June and ran through September. She signed a recording contract with the Bluebird label of RCA Victor and had her first Top Ten hit in January 1941 with "Yes, My Darling Daughter" (music and lyrics by Jack Lawrence, based on a Ukrainian folk song), which she had performed on the *Eddie Cantor Show*, having joined the program in late 1940. She returned to the Top Ten in March with "I Hear a Rhapsody" (music and lyrics by George Fragos, Jack Baker, and Dick Gasparre) and in October with "Jim" (music by Caesar Petrillo and Edward Ross, lyrics by Nelson Shawn). In November she began another 15-minute radio program, *Songs by Dinah Shore*, which ran through April 1942.

Shore scored four Top Ten hits in 1942, the most successful being "Blues in the Night" (music by Harold Arlen, lyrics by Johnny Mercer), which became a signature song for her. At the end of April she moved to Hollywood to pursue a career as a movie actress, but she maintained her presence on radio, launching another 15-minute music program, *In Person, Dinah Shore,* in May; it ran a year. She had three more Top Ten hits in 1943, notably "You'd Be So Nice to Come Home To" (music and lyrics by Cole Porter). From June to August she sang on the radio program *Paul Whiteman Presents*, then in September began her first half-hour series, *The Birdseye Open House*, which ran for three seasons. She made her movie debut in October with a guest appearance in the all-star feature *Thank Your Lucky Stars*. On Dec. 5, 1943, she married movie actor George Montgomery. They had one child and adopted another. They were divorced on May 9, 1963.

Shore had her first onscreen acting role as costar with Danny Kaye in *Up in Arms*, released in March 1944. The next month, she was seen in another all-star film, *Follow the Boys*, singing "I'll Walk Alone" (music by Jule Styne, lyrics by Sammy Cahn); her recording of the song became her first #1 hit in October. At the end of the year she took another acting role in *Belle of the Yukon*, singing "Sleigh Ride in July" (music by James Van Heusen, lyrics by Johnny Burke), which became a Top Ten hit for her in February 1945.

She scored two more Top Ten singles in 1945 as well as two Top Ten albums, *Gershwin Show Hits* in August and *Musical Orchids* in September. In 1946, the year she moved to Columbia Records, she had seven Top Ten hits, among them "Shoo-Fly Pie and Apple Pan Dowdy" (music by Guy Wood, lyrics by Sammy Gallop); another signature song for her, the chart-topping "The Gypsy" (music and lyrics by Billy Reid); and "Doin' What Comes Natur'lly," from the Irving Berlin musical *Annie Get Your Gun*. Though she had largely given up her hopes of movie stardom, her voice was heard in the animated Disney feature *Make Mine Music* in April and she had a cameo in the Jerome Kern film biography *Till the Clouds Roll By* in December, singing "Smoke Gets in Your Eyes" (music by Kern, lyrics by Otto Harbach). In September, having switched sponsors, she was back on radio in *The Ford Show*, which ran during the 1946–47 season.

Shore had four Top Ten hits in 1947, among them "The Anniversary Song" (music and lyrics by Al Jolson and Saul Chaplin, based on the 1880 waltz "Valurile Dunării," by Ion Ivanovici), which hit #1 in March. In September her voice was heard in another animated Disney feature, *Fun and Fancy Free*. In February 1948 she returned to radio, co-starring with Johnny Mercer and Harry James on *Call for Music*, which ran through the end of the season. In October she returned as a regular on *The Eddie Cantor Show*, staying for the 1948–49 season.

Shore scored the biggest hit of her career and the biggest hit of 1948 with her recording of "Buttons and Bows" (music and lyrics by Jay Livingston and Ray Evans), which hit #1 in November and sold a million copies. She was back in the Top Ten in February 1949 with "Lavender Blue (Dilly Dilly)" (music by Eliot Daniel, lyrics by Larry Morey) and again in July in a duet with Buddy Clark on "Baby, It's Cold Outside" (music and lyrics by Frank Loesser). Her recording of "Dear Hearts and Gentle People" (music by Sammy Fain, lyrics by Bob Hilliard) peaked in the Top Ten in January 1950.

Based in N.Y. in 1950, Shore had an extended engagement at the Waldorf-Astoria Hotel, one of her few nightclub appearances, and she made her network television debut as a guest on Ed Sullivan's *Toast of the Town* series. In April she became a regular on the 15-minute weekday radio series *The Jack Smith Show*, staying on the program until December 1952. In the fall of 1950 she switched from Columbia Records back to RCA Victor and quickly scored several hits. "My Heart Cries for You" (music and lyrics by Carl Sigman and Percy Faith) peaked in the Top Ten in January 1951. That same month she joined the Broadway cast of *Call Me Madam* on the cast album, replacing the show's star, Ethel Merman, who was contracted to another label; the result was a Top Ten LP. She then duetted with Tony Martin on "A Penny a Kiss" (music and lyrics by Buddy Kaye and Ralph Care), which hit the Top Ten in March. She scored her final Top Ten hit with "Sweet Violets" (music and lyrics by Cy Cohen and Charles Grean, adapted from a traditional folk song) in August.

In November 1951, Shore first launched *The Dinah Shore Show* as a live, 15-minute television program following the nightly news on Tuesdays and Thursdays. She continued in this format for six years, until July 1957. She returned to film in April 1952, starring in *Aaron Slick from Punkin Creek*. *The Dinah Shore Show* went back on radio in March 1953, running until July 1955; during the 1954–55 season it was a simulcast of the television show. In March 1955 she won the 1954 Emmy Award for Best Female Singer, repeating in the same category the following year. She continued to record for RCA Victor and reached the Top 40 with "Whatever Lola Wants (Lola Gets)" (music and lyrics by Richard Adler and Jerry Ross) in May 1955 and with "Love and Marriage" (music by James Van Heusen, lyrics by Sammy Cahn) in December 1955.

Starting in October 1956, Shore hosted a one-hour version of *The Dinah Shore Show* on television Friday nights once a month. The following year the show moved to Sunday nights and ran weekly for the next six seasons, through May 1963. In March 1957 she reached the Top 40 for the last time with "Chantez-Chantez" (music by Irving Fields, lyrics by Albert Gamse). That same month she won an Emmy for the third straight year, this one awarded for Best Female Personality—Continuing Performance. She won again in 1958 and 1959.

Shore moved to Capitol Records by 1959, but despite some impressive recordings, notably the 1960 LP *Dinah Sings, Previn Plays*, with André Previn, she stopped having hits and left the label in 1962, after which she recorded infrequently. In 1963, following the end of her television series and her first marriage, she married contractor and professional tennis player Maurice Fabian Smith on May 26. They were divorced on Aug. 21, 1964. For the rest of the 1960s she made occasional appearances on television but was otherwise professionally inactive. In August 1970 she returned to television on a regular basis with *Dinah's Place*, a half-hour daytime talk show. She received her sixth Emmy Award when the show won for Outstanding Program Achievement in Daytime for the 1972–73 season and her seventh as Best Host or Hostess in a Talk, Service, or Variety Series for the 1973–74 season. During this period she had a long-term relationship with actor Burt Reynolds, though the two never married and later separated.

When *Dinah's Place* went off network television at the end of the 1973–74 season, Shore turned to syndication and launched *Dinah!*, a 90-minute program that included more musical performances. She won her eighth Emmy Award as Outstanding Host or Hostess in a Talk, Service, or Variety Series for the 1975–76 season. She returned to network television for the summer of 1976 with the variety series *Dinah and Her New Best Friends*. She had two small parts in films, *Oh, God!* (1977) and *H.E.A.L.T.H.* (1979). In 1979 she retitled her show *Dinah! & Friends* and brought on a co-host each week. The show ended in 1980. She turned to live performances in 1981 for the first time since 1950. In 1989 her new talk show, *A Conversation with Dinah*, premiered on the TNN cable network, running through 1991. She died of cancer at 76 in 1994.

WRITINGS: *Someone's in the Kitchen with D.* (1971); *The D. S. Cookbook* (N.Y., 1983).

BIBL.: B. Cassiday, *D.!: A Biography* (N.Y., 1979).—WR

Shore, John, English trumpeter and lutenist; b. c. 1662; d. London, Nov. 20, 1752. He was made a trumpeter-in-ordinary to James II in 1688, and became a musician-in-ordinary in the court band in 1695, succeeding his uncle as Sergeant-trumpeter in 1707. He is the reputed inventor of the tuning fork. Purcell wrote for Shore trumpet obbligatos to many of his songs.—NS/LK/DM

Shorter, Wayne, highly respected jazz and fusion tenor and soprano saxophonist and composer; b. Newark, N.J., Aug. 25, 1933. As a teenager, he worked in Newark with Nat Phipps; Grachan Moncur III was also in the band. Shorter was in the army from approximately 1956–fall 1958; threafter, he was based in Washington, D.C., where he worked gigs with Horace Silver. During one such gig at the Village Vanguard, he first met John Coltrane. In late 1958, Shorter joined Maynard Ferguson's band along with Joe Zawinul. He played in Art Blakey's Jazz Messengers (1959–63) and began attracting notice for his playing and for composing. He played with Miles Davis (1964–70). He brought his freedom in soloing to Davis's band, which inspired the rhythm section to further loosen up; he also wrote such innovative compositions as "E.S.P.," "Iris," "Orbits," "Footprints," "Dolores," "Limbo," "Vonetta," "Prince of Darkness," "Masqualero," "Nefertiti," "Fall," "Pinocchio," "Paraphernalia" and "Sanctuary." Davis called him "the intellectual musical catalyst for the band." In between tours with Davis, Shorter had time to lead a quartet in 1965–67. He left Davis in 1970 and co-founded Weather Report with Zawinul. With this group, he began to concentrate increasingly on the soprano saxophone. Although Shorter's solos were relatively brief, the composing and combined talents made this the fusion band a favorite of musicians. They were also successful with the wider audience. Their 1978

release *Heavy Weather* was the first million-selling jazz/fusion album and its single "Birdland," was a pop-radio and disco hit. The group received five Grammy nominations and an award in 1979 for the album *8:30*. They disbanded in 1985. Shorter also broadened his horizons in the 1970s and 1980s, playing Brazilian music with Milton Nascimento and working with Airto, Chick Corea, Herbie Hancock, Joni Mitchell, Steely Dan, Jim Hall, and Bobby McFerrin, among others. He reunited with his former Davis bandmates and with Freddie Hubbard in 1976, touring as V.S.O.P. and recording several albums. Since then, he has toured less often, putting together new material and a new touring band for each album. His album *Atlantis* was nominated for a Grammy in 1985; in 1986, he received his second Grammy for his composition "Call Sheet Blues." In 1992, V.S.O.P. came together once again, with Wallace Roney replacing Hubbard; the group toured and recorded the 1994 Grammy Award–winner *A Tribute to Miles*. Shorter also received a nomination for his solo on "Pinocchio." During this period, Shorter also played on film soundtracks, acted, and played in the film *Round Midnight* (1986). In 1993, he took a self-prescribed two year vacation, but still contributed saxophone performances on soundtracks for *Glengarry Glen Ross* (1993), *The Fugitive* (1993), and *Losing Isaiah* (1995). He returned to activity in 1995 with his first solo album in seven years, *High Life*. For this album, he wrote down every note, including bass parts and keyboard voicings, except for his solos. Throughout the album, he used synthesizers and computer technology, effectively expanding the size of his band by using sampled sounds. The album and tour—Shroter toured internationally with a large orchestral group that included former Living Colour drummer Will Calhoun and keyboardist Rachel Z—received mixed reviews, with many critics faulting Shorter for his heavy reliance on electronics and his relatively sparse soloing. He was given an NEA American Jazz Masters award in 1998. *Jazz at Lincoln Center* featured two nights of "Speak No Evil: The Music of Wayne Shorter" in April 1998.

On his first recordings of 1959, Shorter already had developed his distinctive buzzy yet warm sound and was already writing interesting compositions. By the mid-1960s, the compositions he wrote with Davis were moody, offbeat, yet still often catchy and singable—his blues in 6/4 time, "Footprints," is a good example. Musicians admired his ability to create tunes like "ESP" that have unique forms and unusual lengths (for example, 14 bars) yet sound natural and uncontrived. His chord sequences have had especially broad influence. They are rather non-intuitive and challenging to solo over, because they are built out of chords that are individually complex and move in unexpected ways from one to the next. In his fondness for sophisticated chord progressions, he recalls Billy Strayhorn, for whom he wrote "Sweet Pea." While with Davis, his playing moved away from the drive of a bop line into lines with more and more spaces. Shorter also loves a kind of "mumbling" articulation, purposely blurring his lines on occasion. While some feel that his improvising became too spacey, too laid back, especially while with

Weather Report, he still has helped many improvisers to discover ways to create more rhythmic plasticity, more variety, and more flexibility in their playing.

DISC.: *Introducing W. S.* (1959); *Second Genesis* (1960); *Wayning Moments* (1962); *Speak No Evil* (1964); *Night Dreamer* (1964); *JuJu* (1964); *Soothsayer* (1965); *All-Seeing Eye* (1965); *Adam's Apple* (1966); *Schizophrenia* (1967); *Super Nova* (1969); *Odyssey of Iska* (1970); *Moto Grosso Feio* (1970); *Native Dancer* (1974); *Atlantis* (1985); *Phantom Navigator* (1987); *Joy Ryder* (1987); *High Life* (1995).—**LP**

Shostakovich, Dmitri (Dmitrievich), preeminent Russian composer of the Soviet generation, whose style and idiom of composition largely defined the nature of new Russian music, father of **Maxim** and grandfather of **Dmitri Shostakovich;** b. St. Petersburg, Sept. 25, 1906; d. Moscow, Aug. 9, 1975. He was a member of a cultured Russian family; his father was an engineer employed in the government office of weights and measures; his mother was a professional pianist. Shostakovich grew up during the most difficult period of Russian revolutionary history, when famine and disease decimated the population of Petrograd. Of frail physique, he suffered from malnutrition; Glazunov, the director of the Petrograd Cons., appealed personally to the Commissar of Education, Lunacharsky, to grant an increased food ration for Shostakovich, essential for his physical survival. At the age of 9, he commenced piano lessons with his mother; in 1919 he entered the Petrograd Cons., where he studied piano with Nikolayev and composition with Steinberg; graduated in piano in 1923, and in composition in 1925. As a graduation piece, he submitted his first Sym., written at the age of 18; it was first performed by the Leningrad Phil. on May 12, 1926, under the direction of Malko, and subsequently became one of Shostakovich's most popular works. He pursued postgraduate work in composition until 1930. His second Sym., composed for the 10th anniversary of the Soviet Revolution in 1927, bearing the subtitle *Dedication to October* and ending with a rousing choral finale, was less successful despite its revolutionary sentiment. He then wrote a satirical opera, *The Nose*, after Gogol's whimsical story about the sudden disappearance of the nose from the face of a government functionary; here Shostakovich revealed his flair for musical satire; the score featured a variety of modernistic devices and included an interlude written for percussion instruments only. *The Nose* was premiered in Leningrad on Jan. 12, 1930, with considerable popular acclaim, but was attacked by officious theater critics as a product of "bourgeois decadence," and quickly withdrawn from the stage. Somewhat in the same satirical style was his ballet *The Golden Age* (1930), which included a celebrated dissonant *Polka*, satirizing the current disarmament conference in Geneva. There followed the third Sym., subtitled *May First* (Leningrad, Jan. 21, 1930), with a choral finale saluting the International Workers' Day. Despite its explicit revolutionary content, it failed to earn the approbation of Soviet spokesmen, who dismissed the work as nothing more than a formal gesture of proletarian solidarity. Shostakovich's next work was to precipitate a crisis in his career, as well as in Soviet music in general; it was an opera to the libretto drawn from a short story by the 19th-century Russian writer Leskov, entitled *Lady Macbeth of the District of Mtzensk*, and depicting adultery, murder, and suicide in a merchant home under the Czars. It was premiered in Leningrad on Jan. 22, 1934, and was hailed by most Soviet musicians as a significant work comparable to the best productions of Western modern opera. But both the staging and the music ran counter to growing Soviet puritanism; a symphonic interlude portraying a scene of adultery behind the bedroom curtain, orchestrated with suggestive passages on the slide trombones, shocked the Soviet officials present at the performance by its bold naturalism. After the Moscow production of the opera, *Pravda*, the official organ of the Communist party, publ. an unsigned (and therefore all the more authoritative) article accusing Shostakovich of creating a "bedlam of noise." The brutality of this assault dismayed Shostakovich; he readily admitted his faults in both content and treatment of the subject, and declared his solemn determination to write music according to the then-emerging formula of "socialist realism." His next stage production was a ballet, *The Limpid Brook* (Leningrad, April 4, 1935), portraying the pastoral scenes on a Soviet collective farm. In this work he tempered his dissonant idiom, and the subject seemed eminently fitting for the Soviet theater; but it, too, was condemned in *Pravda*, this time for an insufficiently dignified treatment of Soviet life. Having been rebuked twice for 2 radically different theater works, Shostakovich abandoned all attempts to write for the stage, and returned to purely instrumental composition. But as though pursued by vengeful fate, he again suffered a painful reverse. His fourth Sym. (1935–36) was placed in rehearsal by the Leningrad Phil., but withdrawn before the performance when representatives of the musical officialdom and even the orch. musicians themselves sharply criticized the piece. Shostakovich's rehabilitation finally came with the production of his 5th Sym. (Leningrad, Nov. 21, 1937), a work of rhapsodic grandeur, culminating in a powerful climax; it was hailed, as though by spontaneous consensus, as a model of true Soviet art, classical in formal design, lucid in its harmonic idiom, and optimistic in its philosophical connotations. The height of his rise to recognition was achieved in his 7th Sym. He began its composition during the siege of Leningrad by the Nazis in the autumn of 1941; he served in the fire brigade during the air raids; then flew from Leningrad to the temporary Soviet capital in Kuibishev, on the Volga, where he completed the score, which was premiered there on March 1, 1942. Its symphonic development is realistic in the extreme, with the theme of the Nazis, in mechanical march time, rising to monstrous loudness, only to be overcome and reduced to a pathetic drum dribble by a victorious Russian song. The work became a musical symbol of the Russian struggle against the overwhelmingly superior Nazi war machine; it was given the subtitle *Leningrad Symphony*, and was performed during World War II by virtually every orch. in the Allied countries. Ironically, in later years Shostakovich intimated that the sym. had little or nothing to do with the events of the siege of Leningrad but actually with the siege of Russia in the grip of the dehumanizing and tyrannical Stalinist regime. After the tremendous emotional appeal of the *Leningrad Symphony*, the 8th Sym., written in 1943, had a lesser impact; the 9th, 10th, and 11th syms. followed (1945, 1953, 1957) without attracting much comment; the 12th Sym. (1960–61), dedicated to the memory of Lenin, aroused a little more interest. But it was left for his 13th Sym. (Leningrad, Dec. 18, 1962) to create a controversy which seemed to be Shostakovich's peculiar destiny; its vocal first movement for solo bass and men's chorus, to words by the Soviet poet Evtushenko, expressing the horror of the massacre of Jews by the Nazis during their occupation of the city of Kiev, and containing a warning against residual anti-Semitism in Soviet Russia, met with unexpected criticism by the chairman of the Communist party, Nikita Khrushchev, who complained about the exclusive attention in Evtushenko's poem to Jewish victims, and his failure to mention the Ukrainians and other nationals who were also slaughtered. The text of the poem was altered to meet these objections, but the 13th Sym. never gained wide acceptance. There followed the remarkable 14th Sym. (1969), in 11 sections, scored for voices and orch., to words by Federico García Lorca, Apollinaire, Rilke, and the Russian poet Kuchelbecker. Shostakovich's 15th Sym., his last (premiered in Moscow under the direction of his son Maxim on Jan. 8, 1972), demonstrated his undying spirit of innovation; the score is set in the key of C major, but it contains a dodecaphonic passage and literal allusions to motives from Rossini's *William Tell Overture* and the Fate Motif from Wagner's *Die Walküre*. Shostakovich's adoption, however limited, of themes built on 12 different notes, a procedure that he had himself condemned as antimusical, is interesting both from the psychological and sociological standpoint; he experimented with these techniques in several other works; his first explicit use of a 12-tone subject occurred in his 12th String Quartet (1968). Equally illuminating is his use in some of his scores of a personal monogram, D.S.C.H. (for D, Es, C, H in German notation, i.e., D, E-flat, C, B). One by one, his early works, originally condemned as unacceptable to Soviet reality, were returned to the stage and the concert hall; the objectionable fourth and 13th syms. were publ. and recorded; the operas *The Nose* and *Lady Macbeth of the District of Mtzensk* (renamed *Katerina Izmailova*, after the name of the heroine) had several successful revivals.

Shostakovich excelled in instrumental music. Besides the 15 syms., he wrote 15 string quartets, a String Octet, Piano Quintet, 2 piano trios, Cello Sonata, Violin Sonata, Viola Sonata, 2 violin concertos, 2 piano concertos, 2 cello concertos, 24 preludes for Piano, 24 preludes and fugues for Piano, 2 piano sonatas, and several short piano pieces; also choral works and song cycles. What is most remarkable about Shostakovich is the unfailing consistency of his style of composition. His entire oeuvre, from his first work to the last (147 opus numbers in all), proclaims a personal article of faith. His idiom is unmistakably of the 20th century, making free use of dissonant harmonies and intricate contrapuntal designs, yet never abandoning inherent tonality; his music is teleological, leading invariably to a tonal climax, often in a triumphal triadic declaration. Most of his works carry key signatures; his metrical structure is governed

by a unifying rhythmic pulse. Shostakovich is equally eloquent in dramatic and lyric utterance; he has no fear of prolonging his slow movements in relentless dynamic rise and fall; the cumulative power of his kinetic drive in rapid movements is overwhelming. Through all the peripeties of his career, he never changed his musical language in its fundamental modalities. When the flow of his music met obstacles, whether technical or external, he obviated them without changing the main direction. In a special announcement issued after Shostakovich's death, the government of the U.S.S.R. summarized his work as a "remarkable example of fidelity to the traditions of musical classicism, and above all, to the Russian traditions, finding his inspiration in the reality of Soviet life, reasserting and developing in his creative innovations the art of socialist realism, and in so doing, contributing to universal progressive musical culture." His honors, both domestic and foreign, were many: the Order of Lenin (1946, 1956, 1966), People's Artist of the U.S.S.R. (1954), Hero of Socialist Labor (1966), Order of the October Revolution (1971), honorary Doctor of the Univ. of Oxford (1958), Laureate of the International Sibelius Prize (1958), and Doctor of Fine Arts from Northwestern Univ. (1973). He visited the U.S. as a delegate to the World Peace Conference in 1949, as a member of a group of Soviet musicians in 1959, and to receive the degree of D.F.A. from Northwestern Univ. in 1973. A postage stamp of 6 kopecks, bearing his photograph and an excerpt from the *Leningrad Symphony*, was issued by the Soviet Post Office in 1976 to commemorate his 70th birthday. A collected edition of his works was publ. in Moscow (42 vols., 1980 et seq.).

WORKS: DRAMATIC: Opera: *The Nose*, op.15 (1927–28; Leningrad, Jan. 12, 1930); *Lady Macbeth of the District of Mtzensk*, op.29 (1930–32; Leningrad, Jan. 22, 1934; rev. as *Katerina Izmaylova*, op.114, 1956–63; Moscow, Jan. 8, 1963); *The Gamblers* (1941–42; unfinished; Leningrad, Sept. 18, 1978). **Operetta:** *Moskva, Cheryomushki*, op.105 (1958; Moscow, Jan. 24, 1959). **Ballet:** *The Golden Age*, op.22 (Leningrad, Oct. 26, 1930); *Bolt*, op.27 (Leningrad, April 8, 1931); *The Limpid Brook*, op.39 (Leningrad, April 4, 1935). **Incidental Music:** *The Bedbug*, op.19 (Moscow, Feb. 13, 1929); *The Shot*, op.24 (Leningrad, Dec. 14, 1929; not extant); *Virgin Soil*, op.25 (Leningrad, May 9, 1930; not extant); *Rule, Britannia!*, op.28 (Leningrad, May 9, 1931); *Conditionally Killed*, op.31 (Leningrad, Oct. 20, 1931); *Hamlet*, op.32 (Moscow, March 19, 1932); *The Human Comedy*, op.37 (Moscow, April 1, 1934); *Hail, Spain*, op.44 (Leningrad, Nov. 23, 1936); *King Lear*, op.58a (1940; Leningrad, March 24, 1941); *Native Country*, op.63 (Moscow, Nov. 7, 1942); *Russian River*, op.66 (Moscow, Dec. 1944); *Victorious Spring*, op.72 (1945; Moscow, May 1946). **Film:** *New Babylon*, op.18 (1928–29); *Alone*, op.26 (1930–31); *Golden Mountains*, op.30 (1931); *Counterplan*, op.33 (1932); *The Tale of the Priest and His Worker Blockhead*, op.36 (1933–34; unfinished; rev. as a comic opera by S. Khentova, 1980); *Love and Hatred*, op.38 (1934); *The Youth of Maxim*, op.41 (1934); *Girl Friends*, op.41a (1934–35); *The Return of Maxim*, op.45 (1936–37); *Volochayev Days*, op.48 (1936–37); *The Vyborg District*, op.50 (1938); *Friends*, op.51 (1938); *The Great Citizen*, op.52 (1937); *The Man with a Gun*, op.53 (1938); *The Great Citizen*, op.55 (1938–39); *The Silly Little Mouse*, op.56 (1939; unfinished); *The Adventures of Korzinkina*, op.59 (1940; not extant); *Zoya*, op.64 (1944); *Simple People*, op.71 (1945); *The Young*

Guard, op.75 (1947–48); *Pirogov*, op.76 (1947); *Michurin*, op.78 (1948); *Encounter at the Elbe*, op.80 (1948); *The Fall of Berlin*, op.82 (1949); *Belinsky*, op.85 (1950); *The Unforgettable Year 1919*, op.89 (1951); *Song of the Great Rivers (Unity)*, op.95 (1954); *The Gadfly*, op.97 (1955); *The First Echelon*, op.99 (1955–56); *Five Days—Five Nights*, op.111 (1960); *Hamlet*, op.116 (1963–64); *A Year Is a Lifetime*, op.120 (1965); *Sofia Perovskaya*, op.132 (1967); *King Lear*, op.137 (1970). **ORCH.:** *Scherzo*, op.1 (1919); *Theme and Variations*, op.3 (1921–22); *Scherzo*, op.7 (1923–24); 15 syms.: No. 1, op.10 (1924–25; Leningrad, May 12, 1926), No. 2, *To October*, with Bass and Chorus in the finale, op.14 (Leningrad, Nov. 5, 1927), No. 3, *The First of May*, with Chorus in the finale, op.20, (1929; Leningrad, Jan. 21, 1930), No. 4, op.43 (1935–36; Moscow, Dec. 30, 1961), No. 5, op.47 (Leningrad, Nov. 21, 1937), No. 6, op.54 (Leningrad, Nov. 5, 1939), No. 7, *Leningrad*, op.60 (1941; Kuibishev, March 1, 1942), No. 8, op.65 (Moscow, Nov. 3, 1943), No. 9, op.70 (Leningrad, Nov. 3, 1945), No. 10, op.93 (Leningrad, Dec. 17, 1953), No. 11, *The Year 1905*, op.103 (Moscow, Oct. 30, 1957), No. 12, *The Year 1917*, op.112, dedicated to the memory of Lenin (Leningrad, Oct. 1, 1961), No. 13, *Babiy Yar*, with Bass and Men's Chorus, op.113 (Moscow, Dec. 18, 1962), No. 14 for Soprano, Bass, Strings, and Percussion, op.135 (Leningrad, Sept. 29, 1969), and No. 15, op.141 (1971; Moscow, Jan. 8, 1972); 2 Pieces for E. Dressel's opera *Der arme Columbus*, op.23 (1929); 2 piano concertos: No. 1 for Piano, Trumpet, and Strings, op.35 (Leningrad, Oct. 15, 1933) and No. 2, op.102 (Moscow, May 10, 1957); *5 Fragments*, op.42 (1935); *Solemn March* for Military Band (1942); 2 violin concertos: No. 1, op.77 (1947–48; Leningrad, Oct. 29, 1955) and No. 2, op.129 (Moscow, Sept. 13, 1967); *3 Pieces for Orchestra* (1947–48); *Festive Overture*, op.96 (1954); 2 cello concertos: No. 1, op.107 (Leningrad, Oct. 4, 1959) and No. 2, op.126 (Moscow, Sept. 25, 1966); *Novorossiisk Chimes: The Flame of Eternal Glory* (1960); *Overture on Russian and Khirghiz Folk Themes*, op.115 (1963; Moscow, Oct. 10, 1965); *Funeral-Triumphal Prelude in Memory of the Heroes of the Battle of Stalingrad*, op.130 (1967); *October*, symphonic poem, op.131 (Moscow, Sept. 26, 1967); *March of the Soviet Militia* for Military Band, op.139 (1970); also 27 suites from various works (1927–65). **CHAMBER:** 2 piano trios: No. 1, op.8 (1923) and No. 2, op.67 (Leningrad, Nov. 14, 1944); 3 Pieces for Cello and Piano, op.9 (1923–24; not extant); 2 Pieces for String Octet, op.11 (1924–25); Cello Sonata, op.40 (Leningrad, Dec. 25, 1934); 15 string quartets: No. 1, op.49 (Leningrad, Oct. 10, 1938), No. 2, op.68 (Leningrad, Nov. 14, 1944), No. 3, op.73 (Moscow, Dec. 16, 1946), No. 4, op.83 (1949; Moscow, Dec. 3, 1953), No. 5, op.92 (1952; Moscow, Nov. 13, 1953), No. 6, op.101 (Leningrad, Oct. 7, 1956), No. 7, op.108 (Leningrad, May 15, 1960), No. 8, op.110 (Leningrad, Oct. 2, 1960), No. 9, op.117 (Moscow, Nov. 20, 1964), No. 10, op.118 (Moscow, Nov. 10, 1964), No. 11, op.122 (Leningrad, May 28, 1966), No. 12, op.133 (Moscow, Sept. 14, 1968), No. 13, op.138 (Leningrad, Dec. 13, 1970), No. 14, op.142 (Leningrad, Nov. 12, 1973), and No. 15, op.144 (Leningrad, Nov. 15, 1974); 3 Pieces for Violin (1940); Piano Quintet, op.57 (Moscow, Nov. 23, 1940); Violin Sonata, op.134 (1968; Moscow, May 3, 1969); Viola Sonata, op.147 (Leningrad, Oct. 1, 1975). **Piano:** *Minuet, Prelude, and Intermezzo* (1919–20; unfinished); *Murzilka* (n.d.); *8 Preludes*, op.2 (1918–20); *5 Preludes* (1919–21); *3 Fantastic Dances*, op.5 (1920–22); Suite for 2 Pianos, op.6 (1922); 2 sonatas: No. 1, op.12 (Leningrad, Dec. 12, 1926) and No. 2, op.61 (Moscow, June 6, 1943); *Aphorisms*, op.13 (1927); *24 Preludes*, op.34 (1932–33); *Children's Notebook*, op.69 (1944–45); *Merry March* for 2 Pianos (1949); *24 Preludes and Fugues*, op.87 (1950–51; Leningrad, Dec. 23, 1952); Concertino

for 2 Pianos, op.94 (1953). **VOCAL: Choral:** *The Oath to the People's Commissar* for Bass, Chorus, and Piano (1941); *Poem of the Motherland*, cantata for Mezzo-soprano, Tenor, 2 Baritones, Bass, Chorus, and Orch., op.74 (1947); *Song of the Forests*, oratorio for Tenor, Bass, Boy's Chorus, Mixed Chorus, and Orch., op.81 (Leningrad, Nov. 15, 1949); *10 Poems* for Chorus and Boy's Chorus, op.88 (1951); *10 Russian Folksong Arrangements* for Soloists, Chorus, and Piano (1951); *The Sun Shines on our Motherland*, cantata for Boy's Chorus, Mixed Chorus, and Orch., op.90 (1952); *2 Russian Folksong Arrangements* for Chorus, op.104 (1957); *Little Paradise*, cantata for 4 Basses, Small Chorus, and Piano (c. 1960; Washington, D.C., Jan. 12, 1989); *The Execution of Stepan Razin* for Bass, Chorus, and Orch., op.119 (Moscow, Dec. 28, 1964); *Loyalty*, 8 ballads for Men's Chorus, op.136 (1970). **Solo Voice:** *2 Fables of Krilov* for Mezzo-soprano and Orch., op.4 (1922; Moscow, Sept. 16, 1981); *6 Romances on Texts of Japanese Poets* for Tenor and Orch., op.21 (1928–32); *4 Romances* for Bass and Piano, op.46 (1936–37; Nos. 1 to 3 orchestrated); *6 Romances* for Bass and Piano, op.62 (1942; orchestrated as opp. 62a and 140); *Patriotic Song* (1943); *Song About the Red Army* (1943; in collaboration with A. Khachaturian); *From Jewish Folk Poetry* for Soprano, Alto, Tenor, and Piano, op.79 (1948; orchestrated as op.79a); *2 Romances* for Man's Voice and Piano, op.84 (1950); *4 Songs* for Voice and Piano, op.86 (1951); *4 Monologues* for Bass and Piano, op.91 (1952); *Greek Songs* for Voice and Piano (1952–53); *5 Romances: Songs of our Days* for Bass and Piano, op.95 (1954); *There Were Kisses* for Voice and Piano (1954); *Spanish Songs* for Mezzo-soprano and Piano, op.100 (1956); *Satires: Pictures of the Past* for Soprano and Piano, op.109 (1960); *5 Romances* for Bass and Piano, op.121 (1965); *Preface to the Complete Collection of My Works and Reflections on this Preface* for Bass and Piano, op.123 (1966); *7 Romances on Poems of A. Blok* for Soprano, Violin, Cello, and Piano, op.127 (1967); *Spring, Spring* for Bass and Piano, op.128 (1967); *6 Romances* for Bass and Chamber Orch., op.140 (1971); *6 Poems of Marina Tsvetayeva* for Alto and Piano, op.143 (1973; orchestrated as op.143a); *Suite* for Bass and Piano, op.145 (1974; orchestrated as op.145a); *4 Verses of Captain Lebyadkin* for Bass and Piano, op.146 (1975). **OTHER:** Orchestrations of several works, including Mussorgsky's *Boris Godunov* (1939–40), *Khovanshchina* (1958), and *Songs and Dances of Death* (1962).

BIBL.: V. Seroff, *D. S.: The Life and Background of a Soviet Composer* (N.Y., 1943); M. Sahlberg-Vatchnadze, *S.* (Paris, 1945); I. Martinov, *D. S.* (Moscow, 1946; second ed., 1956; Eng. tr., 1947); L. Danilevich, *D. S.* (Moscow, 1958); M. Sabinina, *D. S.* (Moscow, 1959); G. Orlov, *Simfonii S.s* (Moscow, 1961–62); H. Brockhaus, *D. S.* (Leipzig, 1962; second ed., abr., 1963); M. Sabinina, *Simfonizm S.a* (Moscow, 1965); K. Laux, *D. S., Chronist seines Volkes* (Berlin, 1966); G. Orlov, *D. S.* (Leningrad, 1966); L. Danilevich, ed., *D. S.* (Moscow, 1967); G. Ordzhonokidze, ed., *D. S.* (Moscow, 1967); N. Kay, *S.* (London, 1971); P. Buske, *D. S.* (Berlin, 1975); L. Tretyakova, *D. S.* (Moscow, 1976); M. Mac-Donald, *D. S.: A Complete Catalogue* (London, 1977); H. Ottaway, *S. Symphonies* (London, 1978); R. Blokker, *The Music of D. S.: The Symphonies* (London, 1978); S. Khentova, *S. v Petrograde-Leningrade* (Leningrad, 1979; second ed., 1979); M. Shaginyan, *D. S.* (On S.; Moscow, 1979); S. Volkov, ed., *Testimony: The Memoirs of D. S.* (London and N.Y., 1979); N. Lukyanova, *D.D. S.* (Moscow, 1980); D. and L. Sollertinsky, *Pages from the Life of D. S.* (N.Y., 1980); D. Hulme, *D. S.: Catalogue, Bibliography and Discography* (Muir of Ord, 1982; second ed., 1991); C. Norris, ed., *S.: The Man and His Music* (London, 1982); E. Roseberry, *S.: His Life and Times* (Tunbridge Wells and N.Y., 1982); F. Streller, *D. S.*

(Leipzig, 1982); J. Devlin, *S.* (Borough Green, 1983); D. Gojowy, *D. S. mit Selbstzeugnissen und Bilddokumenten* (Reinbek bei Hamburg, 1983); J. Hubard, *The First Five Symphonies of D. S.* (diss., Ball State Univ., 1984); D. Fanning, *The Breath of a Symphonist: S.'s Tenth* (London, 1988); K. Kopp, *Form und Gehalt der Symphonien des D. S.* (Bonn, 1990); I. MacDonald, *The New S.* (Boston, 1990); G. Wolter, *D. S., eine sowjetische Tragödie: Rezeptionsgeschichte* (Frankfurt am Main, 1991); E. Wilson, *S.: A Life Remembered* (London, 1994); D. Fanning, ed., *S. Studies* (Cambridge, 1995); M. Koball, *Pathos und Groteske: Die deutsche Tradition in symphonischen Schaffen von D. S.* (Berlin, 1997); L. Mikheeva, *Zhizn D. S.* (Moscow, 1997); E. Stetina, *Die vierte Symphonie von D. S.: Ein zurückbehaltenes Bekenntnis* (Aachen, 1997); A. Ho and D. Feofanov, *S. Reconsidered* (London, 1998). —NS/LK/DM

Shostakovich, Dmitri, Russian pianist, son of **Maxim Shostakovich** and grandson of **Dmitri (Dmitrievich) Shostakovich;** b. Moscow, Aug. 9, 1961. He studied piano with Elena Khoven. He made his debut as a soloist with the State Academic Sym. Orch. in 1978 in Moscow; also toured Italy in 1979. In April 1981 he was soloist with the U.S.S.R. State Radio Orch. during its tour of West Germany, conducted by his father, who then decided not to return to Russia; both applied for resident visas for the U.S., which were granted. In Sept. 1981 he joined his father and Mstislav Rostropovich in a series of concerts with the National Sym. Orch. of Washington, D.C., in celebration of the 75th anniversary of the birth of his grandfather. In subsequent years he also appeared with other U. S. and European orchs. —NS/LK/DM

Shostakovich, Maxim, Russian conductor, son of **Dmitri (Dmitrievich) Shostakovich** and father of **Dmitri Shostakovich;** b. Leningrad, May 10, 1938. He studied piano at the Moscow Cons. with Yakov Flier, and conducting with Gauk and Rozhdestvensky. In 1963 he became asst. conductor of the Moscow Sym. Orch., and in 1966, of the U.S.S.R. State Orch., which he accompanied on its U.S. tour in 1969; then was its principal conductor from 1971 until he defected during the orch.'s tour of West Germany in 1981. He and his son then settled in the U.S. On Memorial Day 1981 he conducted the National Sym. Orch. of Washington, D.C., in a special concert on the West Lawn of the U.S. Capitol; subsequently appeared as a guest conductor throughout North America, Europe, and the Far East. He was principal conductor of the Hong Kong Phil. (1983–85), artistic director of the Hartford (Conn.) Sym. Orch. (1985–86), and music director of the New Orleans Sym. Orch. (1986–91). He has become best known for his obviously authentic interpretations of his father's works.—NS/LK/DM

Shtogarenko, Andrei (Yakovlevich), Ukrainian composer and pedagogue; b. Noviye Kaidaki, near Ekaterinoslov, Oct. 15, 1902; d. Kiev, Sept. 16, 1992. He studied with Bogatyrev at the Kharkov Cons. (graduated, 1936). From 1954 to 1968 he was director of the Kiev Cons., where he also was a prof. from 1960. In 1972 he was made a People's Artist of the U.S.S.R.

WORKS: DRAMATIC: Film scores. **ORCH.:** 6 syms. (1947, rev. 1958; 1965, rev. 1970; 1971; 1973; 1975–76; *Biographical*, 1983); *Partisan Sketches* (1957); Violin Concerto (1969); Piano Concertino (1972); Violin Concertino (1972); *Symphonic Dances* (1982). **OTHER:** *Lenin Walks the Planet*, choral sym. (1958); cantatas; songs; chamber music; piano pieces.

BIBL.: A. Znosco-Borovsky, *A. S.* (Kiev, 1947; second ed., 1951); M. Borvoyk, *A. Y. S.* (Kiev, 1961); G. Vynogradov, *A. S.* (Kiev, 1973).—NS/LK/DM

Shu, Eddie (originally, Shulman, Edward), jazz reed player, trumpeter, harmonica player, singer, composer; b. N.Y., Aug. 18, 1918; d. Tampa, Fla., July 4, 1986. He toured vaudeville circuits as a harmonica-playing ventriloquist. During service in U.S. Army (November 1942–November 1945), Shu played saxophone, clarinet, and trumpet in military bands. After his discharge, he worked with Tadd Dameron, George Shearing, Johnny Bothwell, Buddy Rich, and Les Elgart prior to a period in 1949 when he worked with Lionel Hampton. During the 1950s, Shu was with Charlie Barnet and Chubby Jackson before working in Gene Krupa's Trio from 1954–58. Shu moved to Fla., led his own group, and worked as a solo act. He toured with the Louis Armstrong All-Stars, playing clarinet, in 1964 and 1965. He worked again with Lionel Hampton and Gene Krupa in the 1960s. During the 1970s, Shu did active freelance work based in N.Y.C.

DISC.: *New Stars-New Sounds, Vol. 1* (1949); *E. S.* (1955). —JC/LP

Shuard, Amy, English soprano; b. London, July 19, 1924; d. there, April 18, 1975. She studied at London's Trinity Coll. of Music. Her principal vocal instructors were Ivor Warren, Ernst Urbach, Gustav Sachs, and Eva Turner. In 1948 she gave a series of lecture-recitals in South Africa, and then made her operatic debut as Aida in Johannesburg in 1949. Returning to London, she sang at the Sadler's Wells Opera until 1955. From 1954 to 1974 she was a principal member of London's Covent Garden. She also sang in Italy, Vienna, Bayreuth, San Francisco, and Buenos Aires. In 1966 she was made a Commander of the Order of the British Empire. Her most acclaimed role was Turandot, but she also won admiration for her Brünnhilde, Sieglinde, Lady Macbeth, Santuzza, Elektra, Káta Kabanová, and Jenůfa. —NS/LK/DM

Shulman, Alan, American cellist, teacher, and composer; b. Baltimore, June 4, 1915; d. 1993. He studied cello with Salmond at the Peabody Cons. of Music in Baltimore, and composition with Wagenaar at the Juilliard School of Music in N.Y., graduating in 1937. He was a member of the NBC Sym. Orch. in N.Y. (1937–42; 1945–54), as well as a teacher at Sarah Lawrence Coll. and at the Juilliard School of Music. In 1993 he entered a nursing home.

WORKS: ORCH.: *Theme and Variations* for Viola and Orch. (N.Y., Feb. 17, 1941); *Pastorale and Dance* for Violin and Orch. (N.Y., July 15, 1944); Cello Concerto (1948; N.Y., April 13, 1950); *Waltzes* (1949); *A Laurentian Overture* (1951; N.Y., Jan. 7, 1952); *Popocatepetl*, symphonic picture (1952). **CHAMBER:** *Rendezvous* for Clarinet and Strings (1946); *Threnody* for String Quartet (1950); *Suite Miniature* for Octet of Cellos (1956); *Suite* for Cello (1950); *Top Brass* for 12 Brass Instruments (Portland, Ore., April 25, 1958); *4 Diversions* for a Pride of Cellos (Philadelphia, April 6, 1975); numerous short works for Violin, for Cello, for Piano, etc.—NS/LK/DM

Shumsky, Oscar, esteemed American violinist, conductor, and pedagogue; b. Philadelphia, March 23, 1917; d. Rye, N.Y., July 24, 2000. He commenced violin lessons at an early age and made his debut with Stokowski and the Philadelphia Orch. as a soloist in Suk's *Fantasy* for Violin and Orch. when he was only 8 (March 27, 1925); that same year he began private lessons with Auer, and then continued training with him at the Curtis Inst. of Music in Philadelphia (1928–30), where he subsequently studied with Zimbalist (1930–36). After further private studies with Zimbalist (1936–38), he played in the NBC Sym. Orch. in N.Y. (1939–42); also was first violinist in the Primrose Quartet, and appeared as a soloist with the leading U.S. orchs.; later was solo violinist with the Bach Aria Group. In 1959 he made his debut as a conductor with the Canadian National Festival Orch.; then was music director of the Canadian Stratford Festival (1959–67). In 1942 he became a teacher at the Peabody Cons. of Music in Baltimore; in 1953 he joined the staff of the Juilliard School of Music in N.Y.; also taught at the Curtis Inst. of Music (1961–65) and at the Yale School of Music (from 1975). He gave up teaching in 1981 to concentrate on his performance activities. His son, Eric Shumsky (b. Port Chester, N.Y., Dec. 7, 1953), is a violist who appeared frequently with his father in chamber music concerts. —NS/LK/DM

Shure, Leonard, respected American pianist and teacher; b. Los Angeles, April 10, 1910; d. Nantucket, Mass., Feb. 28, 1995. He was a pupil of Artur Schnabel at the Berlin Hochschule für Musik (graduated, 1928). He made his recital debut in Berlin in 1927; after serving as Schnabel's teaching assistant (1928–33), he made his U.S. debut in Boston in 1933; subsequently appeared as soloist with many U.S. orchs., as a recitalist, and as a chamber music artist. He served on the faculties of the Longy School of Music in Cambridge, Mass., the New England Cons. of Music in Boston, the Mannes Coll. of Music in N.Y., the Cleveland Inst. of Music, the Univ. of Tex. in Austin, and Boston Univ., numbering among his pupils David del Tredici, Gilbert Kalisch, Gary Karr, Ursula Oppens, and Pinchas Zukerman. He was particularly admired for his performances of Beethoven, Schubert, and Brahms.—NS/LK/DM

Siagian, Rizaldi, significant Indonesian performer, composer, and ethnomusicologist; b. Medan, North Sumatra, early 1950s. He played drums and guitar, and also sang in urban pop groups in the late 1960s, then became interested in traditional Sumatran music; studied at the Univ. of North Sumatra (B.A., 1982) and at San Diego State Univ. (M.A., 1985, with a thesis on South Indian drumming); then returned to Indonesia to head the ethnomusicology program at Universitas Sumatera Utara (U.S.U., Univ. of North Sumatra). He participated in various independent mu-

sic groups; in 1981 he appeared at London's Royal Albert Hall with the group Ansambel Bukit Barisan, and in 1989 directed a performance at the National Palace in Jakarta. In 1987 he served as artistic director for the performance of North Sumatran music for the Cultural Festival Celebration of North Sumatra and in The Hague. In 1991 he was engaged to lead a group of Batak musicians from the Lake Toba area of North Sumatra on a tour of the U.S. as part of its "Festival of Indonesia." As a composer, Siagian was first active as an arranger of popular music (1970–80); in 1986 he began composing works that combined modern and traditional musical elements, his intent being to reintegrate North Sumatran traditional instruments into the musical life of North Sumatra and Indonesia. An example of such compositional "conservation" is his resurrection of the Gambus (plucked lute), as in his *Gambus Menjelang Magrib* for Gambus, Voice, Frame Drum, Harmonium, and Violin, and in his *Gambus Kehendak in 7* and *Gambus Binal*, both for Gambus, Malaysian Drum, Taganing, Gong, Lonceng, Harmonium, Violin, Hasapi, Tube Zither, and Voice. He also composed *Lebah*, a dance accompaniment for Tube Zither, Drum, Shawm, Slit Drum, Cymbal, and Voice.—NS/LK/DM

Sibelius, Jean (actually, **Johan Julius Christian**), great Finnish composer whose music, infused with the deeply felt modalities of national folk songs, opened a modern era of Northern musical art; b. Hämeenlinna, Dec. 8, 1865; d. Järvenpää, Sept. 20, 1957. The family name stems from a Finnish peasant named Sibbe, traced back to the late 17th century; the Latin noun ending was commonly added among educated classes in Scandinavia. Sibelius was the son of an army surgeon; from early childhood, he showed a natural affinity for music. At the age of 9, he began to study piano; then took violin lessons with Gustaf Levander, a local bandmaster. He learned to play violin well enough to take part in amateur performances of chamber music. In 1885 he enrolled at the Univ. of Helsingfors (Helsinki) to study law, but abandoned it after the first semester. In the fall of 1885, he entered the Helsingfors Cons., where he studied violin with Vasiliev and Csillag; he also took courses in composition with Wegelius. In 1889 his String Quartet was performed in public, and produced a sufficiently favorable impression to obtain for him a government stipend for further study in Berlin, where he took lessons in counterpoint and fugue with Albert Becker. Later he proceeded to Vienna for additional musical training, and became a student of Robert Fuchs and Karl Goldmark (1890–91). In 1892 he married Aino Järnefelt. From then on, his destiny as a national Finnish composer was determined; the music he wrote was inspired by native legends, with the great Finnish epic *Kalevala* as a prime source of inspiration. On April 28, 1892, his symphonic poem *Kullervo*, scored for soloists, chorus, and orch., was first performed in Helsingfors. There followed one of his most remarkable works, the symphonic poem entitled simply *En Saga*, that is, "a legend"; in it he displayed to the full his genius for variation forms, based on a cumulative growth of a basic theme adorned but never encumbered with effective contrapuntal embellishments. From 1892 to 1900 he taught theory of composition at the Helsingfors Cons. In 1897 the Finnish Senate granted him an annual stipend of 3,000 marks. On April 26, 1899, he conducted in Helsingfors the premiere of his first Sym. He subsequently conducted the first performances of all of his syms., the fifth excepted. On July 2, 1900, the Helsingfors Phil. gave the first performance of his most celebrated and most profoundly moving patriotic work, *Finlandia.* Its melody soon became identified among Finnish patriots with the aspiration for national independence, so that the Czarist government went to the extreme of forbidding its performances during periods of political unrest. In 1901 Sibelius was invited to conduct his works at the annual festival of the Allgemeiner Deutscher Tonkünstlerverein at Heidelberg. In 1904 he settled in his country home at Järvenpää, where he remained for the rest of his life; he traveled rarely. In 1913 he accepted a commission for an orch. work from the American music patron Carl Stoeckel, to be performed at the 28th annual Festival at Norfolk, Conn. For it he contributed a symphonic legend, *Aalotaret* (Nymphs of the Ocean; later rev. as *The Oceanides*). He took his only sea voyage to America to conduct its premiere on June 4, 1914; on that occasion he received the honorary degree of Mus.D. from Yale Univ. Returning to Finland just before the outbreak of World War I, Sibelius withdrew into seclusion, but continued to work. He made his last public appearance in Stockholm, conducting the premiere of his 7th Sym. on March 24, 1924. He wrote 2 more works after that, including a score for Shakespeare's *The Tempest* and a symphonic poem, *Tapiola*; he practically ceased to compose after 1927. At various times, rumors were circulated that he had completed his 8th Sym., but nothing was forthcoming from Järvenpää. One persistent story was that Sibelius himself decided to burn his incomplete works. Although willing to receive journalists and reporters, he avoided answering questions about his music. He lived out his very long life as a retired person, absorbed in family interests; in some modest ways he was even a *bon vivant*; he liked his cigars and his beer, and he showed no diminution in his mental alertness. Only once was his peaceful life gravely disrupted; this was when the Russian army invaded Finland in 1940; Sibelius sent an anguished appeal to America to save his country, which by the perverse fate of world politics became allied with Nazi Germany. But after World War II, Sibelius cordially received a delegation of Soviet composers who made a reverential pilgrimage to his rural retreat. Honors were showered upon him; festivals of his music became annual events in Helsinki; in 1939 the Helsinki Cons. was renamed the Sibelius Academy in his honor; a postage stamp bearing his likeness was issued by the Finnish government on his 80th birthday; special publications—biographical, bibliographical, and photographic—were publ. in Finland. Artistically, too, Sibelius attained the status of greatness rarely vouchsafed to a living musician; several important contemporary composers paid him homage by acknowledging their debt of inspiration to him, Vaughan Williams among them. Sibelius was the last representative of 19th- century nationalistic Romanticism. He stayed aloof from modern developments, but he was not uninterested in reading scores and listening to performances on the radio of works of such men as Schoenberg, Prokofiev, Bartók, and Shostakovich.

The music of Sibelius marked the culmination of the growth of national Finnish art, in which Pacius was the protagonist, and Wegelius a worthy cultivator. Like his predecessors, he was schooled in the Germanic tradition, and his early works reflect German lyricism and dramatic thought. He opened a new era in Finnish music when he abandoned formal conventions and began to write music that seemed inchoate and diffuse but followed a powerful line of development by variation and repetition; a parallel with Beethoven's late works has frequently been drawn. The thematic material employed by Sibelius is not modeled directly on known Finnish folk songs; rather, he re-created the characteristic melodic patterns of folk music. The prevailing mood is somber, even tragic, with a certain elemental sweep and grandeur. His instrumentation is highly individual, with long songful solo passages, and with protracted transitions that are treated as integral parts of the music. His genius found its most eloquent expression in his syms. and symphonic poems; he wrote relatively little chamber music. His only opera, *The Maid in the Tower* (1896), to a text in Swedish, was never publ. He wrote some incidental music for the stage; the celebrated *Valse triste* was written in 1903 for *Kuolema*, a play by Arvid Järnefelt, brother-in-law of Sibelius.

WORKS: DRAMATIC: Opera: *Jungfrun i tornet* (The Maid in the Tower; Helsinki, Nov. 7, 1896). **Incidental Music:** Overture, op.10, and Suite, op.11, to *Karelia* (Helsinki, Nov. 13, 1893); *King Kristian II*, op.27, for a play by A. Paul (Helsinki, Feb. 28, 1898, composer conducting); *Kuolema* (Death) for Strings and Percussion, op.44, for a play by Arvid Järnefelt (Helsinki, Dec. 2, 1903, composer conducting); *Pelléas et Mélisande*, op.46, for Maeterlinck's play (Helsinki, March 17, 1905, composer conducting); *Belshazzar's Feast*, op.51, for a play by H. Procopé (Helsinki, Nov. 7, 1906, composer conducting); *Svanevhit* (Swanwhite), op.54, for Strindberg's play (Helsinki, April 8, 1908, composer conducting); *Ödlan* (The Lizard) for Violin and String Quintet, op.8, for a play by M. Lybeck (1909; Helsinki, April 6, 1910, composer conducting); *Jedermann* for Chorus, Piano, Organ, and Orch., op.83, for Hofmannsthal's play (Helsinki, Nov. 5, 1916); *The Tempest*, op.109, for Shakespeare's play (1925; Copenhagen, March 16, 1926). **Other:** *Näcken* (The Watersprite), 2 songs with Piano Trio, for a play by Wennerberg (1888); *The Language of the Birds*, wedding march for A. Paul's play *Die Sprache der Vögel* (1911); *Scaramouche*, op.71, "tragic pantomime" after the play by P. Knudsen and M. Bloch (1913; Copenhagen, May 12, 1922). **ORCH.:** *Andantino and Menuetto* for Clarinet, 2 Cornets, 2 Horns, and Baritone (1890–91); *Overture* in E major (1890–91); *Scène de ballet* (1891); *En Saga*, tone poem, op.9 (1891–92; Helsinki, Feb. 16, 1893; rev. 1901–02; Helsinki, Nov. 2, 1909); *Menuetto* (1894); *Skogsrået* (The Wood Nymph), tone poem, op.15 (1894); *Vårsång* (Spring Song), tone poem, op.16 (Vaasa, June 21, 1894); *4 Legends*, op.22 (all first perf. in Helsinki, April 13, 1896, composer conducting): No. 1, *Lemminkäinen and the Maidens of the Island* (1895; rev. 1897 and 1939), No. 2, *The Swan of Tuonela* (1893; rev. 1897 and 1900), No. 3, *Lemminkäinen in Tuonela* (1895; rev. 1897 and 1939), and No. 4, *Lemminkäinen's Homeward Journey* (1895; rev. 1897 and 1900); *King Kristian II*, suite from the incidental music, op.27 (1898); *Scènes historiques*, op.25, I (1899; rev. 1911); *Finlandia*, tone poem, op.26 (1899; rev. 1900; Helsinki, July 2, 1900, Kajanus conducting); 7 syms.: No. 1, in E minor, op.39 (Helsinki, April 26, 1899, composer conducting), No. 2, in D major, op.43 (Helsinki, March 8, 1902, composer conducting), No. 3, in C major, op.52 (1904–07; Helsinki, Sept. 25, 1907, composer conducting), No. 4, in A minor, op.63 (1909–11; Helsinki, April 3, 1911, composer conducting), No. 5, in E-flat major, op.82 (Helsinki, Dec. 8, 1915, Kajanus conducting; rev. version, Helsinki, Dec. 14, 1916; rev. version, Helsinki, Nov. 24, 1919), No. 6, in D minor, op.104 (Helsinki, Feb. 19, 1923, composer conducting), and No. 7, in C major, op.105 (Stockholm, March 24, 1924, composer conducting); *Björneborgarnas March* (1900); *Cortège* (1901); Overture in A minor (Helsinki, March 3, 1902, composer conducting); *Romance* in C major for Strings, op.42 (1903; Turku, March 1904, composer conducting); Concerto in D minor for Violin and Orch., op.47 (1903–04; Helsinki, Feb. 8, 1904, Viktor Nováček soloist, composer conducting; rev. version, Berlin, Oct. 19, 1905, Karl Halir soloist, R. Strauss conducting); *Cassazione*, op.6 (1904); *Pelléas et Mélisande*, suite from the incidental music, op.46 (1905); *Pohjola's Daughter*, symphonic fantasia, op.49 (St. Petersburg, Dec. 29, 1906, composer conducting); *Belshazzar's Feast*, suite from the incidental music, op.51 (1906; Helsinki, Sept. 25, 1907); *Pan and Echo*, dance intermezzo, op.53 (1906); *Nightride and Sunrise*, tone poem, op.55 (1907; St. Petersburg, Jan. 1909); *Svanevhit* (Swanwhite), suite from the incidental music, op.54 (1908); *In Memoriam*, funeral march, op.59 (1909; Helsinki, April 3, 1911); *The Dryad*, tone poem (1910), and *Dance Intermezzo* (1907), op.45; *Rakastava* (The Lover) for Strings and Percussion, op.14 (1911); *Scènes historiques*, op.66, II (1912); 2 serenades for Violin and Orch., op.69: No. 1, in D major (1912) and No. 2, in G minor (1913); *The Bard*, tone poem, op.64 (1913; rev. 1914); *Aallottaret* (Nymphs of the Ocean), tone poem, op.73 (1914; second version as *The Oceanides*, 1914; the latter first perf. at the Norfolk [Conn.] Festival, June 4, 1914, composer conducting); 2 pieces for Violin or Cello, and Orch., op.77 (1914); *2 Humoresques* for Violin and Orch., op.87 (1917); *4 Humoresques* for Violin and Orch., op.89 (also numbered as 3–6 in continuation of the preceding; 1917); *Promootiomarssi* (Academic March) (1919); 3 pieces, op.96: No. 1, *Valse lyrique* (1920), No. 2, *Autrefois, Scène pastorale* for 2 Voices and Orch. (1919), and No. 3, *Valse chevaleresque* (1920); *Suite mignonne* for 2 Flutes and Strings, op.98a (1921); *Suite champêtre* for Strings, op.98b (1921); *Suite caractéristique* for Harp and Strings, op.100 (1922); *The Tempest*, concert version of the incidental music, op.109 (1925); *Tapiola*, tone poem, op.112 (N.Y., Dec. 26, 1926, W. Damrosch conducting); *Andante festivo* for Strings and Percussion (1930?; also for String Quartet, 1922); Suite for Violin and Strings, op.117 (n.d.; Lahti, Dec. 8. 1990). **CHAMBER:** *Vattendroppar* (Water Drops) for Violin and Cello (1875–76); *Menuetto* in F major for 2 Violins and Piano (1883); Trio in G major for 2 Violins and Piano (1883); *Andantino* in C major for Cello and Piano (1884?); 2 quartets for 2 Violins, Cello, and Piano: D minor (1884) and C minor (1891); 4 piano trios: A minor (1884?), A minor (1886), D major, *Korpo* (1887), and C major, *Lovisa* (1888); 2 violin sonatas: A minor (1884) and F major (1889); *Andante grazioso* for Violin and Piano (1884–85); 4 string quartets: E-flat major (1885), A minor (1889), B-flat major, op.4 (1890), and D minor, op.56, *Voces intimae* (1909); *Allegro* in D major for Piano Trio (1886); *Andante cantabile* for Violin and Piano (1887); *Andante molto* in F minor for Cello and Piano (1887?); *Fantasia* for Cello and Piano (1887?); Quartet in G minor for Violin, Cello, Harmonium, and Piano (1887?); *Scherzo* for Violin, Cello, and Piano, 4-Hands (1887?); *Tempo di valse* in G minor for Cello and Piano (1887?); *Theme and Variations* in D

minor for Cello (1887?); *Andantino* in G minor for Piano Trio (1887–88); *Allegretto* in C major for Violin and Piano (1888?); *Allegretto* in E-flat major for Violin and Piano (1888?); *Andante-Allegro* in A major for Piano Quintet (1888?); *Moderato maestoso* for Violin and Piano (1888?); *Romance and Epilogue* for Violin and Cello, op.2 (1888; rev. 1911); Suite (Sonata) in D minor for Violin and Piano (1888?); *Theme and Variations* in C-sharp minor for String Quartet (1888); *Theme and Variations* in G minor for String Quartet (1888–89); Suite (Trio) in A major for String Trio (1889); *Tempo di valse* in F-sharp minor for Cello and Piano, *Lulu Waltz* (1889); Quintet in G minor for Piano and Strings (1890); Rondo for Viola and Piano (1893); *Malinconia* for Cello and Piano, op.20 (1900); 2 pieces for Violin or Cello and Piano, op.77: No. 1, *Laetare anima mea. Cantique* (1914–15) and No. 2, *Devotion* (1915); 4 pieces for Violin or Cello and Piano, op.78: No. 1, *Impromptu* (1915), No. 2, *Romance* (1915), No. 3, *Religioso* (1917), and No. 4, *Rigaudon* (1915); 6 pieces for Violin and Piano, op.79: No. 1, *Souvenir* (1915?), No. 2, *Tempo di menuetto* (1915), No. 3, *Danse caractéristique* (1916), No. 4, *Sérénade* (1916), No. 5, *Danse Idyll* (1917), and No. 6, *Berceuse* (1917); Violin Sonata in E major, op.80 (1915); 5 pieces for Violin and Piano, op.81: No. 1, *Mazurka* (1915), No. 2, *Rondino* (1917), No. 3, *Valse* (1917), No. 4, *Aubade* (1918), and No. 5, *Menuetto* (1918); *Novelette* for Violin and Piano, op.102 (1922); *Andante festivo* for String Quartet (1922; also for Strings and Percussion, 1930?); *5 Danses champêtres* for Violin and Piano, op.106 (1925); 4 pieces for Violin and Piano, op.115 (1929): No. 1, *On the Heath*, No. 2, *Ballade*, No. 3, *Humoresque*, and No. 4, *The Bells*; 3 pieces for Violin and Piano, op.116 (1929): No. 1, *Scène de danse*, No. 2, *Danse caractéristique*, and No. 3, *Rondeau romantique*. **KEYBOARD: P i a n o :** More than 150 pieces (1890–1929). **O r g a n :** 2 pieces, op.111: No. 1, *Intrada* (1925) and No. 2, *Sorgmusik Surusoitto* (Funeral Music; 1931). **VOCAL:** *Kullervo*, symphonic poem for Soprano, Baritone, Men's Chorus, and Orch., op.7 (Helsinki, April 28, 1892); *Rakastava* (The Lover) for Men's Chorus, op.14 (1893; Helsinki, April 28, 1894); *Laulu Lemminkäiselle* (A Song for Lemminkäinen) for Men's Chorus and Orch., op.31, No. 1 (1896); *Har du mod?* (Have You Courage?) for Men's Chorus and Orch., op.31, No. 2 (1904); *Atenarnes sång* (The Song of the Athenians) for Men's Voices, Winds, and Percussion, op.31, No. 3 (Helsinki, April 26, 1899); *Tulen synty* (The Origin of Fire) for Baritone, Men's Chorus, and Orch., op.32 (Helsinki, April 9, 1902, composer conducting; rev. 1910); *Vapautettu kuningatar* (The Liberated Queen), cantata for Chorus and Orch., op.48 (Helsinki, May 12, 1906); *Luonnotar* (Spirit of Nature), tone poem for Soprano and Orch., op.70 (1910; Gloucester, Sept. 10, 1913); *Oma maa* (Our Native Land), cantata for Chorus and Orch., op.92 (1918); *Jordens sång* (Song of the Earth), cantata for Chorus and Orch., op.93 (1919); *Maan virsi* (Hymn of the Earth), cantata for Chorus and Orch., op.95 (Helsinki, June 1920, composer conducting); *Väinön virsi* (Väinö's Song) for Chorus and Orch., op.110 (Helsinki, June 28, 1926, Kajanus conducting); *Masonic Ritual Music* for Men's Voices, Piano, and Organ, op.113 (1927–46; rev. 1948); also numerous other choral works, and more than 100 songs composed between 1891 and 1918.

BIBL.: R. Newmarch, *J. S.: A Finnish Composer* (Leipzig, 1906); E. Furuhjelm, *J. S.: Hans tondikting och drag ur hans liv* (Borgå, 1916); W. Niemann, *J. S.* (Leipzig, 1917); C. Gray, *S.* (London, 1931; second ed., 1945); K. Ekman, *J. S.: En konstnärs liv och personlighet* (Stockholm, 1935; Eng. tr., 1935, as *J. S.: His Life and Personality*; fourth Swedish ed., 1959); C. Gray, *S.: The Symphonies* (London, 1935); B. de Törne, *S.: A Close-Up* (London, 1937); R. Newmarch, *J. S.: A Short History of a Long*

Friendship (Boston, 1939; second ed., 1945); B. Sandberg, *J. S.* (Helsinki, 1940); E. Arnold, *Finlandia: The Story of S.* (N.Y., 1941; second ed., 1951); E. Roiha, *Die Symphonien von J. S.: Eine formanalytische Studie* (Jyväskylä, 1941); I. Krohn, *Der Formenbau in den Symphonien von J. S.* (Helsinki, 1942); E. Tanzberger, *Die symphonischen Dichtungen von J. S. (Ein inhalt sund formanalytische Studie)* (Würzburg, 1943); S. Levas, *J. S. ja hänen Ainolansa* (Helsinki, 1945; second ed., 1955); M. Similä, *Sibeliana* (Helsinki, 1945); B. de Törne, *S., i närbild och samtal* (Helsinki, 1945; second ed., 1955); G. Abraham, ed., *S.: A Symposium* (London, 1947; second ed., 1952); I. Hannikainen, *S. and the Development of Finnish Music* (London, 1948); N.-E. Ringbom, *S.* (Stockholm, 1948; Eng. tr., Norman, Okla., 1954); V. Helasvuo, *S. and the Music of Finland* (Helsinki, 1952; second ed., 1957); O. Anderrson, *J. S. i Amerika* (Åbo, 1955); S. Parmet, *S. symfonier* (Helsinki, 1955; Eng. tr., 1959, as *The Symphonies of S.: A Study in Musical Appreciation*); L. Solanterä, *The Works of J. S.* (Helsinki, 1955); H. Johnson, *J. S.* (N.Y., 1959); E. Tanzberger, *J. S.: Eine Monographie* (Wiesbaden, 1962); F. Blum, *J. S.: An International Bibliography on the Occasion of the Centennial Celebrations, 1965* (Detroit, 1965); R. Layton, *S.* (London, 1965; third ed., rev., 1983); E. Tawaststjerna, *J. S.* (5 vols., Helsinki, 1965–88; Eng. tr. by R. Layton, 1976 et seq.); R. Layton, *The World of S.* (London, 1970); B. James, *The Music of J. S.* (East Brunswick, N.J., London, and Mississauga, Ontario; 1983); E. Salmenhaara, *J. S.* (Helsinki, 1984); F. Dahlström, *The Works of J. S.* (Helsinki, 1987); T. Howell, *J. S.: Progressive Techniques in the Symphonies and Tone Poems* (N.Y., 1989); K. Kilpeläinen, *The J. S. Musical Manuscripts at Helsinki University Library: A Complete Catalogue* (Wiesbaden, 1991); E. Tawaststerjna, *J. S.: Aren 1865–1893* (Helsinki, 1992); J. Hepokoski, *S.: Symphony No. 5* (Cambridge, 1993); V. Murtomaki, *Symphonic Unity: The Development of Formal Thinking in the Symphonies of S.* (Helsinki, 1993); G. Schlüter, *The Harold E. Johnson J. S. Collection at Butler University: A Complete Catalogue* (Indianapolis, 1993); G. Goss, *J. S. and Olin Downes: Music, Friendship, Criticism* (Boston, 1995); L. Luyken, "*—aus dem Nichtigen eine Welt shcaffen—": Studien zur Dramaturgie im symphonisehen Spätwerk von J. S.* (Kassel, 1995); E. Englund, *Sibeliuksen varjossa: Katkelmia säveltäjän elämästä* (Helsinki, 1996); G. Goss, ed., *The S. Companion* (Westport, Conn., 1996); E. Salmenhaara, *J. S.: Violin Concerto* (Wilhelmshaven, 1996); G. Goss, *J. S.: A Guide to Research* (N.Y., 1997); G. Rickards, *J. S.* (London, 1997); H. Williams, *S. and His Masonic World: Sounds in "Silence"* (Lewiston, N.Y., 1998).—**NS/LK/DM**

Siboni, Erik (Anthon Valdemar), Danish organist, teacher, and composer of Italian parentage, son of **Giuseppe (Vincenzo Antonio) Siboni;** b. Copenhagen, Aug. 26, 1828; d. Frederiksberg, Feb. 11, 1892. He studied with J.P.E. Hartmann, then with Moscheles and Hauptmann at Leipzig and with Sechter at Vienna. He returned to Copenhagen, and in 1865 became organist and prof. of piano at the Soro Academy. He retired in 1883.

WORKS: DRAMATIC: O p e r a : *Loreley* (Copenhagen, 1859); *Carl den Andens flugt* (Flight of Charles II; Copenhagen, 1861). OTHER: 2 syms.; Piano Concerto (1864); *Otello*, overture (1881); choral works; Piano Quartet (1862); piano pieces. —**NS/LK/DM**

Siboni, Giuseppe (Vincenzo Antonio), Italian tenor and singing teacher, father of **Erik (Anthon Valdemar) Siboni;** b. Forlì, Jan. 27, 1780; d. Copenhagen, March 28, 1839. He made his operatic debut in

Rimini when he was only 17. Following appearances in Florence (1797), Bologna (1798), Genoa (1800), and at Milan's La Scala (1805), he became a principal singer at the King's Theatre in London in 1806, where he was chosen to create roles in several operas by Paër. He continued to sing in Italy, and also fulfilled engagements in Paris, Vienna, Prague, and St. Petersburg. In 1819 he settled in Copenhagen, where he was made director of singing at the Royal Theater and founded the Royal Cons. in 1821.—**NS/LK/DM**

Siciliani, Alessandro, Italian conductor and composer; b. Florence, June 5, 1952. He received training in piano, conducting, and composition at the Milan Cons. and the Accademia di Santa Cecilia in Rome, his principal conducting mentor being Ferrara. He conducted opera throughout Italy, including Rome, Naples, and Palermo; also conducted opera in Barcelona, Marseilles, Nice, Liège, N.Y., Philadelphia, and New Orleans. In 1988 he conducted for the first time at the Metropolitan Opera in N.Y., leading the double bill of *Cavalleria Rusticana* and *Pagliacci*; also appeared as a symphonic conductor with leading orchs. throughout Europe, the U.S., and the Far East. In 1988 he became principal guest conductor of the Teatro Colón in Buenos Aires, and of the Teatro Municipal in São Paulo. He was music advisor (1991–92) and music director (from 1992) of the Columbus (Ohio) Sym. Orch. Among his compositions are a ballet, *L'Amour Peintre*, orch. works, an oratorio, *Giona*, a cantata, etc.—**NS/LK/DM**

Sicilianos, Yorgos, Greek composer; b. Athens, Aug. 29, 1922. He studied harmony with Varvoglis at the Hellenic Cons. and with Sklavos at the Athens Cons. (until 1943); then went to Rome, where he took a course with Pizzetti at the Accademia di Santa Cecilia (1951–53); supplemented his music education at the Paris Cons. (1953–54), where he studied with Milhaud and Aubin. He received a Fulbright scholarship to continue his training with Piston at Harvard Univ., Blacher at the Berkshire Music Center at Tanglewood, and Persichetti at the Juilliard School of Music in N.Y. (1955–56). Upon his return to Greece, he occupied various educational and administrative posts. He was head of music services for the National Broadcasting Inst. (1960–61; 1979), and taught at Pierce Coll. in Athens (from 1967). His style of composition is classical in format, pandiatonic in harmony, and intricately polyphonic in contrapuntal and fugal developments.

WORKS: DRAMATIC: B a l l e t : *The Pearl* (1957); *Tanagra* for 2 Pianos and Percussion (Athens, April 21, 1958; orch. version, Athens, Feb. 5, 1962); *Bacchantes* (Athens, Jan. 11, 1960). ORCH.: Sym. (1941–47); Sym. No. 1 (1955–56; N.Y., March 1, 1958); *Prelude and Dance* (Athens Radio, Sept. 1, 1948); *The Revelation of the Fifth Seal*, symphonic poem (1951; Athens, May 11, 1952); Concertino for 5 Winds and Strings (Rome, June 9, 1953); *Concerto for Orchestra* (Athens, Nov. 28, 1954); *Synthesis* for 2 String Orchs. and Percussion (Athens, Nov. 26, 1962; based on the String Quartet No. 3, 1957–62); Cello Concerto (1963); *Variations on 4 Rhythmical Themes* (1963); *Perspectives* for 4 Orch. Groups (1966); *Episodia* for 17 Instruments (1964–67); *Antiphona* for Strings, Brass, and Percussion (1976). CHAMBER: 4 string quartets (1951; 1954–55; 1957–62; 1967); *Study for Tuba* (1974);

Schemata for 6 Percussion (1976). **P i a n o :** 3 sonatas (1939); *8 Children's Miniatures* (1963); (8) *Études compositionnelles* (1972–73; rev. as 6 études for Piano and Orch., 1975). **VOCAL:** *Stasimon II* for Mezzo-soprano, Women's Voices, and Orch. (1965); *Episodes II* for Double Chorus, Piano, Double Bass, Percussion, and Tape (1971); *Epitaphion: in memoriam Nikos Marangopoulos* for Chorus, Children's Voices, Narrator, and Orch. (1971); *Parable* for Chorus, Flute, Tuba, Percussion, and Tape (1973); *6 Songs* for Mezzo-soprano or Baritone and Piano (1975); *Moonlight Sonata*, cantata for Mezzo-soprano, Clarinet, Viola, and Guitar (1976–77).—**NS/LK/DM**

Sidarta, Otok Bima, active Indonesian composer, teacher, dancer, painter, and journalist; b. Yogyakarta, Java, May 18, 1960. He was born into an artistic family; his father, Bagong Kussudiarja, is a famous choreographer and painter, and his brother, Djaduk Ferianto, a well-known composer. Sidarta studied dance at his father's Pusat Latihan Tari (PLT, Center for Dance Study; 1967) and at Pamulangan Beksa Nyayogyakarta (PBN, 1979), founded by the important choreographer/ dancer Romo Sasminta Mardawa; also studied music at the Yogyakarta high school cons., Sekolah Menengah Karawitan Indonesia (SMKI). From 1980 to 1984 he was active in Calif.; appeared at World Music Festivals at the Calif. Inst. of the Arts in Valencia (1981) and in San Diego (1982); also participated in the Asian Pacific Culture Festival at Loyola Marymount Univ. (1983) and in the activities of the Indonesian Cultural Center, both in Los Angeles. In 1984 he returned to Indonesia, where he founded the group Kelompok Musik Sempu (KMS), which took first place in the "best creativity" category at the Acoustic Music Competition (1984); taught dance and music in Sumatra (1985) and in Kuala Lumpur (1986), following a tour to Malaysia; also was active at his father's Padepokan Seni Bagong Kussudiarja (PSBK, Residential Art Center) in Yogyakarta. In 1987 he participated in the ASEAN workshop on Liturgy and Music in Manila; also performed his own *Meja, meja* (Table, table) at a PSBK concert, "Experimental Arts I," and collaborated on and performed in the collective composition *Antara Tugu Ngejaman* with his brother at the national Pekan Komponis (Composers Festival) in Jakarta. He also founded a group that specialized in children's songs, Sanggar Dolanan Anak-anak Among Siswa. After touring with his father's group in Seoul, Japan, Hong Kong, Singapore, and Malaysia (1988), he founded Pusat Latihan Karawitan Yogyakarta (PLK, Center for the Study of [Javanese] Music). In 1989 he founded and coordinated the first composition festival in Yogyakarta for new music using Javanese gamelan, "Lomba Komposisi Karawitan I," in cooperation with PSBK and the Yogyakarta Arts Council. Sidarta's musical innovations include the addition to the gamelan of hand-held percussion instruments (such as bells, triangles, and claves), as well as the development of new percussion techniques, including placing hanging gongs horizontally on cloth and striking them muted. He also created a personal drumming style that combines Javanese, Sundanese, and original elements. He composed for various venues; from 1984 he created pieces for dance accompaniment, alone and collectively, which included *Kebangkitan Nasional, Lintasan Sejarah*

(ABRI) (Armed Forces) and *Sendratari Kelahiran*; also created works for folk theater, known as ketoprak, which were performed in art centers and on Indonesian National TV (TVRI) in Yogyakarta and Jakarta. His compositions for Javanese gamelan include *Meja, meja* (1987), *Antara Tugu Ngejaman* (with Djaduk Ferianto), and *Sang Pahlawan, Lesehan, Sibab*, and *511* (all 1988). Among his popular songs is *Kemuning* (1983). He was also active as a choreographer, numbering among his dance works *Sasap* (1978), *GothakGathuk* (1979), *Kelahiran* (1981), *Gerka Suara Nusantara* (1981), *Gaung Kaputren, Santyang*, and *Kasonangane* (all 1985), and *Lima Alit* (1988). From 1975 he was active as a painter; his works have been exhibited in Bali and at the Indonesian Consulate in Los Angeles.—**NS/LK/DM**

Sidlin, Murray, American conductor; b. Baltimore, May 6, 1940. He was a student of Galkin and Cheslock (theory) and Harold Rherig (trumpet) at the Peabody Cons. of Music in Baltimore (B.A., 1962; M.M., 1968), of Celibidache (conducting) at the Accademia Musicale Chigiana in Siena (summers, 1961–62), and of Grout and Husa at Cornell Univ. (1963–65). In 1970–71 he was asst. conductor at the Aspen (Colo.) Music Festival. After working with Barzin and the National Orchestral Assn. in N.Y. (1971), he was asst. conductor of the Baltimore Sym. Orch. (1971–73). From 1973 to 1977 he was resident conductor of the National Sym. Orch. in Washington, D.C. From 1977 to 1988 he was music director of the New Haven (Conn.) Sym. Orch. He also was music director of the Tulsa Phil. (1978–80). From 1978 to 1993 he served as director of the Aspen Music Festival conducting fellowship program. He also was music director of the Long Beach (Calif.) Sym. Orch. from 1980 to 1988. From 1987 to 1992 he was conductor of the American Music Concerts for Chevron Corp. In 1994 he became resident conductor of the Ore. Sym. Orch. in Portland.—**NS/LK/DM**

Sidran, Ben, jazz pianist, singer, songwriter, journalist; b. Chicago, Ill., Aug. 14, 1943. He grew up in Racine, Wisc. and started playing piano at age seven. He attended the Univ. of Wisc. (1961–66), and received his B.A. He met Steve Miller and Boz Scaggs there and was a member of an early Miller band, but switched to mainstream jazz. Sidran studied at the Univ. of Sussex in Brighton, England (1967–70), earning a Ph.D. in American Studies. His dissertation was the basis of the book *Black Talk*, published in 1970. He had a weekly program on WMTV in Wisc. (1973–74); by 1975–76, he was producing programs for the nationally aired WTTW-TV production *Soundstage*. He produced *The Jazz Life* (1981–83), a series of one-hour performance videos. He was also active in radio as the host and artistic director of *Jazz Alive* (1981–83) and a contributor of music features to *All Things Considered* on National Public Radio (NPR) (1983–85). From 1985–90, he was host and producer of *Sidran on Record*, an NPR program that featured weekly national interviews with jazz personalities. He hosted *New Visions* (1988–91) on the VH–1 Television Network that won a 1989 Ace Award for "Best Cable Music Series." In 1994, he was music producer and composer for the prize-winning documentary *Hoop Dreams*. He has produced albums by Van Morrison, Mose Allison, Michael Franks, Diana Ross, Jon Hendricks, Tony Williams, Ricky Peterson, Richie Cole, Dominique Eade, and others. He is president of Go Jazz Records. As a performer, since 1970 he has given concerts and lectures at universities, concert halls jazz festivals, clubs, and radio and television studios throughout the U.S., Europe, Japan, Australia and Latin America, including the Newport and Montreux Jazz Festivals. He appears in the film *Survivors* (with Archie Shepp) and did national tours with the Steve Miller Band (1987–90). From 1973–74, he taught at the Univ. of Wisc. He has written columns, articles, and criticism for *Esquire, Rolling Stone, Jazz Magazine* (France), and *Swing Journal* (Japan).

DISC.: *I Lead a Life* (1972); *Puttin' in Time on Planet Earth* (1973); *That's Life I Guess* (1976); *Free in America* (1976); *Live at Montreux* (1978); *The Cat and the Hat* (1980); *Get to the Point* (1981); *Old Songs (for the New Depression)* (1982); *Live with Richard Davis* (1985); *Too Hot to Touch* (1988); *Cool Paradise* (1990); *Life's a Lesson* (1993); *Mr. P's Shuffle* (1996).—**LP**

Siefert, Paul, German organist and composer; b. Danzig, June 28, 1586; d. there, May 6, 1666. He studied with Sweelinck in Amsterdam (1607–09), and then returned to Danzig as asst. organist at the Marienkirche. After serving as organist of the principal church in the Altstadt in Königsberg (1611–16) and as court organist in Warsaw (1616–23), he returned to Danzig as principal organist at the Marienkirche, a position he retained for the rest of his life. He publ. 5 vols. of sacred vocal music (1640–51). Among his instrumental works were *Canzona a 8* in *Psalmorum* (1651) and several chorale variations. —**LK/DM**

Siegel, Janis, jazz singer; b. N.Y., July 23, 1952. She was a member of the all-girl folk groups Young Generation and Laurel Canyon; she later sang with Jon Hendricks and Bobbie McFerrin, and recorded Ilhan Mimaroglu's "Prelude No. 16" and "String Quartet No. 4" (1978), both written for her. Siegel became best known as a member of Manhattan Transfer, a vocal quartet devoted to the performance of harmonic arrangements of jazz and popular music for which she sings alto. Formed originally in 1969, the group was reconstructed in 1972 by original member and bass Tim Hauser (b. Troy, N.Y., Dec. 12, 1941) to include Siegel, tenor Alan Paul (b. Newark, N.J., Nov. 23, 1949), and soprano Laurel Masse (b. 1954); Masse was replaced by Cheryl Bentyne (b. Jan. 17, 1954) in 1979. The group produced numerous critically acclaimed recordings. They also created an experimental TV mini-series (1975) and a video, *Vocalese Live* (1986). They continued to record and tour throughout the 1990s.

DISC.: *Experiment in White* (1982); *At Home* (1988); *Short Stories* (1990); *Slow Hot Wind* (1994). **MANHATTAN TRANSFER:** *Manhattan Transfer* (1975); *Coming Out* (1976); *Pastiche* (1978); *Manhattan Transfer Live* (1978); *Extensions* (1979); *Mecca for Moderns* (1981); *Bodies and Souls* (1983); *Bop Doo-Wop* (1984); *Vocalese* (1985); *Brazil* (1988).—**NS/LP**

Siegel, Jeffrey, American pianist; b. Chicago, Nov. 18, 1942. He was a student of Ganz at the Chicago

Musical Coll., and later of Rosina Lhévinne and Kabos at the Juilliard School in N.Y. (D.M.A., 1971). In 1958 he made his debut as a soloist with the Chicago Sym. Orch. In 1968 he captured the Silver Medal at the Queen Elisabeth of Belgium Competition in Brussels. In subsequent years, he appeared as a soloist with major American and European orchs., and also toured widely as a recitalist. His vast repertoire ranges from Mozart to Dutilleux.—**NS/LK/DM**

Siegl, Otto, Austrian composer, conductor, and pedagogue; b. Graz, Oct. 6, 1896; d. Vienna, Nov. 9, 1978. He was a pupil of Mojsisovics, Kroemer, Kunzel, and Kornauth at the Graz Schule des Steiermärkischen Musikverein (1901–15; 1918–20). In 1921–22 he was a violinist in the Vienna Sym. Orch., and then was asst. conductor of the Graz Opera (1922–24). After serving as music director in Paderborn and Herford, as a choral conductor in Essen and Bielefeld, and as a theory teacher in Hagen, he was a teacher (1933–35) and a prof. (1935–48) at the Cologne Hochschule für Musik. He also was conductor of the chorus at the Univ. and of the Gürzenich choir of Cologne (1934–48). Returning to Vienna, he taught theory at the Academy of Music (from 1948), where he later was head of the theory and conducting depts. (from 1955), and served as a prof. (1958–67). In 1957 he received Austria's Great State Prize for music.

WORKS: ORCH.: Flute Concerto (1955); Cello Concerto (1957); 2 syms. (1958, 1959); Chamber Concerto for Piano and Orch. (1960); Concerto for Clarinet and Strings (1968). **CHAMBER:** 4 cello sonatas (1923, 1923, 1924, 1967); 5 string quartets (*Burleskes,* 1924; 1924; 1932; 1941; *Festliches,* 1956); 2 viola sonatas (1925, 1938); 2 violin sonatas (1925, 1940); 2 string quintets (1940, 1954); Trio for Clarinet, Cello, and Piano (1959); *Quintet-Serenade* for Clarinet, Bassoon, Violin, Viola, and Cello (1961); Sonata for Clarinet and Cello (1965); 2 clarinet sonatas (1965, 1968); Flute Sonata (1968). **VOCAL:** *Missa Mysterium magnum* for Chorus (1926); *Eines Menschen Lied,* cantata for Soloists, Chorus, and Orch. (1931); *Klingendes Jahr,* cantata for Soprano, Men's Chorus, Piano, and String Orch. (1933); *Missa parva* for Soloists, Chorus, and Orch. (1953); *Wort und Wunder,* cantata for Soprano, Chorus, and Orch. (1955); *Missa humilitatis* for Soloists, Chorus, Organ, and Orch. (1959); *Stern des Lebens,* oratorio for Soloists, Chorus, Organ, and Orch. (1959).

BIBL.: W. Trienes, *O. S.* (Mülheim, 1956); W. Suppan, *O. S.* (Vienna, 1966).—**NS/LK/DM**

Siegmeister, Elie, significant American composer and teacher, whose works reflected the national moods and preoccupations from early social trends to universal concepts; b. N.Y., Jan. 15, 1909; d. Manhasset, N.Y., March 10, 1991. He took piano lessons as a youth with Emil Friedberger; in 1925 he entered Columbia Univ. and studied theory and composition with Seth Bingham (B.A., 1927); also took private lessons in counterpoint with Riegger; after training with Boulanger in Paris (1927–32), he received instruction in conducting from Stoessel at the Juilliard School of Music in N.Y. (1935–38). He was active with the Composers Collective of N.Y., for which he wrote songs under the name L.E. Swift; was a founder of the American Composers Alliance in 1937; was founder-conductor of the American

Ballad Singers (1939–46), which he led in performances of American folk songs. He felt strongly that music should express the social values of the people; in his early songs, he selected texts by contemporary American poets voicing indignation at the inequities of the modern world; he also gave lectures and conducted choruses at the revolutionary Pierre Degeyter (composer of the *Internationale*) Club in N.Y. As a result of his multiple musical experiences, Siegmeister developed an individual style of composition ranging from the populist American manner to strong modernistic sonorities employing a sort of euphonious dissonance with intervallic stress on minor seconds, major sevenths, and minor ninths. In his syms. and chamber music, he organized this dissonant idiom in self-consistent modern formulations, without, however, espousing any of the fashionable doctrines of composition, such as dodecaphony. The subject matter of his compositions, especially in the early period, was marked by a strongly national and socially radical character, exemplified by such works as *American Holiday, Ozark Set, Prairie Legend, Wilderness Road*, and *Western Suite*, the last achieving the rare honor of being performed by Toscanini. Siegmeister did not ignore the homely vernacular; his Clarinet Concerto is a brilliant realization of jazz, blues, and swing in a classically formal idiom. Siegmeister achieved an important position as an educator; he taught at Brooklyn Coll. (1934), the New School for Social Research (1937–38), the Univ. of Minn. (1948), and Hofstra Univ. (1949–76), where he also was composer-in-residence (from 1966); in 1976 he became prof. emeritus. He received numerous commissions and awards; held a Guggenheim fellowship in 1978 and in 1990 was elected a member of the American Academy and Inst. of Arts and Letters. In accepting this honor, he stated his *profession de foi* as first formulated in 1943: "My aim is to write as good music as I can that will at the same time speak the language of all our people."

WORKS: DRAMATIC: O p e r a : *Darling Corie* (1952; Hempstead, N.Y., Feb. 18, 1954); *Miranda and the Dark Young Man* (1955; Hartford, Conn., May 9, 1956); *The Mermaid of Lock No. 7* (Pittsburgh, July 20, 1958); *Dublin Song* (St. Louis, May 15, 1963; rev. version as *The Plough and the Stars*, Baton Rouge, La., March 16, 1969); *Night of the Moonspell* (Shreveport, La., Nov. 14, 1976); *The Marquesa of O* (1982); *Angel Levine* (N.Y., Oct. 5, 1985); *The Lady of the Lake* (N.Y., Oct. 5, 1985). **O t h e r :** *Doodle Dandy of the USA*, play with music (N.Y., Dec. 26, 1942); *Sing Out, Sweet Land*, musical (Hartford, Conn., Nov. 10, 1944); *Fables from the Dark Woods*, ballet (Shreveport, April 25, 1976). Also incidental music; film scores, including *They Came to Cordura* (1959). **ORCH.:** *American Holiday* (1933); *Abraham Lincoln Walks at Midnight* (1937); *Ozark Set* (1943; Minneapolis, Nov. 7, 1944); *Prairie Legend* (1944; N.Y., Jan. 18, 1947); *Wilderness Road* (1944; Minneapolis, Nov. 9, 1945); *Western Suite* (N.Y., Nov. 24, 1945); *Sunday in Brooklyn* (N.Y., July 21, 1946); *Lonesome Hollow* (1946; Columbus, Ohio, 1948); 8 syms.: No. 1 (N.Y., Oct. 30, 1947; rev. 1972), No. 2 (1950; N.Y., Feb. 25, 1952; rev. 1971), No. 3 (1957; Oklahoma City, Feb. 8, 1959), No. 4 (1967–70; Cleveland, Dec. 6, 1973), No. 5, *Visions of Time* (1971–75; Baltimore, May 4, 1977), No. 6 (1983; Sacramento, Nov. 4, 1984), No. 7 (1986), and No. 8 (1989; Albany, N.Y., March 30, 1990); *Summer Night* (1947; N.Y., Sept. 27, 1952); *From My Window* (1949; also for Piano); *Divertimento* (1953; Oklahoma City, March 28, 1954); Clarinet Con-

certo (Oklahoma City, Feb. 3, 1956); Flute Concerto (1960; Oklahoma City, Feb. 17, 1961); *Theater Set*, after the film score *They Came to Cordura* (1960; Rochester, N.Y., May 8, 1969); *Dick Whittington and His Cat* for Narrator and Orch. (1966; Philadelphia, Feb. 10, 1968); *5 Fantasies of the Theater* (1967; Hempstead, N.Y., Oct. 18, 1970); Piano Concerto (1974; Denver, Dec. 3, 1976; rev. 1982); *Shadows and Light: Homage to 5 Paintings* (Shreveport, La., Nov. 9, 1975); *Double Concerto: An Entertainment* for Violin, Piano, and Orch. (Columbia, Md., June 25, 1976); Violin Concerto (1977–83; Oakland, Calif., Jan. 29, 1985); *Fantasies in Line and Color: 5 American Paintings* (1981); *From These Shores: Homage to 5 American Authors* (1986; Merillville, Ind., Feb. 13, 1990); *Figures in the Wind* (1990); also works for Band. **CHAMBER:** *Nocturne* for Flute and Piano (1927); *Prelude* for Clarinet and Piano (1927); *Contrasts* for Bassoon and Piano (1929); 3 string quartets (1935, 1960, 1973); *Down River* for Alto Saxophone and Piano (1939); 6 violin sonatas (1951, 1965, 1965, 1971, 1975, 1988); *Song for a Quiet Evening* for Violin and Piano (1955); *Fantasy and Soliloquy* for Cello (1964); Sextet for Brass and Percussion (1965); *American Harp* for Harp (1966); *Declaration* for Brass and Timpani (1976); *Summer* for Viola and Piano (1978); *Ten Minutes* for 4 Players for Wind Quartet (N.Y., Jan. 15, 1989). **P i a n o :** *Theme and Variations No. 1* (1932) and *No. 2* (1967); *Toccata on Flight Rhythms* (1937); 5 sonatas: No. 1, *American* (1944), No. 2 (1964), No. 3 (1979), No. 4, *Prelude, Blues, and Toccata* (1980), and No. 5 (1987; N.Y., Jan. 15, 1988); *Sunday in Brooklyn* (1946); *3 Moods* (1959); *On This Ground* (1971); *3 Studies* (1982); also 4 vols. of educational pieces (1951–77). **VOCAL: C h o r a l :** *Heyura, Ding, Dong, Ding* (1935–70); *John Henry* (1935); *American Ballad Singers Series* (1943); *American Folk Song Choral Series* (1953); *I Have a Dream*, cantata for Baritone, Narrator, Chorus, and Orch., after Martin Luther King Jr. (1967; Omaha, Oct. 7, 1968); *A Cycle of Cities* for Soprano, Tenor, Chorus, and Orch. (Wolf Trap, Va., Aug. 8, 1974); *Cantata for FDR* for Baritone, Chorus, and Wind Ensemble (1981; Denver, May 5, 1982); *Sing Unto the Lord a New Song* for Chorus and Organ (1981). **S o n g s a n d S o n g C y c l e s** (all for Solo Voice and Piano unless otherwise given): *Cortège for Rosenbloom* (1926); *4 Robert Frost Songs* (1930); *The Strange Funeral in Braddock* (1933; also for Baritone and Orch., 1938); *3 Elegies for García Lorca* (1938); *Johnny Appleseed* for Solo Voice (1940; also for Chorus, 1940); *Nancy Hanks* (1941); *For My Daughters* (1952); *Madam to You* (1964); *The Face of War* (1966; also for Voice and Orch., 1967–68; N.Y., May 24, 1968); *Songs of Experience* (1966; rev. for Alto or Bass, Viola, and Piano, 1977); 11 songs to words by e.e. cummings (1970); *Songs of Innocence* (1972); *City Songs* (1977); *3 Minute Songs* (1978); *Brief Introduction to the Problems of Philosophy* (1979); *Ways of Love* for Voice and Chamber Orch. (1983; N.Y., Jan. 15, 1984); *Bats in My Belfry* (1990); *4 Langston Hughes Songs* (1990); *Outside My Window* (1990).

WRITINGS: Ed. with O. Downes, *A Treasury of American Song* (N.Y., 1940; third ed., 1984); *The Music Lover's Handbook* (N.Y., 1943; rev., 1973, as *The New Music Lover's Handbook*; new ed., 1983); *Work and Sing* (N.Y., 1944); *Invitation to Music* (Irvington-on- Hudson, 1961); *Harmony and Melody* (2 vols.; Belmont, Calif., 1965–66).

BIBL.: J. Gallagher, *Structural Design and Motivic Unity in the second, third, and fourth Symphonies of E. S.* (diss., Cornell Univ., 1982).—**NS/LK/DM**

Siegmund-Schultze, Walther, German musicologist; b. Schweinitz, July 6, 1916; d. Halle, March 6, 1993. He studied musicology with Arnold Schmitz at

the Univ. of Breslau (Ph.D., 1940, with the diss. *Mozarts Vokal- und Instrumentalmusik in ihren motivisch-thematischen Beziehungen*); he completed his Habilitation at the Univ. of Halle with his *Untersuchungen zum Brahms Stil und Brahms Bild* in 1951. In 1954 he became a lecturer at the Univ. of Halle; in 1956 he was made a prof. of musicology, director of the musicological faculty, and dean of the philosophy faculty. He was noted for his studies of 18th-century music; his analysis of the styles of Bach, Handel, and Mozart is interesting as an example of Marxist theories applied to music.

WRITINGS: *Die Musik Bachs* (Leipzig, 1953); *Georg Friedrich Händel: Leben und Werk* (Leipzig, 1954; third ed., 1962); *Mozarts Melodik und Stil: Eine Studie* (Leipzig, 1957); *Lehrbriefe für das Fernstudium: Die Musik der Klassik* (Halle, 1964); *Georg Friedrich Händel: Thema mit 20 Variationen* (Halle, 1965); *Die Hauptvertreter der bürgerlichen Musikkultur im 20. Jahrhundert* (Halle, 1966–67); *Johannes Brahms: Eine Biographie* (Leipzig, 1966; second ed., 1974); *Die Musik der sozialistischen Länder (ausser DDR)* (Halle, 1967); *Ziele und Aufgaben der sozialistischen Musikerziehung* (Leipzig, 1967; third ed., 1975); *Die Bach-Händel-Epoche* (Halle, 1968); *Das Musikschaffen der DDR* (Halle, 1969); *Ludwig van Beethoven: Eine Biographie* (Leipzig, 1975; second ed., 1977); *Johann Sebastian Bach* (Leipzig, 1976); *Wolfgang Amadeus Mozart, 1756–1791: Eine kleine Biographie gewidmet allen Freunden von Michaelstein im Mozartjahr 1991* (Michaelstein, 1991).
—NS/LK/DM

Siehr, Gustav, noted German bass; b. Arnsberg, Sept. 17, 1837; d. Munich, May 18, 1896. He studied with Heinrich Dorn and Julius Krause, making his debut in 1863 in Neustrelitz. He then sang in Prague (1865–70), Wiesbaden (1870–81), and at the Munich Court Opera (1881–96). He also appeared at the Bayreuth Festivals, where he created the role of Hagen in *Götterdämmerung* (Aug. 17, 1876). He was particularly distinguished as a Wagnerian interpreter.—NS/LK/DM

Siems, Margarethe, outstanding German soprano; b. Breslau, Dec. 30, 1879; d. Dresden, April 13, 1952. She studied with Orgeni. She made her debut at the Prague May Festival in 1902, and that same year joined the Prague Opera; in 1908 she joined the Dresden Court (later State) Opera, where she was a leading dramatic coloratura soprano until 1920; Strauss chose her to create the roles of Chrysothemis in *Elektra* (Jan. 25, 1909) and the Marschallin in *Der Rosenkavalier* (Jan. 26, 1911) there, and also Zerbinetta in *Ariadne auf Naxos* in Stuttgart (Oct. 25, 1912). In 1913 she made her London debut at Covent Garden. She retired from the operatic stage in Breslau in 1925 but continued to sing in concerts; taught at the Berlin Cons. (1920–26), and then in Dresden and Breslau. In addition to her roles in Strauss's operas, she gained renown for her performances in the operas of Bellini, Donizetti, Verdi, and Wagner.—NS/LK/DM

Siepi, Cesare, admired Italian bass; b. Milan, Feb. 10, 1923. He studied at the Milan Cons. He made his operatic debut as Sparafucile in Schio, near Vicenzo (1941); appeared as Zaccaria in *Nabucco* in Verona (1945) and at his La Scala debut in Milan (1946), where he was

a principal artist until 1958; also appeared with the company during its 1950 visit to London's Covent Garden, where he was a regular singer from 1962 to 1973. On Nov. 6, 1950, he made his Metropolitan Opera debut in N.Y. as Philip II in *Don Carlos*, remaining on its roster until 1973; also sang in other major opera houses on both sides of the Atlantic. An esteemed cantante artist, he excelled in the operas of Mozart and Verdi. —NS/LK/DM

Sierra, Roberto, Puerto Rican composer; b. Vega Baja, Oct. 9, 1953. He began musical training at the Puerto Rico Cons. of Music and at the Univ. of Puerto Rico (graduated, 1976), and then pursued studies in London at the Royal Coll. of Music and the Univ. (1976–78), at the Inst. of Sonology in Utrecht (1978), and with Ligeti at the Hamburg Hochschule für Musik (1979–82). He was asst. director (1983–85) and director (1985–86) of the Cultural Activities Dept. at the Univ. of Puerto Rico, then dean of studies (1986–87) and Chancellor (1987–89) at the Puerto Rico Cons. of Music. From 1989 to 1992 he was composer-in-residence at the Milwaukee Sym. Orch. In 1992 he joined the faculty of Cornell Univ., where he later became a prof. of music.

WORKS: DRAMATIC: *El Mensajero de Plata*, chamber opera (1984); *El Contemplado*, ballet (1987). ORCH.: *Jubilo* (1985); *Glosas* for Piano and Orch. (1987); *Descarga* (1988; Milwaukee, Sept. 28, 1989); *Preámbulo* (Milwaukee, Sept. 28, 1989); *SASIMA* (San Antonio, Feb. 22, 1990); *Idilio* (1990); *A Joyous Overture* (1991); *Concierto Evocativo* for Horn and Orch. (1991); *Tropicalia* (Milwaukee, Nov. 14, 1991); *Of Discoveries* for 2 Guitars and Orch. (Chautauqua, N.Y., July 3, 1992); *Imágenes*, concerto for Violin, Guitar, and Orch. (1993); *Concierto Caribe* for Flute and Orch. (1993); *Evocaciones*, violin concerto (Pittsburgh, Dec. 1, 1994); *Ritmo* (1995); *Saludo* (1995); Concertino for Chamber Orch. and Tape (N.Y., Dec. 15, 1995); *Con madera, metal y cuero* (1998). CHAMBER: *Salsa on the C String* for Cello and Piano (1981); *Bongo-O* for Percussion (1982); *Salsa para vientos* for Wind Quintet (1983); *Cinco bocetos* for Clarinet (1984); *Concierto Nocturnal* for Harpsichord, Flute, Clarinet, Oboe, Violin, and Cello (1985); *Memorias Tropicales* for String Quartet (1985); *Toccata y Lamento* for Guitar (1987); *Essays* for Wind Quintet (1987); *Mano a mano* for 2 Percussionists (1987); *Con Tres* for Clarinet, Bassoon, and Piano (1990); *Trio Tropical* for Violin, Cello, and Piano (1992); *Segunda Crónica del Descubrimiento* for Flute and Guitar (1992); *Tercera Crónica del Descubrimiento* for Flute and Guitar (1992); *Tres Fantasías* for Clarinet, Cello, and Piano (1994); *Ritmorroto* for Clarinet (1995); *Tema y Variaciones* for Clarinet and Piano (1999). KEYBOARD: P i a n o : *Vestigios Rituales* for 2 Pianos (1984); *Tres inventos* (1987); *2 X 3* for 2 Pianos (1994). H a r p s i c h o r d : *Tres miniaturas* (1982); *Con salsa* (1984). VOCAL: *Cantos populares* for Chorus (1983); *Doña Rosita* for Mezzo-soprano and Wind Quintet (1985); *Invocaciones* for Voice and Percussion (1986); *Glosa a la sombra...* for Mezzo-soprano, Viola, Clarinet, and Piano (1987); *Bayoán*, oratorio for Soprano, Baritone, and Orch. (1991; N.Y., Oct. 14, 1994); *Cancionero Setardi* for Soprano, Flute, Clarinet, Violin, Cello, and Piano (1999). OTHER: *entre terceras* for 2 Synthesizers and Computer (1988).—NS/LK/DM

Siface (real name, **Giovanni Francesco Grossi),** famous Italian castrato soprano; b. Chiesina Uzzanese, near Pescia, Feb. 12, 1653; d. (murdered) near

Ferrara, May 29, 1697. He gained renown and his nickname when he appeared as Siface in Cavalli's *Scipione affricano* in Rome in 1671. After singing in the Papal Chapel (1675–79), he was in the service of Francesco II d'Este, Duke of Modena. He also appeared in opera throughout Italy, and in 1687 visited London and sang before King James II in his private chapel. He then pursued his career in Modena, Naples, Parma, Bologna, Milan, and Reggio Emilia. When he became intimate with a female member of the Marsili family, affronted members of the family took revenge by having assassins kill him.—NS/LK/DM

Sigismondi, Giuseppe, Italian librarian, historian, singing teacher, and composer; b. Naples, Nov. 13, 1739; d. there, May 10, 1826. He studied law (degree, 1759), and received instruction in singing, figured bass, and counterpoint, taking lessons with Durante and later with Porpora (1761–67). He wrote comedies for an amateur theater company, and also composed 2 stage pieces, sacred and secular vocal works, and pieces for organ and for harpsichord. However, he became best known as a singing teacher. He served as archivist-librarian at the Pietà dei Turchini Cons. (from 1794). He prepared a 4 vol. MS, *Apoteosi della musica del regno di Napoli in tre ultimi transundati secoli* (1820), which was reworked and publ. by Villarosa as *Memorie dei compositori di musica del regno di Napoli* (Naples, 1840). —NS/LK/DM

Signorelli, Frank, early jazz pianist, composer; b. N.Y., May 24, 1901; d. Brooklyn, N.Y., Dec. 9, 1975. Originally taught piano by his cousin, Pasquale Signorelli. Founding member of the Original Memphis Five (from 1917), worked briefly in the Original Dixieland Jazz Band in 1921, then resumed with the Original Memphis Five. From the mid-1920s, Signorelli did prolific freelance work for radio, the theater, and on records. He left the Original Memphis Five in September 1926, and joined Joe Venuti. Member of Adrian Rollini's short-lived New Yorker Band from September–October 1927. Recorded with Joe Venuti, Ed Lang, and Bix Beiderbecke, among others; in the late 1920s and early 1930s. Signorelli enjoyed great success as a composer. During the mid-1930s, he played in the reformed O.D.J.B., then, starting in summer 1938, he joined Paul Whiteman. During the 1940s and 1950s he continued to play regularly; he worked with Bobby Hackett at Nick's in 1947, then at same venue with Phil Napoleon from the late 1940s. Took part in television shows with specially reformed the Original Memphis Five, During the late 1950s he played solo spots in Greenwich Village. He was inactive from the 1960s to his death.—JC/LP

Sigtenhorst-Meyer, Bernhard van den, Dutch composer; b. Amsterdam, June 17, 1888; d. The Hague, July 17, 1953. He studied at the Amsterdam Cons., and later in Vienna and Paris. He settled in The Hague as a composer and writer.

WRITINGS: *Jan Pieterszoon Sweelinck en zijn instrumentale muziek* (The Hague, 1934; second ed., 1946); *De vocale muziek van Jan Pieterszoon Sweelinck* (The Hague, 1948).

WORKS: 2 string quartets (1919, 1944); Sonata for Solo Cello (1926); 2 violin sonatas (1926, 1938); *6 Miniatures* for Oboe and Piano (1926–46); 2 piano sonatas (1922, 1925); 3 piano sonatinas (1928, 1930, 1948); other piano pieces, including *La Vieille Chine* (1916), *Les Oiseaux* (1917), and *Le Monde de contesbleus* (2 albums; 1926–28).—NS/LK/DM

Sigurbjörnsson, Thorkell, prominent Icelandic composer, pedagogue, and administrator; b. Reykjavík, July 16, 1938. He studied at the Reykjavík Coll. of Music (1948–57), had lessons in composition with R.G. Harris at Hamline Univ. in St. Paul, Minn. (B.A., 1959) and in electronic music with Hiller and composition with Gaburo at the Univ. of Ill. in Urbana (M.M., 1961), and attended sessions in Nice and Darmstadt (1962). Returning to Reykjavík, he was one of the founders of the modern group Musica Nova. He taught at the Reykjavík Coll. of Music (from 1962), becoming a full prof. in 1969, and also was active with the Icelandic State Radio (1966–69). In 1973 he was a creative assoc. at the State Univ. of N.Y. at Buffalo, and in 1975 was a research musician at the Univ. of Calif. in La Jolla. He served as secretary (1969–85) and president (1985–88) of the Icelandic Soc. of Composers. In addition to his work as a composer, pedagogue, and broadcaster, he also appeared as a pianist and conductor. In 1999 he was awarded an honorary doctorate of Fine Arts degree by Hamline Univ.

WORKS: DRAMATIC: *Composition in 3 Scenes*, chamber opera (1964); *Apaspil*, children's opera (1966); *Rabbi*, children's opera (1968); *Thorgeirsboli* (The Bull-man), ballet (1971); *About People*, ballet (1988); *The Girl in the Lighthouse*, opera (1999). **ORCH.:** *Flökt* (Fluctuations; 1961); *Cadenza and Dance* for Violin and Orch. (1967); *Ymur* (1969); *Ys og Thys* (Much Ado), overture (1970); *Laeti* for Orch. and Orch. on Tape (1971); *Mistur* (1972); *Haflög* (1973); *Nidur*, double bass concerto (1974); *Bükolla*, clarinet concerto (1974); *Eurydice* for Flute and Orch. (1978); *Sequences*, violin concerto (1981); *Ulisse ritorna*, cello concerto (1981); *Columbine*, divertimento for Flute and Strings (Falun, Sweden, Dec. 5, 1982); *Diaphony* (1984); Triple Concerto for Violin, Cello, Piano, and Orch. (1984); Concerto for Flute, Strings, and Percussion (1984); *Trifonia* (1990). **CHAMBER:** *Víxl* (Rotation) for Violin, Clarinet, Cello, and Duplicate Instruments on Tape (1962); *Hässelby-Quartet*, string quartet (1968); *Kisum* for Clarinet, Viola, and Piano (1970); *Intrada* for Clarinet, Viola, and Piano (1970); *Happy Music* for Brass Ensemble (1971); *Hylling* (Homage) for Flute, Cello, Piano, Percussion, Tape, and Audience (1974); *4 Better or Worse* for Flute, Clarinet, Cello, and Piano (1975); *Copenhagen Quartet* for String Quartet (1977); *The Pied Piper* for Flute and String Trio (1978); *Bergabesk* for Woodwind Quintet (1979); *Ra's Dozen* for 12 Flutes (1980); *Tema senza variazioni* for Clarinet, Cello, and Piano (1981); *Saman* for 2 Flutes, 2 Oboes, 2 Clarinets, 2 Bassoons, 2 Horns, and Piano (1983); *Drift* for Clarinet and Piano (1984); *Hot Spring Birds* for Flute, Guitar, and Cello (1984); *Hoquetus minor* (Minor Hiccups) for Harpsichord and Percussion (1987); *6 Icelandic Folksongs* for Flute, Violin, and Cello (1988); *Bird of Fate* for Clarinet and String Quartet (1989); *Music from the Court of Thora* for Alto Saxophone, Vibraphone, Harpsichord, and Electric Bass Guitar (1990); Duo for Violin and Cello (1990); *6 Icelandic Folksongs* for Clarinet, Cello, and Piano (1991); *Govertimento* for Flute, Oboe, Clarinet, Horn, Bassoon, and Piano (1991); *Usamo* for Organ, Percussion, and Strings (1992). **VOCAL:** *Ballade* for Tenor, Flute, Viola, and Guitar (1960); *Leikar* for Chorus and Orch.

(1961); *Solstice* for Soprano, Alto, Baritone, Flute, Marimba, and Double Bass (1976); *The Last Flower* for Children's Chorus and Children's Orch. (1983); *A Poem About Settlement* for Tenor and Chamber Orch. (1987); *The Coming* for Chorus (1988); *Immanuel*, oratorio for Soprano, Tenor, Chorus, and Orch. (1999).
—NS/LK/DM

Siki, Béla, distinguished Hungarian pianist and teacher; b. Budapest, Feb. 21, 1923. He studied with Dohnányi and Leo Weiner at the Budapest Academy of Music, and later took lessons with Lipatti in Geneva. In 1945 he made his debut in Budapest; in 1947 he won the Concours International d'Exécutions Musicales in Geneva; then made tours of Australia, Japan, South America, and the U.S. In 1965 he became a prof. of piano at the Univ. of Wash. in Seattle, and in 1980 at the Univ. of Cincinnati Coll.-Cons. of Music. He wrote *Piano Repertoire: A Guide to Interpretation and Performance* (N.Y., 1981). He became especially known for his authoritative performances of the works of Liszt and Bartók.
—NS/LK/DM

Siklós (real name, **Schönwald**), **Albert,** Hungarian cellist, musicologist, pedagogue, and composer; b. Budapest, June 26, 1878; d. there, April 3, 1942. He changed his name to Siklós in 1910. He studied law, and later took courses with Koessler at the Budapest Academy of Music, graduating in 1901; he taught at the Academy from 1910, and gradually became one of its most respected teachers. He was a prolific composer, but few of his works were publ., and there were virtually no performances outside Hungary. He publ. a number of instructive books as well as a music dictionary (1923).

WORKS: DRAMATIC: O p e r a : *Knight Fulkó* (1896); *The House of Moons* (1926; Budapest, Dec. 21, 1927). **B a l l e t :** *The Mirror* (Budapest, March 28, 1923). **ORCH.:** 2 cello concertos (1895, 1902); 3 sym. (1896; *Anlauf*, 1896; 1901); *Symphonie aetherique* for 12 Double Basses (1899); Violin Concerto (1899); overtures; suites. **OTHER:** Chamber music; vocal works; piano pieces; organ music.—NS/LK/DM

Sikorski, Kazimierz, Swiss-born Polish composer and pedagogue, father of **Tomasz Sikorski;** b. Zürich (of Polish parents), June 28, 1895; d. Warsaw, June 23, 1986. He studied composition with Szopski at the Chopin Music H.S. in Warsaw (graduated, 1919); took courses in philosophy at the Univ. of Warsaw (graduated, 1921) and then pursued musicology training with Chybiński at the Univ. of Lwów; completed his musical studies in Paris (1925–27; 1930). He taught at the ód Cons. (1947–54) and the Warsaw Cons. (1951–57), serving as director of the latter (1957–66). Among his many students were Bacewicz, Panufnik, Palester, Serocki, and his own son. He publ. *Instrumentoznawstwo* (The Study of Instruments; Warsaw, 1932; third ed., 1975), *Harmonia* (Harmony; 3 vols., Kraków, 1948–49; fourth ed., 1972), and *Kontrapunkt* (Counterpoint; 3 vols., Kraków, 1953–57).

WORKS: ORCH.: *Suite* for Strings (1917); 6 syms. (1918; 1921; 1953; 1969; 1978–79; 1983); Clarinet Concerto (1947); Concerto for Horn and Small Orch. (1948); *Popular Overture*

(1954); Flute Concerto (1957); Concerto for Trumpet, Strings, 4 Timpani, Xylophone, and Tam-tam (1959); *6 Old Polish Dances* for Small Orch. (1963); *Concerto Polyphonique* for Bassoon and Orch. (1965); Oboe Concerto (1967); Trombone Concerto (1973). **CHAMBER:** 3 string quartets; String Sextet. **VOCAL:** Choruses.—NS/LK/DM

Sikorski, Tomasz, Polish composer and pianist, son of **Kazimierz Sikorski;** b. Warsaw, May 19, 1939; d. there, Nov. 13, 1988. He studied piano with Drzewiecki and composition with his father at the Warsaw Cons.; then took lessons with Boulanger in Paris. As a pianist, he emphasized new music in his programs. His own compositions were in an advanced idiom.

WORKS: DRAMATIC: R a d i o O p e r a : *Przygody Sindbada zeglaraza* (The Adventures of Sinbad the Sailor; 1971). **ORCH.:** *Concerto breve* for Piano, 24 Winds, and 4 Percussionists (1965); *Sequenza I* (1966); *Holzwege* (1972); *Étude* (1972); *Music in Twilight* for Piano and Orch. (1978); *Strings in the Earth* for 15 Strings (1979–80); *Self-portrait* (1983); *Autoritratto* for 2 Pianos and Orch. (1983); *La Notte* for Strings (1984); *Omaggio per quattro pianoforti ed orchestra in memoriam Borges* (1987). **CHAMBER:** *Echoes 2 quasi improvvisazione* for 1 to 4 Pianos, Percussion, and Tape (1961–63); *Architectures* for Piano, Winds, and Percussion (1965); *Intersections* for 36 Percussion Instruments (1968); *Homophony* for 4 Trumpets, 4 Horns, 4 Trombones, Piano, and 2 Gongs (1968); *For Strings* for 3 Violins and 3 Violas (1970); *Bez tytulu* (Untitled) for Piano, Clarinet, Trombone, and Cello (1972); *Other Voices* for Winds and Percussion (1975); *Das Schweigen der Sirenen* for Cello (1986). **P i a n o :** *Sonant* (1967); *Diafonia* for 2 Pianos (1969); *Zerstreutes Hinausschauen* (1971); *Listening Music* for 2 Pianos (1973). **VOCAL:** *Antyfony* for Soprano without Text, Piano, Horn, Chimes, 2 Gongs, 2 Tam-tams, and Tape (1963); *Prologues* for Women's Chorus, 2 Pianos, 4 Flutes, 4 Horns, and 4 Percussionists (1964); *Vox humana* for Chorus, 12 Brasses, 2 Pianos, 4 Gongs, and 4 Tam-tams (1971); *Music from Afar* for Chorus and Orch. (1974); *Sickness Unto Death* for Narrator, 2 Pianos, 4 Trumpets, and 4 Horns (1976).
—NS/LK/DM

Silbermann, family of eminent German organ and piano makers.

(1) Andreas Silbermann, b. Klein-Bobritzsch, Saxony, May 16, 1678; d. Strasbourg, March 16, 1734. He worked with the organ builder Friedrich Ring in Alsace before going to Strasbourg in 1702. He was in Paris from 1704 until 1706, then returned to Strasbourg, where he built the Munster organ there (1713–16) and 33 others.

(2) Gottfried Silbermann, brother of the preceding; b. Klein- Bobritzsch, Jan. 14, 1683; d. Dresden, Aug. 4, 1753. Apprenticed to a bookbinder, he ran away and joined his brother in Strasbourg about 1702 as his helper. During his brother's sojourn in Paris (1704–06), he ran the family business; upon his brother's return to Strasbourg, they worked as partners. After working on his own there and in other cities, he went to Freiberg in 1711. His finest organ was the instrument built for the Katholische Hofkirche in Dresden (3 manuals, 44 stops), begun in 1750 and completed after his death by his pupil Zacharias Hildebrandt. He owed his fame, however, mainly to the manufacture of pianos in Germany, in which field he was a pioneer; the hammer action in his instruments was practically identical with that of Cristofori, the piano inventor. Silbermann also invented the "cembal d'amour," a clavichord with strings of double length, struck in the middle by the tangents, thus yielding the duplicated octave of the tone of the entire string. He supplied 3 pianos to Frederick the Great for Potsdam, and Bach played on them during his visit there in 1747.

(3) Johann Andreas Silbermann, son of **(1) Andreas Silbermann;** b. Strasbourg, May 26, 1712; d. there, Feb. 11, 1783. He received his training from his father. He built 54 organs, and also publ. *Geschichte der Stadt Strassburg* (1775).

(4) Johann Daniel Silbermann, brother of the preceding; b. Strasbourg, March 31, 1717; d. Leipzig, May 9, 1766. He worked with his uncle Gottfried at Freiberg, and continued the manufacture of pianos after the latter's death.

(5) Johann Heinrich Silbermann, brother of the 2 preceding; b. Strasbourg, Sept. 24, 1727; d. there, Jan. 15, 1799. He made pianos at Strasbourg, similar to those of his uncle Gottfried, and introduced them into France. His son, Johann Friedrich Silbermann (b. Strasbourg, June 21, 1762; d. there, March 8, 1817), was an organist and composer; during the Revolution, he wrote a *Hymne à la Paix*; also composed songs.

BIBL.: L. Mooser, *G. S.* (Langensalza, 1857); G. Zschaler, *G. S.* (1898); E. Flade, *Der Orgelbauer G. S.* (Leipzig, 1926); H. Hullemann, *Die Tätigkeit des Orgelbauers G. S. im Reussenland* (Leipzig, 1937); R. Gärtner, *G. S. der Orgelbauer* (Dresden, 1938); J. Wörsching, *Die Orgelbauer Familie S. in Strassburg im Elsass* (Mainz, 1941; second ed., 1960); U. Dähnert, *Die Orgeln G. S.s in Mitteldeutschland* (Leipzig, 1953); E. Flade, *G. S. Ein Beitrag zur Geschichte des deutschen Orgel- und Klavierbau im Zeitalter Bachs* (Leipzig, 1953); W. Müller, *Auf den Spuren von G. S.* (Kassel, 1968); idem, *G. S.: Persönlichkeit und Werk: Eine Dokumentation* (1983); H. Wettstein, *Die Orgelbauerfamilie S.: Bibliographie zu ihrem Leben und Werk* (Buren, the Netherlands, 1989); M. Schaefer, ed., *J.A. S.: Das S.- Archiv: Der Handschriftliche Nachlass des Orgelmachers J.A. S. (1712–1783)* (Winterthur, 1994). —NS/LK/DM

Silcher, (Philipp) Friedrich, German composer; b. Schnait, Württemberg, June 27, 1789; d. Tübingen, Aug. 26, 1860. He studied with his father and with Auberlen, an organist at Fellbach. In 1815 he went to Stuttgart to study piano and composition with K. Kreutzer and Hummel, and in 1817 he was appointed music director at the Univ. of Tübingen, receiving an honorary Ph.D. in 1852. He was an influential promoter of German popular singing and publ. several collections of German folk songs, in which he included his own compositions; of the latter, *Lorelei* (*Ich weiss nicht, was soll es bedeuten*, to words by Heinrich Heine) became so popular that it was often mistaken for a folk song; in all, he wrote about 250 songs. He also publ. *Choralbuch* for 3 voices, 3 books of hymns for 4 voices, and *Tübinger Liedertafel* (men's choruses). A critical ed. of his output was publ. in 1960. He wrote the books *Geschichte des evangelischen Kirchengesanges* (1844) and *Harmonie- und Kompositionslehre* (1851; second ed., 1859).

BIBL.: A. Köstlin, *F. S. und Weber* (Stuttgart, 1877); H. Weber, *F. S., Neujahrsgeschenk an die Zürcherische Jugend von der Allgemeinen Musik-Gesellscaft Zürich,* LXVII (Zürich, 1879); A. Prümers, *P.F. S.* (Stuttgart, 1910); A. Bopp, *F. S.* (Stuttgart, 1916); H. Kleinert and H. Rauschnabel, eds., *F. S.* (Stuttgart, 1935); A. Lämmle, *F. S.* (Mühlacker, 1956); H. Dahmen, *F. S.: Komponist und Demokrat: Eine Biographie* (Stuttgart, 1989); M. Schmid, ed., *F. S., 1789–1860: Studien zu Leben und Nachleben* (Stuttgart, 1989). —NS/LK/DM

Silja, Anja, remarkable German soprano; b. Berlin, April 17, 1935. Her grandmother was the singer Paula Althof. At the age of 8, Anja began vocal training with her grandfather, Egon van Rijn, giving a solo recital in Berlin at the age of 10. In 1956 she sang Rosina at the Berlin Städtische Opera. After appearing at the Braunschweig State Theater (1956–58), she sang at the Württemberg State Theater in Stuttgart (1958), at the Frankfurt am Main Opera (1960–63), and at the Bayreuth Festivals (from 1965). In 1968 she made her U.S. debut as Senta with the Chicago Lyric Opera; her Metropolitan Opera debut followed in N.Y. as Leonore in *Fidelio* on Feb. 26, 1972. In subsequent years, she made appearances with leading North American and European opera houses; also sang in concerts with major orchs. She later was also active as an opera producer. However, she continued to make appearances in opera. In 1995 she gave a stunning portrayal of Janáček's Elina Makropulos at the Glyndebourne Festival and at the London Proms. The breadth of her repertoire is commanding. Wagner's grandson Wieland coached her in the Wagnerian roles, among them Elisabeth, Elsa, Eva, and Senta, which she performed at Bayreuth. She also sang the roles of Salome and Elektra in Strauss's operas, of Marie and Lulu in Berg's operas, and of the sole character in Schoenberg's *Erwartung*. As a matter of course, she mastered the majority of standard soprano roles. She married **Christoph von Dohnányi,** under whose baton she sang in both operatic and concert settings.—NS/LK/DM

Silk, Dorothy (Ellen), English soprano; b. King's Norton, Worcestershire, May 4, 1883; d. Alvechurch, Worcestershire, July 30, 1942. She studied in Birmingham and with Johannes Ress in Vienna. She pursued a fine career as a concert artist, appearing in London and at major English festivals. She also made forays into opera. In addition to her performances of works by English composers, she programmed the music of Schütz and other rarely heard composers.—NS/LK/DM

Sills, Beverly (real name, **Belle Miriam Silverman**), celebrated American soprano and opera administrator; b. N.Y., May 25, 1929. At the age of 3, she appeared on the radio under the cute nickname "Bubbles," and won a prize at a Brooklyn contest as "the most beautiful baby of 1932." At 4, she joined a Saturday morning children's program, and at 7 she sang in a movie. At 10, she had a part on the radio show "Our Gal Sunday." Her natural thespian talent and sweet child's voice soon proved to be valuable financial assets. She did a commercial advertising Rinso White soap, and appeared on an early television program, "Stars of the Future." She began formal vocal studies with Estelle

Liebling when she was 7; also studied piano with Paolo Gallico; in Public School 91 in Brooklyn she was voted most "likely to succeed." In 1947 she made her operatic debut as Frasquita in *Carmen* with the Philadelphia Civic Opera; then toured with several operas companies, and sang with the San Francisco Opera (1953) and the N.Y.C. Opera (1955), quickly establishing herself at the latter as one of its most valuable members. She extended her repertoire to embrace modern American operas, including the title role of Douglas Moore's *The Ballad of Baby Doe*; she also sang in the American premiere of Luigi Nono's avant-garde opera *Intolleranza 1960*. She was a guest singer at the Vienna State Opera and in Buenos Aires in 1967, at La Scala in Milan in 1969, and at Covent Garden in London and the Deutsche Oper in Berlin in 1970. She made her first appearance with the Metropolitan Opera as Donna Anna in a concert production of *Don Giovanni* on July 8, 1966, at the Lewisohn Stadium in N.Y.; her formal debut with the Metropolitan took place at Lincoln Center in N.Y. as Pamira in *Le Siège de Corinthe* on April 7, 1975. At the height of her career, she received well-nigh universal praise, not only for the excellence of her voice and her virtuosity in coloratura parts, but also for her intelligence and erudition, rare among the common run of operatic divas. She became general director of the N.Y.C. Opera in 1979, and made her farewell performance as a singer in 1980. She showed an uncommon administrative talent; during her tenure with the N.Y.C. Opera, she promoted American musicians and broadened the operatic repertoire. In 1988 she retired from her post with the N.Y.C. Opera. In 1994 she was named chairwoman of Lincoln Center. In her personal life, she suffered a double tragedy; one of her 2 children was born deaf, and the other autistic. In 1972 she accepted the national chairmanship of the Mothers' March on Birth Defects. She publ. *Bubbles: A Self-portrait* (N.Y., 1976; second ed., rev., 1981, as *Bubbles: An Encore*) and *Beverly: An Autobiography* (N.Y., 1987). She received (deservedly so) honorary doctorates from Harvard Univ., N.Y.U., and the Calif. Inst. of the Arts. On Nov. 22, 1971, she was the subject of a cover story in *Time*. In 1980 she was awarded the U.S. Presidential Medal of Freedom. In 1998 she was inducted into the National Women's Hall of Fame. Her most notable roles included Cleopatra in Handel's *Giulio Cesare*, Lucia, Elisabeth in *Roberto Devereux*, Anna Bolena, Elvira in *I puritani*, and Maria Stuarda.

BIBL.: M. Kerby, *B. S.: America's Own Opera Star* (N.Y., 1989); B. Paolucci, *B. S.* (N.Y., 1990).—**NS/LK/DM**

Siloti, Alexander, eminent Russian pianist, pedagogue, and conductor; b. near Kharkov, Oct. 9, 1863; d. N.Y., Dec. 8, 1945. He studied piano with Zverev and Nikolai Rubinstein at the Moscow Cons., and theory there with Tchaikovsky (1876–81), winning the gold medal. He made his debut as a pianist in Moscow in 1880; then made a tour in Germany; Liszt accepted him as a student in 1883, and Siloti continued his study with him in Weimar until Liszt's death in 1886. Returning to Russia, he was a prof. of piano at the Moscow Cons. (1888–91); among his students was Rachmaninoff (his first cousin). Between 1891 and 1900 he lived in Ger-

many, France, and Belgium; returned to Russia in 1901 and conducted the concerts of the Moscow Phil. Soc. during the 1901–02 season; in 1903 he organized his own orch. in St. Petersburg; these concerts acquired great cultural importance; Siloti invited Mengelberg and Mottl as guest conductors, and Rachmaninoff, Casals, and Chaliapin as soloists. In 1915 he began a series of popular free concerts, and in 1916 started a Russian Musical Fund to aid indigent musicians. In 1919 he left Russia; in 1922 he settled in N.Y., where he was active principally as a teacher but continued to appear as a soloist with American orchs.; from 1925 to 1942 he was on the faculty of the Juilliard School of Music. He publ. a collection of piano pieces which he ed., with indications of fingering and pedaling; also arranged and ed. concertos by Bach and Vivaldi. He publ. a book of reminiscences of Liszt (St. Petersburg, 1911; Eng. tr., Edinburgh, 1913).—**NS/LK/DM**

Silva, Alan (Treadwell), avant-garde jazz bassist, cellist, leader; b. Bermuda, Jan. 22, 1939. His family moved to Brooklyn, N.Y., when he was five years old. Silva studied piano, violin, and drums in his youth. He studied trumpet for three years with Donald Byrd, then bass in the early 1960s at the N.Y. Coll. of Music, with the N.Y. Symphony players, and with Ollie Richardson. He teamed with Burton Greene in the Free Form Improvisation Ensemble, and participated in the "October Revolution in Jazz" concert series in 1964. He studied with Dixon, playing duets with him before he could read. Silva joined Cecil Taylor (1965–69), touring Europe with him (1966). He also played with Sun Ra, Albert Ayler, Sonny Murray, and Archie Shepp. In Paris in 1969, he formed the Celestial Communication Orch., a group with rotating personnel, and also played with Frank Wright, Bobby Few, and Muhammad Ali (drums). While in Paris in 1970, he formed the Celestial Strings. Since 1972, he has worked with the Frank Wright Quartet and formed his own production company, Center of the World. He lived and worked in both Paris and N.Y. during the 1970s and 1980s, playing and recording with Taylor, Bill Dixon, Andrew Hill, and the Globe Unity Orch.

DISC.: *A. S.* (1968); *Lunar Surface* (1969); *Seasons* (1970); *Solos, Duets* (1975); *Shout* (1978).—**LP**

Silva, Francisco Manuel da, Brazilian conductor and composer; b. Rio de Janiero, Feb. 21, 1795; d. there, Dec. 18, 1865. He began his musical training with José Maurício Nunes Garcia, and later studied counterpoint and composition with Sigismund Neukomm in Rio de Janeiro. He was a singer and then a cellist in the orch. of the royal chapel and chamber until it was disbanded when Emperor Dom Pedro I abdicated in 1831; that same year he wrote the abdication hymn *Hino ao 7 de Abril*, which was adopted as the Brazilian national anthem (with new text) upon the establishment of the Republic in 1889. In 1833 he founded the Sociedade Beneficência Musical. He became conductor of the Sociedade Filarmônica in 1834, served as composer of the imperial chamber (from 1841) and as master composer of the imperial chapel (from 1842), and founded the Rio de Janeiro Cons. (1847). He wrote an opera, *O prestigio da lei*, and much sacred music.

BIBL.: A. de Albuquerque, *Ouviram do Ypiranga, Vida de F.M. d.S.* (Rio de Janeiro, 1959); A. de Andráde, *F.M. d.S. e seu tempo, 1808–65. Uma fase do pássado musical do Rio de Janeiro á luz de novos documentos* (2 vols., Rio de Janeiro, 1967).—**NS/LK/DM**

Silva, Óscar da, Portuguese pianist, teacher, and composer; b. Paranhos, near Oporto, April 21, 1870; d. Oporto, March 6, 1958. He studied at the Lisbon Cons., and in 1892 he went to Leipzig, where he had lessons with Reinecke and Clara Schumann. Returning to Portugal in 1910, he devoted himself mainly to teaching, acquiring a very high reputation as a piano pedagogue. From 1932 to 1952 he lived in Brazil, and then returned to Portugal. He wrote an opera, *Dona Mecia* (Lisbon, July 4, 1901); a symphonic poem, *Alma crucificada*; chamber music; songs; effective piano pieces.

BIBL.: F. Pires, *O.d. S.: Estuo biográfico analítico* (Matosinhos, 1995).—**NS/LK/DM**

Silver, Sheila, talented, prolific, and original American composer; b. Seattle, Wash., Oct. 3, 1946. She studied at the Univ. of Wash. in Seattle (1964–65), then went to Paris for a course at the Inst. for European Studies (1966–67); returned to the U.S. to earn her B.A. degree at the Univ. of Calif. at Berkeley (1968), and then enrolled at the Paris Cons. (1968). She further took courses at the Hochschule für Musik in Stuttgart, where her mentors were Ligeti and Karkoschka. Shuttling back to the U.S. once more, she studied with Shifrin, Berger, and Shapero at Brandeis Univ., completing her Ph.D. in composition there in 1976; she also attended the summer courses in new music in Darmstadt (1970), and studied with Druckman at the Berkshire Music Center at Tanglewood (summer, 1972). There followed a number of grants that enabled her to travel to London and to Italy, where she was awarded the Prix de Rome at the American Academy. The list of awards she has received is most impressive. In 1979 she was appointed instructor in composition at the State Univ. of N.Y. at Stony Brook. During all of her peregrinations, she continued to compose productively; her mature style may be described as enlightened dissonance devoid of ostensible disharmonies.

WORKS: DRAMATIC: O p e r a : *The Thief of Love*, after a Bengali tale (1986). **OTHER:** Film and theater works. **ORCH.:** *Galixidi* (1976; Seattle, Wash., March 1977); *Shirat Sarah* (Song of Sarah) for Strings (1985; Hartford, Conn., Jan. 1987); *Dance of Wild Angels* for Chamber Orch. (1990); *Three Preludes for Orchestra* (1992); Piano Concerto (1996). **CHAMBER:** 2 string quartets: No. 1 (1975; Frankfurt, 1976) and No. 2, *Four Etudes and a Fantasy* (1997); *Dynamis* for Horn (Rome, May 1979); *Theme and Variations* for Bowed Vibraphone (N.Y., April 1981); *Dance Converging* for Viola, Horn, Piano, and Percussion (1987); *G Whiz*, etude for 2 Violins and Marimba (N.Y., May 1988); *Window Waltz* for Bass Clarinet, Horn, Strings, Harpsichord, Piano, and Percussion (N.Y., May 1988); Cello Sonata (N.Y., Nov. 1988); *To the Spirit Unconquered*, trio for Piano, Violin, and Cello (1992); *From Darkness Emerging* for Harp and String Quartet (1995); *Winter Tapestry* for Chamber Ensemble (1998); *Fantasy on an Imaginary Folk Song* for Flute and Harp (1999); *Lullaby* for Bassoon, Piano, and Optional Video (1999; also for String Bass and Piano or Bass Clarinet and Piano, both with Optional Video); *Subway Sunset* for Oboe, Piano, and Optional Video (1999). **P i a n o :** *Fantasy Quasi Theme and Variations* (Washington, D.C., April 1981); *Oh, Thou Beautiful One* (1989); *Six Preludes pour Piano, d'après textes de Baudelaire* (1990). **VOCAL:** *Canto* for Baritone and Chamber Ensemble, after Ezra Pound's "Canto XXXIX" about Ulysses (1979); *Chariessa* for Soprano and Orch., after Sappho (Rome, June 1980; also for Soprano and Piano, 1978); *2 Elizabethan Songs* for Chorus (N.Y., Sept. 1982); *Ek Ong Kar* for Chorus (N.Y., Feb. 1983); *Barechi Nafshi et Adonai (Psalm 104)* for Antiphonal Chorus and Piano (1990); *Transcending, 3 Songs for Michael Dash, in memoriam,* for Baritone and Piano, after Yeats, Emerson, and Dunbar (1995).—**NS/LK/DM**

Silveri, Paolo, Italian baritone; b. Ofena, near Aquila, Dec. 28, 1913. He studied in Milan and at the Accademia di Santa Cecilia in Rome. In 1939 he made his operatic debut as Schwarz in *Die Meistersinger von Nürnberg*. After singing bass roles, he turned to baritone roles after successfully appearing as Germont in Rome in 1944. In 1946 he sang Marcello, Scarpia, and Rossini's Figaro with the Teatro São Carlo of Naples during its visit to London's Covent Garden. He continued to sing at Covent Garden until 1952, both with the resident company and with the visiting La Scala company of Milan as Rigoletto, Count Luna, Amonasro, and Iago. He sang Don Giovanni and Renato with the Glyndebourne company during its visit to the Edinburgh Festival (1948, 1949). From 1949 to 1955 he sang regularly at La Scala. On Nov. 20, 1950, he made his Metropolitan Opera debut in N.Y. as Don Giovanni. He remained on its roster until 1953, singing such roles as Tonio, Marcello, Germont, Escamillo, Rigoletto, and Scarpia. He then pursued his career in Europe. In 1959 he sang the tenor role of Otello in Dublin but then resumed his career as a baritone. His farewell performance took place at the Camden Festival in 1967 as Donizetti's Israele. From 1970 he taught voice in Rome. —**NS/LK/DM**

Silverstein, Joseph, distinguished American violinist and conductor; b. Detroit, March 21, 1932. He received his early instruction in violin from his father, and then studied with V. Reynolds and Zimbalist at the Curtis Inst. of Music in Philadelphia (1945–50) and later with Gingold and Mischakoff. He played in the Houston Sym. Orch., Denver Sym. Orch., and Philadelphia Orch. before joining the Boston Sym. Orch. in 1955, where he was concertmaster (1962–83) and asst. conductor (1971–83). Having won the Queen Elisabeth of Belgium Competition (1959) and the Naumburg Foundation Award (1960), he made solo appearances while retaining his Boston posts. He was also chairman of the violin faculty of the Berkshire Music Center and a teacher at Boston Univ. He appeared as guest conductor with various U.S. orchs. Silverstein served as interim music director of the Toledo (Ohio) Sym. Orch. (1979–80) and principal guest conductor of the Baltimore Sym. Orch. (1981–83). He then was music director of the Utah Sym. Orch. in Salt Lake City (1983–98) and the Chautauqua (N.Y.) Sym. Orch. (1987–89). In 1994–95 he also was music adviser of the Louisville Orch. In 1998–99 he was artistic advisor of the Kansas City Sym. Orch. As both a violinist and conductor, he impressed his auditors by his technical expertise and musical integrity.—NS/LK/DM

Silvestri, Constantin, esteemed Romanian-born English conductor and composer; b. Bucharest, June 13, 1913; d. London, Feb. 23, 1969. He studied piano as a child, making his debut at age 10. After taking courses in piano and composition (with Jora) at the Bucharest Cons., he was active as a pianist. In 1930 he made his debut as a conductor with the Bucharest Radio Sym. Orch.; was a conductor with the Bucharest Opera (from 1935) and music director of the Bucharest Phil. (1947–53); also taught conducting at the Bucharest Cons. (from 1948). In 1956 he went to Paris, and in 1957 settled in England, becoming a naturalized British subject in 1967. In 1961 he became principal conductor of the Bournemouth Sym. Orch., which he led with distinction until his death; took it on a European tour in 1965. In 1963 he made his debut at London's Covent Garden conducting *Khovanshchina*. He was an impassioned if sometimes willful interpreter of the classics. He composed mostly in small forms in an unpretentious, neo-Baroque manner.

WORKS: ORCH.: *Jocuri populare românești din Transilvania* (1929; Bucharest, March 10, 1933); *3 Pieces* for Strings (1933; rev. 1950; Bucharest, Jan. 7, 1951); *Prelude and Fugue* (1955; Bucharest, Nov. 1956). **CHAMBER:** 2 string quartets (1935, 1947); *Sonata breve* for Clarinet and Bassoon (1938; rev. 1957); Violin Sonata (1939); Oboe Sonata (1939); Harp Sonata (1940); piano pieces, including sonatas, suites, and sonatinas. **VOCAL:** Songs.—NS/LK/DM

Silvestrov, Valentin (Vasilievich), Russian composer; b. Kiev, Sept. 30, 1937. He studied with Liatoshinsky at the Kiev Cons. (1958–64). He began to compose in a boldly experimental idiom of Western provenance; wrote piano pieces in the strict 12-tone technique. Although severely reprimanded in the Soviet press, he was not forcibly restrained from continuing to write music in a modernistic manner. After the demise of the Soviet regime, he encountered no obstructive criticism to his chosen means of compositional expression.

WORKS: ORCH.: 6 syms.: No. 1 (1963), No. 2 for Flute, Percussion, Piano, and Strings (1965), No. 3 (1966), No. 4 for Brass Instruments and Strings (1976), No. 5 (1982), and No. 6 (1997); *Monodia* for Piano and Orch. (1965); *Spectrum* for Chamber Orch. (1965); *Meditation* for Cello and Chamber Orch. (1972); Serenade for 2 Violins and Chamber Orch. (1978); *Postlude*, symphonic poem for Piano and Orch. (1984); *Widmung*, violin concerto (1990); *Metamusic* for Piano and Orch. (1992). **CHAMBER:** Piano Quintet (1961); *Quartetto piccolo* for String Quartet (1961); Trio for Flute, Trumpet, and Celesta (1962); *Mysteries* for Alto Flute and Percussion (1964); *Projections* for Harpsichord, Vibraphone, and Bells (1965); *Drama* for Violin, Cello, and Piano (1971); 2 string quartets (1974, 1988); *Postludium* for Cello and Piano (1982); Cello Sonata (1983); *Post Scriptum*, violin sonata

(1990). **Piano:** 3 sonatas (1960, 1975, 1979); *Classical Sonata* (1973); *Kitch Music*, 5 pieces (1977). **VOCAL:** Cantata for Soprano and Chamber Orch. (1973); *Ode to a Nightingale* for Soprano and Chamber Orch. (1983); *Exegi monumentum*, sym. for Baritone and Orch. (1988).—NS/LK/DM

Simai, Pavol, Czech composer; b. Levice, June 29, 1930. He studied with Pál Kadosa in Budapest, with Alexander Moyzes and Jan Cikker in Bratislava, and with Paul Dessau in East Berlin. In 1968 he settled in Sweden.

WORKS: Flute Sonatina (1952); *Zuzuka*, ballet (1954–60); *Mother Speaks*, melodrama for Female Speaker, Flute, Clarinet, Bassoon, Guitar, and Percussion (1959); *Victory* for Orch. (1963); *Meditation* for Contralto and String Quartet (1965); *5: 10* for Clarinet, Violin, Cello, and Piano (1972); Piano Trio (1974); *Violoncellen* for Mezzo-soprano, Cello, and Piano (1975). —NS/LK/DM

Simandl, Franz, Bohemian double-bass player, pedagogue, and composer; b. Blatna, Aug. 1, 1840; d. Vienna, Dec. 13, 1912. He was a double-bass player in the Vienna Court Opera orch. and the Vienna Phil. (1869–1904); also taught at the Vienna Cons. (from 1869). He publ. *Neueste Methode des Kontrabass-Spiels* (in 3 parts) and *30 Etüden für Kontrabass, Die hohe Schule des Kontrabass-Spiels*, a collection of concertos, studies, solo pieces, etc. His original compositions include a *Konzert-stück, Konzert-Etude*, Concerto, fantasias, and minor pieces for his instrument.—NS/LK/DM

Simándy, József, noted Hungarian tenor; b. Budapest, Sept. 18, 1916; d. there, March 4, 1997. Following studies with Emilia Posszert (1943–45), he completed his training at the Budapest Academy of Music. After singing in the Budapest Opera chorus (1940–45), he was a member of the Szeged Opera (1945–47). In 1947 he joined the Budapest Opera, where he distinguished himself in lyric, heroic, and spinto roles. He also sang at the Bavarian State Opera in Munich from 1956 to 1960. His guest engagements took him to many of the major European music centers. From 1978 he was a prof. at the Budapest Academy of Music. In 1953 he received the Kossuth Prize, and in 1962 he was made a Meritorious Artist and in 1964 an Outstanding Artist by the Hungarian government. Among his outstanding portrayals were Florestan, Lohengrin, Don Carlos, Otello, Walther von Stolzing, Don José, Cavaradossi, Des Grieux, and Turiddu. He also was renowned for his roles in operas by Ferenc Erkel.—NS/LK/DM

Simeon, Omer (Victor), early jazz clarinetist, alto and baritone saxophonist; b. New Orleans, La., July 21, 1902; d. N.Y., Sept. 17, 1959. His family moved to Chicago in 1914. He began playing clarinet in Chicago, taking lessons from Lorenzo Tio Jr. from 1918–20. In 1920 Simeon got his first professional work in a band led by his violinist brother: Al Simeon's Hot Six. He worked briefly with Jimmy Bell's Band, then played with Charlie Elgar's Creole Band (1923–spring 1927). He took part in several pick-up recording sessions with Jelly Roll Morton (1926), including "Black Bottom Stomp." In spring 1927, he joined King Oliver's Dixie Syncopators for a brief tour of St. Louis and a residency at the Savoy, N.Y. He left King Oliver in Baltimore during the summer of 1927 to rejoin Charlie Elgar at the Eagle Ballroom, Milwaukee. He returned to N.Y. in the summer of 1928, played with Luis Russell at the Nest Club, then worked for a week with Jelly Roll Morton at the Rose Danceland before returning to Chicago. He performed with Erskine Tate at Metropolitan Theatre (October 1928–30). He gigged around Chicago, then played three months with pianist Jerome Carrington's Orch. at the Regal Theatre (early 1931) before joining Earl Hines. He remained with Earl Hines for ten years, except for a short spell with Horace Henderson (March–August 1938) and briefly with Walter Fuller (1940); he also covered for Buster Bailey with Fletcher Henderson (1936). Simeon worked in Coleman Hawkins's Band from May 1941, then played with Walter Fuller's Orch. (late 1941–summer 1942). He joined Jimmie Lunceford in summer 1942 and remained with the band after the leader's death (1947), working under Eddie Wilcox's leadership until 1950. While with Lunceford, he made small band recordings with Kid Ory (1944–45). He worked regularly with Wilbur de Paris Band from fall 1951 until shortly before dying of throat cancer. Later in life, Simeon signed his name as Omer, however, several early reports give the name as Omar. There is also a report that Simeon Sr. worked as a cigar maker, using the name Omer Simeon.—JC/LP

Simeonov, Konstantin (Arsenievich), Russian conductor; b. Koznakovo, June 20, 1910; d. Kiev, Jan. 3, 1987. He began a career as a singer, then studied conducting at the Leningrad Cons. with Alexander Gauk. He subsequently appeared as a guest conductor throughout the Soviet Union. He served as chief conductor of the Ukrainian Theater of Opera and Ballet in Kiev (1961–66), then occupied a similar post at the Kirov Theater of Opera and Ballet in Leningrad (1966–75); he resumed his Kiev post in 1975. He also appeared as a guest conductor abroad.—NS/LK/DM

Simeonova, Nedyalka, Bulgarian violinist and teacher; b. Khaskovo, Dec. 2, 1901; d. Paris, March 14, 1959. A child prodigy, she studied at a very early age with her father. Following concerts in the U.S. (1913), she pursued training in Dresden with Auer, Rapoldi, and Havemann, and later with Auer in N.Y. (1921–23). Following a successful N.Y. debut in 1923, she toured throughout Europe, the U.S., India, and the Far East. In 1932 she returned to Bulgaria but continued to make tours. From 1946 she also taught violin at the Bulgarian State Cons. in Sofia.—LK/DM

Similä, Martti, Finnish conductor and composer; b. Oulu, April 9, 1898; d. Lahti, Jan. 9, 1958. He studied in Finland, then in Paris and London. He conducted the Helsinki Opera (1927–44) and the Municipal Orch. of Lahti. He made 2 tours in the U.S. as a pianist, in 1923 and 1926; was again in the U.S. in 1957 to lead a memorial concert of the music of Sibelius with the N.Y. Phil. (Dec. 8, 1957). He wrote the book, *Sibeliana* (Helsinki, 1945); also composed orch. music.—NS/LK/DM

Simionato, Giulietta, outstanding Italian mezzo-soprano; b. Forlì, May 12, 1910. She studied with Locatello and Palumbo in Rovigo, winning the bel canto competition in Florence in 1933; she then returned there to sing in the premiere of Pizzetti's *Orsèolo* (May 5, 1935). In 1939 she joined Milan's La Scala, remaining on its roster as one of its principal artists until 1966. In 1947 she made her British debut as Cherubino at the Edinburgh Festival; her first appearance at London's Covent Garden followed, as Adalgisa in 1953. In 1954 she made her U.S. debut at the Chicago Lyric Opera. On Oct. 26, 1959, she made her first appearance at the Metropolitan Opera in N.Y. as Azucena; sang there again in 1960 and 1962. She gave her farewell stage performance as Servilia in *La clemenza di Tito* at Milan's Piccola Scala in 1966. A distinguished coloratura artist, Simionato excelled in the operas of Rossini, Donizetti, Bellini, and Verdi.

BIBL.: J.-J. Hanine Vallaut, *G. S.: Come Cenerentola divenne regina* (Parma, 1987; second ed., rev., 1998).—NS/LK/DM

Simmons, Calvin (Eugene), gifted black American conductor; b. San Francisco, April 27, 1950; d. (drowned) Connery Pond, east of Lake Placid, N.Y., Aug. 21, 1982. He was the son of a longshoreman and a gospel singer. He joined the San Francisco Boys' Choir at age 11, where he received conducting lessons from its conductor, Madi Bacon; then went to the Cincinnati Coll.-Cons. of Music, where he studied conducting with Max Rudolf (1968–70); when Rudolf was appointed to the faculty of the Curtis Inst. of Music in Philadelphia, Simmons joined him there (1970–72); he also took piano lessons with Serkin. He served as a rehearsal pianist and asst. conductor under Adler at the San Francisco Opera (1968–75), where he made his formal debut conducting *Hänsel und Gretel* in 1972. In 1975 he made his British debut at the Glyndebourne Festival. He was asst. conductor of the Los Angeles Phil. and music director of the Young Musicians Foundation orch. (1975–78). In 1979 he was appointed music director of the Oakland (Calif.) Sym. Orch. Before his tragic death in a canoeing accident, he appeared as a guest conductor with increasing success throughout North America. He made his Metropolitan Opera debut in N.Y. in 1978 and his N.Y.C. Opera debut in 1980.

BIBL. R. Wolfe, *The C. S. Story, or, "Don't call me Maestro!"* (Berkeley, 1994).—NS/LK/DM

Simon, Abbey, distinguished American pianist and teacher; b. N.Y., Jan. 8, 1922. He studied with Saperton and Hofmann at the Curtis Inst. of Music in Philadelphia (1932–41), and also took lessons with Godowsky in N.Y. In 1941 he won the Naumberg Award and then launched a major career, appearing as a soloist with the leading U.S. orchs.; made his first tour of Europe in 1949, and subsequently traveled all over the world. He taught at the Ind. Univ. School of Music in Bloomington (1960–74), the Juilliard School in N.Y. (from 1977), and the Univ. of Houston (from 1977). A master of the repertory from Beethoven to Rachmaninoff, he evolved a grand bravura style of pianistic virtuosity in which no technical difficulties seem to exist, no tempi are too fast, no nuance is too subtle. —NS/LK/DM

Simon, Carly, singer-songwriter; b. N.Y.C., June 25, 1945. Achieving several pop and easy-listening hits during the 1970s, Carly Simon cowrote many of her own songs, but her slick, sophisticated style and image bore stark contrast to that of most other 1970s female singer-songwriters. Married to James Taylor from 1972 to 1983, Simon scored her best-remembered hit with late 1972's "You're So Vain" from her most successful album, *No Secrets*, produced by Richard Perry. Her popularity waned in the 1980s, although she managed somewhat of a comeback with 1987's *Coming Around Again*.

Carly Simon was raised in affluence in Riverdale, N.Y., and Stamford, Conn., as the daughter of the cofounder of the Simon and Schuster publishing firm. While attending the exclusive Sarah Lawrence Coll., she began singing folk-style material with her older sister Lucy as the Simon Sisters. She dropped out of college after two years and performed with Lucy in area folk clubs during the early 1960s, signing with Kapp Records in 1963. They scored a minor hit in 1964 with "Winkin', Blinkin' and Nod" and recorded two albums before Lucy's marriage broke up the duo. In 1966 Carly Simon met manager Albert Grossman, who envisioned her as a female Bob Dylan. She recorded with Al Kooper, Mike Bloomfield, and the Band's Rick Danko and Richard Manuel, but the material was never released. Simon served as colead vocalist of the N.Y.–based rock band Elephant's Memory in 1969, and she wrote commercial jingles in 1969 and 1970.

In 1970 Carly Simon began cowriting songs with film critic and writer Jacob Brackman and signed with Elektra Records late in the year. Playing guitar and piano and singing in a powerful contralto voice, she scored a major pop and easy-listening hit with "That's the Way I've Always Heard It Should Be," cowritten with Brackman, from her debut album. A notoriously shy performer, Simon debuted in support of Cat Stevens at the Troubadour in Los Angeles in April 1971 and met singer-songwriter James Taylor, whom she married in November 1972. *Anticipation*, produced by Cat Stevens producer and former Yardbird Paul Samwell-Smith, yielded pop and easy-listening hits with her title song and "Legend in Your Own Time."

Carly Simon recorded her next three albums under producer Richard Perry. The first, *No Secrets*, included "We Have No Secrets" and yielded a top pop and easy-listening hit with "You're So Vain" and a major pop and smash easy-listening hit with "The Right Thing to Do," all of which she wrote. "You're So Vain," recorded with Mick Jagger as backup vocalist, was spurred into popularity by speculation about who inspired the lyric (she finally admitted that it was Warren Beatty). Simon abandoned touring in 1973 and retained a low public profile after the birth of her daughter in January 1974. Nonetheless, *Hotcakes* produced a smash hit with a horrendous remake of Charlie and Inez Foxx's "Mockingbird," recorded with husband James Taylor,

and a major hit with "Haven't Got Time for the Pain," cowritten with Jacob Brackman. *Playing Possum*, her final album under Richard Perry, contained the major hit "Attitude Dancing" and the minor hits "Waterfall" and "More and More."

Appearing with James Taylor on his summer 1975 tour and singing backup on sister Lucy's debut album, Carly Simon's popularity began to wane. In 1977 she scored a smash pop and top easy-listening hit with "Nobody Does It Better" from the James Bond movie *The Spy Who Loved Me*, followed in 1978 by the near-smash "You Belong to Me," cowritten by Simon and Doobie Brother Michael McDonald. Later that year she managed a moderate pop and easy-listening hit with the Everly Brothers' "Devoted to You," in duet with James Taylor. "Jesse" became her final major hit for several years in 1980.

Carly Simon divorced James Taylor in 1983 and her career remained in eclipse until 1986, when "Coming Around Again," on her new label Arista Records, was featured in the movie *Heartburn*. Her first public performance in six years was given on Martha's Vineyard in 1987 and produced an HBO cable television special and live album. Simon next worked on the soundtrack to the movie *This Is My Life*, released on Quincy Jones's Qwest label. Since the mid-1980s she has authored four children's books and is said to be working on a fiction work for adults. In 1993 Carly Simon's opera *Romulus Hunt* premiered at the Kennedy Center in Washington, D.C. (years earlier, sister Joanne had become an opera singer). In 1991 sister Lucy received recognition as the composer of the musical *The Secret Garden*, a Broadway hit in 1991.

DISC.: *C. S.* (1971); *Anticipation* (1971); *No Secrets* (1972); *Hot Cakes* (1974); *Playing Possum* (1975); *Best* (1975); *Another Passenger* (1976); *Boys in the Trees* (1978); *Spy* (1979); *Come Upstairs* (1980); *Torch* (1981); *Hello Big Man* (1983); *Spoiled Girl* (1985); *Coming Around Again* (1987); *Greatest Hits Live* (1988); *My Romance* (1990); *Have You Seen Me Lately?* (1990); *Letters Never Sent* (1994); *Film Noir* (1997); *Bedroom Tapes* (2000). **LUCY SIMON:** *Lucy Simon* (1975); *Stolen Time* (1977); *The Secret Garden (music from Broadway original cast)* (1991). **THE SIMON SISTERS:** *Winkin', Blinkin' and Nod* (1964); *Cuddlebug* (1964). —BH

Simon, Geoffrey, Australian conductor; b. Adelaide, July 3, 1946. He was educated at the Univ. of Melbourne (1964–68), the Juilliard School in N.Y. (1968–69), and Ind. Univ. in Bloomington (1969–72). He also was a student in conducting of Ferrara in Hilversum (1972), Swarowsky in Ossiach, Austria (1973–75), Markevitch in France (1974), and Kempe in London (1974–75). He was asst. conductor of the South Melbourne Sym. Orch. (1966–68), and then music director of the Bloomington (Ind.) Sym. Orch. (1969–72). Returning to London, he was music director of the Australian Sinfonia (1975–79) and the Zemel Choir (1975–78). After conducting and teaching at the Univ. of Wisc. in Milwaukee (1978–82) and at North Tex. State Univ. in Denton (1982–84), he was music director of the Albany (N.Y.) Sym. Orch. (1987–89). In 1991 he became artistic director of Cala Records in London, with which he recorded rarely heard scores from both the past and present; concurrently served as artistic advisor and principal conductor of the Sacramento (Calif.) Sym. Orch. in 1993–94, serving as its music director from 1994 to 1996. His guest conducting engagements have taken him around the globe.—NS/LK/DM

Simon, James, German musicologist and composer; b. Berlin, Sept. 29, 1880; d. in the Auschwitz concentration camp about Oct. 14, 1944. He studied piano with Ansorge and composition with Bruch in Berlin. From 1907 to 1919 he taught at the Klindworth-Scharwenka Cons. in Berlin. He left Germany shortly after the advent of the Nazi regime in 1933, and lived in Zürich; then moved to Amsterdam, where the Hitlerite wave engulfed him after the Nazi invasion of the Netherlands. He was deported to Theresienstadt on April 5, 1944, and from there, on Oct. 12, 1944, was sent to Auschwitz, where he was put to death a few days later. His opera, *Frau im Stein*, was premiered in Stuttgart in 1925. He also wrote a Sym., Piano Concerto, Sextet for Piano and Wind Instruments, choruses, and many songs.—NS/LK/DM

Simon, Prosper-Charles, French organist and pedagogue; b. Bordeaux, Dec. 27, 1788; d. Paris, May 31, 1866. He received music instruction from Franz Beck and studied organ with Father Placide, a Benedictine. After serving as organist at the church of St. Croix (1802–06) and St. Sevrin (1807–08; 1811–25), he settled in Paris as organist of the church of Notre-Dame des Victoires in 1826. He also taught organ and harmony at the Maison Royale of St. Denis from 1827. In 1840 he was made organist of the Basilica of St. Denis. In 1858 he was made a Chevalier of the Legion d'honneur. Simon was highly regarded as an organist and pedagogue. He wrote Vol. 2 of Georges Schmitt's *Nouveau manuel complet de l'organiste* (Paris, 1863).

BIBL.: J. Dumoulin, *Biographie de P.-C. S.* (Paris, 1866). —LK/DM

Simon, Stephen (Anthony), American conductor, composer, and arranger; b. N.Y., May 3, 1937. He studied at the Yale Univ. School of Music (B.M. in piano) and pursued choral studies with Hugh Ross and Julius Herford. From 1963 to 1978 he was music director of the Orch. Soc. of Westchester/County Sym. Orch., and also of the Handel Soc. of N.Y. from 1970 to 1974 and of the Handel Festival at the John F. Kennedy Center for the Performing Arts in Washington, D.C., from 1976 to 1986. In 1986 he became music director of the Washington (D.C.) Chamber Sym. He also was a frequent guest conductor of the Halle Handel Festival in Germany. Simon has become especially well known for his pioneering new programming for young people via works for orch. and narrator, including his own *Casey at the Bat* and *The Tortoise and the Hare*, which he co-authored with his wife Bonnie. They founded Magic Maestro Recordings in 2000 with their young people's series *Stories in Music*.—NS/LK/DM

Simon and Garfunkel, influential folk-pop vocal duo. **MEMBERSHIP:** Paul Simon, gtr., ten. voc. (b.

Newark, N. J., Oct. 13, 1941); and Art Garfunkel, ten. voc. (b. Forest Hills, N.Y., Nov. 5, 1941).

Paul Simon grew up in Queens, N.Y., where he met Art Garfunkel at the age of 11. They began singing and writing songs together in 1955 and, in late 1957, scored a moderate hit with "Hey, Schoolgirl" as Tom and Jerry on Big Records. They appeared on Dick Clark's *American Bandstand*, but subsequent singles for Big, including "Teenage Fool," recorded by Simon as True Taylor, proved unsuccessful. These recordings for Big Records were later included on Pickwick Records' *The Hit Sounds of Simon and Garfunkel*. The two split up after high school to attend different colleges. Garfunkel went to Columbia Univ., whereas Simon attended Queens Coll., where he met Carole King. Simon began writing songs and working as a song promoter for E. B. Marks Publishing while recording demonstration tapes (including one with Carole King, "Just to Be with You," that became a minor pop hit for The Passions in 1959). In the early 1960s, he worked as a songwriter-producer at Amy Records and recorded under a variety of pseudonyms, including Tico and The Triumphs ("Motorcycle"), Jerry Landis ("The Lone Teen Ranger"), and Paul Kane ("He Was My Brother"). Around the same time, Art Garfunkel was recording as Artie Garr on Octavia and Warwick Records.

Paul Simon performed in Greenwich Village folk clubs such as Gerde's Folk City in 1963 and was joined by Garfunkel later in the year. The duo eventually won an audition with Tom Wilson of Columbia Records after Simon returned from Europe in 1964. The audition led to Simon and Garfunkel's debut album, *Wednesday Morning, 3 a.m.*, recorded and released in late 1964. In January 1965, Simon left for England, where he played folk clubs and recorded the British-only album *Paul Simon Songbook*. While there, Simon and Bruce Woodley of The Seekers collaborated on "Someday One Day," a major British hit for The Seekers in 1966, and "Red Rubber Ball," a smash American hit for The Cyrkle in 1966.

A vacationing Art Garfunkel joined Paul Simon in England in the summer of 1965, and, in their absence, Wilson overdubbed rock instrumentation onto "Sounds of Silence" from their debut album. With the advent of folk-rock, the song became a top hit in late 1965. Returning to N.Y., the two hastily recorded *Sounds of Silence* and began touring the college circuit. The album, pervaded by the duo's precise, overdubbed, close-harmony singing, was released as "Homeward Bound" (included on their next album), becoming a smash hit and yielding a smash hit with the alienated "I Am a Rock."

Over the next five years, Simon and Garfunkel were one of the most successful acts in popular music, recording some of the most artistically and commercially successful albums of the era. Strings were utilized for *Parsley, Sage, Rosemary and Thyme*, which included the self-consciously poetic major hit "The Dangling Conversation," the ditty "The 59th Street Bridge Song (Feelin' Groovy)," the satiric "A Simple Desultory Philippic," and the depressing but moving "7 O'Clock News"/"Silent Night." Like its predecessor, *Parsley,*

Sage, Rosemary and Thyme remained on the album charts for nearly three years. The duo subsequently scored major hits with "A Hazy Shade of Winter," "At the Zoo," and "Fakin' It," and performed at the Monterey International Pop Festival in June 1967.

Simon and Garfunkel next worked on the soundtrack to the Mike Nichols's movie *The Graduate*. The album included six instrumental songs by David Grusin, the hit "Scarborough Fair" (based on a 17th-century folk ballad), and the top hit classic "Mrs. Robinson." *Bookends*, their first self-produced album, was perhaps the masterpiece of their career. It included the hits "A Hazy Shade of Winter," "At the Zoo," "Fakin' It," and "Mrs. Robinson" as well as "Save the Life of My Child" and "America." In 1969, Simon and Garfunkel achieved a near-smash hit with the classic "The Boxer," later included on *Bridge Over Troubled Water*. The album also yielded the smash hit "Cecilia," the major hit "El Condor Pasa," recorded with the Peruvian group Los Incas, and included "Keep the Customer Satisfied," "So Long, Frank Lloyd Wright," and "Baby Driver." The album ultimately sold over five million copies in the U.S. "Bridge Over Troubled Water," a top pop, easy-listening, and British hit, was eventually recorded by more than 200 artists.

In early 1970, the Simon and Garfunkel team separated. By then, Art Garfunkel had worked in the Mike Nichols's films *Catch-22* (1969) and *Carnal Knowledge* (1970). In early 1972, Columbia Records issued Paul Simon's debut solo album. Co-produced by Simon, *Paul Simon* confirmed his reputation as one of the consummate songwriting craftsmen of 1970s rock with compositions such as "Duncan" and "Run That Body Down" and the hits "Mother and Child Reunion" (recorded in Jamaica) and "Me and Julio Down by the Schoolyard." He recorded *There Goes Rhymin' Simon* primarily in Muscle Shoals, Ala., and the album contained the smash hits "Loves Me Like a Rock" (recorded with the gospel group The Dixie Hummingbirds) and "Kodachrome," as well as "Something So Right" and "Take Me to the Mardi Gras." Conducting his first solo tour of America and Europe in the 1973, Simon's next album was recorded on the tour.

In the meantime, Art Garfunkel had recorded his debut solo album, *Angel Claire*, which featured easy-listening material such as Jimmy Webb's "All I Know" (a near-smash pop hit) and Van Morrison's "I Shall Sing" (a moderate hit). In 1974, he scored a moderate pop hit with "Second Avenue," and *Breakaway*, produced by Richard Perry, yielded top easy-listening hits with a remake of The Flamingos' 1959 hit "I Only Have Eyes for You," "Break Away," and the duet with Paul Simon, "My Little Town." Garfunkel's 1977 *Watermark* album comprised primarily Jimmy Webb songs, yet yielded a major pop and top easy-listening hit with Sam Cooke's "(What a) Wonderful World," recorded with Paul Simon and James Taylor. Garfunkel conducted his only tour in 1977 and 1978, scored a minor pop hit with a remake of The Skyliners' 1959 hit "Since I Don't Have You," and co-starred in the disconcerting and explicit Nicholas Roeg movie *Bad Timing—A Sexual Obsession*. *Scissors Cut* produced a top British hit with "Bright

Eyes," but yielded only a minor American hit with "A Heart in N.Y." In 1986, Garfunkel appeared in the movie *Good to Go* and recorded the Christmas album *The Animals' Christmas* with Amy Grant.

Paul Simon co-produced his 1975 top album hit *Still Crazy After All These Years*, which yielded a top pop and easy-listening hit with "50 Ways to Leave Your Lover" and a moderate pop hit with the title song. It also included "I Do It for Your Love," "Have a Good Time," a duet with Phoebe Snow on "Gone at Last," and the near-smash pop and top easy-listening duet with Art Garfunkel, "My Little Town." Simon conducted a major international tour in 1975 and 1976 and appeared in Woody Allen's Academy Award–winning 1977 movie *Annie Hall*. Late that year, Columbia issued *Greatest Hits, Etc.*, which compiled many of his hits and included the bonus songs "Slip Slidin' Away" (a smash pop hit) and "Stranded in a Limousine."

By early 1979, Paul Simon had switched to Warner Bros. Records. He subsequently became involved in legal disputes with his former label Columbia while working on his first feature film, *One-Trick Pony*, for Warner. He wrote, scored, and starred in the movie as a musician seeking another hit record after years on the road. Eventually released in October 1980, the movie featured performances by The B-52's, Sam and Dave, and the reunited Lovin' Spoonful, with Lou Reed appearing as Simon's unsympathetic producer. The film proved a commercial failure, but the soundtrack album produced a smash hit with "Late in the Evening" and a moderate hit with the title song.

On Sept. 19, 1981, Paul Simon and Art Garfunkel reunited for a free concert in N.Y.'s Central Park. The performance drew an estimated crowd of 500,000 and resulted in a live double-record and HBO cable television special for the duo. The two began recording an album together and toured for the first time in 12 years in 1982 and 1983. Simon ultimately decided to erase Garfunkel's vocals and release the album as a solo album. Despite the inclusion of the moderate hit "Allergies" and excellent songs such as "Think Too Much" and "The Late Great Johnny Ace," *Hearts and Bones* sold only moderately.

Never a prolific writer, Paul Simon became interested in the music of South Africa in the summer of 1984. In February 1985, he flew to Johannesburg to investigate the music of black South Africans. Using the recorded music of South African groups as a starting point, he began composing lyrics. He formed a basic trio of musicians with guitarist Chikapa "Ray" Phiri, bassist Baghiti Khumalo, and drummer Isaac Mthsli and flew the trio to N.Y. for recordings. Over the next year, he recorded the material for *Graceland* with the trio, the vocal group Ladysmith Black Mambazo, and the band Stimela, among others. With the accordion as the common link, he also recorded "That Was Your Mother" with the zydeco band Rockin' Dopsie and The Twisters and "All Around the World" with Los Lobos. The album produced a major hit with "You Can Call Me Al" and two minor hits with "Graceland" and "Boy in the Bubble" and, amazingly, sold spectacularly, remaining on the album charts for nearly two years and eventually selling over four million copies in the U.S. Although the album reinvigorated Simon's career, it also stirred controversy, inasmuch as Simon had recorded in South Africa during a United Nations cultural boycott of the country.

In 1987, Paul Simon toured internationally with Ladysmith Black Mambazo, Stimela, and South African expatriates Hugh Masekela and Miriam Makeba. Their concert in Zimbabwe, the country's biggest musical event since Bob Marley and The Wailers performed at that country's Independence Day celebration in 1980, resulted in a Showtime cable television special in May.

Paul Simon next immersed himself in the rhythms of Brazil and West Africa. As with *Graceland*, the rhythms preceded the songs for *The Rhythm of the Saints* in an inductive style of songwriting, with poet Derek Walcott as the lyrical inspiration. Regarded as even more ambitious than *Graceland*, *The Rhythm of the Saints* was recorded over a two-year period and featured "Born at the Right Time," "The Cool, Cool River," and "She Moves On," and yielded a minor hit with "The Obvious Child." Simon toured in support of the album and performed a free solo concert in N.Y.'s Central Park that drew 750,000 and was broadcast live on the HBO cable television network. The concert also produced a live album that was issued in 1991. With the lifting of the cultural boycott of South Africa in late 1991, Simon became the first international star to perform in the country in early 1992, although one of the tour's offices was bombed and protesters picketed the concert.

Simon and Garfunkel were inducted into the Rock and Roll Hall of Fame in 1990. They reunited occasionally during the 1990s for benefit concerts and performed at N.Y.'s Paramount Theater in the fall of 1993. In May 1992, Paul Simon married Edie Brickell, vocalist of The New Bohemians from 1986 to 1991. In 1994, he co-produced her *Picture Perfect Morning* album. Simon next enlisted Derek Walcott to co-write the book and lyrics for the musical *Capeman*, based on the true story of a teenage Puerto Rican who murdered two people in N.Y. in 1959. Eventually staged on Broadway in January 1998, the $11 million production closed less than two months later after being panned by critics who nonetheless appreciated the show's mix of pop, salsa, rock, and doo-wop music.

DISC.: SIMON AND GARFUNKEL: *Wednesday Morning, 3 a.m.* (1964); *Sounds of Silence* (1966); *Parsley, Sage, Rosemary and Thyme* (1966); *The Graduate* (soundtrack; 1968); *Bookends* (1968); *Bridge Over Troubled Water* (1970); *The Concert in Central Park* (1982). PAUL SIMON: *Paul Simon* (1972); *There Goes Rhymin' Simon* (1973); *Live Rhymin'* (1974); *Still Crazy After All These Years* (1975); *Greatest Hits, Etc.* (1977/1985); *One-Trick Pony* (soundtrack; 1980/1987); *Hearts and Bones* (1983/1984); *Graceland* (1986); *The Rhythm of the Saints* (1990); *Paul Simon's Concert in the Park 1964–93* (1991); *Songs from The Capeman* (1997). ART GARFUNKEL: *Angel Claire* (1973); *Breakaway* (1975); *Watermark* (1977); *Fate for Breakfast* (1979); *Scissors Cut* (1981); *Lefty* (1988); *Garfunkel* (1988); *Up Until Now* (1993). ART GARFUNKEL AND AMY GRANT: *The Animals' Christmas* (1986/1990).

BIBL.: S. Leigh, *P. S.: Now and Then* (Liverpool, 1973); D. Marsh, *P. S.* (N.Y., 1978); P. Humphries, *P. S., Still Crazy After All*

These Years (N.Y., 1989); J. Morella and P. Barey, *S. and G.: Old Friends, A Dual Biography* (N.Y., 1991); S. Luftig, ed., *The P. S. Companion: Four Decades of Commentary* (N.Y., 1997); V. Kingston, *S. and G.: The Biography* (N.Y., 1998).—BH

Simoneau, Léopold, eminent Canadian tenor, pedagogue, and administrator; b. St.-Flavien, near Quebec City, May 3, 1916. He was a student of Émile Larochelle in Quebec City (1939–41) and of Salvator Issaurel in Montreal (1941–44). In 1941 he made his operatic debut as Hadji in *Lakmé* with the Variétés lyriques in Montreal. In 1943 he sang Don Curzio at the Montreal Festival. After winning the Prix Archambault in 1944, he studied with Paul Althouse in N.Y. (1945–47). He also pursued his career, winning extraordinary success as Ferrando and Tamino in Montreal in 1945. During this period, he also sang in the U.S. In 1949 he made his Paris debut as Mireille at the Opéra-Comique; he continued to sing there, as well as at the Opéra, until 1954. In 1953 he made his first appearance at Milan's La Scala. In 1954 he sang with the Vienna State Opera on its visit to London. He soon acquired a notable reputation as a Mozartian. He also sang widely in the U.S. and Canada as a soloist with the leading orchs. and as a recitalist. On Oct. 18, 1963, he made his Metropolitan Opera debut in N.Y. as Ottavio, but remained on its roster for only that season. In 1964 he chose Ottavio as his farewell to the operatic stage at the Place de arts in Montreal. He sang for the last time in public as a soloist in *Messiah* with the Montreal Sym. Orch. on Nov. 24, 1970. From 1963 to 1967 he taught at the Montreal Cons. In 1967 he became deputy head of the music division of the Ministry of Cultural Affairs of Quebec. In 1971 he served as the first artistic director of the Opéra du Quebec. He taught at the San Francisco Cons. of Music from 1972, and also at the Banff School of Fine Arts from 1973 to 1976. In 1982 he settled in Victoria, British Columbia, and founded Canada Opera Piccola. In 1946 he married **Pierrette Alarie.** In 1959 they were the first recipients of the Prix de musique Calixa-Lavallée. In 1971 he was made an Officer of the Order of Canada. The French government made him an Officier of the Ordre des arts des lettres in 1990.

BIBL.: R. Maheu, *Pierrette Alarie, L. S.: Deux voix, un art* (Montreal, 1988).—NS/LK/DM

Simonelli, Matteo, Italian singer, organist, and composer; b. Rome, c. 1619; d. there, Sept. 20, 1696. He pursued his career in Rome. In 1633 he became a treble in the Cappella Giulia at St. Peter's. He studied with Vincenzo Giovannoni, maestro di cappella at S. Lorenzo in Damaso, where he concurrently served as organist. From 1660 to 1679 he was maestro di cappella at S. Giovanni dei Fiorentini, and from 1662 to 1687 he was a countertenor at the Cappella Sistina. His distinguished works included a Mass for 17 Voices, a Stabat Mater for 5 Voices, 2 Violins, and Organ, and several motets.—LK/DM

Simonetti, Achille, Italian-English violinist and composer; b. Turin, June 12, 1857; d. London, Nov. 19, 1928. He began violin lessons with Francesco Bianchi.

After training with Eugenio Cavallini at the Milan Cons. (1872–73), he returned to Turin to study violin with Giuseppe Gamba and composition with Carlo Pedrotti; then continued his violin training with Sivori in Genoa, and finally studied violin with Danda and composition with Massenet at the Paris Cons. (1881–83). In 1887 he settled in England, where he toured with Maria Roze and Benno Schönberger. He lived in London from 1891; was a member of the London Trio (1901–12) and a prof. of violin at the Irish Royal Academy of Music (1912–19). He was greatly esteemed as both a soloist and chamber music artist. An early champion of the Brahms Violin Concerto, he wrote a cadenza for the work, which he introduced in Dresden (Dec. 11, 1896). He composed numerous pieces for solo violin; his *Madrigale* became world famous.—NS/LK/DM

Simon-Girard, Juliette, French soprano; b. Paris, May 8, 1859; d. Nice, Dec. 1959. She made her debut at the Folies-Dramatiques in Paris, where she created the principal role in *Les Cloches de Cornevilles* on April 19, 1877; then sang at the premieres of *La Fille du Tambour- major* (1879), *Fanfan la tulipe* (1882), and many other operettas; she became particularly successful in Offenbach's repertoire. She married the tenor Nicolas Simon, known as Simon-Max (1855–1923); divorced him in 1894, and married the comedian Huguenet. She then retired to Nice.—NS/LK/DM

Simonis, Jean-Marie, Belgian composer; b. Mol, Nov. 22, 1931. He studied composition with Stekke, Souris, Louel, and Quinet, and conducting with Defossez at the Brussels Cons. He taught there (from 1969) and at the Uccles Academy of Music (from 1971).

WORKS: DRAMATIC: Radio Opera: *Gens de maison* (1962). ORCH.: *Introduction et Danse* for Chamber Orch. (1963); *3 esquisses symphoniques* (1964); *Sinfonia da camera* for Strings (1966); *L'Automne,* symphonic poem (1967); *Scherzetto* for Chamber Orch. (1968); *Evasions* (1982); *Cantilène* for Violin and Orch. (1985); *Espressioni* (1988). CHAMBER: 3 *Pieces* for 4 Clarinets (1965); *Duetti* for Viola and Piano (1968); *Impromptu* for Cello (1968–69); *Séquences* for Clarinet and Piano (1969); *Suggestions* for Flute and 4 Percussionists (1970); *Boutades* for 4 Saxophones (1971); *Résonances* for Percussion and Piano (1979); *Introit et Graduel* for String Quartet and Organ (1984); *Fantasia a due* for Violin and Piano (1986). Piano: *Étude de Concert* (1963); *Mouvements* for 2 Pianos (1971); *Historiettes* (1972); *Impromptu* (1973); *2 animations* (1973); *2 pastourelles* (1973); *Evocations* (1974); *Incantations* (1980). VOCAL: 3 *Motets* for Soprano, Chorus, and Orch. (1961); 3 *Lagu Dolanan* for Soprano and Percussion (1969).—NS/LK/DM

Simonov, Yuri (Ivanovich), prominent Russian conductor; b. Saratov, March 4, 1941. He received training in violin at a Saratov music school, where he made his debut as a conductor of the school orch. when he was only 12. He pursued his studies with Kramarov (viola) and Rabinovich (conducting) at the Leningrad Cons. (1956–68), where he made his formal conducting debut as a student in 1963. In 1966 he won first prize in the U.S.S.R. conducting competition and in 1968 took first prize in the Accademia di Santa Cecilia conducting

competition in Rome. He was conductor of the Kislovodsk Phil. (1967–69) and asst. conductor to Mravinsky and the Leningrad Phil. (1968–69). In 1969 he made his debut at the Bolshoi Theater in Moscow conducting *Aida*. From 1970 to 1985 he was chief conductor of the Bolshoi Theater, where he established a notable reputation for his idiomatic performances of the Russian masterworks. He also restored Wagner's operas to the active repertoire after a hiatus of some 40 years. He conducted the company on acclaimed tours abroad, including visits to Paris, Vienna, N.Y. (Metropolitan Opera, *War and Peace*, 1975), Milan, Washington, D.C., and Japan. During these years, he also appeared as a conductor with the leading Russian orchs. at home and on tours abroad. In 1982 he made his first appearance with a Western opera company when he made his debut at London's Covent Garden with *Eugene Onegin*. He returned to Covent Garden in 1986 to open the season with *La Traviata*. He also appeared with most of the major British orchs. During the 1991–92 season, he conducted the Junge Deutsche Philharmonie and the Buenos Aires Phil. on tours of Europe. He made his debut at the Hamburg State Opera conducting *Don Carlo* during the 1992–93 season. In 1994 he became music director of the Orchestre national de Belgique in Brussels.—NS/LK/DM

Simonsen, Rudolph (Hermann), eminent Danish music historian and composer; b. Copenhagen, April 30, 1889; d. there, March 28, 1947. He studied piano with Agnes Adler and theory with Otto Malling at the Copenhagen Cons. (1907–09), completing his piano studies with Teresa Carreño and Anders Rachlew; also earned a law degree from the Univ. of Copenhagen (1912). He taught at the Copenhagen Cons. from 1916, succeeding Nielsen as director in 1931. Although his compositions reveal the influence of Nielsen, he succeeded in producing works of distinction and individuality, but it is as a compiler of books on music culture and philosophy that he is best known.

WORKS: ORCH.: Piano Concerto (Copenhagen, Nov. 15, 1915); 4 syms.: No. 1, *Zion* (Göteborg, Feb. 4, 1920), No. 2, *Hellas* (Berlin, Sept. 23, 1921), No. 3, *Roma* (1923; Copenhagen, March 5, 1928), and No. 4, *Danmark* (1925; Copenhagen, April 4, 1931). CHAMBER: Piano Quintet (1908); 2 string quartets (1923, 1925); Clarinet Quintet (1929). VOCAL: Works for Chorus and Orch.; songs.

WRITINGS (all publ. in Copenhagen): *Musikkultur* (1927); *Musikhistoriske hovedstrmninger* (1930); *Alenmenneskelige vaerdier: Plato-Spinoza-Goethe* (1940); *Sub specie aeternitatis* (1942); *Musikhistorisk kompendium* (1946).

BIBL.: *Mindeskrift om R. S.* (Copenhagen, 1949). —NS/LK/DM

Simovich, Roman, outstanding Ukrainian composer; b. Sniatin, Feb. 28, 1901; d. Lwów, July 30, 1984. He studied piano and composition with Novák at the Prague Cons. (1933–36). He taught at the Lisenko Institutes in Drogobych and Stanislav (1936–44) and at the Lwów Cons. (from 1944), where he became a prof. in 1963. He was made an Honored Artist of the Ukraine in

1954. His compositions were firmly rooted in the history and lore of the western Ukraine.

WORKS: DRAMATIC: Ballet: *Sopilka Dovbusha* (1948). **ORCH.:** 7 syms. (*Gutsulska*, 1945; *Lemkovsk*, 1947; *Springtime*, 1951; *Heroic*, 1954; *Celestial*, 1955; 1965; 1972); 3 suites; 6 symphonic poems; 4 overtures: *Carnival* (1936), *Youth* (1958), *Ceremonial* (1966), and *Bombastic* (1967); Flute Concerto (1953); Piano Concerto (1971). **CHAMBER:** 2 piano trios (1929, 1935); 2 string quartets (1929, 1950); solo piano pieces. **VOCAL:** 4 vocal symphonic poems: *The Shawl* (1933), *The Word* (1946), *In the Carpathians* (1949), and *The Flowers of Happiness and Freedom* (1959).

BIBL.: A. Tereshchenko, *R. S.* (Kiev, 1973).—**NS/LK/DM**

Simple Minds, popular British new-wave band. **MEMBERSHIP:** Jim Kerr, voc. (b. Glasgow, Scotland, July 9, 1959); Charlie Burchill, gtr., kybd. (b. Glasgow, Scotland, Nov. 27, 1959); Mick McNeil, kybd. (b. Glasgow, Scotland, July 20, 1958); Derek Forbes, bs. (b. Glasgow, Scotland, June 22, 1956); Brian McGee, drm.

Simple Minds started out when John Milarky booked his imaginary band, Johnny and the Self Abusers (J&TSA) at the Dourne Castle Pub in Glasgow during the height of punk's first wave. He convinced several friends and friends of friends to play, including guitarist Charlie Burchill and singer Jim Kerr. It became a standing gig, and the group even released a single that *Melody Maker* called "rank and vile." The band split on the day the single came out. Kerr, Burchill, Brian McGee, and the drummer from J&TSA formed Simple Minds. Their first gig was opening for the English reggae band Steel Pulse. After cutting their teeth in the pubs, with a show that included full make-up, they made a demo that was greeted with much more enthusiasm than the J&TSA's single. They signed to fledgling Zoom records, and John Leckie produced their debut album *Life in a Day*, released in 1979. It reached #30 on the U.K. charts. Zoom lost its deal with Arista, but the company retained Simple Minds, and Zoom's owner became their manager. Later in 1979, the band went on tour with Magazine and then right back into the studio, where they cut *Real to Real Cacophony*. A highly experimental album, it gathered good reviews, but sold poorly. After touring Europe, they released 1980's *Empire and Dance*, which again pleased the critics but found no buyers. Nonetheless, Peter Gabriel asked the band to open for his European tour. They signed to Virgin, and after tumultuous sessions they released two albums simultaneously in 1981, *Sons and Fascination* and *Sister Feelings Call*. After touring Canada and Australia, the albums started selling in those areas, too. The group cut a single, "Promised You a Miracle," that did well in Europe, Australia, and Canada, and even attracted some "alternative" play in the U.S. It was included on the band's next release, *New Gold Dream (81, 82, 83, 84)*. The second single, "Glittering Prizes," was celebrated as a new wave masterpiece.

After touring with U2, they went into the studio with U2's producer at the time, Steve Lillywhite. Informed by Lillywhite's "wide-scream" production methods, the 1984 album *Sparkle in the Rain* entered the U.K. charts at #1. Yet, a U.S. hit continued to elude the group. Kerr,

however, became something of a celebrity. They toured in support of the album with The Pretenders; during the tour's stop in N.Y., Kerr married Pretender's leader Chrissie Hynde. The group wanted to take it easy for a while, but producer Keith Forsey kept calling them. He wanted the group to cut a song for the soundtrack to the movie *The Breakfast Club*. Their label wanted them to do it, their manager wanted them to do it, and so the band went into the studio and cut the track "Don't You Forget about Me." It became the title track for the film and the band had a chart topping single in the U.S. They finally cracked the U.S. market in a big way. Capitalizing on this hit (which the band never really liked) they recorded an album with producers Jimmy Iovine and Bob Clearmountain. 1985's *One upon a Time* became the band's biggest selling album, going gold and hitting #10 in the U.S. The single "Alive and Kicking" hit #3 in the U.S. and was a hit all around the world. After a dearth of success in the U.S., the album produced two more hits as well: "Sanctify Yourself" rose to #14 and "All the Things She Said" hit #28. The band hit the apogee of their success.

Their 1987 followup set, *Live in the City of Light*, once again entered the U.K. charts at #1, the fastest selling live record to that time, but sold only modestly in the U.S. 1989's *Street Fighting Years*, a tough, political album, did even worse in the U.S., though it, too, went to #1 in the U.K. Their 1991 opus *Real Life* became the first Simple Minds album in years not to go to #1 in the U.K. (it stalled at #2). The band was still playing stadiums across Europe and smaller venues in the U.S., where they scored a #40 hit with "See the Lights." On the verge of exhaustion, the band took some time off. In the meantime, a greatest hits record, *Glittering Prizes*, went to the top of the U.K. charts. During the time off, most of the band bowed out, leaving the core of Kerr and Burchill to continue under the Simple Minds name. Keith Forsey returned to the band, requesting they cut another track for a film. This time, the group was so pleased with it, they decided it was too good for the movie (*Super Mario Brothers*) and asked Forsey to produce their next album. 1995's guitar-oriented *Good News from the Next World* featured the core duo and a slew of session players. Kerr put together a recording studio in his home and Simple Minds' dense, textured 1998 album *Neopolis* was recorded there. The band's huge European success has made Kerr a wealthy man; so wealthy, in fact, that he bought his favorite soccer club, Glasgow Celtic, in 1998.

DISC.: *Life in a Day* (1979); *Real to Real Cacophony* (1979); *Empires and Dance* (1980); *Sons and Fascination* (1981); *Sister Feelings Call* (1981); *New Gold Dream* (rec. 1981/1982; rel. 1982); *Sparkle in the Rain* (1984); *Once upon a Time* (1985); *Live in the City of Light* (1987); *Street Fighting Years* (1989); *Themes, Vol. 1* (1990); *Themes, Vol. 2* (1990); *Themes, Vol. 3* (1990); *Themes, Vol. 4* (1990); *Real Life* (1991); *Good News from the Next World* (1995); *Promised Night* (1998); *Neapolis* (1998).—**HB**

Simply Red, named for and led by red-headed, blue-eyed soul singer, Mick Hucknall. **MEMBERSHIP:** Mick Hucknall, voc. (b. Manchester, England, June 8, 1960); Tony Bowers, bs. (b. Oct. 31, 1952); Chris Joyce, drm. (b. Manchester, England, Oct. 11, 1957); Tim

Kellett, kybd. (b. Knaresborough, England, July 23, 1964); Fritz McIntyre, kybd. (b. Birmingham, England, Sept. 2, 1956); Sylvan Richardson, gtr.; Shaun Ward, bs.; Ian Kirkham, wdwnd.

Always more popular at home than in the U.S., Mick Hucknall and the myriad lineups of the group that takes its name from his flaming red mane have nonetheless remained sporadically popular on the American charts. The group has earned a devoted following for its middle-of-the road fusion of pop and soul with tinges of jazz.

Hucknall began performing in a punk band called the Frantic Elevators, formed somewhat after the punk aesthetic had peaked in the late 1970s. When the band ended, Hucknall pursued a more soulful pop sound. He enlisted several former members of Midlands experimental popsters Durutti Column to form the first Simply Red lineup. They were signed to Elektra and recorded *Picture Book*, released in 1985. They hit it big on the U.S. charts with their second single, the Hucknall tune "Holding Back the Years." The song featured Hucknall's shivering countertenor, his strongest suit as a vocalist, and hit #1; the album rose to #16 and went platinum.

The group's sophomore effort, *Men & Women*, was more successful in the U.K. than the U.S. Despite teaming with Motown great Lamont Dozier on two songs, the album only got to #31 in the States, based largely on momentum from the previous record and the minor 1987 hit "The Right Thing" (#27). In the U.K., "Infidelity," their version of Cole Porter's "Ev'ry Time We Say Goodbye," also charted.

Simply Red returned to the top of the U.S. charts with a gold-selling cover of Howard Melvin and the Blue Notes' "If You Don't Know Me by Now" from the group's next album, *A New Flame*, in 1989. In the U.S., the album hit #22 and went gold; the album once again generated two more singles in the U.K. While their next album, *Stars*, didn't make the U.S. Top 40, it did eventually go gold, with the #23 single "Something Got Me Started" leading the way. In the U.K., however, *Stars* was the best-selling album of 1991, topping the charts for 19 weeks and spinning off five hit singles.

For the balance of the 1990s, Simply Red became more or less just the given name for whatever group was backing Hucknall at the time. While continuing to produce major hits in the U.K. and Europe, Hucknall never again was able to crack the U.S. charts.

DISC.: *Picture Book* (1985); *Men & Women* (1987); *A New Flame* (1989); *Stars* (1991); *Life* (1995); *Fairground* (1995); *Blue* (1998); *Love & The Russian Winter* (1999).—**HB**

Simpson (Sympson), Christopher, eminent

English viol player, music theorist, and composer; b. probably in Westonby, near Egton, Yorkshire, c. 1605; d. probably in Holborn, London, between May 5 and July 29, 1669. He fought on the Royalist side in the English Civil War (1643–44) and later entered the service of Sir Robert Bolles as music tutor to the latter's son. His playing, writings, and compositions won him great esteem.

WRITINGS: *The Division-violist, or, An Introduction to the Playing Upon a Ground* (London, 1659; second ed., rev., 1665 as *Chelys minuritionum artificio exornata/The Division-viol, or the Art of Playing Extempore upon a Ground*; third ed., 1712); *The Principles of Practical Musick* (London, 1665; second ed., rev. and aug., 1667 as *A Compendium of Practical Musick*; ed by P. Lord, Oxford, 1970); also annotations to T. Campion in J. Playford, *A Brief Introduction to the Skill of Musick* (London, second ed., 1655).

WORKS: *Airs in The Principles of Practical Musick* (see Writings above); various other airs in MS; divisions in *The Division- violist* (see Writings above); various other divisions in MS; fantasias and fantasia-suites in MS.

BIBL.: M. Meredith, *C. Simpson and the Consort of Viols* (diss., Univ. of Wales, Cardiff, 1969).—**NS/LK/DM**

Simpson, Robert (Wilfred Levick), English

composer and writer on music; b. Leamington, March 2, 1921; d. Tralee, Ireland, Nov. 21, 1997. He studied composition with Howells in London (1942–46) and received his Mus.D. from the Univ. of Durham in 1951. He joined the staff of the BBC as a music producer in 1951, resigning in 1980. He was awarded the Carl Nielsen Gold Medal of Denmark in 1956 and the Bruckner Medal in 1962. In his compositions, Simpson pursued a tonal path.

WORKS: DRAMATIC: Incidental Music To : Ibsen's *The Pretenders* (1965); Milton's *Samson Agonistes* (1974). **ORCH.:** 11 syms.: No. 1 (1951; Copenhagen, June 11, 1953), No. 2 (1955; Cheltenham, July 16, 1957), No. 3 (1962; Birmingham, March 14, 1963), No. 4 (1970–72; Manchester, April 26, 1973), No. 5 (1972; London, May 3, 1973), No. 6 (1976; London, April 8, 1980), No. 7 (1977), No. 8 (1981; London, Nov. 10, 1982), No. 9 (1985; Poole, April 8, 1987), No. 10 (1988), and No. 11 (1990); Violin Concerto (1959; Birmingham, Feb. 25, 1960); Piano Concerto (Cheltenham, July 14, 1967); Flute Concerto (1989); Cello Concerto (1991). **Brass Band :** *Canzona* (1958); *Energy* (1971); *Volcano* (1979); *The 4 Temperaments* (1983); *Introduction and Allegro on a Bass by Max Reger* (1987); *Vortex* (1989). **CHAMBER:** 15 string quartets (1952, 1953, 1954, 1973, 1974, 1975, 1977, 1979, 1982, 1983, 1984, 1987, 1989, 1990, 1991); *Canzona* for Brass (1958); *Variations and Fugue* for Recorder and String Quartet (1958); Trio for Clarinet, Cello, and Piano (1967); Quartet for Clarinet and Strings (1968); Quartet for Horn, Violin, Cello, and Piano (1975); Quintet for Clarinet, Bass Clarinet, and String Trio (1981); Trio for Horn, Violin, and Piano (1984); Violin Sonata (1984); String Trio (1987); String Quintet (1987); Trio for Violin, Cello, and Piano (1988–89). **KEYBOARD: P i a n o :** Sonata (1946); *Variations and Finale on a Theme by Haydn* (1948); Sonata for 2 Pianos (1980); *Variations and Finale on a Theme of Beethoven* (1990). **O r g a n :** *Eppur si muove: Ricercar e Passacaglia* (1985). **VOCAL:** *Media morte in vita sumus* for Chorus, Brass, and Timpani (1975); *Tempi* for Chorus (1985).

WRITINGS (all publ. in London unless otherwise given): *Carl Nielsen, Symphonist* (1952; second ed., rev., 1979); *Bruckner and the Symphony* (1963); *Sibelius and Nielsen* (1965); *The Essence of Bruckner: An Essay towards the Understanding of his Music* (1966; third ed., rev., 1992); ed. *The Symphony* (Harmondsworth, vol. I, 1966; second ed., 1972; vol. II, 1967); *Beethoven Symphonies* (1970); *The Proms and Natural Justice* (1981).

BIBL.: R. Johnson, *R. S.: 50th Birthday Essays* (London, 1971); R. Matthew-Walker, ed., *The Symphonies of R. S.* (London, 1991).—**NS/LK/DM**

Simpson, Thomas, English viol player, music editor, and composer; b. Milton next Sittingbourne, Kent (baptized), April 1, 1582; d. probably there, after 1630. He went to Germany as a youth, and served as a viol player at the Heidelberg court from 1608. He then was at the court of the Count of Holstein-Schaumburg in Buckeburg (c. 1615–21), and subsequently was employed in the royal chapel of Copenhagen as a court musician to King Christian IV (1622–25). An excellent composer of court dances and songs, he brought out *Opusculum* [30] *newer Pavanen, Galliarden, Couranten und Volten, a 5* (Frankfurt am Main, 1610; includes 24 pieces by Simpson), *Opus* [22] *newer Paduanen, Galliarden, Intraden, Canzonen, Ricercaren, a 5* (Frankfurt am Main, 1611; not extant; second ed., Hamburg, 1617), and (50) *Taffel-Consort, a 4* and Basso Continuo (Hamburg, 1621; includes 7 pieces by Simpson).—NS/LK/DM

Simrock, Nikolaus, famous German music publisher; b. Mainz, Aug. 23, 1751; d. Bonn, June 12, 1832. He played the horn in the Electoral Orch. in Bonn until 1794. He began dealing in printed music and instruments in 1780, and in 1785 he opened a music shop in Bonn, selling musical instruments. In 1793 he established a music publ. house with its own printing press. During Beethoven's lifetime, Simrock's catalogue listed 85 of his works, including the *Kreutzer Sonata* and opus nos. 17, 31, 81b, 102, and 107. His son Peter Joseph Simrock (b. Bonn, Aug. 18, 1792; d. Cologne, Dec. 13, 1868) succeeded him and greatly increased the prestige of the house by acquiring the early works of Brahms. He was succeeded by his son "Fritz" (Friedrich August) Simrock (b. Bonn, Jan. 2, 1837; d. Ouchy, near Lausanne, Aug. 20, 1901), who transferred the firm to Berlin in 1870, publ. the works of Brahms, and, at the suggestion of Brahms, added the works of Dvořák to his catalogue. His nephew "Hans" (Johann Baptist) Simrock (b. Cologne, April 17, 1861; d. Berlin, July 26, 1910) reorganized the firm in 1902 as a stock company and established branches in London and Paris. A grandson of Fritz Simrock, Fritz Auckenthaler Simrock (b. Zürich, Nov. 17, 1893; d. Basel, April 19, 1973), headed the firm (1920–29) when it was sold to A.J. Benjamin in Hamburg. In 1951 the Hamburg firm, which also had a branch in London, resumed its original name, N. Simrock Co.

BIBL.: *Verzeichnis des Musikalien-Verlages N. S.* (Berlin, 1893; 3 suppls., 1902–27); W. Ottendorf-Simrock, *Das Haus S.* (Ratingen, 1954); K. Stephenson, *Johannes Brahms und Fritz S., Weg einer Freundschaft. Briefe des Verlegers an den Komponisten* (Hamburg, 1961).—NS/LK/DM

Sims, Ezra, innovative American composer; b. Birmingham, Ala., Jan. 16, 1928. After training at Birmingham Southern Coll. (B.A., 1947) and with G. Ackley Brower at the Birmingham Cons. of Music (1945–48), he was a student of Porter at the Yale Univ. School of Music (B.Mus., 1952). While serving in the U.S. Army, he studied Chinese at its language school (1953). Following his discharge, he pursued his musical training with Kirchner and Milhaud at Mills Coll. in Oakland, Calif. (M.A., 1956). In 1962–63 he was active at the NHK electronic music studio in Tokyo. From 1968 to 1978 he

was music director of the New England Dinosaur Dance Theatre. He taught at the New England Cons. of Music in Boston from 1976 to 1978. From 1977 to 1981 he was president of the Dinosaur Annex Music Ensemble. In 1992–93 he was a guest lecturer at the Salzburg Mozarteum. In 1962 he held a Guggenheim fellowship, and in 1976 and 1978 NEA fellowships. In 1985 he received an award from the American Academy of Arts and Letters. He held a Fulbright research grant in 1992. Sims began to compose tape music early in his career. In 1971 he devised a microtonal system utilizing an assymetrical mode of 18 (later 24) pitches, taken from and made transposable within a 72-note division of the octave, or an unaltered diatonicism. In 1988 he also began to use computer elements in some of his instrumental music.

WORKS: MICROTONAL ORCH.: *Longfellow Sparrow* (1976); *Yʳ Obedᵗ Servᵗ* (1977; rev. 1981); *Pictures for an Institution* for Chamber Orch. (1983); *Night Unto Night* (1984); *Concert Piece* for Viola, Flute, Clarinet, Cello, and Small Orch. (1990; Cambridge, Mass., March 1, 1992). **CHAMBER:** String Octet (1964); *From An Oboe Quartet* for Oboe, Violin, Viola, and Cello (1971); Oboe Quartet for Oboe, Violin, Viola, and Cello (1971–75); *II-Variations* for Oboe, Violin, Viola, and Cello (1973); *Second Thoughts* for 1, 2, or Many Double Basses, with or without Tape (1974); *String Quartet No. 2 (1962)* for Flute, Clarinet, Violin, Viola, and Cello (1974); Flourish for Oboe, Violin, Viola, and Cello (1975); *Twenty Years After* for Violin and Clarinet (1978); *Midorigaoka* for 2 Violins, 2 Violas, and Cello (1978); *and, as I was saying...* for Viola (1979); *All Done From Memory* for Violin (1980); Ruminations for Clarinet (1980); *Two for One* for Violin and Viola (1980); *Phenomena* for Flute, Clarinet, Violin, Viola, and Cello (1981); Sextet for Clarinet, Alto Saxophone, Horn, Violin, Viola, and Cello (1981; also for 3 Clarinets, Violin, Viola, and Cello, 1983); *Solo After Sextet* for Saxophone (1981); Quartet for Flute, Violin, Viola, and Cello (1982); *Brief Elegies* for Flute and Zoomoozophone, with Clarinet and Bassoon (1983); *This Way to the Egress* or *Manners Makyth Man* for Violin, Viola, and Cello (1983); *Tune & Variations* for 1 or 2 Horns (1983); String Quartet No. 4 (1984); *Wedding Winds* for 3 Clarinets (1986); *Chase* for Clarinet (1987); Quintet for Clarinet, 2 Violins, Viola, and Cello (1987); *Solo in 4 Movements* for Cello (1987); *AEDM im memoriam* for Cello (1988); *Flight* for Flute and Electronics (1989); *Night Piece: In Firum Imus Nocte et Consumimur Igni* for Flute, Clarinet, Viola, Cello, and Electronics (1989); Duo for Flute and Cello (1992); *Stanzas* for Flute, 3 Clarinets, Viola, and Cello (1995); Duo for Viola and Cello (1996); *Duo '97* for Clarinet and Viola (1997). **VOCAL:** *In Memoriam Alice Hawthorne* for Tenor, Baritone, Narrator, 4 Clarinets, Horn, and Marimba 4-Hands or 2 Marimbas (1967); *Celebration of Dead Ladies* for Voice, Alto Flute, Basset Clarinet, Viola, Cello, and Percussion (1976); *Elegie-nach Rilke* for Soprano, Flute, Clarinet, Violin, Viola, and Cello (1976); *Aeneas on the Saxophone* for Chorus, 2 Clarinets, Horn, Trombone, Viola, and Double Bass (1977); *Come Away* for Mezzo-soprano, Viola, Clarinet, Alto Flute, Horn, Trombone, and Double Bass (1978); *5 Songs* for Alto and Viola (1979); *Song* for Mezzo-soprano, Clarinet, and Viola, after W.H. Auden (1980); *The Conversions* for Chorus, after Harry Mathews (1985); *Invocation* for Voice, 3 Flutes, Viola, Double Bass, and Quarter-tone Guitar or Sampler Keyboard (1992); *If I Told Him* for Alto and Cello, after Gertrude Stein (1996); *Two Encores* for Mezzo-soprano and Cello (1997). **QUARTER TONE: C h a m - b e r :** *5 Sonate Concertante* for Strings and/or Other Instruments (1961); String Quartet No. 3 (1962). **V o c a l :** *Cantata III* for Mezzo-soprano and Percussion (1963). **MUSIC USING 12-NOTE EQUAL DIVISION OF THE OCTAVE: O r c h . :** *Le Tombeau d'Albers* (1959). **C h a m b e r :** Cello Sonata (1959); String Quartet (1959); *Slow Hiccups* for 2 Equal Melody Instruments (1975). **P i a n o :** Sonatine (1957); *Buchlein for Lyon* (1962). **VOCAL:** *Chanson d'aventure* for Tenor and Harpsichord or Piano (1951; rev. 1975); *Chamber Cantata on Chinese Poems* for Tenor, Flute, Clarinet, Viola, Cello, and Harpsichord (1954); *2 Folk Songs* for Baritone and Piano (1958); *3 Songs* for Tenor and Orch. (1960); *The Bewties of the Futeball* for Children's Chorus, Optional Recorders, Piano, and Metal Idiophones (1974); *What God Is Like To Him I Serve?* for Chorus (1976). **TA P E :** *Sakoku*, music for a television drama (NHK-TV, Tokyo, April 1963); *McDowell's Fault, or The 10th Sunday After Trinity* (1968); *Commonplace Book or A Salute to Our American Container Corp.* (1969); *A Frank Overture. 4 Dented Interludes. And Coda* (1969); *Warts and All* (1969); *Clement Wenceslaus Lothaire Nepomucene, Prince Metternich (1773–1859): In Memoriam* (1970); *Elina's Piece* (1970); *Real Toads* (1970); *Where the Wild Things Are* (1973).—**NS/LK/DM**

Sims, Jon Reed, American conductor; b. Smith Center, Kans., May 6, 1947; d. (of AIDS) San Francisco, July 16, 1984. He studied piano and horn, and was drum major of his high school band, and later attended Wichita State Univ. (B.Mus. and B.A., 1969) and Ind. Univ. (M.Mus., 1972). He studied eurhythmics at the Dalcroze School in N.Y., arts administration at San Francisco's Golden Gate Univ., dance in N.Y., Chicago, and San Francisco, and horn and composition (with Milhaud). He taught in Chicago (1972–74) and San Francisco (1974–78). In 1978 he founded the San Francisco Gay Freedom Day Marching Band & Twirling Corps, which made its debut performance at the Gay Pride Day parade that same year. He then founded in rapid succession the San Francisco Gay Men's Chorus (Nov. 1978), the Golden Gate Performing Arts (an administrative organization, March 1979), Lambda Pro Musica, and the San Francisco Lesbian & Gay Men's Community Chorus; directed the San Francisco Band & Corps until early 1982. Sims's dream was to create a nationwide network of gay and lesbian instrumental and choral ensembles; the San Francisco chorus toured the U.S. in 1981, a public gesture that caused the founding of ensembles nationwide. Gay and lesbian choruses appeared in quick succession in Los Angeles (July 12, 1979), Seattle (Nov. 1979), and Chicago. The first meeting of what was to become GALA (Gay and Lesbian Assn. [of choruses]; Chicago, June 1981) included directors and ensemble founders Jerry Carlson (Chicago Gay Men's Chorus; later director of the Los Angeles Gay Men's Chorus; d. of AIDS, Nov. 1987), Dennis Coleman (Seattle Men's Chorus), Richard Garrin (Chicago's Windy City Gay Chorus), Dick Kramer (San Francisco Gay Men's Chorus), Gary Miller (N.Y.C. Gay Men's Chorus), and Susan Schleef (Chicago's Artemis Singers). The first West Coast conference of GALA included 9 choruses (1982); the first national conference, with 11 choruses (N.Y., 1983), was followed by conferences with 17 (Minneapolis, 1986) and 43 choruses (Seattle, 1989); in 1990 GALA boasted a membership of 88 choruses situated throughout North America and Europe. Most GALA choruses are made up of gay men, although there are a number of lesbian and mixed-voice ensembles; many additional lesbian groups are not GALA members. Following Sims's example, gay and lesbian musical organizations have grown remarkably in number, size, and sophistication; they are important examples of communal expression in American gay and lesbian culture.—**NS/LK/DM**

Sims, Zoot (John Haley), noted jazz tenor saxophonist, leader; b. Inglewood, Calif., Oct. 29, 1925; d. N.Y., March 23, 1985. He made his debut in 1941 and played with various "name" bands, including Benny Goodman's, until he was drafted. He briefly rejoined Goodman, but made his mark with Woody Herman, where he was one of the "four brothers" sax team in the Woody Herman Band (1947–49). While in Herman's band, he struck up a lifetime friendship with Al Cohn; the two worked together until Sims's death. In the late 1950s, Sims often backed beat novelist Jack Kerouac, who was a big fan of Sims's playing. He toured frequently with *Jazz at the Philharmonic*, and was often hired by Goodman for various gigs, including the tour of the Soviet Union (1962). In addition, he freelanced in clubs and recorded in a variety of settings. He later also played some soprano sax. From the 1960s through his death from cancer, he led his own small groups on record in clubs, and on tour. His brother, Ray C. (b. Wichita, Kans., Jan. 18, 1921), was a trombonist who played for long periods with Harry James (1947–57 and 1957–69) as well as playing and singing with Zoot's early 1970s quintet.

DISC.: *Trotting* (1950); *Quartets* (1950); *First Recordings!* (1950); *Zoot!* (1956); *Z. S. Plays Alto, Tenor, and Baritone* (1956); *Tonite's Music Today* (1956); *Plays Four Altos* (1957); *Four Brothers: Together Again* (1957); *Jazz Alive: A Night at the Half Note* (1959); *Live at Ronnie Scott's* (1961); *Two Jims and a Zoot* (1964); *Waiting Game* (1966); *Nirvana* (1974); *and the Gershwin Bros.* (1975); *Nights* (1976); *Zoots Plays Soprano* (1976). Jimmy Rowles: *If I'm Lucky* (1977); *Warm Tenor* (1978). Harry "Sweets Edison: *Just Friends* (1978). *For Lady Day* (1978); *Swinger* (1979); *Passion Flower* (1979); *Blues for Two* (1982); *On the Korner* (rec. 1983; rel. 1994); *Quietly There: Z. S. Plays Johnny Mandel* (1984); *Basie and Zoot* (1985).

BIBL.: A. Astrup, *John Haley Sims (Zoot Sims) Discography* (Lyngby, Denmark, 1980).—**LP**

Šín, Otakar, eminent Czech music theorist and composer; b. Rokytno, Moravia, April 23, 1881; d. Prague, Jan. 21, 1943. He studied composition with V. Novák at the Prague Cons., where he was appointed a prof. of theory in 1920. He publ., in Prague, the textbooks *Uplná nauka o harmonii na základě melodie a rytmu* (A Complete Harmony Course on the Basis of Melody and Rhythm; 1922; 6th ed., rev., 1949), *Nauka o kontrapunktu, imitaci a fuge* (Counterpoint, Imitation and Fugue; 1936; second ed., 1945), and *Všeobecná nauka o hudbé* (A General Music Course; 1949; completed by F. Bartoš and K. Janeček).

WORKS: O R C H . : 2 symphonic poems: *Tillotama* (1908) and *King Menkera* (1916–18); *Radio Overture* (1936); *3 Czech*

Dances for Orch. (1939; also for Nonet). **CHAMBER:** 2 string quartets (1923; 1926–28); Cello Sonata (1934); *Small Suite* for Violin and Piano (1937); *Hunting*, festive greeting for Horns (1938); numerous piano pieces. **VOCAL:** Choruses; songs.

BIBL.: K. Janeček, *O. S.* (Prague, 1944).—**NS/LK/DM**

Sinatra, Frank (actually, Francis Albert),

renowned American singer and actor; b. Hoboken, N. J., Dec. 12, 1915; d. Los Angeles, May 14, 1998. Maintaining his appeal from the height of the Swing Era until his death nearly 60 years later, Sinatra dominated popular music for much of the 20th century. He was universally acknowledged as the paramount interpreter of the American popular song, which he rendered in a pure baritone that employed knowing, exquisitely enunciated phrasing. His personal approach to singing delivered popular music from the frothy, light-hearted style of the 1920s and 1930s to the darker, more complex sounds of the 1950s and beyond. He led the evolution of the Big Band Era into the singer-dominated period of the later 1940s and withstood the emergence of rock 'n' roll with a series of 1950s albums that permanently revived interest in the major songwriters of the 1920s and 1930s. Long after rock had become synonymous with popular music, he continued to perform and record successfully. Of the 150 chart singles he scored as a solo artist between 1942 and 1980, his most successful were "Oh! What It Seemed to Be," "Five Minutes More," and a duet with his daughter Nancy Sinatra, "Somethin' Stupid"; of his 79 chart albums between 1946 and 1998, the biggest hits were *Nice 'n' Easy, Frank Sinatra Sings for Only the Lonely,* and *Come Fly with Me.*

Sinatra was the son of Anthony Martin Sinatra, a fireman, and Natalie Garaventi Sinatra. He sang in the glee club at his high school, then dropped out in his senior year to become a singer. In September 1935 he appeared on Major Bowes's *Original Amateur Hour* radio series as part of the vocal group The Hoboken Four. The group won the amateur contest and toured with the Bowes troupe. Sinatra began to study singing with vocal coach John Quinlan. In the mid-1930s, he performed on local radio and got a job as a singing waiter and master of ceremonies at the Rustic Cabin, a roadhouse in Englewood, N. J., from which radio broadcasts were made. On Feb. 4, 1939, he married Nancy Barbato. They had three children. Two of them, Nancy Sandra Sinatra (b. June 8, 1940) and Franklin Wayne Sinatra, known as Frank Sinatra Jr. (b. Jan. 10, 1944), became singers. Frank and Nancy Sinatra divorced Oct. 29, 1951.

Sinatra was hired by Harry James in June 1939 to be the male singer in his recently formed big band. He made his first recordings on July 13, 1939. None of the records he made with James were hits at the time they were first released. The James band struggled through 1939, and at the end of the year Sinatra received an offer from the more successful Tommy Dorsey to join his band. He made his debut with Dorsey in January 1940. The first Dorsey recording on which he was featured that became a success was "You're Lonely and I'm Lonely" (music and lyrics by Irving Berlin), which reached the hit parade in June. In July, "I'll Never Smile Again" (music and lyrics by Ruth Lowe), on which

Sinatra sang with the vocal group The Pied Pipers, became a #1 hit for Dorsey. In 1982 the recording was inducted into the Grammy Hall of Fame.

Sinatra sang lead vocals on four more Top Ten hits with Dorsey in 1940 and, sometimes with The Pied Pipers and Dorsey's female singer Connie Haines, on eight Top Ten hits in 1941, among them "This Love of Mine," for which he wrote the lyrics to music by Sol Parker and Henry Sanicola. He also performed on Dorsey's various network radio programs, notably the *Fame and Fortune* show of 1940–41. He made his film debut singing "I'll Never Smile Again" with Dorsey in *Las Vegas Nights*, released in March 1941.

While still with Dorsey, Sinatra made a solo recording on Jan. 19, 1942, that included a version of Cole Porter's "Night and Day," which became his first chart record. Nevertheless, he continued to record with Dorsey until the onset of the musicians' union recording ban on Aug. 1, 1942, and sang on two more Top Ten hits before he left Dorsey for a solo career in September, at the time a highly unusual step. In October he launched a 15-minute radio series, *Songs by Sinatra*, on CBS that ran through the end of 1942. Booked as a support act to Benny Goodman at the Paramount Theatre in N.Y., beginning New Year's Eve, 1942, he created a sensation, with teenager girls lining up for blocks and swooning during his performances. Before the end of the eight-week run, he was a star. Meanwhile, his recording with Dorsey of "There Are Such Things" (music and lyrics by Stanley Adams, Abel Baer, and George W. Meyer) had been released, and it hit #1 in January 1943, selling a million copies.

Sinatra became a regular on the radio series *Your Hit Parade* in February 1943, staying with the show until the end of 1944. In April he was seen in the motion picture *Reveille with Beverly*, singing "Night and Day," his first featured film appearance. He added a third radio series in June, performing on *Broadway Bandbox* through October, after which he again appeared on *Songs by Sinatra* through December. As the recording ban continued, record companies began to reissue earlier recordings, resulting in more Sinatra hits: "All or Nothing at All" (music by Arthur Altman, lyrics by Jack Lawrence), recorded and released in 1939 by Harry James, was reissued with Sinatra's name billed in front of James's; it reached the charts in June 1943, hitting the Top Ten and selling a million copies. "In the Blue of the Evening" (music by Alfred A. D'Artega, lyrics by Tom Adair), recorded and released in 1942 by Dorsey with Sinatra on lead vocals, was reissued and went to #1 in August 1943.

Sinatra himself, meanwhile, had signed to Columbia Records and, using a temporary loophole in the recording ban (that closed after the union protested), recorded several sessions employing only a cappella backing. These sessions brought him five Top Ten hits between August 1943 and March 1944, the most popular of which was "You'll Never Know" (music by Harry Warren, lyrics by Mack Gordon).

Sinatra went to Hollywood, where he made his film acting debut (albeit playing himself) in RKO's *Higher and Higher*, released in December 1943. In January 1944 he replaced his *Songs by Sinatra* radio series with the weekly half-hour program *The Frank Sinatra Show*; it ran for a year and a half. He had a more substantial role in his second RKO film musical, *Step Lively*, released in July 1944, then signed to MGM. With the recording ban lifted in the fall of 1944, he returned to the recording studio in November and cut a version of "White Christmas" (music and lyrics by Irving Berlin) that became a Top Ten, million-selling hit, the second most successful rendition of the song after Bing Crosby's. He went on to score nine Top Ten hits in 1945, the most popular being "Saturday Night (Is the Loneliest Night of the Week)" (music by Jule Styne, lyrics by Sammy Cahn) in March. On screen he sang, acted, and danced beside Gene Kelly in *Anchors Aweigh*, released in July, which became one of the biggest box office hits of the year. In September he returned to radio with a weekly series again called *Songs by Sinatra* that ran through June 1947.

Sinatra scored eight Top Ten hits during 1946, including two that reached #1: "Oh! What It Seemed to Be" (music and lyrics by Bennie Benjamin, George David Weiss, and Frankie Carle) and "Five Minutes More" (music by Jule Styne, lyrics by Sammy Cahn). In March his album *The Voice of Frank Sinatra* also topped the charts. In December he appeared in the climax of the Jerome Kern film biography *Till the Clouds Roll By*, singing "Ol' Man River" (lyrics by Oscar Hammerstein II). He had another five Top Ten hits in 1947, including the #1 "Mam'selle" (music by Edmund Goulding, lyrics by Mack Gordon), and his album *Songs by Sinatra* reached the Top Ten. He starred in the film musical *It Happened in Brooklyn*, released in March. In September he returned to *Your Hit Parade*, performing on the show regularly during the 1947–48 and 1948–49 seasons.

A second recording ban kept Sinatra out of the recording studio for most of 1948, and he scored only one Top Ten hit during the year, an a cappella version of "Nature Boy" (music and lyrics by Eden Ahbez) in June. He also reached the Top Ten on the album charts with *Christmas Songs by Sinatra*. He appeared in two film musicals, *The Miracle of the Bells* in March and *The Kissing Bandit* in November. By 1949 it was clear that Sinatra's career was in decline, but he still scored three Top Ten hits during the year, the most successful of which was "Some Enchanted Evening" (music by Richard Rodgers, lyrics by Oscar Hammerstein II) in July. He appeared in two MGM musicals, *Take Me Out to the Ball Game* in March and *Our Town* in December, and he launched a new, 15-minute weekday radio series, *Light-Up Time*, that ran during the 1949–50 season.

Sinatra had another three Top Ten hits in 1950, including his version of "Goodnight Irene" (music and lyrics by Lead Belly), on which he was accompanied by the Mitch Miller Orch. Miller, Columbia's new recording executive, encouraged Sinatra to record more of the novelty material then popular, a move the singer resisted. Meanwhile, he branched out into television, launching the hour-long musical variety series *The Frank Sinatra Show* in October 1950. It ran two seasons, ending in April 1952. Also in October 1950 he began the weekly radio series *Meet Frank Sinatra*, on which he served as a disc jockey. It ran through July 1951.

Sinatra reunited with Harry James for his final Top Ten hit on Columbia, "Castle Rock" (music by Al Sears, lyrics by Ervin Drake and Jimmy Shirl), in September 1951. He married actress Ava Gardner on Nov. 7, 1951. They divorced on July 5, 1957. In December 1951, RKO belatedly released *Double Dynamite*, a film Sinatra had shot in 1948. In March 1952 he appeared in the Universal feature *Meet Danny Wilson*, but the year marked the nadir of his career: for the first time he failed to score a Top Ten hit; he parted ways with his record company; his television series ended; and he was without a radio show or a film contract. He then scored a dramatic comeback.

Signing to Capitol Records, Sinatra returned to the Top Ten with "I'm Walking Behind You" in June 1953. In August he appeared in a non-starring, non-singing, dramatic role in the film *From Here to Eternity*; it was one of the year's biggest box office hits, and he won the Academy Award for Best Supporting Actor. He returned to radio with two new series, the weekly *Rocky Fortune*, a drama in which he played a detective, running from October 1953 to March 1954, and another 15-minute, twice-weekly musical program, *The Frank Sinatra Show*, which ran from November 1953 to July 1955. In February 1954 his recording career was revitalized in earnest with the single "Young-at-Heart" (music by Johnny Richards, lyrics by Carolyn Leigh), which reached the Top Ten and sold a million copies, and the Top Ten LP *Songs for Young Lovers*, the first of his thematically selected concept albums, on which he revived the songs of such writers as Richard Rodgers and Lorenz Hart, George and Ira Gershwin, and Cole Porter in contemporary arrangements by Nelson Riddle. With Riddle, he scored another Top Ten single, the movie theme "Three Coins in the Fountain" (music by Jule Styne, lyrics by Sammy Cahn) in July, and another Top Ten LP in September with *Swing Easy!*, a more up-tempo collection.

His career back on track, Sinatra found success on records, on television, and in film in 1955. In January he starred in a movie named after his recent hit, *Young at Heart*. A single released in April, "Learnin' the Blues" (music and lyrics by Dolores Vicki Silvers), hit #1, and his album of ballads *In the Wee Small Hours*, released in May, also topped the charts. (It was inducted into the Grammy Hall of Fame in 1984.) In June he had a non-singing, co-starring role in *Not as a Stranger*, one of the top box office hits of the year. In September he appeared in a TV musical version of the Thornton Wilder play *On the Town*, singing "Love and Marriage" (music by James Van Heusen, lyrics by Sammy Cahn), which became a Top Ten hit. He earned an Emmy Award nomination for Best Male Singer. In November he appeared in the movie version of the Frank Loesser musical *Guys and Dolls*, which became the highest grossing film of 1956. In December his film *The Tender Trap* generated a Top Ten hit in the title song, "(Love Is) The Tender Trap" (music by Van Heusen, lyrics by Cahn). Also released in December was *The Man with the Golden Arm*, a dramatic film in which Sinatra played a recovering drug addict. It earned him an Academy Award nomination for Best Actor.

Continuing to alternate ballad and up-tempo albums, Sinatra released *Songs for Swingin' Lovers!* in March 1956; it reached the Top Ten and went gold. In August he co-starred with Bing Crosby in Cole Porter's musical version of the play *The Philadelphia Story*: *High Society*, one of the year's biggest box office hits. October saw the release of the single "Hey! Jealous Lover" (music and lyrics by Sammy Cahn, Kay Twomey, and Bee Walker), which became a Top Ten hit, and in November Capitol released the hits compilation *This Is Sinatra!*, which reached the Top Ten and went gold. Sinatra's next ballad album, *Close to You*, became a Top Ten hit upon release in February 1957. It was followed three months later by the up-tempo *A Swingin' Affair!*, a #1 hit, and in September by the ballad album *Where Are You?*, which reached the Top Ten.

Meanwhile, Sinatra co-starred in the dramatic film *The Pride and the Passion*, one of the year's box office hits, released in June. In September his appearance in *The Joker Is Wild* generated the Top Ten hit "All the Way" (music by James Van Heusen, lyrics by Sammy Cahn), and in October he starred in a movie version of the Rodgers and Hart musical *Pal Joey*, another box office hit accompanied by a Top Ten soundtrack album. That same month he launched another TV series, again called *The Frank Sinatra Show*, but it lasted only one season. Thereafter, he never attempted another series, though he made many television specials. He ended the year with the million-selling seasonal album *A Jolly Christmas from Frank Sinatra*.

"Witchcraft" (music by Cy Coleman, lyrics by Carolyn Leigh) became a Top Ten hit for Sinatra in February 1958. Released concurrently, *Come Fly with Me*, an up-tempo album of songs relating to travel, entered the charts, where it peaked at #1. Another hits collection, *This Is Sinatra, Vol. Two*, was released in April and made the Top Ten, and the ballad album *Frank Sinatra Sings for Only the Lonely*, released in September, topped the charts and went gold. His recordings earned Sinatra five nominations at the first Grammy Awards: Album of the Year for both *Come Fly with Me* and *Only the Lonely*, Record of the Year for "Witchcraft," and Best Vocal Performance, Male, for the songs "Come Fly with Me" (music by James Van Heusen, lyrics by Sammy Cahn) and "Witchcraft."

Sinatra's next up-tempo album, *Come Dance with Me!*, was released in January 1959. It reached the Top Ten and went gold, earning him Grammy Awards for Album of the Year and Best Vocal Performance, Male. He also reached the Top Ten during the year with the compilation album *Look to Your Heart* and the ballad album *No One Cares*. Though he had begun to sing less frequently in his movies, he performed "High Hopes" (music by James Van Heusen, lyrics by Sammy Cahn) in the July 1959 release *A Hole in the Head*. His single made the Top 40 and earned a Grammy nomination for Record of the Year.

Sinatra's first appearance in a full-fledged movie musical in two and a half years came in March 1960 with Cole Porter's *Can-Can*, which was one of the biggest box office hits of the year with a Top Ten soundtrack album. Sinatra's next regular album broke the formula of alternating ballad and up-tempo collections: *Nice 'n' Easy*, released in August, contained mid-tempo songs. It became a long-running #1 hit and went gold, and its title track (music by Lew Spence, lyrics by Marilyn and Alan Bergman) made the singles charts. The album earned Sinatra Grammy Award nominations for Album of the Year and Best Vocal Performance, Album, Male, and the single was nominated for Record of the Year, Best Vocal Performance, Single or Track, Male, and Best Performance by a Pop Single Artist.

As his contract with Capitol Records neared completion, Sinatra determined to found his own record company, and he did his first sessions for what became Reprise Records in December 1960 while still owing recordings to Capitol. The result was a series of overlapping releases: six newly released albums during 1961, all of which reached the Top Ten. On Capitol there was *Sinatra's Swingin' Session!!!* in January, the hits collection *All the Way* in March, and *Come Swing with Me!* in July; on Reprise, *Ring-a-Ding Ding!* in April, *Sinatra Swings* in July, and *I Remember Tommy*, an album of remakes of Tommy Dorsey hits, in October. The first single release on Reprise was "The Second Time Around," which reached the charts in February and won the Grammy Award for Record of the Year. Another five Sinatra albums appeared in 1962, but only one, *Sinatra and Strings* on Reprise, made the Top Ten.

Having finished his commitment to Capitol, Sinatra was able to focus on his Reprise releases, and he hit the Top Ten with all three of his 1963 albums: *Sinatra-Basie* backed by Count Basie and His Orch., in January; *The Concert Sinatra*, which, despite its title, was a studio-recorded album of show tunes arranged by Nelson Riddle, in June; and *Sinatra's Sinatra*, featuring new versions of some of Sinatra's more popular Capitol recordings, a gold album released in September. Sinatra sold Reprise to Warner Bros., which retained him as a recording artist.

Sinatra returned to the Top Ten of the LP charts with the March 1964 release *Days of Wine and Roses, Moon River, and Other Academy Award Winners*. His most music-filled film release in years was the comedy *Robin and the 7 Hoods*, released in August, in which he was accompanied by Dean Martin, Sammy Davis Jr., and Bing Crosby.

Sinatra had disdained the emergence of rock 'n' roll in the 1950s, but in the mid-1960s he adapted himself to the lighter aspects of contemporary music and launched a publicity campaign to mark his 50th birthday on Dec. 12, 1965, with surprisingly successful results. *Sinatra '65*, an album compiling stray tracks recorded between 1963 and 1965 and including four recent chart singles, hit the Top Ten in August 1965. That month Sinatra released *The September of My Years*, a ballad album containing reflections on aging. When its single, "It Was a Very Good Year" (music and lyrics by Ervin Drake) became a Top 40 hit, the LP vaulted into the Top Ten, earning a gold record and winning the Grammy Award for Album of the Year. "It Was a Very Good Year" won Sinatra a Grammy for Best Vocal Performance, Male.

Sinatra had meanwhile marked his birthday with a television special, *A Man and His Music*, in November

1965, and a similarly titled double album on which he described his career and re-recorded many of his songs. The TV show won an Emmy for Outstanding Musical Program; the album reached the Top Ten, went gold, and won the 1966 Grammy Award for Album of the Year. Meanwhile, he continued to make nonmusical films. He produced and directed the World War II drama *None but the Brave*, released in February 1965, and starred in another war story, *Von Ryan's Express*, released in June, which was among the top moneymakers of the year.

Sinatra's career renaissance continued in 1966 with the release of the single "Strangers in the Night" (music by Bert Kaempfert, lyrics by Charles Singleton and Eddie Snyder) in April; the song hit #1 and sold a million copies, as did the subsequent LP of the same title. "Strangers in the Night" won Grammy Awards for Record of the Year and Best Vocal Performance, Male. Sinatra married for a third time, to actress Mia Farrow, on July 19, 1966, but the marriage lasted only two years, ending in divorce on Aug. 16, 1968. *Sinatra at the Sands*, a live album made with Count Basie, was released in August and went gold. Sinatra changed pace with the bluesy, boasting single "That's Life" (music and lyrics by Dean Kay and Kelly Gordon), released in November. It hit the Top Ten, as did the gold-selling *That's Life* album that followed in December.

Sinatra's daughter Nancy had launched a successful singing career, and the two recorded a duet, "Somethin' Stupid" (music and lyrics by C. Carson Parks), released in March 1967. It hit #1, sold a million copies, and was nominated for a Grammy Award for Record of the Year. Also released in March was the album *Francis Albert Sinatra and Antonio Carlos Jobim*, a duet record of sambas. It earned Grammy nominations for Album of the Year and Best Vocal Performance, Male. The Brazilian singer/songwriter also joined Sinatra and Ella Fitzgerald on the television special *Frank Sinatra: A Man and His Music + Ella + Jobim*. Broadcast Nov. 13, 1967, it was nominated for an Emmy Award for Outstanding Musical or Variety Program. *Frank Sinatra's Greatest Hits!*, gathering together his recent singles successes, was released in August 1968 and sold a million copies. *Cycles*, on which Sinatra essayed songs written by such contemporary writers as Joni Mitchell and Jimmy Webb, appeared in December and earned a gold record.

In March 1969, Sinatra released "My Way" (music by Claude François and Jacques Revaux, English lyrics by Paul Anka), with a retrospective lyric written for him. Reaching the Top 40, it became his signature song, earning a Grammy nomination for Best Contemporary Vocal Performance, Male, and anchoring a Top Ten, gold-selling album of the same name. He sang it along with other songs on his Nov. 5, 1969, television special *Sinatra*, which was nominated for an Emmy for Outstanding Variety or Musical Program.

Notwithstanding his successes of the 1960s, Sinatra announced his retirement in the spring of 1971. But it lasted only until the fall of 1973, when he returned to action with an album and a television special both entitled *Ol' Blue Eyes Is Back*; the LP went gold. But while he made occasional albums, television specials,

and films, thereafter Sinatra devoted himself primarily to live performing, appearing in concert all over the world and especially in Las Vegas. On July 11, 1976, he married Barbara Jane Blakeley Marx, to whom he remained married for the rest of his life.

Sinatra's first new studio album in six years was *Trilogy: Past, Present, Future*, released in March 1980. An ambitious triple-LP, it found him re-recording old favorites, interpreting recent standards (among them "Theme from *N.Y., N.Y.*" [music by John Kander and Fred Ebb], which became a Top 40 single and another signature song), and undertaking a newly written song cycle by Gordon Jenkins. The set went gold and earned a Grammy nomination for Album of the Year, and "Theme from *N.Y., N.Y.*" was nominated for Grammys for Record of the Year and Best Pop Vocal Performance, Male.

Sinatra continued to give concerts throughout the 1980s and into the 1990s. His 75th birthday in 1990 was marked by the release of several multidisc retrospective albums, including the gold-selling *The Capitol Years* and *The Reprise Collection*, the latter also going gold in a single-disc version, *Sinatra Reprise—The Very Good Years*. Sinatra re-signed to Capitol Records in 1993 and released *Duets*, re-recording some of his best-known songs with such partners as Tony Bennett, Aretha Franklin, Barbra Streisand, and Bono of U2. The album was a multimillion-seller and was followed by a million-selling sequel, *Duets II*, in 1994, which featured Lena Horne, Willie Nelson, Neil Diamond, and Linda Ronstadt, among others. It won the 1995 Grammy Award for Traditional Pop Performance. Sinatra retired from performing in 1995. He died of a heart attack in 1998 at 82.

WRITINGS: *Tips on Popular Singing* (N.Y., 1941).

BIBL.: E. Kahn Jr., *The Voice: The Story of an American Phenomenon* (N.Y., 1947); J. Tarantino, *Sacred Sanctuary of F. S.* (Newark, 1959); J. Deacon, *The F. S. Discography* (Crawley, England, 1961); R. Douglas-Home, *S.* (N.Y., 1962); R. Gehman, *S. and His Rat Pack* (N.Y., 1963); A. Shaw, *S.: Twentieth Century Romantic* (N.Y., 1968); A. Shaw, *S.: Retreat of the Romantic* (London, 1968); R. McKuen, *F. S.: A Man Alone* (Hollywood, 1969); A. Lonstein and V. Marino, *The Compleat S. Discography, Filmography, Television Appearances, Motion Picture Appearances, Radio, Concert Stage Appearances* (Ellenville, N.Y., 1970; 2nd ed., rev. and enl. as *The Revised Compleat S.*, 1979; 3rd ed., 1981); K. Barnes, ed., *S. and the Great Song Stylists* (Sheperton, U.K., 1972); P. Goddard, *F. S.: The Man, the Myth and the Music* (Don Mills, Canada, 1973); B. Hainsworth, *Songs by S.* (Branhope, England, 1973); J. Harvey, *Monsieur S.* (Paris, 1976); H. Lake, *On Stage: F. S.* (Mankato, Minn., 1976); J. Romero, *S.'s Women* (N.Y., 1976); T. Sciacca, *S.* (N.Y., 1976); P. Taylor, *F. S.* (Mankato, Minn., 1976); E. Wilson, *S.: An Unauthorized Biography* (N.Y., 1976); J. Ridgeway, *The Sinatra File* (Birmingham, England, vol. one, 1977; vol. two, 1978; vol. three, 1980); A. Scaduto, *F. S.* (London, 1976); A. Frank, *S.* (N.Y., 1978); J. Howlett, *F. S.* (N.Y., 1979); G. Ringgold and C. McCarty, *The Films of F. S.* (N.Y., 1979; rev. ed., 1989); E. O'Brien and S. Sayers Jr., *The S. Sessions, 1939–80* (Dallas, 1980); P. Ruggeri, *F. S.* (Rome, 1981); N. Goldstein, *F. S.: Ol' Blue Eyes* (N.Y., 1982); R. Peters, *The F. S. Scrapbook* (N.Y., 1982); A. Shaw, *S.: The Entertainer* (N.Y., 1982); A. Lonstein, *S.: An Exhaustive Treatise* (N.Y., 1983); J. Turner, *F. S.: A Personal Portrait* (N.Y., 1983); C. Dureau and L. Christophe, *F. S.* (Paris, 1984); J.

Rockwell, *S.: An American Classic* (N.Y., 1984); D. Jewell, *F. S.: A Celebration* (Boston, 1985); N. Sinatra, *F. S.: My Father* (Garden City, N.Y., 1985); K. Kelley, *His Way: The Unauthorized Biography of F. S.* (N.Y., 1986); B. Adler, *S., the Man and the Myth: An Unauthorized Biography* (N.Y., 1987); S. Britt, *Sinatra the Singer* (London, 1989); C. Garrod, *F. S.* (Zephyrhills, Fla., 1989–90); G. Doctor, *The S. Scrapbook* (N.Y., 1991); G. DeStephano, *F. S.* (Venice, Italy, 1991); R. Ackelson, *F. S.: A Complete Recording History* (Jefferson, N. C., 1992); E. O'Brien and S. Sayers Jr., *S.: The Man and His Music* (Austin, Tex., 1992); V. Marino and A. Furfero, *The Official Price Guide to F. S. Records and CDs* (N.Y., 1993); J. Hodge, *F. S.* (North Dighton, Mass., 1994); R. Pickard, *F. S. at the Movies* (London, 1994); S. Britt, *S.: A Celebration* (N.Y., 1995); R. Coleman, *S.: A Portrait of the Artist* (Washington, D.C., 1995); F. Dellar, *S.: His Life and Times* (London, 1995); W. Friedwald, *S.! The Song Is You: A Singer's Art* (N.Y., 1995); D. Holder, *Completely F.: The Life of F. S.* (London, 1995); L. Irwin, *S.: The Pictorial Biography* (N.Y., 1995); C. Phasey, *Francis Albert S. Tracked Down* (London, 1995); N. Sinatra, *F. S.: An American Legend* (Santa Monica, Calif., 1995); S. Petkov and L. Mustazza, eds., *The F. S. Reader* (N.Y., 1995); E. Vare, ed., *Legend: F. S. and the American Dream* (N.Y., 1995); E. O'Brien, R. Wilson, and S. Mark, *S. 101: The 101 Best Recordings and the Stories behind Them* (N.Y., 1996); D. Clarke, *All or Nothing at All: A Life of F. S.* (N.Y., 1997); E. Hawes, *The Life and Times of F. S.* (Philadelphia, 1997); J. Taraborrelli, *S.: Behind the Legend* (N.Y. 1997); B. Zehme, *The Way You Wear Your Hat: F. S. and the Lost Art of Livin'* (N.Y., 1997); J. Collins, *The Complete Guide to the Music of F. S.* (London, 1998); M. Freedland, *All the Way: A Biography of F. S.* (N.Y., 1998); P. Hamill, *Why S. Matters* (Boston, 1998); D. Hanna, *S.: Ol' Blue Eyes Remembered* (N.Y., 1998); J. Lahr, *S.: The Artist and the Man* (N.Y., 1998); L. Irwin, *S.: A Man Remembered* (Philadelphia, 1998); S. Levy, *Rat Pack Confidential: F., Dean, Sammy, Peter, Joey and the Last Great Showbiz Party* (N.Y., 1998); L. Mustazza, *Ol' Blue Eyes: A F. S. Encyclopedia* (Westport, Conn., 1998); L. Quirk and W. Schoell, *The Rat Pack: The Hey-Hey Days of F. and the Boys* (Dallas, 1998).—**WR**

Sinatra, Nancy, 1960s-era pop icon, daughter of famed crooner **Frank Sinatra;** b. Jersey City, N.J., June 8, 1940. Being the daughter of Frank Sinatra gave Nancy Sinatra a leg up on the entertainment biz. As a four-year-old, she inspired Phil Silvers and Jimmy Van Heusen to write "Nancy (with the Laughing Face)," a Top Ten hit for her dad in 1945. By 19, she was sharing the small screen with dad and Elvis Presley in a group called the Tri-Tones. She married teen sensation Tommy Shaw shortly after and curtailed her own career for a while. In the early 1960s, Nancy made several records for her father's company, Reprise. "Cuff Links & a Tie Clip" cast her as an Annette Funicello wannabe, to the extent of using Funicello's producer Tutti Camarara. She scored a small success with "Like I Do," which charted well in places like Italy and Japan.

By 23, however, Nancy had turned her attention to acting in teen movies, starting with *For Those Who Think Young.* This led to other forgettable films and some TV performances. Her career started to eclipse her husband's, and as she filmed *Marriage on the Rocks,* her own union ended.

Not giving up on recording, Nancy started to explore a different direction, working with country music legend Jimmy Bowen. Although this didn't yield the success she sought, she started to make other changes, segueing from Disney-esque good girl to miniskirted siren. Her transformation was completed when she hooked up with Duane Eddy's songwriting mainstay, Lee Hazelwood. Hazelwood created a sound that perfectly complemented her new bad-girl image. Their first collaboration, "These Boots Were Made for Walking," with its walking bass and swingy beat, zoomed to #1 in the winter of 1966, going gold. She followed this a couple of months later with the #7 "How Does that Grab You, Darlin'?" During that summer, "Friday's Child" went to #36. The *Boots* album also went gold.

By the end of 1966, with another project in the works, Nancy rose to gold with the adult contemporary chart topper (#5 pop) gold record "Sugar Town." The *Sugar* album was banned in Boston for the cover, which featured Sinatra in a very revealing (for the time) bikini. Despite the pop hit, the album only rose to #18.

By 1967, with his daughter's meteoric pop success during the previous year, Frank Sinatra began introducing himself as "Nancy Sinatra's father" during shows. They got together for the duet "Something Stupid." A song more in tune with her dad's oeuvre than her own, it rose to the top to both the pop charts for four weeks and the adult contemporary charts for nine during the spring of that year, going gold. She followed this a month or so later with the #15 "Love Eyes." Teaming with Hazelwood, she recorded the #14 version of the Johnny Cash and June Carter hit "Jackson." Her theme from the James Bond film *You Only Live Twice,* another string-laden ballad with the odd touch of an acid-tinged guitar, didn't quite make the Top 40 (stalling at #44), but she rode "Lightning's Girl" to #24 toward the end of 1967.

Nancy recorded a TV special that co-starred her dad, Dean Martin, and Hazelwood. The album version of the show, *Movin' with Nancy,* hit #37. She started dating the show's choreographer, Hugh Lambert. In 1968 she recorded a duet album with Hazelwood, which produced the #20 single "Lady Bird" and the #26 single "Some Velvet Morning." That album, *Nancy and Lee,* went gold, rising to #13. She continued to act, appearing with Elvis in *Speedway,* among others.

By 1970, Sinatra and Lambert had married and she once again dropped out of show business to become a wife and mother, recording sporadically and with little success. In 1985 her public profile rose once more upon the publication of her book about her father, an antidote to an especially nasty volume by Kitty Kelly. In 1995, with her daughters grown, Sinatra started recording and concertizing again, starting where she left off in 1968 with a country rock record *One More Time.* She announced her comeback with a six-page photo spread in *Playboy* magazine. She toured with a rock band, joined every now and then by Hazelwood. In 1998 she cut a collection of old, rare songs *Sheet Music.* In early 1999 she played a show celebrating the 25th anniversary of the Los Angeles club, the Whiskey a Go Go.

Disc.: *Boots* (1966); *How Does That Grab You?* (1966); *Nancy in London* (1966); *Sugar* (1967); *Country, My Way* (1967); *Movin' with Nancy* (1968); *Nancy & Lee* (1968); *Nancy* (1969); *Woman* (1970); *This Is Nancy Sinatra* (1971); *Sheet Music: Collection of Her Favorite Love...* (1998).—**HB**

Sinclair, Monica, English mezzo-soprano; b. Evercreech, Somerset, March 23, 1925. She studied voice with Marcus Thomson and piano with Harold Craxton at the Royal Academy of Music (1942–44), and voice with Arnold Smith, piano with Olive Bloom, and accompaniment with Charles Lofthouse at the Royal Coll. of Music (1944–48) in London. In 1948 she made her operatic debut as Suzuki with the Carl Rosa Opera Co., a role she also chose for her debut at London's Covent Garden in 1949, where she sang until 1967. In 1954 she appeared as Ragonde in *Le Comte Ory* with the Glyndebourne company during its visit to the Edinburgh Festival, and she continued to make appearances with the Glyndebourne company until 1960. She also made frequent appearances with the Handel Opera Soc. On March 14, 1972, she made her Metropolitan Opera debut in N.Y. as Berkenfield in *La Fille du régiment*. She was best known for her roles in operas by Lully, Mozart, Rossini, and Strauss.—**NS/LK/DM**

Sinding, Christian (August), celebrated Norwegian composer; b. Kongsberg, Jan. 11, 1856; d. Oslo, Dec. 3, 1941. He studied first with L. Lindeman in Norway, then at the Leipzig Cons. (1874–78) with Schradieck (violin), Jadassohn (theory), and Reinecke (orchestration); a government stipend enabled him to continue his studies in Germany, and he spent 2 years (1882–84) in Munich, Berlin, and Dresden; there he wrote his first opera, *Titandros*, much influenced by Wagner. On Dec. 19, 1885, he gave a concert of his works in Oslo; during another stay in Germany, his Piano Quintet was played in Leipzig, with Brodsky and Busoni among the performers (Jan. 19, 1889); Erika Lie-Nissen played his Piano Concerto in Berlin (Feb. 23, 1889). He publ. a number of piano pieces in Germany; of these, *Frühlingsrauschen* became an international favorite. His opera to a German text, *Der heilige Berg* (1914), was not successful. In 1915 he received a life pension of 4,000 crowns "for distinguished service"; on his 60th birthday (1916), the Norwegian government presented him with a purse of 30,000 crowns, a mark of appreciation for "the greatest national composer since Grieg." He was invited by George Eastman to teach at the Eastman School of Music in Rochester, N.Y., during the academic season 1921–22; after this journey, he lived mostly in Oslo. He continued to compose, and toward the end of his life wrote in larger forms; his third Sym. was conducted by Nikisch with the Berlin Phil. in 1921, and his fourth Sym. was performed on his 80th birthday in Oslo (1936). His works aggregate to 132 opus numbers. Most of his music is of a descriptive nature; his lyric pieces for piano and his songs are fine examples of Scandinavian Romanticism, but the German inspiration of his formative years is much in evidence; he was chiefly influenced by Schumann and Liszt. A complete list of Sinding's works was publ. by Ö. Gaukstad in *Norsk Musikkgranskning arbok* (Oslo, 1938).

Works: DRAMATIC: O p e r a : *Titandros* (1884; not perf.); *Der heilige Berg* (1912; Dessau, April 19, 1914). **ORCH.:** 4 syms.: No. 1 (1880–82; Christiania, March 25, 1882), No. 2 (1903–04; Berlin, March 22, 1907), No. 3 (1920; Berlin, Jan. 10, 1921), and No. 4, *Vinter og vår* (1921–36; Oslo, Jan. 11, 1936); *Episodes chevaleresques* (1888); *Rondo infinito* (1886; rev. 1897); Piano Concerto (Berlin, Feb. 23, 1889); 3 violin concertos (1898, 1901, 1917); *Legende* for Violin and Orch. (1900); *Romanze* for Violin and Orch. (1910); *Abendstimmung* for Violin and Orch. (1915). **CHAMBER:** Piano Quintet (1882–84); 2 string quartets (1884, 1904); 3 piano trios (1893, 1902, 1908); 4 violin sonatas (1894, 1895, 1905, 1909); *Scènes de la vie* for Violin and Piano (1900); *Cantus doloris*, variations for Violin and Piano (1906); *Nordische Ballade* for Cello and Piano (1911); etc. **P i a n o :** Sonata (1909); *Fatum*, variations (1909); 5 *Stücke*, op.24 (1894); 7 *Stücke*, op.25 (1895); 6 *Stücke*, op.31 (1896); 6 *Stücke*, op.32 (1896; No. 3 is the celebrated *Frühlingsrauschen*); 6 *Charakterstücke*, op.33 (1896; contains *A la Menuetto* and *Standchen*); 6 *Charakterstücke*, op.34 (1896; contains *Chanson*); 6 *Klavierstücke* (1899; contains *Humoresque*); *Mélodies mignonnes* (1900); 4 *morceaux de salon* (1900; contains *Sérénade*); etc. **VOCAL:** About 250 songs, including *Alte Weisen* (1886), *Lieder und Gesange* (1888; contains *Viel Träume* and *Ein Weib*), *Galmandssange* (1893; contains *Mainat*), and *Nyinger* (1908); several cantatas and other choral works.—**NS/LK/DM**

Singer, George, Czech-born Israeli conductor and composer; b. Prague, Aug. 6, 1908; d. Tel Aviv, Sept. 30, 1980. He studied piano at the Prague Academy of Music with Schulhoff and composition with Zemlinsky. He made his first appearance as an opera conductor in Prague in 1926. In 1930 he received an engagement at the Hamburg Opera, returning to Prague in 1934. When the Nazis invaded Czechoslovakia in 1939, he, being Jewish, was compelled to take refuge in Tel Aviv, where he established himself favorably as a conductor. He also accepted engagements as a conductor in Russia and in the U.S., where he led the N.Y.C. Opera in 1968. Back in Israel, he gave performances of several works of local composers. He was known for his phenomenal facility in sight- reading, performing works perfectly at first reading on the piano and conducting every nuance of an orch. score. He composed some orch pieces.—**NS/LK/DM**

Singer, Hal (actually, **Harold**; aka **Cornbread**), jazz tenor saxophonist, leader; b. Tulsa, Okla., Oct. 8, 1919. His father was a guitarist, and Hal took up violin at age eight; he later played saxophone and clarinet in his high school band. He went to Hampton Inst., Va., in 1937 (where he later obtained degree in agriculture), but also did summer vacation gigs in Oklahoma City with trumpeter James Simpson and in a band led by Charlie Christian's brother Edward. Singer became a professional musician in summer 1938, working first with Ernie Fields's Band; during the following year, he worked with Lloyd Hunter's Serenaders and with Nat Towles. In late 1939 Singer joined the Tommy Douglas Band; in 1941 he became a member of Jay McShann's Band, but left to settle in N.Y. in 1942. He did extensive gigging, then worked with many leaders, including Hot Lips Page (1943), Jay McShann, Roy Eldridge Big Band (1944), Earl Bostic, Don Byas (1945), Henry 'Red' Allen Sextet (summer 1946), Sid Catlett

(1947), Lucky Millinder (early 1948), and six months with Duke Ellington (1948). Through the success of his own best-selling single "Cornbread," he formed his own touring band 1949–58. From 1958–65, he led his own bands in N.Y. clubs, and then moved to Paris. He worked regularly in Europe through the early 1980s, including tours and club work.

DISC.: *Rent Party* (1948); *Blue Stompin'* (1959); *Royal Blue* (1990).—**JC/LP**

Singer, Peter (Alkantara) (actually, Josef Anton),

Austrian organist, music theorist, teacher, instrument maker, and composer; b. Unterhaselgehr, North Tirol, July 18, 1810; d. Salzburg, Jan. 25, 1882. He became a Franciscan monk in 1830, and was made a priest in 1837. He served as organist and choirmaster in Bolzano and Innsbruck (1837–40), and then at the Salzburg Franciscan convent. He wrote over 100 masses, some 40 motets, 15 litanies, numerous Marian hymns, many offertories, etc. In 1839 he invented the "Pansymphonikon," a kind of orchestrion with reeds. He publ. *Metaphysische Blicke in die Tonwelt, nebst einem neuen System der Tonwissenschaft* (Munich, 1847).

BIBL.: Pater Hartmann, *P. S.* (Innsbruck, 1910); V. Keldorfer, *Der Spielmann des Herrn Pater P. S.* (Salzburg, 1952). —**NS/LK/DM**

Singher, Martial (Jean-Paul),

noted French baritone and pedagogue; b. Oloron-Ste. Marie, Aug. 14, 1904; d. Santa Barbara, Calif., March 10, 1990. He received his education as a public-school teacher in Dax, and at the École Normale de Toulouse and the École Normale Supérieure de St. Cloud. He then studied voice with André Gresse at the Paris Cons. (premier prix for singing, 1929; premier prix for opera and opéra-comique singing, 1930; Grand Prix Osiris de l'Institute de France, 1930); also studied voice with Juliette Fourestier. He made his operatic debut in Amsterdam as Orestes in *Iphigénie en Tauride* on Nov. 14, 1930; then joined the Paris Opéra, remaining with it until 1941; also sang at the Opéra-Comique. On Jan. 10, 1940, he married Margareta Busch, daughter of the conductor Fritz Busch. He went to the U.S. in 1941; made his Metropolitan Opera debut in N.Y. on Dec. 10, 1943, as Dapertutto in *Les Contes d'Hoffmann*; subsequently sang the roles of the Count in *Le nozze di Figaro*, Lescaut in *Manon*, and all 4 baritone roles in *Les Contes d'Hoffmann*; remained on the roster, with some interruptions, until 1959. He also sang with the leading orchs. of the U.S., and appeared widely in song recitals. He was on the faculty of the Mannes Coll. of Music in N.Y. (1951–62) and the Curtis Inst. of Music in Philadelphia (1955–68); then was director of the voice and opera dept., and was the opera producer at the Music Academy of the West in Santa Barbara (1962–81). His students included Donald Gramm, John Reardon, James King, Louis Quilico, Judith Blegen, Benita Valente, and Jeannine Altmeyer. He was a particularly distinguished interpreter of the French operatic and song repertoire. He wrote a book useful to vocalists aspiring to an operatic career, *An Interpretive Guide to Operatic Arias: A Handbook for Singers, Coaches, Teachers, and Students* (1983).—**NS/LK/DM**

Singleton, Alvin (Elliot),

black American composer; b. N.Y., Dec. 28, 1940. He took courses in composition and music education at N.Y.U. (B.M., 1967), then continued his study of composition with Powell and Wyner at Yale Univ. (M.M.A., 1971). He received a Fulbright fellowship to study with Petrassi in Rome at the Accademia di Santa Cecilia (1971–72), and in 1981 was awarded an NEA grant. From 1985 to 1988 he served as composer-in-residence of the Atlanta Sym. Orch.; in 1988 he was appointed composer-in-residence at Spelman Coll. in Atlanta.

WORKS: DRAMATIC: O p e r a : *Dream Sequence '76* (1976). **ORCH.:** *Kwitana* for Piano, Double Bass, Percussion, and Chamber Ensemble (1974); *Again* for Chamber Orch. (1979); *A Yellow Rose Petal* (1982); *Shadows* (1987); *After Fallen Crumbs* (1988); *Sinfonia Diaspora* (Portland, Ore., May 5, 1991); *Even Tomorrow* (Birmingham, Ala., Oct. 11, 1991); *56 Blows (Quis Custodiet Custodies?)*, based on the Rodney King beating by the Los Angeles police (1992; Philadelphia, Jan. 13, 1994); *Blueskonzert* for Piano and Orch. (Houston, Sept. 30, 1995). **CHAMBER:** Woodwind Quintet (1969); *Argoru I* for Piano (1970), *II* for Cello (1970), *III* for Flute (1971), *IV* for Viola (1978), *V* for Bass Clarinet (1984), and *VI* for Marimba (1989). **VOCAL:** *Messa* for Soprano, Chorus, Flute, 2 Guitars, Electric Organ, Cello, and Double Bass (1975); *Necessity Is a Mother*, wordless drama (1981); *Between Sisters* for Soprano, Piano, Alto Flute, and Vibraphone (1990).—**NS/LK/DM**

Singleton, Zutty (actually, Arthur James),

early jazz drummer; b. Bunkie, La., May 14, 1898; d. N.Y., July 14, 1975. Singleton was raised in New Orleans; his uncle was Willie "Bontin" Bontemps (bass, guitar, banjo). He worked with local bands in the mid-teens, and then served in the U.S. Navy during World War I. After his discharge, he returned to New Orleans, gigging with various bands, as well as leading his own groups. He worked on Miss. riverboats with Fate Marable from late 1921–23, then returned to New Orleans. He did some pit band work, and then moved to St. Louis to join Charlie Creath for a year (for over 40 years, Singleton was married to Creath's piano-playing sister, Marge). He briefly returned to New Orleans, then moved to Chicago, working with several bands, including several stints in 1927 with Dave Peyton and Jimmie Noone. That fall, he joined Clarence Jones's Band at the Metropolitan Theatre, where he first worked with Louis Armstrong. He contnued to work with Armstrong in various settings, including Carroll Dickerson's Band in later 1928; Singleton played on many of Armstrong's Savoy Ballroom small band recordings. He moved to N.Y. with Dickerson and Louis Armstrong in spring 1929. During the early 1930s, Singleton worked for several other leaders, including Fats Waller, Bubber Miley, and Otto Hardwick. He also accompanied several dance acts, including the Berry Brothers and Bill Robinson, and toured accompanying Norman and Irene Selby (c. 1933). The latter show ended its run in Chicago, where Singleton settled for several years, rejoining Carroll Dickerson in 1934 as well as leading his own small groups. From September 1936–mid-1937, he worked with Roy Eldridge. He then moved back to N.Y. Until 1943, he played at various N.Y. Dixieland-revival clubs, including a stint with Sidney Bechet (winter–November 1938). Singleton then moved to Los Angeles, where he led his own quartet from April 1943; he did film and radio work, and continued to freelance with other leaders through the end of the 1940s. In 1950, he was back in Chicago working with Art Hodes, then with Bobby Hackett (spring 1951) before joining Bernie Billings in Los Angeles (August 1951). He sailed to Europe in November 1951, where he played with various groups through February 1953. He settled in N.Y., working the clubs throughout the 1950s, briefly with Wilbur de Paris (late 1954). In late 1963, together with Tony Parenti, Singleton began a long residency at Ryan's. He left temporarily early in 1969, but soon returned to the same venue (with Max Kaminsky). He briefly returned to New Orleans in June 1969 to play at the Jazz Fest. Singleton was forced to retire from full-time music after suffering a stroke in 1970. His appearances in films include *Stormy Weather* (1943), *New Orleans* (1946), and *Turned-up Toes* (1949).

DISC.: *Battle of Jazz, Vol. 2* (1953); *Zutty and the Clarinet Kings* (1967).—JC/LP

Sinico, Francesco, Italian organist, choirmaster, teacher, and composer; b. Trieste, Dec. 12, 1810; d. there, Aug. 18, 1865. He studied with G. Farinelli. He was an organist and conductor in various churches, and in 1843 he established his own singing school in Trieste, providing excellent training for choral singing. He produced his opera *I Virtuosi di Barcellona* in 1841. His son, Giuseppe Sinico (b. Trieste, Feb. 10, 1836; d. there, Dec. 31, 1907), continued the popular singing classes at the Sinico School in Trieste. He wrote several operas, which he produced there: *Marinella* (Aug. 26, 1854), *I Moschettieri* (March 26, 1859), *Aurora di Nevers* (March 12, 1861), *Alessandro Stradella* (Lugo, Sept. 19, 1863), and *Spartaco* (Nov. 20, 1886). He publ. *Breve metodo teoricopratico di canto elementare.*—NS/LK/DM

Sinigaglia, Leone, Italian composer; b. Turin, Aug. 14, 1868; d. there, May 16, 1944. He was a pupil at the Turin Cons., studying with Giovanni Bolzoni, and later studied in Vienna (1894–1900) with Mandyczewski, and in Prague with Vysoka and Dvořák (1900–01). His first successful work was a violin concerto (1900) dedicated to Arrigo Serato, who played it with considerable success in the principal cities of Germany. His early works were much influenced by Brahms and Dvořák; then he turned for inspiration to the music of his native Piedmont, and in this field achieved a lasting reputation. Toscanini conducted in Turin the premiere of Sinigaglia's suite *Danze piemontesi*, on popular themes (May 14, 1905). Later Sinigaglia publ. a collection of songs (6 albums), *Vecchie canzoni populari del Piemonte*; another work in the folk-song manner is the symphonic suite *Piemonte* (1909; Utrecht, Feb. 16, 1910). He further wrote *Le Baruffe Chiozzotte*, an overture to Goldoni's comedy (Utrecht, Dec. 21, 1907), *Rapsodia piemontese* for Violin and Orch. (1900), *Romanze* for Violin and Orch. (1899), *Variations on a Theme of Brahms* for String Quartet (1901), *Serenade* for String Trio (1906), and Cello Sonata (1923).

BIBL.: C. Mosso and E. Bassi, eds., *L. S., Torino, 1868–1944: Primo centenario della nascita* (Turin, 1968).—NS/LK/DM

Sinopoli, Giuseppe, distinguished Italian conductor and composer; b. Venice, Nov. 2, 1946. He studied organ and harmony as a youth in Messina, then took courses in harmony and counterpoint at the Venice Cons.; also studied medicine at the Univ. of Padua (degree in psychiatry, 1971) while concurrently studying composition privately with Donatoni in Paris; then took a course in conducting with Swarowsky at the Vienna Academy of Music. He organized the Bruno Maderna Ensemble in 1975, and conducted it in performances of contemporary music; was also active as a teacher. After a successful engagement as a guest conductor at the Teatro La Fenice in Venice in 1976, he appeared at the Deutsche Oper in Berlin (1980), the Hamburg State Opera (1980), and the Vienna State Opera (1982). On May 3, 1983, he made his Covent Garden debut in London, conducting *Manon Lescaut*; his Metropolitan Opera debut followed in N.Y. on March 11, 1985, when he led a performance of *Tosca*. He served as chief conductor of the Orchestra dell'Accademia Nazionale di Santa Cecilia in Rome (1983–87). He also was principal conductor of the Philharmonia Orch. of London (1984–94). In 1990 he became Generalmusikdirektor of the Deutsche Oper in Berlin, but abruptly resigned that same year after disagreements with its Intendant, Götz Friedrich. In 1992 he became chief conductor of the Dresden State Orch. and Opera. His training as a psychiatrist led him to probe deeply into the scores he conducted, often resulting in startlingly revealing but controversial interpretations. As a composer, he pursues contemporary modes of expression. Among his works is the opera *Lou Salome* (Munich, May 10, 1981; also 2 suites: No. 1 for Soloists, Chorus, and Orch., 1981, and No. 2 for Orch., 1985).—NS/LK/DM

Siohan, Robert (-Lucien), French conductor, composer, and writer on music; b. Paris, Feb. 27, 1894; d. there, July 16, 1985. He studied at the Paris Cons. (1909–22). In 1929 he founded the Concerts Siohan, which he conducted until 1936; was chorus master at the Paris Opéra (1931–46), and from 1948 to 1962 an instructor in solfège and sight-reading at the Paris Cons.; subsequently served as inspector-general of music in the Ministry of Culture. He received his doctorate at the Sorbonne in Paris in 1954 with the diss. *Théories nouvelles de l'homme* (publ. as *Horizons sonores*, Paris, 1956). Among his compositions are the opera *Le saut dans les etoiles* (1926–27), *Cantique au frère soleil* for Soloists, Chorus, and Orch. (1926), Violin Concerto (1928), Piano Concerto (1939), String Quartet (1922), and *Gravitations* for Viola and Piano (1952). He publ. *Stravinsky* (Paris, 1959; Eng. tr., London, 1966) and *Histoire du public musical* (Lausanne, 1967), as well as numerous articles in French and German publs.—NS/LK/DM

Sipilä, Eero (Aukusti), Finnish composer and teacher; b. Hailuoto, July 27, 1918; d. Kajaani, May 18, 1972. He studied in Helsinki at the Church Music Inst. (graduated, 1943) and the Sibelius Academy (organ diploma, 1945), then taught at the Kajaani training college (1945–72).

WORKS: String Trio (1952); *Partita* for Wind Quartet (1955); *Super flumina Babylonis* and *Miserere*, 2 motets for Chorus (1963);

Te Deum Laudamus for Alto, Baritone, Chorus, and Orch. (1969); *Fugue and Chaconne* for Strings (1969); *Lux aeterna* for String Quartet (1972); *Composition* for Orch. (Kajaani, May 8, 1973); song cycles; organ music.—NS/LK/DM

Siret, Nicholas, French organist and composer; b. Troyes, March 16, 1663; d. there, June 22, 1754. He was born into a musical family. After studies with François Couperin, he succeeded his father as organist at Troyes Cathedral in 1689, a position he held for his entire life. He also served as organist at the churches of St. Jean and St. Madeleine. Siret publ. 2 esteemed vols. of harpsichord music (Paris, c. 1710, 1719).—LK/DM

Sirmen, Maddalena Laura (née **Lombardini**), Italian violinist, singer, and composer; b. Venice, 1735; d. after 1785. She studied at the Cons. dei Mendicanti in Venice and received violin lessons from Tartini in Padua. In 1760 she married Ludovico Sirmen, a violinist, maestro di cappella, and composer at S. Maria Maggiore in Bergamo. After touring with him (1760–68), they scored a notable success at the Concert Spirituel in Paris in 1768. In 1771–72 she appeared in London to great acclaim, but then inexplicably launched a career as a singer of no particular distinction. In 1782 she was the principal singer at the Dresden court. In 1785 she made her last public appearance, as a violinist, at the Concert Spirituel.

WORKS: 6 quartetti, op.3 (Paris, 1769; second ed., London, c. 1775; in collaboration with L. Sirmen); 6 Trios for 2 Violins and Cello Obbligato, op.1 (London, c. 1770); 6 sonates for 2 Violins, op.2 (Paris, c. 1770; as op.4, London, 1773); 6 violin concertos, op.3 (London and Paris, c. 1770; as opp. 2 and 3, Amsterdam, c. 1772); 6 duetti for 2 Violins, op.5 (Paris, 1775). —NS/LK/DM

Širola, Božidar, distinguished Croatian musicologist and composer; b. Žakanj, Dec. 20, 1889; d. Zagreb, April 10, 1956. He studied mathematics and physics at the Univ. of Zagreb. After training in composition from Ivan Zajc, he studied musicology with Robert Lach at the Univ. of Vienna (Ph.D., 1921, with the diss. *Das istrische Volkslied*). He taught mathematics and physics in Zagreb secondary schools, and also was active as a lecturer, critic, ethnomusicologist, and organologist. From 1935 to 1941 he was director of the secondary school of music at the Zagreb Academy of Music, and then was director of the Ethnographic Museum. After Tito consolidated his control of Yugoslavia in 1945, Širola devoted himself to private research. He was a noted authority on Croatian folk music. As a composer, he became best known for his operas and songs.

WRITINGS (all publ. in Zagreb): *Pregled povijesti hrvatske muzike* (Survey of the History of Croatian Music; 1922); with M. Gavazzi, *Muzikološki rad Etnografskog muzeja u Zagrebu* (Musicological Works of the Ethnographic Museum in Zagreb; 1931); *Fućkalice: Sviraljke od kore svježeg drveta* (Fućkalice: Wind Instruments Made From the Bark of Green Wood; 1932); *Sopile i zurle* (Sopilas and Zurlas; 1932); *Sviraljke s udarnim jezičkom* (Wind Instruments with a Beating Reed; 1937); *Hrvatska narodna glazba* (Croatian Folk Music; 1940; second ed., 1942); *Hrvatska umjetnička glasba: Odabrana poglavlja iz povijesti hrvatske glazbe* (Croat-

ian Art Music: Selected Chapters of a History of Croatian Music; 1942).

WORKS: DRAMATIC: O p e r a : *Stanac* (1915); *Citara i bubanj* (The Cittern and the Drum; 1929); *Grabancijaš* (The Student of the Black Arts; 1935); *Mladi gospodin* (The Young Gentleman; 1940); *Kameni svatovi* (The Stone Wedding Guests; 1954). M e l o d r a m a s : *Iz Danteova "Ruja"* (From Dante's "Paradiso"; 1912); *Putnik* (The Traveller; 1919); *Otmica* (The Abduction; 1922); *Šuma Striborova* (1923); *Kameni svatovi* (1935). O p e r e t t a : *Z Griča na Trešnjevku* (1931); *Mecena* (1934). O t h e r : Ballets and incidental music. ORCH.: *Novela od Stanac* (The Story of Stanac), overture (1912); *Symphonic Scherzo* (1912); *Svečana uvertira* (Festival Overture; 1920); *Concerto da camera* for 2 Flutes and Chamber Orch. (1927); *Koncertna uvertira* (1927); *Romanca* for Violin and Strings (1939); *Scherzo i ricercar* for Violin and Strings (1939); *Sinfonietta* for Strings (1939); Sym. (1945); *Sinfonia concertante* for Piano and Orch. (1952); Violin Concerto (1953). CHAMBER: 13 string quartets (*Medimurski*, 1920; *Bodulski*, 1933; 1946; 1946; 1951; 1951; 1951; 1952; *Nizozemski*, 1953; 1955; 1955; 1955; 1955); 3 piano trios (1934, 1937, 1939); Suite for Violin and Harpsichord or Piano (1940); Cello Sonata (1952); 2 violin sonatas (1952, 1955); Rondo for Trumpet and Piano (1954); piano pieces. VOCAL: 6 oratorios (1924, 1926, 1928, 1928, 1929, 1931); choruses; song cycles.—NS/LK/DM

Sirota, Robert, American composer, music educator, and conductor; b. N.Y., Oct. 13, 1949. He was a student in composition of Richard Hoffmann and Joseph Wood, and in piano of Elizabeth Lasley, at the Oberlin (Ohio) Coll. Cons. of Music (B.M., 1971). He also studied composition in Paris with Nadia Boulanger (1969; 1971–72). His composition training was completed with Leon Kirchner and Earl Kim at Harvard Univ. (M.A., 1975; Ph.D., 1979). He was an instructor (1976–79), asst. prof. of music theory and composition (1980–85), acting director (1985), and director (1986–91) of the Boston Univ. School of Music. In 1991–92 he was a lecturer at the Mass. Inst. of Technology, and from 1991 to 1995 he was conductor and mentor for the Choreographer Composer Collaborations Program. From 1992 to 1995 he was chair of the dept. of music and performing arts professions at N.Y.U., where he was an assoc. prof. of music. In 1995 Sirota became director of the Peabody Inst. of the Johns Hopkins Univ. He held a fellowship (1980) and a grant (1992) from the NEA, and in 1983–84 a Guggenheim fellowship. In 1998 he was awarded the Andrew White Medal from Loyola Coll. of Baltimore.

WORKS: DRAMATIC: O p e r a : *Bontshe the Silent* (1978); *The Tailor of Gloucester* (1987); *The Clever Mistress*, after Boccaccio (1988); *Iscariot* (1994). ORCH.: *Scherzo and Adagio* for Strings (1980); Saxophone Concerto (1981); Cello Concerto (1984); Concerto for Organ, Strings, and Percussion (1985); *Dark Dances* for Viola and Chamber Orch. (1995; also for Viola and Piano, 1994); *Cummington Junction* for Chamber Orch. (1998); *In the Fullness of Time* for Organ and Orch. (1999). S y m - p h o n i c B a n d : *Concord Suite* (1984). CHAMBER: 9 *Epigrams* for Flute (1972); *Fantasy* for Cello and Piano (1976); Concerto Grosso for 14 Instruments (1981); *Letters Abroad* for Organ and Piano (1982); *Music* for Chamber Ensemble (1985); *Primal Voice* for Bassoon and 3 Percussionists (1987); *7 Picassos* for Flute, Clarinet, Piano, Violin, Viola, and Cello (1987); Cello Sonata (1988); *Synopses* for Tuba (1990); *Easter Canticles* for Cello and Organ (1993); *Dark Dances* for Viola and Piano (1994; also for Viola and Chamber Orch., 1995); *Prayers and Lamentations* for Cello (1996); Trio for Violin, Cello, and Piano (1998). **KEY-BOARD: P i a n o :** *3 Pieces* (1973–79); *Jerusalem Psalms* for 2 Pianos, 4-Hands, and Optional Narrator (1995). **O r g a n :** *Jeux* (1974); *Night Echoes I* for 2 Organs (1974) and *II* for Organ and Tape (1975); *4 Pieces* (1975); *2 Lenten Chorale Preludes* (1978–79); *Toccata* (1979); *Festival Prelude on "Now Thank We All Our God"* (1985); *Celestial Wind* (19987); *Incantations* (1988); *Psalm 100* (1992). **VOCAL:** *Songs and Spells: A Midsummer Nightscape* for Chorus and Chamber Ensemble, after Shakespeare (1981); *Remembrance*, 4 songs for Soprano, Oboe, Clarinet, Piano, Viola, and Cello, after Shakespeare (1988); Mass for Soloists, Chorus, Organ, and Percussion (1990); *3 Cabaret Songs* for Soprano and Piano, after Millay, Thackeray, and Tennessee Williams (1991); *The Passion of Jesus Christ*, visual oratorio for Soprano, Tenor, Bass, Chorus, Organ, Piano, and 2 Percussion (1998).—**LK/DM**

Sissle, Noble (Lee), early pop/jazz singer, composer, leader; b. Indianapolis, Ind., July 10, 1889; d. Tampa, Fla., Dec. 17, 1975. In 1914, he formed his first band for residency at the Severin Hotel, Indianapolis. He moved to Baltimore in 1915, and worked in Bob Young's Band (with Eubie Blake-Luckey Roberts; occasionally on second piano). Later that year, Sissle led his own band in Coconut Grove, Palm Beach, Fla. He joined Jim Europe's Society Orch. as guitarist-vocalist, then (with Europe) joined the U.S. Army in December 1916. He served as a lieutenant in the famous 369th Division Band, acting as drum major. He returned to the U.S. and continued to tour with Europe until Europe's death in 1919. Sissle then formed a highly successful duo with Eubie Blake; these two worked as partners for many years, producing and composing for a variety of shows, including *Shuffle Along, Chocolate Dandies,* and many others. Many of their songs became standards; "I'm Just Wild About Harry" was revived as a campaign song in 1948 for Harry Truman. In 1926 they played a residency in London at the Kit Kat Club, and then returned to the U.S. that August. During this period, they also recorded and toured in the U.S., and appeared in several short Vitaphone films. Sissle returned to London without Blake in 1928, did a solo act accompanied by pianist Harry Revel, then formed his own band for residency at Les Ambassadeurs in Paris (summer 1928). Through the mid-1930s, he alternated between leading bands in Europe and the U.S. (except for a spell of inactivity following injuries sustained in a car crash during summer 1936). Beginning in 1938, he led the band at Billy Rose's Diamond Horseshoe in N.Y. Sissle continued this residency for over 12 years, but did touring for U.S.O. shows during World War II (including a trip to Europe). During the 1960s he continued to manage his own publishing company. He also continued to lead his own bands and to run his own night-club, Noble's. In 1969, he reunited with Blake to make recordings. He lived in Fla. from the 1970s on; in his later years, he suffered from Alzheimer's disease. Over the years, Noble Sissle employed many famous jazz soloists, including Sidney Bechet, Buster Bailey, Harvey Boone, Johhny Dunn, and Tommy Ladnier.

DISC.: *Noble Sissle and His Sizzling Syncopaters* (1931).

BIBL.: R. Kimball and W. Bolcom, *Reminiscing with Sissle and Blake* (N.Y., 1973).—**JC/LP**

Sitkovetsky, Dmitry, esteemed Russian-born American violinist and conductor; b. Baku, Sept. 27, 1954. He was born into a distinguished family of musicians. His father was the violinist Julian Sitkovetsky and his mother the pianist **Bella Davidovich.** He was taken to Moscow where he studied at the Central Music School (1961–72). In 1966 he won first prize in the Concertino Praha Competition in Prague. After further training with Yankelevich and Bezrodny at the Moscow Cons. (1972–77), he completed his studies with Galamian at the Juilliard School in N.Y. (1977–79). In 1979 he captured first prize in the Fritz Kreisler Competition in Vienna, which led to an auspicious appearance as a soloist with the Berlin Phil. in 1980. He made his U.S. debut as a soloist with the Chicago Sym. Orch. in 1983; that same year, he was awarded an Avery Fisher Career Grant. In 1985 he appeared for the first time at the Salzburg Festival as a soloist with the Polish Chamber Orch. In 1986 he played at the London Promenade Concerts. In 1988 he was a soloist with the N.Y. Phil. From 1992 to 1998 he was artistic advisor of the Seattle International Music Festival. He toured as a soloist with Leppard and the Indianapolis Sym. Orch. on their visit to many of the major European music centers in 1993. In addition to his numerous engagements as a soloist with the world's principal orchs., he has appeared frequently as a recitalist. He has also given duo concerts with his mother. He likewise has devoted a portion of his career to conducting. From 1997 he served as principal conductor and artistic advisor of the Ulster Orch. in Belfast. His repertoire ranges from Bach to Prokofiev. He prepared highly effective transcriptions of Bach's *Goldberg Variations* for String Trio (1984) and String Orch. (1994).—**NS/LK/DM**

Sitsky, Larry, prominent Australian composer, pianist, teacher, and writer on music; b. Tientsin, China (of Russian-Jewish parents), Sept. 10, 1934. He began to study piano at an early age. After emigrating to Australia in 1951, he won a scholarship and studied piano and composition at the New South Wales State Conservatorium of Music in Sydney (graduated, 1956; postgraduate studies, 1956–58). He completed his postgraduate studies with Egon Petri at the San Francisco Cons. of Music (1959–61). From 1961 to 1965 he taught piano at the Queensland State Conservatorium of Music in Brisbane, and concurrently served as a guest lecturer on contemporary music at the Univ. of Queensland. Sitsky was head of keyboard studies (1966–78), of the dept. of composition and electronic music (1978–81), of the dept. of composition and musicology (1981–83), and of the dept. of composition (from 1983) at the Canberra School of Music. In 1993 he was promoted to reader and in 1994 to prof. (personal chair). Under the auspices of the Australian Dept. of Foreign Affairs, he was the first Australian to hold visiting composition fellowships to the Soviet Union (1977) and Communist China (1983). In 1998 he was the composer-in-residence of the Australian Academy of Music. Sitsky held a Fulbright Australian-American fellowship in 1988–89. In 1989 he won the Advance Australia Award, the inaugural prize of the Fellowship of Composers, and the inaugural National Critics' Award. He received the first Higher

Doctorate in Fine Arts from the Australian National Univ. in 1997. In 1998 he was elected a fellow of the Australian Academy of the Humanities. In addition to his books, he has contributed articles to various publications. As a composer, he has written scores that range from the most challenging avant-garde pieces to works of melodious accessibility.

WRITINGS: *Busoni and the Piano: The Music, the Writings, the Recordings: A Complete Survey* (Westport, Conn., 1986); *The Classical Reproducing Piano Roll: A Catalogue-Index* (2 vols., Westport, Conn., 1989); *Music of the Repressed Russian Avant-Garde, 1900–1929* (Westport, Conn., 1993); *Anton Rubinstein: An Annotated Catalog of Piano Works and Biography* (Westport, Conn., 1998).

WORKS: DRAMATIC: O p e r a : *Fall of the House of Usher* (Hobart, Aug. 1965); *Lenz* (1970; Sydney, March 1974); *Fiery Tales* (1975); *Voices in Limbo* (1977); *The Golem* (1980; Sydney, Oct. 14, 1993); *Three Scenes from Aboriginal Life* (1988). **I n c i d e n t a l   M u s i c   T o :** *Faust* (1996). **ORCH.:** 4 *Orchestral Pieces* (1966–74); Woodwind Quintet Concerto (1971); 5 violin concertos (1971, 1983, 1987, 1998, 1998); 6 *Orchestral Songs* for Low Voice and Orch. (1980); *Santana*, concerto for Clarinet and Strings (1981); *Kundalini*, concerto for Trombone, Keyboards, and Percussion (1982); *Concerto for Orchestra* (1984; completion and realization of Busoni's *Fantasia Contrappuntistica*); Guitar Concerto (1984); *Songs and Dances from "The Golem"* (1984); *Suite* for Concert Band (1987); Piano Concerto, *The 22 Paths of the Tarot* (1991; rev. 1994); *At the Gate* (1992); *Sphinx*, cello concerto (1993); *Zohar*, Sephardic Concerto for Mandolin and Small Orch. (1998). **CHAMBER:** Sonata for Solo Violin (1959); 3 sonatas for Solo Flute (1959, 1979, 1994); Woodwind Quartet (1963); *Sinfonia* for 10 Players (1964); Sonata for 2 Guitars (1968); 2 string quartets (1969, 1981); Sonata for Solo Guitar (1974); *Atman: A Song of Serenity* for Piano Trio (1975); *Maherq: Fantasia No. 6 in Memory of John Crocker* for Bassoon (1984); *Agharti*, trio for Baroque Violin, Viola da Gamba, and Harpsichord (1986); *Diabolus in Musica* for Percussion Quartet (1986); Concertino for Mandolin and Wind Quartet (1987); *The Secret Gates of the House of Osiris* for Flute, Viola, Cello, and Piano (1987); *Neconomicon*, 18 aphorisms for Clarinet and Piano (1989); Sonata for Solo Mandolin, *The Three Names of Shiva* (1992); Violin Sonata, *Omnia exeunt in mysterium* (1995); Double Bass Sonata, *Beowulf* (1997); *Enochian Sonata* for 2 Cellos and Piano (1999). **KEYBOARD: P i a n o :** *Fantasia Nos. 1–11* (1962–98); Concerto for 2 Solo Pianos (1967); 12 *Mystical Preludes After the Nuctemeron of Appollonius of Tyana* (1973); *Lotus I* (1995) and *II* (1996). **O r - g a n :** 7 *Meditations on Symbolist Art* (1975). **VOCAL:** Concert Aria for Low Voice, Ensemble, Tapes, and Synthesizer (1972); *A Whitman Cycle* for Low Voice and Piano (1972); *8 Settings After Li-Po* for Low Voice, Flute, Cello, and Piano (1974); *Music in Mirabell Garden* for Soprano and Instruments (1977); *De Profundis* for Baritone, Percussionist, and 2 String Quartets (1982); *Deep in My Hidden Country...*, cantata for Soprano, Flute, Cello, Percussion, and Piano (1984); *In Pace Requiescat* for Soprano and Strings (1989); *The Sound of Drums* for Soprano, Oboe, Harpsichord, and Bassoon (1990); *Shih Ching* (The Book of Songs) for Alto and Piano (1996); *Sonette* for Jazz Singer (1997); *Bone of My Bones* for Voice and Piano (1998); many other pieces.

BIBL.: R. Holmes, P. Shaw, and P. Campbell, *L. S.: A Bio-Bibliography* (Westport, Conn., 1997).—NS/LK/DM

Sitt, Hans, Bohemian violinist, violist, conductor, teacher, and composer; b. Prague, Sept. 21, 1850; d. Leipzig, March 10, 1922. He studied violin at the Prague

Cons., and held various positions as a violinist and conductor of theater orchs. in Breslau, Prague, and Chemnitz. In 1881 he settled in Leipzig, where he organized a series of popular concerts. He was a violist in the Brodsky Quartet, and conducted the Bachverein (1885–1903) and other musical societies. He wrote 3 violin concertos, a Viola Concerto, and 2 cello concertos, and publ. valuable studies for the violin; also *Praktische Violaschule, Schulausgabe neuerer Violinlitteratur* (5 books), and (with Reinecke) *Lyrica*, a collection of 30 Classical and Romantic pieces for violin and piano. —NS/LK/DM

Sivori, (Ernesto) Camillo, renowned Italian violinist and composer; b. Genoa, Oct. 25, 1815; d. there, Feb. 19, 1894. At a very early age he began violin lessons with Restano and then with Giacomo Costa, Paganini's former teacher. After further training with Agostino Dellepiane, he received instruction from Paganini himself (1824). In 1827 he made his debut in Genoa, then performed in London and Paris. Returning to Genoa, he took lessons in composition with Giovanni Serra (1829); played first violin in the theater orch., and taught at the Cons. He made an extensive tour of Europe in 1841–42, and then toured throughout the world during the next 14 years with great success; won notable acclaim during his tours of North and South America (1846–50). From 1855 his career was centered in Europe, where he made regular appearances in France, Italy, Germany, and England. He resided in Paris (1863–92), and then retired to Genoa. Many honors were bestowed upon him, including the French Legion d'honneur in 1886. He was one of the great violin virtuosos of the 19th century; his demanding compositions include 2 violin concertos (both 1841) and numerous solo violin pieces, including the greatly admired *Études-caprices* (1867).

BIBL.: E. James, *C. S.: A Sketch of His Life, Talent, Travels and Successes* (London, 1845; second ed., 1846); G. Da Fieno, *Die due chiarissimi genovesi: Cav. C. S., violinista e comm. F. Romani, poeta lirico* (Milan, 1871); A. Pierrottet, *C. S.* (Milan, 1896); F. Menardi Noguera, *C. S.: La vita, i concerti, le musiche* (Genoa, 1991). —NS/LK/DM

Sixt, Johann Abraham, German organist, harpsichordist, and composer; b. Grafenhausen, Baden-Wurttemberg, Jan. 3, 1757; d. Donaueschingen, Jan. 30, 1797. He was the son of a schoolmaster and organist, Johann Michael Sixt, who gave him his first music lessons; later attended the Stuttgart Karlsschule; was in Vienna in 1784, and received a recommendation from Mozart. After holding minor posts as an organist, he was active in Stuttgart; became a harpsichordist and composer at the Donaueschingen court in 1784. He wrote piano trios, sonatas, and other instrumental works, but of particular interest are his lieder, with long introductions in the accompaniment, setting the mood of the text.—NS/LK/DM

Sixta, Jozef, Slovak composer and teacher; b. Jičín, May 12, 1940. He was a student of Očenaš at the Cons. (1955–60) and of Moyzes at the Academy of Music and Drama (1960–64) in Bratislava, and later worked with

Messiaen and Jolivet in Paris (1971). After teaching at the Cons. (1964–76), he taught at the Academy of Music and Drama in Bratislava. In 1987 and 1990 he won the Ján Levoslav Bella prize. In his works, Sixta has utilized serialism and aleatory with judicious handling of harmonic, chordal, and melodic writing.

WORKS: ORCH.: Suite for Strings (1960); *3 Compositions for Small Orch.* (1963); 2 syms. (1964, 1989); *Asynchronicity* (1968); *Punctum contra punctum* (1971); *4 Orchestral Pieces* (1979). **CHAMBER:** Quintet for Flute, Oboe, Clarinet, Bassoon, and Piano (1961); 2 string quartets (1965, 1983); *Variations* for 13 Instruments (1967); Nonet for 4 Strings and 5 Winds (1970); Quartet for 4 Flutes (1972); *Recitative* for Violin (1974); Octet for 2 Flutes, 2 Oboes, 2 Clarinets, and 2 Bassoons (1977); Trio for 2 Oboes and English Horn (1980); Trio for Clarinet, Cello, and Piano (1981); *Music for 4 Players* for Oboe, Clarinet, Bassoon, and Harpsichord (1988); Trio for Clarinets (1992); *Music* for Flute, Oboe, Marimba, Vibraphone, and Synthesizer (1994). **Piano:** *Phantasia* (1962); *Solo* (1973); Sonata (1985); *Concertante Étude* (1986; also for Harpsichord).—**NS/LK/DM**

Sjögren, (Johan Gustaf) Emil,

Swedish organist and composer; b. Stockholm, June 16, 1853; d. there, March 1, 1918. He studied composition at the Stockholm Cons. with H. Berens, in Berlin with Kiel, and in Vienna with Grädener. In 1891 he was appointed organist at St. John's Church in Stockholm. His importance as a composer rests chiefly on his songs, of which he wrote about 200, to texts in Swedish, French, and German; he also wrote a *Festspel* for Orch. (1892), several choruses, 5 violin sonatas, a Cello Sonata, 2 piano sonatas, and several groups of lyric pieces for piano.

BIBL.: C. Nyblom, *E. S.* (Stockholm, 1916); G. Norlen, W. Peterson-Berger, T. Rangström et al., *E. S. in memoriam* (Stockholm, 1918).—**NS/LK/DM**

Skaggs, Ricky,

bluegrass multi-instrumentalist and bandleader, b. near Cordell, Ky., July 18, 1954. Hailing from a musical family, Ricky Skaggs is one of the few artists who has successfully crossed over from traditional bluegrass to mainstream country while still maintaining his basic sound and style intact. He was one of the first new country stars of the early 1980s who pointed the direction for a return to country's roots in repertoire and style. Although he has not been as consistently popular as some of the more flashy acts who have followed his lead, Skaggs remains an important force in country music today.

A multi-instrumentalist, Skaggs began his career while still in high school with his friend Keith Whitley, performing mandolin-guitar duets in a traditional style derived from country's brother acts. The duo were particularly enamored of the Stanley Brothers sound, and they soon found themselves performing as members of Ralph Stanley's band. Poor pay and a grueling touring schedule led to Skaggs's retirement and brief employment as an electric-company worker in a suburban Washington power plant. There, he began performing with a later version of the progressive bluegrass band, The Country Gentlemen.

In the early 1970s, he joined briefly with J.D. Crowe's groundbreaking bluegrass ensemble, The New South,

along with ace guitarist/vocalist Tony Rice. Determined to modernize and popularize the bluegrass sound, he formed his own progressive band, Boone Creek, with dobro player Jerry Douglas, who has appeared on many of Skaggs's recordings, and singer/guitarist Terry Baucom. By the late 1970s, he was working as a backup musician for Emmylou Harris, helping mold her new traditional approach on landmark albums such as *Roses in the Snow.*

Blessed with a unique, high-tenor voice, Skaggs recorded his first solo album in a contemporary country vein for the bluegrass label, Sugar Hill, while at the same time he made a duet album with Rice featuring just their guitar and mandolin and vocal harmonies in an homage to the 1930s country sound. He was quickly signed to CBS, and had a string of hits in the early 1980s with his unique adaptations of bluegrass and country standards of the 1950s. In fact, his cover of Bill Monroe's "Uncle Pen" in 1984 was the first bluegrass song to hit #1 on the country charts since 1949. He also was one of the first new country artists to tour Europe, scoring great success in England where he performed with diverse artists from Elvis Costello to Nick Lowe.

The mid-1980s found Skaggs teetering on the edge of a more pop-country sound, but basically he has stuck close to his country roots in choice of material and performance. He married country vocalist Sharon White of the Whites, and produced some of their successful recordings of the 1980s. While Skaggs' more recent recordings have not been as successful on the country charts, he continues to be influential as an instrumentalist and producer. He returned to his bluegrass/country swing roots as a member of Mark O'Connor's New Nashville Cats band, which featured another crossover artist from bluegrass, Vince Gill. Skaggs continues to represent bluegrass music on awards programs, often performing with such veterans as Bill Monroe and his old mentor, Ralph Stanley.

DISC.: *Sweet Temptation* (1979); *Waitin' for the Sun to Shine* (1981); *Highways and Heartaches* (1982); *Don't Cheat on Our Hometown* (1983); *Love's Gonna Get Ya!* (1986); *Comin' Home to Stay* (1987); *Kentucky Thunder* (1987); *My Father's Son* (1991); *Solid Ground* (1995); *Bluegrass Rules!* (1997).—**RC**

Skalkottas, Nikos (actually, Nikolaos),

greatly talented Greek composer; b. Chalkis, island of Euboea, March 8, 1904; d. Athens, Sept. 19, 1949. He studied violin with his father, with his uncle, and with a nonrelated violinist at the Athens Cons. (1914–20). In 1921 he went to Berlin, where he continued his violin studies with Hess at the Hochschule für Musik (until 1923); then took lessons in theory with Jarnach (1925–27). The greatest influence on Skalkottas' creative life was Schoenberg, with whom he studied in Berlin (1927–31); Schoenberg, in his book *Style and Idea*, mentions Skalkottas as one of his most gifted disciples. Skalkottas eagerly absorbed Schoenberg's instruction in the method of composition with 12 tones related only to one another, but in his own music applied it in a very individual manner, without trying to imitate Schoenberg's style. In Berlin, Skalkottas also received some suggestions in free composition from Kurt Weill

(1928–29). He returned to Athens and earned his living by playing violin in local orchs., but continued to compose diligently, until his early death from a strangulated hernia. His music written between 1928 and 1938 reflects Schoenberg's idiom; later works are tonally conceived, and several of them are in the clearly ethnic Greek modalities, set in the typical asymmetric meters of Balkan folk music. After his death, a Skalkottas Soc. was formed in Athens to promote performances and publications of his works; about 110 scores of various genres are kept in the Skalkottas Archives in Athens.

WORKS: DRAMATIC: *I lygery kai o charos* (The Maiden and Death), ballet (1938; Athens, May 10, 1940; rev. version, Athens, March 23, 1947); *Me tou mayoa ta maya* (The Spell of May), incidental music (1943–44; orchestrated 1949; London, May 30, 1961); *Henry V*, incidental music to Shakespeare's play (1947–48; not extant). **ORCH.:** 1 unnumbered symphonic suite (1928; not extant); 2 numbered symphonic suites: No. 1 (1935; London, April 28, 1973) and No. 2 (1944; orchestrated 1946–49; London, Jan. 31, 1966); Concerto for Winds and Orch. (1929; Berlin, May 20, 1930; not extant); *Little Suite* for Violin and Chamber Orch. (1929; Berlin, April 6, 1930; not extant); Concerto for Piano, Violin, and Chamber Orch. (Berlin, April 6, 1930; not extant); 3 piano concertos: No. 1 (1931), No. 2 (1937–38; Hamburg, Oct. 12, 1953), and No. 3 (1938–39; London, July 9, 1969); *36 elliniki chori* (36 *greichische Tänze*) (1931–36; reorchestrated, 1948–49); Concertino for 2 Pianos and Orch. (1935; Geneva, June 15, 1952); Violin Concerto (1937–38; Hamburg, May 14, 1962); Cello Concerto (1938; not extant); Concerto for Violin, Viola, Winds, and Double Basses (1939–40; London, July 7, 1969); *10 Musical Sketches* for Strings (1940; Athens, Nov. 6, 1952; also for String Quartet); *Little Suite* for Strings (1942; Zürich, Aug. 30, 1953); *I epistrophi tou Odyssevs* (The Return of Ulysses), overture (1942–43; London, June 23, 1969; also for 2 Pianos, 1943–44); Double Bass Concerto (1942–43); Concerto for 2 Violins and Orch. (1944–45); *Klassiki symphonia* for Winds and Double Basses (1947); Sinfonietta (1948); Piano Concertino (1948); *Mikri chorevtiki suita: 4 chori ya balleto* (Kleine Tanz-Suite: 4 Tanze für Ballett; 1948–49; Athens, May 2, 1949); *Dance Suite* (1948–49); *Nocturne-divertimento* for Xylophone and Orch. (1949); *I thalassa* (The Sea; 1949). **CHAMBER:** 2 string trios (1924, not extant; 1935; Athens, March 20, 1954); 1 unnumbered string quartet (1924; not extant); 4 numbered string quartets: No. 1 (1928; Berlin, June 19, 1929), No. 2 (1929; Athens, Nov. 27, 1930; not extant), No. 3 (1935; Oxford, July 3, 1965), and No. 4 (1940; London, July 13, 1969); Sonata for Solo Violin (1925); 2 violin sonatas (1928, not extant; 1940); *Evkoli mousiki* (Easy Music) for String Quartet (1929; Athens, Nov. 27, 1930; not extant); 4 violin sonatinas (1929, only second movement extant; 1929; 1935; 1935); Octet for Flute, Clarinet, Bassoon, Trumpet, Trombone, and Piano Trio (1929; not extant); Octet for Woodwind Quartet and String Quartet (Berlin, June 2, 1931); Piano Trio (1936); *Der Marsch der kleinen Soldaten, Rondo, Nachstück, Kleiner Choral und Fuge* for Violin and Piano (1937–38); Suite for Cello and Piano (1937–38; not extant); Duo for Violin and Viola (1938); *8 Variationen über ein griechisches Volksthema* for Piano Trio (1938; Athens, March 31, 1950); *9 Greek Dances* for String Quartet (1938–47); *Gavotte, Scherzo, Menuetto cantato* for Violin and Piano (1939); Concertino for Oboe and Piano (1939); *Scherzo* for Piano Quartet (1939–40); 2 quartets for Oboe, Bassoon, Trumpet, and Piano (1940–42; Bamberg, June 15, 1968); Concertino for Trumpet and Piano (1940–42); *6 Greek Dances* for Violin and Piano (1940–47); *Largo* for Cello and Piano (1941–42); *Sonata concertante* for Bassoon and Piano (1943); *Mikri serenate* (Kleine

Serenade) for Cello and Piano (1945); *Bolero* for Cello and Piano (1945); *3 Greek Folksongs* for Violin and Piano (1945–46); *2 Little Suites* for Violin and Piano (1946, 1949); *4 parties* for Violin and Cello (1947); Cello Sonatina (1949); *Zarte Melodie* for Cello and Piano (1949). **Piano:** 2 suites for 2 Pianos (1924–25); Sonatina (1927); *15 Little Variations* (1927); 4 suites (1936, 1940, 1940, 1940); 32 pieces (1940–41). **VOCAL:** Choral piece (1930; not extant); 3 songs for Voice and Piano (1932–38); *Kapote* (Sometime) for Soprano or Baritone and Piano (1938–39); *16 Songs* for Mezzo-soprano and Piano (1941; London, March 18, 1962); *To fengari* (The Moon) for Soprano and Piano (1941–42); *To tragoudi tou kleidona* (The Locksmith's Song) for 2 Sopranos and 2 Mezzo-sopranos (1943–44).—**NS/LK/DM**

Škerjanc, Lucijan Marija, Slovenian pianist, conductor, teacher, writer on music, and composer; b. Graz, Dec. 17, 1900; d. Ljubljana, Feb. 27, 1973. He studied composition in Vienna with Marx and in Paris with d'Indy. He became a music teacher in Ljubljana in 1922, where he was a teacher of composition at the Cons. (1926–40) and at the Academy of Music (1940–70), serving as rector of the latter (1945–47). He was conductor of the Glasbena Matica orch. society (1925–45), and director of the Slovene Philharmonia (1950–55). Much of his music reflects neo-Romantic trends, with some impressionistic colors; in later works he also utilized 12-note techniques.

WORKS: ORCH.: 2 violin concertos (1927, 1944); 5 syms. (1931, 1938, 1940, 1941, 1943); Piano Concerto (1940); Bassoon Concerto (1953); Harp Concerto (1954); Concerto for Clarinet, Strings, Percussion, and Harp (1958); Flute Concerto (1962); Concerto for Piano, Left-hand, and Orch. (1963). **CHAMBER:** 5 string quartets (1917, 1921, 1925, 1935, 1945); Wind Quintet (1925); Piano Trio (1935); String Quintet (1945); *Concertone* for 4 Cellos (1954); other chamber works; piano pieces. **VOCAL:** Songs.—**NS/LK/DM**

Skilton, Charles Sanford, American composer and teacher; b. Northampton, Mass., Aug. 16, 1868; d. Lawrence, Kans., March 12, 1941. He first studied in Germany; after graduating from Yale Univ. (B.A., 1889), he studied in N.Y. with Harry Rowe Shelley (organ) and Dudley Buck (composition); then at the Berlin Hochschule für Musik with Bargiel (1891–93). From 1893 to 1896 he was director of music at the Salem (N.C.) Academy and Coll., and conducted the local orch. there; then filled a similar post at the State Normal School in Trenton, N.J. (1897–1903); in 1903 he was engaged as a prof. of organ and theory at the Univ. of Kans., Lawrence, where he remained most of his life. He made a detailed study of Indian music, and introduced Indian motifs into the traditional forms of the suite and fantasy. His opera *Kalopin* (1927) received the David Bispham Memorial Medal in 1930.

WORKS: DRAMATIC: Opera: *Kalopin* (1927); *The Sun Bride* (NBC, April 17, 1930); *The Day of Gayomair* (1936). **ORCH.:** *Suite Primeval*, on Indian melodies, in 2 parts: *2 Indian Dances* (originally for String Quartet, 1915; Minneapolis, Oct. 29, 1916) and part II (Minneapolis, Nov. 13, 1921); *Autumn Night* (Detroit, Dec. 11, 1930); *Shawnee Indian Hunting Dance* (Detroit, Dec. 11, 1930); *A Carolina Legend*, symphonic poem; *Mt. Oread*, overture. **CHAMBER:** *2 Indian Dances* for String Quartet (1915; orchestrated as part 1 of *Suite Primeval*); Violin Sonatina

(1923); String Quartet (1938). KEYBOARD: P i a n o : *3 Indian Sketches* (1919); *Shawnee Indian Hunting Dance* (1929). O r g a n : *American Indian Fantasy* (1926; also for Orch., 1932). VOCAL: *The Witch's Daughter*, cantata (1918); *The Guardian Angel*, oratorio (1925); *From Forest and Stream* for Women's Chorus (1930).

BIBL.: J. Howard, *C.S. S.* (N.Y., 1929); J. Smith, *C.S. S. (1868–1941), Kansas Composer* (thesis, Univ. of Kans., 1979). —NS/LK/DM

Skinner, Ernest M(artin), American organ builder; b. Clarion, Pa., Jan. 15, 1866; d. Duxbury, Mass., Nov. 27, 1960. He was the founder of the Ernest M. Skinner Co., organ builders, originally of Dorchester, later of Methuen, Mass. Until 1905 the business was carried on by Skinner himself; it was then incorporated, with Skinner as president. From 1917 to 1932 he was technical director of the Skinner Organ Co., which in 1932 was merged with the Aeolian Co. of Garwood, N.J., and became the Aeolian-Skinner Organ Co. He was especially successful in the construction of organ pipes reproducing the exact tone color of the various woodwind instruments and the French horn; among several important inventions is the "duplex windchest," by means of which the stops of 2 manuals are made interchangeable, and the arrangement of placing the stops on swinging sides. The Skinner Co. built the organ in the National Cathedral at Washington, D.C. He publ. *The Modern Organ* (1915; 6th ed., 1945) and *The Composition of the Organ* (1947).

BIBL.: D. Holden, *The Life and Work of E.M. S.* (Richmond, Va., 1985).—NS/LK/DM

Sklavos, George, Greek composer and teacher; b. Brailov, Romania (of Greek parents), Aug. 20, 1888; d. Athens, March 19, 1976. He studied with Armand Marsick at the Athens Cons., where he was an instructor (1913–68). He devoted himself chiefly to the musical theater.

WORKS: D R A M A T I C : O p e r a : *Niovi* (1919); *Lestenisa* (1923; Athens, March 14, 1947); *Kassiani* (1929–36; Athens, Oct. 30, 1959); *Krino st' akroyali* (Lily at the Seashore; 1937–41); *Amphitryon* (1955–60); *St' Ai Yorghi to panyghiri* (At St. George's Fair; 1961–62). O t h e r : Incidental music. ORCH.: *Aetos* (Eagle; 1922); *Arcadian Suite* (1922); *Cretan Fantasy* (1922); *Heroiko poiema* (1926); *2 idylls* (1928); *Nissiotikos gamos* (Marriage on a Greek Island; 1937). VOCAL: Choruses; songs. —NS/LK/DM

Sköld, (Karl) Yngve, Swedish composer; b. Vallby, April 29, 1899; d. Stockholm, Dec. 6, 1992. He studied piano and composition in Stockholm (1915–18), then in Brno (1920–22) and Prague (1922). From 1938 to 1964 he was librarian of the Swedish Composers' Society. His music blends Nordic Romanticism with subdued modernity.

WORKS: ORCH.: 4 syms. (1915, 1937, 1949, 1968); 3 piano concertos (1917, 1946, 1968); *Suite concertante* for Viola and Orch. (1936); *Sinfonia di chiesa* (1939); Violin Concerto (1941); Cello Concerto (1947); Double Concerto for Violin, Cello, and Orch. (1950); *Divertimento* (1951). CHAMBER: Cello Sonata (1927); 4 string quartets (1930, 1955, 1965, 1974); Quintet

for 2 Flutes, Cello, and Piano (1958); Sonata for Viola and Organ (1962); Concertino for 5 Winds, Timpani, and Strings (1963); *Divertimento* for Violin, Viola, and Cello (1971); *Trio domestico* for Piano Trio (1974). P i a n o : 2 sonatas (1963); Sonatina (1970). —NS/LK/DM

Skovhus, Bo(je), admired Danish baritone; b. Århus, May 22, 1962. He received his training at the Århus Cons. (1982–86), the Royal Opera Academy in Copenhagen (1986–88), and with Oren Brown in N.Y. In 1988 he made his operatic debut as Don Giovanni at the Vienna Volksoper, which role he reprised for his first appearance at the Royal Opera in Copenhagen in 1990. In 1991 he made his debut at the Vienna State Opera as Silvio and at the Hamburg State Opera as Guglielmo. Following debuts as Billy Budd at the Cologne Opera in 1992 and as Mozart's Almaviva at the Bavarian State Opera in Munich in 1994, he portrayed Don Giovanni at his first appearance at the Deutsche Oper in Berlin in 1995. In 1997 he sang for the first time at London's Covent Garden as Guglielmo, at the Opéra de la Bastille in Paris as Danilo, and at the San Francisco Opera as Almaviva. After singing Billy Budd at the Houston Grand Opera in 1998, he made his Metropolitan Opera debut on Dec. 24th of that year as Eisenstein. His first engagement at the Dresden State Opera followed in 1999 as Don Giovanni. As a soloist, he appeared with the Berlin Phil., the Chicago Sym. Orch., the Vienna Sym. Orch., the Boston Sym. Orch., the Cleveland Orch., and many others. His recital engagements took him to the principal music centers on both sides of the Atlantic. Among his other roles are Hamlet, Eugene Onegin, Wolfram, Strauss's Olivier, and Wozzeck.—NS/LK/DM

Skram, Knut, Norwegian baritone; b. Saebo, Dec. 18, 1937. He was educated in Mont. and studied voice with George Buckee, in Wiesbaden with Paul Lohmann, in Rome with Luigi Ricci, and in Copenhagen with Kristian Riis. In 1964 he made his operatic debut at the Norwegian Opera in Oslo as Amonasro. After winning first prize in the Munich International Competition in 1967, he made his debut at the Glyndebourne Festival as Mozart's Guglielmo in 1969, where he made return visits until 1976. From 1978 he sang at the Spoleto Festival. In 1979 he made his U.S. debut as Papageno with the Ky. Opera in Louisville. He portrayed Eugene Onegin in Lyons in 1984. During the Berlin State Opera's tour of Japan in 1987, he was engaged as Jochanaan. In 1988 he sang Pizzaro in Buenos Aires and Scarpia in Moscow. He appeared as Hans Sachs in Nice in 1992. In 1996 he sang the Wanderer in *Siegfried* in Oslo. As a concert artist, he appeared frequently as a lieder interpreter.—NS/LK/DM

Skriabin, Alexander (Nikolaievich)
See **Scriabin, Alexander (Nikolaievich)**

Škroup, František Jan, prominent Bohemian conductor and composer, brother of **Jan Nepomuk Škroup**; b. Osice, near Pardubice, June 3, 1801; d.

Rotterdam, Feb. 7, 1862. He received his musical training from his father, the teacher and composer Dominik Josef Skroup (1766–1830). He studied law in Prague. In 1827 he became asst. conductor, and in 1837 principal conductor, at the Estates Theater, Prague, and remained at that post until 1857; he put into performance several Wagner operas for the first time in Prague. He wrote several operas to Czech librettos, which he conducted in Prague: *Dráteník* (The Tinker; Feb. 2, 1826), *Oldřich a Božena* (Dec. 14, 1828), *Libušin snatek* (Libusa's Marriage; April 11, 1835; rev. 1849; April 11, 1850), *Die Geisterbraut* (Nov. 17, 1836), *Drahomira* (Nov. 20, 1848), and *Der Mergeuse* (Nov. 29, 1851). In 1860 he went to Rotterdam as conductor of a German opera troupe. He also scored a success as a composer with his incidental music to Josef Tyl's play *Fidlovačka* (Prague, Dec. 21, 1834), which includes the song *Kde domov můj?* (Where Is My Home?); the latter became so famous that it was mistaken for a folk song and the first part of it was made into the Czech national anthem in 1918. He also wrote sacred music, cantatas, choruses, chamber music, and songs.

BIBL.: J. Plavec, *F. S.* (Prague, 1946).—**NS/LK/DM**

Škroup, Jan Nepomuk, Bohemian conductor, teacher, and composer, brother of **František Jan Škroup;** b. Osice, near Pardubice, Sept. 15, 1811; d. Prague, May 5, 1892. He studied at the Prague Gymnasium, then conducted various orch. concerts and theater productions and served as choirmaster in churches and monasteries in Prague; was choirmaster at St. Vitus Cathedral (1848–87). He wrote the operas *Svédové v Praze* (The Swedish Girl in Prague; 1844), *Der Liebesring* (1860), and *Vineta* (1861); also incidental music, choral works, partsongs, and songs.—**NS/LK/DM**

Skrowaczewski, Stanislaw, eminent Polish-born American conductor and composer; b. Lwów, Oct. 3, 1923. A precocious *wunderkind*, he composed an orch. overture at the age of 8, played a piano recital at 11, and performed Beethoven's third Piano Concerto at 13, conducting the orch. from the keyboard. He studied composition and conducting at the Lwów Cons. and also physics, chemistry, and philosophy at the Univ. of Lwów. The oppressive Nazi occupation of Poland interrupted his studies, and an unfortunate bomb exploded in the vicinity of his house, causing an injury to his hands that interfered with his further activities as a concert pianist. After World War II, he went to Kraków to study composition with Palester and conducting with Bierdiajew. In 1947 he received a French government scholarship that enabled him to study composition with Boulanger and conducting with Kletzki in Paris. He then conducted the Wroclaw Orch. (1946–47), the State Silesian Phil. in Katowice (1949–54), the Kraków Phil. (1954–56), and the National Phil. in Warsaw (1956–59). In 1956 he won first prize in the international conducting competition in Rome. On Dec. 4, 1958, he made his U.S. debut as a guest conductor of the Cleveland Orch., scoring an impressive success. In 1960 he was named music director of the Minneapolis Sym. Orch. (renamed the Minn. Orch. in 1968), and asserted his excellence

both as a consummate technician of the baton and a fine interpreter of the classic and modern repertoire. In 1966 he became a naturalized American citizen. He also made appearances as a guest conductor throughout the world. He made his Metropolitan Opera debut in N.Y. on Jan. 8, 1970, with *Die Zauberflöte*. In 1979 he resigned as music director of the Minn. Orch., and was made its conductor emeritus. He was principal conductor and musical adviser of the Hallé Orch. in Manchester from 1984 to 1990. He also served as music adviser of the St. Paul (Minn.) Chamber Orch. (1987–88) and as artistic advisor of the Milwaukee Sym. Orch. (1995–97).

WORKS: DRAMATIC: Ballet: *Ugo and Parisina* (1949). **OTHER:** Theater and film music. **ORCH.:** 4 syms.: No. 1 (1936), No. 2 (1945), No. 3, for Strings (1947), and No. 4 (1954); *Overture 1947* (1947); *Music at Night*, extracts from the ballet, *Ugo and Parisina* (1949–51); English Horn Concerto (Minneapolis, Nov. 21, 1969; rev. 1998); *Ricercari notturni* for Saxophone and Orch. (1977; Minneapolis, Jan. 19, 1978); Clarinet Concerto (1981); Violin Concerto (Philadelphia, Dec. 12, 1985); Fanfare (1987); Triple Concerto for Violin, Clarinet, Piano, and Orch. (1991); *Gesualdo di Venosa*, arrangement of 6 madrigals for Chamber Orch. (1992); Chamber Concerto, *Ritornelli poi Ritornelli* (1993); *Passacaglia Immaginaria* (1995). **CHAMBER:** 4 string quartets; Trio for Clarinet, Bassoon, and Piano (1982–84); *Fantasie per quattro* for Clarinet, Violin, Cello, and Piano (1984); *Fantasie per sei* for Oboe, Violin, Viola, Cello, Bass, and Piano (Atlanta, April 16, 1989); String Trio (1990); *Fantasie per tre* for Flute, Oboe, and Cello (1992); *Musica a quattro* for Clarinet, Violin, Viola, and Cello (1998). **Piano:** 6 sonatas. **VOCAL:** Songs.—**NS/LK/DM**

Skuherský, František Zdeněk (Xavier Alois), Bohemian conductor, teacher, music theorist, and composer; b. Opočno, July 31, 1830; d. Budweis, Aug. 19, 1892. He first studied medicine, then had music lessons with Kittl in Prague. From 1854 to 1866 he was in Innsbruck, where he conducted the Musikverein. In 1866 he went to Prague as director of the Organ School; also was choirmaster at St. Hastal's and at the Holy Trinity, director of the court chapel, and a teacher of music theory at the Czech Univ. (from 1882). In 1890 he retired. Among his outstanding pupils were J. F. Foerster and Janáček. Skuherský was a leading figure in the reform of church music in his homeland. He publ. several texts on music theory (in Prague): *O formách hudebních* (Musical Form; 1873; second ed., 1884), *Nauka o hudební komposici* (Theory of Musical Composition; 4 vols., 1880–84), and *Nauka o harmonii na vědeckém základě ve formě nejjednodušší* (Theory of Harmony on a Scientific Basis in the Simplest Form; 1885).

WORKS: DRAMATIC: Opera: *Samo* (1854; unfinished); *Der Apostat* (rev. as *Vladimir, bohů zvolenec* [Vladimir, the Gods's Chosen One], Prague, Sept. 27, 1863); *Der Liebesring* (Innsbruck, 1861; Czech version as *Lora*, Prague, April 13, 1868); *Der Rekrut* (Czech version as *Rektor a generál* [Rector and General], Prague, March 28, 1873); *Smrt krále Václava* (King Wenceslas's Death; 1868; unfinished). **ORCH.:** Sym. (n.d.); *Máj* (May), symphonic fantasia (1874; Brünn, April 22, 1877); 3 Fugues (1883–84). **CHAMBER:** Piano Quintet (1871); String Quartet (1871); Piano Trio (1871–72); also piano pieces and organ music. **VOCAL:** Much sacred vocal music; choruses; songs.—**NS/LK/DM**

Slade, a hugely popular band at home in England and Europe, but barely a blip on the pop radar in the U.S. **MEMBERSHIP:** Noddy (real name, Neville) Holder, voc., gtr. (b. Wallsall, England, June 15, 1950); David Hill, gtr. (b. Fleet Castle, England, April 4, 1952); Jim Lea, bs., kybd. (b. Wolverhampton, England, June 14, 1952); Don Powell, drm. (b. Bilston, England, Sept. 10, 1950).

Slade grew out of several bands including Listen, which featured Noddy Holder and Robert Plant on vocals, and the Vendors with guitarist Dave Hill and drummer Don Powell. By November of 1966, the four had come together as the 'N Betweens. They hooked up with Kim Fowley and recorded "You Better Run" in 1968. A year later, they moved from the Midlands to London, where they signed with former Animals bassist Chas Chandler, who managed Jimi Hendrix.

In the late 1960s, Slade had developed a following among the burgeoning soul, reggae and ska crowd. Chandler suggested the band change their name to Ambrose Slade, and they released the *Ballzy* (in the U.S.)/*Beginnings* album in 1969 under that name. After that album stiffed, they dropped the "Ambrose" from their name and released several singles and the *Play It Loud* album, none of which attracted much attention. In 1971 Chandler had them record Little Richard's (via Bobby Marchan) "Get Down and Get with It"—a favorite of the band's live shows—which became their first U.K. chart single. Their next single, "Coz I Luv You," topped the U.K. charts for a month. It became the first in a long line of hit Holder/Lea compositions with bastardized spellings. The group was proclaimed "unhealthy for the educational good of Britain."

They released *Slade Alive!* in 1972, an album *Rolling Stone* called one of the five best live recordings of all time. It hit #2 on the U.K. charts. The singles "Take Me Back 'ome" and "Mama, Weer All Crazee Now" topped the charts across Europe. "Gudbuy T' Jane" hit #2, unable to knock Chuck Berry's "My Ding-A-Ling" out of the #1 spot. Later that year, the *Slayed?* album was released, featuring the tracks "Cum on Feel the Noize" and "Skweeze Me, Pleeze Me", both huge hits in Europe. Unfortunately, drummer Don Powell was in a serious car accident that killed his girlfriend and put him in the hospital for six weeks. The group issued a greatest hits album while he recovered. They also released a single, "Merry Christmas Everybody," that has become a regular seasonal favorite in the U.K.

In 1973 Slade released *Old New Borrowed and Blue*. This album was issued in the U.S. as *Stomp Your Hands/Clap Your Feet*. Not one of the band's better efforts, it failed to capture the attention of U.S. fans, and it would be a decade before the group tried to crack the U.S. market again. Slade continued to have massive success in Europe, however, with tunes like "The Bangin' Man," "Far Far Away," and "Nobody's Fools." However, the advent of punk and disco in the mid-1970s squeezed the market for their brand of anthemic pop out of the charts. They moved from Polydor to Chandler's own label, Barn, releasing the tongue-in-cheek *Whatever Happened to Slade* in 1977. Holder and Lea formed a punk band called the Dummies that

nearly was signed to the leading new-wave label Stiff Records until the label's executives found out the group consisted mostly of members of Slade!

In the 1980s, Slade enjoyed a renaissance. First, they aligned with the new wave of British metal. This association attracted American fans, especially musicians like the Runaways and Quiet Riot. The Runaways recorded "Mama Weer All Crazee Now" in 1980, and Joan Jett re-recorded it when she went solo in 1982. In 1984 Quiet Riot had a #5 gold hit with a cover of "Cum on Feel the Noize." They also covered "Mama Weer All Crazee Now." The band signed to Columbia, and in 1984, Slade released *The Amazing Kamikaze Syndrome*. Called *Keep Your Hands off My Power Supply* in the U.S., the album spawned two minor hits here, including the #20 "Run Runaway." The album reached #33 in the U.S. However, the group didn't get the MTV exposure it took to really put them over and thereafter remained a cult band in the U.S.

By the late 1980s, Slade's European heyday was largely over as well. Nonetheless, the group continued to play out and occasionally record through the 1990s. Noddy Holder became a radio personality and star of an English sitcom. He was named Sir Neville Holder late in the 1990s as well. Lea worked with a band called Whild that got some play in the late 1990s.

DISC.: *Ballzy/Beginnings* (1969); *Play It Loud* (1970); *Slade Alive!* (1972); *Slayed?* (1972); *Sladest* (1973); *Stomp Your Hands, Clap Your Feet* (1974); *Slade in Flames* (1974); *Old New Borrowed & Blue* (1974); *Nobody's Fools* (1976); *Whatever Happened to Slade* (1977); *Alive, Vol. 2* (1978); *Return to Base* (1979); *Slade Alive at Reading '80* (1980); *Till Deaf Do Us Part* (1981); *On Stage* (live; 1982); *The Amazing Kamikaze Syndrome* (1983); *Keep Your Hands off My Power Supply* (1984); *Sladed Alive* (1984); *Rogues Gallery* (1985); *You Boyz Make Big Noize* (1987); *Slade on Stage* (live; 1993); *Crackers* (1994); *Keepin'z Make Big Noize* (1995).—**HB**

Slatkin, Felix, American violinist and conductor, father of **Leonard (Edward) Slatkin**; b. St. Louis, Dec. 22, 1915; d. Los Angeles, Feb. 8, 1963. He studied violin with Zimbalist and conducting with Reiner at the Curtis Inst. of Music in Philadelphia. He was a member of the St. Louis Sym. Orch. (1931–37). In 1937 he went to Los Angeles, where he played in film studio orchs. In 1947 he organized the Hollywood String Quartet, which gave regular performances until it was dissolved in 1961. He also was active as a conductor, especially in programs of light music. In 1939 he married the cellist Eleanor Aller Slatkin (b. N.Y., May 20, 1917; d. Los Angeles, Oct. 12, 1995). She studied with her father and at the Juilliard School of Music in N.Y. At the age of 12 she played at N.Y.'s Carnegie Hall. She was principal cellist in the Warner Brothers studio orch. in Hollywood from 1939 to 1963, and also was a member of the Hollywood String Quartet. From 1968 to 1970 she was head of the string dept. at DePaul Univ. in Chicago.—**NS/LK/DM**

Slatkin, Leonard (Edward), prominent American conductor, son of **Felix Slatkin**; b. Los Angeles, Sept. 1, 1944. He received music training in his youth, studying violin, viola, piano, and conducting, as well as composition with Castelnuovo-Tedesco; after attending Ind. Univ. (1962) and Los Angeles City Coll. (1963), he received valuable advice from Susskind at the Aspen (Colo.) Music School (1964); then studied conducting with Morel at the Juilliard School of Music in N.Y. (Mus.B., 1968). In 1968 he joined the St. Louis Sym. Orch. as asst. conductor to Susskind, and was successively named assoc. conductor (1971), assoc. principal conductor (1974), and principal guest conductor (1975). He made his European debut in London as a guest conductor with the Royal Phil. in 1974. He was music adviser of the New Orleans Phil. (1977–80); also music director of the Minn. Orch. summer concerts (from 1979). In 1979 he became music director of the St. Louis Sym. Orch.; took it on a major European tour in 1985. In 1990 he also became music director of the Great Woods Performing Arts Center in Mansfield, Mass., the summer home of the Pittsburgh Sym. Orch., and in 1991 of the Blossom Music Center, the summer home of the Cleveland Orch. On Oct. 10, 1991, he made his Metropolitan Opera debut in N.Y. conducting *La Fanciulla del West*. In 1992 he was awarded the Elgar Medal. He was named music director designate of the National Sym. Orch. in Washington, D.C., in 1994. After completing his tenure with the St. Louis Sym. Orch. in 1996, he thereafter served as its laureate conductor. In 1996 he assumed his new post as music director of the National Sym. Orch. On Oct. 24, 1997, he led it in the opening of its refurbished concert hall at the Kennedy Center. From 1997 he also was principal guest conductor of the Philharmonia Orch. in London. In 2000 he became chief conductor of the BBC Sym. Orch. while retaining his position with the National Sym. Orch. He appeared widely as a guest conductor of major orchs., both in North America and Europe, demonstrating particular affinity for works of the 19th and 20th centuries. —NS/LK/DM

Slavenski (real name, Štolcer), Josip, outstanding Croatian composer and teacher; b. Čakovec, May 11, 1896; d. Belgrade, Nov. 30, 1955. He studied with Kodály in Budapest and with Novák in Prague. He taught at the Zagreb Cons. (1923–24), then settled in Belgrade, where he taught at the Stankovič Music School; subsequently was a teacher (1937–45) and a prof. (1945–55) at the Academy of Music. About 1930 he adopted the name Slavenski, which he used exclusively in his publ. works. A musician of advanced ideas, he attempted to combine Slavic melodic and rhythmic elements with modern ingredients; he experimented with nontempered scales and devised a "natural" scale of 53 degrees to the octave. His significance was only fully recognized in his homeland after his death.

WORKS: DRAMATIC: Incidental music; film scores. **ORCH.:** *Nocturne* (1916; rev. 1920); *Chaos* (1918–32); *Prasimfonia* ("protosymphony") for Organ, Piano, and Orch. (1919–26); *Balkanophonia*, suite (1927; Berlin, Jan. 25, 1929); Violin Concerto (1927); 2 suites (1929, 1935); *Religiophonia (Simfonija orijenta)* for Solo Voices, Chorus, and Orch. (1934); *Muika za film* (1936); Muzika for Chamber Orch. (1938); *4 balkanske igre* (4 Balkan Dances; 1938); *Simfonijski epos* (1944–46); Piano Concerto (1951; unfinished). **CHAMBER:** 4 string quartets (1923; *Lyric*, 1928; 1938; c. 1949, arr. from the *4 Balkan Dances* for Orch., 1938); *Slavenska*, violin sonata (1924); *Sonata religiosa* for Violin and Organ (1925); Wind Quintet (1930); Piano Trio (1930); piano pieces. **VOCAL:** *Pesme moje majik* (Songs of My Mother) for Alto and String Quartet (1944); choral pieces.—NS/LK/DM

Slavický, Klement, Czech composer; b. Tovačov, Sept. 22, 1910; d. Prague, Sept. 8, 1999. He entered the Prague Cons. in 1927 to study composition with Jirák, and also received training there in conducting, piano, and viola. His advanced training was also completed there as a student of Suk and Talich (1931–33). He subsequently worked at the Czech Radio in Prague. His first Sinfonietta was awarded the prize of the Czech Academy of Sciences and Arts in 1941. In spite of the notable success of his *3 Compositions* for Piano at the Prague Spring Festival in 1947, the Communist regime branded his music as formalistic in 1949 and in 1951 he was forced to leave the Czech Radio. When he refused to join the Communist Party, he was expelled from the Union of Czech Composers and spent many years working outside official musical life. However, his music continued to be heard. With the Soviet-bloc invasion of Czechoslovakia in 1968, Slavický's music was banned for the next decade. His fourth Sinfonietta, *Pax hominibus in universo orbi*, dedicated to the United Nations in honor of its 40th anniversary in 1985, was awarded the U.N. Gold Commemorative Medal. When the Communist regime finally recognized his talent with its title of National Artist in 1989, Slavický refused to accept the title. With the collapse of the Communist regime later that year, he emerged as a respected elder statesman of Czech musical life. In his music, Slavický generally wrote scores notable for their technical complexity and assured handling of instrumental resources. On occasion he also utilized Moravian folk melos.

WORKS: ORCH.: *Fantasy* for Piano and Orch. (1931); 4 sinfoniettas: No. 1 (1940), No. 2 (1962), No. 3, *Concerto for Orchestra* (1980), and No. 4, *Pas hominibus in universo orbi*, for Strings, Keyboard, Percussion, Voice, Reciter, and Organ (1984); *Moravian Dance Fantasies* (1951); *Rhapsodic Variations* (1953). **CHAMBER:** 2 string quartets (1932, 1972); *2 Compositions* for Cello and Piano (1936); Trio for Oboe, Clarinet, and Bassoon (1937); Suite for Oboe and Piano (1959); *Partita* for Violin (1963); *Intermezzi Mattutini* for Flute and Harp (1965); *Trialog* for Violin, Clarinet, and Piano (1966); *Capriccio* for Horn and Piano (1967); *Musica monologica* for Harp (1973); *Poem and Rondo* for Cello and Piano (1973); Violin Sonata, *Friendship* (1974); *Sentenze* for Trombone and Piano (1976); *Playing in 2 and 3* for Young Violinists (1986); *Rhapsody* for Viola (1987); *Musica* for Horn (1988). **KEYBOARD: Piano:** 3 Compositions (1947); Sonata, *Meditation on Life* (1958); *On the Black and White* (1958); *Piano and Youth* (1958); *12 Small Études* (1964); *Études and Essays* (1965); Suite for Piano, 4-Hands (1968); *A Song for the Homeland and Furiat* for Piano, 4-Hands (1971). **Harpsichord:** 3 Studies (1983). **VOCAL:** *To Nature* for High Voice and Orch. (1942); *Lidice* for Double Men's Chorus (1945); *Šohajé*, Moravian love songs for Women's Chorus (1948; rev. 1950–51); *Madrigals* for Chamber Chorus (1959); *Psalms* for Soprano, Alto, Tenor, Bass, Chorus, and Organ (1970); *A Path Towards the Light*, dramatic fresco for Tenor, Reciter, and Men's Chorus (1980); *The Homeland* for Chorus (1982); other choral pieces and songs. —NS/LK/DM

Slavík, Josef, Bohemian violinist and composer; b. Jince, March 26, 1806; d. Budapest, May 30, 1833. He studied violin with Pixis and theory and composition with B. Weber at the Prague Cons. (1816–23). He went to Vienna in 1826, then went on a concert tour. In 1829 he was appointed to the court chapel in Vienna, and became a friend of Schubert, who dedicated to him his Fantasia in C major, D.934, which Slavík performed for the first time on Jan. 20, 1828. Among his own compositions are a Violin Concerto (1823) and *Grand Potpourri* for Violin and Orch. (1826).

BIBL.: J. Pohl, *J. S.: Český houslista* (J. S.: Czech Violinist; Prague, 1906); S. Klima, *J. S.* (Prague, 1956); L. Ginzburg, *J. S.* (Moscow, 1957).—**NS/LK/DM**

Slawson, Wayne, American composer and music theorist; b. Detroit, Dec. 29, 1932. He studied at the Univ. of Mich. (B.A. in mathematics, 1955; M.A. in composition, 1959) and Harvard Univ. (Ph.D. in psychoacoustics, 1965). He was a computer programmer and systems analyst with the U.S. Air Force, the Rand Corp. in Santa Monica, Calif. (1955–57), and the Mitre Corp. in Bedford, Mass. (1959–62), specializing in speech synthesis. He taught at Yale Univ. (1967–72), the Univ. of Pittsburgh (1972–86; prof. from 1984), and the Univ. of Calif. at Davis (from 1986), where he directed the Computer and Electronic Music Studio. He composed MUCH, electronic music from various sources, with Robert Morris (1971–74); developed the music and speech synthesis programs MUSE (1961) and SYNTAL (1969–89); publ. numerous articles on theory and psychoacoustics, his monograph *Sound Color* (Berkeley, 1985) seeking to systematize timbre for analytical and compositional purposes.

WORKS: ORCH.: *Motions* (1973). **CHAMBER:** *5 Turns for 10* for Variable Ensemble (1970); *Pieces* for String Quartet (1970; rev. and aug. as *Limits*, 1977); *Reflections* for Cello and Piano (1975; rev. and aug. as *Rereflections*, 1988); *Variations* for 2 Violins (1977); *Triad* for Clarinet, Horn, and Cello (1984); *Quick Trick* for String Quartet (1987); *Interpolation of Dance* for String Quartet (1992). **VOCAL:** *Music for an Ordination* for Organ and Chorus (1963); *Pity...Not* for Chorus (1974); *Omaggio a Petrarca* for Chorus (1975); *Minglings* for Men's Chorus (1976); *Warm Shades*, octet for Singers and Woodwinds (1993). **COMPUTER:** *Colors* (1981); *Greetings* (1985); *Quatrains Miniatures I-V* (1985); *Swapper I* (1989; rev. and aug. as *If These 2 Tolled*, 1990). **TAPE:** *Wishful Thinking about Winter* (1967); *Death, Love, and the Maiden* (1975); *poor flesh and trees, poor stars and stones* (1977).—**NS/LK/DM**

Sledge, Percy, soul singer who earned the first gold record for Atlantic records; b. Leighton, Ala., Nov. 25, 1940. Percy Sledge's first record was undoubtedly his most famous. "When a Man Loves a Woman," wrought with soul, passion, and emotion, topped the pop charts for two weeks in 1966, sent four weeks atop the R&B charts, and became the first gold record on the walls of Atlantic records. In the process, Sledge helped establish the entire Muscle Shoals, Ala. music scene.

In the early 1960s, Sledge was working on the family farm and as a hospital orderly by day; at night, he sang in a gospel group at the Galilee Baptist Church and with the Esquires, a popular local act in Ala. Ala. music business impresario Quinn Ivy was impressed by Sledge's voice and took him into his studio. Ivy released "When a Man Loves a Woman" independently, then licensed the song to Atlantic records, which ultimately bought Sledge's contract. Over the course of 1966, he put out two more chart singles, "Warm and Tender Love" (#17) and "It Tears Me Up" (#20). However, in 1967, his "Love Me Tender" barely scraped into the Top 40, and in 1968, he had his last pop hit, "Take Time to Know Her," which rose to #11. After that, Sledge all but fell by the pop music wayside. He recorded for Atlantic for another six years without a great deal of success, moving to Capricorn records in the early 1970s. There he scored a minor R&B hit with "I'll Be Your Everything." He split most of the 1970s and 1980s between various day jobs and stints on the road.

In 1987 his version of "When a Man Loves a Woman" turned up as the soundtrack to a commercial for jeans and the soundtrack to the Oliver Stone film *Platoon*. This led to a minor revival that saw him appear on *Saturday Night Live* and other TV shows. In 1989 the R&B foundation made him one of their first Career Achievement winners. Michael Bolton revived "When a Man" again in 1991. Bolton won a Best Pop Vocal Performance, Male Grammy, but somehow managed to forget to acknowledge the original performer and writer of the song while accepting his award. However, the renewed visibility led to Sledge signing with Virgin's Pointblank blues imprint. In 1994, he released *Blue Light*, his first new album in over 20 years. It featured Bobby Womack, Steve Cropper, and Mick Taylor. Four years later, he was recording for a small independent label, issuing the *Wanted Again* album.

DISC.: *Warm & Tender Soul* (1966); *When a Man Loves a Woman* (1966); *The Percy Sledge Way* (1967); *Take Time to Know Her* (1968); *Golden Voice of Soul* (1974); *I'll Be Your Everything* (1974); *It Tears Me Up* (1992); *Percy Sledge* (1994); *Blue Light* (1994); *Wanted Again* (1998).—**HB**

Slenczynska, Ruth, American pianist of precocious talent; b. Sacramento, Calif., Jan. 15, 1925. Her father, a violinist, subjected her to severe discipline when her musical talent was revealed in early childhood; she was only 4 when she began piano lessons with Alma Schmidt-Kennedy; played in public in Berlin at 6 years and with an orch. in Paris at 11. She made a sensation and was acclaimed by European critics as a prodigy of nature; she took lessons with Petri, Schnabel, Cortot, and others in Europe and America, and even played for Rachmaninoff, who became interested in her destiny. However, she developed psychological difficulties with her father, whose promotion of her career became obsessive, and had to cease public appearances; when she played concerts at the age of 15, the critics characterized her performances as mechanical reproductions of the music, seemingly without any personal projection. She then withdrew from public performances; after taking a degree in psychology at the Univ. of Calif. at Berkeley (1954), she resumed her career; also taught at Southern Ill. Univ. at Edwardsville (1964–90). She publ. a book of memoirs (with L. Biancolli), *Forbidden Childhood* (N.Y., 1957), in which she recounted the

troubles of a child prodigy's life; she also brought out a pedagogical ed., *Music at Your Fingertips. Aspects of Pianoforte Technique* (with A. Lingg; N.Y., 1961).
—NS/LK/DM

Slezak, Leo, famous Austrian tenor; b. Mährisch-Schönberg, Moravia, Aug. 18, 1873; d. Egern am Tegernsee, Bavaria, June 1, 1946. He studied with Adolf Robinson; as a youth, sang in the chorus of the Brünn Opera, making his operatic debut there as Lohengrin (March 17, 1896), one of his finest roles. He appeared with the Berlin Royal Opera (1898–99); in 1901 he became a member of the Vienna Opera, where he was active until 1926; also performed frequently in Prague, Milan, and Munich. He made his London debut with marked acclaim as Lohengrin, May 18, 1900, at Covent Garden; not satisfied with his vocal training, he went to Paris, where he studied with Jean de Reszke in 1907. He appeared in America for the first time as Otello with the Metropolitan Opera in N.Y. (Nov. 17, 1909); remained with the company until 1913. He returned to the Vienna Opera as a guest artist, making his farewell appearance in *Pagliacci* on Sept. 26, 1933. Slezak also toured widely as a recitalist of impeccable taste; also made some appearances in films. He was a man of great general culture, and possessed an exceptionally sharp literary wit, which he displayed in his reminiscences, *Meine sämtlichen Werke* (1922) and *Der Wortbruch* (1927); both were later combined in a single vol. (1935; Eng. tr. as *Songs of Motley: Being the Reminiscences of a Hungry Tenor*, London, 1938); he also publ. *Der Rückfall* (1940). A final book of memoirs, *Mein Lebensmärchen*, was publ. posthumously (1948). His son, the film actor Walter Slezak, publ. Slezak's letters, *Mein lieber Bub. Briefe eines besorgten Vaters* (Munich, 1966), and *What Time's the Next Swan?* (N.Y., 1962), alluding to the possibly apocryphal story of the swan failing to arrive in time during one of his father's performances as Lohengrin, thus prompting the non-Wagnerian query from the hapless hero.

BIBL.: L. Kleinenberger, *L. S.* (Munich, 1910).—NS/LK/DM

Slobodianik, Alexander, brilliant Russian pianist; b. Kiev, Sept. 5, 1941. He studied at the Moscow Cons. with Gornostaeva, graduating in 1964. In 1966 he received fourth prize at the Tchaikovsky Competition in Moscow. He subsequently undertook numerous concert tours in Russia and abroad. He was particularly successful during his American tours in the 1970s. Like most Russian pianists who venture abroad, he astounds by his unlimited technical resources, but he is also appreciated for the romantic elan of his playing.
—NS/LK/DM

Slobodskaya, Oda, esteemed Russian soprano; b. Vilnius, Dec. 10, 1888; d. London, July 29, 1970. She studied at the St. Petersburg Cons. She made her operatic debut as Lisa in *The Queen of Spades* at the Maryinsky Theater there in 1917. She also sang the regular repertoire there, including the roles of Marguerite in *Faust* and *Aida*. She emigrated in 1922; sang in Paris, at La Scala in Milan, and in Buenos Aires; eventually settled in London; sang Venus in *Tannhäuser*

at Covent Garden in 1932. She developed an active career in England, establishing herself as an authoritative interpreter of Russian songs in recital; she also joined the faculty of the Guildhall School of Music and proved a sympathetic and effective voice teacher.

BIBL.: M. Leonard, *S.: A Biography of O. S.* (London, 1978).
—NS/LK/DM

Slonimsky, Nicolas (actually, **Nikolai Leonidovich**), legendary Russian-born American musicologist of manifold endeavors, uncle of **Sergei (Mikhailovich) Slonimsky;** b. St. Petersburg, April 27, 1894; d. Los Angeles, Dec. 25, 1995. A self-described failed *wunderkind*, he was given his first piano lesson by his illustrious maternal aunt **Isabelle Vengerova**, on Nov. 6, 1900, according to the old Russian calendar. Possessed by inordinate ambition, aggravated by the endemic intellectuality of his family of both maternal and paternal branches (novelists, revolutionary poets, literary critics, university professors, translators, chessmasters, economists, mathematicians, inventors of useless artificial languages, Hebrew scholars, speculative philosophers), he became determined to excel beyond common decency in all these doctrines. As an adolescent, he wrote out his future biography accordingly, setting down his death date as 1967, but survived. He enrolled in the St. Petersburg Cons. and studied harmony and orchestration with Kalafati and Maximilian Steinberg. He also tried unsuccessfully to engage in Russian journalism. After the Revolution, he made his way south. He was a rehearsal pianist at the Kiev Opera, where he took some composition lessons with Glière (1919), and then in Yalta (1920), where he earned his living as a piano accompanist to displaced Russian singers, and as an instructor at a dilapidated Yalta Cons. He thence proceeded to Turkey, Bulgaria, and Paris, where he became secretary and piano-pounder to Serge Koussevitzky. In 1923 he went to the U.S. and became coach in the opera dept. of the Eastman School of Music in Rochester, N.Y., where he took an opportunity to study some more composition with the visiting prof. Selim Palmgren, and conducting with Albert Coates. In 1925 he was again with Koussevitzky in Paris and Boston, but was fired for insubordination in 1927. He learned to speak polysyllabic English and began writing music articles for the *Boston Evening Transcript* and the *Christian Science Monitor* and ran a monthly column of musical anecdotes of questionable authenticity in *Etude* magazine. He also taught theory at the Malkin Cons. in Boston and at the Boston Cons. Slonimsky conducted the Pierian Sodality at Harvard Univ. (1927–29) and the Apollo Chorus (1928–30). In 1927 he organized the Chamber Orch. of Boston with the purpose of presenting modern works; with it he gave first performances of works by Charles Ives, Edgar Varèse, Henry Cowell, and others. He became a naturalized American citizen in 1931. In 1931–32 he conducted special concerts of modern American, Cuban, and Mexican music in Paris, Berlin, and Budapest under the auspices of the Pan-American Assn. of Composers, producing a ripple of excitement; he repeated these programs at his engagements with the Los Angeles Phil. (1932) and at the Hollywood Bowl (1933), which created such consternation that his conducting career came to a jarring halt. From 1945 to 1947 he was, by accident (the head of the dept. had died of a heart attack), lecturer in Slavonic languages and literatures at Harvard Univ. In 1962–63 he traveled in Russia, Poland, Yugoslavia, Bulgaria, Romania, Greece, and Israel under the auspices of the Office of Cultural Exchange at the U.S. State Dept., as a lecturer in native Russian, ersatz Polish, synthetic Serbo-Croatian, Russianized Bulgarian, Latinized Romanian, archaic Greek, passable French, and tolerable German. Returning from his multinational travels, he taught variegated musical subjects at the Univ. of Calif. at Los Angeles, but was irretrievably retired after a triennial service (1964–67), ostensibly owing to irreversible obsolescence and recessive infantiloquy. However, disdaining the inexorable statistics of the actuarial tables, he continued to agitate and even gave long-winded lecture-recitals in institutions of both dubious and non-dubious learning. In 1987 he received a Guggenheim fellowship. In 1991 he was inducted as an honorary member of the American Academy and Inst. of Arts and Letters for his manifold contributions to music. As a composer, he cultivated miniature forms, usually with a gimmick, e.g., *Studies in Black and White* in "mutually exclusive consonant counterpoint" for Piano (1928; orchestrated as *Piccolo Divertimento*; Los Angeles Phil. New Music Group, Oct. 17, 1983), a song cycle, *Gravestones*, to texts from tombstones in an old cemetery in Hancock, N.H. (1945), and *Minitudes*, a collection of 50 quaquaversal piano pieces (1971–77). His only decent orch. work is *My Toy Balloon* (1942), a set of variations on a Brazilian song, which includes in the score 100 colored balloons to be exploded *f f f* at the climax. He also conjured up a *Möbius Strip-Tease*, a perpetual vocal canon notated on a Möbius band to be revolved around the singer's head; it had its first and last performance at the Arrière-Garde Coffee Concert at UCLA on May 5, 1965, with the composer officiating at the piano non-obbligato. A priority must be conceded to him for writing the earliest singing commercials to authentic texts from the *Saturday Evening Post* advertisements, among them *Make This a Day of Pepsodent, No More Shiny Nose*, and *Children Cry for Castoria* (1925). More "scholarly," though no less defiant of academic conventions, is his *Thesaurus of Scales and Melodic Patterns* (1947), an inventory of all conceivable and inconceivable tonal combinations, culminating in a mind-boggling "Grandmother Chord" containing 12 different tones and 11 different intervals. Beset by a chronic itch for novelty, he coined the term "pandiatonicism" (1937), which, *mirabile dictu*, took root and even got into reputable reference works, including the 15th ed. of the *Encyclopaedia Britannica*. In his quest for trivial but not readily accessible information, Slonimsky blundered into the muddy field of musical lexicography. He publ. the now-classic *Music since 1900*, a chronology of musical events, which actually contains some beguiling serendipities (N.Y., 1937; 5th ed., rev., 1994), took over the vacated editorship (because of the predecessor's sudden death during sleep) of Thompson's *International Cyclopedia of Music and Musicians* (4th to 8th eds., 1946–58), and accepted the editorship of the 5th, 6th, 7th, and 8th eds. of the prestigious *Baker's Biographical Dic-*

tionary of Musicians* (N.Y., 1958, 1978, 1984, 1992). He also abridged this venerable vol. into *The Concise Baker's Biographical Dictionary of Musicians* (N.Y., 1988). In 1978 he mobilized his powers of retrospection in preparing an autobiography, *Failed Wunderkind*, subtitled *Rueful Autopsy* (in the sense of self- observation, not dissection of the body); the publishers, deeming these titles too lugubrious, renamed it *Perfect Pitch* (N.Y., 1988). He also translated Boris de Schloezer's biography of Scriabin from the original Russian (Berkeley and Los Angeles, 1987), which was followed by his *Lectionary of Music*, a compendium of articles on music (N.Y., 1988). His other writings include *Music of Latin America* (N.Y., 1945; several reprints; also in Spanish, Buenos Aires, 1947); *The Road to Music*, ostensibly for children (N.Y., 1947); *A Thing or Two about Music* (N.Y., 1948; inconsequential; also lacking an index); *Lexicon of Musical Invective*, a random collection of pejorative reviews of musical masterpieces (N.Y., 1952); numerous articles for encyclopedias; also a learned paper, *Sex and the Music Librarian*, valuable for its painstaking research; the paper was delivered by proxy, to tumultuous cachinnations, at a symposium of the Music Library Assn., at Chapel Hill, N.C., Feb. 2, 1968. R. Kostelanetz ed. a collection of his writings as *Nicolas Slonimsky: The First Hundred Years* (N.Y., 1994). His much-lamented death, just 4 months before his 102nd birthday, brought to a close one of the most remarkable careers in the annals of 20th century music.—**NS/LK/DM**

Slonimsky, Sergei (Mikhailovich), greatly talented Russian composer, nephew of **Nicolas (Nikolai Leonidovich) Slonimsky;** b. Leningrad, Aug. 12, 1932. A member of a highly intellectual family (his father was a well-known Soviet author; his paternal grandfather, an economist, the author of the first book on Karl Marx in the Russian language; his father's maternal uncle was a celebrated Russian ed. and literary critic; his father's maternal aunt was the noted piano teacher Isabelle Vengerova), he studied at the Leningrad Cons., taking composition with Boris Arapov and Orest Evlakhov (graduated, 1955) and piano with Vladimir Nilsen (graduated, 1956); he also took courses in musicology with F. Rubtzov (folk music) and N. Uspensky (polyphonic analysis). While a student, he wrote a fairy-tale suite, *Frog-Princess*, and in 1951 composed a string quartet on Russian folk motifs. In 1959 he was appointed to the faculty of the Leningrad Cons. For further study of folk music he traveled into the countryside, in the rural regions of Pskov and Novgorod. Concurrently, he explored the technical modalities of new music, in the tradition of Soviet modernism, evolving a considerable complexity of texture in a framework of dissonant counterpoint, while safeguarding the tonal foundation in triadic progressions. Some of his works, such as his opera *Virineya*, represent a contemporary evolution of the Russian national school of composition, broadly diatonic and spaciously songful; his other works tend toward ultramodern practices, including polytonality, microtonality, dodecaphony, tone-clusters, amplified sound, prepared piano, electronic sonorism, aleatory proceedings, and spatial placement of instruments. His *Concerto for Orchestra* employs electronically amplified guitars and solo instruments; even more advanced is his *Antiphones* for String Quartet, employing non-tempered tuning and an "ambulatory" setting, in which the players are placed in different parts of the hall and then walk, while playing, en route to the podium; the piece is especially popular at modern music festivals. A prolific composer, he has written 10 syms. and a remarkably varied catalogue of chamber music pieces which he produces with a facility worthy of Rossini. He also has an easy hand with choral works. Although his natural impulse tends towards the newest sound elements, he proves remarkably successful in gathering and transforming folk motifs and rhythms, as in his Novgorod choruses, composed for the American Festival of Soviet Music of 1988. The most unusual subject, for a Soviet composer, was an opera based on the life and death of the Catholic Queen of Scotland, Mary Stuart. Mary Stuart was first performed in Kuibishev on Oct. 1, 1983, and then subsequently performed in Leningrad and in Leipzig (1984). It was then selected for a gala production at the Edinburgh Festival in Scotland, where it was given on Aug. 22, 1986, by the Leningrad Opera in a performance in the Russian language. The score utilizes authentic Scottish folk songs, suitably arranged in modern harmonies, as well as original themes in the pentatonic scale. The opera received the prestigious Glinka Prize in 1983. Slonimsky encountered considerable difficulties in producing his chamber opera, *The Master and Margarita*, after a novel by Bulgakov, because the subject had to do with mystical religious events. The Soviet authorities delayed its production for nearly 15 years. Finally, with a liberal change in the political climate, the opera was performed, first in East Germany, and, eventually and to considerable acclaim, in Leningrad, on Dec. 1, 1989. Practically all of Slonimsky's music, including the operas, has been publ. Apart from his work as a composer and teacher, he contributes music criticism to Russian magazines; he also publ. a valuable analytic survey of the symphonies of Prokofiev (Leningrad, 1976).

WORKS: DRAMATIC: O p e r a : *Virineya* (Leningrad, Sept. 30, 1967); *The Master and Margarita*, chamber opera, after Bulgakov (1973; Leningrad, Dec. 1, 1989); *Mary Stuart*, opera-ballad (1978–80; Kuibishev, Jan. 31, 1981); *Hamlet* (1992). **B a l - l e t :** *Icarus* (1962–69; Moscow, May 29, 1971). **O t h e r :** Incidental music and film scores. **ORCH.:** *Carnival Overture* (1957); 10 syms.: No. 1 (1958; Leningrad, March 11, 1962), No. 2 (1977; Leningrad, Sept. 21, 1979), No. 3 (Leningrad, Dec. 15, 1982), No. 4, dedicated to the memory of his father (Kuibishev, Oct. 1, 1983), No. 5 (1983; Kuibishev, Oct. 1, 1984), No. 6 (1983; Leningrad, June 21, 1986), No. 7 (1984; Leningrad, June 21, 1986), No. 8 for Chamber Orch. (Vilnius, Sept. 30, 1985), No. 9 (Leningrad, Feb. 18, 1989), and No. 10 (1992); *Choreographic Miniatures* (1964); *Concerto buffo* (1964–65; Leningrad, April 28, 1966); Concerto for Sym. Orch., 3 Electric Guitars, and Solo Instruments (1973; Leningrad, Feb. 9, 1974); *Dramatic Song* (1974); *Festive Music* for Balalaika, Castanets, and Orch. (1975); *Symphonic Motet* (1976); *Quiet Music* (1981; Leningrad, March 7, 1982); *Concerto primaverile* for Violin and String Orch. (Vilnius, Oct. 8, 1983, Sergei Stadler soloist). **CHAMBER:** String Quartet on Russian Themes (1951); 2 Pieces for Viola and Piano (1956); Suite for Viola and Piano (1959); Sonata for Solo Violin (1960); *Chromatic Flute and Humoresque* for Flute (1961); 3 Pieces for Cello (1964); *Dialogues* for Wind Quintet (1964); *Antiphones* for String Quartet (1968); *Sonatina allegro* for Horn and Piano (1974); *Monologue and Toccata* for Clarinet and Piano (1974); *Solo espressivo* for Oboe (1975); *Exotic Suite* for 2 Violins, 2 Electric Guitars, Saxophone, and Percussion (1976; Leningrad, Nov. 3, 1978); *Legend* for Domra and Piano (1976); *Merry Rondo* for Domra and Piano (1976); *Novgorod Dance* for Clarinet, Trombone, Cello, Piano, and Percussion (1980); *Rondo*, on a theme by Gounod, for Trumpet and Piano (1980); *Musica lirica* for Flute, Violin, and Harpsichord (1981); *Dithyramb* for Cello Ensemble and Piano (1982); *In the World of Animals*, children's suite for Cello and Piano (1982); Suite (Seattle, July 1990). **KEY-BOARD: P i a n o :** Sonata (1962); *Three Graces*, suite (1964); *Children's Pieces* (1970); *Coloristic Fantasy* (1972); *Tiny Pieces* for children (1973); *Serenade from a Musical*, street song (1976); *Round Dance and Merry Rumba* (1977); *Charlie Chaplin Whistles On* (1978); *Cat's Lullaby* (1978); *Hungarian March* for Piano, 4-Hands (1980); *Intermezzo in Memory of Brahms* (1980); *Travel Suite* (1981); *Romantic Waltz* (1982); *Variations on a Theme by Mussorgsky* (1984); 3 pieces: *Jump Rope, Blues*, and *Metro* (1984); 24 Preludes and Fugues (1993). **O r g a n :** *Pastorale and Toccata* (1961); *Chromatic Poem* (1969); *Round Dance and Fugue* (1976); *Rondo-Humoresque* (1979). **VOCAL:** *Songs of Freedom*, on Russian folk motifs, for Mezzo-soprano, Baritone, and Piano (1957); *Spring has arrived*, vocal cycle for Voice and Piano, after Japanese poets (1958); *Polish Stanzas*, vocal cycle, after the Polish poet Anthoni Slonimski, first cousin of the composer's father (1963); *Lyric Stanzas*, vocal cycle for Voice and Piano (1964); *Voice from the Chorus*, cantata, after Alexander Blok (1964); *Farewell to a Friend* for Voice and Piano (1966); *Monologues* for Soprano, Oboe, Horn, and Harp (1967); 2 *Russian Songs* for Chorus (1968); 6 *Songs*, after Anna Akhmatova (1969); *Northern Landscapes* for Chorus (1969); *Merry Songs* for Voice and Piano (1971); *Choral Games* for Children's Chorus, Boy Soloist, and 2 Percussion Instruments (1972); *Evening Music* for Chorus (1973); 4 *Songs*, after Osip Mandelstam (1974); 10 *Songs*, after Anna Akhmatova (1974); 4 *Russian Songs* for Chorus (1974); *Virineya*, suite-oratorio from the opera of the same name (1974); *Pesnohorka* (Sing-Chorus) for Contralto, Flute, Oboe, Trumpet, Balalaika, Accordion, 3 Electric Guitars, Castanets, and Vibraphone, on Russian folk songs (1975); *Songs of the Troubadours*, vocal cycle on old French ballads for Soprano, Tenor, 4 Recorders, and Lute (1975); *Songs of Songs* for Soprano, Tenor, Chorus, Oboe, Horn, and Harp (1975); *Bashkir Girl's Song* for Voice, Flute, and 2 Bongos (1977); *Quiet Flows the Don* for Chorus, to words of old Cossack chants, after Sholokhov's novel (1977); 2 *Poems* for Chorus, after Pushkin (1979); Suite from the opera *Mary Stuart* for Chorus and Orch. (1980); 2 *Songs* for Mezzo-soprano and Piano, after Alexander Blok (1980); *White Night* for Chorus (1980); *Morning Song* for Children's Chorus and Snare Drum (1981); *Strophes of Dhammapada* for Soprano, Harp, and Percussion, after the classic Buddhist epic (1983; Leningrad, Feb. 21, 1984); *Song of Leningrad* for Bass, Chorus, and Orch. (1983); *Little Triptych* for Chorus (1983); 2 *Vocalises* for Soprano and Mezzo-soprano (1983); *Railroad* for Chorus, Trumpet, Piano, and Percussion (1983); *White Night in Leningrad* for Chorus (1983); 4 *Strophes* for Chorus, after Sophocles' *Oedipus Colonus* (1983).

BIBL.: A. Milka, *S. S.* (Leningrad, 1976).—NS/LK/DM

Slovák, Ladislav, Slovak conductor; b. Bratislava, Sept. 9, 1919. He studied organ and conducting at the Bratislava Cons. (1938–45) and conducting with Talich at the Bratislava Academy of Music (1949–53). He was music director of Bratislava Radio (from 1949), where he founded and conducted its choir; after serving as an assistant to Mravinsky and the Leningrad Phil. (1953–55), he returned to Bratislava as conductor of the Radio Orch. (1955–61); then was chief conductor of the Slovak Phil. there (1961–81) and of the Prague Sym. Orch. (1972–76). In 1964 he was made an Artist of Merit and in 1977 a National Artist by the Czech government. —NS/LK/DM

Sly and The Family Stone, funk-pop-psychedelic band of the 1960s and early 1970s. **MEMBERSHIP:** Sly Stone, lead voc., kybd., gtr. (b. Sylvester Stewart, Dallas, Tex., March 15, 1944); Rosemary Stewart, pno., voc. (b. Vallejo, Calif., March 21, 1945); Freddie Stewart, gtr., voc. (b. June 5, 1946); Larry Graham, bs., voc. (b. Beaumont, Tex., Aug. 14, 1946); Jerry Martini, sax., clarinet, pno., accordion (b. Boulder, Colo., Oct. 1, 1943); Cynthia Robinson, trpt., voc. (b. Sacramento, Calif., Jan. 12, 1946); and Greg Errico, drm. (b. San Francisco, Calif., Sept. 1, 1946).

As a child, Sylvester Stewart moved to Vallejo, Calif., where he sang with siblings Rose and Freddie in the gospel group The Stewart Four, who recorded "On the Battlefield of My Lord" when Sylvester was four. By then, he was already playing drums and guitar, and he eventually taught himself a number of other instruments, including piano and organ. In 1960, he scored a local hit with "Long Time Ago" and later manned The Stewart Brothers (with Freddie) and The Viscanes, who achieved another local hit with "Yellow River" when he was a high school senior. After graduation, he attended junior college and radio broadcasting school and secured disc jockey positions on San Francisco Bay Area black radio stations KSOL and KDIA. In 1964, Stewart met disc jockey Tom Donahue and soon became staff producer for Donahue's Autumn label. There he wrote and produced Bobby Freeman's smash crossover dance hit "C'mon and Swim" and produced the early hits of The Beau Brummels ("Laugh, Laugh," "Just a Little") while recording local groups such as The Vejtables ("I Still Love You"), The Mojo Men ("Dance with Me"), and The Great Society (with Grace Slick). Brother Freddie formed the soul band The Stone Souls in the mid-1960s, while Sylvester led The Stoners, with trumpeter Cynthia Robinson.

Around 1966, The Stoners and The Stone Souls merged to form Sly and The Family Stone. Developing a regional reputation as a live act, the group was joined by the Stewarts' cousin Larry Graham, a veteran multi-instrumentalist, in 1967. Signed with Epic Records, the group's debut album, *A Whole New Thing*, featured shared and contrasted lead vocals, psychedelic lead guitar, complex horn arrangements, and a funky rhythm sound rooted in Graham's bass playing. *Dance to the Music* produced a near-smash pop and rhythm-and-blues hit with the title song, but *Life* fared poorly. Early 1969's *Stand!*, sometimes labeled as soul music's first concept album and regarded as one of the most influential albums of the era, firmly established the group with black and white audiences. It included the classic "I Want to Take You Higher," "Don't Call Me Nigger, Whitey," the ominous "Somebody's Watching You," and "You Can Make It if You Try." The album yielded a major crossover hit with "Stand!" and a top crossover hit with "Everyday People," backed by the funk classic "Sing a Simple Song."

Sly and The Family Stone scored a smash pop and rhythm-and-blues hit with "Hot Fun in the Summertime" just days before their appearance at the Woodstock Festival in August 1969. One of the most dynamic and electrifying acts at the festival, the group next scored a top pop and R&B hit with "Thank You (Falettinme Be Mice Elf Agin)," backed with "Everybody Is a Star." However, Stewart became mired in legal and drug-related problems and, by 1971, the group had developed a reputation for failing to show up at scheduled concerts, a circumstance that occasionally led to riots, as it did in Chicago. Their next album of new material, the ironically titled *There's a Riot Goin' On*, came more than two years after the release of *Stand!* and revealed a darker, disillusioned side to Sly's songwriting. The album yielded a top pop and rhythm-and-blues hit with "Family Affair" and a major crossover hit with "Runnin' Away."

Sly and The Family Stone subsequently suffered the departures of bassist Larry Graham and drummer Greg Errico. Their next album, 1973's *Fresh*, produced a major pop and smash R&B hit with "If You Want Me to Stay." Sylvester Stewart married Kathy Silva in June 1974 during a concert at Madison Square Garden attended by 23,000 fans. Sly and The Family Stone achieved their last important hit soon thereafter with "Time for Livin'," a moderate pop and near-smash rhythm-and-blues hit.

Upon departure, Larry Graham formed Hot Chocolate, and the group evolved into Graham Central Station. Signed to Warner Bros. Records, the group became one of the era's most popular funk bands, scoring a moderate pop and near-smash R&B hit with "Can You Handle It" in 1974. *Ain't No 'Bout-A-Doubt It*, the group's best-selling album, yielded a moderate pop and top rhythm-and-blues hit with "Your Love" and major R&B hits with "It's Alright" and "The Jam." Subsequent albums sold progressively less well as the group scored rhythm-and-blues hits with "Love," "Now Do-U-Wanta Dance," and "My Radio Sure Sounds Good to Me" through 1978. In 1980, Graham went solo, achieving his biggest success with his debut album *One in a Million You* and its two smash R&B hits "One in a Million You" (a near-smash pop hit) and "When We Get Married." After the 1981 R&B smash "Just Be My Lady," Graham's popularity waned. In 1987, he dueted with Aretha Franklin on her minor R&B hit "If You Need My Love Tonight." Graham Central Station reassembled for a brief Japanese tour in 1992 and ultimately reunited with five of its six original members in 1995 to tour and once again record for Warner Bros.

By 1978, Jerry Martini had joined Rubicon with Jack Blades and Brad Gillis, scoring a major hit with "I'm Gonna Take Care of Everything." In the meantime, Sylvester Stewart's career was in serious trouble. He filed for bankruptcy in 1976 and switched record labels in 1979. In the early 1980s, he toured and recorded with George Clinton's Funkadelic, appearing on 1981's *The Electric Spanking of War Babies*. He recorded his final Sly and The Family Stone album in 1983. Thereafter better known for his legal and drug problems, Stewart unsuccessfully attempted comebacks with Bobby Womack in 1984 and 1987. He managed a minor pop and smash R&B hit in 1986 with "Crazay," recorded with Jesse Johnson of The Time. Sly and The Family Stone were inducted into the Rock and Roll Hall of Fame in 1993.

DISC.: SLY AND THE FAMILY STONE: *A Whole New Thing* (1967); *Dance to the Music* (1968); *Life* (1968); *Stand!* (1969/1986); *Greatest Hits* (1970); *There's a Riot Goin' On* (1971); *Fresh* (1973); *Small Talk* (1974); *High Energy* (1975); *Heard Ya Missed Me, Well, I'm Back* (1976); *Ten Years Too Soon* (1979); *Back on the Right Track* (1979); *Ain't but the One Way* (1983); *Slyest Freshest Funkiest Rarest Cuts* (1996). **SLY STONE:** *High on You* (1975). **GRAHAM CENTRAL STATION:** *Graham Central Station* (1973/1991); *Release Yourself* (1974/1991); *Ain't No 'Bout-A-Doubt It* (1975); *Mirror* (1976); *Now Do U Wanta Dance* (1977); *My Radio Sure Sounds Good to Me* (1978); *Star Walk* (1979); *Graham Central* (1996). **LARRY GRAHAM:** *One in a Million You* (1980); *Just Be My Lady* (1981); *Sooner or Later* (1982); *Victory* (1983); *Fired Up* (1985). **RUBICON:** *Rubicon* (1978).—BH

Smallens, Alexander,

Russian-born American conductor; b. St. Petersburg, Jan. 1, 1889; d. Tucson, Ariz., Nov. 24, 1972. He was taken to the U.S. as a child, and became a American naturalized citizen in 1919. He studied at the Inst. of Musical Art and the Coll. of the City of N.Y. (B.A., 1909), then took courses at the Paris Cons. (1909). He was asst. conductor of the Boston Opera (1911–14), he accompanied the Anna Pavlova Ballet Co. on a tour of South America (1915–18), and he then was on the staff of the Chicago Opera (1919–23) and of the Philadelphia Civic Opera (1924–31). From 1927 to 1934 he was asst. conductor of the Philadelphia Orch., and from 1947 to 1950 music director at Radio City Music Hall in N.Y. In 1934 he conducted the premiere of Gershwin's *Porgy and Bess* in Boston; conducted it on a European tour in 1956. He retired in 1958. —NS/LK/DM

Smalley, Roger,

English pianist, composer, and teacher; b. Swinton, Manchester, July 26, 1943. He studied piano with Antony Hopkins and composition with Peter Racine Fricker and John White at the Royal Coll. of Music in London (1961–65); also took private composition lessons with Goehr and attended Stockhausen's Cologne course for new music (1965). With Tim Souster, he founded the contemporary music ensemble Intermodulation, with which he toured extensively in Europe until 1976. In 1968 he became the first artist- in-residence at King's Coll., Cambridge; in 1974 he was named musician-in- residence at the Univ. of Western Australia, where he became a research fellow (1976) and then senior lecturer. As a pianist, he consistently champions avant- garde music. His compositions are steeped in electronic and aleatory techniques.

WORKS: DRAMATIC: Music Theater: *William Derrincourt*, entertainment for Baritone, Men's Chorus, and Instrumental Ensemble (1978; Perth, Aug. 31, 1979); *The Narrow Road to the Deep North*, "journey" for Baritone and 6 Players (London, Nov. 29, 1983). **ORCH.:** *Variations* for Strings (1964); *Gloria Tibi Trinitas* (1965; rev. 1969; Liverpool, Sept. 30, 1969); *Beat Music* for Percussion, Electric Organ, Viola, Soprano Saxo-

phone, and Orch. (London, Aug. 13, 1971); *Strata* for 15 Solo Strings (1971; London, Feb. 19, 1973); *Konzertstück* for Violin and Orch. (Perth, Feb. 23, 1980); Sym. (1981; London, Aug. 25, 1982); Piano Concerto (Swansea, Aug. 11, 1985); *Strung Out* for 13 Solo Strings (Perth, Feb. 20, 1988). **CHAMBER:** String Sextet (1964); *Missa Parodia II*, nonet (1967); *Pulses* for Brass, Percussion, and Live Electronics (1969; rev. 1986); *Zeitebenen* for Live Electronic Ensemble and Tape (1973); *Echo II* for Cello and Stereo Tape-delay System (1978), *III* for Trumpet and Stereo Tape-delay System (1978), and *IV* for Horn and Stereo Tape-delay System (1983); String Quartet (1979); *Movement* for Flute and Piano (1976–80); *Impulses* for Flute, Trombone, Percussion, Piano, Synthesizer, and Cello (1986); *Ceremony I* for Percussion Quartet (1987); various piano pieces. **VOCAL:** Choral music.

BIBL.: J. Thönell, ed., *Poles Apart: The Music of R. S.* (Perth, 1994).—NS/LK/DM

Small Faces,

popular 1960s-era British band that produced many hits at home but not much abroad; also spawned the Faces and Humble Pie. **MEMBERSHIP:** Steve Marriott, lead gtr., lead voc. (b. Bow, London, England, Jan. 30, 1947; d. Saffron Walden, Essex, England, April 20, 1991); Jimmy Winston (James Langwith), kybd. (b.Stratford, London, April 20, 1945), Ian McLagan, kybd., gtr., voc. (b. England, May 12, 1945); Ronnie Lane, bs., gtr., voc. (b. Plaistow, London, April 1, 1946; d. Trinidad, Colo., June 4, 1997); Kenny Jones, drm. (b. Stepney, London, Sept. 16, 1948).

MEMBERSHIP: The Faces: Rod Stewart, voc. (b. Highgate, London, Jan.10, 1945); Ron Wood, rhythm gtr., bs. (b. Hillingdon, Middlesex, England, June 1, 1947); Ian McLagan, Ronnie Lane, and Kenny Jones. Humble Pie: Peter Frampton, gtr., voc. (b. Beckenham, Kent, England, April 22, 1950); Greg Ridley, bs., voc. (b. Carlisle, Cumberland, England, Oct. 23, ca.1947); Jerry Shirley, drm. (b. England, Feb. 4, 1952); Steve Marriott. Frampton left in October 1971, replaced by David "Clem" Clempson (b. Tamworth, Staffordshire, England, Sept. 5, 1949).

Formed in London as a British rhythm-and-blues band in June 1965, The Small Faces comprised Steve Marriott, Ronnie Lane, Kenny Jones, and Jimmy Winston. Marriott had played the Artful Dodger in the London production of *Oliver!* at age 12 and recorded a solo single for Decca in 1963. Signed to British Decca, The Small Faces recorded one major British-only hit single, "Whatcha Gonna Do about It," before Winston left in late 1965, to be replaced by Ian McLagan. Effervescent and well dressed in performance, The Small Faces quickly became favorites of England's young Mods, scoring smash British-only hits through 1966 with "Sha-La-La-La-Lee," and Marriott and Lane's "Hey Girl," "All or Nothing," and "My Mind's Eye."

The Small Faces began recording for Immediate Records, the new label of Rolling Stones' manager-producer Andrew "Loog" Oldham, in the spring of 1967 and came under his management that summer. Veering toward psychedelia, they achieved a British-only hit with "Here Comes the Nice" and finally penetrated into the American market with "Itchycoo Park," made distinctive through the manipulation of phasing. Although Small Faces' albums had been issued in Great Britain on

Decca in 1966 and 1967, their first American release did not come until 1968 on Immediate. British-only hits continued with "Tin Soldier," "Lazy Sunday," and "Universal," but, following *Ogden's Nut Gone Flake*, regarded as one of the great albums of the late 1960s, Steve Marriott quit the group to form Humble Pie in April 1969 with guitarist Peter Frampton, formerly with The Herd.

Humble Pie signed with Oldham's Immediate label, recording two rather pastoral albums and the smash British-only hit "Natural Born Boogie" for the label before switching to A&M Records in 1970. More effective live than on recordings, the group's first American success came with 1971's live double-record set *Rockin' the Fillmore*, which yielded a minor hit with "I Don't Need No Doctor." Marriott's hard-rock orientation overwhelmed Frampton's more gentle, romantic leanings and, as a consequence, Frampton left the group in October 1971. He was replaced by David "Clem" Clempson, previously with Colosseum. The group's first album with Clempson, *Smokin'*, became their best-seller, containing the favorite "30 Days in the Hole" and producing a minor hit with "Hot 'n' Nasty." Subsequent albums sold progressively less well and the group disbanded in 1975. At the beginning of the 1980s, Marriott reconstituted Humble Pie with guitarist-vocalist Bobby Tench, bassist Anthony Jones, and original Jerry Shirley for two albums on Atlantic Records.

With the dissolution of the first edition of The Small Faces, former members Ronnie Lane, Ian McLagan, and Kenny Jones recruited guitarist Ron Wood and vocalist Rod Stewart from The Jeff Beck Group in June 1969. Signing with Warner Bros. Records, they shortened their name to The Faces, although their debut album, *First Step*, was credited to The Small Faces. Touring America successfully several times in 1970, The Faces broke through with late 1971's *A Nod Is as Good as a Wink...To a Blind Horse*. The album yielded a major hit with "Stay with Me" two months after Stewart's "(I Know) I'm Losing You," recorded with The Faces, became a major hit from his *Every Picture Tells a Story* album.

Following his departure from The Jeff Beck Group, Rod Stewart had secured a solo recording contract with Mercury Records. Thus, he recorded both solo and with The Faces, but his popularity as a solo artist became paramount with *Every Picture Tells a Story*. Stewart continued to record and tour with The Faces through 1975, becoming one of the most popular live bands of the time, but they managed only one more moderate hit with "Cindy Incidentally" in 1973. Ronnie Lane played his final engagement with The Faces that May, to be replaced on bass by Tetsu Yamauchi, formerly with Free. Lane later formed Slim Chance, which recorded three British albums (one released in the U.S.) and scored one British hit with "How Come?" before disbanding in 1977.

In 1974, Ron Wood recorded his first solo album, *I've Got My Own Album to Do*, with Ian McLagan and Rolling Stones guitarist Keith Richards. During the summer of 1975, Wood toured with both The Rolling Stones (as Mick Taylor's replacement) and Rod Stewart and The Faces. Wood's second solo album was released that July. Given the apparent conflicts with Ian McLagan, Wood's increasing involvement with The Rolling Stones, and his own rising popularity, Rod Stewart announced his departure from The Faces in December 1975, effectively ending the career of The Faces.

Steve Marriott recorded a solo album in 1975 and reconstituted The Small Faces with Ian McLagan, Kenny Jones, and bassist-vocalist Rick Wills in June 1976 for two overlooked albums for Atlantic. The Small Faces dissolved in the spring of 1978. By 1979, Kenny Jones had joined The Who and Rick Wills had joined Foreigner. Ian McLagan recorded two solo albums for Mercury and subsequently became a member of The Rolling Stones' touring band.

In 1976, Ronnie Lane reunited with Ron Wood for the soundtrack to the movie *Mahoney's Last Chance*, later recording *Rough Mix* with Pete Townshend of The Who. Wood, an official member of The Rolling Stones since July 1977, released another solo set, *Gimme Some Neck*, recorded with McLagan, Richards, Charlie Watts, and Mick Fleetwood, in the spring of 1979. The album included eight Wood originals and "Seven Days," written for Wood by Bob Dylan. Wood later briefly toured with The New Barbarians, which comprised Richards, McLagan, and jazz bassist Stanley Clarke.

In 1983, Ronnie Lane, diagnosed with multiple sclerosis in 1976, recruited Eric Clapton, Jeff Beck, Jimmy Page, Joe Cocker, Paul Rodgers, and others for a brief tour in support of his Appeal for Action Research into Multiple Sclerosis organization. He then moved to Tex. and toured once again in 1987 and 1990. Steve Marriott's *30 Seconds to Midnight* was released in 1989. On April 20, 1991, after returning from the U.S. where he had been working with Peter Frampton, Marriott died in a house fire at his Saffron Walden cottage in Essex at the age of 44. By then, Kenny Jones had formed The Law with former Bad Company vocalist Paul Rodgers.

DISC.: THE SMALL FACES: *There Are but Four Small Faces* (1968); *Ogden's Nut Gone Flake* (1968); *Archetypes* (1974); *Playmates* (1977); *78 in the Shade* (1978); *By Appointment* (1982); *The Small Faces* (1984); *All or Nothing* (1992). **HUMBLE PIE:** *Town and Country* (1969); *As Safe as Yesterday* (1969); *Humble Pie* (1970); *Rock On* (1971); *Rockin' the Fillmore* (1971); *Smokin'* (1972); *Eat It* (1973); *Thunderbox* (1974); *Street Rats* (1975); *Hot 'n' Nasty: The Anthology* (rec. May 1973; rel. 1994); *On to Victory* (1980); *Go for the Throat* (1981); *The Scrubbers Sessions* (1997). **STEVE MARRIOTT:** *Marriott* (1976); *30 Seconds to Midnight* (1989). **THE FACES:** *First Step* (1970/1993); *Long Player* (1971/1993); *A Nod Is as Good as a Wink...To a Blind Horse* (1971/1993); *Ooh La La* (1973/1993). **ROD STEWART AND THE FACES:** *A Live Concert* (1971); *Coast to Coast: Overture and Beginners* (1973); *Rod Stewart and The Faces* (1975). **RON WOOD:** *I've Got My Own Album to Do* (1974); *Now Look* (1975); *Gimme Some Neck* (1979); *Slide on This* (1992); *Slide on Live* (1998). **RON WOOD AND BO DIDDLEY:** *Live at the Ritz* (1992). **RONNIE LANE/SLIM CHANCE:** *Ronnie Lane/Slim Chance* (1975). **RONNIE LANE AND RON WOOD:** *Mahoney's Last Chance* (soundtrack; 1976). **RONNIE LANE AND PETE TOWNSHEND:** *Rough Mix* (1977). **IAN MCLAGAN:** *Troublemaker* (1980); *Bump in the Night* (1981). **THE LAW (WITH KENNY JONES):** *The Law* (1991).—BH

Smalls, Cliff (actually, **Clifton Arnold**), jazz pianist, trombonist, arranger; b. Charleston, S.C, March 3, 1918. Smalls began playing music as a child; his father was also a musician. During high school, he played in a local group called the Royal Eight. He left Charleston with the Carolina Cotton Pickers, remained with them until joining Earl Hines in summer 1942 (doubling on trombone and second piano); he left Hines in late 1946. Reformed with Billy Eckstine (1948–50) and with Earl Bostic before suffering a serious injury in an auto accident in 1951. Resumed touring in the mid-1950s, worked with trombonist Bennie Green, and with Paul Williams; he also accompanied vocalist Clyde McPhatter. Smalls acted as musical director and accompanist for vocalist Brook Benton for seven years in late 1950s and early 1960s prior to becoming musical director for Smokey Robinson. During the 1960s he also worked with Ella Fitzgerald, and with Reuben Phillips's Big Band at the Apollo Theater, N.Y. During the 1970s Smalls often worked with Sy Oliver's Band; he also did work as an accompanist and made freelance recordings. Toured Europe in Oliver Jackson's trio in the early 1980s.—JC/LP

Smareglia, Antonio, talented Italian composer; b. Pola, Istria, May 5, 1854; d. Grado, Istria, April 15, 1929. He was trained in engineering before turning to music; studied composition with Franco Faccio at the Milan Cons. (1873–77), who became an early champion of his works. He first attracted notice with his opera *Preziosa* (Milan, Nov. 19, 1879); wrote his finest opera for Trieste, *Nozze istriane* (March 28, 1895). In 1903 he was stricken with blindness and was soon reduced to poverty; through the intervention of the Tartini Cons. in Trieste, which made him honorary artistic director in 1921, and the local industrialist Carlo Sai, his fortunes were mended and he was able to present several of his operatic and orch. works. He also engaged in private teaching. After the onset of his blindness, he continued to compose with the assistance of an amanuensis.

WORKS: DRAMATIC: O p e r a : *Preziosa* (Milan, Nov. 19, 1879); *Bianca di Cervia* (Milan, Feb. 7, 1882); *Re Nala* (Venice, Feb. 9, 1887; destroyed by the composer); *Il vassallo di Szigeth* (first perf. as *Der Vasall von Szigeth*, Vienna, Oct. 4, 1889; first perf. in Italian, Pola, Oct. 4, 1930); *Cornil Schut* (first perf. as *Cornelius Schut*, Prague, May 20, 1893; first perf. in Italian, Trieste, Feb. 17, 1900; rev. as *Pittori fiamminghi*, Trieste, Jan. 21, 1928); *Nozze istriane* (Trieste, March 28, 1895); *La falena* (Venice, Sept. 4, 1897); *Oceàna* (Milan, Jan. 22, 1903); *Abisso* (Milan, Feb. 9, 1914). ORCH.: *Leonora, ballata di Burger*, "descriptive sym." (1877); *Oceana Suite* (1902). VOCAL: *Caccia lontana*, melodramatic scene (Milan, Aug. 10, 1875); *Inno a Tartini* for Voices and Band (1896); *Salve regina* for Voices and Piano or Harmonium (1930).

BIBL.: G. Zuccoli, *A. S.* (Trieste, 1922); G. Nacamuli, *A. S.* (Trieste, 1930); A. Smareglia, *Vita ed arte di A. S.: Un capitolo di storia del teatro lirico italiano* (Lugano, 1932; second ed., 1936); M. Smareglia, *A. S. nella storia del melodramma italiano: Accolta di critiche musicali e di altri documenti* (Pola, 1934); V. Levi, *Nozze istriane: Nel centenario della nascita di A. S.* (Trieste, 1954); S. Benco, *Ricordi di A. S.* (Duino, 1968).—NS/LK/DM

Smart, family of prominent English musicians:

(1) **Sir George (Thomas) Smart**, organist, conductor, and composer; b. London, May 10, 1776; d. there, Feb. 23, 1867. He was a chorister in the Chapel Royal under Aryton until 1791; studied organ with Cupuis and composition with Arnold. In 1791 he became organist at St. James's Chapel, Hampstead Road, and also was a violinist in Salomon's concert series. In 1811 he conducted a series of Dublin concerts and was knighted. He was a founder in 1813 of the Phil. Soc. of London, where he was active as a conductor until 1844, leading the first British performance of Beethoven's 9th Sym. in 1826. He also conducted the Lenten oratorio concerts at Covent Garden and Drury Lane (1813–25) and the City Amateur Concerts (1818–22), at which he introduced many works of Mozart and Beethoven. In 1822 he was named organist at the Chapel Royal, and in 1838 was made one of its composers. He toured widely in Europe; his valuable journal relates his conversations with Beethoven in Vienna. He also befriended Weber, who died in his house during his visit to London. His works include 6 anthems, 8 glees, Kyries, Psalm tunes, and chants. He also ed. Gibbons's madrigals (1841) and Handel's *Dettingen Te Deum* (1846–47).

BIBL.: H. and C. Cox, *Leaves from the Journals of Sir G. S.* (London, 1907).

(2) **Henry Smart**, violinist, brother of the preceding; b. London, 1778; d. Dublin, Nov. 27, 1823. He studied violin with W. Cramer, beginning his career at age 14 at the Opera, the Concert of Ancient Music, and the Academy of Ancient Music. He served as concertmaster of the orch. at the Lyceum Theatre (1809–12) and at the Drury Lane Theatre (1812–21); also was active with the Phil. Soc. (from 1813). He opened a piano factory in 1821. He wrote a ballet, *Laurette* (1803).

(3) **Henry Thomas Smart**, organist and composer, son of the preceding;; b. London, Oct. 26, 1813; d. there, July 6, 1879. He was educated at Highgate and received instruction in instrumentation from W.H. Kearns. After serving as organist of the Blackburn parish church (1831–36), he returned to London as organist of St. Philip's Church, Regent Street, in 1836; also was active as a music critic for the *Atlas* and engaged in teaching. He then was organist at St. Luke's, Old Street (1844–64), and at St. Pancras, Euston Road (1864–79). In 1864 he became blind and in 1879 was awarded a government pension, but died without its benefits. His partsongs and organ pieces were especially admired. He also wrote an opera, *Berta, or The Gnome of the Hartzberg* (London, May 26, 1855), an oratorio, *Jacob* (Glasgow, 1873), cantatas, services, anthems, hymn tunes, songs, etc.

BIBL.: J. Broadhouse, *H. S.'s Compositions for Organ* (London, 1880); W. Spark, *H. S.* (London, 1881); D. Hill, *H. S.: Neglected Nineteenth Century Organ Master* (Schagen, 1988). —NS/LK/DM

Smashing Pumpkins, the band that broke out of the "alternative" scene to become pop icons of the 1990s. MEMBERSHIP: Billy Corgan, voc., gtr. (b. Chicago, March 17, 1967); James Iha, gtr. (b. Elk Grove, Ill., March 26, 1968); D'Arcy Wretzky, bs. (b. South Haven,

Mich., May 1, 1968); Jimmy Chamberlain, drm. (b. Joliet, Ill., June 10, 1964).

Through death, drug abuse, and self-doubt, Smashing Pumpkins became one of the most durable bands to emerge during the 1990s. With a sound that combines the sloppy playing/sharp beat dichotomy that fueled the Rolling Stones—along with overdubbed guitars and a touch of heavy metal—they took the alterna-grunge that ruled at the beginning of the decade to another level of success. The Pumpkins did it with a combination of business savvy, showmanship both on stage and in the press, and songs that reached their audience.

Frontman and main songwriter Billy Corgan was the son of a jazz guitarist, but lived with his mother in the suburbs of Chicago. At 19, he moved to Fla. to front a goth-metal band, but returned a couple of years later and took a job at a used record shop. There, he met a Loyola design student named James Iha. The pair started to work on songs together, initially performing and recording with a drum machine. Corgan brought in D'Arcy Wretzky on bass, and the band developed a live following in Chicago. Iha and Wretzky became lovers. The band's name developed as something of a joke. Recalling how British musicians used "Smashing" as an adjective, Corgan thought it would make a great name for the band. How the "Pumpkins" part got added is anyone's guess.

The group earned an opening slot for Jane's Addiction and hired drummer Jimmy Chamberlin. By 1990 they had released their first single, "I Am One," on a Chicago indie label. When the run of the single sold out, they were signed to Sub Pop for the "Tristessa" record. It success inspired a fierce struggle among the various major labels to sign the band. They went to Virgin, initially signing with Virgin's "indie" subsidiary, Caroline. Their first Virgin album, 1991's Gish, took college and modern rock radio by storm, building on the band's following. They supported the album with opening slots on tours with Pearl Jam and the Red Hot Chili Peppers. The song "Drown" on the soundtrack to the movie Singles also helped raise their visibility. However, while on tour Chamberlin became heavily involved with drugs and drink, and Iha and Wretsky went through a messy break up.

Nonetheless, the band stayed together, mostly because Corgan cut the bulk of the tracks for the group's next album by himself, 1993's Siamese Dream. Highly anticipated, it debuted at its peak of #10 on the charts, powered by modern rock hits like the moody "Today" and the largely acoustic "Disarm." Ultimately the album went quadruple platinum. The group spent nearly the whole year on the road, finishing with a headlining stint on the 1994 Lollapalooza tour. The group the retreated into the studio to make a promised two-CD set. The process took nearly two years. As a stopgap, in 1994 the group released a disc of outtakes, Pisces Iscariot. A Pumpkin-hungry audience sent it to #4 and platinum out of the box.

Work on the double-album continued slowly. Recording dozens of songs, they winnowed them down to a 28-track double album, Mellon Collie and the Infinite Sadness, which debuted at #1 in 1995 and shipped

quintuple platinum. The single "Bullet with Butterfly Wings" crossed over pop, reaching #22 on the chart and going gold. Both the Zeppelin-esque hard rock single "Zero" and the quasi-psychedelic "1979" also went gold, without even reaching the pop charts. By a year after its release, the album had gone octuple platinum. The band started playing stadiums and arenas. While on tour, however, the group's road keyboard player, Jonathan Melvoin (brother of Prince side-person Wendy Melvoin), overdosed on heroin supplied and shared by Jimmy Chamberlin. The band fired Chamberlin, first going on the road with former John Mellencamp/John Fogerty drummer Kenny Aronoff. A series of other drummers followed, including Filter's Matt Walker and Dennis Flemion of the Frogs.

The band took a hiatus in the mid-1990s. Iha and Wretzky formed their own Scratchie Records, and Iha released a solo album, Let It Come Down. Corgan wrote some of the music for the film Ransom, and the group contributed some songs to the Batman & Robin soundtrack. During this interim, Corgon's mother died and his marriage ended. Without Chamberlin, the group's 1998 Adore sold relatively poorly, going platinum. Chamberlin returned, clean and sober, but after recording their 2000 effort Machina/The Machines of God, Wretzky parted company with the group. Former Hole bassist Melissa Auf der Maur replaced her. A return to their hard- rock roots, Machina entered the charts at #3. Reflecting the continuing turmoil that has troubled the band, that year the group's manager, Sharon Osbourne (wife of rocker Ozzy Osbourne), quit for "medical reasons," saying "Billy Corgan was making [her] sick." Still, the band persevered.

DISC.: Gish (1991); Siamese Dream (1993); Pisces Iscariot (1994); Mellon Collie and the Infinite Sadness (1995); Adore (1998); Machina/The Machines of God (2000). **BIBL.:** Nick Wise, Smashing Pumpkins (London, 1996); Jim Stapleton, Smashing Pumpkins.—HB

Smend, Friedrich, eminent German musicologist; b. Strasbourg, Aug. 26, 1893; d. Berlin, Feb. 10, 1980. He studied theology at the Univs. of Strasbourg, Tübingen, Marburg, and Münster (Ph.D., 1921, with the diss. Die Acta-Berichte über Bekehrung des Paulus nach ihrem Quellenwert). He was employed at the Univ. of Münster Library (1921–23) and at the Prussian State Library in Berlin (1923–45); was a teacher (1945–46), director of the library (1946–58), a prof. (1949–58), and rector (1954–57) at the Kirchliche Hochschule in Berlin. In 1951 he received an honorary doctorate in theology from the Univ. of Heidelberg and in 1954 an honorary doctorate in philosophy from the Univ. of Mainz. He was an authority on the life and music of Bach.

WRITINGS: Luther und Bach (Berlin, 1947); J.S. Bachs Kirchen-Kantaten (Berlin, 1947–49; second ed., 1950); Johann Sebastian Bach bei seinem Namen gerufen (Kassel and Basel, 1950); Bach in Köthen (Berlin, 1951); Goethes Verhältnis zu Bach (Berlin and Darmstadt, 1955); Bach Studien: Gesammelte Reden und Aufsätze (Kassel, 1969). **BIBL.:** Festschrift für F. S. zum 70. Geburtstag dargebracht von Freunden und Schülern (Berlin, 1963).—NS/LK/DM

Smendzianka, Regina, Polish pianist and teacher; b. Torún, Oct. 9, 1924. She studied at the Pomerian Cons. in Torún, with Sztompka at the Torún Cons., and with Drzewiecki at the Kraków State Coll. of Music (1945–48). After making her formal debut as soloist with the Kraków Phil. in 1947, she toured widely in Europe, the U.S., and the Far East. In 1964 she joined the faculty of the Warsaw Academy of Music, where she later was rector (1972–73) and a prof. (from 1977). Her exhaustive repertoire ranges from Bach to contemporary composers.—NS/LK/DM

Smetáček, Václav, noted Czech oboist, conductor, and teacher; b. Brunn, Sept. 30, 1906; d. Prague, Feb. 18, 1986. He studied oboe with Ladislav Skuhrovský, composition with Jaroslav Kříčka, and conducting with Metod Doležil and Pavel Dědeček at the Prague Cons. (1922–30); also took courses in musicology and aesthetics at the Charles Univ. in Prague (Ph.D., 1933). In 1928 he founded the Prague Wind Quintet, remaining with it until 1955; was also oboist in the Czech Phil. (1930–33). He conducted the Radio Orch. (1934–43) and the Hlahol Choir (1934–46) in Prague; became chief conductor of Prague's FOK Sym. Orch. in 1942; it became the Prague Sym. Orch. in 1952, and he continued to lead it until 1972; he also appeared widely as a guest conductor. He taught at Prague's Cons. and Academy of Music (1945–66). In 1962 he was made an Artist of Merit and in 1976 a National Artist by the Czech government. He was best known for his performances of Czech music, both traditional and contemporary.

BIBL.: L. Šíp, *V. S.* (Prague, 1957).—NS/LK/DM

Smetana, Bedřich, great Bohemian composer; b. Leitomischl, March 2, 1824; d. Prague, May 12, 1884. His talent manifested itself very early, and although his father had misgivings about music as a profession, he taught his son violin; Bedřich also had piano lessons with a local teacher, making his first public appearance at the age of 6 (Oct. 14, 1830). After the family moved to Jindrichův Hradec in 1831, he studied with the organist František Ikavec; continued his academic studies in Jihlava and Německý Brod, then entered the Classical Grammar School in Prague in 1839; also had piano lessons with Jan Batka, and led a string quartet for which he composed several works. His lack of application to his academic studies led his father to send him to the gymnasium in Pilsen, but he soon devoted himself to giving concerts and composing. He met a friend of his school days there, Kateřina Kolářová, whom he followed to Prague in 1843; he was accepted as a theory pupil of Kolářová's piano teacher, Josef Proksch, at the Music Inst. To pay for his lessons, Bedřich Kittl, director of the Prague Cons., recommended Smetana for the position of music teacher to the family of Count Leopold Thun. He took up his position in Jan. 1844, and for 3-1/2 years worked earnestly in the count's service; also continued to study theory and to compose. Bent on making a name for himself as a concert pianist, Smetana left the count's service in the summer of 1847 and planned a tour of Bohemia; however, his only concert in Pilsen proved a financial disaster, and he abandoned his

tour and returned to Prague, where he eked out a meager existence. He wrote to Liszt, asking him to find a publisher for his op.1, the *6 Characteristic Pieces* for piano; Liszt was impressed with the score, accepted Smetana's dedication, and found a publisher. In 1848 Smetana established a successful piano school, and on Aug. 27, 1849, he married Kolářová. In 1850 he became court pianist to the abdicated Emperor Ferdinand. His reputation as a pianist, especially as an interpreter of Chopin, grew, but his compositions made little impression. The death of his children and the poor health of his wife (who had tuberculosis) affected him deeply; he set out for Sweden in 1856; gave a number of successful piano recitals in Göteborg, where he remained. He soon opened his own school, and also became active as a choral conductor. His wife joined him in 1857, but the cold climate exacerbated her condition; when her health declined, they decided to return to Prague (1859), but she died en route, in Dresden, on April 19, 1859. Stricken with grief, Smetana returned to Göteborg. Before his wife's death, he had composed the symphonic poems *Richard III* and *Valdštýnův tabor* (Wallenstein's Camp); he now began work on a third, *Hakan Jarl*. On July 10, 1860, he married Betty Ferdinandi, which proved an unhappy union. During Smetana's sojourn in Sweden, Austria granted political autonomy to Bohemia (1860), and musicians and poets of the rising generation sought to establish an authentic Bohemian voice in the arts. Agitation for the erection of a national theater in Prague arose; although earlier attempts to write operas in a Bohemian vein had been made by such composers as František Škroup and Jiří Macourek, their works were undistinguished. Smetana believed the time was ripe for him to make his mark in Prague, and he returned there in May 1861. However, when the Provisional Theater opened on Nov. 18, 1862, its administration proved sadly unimaginative, and Smetana contented himself with the conductorship of the Hlahol Choral Soc., teaching, and writing music criticism. In his articles he condemned the poor musical standards prevailing at the Provisional Theater. In 1862–63 he composed his first opera, *Braniboři v Čechách* (The Brandenburgers in Bohemia), conducting its successful premiere at the Provisional Theater on Jan. 5, 1866. His next opera, *Prodaná nevěsta* (The Bartered Bride), proved a failure at its premiere in Prague under his direction on May 30, 1866, but eventually it was accorded a niche in the operatic repertoire at home and abroad. Smetana became conductor of the Provisional Theater in 1866. He immediately set out to reform its administration and to raise its musical standards. For the cornerstone laying of the National Theater on May 16, 1868, he conducted the first performance of his tragic opera *Dalibor*, which was criticized as an attempt to Wagnerize the Bohemian national opera. In 1871, when there was talk of crowning Emperor Franz Josef as King of Bohemia, Smetana considered producing his opera *Libuše* for the festivities; however, no coronation took place and the work was withheld. Hoping for a popular success, he composed the comic opera *Dvě vdovy* (The 2 Widows), which proved to be just that at its premiere under his direction on March 27, 1874. Smetana's success, however, was short-lived. By the autumn of 1874 he was deaf and had to resign as conductor of the Provisional Theater. In spite of the bitter years to follow, marked by increasingly poor health, family problems, and financial hardship, he continued to compose. Between 1874 and 1879 he produced his 6 orch. masterpieces collectively known as *Má Vlast* (My Country): *Vyšehrad* (referring to a rock over the river Vltava, near Prague, the traditional seat of the ancient kings of Bohemia), *Vltava* (The Moldau), *Šárka* (a wild valley, near Prague, depicting the legendary story of the maiden Sarka), *Z Českych luhů a hájů* (From Bohemia's Woods and Fields), *Tábor* (the medieval town in southern Bohemia, the seat of the Hussites, and thus the traditional symbol of freedom and religion; the work is based on the chorale *Ye Who Are God's Warriors*), and *Blaník* (the mountain that served as a place of refuge for the Hussites; the previously mentioned chorale serves as the foundation of the work). From 1876 dates his famous String Quartet in E minor, subtitled *Z mého života* (From My Life), which he described as a "remembrance of my life and the catastrophe of complete deafness." His opera *Hubička* (The Kiss) was successfully premiered in Prague on Nov. 7, 1876. It was followed by the opera *Tajemství* (The Secret), which was heard for the first time on Sept. 18, 1878. For the opening of the new National Theater in Prague on June 11, 1881, his opera *Libuše* was finally given its premiere performance. The ailing Smetana attended the opening night and was accorded sustained applause. His last opera, *Čertova stěna* (The Devil's Wall), was a failure at its first hearing in Prague on Oct. 29, 1882. By this time Smetana's health had been completely undermined by the ravages of syphilis, the cause of his deafness. His mind eventually gave way and he was confined to an asylum. At his death in 1884, the nation was plunged into a state of mourning. The funeral cortege passed the National Theater as Smetana was carried to his final resting place in the Vyšehrad cemetery.

Smetana was the founder of the Czech national school of composition, and it was through his efforts that Czech national opera came of age. The centenary of his death in 1984 was marked by numerous performances of his music in Czechoslovakia and a reaffirmation of his revered place in the history of his nation.

WORKS: DRAMATIC: O p e r a (all first perf. in Prague): *Branibroři v Čechách* (The Brandenburgers in Bohemia; 1862–63; Jan. 5, 1866, composer conducting); *Prodaná nevěsta* (The Bartered Bride; 1863–66; May 30, 1866, composer conducting; 2 revs., 1869; final version, 1869–70; Sept. 25, 1870, composer conducting); *Dalibor* (1865–67; May 16, 1868, composer conducting; rev. 1870); *Libuše* (1869–72; June 11, 1881, A. Čech conducting); *Dvě vdovy* (The 2 Widows; March 27, 1874, composer conducting; final version, 1877; March 15, 1878, Čech conducting); *Hubička* (The Kiss; Nov. 7, 1876, Čech conducting); *Tajemství* (The Secret; Sept. 18, 1878, Čech conducting); *Čertova stěna* (The Devil's Wall; 1879–82; Oct. 29, 1882, Čech conducting); *Viola* (sketches begun in 1874; fragment from 1883–84 only). **ORCH.:** Minuet (1842); *Galop bajadérek* (Bajader's Galop; 1842); *Pochod Pražké studentské legie* (March for the Prague Students' Legion; 1848; arranged for Military Band by J. Pavlis); *Pochod Národní gardy* (March for the National Guard; 1848; arranged for Military Band by J. Pavlis); Polka (1849; later known as *Naším devám* [To Our Girls]); Overture (1849); Prelude

(1849; 3 unconnected fragments only); *Frithjof* (1857; unfinished fragment only); *Slavnostní Symfonie* (Festival or Triumphal Sym.; 1853–54; Prague, Feb. 26, 1855, composer conducting); *Plavba vikingu* (The Viking's Voyage; 1857; unfinished fragment only); *Richard III*, symphonic poem after Shakespeare (1857–58; first perf. in an arrangement for 4 Pianos, Göteborg, April 24, 1860; first orch. perf., Prague, Jan. 5, 1862, composer conducting); *Valdštýnuv tabor* (Wallenstein's Camp), symphonic poem after Schiller (1858–59); *Hakon Jarl*, symphonic poem after Oehlenschläger (1860–61; Prague, Feb. 24, 1864, composer conducting); *Doktor Faust*, prelude to a puppet play by M. Kopecký for Chamber Orch. (1862); *Oldřich a Božena*, prelude to a puppet play by M. Kopecký for Chamber Orch. (1863); *Pochod k slavnosti Shakespearove* (March for Shakespeare Festival; 1864); *Fanfáry k Shakespearovu dramatu Richard III* (Fanfares for Shakespeare's Drama *Richard III*; 1867); *Slavnostní predehra* (Ceremonial Prelude; 1868); *Prodaná nevěsta* (The Bartered Bride), tableau vivant for Chamber Orch. (1869); *Rybar* (The Fisherman), tableau vivant after Goethe's *Der Fischar* for Chamber Orch. (1869); *Libušin soud* (Libuše's Judgment), tableau vivant for Chamber Orch. (1869); *Divertissement na slovanské napevy* (Divertissement on Slavonic Songs) for Solo Flugelhorn and Military Band (1869; not extant); *Má Vlast* (My Country), cycle of 6 symphonic poems: 1, *Vyšehrad* (1872–74; Prague, March 14, 1875), 2, *Vltava* (The Moldau; 1874; Prague, April 4, 1875), 3, *Šárka* (1875; Prague, March 17, 1877), 4, *Z Českych luhu a háju* (From Bohemia's Woods and Fields; 1875; Prague, Dec. 10, 1876), 5, *Tábor* (1878; Prague, Jan. 4, 1880), and 6, *Blaník* (1878–79; Prague, Jan. 4, 1880) (first complete perf. of the entire cycle, Prague, Nov. 5, 1882, Čech conducting); *Venkovanka* (The Peasant Woman), polka (1879); *Pražský karneval* (Prague Carnival), introduction and polonaise (1883; Prague, March 2, 1884); *Grosse Sinfonie* (1883–84; sketch for part of the first movement only). **CHAMBER:** Polka for String Quartet (1839–40; not extant); *Osmanen Polka* for String Quartet (1839–40; not extant); 3 string quartets: No 1 (1839–40; not extant), No. 1, *Z mého života* (From My Life; 1876), and No. 2 (1882–83); Waltz for String Quartet (1839–40; first violin part only extant); Overture for String Quartet (1839–40; not extant); Fantasia on motifs from Bellini's *Il Pirata* for String Quartet (1840); Fantasia on *Sil jsem proso* (I Sowed Millet) for Violin and Piano (1842–43); Trio for Piano, Violin, and Cello (1855; rev. 1857); *Z domoviny*, 2 duets for Violin and Piano (1880); also numerous piano pieces. **CHORAL:** *Jesu meine Freude*, chorale (1846); *Ich hoffe auf den Herrn*, fugue (1846); *Lobet den Herrn*, introduction and fugue (1846); *Heilig, Heilig, ist der Herr Zabaoth* for Double Chorus (1846); *Scapulis suis obumbrabit tibi Dominus*, offertory for Chorus, Horns, Strings, and Organ (1846); *Meditabitur in mandatis tuis* (*Offertorium à la Händel*) for Chorus, Horns, Strings, and Organ (1846); *Píseň svobody* (Song of Freedom) for Unison Voices and Piano (1848); *Česká píseň* (Song of the Czechs) for Men's Voices (1860); *Tři jezdci* (The 3 Riders) for Men's Voices (1862); *Odrolilec* (The Renegade) for Double Chorus of Men's Voices (1863); *Rolnická* (Farming) for Men's Voices (1868); *Slavností sbor* (Ceremonial Chorus) for Men's Voices (1870); *Píseň na moři* (Song of the Sea) for Men's Voices (1877); *Má hvězda* (My Star) for Women's Voices (1878); *Přiletěly vlaštorvičky* (The Swallows Have Gone) for Women's Voices (1878); *Za hory slunce zapadá* (The Sun Sets behind the Mountain) for Women's Voices (1878); *Věno* (Dedication) for Men's Voices (1882); *Modlitba* (Prayer) for Men's Voices (1880); *Dvě hesla* (2 Slogans) for Men's Voices (1882); *Naše píseň* (Our Song) for Men's Voices (1883).

BIBL.: K. Teige, *Příspěvky k životopisu a umělecké činnosti mistra B.a Smetany, I: Skladby Smetanovy* (S.'s Works; Prague,

1893) and II: *Dopisy Smetanoy* (S.'s Letters; Prague, 1896); O. Hostinský, *B. S. a jeho boj o moderni českou hudbu* (S. and His Struggle for Modern Czech Music; Prague, 1901; second ed., 1941); W. Ritter, *S.* (Paris, 1907); Z. Nejedlý, *Zpěvohry Smetanovy* (S.'s Operas; Prague, 1908; third ed., 1954); V. Balthasar, *B. S.* (Prague, 1924); V. Helfert, *Tvůrči rozvoj B.a Smetany* (S.'s Creative Development; Prague, 1924; third ed., 1953; Ger. tr., 1956); Z. Nejedlý, *B. S.* (4 vols., Prague, 1924–33; second ed., 7 vols., 1950–54; additional vol. as *S.: Dobá zrání* [S.: The Period of Maturity], Prague, 1962); J. Tiersot, *S.* (Paris, 1926); F. Bartoš, *B. S.* (Prague, 1940); J. Teichman, *B. S.: Život a dilo* (S.: Life and Work; Prague, 1944); O. Šourek, *Komorni skladby B.a Smetany* (S.'s Chamber Music; Prague, 1945); P. Pražák, *Smetanovy zpěvohry* (S.'s Operas; Prague, 1948); M. Malý, *B. S.* (Prague, 1954; Eng. tr., 1956); J. Plavec, *Smetanova tvorba skorova* (S.'s Choral Works; Prague, 1954); H. Boese, *Zwei Urmusikanten: S.—Dvořák* (Zürich, 1955); M. Očadlík, *Klavirni dilo B.a Smetany* (S.'s Piano Works; Prague, 1961); B. Karásek, *B. S.* (Prague, 1966; Eng. tr., 1967); C. Thörnqvist, *S. in Göteborg, 1856–1862* (in Eng.; Göteborg, 1967); B. Large, *S.* (N.Y., 1970); J. Clapham, *S.* (London, 1972); K. Janeček, *Smetanova komorni hudba* (S.'s Chamber Music; Prague, 1979); H. Séguardtová, *B. S.* (Leipzig, 1985); A. Neumayr, *Musik und Medizin: Chopin, S., Tschaikowsky, Mahler* (Vienna, 1991); G. Erismann, *S.: L'éveilleur* (Arles, 1993); M. Ottlová and M. Pospíšil, *B. S. a jeho doba: Vybrane studie* (Prague, 1997).—NS/LK/DM

Smeterlin, Jan, Polish-born English pianist; b. Bielsko, Feb. 7, 1892; d. London, Jan. 18, 1967. He was a child prodigy, making his public debut at the age of 8. After studies with Godowsky in Vienna, he toured throughout Europe and the U.S. (from 1930), eventually settling in London just before the outbreak of World War II; became a naturalized British subject. He was praised for his congenially Romantic interpretations of Chopin's music; celebrated his 50th anniversary as a concert artist at London's Wigmore Hall in 1951. —NS/LK/DM

Smijers, Albert(us Antonius), eminent Dutch musicologist; b. Raamsdonksveer, July 19, 1888; d. Huis ter Heide, near Utrecht, May 15, 1957. He studied music with Averkamp at the Amsterdam Cons. He was trained for the priesthood and was ordained in 1912; then entered the school for church music at Klosterneuburg; later took a course in musicology with Adler at the Univ. of Vienna (Ph.D., 1917, with the diss. *Karl Luython als Motettenkomponist*; publ. in Amsterdam, 1923). He taught at Beekvliet Seminary in Amsterdam until 1929, then at the Amsterdam Cons. (1929–33); in 1930 he was appointed prof. of musicology at the Univ. of Utrecht; formed the Inst. of Musicology there. He brought out 7 vols. of the anthology *Van Ockeghem tot Sweelinck* (Amsterdam, 1939–56), and, in collaboration with C. Van den Borren and others, he publ. *Algemeene Muziekgeschiedenis* (Utrecht, 1938; fourth ed., 1947). He also ed. the collected works of Josquin Des Prez (Amsterdam, 1921–56) and Obrecht (Vols. I-III, Amsterdam, 1953–56). —NS/LK/DM

Smirnov, Dmitri, Russian composer; b. Minsk, Nov. 2, 1948. After training in Frunze, he studied at the Moscow Cons. (1967–72) with Nikolai Sidelnikov (com-

position), Edison Denisov (orchestration), and Yuri Kholopov (analysis). He also received private instruction from Philip Gershkovich. From 1973 to 1980 he was an ed. with the publishing firm Soviet Composer. In 1993 he became a prof. and composer-in-residence at the Univ. of Keele in England. In 1972 he married **Elena Firsova.** While thoroughly grounded in various contemporary styles and techniques, Smirnov has found great inspiration in the tonal world of late Romanticism. He has also been much influenced by the poetry and painting of William Blake, and has set a number of his works to music.

WORKS: DRAMATIC: *Tiriel,* opera (1983–85; Freiburg im Breisgau, Jan. 28, 1989); *The Lamentations of Thel,* opera (1985–86; London, June 9, 1989); film scores. **ORCH.:** 2 *Ricercares* for Strings (1963–83; Moscow, April 11, 1983); 2 piano concertos: No. 1 (1971; Moscow, June 21, 1972) and No. 2 (Moscow, Dec. 25, 1978); Clarinet Concerto (1974; rev. 1977); *Pastorale* (1975; Leningrad, Feb. 14, 1977); Triple Concerto for Alto Saxophone, Double Bass, Piano, and Orch. (Moscow, Dec. 26, 1977); *Fanfares,* symphonic poem (1978); 2 syms.: No. 1, *The Seasons (in Memory of William Blake)* (1980; Riga, Oct. 8, 1981) and No. 2 for 4 Singers, Chorus, and Orch. (1982); *Tiriel-Prologue* (1983); *Mozart Variations* (1987; Moscow, Feb. 2, 1988); Concerto for Violin and 13 Strings (1990); Cello Concerto (1992). **CHAMBER:** *Monologue* for Clarinet (1968); 2 violin sonatas: No. 1 (1969; Moscow, April 20, 1970; rev. 1971) and No. 2 (Moscow, Dec. 26, 1979); 2 *Fugues* for Violin (1970); String Trio (1970; Moscow, Feb. 28, 1971); *Cradle Song* for Oboe and Piano (1972); 4 string quartets: No. 1 (1973), No. 2 (Moscow, Oct. 22, 1985), No. 3 (1993), and No. 4 (1993); *Trio Sacrum* for Percussion (1974); *The Melancholic Minute* for Clarinet and Piano (1975); *Preparations* for Clarinet and Piano (1975); *Canon-Humoresque* for 3 Saxophones (1975); Sonata for Flute and Harp (Moscow, Oct. 6, 1975); *Mirages* for Saxophone Quartet (1975; Moscow, May 6, 1976); *Lyrical Composition* for Flute, Oboe, Violin, Cello, and Harpsichord (1975; Moscow, May 11, 1977); *Solo* for Harp (Limburg, Aug. 1976); Bassoon Sonata (1977; Moscow, Jan. 30, 1978); 3 *Dances* for Xylophone (1977); 2 piano trios: No. 1 (1977; Moscow, Oct. 11, 1980) and No. 2 (1992); Cello Sonata (1978; Moscow, Feb. 24, 1979); 2 *Pieces* for Harp (1978); 9 *Children's Pieces* for Horn and Piano (1979); *Children's Concerto* for Cello and Piano (1980); *Dirge Canons in memoriam Igor Stravinsky* for 13 Players (Moscow, Dec. 14, 1981); *Serenade* for Oboe, Saxophone, and Cello (Moscow, May 25, 1981); 3 *Equale* for 4 Instruments (1981); *Ballade* for Alto Saxophone and Piano (Moscow, April 14, 1982); *Forest Pictures* for Harp (1982); *The Farewell Song* for Viola and Harp (Moscow, Oct. 4, 1982); *Fantasia* for Saxophone Quartet (1982; Moscow, Dec. 12, 1983); *Tiriel* for Baritone Saxophone and Piano (1983; Moscow, April 25, 1984); *Tiriel* for Cello and Piano (1984; Kishinev, March 5, 1987); *Music Greeting to H. S.* for Trumpet (Hamburg, Oct. 16, 1985); *Partita* for Violin (1985; N.Y., Dec. 7, 1987); *Epitaph to Emil Gilels* for Piano and Organ (1985); 7 *Melancholic Waltzes* for Alto Saxophone and Piano (1985; Kiev, Feb. 22, 1986); *Thel-Prologue* for Chamber Ensemble (1985); 2 *Moods* for Guitar (1987); *The Moolight Story* for Piccolo, Bass Clarinet, Violin, Viola, Cello, and Double Bass (1988; London, June 8, 1989); *The Evening Song* for Alto or Tenor Saxophone and Piano (1990); *Trinity Music* for Clarinet, Violin, and Piano (1990); *Jacob's Ladder* for Chamber Ensemble (1990; London, April 17, 1991); *Job's Studies* for Clarinet (1992); *The River of Life* for Chamber Ensemble (1992); *Prayer* for Trumpet and Organ (1992); *Threnody* for Trumpet and Organ (1992); *Orcades* for Flute (1992); Piano Quintet (1992).

KEYBOARD: P i a n o : *12 Melancholic Waltzes* (1965–85); *2 Pieces* (1966); *3 sonatas* (1967, 1980, 1992); *5 Little Pieces* (1968); *Magic Casket* (1969–85); *2 Magic Quadrates* (1971); *Toccata* (1972); *9 Pieces* (1979); *Suite in Baroque Style* (1980; also for Harpsichord); *Epitaph* (1985; also for Organ); *2 Intermezzi* (1987); *The 7 Angels of William Blake* (1988); *The Angels of Albion* (1991); *Magic Music Box*, 50 children's pieces (1993). O r g a n : *Diptych* (1992). VOCAL: *The Handful of Sand* for Voice and 12 Players (1967; rev. 1983; also for Voice and Piano); *2 Choruses* (1968); *12 Chorales* for Chorus (1968–72); *The Ominous Stink* for Bass, Chorus, and Orch. (1969–70); *6 Poems by Alexander Blok* for Voice and Orch. (1972); *Eternal Refuge* for Voice, Organ, Strings, and Percussion (1972; rev. 1981); *6 Haiku of Kabajasi Issa* for Voice, Flute, and Piano (1973); *Cantata in memoriam Pablo Neruda* for Soprano, Tenor, Chorus, Strings, and Percussion (1974); *The Sorrow of Past Days* for Voice, Flute, Violin, Cello, and Percussion (1976); *The Seasons* for Voice, Flute, Viola, and Harp (1979); *The Night Rhymes* for Voice and Orch. (1982); *The Visions of Coleridge* for Voice, Flute, Clarinet, Horn, Percussion, and String Quintet (1987); *Songs of Love and Madness* for Voice, Clarinet, Celesta, Harp, and String Trio (1988); *8-line Poems* for Voice, Flute, Horn, Harp, and String Trio (1989); *A Song of Liberty* for Soprano, Alto, Tenor, Bass, Chorus, and Orch. (1991); *Short Poems* for Soprano and Ensemble (1991); *3 Blake Songs* for Soprano and Ensemble (1991); *Ariel Songs* for Countertenor, 2 Recorders, Cello, and Harpsichord (1993); many solo songs for Voice and Piano.—**NS/LK/DM**

Smirnov, Dmitri (Alexeievich), outstanding Russian tenor; b. Moscow, Nov. 19, 1882; d. Riga, April 27, 1944. He sang in a church choir as a youth, then studied voice with Dodonov and others in Moscow. On Feb. 3, 1903, he made his debut as Gigi in Esposito's *Camorra* at Moscow's Hermitage Theater. In 1904 he was accepted as a member of the Bolshoi Theater there, but interrupted his career by traveling to Paris and Milan for further voice training. Returning to Moscow in 1906, he sang again at the Bolshoi Theater; from 1910 he appeared also with the Maryinsky Opera Theater in St. Petersburg. During the same period, he took part in the famous Russian Seasons in Paris. On Dec. 30, 1910, he made his debut at the Metropolitan Opera in N.Y. in the role of the Duke of Mantua in *Rigoletto*, remaining with the company until 1912; then sang with the Boston Opera (1911); after a tour of Latin America, he appeared at London's Drury Lane (1914) and other European theaters. Although he lived mostly abroad, he revisited Russia in 1926 and 1928 as a guest artist. He later appeared mostly in solo recitals; was also active as a voice teacher; taught at the Athens Cons. and in Riga. In Russia he was regarded as one of the finest lyric tenors of his time, often compared to Caruso; as a bel canto singer, he was praised by Russian and European critics. Apart from the Russian repertoire, in which he excelled, he made a deep impression in such lyrico-dramatic roles as Faust, Don José, Canio, and Rodolfo.—**NS/LK/DM**

Smit, Leo, American pianist, teacher, and composer; b. Philadelphia, Jan. 12, 1921; d. Encinitas, Calif., Dec. 12, 1999. He studied piano with Vengerova at the Curtis Inst. of Music in Philadelphia (1930–32), and took lessons in composition with Nabokov (1935). He made his debut as a pianist at Carnegie Hall in N.Y. in 1939,

and then made tours of the U.S. He also taught at Sarah Lawrence Coll. (1947–49), at the Univ. of Calif. at Los Angeles (1957–63), and at the State Univ. of N.Y. at Buffalo (1962–98). He likewise served as director of the Monday Evening Concerts in Los Angeles (1957–63) and as composer-in-residence at the American Academy in Rome (1972–73) and at Brevard Music Center (1980). His style of composition was neo-Classical, marked by a strong contrapuntal fabric; the influence of Stravinsky, with whom he had personal contact, was pronounced in many of his scores.

WORKS: DRAMATIC: O p e r a : *The Alchemy of Love* (1969); *Magic Water* (1978). M e l o d r a m a : *A Mountain Eulogy* (1975). B a l l e t : *Yerma* (1946); *Virginia Sampler* (N.Y., March 4, 1947; rev. 1960). ORCH.: *The Parcae*, overture (Boston, Oct. 16, 1953); 3 syms.: No. 1 (1956; Boston, Feb. 1, 1957), No. 2 (1965), and No. 3 (1981); *Capriccio* for Strings (Ojai, Calif., May 23, 1958; rev. 1974); Piano Concerto (1968; rev. 1980); *4 Kookaburra Marches* for Orch. and Tape (1972); *Symphony of Dances and Songs* (1981); *Variations* for Piano and Orch. (1981); *Alabaster Chambers* for Strings (1989). CHAMBER: Sextet for Clarinet, Bassoon, and Strings (1940); *Invention* for Clarinet and Piano (1943); *In Woods* for Oboe, Harp, and Percussion (1978); *Delaunay Pochoirs*, 3 pieces for Cello and Piano (1980); Sonata for Solo Cello (1982); *Flute of Wonder*, 3 pieces for Flute and Piano (1983); *Tzadik* for Saxophone Quartet (1983), 12 Instruments (1984), String Quartet (1984), and Piano Trio (1985); *Exequy* for String Trio (1985); piano pieces, including a Sonata for Piano, 4-Hands (1987). VOCAL: *A Choir of Starlings* for 4 Soloists, 2 Oboes, Bassoon, 2 Horns, and String Quintet, after A. Hecht (1951); *Academic Graffiti* for Voice, Clarinet, Cello, Piano, and Percussion, after Auden (1959); *Caedmon (After the Venerable Bede)* for Soloists, Chorus, and Orch. (1972); *Copernicus—Narrative and Credo* for Narrator, Chorus, and Instrumental Ensemble (1973); *From Banja Luka* for Mezzo-soprano and Orch. (1987); many songs.—**NS/LK/DM**

Smith, Bernard (real name, **Bernhard Schmidt**), German-born English organ builder, known as "Father Smith;" b. c. 1630; d. London, Feb. 20, 1708. He was trained in his homeland and was active in Holland before settling in London in 1666. He was organ maker to the king from 1671, a title formally bestowed upon him in 1681. He built or rebuilt some 70 organs.

BIBL.: A. Freeman, *Father S.* (London, 1926).—**NS/LK/DM**

Smith, Bessie (Elizabeth), American blues singer and songwriter; b. Chattanooga, Tenn., April 15, 1894; d. Clarksdale, Miss., Sept. 26, 1937. Smith was the most successful early blues singer on records and a major influence on all the blues and jazz singers who followed her. Her 160 recordings, made between 1923 and 1933, featured such jazz performers as Fletcher Henderson, Louis Armstrong, James P. Johnson, Jack Teagarden, Chu Berry, and Benny Goodman. She sold between five and ten million copies during her lifetime and continued to sell for decades after.

Smith was the daughter of William and Laura Smith, both of whom died during her childhood, leaving her to be raised in poverty by a sister. She sang in school plays and in a girls choir as well as on the streets. She first sang onstage at the age of nine at the Ivory Theatre in Chattanooga in an amateur contest. In 1912 she joined the Moses Stokes vaudeville troupe as a dancer, where she met blues singer Ma Rainey. She performed in vaudeville during the 1910s and early 1920s, gradually achieving prominence. During this period she was seen by record executive Frank Walker at a club in Selma, Ala. When Walker became recording director of Columbia Records in 1923, he sent for her.

Smith's first recording sessions, in February 1923, produced "Down Hearted Blues," released by Columbia on June 7, 1923; it sold 780,000 copies within six months of release, eventually becoming a million-seller. Smith sold two million records during her first year as a recording artist; her other successful records included "Gulf Coast Blues" (the flip side of "Down Hearted Blues"), "Aggravatin' Papa," "Baby Won't You Please Come Home Blues," and "T'ain't Nobody's Biz-Ness If I Do." On the same day that her first record was released, Smith married Philadelphia nightwatchman Jack Gee, apparently her second marriage following the death of Earl Love, whom she had married circa 1920. Smith and Gee adopted a son, Jack Gee Jr., in 1926, but they had separated by 1929.

Smith's success as a recording artist allowed her to become a top star on the black vaudeville circuit, and she toured the country extensively, traveling in her own Pullman railroad car but returning frequently to N.Y. to record. Her most popular records of 1925 included "The St. Louis Blues," "Careless Love Blues," and "I Ain't Gonna Play No Second Fiddle," all of which featured Armstrong on cornet. In 1926 "I Ain't Got Nobody" and "Lost Your Head Blues" (written by Smith) were popular. By 1927, Smith was finding success with such standards as "After You've Gone" and "Alexander's Ragtime Band," as she expanded her repertoire beyond blues to adapt to changing musical tastes. In 1928 her most popular records were "A Good Man Is Hard to Find" and "Empty Bed Blues." The latter was selected for the NARAS Hall of Fame in 1983.

Smith made her Broadway debut in the short-lived musical *Pansy* (N.Y., May 14, 1929) and the following month shot her only film appearance, starring in the 15-minute *St. Louis Blues*. (The film's soundtrack is included on the album *The Final Chapter: The Complete Recordings, Vol. 5*, released by Columbia/Legacy Records in 1996.) Her last successful record was "Nobody Knows You When You're Down and Out," released in August 1929, though Columbia continued to record her and release her records through the end of 1931.

Smith's career went into decline at the end of the 1920s due to several factors, including the death of vaudeville in the face of radio and sound motion pictures and the onset of the Depression. She supported herself in part by making and selling bootleg liquor, but she continued to perform regularly during the early 1930s. Record executive John Hammond brought her back into the recording studio in November 1933 for four sides that turned out to be her final recordings. She was well received during an extended stay at Connie's Inn on Times Square in N.Y. in 1936; she was on tour in

1937 when she was killed in an automobile accident. Shortly after her death, Hammond published an article in *Down Beat* magazine erroneously suggesting that she had bled to death after being refused admittance to a white hospital. This rumor served as the basis for Edward Albee's play *The Death of Bessie Smith*, produced Off-Broadway in 1961; it was not definitively disproved until the publication of Chris Albertson's biography in 1972.

Smith's recordings were periodically reissued and continued to be popular over the years. Columbia issued four volumes of *The Bessie Smith Story* on LP in 1950–51; starting in June 1970, the company reissued all of her recordings on five double-LP sets—*The World's Greatest Blues Singer, Any Woman's Blues, The Empress, Empty Bed Blues,* and *Nobody's Blues but Mine*—that sold in the hundreds of thousands. In the CD era Columbia/Legacy reissued the material as five double-CDs of *The Complete Recordings*, released between 1991 and 1996. Smith was the subject of *Me and Bessie* (N.Y., Oct. 22, 1975), a musical play conceived and written by Will Holt and Linda Hopkins, in which Hopkins portrayed Smith. The play ran on Broadway during the 1975–76 season and toured into 1977.

BIBL.: P. Oliver, *B. S.* (London, 1959); C. Moore, *Somebody's Angel: The Story of B. S.* (N.Y., 1969); C. Albertson, *B.* (N.Y., 1972); C. Albertson and G. Schuller, *B. S.: Empress of the Blues* (N.Y., 1975); E. Brooks, *The B. S. Companion: A Critical and Detailed Appreciation of the Recordings* (N.Y., 1982); E. Feinstein, *B. S.: Empress of the Blues* (N.Y., 1985).—WR

Smith, Buster (Henry), jazz alto saxophonist, clarinetist, arranger, guitarist; b. Alfdorf, Tex., Aug. 24, 1904; d. Dallas, Tex., Aug. 10, 1991. Brother of pianist Boston Smith, he was a mentor and early influence on Charlie Parker. He began playing piano and organ, then switched to clarinet in late teens. Smith worked with the Voddie White Trio (c. 1922), and began doubling on alto sax. Smith gigged with many bands in Dallas, then went to Oklahoma City in 1925 as a member of the Blue Devils, then led by trombonist Emir Coleman, and later by Walter Page. Smith remained in the band until late 1933, then went to Kansas City to join the Bennie Moten-George E. Lee Band. He worked briefly with Buster Moten (1935), then co-led the Barons of Rhythm with Count Basie. Smith left Kansas City late in 1936 to join Claude Hopkins (then in Iowa). Returned to work with Count Basie as staff arranger, worked briefly with Andy Kirk, then returned to Kansas City to lead his own band. He worked with trumpeter Dee "Prince" Stewart early in 1938, then from summer 1938 led his own band again. Left Kansas City in September 1938, moved to N.Y., worked as an arranger for Gene Krupa and Hot Lips Page, and did extensive gigging on alto and clarinet. Led his own band in Va. in 1939, then worked in N.Y. with Don Redman, Eddie Durham, and Snub Mosley, among others. Returned to Kansas City in 1942, formed his own band, which had a long residency at the Club Shangri-La. From the 1940s on, Smith led his own band in Tex., Okla., and Ark.; in 1959 his band recorded an LP in Fort Worth, Tex. He lived in semi-retirement in South Dallas from the 1970s.

DISC.: *The Legendary Buster Smith* (1959).—JC/LP

Smith, Carleton Sprague, distinguished American musicologist; b. N.Y., Aug. 8, 1905; d. Washington, Conn., Sept. 19, 1994. He was educated at Harvard Univ. (M.A., 1928) and at the Univ. of Vienna (Ph.D., 1930, with the diss. *Die Beziehungen zwischen Spanien und Oesterreich im 17. Jahrhundert*). Returning to the U.S., he was an instructor in history at Columbia Univ. (1931–35), then at N.Y.U. (1939–67); he also served as chief of the Music Division at the N.Y. Public Library (1931–43; 1946–59). A linguist, he lectured in South America, in Spanish and Portuguese, on the social history of the U.S. Smith was also a skillful flutist, and often took part in concerts of early and new music.

BIBL.: I. Katz, M. Kuss, and R. Wolfe, eds., *Libraries, History, Diplomacy, and the Performing Arts: Essays in Honor of C.S. S.* (Stuyvesant, N.Y., 1991).—**NS/LK/DM**

Smith, Carl (M.), American country singer and guitarist; b. Maynardsville, Tenn., March 15, 1927. Smith was one of the most successful country singers of the 1950s, performing in a variety of styles, from honky-tonk to ballads and even rockabilly; his biggest hits among the 93 recordings he placed in the country charts between 1951 and 1978 were "Let Old Mother Nature Have Her Way," "(When You Feel Like You're in Love) Don't Just Stand There," and "Hey Joe!"

Smith took up the guitar in his youth and first played in public at an amateur contest when he was 13. At 17 he got a summer job performing on Knoxville radio station WROL. He graduated from high school and enlisted in the navy in 1945, serving until August 1946. He returned to WROL and also performed on other radio stations and in country bands during the next few years. He came to the attention of the *Grand Ole Opry* radio show in Nashville and made his debut on the show in March 1950, also getting a job at the show's home station, WSM.

On May 5, 1950, Smith signed to Columbia Records, making his recording debut on May 11. His first hit came in June 1951 with "Let's Live a Little" (music and lyrics by Ruth Coletharp), and he scored three more hits before the end of the year, including "Let Old Mother Nature Have Her Way" (music and lyrics by Louie Clark and Loys Southerland), which hit #1 in December.

Smith had four more hits in 1952, among them "(When You Feel Like You're in Love) Don't Just Stand There" (music and lyrics by Jack Henley and Ernest Tubb), which topped the charts in March, and "Are You Teasing Me" (music and lyrics by Charlie Louvin and Ira Louvin), which became his third consecutive #1 country hit in July. That month he married singer June Carter of the group Mother Maybelle Carter and the Carter Sisters. Their daughter, Rebecca Carlene Smith (b. Madison, Tenn., Sept. 26, 1955), became a successful singer under the name Carlene Carter. They later divorced.

Smith continued to be a top country recording artist over the next four years. His seven hits in 1953 were led by "Hey Joe!" (music and lyrics by Boudleaux Bryant), which hit #1 in August. Of his five chart entries in 1954, the most successful was "Loose Talk" (music and lyrics

by Freddie Hart and Ann Lucas), which hit #1 in January 1955. He had eight chart songs in 1955, four of which reached the Top Ten, the most popular being "There She Goes" (music and lyrics by Durwood Haddoc, Eddie Miller, and W. S. Stevenson). There was another four Top Ten country hits in 1956, with "You Are the One" (music and lyrics by Pat Patterson) charting the highest.

Smith was a regular on the monthly one-hour network television broadcast of the *Grand Ole Opry* that ran from October 1955 to September 1956. After it concluded, he quit the *Grand Ole Opry* and undertook an extensive package tour underwritten by the Philip Morris cigarette company that lasted a year and a half. He also found time to appear in two films, *The Badge of Marshall Brennan* (1957) and *Buffalo Guns* (1958). In September 1957 he married singer Goldie Hill; they had three children.

Though he regularly reached the country charts, Smith had fewer hits after 1956, making the Top Ten only four more times, with "Why, Why" (1957), "Your Name Is Beautiful" (1957), "Ten Thousand Drums" (1959), and "Deep Water" (1967). From March to September 1961 he was one of the regulars on the musical variety series *Five Star Jubilee*, broadcast on network television once a week. For five years starting in 1964 he hosted the TV series *Carl Smith's Country Music Hall*, which was produced and syndicated in Canada with some U.S. station also picking it up.

Smith left Columbia Records in 1974 and cut back on his activities, but he signed to Hickory Records the following year and continued recording until 1977, when he retired to his ranch near Nashville. He came out of retirement to do the occasional show, and in 1980 he rerecorded his greatest hits for an album promoted on television.

DISC.: *Carl Smith* (9156); *Softly and Tenderly* (1956); *Sentimental Songs* (1957); *Smith's the Name* (1957); *Sunday Down South* (1957); *Let's Live a Little* (1958); *The Carl Smith Touch* (1960); *Easy to Please* (1962); *Tall, Tall Gentleman* (1963); *There Stands the Glass* (1964); *I Want to Live and Love* (1965); *Kisses Don't Lie* (1965); *Man with a Plan* (1966); *The Country Gentleman Sings* (1967); *Satisfaction Guaranteed* (1967); *Country on My Mind* (1968); *Deep Water* (1968); *A Tribute to Roy Acuff* (1969); *Faded Love and Winter Roses* (1969); *I Love You Because* (1970); *The Way I Lose My Mind* (1975); *This Lady Loving Me* (1977); *Old Lonesome Times* (1988).—**WR**

Smith, Chas, American composer and performer; b. West Brookfield, Mass., March 15, 1948. He began playing piano at the age of 8. He played guitar in rock bands (1964–69), and attended N.Y.'s Utica Coll. (1967) and studied jazz composition and arranging at the Berklee School of Music in Boston (1969–70). He studied composition with Powell, Subotnick, Budd, Brown, and Tenney at the Calif. Inst. of the Arts in Valencia (B.F.A., 1975; M.F.A., 1977), where he performed with Michael Le Donne-Bhennet, Michael Jon Fink, and William Hawley at galleries and performance spaces under such ensembles as Ronin, C33, 100 Miles of Sheep Jokes, and Stilllife (1975–80). The Chas Smith Ensemble, formed in 1985, made appearances in various Los Angeles venues. His recordings include *Stilllife* (1981), *Santa Fe* (1982), and *Nakadai* (1987); also played on records by Harold Budd, Jim Fox, and Carole Caroompas and appeared in several rock videos that feature his extensive tattoos, of which he is justly proud; also performed in a number of film soundtracks, including *The Lost Boys* and *Less than Zero*. Smith performs chiefly on the pedal steel guitar, but also plays other stringed instruments, keyboards, and electronics; his music consists of austere meditations on very slowly evolving chords in the Lydian mode. He is a certified welder.

WORKS: *Ontolosis* for Electronics (1974); *Triactus* for Electronics (1975); *Mirage* for Voices, Bells, and Mallet Instruments (1977); *Santa Fe, October 68*, and *After*, all for Pedal Steel Guitar (1979–82); *Scicura* for 2 Pianos, 3 Vibraphones, Marimba, and Wind Instruments (1975; also arranged for Dobro and Pedal Steel Guitar, 1982); *Beatrix* for Pedal Steel Guitar (1983); *James Tenney* for Pedal Steel Guitar (1984); *Nakadai* for Multitrack Pedal Steel Guitar (1985); *A Judas Within: Seduction and Betrayal* for Vibraphone, Marimba, Hammer Dulcimer, Pedal Steel Guitar, Microtonal Chimes, Bowed Rods, and Small Metal Objects (1985–86); *Hollister* for Pedal Steel Guitar (1986).—NS/LK/DM

Smith, Clara, blues singer; b. Spartanburg, S.C., 1894; d. Detroit, Mich., Feb. 2, 1935. Smith had extensive work on the theater circuits from the early 1910s and began her recording career in 1923 with Fletcher Henderson, singing "I Never Miss the Sunshine/Awful Moanin' Blues" (1923) and made several duets with with Bessie Smith: "My Man Blues" (1925), "It's Tight Like That," (1929), and "Papa I Don't Need You Now" (1929). Smith made many records in the 1920s, accompanied by all-star personnel, including Lemuel Fowler, Louis Armstrong, and Coleman Hawkins. She appeared regularly at the Strollers' Club in N.Y. during the early 1930s; played a six-month residency at Orch. Gardens, Detroit, then played dates in Cleveland. Smith died of heart trouble at the Parkside Hospital, Detroit. Clara Smith was not related to Bessie Smith, Trixie Smith (d. Sept. 21, 1943), or Laura Smith (d. Feb. 1932).—JC/LP

Smith, Curtis O(tto) B(ismarck) Curtis- *See* **Curtis-Smith, Curtis O(tto) B(ismarck)**

Smith, Cyril (James), English pianist and teacher; b. Middlesbrough, Aug. 11, 1909; d. London, Aug. 2, 1974. He was a pupil of Herbert Fryer at the Royal Coll. of Music in London. He made his formal debut as a soloist in the Brahms second Piano Concerto in Birmingham (1929). In 1937 he married the pianist Phyllis Sellick, with whom he often appeared in works for 2 pianos from 1941; during a visit to the Soviet Union in 1956, he suffered a stroke that incapacitated his left arm; they subsequently gave concerts for Piano, 3-Hands (from 1957). He taught at the Royal Coll. of Music (1934–74). In 1971 he was made an Officer of the Order of the British Empire. His autobiography was appropriately titled *Duet for Three Hands* (London, 1958). At the apex of his career, he won particular distinction for his performances of Rachmaninoff; he later commissioned new works and arrangements for Piano, 3-Hands. —NS/LK/DM

Smith, David Stanley, American conductor, music educator, and composer; b. Toledo, Ohio, July 6, 1877; d. New Haven, Conn., Dec. 17, 1949. He studied with Horatio Parker at Yale Univ., graduating in 1900. He then took courses in composition with Thuille in Munich and Widor in Paris. Upon his return to the U.S., he obtained a Mus.B. degree at Yale (1903) and was appointed an instructor at the Yale Univ. School of Music; in 1916 he became a prof. there; in 1920 was appointed dean of the School of Music, retiring in 1946. He was conductor of the New Haven Sym. Orch. from 1920 to 1946. In 1910 he was elected a member of the National Inst. of Arts and Letters. His compositions were cast in a conservative mold.

WORKS: DRAMATIC: O p e r a : *Merrymount* (1914). ORCH.: 4 syms.: No. 1 (1910), No. 2 (1917), No. 3 (1928; Cleveland, Jan. 8, 1931, composer conducting), and No. 4 (1937; Boston, April 14, 1939, composer conducting); *Prince Hal*, overture (New Haven, Dec. 1912); *Impressions*, suite (1916); *Fête galante*, fantasy for Flute and Orch. (N.Y., Dec. 11, 1921); *Epic Poem* (1926; Boston, April 12, 1935, composer conducting); *Sinfonietta* for Strings (1931); *1929: A Satire* (1932; N.Y., Nov. 15, 1933); *Requiem* for Violin and Orch. (1939); *Credo*, symphonic poem (1941); 4 Pieces for Strings (1943); *The Apostle*, symphonic poem (1944). CHAMBER: 10 string quartets (1899–1938); *Sonata Pastorale* for Oboe and Piano (1918); Violin Sonata (1923); *Flowers* for 10 Instruments (1924); Piano Quintet (1927); String Sextet (1931); piano pieces, including a Sonata (1929). VOCAL: *Rhapsody of St. Bernard* for Solo Voices, Chorus, and Orch. (1915); *The Vision of Isaiah* for Soprano, Tenor, Chorus, and Orch. (1927); *The Ocean* for Bass, Chorus, and Orch. (1945); song cycles.

BIBL.: E. Goode, *D.S. S. and his Music* (diss., Univ. of Cincinnati, 1978).—NS/LK/DM

Smith, Floyd (Wonderful), jazz guitarist; b. St. Louis, Mo., Jan. 25, 1917; d. Indianapolis, Ind., March 29, 1982. His father was a drummer. Smith began on ukulele, then switched to guitar; studied theory at the Victor Hugo School in St. Louis. He played in Eddie Johnson's Crackerjacks and Dewey Jackson's Band before working in the Jeter-Pillars Orch. (1937–38). He joined the Sunset Royal Orch. in summer 1938, then left to work with the Brown Skin Models before joining Andy Kirk in January 1939. He served in Europe with the U.S. Army during World War II, then returned to Andy Kirk in late 1945. Smith left Kirk in September 1946 to form his own trio which played for several years at the Dusable Club in Chicago. In the mid-1950s he worked with Wild Bill Davis and Chris Columbus, and led his own group to Europe with Bill Doggett in the early 1960s, and again led his own group. During the late 1960s, Smith played in the Hank Marr duo in Atlantic City. He moved to Indianapolis during the 1970s.—JC/LP

Smith, Gregg, American conductor and composer; b. Chicago, Aug. 21, 1931. He studied composition with Leonard Stein, Lukas Foss, and Ray Moreman and conducting with Fritz Zweig at the Univ. of Calif. at Los Angeles (M.A., 1956). In 1955 in Los Angeles he founded the Gregg Smith Singers, a chamber choir, with which he toured and recorded extensively; from 1970, was active with it in N.Y. He also taught at Ithaca Coll., the State Univ. of N.Y. at Stony Brook, the Peabody Cons. of Music in Baltimore, Barnard Coll., and the Manhattan School of Music in N.Y. His repertoire extends from early music to works by contemporary American composers. He ed. the Gregg Smith Choral Series. Smith wrote much vocal music, including 2 operas, choral works, songs, and pieces for chamber orch.—NS/LK/DM

Smith, Hale, black American composer; b. Cleveland, June 29, 1925. He studied piano with Dorothy Price and composition with Marcel Dick at the Cleveland Inst. of Music (B.Mus., 1950; M.Mus., 1952); went to N.Y. in 1958 and was active as a music ed. for publishers, as a jazz arranger, and as a teacher; later was a prof. at the Univ. of Conn. in Storrs (1970–84). His output is remarkable for its utilization of serial procedures with jazz infusions; wrote musical scores for Dizzy Gillespie, Ahmad Jamal, Eric Dolphy, and Abby Lincoln, and worked in various capacities for Quincy Jones, Clark Terry, Oliver Nelson, Miriam Makeba, and Hugh Masekela.

WORKS: DRAMATIC: Chamber Opera: *Blood Wedding* (1953). **ORCH.:** *Orchestral Set* (1952; rev. 1968); *Contours* (Louisville, Oct. 17, 1961); *By Yearning and By Beautiful* for Strings (1964); *Music* for Harp and Orch. (1972); *Ritual and Incantations* (1974); *Innerflexions* (N.Y., Sept. 2, 1977). **CHAMBER:** Duo for Violin and Piano (1953); Cello Sonata (1955); *Epicedial Variations* for Violin and Piano (1956); *3 Brevities* for Flute (1960); *Introductions, Cadenzas and Interludes* for 8 Players (1974); *Variations* for 6 Players (1975); *Variations a due* for Cello, Alto Saxophone, and Flute or Saxophone, or Clarinet ad libitum (1984). **Piano:** *Evocation* (1966); *Anticipations, Introspections and Reflections* (1971). **VOCAL:** *5 Songs* for Voice and Violin (1956); *2 Love Songs of John Donne* for Soprano and 9 Instruments (1958); *Comes Tomorrow,* jazz cantata for Chorus and Accompaniment (1972; rev. 1977); *Toussaint L'Ouverture 1803* for Chorus and Piano (1977); *Symphonic Spirituals* for Soprano and Orch. (1979); *Meditations in Passage* for Soprano, Baritone, and Piano or Orch. (1980).

BIBL.: M. Breda, *H. S.: Biographical and Analytical Study of the Man and His Music* (diss., Univ. of Southern Miss., Harrisburg, 1975).—NS/LK/DM

Smith, Howie, American saxophonist, composer, and teacher; b. Pottsville, Pa., Feb. 25, 1943. He studied saxophone with Donald Sinta and composition with Warren Benson at Ithaca Coll. (B.S.), and composition with Salvatore Martirano and Edwin London at the Univ. of Ill. (M.S.). As a performer, he has worked with musicians and composers as diverse as Mike Nock, Elvis Presley, and John Cage, and with ensembles as different as the Australian quartet Jazz Co-op, Bernard Rands's Sonor, and the Cleveland Orch. He has been a frequent performer with the Cleveland Chamber Sym., and has had a number of works commissioned for him as soloist with that ensemble, including scores by Martirano, London, and David Baker. In 1979 he joined the faculty of Cleveland State Univ. Since 1981 he has presented the annual Concert in Progress in Cleveland, an evening of new compositions and performances for soloists and ensembles as varied as his own interests. As a composer, he has created works for conventional big bands and combos, for string, wind, and percussion ensembles, for electronics, and for mixed media. Among his most important works are *Thandi* (1975) and *The Golden Goose* (1978) for Large Jazz Ensemble, *Song for the Children* for Saxophone, Strings, and Keyboards (1986), *Time/Windows* for Trumpet and Chamber Orch. (1992), *Mobius Strip* for Trumpet and Chamber Sym. (1994), *The Speed of Time* for Solo Saxophone, Saxophones, Synthesizers, Percussion, Voices, and Electronics (1994–95), and *M. & M.* for Jazz Ensemble (1999).—LK/DM

Smith, Jabbo (Cladys), noted jazz trumpeter, trombonist, singer; b. Pembroke, Ga., Dec. 24, 1908; d. N.Y., Jan. 16, 1991. His father died when Smith was four years old; he moved with his mother to Savannah, then at age six was placed in the Jenkins' Orphanage in Charleston, S.C. In the orphanage, he was taught trumpet and trombone; at age 10, he began touring with the orphanage band. He ran away from the institution on several occasions and finally left the orphanage for good when he was 16. He then traveled to Philadelphia and worked there and in Atlantic City before settling in N.Y., where he worked from autumn 1925 until early 1928 and also sat in on a recording session with Duke Ellington (November 1927). Smith joined the James P. Johnson Orch. and toured with the "Keep Shufflin'" revue from February 1928. The show folded in Chicago that November, and Jabbo worked there for various leaders and also led his own recording band. Through the mid-1930s, he worked primarily in Chicago, although he also worked on occasion in Milwaukee—where he set up residence—and Deroit as well as on the road. In 1936, Smith returned to his hometown of Milwaukee and joined Claude Hopkins (then on tour), remaining with him for two years; Smith and Hopkins set up a residency at the Roseland, N.Y., in autumn 1936. From the late 1930s through the mid-1940s Smith worked in N.Y. and Newark, N.J., and then moved back to Milwaukee, where he played with local bands and led his own sextet in the late 1940s. He then left full-time music, but continued to play occasionally in the 1950s. He made a comeback at the Milwaukee Jazz Society concert in June 1961, resumed working with local bands, and made a playing trip to Chicago. He continued day work with a car-hire company in Milwaukee while playing valve trombone and piano at Tina's Lounge in 1966. A proficient pianist, Smith became particularly interested in composing. He made several tours of Europe during the 1970s and 1980s. He made another comeback when he was featured in the Broadway and touring production of *One Mo' Time* in 1978. Although his playing was a shadow of its old quality, he continued to work as a vocalist, particularly after a bout of illness in 1982.

Smith played longer and more complex lines than most trumpeters during the late 1920s and was among the most advanced musicians of his day. For many years, a rumor persisted that there were two Jabbo Smiths; the confusion arose because one of Jabbo Smith's trumpet-playing colleagues was called "Jabbo" Jenkins.

DISC.: "Sweet 'n' Lowdown," "Ace of Rhythm" (both 1929). D. Ellington: "Black and Tan Fantasy" (1927).—JC/LP

Smith, Jennifer, English soprano; b. Lisbon, July 13, 1945. Following training at the Lisbon Cons., she pursued vocal studies with Winifred Radford in London, Pierre Bernac in London and Paris, and Hans Keller in London. In 1966 she made her operatic debut as Carissimi's Jeptha in Lisbon, and then sang in other European cities and in England. In 1979 she appeared as Mozart's Countess at the Welsh National Opera in Cardiff. She portrayed Alphise in the first stage performance of Rameau's *Les Boréades* in Aix-en-Provence in 1982. In 1988 she sang Cybele in the first U.S. performance of Lully's *Atys* in N.Y. She appeared as the Queen of the Night in London in 1989. In 1992 she was engaged as Iphigénie in Gluck's *Iphigénie en Tauride* at the English Bach Festival at London's Covent Garden. In 1995 she sang Elettra in Lisbon. Her concert engagements took her to major European music centers. Among her other important portrayals were roles in operas by Marais, Mondonville, and Purcell.—**NS/LK/DM**

Smith, Jimmy (actually, **James Oscar Jr.**), American jazz organist; b. Norristown, Pa., Dec. 8, 1925. Smith validated the organ as a jazz instrument and popularized jazz organ playing in a series of recordings; he hit the pop charts with 22 albums between 1962 and 1970.

Both of Smith's parents were pianists, and he won a Major Bowes amateur contest on the instrument at the age of nine, later going on to appear on the radio in Philadelphia. He and his father performed together in local clubs in 1942. He served in the navy during World War II, then returned to Philadelphia, where he studied the string bass at the Hamilton School of Music in 1948 and the piano at the Ornstein School of Music in 1949–50. He joined Don Gardner and His Sonotones as a pianist in 1952, later switching to organ. In September 1955 he formed his own organ-guitar-drums trio, and his N.Y. debut at the Bohemia club in 1956 was critically acclaimed. He made his first appearance at the Newport Jazz Festival in 1957.

Smith recorded for Blue Note Records until 1962. His album *Midnight Special*, featuring tenor saxophonist Stanley Turrentine and guitarist Kenny Burrell, spent almost a year in the pop charts, and the single "Midnight Special" was in both the R&B and pop singles charts. Switching to Verve Records, he hit the Top Ten of the LP charts with *Bashin'* (1962), which featured "Walk on the Wild Side" (music by Elmer Bernstein), a Top 40 hit and Grammy nominee for Best Jazz Performance by a Large Group, Instrumental.

Smith continued to place albums in the charts consistently through 1970. In 1974 he formed his own label, Mojo Records. In September 1974 he married his manager, Lola Ward. After touring Europe in June 1975 he cut back on touring and moved to Los Angeles, where he opened his own jazz club. In 1982 he signed to the Elektra-Musician jazz label, run by record executive Bruce Lundvall, and released a new album, *Off the Top*. He followed Lundvall back to Blue Note Records in 1986 and re-signed to Verve Records in 1995.

DISC.: *A new Sound...A New Star: Jimmy Smith at the Organ, Vol. 1–3* (1956); *A Date with Jimmy Smith* (1957); *Plays Pretty Just for You* (1957); *Confirmation* (1957); *Special Guests* (1957); *House Party* (1957); *Groovin' at Small Small's Paradise, Vol. 1, 2* (1957); *The Sermon* (1958); *Softly as a Summer Breeze* (1958); *Home Cookin'* (1958); *Six Views of the Blues* (1958); *Crazy! Baby* (1960); *Back at the Chicken Shack* (1960); *Midnight Special* (1960); *Prayer Meetin'* (1960); *Bashin': The Unpredictable Jimmy Smith* (1962); *I'm Movin' On* (1963); *Bucket!* (1963); *Any Number Can Win* (1963); *Jazz 'Round Midnight: Jimmy Smith* (1963); *The Cat* (1964); *Christmas Cookin'* (1964); *Organ Grinder Swing* (1965); *Peter and the Wolf* (1966); *The Dynamic Duo* (1966); *The Further Adventures of Jimmy and Wes* (1966); *Respect* (1967); *Stay Loose* (1968); *The Boss* (1968); *Groove Drops* (1969); *Jimmy Smith in a Plain Brown Wrapper* (1971); *Root Down* (1972); *Other Side of Jimmy Smith* (1973); *Blacksmith* (1974); *Jimmy Smith* (1975); *Sit on It!* (1976); *It's Necessary* (1977); *Tomorrow's Sounds Today* (1978); *The Cat Strikes Again* (1980); *All the Way I Live* (1981); *Off the Top* (1982); *Keep on Comin'* (1983); *Prime Time* (1989); *Fourmost* (1990); *The Master* (1993); *Sum Serious Blues* (1993); *Damn!* (1995); *Angel Eyes: Ballad & Slow Jams* (1995); *Platinum* (1996).—**WR**

Smith, Joe (actually, **Joseph C.**), jazz trumpeter; b. Ripley, Ohio, June 28, 1902; d. N.Y., Dec. 2, 1937. Brother of **Russell T. Smith**. Joe Smith is best known for his sensitive work with Fletcher Henderson and Bessie Smith in the 1920s. His father was Luke Smith Sr., who led a big brass band in Cincinnati. Smith had six brothers, all trumpet players; the most famous of which was Russell T. Smith; another brother, Luke Jr., died in 1936; two others, George and Charlie, were also professional musicians. A cousin, Clarence Smith, played trumpet with Andy Kirk for a while. Joe was originally taught by his father, gigged with local bands, then left town with a traveling fair. Stranded in Pittsburgh, he carved a unique wooden trumpet mouthpiece from a used cotton spool; for some years afterwards he used this occasionally for special effects. Around 1920, he traveled to N.Y. He then returned to Pittsburgh before traveling to Chicago to join the Black Swan Jazz Masters (directed by Fletcher Henderson). He toured accompanying Ethel Waters from January–July 1922, and then returned briefly to N.Y. A few weeks later, he went out on tour with Mamie Smith's Jazz Hounds, working with her through early 1923, including bookings in Calif. By late 1923, he was back in N.Y., working with various bands and doing extensive gigging and recording sessions (some with Fletcher Henderson). In March 1924, Smith directed the band for the Noble Sissle and Eubie Blake revue *In Bamville* and remained with this show (later renamed *The Chocolate Dandies*) until November 1924. When the revue began touring, Joe remained in N.Y.; in April 1925, he joined Fletcher Henderson on a full-time basis, remaining with the band until October 1928; during this period, he also recorded with many blues singers, notably Bessie Smith. He continued to work with various leaders through the early 1930s, including several stints with McKinney's Cotton Pickers (summer 1929–November 1930; late 1931–early 1932). In early 1933, he was working out of Kansas City, where his health began to fail. Fletcher Henderson rehired him that year, but Smith was unable to play, and returned with Henderson to N.Y., where he was immediately hospitalized, suffering from the symptoms of syphilis. He succumbed to the disease in 1937.—**JC/LP**

Smith, John Christopher (real name, **Johann Christoph Schmidt**), German-born English organist and composer; b. Ansbach, 1712; d. Bath, Oct. 3, 1795. His father, Johann Christoph Schmidt, went to London in 1716 as Handel's treasurer and chief copyist; the son followed in 1720, and received a few lessons from Handel about 1725; after lessons from Pepusch, he studied with Thomas Roseingrave. He wrote his first opera, *Ulysses*, in 1733; after its failure, he gave up the theater. Following a sojourn abroad (1746–48), he became organist at the Foundling Hospital in London in 1754, where he directed the annual performance of *Messiah* (1759–68). He scored a success with his opera *The Enchanter of Love and Magic* (1760), but thereafter devoted himself to composing oratorios; with Stanley, he oversaw the Lenten performances of oratorios at Covent Garden (1760–74). He settled in Bath, where he was active as a teacher; upon his father's death in 1763, he was bequeathed his father's large Handel collection, which, after being granted a royal pension by King George III (1772), he bequeathed to the king; it is now housed in the Royal Music Library at the British Museum.

WORKS (all first perf. in London unless otherwise given): **DRAMATIC: Opera:** *Ulysses* (April 16, 1733); *Rosalinda* (Jan. 4, 1740); *The Seasons* (1740; not perf.); *Issipile* (1743; not perf.); *Il ciro riconosciuto* (1745; not perf.); *Dario* (1746; not perf.); *Artaserse* (1748; unfinished); *The Fairies* (Feb. 3, 1755); *The Tempest* (Feb. 11, 1756); *The Enchanter of Love and Magic* (Dec. 13, 1760); *Medea* (1760–61; unfinished). **Oratorios:** *David's Lamentation over Saul and Jonathan* (1738; Feb. 22, 1740); *Paradise Lost* (1757–58; Feb. 29, 1760); *Judith* (1758; not perf.); *Feast of Darius* (1761–62; not perf.; based on the opera *Dario*); *Rebecca* (March 16, 1764); *Nabal* (March 16, 1764); *Jehosaphat* (1764; not perf.); *Gideon* (Feb. 10, 1769; based on the *Feast of Darius* and works by Handel); *Redemption* (1774; not perf.). **Other Vocal:** *The Mourning Muse of Alexis*, funeral ode (1729); *Thamesis, Isis and Proteus*, cantata; *Daphne*, cantata (1744); *The Foundling Hymn* (1763); *Funeral Service for the Dowager Princess of Wales* (1772); songs. **HARPSICHORD** (all publ. in London): 6 suites, op.1 (1732); 6 suites, op.2 (c. 1735); *6 Suites of Lessons*, op.3 (c. 1755); *6 Lessons*, op.4 (c. 1758); *12 Sonatas*, op.5 (1763).

BIBL.: [W. Coxe], *Anecdotes of George Frederick Handel and J.C. S.* (London, 1799).—NS/LK/DM

Smith, John Stafford, English music scholar, organist, and composer; b. Gloucester (baptized), March 30, 1750; d. London, Sept. 21, 1836. He studied with his father, Martin Smith, organist at Gloucester Cathedral, and later with Boyce and Nares. In 1784 he was made a Gentleman of the Chapel Royal, and in 1802 was made one of its organists; from 1785 he served as lay-vicar at Westminster Abbey; also served as Master of the Children at the Chapel Royal (1805–17). His importance to music history rests upon his work as a music scholar. He acquired an invaluable collection of early music MSS and editions, which included the Mulliner Book and the Old Hall MS. In all, he acquired 2,191 vols. of music, of which 578 were in MS. After his death, the collection was sold at auction and dispersed without a trace. As a composer, he became best known for his glees. In the 5th collection of his glees (1799), he included an arrangement of the tune *To Anacreon in Heaven*, to which Francis Scott Key wrote *The Star-Spangled Banner* (1814); but there were several reasons for questioning whether he was the composer; his authorship was doubted by many reputable American scholars. William Lichtenwanger, in his "The Music of The Star-Spangled Banner: From Ludgate Hill to Capitol Hill," *Quarterly Journal of the Library of Congress* (July 1977), seems to have dispelled these doubts by publ. excerpts from the "Recollections" of Richard John Samuel Stevens, an active member of the Anacreontic Society of London, who states in the rubric for 1777: "The president was Ralph Tomlinson...He wrote the Poetry of the Anacreontic Song; which Stafford Smith set to Music." Smith was an excellent musician. He transcribed into modern notation early MSS for the *History of Music* by Sir John Hawkins, ed. *Musica antiqua*, containing compositions "from the commencement of the 12th to the 18th century" (2 vols., 1812), and publ. *A Collection of Songs of Various Kinds for Different Voices* (1785).

BIBL.: B. Frith, *J.S. S., 1750–1836, Gloucester Composer* (Gloucester, 1950); F. Grameny, *J.S. S., 1750–1836: An Early English Musicologist* (diss., Boston Univ., 1987).—NS/LK/DM

Smith (real name, **Vielehr**), **Julia (Frances)**, American pianist, composer, and writer on music; b. Denton, Tex., Jan. 25, 1911; d. N.Y., April 27, 1989. She studied at North Tex. State Univ. (graduated, 1930), then took courses in piano with Carl Friedberg and received instruction in composition at the Juilliard School of Music in N.Y. (diploma, 1939); also studied at N.Y.U. (M.A., 1933; Ph.D., 1952). She was the pianist of the all-women Orchestrette of N.Y. (1932–39); made tours of the U.S., Latin America, and Europe; taught at the Hartt School of Music in Hartford, Conn. (1941–46).

WRITINGS: *Aaron Copland: His Work and Contribution to American Music* (N.Y., 1955); *Master Pianist: The Career and Teaching of Carl Friedberg* (N.Y., 1963); *Directory of American Women Composers* (Indianapolis, 1970).

WORKS: DRAMATIC: Opera: *Cynthia Parker* (1938; Denton, Feb. 16, 1940; rev. 1977); *The Stranger of Manzano* (1943; Dallas, May 6, 1947); *The Gooseherd and the Goblin* (1946; N.Y., Feb. 22, 1947); *Cockcrow* (1953; Austin, Tex., April 22, 1954); *The Shepherdess and the Chimney Sweep* (1963; Fort Worth, Tex., Dec. 28, 1967); *Daisy* (Miami, Nov. 3, 1973). **ORCH.:** *Episodic Suite* (1936); Piano Concerto (1938; rev. 1971; Dallas, Feb. 28, 1976; arr. for 2 Pianos, 1971); *Folkways Symphony* (1948); *Remember the Alamo* for Symphonic or Full Band and Optional Narrator and Chorus (1965; in collaboration with C. Vashaw). **CHAMBER:** *Cornwall*, piano trio (1955); String Quartet (1964); Suite for Wind Octet (1980); piano pieces. **VOCAL:** Various works, including *Our Heritage* for Double Chorus and Orch. (1958) and *Prairie Kaleidoscope*, song cycle for Soprano and String Quartet (1982).—NS/LK/DM

Smith, Kate (actually, **Kathryn Elizabeth**), American singer and radio personality; b. Greenville, Va., May 1, 1907; d. Raleigh, N. C., June 17, 1986. Smith had her greatest impact as a popular radio host and performer in the 1930s and 1940s, though she also appeared on Broadway, in films, on records, in personal appearances, and on television in a career lasting half a century. She had a wholesome image and was closely identified with the patriotic anthem "God Bless America," which she introduced.

Smith was the daughter of William and Charlotte Hanby Smith; her father owned a news dealership. She was raised in Washington, D.C., and early on showed talent as a singer and dancer, though her parents tried to steer her toward a career in nursing and she did begin training as a nurse after graduating from high school in 1925. But after a year she landed a job in vaudeville locally and was seen by comic actor Eddie Dowling, who cast her as Tiny Little (a humorous reference to her large size) in his musical *Honeymoon Lane* (N.Y., Sept. 20, 1926). It ran 353 performances, and while it was still running Smith began recording for Columbia Records, scoring her first hit with "One Sweet Letter from You" (music by Harry Warren, lyrics by Lew Brown and Sidney Clare) in July 1927.

Smith performed in a touring version of the Vincent Youmans musical *Hit the Deck* in 1929 and returned to N.Y. to star in the De Sylva Brown Henderson show *Flying High* (N.Y., March 3, 1930) with Bert Lahr. Enduring Lahr's jokes about her weight almost drove her out of show business, but she met Columbia Records executive Joseph Martin (Ted) Collins, who became her manager and directed her career toward radio.

Smith first hosted her own network radio series in the spring of 1931 and continued with various programs for the next 20 years. She returned to recording for Columbia in August 1931 and scored a best-selling record with "When the Moon Comes over the Mountain" (music and lyrics by Howard Johnson, Harry Woods, and Kate Smith) in October; it became her radio theme song. She had another best-seller with "River, Stay 'Way from My Door" (music by Harry Woods, lyrics by Mort Dixon) in January 1932. Accompanying her on the record were Guy Lombardo and His Royal Canadians.

Smith's enormous popularity as a radio performer brought her to film for a guest role in Paramount's *The Big Broadcast*, released in October 1932. Paramount signed her and starred her in *Hello, Everybody*, released in January 1933, but the film failed and she returned to radio. On Armistice (now Veterans) Day, 1938, she introduced "God Bless America" (music and lyrics by Irving Berlin) on her radio show. She also recorded it for RCA Victor and scored a Top Ten hit in August 1940. With the U.S. entry into World War II in December 1941 she became a national symbol of patriotism. Her record coupling "Rose O'Day (The Filla-Ga-Dusha Song)" (music and lyrics by Charles Tobias and Al Lewis) and the war-themed "(There'll Be Bluebirds Over) The White Cliffs of Dover" (music by Walter Kent, lyrics by Nat Burton) was a Top Ten hit in February 1942 and sold a million copies. In July 1943 she re-created her introduction of "God Bless America" in the film *This Is the Army*. Her last Top Ten hit came in January 1945 with "Don't Fence Me In" (music and lyrics by Cole Porter), but she continued to reach the pop charts through March 1948, scoring her final hit with "Now Is the Hour" (music and lyrics by Maewa Kaihan, Clement Scott, and Dorothy Stewart).

While continuing two radio series, *Kate Smith Calls* and *Kate Smith Speaks*, Smith launched a weekday afternoon television series on Sept. 25, 1950, *The Kate Smith Hour*. The show ran for four years, through June 18, 1954. On Sept. 19, 1951, it was joined by the weekly variety program *The Kate Smith Evening Hour*, which ran one season, through June 11, 1952. She was less active after the mid-1950s but returned to radio with a program in 1958–59 and to television with a program that ran from Jan. 25 to July 18, 1960; both were called *The Kate Smith Show*.

Smith launched a comeback with a performance at Carnegie Hall on Nov. 2, 1963, which was recorded for an album that reached the charts in December. She also charted with the LPs *The Sweetest Sounds* (1964), *How Great Thou Art* (a 1965 Grammy nominee for Best Gospel Recording), *The Kate Smith Anniversary Album* (1966), and *Kate Smith Today* (1966). She remained active until the mid-1970s, when her health forced her to retire. She died of heart failure at 79 in 1986.

DISC.: *Kate Smith at Carnegie Hall* (1963); *The Sweetest Sounds* (1964); *The Kate Smith Christmas Album* (1966); *How Great Thou Art* (1966); *Kate Smith Today* (1966).

WRITINGS: *Living in a Great Big Way* (1938); *The K. S. Company's Coming Cookbook* (1958); *Upon My Lips a Song* (N.Y., 1960).

BIBL.: R. Hayes, *K. S.: A Biography, with Discography, Filmography and List of Stage Appearances* (Jefferson, N.C., 1995); M. Pitts, *K. S.: A Bio-Bibliography* (Westport, Conn., 1988).—**WR**

Smith, Lawrence Leighton, American conductor and pianist; b. Portland, Ore., April 8, 1936. He studied piano with Ariel Rubstein in Portland and then with Leonard Shure in N.Y. before pursuing his education at Portland State Univ. (B.S., 1956) and at the Mannes Coll. of Music in N.Y. (B.M., 1959). In 1964 he received first prize at the Mitropoulos International Conducting Competition in N.Y., and was then asst. conductor at the Metropolitan Opera in N.Y. (1964–67). He was music director of the Westchester (N.Y.) Sym. Orch. (1967–69) and principal guest conductor of the Phoenix (Ariz.) Sym. Orch. (1971–73), and also was music director of the Austin (Tex.) Sym. Orch. (1972–73). He served as music director of the Ore. Sym. Orch. in Portland (1973–80) and of the San Antonio Sym. Orch. (1980–85). Smith was artistic adviser and principal guest conductor of the N.C. Sym. Orch. in Raleigh (1980–81), music director of the Louisville Orch. (1983–94) and of the Music Academy of the West in Santa Barbara (from 1985), and artistic director of the Philharmonia Orch. of Yale in New Haven (from 1995). In addition to his appearances as a conductor in the U.S. and abroad, he continued to perform as a pianist, especially as an accompanist.—**NS/LK/DM**

Smith, Leland (Clayton), American bassoonist, clarinetist, teacher, computer music publisher, and composer; b. Oakland, Calif., Aug. 6, 1925. He was a student of Milhaud (composition) at Mills Coll. in Oakland, Calif. (1941–43; 1946–47), of Sessions (composition) and Bukofzer (musicology) at the Univ. of Calif. at Berkeley (M.A., 1948), and of Messiaen at the Paris Cons.

(1948–49). After teaching at the Univ. of Calif. at Berkeley (1950–51), Mills Coll. (1951–52), and the Univ. of Chicago (1952–58), he joined the faculty of Stanford Univ. in 1958 and was a prof. there from 1968 until his retirement in 1992. He was one of the founders and director of Stanford's computer music center, and he also served as an advisor to IRCAM in Paris. He pioneered in the development of a computer music publishing system he named SCORE. In 1971 he published what is believed to have been the first score ever printed entirely by a computer without added hand work. Since that time, he has perfected his system to such a high level of excellence that most of the principal music publishers of the world have chosen his SCORE system for their prestige publications. He later worked on projects to use his SCORE system and the Internet for complete music distribution systems. In addition to his lectures on the use of computers in both composing and printing, he publ. the *Handbook of Harmonic Analysis* (1963). In his compositions, Smith has traversed a modern course in which serial procedures are often utilized with occasional excursions into explorations of computer-generated sounds.

WORKS: DRAMATIC: O p e r a : *Santa Claus* (Chicago, Dec. 9, 1955). ORCH.: Sym. (1951); *Concerto for Orch.* (1956); *Divertimento* No. 2 for Chamber Orch. (1957). CHAMBER: Trumpet Sonata (1947); Trio for Flute, Cello, and Piano (1947); Trio for Violin, Trumpet, and Clarinet (1948); *Divertimento* No. 1 for 5 Instruments (1949); Woodwind Quintet (1951); 2 Duets for Clarinet and Bassoon (1953); Sonata for Heckelphone or Viola and Piano (1953); String Trio (1953); Quintet for Bassoon and Strings (1956); Trio for Oboe, Clarinet, and Bassoon (1960); Quartet for Horn, Violin, Cello, and Piano (1961); *Orpheus* for Guitar, Harp, and Harpsichord (1967); piano pieces. VOCAL: 2 motets (1948, 1954); *3 Pacifist Songs* for Soprano and Piano (1951–58); *Advice to Young Ladies* for Women's Voices, Clarinet, Violin, and Cello (1963); *Dona nobis pacem* for Chorus and Chamber Ensemble (1964); *Machines of Loving Grace* for Narrator, Bassoon, and Computer (1970).—NS/LK/DM

Smith, Leonard B(ingley), American cornetist, trumpeter, conductor, arranger, and composer; b. Poughkeepsie, N.Y., Sept. 5, 1915. After training with Ernest S. Williams, he studied at the N.Y. Military Academy, the Ernest Williams School of Music, N.Y.U., and the Curtis Inst. of Music in Philadelphia. He was first trumpeter in the Detroit Sym. Orch. (1936–42), and concurrently played during the summers with the Goldman Band in N.Y. In 1942 he enlisted in the U.S. Navy, serving as cornet soloist with the U.S. Navy Band in Washington, D.C. In 1946 he became founder-conductor of the Detroit Concert Band, which became one of the leading ensmbles of its kind in the U.S. He composed and arranged numerous works for band, and also publ. the manual *The Treasury of Scales* (1952).—NS/LK/DM

Smith, (Joseph) Leo(pold), English-born Canadian cellist, teacher, writer on music, and composer; b. Birmingham, Nov. 26, 1881; d. Toronto, April 18, 1952. A child prodigy, he made his debut at the Birmingham Town Hall at age 8. Following instruction from Priestly in Birmingham and Fuchs in Manchester, he studied at the Royal Manchester Coll. of Music and the Univ. of Manchester (Mus.B., 1902). He played in the Hallé Orch. in Manchester and in the Covent Garden orch. in London before emigrating to Canada in 1910. In 1911 he joined the faculty of the Toronto Cons. and served as the cellist in the Cons. Trio and later the Cons. String Quartet (1929–41). From 1932 to 1940 he was first cellist in the Toronto Sym. Orch., a post he also held in the Toronto Phil. In 1927 he joined the faculty of the Univ. of Toronto, where he was a prof. from 1938 to 1950. From 1950 until his death, he was the chief music critic of the *Toronto Globe and Mail*. In addition to serving as contributing ed. of the *Toronto Cons. Quarterly Review* (1918–35), he publ. the books *Musical Rudiments* (Boston, 1920), *Music of the 17th and 18th Centuries* (Toronto, 1931), and *Elementary Part-Writing* (Oakville, Ontario, 1939). Smith utilized Canadian folk tunes in his compositions, although the English character of his music remained predominant. Among his works were orch. pieces, chamber music, piano pieces, many songs, and folk song arrangements.

BIBL.: P. McCarthy, *L. S.: A Biographical Sketch* (Toronto, 1956).—NS/LK/DM

Smith, Mamie (Robinson), blues singer; b. Cincinnati, Ohio, May 26, 1883; d. N.Y., Oct. 30, 1946. She moved to N.Y. in 1913 with a white vaudeville group, the Four Mitchells. Later she worked in the show *The Smart Set* and appeared at various N.Y. clubs, including Leroy's and Barren Wilkins's. In 1920 she became the first black blues singer to record solo; her version of "Crazy Blues" (musical director Perry Bradford) sold a million copies within six months of issue. Mamie began touring, accompanied by her Jazz Hounds. This group, originally directed by Ocey Williams, featured many jazz musicians in its fluctuating personnel: Coleman Hawkins, Joe Smith, Curtis Mosby, Amos White, etc. Her husband, William Smith, died on May 9, 1928. Smith toured regularly during the 1930s, occasionally accompanied by Fats Pichon's Band, Andy Kirk, etc. She led her own group, the Beale Street Boys, at Town Casino, N.Y. (1936). During the late 1930s and early 1940s she appeared in several films, including *Jail House Blues*, *Paradise in Harlem*, *Murder on Lenox Avenue*, and *Sunday Sinners*. One of her last public appearances was at the Lido Ballroom, N.Y., on Aug. 19, 1944, where she took part in a benefit concert; also appearing on the same bill was Billie Holiday. Mamie suffered a long illness in the Harlem Hospital; her burial took place in the Frederick Douglass Memorial Park, Staten Island, N.Y.—JC/LP

Smith, Patrick J(ohn), American music critic, author, and editor; b. N.Y., Dec. 11, 1932. He was educated at Princeton Univ. (A.B., 1955). He then pursued a career as a music critic, contributing articles to *High Fidelity, Musical America, Musical Quarterly*, and the *Musical Times*. From 1965 to 1985 he was book ed. of *Musical America*; also served as N.Y. music correspondent to the *Times* of London. He was president of the Music Critics Assn. (1977–81); was director of the Opera-Musical Theater Program of the NEA (from

1985). From 1988 to 1998 he was ed.-in-chief of *Opera News*, then ed.-at-large. He publ. *The Tenth Muse, A Historical Study of the Opera Libretto* (N.Y., 1970) and *A Year at the Met* (N.Y., 1983).—NS/LK/DM

Smith, Patti, unique late–1970s female singer-songwriter; b. Chicago, Dec. 31, 1946. Patti Smith attempted to establish her literate and somewhat bizarre poetry as a rock art form when backed by minimalist, hard- driving music. In 1974 she began performing at N.Y. clubs such as Max's Kansas City and CBGB's, serving as inspiration to the soon-to-burgeon punk-rock scene. Winning a cult following on both American coasts for her volatile and personal lyrics, erratic vocal style, and unusual stage antics, Smith finally broke nationally with the 1978 hit "Because the Night," cow-ritten by Smith and Bruce Springsteen. Recording two of the most striking albums of the late–1970s, *Horses* and *Easter*, she retired after 1979's *Wave*, produced by Todd Rundgren. Patti Smith unsuccessfully attempted a comeback with husband Fred "Sonic" Smith of the MC5 in 1988; after his death, she resumed touring in 1995, opening for Bob Dylan on several dates, and she began recording a new album working with guitarist Lenny Kaye.

Patti Smith grew up in southern N.J., moving to N.Y.C. in 1967, where she frequented Pratt Art Coll. She later traveled to Paris with her sister, returning to N.Y. in 1969. There she met playwright Sam Shepard, with whom she wrote the play *Cowboy Mouth*. In February 1971 she began reading her poetry at St. Mark's Church, accompanied by guitarist and rock critic Lenny Kaye. Attracting her initial following as a rock critic for *Creem* magazine, Smith subsequently published two volumes of writing, *Seventh Heaven* and *Witt*, in the early 1970s. Encouraged to write songs and sing by Kaye and Blue Öyster Cult keyboardist Allen Lanier, she coauthored "Career of Evil," which the group included on their 1974 *Secret Treaties* album.

By 1974 Patti Smith was performing in Manhattan clubs such as Max's Kansas City and CBGB's backed by Lenny Kaye and pianist Richard Sohl. She recorded the single "Hey Joe"/"Piss Factory" for Kaye's Mer Records label, becoming one of the focal points of the emerging N.Y. underground rock scene with her literate, passionate, and unusual lyrics, inconsistent vocal delivery, androgynous appearance, and ranting onstage antics. Late in the year, she signed with Arista Records, recording *Horses* under producer-artist John Cale, a former member of the Velvet Underground. Recorded with Lanier, Kaye, Sohl, Ivan Kral (bs., gtr., kybd.), and Jay Dee Daugherty (drm.), the album featured seven originals (she took sole credit for only the title song) and reworked versions of Van Morrison's "Gloria" and Chris Kenner's "Land of 1,000 Dances." The album sold modestly, and Smith made her first national tour in January 1976.

Forming the Patti Smith Group with Lenny Kaye, Ivan Kral, and Jay Dee Daugherty, Patti Smith next recorded *Radio Ethiopia*, but the album's heavy-metal sound overwhelmed her vocals. While on tour in January 1977 she fell off stage in Tampa, Fla., sustaining

broken neck bones that necessitated a six- month period of recovery. In early 1978 she published a poetry collection, *Babel*, her first work released by a major publishing house (Putnam). The Patti Smith Group regrouped with Smith, Kaye, Kral, Daugherty, and keyboardist Bruce Brody for *Easter*. The album included "Rock 'n' Roll Nigger," "Privilege (Set Me Free)," "Till Victory," and "Space Monkey," and yielded a major hit with "Because the Night." *Wave*, produced by Todd Rundgren, featured "Revenge" and a version of the Byrds' "So You Want to Be a Rock 'n' Roll Star," and produced a minor hit with "Frederick." Later in 1979 Patti Smith retired from the music business and moved to Detroit, and in 1980 she married Fred "Sonic" Smith of the MC5.

Patti Smith reemerged in 1988 with *Dream of Life*, recorded with Richard Sohl, Jay Dee Daugherty, and Fred Smith. With Fred and Patti as cosongwriters, the album included "People Have the Power," "Up There Down There," the gentle "Paths That Cross," and the lullaby "The Jackson Song." However, it failed to sell in significant quantities. In late autumn 1995 Smith reemerged for a brief tour opening for Bob Dylan while preparing a new album of original compositions with Lenny Kaye.

DISC.: PATTI SMITH: *Horses* (1975); *Dream of Life* (1988); *Gone Again* (1996); *Peace and Noise* (1997); *Gung Ho* (2000). **THE PATTI SMITH GROUP:** *Radio Ethiopia* (1976); *Easter* (1978); *Wave* (1979).

BIBL.: D. Roach, *P. S.: Rock & Roll Madonna* (South Bend, 1979).—BH

Smith, Pine Top (Clarence), singer, boogie-woogie pianist; b. Troy, Ala., June 11, 1904; d. Chicago, Ill., March 15, 1929. Raised in Birmingham, Ala., Smith worked as an entertainer in various Pittsburgh clubs before playing solo piano on T.O.B.A circuit; he also worked for a time as accompanist for Ma Rainey. He settled in Chicago in the late 1920s and was accidentally shot dead during a dance-hall fracas where he was performing. He gained posthumous fame through his composition "Pinetop's Boogie Woogie"—that he had recorded in 1928.—JC/LP

Smith, Ronald, English pianist, writer on music, and composer; b. London, Jan. 3, 1922. He won the Sir Michael Costa Scholarship for composition and studied at the Royal Academy of Music in London, later completing his training in Paris. In 1942 he made his debut at a London Promenade concert. In 1951 he made his debut on the Continent as a soloist with Ansermet and the Orchestre de la Suisse Romande in Geneva, and subsequently appeared as a soloist with many orchs. He toured Australia in 1975, 1977, 1981, and 1983, the Far East in 1977, the U.S. and Canada in 1982, 1983, and 1987, and Russia in 1985. As a leading interpreter of the music of Alkan, he gave an Alkan centenary concert at London's Wigmore Hall in 1988. He also championed the music of Beethoven, Schubert, Chopin, Liszt, and the Russian masters of the 19th century. He publ. the major study *Alkan, Vol. I: The Enigma* (London, 1976) and

Alkan, Vol. II: The Music (London, 1978). Among his other writings were *Alkan, The Man and His Music* (London, 1975) and *Alkan in Miniature* (London, 1978). He composed several orch. works.—**NS/LK/DM**

Smith, Russell (T.; aka **"Pops"),** jazz trumpeter; b. Ripley, Ohio, 1890; d. Los Angeles, Calif., March 27, 1966. Brother of **Joe Smith**. Taught music by his father, he started on alto horn, then switched to trumpet at age 14. His first professional work was in a Cincinnati theater; he then began touring with the Six Musical Spillers (c. 1910). He settled in N.Y. and joined Ford Dabney at the Ziegfeld Roof Garden. He went to Europe with Joe Jordan in 1914. After returning to the U.S., he joined the Army and served as a musician in the 350th Field Artillery Band (directed by Lt. Tim Brymn); he sailed with this unit to France in 1917. After demobilization, he joined Jim Europe's Band in 1919, then spent four years working mainly with the "Shuffle Along/Bamville" revue. Smith joined Fletcher Henderson regularly in late 1925, and was Henderson's first choice for lead trumpet work until 1942. During this period he also worked for many other leaders, including Claucle Hopkins (1935–36), Benny Carter (1939–40), and Horace Henderson. Smith was with Cab Calloway until summer 1945, then began a long association with Noble Sissle. He retired to Calif. in the 1950s, playing occasionally and doing some teaching.—**JC/LP**

Smith, Stuff (Hezekiah Leroy Gordon), influential jazz violinist, singer; b. Portsmouth, Ohio, Aug. 14, 1909; d. Munich, Germany, Sept. 25, 1967. Dizzy Gillespie credited Smith with showing him how artistry and entertainment could be combined. His father, a barber and part-time boxer, also played all the string instruments and doubled on reeds. When Stuff was seven his father made him his first violin; at age 12 he began playing in his father's band. At that time, the family lived in Masillon, Ohio. Stuff won a music scholarship to study at the Johnson C. Smith Univ. in N.C., He left school in 1924 to tour with the "Aunt Jemima" Revue Band. After two years on the road, he joined Alphonse Trent (then playing in Ky.), and subsequently played with that band during their long residency at the Adolphus Hotel, Dallas. He moved to N.Y. (with Edwin Swayzee) in 1928 to join Jelly Roll Morton, but soon returned to Alphonse Trent's Band because he felt that he couldn't be heard in Morton's band. He made his first recordings with Trent in 1933. After various residencies and tours through the Midwest and Canada, he finally left Trent in Syracuse. He settled in Buffalo and led small groups at clubs there. Early in 1936, his sextet moved from Buffalo to N.Y. for a long residency at the Onyx Club with Jonah Jones and Cozy Cole (during this booking he began to play amplified violin). This was Smith's most famous group, and it recorded on several occasions. The band played in Hollywood from summer 1937 until early 1938; then, facing union problems and a bankruptcy order, Stuff temporarily disbanded his group. He continued to work with various groups back in N.Y., and then in 1945 settled in Chicago, where he formed a new trio to play

at his own restaurant/club. During the 1950s, he was based in Calif., although he also made European tours, notably a 1957 trip with Jazz at the Philharmonic. In the early 1960s, he moved from Calif. to Toronto for a year, and then settled in N.Y. for an extended engagement in 1964; a year later, he went to Europe, touring several countries, and making his home base in Copenhagen. He died in Munich, but was buried in Copenhagen.

DISC.: *Stuff Smith Trio* (1943); *Stuff Smith* (1953); *Have Violin, Will Swing* (1957); *Stuff Smith-Dizzy Gillespie-Oscar Peterson* (1957); *Soft Winds* (1957); *Violins No End* (1957); *Stephane Grappelli with Stuff Smith* (1957); *Cat on a Hot Fiddle* (1959); *Sweet Singin' Stuff* (1959); *Live in paris* (1965); *Live at the Montmartre* (1965); *Swingin' Stuff* (1965); *Hot Violins* (1965); *Stuff Smith* (1965).—**JC/LP**

Smith, Tab (Talmadge), jazz/R&B alto, soprano, tenor, and C-melody saxophonist; b. Kinston, N.C., Jan. 11, 1909; d. St. Louis, Mo., Aug. 17, 1971. His mother and four sisters were all pianists. Smith started on piano, then played C-melody sax before specializing on alto. He played with Ike Dixon's Band in Baltimore and with the Carolina Stompers before joining Eddie Johnson's Crackerjacks (1931–33). After playing on the riverboats with Fate Marable, he rejoined Eddie Johnson. He joined Lucky Millinder in June 1936, and left him in 1938 to join Frankie Newton; Smith played tenor sax with Newton in 1939. After brief stints on tenor with the Teddy Wilson Big Band (spring 1940), and Count Basie, he joined Eddie Durham in August 1940, only to rejoin Lucky Millinder a month later. From December 1940 until spring 1942, he worked with Count Basie, then returned to Lucky Millinder until spring 1944. He formed his own band, which he continued to lead through the 1940s, and which sometimes included singer Wynonie Harris. In 1951, Smith moved back to St. Louis to devote time to his business interests; he also led his band for a residency at a local club. As a result of several best-selling singles, he resumed full- time music in early 1952 and continued leading small groups for several years. During the 1950s, Smith cut many songs for tiny independent labels that were huge R&B hits in the black community and on jukeboxes. In the 1960s, he returned to St. Louis, worked in real estate, played gigs, and taught music. In the last years of his life, he played organ at a steak house in East St. Louis.

DISC.: *Joy at the Savoy* (1944); *Music Styled by T. S.* (1951); *Jump Time* (1951); *Because of You* (1951); *Ace High* (1952).—**JC/LP**

Smith, Warren (Doyle; aka **Smitty),** jazz trombonist; b. Middlebourne, W.Va., May 17, 1908; d. Santa Barbara, Calif., Aug. 28, 1975. He began on piano at age seven. After the family moved to Dallas in 1920, he began lessons from his father on cornet and sax, then specialized on trombone. Smith continued doubling on sax for his first professional work with Harrison's Texans (1924–28) and he had a long period with Abe Lyman (1929–35). He joined Bob Crosby (summer 1936) and remained with that band until May 1940 when he briefly rejoined Abe Lyman. He worked mostly in Chicago from 1941–45, with various leaders, including Wingy Manone, Bud Jacobson, and Paul Jordan. After moving to Calif. in 1945, Smith worked again with Bob Crosby, then for a long time with Peter Daily in the late 1940s. In 1950 he was with Jess Stacy, then he worked briefly with Lu Watters before joining Nappy Lamare's Band (1951). Smith worked for a brief period in N.Y. with Duke Ellington (summer 1955), then with Joe Darensbourg (1957–60) and many others before joining Red Nichols in the early 1960s. He traveled with Nichols to Japan in the summer of 1964. Smith continued to work regularly in Calif. until the month of his death. —JC/LP

Smith, Warren (Jr.), jazz percussionist, vibraphonist; b. Chicago, Ill., May 4, 1934. He came from a musical family: his father (not Warren Doyle Smith) was a clarinetist who played with various jazz bands and taught in Chicago; his mother was a professional harpist and piano player. Smith studied at the Univ. of Ill. (1957) and at the Manhattan School of Music (1958); since then, he has been active around N.Y. He taught in schools, colleges, and universities. He worked with Tony Williams's Lifetime, Sam Rivers's Harlem Ensemble, and as a studio musician. He led the Composer's Workshop Ensemble, recording on the Musicians cooperative Strata-East in the early 1970s; other members included Howard Johnson, Herb Bushler, Jack Jeffers, and Bross Townsend. Smith played with Nat "King" Cole, Gil Evans, George Russell, Charles Mingus, and Elvin Jones, and was a founding member of Max Roach's M'Boom percussion ensemble. He is associate professor at SUNY Purchase, N.Y.

Disc.: *Cricket Poem Song* (1982).—LP

Smith, William O(verton), American clarinetist, composer, and teacher; b. Sacramento, Calif., Sept. 22, 1926. He took up the clarinet as a child. After attending the Juilliard School of Music in N.Y. (1945–46), he pursued his training with Milhaud at Mills Coll. in Oakland, Calif. (1946–47) and with Sessions at the Univ. of Calif. at Berkeley (B.A., 1950; M.A., 1952). He performed with various jazz musicians, including Dave Brubeck. He also played much contemporary music. Smith held the Prix de Paris (1951–53), the American Prix de Rome (1957), and a Guggenheim fellowship (1960). After teaching at the Univ. of Calif. at Berkeley (1952–53), the San Francisco Cons. of Music, and the Univ. of Southern Calif. in Los Angeles (1954–60), he was on the faculty of the Univ. of Wash. in Seattle (1966–88). In his extensive catalog of works, Smith has applied a variety of quaquaversal elements, from jazz to dodecaphony to electronics.

WORKS: ORCH.: Concerto for Trombone and Chamber Orch. (1949); Suite for Concert Band (1954); Concerto for Clarinet and Combo (1957); Concerto for Jazz Soloist and Orch. (1962); *Interplay* for Jazz Combo and Orch. (1964); *Tangents* for Clarinet and Orch. (1965); *Quadri* for Jazz Combo and Orch. (1968); *Agate* for Jazz Soloist and Jazz Orch. (1974); *Theona* for Jazz Combo and Orch. (1975); *Ecco!* for Clarinet and Orch. (1979); *Mu* for Clarinet and Small Orch. (1978); Concerto for Clarinet and Small Orch. (1985); *East Wind* for Wind Ensemble (1990); *Blue Shades* for Clarinet and Wind Ensemble (1993). CHAMBER: Clarinet Sonata (1948); Quintet for Clarinet and String Quartet (1950); 2 string quartets (1952, 1969); 2 trios for

Clarinet, Violin, and Piano (1957, 1984); Quartet for Clarinet, Violin, and Piano (1958); *Explorations* for Jazz Combo and Tape (1963); *Ambiente* for Jazz Ensemble (1970); *Jazz Set* for Flute and Clarinet (1974); *Chronos* for String Quartet (1975); *Janus* for Trombone and Jazz Ensemble (1977); *Eternal Truths* for Wind Quintet (1979); *Pente* for Clarinet and String Quartet (1983); *Oni* for Clarinet, Keyboard, Percussion, and Electronics (1986); *Slow Motion* for Electric Clarinet and Computer Graphics (1987); *Illuminated Manuscript* for Wind Quintet and Computer Graphics (1987); *Serenade* for Clarinet, Violin, and Cello (1989); *Piccolo Concerto* for Flute, Clarinet, Violin, Cello, and Piano (1991); *Jazz Set* for Violin and Wind Quintet (1991); *Jazz Fantasy* for Jazz Improvisors and String Quartet (1992); *Ritual* for Clarinet, Viola, Percussion, Tape, and Projections (1992); *86910* for Clarinet and Digital Delay (1993); *Soli* for Flute, Clarinet, Violin, and Cello (1993); *Studies* for 2 Clarinets and Computers (1994). VOCAL: *My Father Moved Through Dooms of Love* for Chorus and Orch. (1955); *Songs to Myself Alone* for Soprano and Percussion (1970); *1* for Chorus and 6 Instruments (1975); *3* for Soprano, Clarinet, Trombone, and Dancer (1975); *Ilios* for Chorus, Winds, and Dancers (1977); *Manadala I* for Voices and Instruments (1977); *Intermission* for Soprano, Chorus, and Instruments (1978); *Enchantments* for Women's Voices and Flute (1983); *Sudana* for Voices and Oboe (1985); *Psyche* for Voices and Viola (1987); *Alleluia* for Chorus and/or Instruments (1990). —NS/LK/DM

Smith, Willie (actually, **William McLeish**), jazz alto and baritone saxophonist, clarinetist, singer, composer; b. Charleston, S.C., Nov. 25, 1910; d. Los Angeles, Calif., March 7, 1967. He was a brilliant soloist. He began on clarinet at age 12; two years later, he played at local concerts accompanied by his sister on piano. He played in the Boston Serenaders in Memphis (c. 1926). He studied at the Case Technical Coll. before attending Fisk Univ. in Nashville, Tenn. In 1927 he worked in Belmar, N.J., with the Betty Conner Quartet during his summer vacation. While at Fisk, he first met Jimmie Lunceford; after majoring in chemistry, he left the college to join Lunceford in Memphis (summer 1929). Smith played alto sax, wrote arrangements (including an innovative "Mood Indigo"), and sang in the vocal trio. He remained with Lunceford until the summer of 1942, then joined Charlie Spivak. In April 1943 he left Spivak to serve as a musical instructor in the U.S. Navy. After his release in late 1944, he joined Harry James, remaining with him until March 1951 (except for a brief absence in summer 1947). He worked with Duke Ellington for a year, beginning in March 1951. Smith was reportedly criticized for his light skin color. He left in spring 1952 to join Billy May's Orch. In early 1953 he toured Europe with *Jazz at the Philharmonic*, then did a brief tour in the Benny Goodman All-star Band (directed for most of the tour by Gene Krupa). Smith returned to Calif., did brief tours with Billy May, then led his own band at the Oasis Club, Los Angeles. He rejoined Harry James in spring 1954, remaining with him until summer 1963; during this period he also worked regularly with Billy May and other West Coast studio orchestras. After a long period of ill health, Smith joined Johnny Catron's Band in Los Angeles (autumn 1964), worked with Johnny Rivers in Las Vegas during the following year, then returned to studio work. In late

1966 Smith played in N.Y. in a big band specially formed by Charlie Barnet. The last few weeks of his life were spent in the Veterans' Administration Hospital in Los Angeles. He died of cancer.

DISC.: *Alto Sax Artistry* (1950).—**JC/LP**

Smith, Willie "the Lion" (originally, **Bertholoff, William Henry Joseph Bonaparte**), famed stride pianist, composer, singer; b. Goshen, N.Y., Nov. 25, 1897; d. N.Y., April 18, 1973. His mother played piano and organ. He started on organ, then specialized on piano. From 1912, he played many residencies in N.Y. and Atlantic City, N.J., until joining the U.S. Army in November 1916. He saw active service in France, and also played bass drum in Lt. Tim Brymn's Regimental Band; he was demobilized in the U.S. in late 1919. From 1923, Smith began long residencies in N.Y., including Leroy's, Small's, and Garden of Joy. He played many freelance recording sessions, including accompanying Mamie Smith on "Crazy Blues." He toured theatre circuits; was featured in the "Holiday in Dixieland" revue (1922–23); led his own band at the Capitol Palace, Rhythm Club, and Hooper's Club; and also played and acted in the Broadway play *The Four Walls* (1927–28). Smith was the featured pianist at Pod's and Jerry's in the late 1920s and early 1930s; he also toured as an accompanist for Nina Mae McKinney and took part in Clarence Williams's recording sessions. During the 1930s, he was featured at many venues in N.Y., including The Onyx, Adrian's Tap Room, and The Apollo; he recorded with his own groups and worked occasionally in the Milt Herth Trio. In the 1940s, Smith led bands at Man About Town Casablanca, Newark, and the Venetian Room. In late 1949 to early 1950, he toured Europe as a soloist. He played regularly at The Central Plaza sessions and took part in the film *Jazz Dance*. In the 1950s, 1960s, and early 1970s, Smith appeared at many jazz festivals; he toured Europe (1965–66); he performed in Canada, and was the subject of two short films (1966). He wrote over 70 songs, including "Portrait of the Duke," and co-wrote "The Stuff Is Here and It's Mellow." Ellington, one of Willie the Lion's most fervent admirers, dedicated "Portrait of the Lion" to him. He was a very successful teacher, and his pupils included Joe Bushkin, Mel Powell, Howard Smith, Jack O'Brian, and Artie Shaw.

DISC.: *Reminiscing the Piano Greats* (1949); *Lion of the Piano* (1951); *Harlem Memories* (1953); *Grand Piano* (1953); *Compositions of James P. Johnson* (1953); *Lion Roars* (1957); *Legend of Willie Smith* (1957); *Music on My Mind* (1967); *Memoirs of Willie the Lion Smith* (1968); *Relaxin'* (1970); *Live at Blues Alley* (1970).—**JC/LP/MM**

Smith Brindle, Reginald, English composer, teacher, and writer on music; b. Bamber Bridge, Lancashire, Jan. 5, 1917. He studied architecture before serving as a captain in the Royal Engineers (1940–46). He then studied music at the Univ. Coll. of North Wales in Bangor (1946–49; B.Mus.; later Mus.D.), and subsequently with Pizzetti at the Accademia di Santa Cecilia in Rome (1949–52; composition diploma). He also studied privately with Dallapiccola in Florence (1949; 1952–53). From 1956 to 1961 he was active with the RAI.

In 1957 he joined the faculty of the Univ. Coll. of North Wales, serving as a prof. there from 1967 to 1970. From 1970 to 1985 he was prof. of music at the Univ. of Surrey in Guildford. In addition to his many articles in journals, he publ. the books *Serial Composition* (1966), *Contemporary Percussion* (1970), *The New Music* (1975), and *Musical Composition* (1980). He utilized serial techniques in his scores until about 1970, all the while varying his style. Thereafter his path proved ever more eclectic as he refined his personal idiom of musical expression.

WORKS: DRAMATIC: Opera: *The Death of Antigone* (1969). **ORCH.:** Concertino for Guitar and Chamber Orch. (1951); 2 syms. (1954, 1990); *Variations on a Theme by Dallapiccola* (1955); *An Epitaph for Alban Berg* (1955); *Symphonic Variations* (1957); *Cosmos* (1959); *Via Crucis* (1960); *Homage to H.G. Wells* (1960); Clarinet Concerto (1962); *Creation Epic* (1964); *Apocalypse* (1970); *Fons Bonitatis II* (1973); Guitar Concerto (1977); *Le Chant du Monde* (1984); *Recordando el gran maestro* (1987); *Grande Chaconne* (1993). **CHAMBER:** *3 Pieces* for Guitar and Piano (1956); *10-String Music* for Guitar and Cello (1957); *5 Sketches* for Violin and Guitar (1957); *String Quartet Music* (1958); Concerto for 5 Instruments and Percussion (1960); *Segments and Variants* for Wind Quintet (1965); *Andromeda* for Flute (1966); *Orion M42* for Percussion (1967); *Auriga* for Percussion (1967); *Concerto Breve Omnis Terra* for 8 Guitars and Percussion (1971); *Tubal Cain's Heritage* for Trombone and Piano (1973); *Concerto de angelis* for 4 Guitars (1973); *Concerto CumJubilo* for 3 Guitars (1974); *The Walls of Jericho* for Tuba (1975); *The Pillars of Karnak* for 4 Guitars (1979); *Las doces cuerdas* for 2 Guitars (1989); numerous solo guitar pieces. **Organ:** Organ Sym. (1979); *Missa de spiritus flammis* (1980); *Regina caeli* (1986); *The Harmonies of Peace* (1986); *Inner Refrains* (1988); *The Firmament Beyond* (1988).—**NS/LK/DM**

Smither, Howard E(lbert), distinguished American musicologist; b. Pittsburg, Kans., Nov. 15, 1925. He studied at Hamline Univ. in St. Paul, Minn. (A.B., 1950), and at Cornell Univ. with Grout and Austin (M.A., 1952; Ph.D., 1960, with the diss. *Theories of Rhythm in the Nineteenth and Twentieth Centuries, with a Contribution to the Theory of Rhythm for the Study of Twentieth Century Music*); also attended classes of Rudolf von Ficker at the Univ. of Munich (1953–54). He taught at the Oberlin Cons. of Music (1955–60), the Univ. of Kans. (1960–63), and Tulane Univ. (1963–68); in 1968 he was appointed a prof. of music at the Univ. of N.C. at Chapel Hill; served as president of the American Musicological Soc. (1981–82). His major work is the valuable study *A History of the Oratorio* (3 vols., Chapel Hill, 1977–87); also contributed to *The New Grove Dictionary of Music and Musicians*.—**NS/LK/DM**

Smithers, Don (LeRoy), American music historian, trumpeter, cornet player, and wind player; b. N.Y., Feb. 17, 1933. He studied at Hofstra Univ. (B.S., 1957), attended seminars in musicology at N.Y.U. (1957–58), took courses in Renaissance and Reformation history at Columbia Univ. (1958), and completed his training in music history at the Univ. of Oxford (Ph.D., 1967, with the diss. *The Baroque Trumpet:Instruments and Music c. 1600–1700*). In 1965 he co-founded and became the first music director of the Oxford Pro Musica. He also gave many performances as a Baroque trumpeter, cornet player, and Renaissance wind player. After teaching at Syracuse Univ. (1966–75), he taught at the Royal Cons. of Music in The Hague (1975–80). In addition to his numerous articles in books and journals, he publ. *The Music and History of the Baroque Trumpet Before 1721* (1973) and *Number, Symbolism, and Allegory in the Late Works of Johann Sebastian Bach* (1975).—**NS/LK/DM**

Smiths, The, British pop band that brought guitars back to the U.K. charts in the 1980s. **MEMBERSHIP:** Morrissey (real name, Steven Patrick Morrissey), voc. (b. Manchester England, May 22, 1959); Johnny Marr (real name, John Maher), gtr. (b. Manchester, England, Oct. 31, 1963); Mike Joyce, drm. (b. Manchester, England, June 1, 1963); Andy Rourke, bs. (b. Manchester, England, 1963); Craig Gannon, gtr. (b. July 3, 1966).

Enormously literate and cranky, the Smiths flew in the face of the electropop music that dominated the English charts in the mid-1980s. With the sometimes slashing, sometimes shimmering guitars of Johnny Marr and the Ian-Curtis-in-training vocals of Morrissey, they toned down the punk ethic while making guitars cool again. They set the pace for bands like James and Oasis that followed in their considerable wake.

Steven Morrissey, whose parents worked in a hospital and library, displayed a gift for literary allusion and a sardonic streak as wide as the English Channel even before forming a rock band. An occasional critic for England's *Record Mirror*, he also wrote small books on James Dean and The New York Dolls. He was president of the Dolls U.K. fan club. Johnny Marr invited him to write lyrics to his music. They decided their songs were far too singular for anyone but themselves to perform. The duo called themselves the Smiths, in reaction to the pretentious names of groups like Depeche Mode. From the get-go, the ascetic Morrissey—who claimed to be a celibate by choice—juxtaposed radically with the rock star posturing of Marr. It's one of the things that made the group interesting.

Bringing on Marr's old bandmate Andy Rourke to play bass and drummer Mike Joyce, they cut the single "Hand in Glove" for Rough Trade. It became an underground hit. Even before they were able to release another record, the group became embroiled in their first of many controversies. The British tabloids asserted that their song "Reel Around the Fountain" was about child molesting. Morrissey eloquently refuted the charge, establishing himself as the group's spokesperson.

The press did them no harm when they put out their next single, "This Charming Man." With its chiming guitar and tongue-in-cheek lyrics, the song charted in the U.K. at #25. It was followed by "What Difference Does It Make," which rose to #12. However, these chart numbers were not as indicative of the impact the band was making on the English audiences as their eponymous 1984 debut album, which peaked at #2. A remake of "Hand in Glove," recorded with 1960s Mersey-beat star Sandy Shaw, rose into the British Top 40. "Heaven Knows I'm Miserable Now" zoomed into the Top Ten, amidst another bout of controversy regarding the single's B-side, a song about a serial child killer. Again Morrissey proved an eminently quotable spokesperson.

In 1985 the group released a set of non-LP B-sides, singles, and radio sessions called *Hatful of Hollow* that rose to the U.K. Top Ten. They followed this with *Meat Is Murder*. At this point, vegetarian Morrissey forbid the rest of the band to be photographed eating meat. As Morrissey became more austere, Marr became more dissolute.

Rebounding from their sophomore slump, 1986's *The Queen Is Dead* revived the band. It debuted in the U.K. at #2 propelled by some of the group's best material, such as "Big Mouth Strikes Again" and "The Boy with the Thorn in his Side." They briefly added former Aztec Camera guitarist Craig Gannon to the lineup, and almost as quickly fired him when Marr put the band on hiatus while recovering from a car crash. This prompted the first of the group's personnel-inspired lawsuits.

In early 1987 the group went into the studio and recorded *Strangeways Here We Come*, but the experience proved too draining for Marr, who left the group that summer. Morrissey thought about keeping the Smiths together, but ultimately decided to disband the group and go solo. Both Joyce and Rourke joined another Smith, former Fall singer Brix, in her band Adult Net, then worked with Sinead O'Conner. They both played a show in 1989 with Morrissey. Rourke ultimately retired from music, while Joyce became a member of the Buzzcocks. In the mid-1990s, both Rourke and Joyce sued Marr and Morrissey for back royalties; Rourke settled the case, but Joyce went to trial and won.

Not anxious to be "in charge" of anything, Marr became guitarist for the Pretenders for a while. During the 1990s, he moved on to session work, and formed the sporadic super-group Electric with New Order's Bernard Sumner. In the summer of 2000, he finally put his own name on a project with the release of Johnny Marr and the Healers.

In 1988 Morrissey launched his solo career with the musical help of the Smith's producer Steven Street and Durutti Column's Vini Reilly. While the album *Viva Hate* was not as strong as *The Queen Is Dead*, it had several bright moments like "Everyday Is like Sunday" and the brilliant "Suedehead." However, 1991's *Kill Uncle* was a weak follow-up. Later that year, Morrissey began working with a local glam-rockabilly outfit, the Memphis Sinners, and former Polecat's guitarist Boz Boorer. Boorer's old band had once had a hit with a rockabilly version of T-Rex's "Jeepster." They backed Morrissey on his first major post-Smiths tour. Their mixture of roots rock and glam informed Morrissey's next album, 1992's *Your Arsenal*, produced by former Bowie guitarist Mick Ronson. The album earned Morrissey his first ever Top 40 solo record, hitting #21 on the U.S. charts.

The next two years were rough ones for the singer. Both Ronson and video director Tim Broad stopped working with him. Morrissey was also widely criticized in the press for supposed right-wing leanings. A scurrilous biography also appeared, and he was mired in lawsuits with ex-Smiths members. Nonetheless, in 1994 Morrissey released his most successful album, *Vauxhall and I*. The album finally established Morrissey as something greater than a cult artist. The almost folk-rock "The More You Ignore Me, the Closer I Get" became a regular on MTV in the U.S. The album rose to #18 in the U.S. and topped the U.K. charts.

After severing relations with his management, booking agent, and record company, Morrissey came back with the loud, noisy *Southpaw Grammar* in 1995. It garnered critical praise, but didn't sell well. 1997's *Maladjusted* didn't fare much better, and Morrissey was forced to leave a track about the Joyce case off the album to avoid libel problems. But he did tour to much acclaim in 1999, even playing some Smiths songs.

DISC.: THE SMITHS: *The Smiths* (1984); *Hatful of Hollow* (1985); *Meat Is Murder* (1985); *The Queen Is Dead* (1986); *Strangeways Here We Come* (1987); *Rank* (live; 1988). **MORRISSEY:** *Viva Hate* (1988); *Kill Uncle* (1991); *Your Arsenal* (1992); *Beethoven Was Deaf* (live; 1993); *Vauxhall and I* (1994); *Southpaw Grammar* (1995); *Maladjusted* (1997).—**HB**

Smits van Waesberghe, Jos(eph Maria Antonius Franciscus), prominent Dutch musicologist; b. Breda, North Brabant, April 18, 1901; d. Amsterdam, Oct. 9, 1986. He studied at several Jesuit seminaries, and became a priest. In addition to his training in philosophy (1922–26) and theology (1930–35), he also studied music with Louis van Tulder, Marius Monnikendam, and Johan Winnubst. He taught at Canisius Coll. in Nijmegen (1935–37), Ignatius Coll. in Amsterdam (1937–43), the Rotterdam Cons. (1939–43), the Amsterdam Cons. (1944–46), and the Univ. of Amsterdam, where he was a Privatdozent in music and medieval theory (1945–57) and a prof. (1957–71). He served as general secretary of the Koninklije Nederlandse Toonkunstenaars Vereniging (1945–48), founder-secretary of the Nederlandse Toonkunstenaars Raad (from 1948), and president of the Gregoriusvereniging (1958–67).

WRITINGS: *Klokken en klokkengieten in de middeleeuwen* (Tilburg, 1937); *Muziekgeschiedenis der middeleeuwen* (Tilburg, 1936–42); *Het Gregoriaans* (Amsterdam, 1943; Eng. tr., 1946); *Muziek en drama in de middeleeuwen* (Amsterdam, 1943; second ed., 1954); *De uitzonderlijke plaats van de Ars Musica in de ontwikkeling der wetenschappen gedurende de eeuw der Karolingers* (The Hague, 1947); *Handleiding voor het lezen der neumletters van St. Gallen* (Tilburg, 1947); *School en muziek in de Middeleeuwen* (Amsterdam, 1949); *Melodieleer* (Amsterdam, 1950; Eng. tr., 1954); *Cymbala: Bells in the Middle Ages* (Rome, 1951); *De musico et musico-paedogogico Guidone Aretino* (Florence, 1953); *Oud-Nederlands paasspel* (Bussum, 1953); *Het toonkunstenaarsboek van Nederland* (Amsterdam, 1956); with P. Fischer and C. Maas, *The Theory of Music from the Carolingian Era up to 1400* (1961); *Musikerziehung* (Leipzig, 1969); *De muzische mens: Zijn motoriek* (Amsterdam, 1971).

BIBL.: *Organicae voces: Festschrift J. S.v.W. angeboten anlässlich seines 60. Geburtstages* (Amsterdam, 1963); *Dia-pason, de omnibus: Ausgewählte Aufsätze von J. S.v.W.: Festgabe zu seinem 75. Geburtstag* (Buren, 1976).—**NS/LK/DM**

Smoker, Paul (Alva), jazz trumpeter, composer, educator; b. Muncie, Ind., May 8, 1941. He was raised in Davenport, Iowa, from the age of two. He started piano lessons at six and began trumpet at ten, after hearing Harry James on the radio. He played in school bands and orchestras. At age 14, he began playing in the clubs

across the Mississippi River in Rock Island, Ill.; at 19, he played there with Dodo Marmarosa. In music school at the Univ. of Iowa, he was instrumental in organizing the first jazz large ensemble that met on a regular basis; members included David Sanborn, Dale Oehler, and Will Parsons. Smoker was awarded Best Arranger at the 1966 Notre Dame Jazz Fest. He played 20th-century classical music with the Univ. of Iowa Center for New Music and Univ. Orch. He studied trumpet with John Beer at Iowa, and, in 1966, with Doc Severinsen in N.Y. Smoker taught jazz studies and contemporary music at the Univ. of Wisc., Oshkosh (1968–71), Univ. of Iowa (1971–75), Univ. of Northern Iowa (1975–76) and Coe Coll. (1976–90). He formed a trio in 1981 with Ron Rohovit and Phil Haynes. In 1987, he formed Joint Venture, a quartet with Ellery Eskelin, Drew Gress, and Haynes. He began playing solo trumpet concerts in the late 1980s. In 1992, he was a founding member of the Corner Store Syndicate Big Band with Eskelin, Dress, and Haynes, as well as Frank Lacey, Herb Robertson, Don Byron, Andy Laster, Chris Speed, Tim Berne, and others. In 1998, his projects included the Paul Smoker Brass Group, and the Paul Smoker/Vinny Golia Quartet. He has played with Anthony Braxton since 1983, and pianist Borah Bergman since 1989. He has also worked with David Liebman, Art Pepper, Frank Rosolino, and Peter Brotzmann.

DISC.: *QB* (1984); *Alone* (1986); *Come Rain or Come Shine* (1986); *Genuine Fables* (1988); *Halloween '96* (1996). Joint Venture: *Joint Venture* (1987); *Ways* (1989).—**LP**

Smyth, Dame Ethel (Mary), eminent English composer; b. London, April 22, 1858; d. Woking, Surrey, May 8, 1944. She became a pupil of Reinecke and Jadassohn at the Leipzig Cons. in 1877, but soon turned to Heinrich von Herzogenberg for her principal training, following him to Berlin; her String Quintet was performed in Leipzig in 1884. She returned to London in 1888; presented her orchestral *Serenade* (April 26, 1890) and an overture, *Antony and Cleopatra* (Oct. 18, 1890). Her prestige as a composer rose considerably with the presentation of her *Mass* for Solo Voices, Chorus, and Orch. at the Albert Hall (Jan. 18, 1893). After that she devoted her energies to the theater. Her first opera, *Fantasio*, to her own libretto in German, after Alfred de Musset's play, was premiered in Weimar on May 24, 1898; this was followed by *Der Wald* (Berlin, April 9, 1902), also to her own German libretto; it was premiered in London in the same year, and then performed in N.Y. by the Metropolitan Opera on March 11, 1903. Her next opera, *The Wreckers*, was her most successful work; written originally to a French libretto, *Les Naufrageurs*, it was first performed in a German version as *Strandrecht* (Leipzig, Nov. 11, 1906); the composer herself tr. it into Eng., and it was staged in London on June 22, 1909; the score was revised some years later, and produced at Sadler's Wells, London, on April 19, 1939. She further wrote a comic opera, *The Boatswain's Mate* (London, Jan. 28, 1916); a one-act opera, described as a "dance-dream," *Fête galante* (Birmingham, June 4, 1923); and the opera *Entente cordiale* (Bristol, Oct. 20, 1926). Other works are a Concerto for Violin, Horn, and Orch. (London, March 5, 1927); *The Prison* for Soprano, Bass

Chorus, and Orch. (London, Feb. 24, 1931); 2 string quartets (1884; 1902–12); Cello Sonata (1887); Violin Sonata (1887); 2 trios for Violin, Oboe, and Piano (1927); choral pieces, including *Hey Nonny No* for Chorus and Orch. (1911) and *Sleepless Dreams* for Chorus and Orch. (1912); songs; etc. Her music never overcame the strong German characteristics, in the general idiom as well as in the treatment of dramatic situations on the stage. At the same time, she was a believer in English national music and its potentialities. She was a militant leader for woman suffrage in England, for which cause she wrote *The March of the Women* (1911), the battle song of the WSPU After suffrage was granted, her role in the movement was officially acknowledged; in 1922 she was made a Dame Commander of the Order of the British Empire. She publ. a number of books in London, mostly autobiographical in nature: *Impressions That Remained* (2 vols., 1919; new ed., 1945), *Streaks of Life* (1921), *As Time Went On* (1936), and *What Happened Next* (1940). She also wrote some humorous essays and reminiscences: *A Three-legged Tour in Greece* (1927), *A Final Burning of Boats* (1928), *Female Pipings in Eden* (1934), *Beecham and Pharaoh* (1935), and *Inordinate (?) Affection* (1936).

BIBL.: C. St. John, *E. S.: A Biography* (N.Y., 1959); L. Collis, *Impetuous Heart: The Story of E. S.* (London, 1984).—**NS/LK/DM**

Snel, Joseph-François, Belgian violinist, conductor, teacher, and composer; b. Brussels, July 30, 1793; d. Koekelberg, near Brussels, March 10, 1861. He studied violin with Corneille Vander Nicolas in Brussels, then continued his training with Baillot and Dourlen at the Paris Cons. In 1818 he founded in Brussels the Académie de Musique et de Chant (with Mees). He popularized in Belgium the instructional singing methods of Galin and Wilhem; was an inspector of army music schools (1829). He conducted at the Théâtre Royal de la Monnaie (1831–34), and was made conductor of the Société Royale de la Grande-harmonie (1831), maître de chapelle at the Church of St. Michel et Ste. Gudule (1835), and head of the music of the Civic Guard (1837). In 1847 he became a member of the Classe des Beauxarts of the Belgian Royal Academy.

WORKS: DRAMATIC: B a l l e t (all first perf. in Brussels): *Frisac, ou La double noce* (Feb. 13, 1825); *Le page inconstant* (June 27, 1825); *Le cinq juillet* (July 9, 1825; in collaboration with C.-L. Hanssens Jr.); *Pourceaugnac* (Feb. 3, 1826); *Les enchantements de Polichinelle* (March 8, 1829); *Les barricades* (Feb. 3, 1830). **OTHER:** Symphonic concertante; Violin Concerto; 2 clarinet concertos; Clarinet Concertino; various pieces for Wind Band; chamber music; sacred and secular vocal works; piano pieces. —**NS/LK/DM**

Snetzler (Schnetzler), Johann, Swiss organ builder; b. Schaffhausen, April 6, 1710; d. there, Sept. 28, 1785. He was apprenticed to the Passau organ builder Egedacher, with whom he worked on the Passau Cathedral organ (1731–33). After serving as assistant to Müller in Haarlem, he went to England and settled in London about 1746 as an organ builder; constructed the organ for St. Margaret's, King's Lynn (1753–54). He retired about 1781 and returned to his homeland.—**NS/LK/DM**

Snoop Dogg (originally, **Broadus, Calvin**; aka **Snoop Doggy Dogg**), a major voice in gangsta rap, and the first artist to enter the pop charts at #1 with a debut album (b. Long Beach, Calif., Oct. 20, 1972).

Snoop's father was a postal worker who sang and left his family when his son Calvin was still a boy. His parents called Calvin "Snoop" after the dog in the comic *Peanuts*, claiming he looked like a puppy in his younger days.

A good student, Pop Warner Football player, and a sought-after high-school basketball star, Snoop was also a street kid and fell in with one of Los Angeles's notorious gangs, the Crips. He started selling drugs, and shortly after graduating high school, he got arrested and jailed. He spent the next three years in and out of prison. When he was on the streets, he would invent raps with his friend Warren Griffin. They began recording them. Griffin played one of the tapes for his half-brother Andrew Young, better known in the Hood as Dr. Dre of the Los Angeles rap group NWA.

Dre had just left NWA. He concurrently had begun work on solo projects and was putting together a new label with publishing impresario Suge Knight called Death Row records. Dre liked what he heard and asked Snoop to start working with him, first on his debut single "Deep Cover." On Dre's debut album "The Chronic," Snoop's vocals were nearly as prominent as Dre's, especially on the hit "Nuthin' but a 'G' Thang."

Dre produced Snoop's debut album. By this time, he was nearly as well known as his mentor. Thanks to his role in Dre's hits, Snoop's debut album, *Doggystyle*, entered the charts at #1, the first debut album ever to top the charts in its first week. Snoop's debut single, "What's My Name," rose to #8 and sold gold, as did the follow-up single, "Gin and Juice." Like many gangsta rappers, Snoop's work faced criticisms from members of the establishment. While on tour in Europe, a member of the British Parliament urged the body to "kick this evil bastard out" of the continent.

Just as *Doggystyle* came out, Snoop and his bodyguard were charged in the drive-by shooting of a rival gang member. Both were exonerated of the charge, but the trial kept Snoop occupied for well over a year. With the trial over, he went into the studio and produced *Da Doggfather*. This album also entered the charts at #1. However, Death Row records was in chaos: Dr. Dre had left the label, renouncing gangsta rap; the label's biggest star in Dogg's absence, Tupac Shakur was shot to death while cruising with Knight in Las Vegas; and Knight himself was under investigation. Snoop's album sold double platinum, but Death Row was unable to break any singles to give it momentum.

When Knight was imprisoned, Dogg negotiated a deal with Master P's No Limit records. He changed his nom de rap to Snoop Dogg and even toured as part of the alternative-rock Lollapalooza festival. His debut for No Limit, *The Game Is to Be Sold Not to Be Told*, once again entered the charts at #1. However, it also failed to produce any significant hits, although Snoop was the featured rapper on Keith Sweat's #12 "Come and Get with Me."

Snoop's decline in popularity continued into the late 1990s. His 1999 release *No Limit Top Dogg* debuted at a peak of #2, but the single "Woof" did not even crack the Top 50. To make up for his fading popularity, Dogg was investigating other areas. He claimed to be writing an autobiography and was looking into opening a Snoop Dogg theme park called Doggyland in Magnolia, Miss.

DISC.: *Doggystyle* (1993); *Tha Doggfather* (1996); *Da Game Is to Be Sold Not to Be Told* (1998); *No Limit Top Dogg* (1999).—**HB**

Snow, Hank (Clarence Eugene), Canadian-

born American country-music singer, guitarist, and songwriter; b. Brooklyn, Nova Scotia, May 9, 1914; d. Dec. 20, 1999. After establishing himself as a major star in his native Canada in the 1930s and 1940s, Snow shifted his attention to the U.S. and went on to become one of the most successful country-music performers in America during the 1950s. With his distinctive baritone and precise enunciation, he carried on from his primary influence, Jimmie Rodgers, frequently singing songs concerned with travel. He reached the country charts 85 times between 1949 and 1980, his biggest hits being "I'm Moving On," "The Rhumba Boogie," and "I Don't Hurt Anymore."

Snow's father, George Lewis Snow, worked in a sawmill; his musically inclined mother, Marie Alice Boutlier Snow, sang in minstrel shows and played piano for silent films. When he was eight his parents separated, and thereafter he lived variously with his grandparents, with his mother and an abusive stepfather, and with his sisters. From age 12 to 16 he worked on fishing vessels in the Canadian maritime, sometimes singing, playing the harmonica, and dancing to entertain his fellow sailors. During his late teens he worked at various menial jobs while taking up the guitar in emulation of Jimmie Rodgers.

Around 1934 he successfully auditioned at a radio station in Halifax and began a 15-minute weekly show, *Clarence Snow and His Guitar.* Later he was billed as the more Western-sounding "Hank, the Yodeling Ranger," then as "Hank, the Singing Ranger." He began to make other radio appearances and to perform concerts. On Sept. 2, 1935, he married Minnie Blanche Aalders; they had a son, Jimmie Rodgers Snow, who became a country-music singer before turning to the ministry.

Snow made his first recordings, the self-penned "Lonesome Blue Yodel" and "Prisoned Cowboy," for RCA Victor Records on Oct. 29, 1936, beginning an association that would last 45 years. His records were released only in Canada at first, on RCA's Bluebird label. For the rest of the 1930s and into the mid-1940s, he toured eastern Canada, performed on radio, and recorded. In July 1944 he traveled to Philadelphia and first appeared live and performed on radio in the U.S. Late in the year he joined the *Wheeling Jamboree* radio program in Wheeling, W.Va. For the rest of the 1940s he alternated Canadian tours with forays into the U.S. By 1948 he was based in Dallas, where his songs became popular on the radio, leading RCA Victor to begin releasing his records in the U.S.

Snow scored his first country Top Ten hit in the U.S., "Marriage Vow" (music and lyrics by Jenny Lou Car-

son), in December 1949. On Jan. 7, 1950, he joined the *Grand Ole Opry* radio show in Nashville. His appearances were not successful at first. But on March 28, 1950, he recorded his own song, "I'm Moving On," and it went on to become the biggest hit in the history of the country-music charts, hitting #1 in August and remaining at the top for months. He followed it with "The Golden Rocket" (music and lyrics by Hank Snow), which hit #1 in January 1951, and "The Rhumba Boogie" (music and lyrics by Hank Snow), which hit #1 in March 1951.

Snow had three more Top Ten hits in the country charts in 1951 and another five in 1952, the most successful of which were "The Gold Rush Is Over" (music and lyrics by Cindy Walker) and "Lady's Man" (music and lyrics by Cy Coben). He had six country Top Ten hits in 1953, notably "(Now and Then, There's) A Fool Such as I" (music and lyrics by Bill Trader) and "Spanish Fire Ball" (music and lyrics by Dan Welch). He scored another massive hit with "I Don't Hurt Anymore" (music by Don Robertson, lyrics by Jack Rollins), which spent months atop the country charts starting in June 1954, and he scored his fifth #1 on the country charts with "Let Me Go, Lover!" (music and lyrics by Jenny Lou Carson and "Al Hill" [a pseudonym for Kay Twomey, Fred Wise, and Ben Weisman]) in January 1955. There were another six country Top Ten hits in 1955, and starting in October, Snow was among the hosts of a monthly network television version of the *Grand Ole Opry* that ran through September 1956.

Snow scored nine country Top Ten hits between 1956 and 1959, the most successful of which was "The Last Ride" (music by Ted Daffan, lyrics by Robert Halcomb) in the fall of 1959. From 1960 to 1965 he reached the country Top Ten another six times, his biggest hits for the period being "I've Been Everywhere" (music and lyrics by Geoff Mack), which went to #1 in November 1962, and "Ninety Miles an Hour (Down a Dead End Street)" (music by Don Robertson, lyrics by Robertson and Hal Blair) in the fall of 1963; the latter earned him a Grammy Award nomination for Best Country & Western Recording. He also reached the Top Ten of the country LP charts with three albums in 1964: *Railroad Man; More Hank Snow Souvenirs,* which hit #1 in June; and *Songs of Tragedy.*

Snow continued to appear on the *Grand Ole Opry* and to tour successfully, but his record sales diminished after the mid-1960s. He scored a considerable comeback with "Hello Love" (music and lyrics by Betty Jean Robinson and Aileen Mnich), which topped the country charts in April 1974, accompanied by a *Hello Love* LP that went to #1 on the country LP charts in May. He continued to record for RCA Victor and to place records in the country charts until 1980. After he was dropped by the label in 1981, he gave up recording, except for *Brand on My Heart,* a duet album he made with Willie Nelson in 1985. He also cut back on touring, though he continued to appear on the *Grand Ole Opry* into the 1990s.

DISC.: *Hank Snow Sings* (1952); *Just Keep A-Movin'* (1955); *Country and Western Jamboree* (1957); *Hank Snow Sings Sacred Songs* (1958); *Singing Ranger* (1959); *Hank Snow Sings Jimmie*

Rodgers Songs (1960); *Souvenirs* (1961); *Together Again* (1962); *I've Been Everywhere* (1963); *Railroad Man* (1963); *Songs of Tragedy* (1964); *More Hank Snow Souvenirs* (1964); *Reminiscing* (1964); *Your Favorite Country Hits* (1965); *The Guitar Stylings of Hank Snow* (1966); *Christmas with Hank Snow* (1967); *Hits, Hits and More Hits* (1968); *Snow in All Seasons* (1969); *In Memory of Jimmie Rodgers* (1970); *Hank Snow Sings* (1970); *Tracks and Trains* (1971); *The Jimmie Rodgers Story* (1972); *All About Trains* (1975); *Living Legend* (1978); *Lovingly Yours* (1980); *By Request* (1981); *Three Coutnry Gentlemen* (1983).

WRITINGS: With J. Ownbey and B. Burris, *The H. S. Story* (Urbana, Ill., 1994).—**WR**

Snow, Valaida, early jazz trumpeter, singer; b. Chattanooga, Tenn., June 2, 1903; d. N.Y., May 30, 1956. Her mother was a music teacher. She began her professional career (c. 1920) appearing in Atlantic City and Philadelphia; she played a residency at Barren Wilkins's during 1922, then toured with Will Masten's Revue. Throughout the 1920s, she continued to sing, dance, and play trumpet in various shows throughout the U.S. In August 1926, she sailed to Shanghai to work as a specialty act with Jack Carter's Band. After returning to the U.S., she worked in Chicago, then from 1929 toured through Russia, the Middle East, and Europe. After working in the *Grand Terrace Revue* (1933), she was featured in the *Blackbirds of 1934* and traveled with this show to England in August 1934. She then worked with Ananias Berry as a double act in Los Angeles (summer 1935). While in Calif., Snow appeared in two films: *Take It from Me* and *Irresistible You*; she also appeared in the pre-war French film *Alibi*. After touring the Far East again, she played The Apollo, N.Y. (June 1936), returned to Britain, and from September 1936 began extensive touring in Europe, playing France, Belgium, Austria, Switzerland, Holland, Denmark and Sweden. After touring Sweden (summer 1941), she was arrested by the Swedish police and subsequently deported. (She claimed she spent two years in a Nazi concentration camp, but this was never verified; a known heroin user, she may also have been arrested on drug charges.) She resumed her career at The Apollo, N.Y. (April 1943). She did extensive tours of clubs and theatres and then moved to Calif. (1945). From 1946–56, Snow continued to work regularly as a vocalist in concerts, shows, and clubs throughout the U.S., and resumed regular recordings. Her last engagement took place at the Palace Theatre, N.Y.; she collapsed at her home after suffering a cerebral hemorrhage; three weeks later she died in Kings County Hospital, N.Y. Her husband in the mid-1930s was dancer Ananias Berry (d. 1951); she later married Earle Edwards. Her sister, Lavaida, was also a musician.

DISC.: *Swing Is the Thing* (1979).—**JC/LP**

Snowden, Elmer (**Chester**; aka **"Pops"**), early jazz banjoist, guitarist, leader, best remembered for his early association with Duke Ellington; b. Baltimore, Md., Oct. 9, 1900; d. Philadelphia, Pa., May 14, 1973. He played banjo-mandolin and guitar from early childhood. His first professional work with pianist Addie Booze (1914). He joined Eubie Blake (in a dance school) in 1915; remained with the band when it was taken over by pianist Joe Hochester (1916). After Rochester's death in 1919, Snowden moved to Washington and played in a trio led by Duke Ellington. In 1920, he joined pianist Gertie Wells (to whom he was married for some years), played briefly with Claude Hopkins (1921), then formed his own band and began doubling on saxophone. After residencies in Washington and Atlantic City, the band moved to N.Y. in September 1923. There, Snowden led another group, the Washingtonians; then from March 1924 he played in the Broadway Jones Band and was subsequently appointed leader. Later that year, he rejoined the Washingtonians, by that time led by Ellington. After a spell in Ford Dabney's Orch., Snowden once again became a bandleader in autumn 1925, and at one time had five different bands working under his name in and around N.Y. During the late 1920s and early 1930s, he led successful bands at several N.Y. clubs. One of his bands, which included Roy Eldridge, appeared in the Warner Brothers' short film *Smash Your Baggage* (1932). After a dispute with the N.Y. Local 802, Snowden moved to Philadelphia, where his main occupation was teaching saxophone and fretted instruments. He settled his union problems in the early 1940s, and spent the rest of the decade gigging in N.Y. and Philadelphia. From 1950, he worked with his own quartet, which continued touring (in the U.S. and Canada) until 1957. From 1957–60, he was occupied teaching, although he continued to perform on occasion; he then formed a new small group for local club work. In 1963, Snowden moved to Calif.; he played clubs in the San Francisco–Berkeley area and also taught. He toured Europe for George Wein in late 1967. He declined an offer to rejoin Ellington's orch. in the late 1960s, and in 1969, moved back to Philadelphia and continued to play occasionally.

DISC.: *Harlem Banjo* (1960).—**JC/LP**

Sobinov, Leonid (**Vitalievich**), celebrated Russian tenor; b. Yaroslavl, June 7, 1872; d. Riga, Oct. 14, 1934. He was an offspring of a middle-class family with peasant roots (his grandfather was an emancipated serf). He studied law at the Univ. of Moscow, where he also sang in a student choir. In 1892 he began to study voice with Dodonov and appeared professionally in a traveling Italian opera company in Moscow without interrupting his univ. study (1893–94); he graduated in law in 1894, and was appointed asst. advocate to a Moscow lawyer. Turning decisively to singing, he made his debut at the Bolshoi Theater in Moscow in 1897, and retained his connection with it during almost his entire career. In 1901 he also joined the Imperial Maryinsky Theater in St. Petersburg. His successes on the European stage were no less outstanding; he sang at La Scala in Milan (1904–06); from 1909 he also appeared in London, Paris, and Berlin. He was eloquent in the roles of Alfredo in *La Traviata*, Des Grieux in *Manon*, and Faust in Gounod's opera. His performance of Lensky in *Eugene Onegin* remained an unsurpassed model of Russian operatic lyricism. In his solo recitals he could squeeze the last fluid ounce out of Tchaikovsky's melancholy songs. No wonder that he was idolized by Russian audiences, particularly among the young and female; a whole tribe of "Sobinovites" appeared, and long queues formed before his concerts, willing to stand in line for hours in the hope of obtaining scarce tickets. He served as director of the Bolshoi Theater in 1917–18. In 1918–19 he gave recitals in and around Kiev, N. Slonimsky serving occasionally as his accompanist. He retired from the stage in 1924.

BIBL.: M. Lvov, *L. S.* (Moscow, 1951).—NS/LK/DM

Sobolewski, Edward (actually, **Johann Friedrich Eduard**), German-born American violinist, conductor, and composer of Polish descent; b. Königsberg, Oct. 1, 1804; d. St. Louis, May 17, 1872. He was a composition pupil of Zelter in Berlin and of Weber in Dresden (1821–24). He became an opera conductor in Königsberg (1830), and was founder-conductor of the orch. of the Philharmonische Gesellschaft (from 1838) and conductor of the choir of the Academy of Music (from 1843); subsequently was director of music at the Bremen Theater (from 1854). In 1859 he emigrated to the U.S., settling in Milwaukee, then a center of German musical immigrants; was founder-conductor of the Milwaukee Phil. Soc. Orch. (1860). He then settled in St. Louis, where he conducted the Phil. Soc. (1860–66); was prof. of vocal music at Bonham's Female Seminary (from 1869). His works include the operas *Imogen* (1833), *Velleda* (1836), *Salvator Rosa* (1848), *Komala* (Weimar, Oct. 30, 1858), *Mohega, die Blume des Waldes* (Milwaukee, Oct. 11, 1859, to his own libretto, in German, on an American subject dealing with an Indian girl saved by Pulaski from death), and *An die Freude* (Milwaukee, 1859), as well as oratorios, symphonic poems, oratorios and other choral works, songs, etc.—NS/LK/DM

Socarras, Alberto, reed player, saxophonist, flutist, clarinetist, leader; b. Manzanillo, Cuba, Sept. 19, 1908. He may have been the first to play flute on jazz recordings in 1929. Socarras was born in Cuba, where he played with local orchestras; when he moved to the U.S. he began a regular series of recordings with Clarence Williams. He was with the "Blackbirds" shows from 1928 until 1933, including a tour of Europe. Socarras played briefly with Benny Carter in 1933, then formed his own band. In 1934 he visited Europe, this time as musical director of an all-girls' band. He was with Sam Wooding in 1935, then again formed his own band. He worked with Erskine Hawkins for the 1937 Cotton Club Parade, then again formed a for residency at Harlem Uproar House from September 1937. From 1939, he regularly led his own band in N.Y. area clubs. For many years, Socarras specialized in classical flute, and gave a solo performance at Carnegie Hall in 1945. He was solo flutist in the first performance of Eddie Bonnemere's "Missa Hoosierna" (May 1966). Socarras was actively teaching through the 1970s.—JC/LP

Socor, Matei, Romanian composer; b. Iaşi, Sept. 28, 1908; d. Bucharest, May 30, 1980. He studied theory with Castaldi at the Bucharest Cons. (1927–29) and composition with Karg-Elert at the Leipzig Cons.

(1930–33). He then was active as a composer and teacher in his homeland.

WORKS: DRAMATIC: O p e r a : *Conu Leonida fata cu reactiunea* (1976; Bucharest, Dec. 28, 1978). **ORCH.:** Concerto for Clarinet, Horn, Cello, and Orch. (1939); *Passacaglia* for Cello and Chamber Orch. (1944; also for Violin or Cello and Piano); Violin Concerto (1955). **CHAMBER:** Piano Sonata (1932); Concerto for Oboe, Clarinet, Bassoon, Violin, Viola, Cello, and Piano (1936); Wind Sextet (1968). **VOCAL:** *Mama*, poem for Mezzo-soprano, Chorus, and Orch. (1949); choruses; songs. —NS/LK/DM

Söderblom, Ulf, Finnish conductor; b. Turku, Feb. 5, 1930. He received his training from Swarowsky at the Vienna Academy of Music (graduated, 1957). In 1957 he made his debut as a conductor at the Finnish National Opera in Helsinki, where he subsequently conducted regularly. From 1973 to 1993 he was its music director. During his long tenure, he became particularly known for his championship of contemporary operas. In 1983 he took the Finnish National Opera to the U.S. for performances at the Metropolitan Opera in N.Y. He also appeared as a guest conductor with many orchs. in Finland and abroad. On Feb. 25, 1992, he conducted the premiere of Sallinen's *Kullervo* at the Los Angeles Opera. —NS/LK/DM

Soderini, Agostin, esteemed Italian organist and composer who flourished in the late 16th and early 17th centuries. He was organist of Milan's S. Maria della Rosa in 1608. He publ. in *Milan Sacrarum cantionum 8 et 9 Vocibus liber primus* (1599) and *Canzoni a 4 et 8 voci libro primo* (1608).—NS/LK/DM

Söderlind, Ragnar, Norwegian composer; b. Oslo, June 27, 1945. He was a student of Baden (counterpoint), Hukvari (conducting), and Ulleberg (horn) at the Oslo Cons. (1966–67), of Bergman and Kokkonen (composition) at the Sibelius Academy in Helsinki (1967–68), and of Fladmoe (conducting) at the Oslo Cons. (graduate degree, 1976). For all practical purposes, he was autodidact in composition. Söderlind eschewed the predominant avant-garde course blazed by his contemporaries to embrace a style akin to the new Romanticist persuasion. Programmatic elements are found in several of his scores.

WORKS: DRAMATIC: *Esther and the Blue Serenity*, opera (1971–72); *Hedda Gabler*, symphonic/choreographic drama (1978); *Kristin Lavransdatter*, ballet (1982); *Victoria*, ballet music (1985–86); *Rose og Ravn*, opera (1989). **ORCH.:** *Jølsterslått* (1962–63); *Preludium* (1964–65); *Rokkomborre*, symphonic poem (1967); *Polaris*, symphonic vision (1967–69); *Trauermusik* (1968); *Fantasia borealis* (1969); *Sinfonia minimale* for Youth Orch. (1971); *International Rhapsody* (1971–72); *2 Pieces from the Desert* for Oboe and Small Orch. (1973–75); 6 syms.: No. 1 for Soprano and Orch. (1975–79), No. 2, *Sinfonia breve* (1981), No. 3, *Les illuminations symphonique*, for Soprano, Baritone, and Orch. (1984), No. 4 (1991), No. 5, *Kvitsunn* (1995), and No. 6, *Todessahnung* (1998–99); *Amor et labor*, symphonic poem (1979); *Sinfonietta* for Brass and Percussion (1981–88); *Kom Havsvindar, Kom!*, symphonic poem (1982); *Toccata brillante over "Seier'n er Vår"* (1984); *Eystradalir*, nostalgic rhapsody (1984); *Ecstasy* for Strings (1988);

Violin Concerto (1986–87); *The Hour of Love*, tone poem from the ballet *Victoria* (1990); *Nach Bildern von Edvard Munch* (1995). **CHAMBER:** *Elegia I* for Cello (1966) and *II* for Violin (1966); *Intermezzo* for Percussionist (1967); *La poema battutta* for Percussion (1973); *2 Pieces from the Desert: A Study in Arabian Music* for Oboe and Piano (1973); 2 string quartets (1975, 1997); Quintet for 2 Trumpets, Horn, Trombone, and Tuba (1982). **KEYBOARD: P i a n o :** Sonata (1999). **O r g a n :** *Ciacona* (1976–77); *Preludium funèbre* (1991). **VOCAL:** *Pietá* for Voice and String Orch. (1965–77); *Körsbärsblommor* for Baritone, Flute, English Horn, Cello, and 2 Percussion (1967–71); *La mort des pauvres* for Men's Chorus, Percussion, and 4 Trombones ad libitum (1969); *Vaer Utålmodig, Menneske* for Children's or Women's Chorus and Orch. (1977); *Olavs Hymne* (Olav's Hymn) for Voice, Chorus, and Orch. for the 80th birthday of King Olav I (1983); *Septemberlys* for Voice and Orch. (1983); *Nasadiya/Upphavshymnia* for 3 Choruses and Instrumental Ensemble (1984); *Pasjonskantate* for 2 Soloists, Chorus, and Orch. (1989); *Tranströmer-Svit* for Voice, Piano, 2 Percussion, and String Orch. (1991).—NS/LK/DM

Söderman, (Johan) August, Swedish composer; b. Stockholm, July 17, 1832; d. there, Feb. 10, 1876. He studied piano and composition at the Stockholm Cons. (1847–50), then joined Stjernstrom's theater company as director of music and toured with it in Sweden and Finland. Following further studies with E.F. Richter in Leipzig (1856–57), he resumed his post with the Stjernstrom company; later was chorusmaster and deputy director at Stockholm's Royal Theater. He was particularly influenced by the lyric works of Schumann, Wagner, and Liszt, an influence that is combined with Swedish national elements in his theater music. Among his works were the operettas *Urdur, eller Neckens dotter Zigenarhofdingen Zohrab* (Zohrab, the Gypsy Chief; Helsinki, 1852) and *Hin Ondes första lärospan* (The Devil's First Lesson; Stockholm, Sept. 14, 1856); also incidental music to some 80 plays, orch. pieces, choral works, chamber music, and many ballads and songs.

BIBL.: G. Jeanson, *A. S.: En svensk tondiktares liv och verk* (Stockholm, 1926; includes a complete list of works).
—NS/LK/DM

Söderström (-Olow), (Anna) Elisabeth, prominent Swedish soprano; b. Stockholm, May 7, 1927. She studied voice with Andreyeva von Skilondz in Stockholm, and also took courses in languages and literary history at the Univ. of Stockholm, and received a thorough musical education at the Stockholm Royal Opera School. She made her operatic debut as Bastienne in Mozart's *Bastien und Bastienne* at the Drottningholm Court Theater in Stockholm in 1947. She became a member of the Royal Opera there in 1950. She made her first appearance in Salzburg as Ighino in Pfitzner's *Palestrina* in 1955; then at the Glyndebourne Festival as the Composer in *Ariadne auf Naxos* in 1957, becoming one of its most noted singers. She made her Metropolitan Opera debut in N.Y. as Susanna in *Le nozze de Figaro* on Oct. 30, 1959, and remained on its roster until 1964. Subsequently she pursued her career mainly in Europe until returning to the U.S. in 1977 to sing the title role in *Kat'a Kabanová* at the San Francisco Opera. She returned to the Metropolitan Opera in 1983 as Ellen Orford in

Peter Grimes. In 1988 she sang in the premiere of Argento's *The Aspern Papers* in Dallas. In 1990 she was appointed artistic director of the Drottningholm Court Theater. In 1991 she was awarded the Stora Culture Prize. In 1999 she came out of retirement to portray the Countess in *The Queen of Spades* at the Metropolitan Opera. Her extraordinary command of languages made her an outstanding concert and lieder artist, both in Europe and in North America. Among her notable roles were Fiordiligi, Tatyana, Sophie, Marie in *Wozzeck*, the Countess in *Capriccio*, Jenůfa, Emilia Marty in *The Makropoulos Affair*, and the Governess in *The Turn of the Screw*. She publ. a lighthearted autobiography, *I Min Tonart* (1978; Eng. tr., 1979, as *In My Own Key*).
—NS/LK/DM

Soffel, Doris, German mezzo-soprano; b. Hechingen, May 12, 1948. She received training in voice from Marianne Schech in Munich (1968–73). After singing in *Das Liebesverbot* at the Bayreuth Youth Festival in 1972, she sang in Stuttgart from 1973 to 1976. In 1976 she made her first appearance at the Bayreuth Festival as Waltraute, and returned there as Fricka in 1983. She appeared as Puck in *Oberon* at the Bregenz Festival in 1977. She was engaged as Monteverdi's Poppea in Toronto and as Sextus in *La Clemenza di Tito* at London's Covent Garden in 1983. After singing in the premiere of Reimann's *Troades* in Munich in 1986, she portrayed Angelina in *La Cenerentola* at the Berlin State Opera in 1987. In 1991 she appeared in Munich in the premiere of Pendericki's *Ubu Rex*, returning there in 1994 as Preziosilla. She sang Judith in *Bluebeard's Castle* at the Deutsche Oper in Berlin and as Charlotte in *Werther* in Parma in 1995. In 1997 she appeared in recital in London.
—NS/LK/DM

Soffredini, Alfredo, Italian writer on music, teacher, and composer; b. Livorno, Sept. 17, 1854; d. Milan, March 12, 1923. He studied with Mazzucato and Sangalli at the Milan Cons. He ed. Milan's influential *Gazzetta Musicale* (1896–1912), and also taught composition, numbering among his students Mascagni. He composed 8 operas to his own librettos: *Il Saggio* (Livorno, Feb. 3, 1883), 2-act children's opera, *Il piccolo Haydn* (Faenza, Nov. 24, 1889), *Salvatorello* (Pavia, March 25, 1894), *Tarcisio* (Milan, Nov. 23, 1895), *Aurora* (Pavia, April 21, 1897), *La coppa d'oro* (Milan, Jan. 27, 1900), *Graziella* (Pavia, Nov. 15, 1902), and *Il leone* (Cesena, 1914).—NS/LK/DM

Sofronitzky, Vladimir (Vladimirovich), esteemed Russian pianist and teacher; b. St. Petersburg, May 8, 1901; d. Moscow, Aug. 29, 1961. He studied with A. Lebedeva-Geshevich and A. Mikhailovsky in Warsaw, where he began his career while still a child; completed his training with Nikolayev at the Petrograd Cons. (graduated, 1921). He then toured throughout Europe; also was a prof. at the Leningrad Cons. (1936–42) and the Moscow Cons. (1942–61). He was greatly praised for his interpretations of Chopin and Scriabin, and his performances of Liszt, Schumann, and Rachmaninoff were also notable.

BIBL.: V. Delson, *V. S.* (Moscow, 1959); Ya. Milstein, ed., *Vospominaniya o Sofronitskom* (Reminiscences of S.; Moscow, 1970).—NS/LK/DM

Sohal, Naresh (Kumar), Indian composer; b. Harsipind, Punjab, Sept. 18, 1939. He took courses in science and mathematics at Punjab Univ. In 1962 he settled in England and pursued training in harmony and counterpoint at the London Coll. of Music (1965) and in composition with Jeremy Dale Roberts (1965–66). He then conducted research on micro-intervals under Alexander Goehr.

WORKS: ORCH.: *Asht Prahar* (1965; London, Jan. 17, 1970); Concerto for Harmonica, Percussion, and Strings (1966); *Aalaykhyam I* (1970; London, Nov. 27, 1971) and *II* (1972; London, Feb. 5, 1973); *Indra-Dhanush* (1973); *Dhyan I* for Cello and Small Orch. (1974); *Tandavva Nritya: Dance of Destruction and Re-creation* (1984). **CHAMBER:** *Hexand* for 6 Players (1971); *Octal* for 8 Players (1972); *Hexahedron* for 6 Players (1975); 2 brass quintets (1981, 1983). **VOCAL:** *Kavita I* for Soprano and 8 Players (1970), *II* for Soprano, Flute, and Piano (1972), and *III* for Soprano and Electric Double Bass (1972); *Surya* for 5 Soloists, Chorus, Flute, and 3 Percussion (1970); *Inscape* for 6 Solo Voices, Flute, Percussion, and Electronics (1979); *The Wanderer* for Baritone, Chorus, and Orch. (1981; London, Aug. 23, 1982); *From Gitanjali* for Bass-baritone and Orch. (N.Y., Sept. 12, 1985).—NS/LK/DM

Söhngen, Oskar, learned German theologian and musicologist; b. Hottenstein, Dec. 5, 1900; d. Berlin, Aug. 28, 1983. He studied philosophy and theology (Ph.D., 1922) at the Univ. of Bonn; took courses in philosophy and theology (licentiae, 1924) at the Univ. of Marburg, where he also received instruction in musicology from Stephani. He was a priest in Cologne (1926–32), then an adviser to the Evangelical Church Synod (1932–33; 1935–69); also taught at the Berlin Hochschule für Musikerziehung und Kirchenmusik (1935–59). He devoted his efforts to the study and promotion of liturgical music; was an ed. of the journal *Kunst und Kirche.*

WRITINGS: *Pfarrer und Kirchenmusiker: Sinn und Richtlinien einer Arbeitsgemeinschaft* (Kassel, 1933); *Die neue Kirchenmusik: Wandlungen und Entscheidungen* (Berlin, 1937); ed. with C. Mahrenholz, *Handbuch zum Evangelischen Kirchengesangbuch* (Berlin, 1953); *Kämpfende Kirchenmusik: Die Bewährungsprobe der evangelischen Kirchenmusik im Dritten Reich* (Kassel and Basel, 1954); *Theologische Grundlagen der Kirchenmusik* (Kassel, 1958); *Wandel und Beharrung* (Berlin, 1965); *Theologie der Musik* (Kassel, 1967); *Erneuerte Kirchenmusik: Eine Streitschrift* (Göttingen, 1975).—NS/LK/DM

Sojo, Vicente Emilio, Venezuelan conductor, pedagogue, ethnomusicologist, and composer; b. Guatire, Dec. 8, 1887; d. Caracas, Aug. 11, 1974. He studied music at the Academia de Bellas Artes in Caracas (1910). In 1921 he became a prof. of theory at the Escuela Superior de Música in Caracas. In 1937 he founded the Orquesta Sinfónica Venezuela and the choral ensemble Orfeón Lamas, which became of prime importance in the musical culture of Venezuela. Sojo was also active in national ethnomusicology; he col-lected and harmonized several hundred Venezuelan folk songs and church hymns of the colonial period. He composed mainly sacred music, motets, and organ pieces.

BIBL.: R. Fernández, *V.E. S.* (Caracas, 1968)).—NS/LK/DM

Sokola, Miloš, Czech composer; b. Bučovice, Moravia, April 18, 1913; d. Malé Kyšice, Sept. 27, 1976. He studied composition with Petrželka and violin with O. Vávra at the Brno Cons. (1929–38); had further composition studies at the Prague Cons. with Novák (1938–40) and Křička (1942–44). From 1942 to 1973 he was a violinist in the Prague National Theater orch.

WORKS: DRAMATIC: Opera: *Marnotratný syn* (The Prodigal Son; 1948; Olomouc, 1963). **ORCH.:** *9 Variations on a Theme by Vítězslava Kaprálová* (1952; Prague, Feb. 17, 1957; from Kaprálová's *April Preludes*); Violin Concerto (1952); *Devátý kĕvten* (The Ninth of May), symphonic poem (1960); Concerto for Organ and Strings (1971); Piano Concertino (1972). **CHAMBER:** 5 string quartets (1944; with Solo Tenor, 1946; 1955; 1964; 1971); Violin Sonata (1972); Wind Quintet (1973). **KEYBOARD: Piano:** *5 Miniatures* (1931); Sonata (1946); *Valses* (1953); *12 Preludes* (1954); *Suite* for Piano, Left-hand (1972). **Organ:** *Toccata quasi Passacaglia* (1964); *B-A-C-H Studies* (1972); *Andante cantabile* (1973).—NS/LK/DM

Sokoloff, Nicolai, Russian-born American conductor; b. near Kiev, May 28, 1886; d. La Jolla, Calif., Sept. 25, 1965. He was taken to the U.S. as a child, and studied violin with Loeffler in Boston; played violin in the Boston Sym. Orch. In 1907 he went to Europe to complete his studies. After serving as concertmaster of the Russian Sym. Orch. in N.Y., he decided to settle in the U.S. in 1914 and became a naturalized American citizen. He became music director of the San Francisco Phil. in 1914, then served as the first music director of the Cleveland Orch. (1918–33). He was director of the Federal Music Project (1935–38) and music director of the Seattle Sym. Orch. (1938–40); later was music director of the La Jolla Arts Assn.—NS/LK/DM

Soldat, Marie, Austrian violinist; b. Graz, March 25, 1863; d. there, Sept. 30, 1955. She studied in Graz and with Joachim at the Berlin Hochschule für Musik (1879–82), graduating with the Mendelssohn Prize. She made a specialty of the Brahms Violin Concerto, which she performed with great authority. In 1887 she formed in Berlin her own string quartet (all women); in 1899 she married the lawyer Roger, and settled in Vienna, where she formed a new string quartet; also continued to appear as a soloist.—NS/LK/DM

Soler, Josep, Catalan composer; b. Barcelona, March 25, 1935. He studied composition with Leibowitz in Paris (1959) and with Taltabull in Barcelona (1960–64). In 1977 he was appointed to the staff of the Barcelona Cons.

WORKS: DRAMATIC: Opera: *Agamemnon* (1960); *Edipo y Iocasta* (1972; Barcelona, Oct. 30, 1974); *Jesús de Nazaret* (1974–78). **ORCH.:** *Danae* for Strings (1959; rev. 1969; Lisbon, June 23, 1977); *Orpheus* for Piano and Orch. (1965; rev. 1974);

Quetzalcoatl for Flute and Chamber Orch. (1966); 2 syms.: *The Solar Cycle I* (1967) and *II* (1969; rev. 1977); *Diaphonia* for 17 Wind Instruments (1968); Piano Concerto (1969); Cello Concerto (1973); *Requiem* for Percussion and Orch. (1974–75; Kassel, Sept. 18, 1977); *Apuntava l'alba* (1975; Barcelona, Feb. 5, 1976). **CHAMBER:** Trio for 2 Violins and Piano (1961); Piano Trio (1964); 3 string quartets (1966, 1971, 1975); *Lachrymae* for 11 Instruments (1967); String Trio (1968); *Musica triste* for Guitar (1968); Concerto for Harpsichord, Oboe, English Horn, Bass Clarinet, Viola, and Cello (1969); *Sounds in the Night* for 6 Percussionists (1969); *Inferno* for Chamber Ensemble (1970); *Tanido de Falsas* for Guitar and Percussion (1971); *Noche oscura* for Organ and Percussion (1971); *Harmonices mundi*, in 3 vols.: No. 1 for Piano, and Nos. 2 and 3 for Organ (1977). **VOCAL:** *Cantata Ioel Prophetae*, chamber cantata (1960); *3 Erotic Songs* for Chorus (1976); *Shakespeare Lieder* for Tenor and Orch. (1976–77); songs.

BIBL.: A. Medina, *J. S.: Música de la pasión* (Madrid, 1998). —**NS/LK/DM**

Solera, Temistocle, Italian librettist and composer; b. Ferrara, Dec. 25, 1815; d. Milan, April 21, 1878. He ran away from a Viennese boarding school, and worked with a traveling circus. He met Verdi, who accepted his offer to rework the libretto for *Oberto, conte de San Bonifacio* (1839). Solera then provided Verdi with librettos for *I Lombardi alla prima Crociata* (1843), *Giovanna d'Arco* (1845), and *Attila* (1846). He subsequently was active as an impresario in Saragossa, Barcelona, Gibraltar, and Madrid, where he was joined by his wife, the singer Teresa Rosmini. He also was a secret courier between Napoleon III and Cavour. After serving as chief of police in various locales, he went to Paris as an antique dealer. His last days were spent in poverty in Milan. Solera's operas, all to his own librettos, included *Ildegonda* (Milan, March 20, 1840), *Il contadino d'Angleiate* (Milan, Oct. 4, 1841; rev. version as *La fanciulla di Castelguelfo*, Modena, Oct. 23, 1842), *Genio e sventura* (Padua, June 1843), and *La hermana de Palayo* (Madrid, 1845). He also wrote chamber music, sacred pieces, and songs.—**LK/DM**

Soler (Ramos), Antonio (Francisco Javier José), important Catalan composer and organist; b. Olot, Gerona (baptized), Dec. 3, 1729; d. El Escorial, near Madrid, Dec. 20, 1783. He entered the Montserrat monastery choir school in 1736, where his mentors were the maestro Benito Esteve and the organist Beninto Valls. About 1750 he was made maestro de capilla in Lérida; in 1752, was ordained a subdeacon and also became a member of the Jeronymite monks in El Escorial, taking the habit, and then being professed in 1753; was made maestro de capilla in 1757. He also pursued studies with José de Nebra and Domenico Scarlatti. Soler was a prolific composer of both sacred and secular vocal music, as well as instrumental music. Among his works are 9 masses, 5 Requiems, 60 Psalms, 13 Magnificats, 14 litanies, 28 Lamentations, 5 motets, and other sacred works; 132 villancicos (1752–78); 120 keyboard sonatas (100 sonatas and a *Fandango* ed. by F. Marvin, N.Y., 1958–59); 6 quintets for 2 Violins, Viola, Cello, and Organ (1776; ed. by R. Gerhard, Barcelona, 1933); *6 conciertos de dos organos obligados* (ed. in Musica Hispana,

series C, 1952–62, and by S. Kastner, Mainz, 1972); liturgical organ pieces. His writings include *Llave de la modulación, y antigüedades de la música en que se trata del fundamento necessario para saber modular: Theórica, y prática para el más claro conocimiento de qualquier especie de figuras, desde el tiempo de Juan de Muris, hasta hoy, con albunos cánones enigmáticos, y sus resoluciones* (Madrid, 1762; ed. and tr. by M. Crouch, diss., Univ. of Calif., Santa Barbara, 1978), *Satisfacción a los reparos precisos hechos por D. Antonio Roel del Rio, a la Llave de la modulación* (Madrid, 1765), *Carta escrita a un amigo en que le da parte de un diálogo ultimamente publicado contra su Llave de la modulación* (Madrid, 1766), and *Combinacion de Monedas y Calculo manifiesto contra el Libro anónimo inititulado: Correspondencia de la Moneda de Cataluña a la de Castilla* (Barcelona, 1771).

BIBL.: F. Carroll, *An Introduction to A. S.* (diss., Univ. of Rochester, 1960); T. Espinosa, *Selected Unpublished Villancicos of Padre Fray A. S.* (diss., Univ. of Southern Calif., 1969); K. Heimes, *A. S.'s Keyboard Sonatas* (Pretoria, 1969); P. Capdepón Verdú, *El P. A. S. (1729–1783) y el cultivo del villancico en El Escorial* (Madrid, 1993); idem, *Die Villancicos des P. A. S. (1729–1783)* (Frankfurt am Main, 1994).—**NS/LK/DM**

Solerti, Angelo, Italian philologist and music scholar; b. Savona, Sept. 20, 1865; d. Massa Carrara, Jan. 10, 1907. He studied at the Istituto di Studi Superiori in Florence and at the Univ. of Turin (arts degree, 1887). His contributions to the early history of opera are valuable: *Le origini del melodramma: Testimonianze dei contemporanei* (a collection of contemporary documents and prefaces to the earliest operas; Turin, 1903), *Gli albori del melodramma* (3 vols., Milan, 1904–05), *Musica, ballo e drammatica alla corte medicea dal 1600 al 1637: Notizie tratte da un diario (tenuto da Cesare Tinghi), con appendice di testi inediti e rari* (Florence, 1905), and *Ferrara e la Corte Estense nella second metà del secolo XVI* (Città di Castello, 1891).—**NS/LK/DM**

Solié, Jean-Pierre, French tenor, later baritone, and composer; b. Nîmes, 1755; d. Paris, Aug. 6, 1812. He received training in music as a choirboy at Nîmes Cathedral. In 1778 he made his debut as a tenor in Grétry's *La rosière de Salency* in Avignon, and then sang in provincial theaters. In 1782 he appeared at the Comédie-Italienne in Paris. Following engagements in Nancy and Lyons, he returned there to sing secondary roles in 1787 before being made its principal singer in 1789. He composed some 40 stage works, the best known being his opéras-comiques *Le jockey* (Paris, Jan. 6, 1796) and *Le secret* (Paris, April 20, 1796).—**LK/DM**

Sollberger, Harvey (Dene), American flutist, conductor, teacher, and composer; b. Cedar Rapids, Iowa, May 11, 1938. He studied composition with Philip Bezanson and Eldon Obrecht at the Univ. of Iowa (B.A., 1960) and also received instruction in flute from Betty Bang Mather; completed his training in composition with Beeson and Luening at Columbia Univ. (M.A., 1964); held 2 Guggenheim fellowships (1969, 1973). With Charles Wuorinen, he founded the Group for Contemporary Music in N.Y. in 1962; appeared regularly with it as a flutist and conductor; also toured as a flutist and conductor in the U.S. and Europe. He served on the faculties of Columbia Univ. (1965–83), the Manhattan School of Music (1971–83), the Philadelphia Coll. of the Performing Arts (1980–82), and the Ind. Univ. School of Music (1983–92), where he also directed its new-music ensemble. In 1992 he became a prof. of music at the Univ. of Calif. at San Diego. From 1998 he was music director of the La Jolla Sym. Orch. His music reveals an imaginatively applied serial method.

WORKS: *Grand Quartet* for Flutes (1962); *2 Oboes Troping* (1963); *Chamber Variations* for 12 Players and Conductor (1964); *Music for Sophocles' Antigone*, electronic music (1966); *Fanfare Mix Transpose*, electronic music (1968); *As Things Are and Become* for String Trio (1969; rev. 1972); *Musica transalpina*, 2 motets for Soprano, Baritone, and 9 Players (1970); *Elegy for Igor Stravinsky* for Flute, Cello, and Piano (1971); *The 2 and the 1* for Amplified Cello and 2 Percussionists (1972); *Folio*, 11 pieces for Bassoon (1974–76); *Sunflowers* for Flute and Vibraphone (1976); *Flutes and Drums* for 8 Flutes, 8 Percussionists, and 4 Double Basses (1977); *Music for Prepared Dancers* for Dancers, Flute, Violin, and Percussion (1978); *6 Quartets* for Flute and Piano (1981); *The Humble Heart/CAT Scan* for Woodwind Quintet (1982); *Interrupted Night* for 5 Instruments (1983); *Killapata/Chaskapata* for Solo Flute and Flute Choir (1983); *Double Triptych* for Flute and Percussion (1984); *3 or 4 Things I Know about the Oboe*, chamber concerto for Oboe and 13 Players (1986); *original substance/manifests/traces* for Flute, Harp, Guitar, Piano, and Percussion (1987); *Persian Golf* for Strings (1987); *Quodlibetudes* for Flute (1988); *Aurelian Echoes* for Flute and Alto Flute (1989); *...from winter's frozen stillness*, trio for Violin, Cello, and Piano (1990); *Passages* for Soloists, Chorus, and Orch. (1990); *Mutable Duo* for Flute, Clarinet, Violin, Cello, Piano, and Percussion (1991); *The Advancing Moment* for Flute, Clarinet, Violin, Cello, Piano, and Percussion (1993); *CIAO, Arcosanti!* for 8 Instruments (1994); *In Terra Aliena* for 5 Soloists and Orch. (1995).—**NS/LK/DM**

Sollertinsky, Ivan (Ivanovich), brilliant Russian musicologist and music critic; b. Vitebsk, Dec. 3, 1902; d. Novosibirsk, Feb. 11, 1944. He studied Hispanic philosophy at the Univ. of Petrograd (1919–24) and drama at the Inst. for the History of the Arts (graduated, 1923), subsequently pursuing postgraduate courses (1926–29); also took conducting lessons with Malko. He was active as a lecturer and music critic in Leningrad, where he later taught at the Cons. (from 1936). He showed profound understanding of the problems of modern music and was one of the earliest supporters of Shostakovich; publ. numerous articles dealing with Soviet music in general; M. Druskin ed. 4 vols. of his writings (Leningrad, 1946; 1956, second ed., 1963; 1973; 1973).

BIBL.: L. Mikheeva, *I.I. S.* (Leningrad, 1988).—**NS/LK/DM**

Solomon (actually, **Solomon Cutner**), outstanding English pianist; b. London, Aug. 9, 1902; d. there, Feb. 2, 1988. He studied with Mathilde Verne, making a sensational debut as a child prodigy as soloist in Tchaikovsky's first Piano Concerto in London (June 30, 1911); later studied in Paris with Lévy and Dupré, and then resumed his career in 1923, adopting his first name for his concert engagements. In 1926 he made his U.S. debut, and in subsequent years toured all over the world as a soloist with orchs., recitalist, and chamber music artist. His remarkable career was cut short at the height of his interpretative powers when he was stricken by an incapacitating illness in 1955. In 1946 he was made a Commander of the Order of the British Empire. His performances of the classics were particularly esteemed; he eschewed virtuosity for its own sake, opting instead for intellectually insightful and unmannered interpretations of the highest order.—**NS/LK/DM**

Solomon, Izler, American conductor; b. St. Paul, Minn., Jan. 11, 1910; d. Fort Wayne, Ind., Dec. 6, 1987. He took violin lessons with Myron Poliakin in Philadelphia and Michael Press in N.Y.; then studied at Mich. State Coll. (1928–31). He made his debut as a conductor with the Lansing (Mich.) Civic Orch. on March 17, 1932; led that orch. until 1936; then conducted the Ill. Sym. Orch. (1936–42) and the Columbus (Ohio) Phil. (1941–49); was guest conductor of the Israel Phil. during its American tour in 1951. His major post, which established his reputation, was as music director of the Indianapolis Sym. Orch. (1956–75), which he brought to a level of excellence. In his programs he included many modern American works. In 1976 he suffered a stroke, which ended his career.—**NS/LK/DM**

Solomon, Maynard (Elliott), American recording executive and writer on music; b. N.Y., Jan. 5, 1930. He was educated in N.Y. at the H.S. of Music and Art and at Brooklyn Coll. (A.B., 1950), and then pursued postgraduate studies at Columbia Univ. (1950–51). He was co-founder and co-owner of the Vanguard Recording Soc., Inc., of N.Y. (1950–86); was on the faculty of the City Univ. of N.Y. (1979–81) and served as a visiting prof. at the State Univ. of N.Y. at Stony Brook (1988–89), Columbia Univ. (1989–90), and Harvard Univ. (1991–92). In 1978, 1989, and 1995 he won ASCAP-Deems Taylor Awards. In 1999 he was made an honorary member of the American Musicological Soc. He contributed many articles on Beethoven, Schubert, and other composers to the *Musical Quarterly*, *Music & Letters*, *19th Century Music*, *Beethoven Studies*, the *Beethoven-Jahrbuch*, the *Journal of the American Musicological Society*, and other publications, and also served as assoc. ed. of *American Imago*.

WRITINGS: *Marxism and Art* (1973); *Beethoven* (1977; second ed., rev., 1998); *Myth, Creativity and Psychoanalysis* (1978); *Beethoven's Tagebuch 1812–1818* (1983); *Beethoven Essays* (1988); *Mozart: A Life* (1994).—**NS/LK/DM**

Solomon, Yonty, South African-born English pianist and teacher; b. Cape Town, May 3, 1938. He was a pupil of Cameron Taylor at the Univ. of Cape Town (B.Mus., 1958). In 1963 he won the Beethoven International Award and settled in London, where he continued his training with Dame Myra Hess. He later studied with Agosti in Rome and Rosen in the U.S. He appeared as a soloist with orchs. in Europe, North America, South Africa, and Israel, and also gave recitals. Solomon was also active as a prof. at the Royal Coll. of Music and gave various master classes in other locales. In addition to the standard piano literature, he championed many composers of the modern age, among them Janáček, Ives, Schoenberg, Prokoviev, Sorabji, Bennett, and Josephs.—NS/LK/DM

Solothurnmann, Juerg, jazz tenor, alto and soprano saxophonist, musicologist; b. Zurich, April 22, 1943. He grew up in the town of Solothurn, where his first instruments were the accordion, piano, banjo and marching drum. He began his music studies at the Univ. of Bern (1963); in the late 1960s, he became interested in ethnomusicology. At the same time (1968–72), he studied saxophone and jazz theory at the Swiss Jazz School; from 1972–74, he studied at Ind. Univ. He taught jazz history at the Swiss Jazz School in Bern until 1986. Since 1969, he has done jazz programs for Swiss National Radio DRS. Since the mid-1970s, he has performed with blues, jazz-rock and salsa bands, and later with his own jazz ensembles Uepsilon (1976–84), S.A.H. (1985), Alpine Jazz Herd (1982–94), First Aid Band I, II & III (1985–92), At the Crossroads (1988), Agasul Orchester (since 1990), Raw & Cooked (1992–96), Sound & Space (from 1996), The Magic Triangle (from 1995), a project with Harry Tavitian and Corneliu Stroe, and Live According to e. e. cummings with Ellen Christi. Solothurnmann's style is to combine contemporary jazz and Swiss folklore. He is co-founder and longtime board member of the Musiker Kooperative Schweiz (MKS) and the Interessegemeinschaft improvisierte Musik (IGIM) in Bern. In 1992, he organized and directed the Swiss-Spanish Jazz Festival at the Swiss Pavillon within the World EXPO Sevilla. He founded Unit Records (1983), a musician-owned label, and served as its director until 1991. He has won the Zurich Radio Award (1988) and the Big Music Prize 1996 of the Canton Bern.

DISC.: Alpine Jazz Herd: *Swiss Flavor* (1983); Uepsilon: *Head in the Clouds* (1984).—LP

Soloviev, Nikolai (Feopemptovich), Russian music critic, teacher, and composer; b. Petrozavodsk, May 9, 1846; d. Petrograd, Dec. 27, 1916. After completing his studies in composition at the St. Petersburg Cons. (1868–72), he joined its faculty as a teacher of theory (1874–85) and a prof. of composition (1885–1909); also was active as a music critic (from 1870), acquiring a reputation as a determined opponent of the contemporary scene and being highly critical of Tchaikovsky and the national school of composers. He composed the operas *Vakula the Smith* (1875; concert perf., St. Petersberg, 1880), *Cordelia* (St. Petersburg, Nov. 24, 1885; rev. as *Vengeance*, 1898), and *The House at Kolomna* (n.d.). He also orchestrated Act 5 and part of Act 1 of Serov's opera *The Evil Power*. Other works include *Russia and the Mongols*, symphonic picture (1870), *Ey, ukhnem*, orch. fantasy (1882), *Samson*, cantata (1870), and other cantatas, choral pieces, chamber music, piano pieces, and songs.—NS/LK/DM

Soloviev-Sedoy, Vasili (Pavlovich), Russian composer; b. St. Petersburg, April 25, 1907; d. Moscow, Dec. 2, 1979. He learned to play the balalaika, guitar, and piano before pursuing studies at the Mussorgsky Music School (1929–31) and the Leningrad Cons. (1931–36). He was active as a pianist, playing improvisations on the radio and accompanying exercises in the Leningrad Studio of Creative Gymnastics. During World War II, he organized a series of theatrical productions for the Soviet army. He was a member of the Supreme Soviet in the 3rd, 4th, and 5th congresses. In 1975 he was awarded the order of Hero of Socialist Labor. He was regarded in Russia as one of the most expert composers of Soviet songs, some of which acquired immense popularity; one of them, *Evenings at Moscow*, became a musical signature of daily news broadcasts on the Soviet radio. In all, he wrote over 700 songs. He was able to synthesize the melos of Russian folk songs with revolutionary ballads and marching rhythms. His other works include an opera, several operettas, the ballet *Taras Bulba* (Leningrad, Dec. 12, 1940; rev. 1953), a few orch. pieces, film scores, and piano music.

BIBL.: A. Sokhor, *V.P. S.-S.* (Leningrad and Moscow, 1952; second ed., 1967); Yu. Kremlyov, *V.P. S.-S. ocherk zhizni i tvorchestva* (V.P. S.-S.: Outline of His Life and Work; Leningrad, 1960).—NS/LK/DM

Soltesz, Stefan, Hungarian-born Austrian conductor; b. Nyiregyhaza, Jan. 6, 1949. He was a student of Dieter Weber, Hans Swarowsky, Reinhold Schmidt, and Friedrich Cerha at the Vienna Academy of Music. He was a conductor at the Theater an der Wien (1971–73) and the Vienna State Opera (1973–83), and also was an assist. conductor at the Salzburg Festival (1978–79; 1983). After holding the position of first conductor at the Graz Opera (1979–81), the Hamburg State Opera (1983–85), and the Deutsche Oper in Berlin (1985–88), he was Generalmusikdirektor in Braunschweig from 1988 to 1993. In 1992 he made his U.S. debut at the Washington (D.C.) Opera conducting *Otello*. He became music director of the Flanders Opera and principal guest conductor of the Leipzig Opera in 1992. From 1997 he was Generalmusikdirektor in Essen. As a guest conductor, he led various opera companies and orchs. in Europe.—NS/LK/DM

Solti, Sir Georg (real name, **György Stern**), eminent Hungarian-born English conductor; b. Budapest, Oct. 21, 1912; d. Antibes, Sept. 5, 1997. He began to study the piano when he was 6, making his first public appearance in Budapest when he was 12; at 13, he enrolled there at the Franz Liszt Academy of Music, studying piano with Dohnányi and, briefly, with Bartók. He took composition courses with Kodály. He graduated at the age of 18, and was engaged by the Budapest Opera as a répétiteur. He also served as an assist. to Bruno Walter (1935) and Toscanini (1936, 1937) at the Salzburg Festivals. On March 11, 1938, he made a brilliant conducting debut at the Budapest Opera with Mozart's *Le nozze di Figaro*; however, the wave of anti-Semitism in Hungary under the reactionary military rule forced him to leave Budapest (he was Jewish). In 1939 he went to Switzerland, where he was active mainly as a concert pianist; in 1942 he won the Concours International de Piano in Geneva; finally, in 1944, he was engaged to conduct concerts with the orch. of the Swiss Radio. In 1946 the American occupation authorities in Munich invited him to conduct *Fidelio* at the Bavarian State Opera; his success led to his appointment as its Generalmusikdirektor, a position he held from 1946 to 1952. In 1952 he became Generalmusikdirektor in Frankfurt am Main, serving as director of the Opera and conductor of the Museumgesellschaft Concerts. He made his U.S. debut with the San Francisco Opera on Sept. 25, 1953, conducting *Elektra*. He later conducted the Chicago Sym. Orch., the N.Y. Phil., and at the Metropolitan Opera in N.Y., where he made his first appearance on Dec. 17, 1960, with *Tannhäuser*. He was then engaged as music director of the Los Angeles Phil., but he withdrew when the board of trustees refused to grant him full powers in musical and administrative policy. In 1960–61 he was music director of the Dallas Sym. Orch. In the meantime, he made his Covent Garden debut in London in 1959; in 1961 he assumed the post of music director of the Royal Opera House there, retaining it with great distinction until 1971. In 1969 he became music director of the Chicago Sym. Orch., and it was in that capacity that he achieved a triumph as an interpreter and orch. builder, so that the "Chicago sound" became a synonym for excellence. He showed himself an enlightened disciplinarian and a master of orch. psychology, so that he could gain and hold the confidence of the players while demanding from them the utmost in professional performance. Under his direction the Chicago Sym. Orch. became one of the most celebrated orchs. in the world. He took it to Europe for the first time in 1971, eliciting glowing praise from critics and audiences. He subsequently led it on a number of acclaimed tours there, and also took it to N.Y. for regular appearances at Carnegie Hall. He held the additional posts of music adviser of the Paris Opéra (1971–73) and music director of the Orch. de Paris (1972–75), which he took on a tour of China in 1974. He served as principal conductor and artistic director of the London Phil. from 1979 to 1983, and was then accorded the title of conductor emeritus. During all these years, he retained his post with the Chicago Sym. Orch., while continuing his appearances as a guest conductor with European orchs. In 1983 he conducted the *Ring* cycle at the Bayreuth Festival, in commemoration of the 100th anniversary of the death of Richard Wagner. Solti retained his prestigious position with the Chicago Sym. Orch. until the close of the 100th anniversary season in 1990–91, and subsequently held the title of Laureate Conductor. In 1992–93 he served as artistic director of the Salzburg Festival. In 1968 he was made an honorary Commander of the Order of the British Empire; in 1971 he was named an honorary Knight Commander of the Order of the British Empire. In 1972 he became a British subject and was knighted, assuming the title of Sir Georg. In 1992 he was awarded Germany's Grosses Verdienstkreuz mit Stern und Schulterband. In honor of his 80th birthday in 1992 the Vienna Phil. awarded him the first Hans Richter Medal. In 1993 President Clinton awarded him the National Medal of Arts and he was accorded honors at the Kennedy Center in Washington, D.C. With H. Sachs, he wrote a vol. of memoirs (N.Y., 1997). Solti was generally acknowledged as a superlative interpreter of the symphonic and operatic repertoire. He was renowned for his performances of Wagner, Verdi, Mahler, Richard Strauss, and other Romantic masters; he also conducted notable performances of Bartók, Stravinsky, Schoenberg, and other composers of the 20th century. His recordings received innumerable awards.

BIBL.: W. Furlong, *Season with S.: A Year in the Life of the Chicago Symphony* (N.Y. and London, 1974); P. Robinson, *S.* (London, 1979).—**NS/LK/DM**

Soltys, Adam, Polish pedagogue and composer, son of **Mieczyslaw Soltys;** b. Lemberg, July 4, 1890; d. there (Lwów), July 6, 1968. He studied with his father, and later with Georg Schumann in Berlin; also took courses in musicology at the Univ. of Berlin with Kretzschmar and Johannes Wolf (Ph.D., 1921). Returning to Poland, he served as director of the Lwów Cons. (1930–39) and again after World War II. His compositions include 2 syms. (1927, 1946); the symphonic poems *Slowanie* (1949), *O pokoj* (About Peace; 1953), and *Z gór i dolin* (From Mountains and Valleys; 1960); numerous teaching pieces for violin and for piano.—**NS/LK/DM**

Soltys, Mieczyslaw, Polish conductor, teacher, and composer, father of **Adam Soltys;** b. Lemberg, Feb. 7, 1863; d. there (Lwów), Nov. 12, 1929. He studied in Lemberg and Paris. Returning to Lemberg in 1899, he was director of the Cons. and of the Musical Society; also wrote music criticism.

WORKS: DRAMATIC: Opera: *Rzeczpospolita Babińska* (Republic of Babin; 1894; Lemberg, April 27, 1905); *Panie Kochanku* (1890; Lwów, May 3, 1924) *Opowieć kresowa* or *Opowieść ukraińska* (A Ukraine Story; 1909; Lemberg, March 8, 1910); *Nieboska komedia* (1925). **OTHER:** 2 syms.; 3 symphonic poems; *Concerto religioso* for Piano and Orch.; oratorios; choruses; piano pieces; songs; organ music.—**NS/LK/DM**

Solum, John (Henry), American flutist and teacher; b. New Richmond, Wisc., May 11, 1935. He studied flute with William Kincaid in Philadelphia (1953–58) and was a student at Princeton Univ. (B.A., 1957); he also received instruction in harmony, counterpoint, composition, and musicology. He made his debut in 1953. In 1957 he appeared as a soloist with the Philadelphia Orch. In 1959 he made his N.Y. recital debut. In subsequent years, he toured all over the world as a soloist with orchs., as a chamber music artist, and as a recitalist. He taught at Vassar Coll. (1969–71). After teaching at Ind. Univ. (1973) and the Oberlin (Ohio) Coll. Cons. of Music (1976), he again taught at Vassar Coll. (from 1977). From 1979 to 1989 he was co-director of the Bath (England) Summer School of Baroque Music. He also was active with the Conn. Early Music Festival from 1982. His repertoire ranges from Bach, Handel, Telemann, and Vivaldi to Honegger, Ibert, Jolivet, and Sir Malcolm Arnold.—**NS/LK/DM**

Solzhenitsyn, Ignat, Russian-born American pianist and conductor; b. Moscow, Sept. 23, 1972. He is the son of the great Russian novelist Aleksandr Solzhenitsyn, and was reared in Cavendish, Vt. After learning to read music with the help of a neighbor, he began formal piano lessons at age 9 with Chonghyo Shin, and then studied with Luis Batlle. At age 10, he began making appearances as a soloist with orchs. and as a recitalist. When he was 14, he went to London to pursue piano studies with Maria Curcio. In 1989 he made his London debut as a pianist. After some piano instruction from Arrau in N.Y., he studied with Graffman (B.Mus. in piano, 1995) and Mueller (diploma in conducting, 1995) at the Curtis Inst. of Music in Philadelphia. He won critical acclaim as soloist with Rostropovich and the National Sym. Orch. of Washington, D.C., in Moscow in 1993. In 1994 he was awarded an Avery Fisher Career Grant. As a soloist, he has appeared with many orchs. in the U.S. and abroad, including those of Boston, Chicago, Philadelphia, St. Louis, Los Angeles, Seattle, Baltimore, Montreal, Paris, St. Petersburg, and Israel. During the 1999–2000 season, he toured the U.S. as soloist with Daniele Gatti and the Royal Phil. of London. His recital engagements have taken him to most of the principal music centers of the world. In 1993 he began to conduct the Concerto Soloists Chamber Orch. in Philadelphia. After serving as its asst. and assoc. conductor, he became its principal conductor in 1999. He has also appeared as a guest conductor with several U.S. orchs. —NS/LK/DM

Somary, Johannes (Felix), American organist, conductor, and composer; b. Zürich (of American parents), April 7, 1935. He was taken to the U.S. as a child, and received his musical training at Yale Coll. (B.A., 1957) and with Quincy Porter and Keith Wilson at the Yale Univ. School of Music (M.M., 1959). In 1961 he founded the Amor Artis Chorale and Orch., which he conducted in much Baroque music; led the U.S. premieres of Handel's *Esther* in 1961, *Theodora* in 1963, and *Susanna* in 1965; also was a guest conductor in the U.S. and Europe. From 1971 he was chairman of the arts and music dept. at the Horace Mann School in N.Y. He also was conductor of the Fairfield County Chorale (from 1975), the Great Neck Choral Soc. (from 1982), and the Taghkanic Chorale (from 1992). He composed orch. works, choral pieces, songs, and chamber music. —NS/LK/DM

Somer, (Ruth) Hilde, Austrian-born American pianist; b. Vienna, Feb. 11, 1922; d. Freeport, Bahamas, Dec. 24, 1979. She studied with her mother; in 1938 the family went to the U.S. and she enrolled at the Curtis Inst. of Music in Philadelphia as a student of Serkin; also took private lessons with Arrau. She cultivated modern works; commissioned piano concertos from John Corigliano Jr. (San Antonio, April 7, 1968) and Antonio Tauriello (Washington, D.C., June 29, 1968), the second Piano Concerto by Alberto Ginastera (Indianapolis, March 22, 1973), and a "spatial concerto" by Henry Brant (Tucson, Ariz., Nov. 16, 1978). She also gave a series of concerts of piano music by Scriabin, with color images projected upon the screen to suggest Scriabin's own ideas of a synthesis of sounds and colors. —NS/LK/DM

Somers, Harry (Stewart), outstanding Canadian composer and pianist; b. Toronto, Sept. 11, 1925; d. there, March 9, 1999. He studied piano with Dorothy Hornfelt (1939–41), Reginald Godden (1942–43), Weldon Kilburn (1945–48), and E.R. Schmitz (1948) in Toronto, and also attended classes in composition with John Weinzweig (1941–43; 1945–49). He then studied with Milhaud in Paris (1949–50). Returning to Canada, he eked out a meager living as a music copyist, finally receiving commissions in 1960. He also became active as a broadcaster. In 1972 he was made a Companion of the Order of Canada. His historical opera, *Louis Riel*, was performed at the Kennedy Center in Washington, D.C., on Oct. 23, 1975, as part of America's Bicentennial celebration. His musical idiom was quaquaversal, absorbing without prejudice ancient, national, and exotic resources, from Gregorian chant to oriental scales, from simple folkways to electronic sound, all handled with fine expertise.

WORKS: DRAMATIC: *The Fool,* chamber opera for 4 Soloists and Chamber Orch. (1953; Toronto, Nov. 15, 1956); *The Homeless Ones,* television operetta (CBC-TV, Toronto, Dec. 31, 1955); *The Fisherman and His Soul,* ballet (Hamilton, Nov. 5, 1956); *Ballad,* ballet (Ottawa, Oct. 29, 1958); *The House of Atreus,* ballet (1963; Toronto, Jan. 13, 1964); *Louis Riel,* historical opera (Toronto, Sept. 23, 1967); *Improvisation,* theater piece for Narrator, Singers, Strings, any number of Woodwinds, 2 Percussionists, and Piano (Montreal, July 5, 1968); *And,* choreography for Dancers, Vocal Soloists, Flute, Harp, Piano, and 4 Percussionists (CBC-TV, Toronto, 1969); *Death of Enkidu: Part I,* chamber opera, after the epic of Gilgamesh (Toronto, Dec. 7, 1977); *Mario and the Magician,* opera (1991). **ORCH.:** *Scherzo* for Strings (1947); 3 piano concertos: No. 1 (Toronto, March, 1949), No. 2 (Toronto, March 12, 1956), and No. 3 (1994–95); *North Country* for Strings (Toronto, Nov. 10, 1948); *Suite* for Harp and Chamber Orch. (Toronto, Dec. 11, 1952); *The Case of the Wayward Woodwinds* for Chamber Orch. (1950); Sym. No. 1 (1951; Toronto, April 27, 1953); *Passacaglia and Fugue* (1954); *Little Suite for String Orchestra on Canadian Folk Songs* (1955); *Fantasia* (Montreal, April 1, 1958); *Lyric* (Washington, D.C., April 30, 1961); *5 Concepts* (1961; Toronto, Feb. 15, 1962); *Movement* (CBC-TV, Toronto, March 4, 1962); *Stereophony* (Toronto, March 19, 1963); *The Picasso Suite,* light music for Small Orch. (1964; Saskatoon, Feb. 28, 1965); *Those Silent Awe-filled Spaces* (Ottawa, Feb. 2, 1978); *Variations* for Strings (1979); *Elegy, Transformation, Jubilation: In Memoriam Four Suicides* (1981); *Concertante* for Violin, String Orch., and Percussion (1982); Guitar Concerto (1984). **CHAMBER:** 3 string quartets (1943, 1950, 1959); *Suite* for Percussion (1947); *Mime* for Violin and Piano (1948); *Rhapsody* for Violin and Piano (1948); Wind Quintet (1948); Trio for Flute, Violin, and Cello (1950); 2 violin sonatas (1953, 1955); *Movement* for Wind Quintet (1957); Sonata for Solo Guitar (1959); *Theme and Variations* for any combination of Instruments (1964); *Music* for Violin (1974); *Movement* for String Quartet (1982); *Fanfare to J.S. B.* for Brass Quintet (1984); *11 Miniatures* for Oboe and Piano (1994). **Piano:** *Strangeness of Heart* (1942); *Flights of Fancy* (1944); 5 sonatas (*Testament of Youth,* 1945; 1946; 1950; 1950; 1957); *3 Sonnets* (1946); *Solitudes* (1947); *4 Primitives* (1949); *12 x 12,* fugues (1951). **VOCAL:** *5 Songs for Dark Voice* for Contralto and Orch. (Stratford, Ontario, Aug. 11, 1956); *At the Descent from the Cross* for Bass and 2 Guitars (1962); *12 Miniatures* for Soprano, Recorder or Flute, Viola da Gamba, and Spinet (1963); *Crucifixion* for Chorus, English Horn, 2 Trumpets, Harp, and Percussion (1966); *Kuyas* for Soprano, Flute, and Percussion

(1967; adapted from Louis Riel); *Kyrie* for Soloists, Chorus, Flute, Oboe, Clarinet, Cello, 3 Trumpets, Piano, and 6 Percussionists (1970–72); *Voiceplay* for Male or Female Singer/Actor (Toronto, Nov. 14, 1972; Cathy Berberian, soloist); *Zen, Yeats and Emily Dickinson* for Female and Male Narrators, Soprano, Flute, Piano, and Tape (1975); *Chura-churum* for Chorus, Flute, Harp, Piano, 4 Percussion, and 8 Loudspeakers (1985); choruses; songs.

BIBL.: B. Cherney, *H. S.* (Toronto, 1975).—NS/LK/DM

Somervell, Sir Arthur, English music educator and composer; b. Windermere, June 5, 1863; d. London, May 2, 1937. He studied the classics at King's Coll., Cambridge (B.A., 1883), where he also took courses in music with Stanford; after further training at the Berlin Hochschule für Musik (1883–85), he studied at the Royal Coll. of Music in London (1885–87); then received private instruction from Parry. He taught at the Royal Coll. of Music (1893–1901); then was active as an inspector of music. He was knighted in 1929. He was at his best as a composer of vocal music.

WORKS: ORCH.: *Normandy*, symphonic variations (1912); *Thalassa*, sym. (1912); *Highland Concerto* for Piano and Orch. (1921); Violin Concerto (1932). **VOCAL: C h o r a l :** 2 Masses (1891, 1907); *Joan of Arc* (1893); *Ode to the Sea* (1897); *Ode on the Intimations of Immortality* (1907); *Christmas*, cantata (1926). **O t h e r V o c a l :** Song cycles. **OTHER:** Piano pieces; numerous educational pieces for schools; etc.—NS/LK/DM

Somfai, László, Hungarian musicologist; b. Jászladány, Aug. 15, 1934. He studied at the Budapest Academy of Music as a student of Szabolcsi and Bartha, receiving his Ph.D. there in 1959. He served as a music librarian at the National Széchényi Library (1958–62). In 1963 he joined the staff of the Bartók Archives (from 1969 known as the Inst. of Musicology of the Hungarian Academy of Sciences); became its director in 1972. He also taught at the Budapest Academy of Music (from 1969; prof. from 1980) and was ed. of the archive series Documenta Bartókiana (from 1972). In 1986 he became a corresponding member of the American Musicological Soc.

WRITINGS: With D. Bartha, *Haydn als Opernkapellmeister: Die Haydn-Dokumente der Esterházy-Opernsammlung* (Budapest and Mainz, 1960); *Joseph Haydn: Sein Leben in zeitgenössischen Bildern* (Budapest and Kassel, 1966; Eng. tr., 1969); *Anton Webern* (Budapest, 1968); *The Keyboard Sonatas of Joseph Haydn: Instruments and Performance Practice, Genres and Styles* (Chicago, 1995); *Béla Bartók: Composition, Concepts, and Autograph Sources* (Berkeley, 1996).—NS/LK/DM

Somigli, Franca (real name, **Maria Bruce Clark**), American-Italian soprano; b. Chicago, March 17, 1901; d. Trieste, May 14, 1974. She was a pupil of Malatesta, Votto, and Storchio in Milan. After making her operatic debut as Mimi in Rovigo (1926), she sang at Milan's La Scala (1933–44), in Chicago (debut as Maddalena in *Andrea Chénier*, 1934), in Rome (1934–43), at the Salzburg Festivals (1936–39), at Buenos Aires's Teatro Colón (1936–39), and at the Metropolitan Opera in N.Y. (debut as Cio-Cio-San, March 8, 1937). She was married to **Giuseppe Antonicelli**. Among her most prominent roles were Kundry, Sieglinde, Fedora, the Marschallin, Arabella, and Salome.—NS/LK/DM

Somis, Giovanni Battista, eminent Italian violinist, teacher, and composer, brother of **Lorenzo Giovanni Somis;** b. Turin, Dec. 25, 1686; d. there, Aug. 14, 1763. He studied violin with his father, Francesco Lorenzo Somis (1663–1736), a violinist in the Turin ducal orch. known as "Ardy" or "Ardito." About 1696 he joined his father in the ducal orch., then studied with Corelli in Rome (1703–06) under the patronage of the Duke of Savoy; returning to Turin in 1707, he served as solo violinist and director of the ducal chapel until his death. He scored a brilliant success as a soloist at the Concert Spirituel in Paris (April 2 and May 14, 1733). He was the mentor of Pugnani, J.M. Leclair, Guignon, and Guillemain. He was a distinguished composer of chamber music, his solo sonatas being of particular historical interest. Much of his output is not extant.

WORKS: (12) *Sonate da camera* for Violin, and Cello or Harpsichord (Amsterdam, c. 1717; second ed., 1725); (12) *Sonate da camera* for Violin, and Cello or Harpsichord, op.2 (Turin, 1723; ed. in Monumenti Musicali Italiani, II, Milan, 1976); (12) *Sonates* for Violin, and Cello or Harpsichord, op.4 (Paris, 1726); (6) *Sonate a tre* for 2 Violins, and Cello or Harpsichord, op.5 (Paris, 1733); (12) *Sonate da camera* for Violin, Cello, and Harpsichord, op.6 (Paris, 1733); *Ideali trattenimenti da camera* for 2 Violins or Flutes or Descant Viols, op.7 (Paris, n.d.); *6 sonata a tre* for 2 Violins and Cello, op.8 (n.p., n.d.); *12 sonate* for Cello and Bass (Paris, c. 1740); many concertos: 150 for Violin, 3 for 2 Violins, 3 for Flute, 1 for Oboe, and 4 for Trumpet; also 75 sonatas for Violin and Basso Continuo.—NS/LK/DM

Somis, Lorenzo Giovanni, Italian violinist, teacher, and composer, brother of **Giovanni Battista Somis;** b. Turin, Nov. 11, 1688; d. there, Nov. 29, 1775. He studied in Bologna, where he was made a member of the Accademia Filarmonica. After a sojourn in Paris, he returned to Turin as second violin in the ducal chapel (1724–70); his most distinguished student was Felice Giardini. He composed (12) *Sonate* for Violin and Cello or Harpsichord, op.1 (Rome, 1722), (8) *Sonate* for Violin and Cello or Harpsichord, op.2 (Paris, c. 1740; ed. in Monumenti musicali italiani, III, Milan, 1976), and *6 sonate a 2* for Violin and Cello or Harpsichord, op.3 (Paris, c. 1740); also several violin concertos. —NS/LK/DM

Sommer, Hans (real name, **Hans Friedrich August Zincke**), German teacher, writer on music, and composer; b. Braunschweig, July 20, 1837; d. there, April 26, 1922. He studied mathematics at the Univ. of Göttingen (Ph.D., 1858), where he became a prof. of physics; taught mathematics at Braunschweig's Technische Hochschule (1859–84), serving as its director (from 1875). He then devoted himself to music. In 1898 he helped to found the Genossenschaft Deutscher Komponisten, which became the Genossenschaft Deutscher Tonsetzer in 1903. His lyric songs were greatly appreciated in Germany and England.

WORKS: DRAMATIC: O p e r a : *Der Nachtwächter* (Braunschweig, Nov. 22, 1865); *Der Vetter aus Bremen* (1865; not perf.); *Loreley* (Braunschweig, April 11, 1891); *Saint Foix* (Munich, Oct. 31, 1894); *Der Meermann* (Weimar, April 19, 1896); *Augustin* (1898; not perf.); *Münchhausen* (1896–98; not perf.);

Rübezahl und der Sackpfeifer von Neisse (Braunschweig, May 15, 1904); *Riquet mit dem Schopf* (Braunschweig, April 14, 1907); *Der Waldschratt* (Braunschweig, March 31, 1912). **OTHER**: Orch. pieces; choruses for Men's Voices; songs.

BIBL.: E. Valentin, *H. S.* (Braunschweig, 1939). —**NS/LK/DM**

Sommer, Vladimír, Czech teacher and composer; b. Dolní Jiřetín, near Most, Feb. 28, 1921. He studied composition with Janáček at the Prague Cons. (1942–46) and with Bořkovec at the Prague Academy of Music (1946–50). He was music ed. of foreign broadcasts of Radio Prague (1953) and then was creative secretary of the Czech Composers Union (1953–56); taught at the Prague Academy of Music (1953–60) and then at the Charles Univ. in Prague (from 1960), where he was a prof. of theory from 1968 until his retirement in 1987. His music is crafted in a fine, expressive manner.

WORKS: ORCH.: Violin Concerto (Prague, June 13, 1950); *Antigone*, overture (1956–57); Cello Concerto (1956–59); 3 syms.: No. 1, *Vokální symfonie*, for Narrator, Mezzo-soprano, Chorus, and Orch., after Dostoyevsky, Kafka, and Cesare Pavese (1957–59; rev. 1963; Prague, March 12, 1963), No. 2, *Anno mundi ardenti*, for Piano, Timpani, and Strings (1968), and No. 3, *Sinfonia concertante*, for 2 Violins, Viola, Cello, and Chamber Orch. (1968). **CHAMBER**: Sonata for 2 Violins (1948; also for Violin and Viola); 3 string quartets (1950; 1955; 1960–66); Piano Sonata (1954–56). **VOCAL**: *Cantata on Gottwald* for Baritone, Chorus, and Orch. (Prague, Nov. 20, 1949); *Černý Muž* (The Black Man), symphonic poem for Tenor, Bass, and Orch. (1964); *Sinfonia da Requiem: Vokální symfonie No. 2* for Soloists, Chorus, and Orch. (1978); songs.—**NS/LK/DM**

Sommerfeldt, Øistein, Norwegian composer; b. Christiania, Nov. 25, 1919. He studied theory and composition in Paris with Boulanger (1950–56). He was active as a music critic and composer in Oslo.

WORKS: ORCH.: 3 suites (1956; based on Grieg's *Dances for Piano*, op.72); *Miniature Suite* (1958; rev. 1972); *Miniature Overture* (1960); *Adagio, Scherzo, and Finale* (1969); *Sinfonia "La Betulla"* (1974); *Mot en Lengsel*: Piano Concerto in 1 Movement (1976–77); *Intrada*, symphonic prelude (1980); *Eika*, symphonic prelude (1981–83). **CHAMBER**: *Divertimento* for Flute (1960; rev. 1969); *Divertimento* for Bassoon (1960; rev. 1973); *Transformation*, audio-visual score for Chamber Group and Tape (1970); *Divertimento* for Trumpet (1971); Violin Sonata (1971); *Elegy* for Trumpet and Organ (1971); *Suite* for Piano Trio (1973); *Divertimento* for Oboe (1974). **P i a n o**: 5 sonatinas (1956, 1960, 1968, 1970, 1972). **VOCAL**: *Hafrsfjord* for Narrator and Orch. (1972); *3 Lyrical Scenes* for Tenor or Soprano and Orch. (1973);

BIBL.: *Festskrift til O. S.: Til 70-årsdagen 25. november 1989* (Oslo, 1989).—**NS/LK/DM**

Somogi, Judith, American conductor; b. N.Y., May 13, 1937; d. Rockville Centre, N.Y., March 23, 1988. She studied violin, piano, and organ at the Juilliard School of Music in N.Y. (M.M., 1961), and attended courses at the Berkshire Music Center in Tanglewood; later was an assistant to Schippers at the Spoleto Festival and to Stokowski at the American Sym. Orch. in N.Y. In 1974 she made a successful debut with the N.Y.C. Opera conducting *The Mikado*, and subsequently conducted in

San Francisco, San Diego, San Antonio, and Pittsburgh. She made her European debut in Saarbrücken in 1979. After conducting *Madam Butterfly* at the Frankfurt am Main Opera in 1981, she held its position of first conductor from 1982 to 1987.—**NS/LK/DM**

Somogyi, László, Hungarian conductor; b. Budapest, June 25, 1907; d. Geneva, May 20, 1988. He learned to play the violin; after training in composition with Kodály at the Budapest Academy of Music (1930–34), he studied conducting with Scherchen in Brussels (1935). He was a violinist in the Budapest Concert Orch. (1930–39), and then was founder-conductor of the Goldmark Sym. Orch. in Budapest (1939–43), a Jewish ensemble; subsequently he was chief conductor of the Municipal Sym. Orch. (1945–51) and the Sym. Orch. of the Hungarian Radio (1951–56) in Budapest, and also was prof. of conducting at the Academy of Music there (1949–56). In succeeding years, he lived abroad and toured as a guest conductor throughout Europe and the U.S. before serving as music director of the Rochester (N.Y.) Phil. (1964–69). —**NS/LK/DM**

Sonami, Laetitia, talented French composer and performer; b. Paris, Nov. 28, 1957. She studied in France with Eliane Radigue, then moved to the U.S. to pursue her interest in electronic music, first with Joel Chadabe at the State Univ. of N.Y. at Albany, and then in Oakland, Calif., with Robert Ashley and David Behrman at the Center for Contemporary Music (M.F.A., 1981). From 1977 to 1990 she composed works primarily involving voice and electronics, including *Drole de Dimanche* for Home-made Electronics, *Oh-Balihi-Wadou* for Magnetic Tapes and Text, *Passages* for Dancers, Tape, and Slides, *Blue Yonder* for Tape and Dancers, *Migrations* for Tape, and *Dunes* for Tape. Compositions from 1991 involve complex solo performance with the use of live electronics enhanced by personalized controllers, among them the "Lady's Glove," an electronic glove studded with sensors which allow for real-time control of music. Sonami's talent as a performer is formidable and disarming. Critics have variously described her as magical, compelling, humorous, sultry, and electric.

WORKS: *What Happened I* for Voice and Electronic Instruments (1990), *II* for Electronics controlled by the Lady's Glove (1994), and *III* for Live Interactive Video, Voice, and Electronic Music controlled by the Lady's Glove (1997); *Mechanization takes command* for Voice, Electronics, and Slide Projections (1991; in collaboration with P. DeMarinis); *Wilfred wants you to remember us* for Voice and Electronics (1991; rev. 1995, as *The Bench*); *Story Road* for Voice and Synthesizers (1992); *The Manananggal-Women Soignées*, music theater piece (1994; in collaboration with M. Goyette and M. Sumner Carnahan); *...and she keeps coming back for more* for Live Electronics controlled by the Lady's Glove (1995); *Mona Lisa* for Electronics controlled by Body Gestures, Voices, and Live Multi-screen Video Projections (1996; in collaboration with D. Swearinghen, Pamela Z, and Visual Brains); *Nga'i pha yul* for Live Elecronics and Voice (1996; in collaboration with D. Wessel and T. Wagmo); *Has/Had* for Voice and Live Electronics controlled by the Lady's Glove (1997; usually performed with *She Came Back Again*, an adaptation of *...and she keeps coming back for more* [1995], 1997); *Shaky Memories*, sound installation for Automated Rubber Gloves and Music (1998); *Why__dreams like a loose engine (autoportrait)* for Voice, Live Electronics, and Computer-controlled Servo-motors (1998); *Mechanical Songs Between Light and Shadows* for Voice, Live Electronics, Motorized Wash Basins, Computer-controlled Shadows, and Saxophonist (1999); *Mismatch* for Voice and Live Electronics (1999; in collaboration with J. Ingle).—**LK/DM**

Sondheim, Stephen (Joshua), brilliant American composer and lyricist; b. N.Y., March 22, 1930. Of an affluent family, he received his academic education in private schools; composed a school musical at the age of 15. He then studied music at Williams Coll., where he wrote the book, lyrics, and music for a couple of college shows; graduated magna cum laude in 1950. In quest of higher musical learning, he went to Princeton Univ., where he took lessons in modernistic complexities with Babbitt and acquired sophisticated techniques of composition. He made his mark on Broadway when he wrote the lyrics for Bernstein's *West Side Story* (1957). His first success as a lyricist-composer came with the Broadway musical *A Funny Thing Happened on the Way to the Forum* (1962), which received a Tony award. His next musical, *Anyone Can Whistle* (1964), proved unsuccessful, but *Company* (1970), for which he wrote both lyrics and music, established him as a major composer and lyricist on Broadway. There followed *Follies* (1971), for which he wrote 22 pastiche songs; it was named best musical by the N.Y. Drama Critics Circle. His next production, *A Little Night Music*, with the nostalgic score harking back to the turn of the century, received a Tony, and its leading song, "Send in the Clowns," was awarded a Grammy in 1976. This score established Sondheim's characteristic manner of treating musicals; it is almost operatic in conception, and boldly introduces dissonant counterpoint *à la moderne*. In 1976 he produced *Pacific Overtures*, based on the story of the Western penetration into Japan in the 19th century, and composed in a stylized Japanese manner, modeled after the Kabuki theater; he also wrote the score to the musical *Sunday in the Park with George*, inspired by the painting by Georges Seurat entitled "Sunday Afternoon on the Island of La Grande Jatte" (1982; N.Y., May 1, 1984), which received the Pulitzer Prize for drama in 1985. In 1987 his musical *Into the Woods*, based on 5 of the Grimm fairytales, scored a popular success on Broadway. It was followed by the musical *Assassins* in 1990. In 1992 he was selected to receive the National Medal of Arts, but he rejected the medal by stating that to accept it would be an act of hypocrisy in light of the controversy over censorship and funding of the NEA. After the inauguration of Bill Clinton as president in 1993, Sondheim accepted the National Medal of Arts and was honored at the Kennedy Center in Washington, D.C. His musical *Passion* was premiered in N.Y. on April 28, 1994.

BIBL.: C. Zadan, *S. & Co.* (N.Y., 1974; second ed., rev., 1994); M. Adams, *The Lyrics of S. S.: Form and Function* (diss., Northwestern Univ., 1980); D. Cartmell, *S. S. and the Concept Musical* (diss., Univ. of Calif., Santa Barbara, 1983); S. Wilson, *Motivic, Rhythmic, and Harmonic Procedures of Unification in S. S.'s "Company" and "A Little Night Music"* (diss., Ball State Univ., 1983); J. Gordon, *Art Isn't Easy: The Achievement of S. S.* (Carbondale, Ill., 1990; rev. ed., 1992); M. Gottfried, *S.* (N.Y., 1993); J. Gordon, ed., *S. S.: A Casebook* (N.Y., 1997); M. Secrest, *S. S.: A Life* (N.Y., 1998).—**NS/LK/DM**

Sonneck, Oscar G(eorge) T(heodore), eminent American musicologist; b. Jersey City, N.J., Oct. 6, 1873; d. N.Y., Oct. 30, 1928. He attended the Gelehrtenschule in Kiel (1883–89) and the Kaiser Friedrich Gymnasium in Frankfurt am Main (1889–93), where he also took piano lessons with James Kwast; attended the Univ. of Heidelberg and received instruction in musicology from Sandberger at the Univ. of Munich (1893–97); studied composition privately with Melchior and Ernest Sachs in Munich; took courses in composition and orchestration with Iwann Knorr in Frankfurt am Main and in conducting with Carl Schroder at the Sondershausen Cons. (1897–98). After doing research in Italy in 1899, he returned to the U.S. to pursue his interest in early American music. From 1902 to 1917 he was chief of the Music Division of the Library of Congress in Washington, D.C. He then became director of the Publishing Dept. of G. Schirmer in N.Y., managing ed. of the *Musical Quarterly* (of which he had been ed. since its foundation in 1915), and personal representative of the president, Rudolph E. Schirmer; in 1921 he became vice-president of G. Schirmer. He took a leading part in the formation of the Society for the Publication of American Music, and of the Beethoven Assn. in N.Y. Under Sonneck's administration, the Music Division of the Library of Congress became one of the largest and most important music collections in the world. His writings, exhibiting profound and accurate scholarship and embodying the results of original research, laid a real foundation for the scientific study of music in the U.S.; his elaborate catalogues, issued by the Library of Congress, are among the most valuable contributions to musical bibliography. The Sonneck Soc., an organization designed to encourage the serious study of American music in all its aspects, was established in 1975 and named after Sonneck in recognition of his achievements in this area. He was also a composer and a poet, numbering among his works symphonic pieces, a String Quartet, *Rhapsody and Romanze* for Violin and Piano, some vocal works, and piano pieces. He publ. 2 vols. of poems: *Seufzer* (1895) and *Eine Totenmesse* (1898).

WRITINGS: *Protest gegen den Symbolismus in der Musik* (Frankfurt am Main, 1897); *Classification: Class M, Music: Class ML, Literature of Music: Class MT, Musical Instruction: Adopted December, 1902: as in force April, 1904* (Washington, D.C., 1904; second ed., rev., 1917; third ed., 1957); *A Bibliography of Early Secular American Music* (Washington, D.C., 1905; second ed., rev. and enl., 1945 by W. Upton); *Francis Hopkinson, the First American Poet-Composer (1737–1791) and James Lyon, Patriot, Preacher, Psalmodist (1735–1794): Two Studies in Early American Music* (Washington, D.C., 1905); *Early Concert-life in America (1731–1800)* (Leipzig, 1907); *Dramatic Music: Catalogue of Full Scores in the Collection of the Library of Congress* (Washington, D.C., 1908; second ed., 1917); *Report on "The Star-Spangled Banner," "Hail Columbia," "America," "Yankee Doodle"* (Washington, D.C., 1909; second ed., rev. and enl., 1914); *Orchestral Music Catalogue: Scores* (Washington, D.C., 1912); with J. Gregory, *Catalogue of Early Books on Music (before 1800)* (Washington, D.C.,

1913); *Catalogue of Opera Librettos Printed before 1800* (Washington, D.C., 1914); with W. Whittlesey, *Catalogue of First Editions of Stephen C. Foster (1826–1864)* (Washington, D.C., 1915); *Early Opera in America* (N.Y., 1915); *Suum cuique: Essays in Music* (N.Y., 1916); *Catalogue of First Editions of Edward MacDowell (1861–1908)* (Washington, D.C., 1917); *Miscellaneous Studies in the History of Music* (N.Y., 1921); *Beethoven: Impressions of Contemporaries* (N.Y., 1926); *Beethoven Letters in America* (N.Y., 1927).

BIBL.: H. Wiley Hitchcock, *After 100 [!] Years: The Editorial Side of S.* (Washington, D.C., 1974; with complete list of writings and compositions compiled by I. Lowens); W. Lichtenwanger, ed., *O. S. and American Music* (Urbana, Ill., 1983).—**NS/LK/DM**

Sonninen, Ahti, Finnish composer; b. Kuopio, July 11, 1914; d. Helsinki, Aug. 27, 1984. Following graduation from the Kajaani training college, he took courses in theory and composition with Palmgren, Merikanto, Ranta, and Funtek at the Sibelius Academy in Helsinki (1939–47). He taught elementary school (1936–43), then taught in the school music dept. of the Sibelius Academy (from 1957). He followed the tenets of international musical modernism in his technique of composition, but also adhered to subjects from Finnish folklore.

WORKS: DRAMATIC: *Merenkuninkaan tytär* (Daughter of Neptune), opera (1949); *Pessi and Illusia*, ballet (1952); *Ruususolmu* (Wreath of Roses), ballet (1956); *Karhunpeijaiset* (Feast to Celebrate the Killing of a Bear), ritual opera (1968); *Se* (It), ballet farce (Helsinki, Feb. 24, 1972); *Haavruuva* (Lady of the Sea), opera (1971); film scores. **ORCH.:** *East Karelian Suite* (1942); Violin Concerto (1943–45); Piano Concerto (1944–45); *Symphonic Sketches* (1947); *Preludio festivo* (1953); *Under Lapland's Sky*, suite (1954); *Pezzo pizzicato* (1954–55); *Rhapsody* (1957); *4 Partitas* for Strings (1958); *Prelude and Allegro* for Trumpet, Trombone, and Orch. (1961); *Reactions* for Chamber Orch. (1961). **CHAMBER:** *Conference* for Clarinet, Horn, Trumpet, and Trombone (1954); *Theses* for String Quartet (1968); *Divertimento* for Wind Quintet (1970). **Piano:** 5 suites: *In the Big City* (1954), *White Pepper* (1970), *Black Pepper* (1970), *Koli* (1970), and *3 Characters* (1971). **VOCAL:** *7 Songs to Hungarian Folk Poems* for Soprano and Orch. (1939–41); *Midsummer Night* for Soprano and Orch. (1946); *El amor pasa* for Soprano, Flute, and Orch. (1953); *Smith of the Heavens* for Baritone and Orch. (1957); *The Karelian Wedding* for Voice, Chorus, Flute, Accordion, Percussion, Harpsichord, and Tape (1965); *Highway Requiem* for Soprano, Baritone, Chorus, and Orch. (1970); *Forging of the Golden Virgin* for Voices, 2 Percussionists, and Tape (1971); *Finnish Messiah* for Soloists, Mixed and Children's Choruses, and Orch. (1972); *In the Court of the Lamb*, suite for Soloists, Chorus, and Orch. (1972); about 15 cantatas and 100 choruses; about 70 songs with piano.—**NS/LK/DM**

Sonnleithner, family of Austrian musicians and writers:

(1) Christoph Sonnleithner, composer; b. Szegedin, May 28, 1734; d. Vienna, Dec. 25, 1786. He was 2 when he was taken to Vienna, where he received his musical training from his uncle, Leopold Sonnleithner, a choirmaster; he took courses in law and served as a barrister in the employ of Prince Esterházy, becoming associated with Haydn. His works include syms., sacred pieces, and 36 string quartets. His daughter Anna was the mother of the famous poet Grillparzer. He also had 2 sons who were active in music:

(2) Joseph Sonnleithner, librettist and archivist; b. Vienna, March 3, 1766; d. there, Dec. 25, 1835. He acquired material for the emperor's private library, and was ed. of the *Wiener Theater-Almanach* (1794–96). He served as secretary of the Court theaters (1808–14), and also was manager of the Theater an der Wien (until 1807); was one of the founders of the Gesellschaft der Musikfreunde (1812). He wrote some librettos and adapted others, including *Fidelio* for Beethoven and *Faniska* by Cherubini. In 1827 he discovered the famous Antiphonary of St. Gall of the 9th century, in neume notation, probably a copy of the one sent there by Charlemagne in 790. He bequeathed his collection of opera librettos to the Vienna Cons. and his instrument collection and library to the Gesellschaft der Musikfreunde. He was a close friend of Schubert and Grillparzer.

(3) Ignaz (von) Sonnleithner, bass, doctor, and scientist; b. Vienna, July 30, 1770; d. there, Nov. 27, 1831. He appeared as principal bass with the Gesellschaft der Musikfreunde. He held musical soirées in his home (1815–24), at which Schubert tried out several of his vocal works. His son was Leopold von Sonnleithner (b. Vienna, Nov. 15, 1797; d. there, March 4, 1873). A barrister, he was a staunch friend of Schubert and enabled him to publ. the *Erlkönig* (Schubert's first publ. work). A great lover of music, he was active with the Gesellschaft der Musikfreunde, to which he left his musical papers.—**NS/LK/DM**

Sonny and Cher, folk-rock duo of the 1960s; Sonny later became a conservative congressman; Cher continued on as an actress/singer and all-around diva. Salvatore "Sonny" Bono (b. Detroit, Mich., Feb. 16, 1935; d. near South Lake Tahoe, Calif., Jan. 5, 1998); Cher (Cherilyn Sarkisian LaPierre) (b. El Centro, Calif., May 20, 1946).

Sonny Bono moved to Hollywood in 1954 and began his musical career as a songwriter at Specialty Records. Bono's "H.S. Dance" was recorded as the flip-side of Larry Williams's 1957 smash hit "Short Fat Fannie" and Williams later recorded "She Said Yeah," cowritten by Bono and later covered by The Rolling Stones. As a consequence, Bono became an apprentice producer at Specialty while recording unsuccessfully as Don Christy, Sonny Christy, and Ronny Sommers. When Specialty curtailed operations in 1960, he continued to write and record unsuccessfully, although his "Needles and Pins," cowritten with Jack Nitzche, did become a major hit for The Searchers in 1964. In 1962, through Nitzche, Bono met Phil Spector and became his assistant.

Born to Armenian and Cherokee Indian parents, Cher moved to Hollywood as a teenager to pursue an acting career, supplementing her income by singing background vocals on sessions for Phil Spector's Philles label. There she met Bono in 1963 and the couple soon married, later recording as Sonny and Cher for Vault Records and as Caesar and Cleo for Reprise Records. Cher also recorded as Bonnie Jo Mason for Annette Records and as Cherilyn for Imperial Records.

Signed to Atco Records in 1965, Sonny and Cher scored a top pop hit with "I Got You Babe," written, produced and arranged by Sonny, and a major pop hit with "Just You" from their debut album *Look at Us*. Sonny's "Laugh at Me" and the couple's "But You're Mine" became major hits on Atco, as Reprise reissued "Baby Don't Go," a near-smash hit for the couple. Cher, recording solo for Imperial Records, scored major hits with Bob Dylan's "All I Really Want to Do" and "Where Do You Go" in 1965, followed by the smash "Bang Bang (My Baby Shot Me Down)," written by Sonny, in the spring of 1966.

Sonny and Cher became prominent members of Los Angeles's elite hippie set and continued to achieve major hits with "What Now My Love," "Little Man," and Sonny's classic "The Beat Goes On." They appeared in the films *Good Times* (1967) and *Chastity* (1969), and Cher scored a near-smash hit with "You Better Sit Down Kids" in late 1967. Their daughter Chastity was born in Los Angeles on March 4, 1969. Cher switched to Atco Records in 1968, and Sonny and Cher moved to Kapp Records (later MCA Records) in 1971. In 1970, Cher began modeling for *Vogue*, becoming a fashion queen and international celebrity.

In 1970, Sonny and Cher moved to the Las Vegas club circuit, later hosting their own variety show on CBS television from 1971 to 1974. Thereby leaving the rock audience behind in favor of the easy-listening crowd, Sonny and Cher scored near-smash pop and smash easy-listening hits with "All I Ever Need Is You" and "A Cowboy's Work Is Never Done." Cher achieved a succession of pop and easy-listening hits through 1974, including the top pop and smash easy-listening hits "Gypsys, Tramps and Thieves," "Half-Breed," and "Dark Lady."

Sonny and Cher divorced in 1974, and each had their own short-lived network television show in 1974 and 1975, respectively. By 1975, Cher had switched to Warner Bros. Records for the Jimmy Webb–produced *Stars*, but the album and two subsequent for the label failed to produce any major hits. She married Gregg Allman in the summer of 1975, but the relationship lasted all of nine days, and the couple eventually divorced in 1977. The liaison produced one dismal album, *Two the Hard Way*, and one son named Elijah Blue (b. July 10, 1977). Sonny and Cher resumed their professional relationship from 1976 to 1977 for *The Sonny and Cher Show* on CBS television.

Cher returned to performing in Las Vegas casinos and moved to Casablanca Records in 1979, scoring a near-smash pop hit with the disco-style "Take Me Home." Late in the year, she formed the new wave–style band Black Rose with guitarist Les Dudek, but their album failed to sell and the group soon disbanded. In 1979, Sonny moved to Palm Springs, where he opened his own Italian restaurant. He appeared in the 1988 film *Hairspray* with Debbie Harry and served as mayor of Palm Springs from 1988 to 1992. Unsuccessfully campaigning for the Republican Party nomination for the U.S. Senate seat vacated by retiring Alan Cranston, Sonny won election as the representative from Calif.'s 44th District in 1994. Reelected in 1996, he died

in a skiing mishap near South Lake Tahoe, Calif., on Jan. 5, 1998, at the age of 62.

In February 1982, Cher returned to her first career pursuit, acting, by appearing in the Broadway production of *Come Back to the Five and Dime, Jimmy Dean, Jimmy Dean*. She won praise for her straight dramatic role and later starred with Sandy Dennis and Karen Black in the film version. She garnered critical acclaim and an Academy Award nomination for her role in the 1983 film *Silkwood* with Meryl Streep and Kurt Russell and, in 1985, enjoyed well-deserved recognition of her demanding role in *Mask*, with Sam Elliott and Eric Stoltz. She starred in three 1987 films, *Suspect* with Dennis Quaid; *The Witches of Eastwick* with Jack Nicholson; and *Moonstruck* with Nicholas Cage, Danney Aiello, and Olympia Dukakis. In 1988, Cher achieved the pinnacle of any acting career, an Oscar, for her performance in *Moonstruck*.

In 1987, David Geffen convinced Cher to return to recording, and her debut for his label produced major hits with "I Found Someone," written and produced by Michael Bolton, and "We All Sleep Alone," cowritten and coproduced by Jon Bon Jovi. Her 1989 album, *Heart of Stone*, became the best-selling album of her career, selling more than two million copies. It yielded two smash pop and top easy-listening hits with "After All," sung in duet with Peter Cetera, and "If I Could Turn Back Time," plus the near-smash "Just Like Jesse James," and the major hit "Heart of Stone." Cher toured North America in 1990, but that year's film *Mermaids*, with Cher and Winona Ryder, was not well received. Cher's 1991 *Love Hurts* album produced only one major hit with "Love and Understanding." In 1992 and 1994, Cher joined ensemble casts for the films *The Player* and *Ready to Wear*. In 1995 Cher switched to Reprise Records, where she scored hits with "Walking in Memphis" and "One by One." She made her directing debut in 1996 with one of the three short films of HBO's *If These Walls Could Talk* abortion trilogy. In 1999, she made yet another Phoenix-like comeback with her discofied single and album *Believe*. Her tour in support of the album featured many lavish costume changes and was recorded for live broadcast (from Las Vegas) for HBO.

In the 1990s, Sonny and Cher's daughter, Chastity, formed the pop band Ceremony with longtime friend Heidi Shink, using the name Chance, for *Hang Out Your Poetry* on Geffen Records. In 1996, Chastity was appointed media entertainment director for the Gay and Lesbian Alliance Against Defamation. In 1998, Little, Brown published Chastity's book *Family Outing*, which told stories of the "coming out" (as a homosexual) process that she and others experienced. By the late 1990s, Cher's son, Elijah Blue, was singer for the band Deadsy, which released its debut album in 1997.

DISC.: SONNY AND CHER: *Baby, Don't Go* (1965); *Look at Us* (1965); *The Wondrous World of Sonny and Cher* (1966); *In Case You're in Love* (1967); *Good Times* (soundtrack; 1967); *The Two of Us* (1972); *Sonny and Cher Live* (1971); *All I Ever Need Is You* (1972); *Mama Was a Rock 'n' Roll Singer, Papa Used to Write All Her Songs* (1973); *Live in Las Vegas, Vol. 2* (1973). **SONNY:** *Inner Views* (1967). **CHER:** *All I Really Want to Do* (1965); *The Sonny Side of Cher* (1966); *Cher* (1966); *With Love* (1967); *Backstage*

(1968); *Golden Greats* (1968); *3614 Jackson Highway* (1969); *Chastity* (soundtrack; 1969); *This Is Cher* (1970); *Cher* (1971); *Superpak* (1972); *Superpak, Vol. 2* (1972); *Foxy Lady* (1972); *Bittersweet White Light* (1973); *Half-Breed* (1973); *Dark Lady* (1974); *Cher Sings the Hits* (1975); *Stars* (1975); *I'd Rather Believe in You* (1976); *Cherished* (1977); *Take Me Home* (1979); *Prisoner* (1979); *Outrageous* (1989); *I Paralyze* (1982/1990); *Cher* (1987); *Heart of Stone* (1989); *Love Hurts* (1991); *It's a Man's World* (1996); *Believe* (1998). **GREGG ALLMAN AND CHER (ALLMAN AND WOMAN):** *Two the Hard Way* (1977). **BLACK ROSE:** *Black Rose* (1980). **CEREMONY (WITH CHASTITY AND CHANCE):** *Hang Out Your Poetry* (1993). **DEADSY (WITH ELIJAH BLUE):** *Deadsy* (1997).

WRITINGS: S. Bono, *And the Beat Goes On* (N.Y., 1991); Cher, with J. Coplon, *The First Time* (N.Y., 1998).

BIBLIOGRAPHY: V. Pellegrino, *C.!* (N.Y., 1975); J. R. Taraborrelli, *C.: A Biography* (N.Y., 1986); L. J. Quirk, *Totally Uninhibited: The Life and Wild Times of C.* (N.Y., 1991); C. Bono, with B. Fitzpatrick, *Family Outing* (Boston, 1998).

Sontag, Henriette (real name, **Gertrude Walpurgis Sonntag**), celebrated German soprano; b. Koblenz, Jan. 3, 1806; d. Mexico City, June 17, 1854. Her father was the actor Franz Sonntag and her mother the actress and singer Franziska (née Martloff) Sonntag (1798–1865). She studied with her mother, and began appearing in stage plays and operas at age 5. In 1815 she was admitted to the Prague Cons., where she received instruction in singing from Anna Czegka, theory from Josef Triebensee, and piano from Pixis. In 1821 she made her formal operatic debut as the princess in Boieldieu's *Jean de Paris* in Prague; in 1822 she went to Vienna, where she appeared in German and Italian opera. She was chosen by Weber to create the title role in his *Euryanthe* (Oct. 25, 1823), and then was chosen by Beethoven to sing in the first performances of his 9th Sym. and *Missa solemnis* (May 7 and 13, 1824, respectively). She sang in Dresden in 1825, and that same year made her Berlin debut at the Königstädter Theater as Isabella in *L'Italiana in Algeri* (Aug. 3). On May 15, 1826, she made a stunning debut at the Théâtre-Italien in Paris as Rosina in *Il Barbiere di Siviglia*; following engagements in Germany, she returned to Paris in 1828 to win further accolades as Donna Anna and Semiramide. During a visit to Weimar, she won the approbation of Goethe, who penned the poem *Neue Siren* for the "fluttering nightingale" of the operatic stage. On April 19, 1828, she chose the role of Rosina for her British debut at the King's Theatre in London; during her British sojourn, she married Count Carlo Rossi, a Sardinian diplomat, secretly (so as not to jeopardize his career); after the King of Prussia ennobled her as Henriette von Lauenstein, she was able to publicly join her husband in The Hague, her low birth no longer a matter of concern; however, she quit the stage in 1830, and then appeared only in private and concert settings in the cities where her husband was stationed. After her husband lost his diplomatic post at the abdication of the King of Sardinia in 1849, she resumed her stage career with appearances at Her Majesty's Theatre in London. She toured England that same year, and then created the role of Miranda in Halévy's *La tempesta* at Her Majesty's Theatre on June 8, 1850; after further appearances in

London and Paris in 1851, she toured with great success in Germany, then appeared in the U.S. in 1852. In 1854 she toured Mexico as a member of an Italian opera company; on June 11 of that year she made her last appearance as Lucrezia Borgia; the next day she was stricken with cholera and died 5 days later. Her beautiful voice, which ranged from a to e^3, her striking physical appearance, and her natural acting abilities led to her reputation as the equal or superior to all other divas of the age. She was a matchless interpreter of roles in operas by Mozart, Rossini, Donizetti, and Bellini.

BIBL.: T. Gautier, *L'Ambassadrice, Biographie de la comtesse Rossi* (Paris, 1850); J. Gundling, *H. S.* (2 vols., Leipzig, 1861); H. Stümcke, *H. S.* (Berlin, 1913); E. Pirchan, *H. S.: Die Sängerin des Biedermeier* (Vienna, 1946); F. Russell, *Queen of Song: The Life of H. S., Countess de Rossi* (N.Y., 1964).—**NS/LK/DM**

Sonzogno, Edoardo, Italian music publisher; b. Milan, April 21, 1836; d. there, March 14, 1920. He inherited a printing plant and bookstore founded by his grandfather, and in 1874 began to publ. popular eds. of French and Italian music with marked success. In 1883 he inaugurated a series of contests for new operas; the second contest, in 1889, was won by Mascagni (then unknown) with *Cavalleria rusticana*. Sonzogno established his own theater (the Lirico Internazionale) at Milan in 1894. From 1861 until his retirement in 1909 he was sole proprietor of the newspaper *Il Secolo*; was also publisher of the journals *Il teatro illustrato* (1881–92) and *La musica popolare* (1882–92). He was succeeded by his son, Riccardo Sonzogno (1871–1915); upon his death, his cousin, Renzo (1877–1920), who had run his own firm from 1910, took over the business. In 1923 the firm became known as Società Anonima Sonzogno, and is now known as the Società per Azioni Sonzogno. —**NS/LK/DM**

Soomer, Walter, German bass-baritone; b. Liegnitz, March 12, 1878; d. Leipzig, Aug. 1955. He was a student of Hermann Stoeckert and Anna Uhlig in Berlin. In 1902 he made his operatic debut in Kolmar. After singing in Halle (1902–06), he was a member of the Leipzig Opera (1906–27). He also appeared at the Bayreuth Festivals (1906; 1908–14; 1924–25). On Feb. 18, 1909, he made his Metropolitan Opera debut in N.Y. as Wolfram, remaining on its roster until 1911. From 1911 to 1915 he sang in Dresden. In 1927 he became director of his own vocal and opera school in Leipzig. Soomer was best known as a Wagnerian, singing such roles as Hans Sachs, Wotan, Gurnemanz, Kurwenal, and Amfortas.—**NS/LK/DM**

Soot, Fritz (actually, **Friedrich Wilhelm**), distinguished German tenor; b. Wellesweiler-Neunkirchen, Saar, Aug. 20, 1878; d. Berlin, June 9, 1965. He first pursued a career as an actor in Karlsruhe (1901–07); then studied voice with Scheidemantel in Dresden. He made his operatic debut with the Dresden Court Opera as Tonio in *La Fille du régiment* in 1908, remaining on its roster until 1918; during his tenure there, he sang in the first performance of *Der Rosenkavalier* as the Italian Singer (Jan. 26, 1911). His subsequent engagements were in Stuttgart (1918–22), at the Berlin State Opera (1922–44; 1946–52), and at the Berlin Städtische Oper (1946–48). He sang in the premieres of Berg's *Wozzeck*, as well as in works by Pfitzner and Schreker. He excelled in such Wagnerian roles as Tristan, Siegmund, and Siegfried.—NS/LK/DM

Sopeña (Ibáñez), Federico, noted Spanish musicologist; b. Valladolid, Jan. 25, 1917; d. Madrid, May 22, 1991. He studied in Bilbao and Madrid, and later obtained a doctorate in theology at the Università Gregoriana in Rome. He was active as a music critic, and from 1951 to 1956, was director of the Madrid Cons.; was also the founder and publisher of the music magazine *Música*. He publ. (in Madrid) a number of useful monographs of Spanish composers, including *Joaquín Turina* (1943; second ed., 1952) and *Joaquín Rodrigo* (1946; second ed., rev. 1970); also *Historia de la música* (1946; 5th ed., 1974), *La música europea contemporánea* (1952), *Historia de la música española contemporánea* (1958; second ed., 1967), and *Música y literatura* (1974).—NS/LK/DM

Sopkin, Henry, American conductor; b. N.Y., Oct. 20, 1903; d. Stanford, Calif., March 1, 1988. He was reared in Chicago, where he earned degrees in violin at the American Cons. of Music. He was head of its instrumental dept. and also taught at Woodrow Wilson Coll.; in 1944 he became conductor of the Atlanta Youth Sym. Orch., which served as the foundation of the Atlanta Sym. Orch. in 1945, which he conducted until 1966; then taught briefly at the Calif. Inst. of the Arts in Valencia.—NS/LK/DM

Soproni, József, Hungarian composer and pedagogue; b. Sopron, Oct. 4, 1930. He studied with Viski at the Budapest Academy of Music (1949–56). In 1957 he became a teacher at the Béla Bartók School in Budapest. In 1962 he joined the faculty of the Budapest Academy of Music, where he was a prof. from 1977. From 1988 to 1994 he served as its rector.

WORKS: DRAMATIC: Opera: *Antigone* (1987). ORCH.: Concerto for Strings (1953); Viola Concerto (1967); 2 cello concertos (1967, 1984); *Eklypsis* (1969); 5 syms.: No. 1 (1975), No. 2, *The Seasons* (1977), No. 3, *Sinfonia da Requiem*, for Soloists, Chorus, and Orch. (1979–80), No. 4 for Strings and 3 Winds (1994), and No. 5 (1995); Concertino for Flute, Clarinet, Cimbalom, and Orch. (1976); Violin Concerto (1982–83); *Comments on a Theme by Handel* (1985); *3 Pieces* (1987–88); Piano Concerto (1997). CHAMBER: Viola Sonatina (1958); 11 string quartets (1958–99); *Musica da camera No. 1* for Piano Trio (1963) and *No. 2, Capricorn Music*, for Violin, Clarinet, Cello, and Piano (1976); Flute Sonata (1971); *Concerto da camera* for 12 Instruments (1972); Horn Sonata (1976); *Tre pezzi* for Flute and Cimbalom (1977); *6 Bagatelles* for Wind Quintet (1977); *4 Pieces* for Saxophone and Piano (1978); *Late Summer Caprices* for Violin, Viola, Cello, and Piano (1978); *Episodi ritornanti* for 2 Cimbaloms (1979); 2 violin sonatas (1979, 1980); Piano Quintet (1990). KEYBOARD: Piano: *4 Bagatelles* (1957); *7 Piano Pieces* (1963); *Incrustations* (1970); *Invenzioni sul B-A-C-H* (1971); *Note Pages* (4 books, 1974–78); *Quattro intermezzi* (1976); *12 sonatas* (1995–99). Organ: *Meditatio con toccata* (1959); *Livre d'orgue*, 9 pieces (1994). VOCAL: *Carmina polinaesiana*, cantata for Women's Chorus and Chamber Ensemble (1963); *Ovidii metamorphoses*, cantata for Soprano, Chorus, and Orch. (1965); *De aetatibus mundi carmina*, cantata for Soprano, Baritone, Chorus, and Orch. (1968); *Magnificat* for Soloists, Chorus, and Orch. (1989); *Missa Scarbantiensis* for Soloists, Chorus, and Orch. (1991); *Missa choralis* for Soloists, Chorus, and Orch. (1992); *Missa super B- A-C-H* for Chorus, Organ, Trumpet, and Trombone (1992); *Litaniae Omnium Sanctorum* for Soloists, Chorus, and Orch. (1993); *Psalm XXIX* for Chorus, Organ, Trumpet, and Trombone (1993); *Missa Gurcensis* for Chorus and Chamber Ensemble (1994); choruses; song cycles.—NS/LK/DM

Sor (real name, **Sors**), **(Joseph) Fernando (Macari),** celebrated Catalan guitarist and composer; b. Barcelona, Feb. 13, 1778; d. Paris, July 10, 1839. At the age of 11 he entered the school of the monastery of Montserrat, where he studied music under the direction of Anselmo Viola. He wrote a Mass, then attended the Barcelona military academy. In 1799 he went to Madrid, subsequently holding administrative sinecures in Barcelona (from 1808); also was active in the battle against France, but about 1810 accepted an administrative post under the French. When Bonapartist rule was defeated in Spain in 1813, he fled to Paris. There he met Cherubini, Méhul, and others, who urged him to give concerts as a guitarist, and he soon acquired fame. His ballet *Cendrillon* (London, 1822) became quite popular and was given more than 100 times at the Paris Opéra; it was heard at the gala opening of the Bolshoi Theater in Moscow in 1823. Sor was active in Russia from 1823; wrote funeral music for the obsequies of Czar Alexander I in 1825. He returned to Paris via London in 1826, and subsequently devoted himself to performing and teaching. An outstanding guitar virtuoso, he also garnered recognition as a composer; in all, he wrote over 65 works for the guitar, including a number of standard pieces. He also wrote the most important guitar method ever penned.

WORKS: DRAMATIC: Opera: *Telemaco nell'isola de Calipso* (Barcelona, Aug. 25, 1797); *Don Trastullo* (unfinished; not extant). Ballet: *La Foire de Smyrne* (London, 1821; not extant); *Le Seigneur généreux* (London, 1821; not extant); *Cendrillon* (London, 1822); *L'Amant peintre* (London, 1823); *Hercule et Omphale* (Moscow, 1826); *Le Sicilien* (Paris, 1827); *Hassan et le calife* (London, 1828; not extant). OTHER: Various vocal works, including *25 boleros or seguidillas boleras* for 1 to 3 Voices and Guitar or Piano; 33 ariettas for Voice and Piano; Spanish, Italian, and English songs and duets; some sacred music; over 65 guitar pieces, including 3 sonatas, fantasias, variations, divertimentos, studies, etc.; piano pieces; 2 syms.; 3 string quartets; Concertante for Guitar and String Trio; march for Military Band.

BIBL.: M. Rocamora, *F. S.* (Barcelona, 1957); W. Sasser, *The Guitar Works of F. S.* (diss., Univ. of N.C., Chapel Hill, 1960); B. Jeffery, *F. S.: Composer and Guitarist* (London, 1977); B. Piris, *F. S.: Une guitare à l'orée du Romantisme* (Paris, 1989).—NS/LK/DM

Sorabji, Kaikhosru Shapurji (actually, **Leon Dudley**), remarkable English pianist, writer on music, and composer of unique gifts; b. Chingford, Aug. 14, 1892; d. Wareham, Dorset, Oct. 14, 1988. His father was a Parsi, his mother of Spanish-Sicilian descent. He was largely self-taught in music. After appearing with notable success as a pianist in London, Paris,

Vienna (1921–22), Glasgow, and Bombay, he gave up the concert platform and began writing on music. Through sheer perseverance and an almost mystical belief in his demiurgic powers, he developed an idiom of composition of extraordinary complexity, embodying within the European framework of harmonies the Eastern types of melodic lines and asymmetrical rhythmic patterns, and creating an enormously intricate but architectonically stable edifice of sound. His most arresting work is his magisterial *Opus Clavicembalisticum*, completed in 1930, taking about 5 hours to play and comprising 3 parts with 12 subdivisions, including a theme with 49 variations and a passacaglia with 81 variations; characteristically, the score is dedicated to "the everlasting glory of those few men blessed and sanctified in the curses and execrations of those many whose praise is eternal damnation." Sorabji gave its premiere in Glasgow under the auspices of the Active Society for the Propagation of Contemporary Music on Dec. 1, 1930. Wrathful at the lack of interest in his music, Sorabji issued in 1936 a declaration forbidding any performance of his works by anyone anywhere; since this prohibition could not be sustained for works actually publ., there must have been furtive performances of his piano works in England and the U.S. by fearless pianists. Sorabji eventually mitigated his ban, and in 1975 allowed the American pianist Michael Habermann to perform some of his music; in 1976 he also gave his blessing to the English pianist Yonty Solomon, who included Sorabji's works in a London concert on Dec. 7, 1976; on June 16, 1977, Solomon gave in London the first performance of Sorabji's third Piano Sonata. Gradually, Sorabji's music became the cynosure and the lodestone of titanically endowed pianists. Of these, the most Brobdingnagian was the Australian pianist Geoffrey Madge, who gave the second complete performance in history of *Opus Clavicembalisticum* at the 1982 Holland Festival in Utrecht; he repeated this feat at the first American performance of the work at the Univ. of Chicago on April 24, 1983; 2 weeks later he played it in Bonn. True to his estrangement from the human multitudes and music officials, Sorabji took refuge far from the madding crowd in a castle he owned in England; a notice at the gate proclaimed: Visitors Unwelcome. Yet as he approached his 90th birthday, he received at least 2 American musicians who came to declare their admiration, and allowed them to photocopy some of his MSS.

WORKS: ORCH.: 8 indefinitely numbered piano concertos (1915–16; 1916–17; 1917; 1918; 1922; *Simorg-Anka,* 1924; 1924–25; 1927); *Chaleur* (1920); *Opusculum* (1923); *Symphonic Variations* for Piano and Orch. (1951–55); *Opus Clavisymphonicum* for Piano and Orch. (1957–59); *Opusculum Claviorchestrale* for Piano and Orch. (1973–75). **CHAMBER:** 2 piano quintets: No. 1 (1920) and No. 2 (1949–53); *Concertino non Grosso* for 4 Violins, Viola, 2 Cellos, and Piano (1968); *Il tessuto d'Arabeschi* for Flute and String Quartet (1979; Philadelphia, May 2, 1982). **KEYBOARD: P i a n o :** 6 sonatas: No. 0 (1917), No. 1 (1919), No. 2 (1920), No. 3 (1922), No. 4 (1928–29), and No. 5, *Opus Archimagicum* (1934–35); 2 pieces: *In the Hothouse* and *Toccata* (1918, 1920); *Fantaisie espagnole* (1919); *Prelude, Interlude and Fugue* (1920–22); *3 Pastiches:* on Chopin, Bizet, and Rimsky-Korsakov (1922); *Le Jardin parfumé* (1923); *Variations and Fugue on "Dies Irae"* (1923–26); *Valse-Fantaisie (Hommage à Johann*

Strauss) (1925); *Fragment* (1926; rev. 1937); *Djâmî,* nocturne (1928); 4 toccatas: No. 1 (1928), No. 2 (1933–34), No. 3 (1957), and No. 4 (1964–67); *Opus Clavicembalisticum* (Glasgow, Dec. 1, 1930, composer soloist); *Symphonic Variations* (1935–37); 6 solo syms.: No. 1, *Tantrik* (1938–39), No. 2 (1954), No. 3 (1959–60), No. 4 (1962–64), No. 5, *Symphonia Brevis* (1973–75), and No. 6, *Symphonia Magna* (1975–76); *Gulistan,* nocturne (1940); *100 Transcendental Studies* (1940–44); *St. Bertrand de Comminges: "He Was Laughing in the Tower"* (1941); *Concerto per suonare da me solo* (1946); *Sequentia Cyclica on "Dies Irae"* (1949); *Un nido di scatole* (1954); *Passeggiata veneziana* (1956); *Rosario d'arabeschi* (1956); *Fantasiettina* (1961); *Symphonic Nocturne* (1977–78); *Il grido del gallino d'oro* (1978–79); *Evocazione nostalgicaVilla Tasca* (1979); *Opus secretum* (1980–81); *Passeggiata arlecchinesca* (1981–82). **O r g a n :** 3 solo syms.: No. 1 (1924), No. 2 (1929–32), and No. 3 (1949–53). **VOCAL:** Sym. No. 1 for Orch., Chorus, Organ, and Piano (1921–22); *5 sonetti del Michelangelo Buonarroti* for Voice and Chamber Orch. (1923; Toronto, Feb. 2, 1980); *Jâmî,* sym. for Orch., Baritone, Chorus, Organ, and Piano (1942–51); *Symphonic High Mass* for Orch., Solo Voices, Chorus, Organ, and Piano (1955–61); songs.

WRITINGS: *Around Music* (London, 1932); *Mi contra fa: The Immoralisings of a Machiavellian Musician* (London, 1947).

BIBL.: B. Posner, *S.* (diss., Fordham Univ., N.Y., 1975); P. Rapoport, *Opus Est: 6 Composers from Northern Europe* (London, 1978, and N.Y., 1979); idem, ed., *S.: A Critical Celebration* (Aldershot, 1992).—**NS/LK/DM**

Sörenson, Torsten, Swedish organist, teacher, and composer; b. Grebbestad, April 25, 1908; d. Uddevalla, Dec. 29, 1992. He began his training at the Stockholm Musikhögskolan (diplomas as a music teacher and church musician, 1934, and as an organist, 1936). After studies with Torsten Ahlberg (counterpoint) in Göteborg (1936–39), he studied composition with Rosenberg (1942) and Orff (1949). From 1935 he was a church organist in Göteborg, later serving at the Oscar Fredrik Church (1946–75); he also taught theory at the Göteborg Musikhögskolan (1954–76). He composed a number of fine works, ranging from large forces to lieder.

WORKS: ORCH.: *Sinfonietta* for Strings (1946; rev. 1957); Concerto for Organ and Strings (1952); Sym. for Chamber Orch. (1956); *Sinfonia da chiesa* 1 (1958) and 2 (1964–69) for Strings; Concerto for Flute, Strings, and Percussion (1976). **CHAMBER:** 2 trios for Flute, Clarinet, and Oboe (1949, 1959); Sonata for Solo Viola (1956); 3 sonatas for Solo Flute (1962, 1964, 1966); 2 string quartets (1970; *Due contrasti,* 1983); Brass Quintet (1970); *Divertimento* for Flute, Oboe, Violin, and Viola (1976); *Quintafonia* for 5 Instrumentalists (1979); *Sonans* for Piano and Organ (1983); Violin Sonata (1985); *Pezzo d'amore* for Viola d'Amore and 4 Violas (1986). **P i a n o :** Sonata (1956); *Svart-Vitt* (Black and White), 24 pieces (1975); *Dygnets fyra tider,* 4 studies (1975–79); *Floriad,* 15 pieces (1981–82); *Två sånger* (1988). **VOCAL:** *Den underbara Kvarnan* for Baritone and Orch. (1936; rev. 1958); *Hymn om Kristus,* cantata (1950); *Hymnarium,* 56 motets for 1 to 6 Voices and Instruments (1957–62); *Laudate nomen Domini* for Chorus, 17 Winds, and Percussion (1972); *En sang om Herrens boninger* for Soprano, 2 Choruses, and Orch. (1975); *Gud är här tillstädes,* cantata (1978).—**NS/LK/DM**

Soresina, Alberto, Italian composer and teacher; b. Milan, May 10, 1911. He studied with Paribeni and Bossi at the Milan Cons., graduating in 1933; then took a course in composition in Siena with Frazzi. He subsequently was on the faculty of the Milan Cons. (1947–60) and the Turin Cons. (1963–66); then again at the Milan Cons. (from 1967).

WORKS: DRAMATIC: O p e r a : *Lanterna rossa* (1942); *Cuor di cristallo* (1942); *L'amuleto* (Bergamo, Oct. 26, 1954); *Tre sogni per Marina* (1967). **ORCH.:** *Trittico Wildiano* (1939); *Il Santo*, symphonic poem (1940); *2 notturni* for Harp and Strings (1946); *Divertimento* (1956). **CHAMBER:** Concertino for Viola, Cello, and Piano (1953); *Sonatina serena* for Violin and Piano (1956); piano pieces. **VOCAL:** Several works for Voice and Orch., including *La Fanciulla mutata in rio* (1939).—**NS/LK/DM**

Sorge, Georg Andreas,

eminent German organist, music theorist, and composer; b. Mellenbach, Schwarzburg, Thuringia, March 21, 1703; d. Lobenstein, Thuringia, April 4, 1778. He began his music training in Mellenbach with Nicolas Walter, the local Kantor and organist, and his assistant, Caspar Tischer, then continued his studies with Tischer in Schney (Franconia) from 1714 to 1716; returned to Mellenbach to study academic subjects and composition with Pastor Johann Wintzern. After serving as a private tutor in Burg (Vogtland), he was made court and civic organist in Lobenstein when he was 19; he remained there until his death. In 1747 he was elected to membership in Mizler's Societät der Musikalischen Wissenschaften of Leipzig. He won distinction as an authority on organ building, as a music theorist, and as a composer. Although his keyboard music was widely disseminated during his lifetime, his importance now rests upon his contributions to music theory. In his masterwork, *Vorgemach der musicalischen Composition* (Lobenstein, 1745–47), he places prime importance on the triad as the foundation upon which all musical composition is based.

WRITINGS: *Genealogia allegorica intervallorum octavae diatono-chromaticae* (Hof, 1741); *Anweisung zur Stimmung und Temperatur sowohl der Orgelwerk, als auch anderer Instrumente, sonderlich aber des Claviers* (Hamburg, 1744); *Vorgemach der musicalischen Composition, oder: Ausführlich, ordentliche und vor heutige Praxin hinlängliche Anweisung zum General-Bass* (Lobenstein, 1745–47); *Gespräch zwischen einem Musico theoretico und einem Studioso musices von der Prätorianischen, Printzischen, Werckmeisterischen, Neidhardtischen, und Silbermannischen Temperatur wie auch von dem neuen Systemate Herrn Capellmeister Telemanns, zu Beförderung reiner Harmonie* (Lobenstein, 1748); *Ausführliche und deutliche Anweisung zur Rational-Rechnung, und der damit verknüpfften Ausmessung und Abteilung des Monochords* (Lobenstein, 1749); *Gründliche Untersuchung, ob die...Schröterischen Clavier- Temperaturen für gleichschwebend passieren können oder nicht* (Lobenstein, 1754); *Ausweichungs-Tabellen in welchen auf vierfache Art gezeiget wird wie eine jede Tonart in ihre Neben-Tonarten ausweichen könne* (Nuremberg, 1753); *Georg A. Sorgens...zuverlässige Anweisung Claviere und Orgeln behörig zu temperiren und zu stimmen* (Leipzig and Lobenstein, 1758); *Compendium harmonicum oder Kurzer Begriff der Lehre von der Harmonie* (Lobenstein, 1760; also publ. as *Herrn G.A. Sorgens Anleitung zum Generalbass und zur Composition*, Berlin, 1760); *Die geheim gehaltene Kunst von Mensuration von Orgel-Pfeiffen* (MS, c. 1760; facsimile ed. and Eng. tr. in Bibliotheca Organologica, XXIII, Busen, 1977); *Kurze Erklärung des Canonis Harmonici* (Lobenstein, 1763); *Anleitung zur Fantasie oder: Zu der schönen Kunst das Clavier wie auch andere Instrumente aus dem Kopfe zu spielen* (Lobenstein, 1767); *Bei der Einweihung...über die Natur des Orgel-*

Klangs (Hof, 1771); *Der in der Rechen-und Messkunst wohlerfahrne Orgelbaumeister* (Lobenstein, 1773); *Die Melodie aus der Harmonie...hergeleitet* (MS).

BIBL.: M. Frisch, *G.A. S. und seine Lehre von der musikalischen Harmonie* (diss., Univ. of Leipzig, 1954).—**NS/LK/DM**

Soriano, Alberto,

Uruguayan composer and musicologist; b. Santiago del Estero, Argentina, Feb. 5, 1915. He studied violin in Bahia, Brazil. In 1937 he went to Montevideo, where he was prof. of ethnomusicology at the Univ. (1953–69). In his music he makes use of South American melorhythms, while retaining fundamental classical forms. From 1953 to 1969 he was a prof. of enthnomusicology at the Univ. of Montevideo. Among his scholarly publications is *Algunas de las inmanencias etnomusicológicas* (Montevideo, 1967).

WORKS: Piano Concerto (1952); 2 guitar concertos (1952, 1957); *Sinfonietta* for Guitar, Cello, Bassoon, and Flute (1952); *4 rituales sinfónicos* (1953); *Divertimento* for Bassoon and String Orch. (1954); Cello Sonata (1955); Violin Concerto (1956); Violin Sonata (1959); Piano Trio (1961); *Canticos sinfónicos a la Revolución de Cuba* (1961); Concertino for Cello and Orch. (1961); *Pastoral de Sibiu* for Flute and Orch. (1962); *Tríptico de Praga* for Orch. (1962); *Tiempo sinfónico para los caidos en Buchenwald* (1962).—**NS/LK/DM**

Soriano, Francesco,

outstanding Italian composer; b. Soriano, near Viterbo, 1548 or 1549; d. Rome, July 19, 1621. He went to Rome, where he was a choirboy at St. John Lateran; received instruction from Annibale Zoilo, Bartolomeo Roy, G.B. Montanari, and Palestrina. About 1574 he entered the priesthood; was maestro di cappella at S. Luigi dei Francesi by 1580. After serving in a similar capacity to the Gonzaga court in Mantua (1581–86), he returned to Rome as maestro di cappella at S. Maria Maggiore (1587–99; 1601–3), St. John Lateran (1599–1601), and the Cappella Giulia at St. Peter's (1603–20). With Felice Anerio, he was named by a papal commission to complete the revision of the chant books started by Palestrina and Zoilo in 1577; the *Editio medicaea* was finished in 1612 and publ. in 1614. Soriano was a masterful polyphonist.

WORKS: VOCAL: S a c r e d : *Motectorum* for 8 Voices (Rome, 1597); *Missarum liber primus* for 4 to 6 and 8 Voices (Rome, 1609); *Psalmi et motecta* for 8, 12, and 16 Voices and Basso Continuo (organ) (Venice, 1616); *Passio D. N. Jesu Christe secundum quatuor Evengelistas, Magnificat, sequentia fidelium defunctorum, una cum responsoria* for 4 Voices (Rome, 1619). **S e c u l a r :** *Il primo libro di madrigali* for 5 Voices (Venice, 1581); *Il secondo libro di madrigali* for 5 Voices (Rome, 1592); *Il primo libro di madrigali* for 4 to 6 Voices (Rome, 1601); *Il secondo libro di madrigali* (n.p., 1602); *Canoni et oblighi di 110 sorte, sopra l'Ave maris stella* for 3 to 8 Voices (Rome, 1610); other works in contemporary collections.

BIBL.: S. Kniseley, *The Masses of F. S.: A Style-critical Study* (Gainesville, Fla., 1967).—**NS/LK/DM**

Soriano, Gonzalo,

Spanish pianist; b. Alicante, March 14, 1913; d. Madrid, April 14, 1972. He studied with Cabiles in Madrid, and later with Cortot and Landowska at the Paris Cons. He made his debut in

Alicante in 1929; pursued an active career in Europe; also gave concerts in the U.S. and the Far East. He was particularly noted for his congenial performances of Spanish music.—NS/LK/DM

Soro (Barriga), Enrique, prominent Chilean composer, pedagogue, and pianist; b. Concepción, July 15, 1884; d. Santiago, Dec. 2, 1954. He was a son of the Italian composer José Soro Sforza, with whom he studied piano and theory; played in public as a small child. He was granted a stipend by the government of Chile for study in Italy; entered the Milan Cons. at 14; graduated in 1904 with a grand prize in composition. Returning to Chile in 1905, he was appointed inspector of musical education in primary schools; in 1906 he joined the faculty of the Santiago Cons.; from 1919 to 1928 he was its director. He traveled as a pianist; gave concerts in Europe and South America; also publ. a number of works. In 1948 he was awarded the Premio Nacional de Arte.

WORKS: O R C H .: *Andante appassionato* (1915); *Danza fantastica* (1916); *Suite sinfónica,* No. 1, *Pensamientos intimos* (1918) and No. 2 (Santiago, May 9, 1919, composer conducting); *Impresiones líricas* for Piano and Strings (1919); Piano Concerto (1919); *Sinfonía romántica* (1920); *3 preludios sinfónicos* (Santiago, July 18, 1936); *Aires chilenos* (Santiago, 1942); *Suite en estilo antiguo* (Santiago, May 28, 1943). C H A M B E R: String Quartet (1904); Piano Quintet (1919); Piano Trio (1926); Violin Sonata; Cello Sonata. P i a n o : 3 sonatas (1920, 1923, 1942); piano pieces in a salon genre, some of them based on Chilean melorhythms.

BIBL.: L. Giarda, *Analytische Studie über S. 2. Sonate für Violine und Klavier A moll, das Quartett A dur und das Klavierquintett* (Santiago, 1919).—NS/LK/DM

Sotin, Hans, notable German bass; b. Dortmund, Sept. 10, 1939. He was a student of F.W. Hetzel and then of Dieter Jacob at the Dortmund Hochschule für Musik. In 1962 he made his operatic debut as the Police Commissioner in *Der Rosenkavalier* in Essen. After joining the Hamburg State Opera in 1964, he quickly became one of its principal members singing not only traditional roles but creating new roles in works by Blacher, Einem, Penderecki et al. His success led to his being made a Hamburg Kammersänger. In 1970 he made his first appearance at the Glyndebourne Festival as Sarastro. He made his debut at the Chicago Lyric Opera as the Grand Inquisitor in *Don Carlos* in 1971. That same year he sang for the first time at the Bayreuth Festival as the Landgrave, where he subsequently returned with success in later years. On Oct. 26, 1972, he made his Metropolitan Opera debut in N.Y. as Sarastro. From 1973 he sang at the Vienna State Opera. He made his debut at London's Covent Garden as Hunding in 1974. In 1976 he sang for the first time at Milan's La Scala as Baron Ochs. He also appeared as a soloist with the leading European orchs. In 1986 he returned to Covent Garden as Baron Ochs. In 1988 he sang Lodovico in *Otello* at the Metropolitan Opera. In 1992 he appeared as the Landgrave in Berlin. His portrayals of Tannhäuser, Lohengrin, and Gurnemanz at the 1993 Bayreuth Festival elicited critical accolades. He returned there as the Landgrave and Gurnemanz in 1995. In 1998

he was engaged as Pogner at the Metropolitan Opera. In addition to his varied operatic repertoire, Sotin has won distinction for his concert repertoire, most particularly of the music of Bach, Haydn, Beethoven, and Mahler. —NS/LK/DM

Soto de Langa, Francisco, Spanish singer, music editor, and composer; b. Langa, Soria province, 1534; d. Rome, Sept. 25, 1619. He spent most of his life in Rome, where he was a member of the Papal Choir (1562–1611); also was a member of the oratory of St. Filippo Neri (1566–75). In 1575 he became a priest and went to S. Maria in Vallicella. In 1590 he served as interim maestro di cappella of the Papal Choir in Rome. He has been credited with compiling 5 significant vols. of laude spirituale (Rome, 1583–98), which includes several of his own pieces.—NS/LK/DM

Soubies, Albert, French writer on music; b. Paris, May 10, 1846; d. there, March 19, 1918. He studied law and was admitted to the bar, and about the same time became a pupil of Savard, Bazin, and Guilmant at the Paris Cons. In 1876 he became music critic for *Le Soir* and in 1885 began to write for the *Revue de l'Art Dramatique.* In 1874 he revived the famous old *Almanach Duchesne* (publ. between 1752 and 1815), reissuing it as *Almanach des Spectacles* (43 vols. publ. to 1914). His articles were publ. under the name B. de Lamange.

WRITINGS (all publ. in Paris): With C. Malherbe, *L'oeuvre dramatique de Richard Wagner* (1886); with H. de Curzon, *Précis de l'histoire de l'Opéra-Comique* (1887); *Une première par jour: Causeries sur le théâtre* (1888); with C. Malherbe, *Wagner et Meyerbeer: Documents inédits* (1891); with C. Malherbe, *Histoire de l'Opéra-Comique: La seconde Salle Favart* (1892); with C. Malherbe, *Mélanges sur Richard Wagner* (1892); *Soixante-sept ans à l'Opéra en une page* (1893); *Musique russe et musique espagnole* (1894); *La Comédie-Française depuis l'époque romantique* (1895); *Histoire de la musique dans les différents pays d'Europe* (1895); *Histoire du théâtre-lyrique 1851–1870* (1899); with H. de Curzon, *Documents inédits sur le Faust de Gounod* (1912); *Massenet historien* (1913).—NS/LK/DM

Souchon, Edmond (II; aka "Doc"), early jazz guitarist, writer; long-time member of the Six and Seven Eighths Jazz Band; b. New Orleans, Oct. 25, 1897; d. there, Aug. 24, 1968. Raised in New Orleans, he trained to be a doctor in Chicago before returning home. Self-taught on guitar, he was one of the original members of the Six and Seven Eighths Band, a string band that originally had nine members. The original band was active during most of the teens. During the "Dixieland" revival of the late 1940s, the band was reorganized as a quartet, and recorded and toured from 1949 through the early 1960s. Souchon also gigged with other revival bands during this period and led his own ensembles. He was active in sparking interest in New Orleans jazz history, and was one of the first presidents of the New Orleans Jazz Club. He edited its newsletter from 1951 until his death. He also was a key force behind the founding of the National Jazz Foundation in 1942, and a decade later helped establish the New Orleans Jazz Museum.

DISC.: *High Society* (1949).—LP

Soudant, Hubert, Dutch conductor; b. Maastricht, March 16, 1946. He studied trumpet and horn at the Maastricht Cons., and then pursued training in conducting with Fournet and Ferrara. After serving as asst. conductor with the Netherlands Radio in Hilversum (1967–70), he took first prize in the Besançon Competition in 1971, second prize in the Karajan Competition in 1973, and first prize in the Cantelli Competition in Milan in 1975. From 1981 to 1983 he was chief conductor of the Nouvel Orchestre Philharmonique de Radio-France in Paris. He became music director of the Utrecht Sym. Orch. in 1982, and then of the Orch. Sinfonica dell'Emilia Romagna "Arturo Toscanini" in Parma in 1988. In 1995 he became music director of the Mozarteum Orch. in Salzburg and of the Orchestre Philharmonique des Pays de la Loire in Angers.—LK/DM

Souhaitty, Jean-Jacques, French music theorist who flourished in the mid 17th century. He was active in Paris as a Franciscan monk. He was the first to employ number notation, indicating by the numerals 1 to 7 the degrees of the scale, and used this system for popular teaching. He publ. *Nouvelle méthode pour apprendre le plain-chant et la musique* (Paris, 1665; second ed. as *Nouveaux éléments de chant, ou L'essay d'une nouvelle découverte quón a fait dans l'art de chanter,* 1677) and *Essai du chant de l'église par la nouvelle méthode des chiffres* (Paris, 1679).—NS/LK/DM

Soukupová, Věra, Czech mezzo-soprano; b. Prague, April 12, 1932. She was a student in Prague of Kadeřábek and Mustanová-Linková. In 1957 she made her debut at the J.K. Tyl Theater in Plzeň, where she sang until 1960. From 1960 to 1963 she was a member of the Prague National Theater. After capturing first prize in the Rio de Janeiro competition in 1963, she pursued a major career as an opera and concert singer. In 1966 she sang at the Bayreuth Festival. She made her first appearance in Hamburg in 1968. Thereafter she sang with major European opera houses and at major festivals. She became particularly known for her idiomatic performances of roles in 19th and 20th-century Czech operas.—NS/LK/DM

Souliotis, Elena, Greek soprano and mezzo-soprano; b. Athens, May 28, 1943. She studied in Buenos Aires with Alfredo Bonta, Jascha Galperin, and Bianca Lietti, and in Milan with Mercedes Llopart. In 1964 she made her operatic debut as Santuzza at the Teatro San Carlo in Naples. In 1965 she made her U.S. debut as Elena in Boito's *Mefistofele* in Chicago. In 1966 she sang Abigaille in *Nabucco* at Milan's La Scala, appeared as Luisa Miller in Florence, and made her N.Y. debut as Anna Bolena in a concert performance at Carnegie Hall. Her London debut followed in 1968 as Abigaille in a concert performance. She returned to London in 1969 to make her Covent Garden debut as Lady Macbeth, and continued to sing there until 1973. In subsequent years, she sang in various European operatic centers. Among her other roles were Norma, Gioconda, Manon Lescaut, Desdemona, Leonora in *Il Trovatore,* and Aida.
—NS/LK/DM

Soundgarden, "grunge" band that set the stage for Nirvana. **MEMBERSHIP:** Chris Cornell, voc., gtr., drm. (b. Seattle Wash., July 20, 1964); Kim Thayil, gtr. (b. Seattle, Wash., Sept. 4, 1960); Hiro Yamamoto, bs. (b. Okinawa, Japan, Sept. 20, 1968); Matt Cameron, drm. (b. San Diego, Calif., Nov. 28, 1962); Jason Everman, bs. (b. Aug. 16, 1967); Ben "Hunter" Shepherd, bs.

If the musical terrain of Seattle during the 1990s was fertile, Soundgarden was one of the bands that provided the fertilizer. Mixing hard-rock influences like Led Zeppelin with a punk attitude and *Rubber Soul*-era Beatles psychedelic lyricism, the band developed a unique and special sound that took 10 years to reach a pop audience but ultimately became hugely popular.

In the early 1980s, Kim Thayil and Hiro Yamamoto left Ill. to attend Evergreen State Coll. in Olympia, Wash. Lured by the growing scene in Seattle, they never finished school. Instead, Yamamoto started rooming with drummer Chris Cornell, and they began playing together. Yamamoto brought Thayil into the group in 1984, and they named the band Soundgarden, after a sculpture made of metal tubes in a local park that made noise whenever the wind blew. With Cornell both singing and drumming, the band lacked a focal point so they brought in several drummers, settling on Matt Cameron, allowing Cornell to move up front.

The group became a popular attraction on the Seattle scene. They were featured on several local compilations before releasing their first EP, *Screaming Life,* in 1987. The record came out on Seattle's Sub-Pop records, co-run by Bruce Pavitt, a friend of Yamamoto's and Thayil who had come out west with them. They followed this a year later with the *Fopp* EP; its success inspired several major labels to start chasing after them. Instead of taking a big-money deal, they released their full-length debut *Ultramega OK* on southern Calif. punk powerhouse indie SST in 1988 Garnering impressive reviews and decent sales, they signed with A&M to take them to the next level with 1990's *Louder than Love.*

Soon after they made the album, Yamamoto grew tired of the band and returned to school, eventually getting a Masters degree in physical chemistry. The group needed to hire a bassist quickly to prepare for a national tour. They took on former Nirvana guitarist Jason Everman. He lasted for the tour and recorded one track for their next album, a cover of the Beatles "Come Together." Ben "Hunter" Shepherd replaced him for the rest of 1991's *Badmotorfinger.*

Badmotorfinger broke the band, with the thundering tracks "Outshined" and "Jesus Christ Pose" getting hefty amounts of MTV airplay. The album rose to #39 and eventually went double platinum. The band hit the road with Guns 'n' Roses, then became a major attraction on the second Lollapalooza tour. Taking a break, Cornell and Cameron joined Pearl Jam's Eddie Vedder, Stone Gossard, Jeff Ament, and Mike McCready on a tribute album to Andrew Wood, the late singer of Mother Love Bone, a band that featured Gossard and Ament. The album *Temple of the Dog* hit #5, eventually going platinum. Shepherd and Cameron also released an album by their side project, Hater.

With all that exposure, Soundgarden's next album, 1994's *Superunknown*, hardly lived up to its title. The record topped the charts its first week, eventually going triple platinum. The songs "Black Hole Sun" and "Spoonman" became major rock and alternative hits, the latter earning a Grammy for Best Metal Performance and the former earning the Best Hard Rock Performance statuette. The record eventually went quintuple platinum.

The follow-up, 1996's *Down on the Upside*, while maintaining their power and momentum musically, only went platinum. This might have been due to the amount of time the band members were spending on other projects. The group finished touring the album in the winter of 1997 and decided to take a break. By that spring, they had announced the break would be permanent.

DISC.: *Screaming Life* (1987); *Ultramega OK* (1988); *Fopp* (1988); *Louder than Love* (1990); *Badmotorfinger* (1991); *Superunknown* (1994); *Songs from the Superunknown* (1995); *Down on the Upside* (1996).—**HB**

Šourek, Otakar, Czech writer on music; b. Prague, Oct. 1, 1883; d. there, Feb. 15, 1956. He was trained as an engineer, and although he was employed in the Prague City Council works dept. (1907–39), music was his avocation. He wrote music criticism for several publications, including Prague's *Venkov* (1918–41). However, it was as an authority on the life and music of Dvořák that he gained distinction; he devoted fully 40 years to Dvořák research, and served as the first ed. of the composer's collected works.

WRITINGS: *Život a dilo Antonína Dvořáka* (The Life and Works of Dvořák; 4 vols., Prague, 1916–33; vols. I-II, third ed., 1955–56; vols. III-IV, second ed., 1957–58; in Ger. as *Dvořák: Leben und Werk*, one vol., abr. by P. Stefan, Vienna, 1935; Eng. tr. by Y. Vance as *Anton Dvořák*, N.Y., 1941); *Dvořák's Werke: Ein völlstandiges Verzeichnis in chronologischer, thematischer und systematischer Anordnung* (Berlin, 1917; rev. Czech ed., Prague, 1960); *Výlety pana Broučka* (Mr. Brouček's Excursions; Prague, 1920); *Dvořákovy symfonie* (Prague, 1922; third ed., 1948; abr. ed. in Ger. in *Antonin Dvořák Werkanalysen I, Orchesterwerke*, Prague, 1954, and in Eng. in *The Orchestral Works of Antonín Dvořák*, Prague, 1956); *Antonín Dvořák* (Prague, 1929; fourth ed., 1947; Eng. tr., Prague, 1952, as *Antonín Dvořák: His Life and Work*); *Dvořákova citanka* (A Dvořák Reader; Prague, 1929; third ed., 1946; Eng. tr., Prague, 1954); *Dvořák ve vzpomínkach a dopisech* (Prague, 1938; 9th ed., 1951; Eng. tr., Prague, 1954, as *Dvořák: Letters and Reminiscences*; Ger. tr., 1955; Russian tr., 1964); *Smetanova Ma vlast* (Prague, 1940); *Antonin Dvořák přátelům doma* (Dvořák to His Friends at Home; 395 letters; Prague, 1941); *Antonín Dvořák a Hans Richter* (Letters to Richter; Prague, 1942); *Dvořákovy skladby komorni* (Prague, 1943; second ed., 1949; abr. ed. in Ger. in *Antonín Dvořák Werkanalysen II, Kammermusik*, Prague, 1954, and in Eng. in *The Chamber Music of Antonin Dvořák*, Prague, 1956); *Dvořákovy skladby orchestralni* (2 vols., Prague, 1944 and 1946; abr. ed. in Ger. in *Antonin Dvořák Werkanalysen I, Orchesterwerke*, Prague, 1954, and in Eng. in *The Orchestral Works of Antonin Dvořák*, Prague, 1956); *Komorni skladby Bedřicha Smetany* (Smetana's chamber works; Prague, 1945); *Rudolf Karel* (Prague, 1947).—**NS/LK/DM**

Souris, André, prominent Belgian conductor, musicologist, and composer; b. Marchienne-au-Pont, Hain-

aut, July 10, 1899; d. Paris, Feb. 12, 1970. He studied at the Brussels Cons. (1911–18) with Lunssens (harmony) and Closson (music history), and privately with Gilson (composition). In 1925 he began teaching at the Royal Cons. in Brussels; in 1927 he won the Prix Rubens, and traveled to Italy, France, and Austria; conducted the Belgian Radio Orch. (1937–46); from 1949 to 1964 he was a prof. of harmony at the Royal Cons. in Brussels. He was the founder of the quarterly music review *Polyphonie* (1947–54). He collaborated with R. Vannes on the *Dictionnaire des musiciens (compositeurs)* (Brussels, 1947); also ed. works by various composers. His compositions reflect the influence of the French avant-garde of the period between the 2 World Wars; in a few of his later works, he adopted serialism.

WORKS: DRAMATIC: Theater music; radio and film scores. **ORCH.:** *Soliloque* for Strings and Percussion (1923); *Scherzo* (1923); *Musique (Collage)* (1928); *Rêverie* (1931); *Danceries de la Renaissance* (1932); *Canzone* (1932); *Hommage à Babeuf* for Wind Orch. (1934); *Fanfare et scherzo* for Winds and Percussion (1937); *Burlesque* (1938); *Symphonies* (1939); *Suite de danceries No. 2* for Wind Orch. (1943); *Danses mosanes* (1943); *4 Fantasies* for Strings (1960); *Ouverture pour une arlequinade* (1962). **CHAMBER:** *Fantasque* for 4 Instruments (1916); *Fugue* for String Quartet (1917); *2 petits poèmes* for Violin and Piano (1917); *Hymne à l'automne* for Violin and Piano (1919); *Bagatelle* for Violin and Piano (1923); *Berceuse* for Violin and Piano (1924); *Choral, marche et galop* for 2 Trumpets and 2 Trombones (1925); *Burlesque* for Trumpet and Piano (1931); *Fatrasie* for Violin and Piano (1934); *Rengaines* for Woodwind Quintet (1937); *Suite de danceries No. 3* for 2 Trumpets, Horn, and Trombone (1944); *Concert flamand* for Woodwind Quartet (1965); *3 pièces anciennes* for Violin and Viola (1969). **Piano:** *Improvisation* (1917); *Sonatine* (1920); *Echos de Spa* (1934). **VOCAL:** *3 poèmes japonais* for Soprano and String Quartet (1916); *Avertissement* for 3 or 5 Narrators and Percussion (1926); *Quelques airs de Clarisse Juranville* for Alto and 8 Instruments or Piano Quintet (1928); *Alleluia* for Voice and 9 Instruments (1928); *Pastorales wallonnes* for Soprano, Alto, Tenor, Bass, and Orch. (1942); *Comptines pour enfants sinistres* for Soprano, Mezzo-soprano, Violin, Clarinet, and Piano (1942); *8 chansons enfantines* for Voice and Orch. (1943); *La légende de St. Nicolas* for Voice, Celesta, and Orch. (1943); *Le marchand d'images*, rustic cantata for 2 Speakers, Soprano, Alto, Tenor, Bass, Chorus, and Orch., after popular Walloon songs (1944–65); *L'autre voix* for Soprano, Flute, Clarinet, Violin, Cello, and Piano (1948); *5 laude* for Soprano, Alto, Tenor, Bass, and Chorus (1961); *Motet* for 6 Solo Voices and Orch. (1961); *Triptyque pour un violon* for Speaker, Mezzo-soprano, 2 Altos, 2 Baritones, Bass, Organ, and Percussion (1963); choruses; solo songs.—**NS/LK/DM**

Sousa, John Philip, famous American bandmaster and composer; b. Washington, D.C., Nov. 6, 1854; d. Reading, Pa., March 6, 1932. He was the son of a Portuguese father and a German mother. He studied violin and orchestration with John Esputa Jr., and violin and harmony with George Felix Benkert in Washington, D.C.; also acquired considerable proficiency on wind instruments. After playing in the Marine Band (1868–75), he was active in theater orchs.; in 1876 he was a violinist in the special orch. in Philadelphia conducted by Offenbach during his U.S. tour. In 1880 he was appointed director of the Marine Band, which he led with distinction until 1892. He then organized his own band and led it in its first concert in Plainfield, N.J., on Sept. 26, 1892. In subsequent years he gave successful concerts throughout the U.S. and Canada; played at the Chicago World's Fair in 1893 and at the Paris Exposition in 1900; made 4 European tours (1900, 1901, 1903, and 1905), with increasing acclaim, and finally a tour around the world, in 1910–11. His flair for writing band music was extraordinary; the infectious rhythms of his military marches and the brilliance of his band arrangements earned him the sobriquet "The March King"; particularly celebrated is his march The Stars and Stripes Forever, which became famous all over the world; in 1987 a bill was passed in the U.S. Congress and duly signed by President Ronald Reagan making it the official march of the U.S. During World War I, Sousa served as a lieutenant in the Naval Reserve. He continued his annual tours almost to the time of his death. He was instrumental in the development of the Sousaphone, a bass tuba with upright bell, which has been used in bands since the 1890s.

WORKS (in alphabetical order): **DRAMATIC: O p e r - e t t a :** *The American Maid* (1909; Rochester, N.Y., Jan. 27, 1913); *The Bride Elect* (New Haven, Conn., Dec. 28, 1897); *El Capitan* (1895; Boston, April 13, 1896); *The Charlatan* (Montreal, Aug. 29, 1898); *Chris and the Wonderful Lamp* (New Haven, Conn., Oct. 23, 1899); *Desirée* (1883; Washington, D.C., May 1, 1884); *The Free Lance* (1905; Springfield, Mass., March 26, 1906); *The Irish Dragoon* (1915; unfinished); *Katherine* (1879); *The Queen of Hearts* (1885; Washington, D.C., April 12, 1886); *The Smugglers* (Washington, D.C., March 25, 1882). **O t h e r :** Incidental music. **MARCHES:** *Across the Danube* (1877); *America First* (1916); *Anchor and Star* (1918); *Ancient and Honorable Artillery Company* (1924); *The Atlantic City Pageant* (1927); *The Aviators* (1931); *The Beau Ideal* (1893); *The Belle of Chicago* (1892); *Ben Bolt* (1888); *The Black Horse Troop* (1924); *Bonnie Annie Laurie* (1883); *Boy Scouts of America* (1916); *The Bride Elect* (1897); *Bullets and Bayonets* (1918); *El Capitan* (1896); *A Century of Progress* (1931); *The Chantyman's March* (1918); *The Charlatan* (1898); *The Circumnavigators Club* (1931); *Circus March* (n.d.); *Columbia's Pride* (1914); *Comrades of the Legion* (1920); *Congress Hall* (1882); *Corcoran Cadets* (1890); *The Crusader* (1888); *Daughters of Texas* (1929); *The Dauntless Battalion* (1922); *The Diplomat* (1904); *The Directorate* (1894); *Esprit de Corps* (1878); *The Fairest of the Fair* (1908); *The Federal* (1910); *Flags of Freedom* (1918); *La Flor de Sevilla* (1929); *Foshay Tower Washington Memorial* (1929); *The Free Lance* (1906); *From Maine to Oregon* (1913); *The Gallant Seventh* (1922); *George Washington Bicentennial* (1930); *The Gladiator* (1886; the first work to sell a million copies); *Globe and Eagle* (1879); *The Glory of the Yankee Navy* (1909); *Golden Jubilee* (1928); *The Golden Star* (1919); *The Gridiron Club* (1926); *Guide Right* (1881); *Hail to the Spirit of Liberty* (1900); *Hands Across the Sea* (1899); *Harmonica Wizard* (1930); *The High School Cadets* (1890); *Homeward Bound* (n.d.); *The Honored Dead* (1876); *Imperial Edward* (1902); *In Memoriam* (1881; for the assassinated President Garfield); *The Invincible Eagle* (1901); *Jack Tar* (1903); *Kansas Wildcats* (1931); *Keeping Step with the Union* (1921); *King Cotton* (1895); *The Lambs' March* (1914); *The Legionnaires* (1930); *The Liberty Bell* (1893); *Liberty Loan* (1917); *The Loyal Legion* (1890); *Magna Carta* (1927); *The Man Behind the Gun* (1899); *Manhattan Beach* (1893); *March of the Mitten Men* (1923); *March of the Pan-Americans* (1915); *March of the Royal Trumpets* (1892); *Marquette University March* (1924; on receiving an honorary D.M., Nov. 16, 1923); *Mikado March* (1885); *The Minnesota March* (1927); *Mother Goose* (1883); *Mother*

Hubbard March (1885); *National Fencibles* (1888); *The National Game* (1925; for the 50th anniversary of the National League of baseball); *The Naval Reserve* (1917); *New Mexico* (1928); *The New York Hippodrome* (1915); *Nobles of the Mystic Shrine* (1923); *The Northern Pines* (1931); *The Occidental* (1887); *Old Ironsides* (1926); *On Parade* (1892); *On the Campus* (1920); *On the Tramp* (1879); *Our Flirtations* (1880); *The Pathfinder of Panama* (1915); *Pet of the Petticoats* (1883); *The Phoenix March* (1875); *The Picador* (1889); *Powhatan's Daughter* (1907); *President Garfield's Inauguration March* (1881); *The Pride of Pittsburgh* (1901); *The Pride of the Wolverines* (1926); *Prince Charming* (1928); *The Quilting Party March* (1889); *Recognition March* (c. 1880); *Resumption March* (1879); *Review* (1873; his first publ. march); *Revival March* (1876); *Riders for the Flag* (1927); *The Rifle Regiment* (1886); *Right Forward* (1881); *Right—Left* (1883); *The Royal Welch Fusiliers* (No. 1, 1929; No. 2, 1930); *Sable and Spurs* (1918); *Salutation* (1873); *The Salvation Army* (1930); *Semper Fidelis* (1888); *Sesquicentennial Exposition March* (1926); *Solid Men to the Front* (1918); *Sound Off* (1885); *The Stars and Stripes Forever* (1896; made the official march of the U.S. by act of Congress, 1987); *The Thunderer* (1889); *Transit of Venus* (1883); *The Triton* (1892); *Triumph of Time* (1885); *Universal Peace* (probably 1925); *University of Illinois* (1929); *University of Nebraska* (1928); *USAAC March* (1918); *U.S. Field Artillery* (1917); *The Victory Chest* (1918); *The Volunteers* (1918); *The Washington Post* (1889); *Wedding March* (1918); *The White Plume* (1884); *The White Rose* (1917); *Who's Who in Navy Blue* (1920); *The Wildcats* (1930 or 1931); *Wisconsin Forward Forever* (1917); *The Wolverine March* (1881); *Yorktown Centennial* (1881). **OTHER:** Suites for Band; overtures; descriptive pieces; instrumental solos; orch. works; about 76 songs, ballads, hymns; many arrangements and transcriptions.

WRITINGS: AUTOBIOGRAPHICAL: *Through the Years with Sousa* (1910); *Marching Along* (1928). **MANUALS:** *The Trumpet and Drum* (1886); *National Patriotic and Typical Airs of All Lands* (1890). **NOVELS:** *The Fifth String* (1902); *Pipetown Sandy* (1905); *The Transit of Venus* (1919).

BIBL.: M. Simon, *J.P. S., the March King* (N.Y., 1944); A. Lingg, *J.P. S.* (N.Y., 1954); K. Berger, *The March King and His Band* (N.Y., 1957); J. Smart, *The S. Band: A Discography* (Washington, D.C., 1970); W. Stacy, *J.P. S. and His Band Suites: An Analytic and Cultural Study* (diss., Univ. of Colo., 1972); P. Bierley, *J.P. S.: American Phenomenon* (N.Y., 1973; second ed., rev., 1986); idem, *J.P. S.: A Descriptive Catalog of His Works* (Urbana, Ill., 1973; second ed., rev. and aug., 1984, as *The Works of J.P. S.*); J. Newsom, ed., *Perspectives on J.P. S.* (Washington, D.C., 1983); W. Mitziga, *The Sound of S.: J.P. S. Compositions Recorded* (Chicago, 1986).—**NS/LK/DM**

Souster, Tim(othy Andrew James), avantgarde English composer; b. Bletchley, Buckinghamshire, Jan. 29, 1943; d. Cambridge, March 1, 1994. He studied with Rose, Lumsden, and Wellesz at the Univ. of Oxford (B.A., 1964; B.Mus., 1965); in 1964 he attended courses in new music given by Stockhausen and Berio in Darmstadt; received private instruction from Bennett (1965). He was a music producer for the BBC (1965–67). After serving as composer-in-residence at King's Coll., Cambridge (1969–71), he was a teaching assistant to Stockhausen in Cologne (1971–73); later was a research fellow in electronic music at the Univ. of Keele (1975–77); in 1988–89 he was chairman of the Assn. of Professional Composers. He became one of the most articulate exponents of serial, aleatory, and combinatorial ideas, in which electronic media are employed in conjunction with acoustical performances by humans; he expounded these ideas in his writings in the *Listener*, *Tempo*, and other progressive publications. In 1969 he was a co-founder (with Roger Smalley) of the Intermodulation Group, with the aim of presenting works by congenial composers and experimenters; it disbanded in 1976 and he then formed a new group, OdB.

WORKS: *Songs of the Seasons* for Soprano and Viola (1965); *Poem in Depression* for Soprano, Flute, Viola, Cello, and Piano (1965); *Parallels* for 2 Percussion Players (1966); *Metropolitan Games* for Piano Duet (1967); *Titus Groan Music* for Wind Quintet, Electronics, and Magnetic Tape (1969); *Chinese Whispers* for Percussion and 3 Electronic Synthesizers (1970); *Waste Land Music* for Soprano Saxophone, Modulated Piano, Modulated Organ, and Electronic Synthesizer (London, July 14, 1970); *Triple Music II* for 3 Orchs. (London, Aug. 13, 1970); *Song of an Average City* for Small Orch. and Tape (1974); *Afghan Amplitudes* for Keyboards and Synthesizers (1976); Sonata for Cello and Ensemble (1979); *Mareas* for 4 Amplified Voices and Tape (1981); *Paws 3D* for Orch. (1984); *Le Souvenir de Maurice Ravel* for Septet (1984); *Hambledon Hill* for Amplified String Quartet (1985); Concerto for Trumpet, Live Electronics, and Orch. (1988). —**NS/LK/DM**

Soustrot, Marc, French conductor; b. Lyons, April 15, 1949. He studied at the Lyons Cons. (1962–69) and then was a student at the Paris Cons. (1969–76) of Paul Bernard (trombone), Christian Lardé (chamber music), Claude Ballif (analysis), and Manuel Rosenthal and Georges Tzipine (conducting). In 1974 he won the Rupert conducting competition in London, and was Previn's assistant with the London Sym. Orch. from 1974 to 1976. In 1975 he won the Besançon conducting competition. He was made second conductor of l'Orchestre Philharmonique des Pays de la Loire in Angers in 1976, and then was its music director from 1978. From 1986 to 1990 he concurrently served as artistic director of the Nantes Opera. From 1995 he was music director of the Brabant Phil. in Eindhoven and from 1997 he was Generalmusikdirektor of the Orchester der Beethovenhalle and the Opera in Bonn. As a guest conductor, Soustrot appeared with various orchs. and opera houses in Europe.—**NS/LK/DM**

South, Eddie (actually, **Edward Otha**), influential jazz violinist; b. Louisiana, Mo., Nov. 27, 1904; d. Chicago, April 25, 1962. His family moved to Chicago when Eddie was three months old. A child prodigy on violin, South first studied with Charles Elgar, then with Prof. Powers, was later given jazz coaching by Darnell Howard. At 16 South began working in Chicago, continuing to study at the Chicago Coll. of Music. He worked with Charles Elgar, Erskine Tate, and Mae Brady's Orch., then became front man and musical director for Jimmy Wade's Syncopators at Chicago's Moulin Rouge Cafe (c. 1924). South remained with Wade until 1927, worked briefly with Erskine Tate until January 1928, with Gilbert "Little Mike" McKendrick's Quartet, and then went to Europe with his own small group, The Alabamians. They toured several European countries; South also had extensive musical studies in Paris and Budapest. He was mostly in Chicago during the early to mid-1930s, except for a brief period in late

1932 when he was working in Calif. South returned to Europe in 1937; he played long residency at the Club des Oiseaux, Paris, appeared in Holland (early 1938), and returned to the U.S. in May 1938. He continued to lead his own groups (usually a quartet, occasionally big bands) from the late 1930s through the 1950s. South had his own radio series in the 1940s, and regular television shows from Chicago during the 1950s. He suffered from ill health for many years, but continued to work professionally until a few weeks before his death. South, who never used an amplified instrument, was known as "The Dark Angel of the Violin."

DISC.: *Distinguished Violin of Eddie South* (1958); *Dark Angel of the Fiddle* (1958).—**JC/LP**

Southern, Eileen, black American musicologist; b. Minneapolis, Feb. 19, 1920. The Norwegian pianist Meda Zarbell Steele supervised her studies at Chicago Musical Coll. and helped her obtain scholarships at the Univ. of Chicago, where she studied with Scott Goldwaite and Sigmund Levarie (B.A., 1940; M.A., 1941, with the thesis *The Use of Negro Folksong in Symphonic Music*). She then taught at Prairie View State Coll. (1941–42), Southern Univ. (1943–45; 1949–51), Alcorn State Coll. (1945–46), Claflin Univ. (1947–49), and secondary schools in N.Y. (1954–60). She pursued her education at N.Y.U. (Ph.D., 1961, with the diss. *The Buxheim Organ Book*; publ. in 1963). Southern taught at Brooklyn Coll. (1960–68) and York Coll. (1968–75), and also founded the journal *Black Perspective in Music* (1973), which she ed. until 1991. She was prof. of music and chairman of the dept. of Afro-American studies at Harvard Univ. (1975–86). In addition to her articles in journals, she was a contributor to *The New Grove Dictionary of Music and Musicians* (1980) and *The New Grove Dictionary of American Music* (1986). In 1991 she was made an honorary member of the American Musicological Soc.

WRITINGS: *The Music of Black Americans: A History* (N.Y., 1971; second ed., 1984); *Readings in Black American Music* (N.Y., 1971; third ed., 1997); *Biographical Dictionary of Afro-American and African Musicians* (Westport, Conn., 1982); *Afro-American Traditions in Song: An Annotated Bibliography* (1990).

BIBL.: J. Wright and S. Floyd Jr., *New Perspectives on Music: Essays in Honor of E. S.* (Detroit, 1992).—**NS/LK/DM**

Southern, Jeri (actually, **Genevieve Hering**), singer; b. Royal, Nebr., Aug. 5, 1926; d. Los Angeles, Calif., Aug. 4, 1991. Southern sang with Anita O'Day in Chicago and was signed to Decca. She was more popular in Britain than her native country; her version of "When I Fall in Love" sold better in the U.K. than the huge U.S. Doris Day hit. She recorded with Marty Paich and Billy May, but quit in the early 1960s to teach singing, settling in Southern Calif.

DISC.: "When I Fall in Love" (1952); *Intimate Songs* (1954); *Jeri Southern Meets Johnny Smith* (1958); *Jeri Southern at the Crescendo* (1960).—**MM/LP**

Souzay, Gérard (real name, **Gérard Marcel Tisserand**), distinguished French baritone; b. Angers, Dec. 8, 1918. He studied voice with Pierre Bernac,

Claire Croiza, Vanni Marcoux, and Lotte Lehmann, and was a student at the Paris Cons. (1940–45). He made his recital debut in Paris in 1945, his U.S. debut in a recital at N.Y.'s Town Hall in 1950, and his operatic debut as Count Robinson in Cimarosa's *Il Matrimonio segreto* at the Aix-en-Provence Festival in 1957. He made his Metropolitan Opera debut in N.Y. as Count Almaviva in *Le nozze di Figaro* on Jan. 21, 1965. In subsequent years, he toured extensively, mainly as a recitalist. In 1985 he joined the faculty of the Ind. Univ. School of Music in Bloomington; taught at the Univ. of Tex. in Austin in 1986. Souzay won renown as a concert artist; after Bernac, he was esteemed as the foremost interpreter of French art songs; equally acclaimed were his performances of German lieder, which received encomiums from German critics and audiences.

BIBL.: M. Morris, *The Recorded Performances of G. S.: A Discography* (N.Y., 1991).—NS/LK/DM

Sowande, Fela (actually, **Olufela**), Nigerian composer; b. Oyo, May 29, 1905; d. Ravenna, Ohio, March 13, 1987. He studied music in Lagos, then went to London, where he played in a combo in nightclubs; at the same time he took courses at London Univ. and the Trinity Coll. of Music. He served in the Royal Air Force during World War II. In 1944 he composed an *African Suite* for Strings. He returned to Nigeria in 1953, and in 1957 received a grant from the State Dept. to travel in the U.S.; was again in the U.S. in 1961, on a Rockefeller grant, and on June 1, 1961, conducted a group of members of the N.Y. Phil. in Carnegie Hall in a program of his own compositions, among them *Nigerian Folk Symphony*. Upon returning to Nigeria, he joined the staff of the Univ. Coll. at Ibadan. In his music he pursued the goal of cultural integration of native folk material with Western art forms.—NS/LK/DM

Sowerby, Leo, remarkable American composer and organist; b. Grand Rapids, Mich., May 1, 1895; d. Fort Clinton, Ohio, July 7, 1968. He studied piano with Calvin Lampert and theory with Arthur Andersen in Chicago; also had sporadic lessons with Grainger. He learned to play the organ without a teacher, and yet developed a virtuoso technique that enabled him to hold prestigious appointments as a church organist. He was extremely precocious; on Jan. 17, 1917, he presented himself in Chicago in a program grandiloquently billed "Leo Sowerby: His Music," which included such ambitious works as a Piano Concerto, with the composer at the keyboard; a Cello Concerto; and symphonic pieces. During World War I, he served as a bandmaster in the U.S. Army. He completed his musical studies at the American Cons. in Chicago (M.M., 1918). In 1921 he received the American Prix de Rome, the first of its kind to be awarded for composition; he spent 3 years at the American Cons. in Rome. Returning to Chicago, he served as a teacher of composition at the American Cons. (1925–62); also was organist and choirmaster at the Episcopal Cathedral of St. James (1927–62); then was founder-director of the Coll. of Church Musicians at the National Cathedral in Washington, D.C. (1962–68). In 1935 he was elected to membership in the National Inst.

of Arts and Letters. In 1946 he won the Pulitzer Prize in Music for his *Canticle of the Sun*. Sowerby never attempted to discover new ways of making music; his style was eclectic in the positive sense of the word, selecting what appeared to be the best in various doctrines and styles. Hindemith's invidious reference to Sowerby as the fourth B in music, a "sour B," is not appropriate, for Sowerby's music is anything but sour; he certainly knew how to build up sonorous masses, particularly in his vocal compositions.

WORKS: ORCH.: Violin Concerto (1913; rev. 1924); *The Sorrow of Mydath*, symphonic poem (1915); *Rhapsody on British Folk Tunes* (1915); *Comes Autumn Time*, overture (Chicago, Jan. 17, 1917); 2 cello concertos: No. 1 (Chicago, Jan. 17, 1917) and No. 2 (1929–34; N.Y., April 2, 1935); 2 piano concertos: No. 1, with Soprano obbligato (Chicago, Jan. 17, 1917; rev., 1919, without soprano) and No. 2 (1932; Boston, Nov. 30, 1936); *The Irish Washerwoman*, transcription (Chicago, Jan. 17, 1917); *Money Musk*, transcription (1917); *A Set of 4: Suite of Ironics* (Chicago, Feb. 15, 1918); Concerto for Harp and Small Orch. (1919); 5 syms.: No. 1 (Chicago, April 7, 1922), No. 2 (Chicago, March 29, 1929), No. 3 (Chicago, March 6, 1941), No. 4 (Boston, Jan. 7, 1949, Koussevitzky conducting), and No. 5 (1964); *King Estmere*, ballad for 2 Pianos and Orch. (Rome, April 8, 1923); *Rhapsody* for Chamber Orch. (1922); *From the Northland* (Rome, May 27, 1924); *Synconata and Monotony* for Jazz Orch. (1924, 1925; Chicago, Oct. 11, 1925); *Medieval Poem* for Organ and Orch. (Chicago, April 20, 1926); *Prairie*, symphonic poem (Interlochen, Mich., Aug. 11, 1929); *Passacaglia, Interlude and Fugue* (1931–32); *Sinfonietta* for Strings (1933–34); *Theme in Yellow*, after Sandburg (1937); Concerto in C for Organ and Orch. (Boston, April 22, 1938; E. Power Biggs soloist); *Concert Overture* (1941); *Poem* for Viola and Orch. or Organ (1941); *Fantasy on Hymn Tunes* (1943); *Classic Concerto* for Organ and Strings (1944); *Portrait: Fantasy in Triptych* (1946; Indianapolis, Nov. 21, 1953); *Concert Piece* for Organ and Orch. (1951); *All on a Summer's Day* (1954; Louisville, Jan. 8, 1955); untitled work (Concerto No. 2) for Organ and Orch. (1967–68). **CHAMBER:** Quartet for Violin, Cello, Horn, and Piano (1911); 3 unnumbered piano trios (in D, undated; 1911; 1953); 5 unnumbered violin sonatas (in E, 1912, rev. 1916; in G, undated; in B-flat, 1922; in A, *Fantasy Sonata*, 1944; in D, 1959); 2 unnumbered cello sonatas (1912, 1920); Sonata for Solo Violin (1914); *Serenade* for String Quartet (1916); Wind Quintet (1916); Trio for Flute, Viola, and Piano (1919); 2 string quartets (1923–24; 1934–35; both MSS lost); *Pop Goes the Weasel* for Wind Quintet (1927); *Chaconne* for Trombone and Piano (1936); Clarinet Sonata (1938); *Poem* for Viola and Organ (1941); Trumpet Sonata (1945); *Ballade* for English Horn and Organ (1949); *Fantasy* for Trumpet and Organ (1962); *Suite* for Oboe and Piano (1963); *Triptych of Diversions* for Organ, 2 Violins, Double Bass, Oboe, and Percussion (1962); *Dialog* for Organ and Piano (1967); an undated Horn Trio. **KEYBOARD: Piano:** 2 sonatas (1912; 1948, rev. 1965); *Florida*, suite (1929); Suite (1959); Suite for Piano, 4-Hands (1959). **Organ:** Sonata (1914–17); Sym. (1930); Suite (1934); *Church Sonata* (1956); *Sinfonia brevis* (1965); *Bright, Blithe and Brisk* (1967); *Passacaglia* (1967). **VOCAL:** *A Liturgy of Hope* for Soprano, Men's Chorus, and Organ (1917); an untitled oratorio after the Book of Psalms (1924); *The Vision of Sir Launfal*, cantata after James Lowell (1925); *Great Is the Lord* for Chorus, Orch., and Organ (1933); *Forsaken of Man* for Chorus and Organ (1939); *Song for America* for Chorus and Orch. (1942); *The Canticle of the Sun* for Chorus and Orch., after St. Francis (1944; N.Y., April 16, 1945); *Christ Reborn*, cantata for Chorus and Organ (1950; Philadelphia, Nov. 1, 1953); *The Throne of God* for Chorus and Orch. (1956; Washington, D.C., Nov. 18, 1957); *The Ark of the Covenant*, cantata for Chorus and Organ (1959); *Solomon's Garden*, cantata for Tenor, Chorus, and Chamber Orch. (1964); *La Corona* for Chorus and Orch. (1967); numerous anthems, songs, etc.

BIBL.: M. Guiltinan, *The Absolute Music for Piano Solo by L. S.* (diss., Univ. of Rochester, 1977); *L. S.: A Short Biography and a Complete List of His Compositions* (Chicago, 1979); D. Bading, *L. S.'s Works for Organ with Orchestra or Ensemble* (thesis, Univ. of Kans., 1983).—NS/LK/DM

Sowinski, Wojciech (Albert), Polish pianist, teacher, writer on music, and composer; b. Lukaszówka, Podolia, c. 1803; d. Paris, March 5, 1880. He was a pupil of Czerny, Gyrowetz, Leidersdorf, and Seyfried in Vienna, where he made his debut as a pianist in 1828; after touring Italy, France, and England, he settled in Paris as a music teacher in 1830. He publ. the first dictionary of Polish musicians in a Western language, *Les Musiciens polonais et slaves, anciens et modernes. Dictionnaire biographique des compositeurs, chanteurs, instrumentistes, luthiers* (Paris, 1857; in Pol., Paris, 1874), and it is through this publication that his name is remembered. He wrote the operas *Lenore, ou Les morts vont vite, Le Modèle, Une Scène sous la ligne,* and *Zlote gody,* an oratorio, *Saint Adalbert,* several motets, a Sym., overtures on Polish subjects, 2 piano concertos, a Piano Quartet, a Piano Trio, and numerous piano pieces in the salon genre.—NS/LK/DM

Soyer, Roger (Julien Jacques), French bass; b. Paris, Sept. 1, 1939. He began his training with Daum, and then studied with Jouatte and Musy at the Paris Cons., where he won premiers prix in singing (1962) and opera (1963). In 1962 he made his debut at the Piccola Scala in Milan as Poulenc's Tiresias. From 1963 he sang at the Paris Opéra. In 1964 he appeared as Pluto in Monteverdi's *Orfeo* at the Aix-en-Provence Festival, where he sang with much success in subsequent years. In 1968 he made his U.S. debut in Miami as Friar Lawrence in *Roméo et Juliette,* and also appeared at the Wexford Festival in England in *La Jolie Fille.* He made his Metropolitan Opera debut in N.Y. in one of his finest roles, Don Giovanni, on Nov. 16, 1972. He also chose that role for his first appearance at the Edinburgh Festival in 1973. In subsequent years, he sang with principal European opera houses and festivals. He also appeared widely as a concert artist. Among his other admired roles were Don Basilio, Méphistophélès, Ferrando, Colline, and Sulpice.—NS/LK/DM

Spadavecchia, Antonio (Emmanuilovich), Russian composer; b. Odessa, June 3, 1907; d. Moscow, Feb. 7, 1988. He was of Italian descent. After training with Shebalin at the Moscow Cons. (graduated, 1937), he completed his studies with Prokofiev (1944).

WORKS: DRAMATIC: O p e r a : *Ak-Buzat* (The Magic Steed; Ufa, Nov. 7, 1942; rev. 1952; in collaboration with Zaimov); *Khozyaka gostinitsa* (The Inn Hostess; Moscow, April 24, 1949); *Khozhdeniye po mukam* (Pilgrimage of Sorrows; Perm, Dec. 29, 1953); *Ovod* (The Gadfly; Perm, Nov. 8, 1957); *Braviy soldat Shveky* (1963); *Yukki* (1970); *Ognenniye godi* (Ordeal by fire;

1971). **B a l l e t :** *Vragie* (Enemies; Moscow, May 20, 1938); *Bereg schastya* (The Shore of Happiness; Moscow, Nov. 6, 1948; rev. 1955). **O t h e r :** Musical comedies; incidental music; film scores. **ORCH:** *Dzangar,* symphonic suite (1940); *Heroic Overture on Bashkir Songs* (Ufa, Nov. 6, 1942); Piano Concerto (1944). **CHAMBER:** *Romantic Trio* for Violin, Cello, and Piano (1937); String Quartet (1937); *Elegie* for Cello and Piano (1955). **VOCAL:** Songs.—NS/LK/DM

Spaeth, Sigmund, American writer on music; b. Philadelphia, April 10, 1885; d. N.Y., Nov. 11, 1965. He studied piano and violin with A. Bachmann, then attended Haverford Coll. (B.A., 1905; M.A., 1906) and Princeton Univ. (Ph.D., 1910, with the diss. *Milton's Knowledge of Music;* publ. in Princeton, N.J., 1913). He was music ed. of the *N.Y. Evening Mail* (1914–18), education director of the American Piano Co. (1920–27), and president of the National Assn. of American Composers and Conductors (1934–37). Spaeth lectured widely on music, gave popular talks on the radio, was active in musical journalism, and held various posts in educational organizations. He ed. the valuable collections *Read 'em and Weep* (1926; rev. 1945) and *Weep Some More, My Lady* (1927).

WRITINGS (all publ. in N.Y. unless otherwise given): *The Common Sense of Music* (1924); *The Art of Enjoying Music* (1933; rev. 1949); *Music for Everybody* (1934); *Great Symphonies* (Garden City, N.Y., 1936; second ed., rev., 1952); *Stories behind the World's Great Music* (1937); *Music for Fun* (1939); *Great Program Music* (1940); *A Guide to Great Orchestral Music* (1943); *At Home with Music* (Garden City, N.Y., 1945); *A History of Popular Music in America* (1948); *Dedication: The Love Story of Clara and Robert Schumann* (N.Y., 1950); *Opportunities in Music Careers* (1950; second ed., rev., 1966); *Fifty Years with Music* (1959); *The Importance of Music* (1963).—NS/LK/DM

Spalding, Albert, esteemed American violinist; b. Chicago, Aug. 15, 1888; d. N.Y., May 26, 1953. He studied violin with Ulpiano Chiti in Florence and with Juan Buitrago in N.Y. before entering the Bologna Cons. at the age of 14; subsequently received further violin training from Augustin Lefort at the Paris Cons., and studied composition with Antonio Scontrino in Florence. He made his public debut in Paris on June 6, 1905, and his American debut as a soloist with the N.Y. Sym. Orch. on Nov. 8, 1908. Beginning in 1919, he made annual tours of the U.S. and acquired the reputation of a fine artist, even though not necessarily a contagiously flamboyant one. He also made appearances in Europe. On June 20, 1950, he gave his farewell performance in N.Y. In 1926 he was elected to the National Inst. of Arts and Letters and in 1937 to the American Academy of Arts and Letters. He gave the U.S. premieres of the violin concertos of Dohnányi, Elgar, and Barber. His own works include an orch. suite, 2 violin concertos, a String Quartet, a Violin Sonata, various violin pieces, songs, and piano pieces. He publ. an autobiography, *Rise to Follow* (N.Y., 1943), and a fictionalized biography of Tartini, *A Fiddle, a Sword, and a Lady* (N.Y., 1953).
—NS/LK/DM

Spani, Hina (real name, **Higinia Tunon**), Argentine soprano; b. Puan, Feb. 15, 1896; d. Buenos Aires, July 11, 1969. She studied in Buenos Aires and

Milan. She made her operatic debut at La Scala in Milan in 1915 as Anna in Catalani's *Loreley*; also sang in Turin, Naples, and Parma; made many appearances at the Teatro Colón in Buenos Aires (1915–40). From 1946 she taught voice in Buenos Aires, and from 1952 served as director of the School of Music at the Univ. of Buenos Aires. She was highly regarded as a dramatic soprano; her repertoire included more than 70 roles.—**NS/LK/DM**

Spanier, "Muggsy" (Francis Joseph), influential early jazz cornetist; b. Chicago, Nov. 9, 1906; d. Sausalito, Calif., Feb. 12, 1967. He was nicknamed after "Muggsy" McGraw, a baseball manager. Spanier started on drums, but switched to cornet at age 13. He played in Holy Name Cathedral School Band and then, while working as a messenger boy, did semi- professional jobs with Elmer Schobel during 1921. He made his professional debut with Sig Meyers's Band at White City, Chicago (1922), and worked with Meyers until 1924. From late 1925–28, he worked primarily with Floyd Town's Band although he gigged with others. In October 1928, he joined Ray Miller's Orch., where he came to the attention of Ted Lewis; Spanier subsequently joined Ted Lewis in San Francisco in 1929, and remained with him until late 1936 (including a European tour in 1930). Spanier joined Ben Pollack from December 1936 until early 1938, when a near-fatal illness forced his temporary retirement. He resumed regular playing early in 1939, and organized his own band, Ragtimers, which played gigs in Chicago and N.Y. through the end of that year. Spanier rejoined Ted Lewis briefly in late 1939, and then joined Bob Crosby's Band through mid-1941. After that, he formed his own big band, which was active for the next two years, until its membership was depleted because of World War II. Spanier was briefly incapacitated by an injury incurred in car accident, but then led his own sextet in Chicago. He returned to N.Y. in March 1944, and gigged with Art Hodes and others. He then rejoined Ted Lewis from May–August 1944, and played on the west coast (October 1944), until finally he joined Miff Mole at Nick's, N.Y. From mid-1940s through early 1950s, Spanier played club dates in Chicago and N.Y. with various others. From 1951 until summer of 1959 he worked on and off with Earl Hines in San Francisco. In 1957, he made his permanent home in Calif. He continued to lead and tour until 1964, with frequent residencies in San Francisco, and also played a season at Bourbon Street, New Orleans (1961). Not long after being featured at the 1964 Newport Jazz Festival, ill health forced him to retire.

DISC.: *At the Jazz Band Ball* (1929); *Great Sixteen* (1939); *Spanier's Ragtimers* (1944); *Relaxin' at the Touro* (1952); *Rare Custom 45's* (1956); *Hot Horn* (1957); *Spanier in Chicago* (1958); *Columbia, the Gem of the Ocean* (1962); *Great Moments at Newport* (1964).—**JC/LP**

Spano, Robert, American conductor and pianist; b. Conneaup, Ohio, May 7, 1961. He studied conducting with Robert Baustian at the Oberlin (Ohio) Coll. Cons. of Music, where he also received training in piano, violin, and composition; later completed his conducting studies with Max Rudolf at the Curtis Inst. of Music in Philadelphia. In 1989 he became music director of the Opera Theater at Oberlin Coll. From 1990 to 1993 he was asst. conductor of the Boston Sym. Orch.; subsequently toured widely as a guest conductor of major orchs. throughout North America, Europe, and Asia. In 1994 he received the Seaver/NEA conductors award. During the 1994–95 season, he made his debut at London's Covent Garden conducting *Billy Budd*. He was music director designate (1995–96) and then music director (from 1996) of the Brooklyn Phil. In 1999 he also became director of the Tanglewood Music Center conducting program and in 2000 he was named music director of the Atlanta Sym. Orch.—**NS/LK/DM**

Spargo, Tony (originally, **Sbarbaro, Antonio**), early jazz drummer, kazoo player; b. New Orleans, June 27, 1897; d. Forest Hills, N.Y., Oct. 30, 1969. He was on the first jazz recordings as a member of the Original Dixieland Jazz Band. At 14, he began playing drums with the Frayle Brothers' Band, then with Ernest Giardina's Band; he also did parade work in Papa Jack Laine's Reliance Bands. He continued playing with Giardina until 1915, and then joined Merritt Brunies's Band at the Tango Place. He also worked with pianist Carl Randall at the Black Cat Cabaret. Spargo left New Orleans in June 1916 to join The Original Dixieland Jazz Band in Chicago. He continued to work under Nick LaRocca until early 1925, then became leader of The Original Dixieland Jazz Band for residency at The Cinderella Ballroom, N.Y. He led the small unit until early 1927, then led an augmented band at Rose Danceland, N.Y., before working with Lacey Young's Orch. (1927–28). Spargo did a variety of musical work, including another stint leading his own band, then, in 1936, took part in the re-creation of the O.D.J.B. He worked with LaRocca until early 1938, then continued with the O.D.J.B. until 1940. Spargo began playing regularly at Nick's, N.Y., in 1939, and was featured at N.Y.'s World Fair in 1941. In 1943 he toured in Katherine Dunham's Revue, then resumed playing at Nick's. He played in N.Y. with Miff Mole, Big Chief Moore, Pee Wee Erwin, Jimmy Lytell, Tony Parenti, Eddie Condon, and pianist Mike Loscalzo, recording with some of them. He was a regular with Phil Napoleon at Nick's during the early 1950s, and recorded with Connee Boswell in the 1950s. He retired from regular playing in the early 1960s.

Spargo's early playing contrasts sharply with that of his New Orleans contemporaries, Baby Dodds and Zutty Singleton. Spargo's showy technique and exuberant improvisatory style are rooted in the ragtime playing of such drummers as James Lent, Buddy Gilmore, and John Lucas. His earliest recordings, notably "Indiana," "Dixie Jazz Band One-Step," and "Tiger Rag," belie the idea that the equipment and playing techniques of drummers were always restricted in early recording studios. His cymbal, woodblock, cowbells, snare drum, and bass drum are clearly heard on these tracks.

DISC.: Original Dixieland Jazz Band: "Indiana," "Dixie Jazz Band One-Step," "Tiger Rag" (all 1917); "Crazy Blues" (1921); "Fidgety Feet," "Original Dixieland One-Step" (both 1936). E. Condon: "Mandy Make up Your Mind" (1943).—**JC/LP**

Sparnaay, Harry, prominent Dutch bass clarinetist; b. Amsterdam, April 14, 1944. He played tenor saxophone in the Bohemia Jazz Quintet and later in the Theo Deken Orch.; studied clarinet at the Amsterdam Cons., where he eventually turned to the bass clarinet. He had over 100 works written for him (as a soloist or for his chamber duo, Fusion Moderne, which was formed in 1971 with the pianist Polo de Haas) by Berio, Goeyvaerts, Hrisanidis, Kunst, Logothetis, Raxach, Straesser, and others; played in contemporary music festivals.—NS/LK/DM

Spasov, Ivan, Bulgarian composer; b. Sofia, Jan. 17, 1934; d. 1996. He studied composition with Vladigerov at the Bulgarian State Cons. in Sofia (1951–56) and later with Sikorski and Wislocki at the Warsaw Cons.; subsequently devoted himself mainly to teaching and composing. Spasov composed in an advanced style.

WORKS: ORCH.: *Sonata concertante* for Clarinet and Orch. (1959); 3 syms. (1960, 1975, 1978); *Micro-Suite* for Chamber Orch. (1963); *Dances* (1964); *2 Bulgarian Melodies* (1968, 1970); *Competition* for 22 Winds (1969; Plovdiv, May 10, 1973); Cello Concerto (1974); Piano Concerto (1976); *Firework* (1980); Violin Concerto (1980). **CHAMBER:** Clarinet Sonata (1959); Viola Sonata (1960); *Bagatelles* for Flute and Harp (1964); *Episodes* for 4 Instrumental Groups (1965); *Movements I* for 12 Strings (1966) and *II* for 12 Strings and 3 Bagpipes (1968); *10 Groups* for Hunting Horn and Piano (1965); *Musique pour des amis* for String Quartet and Jazz Quartet (1966); String Quartet No. 1 (1973); Cello Sonata (1980); Piano Trio (1981). **P i a n o :** *Games* (1964); *The Art of the Seria* (3 notebooks; 1968, 1969, 1970). **VOCAL:** *Plakat*, oratorio (1958); *Monologues of a Lonely Woman*, monodrama for Soprano, Women's Chorus, Chamber Ensemble, and Tape (1976); *Canti lamentosi* for 2 Sopranos and Chamber Orch. (1979); *23 Lines from Emily Dickenson* for Soprano and Instrumental Ensemble (1989).—NS/LK/DM

Spataro, Giovanni, Italian music theorist and composer; b. Bologna, c. 1458; d. there, Jan. 17, 1541. He studied with Bartolomeo Ramos de Pareia while the latter was in Bologna in 1482. Ramos publ. his *Musica pratica* in 1482, which resulted in an attack from Niccolo Buzio. Spataro countered on his teacher's behalf with his *Honesta defensio* (1491). Gaffurius entered the fray with his *Apologia* (1520), which Spataro answered in his *Errori* (1521). Spataro championed what he saw as the progressive ideas of his teacher. He was active as a member of the choir at S. Petronio from at least 1505, and was installed as maestro di canto in 1512. His only extant works are 6 motets and 1 laude, which are publ. in the Antiquae Musicae Italicae series *Monumenta Bononiensa*, II (1967).

WRITINGS: *Honesta defensio in Nicolai Burtii parmensis opusculum* (Bologna, 1491; ed. in the Antiquae Musicae Italicae series *Monumenta Bononiensa*, II/1, 1967); *Dilucide, et probatissime demonstratione...contra cert frivole et vane excusatio[n]e, da Fra[n]chino Gafurio (maestro de li errori)* (Bologna, 1521); *Errori di Franchino Gafurio da Lodi, da maestro Joanne Spatario, musico bolognese, in sua defensione, e del suo precettore mro. Bartolomeo Ramis hispano subtiliter dimonstrati* (Bologne, 1521); *Tractato di musica, nel quale si tracta de la perfectione de la sesquialtera producta in la musica mensurata* (Venice, 1531).

BIBL.: B. Blackburn, E. Lowinsky, and C. Miller, eds. and trs., *A Correspondence of Renaissance Musicians* (Oxford, 1991). —NS/LK/DM

Spazier, Johann Gottlieb Karl, German pedagogue, writer on music, and composer; b. Berlin, April 20, 1761; d. Leipzig, Jan. 19, 1805. He was a student of philosophy at the Univ. of Halle, then a prof. of philosophy at the Univ. of Giessen; settled in Leipzig in 1800. He composed many songs, some of which became great favorites. Among his writings are *Freymüthige Gedanken über die Gottesverehrung der Protestanten* (Gotha, 1788), *Carl Pilger's Roman seines Lebens von ihm selbst geschrieben: Ein Beitrag zur Erziehung und Kultur des Menschen* (Berlin, 1792–96), and *Etwas über Gluckische Musik und die Oper Iphigenia in Tauris auf dem Berlinischen Nationaltheater* (Berlin, 1795).—NS/LK/DM

Speach, Bernadette (Marie), accomplished American composer, pianist, administrator, presenter, and teacher; b. Syracuse, N.Y., Jan. 1, 1948. She studied piano as a child and at the age of 18 entered the order of the Sisters of St. Joseph of Corondelet, serving as a nun until 1977. She was educated at the Coll. of Saint Rose in Albany, N.Y. (B.S. in music education, 1971), then taught music at parochial schools and composed music, including religious pieces and folk songs for voice and guitar. In 1977 she left the order and entered Columbia Univ., meeting Morton Feldman while on a summer session in Siena, Italy. She then transferred to the State Univ. of N.Y. at Buffalo for composition studies with him as well as with Lejaren Hiller (M.A., 1977; Ph.D., 1979). She also married the jazz guitarist and politically motivated composer Jeffrey Schanzer, with whom she moved to N.Y. in 1984, becoming active as a new music administrator and presenter at such venues as the Alternative Museum (1987–93), Lotus Fine Arts, Inc. (1994), Composers' Forum, Inc. (from 1995), The Kitchen (1998), and the Electronic Music Foundation's new laboratory and performance space, Engine 27 (from 1999). She also lectured widely, and taught at the New School (1994–98). In 1993 she was artist-in-residence with the Minneapolis-based new music ensemble Zeitgeist, and in 1994 with the American Composers Orch. in N.Y. From 1996 she served on the board of the American Music Center. Speach is an accomplished composer whose works span virtually all genres; much of her work has involved jazz elements and improvisation. She has received awards from the NEA (1992), the N.Y. State Council on the Arts (1992), Arts Midwest/Meet the Composer Residency Support Grant (1993), and the N.Y. Foundation for the Arts (1998–99), among others. Among her recordings are a collection of chamber pieces on *Without Borders* (1989) and a collection of improvised solos and duets on *Dualities* (1992).

WORKS: DRAMATIC: D a n c e : *Bone, Burned, Abandon/Creak* (N.Y., June 1, 1990; in collaboration with David Alan Harris); *Almost Tadzio/Overbite Alarm* (N.Y., Feb. 7, 1991; in collaboration with David Alan Harris); *Baobab 4* for Flute, Clarinet, Alto Saxophone, Trombone, Acoustic and Electric Guitar, Bass, 2 Pianos, Balafon, Reciter, 3 Women's Voices, and Dancer (N.Y., April 9, 1994). **I n c i d e n t a l M u s i c T o :** *A Clearing in the Woods* by Arthur Laurents for Piano, Flute, and

Tape (Mattituck, Long Island, N.Y., March 23, 1979). **M u s i c T h e a t e r :** *Gertrude* (Buffalo, N.Y., June 15, 1984); *Light Rail for Subway Track* (N.Y., Nov. 15, 1985). **ORCH.:** *Within* for Piano and Orch. (N.Y., Feb. 15, 1990); *Parallel Windows—Unframed* for Piano and Orch. (1996; N.Y., March 20, 1997). **C H A M B E R :** Wind Trio for Flute, Clarinet, and Bassoon (N.Y., May 5, 1977); *Ode to Thelonius* for Flute, Alto Flute, Oboe, English Horn, Trumpet, Horn, Viola, Cello, Prepared Piano, and Percussion (1978–79; first complete perf., Buffalo, N.Y., May 1, 1979); *A Set of Two* for Cello (1982; Buffalo, N.Y., April 11, 1984); *Moto* for Trombone, Piano, and Percussion (1982; N.Y., April 12, 1983); *Pentamenta* for String Quartet (1982; Buffalo, N.Y., March 13, 1988); *Echange* for Guitar, Piano, and Percussionist (1982; Buffalo, Oct. 28, 1983); *Onde* for Flute and Percussion (1983; Rye, N.Y., Sept. 20, 1984); *Quatri* for Percussion Quartet (1983; Buffalo, N.Y., April 27, 1984); *Trajet* for Trombone and Percussion (Buffalo, N.Y., Nov. 13, 1983); *Pensees I, II, & III* for Guitar (Buffalo, Dec. 4, 1983); *Between the Lines* for Violin, Piano, and Percussion (Buffalo, N.Y., April 9, 1984); *Streamline* for Leroys Jenkins' Sting (N.Y., Jan. 26, 1986); *Spero* for Guitar (N.Y., Oct. 17, 1986); *Shattered Glass* for Percussion (N.Y., Oct. 17, 1986); *Les Ondes Pour Quatre* for String Quartet (Darmstadt, Aug. 7, 1988); *Improvisations* for Piano and Guitar (1986–99); *Boppin' Again* for Chamber/Jazz Ensemble (N.Y., Feb. 3, 1989; also for 10-piece Ensemble, N.Y., May 24, 1991); *Chosen Voices* for Toy Piano and Prepared Guitar (N.Y., June 8, 1991); *Trio des trois I* for Violin, Piano, and Percussion (1991; N.Y., Feb. 19, 1993), *II* for Flute, Harp, and Viola (1991; N.Y., Dec. 9, 1994), and *III* for Piano, Viola, and Cello (1992; New Britain, Conn., April 28, 1993); *Walking Again* for Piano, Flute, Bass, and Traps (N.Y., April 15, 1993; also for Piano, 1992); *Avanzando* for Bass Clarinet, Piano, Marimba, Vibraphone, and Glockenspiel (Minneapolis, Nov. 4, 1993); *From Death Row, This Is Mumia Abu-Jamal* for Piano, 3 Percussionists, and Tape (N.Y., Nov. 16, 1996); *Le Donne* for Chamber Ensemble (N.Y., Feb. 19, 1998). **P i a n o :** *des Sondages* (1981–82; Nos. I-III, Buffalo, Oct. 27, 1981; No. IV, Buffalo, April 17, 1983); *Untitled* (Buffalo, N.Y., Dec. 5, 1982); *To Tango or Not* (N.Y., Feb. 27, 1986); Sonata (N.Y., June 4, 1986); *Inside Out* (N.Y., Oct. 18, 1987); *a page upon which...* (N.Y., Sept. 23, 1989); *Resoundings* for Piano, 4-Hands (N.Y., Dec. 13, 1990); *and so it is...* (N.Y., Dec. 13, 1990); *Walking Again* (N.Y., Feb. 2, 1992; also for Piano, Flute, Bass, and Traps, 1993); *Angels in the Snow* (N.Y., Dec. 9, 1993); *When It Rains, Llueve* (1995; N.Y., Feb. 1, 1996). **VOCAL:** *Lost* for Flute, Horn, Mezzo-soprano, Viola, and Double Bass, after H. Hesse (Siena, Aug. 20, 1976); *Sono I & II* for Soprano, Flute, Clarinets, Alto Saxophone, Trombone, and Percussion, after Liv Ullmann (1981–82; first complete perf., Buffalo, N.Y., April 2, 1982); *It Came to Me in a Dream*, in counterpoint with Ash Wednesday, for Flute, Alto Flute, Guitar, Piano, and Baritone, after T.S. Eliot (N.Y., Sept. 15, 1990); *Telepathy Suite* for Reciter and 20- piece Ensemble (N.Y., March 18, 1988; in collaboration with Thulani Davis); *A Set of Five* for Reciter and Chamber Ensemble (N.Y., Jan. 11, 1989; in collaboration with Thulani Davis); *Complaints* for Speaker, Flute, Bass, Vibraphone, and Traps (N.Y., April 15, 1993); *Woman Without Adornment* for Reciter and Piano (N.Y., Dec. 21, 1994; in collaboration with Thulani Davis; also for Reciter and Chamber Ensemble, N.Y., March 29, 1995); *Anne* for 2 Sopranos, Baritone, String Quartet, and Clarinet (N.Y., Feb. 19, 1998). **ELEC-TRONICS, SAMPLERS, AND/OR TAPE:** *"I Think We Are Small Enough"* for Tape (Buffalo, May 1, 1979); *9/9/89* for Digital Sampler and Tape (Troy, N.Y., March 27, 1990). **—LK/DM**

Speaks, Oley, American baritone and song composer; b. Canal Winchester, Ohio, June 28, 1874; d. N.Y., Aug. 27, 1948. He studied singing with Emma Thursby and composition with Max Spicker and W. Macfarlane. After singing at various churches in N.Y. (1898–1906), he devoted himself entirely to concert singing and composition. He wrote some of the most popular songs in the American repertoire of his day: *On the Road to Mandalay* (1907), *Morning* (1910), *To You* (1910), *Sylvia* (1914), and *The Prayer Perfect* (1930).—**NS/LK/DM**

Specials, The, founding fathers of the second wave of ska. **MEMBERSHIP:** Terry Hall, voc. (b. Coventry, England, March 19, 1959); Jerry Dammers (real name, Gerald Dankin), kybd. (b. India, May 22, 1954); Lynval Golding, gtr. (b. Coventry, England, July 24, 1951); Rodney Radiation (real name Rodney Byer), gtr.; Sir Horace Gentleman (real name, Horace Panter), bs.; Neville Staples, voc., perc.; John Bardbury, drm.

In mid-1970s Britain, while everyone else was playing loud, fast, and angry, the Specials started playing fast, melodic, and smart. They revived a 1960s music popular in Jamaica and among expatriate West Indians in England called ska, and spawned a music that both answered punk and expanded punk's palette. While the original band only lasted two albums before splintering into the cream of England's experimental new wave, members continued to record, write, and play Two-Tone Ska into the new millennium. Ultimately, while they never charted in the U.S. Top 40, they influenced bands from the Mighty Mighty Bosstones to Rancid.

The group began playing as the Coventry Automatics, and later called themselves the Special AKA before settling on the Specials. Initially, they split their set between reggae and punk, but found that the two didn't work well in tandem for them, so fused them together to revive ska. The Clash invited them to open for them on tour, which got the major labels interested. Instead of signing, keyboard player Jerry Dammers started his own label, Two-Tone, in homage to the black-and-white garb their fans wore and, more importantly, on the biracial component of both the band and the audience. Their self-released single "Gangsters" rose to the English Top ten. Then other Two-Tone bands like the Selecter, the Beat, and Madness started making hits, earning the label distribution by Chrysalis.

In 1979 the group released their eponymous, Elvis Costello-produced debut album to considerable praise on both sides of the Atlantic. Mixing ska classics like "Message to You Rudi" and "Monkey Man" to show their roots with their own socially aware tunes like "Concrete Jungle," "Stupid Marriage," and "Too Much Too Soon" (released on EP in the U.K.), the band established a new beachhead for the music. Their horn charts, featuring Rico on trombone, stole a page from bands like the Skatalites for pure jazziness.

By the time they recorded their second album, the tension between the pro-ska factions of the band and the pro-pop segment became audible. *More Specials* featured less ska and more...other stuff. The album began and ended with a ska-ed up version of Herb Magidson and

Carl Sigman's 1949 chestnut "Enjoy Yourself" and built from there, but nothing was as strong as their debut.

While it was evident that the band and the movement was winding down, they took their label out on tour, recording the Two-Tone gestalt for posterity on film and album as *Dance Craze*. The band also released an EP featuring the incredibly powerful and spooky "Ghost Town" about the early 1980 race riots in Brixton. It topped the English charts.

Shortly after the Specials's second album was released in 1980, Hall, Golding, and Staples splintered off to form the avant-pop unit Fun Boys Three. Fun Boys Three released several singles that had middling sales in the U.K., but were startling nonetheless. "The Lunatics Have Taken Over the Asylum" a strange, minimalist dirge, reached the Top 20 in 1982. They duetted with the all-woman trio Bananarama on an old Jimmy Lunceford (via Young James Oliver) tune "It Ain't What You Do (It's the Way That You Do It)" and had another hit with George Gershwin's "Summertime." Their second album, released in 1983, featured "Tunnel of Love" and their version of "Our Lips Are Sealed," a hit Hall wrote with Jane Weidlin of the Go-Gos, who had already had a hit with it.

Meanwhile, Dammers worked close to three years to finish *In the Studio*, which was finally released in 1984. With vocalist Stan Campbell from the Selecter filling in nicely, the album had some classic songs, including "What I Like Most about You Is Your Girlfriend," "Racist Friend," and the political landmark "Free Nelson Mandela." However, the album cost so much money to make Dammers wound up in heavy debt. After that, Dammers left the music scene to pursue his political interests.

The 1990s saw various Specials and related bands working on tour and record. Past members of the Specials hooked up with members of another Two-Tone band, the (English) Beat, and toured as the Special Beat, releasing a couple of live albums in the early 1990s. The Specials with Staples, Golding, Panter, and Radiation (now using his given name of Byer), hit the road mid-decade and released *Guilty 'Til Proved Innocent*, an album of new material in 1998. Two live albums followed.

DISC.: THE SPECIALS: *The Specials* (1979); *More Specials* (1980); *In the Studio* (1984); *Today's Specials* (1996); *Concrete Jungle* (1998); *Guilty 'Til Proved Innocent!* (1998); *Blue Plate Specials Live* (1999); *Ghost Town: Live at Montreux Jazz Festival* (1999). **THE FUN BOY THREE:** *The Fun Boys Three* (1982); *Waiting* (1983); *Old Grey Whistle Test Series* (live; 1995); *Singles* (1995); *Fame* (1999). **SPECIAL BEAT:** *Live* (1992); *Live in Japan* (1994); *Gangsters* (live; 1998); *Tears of a Clown* (live; 1998). —HB

Spector, Phil, the most influential producer in rock and roll who created "teenage symphonies to God"; b. Bronx, N.Y., Dec. 26, 1940. Phil Spector moved to Los Angeles at the age of 13 with his mother and sister. He studied guitar and piano in high school and formed The Teddy Bears in 1958 with Annette Kleinbard and Marshall Leib. Signed to Dore Records, the trio soon scored a top pop and near-smash rhythm-and-blues hit with

Spector's own "To Know Him Is to Love Him," but subsequent recordings for Imperial fared poorly and the group disbanded in 1959. After unsuccessfully recording with The Spectors Three for Trey Records, Spector worked on the West Coast under Lester Sill and Lee Hazlewood and subsequently served as understudy to Jerry Leiber and Mike Stoller in N.Y. He coauthored Ben E. King's solo debut pop and R&B hit, "Spanish Harlem," with Leiber and produced the hits "Corinna, Corinna" for Ray Peterson, "Pretty Little Angel Eyes" for Curtis Lee, and "I Love How You Love Me" for The Paris Sisters.

Phil Spector formed Philles Records with Lester Sill in late 1961. The Crystals were the label's first signing and they soon had pop and rhythm- and-blues hits with "There's No Other" and "Uptown." The so-called "wall-of-sound" technique devised by Spector was launched into international prominence with The Crystals' top pop and smash R&B hit "He's a Rebel," written by Gene Pitney. Following "He's Sure the Boy I Love," The Crystals had smash crossover hit classics with "Da Doo Ron Ron" and "Then He Kissed Me," both cowritten by Spector, Jeff Barry, and Ellie Greenwich.

In late 1962, Phil Spector bought out Lester Sill and assumed total control of Philles Records. Bob B. Soxx and The Blue Jeans (with Darlene Love) followed their near-smash crossover hit "Zip-a-Dee Doo-Dah" with the moderate pop hit "Why Do Lovers Break Each Other's Hearts," while Darlene Love scored moderate pop hits with "(Today I Met) The Boy I'm Gonna Marry" and "Wait 'Til My Bobby Gets Home," all produced by Spector. In mid-1963, Spector signed The Ronettes to Philles Records and they soon had a smash pop and R&B hit with "Be My Baby," written by Spector, Barry, and Greenwich. Other major crossover hits for The Ronettes through 1964 were "Baby, I Love You" and "Walking in the Rain." In late 1963, Philles issued the celebrated Christmas album *A Christmas Gift for You*, featuring Philles artists performing seasonal standards plus Darlene Love's "Christmas (Baby Please Come Home)," written by Spector, Greenwich, and Barry. The album was included as part of 1991's anthology set *Back to Mono*.

During 1964, Phil Spector signed The Righteous Brothers and, at year's end, the duo scored a top pop and smash rhythm-and-blues hit with "You've Lost That Lovin' Feelin'," written by Spector, Barry Mann, and Cynthia Weil. The recording came to be regarded as one of rock's all-time classic singles. The Righteous Brothers subsequently achieved smash pop hits with "Just Once in My Life" (by Spector, Carole King, and Gerry Goffin); "Unchained Melody"; and "Ebb Tide" before switching to Verve Records, where their top pop hit, "(You're My) Soul and Inspiration," mimicked Spector's production style.

In the spring of 1966, Philles Records issued the Spector-Barry-Greenwich epic "River Deep, Mountain High" as recorded by Ike and Tina Turner, but the single failed to become anything more than a minor American pop hit (it was a smash hit in Great Britain), much to Spector's chagrin, as he ostensibly considered it his consummate production effort. Thus rebuffed by the

American public, Spector withdrew from the record business and soon closed Philles Records, ending a stellar chapter in the history of rock music. He married Veronica "Ronnie "Bennett of The Ronettes in 1968, but the couple divorced in 1974.

During the rest of the 1960s, Phil Spector was largely inactive, although he did make a cameo appearance in the film *Easy Rider* and worked for a time at A&M Records, producing one album by The Checkmates. He later salvaged The Beatles' *Let It Be* album and produced George Harrison's *All Things Must Pass* and four albums for John Lennon, including *Imagine*. He left Apple Records in 1973 and formed Warner-Spector Records under the aegis of Warner Bros. Records. The label reissued his *Christmas Album* and issued the two-record set *Greatest Hits*, but productions for Cher ("A Woman's Story"), Cher and Nilsson ("A Love Like Yours Don't Come Knocking Every Day"), and Ronnie Spector (Spector and Nilsson's "Paradise") fared poorly. Forming Phil Spector International in Great Britain in conjunction with Polydor Records, Spector produced Dion's *Born to Be with You* (unreleased in the U.S.) for the label. Spector's later productions for Leonard Cohen (*Death of a Ladies' Man*) and The Ramones (*End of the Century*) failed to reestablish him. Since coproducing Yoko Ono's *Season of Glass* in 1981, Spector has remained largely in seclusion. Inducted into the Rock and Roll Hall of Fame in 1989, Phil Spector emerged to assemble 1991's four-disc set *Back to Mono*, which included the entire *Christmas Album*.

DISC.: *The Early Productions, 1958–61* (1983); *Today's Hits* (1963); *A Christmas Gift to You* (1963); *Phil Spector: Back to Mono (1958–69)* (1991). **THE TEDDY BEARS:** *The Teddy Bears* (1959).

BIBL.: R. Williams, *Out of His Head: The Sound of P. S.* (N.Y., 1972); M. Ribowsky, *He's a Rebel* (N.Y., 1989); J. J. Fitzpatrick and J. E. Fogerty. *Collecting P. S.: The Man, the Legend, and His Music* (St. Paul, Minn., 1991).—**BH**

Speer, Daniel, noted German composer, music theorist, and writer; b. Breslau, July 2, 1636; d. Göppingen, Oct. 5, 1707. He studied at the Maria-Magdalenen-Gymnasium in Breslau, then traveled throughout southeastern Europe, obtaining practical experience in music. After serving as a church musician in Stuttgart (1664–66), he was a schoolteacher and church musician in Göppingen (1667–68); then was active in Gross Bottwar and Leonberg, near Stuttgart. In 1673 he settled in Göppingen as a teacher at the Lateinschule. In 1689 he publ. a pamphlet criticizing the Wurttemberg authorities for their lack of adequate response to the French invasion; for this he was arrested and imprisoned at the Hohenneuffen fortress. Upon his release, he was sent to Waiblingen, near Stuttgart. In 1694 he returned to Göppingen as Kollaborator at the Lateinschule, where he later became Kantor. His most significant work was the treatise *Grund-richtiger...Unterricht der musicalischen Kunst* (Ulm, 1687; second ed., rev. and enl., 1697, as *Grund-richtiger...Unterricht der musicalischen Kunst, oder Vierfaches musicalisches Kleeblatt*; see H. Howery, *A Comprehensive Performance Project in Trombone Literature with an Essay Consisting of a Translation of Daniel Speer's "Vierfaches Musicalisches Kleeblatt,"* diss., Univ. of Iowa,

1971). He composed sacred vocal works and 3 valuable quodlibet collections (1685, 1687, 1688). Among his other works are novels and various political writings. —**NS/LK/DM**

Spelman, Timothy (Mather), American composer; b. Brooklyn, Jan. 21, 1891; d. Florence, Italy, Aug. 21, 1970. He studied with H.R. Shelley in N.Y. (1908), W.R. Spalding and E.B. Hill at Harvard Univ. (1909–13), and Walter Courvoisier at the Munich Cons. (1913–15); he returned to the U.S. in 1915 and was active as director of a military band. After 1918 he went back to Europe with his wife, the poetess Leolyn Everett, settling in Florence. He returned to the U.S. in 1935; in 1947 he went back to Florence. His music was performed more often in Europe than in America; indeed, his style of composition is exceedingly European, influenced by Italian Romanticism and French Impressionism.

WORKS: DRAMATIC: *Snowdrop*, pantomime (Brooklyn, 1911); *The Romance of the Rose*, "wordless fantasy" (Boston, 1913; rev., St. Paul, Minn., Dec. 4, 1915); *La Magnifica*, music drama after Leolyn Everett-Spelman (1920); *The Sea Rovers*, opera (1928); *The Sunken City*, opera (1930); *Babakan*, fantastic comedy (1935); *The Courtship of Miles Standish*, opera after Longfellow (1943). **ORCH.:** *Saint's Days*, suite in 4 movements, including *Assisi, the Great Pardon of St. Francis* (Boston, March 26, 1926); *The Outcasts of Poker Flat*, symphonic poem after Bret Harte (1928); Sym. (1935; Rochester, N.Y., Oct. 29, 1936); *Jamboree*, "pocket ballet" (1945); Oboe Concerto (1954). **CHAMBER:** *5 Whimsical Serenades* for String Quartet (1924); *Le Pavillion sur l'eau* for Flute, Harp, and Strings (1925); *Eclogue* for 10 Instruments (1926); String Quartet (1953); piano pieces, including a sonata (1929). **VOCAL:** *Pervigilium Veneris* for Soprano, Baritone, Chorus, and Orch. (1929; Paris, April 30, 1931); *I Love the Jocund Dance* for Women's Voices and Piano (1938); choruses; songs.—**NS/LK/DM**

Spencer, Émile-Alexis-Xavier, French composer; b. Brussels, May 24, 1859; d. Nanterre, Seine, May 24, 1921. He studied piano in Brussels. In 1881 he went to Paris, where he found his métier as a composer for vaudeville; he was credited with about 4,000 chansonettes, which were popularized by famous singers, among them Yvette Guilbert. His chanson *Jambes de bois* was used by Stravinsky in *Petrouchka* under the impression that it was a folk song; when Spencer brought an action for infringement on his authorship, Stravinsky agreed to pay him part of the royalties for performances.—**NS/LK/DM**

Spencer, Robert, English lutenist, guitarist, singer, and teacher; b. Ilford, May 9, 1932; d. Woodford Green, Essex, Aug. 8, 1997. He studied lute with Walter Gerwig and Julian Bream (1955) and voice at the Guildhall School of Music and Drama in London (1956). Following addition studies at the Dartington School of Music (from 1956), he married the mezzo-soprano Jill Nott-Bower in 1960 and thereafter appeared with her in recitals. He also was a lutenist with the Julian Bream Consort (from 1960) and the Deller Consort (from 1974). He likewise served as prof. of lute at the Royal Academy of Music in London. His repertoire embraced works from the Renaissance to the contemporary era. —**NS/LK/DM**

Spendiarov, Alexander (Afanasii), significant Armenian composer; b. Kakhovka, Crimea, Nov. 1, 1871; d. Yerevan, May 7, 1928. He studied violin as a child; in 1896 he went to St. Petersburg and took private lessons with Rimsky-Korsakov. In his works, he cultivated a type of Russian orientalism in which the elements of folk songs of the peripheral regions of the old Russian Empire are adroitly arranged in the colorful harmonies of the Russian national school. His best work in this manner was an opera, *Almast*, the composition of which he undertook a decade before his death. It was completed and orchestrated by Maximilian Steinberg, and performed posthumously in Moscow on June 23, 1930. Other works were *The 3 Palm Trees*, symphonic tableau (1905), *Crimean Sketches* for Orch. (1903–12), *2 Songs of the Crimean Tatars* for Voice and Orch. (1915; Moscow, Dec. 25, 1927), and *Études d'Eriwan*, on Armenian melodies (1925). A complete ed. of his works was publ. in Yerevan (1943–71).

BIBL.: A. Shaverdian, *A. S.* (Moscow, 1929); G. Tigranov, *A. S.* (Yerevan, 1953); idem, *A. S.* (Moscow, 1959; second ed., 1971); R. Atadjan, *A. S.* (Yerevan, 1971).—NS/LK/DM

Sperontes (real name, **Johann Sigismund Scholze**), German poet and musical anthologist; b. Lobendau, Silesia, March 20, 1705; d. Leipzig, Sept. 27, 1750. He was educated in Liegnitz and then settled in Leipzig, where he was active as a poet and amateur musician. His most important work was the collection of strophic songs publ. as *Singende Muse an der Pleisse* (4 vols., Leipzig, 1736, 1742, 1743, 1745; ed. in Denkmäler Deutscher Tonkunst, XXXV-XXXVI, 1909). It contained 250 poems with 248 musical settings, the latter being almost wholly from pre-existing instrumental and vocal works adapted by Sperontes. Many of these songs were popular in his day, and several entered the standard repertoire.—NS/LK/DM

Sperry, Paul, American tenor; b. Chicago, April 14, 1934. He studied psychology at Harvard Univ., then attended the Sorbonne in Paris; returning to the U.S., he took courses at the Harvard Business School. He then decided upon a career in music, and proceeded to take vocal lessons from a number of coaches, among them Olga Ryss, Michael Trimble, Randolph Mickelson, Martial Singher, Pierre Bernac, Jennie Tourel, and Hans Hotter. He made his debut at Alice Tully Hall in N.Y. on Oct. 8, 1969, then toured throughout the U.S. and Europe. He became chiefly known for his performances of contemporary scores. From 1989 to 1992 he served as president of the American Music Center in N.Y. —NS/LK/DM

Speuy, Henderick (Joostzoon), Netherlands organist and compoer; b. Brielle, c. 1575; d. Dordrecht, Oct. 1, 1625. He settled in Dordrecht as organist of the Grote Kerk and the Augustijnen Kerk in 1595. He publ. a vol. of bicinia for organ or harpsichord as *De psalmen Davids, gestelt op het tabulatuer van het orghel ende claver-cymmel met 2. partijen* (Dordrecht, 1610; ed. by F. Noske, Amsterdam, 1962), which was formerly attributed to Sweelinck and publ. in that composer's collected works (Leipzig, 1899).—LK/DM

Speyer, Wilhelm, German violinist and composer; b. Frankfurt am Main, June 21, 1790; d. there, April 5, 1878. He studied in Offenbach with F. Fränzl (violin) and A. Andre (composition), and later in Paris with Baillot (violin). After extensive travels as a concert violinist, he returned to Frankfurt am Main and embraced a mercantile career, but continued his association with eminent musicians (Spohr, Mendelssohn, etc.) and began to compose. He wrote a great deal of chamber music; his violin pieces were often played, but he achieved lasting popularity with his ballads written in a characteristically Romantic style; of these, *Der Trompeter, Die drei Liebchen,* and *Rheinsehnsucht* were particularly famous. His son Edward (actually Eduard) Speyer (b. Frankfurt am Main, May 14, 1839; d. Shenley, Hertfordshire, Jan. 8, 1934) settled in England in 1859, where he organized the Classical Concerts Society; his second wife was the soprano Antonia Kufferath, whom he married in 1885.

BIBL.: E. Speyer, *W. S., der Liederkomponist* (Munich, 1925); idem, *My Life and Friends* (London, 1937).—NS/LK/DM

Spialek, Hans, Austrian-American orchestrator, arranger, and composer; b. Vienna, April 17, 1894; d. N.Y., Nov. 20, 1983. He took courses at the Vienna Cons. He was drafted into the Austrian army during World War I and taken prisoner by the Russians. In Russia his musical abilities were duly appreciated, and after the Russian Revolution he was given a job at the Bolshoi Theater in Moscow as asst. stage manager (1918–20); concurrently studied at the Cons. with Glière; later he conducted sym. orchs. in Bessarabia (1920–22). He married a Russian singer, Dora Boshoer. In 1923 he went to Germany, and in 1924 reached the U.S. He earned his living as a music copyist; he also supplied orch. interludes and entr'acte music, showing such expertise at organizing the raw materials of American musicals that even before he could master the American tongue he intuitively found the proper instrumentation for the text; and he could work fast to meet the deadlines. Altogether he orchestrated 147 shows, among them 5 by Cole Porter and 11 by Richard Rodgers and Lorenz Hart. With Robert Russell Bennett, he became one of the most reliable arrangers on Broadway. He also composed some orch. works in the approved Broadway style, with such idiosyncratic titles as *The Tall City* (1933) and *Manhattan Watercolors* (1937).—NS/LK/DM

Spice Girls, vocal pop stars of the late 1990s. MEMBERSHIP: Mel "Scary Spice" B. (real name, Melanie Janine Brown) (b. Leeds, England, May 29, 1975); Mel "Sporty Spice" C. (real name, Melanie Jayne Chisolm) (b. Liverpool, England, Jan. 12, 1974); Victoria "Posh Spice" Adams (b. Hertfordshire, England, April 17, 1975); Emma Lee "Baby Spice" Bunton (b. Barnet, England, Jan. 21, 1978); Geri "Ginger Spice" Halliwell (b. Hertfordshire, England, Aug. 18, 1970).

One of the most popular English exports since the Beatles, between 1996 and 1998 the Spice Girls became a pop culture phenomenon. Their images were on girls clothing, Christmas ornaments, and tons of licensed products. However, like many other pop phenomena, the group quickly faded.

The group's members had all been performing around London as singers or dancers since their pre-teens. They met at an audition, answering an ad for "lively girls for a pop act." When that didn't work out, they decided to form their own group and started writing pop ditties.

They took a house together in Berkshire and honed their act. Annie Lennox's manager Simon Fuller signed them and in turn got them a recording contract with Virgin. The band was heavily promoted in the press. Their slogan "Girl Power" appealed to pre-adolescent girls everywhere, as did their colorful costumes. Their debut single, 1996's "Wannabe," with its incredibly catchy rap chorus of "tell me what you want, what you really, really want" debuted at #1 in the English charts. They followed this with "Say You'll Be There." Their third single, "2 Become 1," topped the English charts over the 1997 New Year. A month later, they broke in the U.S. "Wannabe" reached #1 in just four weeks, and their eponymous debut zoomed to the top of the charts as well. They made their live debut before millions on *Saturday Night Live*. Soon, their videos were dominating MTV airplay.

The group followed their smash debut with a second album, *Spiceworld*, and the movie of the same name. Around this time they dumped their manager and decided to manage themselves. The movie *Spiceworld* opened to huge crowds over the 1998 New Year's holiday. The hit "Stop" reached #2 in the U.K., their first single to fall short of #1. In the spring of 1998, Halliwell left the group to go solo, under somewhat mysterious circumstances. Only one single, "Viva Forever" has emerged from the band in her wake. Mel B cut a duet with hip-hop star Missy "Misdemeanor" Elliot, "I Want You Back," which rocketed to the top of the U.K. charts. Halliwell's solo debut, *Schizophonic*, was released in 1999. The singles "Mi Chico Latino," "Bag It Up," and "Lit Me Up" topped the U.K. charts; however, these songs barely made a dent in the U.S.

Disc.: *Spice* (1996); *Spiceworld* (1997).—HB

Spiegel, Laurie, American composer, innovator in computer-music technology, computer artist, and writer; b. Chicago, Sept. 20, 1945. She taught herself mandolin, then guitar and banjo in her youth; majored in social sciences at Shimer Coll. in Mt. Carroll, Ill. (B.A., 1967), before switching to the lute and also studying composition with Michael Cjakowski, Persichetti, and Druckman at the Juilliard School in N.Y. (1969–72) and then at Brooklyn Coll. of the City Univ. of N.Y. (M.A., 1975), where she also studied American music with H. Wiley Hitchcock and Richard Crawford; received additional training in philosophy at the Univ. of Oxford, in classical guitar from John W. Duarte in London, in Renaissance and Baroque lute from Fritz Rikko, and in computer music from Emmanuel Ghent and Max Mathews at Bell Labs (1973–79). She taught composition and/or directed electronic-and-computer-music studios at Bucks County Comm. Coll. in Newton, Pa. (1971–75), Aspen (Colo.) Music School (summers, 1971–73), the Cooper Union for the Advancement of Science and Art in N.Y. (1979–81), and N.Y.U. (1982). Throughout the

1970s, she worked as a composer and music ed. for film and television and also created computer-generated visual art and computer-animation software based on her music software. She served as a consultant to firms involved in information- and signal-processing technology, being a designer of computer systems and software for musical composition and performance; her program *Music Mouse—An Intelligent Instrument* (1986) is widely known and used. In addition to her electronic and computer scores, she has composed works for traditional media. Her realization of Kepler's *Harmony of the Planets* was sent into space as the first cut in the recording *Sounds of Earth* on each of the 2 Voyager spacecrafts in 1977. Her articles on such topics as music and computers, software design and applications, analogies between the musical and visual arts, and music in the media have appeared in a variety of publications; in 1977–78 she served as co-ed. (with Beth Anderson) of *EAR* magazine, a monthly tabloid devoted to the promulgation of new musical ideas. Spiegel has most recently been associated with the revival of Romanticism, tonality, and folk modalities and with the development of visual music, interactive process composition, algorithmic composition, logic-based intelligent instruments, and the use of computers as a performance instruments, compositional tools, and means of distributing music.

WORKS: COMPUTER OR ELECTRONIC: *Orchestras* (1971); *A Tombeau* (1971); *Sojourn* (1971); *Before Completion* (1971); *Mines* (1971); *Harmonic Spheres* (1971); *Return to Zero* (1972); *Sediment* (1972); *Rāga* (1972); *Sunsets* (1973); *Introit* (1973); *2 Fanfares* (1973); *Purification* (1973); *Water Music* (1974); *A Meditation* (1974); *Appalachian Grove* (1974); *The Unquestioned Answer* (1974; also for Harp, 1981); *The Orient Express* (1974); *Pentachrome* (1974); *Patchwork* (1974; rev. 1976); *The Expanding Universe* (1975); *Drums* (1975); *Clockworks* (1975); *Voyages* (1976; rev. with video, 1978); *Music for a Garden of Electronic Delights* (1976); *A Folk Study* (1976); *Kepler's Harmony of the Planets* (1977); Concerto for Digital Synthesizer (1977); *5 Short Visits to Different Worlds* (1977); *An Acceleration* (1978); *Voices Within* (1979); *2 Nocturnes* (1980); *Modes* (1980); *A Quadruple Canon* (1980); *A Canon* (1980); *Phantoms* (1980); *Nomads* (1981); *A Harmonic Algorithm* (1981); *A Cosmos* (1982); *Progression* (1982); *Idea Pieces* (1983); *Harmonic Rhythm* (1983); *Immersion* (1983); *3 Modal Pieces* (1983); *Over Time* (1984); *Cavis Muris* (1986); *Passage* (1987). **OTHER:** *A Deploration* for Flute and Vibraphone (1970); *An Earlier Time* for Guitar (1972); *Waves*, dance piece (1975); *Music for Dance*, dance-video piece (1975); *East River*, dance piece (1976); *Escalante*, ballet (1977); *Evolutions*, music with video (1977); *A Living Painting*, silent visual study (1979); *Hearing Things* for Chamber Orch. (1983); *Over Time*, dance piece (1984); *A Stream* for Mandolin (1984); *Gravity's Joke*, dance piece (1985); *Rain Pieces*, dance suite (1985); *All Star Video*, music for videotape by Nam June Paik (1985); *Song without Words* for Guitar and Mandolin (1986); *Cavis Muris* (1986); *Passage* (1987); *A Harmonic Algorithm* (1988; from the projected *A Musical Offering*); *3 Sonic Spaces* (1989); *Returning East and After the Mountains* (N.Y., Oct. 10, 1990); *3 Movements* for Harpsichord (1990); also computer versions of pieces for Piano or Guitar; incidental music; film and video scores.—**NS/LK/DM**

Spiegelman, Joel (Warren), American pianist, harpsichordist, conductor, and composer; b. Buffalo, N.Y., Jan. 23, 1933. He studied at the Yale School of

Music (1949–50), the Univ. of Buffalo (B.A., 1953), the Longy School of Music at Cambridge, Mass. (1953–54), and Brandeis Univ., where he attended the classes of Shapero, Fine, and Berger (1954–56; 1960–61; M.F.A.); also studied with Boulanger privately in Paris and took courses at the Cons. there (1956–57). He taught at the Longy School of Music (1961–62), Brandeis Univ. (1961–66), and Sarah Lawrence Coll. (from 1966), where he was director of its Studio for Electronic Music and Sound Media. He made tours as a harpsichordist; was director of the N.Y. Electronic Ensemble (1970–73) and conductor of the Russian Orch. of the Americas (1976–79). His output as a composer reveals an eclectic bent.

WORKS: *Ouverture de Saison 1958* for 2 Harps, 2 Flutes, Piano, and Celesta (1958); *2 Fantasies* for String Quartet (1963, 1974); *Kusochki* (Morsels) for Piano, 4-Hands (1966); *3 Miniatures* for Clarinet and Piano (1972); *Chamber Music* for Piano Quartet and Percussion (1973); *Midnight Sun* for Oboe and Tape (1976); *A Cry, a Song, a Dance* for Strings (1978); *How Lovely is Thy Dwelling Place* for Bass, Chorus, and Organ (1982); *Astral Dimensions II—Metamorphosis* for Piano, Violin, and Cello (1983; rev. 1984); *Cicada Images: Moltings* for Soprano, Flute, Piano, Pipa, Erhu, and Percussion (1983).—**NS/LK/DM**

Spies, Claudio, Chilean-born American teacher, conductor, and composer; b. Santiago, March 26, 1925. He settled in the U.S. in 1942 and became a naturalized American citizen in 1966; in 1942 he entered the New England Cons. of Music in Boston and in 1943 became a pupil of Boulanger at the Longy School of Music in Cambridge, Mass.; received private instruction from Shapero (1944–45) and attended the conducting class at the Berkshire Music Center in Tanglewood (summer, 1946); pursued his musical training with Fine, Hindemith, Tillman Merritt, Piston, and Thompson at Harvard Univ. (A.B., 1950), completing his graduate studies there under Piston and Gombosi (M.A., 1954). He was an instructor at Harvard Univ. (1954–57) and a lecturer at Vassar Coll. (1957–58); was asst. prof. (1958–64), assoc. prof. (1964–69), and prof. (1969) at Swarthmore Coll., where he also conducted its orch. (1958–69); was visiting assoc. prof. at Princeton Univ. (1966–67), returning there as prof. in 1970. In 1950–51 he held a John Knowles Paine Traveling Fellowship and in 1956 received the Lili Boulanger Memorial Fund Award; also received the Brandeis Univ. Creative Arts Award (1967) and an NEA fellowship (1975).

WORKS: ORCH.: *Music for a Ballet* (1955); *Tempi* for 14 Instrumentalists (1962); *LXXXV, Eights and Fives* for Strings and Clarinets (1967). **CHAMBER:** *Canon* for 4 Flutes (1959); *Canon* for Violas (1961); *Viopiacem*, duo for Viola and Keyboard Instruments (1965); *Times 2* for Horns (1968); *Half-time* for Clarinet and Trumpet (1981); *Dreimal Sieben...* for Oboe and Piano (1991); *Insieme* for Flute and Violin (1994); *Beisammen* for 2 Oboes or English Horns (1994). **Piano:** *Impromptu* (1963); *Bagatelle* (1970); *A Between-Birthdays Bagatelle for Roger Sessions's 80th–81st* (1977); *Ein Aggregats- Walzer* (1978); *Bagatelle* (1979); *Verschieden* (1980); *Jahrhundertwalzer* (1981). **VOCAL:** *Il cantico de frate solo* for Bass and Orch. (1958); *Proverbs on Wisdom* for Men's Voices, Organ, and Piano (1964); *7 Enzensberger-Lieder* for Baritone, Clarinet, Horn, Cello, and Percussion (1972); *Rilke: Ruhmen* for Soprano, Clarinet, Trumpet, and Piano (1981); *7 Sonnets* for Soprano, Bass, Clarinet, Bass Clarinet, and String Trio (1989).—**NS/LK/DM**

Spies, Hermine, eminent German contralto; b. Lohneberger Hutte, near Weilburg, Feb. 25, 1857; d. Wiesbaden, Feb. 26, 1893. She was a pupil of Stockhausen in Frankfurt am Main, and in 1883 began to give song recitals in Germany. In 1889 she made an appearance in England with excellent success; also sang in Austria, Denmark, and Russia. She excelled as an interpreter of songs by Brahms, who had a high regard for her.

BIBL.: M. Spies, *H. S.: Ein Gedenkbuch für ihre Freunde* (Stuttgart, 1894).—**NS/LK/DM**

Spies, Leo, German conductor and composer; b. Moscow, June 4, 1899; d. Ahrenshoop an der Ostsee, May 1, 1965. He studied with Oskar von Riesemann (1913–15), then continued his training with Schreyer in Dresden and with Kahn and Humperdinck at the Berlin Hochschule für Musik (1916–17). He worked as a répétiteur and conductor in German theaters and with the Universum Film AG; then was in Berlin as conductor of the ballet at the State Opera (1928–35) and the Deutsche Opernhaus (1935–44); subsequently was director of studies and conductor at the Komische Oper (1947–54). In 1956 he was awarded the National Prize of the German Democratic Republic. His compositions followed Romantic lines.

WORKS: DRAMATIC: Ballet: *Apollo und Daphne* (1936); *Der Stralauer Fischzug* (1936); *Seefahrt* (1937); *Die Sonne lacht* (1942); *Pastorale* (1943); *Die Liebenden von Verona* (1944); *Don Quijote* (1944). **Other:** Incidental music. **ORCH.:** *Saltabile* for Strings (1929); Cello Concerto (1940); *Divertimento notturno* for Piano and Orch. (1941); *Fröhliche Ouvertüre* (1951); *Trauermusik* (1951); Violin Concerto (1953); *Orchesterfantasie "Friedrich Engels"* (1955); 2 syms. (1957, 1961); Viola Concerto (1961); *Festmusik* (1964). **CHAMBER:** 2 string quartets (1939, 1961); *Divertimento goldoniano* for 9 Instruments (1939); *Serenade* for 6 Winds, Harp, Percussion, and Double Bass (1946); Sonata for 3 Violins (1958); Trio for 2 Cellos and Piano (1959); 2 sonatas for Wind Quintet (1959, 1963); *Rustikale Fantasien* for 9 Instruments (1962); piano pieces, including 3 sonatas (1917, 1938, 1963). **VOCAL:** Cantatas; choruses; lieder; mass songs. —**NS/LK/DM**

Spiess, Ludovic, Romanian tenor; b. Cluj, May 13, 1938. He studied in Braşov, Bucharest, and with Antonio Narducci in Milan (1965–66). In 1962 he made his operatic debut as the Duke of Mantua in Galaţi. After singing at the Bucharest Operetta Theater (1962–64), he made his first appearance at the Bucharest Opera as Cavaradossi in 1964, where he subsequently sang regularly. In 1967 he made his debut at the Salzburg Festival as Dmitri in *Boris Godunov*. In 1968 he made his first appearances in Zürich as Radamès and at the Vienna State Opera as Dalibor. He sang Calaf at the Verona Arena in 1969. On June 3, 1971, he made his Metropolitan Opera debut in N.Y. as Manrico. He sang Radamès at his Covent Garden debut in London in 1973. He also appeared with many other opera houses in Europe and North and South America. Among his other roles were Florestan, Lohengrin, Otello, Don José, and Rodolfo. **—NS/LK/DM**

Spiess, Meinrad, German music theorist and composer; b. Honsolgen, Aug. 24, 1683; d. Irsee, June 12, 1761. In 1701 he entered the Irsee Benedictine abbey, where he was ordained a priest in 1708. After music training with Giuseppe Antonio Bernabei in Munich (1708–12), he returned to the abbey as music director (until 1749); later served as its prior. In 1743 he was made a member of Mizler's Societat der musikalischen Wissenschaften in Leipzig. He wrote mainly sacred music, much of which is lost. He remains best known for his treatise *Tractatus musicus compositorio-practicus. Das ist, musicalischer Tractat, in welchem alle gute und sichere Fundamenta zur musicalischen Composition aus denen alt- und neuesten besten Autoribus herausgezogen, zusammen getragen, gegen einander gehalten, erklaret, und mit untersetzten Exemplen dermassen klar und deutlich erläutert werden* (Augsburg, 1745).**—NS/LK/DM**

Spilka, František, Czech choral conductor, pedagogue, and composer; b. Štěken, Nov. 13, 1887; d. Prague, Oct. 20, 1960. He studied at the Prague Cons. with Stecker, Knittl, and Dvořák. In 1918 he was appointed administrative director of the Prague Cons. He established the Prague Teachers' Choral Society in 1908, of which he remained choirmaster until 1921, and gave concerts with it in France and England; later directed the Prague singing ensemble Smetana. Spilka developed, together with Ferdinand Vach, a new approach to choral performance, emphasizing sound color.

WORKS: DRAMATIC: Opera: *Stará práva* (Ancient Rights; 1915; Prague, June 10, 1917); *Cain or The Birth of Death* (1917). **ORCH.:** *Rhapsody* (1896); *Overture* (1897). **CHAMBER:** *6 Sonnets* for Violin and Piano (1944); *Rhapsodic Sonata* for Cello and Piano (1946); numerous piano pieces. **VOCAL:** *Jan Hus at the Stake,* oratorio (1907); *Miller's Journeyman,* cantata (1947); choruses; songs.**—NS/LK/DM**

Spinelli, Nicola, Italian pianist, conductor, and composer; b. Turin, July 29, 1865; d. Rome, Oct. 17, 1909. He studied with Sgambati in Rome and at the Naples Cons. under Serrao. In 1889 his opera *Labilia* took second prize in the famous competition instituted by the publisher Sonzogno, when Mascagni won the first prize with *Cavalleria rusticana;* Spinelli's opera was produced in Rome on May 7, 1890, with indifferent success. His next opera, *A basso porto,* was more fortunate; after its initial production in Cologne on April 18, 1894 (in a German version), it was staged in Rome, in Italian (March 11, 1895), and then in Budapest, St. Petersburg, etc.; it was also produced in the U.S. (St. Louis, Jan. 8, 1900; N.Y., Jan. 22, 1900). He toured widely as a pianist from 1889 to 1894. He was then active as a conductor until becoming mentally ill.**—NS/LK/DM**

Spink, Ian (Walter Alfred), noted English musicologist; b. London, March 29, 1932. He studied at London's Trinity Coll. of Music (B.Mus., 1952) and

pursued postgraduate studies at the Univ. of Birmingham (diss., 1957–58, *The English Declamatory Ayre, c. 1620–60*). He served as an overseas examiner for Trinity Coll. of Music (1958–60), then was senior lecturer at the Univ. of Sydney (1962–69); subsequently was head of the music dept. of Royal Holloway Coll. at the Univ. of London (from 1969), where he was a reader (1971–74) and a prof. (from 1974); also was dean of the Faculty of Arts (1973–75; 1983–85) and of the Faculty of Music (1974–78). A learned authority on English lute songs, he ed. the valuable collection English Songs, 1625–1660 for the Musica Britannica series, XXXIII (1971); also authored *An Historical Approach to Musical Form* (London, 1967) and *English Song: Dowland to Purcell* (London, 1974; rev. 1986), and ed. Vol. 3, *The Seventeenth Century,* in *The Blackwell History of Music in Britain* (1992). **—NS/LK/DM**

Spinner, Bob (actually, **Robert Channing**), American dulcimer player; b. Elk Rapids, Mich., Oct. 25, 1932; d. in an automobile accident near there, Oct. 1, 1990. He was born with perfect pitch and built his first hammer dulcimer at the age of 12; as a teen, was known as an exceptional player throughout northern Mich., one of the traditional homes of the instrument, where he performed at community venues. He played banjo, fiddle, piano, and the cymbalom, and performed Hungarian music on both the dulcimer and the cymbalom; played at the Ind. State Fair in 1952, whereupon he was invited to Ind. Univ. to assist with research and restoration of its dulcimer collection. He appeared on the recorded collection *The American Hammer Dulcimer* (1977) and was taped for the Univ. of Mich. video archive. Spinner was a mentor to numerous dulcimer players, among them Michael Masley, Thomas Bauer, and Paul Gifford; also was co-founder of the Everett Dulcimer Club. He owned more than 20 instruments; a favorite was an unusual and partly damaged instrument made by John Brown of Torch Lake Village in 1880, which went with him to his grave.**—NS/LK/DM**

Spinner, Leopold, Austrian composer; b. Lemberg (Galicia), April 26, 1906; d. London, Aug. 12, 1980. He studied at the Univ. of Vienna with Adler, von Ficker, and Lach (Ph.D., 1931, with the diss. *Das Rezitativ in der romantischen Oper bis Wagner*); also studied composition with Pisk (1930) and Webern (1935–38). He settled in London in 1938. He received the Hertzka Prize (1933) and the Henri-le-Boeuf Prize (1936) for his compositions. Most of his works are set in the serial mode. His paper "The Abolition of Thematicism" was publ. posthumously in *Tempo* (Sept. 1983).

WORKS: ORCH.: Sym. for Small Orch. (1933); *Passacaglia* for Winds and Piano Trio (1934; Brussels, April 29, 1936); Concerto for Piano and Chamber Orch. (1948; Paris, May 13, 1949); Violin Concerto (1955); *Concerto for Orchestra* (1957); *Ricercata* (1965); Chamber Sym. (1979; BBC, April 15, 1985). **CHAMBER:** 3 string quartets (1935, 1941, 1952); Violin Sonata (1936); Piano Quintet (1937); Piano Trio (1950); Suite for Clarinet and Piano (1956); Clarinet Sonata (1961); Quintet for Clarinet, Horn, Bassoon, Guitar, and Double Bass (1963). **Piano:** *Fantasy* (1954); *5 Inventions* (1958). **VOCAL:** *Die Sonne sinkt,* cantata (1952); *6 Canons on Irish Folk Songs* for Chorus (1963); many songs.**—NS/LK/DM**

Spinners, The, long-lived Detroit-based black vocal group. **MEMBERSHIP:** Robert Smith, lead and ten. voc. (b. Detroit, April 10, 1937); George W. Dixon, lead and ten. voc.; Billy Henderson, ten. voc. (b. Detroit, Aug. 9, 1939); Henry Fambrough, bar. voc. (b. Detroit, May 10, 1935); Pervis Jackson, bs. voc. (b. New Orleans, La., May 17, 1938). George Dixon was replaced in 1962 by Edgar "Chico" Edwards; Robert Smith was replaced by G. C. Cameron (b. Jackson, Miss.) in 1968, who was replaced in 1972 by Philippe Wynne (b. Detroit, April 3, 1941; d. Oakland, Calif., July 14, 1984), who was replaced by John Edwards (b. St. Louis, Mo., Dec. 25, 1944) in 1977.

The Spinners first recorded in 1961 for Harvey Fuqua's Tri-Phi label before moving with Fuqua to Motown Records, where they languished for seven years. Switching to Atlantic Records in 1972 at the urging of Aretha Franklin, the Spinners were teamed with Philadelphia songwriter-producer Thom Bell. They scored a succession of smooth soul ballad crossover hits such as "I'll Be Around," "Could It Be I'm Falling in Love," and "(One of a Kind) Love Affair," featuring the distinctive lead vocals of Philippe Wynne. Rivaling the O'Jays as America's most popular black vocal group of the era, the Spinners were introduced to the Nev. cabaret circuit by Dionne Warwick. After Wynne's departure in 1977, neither the group nor Wynne as a soloist fared very well, although remarkably the Spinners persevered with lead vocalist John Edwards into the 1990s without a personnel change.

The Spinners were initially formed around 1955 as an a cappella vocal group called the Domingos by five Detroit-area high school students: Robert Smith, George Dixon, Billy Henderson, Henry Fambrough, and Pervis Jackson. During the late 1950s they performed locally, changing their name to the Spinners in 1961. The group signed with former Moonglow Harvey Fuqua's Tri-Phi label, scoring a smash R&B and major pop hit with "That's What Girls Are Made For." They switched to Motown Records when Fuqua joined the company in 1964. After achieving a moderate pop and near-smash R&B hit with "I'll Always Love You" in 1965, they replaced Smith with G. C. Cameron in 1968 and recorded for Motown's subsidiary label V.I.P., hitting in 1970 with "It's a Shame," written and produced by Stevie Wonder.

Leaving Motown in 1972, the Spinners replaced Cameron with charismatic singer Philippe Wynne and signed to Atlantic Records with the help of Aretha Franklin. Placed with Philadelphia soul songwriter-arranger-producer Thom Bell, they soon scored a top R&B and a smash pop hit with "I'll Be Around" and "Could It Be I'm Falling In Love" and an R&B smash with "Ghetto Child," all from their debut album for the label. *Mighty Love* produced three major pop and smash R&B hits with "Mighty Love—Pt. 1," "I'm Coming Home," and "Love Don't Love Nobody—Pt. 1."

Becoming one of the most popular soul groups of the mid-1970s, the Spinners included the top pop and smash R&B hit "Then Came You," recorded with Dionne Warwick, on their album *New and Improved*, which also produced near-smash R&B hits with "Living a

Little, Laughing a Little" and "Sadie." *Pick of the Litter* yielded the top R&B and smash pop hit "They Just Can't Stop It (The Games People Play)" and an R&B near-smash with "Love or Leave." After a top R&B and smash pop hit with the disco-style "The Rubber Band Man" and the R&B smash "You're Throwing a Good Love Away," Philippe Wynne left the Spinners in 1977, to be replaced by John Edwards. Two years later producer-arranger Thom Bell also stopped working with the group. Still, the Spinners managed pop and R&B smashes with the oldies medleys "Working My Way Back to You"/"Forgive Me, Girl" and "Cupid"/"I've Loved You for a Long Time" in 1979–1980, though they never again achieved another major pop hit. Nonetheless, the Spinners remained intact into the 1990s, recording *Down to Business* for Volt in 1989.

Wynne's solo debut, *Starting All Over*, fared dismally, and he soon joined George Clinton's Parliament-Funkadelic aggregation, recording *Jammin'* for Clinton's Uncle Jam label in 1980. While performing at the Oakland, Calif., nightclub Ivey's on July 14, 1984, Philippe Wynne collapsed and died of a heart attack at age 43.

DISC.: THE SPINNERS: *The Original S.* (1968); *Second Time Around* (1970); *Best* (1973); *The S.* (1973); *Mighty Love* (1974); *New and Improved* (1974); *Pick of the Litter* (1975); *Live* (1975); *Happiness Is Being with the S.* (1976); *Yesterday, Today and Tomorrow* (1977); *8* (1977); *Best* (1978); *From Here to Eternally* (1979); *Dancin' and Lovin'* (1979); *Love Trippin'* (1980); *Can't Shake This Feelin'* (1981); *Grand Slam* (1983); *Cross Fire* (1984); *Lovin' Feelings* (1985); *A One of a Kind Love Affair—The Anthology* (1991); *Down to Business* (1989); *Very Best* (1993). **JOHN EDWARDS:** *Life, Love and Living* (1976). **PHILIPPE WYNNE:** *Starting All Over* (1977); *Jammin'* (1980).—**BH**

Spirit, American rock group. **MEMBERSHIP:** (from 1967 to 1971), Mark Andes, bs. (b. Philadelphia, Pa., Feb. 19, 1948), Randy California (Randy Craig Wolfe), gtr. (b. Los Angeles, Calif., Feb. 20, 1951; d. near Molokai, Hawaii, Jan. 2, 1997), Ed Cassidy, drm. (b. Chicago, Ill., May 4, 1923), Jay (John Arden) Ferguson, voc. (b. Burbank, Calif., May 10, 1947), John Locke, kybd. (b. Los Angeles, Calif., Sept. 25, 1943).

Spirit played an eclectic mixture of rock, jazz, and other forms of popular music on a series of critically acclaimed, moderate-selling singles and albums, including the Top 40 hit "I Got a Line on You" and the gold album *Twelve Dreams of Dr. Sardonicus*. After 1971 the group for the most part consisted of California, Cassidy, and various bassists, occasionally joined by other original members, and continued to record and to perform internationally until California's death.

California was the son of Bernice Pearl, whose brother ran the Ash Grove nightclub in Los Angeles. In the early 1960s, Cassidy, a veteran jazz drummer, played at the Ash Grove with his own group, The New Jazz Trio, which included Locke, and with the folk-rock group the Rising Sons, which included Ry Cooder and Taj Mahal. He married Pearl, becoming California's stepfather. He began sitting in with California's group, The Red Roosters, whose members included high school friends Andes and Ferguson, in 1965. In 1966, Cassidy, Pearl, and California moved to N.Y., where the 15-year-old California joined Jimi Hendrix's band Jimmy James and the Blue Flames, who were performing in Greenwich Village; Hendrix dubbed him Randy California to distinguish him from another Randy in the band. When he acquired a manager who wanted to take him to England, Hendrix asked California to come along, but his parents felt he was too young and refused permission.

Late in 1966, Cassidy, Pearl, and California returned to Los Angeles, where Cassidy and California resumed working with Locke under the name Spirits Rebellious, taken from a 1948 novel by Kahlil Gibran. By the spring of 1967, Andes and Ferguson had joined the group, whose name was shortened to Spirit. In August they signed to Ode Records, a start-up label founded by Lou Adler, previously the head of Dunhill Records and producer of The Mamas and the Papas; the label was distributed by Epic Records, a division of the major label CBS Records. Adler produced the group's debut album, *Spirit*, released in January 1968; it spent seven months in the charts, and a single, "Mechanical World" (music and lyrics by Mark Andes and Jay Ferguson), also charted.

Although the hybrid musical style of the first album was well received critically, the group tried for greater commercial appeal by releasing the hard- driving rock song "I Got a Line on You" (music and lyrics by Randy California) as a single in October 1968, in advance of their second album, *The Family That Plays Together*, which appeared in December. The single became a Top 40 hit, while the album spent more than four months in the charts. In January 1969 the group scored and appeared in director Jacques Demy's film *The Model Shop*. Their third album, *Clear*, was released in July and stayed in the charts three months.

Spirit tried to regain its commercial momentum with the release of the ominous "1984" (music and lyrics by Randy California) in December 1969, but although the single reached the charts, it did not become a substantial hit. Work on the fourth album was interrupted in April 1970 when California was injured in a riding accident. In the meantime, Adler parted ways with the group, whose contract was transferred to Epic, with David Briggs, known for his work with Neil Young, taking over as a producer. A new single, "Animal Zoo" (music and lyrics by Jay Ferguson), appeared in July and barely made the charts. The fourth album, *Twelve Dreams of Dr. Sardonicus*, finally appeared in November 1970 and spent three months in the charts while the group toured to promote it.

In June 1971, Andes and Ferguson announced that they were leaving Spirit to form a new group, Jo Jo Gunne, with Andes's brother Matt(hew) as guitarist and drummer Curley Smith. Jo Jo Gunne went on to release four albums on Asylum Records through 1974, the first of which, *Jo Jo Gunne* (1972), featured the Top 40 hit "Run Run Run" (music and lyrics by Jay Ferguson and Matthew Andes). California also left the group, moving to England and, despondent, attempting suicide. Cassidy and Locke added twin brothers guitarist Chris

(John Christian) and bassist Al Staehely and continued to perform as Spirit. This lineup recorded a new album for Epic, *Feedback*,which was released in February 1972 and spent three months in the charts. Cassidy and Locke then left Spirit, and the Staehely brothers briefly performed under the name.

Meanwhile, Spirit's record catalogue continued to be active. *Twelve Dreams of Dr. Sardonicus* sold steadily, finally going gold in 1976. Epic reissued *The Family That Plays Together* in mid-1972 and saw it return to the charts. In mid-1973 the label released a compilation, *The Best of Spirit*, that spent two and a half months in the charts, along with a charting single "Mr. Skin" (music and lyrics by Jay Ferguson), originally released on *Twelve Dreams of Dr. Sardonicus*; a two-disc reissue of the *Spirit* and *Clear* albums also reached the charts in 1973.

Randy California returned to action in November 1972, releasing a solo album, *Kapt. Kopter and the (Fabulous) Twirly Birds*, on Epic, with such sidemen as Cassidy, bassist Larry "Fuzzy" Knight, and, performing under a pseudonym for contractual reasons, former Jimi Hendrix Experience bassist Noel Redding. The album failed to chart, but California, Cassidy, and Knight began performing under the Kapt. Kopter name and recorded a follow-up album, originally titled *The Adventures of Kaptain Kopter & Commander Cassidy in Potatoland*, that Epic rejected. The trio did a European tour billed as Spirit, after which California retired to Hawaii and Cassidy assembled a new Spirit lineup for live performances.

In January 1974, California and Cassidy reunited and began to perform as Spirit with bassist Barry Keene. Signed to Mercury Records, they released the double album *Spirit of '76* in May 1975; it spent two months in the charts and was followed in October by *Son of Spirit*, which charted briefly. With the demise of Jo Jo Gunne, the Andes brothers joined Spirit, as did Locke, for a third Mercury album, *Farther Along*, released in June 1976, and even Ferguson turned up for a July 31, 1976, concert marking a full reunion of the original group. Nevertheless, *Farther Along* only charted for four weeks.

Mark Andes joined Firefall, later becoming a member of Heart; Locke also left, and Ferguson launched a solo career, hitting the Top Ten in 1978 with "Thunder Island" (music and lyrics by Jay Ferguson). California and Cassidy continued to work as Spirit, releasing *Future Games* (January 1977), which reached the charts.

Spirit formed its own Potato Records label to release *Live* in 1979, and Rhino Records belatedly released *Potatoland* in 1981; it reached the British charts. California worked largely as a solo act in the early 1980s, but in early 1984 the original lineup of Spirit reunited to record *Spirit of '84*, consisting largely of remakes of their old songs, for Mercury; the album did not chart. The Spirit album *Rapture in the Chambers*, released by I.R.S. Records in 1989, credited California, Cassidy, and Locke as group members and Mark Andes as a guest artist. *Tent of Miracles*, released by the Dolphin Record Group in 1990, featured California, Cassidy, and Mike Nile. *Chronicles, 1967–92*, was released on the group's own W.E.R.C. C.R.E.W. label and featured recordings from their original demo tape as well as later material. The new *California Blues* album was ready for release when California accidentally drowned in 1997 at the age of 45.

DISC.: *Spirit* (1968); *The Family That Plays Together* (1969); *Clear Spirit* (1969); *Twelve Dreams of Dr. Sardonicus* (1970); *Feedback* (1972); *Farther Along* (1976); *Future Games* (1977); *Live Spirit* (1978); *Journey to Potatoland* (1981); *Spirit of '84* (1984); *Rapture in the Chamber* (1988); *Tent of Miracles* (1990); *Time Circle (1968–72)* (1991).—**WR**

Spisak, Michal, eminent Polish composer; b. Dabrowa Górnicza, Sept. 14, 1914; d. Paris, Jan. 29, 1965. He studied violin and composition at the Katowice Cons. (diplomas in both, 1937), and composition with Sikorski in Warsaw (1935–37). He completed his training with Boulanger in Paris, where he lived for the rest of his life although he continued to be closely associated with his homeland. In 1964 he was awarded the Polish Composers' Union Prize. He was greatly influenced by Boulanger and by the music of Stravinsky.

WORKS: DRAMATIC: O p e r a : *Marynka* (1955). **ORCH.:** *Serenade* (1939); Concertino for Strings (1942); *Aubade* for Small Orch. (1943); *Allegro de Voiron* (1943); Bassoon Concerto (1944; Copenhagen, June 2, 1947); *Toccata* (1944); *Suite* for Strings (1945); Piano Concerto (1947); *2 Symphonies concertante* (1947, 1956); *Etudes* for Strings (1948); *Divertimento* for 2 Pianos and Orch. (1948); Sonata for Violin and Orch. (1950); Trombone Concertino (1951); *Divertimento* (1951); *Andante and Allegro* for Violin and Orch. (1954); *Concerto giocoso* for Chamber Orch. (1957); Oboe Concerto (1962); Violin Concerto (Katowice, Jan. 30, 1976). **CHAMBER:** Quartet for Oboe, 2 Clarinets, and Bassoon (1938); Sonatina for Oboe, Clarinet, and Bassoon (1946); Violin Sonata (1946); Wind Quintet (1948); *Duetto concertante* for Viola and Bassoon (1949); String Quartet (1953); *Suite* for 2 Violins (1957); *Improvvisazione* for Violin and Piano (1962). **P i a n o :** Concerto for 2 Solo Pianos (1942); other pieces. **VOCAL:** Choruses; songs.—**NS/LK/DM**

Spitta, (Julius August) Philipp, eminent German music scholar; b. Wechold, near Hoya, Dec. 27, 1841; d. Berlin, April 13, 1894. He studied piano, organ, and composition in his youth, and in 1860 entered the Univ. of Göttingen as a student of theology, where he later studied classical philology (Ph.D., 1864). He taught Greek and Latin at Reval's Ritter und Domschule (1864–66), at Sondershausen's Gymnasium (1866–74), and at Leipzig's Nikolai-Gymnasium (1874–75), where he was co-founder of the Bach-Verein (1874). In 1875 he settled in Berlin as prof. of music history at the Univ., life-secretary to the Royal Academy of Arts, and a teacher at, and vice-director of, the Hochschule für Musik. As a teacher, he had extraordinary success; among his pupils were O. Fleischer, A. Sandberger, M. Freidlaender, R. Schwartz, M. Seiffert, E. Vogel, K. Krebs, J. Combarieu, and J. Wolf. He was one of the leading spirits in organizing the publication of Denkmäler Deutscher Tonkunst in 1885. With Chrysander and G. Adler, he founded the journal *Vierteljahrsschrift für Musikwissenschaft* in 1884; also contributed to various other journals. He ed. Buxtehude's organ works (2 vols., 1875–76) and the complete works of Schutz (16 vols., 1885–94; supp. vols., 1909, 1927).

WRITINGS: *Ein Lebensbild Robert Schumanns* (Leipzig, 1862); *Johann Sebastian Bach* (2 vols., Leipzig, 1873–80; Eng. tr. by

C. Bell and J. Fuller Maitland, with many additions, 3 vols., London, 1884–85; second ed., 1899; reprint, 2 vols., N.Y., 1951); *Zur Musik* (Berlin, 1892; essays); *Musikgeschichtliche Aufsätze* (Berlin, 1894; collected essays).

BIBL.: H. Riemann, *P. S. und seine Bach-Biographie* (Berlin, 1900); U. Schilling, *P. S.: Leben und Wirken im Spiegel seiner Briefwechsel: Mit einem Inventar des Naclasses und einer Bibliographie der edruckten Werke* (Kassel, 1994); W. Sandberger, *Das Bach-Bild P. S.s: Ein Beitrag zur Geschichte der Bach-Rezeption im 19. Jahrhundert* (Stuttgart, 1997).—**NS/LK/DM**

Spitzmüller (-Harmersbach), Alexander, Freiherr von, Austrian composer; b. Vienna, Feb. 22, 1894; d. Paris, Nov. 12, 1962. His father was the last finance minister of Austria-Hungary. He studied law at the Univ. of Vienna (D.Jur., 1919); later took lessons in composition with Alban Berg and Hans Apostel. In 1928 he went to Paris, where he taught at the Schola Cantorum; also was active in radio broadcasting and as a music critic. In 1959 he was awarded the music prize of the city of Vienna. His early works are in the neo-Classical vein; eventually he followed the method of composition with 12 tones, following its usage by Berg and Webern.

WORKS: DRAMATIC: O p e r a : *Der Diener zweier Herren* (1958). **B a l l e t :** *Le premier amour de Don Juan* (1954); *L'impasse* (1956); *Die Sackgasse* (1957); *Le journal* (1957); *Construction humaine* (1959). **ORCH.:** *Sinfonietta ritmica* (1933); 2 piano concertos (1937, 1953); Sym. (1939); *Der 40. Mai*, suite for Chamber Orch. (1941; Amsterdam, June 12, 1948); *3 hymnes à la Paix* (1947); Sym. for Strings (1954). **OTHER:** Chamber music; choral works.—**NS/LK/DM**

Spivacke, Harold, eminent American musicologist and librarian; b. N.Y., July 18, 1904; d. Washington, D.C., May 9, 1977. He studied at N.Y.U. (B.A., 1923; M.A., 1924) and at the Univ. of Berlin (Ph.D., 1933, with the diss. *Über die objektive und subjektive Tonintensität*); while in Berlin, he took private lessons with d'Albert and Leichtentritt as an American-German Students Exchange Fellow and an Alexander von Humboldt Stiftung Fellow. Returning to the U.S., he joined the staff of the Music Division of the Library of Congress in Washington, D.C., first as asst. chief (1934–37), then as chief (1937–72). He also held numerous advisory positions with the Dept. of State, UNESCO et al. As chief of the Music Division of the Library of Congress, he was responsible for the acquisition of many important MSS by contemporary composers, including a large collection of Schoenberg's original MSS. He also commissioned works from contemporary composers for the Coolidge Foundation at the Library of Congress. He publ. some valuable bibliographical papers, among them *Paganiniana* (Washington, D.C., 1945). In 1939 he was chairman of the Organizing Committee of the National Music Council, and until 1972 was Archivist and a member of the Executive Committee of the Council.—**NS/LK/DM**

Spivak, Charlie (actually, **Charles**), popular jazz trumpeter, leader; b. Kiev, Ukraine, Feb. 17, 1907; d. Greenville, S.C., March 1, 1982. Spivak was brought to the U.S. as an infant and raised in New Haven, Conn. He began on trumpet at the age of 10, and played in the Hill House H.S. Band. After gigging with the local Paragon Band, he joined Don Cavallaro's Orch. He worked mainly with Paul Specht from summer of 1924 until 1930, then with Ben Pollack (1931–34), and with the Dorsey Brothers from late 1934 until spring 1935, when he joined Ray Noble. Spivak did two years' studio work (including a spell with Raymond Scott's Radio Band), then worked with Bob Crosby from January until August 1938. He was with Tommy Dorsey from August 1938 until c. June 1939, then left to work as a trumpeter/straw boss with Jack Teagarden's Band. In November 1939, Spivak left to form his own band, which made its debut in St. Paul with backing from Glenn Miller. They disbanded a year or so later, and Spivak subsequently took over Bill Downer's Band. With this new line-up, he gradually established the band as one of the major commercial successes of the 1940s, featured in many films. He had hits through that decade with arrangements by Sonny Burke, Jimmy Mundy, and Nelson Riddle. The vocal group The Stardusters were part of his unit, and soloists included Dave Tough and Willie Smith. Spivak moved to Fla. in the 1950s, and continued to lead a band until suffering a serious illness in 1963. Once recovered, he led a bands in Las Vegas and Miami. In late 1960s, he settled in Greenville, S.C., where he continued to lead a band at local clubs through the mid-1970s.

Disc.: *Uncollected Charlie Spivak & His Band* (1943); *For Sentimental Reasons* (1947).

Bibl.: C. Garrod, *Charlie Spivak and His Orch.* (Spotswood, N.J.).—JC/MM/LP

Spivakov, Vladimir, notable Russian violinist and conductor; b. Ufa, Sept. 12, 1944. He studied violin with Veniamin Sher at the music school of the Leningrad Cons. (1956–60) and with Yankelevich at the Moscow Cons. (graduated, 1967). He also received training in conducting. After taking prizes in the Long-Thibaud (Paris, third, 1965), Paganini (Genoa, second, 1967), Montreal (first, 1969), and Tchaikovsky (Moscow, second, 1970) competitions, he toured widely as a violin virtuoso. On Feb. 2, 1975, he made his N.Y. debut, and in 1977 he played in London. In 1979 he made his debut as a conductor with the Chicago Sym. Orch. at the Ravinia Festival. That same year, he founded the Moscow Virtuosi, a chamber orch. with which he served as principal soloist, artistic director, and conductor. He led it on many tours abroad and in various recordings. From 1989 he also was artistic director of the Colmar International Festival in France, and from 1999 music director of the Russian National Orch. in Moscow. —NS/LK/DM

Spivakovsky, Tossy, outstanding Russian-American violinist; b. Odessa, Feb. 4, 1907. He studied with Arrigo Serato and Willy Hess at the Berlin Hochschule für Musik. He made his concert debut there at the age of 10; toured Europe (1920–33) and Australia (1933–39). In 1940 he settled in the U.S. and made his N.Y. debut that same year at N.Y.'s Town Hall; then appeared with major American orchs. He taught at the Juilliard School in N.Y. (from 1974). A brilliant virtuoso, his repertory ranged from the classics to contemporary works. As a teacher, he advocated new bowing techniques that proved controversial.

Bibl.: G. Yost, *The S. Way of Bowing* (Pittsburgh, 1949). —NS/LK/DM

Spivey, Victoria (Regina; aka **"Queen Victoria"),** blues vocalist, pianist, organist, ukulele player, songwriter; b. Houston, Tex., Oct. 15, 1906; d. N.Y., Oct. 3, 1976. Raised in Dallas; one of eight children. Spivey played piano at a local theatre from the age of 12, then made her record debut in St. Louis in 1926 (singing her own composition, "Black Snake Blues"). During the following year, she was featured at the Lincoln Theatre, N.Y., then gained an important role in the film *Hallelujah*. She made many recordings during the 1920s and 1930s, accompanied by Louis Armstrong, Henry Allen, Lee Collins, Lonnie Johnson, and other jazz musicians. During the early 1930s, she directed Lloyd Hunter's Serenaders and was featured for a while with Jap Allen's Band, then worked as a solo artist before forming a successful duo with dancer Billy Adams (who was at that time her husband; Spivey had previously been married to trumpeter Reuben Floyd). They toured with Olsen and Johnson's "Hellzapoppin'" show in the late 1940s, and also guested with Henry Allen at The Stuyvesant Casino in 1950. In 1952 she left full-time music and worked for a while as a church administrator. She returned to prominence in the late 1950s, recording and performing mostly on the folk/"blues revival" circuit. She formed her own Spivey Records Company, and issued many albums featuring herself and her contemporaries (and even used a young Bob Dylan as a session harmonica player on some tracks; a photo of the two together appeared on the back of Dylan's *New Morning* album). She continued to perform until shortly before her death.—JC/LP

Spohr, Louis (actually, **Ludewig**), celebrated German violinist, composer, and conductor; b. Braunschweig, April 5, 1784; d. Kassel, Oct. 22, 1859. His name is entered in the church registry as Ludewig, but he used the French equivalent, Louis. The family moved to Seesen in 1786; his father, a physician, played the flute, and his mother was an amateur singer and pianist. Spohr began violin lessons at the age of 5 with J.A. Riemenschneider and Dufour, a French émigré. In 1791 he returned to Braunschweig, where he studied with the organist Carl August Hartung and the violinist Charles Louis Maucourt; also composed several violin pieces. Duke Carl Wilhelm Ferdinand admitted him to the ducal orch. and arranged for his further study with the violinist Franz Eck. In 1802 Eck took him on a tour to Russia, where he met Clementi and Field; returned to Braunschweig in 1803 and resumed his post in the ducal orch. The violin technique and compositional traits of Pierre Rode, whom Spohr met on his return, were major influences on both his compositions and his violin technique. In 1804 Spohr made his first official tour as a violinist to Hamburg (his first actual tour to Hamburg in 1799 proved a failure, and a second, early in 1804, was aborted when his Guarnerius violin was stolen); gave concerts in Berlin, Leipzig, and Dresden. In 1805 he became concertmaster in the ducal orch. at Gotha. On Feb. 2, 1806, he married the harpist Dorette (Dorothea) Scheidler (1787–1834); wrote many works for violin and harp for them to perform together, and also toured with her in Germany (1807). His reputation as a virtuoso established, he began writing compositions in every genre, all of which obtained excellent success. In 1812 he gave a series of concerts in Vienna and was acclaimed both as a composer and as a violinist; was concertmaster in the orch. of the Theater an der Wien until 1815. He then made a grand tour of Germany and Italy, where Paganini heard him in Venice. In 1816 Spohr's opera *Faust*, skillfully employing many devices that foreshadowed developments in later German operas, was performed by Weber in Prague. After a visit to Holland in 1817, he became Kapellmeister of the Frankfurt am Main Opera, where he produced one of his most popular operas, *Zemire und Azor*. In 1820 he and his wife visited England and appeared at several concerts of the London Phil. Soc.; this was the first of his 6 visits to England, where he acquired an immense reputation as a violinist, composer, and conductor; his works continued to be performed there long after his death. On his return trip to Germany, he presented concerts in Paris; his reception there, however, failed to match his London successes, and he proceeded to Dresden, where Weber recommended him for the Kapellmeistership at the court in Kassel; attracted by the lifetime contract, Spohr accepted the post and settled there in 1822, producing his operatic masterpiece, *Jessonda*, which remained popular throughout the rest of the 19th century, in 1823. Following this success were performances of his oratorio *Die letzten Dinge* (1826) and his fourth Sym., *Die Weihe der Töne* (1832), both of which elicited great praise. The *Violinschule*, a set of 66 studies covering every aspect of his violin style, was publ. in 1831. Spohr's wife died on Nov. 20, 1834, and on Jan. 3, 1836, he married the pianist Marianne Pfeiffer, the sister of his friend Carl Pfeiffer, librettist of *Der Alchymist*. In 1837 Spohr began having difficulties with the Electoral Prince of Kassel, who caused the cancellation of a festival in Kassel and forbade Spohr from making a trip to Prague, which the composer made nevertheless to conduct *Der Berggeist*; on his return, he visited Mozart's widow and birthplace in Salzburg. He traveled to England in 1839 for the Norwich Festival, but could not obtain permission from the Prince to return for the performance of his Fall of Babylon in 1842. In 1841, returning from the Lucerne Festival, he received the suggestion from his wife to use 2 orchs. for his 7th Sym. in 3 parts, portraying the mundane and divine elements in life. In 1843, in England, his success was so great that a special concert was given by royal command; it was the first time a reigning English monarch attended a Phil. Concert. In 1844 he received the silver medal from the Société des Concerts in Paris, and a festival honoring him was held in Braunschweig. Spohr never visited the U.S., in spite of the fact that his daughter lived in N.Y. and an invitation to hold a festival in his honor was issued. In 1845 he received a golden wreath from the Berlin Royal

Opera. In 1847 he visited England for the third time, then went to Frankfurt am Main for the German National Assembly. Returning to Kassel, he found himself in an increasingly difficult position because of his dissident political views. The Elector of Hesse refused him further leaves of absence, but Spohr ignored the ban, traveling to Switzerland and Italy. In the litigation that followed with the Kassel court, Spohr was ordered to forfeit part of his yearly income. He was retired from Kassel on Nov. 22, 1857, on a pension despite his lifetime contract. In 1853 he appeared at the New Phil. Concerts in London. Although he fractured his left arm in a fall on Dec. 27, 1857, he conducted *Jessonda* in Prague in July 1858. He conducted his last performance in Meiningen (1859).

Spohr's compositional style was characteristic of the transition period between Classicism and Romanticism. He was technically a master; while some of his works demonstrate a spirit of bold experimentation. In his aesthetics he was an intransigent conservative. He admired Beethoven's early works but confessed total inability to understand those of his last period; he also failed to appreciate Weber. It is remarkable, therefore, that he was an early champion of Wagner; in Kassel he produced *Der fliegende Holländer* (1843) and *Tannhäuser* (1853), despite strenuous opposition from the court. He was a highly esteemed teacher, numbering among his students Ferdinand David and Moritz Hauptmann. His memoirs were publ. posthumously as *Louis Spohrs Selbstbiographie* (2 vols., Kassel, 1860–61; abr. version in Eng., London, 1865, 1878, and 1969; different tr. by H. Pleasants as *The Musical Journeys of Louis Spohr*, Norman, Okla., 1961). A new ed., edited by F. Göthel using the autograph, was publ. as *Lebenserinnerungen* (Tutzing, 1968). The Spohr Soc. was founded in Kassel in 1908, disbanded in 1934, and revived in 1952. A new ed. of his works, *Neue Auswahl der Werke*, edited by F. Göthel, was begun in 1963 (Kassel, Verlag der Spohr-Gesellschaft). A *Thematisch-bibliographisches Verzeichnis der Werke von Louis Spohr*, compiled by F. Göthel, was publ. in Tutzing in 1981.

WORKS: DRAMATIC (all first perf. in Kassel unless otherwise given): **Opera:** *Die Prüfung* (1806); *Alruna, die Eulenkönigin* (1808); *Der Zweikampf mit der Geliebten* (Hamburg, Nov. 15, 1811); *Faust* (1813; Prague, Sept. 1, 1816; rev. 1852; London, July 15, 1852); *Zemire und Azor* (Frankfurt am Main, April 4, 1819); *Jessonda* (July 28, 1823); *Der Berggeist* (March 24, 1825); *Pietro von Abano* (Oct. 13, 1827); *Der Alchymist* (July 28, 1830); *Die Kreuzfahrer* (Jan. 1, 1845). **Oratorios:** *Das jüngste Gericht* (Erfurt, Aug. 15, 1812); *Die letzten Dinge* (March 25, 1826); *Des Heilands letzte Stunden* (Easter 1835); *Der Fall Babylons* (Norwich Festival, Sept. 14, 1842). **ORCH.: 10 Syms.:** No. 1 (Leipzig, June 11, 1811), No. 2 (London, April 10, 1820), No. 3 (Kassel, April 6, 1828), No. 4, *Die Weihe der Töne* (London, Feb. 23, 1835), No. 5 (Vienna, March 1, 1838), No. 6, *Historische Symphonie* (London, April 6, 1840), No. 7, *Irdisches und Gottliches im Menschenleben* (London, May 30, 1842), No. 8 (Kassel, Dec. 22, 1857), No. 9, *Die Jahreszeiten* (London, Nov. 25, 1850), and No. 10 (1847). **Overtures:** C minor (1807); F major (1820); Macbeth (1825); *Die Tochter der Luft*, phantasie in the form of an overture (1836); *Der Matrose* (1838); Concert Overture "im ernsten Styl" (1842). **S o l o   I n s t r u m e n t s   a n d   O r c h .:** 18 violin concertos (c. 1799–1844); Concerto for String Quartet (1845); 4 clarinet concertos; 2 Concertantes for 2 Violins; 2 Concertantes for Harp and Violin. **CHAMBER:** Nonet (1814); Octet (1815); 4 double quartets for Strings; Septet (1854); Sextet (1848); 7 string quintets; Piano Quintet; Quintet for Piano and Winds; 34 string quartets; 5 piano trios; 14 duets for 2 Violins; 3 duets for Piano and Violin; 3 sonatas for Harp and Violin; Piano Sonata; etc. **VOCAL:** *Das befreite Deutschland*, dramatic cantata (Frankenhausen, Oct. 1815); Mass for Double 5-part Chorus; 6 Psalms; Requiem (unfinished); hymns; partsongs; 7 duets; 64 songs; *An sie am Klavier*, sonatina for Voice and Piano (1848).

BIBL.: W. Neumann, *L. S.* (Kassel, 1854); H. Giehne, *Zur Erinnerung an L. S.* (Karlsruhe, 1860); A. Malibran, *L. S.* (Frankfurt am Main, 1860); L. Stierlin, *L. S.* (2 vols., Zürich, 1862–63); M. Hauptmann, *Briefe von M. Hauptmann an L. S. und andere* (Leipzig, 1876; Eng. tr., London, 1892); H. Schletterer, *L. S.* (Leipzig, 1881); L. Nohl, *S.* (Leipzig, 1882); C. Robert, *L. S.* (Berlin, 1883); R. Wassermann, *L. S. als Opernkomponist* (diss., Univ. of Rostock, 1910); H. Glenewinckel, *L. S. Kammermusik für Streichinstrumente* (diss., Univ. of Munich, 1912); F. Göthel, *Das Violinspiel L. S.s* (diss., Univ. of Berlin, 1934); E. von Salburg, *L. S.* (Leipzig, 1936); H. Heussner, *Die Symphonien L. S.s* (diss., Univ. of Marburg, 1956); F. Göthel, *L. S.: Briefwechsel mit seiner Frau Dorette* (Kassel, 1957); D. Mayer, *The Forgotten Master: The Life and Times of L. S.* (London, 1959); D. Greiner, *L. S. Beitrage zur deutschen romantischen Oper* (diss., Univ. of Kiel, 1960); H. Homburg, *L. S.: Bilder und Dokumente seiner Zeit* (Kassel, 1968); S. Johnston, *The Clarinet Concertos of L. S.* (diss., Univ. of Md., 1972); C. Brown, *The Popularity and Influence of S. in England* (diss., Oxford Univ., 1980); P. Katow, *L. S.: Persönlichkeit und Werk* (Luxembourg, 1983); C. Brown, *L. S.: A Critical Biography* (Cambridge, 1984); H. Peters, *Der Komponist, Geiger, Dirigent und Pädagoge L. S. (1784–1859) mit einer Auswahlbibliographie zu Leben und Schaffen* (Braunschweig, 1987); P. Autexier, *La lyre maconne: Haydn, Mozart, S., Liszt* (Paris, 1997).—**NS/LK/DM**

Spontini, Gaspare (Luigi Pacifico), significant Italian opera composer; b. Majolati, Ancona, Nov. 14, 1774; d. there, Jan. 24, 1851. His father, a modest farmer, intended him for the church and gave him into the charge of an uncle, a priest at Jesi, who attempted to stifle his musical aspirations. Spontini sought refuge at Monte San Vito with another relative, who not only found a competent music teacher for him, but effected a reconciliation so that, after a year, he was able to return to Jesi. In 1793 he entered the Cons. della Pietà de' Turchini in Naples, where his teachers were Tritto (singing) and Sala (composition). When he failed to obtain the position of maestrino there in 1795, he quit the Cons. without permission. He rapidly mastered the conventional Italian style of his time; some of his church music performed in Naples came to the attention of a director of the Teatro della Pallacorda in Rome, who commissioned him to write an opera. This was *Li puntigli delle donne*, produced during Carnival in 1796. He served as maestro di cappella at Naples's Teatro del Fondo during Carnival in 1800, and that same year went to Palermo to produce 3 operas. Returning to the mainland in 1801, he produced operas for Rome and Venice before going to Paris in 1803. After eking out an existence as a singing teacher, he found a patron in Joséphine. He first gained success as a composer in Paris with a revised version of his *La finta filosofa* (Feb. 11, 1804); it was followed by *La Petite Maison* (May 12, 1804), which proved unsuccessful. All the same, the poet Etienne de Jouy now approached Spontini to write the music to his libretto *La Vestale*, a task previously turned down by Boieldieu, Cherubini, and Méhul. In the meantime, Spontini brought out 2 more operas without much success: *Milton* (Nov. 27, 1804) and *Julie, ou Le Pot de fleurs* (March 12, 1805). However, he won appointment as composer of Joséphine's private music in 1805; for her he wrote several occasional pieces, including the cantata *L'eccelsa gara* (Feb. 8, 1806), celebrating the battle of Austerlitz. Thanks to Josephine's patronage, *La Vestale* won a triumphant success at its premiere on Dec. 15, 1807, in spite of virulent opposition. Spontini's next opera, *Fernand Cortez* (Nov. 28, 1809), failed to equal his previous success, although the second version (May 8, 1817) won it a place in the repertoire. In 1810 he was awarded the prix décennal for having composed the finest grand opera of the preceding decade; that same year he married Céleste Erard, daughter of Jean-Baptiste Erard, and accepted the post of director of the Théâtre-Italien. Although his artistic policies were successful, his personality clashed with those of his superiors and he was dismissed in 1812. On Aug. 23, 1814, his opera *Pélage, ou Le Roi et la paix*, celebrating the Restoration, was successfully produced. The following month he was named director of Louis XVIII's private music and of the Théâtre-Italien, although soon after he sold his privilege to the latter to Catalani. Having become a favorite of the Bourbons, he was made a French citizen by the king in 1817 and was granted a pension in 1818. In spite of his favored position, his grand opera *Olimpie* proved a dismal failure at its premiere on Dec. 22, 1819. The next year he went to Berlin as Generalmusikdirektor, scoring an initial success with the revised version of *Olimpie* on May 14, 1821. However, his position of eminence quickly waned. He had been placed on an equality with the Intendant of the Royal Theater, and there were frequent misunderstandings and sharp clashes of authority, not mitigated by Spontini's jealousies and dislikes, his overweening self-conceit, and his despotic temper. Partly through intrigue, partly by reason of his own lack of self-control, he was formally charged in criminal court with lèse-majesté in Jan. 1841. On April 2, 1841, while he was conducting the overture to *Don Giovanni*, a riot ensued and Spontini was compelled to leave the hall in disgrace. In July 1841 he was sentenced to 9 months in prison, and soon thereafter was dismissed as Generalmusikdirektor by the king, although he was allowed to retain his title and salary. In May 1842 his sentence was upheld by an appeals court, but the king pardoned him that same month. He then went to Paris, where illness and growing deafness overtook him. In 1844 he was raised to the papal nobility as the Conte di San Andrea. In 1850 he retired to his birthplace to die. Spontini's importance to the lyric theater rests upon his effective blending of Italian and French elements in his serious operas, most notably in *La Vestale* and *Fernand Cortez*. His influence on Berlioz was particularly notable.

WORKS: DRAMATIC: Opera: *Li puntigli delle donne,* farsetta (Rome, Carnival 1796); *Il finto pittore* (Rome?, 1797 or 1798); *Adelina Senese, o sia L'amore secreto,* dramma giocoso (Venice, Oct. 10, 1797); *L'eroismo ridicolo,* farsa (Naples, Carnival 1798); *Il Teseo riconosciuto,* dramma per musica (Florence, 1798); *La finta filosofa,* commedia per musica (Naples, 1799; rev. as a dramma giocoso per musica, Paris, Feb. 11, 1804); *La fuga in maschera,* commedia per musica (Naples, Carnival 1800); *I quadri parlante,* melodramma buffo (Palermo, 1800); *Gli Elisi delusi,* melodramma serio (Palermo, Aug. 26, 1800); *Gli amanti in cimento, o sia Il Geloso audace,* dramma giocoso (Rome, Nov. 3, 1801); *Le metamorfosi di Pasquale, o sia Tutto è illusione nel mondo,* farsa giocosa (Venice, Carnival 1802); *La Petite Maison,* opéra-comique (Paris, May 12, 1804); *Milton,* opéra-comique (Paris, Nov. 27, 1804); *Julie, ou Le Pot de fleurs,* opéra-comique (Paris, March 12, 1805); *La Vestale,* tragédie-lyrique (Paris, Dec. 15, 1807); *Fernand Cortez, ou La Conquète du Mexique,* tragédie-lyrique (Paris, Nov. 28, 1809; second version, Paris, May 8, 1817; third version, Berlin, Feb. 1832); *Pélage, ou Le Roi et la paix,* opera (Paris, Aug. 23, 1814); *Les Dieux rivaux ou Les Fêtes de Cythère,* opéra-ballet (Paris, June 21, 1816; in collaboration with Kreutzer, Persuis, and Berton); *Olimpie,* tragédie-lyrique (Paris, Dec. 22, 1819; rev. as a grosse Oper, Berlin, May 14, 1821); *Nurmahal, oder Das Rosenfest von Caschmir,* lyrisches Drama (Berlin, May 27, 1822); *Alcidor,* Zauberoper (Berlin, May 23, 1825); *Agnes von Hohenstaufen,* lyrisches Drama (Act 1 only, Berlin, May 28, 1827; second version as a grosse historisch-romantische Oper, Berlin, June 12, 1829; rev. version, Berlin, Dec. 6, 1837). **Other Dramatic:** *L'eccelsa gara,* cantata (Paris, Feb. 8, 1806); *Tout le monde a tort,* vaudeville (Malmaison, March 17, 1806); *Lalla Rûkh,* Festspiel (Berlin, May 27, 1822). **OTHER:** Arias and duets, etc.; songs; some choral works; several instrumental pieces.

BIBL.: L. Rellstab, *Über mein Verhältnis als Kritiker zu Herrn S. als Componist und General Musikdirektor* (Leipzig, 1827); E. Oettinger, *S.* (Leipzig, 1843); D. Raoul-Rochette, *Notice historique sur la vie et les oeuvres de M. S.* (Paris, 1852); C. Bouvet, *S.* (Paris, 1930); K. Schubert, *S.s italienische Schule* (Strasbourg, 1932); A. Ghizlanzoni, *G. S.* (Rome, 1951); P. Fragapane, *S.* (Bologna, 1954); A. Belardinelli, *Documenti s.ani inediti* (Florence, 1955); F. Schlitzer, *La finta filosofa di G. S.* (Naples, 1957); P. Fragapane, *S.* (Florence, 1983); A. Mungen, *Musiktheater als Historienbild: G. S.s Agnes von Hohenstaufen als Beitrag zur deutschen Oper* (Tutzing, 1997).—NS/LK/DM

Spooky Tooth, seminal British underground band. **MEMBERSHIP:** Gary Wright, kybd., voc. (b. Creskill, N.J., April 26, 1943); Mike Harrison, kybd., voc. (b. Carlisle, Cumberland, England, Sept. 3, 1945); Luther Grosvenor (aka Ariel Bender), gtr. (b. Evesham, Worcester, England, Dec. 23, 1949); Greg Ridley, bs. (b. Carlisle, Cumberland, England, Oct. 23, 1947); Mike Kellie, drm. (b. Birmingham, England, March 24, 1947). Group disbanded in 1970 and re-formed in 1972 with Gary Wright, Mike Harrison, guitarist-vocalist Mick Jones (b. London, England, Dec. 27, 1944), bassist Chris Stewart, and drummer Bryson Graham; Harrison, Stewart, and Jones left in 1973 and re-formed in 1974 with keyboardist-vocalist Mike Patto (b. Sept. 22, 1946; d. March 4, 1979) and bassist-vocalist Val Burke. The group disbanded for good in 1975.

Formed by Briton Mike Harrison and American Gary Wright, Spooky Tooth was a seminal British underground band, although they never had a hit record.

The group disbanded in 1970 and re-formed in 1972, as original bassist Greg Ridley joined Humble Pie and original guitarist Luther Grosvenor joined Mott the Hoople and later formed Widowmaker. Later member Mick Jones eventually founded Foreigner, and Harrison and Wright pursued solo careers, with Wright scoring the biggest success with *The Dream Weaver* in 1975.

Gary Wright performed as a child actor on television and Broadway, later playing keyboards in a number of high school bands. Graduating from N.Y.U., he traveled to Berlin, Germany, to pursue graduate work, but musical interests prevailed and he formed a band called The New York Times. Invited to England by Traffic's manager, Chris Blackwell, Wright formed Spooky Tooth in 1968 with Mike Harrison, Luther Grosvenor, Greg Ridley, and Mike Kellie of the group Art. Spooky Tooth's debut album featured the contrasting vocal and songwriting styles of Wright and Harrison and was eventually released in the United States in 1971 as *Tobacco Road. Spooky Two* sold modestly, but Ridley left after its release to join Humble Pie, and the band's next album, *Ceremony,* was cocredited to French electronic-music wizard Pierre Henry. Wright left to pursue an inauspicious solo career in 1970, and Spooky Tooth disbanded after *The Last Puff,* recorded with Henry McCullough, Chris Stainton, and Alan Spenner from Joe Cocker's Grease Band.

Like Gary Wright, Luther Grosvenor and Mike Harrison unsuccessfully pursued solo careers, with Grosvenor joining Stealers Wheel, then Mott the Hoople, under the name of Ariel Bender. Wright and Harrison reconstituted Spooky Tooth with Mick Jones in 1972, but none of the new band's three albums sold significantly and the group disbanded in late 1974, with Jones going on to form Foreigner with Lou Gramm and Ian McDonald. In 1976 Grosvenor formed Widowmaker with vocalist John Butler, but the group proved unsuccessful.

Gary Wright's second attempt at a solo career succeeded with 1975's *The Dream Weaver.* He played virtually all parts on the album save drums and occasional guitar, and the album yielded belated smash American pop hits with the eerie title cut and "Love Is Alive." He toured as a major headline act in 1976, but after 1977's *The Light of Smiles* his popularity faded. He scored his last major hit in 1981 with "Really Wanna Know You." In 1995 Gary Wright returned to recording with *First Signs of Life* for the Worldly Music label.

DISC.: SPOOKY TOOTH: *Tobacco Road* (1971); *Spooky Two* (1969); *Ceremony* (1970); *The Last Puff* (1970); *You Broke My Heart ... So I Busted Your Jaw* (1973); *Witness* (1973); *The Mirror* (1974); *Hell or High Water* (1982). **GARY WRIGHT AND SPOOKY TOOTH:** *That Was Only Yesterday* (1976). **GARY WRIGHT:** *Extraction* (1971); *Footprint* (1971); *The Dream Weaver* (1975); *The Light of Smiles* (1977); *Touch and Gone* (1977); *Headin' Home* (1979); *The Right Place* (1981); *Who I Am* (1988); *First Signs of Life* (1995). **MIKE HARRISON:** *Mike Harrison* (1972); *Smokestack Lightning* (1972); *Rainbow Rider* (1976). **LUTHER GROSVENOR:** *Under Open Skies* (1972). **WIDOWMAKER:** *Widowmaker* (1976); *Too Late to Cry* (1977); *Widowmaker* (1992).—BH

Spoorenberg, Erna, Dutch soprano; b. Yogyakarta, Java, April 11, 1926. She studied in Hilversum and Amsterdam. She made her debut in an appearance with Radio Hilversum in 1947. In 1958 she became a leading member of the Netherlands Opera in Amsterdam. She made occasional appearances at various European music centers, but principally was associated with the musical life of the Netherlands; made her first appearance at the Vienna State Opera in 1949 and her U.S. debut in N.Y. in 1967. She was especially esteemed for her roles in operas by Mozart and for her portrayal of Mélisande. She also pursued a successful career as a concert singer.—NS/LK/DM

Spratlan, Lewis, American composer and teacher; b. Miami, Sept. 5, 1940. He studied composition with Wyner, Schuller, and Powell at Yale Univ. (B.A., 1962; M.M., 1965), and then studied with Rochberg and Sessions at the Berkshire Music Center in Tanglewood (1966). He held a Guggenheim fellowship (1980–81). He taught at Bay Path Jr. Coll. (1965–67), Pa. State Univ. (1967–70), and at Amherst Coll. (from 1970), where he was made a prof. in 1980. In 1989 he toured widely in the Soviet Union and Armenia as a guest of the Union of Soviet Composers, during which tour his *Apollo and Daphne Variations* and *Toccapsody* were premiered. In 2000 he won the Pulitzer Prize in Music.

WORKS: DRAMATIC: *Life is a Dream*, opera (1975–77); *Unsleeping City*, dance music (1967). **ORCH.:** 2 Pieces (1971); *Penelope's Knees*, double concerto for Alto Saxophone, Double Bass, and Chamber Orch. (1986); *Apollo and Daphne Variations* (1987; Kislovodsk, Russia, Oct. 4, 1989); Concertino for Violin and Chamber Orch. (1995). **CHAMBER:** *Flange* for 14 Instruments (1965); *Serenade* for 6 Instruments (1970); *Trope-Fantasy* for Oboe, English Horn, and Harpsichord (1970); *Summer Music* for Oboe, Horn, Violin, Cello, and Piano (1971); Woodwind Quintet (1971); *Dance Suite* for Clarinet, Violin, Guitar, and Harpsichord (1973); *Fantasy* for Piano and Chamber Ensemble (1973); *Coils* for Flute, Clarinet, Violin, Viola, Cello, Percussion, and Piano (1980); *Diary Music II* for Chamber Ensemble (1981); String Quartet (1982); *When Crows Gather* for 3 Clarinets, Violin, Cello, and Piano (1986); *A Fanfare for the Tenth* for String Quartet (1988); *Hung Monophonies* for Oboe and 11 Instruments (1990); *Night Music* for Violin, Clarinet, and Percussion (1991); *Sojourner* for 10 Players (2000). **P i a n o :** *Toccapsody* (1989). **VOCAL:** *Missa brevis* for Men's Chorus and Winds (1965); *Cantata Domine* for Men's Chorus, Winds, and Tape (1968); *Structures after Hart Crane* for Tenor, Piano, and Tape (1968); *Moonsong* for Chorus and Ensemble (1969); *3 Carols on Medieval Texts* for Chorus and Ensemble (1971); *3 Ben Jonson Songs* for Soprano, Flute, Violin, and Cello (1974); *Night Songs* for Soprano, Tenor, and Orch. (1976); *Celebration* for Chorus and Orch. (1984); *Wolves* for Soprano, Flute, Clarinet, and Piano (1988); *In Memoriam* for Soloists, Chorus, and Orch. (1993); *A Barred Owl* for Baritone and 5 Instruments (1994); *Psalm 42* for Soprano and 6 Instruments (1996); *Vocalise with Duck* for Soprano and 5 Instruments (1998). **OTHER:** Electronic pieces.—NS/LK/DM

Springfield, Dusty (originally, **O'Brien, Mary Isabel Catherine Bernadette**), one of the great white soul singers of all time; b. London, England, April 16, 1939; d. there, March 2, 1999. Revered among her peers, Dusty Springfield's career was a veritable rollercoaster. She recorded hits that spanned three decades, but also had long periods when her sexy

alto went unheard. And just as she was about to garner some long-due respect, she succumbed to cancer.

Born Mary O'Brien in London, she joined her brother Tom and his friend Tim Field in the folk group the Springfields. Joining the band, she took the stage name Dusty Springfield. Sounding like the U.K.'s version of Peter, Paul and Mary, they soon were one of the best-selling groups in England. By 1962 they had a hit in the U.S. with "Silver Threads and Golden Needles," which hit #20 on the pop charts. With the U.S. success, they went to Nashville to record. When Springfield heard the burgeoning girl-group sound growing out of N.Y.'s Brill Building and Motown records, she abruptly quit the Springfields to pursue a solo career.

Her first single, "I Only Want to Be with You," with it's Motown bounce, girl-group harmonies, and horns proved a welcome addition to the girl-group sound in the U.S., hitting #12 in the U.S. during the winter of 1964, while going top five in the U.K. It was the first song played on the British TV show *Top of the Pops*. Her followup, "Stay Awhile," only got to #38, but in the summer of 1964, "Wishin' and Hopin'," a girl-group pastiche with a vocal worthy of the Exciters, rose to #6, beginning her long association with songwriters Burt Bacharach and Hal David. Dusty also established a reputation for political consciousness, getting expelled from South Africa for refusing to play to segregated audiences. While she didn't chart in the U.S. during 1965, she hosted a TV show that introduced the Motown sound to England.

Dusty made a strong return to the U.S. charts in 1966, with the big, bombastic ballad "You Don't Have to Say You Love Me." The song rose to #4 in the U.S. and topped the U.K. charts during the spring of 1966, and has become a radio standard. She followed that in the fall with the similar "All I See Is You," which went to #20 in the U.S. However, the girl-group sound was beginning to fade. She recorded Bacharach and David's "The Look of Love," the love theme to the James Bond spoof *Casino Royal*, which rose to #22 in 1967.

In need of a change, Springfield signed with Atlantic records, home to one of her musical heroes, Aretha Franklin. Atlantic's production dream team of Jerry Wexler, Tom Dowd, and Arif Mardin took her down to Memphis to make the definitive white soul album. They arguably succeeded with the album, *Dusty in Memphis*. While the single "Son of a Preacher Man" rose to #10, the album barely cracked the Top 100, going out of print for nearly two decades. It became a critic's darling and a minor holy grail for record collectors until Rhino reissued it on CD in the mid-1990s.

Later in 1969, Springfield recorded "Windmills of Your Mind," the theme to the film *The Thomas Crown Affair*. Although it, too, has become a standard, the single only hit #31 at the time. By now, Springfield was living in the U.S. That year she recorded with the Philly soul team Kenny Gamble and Leon Huff. The album, *A Brand New Me*, spawned the title track, which hit #24, but again the album sales were weak. Before leaving Atlantic, she told Wexler about a band making waves in London that he quickly signed to the label: Led Zeppelin.

Leaving Atlantic, Springfield recorded the album *Cameo* for ABC in the early 1970s, which was a total sales disaster. About this time, she took the unusual step of admitting that she was bisexual. This did little to help her career, but subsequently turned her into a star of the gay community. After abandoning her next album, Springfield fell off the pop scene for much of the 1970s, returning only to sing backgrounds on an Anne Murray record. She fought battles with alcohol and drugs.

When Dusty returned to the music scene in 1978, despite having producer Roy Thomas Baker in her corner, listeners no longer seemed interested. All she could manage was a minor British hit "Baby Blue." She moved back to London, and in 1982 got involved with the synthpop explosion that had rekindled Tina Turner's career. A 1984 duet with Spencer Davis garnered some notice in England, while a similar project with Richard Carpenter had the same effect in the U.S.

In 1987, Dusty was contacted by one of Britain's hot new groups, the Pet Shop Boys. They invited her into the studio to cut a few songs. One of them, "What Have I Done to Deserve This?" became a huge international hit. The urban piece of synth-pop topped out at #2 on both the U.S. and U.K. charts. Another Pet Shop Boys collaboration, "Nothing Has Been Proved," was featured on the soundtrack to the movie *Scandal*. The duo produced her 1990 album, *Reputation*. Although it didn't produce any significant singles, it was her best selling album since the early 1960s.

Springfield returned to Tenn. in 1995, recording *A Very Fine Love* in Nashville. Again, peer fans turned out in droves to work with Springfield, including Mary Chapin Carpenter and KT Oslin. However, soon after, Springfield discovered a cancerous lump in her breast and spent much of the next 18 months undergoing treatment. At the same time, her back catalog began to attract attention: "Son of a Preacher Man" made an appearance on the soundtrack to the film *Pulp Fiction*. Springfield's cancer went into remission briefly, only to return in the late 1990s. On March 2, the eve of her sixtieth birthday, her induction into the Rock and Roll Hall of Fame, and being named Dame Dusty Springfield on the Queen's Order of the British Empire list, she died.

DISC.: *I Only Want to Be with You* (1964); *Stay Awhile* (1964); *Dusty* (1964); *Oooooooweeee!!!* (1965); *Ev'rything's Coming Up Dusty* (1965); *You Don't Have to Say You Love Me* (1966); *Where Am I Going* (1967); *The Look of Love* (1967); *Dusty Definitely* (1968); *Dusty in Memphis* (live; 1969); *A Brand New Me* (1970); *This Is Dusty Springfield* (1971); *See All Her Faces* (1972); *Cameo* (1973); *Magic Garden (This Is, Vol. 2)* (1973); *Sings Bacharach & King* (1975); *It Begins Again* (1978); *Living without Your Love* (1979); *White Heat* (1982); *Reputation* (1991); *A Very Fine Love* (1995); *Dusty in Memphis* (deluxe ed., 1999); *Blue for You* (2000). —HB

Springfield, Rick (originally, Springhorpe, Richard),

major pop artist and actor of the 1980s; b. Sydney, Australia, Aug. 23, 1949. While Australians knew him as a singer, American audiences had more trouble accepting Rick Springfield. Most of his initial fans in the U.S. knew of him not from his 1972 hit "Speak to the Sky" but his role nearly a decade later on the soap opera *General Hospital*. However, while his music might have had the air of pre-fab pop rock, he wrote most of his hits and they have held up surprisingly well.

Springfield's father was in the military and moved the family around quite a bit. Springfield spent much of his youth reading and playing the guitar. He finally was in one place long enough in high school to form a band. From there he joined a 1950s revival group before landing in the popular Australian teen band Zoot. After a memorable three-month tour entertaining in Vietnam, Zoot became one of the most popular bands in the Antipodes at the turn of the decade. When the band disbanded, Springfield went solo. He re-recorded one of the band's songs "Speak to the Sky," which became a hit in the U.S., climbing to #14 in 1972, and taking the *Beginnings* album to #35. However, he couldn't follow it up, and subsequent albums didn't do nearly as well. He came to loggerheads with his record company and was enjoined from recording for three years.

Springfield had been taking acting classes and made some guest appearances on television shows as a contract player with Universal. In 1980 he extricated himself from his previous recording contract, signing with RCA. Additionally, he was offered a plum role of single, eligible doctor Noah Drake in the popular soap opera *General Hospital*. His character became one of the most popular on daytime TV. When his RCA debut, *Working Class Dog*, with its humorous cover of a well-dressed pit bull, came out in 1981, it had a ready-made audience. The infectious single "Jessie's Girl" topped the charts, went gold, and won a Best Rock Song Grammy Award. His version of Sammy Hagar's rocker "I've Done Everything for You" rose to #8 and "Love Is Alright Tonight" hit #20. The album went to #7 and platinum.

When Springfield's two careers came into conflict, he gave up *General Hospital*, opting for his first love. *Success Hasn't Spoiled Me Yet* followed less than a year after *Working Class Dog*. The single "Don't Talk to Strangers," infused with that curious post-disco beat very popular among pop artist in the early 1980s, reached #2 for four weeks. The follow-up singles, "What Kind of Fool" and "I Get Excited," didn't fare as well (and were more pedestrian), peaking at #21 and #32 respectively. However the album was #2 for three weeks and also went platinum. The following year's *Living in Oz* also went platinum, rising to #12 on the basis of the #9 hit "Affair of the Heart," the #18 hit "Human Touch," and the #23 "Souls." Ironically, since "Human Touch" dealt with the rise of technology in music, all of the tunes relied a bit more on synthesized keyboards than his previous guitar pop.

In 1984 Springfield tried to bring together his two professions, starring in the film *Hard to Hold* and writing the songs for the soundtrack. His song "Love Somebody"—heavily showing the influence of Bruce Springsteen—hit #5. This was followed by the #26 "Don't Walk Away" and the #20 "Bop 'Til You Drop." The movie did well at the box office, and the album rose to #16 and went platinum. Next, Springfield cut the novelty song "Bruce" about people mistaking him for Springsteen that actually went to #27.

1985's *Tao* featured the minor hits "Celebrate Youth" (#26) and "State of the Heart" (#22). It hit #21 and went gold largely on fan momentum. Three years later, *Rock of Life* featured Springfield's last Top 40 hit, the #22 title track. After that, Springfield dropped off the radar for a while, recovering from a motorcycle accident, a three-year TV syndication contract, and just wanting to stay home and raise his family. He returned in the late 1990s, once again juggling two careers: he made many TV guest appearances and released a new album called *Karma* in 1999.

DISC.: *Just Zoot* (1969); *Zoot Out* (1970); *Beginnings* (1972); *Comic Book Heroes* (1974); *Mission Magic* (1974); *Wait for Night* (1976); *Working Class Dog* (1981); *Success Hasn't Spoiled Me Yet* (1982); *Living in Oz* (1983); *Beautiful Feelings* (1984); *Hard to Hold* (1984); *Tao* (1985); *Rock of Life* (1988); *Karma* (1999).—**HB**

Springsteen, Bruce, foremost rock artist of the 1980s; b. Freehold, N.J., Sept. 23, 1949. **THE E STREET BAND,** backup band. **MEMBERSHIP:** Clarence Clemons, sax. (b. Norfolk, Va., Jan. 11, 1942); David Sancious, kybd.; Danny Federici, kybd.; Gary Tallent, bs.; Vini Lopez, drm. In 1974 David Sancious and Vini Lopez were replaced by Roy Bittan and Max Weinberg (b. Newark, N.J., 1951). Guitarist "Miami" Steve Van Zandt (b. Boston, Nov. 22, 1950) joined in 1975 and left in 1984; he was replaced by guitarist Nils Lofgren (b. Chicago, June 21, 1951). Vocalist Patti Scialfa (b. Long Branch, N.J., June 29, 1953) joined in 1984.

Bruce Springsteen burst upon the rock scene with his outstanding 1975 album *Born to Run*. Although the album became an instant best-seller, Springsteen's credibility was hurt by the bombastic hyperbole that proclaimed him the next Bob Dylan and the savior of rock and roll. He subsequently was embroiled in legal disputes that prevented him from recording, a situation that would have destroyed or at least crippled the career of an artist of lesser talent and fortitude. Springsteen returned to recording in 1978, but he did not achieve massive recognition for his talents until 1984's *Born in the U.S.A.* Suffused with engaging songs of celebration, hope, and disillusionment, the album established Springsteen as the most important rock artist of the 1980s. After its huge success, Springsteen again withdrew from the rock scene and, much to the dismay of his fans, disbanded the E Street Band in 1989. Although his career has not reached its previous heights, he remains one of the most provocative songwriters and performers in rock.

Raised in N.J., Bruce Springsteen took up guitar at 13 and joined a local group, the Castiles, around 1963. In 1966 the band recorded several unreleased singles, later performing at the Cafe Wha in N.Y.'s Greenwich Village. Springsteen next formed a succession of bands (Steel Mill, Doctor Zoom and the Sonic Boom) with whom he performed around N.J. clubs for years, most notably at the Stone Pony in Asbury Park. He turned down a contract offer from Bill Graham's Fillmore Records in 1969 and eventually signed a management contract with Mike Appel in May 1972. Appel arranged an audition with legendary record executive John Hammond, and Springsteen signed with Columbia Records

in June. Recorded in both an acoustic and rock-band setting, his debut album, *Greetings from Asbury Park, New Jersey*, featured "Blinded by the Light" and "Spirit in the Night," hits for Manfred Mann in 1976, and "It's Hard to Be a Saint in the City." However, the album was generally ignored, except by rock critics and his cult following based in the Northeast. Released only months later, *The Wild, the Innocent and the E Street Shuffle* suffered similarly, even though it contained such excellent songs as "4th of July, Asbury Park (Sandy)," a minor hit for the Hollies in spring 1975; "Rosalita (Come Out Tonight)"; and "New York City Serenade."

By 1974 Bruce Springsteen had formed his permanent backup group, the E Street Band, with David Sancious, Gary Tallent, Clarence Clemons, and former Steel Mill members Danny Federici and Vini Lopez. They rigorously toured the East Coast during the year and were spotted by critic Jon Landau, who called Springsteen, in a famous quote, "the future of rock and roll." The band subsequently realigned with Tallent, Clemons, and Federici, plus Roy Bittan and Max Weinberg. In 1975 guitarist "Miami" Steve Van Zandt, a cofounder of Southside Johnny and the Asbury Jukes, joined. This aggregation recorded Springsteen's breakthrough album, *Born to Run*.

The album was launched with massive hype by Columbia; for a 5-day, 10-show run at N.Y.'s Bottom Line in August, a large number of tickets were reserved for so-called media tastemakers. Coproduced by Springsteen, Appel, and Landau, the album quickly produced a major hit with the title song. Springsteen was the first rock star to appear simultaneously on the covers of *Time* and *Newsweek* in October, attesting to his sudden popularity (and the power of Columbia's PR office), although ultimately damaging his credibility with hardcore rock fans. Nonetheless, *Born to Run* included standout songs such as "Tenth Avenue Freeze-Out," "Thunder Road," "Jungleland," and "She's the One." The album became a best-seller, remaining on the charts for more than two years, and it helped spur the sales of Springsteen's first two albums.

Bruce Springsteen soon became embroiled in legal disputes with manager Mike Appel that prevented him for more than a year from recording. He toured with the E Street Band in 1976 and 1977, establishing his reputation as a live performer with marathon three- and four-hour performances. Soon after the resolution of the legal problems in May 1977, Springsteen entered the studio to record a new album under mentor-producer-manager Jon Landau. Issued in mid-1978, *Darkness at the Edge of Town* revealed a growing maturity to Springsteen's songwriting, and aptly showcased the E Street Band. The album included "The Promised Land," "Racing in the Streets," and "Streets of Fire," and yielded moderate hits with "Prove It All Night" and "Badlands." During the year, Patti Smith scored her only major hit with "Because the Night," cowritten with Springsteen, and the Pointer Sisters achieved a smash hit with Springsteen's "Fire."

Touring tirelessly from July to September 1978 and again beginning in November, Springsteen performed at the September 1979 benefit concerts in N.Y. for MUSE

(Musicians United for Safe Energy), and his segment of the resulting movie and album came to be regarded as the highlight of the event. He spent more than a year recording his next album, ostensibly recording more than 50 songs, and upon release the two-record set *The River* was widely praised. Pervaded by songs using the automobile as its primary metaphor ("Stolen Car," "Drive All Night," "Wreck on the Highway," and "Cadillac Ranch"), the set also included Springsteen's first smash hit, "Hungry Heart," and the major hit "Fade Away," as well as "I'm a Rocker," "Independence Day," and "The Price You Pay." The release was accompanied by a three-month nationwide tour, his first in two years. In 1981 and 1982 Springsteen and Steve Van Zandt produced two comeback albums for Gary "U.S." Bonds. Each yielded a major hit: *Dedication* with "This Little Girl," and *On the Line* with "Out of Work."

Although Springsteen recorded the songs for his next album with the E Street Band, he ultimately decided to issue solo acoustic recordings he made as demonstration tapes for the work as *Nebraska* in 1982. A stark folk-style album somewhat reminiscent of a solo Bob Dylan, complete with honking harmonica, the album sold less well than previous albums but included such memorable songs as "Highway Patrolman," "Atlantic City," and the ominous "Johnny 99."

Meanwhile, various members of the E Street Band undertook solo projects. In 1982 Steve Van Zandt recorded *Men without Women* with the 11-piece Disciples of Soul, as Springsteen worked on his next album. Van Zandt's solo album contained his "Under the Gun" and "Till the Good Is Gone" and sold modestly, yielding a minor hit with "Forever." Clarence Clemons formed the 10-piece soul band the Red Bank Rockers with vocalist John "J.T." Bowen for touring and the recording of *Rescue*, which featured Springsteen's "Savin' Up" and the single "A Woman's Got the Power."

In 1984 Columbia issued Bruce Springsteen's masterpiece, *Born in the U.S.A.* It is his most powerful musical statement, as it regards the promise and disappointment of the American dream. A tough but empassioned album, rooted in the belief that rock has the power to change and improve the quality of people's lives, *Born in the U.S.A.* yielded *seven* smash hits: the celebratory "Dancing in the Dark"; the desperate "Cover Me"; the rocking but disillusioned title cut; the gentle "I'm On Fire"; the nostalgic "Glory Days" and "My Hometown"; and the disillusioned "I'm Goin' Down." The album established Springsteen in the top rank of rock artists and ultimately sold 15 million copies in the United States. Between June 1984 and September 1985 he played more than 160 stadium concerts worldwide in support of *Born in the U.S.A.*, introducing new guitarist Nils Lofgren and backup vocalist Patti Scialfa. The tour solidified Springsteen's reputation as rock's most exciting and compelling live performer of the 1980s.

"Miami" Steve Van Zandt had left the E Street Band following the recording of *Born in the U.S.A.* He trimmed the Disciples of Soul down to a five-piece band for the politically charged *Voice of America*. The album featured "I Am a Patriot" and "Undefeated (Everybody Goes Home)" and sold modestly. In 1985 Van Zandt assembled Artists United Against Apartheid to record his song "Sun City" as a protest against South Africa's racial policies. Recorded with 49 major contemporary-music stars, including Bob Dylan, Peter Gabriel, Jackson Browne, Lou Reed, Pete Townshend, Bonnie Raitt, Bono of U2, and Springsteen, the single proved only a moderate hit, although it did much to bring attention to the injustices suffered in South Africa. The single was soon followed by a six-song album, *Sun City*. In late 1985 Columbia issued Clarence Clemons's second album recorded with the Red Bank Rockers, *Hero*, which yielded a major hit with "You're a Friend of Mine," a duet with Jackson Browne.

Bruce Springsteen retained a low profile following the massive tour in support of *Born in the U.S.A.* He added vocals to the "We Are the World" superstar single, a smash pop, R&B, and easy-listening hit, and contributed his "Light of Day" composition, a moderate hit for Joan Jett and the Blackhearts, to the film of the same name. In May 1985 he married actress and model Julianne Phillips. In late 1986 Columbia issued *Live 1975–1985*, which compiled 40 songs recorded live over the past decade. The album yielded a near-smash hit with a cover version of Edwin Starr's "War" and a moderate hit with "Fire." The album sold spectacularly for a live, multirecord set.

Bruce Springsteen eventually reemerged in 1987 with *Tunnel of Love*. Leaving behind his angst-ridden songs of youth and disillusionment, the album investigated the exigencies and vagaries of interpersonal love. Recorded virtually solo by Springsteen, the album was a dark, intimate work, revealing not only his personal growth and maturity but also his leanings toward folk and even country music. It yielded the smash hit "Brilliant Disguise," the near-smash title cut, and the major hit "One Step Up." He briefly toured with the E Street Band in support of the album, performing standardized sets (as opposed to the free-form concerts of the past) in arenas rather than stadiums. His only other performances until 1992 were with the Amnesty International tour of 1988, and a benefit in Los Angeles for the Christic Inst. in November 1990.

In 1987 Manhattan Records issued "Miami" Steve Van Zandt's *Freedom, No Compromise*, which included a duet with Springsteen, "I Am a Native American," and a duet with Ruben Blades, "Bitter Fruit." In 1989 Clarence Clemons toured with Ringo Starr's All-Starr Band and recorded *A Night with Mr. C.* Springsteen and Julianne Phillips divorced in March 1989, and that November he announced his dismissal of the E Street Band (retaining Roy Bittan and Patti Scialfa), much to the dismay of longtime fans. Bassist Gary Tallent became a Nashville producer, and guitarist Nils Lofgren returned to his solo career, touring with Ringo Starr's All-Starr Band in 1995. Drummer Max Weinberg founded his own record label, Hard Ticket, for recordings by his band Killer Joe, and later served as band leader for the house band on television's *Late Night with Conan O'Brien*. Keyboardist Danny Federici subsequently played with the house band at Los Angeles's House of Blues.

In July 1990 Patti Scialfa bore her and Springsteen's first son, Evan James. The couple married in June 1991. Springsteen released two albums of new material in 1992, *Human Touch* and *Lucky Town*. The energetic *Human Touch*, recorded in 1989–1990, yielded the major-hit title song and the minor hit "57 Channels (And Nothin' On)." The introspective *Lucky Town*, recorded in 1991, featured "Living Proof," the ballad "If I Should Fall Behind," and the autobiographical "Better Days" and "Local Hero." To promote the albums, Springsteen appeared on *Saturday Night Live*, his first-ever performance on network television, and gave an interview to *Rolling Stone* magazine. However, the albums sold only modestly, and he later toured with his new band, who were somewhat disappointing in light of the quality of his previous shows with the E Street Band. Springsteen and his new group performed on an MTV show called *Bruce Springsteen Plugged*.

Springsteen returned to the charts with the smash hit "Streets of Philadelphia," from the soundtrack to the 1993 film *Philadelphia*, the first major-studio effort to deal with the issue of AIDS. Springsteen won an Academy Award and four Grammys for this work. Patti Scialfa recorded her solo debut, *Rumble Doll*, for 1993 release, and Springsteen's *Greatest Hits* contained four previously unreleased songs, including the stark "Murder Incorporated," recorded during the *Born in the U.S.A.* sessions. The E Street Band reunited briefly to record a video for the song.

Springsteen returned to the solo semiacoustic format for his 1995 album *The Ghost of Tom Joad*. The title track referred directly to the legacy of social-protest music of singers like Woody Guthrie, who had written his own song based on the main character of John Steinbeck's *Grapes of Wrath*. These contemporary ballads focus on neglected Americans, such as immigrants and the inner-city homeless; the work was met by mixed critical reviews and sold modestly.

DISC.: BRUCE SPRINGSTEEN: *Greetings from Asbury Park, New Jersey* (1973); *The Wild, the Innocent and the E Street Shuffle* (1973); *Born to Run* (1975); *Darkness at the Edge of Town* (1978); *The River* (1980); *Nebraska* (1982); *Born in the U.S.A.* (1984); *Bruce Springsteen and the E Street Band: Live, 1975–85* (1986); *Tunnel of Love* (1987); *Human Touch* (1992); *Lucky Town* (1992); *Greatest Hits* (1995); *The Ghost of Tom Joad* (1995). **TRIBUTE ALBUM:** *Cover Me: A Collection of Bruce Springsteen Songs* (1986). **LITTLE STEVEN AND THE DISCIPLES OF SOUL:** *Men without Women* (1982); *Voice of America* (1984). **ARTISTS UNITED AGAINST APARTHEID:** *Sun City* (1985). **LITTLE STEVEN:** *Freedom, No Compromise* (1987). **CLARENCE CLEMONS AND THE RED BANK ROCKERS:** *Rescue* (1983); *Hero* (1985). **CLARENCE CLEMONS:** *A Night with Mr. C* (1989). **KILLER JOE (WITH MAX WEINBERG):** *Scene of the Crime* (1991). **PATTI SCIALFA:** *Rumble Doll* (1993).

BIBL.: P. Gambaccini, *B. S.: A Photo-Bio* (N.Y., 1979); D. Marsh, *Born to Run: The B. S. Story* (Garden City, N.J., 1979); D. Marsh, *Glory Days* (N.Y., 1987).—**BH**

Sprongl, Norbert, Austrian composer; b. Obermarkersdorf bei Retz, April 30, 1892; d. Mödling, near Vienna, April 26, 1983. He studied at the Vienna Cons.

(graduated, 1933) with J. Marx (composition), N. Kahrer (piano), and R. Lach (theory). Following the development of a style of "free dissonance" modeled after Bartók and Hindemith, he wrote 166 works.

WORKS: ORCH.: 5 piano concertos (1935, 1938, 1952, 1953, 1975); 4 syms. (1941, 1956, 1964, 1969); *Passacaglia* for Piano and Strings (1945); Concerto for Mandolin, Lute, Guitar, and Orch. (1953); 2 violin concertos (1955, 1968); Concerto for Viola, Piano, and Orch. (1960); 2 partitas (1962, 1966); Concerto for Flute, Guitar, and Orch. (1965). **CHAMBER:** Cello Sonata (1937); 2 double bass sonatas (1944, 1960); 2 clarinet sonatas (1948, 1960); Viola Sonata (1955); Viola d'Amore Sonata (1957); Oboe Sonata (1960); Trio for Violin, Guitar, and Double Bass (1964).

BIBL.: R. Stockhammer, *N. S.* (Vienna, 1977).—**NS/LK/DM**

Squarcialupi, Antonio, renowned Italian organist, known as **Antonio degli Organi, Antonio de Bartolomeo**, and **Antonio del Bessa**; b. Florence, March 27, 1416; d. there, July 6, 1480. He was the son of a butcher, Bartolomeo di Giovanni, and adopted the name of the prominent Squarcialupi family of Tuscany about 1457. He pursued his career in Florence, serving as organist of Orsanmichele (1431–33) and at the cathedral of S. Maria del Fiore (1432–80). His name is immortalized through the 15th century MS of Florentine polyphonic music known as the "Squarcialupi Codex," which was once in his possession; it was ed. by J. Wolf (1955).—**NS/LK/DM**

Squeeze, innovative rock band. **MEMBERSHIP:** Chris Difford, voc., gtr. (b. London, England, April 11, 1954); Glenn Tilbrook, voc., gtr. (b. London, England, Aug. 31, 1957); Jools (real name, Julian) Holland, voc., kybd. (b. Jan. 24, 1958); Harry Kakouli, bs.; Gilson Lavis, drm. (b. Bedford, England, June 27, 1951). Other members included: John Bently, bs. (b. London, England, April 15, 1951); Paul Carrack, voc., kybd. (b. Sheffield, England, April 16, 1951); Don Snow, kybd., voc. (b. Kenya, Jan. 13, 1957); Keith Wilkinson, bs., voc. (b. Sept. 24, 1954); Kevin Wilkinson, drm. (b. Swindon, England, c. 1957; d. Baydon, England, July 22, 1999); Andy Metcalf, kybd.; Matt Irving, kybd.; Pete Thomas, drm. (b. Aug. 9); Ashley Soan, drm.; Chris Holland, kybd.; Chris Braide, kybd.; Hillare Penda, bs.

Although their membership roster reads like a revolving door, two elements anchor Squeeze: Glenn Tilbrook and Chris Difford. Together, they've written some of the pithiest songs ever to come out of a rock band. A great live band as well, at their height they could sell out arenas like N.Y.'s Madison Square Garden, although they released but one record that went gold and platinum.

Difford and Tilbrook met in the early 1970s, when Tilbrook answered an ad that Difford had posted looking for a songwriting partner. By 1974, they had put together a band to play the songs, including Gilson Lavis on drums, Jools Holland on keyboards, and Harry Kakouli on bass. Emerging in the pre-punk pub- rock days, they were compatriots of bands like Ducks Deluxe. Although their songs tended to be more highbrow, they were couched in tunes that were immediately infectious. Big Velvet Underground fans (their name derives from a Velvet's album that features neither Lou Reed nor John Cale), they hooked up with Miles Copeland's record company, who in turn hooked them up with Cale to produce some songs. These early recordings came out in 1977 as *Packet of Three* on the band's own Depford Fun City Records.

When they came to America, they had to change their name to U.K. Squeeze to avoid confusion with a band called Tight Squeeze. Cale also produced their eponymous A&M debut album in 1978. It featured wonderful tunes like "Take Me I'm Yours" and the instrumental "Wild Sewerage Tickles Brazil." The group really broke through, as pop in the U.K. and as a college radio phenomenon in the U.S., with their 1979 album *Cool for Cats*. They also regained the right to call themselves Squeeze in the U.S. with the demise of Tight Squeeze. In the U.K., the bouncy, cockney inflected title track and the ballad—in the classic sense of the word—"Up The Junction" rose to #2. Those tunes also earned college and rock radio play in the U.S., along with the tongue in cheek "Slap and Tickle."

The momentum built with 1980's *Argybargy*. While the hits weren't as impressive—"Another Nail in My Heart" and "Pulling Mussels (from the Shell)" were middling hits in the U.K.—those two songs along with "If I Didn't Love You" and "Farfisa Beat" earned college and "new-wave" radio airplay in the U.S. The album actually landed in the bottom half of the U.S. Top 100. This set the stage for the Elvis Costello–produced *East Side Story* in 1981. Perhaps the band's most consistent album, it also had some of their most serious songs. Holland had left the band, replaced by former Ace keyboard player Paul Carrack. He sang the song "Tempted," which hit the U.S. Top 50, and "Labelled with Love" went into the British Top Ten.

Carrack left the band, replaced by former Sincero vocalist Don Snow for 1982's *Sweets from a Stranger*. Although the record was uneven, on the strength of the rock radio hit (#51 pop) "Black Coffee in Bed," the album became their highest U.S. charting record at #32. The band had its first sold-out show at Madison Square Garden. However, they still weren't making any money. Added to that, Lavis was having trouble with his drinking, and the group was tired of spending over a hundred days a year on the road.

During this period in the early 1980s, Difford and Tilbrook made an album by that name, produced by Tony Visconti. They mounted a play, *Labelled with Love*, a theatrical piece with their songs. They wrote songs for other artists as well, with their former bandmate Holland cutting one of their tunes, along with Helen Shapiro and Paul Young. Ironically, the group's best of, *Singles 45 and Under*, became the band's best-selling album, eventually hitting platinum.

By 1985, they had begun to miss the band. They came together with Holland, Lavis, and the bass player from the *Difford and Tilbrook* album, Keith Wilkinson, for a charity gig and reformed the band. The comeback album, *Cosi Fan Tutti Frutti*, was moderately successful, both artistically and financially. They took on a second keyboard man, Andy Metcalf from Robin Hitchcock and the Egyptians. Their next album, 1987's *Babylon and On*,

became the bands best record in terms of actually charting, and perhaps their most consistent since *East Side Story*. For the first time, the band landed not just one but two hits into the U.S. Top 40 (their only songs to make it there): "Hourglass," a funky, fun tune, rose to #15 thanks to heavy play on MTV; the follow-up, "853–5937" hit #32. The album made it to #36.

Unfortunately, they weren't able to capitalize on this success. 1989's *Frank*, despite having strong songs like "She Doesn't Have to Shave," stiffed. A&M dropped the group while they were touring to support the album. Holland left the band to work on his own music projects and his burgeoning career as a host on BBC TV. The group put out a live album on Copeland's IRS records. By the time they were ready to record another studio album, they were signed to Reprise records. Rather than replace Holland right away, they used former Elvis Costello collaborator Steve Nieve, Bruce Hornsby, and Matt Irving on keyboards. However, while they were recording, grunge emerged as the new sound of young America and Reprise was not prepared to promote the record in that environment. When the band went out on tour, they brought back Don Snow and hired Carol Isaacs to play keyboards. Difford and Tilbrook also began to play acoustic duet dates. This led to an appearance on MTV, the first edition of their series of "Unplugged" concerts.

Between albums, Gilson Lavis went to play with Jools Holland's big band. Former Attractions drummer Pete Thomas joined the band along with the return of vocalist Carrack. The band resigned to A&M for 1993's *Some Fantastic Place*, which rose to the mid 20s on the U.K. chart, but didn't make any waves in the U.S. They lost Thomas to Elvis Costello again, and hired former China Crisis drummer Kevin Wilkinson (no relation to Keith). Another strong effort, 1995's *Ridiculous* generated a couple of minor English hits and again was largely ignored in the U.S. With their A&M contract ended, Difford and Tilbrook hired Holland's brother Chris to play keyboards, former Del Amitri drummer Ashely Soan, and bassist Hilaire Penda to record *Domino* for a U.K. indie in 1998. The album never came out in the U.S. A live album followed.

DISC.: *Packet of Three* (1977); *U.K. Squeeze* (1978); *Cool for Cats* (1979); *Argybargy* (1980); *East Side Story* (1981); *Sweets from a Stranger* (1982); *Cosi Fan Tutti Frutti* (1985); *Babylon and On* (1987); *Frank* (1989); *A Round & A Bout* (live; 1990); *Play* (1991); *Some Fantastic Place* (1993); *Ridiculous* (1995); *Domino* (1998); *Live at Royal Albert Hall* (1999).—**HB**

Squire, W(illiam) Barclay, English music librarian; b. London, Oct. 16, 1855; d. there, Jan. 13, 1927. He received his education in Frankfurt am Main and at Pembroke Coll., Cambridge (B.A., 1879; M.A., 1902). In 1885 he was placed in charge of the printed music in the British Museum, retiring as Assistant Keeper in 1920. He compiled catalogues of music for the British Museum (publ. in 1899 and 1912), and also the catalogue of the King's Music Library (3 vols., 1927–29). He ed. (with J. Fuller Maitland) *The Fitzwilliam Virginal Book* (2 vols., London, 1899; reprint, N.Y., 1963), and also ed. Byrd's masses, Purcell's music for harpsichord, and Elizabethan madrigals.—**NS/LK/DM**

Šrámek, Vladimír, Czech composer; b. Kosiče, March 3, 1923. He was a student of Picha at the Prague Cons. After working in the music division of the National Museum in Prague, he joined the staff of the Opera at the National Theater in Prague. In 1977 he became ed. of music at the FILIA. In his early works, Šrámek composed in a traditional style. Later he embraced avant-garde techniques. In his orch. score *The Astronauts* (1959), he introduced the Monophon, an electronic device of his own creation.

WORKS: DRAMATIC: *Driver to Aristofana,* opera (1955); *Flower of Cobalt,* radio opera (1963); *The Pit,* pantomime (1963); *Spectrum I* (1964), *II* (1964), and *III* (1965), music theater; *Light of the World,* pantomime (1964); *The Last Forest,* musical television play (1965). **ORCH.:** *Comedy* for Winds and Percussion (1957); *The Astronauts* (1959); *Metamorphoses I-VII* for Various Instrumental Groups (1961–63); *Swiss Diary* (1966); *Catastrophic Account* (1966); *Delta 12* (1986). **CHAMBER:** Suite for Trombone and Piano (1953); Recorder Sonatina (1955); Suite for Accordion, 2 Clarinets, Trumpet, and Bassoon (1958); *Study* for Flute and Piano (1960); *Tempi* for String Quartet (1960); *Metra symmetrica* for Flute, Oboe, Clarinet, Bassoon, and Horn (1961); *Rondo* for Flute, Oboe, Clarinet, Bassoon, 2 Horns, and 2 Trombones (1961); *Prodomos* for Flute, Bass Clarinet, Trumpet, and Violin (1962); *The Laughter* for Tape- Speaker, Flute, Piano, and Percussion (1962); *Proportioni* for Viola (1964); *Dialogue* for Violin and Viola (1965); *Kaleidoscope* for Violin, Viola, and Cello (1965); *Anticomposizione* for Violin, Viola, and Cello (1966); *Circulus perpetuus* for Flute, Oboe, and Clarinet (1975); Nonetto (1982); *5 Pieces* for 2 Violins, Viola, and Cello (1984); *The Puppet Show Music,* quintet for Flute, Oboe, Clarinet, Bassoon, and Horn (1985); Trio for Oboe, Clarinet, and Bassoon (1986); *Masques,* quintet for Flute, Oboe, Clarinet, Bassoon, and Horn (1986); Quartet for Flute, Oboe, Clarinet, and Bassoon (1986). **OTHER:** *The City,* electronic music (1959); *Sonnet for Sonnet Duo,* electronic music (1966); *The Play* for Monophon (1966).
—NS/LK/DM

Srebotnjak, Alojz, Slovenian composer and pedagogue; b. Postojna, June 27, 1931. He studied with Škerjanc at the Ljubljana Academy of Music (1953–58), with Porrena in Rome (1958–59), with Fricker in London (1960–61), and in Paris (1963). After teaching at the Ljubljana Pedagogical Academy (1964–70), he was a prof. of composition at the Ljubljana Academy of Music (1970–95). In his works, Srebotnjak has made effective use of various modern techniques, including atonality and serialism.

WORKS: DRAMATIC: *The Trumpet and the Devil,* ballet (1980; orch. suite, 1983); incidental music; film scores. **ORCH.:** *Music* for Strings (1955; rev. 1982); *Sinfonietta in due tempe* (1958); *Monologues* for Flute, Oboe, Horn, and Strings (1962); *Kraška Suite* (1964); *Antifona* (1964); *Episodes* (1967); Harp Concerto (1971); Violin Concerto (1975); *Slovenica* (1976); *Macedonian Dances* for Strings (1976; also for Orch. or 2 Oboes, 2 Clarinets, 2 Bassoons, and Percussion); *Ballads* (1977); *Naturae vox* (1981); *Slovenian Folk Dances* for Strings (1982; also for Orch. or Violin and Piano); *Rapsodica* for Strings (1988). **CHAMBER:** 3 violin sonatinas (1954, 1966, 1968); *Allegro, Corale 3 Passacaglia* for String Quartet (1954); *Fantasia Notturna* for 3 Violins, Clarinet, and Harp (1957); *5 Préludes* for Harp (1960); *Serenata* for Flute, Clarinet, and Bassoon (1961); *6 Pieces* for Bassoon and Piano (1963); *Diary* for Piano Trio (1972); *Lamento* for Chamber Ensemble (1976); *Naif,* collage for Instrumental Group (1977); *Macedonica,* collage for Instrumental Group (1978); *Spray,* collage for Instrumental Group (1981); *Improvisation After Tartini* for Violin (1991). **P i a n o :** *Invenzione variata* (1961); *Macedonian Dances* (1972); *Variations on a Theme by Marij Kogoj* (1984); *The Folk Music Player—Folk Melodies* (1988); *Variations on a Theme by Slavko Osterc* (1990); *Variations on a Theme by Lucijan M. Škerjanc* (1996); *Scherzzzando* (1997). **VOCAL:** *Mother* for Voice and Strings (1955); *Letters* for Soprano and Harp (1956); *War Pictures* for Tenor, Viola, Percussion, and Piano (1957); *Requiem for a Hostage* for Chorus, Harp, Timpani, and Tam-tam (1963); *Micro Songs* for Voice and Chamber Ensemble (1964); *Ectasy of Death* for Baritone, Chorus, and Orch. (1965); *A Naive Orpheus* for Chorus and Chamber Ensemble (1973); *Dark Stars, Brighten Up!,* cantata for Baritone, Trumpet, Harp, Timpani, and String Orch. (1989); *Sonnets* for Tenor and Piano (1991); *The Poet's Portrait* for Tenor and Piano (1993); *The Škofja Loka Passion* for Soloists, Chorus, and Orch. (2000); other choral works and songs.**—NS/LK/DM**

Srensen, Bent, Danish composer; b. Borup, July 18, 1958. He studied with Nordholm in Copenhagen (1983–87), and also had lessons with Nrgård. After composing in a tonal style, Srensen embraced a highly personal contemporary means of expression. His Violin Concerto, *Sterbende Gärten* (1992–94), won the Nordic Council Music Prize in 1996. Among his other works are *Lacrimae* for Orch. (1985), 3 string quartets (*Alman,* 1984; *Adieu,* 1986; *Angel's Music,* 1988). piano pieces, and vocal music, including *Cyprianus* for 3 Women's Voices, 2 Clarinets, and Percussion (1983) and *Pop Sange* for Tenor and Piano (1990).**—NS/LK/DM**

Srensen, Søren, distinguished Danish musicologist, organist, and harpsichordist; b. Copenhagen, Sept. 20, 1920. He studied organ with Vider at the Copenhagen Cons. (diploma, 1943) and musicology with Abrahamsen and Larsen at the Univ. of Copenhagen (M.A., 1943; Ph.D., 1958, with the diss. *Diderich Buxtehudes vokale kirkemusik;* publ. in Copenhagen, 1958). In 1943, with L. Friisholhm, he founded Copenhagen's Collegium Musicum, a chamber ensemble with which he made frequent appearances as an organist and harpsichordist; also was organist at Holmens Church (1947–58). He was prof. of musicology and chairman of the musicologial inst. at the Univ. of Århus (from 1958); was co-ed. of the *Dansk Årbog for Musikforskning* (from 1961). Among his many administrative positions were the chairmanships of the Danish Soc. of Organists and Choirmasters (1953–59), the Carl Nielsen Soc. (from 1966), the Danish Council for Research in the Humanities (from 1974), and the State Council of Music Education (from 1986). In 1982 he was awarded Hungary's Bartók Medal. He won notable distinction as an authority on 17th-century music, most particularly that of Buxtehude.

WRITINGS: *Kirkens liturgi* (Copenhagen, 1952; second ed., 1969); ed. with B. Hjelmbor, *Natalicia musicologica Knud Jeppesen* (Copenhagen, 1962); *Renaissancebegrebet i musikhistorien* (Århus, 1964); *Das Buxtehudebild im Wandel der Zeit* (Lübeck, 1973); *Kobenhavns Drengekor gennem 50 år* (Copenhagen, 1974); ed. *Gads musikleksikon* (Copenhagen, 1976; second ed., 1987).
—NS/LK/DM

Srnka, Jiří, Czech composer; b. Pisek, Aug. 19, 1907; d. Prague, Jan. 31, 1982. He took violin lessons at the Prague Cons. under A. Mařák and J. Feld (1922–24), then studied composition there with Šín (1924–28) and Novák (1928–32); had instruction in quarter tone music with Alois Hába (1927–28; 1934–37). He was an asst. conductor and violinist with J. Jezek's Liberated Theater in Prague (1929–35), then became interested in film music, producing over 120 film scores. From 1950 to 1953 he taught classes in film music at the Academy of Musical Arts in Prague.

WORKS: DRAMATIC: Over 120 film scores. ORCH.: *Symphonic Fantasy* (1932); Violin Concerto (1957; Olomouc, Sept. 23, 1958); *Historical Pictures from the Pisek Region* for Amateur String Orch. (1961); *Partita* for Violin and Chamber Orch. (1962); Piano Concerto (1968); Concerto for Flute, Strings, and Piano (1974; Prague, March 8, 1975); *Nocturne* for Strings (1975); *Echo of Songs of the Prachen Region* (1976); *Sinfonietta* (1977); *Mater Dolorosa* for Flute, Harp, and Strings (1977); *Lyrical Symphony* (1979). CHAMBER: 2 string quartets (1928, 1936); Wind Quartet (1928); *Suite* for Violin and Piano (1929); String Quintet (1930); *3 Pieces* for Violin and Piano (1961); *Léto budiž pochváleno* (Summer Be Thou Praised) for String Quartet (1980); *Byl tichý letní večer* (There Was a Quiet Summer Evening) for String Quartet (1980); Nonet (1981). Piano: Suite (1933); *Fantasy* (1934); *2 Quarter-Tone Pieces* (1936); *3 Pieces* (1936). VOCAL: Songs.—NS/LK/DM

Šrom, Karel, Czech composer, writer on music, and administrator; b. Pilsen, Sept. 14, 1904; d. Prague, Oct. 21, 1981. He studied composition with Jan Zelinka and Karel Hába in Prague (1919–25), and also took courses in law at the Univ. (Jur.Dr., 1927). He wrote music criticism (1928–45) and served as head of the music dept. of the Czech Radio (1945–51).

WRITINGS (all publ. in Prague): *Orchestr a dirigent* (1960); *Záhudbi* (Beyond Music; 1965); *Karel Ančerl* (1968).

WORKS: ORCH.: 2 syms. (1930, 1951); *Plivník* (The Gnome), scherzo (1953); *Vzdech na bruslích* (A Sigh on Skates), symphonic allegretto (1957); *Hayaya*, suite for adults and children (1961); Piano Concerto (1961); *Etudes* (1970); *Mala* for Chamber Orch. (1972). CHAMBER: Violin Sonata (1920); 3 string quartets (1923, 1941, 1966); *Scherzo* Trio for String Trio (1943); *Vynajitka* (Fairytale) for Nonet (1952); *Etudes* for Nonet (1959); Concertino for 2 Flutes and String Quintet or String Orch. (1971). Piano: *Whiles*, trifles (1942); *7 Pieces* (1942); *Black Hour*, cycle (1965).—NS/LK/DM

Stabile, Mariano, prominent Italian baritone; b. Palermo, May 12, 1888; d. Milan, Jan. 11, 1968. He studied voice at the Accademia di Santa Cecilia in Rome. He made his operatic debut as Amonasro in Palermo (1909). For a number of seasons he sang in provincial opera houses in Italy. The turning point in his career came when he was engaged by Toscanini to sing Falstaff in Verdi's opera at La Scala (Dec. 26, 1921). He triumphed and the role became his major success; he sang it more than 1,000 times. His guest engagements took him to London's Covent Garden (1926–31), the Salzburg Festivals (1935–39), the Glyndebourne Festivals (1936–39), again in London (1946–49), and the

Edinburgh Festival (1948). He retired in 1960. Among his other notable roles were Don Giovanni, Mozart's and Rossini's Figaro, Don Alfonso, Dr. Malatesta, Iago, Rigoletto, and Scarpia.—NS/LK/DM

Stabinger, Mathias, German flutist, clarinetist, conductor, and composer; b. c. 1750; d. Venice, c. 1815. He was a flutist and clarinetist in Lyons in 1772, and then made his first appearance in Paris that same year. In 1777 he went to Italy, where he brought out the highly successful opera buffa *Le astuzie di Bettina* (Genoa, 1780), which subsequently was performed throughout Europe. In 1781 he was maestro al cembalo at the Warsaw Opera; in 1782 he was active with the Mattei-Orecia opera troupe in St. Petersburg, and then was associated with the Petrovsky Theater in Moscow. After another Italian sojourn (1783–85), he returned to Moscow as director of the orch. at the Petrovsky Theater, where he produced such successful stage works as *Schastlivaya Tonia* (Lucky Tonia; Jan. 14, 1786), *Baba Yaga* (Dec. 2, 1786), *Zhenitba neudachnaya* (The Unfortunate Marriage; Feb. 19, 1788), and *Orphée traversant l'enfer à la recherche d'Eurydice* (Feb. 22, 1792). About 1800 he returned once more to Italy, finally settling in Venice in 1814. He also wrote an oratorio, *Betulia liberata* (Moscow, March 26, 1783), and publ. much chamber music. —NS/LK/DM

Stäblein, Bruno, distinguished German musicologist; b. Munich, May 5, 1895; d. Erlangen, March 6, 1978. He studied musicology with Sanderberger and Kroyer at the Univ. of Munich (Ph.D., 1918, with the diss. *Musicque de Joye: Studien zur Instrumentalmusik des 16. Jahrhunderts*); later completed his Habilitation at the Univ. of Erlangen in 1946 with his *Hymnestudien*. He was a theater conductor in Innsbruck, Coburg, and Regensburg, where he was also active as an adviser in musical studies. He was a prof. and chairman of the seminars in musicology at the Univ. of Erlangen (1956–63); in 1967 he was appointed director of the Society for Bavarian Music History. He ed. the important collection Monumenta Monodica Medii Aevi (Kassel, 1956–70); contributed a number of informative articles on the music of the Middle Ages and the Renaissance; ed. reprints of documentary materials pertaining to these epochs. A Festschrift in his honor, issued for his 70th birthday, contains a complete list of his publs. (Kassel, 1967).—NS/LK/DM

Stäbler, Gerhard, German organist, teacher, and composer; b. Wilhelmsdorf, near Ravensburg, July 20, 1949. He studied at the North West German Music Academy in Detmold (1968–70) and with Nicolaus Huber (composition) and Gerd Zacher (organ) at the Essen Folkwang Hochschule (1970–76). He also attended courses with Stockhausen, Schnebel, Kagel, and Ligeti. In 1982 he won the Cornelius Cardew Memorial Prize in London. He taught at the Essen Folkwang Hochschule from 1982 to 1984, and again from 1989 to 1994. In 1983 and 1986 he worked at the Stanford Univ. computer music center. From 1985 he toured widely in Europe and the U.S. as an organist in programs ranging from Bach and Bull to Ligeti, Cage, and himself. He also gave lectures and taught. From 1986 he worked with Aktiv Musik, a touring concert/lecture series. In 1989 he oversaw "Actik Musik '89" in N.Y. In 1991 he co-founded the Gesellschaft für neue Musik Ruhr. He made a concert and lecture tour of Japan and Korea in 1991. In 1992 he was composer-in-residence at Northwestern Univ. in Chicago, and returned there as a guest prof. in 1993. In 1994 he was awarded a Japan Foundation scholarship; in 1995 he made concert and lecture tours in Brazil and Japan. In his music, Stäbler has charted his own avant-garde, and even radical, course. All the same, he has attempted to reestablish a working relationship with the public. His work is infused with a political and social consciousness.

WORKS: *Dämpfe*, 5-fold chamber music (1968–70); *Mo-ped* for Organ and Motorcycle (1970–71); *drüber...* for 8 Active Screamers, Cello, Synthesizer, and Tape (1972–73); *Gehörsmassage* for Active Audience (1973); *Cage-Mix*, arrangement with Animal Voices (1973–74); *Suchen nach...*, experiments with historical materials for Various Ensembles (1976–80); *Drei Lieder zu Gedichten von Gert Udo Jerns* for Voice, Drum, and Piano (1979–82); *Hitlerchoräle IV-VI* for Chorus and Electronic Organ (1980); *...fürs Vaterland*, 3 songs for Instruments, Voices, and Speaking Chorus (1981–82); *Reisegepäck*, traveling works (1981–84); *Den Toten von Sabra und Chatila* for Voice, Flute, Oboe, Clarinet, and Piano (1982; rev. for Flute, Oboe, Clarinet, Trombone, and Piano, 1988); *Das Sichere ist nicht sicher*, spiraling rondo for 8 Instruments and Tape (1982); *Windows: Elegien* for Chamber Ensemble (1983; various other versions, 1983–85); *Schatten wilder Schmerzen* for Orch. (1984–85); *Die Spieldose* for Percussion, Tape, and Visual Media (1984–85); *California Dreams: Lullaby (poisoned), Shooting Stars, Soul Trap*, and *Crack of Dawn* for Accordion (1986); *Hart auf Hart*, improvisatory music for Ensemble (1986); *rasend still* for Euphonium or Trumpet (1986); *Warnung mit Liebeslied* for Harp, Accordion, and Percussion (1986); *Mit wachen Sinnen* for Chorus and Drums (1986–87); *Ruck-VERSCH^{ei}BEN Zuck* for Accordion and Orch. (1986–88); *...strike the ear...* for String Quartet (1987–88); *auf dem Seil, auf scharf gespanntem Seil* for Flute, Violin, Trombone, and Piano (1987–88); *fallen, fallen...und liegen und fallen* for Soprano or Alto, Accordion, Tuba, and Tape (1988–89); *Nachbeben und Davor* for Cello and Accordion (1988–89); *Oktober* for Flute, Violin, and Double Bass (1989); *Affiliert* for Ensemble (1989–90); *Den Müllfahrern von San Francisco* for 17 Instruments (1989–90); *Co—wie Kobalt* for Double Bass and Orch. (1989–90); *...Im Spalier...* for Brass Quintet (1990); *Ungaretti Lieder* for Mezzo-soprano or Baritone and Percussion (1990); *Zeitsprünge* for Accordion and Percussion (1990); *Sunde. Fall. Beil.*, opera, after Dumas' *Catherine Howard* (1990–91; Munich, May 16, 1992); *Traum 1/9/92* for Saxophone, Cello, Piano, and Ensemble (1992); *CassandraComplex*, music theater, after Christa Wolf (1993–94; Wiesbaden, April 29, 2000); *Beppu*, "Thoughts on 3 Haiku by Matsuo Basho," for Trumpet and Percussion (1994; also for Trombone or Tuba and Percussion); *[Apparat]* for Chorus, Clarinet, Accordion, Double Bass, and 3–6 Percussion (1994–95); *Karas. Krähen.* for Tape (1994–95; also for Vocalists, Sho or Accordion, Double Bass, Percussion, and Tape); *news1*, projected performance with or without a player (1995) and 2 for 11 Vocalists and Projectors (1996); *Radierung* for Oboe (1995); *Spuren* for Saxophone Quartet (1995); *Winkelzüge* for Flute Quartet (1995); *Winter, Blumen* for Countertenor, Violin, Viola, Cello, and Double Bass (1995); *Zeichnung* for Recorders (1995); *INTERNET 3.2* for Mezzo-soprano (Alto), Piano, and Percussion (1995–96); *INTERNET 3.1*

(Fragment) for Mezzo-soprano (Alto), Clarinet, and Percussion (1995–97); *...am Grunde der Moldau wandern die Steine...* for Ensemble or Keyboards and Percussionist (1996); *Belfast Breakfast Songs* for Voice (1996); *Dalím Música mágica para piano* (1996); *INTERNET 1.1, 1.5*, and *1.9* for Piano (all 1996); *Journal 9'1119* for Flutes, Percussion, Tape, and Odors (1996); *MOON'SCAPE* for Flute and Guitar (1996); *POETIC ARCS* for 15 Instruments (1996); *Unstern! Sinistre*, arrangement of Liszt's late piano work for 15 Instruments (1996); *BRIDGES* for Voice and Accordion (1996–97); *INTERNET 1.2* for Accordion (1996–97); *INTERNET 4 (Adriatico)* for Piano(s) and Percussion (1996–97); *[voix(time)]*, multimedia project (1996–98; in collaboration with various artists); *DreiZehn (ThirteeN)* for 11, 17, 19, 23, 29, 31, 37, 41, 43, 47, 53... Performers (1997); *Fall.Zeit* for 1 or 2 Percussionists (1997); *hyacinth—liquids.scent* for Percussion (1997); *INTERNET 4 (N.Y./Francesco Clemente)* for 4 Pianos (1997); *SPEED* for A Group (or Groups) of 3 Vocalists (1997); *TAP* for Organ Pedal (1997); *WOLKEN.BILDER* for Orchestrion (1997); *Ausnahme.Zustand—Musikalischer Diskurs über das Unheil der Automation* for Orch. (1997–98); *TRAMA/GEWEBE* for Chorus (1997–98); *beats* for String Quartet and Percussion (1998); *estratto* for Bassoon and Harmonica (1998); *futuressence 1* for Trombone, Percussion, and Accordion (1998); *HarbourMarks* for Horns, Brass Ensemble, and Percussion (1998); *katalekt* for Cello with a Roundbow, ad libitum (1998); *KRUSTEN/CRUSTS* for Cello (1998); *Luna*, electroacoustic music (1998); *Secrets—Songs on Poems by Wolf Wondratschek* for Alto/Mezzo-soprano, Baritone, and Piano (1998); *SpringLight* for Tape (1998); *MetalSeasons* for Violin, Trumpet, Horn, Trombone, Tuba, Percussion (4 Players), and Airplanes (1998–99); *playmanic* for Playerpianos (1998–99); *Time for Tomorrow*, music for 25 acts for Trombone, Percussion, and 8-Track Tape (1998–99); *EarPlugs I & II* (1999); *elements (edged)—Fragment* for CD/Tape (1999); *frictions (unlimited)—Fragment* for CD/Tape (1999); *...ohne netz und doppelten boden...* for Ensemble (1999); *open sky (1)* for Chamber Orch. (1999; also for Accordion, Strings, and Timpani); *Supreme Particles R111*, interactive environment (1999); *...vom Wasser...* for Soprano and CD/Tape, after Leonardo da Vinci (1999); 5 performance pieces: *HandStreiche, Footprints I & II, AugenTanz, MundStücke*, and *NasenTraum* (all 1999); *energy-light-dream* for Soprano, Orch., and Ensemble of Baritone and Tapes, after Heiner Müller (1999–2000); *...müd des Festen...* for Ensemble and Tape (1999–2000); *spatial ayres* for Soprano, Ensemble, and Tape, after Müller (1999–2000); *Strafkolonie* for Baritone (or Other Voice) and Tenor Drum (2000).—**NS/LK/DM**

Stachowski, Marek, Polish composer and pedagogue; b. Piekary Śląskie, March 21, 1936. He received training in composition (from Penderecki) and in theory at the State Higher School of Music (later the Academy of Music) in Kraków (1963–68). From 1967 he taught composition there, and also served as the Academy's rector from 1993 to 1999. He also taught composition at the Inst. of Musicology at the Jagiellonian Univ. in Kraków from 1979. In 1981 he was granted the state title of prof. He won first prize in the Szymanowski Competition in 1974, was honored with the Minister of Culture and Arts Award, second Class, in 1984, won the Polish Composers' Union Award in 1989, and received the Alfred Jurzykowski Foundation Award of the U.S. in 1990.

WORKS: DRAMATIC: *Najdzielniejszy z rycerzy* (The Bravest Knight), children's opera (Poznań, March 15, 1965); *Magiczne kuranty* (Magic Chimes), children's musical fairytale-ballet (1989; Poznań, April 22, 1990). ORCH.: *Musica con una battuta del tam-tam* (1966; Rotterdam, Sept. 9, 1968); *Ricercar 66* for Concertante Organ and Chamber Orch. (1966); *Sequenze concertanti* (1968); *Irisation* (1969–70; Graz, Oct. 23, 1970); *Musique solennelle* (1973; Warsaw, Sept. 27, 1974); *Poème sonore* (1975; Mönchengladbach, Jun3e 24, 1976); *Divertimento* for Chamber String Orch. (1978; Warsaw, Jan. 6, 1979); *Choreia* (1980; Milton Keynes, Feb. 15, 1981); *Capriccio* (Warsaw, April 13, 1984); Concerto for Cello and Strings (1988; Warsaw, Sept. 20, 1991); *Z księgi nocy* (From the Book of Night; Kraków, Sept. 29, 1990); *Sinfonietta* for Strings (Bad Kissingen, July 7, 1998); Concerto for Viola and Strings (1998; Warsaw, Jan. 24, 1999); *Recitativo e la preghiera* for Cello and Strings (1999). CHAMBER: 3 string quartets: No. 1 (1963; Kraków, March 22, 1996), No. 2 (1972; Kraków, Dec. 18, 1974), and No. 3 (Warsaw, Sept. 17, 1988); *Musica da camera* for Flute, Cello, Harp, and Percussion (1965; Durham, July 21, 1978); *Musica* for String Quartet (1965; Kraków, March 12, 1970); *Audition* for Flute, Cello, and Piano (Kraków, Sept. 18, 1970); *Pezzo grazioso* for Wind Quintet (Graz, Nov. 3, 1982); *Musique en quatre scènes* for Clarinet and String Quartet (Warsaw, Sept. 21, 1987); Chamber Concerto for Flute, Clarinet, Violin, Cello, Percussion, and Piano (Southampton, Sept. 22, 1989); Sonata for Strings (Kraków, June 4, 1991); *Tre intermezzi* for String Trio (1993–93; Kraków, Jan. 17, 1994); *Musica festeggiante* for String Quartet (Kraków, Dec. 6, 1995); *Quodlibet* for Wind Trio (1995; Kraków, May 30, 1996); *Tastar e canzona* for Cello and Piano (Katowice, Sept. 30, 1996); *Jeu parti* for Violin and Piano (1997; Kraków, June 1, 1998); Trio for Clarinet, Cello, and Piano (1999). Piano: *Extensions* (1971; Munich, March 14, 1972); *Odys wśród białych klawiszy* (Odysseus Amidst the White Keys; 1979; Łódź, Nov. 21, 1981); *Cinq petites valses* (1997–98; Katowice, Oct. 22, 1998). VOCAL: *Pięć zmysłów i róża* (Five Senses and the Rose) for Voice and 4 Instruments (1964; Kraków, June 2, 1996); *Neusis II* for 2 Vocal Ensembles, Percussion, Cellos, and Double Basses (1968; Kraków, Feb. 21, 1974); *Chant de l'espoir* for Reciter, Soprano, Baritone, Boy's Chorus, Mixed Chorus, and Orch. (Skopje, July 26, 1969); *Słowa* (Words) for Solo Voices, Chorus, and Orch. (1971); *Śpiewy thakuryjskie* (Thakurian Chants) for Chorus and Orch. (1974; Warsaw, Sept. 24, 1975); *Ptaki* (Birds) for Soprano and Instruments (1976; Wrocław, Feb. 25, 1978); *Symfonia pieśni tęsknotą uświęconych* (Symphony for Songs Sanctified by Nostalgia) for Soprano, Chorus, and Orch. (1981; Kraków, June 10, 1986); *Amoretti* for Voice, Lute, and Viola da Gamba (1981–82; Lisbon, Jan. 21, 1983); *Madrigali dell'estate* for Voice and String Trio (Pontino, June 16, 1984); *Ody safickie* (Sapphic Odes) for Mezzo-soprano and Orch. (1985; Poznań, April 9, 1986); *Jubilate Deo* for Chorus and Organ (1988; Kraków, Feb. 12, 1989).—NS/LK/DM

Stacy, Jess (Alexandria), jazz pianist; b. Bird's Point, Mo., Aug. 11, 1904; d. Los Angeles, Calif., Jan. 1, 1994. He was best known for his work with Benny Goodman 1935–39; his solo on "Sing Sing Sing" at the Carnegie Hall concert in January 1938 is celebrated. Stacy started on drums, then switched to piano, and was mostly self-taught, with some lessons from Florina Morris. He played in a local youth band and on steamboats; while working out of Davenport, Iowa, c. 1924, he gigged with a young Bix Beiderbecke. He mostly work with Joe Kayser's Band out of Ohio and during a residency in Chicago between 1926–28, then did a long spell with various Chicago leaders through the mid-1930s. He also briefly led his own Stacy's Aces

band. In July 1935, on the recommendation of John Hammond, he joined Benny Goodman, remained with him until July 1939 (and took part in many freelance recordings). He returned home for a few months before joining Bob Crosby, playing with him from September 1939–December 1942. He rejoined Goodman and stayed with him until the band temporarily disbanded in March 1944. Stacy then worked briefly with Horace Heidt (March–September 1944) and Tommy Dorsey (November 1944–early 1945), before forming his own short-lived band. He was home during most of 1946, then rejoined Goodman that November, staying with him until March 1947. That May, he relocated to Calif., and formed another short-lived band before joining Billy Butterfield's Band in N.Y for a brief period in 1948. He returned to Calif. where he worked through the 1950s as a solo pianist in various clubs. He had a brief reunion with Benny Goodman for special appearances in December 1959 to January 1960. He then left full-time music, and in 1963 was an employee of the Max Factor Company. He came back to music in 1973, doing the soundtrack for the film *The Great Gatsby*; he received a standing ovation at the 1974 Newport Jazz Festival, and also resumed recording. He continued to perform and record through the 1970s until retiring again.

DISC.: "Blue Notion" (1944); *Tribute to Benny Goodman* (1954); *Return of Jess Stacy* (1964); *Stacy Still Swinging* (1974); *EC-Stacy* (1995).—JC/LP

Stacy, Thomas, American English-horn player; b. Little Rock, Ark., Aug. 18, 1938. He received his training at the Eastman School of Music in Rochester, N.Y. After graduating in 1960, he made his formal debut as a soloist with the Minneapolis Sym. Orch., with which he subsequently was solo English horn. In 1972 he became solo English horn in the N.Y. Phil. He also toured as an English-horn soloist, appearing with many American orchs. Stacy was soloist in the premieres of the English-horn concertos of Skrowaczewski (Minneapolis, Nov. 21, 1969), Persichetti (N.Y., Nov. 17, 1977), and Rorem (N.Y., Jan. 27, 1994).—NS/LK/DM

Stade, Frederica von
See **Von Stade, Frederica**

Staden, Johann, eminent German organist and composer, father of **Sigmund Theophil Staden;** b. Nuremberg (baptized), July 2, 1581; d. there (buried), Nov. 15, 1634. He spent most of his life in his native city, winning particular distinction as an organist by the time he was 18. After serving as court organist in Bayreuth (1604–05), he went with the court to Kulmbach following a disastrous fire; returned to Nuremberg as organist at the Spitalkirche (1616), St. Lorenz (1616–18), and St. Sebald (from 1618). He also was active as a teacher, Kindermann being his most celebrated pupil. Only about half of Staden's extant output has survived in complete form; these include distinguished sacred and secular vocal works as well as instrumental pieces. He was one of Germany's first exponents of the concertato style.—NS/LK/DM

Staden, Sigmund Theophil, esteemed German organist, instrumentalist, music theorist, and composer, son of **Johann Staden**; b. Kulmbach (baptized), Nov. 6, 1607; d. Nuremberg (buried), July 30, 1655. He studied organ, violin, and composition with his father, and after receiving instruction in keyboard instruments, cornett, trombone, bassoon, viola, and composition from Jakob Paumann in Augsburg (1620–23), he was active in Nuremberg as a city musician. He then completed his training with Walter Rowe in Berlin (1627). He returned to Nuremberg in 1627, and was made organist at St. Lorenz in 1634. On many occasions he was called upon to act as Kapellmeister to the city. His *Seelewig* (1644; publ. in *Frauenzimmer Gesprächspiele*, Vol. IV, 1644; ed. in *Monatshefte für Musikgeschichte*, XIII, 1881) is the earliest extant Singspiel, which he wrote in the Italian manner. He also composed incidental music, about 50 lieder, etc.

BIBL.: H. Druener, *S.T. S. 1607–1655* (diss., Univ. of Bonn, 1946); P. Keller, *S.s Oper "Seelewig"* (diss., Univ. of Zürich, 1970). —NS/LK/DM

Stader (originally, **Molnár**), **Maria,** Hungarian-born Swiss soprano; b. Budapest, Nov. 5, 1911; d. Zürich, April 27, 1999. She was orphaned and while still young was sent to Switzerland by the International Red Cross, where she was adopted by a family named Stader. She studied with Ilona Durigo in Zürich, Hans Keller in Karlsruhe, Giannina Arangi-Lombardi in Milan, and Thérèse Behr-Schnabel in N.Y. In 1939 she won first prize in the Geneva International Competition, but the outbreak of World War II that year prevented her from actively pursuing her career. When the War ended in 1945, she began to tour in Europe, principally as a concert artist. During the 1949–50 season, she sang the Queen of the Night at London's Covent Garden. In 1954 she made her U.S. debut as a soloist with the Little Orch. Soc. Her engagements also took her to other North American music centers, as well as to Israel and the Far East. Following her retirement in 1969, she taught voice in Zürich. Her autobiography appeared as *Nehmt meinen Dank*. Stader was especially admired for her interpretations of Bach and Mozart, but she also was esteemed for her performances of works by A. Scarlatti, Gluck, Bruckner, and Mahler.—NS/LK/DM

Stadler, Abbé Maximilian (actually, **Johann Karl Dominik**), prominent Austrian keyboard player, music historian, and composer; b. Melk, Aug. 4, 1748; d. Vienna, Nov. 8, 1833. He began his musical training with Johann Leuthner, a bass at the Melk Benedictine abbey, then went as a choirboy in 1758 to Lilienfeld, where he received instruction in violin, clavichord, and organ; concurrently took music lessons with Albrechtsberger in Melk, and completed his education at the Jesuit Coll. in Vienna in 1762. In 1766 he returned to Melk and became a novice; took his vows in 1767 and was made a priest in 1772; then was head of the abbey's theological studies. After being made chaplain in Wullersdorf in 1783, he was elected prior of Melk in 1784. In 1786 he became abbot of Lilienfeld and in 1789 in Kremsmünster. After a sojourn in Linz (1791–96), he settled in Vienna. In 1803 he was secularized and was given the titular canonry of Linz; was parish priest in Alt-Lerchenfeld (1803–10) and Grossk-

rut (1810–15); then was again active in Vienna. He was esteemed as a keyboard player and composer by his contemporaries; his oratorio *Die Befreyung von Jerusalem* (1813) was widely performed in his day. His *Materialen zur Geschichte der Musik unter den österreichischen Regenten* (c. 1816–25) is duly recognized as the first Austrian history of music. He was a friend of Mozart, and took care of Mozart's MS of the Requiem, which he copied at Mozart's death. When the authenticity of the work was called into question by Gottfried Weber and others, Stadler publ. a pamphlet in its defense, *Vertheidigung der Echtheit des Mozartschen Requiems* (Vienna, 1825; supplement, 1826). His own compositions include, in addition to the above-cited oratorio, a Singspiel, *Das Studenten-Valete* (Melk, Sept. 6, 1781), incidental music, numerous sacred works, secular cantatas, lieder, orch. and chamber music pieces, keyboard works, and completions and arrangements of works by other composers.

WRITINGS: *Anleitung zur musikalischen Composition durch Würfelspiel* (MS, c. 1780); *Erklärung, wir man aus … Ziffer-und Notentabellen eine Menuet herauswürfeln könne* (Vienna, 1781); *Priorats-Ephemeriden* (MS, 1784–86); *Beschreibung der Fragmente aus Mozart's Nachlass* (MS, c. 1798); *Fragmente von Singstücken* (MS, c. 1798); *Fragmente einiger Mozartischen Klavierstucke, die von einem Liebhaber der Musik vollendet worden* (MS; ed. in *Österreichische Musikzeitschrift*, XXI, 1966); *Materialen zur Geschichte der Musik unter den österreichischen Regenten* (MS, c. 1816–25; ed. by K. Wagner, Kassel, 1974); *Eigenhändig geschriebene Selbst-Biographie des Hochwürdigen Herrn Maximilian Stadler* (MS, c. 1816–26; ed. in *Mozart-Jahrbuch* 1957); *Vertheidigung der Echtheit des Mozartschen Requiems* (Vienna, 1825; supplement 1826); *Nachtrag zur Vertheidigung* (Vienna, 1827); *Zweyter und letzter Nachtrag zur Vertheidigung … sammt Nachbericht über die Ausgabe … durch Herrn André in Offenbach, nebst Ehrenrettung Mozart's und vier fremden Briefen* (Vienna, 1827); *Biographische Notizen über Abbé Maximilian Stadler von ihm selbst aufgezeichnet* (MS, c. 1833; ed. in *Mozart-Jahrbuch* 1964).

BIBL.: H. Sabel, *M. S.s weltliche Werke und seine Beziehungen zur Wiener Klassik* (diss., Univ. of Cologne, 1941); K. Wagner, *A.M. S.* (Kassel, 1974).—NS/LK/DM

Stadler, Anton (Paul), famous Austrian clarinetist and basset-horn player; b. Bruck an der Leitha, June 28, 1753; d. Vienna, June 15, 1812. With his brother, Johann (Nepomuk Franz) Stadler (b. Vienna, May 6, 1755; d. there, May 2, 1804), a clarinetist and basset-horn player, he first attracted attention as a soloist with the Vienna Tonkünstler-Sozietät in 1773. After serving Count Dimitri Golitsin, the Russian ambassador to Vienna, they entered the service of the imperial wind band in 1782. They entered the Court Orch. as clarinetists in 1787, Johann taking first position and Anton second. Anton became one of Mozart's closest friends; the composer wrote his Quintet, K.581, and Clarinet Concerto, K.622, for him. After accompanying Mozart to Prague in 1791, where he played the clarinet and basset-horn obbligatos in *La clemenza di Tito* to great applause, he toured widely in Europe as a virtuoso. In 1796 he finally returned to his post in Vienna, being pensioned in 1799; then played for several seasons in the opera orch. In 1806 he made his farewell appearance as a solo artist with the Tonkünstler-Sozietät. Anton was also a competent composer, numbering among his works 10 sets of variations for Clarinet (Vienna, 1810), 12 ländlerische Tänze for 2 Clarinets (Vienna, c. 1823), 3 caprices for Clarinet (Vienna, c. 1825), 6 progressive duets for 2 Clarinets (Vienna, c. 1827), 18 trios for 3 Basset Horns, partitas for 6 Wind Instruments, and other pieces.—NS/LK/DM

Stadlmair, Hans, Austrian conductor and composer; b. Neuhofen an der Krems, May 3, 1929. He received his musical training in Linz and Vienna; eventually settled in Munich. In 1956 he founded the Munich Chamber Orch., with which he traveled on numerous tours in Europe, the U.S., South America, Africa, and Asia. He served as its music director until 1995. As a composer, he wrote mostly instrumental works, in a neo-Baroque manner, among them a Toccata for Strings and Harpsichord (1966), a Trumpet Concerto with Strings (1967), and *Sinfonia serena* for Strings (1970); he also wrote some choral pieces.—NS/LK/DM

Stadlmayr, Johann, eminent German composer; b. probably in Freising, Bavaria, c. 1575; d. Innsbruck, July 12, 1648. He went to Salzburg, where he entered the service of the Archbishop in 1603; in 1604 he was made Vice-Kapellmeister, and soon thereafter Kapellmeister. In 1607 he was called to Innsbruck as Kapellmeister at the Habsburg court of Archduke Maximilian II of the Tirol. After the latter's death, the new archduke, Leopold V, disbanded the Innsbruck court chapel in favor of his Alsatian establishment in 1618. Stadlmayr petitioned Leopold to retain his services, but it was not until 1624 that he was reappointed to his Innsbruck position, which subsequently flourished under his direction. Stadlmayr was a leading composer of music for the Catholic church. Among his works were 4 vols. of Magnificats (1603–18), 7 vols. of masses (1596–1643), hymns, motets, Psalms, etc.

BIBL.: J. Peregrinus (J. Hupfauf), *J. S.* (Salzburg, 1885); F. Daniel, *Die konzertanten Messen J. S.s* (diss., Univ. of Vienna, 1928); B. Hinterleitner, *Die Vokalmessen S.s* (diss., Univ. of Vienna, 1930); K. Gress, *Die Motetten J. S.s im Lichte der Entwicklung der Motette im beginnenden siebzehnten Jahrhundert* (diss., Univ. of Vienna, 1931); H. Junkermann, *The Magnificats of J. S.* (diss., Ohio State Univ., 1966).—NS/LK/DM

Staempfli, Edward, Swiss composer, pianist, and conductor; b. Bern, Feb. 1, 1908. He received training in composition from Jarnach and Maler in Cologne (1929–30) and Dukas in Paris (1930), and in conducting from Scherchen in Brussels (1935). After living in Paris (1930–39), he returned to Switzerland. He went to Heidelberg in 1951 before settling in Berlin in 1954. He made occasional appearances as a pianist and conductor, usually in hs own works. His early music reflected his Parisian sojourn, but later he embraced 12-tone writing.

WORKS: DRAMATIC: O p e r a : *Ein Traumspiel* (1943); *Medea* (1954); *Caligula* (1981–82). **B a l l e t :** Several works. **ORCH.:** 4 piano concertos (1932, 1933, 1954, 1963); 4 violin concertos (1936, 1939, 1941, 1990); 6 syms. (1938–88); Concerto for 2 Pianos and Orch. (1940); *Praeludim und Variationen über ein*

Tessiner Volkslied (1945); *Mouvements concertantes* (1947); *Epitaphe pour Paul Eluard* (1954); *Fantasie* for Strings (1955); *Strophen* (1958); *5 Nachstücke* (1961); *Musik* for 16 Strings (1968); *Tripartita* for 3 Pianos and 23 Winds (1969); *Satze und Gegensatze* for Vibraphone, Piano, Percussion, and 15 Strings (1972); Concerto for Horn, Trumpet, Trombone, and Orch. (1984); *Helles Licht und spate Schatten* (1988); Cello Concerto (1991); *Ornamente III* (1992). **CHAMBER:** 6 string quartets (1926–62); Quartet for Flute and String Trio (1932); 2 piano trios (1932, 1956); Wind Quintet (1934); 2 string trios (1937, 1984); Wind Trio (1949); *Ornamente I* for 2 Flutes, Celesta, and Percussion (1960) and *III* for Oboe, Saxophone, Marimbaphone, Percussion, and Harp (1983); Trio for Violin, Clarinet, and Piano (1985); Duo for Alto Flute and Cello (1987); Quintet for Flute, Violin, Viola, Cello, and Piano (1988); *Why not?*, quartet for Alto Saxophone, Trumpet, Vibraphone, and Piano (1990); Quintet for 2 Violins, Viola, Cello, and Double Bass (1992); piano pieces. **VOCAL:** Oratorios; cantatas; choruses; songs.—NS/LK/DM

Stafford, Jo (Elizabeth), American singer; b. Coalinga, Calif., Nov. 12, 1917. Stafford, a pure-voiced, classically trained contralto, was one of the most successful singers in popular music from the mid-1940s to the mid-1950s. Emerging from earlier work with the vocal group the Pied Pipers and as a bandsinger with Tommy Dorsey, she built a solo career on radio and television appearances and recordings, including 78 chart songs between 1944 and 1957, among them "Candy," "You Belong to Me," and "Make Love to Me!" She also maintained a pseudonymous career as a comedy singer.

Stafford's parents, Grover Cleveland Stafford and Anna York Stafford, moved from Tenn. to Calif. shortly before her birth. She grew up in Long Beach while her father worked in the oil fields. Her mother was an accomplished five-string banjo player. She studied piano as a child and had five years of voice training as an adolescent. When she graduated from high school in 1935, she joined The Stafford Sisters, a vocal group featuring her older sisters, which worked on local radio and sang backgrounds on the soundtracks of film musicals.

The Stafford Sisters were heard in the Fred Astaire film *A Damsel in Distress*, released in November 1937, and appeared in *Gold Mine in the Sky*, released in June 1938. While they were doing backgrounds for the film *Alexander's Ragtime Band* (eventually released in August 1938), Stafford began singing with two all-male vocal groups also working on the picture, the Four Esquires and the Three Rhythm Kings, and when one of her sisters married and retired, breaking up The Stafford Sisters, she and the other two groups formed an octet, The Pied Pipers. She also married one of the members, John Huddleston.

The group caught the attention of Paul Weston (real name Wetstein, 1912–96) and Axel Stordahl, arrangers for Tommy Dorsey's orchestra, and they were hired to appear on Dorsey's radio program in N.Y., debuting on *The Raleigh-Kool Show* on Dec. 28, 1938. They performed on the show for several weeks, then signed to RCA Victor Records and cut a couple of singles on June 6, 1939, but then returned to Calif. where attrition reduced them to a quartet. Dorsey then called to offer them a job with his band and they joined him in Chicago in December 1939.

The Pied Pipers' first notable vocal on a Dorsey recording came with "I'll Never Smile Again" (music and lyrics by Ruth Lowe), on which they accompanied Frank Sinatra; the record hit #1 in July 1940. From 1941 to 1943 they were also featured on such Top Ten hits as "Star Dust" (music by Hoagy Carmichael, lyrics by Mitchell Parish), "Do I Worry?" (music and lyrics by Stanley Cowan and Bobby Worth), "Dolores" (music by Louis Alter, lyrics by Frank Loesser), "Oh! Look at Me Now" (music by Joe Bushkin, lyrics by John De Vries), "Let's Get Away from It All" (music by Matt Dennis, lyrics by Tom Adair), "Just as Though You Were Here" (music by John Benson Brooks, lyrics by Eddie De-Lange), "There Are Such Things" (music and lyrics by Stanley Adams, Abel Baer, and George W. Meyer), and "It Started All Over Again" (music by Carl Fischer, lyrics by Bill Carey).

The Pied Pipers performed on Dorsey's network radio shows, notably the *Fame and Fortune* series of 1940–41, and appeared with the Dorsey band in the films *Las Vegas Nights* (March 1941), *Ship Ahoy* (June 1942), and *DuBarry Was a Lady* (August 1943). Dorsey also occasionally featured Stafford on recordings, giving her first solo with "Little Man with a Candy Cigar" (music by Matt Dennis, lyrics by Townsend Brigham), recorded Feb. 7, 1941. She duetted with Sy Oliver on "Yes, Indeed!" (music and lyrics by Sy Oliver), which peaked in the Top Ten in August 1941.

The Pied Pipers left Dorsey in November 1942. Huddleston went into the army and was replaced by Hal Hooper, one of the original members when the group was an octet. Huddleston and Stafford divorced in 1943. Stafford took a job singing on the musical variety radio series *The Colgate Program* starring Al Jolson through June 1943, but she remained in the Pied Pipers, with whom she appeared on the radio series *Johnny Mercer's Music Shop* from June to September. In August the Pied Pipers appeared in the film *Gals, Incorporated*.

Stafford and The Pied Pipers were each signed to Capitol Records and recorded their first session on Oct. 15, 1943, backed by an orchestra conducted by Paul Weston, Capitol's musical director. Both sides of Stafford's debut solo single, "Old Acquaintance" (music by Franz Waxman, lyrics by Kim Gannon) and "How Sweet You Are" (music by Arthur Schwartz, lyrics by Frank Loesser), reached the charts in January 1944. The Pied Pipers' recording of "Mairzy Doats" (music and lyrics by Milton Drake, Al Hoffman, and Jerry Living-ston) hit the Top Ten in April, but when both sides of Stafford's second Capitol single, "I Love You" (music and lyrics by Cole Porter) and "Long Ago (And Far Away)" (music by Jerome Kern, lyrics by Ira Gershwin), released the same month, took off for the Top Ten, she amicably left the group, which replaced her with June Hutton.

Both Stafford and the Pied Pipers were again featured on the *Music Shop* series, which resumed June 12 and continued through Dec. 8. She returned to the Top Ten with "It Could Happen to You" (music by James

Van Heusen, lyrics by Johnny Burke) in September and her final single with The Pied Pipers, "The Trolley Song" (music and lyrics by Hugh Martin and Ralph Blane), peaked in the Top Ten in December.

In her solo career, Stafford focused on radio and recordings, only rarely giving live performances. The week after leaving the *Music Shop* series in December 1944, she began hosting the weeknight series *The Chesterfield Supper Club* on Tuesdays and Thursdays. She cut back to just Tuesdays in 1948; the show ran through Sept. 2, 1949. She also hosted her own *Jo Stafford Show* from Nov. 9 to Dec. 25, 1945, and again from Nov. 11, 1948, to May 5, 1949. She costarred with Tony Martin on *The Carnation Contented Hour* from Oct. 2, 1949, to Dec. 30, 1951, and also appeared on other shows, notably *Club Fifteen*. She scored four Top Ten hits in 1945, the most successful of which was a duet with Johnny Mercer with the backing of the Pied Pipers on "Candy" (music and lyrics by Mack David, Joan Whitney, and Alex Kramer) that hit #1 in March.

There were another four Top Ten hits in 1946 and four more in 1947, among them "Temptation (Tim-Tayshun)" (music by Nacio Herb Brown, lyrics by Arthur Freed), a novelty performance on which she duetted with comic singer Red Ingle and the Natural Seven under the pseudonym Cinderella G. Stump; the record topped the charts in June 1947 and sold a million copies. Her only Top Ten hit of 1948 came with "Say Something Sweet to Your Sweetheart" (music and lyrics by Sid Tepper and Roy Brodsky), on which she was paired with Gordon MacRae. But her seven Top Ten hits in 1949, the most successful of which was "My Darling, My Darling" (music and lyrics by Frank Loesser), another pairing with MacRae that hit #1 in January, made her second only to Perry Como as the most successful recording artist of the year. She and MacRae also hit the Top Ten of the album charts in April 1949 with their set of songs from Cole Porter's Broadway musical *Kiss Me, Kate*.

In 1950, Stafford enjoyed three Top Ten singles, the most successful of which was "No Other Love," which Paul Weston and Bob Russell based on Chopin's "Etude No. 3 in E." Weston left Capitol for Columbia Records, and Stafford followed him in the fall of 1950; they married in 1952 and had two children, Tim and Amy, both of whom became professional musicians.

The switch in record labels did not affect Stafford's success: she had four Top Ten hits in 1951, notably "Shrimp Boats" (music and lyrics by Paul Mason Howard and Paul Weston); four in 1952, among them the long-running #1 "You Belong to Me" (music and lyrics by Pee Wee King, Redd Stewart, and Chilton Price); one, "Keep It a Secret" (music and lyrics by Jessie Mae Robinson) in 1953; and the chart-topping million-seller "Make Love to Me!" (music by Paul Mares, Leon Rappolo, Ben Pollack, George Brunies, Mel Stitzel, and Walter Melrose, lyrics by Bill Norvas and Allan Cope-land) in 1954. She returned to radio with the weekday *Jo Stafford Show* from Jan. 19 to June 12, 1953, and appeared on the *Chesterfield Supper Club* during the 1954–55 season. And she had a weekly 15-minute television program, *The Jo Stafford Show*, from Feb. 2, 1954 to June 28,

1955; it earned her a 1954 Emmy nomination for Best Female Singer.

Stafford gradually cut back her professional activities from the mid-1950s. In 1957, in addition to her recordings under her own name, she joined Weston as the comically inept musical duo Jonathan and Darlene Edwards, initially on four cuts on his album *The Original Piano Artistry of Jonathan Edwards*. *Jonathan and Darlene Edwards in Paris*, released in 1960, won the Grammy for Best Comedy Performance, Musical. In 1961 she went to England and taped a musical television series for syndication. She re-signed to Capitol Records and rerecorded many of her earlier efforts in stereo, also cutting a religious album, *Sweet Hour of Prayer*, that earned her a 1964 Grammy nomination for Best Gospel or Other Religious Recording (Musical). She recorded for other labels during the 1960s as well. In the 1970s Paul Weston acquired her master recordings from Columbia and set up Corinthian Records to reissue them.

DISC.: *Music of My Life* (1940); *Jo Stafford with Gordon MacRae* (1949); *Autumn in New York* (1950); *Songs of Faith* (1950); *Songs for Sunday Evening* (1950); *American Folk Songs* (1950); *As You Desire Me* (1952); *Starring Jo Stafford* (1953); *Broadway's Best* (1953); *My Heart's in the Highland* (1954); *Garden of Prayers* (1954); *Happy Holiday* (1955); *Soft and Sentimental* (1955); *Guys and Dolls* (1955); *A Girl Named Jo* (1956); *Once Over Lightly* (1957); *Songs of Scotland* (1957); *Swingin' Down Broadway* (1958); *Ballad of the Blues* (1959); *Jo + Jazz* (1960); *Whispering Hope* (1962); *Sweet Hour of Prayer* (1964); *This is Jo Stafford* (1966).—**WR**

Stagno, Roberto (real name, Vincenzo Andriolo),

Italian tenor; b. Palermo, Oct. 11, 1840; d. Genoa, April 26, 1897. He studied with Giuseppe Lamperti in Milan, making his operatic debut as Rodrigo in Rossini's *Otello* in Lisbon (1862); then sang with notable success in Madrid (from 1865), Moscow (1868), and Buenos Aires (from 1879), and throughout Italy. While in Buenos Aires, he became the mentor of the soprano Gemma Bellincioni; their teacher-pupil relationship developed into intimacy, and they subsequently toured widely together. Their daughter, Bianca Stagno-Bellincioni (b. Budapest, Jan. 23, 1888; d. Milan, July 26, 1980), became a singer. Stagno was engaged for the first season of the Metropolitan Opera in N.Y., making his debut there as Manrico in *Il Trovatore* on Oct. 26, 1883; remained there for only that season. In 1884 he appeared at the Paris Théâtre- Italien. He was chosen to create the role of Turiddu in *Cavalleria rusticana* opposite Bellincioni's Santuzza in Rome (1890).

BIBL.: B. Stagno-Bellincioni, *R. S. e Gemma Bellincioni, intimi* (Florence, 1943).—**NS/LK/DM**

Stählin, Jacob von,

German music historian; b. Memmingen, May 10, 1709; d. St. Petersburg, July 6, 1785. He was educated at the Memmingen Lateinschule, the Zittau Gymnasium, and the Univ. of Leipzig; while in Leipzig, he became a friend of Bach. In 1735 he went to Russia, where he worked as a fireworks director and as a teacher of poetry and rhetoric; he held various posts at the imperial court in St. Petersburg. His valuable *Nachrichten von der Musik in Russland* (publ. in J. Haigold's *Beylagen zum neuveranderten Russland*, Riga and Leipzig, 1769–70) was the first study of Russian music, theater, and dance.—**NS/LK/DM**

Stahlman, Sylvia,

American soprano; b. Nashville, March 5, 1929; d. St. Petersburg, Fla., Aug. 19, 1998. She was a student at the Juilliard School of Music in N.Y. and of Toti Dal Monte. Under the name Giulia Bardi, she made her operatic debut at the Théâtre de la Monnaie in Brussels in 1951 as Elvira in *I Puritani*. After singing Lucia, Gilda, Amina, and Dinorah there, she returned to the U.S. and sang at the N.Y.C. Opera in 1956 under her real name. In 1957 she appeared at the San Francisco Opera. From 1958 to 1960 she sang with the Frankfurt am Main Opera. In 1959 she was engaged as Ilia at the Glyndebourne Festival, and then portrayed Sophie at the San Francisco Opera in 1960. In 1964 she appeared as Daphne at the Santa Fe Opera. She also was active as a concert artist. She retired from the operatic stage in 1971.—**NS/LK/DM**

Staier, Andreas,

German fortepianist and harpsichordist; b. Göttingen, Sept. 13, 1955. He studied piano before concentrating his attention on the fortepiano and harpsichord. After training at the Hannover Hochschule für Musik (1974–79), he studied at the Amsterdam Cons. (1980–82). From 1983 to 1986 he was the harpsichordist with Musica Antiqua Köln, with which he traveled throughout Europe, North and South America, Australia, New Zealand, and Southeast Asia. From 1986 he pursued a career as a soloist with the leading period instrument ensembles, as a recitalist, and as a chamber music player. He also taught at the Schola Cantorum Basiliensis in Basel from 1987 to 1995. Among the composers he has revealed a special affinity for are J.S. Bach, D. Scarlatti, Haydn, Mozart, and Schubert. He has also played works by composers infrequently heard, among them Steffan, Dussek, and Salieri.—**LK/DM**

Stainer, Jacob (or Jakob),

esteemed Austrian violin maker; b. Absam, near Hall, Tirol, July 14, 1617?; d. there, Oct. or Nov. 1683. He was trained as a chorister, then apprenticed to a German violin maker who lived in Italy. After traveling to Salzburg, Munich, Venice, and other cities to sell his instruments, he settled in Absam. He was named archprince's servant (purveyor to the court) by Ferdinand Karl, prince of Tirol, in 1656. His fortunes suffered an adverse turn when, in 1669, he was accused of Lutheran leanings, and spent several months in prison; was stricken with bouts of mental instability from 1675, although he continued to make instruments during periods of remission. His instruments were made between 1638 and 1682. He also made alto and tenor viols, cellos, and double basses. His violins were especially admired for their expert craftsmanship and beauty of tone. He was no relation to Markus (Marcus) Stainer (b. Hallein, Salzburg, c. 1633; d. Laufen, Upper Bavaria, Nov. 27, 1693), who was also a fine Austrian violin maker. The latter Stainer settled in Laufen, where he was made a citizen in 1656; his instruments are highly prized.

BIBL.: S. Ruf, *Der Geigenmacher Jacobus S. von Absam im Tirol* (Innsbruck, 1872; second ed., 1892); F. Lentner, *J. S.s Lebenslauf im Lichte archivarischer Forschung* (Leipzig, 1898); Princess de la Tour et Taxis, *Le Violon de J. S.* (Paris, 1910); W. Senn, *J. S., der Geigenmacher zu Absam: Die Lebesgeschichte nach urkundlichen Quellen* (Innsbruck, 1951); W. Salmen, ed., *J. S. und seine Zeit: Bericht uber die J.- S.-Tagung Innsbruck 1983* (Innsbruck, 1984); W. Senn and K. Roy, *J. S.: Leben und Werk des Tiroler Meisters, 1617–1683* (Frankfurt am Main, 1986).—**NS/LK/DM**

Stainer, Sir John, English organist, music scholar, and composer; b. London, June 6, 1840; d. Verona, March 31, 1901. He received organ lessons at an early age from his father, William Stainer, the parish schoolmaster at St. Thomas, Southwark, and although he was blinded in the left eye in an accident when he was 5, he persevered in his music training. He was a probationer (1848–49) and a chorister (1849–54) at St. Paul's Cathedral in London, then served as organist at St. Benedict and St. Peter, Paul's Wharf (1854–56), and subsequently at the Coll. of St. Michael, Tenbury. He continued his education at Christ Church, Oxford (B.Mus., 1860; B.A., 1864; D.Mus., 1865; M.A., 1866). He served as organist at St. Paul's Cathedral (1872–88) and at the National Training School of Music (1876–89), where he also was its principal (1881–89). From 1889 until his death he was a prof. at Oxford Univ. In 1888 he was knighted. He wrote much liturgical music, which has not withstood the test of time. His reputation rests upon his scholarly pursuits.

WORKS: DRAMATIC: Oratorios: *Gideon* (Oxford, 1865); *The Crucifixion* (London, Feb. 24, 1887). **Cantatas:** *The Daughter of Jarius* (Worcester, 1878); *St. Mary Magdalen* (Gloucester, 1887); *Jubilee* (1887); *The Story of the Cross* (1893). **OTHER:** Services; anthems; hymn tunes; madrigals; partsongs; songs; organ music. **EDITIONS:** With H. Bramley, *Christmas Carols, New and Old* (London, 1871); with S. Flood et al., *The Cathedral Psalter* (London, 1874); *Six Italian Songs* (London, 1896); *The Church Hymnary* (Edinburgh, 1898); with J. and E. Stainer, *Early Bodleian Music* (London and N.Y., 1901); with W. Frere and H. Briggs, *A Manual of Plainsong* (London, 1902).

WRITINGS (all publ. in London): *A Theory of Harmony* (1871); with W. Barrett, *A Dictionary of Musical Terms* (1876); *The Organ* (1877); *Music of the Bible, with an Account of the Development of Modern Musical Instruments from Ancient Types* (1879; second ed., 1914, with suppl. by F. Galpin); *Music in Relation to the Intellect and Emotions* (1892); *Dufay and His Contemporaries* (1898).

BIBL.: P. Carlton, *The Life and Influence of Sir J. S.* (diss., Univ. of East Anglia, 1976); idem, *J. S. and the Musical Life of Victorian Britain* (Newton Abbot, 1984).—**NS/LK/DM**

Stainov, Petko, Bulgarian composer; b. Kazanluk, Dec. 1, 1896; d. Sofia, June 25, 1977. Despite an almost complete loss of sight at age 5, he learned to play piano by ear. He studied composition with Wolf and piano with E. Münch in Braunschweig and Berlin (1920–24). Returning to Sofia, he taught piano at the Inst. for the Blind (1927–41); then was director of the National Opera (1941–44) and of the Inst. for Music of the Bulgarian Academy of Sciences (from 1948).

WORKS: ORCH.: *Thracian Dances* (1925–26); *Legend,* symphonic poem (1927; Sofia, Jan. 1, 1928); *Balkan,* overture (1936); 2 syms. (1945, 1948); *Youth Concert Overture* (1952). **VOCAL:** Numerous choruses and choral ballads.

BIBL.: V. Krastev, *P. S.* (Sofia, 1957).—**NS/LK/DM**

Stalvey, Dorrance, American composer; b. Georgetown, S.C., Aug. 21, 1930. He studied clarinet and general music subjects at the Coll. of Music in Cincinnati (M.M., 1955). Prior to his late twenties, his interest was primarily in jazz improvisation. In composition he was wholly self-taught, and thanks to that developed an independent style marked by quaquaversal contrapuntal and harmonic techniques vivified by asymmetrical rhythms. He embraced a variegated career of teaching, composing, and management. He lectured on music history, theory, and analysis, off and on, at various schools; was an asst. prof. (1972–77) and then full prof. (1977–80) in composition at the Immaculate Heart Coll. in Los Angeles. In 1971 he assumed the post of artistic director of the Monday Evening Concerts in Los Angeles, and since 1981 has been music director for the Los Angeles County Museum of Art. He also was active as a radio commentator and conductor. Stalvey received several awards from ASCAP and other musical organizations. His compositions had frequent performances, and astonishingly good reviews from habitually fatigued critics for his special spatial effects in multifarious multimedia productions.

WORKS: *Celebration-Principium* for Brass and Percussion (1967); *Points-Lines-Circles* for Clarinet, Double Bass, Harp, Guitar, and Percussion (1968); *In Time and Not* for Multimedia Ensembles (1970); *Togethers I* for Guitar and Tape (1970), *II* for Percussion and Tape (1970), and *III* for Clarinet and Tape (1970); *Celebration-Sequents I* for Various Instruments (1973), *II* (1976), and *IV* (1980); *Agathlon* for Modern Dance and Instruments (1978); *Ex Ferus* for 6 Cellos or String Sextet (1982); *Pound Songs* for Soprano and Instruments (1985); *Dualities* for Guitar, Soprano, and Instruments (1986–87); *String Quartet 1989* (1989); *Exordium/Genesis/Dawn* for 6 Players (1990). Also theatrical multi-lectures; chamber works (with and without tape); piano solos; composite compositions compounded of combinations of original numbers.—**NS/LK/DM**

Stam, Henk (actually, **Hendrikus Gerardus**), Dutch composer, conductor, teacher, and writer on music; b. Utrecht, Sept. 26, 1922. He studied instrumentation with Hendrik Andriessen and piano with Jan Wagenaar and André Jurres at the Utrecht Cons.; later studied musicology at the Univ. of Utrecht and composition with Fortner in Germany. He taught at the music school in Deventer (1948–54), then was director at the music schools in Zeeland (1954–61) and Rotterdam (1962–72).

WORKS: 5 piano sonatinas (1943, 1946, 1946, 1947, 1953); 2 *Rispetti* for Baritone and String Orch. (1944); 3 string quartets (1947, 1948, 1949); *Histoire de Barbar,* 8 pieces for Piano (1949); *Cassation,* pantomime for 3 Dancers, Violin, Flute, Cello, Trombone, Mezzo-soprano, Baritone, Speaking Voice, and Chamber Orch. (1949); Violin Sonata (1950); Sonata for Solo Violin (1951); *Suite* for Violin and Piano (1953); *Ouverture Michiel de Ruyter* (1957); Cello Sonata (1966); *Tropic* for Flute, Oboe, and Piano (1972); Flute Sonata (1972); *Klachte der Prinsesse van Oranjen* for Chorus and 3 Trumpets ad libitum (1973); *Sonata concertante* for Cello and Piano (1982); *Berceuse pour B.* for Cello and Piano (1983); choruses.—**NS/LK/DM**

Stamaty, Camille (-Marie), Graeco-French pianist, teacher, and composer; b. Rome, March 13?, 1811; d. Paris, April 19, 1870. He was of Greek-French origin; his mother, a Frenchwoman, educated him after the death of his father in 1818, and took him to Paris, where he became a pupil of Kalkbrenner; in 1836 he went to Leipzig, where he studied with Mendelssohn. He returned to Paris the next year and remained there as a pianist and teacher; among his students were Saint-Saëns and Gottschalk. He became well known as a champion of the music of Bach, Mozart, and Beethoven. In 1862 he was made a Chevalier of the Legion d'honneur. He wrote a Piano Concerto, which won the approbation of Schumann, as well as a Piano Trio, various works for piano, including a Sonata, variations, and solo pieces, and a number of didactic works. —NS/LK/DM

Stamitz, family of distinguished Bohemian musicians:

(1) Johann (Wenzel Anton) (Jan Waczlaw or **Václav Antonín) Stamitz,** eminent violinist, teacher, and composer; b. Deutsch-Brod, June 19, 1717; d. Mannheim, March 27, 1757. He most likely began his musical training with his father in Deutsch-Brod; after studies at the Iglau Jesuit Gymnasium (1728–34), he attended the Univ. of Prague (1734–35). About 1741 he entered the service of the Mannheim court, where his first patron was Carl Philipp, margrave of Pfalz. His playing at the coronation of the Emperor Charles VII on Feb. 12, 1742, created a sensation, and Prince Carl Theodor, who in 1743 became Palatine Elector, engaged him as a chamber musician; the court journals reported on his virtuosity in extravagant terms, extolling his ability to perform his own concerto on several different instruments—violin, viola d'amore, cello, and contra-violin solo. In 1743 the Elector made him "first court violinist" in Mannheim; the next year, he married Maria Antonia Luneborn. So widespread was Stamitz's fame that Baron Grimm publ. in Paris a satirical pamphlet, *Le Petit Prophête de Boehmisch-Broda,* ridiculing Stamitz's innovations. By 1746 he was Konzertmeister, and then was promoted to the newly created position of director of instrumental music in 1750, being charged with composing orch. and chamber music for the Mannheim court. On Sept. 8, 1754, he made his debut at the Paris Concert Spirituel; also was engaged as director of La Poupeliniere's private orch. and made some appearances at the Concert Italien. In 1755 he returned to his duties in Mannheim, where the Court Orch. became the finest in Europe under his discerning leadership. Among his outstanding students were Cannabich, W. Cramer, and I. Fränzl, as well as his own sons, Carl and Anton. Stamitz's major contribution to music rests upon his skillful adaptation and expansion of the overture style of Jommelli and his Italian compatriots to the Mannheim school of composition. His most important works are his 58 extant syms. and 10 orch. trios. Among his other extant works are violin concertos, 11 flute concertos, 2 harpsichord concertos, an Oboe Concerto, a Clarinet Concerto, much chamber music, and some sacred vocal pieces. For a selection of his orch. and chamber music, see H. Riemann, ed., Denkmäler der Tonkunst in Bayern, IV, Jg. III/1 (1902), XIII, Jg. VII/2 (1906), and XXVII, Jg. XVI (1915).

BIBL.: P. Gradenwitz, *J. S.: Das Leben* (Brno, 1936; second ed., greatly aug., as *J. S.: Leben, Umwelt, Werke,* 2 vols., Wilhelmshaven, 1984); P. Nettl, *Der kleine "Prophète von Böhmisch-Broda"* (Esslingen, 1953); H.-R. Durrenmatt, *Die Durchführung bei J. S.* (Bern, 1969); E. Wolf, *The Symphonies of J. S.: Authenticity, Chronology and Style* (diss., N.Y.U., 1972); E. Wolf, *The Symphonies of J. S., A Study in the Formation of the Classic Style* (Utrecht, 1981).

His 2 sons were also distinguished musicians:

(2) Carl (Philipp) Stamitz, violinist, violist, viola d'amorist, and composer; b. Mannheim (baptized), May 8, 1745; d. Jena, Nov. 9, 1801. He commenced his training with his father, then studied with Cannabich, Holzbauer, and Richter at the Mannheim court, where he played second violin in the Court Orch. (1762–70). With his brother, Anton, he went to Strasbourg in 1770; by 1771 he was in Paris as court composer and conductor to Duke Louis of Noailles. On March 25, 1772, Carl and Anton made their first appearance at the Concert Spirituel, where Carl performed regularly until 1777; he also made tours as a virtuoso to Vienna in 1772, Frankfurt am Main in 1773, and Augsburg, Vienna, and Strasbourg in 1774. After a London sojourn (1777–79), he went to The Hague, where he made appearances at the court as a violist (1782–84). He then toured extensively in Germany, including appearances in Hamburg, Leipzig, and Berlin in 1786 and in Dresden and Halle in 1787; also performed in Prague in 1787. He served as director of Kassel's Liebhaber concerts (1789–90). In 1795 he settled in Jena as city Kapellmeister and as a music teacher at the Univ. He was a significant composer of orch. music. He wrote at least 51 syms. (28 are extant), some 38 syms. concertantes, and more than 60 concertos, including 15 for Violin, 10 for Clarinet, 7 for Flute, and 7 for Bassoon; many of his concertos are lost. Among his other works are chamber music pieces and vocal music. Some of his works are found in H. Riemann, ed., Denkmäler der Tonkunst in Bayern, XV, Jg. VIII/2 (1907), XXVII, Jg. XV (1914), and XXVIII, Jg. XVI (1915).

BIBL.: F. Kaiser, *C. S. (1745–1801): Biographische Beiträge, das symphonische Werk, thematischer Katalog der Orchesterwerke* (diss., Univ. of Marburg, 1962); D. Thomason, *A Discussion of the Viola d'Amore Music of K. S.* (n.p., 1979); M. Jacob, *Die Klarinettenkonzerte von C. S.* (Wiesbaden, 1991).

(3) Anton (actually, Thadäus Johann Nepomuk) Stamitz, violinist, violist, and composer; b. Deutsch-Brod (baptized), Nov. 27, 1750; d. probably in Paris or Versailles, after 1789. He studied violin with his brother, Carl, and with Cannabich in Mannheim, where he was second violinist in the Court Orch. (1764–70). He then accompanied his brother to Strasbourg, moving on to Paris with him by 1771, where from 1772 he appeared regularly at the Concert Spirituel. He was active in Versailles from 1778, and was the teacher of Rodolphe Kreutzer until 1780; then was a member of the musique du roi from 1782 until disappearing from the musical scene without a trace in 1789. Among his extant compositions are 12 syms., 2 syms. concertantes, over 22 violin concertos, several other concertos, 66 string quartets, many trios, numerous duos, etc.—NS/LK/DM

Stamm, Marvin (Louis), jazz trumpeter, flugelhornist; b. Memphis, Tenn., May 23, 1939. He began his study of music at the age of 12 in junior high school. He continued music at Memphis Central H.S. under the tutelage of A. E. McLain, studying trumpet with Perry Wilson, and freelancing around town. He then attended North Tex. State Univ., where he played in the Lab Band and freelanced around the Dallas–Fort Worth area. Upon graduation, he became Stan Kenton's trumpet soloist for two years, then moved to Reno, Nev., where he worked in show bands until he joined Woody Herman (September 1965–July 1966). He settled in N.Y. in late 1966 and did studio work. He played with the Thad Jones/Mel Lewis Jazz Orch. from 1966 until early 1973. He was also a member of the Duke Pearson Big Band during the band's three year existence (1968–71). Stamm recorded with Quincy Jones, Oliver Nelson, Gary McFarland, Charles Mingus, Freddie Hubbard, Don Sebesky, Stanley Turrentine, Frank Foster, George Benson, Paul McCartney, the Rolling Stones, Paul Simon, Aretha Franklin, James Brown, and Barbra Streisand. He made several tours with Frank Sinatra beginning in 1973. He left the studio scene around 1987, and since that time has worked with John Lewis's American Jazz Orch., the Bob Mintzer Band, the George Gruntz Concert Jazz Band, Louis Bellson's big band and quintet and, at times, with the big bands of composers Maria Schneider and Rich Shemaria. In the late 1990s, he toured primarily as a guest soloist, as well as in a duo with Bill Mays and a quartet with Ed Soph. In 1998, he worked with trumpeter Dennis Najoom in a jazz/classical duo in which they performed compositions commissioned especially for them with an orch. or wind symphony. He visits universities and high schools across the U.S. and abroad as a clinician.

DISC.: *Machinations* (1968); *Stampede* (1983); *Bop Boy* (1990); *Mystery Man* (1992); *Dialogues/Poetry* (1997).—**LP**

Standage, Simon, English violinist, conductor, and teacher; b. High Wycombe, Buckinghamshire, Nov. 8, 1941. He studied at Bryanston School and the Univ. of Cambridge, and subsequently took private lessons with Ivan Galamian in N.Y. (1967–69). Upon his return to England, he became an assoc. member of the London Sym. Orch. and sub-concertmaster of the English Chamber Orch. In 1973 he was appointed principal violin of the English Concert and concertmaster of the Richard Hickox Orch. and City of London Sinfonia. In 1981 he founded the Salomon String Quartet. In 1983 he was appointed teacher of Baroque violin at the Royal Academy of Music. In 1990 he founded with Richard Hickox the Collegium Musicum 90 of London. From 1991 to 1995 he was assoc. director of the Academy of Ancient Music in London. In 1993 he was made prof. of Baroque violin at the Dresden Academy of Early Music. —**NS/LK/DM**

Standford, Patric (John), English composer, writer on music, and teacher; b. Barnsley, Feb. 5, 1939.

He was a student of Edmund Rubbra and Raymond Jones at the Guildhall School of Music and Drama in London (1961–63). After receiving the Mendelssohn Scholarship in 1964, he continued his studies with Malipiero in Italy and with Lutosławski. He taught at the Guildhall School of Music and Drama (1968–80) and also served as chairman of the Composer's Guild of Great Britain (1977–79). From 1979 to 1991 he was chairman of the British Music Information Centre. He was director of the music school at Bretton Hall Coll. (Univ. of Leeds) in Wakefield (1980–93). Standford travels widely as a lecturer and adjudicator, and writes regular features and reviews for British music journals. In 1983 he was awarded the Ernest Ansermet prize of Geneva for his third Sym., and in 1997 the first Kodály Prize of the City of Budapest for his masque *The Prayer of Saint Francis* for Chorus and Orch.

WORKS: DRAMATIC: O p e r a: *Villon* (1972–85). **B a l l e t:** *Celestial Fire* (1968; orch. suite, 1971); *Reflections* (1980). **O t h e r:** Light music for the theater, films, and television. **ORCH.:** 6 syms: No. 1, *The Seasons* (1971–72), No. 2, *Christus-Requiem* for 4 Soloists, Narrator, Chorus, Children's Chorus, and Orch. (1971–72; rev. 1980), No. 3, *Toward Paradise* for Chorus and Orch. (1982; Geneva, June 11, 1986), No. 4, *Taikyoku* for 2 Pianos and Percussion (1975–79), No. 5, with Soprano Solo (Manchester, Jan. 24, 1986), and No. 6 (1998); *Saracinesco,* symphonic poem (1966); *Notte,* poem for Chamber Orch. (1968); *Antitheses* for 15 Strings (1971); Cello Concerto (1974); Violin Concerto (1975); *Variations* (1977; arranged from the Piano Variations, 1969); Piano Concerto (1979); *Dialogues* for Cimbalom and Chamber Orch. (1981); *Folksongs* for Strings (3 sets, 1982, 1985, 1986); *Rage* (1993). **CHAMBER:** 2 string quartets (1965, 1973); *Suite française,* 4 pieces for Wind Quintet (1964); *Cartoons* for Oboe, Clarinet, and Bassoon (1984); Concertino for Piano, Oboe, and String Trio (1986); *Suite humoresque* for Piano, Oboe, Clarinet, and Bassoon (1987); Piano Quartet (1988); *Divertimento* for Violin and Piano (1989). **P i a n o:** *Variations* (1969); Sonata (1979–80); *Faeries* (1987); *3 Nocturnes* (1991). **VOCAL:** 3 motets: *In memoriam Benjamin Britten* for Chorus (1976–77), *Mass* for Chorus and Brass Band (1980), and *O sacrum convivium* for Chorus (1985); *Mass of Our Lady and St. Rochus* for Chorus (1988); *The Inheritor* for Voice and String Quartet (1992); *A Messiah Reborn* for 4 Soloists, Chorus, and Orch., after Handel (1993); *The Prayer of Saint Francis,* masque for Chorus and Orch. (1997).—**NS/LK/DM**

Stanford, Sir Charles Villiers, eminent Irish organist, conductor, pedagogue, and composer; b. Dublin, Sept. 30, 1852; d. London, March 29, 1924. He studied piano, organ, violin, and composition with Michael Quarry at St. Patrick's Cathedral, and with Robert Stewart and Joseph Robinson at the Royal Irish Academy of Music in Dublin. In 1862 he was sent to London, where he studied piano with Ernst Pauer and composition with Arthur O'Leary. In 1870 he entered Queen's Coll., Cambridge, as a choral scholar (B.A., 1874), and then studied composition with Reinecke in Leipzig (1874–76) and with Kiel in Berlin (1876). Stanford was awarded the M.A. degree from Cambridge (1877). In 1883 he was appointed prof. of composition at the Royal Coll. of Music and conductor of the orch. there. In 1887 he also became a prof. of music at Cambridge, holding both positions until his death. He was conductor of the Leeds Festivals from 1901 to 1910, and appeared as guest conductor of his own works in Paris, Berlin, Amsterdam, and Brussels. From 1885 to 1902 he conducted the London Bach Choir. He was knighted in 1902. Stanford was an extremely able and industrious composer in a distinctly Romantic style, yet unmistakably national in musical materials, both Irish and English. In recent years there has been renewed interest in and appreciation of his music, both in England and abroad.

WORKS: DRAMATIC: O p e r a : *The Veiled Prophet of Khorassan* (1877; Hannover, Feb. 6, 1881); *Savonarola* (Hamburg, April 18, 1884); *The Canterbury Pilgrims* (London, April 23, 1884); *Lorenza* (c. 1894; not perf.); *Shamus O'Brian* (London, March 2, 1896); *Christopher Patch (The Barber of Bath)* (c. 1897; not perf.); *Much Ado about Nothing* (London, May 30, 1901); *The Critic, or An Opera Rehearsed* (London, Jan. 14, 1916); *The Traveling Companion* (1919; amateur perf., Liverpool, April 30, 1925; professional perf., Bristol, Oct. 25, 1926). **O t h e r :** Incidental music. **ORCH.:** 7 syms.: No. 1 (1876; London, March 8, 1879), No. 2, *Elegiac* (1880; Cambridge, March 7, 1882, composer conducting), No. 3, *Irish* (London, May 17, 1887), No. 4 (1888; Berlin, Jan. 14, 1889, composer conducting), No. 5, *L'Allegro ed il Penseroso* (1894; London, March 20, 1895, composer conducting), No. 6, "In honour of the life-work of a great artist: George Frederick Watts" (1905; London, Jan. 18, 1906), and No. 7 (1911; London, Feb. 22, 1912); *Suite* for Violin and Orch. (Berlin, Jan. 14, 1889; Joachim, soloist); 3 piano concertos (1896, 1915, 1919); *6 Irish Rhapsodies* (1901- c. 1923); Clarinet Concerto (1902; London, June 20, 1904, composer conducting); *Overture in the Style of a Tragedy* (1904); 2 violin concertos (1904, 1918); *Irish Concertino* for Violin, Cello, and Orch. (1919); *Variations* for Violin and Orch. (1921; also for Violin and Piano). **CHAMBER:** 4 violin sonatas (c. 1880, 1893, c. 1898, 1919); 3 piano trios (1889, 1899, 1918); 8 string quartets (c. 1891-c. 1919); 2 string quintets (1903, c. 1903); various piano pieces, including 5 sonatas (1917–21); organ music. **VOCAL:** *Eden*, oratorio (Birmingham, 1891); *Mass* (London, 1893); *Requiem* (Birmingham, 1897); *Te Deum* (Leeds, 1898); *Stabat Mater* (Leeds, 1907); numerous other works, including 2 *Magnificats* (1872, 1873), anthems, services, choruses, song cycles, and solo songs.

WRITINGS (all publ. in London): *Studies and Memories* (1908); *Musical Composition: A Short Treatise for Students* (1911; 6th ed., 1950); *Brahms* (1912); *Pages from an Unwritten Diary* (1914); *Interludes: Records and Reflections* (1922).

BIBL.: J. Porte, *Sir C.V. S.* (London and N.Y., 1921); J. Fuller Maitland, *The Music of Parry and S.* (Cambridge, 1934); H. Plunket Greene, *C.V. S.* (London, 1935); G. Norris, *S., the Cambridge Jubilee and Tchaikovsky* (Newton Abbot, 1980). —**NS/LK/DM**

Stanislav, Josef, Czech composer and pedagogue; b. Hamburg, Jan. 22, 1897; d. Prague, Aug. 5, 1971. He went in his youth to Prague, where he took lessons in composition with Jeremiáš and Foerster and in piano with Mikeš and Veselý; completed his training in the Cons. master classes of Novák in composition (1922) and of Hoffmeister in piano (1929); also studied with Nejedý at the Univ. He joined the Czech Communist party and was active in various left-wing organizations. His music was banned during the German occupation, but after the liberation in 1945, he played a prominent role in Czech musical life; was a prof. at the Prague Academy of Music (from 1948) and director of the ethnographical and folklore inst. of the Czech Academy of Sciences (from 1953).

WORKS: *Symfonické vypravovani* (Symphonic Narration; n.d.); *Rudoarmějská symfonie* (Red Army Sym.; 1942); Viola Sonata (1920); 3 piano sonatas (1921, 1929, 1944); Viola Sonata (1933); String Quartet (1935); several cantatas; choruses; songs; incidental music.

WRITINGS: *O té lidové a vážné hudbě a lidových hudebnícich* (Folk Music, Art Music, and Folk Musicians; Prague, 1939); *Hudebni kultura, umění a život* (Musical Culture, Art, and Life; Prague, 1940); *Ludvík Kuba* (Prague, 1963).—**NS/LK/DM**

Stanislavsky (real name, **Alexeiev**), **Konstantin (Sergeievich),** famous Russian actor and theater and opera director; b. Moscow, Jan. 17, 1863; d. there, Aug. 7, 1938. He received practical experience by performing in and directing operettas in his family's private theater; studied voice with Komisarzhevsky, but gave up all hope of a career in opera when his voice proved inadequate. Then, with Nemirovich-Danchanko, he founded the Moscow Art Theater in 1898; it became an innovative setting for both stage plays and operas. In 1918 he founded the Bolshoi Theater Opera Studio, which became an independent studio in 1920; it was named the Stanislavsky Opera Theater in his honor in 1926. The Stanislavsky method as applied to opera concentrates upon the musical score as the guiding force of a production, allowing all elements to evolve naturally to present a realistic work of art. He wrote several books on his theater methods.

BIBL.: G. Kristi, *Rabota Stanislavskovo v opernom teatre* (S.'s Work in the Opera Theater; Moscow, 1952); I. Vinogradskaya, ed., *Zhizn i tvorchestvo K.S. Stanislavskovo: Letopis* (The Life and Work of K.S. S.: A Chronicle; Moscow, 1973); E. Hapgood, ed., *S. on Opera* (N.Y., 1975).—**NS/LK/DM**

Stanley, Frank (originally, **Grinsted, William Stanley**), popular American bass singer of the early recording era; b. c. 1869; d. Dec. 12, 1910. Stanley began his career as a banjo player and made his first recordings as accompanist to Arthur Collins, but he was making his own recordings as a singer as early as 1899. He frequently recorded in duets with such partners as Byron Harlan, Corrine Morgan, Henry Burr, and Elise Stevenson. His biggest hits included "Blue Bell" (1904), "Good Evening, Caroline" (with Stevenson; 1909), and "Tramp! Tramp! Tramp!" (from Victor Herbert's *Naughty Marietta*; 1910). In 1906 he replaced Tom Daniels in The Peerless Quartet, taking over as lead singer and even managing the group. His most successful records with the quartet were "Honey Boy" (1907), "By the Light of the Silvery Moon" (1910), and "Silver Bell" (1910). He died of pneumonia at the age of 41. —**WR**

Stanley, John, prominent English organist and composer; b. London, Jan. 17, 1712; d. there, May 19, 1786. Blind from early childhood, he studied organ with Maurice Greene, and soon was able to fill church positions. He composed theater music, and publ. a number of instrumental works. He was the youngest individual ever to take the B.Mus. degree at the Univ. of

Oxford in 1729. In 1779 he succeeded Boyce as Master of the King's Band of Musicians. He enjoyed the friendship and esteem of Handel, after whose death he conducted performances of Handel's oratorios with J.C. Smith. He especially distinguished himself as a composer of keyboard music and cantatas.

WORKS: DRAMATIC: O p e r a : *Teraminta* (not perf.). **M a s q u e :** *The Tears and Triumphs of Parnassus* (London, Nov. 17, 1760). **P a s t o r a l :** *Arcadia, or The Shepherd's Wedding* (London, Oct. 26, 1761). **I n c i d e n t a l   M u s i c :** to J. Hawkesworth's *Oroonoko* (London, Dec. 1, 1759). **O r a t o - r i o s :** *Jephtha* (c. 1751–52); *Zimri* (London, March 12, 1760); *The Fall of Egypt* (London, March 23, 1774). **O T H E R :** Cantatas; various court odes; anthems and hymns; songs; much instrumental music.

BIBL.: G. Williams, *The Life and Works of J. S. (1712–86)* (diss., Univ. of Reading, 1977).—**NS/LK/DM**

Stanley Brothers, The, compelling bluegrass performers. **MEMBERSHIP:** Carter Glen Stanley, voc., gtr. (b. McClure, Va., Aug. 27, 1925; d. there, Dec. 1, 1966); Ralph Edmond Stanley, voc., bjo. (b. McClure, Va., Feb. 27, 1927). The most traditional-sounding of bluegrass bands, The Stanley Brothers with their group The Clinch Mountain Boys brought the high, lonesome mountain singing style to the new bluegrass style.

The Stanleys were raised in rural western Va., where their mother was an old-time banjo player. Both sons began playing the banjo, learning traditional songs like "Little Birdie" in the drop-thumb or clawhammer style. Carter switched to guitar after Ralph became proficient on banjo, and the duo began performing locally. Their first professional work came after World War II with Roy Sykes and The Blue Ridge Boys in 1946; one year later, they left the band, along with mandolinist "Pee Wee" (Darrell) Lambert, to form The Clinch Mountain Boys. It was about this time that they heard the legendary performances of Bill Monroe's Bluegrass Boys, and Ralph adopted the finger- picking style of Earl Scruggs to his banjo playing. The Stanley's band were hired to perform over the radio in Bristol, Tenn., and made their first recordings for the tiny Rich-R-Tone label out of Johnson City.

In 1949, they relocated to take a radio job in Raleigh, N. C., where they were heard by Columbia talent scout Art Slatherley, who signed them to that label. (Supposedly, Monroe left the label because he was angered by Columbia's decision to hire another bluegrass group; he signed to Decca in 1950.) The Stanleys recorded for Columbia for three years, featuring their breathtaking traditional harmonies on traditional mountain ballads and Carter Stanley's compositions in a traditional vein, including the classic "White Dove" and "A Vision of Mother." In 1952, guitarist/vocalist George Shuffler joined the group, a talented flatpicker who would be featured prominently as a soloist in the band for the next decade.

Carter took a job as lead vocalist for Bill Monroe's band briefly in 1952, recording the lead vocals on Monroe's own "Uncle Pen" and the honky-tonk song

"Sugar Coated Love." The brothers reunited in 1953, signing to Mercury, remaining with the label through 1958, and then recording for King/Starday through Carter's death. By this time, they had solidified their sound around lead guitar and banjo, with Ralph's licks limited to a fairly small repertoire. Carter's expressive lead vocals were perfectly complimented either by Ralph's unearthly high mountain tenor or Shuffler's more modern-sounding harmonies.

In the late 1950s and early 1960s, the market for bluegrass music was fairly small, so the Stanleys relocated to Fla. for the winters, hosting a radio program as well as recording for smaller local labels. The folk revival of the 1960s helped revive the Stanleys popularity, and they toured the revival circuit and in Europe. Carter's life was cut short by alcoholism in 1966, and for a while it seemed as if the band would fold.

However, Ralph emerged as an important band leader by the decade's end. He first enlisted vocalist Larry Sparks to fill Carter's shoes, who went on to be one of the 1970s most important progressive bluegrass performers, and then the more traditionally oriented Roy Lee Centers, who sounded eerily like Carter. The band signed with Rebel records, and were popular both on the revival and traditional bluegrass circuits. Centers's murder in 1974 was another blow to Stanley, but he was soon followed by two high school–age musicians whom the elder banjo player had discovered— mandolinist Ricky Skaggs and guitarist Keith Whitley— helping to launch their careers in bluegrass and later the new traditional Nashville music.

The Stanley band has centered for the last two decades on Ralph's banjo, the showy fiddling of Curly Ray Cline, and the bass playing of Jack Cooke, usually augmented by a young guitarist/vocalist and mandolinist. Despite the variability in the talents of the lead vocalists, the sound of Stanley's music remains pretty much unchanged. Ralph Stanley's contribution and influence on Nashville's new country stars was finally acknowledged by the recent release of a two-CD set on which he performs with Ricky Skaggs, Vince Gill, and other new Nashvillians.

The Stanley repertoire has also remained fairly constant since the late 1950s. Their theme song is the "Clinch Mountain Backstep," an instrumental that combines the modality of old-time mountain banjo tunes with the energy and sheen of bluegrass picking. Their repertoire has always combined traditional mountain ballads, including Ralph's powerful vocals on songs like "Man of Constant Sorrow," along with more modern honky-tonk classics, such as "She's More to Be Pitied than Scolded." Drawing on their experience singing in small local churches, the Stanleys have always included both traditional and contemporary gospel songs in their repertoire, and have recorded some of the most memorable gospel LPs in the bluegrass canon.

DISC.: *Country Pickin' and Singin'* (1958); *Everybody's Country Favorties* (1959); *Hymns and Sacred Songs* (1959); *The Stanley Brothers and the Clinch Mountain Boys* (1959); *For the Good People* (1960); *On Radio* (1960); *Sacred Songs from the Hills* (1960); *Long*

Journey Home (1961); Old Time Camp Meeting (1961); The Stanleys in Person (1961); Award Winners (1962); Folk Song Festival (1962); Old Country Church (1963); Hymns of the Cross (1964); Sing and Play Bluegrass Songs for You (1965); Bluegrass Gospel Favorites (1966).—RC

Stapp, Olivia, American soprano; b. N.Y., May 31, 1940. She studied at Wagner Coll. in Staten Island, N.Y. (B.A.) and received vocal training from Oren Brown in N.Y. and Ettore Campogalliani and Rodolfo Ricci in Italy. In 1960 she made her debut as Beppe in L'Amico Fritz at the Spoleto Festival, and then appeared in various operatic centers in Europe and the U.S. In 1972 she made her first appearance at the N.Y.C. Opera as Carmen, and subsequently sang there with fine success. In 1981 she appeared as Elvira in Ernani in Barcelona. She sang Norma in Montreal and Lady Macbeth at the Paris Opéra in 1982. On Dec. 7, 1982, she made her Metropolitan Opera debut in N.Y. as Lady Macbeth. In 1983 she appeared as Turandot at Milan's La Scala. She again sang Lady Macbeth in Geneva and in Venice in 1986. In 1990 she appeared as Shostakovich's Katerina Ismailova in Hamburg. Among her other prominent roles were Lucrezia Borgia, Aida, Elektra, and Tosca. —NS/LK/DM

Starek, Jiří, Czech conductor; b. Mocovice, March 25, 1928. He was educated at the Prague Academy of Music (graduated, 1950). In 1953 he became a conductor with the Czech Radio in Prague, and was concurrently chief conductor of the Collegium Musicum Pragense chamber orch. (1963–68). From 1975 to 1997 he was a prof. and head of the conducting class at the Frankfurt am Main Hochschule für Musik. He was artistic director of the RIAS Sinfonietta in Berlin (1976–80), chief conductor of the Trondheim Sym. Orch. in Norway (1981–84), and principal guest conductor of the West Australian Sym. Orch. in Perth (1988–90). In 1996 he became chief conductor of the Prague State Opera. His guest conducting engagements took him to many opera companies and orchs.—NS/LK/DM

Starer, Robert, esteemed Austrian-born American composer and pedagogue; b. Vienna, Jan. 8, 1924. He entered the Vienna Academy of Music at 13 and studied piano with Victor Ebenstein. Shortly after the Anschluss in 1938, he went to Jerusalem and pursued his training at the Cons. with Rosowsky, Tal, and Partos (until 1943). After service in the British Royal Air Force (1943–46), he emigrated to the U.S. and became a naturalized American citizen in 1957. He pursued postgraduate studies under Jacobi at the Juilliard School of Music in N.Y. (1947–49) and studied with Copland at the Berkshire Music Center in Tanglewood (summer, 1948). From 1949 to 1974 he taught at the Juilliard School of Music; he also taught at the N.Y. Coll. of Music (1959–60) and the Jewish Theological Seminary in N.Y. (1962–63). In 1963 he became an assoc. prof. of music at Brooklyn Coll. of the City Univ. of N.Y., where he was made a full prof. in 1966 and a Distinguished Prof. in 1986. He retired in 1991. He publ. the vol. Rhythmic Training (1969), the autobiography Continuo: A Life in Music (1987), and a book of fiction, The Music Teacher (1997). In 1957 and 1963 he held Guggenheim fellowships, and he also received grants from the NEA and the Ford Foundation. In 1994 he was elected to membership in the American Academy of Arts and Letters, in 1995 he was awarded the Medal of Honor for Science and Art by the President of Austria, in 1996 he received an honorary doctorate from the State Univ. of N.Y., and in 1997 he was honored with a presidential citation from the National Federation of Music Clubs. Starer's music reflects his grounding in the 20th-century Viennese tradition and his study of Arabic scales and rhythms. In some of his works, he utilized aleatory techniques and collage. His output is particularly distinguished by its craftsmanship.

WORKS: DRAMATIC: Opera: The Intruder (N.Y., Dec. 4, 1956); Pantagleize (1967; N.Y., April 7, 1973); Apollonia (1978); The Other Voice, chamber opera (Kingston, Oct. 24, 1998). **Musical Morality Play:** The Last Lover (1974; Katonah, N.Y., Aug. 2, 1975). **Ballet:** The Story of Esther (1960); The Dybbuk (1960); Samson Agonistes (1961); Phaedra (1962); The Sense of Touch (1967); The Lady of the House of Sleep (1968); Holy Jungle (N.Y., April 2, 1974). **ORCH.:** Fantasy for Strings for Violin, Viola, Cello, and String Orch. (1945); 3 piano concertos (1947, 1953, 1972); 3 syms. (1950, 1951, 1969); Prelude and Rondo Giocoso (1953); Concerto a tre for Clarinet, Trumpet, Trombone, and Strings (1954); Ballade for Violin and Orch. (1955); Concerto for Viola, Strings, and Percussion (1958; Geneva, July 3, 1959); Samson Agonistes, symphonic poem after the ballet (1963); Mutabili (Variants for Orchestra) (1965); Concerto for Violin, Cello, and Orch. (1967; Pittsburgh, Oct. 11, 1968); 6 Variations with 12 Notes (1967); Violin Concerto (1979–80; Boston, Oct. 16, 1981); Concerto à quattro for Solo Woodwind and Chamber Orch. (1983); Hudson Valley Suite (1984); Serenade for Trombone, Vibraphone, and Strings (1984); Symphonic Prelude (1984); Cello Concerto (N.Y., May 7, 1988); Concerto for 2 Pianos and Orch. (Seattle, March 4, 1996); Concerto for Piano, 4-Hands, and Orch. (1997). **CHAMBER:** 3 string quartets (1947; Bellington, Wash., Aug. 30, 1995; Miami, July 25, 1996); 5 Miniatures for Brass (1948); Prélude for Harp (1948); Cello Sonata (1951); Dirge for Brass Quartet (1956); Serenade for Brass (1956); Dialogues for Clarinet and Piano (1961); Variants for Violin and Piano (1963); Trio for Clarinet, Cello, and Piano (1964); Woodwind Quartet (1970); Colloquies for Flute and Piano (1974); Mandala for String Quartet (1974); Profiles in Brass for Brass (1974); Annapolis Suite for Harp and Brass Quintet (1982); 6 Preludes for Guitar (1984); Piano Trio (1985); Kaaterskill Quartet (1987); Duo for Violin and Piano (Washington, D.C., Nov. 18, 1988); Angel Voices for Brass and Organ (Bergen, May 29, 1989); Clarinet Quintet (1992); Episodes for Viola, Cello, and Piano (1992; Hartford, Conn., Jan. 23, 1993); Dialogues for Flute and Harp (N.Y., March 23, 1993); Song of Solitude for Cello (Washington, D.C., Nov. 17, 1996); Piano Quintet (1998); Music for a Summer Afternoon for Flute, Violin, Viola, and Cello (1999). **Piano:** 3 sonatas: No. 1 (1949), No. 2 (1965), and No. 3 (N.Y., Nov. 27, 1994); Fantasia concertante (1959); Sketches in Color I (1963) and II (1973); Evanescents (1975); 4 Seasonal Pieces (1985); The Ideal Self (1985). **VOCAL:** Concertino for 2 Voices or 2 Instruments, Violin, and Piano (1948); 5 Proverbs on Love for Chorus (1950); Kohelet for Soprano, Baritone, Chorus, and Orch. (1952); Ariel: Visions of Isaiah for Soprano, Baritone, Chorus, and Orch. or Piano and Organ (1959); Joseph and His Brothers for Narrator, Soprano, Tenor, Baritone, Chorus, and Orch. (1966); Images of Man for Soprano, Mezzo-soprano, Tenor, Baritone, Chorus, Flute, Horn, Cello,

Harp, and Percussion (1973); *Journals of a Songmaker* for Soprano, Baritone, and Orch. (1975); *The People, Yes* for Chorus and Orch. (1976); *Anna Margarita's Will* for Soprano, Flute, Horn, Cello, and Piano (1979); *Transformations* for Soprano, Flute or Clarinet, and Piano (1980); *Voices of Brooklyn* for Solo Voices, Chorus, and Band (1980–84); *Night Thoughts* for Chorus and Synthesizer (1990); *Proverbs for a Son* for Chorus (1991); various other choral pieces and songs. **OTHER:** Many band pieces and didactic works.—**NS/LK/DM**

Stark, Bobby (actually, **Robert Victor**), jazz trumpeter; b. N.Y., Jan. 6, 1906; d. N.Y., Dec. 29, 1945. Stark began on the alto horn at 15, and studied piano and reed instruments before specializing on trumpet. His first professional work was subbing for June Clark at Small's, N.Y. (late 1925); he then played for many bandleaders in N.Y. He worked with Chick Webb on and off during 1926–27. He joined Fletcher Henderson early in 1928 and remained with that band until late 1933, except for a brief spell with Elmer Snowden in early 1932. He performed with Chick Webb from 1934 until 1939, then freelanced awhile. In November 1942, he was in the U.S. Army, but was discharged a year later due to an injury. He returned to N.Y. in late 1943 and gigged with various leaders, including Garvin Bushell and Benny Motion, until his death. Roy Eldridge has acknowledged Stark as an influence.—**JC/LP**

Stark, Robert, eminent German clarinetist; b. Klingenthal, Sept. 19, 1847; d. Wurzburg, Oct. 29, 1922. He studied at the Dresden Cons., then began his career as an orch. player at Chemnitz. From 1873 to 1881 he played the clarinet in Wiesbaden, then was a prof. at the Hochschule für Musik in Wurzburg. He publ. valuable and practical pieces for his instrument, including 3 concertos and *Romanze* for Clarinet and Orch.; also a *Ballade* for Trombone and Orch., *Quintett concertante* for Flute, Oboe, Clarinet, Horn, and Bassoon, and *Serenade* for Oboe and Piano. His instructive works include *Die Kunst der Transposition auf der Klarinette, Grosse theoretisch-praktische Klarinett-Schule*, in 2 parts, followed by part III, *Die hohe Schule des Klarinett-Spieles* (24 virtuoso studies).—**NS/LK/DM**

Starker, János, renowned Hungarian-born American cellist and pedagogue; b. Budapest, July 5, 1924. He made his first public appearance when he was only 6 and at 7 studied cello with Adolf Cziffer at the Budapest Academy of Music and made his solo debut there at the age of 11. After graduating, he served as first cellist of the Budapest Opera orch. (1945–46), then emigrated to the U.S. in 1948. He became a naturalized American citizen in 1954. He held the positions of first cellist in the Dallas Sym. Orch. (1948–49), the Metropolitan Opera Orch. in N.Y. (1949–53), and the Chicago Sym. Orch. (1953–58). Subsequently he embarked upon a solo career. In 1958 he was appointed a prof. of music at the Ind. Univ. School of Music in Bloomington, where he was named Distinguished Prof. of Music in 1965. His 75th birthday was celebrated with a gala concert on Sept. 14, 1999, with Starker as a soloist in the Brahms Double Concerto with the Ind. Univ. Phil. in Bloomington

conducted by Rostropovich. As a recitalist, he achieved renown in performances of Bach's unaccompanied cello suites. He also devoted much attention to modern music, and promoted cello works of Kodály and gave first performances of works by Messiaen, Peter Mennin, Miklós Rozsa, and others. He publ. *An Organized Method of String Playing* (1961).—**NS/LK/DM**

Starr, Ringo (originally, **Starkey, Richard**), drummer, singer, songwriter; b. Dingle, Liverpool, England, July 7, 1940. With his straightforward drumming, undistinguished voice, and infrequent songwriting, Ringo Starr was not expected to do much after the breakup of the Beatles, yet he managed a string of smash singles from 1971 to 1975 with cover songs, Hoyt Axton's "No No Song," and three originals—"It Don't Come Easy," "Back Off Boogaloo," and "Photograph." Enjoying his greatest album success with 1973's *Ringo*, Starr faded from public view in the 1980s, only to return as leader of an all-star rock-and-roll revue, Ringo Starr and His All-Starr Band, for tours in 1989, 1992, and 1995.

Ringo Starr took up drums after high school, eventually joining Rory Storm and the Hurricanes. In 1961 he met Brian Epstein and subsequently joined the Beatles as Pete Best's replacement in August 1962. During the career of the Beatles, Starr was constantly overshadowed by the group's more talented members, developing the image of a cheerful, self-effacing buffoon in concerts and movies. He sang occasional lead vocals on songs such as "I Wanna Be Your Man," "Matchbox," "Honey Don't," "Boys," and the minor hits "Act Naturally" and "What Goes On," and contributed two songs to the group's catalog, "Don't Pass Me By" and "Octopus's Garden." His biggest success as a lead singer came with 1966's "Yellow Submarine" and the classic "With a Little Help from My Friends," perhaps the crowning achievement of his career with the Beatles.

After appearing in a cameo role in the 1969 film *Candy*, Ringo Starr costarred with Peter Sellers in 1970's *The Magic Christian*. His debut solo album, *Sentimental Journey*, was comprised of Tin Pan Alley standards, and his next, *Beaucoups of Blues*, featured country material. In 1971 he scored a smash hit with "It Don't Come Easy," performed at George Harrison's Concert for Bangladesh in August, and appeared in the role of Frank Zappa in Zappa's outlandish movie *200 Motels*. He had a near-smash hit with his own "Back Off Boogaloo" in 1972, and later appeared in the films *Son of Dracula* (with Harry Nilsson), the highly acclaimed *That'll Be the Day*, and the western *Blindman*. He also directed the film documentary of Marc Bolan, *Born to Boogie*.

Recorded under producer Richard Perry, Ringo Starr's first album in three years, *Ringo*, yielded the top hits "Photograph" (cowritten by Starr and George Harrison) and the rock classic "You're Sixteen" (a near-smash hit for Johnny Burnette in 1960) plus the smash "Oh, My, My"; it also contained one song written by each of the former Beatles, including John Lennon's ironic "I'm the Greatest." Perry also produced *Goodnight Vienna*, which included two smash hits, "Only You" (originally popularized by the Platters) and Hoyt Axton's humorous antidrug "No No Song" (backed as a single by Elton John and Bernie Taupin's "Snookero"). The album also produced a moderate hit with John Lennon's "It's All Down to Goodnight Vienna." The compilation set *Blast from Your Past* included "Early 1970," Starr's song about the breakup of the Beatles.

Ringo Starr switched to Atlantic Records for *Ringo's Rotogravure*, which yielded his last major hit, "A Dose of Rock 'n' Roll." After *Ringo the Fourth* he moved to Portrait Records for *Bad Boy* and Boardwalk Records for *Stop and Smell the Roses*, which produced his last moderate hit with George Harrison's "Wrack My Brain." In 1981 Starr costarred in the inane movie *Caveman* opposite Barbara Bach, whom he subsequently married. Joe Walsh produced Starr's 1983 album *Old Wave*, but it was never released in the United States. Starr appeared in Paul McCartney's disastrous 1984 movie *Give My Regards to Broad Street*, and legally prevented the release of recordings made in 1987 under Memphis producer Chips Moman.

Ringo Starr and his wife conquered their alcohol problem in 1988, and Ringo played the diminutive Mr. Conductor in the children's public television show *Shining Time Station* from 1989 to 1991. In 1989 Starr assembled a stellar cast for his first tour in 23 years. The All-Starr Band included guitarists Nils Lofgren and Joe Walsh, keyboardists Billy Preston and Dr. John, saxophonist Clarence Clemons, bassist Rick Danko, and drummers Jim Keltner and Levon Helm. The tour produced a live album on Rykodisc. Ringo's next tour, in 1992, featured holdovers Lofgren and Walsh, multi-instrumentalist Todd Rundgren, guitarist Dave Edmunds, vocalist Burton Cummings, bassist Timothy B. Schmit, and Ringo's drummer son Zak Starkey. Earlier in the year Ringo had recorded *Time Takes Time*, but the album failed to sell despite favorable reviews, a stellar backing cast, and the inclusion of "Weight of the World" and "Don't Go Where the Road Don't Go." When Ringo Starr toured again in 1995, he was accompanied by vocalist Felix Cavaliere, guitarists Randy Bachman and Mark Farner, keyboardist Billy Preston, bassist John Entwistle, and Zak Starkey.

Starr appeared in the 1995 Beatles' TV documentary, and he drummed on the two new tracks recorded by Paul McCartney and George Harrison for the *Anthology* set of Beatles recordings. Always good-humored about his past role as part of the Fab Four, he satirized persistent reunion rumors earlier in the year by appearing in a commercial for Pizza Hut, where he is mistakenly reunited with the Pre-Fab Four, The Monkees!

DISC.: *Sentimental Journey* (1970); *Beaucoups of Blues* (1970); *Ringo* (1973); *Goodnight Vienna* (1974); *Blast from Your Past* (1975); *Ringo's Rotogravure* (1976); *Ringo the Fourth* (1977); *Bad Boy* (1978); *Stop and Smell the Roses* (1981); *Old Wave* (1994); *Starr Struck: Ringo's Best, Vol. 2 (1976–1983)* (1989); *R. S. and His All-Starr Band* (1990); *Time Takes Time* (1992).—**BH**

Staryk, Steven, Canadian violinist and teacher; b. Toronto, April 28, 1932. He studied at the Royal Cons. of Music of Toronto and with Mischakoff, Shumsky, and Schneider in N.Y. (1950–51). He played in the Toronto Sym. Orch. (1950–52) and the CBC Sym. Orch. (1952–56). In 1956 he took second prizes in the Geneva

Competition and the Carl Flesch Competition in London. He was concertmaster of the Royal Phil. in London (1956–60) and of the Concertgebouw Orch. in Amsterdam (1960–63), where he concurrently taught at the Amsterdam Cons. He then was concertmaster of the Chicago Sym. Orch. (1963–67) and a teacher at Northwestern Univ. and the American Cons. He was a prof. at the Oberlin (Ohio) Coll. Cons. of Music (1968–72). Returning to Canada, he was head of the string dept. at the Community Music School of Greater Vancouver (1972–75). From 1975 to 1987 he was a teacher at the Royal Cons. of Music of Toronto. He also taught at the Univ. of Western Ontario (1977–79) and at the Univ. of Toronto (1978–87). From 1982 to 1987 he was likewise concertmaster of the Toronto Sym. In 1987 he became a teacher at the Univ. of Wash. in Seattle, a position he retained until being made prof. emeritus in 1997.—**NS/LK/DM**

Starzer, Josef, outstanding Austrian composer; b. 1726 or 1727; d. Vienna, April 22, 1787. By about 1752 he was a violinist in Vienna's Burgtheater orch., where he began his career as a composer of ballets. During the winter of 1758–59, he went to Russia, where he was active at the Imperial court in St. Petersburg; gave concerts and later was made Konzertmeister and then deputy Kapellmeister and composer of ballet music; served as maitre de chapelle et directeur des concerts in 1763. Returning to Vienna about 1768, he composed several notable ballets; with Gassmann, he helped in 1771 to organize the Tonkünstler-Sozietat, for which he wrote a number of works. In 1779 he retired as a violinist and in 1785 gave up his duties with the society. Starzer was one of the leading Austrian composers of his day, winning distinction not only for his ballets but for his orch. and chamber music; his string quartets have been compared favorably with those of Haydn.

WORKS: DRAMATIC: S i n g s p i e l : *Die drei Pachter.* **B a l l e t :** *Diane et Endimione* (Vienna, c. 1754); *Les Bergers* (Laxenburg, 1755); *Le Misantrope* (Vienna, 1756); *L'Amour venge* (Laxenburg, 1759); *L'Asile de le vertu* (St. Petersburg, 1759; in collaboration with H. Raupach); *Les Nouveaux Lauriers* (St. Petersburg, c. 1759; in collaboration with H. Raupach); *La Victoire de Flore su Borée* (St. Petersburg, 1760); *Siroe* (St. Petersburg, 1760); *Le Jugement de Paris* (St. Petersburg, 1761); *Prométhée et Pandore* (St. Petersburg, 1761); *Le Pauvre Yourka* (Moscow, 1762); *Le Seigneur de village moqué* (Moscow, 1762); *Le Vengeance du dieu de l'amour* (Moscow, 1762); *Apollon et Daphne, ou Le Retour d'Apolon au Parnasse* (St. Petersburg, 1763); *Apollon et Diane* (Vienna, 1763); *Le Retour de la déesse du printemps en Arcadie* (Moscow, 1763); *Les Fêtes hollandoises* (Vienna, 1763); *Pygmalion, ou La Statue animée* (St. Petersburg, 1763); *Acis et Galatée* (St. Petersburg, 1764); *Le Triomphe du printemps* (St. Petersburg, 1766); *Don Quichotte* (Vienna, c. 1768); *Les Moissonneurs* (Vienna, 1770); *Agamemnon* (Vienna, 1771); *Atlante* (Vienna, 1771); *Les Cinque Soltanes* (Vienna, 1771); *Roger et Bradamante* (Vienna, 1771); *Adèle de Ponthieu* (Vienna, 1773); *El Cid* (Vienna, 1774); *Le Ninfe* (Vienna, 1774); *Les Horaces et les Curiaces* (Vienna, 1774); *Les Moissonneurs* (Vienna, 1775); *Montezuma* (Vienna, 1775); *Teseo in Creta* (Vienna, 1775); etc. **ORCH.:** 7 syms.; Violin Concerto (ed. in Diletto Musicale, LXXXII, Vienna, 1964); Concerto for 2 Orchs. (Vienna, March 23, 1779); Concerto for 2 Clarinets, 2 Horns, Bassoon, and Orch. (Vienna, March 14, 1780); *Die Belagerung Wiens*, overture (1799); 6 menuetti; Menu-

etto e contradanze. **CHAMBER:** About 25 string quartets (2 ed. in Denkmäler der Tonkunst in Österreich, XXXI, Jg. XV/2, 1908); 3 string trios; *Musica da camera*, 5 pieces for Chalumeaux or Flutes, 3 C-clarinos, 2 D-clarinos, and Timpani; *Le Matin et le soir*, octet for 2 Oboes, 2 English Horns or Clarinets, 2 Horns, and 2 Bassoons; etc. **VOCAL:** *La passione di Gesù Christo*, oratorio (Vienna, 1778). **OTHER:** Arrangements.
—NS/LK/DM

Stasny, Ludwig, popular Bohemian bandmaster and composer; b. Prague, Feb. 26, 1823; d. Frankfurt am Main, Oct. 30, 1883. He studied at the Prague Cons., then was bandmaster in the Austrian army. He settled in Frankfurt am Main in 1871. He produced 2 operas in Mainz: *Liane* (1851) and *Die beiden Grenadiere* (1879). He was noted for his popular dances (211 opus numbers) and for his potpourris from Wagner's music dramas.
—NS/LK/DM

Stasov, Vladimir (Vasilievich), famous Russian writer on music; b. St. Petersburg, Jan. 14, 1824; d. there, Oct. 23, 1906. He studied foreign languages and art, and also received instruction in music from Antoni Gerke; then continued his training with Adolf Henselt at the so-called Law School for civil servants (1836–43). From 1847 he was active as a book and music reviewer. After an Italian sojourn as secretary to Prince A.N. Demidov (1851–54), he became active at the St. Petersburg Public Library; was made personal assistant to the director in 1856 and then head of the art dept. in 1872. Stasov played a very important role in the emergence of the Russian national school, and was to the end of his days an ardent promoter of Russian music. It was Stasov who first launched the expression "Moguchaya Kuchka" ("mighty little company," in an article publ. on May 24, 1867, in a St. Petersburg newspaper); although he did not specifically name the so-called "Five" (Balakirev, Borodin, Cui, Mussorgsky, and Rimsky-Korsakov), these composers became identified with the cause championed by Stasov. When young Glazunov appeared on the scene, Stasov declared him a natural heir to the Five. His numerous writings, including biographies of Glinka, Mussorgsky, and others, have the value of authenticity. Those publ. between 1847 and 1886 were reissued in book form in honor of his 70th birthday (3 vols., St. Petersburg, 1894); a fourth vol. was brought out in 1905, containing essays written between 1886 and 1904; among them, "Russian Music during the Last 25 Years" and "Art in the 19th Century" are particularly important. His collected works, including articles on art and other subjects, were publ. in Moscow in 1952. Some of his *Selected Essays on Music* were publ. in English (London, 1968).
BIBL.: V. Komarova (his niece), *V.V. S.* (2 vols., Leningrad, 1927); A. Lebedev and A. Solodovnikov, *V. S.* (Moscow, 1966); Y. Olkhovsky, *V. S. and Russian National Culture* (Ann Arbor, 1983).
—NS/LK/DM

Statkowski, Roman, Polish composer and pedagogue; b. Szczpiorna, Jan. 5, 1860; d. Warsaw, Nov. 12, 1925. He studied law at the Univ. of Warsaw, graduating in 1866. He received instruction in music from Zeleński at the Warsaw Music Inst. and then was a pupil of Soloviev (composition) and Rimsky-Korsakov (orchestration) at the St. Petersburg Cons., graduating in 1890. After teaching in Kiev, he became a prof. at the Warsaw Cons. in 1904. He was founder-ed. of the Kwartalnik muzyczny (from 1911). His style represents a blend of German and Russian influences. He wrote the operas *Filenis* (1897; Warsaw, Sept. 14, 1904; won first prize at the London International Opera Contest, 1903) and *Maria* (1903–04; Warsaw, March 1, 1906), as well as *Polonaise* for Orch. (1900), *Symphonic Fantasy* (1900), 5 string quartets, and many solo piano works.
BIBL.: J. Reiss, *S.-Melcer-Mylnarski-Stojowski* (Warsaw, 1949).**—NS/LK/DM**

Staton, Dakota (Aliyah Rabia), dynamic singer whose star rose quickly in the mid-1950s; b. Pittsburgh, Pa., June 3, 1932. Dakota Staton has never attained the notoriety deserving of her talent. She studied at the Filion School of Music in Pittsburgh and sang professionally with her sisters as well as singing with her brother's orchestra. Moving to N.Y., she took part in a jam session at the Baby Grand club, in Harlem, in 1954. She caused a stir and landed a record contract with Capitol in 1955. With the popularity of her first recording, *The Late, Late Show*, she was voted most promising newcomer by *Down Beat*'s readers. In 1958, she recorded with George Shearing. Moving to Europe in 1965, she performed and spent time in England and Germany. She returned to N.Y. in 1970, and has continued to perform and record on into the 1990s. Sometime between the 1950s and the 1990s, she took the name Aliyah Rabia. No matter what names she uses, the gifted singer's power, stage presence, and natural swingability instantly grab audiences.
DISC.: *The Late, Late Show* (1957); *In the Night* (1958); *Time to Swing* (1959); *Round Midnight* (1960); *Dakota at Storyville* (1961); *Live and Swinging* (1963); *Manny Albam Big Band* (1973); *Dakota Staton* (1990); *Dakota Staton with the Manny Albam Big Band* (1990); *Darling Please Save Your Love for Me* (1991); *Isn't This a Lovely Day* (1995).**—SKB**

Staudigl (I), Joseph, distinguished Austrian bass, father of **Joseph Staudigl (II)**; b. Wöllersdorf, April 14, 1807; d. Michaelbeueangrund, near Vienna, March 28, 1861. He was admitted in 1816 to the Wiener Neustadt Gymnasium, where he made his mark as a boy soprano; after studying at the Krems philosophical college (1823–25), he entered the Melk monastery to commence his novitiate; then went to Vienna as a medical student in 1827, but lack of funds soon compelled him to join the chorus of the Kärnthnertortheater. He subsequently sang minor roles before assuming a position as its principal bass; was a member of the Theater an der Wien (1845–48) and the Court Opera (1848–54); appeared at London's Drury Lane (1841), Covent Garden (1842), and Her Majesty's Theatre (1847). He also had a notable career as an oratorio and concert singer, both at home and abroad; sang Elijah in the premiere of Mendelssohn's oratorio (1846). He died insane.**—NS/LK/DM**

Staudigl (II), Joseph, Austrian baritone, son of **Joseph Staudigl (I)**; b. Vienna, March 18, 1850; d.

Karlsruhe, April 1916. He studied with Rokitansky at the Vienna Cons. He sang at the Karlsruhe Court Theater (1875–83), then made his Metropolitan Opera debut in N.Y. as Fernando in *Fidelio* on Nov. 19, 1884; there he also sang Pogner in the U.S. premiere of *Die Meistersinger von Nürnberg* (Jan. 4, 1886). He appeared as Don Giovanni in Salzburg in 1886, then sang in opera and oratorio in Germany. In 1885 he married the Austrian contralto Gisela (née Koppmayer) Staudigl (b. Vienna, date unknown; d. 1929); she studied with Marchesi in Vienna, where she made her debut in a concert in 1879; sang opera in Hamburg (1882–83) and Karlsruhe (1883–84) and at Bayreuth (1886–92), where she appeared as Brangane and Magdalene; also toured as Adriano and the Queen of Sheba with the Metropolitan Opera of N.Y. in 1886; later made another U.S. tour with the Damrosch-Ellis Opera Co. in 1897–98. —NS/LK/DM

St. Clair, Carl, American conductor; b. Hoccheim, Tex., June 5, 1952. He studied opera and orch. conducting with Walter Ducloux at the Univ. of Tex. in Austin, and later worked with Bernstein and Masur. After serving as a conducting fellow at the Tanglewood Music Center (summer, 1985), he was asst. conductor of the Boston Sym. Orch. from 1986 to 1990. He also was music director of the Ann Arbor (Mich.) Sym. Orch. (1985–92) and of the Cayuga Chamber Orch. in Ithaca, N.Y. (1986–91). In 1990 he won the NEA/Seaver Conducting Award. From 1990 he was music director of the Pacific Sym. Orch. in Santa Ana, Calif. He also appeared as a guest conductor throughout North American, Europe, and the Far East.—NS/LK/DM

St. Clair, Cyrus, jazz sousaphone player; b. Cambridge, Mass., 1890; d. N.Y., 1955. His father and uncle were tuba players. He began playing cornet in the Merry Concert Band in Md., later switching to tuba. Around 1925, he moved to N.Y.C., and worked with the Wilbur de Paris Band and Bobby Lee's Cotton Pickers, along with doing club work. From 1926–31, he worked with Charlie Johnson's band; during this period, he also played on many of Clarence Williams's recording sessions, including accompanying Bessie Smith and many other pop-blues singers. St. Clair worked in Cozy Cole's Hot Cinders (1930) and gigged in N.Y. He was musically inactive for several years, and then returned to regular playing on Rudi Blesh's *This Is Jazz* radio series in 1947; he also recorded with Tony Parenti's Ragtimers. St. Clair worked for the Buildings and Grounds Department of Columbia Univ. until shortly before his death.—JC/LP

St. Cyr, Johnny (actually, **John Alexander**), famed early jazz guitarist, banjoist; b. New Orleans, La., April 17, 1890; d. Los Angeles, Calif., June17, 1966. His father, Jules Firmin St. Cyr (died: 1901), played guitar and flute. Johnny began playing on a homemade, "cigar-box" guitar, then graduated to a real instrument. He formed the Consumers' Trio (named after a local brewery), then began gigging with Jules Baptiste and Manuel Gabriel (c. 1905–08). While working during the day as a plasterer, he performed with many legendary New Orleans groups, including Freddie Keppard's Band (and also with Keppard in the Olympia Band), Papa Celestin, Kid Ory, Armand Piron (c. 1914), pianist Arthur Campbell (1915–16), King Oliver's Magnolia Band, and Armand Piron (1917–early 1918). St. Cyr finally gave up his day job to join Fate Marable playing on the riverboats that traveled up and down the Mississippi (summer 1918 until summer of 1920). By fall 1921, he was back in New Orleans, again working as a plasterer for the next two years, he did occasional parade work and played with various leaders. He moved to Chicago in September 1923, played briefly with King Oliver, then spent two months in Darnell Howard's Band before joining Doc Cooke's Dreamland Orch. (from January 1924 until November 1929). During this period he regularly doubled at various late-night clubs including a spell playing with Jimmie Noone at the Apex. However, St. Cyr is best remembered for participating in many freelance recording sessions with Louis Armstrong (the legendary Hot Five and Hot Seven groups) and Jelly Roll Morton, among many others. St. Cyr left Doc Cooke in November 1929, and gigged in Ind. before returning to New Orleans via Chicago. St. Cyr worked as a plasterer throughout the 1930s and 1940s while he continued regular part-time playing. The New Orleans revival of the late 1940s–early 1950s brought him out of retirement; in 1955 he settled in Calif. to work with Paul Barbarin. St. Cyr guested with many bands, played regularly with the New Orleans Creole Jazz Band in Los Angeles (1959), then played with and later led the Young Men of New Orleans during the early 1960s, a gig that included a stint on the miniature river steamer "Mark Twain" at Disneyland. St. Cyr survived a bad car crash during the summer of 1965, but was forced by illness to restrict regular playing during the last years of his life. He died of leukemia in 1966.

Disc.: *Johnny St. Cyr and His Hot Five* (1957).—JC/LP

Stebbins, George C(oles), noted American evangelistic singer, composer, and editor; b. East Carlton, N.Y., Feb. 26, 1846; d. Catskill, N.Y., Oct. 6, 1945. He received instruction in singing schools and learned to play the piano in his youth, then studied singing in Rochester, N.Y., where he sang in a church choir. In 1870 he joined the Lyon & Healy Co. in Chicago, where he also was music director in several Baptist churches; then held similar posts in Boston (1874–76). In 1876 he began appearing as an evangelistic singer with Dwight L. Moody, and became active as a composer of gospel songs and hymns. With Sankey and McGranahan, he ed. Vols. 3 to 6 of the *Gospel Hymns and Sacred Songs* series (1878–91; reprinted as *Gospel Hymns nos. 1–6 Complete*, 1894). Among his best-known hymns are *Jesus Is Tenderly Calling Today* (1883), *Take Time to Be Holy* (1890), and *Have Thine Own Way, Lord* (1907). —NS/LK/DM

Steber, Eleanor, eminent American soprano; b. Wheeling, W.Va., July 17, 1914; d. Langhorne, Pa., Oct. 3, 1990. She studied singing with her mother; then with William Whitney at the New England Cons. of Music in

Boston (Mus.B., 1938) and with Paul Althouse in N.Y. She won the Metropolitan Opera Auditions of the Air in 1940; made her debut with the Metropolitan Opera in N.Y. as Sophie in *Der Rosenkavalier* on Dec. 7, 1940, and remained with the company until 1962; altogether she appeared 286 times in N.Y. and 118 times on tour; she sang 28 leading roles in an extremely large repertoire. She performed brilliantly in the roles of Donna Anna in *Don Giovanni*, Pamina in *Die Zauberflöte*, and the Countess in *Le nozze di Figaro*, as well as in other Mozart operas; her other roles were Violetta, Desdemona, Marguerite, Manon, Mimi, and Tosca; in Wagner's operas she sang Eva in *Die Meistersinger von Nürnberg* and Elsa in *Lohengrin*; she also performed the challenging part of Marie in Berg's opera *Wozzeck*. She sang the title role in the premiere of Samuel Barber's opera *Vanessa* on Jan. 15, 1958. After several years of absence from the Metropolitan Opera, she took part in the final gala performance in the old opera building on April 16, 1966. Her European engagements included appearances at Edinburgh (1947), Vienna (1953), and the Bayreuth Festival (1953). After partial retirement in 1962, she was head of the voice dept. at the Cleveland Inst. of Music (1963–72); taught at the Juilliard School in N.Y. and at the New England Cons. of Music (both from 1971); also at the American Inst. of Music Studies in Graz (1978–80; 1988). She established the Eleanor Steber Music Foundation in 1975 to assist young professional singers. With R. Beatie, she publ. the study *Mozart Operatic Arias* (N.Y., 1988). Her autobiography, written in collaboration with M. Sloat, was publ. posthumously (Ridgewood, N.J., 1992). —NS/LK/DM

Stecker, Karel, Czech pedagogue, writer on music, and composer; b. Kosmanos, near Mladá Boleslav, Jan. 22, 1861; d. Mladá Boleslav, March 13, 1918. He studied law and aesthetics at the Univ. of Prague, then entered the Prague Organ School, joining its faculty in 1885; when it became a part of the Prague Cons. in 1890, he was made a prof. He composed mostly sacred music and organ pieces. He publ. a history of music in the Czech language (2 vols., 1892, 1902), a treatise on musical form (1905), and an interesting essay on nonthematic improvisation (1903).

BIBL.: C. Sychra, *K. S.* (Prague, 1948).—NS/LK/DM

Štědroň, Bohumír, eminent Czech musicologist, brother of **Vladimír Štědroň** and uncle of **Miloš Štědroň**; b. Vyžkov, Oct. 30, 1905; d. Brno, Nov. 24, 1982. He studied theory with Josef Blatný (1925–28) and piano with Vilém Kurz (1926–28); also took courses in history and geography at the Univ. of Brno (graduated, 1929), where he attended Helfert's lectures in musicology; after further training in Italy (1931), he returned to the Univ. of Brno to take his Ph.D. in 1934 with the diss. *Sólové chrámové kantáty G. B. Bassaniho* (G.B. Bassani's Solo Church Cantatas) and to complete his Habilitation in 1945 with his *Chrámová hudba v Brně v XVIII. století* (Church Music in Brno in the XVIIIth Century). He taught music education at a teacher-training college (1931–39), and also was an assistant to Helfert (1932–38); then taught music history at the Brno Cons. (1939–45;

1950–52); in 1945 he became a teacher at the Univ. of Brno, where he subsequently was made asst. lecturer in 1950, lecturer in 1955, and prof. in 1963. He was an authority on the life and music of Janáček. In addition to his important books, he contributed many articles to scholarly journals.

WRITINGS: *Leoš Janáček a Luhačovice* (Leoš Janáček and Luhačovice; Luhacovice, 1939); *Leoš Janáček ve vzpomínkách a dopisech* (Prague, 1945; rev. Ger. tr., 1955; rev. Eng. tr., 1955, as *Leoš Janáček: Letters and Reminiscences*); *Josef Bohuslav Foerster a Moravia* (Brno, 1947); ed. with G. Černušák and Z. Nováček, *Československý hudební slovník osob a instituci* (Czechoslovak Music Dictionary of Places and Institutions; Prague, 1963–65); *Vitežlav Novák v obrazech* (Vitežlav Novák in Pictures; Prague, 1967); *Zur Genesis von Leoš Janáček's Oper Jenůfa* (Brno, 1968; second ed., rev., 1971); *Leoš Janáček: K jeho lidskému a uměleckému profilu* (Leoš Janáček: Personal and Artistic Profile; Prague, 1976).

BIBL.: *Sborník prací filosofické fakulty brněnské univerzitě* (Brno, 1967; dedicated to S. on his 60th birthday).—NS/LK/DM

Štědroň, Miloš, significant Czech composer and musicologist, nephew of **Bohumír Štědroň** and **Vladimír Štědroň**; b. Brno, Feb. 9, 1942. He studied musicology with Racel, Vysloužil, and his uncle Bohumír at the Univ. of Brno (Ph.D., 1967); also studied composition at the Janáček Academy of Music in Brno (1965–70). After working in the music dept. of Brno's Moravian Museum (1963–72), he taught theory at the Univ. of Brno (from 1972). Among his books is a monograph on Monteverdi (Prague, 1985) and a study on Josef Berg (Brno, 1992). He contributed important articles to various journals, many of which deal with the music of Janáček. His own works range from traditional scores to pieces utilizing jazz and pop elements or tape.

WORKS: DRAMATIC: O p e r a : *Aparát* (The Apparatus), chamber opera after Kafka's *In the Penal Colony* (1967); *Kychýnské starosti* (1977); *Josef Fouché- Chameleon* (1984). **B a l - l e t :** *Justina* (1969); *Ballet macabre* (1986). **ORCH.:** *Moto balladico* (1968); *Quiet Platform* (1969); Concerto for Double Bass and Strings (1971); *To the Memory of Gershwin* for Piano and Jazz Orch. (1971); *Diagram* for Piano and Jazz Orch. (1971); *Music for Ballet* for Chamber Orch. (1972); *Kolo* (Wheel), sym. in memory of Yugoslav partisans of World War II (1971–72); Cello Concerto (1975); *Sette Villanelle* for Cello and Strings (1981); *Musica concertante* for Bassoon and Strings (1986); *Lammento* for Viola and Orch. (1987). **CHAMBER:** *Via crucis* for Flute, Bass Clarinet, Piano, Harpsichord, and Percussion (1964); *Dyptich* for Bass Clarinet, Piano, Strings, and Percussion (1967); *Lai* for Bass Clarinet and Timpani (1967); *Utis II* for Bass Clarinet and Tape (1967); *Util II* for Bass Clarinet, Piano, and Tape (1968); *O, Sancta Caecilia* for Double Bass and Tape (1968); *Musica ficta* for Wind Quintet (1968); *Duplum* for Bass Clarinet and Double Bass (1968); *Free Landino Jazz* for Bass Clarinet and Piano (1968); *Affeti graziosi* for Violin and Piano (1969); *Saluti musicali* for Bass Clarinet and Piano (1969); *4 Together (Everyman for Himself)* for Bass Clarinet, Piano, and Jazz Combo (1969); String Quartet (1970); *Seikilos z Moravy* (Seikilos from Moravia) for Bass Clarinet and Piano (1978; in collaboration with A. Parsch); *Old and New Renaissance Poems* for Bass Clarinet, Piano, Strings, and Drums (1980); *Trium vocum* for Flute, Cello, and Drums (1984); *Danze, Canti e lamenti* for String Quartet (1986); solo pieces; piano works. **VOCAL:** *Agrafon* for Madrigal Chorus, Renaissance Instruments, and Jazz Ensemble (1968); *Mourning Ceremony*, cantata for Chorus, Trumpet, Oboe, and Church Bell (Czech Radio, Feb. 21, 1969); Vocal Sym. for Soprano, Bass-baritone, and Orch. (1969); *Verba*, cantata for Chorus and 2 Trumpets (1969); *Jazz trium vocum*, free jazz for Chorus and Jazz Ensemble (1972); *Dolorosa gioia*, madrigal-cantata (1975); *Attendite, populi*, cantata for Chorus and Drums (1982); *Conversations, Tunes, Desires* for Tenor, Lute, and Viola da Gamba (1986); *Ommaggio a Gesualdo: Death of Dobrovský*, cantata-oratorio for 2 Solo Voices, Chorus, and Orch. (1988).—NS/LK/DM

Štědroň, Vladimír, Czech composer, brother of **Bohumír Štědroň** and uncle of **Miloš Štědroň;** b. Vyškov, March 30, 1900; d. Brno, Dec. 12, 1982. He studied law at the Univ. of Prague; simultaneously took lessons in composition with Foerster, Novák, and Suk at the Prague Cons. (1919–23); then studied musicology with Helfert at the Univ. of Brno. He served for many years as a judge, but found time to compose; later was in Prague as a teacher at the Academy of Music, the Univ., and the Cons. (1951–60). His music is couched in an unassuming style inspired by native folk songs.

WORKS: ORCH.: *Fidlovacka*, overture (1916); *Fantastic Scherzo* (1920); *Illusions*, symphonic poem (1936); *Janka*, polka (1962); *Moto balladico* (1967). **CHAMBER:** 2 string quartets (1920; 1940–45); *Variation Fantasy* for String Quartet (1923); *Little Domestic Suite* for 2 Violins and Viola (1937); *Monologe* for Flute (1967); *Monologe* for Horn (1969).—NS/LK/DM

Steel, Christopher (Charles), English composer and teacher; b. London, Jan. 15, 1939; d. Cheltenham, Dec. 31, 1991. He studied composition with John Gardner at the Royal Academy of Music in London (1957–61) and with Harald Genzmer at the Staatliche Hochschule für Musik in Munich (1961–62). He taught at Cheltenham Coll. Junior School (1963–66); was asst. director (1966–68) and director (1968–81) of music at Bradfield Coll., also serving as an instructor; taught at North Hennepin Comm. Coll. in Brooklyn Park, Minn. (1977–78); accepted private students from 1982.

WORKS: DRAMATIC: O p e r a : *The Rescue*, chamber opera (1974); *The Selfish Giant* for Baritone and Children (Westcliffe-on-Sea, July 1981); *The Angry River*, chamber opera for 7 Soloists, Chorus, and Orch. (1989). **ORCH.:** 7 syms., including No. 3, *A Shakespeare Symphony* for Baritone, Chorus, and Orch. (1967), No. 4 (Manchester, Nov. 2, 1983), No. 5, *Romantic Symphony* (Manchester, Oct. 21, 1986), and No. 6, *Sinfonia sacra* for Soprano, Baritone, Chorus, and Orch. (Sheffield, Nov. 22, 1985); Concerto for Organ and Chamber Orch. (1967); Concerto for String Quartet and Orch. (1968); *Overture Island* (1968); *Odyssey*, suite for Concert Brass Band (1973); *6 Turner Paintings*, suite (1974); *Apollo and Dionysus* (1983); *The City of God and the Garden of Earthly Delights* (Reading, April 12, 1986); Cello Concerto (1988); *Sinfonietta Concertante No. 1* for Organ and Strings (1989) and *No. 2* for Small Orch. (1990); *Serenata Concertante* for Trumpet and Strings or Organ (1991). **VOCAL:** 4 cantatas: *Gethsemane* (1964), *Mary Magdalene* (1967), *Paradise Lost* (1972), and *Jerusalem* (1972); Mass (1968); *Piping Down the Valleys Wild*, song cycle for Baritone and Piano (1971); *Passion and Resurrection According to St. Mark* for Soloists, Chorus, and Chamber Orch. (1978); *The Path of Creation* for Baritone, Oboe, Soloists, Chorus, and Orch. (1984); anthems. **OTHER:** Chamber music, piano pieces, and organ works. —NS/LK/DM

Steely Dan, songwriting duo and popular nontouring group. **MEMBERSHIP:** Walter Becker, bs., gtr., voc. (b. N.Y., Feb. 20, 1950); Donald Fagen, kybd., voc. (b. Passaic, N.J., Jan. 1, 1948).

Although posing as a group, Steely Dan was essentially a studio duo comprised of songwriters Walter Becker and Donald Fagen. Composing musically sophisticated, lyrically erudite and oblique songs, Steely Dan immediately came to prominence with their excellent debut album, *Can't Buy a Thrill*, and its two hit singles, "Do It Again" and "Reeling in the Years." Admittedly more influenced by jazz than rock, Becker and Fagen persevered through 1980 as one of the most popular nontouring groups since the Beatles. They scored their biggest artistic and commercial success with their 1977 album, *Aja*, their acknowledged masterpiece. During the 1980s the two pursued a variety of low-key independent endeavors, reuniting in 1993 for one of the most anticipated tours of the year.

Walter Becker and Donald Fagen met while attending Bard Coll. in upstate N.Y. in 1967. Fagen had studied jazz piano in high school, whereas Becker played bass and guitar. The two decided to form a composing team, and after Fagen's graduation and Becker's dismissal, the duo unsuccessfully attempted to sell their songs around N.Y. They formed a short-lived group on Long Island with guitarist Denny Dias and composed and performed the score to the obscure underground movie *You Gotta Walk It Like You Talk It*. Fagen and Becker next joined the backup group for Jay and the Americans and toured with them in 1970 and 1971. Through that group's producer, Gary Katz, they secured employment as staff songwriters for ABC-Dunhill in Los Angeles, but their failure to write hits led to the formation of Steely Dan as a vehicle for their songwriting.

Formed in 1972, Steely Dan was initially comprised of Becker, Fagen, Dias, lead vocalist David Palmer, guitarist Jeff "Skunk" Baxter, and drummer Jim Hodder. Their exceptional debut album, *Can't Buy a Thrill*, featured the disdainful "Dirty Work" and the vaguely political "Change of the Guard" and yielded near-smash hits with "Do It Again" and "Reeling in the Years." Touring infrequently, Steely Dan recorded their second jazz-inflected album without Palmer, as Fagen assumed the lead-vocalist role. *Pretzel Logic* produced a smash hit with "Rikki Don't Lose That Number," but following their 1974 tour, Becker and Fagen dismissed their band, with Baxter soon joining the Doobie Brothers. They retained Denny Dias while recording subsequent albums with session musicians. However, neither *Katy Lied* nor *The Royal Scam* yielded a major hit.

Released in late 1977, *Aja* became Steely Dan's best-selling and most highly regarded album. It ultimately yielded three major hits, with "Peg," "Deacon Blues," and "Josie." They also scored a major hit with "FM (No Static at All)" from the movie *FM* in 1978. The group's next album, *Gaucho*, did not come until 1980, yet it produced two major hits (their last) with "Hey Nineteen" and "Time Out of Mind."

By 1981, Walter Becker and Donald Fagen had parted company. Becker retreated to Hawaii, where he built his own recording studio, while Fagen recorded the autobiographical solo album *The Nightfly*, which yielded a major hit with "I.G.Y. (What a Beautiful World)" and a minor hit with the caustic "New Frontier." During the 1980s Fagen composed songs, wrote a movie column for *Premiere* magazine, and contributed to the soundtrack of the movie *Bright Lights, Big City*. Around 1989 Fagen began performing in clubs around N.Y., later organizing and touring with the N.Y. Rock and Soul Revue in 1991 and 1992. Becker and Fagen reunited to coproduce Fagen's second solo album, *Kamakiriad*, in 1993, and the duo assembled an 11-piece band for their first tour in 19 years. Although the tour sold out, the performances served more as cultural events than as music renaissance. In 1994 Walter Becker recorded his first solo album, *11 Tracks of Whack*, and Steely Dan toured once again.

DISC.: *Can't Buy a Thrill* (1972); *Countdown to Ecstasy* (1973); *Pretzel Logic* (1974); *Katy Lied* (1975); *The Royal Scam* (1976); *Aja* (1977); *Greatest Hits* (1978); *Gaucho* (1980); *Gold* (1982); *Gold (expanded edition)* (1991); *A Decade of S. D.* (1985); *Citizen S. D.: 1972–1980* (1993); *Alive in America* (1995); *Two Against Nature* (2000). **FAGEN/BECKER/DIAS:** *You Gotta Walk It Like You Talk It* (1971). **DONALD FAGEN:** *The Nightfly* (1982); *Kamakiriad* (1993). **WALTER BECKER:** *11 Tracks of Whack* (1994).—**BH**

Stefani, Jan, significant Polish composer of Bohemian descent, father of **Józef Stefani;** b. Prague, 1746; d. Warsaw, Feb. 24, 1829. He studied at Prague's Benedictine school. After an Italian sojourn, he went to Vienna about 1765 as a violinist in Count G. Kinski's orch.; in 1779 he settled in Warsaw as a violinist and conductor in King Stanislaw August Poniatowski's Court Orch.; also was Kapellmeister at the Cathedral and a conductor at the National Theater and later a violinist in its orch. (1799–1811). Stefani's importance rests upon his notable contribution to Polish opera; his masterpiece is *Cud mniemany czyl: Krakowiacy i Górale* (The Supposed Miracle or Krakovians and Highlanders; Warsaw, March 1, 1794). He also was a fine composer of polonaises.

WORKS: DRAMATIC (all first perf. in Warsaw): **O p - e r a :** *Król w kraju rozkoszy* (The King of Cockaigne; Feb. 3, 1787); *Cud mniemany czyli Krakowiacy i Górale* (The Supposed Miracle or Krakovians and Highlanders; March 1, 1794); *Wdieczni poddani czyli Wesele wiejskie* (Thankful Serfs or The Country Wedding; July 24, 1796; also known as *Przjazd pana czyli Szczęśliwi wieśniacy* [The Arrival of the Lord or Happy Country Folk]); *Drzewo zaczarowane* (The Magic Tree; 1796); *Frozyna czyli Siedem razy jedna* (Frozine or 7 Times Dressed Up; Feb. 21, 1806); *Rotmistrz Górecki czyli Oswodobodzenie* (Captain Gorecki or The Liberation; April 3, 1807); *Polka czyli Obleeżnie* (The Polish Woman or The Siege of Trembowla; May 22, 1807); *Stary myśliwy* (The Old Huntsman; Jan. 31, 1808); *Papirius czyli Ciekawość dawnych kobiet* (Papyrus or The Curiosity of Women in Ancient Times; May 15, 1808). **B a l l e t :** *Miłość każdemu wiekowi przstoi* (Love Becomes Every Age; Nov. 4, 1785). **OTHER:** Some 100 polonaises for Orch.; sacred music; songs. —**NS/LK/DM**

Stefani, Józef, Polish composer and conductor, son of **Jan Stefani;** b. Warsaw, April 16, 1800; d. there, March 19, 1867. He was a pupil of his father and of Elsner in Warsaw (1821–24). He conducted ballet at the Warsaw Opera, and wrote a number of light operas, which enjoyed a modicum of success during his lifetime: *Dawne czasy* (April 26, 1826), *Lekcja botaniki* (March 15, 1829), *Figle panien* (Aug. 6, 1832), *Talizman* (Dec. 7, 1849), *Zyd wieczny tulacz* (Jan. 1, 1850), *Piorun* (May 21, 1856), and *Trwoga wieczorna* (posthumous, July 25, 1872). He also wrote church music, which was often performed in religious services in Poland. Many of his works are lost. —**NS/LK/DM**

Stefano, Giuseppe di
See **Di Stefano, Giuseppe**

Stefánsson, Fjölnir, Icelandic composer and educator; b. Reykjavík, Oct. 9, 1930. He was a student of Thórarinsson at the Reykjavík Music School (graduated, 1954) and of Seiber in England (1954–58). Returning to Iceland, he was active as a teacher and later as an educator. He composed a Trio for Flute, Clarinet, and Bassoon (1951); Violin Sonata (1954); Duo for Oboe and Clarinet (1974); *Koplon* for Orch. (1979); Sextet for Flute, Clarinet, Bassoon, Horn, Violin, and Cello (1983); many choral works and songs; numerous arrangements of Icelandic folk songs for chorus.—**NS/LK/DM**

Steffan, Joseph Anton (Josef Antonín Štepán), important Czech composer, harpsichordist, and teacher; b. Kopidlno, Bohemia (baptized), March 14, 1726; d. Vienna, April 12, 1797. His father was organist and schoolmaster in Kopidlno, and Joseph Anton most likely began his musical training under his father's tutelage. When the Prussian army invaded Bohemia in 1741, he fled to Vienna, where he found a patron in Count František Jindřich Šlik, lord of the Kopidlno estate; received instruction in violin from Hammel, his patron's Kapellmeister, whom he later succeeded, and in harpsichord and composition from G.C. Wagenseil, the court composer. He soon established himself as an outstanding harpsichord virtuoso, teacher, and composer; was made Klaviermeister to the princesses Maria Carolina (later Queen of Naples) and Maria Antonia (later Queen of France) in 1766, remaining active at the court until 1775. In subsequent years he taught privately and composed; he died in obscurity. Steffan was a major figure in the development of the Classical style. His keyboard works, including concertos and sonatas, reveal him as a worthy compatriot of Haydn and Mozart. He was the first to publ. lieder collections in Vienna.

WORKS: DRAMATIC: S i n g s p i e l : *Der Doktor Daunderlaun.* **ORCH.:** 10 sinfonie, 4 of which are lost; 6 concertos for Harpsichord or Harp, op.10 (Paris, c. 1773; nos. 3–6 lost); 37 concertos for Harpsichord or Piano, one of which is lost; 2 concertos for 2 Harpsichords, one of which was for long attributed to Haydn. **CHAMBER:** Concertino for Harpsichord, Flute, Violin, and Cello; Concertino for Harpsichord, Flute, Violin, Bass, and 2 Horns; 7 trios for Violin, Cello, and Harpsichord or Piano; Sonata for Violin and Piano; Variations for Violin and Piano; several pieces for Wind Instruments. **KEYBOARD:** 6 *divertimenti* (Vienna, 1756; ed. in Musica Antiqua Bohemica, LXIV, 1964); 6 *sonate*, op.2 (Vienna, c. 1759–60); 40 *preludi per diversi tuoni* (Vienna, 1762); *Parte 1 a del* op.3 *continente 3 sonate* (Vienna, 1763); *Parte 2a...continente 3 sonate* (Vienna, 1771); *Parte 3a* (lost) (Parts 1–2 ed. in Musica Antiqua Bohemica, LXIV [1964]); *Sonata I* (Vienna, 1771), *II* (Vienna, c. 1771), and *III* (Vienna, 1776) (all ed. in Musica Antiqua Bohemica, LXIV [1964]); *6 sonates choisies* for Harpsichord or Piano, *par...Steffann et Rutini* (Paris, 1773–74); *Parte 2a continente 90 cadenze, fermade, e capricci* for Harpsichord or Piano (Vienna, 1783); *25 variationi* for Piano (Vienna, 1785–92); also various other keyboard works, including 21 divertimentos and sonatas (8 of the latter ed. in Musica Antiqua Bohemica, LXX, 1968); several single-movement sonatas; minuets; 5 sets of variations; etc. **VOCAL: S a c r e d** : *Stabat mater* for Voice and Piano (Prague and Vienna, 1782); 2 masses; 2 Christmas pastorellas (1 in collaboration with J.G. Zechner); various hymns. **S e c u l a r** : *Sammlung* [24] *deutscher Lieder*, I (Vienna, 1778); *Sammlung* [25] *deutscher Lieder*, II (Vienna, 1779); *Gesang bei dem Beschlusse der...Prufung der 31 Unteroffiziere und Gemeinen* (Vienna, 1780); *Sammlung* [24] *deutscher Lieder*, IV (Vienna, 1782).

BIBL.: D. Šetková, *Klavírní dílo Josefa Antonína Štěpána* (The Keyboard Works of J.A. S.; Prague, 1965); H. Picton, *The Life and Works of J.A. S. (1726–1797)* (2 vols., N.Y. and London, 1989). —NS/LK/DM

Steffani, Agostino,

eminent Italian composer, churchman, and diplomat; b. Castelfranco, near Venice, July 25, 1654; d. Frankfurt am Main, Feb. 12, 1728. He most likely received his early musical training in Padua, where he was probably a choirboy. In 1667 Elector Ferdinand Maria of Bavaria took him to his court in Munich, where Steffani became a ward of Count von Tattenbach; he sang in *Le pretensioni del sole* (1667) by J.K. Kerll, the court Kapellmeister, who gave him organ lessons (1668–71); then studied composition with Ercole Bernabei, maestro di capella at St. Peter's in Rome (1672–74). In 1674 he returned to Munich with Bernabei, who assumed the post of Kapellmeister; Steffani appears to have taken on the duties of court and chamber organist in 1674, although the court records only list him as such from 1678. In 1680 he became a priest. With the accession of the Elector Maximilian II Emanuel in 1680, he found great favor at the court. In 1681 the position of director of the court chamber music was especially created for him; that same year his first opera, *Marco Aurelio*, to a libretto by his brother Ventura Terzago, was premiered; it was also about this time that he became active as a diplomat for the court. He was made Abbot of Lepsingen in 1683. In 1688 he was called to Hannover by Duke Ernst August to serve as court Kapellmeister; he was in charge of the first permanent Italian opera company there (1689–97); he subsequently was mainly active as a diplomat for the Hannoverian court. In 1691 he was sent to Vienna to assist in creating Hannover as the 9th electorate. In 1693 he was made envoy extraordinary to the Bavarian court in Brussels, where he worked diligently to persuade the Elector Maximilian to support the Emperor rather than Louis XIV as the War of the Spanish Succession loomed in the background; however, his mission failed, and he returned to Hannover in 1702. In 1703 he entered the service of Johann Wilhelm, Palatine Elector, in Düsseldorf; since he had virtually given up composing, a number of his works were circulated from 1709 under the name of one of his

copyists, Gregorio Piva. He began his duties in Düsseldorf in 1703 as privy councillor and president of the Spiritual Council for the Palatinate and the duchies of Julich and Berg; later that year he was named general president of the Palatine government; also was the first rector magnificus (1703–05) and then a curator (from 1705) of the Univ. of Heidelberg. In 1706 he was elected Bishop of Spiga in partibus infedelium (Asia Minor). In 1708–09 he was in Rome to mediate the war between the Pope and the Emperor, which resulted in the Pope making him a Domestic Prelate and Assistant to the Throne. In 1709 he was appointed Apostolic Vicar in northern Germany, and later that year settled in Hannover. He continued to be active at the court there as well, having served as minister and Grand Almoner to the Elector Johann Wilhelm from 1706. His ecclesiastical duties were particularly onerous, but he carried them out faithfully until retiring to Padua in 1722. However, at the insistence of Rome, he returned to Hannover in 1725. In 1727 he received the honor of being elected president of the Academy of Vocal Music in London, the forerunner of the Academy of Ancient Music. This honor renewed his interest in composing, but ill health soon intervened. He died while on his way to Italy. Steffani was an important composer of operas, notably influential in the development of the genre in northern Germany. All the same, his most significant achievement was as a composer of outstanding chamber duets for 2 Voices and Continuo, which had a major impact on Handel.

WORKS: DRAMATIC (all operas unless otherwise given): *Marco Aurelio* (Munich, 1691); Serenata for the wedding of Countess von Preysing (Munich, 1682); *Solone* (Munich, 1685); *Audacia e rispetto* (Munich, 1685); *Servio Tullio* (Munich, 1686); *Alarico il Baltha, cioè L'audace rè de' gothi* (Munich, 1687); *Niobe, regina di Tebe* (Munich, 1688); *Henrico Leone* (Hannover, 1689; German version by G. Schürmann, Braunschweig, 1716); *La lotta d'Hercole con Acheloo*, divertimento drammatico (Hannover, 1689); *La superbia d'Alessandro* (Hannover, 1690); *Orlando generoso* (Hannover, 1691); *Le Rivali concordi* (Hannover, 1692); *La libertà contenta* (Hannover, 1693); *Baccanali*, favola pastorale (Hannover, 1695); *I trionfi del fato* or *Le glorie d'Enea* (Hannover, 1695); *Arminio*, pasticcio (Düsseldorf, 1707); *Amor vien del destino* (Düsseldorf, 1709); *Il Tassilone* (Düsseldorf, 1709). **VO-CAL: S a c r e d** : *Psalmodia vespertina* for 8 Voices and Organ (Rome, 1674); *Sacer Ianus quadrifons* for 3 Voices and Basso Continuo (Munich, 1685); other works, including a Stabat mater for 6 Voices, Strings, and Basso Continuo (1727). **S e c u l a r** : About 75 chamber duets for 2 Voices and Basso Continuo; many cantatas; arias; etc. **INSTRUMENTAL:** *Sonata da camera* for 2 Violins, Viola, and Basso Continuo (Amsterdam, c. 1705).

BIBL.: J. Hawkins, *Memoirs of the Life of A. S.* (London, c. 1749–52); F. Woker, *Aus den Papieren des kurpfälzischen Ministers A. S., Bischofs von Spiga, spätern apostolischen Vicars von Norddeutschland ... 1703–1709: Erste Vereinsschrift der Görresgesellschaft* (Cologne, 1885); idem, *A. S., Bischof von Spiga, i.p.i., apostolischer Vikar von Norddeutschland 1709–28: Dritte Vereinsschrift der Görresgesellschaft* (Cologne, 1886); A. Neisser, *Servio Tullio: Eine Oper aus dem Jahr 1685 von A. S.* (Leipzig, 1902); W. Baxter Jr., *A. S.: A Study of the Man and His Work* (diss., Eastman School of Music, 1957); G. Croll, *A. S. (1654–1728): Studien zur Biographie, Bibli-*

ographie der Opern und Turnierspiele (diss., Univ. of Münster, 1960); C. Timms, *The Chamber Duets of A. S. (1654–1728): With Transcriptions and Catalogue* (diss., Univ. of London, 1976).—**NS/LK/DM**

Steffek, Hanny (actually, **Hannelore**), Austrian soprano; b. Biala, Galicia, Dec. 12, 1927. She received her training at the Vienna Academy of Music and the Salzburg Mozarteum. In 1949 she made her concert debut at the Salzburg Festival, and returned there in 1950 to make her operatic debut in a minor role in *Die Zauberflöte*. She also sang in Graz and Frankfurt am Main, and then was a member of the Bavarian State Opera in Munich (1957–72). In 1959 she made her debut at London's Covent Garden as Sophie. From 1964 to 1973 she sang at the Vienna State Opera. In 1965 she appeared with the visiting Bavarian State Opera at the Edinburgh Festival singing Christine in the first British performance of *Intermezzo*. She also sang with various other European opera houses. In addition to her noted portrayal of Christine, she was admired for such roles as Despina, Blondchen, Papagena, and Ilia. She also was highly successful in Viennese operetta.—**NS/LK/DM**

Steffen, Wolfgang, German composer; b. Neuhaldensleben, April 28, 1923; d. Berlin, Dec. 4, 1993. He studied at the Berlin Cons. (1946–49) and with Tiessen at the Hochschule für Musik there (1949–53); after graduation, he devoted himself principally to the promotion of new music. He was active as a conductor (1947–59); was an honorary and guest prof. at the Berlin Staatliche Hochschule der Künste (from 1974). In 1978 he won the Australian composition prize and in 1979 the Johann Wenzel Stamitz Prize.

WORKS: ORCH.: *Serenade* for Flute and Strings "im alten Stil" (1948); *Sinfonietta* for Strings (1949); *Tanzerische Impression I* for Piano and Orch. (1950) and *II* for Piano, Percussion, and Orch. (1970); *Intrada seria* (1953); *Meditations de la nuit* (1954); *Aus dem Lebensbuch eines Tanzers* (1954); Piano Concerto (1955); Violin Concerto (1966); *Polychromie* for Piano and 10 Instruments (1970; also for Piano and Orch., 1971); *Klangsegmente* for Cymbal, Harp, Harpsichord, and Orch. (1973–74); *Sinfonia da camera* (1976); Chamber Concerto (1978); Concerto for 6 Flutes and Orch. (1979–83); Concertino for Piano and 9 Instruments or Chamber Orch. (1984); *GOSLAR*, symphonic poem (1991). **CHAMBER:** Trio for Oboe, Flute, and Bassoon (1947); *Theme with 8 Variations* for String Quartet (1948); Trio for Clarinet, Cello, and Piano (1959); *Diagram* for Viola or Cello and Piano (1965); Wind Quintet (1966); *Jeu* for Violin and Piano (1967); Trio for Flute, Cello, and Piano (1970); *Triplum 72* for Flute, Piano, and Percussion (1972); *Tetraphonie* for Flute Ensemble (1974); *Trilogie 75* for Bandoneon, Flute, and Percussion (1975); *Music for Piano and 7 Players* (1975); *Meditation* for Violin (1981); Duo for Cello and Accordion (1982); *Piece* for Clarinet (1983); String Trio (1983); *Duo Serenade* for Flute and Piano (1987); *Klangdialog* for Mandolin and Guitar (1989); *Klangspiele* for 6 to 7 Percussionists (1991). **Piano:** *Fantasy* (1947); Sonata (1955); *Reihenproportionen* (1961); *Notturno* for 4-Hands (1968); *Les Spirales* (1969); *Introversion* (1982); *Music* (1985). **VOCAL:** *Nachtwachen* for Chorus, Flute, Oboe, Clarinet, and String Quintet (1954); *Hermann-Hesse-Zyklus* for Chorus, Clarinet, Viola, and Piano (1955); *Botschaft*, oratorio (1975–76); *Augenblicke* for Chorus

(1986); *Kantate nach Gedichten von Gertrud Kolmar* for Soprano, Chorus, and 6 Instruments (1987); *Bilder von Algina* for Baritone or Bass-baritone and Piano (1987; also for Baritone, Piano, and Orch., 1989); songs.—**NS/LK/DM**

Steglich, Rudolf, eminent German musicologist; b. Rats-Damnitz, Feb. 18, 1886; d. Scheinfeld, July 8, 1976. He studied musicology with Sandberger at the Univ. of Munich, with Wolf at the Univ. of Berlin, and with Riemann at the Univ. of Leipzig (Ph.D., 1911, with the diss. *Die Quaestiones in Musica und ihr mutmasslicher Verfasser Rudolf von St. Trond* (1070–1138); publ. in Leipzig, 1911); completed his Habilitation in 1930 at the Univ. of Erlangen with his *Die elementare Dynamik des musikalischen Rhythmus* (publ. in Leipzig, 1930). He was in the German army during World War I; then was active as music critic of the Hannover *Anzeiger* (1919–29); in 1929 he was appointed to the faculty of the Univ. of Erlangen; retired in 1956. He was ed. of the *Händel-Jahrbuch* (1928–33) and of the *Archiv für Musikforschung* (1936–40); ed. the Hallische Händel-Ausgabe (with M. Schneider; from 1955), works by Bach's sons, early German song collections, etc. Steglich was an authority on music of the 18th and 19th centuries.

WRITINGS: *J.S. Bach* (Potsdam, 1935); *Mozarts Flügel klingt wieder* (Nuremberg and Salzburg, 1937); *Robert Schumanns Kinderszenen* (Kassel, 1949); *Wege zu Bach* (Regensburg, 1949); *Über die 'kantable Art' der Musik J.S. Bachs* (Zürich, 1958); *Georg Friedrich Händel* (Wilhelmshaven, 1960); *Tanzrhythmus in der Musik J.S. Bachs* (Wolfenbüttel and Zürich, 1962).—**NS/LK/DM**

Stegmann, Carl David, German tenor, harpsichordist, conductor, and composer; b. Staucha, near Meissen, 1751; d. Bonn, May 27, 1826. He studied with the Staucha organist, then went to Dresden to study with J.F. Zillich; also attended the Kreuzschule there (1766–70) and received instruction from Homilius and H. Weisse. He was active at theaters in Breslau (1772) and Königsberg (1773). After serving as court harpsichordist to the Bishop of Ermeland in Heilsberg (1774), he was active again in Königsberg and then in Gotha. From 1778 to 1783 he won success as a harpsichordist in Hamburg, then went to Bonn as a member of the Grossmann theater company and later was active at the Mainz Court Theater. Stegmann was a skillful composer of both vocal and instrumental works.

WORKS: DRAMATIC: Opera: *Sultan Wampum oder Die Wünsche* (Mainz, March 7, 1791); *Der Roseninsel* (Hamburg, Nov. 24, 1806). **Comic Opera:** *Der Kaufmann von Smirna* (Königsberg, 1773); *Die Rekruten auf dem Lande* (Danzig, 1775); *Das redende Gemahlde* (Königsberg, 1775). **Singspiels:** *Heinrich der Löwe* (Frankfurt am Main, July 15, 1792); *Der Triumph der Liebe oder Das kühne Abentheuer* (Hamburg, Feb. 27, 1796). **Operetta:** *Der Deserteur* (Danzig, 1775). **Ballet:** *Die herrschaftliche Küche* (Danzig, 1775). **Other:** Incidental music. **ORCH.:** Various concertos, including a Concerto for Piano, Oboe, Horn, and Orch. and a Concerto for 2 Pianos, Violin, and Strings. **OTHER:** chamber works; piano pieces; songs.—**NS/LK/DM**

Stegmayer, Ferdinand, Austrian pianist, conductor, and composer, son of **Matthäus Stegmayer;** b.

Vienna, Aug. 25, 1803; d. there, May 6, 1863. He studied with Seyfried, then was chorus master in Linz and Vienna. In 1825 he was made music director of Berlin's Königstädtisches Theater, then was conductor of a German opera troupe in Paris (1829–30). After filling various engagements as a theater conductor in Leipzig, Bremen, and Prague, he settled in Vienna in 1848; was a teacher of singing at the Vienna Cons., and co-founded, with August Schmidt, the Vienna Singakademie (1858). He wrote church music, piano pieces, and songs.
—NS/LK/DM

Stegmayer, Matthäus, Austrian singer, poet, actor, and composer, father of **Ferdinand Stegmayer;** b. Vienna, April 29, 1771; d. there, May 10, 1820. He was a chorister in the Dominican church in Vienna. About 1792 he became a member of the Theater in der Josefstadt, where he assumed major roles and was active as a composer; in 1796 he joined Schikaneder's Freihaus-Theater. He joined the court theater in 1800, where he was active as chorus director and producer; in 1804 he became an actor, chorus master, and composer at the Theater an der Wien, for which he wrote the text to the enormously successful quodlibet *Rochus Pumpernickel* (Jan. 28, 1809) with music provided by Haibel and Seyfried; it was widely performed in German-speaking countries, and was followed by at least 3 sequels.

BIBL.: F. Blitzenetz, *M. S.* (diss., Univ. of Vienna, 1929).
—NS/LK/DM

Stehle, Adelina, outstanding Austrian soprano; b. Graz, 1860; d. Milan, Dec. 24, 1945. She studied in Milan. She made her operatic debut in Broni in 1881 as Amina; then sang in Bologna, Florence, and Venice. In 1890 she joined La Scala in Milan, where she created roles in *Falstaff* as Nanetta, in *Guglielmo Ratcliff* as Maria, and others; also sang in Berlin, Vienna, St. Petersburg, South America, and the U.S. After her marriage to **Edoardo Garbin,** she appeared under the name of Stehle Garbin.
—NS/LK/DM

Stehle, Sophie, German soprano; b. Hohenzollern-Sigmaringen, May 15, 1838; d. Schloss Harterode, near Hannover, Oct. 4, 1921. She made her operatic debut as Emmeline in Weigl's *Schweizerfamilie* in Munich (1860). She was a prominent member of the Munich Court Opera, where she created the roles of Fricka in *Das Rheingold* (Sept. 22, 1869) and Brünnhilde in *Die Walküre* (June 26, 1870). She also distinguished herself in other Wagnerian parts (Elisabeth, Elsa, Eva).—NS/LK/DM

Stehman, Jacques, Belgian composer and music critic; b. Brussels, July 8, 1912; d. Heist-aan-Zee, May 20, 1975. He studied piano with Del Pueyo, composition with Jean Absil, and orchestration with Paul Gilson at the Brussels Cons., then was active as music critic for *Le soir.* He was made a prof. of practical harmony (1954) and of music history (1968) at the Brussels Cons., and also taught at the Chapelle Musicale Reine Elisabeth. His music is cautiously modernistic, with engaging touches of obsolescent jazz.

WORKS: ORCH.: *Symphonie de poche* (1950); *Musique de mai* for Strings (1961); *Dialogues* for Harp and Small Orch. (1964); *Escapades* for Piano and String Orch. (1968); Piano Concerto (1965–72). **CHAMBER:** *Lamento* for Cello and Piano (1947). **P i a n o :** *Burlesques en 6 formes* (1934); *Colloque* for 2 Pianos (1943); *3 rythmes* for 2 Pianos (1955); *Montmartre* for 2 Pianos (1975). **VOCAL:** *Melos* for Mezzo-soprano, Flute, and Strings (1968); songs.—NS/LK/DM

Steibelt, Daniel, renowned German pianist and composer; b. Berlin, Oct. 22, 1765; d. St. Petersburg, Oct. 2, 1823. He studied with Kirnberger (piano and theory), then joined the Prussian Army only to desert and flee his homeland in 1784. He publ. sonatas for Piano and Violin, as opp. 1 and 2 (Munich, 1788), then gave concerts in Saxony and Hannover before proceeding to Paris in 1790. There he found himself in strong competition with Ignaz Pleyel, but won out, and became a favorite piano teacher. His opera *Roméo et Juliette* was produced at the Théâtre Feydeau on Sept. 10, 1793, and, despite the revolutionary turmoil of the time, achieved excellent success. After defrauding his publisher, he left Paris in 1796, going to the Netherlands and then to London. He became a soloist at Salomon's Concerts; played the solo part of his third Piano Concerto (March 19, 1798), with its rousing finale *L'Orage, précédé d'un rondeau pastoral,* which as a piano solo became as popular as *Koczwara's Battle of Prague;* then produced the pasticcio *Albert and Adelaide, or The Victim of Constancy* at Covent Garden (Dec. 11, 1798), to which Attwood also contributed. After returning to Germany in 1799, he was granted an official pardon for his army desertion. In 1800 he visited Dresden, Prague, Berlin, and Vienna, where he challenged Beethoven to a contest of skill, but was easily bested. His next destination was Paris, where he produced Haydn's *Creation* (Dec. 24, 1800), with an orch. of 156 players, in an arrangement by Steibelt himself; Napoleon was present at that performance. A ballet by Steibelt, *Le retour de Zéphire,* was produced at the Paris Opéra on March 3, 1802. He then went to London, where he staged 2 ballets, *Le jugement du berger Paris* (May 24, 1804) and *La belle laitère* (Jan. 26, 1805). Returning once more to Paris, he wrote a festive intermezzo, *La fête de Mars,* to celebrate Napoleon's victory at Austerlitz; it was produced at the Opéra on March 4, 1806. In 1808–09 he presented concerts in Frankfurt am Main, Leipzig, Breslau, and Warsaw on his journey to St. Petersburg to assume his appointment as director of the French Opéra. In 1810 he was made maître de chapelle to the Czar. He composed several works for the French Opéra, but devoted himself mainly to teaching and giving occasional concerts. On March 16, 1820, he gave the premiere of his 8th Piano Concerto in St. Petersburg. His last years were marked by ill health. Although he acquired greath wealth during his career, he squandered his money and died in relative poverty. Much of his large output is now of little interest, although several of his piano concertos and his 3 quintets for Piano and Strings are worthy of note.

BIBL.: G. Müller, *D. S.: Sein Leben und seine Klavierwerke* (Leipzig and Zürich, 1933); K. Hagberg, *D. S.'s Cendrillon: A Critical Edition with Notes on S.'s Life and Works* (diss., Eastman School of Music, 1975).—NS/LK/DM

Steiger, Anna, American soprano; b. Los Angeles, Feb. 13, 1960. She studied at the Guildhall School of Music and Drama in London (1977–83), the National Opera Studio (1985–86), and with Vera Rozsa and Irmgard Seefried. She won the Sir Peter Pears Award in 1982, the Richard Tauber Prize in 1984, and the John Christie Award in 1985. In 1984 she made her operatic debut with Opera 80 as Dorabella. In 1985 she sang Micaëla with the Glyndebourne Touring Opera, and in 1986 she made her Glyndebourne Festival debut as Poppea. She sang Musetta at Opera North in Leeds in 1986. In 1987 she returned to Glyndebourne to create the role of Sashka in the premiere of Osborne's *The Electrification of the Soviet Union.* Following her debut as a Flower Maiden in *Parsifal* at London's Covent Garden in 1987, she portrayed Kristine in *The Makropulos Affair* at the English National Opera in London in 1989. In 1989 she also sang Weill's Jenny in Los Angeles, and in 1990 Ravel's Conception at the N.Y.C. Opera and Despina at the Netherlands Opera in Amsterdam. In 1994 she appeared in Verdi's *Un Giorno di Regno* at the Dorset Opera. She is the daughter of the acclaimed actor Rod Steiger.—NS/LK/DM

Steiger, Rand, American composer and conductor; b. N.Y., June 18, 1957. He attended N.Y.'s H.S. of Music and Art (1972–75), then studied percussion and composition (with Tanenbaum) at the Manhattan School of Music (B.Mus., 1980); attended the Calif. Inst. of the Arts, where he studied with Brown, Mosko, Powell, and Subotnick (M.F.A., 1982); also studied at Yale Univ. with Carter, Druckman, Jolas, and Martino (1981) and at IRCAM in Paris (1982). He taught at the Univ. of Costa Rica (1984–85), the Calif. Inst. of the Arts (1982–87), and the Univ. of Calif. at San Diego (from 1987). He was the first Composer Fellow of the Los Angeles Phil. (1987–88). His works include *Dialogues II* for Marimba and Orch. (1979–80); *Brave New World* for Voices and Electronics (1980); *Quintessence* for 6 Instruments (1981); *Currents Caprice,* electronic film score (1982); *Kennedy Sketches* for Marimba and Vibraphone (1982); *In Nested Symmetry* for 15 Instruments and Electronics (1982); *Hexadecathlon* for Horn and 7 Instruments (1984); *Fanfare erafnaF* for Double Chamber Orch. (1985); *Tributaries* for Chamber Orch. (1986); *Tributaries for Nancarrow* for 6 Computer-controlled Pianos (1987); *Double Concerto* for Piano, Percussion, and Double Chamber Orch. (1987); *Druckman Tributary* for 11 Instruments (1988); *ZLoops* for Clarinet, Piano, and Percussion (1989); *Mozart Tributary* for Clarinet Quintet (1991); *The Burgess Shale* for Orch. (1991). Steiger has conducted and directed new-music performances by SONOR of the Univ. of Calif. at San Diego and the Los Angeles Phil. New Music Group. He is perhaps best known as a member of the Calif. E.A.R. Unit, a highly respected new-music ensemble established at the Calif. Inst. of the Arts in 1981. Other members include cellist Erika Duke-Kirkpatrick (b. Los Angeles, Aug. 1, 1956), who studied with Cesare Pascarella (1971–82) and at the Calif. Inst. of the Arts (B.F.A., 1978; M.F.A., 1982), where she later taught (from 1987); among composers who have written works for her are Subotnick, La Barbara, Powell, and Mosko; she performed as a soloist and in ensembles in the U.S., South America, and Europe. Pianist Lorna Ellen Eder (b. Aberdeen, Wash., April 2, 1953) studied at the Univ. of Puget Sound in Tacoma, Wash. (1971–73), Wash. State Univ. in Pullman (B.Mus., 1975), with Leonid Hambro at the Calif. Inst. of the Arts (M.F.A., 1980), and with Bruno Seidlhofer in Vienna (1975–77). She was a staff accompanist at the Calif. Inst. of the Arts (1980–84); played with the Santa Clarita Chamber Players (1985–90) and in duo recitals with Eugene Fodor (1984–86). Composer, percussionist, and performance artist Art(hur) Jarviven (b. Ilwaco, Wash., Jan. 27, 1956) studied at Ohio Univ. (B.Mus., 1978) and the Calif. Inst. of the Arts (M.F.A., 1981); had percussion lessons from Guy Remonko, John Bergamo, Karen Ervin, and Ruth Underwood, and composition lessons with Subotnick, Brown, and Mosko. He performed with the Los Angeles Phil. New Music Group and the performance-art ensemble Le Momo; also worked with Steve Reich and Frank Zappa. His satiric works, which involve poetry, theater, visual media, and various musical styles, have been performed throughout the U.S.; these include *Vote of Confidence* for Percussion Trio (1979); *Through Birds, through Fire, but Not through Glass* for Percussion Quartet (1979); *Soluble Furniture* for Piano (1980); *Mercury at Right Angles* for Celesta (1980); *Viscous Linings* for Celesta, Viola, Bass Clarinet, and Percussion (1981); *Prosthesis, false piece for anything or nothing* (1981); *Raison d'etre* for Marimba and Vibraphone (1981); *Carbon* for Bass Clarinet (1982); *Deductible Rooms* for Marimba (1982); *Adult Party Games from the Leisure Planet* for Various Ensembles (1985); *Ivan, Where Are You Running To* for 9 Players and Tape (1985); *Electric Jesus* for Juvenile Pianist and Large Ensemble (1985); *Mass Death of a School of Small Herring* for Chamber Orch. (1986); *A Book of 5 Rings* for Pianos and Percussion (1986); *Egyptian 2-Step* for Ensemble (1986); *The 7 Golden Vampires* for 2 Pianos (1987); *35 1/2 Minutes for Gaylord Mowrey* for Piano, Video, and Refreshments (1987); *Goldbeater's Skin* for Clarinet (1987; other versions, 1988); *The Queen of Spades, parts I–III* for 2 Electronic Harpsichords and Percussion (1988–90); *The 15 Fingers of Doctor Wu* for Oboe (1987); *Murphy-Nights* for Ensemble (1989); *The Vulture's Garden* for 4 Players (1990). Percussionist Amy Knoles (b. Milwaukee, Sept. 10, 1959) studied at the Univ. of Wisc. (1977–79) and at the Calif. Inst. of the Arts (B.F.A., 1982), where she later taught. Among the composers whose works she has premiered are Powell, Subotnick, Chatham, and Tower. Violinist and vocalist Robin Lorentz (b. Seattle, Dec. 19, 1956) studied at the Cornish School of Music, the Univ. of Wash. (1977–78), and with Emanuel Zetlin and Yoko Matsuda at the Calif. Inst. of the Arts (B.F.A., 1980); taught at the Kirk Cons. of Music in Pasadena, Calif., and at the Aspen Music Festival (1989, 1990). She was concertmaster for the Ojai Festival (1986, 1988), and assoc. concertmaster for both the San Diego Chamber Players (1988) and the Los Angeles Phil. New Music Group (1987, 1988, 1990). She has performed with the Sterling Consort (1987–90) and the Ensemble of Santa Fe (from 1985). Her solo recording credits include works for television and film, in Irish, Cajun, bluegrass, jazz, and pop-rock styles. She joined the E.A.R. Unit in 1983. Clarinetist and saxophonist Jim Rohrig (b. Long Beach, Calif., Nov. 30, 1954)

studied at the Univ. of Southern Calif. (B.A., 1977) and at the Calif. Inst. of the Arts (M.F.A., 1981; advanced certificate, 1983), where he also taught (1982–83); his teachers included Mitchell Lurie, Michelle Zukovsky, and Douglas Masek. He was a co-founder of the E.A.R. Unit. He has recorded works by Subotnick, La Barbara et al., and is an active member of the performance-art ensemble Le Momo. He has composed incidental music for the stage and has directed and ed. film and video, including those of E.A.R. Unit performances. His in-progress projects include a film documentary of Nicolas Slonimsky. Flutist Dorothy Stone (b. Kingston, Pa., June 7, 1958) studied at the Manhattan School of Music (B.Mus., 1980) and at the Calif. Inst. of the Arts (M.F.A., 1982), her teachers including Harold Bennett, Harvey Sollberger, Thomas Nyfenger, Julius Baker, and Ann Deiner Giles; gave first performances of works by Boulez, Cage, Ferneyhough, and Carter; numerous composers have composed works for her, including Babbitt, Steiger, and Mosko. She composed Wizard Ball for Flute and Electronics, which won several awards. Stone is artistic director and administrative manager of the E.A.R. Unit. She is married to **Stephen Mosko**.
—NS/LK/DM

Steigleder, family of German musicians:

(1) **Utz Steigleder**, organist and composer; b. place and date unknown; d. Stuttgart, Oct. 7 or 8, 1581. He was in the service of Duke Ulrich of Württemberg in Stuttgart from at least 1534, holding the posts of court and abbey organist. His only known work is *Veni Sancte Spiritus* for 6 Voices (ed. in Die Motette, no. 457, Stuttgart, 1963).

(2) **Adam Steigleder**, organist and composer, son of the preceding; b. Stuttgart, Feb. 19, 1561; d. there, Nov. 8, 1633. He studied with S. Lohet (1575–78) and in Rome (1580–83); was organist at the Stuttgart abbey church (1583–92), the Michaeliskirche in Schwabisch Hall (1592–95), and at Ulm Minster (1595–1625); then returned to Stuttgart. His extant works consist of a *Passa e mezo* and a *Toccata primi toni*.

(3) **Johann Ulrich Steigleder**, organist and composer, son of the preceding; b. Schwäbisch Hall, March 22, 1593; d. Stuttgart, Oct. 10, 1635. He was a pupil of his father, and although lame, he served as organist at Lindau's Stephanskirche on Lake Constance (1613–17). In Stuttgart, he was organist at the abbey church (1617–35) and the ducal court (1627–35). He died of the plague. His extant works comprise *Ricercar tabulatura, organis et organoedis* (Stuttgart, 1624) and *Tabulatur-Buch* (Strasbourg, 1627), both ed. in the Corpus of Early Keyboard Music, XIII/1 (1968).

BIBL.: E. Emsheimer, *J.U. S.: Sein Leben und seine Werke* (Kassel, 1928).—NS/LK/DM

Stein, Fritz (actually, Friedrich Wilhelm),

German musicologist; b. Gerlachsheim, Baden, Dec. 17, 1879; d. Berlin, Nov. 14, 1961. He studied theology in Karlsruhe, then took courses in musicology with P. Wolfrum in Heidelberg. Subsequently he went to Leipzig, where he studied various subjects with Krehl, Nikisch, Riemann, and Straube, then completed his musicological training at the Univ. of Heidelberg (Ph.D., 1910, with the diss. *Zur Geschichte der Musik in Heidelberg*; publ. in 1912; new ed., 1921, as *Geschichte des Musikwesens in Heidelberg bis zum Ende des 18. Jahrhunderts*). He went to Jena in 1906 as music director of the Univ. and city organist; in 1913 he was appointed prof. of musicology at the Univ.; was in the German army during World War I and directed a male chorus for the troops at the front. He became a reader in musicology at the Univ. of Kiel in 1920, then was a prof. from 1928 to 1933; in 1933 he became director of the Hochschule für Musik in Berlin, holding this position to the end of World War II in 1945. He achieved notoriety when he discovered in the library of the Univ. of Jena the parts of a sym. marked by an unknown copyist as a work by Beethoven. The sym. became famous as the "Jena Symphony" and was hailed by many as a genuine discovery; the score was publ. by Breitkopf & Hartel in 1911, and performances followed all over the world; Stein publ. his own exegesis of it as "Eine unbekannte Jugendsymphonie Beethovens?" in the *Sammelbände der Internationalen Musik-Gesellschaft* (1911). Doubts of its authenticity were raised, but it was not until 1957 that H.C. Robbins Landon succeeded in locating the original MS, proving that the "Jena Symphony" was in reality the work of Friedrich Witt (1770–1837). Stein publ. a monograph on Max Reger (Potsdam, 1939) and *Max Reger: Sein Leben in Bildern* (a pictorial biography; Leipzig, 1941; second ed., 1956); brought out a thematic catalogue of Reger's works (Leipzig, 1934; definitive ed., 1953); ed. works by Johann Christian Bach, Telemann, Handel, Beethoven, etc.; contributed essays to numerous learned publs. A Festschrift was publ. in his honor on his 60th birthday (1939).—NS/LK/DM

Stein, Horst (Walter), German conductor; b. Elberfeld, May 2, 1928. He studied at the Hochschule für Musik in Cologne, and at age 23 was engaged as a conductor at the Hamburg State Opera; then was on the staff of the State Opera in East Berlin (1955–61). He was deputy Generalmusikdirektor at the Hamburg State Opera (1961–63); after serving as Generalmusikdirektor of the Mannheim National Theater (1963–70), he returned to the Hamburg State Opera as Generalmusikdirektor (1972–77); also was Generalmusikdirektor with the Hamburg State Phil. (1973–76). He subsequently was chief conductor of the Orchestre de la Suisse Romande in Geneva (1980–85), the Bamberg Sym. Orch. (from 1985), and the Basel Sym. Orch. (1987–94). He made many guest conducting appearances in Europe and in North and South America.—NS/LK/DM

Stein, Johann (Georg) Andreas, German keyboard instrument maker; b. Heidelsheim, Palatinate, May 6, 1728; d. Augsburg, Feb. 29, 1792. He worked under Johann David Stein in Strasbourg (1748–49), then was associated with F.J. Späth in Regensburg (1749–50). In 1750 he settled in Augsburg, where he built the organ of the Barfüsserkirche; was appointed organist there in 1757. He spent a few months in Paris in 1758 before returning to Augsburg. He experimented with various types of keyboard instruments, and invented a "polytoni-clavichordium" (1769), a "melodika" (1772), a

"vis-à-vis Flügel" (1777), and a "Saitenharmonika" (1789). The business was carried on by his daughter, Nannette (b. Augsburg, Jan. 2, 1769; d. Vienna, Jan. 16, 1833), and his son, Matthäus Andreas (b. Augsburg, Dec. 12, 1776; d. Vienna, May 6, 1842). In 1794 Nannette married the pianist J.A. Streicher, and the firm was moved to Vienna, where her brother remained a partner until 1802 when he founded his own firm of André Stein. His son, Carl Andreas (b. Vienna, Sept. 4, 1797; d. there, Aug. 28, 1863), carried on his father's business while also pursuing a career as a pianist and composer.

BIBL.: F. Luib, *Biographische Skizze des J.A. S.* (1886); T. Bolte, *Die Musikerfamilien S. und Streicher* (Vienna, 1917); E. Hertz, *J.A. S. (1728–1792): Ein Beitrag zur Geschichte des Klavierbaues* (Berlin, 1937).—**NS/LK/DM**

Stein, Leon, American composer, teacher, and conductor; b. Chicago, Sept. 18, 1910. He studied violin at the American Cons. in Chicago (1922–27), and theory at Crane Jr. Coll. in Chicago (1927–29); took private lessons in composition with Sowerby, in orchestration with DeLamarter, and in conducting with Stock and Lange (1937–40); also studied at De Paul Univ. (B.M., 1931; M.M., 1935; Ph.D., 1949; diss. publ. as *The Racial Thinking of Richard Wagner*, 1950), where he served on its faculty (1931–78); served as dean of its school of music (1966–76); also was director of the Inst. of Music of the Coll. of Jewish Studies (1952–59) and was a conductor of various community orchs. He publ. *Structure and Style: The Study and Analysis of Musical Form* (Evanston, Ill., 1962; third ed., rev. and enl., 1979) and *Anthology of Musical Forms* (Evanston, Ill., 1962). In 1982 he received Chicago's Hall of Fame Award. His music is academic, but not devoid of occasional modernities.

WORKS: DRAMATIC: O p e r a : *The Fisherman's Wife* (1953–54; St. Joseph, Mich., Jan. 10, 1955); *Deirdre,* after Yeats (1956; Chicago, May 18, 1957). **B a l l e t F o r P i a n o :** *Exodus* (Chicago, Jan. 29, 1939); *Doubt* (Chicago, Jan. 21, 1940). **ORCH.:** *Prelude and Fugue* (1935); *Passacaglia* (1936); *Sinfonietta* for Strings (1938); Violin Concerto (1938–39; Chicago, Dec. 3, 1948); 4 syms.: No. 1 (1940), No. 2 (1942), No. 3 (1950–51), and No. 4 (1975); *3 Hassidic Dances* (1940–41; Chicago, April 13, 1942); *Triptych on 3 Poems of Walt Whitman* (1943; Chicago, March 29, 1949); *Great Lakes Suite* for Small Orch. (1943–44); *Rhapsody* for Flute, Harp, and Strings (1954; Chicago, Nov. 8, 1955); *Adagio and Rondo Ebraico* (1957); *A Festive Overture* (1959); *Then Shall the Dust Return* (1971); Cello Concerto (1977; Chicago, June 11, 1983); Concerto for Clarinet and Percussion Ensemble (1979); *Nexus* for Wind Ensemble (1983); *Aria Hebraique* for Oboe and Strings (1984; Los Angeles, April 10, 1994); Concerto for Oboe and Strings (1986; Chicago, Jan. 29, 1988). **CHAM-BER:** Sonata for 2 Violins (1931); Violin Sonata (1932); 5 string quartets (1933, 1962, 1964, 1964, 1967); Woodwind Quintet (1936); *12 Preludes* for Violin and Piano (1942–49); Trio for 3 Trumpets (1953); Quintet for Saxophone and String Quartet (1957); Sextet for Alto Saxophone and Wind Quintet (1958); solo sonatas for Violin (1960), Flute (1968), Horn (1969), Trombone (1969), Trumpet (1969), Bassoon (1969), Oboe (1969), Bass (1970), and Cello (1970); *Trio Concertante* for Saxophone, Violin, and Piano (1961); *Suite* for Saxophone Quartet (1962); Tenor Saxophone Sonata (1967); Trio for Alto Saxophone, Clarinet, and Piano (1969); *3 Pieces* for Clarinet (1969); *Rhapsody* for Alto Saxophone (1969); Suite for Brass Quintet (1975); Quintet for

Harp and String Quartet (1976); *Introduction and Rondo* for Flute and Percussion (1977); Suite for Woodwind Quintet (1978); *Rhapsody* for Cello (1979); Suite for Violin, Viola, and Cello (1980); *Dance ebraico* for Cello and Piano (1982); *Duo Concertante* for Bassoon or Violin and Marimba (1988); Trio Concertante for Violin, Saxophone or Cello, and Piano (1993); numerous solo works and various piano pieces. **VOCAL:** *The Lord Reigneth,* cantata for Tenor, Women's Chorus, and Orch. (1953); choral pieces; songs.—**NS/LK/DM**

Stein, Leonard, eminent American music scholar; b. Los Angeles, Dec. 1, 1916. He attended Los Angeles City Coll. (1933–36) and studied piano privately with Richard Buhlig (1936–39); enrolled in the class of composition and musical analysis with Schoenberg at the Univ. of Southern Calif. (1935–36) and at the Univ. of Calif. at Los Angeles (1936–42); from 1939 to 1942 he was Schoenberg's teaching assistant; received the degrees of B.A. (1939) and M.M. (1941) from the Univ. of Calif. at Los Angeles, and his D.M.A. from the Univ. of Southern Calif. (1965); was the recipient of a Guggenheim fellowship (1965–66). He taught at Occidental Coll. (1946–48); Los Angeles City Coll. (1948–60); Pomona Coll. (1961–62); Univ. of Calif. at Los Angeles (1962–64); Claremont Graduate School (1963–67); Univ. of Calif. at San Diego (1966); and Calif. State Coll. at Dominguez Hills (1967–70); in 1970 he was appointed a member of the music faculty of the Calif. Inst. of the Arts; in 1975 he became adjunct prof. in the School of Music at the Univ. of Southern Calif. in Los Angeles. In 1975 he was elected director of the Arnold Schoenberg Inst. of the Univ. of Southern Calif., and editorial director of the *Journal of the Arnold Schoenberg Inst..* Stein retired in 1991. In addition to his musicological work, he also made occasional appearances as a piansit and conductor. He contributed a number of articles on the proper performance of piano works by Schoenberg; was a member of the editorial board of the complete works of Schoenberg. He ed. Schoenberg's *Nachtwandler* (1969); Piano Concerto (1972); *Ode to Napoleon Bonaparte* (1973); *Brettl-Lieder* (1974); ed. and completed Schoenberg's pedagogical works: *Preliminary Exercises in Counterpoint* (1963); *Models for Beginners in Composition* (rev. of the text, 1972); *Structural Functions of Harmony* (rev., 1969); *Style and Idea. Selected Writings of Arnold Schoenberg* (London, 1975; received the 1976 ASCAP award). —**NS/LK/DM**

Stein, Peter, German opera and theater producer; b. Berlin, Oct. 1, 1937. He was educated in Frankfurt am Main and in Munich. In 1964 he joined the staff of the Munich Kammerspiele. In 1970 he co-founded the Schaubühne in Berlin, and subsequently was its artistic director until 1985. He produced his first opera, *Das Rheingold,* in Paris in 1976. In 1986 he staged *Otello* at the Welsh National Opera in Cardiff, and returned there to produce *Falstaff* in 1988 and *Pelléas et Mélisande* in 1992. From 1992 to 1997 he was director of drama at the Salzburg Festival, where his production of Schoenberg's *Moses und Aron* was mounted in 1996.

BIBL.: M. Patterson, *P. S.: Germany's Leading Theatre Director* (Cambridge, 1981).—**NS/LK/DM**

STEIN

Stein, Richard Heinrich, German music theorist and composer; b. Halle, Feb. 28, 1882; d. Santa Brigida, Canary Islands, Aug. 11, 1942. He studied law and music, and received his Ph.D. from the Univ. of Erlangen in 1911 with the diss. *Die psychologischen Grundlagen der Wundtschen Ethik.* From 1914 to 1919 he lived in Spain; from 1920 to 1932 he taught in Berlin. In 1933 he settled in the Canary Islands. He was a composer of experimental tendencies; his *2 Konzertstücke* for Cello and Piano, op.26 (1906), was the first composition containing quarter tones to be publ. In 1909 he wrote a brochure giving a detailed exposition of his quarter-tone system, and in 1914 he built a quarter-tone clarinet. He composed about 100 piano pieces, about 50 songs, and *Scherzo fantastico* for Orch. He publ. the books *La música moderna* (Barcelona, 1918; in Spanish and German), *Grieg* (1921), and *Tschaikowsky* (1927).—NS/LK/DM

Steinbach, Fritz, eminent German conductor; b. Grünsfeld, June 17, 1855; d. Munich, Aug. 13, 1916. He began his musical training with his brother, Emil Steinbach, then studied at the Leipzig Cons., with V. Lachner in Karlsruhe, and with G. Nottebohm in Vienna. After serving as second conductor in Mainz (1880–86), he was appointed Hofkapellmeister in Meiningen in 1886; later was promoted to Generalmusikdirektor in recognition of his efforts to carry forward Bülow's tradition of excellence; in 1902 he took the Meiningen Orch. to London, where he conducted the Brahms syms. to critical acclaim. In 1903 he went to Cologne as director of the Cons. and as Kapellmeister of the Gürzenich Orch. He retired to Munich in 1914.—NS/LK/DM

Steinberg, Maximilian (Osseievich), significant Russian composer and pedagogue; b. Vilnius, July 4, 1883; d. Leningrad, Dec. 6, 1946. He was a student at the Univ. of St. Petersburg (graduated, 1907) and of Rimsky-Korsakov (composition), Liadov (harmony), and Glazunov (instrumentation) at the St. Petersburg Cons. (graduated, 1908). In 1908 he married Rimsky-Korsakov's daughter and became a teacher of theory and composition at the St. Petersburg Cons. From 1917 to 1931 he was dean of its faculty of composition, and later was its acting rector from 1934 to 1939. Many composers who became prominent in the Soviet era were his pupils. His early compositions reflected the influence of his teachers, but he gradually evolved a personal style distinguished by rhapsodic eloquence with some touches of French Impressionism.

WORKS: DRAMATIC: B a l l e t : *Metamorphoses* (second part perf. in Paris, June 2, 1914). ORCH.: 4 syms.: No. 1 (1907), No. 2 (St. Petersburg, Nov. 27, 1909), No. 3 (Leningrad, March 3, 1929, composer conducting), and No. 4, *Turksib* (Leningrad, Dec. 2, 1933); *In Armenia* (Leningrad, Dec. 24, 1940); Violin Concerto (1946). CHAMBER: 2 string quartets; piano pieces. VOCAL: *La Princesse Maleine* for Women's Chorus and Orch. (1916); *Heaven and Earth* for 6 Soloists and Orch. (1918); songs. OTHER: Arrangements of works by other composers.

BIBL.: A. Rimsky-Korsakov, *M. S.* (Moscow, 1928); V. Bogdanov-Berezovsky, *M. S.* (Moscow, 1947).—NS/LK/DM

Steinberg, (Carl) Michael (Alfred), German-born American music critic; b. Breslau, Oct. 4, 1928. He went to England in 1939 and to the U.S. in 1943, becoming a naturalized American citizen in 1950. He studied music at Princeton Univ. (A.B., 1949; M.F.A., 1951), and then was in Italy (1952–54). Returning to North America, he taught at Princeton Univ., Hunter Coll., Manhattan School of Music, Univ. of Saskatchewan, Smith Coll., Brandeis Univ., Boston Univ., and (from 1968) the New England Cons. of Music in Boston. In 1964 he was appointed music critic of the *Boston Globe*. His criticisms, utterly disrespectful of the most sacrosanct musical personalities, aroused periodic outbursts of indignation among outraged artists, aggrieved managers, and chagrined promoters. In 1969 several Boston Sym. Orch. players petitioned the management to banish him from their concerts. Then, in a spectacular peripeteia, he left the *Boston Globe* in 1976 and was appointed director of publs. for the Boston Sym. Orch. In 1979 he assumed the position of artistic adviser and publications director of the San Francisco Sym., subsequently serving as its program annotator from 1989. He also was artistic advisor of the Minn. Orch. in Minneapolis (1989–92) and program annotator of the N.Y. Phil. (from 1995). He publ. *The Symphony: A Listener's Guide* (Oxford, 1995) and *The Concerto: A Listener's Guide* (N.Y., 1998).—NS/LK/DM

Steinberg, Pinchas, American conductor; b. N.Y., Feb. 12, 1945. He studied violin in N.Y., then pursued musical training at Tanglewood and at Ind. Univ. In 1967 he became a conductor at the Chicago Lyric Opera; in 1971 he conducted in Berlin; subsequently conducted opera in Frankfurt am Main, Stuttgart, Hamburg, London, Paris, and San Francisco. From 1985 to 1989 he was Generalmusikdirektor in Bremen. In 1989 he became chief conductor of the Austrian Radio Sym. Orch. in Vienna.—NS/LK/DM

Steinberg, William (actually, **Hans Wilhelm**), eminent German-born American conductor; b. Cologne, Aug. 1, 1899; d. N.Y., May 16, 1978. He studied piano and violin at home; conducted his own setting for chorus and orch. of a poem from Ovid's *Metamorphoses* in school at the age of 13; then took lessons in conducting with Hermann Abendroth, in piano with Lazzaro Uzielli, and in theory with Franz Bölsche at the Cologne Cons., graduating in 1920, with the Wullner Prize for conducting. He subsequently became assistant to Otto Klemperer at the Cologne Opera, and in 1924 became principal conductor. In 1925 he was engaged as conductor of the German Theater in Prague; in 1929 he was appointed Generalmusikdirektor of the Frankfurt am Main Opera, where he brought out several modern operas, including Berg's *Wozzeck*. With the advent of the Nazi regime in 1933, he was removed from his position and became conductor for the Jewish Culture League, restricted to Jewish audiences. In 1936 he left Germany and became one of the conductors of the Palestine Orch., which he rehearsed and prepared for Toscanini, who subsequently engaged him as an asst. conductor of the NBC Sym. Orch. in N.Y. in 1938. His career as an orch. conductor was then connected with major American orchs. He became a naturalized American citizen in

3464

1944. He was music director of the Buffalo Phil. (1945–52); in 1952 he was appointed music director of the Pittsburgh Sym. Orch.; concurrently, he served as music director of the London Phil. (1958–60) and of the Boston Sym. Orch. (1969–72); he retired from his Pittsburgh post in 1976. He also made many guest conducting appearances with major U.S. and European orchs. His performances were marked by impeccable taste and fidelity to the music; in this respect he was a follower of the Toscanini tradition.—**NS/LK/DM**

Steinberg, Ze'ev (Wolfgang), German-born Israeli violist and composer; b. Düsseldorf, Nov. 27, 1918. He studied with Eldering in Cologne (1933). In 1934 he emigrated to Palestine, where he studied viola and composition with Partos (1940–42). He then became a violist in the Palestine Sym. Orch. (later the Israel Phil.) in Tel Aviv; in 1957, became the violinist in the New Israeli String Quartet; from 1969 to 1972, was a lecturer at the Tel Aviv Academy of Music. His compositions present an agreeable blend of oriental melos, asymmetrical rhythms, and sharp atonal progressions in dissonant counterpoint.

WORKS: Sonata for 2 Violas (1955–56); 3 string quartets (1959; 1969; 1981–82); *6 Miniatures* for Cello and Piano (1961); *4 Bagatelles* for 2 Recorders (1962); *2 concerti da camera*: No. 1 for Viola and String Orch. (1962) and No. 2 for Violin and 8 Instruments (1966); *Purim Variations* on a nursery song for Horn and String Trio (1963); *The Story of Rahab and the Spies*, biblical cantata (1969); *Festive Prologue* for Flute, Oboe, and String Trio (1969); *2 Songs without Words* for Viola, String Quartet, and String Orch. (1970); *a little suite for a big flute* for Bass Flute in C (1972); *Variations and Dance* for Violin (1976); *Prelude and Fughetta* for Flute, Viola, and Harp (1977); *4 Pieces* for Orch. (1985); *7 Pieces* for 11 Instruments (1987); arrangements of works by Vivaldi, Bach, Schubert, and others.—**NS/LK/DM**

Steiner, Emma, American composer and conductor; b. 1850; d. N.Y., Feb. 27, 1928. Her grandfather led the Md. 16th Brigade, which won the battle of North Point (near Fort McHenry, Baltimore) on Sept. 13, 1814, enabling Francis Scott Key to finish the last stanza of *The Star-Spangled Banner*. She wrote 7 light operas, plus ballets, overtures, and songs; purportedly she was also the first woman ever to receive payment for conducting. Conried, the manager of the Metropolitan Opera, is said to have declared that he would have let her conduct a performance had he dared to put a woman armed with a baton in front of a totally male orch. According to unverifiable accounts, she conducted 6,000 performances of 50 different operas. She also organized an Emma R. Steiner Home for the Aged and Infirm Musicians at Bay Shore, Long Island. On Feb. 28, 1925, she conducted a concert at the Metropolitan Opera to commemorate the 50th anniversary of her first appearance as conductor. Her works, of different genres and light consistency, aggregate more than 200 opus numbers. —**NS/LK/DM**

Steiner, Max(imilian Raoul Walter), Austrian-born American composer; b. Vienna, May 10, 1888; d. Los Angeles, Dec. 28, 1971. He studied at the Vienna Cons. with Fuchs and Gradener, and also had some advice from Mahler. At the age of 14, he wrote an operetta. In 1904 he went to England; in 1911 he proceeded to Paris. In 1914 he settled in the U.S.; after conducting musical shows in N.Y., he moved in 1929 to Hollywood, where he became one of the most successful film composers. His music offers a fulsome blend of lush harmonies artfully derived from both Tchaikovsky and Wagner, arranged in a manner marvelously suitable for the portrayal of psychological drama on the screen. Among his film scores, of which he wrote more than 200, are *King Kong* (1933), *The Charge of the Light Brigade* (1936), *Gone with the Wind* (1939), and *The Treasure of Sierra Madre* (1948).

BIBL.: G. Lazarou, *M. S. and Film Music: An Essay* (Athens, 1971).—**NS/LK/DM**

Steinert, Alexander Lang, American pianist, conductor, composer, and arranger; b. Boston, Sept. 21, 1900; d. N.Y., July 7, 1982. He was the son of a piano manufacturer; studied at Harvard Univ., graduating in 1922; then took private lessons in composition with Loeffler in Boston, and with Koechlin and d'Indy in Paris. He lived much of his time in Europe; was active as a conductor and arranger in Hollywood. His music bears the imprint of the French modern school.

WORKS: ORCH.: *Nuit méridionale* (Boston, Oct. 15, 1926); *Leggenda sinfonica* (Rome, 1930); *Concerto sinfonico* for Piano and Orch. (Boston, Feb. 8, 1935, composer soloist); *Rhapsody* for Clarinet and Orch. (1945); *The Nightingale and the Rose* for Speaker and Orch. (Philadelphia, March 31, 1950). CHAMBER: Violin Sonata; Piano Trio; piano pieces. VOCAL: Songs.—**NS/LK/DM**

Steingruber, Ilona, Austrian soprano; b. Vienna, Feb. 8, 1912; d. there, Dec. 10, 1962. She studied piano before taking up vocal training at the Vienna Academy of Music. She sang in performances broadcast by the Austrian Radio (1939–42), making her operatic debut in Tilsit (1942). After World War II, she toured as a concert artist; also sang at the Vienna State Opera (1948–51); then taught in Darmstadt. In 1946 she married **Friedrich Wildgans**.—**NS/LK/DM**

Steinitz, (Charles) Paul (Joseph), English organist and conductor; b. Chichester, Aug. 25, 1909; d. Oxted, April 22, 1988. He studied at the Royal Academy of Music in London, and also privately with George Oldroyd. He then served as church organist in Ashford, Kent (1933–42). In 1947 he organized the South London Bach Soc.; this choral group later became noteworthy under the name of the London Bach Soc. He also served as organist and choirmaster at the Church of St. Bartholomew-the-Great in London (1949–61). In 1969 he founded the Steinitz Bach Players, which he conducted on tours. In 1945 he became a prof. at the Royal Academy of Music in London; also taught at Goldsmiths' Coll., Univ. of London (1948–76). He publ. *Bach's Passions* (London, 1979). In 1985 he was made a member of the Order of the British Empire.—**NS/LK/DM**

Steinpress, Boris (Solomonovich), erudite Russian musicologist; b. Berdyansk, Aug. 13, 1908; d.

Moscow, May 21, 1986. He studied piano with Igumnov at the Moscow Cons., graduating in 1931, and took a postgraduate course there in musicology with Ivanov-Boretsky, completing it in 1936; was a member of its faculty (1931; 1933–36); in 1938 he received the title of candidate of fine arts for his diss. on Mozart's *Le nozze di Figaro*. He taught at the Urals Cons. in Sverdlovsk (1936–37; 1942–43); served as head of the music history dept. of the Central Correspondence Inst. for Musical Education (1939–41), and was senior lecturer and dean of the faculty of history and theory (from 1940). In 1942 he joined the Communist Party. Although engaged primarily in musical encyclopedic work, Steinpress also composed; his patriotic songs were popular in the U.S.S.R. during World War II. From 1938 to 1940 and from 1943 to 1959 he was chief contributor to the music section of the *Great Soviet Encyclopedia*. His publcations are particularly important in musical biography; he decisively refuted the legend of Salieri's poisoning Mozart. His biography of Aliabiev clarifies the story of Aliabiev's life and his internal exile on the false charge of murder in a duel. With I. Yampolsky, he ed. an extremely valuable and accurate one-vol. encyclopedic musical dictionary (Moscow, 1959; second ed., 1966); also with Yampolsky he compiled a useful brief dictionary for music lovers (Moscow, 1961; second ed., 1967). In 1963 he publ. a partial vol. of a monumental work on opera premieres covering the period 1900–40, giving exact dates and names of theaters for all opera productions worldwide.—NS/LK/DM

Steinway & Sons, celebrated family of German-American piano manufacturers. The founder of the firm was **Heinrich Engelhard Steinweg** (b. Wolfshagen, Germany, Feb. 15, 1797; d. N.Y., Feb. 7, 1871; in 1864 he Anglicized his name to Henry E. Steinway). He learned cabinetmaking and organ building at Goslar, and in 1818 entered the shop of an organ maker in Seesen, also becoming church organist there. From about 1820 he became interested in piano making and worked hard to establish a business of his own. He built his first piano in 1836. In 1839 he exhibited one grand and 2 square pianos at the Braunschweig State Fair, winning the gold medal. The Revolution of 1848 caused him to emigrate to America with his wife, 2 daughters, and 4 of his 5 sons: **Charles (actually, Christian Karl Gottlieb) Steinweg** (b. Seesen, Jan. 4, 1829; d. there, March 31, 1865); **Henry (actually, Johann Heinrich Engelhard) Steinweg** (b. Seesen, Oct. 29, 1830; d. N.Y., March 11, 1865); **William (actually, Johann Heinrich Wilhelm) Steinweg** (b. Seesen, March 5, 1835; d. N.Y., Nov. 30, 1896); and **(Georg August) Albert Steinweg** (b. Seesen, June 10, 1840; d. N.Y., May 14, 1877). The management of the German business at Seesen was left in charge of the eldest son, **(Christian Friedrich) Theodore Steinweg** (b. Seesen, Nov. 6, 1825; d. Braunschweig, March 26, 1889). The family arrived in N.Y. on June 29, 1850, and for about 2 years father and sons worked in various piano factories there. On March 5, 1853, they established a factory of their own under the above firm name, with premises on Varick St. In 1854 they won a gold medal for a square piano at the Metropolitan Fair in Washington, D.C. Their remarkable prosperity dates from 1855,

when they took first prize for a square over-strung piano with cast-iron frame (an innovation then) at the N.Y. Industrial Exhibition. In 1856 they made their first grand, and in 1862 their first upright. Among the numerous honors subsequently received may be mentioned first prize at London, 1862; first grand gold medal of honor for all styles at Paris, 1867 (by unanimous verdict); diplomas for "highest degree of excellence in all styles" at Philadelphia, 1876. In 1854 the family name (Steinweg) was legally changed to Steinway. In 1865, upon the death of his brothers Charles and Henry, Theodore gave up the Braunschweig business and became a full partner in the N.Y. firm; he built Steinway Hall on 14th St., which, in addition to the offices and retail warerooms, housed a concert hall that became a leading center of N.Y. musical life. In 1925 headquarters were established in the Steinway Building on 57th St. Theodore was especially interested in the scientific aspects of piano construction and made a study of the acoustical theories of Helmholtz and Tyndall, which enabled him to introduce important improvements. He returned to Germany in 1870. On May 17, 1876, the firm was incorporated and William was elected president; he opened a London branch in 1876, and established a European factory at Hamburg in 1880. In the latter year he also bought 400 acres of land on Long Island Sound and established there the village of Steinway (now part of Long Island City), where since 1910 the entire manufacturing plant has been located. Control and active management of the business, now the largest of its kind in the world, has remained in the hands of the founder's descendants. **Theodore E. Steinway** (d. N.Y., April 8, 1957), grandson of Henry E. Steinway, was president from 1927; also a stamp collector, he was honored by Liechtenstein with his portrait on a postage stamp on Sept. 7, 1972; in 1955 he was succeeded by his son, Henry Steinway. The firm was sold to CBS in 1972, although the Steinway family continued to be closely associated with the business. In 1985 CBS sold the firm to Steinway Musical Properties. In 1988 Steinway & Sons celebrated its 135th anniversary with a special concert in N.Y. and the unveiling of its 500,000th piano. In 1995 the firm was purchased by the Selmer Co.

BIBL.: O. Floersheim, *W. S.* (Breslau, 1894); E. Hubbard, *The Story of the S.s* (East Aurora, N.Y., 1911); T. Steinway, *People and Pianos* (N.Y., 1953; second ed., 1961); C. Ehrlich, *The Piano: A History* (London, 1976); D. Fostle, *The S. Saga: An American Dynasty* (N.Y., 1994); R. Lieberman, *S. & Sons* (New Haven, 1995).—NS/LK/DM

Steinweg, original name of the Steinway family of piano manufacturers. (Christian Friedrich) Theodore Steinway continued the piano-making business established by his father at Seesen until 1852, when he transferred it to Wolfenbüttel; in 1859 he moved it to Braunschweig, carrying it on there until 1865, when he left for America. The business was then taken over by his partners, Grotrian, Helfferich, and Schulz, under the name "Theodore Steinweg Nachfolger." In 1886 Grotrian became sole owner, and the business was carried on by his sons Willi and Kurt, the firm name being "Grotrian-Steinweg."—NS/LK/DM

Stella, Antonietta, Italian soprano; b. Perugia, March 15, 1929. She studied voice with Aldo Zeetti in Perugia. She made her operatic debut in Rome as Leonore in *La forza del destino* in 1951; in 1953 she sang at La Scala in Milan; further engagements were at Covent Garden in London (1955) and at the Vienna State Opera. She made her American debut at the Metropolitan Opera in N.Y. on Nov. 13, 1956, as Aida; after remaining on its roster until 1960, she pursued her career in Europe.—**NS/LK/DM**

Stemper, Frank, American pianist and composer; b. Milwaukee, Oct. 19, 1951. He studied at the Univ. of British Columbia in Vancouver (B.Mus., 1975), the State Univ. of N.Y. at Stony Brook (M.A., 1978), and the Univ. of Calif. at Berkeley (Ph.D., 1981); also with Betsy Jolas at the Paris Cons. (1981, 1983). He was a studio technician at the Univ. of Calif. at Berkeley's Electronic Music Studio (1979–81) and guest composer at the Computer Music Project at the Univ. of Ill. at Urbana (1987; 1988); also appeared as a pianist in classical, jazz, and big-band settings. His music fuses postwar serial techniques with jazz elements.

WORKS: ORCH.: Violin Concerto (1978); *Hoye's Tribute* for Winds (Carbondale, Ill., Oct. 1, 1988). **CHAMBER:** Trio for Oboe, Clarinet, and Bassoon (1974; Vancouver, March 27, 1975); *Off Center to the Left* for Percussion Quartet (1977; Stony Brook, N.Y., Oct. 19, 1978); *Humble Cake* for Flute, Clarinet, Bass Clarinet, Violin, and Cello (1977; Stony Brook, N.Y., April 24, 1978); String Quartet (1982; Carbondale, Ill., March 29, 1988); Double Wind Trio for Oboe, Bassoon, and Piano (1983); *Chameleon* for Clarinet, String Trio, and Piano (Los Angeles, May 13, 1984); *Dreams* for Woodwind Quintet (1984; Bucharest, Feb. 17, 1987); *Memories from Euphoria* for Guitar and Harpsichord (1986); *second Diary* for Clarinet and Piano (1986; Urbana, Ill., April 3, 1988); *Some Things* for Flute, Clarinet, Violin, Cello, and Piano (1987; St. Louis, March 25, 1988); works for Solo Instruments. **VOCAL:** *Written in Response to a Request for a Manifesto on Music, 1952* for Chorus (1980; Berkeley, April 15, 1981); *Seamaster* for Soprano and Chamber Orch. (1981; Milwaukee, May 13, 1983); *My Breakfast with Ronald* for Soprano, Clarinet, and Piano (Raleigh, N.C., March 10, 1985).—**NS/LK/DM**

Stenberg, Jordan, American avant-garde composer; b. Fresno, Calif., May 31, 1947. He studied music theory with Robert Moran at the San Francisco Cons. and worked on electronic problems with Robert Ashley at Mills Coll. In his compositions, he aims at creating an organic expression of cosmic philosophy as formalized by his deep reading of Russian theosophists and Indian psychologists. His zodiacal parameters are sun in Gemini, moon in Scorpio, with Libra rising. In addition to the works listed below, Stenberg composed music for flower conservatories to stimulate the growth of timid plants.

WORKS: *88 Fog-Horn Seconds,* a recording of Foghorns on Electronic Tape (1967); *A Snail's Progress in a Goldfish Bowl* for Strings glissandi within a definite integral of white noise (1968); *Music for 4 Horse-Drawn Carriages,* a literal equestrian exercise (1968); *Mind over Matter,* film opera for Voices and Instruments (1969); *Extension Chords,* to be perf. by nomadic bands on the desert floor during a lunar eclipse or at the winter solstice (1970); *A Stitch in Time* for 11 Acoustical Sources (1970); *The*

Clock Struck One, opera-play for Voices, Instruments, and Dervish Dancers (1970); *Circles, Lines, Planes,* a choreographed acoustical dance notated in the form of an enneagram, to be produced in a canyon by 9 Bagpipers and 9 x 9 Buglers (1970). —**NS/LK/DM**

Stenborg, Carl, Swedish tenor, impresario, and composer; b. Stockholm, Sept. 25, 1752; d. Djurgarden, Aug. 1, 1813. His father, Petter Stenborg, was a theater manager. He began appearing in concerts in Stockholm when he was 14; studied vocal and instrumental music with F. Zellbel, the court Kapellmeister. He appeared as Peleus in F. Uttini's *Thetis och Pelée* for the opening of the Royal Swedish Opera in 1773; was made a court singer and a member of the Academy of Music in 1782; also was active as a conductor and composer at his father's theater, which he managed from 1780 until it was closed in 1799. After leaving the court in 1806, he ran his own theater. His major work was the Singspiel *Gustaf Ericsson i Dalarna* (1784); also wrote incidental music to the dramas *Caspar och Dorothea* (1775) and *Konung Gustaft Adolfs jagt* (1777).

BIBL.: J. Flodmark, *S.ska skadebanorna* (Stockholm, 1893); idem, *Elisabeth Olin och C. S.* (Stockholm, 1903).—**NS/LK/DM**

Stendhal (real name, **Marie-Henri Beyle**), famous French writer; b. Grenoble, Jan. 23, 1783; d. Paris, March 23, 1842. He received some lessons in singing, violin, and clarinet. He served as a military official under Napoleon, taking part in the German and Russian campaigns; from 1815 he lived in Milan, Paris, and Rome, and in 1830 he became French consul at Trieste, from 1831 in Civitavecchia. He became best known as a novelist (*Le Rouge et le noir, La Chartreuse de Parme,* etc.), but also wrote on music; under the name César Bombet, he publ. *Lettres écrites de Vienne, en Autriche, sur le célèbre compositeur Haydn, suivies d'une vie de Mozart, et de considérations sur Métastase et l'état présent de la musique en France et en Italie* (Paris, 1814; Eng. tr., London, 1817; new ed., 1817, as *Vies de Haydn, Mozart et Métastase,* by Stendhal; republ., 1914, by R. Rolland). The life of Haydn is in part tr. from Carpani's *Le Haydine;* the first 4 chapters of the life of Mozart are taken from Schlichtegroll's Necrology (1791), the last 3 from Cramer's *Anecdotes sur Mozart.* In Jan. 1824 Stendhal's life of Rossini was publ. in London as *Memoirs of Rossini,* in a tr. made from the original MS (republ. as *The Life of Rossini,* London, 1956); the French version, considerably expanded, was publ. in Paris as *Vie de Rossini* (1824; second ed., rev., 1922 by H. Prunières; Eng. tr., 1956; second ed., rev., 1970).

BIBL.: A. Paupe, *Histoire des oeuvres de S.* (Paris, 1903); A. Beau, *Das Verhaltnis S.s zur Musik* (diss., Univ. of Hamburg, 1930); D. Maurice, *S.* (Paris, 1931); P. Jourda, *S., L'Homme et l'oeuvre* (Paris, 1934); F. Green, *S.* (Cambridge, 1939). —**NS/LK/DM**

Stenhammar, Per Ulrik, Swedish composer, father of **(Karl) Wilhelm (Eugen) Stenhammar;** b. Tornvalla, Feb. 20, 1828; d. Stockholm, Feb. 8, 1875. He received his primary musical education from A.F. Lindblad. Becoming interested in sacred music, he wrote choral works in Mendelssohn's style; also many solo songs. His oratorio, *Saul och David* (1869), was orchestrated by his son.—**NS/LK/DM**

Stenhammar, (Karl) Wilhelm (Eugen), eminent Swedish pianist, conductor, and composer, son of **Per Ulrik Stenhammar;** b. Stockholm, Feb. 7, 1871; d. there, Nov. 20, 1927. He began to play the piano and to compose in childhood. After attending Richard Andersson's music school, he studied theory with Joseph Dente and organ with Heintze and Lagergren (1888–89); passed the organists' examination privately (1890), and later pursued theory lessons with Emil Sjögren and Andreas Hallén; completed his piano training with Heinrich Barth in Berlin (1892–93). He subsequently toured as a pianist, appearing as a soloist and frequently with the Aulin Quartet. His first large work for Solo Voices, Chorus, and Orch., *I rosengård* (In a Rose Garden; 1888–89; after K.A. Melin's collection of fairy tales, *Prinsessan och svennen*), was performed in Stockholm on Feb. 16, 1892, attracting considerable attention; his love for the theater prompted him to compose 2 music dramas, *Gildet på Solhaug* (1892–93) and *Tirfing* (1897–98), neither of which was successful; he did, however, compose much outstanding incidental music. He made his conducting debut with a performance of his overture *Excelsior!* in 1897. After serving as artistic director of the Phil. Soc. (1897–1900), the Royal Theater (1 season), and the New Phil. Soc. (1904–6) in Stockholm, he went to Göteborg as artistic director of the Orch. Soc.; during his tenure (1906–22), he elevated the musical life of the city; then returned to Stockholm, where he again took charge of the Royal Theater (1924–25) before ill health compelled him to retire. Stenhammar's early compositions reflect his preoccupation with the Romantic movement; the influence of Wagner and Liszt is quite perceptible, but he later developed an individual style based on his detailed study of Classical forms. His ability to absorb and transmute authentic folk melodies is a notable characteristic of many of his works. Among his most outstanding scores are the second Sym., the second Piano Concerto, the Serenade for Orch., several of his string quartets, his choral pieces, and a number of his songs.

WORKS: DRAMATIC: Opera: *Gildet på Solhaug* (The Feast at Solhaug), op.6, after Ibsen (1892–93; first perf. in Ger. as *Das Fest auf Solhaug*, Stuttgart, April 12, 1899; first perf. in Swedish, Stockholm, Oct. 31, 1902); *Tirfing*, op.15 (Stockholm, Dec. 9, 1898). **Incidental Music To:** Strindberg's *Ett drömspel*; H. Bergman's *Lodolezzi sjunger*; Tagore's *Chitra*; Shakespeare's *Romeo and Juliet.* **ORCH.:** 2 piano concertos: No. 1 (1893; Stockholm, March 17, 1894) and No. 2, op.23 (1904–7; Göteborg, April 15, 1908); *Excelsior!*, overture, op.13 (1896); 2 syms.: No. 1 (Stockholm, Dec. 1903) and No. 2, op.34 (1911–15; Göteborg, April 22, 1915); 2 *sentimentala romanser* for Violin and Orch., op.28 (1910); Serenade, op.31 (1911–13; rev. 1919). **CHAMBER:** 6 string quartets: No. 1, op.2 (1894), No. 2, op.14 (1896), No. 3, op.18 (1897–1900), No. 4, op.24 (1905–09), No. 5, op.29 (1910), and No. 6, op.35 (1916); Violin Sonata, op.19 (1899–1900). **Piano:** 2 sonatas (1890, 1895); 3 *fantasier*, op.11 (1895); *Sensommarnätter*, op.33 (1914). **VOCAL:** *I rosengård* for Solo Voices, Chorus, and Orch. (1888–89); *Norrland* for Men's Voices, Mixed Chorus, and Orch.; 3 *körvisor till dikter av J.P. Jacobsen* for Chorus (c. 1890); *Snöfrid* for Solo Voices, Chorus, and Orch., op.5 (1891); *Florez och Blanzeflor* for Baritone and Orch., op.3 (1891); *Ur idyll och epigram av J.L. Runeberg* for Mezzo-soprano and Orch., op.4a (1893); *Ett folk* for Baritone, Chorus, and Orch., op.22 (1904–05); *Midvinter* for Chorus and Orch., op.24 (1907); *Folket i Nifelhem Vårnatt* for Chorus and Orch., op.30 (1911–12); *Sangen* for Solo Voices, Chorus, and Orch., op.44 (1921); also *Ithaka* for Baritone and Orch., op.21; 4 *Stockholmsdikter*, op.38; other songs.

BIBL.: B. Wallner, *W. S. och hans tid* (3 vols., Stockholm, 1991).—**NS/LK/DM**

Stenz, Markus, German conductor; b. Bad Neuenahr, Feb. 28, 1965. He studied at the Cologne Hochschule für Musik and with Gary Bertini and Noam Sheriff. From 1989 to 1992 he was music director of the Montepulciano Festival. In 1990 he conducted the premiere of Henze's *Das verratene Meer* in Berlin. He was engaged to conduct *Le nozze di Figaro* at the Los Angeles Opera in 1994. From 1994 to 1998 he served as principal conductor of the London Sinfonietta. In 1995 he made his debut with the English National Opera conducting *Don Giovanni*, and in 1996 he appeared at the Hamburg State Opera. In 1997 he conducted the premiere of Henze's *Venus und Adonis* in Munich. From 1998 he was chief conductor of the Melbourne Sym. Orch. He also appeared as a guest conductor with many European and North American orchs.—**NS/LK/DM**

Stenzl, Jürg (Thomas), Swiss musicologist; b. Basel, Aug. 23, 1942. He began instruction in recorder and violin in 1949 in Bern; then studied the oboe with Huwler at the Bern Cons. in 1961; attended the Univ. of Bern as a student of musicology with Geering and Dickenmann (Ph.D., 1968, with the diss. *Die vierzig Clausulae der Handschrift Paris, Bibliothéque Nationale, latin 15139 [Saint Victor- Clauselae]*; publ. in Bern, 1970); he also worked with Chailley at the Univ. of Paris (1965) and later completed his Habilitation at the Univ. of Fribourg (1974), where he was a prof. from 1980 to 1992. He was engaged as a visiting prof. at the univs. of Geneva (1976–77; 1979–80), Neuchâtel (1982), Bern (1986–87), and Basel (1987–88), and subsequently served at the Technical Univ. in Berlin (1988–89). In 1992–93 he was artistic director of Universal Edition in Vienna. He then was a prof. at the Graz Hochschule für Musik (until 1996) and program advisor of the Donaueschingen Festival (1995–98). In 1996 he became a prof. and director of the musicological inst. at the Univ. of Salzburg. He was secretary of the Société Suisse de Musicologie (1972–80) and ed. of the *Schweizerische Musikzeitung* (1975–83). He contributed valuable articles and music criticism to various publications, including *Sohlmans Musiklexikon* (1975–79) and *The New Grove Dictionary of Music and Musicians* (1980), and was author of *Von Giacomo Puccini zu Luigi Nono: Italienische Musik, 1922–1952: Faschismus, Resistenza, Republik* (Buren, 1990) and *Luigi Nono* (Reinbek, 1998). Stenzl married Wieland Wagner's daughter Nike in 1991. His expertise ranges from the Middle Ages to contemporary music. —**NS/LK/DM**

Štěpán, Václav, Czech pianist, pedagogue, and writer on music; b. Pečky, near Kolín, Dec. 12, 1889; d. Prague, Nov. 24, 1944. He studied musicology with Nejedlý at the Univ. of Prague (graudated, 1913), and then took courses at the German Univ. of Prague and in Berlin; also studied piano with Josef Čermák in Prague (1895–1908), and later with James Kwast in Berlin and Blanche Selva in Paris. He was active as a pianist from 1908; also taught aesthetics (from 1919) and later piano at the Prague Cons. He was an authority on Suk and Novák; a collection of his major articles on these composers appeared as *Novak à Suk* (Prague, 1945); also publ. *Symbolika z přibuzné zjevy v programni hudbě* (Symbolism and Related Phenomena in Program Music; Prague, 1915). He composed some vocal, chamber, and piano pieces but abandoned composition when he was 30.—**NS/LK/DM**

Stepanian, Aro (Levoni), Armenian composer; b. Elizavetpol, April 24, 1897; d. Yerevan, Jan. 9, 1966. He studied with Gnessin in Moscow (1923–27) and with Shcherbachev and Kushnarian at the Leningrad Cons. (1926–30). He then settled in Yerevan, where he served as president of the Armenian Composers' Union (1938–48). He was one of the leading Armenian composers of his generation.

WORKS: DRAMATIC: O p e r a : *Brave Nazar* (1934; Yerevan, Nov. 29, 1935); *David of Sasun* (1936); *At the Dawn* (1937); *Nune* (1947); *Heroine* (1950). **ORCH.:** 3 syms. (1943, 1945, 1953); 2 piano concertos (1947, 1955); Viola Concerto (1955); Rhapsody for Piano and Orch. (1962). **CHAMBER:** 4 string quartets; 2 violin sonatas; Cello Sonata. **VOCAL:** Numerous choruses and songs.

BIBL.: M. Kazakhian, *A. S.* (Yerevan, 1962); G. Tigranov, *A. S.* (Moscow, 1967).—**NS/LK/DM**

Stephan, (Gustav-Adolf Carl) Rudolf, learned German musicologist; b. Bochum, April 3, 1925. He studied in Heidelberg, receiving instruction in violin at the Cons., in theory with Fortner at the Inst. of Protestant Church Music, and in musicology with Besseler and in philosophy with Jaspers and Hofmann at the Univ. He subsequently studied at the Univ. of Göttingen, where he took courses in philosophy with Hartmann and in musicology with Gerber (Ph.D., 1950, with the diss. *Die Tenores der Motetten Ältesten Stils*); completed his Habilitation there in 1963 with his *Antiphonar-Studien,* and then served on its faculty as a lecturer (1966–67). From 1967 to 1990 he was a prof. at the Free Univ. of Berlin, being made prof. emeritus in 1990. In 1981 he was a visiting prof. at the Univ. of Vienna. He served as editorial director of both the Schönberg-Gesamtausgabe and the Berg-Gesamtausgabe, and as president of the Institut für Neu Musik und Musikerziehung in Darmstadt (1970–76) and of the Gesellschaft für Musikforschung (1980–89). He has written valuable articles on topics ranging from medieval music to Hindemith for a variety of publications.

WRITINGS: *Musik* (Frankfurt am Main, 1957); *Neue Musik* (Göttingen, 1958; second ed., 1973); *Gustav Mahler: Vierte Symphonie G-Dur* (Munich, 1966); *Alexander Zemlinsky: Ein unbe-* *kannter Meister der Wiener Schule* (Kiel, 1978); *Gustav Mahler: Zweite Symphonie C-Moll* (Munich, 1979); *Gustav Mahler: Werk und Interpretation* (Cologne, 1979); *Vom musikalischen Denken* (Mainz, 1985); *Alban Berg: Violinkonzert (1935)* (Munich, 1988); *Die Wiener Schule* (Darmstadt, 1989); A. Riethmüller, ed., *Musiker der Moderne* (Laaber, 1995).

BIBL.: H. Lehr, *Musik für—: Untersuchungen zum Werk R. S.s* (Berlin, 1996).—**NS/LK/DM**

Stephan, Rudi, German composer; b. Worms, July 29, 1887; d. in battle near Tarnopol, Galicia, Sept. 29, 1915. He studied counterpoint with Sekles at the Hoch Cons. in Frankfurt am Main (1905), then went to Munich, where he received instruction in composition from Rudolf Louis and in piano from Heinrich Schwartz (1906–08); also studied philosophy at the Univ. His output is marked by a secure command of harmony and counterpoint with a fine feeling for orch. color. Stephan's tragic death was greatly lamented.

WORKS: DRAMATIC: O p e r a : *Die ersten Menschen* (1911–14; Frankfurt am Main, July 1, 1920). **ORCH.:** *Musik für Orchester* (1912; Jena, June 6, 1913); *Musik für Geige und Orchester* (Berlin, Oct. 10, 1913). **CHAMBER:** *Musik für sieben Saiteninstrumente* (2 violins, viola, cello, double bass, harp, and piano; 1911; Danzig, May 30, 1912). **VOCAL:** *Liebeszauber* for Tenor and Orch. (1909–10; Munich, Jan. 16, 1911; withdrawn; rev. for Baritone and Orch., 1913); 18 songs (1908–14).

BIBL.: K. Holl, *R. S.: Studie zur Entwicklungsgeschichte der Musik am Anfang des 20. Jahrhunderts* (Saarbrücken, 1920; second ed., 1922); A. Machner, *R. S.s Werk* (diss., Univ. of Breslau, 1943). —**NS/LK/DM**

Stephănescu, George, noted Romanian conductor, teacher, and composer; b. Bucharest, Dec. 13, 1843; d. there, April 25, 1925. He studied harmony and piano with Wachmann at the Bucharest Cons. (1864–67), then pursued his training at the Paris Cons. (1867–71), where he studied harmony with Reber, composition with Auber and Thomas, piano with Marmontel, and singing with Delle Sedie. Returning to Bucharest, he taught singing and opera at the Cons. (1872–1904); was a conductor of the Romanian Opera at the National Theater (from 1877), for which he wrote several works in an effort to produce native scores for the stage; also was active as a music critic. Stephănescu was one of the foremost figures in Romanian musical life of his era. He composed the first Romanian sym. (1869). His output reflects his interest in Romanian folk tunes, although he did not directly quote from such sources.

WORKS: DRAMATIC: O p e r a : *Petra* (1902). **O p e r e t t a :** *Peste Dunăre* (Across the Danube; 1880); *Scaiul bărbaților* (Men's Burr; 1885); *Cometa* (1900). **M u s i c a l F a i r y T a l e :** *Sînziana şi Pepelea* (1880). **ORCH.: S y m p h o n i c P o e m s :** *In munti* (In the Mountains; 1888); *In cring* (In the Meadow; 1889); *Intre flori* (1890); *In alte timpuri* (In Old Times; 1895); *Idila* (1902). **O t h e r :** Sym. (1869); *Uverta nationala* (1876). **CHAMBER:** Cello Sonata (1863); Octet (1866); Septet (1870); String Quartet (1870); also a piano sonata (1863). **VOCAL:** Choruses and songs.

BIBL.: G. Stephănescu, *G. S.: Viata în imagini* (G. S.: Life in Pictures; Bucharest, 1962).—**NS/LK/DM**

Stephens, Catherine, noted English soprano and actress; b. London, Sept. 18, 1794; d. there, Feb. 22, 1882. She studied voice with Gesualdo Lanza. After appearing in the English provinces, she sang minor roles with an Italian opera company at London's Pantheon (1822); following additional vocal training with Thomas Welsh, she made her debut at London's Covent Garden as Mandane in Arne's *Artaxerxes* (Sept. 23, 1813); she sang there with much success until 1822. After singing at Drury Lane (1822–28), she returned to Covent Garden and appeared there until her retirement in 1835. In 1838 she married the Earl of Essex. She was highly successful as a concert and oratorio singer, as well as a singer and actress in the theater; sang Susanna in the first performance in English of *Le nozze di Figaro* (1819). Weber's last work, the song *From Chindara's warbling fount I come* (1826), was written for her.—NS/LK/DM

Stephens, John (Elliott), American conductor and composer; b. Washington, D.C., Nov. 6, 1929. He studied at the Catholic Univ. of America in Washington, D.C. (B.M., 1959; M.M., 1962; D.M.A., 1972); also had lessons in 20th-century conducting with Boulez at the Basel Academy of Music (certificate, 1969), and studied composition privately with Wuorinen, Shapey, and Brant. He founded and was music director of the American Camerata for New Music in Washington, D.C., with which he appeared widely and made numerous recordings; taught at George Washington Univ. (1963–74), Catholic Univ. (1967–68), American Univ. (1976–83), and the Univ. of the District of Columbia (from 1983). He produced for radio the acclaimed educational series "New Sounds for Young Ears."

WORKS: String Quartet (1959); *Concert Piece* for Jazz Band (1960); Sym. in 1 Movement (1962); Sextet for Woodwind Quintet and Piano (1963); Chamber Sym. (1964); *Inventions* for Treble Instruments (1965); *Concert Music* for Flutes and Piano (1970); *Cantata* for Narrator, Chamber Chorus, Baritone, Boy's Chorus, and Chamber Ensemble (1972); Songs for Soprano, Flute, Harp, and Strings (1975); *Inventions* for Clarinet (1978); *Creations* for Trombone and String Quartet (1982); *3 for 4* for Harp, Flute/Piccolo, Viola, and Trombone (1984); Double Concerto for Flute, Oboe, Strings, Percussion, and Harp (1988). —NS/LK/DM

Steppenwolf, 1960s-era band led by singer/ songwriter John Kay famed for the song "Born to be Wild" which introduced the term "heavy metal" to rock and roll. **MEMBERSHIP:** John Kay (Joachim Krauledat, Tilsit), gtr., voc. (b. East Germany, April 12, 1944); Goldy McJohn, kybd. (b. May 2, 1945); Michael Monarch, lead gtr. (b. Los Angeles, Calif., July 5, 1950); John Morgan, bass; Jerry Edmonton, drm. (b. Canada, Oct, 24, 1946; d. near Santa Barbara, Calif., Nov. 28, 1993). Later members included bassists Nick St. Nicholas (b. Hamburg, Germany, Sept. 28, 1942) and George Biondo (b. Brooklyn, N.Y., Sept. 3, 1945), and guitarist Larry Byrom (b. Dec. 27, 1948).

Born near-blind, John Kay fled East Germany with his mother in 1958, settling in Canada. He performed as a folk singer in Toronto's Yorkville district in the early 1960s, and moved to N.Y. in 1963 and Santa Monica, Calif., in 1964, to tour the folk club circuit. Back in Toronto in 1966, he and organist Goldy McJohn joined The Sparrow, originally formed in 1965 by Jerry and Dennis Edmonton (also known as Mars Bonfire) and bassist Nick St. Nicholas. Traveling to N.Y., then Los Angeles, The Sparrow signed with Columbia Records, which eventually released an album of their recordings after the success of Steppenwolf. Dennis Edmonton/Mars Bonfire later recorded a neglected album for Columbia Records.

In 1967, John Kay, Goldy McJohn, and Jerry Edmonton moved to Los Angeles and formed Steppenwolf with lead guitarist Michael Monarch and, later, bassist John Morgan. Developing a reputation as a live act on the West Coast, Steppenwolf signed with Dunhill Records. Their debut album yielded a smash hit with the classic biker song, "Born to Be Wild," and included Hoyt Axton's "The Pusher" and Kay's existential "Desperation" and "The Ostrich." "Born to Be Wild" and "The Pusher" were featured in the 1969 cult classic Peter Fonda–Dennis Hopper movie *Easy Rider*. *Steppenwolf the Second* produced another smash hit with the psychedelic "Magic Carpet Ride" and contained Mars Bonfire's "Faster Than the Speed of Life" and Kay's satirical "Don't Step on the Grass, Sam."

At Your Birthday Party yielded a near-smash hit with "Rock Me" and a minor hit with "It's Never Too Late," but subsequent singles by Steppenwolf proved moderate hits at best, and personnel defections began in 1969. Monarch and Morgan left in April, to be replaced by guitarists Larry Byrom and Nick St. Nicholas from the group T.I.M.E. for *Monster*. Nick St. Nicholas left in mid-1970, to be replaced by George Biondo. Steppenwolf disbanded in 1972. John Kay subsequently recorded two overlooked solo albums for Dunhill before reviving Steppenwolf with McJohn, Jerry Edmonton, and Biondo in 1974. They scored a major hit with "Straight Shootin' Woman" on Mums Records. The group disbanded again around 1976, with Kay reconstituting the group as its sole original member in 1980 for touring and recordings on DBX, Qwil, and I.R.S. Records.

DISC.: *Early Steppenwolf* (1969); *Steppenwolf* (1968); *Steppenwolf the Second* (1968); *At Your Birthday Party* (1969); *Monster* (1969); *Live* (1970); *Seven* (1970); *Gold* (1971); *For Ladies Only* (1971); *Rest in Peace* (1972); *Slow Flux* (1974); *Hour of the Wolf* (1975); *Skullduggery* (1976); *Reborn to Be Wild* (1976). **THE SPARROW:** *The Sparrow* (1969). **T.I.M.E. (WITH LARRY BYROM AND NICK ST. NICHOLAS):** *12 Originals* (1968); *Smooth Ball* (1969). **MARS BONFIRE:** *Faster Than the Speed of Life* (1969). **JOHN KAY:** *Forgotten Songs and Unsung Heroes* (1972); *My Sportin' Life* (1973); *All in Good Time* (1978); *Lone Steppenwolf* (1988). **JOHN KAY AND STEPPENWOLF:** *Wolftracks* (1984); *Rock and Roll Rebels* (1987); *Rise and Shine* (1990); *Live at Twenty-Five* (1994).—BH

Steptoe, Roger (Guy), English composer, teacher, and pianist; b. Winchester, Hampshire, Jan. 25, 1953. He studied at the Univ. of Reading (B.A., 1974) and received training in composition from Alan Bush at the Royal Academy of Music in London (1974–76). After serving as composer-in- residence at Charterhouse

School, Surrey (1976–79), he was a prof. of composition at the Royal Academy of Music (1980–91), where he served as administrator of its International Composers Festivals (1986–93). In 1993 he became artistic director of the Landmark Festivals Assn. He also was active as a pianist.

WORKS: DRAMATIC: O p e r a : *King of Macedon* (Surrey, Oct. 18, 1979). **ORCH.:** *2 Miniatures* for Strings (1977; Oxford, May 29, 1982); *Sinfonia concertante* for Violin, Viola, Cello, and Strings (1981; London, June 26, 1982); Concerto for Oboe and Strings (1982; Crewe, Jan. 10, 1984); Concerto for Tuba and Strings (1983; London, Oct. 27, 1986); *Rapsodia sinfonica*, concerto for Violin and Orch. (1987); Sym. (1988); Concerto for Clarinet and Strings (1989); Organ Concerto (1990); Cello Concerto (1991); *Cheers!* (1993). **CHAMBER:** 2 string quartets: No. 1 (1976; London, Jan. 5, 1977) and No. 2 (1985; Aberystwyth, May 5, 1986); Suite for Cello (1977); *Study* for Violin (1978); *2 Impromptus* for Clarinet (1978); Quintet for Clarinet and Strings (1980); *Study* for Guitar (1981); *The Knight of the Sun* for Brass Quintet (1982); *3 Pieces* for Viola and Piano (1982); 2 violin sonatas (1983, 1986); *2 Studies* for Bassoon and Piano (1983); *4 Sonnets* for Brass Quintet (1984); Quartet for Oboe and Strings (1988; Berlin, April 18, 1989); Duo for Oboe and Harp (1991); Piano Trio (1993). **P i a n o :** *3 Preludes* (1976); 2 sonatas (1979, 1988); *Equinox* (1981). **VOCAL:** *2 Madrigals* for Chorus (1976): *2 Introits* for Chorus and Organ (1977, 1985); *The Looking Glass* for Soprano, Oboe, and Piano (1980); *Chinese Lyrics*: set 1 for Soprano and Piano (1982) and set 2 for Mezzo-soprano and Countertenor and Piano (1983); *Another Part of the Forest*, scena for 4 Voices and Piano (1983); *In Winter's Cold Embraces Dye*, cantata for Mezzo-soprano, Tenor, Chorus, and Orch. (1985); *Elegy on the Death and Burial of Cock Robin* for Countertenor and 11 Solo Strings (1988); *Life's Unquiet Dream* for Baritone, Chorus, and Chamber Orch. (1992); *The Passionate Shepherd to his Love* for Children's Voices and Piano (1992); *3 Sonnets to Delia* for Baritone and Piano (1993).—**NS/LK/DM**

Stepton, Rick, trombonist; b. Fitchburg, Mass., Feb. 28, 1942. A third-generation trombonist, he played in local town bands as a youth and the 118th army band in France in the early 1960s. He worked in the "Territory Bands" of Bruce Stevens, Dean Hudson, and Buddy Bair. He performed in the Jimmy Dorsey Orch., studied at Berklee Coll. of Music, and joined Buddy Rich, playing lead with him on and off (1968–76). He also toured with Woody Herman and Maynard Ferguson, and worked with Chuck Mangione, the Canadian jazz-rock band Lighthouse, and the Phil Nimmons Orch. In 1977, he returned to Mass. to teach at Berklee for four years, and subsequently put in nine years of service on the jazz faculty at New England Cons. He has played about 30 Broadway shows in Boston theatres and backed up Natalie Cole, Tony Bennett, and Ella Fitzgerald. In the early 1990s, he was attacked by a dog, leaving him with severe injuries to his face and an almost completely severed lip; he needed reconstructive surgery and months of practice to re-learn how to play the trombone. During the 1990s, he performed with the Orange Then Blue Jazz Orch. and the Herb Pomeroy Orch. He is the leader of the Rick Stepton Quartet.

DISC.: *Blue Collar* (1997); *Inspiration* (1998).—**LP**

Sterkel, Johann Franz Xaver, prominent German pianist, teacher, and composer; b. Würzburg, Dec.

3, 1750; d. there, Oct. 12, 1817. He received a thorough training in music from A. Kette, the court organist, and from Weismandel in Würzburg; also attended the Univ. there. In 1768 he was tonsured and named organist in the collegiate chapter of Neumünster, where he subsequently was made subdeacon (1772), deacon (1773), and priest (1774). In 1778 he was called to Mainz to serve the Liebfrauen chapter and as court chaplain; the Elector then sent him to Italy, where he toured widely as a pianist (1779–82) and produced the opera *Il Farnace* (Naples, Jan. 12, 1782); subsequently returned to Mainz to serve as a canon of his chapter. Beethoven heard him play in Aschaffenburg in 1791 and was greatly impressed by him as a pianist and composer. The French invasion of 1792 wreaked havoc with the Mainz court, but when the city was regained in 1793, Sterkel was named court Kapellmeister; however, continued warfare led to the closing of the royal chapel in 1797 and Sterkel returned to Würzburg, where he was active at the court. About 1802 he went to Regensburg, where he found a patron in Karl Theodor von Dalberg; he founded his own choir school. When his patron was made Grand Duke of Frankfurt am Main in 1810, Sterkel went with him to Aschaffenburg as his music director. The court was disbanded in 1814 and he returned once more to Würzburg in 1815. Sterkel was a prolific composer; his most important works are his chamber music and keyboard pieces.

WORKS: DRAMATIC: O p e r a : *Il Farnace* (Naples, Jan. 12, 1782). **ORCH.:** 22 syms.; 4 overtures; 6 piano concertos. **CHAMBER:** 43 piano or harpsichord trios; 28 piano or harpsichord sonatas; *Grand Quintette* for 2 Violins, 2 Violas, and Cello; Piano Quartet; 6 duos for Violin and Viola. **P i a n o :** Numerous solo pieces, including 13 sonatas, 6 of which are for 4-Hands. **VOCAL:** 4 festival masses, 2 Te Deums, and other sacred music; numerous lieder.

BIBL.: A. Scharnagl, *J.F.X. S.: Ein Beitrag zur Musikgeschichte Mainfrankens* (Würzburg, 1943).—**NS/LK/DM**

Sterling, Antoinette, American contralto; b. Sterlingville, N.Y., Jan. 23, 1850; d. London, Jan. 9, 1904. She studied with Abella in N.Y., Mathilde Marchesi in Cologne, and Pauline Viardot-García in Baden; also took lessons with Manuel García in London. Returning to America (1871), she sang in Henry Ward Beecher's church in Brooklyn; then went to London, where she made her debut at a Covent Garden Promenade Concert (Nov. 5, 1873). She introduced many favorite songs (most of which were composed especially for her), such as Arthur Sullivan's *Lost Chord* (Jan. 31, 1877) and Barnby's *When the Tide Comes In.* In 1875 she toured the U.S.; her permanent home was in London.

BIBL.: M. MacKinlay (her son), *A. S. and Other Celebrities* (London, 1906).—**NS/LK/DM**

Stern, Isaac, outstanding Russian-born American violinist; b. Kremenetz, July 21, 1920. His parents emigrated to the U.S. when he was an infant, and settled in San Francisco. He first studied the piano, and then turned to the violin at the age of 10. After attending the San Francisco Cons., he found his principal mentor in Naoum Blinder. He also had some lessons with Louis

Persinger. While still a youth, Stern appeared in recitals and with orchs. At age 17, he made his N.Y. recital debut at Town Hall on Oct. 11, 1937. It was not until he made his Carnegie Hall recital debut in N.Y. on Jan. 8, 1943, however, that his career began to blossom. He subsequently appeared as a recitalist and as a soloist with orchs. in various U.S. music centers. After making his European debut at the Lucerne Festival in 1948, Stern toured widely around the globe. In 1956 he made an acclaimed tour of the Soviet Union. In 1961 he organized a trio with Eugene Istomin and Leonard Rose, which remained one of the premiere trios of the day until Rose's death in 1983. Stern celebrated the 25th anniversary of his Carnegie Hall debut in 1968. His career continued unabated in succeeding years. In 1979 he toured Communist China, an event featured in the film documentary *From Mao to Mozart: Isaac Stern in China*. His career was chronicled in the subsequent film documentary *Isaac Stern: A Life* (1991). In a career lasting more than 60 years, Stern remained faithful to the creed of those virtuosos to whom fame is a natural adjunct to talent and industry. His repertoire was enormous, encompassing both the great masters of the past and many contemporary composers. In addition to his career in music, Stern maintained a high profile as an advocate of cultural enrichment and human rights. When Carnegie Hall faced the prospect of demolition in 1960, he spearheaded the effort to save the historical edifice for future generations. Thereafter he served as its president. His honors have been numerous. In 1979 he was made an Officier of the Légion d'honneur of France, in 1984 he received the Kennedy Center Honors Award, in 1987 he was given the Wolf Prize of Israel, in 1992 he was awarded the Presidential Medal of Freedom of the U.S., and in 2000 he received the Polar Music Award of Sweden. With C. Potock, he publ. his autobiography as *Isaac Stern: My First 79 Years* (N.Y., 1999).—**NS/LK/DM**

Stern, Julius, eminent German music pedagogue; b. Breslau, Aug. 8, 1820; d. Berlin, Feb. 27, 1883. He studied violin with Lüstner, and later took courses with Maurer, Ganz, and Rungenhagen in Berlin; then studied singing in Dresden (1843) and subsequently in Paris, where he conducted the German Gesangverein. In 1846 he settled in Berlin, where he was founder-conductor of the Sternscher Gesangverein (1847–74); also conducted the Sinfonie-Kapelle (1869–71) and the Reichshalle concerts (1873–75). In 1850 he founded the Berlin Cons. with Kullak and Marx; Kullak withdrew in 1855, and Marx in 1857; thenceforth Stern became the sole head of the institution, now known as the Julius Stern Staatliche Hochschule für Musik; it prospered and acquired the reputation of one of the greatest music schools in Europe. Stern was also a composer, and received commendation from Mendelssohn for his songs. He publ. *Barcarolle* for Voice, Cello, and Piano, *Les Adieux* for Violin and Piano, men's choruses, and songs. His opera, *Ismene*, was not produced. He also wrote singing exercises which were long in use.

BIBL.: R. Stern, *Erinnerungsblätter an J. S.* (Berlin, 1886).
—**NS/LK/DM**

Stern, Leo(pold Lawrence), noted English cellist; b. Brighton, April 5, 1862; d. London, Sept. 10, 1904. His father was a violinist and his mother a pianist. He played drum in the Brighton Sym. Soc. orch. conducted by his father, and in 1877 went to London to study chemistry, but also had cello lessons with Hugo Daubert. He then studied with Pezze and Piatti at the Royal Academy of Music (1883–85), and completed his training with Klengel and Davidov in Leipzig (1885–86). In 1886 he performed in London and other English cities; after touring with Adelina Patti in 1888, he gave concerts with Sauret, Paderewski, Albani, Godard, and Massenet. He was the soloist in the premiere of Dvořák's Cello Concerto (London, March 19, 1896, composer conducting), which he later performed in Leipzig, Prague, and Berlin; after touring North America (1897–98), he returned to London, but ill health compelled him to give up his career. He composed pieces for cello and songs. His second wife was **Suzanne Adams.**—**NS/LK/DM**

Stern, Mike (actually, **Michael**), jazz-fusion guitarist; b. Boston, Mass., Jan. 10, 1953. Married to guitarist Leni Stern. He began playing guitar at age 12. He studied with Pat Metheny at Berklee for three years, then joined Blood, Sweat, and Tears alongside Jaco Pastorius. In the mid-1970s, his fine playing with Bob Berg and others attracted attention in the Boston area. In 1978, he joined Billy Cobham's band; during their gig at the Bottom Line, N.Y., Miles Davis dropped in to listen and offered Stern a spot in his band. He played with Davis for three years. He has also worked with David Sanborn, Steps Ahead, and the Brecker Brothers. He was less active for a few years due to self-described drug problems. In 1993, he was voted *Guitar Player* magazine's "Best Jazz Guitarist." His albums *Between the Lines* and *Is What It Is* earned Grammy nominations. In 1997, his quartet included Dave Weckl, Lincoln Goines, and Bob Sheppard.

DISC.: *Upside Downside* (1986); *Time in Place* (1987); *Jigsaw* (1989); *Odds or Evens* (1991); *Standards (and Other Songs)* (1992); *Is What It Is* (1993); *Between the Lines* (1996); *Give & Take* (1997).
WRITINGS: *Jazz Guitar Solos* (Aebersold, 1992).
BIBL.: G. Varlotta, *Mike Stern Standards* (Aebersold).—**LP**

Sternberg, Constantin, Russian-American pianist, teacher, and composer; b. St. Petersburg, July 9, 1852; d. Philadelphia, March 31, 1924. He studied piano with Moscheles at the Leipzig Cons., and later had lessons with Theodor Kullak; also visited Liszt at Weimar. He toured Russia as a concert pianist; in 1880 he emigrated to the U.S. In 1890 he established the Sternberg School of Music in Philadelphia, and was its director until his death. He was greatly esteemed as a piano teacher. He wrote some 200 salon pieces for piano, and *Danses cosaques* for Violin. He publ. *Ethics and Aesthetics of Piano Playing* (N.Y., 1917) and *Tempo Rubato and Other Essays* (N.Y., 1920).—**NS/LK/DM**

Sternberg, Erich Walter, German-born Israeli composer; b. Berlin, May 31, 1891; d. Tel Aviv, Dec. 15, 1974. He studied law at the Univ. of Kiel (graduated,

1918), and then received training in composition from Leichtentritt and in piano from Praetorius in Berlin. In 1932 he emigrated to Palestine. In 1936 he was a co-founder of the Palestine Orch. (later the Israel Phil.). Many of his works were inspired by biblical subjects.

WORKS: DRAMATIC: *Dr. Dolittle*, children's opera (1937; orch. suite, 1941); *Pacifica, the Friendly Island*, opera for "children and others" (1972–74). **ORCH.:** *Overture to a Comedy* (1932); *Quodlibet* (1935); *Amcha* (Thy People), suite (1936); *Joseph and His Brothers*, suite for Strings (1937); *The 12 Tribes of Israel*, variations (Tel Aviv, May 3, 1942); *Shema Israel* (Hear, O Israel; 1947); *Höre Israel* (1948); *Contrapuntal Study* (1955); *Tewat Noah* (Noah's Ark; 1960). **CHAMBER:** 2 string quartets (1924, 1926); Violin Sonata (1955); Piano Trio; Wind Quintet. **VOCAL:** *The Story of David and Goliath* for Baritone and Orch. (1927); *Kol nidrei* for Baritone and Orch. (1927); *Halochem ha'amitz* (The Garland Soldier) for Baritone and Orch. (1930); *Ami* (My People) for Soprano and Orch. (1945); *Shirim mukdamim* (Early Songs) for Soprano and Orch. (1946); *Ha'orev* (The Raven) for Baritone and Orch. (1949); *Sichot haruach* (Dialogues with the Wind) for Alto and Orch. (1955); *Hachalil bamerchakim* (The Distant Flute) for Alto and Flute (1958); *Shirei nezirūt* (Songs of Resignation) for Baritone and Orch. (1958); *Songs of Hafis* for Voice and Orch. (1959); *Techiat Israel* (The Resurrection of Israel), oratorio (1959); *Tefilot* (Prayers of Humility) for Contralto and Chamber Orch. (1962); *The Sacrifice of Isaac* for Soprano and Orch. (1965); *Love Songs* for Chorus and Orch. (1968); *The Wretched* for Baritone and String Orch. (1969); *My Brother Jonathan* for Chorus and String Orch. (1969); about 100 solo songs.—**NS/LK/DM**

Sternberg, Jonathan, American conductor; b. N.Y., July 27, 1919. He studied at the Juilliard School of Music (1929–31), N.Y.U. (B.A., 1939; graduate study, 1939–40), and the Manhattan School of Music (1946); took conducting lessons with Monteux at his summer school (1946, 1947). In 1947 he made his conducting debut with the Vienna Sym. Orch.; then toured extensively as a guest conductor in Europe, North America, and the Far East. He was music director of the Royal Flemish Opera in Antwerp (1961–62), the Harkness Ballet in N.Y. (1966–68), and the Atlanta Opera and Ballet (1968–69); then was a visiting prof. of conducting at the Eastman School of Music in Rochester, N.Y. (1969–71), a prof. of music at Temple Univ. (1971–89), and a lecturer at Chestnut Hill Coll. (from 1989). —**NS/LK/DM**

Sternefeld, Daniël, Belgian conductor, teacher, and composer; b. Antwerp, Nov. 27, 1905; d. Brussels, June 2, 1986. He studied flute and theory at the Antwerp Cons. (1918–24); then composition with Gilson and conducting with van der Stücken (1928); subsequently took lessons in conducting with Paumgartner, Krauss, and Karajan at the Mozarteum in Salzburg. He was a flutist in the orch. of the Royal Flemish Opera in Antwerp (1929–38); then was its second conductor (1938–44) and principal conductor (1944–48); subsequently was chief conductor of the Belgian Radio and Television Orch. in Brussels (1948–72); also appeared as a guest conductor in Europe and South America. He taught conducting at the Antwerp Cons. (1949–71).

WORKS: DRAMATIC: Opera: *Mater Dolorosa* (1934; Antwerp, 1935). **Ballet:** *Pierlala* (1937); *Antverpia* (1975); *Rossiniazata* (1982). **Other:** Incidental music to various plays. **ORCH.:** *Variations symphoniques* (1928); *Elégie* (1931); *Suite de vieilles chansons flamandes et wallonnes* for Chamber Orch. (1934); 2 syms.: No. 1 (1943) and No. 2, *Bruegelsymfonie* (1981–83); *Frère Jacques*, variations for Brass and Percussion (1955); *Divertimento* for Wind Orch. (1980); *Waaier* (1984). **CHAMBER:** *Étude-passacaglia* for Harp (1979); Quintet for Flute, Oboe, Clarinet, Bassoon, and Horn (1986).—**NS/LK/DM**

Sternfeld, F(riedrich) W(ilhelm), Austrian-born English musicologist; b. Vienna, Sept. 25, 1914; d. Brightwell-cum-Sotwell, near Wallingford, Jan. 13, 1994. He took courses with Lach and Wellesz at the Univ. of Vienna (from 1933); then pursued his training with Schrade at Yale Univ. (Ph.D., 1943, with the diss. *Goethe and Music*); held a Guggenheim fellowship (1954). He taught at Wesleyan Univ. (1940–46) and Dartmouth Coll. (1946–56); also was a member of the Inst. for Advanced Studies at Princeton Univ. (1955). In 1956 he joined the faculty of the Univ. of Oxford, where he served as a reader in music history (1972–81). He also became a naturalized British subject. He was ed. of *Renaissance News* (1946–54) and of the *Proceedings of the Royal Musical Association* (1957–62); publ. the books *Goethe's Relationship to Music: A List of References* (N.Y., 1954), *Music in Shakespearean Tragedy* (London, 1963; second ed., 1967), *Songs from Shakespeare's Tragedies* (London, 1964), and *The Birth of Opera* (Oxford, 1993). He also ed. *A History of Western Music* (London, 1973), with Wellesz, the 7th vol. of *The New Oxford History of Music: The Age of Enlightenment 1745–1790* (Oxford, 1973), and with others, *Essays on Opera and English Music in Honour of Sir Jack Westrup* (Oxford, 1975).—**NS/LK/DM**

Steuerlein, Johann, German organist, poet, and composer; b. Schmalkalden, Thuringia, July 5, 1546; d. Meiningen, May 5, 1613. He studied at the Magdeburg grammar school (1559–62) and at the Univ. of Wittenberg; concurrently served as a chancery clerk in Burgbreitungen; then was town clerk, organist, and Kantor in Wasungen, near Mainingen (1569–89); subsequently was chancellery secretary to the Elector of Saxony in Meiningen (from 1589), where he was made public notary and mayor in 1604; also was crowned poet laureate. He remains best known for the celebrated song *Das alte Jahr vergangen ist* for 6 Voices. He also publ. many vols. of vocal music.—**NS/LK/DM**

Steuermann, Edward (actually, **Eduard**), eminent Polish-American pianist, pedagogue, and composer; b. Sambor, near Lemberg, June 18, 1892; d. N.Y., Nov. 11, 1964. He studied piano with Vilém Kurz in Lemberg and with Busoni in Berlin (1911–12), and theory with Schoenberg (1912–14); also took some composition lessons with Humperdinck. Returning to Poland, he taught at the Paderewski School in Lwów, and concurrently at the Jewish Cons. in Kraków (1932–36). In 1936 he emigrated to the U.S. He taught at the Philadelphia Cons. (1948–63) and at the Juilliard School of Music in N.Y. (1952–64); also gave summer classes at the Salzburg Mozarteum (1953–63) and in Darmstadt (1954; 1957–60). As a recitalist and soloist with major orchs., Steuermann was an ardent champion of new music, particularly of Schoenberg; gave the first performance of Schoenberg's Piano Concerto (1944); made excellent arrangements for piano of Schoenberg's operatic and symphonic works, among them *Erwartung, Die gluckliche Hand, Kammersymphonie No. 1*, and the Piano Concerto; received the Schoenberg Medal from the ISCM in 1952. Although he did not follow Schoenberg's method of composition with 12 tones with any degree of consistency, his music possesses an expressionistic tension that is characteristic of the second Viennese School.

WORKS: ORCH.: *Variations* (1958); *Music for Instruments* (1959–60); Suite for Chamber Orch. (1964). **CHAMBER**: *7 Waltzes* for String Quartet (1946); Piano Trio (1954); *Improvisation and Allegro* for Violin and Piano (1955); String Quartet, *Diary* (1960–61); *Dialogues* for Violin (1963). **P i a n o** : Sonata (1926); Suite (1952). **VOCAL**: *Brecht-Lieder* for Contralto (1945); *3 Choirs* (1956); Cantata for Chorus and Orch., after Kafka (1964); other songs.

BIBL.: A. Ani Netto, *E. S.: Um esboço de figura* (São Paulo, 1991).—**NS/LK/DM**

Stevens, Bernard (George),
English composer; b. London, March 2, 1916; d. Great Maplestead, Essex, Jan. 2, 1983. He studied composition with Dent and Rootham at Cambridge (1934–37) and with Morris and Jacob at the Royal Coll. of Music in London (1937–40), where he was named a prof. of composition in 1948; received his Mus.D. from the Univ. of Cambridge in 1968. He wrote a number of works for various instrumental combinations; his music adheres to traditional concepts of harmony, while the programmatic content is often colored by his radical political beliefs.

WORKS: ORCH.: Violin Concerto (1943); *Ricercar* for Strings (1944); *A Symphony of Liberation* (1945); Cello Concerto (1952); Piano Concerto (1955); Sym. No. 2 (1964); *Choriamb* (1968); *Introduction, Variations and Fugue on a Theme of Giles Farnaby* (1972). **CHAMBER**: Trio for Violin, Horn, and Piano (1966); *Suite* for 6 Instruments (1967); *The Bramble Briar* for Guitar (1974); piano pieces. **VOCAL**: 3 cantatas: *The Harvest of Peace* (1952), *The Pilgrims of Hope* (1956), and *Et resurrexit* (1969); *The Turning World* for Baritone, Chorus, and Orch. (1971).

BIBL.: B. Stevens, ed., *B. S. and His Music: A Symposium* (White Plains, N.Y., 1989).—**NS/LK/DM**

Stevens, Cat (originally, Georgiou, Steven),
popular British singer-songwriter of the first half of the 1970s; b. London, England, July 21, 1947. Cat Stevens utilized a distinctive guitar sound backed by gentle rhythms for his engaging, mellow songs, such as "Wild World," "Peace Train," and "Oh Very Young." Scoring his last major hit at the end of 1974, Cat Stevens abandoned music and converted to the Muslim religion in 1979.

Cat Stevens began writing songs and playing folk music in the mid-1960s while at Hammersmith Art Coll. Signed to Deram Records on the strength of a demonstration tape, he scored major British-only hits with "Matthew and Son," "I'm Gonna Get Me a Gun," and "A Bad Night" in 1967. Restricting his touring to England, Belgium, and France, he worked tirelessly and contracted tuberculosis, resulting in his hospitalization in September 1968 and a protracted period of convalescence. Emerging in spring 1970, Cat Stevens returned to the studio with guitarist Alun Davies to record *Mona Bone Jakon*, his first album for A&M Records. The album produced a British-only hit with "Lady D'Arbanville" and gained him his first recognition in the United States.

Cat Stevens's next album, *Tea for the Tillerman*, included a number of exciting acoustic-guitar songs, such as "Where Do the Children Play," "Hard-Headed Woman," "Longer Boats," and "On the Road to Find Out," and yielded his first major American hit with "Wild World." The intriguing follow-up, *Teaser and the Firecat*, produced a moderate hit with "Moon Shadow" and the top easy-listening and near-smash pop hits "Peace Train" and "Morning Has Broken." Stevens later abandoned his guitar-dominated sound in favor of piano, and despite scoring only a single hit from his next three albums—*Catch Bull at Four, Foreigner*, and *Buddha and the Chocolate Box*—all sold quite well. His major hits through 1975 include the near-smash "Oh Very Young," a smash-hit version of Sam Cooke's "Another Saturday Night," and "Ready." Recording his final album in 1978, Cat Stevens converted to the Muslim religion in 1979, changing his name to Yusef Islam and establishing the relief organization Muslim Aid near London.

DISC.: *Matthew and Son* (1967); *New Masters* (1968); *Very Young and Early Songs* (1971); *Cat's Cradle* (1978); *Mona Bone Jakon* (1970); *Tea for the Tillerman* (1970); *Teaser and the Firecat* (1971); *Catch Bull at Four* (1972); *Foreigner* (1973); *Buddah and the Chocolate Box* (1974); *Greatest Hits* (1975); *Numbers* (1975); *Izitso* (1977); *Back to Earth* (1978); *Footsteps in the Dark: Greatest Hits, Vol. 2* (1984); *C. S.* (1987).

BIBL.: C. Charlesworth, *C. S.* (London, 1985).—**BH**

Stevens, Delores (Elaine),
American pianist and teacher; b. Kingman, Kans., Jan. 29, 1930. She studied with Gordon Terwilliger (1946–48) and Jan Chiapusso (1948–52) at the Univ. of Kans. (B.M., 1952) and also had private study at the Music Academy of the West with Ernst von Dohnányi and Joanna Graudan. From 1968 to 1980 she was a pianist in the Montagnana Trio, which commissioned some 28 works by contemporary composers, including Daniel Lentz, Barney Childs, Per Nrgård et al.; toured with the ensemble in the U.S., England, and Scandanavia (1971–90). She was a founding member of Tandem, a piano/percussion duo; also performed extensively as a soloist, giving premieres of Poul Ruders' Sonata No. 2, Arne Nordheim's *Listen*, and Per Nrgård's *Turn*; toured in the U.S. (1988–95), Japan (1990), Japan (1992, with the Daniel Lentz Group), and Spain (1993). From 1971 she also was a member of the Monday Evening Concerts Ensemble in Los Angeles and pianist and director of the Da Camera Players. She taught at the Calif. Inst. of the Arts, Mount St. Mary's Coll., and at Calif. State Univ. at Dominguez Hills, where she also served as director of piano studies; in 1987 she joined the faculty of the American String Teachers Assn. Chamber Music Inst. From 1988 to 1997 she received annual Solo Touring Grants from the Calif. Arts Council.—**NS/LK/DM**

Stevens, Denis (William), English musicologist and conductor; b. High Wycombe, Buckinghamshire, March 2, 1922. He studied with Sir Thomas Armstrong and Egon Wellesz at the Univ. of Oxford (1940–42; 1947–49). From 1949 to 1954 he was head of pre-Classical music for the BBC in London. After serving as a visiting prof. at Cornell Univ. (1955) and Columbia Univ. (1956), he was active with the BBC (1957–87). In 1960 he introduced the first course in musicology at the Royal Academy of Music in London. He founded the Accademia Monteverdiana in 1961, and subsequently appeared with them on radio, television, and at the Bath, Bordeaux, Edinburgh, Gstaad, Lisbon, London, Lucerne, Salzburg, and Windsor festivals. His interest in developing unfamiliar but outstanding repertoire prompted him to premiere a new edition of Monteverdi's Vespers at London's Westminster Abbey in 1961. In 1962 he taught at the Univ. of Calif. at Berkeley, and then was a distinguished visiting prof. at Pa. State Univ. (1962–64), Columbia Univ. (1965–74), where he gave the first course on an English composer, Henry Purcell, and at the Univ. of Washington in Seattle (1976). He made over 75 recordings while still pursuing scholarly work. He inaugurated the Musica Britannica series with *The Mulliner Book* (1951), and also ed. *Early Tudor Organ Music* (1969), Monteverdi's *Selva morale e spirituale* (1998), and many other editions. In 1984 he was made a Commander of the Order of the British Empire.

WRITINGS: *Thomas Tomkins* (1957); *A History of Song* (1960); ed. with A. Robertson, *The Pelican History of Music* (1960–68); *Monteverdi: Sacred, Secular and Occasional Music* (1978); ed. and tr. *The Letters of Claudio Monteverdi* (1960; rev. ed., 1995); *Musicology in Practice* (1981); *Early Music* (1997); ed. and tr. *Monteverdi: Songs and Madrigals* (1999); *Monteverdi in Venice* (2000).—NS/LK/DM

Stevens, Halsey, significant American composer, teacher, and writer on music; b. Scott, N.Y., Dec. 3, 1908; d. Long Beach, Calif., Jan. 20, 1989. He studied composition with William Berwald at Syracuse Univ. (B.M., 1931; M.M., 1937) and with Bloch at the Univ. of Calif. at Berkeley (1944). He taught at Syracuse Univ. (1935–37) and Dakota Wesleyan Univ. (1937–41); was a prof. and director of the Coll. of Music at Bradley Polytechnic Inst. in Peoria, Ill. (1941–46), and then a prof. at the Univ. of Redlands (1946). In 1946 he joined the faculty of the Univ. of Southern Calif. in Los Angeles, serving in various capacities until his retirement as prof. emeritus in 1976. He was a visiting prof. at Pomona Coll. (1954), the Univ. of Wash. (1958), Yale Univ. (1960–61), the Univ. of Cincinnati (1968), and Williams Coll. (1969). His music is above all a monument of sonorous equilibrium; melodies and rhythms are coordinated in a fine melo-rhythmic polyphony; dissonances are emancipated and become natural consorts of triadic harmony. Tonality remains paramount, while a stream of coloristic passages contributes to the brilliance of the instrumental texture. Stevens wrote only "absolute" music, without resort to the stage; there are no operas or ballets in his creative catalog. He does not apply conventional modernistic devices in his music, designed at its culmination to please the aural sense. Apart from composition, Stevens took great interest in the autochthonous music of the peoples of the earth; he was particularly fascinated by the fieldwork that Bartók undertook in gathering authentic folk songs of southeastern Europe. He mastered the Hungarian language, retraced Bartók's travels, and assembled materials on Bartók's life; the result was his exemplary biography, *The Life and Music of Béla Bartók* (N.Y., 1953; second ed., rev., 1964; third ed., rev., 1993, by M. Gillies). Stevens received numerous grants and honors; he held 2 Guggenheim fellowships (1964–65; 1971–72), a grant from the NEA (1976), and the Abraham Lincoln Award of the American Hungarian Foundation (1978).

WORKS: ORCH.: 3 syms.: No. 1 (1945; San Francisco, March 7, 1946, composer conducting; rev., Los Angeles, March 3, 1950), No. 2 (1945; N.Y., May 17, 1947), and No. 3 (1946); *A Green Mountain Overture* (Burlington, Vt., Aug. 7, 1948; rev. 1953); *Triskelion* (a figure with 3 branches; 1953; Louisville, Feb. 27, 1954); *Sinfonia breve* (Louisville, Nov. 20, 1957); *Symphonic Dances* (San Francisco, Dec. 10, 1958); Cello Concerto (1964; Los Angeles, May 12, 1968); *Threnos: In Memoriam Quincy Porter* (1968); Concerto for Clarinet and Strings (Denton, Tex., March 20, 1969); Double Concerto for Violin, Cello, and String Orch. (Los Angeles, Nov. 4, 1973); Viola Concerto (1975). **CHAMBER:** Piano Trio No. 2 (1945); Quintet for Flute, Violin, Viola, Cello, and Piano (1945; Middlebury, Vt., Aug. 30, 1946); Suite for Clarinet and Piano (1945; rev. 1953); Bassoon Sonata (1949); String Quartet No. 3 (1949); *3 Hungarian Folk Songs* for Viola and Piano (1950); Viola Sonata (1950); Horn Sonata (1953); Trumpet Sonata (1956); Piano Trio No. 3 (1954); *Sonatina piacevole* for Alto Recorder or Flute and Keyboard (1956); Septet for Clarinet, Bassoon, Horn, 2 Violas, and 2 Cellos (Urbana, Ill., March 3, 1957); *Divertimento* for 2 Violins (1958–66); Suite for Viola and Piano (1959); Bass Tuba Sonatina (1960); *12 Slovakian Folk Songs* for 2 Violins (1962); Cello Sonata (1965); Oboe Sonata (1971); *Quintetto "Serbelloni"* for Woodwinds (1972); also works for solo instruments. **Piano:** 3 sonatas (1933–48); *Partita* (1954); *6 preludes* (1956); *Ritratti* (1960); *Fantasia* (1961); numerous other pieces. **VOCAL:** *The Ballad of William Sycamore* for Chorus and Orch. (Los Angeles, Oct. 6, 1955); *2 Shakespeare Songs* for Voice, Flute, and Clarinet (1959); *A Testament of Life* for Tenor, Bass, Chorus, and Orch. (1959); *4 Canciones* for Voice and Piano (1961); *Magnificat* for Chorus and String Orch. (1962); *7 Canciones* for Voice and Piano (1964); *Campion Suite* for Chorus (1967); *Te Deum* for Chorus, Brass Septet, Organ, and Timpani (1967); *Chansons courtoises* for Chorus (1967); *Songs from the Paiute* for Chorus, 4 Flutes, and Timpani (1976).—NS/LK/DM

Stevens, Horace (Ernest), Australian bass-baritone; b. Melbourne, Oct. 26, 1876; d. there, Nov. 18, 1950. He studied at St. Kilda in Melbourne, and then sang as a lay clerk at St. Paul's Cathedral in Melbourne. In 1919 he made his London debut in a Queen's Hall concert, and subsequently became a popular favorite at major English festivals. He also sang in oratorios in the U.S. and appeared with the British National Opera Co. and other English companies. Stevens was particularly successful as a concert artist, excelling as Elijah. In opera he won accolades for his Wagnerian roles.—NS/LK/DM

Stevens, John (Edgar), distinguished English musicologist; b. London, Oct. 8, 1921. He studied classics (1940–41) and English (B.A., 1948) at Magdalene Coll., Cambridge; then pursued training with Dart at the Univ. there (Ph.D., 1953, with the diss. *Early Tudor Song Books*); served on the univ. faculty as a teacher of English (1952–74), reader in English and music history (1974–78), and prof. of medieval and Renaissance English (from 1978). He was made a Commander of the Order of the British Empire in 1980. An erudite scholar, he contributed greatly to the understanding of music from the medieval and Renaissance periods. In addition to his books and articles, he ed. works for the Musica Britannica series. His writings include *Music and Poetry in the Early Tudor Court* (London, 1961; second ed., rev., 1979), *Medieval Romance* (London, 1973), and *Words and Music in the Middle Ages* (London, 1986).—NS/LK/DM

Stevens, Richard John Samuel, English organist and composer; b. London, March 27, 1757; d. there, Sept. 23, 1837. He was a chorister at St. Paul's Cathedral in London. From 1786 to 1810 he served as organist at the Inner Temple, and from 1801 he was a prof. of music at Gresham Coll. He ed. *Sacred Music-...from the Works of the Most Esteemed Composers, Italian and English* (c. 1798–1802). Stevens was one of the finest glee composers of his day. His most celebrated glees were *Ye Spotted Snakes* (1782; rev. 1791), *Sigh No More, Ladies* (1787), *Crabbed Age and Youth* (1790), *Blow, Blow, Thou Winter Wind* (1792), and *The Cloud-Cap't Towers* (1795). He also wrote an opera, the oratorio *Emma, The Captivity,* various keyboard pieces, including 3 sonatas, church music, and songs. M. Argent ed. his *Recollections of R. J. S. Stevens: An Organist in Georgian London* (Basingstoke and London, 1992).—NS/LK/DM

Stevens, Risë, noted American mezzo-soprano; b. N.Y., June 11, 1913. The original family surname was Steenberg. She studied voice with Orry Prado; after graduating from high school, she sang minor roles with the N.Y. Opera-Comique Co. The enterprise soon went bankrupt, and for a while she had to earn her living by dress modeling, before she was offered free singing lessons by Anna Schoen-René at the Juilliard School of Music. She was subsequently sent to Salzburg to study with Marie Gutheil-Schoder at the Mozarteum, and later entered classes in stage direction with Herbert Graf. In 1936 she was engaged by Szell for the Prague Opera as a contralto; she prepared several roles from standard operas, coaching with George Schick. She went on a tour to Cairo, Egypt, with a Vienna opera group, and then sang at the Teatro Colón in Buenos Aires. She made her American debut as Octavian in *Der Rosenkavalier* with the Metropolitan Opera in Philadelphia on Nov. 22, 1938. She greatly extended her repertoire, and added Wagnerian roles to her appearances with the Metropolitan. On Jan. 9, 1939, she married in N.Y. the Czech actor Walter Surovy, who became her business manager. In 1939 she sang at the Glyndebourne Festival in England; on Oct. 12, 1940, she appeared with the San Francisco Opera as Cherubino; in 1941 she joined Nelson Eddy in a film production of the operetta *The Chocolate Soldier,* and in 1944 acted in the movie *Going My Way,* in which she sang the Habanera from *Carmen;* on Dec. 28, 1945, she appeared as Carmen at the Metropolitan Opera, scoring a fine success. Carmen became her most celebrated role; she sang it 75

times with the Metropolitan. She remained with the Metropolitan until 1961. On March 24, 1954, she appeared for the first time at La Scala in Milan. She retired from the stage in 1964. In 1975 she joined the teaching staff at the Juilliard School in N.Y. She also served as president of the Mannes Coll. of Music in N.Y. (1975–78).

BIBL.: K. Crichton, *Subway to the Met: R. S.' Story* (N.Y., 1959).—NS/LK/DM

Stevenson, George (Edward), jazz trombonist; b. Baltimore, June 20, 1906; d. N.Y., Sept. 21, 1970. Stevenson's brother, Cyrus, and his father played piano. At age 15, Stevenson studied saxophone and trombone with A. J. Thomas and joined his Baltimore Concert Band. At 19 he joined pianist Harold Stepteau and his Melody Boys, then organized his own 11-piece Baltimore Melody Boys. They disbanded in 1928 and he moved to N.Y. Through the 1930s and 1940s he worked with various bands, including the Savoy Bearcats (spring 1932), Charlie Johnson (1932–33), Fletcher Henderson (1935), Claude Hopkins (1936), Jack Carter's Orch. (1938), Lucky Millinder (1939–43), Cootie Williams and Roy Eldridge (1944), and Cat Anderson (1947). From 1948 he freelanced with various leaders, continuing to perform through the 1960s. He also briefly led his own band in 1959. His last performances were with Max Kaminsky a year before his death. His trombone style was greatly influenced by Tricky Sam Nanton.—JC/LP

Stevenson, Robert (Murrell), erudite American musicologist, educator, composer, and pianist; b. Melrose, N.Mex., July 3, 1916. He studied at the Univ. of Tex., El Paso (A.B., 1936); then went to N.Y. to study piano with Ernest Hutcheson at the Juilliard School of Music; subsequently entered Yale Univ., studying composition with David Stanley Smith and musicology with Leo Schrade (M.Mus., 1939). In 1939 he had 23 private lessons in composition with Stravinsky in Cambridge, Mass., and in 1940 he took private piano lessons with Artur Schnabel in N.Y.; then attended classes in composition with Hanson at the Eastman School of Music in Rochester, N.Y. (Ph.D., 1942); he later had regular music courses at Harvard Univ. (S.T.B., 1943). He also took graduate degrees in theology from the Harvard Divinity School and the Theological Seminary at Princeton Univ. (Th.M., 1949). He served as chaplain with the U.S. Army (1942–46); received the Army Commendation Ribbon; remained in service as a reserve officer until 1953. He then went to the Univ. of Oxford in England, where he took courses in musicology with Jack Allan Westrup (B.Litt., 1954). While thus occupied, he pursued an active career as a concert pianist; gave his first N.Y. recital on Jan. 5, 1942; gave another recital there on March 20, 1947; in both he included his own compositions; he played in London on Oct. 7, 1953. He taught music at the Univ. of Tex., El Paso from 1941 to 1943 and in 1949; lectured on church music at Westminster Choir Coll. in Princeton, N.J., from 1946 to 1949. In 1949 he was appointed to the music faculty at the Univ. of Calif., Los Angeles; was made a prof. of music in 1961; was named faculty research lecturer in 1981. In 1955–56 he was a visiting asst. prof. at Columbia Univ.; also was a visiting prof. at Ind. Univ. in Bloomington (1959–60) and at the Univ. of Chile in Santiago (1965–66). A widely informed musical scientist, he gave courses at the Univ. of Calif. on music appreciation, special seminars on individual composers, and a highly popular course in 1983 on rock-'n'-roll music. He also presented piano recitals as part of the curriculum. A master of European languages, he concentrated his scholarly energy mainly on Latin American, Spanish, and Portuguese music, both sacred and secular, and his publications on these subjects are of inestimable value; he is also an investigative explorer of Italian Renaissance music. He contributed more than 400 articles to *The New Grove Dictionary of Music and Musicians*, and numerous articles on the Baroque period and on American composers to *Die Musik in Geschichte und Gegenwart*; was its American ed. from 1967 to the completion of the last fascicle of its supplement. He held numerous grants, fellowships, and awards from learned societies: was a recipient of a Gulbenkian Foundation fellowship (1953–54); a Carnegie Foundation Teaching Award (1955–56); Fulbright research awards (1958–59; 1964; 1970–71); Ford Foundation fellowships (1966, 1981); a National Endowment for Humanities fellowship (1974); and a fellowship from the American Philosophical Soc. He was a contributor, beginning in 1976, to the *Handbook of Latin American Studies* at the Library of Congress; from 1978 was ed. of and principal contributor to *Inter-American Music Review*. The versatility of his contributions on various subjects is indeed extraordinary. Thus, he publ. several articles containing materials theretofore unknown about Liszt's piano concerts in Spain and Portugal. He ed., transcribed, and annotated *Vilancicos portugueses for Portugaliae Musica XXIX* (Lisbon, 1976); contributed informative articles dealing with early American composers, South American operas, sources of Indian music, and studies on Latin American composers to the *Musical Quarterly*, *Revista Musical Chilena*, *Journal of the American Musicological Society*, *Ethnomusicology*, and *Inter-American Music Review*. His avowed mission in his work is "to rescue the musical past of the Americas." The honors bestowed upon him, especially in the Spanish-speaking world, are many. In 1988 the Organization of American States created the Robert Stevenson Prize in Latin American Musicology. In April 1990 he was awarded a gold medal in ceremonies at the Prado Museum in Madrid, presided over by the King of Spain, and in Dec. of that year was inducted as an honorary member into the Sociedad Española de Musicologica. Also in 1990, the Sociedad Argentina de Musicologia made him an honorary member, and he was honored by the Comisión Nacional de Cultura de Venezuela. In coordination with the quincentennial of the discovery of America in 1992, Stevenson's book *Spanish Cathedral Music in the Golden Age* (1961) was publ. in Madrid in a Spanish tr. as *La música en las catedrales de España durante el siglo do oro*. Among other assorted distinctions, the mayor of El Paso, Tex. (where Stevenson had resided from age 2 to 18), presented him with a scroll making him an honorary citizen. Stevenson's compositions are marked by kinetic energy and set in vigorous and often acrid dissonant counterpoint. His symphonic 2 *Peruvian*

Preludes were performed by Stokowski with the Philadelphia Orch. on June 28, 1962; the score was later expanded into *3 preludias peruanos* and first performed in Mexico City, on July 20, 1963, with Luis Herrera de la Fuente conducting. Other works include *Nocturne in Ebony* and *A Texas Suite* for Orch.; Clarinet Sonata; 3 piano sonatas: *A Cambridge Sonata*, *A Manhattan Sonata*, and *A New Haven Sonata*. He also wrote *Coronation Concerto* for Organ and *A Sandburg Cantata* for Chorus.

WRITINGS: *Music in Mexico. A Historical Survey* (N.Y., 1952); *Patterns of Protestant Church Music* (Durham, N.C., 1953); *La musica en la catedral de Sevilla, 1478–1606; Documentos para su estudio* (Los Angeles, 1954; Madrid, 1985); *Music before the Classic Era* (London, 1955; second ed., 1958); *Cathedral Music in Colonial Peru* (Lima, 1959); *The Music of Peru: Aboriginal and Viceroyal Epochs* (Washington, D.C., 1960); *Juan Bermudo* (The Hague, 1960); *Spanish Music in the Age of Columbus* (The Hague, 1960); *Music Instruction in Inca Land* (Baltimore, 1960); *Spanish Cathedral Music in the Golden Age* (Berkeley, Calif., 1961; Spanish tr., Madrid, 1992); *Mexico City Cathedral Music, 1600–1750* (Washington, D.C., 1964); *Protestant Church Music in America* (N.Y., 1966); *Music in Aztec and Inca Territory* (Berkeley, 1968); *Renaissance and Baroque Musical Sources in the Americas* (Washington, D.C., 1970); *Foundations of New World Opera, with a Transcription of the Earliest Extant American Opera, 1701* (Lima, 1973); *Christmas Music from Baroque Mexico* (Berkeley, 1974); *Latin American Colonial Music Anthology* (Washington, D.C., 1975); *A Guide to Caribbean Music History* (Lima, 1975); *Antologia de la musica postuguesa 1490–1680* (Lisbon, 1984).—**NS/LK/DM**

Stevenson, Ronald, English pianist and composer; b. Blackburn, Lancashire, March 6, 1928. He studied piano as a child, and began to compose at 14. He took courses in composition and piano at the Royal Manchester Coll. of Music (1945–48), and later studied at the Accademia di Santa Cecilia in Rome on an Italian government scholarship (1955). He was appointed lecturer at the Univ. of Edinburgh (in the Extra-Mural Dept.) in 1962. He was on the music staff at the Univ. of Cape Town (South Africa) from 1963 to 1965. A fervent intellectual, he contributed cultured articles to the *Listener* and other publications, and engaged in a thoroughgoing bio-musical tome on Busoni, with whose art he felt a particular kinship. He publ. a book, *Western Music: An Introduction* (London, 1971). Stevenson adheres to neo-Baroque polyphony; a formidable exemplar is his *Passacaglia on DSCH* for Piano, a Brobdingnagian set of variations in 3 continuous sections, 80 minutes long, derived from the initial D of the first name and the first 3 letters of the last name of Dmitri Shostakovich, in German notation, first performed by Stevenson himself in Cape Town, Dec. 10, 1963. Other works include: *Anger Dance* for Guitar (1965); *Triptych*, on themes from Busoni's opera *Doktor Faust*, for Piano and Orch. (Piano Concerto No. 1; Edinburgh, Jan. 6, 1966, composer soloist); *Scots Dance Toccata* for Orch. (Glasgow, July 4, 1970); *Peter Grimes Fantasy* for Piano, on themes from Britten's opera (1971); *Duo-Sonata* for Harp and Piano (1971); Piano Concerto No. 2 (1972); *Ben Dorain*, choral sym. (1973); Violin Concerto, *The Gypsy* (1973); *Corroboree for Grainger* for Piano and Wind Band (1987); *St. Mary's May Songs* for Soprano and Strings (1988); *Voces Vagabundae* for String Quartet (1990); Cello

Concerto (1995); numerous settings for voice and piano and for chorus of Scottish folk songs; transcriptions of works of Purcell, Bach, Chopin, Berlioz, Busoni, Paderewski, Delius, Britten, Berg, Pizzetti, Grainger, and many others.

BIBL.: M. MacDonald, *R. S.: A Musical Biography* (Edinburgh, 1989).—NS/LK/DM

Stewart, Reginald (Drysdale),

Scottish conductor, pianist, and music educator; b. Edinburgh, April 20, 1900; d. Montecito, Calif., July 8, 1984. After training from H.T. Collinson, choirmaster at St. Mary's Anglican Cathedral in Edinburgh, he studied with Arthur Friedheim and Mark Hambourg in Toronto, and then with Boulanger and Philipp in Paris. From 1921 to 1924 he taught at the Canadian Academy of Music. He also began a career as a pianist and conductor in Canada. From 1929 to 1931 he conducted his own radio orch. From 1933 to 1941 he was conductor of the Toronto Bach Choir, and from 1934 to 1941 was conductor of the Toronto Promenade Sym. Concerts. During these years, he also appeared as a guest conductor and a pianist in Canada and the U.S. From 1941 to 1958 he was head of the Peabody Cons. of Music in Baltimore. He also was music director of the Baltimore Sym. Orch. from 1942 to 1952. In 1962 he joined the faculty of the Music Academy of the West in Santa Barbara, where he later served as head of its piano dept. His career was highlighted in the PBS documentary film *An Evening with Reginald Stewart* (Sept. 28, 1983).—NS/LK/DM

Stewart, Rex (William Jr.),

jazz cornetist, master of the "half-valve" technique (pushing the cornet and/or trumpet valves halfway down to create a wealth of expressive sounds); b. Philadelphia, Feb. 22, 1907; d. Los Angeles, Sept. 7, 1967. His father played violin; his mother was a pianist. The family moved to Georgetown, near Washington, D.C., in 1914. Stewart began on piano and violin, then after two years on alto horn switched to cornet. He played regularly in Danny Doyle's Boys' Band and received tuition from the leader. At 14 he began doing gigs on Potomac riverboats. He left home to do a six-week tour with Ollie Blackwell and his Jazz Clowns; when this band folded he became a member of the Musical Spillers and made his first trip to N.Y. with this act in October 1921. Stewart remained with the Musical Spillers for over a year, playing cornet, trombone, tenor and soprano saxes, and xylophone. He quit the act to do gigs around N.Y., from 1923–25; he then joined Elmer Snowden's Band. Stewart left during the following year to join Fletcher Henderson, with whom he would work, on and off, through early 1933. During this period, he also played with Horace Henderson's Collegians (1927) and McKinney's Cotton Pickers (summer 1931; again early 1932). He performed briefly with Fess Williams in N.Y. in spring 1933, then led his own big band at the Empire Ballroom, N.Y., from c. June 1933 until autumn 1934. He spent a few months in Luis Russell's Band, then joined Duke Ellington in late December 1934. Except for short interludes, he stayed with Duke until April 1943. He played in N.Mex. in Dick Ballou Band (June 1943), gigged with Benny

Carter in Calif. (July 1943), then led his own band in Los Angeles until rejoining Duke Ellington from October 1943 until December 1945. He formed his own "Rextet" early in 1946; the band worked mainly in N.Y. until leaving for Europe in October 1947. They disbanded in Europe and he remained to do extensive work as a soloist, and in that capacity appeared in Australia during summer of 1949. He returned to the U.S. in the spring 1950, gigged around N.Y., and then moved to Troy, N.J. to run his own farm. He led his own band in Boston during the early 1950s, and also worked regularly as a disc jockey on station WROW in Albany, N.Y. Stewart organized and recorded with Fletcher Henderson Reunion Bands in 1957 and 1958. From February 1958 until July 1959 he played at Eddie Condon's Club, and subsequently moved to Calif. He continued disc jockey work on local radio stations and began lecturing and writing on jazz history. He did occasional spells of gigging in the 1960s and appeared at several jazz festivals. He toured Europe as a soloist twice in 1966, returned to play a few concerts in Calif., but by then was devoting most of his time to journalism. Stewart died suddenly from a brain hemorrhage in 1967.

DISC.: *Finesse* (1934); *Americans in Sweden* (1947); *Ellingtonia* (1953); *Dixieland Free-For-All* (1953); *Big Jazz* (1956); *Big Reunion* (1957); *Big Challenge* (1957); *Henderson Homecoming* (1958); *Rendezvous with Rex* (1959); *Porgy and Bess Revisited* (1958); *Chatter Jazz* (1959); *Happy Jazz of Rex Stewart* (1960); *With Henri Chase* (1966). D. Ellington: "Trumpet in Spades," "Boy Meets Horn."

WRITINGS: *Rex Stewart's "Warm-Up" Book* (Leeds Music).—JC/LP

Stewart, Sir Robert (Prescott),

Irish organist, conductor, teacher, and composer; b. Dublin, Dec. 16, 1825; d. there, March 24, 1894. He received training as a chorister at Christ Church Cathedral in Dublin, where he became organist, and at Trinity Coll. in 1844. He was made conductor of the Univ. Choral Soc. in 1846, and then took the Mus.B. and Mus.D. degrees in 1851; in 1852 he became organist at St. Patrick's Cathedral, where he also served as vicar-choral. He was named prof. of music at the Univ. in 1861 and at the Irish Academy of Music in 1871; served as conductor of the Dublin Phil. (from 1873); was knighted in 1872. He wrote orch. pieces, instrumental music, cantatas, services, anthems, odes, glees, and songs.

BIBL.: O. Vignoles, *Memoir of Sir R.P. S.* (London, 1899); J. Culwick, *The Works of Sir R. S.* (Dublin, 1902).—NS/LK/DM

Stewart, Rod,

international star vocalist; b. Highgate, London, England, Jan. 10, 1945. A one-time member of several of the seminal British R&B–style bands of 1963–1966, Rod Stewart first gained recognition as the vocalist for the Jeff Beck Group in the late 1960s. Pursuing a solo recording career while performing and recording with the Faces, one of Britain's finest rock bands of the 1970s, Stewart quickly eclipsed the group's popularity with his *Gasoline Alley* album, arguably his finest, followed by *Every Picture Tells a Story* and the smash hit "Maggie May." After four hitless years in the early 1970s, Stewart became an international star, regaining his commercial success, if little critical acclaim, by recording middle-of-the-road pop and disco material. He has managed to maintain success on the charts through the 1990s, despite his often uneven work on record and stage.

Rod Stewart, born to Scottish parents, attended the same secondary school as did Ray and Dave Davies (later of the Kinks), but dropped out of school at age 16. After working a variety of mundane jobs, he learned guitar and performed as a street singer in Spain and France for a number of months. Upon returning to England, he joined Jimmy Powell and the Five Dimensions as harmonica player; in 1963–1964 he led the group. In 1964 he recorded "Good Morning Little School Girl" for Decca on his own, and joined the R&B band the Hoochie Coochie Men, sharing lead vocals with British blues revivalist "Long" John Baldry. When the group disbanded in autumn 1965, Stewart joined Baldry's Steampacket—which featured Brian Auger and Julie Driscoll—for a year before joining Shotgun Express, whose members included Peter Green and Mick Fleetwood (later of Fleetwood Mac).

In early 1967 Rod Stewart helped form the Jeff Beck Group with former Yardbirds lead guitarist Jeff Beck and bassist-guitarist Ron Wood. Their two albums, *Truth* and *Beck-ola*, served as foundations of the British blues movement and brought Stewart his first recognition. They became widely popular in the United States by means of numerous tours over the next two years, but the group fragmented in mid-1969.

Already signed as a solo artist to Mercury Records, Rod Stewart purused a parallel career with the Faces, which evolved out of the Small Faces and whose leader, Steve Marriott, had left the group to form Humble Pie with Peter Frampton. Even before the Faces had recorded their debut album for Warner Bros., Mercury issued *The Rod Stewart Album*, which contained Mike D'Abo's "Handbags and Gladrags" and the Rolling Stones' "Street Fighting Man." Recording his early solo albums with Wood, Ian McLagan, guitarist Martin Quittenton, and drummer Mickey Waller, Stewart overshadowed the career of the Faces beginning with 1970's *Gasoline Alley*. The album included Elton John and Bernie Taupin's "Country Comfort," Stewart's own "Lady Day," and the title cut, by Stewart and Wood.

Developing an energetic and flashy stage act through successful American tours with the Faces beginning in 1970, Rod Stewart became an international star with *Every Picture Tells a Story* and its classic top-hit single, "Maggie May," written by Stewart and Quittenton. The album also included Stewart's beautiful "Mandolin Wind" and the major hit "(I Know) I'm Losing You," a near-smash hit for the Temptations in 1966–1967. After scoring a major hit with Wood and Stewart's "Stay with Me" by the Faces, Stewart's *Never a Dull Moment* yielded a major hit with Quittenton and Stewart's "You Wear It Well" and a moderate hit with Jimi Hendrix's "Angel"; it also contained "I'd Rather Go Blind." Stewart later became embroiled in legal disputes between Mercury and Warner Bros. that saw his next album, *Smiler*, delayed nearly a year. Ron Wood toured America with the Rolling Stones in 1975, and following the Faces'

subsequent U.S. tour, Rod Stewart announced his departure from the group in December.

Signing with Warner Bros. in spring 1975 and moving to Los Angeles, Rod Stewart recorded *Atlantic Crossing* in Muscle Shoals, Ala. The album seemed to mark a deterioration in the songwriting of Stewart. Nonetheless, his next album, *A Night on the Town*, yielded a top hit with "Tonight's the Night (Gonna Be Alright)" and major hits with Cat Stevens's "The First Cut Is the Deepest" and the poignant "The Killing of Georgie." Stewart conducted a massive worldwide tour in 1976–1977. His next album, *Foot Loose and Fancy Free*, produced the smash hit "You're in My Heart (The Final Acclaim)" and major hits with "I Was Only Joking" and the disco-style "Hot Legs." By then an international celebrity, Stewart again mounted a marathon world tour in support of *Blondes Have More Fun*, which included the facile top pop and smash R&B hit "Do Ya Think I'm Sexy" and the major pop hit "Ain't Love a Bitch."

Foolish Behaviour continued Rod Stewart's reliance on formulaic songs and confirmed his artistic decline. Although his live performances devolved into self-parody, he nonetheless remained a popular concert attraction and singles artist. "Passion" and "Young Turks" became smash hits, and "Tonight I'm Yours (Don't Hurt Me)" and "Baby Jane" became major hits. He seemed to pull out of his descent into mediocrity with 1984's *Camouflage* and resulting tour, thanks to his reunion with Jeff Beck, but the guitarist rescued only "Infatuation" from the album (it produced a second near-smash with the Persuaders' "Some Guys Have All the Luck"), and he left the tour after only seven shows. The banal love song "Love Touch" became a smash hit when used as the theme to the movie *Legal Eagles*. *Out of Order* (1988) yielded four major hits: "Lost in You," "Forever Young," "My Heart Can't Tell Her No" (a smash hit), and "Crazy About Her"; the album went on to sell two million copies.

The Rod Stewart anthology set *Storyteller* produced smash pop and top easy-listening hits with Tom Waits's "Downtown Train" and the Motown standard "This Old Heart of Mine," recorded with Ronnie Isley. He payed further tribute to Motown with the near-smash "The Motown Song" from *Vagabond Heart*, which also produced the smash hit "Rhythm of My Heart" and a major hit with Robbie Robertson's "Broken Arrow." In 1993 Stewart toured with a large string section and performed on the MTV series *Unplugged*, reuniting with ex-bandmate Ron Wood. The album derived from the MTV performance, *Unplugged ... and Seated*, yielded a smash pop and top easy-listening hit with Van Morrison's "Have I Told You Lately" and a major pop hit with Tim Hardin's "Reason to Believe," a song he originally recorded in 1971. In 1994 he was inducted into the Rock and Roll Hall of Fame. Stewart's free 1994–1995 New Year's concert at Copacabana Beach in Rio de Janeiro, Brazil, drew an estimated 3.5 million fans, establishing an attendance record for an open-air concert. *A Spanner in the Works* (1995) followed the semiacoustic style of the MTV show and was his final album for Warner Bros.

DISC.: ROD STEWART AND STEAMPACKET: *R. S. and Steampacket* (1976). **THE JEFF BECK GROUP:** *Truth* (1968); *Beck-ola* (1969); *Truth/Beck-ola* (1975). **THE FACES:** *First Step* (1970); *Long Player* (1971); *A Nod Is as Good as a Wink ... To a Blind Horse* (1971); *Ooh La La* (1973); *Snakes and Ladders: Best* (1976). **ROD STEWART AND THE FACES:** *Coast to Coast: Overture and Beginners* (1973); *R. S. and the Faces* (1975). **ROD STEWART:** *The R. S. Album* (1969); *Gasoline Alley* (1970); *Every Picture Tells a Story* (1971); *Never a Dull Moment* (1972); *Sing It Again, Rod* (1973); *Smiler* (1974); *Best* (1976); *Best, Vol. 2* (1977); *Atlantic Crossing* (1975); *A Night on the Town* (1976); *Foot Loose and Fancy Free* (1977); *Blondes Have More Fun* (1978); *Greatest Hits* (1979); *Foolish Behaviour* (1980); *Tonight I'm Yours* (1981); *Absolutely Live* (1982); *Body Wishes* (1983); *Camouflage* (1984); *R. S.* (1986); *Out of Order* (1988); *Storyteller: The Complete Anthology, 1964–1990* (1989); *Downtown Train: Selections from the "Storyteller" Anthology* (1990); *Vagabond Heart* (1991); *The Mercury Anthology* (1992); *You Wear It Well* (1992); *Vintage* (1993); *Unplugged ... and Seated* (1993); *A Spanner in the Works* (1995); *A Shot of Rhythm and Blues* (1976); *Rod the Mod* (1981).

BIBL.: J. Pidgeon, *R. S. and the Changing Faces* (St. Albans, 1976); G. Tremlett, *The R. S. Story* (London, 1976); T. Ewbank, *R. S.: A Biography* (London, 1992).—**BH**

Stewart, Slam (Leroy Elliott), bassist, singer; b. Englewood, N.J., Sept. 21, 1914; d. Binghamton, N.Y., Dec. 10, 1987. He began playing violin during childhood, switched to bass and worked with local bands (including stint with Sonny Marshall), then studied at Boston Cons. of Music. While in Boston he heard Ray Perry on violin singing and bowing in unison; later, Stewart began successfully experimenting with the idea of singing an octave above his bowed bass work. He worked with Peanuts Holland Band in Buffalo (1936–37), then moved to N.Y., met Slim Gaillard, and formed a duo ("Slim and Slam"). They continued to perform together until Gaillard was drafted into the army in 1942. After their initial success on radio station WNEW, the duo recorded the big-selling "Flat Foot Floogie." Stewart appeared in the 1943 film *Stormy Weather*, then worked mainly with Art Tatum (1943–44), with whom he would work on occasion through the early 1950s. Stewart joined Benny Goodman in February 1945, and for the next nine months did several brief interludes with Goodman. During the 1950s, he worked with the Roy Eldridge Quartet (1953) and pianist Beryl Booker (1955–57), as well as leading his own small groups. Stewart was reunited with Slim Gaillard at Great South Bay Jazz Festival in summer 1958. In the late 1950s and 1960s, he worked mainly as accompanist for vocalist-pianist Rose Murphy (including a European tour). During the mid-1960s he temporarily quit playing because of illness. He returned to performing in late 1968, then settled in Binghamton, N.Y., where he taught at the State Univ. during the 1970s. He toured Europe with Milt Buckner and Jo Jones (April 1971), and worked often with Benny Goodman (1973–75). During 1978 he appeared frequently on television on the *Today* show, often in company with guitarist Bucky Pizzarelli. Stewart remained active through the mid-1980s, touring Europe and also appearing in the U.S. with Illinois Jacquet. Stewart was noted for his unique sound created by singing in a high voice while he soloed with a bow; he

was also one of the most melodic and skillful bassists of his generation and one of the few who took melodic solos before Jimmy Blanton.

DISC.: *Bowin' Singin' Slam* (1945); *Slam Stewart* (1971); *Fish Scales* (1975); *Two Big Mice* (1977); *Dialogue* (1978); *Shut Yo' Mouth!* (1981); "Flat Foot Foogie," "Buck Dance Rhythm."—**JC/LP**

Stewart, Thomas (James), distinguished American baritone; b. San Saba, Tex., Aug. 29, 1928. He studied electrical engineering in Waco, and later went to N.Y., where he became a student of Mack Harrell at the Juilliard School of Music. He made his debut there in 1954 as La Roche in *Capriccio* by Richard Strauss; then sang with the N.Y.C. Opera and the Chicago Opera in bass roles. In 1957 he received a Fulbright grant and went to Berlin. He was engaged as a baritone with the Städtische Oper, where he made his debut there as the Don Fernando in *Fidelio* on March 28, 1958; remained on its roster until 1964, and also sang regularly at London's Covent Garden (1960–78) and at the Bayreuth Festivals (1960–75). He made his Metropolitan Opera debut in N.Y. on March 9, 1966, as Ford in Verdi's *Falstaff*; in 1981 he sang the title role in the American premiere of Reimann's *Lear* with the San Francisco Opera. His other roles were Don Giovanni, Count di Luna in *Il Trovatore*, Escamillo in *Carmen*, Iago in *Otello*, and Wotan. In 1955 he married **Evelyn Lear**, with whom he often appeared in opera and concert settings.—**NS/LK/DM**

Stibilj, Milan, Slovenian composer; b. Ljubljana, Nov. 2, 1929. He studied composition with Karol Pahor at the Ljubljana Academy of Music (1956–61) and with Kelemen at the Zagreb Academy of Music (1962–64); took courses in electronic music at the Univ. of Utrecht (1966–67). He composes in an advanced idiom, exploring the techniques of integral serial organization of musical parameters.

WORKS: ORCH.: *Koncertantna glasba* (Concertante Music) for Horn and Orch. (1959); *Skladbe* (Composition) for Horn and Strings (1959); *Slavcek in vrtnica* (The Nightingale and the Rose), symphonic poem (1961); *Skladja* (Congruences) for Piano and Orch. (1963); *Impressions* for Flute, Harp, and String Quintet or String Orch. (1963); *Verz* (1964); *Indian Summer* for Chamber Orch. (1974). **CHAMBER:** *Anekdote* for Piano (1957); *Sarabanda* for 4 Clarinets (1960); *Assimilation* for Violin (1965); *Contemplation* for Oboe and String Quintet (1966); *Condensation* for Trombone, 2 Pianos, and Percussion (1967); *Zoom* for Clarinet and Bongos (1970). **VOCAL:** *Epervier de ta faiblesse, Domine* for Narrator and 5 Percussionists (1964); *Apokatastasis, Slovenian Requiem* for Tenor, Chorus, and Orch. (1967).—**NS/LK/DM**

Stich, Johann Wenzel (actually, **Jan Václav**), Bohemian horn player, violinist, and composer who assumed the name **Giovanni Punto**; b. Žehušice, near Čáslav, Sept. 28, 1746; d. Prague, Feb. 16, 1803. He was sent by Count Thun to study horn with Josef Matiegka in Prague, Schinderlarž in Munich, and Hampel and Haudek in Dresden. He was in the service of Count Thun in Žehušice (1763–66), and then ran away, eventually making his way to the Holy Roman

Empire, where he took the name Giovanni Punto. He toured in Europe from 1768; also was in the service of the Prince of Hechingen and then of the Mainz court (1769–74). In 1778 in Paris he met Mozart, who was impressed with his virtuosity. In 1781 he played in the band of the Prince- Archbishop of Würzburg. He then went to Paris to serve the Comte d'Artois (later Charles X) in 1782; during the Reign of Terror, he was active as a violinist and conductor at the Théâtre des Variétés Amusantes. In 1799 he went to Munich and in 1800 to Vienna, where he made the acquaintance of Beethoven, who, enchanted by his playing, wrote for him a Sonata for Horn and Piano (op.17), and played it with him at a concert (April 18, 1800). After touring with J.L. Dussek in 1802, he settled in Prague. His extant works comprise 11 horn concertos (Prague, c. 1787–1806), 3 quintets for Horn, Flute or Oboe, Violin, Viola, and Bassoon (Prague, c. 1799), 21 quartets for either Horn, Violin, Viola, and Bassoon, or Horn, Violin, Bassoon, and Cello (Prague, c. 1785–96), 20 trios for 3 Horns (Prague, c. 1800), 56 duos for 2 Horns (Prague, c. 1793–1803), and 6 trios for Flute, Violin and Bassoon (London, c. 1773). He publ. a horn method that was a revision of Hampel's (Paris, c. 1798; third ed., 1798) and a book of horn exercises (Paris, 1795; second ed., 1800).—NS/LK/DM

Stich-Randall, Teresa, admired American soprano; b. West Hartford, Conn., Dec. 24, 1927. She received her training at the Hartt School of Music in Hartford and at Columbia Univ. In 1947 she made her operatic debut as Gertrude Stein in the premiere of Thomson's *The Mother of Us All* in N.Y. She was chosen to create the title role in Luening's *Evangeline* in N.Y. in 1948. She then was engaged to sing with Toscanini and the NBC Sym. Orch. in N.Y. After winning the Lausanne competition in 1951, she made her European operatic debut that year as the Mermaid in *Oberon* in Florence. In 1951–52 she sang at the Basel Opera. In 1952 she made her first appearance at the Salzburg Festival and at the Vienna State Opera. In 1955 she made her debut at the Chicago Lyric Opera as Gilda. From 1955 she appeared regularly at the Aix-en-Provence Festivals. On Oct. 24, 1961, she made her Metropolitan Opera debut in N.Y. as Fiordiligi, remaining on its roster until 1966. She also sang widely in the U.S. and Europe as a concert artist. Her success in Vienna led her to being the first American to be made an Austrian Kammersängerin in 1962. She retired in 1971. Stich-Randall was especially esteemed for her roles in Mozart's operas.—NS/LK/DM

Stiedry, Fritz, eminent Austrian-born American conductor; b. Vienna, Oct. 11, 1883; d. Zürich, Aug. 9, 1968. He studied jurisprudence in Vienna and took a course in composition with Mandyczewski. Mahler recommended him to Schuch in Dresden, and he became his asst. conductor (1907–08); he subsequently was active as a theater conductor in the German provinces, and in Prague. He conducted at the Berlin Opera (1916–23); then led the Vienna Volksoper (1923–25). After traveling as a guest conductor in Italy, Spain, and Scandinavia (1925–28), he returned to Berlin as conductor of the Stadtische Oper (1929–33). With the advent of the Nazi regime in 1933, he went to Russia, where he

conducted the Leningrad Phil. (1934–37). In 1938 he emigrated to the U.S. and became a naturalized American citizen; conducted the New Friends of Music Orch. in N.Y.; on Nov. 15, 1946, he made his Metropolitan Opera debut in N.Y. conducting *Siegfried*, remaining on its roster as one of its most distinguished conductors until 1958. As a conductor, he championed the second Viennese School of composition. He was a close friend of Schoenberg; conducted first performances of his opera *Die glückliche Hand* in Vienna (1924) and his second Chamber Sym. in N.Y. (1940). He also gave fine performances of the operas of Wagner and Verdi. —NS/LK/DM

Stiehl, family of German musicians:

(1) Johann Dietrich (Diedrich) Stiehl, organist; b. Lübeck, July 9, 1800; d. there, June 27, 1873. He studied organ in Lübeck with M. Bauck, whom he succeeded as organist of the Jakobikirche in 1835. He had 2 sons who became musicians:

(2) Carl (Karl) Johann Christian Stiehl, organist, conductor, teacher, and writer on music; b. Lübeck, July 12, 1826; d. there, Dec. 1, 1911. He first studied with his father, and then with Lobe in Weimar; completed his training at the Leipzig Cons. He taught organ and singing and served as a church organist in Jever (1848–58) and Eutin (1858–77); also was music director to the Grand Duke of Oldenburg (1860–77). He returned to Lübeck as a singing teacher in 1877, where he conducted the Singakademie until 1901; also was conductor of the Musikverein, and then founder-director of the Phil. Concerts (1886–96). He likewise wrote music criticism.

WRITINGS: *Zur Geschichte der Instrumentalmusik in Lübeck* (1885); *Lübeckisches Tonkünstler-Lexikon* (1887); *Musikgeschichte der Stadt Lübeck* (1891); *Geschichte des Theaters in Lübeck* (1901).

(3) Heinrich (Franz Daniel) Stiehl, organist, conductor, and composer; b. Lübeck, Aug. 5, 1829; d. Reval, May 1, 1886. He studied with Lobe in Weimar, and later with Moscheles, Gade, and Hauptmann at the Leipzig Cons. In 1853 he went to St. Petersburg as organist at the Lutheran Church and conductor of a German choral society. He was subsequently active in Vienna (1867–69), Italy (1869–72), London (1872–73), and Belfast (1874–77). In 1880 he was engaged as organist at St. Olai's Church in Reval. He wrote in all 172 opus numbers, including 2 light operas: *Der Schatzgräber* and *Jery und Bätely*; also *Die Vision* for Orch., 2 piano quartets, 3 piano trios, Violin Sonata, Cello Sonata, and numerous piano pieces of programmatic content. —NS/LK/DM

Stigelli, Giorgio (real name, **Georg Stiegele**), celebrated German tenor; b. 1815; d. Boschetti, near Monza, July 3, 1868. He made extensive concert tours in Europe, and appeared in America in 1864–65. He composed many songs, among them the popular *Die schönsten Augen.*—NS/LK/DM

Stignani, Ebe, esteemed Italian mezzo-soprano; b. Naples, July 11, 1904; d. Imola, Oct. 6, 1974. She studied voice with Agostino Roche at the Naples Cons. She made her operatic debut as Amneris at the Teatro San Carlo in Naples (1925); then joined Milan's La Scala in 1926, winning great distinction for her roles in Italian operas as well as Gluck's Orfeo, Brangäne, and Ortrud. She made guest appearances at London's Covent Garden, winning success as Amneris (1937, 1939, 1955), Azucena (1939, 1952), and Adalgisa (1952, 1957); also sang in San Francisco (1938, 1948). In 1958 she made her operatic farewell as Azucena at London's Drury Lane. —NS/LK/DM

Still, William Grant, eminent black American composer; b. Woodville, Miss., May 11, 1895; d. Los Angeles, Dec. 3, 1978. His father was bandmaster in Woodville; after his death when Still was in infancy, his mother moved the family to Little Rock, Ark., where she became a high school teacher. He grew up in a home with cultured, middle-class values, and his stepfather encouraged his interest in music by taking him to see operettas and buying him operatic recordings; he was also given violin lessons. He attended Wilberforce Coll. in preparation for a medical career, but became active in musical activities on campus; after dropping out of college, he worked with various groups, including that of W.C. Handy (1916); then attended the Oberlin (Ohio) Coll. Cons. During World War I, he played violin in the U.S. Army; afterward returned to work with Handy, and became oboist in the Shuffle Along orch. (1921); then studied composition with Varèse, and at the New England Cons. of Music in Boston with Chadwick. He held a Guggenheim fellowship in 1934–35; was awarded honorary doctorates by Howard Univ. (1941), Oberlin Coll. (1947), and Bates Coll. (1954). Determined to develop a symphonic type of Negro music, he wrote an *Afro-American Symphony* (1930). In his music he occasionally made use of actual Negro folk songs, but mostly he invented his thematic materials. He married the writer Verna Arvey, who collaborated with him as librettist in his stage works.

WORKS: DRAMATIC: Opera: *Blue Steel* (1934); *Troubled Island* (1941); *A Bayou Legend* (1940; PBS, 1981); *A Southern Interlude* (1943); *Costaso* (1950); *Mota* (1951); *The Pillar* (1956); *Minette Fontaine* (1958); *Highway 1, U.S.A.* (1962; Miami, May 13, 1963). Ballet: *La Guiablesse* (1927); *Sahdji* (1930); *Lennox Avenue* (1937); *Miss Sally's Party* (1940). Incidental Music: *The Prince and the Mermaid* (1965). ORCH.: *Darker America* (1924; Rochester, N.Y., Nov. 21, 1927); *From the Black Belt* (1926); *From the Journal of a Wanderer* (Rochester, N.Y., May 8, 1929); 5 syms.: No. 1, *Afro-American Symphony* (1930; Rochester, N.Y., Oct. 29, 1931), No. 2 in G minor, *Song of a New Race* (Philadelphia, Dec. 19, 1937), No. 3 (1945; discarded; new No. 3, *The Sunday Symphony*; 1958), No. 4, *Autochthonous* (1947; Oklahoma City, March 18, 1951), and No. 5, *Western Hemisphere* (revision of discarded No. 3, 1945; Oberlin, Ohio, Nov. 9, 1970); *Africa* (1930); *A Deserted Plantation* (1933); *Kaintuck (Kentucky)* for Piano and Orch. (1935; Rochester, N.Y., Jan. 16, 1936); *Dismal Swamp* (Rochester, N.Y., Oct. 30, 1936); *Beyond Tomorrow* (1936); *Ebon Chronicle* (Fort Worth, Nov. 3, 1936); *Can'tcha Line 'em* (1940); *Old California* (1941); *Pages from Negro History* (1943); *In Memoriam: The Colored Soldiers Who Died for Democracy* (1943; N.Y., Jan. 5, 1944); *Fanfare for American War Heroes* (1943); *Poem* (Cleveland, Dec. 7, 1944); *Festive Overture* (1944; Cincinnati, Jan.

19, 1945); *Fanfare for the 99th Fighter Squadron* for Winds (1945); *Archaic Ritual* (1946); *Wood Notes* (1947; Chicago, April 22, 1948); *Danzas de Panama* for Strings (1948; also for String Quartet); *Ennanga* for Harp and Orch. or Flute and Strings (1956); *The American Scene* (1957); *Little Red Schoolhouse* (1957); *The Peaceful Land* (1960); *Patterns* (1960); *Los alnados de España* (1962); *Preludes for Strings, Flute, and Piano* (1962); *Threnody in Memory of Jan Sibelius* (1965); *Miniature Overture* (1965); *Choreographic Prelude for Strings, Flute, and Piano* (1970). CHAMBER: Suite for Violin and Piano (1943); *Pastorela* for Violin and Piano (1946); *4 Folk Suites* for Flute, Clarinet, Oboe, Bassoon, Strings, and Piano (1962); *Vignettes* for Oboe, Bassoon, and Piano (1962); piano pieces. VOCAL: *Plain Chant for Americans* for Baritone and Orch. (N.Y., Oct. 23, 1941); *Caribbean Melodies* for Chorus, Piano, and Percussion (1941); *Wailing Woman* for Soprano and Chorus (1946); many songs. OTHER: Band pieces; arrangements of spirituals.

BIBL.: V. Arvey, *W.G. S.* (N.Y., 1939); R. Simpson, *W.G. S.: The Man and His Music* (diss., Mich. State Univ., 1964); R. Haas, ed., *W.G. S. and the Fusion of Cultures in American Music* (Los Angeles, 1972); A. Arvey, *In One Lifetime* (Fayetteville, Ark., 1984); J. Still, M. Dabrishus, and C. Quin, *W.G. S.: A Bio-Bibliography* (Westport, Conn., 1996); J. Still, ed., *W.G. S.: An Oral History* (Flafstaff, Ariz., 1998).—NS/LK/DM

Stillman-Kelley, Edgar
See **Kelley, Edgar Stillman**

Stillman-Kelley, Jessie
See **Kelley, Jessie Stillman**

Stilwell, Richard (Dale), outstanding American baritone; b. St. Louis, May 6, 1942. After studying English at Anderson (Ind.) Coll., he appeared as Silvio in *Pagliacci* with the St. Louis Grand Opera (1962); then studied voice with F. St. Leger and P. Mathen at the Ind. Univ. School of Music in Bloomington (B.A., 1966) and with D. Ferro in N.Y. On April 7, 1970, he made a successful debut as Pelléas with the N.Y.C. Opera. In 1973 he made his British debut as Ulysses in *Il ritorno d'Ulisse in Patria* at the Glyndebourne Festival. He was chosen to create the role of Constantine in Pasatieri's *The Seagull* (Houston, 1974) and the title role in Pasatieri's *Ines de Castro* (Baltimore, 1976). On Oct. 15, 1976, he made his Metropolitan Opera debut in N.Y. as Guglielmo in *Così fan tutte*; scored a major success there as Billy Budd in 1978; also appeared at the Paris Opéra, the Netherlands Opera, the Chicago Lyric Opera, the Washington (D.C.) Opera Soc., and the Berlin Deutsche Oper; likewise sang in concerts with the major U.S. orchs. In 1988 he sang in the premiere of Argento's The Aspern Papers in Dallas. In 1990 he appeared as Sharpless in Lyons. He sang Don Alfonso in Seattle in 1992. In 1994 he was engaged to sing in Barber's *Vanessa* in Dallas. He appeared in *The Ballad of Baby Doe* at the Washington (D.C.) Opera in 1997. In addition to his remarkable portrayal of Pelléas, he also excels as Papageno, Don Giovanni, Figaro in *Il Barbiere di Siviglia*, Don Pasquale, Eugene Onegin, Rodrigo in *Don Carlos*, and Ford in *Falstaff*.—NS/LK/DM

Stirling, Elizabeth, English organist and composer; b. Greenwich, Feb. 26, 1819; d. London, March 25,

1895. She studied organ and piano with Edward Holmes, and harmony with G.A. Macfarren. She was organist of All Saints', Poplar (1839–59), and at St. Andrew's, Undershaft (1859–80). In 1856 she passed the examination for the degree of Mus.Bac. at Oxford (her work was *Psalm 130* for 5 Voices, with Orch.), but, ironically, her earned degree could not be granted to a woman. She made many organ transcriptions from classical works and publ. *6 Pedal-Fugues* and other organ pieces and also part-songs, of which *All among the Barley* won great popularity.—NS/LK/DM

Stitt, Sonny (Edward), jazz alto and tenor saxophonist; b. Boston, Mass., Feb. 2, 1924; d. Washington, D.C., July 22, 1982. Sonny Stitt is often pegged as Charlie Parker's most avid disciple, but he had reached many of the same harmonic and rhythmic insights in the early 1940s independent of Bird. A blazing alto saxophonist with an archetypical bebop sound, Stitt was also a highly charged tenor player, though his approach was strongly influenced by Lester Young. He was capable of breathtaking ballad work on either horn. He landed his first major gig as an alto saxophonist with Tiny Bradshaw in the early 1940s and hooked up briefly with Billy Eckstine's seminal bop big band, playing alongside Gene Ammons and Dexter Gordon. Soon after he moved to New York he worked with Dizzy Gillespie (1945–46) and recorded with Kenny Clarke. Drug problems kept him off the scene for a number of years and when he returned he was playing tenor as a way to distinguish himself from Parker. He co-led one of the first great tenor duel bands with Ammons (1950–52) and began leading his own combos. After Parker's death in 1955 he began playing alto again, touring with Jazz at the Philharmonic and Dizzy Gillespie in the late 1950s, and with Miles Davis in 1960–61. He toured with The Giants of Jazz in 1971–72, a band featuring Gillespie, Monk, Kai Winding, Al McKibbon, and Art Blakey. Though Stitt was a very prolific and consistent musician, rarely turning in a poor performance in his 100 or so albums as a leader, he was often at his best when jousting with other saxophonists or in similar competitive situations.

DISC.: *Sonny Stitt/Bud Powell/J. J. Johnson* (1949); *Prestige First Sessions, Vol. 2* (1951); *At the Hi-Hat* (1954); *Only the Blues* (1957); *Sonny Side Up* (1958); *Stitt Meets Brother Jack* (1962); *Low Flame* (1962); *Night Letter* (1963); *Soul People* (1964); *Tune-Up* (1972); *12!* (1972); *Just in Case You Forgot How Bad He Really Was* (1981); *The Last Sessions, Vols. 1 & 2* (1982); *Stitt Plays Bird* (1988); *Kaleidoscope* (1992); *The Good Life* (1994); *Verve Jazz Masters 50* (1995).—AG

Stivori, Francesco, noted Italian organist and composer; b. Venice, c. 1550; d. probably in Graz, 1605. He was a pupil of Claudio Merulo. After serving as municipal organist in Montagna (1579–1601), he was organist to Archduke Ferdinand of Inner Austria at his Graz court (from 1602). Stivori was a significant figure in the movement to introduce multiple choral writing to Austria. He publ. 7 vols. of madrigals (1583–1605), 6 vols. of motets (1579–1601), and 3 vols. of instrumental pieces (1589–99).—NS/LK/DM

Stobaeus, Johann, eminent German composer; b. Graudenz, July 6, 1580; d. Königsberg, Sept. 11, 1646. In 1595 he went to Königsberg, where from 1599 to 1608 he was a pupil of J. Eccard; also attended the Univ. (from 1600). In 1602 he became a bass in the Electoral Kapelle; served as Kantor at the Cathedral church and school in Kneiphof, Königsberg (1603–26); then was Kapellmeister at the Königsberg court. His extant works comprise *Cantiones sacrae harmoniae* for 4 to 10 Voices, *Item aliquot Magnificat* for 5 to 6 Voices (Frankfurt am Main, 1624), compositions in other collections of the era, and many pieces in MS. See also G. Teschner, ed., *J. Eccard und J. Stobaeus: Preussische Festlieder* for 5 to 8 Voices (Leipzig, 1858).

BIBL.: L. Kamieński, *J. S. z Grudziadz* (Poznan, 1928). —NS/LK/DM

Stock, David (Frederick), American composer and conductor; b. Pittsburgh, June 3, 1939. He studied composition with Lopatnikoff and Haieff, musicology with Dorian, and trumpet at Carnegie-Mellon Univ. (B.F.A., 1962; M.F.A., 1963); took courses with Boulanger, Fournet, and Vaurebourg-Honegger at the École Normale de Musique in Paris (1960–61); attended the Berkshire Music Center at Tanglewood (summer, 1964); engaged in advanced studies with Berger at Brandeis Univ. (M.F.A., 1973). He played trumpet in several orchs.; taught at the Cleveland Inst. of Music (1964–65), Brandeis Univ. (1966–68), and the New England Cons. of Music in Boston (1968–70). From 1970 to 1974 he taught at Antioch Coll. and conducted its chamber orch., and also served as chairman of its music dept. (1971–74). In 1974 he held a Guggenheim fellowship. In 1975 he became conductor of the Pittsburgh New Music Ensemble. He also taught at Carnegie-Mellon Univ. (1976–77) and conducted the Carnegie Sym. Orch. (1976–82); taught at the Univ. of Pittsburgh (1978–86) and Duquesne Univ. (from 1987), where he was later a prof. of music and conductor of the Duquesne Contemporary Ensemble. In 1987–88 he was composer-in-residence of the Pittsburgh Sym. Orch. He received NEA fellowships (1974, 1976, 1978, 1983) and various commissions. His compositions are written in a gratefully accessible style.

WORKS: ORCH.: *Divertimento* (1957); *Capriccio* for Small Orch. (1963); *Symphony in 1 Movement* (1963); *Flashback* (1968); *Inner Space* (1973); *Triflumena* (1978); *Zohar* (1978); *The Philosopher's Stone* for Violin and Chamber Orch. (1980); *A Joyful Noise* (1983; Pittsburgh, May 23, 1985); *Parallel Worlds* for Chamber Orch. (1984); *American Accents* for Chamber Orch. (1984; Los Angeles, Oct. 12, 1985); *Back to Bass-ics* for Strings (1985); *On the Shoulders of Giants* (1986); *Rockin' Rondo* (1987); *Quick Opener* for Chamber Orch. (1987); *Tekiah* for Trumpet and Chamber Orch. (1987); *Fast Break* (1988); *Kickoff* (1990); *Fanfarria* (1993); *Power Play* (1993); *String Set* for Chamber Orch. (1993); *Available Light* for Chamber Orch. (1994). **Wind Ensemble:** *Nova* for Band (1974); *The Body Electric* for Amplified Contrabass, Winds, and Percussion (1977); *The 'Slibert Stomp* (1985); *Evensong* for English Horn and Wind Orch. (1985); *No Man's Land* for Wind Sym. (1988); *The Winds of Summer* for Saxophone and Band (1989); *Earth Beat* for Timpani and Wind Sym. (1992). **CHAMBER:** 3 string quartets (1962–94); *Shadow Music* for 5 Percussion and Harp (1964; rev. 1979); *Serenade* for 5 Instruments for

Flute, Clarinet, Horn, Viola, and Cello (1964); Quintet for Clarinet and Strings (1966); *Triple Play* for Piccolo, Contrabass, and Percussion (1970); *Dreamwinds* for Woodwind Quintet (1975); *Night Birds* for 4 or More Cellos (1975); *Icicles* for Piccolo, Oboe, and Clarinet (1976); *Brass Rubbing* for 6 Trumpets (1976); *Pentacles* for Brass Quintet (1978); *Starlight* for Clarinet and Percussion (1979); *Night* for Clarinet, Violin, and Cello (1980); *Persona* for Clarinet, Violin, Cello, Piano, and Percussion (1980); *Keep the Change* for Any 5 Treble Clef Instruments (1981); *Speaking Extravagantly* for String Quartet (1981); *Sulla Spiaggia* for Alto Flute, English Horn, Bass Clarinet, Electric Piano, and Percussion (1985); *Yerusha* for Clarinet and 7 Players (1986); *Partners* for Cello and Piano (1988); *Sunrise Sarabande* for Recorder Quartet (1988); *Sax Appeal* for Saxophone Quartet (1990); *Sonidos de la Noche* for Clarinet, Violin, Cello, and Piano (1994). **VOCAL:** *Scat* for Soprano, Flute, Bass Clarinet, Violin, and Cello (1971); *Spirits* for Chorus or Soloists, Harp and/or Electric Piano, and Percussion (1976); *Upcountry Fishing* for Voice and Violin (1982); *Dor L'Dor* for Chorus (1990); *Beyond Babylon* (1994).—NS/LK/DM

Stock, Frederick (actually, Friedrich August),

respected German-born American conductor; b. Jülich, Nov. 11, 1872; d. Chicago, Oct. 20, 1942. He was first trained in music by his father, a bandmaster; then studied violin with G. Japha and composition with Wüllner, Zöllner, and Humperdinck at the Cologne Cons. (1886–91). From 1891 to 1895 he was a violinist in the Cologne municipal orch. In 1895 he was engaged as a violist in Theodore Thomas's newly organized Chicago Orch., becoming his asst. conductor in 1901; following Thomas's death in 1905, he inherited the orch., which took the name of the Theodore Thomas Orch. in 1906; it became the Chicago Sym. Orch. in 1912, with Stock serving as its conductor until his death, the 1918–19 season excepted. In 1919 he became a naturalized U.S. citizen. As a conductor, Stock was extremely competent, even though he totally lacked that ineffable quality of making orch. music a vivid experience in sound; but he had the merit of giving adequate performances of the classics, of Wagner, and of the German Romantic school. He also programmed several American works, as long as they followed the Germanic tradition. The flowering of the Chicago Sym. Orch. was to be accomplished by his successors Reiner and Solti. Stock was also a composer; wrote 2 syms., a Violin Concerto (Norfolk Festival, June 3, 1915, E. Zimbalist soloist, composer conducting), and some chamber music.

BIBL.: P. Otis, *The Chicago Symphony Orchestra* (Chicago, 1925); W. Holmes, "F. S.," *Le Grand Baton*, VI/2 (1969). —NS/LK/DM

Stockhausen, family of prominent German musicians:

(1) Franz (Anton Adam) Stockhausen, harpist, teacher, and composer; b. Cologne, Sept. 1, 1789; d. Colmar, Sept. 10, 1868. He went to Paris about 1812, and from 1825 he toured Europe in concerts with his wife, the soprano Margarethe (née Schmuck) Stockhausen (b. Gebweiler, March 29, 1803; d. Colmar, Oct. 6, 1877), who had been a pupil of Gioseffo Catrufo at the Paris Cons.

In 1840 they settled in Alsace. He composed harp pieces, some vocal music, and various arrangements for his instrument. They had 2 sons who became musicians:

(2) Julius (Christian) Stockhausen, esteemed baritone, conductor, and pedagogue; b. Paris, July 22, 1826; d. Frankfurt am Main, Sept. 22, 1906. He began his music training at an early age with his parents; studied piano with Karl Kienzl and also received instruction in organ, violin, and cello. In 1843 he went to Paris to study with Cramer, then continued his training at the Cons. (from 1845), and also received private lessons in harmony from Matthäus Nagillers and in singing from Manuel García. In 1848 he sang in *Elijah* in Basel, and in the next year sang before Queen Victoria in London; then toured widely in Europe as a concert singer. He was second baritone at the Mannheim Court Theater (1852–53), then a member of the Paris Opéra-Comique (1856–59). In 1863 he became conductor of the Hamburg Phil. Soc. and Singakademie, which positions he held until 1867; then was conductor of the Berlin Sternscher Gesangverein (1874–78). Settling in Frankfurt am Main, he taught voice at the Hoch Cons. (1878–80; 1883–84); also taught at his own school (from 1880). He publ. *Gesangs-methode* (2 vols., 1886–87; also in Eng.). He was a distinguished interpreter of the lieder of Schubert and Brahms; the latter was a close friend.

BIBL.: J. Wirth-Stockhausen, *J. S.: Der Sänger des deutschen Liedes* (Frankfurt am Main, 1927).

(3) Franz Stockhausen, pianist, conductor, and teacher; b. Gebweiler, Jan. 30, 1839; d. Strasbourg, Jan. 4, 1926. He began his music studies with his parents, and after piano lessons from Alkan in Paris, he pursued training with Moscheles, Richter, Hauptmann, and Davidov at the Leipzig Cons. (1860–62). He was music director in Thann, Alsace (1863–66), then went to Strasbourg, where he was conductor of the Société de Chant Sacré (1868–79), music director at the Cathedral (from 1868), and director of the Cons. and city concerts (1871–1908).—NS/LK/DM

Stockhausen, Karlheinz,

outstanding German composer; b. Modrath, near Cologne, Aug. 22, 1928. He was orphaned during World War II and was compelled to hold various jobs to keep body and soul together; all the same, he learned to play the piano, violin, and oboe; then studied piano with Hans Otto Schmidt-Neuhaus (1947–50), form with H. Schröder (1948), and composition with Frank Martin (1950) at the Cologne Staatliche Hochschule für Musik; also took courses in German philology, philosophy, and musicology at the Univ. of Cologne. After studies in Darmstadt (1951), he received instruction in composition from Messiaen in Paris (1952); subsequently studied communications theory and phonetics with Werner Meyer-Eppler at the Univ. of Bonn (1954–56). He was active at the electronic music studio of the West German Radio in Cologne (from 1953); also was a lecturer at the Internationalen Ferienkurse für Musik in Darmstadt (until 1974) and was founder-artistic director of the Cologne Kurse für Neue Musik (1963–68); likewise served as prof. of composition at the Cologne Hochschule für Musik (1971–77). He was made a member of the Swedish Royal Academy

(1970), the Berlin Academy of Arts (1973), and the American Academy and Inst. of Arts and Letters (1979); also was made a Commandeur dans l'Ordre des Arts et des Lettres of France (1985) and an honorary member of the Royal Academy of Music in London (1987). He investigated the potentialities of *musique concrète* and partly incorporated its techniques into his own empiric method of composition, which from the very first included highly complex contrapuntal conglomerates with uninhibited applications of non-euphonious dissonance as well as recourse to the primal procedures of obdurate iteration of single tones; all this set in the freest of rhythmic patterns and diversified by constantly changing instrumental colors with obsessive percussive effects. He further perfected a system of constructivist composition, in which the subjective choice of the performer determines the succession of given thematic ingredients and their polyphonic simultaneities, ultimately leading to a totality of aleatory procedures in which the ostensible application of a composer's commanding function is paradoxically reasserted by the inclusion of prerecorded materials and by recombinant uses of electronically altered thematic ingredients. He evolved energetic missionary activities in behalf of new music as a lecturer and master of ceremonies at avant-garde meetings all over the world; having mastered the intricacies of the English language, he made a lecture tour of Canadian and American univs. in 1958; in 1965, was a visiting prof. of composition at the Univ. of Pa.; was a visiting prof. at the Univ. of Calif. at Davis in 1966–67; in 1969, gave highly successful public lectures in England that were attended by hordes of musical and unmusical novitiates. Stockhausen is a pioneer of "time-space" music, marked by a controlled improvisation, and adding the vectorial (i.e., directional) parameter to the 4 traditional aspects of serial music (pitch, duration, timbre, and dynamics), with performers and electronic apparatuses placed in different parts of the concert hall; such performances, directed by himself, were often accompanied by screen projections and audience participation; he also specified the architectural aspects of the auditoriums in which he gave his demonstrations. His annotations to his own works were publ. in the series entitled *Texte* (6 vols., Cologne, 1963–88). See also R. Maconie, ed., *Stockhausen on Music: Lectures and Interviews* (London and N.Y., 1989).

WORKS: *Chöre für Doris* (1950); *Drei Lieder* for Contralto and Chamber Orch. (1950); *Choral* (1950); Violin Sonatine (1951); *Kreuzspiel* for Oboe, Bass Clarinet, Piano, and 3 Percussion (1951); *Formel* for Orch. (1951); *Etude*, concrete music (1952); *Spiel* for Orch. (1952); *Schlagtrio* for Piano and Kettledrums (1952); *Punkte* for Orch. (1952; rev. 1962); *Kontra- Punkte* for 10 Instruments (Cologne, May 26, 1953); *Klavierstücke I- IV* (1952–53); *Studie I* (1953) and *II* (1954), electronic music; *Klavierstücke V-X* (1954–55); *Zeitmasse* for 5 Woodwinds (1955–56); *Gruppen* for 3 Orchs. (1955–57; Cologne, March 24, 1959); *Klavierstücke XI* (1956); *Gesang der Junglinge*, electronic music, after the Book of Daniel, dealing with the ordeal of 3 monotheistic Hebrew youths in the Babylonian fiery furnace, scored for 5 groups of loudspeakers surrounding the audience (Cologne, May 30, 1956); *Zyklus* for Percussion (1959); *Carré* for 4 Orchs. and Choruses (Hamburg, Oct. 28, 1960); *Refrain* for 3 Performers (1959); *Kontakte* for Electronics (1959–60); *Kontakte* for Electronics, Piano, and Percussion (Cologne, June 11, 1960); *Originale*, music theater (1961); *Momente* for Soprano, 4 Choruses, and 13 Instrumentalists (1962–64); *Plus-Minus* for Clarinet, Trombone, Cello, and 3 Pianos (1963; Warsaw, Sept. 25, 1968); *Mikrophonie I* for 6 Performers (1964) and *II* for 12 Singers, Hammond Organ, 4 Ring Modulators, and Tape (1965); *Mixtur* for Orch., Sinus Generator, and Ring Modulator (1964); *Stop* for Orch. (1965); *Solo* for Melody Instrument (1965–66); *Telemusik*, electronic music (1966; Warsaw, Sept. 23, 1968); *Adieu* for Wind Quintet (1966); *Hymnen*, electronic and concrete music (Cologne, Nov. 30, 1967); *Prozession* for Ensemble (1967); *Stimmung* for 6 Vocalists (1968); *Kurzwellen* for 6 Performers (1968); *Aus den Sieben Tagen*, 15 pieces in graphic notation for various ensembles (1968); *Spiral* for Soloist and Short-wave Transmitter (1968); *Für kommende Zeiten*, 17 texts of "intuitive music" (1968–70); *Dr. K.-Sextett* (1969); *Fresco* for 4 Orchs. (1969); *Pole* for 2 Performers or Singers, and Short-wave Transmitter (1969–70); *Expo* for 3 Instrumentalists or Singers and Short-wave Transmitter (1969–70); *Mantra* for 2 Pianos (Donaueschingen, Oct. 18, 1970); *Sternklang*, "park music" for 5 Groups (1971); *Trans* for Orch. (1971); *Alphabet für Liège*, 13 musical pictures for Soloist and Duo Performers (1972); "*Am Himmel wandre ich...*," Indian lieder for 2 Soloists and Orch. (Donaueschingen, Oct. 20, 1974); *Herbstmusik* for 4 Performers (1974); *Musik im Brauch* for Percussion and Musical Clocks (1975); "*Atmen gibt das Leben...*," choral opera with Orch. or Tape (1975–77); *Sirius*, electronic music, dedicated to American pioneers on earth and in space (1975–77); *Tierkreis* for Various Instruments and Voices (4 versions, 1975–81); *Harlekin* for Clarinet (1975); *Amour*, 5 pieces for Clarinet (1976); *Jubilaum* for Orch. (1977; N.Y., Sept. 10, 1981); *In Freundschaft* for 11 Solo Instruments (1977); *Licht*, projected cycle of 7 operas, 1 for each day of the week: *Dienstag aus Licht* (1977–91); *Donnerstag aus Licht* (1978–80; Milan, April 3, 1981); *Samstag aus Licht* (1981–83; Milan, May 25, 1984); *Montag aus Licht* (1985–88; Milan, May 7, 1988).

BIBL.: K. Wörner, *K. S., Werk und Wollen* (Cologne, 1963; Eng. tr. as *S., Life and Work*, London, 1973); C. Cardew, *S. Serves Imperialism*, a rambling diatribe by a disenchanted follower who became a militant Maoist (London, 1974); J. Cott, *S., Conversations with the Composer* (N.Y., 1973, and London, 1974); J. Harvey, *The Music of S.* (London, 1975); R. Maconie, *S.* (London, 1976); B. Sullivan and M. Manion, *S. in Den Haag* (The Hague, 1983); H.-J. Nagel, ed., *S. in Calcutta* (Calcutta, 1984); M. Tannenbaum, *Intervisto sul genio musicale* (Rome, 1985; Eng. tr., 1987, as *Conversations with S.*); *S.: 60. Geburtstag: 22. August 1988* (n.p., 1988); M. Kurtz, *S.: Eine Biographie* (Kassel and Basel, 1988; Eng. tr., 1992, as *S.: A Biography*); C. von Blumröder, *Die Grundlegung der Musik K. S.s* (Stuttgart, 1993); W. Hopp, *Kurzwellen von K. S.: Konzeption und musikalische Poiesis* (Mainz, 1998).—NS/LK/DM

Stockhoff, Walter William, American composer; b. St. Louis, Nov. 12, 1876; d. there, April 1, 1968. He was largely autodidact, and began to compose early in life. In his music he was influenced mainly by German Romantic composers, but his thematic material was distinctly American. In some of his early piano music he made use of modernistic devices, such as the whole- tone scale, cadential triads with the added sixth, etc. Busoni wrote an enthusiastic article about him (1915) in which he described him as one of America's most original composers. The orch. version of his piano suite *To the Mountains* was premiered under the title

American Symphonic Suite (Frankfurt am Main, Dec. 10, 1924). Several of his piano works and some chamber music were publ. Other works include *5 Dramatic Poems* for Orch. (1943), Piano Sonata, *Metamorphoses* for Piano, etc.—NS/LK/DM

Stockmann, (Christine) Doris, German ethnomusicologist; b. Dresden, Nov. 3, 1929. She studied piano, opera production, and music theory at the Dresden Hochschule für Musik (1947–49) and musicology with Dräger, Meyer, and Vetter at Humboldt Univ. in Berlin; then studied ethnography, folklore, and linguistics with Steinitz there, taking her doctorate in 1958 with the diss. *Der Volksgesang in der Altmark* (publ. in Berlin, 1962). She became scientific assistant in ethnomusicology at the Inst. for German Folklore of the Academy of Sciences in Berlin (1953); lectured at Humboldt Univ. (1967–68) and at the univs. in Uppsala (1965) and Göteborg (1969). She publ. extensively, alone and with her husband, **Erich Stockmann,** on German and European folk music, particularly in their medieval and contemporary forms.—NS/LK/DM

Stockmann, Erich, German ethnomusicologist; b. Stendal, March 10, 1926. He studied musicology and German at the Univ. of Greifswald (1946–49) and musicology with Dräger, Meyer, and Vetter at Humboldt Univ. in Berlin (Ph.D., 1953, with the diss. *Der musikalische Sinn der elektro-akustischen Musikinstrumente*). After serving as ethnomusicologist at the Inst. for German Folklore of the Academy of Sciences in Berlin, he became a lecturer in ethnomusicology and organology at Humboldt Univ. (1957). He was largely responsible for the development of the ethnomusicological research center of the Berlin Academy of Sciences, leading its first expedition to collect folk music in Albania (1957). He ed. several series, including the Handbüchern der Europäischen Volksmusikinstrumente (Leipzig, 1967 et seq.), Annual Bibliography of European Ethnomusicology (Bratislava, 1967 et seq.), and Studia Instrumentorum Musicae Popularis (Stockholm, 1969 et seq.); also publ. extensively, alone and with his wife, **Doris Stockmann,** on European folk music and instruments.—NS/LK/DM

Stoeckel, Carl, American music patron, son of **Gustave J(acob) Stoeckel;** b. New Haven, Conn., Dec. 7, 1858; d. Norfolk, Conn., Nov. 1, 1925. His contribution to American musical culture was the establishment in 1902 of the summer festivals on his estate in Norfolk. He offered cash prizes to composers who appeared at the festival in performances of their own works. Sibelius composed his tone poem *Aallottaret* especially for the Norfolk Festival, and conducted its world premiere there in its second version as *The Oceanides* in 1914. Among other composers represented were J.A. Carpenter, G.W. Chadwick, S. Coleridge-Taylor, H.F. Gilbert, P. Grainger, H.K. Hadley, E.S. Kelly, C.M. Loeffler, H. Parker, D.S. Smith, C.V. Stanford, and Deems Taylor.—NS/LK/DM

Stoeckel, Gustave J(acob), German-American organist, pedagogue, and composer, father of **Carl Sto-**

eckel; b. Maikammer, Bavarian Palatinate, Nov. 9, 1819; d. Norfolk, Conn., May 14, 1907. He studied in Speyer and Kaiserslauten. After serving as a school principal in Landstuhl and as organist at Speyer Cathedral, he left his homeland in the wake of the 1848 revolution and settled in Norfolk as a private teacher. He then was "Instructor of Vocal Art, Organist, and Chapelmaster" at Yale Univ. (1855–96), where he also was the first Battell Prof. of Music (1890–96). He founded the New Haven Phil. Soc. and was co-founder of the Mendelssohn Soc.; also was active with male glee clubs, becoming known as the father of the American glee-club tradition. He wrote many fine glee-club arrangements. Other works include 6 operas, a Sym., choral works, songs, and piano pieces.

BIBL.: D. Smith, *G.J. S., Yale Pioneer in Music* (New Haven, 1939).—NS/LK/DM

Stoessel, Albert (Frederic), distinguished American violinist, conductor, teacher, and composer; b. St. Louis, Oct. 11, 1894; d. (fatally stricken while conducting the premiere of Walter Damrosch's Dunkirk) N.Y., May 12, 1943. He began his musical studies in St. Louis, then received training in violin with Willy Hess and in theory with Kretzschmar at the Berlin Hochschule für Musik, where he also studied conducting. In 1914 he appeared as a violin soloist in Berlin; after touring in Europe, he returned to St. Louis and performed as a soloist there. During World War I he was a military bandmaster in the U.S. Army (1917–19), serving as director of the school for bandmasters of the American Expeditionary Force in France. Returning to the U.S., he appeared as a violin soloist with the Boston Sym. Orch. and toured with Caruso in 1920. He settled in N.Y. in 1921 as Walter Damrosch's successor as conductor of the Oratorio Soc.; also was named director of music at the Chautauqua Institution (1923) and conductor of the Worcester (Mass.) Music Festival (1925); likewise appeared widely as a guest conductor. In 1923 he founded the music dept. at N.Y.U., which he headed until 1930; was director of the opera and orch. depts. at the Juilliard Graduate School (from 1927), where he conducted a number of premieres of American works. He was elected a member of the National Inst. of Arts and Letters in 1931. He publ. *The Technic of the Baton* (N.Y., 1920; second ed., rev. and enl., 1928).

WORKS: *5 Miniatures* for Violin and Piano (1917); *Suite antique* for 2 Violins and Piano (1917; arranged for 2 Violins and Chamber Orch.); Violin Sonata (1919); *Hispania Suite* for Piano (1920; arranged for Orch., 1927); *Cyrano de Bergerac*, symphonic portrait (1922); *Flitting Bats* for Violin and Piano (1925); *Concerto Grosso* for Piano obbligato and Strings (1935); *Early Americana*, orch. suite (1935); *Garrick*, opera (1936; N.Y., Feb. 24, 1937); choral works; songs; piano pieces; transcriptions.

BIBL.: C. McNaughton, *A. S., American Musician* (diss., N.Y.U., 1957).—NS/LK/DM

Stöhr, Richard, Austrian-American pedagogue and composer; b. Vienna, June 11, 1874; d. Montpelier, Vt., Dec. 11, 1967. He studied medicine in Vienna (M.D., 1898), but then turned to music and studied with Robert Fuchs and others at the Vienna Cons. In 1903 he was appointed instructor in theory there, and during his long tenure had many pupils who later became celebrated (Artur Rodzinski, Erich Leinsdorf et al.). In 1938 he was compelled to leave Vienna and settled in the U.S., where he taught at the Curtis Inst. of Music in Philadelphia (1939–42); then taught music and German at St. Michael's Coll. in Winooski, Vt. (1943–50). He wrote 4 operas, 4 syms., *Vermont Suite* for Orch. (1954), much chamber music, and piano pieces. He publ. a popular manual, *Praktischer Leitfaden der Harmonielehre* (Vienna, 1909; 21st ed., 1963); also *Praktischer Leitfaden des Kontrapunkts* (Hamburg, 1911) and *Musikalische Formenlehre* (Leipzig, 1911; rev. 1933, as *Formenlehre der Musik*); *Modulationslehre* (1932).

BIBL.: H. Sittner, *R. S., Mensch, Musiker, Lehrer* (Vienna, 1965).—NS/LK/DM

Stoin, Elena, Bulgarian ethnomusicologist, daughter of **Vassil Stoin;** b. Samokov, April 12, 1915. She graduated from the Bulgarian State Academy of Music in Sofia (1938), then taught music in various schools until 1945; became research assistant at the Ethnographical Museum in Sofia (1946) and also worked in the folk-music dept. of the Music Inst. of the Bulgarian Academy of Sciences (from 1950), becoming a senior research fellow (1970). She lectured widely in Eastern Europe on Bulgarian folk music; her folk- song collections include *Sbornik narodini pesni ot Samokov i Samokovsko* (Collection of Folk Songs from Samokov and the Samokov Region; Sofia, 1975), to which her father had contributed.—NS/LK/DM

Stoin, Vassil, Bulgarian ethnomusicologist, father of **Elena Stoin;** b. Samokov, Dec. 5, 1880; d. Sofia, Dec. 5, 1938. He taught himself violin at the age of 10, and after graduating from the seminary in Samokov (1897), he taught in neighboring villages until 1907, meanwhile recording folk songs. He studied at the Brussels Cons. (1907–10) and taught music in Sofia, Samokov, and other regions (1911–22), organizing and conducting choirs and orchs. He taught in several schools in Sofia (1922–25), and began lecturing on folk music at the Bulgarian State Academy of Music, becoming a prof. in 1927 and director in 1931. He founded the folk-music dept. of the National Ethnographic Museum (1926). Stoin was one of the first ethnomusicologists to study Bulgarian folk song, transcribing over 9,000 songs and publishing several collections; he laid a foundation for future studies, particularly those of his daughter. His books include *Hypothèse sur l'origine bulgare de la diaphome* (Sofia, 1925), *Balgarskata narodna muzika, metrika i ritmika* (Bulgarian Folk Music, Meter, and Rhythm; Sofia, 1927), and *Bulgarska narodna muzika* (Bulgarian Folk Music; Sofia, 1956).—NS/LK/DM

Stojanović, Peter Lazar, Yugoslav violinist, teacher, and composer; b. Budapest, Sept. 6, 1877; d. Belgrade, Sept. 11, 1957. He studied violin with Hubay at the Budapest Cons. and with J. Grun at the Vienna Cons., where he also received training in composition. In 1913 he established his own school for advanced violin playing in Vienna. In 1925 he settled in Belgrade and became a prof. at the Stankovic Music School; was its director from 1925 to 1928; from 1937 to 1945 he was a prof. of violin at the Belgrade Academy of Music. He publ. *Schule der Skalentechnik* for Violin. His works include the operas *A Tigris* (The Tiger; Budapest, Nov. 14, 1905), *Das Liebchen am Dache* (Vienna, May 19, 1917), and *Der Herzog von Reichsstadt* (Vienna, Feb. 11, 1921); 2 ballets; 2 symphonic poems: *Heldentod* (1918) and *Sava* (1935); 7 violin concertos; 2 cello concertos; 2 viola concertos; Flute Concerto; Horn Concerto; chamber music, including a Piano Trio, a Piano Quartet, and a Piano Quintet.—NS/LK/DM

Stojowski, Sigismund (actually, **Zygmunt Denis Antoni**), noted Polish-born American pianist, pedagogue, and composer; b. Strzelce, May 14, 1869; d. N.Y., Nov. 5, 1946. He was a pupil of Zeleński in Kraków and of Diémer (piano) and Delibes (composition) at the Paris Cons. (1887–89), winning first prize for piano playing and composition; later he took a course with Paderewski. He remained in Paris until 1906, when he emigrated to the U.S. as head of the piano dept. at the Inst. of Musical Art in N.Y. (until 1912); later held a similar position at the Von Ende School of Music in N.Y.; taught at the Juilliard Summer School for several years. He became a naturalized American citizen in 1938. In his prime he was extremely successful as a concert pianist, and in his later years was greatly esteemed as a pedagogue.

WORKS: ORCH.: 2 piano concertos: No. 1 (Paris, 1891, composer soloist) and No. 2, *Prologue, Scherzo and Variations* (London, June 23, 1913, composer soloist); Sym. (1899); Violin Concerto (1900); *Romanza* for Violin and Orch. (1901); *Rapsodie symphonique* for Piano and Orch. (1904); Cello Concerto (1922). **OTHER:** Chamber works, including a Piano Quintet, 2 cello sonatas, and 2 violin sonatas; piano pieces; choral works.—NS/LK/DM

Stoker, Richard, English composer and author; b. Castleford, Yorkshire, Nov. 8, 1938. He attended the Huddersfield School of Music and School of Art in Yorkshire (1953–58) and studied with Eric Fenby. After further training with Berkeley at the Royal Academy of Music in London (1958–62), he completed his studies with Boulanger in Paris (1962–63). From 1963 to 1987 he taught composition at the Royal Academy of Music. He also was ed. of the journal *Composer* (1969–80). He publ. the autobiographical vols. *Open Window—Open Door* (1985) and *Between the Lines* (1994). His other writings include novels *Tanglewood* (1993) and *Diva* (1995), as well as a collection of short stories (1995). Stoker has composed in various genres producing scores of both a serious and more popular nature. He has utilized a modified serial technique in some of his works, but tonal elements are always in evidence.

WORKS: DRAMATIC: *Johnson Preserv'd*, opera (1966; London, July 4, 1967); *My Friend—My Enemy*, ballet (1970); *Garden Party*, ballet (1973); *Thérèse Raquin*, opera (1979); *Prospero's Magic Island*, musical (1980); film and television scores. **ORCH.:** *Antic Hay*, overture (1960); *A Purcell Suite* (1960); *Petite Suite* for Small Orch. (1961); *Serenade* (1964); *4 Countries*, suite for Strings (1965); *French Suite* for Strings (1966); *Feast of

Fools, overture (1967); *Little Symphony* for Youth Orch. (1969); *Chorale* for Strings (1970); *Antiphons and Responses* for Recorder Consort and Orch. (1972); *Movement from Bouquet for Lennox* (1979); *Variations, Passacaglia, and Fugue* for Strings (1980); Piano Concerto (1983); *Locations* for Strings (1990); *Chinses Canticle* (1992). **CHAMBER:** 3 string quartets (1961, 1964, 1968); Wind Quintet (1962); 2 violin sonatas (1962, 1970); 3 piano trios (1963, 1968, 1974); Terzetto for Clarinet, Viola, and Piano (1964); Sextet (1965); *Litany, Sequence, and Hymn* for Brass Quartet (1968); *Sinfonia for Sax* for Saxophone Quartet (1969); *Polemics* for Oboe and String Trio (1970); Trio Sonata for Flute, Violin, and Organ or Piano (1972); Sonata for 2 Guitars (1975); Concerto for 2 Guitars and Tape (1976); Duo for Cello and Piano (1978); *Ostinato* for Guitar and Cello (1993); *Partita* for Mandolin and Harp (1993); piano pieces, including 2 sonatas (1962, 1992); organ music, including an Organ Sym. (1969). **VOCAL:** *Ecce Homo*, cantata for Speaker, Tenor, Baritone, Chorus, and Orch. (1964); *Proverbs* for Chorus and Organ or Ensemble (1970); *Benedictus* for Chorus and Orch. or Organ (1972); *The Scholars* for Voice and Ensemble (1992); numerous choruses and solo songs.—NS/LK/DM

Stokes, Eric (Norman), American composer and teacher; b. Haddon Heights, N.J., July 14, 1930; d. in an automobile accident in Minneapolis, March 16, 1999. He studied at Lawrence Coll. (B.M., 1952), with Carl McKinley and Francis Judd Cooke at the New England Cons. of Music in Boston (M.M., 1956), and with Argento and Fetler at the Univ. of Minn. (Ph.D., 1964). In 1961 he joined the faculty of the Univ. of Minn., where he was a prof. from 1977 until his retirement in 1988. He also founded its electronic music laboratory and the First Minn. Moving and Storage Warehouse Band, a contemporary music ensemble, in 1971. In addition to his varied musical activities, he also wrote poetry and was engaged in environmental causes. In his music, Stokes was principally influenced by Ives, Cage, and Brant. His early interest in collage and mixed media scores prompted him to pursue an eclectic experimental course, producing works leavened with imagination, lyricism, and wit.

WORKS: DRAMATIC: *Horspfal*, opera (Minneapolis, Feb. 15, 1969); *Lampyridae*, theater piece (1973); *Happ or Orpheus in Clover*, micro-opera (1977); *The Jealous Cellist*, opera (Minneapolis, Feb. 2, 1979); *Rock & Roll*, theater piece (Minneapolis, June 13, 1980); *Itaru the Stonecutter*, opera (Roseville, Minn., March 25, 1982); *Tag*, theater piece (1982; Minneapolis, May 6, 1992); *We're Not Robots, You Know*, musical (1986; television premiere, Minneapolis, May 26, 1988); *Apollonia's Circus*, opera (Minneapolis, May 13, 1994). **ORCH.:** *A Center Harbor Holiday* (Center Harbor, N.H., July 18, 1963); *Sonatas* for Strings (1966; Monnickendam, the Netherlands, July 10, 1970); *On the Badlands—Parables* for Chamber Orch. (St. Paul, Minn., June 3, 1972); *5 Verbs of Earth Encircled* for Narrator and Chamber Orch. (1973); *The Continental Harp and Band Report* (1974–75; Minneapolis, March 5, 1975); *Pack-Rat (2-step) Slow (March) Drag* for Chamber Orch. (1976; St. Paul, Minn., Jan. 12, 1977); *The Spirit of Place Among the People* for Orch. and Audience (Minneapolis, July 2, 1977); 5 syms.: No. 1 (Aptos, Calif., Aug. 31, 1979), No. 2 (1981; Rochester, N.Y., Feb. 11, 1982), No. 3, *Captions on the War Against Earth* (1989; Kansas City, Mo., Jan. 1, 1990), No. 4, *The Ghost Bus to Eldorado* (1990; N.Y., Jan. 6, 1991), and No. 5, *Native Dancer* (Anchorage, Oct. 26, 1991); *Prairie Drum* for Chamber Orch. (St. Donats Castle, Wales, Aug. 30, 1981); *Concert Music*

for Piano and Orch. (San Francisco, Dec. 3, 1982); *The Greenhouse Effect* for Chamber Orch. (Minneapolis, March 8, 1983); *Cotton Candy* (Minneapolis, June 19, 1986); *Stages (Homage to Kurt Weill)* (St. Donats Castle, Wales, Aug. 27, 1988); *Prophet Bird* for Chamber Orch., after Robert Schumann (St. Paul, Minn., Oct. 1, 1992); *Fanfare of Rings*, for the 100th anniversary of the Cincinnati Sym. Orch. (1994; Cincinnati, Nov. 24, 1995); *Stipplings on Motley* for Chamber Orch. (St. Donats Castle, Wales, Aug. 17, 1995). **CHAMBER:** Trio for Clarinet, Cello, and Piano (1955; rev. 1963); *Expositions* for 9 Instruments (Vienna, April 8, 1970); *Eldey Island* for Wind Instrument and Tape (1971); *Circles in a Round* for Piano(s) and Optional Tape(s) (1972; Appleton, Wisc., Nov. 14, 1974); *Spring Song* for 5 Players and Spring Instruments (Minneapolis, June 13, 1980); Wind Quintet No. 2 (Minneapolis, May 1, 1981); *Tintinnabulary* for 2 Percussionists (1983); *Susquehannas* for Clarinet, Piano, and 2 Percussion (Minneapolis, March 2, 1985); *Brazen Cartographies* for Brass Quintet (Philadelphia, Nov. 6, 1988); *The Lyrical Pickpocket* for Flute, Oboe, Bassoon, and Toy Piano (Minneapolis, March 25, 1990); *Neon Nocturnes* for 8 Trombones (Kalamazoo, June 14, 1990); *Whittlings* for 4 Players (1992; St. Paul, Minn., March 13, 1993); *The Pickpocket is Lyrical Two* for Clarinet, Keyboard, and 2 Percussion (St. Paul, Minn., March 25, 1995); *Tantamounts* for 4 Flutes and String Quartet (N.Y., Aug. 15, 1996); *Shadows* for 2 Alto Saxophones (Minneapolis, April 21, 1996). **VOCAL:** *Smoke and Steel* for Tenor, Men's Chorus, and Orch. (Boston, May 14, 1958; rev. 1989); *The River's Minute by the Far Brook's Year* for Narrator, Chorus, and Orch. (Minneapolis, Nov. 18, 1981); *Peppercorn Songs* for Chorus and Piano or Optional Ensemble (Minneapolis, May 13, 1984); *Wondrous World* for Chorus and Tape (1984; East Berlin, Oct. 11, 1985); *Harbor Dawn and Proems* for Narrator, Chorus, and Orch. (St. Paul, Minn., May 8, 1986); *Firecho* for 5 or More Soloists and Optional Percussion (Minneapolis, Aug. 23, 1987); *Mermaids Stand by the King of the Sea* for Narrator, Chorus, and Orch. (St. Paul, Minn., Sept. 12, 1991); *Song Circle* for Soprano, Flute, and Harp (1993; N.Y., Jan. 16, 1994); *Pied Beauty* for Chorus, 2 Trumpets, 2 Horns, Timpani, and Organ (1997).—NS/LK/DM

Stokowski, Leopold (Anthony), celebrated, spectacularly endowed, and magically communicative English-born American conductor; b. London (of a Polish father and an Irish mother), April 18, 1882; d. Nether Wallop, Hampshire, Sept. 13, 1977. He attended Queen's Coll., Oxford, and the Royal Coll. of Music in London, where he studied organ with Stevenson Hoyte, theory with Walford Davies, and composition with Sir Charles Stanford. At the age of 18, he obtained the post of organist at St. James, Piccadilly. In 1905 he went to America and served as organist and choirmaster at St. Bartholomew's in N.Y.; he became a naturalized American citizen in 1915. In 1909 he was engaged to conduct the Cincinnati Sym. Orch.; although his contract was for 5 years, he obtained a release in 1912 in order to accept an offer from the Philadelphia Orch. This was the beginning of a long and spectacular career as a sym. conductor; he led the Philadelphia Orch. for 24 years as its sole conductor, bringing it to a degree of brilliance that rivaled the greatest orchs. in the world. In 1931 he was officially designated by the board of directors of the Philadelphia Orch. as music director, which gave him control over the choice of guest conductors and soloists. He conducted most of the repertoire by heart, an impressive accomplishment at the time; he changed the seating of the orch., placing violins to the left and cellos to the right. After some years of leading the orch. with a baton, he finally dispensed with it and shaped the music with the 10 fingers of his hands. He emphasized the colorful elements in the music; he was the creator of the famous "Philadelphia sound" in the strings, achieving a well-nigh bel canto quality. Tall and slender, with an aureole of blond hair, his figure presented a striking contrast with his stocky, mustachioed German predecessors; he was the first conductor to attain the status of a star comparable to that of a film actor. Abandoning the proverbial ivory tower in which most conductors dwelt, he actually made an appearance as a movie actor in the film *One Hundred Men and a Girl*. In 1940 he agreed to participate in the production of Walt Disney's celebrated film *Fantasia*, which featured both live performers and animated characters; Stokowski conducted the music and in one sequence engaged in a bantering colloquy with Mickey Mouse. He was lionized by the Philadelphians; in 1922 he received the Edward Bok Award of $10,000 as "the person who has done the most for Philadelphia." He was praised in superlative terms in the press, but not all music critics approved of his cavalier treatment of sacrosanct masterpieces, for he allowed himself to alter the orchestration; he doubled some solo passages in the brass, and occasionally introduced percussion instruments not provided in the score; he even cut out individual bars that seemed to him devoid of musical action. Furthermore, Stokowski's own orch. arrangements of Bach raised the pedantic eyebrows of professional musicologists; yet there is no denying the effectiveness of the sonority and the subtlety of color that he succeeded in creating by such means. Many great musicians hailed Stokowski's new orch. sound; Rachmaninoff regarded the Philadelphia Orch. under Stokowski, and later under Ormandy, as the greatest with which he had performed. Stokowski boldly risked his popularity with the Philadelphia audiences by introducing modern works. He conducted Schoenberg's music, culminating in the introduction of his formidable score Gurrelieder on April 8, 1932. An even greater gesture of defiance of popular tastes was his world premiere of *Amériques* by Varèse on April 9, 1926, a score that opens with a siren and thrives on dissonance. Stokowski made history by joining the forces of the Philadelphia Orch. with the Philadelphia Grand Opera Co. in the first American performance of Berg's masterpiece *Wozzeck* (March 31, 1931). The opposition of some listeners was now vocal; when the audible commotion in the audience erupted during his performance of Webern's Sym., he abruptly stopped conducting, walked off the stage, then returned only to begin the work all over again. From his earliest years with the Philadelphia Orch., Stokowski adopted the habit of addressing the audience, to caution them to keep their peace during the performance of a modernistic score, or reprimanding them for their lack of progressive views or for coughing during the music; once he even took to task the prim Philadelphia ladies for bringing their knitting to the concert. In 1933 the board of directors took an unusual step in announcing that there would be no more "debatable music" performed by the orch.; Stokowski refused to heed this

proclamation. Another eruption of discontent ensued when he programmed some Soviet music at a youth concert and trained the children to sing the Internationale. Stokowski was always interested in new electronic sound; he was the first to make use of the Theremin in the orch. in order to enhance the sonorities of the bass section. He was instrumental in introducing electrical recordings. In 1936 he resigned as music director of the Philadelphia Orch.; he was succeeded by Eugene Ormandy, but continued to conduct concerts as co-conductor of the orch. until 1938 and then occasionally until 1941. From 1940 to 1942 he took a newly organized All-American Youth Orch. on a tour in the U.S. and in South America. During the season 1942–43 he was assoc. conductor, with Toscanini, of the NBC Sym. Orch.; he shared the season of 1949–50 with Mitropoulos as conductor of the N.Y. Phil.; from 1955 to 1960 he conducted the Houston Sym. Orch. In 1960 he made a triumphant return to the Philadelphia orchestra after an absence of nearly two decades, prefacing his concert with remarks that began "As I was saying 19 years ago..." In 1962 he organized in N.Y. the American Sym. Orch. and led it until 1972; on April 26, 1965, at the age of 83, he conducted the orch. in the first complete performance of the fourth Sym. of Charles Ives. In 1973 he went to London, where he continued to make recordings and conduct occasional concerts until his death; he also appeared in television interviews. He died in his sleep at the age of 95; rumor had it that he had a contract signed for a gala performance on his 100th birthday in 1982. Stokowski was married 3 times: his first wife was **Olga Samaroff**, whom he married in 1911; they were divorced in 1923; his second wife was Evangeline Brewster Johnson, heiress to the Johnson and Johnson drug fortune; they were married in 1926 and divorced in 1937; his third marriage, to Gloria Vanderbilt, produced a ripple of prurient newspaper publicity because of the disparity in their ages; he was 63, she was 21; they were married in 1945 and divorced in 1955. Stokowski publ. *Music for All of Us* (N.Y., 1943), which was translated into the Russian, Italian, and Czech languages.

BIBL.: E. Johnson, ed., *S.: Essays in Analysis of His Art* (London, 1973); P. Robinson, *S.* (N.Y., 1977); A. Chasins, *L. S.: A Profile* (N.Y., 1979); O. Daniel, *S.: A Counterpoint of View* (N.Y., 1982); P. Opperby, *L. S.* (Tunbridge Wells and N.Y., 1982); W. Smith, *The Mystery of L. S.* (Rutherford, N.J., 1990). —NS/LK/DM

Stoliarsky, Piotr (Solomonovich), significant Russian violin pedagogue; b. Lipovets, near Kiev, Nov. 30, 1871; d. Sverdlovsk, April 29, 1944. He began his violin training with his father, then studied with S. Barcewica at the Warsaw Cons. and with E. Mlynarski and Josef Karbulka at the Odessa Music School (graduated, 1898). He played violin in the Odessa Opera orch. (1898–1914), and also taught in his own music school (from 1911). In 1920 he joined the faculty of the Odessa Cons., where he was made a prof. in 1923; opened another school for talented youths that was the first of its kind in the Soviet Union (1933). His role in musical pedagogy was similar to that of Auer in training students from limited backgrounds to attain international stature as virtuosi; among his notable pupils were Oistrakh, Gilels, and Milstein.—NS/LK/DM

Stolpe, Antoni, gifted Polish pianist and composer; b. Pulawy, near Lublin, May 23, 1851; d. Merano, Sept. 7, 1872. He studied piano with his father, Eduard Stolpe, then pursued composition studies with Freyer and Moniuszko at the Warsaw Music Inst., graduating with first prize in 1867; subsequently studied composition with Kiel and piano with Kullak in Berlin, and then taught piano there at the Stern Cons. until ill health forced him to abandon his career. His early death was lamented as a major loss for Polish music.

WORKS: Sym. (1867); Symphonic Overture (1868); Concerto Overture (1869); Piano Concerto (1869); 2 string quartets (1866, 1869); Piano Sextet (1867); 2 piano sonatas (1867, 1872); String Quintet (1868); Piano Trio (1869); *Variations* for String Quartet (1872); various piano pieces; *Credo* for Mixed Voices, Organ, and String Quintet (1867); songs.—NS/LK/DM

Stoltz, Rosine (real name, **Victoire Noël**), famous French mezzo-soprano; b. Paris, Feb. 13, 1815; d. there, July 28, 1903. She was the daughter of a janitor, and was sent by Duchess de Berri to a convent, and in 1826 to the Choron School, which she entered under the name of Rosine Niva; it was under that name that she began her career as a concert artist; then used the name of Mlle. Ternaux, and later Mlle. Héloïse Stoltz (the latter being derived from her mother's maiden name, Stoll). In 1832 she made her stage debut as Victoire Ternaux at the Théâtre Royal de la Monnaie in Brussels; after appearances in Spa, Antwerp, Amsterdam, and Lille, she obtained her first important engagement as Alice in *Robert le diable* at the Théâtre Royal de la Monnaie in Brussels in 1835; the next year she sang Rachel in *La Juive* there, and in 1837 married Alphonse Lescuyer, the theater's director. She made her debut at the Paris Opéra as Rachel on Aug. 25, 1837; subsequently appeared there in many premieres, including operas by Halévy; also created the roles of Ascanio in Berlioz's *Benvenuto Cellini* (Sept. 3, 1838), and Léonore in *La Favorite* (Dec. 2, 1840) and Zaida in *Dom Sébastien* (Nov. 13, 1843), both by Donizetti. She became intimate with Leon Pillet, manager of the Opéra from 1844, and through him wielded considerable influence on appointments of new singers; after a series of attacks in the press, accusing her of unworthy intrigues, she resigned in March 1847. She fought for vindication through 3 obviously inspired pamphlets (C. Cantinjou, *Les Adieux de Madame Stoltz*; E. Perignon, *Rosine Stoltz*; and J. Lemer, *Madame Rosine Stoltz*), all publ. in 1847. At the invitation of the Brazilian Emperor Don Pedro (who was romantically attached to her) she made 4 tours of Brazil between 1850 and 1859, at a salary of 400,000 francs a season. In 1854 and 1855 she once again sang at the Paris Opéra. In 1860 she made her farewell operatic appearance in Lyons, and then sang in concerts for several seasons before retiring. Ernst II of Württemberg named her Baroness Stoltzenau and Countess of Ketschendorf in 1865. She subsequently was made Duchess of Lesignano upon her marriage to Duke Carlo Lesignano in 1872, and then married the Spanish prince Manuel Godoi Bassano de la Paix in 1878. She publ. 6 songs (not composed by her, in all probability), and her name (as Princesse de Lesignano) was used as author of a learned vol., *Les Constitutions de tous les pays civilisés* (1880), which was written in her behalf. The mystifying aspects of her private life and public career are recounted by G. Bord in *Rosine Stoltz* (Paris, 1909) and by A. Pougin in "La Vérité sur Madame Stoltz," *Le Ménestrel* (Aug. 28, 1909, et seq.).—NS/LK/DM

Stoltzer, Thomas, important German composer; b. Schweidnitz, Silesia, c. 1480; d. (drowned in the Taja) near Znaim, Moravia, Feb. (?) 1526. He may have studied with Heinrich Finck, whose works he knew well. In 1519 became a priest in Breslau, where he held a benefice at St. Elisabeth's and was vicarius discontinuus at the Cathedral; was named magister capellae at the Hungarian royal court in Ofen by Ludwig II in 1522, where he composed his most important works. Stoltzer was one of the leading composers of sacred music of his era; his 14 Latin and 4 German Psalm motets are of a very high order. His *Octo tonorum melodiae*, 8 5-part instrumental fantasias arranged according to the church modes, is most likely the earliest motet-style cycle for instruments. Among his other works are masses, Magnificats, antiphons, hymns, Psalms, introits, sequences, responsories, and sacred and secular lieder. A number of his works were publ. in collections of his day; see also H. Albrecht and O. Gombosi, eds., *Thomas Stoltzer: Sämtliche lateinische Hymnen und Psalmen*, Denkmäler Deutscher Tonkunst, LXV (1931), and H. Albrecht and L. Hoffmann-Erbrecht, eds., *Thomas Stoltzer: Ausgewählte Werke*, I–II, ibid., XXII (1942) and LXVI (1969).

BIBL.: L. Hoffmann-Erbrecht, *T. S.: Leben und Schaffen* (Kassel, 1964).—NS/LK/DM

Stoltzman, Richard (Leslie), outstanding American clarinetist; b. Omaha, July 12, 1942. He began clarinet lessons when he was 8 and gained experience playing in local jazz settings with his father, an alto saxophonist. He then studied mathematics and music at Ohio State Univ. (B.Mus., 1964); also studied clarinet with Robert Marcellus; after studies at Yale Univ. (M.Mus., 1967), he completed his clarinet training with Harold Wright at the Marlboro Music School and with Kalman Opperman in N.Y.; pursued postgraduate studies at Columbia Univ.'s Teachers Coll. (1967–70). He played in many concerts at Marlboro; also founded the group Tashi ("good fortune" in Tibetan) with pianist Peter Serkin, violinist Ida Kavafian, and cellist Fred Sherry in 1973, and toured widely with the group; likewise taught at the Calif. Inst. of the Arts (1970–75). He made his N.Y. solo recital debut in 1974; after being awarded the Avery Fisher Prize in 1977, he pursued an international career as a virtuoso; appeared as soloist with major orchs., as a chamber music artist, and as a solo recitalist. In 1982 he became the first clarinetist ever to give a solo recital at N.Y.'s Carnegie Hall. In 1986 he received the Avery Fisher Artist Award. In 1989 he made his debut at the London Promenade Concerts as soloist in the Mozart Clarinet Concerto. He maintains an extensive repertoire, ranging from the classics to the avant-garde, and including popular music genres; he has also commissioned works and made his own transcriptions.—NS/LK/DM

Stolz, Robert (Elisabeth), noted Austrian conductor and composer; b. Graz, Aug. 25, 1880; d. Berlin, June 27, 1975. His father was the conductor and pedagogue Jacob Stolz and his mother the pianist Ida Bondy; after initial studies with them, he was a pupil of R. Fuchs at the Vienna Cons. and of Humperdinck in Berlin. He became a répétiteur in Graz in 1897, and after serving as second conductor in Marburg an der Drau (1898–1902), he was first conductor in Salzburg (1902–03) and at the German Theater in Brünn (1903–05). From 1905 to 1917 he was chief conductor of the Theater an der Wien, where he conducted the premieres of many Viennese operettas. He became successful as a composer of popular songs in the Viennese tradition; his first success as an operetta composer came with his *Der Tanz ins Glück* (Vienna, Oct. 18, 1921). In 1924 he went to Berlin, where he eventually won success as a composer for film musicals. His disdain for the Nazi regime led him to leave Germany in 1936 and then Austria in 1938, but not before he helped to smuggle numerous Jews out of the clutches of the Nazis prior to leaving for Paris in 1938. In 1940 he went to the U.S. and was active as a conductor and as a composer for Hollywood films. In 1946 he returned to Vienna, where he conducted and composed until his last years. He possessed an extraordinary facility for stage music and composed about 65 operettas and musicals in a typical Viennese manner; of these the most famous is *2 Herzen im 3/4 Takt* or *Der verlorene Walzer* (Zürich, Sept. 30, 1933). Other operettas are: *Die lustigen Weiber von Wien* (Munich, 1909); *Das Glücksmädel* (1910); *Das Lumperl* (Graz, 1915); *Lang, lang, ist's her* (Vienna, March 28, 1917); *Die Tanzgräfin* (Vienna, May 13, 1921); *Mädi* (Berlin, April 1, 1923); *Ein Ballroman oder Der Kavalier von zehn bis vier* (Vienna, Feb. 29, 1924); *Eine einzige Nacht* (Vienna, Dec. 23, 1927); *Peppina* (1931); *Wenn die kleinen Veilchen bluhen* (The Hague, April 1, 1932); *Venus im Seide* (Zürich, Dec. 10, 1932); *Der verlorene Walzer* (Zürich, Sept. 30, 1933); *Gruzi* (Zürich, 1934); *Frühling im Prater* (Vienna, Dec. 22, 1949); *Karneval in Wien* (1950); *Trauminsel* (Bregenz, July 21, 1962); *Frühjahrs-Parade* (Vienna, March 25, 1964). He wrote about 100 film scores and nearly 2,000 lieder. His other works include waltzes, marches, and piano pieces. After he was forced to leave Austria, he composed a funeral march for Hitler (at a time when Hitler was, unfortunately, very much alive).

BIBL.: G. Holm, *Im Dreivierteltakt durch die Welt* (Linz, 1948); W.-D. Brümmel and F. van Booth, *R. S.: Melodie eines Lebens* (Stuttgart, 1967); O. Herbrich, *R. S.: König der Melodie* (Vienna and Munich, 1975).—NS/LK/DM

Stolz, Teresa (real name, **Teresina Stolzová**), renowned Bohemian soprano; b. Elbekosteletz, June 5, 1834; d. Milan, Aug. 23, 1902. She was born into a musical family; her twin sisters, Francesca and Ludmila, also became sopranos; they were intimate with the composer Luigi Ricci, who had a child by each of them; Ludmila later became his wife. Teresa studied at the Prague Cons. and then with Ricci in Trieste (1856), making her operatic debut in 1857 in Tiflis, where she sang regularly during the next 5 seasons; also appeared in Odessa and Constantinople. In 1863 she sang in Turin, and thereafter appeared with brilliant success in the major Italian opera centers. She was closely associated with Verdi from 1872 to 1876, leading some writers to speculate that she was his mistress. She was without question one of the greatest interpreters of Verdi's heroines, excelling particularly as Aida and Leonora; she also sang in the premiere of his Requiem (1874). After singing in St. Petersburg (1876–77), she made her farewell appearance as a soloist in the Requiem at Milan's La Scala on June 30, 1879. Her vocal gifts were extraordinary and her range extended from g to c#[3].

BIBL.: J. Šolín, *T. S.ová: Proní a nejslavější Aida* (T. S.: The First and Most Celebrated Aida; Mlnik, 1944; second ed., 1946); U. Zoppi, *Mariani, Verdi e la S.* (Milan, 1947).—NS/LK/DM

Stolze, Gerhard, German tenor; b. Dessau, Oct. 1, 1926; d. Garmisch-Partenkirchen, March 11, 1979. He studied voice in Dresden and Berlin. He made his operatic debut as Augustin Moser in *Die Meistersinger von Nürnberg* at the Dresden State Opera in 1949. From 1951 he made regular appearances at the Bayreuth Festivals; also sang at the Vienna State Opera, and from 1953 to 1961 at the Berlin State Opera. He established his reputation as a Wagnerian singer, but also sang leading parts in German contemporary operas, including Satan in Martin's *Le Mystère de la Nativité* (1960).—NS/LK/DM

Stölzel (also **Stözl, Stöltzel**), **Gottfried Heinrich,** eminent German composer; b. Grundstädtl, near Schwarzenberg, Erzegebirge, Jan. 13, 1690; d. Gotha, Nov. 27, 1749. He began his musical training with his father, and at age 13 he entered the Schneerberg grammar school, where he received musical instruction from the Kantor, Christian Umlaufft. After attending the Gera Gymnasium, where he was encouraged by the Kapelle director, Emanuel Kegel, he went to Leipzig to study at the Univ. (1707); however, he soon turned to music and found a mentor in Melchior Hofmann, whom he served as copyist; his first compositions were performed under his teacher's name. He went to Breslau in 1710 and taught singing and keyboard; also brought out his first stage work there, *Narcissus*. After traveling throughout Italy (1713–15), he was active as a composer in Prague (1715–17) and in Bayreuth (1717–18). In 1718 he became Kapellmeister at the Gera court; in 1719 he went to the Saxe-Gotha court, where he then held the post of Kapellmeister from 1720 until his death. In addition to composing, he devoted much time to teaching. He also wrote the first significant treatise on recitative, *Abhandlung vom Recitativ* (MS; ed. by W. Steger, *Gottfried Heinrich Stolzel's "Abhandlung vom Recitativ,"* diss., Univ. of Heidelberg, 1962). In 1739 he was elected to membership in Mizler's Societät der Musikalischen Wissenschaften. A great portion of his music, including his stage and sacred vocal works, is lost.

BIBL.: W. Schmidt-Weiss, *G.H. S. als Instrumentalkomponist* (diss., Univ. of Munich, 1938); W. Steger, *G.H. S.s "Abhandlung vom Recitativ"* (diss., Univ. of Heidelberg, 1962); F. Hennenberg, *Das Kantatenschaffen von G.H. S.* (diss., Univ. of Leipzig, 1965; publ. in a rev. and abr. ed., Leipzig, 1976).—NS/LK/DM

Stone, Carl, innovative American composer and performer; b. Los Angeles, Feb. 10, 1953. He studied with Tenney and Subotnick at the Calif. Inst. of the Arts in Valencia (B.F.A., 1975). He served as music director of KPFK Radio in Los Angeles (1978–81) and as director of Meet the Composer/Calif. (from 1981); in 1985, was co-artistic director of the 7th New Music America Festival. Among his awards are an NEA grant (1981–82), tour support awards from the Calif. Arts Council (1984–90), and annual ASCAP awards (from 1985); in 1989 he was funded by the Asian Cultural Council for 6 months' residence in Japan. From 1992 to 1995 he served as president of the American Music Center. Stone composes exclusively electroacoustic music, often employing natural sounds and occasional fragments of familiar pieces, as in his *Sonali* (1988; *Die Zauberflöte*), *Hop Ken* (1987; Mussorgsky's *Pictures at an Exhibition*), and *Shing Kee* (1986; recording of a Japanese pop star singing a Schubert lied); Stone inscrutably manipulates his Macintosh computer in solo performances to create sensuous, playful, and often enigmatic real-time compositions. He is also an ethnic foods enthusiast (see J. Gold, "Carl Stone: Between Bytes," in *Los Angeles Times*, Aug. 19, 1990), naming many of his pieces after favorite restaurants. He has performed extensively in the U.S., Canada, Europe, Asia, Australia, South America, and the Near East; among choreographers who have used his music are Bill T. Jones, Ping Chong, and Blondell Cummings. His *Ruen Pair* (1993) was created as part of a (Paul Dresher) consortium commission from the Meet the Composer/Reader's Digest Fund; his untitled collaborative work with Kuniko Kisanuki for Electronics and Dancer (1995) was commissioned by the Aichi-ken Cultural Center in Nagoya, Japan. In 2000 he served as guest artistic director of the Other Minds Festival in San Francisco.

WORKS: TAPE: *LIM* (1975); *Maneeya* (1976); *Sukothai* (1979); *Unthaitled* (1979); *Chao Praya* (1980); *A Tip* (1980); *Thoughts in Stone* (1980); *Woo Lae Oak* (1980); *Jang* (1983). **ELECTRONICS:** *Busobong* (1980); *Kuk II Kwan* (1981); *Green Card March* (1981); *Dong II Jang* (1982); *Vault*, soundtrack (1982); *Woo Lae Oak* (1982); *Hama* (1983); *Torung* (1983); *Fanfare for Pershing Square* (1984); *Ho Ban* for Piano and Electronics (1984; also for Solo Piano, 1990); *Spalding Gray's Map of LA*, soundtrack (1984); *Mae Yao* (in 2 parts; 1984; also for Electronics and Percussion, 1989); *Rime* (1984); *Se Jong* (1984); *Shibucho* (1984); *Wave-Heat* (1984); *Everett & Jones* (1985); *Pho Bác* (1985); *Chia Heng* (1986); *Kappa* (1986); *Imae* (1986); *Samanluang* (1986); *Shing Kee* (1986); *Thanh My* (1986); *Vim* (1986); *Audible Structure* (1987); *Hop Ken* (1987; also for Electronics and Percussion, 1989); *Wall Me Do* (1987); *Amaterasu* (1988); *Amaterasu's Dance* (1988); *Jang Toh* (1988); *Mae* (1988); *Nekai* (1988); *Sonali* (1988); *Zang* (1988); *Zhang Toh* (1988); *Gadberry's* (1989; also for Electronics and Percussion); *Jakuzure* (1989; also *Jakuzure II* for Koto and Electronics and *Jakuzure III* for Flute and Electronics, 1991); *Keika* (1989); *Kokami* (1989); *Kong Joo* (1989; also for Electronics and Percussion); *She Gol Jib* (1989); *Chao Nue* (1990); *Mom's* (1990); *Banteay Srey* (1991); *Janken Pon* (1991); *Noor Mahal* (1991);

Recurring Cosmos (in 2 parts; 1991; also as a soundtrack); *Rezukuja* for Bass Marimba and Electronics (1991); *She Gol Jib* for Flute and Electronics (1991); *Dur-Pars*, soundtrack (1993); *Ruen Pair* for Violin, Clarinet, 2 Keyboards, Marimba, Drums, and Computer (1993); *Mae Ploy* for String Quartet and Electronics (1994); *Nyala* for Electronics (1995); an untitled collaborative work (with Kuniko Kisanuki) for Electronics and Dancer (1995); *Sudi Mampir* for Electronics (1995); *Wei-fun* for Audio Samples and Computer-generated Images (1996); *Music for the Noh Project* for Electronics and Noh Musicians (1996).—NS/LK/DM

Stone, Jesse, jazz pianist, arranger; b. Atchinson, Kans., 1901; d. Altamonte Springs, Fla., April 1, 1999. Raised in St. Joseph and Kansas City, Mo., Stone led his own Blues Serenaders from 1920; he later organized Blue Moon Chasers working in and around Dallas, Tex. He worked with George E. Lee in Kansas City, and then helped Terrence Holder organize new Clouds of Joy (1929). He was musical director for George E. Lee (1930–31), then co-director of Tharnon Hayes's Kansas City Rockets (1932–34). He led his own band, The Cyclones, in Chicago from 1935, and had residencies at the Morocco Club, etc. He continued to lead his own bands in the 1940s, and did a U.S.O. overseas tour. From the early 1950s Stone worked mainly as an A&R man for recording companies. He composed popular jazz pieces ("Idaho") and major R&B hits ("Shake, Rattle, and Roll" and "Money Honey").—JC/LP

Stone, Kurt, German-American musicologist; b. Hamburg, Nov. 14, 1911; d. Wilmington, N.C., June 15, 1989. He studied music in Hamburg and Copenhagen. He went to N.Y. in 1938 as a teacher at the Dalcroze School of Music; also worked for various music publishers from 1942; contributed knowledgeable articles on modern music and composers to various periodicals. With his wife, he ed. *The Writings of Elliott Carter* (1977); publ. *Music Notation in the Twentieth Century: A Practical Guide* (1980).—NS/LK/DM

Stoquerus, Gaspar (real name probably **Caspar Stocker**), German music theorist who flourished in the second half of the 16th century. He was active in Italy and then in Spain, where he studied with Francisco de Salinas at the Univ. of Salamanca. He wrote *De musica verbali* (c. 1570; ed. and tr. by A. Rotola as *The Two Books on Verbal Music*, Lincoln, Nebr., 1988), the only extant Renaissance treatise devoted entirely to text placement in vocal polyphony.—LK/DM

Storace, family of Italian-English musicians:

(1) Stephen (Stefano) Storace, double-bass player; b. Torre Annunziata, c. 1725; d. c. 1781. By 1748 he was in Dublin, where he played in the Smock Alley Theatre band. By 1758 he was in London, where he tr. several works for performance at Marylebone Gardens. He played in the band at the King's Theatre, and also at the 3 Choirs Festival (1759–70), then took his family to Italy in 1778. He had 2 children who became musicians:

(2) Stephen (John Seymour) Storace, noted composer; b. London, April 4, 1762; d. there, March 19, 1796. He entered the Cons. di S. Onofrio in Naples about 1776, where he studied violin, then followed his sister to Vienna, where he became acquainted with Mozart. Two of his operas to Italian librettos were produced in Vienna with satisfying success: *Gli sposi malcontenti* (June 1, 1785) and *Gli equivoci* (Dec. 27, 1786). In 1787 he returned to London, where he produced another Italian opera, *La Cameriera astuta* (March 4, 1788), and a number of English operas, among which *The Haunted Tower* (Nov. 24, 1789) became extremely successful. His finest work for the stage, *The Pirates*, was premiered at the King's Theatre on Nov. 21, 1792. During the 1792–93 season, he was in charge of the Italian opera productions at the Little Theatre and at Drury Lane. In addition to his many stage works, he also composed other vocal works and instrumental pieces.

BIBL.: J. Girdham, *English Opera in Late Eighteenth-Century London: S. S. at Drury Lane* (Oxford, 1997).

(3) **Nancy (Ann** or **Anna Selina) Storace,** celebrated soprano; b. London, Oct. 27, 1765; d. there, Aug. 28, 1817. She studied in London with Sacchini and Rauzzini. She began her career singing in concerts as a child, and appeared at Hereford's 3 Choirs Festival in 1777; the following year she was taken by her parents to Italy, where she began her operatic career in Florence in 1780; then sang in Parma (1781) and Milan (1782). In 1783 she went to Vienna as prima donna, excelling in the performance of comic operas. She married the English composer John Abraham Fisher, but the marriage did not last. She created the role of Susanna in Mozart's *Le nozze di Figaro* (May 1, 1786). In 1787 she returned to London and sang at the King's Theatre until it was destroyed by fire in 1789; then sang at Drury Lane until 1796, appeared in Handel's oratorios, and sang at the King's Theatre in 1793. In 1797 she toured Europe with the tenor John Braham, who became her lover. She continued to sing in London playhouses until her retirement from the stage in 1808. She and Braham lived together until 1816.

BIBL.: G. Brace, *Anna... Susanna: Anna Storace, Mozart's First Susanna: Her Life, Times, and Family* (London, 1991). —NS/LK/DM

Storchio, Rosina, Italian soprano; b. Venice, May 19, 1876; d. Milan, July 24, 1945. She studied at the Milan Cons.; then made her operatic debut at Milan's Teatro del Verme as Micaëla in *Carmen* in 1892. In 1895 she made her first appearance at Milan's La Scala as Sophie in *Werther*; in 1897 she sang in the premiere of Leoncavallo's *La Bohème* in Venice; returning to Milan, she appeared in the title role of Leoncavallo's *Zazà* at the Teatro Lirico in 1900; then appeared at La Scala (from 1902), where she sang in the premieres of several operas, including the title role of *Madama Butterfly* (Feb. 7, 1904); continued to appear there until 1918. After a series of tours in South America and in Europe, she was briefly engaged at N.Y.'s Manhattan Opera House and at the Chicago Grand Opera (1920–21); then retired from the stage. She was paralyzed during the last years of her life as a result of an apoplectic stroke. —NS/LK/DM

Story, Liz, American pianist and composer; b. Los Angeles, Oct. 28, 1956. She began playing piano at an early age, tackling Mozart's 11th concerto at the age of 11; when she was in high school, her family moved to Germany, where she studied languages, philosophy, and poetry. On returning to the U.S., she studied at Hunter Coll. (1977) and the Juilliard School in N.Y. (1978–79); heard jazz pianist Bill Evans, and recognized her own interest in improvisation. She began studying with Sanford Gold, returning to Los Angeles to study at the Univ. of Calif. and at the Dick Grove Music Workshops (1980–81). Her compositions are in reality new-age improvisations with impassioned gestures; among her recordings are *Solid Colors* (1982), *Unaccountable Effect* (1985), *Part of Fortune* (1986), *Escape of the Circus Ponies* (1990), *My Foolish Heart* (1992), *The Gift* (1994), *Liz Story* (1996), and *17 Seconds to Anywhere* (1998). —NS/LK/DM

Stott, Kathryn (Linda), remarkable English pianist; b. Nelson, Lancashire, Dec. 10, 1958. She was a student of Perlemuter and Boulanger at the Yehudi Menuhin School of Music in Stoke d'Abernon, and then of Kendall Taylor at the Royal Coll. of Music in London. In 1978 she won a prize at the Leeds Competition and made her debut at the Purcell Room in London. She then was engaged as a soloist with the principal British orchs. and with orchs. abroad, and also appeared as a recitalist and chamber music player in England and beyond. In 1995 she was artistic director of a Fauré festival in Manchester, the success of which led the French government to name her a Chevalière de l'Ordre des Arts et des Lettres that same year. Her collaboration with Yo-Yo Ma in a recording of works by Piazzolla in 1997 won a Grammy Award. That same year, she was soloist in the premiere of Maxwell Davies's Piano Concerto with the Royal Phil. of London. In 1998 she was artistic director of the "Out of the Shadows" festival in Liverpool, where she showcased the music of Fanny Mendelssohn and Clara Schumann, and where she appeared as soloist in the rarely performed Piano Concerto of the latter composer with the Royal Liverpool Phil. She was artistic director in 2000 of the "Piano 2000" festival in Manchester in which several modern works were highlighted. While Stott has not neglected works from the standard repertoire, she has done much to extend the repertoire to include neglected composers and contemporary scores. Her discerning and idiomatic recording of the complete solo piano music of Fauré is a notable example of her keyboard artistry, while her performances of such modern composers as John Adams, James Macmillan, Paul Schoenfield, and Marc Yeats have secured her reputation as a committed proponent of the music of her own era. —LK/DM

Stout, Alan (Burrage), significant American composer and teacher; b. Baltimore, Nov. 26, 1932. He studied composition with Henry Cowell at the Peabody Cons. of Music in Baltimore and took courses at Johns Hopkins Univ. (B.S., 1954); sporadically had composition lessons with Riegger in N.Y. (1951–56); pursued postgraduate studies at the Univ. of Copenhagen (1954–55); then had lessons with John Verrall at the Univ. of Wash. (1958–59), acquiring an M.A. in music and in Swedish language. From 1959 to 1962 he was employed in the music dept. of the Seattle Public Library; in 1963 he was appointed to the music faculty of Northwestern Univ.; in 1973 he was a visiting lecturer at the Stockholm Musikhögskolan. Besides his primary activities as a composer and a teacher, he also performed valuable service in editing (with some conjectural reconstruction) fragmentary pieces by Ives, to prepare them for practical performance.

WORKS: ORCH.: *3 Hymns* (1953–54); *Intermezzo* for English Horn, Percussion, and Strings (1954); *Pieta* for String or Brass Orch. (1957); 4 syms.: No. 1 (1959), No. 2 (1951–66; Chicago, Aug. 4, 1968), No. 3 for Soprano, Men's Chorus, and Orch. (1959–62), and No. 4 (1962–71; Chicago, April 15, 1971); *Serenity* for Solo Cello or Bassoon, Percussion, and Strings (1959); *Ricercare and Aria* for Strings (1959); *Movements* for Violin and Orch. (1962; Fish Creek, Wisc., Aug. 17, 1966); *Fanfare for Charles Seeger* (1972); *Pulsar* for 3 Brass Choirs and Timpani (1972); *Nimbus* for 18 Strings (1979); *Pilvia* (1983). CHAMBER: 10 string quartets (1952–53; 1952; 1954; 1954; 1957; 1959; 1960; 1960; 1962; 1962); *Solemn Prelude* for Trombone and Organ (1953); Quintet for Clarinet and String Quartet (1958); *Triptych* for Horn and Organ (1961); *Suite* for Flute and Percussion (1962); *Toccata* for Saxophone and Percussion (1965); Cello Sonata (1966); *Music* for Oboe and Piano (1966); *Music* for Flute and Harpsichord (1967); *2 Movements* for Clarinet and String Quartet (1968); *Recitative, Capriccio and Aria* for Oboe, Harp, and Percussion (1970); *Suite* for Saxophone and Organ (1973); Concertino for Clarinet and Chamber Ensemble (1978); *Meditation* for Tenor Saxophone and Organ (1982); Brass Quintet (1984). KEYBOARD: Piano: *Varianti* (1962); *Fantasia* (1962); Suite (1964–67); Sonata for 2 Pianos (1975); *Waltz* (1977). Organ: *8 Chorales* (1960); *Study in Densities and Durations* (1966–67); *3 Chorales* (1967); *Study in Timbres and Interferences* (1977); *Study in Timbres and Interferences* for Fully Mechanical Organ (1978). VOCAL: *2 Hymns* for Tenor and Orch. (1953); *Passion*, oratorio (1953–75; Chicago, April 15, 1976); *Die Engel* for Soprano, Flute, Piano, Percussion, and Brass (1957); *2 Ariel Songs* for Soprano and Chamber Ensemble (1957); *Elegiac Suite* for Soprano and Strings (1959–61); *Laudi* for Soprano, Baritone, and Small Orch. (1961); *Canticum canticorum* for Soprano and Chamber Ensemble (1962); *George Lieder* for High Baritone and Orch. (1962; rev. 1965 and 1970; Chicago, Dec. 14, 1972); *Christmas Poem* for Soprano and Chamber Ensemble (1962); *Prologue*, oratorio (1963–64); *Nattstycken* (Nocturnes) for Narrator, Contralto, and Chamber Ensemble (Chicago, Nov. 10, 1970); *Dialogo per la Pascua* for Soloists, Chorus, and 8 Instruments (1973); *O Altitudo* for Soprano, Women's Chorus, Solo Flute, and Instrumental Ensemble (1974); *5 visages de Laforgue* for Voice and Chamber Orch. (1978); *Triptych* for Soloists, Children's Chorus, and Orch. (1981); choruses, including *The Great Day of the Lord*, with Organ (1956).—NS/LK/DM

Stoutz, Edmond de, Swiss conductor; b. Zürich, Dec. 18, 1920; d. there, Jan. 28, 1997. He received training in law at the Univ. and in piano, cello, oboe, percussion, and composition at the Hochschule für Musik in Zürich. He completed his musical studies in Salzburg and Vienna, and began his career as a cellist in various ensembles in Zürich. In 1954 he founded the Zürich Chamber Orch., with which he toured widely as a conductor. In 1962 he also founded the Zürich Concert Choir. He retired in 1996. In addition to scores of the past, he invariably included works by contemporary composers in his programs.—NS/LK/DM

Stoyanov, Pencho, Bulgarian composer; b. Sofia, Feb. 9, 1931. He studied composition with Vladigerov at the Bulgarian State Cons. in Sofia, graduating in 1954. He then took courses at the Moscow Cons. Returning to Bulgaria, he taught at the Cons. in Sofia. He publ. theoretical texts, including *Interaction between the Musical Forms* (Sofia, 1975).

WORKS: ORCH.: 4 syms. (1958, 1971, 1971, 1975); *Divertimento* for Strings (1959); 2 violin concertos (1961, 1965); *2 Rhapsodies* (1963, 1969). CHAMBER: 2 violin sonatas (1953, 1970); 3 string quartets (1953, 1959, 1977); Concertino for Flute, Clarinet, and Bassoon (1969); Piano Quintet (1975); Piano Sonata (1965).—NS/LK/DM

Stoyanov, Veselin, Bulgarian composer; b. Shumen, April 20, 1902; d. Sofia, June 29, 1969. He studied piano with his brother Andrei Stoyanov at the Sofia Cons, graduating in 1926; then went to Vienna, where he studied with Joseph Marx and Franz Schmidt. In 1937 he was appointed prof. at the Cons. in Sofia; was director of the Cons. in 1943–44 and from 1956 to 1962.

WORKS: DRAMATIC: Opera: *Jensko zarstwo* (Kingdom of Women; Sofia, April 5, 1935); *Salambo* (Sofia, May 22, 1940); *Hitar Petar* (The Wise Peter; 1952; Sofia, 1958). Ballet: *Papessa Joanna* (1966; Sofia, Oct. 22, 1968). ORCH.: *Capriccio* (1934); *Bai Ganju* (Uncle Ganju), grotesque suite (1941); 3 piano concertos (1942, 1953, 1966); *Karwawa pessen* (Bloody Song; 1947); Violin Concerto (1948); Cello Concerto (1960); 2 syms.: No. 1 (1962) and No. 2, *Weliki Preslaw* (The Great Preslaw; 1969). CHAMBER: 3 string quartets (1933, 1934, 1935); Violin Sonata (1934); also piano works, including a Sonata (1930), Suite (1931), and *3 Pieces* (1956). VOCAL: *Da bade den* (Let There Be Day), cantata (1952); choral works.—NS/LK/DM

Stracciari, Riccardo, Italian baritone; b. Casalecchio di Reno, near Bologna, June 26, 1875; d. Rome, Oct. 10, 1955. He studied with Ulisse Masetti in Bologna, where he made his operatic debut as Marcello in 1898. He was a member of La Scala in Milan (1904–06); also sang at Covent Garden in London (1905). He made his debut at the Metropolitan Opera in N.Y. on Dec. 1, 1906, as Germont *père*; remained on the roster until 1908; then returned to Europe, continuing his career there and in South America. He returned to the U.S. to sing with the Chicago Opera (1917–19) and in San Francisco (1925); continued to make appearances in Italy until 1944; also was active as a teacher from 1926, his most eminent student being Boris Christoff. He sang all the major baritone roles in the operatic repertoire, his most famous being Rossini's Figaro, which he sang more than 900 times.—NS/LK/DM

Strada, Anna Maria, famous Italian soprano who flourished in the first half of the 18th century, also known under her married name as **Anna Maria Strada del Pò**. She was born in Bergamo. After serving Count Colloredo, governor of Milan, and singing in Venice (1720–21), she appeared in Naples (1724–26). She then was engaged by Handel for his opera and oratorio seasons in England, making her debut in London as Adelaide in the premiere of his *Lotario* in 1729, and remaining as his principal soprano until 1737. Handel also composed the following roles for her: Partenope (1730), Cleofide in *Poro* (1731), Fulvia in *Ezio* (1732), Elmira in *Sosarme* (1732), Angelica in *Orlando* (1733), Deborah (1733), Josabeth in *Athalia* (1733), Arianna (1734), Erato in *Terpsicore* (1734), Ginevra in *Ariodante* (1735), Alcina (1735), the soprano part in *Alexander's Feast* (1736), Atalanta (1736), Tusnelda in *Arminio* (1737), Arianna in *Giustino* (1737), Berenice (1737), and Bellezza in *Il trionfo del tempo* (1737). In 1738 she was called to Breda to sing for the Princess of Orange; after appearances with Senesino in Naples (1739–40), she retired to Bergamo.—NS/LK/DM

Stradal, August, Bohemian pianist; b. Teplitz, May 17, 1860; d. Schönlinde, Germany, March 13, 1930. He studied composition with Bruckner at the Vienna Cons. and piano with Door; was a pupil of Liszt in 1884, and became an ardent propagandist for Liszt's piano music. He gave concerts in Germany, Austria, France, and England, and also made arrangements of Liszt's orch. works; also of works by Bach, Frescobaldi, etc. His original compositions consist of piano pieces (*Ungarische Rhapsodie*, etc.) and songs. He wrote *Erinnerungen an Franz Liszt* (Bern, 1929).

BIBL.: H. Stradal, *A. S.s Lebensbild* (Bern, 1934). —NS/LK/DM

Stradella, Alessandro, important Italian composer; b. Nepi, near Viterbo, 1639; d. (murdered) Genoa, Feb. 25, 1682. He was a scion of nobility, and received his early training in Bologna. In 1667 he went to Rome, where he composed oratorios, prologues, intermezzos for opera, etc. He led a tempestuous life, replete with illicit liaisons, flights from personal vendettas, and some criminal acts. In Rome he attempted to embezzle funds from the Roman Catholic church, and in 1669 fled the city to avoid exposure. He returned to Rome after the affair calmed down, but again got in trouble when he aroused the enmity of Cardinal Alderan Cibo. In 1677 he was forced to flee Rome again, and he went to Venice, where he became involved in a torrid affair with the fiancee of the Venetian nobleman Alvise Contarini; he persuaded the lady to accompany him to Turin, and the outraged bridegroom and a band of assassins followed in hot pursuit. Stradella escaped and fled to Genoa. There he became entangled with a married woman, a sister of the Lomellini brothers, who had a high social standing in the town. This time Stradella failed to evade the vengeful brothers, who hired an experienced murderer to kill him; the bloody deed was done on Feb. 25, 1682. A rather successful opera, *Alessandro Stradella* by Flotow (Hamburg, 1844), dramatized his stormy life and death; other operas on Stradella were composed by Niedermeyer (Paris, 1837) and Sinico (Lugo, 1863).

As a composer, Stradella left an important legacy, both in opera and in instrumental writing. His operas *La forza dell'amor paterno, Le gare dell'amore eroico,* and *Il Trespole tutore* were staged in Genoa (1678–79); he also composed the oratorio *La Susanna* and a wedding serenade, *Il barcheggio,* for Duke Francesco d'Este of Modena (1681). Other operas were *Il moro per amore, Il Corispero,* and *Doriclea.* His oratorios include *S. Giovanni*

Battista and *S. Giovanni Crisostomo;* another oratorio, *S. Editta, vergine e monaca, regina d'Inghilterra,* remained unfinished. He wrote about 25 sinfonias (sonatas), most of them for violin with basso ostinato, motets, arias, and canzonettas. An ed. of his oratorios was begun in 1969, under the editorship of L. Bianchi.

BIBL.: A. Catelani, *Delle opere di A. S. esistenti nell'archivio musicale della R. Biblioteca Palatina di Modena* (Modena, 1866); H. Hess, *Die Opern A. S.'s,* in *Publicationen der Internationalen Musik-Gesellschaft,* supplement, II/3 (1906); F. Crawford, *S.* (London, 1911); A. Gentili, *A. S.* (Turin, 1936); G. Roncaglia, *Il genio novatore di A. S.* (Modena, 1941); O. Jander, *A Catalogue of the Manuscripts of Compositions by A. S. Found in European and American Libraries* (Wellesley, Mass., 1960; second ed., rev., 1962); R. Giazotto, *Vita di A. S.* (2 vols., Milan, 1962); O. Jander, *A. S. and His Minor Dramatic Works* (diss., Harvard Univ., 1962); L. Bianchi, *Carissimi, S., Scarlatti e l'oratorio musicale* (Rome, 1969); C. Gianturco, *The Operas of A. S. (1644–1682)* (diss., Univ. of Oxford, 1970); idem, ed., *A. S. e Modena* (Modena, 1983); C. Gianturco and E. McCrickard, *A. S. (1639–1682): A Thematic Catalog of His Compositions* (Stuyvesant, N.Y., 1991). —NS/LK/DM

Stradivari (Latinized as **Stradivarius**), **Antonio,** celebrated Italian violin maker; b. probably in Cremona, 1644; d. probably there, Dec. 18, 1737. He was a pupil of Niccolò Amati in the early 1660s. His earliest known violin dates from 1666; he may have worked for Amati and others from 1666 before purchasing the house that contained his workshop from 1680. His finest instruments were made in the period from 1700 to 1725, but he still worked up to the year of his death; he made his last instrument at the age of 92. His label reads: "Antonius Stradivarius Cremonensis. Fecit Anno...(A x S)." His cellos command even higher prices than the violins, and violas the highest of all, for he made very few of them. Stradivari had 11 children; of them Francesco (b. Feb. 1, 1671; d. May 11, 1743) and Omobono (b. Nov. 14, 1679; d. July 8, 1742) were his co-workers. Stradivari also made viols of early types, guitars, lutes, mandolins, etc.

BIBL.: F.J. Fétis, *A. S., Luthier célèbre* (Paris, 1856; Eng. tr., London, 1864); P. Lombardini, *Cenni sulla celebre scuola Cremonense degli stromenti ad arco e sulla famiglia del sommo A. S.* (Cremona, 1872); A. Reichers, *The Violin and the Art of Its Construction; A Treatise on S.* (1895); H. Petherick, *A. S.* (London, 1900); W.H., A.F., and A.E. Hill, *A. S. His Life and Work* (London, 1902); A. Mandelli, *Nuove indagini su A. S.* (Milan, 1903); H. Herrmann, *Geschichte und Beschreibung von zwei Meisterwerken des A. S.* (N.Y., 1929); R. Bacchetta, *S.* (1937); G. Hoffmann, *S. l'enchanteur* (Paris, 1938); W. Orcutt, *The S. Memorial at Washington, D.C.* (Washington, D.C., 1938); M. Boger, *Das Geheimnis des S.* (Berlin, 1944); D. Balfoort, *A. S.* (Amsterdam, 1945; also in Eng.); E. Doring, *How Many Strads?...A Tabulation of Works Believed to Survive, Produced in Cremona by A. S. between 1666 and 1737* (Chicago, 1945); G. Ottani, *S.* (Milan, 1945); H. Goodkind, *Violin Iconography of A. S. 1644–1737* (Larchmont, N.Y., 1972); S. Sacconi, *I "segreti" di S.* (Cremona, 1972); E. Santoro, *A. S.* (Cremona, 1987).—NS/LK/DM

Straesser, Joep, Dutch composer and teacher; b. Amsterdam, March 11, 1934. He studied musicology at the Univ. of Amsterdam (1952–55), then took organ lessons with Van der Horst (1956–59) and theory lessons with Felderhof (1959–61) at the Amsterdam Cons.; also received instruction in composition from Ton de Leeuw (1960–65). He was a church organist (1953–61). From 1962 to 1989 he taught at the Utrecht Cons.

WORKS: *5 Close-ups* for Piano (1960–61; rev. 1973); *Music for Oboe Quartet* (1962); *Psalmus* for Men's Chorus, Winds, and Percussion (1963); *22 Pages* for Wind Orch., Percussion, and 3 Men's Voices, after John Cage essays (Hilversum, Sept. 14, 1965); String Quartet No. 2 (1966); *Chorai* for 48 Strings and Percussion (1966; Hilversum, Sept. 14, 1967; re-composed in 1974 for Full Orch. and retitled *Chorai Revisited*); *Duet* for 2 Cellos (1967); *Seismograms* for 2 Percussionists (1967; rev. 1979); *Adastra*, music for ballet (1967); *Summer Concerto* for Oboe and Chamber Orch. (1967; Graz, Oct. 24, 1969); *Ramasasiri* (Traveling Song) for Soprano, Flute, Vibraphone, Piano, and 2 Percussionists, on texts in the Papuan language (1967–68); *Musique pour l'homme* for Soprano, Alto, Tenor, Bass, and Orch. (1968; Amsterdam, Dec. 9, 1968); *Missa* for Chorus and Wind Instruments (1969); *Intersections I* for Wind Quintet and 5 Instrumental Groups spatially positioned (1969), *II* for 100 or More Musicians (1970; Amsterdam, April 3, 1971; except for percussionists, all orch. members improvise freely), *III* for Piano (1971), *IV* for Oboe, Violin, Viola, and Cello (1972), *V (A Saxophone's World)* for 4 Saxophones (1974; rev. 1979), and *V–2* for Bass Clarinet and Piano (1975); *Sight-Seeing I, II, III* for Flute and Prepared Piano (1969), *IV* for Double Bass (1970), and *V (Spring Quartet)* for String Quartet (1971); *Emergency Case* for Flute, Piano, and Percussion (1970); *Enclosures* for Winds and Percussion (1970; as a ballet, Rotterdam, Oct. 3, 1971); *Eichenstadt und Abendstern*, 6 songs for Soprano and Piano (1972); *Encounters* for Bass Clarinet and 6 Percussionists (1973); *Chorai Revisited* for Orch. (1975); *Intervals I* for Chamber Chorus, Flute, Cello, and Harp (1975–76), *II* for Chorus and Instruments (1979), and *III: Longing for the Emperor*, 5 songs for Soprano, Clarinet, Mandolin, Guitar, Percussion, Viola, and Double Bass, after early Japanese texts (1981); *3 Psalms* for Chorus and Organ (1976); "*Just a moment...*" for Piano Trio (1978); "*Just a moment again...*" for Piano, 2 Percussion, and Strings (1978); *Fusian a six*, symphonic music (1980); *Signals and Echoes* for Bass Clarinet and Orch. (1982); *Winter Concerto* for Soprano Saxophone and Orch. (1984); *Ueber Erich M.*, Singspiel (1985–86); *Verzauberte Lieder* for Chorus and Orch. (1986); *Triplum* for Violin, Viola, and Cello (1986); *Faites vos jeux* for Organ (1986); *Motetus* for Chorus (1987); Chamber Concerto I for Cello, Winds, Harp, and Percussion (1991), II for Harp and Chamber Orch. (1993), and III for Flute and Chamber Orch. (1993); Sym. No. 3 (1992).—NS/LK/DM

Strakosch, Maurice, Bohemian pianist and impresario; b. Gross-Seelowitz, near Brünn, Jan. 15, 1825; d. Paris, Oct. 9, 1887. He studied with Sechter at the Vienna Cons., then traveled as a pianist in Europe. He went to N.Y. in 1848 as a teacher, and from 1856 he was active mainly as an impresario. He was the brother-in-law of **Adelina Patti**, and managed her concerts; he, his wife, and Ole Bull toured the U.S. (1852–54). Returning to N.Y., he, his brother Max Strakosch (b. Gross-Seelowitz, Sept. 27, 1835; d. N.Y., March 17, 1892), and Bull organized a brief opera season at the Academy of Music in 1855. He then ran his own company (1856–57), which merged with Bernard Ullman's company in 1857; their partnership lasted until 1860, when he again became Patti's manager. In 1861 he went to Europe with the Pattis, and remained Patti's manager until 1868; also

continued to work with his brother, who remained in the U.S. Maurice remained active as a pianist, making tours of Europe and the U.S. with Bull. He also composed, producing the opera *Giovanna di Napoli*. He wrote *Souvenirs d'un impresario* (Paris, second ed., 1887) and *Ten Commandments of Music for the Perfection of the Voice* (1896).—NS/LK/DM

Strang, Gerald, inventive American composer; b. Claresholm, Canada, Feb. 13, 1908; d. Loma Linda, Calif., Oct. 2, 1983. He studied at Stanford Univ. (B.A., 1928) and at the Univ. of Southern Calif. in Los Angeles (Ph.D., 1948); also took private lessons in composition with Toch and Schoenberg, and served as Schoenberg's assistant at the Univ. of Calif. at Los Angeles (1936–38). He taught at Long Beach City Coll. (1938–43; 1945–58); in 1958 he founded the music dept. at San Fernando Valley State Coll. (later Calif. State Univ.) at Northridge, where he taught until 1965; then was chairman of the music dept. at Calif. State Univ. at Long Beach (1965–69); subsequently taught electronic music at the Univ. of Calif. (1969–74). His music is strongly formal, with a unifying technical idea determining the content. An intelligent, energetic, and astute musical technician, he experimented successfully with the new resources available in the fields of acoustics, electronics, and computers; he was also active as an ed. of modern works and was for many years an assoc. of Henry Cowell in editing Cowell's *New Music Quarterly*. The titles of his compositions give clues to their formative semiotics; thus his piano piece *Mirrorrorrim* is an obvious palindrome or cancrizans. His series of 4 *Synclavions* is an electronic synthesis of keyboard variations. Similarly suggestive are his various pieces bearing such titles as *Compusitions* (= computerized compositions) and *Synthions* (= synthetic ions). Strang was also active in the field of acoustics, and served as a consultant on some 25 newly built auditoriums in Calif. and elsewhere.

WORKS: ORCH.: Suite for Chamber Orch. (1934–35); 2 syms. (1938–42; 1946–47); *Canzonet* for Strings (1942); *Overland Trail* (1943); Overture (1943); Concerto Grosso (1950); Cello Concerto (1951). **CHAMBER:** Clarinet Sonatina (1932); Quintet for Clarinet and Strings (1933); String Quartet (1934); *Percussion Music* for 3 Percussion (1935); *Divertimento* for 4 Woodwinds or Strings (1948); Violin Sonata (1949); Flute Sonata (1951); *Variations* for 4 Woodwinds or Strings (1956); piano pieces. **OTHER:** Tape and electronic pieces.

BIBL.: M. Berman, *G. S.: Composer, Educator, Acoustician* (thesis, Calif. State Univ., Long Beach, 1977).—NS/LK/DM

Strangways, A(rthur) H(enry) Fox
See **Fox Strangways, A(rthur) H(enry)**

Stransky, Josef, Bohemian conductor; b. Humpoletz, near Deutschbrod, Sept. 9, 1872; d. N.Y., March 6, 1936. While studying medicine (M.D., Univ. of Prague, 1896), he also studied music in Leipzig with Jadassohn and in Vienna with R. Fuchs, Bruckner, and Dvořák. In 1898 he was engaged by A. Neumann as first Kapellmeister at the Landestheater in Prague; in 1903 he went in a similar capacity to the Stadttheater in Hamburg; in

1910 he resigned from the Hamburg opera to devote himself to concert work; in the autumn of 1911 became Mahler's successor as conductor of the N.Y. Phil. Soc.; a position he held until 1923. A bequest of $1,000,000 to the society (by Joseph Pulitzer, 1912) enabled Stransky to carry out successfully the sweeping reforms instituted by his illustrious predecessor (chief of which was a system of daily rehearsals during the season of 23 weeks). In 1924 he gave up his musical career and spent the rest of his life as an art dealer. He wrote an operetta, *Der General*, which was produced in Hamburg, orch. works, instrumental pieces, and songs.

BIBL.: H. Shanet, *Philharmonic. A History of New York's Orchestra* (Garden City, N.Y., 1975).—NS/LK/DM

Straram, Walther, French conductor; b. London (of French parents), July 9, 1876; d. Paris, Nov. 24, 1933. He was educated in Paris. He played violin in Paris orchs., then was choirmaster at the Opéra-Comique there; later traveled to America as assistant to André Caplet at the Boston Opera Co. Returning to Paris, he established the Concerts Straram, which enjoyed a fine reputation. He conducted the first performance of Ravel's *Bolero* for Ida Rubinstein (dance recital, Nov. 22, 1928).—NS/LK/DM

Strassburg, Robert, American conductor, teacher, and composer; b. N.Y., Aug. 30, 1915. He studied composition with Marion Bauer at N.Y.U., then enrolled at Harvard Univ. (M.A., 1950). He was conductor and founder of the All-Miami Youth Sym. (1957–60). In 1961 he joined the faculty of the Univ. of Judaism in Los Angeles; from 1966 he was on the faculty of Calif. State Coll. His works include *4 Biblical Statements* for Strings (1946), *Fantasy and Allegro* for Violin and Orch. (1947), *Torah Sonata* for Piano (1950), *Chelm*, folk opera (1956), and *Tropal Suite* for Strings (1967). He is the author of a monograph, *Ernest Bloch, Voice in the Wilderness* (Los Angeles, 1977).—NS/LK/DM

Stratas, Teresa (real name, **Anastasia Stratakis**), outstanding Canadian soprano; b. Toronto, May 26, 1938. She was born into a family of Greek immigrant restaurateurs. At 12, she began voice training and, at 13, appeared on the radio singing pop songs. In 1954 she entered the Royal Cons. of Music of Toronto to study with Irene Jessner, and in 1959 was awarded her Artist Diploma. In 1958 she sang Nora in Vaughan Williams's *Riders to the Sea* in Toronto. On Oct. 13, 1958, she made her professional operatic debut as Mimi at the Toronto Opera Festival. In 1959 she was a co-winner in the Metropolitan Opera Auditions, which led to her debut with the company in N.Y. on Oct. 28, 1959, as Poussette in *Manon*. She continued to sing at the Metropolitan, winning her first notable success as Liù in 1961. On Aug. 19, 1961, she created the title role in Peggy Glanville-Hicks's *Nausicaa* in Athens. On June 18, 1962, she made her debut at Milan's La Scala as Queen Isabella in the posthumous premiere of Falla's *Atlántida*. She appeared as Desdemona in *Otello* at Expo '67 in Montreal in 1967. In 1974 she starred as Salome in the film version conducted by Karl Böhm. On May 28, 1979,

she sang the title role in the first performance of the complete version of Berg's *Lulu* in Paris. She sang Violetta in Zeffirelli's film version of *La Traviata* in 1983. In 1986 she appeared on Broadway. On Dec. 19, 1991, she sang Marie Antoinette in the premiere of Corigliano's *The Ghosts of Versailles* at the Metropolitan Opera. In 1992 she appeared as Mélisande in Chicago. Stratas was made an Officer of the Order of Canada in 1972. A film portrait of her was made by Harry Rasky as *StrataSphere*. Stratas's remarkable lyric voice made her interpretations of such roles as Cherubino, Zerlina, Lisa in *The Queen of Spades*, Marguerite in *Faust*, Micaëla, Liù, and Weill's Jenny particularly memorable.

BIBL.: H. Rasky, *S.: An Affectionate Tribute* (Oxford, 1989). —NS/LK/DM

Strategier, Herman, Dutch composer, organist, and teacher; b. Arnhem, Aug. 10, 1912; d. Doorwerth, Oct. 26, 1988. He studied music with his father, a church organist, and with H. Andriessen. He succeeded his father as organist at St. Walpurgis at Arnhem in 1935, but the church was destroyed in war action in 1944. He taught at the Inst. for Catholic Church Music in Utrecht (1939–63); also taught there at the Cons. and at the Univ., and likewise at the Univ. of Rotterdam. He was notable mainly as a composer of liturgical music of the Roman Catholic rite.

WORKS: ORCH.: *Divertimento* for Strings and 4 Winds (1937); Flute Concerto (1943); *Haarlem-suite* (1945–47); *Ramiro-suite* (1946); Piano Concerto (1947–48); Sym. No. 1 (1949); Clarinet Concertino (1950); *Musique pour faire plaisir* for Strings (1950); *Intrada sinfonica* (1954); *Rondo giocoso* (1955); *Rapsodia elegiaca* (1956); *Turandot-suite* (1956); *Kadullen Varieties* for Flute, Bassoon, and Strings (1958); *Triptych* for Piano and Wind Orch. (1960); Accordion Concerto (1969); *Concertante Speelmuziek* for Flute, Bassoon, and Orch. (1970); *Intrada festiva* (1976); Sonatine (1978); Basset Horn Concerto (1981); *Cassation* (1983). **CHAMBER:** 3 string quartets (1935, 1936, 1937); *3 pieces* for Oboe and String Quartet (1937); Sextet for Piano and Wind Quintet (1951); Suite for Harp (1961); Quartet for Flute, Violin, Viola, and Cello (1968); *Curven* for Accordion and String Quartet (1970); *Divertissement* for Oboe, Clarinet, and Bassoon (1970); Suite for Piano and Harpsichord (1973); Piano Trio (1974); *Sonata da camera* for Flute, Oboe, Violin, Viola, Cello, and Piano (1978); *5 Pieces* for Harp (1986). **KEYBOARD: Piano:** Suite for Piano, 4-Hands (1945); Sonata (1948); Sonatina (1951); *Tema con variazioni* for Piano, 4-Hands (1952); *Elegie* (1954); *4 pièces brèves* for Piano, 4-Hands (1973); *3 Speelmuziekjes* (1974); *6 études* (1974); *Zes preludes* (1986). **Organ:** *Preludium, Intermezzo and Theme with Variations* (1939); *Ritornello capriccioso* (1944); *Toccatina* (1951); *Chaconne* (1955); *Voluntary* (1975). **VOCAL:** *Stabat Mater* for Chorus and Small Orch. (1939); *Septem cantica* for Mezzo-soprano and Piano (1941); *4 Drinkleideren* for Baritone and Orch. (1945); *Van der mollenfeeste*, old ballad for Chorus and Small Orch. (1947–48); *Henric van Veldeke* for Narrator, Baritone, and Orch. (1952); *5 Minneliederen* for Middle Voice, Flute, and Small String Orch. (1952); *Koning Swentibold*, oratorio (1955); *Arnhemsche Psalm* for Narrator, Soloists, Chorus, and Orch. (1955); *Rembrandt Cantata* (1956); *Requiem* for Chorus, Wind Quintet, and Strings (1961); *Ballade van de Maagd van Wognum* for Chorus and Orch. (1965); *Plaisanterie* for Chorus and Orch. (1966); *Te Deum* for Soprano, Alto, Chorus, and Orch. (1967); *Colloquia familiaria* for Soprano, Chorus, and String Orch. (1969); *Zoo, Buddingh'zoo* for Baritone, Chorus, and Small Orch. (1970);

Ligeia or The Shadow Out of Time for Chorus, Flute, 6 Percussionists, Organ, and Harp (1973); *De hond* (De Schoolmeester) for Children's Chorus and Orch. (1979); *Hasseltsch meilied* for Chorus and Orch. (1981); *Lof van Walcheren* for Chorus and Orch. (1982); *Hazerswoude* for Chorus and Orch. (1984); choruses; songs.—NS/LK/DM

Straube, (Montgomery Rufus) Karl (Siegfried), prominent German organist, choral conductor, and pedagogue; b. Berlin, Jan. 6, 1873; d. Leipzig, April 27, 1950. He was a scion of an established ecclesiastical family; his father was an organist and instrument maker in Berlin; his mother was an Englishwoman who was a piano student of Sir Julius Benedict. He studied organ with his father, Dienel, Reimann, and others in Berlin, where he became deputy organist at the Kaiser-Wilhelm-Gedächtniskirche in 1895. From 1897 to 1902 he was organist at the Cathedral of Wesel; in 1902 he became organist at the Thomaskirche in Leipzig; in 1903 he was appointed conductor of the Bachverein there, and in 1907 became a prof. at the Cons. and organist ex officio at the Gewandhaus. In 1918 he became cantor at the Thomaskirche. At his suggestion the Gewandhaus Chorus and the Bachverein were united in 1919, and he conducted the combined choir until 1932. He conducted the Handel Festival in 1925, leading to the formation of the Handel Soc. In his teaching, he followed the great tradition of Leipzig organists, traceable to Bach. Among Straube's numerous collections of organ and choral pieces are *Alte Orgelmeister* (1904); *45 Choralvorspiele alter Meister* (1907); *Alte Meister des Orgelspiels* (2 vols., 1929); *Ausgewahlte Gesänge des Thomanerchors* (1930); he brought out eds. of several works of Bach, Handel, and Liszt. His *Briefe eines Thomaskantors* was publ. posthumously (Stuttgart, 1952).

BIBL.: J. Wolgast, *K. S.* (Leipzig, 1928); *K. S. zu seinem 70. Geburtstag* (Leipzig, 1943); G. Hartmann, *K. S. und seine Schule: "Das Ganze ist ein Mythos"* (Bonn, 1991).—NS/LK/DM

Straus, Oscar (Nathan), noted Austrian-born French operetta composer and conductor; b. Vienna, March 6, 1870; d. Bad Ischl, Jan. 11, 1954. (His name was spelled "Strauss" on his birth certificate; he cut off the second *s* to segregate himself from the multitudinous musical Strausses.) He studied privately in Vienna with A. Prosnitz and H. Gradener, and with Max Bruch in Berlin. From 1893 to 1900 he conducted at various theaters in Austria and Germany. In 1901 he became conductor of the artistic cabaret Uberbrettl in Berlin, and wrote a number of musical farces for it. He remained in Berlin until 1927; then lived in Vienna and Paris; on Sept. 3, 1939, he became a naturalized French citizen. In 1940 he went to America; lived in N.Y. and Hollywood until 1948, when he returned to Europe. He was one of the most successful composers of Viennese operettas. His most celebrated production was *Der tapfere Soldat*, based on G.B. Shaw's play *Arms and the Man* (Vienna, Nov. 14, 1908; in N.Y. as *The Chocolate Soldier*, Nov. 13, 1909; London, Sept. 10, 1910; numerous perfs. all over the world). Other operettas were: *Die lustigen Nibelungen* (Vienna, Nov. 12, 1904); *Hugdietrichs Brautfahrt* (Vienna, March 10, 1906); *Ein Walzertraum* (Vienna, March 2, 1907; rev. 1951); *Didi* (Vienna, Oct. 23, 1909); *Das Tal der Liebe* (Berlin and Vienna, simultaneously, Dec. 23, 1909); *Mein junger Herr* (Vienna, Dec. 23, 1910); *Die kleine Freundin* (Vienna, Oct. 20, 1911); *Love and Laughter* (London, 1913); *Rund um die Liebe* (Vienna, Nov. 9, 1914; in N.Y. as *All around Love*, 1917); *Die himmelblaue Zeit* (Vienna, Feb. 21, 1914); *Die schöne Unbekannte* (Vienna, Jan. 15, 1915; in N.Y. as *My Lady's Glove*, 1917); *Der letzte Walzer* (Berlin, Feb. 12, 1920); *Mariette, ou Comment on écrit l'histoire* (Paris, Oct. 1, 1928); *Eine Frau, die weiss was sie will* (Berlin, Sept. 1, 1932); *Drei Walzer* (Zürich, Oct. 5, 1935); *Die Musik kommt* (Zürich, 1948; rev. as *Ihr erster Walzer*, Munich, May 16, 1952); *Bożena* (Munich, May 16, 1952). Among his other works were ballets, film scores, orch. music, chamber pieces, choruses, about 500 cabaret songs, and piano pieces.

BIBL.: B. Grun, *Prince of Vienna: The Life, the Times, and the Melodies of O. S.* (London, 1955); F. Mailer, *Weltburger der Musik: Eine O.-S.-Biographie* (Vienna, 1985).—NS/LK/DM

Strauss, family of celebrated Austrian musicians:

(1) Johann (Baptist) Strauss (I), violinist, conductor, and composer, known as "The Father of the Waltz"; b. Vienna, March 14, 1804; d. there, Sept. 25, 1849. He was born into a humble Jewish family of Hungarian descent. Called "black Schani," he made a concerted effort to conceal his Jewish origins (when the ancestry of the family was realized by the chagrined Nazis a century later, they falsified the parish register at St. Stephen's Cathedral in 1939 to make the family racially pure). His father was an innkeeper who apprenticed him to a bookbinder, but his musical talent revealed itself at an early age; after Strauss ran away, his parents consented to his becoming a musician. He studied violin under Polyschansky and harmony under Seyfried, and at 15 became a violist in Michael Pamer's dance orch., where he found a friend in Josef Lanner. In 1819 he became a member of the latter's small band, and later served as second conductor of Lanner's orch. (1824–25). In 1825 he organized his own orch., which quickly became popular in Viennese inns. He composed his first waltz, *Täuberln-Walzer*, in 1826. His reputation was secured with his appearances at the Sperl, where Pamer served as music director. His renown spread, and his orch. increased rapidly in size and efficiency. From 1833 he undertook concert tours in Austria, and in 1834 was appointed bandmaster of the first Vienna militia regiment. His tours extended to Berlin in 1834, and to the Netherlands and Belgium in 1836; in 1837–38 he invaded Paris with a picked corps of 28, and had immense success both there and in London. In 1846 he was named k.k. (i.e., *kaiserlich und königlich*, or imperial and royal) Hofball-musikdirektor. After catching scarlet fever from one of his children, he died at the age of 45. Among his publ. waltzes, the *Lorelei-, Gabrielen-, Taglioni-, Cäcilien-, Victoria-, Kettenbrücken-,* and *Bajaderen-Walzer* are prime favorites; also popular are his *Elektrische Funken, Mephistos Höllenrufe,* and the *Donau-Lieder*. He also wrote 33 galops, 14 polkas, 33 quadrilles, cotillions and contredances, 23 marches, and 9 potpourris. He had 3 sons who carried on the family musical tradition:

(2) Johann (Baptist) Strauss (II), greatly renowned violinist, conductor, and composer, known as "The Waltz King"; b. Vienna, Oct. 25, 1825; d. there, June 3, 1899. His father intended him for a business career, but his musical talent manifested itself when he was a mere child. At the age of 6 he wrote the first 36 bars of waltz music that later was publ. as *Erster Gedanke*. While he was still a child, his mother arranged for him to study secretly with Franz Amon, his father's concertmaster. After his father left the family in 1842, he was able to pursue violin training with Anton Kohlmann. He also studied theory with Joseph Drechsler until 1844. He made his first public appearance as conductor of his own ensemble at Dommayer's Casino at Hietzing on Oct. 15, 1844. His success was instantaneous, and his new waltzes won wide popularity. Despite his father's objections to this rivalry in the family, Johann continued his concerts with increasing success. After his father's death in 1849, he united his father's band with his own. He subsequently made regular tours of Europe (1856–86). From 1863 to 1871 he was k.k. Hofballmusik-direktor in Vienna. In 1872 he accepted an invitation to visit the U.S., and directed 14 "monster concerts" in Boston and 4 in N.Y. He then turned to the theater. His finest operetta is *Die Fledermaus*, an epitome of the Viennese spirit that continues to hold the stage as one of the masterpieces of its genre. It was first staged at the Theater an der Wien on April 5, 1874, and within a few months was given in N.Y. (Dec. 29, 1874); productions followed all over the world. It was performed in Paris with a new libretto as *La Tzigane* (Oct. 30, 1877); the original version was presented there as *La Chauve-souris* on April 22, 1904. Also very successful was the operetta *Der Zigeunerbaron* (Vienna, Oct. 24, 1885). All his operettas were first produced in Vienna, with the exception of *Eine Nacht in Venedig* (Berlin, Oct. 3, 1883). A complete list of the Vienna productions includes: *Indigo und die vierzig Räuber* (Feb. 10, 1871); *Der Carneval in Rom* (March 1, 1873); *Cagliostro in Wien* (Feb. 27, 1875); *Prinz Methusalem* (Jan. 3, 1877); *Blindekuh* (Dec. 18, 1878); *Das Spitzentuch der Königin* (Oct. 1, 1880); *Der lustige Krieg* (Nov. 25, 1881); *Simplicius* (Dec. 17, 1887); *Ritter Pázmán* (Jan. 1, 1892); *Fürstin Ninetta* (Jan. 10, 1893); *Jabuka, oder Das Apfelfest* (Oct. 12, 1894); *Waldmeister* (Dec. 4, 1895); *Die Göttin der Vernunft* (March 13, 1897). Although Strauss composed extensively for the theater, his supreme achievement remains his dance music. He wrote almost 500 pieces (498 opus numbers). Of his waltzes, the greatest popularity was achieved by *An der schönen blauen Donau*, op.314 (1867), whose main tune became one of the best known in all music. Brahms wrote on a lady's fan the opening measures of it, and underneath: "Leider nicht von Brahms" ("Alas, not by Brahms"). Wagner, too, voiced his appreciation of the music of Strauss. He contracted 3 marriages: to the singer Henriette Treffz, the actress Angelika Dittrich, and Adele Strauss, the widow of the banker Anton Strauss, who was no relation to Johann's family. Strauss also composed numerous quadrilles, polkas, polka-mazurkas, marches, galops, etc., as well as several pieces in collaboration with his brothers. F. Racek began editing a complete ed. of his works in Vienna in 1967.

(3) Josef Strauss, conductor and composer; b. Vienna, Aug. 22, 1827; d. there, July 21, 1870. He studied theory with Franz Dolleschal and violin with Franz Anton. He was versatile and gifted, and at various times wrote poetry, painted, and patented inventions. He first appeared in public conducting in Vienna a set of his waltzes (July 23, 1853), and later regularly appeared as a conductor with his brother Johann's orch. (1856–62). Their younger brother Eduard joined them in 1862, but Johann left the orch. in 1863 and Josef and Eduard continued to conduct the family orch. He wrote 283 opus numbers, many of which reveal a composer of remarkable talent. Among his outstanding waltzes are *Perlen der Liebe*, op.39 (1857), *5 Kleebald'ln*, op.44 (1857), *Wiener Kinder*, op.61 (1858), *Schwert und Leier*, op.71 (1860), *Friedenspalmen*, op.207 (1867), and *Aquarellen*, op.258 (1869). He also wrote polkas, quadrilles, marches, and other works.

(4) Eduard Strauss, conductor and composer; b. Vienna, March 15, 1835; d. there, Dec. 28, 1916. He studied theory and composition with Gottfried Preyer and Simon Sechter, violin with Amon, and harp with Parish-Alvars and Zamara. After playing harp in his brother Johann's orch., he made his debut as a conductor and composer with it at the Wintergarten of the Dianabad-Saal on April 6, 1862. After Johann left the orch. in 1863, Eduard and his other brother Josef shared the conductorship of the orch. until the latter's death in 1870. From 1870 to 1878 he was k.k. Hofballmusikdirektor. He subsequently made annual tours of Europe as a guest conductor, and also with his own orch., and in 1890 and 1900–01 he toured throughout the U.S. In 1901 he retired. He wrote some 300 works, but they failed to rival the superior works of his brothers. His memoirs were publ. in 1906. His son, Johann (Maria Eduard) Strauss (III) (b. Vienna, Feb. 16, 1866; d. Berlin, Jan. 9, 1939), was also a conductor and composer; after working as an accountant in the education ministry, he won success as a composer with the operetta *Katze und Maus* (Vienna, Dec. 1898); from 1900 he was active as a conductor, serving as k.k. Hofballmusikdirektor (1901–5); subsequently pursued his career mainly in Berlin. He also wrote some waltzes, the most popular being *Dichterliebe*. His nephew, Eduard (Leopold Maria) Strauss (b. Vienna, March 24, 1910; d. there, April 6, 1969), was a conductor and the last representative of the great family tradition. He studied at the Vienna Academy of Music, and made his conducting debut in Vienna in 1949. He subsequently led concerts there regularly, and also toured with the Vienna Johann Strauss Orch. and as a guest conductor.

BIBL.: L. Scheyrer, *Johann S.'s musikalische Wanderung durch das Leben* (Vienna, 1851); L. Eisenberg, *Johann S.: Ein Lebensbild* (Vienna, 1894); C. Flamme, *Verzeichnis der sämtlichen im Druck erschienenen Kompositionen von Johann S. (Vater), Johann S. (Sohn), Josef S. und Eduard S.* (Leipzig, 1898); R. von Procházka, *Johann S.* (Berlin, 1900; second ed., 1903); F. Lange, *Joseph Lanner und Johann S.: Ihre Zeit, ihr Leben und ihre Werke* (Vienna, 1904; second ed., 1919); R. Specht, *Johann S.* (Berlin, 1909; second ed., 1922); F. Lange, *Johann S.* (Leipzig, 1912); E. Neumann, *Die Operetten von Johann S.: Ihre Formen und das Verhältnis von Text und Musik* (diss., Univ. of Vienna, 1919); J. Schnitzer, *Meister Johann: Bunte Geschichten aus der Johann S.-Zeit* (Vienna, 1920); E.

Decsey, *Johann S.* (Stuttgart, 1922; second ed., rev., 1948, by E. Rieger); K. Kobald, *Johann S.* (Vienna, 1925); S. Loewy, *Rund um Johann S.: Momentbilder aus einen Künstlerleben* (Vienna, 1925); H. Jacob, *Johann S. und das neunzehnte Jahrhundert: Die Geschichte einer musikalischen Weltherrschaft* (Amsterdam, 1937; third ed., rev., 1962); H. Sündermann, *Johann S.: Ein Vollender* (Brixlegg, 1937; third ed., 1949); W. Jaspert, *Johann S.: Sein Leben, sein Werk, seine Zeit* (Vienna, 1939; second ed., 1949); M. Kronberg, *Johann S.* (Paris, 1939); A. Witeschnik, *Die Dynastie S.* (Vienna and Leipzig, 1939; third ed., 1958); E. Schenk, *Johann S.* (Potsdam, 1940); D. Ewen, *Tales from the Vienna Woods: The Story of Johann S.* (N.Y., 1944); P. Ruff, *Johann-S.- Festschrift: Juni-September 1949* (Vienna, 1949); W. Reich, ed., *Johann S.-Brevier: Aus Briefen und Erinnerungen* (Zürich, 1950); J. Pastene, *Three-quarter Time: The Life and Music of the S. Family of Vienna* (N.Y., 1951); H. Jacob, *Johann S. Vater und Sohn* (Hamburg, 1953); M. Schönherr and K. Reinöhl, *Johann S. Vater: Ein Werkverzeichnis* (Vienna, 1954); A. Weinmann, *Verzeichnis sämtlicher Werke von Johann S. Vater und Sohn* (Vienna, 1956); F. Grasberger, *Die Walzer-Dynastie S.: Eine Ausstellung zum Neujahrskonzert der Wiener Philharmoniker* (Vienna, 1965–66); H. Jäger-Sustenau, *Johann S.: Der Walzerkönig und seine Dynastie, Familiengeschichte, Urkunden* (Vienna, 1965); A. Weinmann, *Verzeichnis sämtlicher Werke von Josef und Eduard S.* (Vienna, 1967); H. Fantel, *Johann S.: Father and Son, and Their Era* (Newton Abbot, 1971); O. Schneidereit, *Johann S. und die Stadt an der schönen blauen Donau* (Berlin, 1972); J. Wechsberg, *The Waltz Emperors* (London, 1973); F. Endler, *Das Walzer-Buch: Johann S.: Die Aufforderung zum Tanz* (Vienna, 1975); F. Mailer, *Das kleine Johann S. Buch* (Salzburg, 1975); M. Prawy, *Johann S.: Weltgeschichte im Walzertakt* (Vienna, 1975); F. Racek, *Johann S. zum 150. Geburtstag: Ausstellung der Wiener Stadtbibliothek 22. Mai bis 31. Oktober 1975* (Vienna, 1975); F. Mailer, *Joseph S.: Genie wider Willen* (Vienna and Munich, 1977; Eng. tr. as *Joseph S.: Genius against His Will*, Oxford, 1985); M. Schönherr, *Lanner, S., Ziehrer: Synoptic Handbook of the Dances and Marches* (Vienna, 1982); P. Kemp, *The S. Family: Portrait of a Musical Dynasty* (Tunbridge Wells, 1985); N. Linke, *Musik erobert die Welt, oder, Wie die Wiener Familie S. die "Unterhaltungsmusik" revolutionierte* (Vienna, 1987); M. Prawy, *Johann S.* (Vienna, 1991); L. Finscher and A. Riethmüller, *Johann S.: Zwischen Kunstanspruch und Volksvergnügen* (Darmstadt, 1995); A. Mayer, *Johann S.: Ein Pop-Idol des 19. Jahrhunderts* (Vienna, 1998); K. Dieman-Dichtl, *Freut euch des Lebens: Die S.-Dynastie und Niederösterreich* (St. Pölten, 1999); W. Sinkovicz and K. Knaus, *Johann S.* (Vienna, 1999).—NS/LK/DM

Strauss, Christoph, eminent Austrian organist and composer; b. probably in Vienna, c. 1577; d. there, June 1631. He was born into a musical family long associated with the Hapsburg court. In 1594 he entered its service, becoming organist of the court church of St. Michael in 1601. After serving as administrator of the imperial estate of Kattenburg (1614–17), he was director of the court music from 1617 until he was removed in 1619 by the new Emperor, Ferdinand II. In 1626 he finally obtained the post of director of music at St. Stephen's Cathedral, where he remained until his death. He was one of the foremost Austrian composers of his time. He publ. *Nova ac diversimoda sacrarum cantionum compositio seu* [36] *motettae* for 5 to 10 Voices and Instruments (Vienna, 1613) and *Missae* for 8 to 20 Voices, Instruments, and Basso Continuo (organ) (Vienna, 1631).—NS/LK/DM

Strauss, Franz (Joseph), German horn player and composer, father of **Richard (Georg) Strauss;** b. Parkstein, Feb. 26, 1822; d. Munich, May 31, 1905. Until his retirement in 1889 he was solo hornist at the Hofoper in Munich. Although a violent opponent of Wagner, the master valued him highly, and entrusted to him at the premieres of *Tristan und Isolde, Die Meistersinger von Nürnberg,* and *Parsifal* the important solo passages. Until 1896 he was a prof. of his instrument at the Akademie der Tonkunst, and from 1875 to 1896 conducted an excellent amateur orch., the Wilde Gungl, in Munich. He wrote a Horn Concerto in C minor (op.8), *Nocturne* (op.7) and *Empfindungen am Meere* (op.12) for Horn and Piano, and 17 *Konzertetüden* and *Übungen für Naturhorn* (2 books).—NS/LK/DM

Strauss, Isaac, French violinist, conductor, and composer; b. Strasbourg, June 2, 1806; d. Paris, Aug. 9, 1888. He went to Paris and learned to play the violin before completing his musical training at the Cons. (1826–28). After playing violin in the orch. of the Théâtre-Italien until 1843, he conducted a spa orch. in Vichy until 1863. He also was music director of the court balls (1852–70) and of the Opéra balls (1870–72) in Paris. Strauss became highly successful as a conductor and composer of light music, producing many popular waltzes, polkas, galops, and quadrilles. Some of his works were given the same titles as those by Johann Strauss Sr., which led to considerable confusion. —LK/DM

Strauss, Richard (Georg), great German composer and distinguished conductor, one of the most inventive music masters of his era, son of **Franz (Joseph) Strauss;** b. Munich, June 11, 1864; d. Garmisch-Partenkirchen, Sept. 8, 1949. Growing up in a musical environment, he studied piano as a child with August Tombo, harpist in the Court Orch.; then took violin lessons from Benno Walter, its concertmaster, and later received instruction from the court conductor, Friedrich Wilhelm Meyer. According to his own account, he began to improvise songs and piano pieces at a very early age; among such incunabula was the song *Weihnachtslied,* followed by a piano dance, *Schneiderpolka.* On March 30, 1881, his first orch. work, the Sym. in D minor, was premiered in Munich under Hermann Levi. This was followed by the Sym. in F minor, premiered on Dec. 13, 1884, by the N.Y. Phil. under Theodore Thomas. Strauss also made progress as a performing musician; when he was 20 years old, Hans von Bülow engaged him as asst. conductor of his Meiningen Orch. About that time, Strauss became associated with the poet and musician Alexander Ritter, who introduced him to the "music of the future," as it was commonly called, represented by orch. works of Liszt and operas by Wagner.

In 1886 Strauss received an appointment as the third conductor of the Court Opera in Munich. On March 2, 1887, he conducted in Munich the first performance of his symphonic fantasy, *Aus Italien.* This was followed by the composition of his first true masterpiece, the symphonic poem *Don Juan,* in which he applied the thematic ideas of Liszt; he conducted its premiere in Weimar on

Nov. 11, 1889; it became the first of a series of his tone poems, all of them based on literary subjects. His next tone poem of great significance in music history was *Tod und Verklärung*; Strauss conducted it for the first time in Eisenach on June 21, 1890, on the same program with the premiere of his brilliant *Burleske* for Piano and Orch., featuring Eugen d'Albert as soloist. There followed the first performance of the symphonic poem *Macbeth*, which Strauss conducted in Weimar on Oct. 13, 1890. In these works, Strauss established himself as a master of program music and the most important representative of the nascent era of musical modernism; as such, he was praised extravagantly by earnest believers in musical progress and damned savagely by entrenched traditionalists in the press. He effectively adapted Wagner's system of leading motifs (leitmotifs) to the domain of symphonic music. His tone poems were interwoven with motifs, each representing a relevant programmatic element. Explanatory brochures listing these leading motifs were publ. like musical Baedekers to guide the listeners. Bülow, ever a phrasemaker, dubbed Strauss "Richard the third," Richard the first being Wagner but no one worthy of direct lineage as Richard the second in deference to the genius of the master of Bayreuth.

Turning to stage music, Strauss wrote his first opera, *Guntram*, for which he also composed the text; he conducted its premiere in Weimar on May 10, 1894, with the leading soprano role performed by Pauline de Ahna; she was married to Strauss on Sept. 10, 1894, and remained with him all his life; she died on May 13, 1950, a few months after Strauss himself. While engaged in active work as a composer, Strauss did not neglect his conducting career. In 1894 he succeeded Bülow as conductor of the Berlin Phil., leading it for a season. Also in 1894 he became asst. conductor of the Munich Court Opera; he became chief conductor in 1896. In 1896–97 he filled engagements as a guest conductor in European music centers. His works of the period included the sparkling *Till Eugenspiegels lustige Streiche* (Cologne, Nov. 5, 1895), *Also sprach Zarathustra*, a philosophical tone poem after Nietzsche (Frankfurt am Main, Nov. 27, 1896, Strauss conducting), and *Don Quixote*, variations with a cello solo, after Cervantes (Cologne, March 8, 1898). In 1898 Strauss became a conductor at the Berlin Royal Opera; in 1908 he was made its Generalmusikdirektor, a position he held until 1918. He conducted the first performance of his extraordinary autobiographical tone poem *Ein Heldenleben* in Frankfurt am Main on March 3, 1899; the hero of the title was Strauss himself, while his critics were represented in the score by a cacophonous charivari; for this exhibition of musical self-aggrandizement, he was severely chastised in the press. There followed his first successful opera, *Feuersnot* (Dresden, Nov. 21, 1901).

In June 1903 Strauss was the guest of honor of the Strauss Festival in London. It was also in 1903 that the Univ. of Heidelberg made him Dr.Phil., *honoris causa*. For his first visit to the U.S., he presented to the public the premiere performance of his *Symphonia domestica* at Carnegie Hall in N.Y. on March 21, 1904. The score represented a day in the Strauss household, containing an interlude describing, quite literally, the feeding of the newly born baby. The reviews in the press reflected

aversion to such a musical self-exposure. There followed his opera *Salome*, to the German tr. of Oscar Wilde's play. Schuch led its premiere in Dresden on Dec. 9, 1905. *Salome* had its American premiere at the Metropolitan Opera in N.Y. on Jan. 22, 1907; the ghastly subject, involving intended incest, 7-fold nudity, and decapitation followed by a labial necrophilia, administered such a shock to the public and the press that the Metropolitan Opera took it off the repertoire after only 2 performances. Scarcely less forceful was Strauss's next opera, *Elektra*, to a libretto by the Austrian poet and dramatist Hugo von Hofmannsthal, in which the horrors of matricide were depicted with extraordinary force in unabashedly dissonant harmonies. Schuch conducted its premiere in Dresden on Jan. 25, 1909.

Strauss then decided to prove to his admirers that he was quite able to write melodious operas to charm the musical ear; this he accomplished in his next production, also to a text of Hofmannsthal, *Der Rosenkavalier*, a delightful opera-bouffe in an endearing popular manner; Schuch conducted its premiere in Dresden on Jan. 26, 1911. Turning once more to Greek mythology, Strauss wrote, with Hofmannsthal again as librettist, a short opera, *Ariadne auf Naxos*, which he conducted for the first time in Stuttgart on Oct. 25, 1912. In June 1914 Strauss was awarded an honorary D.Mus. degree from the Univ. of Oxford. His next work was the formidable, and quite realistic, score *Eine Alpensinfonie*, depicting an ascent of the Alps, and employing a wind machine and a thunder machine in the orch. to illustrate an Alpine storm. Strauss conducted its first performance with the Dresden Court Orch. in Berlin on Oct. 28, 1915. Then, again with Hofmannsthal as librettist, he wrote the opera *Die Frau ohne Schatten* (Vienna, Oct. 10, 1919), using a complex plot, heavily endowed with symbolism.

In 1917 Strauss helped to organize the Salzburg Festival and appeared there in subsequent years as conductor. In 1919 he assumed the post of co-director with Franz Schalk of the Vienna State Opera, a position he held until 1924. In 1920 he took the Vienna Phil. on a tour of South America; in 1921 he appeared as a guest conductor in the U.S. For his next opera, *Intermezzo* (Dresden, Nov. 4, 1924), Strauss wrote his own libretto; then, with Hofmannsthal once more, he wrote *Die ägyptische Helena* (Dresden, June 6, 1928). Their last collaboration was *Arabella* (Dresden, July 1, 1933).

When Hitler came to power in 1933, the Nazis were eager to persuade Strauss to embrace the official policies of the Third Reich. Hitler even sent him a signed picture of himself with a flattering inscription, "To the great composer Richard Strauss, with sincere admiration." Strauss kept clear of formal association with the Führer and his cohorts, however. He agreed to serve as president of the newly organized Reichsmusikkammer on Nov. 15, 1933, but resigned from it on July 13, 1935, ostensibly for reasons of poor health. He entered into open conflict with the Nazis by asking Stefan Zweig, an Austrian Jew, to provide the libretto for his opera *Die schweigsame Frau*; it was duly premiered in Dresden on June 24, 1935, but then taken off the boards after a few performances. His political difficulties grew even more disturbing when the Nazis found out that his daughter-in-law was Jewish. Zweig himself managed to escape Nazi horrors, and emigrated to Brazil, but was so afflicted by the inhumanity of the world that he and his wife together committed suicide.

Strauss valiantly went through his tasks; he agreed to write the *Olympische Hymne* for the Berlin Olympic Games in 1936. On Nov. 5, 1936, he was honored with the Gold Medal of the Royal Phil. Soc. in London; the next day he conducted the visiting Dresden State Opera in a performance of his *Ariadne auf Naxos* at Covent Garden. For his next opera, he chose Joseph Gregor as his librettist; with him Strauss wrote *Daphne* (Dresden, Oct. 15, 1938), which was once more a revival of his debt to Greek mythology. For their last collaboration, Strauss and Gregor wrote the opera *Die Liebe der Danae*, also on a Greek theme. Its public dress rehearsal was given in Salzburg on Aug. 16, 1944, but by that time World War II was rapidly encroaching on devastated Germany, so that the opera did not receive its official premiere until after Strauss's death. The last opera by Strauss performed during his lifetime was *Capriccio*. Its libretto was prepared by the conductor Clemens Krauss, who conducted its premiere in Munich on Oct. 28, 1942. Another interesting work of this period was Strauss's Horn Concerto No. 2, first performed in Salzburg on Aug. 11, 1943.

During the last weeks of the war, Strauss devoted himself to the composition of *Metamorphosen*, a symphonic work mourning the disintegration of Germany; it contained a symbolic quotation from the funeral march from Beethoven's *Eroica* Sym. He then completed another fine score, the Oboe Concerto. In Oct. 1945 he went to Switzerland.

In Oct. 1947 Strauss visited London for the Strauss Festival and also appeared as a conductor of his own works. Although official suspicion continued to linger regarding his relationship with the Nazi regime, he was officially exonerated of all taint on June 8, 1948. A last flame of creative inspiration brought forth the deeply moving *Vier letzte Lieder* (1948), for Soprano and Orch., inspired by poems of Herman Hesse and Eichendorff. With this farewell, Strauss left Switzerland in 1949 and returned to his home in Germany, where he died at the age of 85. Undeniably one of the finest master composers of his era, Strauss never espoused extreme chromatic techniques, remaining a Romanticist at heart. His genius is unquestioned as regards his tone poems from *Don Juan* to *Ein Heldenleben* and his operas from *Salome* to *Das Rosenkavalier*, all of which have attained a permanent place in the repertoire, while his *Vier letzte Lieder* stand as a noble achievement of his Romantic inspiration. In 1976 the Richard-Strauss-Gesellschaft was organized in Munich.

WORKS: DRAMATIC: Opera: *Guntram*, op.25 (1892–93; Hoftheater, Weimar, May 10, 1894, composer conducting; rev. version, with score cut by one third, 1934–39; Deutsches Nationaltheater, Weimar, Oct. 29, 1940); *Feuersnot*, op.50 (1900–01; Hofoper, Dresden, Nov. 21, 1901, Ernst von Schuch conducting); *Salome*, op.54 (1903–05; Hofoper, Dresden, Dec. 9, 1905, Schuch conducting); *Elektra*, op.58 (1906–08; Hofoper, Dresden, Jan. 25, 1909, Schuch conducting); *Der Rosen-*

kavalier, op.59 (1909–10; Hofoper, Dresden, Jan. 26, 1911, Schuch conducting); *Ariadne auf Naxos* "zu spielen nach dem *Bürger als Edelmann* des Moliere," op.60 (1911–12; Hoftheater, Stuttgart, Oct. 25, 1912, composer conducting; rev. version, with prologue, 1916; Hofoper, Vienna, Oct. 4, 1916, Franz Schalk conducting); *Die Frau ohne Schatten*, op.65 (1914–18; Staatsoper, Vienna, Oct. 10, 1919, Schalk conducting); *Intermezzo*, op.72 (1918–23; Staatsoper, Dresden, Nov. 4, 1924, Fritz Busch conducting); *Die ägyptische Helena*, op.75 (1923–27; Staatsoper, Dresden, June 6, 1928, Fritz Busch conducting; rev. version, 1932–33; Festspielhaus, Salzburg, Aug. 14, 1933); *Arabella*, op.79 (1929–32; Staatsoper, Dresden, July 1, 1933, Clemens Krauss conducting; rev. version, Munich, July 16, 1939); *Die schweigsame Frau*, op.80 (1933–34; Staatsoper, Dresden, June 24, 1935, Karl Böhm conducting); *Friedenstag*, op.81 (1935–36; Nationaltheater, Munich, July 24, 1938, Krauss conducting); *Daphne*, op.82 (1936–37; Staatsoper, Dresden, Oct. 15, 1938, Böhm conducting); *Die Liebe der Danaë*, op.83 (1938–40; public dress rehearsal, Festspielhaus, Salzburg, Aug. 16, 1944, Krauss conducting; official premiere, Festspielhaus, Salzburg, Aug. 14, 1952, Krauss conducting); *Capriccio*, op.85 (1940–41; Bayerische Staatsoper, Munich, Oct. 28, 1942, Krauss conducting). **Ballet and Other Dramatic Works:** *Romeo und Julia*, incidental music to Shakespeare's drama (Nationaltheater, Munich, Oct. 23, 1887); *Josephslegende*, op.63 (1912–14; Opéra, Paris, May 14, 1914, composer conducting); *Der Bürger als Edelmann*, incidental music to Hofmannsthal's version of Molière's drama, op.60 (1917; Deutsches Theater, Berlin, April 9, 1918); *Schlagobers*, op.70 (1921–22; Staatsoper, Vienna, May 9, 1924, composer conducting); *Verklungene Feste*, after Couperin (1940; Nationaltheater, Munich, April 5, 1941, Krauss conducting); *Des Esels Schatten*, comedy for music (1949; Hellbrunn Castle, near Salzburg, July 31, 1982, Ernst Märzendorfer conducting). **ORCH.:** Overture for the Singspiel *Hochlands Treue* (1872–73); *Festmarsch* in E-flat major, op.1 (1876; Munich, March 26, 1881, Franz Strauss conducting); Concert Overture in B minor (1876); Serenade in G major (1877); Overture in E major (1878); *Romanze* in E-flat major for Clarinet and Orch. (1879); Overture in A minor (1879); Sym. in D minor (1880; Munich, March 30, 1881, Hermann Levi conducting); Violin Concerto in D minor, op.8 (1880–82; Vienna, Dec. 5, 1882, Benno Walter violinist, composer pianist; official premiere, Leipzig, Feb. 17, 1896, Alfred Krasselt violinist, composer conducting); Serenade in E-flat major for 13 Wind Instruments, op.7 (1881; Dresden, Nov. 27, 1882, Franz Wüllner conducting); Horn Concerto No. 1 in E-flat major, op.11 (1882–83; Meiningen, March 4, 1885, Gustav Leinhos soloist, Hans von Bülow conducting); Overture in C minor (Munich, Nov. 28, 1883, Levi conducting); *Romanze* in F major for Cello and Orch. (1883); *Lied ohne Worte* in E-flat major (1883); Sym. in F minor, op.12 (1883–84; N.Y., Dec. 13, 1884, Theodore Thomas conducting); Suite in B-flat major for 13 Wind Instruments, op.4 (Munich, Nov. 18, 1884, composer conducting); *Der Zweikampf—Polonaise* in B-flat major for Flute, Bassoon, and Orch. (1884); *Festmarsch* in D major (1884; Munich, Jan. 8, 1885, Franz Strauss conducting; rev. 1888); *Burleske* in D minor for Piano and Orch. (1885–86; Eisenach, June 21, 1890, Eugen d'Albert soloist, composer conducting); *Aus Italien*, symphonic fantasy, op.16 (1886; Munich, March 2, 1887, composer conducting); *Macbeth*, tone poem after Shakespeare's drama, op.23 (1886–88; rev. 1889–90; Weimar, Oct. 13, 1890, composer conducting; rev. 1891); *Don Juan*, tone poem after Lenau, op.20 (1888–89; Weimar, Nov. 11, 1889, composer conducting); *Tod und Verklärung*, tone poem, op.24 (1888–89; Eisenach, June 21, 1890, composer conducting); *Festmarsch* in C major

(Munich, Feb. 1, 1889, Franz Strauss conducting); Fanfare for A.W. Iffland's drama *Der Jäger* (1891); *Festmusik "Lebende Bilder"* for the golden wedding anniversary of the Grand Duke and Duchess of Weimar (Weimar, Oct. 8, 1892, composer conducting); *Till Eulenspiegels lustige Streiche, nach alter schelmenweise—in Rondeauform*, op.28 (1894–95; Cologne, Nov. 5, 1895, Wüllner conducting); *Also sprach Zarathustra*, tone poem after Nietzsche, op.30 (1895–96; Frankfurt am Main, Nov. 27, 1896, composer conducting); *Don Quixote, fantastische Variationen über ein Thema ritterlichen Charakters* for Cello and Orch., op.35 (1896–97; Cologne, March 8, 1898, Wüllner conducting); *Ein Heldenleben*, tone poem, op.40 (1897–98; Frankfurt am Main, March 3, 1899, composer conducting); *Symphonia domestica*, op.53 (1902–03; N.Y., March 21, 1904, composer conducting); *Zwei Militärmärsche*, op.57 (1906; Berlin, March 6, 1907, composer conducting); *Feierlicher Einzug der Ritter des Johanniter-Ordens* for Brass and Timpani (1909); *Festliches Präludium* for Orch. and Organ, op.61 (for the dedication of the Konzerthaus, Vienna, Oct. 19, 1913, Ferdinand Löwe conducting); *Eine Alpensinfonie*, op.64 (1911–15; Berlin, Oct. 28, 1915, composer conducting); *Der Bürger als Edelmann*, suite, op.60 (1918; Vienna, Jan. 31, 1920, composer conducting); *Tanzsuite aus Klavierstücken von François Couperin* for Small Orch. (Vienna, Feb. 17, 1923, Krauss conducting); *Wiener Philharmoniker Fanfare* for Brass and Timpani (Vienna, March 4, 1924); *Fanfare zur Eröffnung der Musikwoche der Stadt Wien im September 1924* for Brass and Timpani (Vienna, Sept. 14, 1924); *Parergon zur Symphonia domestica* for Piano, Left-hand, and Orch., op.73 (1924; Dresden, Oct. 16, 1925, Paul Wittgenstein soloist, Fritz Busch conducting); *Militärmarsch* in F major for the film *Der Rosenkavalier* (1925; Dresden, Jan. 10, 1926, composer conducting); *Panathenäenzug, symphonische Etüden in Form einer Passacaglia* for Piano, Left-hand, and Orch., op.74 (1927; Vienna, March 11, 1928, Wittgenstein soloist, Schalk conducting); *Vier sinfonische Zwischenspiele aus Intermezzo* (BBC, London, May 24, 1931); *München, "ein Gelegenheitswalzer"* (for the film *München*, 1939; Munich, May 24, 1939; rev. 1945 as *München, "ein Gedächtniswalzer"*; Vienna, March 31, 1951); *Festmusik zur Feier des 2600jährigen Bestehens des Kaiserreichs Japan*, op.84 (Tokyo, Dec. 7, 1940); *Divertimento, Klavierstücke von Couperin* for Small Orch., op.86 (1940–41; Vienna, Jan. 31, 1943, Krauss conducting); Horn Concerto No. 2 in E-flat major (1942; Salzburg, Aug. 11, 1943, Gottfried Freiberg soloist, Böhm conducting); *Festmusik der Stadt Wien* for Brass and Timpani (1943; second version as *Fanfare der Stadt Wien*, Vienna, April 9, 1943, composer conducting); Sonatina No. 1 in F major, "Aus der Werkstatt eines Invaliden," for 16 Wind Instruments (1943; Dresden, June 18, 1944, Karl Elmendorff conducting); *Erste Walzerfolge aus Der Rosenkavalier* (1944; London, Aug. 4, 1946, Erich Leinsdorf conducting); *Metamorphosen* for 23 Solo Strings (1945; Zürich, Jan. 25, 1946, Paul Sacher conducting); Sonatina No. 2 in E-flat major, "Fröhlische Werkstatt," for 16 Wind Instruments (1944–45; Winterthur, March 25, 1946, Hermann Scherchen conducting); Oboe Concerto in D major (1945–46; Zürich, Feb. 26, 1946, Marcel Saillet soloist, Volkmar Andreae conducting); *Symphonische Fantasie aus Die Frau ohne Schatten* (1946; Vienna, June 26, 1947, Böhm conducting); *Duett-Concertino* for Clarinet, Bassoon, Strings, and Harp (1947; Radio Svizzera Italiana, Lugano, April 4, 1948); *Symphonisches Fragment aus Josephslegende* (1948; San Antonio, Feb. 26, 1949, Max Reiter conducting). **CHAMBER:** String Quartet in A major, op.2 (1880; Munich, March 14, 1881); Cello Sonata in F major, op.6 (1880–83; Nuremberg, Dec. 8, 1883); Piano Quartet in C minor, op.13 (1883–84; Weimar, Dec. 8, 1885); Violin Sonata in E-flat major, op.18 (1887; Munich, Oct. 3, 1888); Allegretto in

E major for Violin and Piano (1948). **P i a n o :** *5 Klavierstücke*, op.3 (1880–81); Sonata in B minor, op.5 (1880–81); *5 Stimmungsbilder*, op.9 (1882–84). **VOCAL: C h o r a l :** Chorus for *Elektra* of Sophocles (1881); *Wanderers Sturmlied* for Chorus and Orch., op.14 (1884; Cologne, March 8, 1887, composer conducting); *Taillefer* for Soprano, Tenor, Baritone, Chorus, and Orch., op.52 (Heidelberg, Oct. 26, 1903, composer conducting); *Bardengesang* for Men's Chorus and Orch., op.55 (1905; Dresden, Feb. 6, 1906); *Deutsche Motette* for Soprano, Alto, Tenor, Bass, and Chorus, op.62 (Berlin, Dec. 2, 1913); *Die Tageszeiten* for Men's Chorus and Orch., op.76 (Vienna, July 21, 1928); *Olympische Hymne* for Chorus and Orch. (1934; Berlin, Aug. 1, 1936, composer conducting); *Die Göttin im Putzzimmer* for Chorus (1935; Vienna, March 2, 1952, Krauss conducting); *An dem Baum Daphne*, epilogue to *Daphne*, for Chorus (1943; Vienna, Jan. 5, 1947, Felix Prohaska conducting). **S o n g s** (source of text precedes date of composition): *Weihnachtslied* (C. Schubart; 1870); *Einkehr* (Uhland; 1871); *Winterreise* (Uhland; 1871); *Waldkonzert* (J. Vogel; 1871?); *Der böhmische Musikant* (O. Pletzsch; 1871?); *Herz, mein Herz* (E. Geibel; 1871); *Der müde Wanderer* (A. Hoffman von Fallersleben; 1873?); *Husarenlied* (von Fallersleben; 1873?); *Der Fischer* (Goethe; 1877); *Die Drossel* (Uhland; 1877); *Lass ruhn die Toten* (A. von Chamisso; 1877); *Lust und Qual* (Goethe; 1877); *Spielmann und Zither* (T. Körner; 1878); *Wiegenlied* (von Fallersleben; 1878); *Abend- und Morgenrot* (von Fallersleben; 1878); *Im Walde* (Geibel; 1878); *Der Spielmann und sein Kind* (von Fallersleben; 1878; orchestrated); *Nebel* (Lenau; 1878?); *Soldatenlied* (von Fallersleben; 1878?); *Ein Röslein zog ich mir im Garten* (von Fallersleben; 1878?); *Waldegesang* (Geibel; 1879); *In Vaters Garten heimlich steht ein Blümchen* (Heine; 1879); *Die erwachte Rose* (F. von Sallet; 1880); *Begegnung* (O. Gruppe; 1880); *John Anderson, mein Lieb* (Burns; F. Freiligrath, tr.; 1880); *Rote Rosen* (K. Stieler; 1883); *Acht Lieder aus Letzte Blätter*, op.10 (H. von Gilm; 1885): *Zueignung* (orchestrated, 1940), *Nichts*, *Die Nacht*, *Die Georgine*, *Geduld*, *Die Verschwiegenen*, *Die Zeitlose*, and *Allerseelen*; *Wer hat's gethan?* (Gilm; 1885); *Fünf Lieder*, op.15 (1884–86): *Madrigal* (Michelangelo), *Winternacht* (Schack), *Lob des Leidens* (Schack), *Aus den Liedern der Trauer (Dem Herzen ähnlich)* (Schack), and *Heimkehr* (Schack); *Sechs Lieder*, op.17 (Schack; 1885–87): *Seitdem dein Aug' in meines schaute*, *Ständchen*, *Das Geheimnis*, *Aus den Liedern der Trauer (Von dunklem Schleier umsponnen)*, *Nur Muth!*, and *Barkarole*; *Sechs Lieder aus Lotusblättern*, op.19 (Schack; 1885–88): *Wozu noch, Mädchen, soll es frommen*, *Breit über mein Haupt dein schwarzes Haar*, *Schön sind, doch kalt die Himmelssterne*, *Wie sollten wir geheim sie halten*, *Hoffen und wieder versagen*, and *Mein Herz ist stumm, mein Herz ist kalt*; *Schlichte Weisen*, op.21 (F. Dahn; 1887–88): *All' mein Gedanken, mein Herz und mein Sinn*, *Du meines Herzens Krönelein*, *Ach Lieb, ich muss nun scheiden*, *Ach weh, mir unglückhaften Mann*, and *Die Frauen sind oft fromm und still*; *Mädchen-blumen*, op.22 (Dahn): *Kornblumen* (1888), *Mohnblumen* (1888), *Efeu* (1886–88), and *Wasserrose* (1886–88); *Zwei Lieder*, op.26 (Lenau; 1891): *Frühlingsgedränge* and *O wärst du mein*; *Vier Lieder*, op.27 (1894): *Ruhe, meine Seele* (K. Henckell; orchestrated, 1948), *Cäcilie* (Hart; orchestrated, 1897), *Heimliche Aufforderung* (J. Mackay), and *Morgen* (Mackay; orchestrated, 1897); *Drei Lieder*, op.29 (Bierbaum; 1895): *Traum durch die Dämmerung*, *Schlagende Herzen*, and *Nachtgang*; *Wir beide wollen springen* (Bierbaum; 1896); *Drei Lieder*, op.31: *Blauer Sommer* (Busse; 1896), *Wenn* (Busse; 1895), and *Weisser Jasmin* (Busse; 1895); added song, *Stiller Gang* (Dehmel; 1895); *Fünf Lieder*, op.32 (1896): *Ich trage meine Minne* (Henckell), *Sehnsucht* (Liliencron), *Liebeshymnus* (Henckell; orchestrated, 1897), *O süsser Mai* (Henckell), and *Himmelsboten (Des Knaben Wunderhorn)*; *Vier Gesänge*, op.33, for Voice and Orch.: *Verführung* (Mackay; 1896),

Gesang der Apollopriesterin (E. von und zu Bodman; 1896), *Hymnus* (1896), and *Pilgers Morgenlied* (Goethe; 1897); *Vier Lieder*, op.36: *Das Rosenband* (Klopstock; orchestrated, 1897), *Für funfzehn Pfennige* (Des Knaben Wunderhorn; 1897), *Hat gesagt—bleibt's nicht dabei* (Des Knaben Wunderhorn; 1898), and *Anbetung* (Rückert; 1898); *Sechs Lieder*, op.37: *Glückes genug* (Liliencron; 1898), *Ich liebe dich* (Liliencron; 1898; orchestrated, 1943), *Meinem Kinde* (Falke; 1897; orchestrated, 1897), *Mein Auge* (Dehmel; 1898; orchestrated, 1933), *Herr Lenz* (Bodman; 1896), and *Hochzeitlich Lied* (A. Lindner; 1898); *Fünf Lieder*, op.39 (1898): *Leises Lied* (Dehmel), *Junghexenlied* (Bierbaum), *Der Arbeitsmann* (Dehmel), *Befreit* (Dehmel; orchestrated, 1933), and *Lied an meinen Sohn* (Dehmel); *Fünf Lieder*, op.41 (1899): *Wiegenlied* (Dehmel; orchestrated, 1916), *In der Campagna* (Mackay), *Am Ufer* (Dehmel), *Bruder Liederlich* (Liliencron), and *Leise Lieder* (Morgenstern); *Drei Lieder*, op.43 (1899): *An Sie* (Klopstock), *Muttertändelei* (G. Bürger; orchestrated, 1900), and *Die Ulme zu Hirsau* (Uhland); *Zwei grössere Gesänge*, op.44, for Voice and Orch. (1899): *Notturno* (Dehmel) and *Nächtlicher Gang* (Rückert); *Weihnachtsgefühl* (Greif; 1899); *Fünf Lieder*, op.46 (Rückert): *Ein Obdach gegen Sturm und Regen* (1900), *Gestern war ich Atlas* (1899), *Die sieben Siegel* (1899), *Morgenrot* (1900), and *Ich sehe wie in einem Spiegel* (1900); *Fünf Lieder*, op.47 (Uhland; 1900): *Auf ein Kind, Des Dichters Abendgang* (orchestrated, 1918), *Rückleben, Einkehr*, and *Von den sieben Zechbrüdern*; *Fünf Lieder*, op.48 (1900): *Freundliche Vision* (Bierbaum; orchestrated, 1918), *Ich schwebe* (Henckell), *Kling!* (Henckell), *Winterweihe* (Henckell; orchestrated, 1918), and *Winterliebe* (Henckell; orchestrated, 1918); *Acht Lieder*, op.49: *Waldseligkeit* (Dehmel; 1901; orchestrated, 1918), *In goldener Fülle* (P. Remer; 1901), *Wiegenliedchen* (Dehmel; 1901), *Das Lied des Steinklopfers* (Henckell; 1901), *Sie wissen's nicht* (O. Panizza; 1901), *Junggesellenschwur* (Des Knaben Wunderhorn; 1900), *Wer lieben will* (C. Mündel; 1901), and *Ach, was Kummer, Qual und Schmerzen* (Mündel; 1901); *Zwei Gesänge*, op.51, for Voice and Orch.: *Das Thal* (Uhland; 1902) and *Der Einsame* (Heine; 1906); *Sechs Lieder*, op.56: *Gefunden* (Goethe; 1903), *Blindenklage* (Henckell; 1903–06), *Im Spätboot* (Meyer; 1903–06), *Mit deinen blauen Augen* (Heine; 1903–06), *Frühlingsfeier* (Heine; 1903–06; orchestrated, 1933), and *Die heiligen drei Könige aus Morgenland* (Heine; 1903–06; orchestrated, 1906); *Der Graf von Rom* (no text; 1906); *Krümerspiegel*, op.66 (A. Kerr; 1918): *Es war einmal ein Bock, Einst kam der Bock als Bote, Es liebte einst ein Hase, Drei Masken sah ich am Himmel stehn, Hast due ein Tongedicht vollbracht, O lieber Künstler sei ermahnt, Unser Feind ist, grosser Gott, Von Händlern wird die Künst bedroht, Es war mal eine Wanze, Die Künstler sind die Schöpfer, Die Händler und die Macher*, and *O Schöpferschwarm, o Händlerkreis*; *Sechs Lieder*, op.67 (1918): *1, Lieder der Ophelia* (Shakespeare; K. Simrock, tr.): *Wie erkenn ich mein Treulieb vor andern nun?, Guten Morgen, 's ist Sankt Valentinstag*, and *Sie trugen ihn auf der Bahre bloss; 2, Aus den Büchern des Unmuts der Rendsch Nameh* (Goethe): *Wer wird von der Welt verlangen, Hab' ich euch denn je geraten*, and *Wanderers Gemütsruhe; Sechs Lieder*, op.68 (Brentano; 1918): *An die Nacht, Ich wollt' ein Sträusslein binden, Säusle, liebe Myrthe, Als mir dein Lied erklang*, and *Amor* (all 5 orchestrated, 1940); *Lied der Frauen* (orchestrated, 1933); *Fünf kleine Lieder*, op.69 (1918): *Der Stern* (A. von Arnim), *Der Pokal* (Arnim), *Einerlei* (Arnim), *Waldesfahrt* (Heine), and *Schlechtes Wetter* (Heine); *Sinnspruch* (Goethe; 1919); *Drei Hymnen von Friedrich Hölderlin*, op.71, for Voice and Orch. (1921): *Hymne an die Liebe, Rückkehr in der Heimat*, and *Die Liebe; Durch allen Schall und Klang* (Goethe; 1925); *Gesänge des Orients*, op.77 (Bethge, tr.; 1928): *Ihre Augen* (Hafiz), *Schwung* (Hafiz), *Liebesgeschenke* (Die chinesische Flöte), *Die Allmächtige* (Hafiz), *Huldigung* (Hafiz); and *Wie etwas sei leicht* (Goethe;

1930); *Vom künftigen Alter*, op.87 (Rückert; 1929); *Erschaffen und Beleben* (Goethe; 1922); *Und dann nicht mehr* (Rückert; 1929); *Im sonnenschein* (Rückert; 1935); *Zugemessne Rhythmen* (Goethe; 1935); *Das Bachlein*, op.88 (1933; orchestrated, 1935); *Blick vom oberen Belvedere* (J. Weinheber; 1942); *Sankt Michael* (Weinheber; 1942); *Xenion* (Goethe; 1942); *Vier letzte Lieder* for Voice and Orch. (1948): *Frühling* (Hesse), *September* (Hesse), *Beim Schlafengehen* (Hesse), and *Im Abendrot* (Eichendorff) (London, May 22, 1950, Kirsten Flagstad soloist, Wilhelm Furtwängler conducting); *Malven* (B. Knobel; 1948; N.Y., Jan. 10, 1985). **SPEAKER AND PIANO:** *Enoch Arden*, after Tennyson, op.38 (Munich, March 24, 1897); *Das Schloss am Meer*, after Uhland (Berlin, March 23, 1899). **ARRANGEMENTS, ETC.:** Strauss prepared a cadenza for Mozart's C- minor Piano Concerto, K.491 (1885); arranged Gluck's *Iphigénie en Tauride* (1899; Hoftheater, Weimar, June 9, 1900); made a new version of Beethoven's *Die Ruinen von Athen* with Hugo von Hofmannsthal (Staatsoper, Vienna, Sept. 20, 1924, composer conducting); made a new version of Mozart's *Idomeneo* with Lothar Wallerstein (1930; Staatsoper, Vienna, April 16, 1931, composer conducting).

BIBL.: WORKS, SOURCE MATERIAL: There is no complete ed. of Strauss's works. A critical edition of his stage works was publ. in 18 vols. in 1996 and of his orchestral works in 12 vols. in 1999 by the Verlag Dr. Richard Strauss of Vienna and C.F. Peters Musikverlag of Frankfurt am Main. The standard thematic catalog was prepared by E.H. Mueller von Asow, *R. S.: Thematisches Verzeichnis* (3 vols., Vienna, 1954–74). See also F. Trenner, *S. R.: Werkverzeichnis* (Munich, 1993). Many of his writings may be found in W. Schuh, ed., *R. S.: Betrachtungen und Erinnerungen* (Zürich, 1949; Eng. tr., N.Y., 1953; second Ger. ed., rev., 1957). The major bibliographical source is *R.-S.-Bibliographie* (2 vols., Vienna; Vol. I, 1882–1944, ed. by O. Ortner, 1964; Vol. II, 1944–1964, ed. by G. Brosche, 1973). Other sources include the following: R. Specht, *R. S.: Vollständiges Verzeichnis der im Druck erschienen Werke* (Vienna, 1910); J. Kapp, *R. S. und die Berliner Oper* (Berlin, 1934–39); E. Wachten, *R. S., geboren 1864: Sein Leben in Bildern* (Leipzig, 1940); R. Tenschert, *Anekdoten um R. S.* (Vienna, 1945); idem, *R. S. und Wien: Eine Wahlverwandtschaft* (Vienna, 1949); E. Roth, ed., *R. S.: Bühnenwerk* (Ger., Eng., and French; London, 1954); W. Schuh, *Das Bühnenwerke von R. S. in den unter Mitwirkung des Komponisten geschaffenen letzten Münchner Inszenierungen* (Zürich, 1954); F. Trenner, *R. S.: Dokumente seines Lebens und Schaffens* (Munich, 1954); R. Petzoldt, *R. S.: Sein Leben in Bildern* (Leipzig, 1962); F. Dostal, ed., *Karl Böhm: Begegnung mit R. S.* (Vienna, 1964); F. Grasberger and F. Hadamowsky, eds., *R.-S.-Ausstellung zum 100. Geburtstag* (Vienna, 1964); F. Hadamowsky, *R. S. und Salzburg* (Salzburg, 1964); W. Schuh, *Ein paar Erinnerungen an R. S.* (Zürich, 1964); W. Schuh and E. Roth, eds., *R. S.: Complete Catalogue* (London, 1964); W. Thomas, *R. S. und seine Zeitgenössen* (Munich, 1964); F. Grasberger, *R. S.: Höhe Kunst, erfülltes Leben* (Vienna, 1965); W. Deppisch, *R. S. in Selbstzeugnissen und Bilddokumenten* (Reinbek, 1968); F. Grasberger, *R. S. und die Wiener Oper* (Vienna, 1969); A. Jefferson, *R. S.* (London, 1975); F. Trenner, *Die Skizzenbücher von R. S. aus dem R.-S.-Archiv in Garmisch* (Tutzing, 1977); idem, *R. S. Werkverzeichnis* (Vienna, 1985). **CORRESPONDENCE:** F. Strauss, ed., *R. S.: Briefwechsel mit Hugo von Hofmannsthal* (Berlin, 1925; Eng. tr., N.Y., 1927); *R. S. et Romain Rolland: Correspondance, fragments de journal* (Paris, 1951; Eng. tr., 1968); F. von Schuch, *R. S., Ernst von Schuch und Dresdens Oper* (Leipzig, 1952; second ed., 1953); W. Schuh, ed., *R. S. und Hugo von Hofmannsthal: Briefwechsel: Gesamtausgabe* (Zürich, 1952; second ed., rev., 1955; Eng. tr.,

1961, as *A Working Friendship: The Correspondence between R. S. and Hugo von Hofmannsthal*); idem, ed., *R. S.: Briefe an die Eltern 1882–1906* (Zürich, 1954); R. Tenschert, ed., *R. S. und Joseph Gregor: Briefwechsel 1934–1949* (Salzburg, 1955); W. Schuh, ed., *R. S., Stefan Zweig: Briefwechsel* (Frankfurt am Main, 1957; Eng. tr., 1977, as *A Confidential Matter: The Letters of R. S. and Stefan Zweig 1931–1935*); D. Kämper, ed., *R. S. und Franz Wüllner im Briefwechsel* (Cologne, 1963); G. Kende and W. Schuh, eds., *R. S., Clemens Krauss: Briefwechsel* (Munich, 1963; second ed., 1964); A. Ott, ed., *R. S. und Ludwig Thuille: Briefe der Freundschaft 1877–1907* (Munich, 1969); W. Schuh, ed., *R. S.: Briefwechsel mit Willi Schuh* (Zürich, 1969); G. Brosche, ed., *R. S., Clemens Krauss Briefwechsel: Gesamtausgabe* (Tutsing, 1997). **BIOGRAPHI-CAL:** A. Seidl and W. Klatte, *R. S.: Eine Charakterskizze* (Prague, 1896); G. Brecher, *R. S.: Eine monographische Skizze* (Leipzig, 1900); E. Urban, *R. S.* (Berlin, 1901); R. Batka, *R. S.* (Charlottenburg, 1908); E. Newman, *R. S.* (London, 1908); M. Steinitzer, *R. S.* (Berlin, 1911; final ed., enl., 1927); H. Finck, *R. S.: The Man and His Works* (Boston, 1917); R. Specht, *R. S. und sein Werk* (2 vols., Leipzig, 1921); R. Muschler, *R. S.* (Hildesheim, 1924); S. Kallenberg, *R. S.: Leben und Werk* (Leipzig, 1926); J. Cooke, *R. S.: A Short Biography* (Philadelphia, 1929); W. Hutschenruyter, *R. S.* (The Hague, 1929); E. Gehring, ed., *R. S. und seine Vaterstadt: Zum 70. Geburtstag am 11. Juni 1934* (Munich, 1934); F. Gysi, *R. S.* (Potsdam, 1934); W. Brandl, *R. S.: Leben und Werk* (Wiesbaden, 1949); E. Bücken, *R. S.* (Kevelaer, 1949); K. Pfister, *R. S.: Weg, Gestalt, Denkmal* (Vienna, 1949); C. Rostand, *R. S.* (Paris, 1949; second ed., 1965); O. Erhardt, *R. S.: Leben, Wirken, Schaffen* (Olten, 1953); E. Krause, *R. S.: Gestalt und Werk* (Leipzig, 1955; third ed., rev., 1963; Eng. tr., 1964); I. Fabian, *R. S.* (Budapest, 1962); H. Kralik, *R. S.: Weltbürger der Musik* (Vienna, 1963); W. Panofsky, *R. S.: Partitur eines Lebens* (Munich, 1965); G. Marek, *R. S.: The Life of a Non-Hero* (N.Y., 1967); A. Jefferson, *The Life of R. S.* (Newton Abbot, 1973); M. Kennedy, *R. S.* (London, 1976; second ed., rev., 1983; rev. and aug., 1995); W. Schuh, *R. S.: Jugend und Meisterjahre: Lebenschronik 1864–98* (Zürich, 1976; Eng. tr. as *R. S.: A Chronicle of the Early Years 1864–98*, Cambridge, 1982); K. Wilhelm, *R. S. persönlich: Eine Bildbiographie* (Munich, 1984; new ed., 1999); T. Ashley, *R. S.* (London, 1999); M. Kennedy, *R. S.: Man, Musician, Enigma* (Cambridge, 1999). **CRITICAL, ANALYTICAL:** G. Jourissenne, *R. S.: Essai critique et biographique* (Brussels, 1899); E. Urban, *S. contra Wagner* (Berlin, 1902); O. Bie, *Die moderne Musik und R. S.* (Berlin, 1906); L. Gilman, *S.' Salome: A Guide to the Opera* (N.Y., 1906); J. Manifarges, *R. S. als Dirigent* (Amsterdam, 1907); E. Schmitz, *R. S. als Musikdramatiker: Eine aesthetisch-kritische Studie* (Munich, 1907); E. von Ziegler, *R. S. und seine dramatischen Dichtungen* (Munich, 1907); P. Bekker, *Das Musikdrama der Gegenwart* (Stuttgart, 1909); E. Fischer-Plasser, *Einführung in die Musik von R. S. und Elektra* (Leipzig, 1909); G. Gräner, *R. S.: Musikdramen* (Berlin, 1909); F. Santoliquido, *Il dopo-Wagner: Claude Debussy e R. S.* (Rome, 1909); O. Hübner, *R. S. und das Musikdrama: Betrachtungen über den Wert oder Unwert gewisser Opernmusiken* (Leipzig, 1910); E. Hutcheson, *Elektra by R. S.: A Guide to the Opera with Musical Examples from the Score* (N.Y., 1910); M. Steinitzer, *S.iana und Anderes* (Stuttgart, 1910); H. Daffner, *Salome: Ihre Gestalt in Geschichte und Künst* (Munich, 1912); A. Seidl, *S.iana: Aufsätze zur R.S.—Frage auf drei Jahrzehnten* (Regensburg, 1913); O. Bie, *Die neuere Musik bis R. S.* (Leipzig, 1916); H. von Waltershausen, *R. S.: Ein Versuch* (Munich, 1921); R. Rosenzweig, *Zur Entwicklungsgeschichte des S.'schen Musikdramas* (diss., Univ. of Vienna, 1923); W. Schrenk, *R. S. und die neue Musik* (Berlin, 1924); E. Blom, *The Rose Cavalier* (London, 1930); T. Armstrong, *S.' Tone Poems* (London, 1931); G.

Röttger, *Die Harmonik in R. S.' Der Rosenkavalier: Ein Beitrag zur Entwicklung der romantische Harmonik nach Richard Wagner* (diss., Univ. of Munich, 1931); E. Wachten, *Das psychotechnische Formproblem in den Sinfonischen Dichtungen von R.S. (mit besonderer Berücksichtigung seiner Bühnenwerk)* diss., Univ. of Berlin, 1932; publ. in an abr. ed., Berlin, 1933); K.-J. Krüger, *Hugo von Hofmannsthal und R. S.: Versuch einer Deutung des künstlerisschen Weges Hugo von Hofmannsthals, mit einem Anhang; erstmalige Veröffentlichung der bischer ungedruckten einzigen Vertonung eines Hofmannsthalschen Gedichtes durch R. S.* (Berlin, 1935); H. Röttger, *Das Formproblem bei R. S. gezeigt an der Oper Die Frau ohne Schatten, mit Einschluss von Guntram und Intermezzo* (diss., Univ. of Munich, 1935; publ. in an abr. ed., Berlin, 1937); J. Gregor, *R. S.: Der Meister der Oper* (Munich, 1939; second ed., 1942); G. Becker, *Das Problem der Oper an Hand von R. S.' Capriccio* (diss., Univ. of Jena, 1944); R. Tenschert, *Dreimal sieben Variationen über das Thema R. S.* (Vienna, 1944; second ed., 1945); O. Gatscha, *Librettist und Komponist: Dargestellt an den Opern R. S.'* (diss., Univ. of Vienna, 1947); A. Pryce-Jones, *R. S.: Der Rosenkavalier* (London, 1947); W. Schuh, *Über Opern von R. S.* (Zürich, 1947); F. Trenner, *Die Zusammenarbeit von Hugo von Hofmannsthal und R. S.* (diss., Univ. of Munich, 1949); D. Lindner, *R. S./Joseph Gregor: Die Liebe der Danae: Herkunft, Inhalt und Gestaltung eines Opernwerkes* (Vienna, 1952); R. Schopenhauer, *Die antiken Frauengestalten bei R. S.* (diss., Univ. of Vienna, 1952); G. Hausswald, *R. S.: Ein Beitrag zur Dresdener Operngeschichte seit 1945* (Dresden, 1953); W. Wendhausen, *Das stilistische Verhältnis von Dichtung und Musik in der Entwicklung der musikdramatischen Werke R. S.'* (diss., Univ. of Hamburg, 1954); G. Kende, *R. S. und Clemens Krauss: Eine Künstlerfreundschaft und ihre Zusammenarbeit an Capriccio (op.85): Konversationsstück für Musik* (Munich, 1960); N. Del Mar, *R. S.: A Critical Commentary on His Life and Works* (3 vols., London, 1962, 1969, and 1972; reprint with corrections, 1978); A. Jefferson, *The Operas of R. S. in Britain, 1910–1963* (London, 1963); A. Natan, *R. S.: Die Opern* (Basel, 1963); A. Berger, *R. S. als geistige Macht: Versuch eines philosophischen Verständnisses* (Gisch, 1964); L. Lehmann, *Five Operas and R. S.* (N.Y., 1964; publ. in London, 1964, as *Singing with R. S.*); W. Mann, *R. S.: A Critical Study of the Operas* (London, 1964); K. Pörnbacher, *Hugo von Hofmannsthal/R. S.: Der Rosenkavalier* (Munich, 1964); W. Schuh, *Hugo von Hofmannsthal und R. S.: Legende und Wirklichkeit* (Munich, 1964); A. Goléa, *R. S.* (Paris, 1965); R. Gerlach, *Tonalität und tonale Konfiguration im Oeuvre von R. S.: Analysen und Interpretationen als Beiträge zum Verständnis von tonalen Problemen und Formen in sinfonischen Werken und in der "Einleitung" und ersten Szene des Rosenkavalier* (diss., Univ. of Zürich, 1966; publ. as *Don Juan und Rosenkavalier*, Bern, 1966); R. Schäfer, *Hugo von Hofmannsthals Arabella* (Bern, 1967); W. Gruhn, *Die Instrumentation in den Orchesterwerken von R. S.* (diss., Univ. of Mainz, 1968); W. Schuh, *Der Rosenkavalier: 4 Studien* (Olten, 1968); J. Knaus, *Hugo von Hofmannsthal und sein Weg zur Oper Die Frau ohne Schatten* (Berlin, 1971); W. Schuh, ed., *Hugo von Hofmannsthal, R. S.: Der Rosenkavalier: Fassungen, Filmszenarium, Briefe* (Frankfurt am Main, 1971); A. Abert, *R. S.: Die Opern: Einführung und Analyse* (Hannover, 1972); A. Jefferson, *The Lieder of R. S.* (London, 1972); W. Colson, *Four Last Songs by R. S.* (diss., Univ. of Ill., 1974); D. Daviau and G. Buelow, *The "Ariadne auf Naxos" of Hugo von Hofmannsthal and R. S.* (Chapel Hill, 1975); B. Peterson, *Ton und Wort: The Lieder of R. S.* (Ann Arbor, 1979); K. Forsyth, *Ariadne auf Naxos by Hugo von Hofmannsthal and R. S.: Its Genesis and Meaning* (Oxford, 1982); R. Hartmann, *R. S.: The Staging of His Operas and Ballets* (Oxford, 1982); R. Schlötter, *Musik und Theater im "Rosenkavalier" vom R. S.* (Vienna, 1985); H. Wajemann, *Die Chorkomposi-*

tionen von R. S. (Tutzing, 1986); G. Splitt, *R. S. 1933–1935: Ästhetik und Musikpolitik zu Beginn der nationalsozialistischen Herrschaft* (Pfaffenweiler, 1987); C. Osborne, *The Complete Operas of R. S.* (London, 1988); E.-M. Axt, *Musikalische Form als Dramaturgie: Prinzipien eines Spätstils in der Oper "Friedenstag" von R. S. und Joseph Gregor* (Munich, 1989); B. Gilliam, *R. S.'s Elektra* (Oxford, 1991); D. Greene, *Listening to S. Operas: The Audience's Multiple Standpoints* (N.Y., 1991); W. Krebs, *Der Wille zum Rausch: Aspekte der musikalischen Dramaturgie von R. S.' "Salome"* (Munich, 1991); B. Gilliam, ed., *R. S. and His World* (Princeton, 1992); idem, ed., *R. S.: New Perspectives on the Composer and His Work* (Durham, N.C., 1992); B. Meier, *Geschichtliche Signaturen der Musik bei Mahler, S. und Schönberg* (Hamburg, 1992); A. Unger, *Welt, Leben und Kunst als Themen der "Zarathustra-Kompositionen" von R. S. und Gustav Mahler* (Frankfurt am Main, 1992); J. Williamson, *S.: Also sprach Zarathustra* (Cambridge, 1993); J. Liebscher, *R. S.: Also sprach Zarathustra: Tondichtung (frei nach Friedr. Nietzsche) für grosses Orchester op.30* (Munich, 1994); J. Schaarwächter, *R. S. und die Sinfonie* (Cologne, 1994); S. Bayerlein, *Musikalische Psychologie der drei Frauengestalten in der Oper Elektra von R. S.* (Tutzing, 1996); R. Bayreuther, *R. S.' Alpensinfonie: Entstehung, Analyse und Interpretation* (Hildesheim, 1997); V. Beci, *Der ewig Moderne: R. S. 1864–1949* (Düsseldorf, 1998).—NS/LK/DM

Stravinsky, Feodor (Ignatievich), distinguished Russian bass of Polish descent, father of **Igor (Feodorovich) Stravinsky;** b. Noviy Dvor, near Rechitza, June 20, 1843; d. St. Petersburg, Dec. 4, 1902. While pursuing the study of law, he appeared in concerts with such success that he decided to study voice; in 1869 he became a student at the St. Petersburg Cons., where he received vocal training from Camillo Everardi (1871–73). On Sept. 3, 1873, he made his formal operatic debut as Count Rodolpho in *La Sonnambula* in Kiev, where he continued to sing until 1876. He became a member of the Russian Imperial Opera at St. Petersburg in 1876 and established himself as one of the greatest Russian basses before Chaliapin; his interpretation of heroic and comical characters in Russian operas evoked unbounded praise from the critics. He was famous as Méphistophélès in Gounod's *Faust*, and was distinguished not only for the power of his voice, but also for his dramatic talent on the stage. Altogether, he made 1,235 appearances in 64 operatic roles.—NS/LK/DM

Stravinsky, Igor (Feodorovich), great Russian-born French, later American composer, one of the supreme masters of 20th-century music, whose works exercised the most profound influence on the evolution of music through the emancipation of rhythm, melody, and harmony, son of **Feodor (Ignatievich) Stravinsky** and father of **(Sviatoslav) Soulima Stravinsky;** b. Oranienbaum, near St. Petersburg, June 17, 1882; d. N.Y., April 6, 1971. He was brought up in an artistic atmosphere; he often went to opera rehearsals when his father sang, and acquired an early love for the musical theater. He took piano lessons with Alexandra Snetkova, and later with Leokadia Kashperova, who was a pupil of Anton Rubinstein; but it was not until much later that he began to study theory, first with Akimenko and then with Kalafati (1900–03). His progress in composition was remarkably slow; he never entered a music school or a cons., and never earned an academic degree in music. In 1901 he enrolled in the faculty of jurisprudence at Univ. of St. Petersburg, and took courses there for 8 semesters, without graduating; a fellow student was Vladimir Rimsky-Korsakov, a son of the composer. In the summer of 1902 Stravinsky traveled in Germany, where he met another son of Rimsky-Korsakov, Andrei, who was a student at the Univ. of Heidelberg; Stravinsky became his friend. He was introduced to Rimsky-Korsakov, and became a regular guest at the latter's periodic gatherings in St. Petersburg. In 1903–04 he wrote a piano sonata for the Russian pianist Nicolai Richter, who performed it at Rimsky-Korsakov's home. In 1905 he began taking regular lessons in orchestration with Rimsky-Korsakov, who taught him free of charge; under his tutelage, Stravinsky composed a Sym. in E-flat major; the second and third movements from it were performed on April 27, 1907, by the Court Orch. in St. Petersburg, and a complete performance of it was given by the same orch. on Feb. 4, 1908. The work, dedicated to Rimsky-Korsakov, had some singularities and angularities that showed a deficiency of technique; there was little in this work that presaged Stravinsky's ultimate development as a master of form and orchestration. At the same concert, his *Le Faune et la bergère* for Voice and Orch. had its first performance; this score revealed a certain influence of French Impressionism. To celebrate the marriage of Rimsky-Korsakov's daughter Nadezhda to the composer Maximilian Steinberg on June 17, 1908, Stravinsky wrote an orch. fantasy entitled *Fireworks*. Rimsky-Korsakov died a few days after the wedding; Stravinsky deeply mourned his beloved teacher and wrote a funeral song for Wind Instruments in his memory; it was first performed in St. Petersburg on Jan. 30, 1909. There followed a *Scherzo fantastique* for Orch., inspired by Maeterlinck's book *La Vie des abeilles*. As revealed in his correspondence with Rimsky-Korsakov, Stravinsky had at first planned a literal program of composition, illustrating events in the life of a beehive by a series of descriptive sections; some years later, however, he gratuitously denied all connection of the work with Maeterlinck's book.

A signal change in Stravinsky's fortunes came when the famous impresario Diaghilev commissioned him to write a work for the Paris season of his company, the Ballets Russes. The result was the production of his first ballet masterpiece, *The Firebird*, staged by Diaghilev in Paris on June 25, 1910. Here he created music of extraordinary brilliance, steeped in the colors of Russian fairy tales. There are numerous striking effects in the score, such as a glissando of harmonics in the string instruments; the rhythmic drive is exhilarating, and the use of asymmetrical time signatures is extremely effective; the harmonies are opulent; the orchestration is coruscating. He drew 2 orch. suites from the work; in 1919 he reorchestrated the music to conform to his new beliefs in musical economy; in effect he plucked the luminous feathers off the magical firebird, but the original scoring remained a favorite with conductors and orchs. Stravinsky's association with Diaghilev demanded his presence in Paris, which he made his home beginning in 1911, with frequent travels to Switzerland. His second ballet for Diaghilev was *Pétrouchka*, premiered in Paris on June 13, 1911, with triumphant success. Not only was the ballet remarkably effective on the stage, but the score itself, arranged in 2 orch. suites, was so new and original that it marked a turning point in 20th-century music; the spasmodically explosive rhythms, the novel instrumental sonorities, with the use of the piano as an integral part of the orch., the bold harmonic innovations in employing 2 different keys simultaneously (C major and F-sharp major, the "Pétrouchka Chord") became a potent influence on modern European composers. Debussy voiced his enchantment with the score, and young Stravinsky, still in his 20s, became a Paris celebrity. Two years later, he brought out a work of even greater revolutionary import, the ballet *Le Sacre du printemps* (Rite of Spring; Russian title, *Vesna sviashchennaya*, literally Spring the Sacred); its subtitle was "Scenes of Pagan Russia." It was premiered by Diaghilev with his Ballets Russes in Paris on May 29, 1913, with the choreography by Nijinsky. The score marked a departure from all conventions of musical composition; while in Petrouchka the harmonies, though innovative and dissonant, could still be placed in the context of modern music, the score of *Le Sacre du printemps* contained such corrosive dissonances as scales played at the intervals of major sevenths and superpositions of minor upon major triads with the common tonic, chords treated as unified blocks of sound, and rapid metrical changes that seemingly defied performance. The score still stands as one of the most daring creations of the modern musical mind; its impact was tremendous; to some of the audience at its first performance in Paris, Stravinsky's "barbaric" music was beyond endurance; the Paris critics exercised their verbal ingenuity in indignant vituperation; one of them proposed that *Le Sacre du printemps* should be more appropriately described as *Le Massacre du printemps*. On May 26, 1914, Diaghilev premiered Stravinsky's lyric fairy tale *Le Rossignol*, after Hans Christian Andersen. It too abounded in corrosive discords, but here it could be explained as "Chinese" music illustrative of the exotic subject. From 1914 to 1918 he worked on his ballet *Les Noces* (Russian title, *Svadebka*; literally, Little Wedding), evoking Russian peasant folk modalities; it was scored for an unusual ensemble of chorus, soloists, 4 pianos, and 17 percussion instruments.

The devastation of World War I led Stravinsky to conclude that the era of grandiose Romantic music had become obsolete, and that a new spirit of musical economy was imperative in an impoverished world. As an illustration of such economy, he wrote the musical stage play *L'Histoire du soldat*, scored for only 7 players, with a narrator. About the same time, he wrote a work for 11 instruments entitled *Ragtime*, inspired by the new American dance music. He continued his association with Diaghilev's Ballets Russes in writing the ballet *Pulcinella*, based on themes by Pergolesi and other 18th-century Italian composers. He also wrote for Diaghilev 2 short operas, *Renard*, to a Russian fairy tale (Paris, May 18, 1922), and *Mavra*, after Pushkin (Paris, June 3, 1922). These 2 works were the last in which he used Russian subjects, with the sole exception of an orch. *Scherzo à la russe*, written in 1944. Stravinsky had now entered the period usually designated as neo-

Classical. The most significant works of this stage of his development were his Octet for Wind Instruments and the Piano Concerto commissioned by Koussevitzky. In these works, he abandoned the luxuriant instrumentation of his ballets and their aggressively dissonant harmonies; instead, he used pandiatonic structures, firmly tonal but starkly dissonant in their superposition of tonalities within the same principal key. His reversion to old forms, however, was not an act of ascetic renunciation but, rather, a grand experiment in reviving Baroque practices, which had fallen into desuetude. The Piano Concerto provided him with an opportunity to appear as soloist; Stravinsky was never a virtuoso pianist, but he was able to acquit himself satisfactorily in such works as the Piano Concerto; he played it with Koussevitzky in Paris on May 22, 1924, and during his first American tour with the Boston Sym. Orch., also under Koussevitzky, on Jan. 23, 1925. The Elizabeth Sprague Coolidge Foundation commissioned him to write a pantomime for string orch.; the result was *Apollon Musagète*, given at the Library of Congress in Washington, D.C., on April 27, 1928. This score, serene and emotionally restrained, evokes the manner of Lully's court ballets. He continued to explore the resources of neo-Baroque writing in his *Capriccio* for Piano and Orch., which he performed as soloist, with Ansermet conducting, in Paris, on Dec. 6, 1929; this score is impressed by a spirit of hedonistic entertainment, harking back to the *style galant* of the 18th century; yet it is unmistakably modern in its polyrhythmic collisions of pandiatonic harmonies. Stravinsky's growing disillusionment with the external brilliance of modern music led him to seek eternal verities of music in ancient modalities. His well-nigh monastic renunciation of the grandiose edifice of glorious sound to which he himself had so abundantly contributed found expression in his opera-oratorio *Oedipus Rex*; in order to emphasize its detachment from temporal aspects, he commissioned a Latin text for the work, even though the subject was derived from a Greek play; its music is deliberately hollow and its dramatic points are emphasized by ominous repetitive passages. Yet this very austerity of idiom makes *Oedipus Rex* a profoundly moving play. It had its first performance in Paris on May 30, 1927; its stage premiere took place in Vienna on Feb. 23, 1928. A turn to religious writing found its utterance in Stravinsky's *Symphony of Psalms*, written for the 50th anniversary of the Boston Sym. Orch. and dedicated "to the glory of God." The work is scored for chorus and orch., omitting the violins and violas, thus emphasizing the lower instrumental registers and creating an austere sonority suitable to its solemn subject. Owing to a delay of the Boston performance, the world premiere of the *Symphony of Psalms* took place in Brussels on Dec. 13, 1930. In 1931 he wrote a Violin Concerto commissioned by the violinist Samuel Dushkin, and performed by him in Berlin on Oct. 23, 1931. On a commission from the ballerina Ida Rubinstein, he composed the ballet *Perséphone*; here again he exercised his mastery of simplicity in formal design, melodic patterns, and contrapuntal structure. For his American tour he wrote *Jeu de cartes*, a "ballet in 3 deals" to his own scenario depicting an imaginary game of poker (of which he was a devotee).

He conducted its first performance at the Metropolitan Opera in N.Y. on April 27, 1937. His concerto for 16 instruments entitled *Dumbarton Oaks*, named after the Washington, D.C., estate of Mr. and Mrs. Robert Woods Bliss, who commissioned the work, was first performed in Washington, on May 8, 1938; in Europe it was played under the noncommittal title Concerto in E-flat; its style is hermetically neo-Baroque. It is germane to note that in his neo-Classical works Stravinsky began to indicate the key in the title, e.g., *Serenade* in A for Piano (1925), Concerto in D for Violin and Orch. (1931), Concerto in E-flat (*Dumbarton Oaks*, 1938), Sym. in C (1938), and Concerto in D for String Orch. (1946).

With World War II engulfing Europe, Stravinsky decided to seek permanent residence in America. He had acquired French citizenship on June 10, 1934; in 1939 he applied for American citizenship; he became a naturalized American citizen on Dec. 28, 1945. To celebrate this event, he made an arrangement of the *Star-Spangled Banner*, which contained a curious modulation into the subdominant in the coda. He conducted it with the Boston Sym. Orch. on Jan. 14, 1944, but because of legal injunctions existing in the state of Mass. against intentional alteration, or any mutilation, of the national anthem, he was advised not to conduct his version at the second pair of concerts, and the standard version was substituted. In 1939–40 Stravinsky was named Charles Eliot Norton lecturer at Harvard Univ.; about the same time, he accepted several private students, a pedagogical role he had never exercised before. His American years form a curious panoply of subjects and manners of composition. He accepted a commission from the Ringling Bros. to write a *Circus Polka* "for a young elephant." In 1946 he wrote *Ebony Concerto* for a swing band. In 1951 he completed his opera *The Rake's Progress*, inspired by Hogarth's famous series of engravings, to a libretto by W.H. Auden and C. Kallman. He conducted its premiere in Venice on Sept. 11, 1951, as part of the International Festival of Contemporary Music. The opera is a striking example of Stravinsky's protean capacity for adopting different styles and idioms of composition to serve his artistic purposes; *The Rake's Progress* is an ingenious conglomeration of disparate elements, ranging from 18th-century British ballads to cosmopolitan burlesque. But whatever transmutations his music underwent during his long and productive career, he remained a man of the theater at heart. In America he became associated with the brilliant Russian choreographer Balanchine, who produced a number of ballets to Stravinsky's music, among them his *Apollon Musagète*, Violin Concerto, Sym. in 3 movements, *Scherzo à la russe*, *Pulcinella*, and *Agon*. It was in his score of *Agon* that he essayed for the first time to adopt the method of composition with 12 tones as promulgated by Schoenberg; *Agon* (the word means "competition" in Greek) bears the subtitle "ballet for 12 tones," perhaps in allusion to the dodecaphonic technique used in the score. Yet the 12-tone method had been the very antithesis of his previous tenets. In fact, an irreconcilable polarity existed between Stravinsky and Schoenberg even in personal relations. Although both resided in Los Angeles for several years, they never met socially; Schoenberg once wrote a canon in which he

ridiculed Stravinsky as Herr Modernsky, who put on a wig to look like "Papa Bach." After Schoenberg's death, Stravinsky became interested in examining the essence of the method of composition with 12 tones, which was introduced to him by his faithful musical factotum Robert Craft; Stravinsky adopted dodecaphonic writing in its aspect of canonic counterpoint as developed by Webern. In this manner he wrote his *Canticum sacrum ad honorem Sancti Marci nominis*, which he conducted at San Marco in Venice on Sept. 13, 1956. Other works of the period were also written in a modified 12-tone technique, among them *The Flood*, for Narrator, Mime, Singers, and Dancers, presented in a CBS-TV broadcast in N.Y. on June 14, 1962; its first stage performance was given in Hamburg on April 30, 1963.

Stravinsky was married twice; his first wife, Catherine Nosenko, whom he married on Jan. 24, 1906, and who bore him 3 children, died in 1939; on March 9, 1940, Stravinsky married his longtime mistress, Vera, who was formerly married to the Russian painter Serge Sudeikin. She was born Vera de Bosset in St. Petersburg, on Dec. 25, 1888, and died in N.Y. on Sept. 17, 1982, at the age of 93. An ugly litigation for the rights to the Stravinsky estate continued for several years between his children and their stepmother; after Vera Stravinsky's death, it was finally settled in a compromise, according to which 2/9 of the estate went to each of his 3 children and a grandchild and 1/9 to Robert Craft. The value of the Stravinsky legacy was spectacularly demonstrated on Nov. 11, 1982, when his working draft of *Le Sacre du printemps* was sold at an auction in London for the fantastic sum of $548,000. The purchaser was Paul Sacher, the Swiss conductor and philanthropist. Even more fantastic was the subsequent sale of the entire Stravinsky archive, consisting of 116 boxes of personal letters and 225 drawers containing MSS, some of them unpubl. Enormous bids were made for it by the N.Y. Public Library and the Morgan Library, but they were all outbid by Sacher, who offered the overwhelming purse of $5,250,000, which removed all competition. The materials were to be assembled in a specially constructed 7- story Sacher Foundation building in Basel, to be eventually opened to scholars for study.

In tribute to Stravinsky as a naturalized American citizen, the U.S. Postal Service issued a 2-cent stamp bearing his image to mark his centennial in 1982, an honor theretofore never granted to a foreign-born composer (the possible exception being Victor Herbert, but his entire career was made in America).

Few composers of his day escaped the powerful impact of Stravinsky's music; ironically, it was his own country that rejected him, partly because of the opposition of Soviet ideologues to modern music in general, and partly because of Stravinsky's open criticism of Soviet ways in art. But in 1962 he returned to Russia for a visit, and was welcomed as a prodigal son; as if by magic, his works began to appear on Russian concert programs, and Soviet music critics issued a number of laudatory studies of his works. Yet it is Stravinsky's early masterpieces, set in an attractive colorful style, that continue to enjoy favor with audiences and performers, while his more abstract and recursive scores are appreciated mainly by specialists.

WORKS: DRAMATIC: *Le Rossignol*, "lyric tale" in 3 acts, after Hans Christian Andersen (1908–14; Paris Opéra, May 26, 1914, Monteux conducting; in 1917 the second and third acts were scored as a ballet, *Le Chant du rossignol*; Paris Opéra, Feb. 2, 1920; also, in 1917, fragments from the second and third acts were used for a symphonic poem under the same title); *L'Oiseau de feu* (The Firebird), ballet (Paris Opéra, June 25, 1910; 3 suite versions: 1911, 1919, and 1945; 2 sections arranged for Violin and Piano, 1926); *Pétrouchka*, ballet (Paris, June 13, 1911, Monteux conducting; rev. 1946; excerpts officially designated as a "suite" in 1946); *Le Sacre du printemps*, ballet, "scenes of pagan Russia" (1911–13; Paris, May 29, 1913, Monteux conducting; first concert perf., Moscow, Feb. 18, 1914, Serge Koussevitzky conducting; first Paris concert perf., April 5, 1914, Monteux conducting); *Renard*, burlesque chamber opera (1915–16; Paris, May 18, 1922); *L'Histoire du soldat*, ballet with Narrator and 7 Instrumentalists (Lausanne, Sept. 28, 1918; concert suite with original instrumentation, London, July 20, 1920, Ansermet conducting; also *Petite suite* for Violin, Clarinet, and Piano extracted from the score, 1919); *Pulcinella*, ballet "after Pergolesi" with solos, trios, and a duet for Soprano, Tenor, and Bass (Paris Opéra, May 15, 1920; an orch. suite was extracted from it in 1922, and first perf. in Boston, Dec. 22, 1922, rev. 1947; 2 chamber pieces, *Suite italienne*); *Les Noces* (The Wedding), ballet-cantata, subtitled "choreographic Russian scenes," revision for Soloists, Chorus, 4 Pianos, and 17 Percussion Instruments (1921–23; Paris, June 13, 1923; orig. scored with Full Orch., 1914–17); *Mavra*, comic opera, after Pushkin (Paris Opéra, June 3, 1922); *Oedipus Rex*, opera-oratorio, after Sophocles (concert perf., Paris, May 30, 1927; stage perf., Vienna, Feb. 23, 1928; rev. 1948); *Apollon Musagète*, classic ballet for String Orch. (Washington, D.C., April 27, 1928; rev. 1947); *Le Baiser de la fée*, ballet on themes of Tchaikovsky (Paris Opéra, Nov. 27, 1928; in 1934 several sections were collected for an independent symphonic piece called *Divertimento*; entire ballet rev. 1950); *Perséphone*, melodrama in 3 parts for Female Narrator, Tenor, Chorus, and Orch., after André Gide (1933; Paris Opéra, April 30, 1934; rev. 1949); *Jeu de cartes*, "ballet in 3 deals" (1935–37; N.Y., April 27, 1937); *Orpheus*, ballet (1946–47; N.Y., April 28, 1948); *The Rake's Progress*, opera, after Hogarth W.H. Auden and C. Kallman (1948–51; Venice, Sept. 11, 1951, composer conducting); *Agon*, ballet for 12 Dancers (1954–57; Los Angeles, June 17, 1957); *Noah and the Flood*, also called *The Flood*, biblical spectacle narrated, mimed, sung, and danced (CBS-TV, N.Y., June 14, 1962; first stage perf., Hamburg, April 30, 1963). **ORCH.:** Sym. in E-flat major, op.1 (1905–07; first partial perf., second and third movements only, St. Petersburg, April 27, 1907; first complete perf., St. Petersburg, Feb. 4, 1908; rev. version, Montreux, Switzerland, April 2, 1914); *Scherzo fantastique*, op.3 (1907; St. Petersburg, Feb. 6, 1909); *Fireworks*, op.4 (St. Petersburg, June 17, 1908; reorchestrated and first perf. in St. Petersburg, Jan. 22, 1910); *Chant funèbre* for Wind Instruments, on the death of Rimsky-Korsakov (1908; St. Petersburg, Jan. 30, 1909; score lost); 2 suites for Small Orch.: No. 1 (1917–25; orch. arrangement of Nos. 1–4 of the *5 pièces faciles* for Piano, 4-Hands: Andante, Napolitana, Española, and Balalaika) and No. 2 (1921; orch. arrangement of *3 pièces faciles* and No. 5 of *5 pièces faciles* for Piano, 4-Hands: March, Waltz, Polka, and Galop); *Symphonies of Wind Instruments*, in memory of Debussy (1918–20; London, June 10, 1921; rev. 1945–47); *Le Chant du rossignol*, symphonic poem after the opera *Le Rossignol* (Geneva, Dec. 6, 1919); Concerto for Piano, with Wind Instruments, Double Basses, and Percussion (Paris, May 22, 1924; rev. 1950); 4 études: *Danse, Excentrique, Cantique*, and *Madrid* (1928; orch.

arrangement of 3 pieces for String Quartet, and Étude for Pianola; Berlin, Nov. 7, 1930; rev. 1952); *Capriccio* for Piano and Orch. (Paris, Dec. 6, 1929; rev. 1949); Concerto in D for Violin and Orch. (Berlin, Oct. 23, 1931; adapted in 1940 for Balanchine's ballet *Balustrade*); *Divertimento* (sections of the ballet *Le Baiser de la fée*, combined in 1934); *Praeludium* for Jazz Ensemble (1936–37; rev. version, Los Angeles, Oct. 19, 1953); Concerto in E-flat, *Dumbarton Oaks*, for Chamber Orch. (Washington, D.C., May 8, 1938); Sym. in C (1938–40; Chicago, Nov. 7, 1940); *Tango*, arrangement by Felix Günther of the piano piece (Philadelphia, July 10, 1941, Benny Goodman conducting; Stravinsky's own orchestration, Los Angeles, Oct. 19, 1953); *Danses concertantes* for Chamber Orch. (Los Angeles, Feb. 8, 1942); *Circus Polka* for Piano (commissioned by the Ringling Bros. Circus, to accompany the elephant numbers; arranged for Band by David Raksin, 1942; arranged by Stravinsky for sym. orch., Cambridge, Mass., Jan. 13, 1944, composer conducting); *4 Norwegian Moods* (1942; Cambridge, Mass., Jan. 13, 1944, composer conducting); Sym. in 3 movements (1942–45; N.Y., Jan. 24, 1946); *Ode* (Boston, Oct. 8, 1943); *Scènes de ballet* (orig. composed for Billy Rose's Broadway show *The Seven Lively Arts*, Philadelphia, Nov. 24, 1944; rev. for concert performance, N.Y., Feb. 3, 1945); *Scherzo à la russe* (1944; San Francisco, March 22, 1946; orig. for Big Jazz Band); *Ebony Concerto* for Clarinet and Swing Band (1945; N.Y., March 25, 1946); Concerto in D for String Orch., *Basler* (1946; Basel, Jan. 21, 1947); *Greeting Prelude* ("Happy Birthday," written for Monteux's 80th birthday; Boston, April 4, 1955); *Tres Sacrae Cantiones* for Chamber Orch., after Gesualdo (1957–59); *Movements* for Piano and Orch. (1958–59; N.Y., Jan. 10, 1960); *Monumentum pro Gesualdo di Venosa ad CD Annum*, instrumental surrealization of 3 madrigals by Gesualdo for 4 Wind Instruments, 8 Brass, and Strings (Venice, Sept. 27, 1960); *Variations: Aldous Huxley, In Memoriam* (1963–64; Chicago, April 17, 1965; as a ballet, N.Y., March 31, 1966); *Canon*, from finale of *The Firebird*, in memory of Monteux (Toronto, Dec. 16, 1965). **CHAMBER:** 3 pieces for String Quartet (1914); *Ragtime* for 11 Instruments (1918; London, April 27, 1920); *Petite suite* for Violin, Clarinet, and Piano (1919; arranged from *L'Histoire du soldat*); 3 pieces for Clarinet (Lausanne, Nov. 8, 1919); Concertino for String Quartet (1920; rev. for 12 Instruments, 1952); Octet for Wind Instruments (Paris, Oct. 18, 1923); *Duo concertant* for Violin and Piano (Berlin, Oct. 28, 1932); *Russian Dance* for Violin and Piano, from *Pétrouchka* (1932); *Suite italienne* No. 1 for Cello and Piano, and No. 2 for Violin and Piano (both from *Pulcinella*; 1932, 1934); *Pastorale* for Violin, Oboe, English Horn, Clarinet, and Bassoon (1933; arrangement of vocal *Pastorale*); *Divertimento* for Violin and Piano, based on material from *Le Baiser de la fée* (1934); *Élégie* for Violin and Viola (1944); Septet for Piano, and String and Wind Instruments (1952; Washington, D.C., Jan. 24, 1954); *Epitaphium for Prince Max of Fürstenberg* for Flute, Clarinet, and Harp (Donaueschingen, Oct. 17, 1959); Double Canon for String Quartet (1959); 8 instrumental miniatures for 15 Players (Toronto, April 29, 1962; instrumentation of *Les Cinq Doigts* for Piano); *Fanfare for a New Theater* for 2 Trumpets (N.Y., April 19, 1964). **PIANO:** 2 sonatas (1903–04; 1924); 4 *Études*, op.7 (1908); *Le Sacre du printemps* for Piano, 4-Hands (1912); *3 pièces faciles* for Piano, 4-Hands (1915); *5 pièces faciles* for Piano, 4-Hands (1917); *Étude* for Pianola (1917); *Piano-Rag-Music* (1919); 3 movements from *Pétrouchka* (1921); *Les Cinq Doigts* (1920–21); *Serenade* in A (1925); Concerto for 2 Solo Pianos (1931–35; Paris, Nov. 21, 1935); *Tango* (1940); *Circus Polka* (1942); Sonata for 2 Pianos (Edgewood Coll. of the Dominican Sisters, Madison, Wisc., Aug. 2, 1944). **VOCAL:** *Le Faune et la bergère* for Mezzo-soprano and Orch. (1906; St.

Petersburg, Feb. 4, 1908); *Pastorale*, "song without words" for Soprano and Piano (1908; also for Soprano, Oboe, English Horn, Clarinet, and Bassoon, 1923); *2 Poems of Verlaine* for Baritone and Piano (1910; with Orch., 1951); *2 Poems of Balmont* for High Voice and Piano (1911; also for High Voice and Chamber Orch., 1954); *Le Roi des étoiles* (Zvezdoliki), cantata for Men's Chorus and Orch. (1912; Brussels Radio, April 19, 1939); 3 poems from the Japanese for Soprano, 2 Flutes, 2 Clarinets, Piano, and String Quartet (1912–13); *Pribaoutki* (Peasant Songs) for Voice and 8 Instruments (1914; Vienna, June 6, 1919); *The Saucer*, 4 Russian songs for Women's Voices (1914–17; as *4 Russian Peasant Songs*, with 4 Horns added, 1954); *Berceuses du chat*, suite of 4 songs for Woman's Voice and 3 Clarinets (1915–16; Vienna, June 6, 1919); *Paternoster* for Chorus (1926); *Symphony of Psalms* for Chorus and Orch. (Brussels, Dec. 13, 1930); *Credo* for Chorus (1932); *Ave Maria* for Chorus (1934); *Tango* for Wordless Voice and Piano (1940); *Babel* for Male Narrator, Men's Chorus, and Orch. (1944; Los Angeles, Nov. 18, 1945; 7th and final movement of *Genesis Suite*, in collaboration with Schoenberg, Shilkret, Tansman, Milhaud, Castelnuovo-Tedesco, and Toch); Mass for Men's and Boy's Voices and 10 Wind Instruments (1944–48; Milan, Oct. 27, 1948); Cantata for Soprano, Tenor, Women's Chorus, and 5 Instruments (Los Angeles, Nov. 11, 1952); 3 songs for Mezzo-soprano, Flute, Clarinet, and Viola, after Shakespeare (1953; Los Angeles, March 8, 1954); *In Memoriam Dylan Thomas* for Tenor, String Quartet, and 4 Trombones (Los Angeles, Sept. 20, 1954); *4 Russian Songs* for Soprano, Flute, Guitar, and Harp (1954); *Canticum sacrum ad honorem Sancti Marci nominis* for Tenor, Baritone, Chorus, and Orch. (Venice, Sept. 13, 1956, composer conducting); arrangement for Chorus and Orch. of J.S. Bach's *Choral-Variationen über das Weihnachtslied "Vom Himmel hoch da komm' ich her"* (Ojai, May 27, 1956, Robert Craft conducting); *Threni* for 6 Solo Voices, Chorus, and Orch., after Jeremiah (Venice, Sept. 23, 1958); *A Sermon, a Narrative and a Prayer*, cantata for Speaker, Alto, Tenor, Chorus, and Orch. (1960–62; Basel, Feb. 23, 1962); *The Dove Descending Breaks the Air*, anthem, after T.S. Eliot (Los Angeles, Feb. 19, 1962, Craft conducting); *Elegy for J.F.K.* for Mezzo-soprano or Baritone, 2 Clarinets, and Corno di Bassetto (Los Angeles, April 6, 1964); *Abraham and Isaac*, sacred ballad for Baritone and Chamber Orch., after Hebrew texts (1962–64; Jerusalem, Aug. 23, 1964); *Introitus (T.S. Eliot in Memoriam)* for 6 Men's Voices, Harp, Piano, Timpani, Tam-tams, Viola, and Double Bass (Chicago, April 17, 1965); *Requiem Canticles* for 4 Vocal Soloists, Chorus, and Orch. (Princeton, N.J., Oct. 8, 1966); *The Owl and the Pussycat* for Voice and Piano, after Lear (Los Angeles, Oct. 31, 1966). **N o n d e s c r i p t :** *Do Not Throw Paper Towels in Toilet* for Treble Voice Unaccompanied, to text from poster in men's room at Harvard Univ. (dated Dec. 16, 1939).

WRITINGS: *Chroniques de ma vie* (2 vols., Paris, 1935; Eng. tr., 1936, as *Chronicles of My Life*); *Poetique musicale* (Paris, 1946; Eng. tr., 1948, as *Poetics of Music*); with R. Craft, *Conversations with Igor Stravinsky* (N.Y., 1958), *Memories and Commentaries* (N.Y., 1959), *Expositions and Developments* (N.Y., 1962), *Dialogues and a Diary* (N.Y., 1963), *Themes and Episodes* (N.Y., 1967), and *Retrospections and Conclusions* (N.Y., 1969); *Themes and Conclusions*, amalgamated and ed. from *Themes and Episodes* and *Retrospections and Conclusions* (1972); R. Craft, ed., *Stravinsky: Selected Correspondence* (2 vols., N.Y., 1982, 1984). A sharp debate raged, at times to the point of vitriolic polemical exchange, among Stravinsky's associates as to the degree of credibility of Craft's reports in his dialogues, or even of the factual accounts of events during Stravinsky's last years of life. Stravinsky was never a master of the English language; yet Craft quotes him at length as delivering literary paragraphs of impeccable English prose. Craft admitted that he enhanced Stravinsky's actual words and sentences (which were never recorded on tape), articulating the inner, and at times subliminal, sense of his utterances. Craft's role was made clear beyond dispute by Stravinsky himself, who, in a letter to his publishing agent dated March 15, 1958, urged that the title of the book be changed to *Conversations with Igor Stravinsky* by Robert Craft, and emphatically asserted that the text was in Craft's language, and that in effect Craft "created" him.

BIBL.: A. Casella, *S.* (Rome, 1926); B. de Schloezer, *I. S.* (Paris, 1926); J. Vainkop, *I. S.* (Leningrad, 1927); V. Belaiev, *I. S.'s Les Noces: An Outline* (London, 1928); I. Glebov, *S.* (Leningrad, 1929); C. Ramuz, *Souvenirs sur I. S.* (Paris, 1929; rev. ed., Lausanne, 1946); P. Collaer, *S.* (Brussels, 1930); E. White, *S.'s Sacrifice to Apollo* (London, 1930); H. Fleischer, *S.* (Berlin, 1931); A. Schaeffner, *I. S.* (Paris, 1931); J. Handschin, *I. S.* (Zürich, 1933); D. de Paoli, *I. S.* (Turin, 1934); M. Armitage, ed., *S., a compendium of articles* (N.Y., 1936); M. Fardell, *S. et les Ballets Russes* (Nice, 1941); G. Malipiero, *S.* (Venice, 1945); A. Casella, *S.* (Brescia, 1947); E. White, *S.: A Critical Survey* (London, 1947); T. Stravinsky, *Le Message d'I. S.* (Lausanne, 1948; Eng. tr., 1953, as *The Message of I. S.*); A. Tansman, *I. S.* (Paris, 1948; Eng. tr., 1949); E. Corle, ed., *I. S.* (N.Y., 1949); M. Lederman, ed., *S. in the Theater* (N.Y., 1949); F. Onnen, *S.* (Stockholm, 1949; Eng. tr.); R. Myers, *Introduction to the Music of S.* (London, 1950); W.H. Auden et al., *I. S.* (Bonn, 1952); H. Strobel, *I. S.* (Zürich, 1956; Eng. tr., 1956, as *S.: Classic Humanist*); H. Kirchmeyer, *I. S.: Zeitgeschichte im Persönlichkeitsbild* (Regensburg, 1958); R. Vlad, *S.* (Rome, 1958; Eng. tr., 1960; third ed., 1979); R. Siohan, *S.* (Paris, 1959; Eng. tr., 1966); F. Herzfeld, *I. S.* (Berlin, 1961); P. Lang, ed., *S.: The Composer and His Works* (London, 1966); E. White, *S.: The Composer and His Works* (Berkeley, 1966; second ed., 1979); A. Boucourechliev, ed., *S.* (Paris, 1968); *The Rite of Spring: Sketches, 1911–1913* (London, 1969); A. Dobrin, *I. S.: His Life and Time* (London, 1970); B. Boretz and E. Cone, eds., *Perspectives on Schoenberg and S.* (N.Y., 1972); P. Horgan, *Encounters with S.* (N.Y., 1972; rev. ed., 1989); L. Libman, *And Music at the Close: S.'s Last Years, A Personal Memoir* (N.Y., 1972); T. Stravinsky, *Catherine and I. S.: A Family Album* (N.Y., 1973); V. Stravinsky and R. Craft, *S.* (N.Y., 1975); idem, *S. in Pictures and Documents* (N.Y., 1976); A. Boucourechliev, *I. S.* (Paris, 1982; Eng. tr., 1987); P. Griffiths, *I. S.: The Rake's Progress* (Cambridge, 1982); H. Keller and M. Cosman, *S. Seen and Heard* (London, 1982); A. Schouvaloff and V. Borovsky, *S. on Stage* (London, 1982); L. Andriessen and E. Schonberger, *Het Apollinisch Uurwerk* (Amsterdam, 1983; Eng. tr., 1989, as *The Apollonian Clockwork: On S.*); C. Joseph, *S. and the Piano* (Ann Arbor, 1983); M. Ruskin, *I. S.: His Personality, Works and Views* (Cambridge, 1983); V. Scherliess, *I. S. und seine Zeit* (Laaber, 1983); P. van den Toorn, *The Music of I. S.* (London, 1983); J. Pasler, ed., *Confronting S.: Man, Musician, and Modernist* (Berkeley, 1986); E. Haimo and P. Johnson, eds., *S. Retrospectives* (Lincoln, Nebr., 1987); J. Kobler, *Firebird: A Biography of S.* (N.Y., 1987); P. van den Toorn, *S. and the Rite of Spring: The Beginnings of a Musical Language* (Berkeley, 1987); S. Walsh, *The Music of S.* (London and N.Y., 1988); A. Pople, *Skryabin and S. 1908–1914: Studies in Theory and Analysis* (N.Y. and London, 1989); C. Goubault, *I. S.* (Paris, 1991); V. Stemann, *Das epische Musiktheater bei S. und Brecht: Studien zur Geschichte und Theorie* (N.Y., 1991); P. Stuart, *I. S.—the Composer in the Recording Studio: A Comprehensive Discography* (N.Y., 1991); C. Migliaccio, *I balletti di I. S.* (Milan, 1992); G. Vinay, ed., *S.* (Bologna, 1992); S. Walsh, *S.: Oedipus Rex* (Cambridge, 1993); W. Burde, *I. S.* (Stuttgart, 1995); M. Marnat, *S.* (Paris, 1995); R. Sievers, *I. S.: Trois pièces* pour quatour à cordes: Analyse und Deutung (Wiesbaden, 1996); J. Cross, The S. Legacy (N.Y., 1998); A. Wachtel, ed., Petrushka: Sources and Contexts (Evanston, Ill., 1998); S. Walsh, S., Vol. I: A Creative Spring: Russia and France 1882–1934 (N.Y., 1999). —NS/LK/DM

Stravinsky, (Sviatoslav) Soulima, Russian-American pianist, teacher, and composer, son of **Igor (Feodorovich) Stravinsky;** b. Lausanne, Sept. 23, 1910; d. Sarasota, Fla., Nov. 28, 1994. He received training in piano from Philipp and in theory and composition from Boulanger in Paris. In 1934 he made his Paris debut as a pianist, and subsequently established himself as an authoritative interpreter of his father's piano music. In 1939 he joined the French Army and remained in France during World War II. In 1948 he settled in the U.S., where he appeared as soloist in his father's works with his father conducting. From 1950 to 1978 he taught piano at the Univ. of Ill. School of Music. Among his compositions were several chamber pieces, including 3 string quartets and a Cello Sonata. He prepared eds. of various Mozart piano concertos, for which he also composed cadenzas.—NS/LK/DM

Strayhorn, Billy (actually, **William Thomas**), jazz composer, arranger, and pianist; b. Dayton, Ohio, Nov. 29, 1915; d. N.Y., May 31, 1967. Strayhorn's career was inextricably linked to that of Duke Ellington, from their meeting in 1938 to Strayhorn's death. Strayhorn wrote music for Ellington's orchestra, both by himself and in collaboration with Ellington; he wrote arrangements of other composers' works; and he occasionally played piano with the Ellington band in concert and on records. His notable compositions include "Lush Life," "Take the 'A' Train," and "Satin Doll" (music also by Ellington, lyrics by Johnny Mercer).

Strayhorn's parents were James Nathaniel Strayhorn, a janitor, and Lillian Young Strayhorn. Shortly after his birth, the family moved to Montclair, N. J., and in 1920 relocated to the Pittsburgh area, eventually settling in Pittsburgh itself. Strayhorn began to play the piano as a child during summer vacations spent with his grandparents in Hillsborough, N. C. He delivered newspapers and worked in a drugstore to save the money to buy a piano. He played in and wrote compositions for his high school orchestra, then attended the Pittsburgh Musical Inst. during the 1936–37 school year, studying piano and music theory. In June 1937 he formed a small jazz group, eventually named The Mad Hatters, which lasted into the fall of 1938, when he began to perform as a solo pianist in clubs. He also wrote arrangements for local bands.

Strayhorn was introduced to Ellington while the bandleader was appearing in Pittsburgh in December 1938. Ellington hired him and he moved to N.Y. He did his first arrangements for a recording session led by Ellington saxophonist Johnny Hodges on Feb. 27, 1939, and on March 21, Ellington first recorded a Strayhorn composition, "Something to Live For." Though it was a song Strayhorn had written before meeting Ellington, it was copyrighted as having been written jointly, initiating a common procedure of crediting Strayhorn's works

to him and Ellington, or even to Ellington alone, as documented by Strayhorn's biographer David Hajdu.

An acknowledged homosexual, Strayhorn began living with pianist Aaron Bridgers in 1939 and they remained together until Bridgers moved to Paris in 1947. Strayhorn lived with Francis Goldberg, a cook, from 1958 to 1959. Though they did not live together he formed a relationship with graphic designer Bill Grove that lasted from 1964 until his death.

Strayhorn arranged "Flamingo" (music by Ted Grouya, lyrics by Edmund Anderson), which became a hit for Ellington in June 1941. The following month Ellington reached the charts with "Take the 'A' Train," which Strayhorn had written upon his arrival in N.Y.; it became Ellington's theme song. Though only cocredited for orchestrations and a few songs, Strayhorn apparently made a major contribution to the Ellington revue Jump for Joy (Los Angeles, July 10, 1941). "My Little Brown Book," a song Strayhorn had written for a high school revue in 1935, became a Top Ten R&B hit for Ellington in June 1944. Ellington also reached the R&B Top Ten that December with "I Don't Mind," for which he had written the music with lyrics by Strayhorn. Strayhorn again was credited only with orchestrations for the Ellington-composed Broadway musical Beggar's Holiday (N.Y., Dec. 26, 1946), though he apparently wrote some of the music as well.

The downturn in the big band business in the late 1940s reduced Ellington's creative activities and thus Strayhorn's participation in them, though his biographer suggests he also became disillusioned about his lack of credit for his work. Strayhorn made his formal recording debut in 1951 with the ten-inch album Billy Strayhorn Trio, released on Ellington's Mercer Records label and featuring both men on piano and two bass players on alternating tracks. During the early and mid-1950s Strayhorn wrote incidental music for Off-Broadway and worked on a musical that was never produced. He also did occasional recording sessions.

In 1956, Ellington, with a new Columbia Records contract and a celebrated appearance at the Newport Jazz Festival, made a major comeback, resulting in increased opportunities for new compositions. He and Strayhorn went back to working together regularly, and they wrote a series of pieces, many of which still were credited solely to Ellington. A Drum Is a Woman, intended as a history of jazz, was written for a television special and broadcast on CBS on May 8, 1957. Such Sweet Thunder was a suite based on Shakespeare and commissioned by the Stratford, Ontario, Shakespeare Festival, where it was performed on Sept. 5, 1957. Strayhorn also participated in the composition of the scores for the films Anatomy of a Murder (1959) and Paris Blues (1961), credited to Ellington. Strayhorn supervised the orchestra for the Ellington-composed musical My People, performed in Chicago at the Century of Negro Progress exhibition in August and September 1963.

Strayhorn's only real solo album, The Peaceful Side, was released by United Artists in 1961. He made his solo concert debut on June 6, 1964, at the New School for Social Research in N.Y. He was nominated for a 1964 Grammy Award for Best Instrumental Arrangement for

"A Spoonful of Sugar" (music and lyrics by Richard M. and Robert B. Sherman) from Ellington's album of the music from the film *Mary Poppins*. With Ellington, Strayhorn earned a second Grammy nomination the following year for Best Original Jazz Composition for "Virgin Islands Suite" from the 1965 Ellington album *Concert in the Virgin Islands*. He died of esophageal cancer at 51 in 1967. Ellington paid tribute to him later that year with an album of his compositions, *...And His Mother Called Him Bill*. Much of his music, with and without Ellington, was heard in the Broadway revue *Sophisticated Ladies* (N.Y., March 1, 1981).

DISC.: *Billy Strayhorn Septet* (1958); *Billy Strayhorn/Johnny Dankworth* (9158); *The Peaceful Side* (1961); *Lush Life* (1964); *Billy Strayhorn Songbook* (1997).

BIBL.: D. Hajdu, *Lush Life: A Biography of B. S.* (N.Y., 1996). —WR